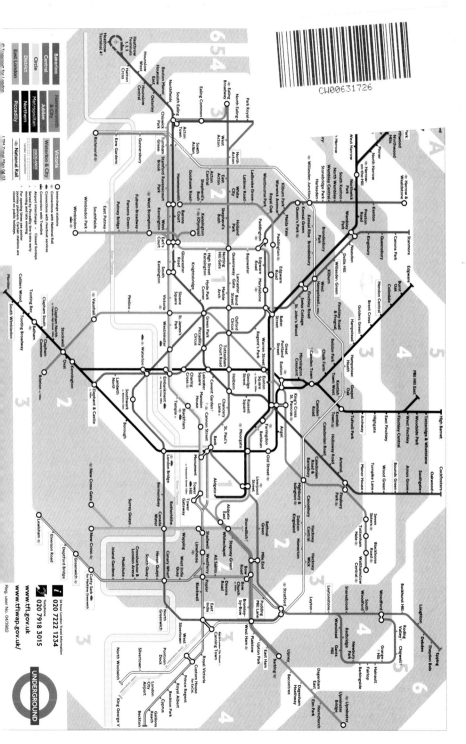

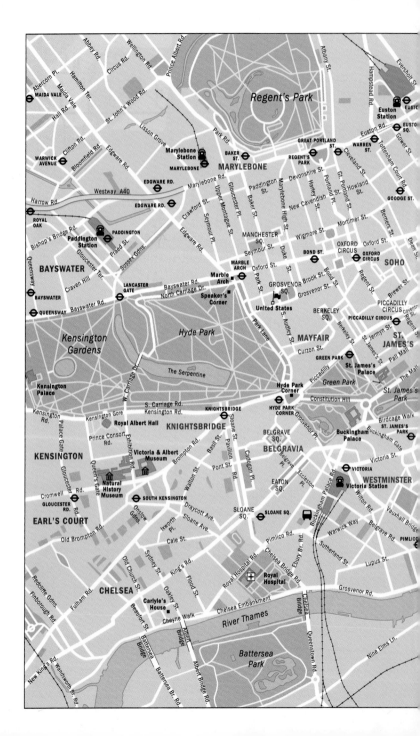

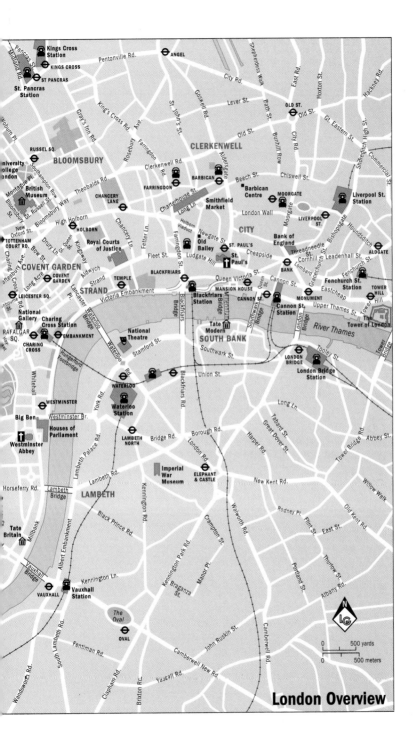

London Overview

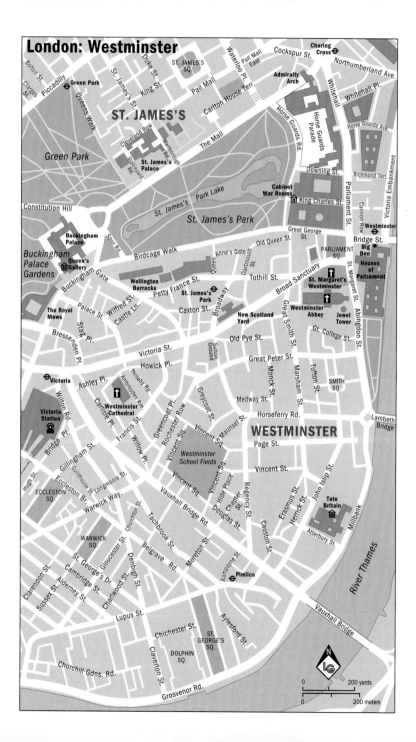

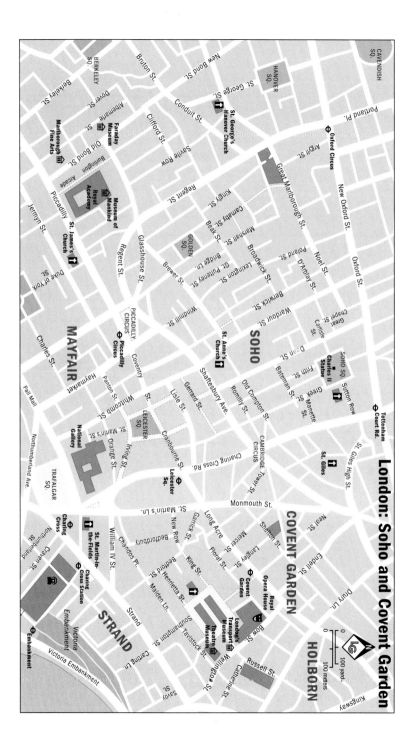

London: Soho and Covent Garden

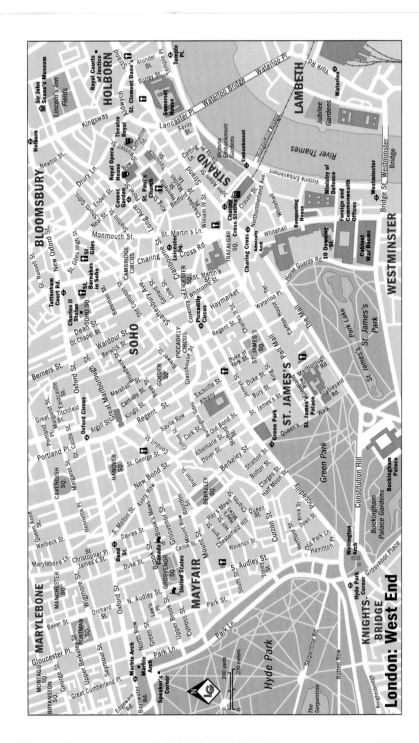

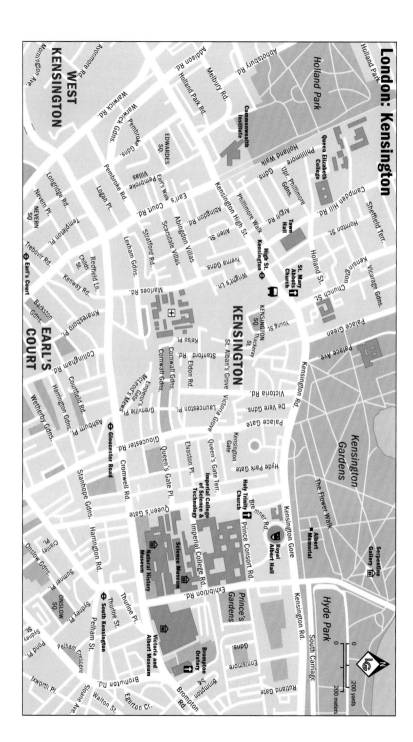

London: Kensington

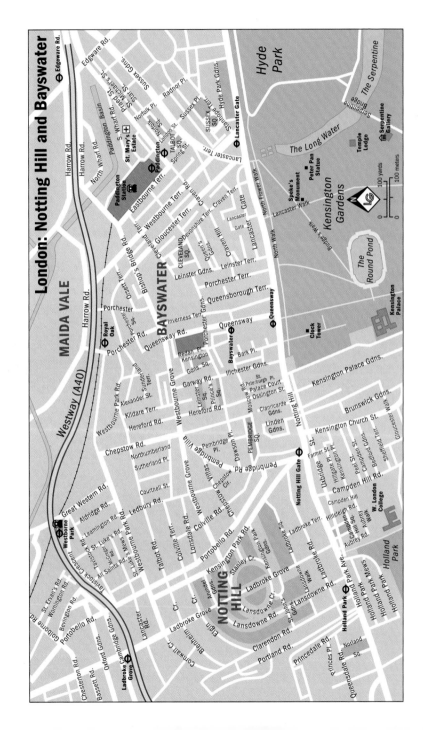

London: Notting Hill and Bayswater

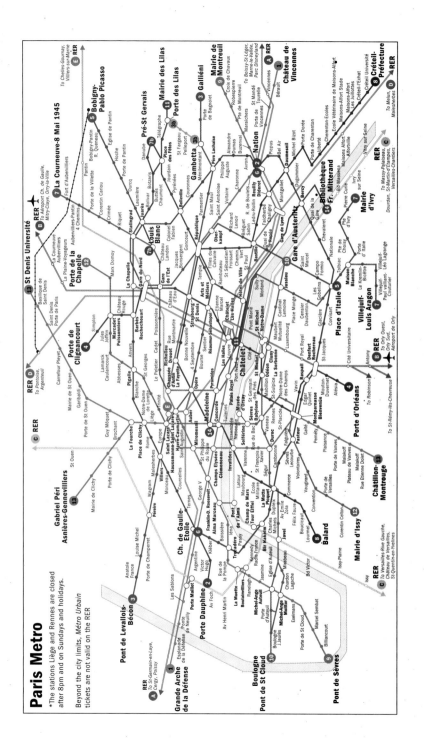

Paris Metro

*The stations Liège and Rennes are closed after 8pm and on Sundays and holidays.

Beyond the city limits, *Métro Urbain* tickets are not valid on the RER

Paris: Overview and Arrondissements

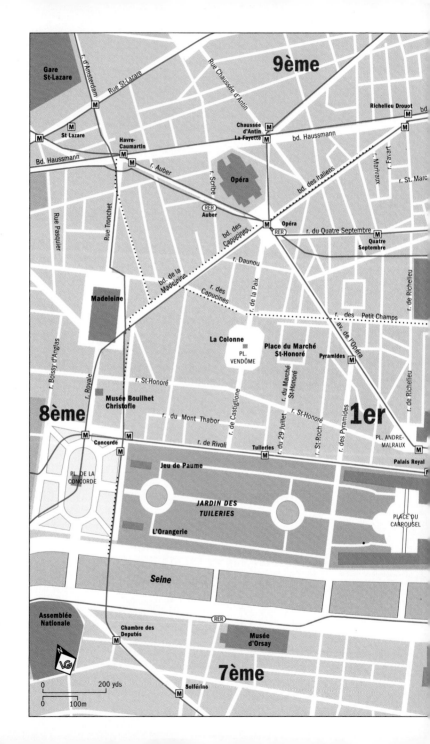

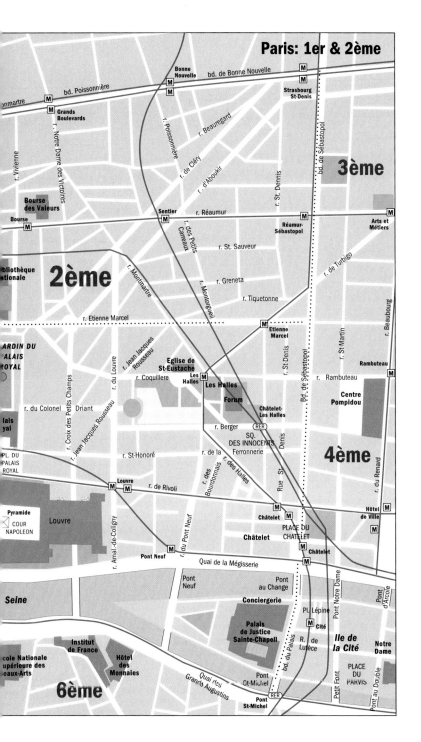

Paris: 1er & 2ème

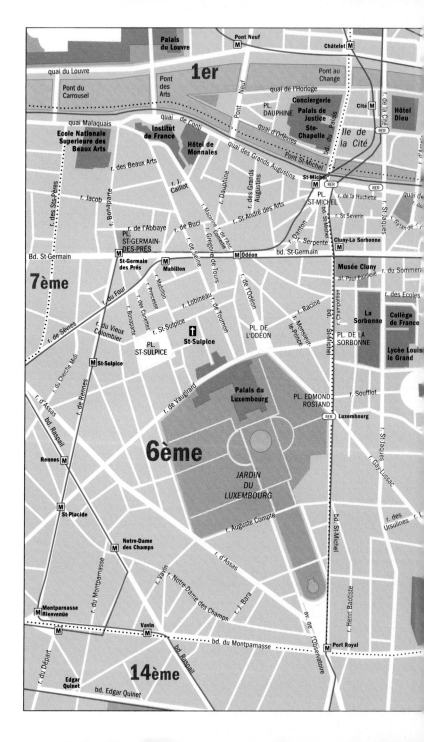

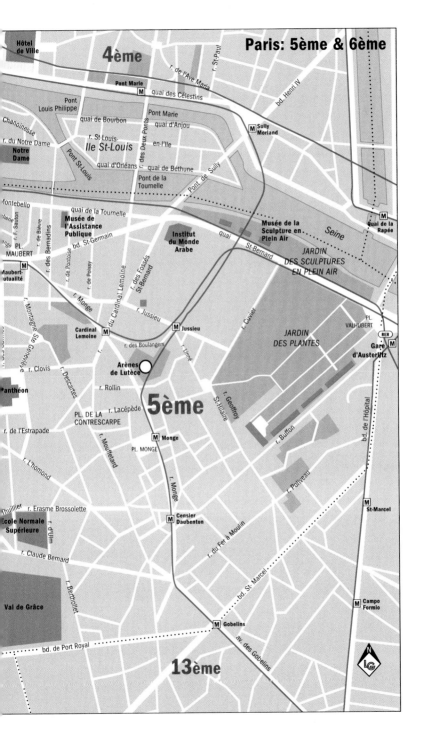

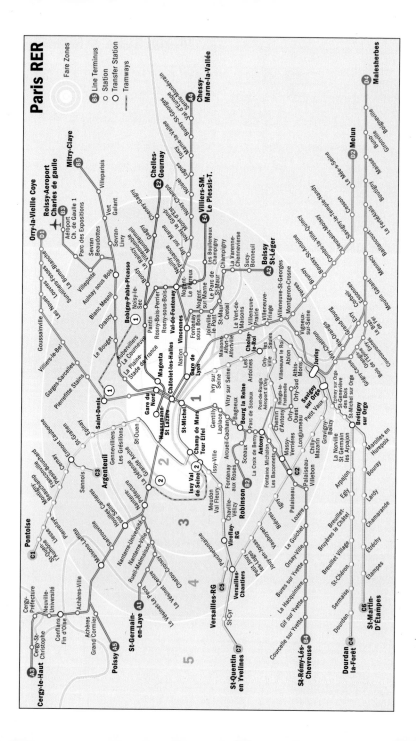

Paris RER

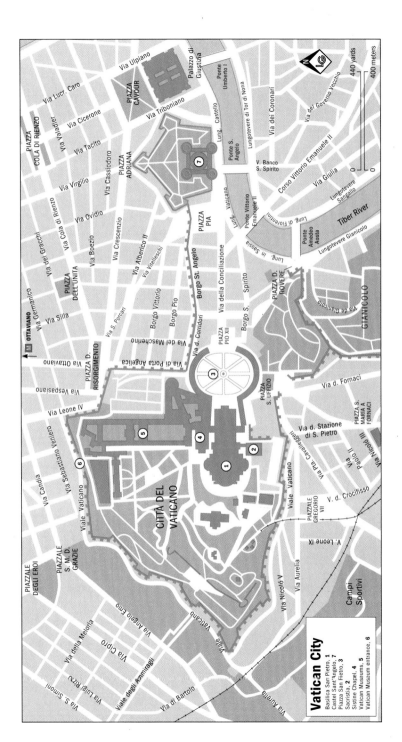

Vatican City

Basilica San Pietro, **1**
Castel Sant'Angelo, **7**
Piazza San Pietro, **3**
Sacristia, **2**
Sistine Chapel, **4**
Vatican Museums, **5**
Vatican Museum entrance, **6**

Rome Mass Transit

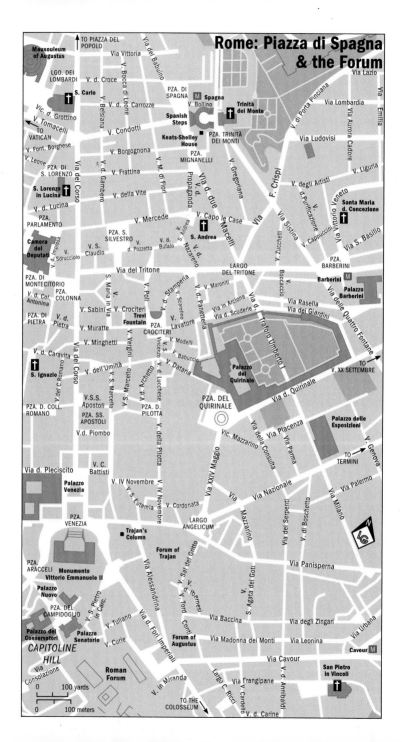

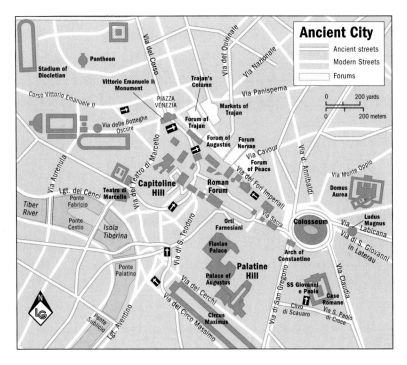

Ancient City

Ancient streets
Modern Streets
Forums

0   200 yards
0   200 meters

Stadium of Diocletian
Pantheon
Via del Corso
Via del Quirinale
Via Nazionale
Vittorio Emanuele II Monument
Trajan's Column
Via Panisperna
Corso Vittorio Emanuele II
PIAZZA VENEZIA
Markets of Trajan
Via delle Botteghe Oscure
Forum of Trajan
Forum of Augustus
Forum Nervae
Via Cavour
Forum of Peace
Via dei Fori Imperiali
Via Aurenuia
Via d. Annibaldi
Lgt. dei Cenci
Via del Teatro di Marcello
Capitoline Hill
Roman Forum
Via Monte Oppio
Domus Aurea
Tiber River
Ponte Fabricio
Teatro di Marcello
Ludus Magnus
Via Labicana
Ponte Cestio
Isola Tiberina
Via di S. Teodoro
Orti Farnesiani
Via Sacra
Colosseum
Via di S. Giovanni in Laterau
Flavian Palace
Arch of Constantine
Ponte Palatino
Palace of Augustus
Palatine Hill
Via Claudia
Ponte Subicio
Lgt. Aventino
Via dei Cerchi
Via dei Circo Massimo
Circus Maximus
Via di San Gregorio
SS Giovanni e Paolo
Case Romane
Clivo di Scauaro
Via S. Paolo di Croce
N
LG

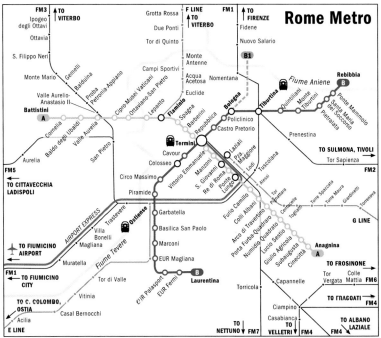

Rome Metro

FM3
Ipogeo degli Ottavi
TO VITERBO
Grotta Rossa
F LINE
TO VITERBO
FM1
TO FIRENZE
Ottavia
Due Ponti
Fidene
S. Filippo Neri
Tor di Quinto
Nuovo Salario
Monte Antenne
B1
Monte Mario
Campi Sportivi
Gemelli
Baldulina
Acqua Acetosa
Nomentana
Rebibbia
B
Valle Aurelio-Anastasio II
Proba Petronia-Apiano
Cipro-Musei Vaticani
Euclide
Fiume Aniene
Ponte Mammolo
Santa Maria del Soccorso
Battistini
A
Ottaviano-San Pietro
Lepanto
Flaminio
Bologna
Tiburtina
Quintiliani
Monte Tiburtini
Pietralata
Cornelia
Baldo degli Ubaldi
Valle Aurelia
San Pietro
Spagna
Barberini
Repubblica
Policlinico
Castro Pretorio
Prenestina
TO SULMONA, TIVOLI
Tor Sapienza
FM5
TO CITTAVECCHIA LADISPOLI
Aurelia
Termini
Cavour
Colosseo
Vittorio Emmanuele
Manzoni
S. Giovanni
Re di Roma
Ponte Lungo
Laziali
Pza. Maggiore
Lodi
Tuscolana
Alessi
FM2
Circo Massimo
Piramide
AIRPORT EXPRESS
Trastevere
Ostense
Furio Camillo
Colli Albani
Arco di Travertino
Porta Furba-Quadraro
Numidio Quadrato
Lucio Sestio
Giulio Agricola
Subaugusta
Cinecitta
Tor Pignatara
Malatesta
Centocelle
Togliatti
Torre Spaccata
Torre Maura
Giardinetti
Tor Vergata
Torrenova
G LINE
TO FIUMICINO AIRPORT
Villa Bonelli
Magliana
Fiume Tevere
Garbatella
Basilica San Paolo
Marconi
EUR Magliana
Anagnina
A
TO FROSINONE
Muratella
FM1
TO FIUMICINO CITY
Tor di Valle
Vitinia
C/IR Palasport
EUR Fermi
Laurentina
B
Torricola
Capannelle
Colle Mattia
FM6
TO LUGOATI
FM4
TO C. COLOMBO, OSTIA
Casal Bernocchi
Acilia
E LINE
TO NETTUNO
FM7
Ciampino
Casabianca
TO VELLETRI
FM4
TO ALBANO LAZIALE
FM4

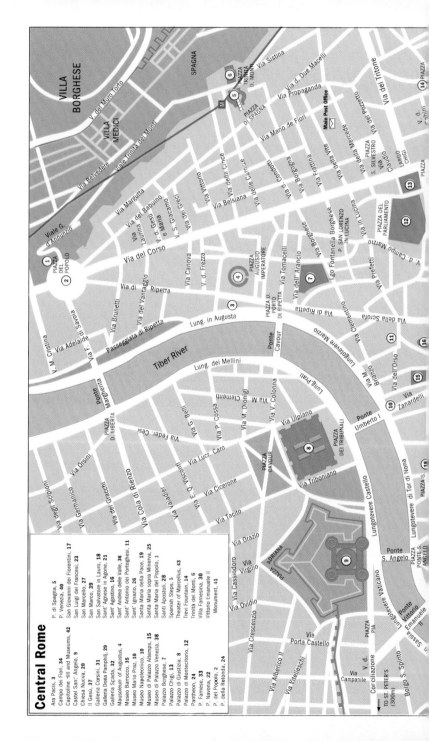

Central Rome

Ara Pacis, **3**
Campo dei Fiori, **34**
Capitoline -Hill and Museums, **42**
Castel Sant' Angelo, **9**
Chiesa Nuova, **20**
Il Gesù, **37**
Galleria Corsini, **31**
Galleria Doria Pamphilj, **29**
Galleria Spada, **32**
Mausoleum of Augustus, **4**
Museo Barrocco, **35**
Museo Mario Praz, **10**
Museo Napoleonico, **10**
Museo di Palazzo Altemps, **15**
Museo di Palazzo Venezia, **38**
Palazzo Borghese, **7**
Palazzo Chigi, **13**
Palazzo di Giustizia, **8**
Palazzo di Montecitorio, **12**
Pantheon, **24**
P. Farnese, **33**
P. Navona, **22**
P. del Popolo, **2**
P. della Retonda, **24**

P. di Spagna, **5**
P. Venezia, **40**
San Giovanni dei Fiorentini, **17**
San Luigi dei Francesi, **23**
San Marcello, **27**
San Marco, **39**
San Salvatore in Lauro, **18**
Sant' Agnese in Agone, **21**
Sant' Agostino, **16**
Sant' Andrea delle Valle, **36**
Sant' Antonio dei Portoghesi, **11**
Sant' Ignazio, **26**
Santa Maria della Pace, **19**
Santa Maria sopra Minerva, **25**
Santa Maria del Popolo, **1**
Santi Apostoli, **28**
Spanish Steps, **5**
Theater of Marcellus, **43**
Trevi Fountain, **14**
Trinità dei Monti, **6**
Villa Farnesina, **30**
Vittorio Emanuele II
Monument, **41**

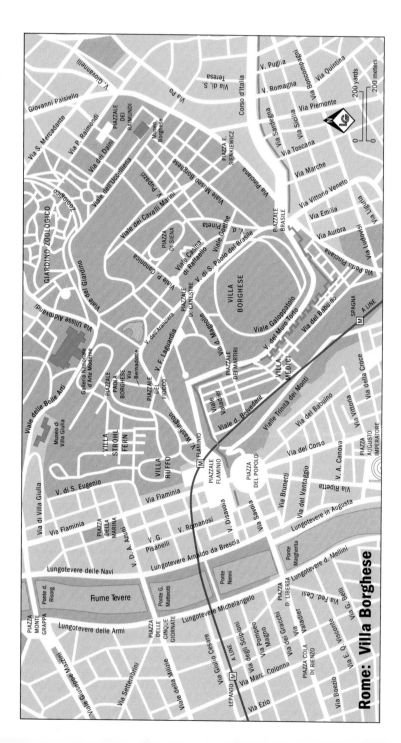

Rome: Villa Borghese

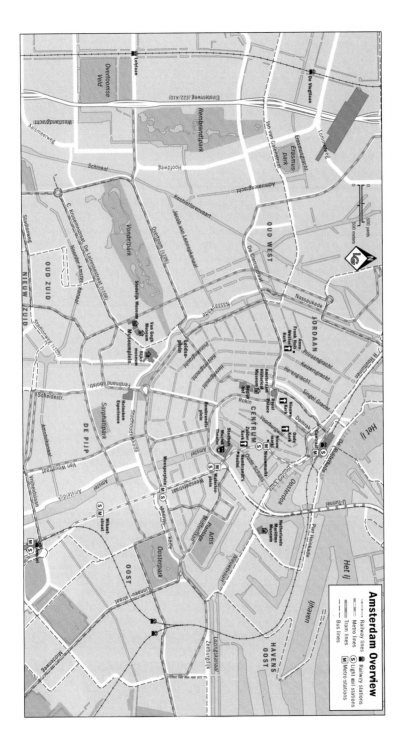

Amsterdam Overview

- Railway lines
- Metro lines
- Light rail stations
- Tram lines
- Bus lines
- Metro stations

0 500 yards
0 500 metres

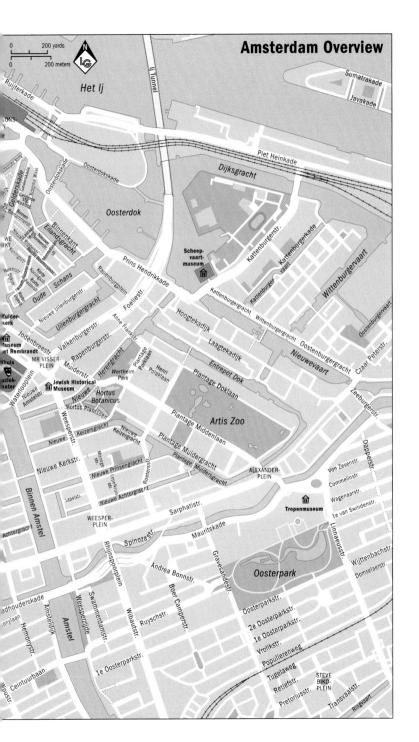

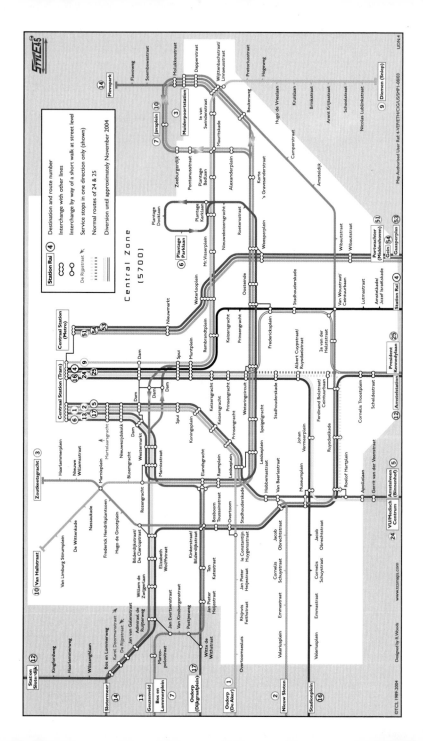

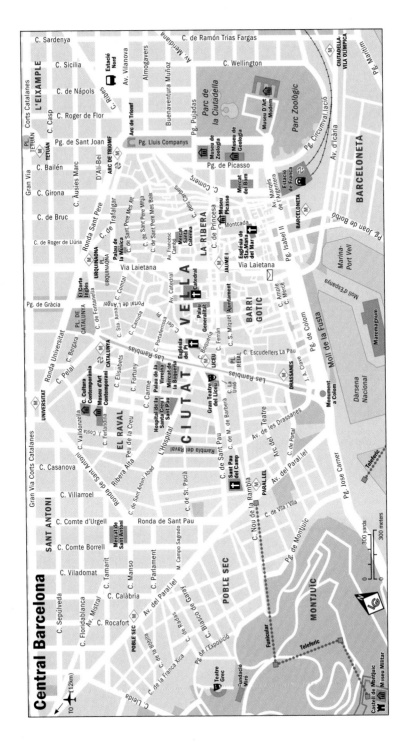

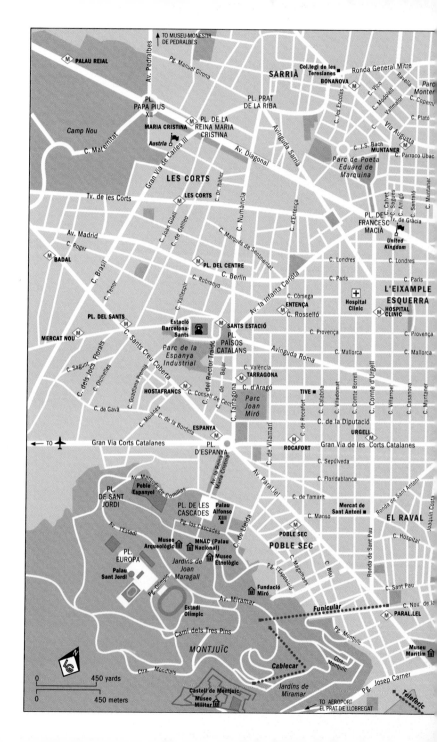

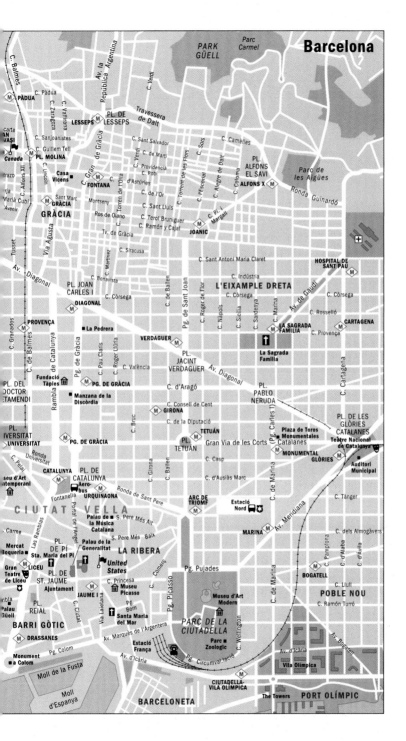

Barcelona Metro

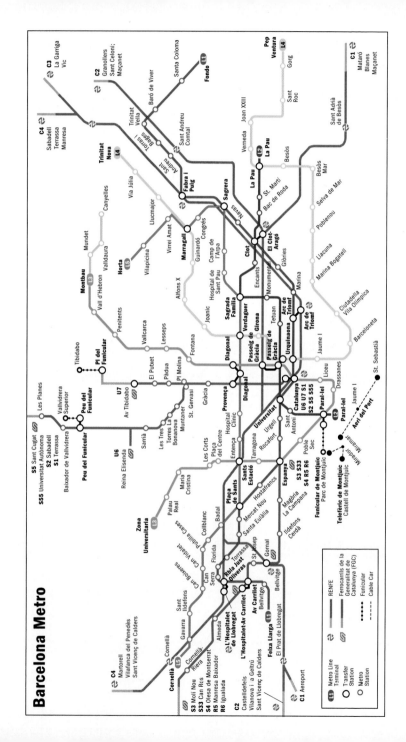

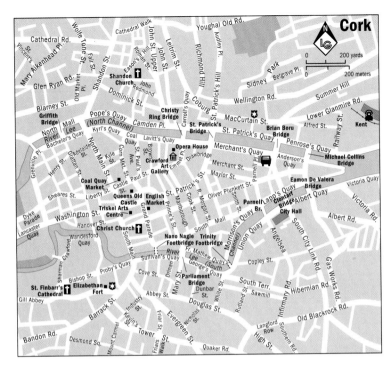

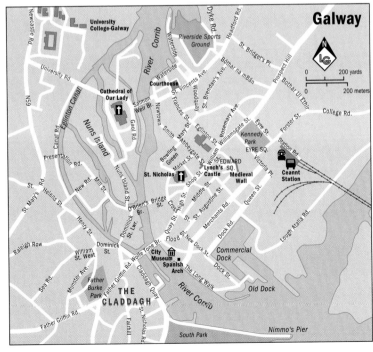

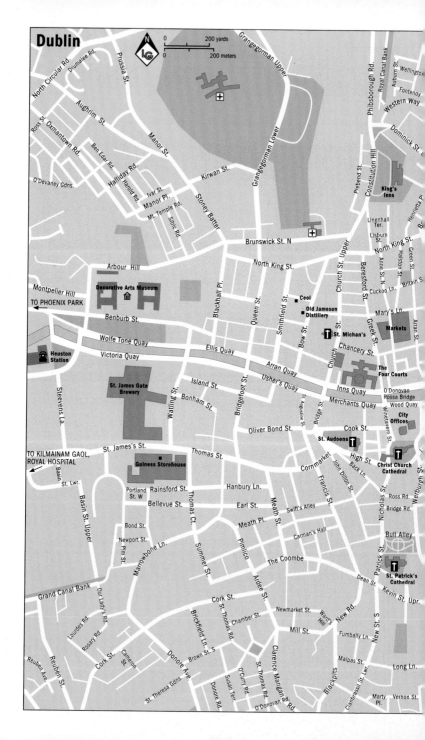

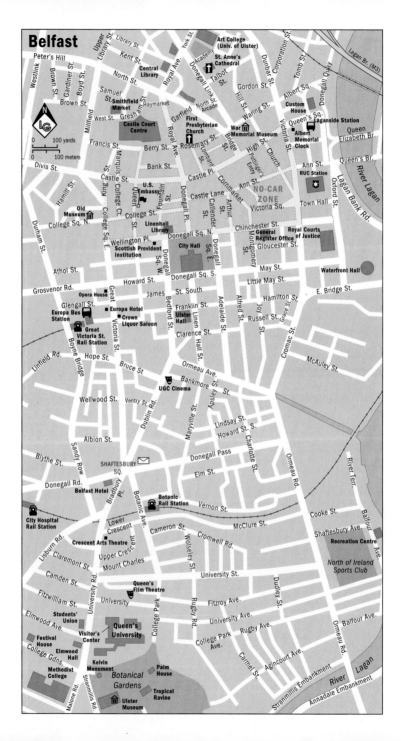

Berlin Transit

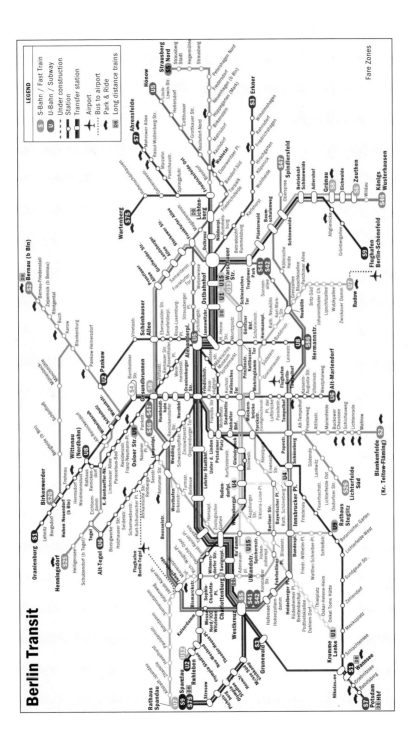

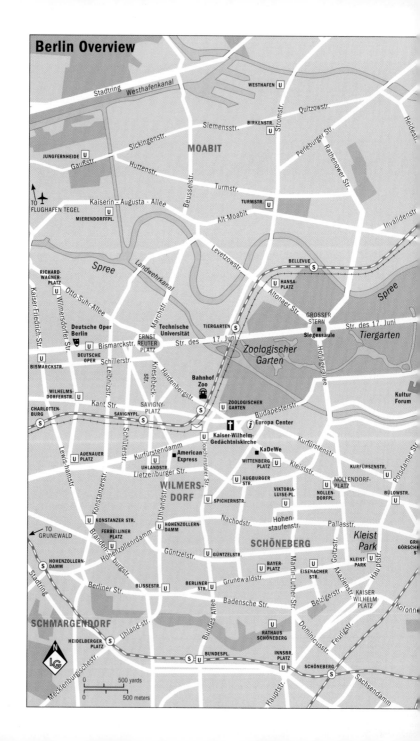

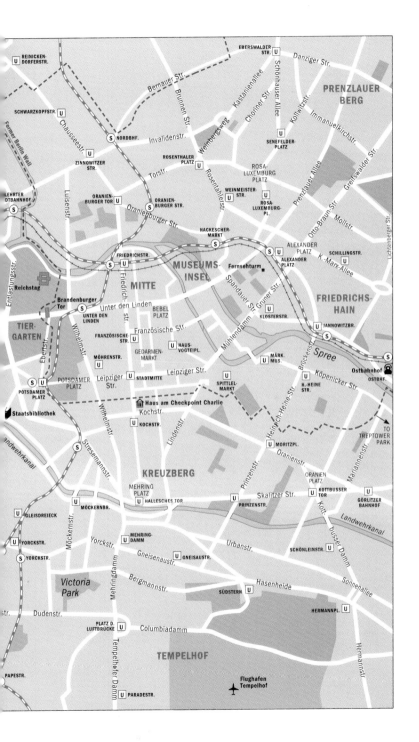

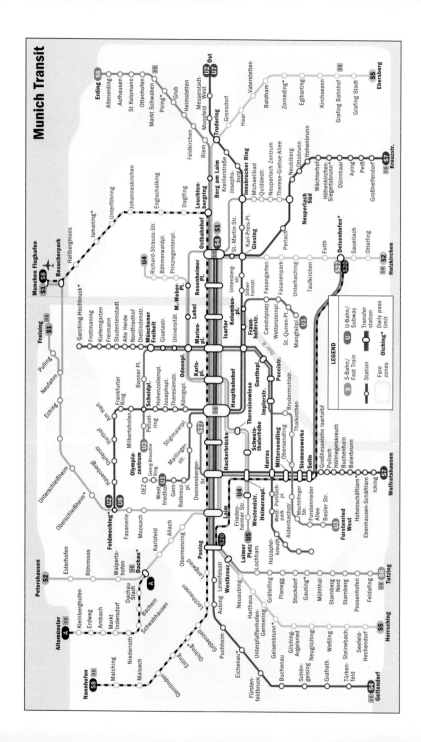

Munich Transit

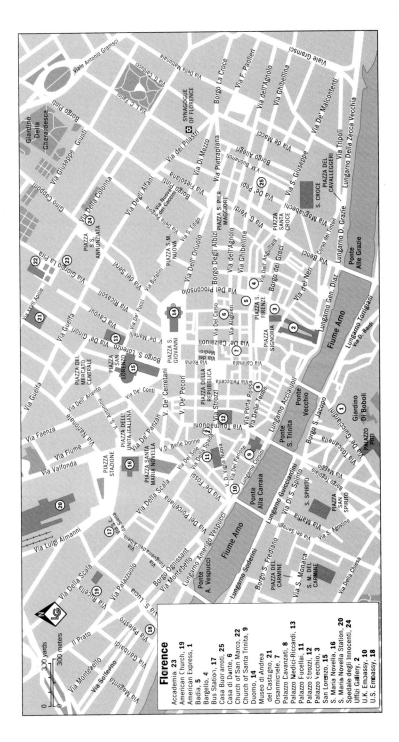

Florence

Accademia **23**
American Church, **19**
American Express, **1**
Badia, **5**
Bargello, **4**
Bus Station, **17**
Casa Buonarroti, **25**
Casa di Dante, **6**
Church of San Marco, **22**
Church of Santa Trinita, **9**
Duomo, **14**
Museo di Andrea
del Castagno, **21**
Orsanmichele, **7**
Palazzo Cavanzati, **8**
Palazzo Medici-Riccardi, **13**
Palazzo Fucellai, **11**
Palazzo Strozzi, **12**
Palazzo Vecchio, **3**
San Lorenzo, **15**
S. Maria Novella, **16**
S. Maria Novella Station, **20**
Spedale degli Innocenti, **24**
Uffizi Gallery, **2**
U.K. Embassy, **10**
U.S. Embassy, **18**

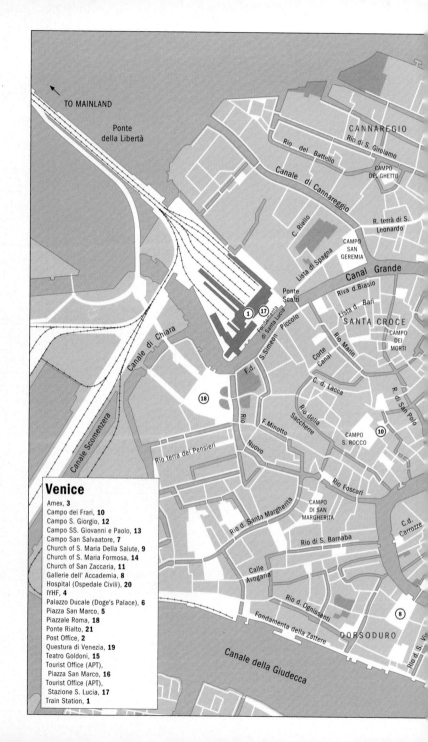

Venice

Amex, **3**
Campo dei Frari, **10**
Campo S. Giorgio, **12**
Campo SS. Giovanni e Paolo, **13**
Campo San Salvaatore, **7**
Church of S. Maria Della Salute, **9**
Church of S. Maria Formosa, **14**
Church of San Zaccaria, **11**
Gallerie dell' Accademia, **8**
Hospital (Ospedale Civili), **20**
IYHF, **4**
Palazzo Ducale (Doge's Palace), **6**
Piazza San Marco, **5**
Piazzale Roma, **18**
Ponte Rialto, **21**
Post Office, **2**
Questura di Venezia, **19**
Teatro Goldoni, **15**
Tourist Office (APT),
 Piazza San Marco, **16**
Tourist Office (APT),
 Stazione S. Lucia, **17**
Train Station, **1**

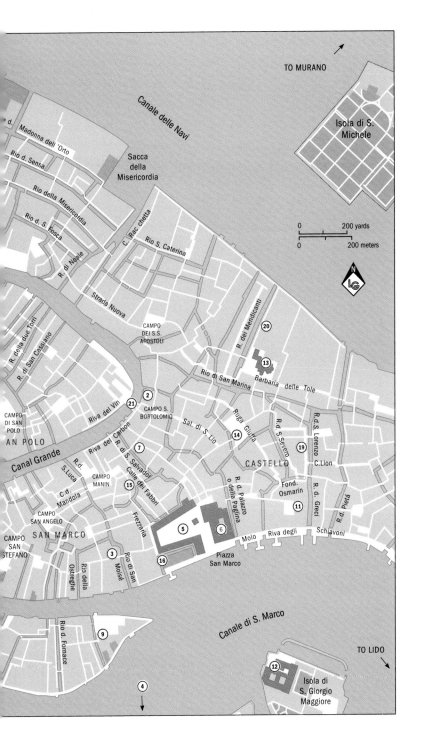

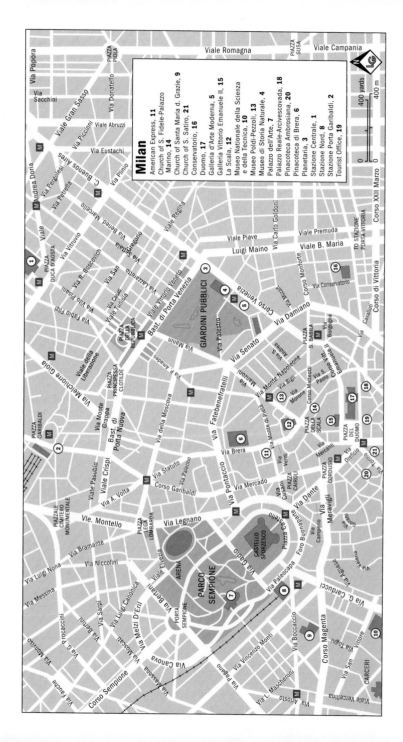

Milan

American Express, **11**
Church of S. Fidele-Palazzo
Marino, **14**
Church of Santa Maria d. Grazie, **9**
Church of S. Satiro, **21**
Conservatorio, **16**
Duomo, **17**
Galleria d'Arte Moderna, **5**
Galleria Vittorio Emanuele II, **15**
La Scala, **12**
Museo Nazionale della Scienza
e della Tecnica, **10**
Museo Poldi-Pezzoli, **13**
Museo di Storia Naturale, **4**
Palazzo dell'Arte, **7**
Palazzo Reale-Arcivescovada, **18**
Pinacoteca Ambrosiana, **20**
Pinacoteca di Brera, **6**
Planetaria, **3**
Stazione Centrale, **1**
Stazione Nord, **8**
Stazione Porta Garibaldi, **2**
Tourist Office, **19**

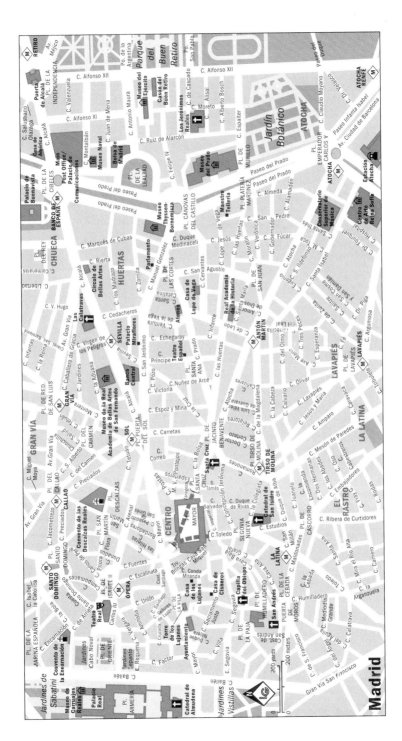

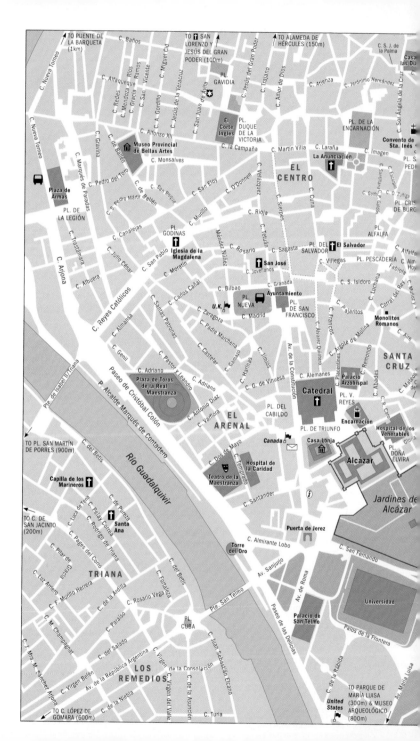

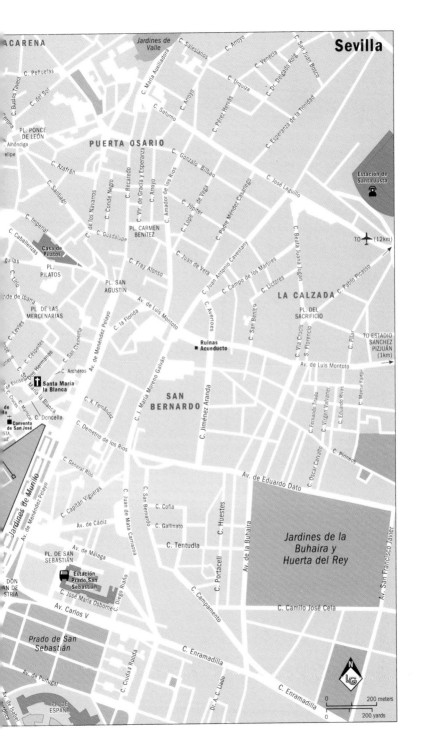

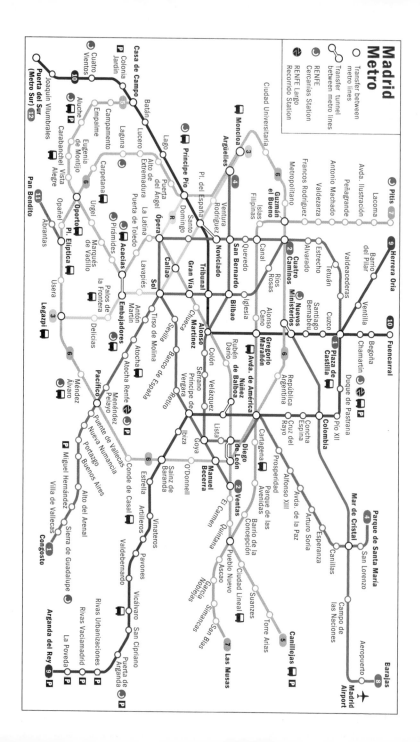

LET'S GO

■ THE RESOURCE FOR THE INDEPENDENT TRAVELER

"The guides are aimed not only at young budget travelers but at the indepedent traveler; a sort of streetwise cookbook for traveling alone."
—The New York Times

"Unbeatable; good sight-seeing advice; up-to-date info on restaurants, hotels, and inns; a commitment to money-saving travel; and a wry style that brightens nearly every page."
—The Washington Post

"Lighthearted and sophisticated, informative and fun to read. [Let's Go] helps the novice traveler navigate like a knowledgeable old hand."
—Atlanta Journal-Constitution

"A world-wise traveling companion—always ready with friendly advice and helpful hints, all sprinkled with a bit of wit."
—The Philadelphia Inquirer

■ THE BEST TRAVEL BARGAINS IN YOUR PRICE RANGE

"All the dirt, dirt cheap."
—People

"Anything you need to know about budget traveling is detailed in this book."
—The Chicago Sun-Times

"Let's Go follows the creed that you don't have to toss your life's savings to the wind to travel—unless you want to."
—The Salt Lake Tribune

■ REAL ADVICE FOR REAL EXPERIENCES

"The writers seem to have experienced every rooster-packed bus and lunar-surfaced mattress about which they write."
—The New York Times

"A guide should tell you what to expect from a destination. Here Let's Go shines."
—The Chicago Tribune

"[Let's Go's] devoted updaters really walk the walk (and thumb the ride, and trek the trail). Learn how to fish, haggle, find work—anywhere."
—Food & Wine

LET'S GO PUBLICATIONS

TRAVEL GUIDES
Alaska 1st edition **NEW TITLE**
Australia 2004
Austria & Switzerland 2004
Brazil 1st edition **NEW TITLE**
Britain & Ireland 2004
California 2004
Central America 8th edition
Chile 1st edition
China 4th edition
Costa Rica 1st edition
Eastern Europe 2004
Egypt 2nd edition
Europe 2004
France 2004
Germany 2004
Greece 2004
Hawaii 2004
India & Nepal 8th edition
Ireland 2004
Israel 4th edition
Italy 2004
Japan 1st edition **NEW TITLE**
Mexico 20th edition
Middle East 4th edition
New Zealand 6th edition
Pacific Northwest 1st edition **NEW TITLE**
Peru, Ecuador & Bolivia 3rd edition
Puerto Rico 1st edition **NEW TITLE**
South Africa 5th edition
Southeast Asia 8th edition
Southwest USA 3rd edition
Spain & Portugal 2004
Thailand 1st edition
Turkey 5th edition
USA 2004
Western Europe 2004

CITY GUIDES
Amsterdam 3rd edition
Barcelona 3rd edition
Boston 4th edition
London 2004
New York City 2004
Paris 2004
Rome 12th edition
San Francisco 4th edition
Washington, D.C. 13th edition

MAP GUIDES
Amsterdam
Berlin
Boston
Chicago
Dublin
Florence
Hong Kong
London
Los Angeles
Madrid
New Orleans
New York City
Paris
Prague
Rome
San Francisco
Seattle
Sydney
Venice
Washington, D.C.

COMING SOON:
Road Trip USA

WESTERN EUROPE

2004

Tabby George Editor

Emilie S. FitzMaurice Associate Editor
David Hambrick Associate Editor
Paul G. Kofoed Associate Editor
Matthew C. Lynch Associate Editor
Rebecca Pargas Associate Editor
Christopher J. Reisig Associate Editor

Researcher-Writer
Sloan Eddleston

Tim Szetela Map Editor
Matthew K. Hudson Managing Editor

Macmillan

HELPING LET'S GO

If you want to share your discoveries, suggestions, or corrections, please drop us a line. We read every piece of correspondence, whether a postcard, a 10-page email, or a coconut. **Address mail to:**

Let's Go: Western Europe
67 Mount Auburn Street
Cambridge, MA 02138
USA

Visit Let's Go at **http://www.letsgo.com,** or send email to:

feedback@letsgo.com
Subject: "Let's Go: Western Europe"

In addition to the invaluable travel advice our readers share with us, many are kind enough to offer their services as researchers or editors. Unfortunately, our charter enables us to employ only currently enrolled Harvard students.

Published in Great Britain 2004 by Macmillan, an imprint of Pan Macmillan Ltd.
20 New Wharf Road, London N1 9RR
Basingstoke and Oxford
Associated companies throughout the world
www.panmacmillan.com

Maps by David Lindroth copyright © 2004 by St. Martin's Press.

Published in the United States of America by St. Martin's Press.

ISBN: 1 4050 3323 1
First edition
10 9 8 7 6 5 4 3 2 1

Let's Go: Western Europe is written by Let's Go Publications, 67 Mount Auburn Street, Cambridge, MA 02138, USA.

ABOUT LET'S GO

GUIDES FOR THE INDEPENDENT TRAVELER

Budget travel is more than a vacation. At *Let's Go*, we see every trip as the chance of a lifetime. If your dream is to grab a knapsack and a machete and forge through the jungles of Brazil, we can take you there. Or, if you'd rather enjoy the Riviera sun at a beachside cafe, we'll set you a table. If you know what you're doing, you can have any experience you want—whether it's camping among lions or sampling Tuscan desserts—without maxing out your credit card. We'll show you just how far your coins can go, and prove that the greatest limitation on your adventure is not your wallet, but your imagination. That said, we understand that you may want the occasional indulgence after a week of hostels and kebab stands, so we've added "Big Splurges" to let you know which establishments are worth those extra euros, as well as price ranges to help you quickly determine whether an accommodation or restaurant will break the bank. While we may have diversified, our emphasis will always be on finding the best values for your budget, giving you all the info you need to spend six days in London or six months in Tasmania.

BEYOND THE TOURIST EXPERIENCE

We write for travelers who know there's more to a vacation than riding double-deckers with tourists. Our researchers give you the heads-up on both world-renowned and lesser-known attractions, on the best local eats and the hottest nightclub beats. In our travels, we talk to everybody; we provide a snapshot of real life in the places you visit with our sidebars on topics like regional cuisine, local festivals, and hot political issues. We've opened our pages to respected writers and scholars to show you their take on a given destination, and turned to lifelong residents to learn the little things that make their city worth calling home. And we've even given you Alternatives to Tourism—ideas for how to give back to local communities through responsible travel and volunteering.

OVER FORTY YEARS OF WISDOM

When we started, way back in 1960, Let's Go consisted of a small group of well-traveled friends who compiled their budget travel tips into a 20-page packet for students on charter flights to Europe. Since then, we've expanded to suit all kinds of travelers, now publishing guides to six continents, including our newest guides: *Let's Go: Japan* and *Let's Go: Brazil*. Our guides are still annually researched and written entirely by students on shoe-string budgets, adventurous travelers who know that train strikes, stolen luggage, food poisoning, and marriage proposals are all part of a day's work. Even as you read this, work on next year's editions is well underway. Whether you're reading one of our new titles, like *Let's Go: Puerto Rico* or *Let's Go Adventure Guide: Alaska*, or our original best-seller, *Let's Go: Europe*, you'll find the same spirit of adventure that has made *Let's Go* the guide of choice for travelers the world over since 1960.

GETTING IN TOUCH

The best discoveries are often those you make yourself; on the road, when you find something worth sharing, please drop us a line. We're Let's Go Publications, 67 Mt. Auburn St., Cambridge, MA 02138, USA (feedback@letsgo.com).

For more info, visit our website: www.letsgo.com.

CONTENTS

DISCOVER WESTERN EUROPE 1

ESSENTIALS 11

TRANSPORTATION 38

ALTERNATIVES TO TOURISM 56

ANDORRA 73

AUSTRIA (ÖSTERREICH) 77

BELGIUM (BELGIQUE, BELGIË) 117

BRITAIN 140

IX

SWITZERLAND (SCHWEIZ, SUISSE, SVIZZERA) 962

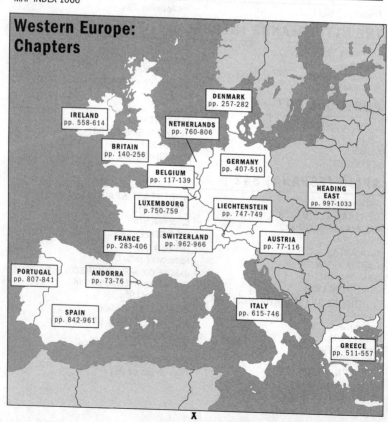

Western Europe:
Chapters

DENMARK
pp. 257-282

IRELAND
pp. 558-614

NETHERLANDS
pp. 760-806

BRITAIN
pp. 140-256

GERMANY
pp. 407-510

BELGIUM
pp. 117-139

HEADING
EAST
pp. 997-1033

LUXEMBOURG
p. 750-759

LIECHTENSTEIN
pp. 747-749

FRANCE
pp. 283-406

SWITZERLAND
pp. 962-966

AUSTRIA
pp. 77-116

PORTUGAL
pp. 807-841

ANDORRA
pp. 73-76

SPAIN
pp. 842-961

ITALY
pp. 615-746

GREECE
pp. 511-557

HOW TO USE THIS BOOK

If you're reading this, you no doubt find yourself about to embark on a grand tour of Western Europe. *Let's Go* is here to lead you to the grandest cathedrals, the cleanest hostels, and the finest €1.75 wines. Things are changing in Western Europe: You can now move from country to country without changing Deutschmarks to lire to francs and you are more likely to find an Internet terminal than a coin-operated pay phone. It's our job to keep up. We understand the time, money, and effort you have spent on this trip and we are here to make it as smooth (and memorable) as possible. So relax! *Let's Go: Western Europe 2004* is on your team and we'll guide you on your travels through the ever-evolving region of Western Europe.

ORGANIZATION. *Let's Go: Western Europe 2004* is arranged to make the information you need easy to find. The **Discover** chapter offers highlights of the regions, tips on when to travel (including a calendar of festivals), and suggested itineraries. The **Essentials** chapter details the nitty gritty of passports, money, communications, and more—everything you'll need to plan your trip and stay safe on the road. The **Transportation** section provides information on traveling to, from, and within Western Europe, while **Alternatives to Tourism** gives advice on how to work or volunteer your way through your journey. Next come the 16 jam-packed **country chapters,** alphabetized from Andorra to Switzerland; each country chapter begins with Life and Times section, detailing history and culture; and essential information pertinent to that country. Don't miss the **Heading East** section, which will lead you on quick jaunts to Prague and Budapest. At the back of the book is a **language appendix** (p. 1034), a crash course in local languages. The black tabs on the side of the book separate the chapters and should help to navigate your way through.

PRICE RANGES AND RANKINGS. We list establishments in order of value from best to worst. Our absolute favorites are denoted by the Let's Go thumbs-up (🎒). Since the best value does not always mean the cheapest price, we have incorporated a system of **price ranges (❶❷❸❹❺)** into our coverage of accommodations and restaurants. At a glance, you can compare the costs of a night's stay in towns a mile apart or halfway across the country. The price ranges for each country can be found in the introductory sections of the country chapters, and for more information about what to expect from each ranking, see p. xxii.

NEW FEATURES. Long-time readers will notice a number of other changes in *Let's Go: Western Europe 2004*, most notably the sidebars that accompany much of our coverage. At the end of the book, you'll find a series of longer **Scholarly Articles** focused on issues affecting Western Europe as a whole. Whether read on a long train ride or a quiet hostel, we hope these articles will entertain as well as inform.

ENJOY YOUR TRIP. Need we say more?

A NOTE TO OUR READERS

The information for this book was gathered by *Let's Go* researchers from May through August of 2003. Each listing is based on one researcher's opinion, formed during his or her visit at a particular time. Those traveling at other times may have different experiences since prices, dates, hours, and conditions are always subject to change. You are urged to check the facts presented in this book beforehand to avoid inconvenience and surprises.

ACKNOWLEDGMENTS

TEAM EUROPE THANKS: Matt Hudson, for being everything good and right in a managing editor—trusting, competent, and supportive to the end. Our mapper Tim, for careful work and a calm presence. Our beloved podmates, Eastern Europe, who preached Cyrillic like a preacher, full of ecstasy and fire. Europe RWs Dave, Defne, and Sloan, for outstanding attitude, excellent research, and valued friendship. Prod for so, so much help. Country guides, whose hard work and dedication made this book possible—and so much better.

TABBY THANKS: Above all my AEs, who made a top-notch team and dear friends: Becca for constant cheerfulness; Chris for smart work; Dave, whose patience is limitless; Emilie, the most can-do person I know; Matt for breaking the tension at all the right moments; and Paul for vegan-tastic chillness and a grounding perspective. Matt Hudson, an outstanding ME and a better friend. Mom, Dad, and Maggie for so much love; all of my friends, who fill my life with happiness.

EMILIE THANKS: Tabby, for her expert navigation and graceful leadership; Becca, Chris, Dave, Matt & Paul, for making me forget I was at work; my RWs, Dave, Defne, and Sloan, for their unfaltering devotion to the books; EEUR, for keeping us sane late at night; my family, for conceiving me in the spirit of travel; and always Dan, who is the sunlight in my growing.

DAVE THANKS: Tabby for dedication and supportive leadership; Chris, Emilie, Paul, Matt L., and Becca for making this a wonderful experience; the EEUR team for help and humor; Betsy and John for friendship and fun times; Mom and Dad for love; and Amy for being a fantastic and fabulous sister.

MATT THANKS: Tabby for commandeering the ship/train; Chris, Emilie, Paul, Becca, and Dave for being good neighbors; Mom, Dad, Adam and Abbie for everything; Christine for countless lunches, Thompson for Euro-advice, Leigh for always keeping in touch, and Ravs for always keeping it real.

PAUL THANKS: Tabby for bumps and sets; the boat crew for blood-curdling monkeys, communal food, and wisdom; Mom and Dad for roadtrips and words, background and foreground; Russ, Seana, and Eric for family matters; Reid, who likes to ride his bicycle; Wendy: Yawp!; and Ruthy, for the spring in my step.

BECCA THANKS: Tabby for amazing dedication; the W/EUR team—Chris, Dave, Emilie, Matt H., Matt L., and Paul—for being fabulous; HPF and my roomies for belly-aching laughs; Jorge for walks; Dan for duets; Mama, Papa, Rafa, Ate Rica & Mike, for patience (Mahal ko kayo!); and George, ever curious, forever listening.

CHRIS THANKS: Tabby for always leading by example; thank you for this incredible opportunity, Becca, Dave, Emilie, Matt, Matt H., and Paul—you made this a great summer; may you never have to format again. Pat, for sanity through it all; Mom and John, for always being there; And Gena, always my silver lining.

TIM THANKS: The Europod for leading me through this continent; Mapland for all of the work you've put into making and editing the maps throughout this guide. And thanks always to April, Tony, Rachel, Mom, and Dad.

RESEARCHER-WRITERS

Sloan Eddleston — *Belgium, Luxembourg, Denmark*

Let's Go's ambassador of good will to Belgium, Luxembourg, and Denmark, Sloan befriended his way across the continent. Always sociable and high-spirited, Sloan's adventures on the road translated into copy that hums with energy and humor. Working tirelessly through the end of his route, Sloan's best work was in Copenhagen, where he expanded coverage and sought the very best the city has to offer.

REGIONAL EDITORS AND RESEARCHER-WRITERS

LET'S GO: AMSTERDAM

Andrew A. M. Crawford	*Editor*
Miranda I. Lash	*Associate Editor*
Irin Carmon	*Researcher-Writer*
John Hulsey	*Researcher-Writer*
Linda Li	*Researcher-Writer*

LET'S GO: AUSTRIA AND SWITZERLAND

Patrick Blanchfield	*Editor*
Chris Townsend	*Associate Editor*
Brent A. Butler	*Researcher-Writer*
Alison Giordano	*Researcher-Writer*
Helen Human	*Researcher-Writer*
Patrick Salisbury	*Researcher-Writer*
Lacey Whitmire	*Researcher-Writer*

LET'S GO: BARCELONA

Stef Levner	*Editor*
Megan Moran-Gates	*Associate Editor*
Scott Michael Coulter	*Researcher-Writer*
Emilie Faure	*Researcher-Writer*
Manuela S. Zoninsein	*Researcher-Writer*

LET'S GO: BRITAIN

Charlotte Douglas	*Editor*
Chloe Schama	*Associate Editor*
Jennifer Cronan	*Researcher-Writer*
Brandon Fail	*Researcher-Writer*
Leslie Jamison	*Researcher-Writer*

Joshua Rosaler	*Researcher-Writer*
Matthew Sussman	*Researcher-Writer*
Thomas Wright	*Researcher-Writer*

LET'S GO: EASTERN EUROPE	*Editor*
Clay H. Kaminsky	*Associate Editor*
Summer Bailey	*Associate Editor*
Lauren Truesdel	*Associate Editor*
Barbara Helen Urbanczyk	*Researcher-Writer*
Natalie Vaz MacLean	*Researcher-Writer*
Lauren Rivera	

LET'S GO: FRANCE	*Editor*
Brianna Cummings	*Associate Editor*
Tim Caito	*Associate Editor*
Emily Porter	*Researcher-Writer*
Gilmara Ayala	*Researcher-Writer*
Marit Dewhurst	*Researcher-Writer*
Robert Hodgson	*Researcher-Writer*
Ian MacKenzie	*Researcher-Writer*
Robin McNamara	*Researcher-Writer*
Priya Mehta	*Researcher-Writer*
Sarah Seltzer	

LET'S GO: GERMANY	*Editor*
Thomas L. Miller	*Associate Editor*
Leigh K. Pascavage	*Researcher-Writer*
Tim Attinucci	*Researcher-Writer*
Emily Carmichael	*Researcher-Writer*
Susanne Chock	*Researcher-Writer*
Makato Kuroda	*Researcher-Writer*
Sergio Rafael Martinez	*Researcher-Writer*
Jim Murrett	*Researcher-Writer*
Gretchen Weingarth	

LET'S GO: GREECE	*Editor*
Joel August Steinhaus	*Associate Editor*
Christina Zaroulis	*Researcher-Writer*
Deirdre Foley-Mendelssohn	*Researcher-Writer*
Alexa H. Hirschfeld	*Researcher-Writer*
Alex Ioannidis	*Researcher-Writer*
Allison Melia	

XV

CONTRIBUTING WRITERS

Derek Glanz *Knockin' on EU's Door (p. 1047)*

Derek Glanz is currently earning a Ph.D. in political science and was an editor for *Let's Go: Spain and Portugal 1998*.

Dr. Brian Palmer & Kathleen Holbrook

Europe in Black and White (p. 1049)

Dr. Brian Palmer lectures on ethnography and ethics, and Kathleen Holbrook researches globalization and human values. They were voted Harvard's best young faculty member and teaching fellow, respectively, for a course which the New York Times nicknamed "Idealism 101."

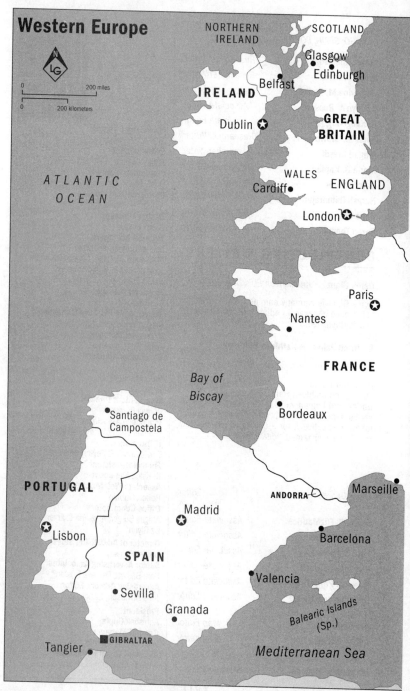

Western Europe

NORTHERN IRELAND

SCOTLAND

Glasgow

Edinburgh

Belfast

IRELAND

GREAT BRITAIN

Dublin

WALES

Cardiff

ENGLAND

ATLANTIC OCEAN

London

Paris

Nantes

FRANCE

Bay of Biscay

Bordeaux

Santiago de Campostela

PORTUGAL

ANDORRA

Marseille

Madrid

Lisbon

Barcelona

SPAIN

Valencia

Sevilla

Granada

Balearic Islands (Sp.)

Tangier

GIBRALTAR

Mediterranean Sea

0   200 miles

0   200 kilometers

Rail prices and times are subject to wide variation, and student or other discounts may be available. This map gives only a general picture of train travel in Europe. Consult *Thomas Cook's European Timetable* for accurate schedule info.

NORTHERN IRELAND

SCOTLAND

Glasgow
$47
3½hr.
Edinburgh

Belfast

$122
5hr.

$22
2½hr.

Dublin

IRELAND

GREAT BRITAIN

ENGLAND

$130
5¾hr.

WALES

Cardiff

London

Amsterdam

$109-149
3hr.

Brussels

$109-149
3hr.

BELGIUM

$68
1¾hr.

$108
7hr.

Paris

$84
4½hr.

Nantes

$78
3¾hr.

$60
3hr.

$78
2¼hr.

Bay of Biscay

$99
10½-14hr.

Lyon

Bordeaux

$48
3hr.

FRANCE

Santiago de Campostela

San Sebastián

$84
7¼hr.

$64
7hr.

$36
2¾hr.

$52
7½hr.

$39
1½hr.

ANDORRA

Marseille

PORTUGAL

Madrid

$56
7hr.

Lisbon

$50
10½hr.

Barcelona

SPAIN

$48-85
1¾hr.

$39
1½hr.

$50
4hr.

Valencia

Palma

Seville

$10-23
1½hr.

Córdoba

Balearic Islands (Sp.)

$23
4½hr.

$27
4½hr.

Granada

Algeciras

GIBRALTAR

Mediterranean Sea

ATLANTIC OCEAN

0   300 miles
0   300 kilometers

XX

Rail Planner

North
Sea

DENMARK

Copenhagen ✪

Baltic
Sea

Hamburg

$79
6hr.

$62
2½hr.

NETHERLANDS ✪

$108
7hr.

Berlin ✪

$46
3hr.

GERMANY

Cologne

$10 ½hr.

$99
4hr.

Bonn

$36 2hr.

Frankfurt

LUXEMBOURG

Prague ✪

**CZECH
REPUBLIC**

$91
3½hr.

$107
8hr.

$59
5¼hr.

$45
5hr.

$37
5hr.

LIECHTENSTEIN

$130
8½hr.

Munich

$66
5hr.

Vienna ✪

Zurich

$66
4¼hr.

Bern ✪

$30
1¼hr.

AUSTRIA

Budapest ✪

SWITZERLAND

Geneva

HUNGARY

Milan

$16
1½hr.

Verona

$27
3hr.

$21
2½hr.

Venice

$24
3hr.

Nice

Florence

MONACO

**SAN
MARINO**

Adriatic Sea

$27
2hr.

ITALY

Corsica
(Fr.)

Rome ✪

$21
2hr.

Sardinia
(It.)

Naples

$21
5hr.

Brindisi

Thessaloniki

$49
6hr.

Aegean
Sea

Tyrrhenian
Sea

$23
2hr.

GREECE

Palermo

$22
3½hr.

Messina

Ionian
Sea

Athens ✪

Sicily

PRICE RANGES >> WESTERN EUROPE

Our researchers list establishments in order of value from best to worst; our favorites are denoted by the *Let's Go* thumbs-up (🖑). Since the best value does not always come at the cheapest price, we have incorporated a system of price ranges to tell you how an establishment compares to others in the same country on a strictly cost-related basis. Our price ranges are based on a rough estimation of what you will pay. For **accommodations,** we base our price range on the cheapest amount a single traveler can spend for a one-night stay. For **restaurants** and other dining establishments, we approximate the average amount that you will pay for a meal in that restaurant. The table below tells you what you will *typically* find in Western Europe at the corresponding price range; keep in mind that a particularly expensive ice cream stand may still only be marked a ❷, depending on what you will spend.

ACCOMMODATIONS	WHAT YOU'RE *LIKELY* TO FIND
❶	Camping; most dorm rooms, such as you'll find in HI or other hostels, or university dorm rooms. Expect bunk beds and a communal bath; you may have to provide or rent towels and sheets.
❷	Upper-end hostels or small hotels. You may have a private bathroom, or there may be a sink in your room and a communal shower in the hall.
❸	A small room with a private bath. Should have decent amenities, such as a phone and TV. Breakfast may be included in the price of the room.
❹	Similar to 3, but may have more amenities or be in a more convenient or touristed area.
❺	Large hotels or upscale chains. If it's a 5 and it doesn't have the perks you want, you've paid too much.

FOOD	WHAT YOU'RE *LIKELY* TO FIND
❶	Mostly street-corner stands, pizza places, or fast-food joints. Rarely ever a sit-down meal.
❷	Sandwiches, appetizers at a bar, or low-priced entrees. You may have the option of sitting down or getting take-out.
❸	Mid-priced entrees, possibly coming with soup or salad. A tip will bump you up a couple dollars, since you'll probably have a waiter or waitress.
❹	A somewhat fancy restaurant or a steakhouse. Either way, you'll have a special knife. Few restaurants in this range have a dress code, but some may look down on t-shirt and jeans.
❺	Upscale restaurant, generally specializing in regional fare, with a decent wine list. Slacks and dress shirts may be expected.

DISCOVER WESTERN EUROPE

The most popular tourist destination in the world, Western Europe offers as many unique journeys as it has travelers to take them. Europe's fame is age-old, and some things never change. Aspiring writers still spin impassioned romances in Parisian alleyways; a cool glass of *sangría* at twilight on the Plaza Mayor tastes as sweet as ever; and iconic treasures, from the leaning tower at Pisa to the behemoth slabs of Stonehenge, inspire wonder in yet another generation. But against this ancient backdrop plays a continent at the beginning of a new act. With the emergence of the European Union, these distinct nations are more intimately connected than ever before.

The proliferation of small, international airlines is setting the stage for a new breed of budget jetsetting, as backpackers trade in their railpasses for standby tickets. While airplanes etch interconnecting patterns across the sky and a common currency passes through hands and across borders below, clusters of Internet cafes weave a virtual web all their own. Western Europe is everything it always has been and much more; and now, it's easier than ever to experience it.

With over 300 pages of new, in-depth coverage of the must-see cities, *Let's Go: Western Europe 2004* will not only take you to the well-photographed classics of European travel, but also the unique bistros and jazz dives that created and sustain the continent's cultural legacy. With these additions, you'll find the tiny beer garden where monks rolling barrels of ale pass in front of Munich's silhouetted cathedral; the eccentric, hole-in-the-wall boutique off a small alleyway in the shadow of Big Ben; and the Greek *taverna* where a glass of ouzo on the patio is accompanied by the perfect vista of the towering Acropolis. Whether your destination is ancient or cutting-edge, monumental or unassuming, world-renowned or nearly undiscovered—we'll take you there. So what are you waiting for? Create your web-based email account, grab your pack, and let's go.

FIGURES AND FACTS

POPULATION: 371,100,000.

LAND MASS: 2.5 million sq. km, almost equal to the Sahara Desert.

HIGHEST POINT: Mont Blanc, France (4807m above sea level).

LOWEST POINTS: Lemmefjord, Denmark and Prins Alexander Polder, The Netherlands (7m below sea level), and MC Solaar.

FACT: Every year the average Western European drinks 82L of beer and 17L of wine and consumes 19kg of cheese.

FACT: If a colony of honeybees has an average wing length of larger than 9.5mm, it is known as a European colony.

FACT: The world's largest pair of jeans (23m long) was created by Lee Jeans Europe and displayed at the Atomium in Brussels, Belgium in 1992.

WHEN TO GO

Traveling during the off season (mid-Sept. to June) brings cheaper airfares and accommodations and frees you from the tourist hordes. The flip side is that many attractions, hostels, and tourist offices close in the winter, and in some rural areas local transportation dwindles to a trickle or shuts down altogether. Most of Western Europe's best festivals also take place during the summer months.

Av. Temp., Precipitation	January			April			July			October		
	°C	°F	in	°C	°F	in	°C	°F	in	°C	°F	in
Amsterdam	3	38	3.1	8	47	1.5	17	62	2.9	11	51	4.1
Athens	10	50	1.9	15	59	0.9	27	81	0.2	19	67	2.1
Berlin	−1	31	1.6	8	46	1.6	18	65	2.0	9	49	1.0
Copenhagen	1	33	1.7	6	43	1.6	17	62	2.6	9	49	2.1
Dublin	6	42	2.5	8	47	1.9	16	60	2.6	11	51	2.9
London	4	39	3.1	8	46	2.1	17	62	1.8	11	51	2.9
Madrid	6	42	1.8	12	53	1.8	24	76	0.4	14	58	1.8
Paris	4	39	0.2	10	50	0.2	19	67	0.2	12	53	0.2
Prague	−2	29	0.8	7	45	1.4	17	63	2.6	8	47	1.2
Rome	8	47	3.2	13	55	2.6	75	75	0.6	18	64	4.5
Vienna	0	32	1.5	9	49	2.0	20	68	2.9	11	51	1.9

WHAT TO DO

Let's be honest—we've never met you, we don't know where we'd take you on our first date, and we certainly don't know what'll make your dream vacation. So we've compiled a few launching pads from which you can start drawing up a custom itinerary: **Themed categories** to let you know where to find your museums, your mountains, your madhouses; **Let's Go Picks** to point you toward some of the quirkiest gems you could uncover; and **suggested itineraries** to outline the common paths across Europe. After getting a general idea of the continent, turn to the country-specific **Discover** sections at the beginning of each chapter for more detailed info.

MUSEUM MANIA

Europe's most precious artifacts reside in her museums; nearly every city houses a sculpture, a painting, or a relic recognized the world over. **London** (p. 151) is packed with artistic gems, not least of which are the imperialist spoils at the British Museum and the striking Tate Modern Gallery. On the other side of the Channel, **Paris** (p. 293) is equally well-stocked—although you could spend half your life at the Louvre, you'd have to take some breaks to visit the Musée d'Orsay, the Musée Rodin, and the endearingly garish Pompidou Centre. For museums designed with as much artistic inspiration as their collections, try Spain's Guggenheim Museum in **Bilbao** (p. 951), and the Dalí Museum in **Figueres** (p. 939). **Madrid** (p. 908) preserves the world's largest collection of paintings in the Prado, while the Reina Sofía shelters Picasso's overpowering *Guernica*.

Florence (p. 710) was the home of the Renaissance and still retains many of its masterworks in the Uffizi and the Accademia. The Vatican Museum in **Rome** (p. 626) houses the Sistine Chapel and other priceless works. Celebrate Germany's

---

■ LET'S GO PICKS: NOT YOUR MIDDLE SCHOOL FIELDTRIP

HEY NOW, YOU'RE A ROCKSTAR: Experience sex, drugs, and rock 'n' roll at Copenhagen's **Museum Erotica** (p. 268), Liverpool's **The Beatles Story** (p. 221), and Amsterdam's **Cannabis College** (p. 785).

CRIME AND PUNISHMENT: First hit Rome's **Museo Criminologico** (p. 654), which displays the tools of Italy's terrorists, spies, and druggies; then head to the **Museo Della Tortura** (p. 727) in San Gimignano, Italy, for a lesson in Medieval torture devices.

MOST MEMORABLE (UNTIL THE MORNING): Learn as you drink at Dublin's **Guinness Brewery** (p. 576) and Amsterdam's **Heineken Experience** (p. 784).

---

reunification at the East Side Gallery in **Berlin** (p. 418), built around the longest remaining stretch of the Wall. **Munich** (p. 492) boasts the technological Deutsches Museum and the twin Pinakotheks; if those don't raise your spirits, try **Hamburg**'s Erotic Art Museum (p. 460). The biggest sin you could commit in **Amsterdam** (p. 767) would be to overlook the Rijksmuseum and the van Gogh Museum. **Budapest**'s Museum of Fine Arts houses little-seen but nonetheless spectacular works by Raphael, Rembrandt, and the rest of the usual suspects (p. 1013).

RUINS AND RELICS

For those who prefer to meet history outside of a museum case, Europe's castles, churches, and ruins are a dream come true. In **London** (p. 151), royals wander around Buckingham Palace, while choirboys croon at Westminster Abbey. Venture away from the city to ponder the mysteries of **Stonehenge** (p. 198). Nobody could miss **Paris**'s (p. 293) breathtaking Cathédrale de Notre-Dame. Elsewhere in France, the *châteaux* of the **Loire Valley** (p. 341) and Normandy's fortified abbey of **Mont-St-Michel** (p. 336) are must-sees, as is the fortress of **Carcassonne** (p. 354). Manmade treasures are strewn throughout Spain, including the largest Gothic cathedral in the world in **Seville** (p. 892) and the luxurious Palacio Real in **Madrid** (p. 854). **Barcelona** (p. 916) sports fanciful Modernism, headlined by Antoni Gaudí's La Sagrada Família and Park Gaudí. Muslim-infused Andalucía offers the mosque in **Córdoba** (p. 887) and the Alhambra in **Granada** (p. 906).

Germany's marvels include the cathedral at **Cologne** (p. 472) and the pure gold tea house at **Potsdam**'s breathtaking Schloß Sans Souci (p. 447). Go crazy in Mad King Ludwig's castles (p. 510). In **Denmark,** (p. 275) an optical illusion makes Egeskov Slot seem to float on water. **Rome** (p. 626) practically invented architecture, beginning with the Pantheon, Colosseum, and Forum. In Greece, the crumbling Acropolis—the foundation of Western civilization—towers above **Athens** (p. 519).

■ LET'S GO PICKS: PEOPLE MAKE THE DARNDEST THINGS

REALLY, REALLY, RIDICULOUSLY NOT NEW: Ireland's **Newgrange** tomb, and the bones inside it, have been around since the 4th millennium BC (p. 575).

MOST LIKELY TO BE GONE 'TIL NOVEMBER: Sweden's **IceHotel** melts away each April, only to be built anew by the craftiest team of ice sculptors in the world.

BEST WAY TO JUST EAT IT: Head to the Szabó Marzipan **Museum and Confectionary** in Budapest, where it don't matter if you're black or a **white chocolate statue of Michael Jackson** (p. 541).

BADDEST TO THE BONE: See what remains of Évora's **Capela dos Ossos** (Chapel of Bones), built by Franciscan monks from the bones of 5000 people.

THE GREAT OUTDOORS

You've seen the Eiffel Tower. You've been to the British Museum. Now it's time to heed the call of the wild. Britain brims with national parks; our favorite is the **Lake District** (p. 228). For jagged peaks and crashing waves, head north to Scotland; the **Outer Hebrides** (p. 219) are particularly breathtaking. Ireland's **Ring of Kerry** (p. 591) is home to secluded Irish villages, and **Killarney National Park** (p. 590) features spectacular mountains. The majestic Pyrenees are the setting for Spain's **Parque Nacional de Ordesa** (p. 941). **Grenoble** (p. 384), in the French Alps, brims with hiking opportunities and tempts skiers with some of the world's steepest slopes. North of Sicily, the **Aeolian Islands** (**p. 744**) boast pristine beaches, dramatic volcanoes, and bubbling thermal springs. **Kitzbühel** (**p. 114**), in Austria, provides the challenges of world-class hiking and skiing. For fresh Swiss Alpine air, conquer the **Matterhorn** (p. 986) or take up adventure sports in **Interlaken** (p. 984). Hike through Germany's eerie **Black Forest** (p. 490), which inspired the Brothers Grimm.

▓ LET'S GO PICKS: LIVING ON THE EDGE

BEST WAYS TO HANG OUT: Cliff-diving is so much more fun when you're naked, according to Corfu's **Pink Palace** (p. 546).

SO HOT RIGHT NOW. If you can't take the heat, then don't tour the active volcano on the Italian island of **Stromboli** (p. 745).

THE FAST AND THE FURIOUS: Get your heart rate up fleeing the angry *toros* during the festival of **San Fermines** (Running of the Bulls; p. 944) in Pamplona.

BEST PLACE TO GO TO EXTREMES. Try sky diving, paragliding, canyoning, river rafting, or bungee jumping in **Interlaken,** Switzerland (p. 984).

BACKPACKERS GONE WILD

When the museums close and the sun sets over the mountains, Europe's wildest parties are just beginning. **Edinburgh** (p. 238) has the highest concentration of pubs in Europe. When you're all crawled out, join the students of **Oxford** (p. 202) for a night of punting. Or, try sipping a strawberry daiquiri in Portugal's **Lagos** (p. 835), or along Spain's **Costa del Sol,** where hip clubs line the beaches of **Marbella** (p. 905). Don't miss the **Balearic Islands**—some clubs on **Ibiza** (p. 957) open at 8am. For the true Spanish experience, join *la Movida* in **Madrid** (p. 854) or try getting into the chic clubs of **Barcelona** (p. 916). Afterward, flaunt your way to the one and only **French Riviera** (p. 366), then let dynamic **Milan** (p. 662) introduce you to Italian style. Head to the Greek islands for the beautiful beaches of **Corfu** (p. 546) and for **Ios** (p. 550), a frat party run amok. **Prague** (p. 998) and **Munich** (p. 492) know that discriminating drinkers don't need a beach to get sloshed, and **Amsterdam** (p. 767)... trust us, it knows everything it needs—and more than you want—to know.

▓ LET'S GO PICKS: BACKPACKERS GONE WILD II

BREAKFAST OF CHAMPIONS: The ravers at **Space** (p. 957) in Ibiza, Spain, begin at 8am and don't stop until 5am the next morning.

EU COME HERE OFTEN? In **Brussels,** Belgium, official seat of the European Parliament, a different country throws an international bash each week.

SHORTEST DISTANCE BETWEEN KEG AND BED: The bungalow city of **Na Vlachovce** in Prague (p. 998), combines the best of two worlds, offering cozy bedding in romantic two-person *Budvar* barrels.

FÊTES! FESTAS! FESTIVALS!

COUNTRIES	APR. – JUNE	JULY – AUG.	SEPT. – MAR.
AUSTRIA AND SWITZERLAND	**Vienna Festival** (mid-May to mid-June)	**Salzburger Festspiele** (late July to late Aug.) **Open-Air St. Gallen** (late June)	**Fasnacht** (Basel; Mar. 1-3) **Escalade** (Geneva; early Dec.)
BELGIUM	**Festival of Fairground Arts** (Wallonie; late May)	**International Bathtub Regatta** (Dinant; mid-Aug.)	**Gentse Feesten** (10 Days Off; Ghent; late July)
BRITAIN AND IRELAND	**Bloomsday** (Dublin; June 16) **Wimbledon** (London; late June)	**Edinburgh Int'l Festival** (Aug.15-Sept. 4) **Fringe Festival** (Aug. 3-25)	**Matchmaking Festival** (Lisdoonvarna; Sept.) **St. Patrick's Day** (Mar. 13)
DENMARK	**Roskilde Music Festival** (late June)	**Copenhagen Jazz Festival** (early July)	**Fastelavn (Carneval)** (Feb.-Mar.)
FRANCE	**Cannes Film Festival** (May)	**Festival d'Avignon** (July-Aug.) **Bastille Day** (July 14) **Tour de France** (July)	**Carnevale** (Nice, Nantes; Feb.)
GERMANY	**May Day** (Berlin; May 1) **Christopher St. Day** (late June)	**Love Parade** (Berlin; mid-July) **Rhine in Flames Festival** (Rhine Valley; Aug. 9)	**Fasching** (Munich; Jan. 7-Feb. 4) **Oktoberfest** (Munich; Sept. 18-Oct. 3)
GREECE	**St. George's Day** (Apr. 23)	**Feast of the Assumption of the Virgin Mary** (Aug. 15)	**Carnival** (early Feb.) **Feast of St. Demetrius** (Oct. 26)
ITALY	**Maggio Musicale** (Florence; late Apr. to mid-June) **Scoppio del Carro** (Florence; Easter Su)	**Il Palio** (Siena; July 2 and Aug. 16) **Umbria Jazz Festival** (July)	**Carnevale** (late Feb.) **Festa di San Gennaro** (Naples; Dec. 16, Sept. 19, May 7) **Dante Festival** (Ravenna; mid-Sept.)
THE NETHERLANDS	**Queen's Day** (Apr. 30) **Holland Festival** (June)	**Gay Pride Parade** (Aug.)	**Flower Parade** (Aalsmeer; Sept.) **Cannabis Cup** (Nov.)
PORTUGAL	**Burning of the Ribbons** (Coimbra; early May)	**Feira Internacional de Lisboa** (June) **Feira Popular** (mid-July)	**Carnival** (Mar. 4) **Semana Santa** (Apr. 4-11)
SPAIN	**Feria de Abril** (Sevilla; late Apr.)	**San Fermines** (Pamplona; July 6-14)	**Semana Santa** (Apr. 4-11) **Las Fallas** (Valencia; Mar.) **Carnaval** (Mar.)

DISCOVER

DISCOVER

SUGGESTED ITINERARIES

There is no formula for the perfect itinerary in Western Europe. Here we humbly suggest a few routes—just to give you an idea of what is possible. **The Basics** below outlines our skeletal suggestions for the best of Europe. We've also included some regional itineraries to help you plan a few extra forays. These other itineraries can be thought of as **Building Blocks** to tack onto a basic route. For more in-depth suggestions, see the **Suggested Itineraries** sections in individual country chapters.

THE BASICS

THE GRAND TOUR: BEST OF WESTERN EUROPE IN 1 MONTH

Start out in **London,** spinning from theaters to museums to pubs (4 days, p. 151). Chunnel to the world-class galleries and chic shops of **Paris** (4 days, p. 293), and slip south to daring and colorful **Barcelona** (2 days, p. 916). Return to France for an all-night party in **Nice** (1 day, p. 369); recover in the blissful **Cinque Terre** on the Italian Riviera (1 day, p. 678). Prop up the leaning tower of **Pisa** (1 day, p. 727), be enchanted by Renaissance art in **Florence** (2 days, p. 710), and don your toga in **Rome** (3 days, p. 626). Float down the canals of **Venice** by gondola (2 days, p. 686) on your way to the opera in **Vienna** (2 days, p. 84). Sip absinthe in starlet **Prague** (2 days, p. 998) and sample the frothy brew in **Munich** (2 days, p. 492) before heading up to funky **Berlin** (2 days, p. 418). Indulge in **Amsterdam** (2 days, p. 767), and then relax with a day in the EU capital, **Brussels** (p. 122).

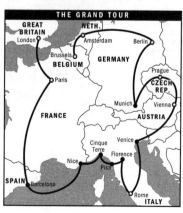

THE GRAND TOUR

GREAT BRITAIN
London
NETH.
Amsterdam
Berlin
Brussels
BELGIUM
GERMANY
Paris
Prague
CZECH REP.
Munich
Vienna
FRANCE
AUSTRIA
Cinque Terre
Venice
Florence
Nice
Pisa
SPAIN
Barcelona
Rome
ITALY

THE BEST OF WESTERN EUROPE IN 9 WEEKS

From **London** (4 days, p. 151), meander the halls of **Cambridge** (1 day, p. 211) or **Oxford** (1 day, p. 202), then catch a play in Shakespeare's **Stratford-Upon-Avon** (1 day, p. 208), before heading to **Dublin,** home to Joyce and Guinness (2 days, p. 568). Chunnel from London to **Paris** (4 days, p. 293) and then gape at **Versailles** (1 day, p. 332). From the castle-dotted **Loire Valley** (1 day, p. 334), go test your taste buds in the vineyards of **Bordeaux** (1 day, p. 347). Proceed to the Iberian peninsula to rage in the clubs of **Madrid** (2 days, p. 854), and bask on the beaches of **Lisbon** (2 days, p. 814). After heading back east to **Barcelona** (3 days, p. 916), spend a day each in festive **Avignon** (p. 356), **Aix-en-Provence** (p. 359), and **Nice** (p. 369). Next replenish in the **Cinque Terre** (2 days, p. 678), send postcards from **Pisa** (1 day, p. 727), and continue on to **Florence** (2 days, p. 710). Stop at the stunning *duomo* in **Siena** (1 day, p. 725) en route to **Rome** (3 days, p. 626). Glide through **Venice** (2 days, p. 686) on your way to posh **Milan** (1 day, p. 662). Grapple the Matterhorn from **Zermatt** (1 day, p. 986), and conquer the Swiss Alps around **Interlaken** (1 day, p. 984). Be a diplomat for a day in **Geneva** (1 day, p. 987), and stock up on chocolate in **Zurich** (1 day, p. 974). Satiate your urge for *The Sound of Music* in **Salzburg** (1 day, p. 101) and waltz your way through **Vienna** (2 days, p. 84), then kick back for 2 days in either the baths of **Budapest** (p. 1013) or the bars of **Prague** (p. 998). From **Munich,** take a sobering daytrip to **Dachau** (3 days, p. 492). Move up the pastoral **Romantic Road** (2 days, p. 508), then cruise down

THE BEST OF WESTERN EUROPE IN 9 WEEKS

the spectacular **Rhine River** (1 day, p. 484). From **Berlin** (2 days, p. 418) and reckless **Hamburg** (1 day, p. 460), head north to cosmopolitan **Copenhagen** (2 days, p. 262) and continue on to **Amsterdam** (3 days, p. 767). Spend a day each in **Brussels** (p. 122) and **Bruges** (p. 130) before heading home.

BUILDING BLOCKS

THE BEST OF THE MEDITERRANEAN IN 6 WEEKS
Begin in the flower-filled *terrazas* of **Seville** (2 days, p. 892) before basking on the soft-sand beaches of **Cádiz** (2 days, p. 902). Stand on the imposing Rock of **Gibraltar** (1 day, p. 903) en route to partying with the beautiful people in the Costa del Sol resort town of **Marbella** (1 day, p. 905). Skip inland to **Granada** (2 days, p. 906), and wind your way through Moorish fortresses. From **Valencia** (2 days, p. 913), hop around the **Balearic Islands** between **Ibiza**'s foam parties and **Menorca**'s raw beaches (3 days, p. 957). Ferry to vibrant **Barcelona** (3 days, p. 916), before hitting the **Costa Brava** and the Dalí museum in **Figueres** (2 days, p. 939). Head to France's *provençal* **Nîmes** (1 day, p. 355) and follow van Gogh's traces through **Arles** (1 day, p. 358). More fun awaits in **Avignon** (1 day, p. 356), before you revel in **Aix-en-Provence** (1 day, p. 359). Taste the *bouillabaisse* in **Marseilles** (1 day, p. 359), and move on to all that glitters on the Côte d'Azur: **Cannes** (2 days, p. 367) is the star-studded diamond, and **Nice** (2 days, p. 369) is the party haven.

Explore the gorgeous clifftop villages of the **Corniches** (1 day, p. 378) before hitting the world-famous casinos of **Monte-Carlo** (1 day, p. 378). Take a breather by relaxing in the placid waters of **Finale Ligure** (1 day, p. 676) and hiking through the colorful villages of Italy's **Cinque Terre** (1 day, p. 678). Admire the architecture of **Genoa** (1 day, p. 674) before oohing and aahing over **Florence**'s magnificent art collection (3 days, p. 710). Check out the two-toned *duomo* of **Siena** (2 days, p. 725) and indulge your gladiatorial fantasies in capital city **Rome** (4 days, p. 626).

THE BEST OF SOUTHERN ITALY AND GREECE IN 4 WEEKS

View the rubble of the toga-clad empire, the cathedrals of high Christianity, and the art of the Renaissance in **Rome** (5 days, p. 626). From **Naples** (2 days,

p. 731), home to the world's best pizza and pickpockets, daytrip to **Pompeii** (1 day, p. 738) and check out lifelike Roman remains buried in AD 79. Then escape to the sensuous paradise of **Capri** (2 days, p. 741). Hop off the boot Brindisi, from which overnight ferries go to Greece (1 day). Get off at **Corfu** (1 day, p. 546), beloved by literary luminary Oscar Wilde and partiers alike, or continue on to **Patras** (1 day, p. 536). Wrestle in **Olympia** (1 day, p. 536) before beginning your Peloponnesian adventure with a survey of the ancient ruins in **Napflion, Mycenae,** and **Epidavros** (3 days, p. 539). Get initiated in the "mysteries of love" in equally ruinous **Corinth** (1 day, p. 540). On to chaotic **Athens**, a jumble of things ancient and modern (2 days, p. 519). Succumb to your longing in the Cyclades: party all night long on **Mykonos** (1 day, p. 548) and repent the morning after at the Tem-

ple of Apollo in **Delos** (1 day, p. 549), before continuing on to the earthly paradise of **Santorini** (2 days, p. 551). Catch the ferry to **Crete,** where chic **Iraklion** and **Knossos,** home to the Minotaur, await (2 days, p. 552). Base yourself in **Rethymno** or **Hania** and hike the **Samaria Gorge** (2 days, p. 553).

THE BEST OF BRITAIN AND IRELAND IN 3 WEEKS
From **London** (4 days, p. 151), get studious in **Cambridge** (1 day, p. 211) and **Oxford** (1 day, p. 202), then take to the **Cotswolds** (1 day, p. 210). Love all things Shakespeare in **Stratford-Upon-Avon** (1 day, p. 208), and move on to party in **Manchester** (1 day, p. 216). Trip down Penny Lane in **Liverpool** (1 day, p. 220), home of the Beatles. Cross the Irish Sea to **Dublin** (3 days, p. 568), the latest international favorite, and daytrip to the **Wicklow Mountains** (1 day, p. 581). Run the **Ring of Kerry** (2 days, p. 591) circuit before listening to *craic* in **Galway** (2 days, p. 596), the culture capital. Take in the murals at **Belfast** (2 days, p. 604) and from there it's back across the Irish Sea to **Stranraer,** energetic **Glasgow** (1 day, p. 248), and nearby **Loch Lomond.** Then jump over to historic and exuberant **Edinburgh** (3 days, p. 238). The **Lake District** (2 days, p. 228) offers scenic diversions, and historic **York** (1 day, p. 223) completes the journey. Return to London to kick back with a West End play and a glass of Tetley's bitter.

THE BEST OF SPAIN AND PORTUGAL IN 5 WEEKS
Hop off the Paris-Madrid train at gorgeous **San Sebastián** (2 days, p. 946), and check out the new Guggenheim in **Bilbao** (1 day, p. 951) before heading to **Madrid** for urban fun (4 days, p. 854). Daytrip to the austere palace of **El Escorial** (1 day, p. 873) and the medieval streets of **Toledo** (1 day, p. 874). Visit the university town of **Salamanca** (1 day, p. 881) and then cross the border into Portugal, heading up to the unpretentious **Porto** (2 days, 838). Marvel at the painted tiles in **Lisbon** (3 days, p. 814) with a daytrip to the town of **Sintra** (1 day, p. 828). Bake in the sun along the Algarve in **Lagos** (3 days, p. 831), where hordes of visitors dance the night away. Sleep off your hangover on the 7hr. express bus from Lagos to **Seville** (2 days, p. 892) and prepare for a romantic stroll along the Guadalquivir River. Delve deeper into Arab-influenced Andalucía—don't miss the Mezquita in **Córdoba** (2 days, p. 887) and the Alhambra in **Granada** (2 days, p. 906). From Granada head up the Mediterranean Coast to stop in **Valencia** (1 day, p. 913) for the *paella* and oranges. Move on to northeastern Spain and hit sunny **Costa Brava** (2 days, p. 939), artsy **Figueres** (1 day, p. 939), and medieval **Girona** (1 day, p. 940). Finish up your journey in colorful **Barcelona** (4 days, p. 916).

THE BEST OF FRANCE IN 3 WEEKS
You'll need at least five days to see the sights and shops of **Paris** (p. 293)—then spend another day in **Versailles** (p. 332). Then travel to **Tours** (2 days, p. 343) in the Loire Valley to explore beautiful châteaux. For a change of pace, visit the 17,000-year-old cave paintings of **Les-Eyzies-de-**

THE BEST OF BRITAIN AND IRELAND

THE BEST OF SPAIN AND PORTUGAL

Tayac (1 day, p. 346) and stroll through the golden streets of **Sarlat** (1 day, p. 346). Sniff, swirl, and spit in **Bordeaux** (2 days, p. 347) before following the pilgrims to miraculous **Lourdes** (1 day, p. 351). Zip southward for some Franco-Spanish flavor in **Toulouse** (1 day, p. 352). Head east to reach the magnificent Roman ruins of **Nîmes** (1 day, p. 355), the birthplace of denim. The stunning Gothic fortifications of the Palais des Papes cast shadows over festive **Avignon** (1 day, p. 356). Students have been partying in elegant **Aix-en-Provence** (1 day, p. 359) for 600 years, but for non-stop action go to **Nice** (3 days, p. 369), undisputed capital of the Riviera. For a change of scenery, climb into the Alps to reach dynamic **Grenoble** (2 days, p. 384). **Strasbourg** (1 day, p. 397) offers a pleasant blend of French and German culture. Finish off in style with a tasting at one of the many champagne *caves* in **Reims** (1 day, p. 403).

THE BEST OF GERMANY, AUSTRIA, AND SWITZERLAND IN 5 WEEKS

Spend five days raging in **Berlin**'s chaotic nightclubs and recovering in the capital's museums and cafes (4 days, p. 418). Move north, where **Hamburg** fuses port town burliness with cosmopolitan flair (2 days, p. 460), before admiring Germany's greatest cathedral in **Cologne** (1 day, p. 472). Meander through **Bonn** (1 day, p. 477) and explore Germany's oldest university in **Heidelburg** (1 day, p. 486). Drool over Porsches and Mercedes-Benzes in ultramodern **Stuttgart** (1 day, p. 490), then relive your favorite Grimms' fairy tales in the **Black Forest** (1 day, p. 490). Cross into Switzerland and enjoy medieval sights in **Basel** (1 day, p. 971) before stopping for pastries in **Neuchâtel** (1 day, p. 995). Play world leader in **Geneva** (2 days, p. 987), shimmy over to capital city **Bern** (1 day, p. 968), and listen to jazz in **Montreaux** (1 day, p. 994). Ogle the Matterhorn from **Zermatt** (1 day, p. 986), and explore the Alps from **Interlaken** (2 days, p. 984). Take a train to the fairytale hamlet of **Lucerne** (1 day, p. 973) before tasting the nightlife in **Zurich** (1 day, p. 974). Skip over to Austria for skiing in **Innsbruck** (1 day, p. 110). Follow Mozart's footsteps in **Salzburg** (2 days, p. 101), then take in the enormous charm of **Vienna** (3 days, p. 84). Head back into Germany to **Munich** (1 day, p. 492) for boisterous beer halls and a day-trip to mad King Ludwig's Castles (1 day, p. 503). Admire the scenery along the **Romantic Road** (2 days, p. 508), but save the last dance for **Dresden** (1 day, p. 448).

THE BEST OF FRANCE

THE BEST OF GERMANY, AUSTRIA, AND SWITZERLAND

ESSENTIALS

ENTRANCE REQUIREMENTS.

Passport (p. 11): Almost always required to visit a Western European country.

Visa (p. 12): Typically, Western European countries require visas for citizens of South Africa, but not for citizens of Australia, Canada, Ireland, New Zealand, the UK, or the US (for stays shorter than 90 days).

Immunizations (p. 20): Travelers to Western Europe should be up to date on vaccines for measles, mumps, rubella, diphtheria, tetanus, pertussis, polio, haemophilus influenza B, hepatitis A, and hepatitis B.

Work Permit (p. 12): Required for all foreigners planning to work in Western Europe, except for citizens of countries in the EU.

Driving Permit (p. 59): Drivers in Western Europe need an International Driving Permit.

DOCUMENTS AND FORMALITIES

Information on European **consular services** at home, foreign consular services in Europe, and specific entry requirements is located in individual country chapters; it can also be found at at www.towd.com or www.embassyworld.com.

PASSPORTS

REQUIREMENTS. Citizens of Australia, Canada, Ireland, New Zealand, South Africa, the UK, and the US need valid passports to enter Western European countries and to reenter their own country. Most countries do not allow entrance if the holder's passport expires in under six months. Returning home with an expired passport is illegal and may result in a fine.

ONE EUROPE. The idea of European unity has come a long way since 1958, when the European Economic Community (EEC) was created in order to promote solidarity and cooperation. Since then, the EEC has become the European Union (EU), with political, legal, and economic institutions spanning 15 member states: Austria, Belgium, Denmark, Finland, France, Germany, Greece, Ireland, Italy, Luxembourg, The Netherlands, Portugal, Spain, Sweden, and the UK. In 1999, the EU established **freedom of movement** across 15 European countries—the entire EU minus Ireland and the UK, but plus Iceland and Norway. This means that border controls between participating countries have been abolished and visa policies harmonized. While you're still required to carry a passport (or government-issued ID card for EU citizens) when crossing an internal border, once you've been admitted into one country, you're free to travel to all participating states. Britain and Ireland have also formed a **common travel area,** abolishing passport controls between the UK and the Republic of Ireland. This means that the only time you'll see a border guard within the EU is while traveling between the British Isles and the Continent.

NEW PASSPORTS. Citizens of Australia, Canada, Ireland, New Zealand, the UK, and the US can apply for a passport at most post offices, passport offices, or courts of law. Citizens of South Africa can apply for a passport at any Home Affairs office. Any new passport or renewal application must be filed well in advance of the departure date, although most passport offices offer rush services for a very steep fee.

PASSPORT MAINTENANCE. Be sure to photocopy the page of your passport with your photo, as well as any other important documents. Carry one set of copies in a safe place, apart from the originals, and leave another set at home. Consulates also recommend that you carry an expired passport or an official copy of your birth certificate in a part of your baggage separate from other documents.

If you lose your passport, immediately notify the local police and the nearest embassy or consulate of your home government. To expedite its replacement, you will need to know all information previously recorded and show ID and proof of citizenship. In some cases, a replacement may take weeks to process, and it may be valid only for a limited time. Any visas stamped in your old passport will be irretrievably lost. In an emergency, ask for immediate temporary traveling papers that will permit you to reenter your home country. More detailed info regarding lost and stolen passports is available at www.usembassy.it/cons/acs/passport-lost.htm.

VISAS

Some countries require a visa—a stamp, sticker, or insert in your passport specifying the purpose of your travel and the permitted duration of your stay—in addition to a valid passport for entrance. Most standard visas cost US$10-70, are valid for one to three months, and must be validated within six months to one year from the date of issue. Almost none of the countries covered by *Let's Go: Western Europe* require visas for citizens of Australia, Canada, Ireland, New Zealand, the UK, or the US for stays shorter than three months; the exception is Australians and Canadians traveling to Prague or Budapest. All European countries, except for Ireland, Switzerland, and the UK, require visas for South African citizens. Travelers to Andorra should contact a French or Spanish embassy for more info, while those going to Liechtenstein should contact a Swiss embassy. Check with the nearest embassy or consulate of your desired destination for up-to-date info. US citizens can consult www.travel.state.gov/foreignentryreqs.html or contact the **Center for International Business and Travel** (**CIBT;** US ☎800-925-2428; www.cibt.com), which secures visas for travel to almost all countries for a service charge. The visa requirements above only apply to stays shorter than three months. If you plan to stay longer than 90 days, or if you plan to work or study abroad, your requirements will be different.

IDENTIFICATION

When you travel, always carry two or more forms of identification on your person, including at least one photo ID; a passport combined with a driver's license or birth certificate is usually adequate. Never carry all your forms of ID together; split them up in case of theft or loss, and keep photocopies in your luggage and at home.

TEACHER, STUDENT, AND YOUTH IDENTIFICATION. The **International Student Identity Card (ISIC),** the most widely accepted form of student ID, provides discounts on some sights, accommodations, and transport; access to a 24hr. emergency helpline (in North America call ☎877-370-4742; elsewhere call US collect ☎+1 715-345-0505); and insurance benefits for US cardholders (see **Insurance,** p. 21). Applicants must be degree-seeking students of a secondary or post-secondary school and must be at least 12 years old. Because of the proliferation of fake ISICs, some services (particularly airlines) require additional proof of student identity.

The **International Teacher Identity Card (ITIC)** offers teachers the same insurance coverage as well as similar but limited discounts. For travelers who are 25 years old or under but are not students, the **International Youth Travel Card (IYTC)** also offers many of the same benefits as the ISIC. Similarly, the **International Student Exchange ID Card (ISE)** provides discounts, medical benefits, and the ability to purchase student airfares.

Each of these identity cards costs US$22 or equivalent. ISIC and ITIC cards are valid for roughly one and a half academic years; IYTC cards are valid for one year from the date of issue. Many student travel agencies (p. 43) issue the cards; for a list of issuing agencies, or for more info, contact the **International Student Travel Confederation (ISTC)**, Herengracht 479, 1017 BS Amsterdam, The Netherlands (☎ +31 20 421 28 00; www.istc.org).

CUSTOMS

Upon entering a country, you must declare certain items from abroad and pay a duty on the value of those articles if they exceed the allowance established by that country's customs service. Note that goods and gifts purchased at duty-free shops abroad are not exempt from duty or sales tax; "duty-free" merely means that you need not pay a tax in the country of purchase. Duty-free allowances were abolished for travel between EU member states on June 30, 1999, but still exist for those arriving from outside the EU. Upon returning home, you must declare all articles acquired abroad and pay a duty on the value of articles in excess of your home country's allowance. In order to expedite your return, make a list of any valuables brought from home and register them with customs before traveling, and be sure to keep receipts for all goods acquired while abroad.

CUSTOMS IN THE EU. Travelers in the countries that are members of the EU (Austria, Belgium, Denmark, Finland, France, Germany, Greece, Ireland, Italy, Luxembourg, The Netherlands, Portugal, Spain, Sweden, and the UK) are afforded freedom of movement for themselves—and their goods. This means that there are no customs controls at internal EU borders (i.e., you can take the blue customs channel at the airport), and travelers are free to transport whatever legal substances they like as long as it is for their own personal (non-commercial) use—up to 800 cigarettes, 10L of spirits, 90L of wine (60L of sparkling wine), and 110L of beer. You should also be aware that duty-free allowances were abolished on June 30, 1999 for travel between EU member states; however, travelers between the EU and the rest of the world still get a duty-free allowance when passing through customs.

MONEY

CURRENCY AND EXCHANGE

As a general rule, it's cheaper to convert money in Western Europe than at home. However, you should bring enough foreign currency for the first few days of a trip to avoid being cashless if you arrive after bank hours or on a holiday.

When changing money abroad, try to go only to banks or change bureaus that have at most a 5% margin between their buy and sell prices. Since you lose money with every transaction, convert large sums (unless the currency is depreciating rapidly), but no more than you'll need. Use **ATM, debit,** or **credit cards** for the lowest exchange rates.

THE EURO. The official currency of 12 members of the EU—Austria, Belgium, Finland, France, Germany, Greece, Ireland, Italy, Luxembourg, The Netherlands, Portugal, and Spain—is now the euro. The currency has some important—and positive—consequences for travelers hitting more than one euro-zone country. First, money-changers across the euro-zone are obliged to exchange money at the official, fixed rate, and at no commission (though they may still charge a small service fee). Second, euro-denominated traveler's checks allow you to pay for goods and services across the euro-zone, again at the official rate and commission-free. At the time of printing, **€1=US$1.093=CAD$1.513=AUS$1.707= NZ$1.911=ZAR7.992.** For more info, check a currency converter site such as www.xe.com or www.europa.eu.int.

If you use traveler's checks or bills, carry some in small denominations (the equivalent of US$50 or less) for times when you are forced to exchange money at disadvantageous rates, but bring a range of denominations since charges may be levied per check cashed. Store your money in a variety of forms; ideally, at any given time you will be carrying some cash, some traveler's checks, and an ATM and/or credit card. All travelers should also consider carrying some US dollars (about US$50 worth), which are often preferred by local tellers.

For more info on currency and exchange rates, see individual country chapters.

CREDIT, DEBIT, AND ATM CARDS

Where they are accepted, credit cards often offer superior exchange rates—up to 5% better than the retail rate used by banks and other currency exchange establishments. Credit cards may also offer services such as insurance or emergency help, and are sometimes required to reserve hotel rooms or rental cars. **MasterCard** (a.k.a. EuroCard or Access in Europe) and **Visa** (a.k.a. Carte Bleue or Barclaycard) are widely-accepted; **American Express** cards work at some ATMs and at AmEx offices and major airports.

Automatic Teller Machine (ATM) cards are commonplace in Western Europe. Depending on the system that your home bank uses, you can most likely access your personal bank account from abroad. ATMs get the same wholesale exchange rate as credit cards, but there is often a limit on the amount of money you can withdraw per day (around US$500), and unfortunately computer networks sometimes fail. There is typically also a surcharge of US$1-5 per withdrawal.

Debit cards are as convenient as credit cards but have a more immediate impact on your funds. A debit card can be used wherever its associated credit card company (usually MasterCard or Visa) is accepted, yet the money is withdrawn directly from the holder's checking account. Debit cards often also function as ATM cards and can be used to withdraw cash from associated banks and ATMs throughout Europe. Ask your local bank about obtaining one.

The two major international money networks are **Cirrus** (to locate ATMs US ☎ 800-424-7787 or www.mastercard.com) and **Visa/PLUS** (to locate ATMs US ☎ 800-843-7587 or www.visa.com). Most ATMs charge a transaction fee that is paid to the bank that owns the ATM.

TRAVELER'S CHECKS

Traveler's checks are a relatively safe and convenient means of carrying funds. American Express and Visa are the most widely recognized brands. Many banks and agencies sell them for a small commission. Check issuers provide refunds if

PIN NUMBERS AND ATMS. To use a cash or credit card to withdraw money from a cash machine (ATM) in Western Europe, you must have a four-digit Personal Identification Number (PIN). If your PIN is longer than four digits, ask your bank whether you can just use the first four, or whether you'll need a new one. Credit cards don't usually come with PINs, so if you intend to hit up ATMs in Europe with a credit card to get cash advances, call your credit card company before leaving to request one. People with alphabetic, rather than numerical, PINs may also be thrown off by the lack of letters on European cash machines. The following handy chart gives the corresponding numbers to use: 1=QZ; 2=ABC; 3=DEF; 4=GHI; 5=JKL; 6=MNO; 7=PRS; 8=TUV; and 9=WXY. Note that if you mistakenly punch the wrong code into the machine three times, it will swallow your card for good.

ESSENTIALS

the checks are lost or stolen, and many provide services such as toll-free refund hotlines, emergency message services, and stolen credit card assistance. They are readily accepted across Europe. Ask about toll-free refund hotlines and the location of refund centers when purchasing checks, and always carry emergency cash.

American Express: Checks available with commission at select banks, at AmEx offices, and online (www.americanexpress.com; US residents only). AmEx cardholders can also purchase checks by phone (☎888-269-6669). *Cheques for Two* can be signed by either of 2 people traveling together. For purchase locations or more info contact AmEx's service centers: in the US and Canada ☎800-221-7282; in the UK ☎08 0587 6023; in Australia ☎0800 688 022; in New Zealand ☎0508 555 358; elsewhere US collect ☎+1 801-964-6665.

Visa: Checks available (generally with commission) at banks worldwide. For the location of the nearest office, call Visa's service centers: in the US ☎800-227-6811; in the UK ☎08 0051 5884; elsewhere UK collect ☎+44 020 7937 8091.

GETTING MONEY FROM HOME

If you run out of money while traveling, the easiest and cheapest solution is to have someone back home make a deposit to your credit card or cash (ATM) card. Failing that, consider one of the following options.

WIRING MONEY. It is possible to arrange a **bank money transfer,** which means asking a bank back home to wire money to a bank in Europe. This is the cheapest way to transfer cash, but it's also the slowest, usually taking several days or more. Note that some banks may only release your funds in local currency, potentially sticking you with a poor exchange rate; inquire about this in advance. Money transfer services like **Western Union** are faster and more convenient than bank transfers— but also much pricier. Western Union has many locations worldwide. To find one, visit www.westernunion.com, or call: in Australia ☎800 501 500, in Canada ☎800-235-0000, in New Zealand ☎800 270 000, in South Africa ☎0860 100 031, in the UK ☎0800 833 833, or in the US ☎800-325-6000. Money transfer services are also available at **American Express** and **Thomas Cook** offices.

US STATE DEPARTMENT (US CITIZENS ONLY). In dire emergencies only, the US State Department will forward money within hours to the nearest consular office, which will then disburse it according to instructions for a US$15 fee. If you wish to use this service, you must contact the Overseas Citizens Service division of the US State Department (☎202-647-5225; Su, nights, and holidays ☎202-647-4000).

COSTS

The cost of your trip will vary considerably depending on where you go, how you travel, and where you stay. The most significant expenses will probably be your round-trip (return) **airfare** to Europe (p. 43) and a **railpass** or **bus pass** (p. 51). Before you go, spend some time calculating a reasonable per-day **budget** that will meet your needs.

STAYING ON A BUDGET. To give you a general idea, the typical first-time, under-26 traveler planning to spend most of their time in Western Europe and then tack on a quick jaunt into Eastern Europe, sleeping in hostels and traveling on a two-month unlimited Eurail pass, can probably expect to spend about US$2000, plus cost of plane fare (US$300-800), railpass (US$882), and backpack (US$150-400). Don't forget to factor in emergency reserve funds (at least US$200).

SAVING MONEY. Some simple ways to save include searching out opportunities for free entertainment, splitting accommodation and food costs with trustworthy fellow travelers, and buying food in supermarkets rather than eating out. Bring a **sleepsack** (p. 22) to save on sheet charges in hostels, and do your **laundry** in the sink (unless you're explicitly prohibited from doing so). With that said, don't go over-board with your budget obsession. Though staying within your budget is important, don't do so at the expense of your health or a great travel experience.

TAXES. The EU imposes a **value-added tax (VAT)** on goods and services, usually included in the sticker price. Non-EU citizens visiting Europe may obtain a **refund** for taxes paid on *unused* retail goods, but not for taxes paid on services. As the VAT is 15-25%, it might be worthwhile to file for a refund. To do so, you must obtain **Tax-free Shopping Cheques,** available from shops sporting the Europe Tax-free Shopping logo, and save your receipts. Upon leaving the EU, present your goods, invoices, and passport to customs and have your checks stamped. Then go to an ETS cash refund office or file for a refund once back home. Keep in mind that goods must be taken out of the country within three months of the end of the month of purchase, and that some stores require minimum purchase amounts to become eligible for a refund.

TIPPING AND BARGAINING. In most Western European countries, the 5-10% gratuity is already included in the food service bill, but an additional 5-10% tip for very good service is often also polite. Note that in Germany, the tip is handed directly to the server instead of being left on the table. For other services such as taxis or hairdressers, a 10-15% tip is recommended. Watch other customers to guage what is appropriate. Bargaining is useful in Greece and outdoor markets in Italy, Britain, and Ireland. See individual country chapters for specific info.

SAFETY AND SECURITY

PERSONAL SAFETY

EXPLORING. Respecting local customs (in many cases, dressing more conservatively) may placate would-be hecklers. Familiarize yourself with your surroundings before setting out. Check maps in shops and restaurants rather than on the street. Never admit that you are traveling alone, and be sure someone at home knows your itinerary. When walking at night, stick to busy, well-lit streets and avoid dark alleyways. If you feel uncomfortable, leave as quickly as possible.

SELF-DEFENSE. There is no sure-fire way to avoid all the threatening situations you might encounter when you travel, but a good self-defense course will give you concrete ways to react to unwanted advances. **Impact, Prepare, and Model Mugging** can refer you to local self-defense courses in the US (☎ 800-345-5425). Visit the website at www.impactsafety.org for a list of nearby chapters. Group workshops (2-3hr.) start at US$50; full courses (20-24hr.) run US$350-500.

TERRORISM AND CIVIL UNREST. In the wake of 9/11, exercise increased vigilance near embassies and be wary of big crowds and demonstrations. Keep an eye on the news, heed travel warnings, and comply with security measures.

Overall, risks of civil unrest tend to be localized and rarely directed toward tourists. Though the peace process in Northern Ireland is progressing, tension tends to surround the July "marching season." Notoriously violent separatist movements include ETA, a Basque group that operates in southern France and Spain, and FLNC, a Corsican separatist group in France. The November 17 group in Greece is known for anti-Western acts, though they do not target tourists.

TRAVEL ADVISORIES. The following government offices provide travel info and advisories by phone or via the web:

Australian Department of Foreign Affairs and Trade: ☎ 13 0055 5135; www.dfat.gov.au.

Canadian Department of Foreign Affairs and International Trade (DFAIT): In Canada and the US ☎ 800-267-6788; www.dfait-maeci.gc.ca. Call for their free booklet, *Bon Voyage...But.*

New Zealand Ministry of Foreign Affairs: ☎ 64 4439 8000; www.mft.govt.nz.

United Kingdom Foreign and Commonwealth Office: ☎ 087 0606 0290; www.fco.gov.uk.

US Department of State: ☎ 888-407-4747; www.travel.state.gov. For the booklet *A Safe Trip Abroad,* call ☎ 202-512-1800.

FINANCIAL SECURITY

PROTECTING YOUR VALUABLES. There are a few steps you can take to minimize the financial risk associated with traveling. First, **bring as little with you as possible.** Second, buy a combination **padlock** to secure your belongings either in your pack or in a hostel or train station locker. Third, **carry as little cash as possible.** Keep your traveler's checks and ATM/credit cards in a **money belt**—not a "fanny pack"—along with your passport and ID cards. Finally, **keep a small cash reserve separate from your primary stash.** This should be about US$50 sewn into or stored in the depths of your pack, along with your traveler's check numbers and important photocopies.

CON ARTISTS AND PICKPOCKETS. In large cities **con artists** often work in groups and employ small children. Beware of certain classic scams, including sob stories that require money, rolls of bills "found" on the street, and mustard spilled (or gum spit) onto your shoulder to distract you while they snatch your bag. Don't ever let your bags out of sight. Beware of **pickpockets** in city crowds, especially on public transportation. Also, be alert in public telephone booths: If you must say your calling card number, do so very quietly; if you punch it in, make sure no one can look over your shoulder. Cities such as Rome, Paris, London, and Amsterdam have higher rates of petty crime.

ESSENTIALS

ACCOMMODATIONS AND TRANSPORTATION. Never leave your belongings unattended; crime can occur in even the most demure-looking hostel or hotel. Be particularly careful on **buses** and **trains**, as sleeping travelers are easy prey for thieves. When traveling with others, sleep in shifts. When alone, never stay in an empty compartment; use a lock to secure your pack to the luggage rack. Try to sleep on top bunks with your luggage stored above you (if not in bed with you), and keep important documents and other valuables on your person. If traveling by **car**, don't leave valuables in sight while you are away.

DRUGS AND ALCOHOL

Drug and alcohol laws vary widely throughout Europe. In The Netherlands you can buy "soft" drugs on the open market; in much of Eastern Europe drug possession may lead to a heavy prison sentence. If you carry **prescription drugs,** you must carry both a copy of the prescriptions themselves and a note from a doctor, especially at border crossings. **Public drunkenness** is culturally unacceptable and against the law in many countries; it can also jeopardize your safety.

TROUBLE WITH THE LAW. Travelers who run into trouble with the law, knowingly or not, do not retain the rights of their home country; instead, they have the same rights as a citizen of the country they are visiting. The law mandates that police notify the embassy of a traveler's home country if he or she is arrested. In custody, a traveler is entitled to a visit from a consular officer. US citizens should check the Department of State's website (www.travel.state.gov/arrest.html) for more info.

HEALTH AND INSURANCE

BEFORE YOU GO

In your **passport,** write the names of any people you wish to be contacted in case of a medical emergency, and list any allergies or medical conditions. While most prescription and over-the-counter **drugs** are available throughout Europe, matching a prescription to a foreign equivalent is not always easy, safe, or possible, so carry up-to-date, legible prescriptions or a statement from your doctor stating the medication's trade name, manufacturer, chemical name, and dosage. See www.rxlist.com to figure out what to ask for at the pharmacy counter. While traveling, be sure to keep all medication with you in your carry-on luggage. For tips on packing a basic **first-aid kit** and other health essentials, see p. 22.

IMMUNIZATIONS AND PRECAUTIONS. Travelers over two years old should be sure that the following vaccines are up to date: MMR (for measles, mumps, and rubella); DTaP or Td (for diptheria, tetanus, and pertussis); IPV (for polio); and Hib (for haemophilus influenza B). For travelers going to Eastern or Southern Europe, the hepatitis A and typhoid vaccines are recommended; those in contact with blood or other fluids should also consider HBV shots (for hepatitis B). Some countries may deny entrance to travelers arriving from parts of South America and sub-Saharan Africa without a certificate of vaccination for yellow fever. For more **region-specific information** on vaccination requirements, as well as recommendations on immunizations and prophylaxis, consult the CDC (see below) in the US or the equivalent in your home country.

USEFUL ORGANIZATIONS AND PUBLICATIONS. The US **Centers for Disease Control and Prevention** (**CDC**; US ☎877-394-8747; www.cdc.gov/travel) maintains an international travelers' hotline and an informative website. The **World Health Organization** (**WHO**; www.who.int/ith) provides disease maps and the free booklet *International Travel and Health*. For the most in-depth country recommendations and a list of travel medicine providers, register with **Travel Health Online** (www.tripprep.com). Consult the appropriate government agency of your home country for consular info sheets on health, entry requirements, and other issues for various countries (see the listings in the box on **Travel Advisories**, p. 17).

For info on medical evacuation services and travel insurance firms, see the US government's website (www.travel.state.gov/medical.html) or the **British Foreign and Commonwealth Office** (www.fco.gov.uk). For detailed info on travel health, including a country-by-country overview of diseases, try the *International Travel Health Guide*, by Stuart Rose, MD (US$12.95; www.travmed.com).

MEDICAL ASSISTANCE ON THE ROAD. Health care in Western Europe tends to be quite accessible and of high quality. All EU citizens can receive free first-aid and emergency services by presenting an **E111 form** (available at post offices).

If you are concerned about access to medical support while traveling, contact one of these services: **GlobalCare, Inc.** (US ☎800-860-1111; www.globalems.com), which provides 24hr. international medical assistance and medical evacuation resources; or the **International Association for Medical Assistance to Travelers** (**IAMAT**; US ☎716-754-4883, Canada ☎416-652-0137; www.iamat.org), which has free membership, lists English-speaking doctors worldwide, and offers detailed info on immunization requirements and sanitation. If your regular insurance policy does not cover travel abroad, you may wish to purchase additional coverage (p. 21).

Those with medical conditions (diabetes, allergies, epilepsy, heart conditions) may want to get a stainless-steel **Medic Alert** ID tag (first year US$35, US$20 thereafter), which identifies the condition and gives a 24hr. collect-call number. Contact the Medic Alert Foundation (US ☎888-633-4298; www.medicalert.org).

For emergencies and quick info on health and other travel warnings, contact a passport agency, embassy, or consulate abroad; US citizens can also call the **Overseas Citizens Services** (US ☎202-647-5225; after-hours US ☎202-647-4000).

ONCE IN WESTERN EUROPE

ENVIRONMENTAL HAZARDS

Heat exhaustion and dehydration: Heat exhaustion can lead to fatigue, headaches, and wooziness. Avoid it by drinking plenty of fluids, eating salty foods (e.g. crackers), and avoiding dehydrating beverages (that contain alcohol or caffeine). Continuous heat stress can eventually lead to heatstroke, characterized by fever, severe headache, and extreme confusion. Victims should be cooled off with wet towels and taken to a doctor.

High altitude: Allow your body a couple of days to acclimate before exerting yourself above 8000 ft. Alcohol is more potent and UV rays are stronger at high elevations.

Hypothermia and frostbite: A rapid drop in body temperature is the clearest sign of overexposure to cold. Victims may also shiver, feel exhausted, have poor coordination or slurred speech, hallucinate, or suffer amnesia. *Do not let hypothermia victims fall asleep.* To avoid hypothermia, keep dry, wear layers, and stay out of the wind. When the temperature is below freezing, watch out for frostbite. If skin turns white, waxy, and cold, do not rub the area. Drink warm beverages, get dry, and slowly warm the area with dry fabric or steady body contact until a doctor can be found.

ESSENTIALS

INSECT-BORNE DISEASES

Many diseases are transmitted by insects—mainly mosquitoes, fleas, ticks, and lice—especially when hiking and camping in wet or forested areas. **Mosquitoes** are most active from dusk to dawn. Wear pants and long sleeves, tuck pants into socks, and sleep in a mosquito net. Use insect repellents such as DEET and spray gear and clothing with permethrin. **Ticks** can give you **Lyme disease,** which is marked by a two-inch bull's-eye on the skin. If you find a tick attached to your skin, grasp it with tweezers as close to the skin as possible and apply slow, steady traction. Left untreated, Lyme disease can cause problems in joints, the heart, and the nervous system. Antibiotics are effective if administered early. Ticks can also give you **encephalitis,** a viral infection. Symptoms can range from headaches and flu-like symptoms to swelling of the brain, but the risk of contracting the disease is relatively low.

FOOD- AND WATER-BORNE DISEASES

Unpeeled fruit and vegetables and tap water should be safe in most of Western Europe. In Southern and Eastern Europe, be cautious of ice cubes and anything washed in tap water, like salad. Other sources of illness are raw meat, shellfish, unpasteurized milk, and sauces containing raw eggs. Buy bottled water, or purify your own water by bringing it to a rolling boil or treating it with **iodine tablets.**

Traveler's diarrhea: Results from drinking untreated water or eating uncooked foods. Symptoms include nausea, bloating, and urgency. Try quick-energy, non-sugary foods with protein and carbohydrates to keep your strength up. Over-the-counter antidiarrheals (e.g. Imodium) may counteract the problems. The most dangerous side effect is dehydration; drink sweetened, uncaffeinated beverages, and eat salted crackers. If you develop a fever or your symptoms don't go away after 4-5 days, consult a doctor. Consult a doctor immediately for treatment of diarrhea in children.

Mad Cow Disease: The human variant, Cruetzfeldt-Jakob disease (nvCJD), is an invariably fatal brain disease. Even in the UK, where the risk is highest, only 1 in 10 billion servings of meat are contaminated. Milk and milk products do not pose a risk.

Parasites: Microbes, tapeworms, etc. that hide in unsafe water and food. **Giardiasis,** for example, is acquired by drinking untreated water from streams or lakes. Symptoms include swollen glands or lymph nodes, fever, rashes or itchiness, and digestive problems. To avoid parasites, boil water, wear shoes, and eat only cooked food.

OTHER INFECTIOUS DISEASES

Hepatitis B: A viral infection of the liver transmitted via bodily fluids or needle-sharing. Symptoms may not surface until years after infection. A three-shot vaccination sequence is recommended for health-care workers, sexually-active travelers, and anyone planning to seek medical treatment abroad; it must begin six months before traveling.

Hepatitis C: Like hepatitis B, but transmitted primarily through exchanges of blood. IV drug users, recipients of blood transfusions and tattoos, those with occupational exposure to blood, and hemodialysis patients are at the highest risk, but the disease can also be spread through sexual contact or by sharing items like razors and toothbrushes that may have traces of blood.

Rabies: Transmitted through the saliva of infected animals; fatal if untreated. By the time symptoms (thirst and muscle spasms) appear, the disease is in its terminal stage. If you are bitten, wash the wound thoroughly, seek immediate medical care, and try to have the animal located. A rabies vaccine, which consists of 3 shots given over a 21-day period, is available but only semi-effective.

AIDS, HIV, AND STIS

For detailed info on **Acquired Immune Deficiency Syndrome (AIDS)** in Europe, call the CDC's 24hr. hotline at US ☎ 800-342-2437, or contact the **Joint United Nations Programme on HIV/AIDS (UNAIDS)** (Switzerland ☎ 22 791 3666; www.unaids.org).

Sexually-transmitted infections (STIs) such as **gonorrhea, chlamydia, HPV, syphilis,** and **herpes** are easier to catch than HIV and can be just as deadly. Hepatitis B and C can also be transmitted sexually (p. 20). Though condoms may protect you from some STIs, oral or even tactile contact can lead to transmission of others. If you think you may have contracted an STI, see a doctor immediately.

WOMEN'S HEALTH

Women traveling in unsanitary conditions are vulnerable to **urinary tract and bladder infections,** common and very uncomfortable bacterial conditions that cause a burning sensation and painful (sometimes frequent) urination. Over-the-counter medicines can sometimes alleviate symptoms, but if they persist, see a doctor.

Vaginal yeast infections may flare up in hot and humid climates. Wearing loosely fitting clothing and cotton underwear will help, as will over-the-counter remedies like Monistat or Gynelotrimin. Bring supplies from home if you are prone to infection, as they may be difficult to find on the road.

Since **tampons, pads,** and reliable **contraceptive devices** are sometimes hard to find when traveling, bring supplies with you.

INSURANCE

Travel insurance generally covers four basic areas: medical problems, property loss, trip cancellation/interruption, and emergency evacuation. Although your regular insurance policies may well extend to travel-related accidents, you should consider purchasing travel insurance if the cost of potential trip cancellation/interruption or emergency medical evacuation is greater than you can absorb. Prices for travel insurance purchased separately generally run about US$50 per week for full coverage, while trip cancellation/interruption may be purchased separately at a rate of about US$5.50 per US$100 of coverage.

Medical insurance (especially university policies) often covers costs incurred abroad; check with your provider. **US Medicare** does not cover foreign travel. Canadians are protected by their home province's health insurance plan for up to 90 days after leaving the country; check with the provincial Ministry of Health or Health Plan Headquarters for details. Australians traveling in Finland, Italy, The Netherlands, Sweden, or the UK are entitled to many of the services that they would receive at home as part of the Reciprocal Health Care Agreement. **Homeowners' Insurance** (or your family's coverage) often covers theft during travel and loss of travel documents (passport, plane ticket, railpass, etc.) up to US$500.

ISIC and **ITIC** (p. 12) provide basic insurance benefits, including US$100 per day of in-hospital sickness for up to 60 days, US$3000 of accident-related medical reimbursement, and US$50,000 for emergency evacuation. Cardholders have access to a toll-free 24hr. helpline (run by insurance provider **TravelGuard**) for medical, legal, and financial emergencies overseas (US and Canada ☎877-370-4742, elsewhere call US collect ☎715-342-4104). **American Express** (US ☎800-338-1670) grants most cardholders automatic car rental insurance (collision and theft, but not liability) and ground travel accident coverage of US$100,000 on flight purchases made with the card.

INSURANCE PROVIDERS. STA (p. 43) offers a range of plans that can supplement your basic coverage. Other US and Canadian providers include **Access America** (☎866-807-3982; www.accessamerica.com), **Travel Guard** (☎800-826-4919; www.travelguard.com), and **International Student Insurance (ISI;** ☎877-328-1565). The UK has **Columbus Direct** (☎084 5330 8518; www.columbusdirect.net), and Australia has **AFTA** (☎02 9264 3299; www.afta.com.au).

PACKING

Pack light: Lay out only what you absolutely need, then take half as many clothes and twice as much money. If you plan to do a lot of hiking, also see **Camping and the Outdoors** (p. 24) for tips on what to pack.

LUGGAGE. If you plan to cover most of your itinerary by foot, a sturdy **frame backpack** is unbeatable. (For the basics on buying a pack, see p. 25.) Toting a **suitcase** or **trunk** is fine if you plan to live in one or two cities and explore from there, but a very bad idea if you're going to be moving around a lot. In addition to your main piece of luggage, a **daypack** (a small backpack or courier bag) is a must.

CLOTHING. No matter when you're traveling, it's always a good idea to bring a **warm jacket** or wool sweater, a **rain jacket** (Gore-Tex is both waterproof and breathable), sturdy shoes or **hiking boots, and thick socks. Flip-flops** or waterproof sandals are must-haves for grubby hostel showers. You may also want to add one outfit beyond jeans and a t-shirt, and maybe a nicer pair of shoes if you have the room. If you plan to visit any religious or cultural sites, remember that you'll need something besides tank tops and shorts to be respectful.

SLEEPSACK. Some hostels require that you either provide your own linen or rent sheets from them. Save cash by making your own sleepsack: Fold a full-size sheet in half the long way, then sew it closed along the long side and one short side. Remember: a sleeping bag is *not* a sleepsack, and will not pass for one.

ELECTRONICS. In Western Europe, electricity is 230V AC, enough to fry any 120V North American appliance. Americans and Canadians should buy an adapter (which changes the shape of the plug; US$10) and a converter (which changes the voltage; US$10-15). Don't make the mistake of using only an adapter (unless appliance instructions state otherwise). New Zealanders, South Africans, and Australians won't need a converter, but will require an adapter. The website www.kropla.com/electric.htm has comprehensive info on what you'll need.

FIRST-AID KIT. For a basic first-aid kit, pack: Bandages, pain reliever, antibiotic cream, a thermometer, a Swiss Army knife, tweezers, moleskin, decongestant, motion-sickness remedy, upset-stomach or diarrhea medication (Pepto Bismol or Imodium), an antihistamine, sunscreen, insect repellent, and burn ointment.

FILM. Film and developing in Western Europe are expensive, so consider bringing enough film for your entire trip and developing it at home. Less serious photographers may want to bring a **disposable camera** or two rather than an expensive permanent one. Despite disclaimers, airport security X-rays *can* fog film, so buy a lead-lined pouch at a camera store or ask security to hand-inspect it. Always pack film in your carry-on luggage, since higher-intensity X-rays are used on checked luggage.

OTHER USEFUL ITEMS. For safety purposes, you should bring a **money belt** and small **padlock.** Basic **outdoors equipment** (plastic water bottle, compass, waterproof matches, pocketknife, sunglasses, sunscreen, hat) may also prove useful. Quick repairs of torn garments can be done with a needle and thread; also consider bringing electrical tape for patching tears. Other things you're liable to forget: an **umbrella,** sealable **plastic bags** (for damp clothes, soap, food, etc.), an **alarm clock,** safety pins, rubber bands, a flashlight, **earplugs,** and garbage bags.

IMPORTANT DOCUMENTS. Don't forget your passport, traveler's checks, ATM and/or credit cards, and adequate ID (p. 12). Also check that you have any of the following that might apply to you: a hosteling membership card (p. 23); driver's license; travel insurance forms; and/or rail or bus pass (p. 50).

ACCOMMODATIONS

HOSTELS

In the summer Western Europe is overrun by young budget travelers, many of whom frequent hostels, which allow people from around the world to meet and learn about places to visit. Hostels are generally laid out dorm-style, often with large single-sex rooms and bunk beds, a common bathroom, and a lounge down the hall. Some offer private rooms for families and couples. Other amenities may include kitchens and utensils, bike or moped rentals, storage areas, Internet access, and laundry facilities. There can be drawbacks: some hostels close during certain daytime "lockout" hours, have a curfew, don't accept reservations, impose a maximum stay, or, less frequently, require chores. A bed in a hostel averages around US$10-25 in Western Europe.

HOSTELLING INTERNATIONAL

Joining the youth hostel association in your own country (see below) automatically grants you membership privileges in **Hostelling International (HI)**, a federation of national hostelling associations. HI's umbrella organization's website (www.iyhf.org), which lists the web addresses and phone numbers of all national associations, is a great place to begin researching hostelling in a specific region. HI hostels are scattered throughout Europe and are typically less expensive than private hostels. Many accept reservations via the **International Booking Network** (US ☎202-783-6161; www.hostelbooking.com). Other comprehensive hostelling websites include www.hostels.com and www.hostelplanet.com. All of these sites offer online reservations, but still call a few days ahead to confirm.

Most HI hostels also honor **guest memberships.** You'll get a blank card with space for six validation stamps; each night you'll pay a nonmember supplement (one-sixth the membership fee) and earn one guest stamp. Six stamps grants you full membership. This system works well in most of Western Europe, but in some countries you may need to remind the hostel reception. Most student travel agencies (p. 43) sell HI cards, as do the national hostelling organizations listed below. All prices listed below are valid for **one-year memberships.**

Australian Youth Hostels Association (AYHA), Level 3, 10 Mallett St., Camperdown NSW 2050 (☎02 9565 1699; www.yha.org.au). AUS$52, under-18 AUS$16.

Hostelling International-Canada (HI-C), 400-205 Catherine St., Ottawa, ON K2P 1C3 (☎800-663-5777 or 613-237-7884; www.hihostels.ca). CDN$35, under-18 free.

Hostelling International Northern Ireland (HINI), 22-32 Donegall Rd., Belfast BT12 5JN, Northern Ireland (☎048 9031 5435; www.hini.org.uk). UK£10, under-18 UK£6.

Youth Hostels Association of New Zealand (YHANZ), P.O. Box 436, Level 1 Moorehouse City, 166 Moorehouse Ave., Christchurch 1 (☎03 379 9970; yha.org.nz). NZ$40, under-18 free.

Hostels Association of South Africa, 3rd fl. 73 St. George's House, P.O. Box 4402, Cape Town 8001 (☎021 424 2511; www.hisa.org.za). ZAR79, under-18 ZAR40.

Youth Hostels Association (England and Wales) Ltd., Trevelyan House, Dimple Rd., Matlock, Derbyshire DE4 3YH, UK (☎016 2959 2600; www.yha.org.uk). UK£13.50, under-18 UK£6.75.

An Óige (Irish Youth Hostel Association), 61 Mountjoy St., Dublin 7 (☎01 830 4555; www.irelandyha.org). IR€25, under-18 IR€10.50.

Scottish Youth Hostels Association (SYHA), 7 Glebe Crescent, Stirling FK8 2JA (☎017 8689 1400; www.syha.org.uk). UK£6, under-18 UK£2.50.

Hostelling International-American Youth Hostels (HI-AYH), 733 15th St. NW, #840, Washington, D.C. 20005 (☎202-783-6161; www.hiayh.org). US$28, under-18 free.

OTHER TYPES OF ACCOMMODATIONS

HOTELS, GUESTHOUSES, AND PENSIONS. In Northern Europe, **hotels** generally start at a hefty US$35 per person. Elsewhere, couples and larger groups can get by fairly well. You'll typically share a hall bathroom; a private bathroom or hot shower will cost extra. Some hotels offer "full pension" (all meals) or "half pension" (no lunch). Smaller **guesthouses** and **pensions** are often cheaper than hotels. Many hotels now offer online reservations. Be sure to indicate your night of arrival and the number of nights you plan to stay. The manager will send a confirmation and may request payment for the first night. Not all establishments take reservations, and few accept checks in foreign currency. For letters, enclosing two **International Reply Coupons** will ensure a prompt reply (each US$1.75; available at any post office).

BED AND BREAKFASTS (B&BS). For a cozy alternative to impersonal hotel rooms, B&Bs (private homes with rooms available to travelers) range from the acceptable to the sublime. B&Bs are particularly popular in Britain and Ireland, where rooms average UK£20/€30 per person. For more info on B&Bs, see InnFinder (www.inncrawler.com) or InnSite (www.innsite.com).

UNIVERSITY DORMS. Many colleges and universities open their residence halls to travelers when school is not in session; some do so even during term-time. Getting a room may take a couple of phone calls and require advanced planning, but rates tend to be low, and many offer free local calls.

HOME EXCHANGES. Home exchange offers the traveler various types of homes (houses, apartments, condominiums, villas, even castles in some cases), plus the opportunity to live like a native and to cut costs. For more information, contact **HomeExchangecCom** (☎ 800-877-8723; www.homeexchange.com) or **Intervac International Home Exchange** (☎ 800-756-4663; www.intervac.com).

CAMPING AND THE OUTDOORS

Organized campgrounds exist just outside most European cities. Showers, bathrooms, and a small restaurant or store are common; some have more elaborate facilities. Prices are low, usually running US$5-15 per person plus additional charges for tents and/or cars. While camping is cheaper than hostelling, the cost of transportation to the campsites can add up. Some parks or public land allow **free camping**, but check local regulations before you set up camp.

USEFUL PUBLICATIONS AND RESOURCES. An excellent resource for travelers planning on camping or spending time in the outdoors is the **Great Outdoor Recreation Pages** (www.gorp.com). Campers heading to Europe should consider buying an **International Camping Carnet.** Similar to a hostel membership card, it's required at a few campgrounds and provides discounts at others. It is available in North America from the **Family Campers and RVers Association** (www.fcrv.org) and in the UK from **The Caravan Club** (see below). For info about camping, hiking, and biking, contact the publishers listed below to receive a **free catalog.**

The Caravan Club, East Grinstead House, East Grinstead, West Sussex RH19 1UA (UK ☎ 013 4232 6944; www.caravanclub.co.uk). For UK£30, members receive equipment discounts, a 700-page directory and handbook, and a monthly magazine.

The European Federation of Campingsite Organizations, EFCO Secretariat, 6 Pullman Court, Great Western Rd., Gloucester GL1 3ND (UK ☎ 014 5252 6911; www.campingeurope.com). The website has links to campsites in most European countries.

CAMPING AND HIKING EQUIPMENT

WHAT TO BUY... Good camping equipment is both sturdy and light. It is generally more expensive in Australia, New Zealand, and the UK than in North America.

Sleeping Bag: Most sleeping bags are rated by season ("summer" 30-40°F at night; "four-season" or "winter" often means below 0°F). They are made either of **down** (warmer and lighter, but more expensive and miserable when wet) or of **synthetic** material (heavier, more durable, and warmer when wet). Prices range from US$80-210 for a summer synthetic to US$250-300 for a good down winter bag. **Sleeping bag pads** include foam pads (US$10-20), air mattresses (US$15-50), and Therm-A-Rest self-inflating pads (US$45-80). Bring a **stuff sack** to store your bag and keep it dry.

Tent: The best tents are free-standing (with their own frames and suspension systems), set up quickly, and require staking only in high winds. Low-profile dome tents are the best all-around. Good 2-person tents start at US$90, 4-person at US$300. Seal the seams of your tent with waterproofer, and make sure it has a rain fly. Other tent accessories include a **battery-operated lantern**, a **plastic groundcloth**, and a **nylon tarp.**

Backpack: Internal-frame packs mold better to your back, keep a lower center of gravity, and flex adequately to allow you to hike difficult trails. **External-frame packs** are more comfortable for long hikes over even terrain, as they keep weight higher and distribute it more evenly. Make sure your pack has a strong padded hip-belt to transfer weight to your legs. Any serious backpacking requires a pack of at least 4000 cubic inches, plus 500 cubic inches for sleeping bags in internal-frame packs. Sturdy backpacks cost anywhere from US$125-420. This is one area in which it doesn't pay to economize. Fill up any pack with something heavy and walk around the store with it to get a sense of how it distributes weight before buying it. Either buy a **waterproof backpack cover,** or store all of your belongings in plastic bags inside your pack.

Boots: Be sure to wear hiking boots with good **ankle support.** They should fit snugly and comfortably over one or two pairs of wool socks and thin liner socks. Break in boots over several weeks first to avoid blisters.

Other Necessities: Synthetic layers, like those made of polypropylene, and a **pile jacket** will keep you warm even when wet. A **"space blanket"** will help you to retain your body heat and doubles as a groundcloth (US$5-15). Plastic **water bottles** are virtually shatter- and leak-proof. Bring **water-purification tablets** for when you can't boil water. For those places that forbid fires or the gathering of firewood (virtually every organized campground in Europe), you'll need a **camp stove** (the classic Coleman starts at US$40) and a propane-filled **fuel bottle** to operate it. Also, don't forget a **first-aid kit, pocketknife, insect repellent, calamine lotion,** and **waterproof matches** or a **lighter.**

...AND WHERE TO BUY IT. The mail-order/online companies listed below offer lower prices than many retail stores, but a visit to a local camping or outdoors store will give you a good sense of the look and weight of certain items.

Campmor, 28 Parkway, P.O. Box 700, Upper Saddle River, NJ 07458 (US ☎888-226-7667; elsewhere US ☎201-825-8300; www.campmor.com).

Discount Camping, 880 Main North Rd., Pooraka, South Australia 5095, Australia (☎08 8262 3399; www.discountcamping.com.au).

Eastern Mountain Sports (EMS), 1 Vose Farm Rd., Peterborough, NH 03458 (☎888-463-6367 or 603-924-9571; www.ems.com).

L.L. Bean, Freeport, ME 04033 (US and Canada ☎800-441-5713; UK ☎08 0089 1297; elsewhere, call US ☎207-552-3028; www.llbean.com).

Mountain Designs, 51 Bishop St., Kelvin Grove, Queensland 4059, Australia (☎07 3856 2344; www.mountaindesigns.com).

ESSENTIALS

Recreational Equipment, Inc. (REI), Sumner, WA 98352 (☎800-426-4840 or 253-891-2500; www.rei.com).

YHA Adventure Shop, 152-160 Wardour St., London WIF 8YA, UK (☎020 7025 1900; www.yhaadventure.com).

CAMPERS AND RVS

Renting an RV is more expensive than tenting or hosteling, but it's cheaper than staying in hotels and renting a car (see **Renting,** p. 60), and the convenience of bringing along your own accomodations makes it an attractive option, although navigating some streets may prove difficult. Rates vary widely by region, season (July and Aug. are the most expensive months), and type of RV. **Motorhome.com** (www.motorhome.com/rentals.html) lists rental companies for several European countries. **Auto Europe** (US ☎888-223-5555; UK ☎0800 169 9797; www.autoeurope.com) rents RVs in Britain, France, and Germany.

ORGANIZED ADVENTURE TRIPS

Organized **adventure tours** offer another way of exploring the wild. Activities include hiking, biking, skiing, canoeing, kayaking, rafting, climbing, photo safaris, and archaeological digs. Tourism bureaus can suggest parks, trails, and outfitters; stores and organizations that specialize in camping and outdoor equipment like REI and EMS are also good resources (see above). The **Specialty Travel Index** (☎888-624-4030 or 415-455-1643; www.specialtytravel.com) compiles tours worldwide.

ENVIRONMENTALLY RESPONSIBLE TOURISM. The idea behind responsible tourism is to leave no trace of human presence behind. A campstove is a safer way to cook than using vegetation, but if you must make a fire, keep it small and use only dead branches or brush. Make sure your campsite is at least 150 ft. (50m) from water supplies or bodies of water. If there are no toilet facilities, bury human waste (but not paper) at least four inches (10cm) deep and above the high-water line, and 150 ft. or more from any water supplies and campsites. Pack your trash in a plastic bag and carry it until you reach the next trash receptacle. For more info, contact any of the organizations listed below.

Earthwatch, 3 Clock Tower Pl. #100, Box 75, Maynard, MA 01754 (☎800-776-0188 or 978-461-0081; www.earthwatch.org).

International Ecotourism Society, 733 15 St. NW #1000, Washington, D.C. 20005 (☎202-347-9203; www.ecotourism.org).

National Audubon Society, Nature Odysseys, 700 Broadway, New York, NY 10003 (☎212-979-3000; www.audubon.org).

Tourism Concern, Stapleton House, 277-281 Holloway Rd., London N7 8HN, UK (☎020 7753 3330; www.tourismconcern.org.uk).

COMMUNICATION

BY MAIL

SENDING MAIL HOME FROM WESTERN EUROPE. Airmail is the best way to send mail home from Europe. From Western Europe to North America, airmail averages seven days; from Central or Eastern Europe, allow anywhere from seven days to three weeks. **Aerogrammes,** printed sheets that fold into envelopes and travel via airmail, are available at post offices. Write "par avion" (or *por avion,* *mit Luftpost, via aerea,* etc.) on the front. Most post offices will charge exorbitant fees or simply refuse to send aerogrammes with enclosures. **Surface mail** is by far the cheapest and slowest way to send mail. It takes one to three months to cross the Atlantic and two to four to cross the Pacific—so it's good for items you won't need to see for a while, such as souvenirs or other articles you've acquired along the way that are weighing down your pack. Check the beginning of each chapter for more specific info on postal service in each country.

SENDING MAIL TO WESTERN EUROPE. Mark envelopes "airmail" in your country's language; otherwise, your letter or postcard will not arrive. In addition to the standard postage system, **Federal Express** (Australia ☎ 13 26 10; Canada and US ☎ 800-247-4747; New Zealand ☎ 0800 733 339; UK ☎ 0800 123 800; www.fedex.com) has express mail services from most home countries to Europe.

> **Australia:** www.auspost.com.au/pac. Allow 5-7 days for regular airmail to Europe. Postcards up to 20g cost AUS$1 and letters up to 50g cost AUS$1.65; packages up to 0.5kg AUS$14, up to 2kg AUS$50.
>
> **Canada:** www.canadapost.ca/personal/rates/default-e.asp. Allow 4-7 days for regular airmail to Europe. Postcards and letters up to 30g cost CDN$1.25; packages up to 0.5kg CDN$10.65, up to 2kg CDN$35.55.
>
> **Ireland:** www.letterpost.ie. Allow 2-3 days for regular airmail to the UK and Western Europe. Postcards and letters up to 50g cost €0.41 to the UK, €0.71 to the continent. **International Swiftpost** zips letters to some major European countries for an additional €3.60 on top of priority postage.
>
> **New Zealand:** www.nzpost.net.nz/nzpost/control/ratefinder. Allow 6-12 days for airmail to Europe. Postcards cost NZ$1.50; letters up to 200g NZ$2-5; small parcels up to 0.5kg NZ$17.23, up to 2kg NZ$55.25.
>
> **UK:** www.royalmail.com/international/calculator. Allow 2-3 days for airmail to Europe. Letters up to 20g cost UK£0.38; packages up to 0.5kg UK£2.78, up to 2kg UK£9.72. **UK Swiftair** delivers letters a day faster for an extra UK£3.30.
>
> **US:** www.usps.com. Allow 4-7 days for regular airmail to Europe. Postcards/aerogrammes cost US$0.70; letters under 1oz. US$0.80; packages under 1lb. US$14; larger packages up to 5lb. $22.75. **Global Express Mail** takes 3-5 days; ½lb. costs US$23, 1lb. US$26. **US Global Priority Mail** delivers flat-rate envelopes to Europe in 4-6 days for US$5-9.

RECEIVING MAIL IN WESTERN EUROPE. There are several ways to pick-up letters while traveling abroad. Mail can be sent via **Poste Restante** (General Delivery; *Lista de Correos, Fermo Posta, Postlagernde Briefe,* etc.) to almost any city or town in Europe with a post office. See individual country chapters to find out how to address *Poste Restante* letters. The mail will go to a special desk in the central post office, unless you specify a post office by street address or postal code. It's best to use the largest post office, since mail may be sent there regardless. It is usually safer and quicker, though more expensive, to send mail express or registered. Bring your passport (or other photo ID) for pick-up; there may be a small fee. If the clerks insist that there is nothing for you, check under your first name as well. *Let's Go* lists post offices in the **Practical Information** section for each city and most towns.

American Express travel offices offer a free **Client Letter Service** (mail held up to 30 days and forwarded upon request) for cardholders who contact them in advance. Address the letter as you would for Poste Restante. Some offices offer these services to non-cardholders (especially AmEx Traveler's Cheque holders), but call ahead. *Let's Go* lists AmEx office locations for most large cities in **Practical Information** sections; for a complete, free list, call US ☎ 800-528-4800.

BY TELEPHONE

TIME DIFFERENCES. All of Europe falls within three hours of **Greenwich Mean Time (GMT).** For more info, consult the **time zone chart** on the inside back cover. GMT is five hours ahead of New York time, eight hours ahead of Vancouver and San Francisco time, two hours behind Johannesburg time, 10 hours behind Sydney time, and 12 hours behind Auckland time. Some countries ignore **daylight savings time;** fall and spring switchover times vary.

 PLACING INTERNATIONAL CALLS. To call Europe from home or to call home from Europe, dial:

1. The **international dialing prefix.** To dial out of **Australia,** dial 0011; **Canada** or the **US,** 011; the **Republic of Ireland, New Zealand,** or the **UK,** 00; **South Africa,** 09. See the inside back cover for a full list of dialing prefixes.
2. The **country code** of the country you want to call. To call **Australia,** dial 61; **Canada** or the **US,** 1; the **Republic of Ireland,** 353; **New Zealand,** 64; **South Africa,** 27; the **UK,** 44. See the back cover for a full list of country codes.
3. The **city/area code.** *Let's Go* lists the city/area codes for cities and towns opposite the city or town name within each country's chapter, next to a ☎. If the first digit is a zero (e.g., 020 for London), omit the zero when calling from abroad (e.g., dial 20 from Canada to reach London).
4. The **local number.**

CALLING HOME FROM WESTERN EUROPE. A **calling card** is probably cheapest. Calls are billed collect or to your account. *Let's Go* has recently partnered with **ekit.com** to provide a calling card that offers a number of services, including email and voice messaging. Before purchasing a calling card, be sure to compare rates, and make sure it serves your needs; for instance, a local phonecard is generally better for local calls. For more info, visit www.letsgo.ekit.com. You can also purchase cards from your national telecommunications companies. Keep in mind that phone cards can be problematic in Russia, Ukraine, Belarus, and Slovenia—double-check with your provider before setting out. You can often make **direct international calls** from pay phones, but without a calling card, you may need to continually add more change. Where available, **prepaid phone cards** and occasionally major credit cards can be used for direct international calls, but they are still less cost-efficient. Placing a **collect call** through an international operator is a more expensive alternative.

CALLING WITHIN WESTERN EUROPE. Many travelers are opting to buy mobile phones for placing calls within Europe. (For more info, see **Cell Phones in Europe** below.) Beyond that, perhaps the easiest way to call within a country is to use a coin-operated phone. However, much of Europe has switched to a **prepaid phone card** system, and in some countries you may have a hard time finding any coin-operated phones at all. Prepaid phone cards (available at newspaper kiosks and tobacco stores) carry a certain amount of phone time depending on the card's denomination. The computerized phone will tell you how much time, in units, you have left on your card. Another kind of prepaid telephone card comes with a Personal Identification Number (PIN) and a toll-free access number. Instead of inserting the card into the phone, you call the access number and follow the directions on the card. These cards can be used to make international as well as domestic calls. Phone rates tend to be highest in the morning, lower in the evening, and lowest on Sunday and late at night.

ESSENTIALS

CELL PHONES IN EUROPE. Cell phones are an increasingly popular option for travelers calling within Europe. In addition to greater convenience and safety, mobile phones often provide an economical alternative to expensive landline calls. Unlike North America, virtually all areas of Europe receive excellent coverage, and the widespread use of the **Global System for Mobiles (GSM)** allows one phone to function in multiple countries. A small chip called a **Subscriber Identity Module Card (SIM or "smart card")** can be purchased from carriers in any European country to provide a local number for any GSM phone. However, some companies lock their phones to prevent switches to competitor carriers, so inquire about using the phone in other countries before buying. Phones in Europe cost around US$100, and instead of requiring a service contract, they often run on prepaid minutes that are easily purchased in many locations. Frequently, incoming calls are free. For more info about GSM phones, try these sites: www.vodafone.com, www.orange.co.uk, www.roadpost.com, www.cellularabroad.com, www.t-mobile.com, and www.planetomni.com.

BY EMAIL AND INTERNET

Email is popular and easily accessible in Western Europe. Take advantage of **web-based email accounts.** If you don't already have one, free services (e.g., www.hotmail.com and www.yahoo.com) are a convenient option, although they can be susceptible to spam. While it's sometimes possible to forge a remote link with your home server, in most cases this is a much slower and more expensive option. Travelers with laptops can call an Internet service provider via a **modem,** and long-distance phone cards specifically intended for such calls can defray normally high phone charges; check with your long-distance provider to see about this option. A handful of large European cities (e.g., Paris) are in the process of making **wireless Internet** available in a variety of public places. **Internet cafes** and the occasional free Internet terminal at a public library or university are listed in the **Practical Information** sections of major cities. For lists of additional cybercafes in Europe, check www.cybercaptive.com or www.netcafeguide.com.

SPECIFIC CONCERNS

WOMEN TRAVELERS

Women traveling on their own inevitably face some additional safety concerns, but it's still possible to be adventurous without taking undue risks. If you are concerned, consider staying in hostels with **single rooms** that lock from the inside or in religious organizations with rooms for women only. Communal **showers** in some hostels are safer than others; check them before settling in. Stick to centrally located accommodations and avoid solitary late-night treks or public transportation rides. Always carry extra money for a phone call, bus, or taxi. **Hitchhiking** is never safe for women, or even for two women traveling together. Choose **train compartments** occupied by women or couples; ask the conductor to put together a women-only compartment if he or she doesn't offer to do so first. Look as if you know where you're going and approach older women or couples for directions if you're lost or uncomfortable.

In general, the less you look like a tourist, the better. Consider wearing skirts rather than shorts to blend in; avoid baggy jeans, T-shirts, and sneakers, since they may make it obvious that you're a foreigner. Try to dress conservatively, especially in rural areas. Wearing a conspicuous **wedding band** may help prevent unwanted overtures; some travelers report that carrying pictures of a "husband" or "children" is extremely useful to help document marriage status.

Your best answer to verbal harassment is no answer at all. The extremely persistent can often be dissuaded by a firm, loud, and very public "Go away!" in the appropriate language (see **Language Basics,** p. 1034). Don't hesitate to seek out a police officer or passerby if you are being harassed or feel threatened. Memorize the emergency numbers in places you visit, and consider carrying a whistle or airhorn on your keychain. A **self-defense course** will both prepare you for a potential attack and raise your awareness and confidence (p. 17). It's also a good idea to be conscious of the health concerns that women face when traveling (p. 21).

USEFUL ORGANIZATIONS

Journeywoman, 50 Prince Arthur Av., Toronto, Canada, M5R 1B5 (Canada ☎416-929-7654; www.journeywoman.com). Posts an online newsletter and other resources providing female-specific travel tips.

Women Traveling Together, 1642 Fairhill Drive, Edgewater, MD 21037 (US ☎410-956-5250; www.women-traveling.com). Places women in small groups to explore the world.

PUBLICATIONS

Active Women Vacation Guide, Evelyn Kaye. Blue Panda Publications (US$18).

A Foxy Old Woman's Guide to Traveling Alone: Around Town and Around the World, Jay Ben-Lesser. Crossing Press (US$11).

A Journey of One's Own: Uncommon Advice for the Independent Woman Traveler, Thalia Zepatos. Eighth Mountain Press (US$17).

Gutsy Women: More Travel Tips and Wisdom from the Road, Marybeth Bond. Travelers' Tales Guides, Inc. (US$13).

Safety and Security for Women Who Travel, Sheila Swan. Travelers' Tales Guides, Inc. (US$13).

The Single Woman's Travel Guide, Jacqueline Simenauer, Doris Walfield. Kensington Publishing (US$13).

SOLO TRAVELERS

There are many benefits to traveling alone, among them greater independence and more opportunities to interact with native residents. On the other hand, a solo traveler is more vulnerable to harassment and street theft. Lone travelers need to be well-organized and look confident at all times. Try not to stand out as a tourist, and be especially careful in deserted or very crowded areas. If questioned, never admit you are traveling alone. Maintain regular contact with someone at home who knows your itinerary. The **Travel Companion Exchange,** P.O. Box 833, Amityville, NY 11701 (US ☎631-454-0880; www.travelcompanions.com) links solo travelers with companions who have similar travel habits; subscribe to their bimonthly newsletter for more info (US$48). **Contiki Holidays** (☎888-CONTIKI; www.contiki.com) offers a variety of European packages designed for 18- to 35-year-olds. Tours include accommodations, transportation, guided sightseeing, and some meals; most average about $65 per day. The books and organizations listed below provide info and services for the lone traveler.

USEFUL ORGANIZATIONS

American International Homestays, P.O. Box 1754, Nederland, CO 80466 (US ☎303-258-3234; www.aihtravel.com). Arranges lodgings with host families across the world.

Connecting: Solo Travel Network, 689 Park Road, Unit 6, Gibsons, BC V0N 1V7 (US ☎604-886-9099; www.cstn.org; membership US$35, internet membership US$25). Offers solo travel tips, host information, and individuals looking for travel companions.

PUBLICATIONS

Traveling Solo, Eleanor Berman. Globe Pequot Press (US$18).

Travel Alone & Love It: A Flight Attendant's Guide to Solo Travel, Sharon B. Wingler. Chicago Spectrum Press (US$15).

OLDER TRAVELERS

Senior citizens are eligible for discounts on transportation, museums, theaters, restaurants, and accommodations. If you don't see a senior citizen price listed, ask, and you might be surprised. However, keep in mind that some hostels, particularly in Germany, do not allow guests over age 26; so call ahead to check. The following books and organizations offer more info for older travelers.

TOUR AGENCIES

+Elderhostel, 11 Ave. de Lafayette, Boston, MA 02111 (US ☎877-426-8056; www.elderhostel.org). Organizes one- to four-week "educational adventures" throughout Europe on varied subjects for ages 55+.

The Mature Traveler, P.O. Box 15791, Sacramento, CA 95852 (US ☎800-460-6676; www.thematuretraveler.com). Deals, discounts, and travel packages for the 50+ traveler. Subscription US$30.

Walking the World, P.O. Box 1186, Fort Collins, CO 80522 (US ☎800-340-9255; www.walkingtheworld.com). Organizes trips for 50+ travelers to many places in Europe.

PUBLICATIONS

No Problem!: Worldwise Travel Tips for Mature Adventurers, by Janice Kenyon. Orca Book Publishers (US$16).

Unbelievably Good Deals and Great Adventures That You Absolutely Can't Get Unless You're Over 50, by Joan Rattner Heilman. McGraw-Hill/Contemporary Publishing (US$13).

BI-GAY-LESBIAN TRAVELERS

Attitudes toward bisexual, gay, and lesbian travelers are particular to each region in Europe. Acceptance is generally highest in large cities and The Netherlands, and generally lower in eastern nations. Listed below are contact organizations, mail-order bookstores, and publishers that offer materials addressing some specific concerns. **Out and About** (www.planetout.com) offers a biweekly newsletter as well as a comprehensive website.

USEFUL ORGANIZATIONS

Giovanni's Room, 1145 Pine St., Philadelphia, PA 19107 (US ☎215-923-2960; www.queerbooks.com). An international lesbian/feminist and gay bookstore with mail-order service (carries many of the publications listed below).

International Lesbian and Gay Association (ILGA), 81 r. Marché-au-Charbon, B-1000 Brussels, Belgium (☎02 502 2471; www.ilga.org). Provides political info, such as the homosexuality laws of specific countries.

PUBLICATIONS

*Damron Men's Travel Guide, Damron Women's Traveler, Damron's Accommodations,*and *Damron Amsterdam Guide.* Damron Travel Guides (US$16-22). For more info, call US ☎800-462-6654 or visit www.damron.com.

Ferrari Guides' Gay Travel A to Z, Ferrari Guides' Men's Travel in Your Pocket, and *Ferrari Guides' Inn Places.* Ferrari Publications (US$16-20).

Spartacus International Gay Guide 2003-2004, Bruno Gmunder Verlag (US$33).

The Gay Vacation Guide: The Best Trips and How to Plan Them, Mark Chesnut. Kensington Publishing Corp. (US$15).

TRAVELERS WITH DISABILITIES

Western European countries vary in accessibility to travelers with disabilities. Some national and regional tourist boards provide directories on the accessibility of various accommodations and transportation services. If these services are not available, contact institutions of interest directly. It is essential that those with disabilities inform airlines, hotels, restaurants, and other facilities of their needs when making reservations, as some time may be needed to prepare special accommodations. **Guide dog owners** should inquire as to the quarantine policies of each destination country. At the very least, you will need to provide a certificate of immunization against rabies.

Rail is probably the most convenient form of transportation for disabled travelers in Western Europe: Many stations have ramps, and some trains have wheelchair lifts, special seating areas, and specially equipped toilets. In general, the countries with the most **wheelchair-accessible rail networks** are: Denmark, France, Germany, Ireland, Italy, The Netherlands, Sweden, and Switzerland. Austria and Britain offer accessibility on selected routes. Greece and Spain's rail systems have limited accessibility. For those who wish to rent cars, some major **car rental agencies** (Hertz, Avis, and National) offer hand-controlled vehicles.

USEFUL ORGANIZATIONS

Mobility International USA (MIUSA), P.O. Box 10767, Eugene, OR 97440 (US ☎541-343-1284, voice and TDD; www.miusa.org). Sells *A World of Options: A Guide to International Educational Exchange, Community Service, and Travel for Persons with Disabilities* (US$35).

Moss Rehab ResourceNet (www.mossresourcenet.org). An Internet resource for international travel accessibility and other travel-related tips for those with disabilities.

Society for Accessible Travel and Hospitality (SATH), 347 Fifth Ave., #610, New York, NY 10016 (US ☎212-447-7284; www.sath.org). An advocacy group that publishes free online travel info and the travel magazine *OPEN WORLD* (US$18, free for members). Annual membership US$45; students and seniors US$30.

TOUR AGENCIES

Accessible Europe, Viale Londra, Rome, Italy 00142 (Italy ☎067 158 2945; www.accessibleurope.com). A European travel group that specializes in arranging individual and group vacations and tours for the physically disabled.

The Campanian Society, P.O. Box 167, Oxford, OH 45056 (US ☎513-524-4846; www.campanian.org). An excellent organization that specializes exclusively in arranging group vacations for the visually impaired. Special emphasis is placed on its educational component, via tactile experience, audio description, and lectures.

The Guided Tour Inc., 7900 Old York Rd., #114B, Elkins Park, PA 19027 (US ☎800-783-5841 or 215-782-1370; www.guidedtour.com). Organizes travel programs for persons with developmental and physical challenges around Ireland, London, and Rome.

PUBLICATIONS

European Holidays and Travel Abroad, Royal Association for Disability and Rehabilitation (US$5).

Around the World Resource Guide, Patricia Smither. Access for Disabled American Publishing (US$20).

Wheelchair Around the World, Patrick D. Simpson. Ivy House Publishing Group (US$25).

MINORITY TRAVELERS

In general, minority travelers will find a high level of tolerance in large cities; the small towns and the countryside are more unpredictable. Travelers with darker skin may face regional intolerance, though most minority travelers, especially those of African or Asian descent, will usually meet with more curiosity than hostility. Anti-Semitism is still a problem in many countries and anti-Muslim sentiment has increased in many places; travelers of Arab ethnicity may be treated suspiciously. Sad to say, it is generally best to be discreet about your religion. Skinheads are on the rise in Europe, and minority travelers, especially Jews and blacks, should regard them with caution. Still, attitudes will vary from country to country and town to town; travelers should use common sense—consult **Safety and Security** (p. 16) for tips on how to avoid unwanted attention.

TRAVELERS WITH CHILDREN

Needless to say, family vacations often require a slower pace and more planning; not all establishments are built for children. If you pick a B&B or a small hotel, call ahead and verify that it's child-friendly. If you rent a car, make sure the rental company provides a car seat for younger children. **Always have your child carry some sort of ID** in case of an emergency, or in case he or she gets lost.

Museums, tourist attractions, accommodations, and restaurants often offer discounts for children. Children under two generally fly for 10% of the adult airfare on international flights (this does not necessarily include a seat). International fares are usually discounted 25% for children from two to 11. Check with your airline, though, to confirm their specific child policy.

DIETARY CONCERNS

Vegetarians should have no problem finding suitable cuisine in most of Western Europe. Particularly in city listings, *Let's Go* notes many restaurants that offer good vegetarian selections. For info on vegetarian and vegan options throughout Europe, check www.vegdining.com.

Travelers who keep **kosher** should contact synagogues in larger cities for info on food options. Your own synagogue or college Hillel should have access to lists of Jewish institutions across the globe. If you are strict in your observance, you may have to prepare your own food on the road. The website www.kashrut.com/travel provides contact info and further resources, while www.shamash.org/kosher catalogues kosher restaurants worldwide.

USEFUL ORGANIZATIONS

North American Vegetarian Society, P.O. Box 72, Dolgeville, NY 13329 (US ☎518-568-7970; www.navs-online.org). Offers resources and publications.

The Vegan Traveller (www.vegan-traveller.com). An internet resource center with info on a number of vegan establishments throughout Europe.

PUBLICATIONS

The Vegan Travel Guide: Places to Stay and Places to Eat for Vegans, Vegetarians, and the Dairy Intolerant, The Vegan Society (US$9).

Vegetarian Europe, Alex Bourke (US$17).

OTHER RESOURCES

Let's Go tries to cover all aspects of budget travel, but we can't include *everything.* Listed below are organizations and websites for your own research.

TRAVEL PUBLISHERS AND BOOKSTORES

Adventurous Traveler Bookstore, 702 H St. NW, Ste. 200, Washington, D.C. 20001 (US☎202-654-8017; www.adventuroustraveler.com), offers information and gear for outdoor and adventure travel.

Hippocrene Books, Inc., 171 Madison Ave., New York, NY 10016 (☎212-685-4371; orders 718-454-2366; www.hippocrenebooks.com). Publishes travel guides, as well as foreign language dictionaries and learning guides. Free catalog.

Hunter Publishing, 130 Campus Dr., Edison, NJ 08818 (☎800-255-0343; www.hunter-publishing.com). Has an extensive catalog of travel guides and diving and adventure travel books.

Rand McNally, 8255 N. Central Park Ave., Skokie, IL 60076 (☎800-275-7263; elsewhere call US ☎847-329-6656; www.randmcnally.com), publishes a number of comprehensive road atlases (from US$10).

THE WORLD WIDE WEB

Almost every aspect of budget travel is accessible via the web. With a few minutes at the keyboard, you can make a hostel reservation, get advice from other travelers, or find out exactly how much a train from Paris to Munich costs.

Listed below are some budget travel sites to start off your surfing; other relevant websites are listed throughout the book. Because web-site turnover is high, use search engines (such as www.google.com) to strike out on your own.

LEARNING THE ART OF BUDGET TRAVEL

Backpacker's Ultimate Guide: www.bugeurope.com. Tips on packing, transportation, and where to go. Also tons of country-specific travel info.

Backpack Europe: www.backpackeurope.com. Helpful tips, a bulletin board, and links.

How to See the World: www.artoftravel.com. A compendium of great travel tips, from cheap flights to self-defense to interacting with local culture.

Travel Library: www.travel-library.com. A fantastic set of links for general information and personal travelogues.

TripSpot: www.tripspot.com/europefeature.htm. An outline of links to help plan trips, transportation, accommodations, and packing.

ESSENTIALS

DESTINATION GUIDES

Atevo Travel: www.atevo.com/guides/destinations. Detailed introductions, transportation tips, and suggested itineraries. Free travel newsletter.

Columbus Travel Guides: www.travel-guides.com/region/eur.asp. Well-organized site with info on geography, governments, communication, health precautions, economies, and useful addresses.

In Your Pocket: www.inyourpocket.com. Extensive virtual guides to select Baltic and Eastern European cities.

MyTravelGuide: www.mytravelguide.com. Country overviews, with everything from history to transportation to local newspapers and weather.

OTHER HELPFUL PAGES

CIA World Factbook: www.odci.gov/cia/publications/factbook/index.html. Vital statistics on European geography, governments, economies, and politics.

Lycos: http://travel.lycos.com. General introductions to cities and regions throughout Europe, accompanied by links to applicable history, news, and local tourism sites.

WWW.LETSGO.COM Our newly designed website now features the full online content of all of our guides. In addition, trial versions of all nine City Guides are available for download on Palm OS™ PDAs. Our website also contains our newsletter, links for photos and streaming videos, online ordering of our titles, info about our books, and a travel forum buzzing with stories and tips.

TRANSPORTATION

GETTING TO WESTERN EUROPE

BY PLANE

When it comes to airfare, a little effort can save you a bundle. If your plans are flexible enough to deal with the restrictions, courier fares are the cheapest. Standby seats and tickets bought from consolidators are also good deals, but last-minute specials, charter flights, and airfare wars often generate even lower rates. The key is to hunt around, be flexible, and ask persistently about discounts. Students, seniors, and those under 26 should never pay full price for a ticket.

AIRFARES

Airfares to Western Europe peak between mid-June and early September; holidays are also expensive. The cheapest times to travel are November to mid-December and early January to March. Midweek (Monday to Thursday morning) round-trip flights run US$40-50 cheaper than weekend flights, but they are generally more crowded and less likely to permit frequent-flier upgrades. Flights without a fixed return date ("open return") or those that arrive and depart from different cities ("open jaw") can be pricier. Patching one-way flights together is the most expensive way to travel. Flights between Europe's capitals or regional hubs—London, Paris, Amsterdam, and Frankfurt—tend to be cheaper. For deals on continental flights to England and other destinations in Europe, try **Ryanair** (www.ryanair.com), **Basiq** (www.basiqair.com), and **Sterling European** (www.sterlingticket.com). For deals flying from England, try Ryanair flights departing from London's **Stansted Airport.**

If Western Europe is only one stop on a more extensive globe-hop, consider a round-the-world (RTW) ticket. Tickets usually include at least five stops and are valid for about a year; prices range from US$1200-5000. Try **Northwest Airlines/KLM** (US ☎800-447-4747; www.nwa.com) or **Star Alliance**, a consortium of 22 airlines including United Airlines (US ☎800-241-6522; www.star-alliance.com).

BUDGET AND STUDENT TRAVEL AGENCIES

While knowledgeable agents specializing in flights to Western Europe can make your life easier and help you save, they get paid on commission, so they may not spend the time to find you the lowest possible fare. Travelers holding **ISIC and IYTC cards** (p. 13) qualify for big discounts from student travel agencies. Most flights from budget agencies are on major airlines, but in peak season some may sell seats on less reliable chartered aircraft.

CTS Travel, 30 Rathbone Pl., London W1T 1GQ, UK (☎020 7290 0630; www.ctstravel.co.uk). A British student travel agency with offices in 39 countries including the US, Empire State Building, 350 Fifth Ave., Ste. 7813, New York, NY 10118 (☎877-287-6665; www.ctstravelusa.com).

STA Travel, 7890 S. Hardy Dr., Ste. 110, Tempe, AZ 85284 (☎800-781-4040, 24hr. reservations and info; www.sta-travel.com). A student and youth travel organization with over 150 offices worldwide (check their website for a listing of all offices),

FLIGHT PLANNING ON THE INTERNET.
Many airline websites offer special last-minute deals, although some may require membership logins or email subscriptions. Try www.icelandair.com, www.airfrance.com, www.lufthansa.de, and www.britishairways.com. (For a great set of links to practically every airline in every country, see www.travelpage.com.)

Other websites do the legwork and compile the deals for you—try www.best-fares.com, www.flights.com, www.lowestfare.com, www.onetravel.com, and www.travelzoo.com.

▨ **StudentUniverse** (www.studentuniverse.com), **STA** (www.sta-travel.com), and **Orbitz.com** provide quotes on student tickets, while **Expedia** (www.expedia.com) and **Travelocity** (www.travelocity.com) offer full travel services. **Priceline** (www.priceline.com) allows you to specify a price, and obligates you to buy any ticket that meets or beats it; be prepared for antisocial hours and odd routes. **Skyauction** (www.skyauction.com) allows you to bid on both last-minute and advance-purchase tickets.

An indispensable resource on the Internet is the *Air Traveler's Handbook* (www.cs.cmu.edu/afs/cs/user/mkant/Public/Travel/airfare.html), a comprehensive listing of links to everything you need to know before you board a plane.

One last note: To protect yourself, make sure any website you use has a secure server before handing over any credit card details.

including US offices in Boston, Chicago, L.A., New York, San Francisco, Seattle, and Washington, D.C. Tickets, travel insurance, railpasses, and more. In the UK, 11 Goodge St., **London** W1T 2PF (☎020 7436 7779); in New Zealand, Shop 2B, 182 Queen St., **Auckland** (☎09 309 0458); in Australia, 366 Lygon St., **Carlton** Vic 3053 (☎03 9349 4344).

Travel CUTS (Canadian Universities Travel Services Limited), 187 College St., Toronto, ON M5T 1P7 (☎416-979-2406; www.travelcuts.com). Offices in Canada, the US, and elsewhere. Also in the UK, 295-A Regent St., **London** W1B 2H9 (☎020 7255 2191).

USIT, 19-21 Aston Quay, Dublin 2 (☎01 602 1600; www.usitworld.com). Ireland's leading student/budget travel agency has 22 offices throughout Northern Ireland and the Republic of Ireland. Offers programs to work in North America.

Wasteels, Skoubogade 6, 1158 Copenhagen K. (☎3314 4633; www.wasteels.com). A huge chain with 180 locations across Europe. Sells Wasteels BIJ tickets discounted 30-45% off regular fare, 2nd-class international point-to-point train tickets with unlimited stopovers for those under 26 (sold only in Europe).

COMMERCIAL AIRLINES

The commercial airlines' lowest regular offer is the **APEX** (Advance Purchase Excursion) fare, which provides confirmed reservations and allows "open-jaw" tickets. Generally, reservations must be made seven to 21 days ahead of departure, with seven- to 14-day minimum-stay and up to 90-day maximum-stay restrictions. These fares carry hefty cancellation and change penalties (fees rise in summer). Book peak-season APEX fares early; by May you will have a hard time getting your desired departure date. Use **Expedia** (www.expedia.com) or **Travelocity** (www.travelocity.com) to get an idea of the lowest published fares, then use the resources outlined here to try and beat those fares. Low-season fares should be appreciably cheaper than the **high-season** (mid-June to August) ones listed here.

TRAVELING FROM NORTH AMERICA

Basic round-trip fares to Western Europe are generally cheapest from the East Coast and range from roughly US$200-750: to Frankfurt, US$300-750; London, US$200-600; Paris, US$250-700. Standard commercial carriers like American (☎800-433-7300; www.aa.com) and United (☎800-241-6522; www.ual.com) will probably offer the most convenient flights, but they may not be the cheapest, unless you manage to grab a special promotion or airfare war ticket. You will probably find flying one of the following "discount" airlines a better deal, if any of their limited departure points is convenient for you.

Icelandair: US ☎800-223-5500; www.icelandair.com. Stopovers in Iceland for no extra cost on most transatlantic flights. New York to Frankfurt May-Sept. US$500-780; Oct.-May US$390-$450.

Finnair: US ☎800-950-5000; www.us.finnair.com. Cheap round-trip fares from San Francisco, New York, and Toronto to Helsinki. Connections throughout Europe.

Martinair: US ☎800-627-8462; www.martinairusa.com. Fly from California or Florida to Amsterdam mid-June to mid-Aug. US$880; mid-Aug. to mid-June US$730.

TRAVELING FROM THE UK AND IRELAND

Because many carriers fly from the British Isles to the continent, we only include discount airlines or those with cheap specials here. The **Air Travel Advisory Bureau** in London (☎020 7636 5000; www.atab.co.uk) provides referrals to travel agencies and consolidators that offer discounted airfares out of the UK.

Aer Lingus: Ireland ☎081 836 5000; UK ☎084 5084 4444; www.flyaerlingus.com. Round-trip tickets from Dublin, Shannon, and Cork to Amsterdam, Brussels, Düsseldorf, Frankfurt, Madrid, Milan, Munich, Paris, Rome, Stockholm, and Zurich (€40-135).

British Midland Airways: UK ☎087 0607 0555; www.flybmi.com. Departures from throughout the UK. Discounted online fares including London to Brussels (UK£83), Madrid (UK£118), Milan (UK£126), and Paris (UK£84).

easyJet: UK ☎087 0600 0000; www.easyjet.com. London to Amsterdam, Athens, Barcelona, Geneva, Madrid, Nice, and Zurich (from UK£30). Online ticketing.

KLM: UK ☎087 0507 4074; www.klmuk.com. Cheap round-trip tickets from London and elsewhere direct to Amsterdam, Brussels, Frankfurt, and Zurich; via Amsterdam Schiphol Airport to Düsseldorf, Milan, Paris, Rome, and elsewhere.

Ryanair: Ireland ☎081 830 3030; UK ☎087 0156 9569; www.ryanair.ie. From Dublin, London, and Glasgow to destinations in France, Germany, Ireland, Italy, Scandinavia, and elsewhere. Deals from as low as UK£9 on limited weekend specials.

TRAVELING FROM AUSTRALIA AND NEW ZEALAND

Air New Zealand: New Zealand ☎0800 737 000; www.airnz.co.nz. From Melbourne, Auckland, and elsewhere to Frankfurt, London, Paris, Rome, and beyond.

Qantas Air: Australia ☎13 13 13; New Zealand ☎0800 808 767; www.qantas.com.au. Flights from Australia and New Zealand to London AUS$2400-3000.

Singapore Air: Australia ☎13 10 11; New Zealand ☎0800 808 909; www.singaporeair.com. Flies from Auckland, Sydney, Melbourne, and Perth to Amsterdam, Brussels, Frankfurt, London, and more.

Thai Airways: Australia ☎13 0065 1960; New Zealand ☎093 770 268; www.thaiair.com. Auckland, Sydney, and Melbourne to Rome, Frankfurt, London, and more.

TRAVELING FROM SOUTH AFRICA

Air France: South Africa ☎0860 340 340; www.airfrance.com/za. Johannesburg to Paris; connections throughout Europe.

British Airways: South Africa ☎0860 011 747; www.british-airways.com/regional/sa. Johannesburg to London; connections to the rest of Western Europe from ZAR3400.

Lufthansa: South Africa ☎0861 842 538; www.lufthansa.co.za. From Cape Town, Durban, and Johannesburg to Germany and elsewhere.

Virgin Atlantic: South Africa ☎0113 403 400; www.virgin-atlantic.co.za. Flies to London from both Cape Town and Johannesburg.

AIR COURIER FLIGHTS

Those who travel light should consider courier flights. Couriers help transport cargo on international flights by using their checked luggage space for freight. Usually, couriers must travel with carry-ons only and must deal with complex flight restrictions. Most flights are round-trip with short fixed-length stays (usually one week) and a limit of one ticket per issue. Most flights also operate only out of major gateway cities, mostly in North America. Generally, you must be over 21 (in some cases 18). In summer, the most popular destinations usually require an advance reservation of about two weeks (you can usually book up to two months ahead). Super-discounted fares are common for "last-minute" flights (three to 14 days ahead).

TRAVELING FROM NORTH AMERICA. Round-trip courier fares from the US to Europe run about US$200-500. Most flights leave from New York, Los Angeles, San Francisco, or Miami in the US; and from Montreal, Toronto, or Vancouver in Canada. The organizations below provide their members with lists of opportunities and courier brokers worldwide for an annual fee (typically US$50-60). Alternatively, you can contact a courier broker directly; most charge registration fees.

Air Courier Association, 350 Indiana St., Ste. 300, Golden, CO 80401 (US ☎800-282-1202; elsewhere call US ☎303-279-3600; www.aircourier.org). Ten departure cities throughout the US and Canada to London, Madrid, Paris, Rome, and throughout Western Europe (high-season US$150-360). One-year membership US$39.

International Association of Air Travel Couriers (IAATC), P.O. Box 980, Keystone Heights, FL 32656 (☎352-475-1584; www.courier.org). From nine North American cities to Western European cities, including London, Madrid, Paris, and Rome. One-year membership US$45-50.

Global Courier Travel, P.O. Box 3051, Nederland, CO 80466 (☎866-470-3061; www.globalcouriertravel.com). Searchable online database. Departures from the US and Canada to Amsterdam, Athens, Brussels, Copenhagen, Frankfurt, London, Madrid, Milan, Paris, and Rome. Lifetime membership US$40, 2 people US$55.

FROM THE UK, IRELAND, AUSTRALIA, AND NEW ZEALAND. The minimum age for couriers from the **UK** is usually 18. **Brave New World Enterprises,** P.O. Box 22212, London SE5 8WB (www.courierflights.com) publishes a directory of all the companies offering courier flights in the UK (UK£10, in electronic form UK£8). **Global Courier Travel** (see above) also offers flights from London and Dublin to continental Europe. **British Airways Travel Shop** (☎087 0240 0747; www.batravelshops.com) arranges some flights from London to destinations in continental Europe (specials may be as low as UK£60; no registration fee). From **Australia** and **New Zealand, Global Courier Travel** (see above) often has listings from Sydney and Auckland to London and occasionally Frankfurt.

STANDBY FLIGHTS

Traveling standby requires considerable flexibility in arrival and departure dates and cities. Companies dealing in standby flights sell vouchers rather than tickets, along with the promise to get to your destination (or near your destination) within a certain window of time (typically one to five days). You call in before your specific window of time to hear your flight options and the probability that you will be able to board each flight. You can then decide which flights you want to try to make, show up at the appropriate airport at the appropriate time, present your voucher, and board if space is available. Vouchers can usually be bought for both one-way and round-trip travel. You may receive a monetary refund only if every available flight within your date range is full; if you opt not to take an available (but perhaps less convenient) flight, you can only get credit toward future travel. Carefully read agreements with any company offering standby flights. To check on a company's service record in the US, call the Better Business Bureau (☎212-533-6200; www.bbb.org). It is difficult to receive refunds, and vouchers will not be honored when an airline fails to receive payment in time.

TICKET CONSOLIDATORS

Ticket consolidators, or **"bucket shops,"** buy unsold tickets in bulk from commercial airlines and sell them at discounted rates. The best place to look is in the Sunday travel section of any major newspaper, where many bucket shops place tiny ads. Call quickly, as availability is typically very limited. Not all bucket shops are reliable, so insist on a receipt that gives full details of restrictions and refunds, and pay by credit card (in spite of the 2-5% fee) so you can stop payment if you never receive your tickets. For more info, see www.travel-library.com/air-travel/consolidators.html. Keep in mind that these are just suggestions to get you started in your research; *Let's Go* does not endorse any of these agencies. As always, be cautious, and research companies before giving them your credit card number.

TRAVELING FROM NORTH AMERICA. Travel Avenue (☎800-333-3335; www.travelavenue.com) searches for the best available published fares and then uses several consolidators to attempt to beat that fare. **NOW Voyager,** 74 Varick St., Ste. 307, New York, NY 10013 (☎212-431-1616; www.nowvoyagertravel.com) arranges discounted flights, mostly from New York, to Barcelona, London, Madrid, Milan, Paris, and Rome. Other consolidators worth trying are **Pennsylvania Travel** (☎877-251-6866; www.patravel.com), **Rebel** (☎800-227-3235; www.rebeltours.com), and **Cheap Tickets** (☎800-377-1000; www.cheaptickets.com). Yet more consolidators on the web include the **Internet Travel Network** (www.itn.com), **Flights.com** (www.flights.com), and **TravelHUB** (www.travelhub.com).

TRAVELING FROM THE UK, AUSTRALIA, AND NEW ZEALAND. In the UK, the **Air Travel Advisory Bureau** (☎020 7636 5000; www.atab.co.uk) has the names of reliable consolidators and discount flight specialists. From Australia and New Zealand, look for consolidator ads in the travel section of the *Sydney Morning Herald.*

CHARTER FLIGHTS

Charters are flights a tour operator contracts with an airline to fly extra loads of passengers during peak season. Charter flights fly less frequently than major airlines, make refunds particularly difficult, and are almost always fully booked. Schedules and itineraries may also change or be cancelled at the last moment (as late as 48 hours before the trip, and without a full refund), and check-in, boarding, and baggage claim are often pretty slow. However, they can also be cheaper.

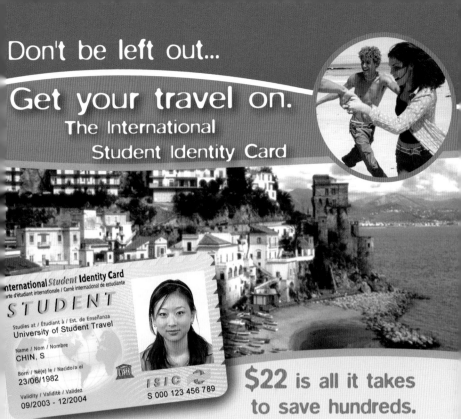

enough already...
Get a room.

Book your next hotel with the people who know what you want.

Discount clubs and fare brokers offer members savings on last-minute charter and tour deals. Study contracts closely; you don't want to end up with an unwanted overnight layover. **Travelers Advantage,** Trumbull, CT (☎203-365-2000; www.travelersadvantage.com; US$60 annual fee includes discounts and cheap flight directories) specializes in European travel and tour packages.

BY CHUNNEL FROM THE UK

Traversing 27 miles under the sea, the Chunnel is undoubtedly the fastest, most convenient, and least scenic route from England to France.

BY TRAIN. Eurostar, Eurostar House, Waterloo Station, London SE1 8SE (UK ☎0990 186 186; US ☎800-387-6782; elsewhere call UK ☎020 7928 5163; www.eurostar.com; www.raileurope.com) runs frequent trains between London and the continent. Ten to 28 trains per day run to Paris (3hr., US$75-159 2nd-class), Brussels (4hr., US$75-159 2nd-class), and Disneyland Paris. Routes include stops at Ashford in England, and Calais and Lille in France. Book at major rail stations in the UK, at the office above, by phone, or on the web.

BY BUS. Both **Eurolines** and **Eurobus** provide bus-ferry combinations (p. 50).

BY CAR. Eurotunnel, Customer Relations, P.O. Box 2000, Folkestone, Kent CT18 8XY (UK ☎080 0096 9992; www.eurotunnel.co.uk) shuttles cars and passengers between Kent and Nord-Pas-de-Calais. Round-trip fares for vehicle and all passengers range from UK£100-210 with car, UK£259-636 with campervan. Same-day round-trip costs UK£110-150, five-day round-trip UK£139-195. Book online or via phone. Travelers with cars can also look into sea crossings by ferry (see below).

BY BOAT FROM THE UK AND IRELAND

The fares below are **one-way** for **adult foot passengers** unless otherwise noted. Though standard round-trip fares are usually just twice the one-way fare, **fixed-period returns** (usually within five days) are almost invariably cheaper. Ferries run **year-round** unless otherwise noted. **Bikes** are usually free, although you may have to pay up to UK£10 in high season. For a **camper/trailer** supplement, you will have to add UK£20-140 to the "with car" fare. A directory of ferries in this region can be found at www.seaview.co.uk/ferries.html.

P&O Stena Line: UK ☎087 0600 0611; from Europe, call UK ☎130 486 4003; www.posl.com. **Dover** to **Calais, France** (1¼hr., 30 per day, UK£24).

Hoverspeed: UK ☎087 0240 8070; www.hoverspeed.co.uk. **Dover** to **Calais** (35-55min., every hr., UK£24) and **Ostend, Belgium** (2hr., 5-7 per day, UK£28). **Newhaven** to **Dieppe, France** (2¼-4¼hr., 1-3 per day, UK£28).

DFDS Seaways: UK ☎087 0533 3000; www.dfdsseaways.co.uk. **Harwich** to **Hamburg** (20hr.) and **Esbjerg, Denmark** (19hr.). **Newcastle** to **Amsterdam** (14hr.); **Kristiansand, Norway** (19hr.); and **Gothenburg, Sweden** (22hr.).

Brittany Ferries: UK ☎087 0366 5333; France ☎08 25 82 88 28; www.brittany-ferries.com. **Plymouth** to **Roscoff, France** (6hr.; in summer 1-3 per day, off-season 1 per week; UK£20-58) and **Santander, Spain** (24-30hr., 1-2 per week, round-trip UK£80-145). **Portsmouth** to **St-Malo** (8¾hr., 1-2 per day, €23-49) and **Caen, France** (6hr, 1-3 per day, €21-44). **Poole** to **Cherbourg, France** (4¼hr., 1-2 per day, €21-44). **Cork** to **Roscoff, France** (13½hr., Apr.-Sept. 1 per week, €52-99).

P&O North Sea Ferries: UK ☎087 0 29 6002; www.ponsf.com. Daily ferries from **Hull** to **Rotterdam, The Netherlands** (13½hr.) and **Zeebrugge, Belgium** (14hr.). Both UK£38-48, students UK£24-31, cars UK£63-78. Online bookings.

Fjord Line: Norway ☎55 54 88 00; UK ☎019 1296 1313; www.fjordline.no. **Newcastle** to **Stavanger** (19hr.) and **Bergen** (26hr.), **Norway** (UK£50-110, students £25-110). Also from **Bergen** to **Egersund, Norway** and **Hanstholm, Denmark.**

Irish Ferries: Ireland ☎189 031 3131; France ☎01 44 88 54 50; UK ☎087 0517 1717; www.irishferries.ie. **Rosslare, Ireland** to **Cherbourg** and **Roscoff, France** (17-18hr., Apr.-Sept. 1-9 per week, €60-120, students €48) and **Pembroke, UK** (3¾hr., €25-39/€19). **Holyhead, UK** to **Dublin** (2-3hr., round-trip £20-31/£15).

Stena Line: UK ☎412 3364 6826; www.stenaline.co.uk. **Harwich** to **Hook of Holland** (5hr., UK£26). **Fishguard** to **Rosslare** (1-3½hr.; UK£18-21, students £14-17). **Holyhead** to **Dublin** (4hr., UK£23-27/£19-23) and **Dún Laoghaire, Ireland** (1-3½hr., £23-27/£19-23). **Stranraer** to **Belfast** (1¾-3¼hr., UK£14-36/£10).

GETTING AROUND WESTERN EUROPE

Fares on all modes of transportation are either **one-way** (single) or **round-trip** (return). **"Period returns"** require a return trip within a specific number of days. **"Day returns"** require a same-day return trip. Unless stated otherwise, *Let's Go* always lists one-way fares for trains and buses. Round-trip fares on trains and buses in Western Europe are simply double the one-way fare.

BY PLANE

Budget flights are increasingly common and have come to rival trains for affordable and convenient continental travel. Student travel agencies sell cheap tickets, and budget fares are frequently available in the spring and summer on high-volume routes between Northern Europe and areas of Greece, Italy, and Spain; consult budget travel agents and local newspapers. For info on cheap flights from Britain to the continent, see **Traveling from the UK**, p. 40.

The **Star Alliance European Airpass** offers low Economy Class fares for travel within Europe to more than 200 destinations in 43 countries. The pass is available to transatlantic passengers on Star Alliance carriers, including Air Canada, Austrian Airlines, BMI British Midland, Lufthansa, Mexicana, Scandinavian Airlines System, Thai Airways, United Airlines, and Varig, as well as on certain partner airlines. Prices are based on mileage between destinations.

In addition, a number of European airlines offer coupon packets that considerably discount the cost of each flight leg. Most are available only as tack-ons to their transatlantic passengers, but some are available as stand-alone offers. Most must be purchased before departure, so research in advance.

Austrian Airlines: US ☎800-843-0002; www.austrianair.com/greatdeals/europe_airpass.html. "European Airpass" available in the US to Austrian Airlines transatlantic passengers (min. 3 cities; max. 10). Prices based on distance.

BMI: www.flybmi.com. "Discover Europe Airpass" permits travelers to change departure dates and times allowing for flexible travel among any of 25 European destinations.

Europe by Air: US ☎888-387-2479; www.europebyair.com. Coupons good on 30 partner airlines to 150 European cities in 30 countries. Must be purchased prior to arrival in Europe. US$99 each, excluding airport tax. Also offers 15- and 21-day unlimited passes; US$699-899.

Iberia: US ☎800-772-4642; www.iberia.com. "Europass" allows Iberia passengers flying from the US to Spain to tack on additional destinations in Europe.

KLM/Northwest: US ☎800-800-1504; www.nwavacations.com. "Passport to Europe," available to US transatlantic passengers, connects 90 European cities (3-city min., 12-city max.). US$100 each.

TRANSPORTATION

Lufthansa: US ☎ 800-399-5838; www.lufthansa.com. "Discover Europe" available to US travelers on transatlantic Lufthansa flights (3 cities min., 9 max.). US$119 each for the first three cities, US$99 each for additional cities.

Scandinavian Airlines: US ☎ 800-221-2350; www.scandinavian.net. One-way coupons for travel within Scandinavia or all of Europe. US$75-155, 8 coupons max. Most are available only to transatlantic Scandinavian Airlines passengers, but some United and Lufthansa passengers also qualify.

BY TRAIN

Trains in Western Europe are generally comfortable, convenient, and reasonably swift. Second-class compartments, which seat two to six, are great places to meet fellow travelers. For long trips, make sure you are in the correct car, as trains sometimes split at crossroads. Towns listed in parentheses on European train schedules require a train switch at the town listed immediately before the parenthesis. For safety tips on train travel, see p. 18.

You can either buy a **railpass,** which allows you unlimited travel within a particular region for a given period of time, or rely on buying individual **point-to-point** tickets as you go. Almost all countries give students or youths (usually defined as anyone under 26) direct discounts on regular domestic rail tickets, and many also sell a student or youth card that provides 20-50% off all fares for up to a year.

RESERVATIONS. While seat reservations (usually US$3-10) are required only for selected trains, you are not guaranteed a seat without one. You should strongly consider reserving in advance during peak holiday and tourist seasons (at the very latest, a few hours ahead). You will have to purchase a **supplement** (US$10-50) or special fare for high-speed or high-quality trains such as Spain's AVE, Cisalpino trains in Switzerland/Italy/Germany, Finland's Pendolino S220, Italy's ETR500 and Pendolino, Germany's ICE, and certain French TGVs. InterRail holders must also purchase supplements (US$10-25) for trains like EuroCity, InterCity, Sweden's X2000, and many French TGVs; supplements are unnecessary for Eurailpass and Europass holders.

OVERNIGHT TRAINS. On night trains, you won't waste valuable daylight hours traveling, and you can avoid the hassle and expense of staying at a hotel. However, the main drawbacks include discomfort, sleepless nights, and the lack of scenery. **Sleeping accommodations** on trains differ from country to country, but typically you can either sleep upright in your seat (for free) or pay for a separate space. **Couchettes** (berths) typically have four to six seats per compartment (about US$20 per person); **sleepers** (beds) in private sleeping cars offer more privacy and comfort, but are considerably more expensive (US$40-150). If you are using a railpass valid only for a restricted number of days, inspect train schedules to maximize the use of your pass: an overnight train or boat journey uses up only one of your travel days if it departs after 7pm.

SHOULD YOU BUY A RAILPASS? Railpasses were conceived to allow you to jump on any train in Europe, go wherever you want whenever you want, and change your plans at will. In practice, it's not so simple. You still must stand in a line to validate your pass, pay for supplements, and fork over cash for seat and couchette reservations. More importantly, railpasses don't always pay off. If you are planning to spend extensive time on trains, hopping between big cities, a railpass will probably be worth it. But in many cases, budget flights or point-to-point tickets (especially if you are under 26) may prove a cheaper option.

You may find it tough to make your railpass pay for itself in Belgium, Greece, Ireland, Italy, Luxembourg, The Netherlands, Portugal, Spain, or Eastern Europe, where train fares are reasonable, distances short, or buses preferable. If, however, the total cost of your trips nears the price of the pass, the convenience of avoiding ticket lines may be worth the difference.

MULTINATIONAL RAILPASSES

EURAILPASS. Eurail is valid in most of Western Europe: Austria, Belgium, Denmark, Finland, France, Germany, Greece, Hungary, Ireland, Italy, Luxembourg, The Netherlands, Norway, Portugal, Spain, Sweden, and Switzerland. It is not valid in the UK. Standard **Eurailpasses,** valid for a consecutive given number of days, are best for those planning to spend extensive time on trains every few days. **Flexipasses,** valid for any 10 or 15 days within a two-month period, are more cost-effective for those traveling longer distances less frequently. The **Selectpass,** which replaces the Europass, allows five to 15 travel days within a two-month period, in three to five pre-selected, contiguous countries. (For the purpose of the Selectpass, Belgium, The Netherlands, and Luxembourg are considered one country.) **Saverpasses** provide first-class travel for travelers in groups of two to five (prices are per person). **Youthpasses** provide parallel second-class perks for those under 26. Youth and Saver versions of all passes are available.

Passholders receive a timetable for major routes and a map with details on ferry, steamer, bus, car rental, hotel, and Eurostar (p. 44) discounts. Passholders often also receive reduced fares or free passage on many bus and boat lines.

SHOPPING AROUND FOR A EURAIL PASS. Eurail passes are designed by the EU itself and can be bought only by non-Europeans, almost exclusively from non-European distributors. These passes must be sold at uniform prices determined by the EU. However, some travel agents tack on a US$10 handling fee, and others offer certain bonuses with purchase, so shop around. Also, keep in mind that pass prices usually go up each year, so if you're planning to travel early in the year, you can save by purchasing before January 1 (you have three months from the purchase date to validate your pass in Europe).

It is best to buy your Eurail or Europass before leaving; only a few places in major European cities sell them, and at a marked-up price. You can get a replacement for a lost pass only if you have purchased insurance on it under the Pass Protection Plan (US$14). Passes are available through travel agents and student travel agencies like STA (p. 38). Several companies specialize in selecting and distributing appropriate railpasses; try **Rail Europe** (US ☎ 888-382-7245; www.raileurope.com) or **Railpass.com** (US ☎ 877-724-5727; www.railpass.com).

EURAILPASSES	15 DAYS	21 DAYS	1 MONTH	2 MONTHS	3 MONTHS
Eurailpass	US$588	US$762	US$946	US$1338	US$1654
Eurailpass Saver	US$498	US$648	US$804	US$1138	US$1408
Eurailpass Youth	US$414	US$534	US$664	US$938	US$1160

SELECTPASSES		5 DAYS	6 DAYS	8 DAYS	10 DAYS	15 DAYS
Selectpass:	3-country	US$356	US$394	US$470	US$542	N/A
	4-country	US$398	US$436	US$512	US$584	N/A
	5-country	US$438	US$476	US$552	US$624	US$794
Saver:	3-country	US$304	US$336	US$400	US$460	N/A
	4-country	US$340	US$372	US$436	US$496	N/A
	5-country	US$374	US$406	US$470	US$530	US$674
Youth:	3-country	US$249	US$276	US$329	US$379	N/A
	4-country	US$279	US$306	US$359	US$409	N/A
	5-country	US$307	US$334	US$387	US$437	US$556

FLEXIPASS	10 DAYS IN 2 MONTHS	15 DAYS IN 2 MONTHS
Flexipass	US$694	US$914
Flexipass Saver	US$592	US$778
Flexipass Youth	US$488	US$642

TRANSPORTATION

OTHER MULTINATIONAL PASSES. If your travels will be limited to one area, consider regional passes. The **France'n Italy pass** lets you travel in France and Italy for four days in a two-month period (standard US$239, saver US$209, youth US$199). The **Scanrail pass,** which covers rail travel in Denmark, Finland, Norway, and Sweden, is available both in the UK and the US (five days of 2nd-class travel in a two month period US$286, under-26 US$199, seniors US$253; 10 days in two months US$382/267/339; 21 consecutive days US$443/309/392). The **Benelux Tourrail pass** for Belgium, Luxembourg, and The Netherlands is available in the UK, in the US, and at train stations in Belgium and Luxembourg, but not in The Netherlands (five days of 2nd-class travel in a one month period US$163, under-26 US$109).

INTERRAIL PASS. If you have lived for at least six months in any European country, **InterRail passes** prove an economical option. There are eight InterRail **zones.** The pass allows either 21 consecutive days or one month of unlimited travel within one, two, three, or all of the eight zones; the cost is determined by the number of zones the pass covers (UK£219-379). The **Under-26 InterRail pass** (UK£149-265) provides the same services as the InterRail pass, as does the new **Child pass** (ages 4-11 UK£110-190). Passholders receive **discounts** on rail travel, Eurostar journeys, and most ferries to Ireland, Scandinavia, and the rest of Europe. Most exclude **supplements** for high-speed trains. Tickets and info are available from travel agents, at major train stations, or online (www.railpassdirect.co.uk).

DOMESTIC RAILPASSES

If you are planning to spend a significant amount of time in one country or region, a national pass will probably be more cost-efficient than a multinational pass. Several national passes offer companion fares, allowing two adults traveling together to save about 50% on the price of one pass. However, they are often limited and, unlike Eurail, don't provide free or discounted travel on many private railways and ferries. Some of these passes can be bought only in Europe, some only outside of Europe; check with a railpass agent or with national tourist offices.

NATIONAL RAILPASSES. The domestic analogs of the Eurailpass, national railpasses (called "flexipasses" in some countries) are valid either for a given number of consecutive days or for a specific number of days within a given period. Usually, they must be purchased before you leave your home country. Though national passes will usually save frequent travelers money, in some cases you may find that they are actually more expensive than point-to-point tickets. Regional passes are also available for areas where the main pass is not valid. For more info, contact Rail Europe (p. 47).

EURO DOMINO. Like the InterRail pass, the **Euro Domino pass** is available to anyone who has lived in Europe for at least six months; however, it can only be used in one country. The pass is available for three to eight days of travel within a one-month period in one of 29 European countries. **Supplements** for many high-speed trains (e.g., French TGV, German ICE, and Swedish X2000) are included, though you must pay for **reservations.** The pass must be bought within your country of residence. Contact your national rail company for more info.

RAIL-AND-DRIVE PASSES

In addition to simple railpasses, many countries (as well as Europass and Eurail) offer rail-and-drive passes, which combine car rental with rail travel—a good option for travelers who wish both to visit cities accessible by rail and to make side trips into the surrounding areas.

TRANSPORTATION

DISCOUNTED RAIL TICKETS

For travelers under 26, **BIJ** tickets (e.g., **Wasteels, Eurotrain,** and **Route 26**) are great alternatives to railpasses. Available for international trips within Europe, travel within France, and most ferry services, they knock 20-40% off regular second-class fares. Issued for a specific international route between two points, they must be used in the direction and order of the designated route and must be bought in Europe. However, tickets are good for 60 days after purchase and allow a number of stopovers along the normal direct route of the train journey. The equivalent for those over 26, **BIGT** tickets provide a 20-30% discount on first- and second-class international tickets for business travelers, temporary residents of Europe, and their families. Both types of tickets are available from European travel agents, at Wasteels or Eurotrain offices (usually in or near train stations), or directly at the ticket counter in some stations. For more info, see www.wasteels.com.

FURTHER RESOURCES ON TRAIN TRAVEL.
Point-to-Point Fares and Schedules: www.raileurope.com/us/rail/ fares_schedules/index.htm. Allows you to calculate whether buying a railpass would save you money.
European Railway Servers: http://mercurio.iet.unipi.it/misc/timetabl.html. Links to railway servers throughout Europe.
Info on Rail Travel and Railpasses: www.eurorail.com; www.raileurope.com.
Thomas Cook European Timetable, updated monthly, covers all major and most minor train routes in Europe. In the US, order it from Forsyth Travel Library. (☎800-367-7984; www.forsyth.com. US$28.95.) In Europe, find it at any Thomas Cook Money Exchange Center. Alternatively, buy directly from Thomas Cook (www.thomascookpublishing.com).
On the Rails Around Europe: A Comprehensive Guide to Travel by Train, Melissa Shales. Thomas Cook Ltd. (US$18.95).
Europe By Eurail 2003, Laverne Ferguson-Kosinski. Globe Pequot Press (US$18.95).

BY BUS

Though European trains and railpasses are extremely popular, buses may prove a better option. In Spain, buses are on par with trains; in Britain, Greece, Ireland, and Portugal, bus networks are more extensive, more efficient, and often more comfortable than train routes; and in Iceland and parts of northern Scandinavia, bus service is the only ground transportation available. In the rest of Europe, scattered offerings from private companies can be inexpensive but sometimes unreliable. Often cheaper than railpasses, **international bus passes** typically allow unlimited travel on a hop-on, hop-off basis between major European cities. In general, these services tend to be more popular among non-American backpackers.

Eurolines, 4 Cardiff Rd., LU1 1PP Luton (UK☎015 8241 5841; www.eurolines.com). The largest operator of Europe-wide coach services, Eurolines offers unlimited peak-season 30-day (UK£259, under-26 UK£209) or 60-day (UK£299/229) travel between 30 major European cities in 16 countries; off-season prices are lower. Euroexplorers mini-passes offer stops at select cities across Europe (UK£55-75).

Busabout, 258 Vauxhall Bridge Rd., London SW1V 1BS (UK ☎020 7950 1661; www.busabout.com) covers 60 European cities. Sells 2 week, consecutive-day passes (US$339, students US$309) and season passes (US$1149/1039). Flexipasses valid for 7 days out of 1 month (US$339/309) or 24 days out of 4months (US$909/809) also available.

BY CAR

Cars offer speed, freedom, access to the countryside, and an escape from the town-to-town monotony of trains. Before setting off, know the laws of the countries in which you'll be driving (e.g., both seat belts and headlights must be on at all times in Scandinavia, and remember to keep left in Ireland and the UK). For an informal primer on European road signs and conventions, check out www.travlang.com/signs. Scandinavians and Western Europeans use unleaded **gas** almost exclusively, but it's not available in many gas stations in Eastern Europe.

SAFETY. Cheaper rental cars tend to be less reliable and harder to handle on difficult terrain. Less expensive 4WD vehicles in particular tend to be more topheavy and are more dangerous when navigating bumpy roads. Road conditions in Eastern Europe are often poor, and many travelers prefer public transportation. Western European roads are generally excellent, but keep in mind that each area has its own hazards. In Scandinavia, for example, you'll need to watch for moose and elk (particularly in low light), while on the Autobahn, cars driving 150kph will probably pose more of a threat. Road conditions fluctuate with seasons; winter weather will make driving difficult in some countries, while in others, spring thaws cause flooding due to melted ice. Roads in mountainous areas are often steep and curvy, and may be closed in the winter. The **Association for Safe International Road Travel (ASIRT)**, 11769 Gainsborough Rd., Potomac, MD 20854 (US ☎301-983-5252; www.asirt.org) can provide specific info about road conditions. ASIRT considers road travel to be relatively safe in most of Western Europe and slightly less safe in developing nations due to poorly maintained roads and inadequately enforced traffic laws. Carry emergency equipment with you (see **Driving Precautions,** p. 52) and know what to do in case of a breakdown.

DRIVING PERMITS AND CAR INSURANCE

INTERNATIONAL DRIVING PERMIT (IDP). If you plan to drive a car while in Europe, you must be over 18 and have an International Driving Permit (IDP), although certain countries (such as the UK) allow travelers to drive with a valid American or Canadian license for a limited number of months. It may be a good idea to get one anyway, in case you're in an accident or stranded in a smaller town where the police may not speak English; info on the IDP is also printed in French, Spanish, Russian, German, Arabic, Italian, Scandinavian, and Portuguese.

Your IDP, valid for one year, must be issued in your own country before you depart. An application for an IDP usually requires one or two passport photos, a valid local license, and a fee (about US$10). To apply, contact the national or local branch of your home country's automobile association.

CAR INSURANCE. If you rent, lease, or borrow a car, you will need a **green card,** or **International Insurance Certificate,** to certify that you have liability insurance and that it applies abroad. Green cards can be obtained at car rental agencies, from car dealers (for those leasing cars), from some travel agents, and at some border crossings. Rental agencies may require the purchase of theft insurance in countries that are considered high-risk. Remember that if you are driving a conventional vehicle on an **unpaved road,** you are almost never covered by insurance; ask about this before leaving the rental agency. Always ask if prices quoted include tax and **insurance** against theft and collision; some credit card companies cover the deductible on collision insurance, allowing their customers to decline the collision damage waiver. Be aware that cars rented on **Amcrioan Exprocc** or **Visa/Mastercard Gold or Platinum** credit cards in Europe might *not* carry the automatic insurance that they would in some other countries; check with your credit card company.

DRIVING PRECAUTIONS. When traveling in the summer or in the desert, bring substantial amounts of water (5L of **water** per person per day) for drinking and for the radiator. For long drives to unpopulated areas, register with police before beginning your trek, and again upon arrival at your destination. Check with the local automobile club for details. When traveling long distances, make sure tires are in good condition and have enough air, and get good maps. A **compass** and a **car manual** can also be very useful. You should always carry a **spare tire** and a **jack, jumper cables, extra oil, flares,** a **flashlight,** and **heavy blankets** (in case your car breaks down at night or in the winter). If you don't know how to **change a tire,** learn before heading out, especially if you are planning to travel in deserted areas. Blowouts on dirt roads are exceedingly common. If you do have a breakdown, **stay with your car;** if you wander off, there's less likelihood that trackers will find you.

RENTING A CAR

Although a single traveler won't save by renting a car, four usually will. If you can't decide between train and car travel, you may benefit from a combination of the two; RailEurope and other railpass vendors offer rail-and-drive packages (p. 49). Fly-and-drive packages are also often available from travel agents or airline/rental agency partnerships.

You can rent a car from a US-based firm (e.g., Alamo, Avis, Budget, or Hertz) with European offices, from a European-based company with local representatives (Europcar), or from a tour operator (Auto Europe, Europe By Car, and Kemwel Holiday Autos) that will arrange a rental for you from a European company at its own rates. Multinationals offer greater flexibility, but tour operators often strike better deals. Rates vary widely by country; expect to pay US$80-400 per week, plus tax (5-25%), for a tiny car. Reserve ahead and pay in advance if possible. Picking up your car in Belgium, Germany, or The Netherlands is usually cheaper than renting in Paris. Particularly during the summer, rental in parts of Eastern Europe and Scandinavia, as well as in Denmark, Ireland, and Italy, might be more expensive; some companies charge extra fees for traveling into Eastern Europe. It is always less expensive to reserve a car from the US than from Europe.

Some chains allow you to choose a drop-off location different from your pick-up city, but there is often a minimum rental period and an extra charge. Expect to pay more for larger cars and for 4WD. Cars with **automatic transmission** are far more expensive than manuals (stick shift), and are more difficult to find in most of Europe. It is virtually impossible to obtain an automatic 4WD. Many rental packages offer unlimited kilometers, while others offer 200km per day with a surcharge of around US$0.15 per kilometer after that. Return the car with a full tank of **gasoline** to avoid high fuel charges in the end. Gas is generally most expensive in Scandinavia; in any country, fuel tends to be cheaper in cities than in outlying areas.

Ask about discounts and check the terms of insurance, particularly the size of the deductible. Minimum age varies from country to country but is usually 21-25; some companies charge those aged 21-24 additional insurance. In general, all you need to rent a car is a license from home and proof that you've had it for a year. Car rental in Europe is available through these agencies:

Auto Europe: US and Canada ☎888-223-5555; www.autoeurope.com.

Avis: Australia ☎136 333; Canada ☎800-272-5871; New Zealand ☎0800 655 111; UK ☎087 0606 0100; US ☎800-230-4898; www.avis.com.

Budget: US and Canada ☎800-527-0700; UK ☎014 4228 0181; www.budgetrentacar.com.

Europe by Car: US ☎800-223-1516; www.europebycar.com.

Europcar International: France ☎55 66 83 00; US ☎877-506-0070; www.europ-car.com.

Hertz: Australia ☎9698 2555; Canada ☎800-263-0600; UK ☎087 0844 8844; US ☎800-654-3001; www.hertz.com.

Kemwel: US ☎877-820-0668; www.kemwel.com.

LEASING A CAR

For longer trips, leasing can be cheaper than the daily cost of renting; it is often the only option for those ages 18-21. The cheapest leases are agreements to buy the car and then sell it back to the manufacturer at a prearranged price. As far as you're concerned, though, it's a lease and doesn't entail enormous financial trans-actions. Leases generally include insurance coverage and are not taxed. The most affordable ones usually originate in Belgium, France, or Germany. Expect to pay around US$1100-1800 (depending on the size of the car) for 60 days. Contact **Auto Europe, Europe by Car,** or **Kemwel** (see above) for more info.

BUYING A CAR

If you're brave and know what you're doing, **buying** a used car or van in Western Europe and selling it just before you leave can provide the cheapest wheels for longer trips. Check with consulates for import-export laws concerning used vehi-cles, registration, and safety and emission standards.

BY FERRY

Most European ferries are slow but inexpensive and quite comfortable; even the cheapest ticket typically includes a reclining chair or couchette. Plan ahead and reserve tickets in advance, or you may spend days waiting in port for the next sail. Fares jump sharply in July and August—ask for discounts. ISIC holders (p. 13) can often get student fares, and Eurailpass holders (p. 47) get many discounts and free trips. Occasional port taxes should run less than US$10. For more info, consult the *Official Steamship Guide International* (available at travel agencies), or www.youra.com/ferry.

ENGLISH CHANNEL AND IRISH SEA FERRIES. Ferries are frequent and depend-able. The main route across the **English Channel,** from England to France, is Dover-Calais. The main ferry port on the southern coast of England is Portsmouth, which has connections to France and Spain. Ferries also cross the **Irish Sea,** connecting Northern Ireland with Scotland and England, and the Republic of Ireland with Wales. For more info on sailing (or "hovering") in this region, see **By Boat from the UK and Ireland,** p. 44, or www.ferrybooker.com.

NORTH AND BALTIC SEA FERRIES. Ferries in the **North Sea** are reliable and cheap. For info on ferries heading across the North Sea to and from the UK, see p. 44. **Baltic Sea** ferries service routes between Poland and Scandinavia.

Polferries: Poland ☎48 94 35 52 102; www.polferries.se. Ferries run from Poland to Denmark and Sweden.

Color Line: Norway ☎47 22 94 44 00; www.colorline.com. Offers ferries from Norway to Denmark, Germany, and Sweden.

Silja Line: US sales ☎800-533-3755; Finland ☎09 18041; www.silja.com. Helsinki to Stockholm (16hr.) and Rostock, Germany (23-25hr., June to mid-Sept.). Also Turku to Stockholm (10hr.).

DFDS Seaways: US ☎800-533-3755; www.seaeurope.com. Offers routes within Scandi-navia and from Scandinavia to England or Germany.

AEGEAN FERRIES. Companies such as **Superfast Ferries** (US ☎954-771-9200; www.superfast.com) offer routes across the **Adriatic and Ionian Seas** from Ancona and Bari, Italy to Patras and Igoumenitsa, Greece. **Eurail** is valid on certain ferries between Brindisi, Italy and Patras, Greece. Countless ferry companies operate these routes simultaneously; websites such as www.ferries.gr list various schedules. See specific country chapters for more info.

BY BICYCLE

Biking can be a very enjoyable way to explore Western Europe. Many airlines will count your bike as your second free piece of luggage; a few charge extra (up to US$110 one-way). Bikes must be packed in a cardboard box with the pedals and front wheel detached; airlines often sell **bike boxes** at the airport (US$10). Most ferries let you take your bike for free or for a nominal fee, and you can always ship your bike on trains. If your touring will be confined to one or two regions, renting a bike beats bringing your own. Some youth hostels rent bicycles for low prices. In Switzerland, train stations rent bikes and often allow you to drop them off elsewhere; check train stations throughout Europe for similar deals.

EQUIPMENT. In addition to **panniers** to hold your luggage, you'll need a good **helmet** (from US$25) and a U-shaped **Citadel** or **Kryptonite lock** (from US$30). For equipment, **Bike Nashbar,** 6103 State Rte. 446, Canfield, OH 44406 (US ☎800-627-4227; www.nashbar.com), beats all competitors' offers and ships anywhere in the US or Canada. For more info, purchase *Europe by Bike,* by Karen and Terry Whitehill. (US ☎800-553-4453; www.mountaineersbooks.org. US$14.95.)

BIKE TOURS. If you'd rather not strike out on your own, **Blue Marble Travel** (Canada ☎519-624-2494; France ☎42 36 02 34; US ☎215-923-3788; www.bluemarble.org) offers bike tours throughout Europe for small groups of travelers ages 20-49. **CBT Tours** (☎800-736-2453; www.cbttours.com) offers full-package biking, mountain biking, hiking, and multisport tours (US$1500-2500) to Belgium, the Czech Republic, England, France, Germany, Italy, Ireland, The Netherlands, Scotland, and Switzerland. **Cycle Rides** (UK ☎012 2542 8452; www.cycle-rides.co.uk) offers various one- to two-week tours throughout Europe. **EURO Bike and Walking Tours** (☎800-321-6060; www.eurobike.com) gives dozens of six-day to five-week bike tours across Central and Western Europe.

BY MOPED AND MOTORCYCLE

Motorized bikes and **mopeds** use little gas, can be put on trains and ferries, and are a good compromise between the cost of car travel and the limited range of bicycles. However, they're uncomfortable for long distances, dangerous in the rain, and unpredictable on rough roads and gravel. Always wear a helmet and never ride with a backpack. If you've never been on a moped before, a twisting Alpine road is not the place to start. Expect to pay about US$20-35 per day; try auto repair shops, and remember to bargain. **Motorcycles** can be much more expensive and normally require a license, but are better for long distances. Before renting, ask if the quoted price includes tax and insurance to avoid unexpected fees. Do not offer your passport as a deposit; if you have an accident or experience mechanical failure you may not get it back until all repairs are covered. Pay ahead of time instead. For more info, try: *Motorcycle Journeys through the Alps and Corsica,* by John Hermann (US$24.95); *Motorcycle Touring and Travel,* by Bill Stermer (US$19.95); or *Europe by Motorcycle,* by Gregory W. Frazier (US$19.95).

BY FOOT

Western Europe's grandest scenery can often be seen only by foot. *Let's Go* describes many daytrips in town listings for the pedestrian-inclined, but native inhabitants, hostel proprietors, and fellow travelers are often the best source of tips. Many European countries have hiking and mountaineering organizations; alpine clubs in Austria, Germany, Italy, and Switzerland, as well as tourist organizations in Scandinavia, provide simple accommodations in idyllic settings.

BY THUMB

 Let's Go strongly urges you to consider the risks before choosing to hitchhike. We do not recommend hitchhiking as a safe means of transportation, and none of the information presented here is intended to do so.

Never hitchhike before carefully considering the risks involved. Hitchhiking means entrusting your life to a stranger, and risking theft, assault, sexual harassment, and unsafe driving. Despite the dangers, there are advantages to hitchhiking when it is safe: It allows you to meet local people and get where you're going, especially in Northern Europe and Ireland, where public transportation is spotty. The choice, however, remains yours.

Conscientious hitchhikers avoid getting in the back of two-door cars (or any car they wouldn't be able to get out of in a hurry) and never let go of their backpacks. If you ever feel threatened, insist on being let off immediately. Acting as if you are going to open the car door or vomit will usually get a driver to stop. Hitchhiking at night can be particularly dangerous; experienced hitchhikers stand in well-lit places and expect drivers to be leery of nocturnal thumbers. For women traveling alone, hitchhiking is just too dangerous. A man and a woman are a safer combination; two men will have a harder time getting a ride.

Experienced hitchhikers pick a spot outside of built-up areas, where drivers can stop, return to the road without causing an accident, and have time to look over potential passengers as they approach. Hitchhiking (or even standing) on superhighways is usually illegal: One may only thumb at rest stops or at the entrance ramps to highways. Most Europeans signal with an open hand, not a thumb; many write their destination in a sign in large, bold letters and draw a smiley-face under it. Finally, success will depend on appearance. Drivers prefer hitchhikers who are neat and wholesome-looking, and are often wary of people wearing sunglasses.

Britain and **Ireland** are the easiest places in Europe to get a lift. Hitchhiking in **Scandinavia** is slow but steady. Hitchhiking in **Southern Europe** is generally mediocre; **France** is the worst. In some **Central and Eastern European** countries, drivers may expect to be paid. Most Western European countries offer a **ride service,** which pairs drivers with riders; the fee varies according to destination. **Eurostop International (Verband der Deutschen Mitfahrzentralen** in Germany and **Allostop** in France) is one of the largest ride service providers in Europe. Riders and drivers can enter their names on the Internet through the **Taxistop** website (www.taxistop.be). Not all organizations screen drivers and riders; ask in advance.

ALTERNATIVES TO TOURISM

In 2002, nearly 700 million trips were made across international borders, and that number is projected to rise to one billion by 2010; that's quite a change from the 1.7 million trips taken when *Let's Go: Europe* was first published in 1961. The dramatic rise in tourism has created an interdependence between the economy, environment, and culture of Europe and the tourists it hosts. In fact, no continent hosts more: with over 400 million arrivals last year, Europe welcomes a larger number of visitors anually than all other destinations combined.

At *Let's Go*, we aim to foster a mutually beneficial relationship between traveler and destination. We've watched the growth of the "ignorant tourist" stereotype with dismay, knowing that the majority of travelers care passionately about the state of the communities and environments they explore—but also knowing that even conscientious tourists can inadvertently damage natural wonders and cultural enclaves. We feel the philosophy of **sustainable travel** is among the most important travel tips we can impart to our readers. Through sensitivity to local communities, today's travelers can be a powerful force in preserving and restoring this fragile world.

Two rising trends in sustainable travel are ecotourism and community-based tourism. **Ecotourism** focuses on the conservation of natural habitats and the promotion of local economies without exploitation or overdevelopment. **Community-based tourism** aims to channel tourist dollars into the local economy by emphasizing tours and cultural programs run by members of the host community, often to the benefit of disadvantaged groups.

Volunteer opportunities range from conservation to humanitarian projects, and can be completed on an infrequent basis or as the main component of your trip.

There are many other ways to integrate with the communities you visit. **Studying** at a college or language program is one popular option. Many travelers also structure trips around the **work** they can get along the way, which often consists of odd jobs as they go or full-time stints in larger cities.

For more info about sustainable tourism visit www.worldsurface.com, which features photos and personal stories of volunteer experiences. More general info is available at www.sustainabletravel.org. For those who would prefer hands-on involvement, Earthwatch International, Operation Crossroads Africa, and Habitat for Humanity offer fulfilling volunteer opportunities around the world.

VOLUNTEERING

Many people who volunteer in Europe do so on a short-term basis at organizations that make use of drop-in or once-a-week volunteers. The best way to find opportunities that match up with your interests is to check with local or national volunteer centers, which generally provide extensive lists of options.

More intensive volunteer services may charge you a fee to participate. These costs can be surprisingly hefty (although they frequently cover airfare and most, if not all, living expenses). Most people choose to go through a parent organization that takes care of logistical details and frequently provides a group environment and support system. There are two main types of organizations—religious and secular—although there are rarely restrictions on participation in either.

A NEW PHILOSOPHY OF TRAVEL

We at *Let's Go* have watched the growth of the 'ignorant tourist' stereotype with dismay, knowing that the majority of travelers care passionately about the state of the communities and environments they explore—but also knowing that even conscientious tourists can inadvertently damage natural wonders, rich cultures, and impoverished communities. We believe the philosophy of **sustainable travel** is among the most important travel tips we could impart to our readers, to help guide fellow backpackers and on-the-road philanthropists. By staying aware of the needs and troubles of local communities, today's travelers can be a powerful force in preserving and restoring this fragile world.

Working against the negative consequences of irresponsible tourism is much simpler than it might seem; it is often self-awareness, rather than self-sacrifice, that makes the biggest difference. Simply by trying to spend responsibly and conserve local resources, all travelers can positively impact the places they visit. Let's Go has partnered with **BEST (Business Enterprises for Sustainable Travel;** see www.sustainabletravel.org), which recognizes businesses that operate based on the principles of sustainable travel. Below, they provide advice on how ordinary visitors can practice this philosophy in their daily travels, no matter where they are.

TIPS FOR CIVIC TRAVEL: HOW TO MAKE A DIFFERENCE

Travel by train when feasible. Rail travel typically requires only half the energy per passenger mile that planes do.

Use public mass transportation whenever possible; outside of cities, take advantage of group taxis or vans. Bicycles are an attractive way of seeing a community firsthand. And enjoy walking—purchase good maps of your destination and ask about on-foot touring opportunities.

When renting a car, ask whether fuel-efficient vehicles are available. Honda and Toyota produce cars that use hybrid engines powered by electricity and gasoline, thus reducing emissions of carbon dioxide.

Reduce, reuse, recycle—use electronic tickets, recycle papers and bottles wherever possible, and avoid using containers made of styrofoam. Refillable water bottles and rechargable batteries both efficiently conserve expendable resources.

Be thoughtful in your purchases. Take care not to buy souvenir objects made from trees in old-growth or endangered forests, such as teak, or items made from endangered species, like ivory or tortoise-shell jewelry. Ask whether products are made from renewable resources.

Buy from local enterprises, such as street vendors. In developing countries and low-income neighborhoods, many people depend on the "informal economy" to make a living.

Be an on-the-road-philanthropist. If you are inspired by the natural environment of a destination or enriched by its culture, join in preserving their integrity by making a charitable contribution to a local organization.

Spread the word. Upon your return home, tell friends and colleagues about places to visit that will benefit greatly from their tourist dollars, and reward sustainable enterprises by recommending their services. Travelers can not only introduce friends to particular vendors but also to local causes and charities that they might choose to support when they travel.

Opportunities for volunteer work are more abundant in Eastern Europe than in other areas of the continent. Habitat for Humanity and Peace Corps placements, for example, are not usually available in Western Europe.

ONLINE DIRECTORIES

www.alliance-network.org. Umbrella website bringing together various international service organizations from around the world.

www.idealist.org. Provides extensive listings of service opportunities.

www.volunteerabroad.com. Searchable database of opportunites around the world.

www.worldvolunteerweb.org. Allows organizations around the world to advertise volunteer opportunities and events.

PROGRAMS

MULTI-COUNTRY

Archaeological Institute of America, 656 Beacon St., Boston, MA 02215 (☎617-353-9361; www.archaeological.org). The *Archaeological Fieldwork Opportunities Bulletin*, available on their website, lists field sites throughout Europe.

Business Enterprises for Sustainable Travel, (www.sustainabletravel.org). Supports travel that helps communities preserve natural and cultural resources and create sustainable livelihoods. Has listings of local programs, innovative travel opportunities, and internships.

Doctors Without Borders, 333 7th Ave., 2nd fl., New York, NY 10001 (☎212-679-6800; www.doctorswithoutborders.org/volunteer). Medical and non-medical volunteer assignments wherever there is need.

Earthwatch Institute, 3 Clocktower Pl., Ste. 100, Box 75, Maynard, MA 01754 (☎800-776-0188; www.earthwatch.org). Arranges 1- to 3-week programs to promote conservation of natural resources. Fees vary based on program location and duration, costs average $1700 plus airfare.

Elderhostel, Inc., 11 Ave. de Lafayette, Boston, MA 02111-1746 (☎877-426-8056; fax 877-426-2166; www.elderhostel.org). Sends volunteers age 55 and over to destinations in Europe to work in conservation, research, teaching, and other programs.

Global Volunteers, 375 E. Little Canada Rd., St. Paul, MN 55117 (☎800-487-1074). A variety of 1- to 3-week volunteer programs throughout Europe. Fees range from US$1295-2395 including room and board, but not airfare.

Habitat for Humanity International, 121 Habitat St., Americus, GA 31709 (☎229-924-6935, ext. 2551; www.habitat.org). Volunteers build houses in over 87 countries. Program durations range from 2 weeks to 3 years. Short-term programs in Europe, including airfare, room, board, and insurance, cost from US$1800-2600.

Oxfam International, 266 Banbury Rd., Ste. 20, Oxford, OX2 7DL, UK (☎18 65 31 39 39; www.oxfam.org). Runs poverty relief campaigns.

Service Civil International Voluntary Service (SCI-IVS), SCI USA Main Office, 5474 Walnut Level Rd., Crozet, VA 22932 (☎206-350-6585; www.sci-ivs.org). Arranges placement in outdoor work camps throughout Europe. 18+. Registration fee US$175.

Simon Wiesenthal Center, 64 av. Marceau, 75008 Paris (☎01 47 23 76 37; www.wiesenthal.org). Fights anti-Semitism and Holocaust denial throughout Europe. Small, variable donation required for membership.

United Nations High Commission for Refugees (UNHCR), Case Postale 2500, CH-1211 Genève 2 Dépôt, Switzerland (☎22 739 8111; www.unhcr.org). Gladly provides advice on how and where to help.

Before handing your money over to any volunteer or study abroad program, make sure you know exactly what you're getting into. It's a good idea to get the name of **previous participants** and ask them about their experience, as some programs sound much better on paper than in reality. The **questions** below are a good place to start:

—Will you be the only person in the program? If not, what are the other participants like? How old are they?

—Is room and board included? If so, what is the arrangement? Will you be expected to share a room? A bathroom? What are the meals like? Do they fit any dietary restrictions?

—Is transportation included? Are there any additional expenses?

—How much free time will you have? Will you be able to travel around the island?

—What kind of safety network is set up? Will you still be covered by your home insurance? Does the program have an emergency plan?

Volunteers for Peace, 1034 Tiffany Rd., Belmont, VT 05730 (☎802-259-2759; www.vfp.org). Arranges placement in work camps throughout Europe. Membership required for registration. Programs average US$200-500 for 2-3 weeks.

World Wide Opportunities on Organic Farms (WWOOF), Main Office, P.O. Box 2675, Lewes BN7 1RB, UK (www.wwoof.org). Arranges volunteer work with organic and eco-conscious farms around the world.

BRITAIN

The National Trust, Volunteering and Community Involvement Office, Rowan, Kembrey Park, Swindon, Wiltshire, SN2 8YL (☎08706 095 383; www.nationaltrust.org.uk/volunteers). Arranges numerous volunteer opportunities, including Working Holidays.

Royal Society for the Protection of Birds (RSPB), UK Headquarters, The Lodge, Sandy, Bedfordshire SG19 2DL (☎01767 680 551; www.rspb.org.uk). Hundreds of volunteer opportunities at sites throughout the UK that range from a day constructing nestboxes in East Anglia to week-long bird surveys off the Pembrokeshire coast to several months monitoring invertebrates in the Highlands. Work available for all levels of experience.

FINLAND

World Wildlife Federation of Finland, (www.wwf.fi/work_camps.html). Offers conservation work camps throughout Finland.

FRANCE

Club du Vieux Manoir, Abbaye Royale du Moncel, 60700 Pontpoint (☎03 44 72 33 98; cvmclubduvieuxmanoir.free.fr). Offers year-long and summer programs restoring castles and churches throughout France. €14 membership/insurance fee; €16 per day, including food and tent.

L'Arche les Sapins, Domaine des Abels, Lignières-Sonneville, 16130 Charente (☎05 45 80 50 66; www.archesapins.org). Small Christian community of adults with learning disabilities. Volunteers help with daily tasks and individual care. Knowledge of French required.

Organisation Mondiale de Protection de la Nature, 188 r. de la Roquette, 75011 Paris (☎01 55 25 84 67; www.wwf.fr). Offers various opportunities for environmental activism around France and the EU. €30 membership fee.

REMPART, 1 r. des Guillemites, 75004 Paris (☎01 42 71 96 55, www.rempart.com). Enlists volunteers to care for endangered monuments. Membership fee €35; most projects charge €5-8 per day.

UNAREC, 33 r. Campagne Première, 75014 Paris (☎01 45 38 96 26; www.unarec.org). Work camps provide assistance to communities facing various problems, often economic. Separate camps for adults and for adolescents (ages 14-16).

GREECE

The 2004 Summer Olympics and Paralympic Games, (www.athens2004.gr). Seeking upwards of 60,000 volunteers to assist with the running of the Games between May and September 2004. Placements are available at competition and non-competition venues; knowledge of foreign languages strongly desired.

Archelon Sea Turtle Protection Society, Solomou 57, GR-104 32, Athens (☎/fax 210 523 1342; www.archelon.gr). Non-profit group devoted to studying and protecting sea turtles on the beaches of Zakynthos, Crete, and the Peloponnese. Hires for seasonal field work and year-round work at the rehabilitation center. €100 participation fee.

Bridges of Friendship, Menekratous 14, GR-116 36 Athens (☎210 902 1111; inst-phil@hol.gr). This NGO is devoted to issues of homelessness.

Conservation Volunteers Greece, Omirou 15, GR-14562, Kifissia (☎010 623 1120; users.otenet.gr/~cvgpeep). Young volunteers (ages 18-30) participate in 1- to 3-week community programs in remote areas of Greece. Projects range from reforestation to preserving archaeological sites. Lodging provided.

Earth, Sea and Sky Ionian Nature Conservation, PO Box 308, Lincoln, England LN4 2GQ (www.earthseasky.org). Based on the island of Zakynthos, promotes awareness on sustainable tourism and conservation. Although particularly concerned with issues of the sea turtle, organizes a variety of volunteer programs and green activities.

GERMANY

AIDS Take Care, Schlossstr. 15, 82269 Getendorf/Munich (☎8193 93000; fax 950754). Based in Germany, this organization supports AIDS education and patient treatment throughout the world.

Jugend Umwelt Projektwerkstaat (JUP), Turmstr. 14a, D-23843 Bad Oldesloe (☎04531 4512; http://projektwerkstaat.de). Organizes stays at works camps in Germany geared toward protecting the environment.

IRELAND

Kilcranny House, 21 Cranagh Rd., Coleraine BT51 3NN (☎028 7032 1816; www.kilcrannyhouse.org). A residential, educational, and resource center that provides a safe space for Protestants and Catholics to interact and explore issues of non-violence, prejudice awareness, and conflict resolution. Volunteering opportunities range from 6 months to 2 years. Drivers (25+) preferred. UK£20/week for room and board.

Mental Health Ireland, Mensana House, 6 Adelaide St., Dún Laoghaire, Co. Dublin (☎01 284 1166; www.mentalhealthireland.ie). Volunteer activities include fundraising, housing, "befriending," and promoting mental health in various regions of Ireland. Opportunities listed in their online newsletter, *Mensana News.*

Northern Ireland Volunteer Development Agency, 4th fl., 58 Howard St., Belfast, BT1 6PG (☎0289 023 6100; volunteering-ni.org). Helps arrange individual and group volunteer efforts in Northern Ireland.

Volunteering Ireland, Coleraine House, Coleraine St., Dublin 7 (☎01 872 2622; www.volunteeringireland.com). Offers opportunities for individuals or groups in various volunteering and advocacy settings.

ITALY

Italian League for the Protection of Birds (LIPU), V. Trento, 49-43100 Parma (☎0521 27 30 43; www.lipu.it). Places volunteers in data collection and research, conservation, nesting site surveillance, and environmental education work camps. Also offers administrative positions throughout Italy. Programs from 1 week to 1 month. Knowledge of Italian is useful. Required skills vary depending on assignment.

Italian Association for Education, Exchanges, and Intercultural Activities (AFSAI), Viale dei Colli Portuensi, 345, 00151 Rome (☎39 06 537 0332; www.afsai.it). In association with the European Voluntary Service program, financed by the EU. Arranges 1-year projects in community and social work, usually with the elderly or disabled, for volunteers ages 18-25. Mandatory 2-3 week language and immersion camp prior to placement.

THE NETHERLANDS

SIW Internationale, Vjiwillgersprojekten, Willemstraat 7, 3511 RJ Utrecht (☎231 77 21; www.siw.nl). Organizes projects in The Netherlands for volunteers from other countries.

SPAIN

Amerispan, PO Box 58129, Philadelphia, PA 19102, USA (☎800-879-6640; www.amerispan.com). Offers several volunteer programs in Spain. Minimun stay 12 weeks. 23+.

STUDYING ABROAD

Study-abroad programs range from basic language and culture courses to college-level classes, often for credit. In order to choose a program that best fits your needs, you will want to research all you can before making your decision—determine costs and duration, as well as what kind of students participate in the program and what sort of accommodations are provided.

In programs that have large groups of students who speak the same language, there is a trade-off. You may feel more comfortable in the community, but you will not have the same opportunity to practice a foreign language or to befriend other international students. For accommodations, dorm life provides a better opportunity to mingle with fellow students, but there is less of a chance to experience the local scene. If you live with a family, there is a potential to build lifelong friendships with natives and to experience day-to-day life in more depth, but conditions can vary greatly from family to family.

UNIVERSITIES

Some American schools still require students to pay them for credits obtained elsewhere. Most university-level study-abroad programs are meant as language and culture enrichment opportunities, and therefore are conducted in the local language. Still, many programs do offer classes in English and beginner- and lower-level language courses. Those relatively fluent in a foreign language, on the other hand, may find it cheaper to enroll directly in a university abroad, although getting college credit may be more difficult. The following is a list of organizations that can help place students in university programs abroad or have their own branches in Europe.

ONLINE DIRECTORIES

The following websites are good resources for finding programs that cater to your particular interests. Each has links to various study abroad programs broken down by a variety of criteria, including desired location and focus of study.

ALTERNATIVES TO TOURISM

www.studyabroad.com. A great starting point for finding college or high school level programs in foreign languages or specific academic subjects. Also maintains a page of links to several other useful websites.

www.petersons.com/stdyabrd/sasector.html. Lists summer and full-year study-abroad programs at accredited institutions that usually offer cross-credit.

www.westudyabroad.com/europe.htm. Lists language and college-level programs in a number of European countries.

PROGRAMS

MULTI-COUNTRY

American Institute for Foreign Study, River Plaza, 9 W. Broad St., Stamford, CT 06902 (☎800-727-2437, ext. 5163; www.aifsabroad.com). Organizes programs for college study at universities in Austria, Britain, the Czech Republic, France, Ireland, Italy, The Netherlands, Poland, Russia, and Spain.

American Field Service (AFS), 71 W. 23rd St., 17th fl., New York, NY 10010 (☎212-807-8686; www.afs.org), has branches in over 50 countries. Summer-, semester-, and year-long homestay exchange programs for high school students and graduating seniors in the Czech Republic, Hungary, Latvia, Russia, and the Slovak Republic. Community service programs also offered for young adults, 18+. Teaching programs available for current and retired teachers. Financial aid available.

Arcadia University for Education Abroad, 450 S. Easton Rd., Glenside, PA 19038 (☎866-927-2234; www.arcadia.edu/cea). Operates programs in Britain, Greece, Ireland, Italy, and Spain. Costs range from US$2300 (summer) to US$31,000 (full-year).

Central College Abroad, Box 0140, 812 University, Pella, IA 50219 (☎800-831-3629 or 641-628-5284; www.central.edu/abroad). Offers internships, as well as summer-, semester-, and year-long programs in Austria, Britain, France, The Netherlands, and Spain. US$30 application fee.

Council on International Educational Exchange (CIEE), 7 Custon House St., 3rd fl., Portland, ME 04101 (☎800-407-8839; www.ciee.org). Sponsors academic, internship, volunteer, and work programs in Belgium, Britain, the Czech Republic, France, Hungary, Italy, The Netherlands, Poland, Russia, Spain, and Turkey.

International Association for the Exchange of Students for Technical Experience (IAESTE), 10400 Little Patuxent Pkwy. Ste. 250, Columbia, MD 21044 (☎410-997-2200; www.aipt.org). 8- to 12-week programs in Britain, Finland, France, Germany, Ireland, Sweden, and Switzerland for college students who have completed 2 years of technical study. US$25 application fee.

International Association of Students in Economic and Business Management (AIESEC), (http://us.aieseconline.net). The "world's largest student organization," with 43 locations throughout the US. Places students in international "traineeships." US$45 non-refundable application fee. Program $US455.

Institute for the International Education of Students (IES), 33 N. LaSalle St., 15th fl., Chicago, IL 60602, USA (☎800-995-2300; www.IESabroad.org). Offers year-long, semester, and summer programs in Austria, England, France, Germany, Ireland, Italy, The Netherlands, and Spain for college students. Internship opportunities. US $50 application fee. Scholarships available.

School for International Training, College Semester Abroad, Admissions, Kipling Rd., P.O. Box 676, Brattleboro, VT 05302 (☎888-272-7881; www.sit.edu). Socially-themed semester-long programs in the Balkans, the Czech Republic, France, Germany, Ireland, The Netherlands, Russia, Spain, and Switzerland. US$12,050-13,700. Also runs **Experiment in International Living** (☎800-345-2929; www.usexperiment.org), 3- to 5-week summer programs that offer high school students cross-cultural homestays, community service, ecological adventure, and language training in Britain, France, Germany, Ireland, Italy, Poland, Spain, and Switzerland. US$2700-5000.

SUNY Cortland International Programs, Old Main, Room B-15, PO Box 2000, Cortland, NY 13045 (☎607-753-2209; www.cortland.edu/html/ipgms.html). Semester- and year-long academic programs and internship placements in Britain, France, Germany, Ireland, and Spain.

Webster University in Geneva and Vienna, Study Abroad Office, Webster University, 470 E. Lockwood, St. Louis, MO, 63119 (☎800-984-6857 or 314-968-6900; www.webster.edu/intl/sa). Semester- and year-long programs in Austria, Britain, The Netherlands, and Switzerland. All courses are taught in English and are fully accredited.

Youth for Understanding International Exchange (YFU), 6400 Goldsboro Rd., Ste. 100, Bethesda, MD 20817 (☎866-493-8872; www.yfu.org). Places US high school students with host families throughout Europe for a year, semester, or summer. US$75 application fee plus $500 enrollment deposit.

AUSTRIA

European University Center for Peace Studies (EPU), Rochusplatz 1, A-7461 Stadtschlaining (☎(33) 55 24 98; www.aspr.ac.at/welcome.htm). Winner of the 1995 UNESCO Prize for Peace Education, EPU offers Masters degrees and certificates in peace and conflict resolution and conflict transformation.

Johannes Kepler University (JKU), Linz, Altenbergerstr. 69, A-4040 Linz (☎(732) 24 68; www.students.jku.edu/e204/exchange/content). Semester-long and year-long study available through exchange programs with participating institutions. Offers study in a full array of academic disciplines.

BRITAIN

The British Council, 10 Spring Gardens, London SW1A 2BN (☎0207 930 8466; www.britishcouncil.org). Invaluable source of info for those wishing to study in the UK.

Hansard Scholar Programme, LSF, 2nd Floor, 9 Kingsway, London WC2B 6XF (☎020 7955 7459; www.hansard-society.org.uk/scholars.htm). Combines classes at the London School of Economics with internships in British government.

University of Oxford, Colleges Admissions Office, Wellington Square, Oxford OX1 2JD (☎0186 528 8000; www.admissions.ox.ac.uk/int). The oldest English-speaking university accepts visiting students for semester- and year-long programs.

University of St. Andrews, Director of Admissions, Butts Wynd, St. Andrews, Fife, Scotland KY16 9AJ (☎13 34 46 33 23; http://www.st-andrews.ac.uk). Offers summer, semester, and year programs for international students.

FRANCE

Agence EduFrance, 173 bd. St-Germain, 75006 Paris (☎01 53 63 35 00; www.edufrance.fr). A one-stop resource for North Americans thinking about attaining a degree in France. Info on courses, costs, grant opportunities, and related topics.

American University of Paris, 31 av. Bosquet, 75007 Paris (☎01 40 62 07 20; www.aup.fr). Offers US-accredited degrees and summer programs in English on its Paris campus. Intensive French language courses available.

Cordon Bleu Paris Culinary Arts Institute, 8 r. Léon Delhomme, 75015 Paris (☎01 53 68 22 50; www.cordonbleu.edu). The *crème de la crème* of French cooking schools. A full-year diploma course will run you about €29,500, but Gourmet Sessions are also available, ranging from half-days to 4 weeks.

L'Institut Paul Bocuse Hôtellerie et Art Culinaires de Lyon (Lyon Culinary Arts and Hotel Management School), Château de Vivier—BP25, 69131 Lyon-Ecully Cedex (☎04 72 18 02 20; www.each-lyon.com). Premier school located in France's capital of *haute cuisine*. Offers 5-day to 16-week summer courses in French and English for amateurs (€1670-7000). Individual day courses range from €62-76.

Lacoste School of Art, P.O. Box 3146, Savannah, GA 31401, USA (☎912-525-5803; www.scad.edu/lacoste). Based in the tiny medieval town of Lacoste in Provence, this school is administered by the Savannah College of Art and Design. Summer and fall courses in architecture, painting, and historical preservation. Tuition US$4000-6500; room and board US$3150-3350.

Painting School of Montmiral, r. de la Porte Neuve, 81140 Castelnau de Montmiral, Tarn (☎/fax 05 63 33 13 11; www.painting-school.com). Teaches 2-week classes at amateur, student, teacher, and professional levels in English or French. €1550, including accommodations and half-board.

Pont Aven School of Art, 5 pl. Paul Gaugin, 29930 Pont Aven (☎02 98 09 10 45; US ☎401-272-5445; www.pontvensa.org). English-speaking school in Brittany offers studio courses in painting and sculpture, art history, and French language. 4- and 6-week sessions €3500-6500, including room and board.

Université Paris-Sorbonne, 1 r. Victor Cousin, 75005 Paris (☎01 40 46 25 49; www.paris4.sorbonne.fr). The grand-daddy of French universities, was founded in 1253 and is still going strong. Inscription into degree courses costs about €300 per year. Also offers 3- to 9-month programs for visiting students.

GERMANY

Deutscher Akademischer Austauschdienst (DAAD), 871 United Nations Plaza, New York, NY 10017, USA (☎212-758-3223; www.daad.org). Info on language instruction, exchanges, and a wealth of scholarships for study in Germany. The place to contact if you want to enroll in a German university; distributes applications and the valuable *Academic Study in the Federal Republic of Germany*.

German American Partnership Program (GAPP), Goethe-Institut Inter Nationes New York, 1014 Fifth Ave., New York, NY 10028 (☎212-439-8700; www.goethe.de/uk/ney/gapp/index.htm). For high school students and classes interested in exchanges, homestays, and study in Germany. GAPP subsidizes travel, housing, and food costs for qualified groups and individuals.

GREECE

American School of Classical Studies (ASCSA), Souidias 54, 10676 Athens (☎210 72 36 313; www.ascsa.org). Offers a variety of archaeological and classical studies programs to undergraduates, graduate students, and doctoral candidates. Visit the website to find a list of publications and links to other archaeological programs.

Art School of the Aegean, P.O. Box 1375, Sarasota, FL 34230, USA (☎941-351-5597; www.artschool-aegean.com). Offers 2- to 3-week summer programs in painting and ceramics from US$1700.

The Athens Centre, Archimidous 48, Athens 11636 (☎210 701 2268; www.athenscentre.gr). Semester and quarter programs on Greek civilization in affiliation with US universities. Also offers 4- to 6-week summer Classics programs, a summer theater program, and modern Greek language programs on the isle of Spetses.

College Year in Athens, P.O. Box 390890, Cambridge, MA 02139, USA (US ☎617-868-8200; Greece ☎210 7560 749; www.cyathens.org). Runs semester- and year-long academic programs for undergraduates. Also offers summer programs, including a 3-week intensive course in modern Greek on Paros, a 6-week study-travel program, and two 3-week modules covering different subjects each year.

Deree College, 6 Gravias, GR-153 42 Agia Paraskevi, Athens (☎210 600 9800; www.acg.edu). Part of the American College of Greece. Bachelor's degree offered in a wide variety of subjects; classes taught in English. Open to students of all international backgrounds, including Greek students.

IRELAND

Irish Studies Summer School, at **usit NOW,** New York Student Center, 895 Amsterdam Ave., New York, NY 10025, USA (☎212-663-5435; usitnow.com). 7-week program offering courses in Irish culture and history.

National University of Ireland, Galway, University Rd., Galway (☎091 524 411; www.nuigalway.ie). Offers half- and full-year opportunities for junior-year students who meet the college's entry requirements. Summer school courses offered July-Aug. include Irish studies, education, and creative writing.

Queen's University Belfast, University Rd., Belfast BT7 1NN (International Office ☎028 9033 5088; www.qub.ac.uk). Study abroad in Belfast for a semester or year. 4-week **Introduction to Northern Ireland** program in Jan. covers the political, social, and economic questions unique to the North.

Trinity College Dublin, Office of International Student Affairs (☎01 608 2011, ext. 2683; www.tcd.ie/isa). Offers a 1-year program of undergraduate courses for visiting students.

University College Cork. Students from around the world are encouraged to enroll through **Cultural Experiences Abroad,** 1400 E. Southern Ave., Ste. B-108, Tempe, AZ 85282, USA (☎800-266-4441; www.gowithcea.com), for semester- or year-long programs in various disciplines.

University College Dublin, International Summer School, Newman House, 86 St. Stephen's Green, Dublin (☎01 475 2004; www.ucd.ie/summerschool). Offers a 2-week international summer course examining Irish culture and tradition.

University of Ulster, Shore Rd., Newtownabbey, Antrim, BT37 0QB, Northern Ireland (☎08 700 400 700; www.ulst.ac.uk). Offers semester- or year-long programs for visiting international students.

ITALY

John Cabot University, V. della Lungara, 233, 00165 Rome (☎39 06 681 9121; US ☎866-227-0122; www.johncabot.edu). Offers a 4-year Bachelor of Arts degree and semester and summer courses.

American University of Rome, V. Pietro Roselli, 4, 00153 Rome (☎39 06 5833 0919; www.aur.edu). Offers courses in English on international business, international relations, and Italian civilization and culture. From US$5200 per semester.

Brown University, Study Abroad Office of International Programs, Brown University, Box 1973, RI 02912, USA (☎401-863-3555; www.brown.edu/Administration/OIP). Academic programs in Britain, the Czech Republic, Denmark, France, Germany, Italy, Poland, and Sweden. 4 full-year university classes required. US$13,900 per semester; US$27,000 per year.

Institute for the International Education of Students: Study Abroad Italy, 33 N. LaSalle St., 15th fl., Chicago, IL 60602, USA (☎800-995-2300; www.IESabroad.org). Arranges semester- and year-long programs in Austria, Britain, France, Germany, Ireland, Italy, The Netherlands, and Spain.

The International Kitchen, 1 IBM Plaza, 330 N. Wabash #3005, Chicago, IL 60611, USA (☎312-726-4525; www.theinternationalkitchen.com). Leading provider of cooking school vacations to Italy and France. Traditional cooking instruction in beautiful settings for groups of 8-12. Program locations include Amalfi Coast, Liguria, and Tuscany. Courses run 2-7 nights. Prices vary.

ALTERNATIVES TO TOURISM

Study Abroad Italy, 7151 Wilton Ave., Ste. 202, Sebastopol, CA 95472, USA (☎707-824-8965; www.studyabroad-italy.com). Arranges enrollment in schools in Florence, Sicily, and Perugia, as well as travel, student visas, housing, and academic advising. US$8000-10,000 per semester.

THE NETHERLANDS

University of Amsterdam, Office of Foreign Relations, Binnengasthuisstraat 9, 1012 ZA Amsterdam (☎525 8080; www.uva.nl/english). Programs for economics, philosophy, history, linguistics, film studies, and international affairs. Open to college and graduate students. Students live either in university dormitories or apartments.

Amsterdam Maastricht Summer University, P.O. Box 53066, 1007 RB Amsterdam (☎620 0225; www.amsu.edu). Located on Keizersgracht 324, Summer University offers courses in cultural studies and art history, economics and politics, health sciences and medicine, language, law and public policy, media studies and information science, and performing arts.

Keizer Culinair, Keizersgracht 376, 1016 GA Amsterdam (☎427 92 76; www.keizerculinair.nl). Choose between a sumptuous Dutch or Italian 5-course feast—then learn to cook it and eat it—at this school. Located in a lovely canal house. An intensive workshop focuses on specialty skills, while the extended course lasts 5 weeks.

PORTUGAL

Universidade de Lisboa, Al. da Universidade, Cidade Universitária, 1600-214 Lisbon (☎217 96 37 59; www.ul.pt). Allows direct enrollment of foreign students in most of its divisions. Free Portuguese language classes for enrolled foreign students.

SPAIN

Universidad Complutense de Madrid, Vicerrectorado de Relaciones Internacionales, Isaac Peral, 28040 Madrid (☎913 94 69 20; www.ucm.es). Largest university in Spain. Hosts 3500 foreign students annually. Opportunities for study in a variety of fields with or without a specific study abroad program.

SWITZERLAND

Eidgenössische Technische Hoschschule (ETH; Swiss Federal Institute of Technology), Student Exchange Office, ETH Zentrum, CH-8092 Zurich (☎(01) 632 61 61; www.mobilitaet.ethz.ch). ETH is a member of the TransAtlantic Science Student Exchange Program (TASSEP), and provides study abroad to students at specific institutions in Australia, Canada, the EU, and the US. Exchanges are generally cheap; inquire with your university to determine if your school participates.

LANGUAGE SCHOOLS

Unlike American universities, language schools are often independently run international or local divisions of foreign universities that rarely offer college credit. Language schools are a good alternative to university study if you desire a more intense focus on the language or a slightly less-rigorous courseload. These programs are also good for high school students that might not feel comfortable with older students in a university program.

MULTI-COUNTRY

Eurocentres, 101 N. Union St., Ste. 300, Alexandria, VA 22314, USA (☎703-684-1494; www.eurocentres.com) or in Europe, Head Office, Seestr. 247, CH-8038 Zurich, Switzerland (☎41 1 485 50 40; fax 481 61 24). Language programs for beginning to advanced students with homestays in Britain, France, Germany, Italy, and Spain.

Language Immersion Institute, 75 South Manheim Blvd., SUNY-New Paltz, New Paltz, NY 12561, USA (☎845-257-3500; www.newpaltz.edu/lii). 2-week summer language courses and some longer overseas courses in France, Italy, and Spain. Program fees are around US$1000 for a 2-week course.

LanguagesPLUS, 413 Ontario St., Toronto, Ontario M5A 2V9, Canada (US ☎888-526-4758; international 416-925-7117; www.languagesplus.com), runs 2- to 12-week programs in Britain, France, Germany, Ireland, Italy, and Spain. 18+. US$350-3000; includes tuition and accommodations with host families or apartments.

AUSTRIA

University of Vienna Language Center, Alser Str. 23/12, A-1080 Vienna (☎42 77 18 277; www.univie.ac.at/wihok). Offers German courses for beginners and advanced students, as well as lectures on German and Austrian culture. Tuition for a 5-week summer course €280. Longer courses (trimesters and semesters) also offered.

BRITAIN

Clì—The New Gaels, North Tower, The Castle, Inverness IV2 3EU (☎01463 226 710; www.cli.org.uk). Organization for the promotion of Scottish Gaelic culture. Language courses offered; searchable database of Gaelic centers and classes online.

Sabhal Mór Ostaig, Teangue, Isle of Skye, IV44 8RQ (☎01471 888 000; www.smo.uhi.ac.uk). College on the Isle of Skye offers long- and short-term courses in Gaelic language and culture. Fees for short-term Gaelic classes £125-200.

The University of Edinburgh, Office of Lifelong Learning, 11 Buccleuch Pl., Edinburgh EH8 9LW (☎0131 650 4400 or 0131 662 0783; www.lifelong.edu.ac.uk). Has a wide range of short-term classes including language courses.

School of Welsh, Trinity College Carmarthen, Wales SA31 3EP (☎0126 676 746; www.trinity-cm.ac.uk). Offers Welsh language courses of varying intensity from 1 day to 30 weeks.

Acen, Ivor House, Bridge St., Cardiff, Wales CF10 2EE (☎029 2030 0808; www.acen.co.uk). Promotes the Welsh language through classes and publications; has contacts with organizations and schools throughout Wales.

DENMARK

AOF, Amager, 21 Lyongate, 2300 Copenhagen S (☎32 86 03 04 or 39 16 82 00). Non-Danes over 18 years of age living in Denmark are eligible for free language instruction. Also provides educational and vocational advisors to help navigate Danish employment requirements and opportunities.

K.I.S.S., 2 Nørrebrogade, 2200 Copenhagen N (☎35 36 25 55). A super-efficient school that places emphasis on spoken communication and pronunciation. 3-week courses covering 10 levels of proficiency, and an 11th level culminating in the Danish Test 2 fluency exam. Instruction is free for non-native residents, but there is a waiting list.

H.O.F., 26 Købmagergade, 1150 Copenhagen K (☎33 11 88 33). Privately-run school offering morning, afternoon, and evening classes 2-3 times per week. 30 2-3hr. classes cost 775kr; basic instruction takes approximately 2 months and costs 1600kr.

FRANCE

Alliance Française, Ecole Internationale de Langue et de Civilisation Française, 101 bd. Raspail, 75270 Paris Cédex 06 (☎01 42 84 90 00; www.alliancefr.org). Instruction at all levels, with courses in legal and business French. Courses are 1-4 months in length. €267 for 16 2hr. sessions; €534 for 16 4hr. sessions.

Cours de Civilisation Française de la Sorbonne, 47 r. des Ecoles, 75005 Paris (☎01 40 46 22 11; www.fle.fr/sorbonne). Courses in the French language at all levels, along with a comprehensive lecture program of French cultural studies taught by Sorbonne professors. Must be at least 18 and at *baccalauréat* level. Semester- and year-long courses during the academic year and 4-, 6-, 8-, and 11-week summer programs.

Institut de Langue Française, 3 av. Bertie-Albrecht, 75008 Paris (☎01 45 63 24 00; www.inst-langue-fr.com). Culture, literature, and specialized language courses. Offers 4-week to year-long programs, 6-20hr. per week. From €185.

Institut Parisien de Langue et de Civilisation Française, 87 bd. de Grenelle, 75015 Paris (☎01 40 56 09 53; www.institut-parisien.com). French language, fashion, culinary arts, and cinema courses. Intensive language courses from €125-375 per week.

GERMANY

Deutscher Akademischer Austauschdienst (DAAD), see p. 64.

Goethe-Institut, Dachauer Str. 122, 80637 München, mailing address Postfach 190419, 80604 München (☎089 15 92 10; www.goethe.de). Runs numerous German language programs in Germany and abroad; also orchestrates high school exchange programs in Germany. 8-week intensive summer course €3350; with room €4550.

GREECE

School of Modern Greek Language at the Aristotle University of Thessaloniki, Thessaloniki 54006 (☎310 99 7571; www.auth.gr/smg). Summer, winter, and intensive programs offered in conjunction with philosophy classes.

ITALY

Centro Fiorenza, V. S. Spirito, 14, 50125 Florence (☎055 239 8274; www.centrofiorenza.com). Language courses from 10-50 hours per week starting at €330. Accommodations are homestays or student apartments. Also offers courses on the island of Elba, although the accomodations are considerably more expensive.

Istituto Zambler Venezia, Campo S. Margherita, 3116A, Dorsoduro, Venice (☎041 522 4331; www.istitutovenezia.com). 1- to 10-week language, cooking, and art courses. Based in a 16th-century *palazzo* in the heart of Venice. €160-1980.

Italiaidea, V. dei due Macelli, 47/I fl., 00187 Rome (☎066 994 1314; www.italiaidea.com). Italian language and culture courses from €450 for a 4-week program.

Koinè, V. de Pandolfini, 27, I-50122 Florence (☎055 21 38 81; www.koinecenter.com). Language courses (group and individual intensive), cultural lessons, wine tastings, and cooking classes. Courses offered year-round in Bologna, Florence, and Lucca; summer programs in Cortona and Orbetello. 20 hr. group language lessons from €195 per week; additional fee for housing.

PORTUGAL

CIAL Centro de Linguas, Av. de República, 41-8° Esq., 1050-187 Lisbon (☎217 940 448; www.cial.pt). Portuguese language courses for all levels in Lisbon and Faro.

SPAIN

Institute of Spanish Studies, El Bachiller 13, 46010 Valencia (☎96 36 96 168; www.spanish-studies.com). Located in Valencia. Offers a range of courses in history, Spanish language, and literature. Students live with host families.

Don Quijote, Pl. San Marcos 7, 37002 Salamanca (☎923 26 88 60; www.donquijote.org). Offers Spanish language courses for all levels in Barcelona, Granada, Madrid, Málaga, Salamanca, Seville, and Valencia.

SWITZERLAND

University of Geneva Summer Courses, r. de Candolle 3, CH-1211 Geneva 4 (☎22 705 74 34; www.unige.ch/lettres/elcf/coursete/courangl.html). Teaches French language and civilization at all levels and offers excursions to Geneva and its surroundings. 17+. Tuition for a 3-week summer course 500SFr.

WORKING

As with volunteering, work opportunities tend to fall into two categories. Some travelers want long-term jobs that allow them to get to know another part of the world as a member of the community, while other travelers seek out short-term jobs to finance the next leg of their travels. International English-language newspapers, such as the International Herald Tribune (www.int.com), often list long- and short-term job opportunities in their classifieds sections.

Acquiring the appropriate work permits will be much easier for EU citizens than for others. Non-EU citizens planning to work in Europe must carefully research country-specific requirements and limitations before their departure.

LONG-TERM WORK

If you're planning to spend a substantial amount of time (more than three months) working in Europe, search for a job well in advance. International placement agencies are often the easiest way to find employment abroad, especially for teaching English. **Internships,** usually for college students, are a good way to segue into working abroad, although they are often unpaid or poorly paid (many say the experience, however, is well worth it). Be wary of advertisements or companies that claim the ability to get you a job abroad for a fee—often times the listings are out of date, or available online or in newspapers. It's best, if going through an organization, to use one that's reputable.

MULTI-COUNTRY

Council Exchanges, 633 Third Ave., New York, NY (☎800-407-8839; www.councilexchanges.org). Charges a US$300-475 fee for arranging 3- to 6-month work authorizations in France, Germany, and Ireland.

Escapeartist.com, (http://jobs.escapeartist.com). International employers post directly to this website; various European jobs advertised.

Go Jobsite, (www.gojobsite.com). Lists jobs in Britain, France, Germany, Ireland, Italy, and Spain.

International Co-operative Education, 15 Spiros Way, Menlo Park, CA 94025 (☎650-323-4944; www.icemenlo.com). Finds summer jobs for students in Belgium, Finland, Germany, and Switzerland. Costs include a US$200 application fee and a US$600 placement fee.

International Employment Gazette, 423 Townes St., Greenville, SC 29601 (☎800-882-9188; www.intemployment.com). An online subscription service that publishes available overseas jobs every 2 weeks. US$20 per month.

ResortJobs.com, (www.resortjobs.com). Searchable database of service and entertainment jobs at resorts around the world.

StepStone, UK office: StepStone ASA, 2 Bell Court, Leapale Lane, Guildford, Surrey GU1 4LY, Great Britain (☎44 14 83 73 94 50; fax 44 14 83 73 94 99; www.stepstone.com). An online database covering international employment openings for most of Europe. Several search options and a constantly changing list of openings.

 WORK AND STUDY VISA INFORMATION. Work and study visas for most countries can be acquired only with the help of a sponsoring organization in that country; non-EU nationals looking for work may have a hard time getting permission, and, if they do secure a permit, it may be valid for only 3-6 months. The organizations listed under **Long-Term Work** (see p. 69) may be able to find sponsors, while the **Center for International Business and Travel** (CIBT; see p. 12) can help expedite the visa process. Study-abroad programs or universities should have no problems sponsoring study visas; check before applying to an institution. Citizens of the EU are free to work in any EU member country, but they may need special permits. Contact the consulate of the country in which you want to work for more info.

BRITAIN

Anders Glaser Wills, Capital House, 1 Houndwell Pl., Southampton, S014 1HU (☎023 8022 3511; andersglaserwills.com). An international job placement agency with 11 offices in Britain.

Fruitful Ltd., Unit 3 Ind. Est., Honeybourne, Evesham, Worcester, WR117QF (☎01386 83255; www.fruitfuljobs.com). Sets up farm work for backpackers and students in the UK; online application available.

FRANCE

French-American Chamber of Commerce (FACC), International Career Development Programs, 1350 Ave. of the Americas, 6th fl., New York, NY 10019, USA (☎212-765-4460). Offers *Work In France* programs, internships, teaching, and public works.

Agence Nationale Pour l'Emploi (ANPE), 4 impasse d'Antin, 75008 Paris (☎01 43 59 62 63; www.anpe.fr). National employment agency has offices throughout France. Comprehensive website with specific info on employment opportunities.

Centre d'Information et de Documentation Jeunesse (CIDJ), 101 quai Branly, 75740 Paris (☎01 44 49 12 00; www.cidj.asso.fr). An invaluable state-run youth center provides info on education, employment, and careers. English spoken. Jobs are posted on the bulletin boards outside. Open M, W, F 10am-6pm; Tu and Th 10am-7pm; Sa 9:30am-1pm.

IRELAND

Working Ireland, 26 Eustace St., Templebar, Dublin 2 (☎01 677 0300; www.workingireland.ie). Multi-tasking agency arranges accommodations and job placement throughout the country. They also help you collect tax refunds and arrange travel home.

ITALY

American Chamber of Commerce in Italy, V. Cantù 1, 20123, Milan (☎02 869 0661; www.amcham.it). Lists employment opportunities and allows job seekers to post resumes. Membership (US$400 for non-residents) gives access to networking, trade fairs, economics info, and professional discounts.

Italian Chambers of Commerce Abroad, (www.italchambers.net). **Australia:** Adelaide, Brisbane, Melbourne, Perth, Sydney. **Canada:** Toronto, Vancouver, Winnipeg. **UK:** London. **US:** Chicago, Houston, Los Angeles, New York.

Recruitaly, (www.recruitaly.it). Directory of Italian corporations seeking to employ foreign college graduates. Useful info about labor laws and documentation.

THE NETHERLANDS

Undutchables, P.O. Box 57204, 1040 BC Amsterdam (☎623 13 00; www.undutchables.nl). The most useful job agency for foreigners, recruiting for work that requires command of a language other than Dutch. Temporary and permanent jobs available.

Other temp agencies: Content, Van Baerlestraat 83 (☎676 44 41); **Manpower** (☎305 56 55); **Randstad,** Dam 4 (☎626 22 13).

SPAIN

Trabajos, (www.trabajos.com). Provides job listings for all regions of Spain.

TEACHING ENGLISH

Teaching jobs abroad are rarely well-paid, although some private American schools can pay competitive salaries. Volunteering as a teacher is also a popular option; programs often provide a daily stipend to help with living expenses. In almost all cases, you must have at least a bachelor's degree to be a full-fledged teacher, although college undergraduates can get summer positions tutoring.

Many schools require teachers to have a **Teaching English as a Foreign Language** (TEFL) certificate. This does not necessarily exclude you from finding a teaching job, but certified teachers often find higher paying jobs. Native English speakers working in private schools are most often hired for immersion classrooms where only English is spoken. Those volunteering or teaching in public schools, or poorer areas, are more likely to be working in both English and the local language. Placement agencies or university fellowship programs are the best resources for finding teaching jobs in Europe. The alternative is to make contacts directly with schools or just to try your luck once you get there. The following organizations specialize in placing teachers in Europe.

Fulbright English Teaching Assistantship, U.S. Student Programs Division, Institute of International Education, 809 United Nations Plaza, New York, NY 10017-3580 (☎212-984-5330; www.fulbrightexchanges.org). Competitive program sends college graduates to teach in Switzerland.

International Schools Services (ISS), 15 Roszel Rd., Box 5910, Princeton, NJ 08543 (☎609-452-0990; www.iss.edu). Hires teachers for more than 200 schools worldwide. Teaching experience recommended. 2-year commitment expected.

Office of Overseas Schools, US Department of State, Rm. H328, SA-1, Washington, DC 20522 (☎202-261-8200; www.state.gov/m/a/os/c6776.htm). Maintains a list of schools and agencies that arrange placement for Americans to teach abroad.

Teaching English as a Foreign Language (TEFL), TEFL Professional Network Ltd., 72 Pentyla Baglan Rd., Port Talbot SA12 8AD, UK (www.tefl.com). Maintains the most extensive database of openings throughout Europe. Offers job training and certification.

AU PAIR WORK

Au pairs are typically women, aged 18-27, who work as live-in nannies, caring for children and doing light housework in foreign countries in exchange for room, board, and a small spending allowance or stipend. Most former au pairs speak favorably of the experience as a chance to get to know a country without the high expenses of traveling. Drawbacks, however, include long hours and somewhat mediocre pay: au pairs in Europe typically work 25-35 hours per week and receive $200-350 per month. Much of the au pair experience really does depend on the host family. The agencies below help place au pairs.

Accord Cultural Exchange, 3145 Geary Blvd., San Francisco, CA 94118, USA (☎415-386-6203; www.aupairsaccord.com).

L'Accueil Familial des Jeunes Etrangers, 23 r. du Cherche-Midi, 75006 Paris, France (☎01 42 22 50 34; www.afje-paris.org).

Au Pair in Europe, P.O. Box 68056, Blakely Postal Outlet, Hamilton, Ontario, Canada L8M 3M7 (☎905-545-6305; www.princeent.com/aupair).

Au Pair Italy, V. Demetrio Martinelli, 11/d, Bologna 40133, Italy (☎39 05 138 3466; www.aupairitaly.com).

Childcare International, Ltd., Trafalgar House, Grenville Pl., London NW7 3SA, UK (☎44 020 8906 3116; www.childint.co.uk).

Mix Culture Au Pair Service, V. Nazionale 204, Rome 00184, Italy (☎39 06 4788 2289; fax 4782 6164; http://web.tiscali.it/mixcultureroma/index.htm).

Working Abroad, InterExchange, 161 Sixth Ave., New York, NY 10013, USA (☎212-924-0446; www.interexchange.org).

ALTERNATIVES TO TOURISM

SHORT-TERM WORK

Traveling for long periods of time can get expensive, so picking up odd jobs for a few weeks at a time is a good way to subsidize the next leg of a trip. Another option is to work several hours a day at a hostel in exchange for free or discounted room and/or board. Most often, these short-term jobs are found by word of mouth, or simply by talking to the owner of a hostel or restaurant. Due to the high turnover in the tourism industry, places are often eager for help.

The availability and legality of temporary work vary widely across Europe. If you are interested in working your way through the continent, we recommend picking up *Let's Go* city and country guides. These books contain thorough information on local work opportunities at specific hostels and restaurants, and are updated yearly.

FURTHER READING ON ALTERNATIVES TO TOURISM

Alternatives to the Peace Corps: A Directory of Third World and U.S. Volunteer Opportunities, by Joan Powell. Food First Books, 2001 (US$10).

How to Get a Job in Europe, by Matherly and Sanborn. Planning Communications, 2003 (US$23).

How to Live Your Dream of Volunteering Overseas, by Collins, DeZerega, Heckscher, and Lappe. Penguin Books, 2002 (US$17).

International Directory of Voluntary Work, by Victoria Pybus. Peterson's Guides and Vacation Work, 2003 (US$20).

International Jobs, by Kocher and Segal. Perseus Books, 2003 (US$19).

Overseas Summer Jobs 2002, by Collier and Woodworth. Peterson's Guides and Vacation Work, 2002 (US$18).

Work Abroad: The Complete Guide to Finding a Job Overseas, by Hubbs, Griffith, and Nolting. Transitions Abroad Publishing, 2002 ($20).

Work Your Way Around the World, by Susan Griffith. Worldview Publishing Services, 2003 (US$20).

Invest Yourself: The Catalogue of Volunteer Opportunities. The Commission on Voluntary Service and Action (☎ 718-638-8487).

ALTERNATIVES
TO TOURISM

ANDORRA

The forgotten country sandwiched between France and Spain, Andorra (pop. 65,000; 464 sq. km), has had its democratic constitution for only ten years; it spent its first 12 centuries caught in a tug-of-war between the Spanish Counts of Urgell, the Church of Urgell, and the French King. Catalán is the official language, but French and Spanish are widely spoken. All establishments were once required to accept *pesetas* and *francs*, but the country's now on the euro system. Because of Andorra's diminutive size, one day can include sniffing aisles of duty-free perfume, hiking through a pine-scented valley, and relaxing in a luxury spa.

▚ TRANSPORTATION AND PRACTICAL INFORMATION

The only way to get to Andorra is by car or bus. All traffic from Spain enters through the town of La Seu d'Urgell; the gateway to France is Pas de la Casa. **Andor-Inter/Samar** buses (Andorra ☎82 62 89; Madrid ☎914 68 41 90; Toulouse ☎561 58 14 53) run from Andorra la Vella to **Madrid** (9hr.; Tu and F-Su 11am, W-Th and Su 10pm; €35), as does **Eurolines** (Andorra ☎80 51 51; Madrid ☎915 06 33 60; Tu-Th and Su 11:30am, F and Su 10pm; €33). **Alsina Graells** (Andorra ☎82 65 67) runs to **Barcelona** (4hr., 5 per day, €18), as does **Eurolines** (3¼hr., 5 per day, €19). To go anywhere in Spain other than Madrid or Barcelona, first go to the town of La Seu d'Urgell on a **La Hispano-Andorra** bus (☎82 13 72; 30min., 5-7 per day, €2.50), departing from Av. Meritxell 11. From La Seu, Alsina Graells buses continue into Spain via Puigcerdà (1hr., 2 per day, €3.60) and Lérida (2½hr., 2 per day, €10.10). **Driving** in Andorra la Vella is an adventure for some, a nightmare for others. Navigating the crowded and twisting streets, which often lack signs, can prove a maddening chore; it's best to ditch the car in one of the many parking lots as soon as possible. Efficient intercity buses connect the villages along the three major highways that converge in Andorra la Vella. Since most towns are only 10min. apart, the country's cities can be seen in a single day via public transportation. **Bus** stops are easy to find; rides cost €0.70-1.70. All buses make every stop in the city. Making an international **telephone call** in Andorra is a chore; you'll have to buy a STA *teletarjeta* (telecard) at the tourist office (p. 74) or the post office (€3 minimum). For directory assistance dial ☎111 or 119 (international). *Let's Go* uses the same **price diversity** range in Andorra as in Spain (p. 853).

SUGGESTED ITINERARIES

THE BEST OF (OKAY, ALL OF) ANDORRA IN THREE DAYS

First, spend, spend, spend in the duty-free shops of **Andorra la Vella** (1 day, p. 74). Then hike Andorra's mountains, including its tallest peak, **Pic Alt de la Coma Pedrosa** (2946m) in nearby (and what isn't?) **La Massana** (1 day, p. 76). Afterward, nurse sore muscles in **Escaldes-Engordany** (1 day, p. 75) at Europe's largest spa resort, Caldea-Spa.

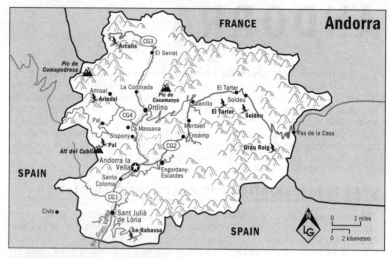

ANDORRA LA VELLA

Andorra la Vella (pop. 20,760), the country's capital, is little more than Spain and France's shopping mall. Effectively a single cluttered road flanked by shop after duty-free shop, this city is anything but *vella* (old); most of the old buildings have been upstaged by shiny new electronics and sporting goods stores. After shopping, you're best off escaping to the countryside.

■ 🔁 **ORIENTATION AND PRACTICAL INFORMATION.** Coming from Spain, visitors first pass through Sant Juliá de Lória and then tiny Santa Coloma, which runs directly into Andorra la Vella. The main thoroughfare **Avinguda Santa Coloma** becomes **Av. Príncep Benlloch** several blocks into the city, which in turn becomes **Av. Meritxell** at Pl. Príncep Benlloch before continuing on as the highway to parishes northeast of the capital. There are several **tourist offices** scattered throughout Andorra la Vella; the largest is on Pl. de la Rotonda. From Spain, take Av. Meritxell until it crosses the river. At the bridge Pl. de la Rotonda will be on your right. Their multilingual staff offers free *Sports Activities* and *Hotels i Restaurants* guides. (☎82 71 17. July-Aug. open M-Sa 9am-9pm, Su 9am-7pm. Sept.-June open daily 9:30am-1:30pm, 3:30-7:30pm.) In a **medical emergency** call ☎116 or the **police,** Prat de la Creu 16 (☎87 20 00). For **weather and ski conditions,** call Ski Andorra (☎86 43 89). The **post office,** Carrer Joan Maragall, 10, is across the river from Pl. Princep Benlloch. (☎902 19 71 97. **Lista de Correos** upstairs. Open M-F 8:30am-2:30pm, Sa 9:30am-1pm.) **Internet** is available at **Future@Point,** C. de La Sardana 6. (☎82 82 02. €1.20/15min. Open M-Sa 10am-11pm, Su 10am-10pm. MC/V.)

🔁🔁 **ACCOMMODATIONS AND FOOD. Hostal del Sol ❶,** Pl. Guillemó 3, provides decent rooms and friendly service. From Spain, take Av. Príncep Benlloch until you pass the **Teatre Comunal** on your right. At the next intersection, bear left onto C. Doctor Nequi. Watch for the fountain of Pl. Guillemó on your left. (☎82 37 01. €13 per person. MC/V.) You don't exactly rough it at shaded **Camp-**

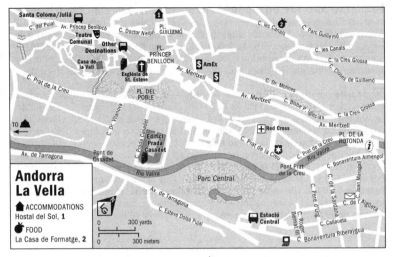

Santa Coloma/Juliá

C. del Pujal Av. Princep Benlloch C. Doctor Nequi PL. GUILLEMÓ

Teatre Comunal

Other Desinations

Casa de la Vall

Església de St. Esteve

PL. PRÍNCEP BENLLOCH

Av. Meritxell AmEx

C. Prat de la Creu

C. Dr. Vilanova

PL. DEL POBLE

Edifici Prada Casadet

C. Prada Casadet

Pont de Casadet

Av. de Tarragona

Riu Valira

C. les Canals C. Parc Guillemó

C. les Canals

C. la Creu Grossa

C. Closes de Guillemó

C. Dr. Molines

Av. Meritxell C. Bisba P. Iglesias

C. la Creu Grossa

Red Cross Av. Meritxell

PL. DE LA ROTONDA

C. Prat de la Creu Riu Valira

C. Prat de la Creu

C. Bonaventura Armengol

Pont Prat de la Creu

C. Pere d'Urg

C. de la Sardana

C. de l'Alzineta

C. Joan Maragall

Andorra La Vella

▲ ACCOMMODATIONS
Hostal del Sol, 1

🍴 FOOD
La Casa de Formatge, 2

0   300 yards
0   300 meters

Parc Central

Av. de Tarragona

C. Esteve Dolsà Pujal

Estació Central

C. Roger Bernat III

C. Callaueta

C. Bonaventura Riberaygua

---

ing Valira ❶, Av. Salou, behind the Estadi Comunal d'Andorra la Vella, which has video games, hot showers, and an indoor pool. (☎82 23 84. €4.50 per person, per tent, and per car. Call ahead. Handicap accessible.) Try the two-story cheese shop extravaganza ◪**La Casa del Formatge,** C. les Canals 4. From Spain, take your first left after Pl. Príncep Benlloch, and then turn left on C. les Canals. (Entrees €5-10. Open M-F 10am-8pm, Sa 9:30am-9pm, Su 9:30am-7pm.)

🛈 EXCURSIONS. The best thing to do in Andorra la Vella is drop your bags in a hostel and get out. **Caldea-Spa,** bordering **Escaldes-Engordany,** is the largest in Europe, with luxurious treatments and prices to match. (☎80 09 99. €25 for 3hr., plus fees for each service. Open daily 9am-11pm.) Housed within the Caldea-Spa complex is the ◪**MicroArt Museum,** which houses an amazing collection of Chinese and Ukrainian miniature art. Using yogic breathing to steady his hand, micromaster Nikolai Siadristy created amazingly small, often microscopic objects, including the tiniest inscription ever made. A grain of rice has never been so enthralling. (Open daily 9am-9pm. €3.) If you have no patience for the miniscule, visit **Canillo** for some fun in the colossal **Palau de Gel D'Andorra,** a recreational complex with swimming pool, squash courts, and an ice-skating rink ("ice disco" or "ice-rink go-carts" by night), which hosts ice-rink go-carts on Friday nights. (☎80 08 40. Open daily 10am-11:30pm; each facility has its own hours. €5.50-8 each. €12.20 for all in 1 day. Ice-rink go-carts F 10:30-midnight. €13. Equipment rental €2.30-€4.50.) For shopping, check out one of the three-story supermarket monstrosities in nearby Santa Coloma, or the **Grans Magatzems Pyrénées,** Av. Meritxell 11, the country's biggest department store, where an entire aisle is dedicated to chocolate bars. (Open Sept.-July M-F 9:30am-8pm, Sa 9:30am-9pm, Su 9:30am-7pm; Aug. and holidays M-Sa 9:30am-9pm, Su 9:30am-7pm.) Nowhere is Andorra's contrast of old and new better on display than at the **Santuari de Meritxell,** in Canillo, which incorporates medieval, Islamic, and ultramodern elements. The Santuari houses a permanent collection dedicated to the patron saint of Andorra: The Virgen of Meritxell. (☎85 12 53. Open Su-M and W-Sa 9:15am-1pm and 3-6pm. Free admission and guided tours July-Oct.)

⚑ HIKING AND THE OUTDOORS. The tourist office brochure *Sports Activities* has 52 suggested hiking itineraries, as well as cabin and *refugios* listings. La Massana is home to Andorra's tallest peak, **Pic Alt de la Coma Pedrosa** (2946m). For organized hiking trips, try the **La Rabassa Sports and Nature Center** (☎32 38 68), in southwest Andorra. In addition to *refugio*-style accommodations, the center has mountain biking, guided hikes, horseback riding, archery, and other field sports.

⛷ SKIING. With five outstanding resorts, Andorra offers skiing opportunities galore. (Nov.-Apr.; €30-40.) **Pal** (☎73 70 00), 10km from La Massana, is accessible by bus from La Massana (5 per day, last returning at 5pm; €1.50). Seven buses run daily from La Massana to nearby **Arinsal**, the last returning at 6:45pm (€1). On the French border, **Pas de la Casa Grau Roig** (☎80 10 60) offers 600 hectares of skiable land, lessons, two medical centers, night skiing, and 27 lifts serving 48 trails for all levels of ability. **Soldeu-El Tarter** (☎89 05 00) occupies 840 hectares of skiable area between Andorra la Vella and Pas de la Casa. **Free buses** pick up skiers from their hotels in Canillo. The more horizontal **La Rabassa** (☎32 38 68) is Andorra's only cross-country ski resort, offering sleighing, skiing, and horse rides. Call **SKI Andorra** (☎86 43 89; www.skiandorra.ad) or the tourist office with any questions.

AUSTRIA
(ÖSTERREICH)

At the peak of Habsburg megalomania, the Austrian Empire was one of the largest in history, encompassing much of Europe from Poland and Hungary in the east to Spain in the west. Although the mighty empire crumbled during World War II, Austria remains a complex, multiethnic country. Drawing on centuries of Habsburg political maneuvering, Austria has become a skillful mediator between Eastern and Western Europe, connecting its eight bordering countries. Today, Austria owes much of its allure to the overpowering Alps, which dominate two-thirds of its surface. The mention of Austria evokes images of onion-domed churches set against snow-capped alpine peaks, castles rising from lush meadows of golden flowers, and 12th-century monasteries towering over the majestic Danube.

LIFE AND TIMES

HISTORY

HOLY ROMANS AND HABSBURGS (800-1740). Austria had its first taste of imperialism in the mid-9th century when **Charlemagne,** founder of the Holy Roman Empire, expanded his kingdom eastward. When he died, the kingdom collapsed and was overrun by pillaging tribes. After driving them out, Holy Roman Emperor **Otto II** entrusted the Bavarian Margrave Liutpoldus (a.k.a. **Leopold of Babenberg**) with the defense of these territories. During his reign, Austria gained its name: *Ostarrichi* (Old High German for *Österreich*), which meant "Eastern Realm."

SUGGESTED ITINERARIES

THREE DAYS Spend all three days in **Vienna** (p. 84), the Imperial headquarters of romance. From the stately **Staatsoper** to the glittering **Musikverein,** the majestic **Hofburg** to the simple **Kirche am Steinhof,** Vienna's attractions will leave you with enough sensory stimulation to last until your next vacation.

ONE WEEK Begin in the Western Austrian mountain town of **Kitzbühel** (1 day; p. 114) to take advantage of its hiking and skiing opportunities. Stop in **Salzburg** (2 days; p. 101) to see the home of Mozart and *The Sound of Music*. Move on to the Salzkammergut region to wonder at the **Dachstein Ice Caves** (1 day; p. 109). End by basking in the glory of **Vienna** (3 days).

TWO WEEKS Start in **Innsbruck,** where museums and mountains meet (2 days; p. 110), then swing by **Kitzbühel** (2 days). Spend another two days wandering **Hohe Tauern National Park** (p. 109), visiting the Krimml Waterfalls and the Großglockner Hochalpenstraße. Next, tour **Hallstatt** and its nearby ice caves (2 days; p. 108). Follow your ears to **Salzburg** (3 days), then check out rural Austria in **Grünau** (1 day; p. 109). Head to **Graz** (1 day; p. 115) for its throbbing nightlife. Finally, make your way to **Vienna** for a grand finale of romance, waltzes, and high coffeehouse culture (4 days).

AUSTRIA

Unfortunately for the dynasty, the last Babenberg died childless. Into this vacuum, hands bloodied, rushed **Rudolf of Habsburg.** Six centuries of Habsburg rule proved the wedding vow an able companion to the sword; receiving The Netherlands from his wife, **Maximilian I** is credited with the adaptation of Ovid's couplet: *"Bella gerant alii, tu felix Austria nube"* ("Let other nations go to war; you, lucky Austria, marry"). His son **Philip** married into Spanish lines, endowing his grandson, **Charles V**, with an empire that encompassed Austria, Burgundy, The Netherlands, Spain, Spanish America, and Italian possessions.

Despite this breadth, Martin Luther's **Protestant Reformation** shook the Habsburg base in the 16th and 17th centuries. Peasants left the Catholic Church *en masse*, and Protestant nobles doggedly fought the Habsburgs in the **Thirty Years' War** (1618-1648). Soon after, the Ottoman Turks besieged Vienna until **Prince Eugene of Savoy** drove them out. The plucky Eugene came through again when he triumphed over the French in the **War of Spanish Succession.**

CASTLES CRUMBLE (1740-1914). But like a house of cards, the Habsburg empire grew tenuous as it grew up. When **Maria Theresa** ascended the throne in 1740, her neighbors were eager to rein in Habsburg power. The marriage of her daughter **Marie Antoinette** to the future **Louis XVI,** an attempt to forge an alliance with France, was quickly negated by the **French Revolution.** After the Revolution, **Napoleon Bonaparte** secured French possession of many Austrian territories. French troops even invaded Vienna, where Napoleon took up residence in Maria Theresa's favorite palace, **Schönbrunn** (p. 97), and married her granddaughter.

Napoleon's success led to the official establishment of the Austrian empire. In 1804, Franz II renounced his claim to the now-defunct Holy Roman crown and proclaimed himself **Franz I,** Emperor of Austria. During the Congress of Vienna, which redrew the map of Europe after Napoleon's defeat, Austrian Chancellor **Clemens von Metternich** reconsolidated Austrian power. Calm prevailed until the spring of 1848, when the French philosophy of **middle-class revolution** reached Austria. Students and workers revolted and seized the palace, demanding a written constitution and freedom of the press. The movement was divided and the rebellion quashed. Nevertheless, the emperor was eventually pressured to abdicate in favor of his nephew, **Franz Josef I,** whose 68-year reign was one of Austria's longest.

Austria's political status continued to shift throughout Franz Josef's life. Prussia, under **Otto von Bismarck,** dominated European politics, defeating Austria in 1866 and establishing a dual **Austro-Hungarian monarchy.** Although Franz Josef was one of the more enlightened leaders of the day, and made male suffrage universal by 1907, the nationalist sentiments of the Slavic underclass grew unchecked.

CURRENTS OF MODERNITY (1914-1945). Brimming with ethnic tension and locked into a rigid system of alliances from 19th-century wars, the Austro-Hungarian Empire was highly combustible material. The spark was the assassination of Austrian archduke and heir **Franz Ferdinand** in June 1914 by a Serbian nationalist in Sarajevo. Austria's declaration of war against Serbia set off a chain reaction that pulled most of Europe into the conflict, beginning **World War I.** Franz Josef died in 1916, leaving the throne to his reluctant grandnephew Karl I, who struggled in vain to preserve the Empire. Despite his valiant efforts, monarchy was a lost cause. On November 11, 1918, Karl finally made peace, but only after the 640-year-old Habsburg dynasty was snuffed by the establishment of the **First Republic of Austria.**

Between 1918 and 1938, Austria had its first, bitter taste of parliamentary democracy. The Republic suffered massive inflation, unemployment, and near economic collapse, but was stabilized by the mid-1920s. In 1933, the weak coalition government gave way when **Engelbert Dollfuss** declared martial law in order to protect Austria from Hitler. Two years later Dollfuss was assassinated by Austrian **Nazis.** The well-known conclusion to the tale of the First Republic is the Nazi

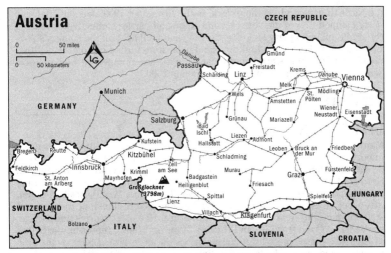

Austria

annexation of Austria. In 1938, the new Hitler-appointed Nazi chancellor invited German troops into Austria. While **World War II** raged, tens of thousands of Jews, political dissidents, disabled and mentally challenged people, Roma (Gypsies), and homosexuals were sent to Nazi concentration camps.

After Soviet troops brutally liberated Vienna in 1945, Allied troops divided Austria into four zones of occupation. During the occupation, the Soviets tried to make Austria a Communist state, but having failed, they finally settled for stripping their sector of any moveable infrastructure. Despite Russian plundering and severe famines in the late 1940s, the American **Marshall Plan** helped to jump-start the Austrian economy, laying the foundation for Austria's present prosperity.

The **Federal Constitution** (1945) and the **State Treaty** (1955), which established Austrian independence and sovereignty, formed the basis for the current Austrian nation, frequently referred to as the **Second Republic.** These documents provided a president (head of state), who is elected for six-year terms, a chancellor (head of government), usually the leader of the strongest party, a bicameral parliamentary legislature, and strong provincial governments. Until very recently, the government has been dominated by two parties, the **Social Democratic Party** (SPÖ) and the **People's Party** (ÖVP). The two parties built one of the world's most successful industrial economies, with enviably low unemployment and inflation rates.

TODAY

THE EUROPEAN UNION. During the 1990s, the country moved toward stronger European unification; current President **Thomas Klestil** was elected on a European integration platform in 1994. In 1995, the country joined the European Union (EU), after citizens accepted membership through a national referendum. Austria adopted the **euro** in January of 2002, phasing out its *Schilling* by July, 2002.

HAIDER AND THE FREEDOM PARTY. In the past few years, Austria has garnered international attention from the political gains made by the far-right **Freedom Party** (FPÖ). This party is infamous primarily for its founder, **Jörg Haider,** who maintains a strong anti-immigrant stance and who has made many remarks that have been seen as sympathetic to Nazi beliefs. Haider has referred to the Nazi camps with euphemisms, and called for Austrian military men who fought for the Nazis to have pride in their work. In the November 1999 elections, Haider's party claimed 27% of the vote (second among all parties), effectively breaking the traditional two-party lock that the SPÖ and ÖVP held on the country's politics since WWII. One-hundred thousand protestors turned out on the day that members of the FPÖ were sworn in, and the EU levied unprecedented political sanctions against Austria, which were lifted in 2000.

THE ARTS

LITERATURE

Many of Austria's great writers were immigrants, but native Austrians have made important contributions to the literary scene as well. The *Song of the Nibelungs* (c. 1200), of unknown authorship, is one of the most impressive heroic epics in German. In the 19th century, **Johann Nestroy** wrote biting comedies and satires that lampooned social follies, such as *The Talisman* (1840). **Adalbert Stifter,** often called Austria's greatest novelist, employed classical themes and strongly metaphysical descriptions of nature. His short stories and novels, such as *The Condor* (1840) and *Indian Summer* (1857), represent the height of Austria's classical style. A classicist with a more lyrical flare, **Franz Grillparzer** penned pieces about the conflict between a life of thought and a life of action in such plays as *The Waves of the Sea and Love* (1831).

Around 1890, the atmosphere of "merry apocalypse" transformed Austrian literature. The literature dating from this second heyday of Austrian culture, known as the **fin de siècle**, is legendary. **Karl Kraus** unmasked the crisis, **Arthur Schnitzler** dramatized it, **Hugo von Hofmannsthal** ventured a cautious eulogy, and **Georg Trakl** commented on its collapse in feverish verse. The cafe provided the backdrop for the *fin de siècle* literary landscape. Meanwhile, the world's most famous psychoanalyst, **Sigmund Freud,** developed his theories of sexual repression and the subconscious—and no young man has looked at his mother in the same way since.

Many of Austria's literary titans, including **Marie von Ebner-Eschenbach** and **Franz Kafka,** lived within the Habsburg protectorate of Bohemia. Ebner-Eschenbach is often called the greatest female Austrian writer, known for her vivid individual portraits and her defense of women's rights. Kafka proved master of the surreal in *The Metamorphosis* (1915), a bizarre tale about waking up and really not feeling like yourself. When the Austro-Hungarian monarchy itself awoke a democracy, novelists **Robert Musil** and **Joseph Roth** were there to chart the transformation. More recently, **Ingeborg Bachman** has gingerly examined the complexities of womanhood, while **Thomas Bernhard** has insightfully critiqued Austrian society.

MUSIC

The first major musician of Viennese classicism was **Josef Haydn,** whose oratorio *The Creation* (1798) is a choral standard, but the work of **Wolfgang Amadeus Mozart** represents the pinnacle of the time period. A child prodigy and brilliant composer, he produced such well-known pieces as *A Little Night Music* (1787) and the unfinished *Requiem*. His work has been proclaimed to be "the culmination of all beauty in music." Although German-born, **Ludwig van Beethoven** lived in Vienna for much of his life and composed some of his most famous works there. In the 19th century, **Johannes Brahms** straddled musical traditions and **Anton Bruckner** created complicated orchestrations that earned him recognition as one of the world's greatest symphonic masters. Between **Johann Strauss the Elder** and his son, **Johann Strauss the Younger,** the Strauss family kept Vienna on its toes for much of the century by composing exhilarating **waltzes** that broke free from older, more formal dances. In the modern era, **Arnold Schönberg** rejected tonal keys, producing a highly abstracted sound. **Anton von Webern** and **Alban Berg** were both students of Schönberg and suffered under Nazi occupation for their "degenerate art."

THE VISUAL ARTS

Landlocked in the middle of Europe and rolling with cash, the Habsburgs married into power and bought into art. Truly Austrian art emerged in the works of **Gustav Klimt** and his followers, who founded the **Secession movement.** Secessionists sought to create space and appreciation for symbolism, Impressionism, and other artistic styles. This can be seen in Klimt's later paintings, such as *The Kiss* (1908), which combine naturalistic portraits with abstractly patterned backgrounds. **Oskar Kokoschka** and **Egon Schiele** revolted against "art *qua* art," seeking to present the energy formerly concealed behind the Secession's surface. Schiele's works are still controversial today for their depictions of tortured figures destroyed by their own bodies or by debilitating sexuality.

In 1897, the new artists split from the old as proponents of modernism took issue with the Viennese Academy's conservatism. This gave rise to the **Jugendstil** (a.k.a. **Art Nouveau**) movement, which formulated the ethic of function over form, an idea embraced by Vienna's artistic elite and most notably by the guru of architectural modernism, **Otto Wagner.**

The spring of architecture in Austria flowered in **Baroque** style. With ornate forms teased into grand entrances, dreamy vistas, and overwrought, cupid-covered facades, the Baroque invokes what was then the most popular art form in Europe—music. This style is exhibited exquisitely in the **Schönbrunn** (p. 97) and **Hofburg** (p. 96) palaces. Austria's 19th-century conservative modernism is showcased by the Ringstraße, the broad boulevard that encircles Vienna; this taste came to be known as the **Ringstraße Style.** In the 1920s and early 1930s, the Social Democratic administration built thousands of apartments in large **municipal projects,** in a style reflecting the newfound assertiveness of workers' movements and the ideals of **urban socialism.** The most outstanding project of the era is the **Karl-Marx-Hof** in Vienna. The huge structure, completed in 1930, extends over 1km and consists of 1600 apartments clustered around several courtyards.

ESSENTIALS

WHEN TO GO

November to March is peak ski season; prices in western Austria double and travelers need reservations months in advance. The situation reverses in the summer, when the flatter eastern half fills with vacationers. Sights and accommodations are cheaper and less crowded in the shoulder season (May-June and Sept.-Oct.). However, some Alpine resorts close in May and June—call ahead. The Vienna State Opera, the Vienna Boys' Choir, and many major theaters throughout Austria don't have any performances during July and August.

AUSTRIA

DOCUMENTS AND FORMALITIES

VISAS. EU Citizens do not need a visa. Citizens of Australia, Canada, New Zealand, South Africa, and the US do not need a visa for stays of up to 90 days.

EMBASSIES. All foreign embassies in Austria are in Vienna (p. 88). Austrian embassies at home include: **Australia,** 12 Talbot St., Forrest, Canberra ACT 2603 (☎(612) 6295 1533; www.austriaemb.org.au); **Canada,** 445 Wilbrod St., Ottawa, ON K1N 6M7 (☎613-789-1444; www.austro.org); **Ireland,** 15 Ailesbury Court, 93 Ailesbury Rd., Dublin 4 (☎(353) 1 269 4577); **New Zealand,** Level 2, Willbank House, 57 Willis St., Wellington (☎04 499 6393; austria@ihug.co.nz); **South Africa,** 1109 Duncan St., Momentum Office Park, Brooklyn, Pretoria 0011 (☎(012) 45 29 155; autemb@mweb.co.az); **UK,** 18 Belgrave Mews West, London SW1X 8HU (☎(020) 7235 3731; www.austria.org.uk); **US,** 3524 International Ct. NW, Washington, D.C. 20008 (☎202-895-6700; www.austria.org).

TRANSPORTATION

BY PLANE. The only major international airport is Vienna's Schwechat Flughafen (VIE). European flights also land in Linz, Innsbruck, Salzburg, Graz, and Klagenfurt. From London-Stansted, **Ryanair** flies to the latter three (☎3531 249 7851; www.ryanair.com).

BY TRAIN. The **Österreichische Bundesbahn** (ÖBB), Austria's federal railroad, operates an efficient system with fast and comfortable trains. **Eurail, InterRail,** and **Europe East** are valid in Austria; however, they do not guarantee a seat without a reservation (US$11). The **Austrian Railpass** allows three days of travel within any 15-day period on all rail lines; it also entitles holders to 40% off on bike rental at train stations (2nd-class US$107, each additional day US$15).

BY BUS. The efficient Austrian bus system consists mainly of orange **Bundes-Buses,** which cover areas inaccessible by train. They usually cost about as much as trains, but railpasses are not valid. Buy tickets at the station or from the driver. For bus info, call ☎(0222) 711 01 between 7am-7pm.

BY CAR. Driving is a convenient way to see more isolated parts of Austria, but gas is costly, an international license is required, and some small towns prohibit cars. The roads are well-maintained and well-marked, and Austrian drivers are quite careful. **Mitfahrzentrale** (ride-sharing services) in larger cities pair drivers with riders for a small fee. Riders then negotiate fares with the drivers. Be aware that not all organizations screen their drivers or riders; ask in advance.

BY BIKE. Bikes are a great way to get around Austria; roads are generally smooth and safe. Many train stations rent bikes and allow you to return them to any participating station. Consult local tourist offices for bike routes and maps.

TOURIST SERVICES AND MONEY

EMERGENCY	Police: ☎133. Ambulance: ☎144. Fire: ☎122.

TOURIST OFFICES. Virtually every town has a tourist office marked by a green "i" sign. Most brochures are available in English. Visit www.austria-tourism.at for more Austrian tourist info.

MONEY. On January 1, 2002, the **euro** (€) replaced the **Schilling** (ATS) as the unit of currency in Austria. For more info, see p. 14. As a general rule, it's cheaper to exchange money in Austria than at home. Railroad stations, airports, hotels, and most travel agencies offer exchange services, as do banks and currency exchanges. If you stay in hostels and prepare most of your own food, expect to spend anywhere from €30-60 per person per day. Accommodations start at about €12, while a basic sit-down meal usually costs around €10. Menus will say whether service is included (*Preise inclusive* or *Bedienung inclusiv*); if it is, you don't have to **tip**. If it's not, leave a tip up to 10%. Austrian restaurants expect you to seat yourself, and servers will not bring the bill until you ask them to do so. Say *Zahlen bitte* (TSAHL-en BIT-uh) to settle your accounts, and don't leave tips on the table. Be aware that some restaurants charge for each piece of bread that you eat during your meal. Don't expect to bargain except at flea markets and the Naschmarkt in Vienna. Austria has a 10-20% **value-added tax (VAT)**, which is applied to purchased goods. You can get refunds for purchases of over €75 at one store.

COMMUNICATION

TELEPHONES. Wherever possible, use a calling card for international phone calls, as the long-distance rates for national phone services are often exorbitant. Prepaid phone cards and major credit cards can be used for direct international calls, but they are still less cost-efficient. For info on cell phones, see p. 36. Direct dial access numbers include: **AT&T**, ☎(0800) 20 02 88; **British Telecom**, ☎(0800) 20 02 09; **Canada Direct**, ☎(0800) 20 02 17; **Ireland Direct**, ☎(0800) 40 00 00; **MCI**, ☎(0800) 20 02 35; **Sprint**, ☎(0800) 20 02 36; **Telecom New Zealand**, ☎(0800) 20 02 22; **Telkom South Africa**, ☎(0800) 20 02 30.

PHONE CODES	Country code: 43. International dialing prefix: 00 (from Vienna, 900). From outside Austria, dial int'l dialing prefix (see inside back cover) + 43 + city code + local number. To call **Vienna** from outside Austria, dial int'l dialing prefix + 43 + 1 + local number.

MAIL. Letters take 1-2 days within Austria. Airmail to North America takes 4-7 days, up to 9 days to Australia and New Zealand. Mark all letters and packages "mit Flugpost." Aerogrammes are the cheapest option. *Let's Go* lists the addresses for mail to be held (*Postlagernde Briefe*) in the practical information of big cities.

LANGUAGE. German is the official language. English is the most common second language; outside of cities and among older residents, English is less common. For basic German words and phrases, see p. 1036.

ACCOMMODATIONS AND CAMPING

AUSTRIA	❶	❷	❸	❹	❺
ACCOMMODATIONS	under €9	€9-15	€16-30	€31-70	over €70

Always ask if your lodging provides a **guest card** (*Gästekarte*), which grants discounts on activities, museums, and public transportation. The **Österreiches Jugendherbergsverband-Hauptverband** (ÖJH) runs the over 80 HI **hostels** in Austria. Because of the rigorous standards of the national organizations, these are usually very clean and orderly. Most charge €12-22 per night for dorms; non-HI members usually pay a surcharge. **Independent hostels** vary in quality, but often have more personality and foster a more lively backpacking culture. **Hotels** are expensive (singles €40-100; doubles €80-150). The cheapest have *Gasthof*, *Gästehaus*, or *Pension-Garni* in the name. Renting a **Privatzimmer** (room in a family home) is an inexpensive and friendly option. Rooms range from €20-50 a night; contact the local tourist office for a list. Slightly more expensive, **Pensionen** are similar to American and British bed-and-breakfasts. **Camping** in Austria is less about getting out into nature than about having a cheap place to sleep; most sites are large plots glutted with RVs and are open in summer only. Prices run €4-6 per person and €4-8 per tent. In the high Alps, hikers and mountaineers can retire to the famously well-maintained system of **mountain huts** (*Hütten*).

FOOD AND DRINK

AUSTRIA	❶	❷	❸	❹	❺
FOOD	under €5	€5-10	€11-16	€17-25	over €25

Loaded with fat, salt, and cholesterol, traditional Austrian cuisine is a cardiologist's nightmare but a delight to the palate. Staple foods include pork, veal, sausage, eggs, cheese, bread, and potatoes. Austria's best known dish, *Wienerschnitzel*, is a breaded meat cutlet (usually veal or pork) fried in butter. Vegetarians should look for *Spätzle* (noodles), *Eierschwammerl* (yellow mushrooms), or anything with the word "Vegi" in it. The best supermarkets are Billa and Hofer, where you can buy cheap rolls, fruits, and veggies. Natives nurse their sweet tooth with *Kaffee und Kuchen* (coffee and cake). Try *Sacher Torte*, a rich chocolate cake layered with marmalade; *Linzer Torte*, a light yellow cake with currant jam; *Apfelstrudel;* or just about any pastry. Austrian beers are outstanding—try *Stiegl Bier*, a Salzburg brew; *Zipfer Bier* from Upper Austria; and Styrian *Gösser Bier*.

HIKING AND SKIING. Nearly every town has **hiking** trails in its vicinity; consult the local tourist office. Trails are usually marked with either a red-white-red marker (only sturdy boots and hiking poles necessary) or a blue-white-blue marker (mountaineering equipment needed). Most mountain hiking trails and mountain huts are open only from late June to early September because of snow in the higher passes. Western Austria is one of the world's best **skiing** regions; the areas around Innsbruck and Kitzbühel are saturated with lifts and runs. High season normally runs from mid-December to mid-January and from February to March. Tourist offices provide information on regional skiing and can suggest budget travel agencies that offer ski packages.

HOLIDAYS AND FESTIVALS

Holidays: Just about everything closes down on public holidays, so plan accordingly. New Year's Day (Jan. 1); Epiphany (Jan. 6); Good Friday (Apr. 9); Easter Monday (Apr. 12); Labor Day (May 1); Ascension (May 20); Corpus Christi (June 19); Assumption Day (Aug. 15); Austrian National Day (Oct. 26); All Saints' Day (Nov. 1); Immaculate Conception (Dec. 8); Christmas (Dec. 25); Boxing Day (Dec. 26).

Festivals: Vienna celebrates **Fasching** (Carnival) during the first 2 weeks of February. Austria's most famous summer music festivals are the **Wiener Festwochen** (mid-May to mid-June) and the **Salzburger Festspiele** (late July to late Aug.).

VIENNA (WIEN)   ☎01

From its humble origins as a Roman camp along the Danube, Vienna (pop. 1,500,000) was catapulted by war, marriage, and Habsburg maneuvering into the political lynchpin of the continent. Meanwhile, music saved its soul; the melodies of Mozart and Beethoven, Mahler and Schönberg have made Vienna an everlasting arbiter of high culture. So high, at times, that it seemed inflated; during its *fin-de-siècle* coffeehouse phase, bohemian Viennese self-mockingly referred to their city as the "merry apocalypse." This smooth veneer of Straussian waltzes and *Gemütlichkeit* (good nature) concealed a darker side expressed in Freud's theories, and later in Musil's *Man Without Qualities*. Although the city has a reputation for living absent-mindedly in its grand past, the recently opened *MuseumsQuartier*, an ultra-modern venue for architecture, film, theater, and dance, proves that Vienna is still writing its own dynamic brand of history.

⊠ INTERCITY TRANSPORTATION

Flights: The **Wien-Schwechat Flughafen** (VIE; ☎ 700 72 22 33) is home to **Austrian Airlines** (☎ 051 76 60; www.aua.com). The airport is 18km from the city center; the cheapest way to reach the city is S7 Flughafen/Wolfsthal, which stops at **Wien Mitte** (30min., every 30min. 5am-11pm, €3). The heart of the city, **Stephansplatz**, is a short Metro ride from Wien Mitte on the U3 line. The **Vienna Airport Lines Shuttle Bus,** which runs between the airport and the City Air Terminal, at the Hilton opposite Wien Mitte, is more convenient, but also more expensive. (☎ 93 00 00 23 00. Every 20min. 6:30am-11:10pm, every 30min. midnight-6am; €5.80.) **Buses** connect the airport to the *Südbahnhof* and *Westbahnhof* (see below) every 30min. 8:25am-6:55pm and every hr. from 5:30-8:25am and 6:55pm-12:10am.

Trains: Vienna has two main train stations with international connections. For general train info, dial ☎ 05 17 17 (24hr.) or check www.oebb.at.

Westbahnhof, XV, Mariahilferstr. 132. Most trains head west, but a few go east and north. To: **Amsterdam** (14½hr., daily, €159); **Berlin Zoo** (11hr., daily, €123); **Budapest** (3-4hr., 3 per day, €38); **Hamburg** (9½hr., 2 per day, €125); **Innsbruck** (5-6hr., 2 per day, €49); **Munich** (4½hr., 5 per day, €63); **Paris** (14hr., 2 per day, €13); **Salzburg** (3½hr., every hr., €37); **Zurich** (9¼hr., 3 per day, €78). **Info counter** open daily 7am-10pm.

Südbahnhof, X, Wiedner Gürtel 1a. Trains generally go south and east. To: **Graz** (2¾hr., every hr., €27); **Kraków** (7-8hr., 3 per day, €46); **Prague** (4½hr., 5 per day, €46); **Rome** (14hr., daily, €101); **Venice** (9-10hr., 3 per day, €72). **Info counter** open daily 6:30am-9pm.

Buses: Buses in Austria are seldom cheaper than trains; compare prices before buying a ticket. **City bus terminals** at Wien Mitte/Landstr., Hütteldorf, Heiligenstadt, Floridsdorf, Kagran, Erdberg, and Reumannpl. **BundesBuses** run from these stations. Ticket counters open M-F 6am-5:50pm, Sa-Su 6am-3:50pm. Many international bus lines also have agencies in the stations. For info, call BundesBus (☎ 711 01; 7am-10pm).

Hitchhiking: Those headed for Salzburg take U4 to Hütteldorf; the highway is 10km farther. Hitchhikers traveling south often ride tram #67 to the last stop and wait at the rotary near Laaerberg. *Let's Go* does not recommend hitchhiking.

⊠ ORIENTATION

Vienna is divided into 23 **districts** (*Bezirke*). The first is the *Innenstadt* (city center), defined by the **Ringstraße** on three sides and the Danube Canal on the fourth. The Ringstraße (or "Ring") consists of many different segments, each with its own name, such as Opernring or Kärntner Ring. Many of Vienna's major attractions are in District I and immediately around the Ringstraße. Districts II-IX spread out from the city center following the clockwise traffic of the Ring. The remaining districts expand from yet another ring, the **Gürtel** ("belt"). Like the Ring, this major thoroughfare has numerous segments, including Margaretengürtel, Währinger Gürtel, and Neubaugürtel. Street signs indicate the district number in Roman or Arabic numerals *before* the street and number. **Let's Go includes district numbers for establishments in Roman numerals before the street address.**

Vienna (Wien)

🏠🏕️ ACCOMMODATIONS

Aktiv Camping Neue Donau, **18**
Believe It Or Not, **37**
Camping Wien Süd, **69**
Camping Wien-West, **63**
Hostel Panda and Lauria Apartments, **39**
Hostel Ruthensteiner (HI), **61**
Hotel Zur Wiener Staatsoper, **46**
Jugendgästehaus Wien Brigittenau (HI), **9**
Katholisches Studentenhaus, **5**
Kolpinghaus Wien-Meidling, **68**
Mytheng./Neustiftg. (HI), **38**
Pension Hargita, **59**
Pension Kraml, **57**
Pension Reimer, **54**
Porzellaneum der Wiener Universität, **6**
Studentenwohnheim der
  Hochschule für Musik (HI), **43**
Turmherberge Don Bosco, **48**
Westend City Hostel, **60**
Wombats City Hostel, **62**

Ⓤ1 Ⓤ2 Ⓤ3 Ⓤ4
U-Bahn (subway)
Routes 1-4

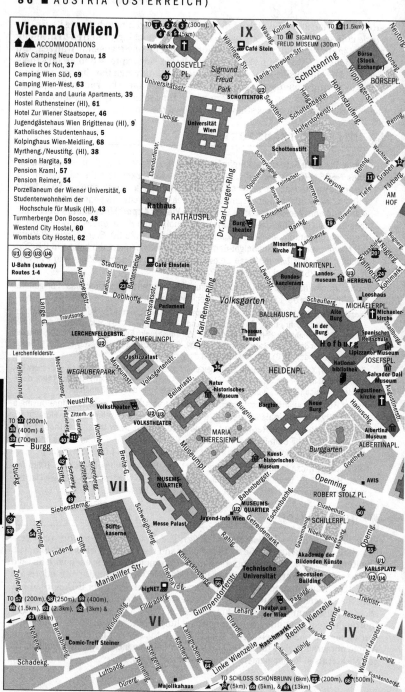

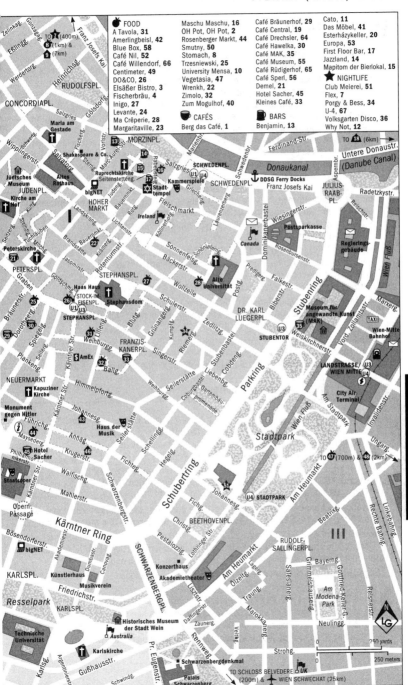

FOOD
A Tavola, **31**
Amerlingbeisl, **42**
Blue Box, **58**
Café Nil, **52**
Café Willendorf, **66**
Centimeter, **49**
DO&CO, **26**
Elsäßer Bistro, **3**
Fischerbräu, **4**
Inigo, **27**
Levante, **24**
Ma Crêperie, **28**
Margaritaville, **23**
Maschu Maschu, **16**
OH Pot, OH Pot, **2**
Rosenberger Markt, **44**
Smutny, **50**
Stomach, **8**
Trzesniewski, **25**
University Mensa, **10**
Vegetasia, **47**
Wrenkh, **22**
Zimolo, **32**
Zum Mogulhof, **40**

CAFÉS
Berg das Café, **1**

Café Bräunerhof, **29**
Café Central, **19**
Café Drechsler, **64**
Café Hawelka, **30**
Café MAK, **35**
Café Museum, **55**
Café Rüdigerhof, **65**
Café Sperl, **56**
Demel, **21**
Hotel Sacher, **45**
Kleines Café, **33**

BARS
Benjamin, **13**

Cato, **11**
Das Möbel, **41**
Esterházykeller, **20**
Europa, **53**
First Floor Bar, **17**
Jazzland, **14**
Mapitom der Bierlokal, **15**

NIGHTLIFE
Club Meierei, **51**
Flex, **7**
Porgy & Bess, **34**
U-4, **67**
Volksgarten Disco, **36**
Why Not, **12**

AUSTRIA

█ LOCAL TRANSPORTATION

Public transportation: call ☎ 790 91 00 for general info. The **subway** (U-Bahn), **tram** (Straßenbahn), **elevated train** (S-Bahn), and **bus** lines operate under one ticket system. A **single fare** (€2 on board; €1.50 in advance from a ticket machine, ticket office, or tobacco shop) lets you travel to any destination in the city and switch from bus to U-Bahn to tram to S-Bahn, as long as your travel is uninterrupted. To **validate a ticket,** punch it in the machine upon entering the first vehicle, but don't stamp it again when you switch trains. Otherwise, plainclothes inspectors may fine you €60. Other ticket options (available at the same places as pre-purchased single tickets) are a **24hr. pass** (€5), a **3-day "rover" ticket** (€12), a **7-day pass** (€12.50; valid M 9am to the next M 9am), or an **8-day pass** (€24; valid any 8 days, not necessarily consecutive; valid also for several people traveling together). The **Vienna Card** (€16.90) offers free travel for 72hr. as well as discounts at sights and events. Regular trams and subway cars stop running between midnight and 5am. **Nightbuses** run every 30min. along most routes; "N" signs designate night bus stops. (Single fare €1.50; day transport passes not valid.) A complete night bus schedule is available at bus counters in U-Bahn stations.

Taxis: ☎ 313 00, 401 00, 601 60, or 814 00. Stands at *Westbahnhof, Südbahnhof,* Karlspl. in the city center, and by the Bermuda Dreieck for late-night revelers. Accredited taxis have yellow-and-black signs on the roof. Rates generally run €2 plus €0.20 per km; slightly more expensive holidays and from 11pm-6am.

Car Rental: Avis, I, Opernring 3-5 (☎ 587 62 41). Open M-F 7am-8pm, Sa 8am-2pm, Su 8am-1pm. **Hertz** (☎ 700 73 26 61), at the airport. Open M-F 7:15am-11pm, Sa 8am-8pm, Su 8am-11pm.

Bike Rental: Pedal Power, II, Ausstellungsstr. 3 (☎ 729 72 34). Rents bikes (€4 per hr., €32 for 24hr. with delivery) and offers bike tours (€19-23). Student and Vienna Card discounts. Open May-Oct. daily 8am-8pm. Pick up *Vienna By Bike* at the tourist office.

█ PRACTICAL INFORMATION

Main Tourist Office: I, Albertinapl. (☎ 21 11 40). Follow Operng. up 1 block from the Opera House. The staff gives a free map of the city and the pamphlet *Youth Scene,* and books rooms for a €3 fee plus a 1-night deposit. Open daily 9am-7pm.

Embassies and Consulates: Australia, IV, Mattiellistr. 2 (☎ 512 85 80). **Canada,** I, Laurenzerberg 2 (☎ 531 38 30 00). **Ireland,** I, Rotenturmstr. 16 (☎ 715 42 46). **New Zealand,** XIX, Karl-Tomay-g. 34 (☎ 318 85 05). **South Africa,** XIX, Sandg. 33 (☎ 32 06 49 30). **UK,** III, Jauresg. 10 (☎ 716 13 51 51). **US,** IX, Boltzmanng. 16 (☎ 313 39).

Currency Exchange: The 24hr. exchange at the **main post office** has excellent rates and an €8 fee for up to US$1100 in traveler's checks. Otherwise, **ATMs** are your best bet.

American Express: I, Kärntnerstr. 21-23 (☎ 515 40), down the street from Stephanspl. Cashes AmEx and Thomas Cook (min. €7 commission) checks, sells theater tickets, and holds mail for 4 weeks. Open M-F 9am-5:30pm, Sa 9am-noon.

Luggage Storage: Lockers are €2 per 24hr. at all train stations.

> **! CRIME IN THE CITY.** Vienna is a gentle giant, but it still knows crime. Pickpockets abound on the U-Bahn, and **Karlsplatz** is home to many pushers and junkies. Be especially cautious in districts **X** and **XIV**, as well as in **Prater Park** and in Vienna's Red Light District, which covers sections of the Gürtel.

Bookstores: Shakespeare & Company, I, Sterng. 2. Great British magazine selection. Open M-Sa 9am-7pm. The **British Bookshop**, I, Weihburgg. 24, has an extensive travel section. Open M-F 9:30am-6:30pm, Sa 9:30am-5pm. Branch at VI, Mariahilferstr. 4.

Bi-Gay-Lesbian Resources: Pick up the *Vienna Gay Guide* (www.gayguide.at), *Extra Connect*, or *Bussi* from any tourist office or gay bar, cafe, or club. **Rosa Lila Villa**, VI, Linke Wienzeile 102 (☎587 17 89), is a favored resource and social center for homosexual Viennese and visitors alike. Friendly staff speaks English. Open M-F 5-8pm.

Laundromat: Most hostels offer laundry service for €4-6. **Schnell und Sauber**, VII, Westbahnhofstr. 60. Wash €4.50, dry €1 per 20min. Soap included. Open 24hr.

EMERGENCY AND COMMUNICATION

Police: ☎133. **Ambulance:** ☎144. **Fire:** ☎122.

Medical Assistance: Allgemeines Krankenhaus (hospital), IX, Währinger Gürtel 18-20 (☎404 00 19 64). **Emergency care:** ☎141.

Crisis Hotlines: All have English speakers. **24hr. immediate help:** ☎717 19. **Rape Crisis Hotline:** ☎523 22 22. M 1-6pm, Tu 10am-3pm, W 1am-6pm, Th 3-8pm.

24hr. Pharmacy: ☎15 50. Consulates have lists of English-speaking doctors, or call **Wolfgang Molnar** (☎330 34 68).

Internet Access: bigNET.internet.cafe, I, Kärntnerstr. 61 or I, Hoher Markt 8-9 (€3.70 per 30min.). **Jugend-Info des Bundesministeriums**, I, Franz-Josefs-Kai 51. Open M-F 11am-6pm. **Cafe Stein**, IX, Wahringerstr. 6-8 (€4 per 30min.).

Post Offices: Hauptpostamt, I, Fleischmarkt 19. Open 24hr. Branches throughout the city and at the train stations; look for the yellow signs with the trumpet logo. Address mail to be held: SURNAME, Firstname, *Postlagernde Briefe*, Hauptpostamt, Fleischmarkt 19, A-1010 Wien AUSTRIA. **Postal Codes:** 1st district A-1010, 2nd A-1020, 3rd A-1030, etc., to the 23rd A-1230.

▛ ACCOMMODATIONS AND CAMPING

Hunting for cheap rooms in Vienna during peak tourist season (June-Sept.) can be unpleasant; call for reservations at least five days in advance. Otherwise, plan on calling between 6 and 9am to put your name down for a reservation. If full, ask to be put on a waiting list. The summer crunch for budget rooms is slightly alleviated in July, when university dorms convert into makeshift hostels.

HOSTELS

▓ **Hostel Ruthensteiner (HI)**, XV, Robert-Hamerlingg. 24 (☎893 42 02). Exit *Westbahnhof*, turn right onto Mariahilferstr., and continue until Haidmannsg. Turn left, then right on Robert-Hamerlingg. Knowledgeable staff, spotless rooms, a rose-filled courtyard, and a kitchenette. Breakfast €2.50. Sheets included (except for 10-bed dorms). Internet €2 for 25min. 4-night max. stay. Reception 24hr. "The Outback" summer dorm €11; 4- to 10-bed dorms €10-12; singles €18-22; doubles €36-44. AmEx/MC/V. ❷

Wombats City Hostel, XIV, Grang. 6 (☎897 23 36). Exit *Westbahnhof*, turn right on Mariahilferstr., right on Rosinag., and left on Grang. While near train tracks and auto-body shops, Wombats compensates with a pub and other perks. Internet €1 per 12min. Bike or in-line skate rental €8 per day. 2-, 4-, and 6-bed dorms €14-36 per person. ❷

Believe It Or Not, VII, Myrtheng. 10, Apt. #14 (☎526 46 58). Take U6 to Burgg./ Stadthalle, then bus #48A (dir.: Ring) to Neubaug. Walk back on Burgg. 1 block and take the 1st right on Myrtheng. A converted apartment, with kitchen and 2 bunkrooms. Min. 2-night stay. Reception 8am-1pm. Easter-Oct. €12.25; Nov.-Easter €7.50-10. ❶

Hostel Panda, VII, Kaiserstr. 77, 3rd fl. (☎522 25 55). U6: Burgg. Small, old-fashioned, *Jugendstil,* co-ed rooms. Kitchen and TV. Check-in until 11pm. Bring lock for lockers. Dorms Easter-Oct. €12.50; Nov.-Easter €9. €3.50 surcharge for 1-night stays. ❷

Westend City Hostel, VI, Fügerg. 3. Near Westbahnhof. Exit on Äussere Mariahilferstr., cross the large intersection, go right on Mullerg. and left on Fügerg. Very plain, but its location is ideal. Breakfast included. Internet €2.60 per 30min. Reception 24hr. Check-out 10:30am. Curfew 11:30pm. 12-bed dorms €16; 8-10 bed dorms €17; 4-6 bed dorms €18; singles €38.50; doubles €23. ❷

Kolpinghaus Wien-Meidling, XIII, Bendlg. 10-12 (☎813 54 87). U6: Niederhofstr. Head right on Niederhofstr. and take the 4th right onto Bendlg. Institutional hostel with 202 beds. Breakfast €3.80. Showers in all rooms. Reception 24hr. Check-out 9am. 8- and 10-bed dorms €11.40; 4- and 6-bed dorms €12.80-14.60. AmEx/MC/V. ❷

Turmherberge Don Bosco (HI), III, Lechnerstr. 12 (☎713 14 94). Take U3 to Kardinal-Nagl-Pl., take the exit facing the park, walk through the park, and turn right on Erdbergstr.; Lechnerstr. is the 2nd left. The cheapest beds in town, in a former bell tower. Curfew 11:45pm. Open Mar.-Nov. Dorms €6. ❶

Myrthengasse (HI), VII, Myrtheng. 7, and **Neustiftgasse (HI),** VII, Neustiftg. 85 (☎523 63 16). These simple, modern hostels, both under the same management, are a 20min. walk from the *Innenstadt.* Rooms separated by sex. Breakfast included. Locks €3.65. Reception 24hr. at Myrtheng. Curfew 1am. 4- to 6-bed dorms with shower €15; 2-bed dorms with shower €17.50. Nonmembers add €3.50. AmEx/MC/V. ❷

Jugendgästehaus Wien Brigittenau (HI), XX, Friedrich-Engels-Pl. 24 (☎332 82 9). U1 or 4 to Schwedenpl., then tram N to Floridsdorferbrücke. Excellent facilities for the disabled, but it's 25min. from the city center. Breakfast included. Free Internet. 5-night max. stay. Reception 24hr. Lockout 9am-1pm. 24-bed dorms (men only) €12.15; 4-bed dorms €15-17; doubles with bath €30-34. Nonmembers add €3.50. ❷

HOTELS AND PENSIONS

▩ **Pension Hargita,** VII, Andreasg. (☎526 19 28). U3: Zieglerg. and exit on Andreasg. Hardwood floors, seafoam walls, cozy beds, and quiet. Breakfast €3. Reception 8am-10pm. Singles €31, with shower €50; doubles €45/52; triples €63/71. MC/V. ❹

Pension Kraml, VI, Brauerg. 5 (☎587 85 88). U3: Zierierg. Exit on Otto-Bauerg., take 1st left, then 1st right. Near the Naschmarkt. Large rooms, a lounge, and cable TV. Breakfast included. Singles €26; doubles €48, with shower €65; triples €65/85. Apartment with bath €100-115 for 3-5 people. ❸

Lauria Apartments, VII, Kaiserstr. 77, Apt. #8 (☎522 25 55). From *Westbahnhof,* take tram #5 to Burgg. The 'Breakfast Club' meets Vienna in this small, but comfortable cluster of apartments. Fully equipped kitchens. Lockers and TV included. 2-night min. Reception 8am-2pm. Lockout 10am-2pm. Dorms €13; singles €35; doubles €46, with shower €60; triples €75-120. ❷

Pension Reimer, IV, Kircheng. 18 (☎523 61 62). Centrally located with huge, comfortable rooms that are always clean. Breakfast included. Singles €31-38; doubles €50-56, with bath €60-64. ❹

Hotel Zur Wiener Staatsoper, I, Krugerstr. 11 (☎513 12 74 75). From Karlspl., exit Oper and follow Kärtnerstr. toward the city center; turn right on Krugerstr. Simple elegance and a prime location. Breakfast included. Singles €76-95; doubles €109-135; triples €131-146. AmEx/MC/V. ❺

UNIVERSITY DORMITORIES

From July through September, many university dorms become hotels, usually with singles, doubles, and a few triples and quads. These rooms don't have much in the way of character, but showers and sheets are standard, and their cleanliness and relatively low cost make them particularly suited to longer stays.

Studentenwohnheim der Hochschule für Musik, I, Johannesg. 8 (☎514 84). Walk 3 blocks down Kärntnerstr. from Stephansdom and turn left on Johannesg. Music student clientele; 23 practice rooms equipped with grand pianos (€5 per hr.). Breakfast included. Reception 24hr. Reserve in advance. Singles €33-36; doubles €58-70; triples €66; quads €80; quints €100. ❹

Porzellaneum der Wiener Universität, IX, Porzellang. 30 (☎317 728 20). From *Südbahnhof*, take tram D (dir.: Nußdorf) to Fürsteng. Great location in the student district. Reception 24hr. Call ahead. Singles €16-18; doubles €30-35; quads €56-64. ❸

Katholisches Studentenhaus, XIX, Peter-Jordanstr. 29 (☎369 55 85). U6: Nußdorferstr., then bus #35A or tram #38 to Hardtg. In a calm, quiet district. Free Internet. Reception daily until 10pm. Singles €18; doubles €30. ❸

CAMPING

Wien-West, Hüttelbergstr. 80 (☎914 23 14). Take U4 to *Hütteldorf*, then bus #14B or 152 (dir.: Campingpl.) to Wien West. Crowded but clean. 8km from the city center. Hikes go through the Vienna Forest. Laundry, groceries, and cooking facilities. Reception daily 7:30am-9:30pm. Open Apr.-Oct. €5-6 per person, €3 per tent. ❶

Aktiv Camping Neue Donau, XXII, Am Kleehäufel 119 (☎202 40 10), is 4km from the city center and adjacent to Neue Donau beaches. U1: Kaisermühlen, then bus #91a to Kleehäufel. Boat and bike rentals. Laundry, supermarket, kitchen, and showers. Open mid-May to mid-Sept. €5.50 per person, €3 per tent. ❶

Wien Süd, Breitenfurterstr. 269 (☎867 36 49). U6: Philadelphiabrücke, then bus #62A to Wien Süd. This former imperial park encompasses 25 sq. km of woods and meadows. Laundry, cafe, playground, supermarket, and kitchen. July-Aug. €5 per person; May-June and Sept. €3.50. €5 per person, €3 per tent. Camper €5, tent €3. ❶

▐▌ FOOD

In 1822, Washington Irving said of Vienna: "Here the people think only of sensual gratifications." Today, that still rings true. The Viennese don't eat to live, they live to eat. Decadent pastries like *Apfelstrudl*, cheesecakes, tortes, *Buchteln* (warm cake with jam in the middle), *Palatschinken*, *Krapfen*, and *Mohr im Hemd* have all helped put Vienna on the culinary map. The restaurants near Kärntnerstr. are expensive—a cheaper area is the neighborhood north of the university, near the Votivkirche (U2: Schottentor), where Universitätsstr. and Währingerstr. meet. Cafes with cheap meals also line **Burggasse** in district VI. The area radiating from the Rechte and Linke Wienzeile near Naschmarkt (U4: Kettenbrückeg.) has cheap restaurants. The **Naschmarkt** has the city's biggest market, while **Brunnenmarkt** (U6: Josefstädterstr.) has a Turkish flair. Supermarket chains include **Zielpunkt, Hofer,** and **Spar.** Kosher groceries are available at the **Kosher Supermarket,** II, Hollandstr. 10 (☎216 96 75).

INSIDE THE RING

▩ **DO&CO,** I, Stephanspl. 12, 7th fl. (☎535 39 69). Set above the Stephansdom, this modern gourmet restaurant offers both traditional Austrian dishes and other international specialties like Thai noodles and Uruguay beef (€19-23.50). Reservations recommended. Open daily noon-3pm and 6pm-midnight. ❹

▩ **Ma Crêperie,** I, Grünangerg. 10. Off Singerstr. near Stephanspl. The sensual decor of this restaurant complements the sumptuous crepes, both sweet and savory (€3-18). Try the *Himbeer* (raspberry) soda (€2). Open daily 11am-midnight. AmEx/MC/V. ❸

▩ **Wrenkh,** I, Bauernmarkt 10. The delicious and creative cuisine at this strictly vegetarian restaurant ranges from Japanese springrolls to spinach gnocchi (€4-18) and fresh fruit juices to original mixed drinks (€3-8). Open daily 11:30am-11pm. AmEx/MC/V. ❷

AUSTRIA

Trzesniewski, I, Dorotheerg. 1, 3 blocks down the Graben from Stephansdom. This famous stand-up establishment has been serving petite open-faced sandwiches for over 80 years. A filling lunch (6 sandwiches and a mini-beer) costs about €5. This was Kafka's favorite place to eat. Open M-F 8:30am-7:30pm, Sa 9am-5pm. ❷

Smutny, I, Elisabethstr. 8. Off Karlspl. A delicious traditional Austrian restaurant offering schnitzel and goulash. Entrees €5-8. ❸

A Tavola, I. Weihburgg. 3. U1: Stephansplatz. Walk down Härtnerstr. and make a left onto Weihburgg. Enjoy homemade pasta dishes with beef, seafood, or pheasant (€8-16) in the romantic, candlelit vaults of the city tavern. Italian wines by the glass (€3-5). Open M-Sa noon-2:30pm and 6pm-midnight. AmEx/MC/V. ❸

Maschu Maschu, I, Rabensteig 8. In Bermuda Dreieck. Filling and super-cheap falafel and schwarma (€3 each). Open M-W 11:30am-midnight, Th-Sa 11:30am-3am. ❶

Levante, I, Wallnerstr. 2. Walk down Graben away from Stephansdom, turn left on Kohlmarkt and right onto Wallnerstr. Greek-Turkish franchise featuring street-side dining and some vegetarian dishes. Entrees €7-12. Open daily 1-11:30pm. ❷

Margaritaville, I, Bartensteing. 3. Take U2: Lerchenfelderstr., exit onto Museumstr., and cut across the triangular green to Bartensteing. Authentic Tex-Mex among Spanish-speakers. Entrees €8-20. Open M-F and Su 4pm-midnight, Sa 11am-midnight. ❸

Café MAK, I, Stubenring 3-5, inside the Museum für Angewandte Kunst. Tram #1 to Stubenring. Funky Bauhaus furniture and international cuisine. Techno parties on Sa nights in July. Entrees €8-15. Open Su and Tu-Sa 10am-2am. MC/V. ❸

Inigo, I, Bäckerstr. 18. Founded by a Jesuit priest as part of a social reintegration program, Inigo provides employment and training for people who are long-term unemployed. International and vegetarian options (€5-10) and a salad bar (€3-7). Open July-Aug. M-F 8:30am-11:30pm; Sept.-June daily 8:30am-11:30pm. AmEx/MC/V. ❷

Zimolo, I, Ballg. 5. Near Stephanspl. off Weihburgg. Good Italian food; sexy ambience. Entrees €7-19. Open M-Sa noon-2:30pm and 6-11pm. AmEx/MC/V. ❸

Rosenberger Markt, I, Mayserderg. 2. Off Kärntnerstr. Salad, fruit, waffles, antipasto, potatoes, and pasta bars. You pay by the size of your plate, not by weight, so pile high. Salads €2.40-6. Waffles €3.60-4.30. Veggie dishes €3.60-7. Open 11am-11pm. ❷

OUTSIDE THE RING

OH Pot, OH Pot, IX, Währingerstr. 22. U2: Schottentor. This adorable eatery serves filling "pots," stew-like veggie or meat concoctions (€7-10). Fusion fare from Chilean to Ethiopian. Open M-F 10am-3pm and 6pm-midnight, Sa-Su 6pm-midnight. AmEx/MC/V. ❷

Centimeter, IX, Liechtensteinstr. 42. Tram D to Bauernfeldpl. This chain offers huge portions of greasy Austrian fare and an unbelievable selection of beers. You pay by the centimeter. Open M-F 10am-2am, Sa 11am-2am, Su 11am-midnight. AmEx/MC/V. ❷

Elsäßer Bistro, IX, Währingerstr. 32. U2: Schottentor. In the palace that houses the French Cultural Institute—walk into the garden and follow your nose to an extravagant meal (€14) and exquisite French wines. Open M-F 11am-3pm and 6:30-11pm. ❹

Vegetasia, III, Ungarg. 57. Take the O tram to Neulingg. A vegetarian nirvana, this cozy Taiwanese restaurant offers seitan and many forms of soy. Lunch buffet M-Sa €6.50. Open daily 11:30am-3pm and 5:30-11:30pm. Closed Tu evenings. AmEx/MC/V. ❷

Café Nil, VII, Siebensterng. 39. Enjoy vegetarian dishes (€6-12) with tortured writers at this Middle Eastern haunt. Breakfast until 3pm. Open daily 10am-midnight. ❷

Blue Box, VII, Richterg. 8. U3: Neubaug. Blue Box is a restaurant by day and a club by night. Dishes are fresh and original (€3.50-7), and DJs spin the latest trance and trip-hop. Open M 6pm-2am, Tu-Su 10am-2am. ❷

Café Willendorf, VI, Linke Wienzeile 102. Take U4 to Pilgramg. and look for the pink building which also houses the **Rosa Lila Villa,** the center of gay life in Vienna. Artsy fare (€7-13), relaxed atmosphere. Open M-Th 6pm-1am, F-Sa 6pm-2pm. ❸

University Mensa, IX, Universitätsstr. 7, on the 7th fl. of the university building, between U2 stops Rathaus and Schottentor. Ride the old-fashioned *Pater Noster* elevator (no doors and never stops, so jump in and out) to the 6th fl. and take the stairs up. Not much atmosphere, but the food is cheap. Typical cafeteria meals €4. Open Sept.-June M-F 11am-2pm, but snack bar open 8am-3pm. ❶

Fischerbräu, XIX, Billrothstr. 17. U6 to Nußdorfer Str., exit on Wahringer Gurtel, continue until Döblinger Hauptpl., take a left, and left again onto Billrothstr. Try the home-brewed beer (€2.50-5), veal sausage (€4.60), or chicken salad (€6.50). Blues brunch Sa noon-3pm. Open M-F 4pm-1am, Sa-Su 11am-1am. Jazz brunch Su 11am-3pm. ❷

Café Rüdigerhof, V, Hamburgerstr. 20. U4: Kettenbrückeng., off Rechte Wienzeile. Designed by students of Otto Wagner, this *Jugendstil* cafe is adorned with floral patterns and leather couches (a gift from King Hussein to the owner). Traditional meat and fish dishes (€5-7). Delicious iced coffee €3.50. Open daily 10am-2am. MC/V. ❷

Café Drechsler, VI, Linke Wienzeile 22. U4: Kettenbrückeng. Or, from Karlspl., head down Operng. and continue on Linke Wienzeile. This is *the* place to be the morning after. Early birds and night owls roost over pungent cups of *Mokka*. Huge portions, hearty food (€4.70-8.50). Open M-F 3am-8pm, Sa 3am-6pm. ❷

Zum Mogulhof, VII, Burgg. 12. Ample portions of delicious Indian food. Vegetarian and meat dishes €8-12. Open daily 11:30am-2:30pm and 6-11:30pm. AmEx/MC/V. ❷

Amerlingbeisl, VII, Stiftg. 8. U3: Neubaug. Rain or snow, the retractible hydraulic roof lets you eat in the courtyard. Entrees €6-8. Open daily 9am-2am. ❷

Stomach, IX, Seeg. 26. Take tram D to Seeg. Sophisticated Austrian cooking with a Styrian kick. 20-something crowd. Entrees €14. Open Su 10am-10pm, W-Sa 4pm-midnight. Reservations recommended. MC/V. ❹

☕ COFFEEHOUSES

In Vienna, the coffeehouse is not simply a place to resolve your midday caffeine deficit. For years these establishments were havens for artists, writers, and thinkers who stayed into the night: Peter Altenberg, "the cafe writer," scribbled lines; Oskar Kokoschka brooded alone; exiled Lenin and Trotsky played chess; Theodor Herzl planned for a Zionist Israel; and Kafka came to visit the Herrenhof. The original literary haunt was **Café Griensteidl**, but after it was demolished the torch passed to **Café Central** and then to **Café Herrenhof.** Cafes still exist under all these names, but only Café Central looks like it used to. Most also serve hot food, but don't order anything but pastries with your *Melange* (Viennese coffee) unless you want to be really gauche. The most serious dictate of coffeehouse etiquette is that you linger; the waiter (*Herr Ober*) will serve you when you sit down, then leave you to sip, read, and cogitate. When you're ready to leave, just ask to pay: *"Zahlen bitte!"* Vienna has many coffeehouses; the best are listed below.

■ **Café Central**, I, at the corner of Herreng. and Strauchg. inside Palais Fers. Arched ceilings, wall frescoes, and every bit the Mecca of the cafe world. Open M-Sa 8am-10pm, Su 10am-6pm. AmEx/MC/V.

■ **Kleines Café**, I, Franziskanerpl. 3. Turn off Kärntnerstr. onto Weihburg. and follow it to the Franziskanerkirche. This tiny, cozy cafe features courtyard tables and salads that are minor works of art (€6.50). Open M-Sa 10am-2am, Su 1pm-2am.

■ **Demel**, I, Kohlmarkt 14. 5min. from the Stephansdom down Graben. The most lavish Viennese *Konditorei*, Demel was confectioner to the imperial court until the Empire dissolved. All of the chocolate is made fresh every morning, and the desserts are legendary. Open daily 10am-7pm. AmEx/MC/V.

Café Sperl, VI, Gumpendorferstr. 11. U2: Museumsquartier. Walk 1 block on Getreidemarkt and turn right on Gumpendorferstr. One of Vienna's oldest and most elegant cafes. Coffee €2-4.50. Cake €2.50-4. Sept.-June live piano Sa after 5pm. Open July-Aug. M-Sa 7am-11pm; Sept.-June M-Sa 7am-11pm, Su 11am-8pm.

ON THE MENU

VIENNA'S ORIGINAL TORTE

Viennese *Sacher Torte*, the city's renowned chocolate confection, was created by 16-year-old Franz Sacher in 1832. At the time, Sacher was studying as a pastry apprentice under the head chef for Vienna's Prince Metternich. The prince, hoping to impress his guests, commissioned the head chef to make a new pastry of exceptional sweetness. However, the head chef fell ill, and Sacher was forced to take the reigns. The result became an instant sensation the world over.

The dessert itself is an airy cake with an apricot jam filling, coated in a creamy chocolate glaze. Cafes all over Vienna serve the dessert, generally with a side of *Schlagobers* (unsweetened whipped cream). Legal battles have ensued over claims to the "authentic" version; Demel Konditorei, one of Vienna's leading pastry houses, claims that the Sacher family sold them the recipe. However, the "Original Sacher-Torte" is made only at the Hotel Sacher, which was founded in 1876 by Franz's son Eduard. The hotel makes around 270,000 *Sacher Torten* each year, always by hand, from a recipe they claim is still a tighly-guarded secret. Thankfully, the cake can be stored for relatively long periods of time (some even say it gets better with age), allowing the famous pastry to be shipped all over the world.

Café Hawelka, I, Dorotheerg. 6, off Graben. Well-worn and glorious. Josephine and Leopold Hawelka put this legendary cafe on the map in 1939. Today, at 90 and 92 years respectively, they still make a mean *Buchteln* (bohemian doughnut with plum marmelade; fresh at 10pm; €3). Open M and W-Sa 8am-2am, Su 4pm-2am.

Hotel Sacher, I, Philharmonikerstr. 4, behind the opera. This historic site has served world-famous *Sachertorte* for years. Cafe open daily 11am-11:30pm. Bakery open daily 9am-11:30pm. AmEx/MC/V.

Café Museum, I, Operng. 7, near the opera. Built in 1899 by Adolf Loos in a plain, spacious style with striking curves, this cafe attracts a mixed bag of artists, lawyers, students, and chess players. Exceptional coffees (€2.50-8). Open daily 8am-midnight.

Café Bräunerhof, I, Stallburgg. 2. A delightful cafe in a small alley near the Hofburg with an excellent selection of newspapers. Bread, cheese and cold cuts, and Austrian salads (€5-10). *Melange* €3. Open M-F 7:30am-8:30pm, Sa 7:30am-6pm, Su 10am-6pm.

Berg das Café, IX, Bergg. 8. Take U2 to Schottentor, and take a right off Währingerstr. onto Bergg. Casual cafe by day and super-swank gay bar by night, this place is always crowded. Wonderful food, desserts, and music in a relaxed atmosphere. It recently merged with nearby gay and lesbian bookstore **Das Löwenherz,** so you can browse while you drink your *Melange* (€2.40). Open 10am-1am.

Café Stein, IX, Währingerstr. 6, near Schottentor. Intimate, lively, and hip. At night DJs spin. Breakfast until 8pm. Open M-Sa 7am-1am, Su 9am-1am.

⚡ HEURIGEN (WINE TAVERNS)

Heurigen, marked by a hanging branch of evergreen at the door, sell wine and savory Austrian buffet-style delicacies. The wine, also called *Heuriger,* is from the most recent harvest and is typically grown and pressed by the owner himself. Good *Heuriger* is white, fruity, and full of body—*Grüner Veltliner* is a good representative of the variety; avoid reds. *G'spritzer* (wine and soda water, served separately, then mixed) is a popular way of enjoying *Heuriger.* Half of the pleasure of visiting a *Heuriger,* however, comes from the atmosphere. Worn picnic benches and old shade trees provide an ideal spot to converse, or listen to *Schrammelmusik* (sentimental folk songs played by elderly musicians). The buffets make for simple, inexpensive meals. For traditional fare, try *Brattfett* or *Liptauer,* a soft, paprika-flavored cheese served on *Schwarzbrot* (black bread).

Open during summer, *Heurigen* cluster in the northern, western, and southern Viennese suburbs, where the grapes grow. The most famous region, **Grinzing**, in district XIX, produces a uniquely strong wine. Unfortunately, that's where the tour buses go; you'll find better atmosphere and prices in the hills of **Sievering, Neustift am Walde** (both in district XIX), and **Neuwaldegg** (in XVII). Authentic, jolly *Heurigen* abound on Hochstr. in **Perchtoldsdorf**, southwest of the city. To reach Perchtoldsdorf, take U4 to Hietzing and tram #6 to Rodaun. Walk down Ketzerg. until Hochstr. and continue for a few minutes. True *Heuriger* devotees make the trip to the celebrated village of **Gumpoldskirchen**. Take the S-Bahn from the *Südbahnhof*. Most vineyard taverns are open daily from 4pm to midnight.

■ **Buschenschank Heinrich Niersche**, XIX, Strehlg. 21. Take U6 to Währingerstr., then tram #41 to Pötzleing. Walk up Pötzleing. until it becomes Khevenhuller Str. and turn right on Strehlg. An oasis of green grass and cheerful voices in a quiet neighborhood. *Weiße G'spritzzer* (white wine spritzer) €1.45. Open M and W-Su 3pm-midnight.

■ **Zum Krottenbach'l**, XIX, Krottenbachstr. 148. U6 to Nußdorferstr., then bus #35A (dir.: Salmannsdorf) to Kleingartenverein. A traditional atmosphere, where everything is made of gnarled wood. Larger but more touristy and family-oriented than Buschenschank. 0.25L of wine about €2. Open daily 3pm-midnight.

Weingut Heuriger Reinprecht, XIX, Cobenzlg. 22. Take U4 to Heiligenstadt then bus #38A to Grinzing. *Schrammel* musicians stroll from table to table under the ivy trellis. In early June, try *Frische Erdbeerbowle* (sparkling wine and strawberries). Open Mar.-Nov. daily 3:30pm-midnight. AmEx/MC/V.

◙ SIGHTS

Vienna's streets are by turns stately, cozy, scuzzy, and grandiose; expect contrasts around every corner. Don't miss the **Hofburg, Schloß Schönbrunn, Schloß Belvedere**, or any of the buildings along the **Ringstraße**. To wander on your own, grab the brochure *Vienna from A to Z* (with Vienna Card €4) from the tourist office. The range of available **tours** is overwhelming—there are 42 themed walking tours alone, detailed in the brochure *Walks in Vienna*. Contact **Vienna-Bike**, IX, Wasag. (☎319 12 58), for **bike rental** (€5) or **cycling tours** (€20). **Bus tours** (from €30) are given by **Vienna Sightseeing Tours**, III, Stelzhamerg. 4/11 (☎712 46 83), and **Cityrama**, I, Börgeg. 1. (☎534 13).

INSIDE THE RING
District I is Vienna's social and geographical epicenter; with its Romanesque arches, Gothic portals, *Jugendstil* apartments, and modern *Haas Haus*, it's also a gallery of the history of aesthetics.

STEPHANSPLATZ, GRABEN, AND PETERSPLATZ. Right in the heart of Vienna, this square is home to the massive **Stephansdom** (St. Stephen's Cathedral), Vienna's most treasured symbol. For a view of Vienna, take the elevator up the North Tower or climb the 343 steps of the South Tower. *(North Tower open Apr.-June and Sept.-Oct. daily 8:30am-4pm. €3.50. South Tower open daily 9am-5:30pm. €2.50.)* Downstairs, skeletons of thousands of plague victims fill the **catacombs**. The **Gruft** (vault) stores all of the Habsburg innards. *(Tours M-Sa every 30min. 10-11:30am and 1-4:30pm, Su and holidays 1:30-4:30pm. €3.)* From Stephanspl., follow **Graben** for a landscape of *Jugendstil* architecture, including the **Ankerhaus** (#10), Otto Wagner's red-marble **Grabenhof**, and the underground public toilet complex designed by Adolf Loos. Graben leads to **Petersplatz** and the 1663 **Postsäule** (Plague Column), which was built in celebration of the passing of the Black Death. *(U1 or 3 to Stephanspl.)*

AUSTRIA

AUSTRIAN GRAFFITI Scratched into the stones near the entrance of the Stephansdom is the abbreviation "05." It's not a sign of hoodlums up to no good but rather a reminder of a different kind of subversive activity. During WWII, "05" was the secret symbol of Austria's resistance movement against the Nazis. The capital letter "O" and the number "5," for the fifth letter of the alphabet, form the first two letters of "Oesterreich"—meaning Austria. Recently, the monogram has received new life. Every time alleged Nazi collaborator and ex-president of Austria Kurt Waldheim attends Mass, the symbol is highlighted in chalk. Throughout the city, "05" has also been appearing on buildings and flyers in protest of the anti-immigration policies of Jörg Haider and the Freedom Party.

HOHER MARKT AND STADTTEMPEL. Once both a market and an execution site, **Hoher Markt** was the heart of the Roman encampment, Vindobona. Roman ruins lie beneath the shopping arcade across from the fountain. *(From Stephanspl., walk down Rotenturmstr. and turn left on Lictenstr. Open Su and Tu-Sa 9am-12:15pm and 1-4:40pm. €1.80, students €0.70.)* The biggest draw is the 1914 *Jugendstil* **Ankeruhr** (clock), whose 3m figures—from Marcus Aurelius to Maria Theresia—rotate past the Viennese coat of arms accompanied by the tunes of their times. *(1 figure per hr. At noon all figures appear. Follow Judeng. from Hoher Markt to Ruprechtspl.)* Hidden on Ruprechtspl. at Seitenstetteng. 2, the **Stadttempel** is the only synagogue in Vienna to escape Nazi destruction during *Kristallnacht*. *(Bring passport. Open M-Th. Free.)*

AM HOF AND FREYUNG. Once a medieval jousting square, **Am Hof** now houses the **Kirche am Hof** (Church of the Nine Choirs of Angels) and **Collalto Palace,** where Mozart gave his first public performance. *(From Stephanspl., walk down Graben until it ends, go right and continue on Bognerg.; Am Hof is on the right.)* Just west of Am Hof is **Freyung,** the "square" with the **Austriabrunnen** (Austria Fountain) in the center. *Freyung* (sanctuary) took its name from the **Schottenstift** (Monastery of the Scots), where fugitives could claim asylum in medieval times. It was once used for public executions, but the annual **Christkindl** market held here blots out such unpleasant memories with baked goods and Christmas cheer.

HOFBURG. The sprawling **Hofburg** was the winter residence of the Habsburgs. Construction began in 1275, and additions continued until the end of the family's reign in 1918. Coming through the Michaelertor, you'll first enter the courtyard called **In der Burg** (within the fortress). On your left is the red-and-black-striped **Schweizertor** (Swiss Gate), erected in 1552. The **Silberkammer,** on the ground floor, displays the gold, silver, goblets, and 100 ft. gilded candelabra that once adorned the imperial table. *(Open 9am-5pm. €7, students €6.)*

Behind the Schweizertor lies the **Schweizerhof,** the inner courtyard of the **Alte Burg** (Old Fortress), which stands on the same site as the original 13th-century palace. Take a right at the top of the stairs for the Gothic **Burgkapelle** (chapel), where the members of the **Wiener Sängerknaben (Vienna Boys' Choir)** raise their heavenly voices every Sunday (p. 100). Beneath the stairs is the entrance to the **Weltliche und Geistliche Schatzkammer,** containing the Habsburg jewels, crowns, and Napoleon's cradle. *(Open M and W-Su 10am-6pm. €7, students €5. Free audio guide available in English.)* Northeast of the Alte Burg, the **Stallburg** is home to the Lipizzaner stallions and the **Spanische Reitschule** (Spanish Riding School). The cheapest way to see the steeds is to watch them train. *(From mid-Feb. to June and late Aug. to early Nov. Tu-F 10am-noon, except when the horses tour. Tickets sold at the door at Josefspl., Gate 2. €11.60, children €5.)*

Built between 1881 and 1913, the **Neue Burg** is the youngest wing of the palace. The double-headed golden eagle crowning the roof symbolizes the double empire of Austria-Hungary. Today, the Neue Burg houses Austria's largest library, the **Österreichische Nationalbibliothek.** *(Open July-Aug. and Sept. 23-30 M-F 9am-3:45pm, Sa 9am-12:45pm; closed Sept. 1-22; Oct.-June M-F 9am-7pm, Sa 9am-12:45pm.)*

High masses are still held in the 14th-century **Augustinerkirche** (St. Augustine's Church) on Josefspl. The hearts of the Habsburgs are stored in urns in the **Herzgrüftel**. *(To reach Hofburg, head through the Michaelertor in Michaelerpl. Mass 11am. Open M-Sa 10am-6pm, Su 11am-6pm. Free.)*

OUTSIDE THE RING

Some of Vienna's most famous modern architecture is outside the Ring, where 20th-century designers found more space to build. This area is also home to a number of Baroque palaces and parks that were once beyond the city limits.

KARLSPLATZ AND NASCHMARKT. Karlspl. is home to Vienna's most beautiful Baroque church, the **Karlskirche**, an eclectic masterpiece combining a Neoclassical portico with a Baroque dome and towers on either side. *(U1, 2, or 4 to Karlspl. Open M-F 7:30am-7pm, Sa 8:30am-7pm, Su 9am-7pm. Free.)* West of Karlspl., along Linke Wienzeile, is the colorful **Naschmarkt** food bazaar. On Saturdays, the Naschmarkt becomes a massive flea market. *(Open M-F 6am-6:30pm, Sa 6am-2pm.)*

SCHLOß BELVEDERE. The **Schloß Belvedere** was originally the summer residence of Prince Eugène of Savoy, one of Austria's greatest military heroes. The grounds, stretching from Schwarzenberg Palace to the *Südbahnhof*, contain three excellent museums (p. 98) and an equal number of spectacular sphinx-filled gardens. *(Take tram D or #71 one stop past Schwarzenbergpl.)*

SCHLOß SCHÖNBRUNN. From its humble beginnings as a hunting lodge, **Schönbrunn** ("beautiful brook") was Maria Theresia's favorite residence. The **Grand Tour** passes through the **Great Gallery**, where the Congress of Vienna met, and the **Hall of Mirrors**, where 6-year-old Mozart played. If you take the shorter **Imperial Tour**, you'll miss these. *(U4: Schönbrunn. Palace open July-Aug. daily 8:30am-7pm; Apr.-June and Sept.-Oct. 8:30am-5pm; Nov.-Mar. 8:30am-4:30pm. Imperial Tour €8, students €7.40. Grand Tour €10.50/8.60. Audioguides included.)* As impressive as the palace itself are the classical **gardens** behind it, which extend nearly four times the length of the palace and contain the **Schmetterlinghaus** (Butterfly House) and a hodgepodge of other attractions. *(Park open 6am-dusk. Free.)*

ZENTRALFRIEDHOF. The Viennese like to describe the Central Cemetery as half the size of Geneva but twice as lively. **Tor I** (Gate 1) leads to the old **Jewish Cemetery**. Many of the headstones are cracked and neglected because the families of most of the dead have left Austria. Behind **Tor II** (Gate 2) are Beethoven and Strauss, and an honorary monument to Mozart, whose true resting place is an unmarked pauper's grave in the **Cemetery of St. Mark**, III, Leberstr. 6-8. **Tor III** (Gate 3) leads to the Protestant section and the new Jewish cemetery. *(XI, Simmeringer Hauptstr. 234. Take S7 to Zentralfriedhof or tram #71 from Schwarzenbergpl. Open May-Aug. daily 7am-7pm; Mar.-Apr. and Sept.-Oct. 7am-6pm; Nov.-Feb. 8am-5pm.)*

🎋 GARDENS AND PARKS

The Viennese have gone to great lengths to brighten the urban landscape with leafy green spaces. There are several parks along the Ring (including the **Stadtpark, Resselpark, Burggarten,** and **Volksgarten**), as well as many in the suburbs. The gardens of **Schloß Schönbrunn** and **Schloß Belvedere** are particularly beautiful.

ALONG THE RING. Established in 1862, the **Stadtpark** (City Park) was the first municipal park outside the former city walls. The oft-photographed **Johann-Strauss-Donkmal** monument is in the center of the park. *(U4: Stadtpark.)* Clockwise up the Ring, past the Staatsoper, the gorgeous greenhouses of **Burggarten** (Palace Garden) were reserved for the imperial family until 1918. Abutting the Hofburg, the romantic **Volksgarten** (People's Garden) is best viewed at sunset.

AUGARTEN. Northeast of downtown is Vienna's oldest public park. Originally a formal French garden, the Augarten was given a Baroque face-lift and opened to all by Kaiser Josef II in 1775. The WWII Flaktürme (anti-aircraft towers) that now dominate the center of the park make it less fashionable than it was. *(Take tram #31 up from Schottenring or tram N to Obere Augartenstr. and head left down Taborstr.)*

ON THE DANUBE. The narrow **Donauinsel** island has miles of bike paths, soccer fields, and restaurants. The northern shore, along the Alte Donau, is lined with beaches. *(U1: Donauinsel. Open May-Sept. M-F 9am-8pm, Sa-Su 8am-8pm. Beach €4.)* For a view of Vienna at its best, go after sundown to **Donaupark** and take the elevator up to the revolving restaurant in the **Donauturm** (Danube Tower) near the UN complex. *(U1: Kaisermühlen, exit towards Schüttaustr., and follow signs to the park. Tower open daily 10am-midnight. €5.20, students €4.20.)* The area also hosts the **Donauinsel Fest,** the largest open-air festival in Europe (see **Festivals,** below).

▥ MUSEUMS

Vienna owes its vast selection of masterpieces to the acquisitive Habsburgs and to the city's own crop of art schools and world-class artists. An exhaustive list is impossible to include here, but the tourist office's free *Museums* brochure lists all opening hours and admission prices. All museums run by the city of Vienna are **free on Friday** before noon (except on public holidays). If you're going to be in town for a while, invest in the **Museum Card** (ask at any museum ticket window).

■ **ÖSTERREICHISCHE GALERIE (AUSTRIAN GALLERY).** The Upper Belvedere houses European art of the 19th and 20th centuries, including Klimt's *The Kiss.* The Lower Belvedere contains the **Austrian Museum of Baroque Art** and the **Austrian Museum of Medieval Art,** which showcase an extensive collection of sculptures and altarpieces. *(III, Prinz-Eugen-Str. 27, in the Belvedere Palace behind Schwarzenbergpl. Walk up from the Südbahnhof, then take tram D to Schloß Belvedere or tram #71 to Unteres Belvedere. Both Belvederes open Tu-Su 10am-6pm. €7.50, students €5.)*

■ **KUNSTHISTORISCHES MUSEUM (MUSEUM OF FINE ARTS).** The world's 4th-largest art collection features Venetian and Flemish paintings, Classical art, and an Egyptian burial chamber. The **Ephesos Museum** exhibits findings of excavations in Turkey, the **Hofjagd- und Rustkammer** is the 2nd-largest collection of arms in the world, and the **Sammlung alter Musikinstrumente** includes Beethoven's harpsichord and Mozart's piano. *(U2: Museumsquartier. Across from the Burgring and Heldenpl. on Maria Theresia's right. Open Su and Tu-Sa 10am-6pm. €9, students €6.50. 1st audio guide free.)*

MUSEUMSQUARTIER. At 60 sq. km, it's one of the ten biggest art districts in the world. Central Europe's largest collection of modern art, the ■ **Museum Moderner Kunst,** highlights Classical Modernism, Pop Art, Photo Realism, Fluxus, and Viennese Actionism in a building made from basalt lava. 20th-century masters include Kandinsky, Klee, Magritte, Miró, Motherwell, Picasso, Pollock, and Warhol. *(Open Su, Tu-W, and F-Sa 10am-7pm; Tu 10am-7pm; Th 10am-9pm. €8, students €6.50.)* The **Leopold Museum** has the world's largest Schiele collection, plus works by Egger-Lienz, Gerstl, Klimt, and Kokoschka. *(Open M, W-Th, and Sa-Su 10am-7pm, F 10am-9pm; €9, students €5.50.)* Themed exhibits of contemporary artists fill **Kunsthalle Wien.** *(Open M-W and F-Su 10am-7pm, Th 10am-10pm. Exhibition Hall 1 €6.50, students €5; Exhibition Hall 2 €5/3.50; both €8/6.50; students €2 on M. Take U2 to Museumsquartier.)*

ALBERTINA. First an Augustinian monastery and then the largest of the Habsburg residences, the Albertina now houses the **Collection of Graphic Arts.** Michelangelo, Picasso, and Dürer are among the diamonds in the rough of 65,000 drawings and 1 million prints. *(Open M-Tu and Th-Su 10am-6pm, W 10am-9pm.)*

HISTORISCHES MUSEUM DER STADT WIEN (VIENNA HISTORICAL MUSEUM).
This collection of historical artifacts and paintings documents Vienna's evolution from a Roman encampment, through the Turkish siege, to the subsequent 640 years of Habsburg rule. *(IV, Karlspl., to the left of the Karlskirche. Open Su and Tu-Sa 9am-6pm. €3.50, students €1.50. Free after 3pm on F.)*

KUNST HAUS WIEN. Artist-environmentalist Friedenreich Hundertwasser built this museum without straight lines—even the floor bends. In addition to his work, it hosts contemporary art from around the world. *(III, Untere Weißgerberstr. 13. U1 or 4 to Schwedenpl., then tram N to Hetzg. Open daily 10am-7pm. €8, students €6; M half-price.)*

HAUS DER MUSIK. Science meets music in this *über*-interactive museum. Experience the physics of sound, learn about famous Viennese composers, and play with a neat invention called the Brain Opera. *(I, Seilerstatte 30, near the opera house. Open daily 10am-10pm. Adults €10, students €8.50.)*

JÜDISCHES MUSEUM (JEWISH MUSEUM). Jewish culture and history told through holograms and more traditional displays. Temporary exhibits focus on prominent Jewish figures and contemporary Jewish art. *(I, Dorotheerg. 11. Near Stephanspl. Open M-W, F and Su 10am-6pm; Th and Sa 10am-8pm. €5, students €3.)*

ÖSTERREICHISCHES MUSEUM FÜR ANGEWANDTE KUNST (MAK). Dedicated to beautiful design, from the smooth curves of Thonet bentwood chairs to the intricacies of Venetian glass. Klimt lovers will warm to *The Embrace. (I, Stubenring 5. U3: Stubentor. Open Su and W-Sa 10am-6pm, Tu 10am-midnight. €7, students €3.30.)*

SIGMUND FREUD HAUS. The famed couch is not here, but Freud's former home has lots of photos and documents, including his report cards and circumcision certificate. *(IX, Bergg. 19. U2: Schottentor; walk up Währingerstr. to Bergg. Open July-Sept. daily 9am-6pm; Oct.-June 9am-5pm. €5, students €3.)*

♫▣ ENTERTAINMENT AND FESTIVALS

While Vienna offers all the standard entertainment in the way of theater, film, and festivals, the heart of the city beats to music. All but a few of classical music's marquee names lived, composed, and performed in Vienna. Mozart, Beethoven, and Haydn wrote their greatest masterpieces in Vienna, creating the **First Viennese School;** a century later, Schönberg, Webern, and Berg teamed up to form the **Second Viennese School.** Every Austrian child must learn to play an instrument during schooling, and the Vienna **Konservatorium** and **Hochschule** are world-renowned conservatories. All year, Vienna has performances ranging from the above-average to the sublime, with many accessible to the budget traveler. Note that the venues below have **no performances in July and August.**

Vienna hosts an array of important annual **festivals,** mostly musical. The **Vienna Festwochen** (mid-May to mid-June) has a diverse program of exhibitions, plays, and concerts. (☎58 92 20; www.festwochen.or.at.) The Staatsoper and Volkstheater host the annual **Jazzfest Wien** during the first weeks of July, featuring many famous acts. (☎503 5647; www.viennajazz.org.) The Social Democrats host the late-June **Danube Island Festival,** which draws millions of party-goers annually for fireworks and rock, jazz, and folk concerts. From mid-July to mid-August, the **Im-Puls Dance Festival** (☎523 55 58; www.impuls-tanz.com) attracts some of the world's greatest dance troupes and offers seminars to enthusiasts. In mid-October, the annual city-wide film festival, the **Viennale,** kicks off.

Staatsoper, I, Opernring 2 (www.wiener-staatsoper.at). Vienna's premiere opera performs nearly every night Sept.-June. No shorts allowed. 500 standing-room tickets are available for every performance (1 per person; €2-3.50), but plan on getting there 2hr.

before curtain. The box office (Bundestheaterkasse; ☎514 44 78 80), I, Hanuschg. 3, around the corner from the opera, sells tickets in advance. Seats €10-180. Open M-F 8am-6pm, Sa-Su 9am-noon; 1st Sa of each month 9am-5pm.

Wiener Philharmoniker (Vienna Philharmonic Orchestra) plays in the **Musikverein**, Austria's premiere concert hall. Even if you only want standing room tickets, visit the box office (Bösendorferstr. 12 or www.wienerphilharmoniker.at) well in advance.

Wiener Sängerknaben (Vienna Boys' Choir) sings during mass every Su at 9:15am (mid-Sept. to the first week of June) in the Hofburgkapelle (U3: Herreng.). Despite rumors to the contrary, standing room is free; arrive before 8am.

Volksoper (People's Opera), IX, Währingerstr. 78, specializes in lighter comedic opera, operettas, dance troupes, and musicals. While the theater is less elaborate, the music is fantastic and the performances diverse. Go 45min. before the show to get the best seats in the house for €7. Tickets €7-250.

🎵 NIGHTLIFE

With one of the highest bar-to-cobblestone ratios in the world, Vienna is a great place to party, whether you're looking for a quiet evening with a glass of wine or a wild night in a disco. Take U1 or 4 to Schwedenpl., which will drop you within blocks of the **Bermuda Dreieck** (Bermuda Triangle), an area packed with lively, crowded clubs. If you make it out, head down **Rotenturmstraße** toward Stephansdom or walk around the areas bounded by the Jewish synagogue and Ruprechtskirche. Slightly outside the Ring, the streets off **Burggasse** and **Stiftgasse** in District VII and the **university quarter** (Districts XIII and IX) have tables in outdoor courtyards and loud, hip bars.

Viennese nightlife starts late, often after 11pm. For the scoop, pick up a copy of the indispensable **Falter** (€2), which prints listings of everything from opera and theater to punk concerts and updates on the gay and lesbian scene.

BARS

Das Möbel, VII, Burgg. 10. U2 or 3 to Volkstheater. Metal couches, car-seat chairs, and Swiss-army tables are filled by an artsy crowd. Open M-F noon-1am, Sa-Su 10am-1am.

Cato, I, Tiefer Graben 19. U3: Herreng. Turn right on Strauchg. and continue onto Tiefer Graben. By night's end the warm hostess, Anna Maria, will have you singing. Try the Sekte Cuvee, a dry spirit from Burgenland (€4). Open Su-Th 6pm-2am, F-Sa 6pm-4am.

Europa, VII, Zollerg. 8. Buy a drink, sidle back to the neon-lit alcoves, and strike a pose. The hip 20-something crowd hangs out late after long nights of clubbing. Mai Tai €6.50. Open daily 9am-5am.

Benjamin, I, Salzgries 11. Punk rock and tequila shots (€1.60). Open daily 7pm-2am.

Mapitom der Bierlokal, I, Seitenstetteng. 1. Right in the center of the Bermuda Triangle, this bar has large tables clustered in a warehouse-style interior. Beer and drinks about €3. Open Su-Th 5pm-3am, F-Sa 5pm-4am.

Jazzland, I, Franz-Josefs-Kai 29. U1: Schwedenpl. Live jazz and smoke mingle above the thirty-to-fifty something crowd. Music 9pm-1am. Cover €3.60. Open Tu-Sa 7pm-2am.

Esterházykeller, I, Haarhofg. 1, off Naglerg. U3: Herrengasse. One of Vienna's least expensive, most relaxed wine cellars. Open in summer M-F 4-11pm; off-season M-F 11am-11pm, Sa-Su 4-11pm.

First Floor Bar, I, Seitstentteng. 5. Martinis (€6-7), Cuban cigars (€4-20), and abundant swank. Open Su-Th 8pm-4am, F-Sa 7pm-4am. AmEx/MC/V.

CLUBS

■ **U-4**, XII, Schönbrunnerstr. 222. (www.clubnet.at) U4: Meidling Hauptstr. In the late 80s, U-4 hosted Nirvana and Hole before they were famous. 2 dance areas and multiple bars. Check in advance for theme nights. Cover €8. Open daily 10pm-5am.

■ **Porgy & Bess**, I, Riemerg. 11. (www.porgy.at) U1: *Stubentor*. The best jazz club in Vienna. Prices vary—shows generally €15-20. Open M-Sa 7pm-late, Su 8pm-late. MC/V.

Volksgarten Disco, I, Volksgarten. U2: *Volkstheater*. Hip-hop and a teenage crowd F; house and a somewhat older crowd Sa. Cover €6-13. Open Su and Th-Sa 10pm-5am.

Flex, I, Donaulände, near the Schottenring U-Bahn station. Dance, grab a beer (€4), or bring your own and sit by the river like everyone else. DJs start spinning at 10pm. Cover €6-10, free after 3am. Open May-Sept. daily 8pm-4am.

Why Not, I, Tiefer Graben 22. Gays and lesbians meet and greet at this disco and bar. Sa drink specials from €3.50. Cover €8. Open F-Sa from 11pm.

Club Meierei, III, Stadtpark. U4: Stadtpark. Located in the park, Meierei has no neighbors and thus more freedom to party loudly. It's rented to different owners and renamed each night; house music Th. Beer €3.50. Cover €10. Open W-Sa 10pm-late.

SALZBURGER LAND
AND UPPER AUSTRIA

Salzburger Land derives its name from the German *Salz* (salt), and it was this white gold that first drew visitors to the region. Combined with Upper Austria, this region encompasses the shining lakes and rolling hills of the Salzkammergut, where Salzburg and Hallstatt are among the more enticing destinations.

SALZBURG ☎ 0662

Backdropped by mountains and graced with Baroque wonders, Salzburg (pop. 140,000) offers both spectacular sights and a rich musical culture. Mozart's birthplace and the setting of *The Sound of Music*, Salzburg now carries on this legacy with aplomb. The city's adoration of classical music and the arts reaches a dizzying climax every summer during the **Salzburger Festspiele**, a five-week music festival featuring hundreds of operas, plays, and open-air performances.

▌ TRANSPORTATION

Trains: Hauptbahnhof, in Südtirolerpl. (24hr. reservations ☎05 17 17). To: **Graz** (4hr., 8 per day, €37); **Innsbruck** (2hr., 11 per day, €30); **Munich** (2hr., 30 per day, €26); **Vienna** (3½hr., 26 per day, €37); **Zurich** (6hr., 7 per day, €65).

Public Transportation: Get bus info. at the **Lokalbahnhof** (☎44 80 61 66), next to the train station. Single tickets (€1.70) available at automatic machines or from the drivers. Books of **five tickets** (€7), **daypasses** (€3.20), and **week passes** (€9) available at machines, the ticket office, or *Tabak* shops (newsstand/tobacco shops). Punch your ticket when you board in order to validate it or risk a €36 fine. Buses usually make their last run at 10:30-11:30pm, but **BusTaxi** fills in when the public buses stop. Get on at Hanuschpl. or Theaterg. and tell the driver where you need to go (every 30min. Su-Th 11:30pm-1:30am, F-Sa 11:30pm-3am; €3 for anywhere within the city limits).

AUSTRIA

✈ 🛈 ORIENTATION AND PRACTICAL INFORMATION

Just a few kilometers from the German border, Salzburg covers both banks of the **Salzach River.** Two hills abut the river: the **Mönchsberg** over the **Altstadt** (old city) on the south side and the **Kapuzinerberg** by the **Neustadt** (new city) on the north side. The *Hauptbahnhof* is on the northern side of town beyond the *Neustadt;* buses #1, 5, 6, 51, and 55 connect it to downtown. On foot, turn left out of the station onto Rainerstr. and follow it straight under the tunnel and on to Mirabellpl.

Tourist Office, Mozartpl. 5 (☎88 98 73 30), in the *Altstadt.* From the station, take bus #5, 6, 51, or 55 to Mozartsteg, head away from the river and curve right around the building into Mozartpl. The office gives free hotel maps, guided tours of the city (daily 12:15pm, €8), and sells the **Salzburg Card,** which grants admission to all museums and sights as well as unlimited public transportation (24hr. card €19; 48hr. €27; 72hr. €33). Room reservation service €2.20. Open daily 9am-6pm.

Currency Exchange: Banks offer better rates for cash than AmEx offices but often charge higher commissions. Banking hours M-F 8am-12:30pm and 2-4:30pm. The train station's exchange is open M-F 8:30am-5pm, Sa 8:30am-2:30pm.

American Express: Mozartpl. 5 (☎80 80). Provides all banking services; no commission on AmEx checks. Holds mail and books tours. Open M-F 9am-5:30pm, Sa 9am-noon.

Luggage Storage: At the train station. 24hr. lockers €2-3.50.

Bi-Gay-Lesbian Resources: Homosexual Initiative of Salzburg (HOSI), Müllner Hauptstr. 11 (☎43 59 27), hosts regular workshops and meetings, and offers a list of bars available upon request at the tourist office.

Emergencies: Police: ☎133. **Ambulance:** ☎144. **Fire:** ☎122.

Pharmacies: Elisabeth-Apotheke, Elisabethstr. 1a (☎87 14 84). Pharmacies in the city center open M-F 8am-6pm, Sa 8am-noon. There are always 3 pharmacies open for emergencies; check the list on the door of any closed pharmacy.

Internet Access: Internet Café, Mozartpl. 5 (☎84 48 22), near the tourist office. €0.15 per min. Open Sept.-June daily 9am-10pm, July-Aug. 9am-midnight. **Piterfun Internetc@fe,** Ferdinand-Porsche-Str. 7, across from the train station, has a rave ambience. 15min. €1.80, 30min. €2.90, 60min. €5. Open daily 10am-10pm.

Post Office: At the train station (☎88 30 30). Address mail to be held: Firstname SURNAME, *Postlagernde Briefe,* Bahnhofspostamt, **A-5020** Salzburg, AUSTRIA. Open M-F 7am-8:30pm, Sa 8am-2pm, Su 1-6pm.

⌂ ACCOMMODATIONS

Although hostels are plentiful, other housing in the city center is expensive; other affordable options lie on the outskirts of town or just outside it on **Kasern Berg.**

IN SALZBURG

Be wary of hotel hustlers at the station. Instead, ask for the tourist office's list of *Privatzimmern* (private rooms) or the *Hotel Plan* (which has info on hostels). From mid-May to mid-September, hostels fill by mid-afternoon; call ahead, and be sure to make reservations during the *Festspiele* (p. 106).

■ **Stadtalm,** Mönchsberg 19c (☎/fax 84 17 29). Take bus #1 (dir.: Maxglan) to Mönchsbergaufzug, go down the street and through the stone arch on the left to the Mönchsberglift (elevator), and ride up (daily 9am-11pm, round-trip €2.40). At the top, turn right, climb the steps, and follow signs for Stadtalm. The view is princely. Breakfast included. Shower €0.80 per 4min. Reception 9am-9pm. Curfew 1am. Open Apr.-Sept. Dorms €13. AmEx/MC/V. ❷

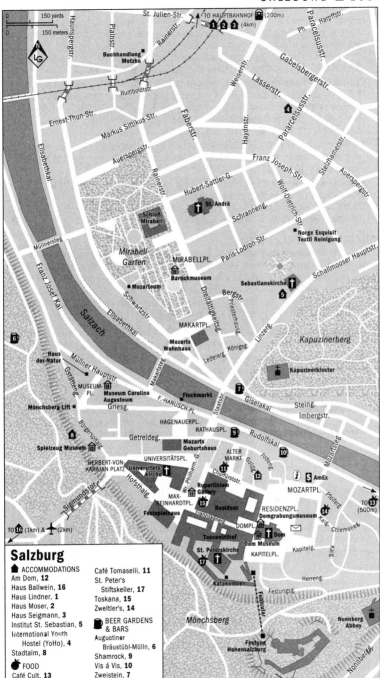

Salzburg

ACCOMMODATIONS
Am Dom, 12
Haus Ballwein, 16
Haus Lindner, 1
Haus Moser, 2
Haus Seigmann, 3
Institut St. Sebastian, 5
International Youth
  Hostel (YoHo), 4
Stadtalm, 8

FOOD
Café Cult, 13

Café Tomaselli, 11
St. Peter's
  Stiftskeller, 17
Toskana, 15
Zweitler's, 14

BEER GARDENS & BARS
Augutiner
  Bräustübl-Mülln, 6
Shamrock, 9
Vis á Vis, 10
Zweistein, 7

Institut St. Sebastian, Linzerg. 41 (☎87 13 86). From the station, bus #1, 5, 6, 51, or 55 to Mirabellpl.; continue in the same direction as the bus, turn left onto Bergstr., and left again onto Linzerg.; the hostel is through the arch. Breakfast included. Sheets €2 for dorms. Laundry €3. Reception 8am-noon and 4-9pm. Dorms €15; singles €21, with shower €33; doubles €40/54; triples €60/69; quads €72/84. ❷

International Youth Hotel (YoHo), Paracelsusstr. 9 (☎87 96 49; www.yoho.at). With a frat-party atmosphere, this hostel is a no-frills place to crash. Breakfast €3-4. Dinner entrees (with veggie options) €5-6. Happy Hour 6-7pm with .5L Stiegl €1.50, other brews €2.50. Lockers in the hall €0.10-1. Dorms €15; doubles €20, with shower €23; quads €68/80. MC/V. ❷

Am Dom, Goldg. 17 (☎84 27 55; bach@salzburg.co.at). Unbeatable location, across the square from the *Dom.* Historic, wood-paneled, traditional Austrian hotel. Singles €68; doubles €94. MC/V. ❹

Haus Ballwein, Moostr. 69a (☎/fax 82 40 29; haus.ballwein@gmx.net). Take bus #1 to Hanuschpl., then bus #60 south to *Gsengerweg.* With balconies overlooking quiet fields and distant mountains, this is the perfect reprieve from city life. Breakfast included. Bicycle rental €7 per day. Singles €22; doubles €38-50. No credit cards. ❸

OUTSIDE OF SALZBURG

The rooms on **Kasern Berg** are officially outside Salzburg, which means the tourist office can't recommend them, but the personable hosts and bargain prices make these *Privatzimmer* (rooms in a family home) a terrific housing option. Expect rolling fields and a reliance on public transportation. All northbound trains run to Kasern Berg (4min.; every 30min. 6:15am-11:15pm; €1.60; Eurail valid). Get off at Salzburg-Maria Plain and take the only road uphill. Most don't accept credit cards.

Haus Lindner, Panoramaweg 5 (☎45 66 81). Offers homey rooms, some with mountain views. Breakfast included. Call for pickup from the station. €16 per person. ❷

Haus Moser, Turnerbühel (☎45 66 76). Climb up the steep hidden stairs on the right side of Kasern Berg road across from German Kapeller. A charming couple offers comfortable rooms in their cozy, dark-timbered home. Breakfast and laundry included. €15 per person. Cheaper after 1st night. ❷

Haus Seigmann, Kasern Bergstr. 66 (☎45 00 01). Snug comforters and balconies overlooking the valley. Afternoon tea served on the hillside patios. About €15 per person (negotiable). Reservations recommended in the summer. MC/V. ❷

🔾 FOOD

Countless beer gardens and pastry-shop patios make Salzburg a great place for outdoor dining. Local specialties include *Salzburger Nockerl* (egg whites, sugar, and raspberry filling baked into three mounds that represent the three hills of Salzburg), *Knoblauchsuppe* (a rich cream soup loaded with croutons and garlic), and the world-famous *Mozartkugeln* (hazelnuts coated in marzipan, nougat, and chocolate). **Supermarkets** cluster on the Mirabellpl. side of the river, and **open-air markets** are held on Universitätpl. (Open M-F 6am-7pm, Sa 6am-1pm.)

Zweltler's, Kaig. 3. Near the tourist office on Mozartpl. Try the tasty *Spinatnockerl* (spinach baked into a pan with cheese and parsley, €6.50) or the classic *Wienerschnitzel* (€9.70). For added excitement local customers yell suggestions to the chef on second floor. Open daily 6pm-1am, during the *Festspiele* also 11am-2pm. ❸

St. Peter's Stiftskeller, St.-Peter-Bezirk 1/4. Tucked away behind the fortress at the foot of the cliffs is the oldest restaurant in Central Europe, established in 803. Most dishes are €18-20, but a few run cheaper. Open M-F 11am-midnight, during the *Festspiele* until 1am. MC/V. ❹

Toskana, Sigmund Haffnerg. 11. This college cafeteria has the cheapest eats in the *Altstadt*. Entrees €4. Open July-Aug. M-F 9am-3pm; Sept.-June M-Th 8:30am-5pm, F 8:30am-3pm. ❶

Café Tomaselli, Alter Markt 9. Indulge. The delectable drinks (€4-6) and desserts (€4-7) here have been a favorite with wealthier Salzburgers since 1705. Open M-Sa 7am-9pm, Su 8am-9pm. ❷

Café Cult, Hellbrunnerstr. 3 (☎84 56 01). In the Kunstlerhaus building. This Mediterranean cafe is popular with the artistic set of Salzburg. Eat on the glass terrace overlooking the river. Entrees €6-9. Open M-F 9am-11pm, Sa 8am-3pm. No credit cards. ❷

🎦 SIGHTS

THE ALTSTADT

FESTUNG HOHENSALZBURG. Built between 1077 and 1681 by the ruling archbishops, Hohensalzburg Fortress, which looms over Salzburg from atop Mönchsberg, is the largest completely preserved castle in Europe—partly because it was never successfully attacked. The castle contains formidable Gothic state rooms, the fortress organ (nicknamed the "Bull of Salzburg" for its off-key snorting), and a watchtower that affords an unmatched view of the city and mountains. The **Burgmuseum** inside the fortress displays medieval instruments of torture and has side-by-side histories of Salzburg, the fortress, and the world. *(Take the trail or the Festungsbahn funicular up to the fortress from Festungsg. Funicular every 10min. 9am-9pm. Ascent €5.60, round-trip €8.50; includes entrance to fortress. Grounds open mid-June to mid-Sept. daily 8:30am-8pm; mid-Sept. to mid-Mar. 9am-5pm; mid-Mar. to mid-June 9am-6pm. Interior open mid-June to mid-Sept. daily 9am-5:30pm; mid-Sept. to mid-Mar. 9am-4:30pm; mid-Mar. to mid-June 9:30am-5pm. If you walk up, entrance to fortress is €3.60; **combo ticket** including fortress, castle interiors, and museums €7.20.)*

MOZARTS GEBURTSHAUS. Mozart's birthplace holds an impressive collection of the child genius' belongings, including his first viola and violin and a pair of keyboardish instruments. Several rooms recreate his young years as a traveling virtuoso. Come before 11am to avoid the crowd. *(Getreudeg. 9. Open July-Aug. daily 9am-6:30pm; Sept.-June 9am-5:30pm. €5.50, students and seniors €4.50.)*

UNIVERSITY CHURCH. In Mozart's backyard stands the **Universitätskirche,** one of the largest Baroque chapels on the continent and designer Fischer von Erlach's masterpiece. Sculpted clouds coat the nave, while pudgy cherubim (lit by pale natural light from the dome) frolic all over the church's immense apse.

TOP TEN LIST

TOP 10 CAFES IN AUSTRIA

Although Vienna is the heart of Austrian cafe culture, many other cities (Salzburg especially) have serious contenders.

1. **Café Demel, Vienna** (p. 93). Once confectioner for the Hapsburg Imperial Court.

2. **Café Hawelka, Vienna** (p. 94). A down-to-earth family-owned-and-operated cafe.

3. **Café Tomaselli, Salzburg** (p. 105). A classy cafe in business for well over 200 years.

4. **Café Traxlmayr, Linz.** A crowded, elegant cafe where you can try the city's delicious *Linzer Torte*.

5. **Café Central, Vienna** (p. 93). Former haunt of Europe's most famous writers, artists, and intellectuals.

6. **Café-Konditorei Grendler, Zell am Ziller.** Award-winning desserts are served on the banks of a mountain river.

7. **Café Stein, Vienna** (p. 94). A busy modern alternative to the more classical cafés in Vienna.

8. **Hofgarten Café, Innsbruck** (p. 113). In the middle of Innsbruck's large public park.

9. **Café Willendorf, Vienna** (p. 92). An artsy, racy cafe at the heart of Vienna's gay and lesbian scene.

10. **Café-Konditorei Hagmann, Krems.** Serves wonderful desserts with true Danube charm.

TOSCANINIHOF, CATACOMBS, AND THE DOM. Steps lead from **Toscaninihof,** the courtyard of **St. Peter's Monastery,** up the Mönchsberg cliffs. **Stiftskirche St. Peter,** a church within the monastery, features a marble portal from 1244. In the 18th century, the building was remodeled in Rococo style. *(Open daily 9am-12:15pm and 2:30-6:30pm.)* Near the far end of the cemetery, against the Mönchsberg, is the entrance to the **Catacombs.** In the lower room (St. Gertrude's Chapel), a fresco commemorates the martyrdom of Thomas á Beckett. *(Open May-Sept. Tu–Su 10:30am-5pm; Oct.-Apr. W-Su 10:30am-3:30pm. €1, students €0.60.)* The exit at the other end of the cemetery leads to the immense baroque **Dom** (cathedral), where Mozart was christened in 1756 and later worked as concert master and court organist. The square leading out of the cathedral, **Domplatz,** features a statue of the Virgin Mary and figures representing Wisdom, Faith, the Church, and the Devil. *(Free, but donation requested.)*

RESIDENZ. The archbishops of Salzburg have resided in the magnificent Residenz since 1595. Stunning baroque **Prunkräume** (state rooms) have gigantic ceiling frescoes, gilded furniture, Flemish tapestries from the 1600s, and ornate stucco work. A **gallery** exhibits 16th- to 19th-century art. *(Open daily 10am-5pm. €7.30, students €5.50; audio guide included.)*

FESTSPIELHAUS. Once the riding school for the archbishops' horses, it now hosts many of the big-name events of the *Festspiele* in its two opera houses. (☎84 90 97. *Down Wiener-Philharmonikerg. from Universitätspl. Tours at 2pm. €5, under 13 €2.90.)* Opposite the *Festspielhaus,* the **Rupertinum Gallery** exhibits modern painting, sculpture, and photography in a graceful building remodeled by Friedensreich Hundertwasser. (☎80 42 23 36. *Open mid-July to Sept. Su, Tu and Th-Sa 9am-5pm, W 10am-9pm; Oct. to mid-July Su, Tu and Th-Sa 10am-5pm, W 10am-9pm. €8, students €4.50.)*

THE NEUSTADT

MIRABELL PALACE AND GARDENS. Mirabellpl. holds the marvelous **Mirabell Schloß,** which the supposedly celibate Archbishop Wolf Dietrich built for his mistress and their ten children in 1606. Behind the palace, the delicately cultivated **Mirabellgarten** is a maze of seasonal flower beds and groomed shrubbery. The Mirabellgarten contains a wooden, moss-covered shack called the **Zauberflöten-häuschen,** where Mozart allegedly composed *The Magic Flute* in just five months.

MOZARTS WOHNHAUS. Mozart moved here at age 17 with his family, staying from 1773-1780. Hear excerpts from his music alongside original scores. *(Makartpl. 8. Open July-Aug. daily 9am-6:30pm; Sept.-June 9am-5:30pm.)*

🎵 ENTERTAINMENT

Max Reinhardt, Richard Strauss, and Hugo von Hofmannsthal founded the renowned **Salzburger Festspiele** in 1920. Ever since, Salzburg has become a musical mecca from late July to the end of August. On the eve of the festival's opening, over 100 dancers don regional costumes and perform a *Fackeltanz* (torchdance) on Residenzpl. Operas, plays, films, concerts, and tourists overrun every available public space. Info and tickets for *Festspiele* events are available through the *Festspiele Kartenbüro* (ticket office) and *Tageskasse* (daily box office) in Karajanpl., against the mountain and next to the tunnel. (Open M-F 9:30am-3pm; July 1-July 22 M-Sa 9:30am-5pm; July 23-end of festival daily 9:30am-6:30pm.)

Even when the *Festspiele* are not on, many other concerts and events occur around the city. The **Salzburg Academy of Music and Performing Arts** performs a number of concerts on a rotating schedule in the **Mozarteum** (next to the Mirabell gardens), and the **Dom** has a concert program in July and August. (€8.75, students €7.30.) In addition, from May through August there are **outdoor performances,** including concerts, folk-singing, and dancing, around the Mirabellgarten. The tourist office has leaflets on scheduled events, but an evening stroll through the park might answer your questions just as well. **Mozartplatz** and **Kapitelplatz** are also popular stops for talented street musicians and touring school bands.

PUBS AND BEER GARDENS

Munich may be known as the world's beer capital, but much of that liquid gold flows south to Austria's pubs and *Biergärten* (beer gardens). These lager oases cluster in the city center by the Salzach River. The more boisterous stick to Rudolfskai between the Staatsbrücke and Mozartsteg. Elsewhere, especially along Chiemseeg. and around Anton-Neumayr-Pl., you can throw back a few drinks in a more reserved *Beisl* (pub). Refined bars with older patrons can be found along Steing. and Giselakai on the other side of the river. The gargantuan **Augustiner Bräustübl-Mülln,** Augustinerg. 4, has been serving home-brewed beer, *Biergarten* style, since 1621. (Open M-F 3-11pm, Sa-Su 2:30-11pm.) Settle into an armchair at the chic **Vis à Vis,** Rudolfskai 24. (Open daily 7:30pm-4am.) A relaxed and friendly Irish pub, **Shamrock,** Rudolfskai 11, has plenty of room and nightly live music. (Open Su noon-2am, M-Th 3pm-2am, F-Sa noon-4am.) **Zweistein,** Giselakai 9, is the center of Salzburg's gay and lesbian scene. (Open M-W 6pm-4am, Th-Su 6pm-5am.)

DAYTRIPS FROM SALZBURG

HELLBRUNN. Just south of Salzburg lies the unforgettable **Lustschloß Hellbrunn,** a sprawling estate with a large palace, fish ponds, flower gardens, and the **Wasserspiele,** elaborate water-powered figurines and a booby-trapped table that spouts water on surprised guests. Pictures of you getting sprayed are available at the end of the tour. (Open May-June and Sept. daily 9am-5:30pm; July-Aug. 9am-10pm; Apr. and Oct. 9am-4:30pm. Ticket for castle tour, gardens, and Wasserspiele €7.50, students €5.50.) Take bus #55 (dir.: Rif; 30 min.) to Hellbrun from the train station, Mirabellpl., or Mozartsteg.

After you dry off, continue on bus #55 to St. Leonhard, where Charlemagne supposedly rests under Untersberg Peak, prepared to return and reign over Europe when duty calls. A cable car glides over the rocky cliffs to the summit, and from there hikes lead off into the distance. On top is a memorial cross and unbelievable mountain scenery. (Open July-Sept. daily 8:30am-5:30pm; Mar.-June and Oct. 8:30am-5pm; Dec.-Feb. 9am-4pm. Round-trip €17.)

NO WORK, ALL PLAY

START YOUR ENGINES...

At the end of May Salzburg shuts down in recognition of *Christi Himmelfahrt,* the Catholic holiday of the Ascension. Although the holiday is a celebration of Jesus's return to heaven, part of Salzburg's observance may seem surprising. At the end of May, antique race cars pour into Residenzpl., revving their engines and parading around town for three days. In 2003 the Gaisberg Race for classic motor cars, which ran from 1929 to 1969, was resurrected by a group of farsighted politicians and antique car lovers. The race is a "regularity contest," meaning that racers try to match their own times. The 8652m course runs from the city center to the Gaisberg, one of three hills overlooking Salzburg. Beaming from their cars, models 1910 to 1970, the owners make the 672m climb. The event allows car collectors a chance to show off their babies, and gives Salzburgers and tourists an excuse to gather in the *Altstadt* and see some really cool cars. While admiring the competitors' automobiles, spectators enjoy the live music and the food stands set up around the edges of Residenzpl.

In 2004, *Christi Himmelfahrt* falls on Thursday, May 20. The festivities last for three days, through Saturday. For more info, check out the Gaisberg Race's site: www.src.co.at.

HALLSTATT ☎ 06134

Teetering on the banks of the Hallstättersee, tiny Hallstatt (pop. 960) seems to defy gravity by clinging to the face of a stony slope. It is easily the most striking lakeside village in the Salzkammergut, if not in all of Austria.

■ TRANSPORTATION. Buses are the cheapest way (€12) to get to Hallstatt from Salzburg, but require layovers in both Bad Ischl and Gosaumühle. The **train station,** across the lake, is not staffed. All trains come from Attnang-Puchheim in the north or Stainach-Irdning in the south. **Trains** run hourly to Bad Ischl (30min., €3) and Salzburg via Attnang-Puchheim (2½hrs., €17).

⚠ PRACTICAL INFORMATION. The **tourist office,** Seestr. 169, finds rooms and offers help with the town's confusing system of street numbers. (☎82 08. Open July-Aug. M-F 9am-5pm, Sa 10am-4pm, Su 10am-2pm; Sept.-June M-Tu and Th-F 9am-noon and 2-5pm, W 9am-noon.) There is an **ATM** next to the post office. The **post office,** Seestr. 160, is below the tourist office. (Open M-Tu and Th-F 8am-noon and 1:30-5:30pm, W 8am-noon.) **Postal Code:** A-4830.

⌂⌂ ACCOMMODATIONS AND FOOD. To reach **Gästehaus Zur Mühle ❷,** Kirchenweg 36, from the tourist office, walk uphill, heading for a short tunnel at the upper right corner of the square; it's right at the end of the tunnel by the waterfall. (☎83 18. Breakfast €2.50. Reception 10am-2pm and 4-10pm. Closed Nov. Dorms €10.) **Frühstückspension Sarstein ❸,** Gosamühlstr. 83, offers glorious views as well as a beachside lawn. From the ferry landing, turn right on Seestr. and walk 10min. (☎82 17. Breakfast included. Showers €1 per 10min. Singles €18; doubles €36.) To get to **Camping Klausner-Höll ❶,** Lahnstr. 201, turn right out of the tourist office and follow Seestr. for 10min. (☎832 24. Breakfast €4-8. Showers included. Laundry €8. Gate closed daily noon-3pm and 10pm-7:30am. Open mid-Apr. to mid-Oct. €5.80; tent €3.70; car €2.90.) The cheapest eats are at the **Konsum supermarket** across from the bus stop; the butcher's counter prepares sandwiches on request. (Open M-Tu and Th-F 7:30am-noon and 3-6pm, W and Sa 7:30am-noon.)

◐◑ SIGHTS AND HIKING. Back when Rome was still a village, the "white gold" from the salt mines made Hallstatt a world-famous settlement; the 2500-year-old **Salzbergwerk** is the oldest salt mine in the world. Take the guided tour (1hr., in English and German), and zip down a wooden mining slide on a burlap sack to an eerie lake deep inside the mountain. (☎200 2400. Open daily May-Sept. 9:30am-4:30pm; Oct. 9:30am-3pm. €14.50; students €8.70.) In the 19th century, Hallstatt was also the site of an immense and well-preserved Iron Age archaeological find. The **charnel house** next to St. Michael's Chapel is a bizarre repository filled with the remains of over 610 villagers dating from the 16th century on; the latest were added in 1995. The dead were previously buried in the mountains, but villagers soon ran out of space and transferred older bones to the charnel house to make room for more corpses. From the ferry dock, follow the signs marked *Katholische Kirche.* (Open daily June-Sept. 10am-6pm; May and Oct. 10am-4pm. €1.)

Hallstatt offers some of the most spectacular day hikes in the Salzkammergut. The tourist office offers an excellent Dachstein **hiking guide** in English (€6), which details 38 hikes in the area, as well as **bike** trail maps (€7). The **Salzbergwerk hike** is a simple 1hr. gravel hike leading to the salt-mine tour; walk to the Salzbergbahn and take the road to the right upward, turning at the black and yellow Salzwelten sign. The **Waldbachstrub Waterfall hike** is a light 1¾hr. walk along a tumbling stream and up to a spellbinding waterfall. From the bus station, follow the brown Malerweg signs near the supermarket and continue to follow them until the Waldbach-strub sign appears (about 40min.). The waterfall is in the **Echental**, a valley carved out millennia ago by glaciers and now blazed with trails leading deep into the valley. The **Gangsteig**, a slippery, primitive stairway, carved into the side of a cliff, requires sturdy hiking shoes and a strong will to climb.

DAYTRIPS FROM HALLSTATT: DACHSTEIN ICE CAVES. Above **Obertraun**, opposite the lake from Hallstatt, the famed **Riesenhöhle** (Giant Ice Cave) is part of the largest system of ice caves in the world. Slide by its frozen waterfalls and palaces on a sheet of green ice. The Riesenhöhle and the **Mammuthöhle** (Mammoth Cave) are up on the mountain, while the **Koppenbrüllerhöhle**, a giant spring, is in the valley. Mandatory tours are offered in English and German; you'll be assigned to a group at the Schönbergalm station. The cave temperatures are near freezing, so wear good footwear and something warm. (☎ (06131) 84 00. Open May to mid-Oct. daily 9am-5pm. Admission to each cave €8, children €4.80.)

From Hallstatt, walk to the Lahn station by heading down Seestr. with the lake to your left, and catch the **bus** to Obertraun (10min., every hr. 9am-5pm, €1.40). Stop at Dachstein, then ride the cable car up to Schönbergalm to reach the ice and mammoth caves. (Every 15min. 8:40am-5:30pm, round-trip €13.) The Koppen-brüller cave is a 15min. walk from the Dachstein bus stop in Obertraun.

GRÜNAU ☎07616

Poised below the picturesque **Totes Gebirge** (Dead Mountains), Grünau (pop. 2100) is ideal for almost any kind of outdoor activity. The real reason to visit is ☒**The Treehouse ❷**, Schindlbachstr. 525, a backpacker's dream resort. The incredibly friendly staff organizes adventure tours, including **canyoning** (€50), **bungee jumping** (€95, only on weekends), and **horseback riding** (€9.50 per hr.). To strike out on your own, rent a **mountain bike** (€6 per day) or ask the staff about **hiking** trails. For winter visitors, the ski lift is a 5min. walk from the front door, and snow gear (jackets, snowsuits, gloves, etc.) is provided free of charge. Day ski-lift passes are €20.50, and **skis** and **snowboards** are available for rent (€13 and up).

Regular **trains** service Grünau from Wels, on the Vienna-Salzburg rail line (1hr., 6:45am-8:45pm, €6). Call ahead to The Treehouse to be picked up free of charge. Rooms feature private showers and goosedown blankets, and amenities include a TV room with hundreds of English-language movies, book-exchange library, sauna, basketball and tennis courts, **Internet** (€0.10 per min.), and two in-house bars for nighttime revelry. (☎ 84 99. Breakfast included. 3-course dinners €7. 6-bed dorms €14.50; doubles €37; triples €51.50; quads €66. AmEx/MC/V.)

HOHE TAUERN NATIONAL PARK

The enormous Hohe Tauern range, part of the Austrian Central Alps and the largest national park in Europe, boasts 246 glaciers and 304 mountains over 3000m. Preservation is a primary goal, so there are no large campgrounds or recreation areas. The best way to explore this rare preserve is to take one of the many hikes, which range from pleasant ambles to difficult mountain ascents. *An Experience in Nature*, available at park centers and most area tourist offices, plots and briefly describes 84 different hikes. The center of the park is Franz-Josefs-Höhe and the Pasterze glacier, which hovers right above the town of Heiligenblut. Aside from the skiing and hiking, the main tourist attractions are the Krimml Waterfalls, in the northwestern corner near Zell am See, and the Großglockner Hochalpenstraße, a high mountain road that runs between Heiligenblut and Bruck.

AUSTRIA

E TRANSPORTATION. Trains arrive in **Zell am See** from: Innsbruck (1½-2hr., 3:45am-9:25pm, €20); Kitzbühel (45min., 7:15am-11:30pm, €8.10); and Salzburg (1½hr., 1-2 per hr., €13). From Zell am See, a rail line runs west along the northern border of the park, terminating in Krimml (1½hr., 6am-10:55pm, €6.80); a bus also runs directly to the Höhe (2hr., 2 per day, €10). The park itself is crisscrossed by **bus** lines that operate on a complicated timetable.

FRANZ-JOSEFS-HÖHE. This tourist center, stationed above the Pasterze glacier, has an amazing view of the Großglockner (3798m). The Höhe has its own **park office** in the parking area. (☎(04824) 27 27. Open daily 10am-4pm.) The free elevator next to the info center leads to the **Swarovski Observation Center,** a crystal-shaped building with binoculars for viewing the surrounding terrain. (Open daily 10am-4pm. Free.) The **Gletscherweg** (3hr.) hike is like walking on the moon.

HEILIGENBLUT. The closest town to the highest mountain in Austria and a great starting point for hikes, Heiligenblut (pop. 1,200) is a convenient base for exploration of the region. Heiligenblut can be reached by **bus** from Franz-Josefs-Höhe (30min., €3.60) and Lienz (1 hr., 2-6 per day, €6). The **tourist office,** Hof 4, up the street from the bus stop, dispenses info about rooms, hikes, and park transportation. (☎04824 20 01 21. Open July-Aug. M-F 8:30am-6pm, Sa 9am-noon and 4-6pm; Sept.-June M-F 8:30am-noon and 2:30-6pm, Sa 9am-noon and 4-6pm.) To reach the **Jugendgästehaus Heiligenblut (HI) ❸,** Hof 36, take the path down from the wall behind the bus stop parking lot. (☎04824 22 59. Breakfast included. Reception daily 7-10am and 5-9pm. Dorms €20, under-27 €15; singles €27/22.)

KRIMML. Over 400,000 visitors per year arrive here to see the extraordinary Krimml Waterfalls, a set of three cascades spanning 380m. (8am-6pm €1.50; free after 6pm.) These waterfalls are usually enjoyed as a daytrip from Zell am See; **buses** run from Zell am See (1½ hr., 5:45am-8:55pm, €7.50) to *Maustelle Ort,* the start of the path to the falls. The trail, called the **Wasserfallweg** (4km), maintains a constant upward pitch. The first set of falls are accessible almost directly from the entrance; it's about 30min. from the first to the second set of falls, and an additional 30min. to the third set. To reach the **tourist office,** Oberkrimml 37, follow the road from the Krimml Ort bus stop and turn right down the hill in front of the church. (☎723 90. Open M-F 8am-noon and 2:30-5:30pm, Sa 8:30-10:30am.)

TYROL (TIROL)

Tyrol's mountains overwhelm the average mortal with their superhuman scale. Craggy summits rising in the northeast and south cradle four-star resorts and untouched valleys like the Ötzal and Zillertal. In eastern Tyrol, the mighty Hohe Tauern range is protected as a national park. The region is a mountain playground, and Innsbruck is its swing set.

INNSBRUCK ☎0512

The 1964 and 1976 winter Olympics were held in Innsbruck (pop. 128,000), bringing international recognition to this beautiful mountain city. The nearby Tyrolean Alps await skiers and hikers, and the tiny cobblestone streets of the *Altstadt* are peppered with fancy facades and relics of the Habsburg Empire.

Innsbruck

▲■ ACCOMMODATIONS

Camping Innsbruck
  Kranebitten, **9**
Gasthof Innbrücke, **5**
Hotel Fritz Prior-
  Schwedenhaus (HI), **1**
Jugendherberge
  Innsbruck (HI), **3**
Pension Paula, **2**

🍖 FOOD

Gasthof Weißes Lamm, **6**
Noi Original Thaiküche, **4**
Salute Pizzeria, **7**
Theresianbräu, **8**

0 ⊢——⊣ 200 yards
0 ⊢——⊣ 200 meters

Waltherpark
Herreng.
Herzog-Otto-Str.
Badg.
Dom St. Jakob
Rennweg
Hölblinghaus ■
Pfarrg.
Hofburg
Goldenes 🏛 **Maxilianeum**
Dachl
Hofg.
Herzog-Friedrich-Str.
Hotel
Goldener **Stadtturm** 🏛
Adler
Rieseng. **Hofkirche**
Seilerg. Schlosserg. Stift.g. **Tiroler**
Markgraben Burggraben **Volkskunst-**
ⓘ **museum**

Alpenzoo
Weyerburgg.
Inn
Hoher Weg
Inn
Rennweg
1
2
St. Nikolas
Elisabethstr.
Falkstr.
TO **3**
(1.5km)
Schillerstr.
Kaiserjägerstr.
Bienerstr.
Claudiastr.
Innsbr.
Karl-Kapferer-Str.
Innsteg
Siebererstr.
Kochstr.
Bus Info ⓘ
Center
Hofgarten
St.-Nikolaus-G.
Walterpark
Herzog-Otto-Str.
Congress ✚
HÖTTING
Höttingerg.
5
SEE INSET
Landes-
theater
UK **Kapuziner-**
kirche
6
Inn-
Brücke
Hofburg
Universitätsstr.
Angerzelle
Mentlhardstr.
Etzel Str.
Jahnstr.
Dreiheiligenstr.
Ingenieur
Sill
BRÜCKEN-
PLATZ
Kürnerstr.
PRADL
Mariahilfstr.
ⓘ
Burggraben
Tiroler
Landesmuseum
Ferdinandeum 🏛
Museumstr.
Weinhartstr.
Bruneckerstr.
König Laurin Str.
Pradlerstr.
Kornerstr.
Defreggerstr.
Stadt
Park
Höttinger Au
Inn
Herzog Sigmund Ufer
Volksgarten
■ **M-Preis**
Burgerstr.
Maria-Theresien-Str.
Erlerstr.
Meranerstr.
W.-Greil-Str.
Adamg.
Meinhardstr.
Brixnerstr.
BOZNERPL.
Bubblepoint **Hertz**
Waschsalon
Landhaus ■**ÖAV**
Universitäts-
brücke
Blasius-Huber-Str.
7
Innrain
Anichstr.
Kaiser Josef Str.
Stainerstr.
8
Salurnerstr.
■ **Denzel Cars**
SÜDTI-
ROLERPL.
Haupt-
bahnhof 🚌
ⓘ
Amraserstr.
Hunoldstr.
Sillufer
Anton Eder-Str.
Anzengruberstr.
University
Library
TO HOMOSEXUELLE
INITIATIVE TIROL (2km)
Maximilianstr.
M-Preis
Sport Neuner
Müllerstr.
Templstr.
Andreas-Hofer-Str.
Triumphpforte ⌐
Heiliggeiststr.
Schopfstr.
Peter-Mayr-Str.
Fritz-Pregl-Str.
Speckbacherstr.
Michael-Gaismayr-Str.
WILTEN
Leopoldstr.
Frauenzentrum
Innsbruck ■
Liebenggstr.
Südbahnstr.
Westfriedhof
Franz-Fischer-Str.
Stafflerstr.
Neuhauserstr.
Tschamlerstr.
Anton Melzer Str.
Olympiabrücke
Olympiastr.
Olympic Ice
Stadium
Karwendel str.
Egger-Lienz-Str.
Westbahnhof ■🚂
Feldstr.
Grassmayr
Bell-Foundry ■
Basilika
Wilten 🏛
Fritz Konzert-Str.
Stiftskirche
Wilten 🏛
TO **9** (5km)
Pastorstr.
TO SCHLOSS AMBRAS (2km) →
Ⓐ12
Autobahn
Ⓐ12

AUSTRIA

🔲 🛈 TRANSPORTATION AND PRACTICAL INFORMATION

Trains: Hauptbahnhof, Südtirolerpl. (☎05 17 17). To: **Munich** (2hr., 13 per day, €32); **Rome** (8½-9½hr., 2 per day, €60); **Salzburg** (2½hr., 13 per day, €30); **Vienna Westbahnhof** (5½-7hr., 10 per day, €47); **Zurich** (4hr., 4 per day, €44).

Public Transportation: The **IVB** Office, Stainerstr. 2 (☎530 17 99), near Maria-Theresien-Str., has bus schedules. Open M-F 7:30am-6pm. The main bus station is in front of the entrance to the train station. Most buses stop running at 10:30 or 11:30pm, but 3 *Nachtbus* lines continue through the night.

Bike Rental: Sport Neuner, Maximillianstr. 23 (☎56 15 01). Mountain bikes and helmets €20 per day, €16 per half day. Open M-F 9am-6pm, Sa 9am-noon.

Tourist Office: Innsbruck Tourist Office, Burggraben 3, 3rd fl. (☎598 50). Off the end of Museumstr. Sells maps (€1) and the **Innsbruck Card,** which provides unlimited access to public transportation and most museums. (24hr. card €21, 48hr. €26, 72hr. €31.) Open M-F 8am-6pm, Sa 8am-noon.

Laundromat: Bubblepoint Waschsalon, Brixnerstr. 1 (☎56 50 07 14). 7kg wash €4, dryer €1 per 10min. Open M-F 8am-10pm, Sa-Su 8am-8pm.

Police: ☎133. **Ambulance:** ☎144 or 142. **Fire:** ☎122.

Internet Access: International Telephone Discount, Bruneckstr. 12 (☎59 42 72 61). Turn right from the *Hauptbahnhof;* it's on the left, just past the end of Südtirolerpl. €0.11 per min. Open daily 9am-11pm.

Post Office: Maximilianstr. 2 (☎500 79 00). Open M-F 7am-11pm, Sa 7am-9pm, Su 8am-9pm. Address mail to be held: Firstname SURNAME, *Postlagernde Briefe,* Hauptpostamt, Maximilianstr. 2, **A-6020** Innsbruck AUSTRIA.

🔲 ACCOMMODATIONS

Inexpensive accommodations are scarce in June, when some hostels close. The opening of student dorms to backpackers in July and August somewhat alleviates the crush. Visitors should join the free **Club Innsbruck** by registering at any Innsbruck accommodation. Membership gives discounts on skiing, bike tours, and the club's hiking program.

Pension Paula, Weiherburgg. 15 (☎29 22 62). Take bus D to *Schmelzerg.* and head uphill. Escape the city rumble. Beautiful views across the valley. Breakfast included. Singles €27, with shower €33; doubles €45/54; triples €60/70; quads €80. ❸

Gasthof Innbrücke, Instr. 1 (☎28 19 34). From the *Altstadt,* cross the Innbrücke. The 575-year-old inn has a riverside and mountain view. Breakfast included. Singles €27, with shower €35; doubles €45/60; quads €110. ❸

Jugendherberge Innsbruck (HI), Reichenauer Str. 147 (☎34 61 79). From the train station, take tram 3 to *Sillpark* and bus O to *Jugendherberge.* Bike rental €11 per day. Breakfast included. Reception daily 5-10pm. 6-bed dorms €12; 4-bed dorms €15; singles with shower €28; doubles with shower €41. Nonmembers add €3. ❷

Hostel Fritz Prior-Schwedenhaus (HI), Rennweg 17b (☎58 58 14). From the station, take tram 4 to *Handelsakademie,* continue to the end and across Rennweg to the river. Spacious rooms with private bath. Sheets €3.10. Reception daily 7-9:30am and 5-10:30pm. Check-in before 6pm. Lockout 9am-5pm. Open July-Aug. and Dec. 27-Jan. 5. Dorms €10; doubles €28; triples €42. ❷

Camping Innsbruck Kranebitten, Kranebitter Allee 214 (☎28 41 80). Take bus O to *Technik* and then bus LK to *Klammstr.* Walk downhill to the right. Pleasant grounds in the shadow of a snow-capped mountain. Restaurant open 8-11am and 4pm-midnight. Showers included. If reception is closed, find a site and check in the next morning. €5 per person, €3 per tent, €3 per car. Bicycle €5 per day. Electricity €3. ❶

FOOD

The delicatessen on glamorous Maria-Theresien-Str. are good but overpriced. From the *Altstadt*, cross the Inn River to Innstr., in the university district, for ethnic restaurants and cheap pizzerias. There are **M-Preis Supermarkets** at Museumstr. 34 and across from the train station. (Open M-F 7:30am-6:30pm, Sa 7:30am-5pm.)

Theresianbräu, Maria-Theresien-Str. 51, is built around giant copper brewing kettles. Try the dark house lager (.5L stein €3.30) alongside traditional meals such as *Käsespatzl* (homemade noodles with cheese; €6.80). Fondue for 2 or more is available after 6pm. Open M-W 10:30am-1am, Th-Sa 10:30am-2am, Su 10:30am-midnight. MC/V. ❷

Salute Pizzeria, Innrain 35, on the side of the street farthest from the river. A popular student hangout. Some of the best and least expensive pizza in town (€3-8). Pasta €4.50-6.50. Salad €3-4.50. Open 11am-midnight. ❷

Noi Original Thaiküche, Kaiserjägerstr. 1. Cooks up Thai soups (€4-8.40) and spicy dishes from the wok (€8-11). Open M-F 11:30am-3pm and 6-11pm, Sa 6-11pm. ❷

Gasthof Weißes Lamm, Mariahilfstr. 12, 2nd fl. Serves Austrian fare to a mostly local crowd. Open M-W and F-Su noon-2pm and 6-10pm. MC/V. ❸

◉ SIGHTS

THE OLD TOWN. The *Altstadt* is a cobbled mix of old buildings, churches, and museums on the river. Its centerpiece is the Goldenes Dachl (Golden Roof) on Herzog Friedrichstr., a gold-shingled balcony commemorating Maximilian. The nearby 15th-century *Helbinghaus* is graced with pale green floral detail and intricate stucco work. Its contemporary, Hotel Goldener Adler (Golden Eagle Inn), has hosted Camus, Goethe, Heine, Maximilian, Mozart, Sartre, and Wagner. Innsbruck's most distinctive street is Maria-Theresien-Straße, which begins at the edge of the *Altstadt* and runs south. The street, lined by Baroque buildings, gives a clear view of the Nordkette mountains. At its far end stands the Triumphpforte (Triumphal Arch), built in 1765 to commemorate the betrothal of Emperor Leopold II. Up the street, the Annasäule (Anna Column) commemorates the Tyroleans' victory on St. Anne's Day (July 26, 1703) after a bloody Bavarian invasion.

DOM ST. JAKOB. The unassuming gray facade of the Dom St. Jakob conceals a riot of pink-and-white High Baroque ornamentation within. *Trompe l'oeil* ceiling murals depict the life of St. James. The cathedral's prized possession is the small altar painting of *Our Lady of Succor* by Lukas Cranach the Elder. (*1 block behind the Goldenes Dachl. Open Apr.-Sept. daily 7:30am-7:30pm; Oct.-Mar. 8am-6:30pm. Free.*)

HOFBURG. The imperial palace was built in 1460 but completely remodeled under Maria Theresia. Imposing furniture, large portraits, and elaborate chandeliers fill the rooms. Don't miss the gilded Augusta Family tableau in the Audience Room, depicting the whole Habsburg gang in gold medallions. (*Behind the Dom St. Jakob. Open daily 9am-5pm. English guidebook €1.80. €5.45, students €3.65.*)

HOFKIRCHE. Twenty-eight bronze statues of Habsburg saints and Roman emperors line the nave, and the elegant Silver Chapel holds the corpse of Archduke Ferdinand II. (*In the Volkskunstmuseum building. Open M-Sa 9am-5pm, Su noon-5pm.*)

HOFGARTEN. The imperial garden is a beautiful park complete with ponds, a concert pavilion, and an oversized chess set. (*Walk down Museumstr. toward the river, turning right onto Burggraben and continuing as it becomes Rennweg. Open daily 6am-10:30pm. Free.*)

AUSTRIA

ALPINE ZOO. The highest-altitude zoo in Europe has every vertebrate species indigenous to the Alps: Bears, pine martens, golden eagles, and a bearded vulture with a 3m wingspan. *(Weherfurgg. 37.* ☎ *29 23 23. A bus leaves for the zoo from in front of the Landestheater every hr. 10am-5pm in summer. Open daily Apr.-Sept. 9am-6pm; Oct.-Mar. 9am-5pm. €5.80, students and seniors €4, ages 6-15 €2.90.)*

TIROLER VOLKSKUNSTMUSEUM. Exhaustive collections of kitchen and farm tools, peasant costumes, and period rooms present local culture over the centuries. *(At the head of Rennweg. Open M-Sa 9am-5pm, Su 9am-noon. €4.35, students €2.25.)*

🥾 🎿 HIKING AND SKIING

A ■Club Innsbruck membership (see Accommodations, above) lets you in on one of the best deals in Austria. The club's excellent and very popular **hiking** program provides free guides, transportation, and equipment (including boots). Participants meet in front of the Congress Center (June-Sept. daily 9am), board a bus, and return after a moderate hike around 4 or 5pm. Free nighttime lantern hikes also leave Tuesday at 7:45pm; the 30min. hike near Igls culminates in a party with traditional Austrian song and dance, in which *everyone* ends up taking part (willing or not). To hike on your own, take the J-line bus to *Patscherkofel Seilbahnen* (20min.). The lift provides access to moderate 1½-5hr. hikes near the bald summit of the Patscherkofel. (Open 9am-noon and 12:45-4:30pm; round-trip €15.)

For Club-led **ski excursions,** take the complimentary ski shuttle (schedules at the tourist office) to any cable car. The **Innsbruck Gletscher Ski Pass** (available at all cable cars) is valid for all 59 lifts in the region (with Club Innsbruck membership: 3-day €85, 6-day €150). The tourist office also rents **ski equipment** (€19-32 per day). One day of winter glacier skiing costs €32. Both branches of **Innsbruck-Information,** Burggraben 3, offer summer ski packages (bus, lift, and rental €47).

▶ DAYTRIPS FROM INNSBRUCK

SCHLOß AMBRAS. In the late 16th century, Ferdinand II transformed a royal hunting lodge into one of Austria's most beautiful castles, ■Schloß Ambras, and filled it with vast collections of art, armor, weapons, and trinkets. Don't miss the famous **Spanischer Saal** (Spanish Hall) and the impressive **Portrait Gallery** (open in summer only). The **gardens** outside vary from manicured shrubs with modern sculptures to shady, forested hillsides. (Schloßstr. 20. Open Apr.-Oct. daily 10am-5pm; Dec.-Mar. closed Tu. Apr.-Oct. €7.50, students €5.50; Dec.-Mar. €4.50/3.) From Innsbruck, take tram 3 or 6 (dir.: Igls) to Schloß Ambras (20min., €1.60).

KITZBÜHEL   ☎ 05356

Everyone in Kitzbühel (pop. 8,500) is merely catching his breath before the next run; the town's **ski area,** the **Ski Circus,** is one of the best in the world. A one-day **ski pass** (€33) or a 3- or 6-day summer **vacation pass** (€35/48) include all 64 lifts and the shuttles that connect them; purchase either at any lift. In the summer, 77 **hiking trails** snake up the mountains; trail maps are free at the tourist office.

Trains leave from the *Hauptbahnhof* for Innsbruck (1hr., every 2hr., €12); Salzburg (2½hr., 9 per day, €21); and Vienna (6hr., 3 per day, €42). To reach the *Fußgängerzone* (pedestrian zone) from the *Hauptbahnhof*, head straight down Bahnhofstr.; turn left at the main road, turn right at the traffic light, and follow the road uphill. The **tourist office,** Hinterstadt 18, is near the *Rathaus* in the *Fußgängerzone*. (☎ 62 15 50. Open July-Aug. and Christmas to mid-Mar. M-F 8:30am-6:30pm, Sa 8:30am-noon and 4-6pm, Su 10am-noon and 4-6pm; Nov.-Christmas and mid-Mar. to June M-F 8:30am-12:30pm and 2:30-6pm, Sa 8:30am-noon.)

Make sure to pick up a free **guest card**, which provides guided hikes (Jun.-Oct. M-F 8:45 am) and informative tours (M 10am) in English. **Hotel Haselberger ❹**, Maurachfeld 4, is seconds from the *Hahmennkammerbahn* ski lift. (☎628 66. Breakfast included. In summer €35 per person; in winter €44. AmEx/MC/V.) Nearby **Chizzo ❸**, Josef Herold-Str. 2, helps skiers recuperate with hearty Tyrolean fare. (Open daily 11am-midnight.) **SPAR supermarket**, Bichlstr. 22, is at the intersection with Ehrenbachg. (Open M-F 8am-7pm, Sa 7:30am-1pm.) **Postal Code:** A-6370.

STYRIA (STEIERMARK)

Many of southern Austria's folk traditions live on in this, "the Green Heart of Austria." Even its largest city, Graz, remains relatively untouristed. Circumnavigate crumbling medieval strongholds, salivate at the Lipizzaner studs, and drink of the wine from the Styrian vine.

GRAZ   ☎0316

Graz's under-touristed *Altstadt* has an unhurried Mediterranean feel, picturesque red-tiled roofs, and Baroque domes. The second largest of Austria's cities, Graz (pop. 226,244) offers a sweaty, energetic nightlife thanks to the 45,000 students at Karl-Franzens-Universität.

▐ TRANSPORTATION. From the **Hauptbahnhof**, trains run to: Innsbruck (6hr., 7 per day, €44); Munich (6½hr., 4 per day, €63); Salzburg (4¼hr., €37); Vienna *Südbahnhof* (2½hr., 16 per day, €25); and Zurich (10hr., 10pm, €74).

▐ PRACTICAL INFORMATION. From the train station, go down Annenstr. and cross the main bridge to reach **Hauptplatz**, the center of town. Five minutes away is **Jakominiplatz**, the hub of the public transportation system. **Herrengasse**, a pedestrian street lined with cafes and boutiques, connects the two squares. The **University** is tucked away past the *Stadtpark*, in the northeast part of Graz. The **tourist office**, Herreng. 16, has free city maps and a walking guide of the city. The staff offers English-language **tours** of the *Altstadt* (2hr.; Apr.-Oct. Su, Tu-W, and F-Sa 2:30pm; €7.50) and makes room reservations for free. (☎807 50. Open June-Sept. M-F 9am-7pm, Sa 9am-6pm, Su 10am-4pm; Oct.-May M-F 9am-6pm, Sa 9am-3pm, Su 10am-3pm.) **Postal Code:** A-8010.

▐▐ ACCOMMODATIONS AND FOOD. In Graz, most hotels, guesthouses, and pensions are pricey and far from the city center. Luckily, the web of local transportation provides a reliable and easy commute to and from the outlying neighborhoods. To reach **Jugendgästehaus Graz (HI) ❸**, Idlhofg. 74, from the station, cross the street, head right on Eggenberger Gürtel, turn left on Josef-Huber-G., then take the first right; the hostel is through the parking lot on your right. Buses #31 and 32 run here from Jakominipl. (☎71 48 76. All rooms with bath. Breakfast included. Laundry €3. **Internet** €1.50 per 20min. Reception daily 7am-10pm. Dorms €19.50; singles €26.50; doubles €42.50. Discount for longer stays. MC/V.) **Hotel Strasser ❸**, Eggenberger Gürtel 11, is 5min. from the train station. Exit, cross the street, and head right on Eggenberger Gürtel. (☎71 39 77. Breakfast included. Singles €29, with shower €36; doubles €45/54; triples with shower €66. AmEx/DC/MC/V.)

Find an inexpensive meal on **Hauptplatz**, where concession stands sell sandwiches, *Wurst* (€1.50-3), and other fast food. Cheap student hangouts line **Zinzendorfgasse** near the university. **Braun de Praun ❹**, Morellenfeldg. 32, is unafraid of a little culinary experimentation. Main dishes include curry pork with glazed banana and almond-raisin rice (€12.50) and chicken "mexicano" (€12.50), but the numerous local dishes, Biergarten ambience, and Lederhosen-clad waiters keep it firmly rooted in Graz. (☎32 20 03. Open M-Sa 8am-2am. AmEx/MC/V.) **Gasthaus Alte Münze ❸**, Schloßbergpl. 8, serves scrumptious Styrian specialties in a traditional setting. (Open M and Su 10am-7pm, Tu-Sa 8am-midnight.) A grocery store, **Merkur**, is to your left as you exit the station. (Open M-Th 8am-7pm, F 7:30am-7:30pm.)

◖◗ SIGHTS AND NIGHTLIFE. The tourist office, in the **Landhaus**, is itself a sight; the building was remodeled by architect Domenico dell'Allio in 1557 in the Lombard style. The **Landeszeughaus** (Provincial Arsenal), Herreng. 16, details the history of Ottoman attacks on the arsenal and has enough spears, muskets, and armor to outfit 28,000 burly mercenaries. (Open Su and Tu-Sa 10am-6pm. €1.50.) North of Hauptpl., the wooded **Schloßberg** (Castle Mountain) rises 123m above Graz. The hill is named for the castle that stood there from 1125 until 1809, when it was destroyed by Napoleon's troops. Even without the castle, it remains a beautiful city park. Climb the zig-zagging stone steps of the **Schloßbergstiege**, built by Russian prisoners during WWI, for sweeping views of the vast Styrian plain.

The hub of after-hours activity is the so-called **Bermuda Triangle**, an area of the old city behind Hauptpl. and bordered by Mehlpl., Färberg., and Prokopig. At **Kulturhauskeller**, Elisabethstr. 30, the dance music throbs. (No sports or military clothing. 19+. Cover €2. Open Tu-Sa 9pm-late.) At the artsy grad-student hangout, **Café Harrach**, Harrachg. 26, most everyone tosses back white wine spritzers. (Open M-F 9am-midnight, Sa-Su 5pm-midnight.)

▶ DAYTRIP FROM GRAZ: LIPIZZANER STUD FARM. The **Gestüt Piber** (Piber Stud Farm) is home to the world-famous **Lipizzaner** horses, whose delicate footwork and snow white coats are the pride of the Spanish Riding School in Vienna. Born either solid black or brown, they become progressively paler, reaching a pure white color sometime between the age of five and ten. The rolling green hills of Piber are home to the mares, their foals, and trained stallions in retirement. On a 1hr. tour of the stud farm, you can see the horses up close in the stables and visit the carriage house and the Lippizaner museum in the 300-year-old Piber castle. (☎03144 33 23. Open Apr.-Oct. daily 9-10:30am and 1:30-3:30pm. €10, students €5.) The horse farm is 1km outside **Köflach**. Take the **train** from Graz (50 min., 8 per day 6am-2pm, €5.40), then the **bus** (€1.60) to Piber. Sign up at the tourist office in Graz for a ride and English-language tour. (Sa 2pm. €24, children €9.)

BELGIUM
(BELGIQUE, BELGIË)

Situated between France and Germany, Belgium rubs shoulders with some of Western Europe's most powerful cultural and intellectual traditions. Travelers too often mistake Belgium's subtlety for dullness, but its cities offer some of Europe's finest art and architecture, and its castle-dotted countryside provides a beautiful escape for hikers and bikers. While Brussels, the nation's capital and home to the head offices of NATO and the European Union, is a flagship for international cooperation, regional tension persists within Belgium's borders between Flemish-speaking Flanders and French-speaking Wallonie. But some things transcend politics: from the deep caves of the Ardennes to the white sands of the North Sea coast, Belgium's diverse beauty is even richer than its chocolate.

LIFE AND TIMES

HISTORY

Belgium's strategic location between several European powers has long been coveted by military and political leaders, including **Julius Caesar** and **Charlemagne**. In 843, the Treaty of Verdun split Flanders, the Dutch-speaking province in the north, and Wallonie, the French-speaking province in the south. Commercial and urban development were at the core of both regions. The 14th century witnessed a golden period of prosperity and culture in the Belgian region, with a boom in the textile industry and the artistic advances of the **Northern Renaissance.** Belgium was united again in the 15th century under control of the **Dukes of Burgundy.** Over the next several centuries, the territory passed through the hands of the Spanish, the Austrians, the French, and finally the Dutch. Only in 1830 did Belgium gain independence by popular **revolution** from the Kingdom of The Netherlands. The newly freed Belgians established a constitutional monarchy, selecting **Leopold I** of Saxe-

SUGGESTED ITINERARIES

THREE DAYS Spend two days in **Brussels** (p. 122). Victor Hugo declared the **Grand-Place**, the heart of the city, to be "the most beautiful square in the world." Witness Brussels's **Mannekin Pis,** a statue of a cherubic boy continuously urinating. Check out the art at the **Musées Royaux des Beaux Arts** (p. 127) and the **Belgian Comic Strip Centre** (p. 127), then visit all of Europe's major sights in record time at **Mini-Europe** (p. 128). Spend the third day exploring the cobblestoned streets and canals of romantic **Bruges** (p. 130).

ONE WEEK After three days in **Brussels,** head to **Antwerp** and stroll along the Meir for

tasty beer and fine chocolates (1 day; p. 135). Spend a day in vibrant **Ghent** (p. 136), then move on to **Bruges** to climb the 366 steps of the Gothic Belfort (2 days; p. 130).

BEST OF BELGIUM, 11 DAYS After your week in **Brussels, Antwerp, Ghent,** and **Bruges,** visit **Ypres** to remember victims of WWI (1 day; p. 137). Head south to explore the castle-dotted **Wallonie** region, where you can hike, bike, kayak, and spelunk among the citadels and grottoes of Namur and Dinant (1 day; p. 139). Don't miss the glittering gold treasury in the cathedral of **Tournai** (1 day; p. 138).

117

Coburg as their first king. In 1839, the European powers declared Belgium a perpetually neutral state. After gaining its independence, Belgium was a pioneer in European industrialization. Development of the coal and iron industries increased tension between the regions, as Wallonie had greater natural resources and prosperity. Other major projects in the 19th century included **colonial expansion** in Africa, most notably in the present-day **Congo.** Despite these international successes, Belgium experienced internal discontent due to poor labor conditions, prompting major social reforms under **King Leopold II.**

German armies invaded during both World Wars, flagrantly violating Belgium's neutral status. In WWI, under **King Albert I,** the outmatched Belgian army courageously fought the German invaders from the trenches for the entire four years of the war. The **Treaty of Versailles,** the settlement of WWI, granted Belgium monetary and territorial reparations as compensation for the widespread devastation resulting from German occupation. In WWII, **King Leopold III**'s rapid **surrender** shocked not only the Belgians, but the British and the French as well, as they were suddenly faced with the advancing German army. Belgium's post-war economic recovery was impressively swift, for its second wartime destruction was relatively limited. Of greater concern was the political disorganization upon the return of King Leopold III from Austria in 1950, where he had been sent during Nazi rule. Popular disapproval of his alleged defeatism led to his abdication in 1951.

TODAY

With the exception of the brief period after the Treaty of Versailles when Belgium was allied with France, the country has maintained a neutral political stance while remaining at the forefront of international affairs. Most significantly, Belgium is the seat of the **European Union.** Belgian government in the 19th and 20th centuries was largely dominated by the French-speaking minority, despite cries of injustice from the Flemish population. To ease tensions between these two groups, the constitution has undergone several revisions granting more autonomy to each of the three distinctive linguistic and cultural communities: **Flemish** in the north, **French** in the south, and **German** in the east. The Belgian king, currently **Albert II,** is the official head of state, but he is accountable to the democratically elected **parliament.** Day-to-day government is run by his appointed prime minister, **Guy Verhofstadt.**

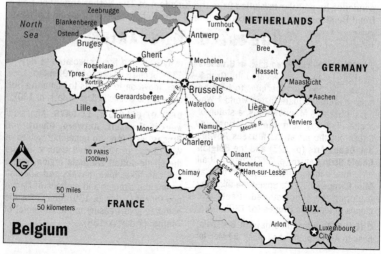

Belgium

THE ARTS

LITERATURE

In the 20th century, Belgian talent made its presence known in the world of **comic strips** and **detective novels**. In Brussels, museums are dedicated to the history of cartooning, where tribute is paid to the work of **Georges Remi**, better-known as **Hergé**, creator of **Tintin** (p. 127), and to **Peyo**, father of the **Smurfs**. The enigmatic **Georges Simenon** authored a 76-novel mystery series around the cunning **Commissaire Maigret**, another famous Belgian creation of the past century. **Henri Michaux** stretched the bounds by even Surrealist standards. His poetry explored the inner self and blurred the boundary between fantasy and reality.

MUSIC

César Franck, the influential **Romantic** musician and organist, is Belgium's best-known composer. His symphonies and sonatas combined technical expertise with emotional energy. **Adolphe Sax**, born in **Dinant** (p. 139), a musical instrument inventor, introduced the **saxophone** to the world. **Jacques Brel** was the voice of the nation; his most famous ballad, *Ne me quitte pas* (1959), has been covered by **Sting**, among countless other musicians.

THE VISUAL ARTS

ARCHITECTURE. A native of Ghent, **Victor Horta** led Belgium's Art Nouveau movement around the turn of the century. His use of abstracted shapes and modern materials was widely influential among later architects. Horta's works can be seen throughout Belgium and at the Musée Horta, in Brussels (p. 128).

ON THE CANVAS. Despite representing a school of painting known as the Flemish Primitives, **Jan van Eyck** in fact transformed the future of painting, working with layers of oil paint to produce luminous depth and amazing detail. His most well-known painting is the *Adoration of the Mystic Lamb* (1432), the altarpiece of **St. Bavo's Cathedral** in Ghent (p. 136). **Pieter Bruegel the Elder** shifted artistic focus from the sacred to the secular, choosing to depict commonplace scenes over grand themes. **Peter Paul Rubens** was Antwerp's most famous artistic son; his paintings are distinctive for their religious symbolism, reflecting the turbulent climate of the **Counter-Reformation**, and for their fluid incorporation of the Italian Renaissance style. Ruben's assistant, **Anthony van Dyck**, was also a prominent member of the Flemish school of painting. Van Dyck's elegant portraits of the aristocracy gained him widespread renown and influenced **portraiture** style across the continent. In the 20th century, the leader of the **Surrealists** was **René Magritte**, who attempted to bring new and unusual meaning to ordinary household objects such as pipes, apples, instruments, chairs, and his most famous icon, the bowler-hatted man.

BELGIUM

FACTS AND FIGURES

Official Name: Kingdom of Belgium.	**Land Area:** 32,547 sq. km.
Capital: Brussels.	**Time Zone:** GMT +1.
Major Cities: Antwerp, Ghent, Charleroi.	**Language:** Flemish, French, German.
Population: 10,300,000.	**Religions:** Roman Catholic (75%).

ESSENTIALS

WHEN TO GO

Belgium, temperate and rainy, is best visited May to September, when temperatures average 13-21°C (54-72°F) and precipitation is the lowest. Winter temperatures average 0-5°C (32-43°F). Bring a sweater and umbrella whenever you go.

DOCUMENTS AND FORMALITIES

VISAS. EU citizens do not need a visa. Citizens of Australia, Canada, New Zealand, South Africa, and the US do not need a visa for stays of up to 90 days.

EMBASSIES. All foreign embassies are in Brussels (p. 122). For Belgian embassies at home: **Australia,** Arkana St., Yarralumla, Canberra, ACT 2600 (☎02 62 70 66 66; fax 62 70 66 06); **Canada,** 80 Elgin St., 4th fl., Ottawa, ON K1P 1B7 (☎613-236-7267; fax 613-236-7882); **Ireland,** 2 Shrewsbury Rd., Ballsbridge, Dublin 4 (☎353 269 20 82; fax 283 84 88); **New Zealand,** Willis Corroon House, 12th fl., Willeston St. 1-3, PB 3379, Wellington (☎04 472 95 58; fax 471 27 64); **South Africa,** 625 Leyds St., Muckleneuk, Pretoria 0002 (☎12 44 32 01; fax 12 44 32 16); **UK,** 103-105 Eaton Sq., London SW1W 9AB (☎020 470 37 00; www.belgium-embassy.co.uk); **US,** 3330 Garfield St NW, Washington, D.C. 20008 (☎202-333-6900; www.diplobel.org/us).

TRANSPORTATION

BY PLANE. Several major airlines fly into **Brussels** from Europe, North America, and Africa. **SN Brussels Airlines** (Belgium ☎070 35 11 11, UK ☎0870 735 23 45; www.brussels-airlines.com) has taken over the service of Sabena airlines. Budget airline **RyanAir** (☎353 819 30 30 30; www.ryanair.com) flies into Charleroi Brussels South Airport from across Europe.

BY TRAIN AND BUS. The extensive and reliable **Belgian Rail** (www.b-rail.be) network traverses the country. **Eurail** is valid in Belgium. A **Benelux Tourrail Pass** allows five days of unlimited **train** travel in a one-month period in Belgium, The Netherlands, and Luxembourg (p. 49). The best deal for travelers under 26 may be the **Go Pass,** which allows 10 trips over one year in Belgium and may be used by more than one person (€40); the equivalent for travelers over 26 is the **Rail Pass** (€60). Because the train network is so extensive, **buses** are used primarily for municipal transport (€1-2).

BY FERRY. P&O European Ferries (UK ☎087 05 20 20 20, Belgium ☎027 10 64 44; www.poferries.com) cross the Channel from **Zeebrugge,** north of Bruges, to **Hull, England** (11hr., departure at 7pm, from $46).

BY CAR, BIKE, AND THUMB. Belgium honors most foreign driver's licenses, including those from Australia, Canada, the EU, and the US. **Speed limits** are 120kph on motorways, 90kph on main roads, and 50kph elsewhere. **Fuel** costs about €1 per liter. **Biking** is popular, and many roads have bike lanes (which you are required to use). In addition to being illegal, **hitchhiking** is not common in Belgium, and *Let's Go* does not recommend it as a safe means of transport.

EMERGENCY	Police: ☎101. Ambulance: ☎105. Fire: ☎100.

TOURIST SERVICES AND MONEY

TOURIST OFFICES. Bureaux de Tourisme, marked by green-and-white or blue signs labelled "i," are supplemented by **Infor-Jeunes/Info-Jeugd,** a service that helps young people secure accommodations. For info, contact the main office of the **Belgian Tourist Office,** Grasmarkt 63 (☎025 04 30 90; www.visitbelgium.com). The weekly English-language *Bulletin* (€2.15 at newsstands) lists everything from movies to job openings.

MONEY. On January 1, 2002, the **euro** (€) replaced the **Belgian Franc** as the unit of currency in Belgium. The Belgian Franc can still be exchanged at a rate of 44.34BF to €1. For exchange rates and more info on the euro, see p. 14. Expect to pay €13-16 for a hostel bed, €23-50 for a hotel room, €7-13 for a day's groceries, and €5-13 for a cheap restaurant meal. A barebones day in Belgium might cost €19-30; a slightly more comfortable day might cost €32-45. The European Union imposes a **value-added tax (VAT)** on goods and services purchased within the EU, which is included in the price (p. 16). Restaurants and taxis usually include a **service charge** (16%) in the price, but tip for exceptional service. Rounding up is also common practice.

BUSINESS HOURS. Banks are generally open Monday through Friday 9am-4pm, but some take a lunch break noon-2pm. **Stores** are open Monday to Saturday 10am to 6 or 7pm; during the summer some shops are open Sunday. Most **sights** are open Sundays but closed Mondays except in Bruges and Tournai, where museums are closed Tuesday or Wednesday. Most stores close on holidays; museums stay open during all except for Christmas, New Year's, and Armistice Day (Nov. 11).

COMMUNICATION

TELEPHONES. Most public phones require a phone card (€5), available at post offices, supermarkets, and magazine stands. Coin-operated phones are rare and more expensive. Calls are cheapest from 6:30pm-8am and on weekends. Mobile phones are an increasingly popular and economical alternative (p. 30). For operator assistance within Belgium, dial ☎12 07 or 13 07; for international assistance, ☎12 04 or 13 04 (€0.25). International direct dial numbers include: AT&T, ☎0800 100 10; British Telecom, ☎0800 100 24; Canada Direct, ☎0800 100 19 or 0800 700 19; Ireland Direct, ☎0800 10 353; MCI, ☎0800 100 12; Sprint, ☎0800 100 14; Telecom New Zealand, ☎0800 100 64; Telkom South Africa, ☎0800 100 27; Telstra Australia, ☎0800 100 61.

MAIL. A postcard or letter (up to 50g) sent to a destination within Belgium costs €0.41-0.49, within the EU €0.47-.52, and to the rest of the world €0.74-.84. Most post offices open Monday to Friday 9am to 4 or 5pm (sometimes with a midday break) and sometimes on Saturdays 9 or 10am to noon or 1pm.

INTERNET ACCESS. There are cybercafes in the larger towns and cities in Belgium. For access to the web, expect to pay €2.50-3.25 per 30min. Many hostels have Internet access for around €0.07-0.10 per min.

LANGUAGES. Belgium is a multilingual nation, with several official languages. Flemish (a variation of Dutch) is spoken in Flanders, the northern half of the country; French is spoken in Wallonie, the southern region; and German is spoken in a small enclave in the west. Both Flemish and French are spoken in Brussels. Most people, especially in Flanders, speak English. For basic French words and phrases, see p. 1035; for German, see p. 1036.

BELGIUM

| PHONE CODES | Country code: 32. International dialing prefix: 00. |

ACCOMMODATIONS AND CAMPING

BELGIUM	❶	❷	❸	❹	❺
ACCOMMODATIONS	under €10	€10-17	€18-26	€27-33	over €33

There is a wide range of accommodations throughout Belgium; however, **hotels** are fairly expensive, with "trench-bottom" singles from €22 and doubles around €30-35. Belgium's 31 **HI youth hostels**, which charge about €13 per night, are generally modern and many boast cheap bars. **Private hostels**, however, often cost about the same but are much nicer. Most receptionists speak some English, and reservations are a good idea, particularly in the summer and on weekends. **Campgrounds** charge about €4 per night. An **international camping card** is not required in Belgium.

FOOD AND DRINK

BELGIUM	❶	❷	❸	❹	❺
FOOD	under €5	€5-8	€8-10	€11-15	over €15

Belgian cuisine, a combination of French and German traditions, is praised throughout Western Europe, but an authentic evening meal may cost as much as that night's accommodations. Seafood, fresh from the coast, is served in a variety of dishes. **Moules** or **mosselen** (steamed mussels), regarded as the national dish, are usually tasty and reasonably affordable (€14 is the cheapest, usually €17-20). Often paired with mussels are **frites** (french fries), actually a Belgian invention, which they dip in mayonnaise and consume in abundance. Belgian **beer** is both a national pride and a national pastime; more varieties—over 300, ranging from ordinary **Pilsners** to religiously brewed **Trappist** ales—are produced here than in any other country. Prices range from as little as €1 for regular or quirky blonde up to €3 for other varieties. Leave room for Belgian **waffles** (*gaufres*)—soft, warm, glazed ones on the street (€1.50) and thin, crispier ones piled high with toppings at cafes (€2-5)—and for the famous brands of **chocolate**, from Leonidas to Godiva.

HOLIDAYS & FESTIVALS

Holidays: New Year's Day (Jan. 1); Easter (Apr. 11); Easter Monday (Apr. 12); Labor Day (May 1); Ascension Day (May 20); Whit Sunday and Monday (May 30-31); Independence Day (July 21); Assumption Day (Aug. 15); All Saints Day (Nov. 1); Armistice Day (Nov. 11); Christmas (Dec. 25).

Festivals: Ghent hosts the **Gentse Feesten**, also know as 10 Days Off (July 17-26). Wallonie hosts a slew of quirky and creative carnivals, including the **Festival of Fairground Arts** (late May), **Les Jeux Nautiques** (early Aug.), the **International French-language Film Festival** (early Sept.), and the **International Bathtub Regatta** (mid-Aug.).

BRUSSELS (BRUXELLES, BRUSSEL) ☎ 02

Beyond the international traffic resulting from the city's association with NATO and the EU, Brussels (pop. 1,200,000) has a relaxed and witty local character best embodied in its two boy heroes, Tintin and the Mannekin Pis. In the late 1920s, cartoonist Hergé created a comic strip hero, Tintin, who, followed by his faithful white dog Snowy, righted international wrongs long before Brussels became the capital of the EU. The cherubic Mannekin Pis perpetually pees three blocks from the Grand Place, ruining any semblance of formality created by international politics. The museums of Brussels are rich with collections of Flemish masters, modern art, and antique sculptures, but you don't need to go inside for a visual feast—many of the city's restaurants, lounges, and movie theaters were built in the style of Art Nouveau architect Victor Horta.

TRANSPORTATION

Flights: Brussels International Airport (BRU; ☎753 42 21 or 723 31 11; www.brusselsairport.be) is 14km from the city. See www.flysn.be for info on **SN Brussels Airline,** the Belgian national carrier. Trains run to the airport from Gare du Midi (25min., every 20min., €2.50), stopping at Gare Centrale and Gare du Nord. Another option is to take bus #12 to the airport (every 30min.; 5am-11pm, Sept.-June until midnight; €3). **Charleroi Brussels South** (CRL; ☎71 25 12 11; www.charleroi-airport.com) is 46km outside the city, between Brussels and Charleroi. Buses run to the airport from r. de France just outside the Gare du Midi in Brussels (2½hr. before each flight, €10). Buses head to Brussels and Charleroi from outside the main terminal 30min. after each flight (€10).

Trains: Info ☎555 25 55. All international trains stop at the **Gare du Midi;** most also stop at the **Gare Centrale** (near Grand Place) or the **Gare du Nord** (near the Botanical Gardens). To: **Amsterdam** (3hr.; M-F €57, Sa-Su €38); **Antwerp** (45 min.; M-F €11, Sa-Su €7); **Bruges** (45min.; M-F €22, Sa-Su €14); **Cologne** (2¾hr.; €36, under-26 €18); **Luxembourg City** (1¾hr., €31); **Paris** (1½hr.; €66, under-26 €33). **Eurostar** goes to **London** (2¾hr.; from €79, under-26 from €60, discount with Eurail or Benelux pass).

Public Transportation: The **Métro (M), buses,** and **trams** run daily 6am-midnight. 1hr. ticket €1.40, day pass €3.70, 5 trips €6.40, 10 trips €9.20. All three are run by the **Société des Transports Intercommunaux Bruxellois (STIB),** Gare du Midi (☎515 20 00; www.stib.irisnet.be). Open M-F 7:30am-5:30pm. **Branch offices** at the *Porte de Namur* and *Rogier* metro stops. Open M-Sa 10am-6pm.

Bus: De Boeck offers a tourist bus that allows you to get on and off at any of 14 major sites. Tickets are good for 24hr.; purchase them aboard the big blue bus. (☎513 77 44; www.brussels-city-tours.com. €14, students €12.)

Hitchhiking: Hitchhiking is illegal on highways in Belgium. *Let's Go* does not recommend hitchhiking as a reliable means of transport.

ORIENTATION AND PRACTICAL INFORMATION

Most major attractions are clustered around **Grand Place,** between the **Bourse** (Stock Market) to the west and the **Parc de Bruxelles** to the east. Two **Métro** lines circle the city, while efficient trams run north to south. Signs in Brussels list both the French and Flemish street names. *Let's Go* gives the French name for all addresses. A **tourist passport** (*Carte d'un Jour;* €7.45), which includes two days of public transit and discounted museum admissions, is sold at the BITC (see below).

Tourist Offices: National, Belgian Tourist Office, Grasmarkt 63 (☎504 30 90; www.visitbelgium.com), one block from Grand Place. Books rooms all over Belgium and offers the free copies of *What's On.* Open July-Aug. M-F 9am-7pm, Sa-Su 9am-1pm and 2-7pm; Sept.-June M-F 9am-6pm, Sa-Su 9am-1pm and 2-6pm; Nov.-Apr. closed Su afternoon. **Brussels International-Tourism and Congress** (BITC; ☎513 89 40; www.brusselsinternational.be), on Grand Place, in the Town Hall.

Tour: City Sightseeing, in Gare Centrale (☎466 11 11), offers a 1½hr. bus tour that passes all the major attractions. Daily 10am-8pm. €12, students €11.

Budget Travel: Infor-Jeunes Bruxelles, 155 r. Van Arteveld (☎514 41 11; bruxelles@inforjeunes.be). Budget travel info for students. Open M-F 10am-5:30pm.

Embassies and Consulates: Australia, 6-8 r. Guimard, 1040 (☎286 05 00; fax 230 68 02). **Canada,** 2 av. Tervuren, 1040 (☎741 06 11; fax 741 06 43). **Ireland,** 50 r. Wiertz 1050 (☎235 66 76; fax 230 53 12). **New Zealand,** 1 de Meeussquare, 1000 (☎512 10 40). **South Africa,** 26 r. de la Loi (☎285 44 00; fax 285 44 02). **UK,** 85 r. d'Arlon, 1040 (☎287 62 11; fax 287 63 55). **US,** 27 bd. du Régent, 1000 (☎508 21 11; www.usinfo.be). Open M-F 9am-noon.

Currency Exchange: Many exchange booths near Grand Place stay open until 11pm. Most banks and booths charge a commission (€2.50-3.75) to cash checks. **CBC-Automatic Change,** 7 Grand-Place (☎547 12 11) exchanges cash and checks and is open 24hr. Exchange booths are also available in the train stations.

Bi-Gay-Lesbian Resources: Call ☎736 26 81 for info on local events. Staffed Tu 8-10pm, W and F 8-11pm. The tourist office offers a guide to gay nightlife.

English-Language Bookstore: Sterling Books, Wolvengracht 38 (r. du Fossé aux Loups). Open M-Sa 10am-7pm, Su noon-6:30pm.

Laundromat: Primus Wash, 50 r. Haute, around the corner from the Jeugdherberg Bruegel. Gare Centrale. Wash €3.50, dry €0.50 per 10min. Open daily 7am-11pm.

Emergencies: Medical: ☎100. **Police:** ☎101. From a **Mobile Phone:** ☎112.

Pharmacy: Neos-Bourse Pharmacie (☎218 06 40), bd. Anspach at r. du Marché aux Polets. M: Bourse. Open M-Sa 8:30am-6:30pm.

Medical Assistance: Free Clinic, 154a Chaussée de Wavre (☎512 13 14). Ignore the name—you'll have to pay. Open M-F 9am-6pm, Sa 10am-noon. **Centre Hospitalier Universitaire St. Pierre,** 322 r. Haute (☎535 31 11). **Medical Services,** (☎479 18 18). Doctors on call 24hr.

Internet Access: easyEverything, pl. de Brouckère (www.easyeverything.com). Approx. €1.50 per hr., rates vary by time of day. Open 9am-1:30am.

Post Office: pl. de la Monnaie, Centre Monnaie, 2nd fl. (☎226 21 11). M: de Brouckère. Open M-F 8am-6pm, Sa 9:30am-3pm. Address mail to be held: Firstname SURNAME, Poste Restante, pl. de la Monnaie, **1000** Bruxelles, BELGIUM.

ACCOMMODATIONS

Accommodations can be difficult to find in Brussels, especially on weekends and in June and July. In general, accommodations are well-kept and centrally located. If a hotel or hostel is booked, the staff will usually call other establishments on behalf of prospective guests.

Sleep Well, 23 r. du Damier (☎218 50 50; www.sleepwell.be), near Gare du Nord. M: Rogier. Nice, newly refurbished rooms and a grand lobby. Breakfast included. Internet €2 per 30min. Lockout 11am-3pm. Dorms €14-19; singles €26; doubles €41; triples €60. Reduced price after 1st night. 5% ISIC discount. ❷

Centre Vincent Van Gogh-CHAB, 8 r. Traversière (☎217 01 58; www.ping.be/chab). M: Botanique. Exit on r. Royale, head right and turn right onto Chausée d'Haecht which becomes r. Traversière. Newly renovated clean rooms, chic lobby. Breakfast included. Sheets €3.60. Laundry €4.50. Internet access. Reception daily 7:30am-2am. Under-35 only. Dorms €12-14; singles €22; doubles €32. ❷

Auberge de Jeunesse "Jacques Brel" (HI), 30 r. de la Sablonnière (☎218 01 87), on pl. des Barricades. M: Botanique. Follow r. Royale, with the botanical gardens to your right, and take the 1st left onto r. de la Sablonnière. Clean, spacious rooms. Breakfast included. Sheets €3.25. Reception daily 8am-1am. HI members only. Dorms €13; singles €23; doubles €35; triples €44. ❷

Hotel Des Eperonniers, 1 r. des Eperonniers (☎513 53 66). Great location close to Grand Place. Well-kept rooms. Breakfast €3.75. Reception daily 7am-midnight. Singles €40-55; doubles €47-70. ❺

Hôtel Pacific, 57 r. Antoine Dansaert (☎511 84 59). M: Bourse. Basic rooms in an excellent location. Breakfast included. Reception daily 7am-midnight. Singles €35; doubles €55; triples €75. ❻

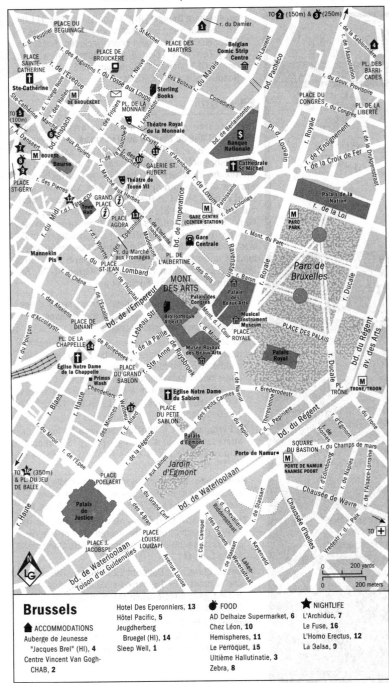

Brussels

ACCOMMODATIONS
Auberge de Jeunesse
  "Jacques Brel" (HI), **4**
Centre Vincent Van Gogh-
  CHAB, **2**

Hotel Des Eperonniers, **13**
Hôtel Pacific, **5**
Jeugdherberg
  Bruegel (HI), **14**
Sleep Well, **1**

FOOD
AD Delhaize Supermarket, **6**
Chez Léon, **10**
Hemispheres, **11**
Le Perroquet, **15**
Ultième Hallutinatie, **3**
Zebra, **8**

NIGHTLIFE
L'Archiduc, **7**
Le Fuse, **16**
L'Homo Erectus, **12**
La Salsa, **9**

BELGIUM

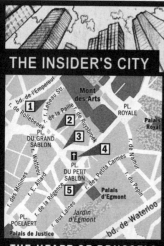

THE INSIDER'S CITY

THE HEART OF BRUSSELS

Antique galleries, beautiful buildings, and the best chocolate shop in the city make up a quintessentially Belgian neighborhood.

1 The splendid **Hotel Frison**, r. Lebeau 37, designed by Art Nouveau architect Victor Horta in 1894, now houses the **Gallery J. Visser.**

2 Splurge on some of the best chocolate in the city at **Wittamer**, pl. du Grand Sablon 6.

3 Surrounded by 16th- to 19th-century houses, the **Place du Grand Sablon** is enlivened every Saturday by an antique market.

4 View the stained glass windows of the flamboyantly Gothic **Cathédral de Notre Dame du Sablon**, r. Bodenbroeck 6.

5 The bronze statues on the balustrades around **Place du Petit Sablon**, r. de la Régence, depict the ancient trades of Brussels, while the fountain memorializes the fight against Spanish tyranny.

Jeugdherberg Bruegel (HI), 2 r. de St-Esprit (☎511 04 36; jeugdherberg.bruegel@ping.be). Near pl. de la Chappelle. Breakfast and sheets included. Reception daily 7am-1am. Lockout 10am-2pm. Curfew 1am. Dorms €13; singles €23; doubles €36; quads €60. Nonmembers add €2.50. ❷

🍴 FOOD

Inexpensive restaurants cluster around **Grand Place**, and **Rue du Marché aux Fromages**, to the south of Grand Place, offers cheap Middle Eastern food. Shellfish, paella, and other seafood are served up on **Rue des Bouchers**, a sight of its own at night with narrow streets and sparkling lights. Cheaper seafood can be found at the small restaurants on **Quai aux Briques**, in the Ste-Catherine area behind pl. St-Géry. **Belgaufra** peddles waffles from nearly every streetcorner, and **Panos** offers quick and tasty sandwiches across the city. The giant **AD Delhaize supermarket** is on the corner of bd. Anspach and r. du Marché aux Polets. (M: Bourse. Open M-Th, Sa 9am-9pm, F 9am-4pm, Su 9am-6pm.)

Chez Léon, 18 r. des Bouchers. Serving seafood and other local dishes for over a century. *Moules frites* €13-22. Open daily noon-11pm. ❹

Maison Antoine, 1 pl. Jourdan. M: Schuman. From the rotary, walk down r. Froissart; it's the brown kiosk in the middle of pl. Jourdan. The best *frites* in town. Also offers tasty sandwiches and fried kebabs. Cones of *frites* (€1.60-1.80) with a huge selection of sauces (€0.50 each). Open Su-Th 11:30am-1am, F-Sa 11:30am-2am. ❶

Le Perroquet, 31 r. Watteau. Sit down for lunch, an afternoon beer, or a late-night pastry. Selection of salads and delicious pitas from €5. Open daily 10:30am-1am. ❷

Hemispheres, 65 r. de l'Ecuyer. Delicious Middle Eastern and Asian cuisine. Vegetarian meals €7-10. Open M-F noon-3pm and 6:30-10:30pm, Sa 6:30pm-midnight. ❸

Zebra, 33-35 pl. St-Géry. Although known for its drinks, this chic, centrally located cafe also serves light, tasty sandwiches and pastas (€2-5). Open daily 10am-1am. ❶

Bonsoir Clara, r. A. Dansaert 22-26. Pricey French cuisine (entrees €13-16) served amid enchanting multicolored glass panels. Open M-F noon-2:30pm and 7-11:30pm; Sa-Su 7-11:30pm. ❹

Arcadi Cafe, 1b r. d'Arenberg. Huge selection of quiches, sandwiches, and pastries (€3-6). Lots of vegetarian choices. Open daily 7:30am-11pm. ❶

Ultième Hallutinatie, 316 r. Royale. Housed in an Art Nouveau house with stained glass and a garden. Restaurant in the front and a cheaper tavern and outdoor patio in back. Salads, pastas, and omelettes in the tavern from €6.20. Open M-F noon-2:30pm and 7:30-10:30pm, Sa 6pm-11pm. ❷

🎯 SIGHTS

GRAND PLACE AND ENVIRONS. Victor Hugo once called the gold-trimmed **Grand-Place** "the most beautiful square in the world." During the incredible flower display (around Aug. 15), it's especially easy to see why. A flower market fills the place each morning, and at night the **Town Hall** is illuminated by 800 multi-colored floodlights set to classical music. *(Apr.-Aug. and Dec. daily around 10 or 11pm. Tours available. Inquire at the Town Hall for info. ☎ 279 43 65.)* Three blocks behind the Town Hall, on the corner of r. de l'Etuve and r. du Chêne, is Brussels's most giggled-at sight, the **Mannekin Pis,** a statue of an impudent boy (with an apparently gargantuan bladder) continuously urinating. The most commonly told story claims that it commemorates a boy who ingeniously defused a bomb destined for Grand Place. In reality, the fountain was installed to supply the neighborhood with drinking water during the reign of Archduke Albert and Archduchess Isabelle. Locals have created hundreds of outfits for him, competitively dressing him in the ritual coats of different organizations and regions, each with a strategically placed hole for his you-know-what. His wardrobe is on display across from the Town Hall on the third floor of the **Museum of the City of Brussels (Maison de Roi),** which also traces the history of Brussels, albeit only in Dutch and French. *(Open Su and Tu-Sa 10am-5pm. €3, students €2.50.)* In the glorious **Galerie Saint-Hubert** arcade, one block behind Grand Place, you can window-shop for everything from square umbrellas to marzipan frogs. Built over the course of six centuries, the magnificent **Cathédral Saint-Michel** is an excellent example of the Gothic style with a touch of Romanesque architecture. *(Pl. St-Gudule, just north of Gare Centrale. Open daily 7am-7pm. Free.)*

MONT DES ARTS. The 🏛**Musées Royaux des Beaux-Arts** houses the **Musée d'Art Ancien,** the **Musée d'Art Moderne,** a sculpture gallery, and temporary exhibitions. Together the museums showcase a huge collection of Belgian art spanning the centuries, including Bruegel the Elder's *Landscape with the Fall of Icarus* and pieces by Rubens and Brussels native René Magritte. Other masterpieces not to be missed are David's *Death of Marat* and paintings by Delacroix, Ingres, Gauguin, van Gogh, and Seurat. The panoramic view of Brussels's cityscape from the fourth floor of the 19th-century wing is alone worth the admission fee. *(3 r. de la Régence. M: Parc. ☎ 508 32 11. Open Su and Tu-Sa 10am-5pm. Some wings close noon-2pm. €5, students €3.50; 1st W of each month 1-5pm free. Audioguide €2.50.)* The **Musical Instrument Museum (MIM),** located in an Art Nouveau building, houses over 1500 instruments. Stand in front of any instrument and your headphones automatically play a sample of its music. There is a fabulous panoramic view of the city from a corner turret on the third floor and in the restaurant upstairs. *(2 r. Montagne de la Cour. One block from the Musées des Beaux-Arts. ☎ 545 01 30. Open Tu-W and F 9:30am-5pm, Th 9:30am-8pm, Sa-Su 10am-5pm. €5, students €3.50; headphones included. 1st W of each month 1-5pm free.)*

BELGIAN COMIC STRIP CENTRE. This museum, in the "Comic Strip Capital of the World," pays homage to *les bandes dessineés* with hundreds of Belgian comics. The **museum library,** in a renovated Art Nouveau warehouse, features a reproduction of Tintin's rocket ship and works by over 700 artists. For Tintin souvenirs, check out the museum store or the Tintin Boutique near Grand Place. *(20 r. des Sables. M: Rogier. From Gare Centrale, take bd. de l'Impératrice until it becomes bd. de Berlaimont, and turn left onto r. des Sables. ☎ 219 19 80. Open Su and Tu-Sa 10am–6pm. €6.20, students €5.)*

INTERNATIONAL MAN OF MYSTERY Tintin (pronounced "tan-tan") is the greatest comic-strip hero of the French-speaking world. From Nice to Quebec City, he remains perpetually young to fans who play hardball at auctions for Tintin memorabilia. His creator, Georges Rémi (whose pen-name "Hergé" is his initials pronounced backwards) sent him to the Kremlin, Shanghai, the Congo, outer space, and the wilderness of... Chicago. Countless dissertations and novels have been written about Tintin's possible androgyny; many also say that Indiana Jones was Tintin made into a man. When former French president Charles de Gaulle was asked whom he feared the most, he replied, "Tintin is my only international competitor."

PARKS AND SQUARES. The **Botanical Gardens** on r. Royale are beautiful in summer. The **Parc de Bruxelles,** just behind Gare Centrale, and the **Parc Leopold,** amidst the EU buildings, are pleasantly green sanctuaries that provide a nice spot for a walk or jog. The charming hills around the **Place du Grand Sablon** are home to antique markets, art galleries, and cafes. Around **Place au Jeu de Balle,** you can practice the fine art of bargaining at the morning **flea market.**

OTHER SIGHTS. The enormous **Musées Royaux d'Art et d'Histoire** showcases artifacts from a wide variety of eras—Roman torsos without heads, Syrian heads without torsos, and Egyptian caskets with feet. The eerily illuminated *Salle au Tresor* (Treasure Room) and the Greco-Roman collection are the museum's main attractions. *(10 Parc du Cinquantenaire. M: Mérode. From the station, it's next to the big arch. ☎741 72 11. Open Tu-F 9:30am-5pm, Sa-Su 10am-5pm. €4, students €3.)* Next door, the **Royal Museum of the Army and Military History** contains a huge exhibit of WWI paraphenalia, including tanks, cannons, and uniforms, that bring to life the most important moments in Belgian history. *(3 Parc du Cinquantenaire. ☎737 78 33. Open Su and Tu-Sa 9am-noon and 1-4:45pm. Free.)* The **European Parliament Building** has been called the *Caprice des Dieux* ("Whim of the Gods"), perhaps because of its exorbitant cost. A quick tour allows you to visit the Parliament floor. *(43 r. Wiertz. M: Schuman. ☎284 34 53; www.europarl.eu.int. Tours M-Th 10am and 3pm, F 10am.)* **Mini-Europe,** an open-air exhibit of European landmarks replicated at one-twenty-fifth of their actual size, may be a perfect solution for travelers pressed for time. Also housed in the **Bruparck** entertainment complex are the **Kinepolis cinema and IMAX,** (the largest movie theater in Europe), and the **Oceade** water park. *(☎478 08 50; www.bruparck.com. Hours vary, but generally open daily 9:30am-5pm. Call or check website for info.)* Twentieth-century master architect Baron Victor Horta's graceful home, today the **Musée Horta,** is a skillful application of his Art Nouveau style to a domestic setting. *(25 r. Américaine. M: Horta. Take a right out of the stop, walking uphill on ch. de Waterloo (7min.), then turn left onto ch. de Charleroi and right onto r. Américaine. ☎543 04 90. Open Su and Tu-Sa 2-5:30pm. €5, students €3.70.)* The **Atomium,** a shining 102m monument of aluminum and steel built for the 1958 World's Fair, represents an iron crystal magnified 165 billion times. An elevator takes visitors to the top. *(Bd. du Centenaire. M: Huysel. ☎475 47 77; www.atomium.be. Open Apr.-Aug. daily 9am-8pm; Sept.-Mar. 10am-6pm. €6.)*

🎵 🎭 ENTERTAINMENT AND NIGHTLIFE

For information on events, check the weekly *What's On,* available from the tourist office. The flagship of Brussels's theater network is the beautiful **Théâtre Royal de la Monnaie,** on pl. de la Monnaie. The theater is renowned throughout the world for its opera and ballet. Its performance of the opera *Muette de Portici* in August 1830 inspired the audience to take to the streets and begin the revolt that led to Belgium's independence. (M: de Brouckère. Info ☎229 12 00, tickets 70 233 939; www.lamonnaie.be. Tickets €8-75.) The **Théâtre Royal de Toone VII,** 21 petite r. des

Bouchers, is a seventh generation puppet theater that stages marionette performances, a distinctly Belgian art form. The theater also houses a unique bar. (☎513 54 86. Shows generally in French; German, Flemish, and English available upon request. Tu-Sa 8:30pm. €10, students €7.) In summer, **concerts** are held on Grand Place, on pl. de la Monnaie, and in the parc de Bruxelles.

On summer nights, **Grand Place** and the **Bourse** come to life with street performers and live concerts. Students crowd in bars at **Zebra** and other hopping cafes around **Place Saint Géry**. Gay nightlife centers around r. des Pierres, next to the Grand Place, and **L'Homo Erectus**, 57 r. des Pierres, is always hot. (Open Su-Th 1pm-3am, F-Sa 1pm-5am.) **L'Archiduc**, 6 r. A. Dansaert, is a pricey but casual Art Deco jazz bar. (Open daily 4pm-late.) For dancing, try **La Salsa**, r. Borgval 9, which offers daily salsa lessons. (Lessons 8pm-11pm. Open daily 8pm-late.) **Le Fuse**, 208 r. Blaes, is one of Belgium's trendiest clubs. (Open daily 10pm-late.)

▶ DAYTRIPS FROM BRUSSELS

WATERLOO. At Waterloo, the Allied troops, commanded by the Duke of Wellington, and the Prussians, led by Marshal Blücher, encountered the French army on June 18th, 1815. It took only nine hours to defeat Napoleon, but 50,000 men were killed in the process. **The Lion's Mound** (*Butte Du Lion*), 5km outside of town, is a huge hill that overlooks the site of Napoleon's last battle. (Open Apr.-Sept. daily 9:30am-6:30pm; Oct. 9:30am-5:30pm; Nov.-Feb. 10:30am-4pm; Mar. 10am-5pm. €1.) **Guides 1815** offers a guided walking tour of the battlefields leaving from the Lion's Mound Visitors Center. (1hr. Apr-Sept. Sa-Su only. €3.) The informative **Musée Wellington,** 147 ch. de Bruxelles, was the British general's headquarters and is now home to battle artifacts. (Open Apr.-Sept. daily 9:30am-6:30pm; Oct.-Mar. 10:30am-5pm. €5, students €4. Audioguide included.)

Waterloo Station is far from most sights. The best option is to take a **train** from Brussels's Gare du Midi to Braine L'Alleud station (15min., every hr., €3), and return on **bus** W, hopping off at *Eglise* (a church in the center of Waterloo near the Musée Wellington) and *Route de Nivelles* (a gas station near Lion's Mound). The reverse route is also possible. Across the street from the Musée Wellington is the **tourist office**, 218 ch. de Bruxelles. (☎02 354 99 10. Open Apr.-Sept. daily 9:30am-6:30pm; Oct.-Mar. 10:30am-5pm.) There are several cheap restaurants along Chaussée de Bruxelles, including **L'Amusoir ❷**, 121 ch. de Bruxelles. (Lunch €7.35. Open daily noon-2:30pm and 6pm-10:30pm.)

MECHELEN (MALINES). Just north of Brussels, Mechelen (pop. 78,000), once the ecclesiastical capital of Belgium, is best known today for its abundance of treasure-filled churches and its grim role in the Holocaust. The stately **St. Rumbold's Cathedral,** down Consciencestr. from the Centraal station, features gorgeous stained-glass windows and the Gothic **St. Rumbold's Tower**, which rises 97m over the **Grote Markt** and houses two carillons (sets of 49 bells) that offer recitals. (Climb the tower July-Aug. M 2:15pm and 7:15pm, Tu-Su 2:15pm; June and Sept. M 7:15pm, Sa-Su and holidays 2:15; €2.50. Carillon recitals June-Sept. M 11:30am and 8:30pm, Sa 11:30am, Su 3pm.) Architectural gems, including the **Stadhuis** (city hall), line the Grote Markt. (Stadhuis open daily July-Aug. Required tour 2pm.) The 15th-century **Church of St. John** boasts Rubens's magnificent 17th-century triptych *The Adoration of the Magi.* (Open Su and T-Sa 1:30-5pm.) To reach the **Jewish Museum of Deportation and Resistance,** 153 Goswin de Stassartstr, follow Wollemarkt from behind St. Rumbold's; it becomes Goswin de Stassartstr. The museum is housed in the 18th-century military barracks used as a temporary holding spot for Jews en route to Auschwitz-Birkenau during the Holocaust. (Open Su-Th 10am-5pm, F 10am-1pm. Free. Tours by request.) The **botanical gardens** along the Dilje River are a great place to stop for a picnic.

Trains arrive from Brussels (15min., every 5-10min., €3.30) and Antwerp (15min., every 5-15min., €2.90). The **tourist office** near the Stadhuis books rooms. (☎015 29 76 55; www.mechelen.be. Open Easter-Oct. M-F 8am-6pm, Sa-Su 9:30am-12:30pm and 1:30-5pm; Nov.-Easter reduced hours.) Restaurants cluster around the Grote Markt. Try the white *asperge* (asparagus), a regional specialty. **Postal Code:** 2800.

FLANDERS (VLAANDEREN)

In Flanders, the Flemish-speaking part of Belgium, you can sample the nightlife in Antwerp, relax in romantic Bruges, and sate your castle-cravings in Ghent. Historically, the mouth of the Schelde River at Antwerp provided the region with a major port, and the production and trade of linen, wool, and diamonds created great prosperity. During it's Golden Age in the 16th century, Flanders's commercial centers were among the largest cities in Europe and its innovative artists inspired the Northern Renaissance. Today, the well-preserved cities of Flanders, rich in masterful oil painting and inspiring Gothic architecture, are Belgium's biggest attractions.

BRUGES (BRUGGE)   ☎050

Famed for its lace and native Jan van Eyck, Bruges (pop. 116,000) is also the most touristed city in Belgium and one of the most romantic cities in Europe. Canals carve their way through rows of stone houses and cobblestone streets to reveal the breathtaking Gothic Markt. The city remains one of the best-preserved examples of Northern Renaissance architecture. Its beauty, however, belies the destruction sustained in World War I; eight decades after the war, farmers still uncover 200 tons of artillery every year as they plough their fields.

▛▜ TRANSPORTATION AND PRACTICAL INFORMATION

Bruges is enclosed by a circular canal, with its main train station, **Stationsplein,** just beyond its southern extreme. The compact historic district is entirely accessible on foot. The dizzying **Belfort** (belfry) towers high over the center of town, presiding over the handsome **Markt.** The windmill-lined **Kruisvestraat** and serene **Minnewater Park** are great for a walk or picnic.

Trains: Leave from **Stationsplein** (☎38 23 82; open daily 4:30am-11pm), a 15min. walk south of the city, for: **Brussels** (50min., 2-6 per hr., €11); **Antwerp** (1¼hr., 2-6 per hr. €12); **Ghent** (25min., 3-10 per hr., €4.80); **Ostend** (17min., 3-5 per hr., €3); **Zeebrugge** (10min., every hr., €2.20).

Bike Rental: At the train station (☎30 23 29). €6.50 per half-day, €9 per day. **'t Koffie,** off the Markt by the belfry. €6 four hours, €9 per day; students €6 per day. Open daily 9am-11pm. Many hostels and hotels also rent bikes for around €9 per day.

Tourist Office: Burg 11 (☎44 86 86; www.brugge.be). From the train station, head left to 't Zand, turn right on Zuidzandstr., and walk through the Markt to Breidelstr. (20min.). Books rooms (€2.50 service fee, €20 deposit) and sells maps (€0.20) and info guides (€1). Open Apr.-Sept. M-F 9:30am-6:30pm, Sa-Su 10am-12:30pm and 2-6:30pm; Oct.-Mar. M-F 9:30am-5pm, Sa-Su 9:30am-1pm and 2-5:30pm. **Branch** office at the train station. Open Tu-Sa 10am-1pm and 2-4pm.

Tours: The tourist office leads **walking tours** (June Sa-Su 2:30pm, July-Aug. daily 3pm; €3.75). Five companies offer **boat tours** that traverse Bruges's canals (every 30min., €5.20); ask at the tourist office or pick up tickets at the booth on the bridge between Wollestr. and Dijver. **Bike tours** are also available through two main companies. **Quasimundo Tours** offers four different tours, including one through the countryside and another at dusk. Bike tours depart daily from the Burg. (☎33 07 75; www.quasimundo.com; Tours Mar.-Oct. €18, under-26 €15.) **Pink Bear Bicycle Company** guides two fun and informative bike tours, one to the neighboring town of Damme and another through the countryside; both leave daily from the Markt. (☎61 66 86; www.pinkbear.freeservers.com. €17, under-26 €15.) Finally, two companies offer daytrips by car to explore the WWI battle site at **Flanders Field** in Ypres (p. 137): **Quasimodo** (☎0800 975 25; www.quasimodo.be) €45, students €38; and **Daytours** (☎0800 991 33; www.visitbruges.com) €59, students €50.

ATMs: Two in the Markt, Vlamingstr. 18 and 78, and at Simon Stevenplein.

Luggage Storage: At the train station. €1.50-3.30. **Lockers** at the tourist office. €1. Only accessible during regular hours.

Laundromat: Belfort, Ezelstr. 51. Wash €2.50-3.50, dry €1. Open daily 7am-10pm.

Emergencies: ☎100. **Police:** ☎101. Police station at Hauwerstr. 7 (☎44 88 44).

Pharmacies: Apotheek Dryepondt, Wollestr. 7. Open M-F 9am-12:30pm and 2-6:30pm, Sa until 6pm. **Apotheek K. Dewolf,** Zuidzandstr. 1. Open M-F 9am-12:30pm and 2-6:30pm, Sa until 6pm.

Hospitals: A. Z. St.-Jan (☎41 21 11; not to be confused with Oud St-Janshospitaal, a museum), St.-Lucas (☎36 91 11), St.-Franciscus Xaverivskliniek (☎47 04 70). Call tourist office for doctors on call.

Internet Access: The Coffee Link, Mariastr. 38 (☎34 99 73), in the Oud St-Janshospitaal. €1.25 for first 15min., €0.07 per min. thereafter. Open daily 10am-8pm. Many hostels (see below) also offer access open to all.

Post Office: Markt 5. Address mail to be held: Firstname SURNAME, *Poste Restante*, Markt 5, **8000** Brugge, BELGIUM. Open M-F 9am-7pm, Sa 9:30am-12:30pm.

◤ ACCOMMODATIONS

Despite Bruges's popularity, reasonably-priced accommodations are available just blocks from the city center. Reserve in advance, as rooms can be hard to come by on weekends.

▨ **De Passage,** Dweersstr. 26 (☎34 02 32). Ideal location, friendly service, great rooms, and a popular cafe. Free beer with dinner and a free t-shirt after a 3-night stay. Breakfast €3. Reception daily 8:30am-11pm. Dorms €12; singles €22; doubles €40. ❷

▨ **Hotel Lybeer,** Korte Vuldersstr. 31 (☎33 43 55; hotellybeer@hotmail.com). Great location. Old-fashioned charm with modern comforts. Backpacker-friendly. Breakfast included. Free Internet access. Reception daily 7:30am-midnight. Singles €25; doubles €43; triples €57; quads €89. ❸

't Keizershof, Oostmeers 126 (☎33 87 28; hotel.keizershof@12move.be). Pretty, comfortable rooms on a quiet street. Breakfast included. Laundry €8. Singles €25; doubles €38; triples €60; quads €70. ❸

Bauhaus International Youth Hotel, Langestr. 133-137 (☎34 10 93; info@bauhaus.be). Cybercafe and popular bar. Nearby laundromat. Breakfast €2. Reception Su-Th 8am-1am, F-Sa 8am-3am. Dorms €11-23; doubles €25-35. ❷

Charlie Rockets, Hoogstr. 19 (☎33 06 60; info@charlierockets.com). Central location. Packed restaurant and bar. Breakfast included. Reception daily 8am-4am. In summer, email reservation required. Dorms €14; doubles €42. ❷

Hotel Cordoeanier, Cordoeanier 16-18 (☎34 61 11; www.cordoeanier.be). From top of the Markt, follow Philipstockstr. and take the first left onto Cordoeanier; follow street around to the hotel. Quaint lobby, comfortable rooms with TV and telephone, and perfect location. Breakfast buffet included. Internet access. Singles €52; doubles €62; triples €72; quads €85; quints €98. ❺

Europa International Youth Hostel (HI), Baron Ruzettelaan 143 (☎35 26 79; brugge@vjh.be). Quiet, away from the Markt and the nightlife. Breakfast and sheets included. Key deposit €5. Internet access €0.08 per min. Reception daily 7:30-10am and 1-11pm. Dorms €13; nonmembers add €2.50. ❷

Camping: St-Michiel, Tillegemstr. 55 (☎38 08 19). From the station, take bus #7 to Jagerstr. Face the road, head left and then turn left on Jagerstr. Bear left at the first intersection, staying on Jagerstr. and going around the rotary to Tillegemstr. €2.90 per person, €3.40 per tent. Showers €2. ❶

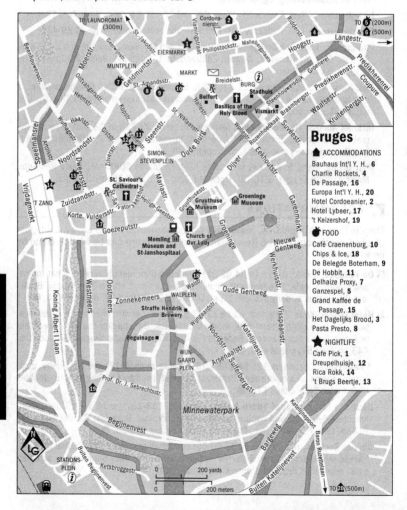

Bruges

♦ ACCOMMODATIONS
Bauhaus Int'l Y. H., **6**
Charlie Rockets, **4**
De Passage, **16**
Europa Int'l Y. H., **20**
Hotel Cordoeanier, **2**
Hotel Lybeer, **17**
't Keizershof, **19**

◉ FOOD
Café Craenenburg, **10**
Chips & Ice, **18**
De Belegde Boterham, **9**
De Hobbit, **11**
Delhaize Proxy, **7**
Ganzespel, **5**
Grand Kaffee de Passage, **15**
Het Dagelijks Brood, **3**
Pasta Presto, **8**

★ NIGHTLIFE
Cafe Pick, **1**
Dreupelhuisje, **12**
Rica Rokk, **14**
't Brugs Beertje, **13**

BELGIUM

🍴 FOOD

Inexpensive food can be hard to find in Bruges, but seafood lovers should splurge at least once on Belgium's famous *mosselen* (mussels; usually €15-22) or buy fresh (raw) seafood at the **Vismarkt.** From the Burg, cross the river and turn left. (Open Tu-Sa 8am-1pm.) For a market with cheaper fare, head to **Delhaize Proxy,** Noordzandstr. 4, near the Markt. (Open M-Sa 9am-7pm.)

Ganzespel, Ganzestr. 37. Quiet restaurant serves up generous and delicious portions of traditional Belgian fare. Menu €7.35. Entrees €5-15. Open Su and W-Sa 6-10pm. ❷

Pasta Presto, St. Amandsstra. 17. Nicely priced Italian fare. Just off the Markt. Takeout available. Menu €6.75. Pasta with choice of nine sauces €2.50. Open M and W-Su 11:30am-9:30pm. ❷

Het Dagelijks Brood, Philipstockstr. 21. Sandwiches, quiches, salads, pastries, and organic yogurt served at a big wooden table. Great for breakfast and lunch. Open M, W-Su 7:30am-6pm. ❷

Grand Kaffee de Passage, Dweerstr. 26-28. Attached to De Passage hotel. Traditional Belgian cuisine with good vegetarian options (€4.50-14). Open daily 6am-11:30pm. ❷

Chips and Ice, Katelijnestr. 32. Cheapest sandwiches (€2.25-3) around. Great for a quick lunch. Open daily 9:30am-7pm. ❷

Café Craenenburg, Markt 16. Grab a quick bite to eat on the outdoor terrace. (€9.70-12.30) Pricey, but has a stunning view. Open M-Tu and Th-Sa 7:30am-1am, W 7am-1am, Su 8am-1am. ❹

De Hobbit, Kemelstr. 8. Big portions of hearty food, from pasta (€6) to meat (€15) and salads (€9-14). Open daily 6pm-1am. ❹

De Belegde Boterham, Kleine St-Amandstr. 5. Serves salads (€8.50-10) and sandwiches (€5.50-7.50). Open M-Sa noon-5pm. ❸

👁 SIGHTS

Lined with gorgeous canals, and small enough to be explored on a short walk, Bruges is best seen on foot. Avoid visiting Bruges on Mondays, when all the museums are closed. If you plan to visit many museums, consider a cost-saving combination ticket (€15; includes admission to five museums).

MARKT AND BURG. Over the **Markt** looms the **Belfort,** an 88m medieval bell tower. During the day, climb its dizzying 366 steps for a great view; return at night, when the tower serves as the city's torch. *(Belfort open Su and Tu-Sa 9:30am-5pm. Tickets sold until 4:15pm. €5, students €3. Bell concerts Oct.-June 15 W and Sa-Su 2:15pm; June 15-Sept. Su only.)* Behind the Markt, the **Burg** is dominated by the massive, yet finely detailed Gothic facade of the **Stadhuis** (City Hall). Inside, the building's attractions include paintings, wood carvings, and a gilded hall where many residents of Bruges still get married. *(Open Su and Tu-Sa 9:30am-4:30pm. €2.50, students €1.50. Audioguide included.)* Hidden in a corner of the Burg next to the Stadhuis, the **Basilica of the Holy Blood** houses a relic that allegedly holds the blood of Christ. *(Basilica open Apr.-Sept. daily 9:30-11:50am and 2-5:50pm; Oct.-Mar. 10am-noon and 2-4pm; closed W afternoon. Free. Worship of the Relic F 11:50am, 5:50pm, 10-11am, and 3-4pm. €1.50.)*

MUSEUMS. From the Burg, follow Wollestr. left and then head right on Dijver to reach the **Groeninge Museum,** which has a comprehensive collection of Belgian and Dutch paintings from the last six centuries. Highlights include Hieronymous Bosch's fantastically lurid ■ *Last Judgment,* and works by Bruges-based Jan Van Eyck and Bruges-born Hans Memling. *(Dijver 12. Open Su and Tu-Sa 9:30am-5pm;*

€8, students €5.) Formerly a palace, the nearby **Gruuthuse Museum** houses a large collection of intricate 16th- and 17th- century tapestries, along with other artifacts dating to the 6th century. The museum's small chapel, which protrudes into the Church of Our Lady (see below), was built so that the Palace residents could attend church services from the comfort of their home. (Dijver 17. Open Su and Tu-Sa 9:30am-5pm; €6, students €4.) Continue on Dijver as it becomes Gruuthusestr. and walk under the stone archway to enter the **Memling Museum**, housed in **St-Jan-shospitaal**, one of the oldest surviving medieval hospitals in Europe. The museum reconstructs everyday life in the hospital and has several paintings by Hans Memling. (Mariastr. 38. Open Su and Tu-Sa 9:30am-5pm; €8, students €5.)

OTHER SIGHTS. The 14th century **Church of Our Lady**, at Mariastr. and Gruuthus-estr., contains Michelangelo's *Madonna and Child* as well as frescoed fragments of the 16th-century tombs of Mary of Burgundy and Charles the Bold. (Open M-F 9am-12:20pm and 1:30-4:50pm, Sa 9am-12:30pm and 1:30-3:50pm, Su 1:30-4:50pm. Church free. Tomb viewing €2.50, students €1.50.) Beer aficionados will enjoy the informative tour (and free sample) at the **Straffe Hendrik Brewery**, a beer museum and brewery built in 1856. (From the Church of Our Lady, turn left, follow Mariastr., turn right onto Wijngaard-str., and turn right onto Welplein. Tours 45min. Apr.-Sept. 11am, noon, 2, 3, and 4pm; Oct.-Mar. 11am and 3pm.) A short hike away, the 230-year-old windmill **St-Janshuismolen** is still used to grind flour in the summer months. (From the Burg, follow Hoogstr., which becomes Langestr., and turn left at the end on Kruisvest. It's the second windmill. Open May-Sept. daily 9:30am-12:30pm and 1:30-5pm. €1, students €0.50.) The **Beguinage**, a grassy cove encircled by medieval cloisters inhabited by Benedictine nuns, displays items used in ancient Flemish households. (From Simon Stevenplein, follow Mariastr., turn right onto Wijngaardstr.; at the canal, turn right and cross the footbridge. Open daily Mar.-Nov. 10am-noon and 1:45-5:30pm; Gate closes at sunset. Adults €2, students €1.) The **Minnewater** (Lake of Love), on the southern end of the city, is a beautiful park perfect for an afternoon picnic; you'd never know it was once used as an ammunition dump.

■ NIGHTLIFE

The best nighttime activity in Bruges is a walk through the city's romantic streets and over its cobblestoned bridges. There are some more lively late-night options, however, including the popular **bar** at the Bauhaus Hostel (see above) or the 300 varieties of beer at **'t Brugs Beertje**, Kemelstr. 5, off Steenstr. (Open Su-Tu and Th 4pm-1am, F-Sa 4pm-2am.) Next door, the candlelit **Dreupelhuisje** serves tantalizingly fruity *jenever*, a flavored Dutch gin. Be careful—the flavors mask a very high alcohol content. (Open Su, Tu and Th-Sa 6pm-1am.) Behind the Markt, **Cafe Pick** is a lively spot popular with young locals, and often offers late-night happy hour specials. (Open Su-Tu 10:30am-2am, W-Sa 10:30am-late. 2 for 1 beer special W and F 11pm-midnight, 2 for 1 spirits Su 10pm-midnight.) A 20-something crowd dances to pulsing music at **Rica Rokk**, 't Zand 6. (Beer from €1.60. Open daily 9:30am-5am.)

■ DAYTRIPS FROM BRUGES

OSTEND (OOSTENDE). On the coast of the North Sea, Ostend is a beach town with a promenade lined with restaurants and bars. The pier and **Viserkaai** (Fisherman's Quay) mark the entrance to the harbor that brings in most of the fresh fish sold in the country. Near the bustling **Vitrap** (Fishmarket), vendors set up stands selling steaming bowls of *caricoles* (sea snails) and fresh seafood galore. To get to the main **beach**, cross the bridge directly in front of the station, turn right on Visserkaai and follow the promenade for 20min.

Trains run to Ostend from Bruges (15min., 3 per hr., €3). To get to the **tourist office** (☎70 11 99; www.oostende.be), follow the directions to the beach, but walk on the promenade for only 10min. and turn left onto Langestr.; follow it to the end.

Don't even bother asking for a menu at **Taverne Koekoek** ❶, Langestr. 38-40, because they only do one thing: perfectly spiced, divine rotisserie chicken. (Half-chicken €4.90. Open 24hr.)

ANTWERP (ANTWERPEN, ANVERS) ☎03

Home to the Golden Age master painter Rubens, Antwerp (pop. 450,000) is distinctly cosmopolitan. Its main street, the Meir, showcases trendy clothing, diamond jewelry, and delectable chocolate.

🖃🛈 TRANSPORTATION AND PRACTICAL INFORMATION. Trains go from Berchem Station to: Amsterdam (2hr., €24); Brussels (1hr., €6); and Rotterdam (1hr., €16). To get from Berchem station to the **tourist office**, Grote Markt 15, take tram #8 (all trams €1) to Groenplaats. (☎232 01 03; www.visitantwerpen.be. Open M-Sa 9am-6pm, Su 9am-5pm). **Postal Code: 2000.**

🖾🛏 ACCOMMODATIONS AND FOOD. To get to ▨**Bed & Breakfast 26,** Pelgrimsstr. 26, from Groenpl., take Reyndersstr. away from Hilton, and turn right onto Pelgirmsstr.; it's the third building on left. Beautiful rooms, appealing showers, and a personable owner. (☎42 83 69. M: Groenpl. Breakfast included. Reserve in advance. Singles €25, with private bath €35; doubles €50/60.) The **New International Youth Hotel and Hostel** ❷, Provinciestr. 256, is a 15min. walk from the train station, on the corner of De Boeystr. and Provinciestr. Or, take tram #2 or 15 to Plantin, follow Plantin de Moretus under the bridge, and turn right on Baron Joostensstr., left on Van Den Nestlei, and right on De Boeystr. Rooms are clean and carpeted. (☎230 05 22. Breakfast included. Sheets €3.50. No lockout. Dorms €14; singles €29; doubles €44-55; quads €71-85.) To get to the conveniently located **Scoutel** ❹, Stoomstr. 3, from Centraal station, turn left on Pelikaanstr., take first left under bridge; once through, the entrance is on the right. (☎226 46 06; www.vvksm.be. Breakfast and sheets included. Reception daily 8am-7pm. Singles €27, under-26 €25; doubles €44/39; quads €71/62.) Farther from the center is **Jeugdherberg Op-Sinjoorke (HI)** ❷, Eric Sasselaan 2. From Groenplaats, take tram #2 (dir.: Hoboken) to *Bouwcentrum*. From the tram stop, walk toward the fountain, take a left, and follow the yellow signs. (☎238 02 73; www.vjh.be. Breakfast included. Reception 7am-10am, 4pm-midnight. Lockout 10am-4pm. Dorms €13; doubles €18. Nonmembers add €3.) You can **camp** near the Jeugdherberg Op-Sinjoorke at the well-kept **Sted. Kamp Vogelzangan** ❶. Follow the directions above to *Bouwcentrum*; when you get off the tram, walk away from the fountain, and take the first left; the campground is on the left. (Max. stay 28 days. Open Apr.-Sept. 3. €2.50 per person, €1 per car; €1.25 per tent. Electricity €2.50. No credit cards.) The **Grote Markt** and **Groenplaats** are surrounded by numerous restaurants. **Suikerrui,** off Grote Markt, is the street for those seeking seafood. For hearty pizza (€4.50-10) and friendly, multilingual service just off Groenpl., visit **Pizzeria Ristorante Da Giovanni** ❷, Jan Blomstr. 8. (Open daily 11am-1am. 20% student discount.) **Spaghettiworld** ❸, Oude Koornmarkt 3, has funky decor and a large selection of large, inexpensive pasta dishes. (Pasta €7-12. Open Su 4-11pm, Tu-F 7am-11pm, Sa noon-11pm.) The **GB supermarket** is off Groenpl. (Open M-Th and Sa 8:30am-8pm, F 8:30am-9pm.)

◨🎭 SIGHTS AND NIGHTLIFE. Many of Antwerp's best sights are free. Its main street, the **Meir,** is great for window shopping. In the city's historic center, the **Cathedral of Our Lady,** Groenpl. 21, boasts a magnificent Gothic tower and Rubens's *Descent from the Cross.* (Open M-F 10am-5pm, Sa 10am-3pm, Su 1-4pm. €2.) Nearby, the dignified Renaissance **Stadhuis** (City Hall) is well worth visiting. (Tours by request only ☎220 80 20. €0.75.) Take tram #11 to see the fanciful and eclectic Golden Age mansions lining the **Cogels Osylei.**

BELGIUM

If you're museum-bound, try to plan your trip to Antwerp on Friday; admission is free at all museums. A stroll down the promenade by the Schelde River leads to the 13th-century **Steen Castle,** which houses the extensive collections of the **National Maritime Museum.** (Open Su and Tu-Sa 10am-4:45pm. €4, students €2.) The **Royal Museum of Fine Arts,** Leopold De Waelpl. 1-9, has one of the world's finest collections of Old Flemish Master paintings. (Open Su and Tu-Sa 10am-5pm. €8, under-25 €2.) The **Mayer van den Bergh Museum,** Lange Gasthuisstr. 19, formerly a private collection with works from the 14th to 16th centuries, showcases Bruegel's *Mad Meg.* (Open Su and Tu-Sa 10am-5pm. €4, students €2.) The **Rubens Huis,** Wapper 9, off Meir, was built by Antwerp's favorite son and is filled with his works. (Open Su and Tu-Sa 10am-5pm. €5, students €2.50.) The **Diamant Museum,** Kon. Astridplein 19, explores every facet of the precious gem, from its unique creation to Antwerp's historic role as the world's diamond center. (Open May-Oct. daily 10am-6pm; Nov.-Apr. 10am-5pm. €5, students €3. Audioguide included.)

Although mostly in Dutch, *Weekly Up* magazine (free at any tourist office) provides nightlife and movie information. Bars abound behind the cathedral, but a trendy scene has emerged in the southern part of the city, near the Royal Arts Museum. For live jazz and a chill atmosphere, visit **De Muze,** Melkmarkt 15, a bar that has remained popular since the 60s. Sample the local *elixir d'Anvers* (a strong, sugary drink) amidst traditionally dressed Flemish bartenders in the candlelit, 15th-century **Pelgrom,** Pelgrimstr. 15. (Open daily noon-late.) Over 600 Flemish religious figurines hang out with drinkers at **'t Elfde Gebod,** Torfburg 10, next to the cathedral. (Beer €1.75-3. Open M-F noon-1am, Sa-Su noon-2am.) Gay nightlife clusters around **Van Schoonhovenstraat,** just north of Centraal Station.

GHENT (GENT)   ☎ 09

Once the heart of the Flemish textile industry, modern Ghent (pop. 225,000) celebrates the memory of its industrial past. Awe-inspiring buildings in the city's main square stand in proud testament to its former grandeur, and the **Gentse Feesten,** the "10 Days Off" celebration, commemorates the first vacation granted to laborers in 1860. During the festivities, the streets fill with performers, live music, carnival rides, great food and loads and loads of beer; the celebration also brings 11 nights of international DJs. (July 17-26, 2004. Info ☎ 269 46 00.)

⊟⊅ TRANSPORTATION AND PRACTICAL INFORMATION. Trains run from St-Pietersstation (accessible by tram #1 or 12) to: Antwerp (40min., €7); Brussels (40min., €6.60); and Bruges (20min., €4.80). The **tourist office,** Botermarkt 17A, is in the crypt of the belfry. (☎ 266 52 32. Open Apr.-Oct. daily 9:30am-6:30pm; Nov.-Mar. 9:30am-4:30pm.) **Postal Code:** 9000.

⊓⊡ ACCOMMODATIONS AND FOOD. To reach **De Draeke (HI) ❷,** St-Widostr. 11, from the station, take tram #1, 10, or 11 to Gravensteen (15min.). Facing the castle, head left over the canal, then go right on Gewad and turn right on St-Widostr. In the shadow of a castle, it's the only hostel in town. (☎ 233 70 50. Breakfast and sheets included. Internet access €0.08 per min. Reception daily 7am-11pm. Dorms €16; singles €24; doubles €38. Nonmembers add €3.) For a listing of private rooms, visit the tourist office. To get to **Camping Blaarmeersen ❶,** Zuiderlaan 12, take bus #9 from St-Pietersstation and ask the driver to connect you to bus #38 to Blaarmeersen. When you get off, take the first street on your left to the end. (☎ 266 81 60. Open Mar. to mid-Oct. In summer, €4 per person, €4 per tent; off-season, €3.30 per person, €3.30 per tent.) **Oudburg,** near Patershol, has many inexpensive kebob and pita restaurants. Also try **St-Pietersnieuwstraat,** by the university. **Magazyne ❶,** Penitentenstr. 24, is a great place for cheap and hearty fare, with good vegetarian options. (Open M-F noon-2pm and 6-11pm, Sa-Su 6-11pm.) **Pain Perdu ❸**, Walpoortstr. 9, serves tasty sandwiches and salads. (Open M-F 8:30am-6:30pm, Sa 9am-6:30pm, Su 9am-2:30pm.)

◙ 🖪 SIGHTS AND NIGHTLIFE. The **Leie canal** runs through the center of the city and wraps around the **Gravensteen**, St-Veerlepl. 11, a medieval fortress whose shadowy halls and spiral staircases will give you chills before you even reach the crypt, dungeon, and torture chamber. (Open Apr.-Sept. daily 9am-5:15pm; Oct.-Mar. 9am-4:15pm. €6, students €1.20.) The castle is near the historic **Patershol** quarter and **Vrijmarkt**, a network of funky and well-preserved 16th- to 18th-century houses. A block away on Limburgstr., the elaborately decorated 14th- to 16th-century **▨Saint Bavo's Cathedral** boasts van Eyck's *Adoration of the Mystic Lamb* and Rubens's *St. Bavo's Entrance into the Monastery of Ghent*. (Cathedral open Apr.-Oct. daily 8:30am-6pm; Nov.-Mar. M-Sa 8:30am-5pm, Su 1-6pm. Free. Crypt and *Mystic Lamb* open Apr.-Oct. M-Sa 9:30am-5pm, Su 1-5pm; Nov.-Mar. M-Sa 10:30am-4pm, Su 1-4pm. €2.50. Audioguide included.) Walk across **Saint Michael's Bridge** and along the **Graslei**, a medieval port-street, to see the handsomely preserved guild houses. The **▨Church of St. Nicholas**, absolutely striking from the exterior, is also worth a look inside. (Open M 2:30-5pm, Tu-Su 10am-5pm. Free.) The **Museum voor Sierkunst** (Museum of Decorative Arts), nearby on Jan Breydelstr., has a large collection of Art Nouveau designs as well as more contemporary furniture. (Open Su and T-Sa 9:30am-5pm. €2.50, students €1.20.) The **Museum voor Schone Kunsten** (Museum of Fine Arts), in Citadel Park, has a collection of 14th- to 16th-century Flemish works. (Open Su and Tu-Sa 10am-6pm. €2.50, students €1.20.) The **Stedelijk Museum voor Actuele Kunst** (SMAK; Municipal Museum for Contemporary Art) is also located in Citadel Park. (Open Su and Tu-Sa 10am-6pm. €5, students €2.50.) **Korenmarkt** and **Vrijdagmarkt** are filled with restaurants and pubs. Beer-lovers flock to **Dulle Griet**, in Vrijdagmarkt, which serves over 250 types of beer. (Open M 4:30pm-12:30am, Tu-Sa noon-12:30am, Su noon-7:30pm.)

YPRES (IEPER)   ☎57

"We are the dead. Short days ago/We lived, felt dawn, saw sunset glow/Loved and were loved, and now we lie/In Flanders fields." Canadian soldier John McCrae wrote these famous lines during WWI at the Battle of Ypres Salient. What the Germans believed would be a quick, sweeping victory quickly became a vicious stalemate that defined the horrors of WWI; chemical warfare was used for the first time in Western history. In four years of intense fighting, 450,000 people died here. Ypres (pop. 35,000), once a medieval textile center, was completely destroyed by the long combat, but was rebuilt as a near-perfect replica of its former self. Today, the town is surrounded by over 150 **British cemeteries** and filled with memorial sites, drawing soldiers' families as well as many British tourists and school groups.

In the **Cloth Hall**, one of the grand medieval guild halls that preside over **Grote Markt**, the **Flanders Field Museum**, Grote Markt 34, documents the gruesome history and bloody battles of the Great War. (Open Apr.-Sept. daily 10am-6pm; Oct.-Mar. Su and Tu-Sa 10am-5pm. €7.50.) Next door stands the splendid Gothic **Saint Martin's Cathedral.** Cross the street in front of St. Martin's and head right to reach the Anglican **Saint George's Memorial Church**, Elverdingsestr. 1. Each brass plaque and kneeling pillow in the church commemorates a specific individual or unit. (Both churches open daily except during services. Free.) Across the *markt*, the names of 54,896 British soldiers who were lost in the trenches are inscribed on the somber **Menin Gate.** At 8pm each evening, the **Last Post** bugle ceremony honors those who defended Ypres. You can easily walk the circumference of Ypres along the old ramparts. From Menin Gate, take the **Rose Coombs Walk** to visit the nearby **Ram-**

parts **Cemetery,** where row upon row of white crosses face the river. The battle-fields are largely inaccessible by foot, so **car tours** are a good, if pricey option. Two companies, **Flanders Battlefield Tours** (☎360 460. www.ypres-fbt.be; €16-22), and **Salient Tours** (☎214 657. www.salienttours.com; €15- 21), offer informative tours that traverse the surrounding battlefields.

Trains run to: Bruges via Courtrai (2hr., €9); Ghent (1hr., €8.50); and Brussels (1½hr., €14). To get to the **Visitors Center,** housed in the Cloth Hall in Grote Markt from the train station, head straight down Stationsstr., turn left onto Tempelstr., then turn right onto Boterstr. (☎22 85 84; www.ieper.be. Open Apr.-Sept. M-Sa 9am-6pm, Su 10am-6pm; Oct.-Mar. M-Sa 9am-5pm, Su 10am-5pm.) **The Hortensia ❺,** Rijselsestr. 196, is a bed & breakfast with great rooms and a friendly owner. From the Grote Markt, turn onto Rijselsestr. and continue for 10min. (☎21 24 06. Singles €46, doubles €54, triples €69.) Many restaurants line the **Grote Markt,** including **I'nt Klein Stadhuis ❸,** a traditional pub and restaurant with a terrace. The **Super GB** grocery store is at Vandepeereboomplein 15. (Open M-Sa 9am-7pm.)

WALLONIE

Wallonie, the French-speaking region of Belgium, enjoys less wealth than its Flem-ish counterpart; nonetheless, its bigger towns boast interesting histories, partially thanks to their oft-coveted citadels. The towns in the **Ardennes** offer a relaxing hideaway, with hiking trails through deep forests and beautiful landscapes. The most exceptional area lies in the southeast corner, where gorgeous train rides sweep through peaceful farmland. Although nature-lovers will probably want to spend a night in this part of the Wallonie wilderness, those pressed for time can enjoy the scenery from a train on the way to Brussels, Paris, or Luxembourg.

TOURNAI   ☎069

The first city liberated by Allied forces, Tournai's (pop. 68,000) medieval old town has a history of being bounced between various empires; it was once a Roman trading post and the former capital of Gaul. The city's most spectacular sight is the 800-year-old **Cathedral of Our Lady,** known for its five steeples and **treasure room.** (Treasure room open in summer daily 10am-noon and 2-5pm, Su until 7:15pm; off-season 10:15-11:45am and 2-3:30pm. €1.) Climb the **belfry** for a stunning view. (Open Mar.-Oct. Su 11am-1pm and 2-6:30pm, Tu-Sa 10am-1pm and 2-5:30pm; Nov.-Feb. Su 2-5pm, Tu-Sa 10am-noon; €2.) Designed by Victor Horta, the **Museum of Fine Arts,** enclos St-Martin, is an Art Nouveau building that houses a small collec-tion of Flemish paintings. (Open Apr.-Oct. M and W-Su 9:30am-noon and 2-4:30pm; Nov.-Mar. M and W-Su 10am-noon and 2-5pm, Su 2-5pm. €3, students €2.)

Trains arrive at pl. Crombez (☎88 62 23) from Brussels's Gare du Midi (1hr., €9.60). To get to the **tourist office,** 14 Vieux Marché Aux Poteries, exit the station, walk straight to the city center (10min.), and go around the left side of the cathe-dral. (☎22 20 45; www.tournai.be. Open Apr.-Oct. M-F 8:30am-6pm, Sa-Su 10am-noon and 2-6pm; Nov.-Mar. M-F 8:30am-6pm, Sa-Su 2-6pm. To get to the **Auberge de Tournai (HI) ❷,** 64 r. St-Martin, continue straight up the hill from the tourist office or take bus #7 or 88 (€1.10) from the station. (☎21 61 36. Breakfast and sheets included. Reception daily 8am-noon and 5-10pm. Reservations required during off-season. Closed Jan. Dorms €13; singles €23; doubles €36. Nonmembers add €2.50.) The area around **Grand Place** has plenty of options for cheap food.

NAMUR
☎ 081

The quiet and friendly city of Namur (pop. 105,000), in the heart of Wallonie, is the last sizable outpost before the wilderness of the Ardennes. Given the proximity of opportunities for **hiking, biking, caving,** and **kayaking,** it is the most convenient base for exploration. The foreboding **citadel,** on top of a cliff to the south, was built by the Spanish in the Middle Ages, expanded by the Dutch in the 19th century, the site of a bloody battle in WWI, and occupied until 1978. (Open daily 11am-5pm. €6.)

Trains link Namur to Brussels (1hr., €6.60). Two **tourist offices,** one a few blocks left of the train station at sq. Leopold (☎24 64 49; open daily 9:30am-6pm), and the other in the **Hôtel de Ville,** r. de Fer (☎24 64 44, www.ville.namur.be; open M-F 8am-4:30pm), help plan excursions. To enjoy a lake-front view, take bus #3 to the **Auberge Félicien Rops (HI) ❷,** 8 av. Félicien Rops. (☎22 36 88; namur@laj.be. Bikes €13 per day. Breakfast and sheets included. Laundry €6.50. Reception daily 7:30am-1am. Lockout 11am-3pm. Dorms €13-15. Nonmembers add €2.50.) To **camp** at **Les Trieux ❶,** 99 r. des Tris, 6km away in Malonne, take bus #6. (☎44 55 83. Open Apr.-Oct. €2.50 per person, €3.75 per tent.) Restaurants cluster in the small square of **Place Marché-aux-legumes** on r. St-Jean.

DINANT

The tiny town of Dinant (pop. 13,000) boasts wonders disproportionate to its size. An imposing **citadel** towers over the Meuse River. (☎22 36 70. Citadel open Mar.-Sept. daily 10am-6pm. Required tour in French and Dutch, 45min., every 35min., €5.50.) Bring a jacket to tour the cascade-filled caves of the **Grotte Merveilleuse,** 142 rte. de Phillippeville. Rich with stalagmites and stalagtites, the cave lives up to its name—it is indeed marvellous. (Open Apr.-Oct. daily 10-11am and 1-5pm; Nov.-Mar. 11am and 1-4pm. Tours every hr. €5, students €4.50.) The 📧**Leffe Abbey,** a brew of beer and religion, offers enlightening tours for the adventurous beer pilgrim. (Tours May-Aug. Su and W 3pm.) Dinant is also a good base for **outdoor** excursions. **Dakota Raid Adventure,** r. Cousot 6 (☎22 32 43), leads rock-climbing and kayaking daytrips in the area. Dinant is accessible by **train** from Brussels (1hr., €9.60) or by **bike** from Namur; on summer weekends, take a one-way river cruise from Namur (3hr.). With your back to the train station, turn right, take the first left, and then the very next left to reach the **tourist office,** Quai Cadoux 8 (☎082 22 28 70), which plans excursions and books rooms.

🗺 **DAYTRIP FROM DINANT: ROCHEFORT** . Rochefort (pop. 10,000), a charming town with hospitable residents, is hidden within the rolling hills and woods of the Lesse Valley. Hike up to the crumbled **Château Comtal** for a breathtaking view of the Northern Ardennes. (☎084 21 44 09. Site open Apr.-Oct. daily 10am-6pm. €1.80.) Also visit the **Grotte de Lorette,** one of Wallonie's many spectacular caves. (☎084 21 20 80. Tours July-Aug. daily 10:30am-noon and 1-5:30pm, every 45min.) To reach Rochefort, take the **train** from Namur to Jemelle (40min., every 40min., €6.60) and **bus** #29 from Jemelle (every hr., usually 34min. after the hr., €1.10). The **tourist office,** 5 r. de Behogne, sells hiking maps. (☎084 34 51 72. Open M-F 8am-5pm, Sa-Su 9:30am-5pm.)

BELGIUM

BRITAIN

Having spearheaded the Industrial Revolution, colonized two-fifths of the globe, and won every foreign war in its history but two, Britain seems intent on making the world forget its tiny size. But this small island nation is just that: Small. The rolling farms of the south and the rugged cliffs of the north are only a day's train ride apart, and people as diverse as London clubbers, Cornish miners, Welsh students, and Gaelic monks all occupy a land area half the size of Spain. Beyond the stereotypical snapshots of Merry Olde England—gabled cottages with flowery borders, tweed-clad farmers shepherding their flocks—Britain today is a cosmopolitan destination driven by international energy. Though the sun may have set on the British Empire, its legacy survives in multicultural urban centers and a dynamic arts and theater scene. Brits eat kebab as often as they do scones, and five-story dance clubs in post-industrial settings draw as much attention as fairy-tale country homes with picturesque views.

Travelers should be aware that names hold political force. "Great Britain" refers to England, Scotland, and Wales; the political term "United Kingdom" refers to these nations as well as Northern Ireland. *Let's Go* uses the term "Britain" to refer to England, Scotland, and Wales because of legal and monetary distinctions.

LIFE AND TIMES

HISTORY

EARLY INVADERS. Once connected to the European continent by a land bridge, Britain has been inhabited for nearly half a million years. Little is known about the island's prehistoric residents, besides the utterly mysterious stone circles they left behind at **Stonehenge** (p. 198) and **Avebury** (p. 198). By the end of the first century, the Romans held all of "Britannia" (England and Wales); you can still see the remnants of their rule at **Hadrian's Wall,** a coast-to-coast fortification

SUGGESTED ITINERARIES

THREE DAYS Spend it all in **London** (p. 151), the city of tea, royalty, and James Bond. After a stroll through **Hyde Park,** head to **Buckingham Palace** for the changing of the guard. View the renowned collections of the **British Museum** and the **Tate Modern.** Spend a night at **Shakespeare's Globe Theatre** and have a drink or two in the **East End.**

ONE WEEK Begin in **Oxford** (1 day; p. 202) and travel north to Scotland for one day in **Glasgow** (p. 248). Then head over for two days in lively **Edinburgh** (p. 238) before going to **London** (3 days).

BEST OF BRITAIN, THREE WEEKS Start in **London** (4 days), where you'll carouse the museums, theaters, and clubs. Tour the college greens in **Oxford** (2 day), then amble through the rolling hills of the **Cotswolds** (1 day; p. 210). Don't miss Shakespeare's hometown, **Stratford-upon-Avon** (1 day; p. 208), or that of the Beatles, **Liverpool** (1 days; 220). Head to **Manchester** for its nightlife (1 day; p. 216) before moving on to **Glasgow** (1 day) and nearby **Loch Lomond** (1 day; p. 252). Exuberant **Edinburgh** will keep you busy, especially during festival season (4 days). Finally, enjoy the beautiful **Lake District** (2 days; p. 228), historic **York** (1 day, p. 223), and the hallowed halls of **Cambridge** (2 day; p. 211).

BRITAIN

designed to keep out unfriendly neighbors. The 4th century saw the decline of the Roman Empire, leaving Britannia vulnerable to raids. This allowed the Angles and Saxons to establish their own kingdoms in the south.

CHRISTIANITY AND THE NORMANS. Christianity caught on in 597 when **August-ine** converted King Æthelbert and founded England's first papal church at **Can-terbury** (p. 195). Christianity continued to flourish in England even after Edward the Confessor, the last Anglo-Saxon king, lost his throne to an up-and-coming Norman named Will. Better known as **The Conqueror,** William I invaded in 1066, and won the pivotal **Battle of Hastings** for the crown. William introduced **feudalism** to Britain, doling out vast tracts of land to the royals and sub-jugating English tenants to French lords.

PLANTAGENETS AND TUDORS. In 1215, noblemen forced King John to sign the **Magna Carta** (p. 198), the document that inspired modern English democracy; the first 'modern' **Parliament** convened 80 years later. While English kings expanded the nation's boundaries, the **Black Death** ravaged its population, kill-ing more than one-third of all Britons between 1348 and 1361. Many more fell in the **Hundred Years' War,** a costly squabble over the French throne. The **Wars of the Roses** (1455-1485)—a lengthy crisis of royal succession between the houses of Lancaster and York—culminated when Richard of York put his nephew, boy-king Edward V, in the Tower of London for safe-keeping. When Edward disappeared, Uncle Dick was conveniently crowned Richard III.

REFORMATION, REPUBLICANISM, AND RESTORATION. **Henry VIII,** crowned in 1509, converted Britain from Roman Catholicism to Protestantism; **Elizabeth I** cemented the success of the reformation. The first union of England, Wales, and Scotland effectively took place in 1603, when **James VI** of Scotland ascended to the throne as **James I** of England. The monarchy was abolished during the **English Civil Wars** (1642-1651), and the first British Commonwealth was founded in 1649. **Oliver Cromwell** emerged as the charismatic but hopelessly despotic mil-itary leader of the new Commonwealth. Much to the relief of the masses, the Republic collapsed under the lackluster leadership of Cromwell's son Richard. **Charles II** returned to power unconditionally in 1660. Debate raged over whether to exclude Charles's fervently Catholic brother **James II** from the suc-cession, which established England's first political parties: the **Whigs,** who insisted on exclusion, and the **Tories,** who supported hereditary succession.

PARLIAMENT AND THE CROWN. James II took the throne in 1685, but lost it three years later to his son-in-law, Dutch Protestant **William of Orange.** After James fled to France, William and his wife Mary wrote the **Bill of Rights** to ensure the Protestantism of future kings. The ascension of William and Mary marked the end of a century of upheaval and the debut of a more liberal age in which Britain rose to economic and political predominance. By the end of the **Seven Years' War** (1756-1763), Britain controlled Canada and the 13 colonies to the south, as well as much of the Caribbean. Meanwhile, Parliament prospered thanks to the inef-fectual leadership of the Hanoverian kings, **Georges I, II, and III,** and the office of Prime Minister soon eclipsed the monarchy as the seat of power.

EMPIRE AND INDUSTRY. During the 18th and 19th centuries, Britain came to rule more than one quarter of the world's population and two-fifths of its land. The **Napoleonic Wars** (1800-1815) revived the Anglo-French rivalry, and added significantly to Britain's colonies, which by 1858 included Australia, India and South Africa. The **Industrial Revolution** continued to fuel Britain as a world power. Massive portions of the rural populace, pushed off their land and lured

BRITAIN

BRITAIN

Britain

FRANCE

North Sea

English Channel

Irish Sea

Celtic Sea

ENGLAND

WALES

IRELAND

CHANNEL

TO ROTTERDAM, ZEEBRUGGE
TO HOEK VAN HOLLAND, ESBJERG, HAMBURG, OSLO
TO DUNKERQUE
TO DIEPPE
TO LE HAVRE, CHERBOURG
TO CHERBOURG, GUERNSEY, JERSEY
TO CHERBOURG
TO SANTANDER, ROSCOFF
TO LE HAVRE, CHERBOURG
TO LE HAVRE
TO LE HAVRE, CHERBOURG

Calais
Boulogne
Dover
Ramsgate
Canterbury
Folkestone
Eastbourne
Newhaven
Brighton
Chichester
Portsmouth
Isle of Wight
Bournemouth
Weymouth
Southampton
Winchester
South Downs
Windsor
Heathrow
Gatwick
Stansted
London
Southend
Great Yarmouth
Felixstowe
Harwich
Ipswich
Colchester
Bury St. Edmunds
Cambridge
Ely
Norwich
NORFOLK BROADS NATL. PARK
King's Lynn
The Fens
Peterborough
Stamford
Northampton
Chiltern Hills
Oxford
Stonehenge
Salisbury
Cotswolds
Cheltenham
Gloucester
Stratford-upon-Avon
Worcester
Birmingham
Wolverhampton
Shrewsbury
Hereford
Cambrian Mts.
BRECON BEACONS NATL. PARK
Carmarthen
Cardiff
Cardiff Airport
Swansea
Tenby
PEMBROKESHIRE COAST NATL. PARK
Fishguard
Milford Haven
Aberystwyth
Machynlleth
Llŷn Peninsula
SNOWDONIA NATL. PARK
Mt. Snowdon
Bangor
Isle of Anglesey
Holyhead
Wrexham
Chester
Crewe
Stoke-on-Trent
Nottingham
Leicester
Derby
PEAK DISTRICT NATL. PARK
Sheffield
Manchester
Liverpool
Southport
Blackpool
Fleetwood
Heysham
LAKE DISTRICT NATL. PARK
Windermere
Isle of Man
Peel
Douglas
Leeds
York
YORKSHIRE DALES NATL. PARK
Kingston-Upon-Hull
Grimsby
Skegness
Lincoln
NORTH YORK MOORS NATL. PARK
Scarborough
Whitby
Middlesbrough
Darlington
Durham

Bath
Bristol
R. Severn
Minehead
EXMOOR NATL. PARK
Barnstaple
Taunton
Dorchester
Exeter
DARTMOOR NATL. PARK
Bodmin
Padstow
Newquay
St. Ives
Penzance
Truro
Falmouth
Plymouth
Isles of Scilly

Dublin
Newry
Dundalk
Drogheda
Boyne Valley
Mullingar
Athlone
Kildare
Wicklow
Wexford
Rosslare Harbour
Kilkenny
Waterford
Portlaoise
Roscommon
Shannon
Limerick
Mallow
Cork
Clonakilty
Skibbereen
Kenmare
Bantry
Killarney
KILLARNEY NATL. PARK
Tralee
Doolin
Galway
Aran Islands
Westport
Ballina
Sligo
Lough Derg

30 miles
30 kilometers

BRITAIN

by growing opportunities in industrial employment, migrated to towns like **Manchester** (p. 216) and **Sheffield.** The **Gold Standard,** which Britain adopted in 1821, established the pound's value with gold as an international financial system, securing Britain's economic supremacy.

THE VICTORIAN ERA. The long and stable rule of **Queen Victoria** (1837-1901) set the tone for foreign and domestic politics and even stylistic mores. A series of **Factory** and **Reform Acts** throughout the century limited child labor, capped the average workday, and made sweeping changes in voting rights. By 1906, trade unions found a political voice in the **Labour Party.** Yet pressures to alter the position of other marginalized groups proved ineffectual, as the rich and bohemian embraced *fin-de-siecle* decadence; women, for instance, would have to wait for the vote until after the trauma of **World War I.**

THE WORLD WARS. The **Great War,** as WWI was known until 1939, brought British military action back to the European stage, scarred the national spirit with the loss of a generation of young men, and dashed Victorian dreams of a peaceful, progressive society. The 1930s brought **depression** and mass unemployment, and tensions in Europe escalated once again with the German reoccupation of the Rhineland. Britain declared war on September 3, 1939. Even the Great War failed to prepare the British Isles for the utter devastation of **World War II.** German air raids began the prolonged **Battle of Britain** in the summer of 1940, and English cities were further demolished by thunderous **Blitzkriegs.** The fall of France precipitated the creation of a war cabinet, led by the eloquent **Winston Churchill.** With the 1944 **D-Day Invasion** of Normandy, the tide of the war changed; peace came to Europe in May 1945.

THE POST-WAR YEARS. With increasing immigration from former colonies and a growing rift between the rich and poor, post-war Britain faced economic and cultural problems that still rankle today. Britain joined the **European Economic Community (EEC)** in 1971, a move that received a rocky welcome from many Britons. It was against this backdrop that Britain grasped for change, electing "Iron Lady" **Margaret Thatcher** as Prime Minister. Her policies brought dramatic prosperity to many but sharpened the divide between the haves and have-nots. Aggravated by her resistance to the EEC, the Conservative Party conducted a vote of no confidence that led to Thatcher's 1990 resignation and the election of **John Major.** In 1993, the Major government suffered its first embarrassment when the British pound toppled out of the EEC's monetary regulation system. Major remained unpopular, and by 1995 his ratings were so low that he resigned as Party leader to force a leadership election. He won the election, but the Conservatives lost parliamentary seats and continued to languish in the polls.

TODAY

HOW BRITANNIA IS RULED. Since the 1700s the monarch has served in a purely symbolic role, leaving real power to **Parliament,** which consists of the **House of Commons,** with its elected Members of Parliament (MPs), and the **House of Lords,** most of whom are government-appointed Life Peers. All members of the executive branch, which includes the **Prime Minister** and the **Cabinet,** are also MPs; this fusing of legislative and executive functions, called the "efficient secret" of the British government, ensures the quick passage of the majority party's programs into bills. The two main parties are **Labour** and the **Conservatives,** representing roughly the left and the right respectively.

CURRENT EVENTS. Under the leadership of charismatic **Tony Blair,** the Labour Party reduced ties with unions, refashioned itself into the alternative for discontented voters, and finally began to rise in popularity. In 1999, however, Blair earned the title of "little Clinton" for his blind conformance to American foreign policy. After the September 11th attacks of 2002, Britain again gave its unilateral support to the US. Blair's detractors believe that Britain's refusal to adopt the **euro** is another sign that his sympathies with the US are greater than those with Europe. Throughout 2002, the British government prepared for the perhaps-inevitable currency switch-over, conducting five "tests" to see if Britain and the euro are compatible. The issue could go before the voters in a referendum in 2003.

Blair's Labour government has also initiated domestic devolution in Scotland and Wales. The Scots voted in a 1997 referendum to have their own Parliament, which opened in 1999, and the Welsh opened their National Assembly in 1999. Progress has been more halting in the latest attempts at Northern Irish autonomy; the British government suspended Belfast's **Stormont Assembly** in 2000, hoping to instigate the decommissioning of arms by the IRA and their Unionist counterparts. A lack of progress satisfactory to either side led to a year of violence throughout 2001 and into 2002. The Good Friday Agreement leads a precarious existence between cease-fires, election outcomes, and disarmament promises.

THE ARTS

LITERATURE

Geoffrey Chaucer tapped into the spirited side of Middle English; his *Canterbury Tales* (c. 1387) remain some of the funniest stories in the English canon. English literature flourished under the reign of Elizabeth I. The era's greatest contributions were dramatic, with the appearance of the first professional playwrights. The son of a glove-maker from Stratford-upon-Avon (p. 208), **William Shakespeare** looms over all of English literature. The British Puritans of the late 16th and early 17th centuries produced a huge volume of obsessive and beautiful literature, including **John Milton**'s epic *Paradise Lost* (1667). In 1719, **Daniel Defoe** inaugurated the era of the English novel with his popular island-bound *Robinson Crusoe*. By the end of the century, **Jane Austen** had perfected the narrative technique; most of her great novels were written in a cottage near Winchester (p. 197).

The Romantic movement of the early 1800s found its greatest expression in poetry. The watershed *Lyrical Ballads* by **William Wordsworth** and **Samuel Taylor Coleridge** included classics like "Lines Composed a Few Miles above Tintern Abbey" (p. 233) and "The Rime of the Ancient Mariner." Victorian poverty and social change spawned the classic, sentimental novels of **Charles Dickens.** In the early 20th century, **Virginia Woolf** tried to capture the spirit of time and the mind in her novels; she and the Irish expatriate **James Joyce** were among the most groundbreaking practitioners of **Modernism.** One of Modernism's poetic champions was **T.S. Eliot;** his influential poem "The Waste Land" (1922) portrays London as a fragmented and barren desert awaiting redemption. The end of the Empire and the growing gap between the classes splintered British literature in a thousand directions. Postcolonial voices like **Salman Rushdie** and 2002 Nobel laureate **V.S. Naipaul** have become an important literary force, and England continues to produce acclaimed works from writers like **A.S. Byatt** and **Martin Amis.**

Britain has also produced volumes of children's literature. **Lewis Carroll's** *Alice's Adventures in Wonderland* (1865) and **C.S. Lewis**'s *Chronicles of Narnia* (1950-1956) have enchanted for generations. **J.R.R. Tolkien** wrote fanciful tales of elves, wizards, short folk, and rings (*The Hobbit*, 1934; *Lord of the Rings*, 1954-56), and recently, **J.K. Rowling** has swept the world with her tale of juvenile wizardry in the blockbuster *Harry Potter* series.

BRITAIN

MUSIC

During the Renaissance, English ears were tuned to cathedral anthems, psalms, madrigals, and the odd lute performance. **Henry Purcell** (1659-1695) rang in the Baroque with instrumental music for Shakespeare's plays as well as England's first great opera, *Dido and Aeneas*. The 18th century welcomed the visits of the foreign geniuses Mozart, Haydn, and **George Frideric Handel**, a German composer who wrote operas in the Italian style but spent most of his life in Britain. Today's audiences are probably familiar with the operettas of **W.S. Gilbert** (1836-1911) and **Arthur Sullivan** (1842-1900); the pair were rumored to hate each other, but managed to produce gems such as *The Mikado* and *The Pirates of Penzance*. The world wars provoked **Benjamin Britten**'s (1913-1976) heartbreaking *War Requiem* and **Michael Tippett**'s (1905-1998) humanitarian oratorio, *A Child of Our Time*. Later 20th-century trends, including **Andrew Lloyd Webber**'s blend of opera, popular music, and falling chandeliers, demonstrate the commercially lucrative shift of British musical influence.

The **British Invasion** groups of the 1960s infiltrated the world with daring, controversial sound. The **Beatles** were the ultimate trendsetters, still influential more than three decades after their break-up. The edgier lyrics and grittier sound of the **Rolling Stones** shifted teens' thoughts from "I Wanna Hold Your Hand" to "Let's Spend the Night Together." Over the next 20 years, England imported the Urban "mod" sound of **The Who** and guitar gurus Eric Clapton of **Cream** and Jimmy Page of **Led Zeppelin**. In the mid-1970s, British rock schismed, as the theatrical excesses of **glam rock** performers like **Elton John** and **David Bowie** contrasted with the conceptual, album-oriented **art rock** emanating from **Pink Floyd**. Punk rock bands like **The Clash** emerged from Britain's industrial centers as a counter to self-indulgence.

British bands continued to achieve popular success on both sides of the Atlantic thanks to the 1980s advent of America's Music Television. **Dire Straits, Duran Duran**, the **Eurythmics, Boy George, Tears for Fears**, and the **Police** have all enjoyed many top-10 hits. England's influence on dance music is still significant; it boasts such stars as the **Chemical Brothers** and **Fatboy Slim**. Beatlesesque bands the **Verve** and **Oasis** cherish dreams of rock 'n' roll stardom, while the tremendous popularity of American grunge rock inspired a host of poseurs in the UK, reaching maturity with Oxford's conceptual innovators, **Radiohead**.

THE VISUAL ARTS

ARCHITECTURE. The cathedrals and castles of England's skyline trace a history of foreign conquests. Houses of worship began as stone, but gave way to cathedrals like **Winchester** (p. 197). The Normans introduced Romanesque architecture, and the Gothic period ushered in intricate buildings like the **Salisbury** (p. 198) cathedral and **King's College Chapel** in Cambridge (p. 211). Christopher Wren's dome on **St. Paul's Cathedral** (p. 171) attests to the capabilities of Renaissance architecture. Early domestic architecture progressed from the stone dwellings of pre-Christian folk to Roman forts and villas to squat Norman castles like the **Tower of London** (p. 171). The Renaissance was ushered in with sumptuous Tudor homes like Henry VIII's **Hampton Court** (p. 180). The **Arts and Crafts** movement was an architectural revival during the Victorian period that gave us the neo-Gothic **Houses of Parliament** (p. 169) and the neo-Classical **British Museum** (p. 181). Today, **Richard Rogers** and **Norman Foster** vie for bragging rights as England's most influential architect, littering London with several tributes to the millennium (p. 173).

FILM. British film has endured an uneven history, marked by cycles of relative independence from Hollywood followed by increasing drains of talent to America. The Royal Shakespeare Company has produced a heavyweight set of alumni, like **Dame Judi Dench** and **Sir Ian McKellen**, who then made the transition to celluloid. Earlier

Shakespeare impresario **Laurence Olivier** worked both sides of the camera in *Henry V* (1944); his *Hamlet* (1948) is still the hallmark Dane. Master of suspense **Alfred Hitchcock** snared audiences with films produced in both Britain and the US. The 1960s phenomenon of "swingin' London" created new momentum for the British film industry and jump-started international interest in British culture. American **Richard Lester** made pop stars into film stars in the Beatles' *A Hard Day's Night* (1963), and Scot **Sean Connery** downed the first of many martinis as James Bond in *Dr. No* (1962).

Elaborate costume drama and offbeat independent films have come to represent contemporary British film. **Kenneth Branagh** has focused his talents on adapting Shakespeare for the screen, with glossy, acclaimed works like *Hamlet* (1996). A new entry into the world of blockbusterdom is the *Harry Potter* franchise, which kicked off in 2001.

ON THE CANVAS. Secular patronage and court painters followed Britain's early, religiously-oriented art. Portrait artist **Thomas Gainsborough** propagated an interest in landscape painting, which peaked in the 19th century with his contemporaries **J.M.W. Turner** and **John Constable.** The Victorian era of revival saw movements like **Dante Gabriel Rossetti's** (1828-82) Italian-inspired, damsel-laden Pre-Raphaelite school. Modernist trends from the Continent, like cubism and expressionism, were picked up by **Wyndham Lewis** (1882-1957) and **Henry Moore** (1898-1986). WWII inspired experimental works by **Francis Bacon** and **Lucian Freud.** The precocious **Young British Artists (YBAs)** of the 1990s include sculptor **Rachel Whitbread** and multi-media artist **Damien Hirst.**

FACTS AND FIGURES

Official Name: United Kingdom of Great Britain and Northern Ireland.

Capital: London.

Major Cities: Cardiff, Glasgow, Edinburgh, Liverpool, Manchester.

Population: 59,800,000.

Land Area: 241,590 sq. km.

Time Zone: GMT.

Language: English; also Welsh, Scottish, and Gaelic.

Religions: Anglican and Roman Catholic (72%), Muslim (3%), other (25%).

ESSENTIALS

WHEN TO GO

It may be wise to plan around the high season (June-Aug.). Spring or autumn (Apr.-May and Sept.-Oct.) are more appealing times to visit; the weather is still reasonable and flights are cheaper, though there may be fewer services in rural areas. If you intend to visit the large cities and linger indoors at museums and theaters, the off season (Nov.-Mar.) is most economical. Keep in mind, however, that sights and accommodations often close or run reduced hours, especially in rural regions. Another factor to consider is hours of daylight—in Scotland, summer light lasts almost to midnight, but in winter the sun may set as early as 3:45pm. Regardless of when you go, it will rain; have warm, waterproof clothing on hand.

DOCUMENTS AND FORMALITIES

VISAS. EU citizens do not need a visa. Citizens of Australia, Canada, New Zealand, South Africa, and the US do not need a visa for stays up to six months.

EMBASSIES. Foreign embassies for Britain are in London (p.151). For British embassies and high commissions at home, contact: **Australia,** British High Commission, Commonwealth Ave., Yarralumla, Canberra, ACT 2606 (☎02 6270 6666;

www.uk.emb.gov.au); **Canada,** British High Commission, 80 Elgin St., Ottawa, ON K1P 5K7 (☎613 237 1530; www.britain-in-canada.org); **Ireland,** British Embassy, 29 Merrion Rd., Ballsbridge, Dublin 4 (☎01 205 3700; www.britishembassy.ie); **New Zealand,** British High Commission, 44 Hill St., Thorndon, Wellington 1 (☎04 924 2888; www.britain.org.nz); **South Africa,** British High Commission, 91 Parliament St., Cape Town 8001 (☎021 405 2400); **US,** British Embassy, 3100 Massachusetts Ave. NW, Washington, D.C. 20008 (☎202-588-6500; www.britainusa.com).

TRANSPORTATION

BY PLANE. Most flights into Britain that originate outside Europe land at London's Heathrow and Gatwick airports (p. 151). Some fly directly to regional airports such as Manchester or Edinburgh (p. 238).

BY TRAIN. For info on getting to Britain from the Continent, see p. 44. Britain's train network is extensive. Prices and schedules often change; get up-to-date information from **National Rail Inquiries** (☎(08457) 484 950) or online at **Railtrack** (www.railtrack.co.uk; schedules only). The **BritRail Pass,** sold only outside of Britain, allows unlimited travel in England, Wales, and Scotland (8-day US$270, under-26 US$219; 22-day US$515/360). In Canada and the US, contact **Rail Europe** (Canada ☎800-361-7245; US ☎877-456-7245; www.raileurope.com). Rail discount cards, available at rail stations and through travel agents, grant 33% off most fares and are available to those ages 16-25 and full-time students (£18), seniors (£18), and families (£20). **Eurail** is not valid in Britain.

BY BUS. The British distinguish between **buses,** which cover short local routes, and **coaches,** which cover long distances; *Let's Go* uses the term "buses" to refer to both. **National Express** (☎(08705) 808 080; www.goby-coach.co.uk) is the principal long-distance coach service operator in Britain, although **Scottish Citylink** (☎(08705) 505 050) has coverage in Scotland. **Discount Coachcards** (£9) are available for seniors over 50, students, and young persons ages 16-25; they reduce fares on National Express by about 30%. The **Tourist Trail Pass** offers unlimited travel for a number of days within a given period (2 days out of 3 £49, students, seniors, and children £39; 5 of 30 £85/69; 8 of 30 £135/99; 15 of 30 £190/145).

BY FERRY. Several ferry lines provide service between Britain and the Continent. Ask for discounts; ISIC holders can sometimes get student fares, and Eurail pass-holders can get reductions and free trips. Book ahead June through August. For information on boats from Wales to Dublin and Rosslare, Ireland, see p. 230; from England to the Continent, see p. 44.

BY CAR. To drive, you must be 17 and have a valid license from your home country. Britain is covered by a high-speed system of **motorways** ("M-roads") that connect London with other major cities. Visitors may not be accustomed to driving on the left, and automatic transmission is rare (and more expensive) in rental cars. Roads are well-maintained, but parking in London is impossible and traffic is slow.

BY BIKE AND BY THUMB. Much of Britain's countryside is well suited for **biking.** Many cities and villages have bike rental shops and maps of local cycle routes. Large-scale Ordnance Survey maps, often available at tourist offices, detail the extensive system of long-distance **hiking** paths. Tourist offices and National Park Information Centres can provide extra information about routes. Hitchhiking is illegal on M-roads; *Let's Go* does not recommend hitchhiking.

EMERGENCY	Police: ☎999. Ambulance: ☎999. Fire: ☎999.
PHONE CODES	Country code: 44. International dialing prefix: 00. From outside Britain, dial int'l dialing prefix (see inside back cover) + 44 + city code + local number.

TOURIST SERVICES AND MONEY

TOURIST OFFICES. Visit Britain, formerly the **British Tourist Authority** (www.visit-britain.com) is an umbrella organization for four separate UK tourist boards outside the United Kingdom.

British Tourist Offices at Home: Australia, Level 2, 15 Blue Street, North Sydney, NSW 2060 (☎02 9377 4400; www.visitbritain.com/au); **Canada,** 5915 Airport Rd., Ste. 120, Mississauga, ON L4V 1T1 (☎888-847-4885; www.visitbritain.com/ca); **New Zealand,** P.O. Box 105-652, Auckland (☎09 303 1446; ww.visitbritain.com/nz); **South Africa,** Lancaster Gate, Hyde Park Ln., Hyde Park, 2196 (☎011 325 0343; www.visit-britian.com/za); **US,** 551 5th Ave., 7th fl., New York, NY 10176 (☎800-462-2748 or 212-986-2266; www.travelbritain.org).

MONEY. The **pound sterling** is the main unit of currency in the United Kingdom. It is divided into 100 pence, issued in standard denominations of 1p, 2p, 5p, 10p, 20p, 50p, and £1 in coins, and £5, £10, £20, and £50 in notes. Scotland has its own bank notes, which can be used interchangeably with English currency, though you may have difficulty using Scottish £1 notes outside Scotland. As a general rule, it is cheaper to exchange money in Britain than at home. Expect to spend anywhere from £25-50 per day. London in particular is a budget-buster, with the bare minimum for accommodations, food, and transport costing £30-40. The European Union imposes a **value-added tax (VAT)** on goods and services purchased within the EU, which is included in the price (p. 16). **Tips** are often included in the bill, sometimes as a "service charge." If gratuity is not included, you should tip 10-15%. Tipping the bartender is not expected, though a pub waiter should be tipped. Taxi drivers should receive a 10-15% tip, and bellhops and chambermaids usually expect between £1 and £3. Aside from open-air markets, don't expect to **bargain.**

COMMUNICATION

TELEPHONES. Most public pay phones in Britain are run by **British Telecom (BT).** BT no longer offers phonecards, but charge cards can be purchased that bill directly to your credit card. Public phones charge a minimum of 10p and don't accept 1p, 2p, or 5p coins. Mobile phone are an increasingly popular and economical alternative (p. 30). For **operator assistance** within Britain, dial ☎192. International direct dial numbers include: **AT&T,** ☎0800 013 0011; **British Telecom,** ☎0800 345 144; **Canada Direct,** ☎0800 890 016; **MCI,** ☎0800 890 222; **Sprint,** ☎0800 890 877; and **Telkom South Africa,** ☎0800 890 027.

BRITISH POUNDS (£)	AUS$1 = UK£0.41	UK£1 = AUS$2.41
	CDN$1 = UK£0.46	UK£1 = CDN$2.20
	EUR€1 = UK£0.69	UK£1 = EUR€1.44
	NZ$1 = UK£0.37	UK£1 = NZ$2.70
	ZAR1 = UK£0.09	UK£1 = ZAR11.70
	US$1 = UK£0.64	UK£1 = US$1.57

BRITAIN

MAIL. To send a postcard or letter within Europe costs £0.37; a postcard to any other international destination costs £0.40, while a letter costs £0.65. Address mail to be held according to the following example: Firstname SURNAME, *Poste Restante*, New Bond St. Post Office, Bath BA1 1A5, UK.

INTERNET ACCESS. Britain is one of the world's most wired countries. Cybercafes can be found in larger cities. They cost £4-6 per hour, but you often pay for only the time used, not for the whole hour. Online guides to cybercafes in Britain and Ireland, updated daily, include the **Cybercafe Search Engine** (http://cybercaptive.com) and **Cybercafes.com** (www.cybercafes.com).

ACCOMMODATIONS AND CAMPING

BRITAIN	❶	❷	❸	❹	❺
ACCOMMODATIONS	£10-19	£10-19	£20-30	£31-59	over £60

Hostels are run by the **Youth Hostels Association (YHA) of England and Wales** (www.yha.org.uk) and the **Scottish Youth Hostels Association** (**SYHA;** www.syha.org.uk). Unless noted as "self-catering," the YHA hostels listed in *Let's Go* offer cooked meals at standard rates (breakfast £3.20, small/standard packed lunch £2.80/£3.65, evening meal £4.15, and children's meals £1.75-2.70). Hostel dorms will cost around £9 in rural areas, £13 in larger cities, and £15-20 in London. You can book **B&Bs** by calling directly, or by asking the local tourist office to help you find accommodations. Tourist offices usually charge a 10% deposit on the price for the first night or the entire stay, deductible from the amount you pay the B&B proprietor; often a flat fee of £1-3 is added on. **Campsites** tend to be privately owned and cost £3-10 per person per night. It is illegal to camp in national parks, since much of their land is privately owned.

FOOD AND DRINK

BRITAIN	❶	❷	❸	❹	❺
FOOD	under £5	£5-9	£10-14	£15-20	over £21

Most Britons like to start their day off heartily with the famous, cholesterol-filled, meat-anchored English breakfast, served in most B&Bs across the country. The best native dishes for lunch or dinner are roasts—beef, lamb, and Wiltshire hams—and puddings, including the standard Yorkshire. The ploughman's lunch, served in pubs, consists of cheese, bread, and pickles. Fish and chips (french fries) are traditionally drowned in malt vinegar and salt. To escape English food, try Chinese, Greek, or Indian cuisine. British "tea" refers to both a drink and a social ritual. The refreshment is served strong and milky. An afternoon tea might include cooked meats, salad, sandwiches, and pastries. Cream tea, a specialty of Cornwall and Devon, includes toast, shortbread, crumpets, scones, jam, and clotted cream.

HOLIDAYS AND FESTIVALS

Holidays: New Year's Day (Jan. 1); Good Friday (Apr. 9); Easter Sunday and Monday (Apr. 11 and 12); May Day (May 1); Bank Holiday (May 31); and Christmas (Dec. 25).

Festivals: One of the largest festivals in the world is the **Edinburgh International Festival** (Aug. 10-30); also highly recommended is the **Fringe Festival** (Aug. 3-25). Manchester's Gay Village hosts **Mardi Gras** (late Aug.). Muddy fun abounds at the **Glastonbury Festival,** Britain's biggest homage to rocks (June 27-29).

ENGLAND

In a land where the stately once prevailed, conservatism has been booted in two successive elections and a wild profusion of the avant-garde has emerged from hallowed academic halls. The country that once determined the meaning of "civilised" now takes many of its cultural cues from former fledgling colonies. The vanguard of art, music, film, and eclecticism, England is a youthful, hip nation looking forward. But traditionalists can rest easy; for all the moving and shaking in the large cities, around the corner there are handfuls of quaint towns, dozens of picturesque castles, and scores of comforting cups of tea.

LONDON   ☎ 020

London offers the visitor a bewildering array of choices: Leonardo at the National or Hirst at Tate Modern; tea at Brown's or chilling in the Fridge; Rossini at the Royal Opera or Les Mis at the Palace; Bond Street couture or Covent Garden cutting-edge—you could spend your entire stay just deciding what to do and what to leave out. The London "buzz" is continually on the move—every few years a previously disregarded neighborhood explodes into cultural prominence. In the 1960s Soho and Chelsea swung the world; the late 80s saw grunge rule the roost from Camden; and in the 90s the East End unleashed Damien Hirst and the Britpack artists. More recently, South London has come to prominence with the cultural rebirth of the South Bank and the thumping nightlife of a recharged Brixton.

■ INTERCITY TRANSPORTATION

Flights: Heathrow (LON; ☎(0870) 000 0123) is London's main airport. The **Piccadilly Line** heads from the airport to central London (45min.-1hr.; every 4-5min.; £3.70, under-16 £1.50). The expensive **Heathrow Express** train speeds to Paddington (15min.; every 15min.; £14, round-trip £25). From **Gatwick Airport** (LGW; ☎(0870) 000 2468), the **Gatwick Express** heads to Victoria (30min., every 15min., round-trip £22), as do cheaper **Connex** commuter trains (40min.; £8.20, round-trip £17).

Trains: London has 8 major stations: **Charing Cross** (serves south England); **Euston** (the northwest); **King's Cross** (the northeast); **Liverpool Street** (East Anglia); **Paddington** (the west and south Wales); **St. Pancras** (the Midlands and the northwest); **Victoria** (the south); and **Waterloo** (the south, the southwest and the Continent). All stations are linked by the Underground (Tube). Itineraries involving a change of stations in London usually include a cross-town transfer by Tube. Get info at the station ticket office or from the **National Rail Enquiries Line** (☎(08457) 484 950; www.britrail.com).

Buses: Long-distance buses (known as **coaches** in the UK) arrive in London at **Victoria Coach Station,** 164 Buckingham Palace Rd. (☎7730 3466). Tube: Victoria. Some services stop at nearby **Eccleston Bridge,** behind Victoria train station.

■ ORIENTATION

The heart of London is the vaguely defined **West End,** which stretches east from Park Lane to Kingsway and south from Oxford St. to the River Thames; within this area you'll find aristocratic **Mayfair,** the shopping streets around **Oxford Circus,** the bars and clubs of **Soho,** and the street performers and boutiques of **Covent Garden.** Heading east of the West End, you'll pass legalist **Holborn** before hitting the ancient **City of London** (a.k.a. "the City"), the site of the original Roman settlement and home to St. Paul's Cathedral and the Tower of London. The City's eastern border jostles the ethnically diverse, working-class **East End.**

Westminster encompasses the grandeur of **Trafalgar Square** and extends south along the Thames; this is the heart of royal and political London, with the Houses of Parliament, Buckingham Palace, and Westminster Abbey. Farther west lies rich, snooty **Chelsea.** Across the river from Westminster and the West End, the **South Bank** has an incredible variety of entertainment and museums. The enormous expanse of **Hyde Park** lies to the west of the West End; along its southern border lies chic **Knightsbridge** and posh **Kensington.** North of Hyde Park is the media-infested **Notting Hill** and the B&B-filled **Bayswater.** Bayswater, Mayfair, and **Marylebone** meet at Marble Arch, on Hyde Park's northeast corner; from there, Marylebone stretches west to meet academic **Bloomsbury,** north of Soho and Holborn. **Camden Town, Islington, Hampstead,** and **Highgate** lie to the north of Bloomsbury and the City. A good street atlas is essential for efficient navigation; the best is ▣**London A to Z,** available at bookstores and newsstands (£5).

⌐ LOCAL TRANSPORTATION

Public Transportation: Run by Transport for London (TfL; 24hr. info ☎7222 1234; www.tfl.gov.uk). Pick up maps at all Tube stations. TfL **Information Centres** at Euston; Heathrow Terminals 1, 2, and 3; Liverpool St.; Oxford Circus; Paddington; Picadilly Circus; St. James's Park; and Victoria also offer guides.

Underground: The Underground (a.k.a. the **Tube**) network is divided into 6 concentric zones; fares depend on the number of zones crossed. Buy your ticket before you board and pass it through automatic gates at both ends of your journey. A one-way trip in Zone 1 costs £1.60. The Tube runs approximately 5:30am-12:30am, depending on the line; always check the last train times. See the color maps section of this book.

Buses: Divided into 4 zones. Zones 1-3 are identical to the Tube zones. Fares 70p-£1. Buses run 6am-midnight, after which a limited network of **Night Buses,** prefixed by an "N," take over.

Passes: The **Travelcard** is valid for travel on all TfL services. Daily, weekend, weekly, monthly, and annual cards. 1-day Travelcard from £5.10 (Zones 1-2). Passes expire at 4:30am the morning after their printed expiration date.

Licensed Taxicabs: An illuminated "taxi" sign on the roof of a black cab signals availability. Expensive, but drivers know their stuff. Tip 10%. For pick-up (min. £2 extra charge), call **Computer Cabs** (☎7286 0286), **Dial-a-Cab** (☎7253 5000), or **Radio Taxis** (☎7272 0272).

Minicabs: Private cars. Cheaper than black cabs, but less reliable—stick to a reputable company. **Teksi** (☎7267 0267) offers 24hr. pick-up anywhere in London.

◪ PRACTICAL INFORMATION

TOURIST, FINANCIAL, AND LOCAL SERVICES

Tourist Offices: Britain Visitor Centre, 1 Regent St. (www.visitbritain.com). Tube: Oxford Circus. Open M 9:30am-6:30pm, Tu-F 9am-6:30pm, Sa-Su 10am-4pm. **London Visitor Centres** (www.londontouristboard.com). Tube branches at: **Heathrow Terminals 1, 2,** and **3** (open Oct.-Aug. daily 8am-6pm; Sept. M-Sa 9am-7pm and Su 8am-6pm); **Liverpool Street** (open June-Sept. M-Sa 8am-7pm, Su 8am-6pm; Oct.-May daily 8am-6pm); **Victoria** (open Easter-Sept. M-Sa 8am-8pm, Su 8am-6pm; Oct.-Easter daily 8am-6pm); **Waterloo** (open daily 8:30am-10:30pm).

Embassies: Australia, Australia House, Strand (☎7379 4334). Tube: Temple. Open M-F 9:30am-3:30pm. **Canada,** MacDonald House, 1 Grosvenor Sq. (☎7258 6600). Tube: Bond St. Open M-F 9am-5pm. **Ireland,** 17 Grosvenor Pl. (☎7235 2171). Tube: Hyde Park Corner. Open M-F 9:30am-4:30pm. **New Zealand,** New Zealand House, 80

Haymarket (☎ 7930 8422). Tube: Piccadilly Circus. Open M-F 10am-5pm. **South Africa,** South Africa House, Trafalgar Sq. (☎ 7451 7299). Tube: Charing Cross. Open M-F 9am-5pm. **US,** 24 Grosvenor Sq. (☎ 7499 9000). Tube: Bond St. Open M-F 8:30am-5:30pm. Phones answered 8am-10pm.

Financial Services: The best rates for **currency exchange** are found at banks, such as **Barclays, HSBC, Lloyd's,** and **National Westminster** (NatWest). **Branches** open M-F 9:30am-4:30pm. Call ☎ (0800) 521 313 for the nearest **American Express** location.

Bi-Gay-Lesbian Resources: London Lesbian and Gay Switchboard (☎ 7837 7324). 24hr. advice and support service.

EMERGENCY AND COMMUNICATIONS

Emergency: Medical, Police, and **Fire ☎ 999;** no coins required.

Hospitals: Charing Cross (☎ 8846 1234), on Fulham Palace Rd.; enter on St. Dunstan's Rd. Tube: Baron's Ct. or Hammersmith. **Royal Free** (☎ 7794 0500), on Pond St. Tube: Belsize Park. **St. Thomas's** (☎ 7928 9292), on Lambeth Palace Rd. Tube: Waterloo. **University College Hospital** (☎ 7387 9300), on Grafton Way. Tube: Warren St.

Pharmacies (Chemists): Most pharmacies keep standard hours (usually M-Sa 9:30am-5:30pm). Late-night and 24hr. chemists are rare; one 24hr. option is **Zafash Pharmacy,** 233 Old Brompton Rd. (☎ 7373 2798). Tube: Earl's Ct.

Police: London is covered by two police forces: The **City of London Police** (☎ 7601 2222) for the City, and the **Metropolitan Police** (☎ 7230 1212) for the rest. There is at least one police station in each borough open 24hr. Call to locate the nearest one.

Internet Access: Try the ubiquitous **easyEverything** (☎ 7241 9000). Locations include: 9-16 Tottenham Court Rd. (Tube: Tottenham Court Rd.); 456/459 The Strand (Tube: Charing Cross); 358 Oxford St. (Tube: Bond St.); 9-13 Wilson Rd. (Tube: Victoria); 160-166 Kensington High St. (Tube: High St. Kensington). Prices (from £1per hr.; £2 min. charge) vary with demand. All open 24hr.

Post Office: Post offices are everywhere; call ☎ (08457) 740 740 for locations. When sending mail to London, be sure to include the full postal code, since London has 7 King's Roads, 8 Queen's Roads, and many other opportunities for misdirected mailings. The largest office is the **Trafalgar Square Post Office,** 24-28 William IV St. (☎ 7484 9304). Tube: Charing Cross. All mail sent *Poste Restante* to unspecified post offices ends up here. Open M-Th and Sa 8am-8pm, F 8:30am-8pm. **Postal Code:** WC2N 4DL.

⌐ ACCOMMODATIONS

No matter where you plan to stay, it is essential to plan ahead, especially in summer; London accommodations are almost always booked solid. Be sure to check the cancellation policy before handing over the deposit; some are non-refundable. **Hostels** are not always able to accommodate every written request for reservations, much less on-the-spot inquiries, but they frequently hold a few beds—it's always worth checking. Sheets are included at all YHA hostels, but towels are not; buy one from reception (£3.50). YHA hostels also sell discount tickets to theaters and major attractions. No YHA hostels have lockouts or curfews. The best deals in town are **student residence halls,** which often rent out rooms over the summer and, less frequently, Easter vacations—you can often get a single for a little more than the price of a hostel bed. Book as early as possible. Don't expect luxury, although rooms are generally clean and well equipped. The term **"Bed and Breakfast"** encompasses accommodations of wildly varying quality and personality, often with little relation to price. Be aware that in-room showers are often prefabricated units jammed into a corner.

BRITAIN

London

● SIGHTS

Albert Memorial, **9**	B4
Apsley House, **26**	C4
The Barbican, **73**	E3
British Library, **39**	D2
British Museum, **42**	D3
Buckingham Palace, **28**	C4
Cabinet War Rooms, **56**	D4
Chelsea Physic Garden, **21**	C5
Chinatown, **47**	D4

Courtaud Institute Galleries, **51**	D4
Design Museum, **86**	F4
The Gilbert Collection, **52**	D4
Guildhall, **81**	E3
Hayward Gallery, **62**	D4
The Houses of Parliament, **58**	D4
ICA, **54**	D4
Imperial War Museum, **67**	E5
Kensington Palace, **8**	B4
London Eye, **61**	D4
London Planetarium, **23**	C3

London Transport Museum, **46**	D3
Madame Tussaud's, **24**	C3
Marble Arch, **20**	C3
Millennium Bridge, **76**	E4
Monument, **82**	F4
Museum of London, **74**	E3
National Gallery, **49**	D4
Natural History Museum, **13**	B5
National Portrait Gallery, **48**	D4
Royal Academy, **34**	D4
Royal Albert Hall, **10**	B4
Royal Courts of Justice, **65**	E3

BRITAIN

D E F

The Royal Hospital, **22**	C5	St. Paul's Cathedral, **75**	E3	The Temple, **66**	E3
The Royal Mews, **29**	C4	St. Paul's Church, **45**	D3	Theatre Royal, Dury Lane, **44**	D3
Royal Opera House, **43**	D3	Savile Row, **33**	D3	Tower Bridge, **85**	F4
St. Bartholomew the Great, **72**	E3	Science Museum, **14**	B5	The Tower of London, **84**	F4
St. Bride's, **69**	E3	Shakespeare's Globe		Trafalgar Square, **53**	D4
St. Etheldreda's, **68**	E3	Theatre, **78**	E4	University College London, **41**	D2
St. James's Palace, **35**	D4	Sir John Soane's Museum, **64**	E3	Victoria and Albert Museum, **15**	B5
St. John's Square, **71**	E3	Smithfield Market, **70**	E3	The Wallace Collection, **25**	C3
St. Margaret's Westminster, **57**	D4	South Bank Centre, **63**	D4	The Wellington Arch, **27**	C4
St. Martin-in-the-Fields, **50**	D4	Southwark Cathedral, **83**	E4	Westminster Abbey, **59**	D4
St. Mary-le-Bow, **80**	E3	Tate Britain, **60**	D5	Westminster Cathedral, **36**	D5
St. Pancras Station, **40**	D2	Tate Modern, **77**	E4	Whitehall, **55**	D4

⊖ Underground (The Tube)

🏠 ACCOMMODATIONS

Abbey House Hotel, **2**	B4	Luna Simone Hotel, **37**	D5
Admiral Hotel, **19**	B3	Melbourne House, **38**	D5
Alexander Hotel, **31**	C5	Oxford Hotel, **4**	B5
Amsterdam Hotel, **1**	A5	Quest Hotel, **6**	B3
Balmoral House Hotel, **18**	B3	Swiss House Hotel, **12**	B5
Cardiff Hotel, **17**	B3	Travel Inn County Hall, **32**	D3
Five Sumner Place Hotel, **16**	B5	Westminster House Hotel, **30**	C5
Garden Court Hotel, **5**	B3	Vicarage Private Hotel, **3**	B4
Hyde Park Hostel, **7**	B4	YHA Earl's Court, **11**	B5
LSE Bankside House, **79**	E4		

BRITAIN

BAYSWATER

The streets between **Queensway** and **Paddington** station house London's highest concentration of cheap accommodations, with countless hostels, B&Bs, and budget hotels. The neighborhood is fairly central, with plenty of nearby restaurants, but accommodations vary in quality—be sure to see a room first.

HOSTELS

Hyde Park Hostel, 2-6 Inverness Terr. (☎7229 5101; www.astorhostels.com). Tube: Queensway or Bayswater. Crowded backpacker hostel with flimsy mattresses, but tons of fun. Big dorms are more spacious. Kitchen, bar, and lounge available. Continental breakfast and sheets included. Laundry facilities. Internet access. Ages 16-35 only. Reserve at least 2 weeks ahead. Dorms £11-17.50; doubles £42-45. MC/V. ❷

Quest Hostel, 45 Queensborough Terr. (☎7229 7782; www.astorhostels.com). Tube: Queensway or Bayswater. Offers good beds and more personal space, but dorms without bath could be 2 floors from a shower. Kitchen available. Continental breakfast and sheets included. Laundry facilities. Dorms £14-16; doubles £40. MC/V. ❷

Leinster Inn, 7-12 Leinster Sq. (☎7729 9641; www.astorhostels.com). Tube: Bayswater. A basic hostel with everything you need, including a kitchen, bar, and pool room. Breakfast and sheets included. Laundry facilities. Internet access. 4- to 8-bed dorms £14, with shower £18; singles £25/29; doubles £35/40; triples £57/60. MC/V. ❷

B&BS AND HOTELS

Admiral Hotel, 143 Sussex Gdns. (☎7723 7309; www.admiral-hotel.com). Tube: Paddington. Beautifully kept B&B. 19 summery, non-smoking rooms with bath and tea kettle. Singles £45; doubles £65; triples £90; quads £100; quints £120. MC/V. ❹

Balmoral House Hotel, 156-157 Sussex Gdns. (☎7723 4925; www.balmoralhousehotel.co.uk). Tube: Paddington. Classy establishment with low prices. All rooms with bath, kettle, and hair dryer. English breakfast included. Singles £40; doubles £65; triples £80; quads £100; quints £120. MC/V (5% surcharge). ❹

Cardiff Hotel, 5-9 Norfolk Sq. (☎7723 9068; www.cardiff-hotel.com). Tube: Paddington. All rooms have kettle and phone. Enthusiastic staff and elegant, reasonably sized rooms. Singles are small. English breakfast included. 48hr. cancellation policy. Singles with shower £49, with bath £55-69; doubles with bath £79; triples with bath £90; quads with bath £110. MC/V. ❹

Garden Court Hotel, 30-31 Kensington Gdns. Sq. (☎7229 2553; www.gardencourthotel.co.uk). Tube: Bayswater. Rooms vary widely in size (the quad is tiny), but all are tastefully decorated. English breakfast included. Singles £39, with bath £58; doubles £58/88; triples £72/99; quad £82/120. MC/V. ❹

Vancouver Studios, 30 Prince's Sq. (☎7243 1270; www.vienna-group.co.uk/vancouver). Tube: Bayswater. Fully-serviced studios. The light, airy rooms are large, with kitchenette, hair dryer, phone, TV, and daily maid service; all have private bath and laundry access. Studio for singles £75; doubles £97 (small), £112 (large); triples £137. Single studio Su and F-Sa £60. AmEx/MC/V. ❺

BLOOMSBURY AND MARYLEBONE

Bloomsbury's proximity to Soho makes it well suited for those who want to stay near nightlife. The neighborhood is also close to the British Museum and plenty of cheap restaurants. Many B&Bs are on busy roads, so be wary of noise levels. The area becomes seedier closer to King's Cross.

HOSTELS AND STUDENT RESIDENCES

The Generator, Compton Pl. (☎7388 7655; www.the-generator.co.uk), off 37 Tavistock Pl. Tube: Russell Sq. In a former police barracks, this is the ultimate party hostel. Basement dorms have lockers and military-style bathrooms. Bar and cafeteria. Internet access. Dorms are 18+. Reserve ahead for weekends. Dorms £15-17; singles £42; doubles £53; triples £68; quads £90. MC/V. ❷

Ashlee House, 261-265 Gray's Inn Rd. (☎7833 9400; www.ashleehouse.co.uk). Tube: King's Cross St. Pancras. Not the best neighborhood, but convenient to nightlife. Quiet and friendly. Steel bunks crammed into clean, bright rooms. Kitchen available. Continental breakfast included. Towels £1. Laundry facilities. Internet access. Dorms £15-19; singles £36; doubles £48. Oct.-Apr. reduced prices. ❷

Indian YMCA, 41 Fitzroy Sq. (☎7387 0411; www.indianymca.org). Tube: Warren St. Standard rooms with desk, phone, and shared bathrooms. Continental breakfast and Indian dinner included. Laundry facilities. Reservations essential. Dorms £20; singles £34; doubles £49, with bath £55. AmEx/MC/V. ❸

Pickwick Hall International Backpackers, 7 Bedford Pl. (☎7323 4958). Tube: Russell Sq. or Holborn. 3- to 4-bed single-sex "dorms." Rooms are clean and recently redecorated by the friendly owner. No smoking, no food in dorms, no guests. Kitchen available. Continental breakfast and sheets included. Laundry facilities. Reception 8am-10pm. Reserve 6 weeks ahead for summer. Singles £25; doubles £50 with bathroom; triples £66 with bathroom. Discounts for longer stays. AmEx/MC/V. ❶

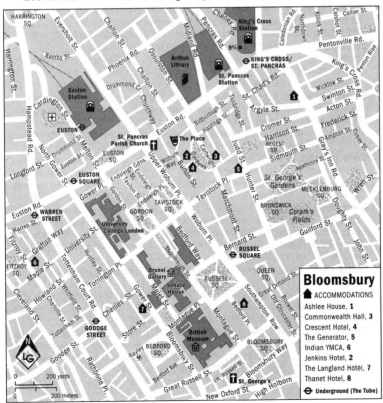

Bloomsbury

🔺 ACCOMMODATIONS

Ashlee House, **1**
Commonwealth Hall, **3**
Crescent Hotel, **4**
The Generator, **5**
Indian YMCA, **6**
Jenkins Hotel, **2**
The Langland Hotel, **7**
Thanet Hotel, **8**

⊖ Underground (The Tube)

BRITAIN

International Student House, 229 Great Portland St. (☎ 7631 8300; www.ish.org.uk). Tube: Great Portland St. A thriving international metropolis. 3 bars, cafeteria, fitness center. Continental breakfast included with private rooms; with dorms £2. Laundry facilities. Internet access. Key deposit £10. Reserve at least 1 month ahead. Dorms £12; singles £31, with bath £33; doubles £50/52; triples £60; quads £72. MC/V. ❷

Commonwealth Hall, 1-11 Cartwright Gdns. (☎ 7685 3500; cwh@lon.ac.uk). Tube: Russell Sq. Basic student-residence singles. English breakfast included. July-Aug. reserve at least 3 months ahead; no walk-ins. Open Mar. 22-Apr. 26 and mid-June to mid-Sept. Singles £23, with dinner £27; UK students £20 (dinner included). MC/V. ❸

Carr-Saunders Hall, 18-24 Fitzroy St. (☎ 7580 6338; www.lse.ac.uk/vacations). Tube: Warren St. Larger rooms than most student halls, with sink and phone. English breakfast included. July-Aug. reserve 6-8 weeks ahead. Open Mar. 22-Apr. 26 and mid-June to mid-Sept. Singles in summer £27; off-season £45/40, with bath £50/45. Discounts for stays over 5 weeks. MC/V. ❸

B&BS AND HOTELS

🏨 **Jenkins Hotel,** 45 Cartwright Gdns. (☎ 7387 2067; www.jenkinshotel.demon.co.uk), enter on Barton Pl. Tube: Euston. Bright, airy, non-smoking rooms with antique-style furniture, phone, fridge, hair dryer, and safe. Guests can use tennis courts. English breakfast included. Reserve 1-2 months ahead. Singles £52, with bath £72; doubles with bath £85; triples with bath £105. MC/V. ❹

🏨 **The Langland Hotel,** 29-31 Gower St. (☎ 7636 5801; www.langlandhotel.com). Tube: Goodge St. Family atmosphere, and sparkling bathrooms cleaned twice a day. All rooms with fan. Singles £40, with bath £55; doubles £50/75; triples £70/90; quads £90/110; quints £100. Discounts for students and in off-season. AmEx/MC/V. ❹

Crescent Hotel, 49-50 Cartwright Gdns. (☎ 7387 1515; www.crescenthoteloflondon.com). Tube: Russell Sq. Artistic rooms in a family-run atmosphere. All rooms with phone and wash stand. Singles £46, with bath £51-73; doubles with bath £89; triples with bath £99; quads with bath £108. Discounts for longer stays. MC/V. ❹

Edward Lear Hotel, 28-30 Seymour St. (☎ 7402 5401; www.edlear.com). Tube: Marble Arch. Clean, cheerful rooms in a pretty location. Each room has phone and kettle. English breakfast included. Free Internet. Singles £48, with shower £60; doubles £67/74, with full bath £83; triples £79/89/99; family quad with shower £99, with full bath £105. 10% discount for stays of 3-4 nights, 15% for 5 nights. MC/V. ❹

Hadleigh Hotel, 24 Upper Berkeley St. (☎ 7262 4084). Tube: Marble Arch. Spacious rooms equipped to executive standards, with bath, phone, kettle, extra sink, minibar, safe, and iron. Continental breakfast included. Reserve 1 month ahead for summer. Singles £65; doubles £75-85; triples £95; 2-bedroom flat £138. AmEx/MC/V. ❺

Thanet Hotel, 8 Bedford Pl., Russell Sq. (☎ 7636 2869; www.thanethotel.co.uk). Tube: Russell Sq. or Holborn. Airy, well-kept rooms in the small, family-run B&B have TV, hair dryer, kettle, and phone. Rooms at the back have a view of the garden. All rooms have private bath. English breakfast included. Reserve 1 month in advance. Singles £69; doubles £94; triples £102; quads £112. AmEx/MC/V. ❺

George Hotel, 58-60 Cartwright Gdns. (☎ 7387 8777; www.georgehotel.com). Tube: Russell Sq. Meticulous rooms with phone, kettle, and sink. Front-facing 1st-floor rooms are best, with high ceilings and tall windows. Internet access. Singles £50, with shower £65, with bath £75; doubles £70/77/90; triples £83/92/105; quads £95. Nov.-June discounts for longer stays. MC/V. ❹

Mentone Hotel, 54-56 Cartwright Gdns. (☎ 7387 3927; www.mentonehotel.com). Tube: Russell Sq. Bright, clean rooms furnished in a variety of styles, with phone and kettle. All rooms with bath. English breakfast included. Free Internet access. Reserve 1-2 weeks ahead. Apr.-Sept. singles £60; doubles £85; triples £95; quads (2 double beds) £105. Oct.-Mar. £55/75/85/95. Discounts for stays over 1 week. AmEx/MC/V. ❹

Royal National Hotel, Bedford Way (☎7637 2488; reservations ☎7278 7871; www.imperialhotels.co.uk). Tube: Russell Sq. London's largest hotel, with 2 lobbies and long corridors. Recently redecorated and meticulously clean. All rooms have bath. Continental breakfast included. Singles £66; doubles £85; triples £102.50. MC/V. ❺

CLERKENWELL

City University Finsbury Residences, 15 Bastwick St. (☎7040 8811; www.city.ac.uk/ems). Tube: Barbican. Student residence with a tower-block facade but renovated interior. Short walk to City sights, Islington restaurants, and Clerkenwell nightlife. Breakfast included. Dinner £4.70. Open June to mid-Sept. Dorms £21, students £19. MC/V. ❸

Rosebery Hall, 90 Rosebery Ave. (☎7278 3251). Tube: Angel. Exit left from the Tube, cross the street, and take the second right onto Rosebery Ave. (10min.). Modern student residence by a sunken garden. English breakfast included. Reserve at least 6 weeks ahead; cancellation fee £10. Open Easter vacation and mid-June to mid-Sept. Singles £26-31; doubles £35-46, with bath £58; triples £55. MC/V. ❸

KENSINGTON

▨ **Five Sumner Place Hotel,** 5 Sumner Pl. (☎7584 7586; www.sumnerplace.com). Tube: South Kensington. The amenities of a luxury hotel with the charm of a converted Victorian, plus an unbeatable location. Spacious rooms have large windows, private bath, fridge, phone, and hair dryer. English breakfast included. Book 1 month ahead in summer. Singles £85; doubles £130. AmEx/MC/V. ❺

▨ **Swiss House Hotel,** 171 Old Brompton Rd. (☎7373 2769; www.swiss-hh.demon.co.uk). Tube: Gloucester Rd. or South Kensington. Large rooms all with phone, fan, and bath. Continental breakfast included; English breakfast £6.50. In summer, reserve 1 month ahead. Singles £51-71; doubles £89-104; triples £120; quads £134. AmEx/MC/V. ❹

Vicarage Private Hotel, 10 Vicarage Gate (☎7229 4030; www.londonvicaragehotel.com). Tube: High St. Kensington. Beautifully kept house with charming rooms. English breakfast included. Reserve 2 months ahead. Singles £46, with bath £75; doubles £76/100; triples £95/130; quads £102/140. ❹

Abbey House Hotel, 11 Vicarage Gate (☎7727 2594; www.abbeyhousekensington.com). Tube: High St. Kensington. Spacious pastel rooms with desk and sink. Very helpful staff. English breakfast included. Singles £45; doubles £74; triples £90; quads £100. Winter discounts. ❹

YHA Holland House, Holland Walk (☎7937 0748; hollandhouse@yha.org.uk). Tube: High St. Kensington. Split between a 17th-century mansion and an ugly 1970s unit; dorms in both are similar and standard. Kitchen available. Breakfast included. Internet access. Book 2-3 weeks ahead in summer. £21, under-18 £18. AmEx/MC/V. ❷

EARL'S COURT

West of fashionable Kensington, Earl's Court feeds on budget tourism. The area is especially popular with Australian travelers. Be careful at night, and be cautious of guides trying to lead you from the station to a hostel. Some B&Bs conceal grimy rooms behind fancy lobbies and well-dressed staff; always ask to see a room.

▨ **Oxford Hotel,** 24 Penywern Rd. (☎7370 1161; www.the-oxford-hotel.com). 3min. from the Connex train to Heathrow or Gatwick. Large rooms with enormous windows afford grand views of the gardens. Continental breakfast included. Reserve 2-3 weeks ahead. Singles with shower £36, with bath £50; doubles £57/67; triples £69/79; quads £87/93; quints £105/115. Discounts for longer stays. AmEx/MC/V. ❹

Amsterdam Hotel, 7 Trebovir Rd. (☎7370 2814; www.amsterdam-hotel.com). Tube: Earl's Court. Suites include kitchenette and lounge. All rooms have private bath, kettle, and phone. Continental breakfast included. Singles £74-82; doubles £84-98; triples £108-112. Suites: Studios £98-101; doubles £102-115; triples £129-140; 2-bedroom £150-160. Discounts for longer stays. AmEx/MC/V. ❺

YHA Earl's Court, 38 Bolton Gdns. (☎7373 7083; earlscourt@yha.org.uk). Tube: Earl's Court. Rambling Victorian townhouse better equipped than most YHAs. Garden. Bright single-sex dorms. Breakfast included for doubles. Sheets included. Reserve at least 1 month ahead. Dorms £19; doubles £52; quads £76. AmEx/MC/V. ❷

Mowbray Court Hotel, 28-32 Penywern Rd. (☎7373 8285; www.m-c-hotel.mcmail.com). Large B&B with elevator and bar. Rooms include trouser press, hair dryer, safe, phone, and bath. Continental breakfast included. Reserve 1 week ahead. Singles £45, with bath £52; doubles £56/67; triples £69/80; quads £84/95; quints £100/110; sextuples £115/125. Discounts for stays over 7 nights. AmEx/MC/V. ❹

THE SOUTH BANK

Though the South Bank has some of the best views in the city, its cheaper hotels don't—still, where else in London could you roll out of bed and be breakfasting by the Thames in five minutes?

■ **Travel Inn County Hall,** Belvedere Rd. (☎(0870) 238 3300; www.travelinn.co.uk). Tube: Westminster or Waterloo. No grand views, but you're seconds from the South Bank and Westminster. Clean rooms near restaurant and bar. Prices by the room make it a great deal for families. Breakfast £5, English £6. Reserve 1 month ahead. Singles/doubles and family rooms (2 adults and 2 children) M-Th £83, F-Su £80. AmEx/MC/V. ❺

LSE Bankside House, 24 Sumner St. (☎7107 5750; www.lse.ac.uk/vacations). Tube: Southwark or London Bridge. One of London School of Economics' well-kept student halls, behind Tate Modern. Elevator, games room, restaurant, and bar. English breakfast included. Laundry facilities. Open July 6-Sept. 20 in 2004. Singles £28, with bath £44; doubles with bath £50; triples with bath £63; quads with bath £84. MC/V. ❸

THE WEST END

■ **High Holborn Residence,** 178 High Holborn (☎7379 5589; www.lse.ac.uk/vacations). Tube: Holborn. Comfortable and modern, this is London School of Economics' best student residence. Suites of 4-5 rooms share phone, kitchen, and bath. Continental breakfast included. Laundry facilities. Open mid-June to late Sept. Singles £30; doubles £48, with bath £58; triples with bath £68. MC/V. ❸

Seven Dials Hotel, 7 Monmouth St. (☎7240 0823; fax 7681 0792). Tube: Covent Garden. Fantastic location and good amenities compensate for smaller rooms. Front rooms are better. English breakfast included. Reserve well ahead. Singles £65, with shower £75, with bath £85; doubles £75/85/95; triple with bath £115. AmEx/MC/V. ❺

YHA Oxford Street, 14-18 Noel St. (☎(0870) 770 5984; www.yha.org). Tube: Oxford Circus. Limited facilities, but an unbeatable location for Soho nightlife. Continental breakfast £3.40. Reserve 1 month ahead. Dorms £24, under-18 £20; doubles £26. ❸

WESTMINSTER

Quiet **Pimlico,** south of Victoria station, is full of budget hotels; **Belgrave Road** has the highest number. Quality tends to improve farther from the station. Though the area is fairly close to major sights such as Parliament and Buckingham Palace, there's little in the way of restaurants or nightlife.

▨ **Alexander Hotel,** 13 Belgrave Rd., SW1V 1RB (☎ 7834 9738; www.alexanderhotel.co.uk). Tube: Victoria. Rooms are lavishly furnished with quality fittings, oak dressers, and comfy beds. Sunny breakfast room. Prices vary according to demand. Singles £45; doubles £65; triples from £75; quads and quints £120. MC/V. ❹

▨ **Westminster House Hotel,** 96 Ebury St. (☎ 7730 7850; www.westminsterhousehotel.co.uk). Tube: Victoria. The welcoming proprietors keep the 10 rooms spotless. Almost all with private bath. English breakfast included. Singles £50, with bath £55; doubles £70/80; triples with bath £90; quads with bath £100. AmEx/MC/V. ❹

Melbourne House, 79 Belgrave Rd. (☎(020) 7828 3516; www.melbournehousehotel.co.uk). Tube: Pimlico. Clean and recently refurbished with friendly staff. Non-smoking. Phones in rooms. Basement double has a bathtub for 2. Continental breakfast included. Reserve 2 weeks ahead. Singles £30, with bath £55; doubles with bath £75; triples with bath £95; quad with bath £110. MC/V (payment on arrival). ❸

Luna Simone Hotel, 47-49 Belgrave Rd. (☎ 7834 5897). Tube: Victoria. Modern rooms with TV and phone are concealed by a Victorian facade. English breakfast included. Singles £40, with bath £60; doubles £60/80; triples with bath £110. Off-season discounts for longer stays. MC/V. ❹

James and Cartref House, 108 and 129 Ebury St. (☎ 7730 7338; www.jamesandcartref.co.uk). Tube: Victoria. Sparkling rooms and well-kept hallways. All rooms come with kettle, hair dryer, and fan. English breakfast included. Reserve with 1-night deposit. Singles £52, with bath £62; doubles £70/85; triples £95/110; family room (1 double and 2 bunks for under-12s) with bath £135. AmEx/MC/V. ❹

Morgan House, 120 Ebury St. (☎ 7730 2384; www.morganhouse.co.uk). Tube: Victoria. Small rooms with kettle and phone for incoming calls (pay phone downstairs); a few have fireplaces. English breakfast included. Reserve 2-3 months ahead. Singles £46; doubles £66/86; triples £110; quad with bath £122. MC/V. ❹

Georgian House Hotel, 35 St. George's Dr. (☎ 7834 1438; www.georgianhousehotel.co.uk). Tube: Victoria. Large rooms with phone, hair dryer, and kettle. "Student" rooms are smaller. English breakfast included. Internet access. Reserve 1 month ahead for Sa-Su and student rooms. Singles £39, students £29, with bath £50; doubles £53/45/69; triples £73/67/87; quads students £77, with bath £97. MC/V. ❹

▢ FOOD

Forget stale stereotypes: In terms of quality and choice, London's restaurants offer a gastronomic experience as diverse, stylish, and satisfying as you'll find, albeit an expensive one. An entree under £10 is regarded as "cheap"; add drinks and service and you're nudging £15. Special offers at lunchtime and in the early evening make it possible to dine in style and stay on budget. Pubs offer hearty staples, but many of the best budget meals are found in ethnic restaurants. For the best ethnic food, head to the source: Whitechapel for Bengali *baltis*, Islington for Turkish *meze*, Marylebone for Lebanese *schwarma*, and Soho for Cantonese *dim sum*.

BAYSWATER

▨ **Aphrodite Taverna,** 15 Hereford Rd. (☎ 7229 2206). Tube: Bayswater. The owners' 20 years of experience is everywhere apparent in this warm Greek restaurant. Entrees £7-10. Chef specials £10-24. The cafe next door has some cheaper specialties. Restaurant open M-Sa noon-midnight. Cafe open daily 8am-5pm. AmEx/MC/V. ❷

▨ **La Bottega del Gelato,** 127 Bayswater Rd. (☎ 7243 2443). Tube: Queensway. Now in his 70s, Quinto Barbieri still makes the best *gelati* this side of the Rubicon. Scoops from £1.60. Open daily 10am-7pm, later in summer. Cash only. ❶

Alounak Kebab, 44 Westbourne Grove (☎ 7229 0416). Tube: Bayswater. A discreet gem among the Persian restaurants in the area. All the dishes, including the kebabs (from £5.60), are served with saffron rice or *taftoon* bread. Open daily noon-11pm. MC/V. ❷

Durbar Tandoori, 84 Westbourne Grove (☎ 7727 1947; www.durbartandoori.co.uk). Tube: Bayswater. Durbar's claim to fame is the extraordinary cooking of Shamin Syed, former International Indian Chef of the Year. Curries start at £5. Set menu for 2, £22. Open M-Th and Sa-Su noon-3pm and 6pm-midnight. MC/V. ❷

BLOOMSBURY AND MARYLEBONE

▨ **ECCo (Express Coffee Co.),** 46 Goodge St. (☎ 7580 9250). 11-inch thin-crust pizzas, made to order, cost an incredible £3.50. Sandwiches and baguettes from £1.50. Rolls 50p. Buy any hot drink before noon and get a free croissant. Pizzas available after noon. Open M-Sa 7am-11pm, Su 9am-11pm. ❶

▨ **Mandalay,** 444 Edgware Rd. (☎ 7258 3696). Tube: Edgware Rd. Looks ordinary, tastes extraordinary; this Burmese restaurant's wall is plastered with awards. Great lunch specials (curry and rice £3.70; 3-courses £6). Entrees £3-5. No smoking. Open M-Sa noon-2:30pm and 6-10:30pm. AmEx/MC/V. ❶

▨ **Patogh,** 8 Crawford Pl. (☎ 7262 4015). Tube: Edgware Rd. Out of proportion portions in the tiny Iranian space; order 'bread' and get a 14 in. flatbread with sesame seeds and subtle spices, just £1.50. Entrees £4-6. Open daily noon-midnight. Cash only. ❶

▨ **Vats,** 51 Lambs Conduit St. (☎ 7242 8963). Tube: Russell Sq. Small front conceals a long romantic wine bar. Food is pricey (entress £10-16), but delicious and innovative. "Good ordinary claret" £3.50 per glass and £14.50 per bottle; Burgundy from £16. Open M-Sa noon-11:30pm; kitchen open noon-2:30pm and 6-9:30pm. AmEx/MC/V. ❸

Diwana Bhel Poori House, 121-123 Drummond St. (☎ 7387 5556). Tube: Euston or Euston Sq. No frills or frippery here—just great, cheap South Indian vegetarian food. Lunch buffet £6, served daily noon-2:30pm. *Thali* set meals £4-6. Open daily noon-11:30pm. AmEx/MC/V. ❷

Giraffe, 6-8 Blandford St. (☎ 7935 2333; www.giraffe.net). Tube: Bond St. Second branch of the world-food micro-chain, with modern decor, and great music. Communal tables. Entrees £7-10. Open daily noon-midnight. AmEx/MC/V. ❷

Ranoush Juice, 43 Edgware Rd. (☎ 7723 5929). Tube: Marble Arch. This tiny arm of the Maroush restaurant empire is commonly regarded as the best Lebanese joint on the Edgware Rd. Lamb kebabs £2.50-4. Open daily 9:30am-3am. ❶

CHELSEA

▨ **Chelsea Bun,** 9a Limerston St. (☎ 7352 3635). Airy, casual diner that serves heaping portions. Early-bird specials available 7am-noon (£2-3). Sandwiches (£1.60-3.20) and breakfasts (from £3.70) served until 6pm. Burgers, omelettes, pasta, and salads £6-8. Open M-Sa 7am-11:30pm, Su 9am-7pm. MC/V. ❶

▨ **Chelsea Kitchen,** 98 King's Rd. (☎ 7589 1330). Dimly lit diner booths provide intimacy and a quietly decadent feel. Entrees, like the roast chicken and mozzarella salad, run about £4; wine is £1.50 per glass and £6.80 per bottle. Open daily 7am-midnight; breakfast served until 11:30am. MC/V. ❷

Bluebird, 350 King's Rd. (☎ 7559 1222). Designer food emporium includes an outdoor cafe and restaurant. Cafe food £6-11. Restaurant fare £16-20. Cafe open M-Sa 8am-11pm, Su 10am-6pm; restaurant open M-F noon-3pm and 6-11pm, Sa 11am-3:30pm and 6-11pm, Su 11am-3:30pm and 6-10pm. AmEx/MC/V. ❷

La Lune, 250 King's Rd. (☎ 7351 5351), entrance on Sydney St. Relaxed and chic cafe, restaurant, and juice bar. French-inspired sandwiches are the centerpiece (£6-10). Smoothies £3. Open daily 9:30am-5pm. MC/V. The **Phât Phúc** noodle bar shares the seating, serving entrees for just £5. Open daily noon-5pm. MC/V. ❷

Buonasera, at the Jam, 289a King's Rd. (☎ 7352 8827). The bunk-style seating makes for a worthwhile experience in itself. Fish and vegetables are bought fresh daily. Grilled fish and steak £8-11.50. Pasta dishes £5-6. Reserve ahead for dinner. Open Tu-F noon-3pm and 6pm-midnight, Sa-Su noon-midnight. MC/V. ❷

THE CITY OF LONDON

▨ **Cafe Spice Namaste,** 16 Prescot St. (☎ 7488 9242). Tube: Tower Hill. The standard-bearer for a new breed of Indian restaurants. The menu features Goan and Parsee specialities. Meat dishes are pricey (£11-13), but vegetarian meals are a bargain (£7-8). Open M-F noon-3pm and 6:15-10:30pm, Sa 6:30-10pm. AmEx/MC/V. ❷

Futures, 8 Botolph Alley (☎ 7623 4529), off Botolph Ln. Tube: Monument. Suits besiege this tiny takeaway for breakfast (pastries 80p, porridge £1) and later for a variety of vegetarian dishes (£2-4). Open M-F 7:30-10am and 11:30am-3pm. ❶

The Place Below, Cheapside (☎ 7329 0789), in the basement of **St. Mary-le-Bow** (p. 172). Tube: St. Paul's or Mansion House. Fantastic vegetarian restaurant. Fresh sandwiches £3-5. Porridge £1.20. Entrees £4-6. Open M-F 7:30am-3:30pm. Cash only. ❶

HOLBORN AND CLERKENWELL

▨ **Bleeding Heart Tavern** (☎ 7404 0333), corner of Greville St. and Bleeding Heart Yard. Tube: Farringdon. Laid-back upstairs pub and cozy restaurant below. Restaurant decor provides a romantic backdrop to hearty English fare, including spit-roasted pork with crackling. Entrees £8-10. Open M-F noon-2:30pm and 6-10:30pm. AmEx/MC/V. ❷

▨ **St. John,** 26 St. John St. (☎ 7251 0848). Tube: Farringdon. St. John has won countless prizes for its eccentric English cuisine. Prices in the posh restaurant are high (entrees from £13), but you can enjoy similar bounty in the smokehouse bar. Excellent lamb sandwich £5. Roast bone-marrow salad £6. A bakery at the back of the bar churns out fresh loaves for £2.50. Open M-Sa 11am-11pm. MC/V. ❷

Bleeding Heart Bistro and Restaurant, Bleeding Heart Yard (Bistro ☎ 7242 8238; Restaurant ☎ 7242 2056). Tube: Farringdon. Around the corner from the Tavern (follow the signs). Among London's finest French restaurants. The Bistro features a prix-fixe menu of 3 courses for around £20. Entrees £8-16. Entrees at the Restaurant £11-19. Both open M-F 11:30am-2:30pm and 6-10:30pm. AmEx/MC/V. ❹

Woolley's, 33 Theobald's Rd. (☎ 7405 3028). Rear entrance on Lamb's Conduit Passage. Tube: Holborn. Narrow take-out joint in two parts: Salads (£1.50-3.70) and jacket potatoes (£2.50-3.50) are dished out from the Theobald's Rd. side, while Lamb's Conduit supplies fresh sandwiches (£2-3). Open M-F 7:30am-3:30pm. Cash only. ❶

KENSINGTON AND EARL'S COURT

▨ **Zaika,** 1 Kensington High St. (☎ 7795 6533). Tube: High St. Kensington. London's best Indian restaurant: Elegant decor, attentive service, and sophisticated food. Appetizers £3-10. Entrees £13-23. Desserts £4-5. 2-course min. for dinner. Lunch fixed menu £12 for 2 courses, £14 for 3. 5-course dinner menu £38, with wine £57. Reservations recommended. Open M-Sa noon-2:45pm and 6:30-10:45pm, Su 6:30-9:45pm. MC/V. ❸

Raison d'Être, 18 Bute St. (☎ 7584 5008). Tube: South Kensington. This comfortable, quiet cafe offers a bewildering range of filled *baguettes* and foccacia (£2.20-5) as well as *salades composées* (£3.50-4.70) and other light dishes. Open M-F 8am-6pm, Sa 9:30am-4pm. Cash only. ❶

Crush, 27 Kensington High St. (☎ 7376 9786). Tube: High St. Kensington. Fresh-squeezed smoothies and juices (£2.50-3.70) with optional vitamin boosters. Cheery, colorful interior: Comfy couches, bright chairs, and a giant fruit mural. Open M-W and F 8:30am-6pm, Th 8:30am-7pm, Sa 9am-6pm, Su 10am-6pm. ❶

KNIGHTSBRIDGE AND BELGRAVIA

■ **Jenny Lo's Teahouse,** 14 Eccleston St. (☎ 7259 0399). Tube: Victoria. Stripped-down Chinese fare at communal tables. *Cha shao* (pork noodle soup) £5.50. Teas (from 65p) are blended in-house and served in hand-turned stoneware. £5 min. Open M-F 11:30am-3pm and 6-10pm, Sa noon-3pm and 6-10pm. ❷

Gloriette, 128 Brompton Rd. (☎ 7584 1182). Tube: Knightsbridge. This venerable *pâtisserie* offers hot meals in a bright cafe atmosphere. Leaf teas £2 per pot. Delicious cakes and pastries £3-3.60. Sandwiches £5-7. Entrees £5. 2- and 3-course set meals £9 and £11. Open M-F 7am-8pm, Sa 7am-7pm, Su 9am-5pm. AmEx/MC/V. ❷

Goya, 2 Eccleston Pl. (☎ 7730 4299; www.goya-restaurant.co.uk). Tube: Victoria. London's most carefully prepared *tapas* menu (£3.50-6 per dish), served in a spacious, tiered dining room. Order 2-3 *tapas* per person. Other Spanish entrees £10-15. Open daily 11:30am-11:30pm. AmEx/MC/V. ❷

NOTTING HILL

■ **George's Portobello Fish Bar,** 329 Portobello Rd. (☎ 8969 7895). Tube: Ladbroke Grove. Choose from the fillets on display or ask them to fry up a new one (£4-5), add a generous helping of chunky chips (£1), and wolf it down outside (no inside seating). Open M-F 11am-midnight, Sa 11am-9pm, Su noon-9pm. ❷

■ **Books for Cooks,** 4 Blenheim Crescent (☎ 7221 1992). Tube: Ladbroke Grove. The chef-owner "tests" recipes from new titles. Offerings change daily, but rely on the cakes (£2). Kitchen open M-Sa 10am-2:30pm. Bookstore open Tu-Sa 10am-6pm. MC/V. ❶

Lisboa Patisserie, 57 Golborne Rd. (☎ 8968 5242). Tube: Ladbroke Grove. Tiny Iberian bakery-cum-cafe, packed with Portuguese and Moroccan men chatting football over their coffee (80p). Broad selection of cakes and pastries (from 45p)—don't miss the Portuguese custard pie. Open M-Sa 8am-8pm, Su 8am-7pm. Cash only. ❶

The Grain Shop, 269a Portobello Rd. (☎ 7229 5571). Tube: Ladbroke Grove. Generous homemade takeaway bakes and salads; mix as many dishes as you like for a small (£2.25), medium (£3.45), or gut-bustingly large (£4.60) box. Organic breads baked on-site (£1-2). Food available noon-6pm. Open M-Sa 9am-6pm. MC/V. ❶

THE SOUTH BANK

■ **Cantina del Ponte,** 36c Shad Thames (☎ 7403 5403), Butlers Wharf. Tube: Tower Hill or London Bridge. Amazing riverside location and high-quality Italian food. Bargain fixed menu £11 for 2 courses, £13.50 for 3 (available M-F noon-3pm and 6-7:30pm). Pizzas £7-8. Entrees £12-15. Live Italian music Tu and Th evenings. Open M-Sa noon-3pm and 6-10:45pm, Su noon-3pm and 6-9:45pm. AmEx/MC/V. ❸

■ **Tas,** 72 Borough High St. (☎ 7403 7200; Tube: London Bridge) and 33 The Cut (☎ 7928 2111; Tube: Southwark). Stylish and affordable Turkish food. Stews and baked dishes—many vegetarian—outshine the kebabs. Entrees £6-8. Live music from 7:30pm. Reservations essential. Open M-Sa noon-11:30pm, Su noon-10:30pm. AmEx/MC/V. ❷

■ **People's Palace,** Royal Festival Hall (☎ 7928 9999). Tube: Waterloo. Despite the Stalinist name, this is the swankiest of the Festival Hall's many eateries. Fantastic location with windows overlooking the river. Dinner is pricey (entrees from £13), but luncheon dishes (served noon-3pm) are all £8. Open daily noon-3pm and 5:30-11pm. MC/V. ❷

Café 7, Tate Modern, Bankside (☎ 7401 5020). Tube: Southwark. On the top floor of Tate Modern; windows on both sides provide stunning views of the city and south London. Artistically presented modern British cuisine. Entrees £8-10. Lunch sandwiches start at £5.50. Open M-Th and Su 10am-5:30pm, F-Sa 10am-9:30pm. AmEx/MC/V. ❷

Cubana, 48 Lower Marsh (☎ 7928 8778; www.cubana.co.uk.). Tube: Waterloo. Look for the giant salsa dancer. Generous *tapas* (£3.50-5) and entrees (£7-10) take second place to the spiky cocktails (£5, 2-pint jug £15). At lunch, get 2 *tapas* for £5, a 2-course meal for £6, and 3 courses for £8. Happy Hour 5-6:30pm. Open M-Th noon-midnight, F noon-1am, Sa 6pm-1am. AmEx/MC/V. ❷

Gourmet Pizza Co., Gabriel's Wharf, 56 Upper Ground (☎ 7928 3188). Tube: Southwark or Waterloo. On the embankment, this adventurous pizzeria offers "tradition with imagination" in the form of pizzas with unexpected toppings (£6-9). Reserve for dinner. Open M-Sa noon-11pm, Su noon-10:30pm. AmEx/MC/V. ❷

THE WEST END

▨ **Masala Zone,** 9 Marshall St. (☎ 7287 9966). Tube: Oxford Circus. Masala Zone's dramatically lit interior has a modern edge, but the food stems firmly from a South Indian tradition, with an emphasis on *masala* or spices. Typical favorites £5-6. *Tapas*-style "street food" £2.80-4.40. Open M-F noon-2:45pm and 5:30-11pm, Sa 12:30-3pm and 5-11pm, Su 12:30-3:30pm and 6-10:30pm. MC/V. ❷

▨ **busaba eathai,** 106-110 Wardour St. (☎ 7255 8686). Tube: Tottenham Court Rd. Wildly popular Thai eatery. Great food (£5-8) at shared tables in a cozy, wood-paneled room. Open M-Th noon-11pm, F-Sa noon-11:30pm, Su noon-10pm. AmEx/MC/V. ❷

▨ **Mô,** 23 Heddon St. (☎ 7434 3999). Tube: Piccadilly Circus. A little piece of Morocco. Mix and match *tapas*-style dishes £6-7.50. Wash it down with sweet mint tea (£2). No reservations, but very popular—arrive early or late. Open M-W 11am-11pm, Th-Sa noon-midnight. AmEx/MC/V. ❷

Ophim, 139 Wardour St. (☎ 7434 9899; www.ophim.com). Sample the entrees, then get unlimited portions of whatever you like best. All-you-can-eat lunch £7.50. Dinner £13.50. Hookahs and red-tinted booths in downstairs lounge. Open daily noon-3pm and 5pm-midnight. AmEx/MC/V. ❷

Mr. Kong, 21 Lisle St. (☎ 7437 7341). You can't go wrong at Mr. Kong. Deep-fried Mongolian lamb £6.50. Pig's knuckles £9. £7 min. Open daily noon-3am. AmEx/MC/V. ❷

Café Emm, 17 Frith St. (☎ 7437 0723). Generous portions in an unpretentious bistro setting. Entrees (£6-8) range from enormous salads to rump steak. Open M-Th noon-2:30pm and 5:30-10:30pm, F noon-2:30pm and 5-11:30pm, Sa 1-4pm and 5-11:30pm, Su 1-4pm and 5-11:30pm. ❷

Itsu, 103 Wardour St. (☎ 7479 4794). The perfection of *kaiten-sushi* (conveyor-belt sushi) in a stylish retro-modern interior. Entrees and sushi £3-7. Expect to spend £15 a person. Open M-Th noon-11pm, F-Sa noon-midnight, Su 1-10:30pm. AmEx/MC/V. ❹

Gordon's Wine Bar, 47 Villiers St. (☎ 7930 1408). Tube: Embankment or Charing Cross. The honeycomb of candle-lit vaults drips with atmosphere. Choose an entree, then pile it on from the self-serve salad bar for £7-9. Sherry and port from wood barrels £3 per glass. Wine £3.60. Open M-Sa 11am-11pm, Su noon-10pm. MC/V (£10 min.). ❷

Carluccio's, St. Christopher's Pl. (☎ 7935 5927; www.carluccios.com). Tube: Bond St. Refined Italian cooking in a bright and bustling environment. Antipasti £4-7. Entrees £5-11. Sandwiches and *calzone* for takeaway £3-4. Open M-F 8am-11pm, Sa 10am-11pm, Su 11am-10pm. AmEx/MC/V. ❷

L'Autre, 5b Shepherd St., in Shepherd's Market (☎ 7499 4680). Tube: Hyde Park Corner or Green Park. London's only Polish-Mexican bistro. Polish fare £9-13. Mexican food £8-12. Open M-F noon-2pm and 5:30-10:30pm, Sa-Su 5:30-10:30pm. AmEx/MC/V. ❷

Tamarind, 20 Queen St. (☎ 7629 3561). Tube: Green Park. 1 of only 2 Indian restaurants in the UK to receive a Michelin star, and the award-winning North Indian cuisine won't break the bank. Vegetarian dishes start at £6. Kebabs £13-22. 3-course set lunch £16.50. Open M-Sa noon-2:45pm and 6-11:15pm, Su 6-10:30pm. AmEx/MC/V. ❷

BRITAIN

WESTMINSTER

▨ **Goya,** 34 Lupus St. (☎7976 5309). Tube: Pimlico. Corner bar where earnest Spanish waiters serve delicious *tapas* to a chattering crowd. Most *tapas* £4-5; 2-3 per person is enough. Open daily noon-11:30pm. AmEx/MC/V. ❸

NORTH LONDON

▨ **Tartuf,** 88 Upper St. (☎7288 0954). Tube: Angel. Have a fantastic cutlery-free experience with an Alsatian *tarte flambée* (£5-6), a cross between a crepe and a pizza, only much tastier. Before 3pm get 1 savory and 1 sweet *tarte* for £7. All-you-can-eat £12. Open M-Th 6-11pm, Sa noon-midnight, Su noon-11pm. MC/V. ❷

▨ **Gallipoli,** 102 Upper St., and **Gallipoli Again,** 120 Upper St. (☎7359 0630). Tube: Angel. Tiled walls and hanging lamps complement Turkish delights like "Iskender Kebap": Grilled lamb with yogurt and marinated pita bread (£6). Make reservations F-Sa. Open M-Th 10:30am-11pm, F-Sa 10:30am-midnight, Su 10:30am-11pm. MC/V. ❷

Le Crêperie de Hampstead, 77 Hampstead High St. Tube: Hampstead. Watch as delicate crepes like Mushroom Garlic Cream (£3) and Banana Butterscotch Cream Dream (£2.60) are prepared before your eyes. 40p extra gets you gooey Belgian chocolate instead of syrup. Open M-Th 11:45am-11pm, F-Su 11:45am-11:30pm. Cash only. ❶

Carmelli Bakery, 128 Golders Green Rd. (☎8455 2074). Tube: Golders Green. The golden, egg-glazed *challah* (£1.30-1.90) is considered the best in London; the bagels and sinfully good pastries (£1.50) aren't far behind. Packed F afternoons. Hours vary, but usually open daily 6am-1am, Th and Sa open 24hr. ❶

Mango Room, 10-12 Kentish Rd. (☎7482 5065). Tube: Camden Town. Small Caribbean menu uses plenty of mango, avocado, and coconut and has an array of potent tropical drinks. Entrees £9-21. Reserve for weekends. Open M 6pm-midnight, Tu-Sa noon-3pm and 6pm-midnight, Su noon-11pm. MC/V. ❷

Le Mercury, 140a Upper St. (☎7354 4088). This sunny little corner restaurant offers delicious and delightfully presented French food. Entrees from £6. Reservations recommended for evenings. Open daily noon-12:30am. MC/V. ❷

Giraffe, 46 Rosslyn Hill (☎7435 0343). With a menu as deliberately international as the world music they play, Giraffe orients itself toward young citizens of the world. Entrees £7-10. M-F 5-7pm get 2 courses for £7 (7-11pm, £9) and 2-for-1 drinks. Family-friendly. Open M-F 8am-11:30pm, Sa 9am-11:30pm, Su 9am-11pm. AmEx/MC/V. ❷

Al Casbah, 42 Hampstead High St. (☎7431 6356). The Moroccan chef cooks up an array of *tajine* meat casseroles (£15-16) and couscous dishes (£14.50-17.50) large enough for two. Open daily 10am-11pm. MC/V. ❹

Galangai Thai Canteen, 29-31 Parkway (☎7485 9930). Simple and sleek with a spicy edge, this Thai restaurant certainly does not look anything like a canteen. Pad thai £5.20. Entrees like deep-fried tilapia fish run from £5-7. Open M-F noon-3pm and 6-11pm, Sa 1:30-11:30pm, Su 1-10pm. MC/V. ❷

Marine Ices, 8 Haverstock Hill (☎7482 9003). Tube: Chalk Farm. The Mansi family supplies superb *gelati* to 1500 restaurants. Get it at the source for £1.50 for a single scoop. Open M-Sa 10:30am-11pm, Su 11am-10pm. MC/V. ❶

SOUTH LONDON

▨ **Bug** (☎7738 3366) in the crypt of St. Matthew's Church, Brixton Hill. Tube: Brixton. Eerie lighting gives a gothic atmosphere. Prices for the mostly vegetarian and fish entrees are high (£9-11), but Sunday's "Bug Roast" gets you 2 courses for £13.50. Reservations essential. Open Su 1-9pm, Tu-Th 5-11pm, F-Sa 5-11:30pm. MC/V. ❸

▨ **Café Bar and Juice Bar,** 407 Coldharbour Ln. (☎ 7738 4141). Tube: Brixton. Plop into a deep leather chair or perch atop a (surprisingly ergonomic) upended bucket in the makeshift bar. Exceptional smoothies, soups, organic quiches, and generous open sandwiches all £4-4.50. Open daily 10am-midnight. MC/V. ❷

EAST LONDON

▨ **Goddard's Pie & Mash,** 45 Greenwich Church St. (☎ 8293 9313). DLR: Cutty Sark. Goddard's has been serving the good folk of Greenwich since 1890. All the original London working-class favorites: Pies 95p (takeaway), eat-in lunch special pie with mash £2. Fruit pie and ice cream £1.20. Eels, jellied and otherwise £2-4. Open M-F 10am-6:30pm, Sa-Su 10am-8pm. Cash only. ❶

Aladin, 132 Brick Ln. (☎ 7247 8210). One of Brick Ln.'s more popular balti joints—even the Prince of Wales has been here. Entrees from £3-7. Open M-Th and Su noon-11:30pm, F-Sa noon-midnight. Cash only. ❷

Beigel Bake, 159 Brick Ln. (☎ 7729 0616). The neighborhood has changed, but the prices haven't—bagels at 12p each. Also platzels, filled bagels, brownies, and pastries, all under £1. Open 24hr. Cash only. ❶

Yelo, 8-9 Hoxton Sq. (☎ 7729 4629). Tube: Old St. This Thai restaurant offers good service and generous portions. Noodles, curries, rice dishes, and salads for £4-5. Open M-Th noon-3pm and 6-11pm, F noon-3pm and 6-11pm, Sa 2-11pm, Su 2-10:30pm. ❷

WEST LONDON

▨ **Café Zagora,** 38 Devonshire Rd. (☎ 8742 7922). Tube: Turnham Green. From the Tube, walk south to Chiswick High St.; turn right, then left onto Devonshire Rd. Oozes elegance, from the attentive, discreet service to the warm North African interior. Inexpensive Lebanese-Moroccan cuisine. Appetizers £2.50-4. Entrees £6.50-13. Excellent desserts £3.50. Open daily 5-11pm. MC/V. ❷

▨ **The Gate,** 51 Queen Caroline St. (☎ 8748 6932). Tube: Hammersmith. Go through the gate and up the external stairs on the right. One of London's top vegetarian restaurants, with an interesting, tasty menu. Plenty of vegan options. Appetizers £4-5. Entrees £8-10. Reserve for dinner. Open M-F noon-3pm and 6-11pm, Sa 6-11pm. AmEx/MC/V. ❷

Maison Blanc, 26-28 Turnham Green Terr. (☎ 8995 7220). Tube: Turnham Green. Delightful little *patisserie/boulangerie,* featuring freshly made pastries and breads, with an emphasis on quality ingredients. Croquettes £3-5. Open daily 8am-6pm. MC/V. ❶

AFTERNOON TEA

Afternoon tea provides a great chance to lounge in sumptuous surroundings that at any other time would be beyond all but a king's budget. Note that you'll often need to book in advance, especially for weekends, and that many hotels have a strict dress code.

▨ **Brown's,** Albemarle St. (☎ 7493 6020). Tube: Green Park. Opened by Byron's butler in 1837, London's first luxury hotel still oozes old-fashioned charm. Set tea £25. No jeans or sneakers. M-F sittings 2, 3:45, and 5:30pm (book 1 week ahead for Th-F); Sa-Su tea 3-4:45pm (no reservations). AmEx/MC/V.

▨ **The Lanesborough,** Hyde Park Corner (☎ 7259 5599). Tube: Hyde Park Corner. For sheer opulence, the Oriental-fantasy interior of The Lanesborough out-ritzes The Ritz. Set tea £25. Champagne tea £27. Dress code: Smart casual. £9.50 per person min.

Fortnum & Mason, 181 Piccadilly (☎ 7734 8040). This locally popular patio restaurant overlooks the food hall of the Royals' official grocery store. Relatively affordable "special" tea (£12) served M-Sa 3-5:45pm. AmEx/MC/V.

St. Martin's Lane Hotel, 45 St. Martin's Ln. (☎7300 5588). Tube: Leicester Sq. This post-modern hotel goes for avant-garde. Bewilder your taste buds with "Asian" (bento) or "Eurasian" tea (£14.50). Casual dress. Tea served daily 3-5pm. AmEx/MC/V.

The Orangery, Kensington Palace (☎7938 1406). Tube: High St. Kensington. This airy Neoclassical building behind Kensington Palace is popular for afternoon teas (from £8) served to a tourist-heavy clientele. Open daily noon-3pm for lunch, 3-6pm for tea. MC/V.

The Ritz, on Piccadilly (☎7493 8181). Tube: Green Park. The world's most famous tea (£31). Reserve 6 weeks ahead for M-F, 3 months for Sa-Su. Daily sittings at noon, 3:30, and 5pm. No jeans or sneakers; jacket and tie preferred for men. AmEx/MC/V.

👁 SIGHTS

ORGANIZED TOURS

The classic London **bus tour** is on an open-top double-decker; in good weather, it's undoubtedly the best way to get a good overview of the city. Tickets for the **Big Bus Company,** 48 Buckingham Palace Rd., are valid for 24hr. on three hop-on, hop-off routes, with 1hr. walking tours and a short Thames cruise included. (☎7233 9533; www.bigbus.co.uk. Tube: Victoria. £16, children £6.) For a more in-depth account, you can't beat a **walking tour** led by a knowledgeable guide. **Original London Walks** is the biggest walking-tour company, running 12-16 walks per day, from the "Beatles Magical Mystery Tour" to the nighttime "Jack the Ripper's Haunts" and guided visits to larger museums. Most walks last 2hr. and start from Tube stations. (☎7624 3978; www.walks.com. £5, students and seniors £4. Under-16 free.)

WESTMINSTER

The City of Westminster, now a borough of London, has been the seat of British power for over a thousand years. William the Conqueror was crowned in Westminster Abbey on Christmas Day, 1066, and his successors built the Palace of Westminster that would one day house Parliament.

BUCKINGHAM PALACE

Originally built for the Dukes of Buckingham, Buckingham House was acquired by George III in 1762 and converted into a full-scale palace by George IV. During the summer opening of the **State Rooms,** visitors have access to the **Throne Room,** the **Galleries** (with works by Rubens and Rembrandt), and the **Music Room,** where Mendelsohn played for Queen Victoria, among others. In the opulent **White Room,** the large mirrored fireplace hides a door used by the Royal Family at formal dinners. Since 2001, Queen Elizabeth has also allowed visitors into the **gardens.** (The Mall; entrance to State Rooms on Buckingham Palace Rd. Tube: Victoria, Green Park, or St. James's Park. ☎7839 1377. State Rooms open Aug.-Sept. daily 9:30am-4:30pm. Ticket Office in Green Park ☎7321 2233. Open late July to Sept. £12, students and seniors £10, under-17 £6.)

CHANGING OF THE GUARD. The Palace is protected by a detachment of Foot Guards in full dress uniform. Accompanied by a band, the "New Guard" starts marching down Birdcage Walk from Wellington Barracks around 10:30am, while the "Old Guard" leaves St. James's Palace around 11:10am. When they meet at the gates of the palace, the officers touch hands, symbolically exchanging keys, et voilà, the guard is changed. Show up well before 11:30am and stand directly in front of the palace, or use the steps of the Victoria Monument as a vantage point. For a less crowded close-up of the marching guards, stand along the Mall between the Victoria Memorial and St. James's Palace. (Daily Apr.-Oct., varies Nov.-Mar. Dependent on whether the Queen is in residence, the weather, and state functions. Free.)

OTHER PALACE SIGHTS. The **Royal Mews**' main attraction is the collection of coaches, from the "glass coach" used to carry Diana to her wedding to the four-ton Gold State Coach and the carriage horses. *(Buckingham Palace Rd. Tube: St. James's Park or Victoria. Open Apr.-Sept. M-Th 11am-4pm. £5.)*

WESTMINSTER ABBEY

On December 28, 1065, Edward the Confessor, the last Saxon King of England, was buried in the church of the West Monastery; a year later, the Abbey saw the coronation of William the Conqueror, thus establishing the Abbey's twin traditions as the figurative birthplace and literal resting place of royalty. It was this connection that allowed Westminster, uniquely among England's great monasteries, to escape wholesale destruction by Henry VIII.

Early English kings are buried around the Confessor's tomb in the **Shrine of St. Edward,** behind which the **Coronation Chair** stands at the entry to the Tudor **Lady Chapel. Poet's Corner** begins with Geoffrey Chaucer, buried in 1400; plaques at his feet commemorate both poets and prose writers, as does the stained-glass window above. At the center of the Abbey, the **Sanctuary** holds the altar, where coronations and royal weddings are held. The simple grave of **Winston Churchill** is just beyond the **Tomb of the Unknown Warrior.** The **Old Monastery** houses the **Great Cloister,** festooned with monuments and plaques, from which passages lead to the **Chapter House,** the original meeting place of Parliament, the **Pyx Chamber** and the **Abbey Museum,** which features an array of royal funeral effigies. The pleasant **gardens** are reached from the Cloisters. *(Parliament Sq.; enter the Old Monastery, cloister, and garden from Dean's Yard, behind the Abbey. ☎ 7222 5152. Tube: Westminster. Abbey open M-Tu and Th-F 9:30am-3:45pm, W 9:30am-7pm, Sa 9:30am-1:45pm, Su for services only. £6, students, seniors, and under-16 £4. Services free. Museum open daily 10:30am-4pm. Chapter House open Apr.-Oct. daily 9:30am-4:45pm; Nov.-Mar. 10am-4pm. Chapter House £1. Cloisters open daily 8am-6pm. Cloisters and garden free.)*

THE HOUSES OF PARLIAMENT

The Palace of Westminster, as the building in which Parliament sits is officially known, has been at the heart of English governance since the 11th century, when Edward the Confessor established his court here. William the Conqueror found the site to his liking, and under the Normans the palace was greatly extended. Westminster Hall aside, little of the Norman palace remained after the massive fire of October 16, 1834; the rebuilding started in 1835 under the joint command of Charles Barry and Augustus Pugin.

THE LOCAL STORY

THE STRONG SILENT TYPE

After 18 years of stony silence, Simon Knowles of the Queen's Guard finally speaks out.

LG: Your uniforms look pretty heavy. Are they comfortable?

A: They're not comfortable at all. The uniform weighs about 3 stone [about 45 lb.] in all.

LG: How do you overcome the itches, sneezes, and bees?

A: Inherent discipline is instilled in every British soldier during training. We know not to move a muscle while on parade no matter what the provocation or distraction—unless, of course, it is a security matter. But our helmets are akin to wearing a boiling kettle on your head; to relieve the pressure, sometimes we use the back of our sword blade to ease the back of the helmet forward.

LG: How do you make the time pass while on duty?

A: The days are long. Smarter men work on horseback in the boxes in shifts from 10am-4pm; less smart men work on foot from 7am-8pm. Some guys count the number of buses that drive past. Unofficially, there are lots of pretty girls around here, and we are allowed to move our eyeballs.

LG: What has been your funniest distraction attempt?

A: One day a taxi pulled up, and out hopped 4 Playboy bunnies, who then posed for a photo shoot right in front of us. You could call that a distraction if you like.

The ostentatious **House of Lords** is dominated by the **Throne of State**. The Lord Chancellor presides from the giant red **Woolsack**. In contrast is the restrained **House of Commons**, with simple green-backed benches under a plain wooden roof. The **Speaker** sits at the rear of the chamber, with government MPs to his right and the opposition to his left. With seating for only 437 out of 635 MPs, things get hectic when all are present. *(Parliament Sq. Tube: Westminster. ☎ 7219 4272. Debates open to the public while Parliament is in session (Oct.-July). M-Th after 6pm and F are least busy. Advance tickets required for Prime Minister's Question Time (W 3-3:30pm). Lords usually sits M-W from 2:30pm, Th 3pm, occasionally F 11:30am; closing times vary. Commons sits M-W 2:30-10:30pm, Th 11:30am-7:30pm, F 9:30am-3pm. Free. Tours Aug.-Sept. M-Sa 9:15am-4:30pm; reserve through Firstcall (☎ (0870) 906 3773). £7, students £3.50.)*

OUTSIDE THE HOUSES. A statue of Oliver Cromwell stands in front of the midpoint of the complex, **Westminster Hall,** the only statue to survive the 1834 fire. During its centuries as a court of law, famous defendants included Saint Thomas More and Charles I. The **Clock Tower** is universally miscalled **Big Ben,** which actually refers only to the bell within; it's named after the robustly proportioned Sir Benjamin Hall, who served as Commissioner of Works when the bell was cast in 1858.

OTHER WESTMINSTER SIGHTS

WHITEHALL. A long stretch of imposing facades housing government ministries, Whitehall is synonymous with the British civil service. From 1532 until a fire in 1698, Whitehall was the main royal palace. All that remains is Inigo Jones's **Banqueting House,** which features magnificent ceiling paintings by Rubens. Charles I was executed on a scaffold outside the house in 1649. *(Whitehall. Tube: Westminster. Open M-Sa 10am-5pm; last admission 4:30pm. £4, students and seniors £3.)* Opposite Banqueting House, tourists line up to be photographed with the Household Cavalry at **Horseguards;** the guard is changed Monday to Friday at 11am and Saturday at 10am. Just off Whitehall, King James St. leads to the ■**Cabinet War Rooms** (p 184). Current Prime Minister Tony Blair lives on **Downing Street,** separated from Whitehall by steel gates. The Prime Minister traditionally lives at #10, but Blair's family is so big that he's had to swap with the Chancellor, Gordon Brown, at #11.

WESTMINSTER CATHEDRAL. Westminster, London's first Catholic cathedral after Henry VIII espoused Protestantism, was started in 1887; in 1903, money ran out, leaving the interior only partially completed. The blackened brick domes contrast dramatically with the swirling marble of the lower walls and the magnificence of the side chapels. An elevator carries visitors up the striped 90m **bell tower.** *(Cathedral Piazza, off Victoria St. Tube: Victoria. Cathedral open daily 7am-7pm. Suggested donation £2. Bell tower open daily 9am-5pm. £3, students and seniors £1.50.)*

ST. MARGARET'S WESTMINSTER. Literally in Westminster Abbey's shadow, St. Margaret's was built for local residents by Abbey monks sick of sharing their church with laymen. It's the official worshipping place of the House of Commons—the first few pews are cordoned off for the Speaker, Black Rod, and other dignitaries. Don't miss the extraordinary grey-hued 1966 Piper Windows. *(Parliament Sq. Tube: Westminster. Open M-F 9:30am-3:45pm, Sa 9:30am-1:45pm, Su 2-5pm. Free.)*

TRAFALGAR SQUARE AND THE STRAND

John Nash suggested the design of **Trafalgar Square** in 1820 to commemorate Nelson's 1805 victory over Napoleon's navy at the Battle of Trafalgar. But it took years to take on its current appearance: Nelson only arrived in 1843, the bronze lions in 1867. The reliefs at the column's base are cast from captured French and Spanish cannons. Every December, the square hosts a giant **Christmas Tree,** donated by Norway to thank the British for assistance against the Nazis. *(Tube: Charing Cross.)*

ST. MARTIN-IN-THE-FIELDS. James Gibbs's 1720s creation was the model for countless Georgian churches in Britain and America. It's still the Queen's parish church; look for the royal box to the left of the altar. The **crypt** downstairs has a life of its own, home to a cafe, bookshop, art gallery, and the **London Brass Rubbing Centre.** *(St. Martin's Ln., in the northeast corner of Trafalgar Sq. Tube: Leicester Sq. Brass Rubbing Centre open M-Sa 10am-6pm. Rubbings £3-15.)*

THE CITY OF LONDON

Until the 18th century, the City *was* London; the rest was merely outlying villages. Yet its modern appearance belies a 2000-year history; what few buildings survived the Great Fire of 1666 and WWII bombings are now overshadowed by giant temples of commerce. Of the 300,000 who work here, only 8000 people call the City home. The **City of London Information Centre,** in St. Paul's Churchyard, offers acres of leaflets and maps, sells tickets to sights and shows, and provides info on a host of traditional municipal events. *(☎ 7332 1456. Tube: St. Paul's. Open Apr.-Sept. daily 9:30am-5pm; Oct.-Mar. M-F 9:30am-5pm, Sa 9:30am-12:30pm.)*

ST. PAUL'S CATHEDRAL

Christopher Wren's masterpiece is the fifth cathedral to occupy the site; the original was built in AD 604. Wren's succeeded "Old St. Paul's," begun in 1087, whose steeple was just one-third higher than the current 111m dome. After three designs were rejected by the bishops, Wren, with Charles II's support, just started building—sneakily, he had persuaded the king to let him make "necessary alterations" as work progressed, and the building that emerged from the scaffolding in 1708 bore little resemblance to the model Charles II had approved.

With space to seat 2500 worshippers, the **nave** is festooned with monuments to great Britons; the tombs, including those of Nelson, Wellington, and Florence Nightingale, are all downstairs, in the **crypt.** Christopher Wren lies beneath the epitaph *Lector, si monumentum requiris circumspice* ("Reader, if you seek his monument, look around"). To see the inside of the second-tallest freestanding **dome** in Europe (after St. Peter's in the Vatican), climb the 259 steps to the **Whispering Gallery.** From here, 119 more steps lead to **Stone Gallery,** on the outer base of the dome, and it's another 152 to the summit's **Golden Gallery.** Back inside, the mosaic of *Christ Seated in Majesty* overlooks the **High Altar.** *(St. Paul's Churchyard. ☎ 7246 8348; www.stpauls.co.uk. Tube: St. Paul's. Open M-Sa 8:30am-4pm; open for worship daily 7:15am-6pm. £6, students and seniors £5, children £3. Worshippers free. Audio tours £3.50, students and seniors £3. 1½hr. tours M-F 4 per day; £2.50, students £2.)*

THE TOWER OF LONDON

The Tower of London, palace and prison of English monarchs for over 900 years, is steeped in blood and history. Conceived by William the Conqueror in 1067 to provide protection *from* rather than *to* his new subjects, the original wooden palisade was replaced by a stone structure in 1078 that over the next 20 years would grow into the **White Tower.** Colorfully dressed Yeomen Warders, or "Beefeaters" (a reference to their former daily allowance of meat), serve as guards and guides.

From the western entrance near the **Middle Tower,** you pass over the old moat, now a garden, entering the **Outer Ward** though **Byward Tower.** Just beyond Byward Tower is a massive **Bell Tower,** dating from 1190; the curfew bell has been rung nightly for over 500 years. The stretch of the Outer Ward along the Thames is **Water Lane,** which until the 16th century was adjacent to the river. **Traitor's Gate** was built by Edward I for his personal use, but it is now associated with the prisoners who passed through it on their way to execution at **Tower Green.** Some of the victims are buried in the **Chapel Royal of St. Peter and Vincula,** including Catholic martyr Saint Thomas More and Henry VIII's wives

Catherine Howard and Anne Boleyn. **White Tower** is now home to a huge display of arms and armor from the Royal Armory. Across the green is the **Bloody Tower,** so named because Richard III allegedly imprisoned and murdered his nephews here before usurping the throne in 1483.

The most famous sights in the Tower are the **Crown Jewels;** moving walkways ensure no awestruck gazers hold up the queue. While the eye is naturally drawn to the **Imperial State Crown,** featuring the Stuart Sapphire along with 16 others, 2876 diamonds, 273 pearls, 11 emeralds, and a mere five rubies, don't miss the **Sceptre with the Cross,** topped with the First Star of Africa, the largest quality-cut diamond in the world. This was hewn from an even larger monster, the 3106-carat Cullinan diamond. Other famous gems include the **Koh-i-Noor,** set into the **Queen Mother's Crown;** legend claims the stone will bring luck only to women. Numerous retired crowns and other treasures are displayed in the **Martin Tower,** at the end of **Wall Walk.** *(Tower Hill.* ☎ *7709 0765; www.hrp.org.uk. Tube: Tower Hill. Open Mar.-Oct. M-Sa 9am-5:30pm, Su 10am-5:30pm; Nov.-Feb. M 10am-4:30pm, Tu-Sa 9am-4:30pm. £12, students and seniors £9. Tickets also sold at Tube stations; buy them in advance to avoid horrendous lines. Audio tours £3. 1hr. tours every 90min. M-Sa 9:30am-3:30pm, Su 10am-3:30pm. Free.)*

OTHER CITY OF LONDON SIGHTS

■ **MONUMENT.** Raised in 1677, Christopher Wren's 202 ft. column stands exactly that distance from the bakery on Pudding Lane where the Great Fire started in 1666. The view of the surrounding city from the top is astounding. *(Monument St. Tube: Monument. Open daily 9:30am-5pm. £2.)*

ALL HALLOWS-BY-THE-TOWER. Holding its own against a vast new Norman Foster development, All Hallows bears the marks of its longevity with pride. The undercroft is home to an array of archaeological finds, including Roman pavements and some striking Celtic carvings. *(Byward St. Tube: Tower Hill. Church open M-F 9am-5:45pm, Sa-Su 10am-5pm. Crypt open M-Sa 10:30am-4pm, Su 1-4pm.)*

GUILDHALL. In this vast Gothic hall, representatives from the City's 102 guilds, from the Fletchers (arrow-makers) to the Information Technologists, meet at the **Court of Common Council,** under the Lord Mayor. The Court meets the third Thursday of every month. *(Off Gresham St. Tube: St. Paul's. Open May-Sept. daily 10am-5pm, Sa-Su 10am-4pm; Oct.-Apr. closed Su. Free.)*

TOWER BRIDGE. This iconic symbol of London is often mistaken for its plain upriver sibling, London Bridge—the story goes that when an Arizona millionaire bought the previous London Bridge and shifted it stone-by-stone to the US, he thought he was getting Tower Bridge. The **Tower Bridge Experience** offers a cutesy introduction to the history and technology of the unique lifting mechanism, though the view isn't all it's cracked up to be. *(Tube: Tower Hill. Open daily 9:30am-6pm; last admission 5pm. £4.50, students and seniors £3.)*

WREN CHURCHES. Aside from St. Paul's Cathedral, the City's greatest architectural treasures are the 22 surviving churches designed by Christopher Wren to replace those lost in the Great Fire of 1666. The most famous is **St. Mary-le-Bow;** traditionally, the term "cockney" is reserved for those born within range of its bells. For the past 800 years, the Archbishop of Canterbury has sworn in bishops in the 11th-century crypt, whose "bows" (arches) gave the church its epithet. *(On Cheapside, near Bow Ln. Tube: St. Paul's. Open M-F 7:30am-6pm. Free.)* **St. Stephen Walbrook,** built from 1672-1679, was Wren's personal favorite. A plain exterior gives no inkling of the wide dome that floats above Henry Moore's 1985 mysterious free-form altar. *(39 Walbrook. Tube: Bank. Organ concert F 12:30pm. Open M-Th 9am-4pm. Free.)*

THE SOUTH BANK

From the Middle Ages until Cromwell's arrival, the South Bank was London's center of amusement; banished from the strictly regulated City, all manner of illicit attractions sprouted in "the Borough" at the southern end of London Bridge. Today, the South Bank is once again at the heart of London entertainment, with some of the city's top concert halls, theaters, cinemas, and galleries.

■ **LONDON EYE.** At 135m, the London Eye is the world's biggest observational wheel. The ellipsoid glass "pods" give uninterrupted views at the top of each 30min. revolution; on clear days, Windsor is visible to the west. *(Jubilee Gardens, between County Hall and the Festival Hall. Tube: Waterloo. Open late May to early Sept. daily 9:30am-10pm; Apr. to early May and late Sept. 10:30am-8pm; Oct.-Mar. 10:30am-7pm; Ticket office, on the corner of County Hall, open daily 8:30am-6:30pm. £11, under-16 £6.)*

THE SOUTH BANK CENTRE. Sprawling on either side of Waterloo Bridge, this concrete complex is Britain's premier cultural center. Its nucleus is the **Royal Festival Hall**, a classic piece of white 1950s architecture. Nearby, the **Purcell Room** and **Queen Elizabeth Hall** host smaller concerts, while just behind, the spiky ceiling of the **Hayward Gallery** shelters excellent modern art exhibitions. The **National Film Theatre,** on the embankment beneath the bridge, offers London's most varied cinematic fare, while the **National Theatre** (p. 185) looms past the bridge. To find out how one of the world's largest, most modern theaters operates, join a backstage tour. *(On the riverbank between Hungerford and Waterloo Bridges. Tube: Waterloo. Tours M-Sa 10:15am, 12:15, and 5:15pm. £5, students £4.30.)*

TATE MODERN AND THE MILLENNIUM BRIDGE. Squarely opposite each other on Bankside are the biggest success and most abject failure of London's millennial celebrations. **Tate Modern** (p. 182), created from the shell of the Bankside power station, is as visually arresting as its contents are thought-provoking. The **Millennium Bridge,** built to link the Tate to the City, was completed six months too late for the Y2K festivities and, following a literally shaky debut, has only recently been stabilized. *(Queen's Walk, Bankside. Tube: Southwark.)*

SHAKESPEARE'S GLOBE THEATRE. In the shadow of Tate Modern, the half-timbered Globe, opened in 1997, sits just 200m from where the original burned down in 1613. Try to arrive in time for a tour of the theater itself, given on mornings during the performance season and 10am-5pm otherwise. Tours include the **Rose Theatre,** where both Shakespeare and Marlowe performed; not much of it is left. *(Bankside. Tube: Southwark. Open May-Sept. daily 9am-noon and 1-4pm; Oct.-Apr. 10am-5pm. £8, students £6.50. See also p. 185.)*

OTHER SOUTH BANK SIGHTS. The giant **HMS Belfast** was used in the bombardment of Normandy during D-Day and then to support UN forces in Korea before graciously retiring in 1965. Kids love clambering over the decks and aiming the anti-aircraft guns. Dozens of narrow passages, steep staircases, and ladders make exploring the boat a physical challenge. *(At the end of Morgans Ln., off Tooley St. Tube: London Bridge. Open Mar.-Oct. daily 10am-6pm; Nov.-Feb. 10am-5pm. £6, students and seniors £4.40.)* The giant curved facade of **County Hall,** almost opposite the Houses of Parliament, houses two of London's most-advertised sights, the **London Aquarium** and **Dalí Universe.** *(Westminster Bridge Rd. Tube: Westminster. Aquarium open daily 10am-6pm; last admission 5pm. £8.80, students £6.50. Dalí open daily 10am-5:30pm. £8.50, students £7.50.)* ■**Vinopolis** is a Dionysian fantasy land offering patrons an interactive tour of the world's wine regions. *(1 Bank End. Tube: London Bridge. Open M and Sa 11am-9pm, Tu-F and Su 11am-6pm. £11.50, seniors £10.50.)* The **London Dungeon** is a grim tourist-trap whose most effective instrument of torture is the obscenely long queue. *(28-34 Tooley St. Tube: London Bridge. Open mid-July to Aug. daily 10:30am-8pm; Apr. to mid-July and Sept.-Oct. 10:30am-5:30pm; Nov.-Mar. 10:30am-5pm. £11, students £9.50.)*

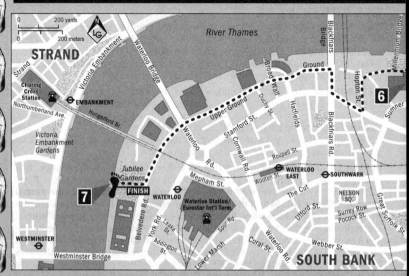

The timeless, understated grace of the Thames, best viewed from the spaceship-like pods of the London Eye, proves that both the area's rich past and its dynamic future fuel its current appeal. Once a rather seedy neighborhood, the South Bank is now home to London's densest concentration of cultural centers, varying from the cutting-edge design of the Tate Modern, which showcases the

Distance: 4km (2½ mi.)

When To Go: Start early morning

Start: Tower Hill Underground

Finish: Westminster Underground

Call Ahead: 5 and 7

best of British contemporary art, to the storied grandeur of Shakespeare's Globe Theatre, which celebrates British artistic traditions of a more mature vintage. Meanwhile, the Jubilee Line Extension, with its acclaimed underground architecture (including a revamped interior at London Bridge), makes transportation to the area easy and enjoyable.

1 TOWER OF LONDON. Begin your trek to the Tower early to avoid the crowds. Tours given by the Yeomen Warders meet every 90min. near the entrance. Listen as they expertly recount tales of royal conspiracy, treason, and murder. See the **White Tower,** once both fortress and residence of kings. Shiver at the executioner's stone on the tower green and pay your respects at the Chapel of St. Peter ad Vinculum, which holds the remains of 3 queens. Get the dirt on the gemstones at **Martin Tower,** then wait in line to see the **Crown Jewels.** The jewels include such glittering lovelies as the First Star of Africa, the largest cut diamond in the world (p. 171).

2 TOWER BRIDGE. An engineering wonder that puts its plainer sibling, the London Bridge, to shame. Marvel at its beauty, but skip the **Tower Bridge Experience.** Better yet, call ahead to inquire when the Tower drawbridge is lifted (p. 172).

3 DESIGN MUSEUM. On Butler's Wharf, let the Design Museum introduce you to the latest innovations in contemporary design, from marketing to movements in haute couture. See what's to come in the forward-looking Review Gallery or home in on individual designers and products in the Temporary Gallery (p. 183). From the Design Museum, walk along the **Queen's Walk,** where you will find the **HMS Belfast,** launched upon Normandy, France on D-Day, 1944.

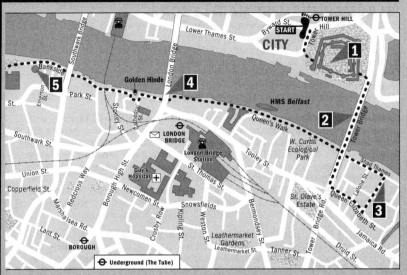

5 LONDON BRIDGE. See the fifth incarnation of a London classic, hopefully more sturdy than its predecessors. The 1832 Old London Bridge is now relocated in Lake Havasu City, Arizona. The **Golden Hinde,** a full-size and functional replica of Sir Francis Drake's 16th-century war ship, is docked on the other side of London Bridge.

5 SHAKESPEARE'S GLOBE THEATRE. In *Henry IV, Part II,* Shakespeare's Davy declares "I hope to see London once ere I die." In time, he may see it from the beautiful recreation of Will's most famous theater. Excellent exhibits reveal the secrets of stage effects, explain how Shakespearean actors dressed, and describe the painstaking process of rebuilding of the theater using only 17th-century methods. You might be able to catch a matinee performance if you time your visit right. Call ahead for tour and show times (p. 173).

6 TATE MODERN. It's hard to imagine anything casting a shadow over Shakespeare's Globe Theatre, but the massive former Bankside Power Station does just that. One of the world's premier modern art museums, the Tate's arrangements create a conceptual spin by juxtaposing well-known masterpieces with works by emerging British artists. Be sure to catch one of the informative tours and don't forget to ogle the rotating installation in the Turbine Room (p. 182).

Having quenched your theatrical and artistic thirsts, sate your stomach at **Cafe 7** and the **East Room** of the Tate Modern, which offer meals and snacks respectively, not to mention fabulous views of the City. As a cheaper alternative, check out the cafes, bars, and boutiques of colorful **Gabriel's Wharf.** If you missed the top floor of the Tate Modern, go to the public viewing gallery on the 8th floor of the **OXO Tower** Wharf.

Pass by the **South Bank Centre** on your way to the London Eye. Established as a primary cultural center in 1951, it now exhibits a range of music from Philharmonic extravaganzas to low-key jazz. Call ahead for dates and times (p. 173).

7 LONDON EYE. Neé the Millennium Wheel, the London Eye has shed its Millennial maiden name thanks in large part to its notorious siblings—the wobbly "Bridge" and the all too visible "Dome". The London Eye has now firmly established itself as one of London's top attractions, offering amazing 360° views from its glass capsules. If you time it right, you can see all of London illuminated by the sunset. Book in advance to avoid long queues (p. 173).

WALKING TOUR

BLOOMSBURY AND MARYLEBONE

Marylebone's most famous resident (and address) never existed. 221b Baker St. was the fictional lodging house of Sherlock Holmes, but 221 Baker St. is actually the headquarters of the Abbey National Bank. Bloomsbury's intellectual reputation was bolstered in the early 20th century when Gordon Sq., east of Marylebone, resounded with the philosophizing and womanizing of the **Bloomsbury Group,** an early 20th-century coterie of intellectuals that included John Maynard Keynes, Bertrand Russell, Lytton Strachey, and Virginia Woolf.

■**BRITISH LIBRARY.** Since its 1998 opening, the new British Library has won acclamation from visitors and users alike. The 325km of underground shelving can hold up to 12 million books. The library also houses a dramatic glass cube containing the 65,000 volumes of George III's **King's Library,** and a stunning display of books, manuscripts, and artifacts, from the 2nd-century *Unknown Gospel* to Joyce's handwritten draft of *Finnegan's Wake.* *(96 Euston Rd.* ☎ *7412 7332. Tube: King's Cross. Open M and W-F 9:30am-6pm, Tu 9:30am-8pm, Sa 9:30am-5pm, Su 11am-5pm. Free. Tours M, W, and F 3pm; Sa 3pm and 10:30am. £5, students and seniors £3.50. Tours Tu 6:30pm, Su 11:30am and 3pm. £6, students £4.50. Reservations recommended.)*

■**REGENT'S PARK.** London's most attractive and popular park, with a wide range of landscapes from soccer-scarred fields to Italian-style formal gardens. The exclusive-sounding **Inner Circle** road separates the flower-filled **Queen Mary's Gardens** from the park without. On the northern edge of the Inner Circle, ■**St. John's Lodge Gardens**—a blaze of lavender entered through an easy-to-miss gate on the Inner Circle itself—remain open to the public. The Holme, overlooking the lake on the western side of the Inner Circle, was designed in 1818 by the 18-year-old prodigy Decimus Burton. *(500 acres stretching north from Marylebone Rd. to Camden Town. Tube: Baker St., Regent's Park, Great Portland St., or Camden Town. Open daily 6am-dusk. Free.)*

ACADEMIA. The strip of land along **Gower Street** and immediately to its west is London's academic heartland. Established in 1828, **University College London** was the first in Britain to admit Catholics, Jews, and women. The embalmed body of founder **Jeremy Bentham** has been on display in the South Cloister since 1850. *(Main entrance on Gower St. South Cloister entrance through the courtyard. Tube: Warren St.)* Now the administrative headquarters of the University of London, **Senate House** was the model for the Ministry of Truth in *1984;* George Orwell worked there as part of the BBC propaganda unit in WWII. *(At the southern end of Malet St. Tube: Goodge St.)*

HOLBORN AND CLERKENWELL

Squeezed between the capitalism of the City and the commercialism of the West End, Holborn is historically the home of two of the world's least-loved professions—lawyers and journalists.

INNS OF COURT. These venerable institutions house the chambers of practicing barristers and provide apprenticeships for law students. Most were founded in the 13th century when a royal decree barred the clergy from the courts, giving rise to a class of professional advocates. Most impressive of the four Inns is the ■**Temple,** south of Fleet St. *(Between Fleet St., Essex St., Victoria Embankment, and Temple Ave./Bouvier St. Numerous passages lead from these streets into the Temple. Tube: Temple.)* The 12th-century **Temple Church** is the finest round church in England. *(Open W-Th 11am-4pm, Sa 10am-2:30pm, Su 12:45-4pm. Free.)* Shakespeare premiered *Twelfth Night* in front of Elizabeth I in **Middle Temple Hall,** whose large wooden dining table is made from the hatch of Sir Francis Drake's *Golden Hinde.* According to Shakespeare's *Henry VI,* the red-and-white flowers of the War of the Roses were plucked in **Middle Temple Garden,** south of the hall. *(Garden open May-Sept. M-F noon-3pm. Free.)*

▨ ST. ETHELDREDA'S. The mid-13th-century church of St. Etheldreda is the sole surviving edifice of its age in London, barely: The upper church was badly damaged in WWII. Inside, the surprisingly high ceiling swallows up the bustle of the streets, and the enormous stained-glass windows make this one of London's most beautiful churches. *(Ely Pl. Tube: Farringdon. Open daily 7:30am-7pm. Free.)*

SOMERSET HOUSE. A magnificent Palladian structure completed in 1790, Somerset House was London's first intended office block. Originally home to the Royal Academy and the Royal Society, the building now harbors the magnificent ▨**Courtauld Institute** (p. 183). From mid-December to mid-January, the central **Fountain Courtyard** is iced over to make an open-air rink. *(On the Strand. Tube: Charing Cross. Courtyard open daily 7:30am-11pm. Free. Tours Sa 1:30 and 3:45pm. £2.80.)*

FLEET STREET. Named for the river (now underground) that flows from Hampstead to the Thames, Fleet Street's association with publishing goes back to the days when Wyken de Worde relocated from Westminster to the precincts of **St. Bride's** church, ever since known as "the printer's cathedral." Christopher Wren's odd steeple is the original inspiration for the tiered wedding cake, invented by a local baker. *(On St. Bride's Ave., just off Fleet St. Tube: Temple. Open daily 8am-4:45pm. Free.)*

ROYAL COURTS OF JUSTICE. This elaborate neo-Gothic structure—easily mistaken for a cathedral—straddles the official division between Westminster and the City of London; the courtrooms are open to the public during cases. *(Where the Strand becomes Fleet St. Tube: Temple. Open M-F 9am-4:30pm. Cases start at 10am.)*

KENSINGTON

Nobody took much notice of Kensington before 1689, when the newly crowned William III and Mary II moved into Kensington Palace. Then, in 1851, the Great Exhibition brought in enough money to finance the museums and colleges of South Kensington. Now the neighborhood is home to London's most expensive stores, including Harrods and Harvey Nichols, and it's hard to imagine the days when the area was known for its taverns and its highwaymen.

KENSINGTON PALACE. Remodeled by Christopher Wren for William III and Mary II, parts of the palace are still in use today as a royal residence. Princess Diana lived here until her death. The **Royal Ceremonial Dress Collection** features 19th-century court costumes along with the Queen's demure evening gowns and some of Diana's sexier numbers. Hanoverian economy is evident in the *trompe l'oeil* decoration in the **State Apartment,** carried out by William Kent for George I. *(On the western edge of Kensington Gardens; enter through the park. Tube: High St. Kensington. Open Mar.-Oct. daily 10am-6pm; Nov.-Feb. 10am-5pm. £11, students and seniors £8.)*

HYDE PARK AND KENSINGTON GARDENS. Surrounded by London's wealthiest neighborhoods, giant Hyde Park has served as the model for city parks around the world, including Central Park in New York and Bois de Boulogne in Paris. **Kensington Gardens,** to the west, is contiguous with Hyde Park. The 41-acre **Serpentine** was created in 1730; innumerable people pay to row and swim here. At the northeastern corner of the park, near Marble Arch, proselytizers, politicos, and flat-out crazies dispense their knowledge to bemused tourists at **Speaker's Corner** on Sundays. *(Tube: Queensway, Lancaster Gate, Marble Arch, Hyde Park Corner, or High St. Kensington. Hyde Park open daily 5am-midnight. Kensington Gardens open dawn-dusk. Both free.)*

LEIGHTON HOUSE. The home of painter Lord Fredric Leighton (1830-1896) is a perfect example of all that is endearing and ridiculous in Victorian tastes. The centerpiece is the **Arab Hall,** a Moorish extravaganza of tilework and mosaics complete with fountain and carpets; the walls bear one of Europe's best collections of medieval Arabian tile. *(12 Holland Park Rd. Tube: High St. Kensington. Open daily 11am-5:30pm. Free. 50min. tours W-Th noon; £3. 60min. audio guide available; £3.)*

KNIGHTSBRIDGE

APSLEY HOUSE AND WELLINGTON ARCH. Apsley House, with the convenient address of "No. 1, London," was bought in 1817 by the Duke of Wellington. On display is Wellington's outstanding collection of art, much of it given in gratitude by European royalty following the battle of Waterloo. The majority of the paintings hang in the **Waterloo Gallery.** *(Hyde Park Corner. Tube: Hyde Park Corner. Open Su and Tu-Sa 11am-5pm. £4.50, students £3. Seniors and children free.)* Across from Apsley House, the **Wellington Arch** was built in 1825. In 1838 it was dedicated to the Duke of Wellington; later, to the horror of its architect, Decimus Burton, an enormous statue of the Duke was placed on top. The arch offers scenic views. *(Hyde Park Corner. Tube: Hyde Park Corner. Open Apr.-Sept. Su and W-Sa 10am-5:30pm; Oct. Su and W-Sa 10am-5pm; Nov.-Mar. Su and W-Sa 10am-4pm. £2.50, students and seniors £2.)*

THE WEST END

MAYFAIR AND ST. JAMES'S

Home to Prince Charles, the Ritz, and exclusive gentlemen's clubs, this is London's aristocratic quarter. On **Jermyn Street,** one block south of Piccadilly, stores cater to the tastes of the English squire, with hand-cut suits and hunting gear.

BURLINGTON HOUSE. The only one of Piccadilly's aristocratic mansions that stands today, Burlington House was built in 1665. Today, it houses numerous regal societies, including the **Royal Academy,** heart of the British artistic establishment and home to some excellent exhibitions (p. 183).

ST. JAMES'S PALACE. Built in 1536, St. James's is London's only remaining purpose-built palace; Prince Charles lives here. The only part of the palace open to the public is the **Chapel Royal,** open for Sunday services from October to Easter at 8:30 and 11am. *(Between the Mall and Pall Mall. Tube: Green Park.)* From Easter to September, services are held in **Queen's Chapel,** across Marlborough Rd.

REGENT STREET. Originally designed by John Nash in the 19th century to link Regent's Park in the north to the Prince Regent's residence in St. James's, Regent St. is divided into two parts. "Upper" Regent St., between Oxford Circus and Piccadilly Circus, is known for its elegant shopping; "Lower" Regent St., running south from Piccadilly Circus, terminates at **Waterloo Place,** where a column topped with the "Grand Old" Duke of York overlooks St. James's Park.

SOHO

Soho's first settlers were French Huguenots fleeing religious persecution in the 17th century. These days, a concentration of gay-owned restaurants and bars has turned **Old Compton Street** into the heart of gay London.

PICCADILLY CIRCUS. In the glow of lurid neon signs, five of the West End's major arteries merge and swirl round the **Statue of Eros,** dedicated to the Victorian philanthropist, Lord Shaftesbury. Eros originally pointed down Shaftesbury Ave., but recent restoration work has put his aim significantly off. *(Tube: Piccadilly Circus.)*

LEICESTER SQUARE. Amusements at this entertainment nexus range from London's largest cinema to the **Swiss Centre** glockenspiel, whose atonal renditions of Beethoven's *Moonlight Sonata* are enough to make even the tone-deaf weep. *(Rings M-F noon, 6, 7, and 8pm; Sa-Su noon, 2, 4, 5, 6, 7, and 8pm.)* Be true to your inner tourist by having your name engraved on a grain of rice and sitting for a caricature. *(Tube: Leicester Sq. or Piccadilly Circus.)*

BRITAIN

CHINATOWN. The pedestrian, tourist-ridden **Gerrard Street,** with dragon gates and pagoda-capped phone booths, is the heart of London's tiny slice of Canton, but gritty **Lisle Street,** one block to the south, has a more authentic feel. Chinatown is most exciting during the raucous Chinese New Year in February. *(Between Leicester Sq., Shaftesbury Ave., and Charing Cross Rd.)*

COVENT GARDEN
The Covent Garden piazza, designed by Inigo Jones in the 17th century, is one of the few parts of London popular with locals and tourists alike. On the very spot where England's first Punch and Judy show was performed, street entertainers delight the thousands who flock here year round. *(Tube: Covent Garden.)*

THE ROYAL OPERA HOUSE. The Royal Opera House reopened in 2000 after a major expansion. After wandering in the ornate lobby of the original 1858 theater, head up to the enormous **Floral Hall.** Then take the escalator to reach the **terrace,** which offers scenic views. *(Bow St. ☎7304 4000. Open daily 10am-3:30pm. Backstage tours M-Sa 10:30am, 12:30, and 2:30pm. Reservations essential. £8, students and seniors £7.)*

THEATRE ROYAL DRURY LANE. Founded in 1663, this is the oldest of London's surviving theaters; David Garrick ruled the roost here in the 18th century. The theater even has a ghost—a corpse and dagger were found bricked up in a wall in the 19th century. This and other pieces of Drury Lane lore are brought back to life in the actor-led backstage tours. *(Entrance on Catherine St. Tours M-Tu and Th-F 2:15 and 4:45pm, W and Sa 10:15am and noon. £8.50, children £6.50.)*

NORTH LONDON
CAMDEN TOWN
An island of good, honest tawdriness in an increasingly affluent sea, Camden Town has thrown off attempts at gentrification thanks to the ever-growing **Camden Markets** (p. 191). On weekends, the market presents a variety of life unmatched even by **London Zoo,** just up the **Regent's Canal** from the market's center.

LONDON ZOO. Thousands of little critters from around the world run freely, their guardians trying frantically to keep up, as the animals look on with indifference from their enclosures. For daily activities, check the *Daily Events* leaflet. *(Main gate on Outer Circle, Regent's Park. Tube: Camden Town. 12min. walk from the Tube station or a quick jaunt on bus #274. Open Apr.-Oct. daily 10am-5:30pm; Nov.-Mar. 10am-4:30pm. £12, students and seniors £10.20, under-16 £9.)*

HAMPSTEAD
Hampstead first caught the attention of well-heeled Londoners in the 17th century. In the 1930s, residents such as Sigmund Freud, Barbara Hepworth, Aldous Huxley, and Piet Mondrian lent the area a cachet that grows to this day.

HAMPSTEAD HEATH. Hampstead Heath is one of the last remaining commons in England, open to all since 1312. **Parliament Hill** is the highest open space in London, with excellent views of the city. Farther north, ▩**Kenwood House** is a picture-perfect 18th-century country estate, designed by Robert Adams for the first Earl of Mansfield and home to the impressive **Iveagh Bequest** of Old Masters, including works by Botticelli, Rembrandt, Turner, and Vermeer. *(Tube: Hampstead. A 20min. walk from the station. Kenwood House open Apr.-Sept. daily 8am-8:30pm, Oct.-Mar. 8am-4pm.)*

EAST LONDON
THE EAST END AND DOCKLANDS
The boundary between the East End and the City of London is as sharp today as it was when Aldgate and Bishopsgate were literal gateways in the wall separating the rich and powerful City from the poorer quarters to the east. **Whitechapel**

is the oldest part of the East End. In the 19th century, it was thronged with Jewish refugees from Eastern Europe; today it's the heart of London's Bangladeshi community, which centers around **Brick Lane. Christ Church,** on Commercial St., opposite Spitalfields market, is Nicholas Hawksmoor's largest, and is considered by many to be his masterpiece; it is slowly being restored to its former glory. *(Tube: Liverpool St. Open M-F 12:30-2:30pm.)*

The area of the East End along the river is known as the **Docklands.** This manmade archipelago of docks was for centuries the commercial heart of the British Empire. In 1981, the government decided to redevelop the area; the showpiece of the regeneration is **Canary Wharf,** with Britain's highest skyscraper, the 244m pyramid-topped **One Canada Square.** Under the tower, the **Canada Place** and **Cabot Square** malls draw shoppers from all over London. *(Tube: Canary Wharf.)*

GREENWICH

Greenwich's position as the "home of time" is connected to its maritime heritage—the Royal Observatory, site of the Prime Meridian, was founded to produce star charts once essential to navigation. The most pleasant way of getting to Greenwich is by boat. **Westminster Passenger Association** boats head from Westminster Pier. *(1hr., call ☎7930 9033 for schedule. Round-trip £6.30.)* TfL Travelcard holders get 33% off riverboat fares. The **Greenwich Tourist Information Centre** is in Pepys House, 2 Cutty Sark Gdns. *(☎(0870) 608 2000. Open daily 10am-5pm.)*

ROYAL OBSERVATORY. Charles II founded the Royal Observatory in 1675 to develop a method for calculating longitude at sea; the **Prime Meridian** (which marks 0° longitude) started out as the axis along which the astronomers' telescopes swung. Next to the Meridian is Christopher Wren's **Flamstead House,** whose **Octagon Room** features long windows designed to accommodate telescopes. The **Observatory Dome,** next to the Meridian Building's telescope display, houses a 28 in. telescope constructed in 1893. It hasn't been used since 1954, but you can get a peek at the stars at the **Planetarium.** *(Greenwich Park. Open daily 10am-5pm. Free.)*

CUTTY SARK. Even landlubbers will appreciate the **Cutty Sark,** the last of the great tea clippers. Launched in 1869, she was the fastest ship of her time, making the trip to and from China in only 120 days. *(King William Walk, by Greenwich Pier. Open daily 10am-5pm; last admission 4:30pm. £4; students, seniors, and under-16 £3.)*

ROYAL NAVAL COLLEGE. On the site of Henry VIII's Palace of Placentia, the Royal Naval College was founded by William III in 1694 as the Royal Hospital for Seamen. In 1998, the University of Greenwich moved in. Don't miss the **Painted Hall** and the **Chapel,** which shelters Benjamin West's painting of a shipwrecked St. Paul. *(King William Walk. Open daily 12:30-5pm. Free.)*

WEST LONDON

■ HAMPTON COURT PALACE. Although a monarch hasn't lived here for 250 years, Hampton Court still exudes regal charm. Cardinal Wolsey built the first palace here in 1514, showing the young Henry VIII how to act the part of a ruler. In 1689, William III and Mary II employed Christopher Wren to bring Hampton Court up to date. In addition to touring the sumptuous rooms of the palace, including Henry's **State Apartments** and William's **King's Apartments,** be sure to leave time for the vast gardens, including the devilishly difficult **maze.** Take the train from Waterloo (35min., every 30min., round-trip £4) or a boat from Westminster Pier (4hr.; 4 per day; £10, round-trip £14); to leave time to see the palace, take the boat one way and return by train. *(Open mid-Mar. to late Oct. M 10:15am-6pm, Tu-Su 9:30am-6pm; mid-Mar. closes 4:30pm. £11, students £8.30. Maze only £3. Gardens only free.)*

KEW GARDENS. The Kew Gardens (a.k.a. the Royal Botanic Gardens) feature thousands of flowers, fruits, trees, and vegetables from around the globe. The three **conservatories,** housing a staggering variety of plants ill-suited to the English climate, are the highlight of the gardens. Most famous is the steamy **Palm House,** home to "The Oldest Pot Plant In The World," which is not at all what it sounds like but interesting nonetheless. The **Temperate House** is the largest ornamental glasshouse in the world. The interior of the **Princess of Wales Conservatory** is divided into 10 different climate zones, including one entirely devoted to orchids. *(Main entrance at Victoria Gate. Tube: Kew Gardens. Open Apr.-Aug. M-F 9:30am-6:30pm, Sa-Su 9:30am-7:30pm; Sept.-Oct. daily 9:30am-6pm; Nov.-Jan. 9:30am-4:15pm; Feb.-Mar. 9:30am-5:30pm. Glasshouses close Feb.-Oct. 5:30pm, Nov.-Mar. 3:45pm. £6.50, "late entry" (45min. before the glasshouses close) £5.50; students and seniors £5.50.)*

🏛 MUSEUMS

Centuries spent as the capital of an empire, together with a decidedly English penchant for collecting, have given London a spectacular set of museums. Art lovers, history buffs, and amateur ethnologists won't know which way to turn when they arrive. And there's even better news for museum lovers: In celebration of the Queen's Golden Jubilee, all major museums are free indefinitely.

▨ BRITISH MUSEUM

The funny thing about the British Museum is that there's almost nothing British in it. The **Western Galleries** house the most famous items in the collection. Room 4 harbors Egyptian sculpture, including the **Rosetta Stone,** and Room 18 is entirely devoted to the Athenian **Elgin Marbles.** Other highlights include giant Assyrian and Babylonian **reliefs,** the Roman **Portland Vase,** and bits and bobs from two Wonders of the Ancient World, the **Temple of Artemis** at Ephesus and the **Mausoleum of Halikarnassos.** The **Northern Galleries** feature eight rooms of mummies and sarcophagi and nine of artifacts from the ancient Near East, including the **Oxus Treasure** from Iran. The northern wing also houses the excellent African and Islamic galleries, the giant Asian collections, and the Americas collection. The upper level of the **South** and **East Galleries** is dedicated to ancient and medieval Europe, some of which is actually British. Famous remains include the preserved body of **Lindow Man,** an Iron Age Celt (Room 50), along with treasures excavated from the **Sutton Hoo Burial Ship** (Room 41). Room 42 is home to the enigmatic **Lewis Chessmen,** an 800-year-old chess set mysteriously abandoned in Scotland. *(Great Russell St., Bloomsbury. Rear entrance on Montague St. ☎ 7323 8000; www.thebritishmuseum.ac.uk. Tube: Tottenham Court Rd., Russell Sq., or Holborn. Great Court open M-W and Su 10am-5:30pm, Th-Sa 9am-9pm. Galleries open daily 10am-5:30pm. Suggested donation £2. Temporary exhibitions average £7, students £3.50. Audio tours £2.50. 1½hr. highlights tour M-Sa 10:30am and 1pm, Su 11am, 12:30, 1:30, 2:30, and 4pm. £7, students £4.)*

▨ NATIONAL GALLERY

The National Gallery was founded by an Act of Parliament in 1824, with 38 paintings displayed in a townhouse; it grew so rapidly in size and popularity that a new gallery was constructed in 1838. The new **Sainsbury Wing** houses the oldest, most fragile paintings, including the 14th-century English Wilton Diptych, Botticelli's Venus and Mars, and the Leonardo Cartoon, a detailed preparatory drawing by Leonardo da Vinci for a never-executed painting. The **West Wing** displays paintings from 1510-1600 and is dominated by Italian High Renaissance and early Flemish art. Rome and Florence fight it out in Room 8, with versions of the Madonna and Child by Raphael and Michelangelo. The **North Wing** spans the 17th century, with an exceptional array of Flemish work. Room 23 boasts no fewer than 17 Rembrandts;

the famous *Self Portrait at 63* gazes knowingly at his *Self Portrait at 34*. The **East Wing,** home to paintings from 1700-1900, is the most popular in the gallery, thanks to an array of Impressionist works including van Gogh's Sunflowers and Cézanne's *Bathers* in Room 45, and two of Monet's *Waterlilies* in Room 43. Room 34 serves as a reminder that there was art on the British side of the Channel, with six luminescent Turners. *(Main entrance on north side of Trafalgar Sq., Westminster. ☎ 7747 2885; www.nationalgallery.org.uk. Tube: Charing Cross or Leicester Sq. Open M-Tu and Th-Sa 10am-6pm; W 10am-9pm, Sainsbury Wing special exhibitions until 10pm. Free; some temporary exhibitions £5-7, students £2-3. Audio tours free; suggested donation £4. 1hr. gallery tours start at Sainsbury Wing info desk daily 11:30am and 2:30pm, W also 6:30pm. Free.)*

◪ TATE MODERN

Since opening in May 2000, Tate Modern has been credited with single-handedly reversing the long-term decline in museum attendance in Britain. The largest modern art museum in the world, its most striking aspect is the building, formerly the Bankside power station. A conversion by Swiss firm Herzog and de Meuron added a seventh floor with wraparound views of north and south London, and turned the old **Turbine Hall** into an immense atrium that often overpowers the installations commissioned for it. The Tate has been criticized for its controversial curatorial method, which groups works according to themes rather than period or artist: The four divisions are **Landscape/Matter/Environment** and **Still Life/Object/Real Life** on level 3 and **Nude/Body/Action** and **History/Memory/Society** on level 5. Even skeptics admit that this arrangement throws up some interesting contrasts, such as the nascent geometry of Cézanne's *Still Life with Water Jug* overlooking the checkerboard tiles of Carl André's *Steel Zinc Plain*, and the juxtaposition of Monet's *Waterlilies* with Richard Long's energetic *Waterfall Line*. The main achievement of the thematic display is that it forces visitors into contact with an exceptionally wide range of art. It's now impossible to see the Tate's more famous pieces, which include Marcel Duchamp's *Large Glass* and Picasso's *Weeping Woman*, without also confronting challenging and invigorating works by little-known contemporary artists. *(Bankside, The South Bank. Main entrance on Holland St. ☎ 7887 8006; www.tate.org.uk. Tube: Blackfriars. Open M-Th and Su 10am-6pm, F-Sa 10am-10pm. Free. Special exhibitions £5-7; students £4-6. Audio tours £1. Free tours meet on the gallery concourses: Landscape/Matter/Environment 3pm, level 3; Still Life/Object/Real Life 2pm, level 3; Nude/Body/Action 11am, level 5; History/Memory/Society noon, level 5.)*

TATE BRITAIN

The original Tate opened in 1897 as a showcase for modern British art. Before long, it had expanded to include contemporary art from all over the world, as well as British art from the Middle Ages on. Despite many expansions, it was clear that the dual role was too much for one building; the problem was resolved with the relocation of almost all the contemporary art to the new Tate Modern at Bankside (see above). At the same time, the original Tate was rechristened and rededicated to British art. The **Clore Gallery** continues to display the Turner Bequest of 282 oils and 19,000 watercolors; other painters featured heavily are William Blake, John Constable, Lucien Freud, David Hockney, and Dante Gabriel Rossetti. Despite the Tate Modern's popular explosion, the annual **Turner Prize** for contemporary art is still held here. *(Millbank, near Vauxhall Bridge, Westminster. ☎ 7887 8008; www.tate.org.uk. Tube: Pimlico. Open daily 10am-5pm. Free. Special exhibitions £3-9. Audio tours £3. Highlights tour M-F 11:30am, Sa 3pm. Free.)*

VICTORIA & ALBERT MUSEUM

Founded in 1852 to encourage excellence in art and design, the V&A is the largest museum of the decorative arts in the world—as befits an institution dedicated to displaying "the fine and applied arts of all countries, all styles, all periods." The subject of a £31 million renovation, the vast **British Galleries** hold a series of recreated rooms from every period between 1500 and 1900, mirrored by the vast **Dress Collection,** a dazzling array of the finest haute couture through the ages. The ground-floor **European** collections range from 4th-century tapestries to Alfonse Mucha posters; if you only see one thing in the museum, make it the **Raphael Gallery,** hung with paintings commissioned by Leo X in 1515. The **Sculpture Gallery,** home to Canova's Three Graces (1814-17), is not to be confused with the **Cast Courts,** a plaster-cast collection of the world's sculptural greatest hits, from Trajan's *Column* to Michelangelo's *David.* The V&A's **Asian** collections are particularly formidable—if the choice of objects occasionally seems to rely on national cliches (Indian carvings, Persian carpets, Chinese porcelain, Japanese ceramics), it says more about how the V&A has formed opinion than followed it. In contrast to the geographically themed ground floor, the **upper levels** are mostly arranged in specialist galleries devoted to everything from jewelry to musical instruments to stained glass. An exception to the materially themed arrangements is the large **20th-century** collections, featuring design classics from Salvador Dalí's 1936 "Mae West" sofa lips to a pair of 1990s rubber hot pants. The six-level **Henry Cole wing** is home to a collection of **British paintings,** including some 350 works by Constable and numerous Turners. Also on display are a number of Rodin bronzes, donated by the artist in 1914, and a collection of **miniature portraits,** including Holbein's Anne of Cleves. The **Frank Lloyd Wright gallery** contains a full-size recreation of the office commissioned by Edgar J. Kauffmann for his Pittsburgh department store in 1935. *(Main entrance on Cromwell Rd., Kensington. ☎ 7942 2000; www.vam.ac.uk. Tube: South Kensington. Open M-Tu and Th-Su 10am-5:45pm, W and last F of month 10am-10pm. Free. Tours daily 10:30, 11:30am, 1:30, and 2:30pm. Gallery talks daily 1pm. Free. Talks, tours, and live music W from 6:30pm; last F of month also fashion shows, debates, and DJs.)*

OTHER MUSEUMS AND GALLERIES

British Library Galleries, 96 Euston Rd. (☎ 7412 7332). Tube: King's Cross. A stunning display of texts, from the 2nd-century *Unknown Gospel* to the Beatles' hand-scrawled lyrics. Other highlights include a Gutenberg Bible and pages from da Vinci's notebooks. Open M and W-F 9:30am-6pm, Tu 9:30am-8pm, Sa 9:30am-5pm, Su 11am-5pm. Free.

Museum of London, London Wall, The City of London (☎ 7600 3699). Tube: Barbican. Enter through the Barbican. The engrossing collection traces the history of London from its foundations to the present day, with a particular focus on Roman objects. Open M-Sa 10am-6pm, Su noon-6pm; last admission 5:30pm. Free.

Courtauld Institute, Somerset House, The Strand, Westminster (☎ 7848 2526). Tube: Charing Cross. Small, outstanding collection. 14th- to 20th-century abstractions, focusing on Impressionism. Manet's *A Bar at the Follies Bergères,* van Gogh's *Self Portrait with Bandaged Ear,* and Cézanne's *The Card Players.* Open M-Sa 10am-6pm. £5, students £4. Free M 10am-2pm.

Natural History Museum, on Cromwell Rd., Kensington (☎ 7942 5000). Tube: South Kensington. Cathedral-like building home to an array of minerals and stuffed animals. Highlights include a frighteningly realistic T-Rex and the engrossing, interactive *Human Biology* gallery. Open M-Sa 10am-5:50pm, Su 11am-5:50pm. Free.

Royal Academy of Art, Burlington House, Piccadilly, The West End (☎ 7300 8000). Tube: Piccadilly Circus. Founded in 1768 as both an art school and meeting place for Britain's foremost artists. Outstanding exhibitions on all manner of art. Open M-Th and Sa-Su 10am-6pm, F 10am-10pm. Around £7; seniors £6, students £5.

Design Museum, 28 Shad Thames, Butler's Wharf (☎ 7403 6933). Tube: Tower Hill or London Bridge. This contemporary museum explores the development of mass-market design with a constantly changing selection of objects; most fun are the funky chairs that you can try out. Open daily 10am-5:45pm, last admission 5:15pm. £6, concessions £4.

Dulwich Picture Gallery, Gallery Rd., Dulwich (☎8693 5254). 10min. from North or West Dulwich rail station, or bus P4 from Tube: Brixton. Designed by Sir John Soane, this marvelous array of Old Masters was England's first public art gallery. Rubens and van Dyck feature prominently, as does Rembrandt's *Portrait of a Young Man.* Open Su 11am-5pm, Tu-F 10am-5pm, Sa 11am-5pm. £4, seniors £3. Students and children free; free for all F.

Cabinet War Rooms, Clive Steps, Westminster (☎7766 0130). Tube: Westminster. The rooms where Churchill and his ministers, generals, and support staff lived and worked underground from 1939 to 1945. Highlights include the small room containing the top-secret trans-atlantic hotline—the official line was that it was Churchill's personal toilet. Open Apr.-Sept. daily 9:30am-6pm; Oct.-Mar. 10am-6pm. £7, students and seniors £5.50.

The Gilbert Collection, Somerset House, The Strand (☎7420 9400). Tube: Charing Cross or Temple. Pick up a free audio guide and magnifying glass as you enter—the latter is invaluable for studying the displays of micro-mosaics and ornate snuffboxes. Open daily 10am-6pm. £5, concessions £4. Children free; free to all after 4:30pm.

London's Transport Museum, Covent Garden Piazza, The West End (☎7565 7299). Tube: Covent Garden. Informative *and* fun. Kids and adults will find themselves engrossed in the history of London's public transportation system. Open M-Th and Sa-Su 10am-6pm, F 11am-6pm. £6, students and seniors £4.50. Under-16 free.

Wallace Collection, Manchester Sq., Marylebone (☎7563 9500). Tube: Bond St. Palatial Hertford House holds a stunning array of porcelain, medieval armor, and weaponry. Open M-Sa 10am-5pm, Su noon-5pm. Free.

Science Museum, Exhibition Rd., Kensington (☎(0870) 870 4868). Tube: South Kensington. A mix of state-of-the-art interactive displays and priceless historical artifacts, encompassing all forms of technology. Open daily 10am-6pm. Free.

The Iveagh Bequest, Kenwood House (☎8348 1286). Tube: Hampstead. A large collection bequeathed by Edward Guinness, Earl of Iveagh. The Kenwood setting and the magnificent pictures make it one of London's finest small galleries. Highlights include works by Botticelli, Rembrandt, Turner, and Vermeer. Open Apr.-Sept. M-Tu, Th, and Sa-Su 10am-6pm; W and F 10:30am-6pm. Oct. M-Tu, Th, and Sa-Su 10am-5pm; W and F 10:30am-5pm. Nov.-Mar. M-Tu, Th, and Sa-Su 10am-4pm; W and F 10:30-4pm. Free.

Imperial War Museum, Lambeth Rd., South London (☎7416 5320). Tube: Lambeth North. The commendably un-jingoistic exhibits follow every aspect of war from 1914 on, covering conflicts large and small. The largest and most publicized display, the Holocaust Exhibition, graphically documents Nazi atrocities. Open daily 10am-6pm. Free.

Institute of Contemporary Arts (ICA), Nash House, The West End (☎7930 3647). Tube: Charing Cross. Down the road from Buckingham Palace—convenient for attacking the establishment. Open M noon-11pm, Tu-Sa noon-1am, Su noon-10:30pm; galleries close 7:30pm. M-F £1.50, Sa-Su £2.50.

National Maritime Museum, Trafalgar Rd., Greenwich, East London (☎8858 4422). Docklands Light Railway: Cutty Sark. Broad-ranging, child-friendly displays cover almost every aspect of seafaring history. The naval portraits in the neighboring Queen's House take second place to Inigo Jones's architecture. Open June to early Sept. daily 10am-6pm; late Sept. to May 10am-5pm. Free.

Whitechapel Art Gallery, Whitechapel High St. (☎7522 7888). Tube: Aldgate East. At the forefront of the East End's art scene, Whitechapel hosts excellent, often controversial, shows of contemporary art. Open Su, Tu-W, and F-Sa 11am-6pm, Th 11am-9pm. Free.

Sir John Soane's Museum, 13 Lincoln's Inn Fields, Holborn. Tube: Holborn. Architect John Soane built this intriguing museum for his own art collection. Open Tu-Sa 10am-5pm; first Tu of the month also 6-9pm. Suggested donation £1.

The Hermitage Rooms, Somerset House, The Strand (☎ 7485 4630). Tube: Charing Cross or Temple. A unique chance to get a taste of the renowned Hermitage art museum without going to St. Petersburg. The paintings are on loan from Russia and are exchanged. Open daily 10am-6pm. £6, concessions £4. Under-16 free.

National Portrait Gallery, St. Martin's Pl., Westminster (☎ 7312 2463). Tube: Charing Cross. The artistic Who's Who of Britain. Began in 1856 as "the fulfillment of a patriotic and moral ideal." Open M-W and Sa-Su 10am-6pm, Th-F 10am-9pm. Free.

🖈 ENTERTAINMENT

The West End is the world's theater capital, supplemented by an adventurous "Fringe" and a justly famous National Theatre. New bands spring eternal from the fountain of London's many music venues. Whatever you're planning to do, the listings in *Time Out* (£2.20, every W) are indispensable.

THEATER

The stage for a dramatic tradition over 800 years old, London theaters maintain unrivaled breadth of choice. At a **West End** theater (a term referring to all the major stages, whether or not they're actually in the West End), you can expect a professional (if mainstream) production and top-quality performers. **Off-West End** theaters tend to present more challenging works, while remaining as professional as their West End brethren. The **Fringe** refers to scores of smaller venues, often just rooms in basements with a few benches and a team of dedicated amateurs. **tkts,** on the south side of Leicester Sq., is run jointly by London theaters and is the only place where you can be sure your discount tickets are genuine. You can only buy on the day of the performance, in person and in cash, and with no choice in seating. There's no way of knowing in advance which shows will have tickets, but you can expect a wide range. There's a £2.50 booking fee per ticket but no limit on the number you can buy. (Open M-Sa 10am-7pm, Su noon-3pm. Most tickets £15-25.)

WEST END AND REPERTORY COMPANIES

▨ **Shakespeare's Globe Theatre,** 21 New Globe Walk (☎ 7401 9919). Tube: Southwark or London Bridge. A faithful reproduction of the original 16th-century playhouse. Opt for backless wooden benches or stand as a "groundling." For **tours,** see p. 173. Performances mid-May to late Sept. Su 6:30pm, Tu-Sa 7:30pm; June Su 1 and 6:30pm, Tu-Sa 2 and 7:30pm. Box office open M-Sa 10am-6pm, and at 8pm on performance days. Seats £12-27, concessions £10-24; standing £5.

Barbican Theatre, main entrance on Silk St. (☎ 7638 8891). A huge, futuristic auditorium with steeply raked, forward-leaning balconies. Hosts touring companies and short-run shows, as well as frequent contemporary dance performances. **The Pit** is largely experimental, while **Barbican Hall** houses the London Symphony Orchestra (p. 187). Tickets £6-30. Student and senior standbys from 9am day of performance.

National Theatre, just down river of Waterloo bridge (info ☎ 7452 3400; box office 7452 3000; www.nationaltheatre.org.uk). Tube: Waterloo or Embankment. At the forefront of British theater since opening under the direction of Laurence Olivier in 1976. Popular musicals and hit plays, which often transfer to the West End, subsidize experimental works. The **Olivier** stage seats 1080, the **Lyttelton** is a proscenium theater, and the **Cottesloe** offers flexible staging for experimental dramas. Box office open M-Sa 10am-8pm. Tickets £10-30; from 10am day of performance £10; standby (2hr. before curtain) £15; standing places, only if all seats sold, £6. Concessions available.

Open-Air Theatre, Inner Circle, Regents Park (☎ 7486 2431; www.open-air-the-atre.org.uk). Tube: Baker St. Bring blankets and waterproofs—performances take place rain or shine. Program runs early June to early Sept., and includes 2 Shakespeare works, a musical, and a children's production. Barbeque before evening shows. Performances M-Sa 8pm (matinees most Th and every Sa 2:30pm). Children's performances M-W, F, and occasionally Th 2:30pm; Sa 11am. £8.50-25, children half-price with adult ticket, student and senior standbys from 1hr. before curtain £8.

Royal Court Theatre, Sloane Sq. (☎ 7565 5000). Called "the most important theater in Europe," dedicated to new writing and innovative interpretations of classics. Main stage £7.50-26, concessions £9, standing room 1hr. before curtain 10p. Upstairs £12.50-15, concessions £9. M all seats £7.50.

Sadler's Wells, Rosebery Ave. (☎ 7863 8000). Tube: Angel. London's premier dance space, with everything from classical ballet to contemporary tap, plus occasional operas. £10-45; student, senior, and child standbys 1hr. before curtain £10-18.50 (cash only). Box office open M-Sa 9am-8:30pm.

MAJOR FRINGE THEATERS

The Almeida, Almeida St. (☎ 7359 4404). Tube: Angel or Highbury & Islington. Top fringe in London, if not the world. Hollywood stars, including Kevin Spacey and Nicole Kidman, queue up to prove their acting cred here. Will open in spring 2003 following renovations. Show times and prices to be announced.

Donmar Warehouse, 41 Earlham St. (☎ 7369 1732). Tube: Covent Garden. Serious contemporary theater. £14-35; concessions standby £12, 30min. before curtain.

Young Vic, 66 The Cut (☎ 7928 6363). Tube: Waterloo. With only 8 rows of seats surrounding the flat stage, Vic can be unnervingly intimate. Box office open M-Sa 10am-8pm. £19, seniors £12.50, students and children £4-9.50.

CINEMA

The heart of the celluloid monster is **Leicester Square** (p. 178), where the latest releases premiere a day before hitting the city's chains. The dominant mainstream cinema chain is **Odeon** (☎ (0870) 5050 007). Tickets to West End cinemas begin at £8; weekday matinees before 5pm are usually cheaper. For less mainstream offerings, try the ⊠**Electric Cinema,** 191 Portobello Rd. (Tube: Ladbroke Grove), for the combination of Baroque stage splendor and the buzzing effects of a big screen. For an extra special experience, choose a luxury armchair or 2-seat sofa. (☎ 7908 9696; tickets 7229 8688. Late-night reruns Sa 11pm; classics, recent raves, and double bills Su 2pm. M £7.50, Tu-Su £12.50; 2-seat sofa M £20, Tu-Su £30; Su double bills £7.50.) ⊠**Riverside Studios,** Crisp Rd. (Tube: Hammersmith) shows a wide and extraordinary range of excellent foreign and classic films. (☎ 8237 1111; £5.50, concessions £4.50.) The **National Film Theatre** (NFT), on the South Bank, underneath Waterloo Bridge (Tube: Waterloo, Embankment, or Temple), promises a mind-boggling array of films—six different movies hit the three screens every evening, starting around 6pm (☎ 7928 3232; £7.20, concessions £5.50). **The Prince Charles,** Leicester Pl. (Tube: Leicester Sq.), will let you *Sing-a-long-a-Sound-of-Music,* with Von Trappists dressed as everything from nuns to "Ray, a drop of golden sun." (☎ 7957 4009 or 7420 0000. Su 2pm, F 7:30pm; £12.50, children £8.)

COMEDY

Capital of a nation famed for its sense of humor, London takes comedy seriously. On any given night, you'll find at least ten comedy clubs in operation: Check listings in *Time Out* or a newspaper to get up to speed. Summertime giggle-seekers should note that London empties of comedians in **August,** when most head to Edinburgh to take part in the annual festival; that means **July** provides plenty of comedians trying out their material. A young Robin Williams performed frequent impromptu acts at the ▨**Comedy Store,** 1a Oxendon St. (Tube: Piccadilly Circus), the UK's top comedy club and sower of the seeds that gave rise to *Ab Fab, Whose Line is it Anyway?*, and *Blackadder.* Tuesday is contemporary satire, Wednesday and Sunday improv, Thursday through Saturday stand-up. (TicketMaster ☎ (0870) 060 2340. Shows Su and Tu-Sa 8pm, F-Sa also midnight. Book ahead. 18+. £12-15, concessions £8.) East London's ▨**Comedy Cafe,** 66 Rivington St., is a sure bet for a good laugh. (☎ 7739 5706. Reserve F-Sa. Doors 7pm, show 9pm. W free try-out night. Th £5, F £10, Sa £14.)

MUSIC

ROCK AND POP

Birthplace of the Stones, the Sex Pistols, Madness, and the Chemical Brothers, home to Madonna (sort of) and McCartney, London is a town steeped in rock.

▨ **The Water Rats,** 328 Grays Inn Rd. (☎ 7837 7269). Tube: King's Cross St. Pancras. Pub-cafe by day, stomping ground for top new talent by night. Cover £5, with band flyer £4. Open for coffee M-F 8am-noon. Music M-Sa 8pm-late.

Brixton Academy, 211 Stockwell Rd. (Ticketweb ☎ 7771 2000). Tube: Brixton. 1929 ex-theater; sloping floor ensures everyone can see the band. Covers all bases, from the Pogues to Senegalese stars. 4300 capacity. Box office open only on performance evenings. £15-30. Cash only at the door.

Dublin Castle, 94 Parkway (☎ 8806 2668). It's madness in the back room every Tu, with a blur of record execs and talent scouts on the lookout for the next big thing at *Club Fandango.* 3 bands nightly 8:45-11pm; doors open 8:30pm. £5, students £4.

Forum, 9-11 Highgate Rd. (☎ 7284 1001; box office 7344 0044). Tube: Kentish Town. Turn right and cross the road. Lavish Art Deco theater with great sound and views. Bjork, Jamiroquai, Oasis, Van Morrison, and others have played this 2000-capacity space.

London Astoria (LA1), 157 Charing Cross Rd. (☎ 7344 0044). Tube: Tottenham Court Rd. Once a pickle factory, London Astoria is now devoted to full-time rock. Su-W sees hometown acts and the popular G-A-Y club night (p. 194). Cover £5-25.

CLASSICAL

Home to four world-class orchestras, three major concert halls, two opera houses, two ballet companies, and more chamber ensembles than you could Simon Rattle your baton at, London is ground zero for serious music—and there's no need to break the bank. To hear some of the world's top choirs for free, head to Westminster Abbey (p. 169) or St. Paul's Cathedral (p. 171) for **Evensong.**

Barbican Hall (see **Barbican Theatre,** p. 185). Tube: Barbican. One of Europe's leading concert halls. Home to the **London Symphony Orchestra.** Tickets £6-33.

English National Opera, the Coliseum, St. Martin's Ln. (☎ 7632 8300; www.eno.org). Tube: Charing Cross or Leicester Sq. In London's largest theater, re-opening in January 2004 for its centennial celebration. Known for innovative productions of the classics and contemporary, avant-garde work. Box office open M-Sa 10am-8pm. £5-55, under-18 half-price with adult. Cheap standbys bookable on performance days, by phone from 9am.

The Proms, at the Royal Albert Hall. This summer season of classical music has been held since 1895, with concerts every night from mid-July to mid-Sept. "Promenade" refers to the tradition of selling dirt-cheap standing tickets, but it's the presence of up to 1000 dedicated prommers that gives the concerts their unique atmosphere. Tickets (£5-30) go on sale in May; standing room (£4) from 1½hr. before the concert.

Royal Opera House, Bow St. (☎ 7304 4000). Tube: Covent Garden. Known as "Covent Garden" to the aficionado, the Opera House is also home to the **Royal Ballet.** Box office open daily 10am-8pm. Best seats start at £100, but standing room and restricted-view upper balcony can be under £5. Concessions standby 4hr. before curtain £12.50-15. 67 seats from 10am day of performance £10-40.

South Bank Centre, on the South Bank (☎ 7960 4201). Tube: Waterloo or Embankment. All manner of serious music is on the program here; the **London Philharmonic** is the orchestra-in-residence for the **Royal Festival Hall.** Tickets for all events at the Festival Hall box office (open daily 11am to 8 or 9pm); **Queen Elizabeth Hall** and **Purcell Room** box offices open 45min. before curtain. Some concessions; standbys may also be released 2hr. before performance (check ☎ 7921 0973).

Wigmore Hall, 36 Wigmore St. (☎ 7935 2141; www.wigmore-hall.org.uk). Tube: Oxford Circus. London's premier chamber music venue, in a beautiful setting with excellent acoustics. Occasional jazz. £1 fee for phone bookings. Concerts most nights 7:30pm, no concerts July-Aug. £8-20, student and senior standbys 1hr. before curtain £8-10 (cash only). Daytime concerts Su 11:30am (£10) and M 1pm (£8, seniors £6).

JAZZ, FOLK, AND WORLD

This isn't Chicago, but top **jazz** clubs still pull in big-name performers. **Folk** (which in London usually means ▓**Irish trad**) and **world** music keep an even lower profile, mostly restricted to pubs and community centers. International performers occasionally make appearances at major concert halls such as the **South Bank Centre,** the **Barbican,** and the **Wigmore Hall** (see above).

▓ **606 Club,** 90 Lots Rd. (☎ 7352 5953; www.606club.co.uk). Hard to find; look for the brick arch with a light bulb and ring the doorbell. The intrepid will be rewarded with brilliant British and European jazz in a smoky basement venue. M-W doors open 7:30pm, music 8pm-late; Th doors 8pm, music 9:30pm-late; F-Sa doors 8pm, music 10pm-2am; Su (vocalists) doors 8pm, music 8:30pm-midnight.

Ronnie Scott's, 47 Frith St. (☎ 7439 0747). Tube: Tottenham Court Rd. or Piccadilly Circus. London's oldest and most famous jazz club. 2 bands alternate 4 sets M-Sa, opener at 9:30pm and headline around 11pm. Reservations essential. Food £5-25. Cocktails £7-8. Cover M-Th £15, F-Sa £25, Su £8-12; students M-W £10. Box office open M-Sa 11am-6pm. Club open M-Sa 8:30pm-3am, Su 7:30-11pm. AmEx/MC/V.

SPECTATOR SPORTS

FOOTBALL. From late August to May, over half a million people attend professional football (soccer) matches every Saturday, dressed with fierce loyalty in team colors. Though violence at stadiums has plagued the game for years, the atmosphere has become much tamer now. The big three London teams are: **Arsenal,** Highbury Stadium, Avenell Rd. (☎ 7413 3366; Tube: Arsenal, Zone 2); **Chelsea,** Stamford Bridge, Fulham Rd. (☎ 7386 7799; Tube: Fulham Broadway, Zone 2); and **Tottenham Hotspur,** White Hart Ln. (☎ 8365 5000; Tube: Seven Sisters, Zone 3 or DRL: White Hart Ln.). Tickets are £10-40, but they are never easy to get on short notice.

RUGBY. Rugby was allegedly created when an inspired (or confused) Rugby School student picked up a regular football and ran it into the goal. Never as popular in London as it is in the north, locals still turn out to support the four big London teams who play their season from August to May on weekends: **London Wasps** (☎ 8993 8298); **NEC Harlequins** (☎ 8410 6000); **Saracens** (☎ 0192 347 5222); and **London Broncos** (☎ 090683 3303). Late winter bring the **Six Nations Championship** (featuring England, France, Ireland, Italy, Scotland, and Wales.). Tickets for matches at **Twickenham** (☎ 8892 2000; DRL: Twickenham) are nearly impossible to get.

CRICKET. London's two cricket grounds stage both county and international contests. **Lord's,** on St. John's Wood Rd., is the home of the **Marylebone Cricket Club** (MCC), the established governing body of cricket. (☎7432 1066. Tube: St. John's Wood.) The **Oval,** on Kennington, also fields matches. (☎7582 7764. Tube: Oval.) Every summer a touring nation plays England in a series of matches, including a customary thrashing every four years at the hands of the **Australian Cricket Team.**

TENNIS. Every year for two weeks in late June and early July, tennis buffs the world over focus their attention on **Wimbledon.** Reserve months ahead or arrive by 6am (gates open 10:30am) to secure one of the 500 Centre and #1 court tickets sold every morning; otherwise, settle for a "grounds" ticket for the outer courts. (All England Lawn Tennis Club. ☎8971 2473. Tube: Southfields. DRL: Wimbledon. Grounds £9-11; after 5pm £5. Show courts £19-60.)

▟ SHOPPING

From its earliest days, London has been a trading city, its wealth and power built upon almost two millennia of commerce. Today, even more so than at the height of the Empire, London's economy is truly international—and thanks to the fundamentally eclectic nature of Londoners' diverse tastes, the range of goods is unmatched anywhere. From Harrods's proud boast to supply "all things to all people" to outrageous club wear in Camden, you could shop for a lifetime.

DEPARTMENT STORES

▨ Hamley's, 188-189 Regent St. (☎7734 3161). Tube: Bond St. 7 floors filled with every conceivable toy and game; dozens of strategically placed product demonstrations. Open M-F 10am-8pm, Sa 9:30am-8pm, Su noon-6pm. AmEx/MC/V.

Selfridges, 400 Oxford St. (☎(0870) 837 7377). Tube: Bond St. The total department store. Covers everything from traditional tweeds to space-age clubwear. 14 eateries, hair salon, **bureau de change,** and hotel. Open M-W 10am-7pm, Th-F 10am-8pm, Sa 9:30am-7pm, Su noon-6pm. AmEx/MC/V.

Liberty, 210-220 Regent St. (☎7734 1234). Tube: Oxford Circus. Focus on top-quality design and handicrafts. Enormous hat department and a whole hall of scarves. Open M-W 10am-6:30pm, Th 10am-8pm, F-Sa 10am-7pm, Su noon-6pm. AmEx/MC/V.

Fortnum & Mason, 181 Piccadilly (☎7734 8040). Tube: Green Park or Piccadilly Circus. London's smallest, snootiest department store, est. 1707. Famed for its sumptuous food hall. Open M-Sa 10am-6:30pm. AmEx/MC/V.

Harrods, 87-135 Old Brompton Rd. (☎7730 1234). Tube: Knightsbridge. The only thing bigger than the bewildering store is the mark-up on the goods—no wonder only tourists and oil sheikhs actually shop here. Open M-Sa 10am-7pm. AmEx/MC/V/your soul.

Harvey Nichols, 109-125 Knightsbridge (☎7235 5000). Tube: Knightsbridge. Bond St., Rue St-Honoré, and Fifth Avenue all rolled up into 5 floors of fashion, from the biggest names to the hippest contemporary unknowns. Open M-Tu and Sa 10am-7pm, W-F 10am-8pm, Su noon-6pm. AmEx/MC/V.

MAJOR CHAINS

As with any large city, London retailing is dominated by chains. Fortunately, local shoppers are picky enough that buying from a chain doesn't mean abandoning the flair and quirky stylishness for which Londoners are famed. Most chains have a flagship on or near Oxford St. Different branches have slightly different hours, but almost all the stores listed below are open daily 10am 7pm, starting later (noon) on Su and staying open an hour later one night of the week (usually Th).

■ **Karen Millen** (☎(01622) 664 032). 8 locations including 262-264 Regents St. (Tube: Oxford Circus) and 22-23 James St. (Tube: Covent Garden). Best known for embroidered brocade suits and evening gowns, but edging towards a more casual line.

■ **Lush** (☎(01202) 668 545). 6 locations, including Garden Piazza (Tube: Covent Garden) and 40 Carnaby St. (Tube: Oxford Circus). All-natural cosmetics that look good enough to eat; soap is hand-cut from blocks masquerading as cakes and cheeses (£3-5) and guacamole-like facial masks are scooped from tubs.

FCUK (☎ 7529 7766). Flagship at 396 Oxford St. (Tube: Bond St.) Home of the advertising coup of the 90s, FCUK offers an extensive collection of items with their vaguely offensive, mildly subversive moniker. AmEx/MC/V.

Jigsaw (☎8392 5678). Flagship at 126 New Bond St. (Tube: Bond St.). The essence of Britishness, distilled into quality mid-priced womenswear. AmEx/MC/V.

Muji (☎ 7287 7323). Flagship at 41 Carnaby St. (Tube: Oxford Circus.) Minimalist lifestyle stores, with a Zen take on everything from clothes to kitchenware. AmEx/MC/V.

Topshop/Top Man/Miss Selfridge (☎ 7927 0000). Flagship at 214 Oxford St. (Tube: Oxford Circus.) Over-25s will feel middle-aged. Topshop sells strappy shoes and skimpy clubwear on 3 floors. Miss Selfridge has an even younger, girlier feel; Top Man is all shiny Ts and cargo pants. 10% student discount. AmEx/MC/V.

SHOPPING BY NEIGHBORHOOD

CENTRAL LONDON

OXFORD AND REGENT STREETS. Oxford St. is London's shopping center. The atmosphere is incredible in the department stores and mainstream chains of Oxford St. and Regent St. Fashionable boutiques line pedestrian **South Molton Street,** stretching south into Mayfair from the Bond St. Tube, and **Foubert's Place,** near youth-oriented Carnaby St. The area also has a number of excellent shops.

MAYFAIR. Mayfair's aristocratic pedigree is evident in the scores of high-priced shops, many bearing Royal Warrants to indicate their status as official palace suppliers. **Bond Street** is the location of choice for the biggest names. Less mainstream designers set up shop on **Conduit Street,** where Old Bond St. meets New Bond St.; here you'll find Vivienne Westwood, Alexander McQueen, and Yohji Yamamoto. Cheap (relatively speaking) duds abound at **Paul Smith Sale Shop,** 23 Avery Row (Tube: Bond St.); find a smallish range of last-season and clearance items from the master of modern British menswear. Exclusive **Sotheran's of Sackville Street,** 2-5 Sackville St. (☎ 7439 6151; Tube: Piccadilly Circus), founded in 1761, has a charming staff and plenty of affordable books, while the **Waterstone's** at 203-206 Piccadilly (☎ 7851 2400; Tube: Piccadilly Circus) is Europe's largest bookshop.

SOHO. Despite its eternal trendiness, Soho has never been much of a shopping destination. The main exception is the record stores of **D'Arblay Street** and **Berwick Street** including: **Reckless Records,** 26 and 30 Berwick St. (☎ 7437 3362 and 7437 4271); **Sister Ray,** 94 Berwick St. (☎ 7287 8385); and top DJ hangout **Uptown Records,** 3 D'Arblay St. (☎ 7434 3639; all Tube: Oxford Circus). Keeping up the musical theme are the excellent instrument and equipment shops of **Denmark Street.**

COVENT GARDEN. Covent Garden is increasingly mainstream, though there are enough quirky shops left to make it worth a look. North of the piazza, **Floral Street** is firmly established as the area's smartest thoroughfare. Ever-popular **Neal Street** is a top destination for funky footwear and mid-priced clubwear, though the fashion focus has shifted to nearby **Shorts Gardens, Earlham Street,** and **Monmouth Street** A best bet for women's clothing is ■**Apple Tree,** 51 and 62 Neal St. (☎ 7836 6088), which offers colorful clothing. Treat your feet at **Office,** 57 Neal St. (☎ 7379 1896), the largest outlet of London's foremost fashion footwear retailer.

BLOOMSBURY. Besides intellectuals, Bloomsbury's main commodity is **books.** The streets around the British Museum in particular are crammed with specialist and cut-price booksellers, like **Unsworths,** 12 Bloomsbury St. (☎7436 9836; Tube: Tottenham Court Rd.). For a blast from the past, the small selection of vintage clothes in ▨**Delta of Venus,** 151 Drummond St. (☎7387 3037; Tube: Warren St. or Euston), is unbeatable and spans the 1960s to the early 80s. For a blast into the future, head to **Tottenham Court Road** for electronics.

CHELSEA AND KNIGHTSBRIDGE. No serious shopper can ignore Chelsea. If **Sloane Square** is too sloaney ("preppy," to Americans), the **King's Road,** with one-off boutiques at all price ranges, is all things to all shoppers. The main shopping arteries of **Knightsbridge** are the **Old Brompton Road,** with upmarket chains, and **Sloane Street,** full of exclusive boutiques. **World's End,** 430 King's Rd. (☎7352 6551) gave birth to the Sex Pistols, but has since gone mainstream. ▨**Steinberg & Tolkein,** 193 King's Rd. (☎7376 3660) offers London's largest collection of vintage clothing.

NOTTING HILL. The best reason to visit Notting Hill is **Portobello Market,** which brings an influx of color and vivacity to an otherwise gentrified area. The "Market" is actually several distinct markets occupying different parts of the street and operating on different days; Saturdays, when all come together in a mile-long row, is the best day to visit. The **antiques market,** north along Portobello from Chepstow Villas to Elgin Cres. (Tube: Notting Hill Gate; open Sa 7am-5pm) sells cheapish bric-a-brac, little of it truly rare or very old; the **general market,** from Elgin Cres. to Lancaster Rd. (Tube: Westbourne Park or Ladbroke Grove; open M-W 8am-6pm, Th 9am-1pm, F-Sa 7am-7pm) sells food, flowers, and household essentials; and the **clothes market,** north of Lancaster Rd. (Tube: Ladbroke Grove; open F-Sa 8am-3pm) has a wide selection of secondhand clothes, New Age bangles, and cheap clubwear. Also in the area is **The Travel Bookshop,** 13-15 Blenheim Cres. (☎7229 5260), the specialist bookshop featured in *Notting Hill.* **Dolly Diamond,** 51 Pembridge Rd. (☎7792 2479; Tube: Notting Hill Gate), allows you to choose "your" look from a selection of classic 50s-70s clothes and elegant 20s-40s evening gowns.

NORTH LONDON

In **Camden Town,** you'll find hundreds of identical stores flogging the same chunky shoes and leather trousers they've been selling for years. Arrive early and have a game plan—amid the dross there are genuine bargains and incredible finds. The **Camden markets** are located off Camden High St. and Chalk Farm Rd. (Tube: Camden Town). The **Stables Market** (most shops open daily) is nearest Chalk Farm and the best of the bunch, offering good vintage clothes plus some of the most outrageous club- and fetish-wear ever made. **Camden Canal Market** (open F-Su) is down the tunnel opposite Camden Lock, and starts out promisingly with jewelry and watches, but degenerates rapidly into sub-par clubbing duds and tourist trinkets. **Camden Lock Market** (most stalls open F or Sa-Su), located between the railway bridge and the canal, is arranged around a food-filled courtyard on the Regent's Canal. **The Camden Market** (open F-Su), nearest to Camden Tube and correspondingly the most crowded and least innovative, offers jeans, sweaters, and designer fakes. Our favorite Camden shop is ▨**Cyberdog/Cybercity,** arch 14 of the Stables Market (☎7482 2842), with unbelievable club clothes for superior life forms. Try on the fluorescent body-armor, or steel corsets with rubber breast-hoses.

Meanwhile in **Islington,** the **Camden Passage,** Islington High St., behind "The Mall" antiques gallery on Upper St., is *the* place for antiques, especially prints and drawings. Shops outnumber stalls. (Tube: Angel. Most open W and Sa 8:30am-6pm.)

BRITAIN

EAST LONDON

In East London, the street-market tradition is alive and well, helped along by large immigrant communities. The **Brick Lane Market** (Tube: Shoreditch or Aldgate East; open Su 8am-2pm) has a South Asian flair, with food, rugs, spices, bolts of fabric, and strains of sitar, while the **Petticoat Lane Market** (Tube: Liverpool St., Aldgate, or Aldgate East; open Su 9am-2pm) has block after block of cheap clothing.

■ NIGHTLIFE

The **West End**—especially **Soho**—is the scene of much of Central London's after-dark action, from the glitzy Leicester Sq. tourist traps, like the Hippodrome and Equinox, to semi-secret underground clubs. The other major axes of London nightlife are East London's **Shoreditch** and **Hoxton** (known as Shoo) and South London's **Brixton,** which is quickly becoming London's top neighborhood for nightlife.

PUBS

Pubs might close at 11pm, but they're still an essential part of the London social scene. There are thousands of pubs in London; these are some of our favorites.

■ **Ye Olde Mitre Tavern,** 1 Ely Ct. Between Ely Pl. and Hatton Garden. Tube: Chancery Ln. To find the alley where this pub hides, look for the street lamp on Hatton Garden bearing a sign of a mitre. This classic pub was built in 1546 by the Bishop of Ely. With dark oak beams and spun glass, the two pint-sized rooms are perfect for nestling up to a bitter. Arguably London's finest pub. Open M-F 11am-11pm.

■ **The Wenlock Arms,** 26 Wenlock Rd. Tube: Old St. or Angel. One of the best-kept secrets in London, this fantastic pub is the real deal, with an unbeatable array of real ales and the best hot salt beef sandwich in the city (£3). Food served "until we run out of bread." Open Tu-F 11am-7pm, Sa 10am-4pm. MC/V.

■ **Ye Olde Cheshire Cheese,** Wine Office Ct. By 145 Fleet St. Tube: Blackfriars or St. Paul's. One-time haunt of Charles Dickens, Theodore Roosevelt, and Mark Twain. Open M-F 11am-11pm, Sa 11am-3pm and 5:30-11pm, Su noon-3:30pm. AmEx/MC/V.

The Eagle, 159 Farringdon Rd. Tube: Farringdon. The original gastropub. The Eagle offers tasty Mediterranean dishes (£10) and a down-to-earth atmosphere that appeals to both tourists and locals. Open M-F 12:30-3pm and 6:30-10pm, Sa 12:30-2:30pm and 6:30-10:30pm, Su 12:30-3:30pm. MC/V.

The Royal Oak, 44 Tabard St. Tube: Borough. Voted the Best Pub of 2003 by the Campaign for Real Ale, the Royal Oak is one of the most pleasant establishments in London. Open M-F 11:30am-11pm. MC/V.

The Jerusalem Tavern, 55 Britton St. Tube: Farringdon. Offers three seating areas and many little niches, including a small balcony. Broad beer selection with specialty ales (£2.40) like grapefruit, cinnamon and apple, and the delicious Suffolk Gold. Open M-F 11am-11pm. MC/V.

The George Inn, 77 Borough High St. Tube: London Bridge. The only remaining galleried inn in London. A tiny interior leads out into a popular patio. Excellent ale and rich history. Open M-Sa 11am-11pm, Su noon-10:30pm. AmEx/MC/V.

The Scarsdale, 23a Edwards Sq. Tube: High St. Kensington. Built by a French speculator to house Napoleon's officers following the inevitable conquest of Britain, it's now a picture-perfect pub. Elaborate entrees (£10-16) served noon-3pm and 6-10pm. Bar food £6-9. Open daily noon-11pm. MC/V.

BARS

An explosion of **club-bars** has invaded the previously forgotten gap between pubs and clubs, offering seriously stylish surroundings and top-flight DJs together with plentiful lounging space. Club-bars are usually open from noon or early evening, allowing you to skip the cover charge by arriving early and staying put. They tend to close earlier than clubs, usually between midnight and 2am.

■ **Filthy MacNasty's Whisky Café,** 68 Amwell St. Tube: Angel. This Irish pub is frequented by a galaxy of stars—the drop-in list includes Johnny Depp, Ewan McGregor, Kate Moss, and U2. Live music most Th. Occasional readings fulfill the erudite bad-boy atmosphere. 32 different whiskies (around £2). Open M-Sa noon-11pm, Su noon-10:30pm.

■ **The Market,** 240A Portobello Rd. Tube: Ladbroke Grove. The loudest spot on Portobello, The Market has a rowdy, unpretentious atmosphere. Cuban punch £3. Jazz Su 5-8pm. Open M-Sa 11am-11pm, Su noon-12:30am.

Freud, 198 Shaftesbury Ave. The sand-blasted walls occasionally echo to live jazz (M starting at 4pm). Cocktails from £3.40. Bottled beers less than £3. Light meals noon-4:30pm (£3.50-6). Open M-Sa 11am-11pm, Su noon-10:30pm. MC/V.

Cafe Kick, 43 Exmouth Market Tube: Farringdon. Dedicated to the twin goals of drinking and soccer, this jovial cafe-bar is dominated by multiple foosball tables (50p per game). Happy Hour daily 4-7pm (beer £1.50). Beers and cocktails £2.50-5.50. Open M-Sa 11:30am-11pm, Su noon-11pm.

The Social, 5 Little Portland St. Tube: Oxford Circus. This small DJ-driven bar packs a happening crowd into its maze of narrow spaces. Cocktails £5.10. Shooters £3. DJs nightly from 7pm. Open M-Sa noon-11pm.

Point 101, 101 New Oxford St. Tube: Tottenham Court Rd. Retro look, with long vinyl booths in the balcony bar. Nightly DJs, starting around 9pm, tend toward chill-out jazz and soul. Open M-Th 8am-2am, F-Sa 8am-2:30am, Su 8am-11:30pm. AmEx/MC/V.

NIGHTCLUBS

Every major DJ in the world either lives in London or makes frequent visits. The UK has taken the lead in developing new types of dance music. Even weekly publications have trouble keeping up with the club scene—*Time Out* (W, £2.20), the Londoner's clubbing bible, only lists about half the happenings any given night. The scene revolves around promoters and the nights they organize rather than the clubs themselves; top nights come, go, and move around unpredictably. To stay on top of things, comb through *Time Out*, which also prints the "TOP" pass, giving you discounts on many of the week's shenanigans.

Working out how to get home afterwards is crucial; the Tube and regular buses stop shortly after **midnight,** and after **1am** black cabs are rare. If there's no convenient **Night Bus** home, ask the club in advance if they can order a **minicab** for you; otherwise, order your own before you leave. Although it's technically illegal for minicabs to ply for hire, whispered calls of "taxi" or honking horns signal their presence—but there's no guarantee that the driver is reputable. Agree on a price before you get in, and never ride alone.

DRESS. Clubs tend to fall into one of two categories: Those for dancing, and those for posing. In the former, dress codes are generally relaxed; jeans, stylish t-shirts, and trainers, though women are usually expected to make more of an effort. At posers' clubs, however, dress is crucial. If you're not sure what to wear, call the club beforehand; otherwise, black and slinky is usually safe.

■ **Fabric,** 77a Charterhouse St. Tube: Farringdon. One of London's premier clubs, Fabric is as large and loud as it gets, featuring a vibrating main dance floor that is actually one giant speaker. Cover F £12, Sa-Su £15.

■ **Tongue&Groove,** 50 Atlantic Rd. Tube: Brixton. Soak up the brothel chic—huge black leather sofas and red lighting—and anticipate ecstatic early-morning partying. Cover £3-4. Open daily 9pm-5am.

■ **Bug Bar,** Crypt, St. Matthew's Church Tube: Brixton. The antithesis of most self-labeled "cool" nightspots, the intimate space in this whitewashed former church crypt holds an extremely laid-back, friendly crowd. Cover under £7. Open W-Th 7pm-1am, F-Sa 8pm-3am, Su 7pm-2am.

Strawberry Moons, 15 Heddon St. Tube: Piccadilly Circus or Oxford Circus. Eccentric club with theatrical lighting effects, an animatronic talking moose head, a "time machine," and a staff that performs impromptu dance routines. Cover under £10. Open M and W 5pm-11pm, Tu and Th-Sa 5pm-3am.

Notting Hill Arts Club, 21 Notting Hill Gate. Tube: Notting Hill Gate. With turntables on folding tables, 1 dance floor, and no decoration beyond projections and art left over from daytime exhibitions, this no-frills basement still manages to rock the house. Acts vary daily. Cover M £4, free before 9pm; Tu-Th £5, free before 8pm; F £6, free before 8pm; Sa-Su £5, free before 6pm. Open M-W 6pm-1am, Th-F 6pm-2am, Sa 4pm-2am, Su 4pm-12:30am.

Scala, 275 Pentonville Rd. Tube: King's Cross. The huge main floor embraces its movie-theater past: DJs spin from the projectionist's box, tiered balconies make great people-watching, and giant screens pulse with wild visuals. Dress up. Cover £7-13.

Ministry of Sound, 103 Gaunt St. Tube: Elephant and Castle. Take the exit for South Bank University. Mecca for serious clubbers worldwide—arrive before it opens or queue all night. Emphasis on dancing rather than decor, with a massive main room, smaller second dance floor, and overhead balcony bar. Dress well, especially on Sa. F garage and R&B (10:30pm-5am; £12); Sa US and vocal house (11pm-8am; £15).

Bar Rumba, 36 Shaftesbury Ave. Tube: Piccadilly Circus. Fresh, young crowd makes good use of the industrial-strength interior. Cover £3-12. Open M-Th 9pm-3am, F 9pm-4am, Sa 9pm-5am, Su 8pm-1:30am.

Madame Jojo's, 8-10 Brewer St. Tube: Piccadilly Circus. Intimate bordello-style red-hued club, with a sunken dance floor inviting grand entrances down the staircase. Th deep beats (cover £5-7).

GAY AND LESBIAN NIGHTLIFE

London has a very visible gay scene, ranging from flamboyant to mainstream. *Time Out* devotes a section to gay listings, and gay newspapers include the *Pink Paper*. *Boyz* magazine, free from gay bars, and the *Ginger Beer* website (www.gingerbeer.co.uk) track gay and lesbian nightlife respectively. Soho—especially **Old Compton Street**—is the heart of gay London, with much smaller scenes in Islington, Earl's Court, and Brixton.

■ **G-A-Y** (☎ 7434 9592; www.g-a-y.co.uk). M and Th at the Mean Fiddler, 165 Charing Cross Rd.; F-Sa at the London Astoria, 157 Charing Cross Rd. Tube: Tottenham Court Rd. London's biggest gay and lesbian night, 4 nights a week. Cover under £11. Open M, Th, F until 4am, Sa until 5am.

The Box, 32-34 Monmouth St. (☎ 7240 5828). Recently renovated, this spacious gay/mixed bar-brasserie is popular with a stylish media/fashion crowd. Open M-Sa 11am-11pm, Su 7-10:30pm. MC/V.

Vespa Lounge, St. Giles Circus (☎ 7836 8956). Tube: Tottenham Court Rd. Relaxed lesbian lounge bar with comfy seats, pool table. Thai food from downstairs Conservatory restaurant. Gay men welcome as guests. Open M-Sa 6pm-midnight.

⚡ DAYTRIP FROM LONDON

WINDSOR AND ETON. The town of Windsor and the attached village of Eton are consumed by two bastions of the British class system, **Windsor Castle** and **Eton College.** Within the ancient stone walls of Windsor Castle lie some of the most sumptuous rooms and rarest artwork in Europe. When the Queen is home, the Royal Standard flies in place of the Union Jack. During these times, large areas of the castle are unavailable to visitors, usually without warning. The **Changing of the Guard** takes place in front of the Guard Room at 11am on most days. (24hr. info ☎01753 831 118. Castle open Apr.-Oct. daily 10am-4pm; Nov.-Mar. 10am-3pm. £11.50, seniors £9.50, under-17 £6, families £29.) **Eton College,** founded by Henry VI in 1440, is still England's preeminent public (or private in the American system) school. The best way to see Eton, 10min. down Thames St. from the town center, across the river, is to wander around the schoolyard, a central quad complete with a statue of Henry VI. (☎01753 671 177. Open July-Aug. and late Mar. to mid-Apr. daily 10:30am-4:30pm; other times 2-4:30pm. £3, under-16 £2.25.)

Two train stations are near Windsor Castle; follow the signs. **Trains** (☎08457 484 950) pull into Windsor and Eton Central from London Paddington via Slough (50min., 2 per hr., round-trip £6.90). Trains arrive at Windsor and Eton Riverside from London Waterloo (50min., 2 per hr., round-trip £6.90). Green Line **buses** (☎8668 7261) make the trip from London, leaving from Eccleston Bridge (#700 and 702; 1-1½hr., round-trip £5.50-6.70).

SOUTHERN ENGLAND

Southern England's history has deep continental roots. Early Britons settled the pastoral counties of Kent, Sussex, and Hampshire after crossing the Channel. Later, William the Conqueror left his mark in the form of awe-inspiring cathedrals, many built around settlements begun by Romans. During WWII, German bombings uncovered long-buried evidence of an invasion by Caesar. This historic landscape has in turn had a profound influence on the country's national identity, inspiring such British literati as Geoffrey Chaucer, Jane Austen, and E.M. Forster. For detailed info on transport options to the Continent, see p. 48.

CANTERBURY ☎01227

Archbishop Thomas à Becket met his demise at ⚡**Canterbury Cathedral** in 1170 after an irate Henry II asked, "Will no one rid me of this troublesome priest?" Later, in his famed *Canterbury Tales*, Chaucer captured the irony of tourists visiting England's most famous execution site. (☎762 862. Open M-Sa 9am-5pm, Su 12:30-2:30pm and 4:30-5:30pm. £3, students £2. Audio tour £2.50.) **The Canterbury Tales,** on St. Margaret's St., is a museum that simulates the journey of Chaucer's pilgrims. (☎479 227. Open July-Aug. daily 9am-5:30pm; Mar.-June and Sept.-Oct. 9:30am-5:30pm; Nov.-Feb. Su-F 10am-4:30pm, Sa 9:30am-5:30pm. £6, students £5.50.) On Stour St., the **Canterbury Heritage Museum** tells the history of Canterbury from medieval times to WWII. (☎452 747. Open June-Oct. M-Sa 10:30am-5pm, Su 1:30-5pm; Nov.-May M-Sa 10:30am-5pm. £2.60, students £1.70.) For a quiet break, walk to the riverside gardens of England's first Franciscan friary, **Greyfriars,** Stour St. (Open in summer M-F 2-4pm. Free.)

Trains from London Victoria arrive at Canterbury's **East Station** (1¾hr., 2 per hr., day return £17), while trains from London Charing Cross and Waterloo arrive at **West Station** (1½hr., every hr., day return £17). National Express **buses** (☎(08705) 808 080) arrive from London at St. George's Ln. (2hr., 2 per hr., £11). The **tourist**

office is in the Buttermarket, 12-13 Sun St., and books rooms for a £2.50 fee and 10% deposit. (☎378 100. Open M-Sa 9:30am-5pm, Su 10am-4pm.) **B&Bs** cluster near West Station, around **High Street,** and on **New Dover Road.** For a relaxing stay, try ☒**Kipps, A Place to Sleep ❷,** 40 Nunnery Fields, home to a social, yet not overbearing, atmosphere. The friendly management offers a kitchen, comfortable lounge, and a great movie selection. (☎786 121. Laundry £3. Key deposit £10. Internet £1 per 30min. Dorms £11-13; singles £18; doubles £30.) The **YHA Canterbury ❷,** 54 New Dover Rd., is in a beautiful old house. (☎462 911. Kitchen available. **Bureau de change.** Breakfast included. Internet £2.50 per 30min. Reception 7:30-10am and 1-11pm. Book at least 2 weeks ahead in summer. Dorms £15, under-18 £12.) The **Camping and Caravanning Club Site ❶,** on Bekesbourne Ln., has good facilities. (☎463 216. Electricity and showers. £4-5.50 per person. £5 per tent.) ☒**Marlowe's ❷,** 55 St. Peter's St., serves an eclectic mix of English and Mexican food. (Entrees €7-10. Open M-Sa 9am-10:30pm, Su 10am-10:30pm.) There's a **Safeway** supermarket on St. George's Pl. (☎769 335. Open M-F 8am-8pm, Su 10am-4pm.) **Postal Code:** CT1 2BA.

BRIGHTON ☎01273

According to legend, the future King George IV sidled into Brighton (pop.180,000) for some decidedly common hanky-panky around 1784. Today, Brighton is still the unrivaled home of the "dirty weekend"—it sparkles with a tawdry luster all its own. Before indulging, check out England's long-time obsession with the Far East at the excessively ornate **Royal Pavilion,** on Pavilion Parade, next to Old Steine. Rumor has it that King George IV wept tears of joy upon entering it, proving that wealth does not give you taste. (☎290 900. Open daily Apr.-Sept. 9:30am-4:30pm; Oct.-Mar. 10am-4:30pm. Admission £5.80, students £4. Guided tours daily 11:30am-2:30pm.) Around the corner on Church St. stands the **Brighton Museum and Art Gallery,** showcasing Art Nouveau paintings, English pottery, and Art Deco pieces, as well as an extensive Brighton historical exhibit that thoroughly explains the phrase "dirty weekend." (Open Tu 10am-7pm, W-Sa 10am-5pm, Su 2-5pm. Free.) Before heading out to the rocky **beach,** stroll the **Lanes,** a jumble of 17th-century streets that form the heart of Old Brighton.

Brighton has plenty of nightlife options; for tips, pick up *The Punter* or *What's On* at music stores, newsstands, and pubs. Purify yourself at ☒**Font and Firkin,** Union St., in the Lanes, where the altar in this former parish house now honors the gods of rock. Live entertainment and good food make this a place worthy of devotion. (Music W, F-Sa. Open M-Sa 11:30am-11pm, Su noon-10:30pm.) Sample the dark rum concoction at the trendy pub **Mash Tun,** 1 Church St., which attracts an eclectic student crowd. (Open M-Sa noon-11pm, Su noon-10:30pm.) Most **clubs** are open M-Sa 9pm-2am. Brighton native Fatboy Slim still mixes occasionally at **The Beach,** 171-181 King's Rd., a popular shore-side club. (Cover £4-10.) **Casablanca,** on Middle St., plays live jazz to a predominantly student crowd. **Event II,** on West St., is crammed with the down-from-London crowd looking for thrills. **Zanzibar,** 129 James St., for drinks and nightly entertainment.

Trains (☎(08457) 484 950) leave from Brighton Station at the northern end of Queen's Rd. for London (1¼hr., 6 per hr., £12) and Portsmouth (1½hr., every hr., £12). National Express **buses** (☎(08705) 808 080) arrive at Pool Valley from London (2hr., 15 per day, round-trip £8). The **tourist office** is at 10 Bartholomew Sq. (☎(0906) 711 2255; www.visitbrighton.com. Open Apr.-Sept. M-F 9am-5pm, Sa 10am-5pm; Oct.-Mar. M-F 9am-5pm, Sa 10am-5pm, Su 10am-4pm.) Rest at **Baggies Backpackers ❷,** 33 Oriental Pl., which has exquisite murals, frequent live music, and many spontaneous parties. Head west of West Pier along King's Rd., and Oriental Pl. is on the right. (☎733 740. Dorms £12; doubles £30.) The rowdy **Brighton Backpackers Hostel ❷,** 75-76 Middle St., features a downstairs lounge that functions as an all-night party spot. A quieter annex faces the ocean. (☎777 717. Dorms £11-

12; doubles £25-30.) **Bombay Aloo ❶**, 39 Ship St., is an inventive Indian/vegetarian restaurant that serves an unbeatable all-you-can-eat special. (Vegetarian special £5. Entrees £3-7. Open noon-midnight.) **Postal Code:** BN1 1BA.

PORTSMOUTH ☎023

Set Victorian seaside holidays against prostitutes, drunkards, and a lot of bloody cursing sailors, and the 900-year history of Portsmouth (pop. 190,500) will emerge. On the **seafront,** visitors relive D-Day, explore warships, and learn of the days when Britannia truly ruled the waves. War buffs and historians will want to plunge head-first into the unrivaled ◙**Portsmouth Historic Dockyard,** in the Naval Base, which houses a fleet of Britain's most storied ships, including Henry VIII's *Mary Rose,* the HMS *Victory,* and the HMS *Warrior.* The entrance is next to the tourist office on the Hard. (Ships open Mar.-Oct. daily 10am-5:30pm; Nov.-Feb. 10am-4:45pm. Individual site tickets £9.50. Combination ticket £15, seniors and children £12.) The ◙**D-Day Museum,** on Clarence Esplanade, leads visitors through life-size dioramas of the 1944 invasion. (Open Apr.-Sept. daily 10am-5:30pm; Oct.-Mar. 10am-5pm. £5, students £3, seniors £3.75.)

Trains (☎(08457) 484 950) run to Southsea Station, on Commercial Rd., from London Waterloo (1½hr., 4 per hr., £21). National Express **buses** (☎(08705) 808 080) arrive from London (2½hr., every 2hr., £17) and Salisbury (2½hr., every 2hr., £17). The **tourist office** is on the Hard, next to the dockyard. (☎9282 6722; www.visitportsmouth.co.uk. Open daily 9:30am-5:45pm.) Moderately priced B&Bs (around £20) clutter **Southsea,** 2½km east of the Hard along the coast. Take any Southsea bus and get off at the Strand to reach the ◙**Portsmouth and Southsea Backpackers Lodge ❶,** 4 Florence Rd., which offers immaculate rooms, energetic owners, and a pan-European crowd. (☎/fax 9283 2495. Internet £1 per 30min. Dorms £12; doubles £26, with bath £29.) **Birchwood Guest House ❷,** 44 Waverly Rd., has bright, spacious rooms, an ample breakfast, and a lounge with digital cable and a bar. (☎9281 1337. Prices vary with season; call for rates.) The owner of the **Brittania Guest House ❸,** 48 Granada Rd., loves to share his maritime interests with guests. (☎814 234. Full breakfast included. Singles £20; doubles £40-45.) **Country Kitchen ❶,** 59a Marmion Rd., serves savory vegetarian and vegan entrees. (£4-6. Open daily 9:30am-5pm.) **Pubs** near the Hard provide sailors with galley fare and grog. **Postal Code:** PO1 1AA.

WINCHESTER ☎01962

Having once been the center of William the Conqueror's kingdom, Winchester (pop. 32,000) revels in its storied past. Duck under the archway, pass through the square, and behold the 900-year-old **Winchester Cathedral,** 5 the Close. The 169m long cathedral is the longest medieval building in Europe; the interior holds magnificent tiles and Jane Austen's tomb. The 12th-century Winchester Bible also resides in the library. (☎857 225. Cathedral open daily 7:15am-5:30pm; east end closes 5pm. Suggested donation £3.50, students £2.50. Free tours 10am-3pm.) About 25km north of Winchester is the meek village of **Chawton,** where Jane Austen lived. It was in her cottage that she penned *Pride and Prejudice, Emma, Northanger Abbey,* and *Persuasion,* among others. Many of her manuscripts are on display. Take Hampshire **bus** #X64 (M-Sa 11 per day, round-trip £5.30), or the London and Country bus #65 from the bus station (Su); ask to be let off at the Chawton roundabout, and follow the signs. (☎0142 083 262. Open Mar.-Dec. daily 11am-4pm; Jan.-Feb. Sa-Su only, call for hours. £4, seniors £3, under-18 50p.)

Trains (☎08547 484 950) arrive at Winchester's Station Hill, at City Rd. and Sussex St., from London Waterloo (1hr., 3 or 4 per hr., £20) and Portsmouth (1hr., every hr., £7). National Express **buses** (☎08705 808 080) run from London via Heathrow (1½hr., 7 per day, £12) and Oxford (2½hr., 2 per day, £6.80). The

tourist office, the Guildhall, Broadway, is across from the bus station. (☎840 500; www.winchester.gov.uk. Open May-Sept. M-Sa 9:30am-5:30pm, Su 11am-4pm; Oct.-Apr. M-Sa 10am-5pm.) Just a 10min. walk from town is the **Farrells B&B ❸,** 5 Ranelagh Rd., off Christchurch Rd. With large, well-kept rooms, friendly owners, and furniture a mother would rave about, this B&B feels instantly welcoming. (☎/fax 869 555. Singles £22, with bath £25; doubles £44.) The **YHA Winchester ❶,** 1 Water Ln., is located in an 18th-century watermill, and offers creative bed arrangements between the mill's roof beams. (☎853 723. Kitchen available. Lockout 10am-5pm. Curfew 11pm. Open from late Mar. to early Nov. daily; late Nov. to early Mar. weekends only. Dorms £11, students £10, under-18 £7.) **Royal Oak ❶,** on Royal Oak Passage, next to Godbegot House off High St., is yet another pub touting itself as the UK's oldest. The locally brewed hogshead cask ale (£1.75) is delicious. (Pub food £3-6. Open daily 11am-11pm.) A **Sainsbury's** supermarket is on Middle Brook St., off High St. (Open M-Sa 7am-8pm, Su 11am-5pm.) **Postal Code:** SO23 8WA.

SALISBURY
☎01722

Salisbury (pop. 37,000) centers around ■**Salisbury Cathedral** and its astounding 123m spire. The bases of the pillars actually bend inward under 6400 tons of limestone; the chapel houses the oldest functioning mechanical clock, which has ticked 500 million times in the last 600 years. (☎555 120. Open June-Aug. M-Sa 7:15am-8:15pm, Su 7:15am-6:15pm; Sept.-May daily 7:15am-6:15pm. Suggested donation £3.50, students and seniors £2.50. Check for free tour times.) The roof and tower tours are worthwhile. (May-Sept. M-Sa 11am, 2, 3pm, Su 4:30pm; June-Aug. also M-Sa 6:30pm. £3, students £2. Call ahead.) Nearby, one of 4 surviving copies of the **Magna Carta** rests in the **Chapter House.** (Open June-Aug. M-Sa 9:30am-5:30pm, Su noon-5:30pm; Sept.-May daily 9:30am-5:30pm. Free.)

Trains arrive at South Western Rd. from London (1½hr., every hr., £22-30) and Winchester (1½hr., £9.90). National Express **buses** (☎08705 808 080) pull into 8 Endless St. from London Victoria (2¾hr.; 4 per day; £12.20, round-trip £14); Wilts & Dorset buses (☎336 855) arrive from Bath (#X4; every hr. from 7am-6pm, £4). The **Tourist Information Centre** is on Fish Row in the Guildhall. (☎334 956. Open June-Sept. M-Sa 9:30am-6pm, Su 10:30am-4:30pm; Oct.-Apr. M-Sa 9:30am-5pm; May M-Sa 9:30am-5pm, Su 10:30am-4:30pm.) From the TIC, head left on Fish Row, turn right on Queen St., go left on Milford St., and then under the overpass to find the **YHA Salisbury ❷,** in Milford Hill House, on Milford Hill, which offers 4 kitchenettes, a TV lounge, and a cafeteria. (☎327 572. Breakfast included. Internet access £2.50 per 30min. Lockout 10am-1pm. Reservations recommended. Dorms £15; under-18 £12.) **Matt and Tiggy's ❷,** 51 Salt Ln. just up from the bus station, is a welcoming 450-year-old house with warped floors and exposed ceiling beams. (☎327 443. Dorms £11-12.) At ■**Harper's "Upstairs Restaurant" ❷,** 6-7 Ox Rd., inventive international and English dishes (£6-10) make hearty meals and the "8B48" (2 courses for £8 before 8pm) buys a heap of food. (Open M-F noon-2pm and 6-9:30pm, Sa noon-2pm and 6-10pm, Su 6-9pm.) **Postal Code:** SP1 1AB.

▶ DAYTRIP FROM SALISBURY: STONEHENGE AND AVEBURY. A sunken colossus amid swaying grass and indifferent sheep, **Stonehenge** stands unperturbed by winds whipping at 80km per hour and legions of people who have visited for over 5000 years. The monument has retained its present shape since about 1500 BC; before that it was a complete circle of 7m-tall stones weighing up to 45 tons. Though fantastical attributions of Stonehenge's erection, ranging from Merlin to extraterrestrials, have helped build an attractive mythology around the site, the more plausible explanation—Neolithic builders using still

BRITAIN

unknown methods—is perhaps the most astonishing of all. You may admire Stonehenge for free from nearby Amesbury Hill, 2½km up A303, or pay admission at the site. (☎01980 624 715. Open daily June-Aug. 9am-7pm; mid-Mar. to May and Sept. to mid-Oct. 9:30am-6pm; mid-Oct. to mid-Mar. 9:30am-4pm. £4.40, students £3.30.) For those looking for less touristy stone circles, the neighboring megaliths at **Avebury** are a good alternative. With stones that date from 2500 BC, Avebury's titans are older and larger than their favored cousins at Stonehenge. Wilts & Dorset **buses** (☎336 855) connect from Salisbury's center and train station, and run to both sites (#3, 5, and 6; round-trip £4-6). An **Explorer** ticket (£6) allows travel all day on any bus.

BATH ☎01225

A place of pilgrimage and an architectural masterwork, Bath (pop. 83,000) has been a must-see for travelers since AD 43. In 1701, Queen Anne's trip to the springs re-established the city as a prominent meeting place for artists, politicians, and intellectuals, and the city quickly became a social capital second only to London. No longer an upper-crust resort, today Bath now plays host to crowds of tourists eager to appreciate its historic sites and still-preserved elegant charm.

⛏⁊ TRANSPORTATION AND PRACTICAL INFORMATION. Trains leave from Bath for: Bristol (15min., 4 per hr., £4.60); Exeter (1¼hr., every hr., £23); and London Paddington (1½hr., 2 per hr., £32). National Express **buses** (☎(08705) 808 080) run to London (3hr., every hr., £14) and Oxford (2hr., daily, £11). The train and bus stations are near the south end of Manvers St.; walk toward the town center and turn left on York St. to reach the **tourist office**, in Abbey Chambers. (☎(0870) 444 6442. Open May-Sept. M-Sa 9:30am-6pm, Su 10am-4pm; Oct.-Apr. M-Sa 9:30am-5pm, Su 10am-4pm.) **Postal Code:** BA1 1AJ.

⛏⛤ ACCOMMODATIONS AND FOOD. Many **B&Bs** cluster on Pulteney Rd., Pulteney Gdns., and Crescent Gdns. The **International Backpackers Hostel ❷**, 13 Pierrepont St., which has musically themed rooms, is up the street from the stations. (☎446 787. Laundry £2.50. **Internet** access. Dorms £12; doubles £30.) To get to the friendly **Toad Hall Guest House ❸**, 6 Lime Grove, go across Pulteney Bridge and through Pulteney Gdn. (☎423 254. Breakfast included. Singles £22-25; doubles £40-45.) **Marlborough House ❹**, 1 Marlborough Ln., has themed rooms ranging in style from Georgian to the orientalist "Bamboo." (☎318 175. Breakfast included. Singles £33-43; doubles £75-85.) To reach **Newton Mill Camping ❶**, 4km west on Newton Rd., take bus #5 from the station to Twerton and ask to be let off at the campsite. (☎333 909. Showers free. Tents £4.30-12.) **Demuths Restaurant ❸**, 2 North Parade Passage, has creative vegetarian dishes; the chocolate fudge cake (£4.80) is delicious. (Entrees £8-12. Open Su-F 10am-5:30pm and 6:30-9:30pm, Sa 9am-5:30pm and 6-10:30pm.) Fantastic pan-Asian noodles at **f.east ❷**, 27 High St., range from £7-9. (Open M-Sa noon-11pm, Su noon-5pm.) **Guildhall Market,** between High St. and Grand Parade, has fresh fruit and vegetables. (Open daily 9am-5:30pm.)

◙ SIGHTS. For 400 years, Bath flourished as a Roman city, its bubbling hot springs making the town a pilgrimage site for those seeking religious miracles and physical healing. The **▨Roman Baths Museum** showcases the complexity of Roman architecture and engineering, which included central heating and internal plumbing. (Open July-Aug. daily 9am-10pm; Apr.-June and Sept. 9am-6pm; Oct.-Mar. 9:30am-5pm; last admission 1hr. before closing. Admission £8.50, seniors and students £7.50, children £4.80. Audio tour included.) Nearby, the towering 15th-century **Bath Abbey** has a whimsical west facade with several angels climbing ladders up to heaven and, curiously enough, two climbing down. (Open Apr.-Oct. M-Sa 9am-6pm, Su 1-2:30pm and 4:30-5:30pm; Nov.-Mar. M-Sa 9am-4pm, Su between services. Requested donation £2.50.) Head north up Stall St., turn left on Westgate St., and turn right on Saw Close to reach Queen Sq.; **Jane Austen** lived at #13. Continue up Gay St. to **The Circus,** where Thomas Gainsborough, William Pitt, and David Livingstone lived. To the left down Brock St. is the **Royal Crescent,** a half-moon of Gregorian townhouses bordering **Royal Victoria Park.** The **botanical gardens** nurture 5000 species of plants. (Open M-Sa 9am-dusk, Su 10am-dusk. Free.) The dazzling **Museum of Costume,** on Bennet St. left of the Circus, will satisfy any fashion fetish. (Open daily 10am-5pm. £6; joint ticket with Roman Baths £11.)

GLASTONBURY
☎ 01458

The seat of Arthurian legend and the reputed cradle of Christianity in England, Glastonbury (pop. 6,900) is an amalgam of myth and religion. Legend has it that Joseph of Arimathea founded ■**Glastonbury Abbey,** on Magdelene St., in AD 63. The abbey was destroyed during the English Reformation, but the colossal pile of ruins that remains still invokes the grandeur of the original church. For Arthurian buffs, **Glastonbury Tor** is a must-see. Once an island, the 160m Tor is reputedly the site of the Isle of Avalon, where King Arthur sleeps until his country needs him. To reach the Tor, take the bus in summer (£1), or turn right at the top of High St. onto Lambrook, which becomes Chilkwell St.; turn left onto Wellhouse Ln. and follow the path up the hill. On your way, visit the **Chalice Well,** on Chilkwell St., where it is said that Joseph of Arimathea washed the Holy Grail. Legend holds that the well once ran red with Christ's blood. Pilgrims of a different sort flock to the annual summertime **Glastonbury Festival,** Britain's largest music event. The week-long concert takes place at the end of June and has featured some of the world's biggest bands. (Tickets ☎ (0115) 912 9129; www.glastonburyfestivals.co.uk.)

No trains serve Glastonbury, but First **buses** (☎ (01934) 429 336) run from Bath via Wells (1¼hr., every hr., £4). From the bus stop, turn right on High St. to reach the **tourist office,** the Tribunal, 9 High St., which books rooms for a £3 fee. (☎ 832 954; fax 832 949. Open Apr.-Sept. Su-Th 10am-5pm, F-Sa 10am-5:30pm; Oct.-Mar. Su-Th 10am-4pm, F-Sa 10am-4:30pm.) **Glastonbury Backpackers** ❷, at the corner of Magdalene St. and High St., has a lively cafe bar and friendly staff; both compliment a great location. (☎ 833 353. Breakfast £2-5. **Internet** £1 per 30min. Dorms £12; doubles £30, with bath £35.) **Postal Code:** BA6 9HG.

THE CORNISH COAST

With lush cliffsides stretching out into the Atlantic, Cornwall's terrain doesn't feel quite like England. Indeed, its isolation made it a favored place for Celtic migration in the face of Saxon conquest; though the Cornish language is no longer spoken, the area remains protective of its distinctive past. England's southwest tip has some of the broadest, sandiest beaches in northern Europe, and the surf is up year-round, whether or not the sun decides to break through.

NEWQUAY. Known to the locals as "the new California," Newquay (pop. 30,000) is an incongruous slice of surfer culture in the middle of Cornwall. Winds descend on **Fistral Beach** with a vengeance, creating what some consider the best surfing conditions in Europe. The enticing **Lusty Glaze Beach** beckons from the bay side. Drink up at **The Chy,** 12 Beach Rd., a chic loft with the hippest interior in Newquay. (open M-Sa 10am-2am, Su 10am-12:30am.) Then, dance at **Tall Trees,** 12 Beach Rd. (Cover £2-6. Open mid-Mar. to mid-Sept. M-Sa 9pm-2am; mid-Sept. to mid.-Mar. W-Sa 9pm-2am.) All **trains** (☎ (08457) 484 950) to Newquay come from Par (50min., 4-

5 per day, £4.30). From Par, trains connect to Plymouth (1hr., 15 per day, £6.80) and Penzance (2hr., 12 per day, £9.10). First (☎ (0870) 608 2608) **buses** arrive from St. Ives (2¼hr., 4 per day, £4.50). National Express (☎ (08705) 808 080) runs to London (6hr., 2-4 per day, £32). The **tourist office** is on Marcus Hill, a block from the bus station. (☎ (01637) 854 020. Open June-Sept. M-Sa 9:30am-5:30pm, Su 9:30am-3:30pm; Oct.-May M-F 9:30am-4:30pm, Sa 9:30am-12:30pm.) **Original Backpackers ❷**, 16 Beachfield Ave., has a fantastic location off Bank St. and near Central Sq., facing the beach. (☎ (01637) 874 668. £12 per person, £49 per week.)

PENZANCE. Penzance is the very model of an ancient English pirate town. A Benedictine monastery, **St. Michael's Mount,** was built on the spot where St. Michael appeared in AD 495. The interior is modest, but the grounds are lovely and the 30-story views are captivating. (Open July-Aug. 10:30am-5:30pm and most weekends; Apr.-Oct. M-F 10:30am-5:30pm; Nov.-Mar. M, W, and F by guided tours only. £4.80.) During low tide, visitors can walk to the mount; during high tide, take ferry bus #2 or 2A to Marazion Sq. and catch a ferry (£1). Penzance boasts an impressive number of art galleries; pick up the *Cornwall Gallery Guide* (£1) at the tourist office. **Trains** (☎ (08457) 484 950) go to London (5½hr., 7 per day, £56) and Plymouth (2hr., every hr., £11). National Express (☎ (08705) 808 080) **buses** also run to London (8hr., 8 per day, £29) and Plymouth (3hr., 2 per hr., £6). The **tourist office** is between the train and bus stations on Station Rd. (☎ (01736) 362 207. Open May-Sept. M-Sa 9am-5:30pm, Su 10am-1pm; Oct.-Apr. M-F 9am-5pm, Sa 10am-1pm.) ◪**Blue Dolphin Penzance Backpackers ❷**, on Alexandra Rd., is relaxed and well-kept. (☎ (01736) 363 836; fax 363 844. **Internet** 5p per min. Dorms £10; doubles £24.) ◪**The Turk's Head ❷**, 49 Chapel St., is a pub once sacked by pirates.

ST. IVES. St. Ives (pop. 11,400) is 15km north of Penzance, on a spit of land edged by pastel beaches and azure waters. The town drew a colony of painters and sculptors in the 1920s; Virginia Woolf's *To the Lighthouse* is thought to refer to the Godrevy Lighthouse in the distance. The *Cornwall Gallery Guide* (£1) will help you navigate the dozens of galleries here, but St. Ives's real attractions are its beaches. ◪**Porthminster Beach,** downhill from the train station, is a magnificent stretch of white sand and tame waves. **Trains** (☎ (08457) 484 950) to St. Ives usually pass through or change at **St. Erth** (15min., every hr., £1.60), though direct service is occasionally available. National Express (☎ (08705) 808 080) **buses** go to Plymouth (3hr., 4 per day) and Penzance (20min., 4 per day). First (☎ (0870) 608 2608) buses #15, 16, and X17 go to Penzance (30min., 2 per hr., £2.40); bus #301 runs to Newquay (2¼hr., 4 per day, £4.50). The **tourist office** is in The Guildhall on Street-an-Pol. From the stations, walk down to the foot of Tregenna Hill and turn right. (☎ (01736) 796 297. Open Easter-Sept. M-Sa 9:30am-6pm, Su 10am-4pm; Oct.-Easter M-F 9am-5pm.) **St. Ives International Backpackers ❷,** The Stenmack, is in a 19th-century Methodist church. (☎ (01736) 799 444. **Internet** £1 per 15min. Dorms £9-13.)

EAST ANGLIA AND THE MIDLANDS

The rich farmland and watery flats of East Anglia stretch northeast from London, cloaking the counties of Cambridgeshire, Norfolk, and Suffolk, as well as parts of Essex. Literally England's newest landscape, the vast plains of the fens were drained as late as the 1820s. Mention of The Midlands inevitably evokes grim urban images, but there is a unique heritage and quiet grandeur to this smoke-stacked pocket. Even Birmingham, the region's much-maligned center, has its saving graces, among them a lively nightlife and the Cadbury chocolate empire.

BRITAIN

OXFORD
☎ 01865

A near-millennium of scholarship at Oxford (pop. 120,000) has seen the education of 25 British prime ministers and numerous other world leaders. A scholarly community initially formed in the 11th century by Henry II, Oxford is not only Britain's first university, but the world's as well. The university's distinguished spires have since inspired the imaginations of luminaries such as Lewis Carroll and C.S. Lewis. Today trucks barrel, buses screech, and bicycles scrape past the pedestrians choking the streets. Despite the touring crowds, Oxford has an irrepressible grandeur and pockets of sweet quiet that lift the spirits: The basement room of Blackwell's Bookshop, the impeccable galleries of the Ashmolean, the serene lily ponds of the Botanic Garden, and the perfectly maintained quadrangles of Oxford's 39 colleges.

▐ TRANSPORTATION

Trains: Botley Rd., down Park End. Ticket office open M-F 6am-8pm, Sa 6:45am-8pm, Su 7:45am-8pm. Trains (☎ (08457) 484 950) from Birmingham (1½hr., every hr., £22-37); Glasgow (6½ hr., 8 per day, £86); London Paddington (1hr., 2-4 per hr., round-trip £15); Manchester (3hr., 13 per day, £50).

Buses: Bus Station, Gloucester Green. **Stagecoach** (☎ (01604) 620 077) runs from Cambridge (3hr.; every hr.; day return £8.75, concessions £6.50) and operates the **Oxford Tube** (☎ 772 250) to London (2hr.; every 12min.; next-day return £10, students £7.50). The **Oxford Bus Company** runs **CityLink** (☎ 785 400) from: Gatwick (2hr.; every hr. during the day, every 2hr. at night; £21); Heathrow (1½hr., 2 per hr., round-trip £14); London (1¾hr., 3 per hr., next-day return £10). **National Express** (☎ (08705) 808 080) travels from Cambridge (4hr., every 2hr., £16) and London (1¾hr., 3 per hr., £8).

Public Transportation: Most local services board around Carfax. The **Oxford Bus Company Cityline** (☎ 785 410) and **Stagecoach Oxford** (☎ 772 250) offer swift and frequent service to Iffly Rd. (#3 or 4 to Rose Hill), Banbury Rd. (#2A, 2B, 2C, 2D), Abingdon Rd. (#X3,16, 35, 35a), Cowley Rd. (#5, 5A, 52), and elsewhere. Fares are low (most 80p-£1.20)

Taxis: Radio Cars (☎ 242 424). **ABC** (☎ 770 077).

◀▌ ▐ ORIENTATION AND PRACTICAL INFORMATION

Queen Street becomes **High Street,** and **Cornmarket Street** becomes **Saint Aldates** at **Carfax Tower,** the center of the original city. The colleges are all within a mile of each other, mainly east of Carfax along High St. and **Broad St.** The *Oxford Cyclists' Guide* (£1.50), at the TIC, is excellent for both cyclists and pedestrians who wish to explore the city.

Tourist Information Centre: 15-16 Broad St. (☎ 726 871; www.visitoxford.org). A pamphleteer's paradise. The busy staff books rooms for £4 and a refundable 10% deposit. Visitors' guide £1, monthly *In Oxford* guide free, accommodation list £1.10, restaurant guide free. Open M-Sa 9:30am-5pm, Su and bank holidays 10am-3:30pm. Last room booking 4:30pm.

Financial Services: Banks line Cornmarket St. **Marks and Spencer,** 13-18 Queen St. (☎ 248 075), has a **bureau de change** upstairs in the back. Free. Open M-W and F 8am-7pm, Th 8am-8pm, Sa 7:30am-7pm, and Su 11am-5pm. **American Express,** 4 Queen St. (☎ 207 101). Open M-F 9am-5:30pm, Sa 9am-5pm. **Thomas Cook,** 5 Queen St. (☎ 447 000). Open M-Sa 9am-5:30pm.

Laundromat: 127 Cowley Rd. Small load £2.60, large load £3.90; dry £2.60.

Police: St. Aldates and Speedwell St. (☎ 266 000).

Hospital: John Radcliffe Hospital, Headley Way (☎ 741 166). Bus #13 from outside the general post office.

Internet Access: **Pickwick Papers,** 90 Gloucester Green (☎ 722 849), next to the bus station. £1 per 30min. Open M 5am-7pm, Tu-Sa 5am-9pm, Su 7am-6pm. **Mice's,** 119 High St. £1 per 30min. Open M-Sa 9am-11pm, Su 10am-11pm.

Post Office: 102-104 St. Aldates (☎ (08457) 223 344). **Bureau de change.** Open M-Sa 9am-5:30pm. **Postal Code:** OX1 1ZZ.

ACCOMMODATIONS

Book at least a week ahead from June to September, and be prepared to mail in a deposit or give a credit card number. **B&Bs** line the main roads out of town and are reachable by bus or a 15-45min. walk. Wherever you go, expect to pay at least £25 per person. If it's late and you're homeless, call the **Oxford Association of Hotels and Guest Houses** at one of the following numbers: ☎ 721 561 (East Oxford), 862 280 (West Oxford), 554 374 (North Oxford), or 244 268 (South Oxford).

Heather House, 192 Iffley Rd. (☎/fax 249 757). A 20min. walk from Magdalen Bridge, or take the bus marked Rose Hill from the bus or train stations or Carfax Tower. Proprietress Vivian offers sparkling, modern rooms, replete with TV, phone, coffee, and tea in every room. Singles £33; doubles £66. Lower for longer stays. ❹

Oxford Backpackers Hostel, 9a Hythe Bridge St. (☎ 721 761). Between the bus and train stations, this lively independent hostel fosters the best of backpacker social life with an inexpensive bar, pool table, constant music, and colorful murals. Sheets provided, but no towels. Laundry facilities £2. Internet access 50p per 10min. Guests must show passport. Dorms £13-14. ❷

YHA Oxford, 2a Botley Rd. (☎ 727 275). An immediate right from the train station onto Botley Rd. Superb location and bright surroundings. Facilities include kitchen, breakfast, lockers (£1) and lockable wardrobes in every room. Towels £1. Laundry £3. Internet 50p per 10min. 24hr. security. 4- and 6-bed dorms £19, under-18 £14; doubles £46; families £51-92. Students £1 off. ❷

Newton House, 82-84 Abingdon Rd. (☎ 240 561), 75km from town. Take any Abingdon bus across Folly Bridge. Affable proprietress and dark wardrobes await Narnia fans. Recently renovated; all rooms have TV and phone. Doubles £58-64. ❹

Camping: Oxford Camping and Caravaning, 426 Abingdon Rd. (☎ 244 088) behind the Touchwoods camping store. Toilet and laundry facilities. Reception 7am-11pm. Pitch £4.60. Electricity £2.60. £3.80-5 per person. Nonmember charge £5.60. ❶

FOOD

The proprietors of Oxford's bulging eateries know they have a captive market; students fed up with fetid college food are easily seduced by a bevy of budget options. If you're cooking for yourself, try the **Covered Market** between Market St. and Carfax, which has fresh produce, deli goods, and breads. (Open M-Sa 8am-5:30pm.) **Gloucester Green Market** abounds with tasty treats, well-priced wares, and fabulous trinkets. (Open W 6am-3:30pm.)

Across Magdalen Bridge, cheap restaurants along the first four blocks of **Cowley Road** serve Chinese, Lebanese, and Polish food, as well as generic fish 'n' chips. Keep an eye out for after-hours **kebab vans,** usually at Broad St., High St., Queen St., and St. Aldates.

Kazbar, 25-27 Cowley Rd. (☎ 202 920). This tapas bar is a local favorite. Spanish-style decor and mood lighting create a posh atmosphere. Tasty tapas £2-4.50. Lunch deal includes 2 tapas and drink (M-F noon-4pm; £5). Open daily noon-11pm. ❶

The Nosebag, 6-8 St. Michael's St. (☎ 721 033). Cafeteria-style service in a 15th-century stone building, with great vegan and vegetarian options and tasty homemade soups. Lunch under £6.50, dinner under £8. Open M-Th 9:30am-10pm, F-Sa 9:30am-10:30pm, Su 9:30am-9pm. **The Saddlebag Cafe** on the ground floor sells sandwiches and salads (£3-5.25). Open M-Su 9:30am-5:30pm. Sandwiches served until 5pm. ❷

Chiang Mai, 130a High St. (☎ 202 233), tucked in an alley; look for the small blue sign. Broad Thai menu served in quaint 14th-century home. Adventurous patrons opt for the jungle curry with wild rabbit (£7). Appetizers £5-7. Entrees £7-10. Open M-Sa noon-2pm and 6-11pm, Su noon-1pm and 6-10pm. F-Sa seatings at 6 and 9pm; reservations recommended. ❷

Mick's Cafe, Cripley Rd. (☎ 728 693), off Botley Rd. next to the train station. A little diner with big breakfasts of bigger value. Combination platters (choice of eggs, sausage, bacon, beans, toast, and more; £2.70-5) and a distinct ambience (murals of the staff) make Mick's popular with locals and students. Open M-F 6am-2pm, Sa 7am-1pm, Su 8am-1pm. ❶

◆ SIGHTS

The TIC sells a map (£1) and the *Welcome to Oxford* guide (£1) listing the colleges' visiting hours, but these can be rescinded without explanation or notice. Some colleges charge admission. Don't bother trying to sneak into Christ Church outside opening hours, even after hiding your backpack and copy of *Let's Go:* bouncers sporting bowler hats (affectionately known as "bulldogs") and stationed 50 ft. apart will squint their eyes and kick you out. Other colleges have been found less vigilant near the back gates. Coddle the porters or you will get nowhere.

CHRIST CHURCH COLLEGE

Just down St. Aldates St. from Carfax. ☎ *286 573. Open M-Sa 9-11:45am and 2:30-5:15pm, Su 9:45-11:45am and 2:30-4:45pm. No entry after 4pm. Chapel services Su 8am, 10am, 11:15am, and 6pm; weekdays 6pm. £4, concessions £3.*

An intimidating pile of stone, "The House" has Oxford's grandest quad and its most socially-distinguished students; it's been responsible for the education of 13 past prime ministers. Charles I made Christ Church his capital for three and a half years during the Civil Wars and escaped dressed as a servant when the city was besieged. Today, the dining hall and Tom Quad serve as shooting locations for the *Harry Potter* films.

CHRIST CHURCH CHAPEL. In AD 730, Oxford's patron saint, St. Fridesweide, built a nunnery here in honor of two miracles: the blinding of a troublesome suitor and his subsequent recovery. A stained-glass window (c. 1320) depicts Thomas à Becket kneeling moments before being gorily dispatched in Canterbury Cathedral. A rather incongruous toilet floats in the background of a window showing St. Fridesweide's death, and the White Rabbit frets in the stained glass of the hall.

TOM QUAD. The site of undergraduate lily-pond dunking, Tom Quad adjoins the chapel grounds. The quad takes its name from Great Tom, the seven-ton bell in Tom Tower that has faithfully rung 101 strokes (the original number of students) at 9:05pm (the original undergraduate curfew) every evening since 1682. Nearby, the fan-vaulted college hall displays portraits of some of Christ Church's most famous alums—Sir Philip Sidney, William Penn, John Ruskin, John Locke, and a bored-looking W.H. Auden in a corner by the kitchen.

Oxford

▲ ACCOMMODATIONS
Heather House, **13**
Newton House, **11**
Oxford Backpackers
Hostel, **5**
YHA Youth Hostel, **4**

🍴 FOOD
Chiang Mai, **10**
Kazbar, **12**
Mick's Cafe, **3**
The Nosebag, **7**

★ NIGHTLIFE
The Bridge, **6**
Freud, **2**

🍺 PUBS
The Kings Arms, **8**
The Old
Bookbinders, **1**
Turf's Tavern, **9**

◯ COLLEGES
All Souls College, **T**
Balliol College, **H**
Brasenose College, **S**
Christ Church, **Z**
Corpus Christi
College, **AA**
Exeter College, **O**
Hertford College, **P**
Jesus College, **N**
Keble College, **B**
Lincoln College, **R**
Magdalen College, **X**
Harris Manchester
College, **K**

Mansfield College, **F**
Merton College, **BB**
New College, **Q**
Nuffield College, **L**
Oriel College, **V**
Pembroke College, **Y**
Queen's College, **U**
Regent's Park College, **C**
Somerville College, **A**
St. Catherine's
College, **DD**
St. Cross College, **D**
St. Hilda's College, **CC**
St. John's College, **E**
St. Peter's College, **M**
Trinity College, **I**
University College, **W**
Wadham College, **J**
Worcester College, **G**

BRITAIN

OTHER COLLEGES

MERTON COLLEGE. Merton has a fine garden and a library housing the first printed Welsh Bible. Tolkien lectured here, inventing the language of Elvish in his spare time. The college's **Mob Quad** is Oxford's oldest and least impressive, dating from the 14th century, but nearby **St. Alban's Quad** has some of the university's best gargoyles. Residents of Crown Prince Narahito's native Japan visit daily to identify the rooms he inhabited in his Merton days. *(Merton St. ☎ 276 310. Open to tours only, daily 2-4pm. £2.)*

UNIVERSITY COLLEGE. This soot-blackened college from 1249 vies with Merton for the title of oldest, claiming Alfred the Great as its founder. Percy Bysshe Shelley was expelled for writing the pamphlet *The Necessity of Atheism* but has since been immortalized in a prominent monument, to the right as you enter. Bill Clinton spent his Rhodes days here. *(High St. ☎ 276 676. Open to tours only.)*

ORIEL AND CORPUS CHRISTI COLLEGES. Oriel College (a.k.a. "The House of the Blessed Mary the Virgin in Oxford") is wedged between High St. and Merton St. and was once the turf of Sir Walter Raleigh. *(☎ 276 555. Open to tours only, daily 2-5pm. Free.)* South of Oriel, **Corpus Christi College,** the smallest of Oxford's colleges, surrounds a sundialed quad. The garden wall reveals a gate built for visits between Charles I and his queen, residents at adjacent Christ Church and Merton during the Civil Wars. *(☎ 276 693. Open to tours only.)*

ALL SOULS COLLEGE. Only Oxford's best are admitted to this prestigious graduate college. Candidates who survive the admission exams are invited to dinner, where it is ensured that they are "well-born, well-bred, and only moderately learned." All Souls is also reported to have the most heavenly wine cellar in the city. **The Great Quad,** with its fastidious lawn and two spare spires, may be Oxford's most serene. *(Corner of High St. and Catte St. ☎ 279 379. Open M-F 2-4pm. Closed Aug. Free.)*

QUEEN'S COLLEGE. Around since 1341, Queen's was rebuilt by Wren and Hawksmoor in the 17th and 18th centuries in the distinctive Queen Anne style. A trumpet call summons students to dinner, where a boar's head graces the table at Christmas. The latter tradition supposedly commemorates an early student who, attacked by a boar on the outskirts of Oxford, choked his assailant to death with a volume of Aristotle. Alumni include starry-eyed Edmund Halley, the more earthly Jeremy Bentham, and actor Rowan Atkinson. *(High St. ☎ 279 121. Open to tours only.)*

MAGDALEN COLLEGE. With extensive grounds and flower-laced quads, Magdalen (MAUD-lin) is considered Oxford's handsomest college. It boasts a deer park flanked by the Cherwell and Addison's Walk. The college's decadent spiritual patron is alumnus Oscar Wilde. *(On High St. near the Cherwell. ☎ 276 000. Open daily 1-6pm. £3, concessions £2.)*

TRINITY COLLEGE. Founded in 1555, Trinity has a splendid Baroque chapel with a limewood altarpiece, cedar lattices, and cherubim-spotted pediments. *(Broad St. ☎ 279 900. Open M-F 10am-noon and 2-4:30pm. £1, concessions 50p.)*

BALLIOL COLLEGE. Students at Balliol preserve the semblance of tradition by hurling abuse over the wall at their conservative Trinity College rivals. Matthew Arnold, Gerard Manley Hopkins, Aldous Huxley, and Adam Smith were all sons of Balliol's mismatched spires. The interior gates of the college bear scorch marks from the immolations of 16th-century Protestant martyrs. *(Broad St. ☎ 277 777. Open daily 2-5pm during term, Su only in summer. £1. Students and children free.)*

NEW COLLEGE. This is the self-proclaimed first *real* college of Oxford; it is here William of Wykeham in 1379 dreamed up a college that would offer a comprehensive undergraduate education under one roof. The bell tower has gargoyles of the

Seven Deadly Sins on one side, the Seven Virtues on the other—all equally grotesque. *(New College Ln. Use the Holywell St. gate. ☎ 279 555. Open daily Easter to mid-Oct. 11am-5pm; Nov.-Easter 2-4pm. £1.50 in the summer, free otherwise.)*

SOMERVILLE COLLEGE. With alumnae including Indira Gandhi and Margaret Thatcher, Somerville is Oxford's most famous once-women's college, though women were not granted degrees at all until 1920; Cambridge held out until 1948. Today, all of Oxford's colleges are coed with the exception of St. Hilda's, which remains women-only. *(Woodstock Rd. From Carfax, head down Cornmarket St,. which becomes Magdalen St., St. Giles, and Woodstock Rd. ☎ 270 600. Open daily 2-5:30pm. Free.)*

OTHER SIGHTS

■ASHMOLEAN MUSEUM. The grand Ashmolean, the finest collection of arts and antiquities outside London, was Britain's first public museum when it opened in 1683. It houses sketches by Michelangelo and Raphael, the gold coin of Constantine, and the Alfred Jewel, as well as works by favorites da Vinci, Monet, Manet, van Gogh, Rodin, and Matisse. *(Beaumont St. ☎ 278 000. Themed tours £1.50. Open Tu-Sa 10am-5pm, Su 2-5pm; in summer until 7:30pm on Th. Free.)*

BODLEIAN LIBRARY. Oxford's principal reading and research library has over five million books and 50,000 manuscripts and receives a copy of every book printed in Great Britain. If you can prove you're a scholar (a student ID may be sufficient, but a letter of introduction from your college is encouraged) and present two passport photos, the Admissions Office will issue a two-day pass ($3). No one has ever been permitted to take out a book, not even Cromwell. Well, especially not Cromwell. *(Catte St. ☎ 277 224. Library open M-F 9am-6pm, Sa 9am-1pm. Tours leave from the Divinity School, across the street; in summer M-F 4 per day, Sa 2 per day; in winter 2 per day. Tours £3.50.)*

BLACKWELL'S BOOKSTORE. Guinness lists this as the largest four-walled space devoted to bookselling anywhere in the world; the staff boasts of six miles of bookshelves. The basement room swallows the building and underpins the foundations of Trinity College next door. *(53 Broad St. ☎ 333 606. Open M and W-Sa 9am-6pm, Tu 9:30am-6pm, Su 11am-5pm.)*

SHELDONIAN THEATRE. This Roman-style auditorium was designed by a teenaged Christopher Wren. Graduation ceremonies, conducted in Latin, take place in the Sheldonian, as do everything from student recitals to world-class opera performances. *(Broad St. ☎ 277 299. Open roughly M-Sa 10am-12:30pm and 2-4:30pm; in winter, until 3:30pm. £1.50, under-15 £1. Purchase tickets for shows (£15) from Oxford Playhouse. Box office open M-Tu and Th-Sa 9:30am-6:30pm, W 10am-6:30pm.)*

CARFAX TOWER. The tower marks the center or the original city. A hike up its 99 (very) narrow spiral stairs affords a fantastic city vista from the only present-day remnant of medieval St. Martin's Church. *(Corner of Queen St. and Commarket St. ☎ 792 653. Open Apr.-Oct. M-Sa 10am-5pm, Su 11am-5pm. £1.40, under-16 70p.)*

PUNTING. A traditional pastime in Oxford is punting on the Isis. Before venturing out, punters receive a tall pole, a small oar, and an advisory against falling into the river. Magdalen Bridge Boat Co. rents **boats** for the day. *(Magdalen Bridge. ☎ 202 643. £12 per hour. Deposit and ID required. Open Apr.-Oct. daily 7:30am-9pm.)*

🎵 🎭 ENTERTAINMENT AND NIGHTLIFE

Check *This Month in Oxford* (free at the TIC) for upcoming events. *Daily Information*, posted in the TIC, most colleges, some hostels, and online (www.dailyinfo.co.uk) provides pointers.

PUBS

Pubs far outnumber colleges in Oxford; some even consider them the city's prime attraction. Most open by noon, begin to fill around 5pm, and close at 11pm (10:30pm on Sundays). Be ready to pub crawl—many pubs are so small that a single band of merry students will squeeze out other patrons, while just around the corner others have several spacious rooms.

■ **Turf's Tavern,** 4 Bath Pl. (☎243 235), off Holywell St. Arguably the most popular student bar in Oxford (they call it "the Turf"), this 13th-century pub is tucked in the alley of an alley, against ruins of the city wall. Choose from 11 ales. Hot food served in back room daily noon-7:30pm. Open M-Sa 11am-11pm, Su noon-10:30pm.

The Old Bookbinders, 17/18 Victor St. (☎553 549), walk up Walton St., left on Jericho St. until Victor St. This crowded little pub provides a neighborhood feel. Occasional beer fests feature over 25 ales. Food served 6-9:30pm. Open M-Su 10:30pm.

The Kings Arms, 40 Holywell St. (☎242 369). Oxford's unofficial student union. The coffee room at the front lets quieter folk avoid the merry masses at the back. Coffee bar closes 5:30pm. Open M-Sa 10:30am-11pm, Su 10:30am-10:30pm.

CLUBS

Though public transit in Oxford shuts down sometime after 11pm, nightlife can last all night long. After happy hour at the pubs, head up **Walton Street** or down **Cowley Road** for late-night clubs and a mix of ethnic restaurants and exotic shops.

Freud, 119 Walton St. (☎311 171), in former St. Paul's Church. Cafe by day, collegiate cocktail bar by night. Open Su-Tu 11am-midnight, W-Sa 11am-2am.

The Bridge, 6-9 Hythe Bridge St. (☎342-526; www.bridgeoxford.co.uk). Dance to R&B, and hip hop; dance and cheese on 2 floors. Erratically frequented by big student crowds. Cover £5-7. Open M-Sa 9pm-2am.

MUSIC AND THEATERS

The City of Oxford Orchestra, (☎744 457). Plays a subscription series at the Sheldonian and in college chapels during summer. Tickets £10-20.

The Oxford Playhouse, 11-12 Beaumont St. (☎798 600). Hosts amateur and professional plays as well as music and dance performances. Box office opens M-Tu and Th-F at 9:30am, W at 10am, and closes after curtain. The playhouse also sells tickets at an 85% discount for venues all over city, including the **New College Choir** (☎305 305; www.ticketsoxford.com), one of the best boy choirs around. Box office open M, Tu and Th-Sa 9:30am-6:30pm, Su 10am-6:30pm or 30 min before last show.)

STRATFORD-UPON-AVON   ☎ 01789

Former native William Shakespeare is now the area's industry; you'll find even the vaguest connections to the Bard fully exploited. Of course, all the perfumes of Arabia will not sweeten the exhaust from tour buses, but beyond the "Will Power" t-shirts, the aura of Shakespeare remains—in the quite grace of the Avon and the pin-drop silence before a soliloquy in the Royal Shakespeare Theatre.

▐ HENCE, AWAY! Thames **trains** (☎08457 484 950) arrive from: Birmingham (1hr., every hr., £3.80); London Paddington (2¼hr., 7 per day, £23); and Warwick (25min., 7 per day, £2.80). National Express (☎08705 808 080) runs **buses** from London Victoria (3hr., 3 per day, £13).

▐ WHO IS'T THAT CAN INFORM ME. The **tourist office,** Bridgefoot, across Warwick Rd., offers maps and a free lodgings guide. (☎293 127. Open Apr.-Oct. M-Sa 9am-5pm, Su 10:30am-4:30pm; Nov.-Mar. M-Sa 9am-5pm.) Surf the **Internet** at **Cyber Junction,** 28 Greenhill St. (£3 per 30min., £5 per hr.; students £2.50/4.) **Postal Code:** CV37 6PU.

TO SLEEP, PERCHANCE TO DREAM...AND FOOD. To B&B or not to B&B? Bed and Breakfasts line Evesham Place, Evesham Road, Grove Road, and Shipston Road, but reservations are still a must. The **YHA Stratford ❷**, Wellsbourne Rd., is located 3km from Clopton Bridge. Follow B4086 35min. from the town center, or take bus X18 from Bridge St. The hostel includes B&B amenities like breakfast, a kitchen, and Internet access (£1 per 15min.), all housed within a gorgeous 200 year-old house. (☎297 093. Midnight lockout. Dorms £17, under-18 £12.) **Carlton Guest Houes ❸**, 22 Evesham Pl., has spacious rooms and spectacular service. (☎293 548. Singles £20-26; doubles £40-52.) **Melita Hotel ❹**, 37 Shipston Rd., is an upscale B&B that offers its patrons a lovely garden and an "honesty bar," where guests can help themselves to a drink. (☎292 432. Breakfast included. Singles £39; doubles £72.) **Riverside Caravan Park ❶**, Tiddington Rd., 1½km east of Stratford on B4086, has **camping** with beautiful but crowded views of the Avon. (☎292 312. Open Easter-Oct. Free electricity and showers. Tent and up to 4 people £10.)

Opposition ❸, 13 Sheep St., is a bistro that receives rave reviews from locals for its varied cuisine. The lasagne (£9) and lamb steak (£12) are definitely worth a try. (Open M-Sa noon-2pm and 5-10pm, Su noon-2pm and 6-9pm.) **Hussain's Indian Cuisine ❷**, 6a Chapel St., has fantastic *chicken tikka masala;* keep an eye out for regular Ben Kingsley. (Lunch £6. Main dishes from £6.50. Open M-W 5pm-midnight, Th-Su 12:30-2:30pm and 5pm-midnight.) A great place for delicious breads, sandwiches, and pastries is **Le Petit Croissant ❶**, 17 Wood St. (Baguettes from 80p. Sandwiches £1.80-2.50. Open M-Sa 8:30am-6pm.) A **Safeway** supermarket is on Alcester Rd. (Open M-W and Sa 8am-9pm, Th-F 8am-10pm, Su 10am-4pm.)

DRINK DEEP ERE YOU DEPART (FOR THE SIGHTS). Traffic at the Shakespeare sights peaks around 2pm, so try to hit them before 11am or after 4pm. Die-hard fans can buy a ticket for admission to all five official Shakespeare properties: Anne Hathaway's cottage, Mary Arden's House and Countryside Museum, Shakespeare's Birthplace, New Place and Nash's House, and Hall's Croft (£13, students and seniors £12). You can also buy a ticket that covers only the latter three sights (£9, students and seniors £8). **Shakespeare's Birthplace**, on Henley St., is part period re-creation and part exhibition of Shakespeare's life and works. (Open summer M-Sa 9am-5pm and Su 9:30am-5pm; mid-season M-Sa 10am-5pm and Su 10:30am-5pm; winter M-Sa 10am-4pm and Su 10:30am-4pm.) **New Place**, on High St., was Stratford's finest home when Shakespeare bought it in 1597. Only the foundation remains—it can be viewed from **Nash's House,** which belonged to the husband of Shakespeare's granddaughter. **Hall's Croft** and **Mary Arden's House** also capitalize on connections to Shakespeare's extended family, but also provide exhibits of what life was like in Elizabethan times. Pay homage to Shakespeare's grave in the **Holy Trinity Church,** on Trinity St. (Admission £1).

Get thee to a performance by the world-famous ■**Royal Shakespeare Company;** recent sons include Kenneth Branagh and Ralph Fiennes. Tickets for all three theaters—the Royal Shakespeare Theatre, the Swan Theatre, and the Other Place—are sold through the box office in the foyer of the Royal Shakespeare Theatre, on Waterside. (☎403 403, 24hr. ticket hotline ☎(0870) 609 1110; www.rsc.org.uk. Open M-Sa 9:30am-8pm. Tickets £5-40; highly demanded student standbys £8-12. Tours M-Sa 1:30, 5:30pm, and Su noon, 1, 2, 3, 5:30pm. £4, students and seniors £3.)

DAYTRIP FROM STRATFORD: WARWICK CASTLE. Climb to the top of the towers of one of England's finest medieval castle and see the countryside unfold like a vision of medieval times. The castle dungeons are filled with life-size wax soldiers preparing for battle, while "knights" and "craftsmen" talk about their trades. Make sure to catch the castle's seasonal events, such as summer jousting tournaments and fireworks displays. (Open Apr.-Sept. daily 10am-6pm; Oct.-Mar. 10am-5pm; £13, students £9.80; early Sept. to early May £1-2 discount.) **Trains** arrive from Birmingham (40min., 2 every hr., £3.80) and Stratford (20-40min., every 2hr., £2.80).

BRITAIN

THE COTSWOLDS

The Cotswolds have deviated little from their etymological roots - "Cotswolds" means "sheep enclosure in rolling hillsides." Grazing sheep and cattle roam 2,000 square kilometers of vivid, verdant hills, which hide tiny towns barely touched by modern times. These old Roman settlements and tiny Saxon villages, hewn from the famed Cotswold stone, demand a place on any itinerary, although their relative inaccessibility via public transportation will necessitate extra effort to get there.

☐ TRANSPORTATION. Useful gateway cities are Cheltenham, Oxford, and Bath. **Moreton-in-Marsh** is one of the bigger villages and has **trains** to Oxford (30min., every hr., £7.90) and London (1½hr., every 1-2hr., £25). The Cotswolds are much easier to reach by **bus.** *Getting There,* a pamphlet that details bus information in The Cotswolds, is available free from the Cheltenham tourist office. **Pulham's Coaches** (☎(01451) 820 369) run from Cheltenham to Moreton-in-Marsh (1hr.; M-Sa 8 per day, Su daily; £1.70) via Stow-on-the-Wold (50min., £2).

Local roads are perfect for biking. **The Toy Shop,** on High St. in Moreton-in-Marsh, rents bikes. (☎(01608) 650 756. Open M and W-Sa 9am-1pm and 2-5pm. £12 per day.) Visitors can also experience the Cotswolds as the English have for centuries by treading footpaths from village to village. **Cotswold Way,** spanning 160km from Bath to Chipping Camden, gives hikers glorious vistas of hills and dales. The *Cotswold Events* booklet lists anything from music festivals and antique markets to cheese-rolling and woolsack races along the Cotswold Way. A newer way of seeing the region, the **Cotswold Experience** is a full-day bus tour that starts in Bath and visits five of the most scenic villages. (☎(01225) 477 101. £22, students £18.)

WINCHCOMBE, MORETON-IN-MARSH, STOW-ON-THE-WOLD. 10km north of Cheltenham on A46, **Sudeley Castle,** once the manor of King Ethelred the Unready, crowns the town of **Winchcombe.** (Open Mar.-Oct. daily 11am-5pm. £6.70.) The Winchcombe **tourist office** is in Town Hall. (☎(01242) 602 925. Open Apr.-Oct. M-Sa 10am-5pm, Su 10am-4pm, closed 1-2pm; Nov.-Mar. sa-Su 10am-4pm.) With a train station, relatively frequent bus service, and bike shop, **Moreton-in-Marsh** is a convenient base for exploring the Cotswolds. The **tourist office** is in the District Council Building. (☎(01608) 650 881. Open M 8:45am-4pm, Tu-W 8:45am-5:15pm, Th 8:45am-7:30pm, F 8:45am-4:45pm, Sa 9:30am-1pm.) **Warwick House B&B ❸,** on London Rd., offers many luxuries, including a pleasant garden and access to a nearby gym. Book 2 weeks in advance. (☎(01608) 650 733. www.snoozeandsizzle.com. Singles £21-25; doubles £42-50.) **Stow-on-the-Wold,** the self-proclaimed "Heart of the Cotswolds," sits atop a hill, offering visitors fine views and a sense of the Cotswold pace of life. The **tourist office** is in Hollis House on The Square. (☎(01451) 831 082. Open Easter-Oct. M-Sa 9:30am-5:30pm; Nov.-Easter M-Sa 9:30am-4:30pm.) The **YHA youth hostel ❷** is near the tourist office on The Square. (☎(01451) 830 497. Open mid Feb.-Oct. daily; Nov.-Dec. F-Sa. Dorms £13, under-18 £9.)

BIRMINGHAM
☎0121

As the industrial heart of the Midlands, Birmingham (pop. 1.2 million) is steadily overcoming its reputation for lack of urban charm. At night, the city truly comes alive, fueled by world-class entertainers and a young university crowd. Twelve minutes south of town by rail lies ▪**Cadbury World,** an unabashed celebration of the famed chocolate company. Take a train from New St. to Bournville, or bus #83, 84, or 85 from the city center. (☎451 4159. Open daily 10am-3pm; closed certain days, so call ahead to confirm. £8.80, students and seniors £7, children £6.60.) The **Birmingham Jazz Festival** (☎454 7020) brings over 200 jazz singers and instrumentalists to town during the first two weeks of July; try to book through the tourist office during this time. **Broad St.** is lined with trendy cafe-bars and clubs. Pick up the bimonthly *What's On* to discover the hotspots. **Stoodibakers,** 192 Broad St., has a dark decor set against a futuristic warehouse motif. (Cover £4 F-Sa after 9:30pm.) A thriving gay-friendly scene has arisen around **Essex St.** Head to **Nightingale,** Kent. St, for a predominantly gay clientele enjoying 2 dance floors, 5 bars, and a jazz lounge. (Cover £6 Sa. Open Su-Th 5pm-2am, F 5pm-4am, Sa 5pm-7am.)

Birmingham is the center of a web of train and bus lines between London, central Wales, southwest England, and all destinations north. **Trains** arrive in New St. Station (☎(08457) 484 950) from: Liverpool Lime St. (1½hr., 1-2 per hr., £19); London Euston (2hr., 4 per hr., £30); Manchester Piccadilly (2½hr., every hr., £19); and Oxford (1¼hr., 2 per hr., £19). National Express **buses** (☎08705 808 080) arrive in Digbeth Station from: Cardiff (3hr., 3 per day, £19); Liverpool (2½hr., every hr., round-trip £9.30); London (3hr., every hr., £13); and Manchester (2½hr., every 2hr., round-trip £10). The **tourist office,** in the Bullring, makes room reservations. (☎202 5099. Open M-Sa 9:30am-5:30pm, Su 10:30am-4:30pm.) Despite its size, Birmingham has no hostels, and inexpensive B&Bs are rare. **Hagley Road** is your best bet. To reach **Wentworth Hotel ❹,** 103 Wentworth Rd., turn right onto Lonsdale Rd. from Harbone swimming bath and then left onto Wentworth Rd. The hotel provides luxurious baths in most rooms, a comfy lounge, and bar downstairs. (☎427 4546. Breakfast included. Singles £32; doubles £54.) **Thai Edge ❸,** 7 Oozells Sq., serves up big portions of delicious Thai specialities. (Entrees £6-15. Open Su-Th 5:30pm-11:30pm, F-Sa-5:30pm-midnight.) **Postal Code:** B2 4AA.

CAMBRIDGE   ☎01223

In contrast to metropolitan Oxford, Cambridge is determined to retain its pastoral academic robes. As the tourist office will tell you, the city manages (rather than encourages) visitors. No longer the exclusive preserve of upper-class sons, the university now welcomes women and state-school pupils; during May Week, which marks term's end, Cambridge shakes off its reserve with gin-soaked glee.

▐ TRANSPORTATION

Trains: Station Rd. (☎(08457) 484 950), To: **London King's Cross** (45min., 2 per hr., £16) and **London Liverpool Street** (1¼hr., 2 per hr., £16).

Buses: Drummer St. **National Express** (☎(08705) 808 080) arrives from **London** (2hr., 2 per hr., from £9). **Stagecoach** (☎(01604) 676 060) buses go to **Oxford** (3hr., every hr., from £6).

Public Transportation: Cambus (☎423 554) runs from the train station to the city center (£1) and around town (£1-2). **Whippet Coaches** (☎(01480) 423 792) runs daytrips. **Cabco** (☎312 444) and **Camtax** (☎ 313 131) taxis are both 24hr.

Bike Rental: Mike's Bikes, 28 Mill Rd. (☎312 591). £8 per day, £10 per week. £50 deposit. Open M-Sa 9am-6pm, Su 10am-4pm.

◪ ▐ ORIENTATION AND PRACTICAL INFORMATION

Cambridge has two main avenues. One, the main shopping street, starts at **Magdalene Bridge** (MAUD-lin) and becomes **Bridge Street, Sidney Street, St. Andrew's Street, Regent Street,** and finally **Hills Road.** The other—first **St. John's Street,** then **Trinity Street, King's Parade,** and **Trumpington Street**—is the academic thoroughfare. The two streets cross at **St. John's College.** From the bus station at **Drummer Street,** a quick walk down **Emmanuel Street** will land you right in the shopping district near the tourist office. To get to the city center from the train station on **Station Road,** turn right onto Hills Rd., and continue straight ahead.

Tourist Office: Wheeler St. (☎(09065) 862 526, calls cost 60p per min.), just south of Market Sq. Books rooms for a £3 fee and 10% deposit. Open Apr.-Oct. M-F 10am-5:30pm, Sa 10am-5pm, Su 11am-4pm; Nov.-Mar. M-F 10am-5:30pm, Sa 10am-5pm.

Financial Services: Banks line Market Sq. and St. Andrew's St. **Thomas Cook,** 8 St. Andrew's St. (☎366 141). Open M-Tu and Th-Sa 9am-5:30pm, W 10am-5:30pm. **American Express,** 25 Sidney St. (☎(08706) 001 060). Open M-Tu and Th-F 9am-5:30pm, W 9:30am-5:30pm, Sa 9am-5pm.

Laundromat: Clean Machine, 22 Burleigh St. (☎578 009). Open daily 9am-8:30pm.

Emergency: ☎999; no coins required. **Police:** (☎358 966), on Parkside.

Hospital: Addenbrookes, Long Rd. (☎245 151). Catch Cambus C1 or C2 from Emmanuel St. (£1) and get off where Hills Rd. intersects Long Rd.

Internet Access: International Telecom Centre, 2 Wheeler St. (☎357 358), across from the tourist office. £1 for first 33min., then 3-4p per min.; £1 minimum. As low as 50p per hr. with student ID. Open daily 9am-10pm.

Post Office: 9-11 St. Andrew's St. (☎323 325). Open M-Sa 9am-5:30pm. **Postal Code:** CB2 3AA.

▐ ACCOMMODATIONS

Rooms are scarce in Cambridge, which makes prices high and quality low. Most **B&Bs** aren't in the town center; those around **Portugal Street** and **Tenison Road** are often open only in July and August. Check the list at the tourist office, or pick up their guide to accommodations (50p).

Warkworth Guest House, Warkworth Terr. (☎363 682). Elegantly decorated old home with sunny, ensuite rooms. Near the bus station for those who wish to skip the walk to the city center. Packed lunch on request. Singles £40; doubles from £60. ❹

Tenison Towers Guest House, 148 Tenison Rd. (☎566 511). Fresh flowers grace airy rooms in this welcoming house 2 blocks from the train station. Proprietress Mrs. Chance keeps an impeccable house, and her breakfast includes homemade bread and marmalade. Singles £20-25; doubles £40-50. ❸

YHA Cambridge, 97 Tenison Rd. (☎354 601), offers a relaxed, welcoming atmosphere. Rock music pervades their well-equipped kitchen and lounge. **Bureau de change.** Breakfast £3.50. Laundry facilities. Internet 50p per 7min. In summer, reserve several weeks ahead. Dorms £16, under-18 £12. ❷

Home from Home B&B, 78 Milton Rd. (☎323 555). A 20min. walk from the city center. Rooms are spotless and well-stocked with biscuits, cocoa, and mini-toiletries. Singles £35-40; doubles £50-60; apartments with kitchens and lounge £350 per week. ❸

Regency Guest House, 7 Regent Terr. (☎329 626), a 5min. walk from the city center. Regency offers bright, spacious rooms, many of which overlook the park outside. Singles £48; doubles £68. ❹

Highfield Farm Camping Park, Long Rd. (☎262 308), Comberton. Head west on A603 (4.5km), then right on the B1046 to Comberton (1.5km), or take Cambus #102 or 103 from the Drummer St. bus station to Westfield Rd. (every 45min.). Open Mar.-Oct. Call ahead. £4-5 per person with tent. ❶

◖ FOOD

Market Square has bright pyramids of fruit and vegetables. (Open M-Sa 9:30am-4:30pm.) Students buy their gin and cornflakes at **Sainsbury's,** 44 Sidney St. (Open M-F 8am-9pm, Sa 7:30am-9pm, Su 11am-5pm.) South of town, **Hills Road** and **Mill Road** brim with good, budget options.

TO PETERBOROUGH (A14)
Shelly Row
Alpha Rd.
Herford St.
Chesterton Rd.
TO 2 & ELY (A10)
Pretoria Rd.
Kimberley Rd.
Aylestone Rd.
De Freville Ave.

Open Air Swimming Pool

Castle St.
Chesterton Ln.
Park Parade
River Cam
Midsummer Common

Kettle's Yard
A1303
Northampton St.
Pound Hill
Magdalene St.
Quayside

Jesus Green

The Backs

A

Tyrell's Punts

Portugal Pl.
Round Church St.
Bridge St.
St. John's St.

B

C

North Terr.
Brunswick Terr.
TO NEWMARKET & A45

TO ROBINSON COLLEGE (200yd)

E

G

Senate House

D

Malcolm St.
Manor Rd.
Jesus Ln.
Victoria Ave.
Maids Causeway
Newmarket Rd.
Grafton Shopping Centre
Burleigh St.

Green St.
Trinity St.
Sussex St.
King St.

5

Christ's Pieces

Short St.
New Sq.
Friar St.
Fitzroy St.
Eden St.
City Rd.
Adam and Eve St.

MARKET SQ.
Petty Cury
Arts Theatre
LION YARD

F

Hobson St.
Sidney St.

6

Elm St.
Orchard St.
Clarendon St.
Emmanuel Rd.
Melbourne Pl.
Prospect Row
Warkworth St.
Prospect Terr.

King's Parade
Bene't St.
Wheeler St.
Corn Exchange St.

7
8

9

Zoology Museum

Drummer St.
Emmanuel St.
St. Andrew's St.
Downing St.

Geology Museum/ Museum of Archaeology

L

Parker St.
Parkside

14

East Rd.

Queen's Rd.
River Cam

H

I

J

K

Pembroke St.
Mill Ln.

N

Downing Pl.
Downing St.

13

Park Terr.
Regent Terr.

Parker's Piece

Gonville Pl.
Gresham Rd.

Mike's Bikes

Mill Rd.

Scudamore's Punts

M

10
11
12

Little St. Mary's Ln.

O

P

Regent St.
Hills Rd.

15

Cricket Grounds

Sidgwick Ave.
Silver St.
Mill Pond

Trumpington St.
Tennis Court Rd.

Malting Ln.
Sheep's Green
The Fen

Newnham Rd.
TO A603 & GRANTCHESTER

Llamas Land

Fitzwilliam Museum

Lensfield Rd.
Scott Polar Research Institute
Union Rd.

Harvey Rd.
St. Paul's Rd.
Cambridge Pl.
Glisson Rd.
Lyndewode Rd.

Tenison Ave.

16

Fen Causeway
Brookside
Trumpington Rd.
Penton St.

Coronation St.
Russell St.
Norwich St.

17

Bateman St.
Botanic Gardens

Station Rd.
Tenison Rd.
Hills Rd.

0 — 250 yards
0 — 250 meters
TO LONDON, M11, A10

TO 18 (100yd)

N

Cambridge

BRITAIN

Dojo's Noodle Bar, 1-2 Miller's Yard, Mill Ln. (☎363 471). Whips out enormous plates of noodles for less than £6. Open M-Th noon-2:30pm and 5:30-11pm, F-Su noon-4pm and 5:30-11pm. ❶

Rainbow's Vegetarian Bistro, 9a King's Parade (☎321 551). A tiny, creative nook that features delicious international vegan and vegetarian fare. All entrees £7.30. Open M-Sa 11am-11pm. ❷

Nadia's, 11 St. John's St. (☎568 336) and 16 Silver St. An uncommonly good bakery serving wonderful flapjacks and quiches (90p-£1.20). Takeaway only. Sandwiches £2. Muffins 90p. Open daily 8am-5pm. ❶

Tatties, 11 Sussex St. (☎323 399). Dedicated to one of the most popular dishes in England, jacket potatoes. Fillings range from butter (£2) to Philly cheese and smoked salmon (£5.75). Open M-Sa 8:30am-6pm, Su 10am-5pm. ❶

Hobbs's Pavillion, Parker's Piece (☎367 480), off Park Terr. Renowned for imaginative, rectangular pancakes, Hobbs's offers views across Parker's Piece, jaunty jazz, and a Mars bar and ice cream pancake (£4). Dinner is standard English fare (£9-14). Open Tu-Sa noon-2:15pm and 6-9:45pm. ❸

Restaurant 22, 22 Chesterton Rd. (☎351 880). Offers a 3-course, top-notch set menu that changes monthly (£24.95). Reservations necessary. Open Tu-Sa 7-9:45pm. ❺

🔘 SIGHTS

Cambridge is an architect's dream—it packs some of the most breathtaking examples of English architecture into less than 3 square kilometers. It's most exciting to behold during the university's three eight-week terms: Michaelmas (Oct.-Dec.), Lent (Jan.-Mar.), and Easter (Apr.-June). If you only have time for a few colleges, **Trinity, King's, St. John's, Queens',** and **Christ's** should top your list. Most of the colleges are open daily from 9am to 5:30pm, but hours can often vary; it's best to call ahead. A few are closed to sightseers during the Easter term, and virtually all are closed during exams (mid-May to mid-June).

TRINITY COLLEGE. Founded in 1546 by Henry VIII, the college is legendary for its incredible wealth. Trinity is now Britain's third largest landowner, behind Queen Elizabeth II and the Church of England; it is said that you can walk from Cambridge to Oxford without stepping off Trinity land. Illustrious alumni of the college include: Byron, Nabokov, Tennyson, and Wittgenstein. Sir Isaac Newton, who lived in E-entry for 30 years, originally measured the speed of sound here by stamping his foot in the cloister along the north side of the **Great Court**—the largest courtyard in Cambridge. The college also houses the stunning **Wren Library,** home to A.A. Milne's handwritten manuscript of *Winnie the Pooh* and Newton's own copies of the *Principia. (Trinity St. ☎338 400. Chapel and courtyard open daily 10am-5pm. Wren Library open M-F noon-2pm. Easter-Oct. £2, concessions £1. Nov.-Easter free.)*

KING'S COLLEGE. E.M. Forster's alma mater dominates King's Parade St. from street level to skyline. The college was founded by Henry VI in 1441 as a partner to Eton, and until 1861 it did not accept students from any other school. Surprisingly, King's is now the most socially liberal of the Cambridge colleges, each year drawing the most students from state schools. As a result, Cambridge's best-known college is also its least traditional—there are no formal dinners or white-tie balls, and its interior corridors are coated with lurid graffiti. Little of this is noticeable to visitors who descend in droves to **King's College Chapel,** a spectacular Gothic monument. Rubens's magnificent *Adoration of the Magi* hangs behind the altar. *(On King's Parade. ☎331 100. Open M-Sa 9:30am-4:30pm, Su 10am-5pm. Tours arranged through the tourist office. £3.50, students £2.50. Under-12 free.)*

ST. JOHN'S COLLEGE. Established in 1511 by Lady Margaret Beaufort, mother of Henry VIII, St. John's is one of the seven colleges founded by women. A copy of Venice's **Bridge of Sighs** connects the older part of the college to the neo-Gothic extravagance of **New Court.** The **School of Pythagoras,** a 12th-century pile of wood and stone, supposedly the oldest complete building in Cambridge, hides in St. John's Gardens. The college also boasts the longest room in the city—the Fellows' Room in Second Court spans 28m and was the site of some D-Day planning. *(St. John's St. ☎ 338 600. Open M-F 10am-5:30pm, Sa-Su 9:30am-5:30pm. £2, students £1.20.)*

QUEENS' COLLEGE. Queens' has the only unaltered Tudor courtyard in Cambridge. The **Mathematical Bridge,** despite rumors to the contrary, has always been supported by screws and bolts, not just mathematical principle. *(Silver St. ☎ 335 511. Open Mar.-Oct. daily 10am-4:30pm. Closed during exams. £1.)*

CHRIST'S COLLEGE. Founded as "God's house" in 1448, Christ's has won fame for gorgeous gardens and its association with John Milton. Charles Darwin studied at Christ's before dealing a blow to its religious origins. *(St. Andrews St. ☎ 334 900. Gardens open in summer M-F 9:30am-noon; term-time M-F 9am-4:30pm. Free.)*

◪FITZWILLIAM MUSEUM. A welcome break from academia, the Fitzwilliam Museum fills an immense Neoclassical building, constructed in 1875 to house Viscount Fitzwilliam's collection. An eclectic mix of Chinese, Egyptian, Greek, and Japanese treasures surrounds a muster of 16th-century German armor downstairs. Upstairs, five galleries feature works by Brueghel, Monet, and Rubens, including a room with books and woodcuttings by William Blake. *(Trumpington St. ☎ 332 900. Open Tu-Sa 10am-5pm, Su 2:15-5pm. Suggested donation £3. Tours Su 2:45pm. £3.)*

◪KETTLE'S YARD. This museum used to be the home of Tate curator Jim Ede; now visitors wander through the house and admire his early 20th-century collection. The gallery rotates exhibits. *(☎ 352 124. House open Apr.-Sept. Su and Tu-Sa 1:30-4:30pm; Oct.-Mar. Su and Tu-Sa 2-4pm. Gallery open Su and Tu-Sa 11:30am-5pm. Free.)*

🎭 🎷 ENTERTAINMENT AND NIGHTLIFE

The best source of info on student activities is the student newspaper *Varsity* (20p); the tourist office also has useful brochures. **Punts** (gondola-like boats) are a favored form of entertainment in Cambridge. Beware that punt-bombing—jumping from bridges into the river alongside a punt, thereby tipping its occupants into the Cam—has evolved into an art form. **Tyrell's,** on Magdalene Bridge, rents boats. *(☎ (01480) 394 941. £12 per hr. plus a £40 deposit.)*

PUBS

Pubs constitute the core of Cambridge nightlife, but clubs and bars are also on the curriculum. Most pubs stay open from 11am to 11pm with reduced hours on Sunday. **King Street** has a diverse collection of pubs and used to host the **King Street Run,** in which contestants ran the street, stopping at each of the 13 pubs to down a pint. The winner was the first to cross the finish line on his own two feet.

- **The Eagle,** 8 Benet St. (☎ 505 020), is Cambridge's oldest pub. Watson and Crick once rushed in to announce their discovery of the DNA double helix—unimpressed, the barmaid insisted they settle their four-shilling tab before she'd serve them a toast. Check the ceiling to see the burned-in initials of British and American WWII pilots.

- **The Mill,** 14 Mill Ln. (☎ 357 026), off Silver St. Bridge. Patrons infiltrate the riverside park on spring nights for punt- and people-watching. In summer, the Mill becomes a hot spot for international youth. Come in during the week to win free drinks on quiz nights.

The Anchor, Silver St. (☎353 554). An undergrad watering hole crowded day and night. Savor a pint while watching amateur punters collide under Silver St. Bridge. Open M-Sa 11am-11pm, Su noon-10:30pm.

The Champion of the Thames, 68 King St. (☎352 043). Making friends is pretty much unavoidable in this tiny pub that prides itself on a fine selection of real ales.

CLUBS

The Kambar Club, 1 Wheeler St., attracts crowds on Saturday with the only regular indie rock night in town. Garage, goth, electronica, and drum 'n bass music also find places in their weekly sets. Open M-Sa 10pm-2:30am.

Club Fez, 15 Market Passage, moves to a wide variety of music, ranging from Latin to trance. Enjoy the Moroccan-themed surroundings, complete with comfy floor cushions. Cover £2-8. Open M-Tu 9pm-2:30am, W-Sa 9pm-2am, Su 8pm-midnight.

The Junction, Clifton Rd., is a music/theater/dance venue that turns into a club on weekends. A rotating schedule includes 7-11pm "teen nights," as well as a monthly gay/lesbian night.

NORTHERN ENGLAND

The north's innovative music and arts scenes are world-famous: Liverpool and Manchester alone produced four of *Q Magazine's* ten biggest rock stars of the century. Its principal urban areas may have grown out of the wool and coal industries, bearing 19th-century scars to prove it, but their newly refurbished city centers have redirected their energies toward accommodating visitors. Find respite from city life in the Peak District to the east or the Lake District to the north.

MANCHESTER ☎0161

The Industrial Revolution transformed the unremarkable village of Manchester (pop. 2.5 million) into Britain's second-largest urban area. A center of manufacturing in the 19th century, the city became a hotbed of liberal politics, its deplorable working-class conditions arousing the indignation of everyone from Frederic Engels (who called it "Hell on Earth") to John Ruskin (who called it a "devil's darkness"). Now teeming with electronic beats and post-industrial glitz, Manchester has risen from factory soot to savor its reputation as one of the hippest spots in England. Though dodgy in parts, the city is undergoing a gradual gentrification and is accessible to the street smart. Thousands are drawn to its vibrant arts and nightlife scenes, proving that it's not just the pretty who are popular.

▐ TRANSPORTATION

Flights: Manchester International Airport (MAN; ☎489 3000). Trains (15-20min., 6-7 per hr., £2.35) and buses #44 and 105 run to Piccadilly Station.

Trains: Manchester Piccadilly, London Rd., and **Manchester Victoria,** Victoria St., have trains (☎08457 484 950) that leave from: Birmingham (1¾hr., 2 per hr., £17); Chester (1hr., every hr., £9); Edinburgh (4hr., every hr., £46); Liverpool (50min., 2 per hr., £7.80); London Euston (2½-3hr., every hr., £49); York (40min., 2 per hr., £18). Connections are made via Metrolink. Travel center open M-Sa 8am-8:30pm, Su 11am-7pm. Additional service to local areas available at the **Deansgate** and **Oxford Road** stations.

Buses: National Express (☎08705 808 080) buses go from Chorlton St. to Liverpool (50min., every hr., £5) and London (4-5hr., 7 per day, £19).

Public Transportation: Piccadilly Gardens is home to about 50 bus routes. Pick up a free route map from the TIC. **Buses** run until 11:30pm, some lines until 2:30am on weekends. Office open M-Sa 7am-6pm, Su 10am-6pm. All-day ticket £3.30.

Taxis: Mantax (☎230 333) or **Radio Cars** (☎236 8033).

ORIENTATION AND PRACTICAL INFORMATION

The city center is an odd polygon formed by Victoria Station to the north, Piccadilly Station to the east, the canals to the south, and the River Irwell to the west. The many byways can be tricky to navigate, but the area is fairly compact, and Mancunians are generally helpful.

Tourist Information Centre: Manchester Visitor Centre, Town Hall Extension, Lloyd St. (☎234 3157, 24hr. info ☎(0891) 715 533). Staff books accommodations (£2.50 plus 10% deposit) and can sometimes get special rates. Free literature includes the *Manchester Pocket Guide*, the *Greater Manchester Network Map*, and *What's On*, which lists local events. Open M-Sa 10am-5pm, Su 10:30am-4:30pm.

Financial Services: Thomas Cook, 23 Market St. (☎910 8787). Open M-W and F-Sa 9am-5:30pm, Th 10am-5:30pm, Su 11am-5:30pm. **American Express,** 10-12 St. Mary's Gate (☎833 0121). Open M-F 9am-5pm.

Police: Chester House, Bootle St. (☎872 5050).

Pharmacy: Boots, 32 Market St. (☎832 6533). Open M-W 8am-6pm, Th 8am-8pm, F 8am-6:30pm, Sa 9am-6m, Su 11am-5pm.

Hospital: Manchester Royal Infirmary, 13 Oxford Rd. (☎276 1234).

Internet Access: Central Library, St. Peter's Sq. (☎234 1966). Free for first hr. Open M-Th 10am-8pm, F-Sa 10am-5pm. **Internet Exchange,** 1-3 Piccadilly Sq. (☎833 8111), 2nd fl. of Coffee Republic. £1 per 15min. or £1 per hr. with £2 membership. Open M-F 7:30am-6:30pm, Sa 8am-6:30pm, Su 9:30am-5:30pm.

Post Office: 26 Spring Gdns. (☎839 0687). Open M-F 9am-5:30pm, Sa 8am-6:30pm, Su 9:30am-5:30pm. *Poste Restante* (☎834 8605) has a separate entrance. Open M-F 6am-1pm, Sa 6am-12:30pm. **Post Code:** M1 1NS.

ACCOMMODATIONS

Cheap stays in the city center are hard to find, though summer offers the possibility of decently priced student housing. The highest concentration of budget lodgings is 3-5km south in the suburbs of **Fallowfield, Withington,** and **Didsbury;** take bus #40, 42, or 157. Browse the free booklet *Where to Stay* (at the TIC) for listings.

YHA Manchester, Potato Wharf, Castlefield (☎(0870) 770 5950; www.yhamanchester.org.uk). Take the metro to G-Mex Station or bus #33 from Piccadilly Gardens toward Wigan to Deansgate. Raising hosteling to swanky heights. Friendly staff and good security. Lockers £1-2. Laundry £1.50. Internet 50p per 6min. Reception 7am-11pm. Dorms £19; doubles £32-42; quads £68-78; quints £97. ❷

Jurys Inn Manchester, 56 Great Bridgewater St. (☎953 8888). Enormous rooms, luxurious baths, and professional service. A double and single bed in every room. Hardly a deal for solo travelers, but a bargain for those with companions. £73 per room, weekend specials subject to availability. ❺

Student Village, Lower Chatham St. (☎236 1776). Dorm-style accommodations; groups of 3-7 single rooms share common space, kitchens, and bathrooms. Open mid-June to Sept. Singles £17, students £15. ❷

Burton Arms, 31 Swan St. (☎/fax 834 3455). Basic rooms above a pub on a busy street. A 15min. walk from both train stations and St. Peter's Sq. Full English breakfast £3. Singles £25; doubles £40, with bath £60; triples £60/90. ❸

University of Manchester: Call the **University Accommodation Office** (☎275 2888, open M-F 9am-5pm) to find out which dorms are available for lodging during summer vacation (mid-June to mid-Sept). 3-7 day minimum stay. Reserve a week or more in advance with deposit. From £42 per week. Dorms offering lodgings include **Hume Hall** (☎275 0210) and **Hardy Farm** (☎861 9913). ❶

🖰 FOOD

Outwit the pricey **Chinatown** restaurants by eating the multi-course "Businessman's Lunch" offered by most (M-F noon-2pm, £4-8). Better yet, visit **Curry Mile,** a stretch of Asian restaurants on Wilmslow Rd., for quality eats. A **Tesco supermarket** is at 55-66 Market St. (☎941 9400. Open 24hr.)

🔳 **Tampopo Noodle House,** 16 Albert Sq. (☎819 1966). This spartan noodle house is one of Manchester's favorites. Noodles from Thailand, Malaysia, Indonesia, and Japan are well-priced (£4-8), quick, and delicious. Try the *Pad Krapow* with prawns and chilis. Open daily noon-11pm. ❷

Dimitri's, Campfield Arcade, Deansgate (☎839 3319), in an alley off Bridgegate St. Greek delicacies for plebeians and soap-opera divas alike (there's a TV studio next door). 2 appetizers make a meal (£3.65-5.45). 20% off drinks during happy hour (5-7pm). Open daily 11am-11:30pm. ❸

Tribeca, 50 Sackville St. (☎236 8300). Serves a wide variety of cuisines, from BBQ ribs to bangers and mash. Take your meal on one of the seductive beds downstairs. Appetizers £3-5.40. Entrees £7-13. Open Su-M noon-12:30am, Tu-Sa noon-2:00am. ❸

Camel One, 107 Wilmslow Rd. (☎257 2282). A simple eatery with an extensive Indian menu. Banner claims "Voted #1 in England." Kebab sandwiches made to order. Dishes £2-5.50. Open daily 10am-7pm. ❶

Gaia, 46 Sackville St. (☎228 1002). Skilled chefs prepare brilliant British fusion cuisine with Mediterranean flavor. Renaissance decor features velvet curtains and candlelight. Appetizers £3-5. Entrees £8-13. Open M-Th and Su noon-midnight, F-Sa noon-2am. ❸

🔄 SIGHTS

Few of Manchester's buildings are notable—postcards mostly portray the fronts of trams—but an exception is the neo-Gothic **Manchester Town Hall,** at Albert St. Behind the Town Hall Extension, the **Central Library** is the city's jewel. One of the largest municipal libraries in Europe, the domed building has a music and theater library, a language and literature library, and the UK's second-largest Judaica collection. The **John Rylands Library,** 150 Deansgate, keeps rare books; its most famous holding is the St. John Fragment, a piece of New Testament writing from the 2nd-century. (☎834 5343. Open M-F 10am-5pm, Sa 10am-1pm. Free. Tours W at noon.) The **Royal Exchange Theater** (☎833 9333) has returned to St. Ann's Sq., a few years after an IRA bomb destroyed the original building. The theater stages Shakespearean productions, as well as premieres of original works. (Box office open M-Sa 9:30am-7:30pm. Tickets £7.25, concessions £6.50 when booked 3 days in advance.) Also recently reopened after a three-year, £35 million renovation, the **Manchester Art Gallery,** on Nicholas St., holds Rossetti's stunning *Astarte Syriaca* among its gigantic collection. (☎235 8888. Open Su and Tu-Sa and bank holidays 10am-5pm. Admission free. Free audio tours.) In the **Museum of Science and Industry,** Liverpool Rd., in Castlefield, working steam engines and looms provide a dramatic illustration of Britain's industrialization that is interesting for adults and children alike. (☎832 2244. Open daily 10am-5pm. Museum free. Special exhibits £3-5.) The Spanish and Portuguese synagogue-turned-**Jewish Museum,** 190 Cheetham Hill Rd., traces the history of the city's sizeable Jewish community and offers city tours. (☎834 9879. Open M-Th 10:30am-4pm, Su 10:30am-5pm. £3.65, families £8.95, concessions £2.75.) Loved and reviled, Manchester United is England's reigning football team. The **Manchester United Museum and Tour Centre,** Sir Matt Busby Way, at the Old Trafford football stadium, displays memorabilia from the club's inception in 1878 to its recent trophy-hogging success. The museum's fervor may just convert you. (From the Old Trafford Metrolink stop, follow signs up Warwick Rd. ☎0870 442 1994. Open daily 9:30am-5pm. Tours every 10min. 9:40am-4:30pm. Museum £5.50, families £15.50, concessions £3.75; with tour £8.50/23.50/5.80.)

⚑ NIGHTLIFE

CAFE-BARS
Many of Manchester's excellent lunchtime spots morph into pre-club drinking venues or even become clubs themselves.

> **The Temple** (☎278 1610), on Bridgewater St., literally. An entrance in the middle of the street leads downstairs to a small, smoky bar, once home to a toilet. Locals squeeze in for drinks before clubbing. Try the Belgian Gay Boy (£3.50), a mysterious concoction served in a pint. Open M-Sa noon-11pm, Su 5-10:30pm.

> **The Lass O'Gowrie,** 36 Charles St. (☎273 6932). Traditional pubs aren't at all passé when the evening crowd is this lively. BBC personalities trickle in from the neighboring studio. Good food at amazing prices (£2-5). Open M-Sa 11am-11pm, Su noon-10:30pm. Kitchen open M-F noon-5pm and Sa-Su noon-3pm.

CLUBS
Manchester's clubbing and live music scene remains a national trendsetter. Centered around **Oldham Street,** the **Northern Quarter** is the city's youthful outlet for live music; its alternative vibe and underground shops attracting a hip crowd. Partiers flock to **Oxford Street** for late-night clubbing and reveling. Don't forget to collect flyers—they'll often score you a discount. At night, streets in the Northern Quarter are dimly lit. If you're crossing from Piccadilly to Swan St. or Great Ancoats St., use Oldham St., where the neon-lit clubs (and their bouncers) provide reassurance. There's no shame in short taxi trips at night in this town.

> 🎵 **Music Box,** Oxford Rd. (☎273 3435). A small, underground venue that hosts live bands and enormously popular parties. Check posters outside for details; monthly Electric Chair and events by Mr. Scruff receive rave reviews from local partiers. Cover £5-8. Open Th-Sa at 10pm, closes between 3am and 6am, depending on the event.

> **Revolution,** Arch 7, Whitworth St. West (☎839 7569). Revolution leads an army of upstart bars and clubs on Deansgate. Bar on the ground floor leads downstairs to small dance floor below. Red decor (look for the bust of Lenin) is a tasteful backdrop to funk, house, old school, and R&B tunes. 150 vodkas. No cover unless special promotion. Open daily noon-2am.

THE GAY VILLAGE
Gay and lesbian clubbers will want to check out the Gay Village, northeast of Princess St. Evening crowds fill the bars lining Canal St., in the heart of the area, which is also lively and lovely during the day.

THE LOCAL STORY

Essential, 8 Minshull St. (☎237 0077), at the corner of Bloom St., off Portland St. Arguably the most popular club in the Gay Village. Dress smart casual. Cover £3-8. Open F 10:30pm-5am, Sa 10:30pm-6am, Su 10:30pm-3am.

Cruz 101, 101 Princess St. (☎950 0101). Fun and sexy cruisers teach a lesson in attitude here. Commercial dancers get bodies moving. Dress smart causal. Cover M, W, Th £2; F £3; Sa £5. Open W-Sa 10pm-2am.

LIVERPOOL ☎0151

Legendary nightlife, a multitude of free museums, and restaurants on every block make Liverpool, hometown of the Beatles, a great destination for travelers. Scousers—as Liverpudlians are colloquially known—are usually happy to introduce you to their dialect and to discuss the relative merits of Liverpool's two football teams.

▐ TICKET TO RIDE. Trains (☎(08457) 484 950) arrive at Lime Street Station from: Birmingham (1¾hr., 2-5 per day, £19); Chester (45min., 2 per hr., £3.40); London Euston (3hr., 10-24 per day, £49); and Manchester Piccadilly (1hr., 2-3 per hr., £7.50). National Express **buses** (☎(08705) 808 080) head from Norton Street Coach Station to: Birmingham (2½hr., 5 per day, £9.30); London (4½hr., 5-6 per day, £19); and Manchester (1hr., 1-2 per hr, £5). The Isle of Man Steam Packet Company (☎(08705) 523 523) runs **ferries** from Princess Dock to Dublin.

▟ HELP! The main **tourist office,** in Queen Square Centre, gives away the handy *Visitor Guide to Liverpool and Merseyside,* and books beds for a 10% deposit. (☎(0906) 680 6886; calls charged 25p per min. Open M and W-Sa 9am-5:30pm, Tu 10am-5:30pm, Su 10:30am-4:30pm.) Expert guide Phil Hughes runs personalized **Beatles tours** (☎228 4565) for the lucky eight that fit in his van. Surf the **Internet** for free at the **Central Library,** on William Brown St. (Open M-Th 9am-8pm, F 9am-7pm, Sa 9am-5pm, Su noon-4pm.) **Postal Code:** L1 1AA.

▐▐ A HARD DAY'S NIGHT. Budget hotels are mostly located around **Lord Nelson Street,** next to the train station, and **Mount Pleasant,** one block from Brownlow Hill. At **▧Embassie Backpackers ❶,** relax by using some of the numerous amenities (including a pool table, three lounges, and a kitchen), or simply sit back for a chat over free toast, tea, or a pint. (☎707 1089. Laundry facilities. Dorms £14 for the first night, £13 for each additional night.) Clean rooms and a relaxing bar await at **Aachen Hotel ❸,** 89-91 Mt. Pleasant, the winner of numerous awards. (☎709 3477. Breakfast included. Singles £28-38; doubles £46-54.) **YHA Liverpool ❷,** 24 Tabley St., off The Wapping, has upscale rooms on three Beatles-themed floors. (☎709 8888. Kitchen available. Breakfast included. Laundry facilities. Internet access. Dorms £19, under-18 £14.) The **International Inn ❷,** 4 South Hunter St., is clean and fun. Enjoy the lounge and adjoining cafe. (☎709 8135. Dorms £15; doubles £36.)

Trendy cafes and well-priced Indian restaurants line **Bold Street** and **Hardman Street,** while fast-food joints crowd **Hardnon Street** and **Berry Street.** Many eateries stay open until 3am. ◪**Country Kitchen ❶,** Drury Ln., dishes out cheap and delicious meals. Toasties, salads, and pasta cost a mere £1, and soup is just 75p. (☎236 0509. Open daily 7:30am-3:30pm.) **Simply Heathcotes ❹,** 25 The Strand, Beetham Plaza, is simply elegant. Try the breaded veal escalope. (Entrees around £15. Open M-F noon-2:30pm and 6-10pm, Sa 6-11pm, Su noon-2:30pm and 6-9:30pm.) **Tavern Co. ❷,** in Queen Sq., near the tourist office, serves burritos and taco salads (£5-7) in a wine-bar atmosphere. (Open M-Sa noon-11pm, Su 10:30am-10:30pm.)

◪ **MAGICAL MYSTERY TOUR.** The tourist office's **Beatles Map** (£2.50) leads visitors through Beatles-themed sights, including **Strawberry Fields** and **Penny Lane.** At Albert Dock, **The Beatles Story** pays tribute to the group's work with a re-creation of the Cavern Club and a yellow submarine. (Open Apr.-Oct. daily 10am-6pm; Nov.-Mar. 10am-5pm. £8, students £5.50.) The intimate Liverpool branch of the **Tate Gallery,** also on Albert Dock, contains a select range of 20th-century artwork. (Open Su and Tu-Sa 10am-6pm. Free. Special exhibits £4.) The Anglican **Liverpool Cathedral,** on Upper Duke St., boasts the highest Gothic arches ever built and the heaviest bells in the world. Climb to the top of the 100m tower for a view stretching to Wales. (Cathedral open daily 8am-6pm. Suggested donation £2.50. Tower open M-Sa 11am-4pm, weather permitting. £2.50.) Neon-blue stained glass casts a glow over the interior of the **Metropolitan Cathedral of Christ the King,** on Mt. Pleasant. Note the many modern sculptures that fill the chapels. (Open in summer M-F 7:30am-6pm, Sa-Su 8:30am-6pm; off-season M-F 8am-6pm, Sa 8:30am-6pm, Su 8:30am-5pm. Free.) The **Liverpool** and **Everton football clubs**—intense rivals—offer tours of their grounds. Bus #26 runs from the city center to both stadiums. (Book in advance. Everton ☎330 2277; tour £5.50. Liverpool ☎260 6677; tour £8.50.)

LG: Sort of Pollock-style...
A: Heh. Yeah...

LG: And how did you become their manager?
A: I put this big rock 'n' roll show on. They came and saw me the next day and said, "Hey Al? When are you going to do something for us like?" And I said to them, "Look, there's no more painting to be done." And they said, "No, we've got a *group.*" I said, "I didn't know that." And they said, "Well, will you manage us?" By then I had got to know them, and they were quite nice personalities—very witty. And I go, "Oh yeah, this could be fun." And then I managed them.

Williams felt that it was their stint in Hamburg, and not Liverpool, that made the Beatles. He describes his falling out with the group as a disagreement over—what else?—contract disputes and general rock-star ingratitude.

A: I wrote them a letter saying that they appeared to be getting more than a little swell-headed and "Remember, I managed you when nobody else wanted to know you. But I'll fix it now so that you'll never ever work again."

LG: Uh-oh.
A: So that's my big mistake, yeah. Heh. And on that note, we'll finish.

⚡ COME TOGETHER. Consult the *Liverpool Echo*, an evening paper sold by street vendors, for up-to-date information on nightlife. **Slater Street** in particular brims with £1 pints, while on weekend nights, the downtown area—especially **Matthew Street, Church Street,** and **Bold Street**—overflows with young clubbers. John Lennon once said that the worst thing about fame was "not being able to get a quiet pint at the Phil." Fortunately, the rest of us can sip in solitude at **The Philharmonic,** 36 Hope St. (Open M-Sa noon-11pm, Su noon-10:30pm.) **The Jacaranda,** on Slater St., the site of the Beatles' first paid gig, has live bands and a dance floor. (Open M-Sa noon-2am, Su noon-10:30pm.) **Medication,** in Wolstonholme Sq., offers the wildest student night in town. (Students only; bring ID. Cover £5. Open W 10am-2am.) **The Cavern Club,** 10 Matthew St., is on the site where the Fab Four gained prominence; today it draws locals for live bands. (No cover until 10pm, 10-11pm £2, 11pm-2am £4. Club open M-W 6pm-midnight, Th 6pm-2am, F-Sa 6pm-2:30am. Pub open M-Sa from noon, Su noon-11:30pm.)

PEAK DISTRICT NATIONAL PARK

A green cushion among England's industrial giants of Manchester, Sheffield, and Nottingham, Britain's first national park sprawls across 1400sq. km of rolling hills and windswept moors, offering a playground for its 22 million urban neighbors.

📋 TRANSPORTATION AND PRACTICAL INFORMATION. The invaluable *Peak District Timetable* (60p), available at tourist offices, has transport routes and a map. Two **train** lines originate in Manchester and enter the park from the west: one stops at Buxton, near the park's edge (1hr., every hr., £5.70), and the other crosses the park (1½hr., 9-17 per day) via Edale (£6.70), Hope, and Hathersage, terminating in Sheffield (£11). Trent (☎(01773) 712 2765) **bus** TP, the "Transpeak," departs from Manchester to Nottingham (3hr., 6 per day), stopping at Buxton, Bakewell, Matlock, Derby, and other towns in between. First PMT (☎(01782) 207 999) #X18 leaves from Sheffield for Bakewell (45min., M-Sa 5 per day). First Mainline (☎(01709) 515 151) #272 and Stagecoach East Midland (☎(01246) 211 007) #273 and 274 depart from Sheffield to Castleton (40-55min., 12-15 per day). The **Derbyshire Wayfarer,** available at tourist offices, allows one day of train and bus travel through the Peak District as far as Sheffield and Derby (£7.50).

The **National Park Information Centres** (NPICs) at Bakewell, Castleton, and Edale offer walking guides. Info is also available at **tourist offices** in Buxton (☎(01298) 25 106) and Matlock Bath (☎(01629) 55 082). There are 20 **YHA Youth Hostels ❷** in the park (Dorms £8-15). For Bakewell, Castleton, and Edale, see below; the Buxton YHA, Harpur Hill Rd., can be reached at ☎(0870) 770 5738, while the Matlock YHA, 40 Bank Rd., can be contacted at ☎(01629) 582 983. To stay at the 13 **YHA Camping Barns ❶** throughout the park (£4 per person), book ahead at the **Camping Barns Reservation Office,** 6 King St., Clitheroe, Lancashire BB7 2EP (☎(0870) 770 6113). The park operates six **Cycle Hire Centres** (£12.50 per day); a free brochure, *Peak Cycle Hire,* available at NPICs, includes phone numbers, hours, and locations.

CASTLETON. The main attraction in Castleton (pop. 705) is ⚡**Treak Cliff Cavern,** which hides seams of Blue John, a mineral found only in these hills. (40min. tours every 15-30min. Open Easter-Oct. daily from 10am, last tour between 4-5pm.; Nov.-Feb. 10am-3:20pm; Mar.-Easter 10am-4:20pm. £5.60, students £4.50.) Castleton lies 3.2km west of **Hope.** The Castleton **NPIC** is on Buxton Rd. (☎(01433) 620 679. Open Apr.-Oct. daily 10am-1pm and 2-5:30pm; Nov.-Mar. Sa-Su 10am-5pm.) **YHA Castleton ❷** is in Castleton Hall, a pretty country house in the heart of town. (☎(01433) 620 235. Kitchen available. **Internet** access. Book 2-3 weeks in advance. Open Feb. to late Dec. Dorms £12-14, under-18 £9-10.)

BAKEWELL AND EDALE. The town of Bakewell, 50km southeast of Manchester, is the best base from which to explore the region; several scenic walks through the **White Peaks** begin nearby. Bakewell's **NPIC** is in Old Market Hall, at Bridge St. (☎(01629) 813 227. Open Mar.-Oct. daily 9:30am-5:30pm; Nov.-Feb. 10am-5pm.) The cozy **YHA Bakewell ❷,** on Fly Hill, is 5min. from the town centers. (☎(01629) 812 313. Open Mar.-Oct. M-Sa; Nov.-Feb. daily. Dorms £11, under-18 £7.)

The northern Dark Peak area contains some of the wildest and most rugged hill country in England. The area around **Edale** is spectacular, and the National Park Authority's *8 Walks Around Edale* (£1.20) details nearby trails. The town offers little other than a church, cafe, pub, school, and the nearby **YHA youth hostel ❷,** Rowland Cote. (☎(01433) 670 302. Dorms £11.50, under-18 £8.30.)

YORK ☎01904

Although its well-preserved city walls have foiled many, York (pop. 105,000) fails to impede its present-day hordes of visitors. Today, marauders brandish cameras instead of swords, and the plunder is now York's compact collection of rich historical sights, including Britain's largest Gothic cathedral.

▄ TRANSPORTATION

Trains: York Station, Station Rd. Ticket office open M-Sa 5:45am-10:15pm, Su 7:30am-10:10pm. Trains (☎(08457) 484 950) arrive from: **Edinburgh** (2½hr., 2 per hr., £60); **London King's Cross** (2hr., 2 per hr., £64); **Manchester Piccadilly** (1½hr., 2 per hr., £17); and **Newcastle** (1hr., 2 per hr., £18).

Buses: There are **bus stations** at Rougier St., Exhibition Sq., Station Rd., and on Piccadilly St. **National Express** (☎(08705) 808 080) arrives from: **Edinburgh** (5½hr., daily, £36); **London** (5hr., 3 per day, £31); and **Manchester** (2¾hr., 3 per day, £12).

Local Transportation: Call **First York** (☎622 992, bus times ☎551 400) for info. Ticket office open M-F 9am-5pm. **Yorkshire Coastliner** (☎(0113) 244 8976 or (01653) 692 556) runs buses from the train station to Castle Howard (p. 227).

Bike Rental: Bob Trotter, 13 Lord Mayor's Walk (☎622 868). Open M-Sa 9am-5:30pm, Su 10am-4pm. From £10 per day, plus £50 deposit.

▄ ▐ ORIENTATION AND PRACTICAL INFORMATION

York's streets are generally short, winding, and unlabeled, and the longer ones change names every block or so. Fortunately, most attractions lie within the city walls, so you can't get too lost, and the **York Minster** (cathedral), visible from almost anywhere, provides an easy reference point. The **River Ouse** (OOZE) cuts through the city, curving from west to south. The city centre lies between the Ouse and the Minster; **Coney Street, Parliament Street,** and **Stonegate** are the main thoroughfares.

Tourist Office: Exhibition Sq. (☎621 756; www.york-tourism.co.uk). Sells the *York Visitor Guide* (£1), a detailed map of the city, and *Snickelways of York* (£5), an off-beat self-tour guide. A **branch** is located in the train station. Open June-Oct. M-Sa 9am-6pm, Su 10am-5pm; Nov.-May daily 9am-5pm.

Financial Services: Banks line Coney St. **Thomas Cook,** 4 Nessgate (☎881 400) is open M-W and F-Sa 9am-5:30pm, Tu 10am-5:30pm. **American Express,** 6 Stonegate (☎676 501) is open M-Tu, Th-F 9am-5:30pm, W 9:30am-5:30pm, Sa 9am-5pm. The **Bureau de Change** is open during business hours.

Laundromat: Haxby Road Washeteria, 124 Haxby Rd. (☎623 379). £5.80 for one load, including wash and dry. Open M-F 8am-6pm, Sa 9am-5:30pm, Su 9am-4:30pm. Last wash 2hr. before closing.

Police: Fulford Rd. (☎631 321).

Hospital: York District Hospital (☎631 313), off Wigginton Rd. Take bus #1 or 18 from Exhibition Sq. and ask for the hospital stop.

Internet Access: Cafe of the Evil Eye, 42 Stonegate (☎640 002). £2 per hr.

Post Office: 22 Lendal (☎617 285). **Bureau de Change.** Open M-Tu 8:30am-5:30pm, W-Sa 9am-5:30pm. **Postal Code:** YO1 8DA.

ACCOMMODATIONS

B&Bs are concentrated on the side streets along **Bootham** and **Clifton,** in the Mount area down **Blossom Street,** and on **Bishopsthorpe Road,** south of town. Book ahead in summer, when competition for all types of accommodations can be fierce.

■ **York Backpackers,** 88-90 Micklegate (☎627 720; fax 339 350). Fun atmosphere abounds in this stately 18th-century mansion. Their "Dungeon Bar" is usually open 5 nights per week, long after the pubs close. Kitchen and laundry facilities available. Internet £1 per 20min. Dorms £13-14; doubles £34. ❶

■ **Avenue Guest House,** 6 The Avenue (☎620 575; www.avenuegh.fsnet.co.uk), off Clifton on a quiet, residential side street. Enthusiastic hosts provide immaculate rooms with soft beds. Singles £20-22; doubles £38-42, with bath £42-46. ❷

Alexander House, 94 Bishopthorpe Rd. (☎625 016), 5min. from the train station. Luxurious rooms have flowers and king-sized beds. Singles £55-59; doubles £65-70. ❹

Foss Bank Guest House, 16 Huntington Rd. (☎635 548). Walk or take bus #12 or 13 from the train station. Offers comfortable beds in particularly swanky doubles. All rooms with shower and sink, some with bathtub and TV. Singles £22-25; doubles £42-52. Discount for *Let's Go* users. ❸

Queen Anne's Guest House, 24 Queen Anne's Rd. (☎629 389), a short walk down Bootham from Exhibition Sq. The friendly proprietress offers spotless rooms and a regal breakfast. Singles £18-20; doubles £32-42. Discount for *Let's Go* users. ❷

YHA York, Water End (☎653 147), Clifton. From Exhibition Sq., walk about 1km on Bootham and take a left at Water End. Excellent facilities, including smoking room, TV lounge, and well-decorated dining room. Lockout 10am-1pm. Dorms £17, under-18 £12; singles £22; doubles £37; family rooms £59-68. ❷

York Youth Hotel, 11-13 Bishophill Senior (☎625 904). Well located hostel catering primarily to groups. Laundry facilites available. Key deposit £3. Reception 24hr. Dorms £11-14; singles £22; doubles £16-20. ❷

Riverside Caravan and Camping Park, Ferry Ln. (☎705 812), Bishopthorpe, 3km south of York off A64. Take bus #11 or 11Y from the bus station and ask the driver to let you off at the campsite (2 per hr., round-trip £1.20). Pleasant riverside site. July-Aug. £8 for tent and 2 people; Sept.-June £7. ❶

FOOD

Greengrocers peddle their produce at **Newgate market** between Parliament St. and Shambles. (Open Apr.-Dec. M-Sa 9am-5pm, Su 9am-4:30pm; Jan.-Mar. M-Sa 9am-5pm.) Food and nightlife converge in York, as its city centre is filled with packed **pubs,** all of which serve bar meals during the day.

Oscar's Wine Bar and Bistro, 8 Little Stonegate (☎652 002). This popular spot combines a chic courtyard and lively mood with massive portions of pub favorites. Open M-Sa 11:30am-11pm, Su noon-10:30pm. ❷

TO 1 (.25mi)

Grosvenor Rd. Bridge Ln. Hospital Ln.

0 — 300 yards
0 — 300 meters

Grosvenor Rd.

The Avenue

Burton Stone Ln.

St. Peter's Gr.

St. Olave's Rd.

Clifton

Bootham Cres.

Grosvenor Terr.

York District
Hospital

Union Terr.

Lowther St.

St. Penley's Grove St.

Brook St. Garden St.

Clarence St.

De Grey Terr.

Lord Mayor's Walk

St. John's St.

Groves Ln.

Huntington
Rd.

Monkgate

Queen Anne's Rd.

Bootham Terr.

Bootham

Saint Mary's

Claremont Terr.

Portland St.

Bootham Row

Gillygate

City Wall

Dean's
Park

Ogleforth

St. Maurice's Rd.

Jewbury Rd.

Foss
Bank

Cricket
Ground

Sycamore Terr.

Longfield Terr.

Almery Terr.

Marygate

High Petergate

EXHIBITION
SQUARE

York City
Art Gallery

St. Leonard's Pl.

Theatre
Royal

York
Minster

College St.

Deangate

Aldwark

St. Andrewgate

St. Saviourgate

Aldwark St.

Peasholme
Green

St. Mary's
Abbey (Ruins)

Yorkshire
Museum

Museum
Gardens

Dame Judi Dench Walk

Museum St.

Lendal

Duncombe
Pl.

Minster Yard

Blake St.

Stonegate

Low Petergate

Goodramgate

Grape Ln.

Swinegate

Church St.

KING'S
SQUARE

THE
SHAMBLES

The Stonebow

Carmelite St.

YorkBoat

Lendal
Bridge

ST. HELEN'S
SQUARE

New St.

Davygate

Feasegate

Market St.

Parliament St.

Pavement

Fossgate

Piccadilly

River Foss

Walmgate

Leeman Rd.

Station Ave.

Station Rd.

Roughier St.

Wellington Row

North St.

Tanner Row

George Hudson St.

St. Martin's Ln.

Bridge St.

Coney St.

Nessgate

Copperg ate

Castlegate

Jorvik
Viking
Centre

Ouse
Bridge

Queen's Staith

King's Staith

York
Dungeon

Clifford's Tower

York Castle
Museum

Micklegate

Toft Green

Priory St.

Trinity Ln.

Fetter Ln.

Bishophill Junior

Bishophill Senior

Victor St.

Hampden St.

Cromwell Rd.

Skeldergate

River Ouse

Clifford St.

Skeldergate
Bridge

Tower St.

George St.

Margaret St.

Lead
Mill Ln.

Hope
St.

Paragon St.

City Wall

Queen St.

Blossom St.

Nunnery Ln.

City Wall

The Crescent

S. Parade

Scarcroft Ln.

Moss St.

Dale St.

Swan St.

Newton Terr.

Price's Ln.

St. Benedict Rd.

Kyme St.

Balie Hill Terr.

Baile Hill Terr.

Clementhorpe

Terry Ave.

Fishergate

Cemetery Rd.

Fulford Rd.

TO
B1224

Holgate Rd.

The Mount

Park St.

Scarcroft Rd.

Bishopthorpe Rd.

Darnborough St.

Vine Cherry

TO A64 &

BRITAIN

York

ACCOMMODATIONS

Alexander House, **14**
Avenue Guest House, **2**
Foss Bank Guest House, **4**
Queen Anne's Guest House, **3**
YHA York, **1**
York Backpackers, **11**
York Youth Hotel, **12**

FOOD

Oscar's Wine Bar
and Bistro, **7**
El Piano, **6**
Rubicon, **8**
Ye Olde Starre, **5**

NIGHTLIFE

Fibber's, **9**
The Gallery, **13**
Toff's, **10**

Rubicon, 5 Little Stonegate (☎676 076). This hip vegetarian restaurant has exotic international options, as well as vegan and gluten-free dishes. Sandwiches £4.50. Entrees £7-9. Open daily 11:30am-10pm. ❷

Betty's, 6-8 Helens Sq. Traditional teas services (£5-9) are offered in a refined atmosphere. Entrees £3-12. Open daily 9am-9pm. ❷

Ye Olde Starre, 40 Stonegate (☎623 063). The city's oldest pub, with a license that dates to 1644. Pub fare (£4-7) includes Guinness pie, *chili con carne,* and Yorkshire pudding. Open M-Sa 10am-11pm, Su noon-10:30pm. ❶

El Piano, 15-17 Grape Ln. (☎610 676). Laid-back atmosphere and colorful decorations make this vegetarian restaurant an ideal place to relax. *Tapas* £3. Entrees £8-13. Open M-Sa 10am-midnight, Su noon-midnight. ❷

👁 🏛 SIGHTS AND ENTERTAINMENT

The best introduction to York is the 4km walk along its **medieval walls.** Beware of the tourist stampede, which slows only in the early morning and just before the walls and gates close at dusk. A free 2hr. **walking tour** is offered daily by the **Association of Voluntary Guides** (☎630 284); tours leave from the York City Art Gallery, across from the tourist office. Everything in York converges at the ⬛**York Minster,** the largest Gothic cathedral in Britain. If the interior seems to glitter, it's because an estimated half of all the medieval stained glass in England lines the walls; the **Great East Window** depicts the beginning and end of the world in over 100 scenes. Climb the 275 steps to the top of **Central Tower** for a view over York's rooftops. (Cathedral open daily 9:30am-6:30pm. £2.50, children £1.) After having seen the heights of the Minster, check out its depths. The **Undercroft, Treasury,** and **Crypt** are filled with interesting sights, including the spot where Constantine the Great was proclaimed emperor and the 12th-century **Doomstone** upon which the cathedral was built. (Open daily 9:30am-6:30pm. £2.50, concessions £1.50.)

The ⬛**York Castle Museum,** at the Eye of York, between Tower St. and Picadilly St., is arguably Britain's premier museum dedicated to everyday life. It contains **Kirkgate,** an intricately reconstructed Victorian shopping street complete with carriage, and **Half Moon Court,** its Edwardian counterpart. (Open daily 9:30am-5pm. £6, concessions £3.50.) The **Jorvik Viking Centre,** on Coppergate, is one of the busiest places in York; visit early or late to avoid lines, or call at least 24hr. in advance. Visitors pass through the York of AD 948 in floating "time cars," past authentic artifacts, eerily life-like mannequins, and painfully accurate smells. (☎643 211. For advance booking, call ☎543 403; M-F 9am-5pm. Open Apr.-Oct. daily 9am-5:30pm; Nov.-Mar. daily 10am-4:30pm. £7.20, concessions £6.10.) Hidden within the four gorgeous hectares of the **Museum Gardens,** the **Yorkshire Museum** presents Roman, Anglo-Saxon, and Viking artifacts, as well as the £2.5 million **Middleham Jewel** from circa 1450. In the gardens, peacocks strut among the haunting ruins of **St. Mary's Abbey,** once the most influential Benedictine monastery in northern England. (Enter from Museum St. or Marygate. Open daily 10am-5pm. £4, students £2.50, families £10. Gardens and abbey free.) **Clifford's Tower,** Tower St., is one of the last remaining pieces of **York Castle,** and a chilling reminder of the worst outbreak of anti-Semitic violence in English History. In 1190, Christian merchants tried to erase their debts by destroying York's Jewish community. 150 Jews took refuge in the tower, where—faced with the prospect of starvation or butchery— they committed mass suicide. The wall walk provides information on the pogrom and the history of the castle. (Open July-Aug. daily 9am-7pm; Sept. and Apr.-June 10am-6pm; Oct. 10am-5pm; Nov.-Mar. 10am-4pm. £2.50, concessions £2.)

The monthly *What's On* and *Artscene* guides, available at the tourist office, publish info on live music, theater, cinema, and exhibitions. In **King's Square** and on **Stonegate**, barbershop quartets share the pavement with jugglers, magicians, and politicians. **The Gallery,** 12 Clifford St., has two dance floors and six bars. (Cover £1.50-7.50. Open daily 9:30pm-2:30am.) The excellent **Toff's,** 3-5 Toft Green, plays mainly house and dance music. (No sneakers. Cover £3.50-7. Open M-Sa 9pm-2am. Gay-friendly "Alternative Sundays" 9pm-1am.) **Fibber's,** Stonebow House, the Stonebow, has quality live music playing nightly at 8pm. In July, the **York Early Music Festival** celebrates composer Henry Purcell (☎ 658 338).

▶ DAYTRIP FROM YORK

■ **CASTLE HOWARD.** The Baroque Castle Howard, still inhabited by the Howard family, presides over four square kilometers of stunning grounds that teem with gardens, fountains, and lakes. The Castle made its TV debut in the BBC adaptation of Evelyn Waugh's *Brideshead Revisited.* The **long gallery** provides a dazzling and dwarfing promenade between enormous windows and shelves stuffed with books. Be sure to see the domed **Temple of the Four Winds,** with a hilltop perch that offers views of grassy fields, still waters, and lazy cows.

The castle is located 24km northeast of York. Yorkshire Coastliner **bus** #840 runs to the castle once in the morning and once in the afternoon, and bus #842 takes passengers back twice in the afternoon (40min., round-trip £4.40). Reduced admission with bus ticket. (☎ (01653) 648 333. Castle open mid-Feb. to Nov. daily 11am-4:30pm. Gardens open daily 10am-6:30pm. Both £9, concessions £8. Gardens only £6.)

NEWCASTLE-UPON-TYNE   ☎ 0191

The largest city in the northeast, Newcastle (pop. 278,000) has emerged into the 21st century determined to forge itself a new identity. Ambitious building efforts have lent the city genuine daytime energy, and its nightlife is hotter than ever as locals, students, and tourists continue to flock to its pubs and cafes. A combination of hoary old and resilient new, Newcastle's monuments blend well with the city. The largely intact **Castle Garth Keep,** at the foot of St. Nicholas St., is all that remains of the 12th-century New Castle complex. Oddly enough, the city derives its name from a castle that existed over 100 years earlier. (☎ 232 7938. Open Apr.-Sept. daily 9:30am-5:30pm; Oct.-Mar. 9:30am-4:30pm. Admission £1.50, concessions 50p.) The **BALTIC Centre for Contemporary Art,** housed in a renovated grain warehouse, is the largest center for contemporary art outside of London. This stunning yet simplistically designed museum rises seven stories above the Tyne and showcases current artists at the cutting edge of their fields. (☎ 478 1810. Open M-W and F-Sa 10am-7pm, Th 10am-10pm, Su 10am-5pm. Free.) Treat yourself to an evening at the lush gilt-and-velvet **Theatre Royal,** 100 Grey St., undoubtedly northern England's premier stage. The **Royal Shakespeare Company** makes a month-long stop here each fall, complementing other top-notch performances. (☎ 232 2061. Call for performance times.) Rowdy **Bigg Market** features the highest concentration of pubs in England, while **Quayside** (KEY-side) is slightly more relaxed and attracts local students. **Chase,** 10-15 Sandhill, is a flashy pub, while nearby **Offshore 44,** 40 Sandhill, has a tropical theme. (Both open M-Sa 11am-11pm and Su noon-6pm.) The hottest dance club is **The Tuxedo Princess,** on a cruise ship under the Tyne Bridge. (Open M and W-Sa 7:30pm-2am.) For a happening gay and lesbian scene, head to Waterloo St. for a night of drinking and dancing at **The Powerhouse.** (Open M, Th, and Su 10:30pm-2am, F-Sa 10pm-3am.)

BRITAIN

Trains leave from Neville St. for Edinburgh (1½hr., approx. every hr., £36) and London King's Cross (3½hr., every hr., £83). National Express **buses** (☎(08705) 808 080) leave Percy St. for Edinburgh (3hr., 4 per day, £14) and London (7hr., 4 per day, £24). The **tourist office** is on 132 Grainger St., facing Grey's Monument. (☎277 8000. Open June-Sept. M-W and F 9:30am-5:30pm, Th 9:30am-7:30pm, Sa 9am-5pm, Su 10am-4pm; Oct.-May M-W and F 9:30am-5:30pm, Th 9:30am-7:30pm, Sa 9am-5pm.) To get to the friendly **YHA Newcastle ❷**, 107 Jesmond Rd., take the Metro to Jesmond, turn left onto Jesmond Rd., and walk past the traffic lights. Call well in advance. (☎281 2570. **Internet** access. Open mid-Jan. to mid-Dec. Dorms £12, under-18 £8.30.) **University of Northumbria ❷**, Sandyford Rd., offers standard dorm accommodations, but its proximity to the city center is a plus. Some rooms come with partial kitchen. (☎227 3215. Breakfast included. Open June-Aug. Singles mid-week £23, weekends £28.) **Gershwins ❷**, 54 Dean St., is a cool underground grotto restaurant that serves continental cuisine at a great price. (2-course dinner with wine £7-11. Open M-Sa 11:30am-2:30pm and 5:30-10:30pm.) **Postal Code:** NE1 7AB.

LAKE DISTRICT NATIONAL PARK

Quite possibly the loveliest place in England, the Lake District owes its beauty to a thorough glacier-gouging during the last ice age. Jagged peaks and windswept fells stand in desolate splendor as hillside rivers pool in serene mountain lakes. Use Windermere, Ambleside, Grasmere, and Keswick as bases from which to ascend into the hills—the farther west you go from the A591, which connects these towns, the more countryside you'll have to yourself.

The **National Park Visitor Centre** is in **Brockhole,** halfway between Windermere and Ambleside. (☎(01539) 446 601. Open Apr.-Oct. daily 10am-5pm.) **National Park Information Centres** book accommodations and dispense free information and town maps. Although B&Bs line every street in every town and there's a hostel around every bend, lodgings do fill up in summer; book ahead.

▤ TRANSPORTATION. Trains (☎(08457) 484 950) run to Oxenholme, the primary gateway to the lakes, from: Birmingham (2½hr., 1 every 2hr., £42); Edinburgh (2½hr., 6 per day, £39); London Euston (4hr., 11-16 per day, £63); and Manchester Piccadilly (1½hr., 9-10 per day, £13). A short line covers the 16km between Windermere and Oxenholme (20min., every hr., £3.20). There is also direct service to Windermere from Manchester Piccadilly (2hr., 1-6 per day, £13). National Express **buses** (☎(08705) 808 080) arrive in Windermere from Birmingham (4½hr., daily, £25) and London (7½hr., daily, £26), and continue north through Ambleside and Grasmere to Keswick. **Stagecoach in Cumbria** (☎(0870) 608 2608) is the primary operator of bus service in the region; a complete timetable, *The Lakeland Explorer*, is available at tourist offices. An **Explorer** ticket offers unlimited travel on all area Stagecoach buses (1-day £7.50, children £5.30; 4-day £17/13). The Ambleside YHA Youth Hostel offers a convenient **minibus** service (☎(01539) 432 304) between hostels (2 per day, £2.50) as well as free service from the Windermere train station to the Windermere and Ambleside hostels.

WINDERMERE AND BOWNESS. Windermere and its sidekick **Bowness-on-Windermere** fill to the gills with vacationers in summer, when sailboats and waterskiers swarm the lake. At **Windermere Lake Cruises** (☎(01539) 443 360), at the north end of Bowness Pier, boats sail north to Waterhead Pier in Ambleside (30min., round-trip £6.40) and south to Lakeside (40min., round-trip £6.60). Lakeland Experience **buses** to Bowness (#599; 3 per hr., £1) leave from the train station. The **tourist office** is next door. (☎(01539) 446 499. Open July-Aug. daily 9am-7:30pm; Easter-June and Sept.-Oct. 9am-6pm; Nov.-Easter 9am-5pm.) The local **National Park Information Centre,** on Glebe Rd., is beside Bowness Pier. (☎(01539) 442 895. Open July-Aug.

daily 9:30am-6pm; Apr.-June and Sept.-Oct. daily 9am-5:30pm; Nov.-Mar. F-Su 10am-4pm.) **Brendan Chase ❷**, 1-3 College Rd., is family friendly, with large and attractive rooms. (☎ (01539) 445 638. Singles £13-25, doubles £26-50.) To get to the spacious **YHA Windermere ❷**, Bridge Ln., 1.5km north of Windermere off A591, catch the YHA shuttle from the train station. This hostel offers panoramic views of the lake, and rents bikes. (☎ (01539) 443 543. Open Feb.-Nov. daily; early Dec. F-Sa only. Dorms £12, under-18 £8.30.) **Camp** at **Park Cliffe ❷**, Birks Rd., 7km south of Bowness. Take bus #618 from Windermere. (☎ (01529) 531 344. £11-12 per tent.)

AMBLESIDE. About 2km north of Lake Windermere, Ambleside offers an attractive and convenient starting place for a day's trip to just about anywhere in the park. Splendid views of higher fells can be had from the top of **Loughrigg** (a moderately difficult 11km round-trip hike); 1.5km from town is the lovely waterfall **Stockghyll Force.** The tourist office has guides to these and other walks. Lakeslink **bus** #555 (☎ (01539) 432 231) leaves from Kelsick Rd. for Grasmere, Keswick, and Windermere (every hr., £2-6.50). The **tourist office** is located in the Central Building on Market Cross. (☎ (01539) 432 582. Open daily 9am-5pm.) To reach the **National Park Information Centre,** on Waterhead, walk south on Lake Rd. or Borrans Rd. from town to the pier. (☎ (01539) 432 729. Open Easter-Oct. daily 9:30am-5:30pm.) Bus #555 conveniently stops in front of ▧**YHA Ambleside ❷**, 1.5km south of Ambleside and 5km north of Windermere, an extremely social spot with superbly refurbished rooms, great food, and swimming off their pier. (☎ (01539) 432 304. Bike rentals. **Internet** £2.50 per 30min. Dorms £14, under-18 £10.)

GRASMERE. The peace that Wordsworth enjoyed in the village of Grasmere is still tangible on quiet mornings. The 17th-century **Dove Cottage,** 10min. from the center of town, was Wordsworth's home from 1799 to 1808 and remains almost exactly as he left it; next door is the outstanding **Wordsworth Museum.** (Both open mid-Feb. to mid-Jan. daily 9:30am-5pm. £5.50, students £4.70.) The **Wordsworth Walk** (9.5km) circumnavigates the two lakes of the Rothay River, passing the cottage, the poet's grave in St. Oswald's churchyard, and **Rydal Mount,** where Wordsworth lived until his death. (Rydal open Mar.-Oct. daily 9:30am-5pm; Nov.-Feb. W-M 10am-4pm. £4, students £3.25.) **Bus** #555 stops in Grasmere every hour on its way south to Ambleside or north to Keswick. The combined **tourist office** and **National Park Information Centre** is on Redbank Rd. (☎ (01539) 435 245. Open Easter-Oct. daily 9:30am-5:30pm; Nov.-Easter F-Su 10am-4pm.) **YHA Butterlip How ❷**, 140m up Easedale Rd., is situated in a large Victorian house, and has **Internet** access. (Open Mar.-Oct. Su and Tu-Sa; Nov.-Feb., call for availability. £13, under-18 £9.) Sarah Nelson's famed **Grasmere Gingerbread Shop ❶**, a staple since 1854, is a bargain at 30p in Church Cottage, outside St. Oswald's Church. (Open Easter-Nov. M-Sa 9:15am-5:30pm, Su 12:30-5:30pm; closes earlier in winter.)

KESWICK. Between towering Skiddaw peak and the northern edge of Lake Derwentwater, Keswick (KEZ-ick) rivals Windermere as the Lake District's tourist capital. A standout 6km day-hike from Keswick culminates with the eerily striking **Castlerigg Stone Circle,** a 5000-year-old neolithic henge. Another short walk hits the beautiful **Friar's Crag,** on the shore of Derwentwater, and **Castlehead,** a viewpoint encompassing the town, the lakes, and the peaks beyond. Both of these walks are fairly easy, although they do have their more strenuous moments. Maps and information on these and a wide selection of other walks are available at the **National Park Information Centre,** in Moot Hall, Market Sq. (☎ (01768) 772 645. Open Apr.-Oct. daily 9:30am-5:30pm; Nov.-Mar. 9:30am-4:30pm.) **YHA Derwentwater ❷**, in Barrow House, Borrowdale, is in a 200-year-old house with its own waterfall. Take bus #79 (every hr.) 3km south out of Keswick. (☎ (01768) 777 246. Open Feb. to early Oct. daily; Dec.-Jan F-Sa only. Dorms £11.50, under-18 £8.)

WALES

Wales may border England, but if many of the 2.9 million Welsh people had their way, it would be floating oceans away. Ever since England solidified its control over the country with the murder of Prince Llewelyn ap Gruffydd in 1282, relations between the two have been marked by a powerful unease. Wales clings steadfastly to its Celtic heritage, as the Welsh language endures in conversation, commerce, and literature. As coal, steel, and slate mines fell victim to Britain's faltering economy in the mid-20th century, Wales turned its economic eye from heavy industry to tourism. Travelers come for the sandy beaches, grassy cliffs, brooding castles, and dramatic mountains that typify the rich landscape of this corner of Britain.

■ FERRIES TO IRELAND

Irish Ferries (☎(08705) 171 717; www.irishferries.ie) sail to Dublin, Ireland, from Holyhead (2-3½hr., 3-4 per day, round-trip £40-65) and to Rosslare, Ireland, from Pembroke (4hr., round-trip £25-39, students £19). **Stena Line** (☎(08705) 707 070; www.stenaline.co.uk) runs from Holyhead to Dublin (4hr., £24-28) and Dún Laoghaire, Ireland (1-3½hr., £26).

CARDIFF (CAERDYDD) ☎029

The "Come on, Cardiff!" signs that flutter all around the city speak to the vigor with which Cardiff (pop. 325,000) is trying to reinvent itself. Formerly the main port of call for Welsh coal, Cardiff is now the port of arrival for a colorful international population. Calling itself "Europe's Youngest Capital," Cardiff offers its rich history alongside a spruced-up set of modern sensibilities.

■ TRANSPORTATION AND PRACTICAL INFORMATION. Trains (☎(08457) 484 950) arrive at Central Station, Central Sq., from: Bath (1-1½hr., 1-3 per hr., £12); Birmingham (2¼hr., 1-3 per hr., £22); Edinburgh (7hr., 7 per hr., £96); London Paddington (2hr., every hr., £47). Ticket office open M-Sa 5:45am-9:30pm, Su 6:45am-9:30pm. National Express **buses** (☎(08705) 808 080) leaves from Wood St. for: Birmingham (2¼hr., 1-3 per hr., £22); London (3½hr., 6 per day, £17); and Manchester (5½hr., 4 per day, £25). Pick up a free *Wales Bus, Rail, and Tourist Map and Guide* at the TIC. Cardiff Bus (Bws Caerdydd), St. David's House, Wood St. (☎2066 6444), runs green city buses. (Service ends M-Sa at 11:20pm, Su 11pm. 60p-£1.50, week-long pass £16.) The **tourist office,** 16 Wood St. (☎2022 7281; www.visitcardiff.info), opposite the bus station, provides a free accommodations list and a map. It also books rooms for a £1 fee and a 10% deposit. (Open July-Aug. M-Sa 9am-6pm, Su 10am-4pm; Sept.-June M-Sa 9am-5pm, Su 10am-4pm.) Surf the **Internet** at the Internet Exchange, 8 Church St. (☎2074 6048). £4 per hr., £1 minimum. Open M-Th 9am-9pm, F-Sa 9am-8pm, Su 11am-7pm.) **Postal Code:** CF10 2SJ.

■ ACCOMMODATIONS AND FOOD. Budget accommodations in Cardiff is an oxymoron, but the TIC lists reasonable B&Bs (£18-20) on the outskirts of the city. Many of the B&Bs on lovely **Cathedral Road,** a short ride on bus #32, are expensive; better bargains await on side streets. ■**Cardiff International Backpacker ②,** 98 Neville St. (☎2034 5577), has a Happy Hour (Su-Th 7-9pm) and a rooftop patio, complete with hammocks and lanterns, that set the scene for this backpackers' heaven. Only international students in summer. (Dorms £15; doubles £36; triples £44.) For a change of pace, try **Annedd Lon ③,** 157-159 Cathedral

Wales

ENGLAND

TO DUBLIN

Irish Sea

Amlwch

Birkenhead

Liverpool

Holyhead

Isle of
Anglesey

Conwy
Bay

Llandudno

Dee Estuary

R. Mersey

M53

M56

Holy
Island

Penmon
Beaumaris

Conwy

Holywell

A5

A55

A55

Chester

Llanfair P.G.

Bangor

Trefriw

Menai Strait

Caernarfon

Llanrwst

Caernarfon Bay

Llanberis

Capel
Curig

Betws-
y-Coed

Wrexham

A470

Mt.
Snowdon

Blaenau
Ffestiniog

Corwen

Llangollen

Porthmadog

Dee

Oswestry

A5

Pwllheli

Criccieth

Portmeirion

Cefrog

LLYN
PENINSULA

Harlech

Lake Bala

Tanat

Severn

Aberdaron

Absersoch

Snowdonia
National Park

Lake
Vyrnwy

Barmouth

Dolgellau

Welshpool

A470

Shrewsbury

Cader
Idris

Dovey

Cardigan
Bay

Aberdyfi

Machynlleth

Newtown

Borth

Severn

A49

Aberystwyth

A470

Ludlow

Knighton

Aberaeron

Rhayader

Llandrindod
Wells

Lampeter

A487

Teifi

Builth Wells

Wye

Cardigan

Llanwrtyd
Wells

Hereford

TO ROSSLARE

Fishguard

A483

Hay-on-Wye

Pembrokeshire
Coast Nat'l Park

Llandovery

Brecon

A49

St. David's

Carmarthen

Llandeilo

Brecon Beacons
National Park

A40

St.
Bride's
Bay

Haverfordwest

A40

A40

Abergavenny

Monmouth

Merthyr
Tydfil

A40

Pembroke

Tenby

Aberdare

Pontypool

Tintern

Manorbier

Llanelli

Tawe

Cwmbran

A449

Carmarthen
Bay

Swansea

Port Talbot

Newport

Chepstow

GOWER
PENINSULA

Mumbles

Bridgend

M4

Cardiff

R. Severn

Swansea
Bay

Mouth
of the
Severn

Bristol

TO CORK

Barry

Bristol
Channel

ENGLAND

├──┤ Wide gauge rail
╫╫╫╫ Narrow gauge rail

0   20 miles
0   20 kilometers

BRITAIN

Rd. (☎2022 3349; fax 2064 0885), 15min. from Cardiff Castle, a pair of Victorian houses that provide a peaceful respite from the city. (Singles £20; doubles £40); rooms in 157, the upscale half, include private bath and British breakfast (singles £30; doubles £45). **Acorn Camping and Caravanning ❶**, Rosedew Farm, Ham Ln. South, Llantwit Major (☎01446 794 024), is 1hr. by bus X91 from Central Station, and a 15min. walk from the Ham Ln. stop. (Electricity £2. Mar.-Nov. £6 per night, Dec.-Feb. £5.50.)

Cardiff's downtown is full of coffee shops and pubs. ◪**Europa Cafe ❶**, 25 Castle St. (☎2066 7776), across from Cardiff Castle, has a funky yet comfortable interior. It also sponsors writers' group meetings and occasional live music performances. (Drinks £1-3. Open Su-Tu 11am-6pm, W-Sa 11am-11pm.) ◪**Celtic Cauldron Wholefoods ❶**, 47-49 Castle Arcade (☎2038 7185), delivers a bold synthesis of traditionally hearty Welsh cuisine (£2-5) and assorted ethnic traditions. Staples like Laverbread and Welsh Rarebit are offered alongside novelties like samosas and lentil stew. (Open in summer M-Sa 8:30am-9pm; winter M-Sa 8:30am-6pm, Su 11am-4pm.) Budget travelers looking for food on the go should scavenge the stalls of **Central Market,** between St. Mary St. and Trinity St. (Open daily 10am-4pm.)

◨◪ SIGHTS AND ENTERTAINMENT. The interior of ◪**Cardiff Castle** is no less flamboyant than the strutting peacocks within its gates. Visit the museums of the **Welsh Regiment** and **The 1st Queen's Dragoon Guards,** enjoy a medieval supper, and watch falconry demonstrations featuring owls Billy and Floyd during winter and spring. The keep also offers sweeping views of the city. *(Castle St. ☎2087 8100. Open Mar.-Oct. daily 9:30am-6pm; Nov.-Feb. 9:30am-3:30pm. £5.50, students £4.20. Free tours Mar.-Oct. every 20min.; Nov.-Feb. 5 tours per day. Last tour 5pm.)* The **National Museum and Gallery** houses an eclectic mix of exhibits, from an audiovisual narrative of Welsh geologic evolution to a skylit display of Celtic stone monuments. *(Located at Cathay's Park, next to the Civic Centre. ☎2039 7951. Open Su and Tu-Sa 10am-5pm. Free. Illustrated guidebook £1.)* The stately Cardiff **Civic Centre** is set against the lawns of Cathays Park. Find the Functions Office, upstairs in City Hall, to pick up a brochure. In the Hall of Welsh Heroes, St. David, patron saint of Wales, is flanked by Owain Glyndŵr, the rebel leader who razed Cardiff in 1404. *(North Rd. across from the castle. ☎2087 1727. Open M-F 9am-6pm. Free.)*

After 11pm the majority of Cardiff's popular downtown pubs stop serving alcohol, and the action migrates to an array of nearby clubs, most located on or around **St. Mary Street.** Have a drink at **The Owain Glyndŵr**, St. John's Sq., and sample one of their 5 cask beers (£2.20 a pint) in an oak and brown leather interior. (Open M-Th 11am-11pm, F-Sa noon-1am.) **Clwb Ifor Bach** (The Welsh Club), 11 Womanby St. (☎2023 2199), is a manic club offering everything from Motown tunes to games. (Cover £2.50-10. Open M-Th until 2am, F-Sa until 3am; occasionally closed M.)

▨ DAYTRIPS FROM CARDIFF: CAERPHILLY CASTLE AND THE MUSEUM OF WELSH LIFE. Thirteen kilometers north of Cardiff, **Caerphilly Castle** will enchant romantics and history buffs alike. Begun in 1268 by Norman warlord Gilbert de Clare, its stone walls, catapults, and pivoting drawbridges made it the most technologically advanced fortification of its time. Take the train (30min., M-Sa 2 per hr., £2.60) or hourly bus #24 or 25 from Central Station stand C1. (☎2088 3143. Open June-Sept. daily 9:30am-6pm; Apr.-May and Oct. daily 9:30am-5pm; Nov.-Mar. M-Sa 9:30am-4pm, Su 11am-4pm. £2.50, students £2.) Lying 6.5km west of Cardiff, the open-air **Museum of Welsh Life** is home to more than 40 authentic buildings from all corners of Wales, reassembled into an interactive display of Welsh history. (☎2057 3500. Open June-Sept. daily 10am-5pm. Free.) Bus #320 runs to the museum (20min., every hr., £1.20) from Central Station.

WYE VALLEY   ☎ 01291

Crossing and recrossing the oft-troubled Welsh-English border, the Wye River (Afon Gwy) cuts through a tranquil valley, its banks riddled with trails, abbeys, and castles rich in legend. The past is palpable in the towns and clusters of homes and farms, from Tintern Abbey to the George Inn Pub.

⌐ TRANSPORTATION

The valley is best entered from the south, at Chepstow. **Trains** go to Chepstow from Cardiff and Newport (40min., 7-8 per day). National Express **buses** (☎ (08705) 808 080) arrive from Cardiff (50min., 7 per day) and London (2¼hr., 10 per day). There is little Sunday bus service in the valley. For schedules, pick up *Discover the Wye Valley on Foot and by Bus* in tourist offices.

Hiking grants the most stunning views of the valley. The 219km **Wye Valley Walk** treks north from Chepstow, through Hay-on-Wye, and on to Prestatyn along wooded cliffs and farmland. **Offa's Dyke Path** consists of more than 293km of hiking and biking paths along the length of the Welsh-English border. For information, consult the **Offa's Dyke Association** (☎ (01547) 528 753).

CHEPSTOW AND TINTERN. Chepstow's strategic position at the mouth of the river and the base of the English border made it an important fortification in Norman times. **Castell Casgwent,** Britain's oldest datable stone castle, offers stunning views of the Wye from its tower walls. (☎ 624 065. Open June-Sept. daily 9:30am-6pm; Oct. and Apr.-May daily 9:30am-5pm; Nov.-Mar. M-Sa 9:30am-4pm, Su 11am-4pm. ₤4, students ₤3.) **Trains** arrive on Station Rd.; **buses** stop in front of Somerfield supermarket. Purchase tickets at **The Travel House,** 9 Moor St. (☎ 623 031. Open M-Sa 9am-5:30pm.) The **tourist office** is on Bridge St. (☎ 623 772. Open Apr.-Oct. daily 10am-5:30pm; Nov.-Mar. 10am-4:30pm.) Visit **Mrs. Presley ❸,** 30 Kingsmark Ave., for beautiful rooms and a conservatory. (☎ 624 466. Singles ₤20; doubles ₤40.) **Postal Code:** NP16 5DA.

Eight kilometers north of Chepstow on A466, the haunting arches of ▨**Tintern Abbey** "connect the landscape with the quiet of the sky"—as described in Wordsworth's famous poem, written just a few kilometers away. (☎ 689 251. Open June-Sept. daily 9:30am-6pm; Apr.-May and Oct. daily 9:30am-5pm; Nov.-Mar. M-Sa 9:30am-4pm, Su 11am-4pm. ₤2.50.) A 2½km hike will get you to **Devil's Pulpit,** from which Satan is said to have tempted the monks as they worked in the fields. A couple kilometers to the north on A466, the **tourist office** is housed in a train carriage at the Old Station. (☎ 689 566. Open Apr.-Oct. daily

THE LOCAL LEGEND

WHEN GAULS ATTACK!

The most recent (and perhaps least-known) of the UK's many invasions took place in 1797, when a fleet of Frenchmen landed just outside of Fishguard. They were an unruly bunch of ex-cons who had been dredged up from various French jails expressly for the purposes of the expedition. They arrived under the unsteady command of one General Tate, his only relevant military qualification being a uncertain familiarity with the coast of Pembrokeshire.

Upon landing, his men set up their headquarters in a local farmhouse stocked with provisions for an upcoming wedding. They proceeded to raid all of its liquor (as well as the liquor stashes of neighboring farmhouses), and they kept themselves hopelessly drunk for the rest of their "attack." Many of their number were captured by local citizens; Jemima Nicholas, a 47-year-old cobbler, managed to take 12 French soldiers hostage wielding only a hay-fork and the bottle of whiskey she had used to fortify herself for the assault.

Tate's troops were eventually bested by a troop of red-cloaked Welsh women, whom they mistook for soldiers and to whom they promptly surrendered. The women had actually just been gathering to watch the spectacle of their inebriation. A formal treaty of surrender was signed at the Royal Oak Inn, which is now (appropriately enough) a pub in town.

10:30am-5:30pm.) **YHA St. Briavel's Castle ❷**, 6.5km northeast of Tintern across the English border, occupies a 12th-century fortress. While a unique experience, St. Briavel's is somewhat remote, and should only be booked by those willing to walk uphill. From A466 (bus #69 from Chepstow) or Offa's Dyke, follow signs for 3.25km from the edge of the bridge. (☎(01594) 530 272. Dorms £11.55, under-18 £8.30.) The cozy **Holmleigh B&B ❷** is near the edge of Tintern Village on A466. (☎689 521. £16.50 per person.) Try **The Moon and Sixpence ❷**, next to Holmleigh B&B, for an astonishing array of dishes in a traditional pub atmosphere.

BRECON BEACONS NATIONAL PARK

The *Parc Cenedlaethol Bannau Brycheiniog* encompasses 837 dramatic square kilometers of barren peaks, well-watered forests, and windswept moors. The park is divided into four regions: **Brecon Beacon,** where King Arthur's fortress is thought to have once stood; **Fforest Fawr,** with the spectacular waterfalls of Ystradfellte; the eastern **Black Mountains;** and the remote western **Black Mountain** (singular). Brecon, on the fringe of the park, makes a pleasant touring base.

⊡ TRANSPORTATION. Trains (☎08457 484 950) run from London Paddington to Abergavenny at the park's southeastern corner and to Merthyr Tydfil on the southern edge. National Express (☎08705 808 080) **bus** #509 runs from London (5hr., daily, £19) via Cardiff (1¼hr., £3). Stagecoach Red and White (☎01633 838 856) buses arrive from Abergavenny and Newport (#21; M-Sa, 6 per day; £3-4.50.)

BRECON (ADERHONDDU). Just north of the mountains, Brecon is the park's best hiking base. **Buses** arrive at the **Bulwark** in the central square. The **tourist office** is in the Cattle Market parking lot; walk through Bethel Square off Lion St. (☎(01874) 622 485. Open daily 9:30am-5pm.) The **National Park Information Centre** (☎(01874) 623 156) is in the same building. **Mulberry House ❷**, 3 Priory Hill, across from the cathedral, is in a former monks' habitation. (☎624 461. £18 per person.) Camp at **Brynich Caravan Park ❶**, 2.5km east on the A40, signposted from the A40-A470 roundabout. (☎(01874) 623 325. Open Easter-Oct. £5 per person, £11 for 2 people with car.)

FFOREST FAWR. Rivers tumble through rapids, gorges, and spectacular falls near Ystradfellte, about 11km southwest of the Beacons. The **YHA Ystradfellte ❶** is a perfect launching pad for those willing to walk there. (☎(01639) 720 301. Open mid-July to Aug. daily; Apr. to mid-July and Sept.-Oct. M-Tu and F-Sa. Dorms £9, under-18 £6.50.) From the hostel, 16km of trails pass **Fforest Fawr,** the headlands of the Waterfall District, on their way to the somewhat touristy **Dan-yr-Ogof Showcaves** (Open Apr.-Oct. daily 10:30am-5pm. £8.50, children £5.50.) Stagecoach Red and White **bus** #63 (1½hr., 2-3 per day) stops at the hostel and caves en route to Brecon.

THE BLACK MOUNTAINS. Located in the easternmost section of the park, the Black Mountains are a group of long, lofty ridges offering 130sq. km of solitude, linked by unsurpassed ridge-walks. Begin forays from **Crickhowell,** or travel the eastern boundary along **Offa's Dyke Path,** which is dotted with a handful of impressive ruins. The **YHA Capel-y-ffin ❶** (kap-EL-uh-fin), along Offa's Dyke Path, is 13km from Hay-on-Wye. Take Stagecoach Red and White **bus** #39 from Hereford to Brecon, stop before Hay, and walk uphill. (☎(01873) 890 650. Lockout 10am-5pm. Open July-Sept. daily; Oct.-Dec. and Mar.-June M-Tu and F-Sa. Dorms £9, students £8, under-18 £6.)

THE BRECON BEACONS. These peaks at the center of the park lure hikers with pastoral slopes. The most convenient route to the top begins at **Storey Arms** (a carpark on A470) and offers views of **Llyn Cwm Llwch** (HLIN koom hlooch), a 610m deep glacial pool. Because this route is the most convenient, however, it is also the most overcrowded. Consult guides at the National Park Information Centres (in Brecon or Abergavenny) for recommendations on alternate trails.

ST. DAVID'S (TYDDEWI) ☎ 01437

An evening walk in St. David's (pop. 1,700), a major medieval pilgrimage site, inevitably leads to ■St. **David's Cathedral,** where visitors and locals gather to watch the sunset. Its history dates to the 6th-century, when it was built with hopes that the defendable church would offer some protection from marauding pirates. Legend has it that the bones of St. David are still kept in the cathedral's relinquary. (Cathedral open daily 6am-5:30pm. Suggested donation £2.) The **Bishop's Palace,** across the stream from the cathedral, features over 150 carvings of fantastic beasts and human heads. (☎ 720 517. Open June-Sept. daily 9:30am-6pm; Apr.-May and Oct. 9:30am-5pm; Nov.-Mar. M-Sa 9:30am-4pm, Su noon-2pm. £2.)

To reach St. David's from Cardiff, take the **train** to Haverfordwest (2½hr., 2 per day), and then take Richards Bros. **bus** #411 (50min., 2-5 per day). The **tourist office** is on the Grove. (☎ 720 392; www.stdavids.co.uk. Open Easter-Oct. daily 9:30am-5:30pm; Nov.-Easter M-Sa 10am-4pm.) Beautiful **Alandale ❸,** 43 Nun St., has friendly proprietors whose warmth and filling breakfasts will make your stay worthwhile. (☎ 720 404. Singles £28; doubles £56.) For excellent Welsh food, head to **Cartref ❷,** in Cross Sq. Try the Celtic pie (£9.30), a Welsh dish that combines cheese, oats, flan, and bread. (Dinner from £10. Open June-Aug. daily 11am-3pm and 6-8:30pm; Mar.-May 11am-2:30pm and 6:30-8:30pm.) **Postal Code:** SA62 6SW.

SNOWDONIA NATIONAL PARK

Snowdonia's craggy peaks actually yield surprisingly diverse terrain—pristine mountain lakes etch glittering blue outlines onto fields of green, while desolate slate cliff-faces slope into thickly wooded hills. Rough and handsome, England and Wales's highest mountains stretch across 2175 square kilometers, from forested Machynlleth to sand-strewn Conwy. Although these lands lie largely in private hands, endless public footpaths accommodate droves of visitors.

⊟ 🖪 TRANSPORTATION AND PRACTICAL INFORMATION. Trains (☎ (08457) 484 950) stop at several large towns on the park's outskirts, including Conwy (p. 237). The **Conwy Valley Line** runs through the park from Llandudno through Betws-y-Coed to Blaenau Ffestiniog (1hr., 2-7 per day). At Blaneau Ffestiniog the Conwy Valley Line connects with the narrow-gauge **Ffestiniog Railway** (p. 236), which runs through the mountains to Porthmadog, meeting the Cambrian Coaster to Llanberis and Aberystwyth. **Buses** run to the interior of the park from Conwy and Caernarfon; consult the *Gwynedd Public Transport Maps and Timetables*, available in all regional tourist offices. The **Snowdonia National Park Information Headquarters,** Penrhyndeudraeth, Gwynedd (☎ (01766) 770 274), provides hiking info and can best direct you to the eight quality **YHA hostels** in the park and the region's other **tourist offices** (www.gwynedd.gov.uk).

🔄 HIKING. The highest peak in England and Wales, **Mount Snowdon** (*Yr Wyddfa;* "the burial place") is the park's most popular destination, measuring 1085m. Six paths of varying difficulties wind their way up Snowdon; tourist offices and National Park Information Centres can provide guides on these ascents. Weather on Snowdonia's exposed mountains shifts unpredictably. No matter how beautiful the weather is below, it will be cold and wet in the high mountains. Pick up the *Ordnance Survey Landranger* Map #115 (£6) and *Outdoor Leisure* Map #17 (£7), as well as individual path guides at tourist offices and park centers. Contact **Mountaincall Snowdonia** (☎ (09068) 500 440; 36-48p per min.) for local forecasts and ground conditions. Weather forecasts are also posted in Park Information Centres.

LLANBERIS. Llanberis owes its outdoorsy bustle to the popularity of Mt. Snowdon, whose ridges and peaks unfold just south of town. The immensely popular **Snowdon Mountain Railway** has been taking visitors to Snowdon's summit since 1896. (☎(0870) 458 0033. Open mid-Mar. to Oct. Round-trip £18.) KMP (☎(01286) 870 880) **bus** #88 runs from Caernarfon (25min., 1-2 per hr., £1.50). The **tourist office** is at 41b High St. (☎(01286) 870 765. Open Easter-Oct. daily 9:30am-5:30pm; Nov.-Easter Su, W, and F-Sa 11am-4pm.) Plenty of sheep keep hostelers company at the **YHA Llanberis ❷**. (☎(0870) 770 5928. Curfew 11:30pm. Open Apr.-Oct. daily; Nov.-Mar. Su-Th. Dorms £11.50, under-18 £8.30.)

HARLECH   ☎ 0 1 7 6 6

This tiny coastal town just south of the Llyn Peninsula commands panoramic views of sea, sand, and Snowdonian summits. High above the sea and sand dunes is ▧**Harlech Castle,** another of Edward I's Welsh castles; this one served as the insurrection headquarters of Welsh rebel Owain Glyndŵr. (Open June-Sept. daily 9:30am-6pm; May and Oct. 9:30am-5pm; Nov.-Mar. M-Sa 9:30am-4pm, Su 11am-4pm. £3, students £2.50.) Harlech lies midway on the Cambrian Coaster line; **trains** arrive from Machynlleth (1¼-1¾hr., 3-7 per day, £8.20) and connect to Pwllheli and other spots on the Llyn Peninsula. The **Day Ranger** pass allows unlimited travel on the Coaster line for one day (£4-7). The **tourist office,** 1 Stryd Fawr, doubles as a **Snowdonia National Park Information Centre.** (☎780 658. Open daily 10am-1pm and 2-6pm.) Enjoy spacious rooms and breakfast served in a glassed-in patio with views of the ocean and castle at **Arundel ❷**, Stryd Fawr. Call ahead for pick-up. (☎780 637. Singles £15; doubles £30.) At the **Plâs Cafe ❷**, Stryd Fawr, guests linger over long afternoon tea (£1-4) and sunset dinners (from £7) while enjoying sweeping ocean views from the grassy patio. (☎780 204. Open Mar.-Oct. daily 9:30am-8:30pm; Nov.-Feb. 9:30am-5:30pm.) **Postal Code:** LL46 2YA.

LLYN PENINSULA   ☎ 0 1 7 6 6

The seclusion and sublime tranquility of the Llyn have brought visitors to reverence since the Middle Ages, when holy men made pilgrimages across it on their way to Bardsey Island, just off the western tip of the peninsula. Today, sun worshippers make the pilgrimage to the endless beaches that line the southern coast. **Porthmadog,** on the southeastern part of the peninsula, is the main gateway. This travel hub's principal attraction is the charming **Ffestiniog Railway** (☎516 073; call for hours.), which runs from Harbour Station on High St. into the hills of Snowdonia (1¼hr., 2-10 per day, round-trip £14). **Trains** run from Aberystwyth (1½-2hr., 3-7 per day). TrawsCambria **bus** #701 travels once a day to Aberystwyth (2hr.) and Cardiff (7hr.). Express Motors bus #1 stops in Porthmadog on its way from Blaenau Ffestiniog to Caernarfon (M-Sa every hr. until 10:25pm). The **tourist office** is on High St. by the harbor. (☎512 981. Open Easter-Oct. daily 10am-6pm; Nov.-Easter 10am-5pm.) The birthplace of Lawrence of Arabia is now the huge and comfortable **Snowdon Backpackers Hostel ❷**, complete with a cafe, a kitchen, and a bar. (☎515 354. Dorms £12-13; doubles £29-33.) **Postal Code:** LL49 9AD.

CAERNARFON   ☎ 0 1 2 8 6

Majestic and fervently Welsh, the walled city of Caernarfon (car-NAR-von) has a world-famous castle at its prow and mountains in its wake. Built by Edward I beginning in 1283, the ▧**Caernarfon Castle** was left unfinished when Eddie ran out of money, yet it is still an architectural feat. (☎677 617. Open June-Sept. daily 9:30am-6pm; Apr.-May and Oct. 9:30am-5pm; Nov.-Mar. M-Sa 9:30am-4pm, Su 11am-4pm. £4.50, students £3.50.) Arriva Cymru **buses** #5 and 5x arrive from Conwy (☎(08706) 082 608; 1¼hr., 1-3 per hr.). TrawsCambria bus #701 arrives daily from Cardiff (7½hr.). National Express bus #545 arrives daily from London (☎ (08705) 808 080; 9hr, daily). The **tourist office** is on Castle St. (☎ 672 232. Open Apr.-Oct. daily 9:30am-5:30pm; Nov.-Mar. Th-Tu 9:30am-4:30pm.) ▓**Totter's Hostel** ❷, 2 High St., has huge rooms, free bikes, a comfortable living room, and a full kitchen. (☎ 672 963. Dorms £11.) **Hole-in-the-Wall Street** offers a tremendous collection of bistros, cafes, and restaurants from which to choose. Try the Welsh lamb (£11) at **Stones Bistro** ❸, 4 Hole-in-the-Wall St., a crowded, candle-lit eatery near Eastgate. (Open Tu-Sa 6-11pm.) **Postal Code:** LL55 2ND.

CONWY   ☎ 01492

The central attraction of this tourist mecca is the 13th-century ▓**Conwy Castle,** another link in Edward I's chain of impressive North Wales fortresses. (Open June-Sept. daily 9:30am-6pm; Apr.-May and Oct. 9:30am-5pm; Nov.-Mar. M-Sa 9:30am-4pm, Su 11am-4pm. £3.50, students £3. Tours £1.) Arriva Cymru **buses** #5 and 5X stop in Conwy on their way to Caernarfon from Bangor (☎ (08706) 082 608; 1-2 per hr.). National Express buses (☎ (08705) 808 080) arrive from: Liverpool (2¾hr., daily); Manchester (4hr., daily); and Newcastle (10hr., daily). The **tourist office** is at the castle entrance. (☎ 592 248. Open Easter-Oct. daily 9:30am-6pm; Nov.-Easter Th-Sa 10am-4pm.) For a good night's sleep, try the ▓**Swan Cottage** ❷, 18 Berry St. Tucked into an old 16th-century building near the center of town, this cottage has cozy rooms and timber ceilings. (☎ 596 840. Singles £17; doubles £34.) **Bistro Conwy** ❷ serves truly inspired Welsh fare on humble wooden plates. (☎ 596 326. Lunch £5-9. Dinner £13. Open Su-M 11:30am-2pm, Tu-Th 11:30am-2pm and 7-9pm, F-Sa 11:30am-2pm and 7-9:30pm.) **Postal Code:** LL32 8DA.

SCOTLAND

A little over half the size of England but with just a tenth of the population, Scotland possesses open spaces and wild natural splendor its southern neighbor cannot hope to rival. The craggy, heathered Highlands, the silver beaches of the west coast, and the luminescent mists of the Hebrides elicit any traveler's awe, while farmlands to the south and peaceful fishing villages on the east coast harbor a gentler beauty. Scotland at its best is a world apart from the rest of the UK. Before reluctantly joining with England in 1707, the Scots defended their independence, bitterly and heroically, for hundreds of years. Since the union, they have nurtured a separate identity, retaining control of schools, churches, and the judicial system. In 1999, the Scots finally regained a separate parliament, which gave them more power over domestic tax laws and strengthened their national identity.

▐ TRANSPORTATION

Bus travel from London is generally cheaper than **train** fares. **British Airways** (☎ (08457) 773 3377) sells a limited number of APEX round-trip tickets from £70. **British Midland** (☎ (0870) 607 0555) also offers a round-trip Saver fare from London to Glasgow (from £70). Scotland is linked by **ferry** to Northern Ireland. From **Stranraer,** Stena Line (☎ (08705) 707 070) sails to Belfast (£15-24).

In the **Lowlands** (south of Stirling and north of the Borders), train and bus connections are frequent. In the **Highlands,** trains snake slowly on a few restricted routes, bypassing the northwest almost entirely, and many stations are unstaffed or nonexistent—buy tickets on board. A great money-saver is the **Freedom of Scotland Travelpass.** It allows unlimited train travel as well as transportation on most Caledonian MacBrayne ferries, with discounts on some other ferry lines.

Purchase the pass *before* traveling to Britain, at any BritRail distributor (p. 148). Buses tend to be the best way to travel; **Scottish Citylink** (☎ (08705) 505 050) provides most intercity service. **MacBackpackers** (☎ (0131) 558 9900; www.macbackpackers.com) and **HAGGiS** (☎ (0131) 557 9393; www.radicaltravel.com) run hop-on/hop-off tours that let you travel Scotland at your own pace.

EDINBURGH ☎ 0131

A city of elegant stone set among rolling hills and ancient volcanoes, Edinburgh (ED-in-bur-ra; pop. 500,000) is the jewel of Scotland. Since David I granted it burgh (town) status in 1130, Edinburgh has been a site of cultural significance—the seeds of the Scottish Reformation were sown here as well as the philosophies of the Scottish Enlightenment. The medieval Stuarts made Edinburgh a center of poetry and music. That tradition lives on today during the festivals each August, when the city becomes a theatrical, musical, and literary magnet, drawing international talent and enthusiastic crowds. At the beginning of the 21st century, Edinburgh's star appears only to be on the rise. Today's city continues to be a cultural beacon, its medieval spires calling travelers to the cosmopolitian mecca beneath.

▚ TRANSPORTATION

Flights: Edinburgh International Airport (EDI; ☎ 333 1000), 11.25km west of the city center. **Lothian Buses' Airlink** (☎ 555 6363) runs shuttles to the airport from Waverley Bridge (25min., £3.30). **Airsaver** gives you 1 trip on Airlink plus 1 day unlimited travel on local Lothian Buses (£4.20, children £2.50).

Trains: Waverley Station straddles Princes St., Market St., and Waverley Bridge. Trains (☎ (08457) 484 950) arrive from: **Aberdeen** (2½hr.; M-Sa every hr., Su 8 per day; £32); **Glasgow** (1hr., 2 per hr., £7.80-8.60); **Inverness** (3½hr., every 2hr., £32); **London King's Cross** (4¾hr., 2 per hr., £83-89); **Stirling** (50min., 2 per hr., £5.30).

Buses: The **bus station** is on the east side of St. Andrew's Sq. **National Express** (☎ (08705) 808 080) arrives from **London** (10hr., 5 per day, £29). **Scottish Citylink** (☎ (08705) 505 050) arrives from: **Aberdeen** (4hr., every hr., £15); **Glasgow** (1hr., 2-4 per hr., £3.80); and **Inverness** (4½hr., 8-10 per day, £15). A bus-ferry route via Stranraer goes to **Belfast** (2 per day, £20) and **Dublin** (daily, £28).

Public Transportation: Lothian Buses (☎ 555 6363; www.lothianbuses.co.uk) provide most services. Exact change required (50p-£1). Buy a 1-day **Daysaver** ticket (all day M-F £2.50; after 9:30pm M-F and all day Sa or Su £1.80) from any driver or from the **Travelshops** on Hanover St. and Waverley Bridge. **Night buses** cover selected routes after midnight (£2). **First Edinburgh** also operates locally. **Traveline** (☎ (0800) 232 323) has info on all public transport.

Bike Rental: Biketrax, 11 Lochrin Pl. (☎ 228 6633). Mountain bikes £10 per day. Open M-F 9:30am-6pm, Sa 9:30am-5pm, Su noon-5pm.

✈ ▚ ORIENTATION AND PRACTICAL INFORMATION

Edinburgh is a glorious city for walking. **Princes Street** is the main thoroughfare in **New Town**, the northern section of Edinburgh. From there you can view the impressive stone facade of the towering **Old Town**, the southern half of the city. **The Royal Mile** (Castle Hill, Lawnmarket, High St., and Canongate) is the major road in the Old Town and connects **Edinburgh Castle** in the west to the **Palace of Holyroodhouse** in the east. **North Bridge, Waverley Bridge,** and **The Mound** connect Old and New Town. Greater Edinburgh stretches well beyond Old and New Town; **Leith,** 3.2km northeast, is the city's seaport on the Firth of Forth.

Tourist Office: 3 Princes St. (☎473 3800), Waverley Market, on the north side of the Waverley Station complex. Books rooms for a £3 fee and 10% deposit, and offers excellent free maps and pamphlets. **Bureau de change.** Open July-Aug. M-Sa 9am-8pm, Su 10am-8pm; Sept. and May-June M-Sa 9am-7pm, Su 10am-7pm; Oct.-Apr. M-W 9am-5pm, Th-Sa 9am-6pm, Su 10am-5pm. In summer, look for the blue-jacketed **Guiding Stars,** who roam the city and can answer questions in several languages.

Budget Travel: STA Travel, 27 Forrest Rd. (☎226 7747). Open M-W 10am-6pm, Th 10am-7pm, F 10am-5:30pm, Sa 10am-5pm.

Financial Services: Thomas Cook, 52 Hanover St. (☎226 5500). Open M-F 9am-6pm, Sa 9am-5:30pm and Su 11am-5pm. **American Express,** 139 Princes St. (☎718 2505 or ☎(08706) 001 600). Open M-F 9am-5:30pm, Sa 9am-4pm.

Bi-Gay-Lesbian Resources: Pick up *Gay Information* at the tourist office or drop by the **Edinburgh Lesbians, Gays, and Bisexuals Centre,** 58a Broughton St. (☎478 7069).

Emergency: ☎999 or 112; no coins required. **Police:** 5 Fettes Ave. (☎311 3131).

Hospital: Royal Infirmary of Edinburgh, Old Dalkeith Rd. (**emergencies** ☎536 4000, otherwise ☎536 1000).

Internet Access: easyInternet Cafe, 58 Rose St. (☎220 3577). £1 per 30min. Open daily 8am-11pm. **Internet Cafe,** beside Platform 1, Waverley Station. £1 per 20min. Open M-F 7:30am-9pm, Sa-Su 8am-9pm.

Post Office: (☎556 9546), in the St. James Shopping Centre, New Town. Open M 9am-5:30pm, Tu-F 8:30am-5:30pm, Sa 8:30am-6pm. **Postal Code:** EH1.

ACCOMMODATIONS

Edinburgh accommodations run the gamut and offer good options for every type of traveler. In the city center, **hostels** and **hotels** are the only options; **B&Bs** and **guest houses** reside on the city's outer edges. It's a good idea to book ahead in summer, and absolutely essential to be well ahead of the game during festival-time (late July to early Sept.). The TIC's booking service can help during those busy periods when many people sublet their apartments for longer stays.

High St. Hostel, 8 Blackfriars St. (☎557 3984). Good facilities, party atmosphere, and convenient Royal Mile location have made this hostel a long-time Edinburgh favorite. Continental breakfast £1.90. Dorms £11-13. ❷

Brodies 2, 93 High St. (☎556 6770). Currently the best value accommodation along the Royal Mile. Offers a luxurious common room, a spotless kitchen, stainless steel showers, and heavenly beds. Dorms £11-17; doubles £34-45; quads from £55. ❷

Merlin Guest House, 14 Hartington Pl., Bruntsfield (☎229 3864), southwest of the Royal Mile. Comfortable, well-priced rooms in a leafy-green neighborhood. £15-23 per person; student discounts available in the off-season. ❷

Ardenlee Guest House, 9 Eyre Pl. (☎556 2838), at the northern edge of New Town. Walk or take northbound bus #23 or 27 from Hanover St. to the corner of Dundas St. and Eyre Pl. Near the Royal Botanic Garden, this friendly guest house offers large, comfortable rooms. No smoking. £30-40 per person. ❸

Castle Rock Hostel, 15 Johnston Terr. (☎225 9666), just steps from the castle. Regal views and top-notch common areas. Continental breakfast £1.60. Internet 80p per 30min. Dorms £11-13. ❷

Brodies Backpackers, 12 High St. (☎/fax 556 6770; www.brodieshostels.co.uk). Under the same management as Brodies 2. Relaxed, fun environment at this relatively small Royal Mile hostel. Free Internet. Dorms £11-17; £59-89 weekly. ❷

Premier Lodge, 94 Grassmarket (☎(0870) 990 6400). A chain hotel lacking in character but comfortable and well-located. £50 per room. ❹

Edinburgh

⌂ ACCOMMODATIONS

Ardenlee Guest House, **1**
Ardmor House, **2**
Argyle Backpackers, **32**
Brodies 2, **13**

Brodies Backpackers, **24**
Castle Rock Hostel, **16**
Edinburgh Backpackers, **12**
Gifford House, **33**
High St. Hostel, **23**
Merlin Guest House, **31**
Premier Lodge, **17**

TO ROYAL BOTANIC GARDENS

Raeburn Pl.
Henderson Row

Dean St.

Clarence St.
St. Stephen St.
Circus Lane
Royal
N. W. Circus Pl.
N. W. Circus

Deanhaugh St.
Hamilton Pl.

Dean Terr.

India Pl.
Doune Terr.

Howe St.

DEAN VILLAGE

Belgrave Cres.

Dean Path

Water of Leith

Moray Pl.

Gloucester Ln.

India St.

Heriot Row

Queen Street Gardens

NEW TOWN

TO SCOTTISH NATIONAL GALLERY OF MODERN ART & DEAN GALLERY (220yd)

Belford Rd.

Dean Bridge

Ainslie Pl.

Stuart Pl.

Georgian House

Queen St.

Young St.
Hill St.
Thistle

Frederick St.

Randolph Cres.

Drumsheugh Gdns.

Queensferry St.

CHARLOTTE SQ.

Charlotte St.

George St.

Rose St.

Douglas Cres.
Douglas Gdns.

Eglinton Cres.
Glencairn Cres.

Chester St.

Melville St.

Alva St.

WEST END

AmEx $

Princes St.

Palmerston Pl.

Manor Pl.

William St.

Coates Cres.

Shandwick Pl.

Rutland St.

West Princes Street Gardens

Kings Stables Rd.

Edinburgh Castle

TO ↑ EDINBURGH INTL. AIRPORT (6.5mi)

Grosvenor St.

West Maitland St.

Canning St.

Haymarket HAYMARKET Terr.

Haymarket Station

Dalry Rd.

Morrison St.

West Approach Rd.

Canada

Cambridge St.

Castle Terr.

Castle Hill

Castlehill

Royal Lyceum Theatre

Traverse Theatre

Grindlay St.

Johnston Terr.

The Filmhouse

Morrison St.

Bread St.

Lady Lawson St.

West Port

Grassmarket

West Approach Rd.

Grove St.

Gardner's Cres.

Fountainbridge

Lothian Rd.

Earl Grey St.

High Riggs

Lawson St.

Lauriston Pl.

FOUNTAINBRIDGE

Dundee St.

Gilmore Park

W. Tollcross

TOLLCROSS

Home St.

Brougham St. Pl.

Lauriston Gdns.

Chalmers St.

Lochrin Pl.
Biketrax

Tarvit St.
King's Theatre

TOLLCROSS

North Meadow Walk

Gilmore Pl.

Leamington Terr.

Gillespie Cr.

Leven St.

Whitehouse Loan

Melville Dr.

The Meadows

Hartington Pl.

Viewforth

Hartington Gdns.

Bruntsfield Links

Bruntsfield Pl.

Warrender Park Terr.

Montpelier Park

Warrender Park Rd.

Spottiswoode St.

Arden St.

Marchmont Rd.

Marchmont Cres.

Sciennes Rd.

Argyle Pl.

0   200 yards
0   200 meters

Forbes Rd.

Bruntsfield Pl.

BRUNTSFIELD

Bruntsfield Cres.

BRITAIN

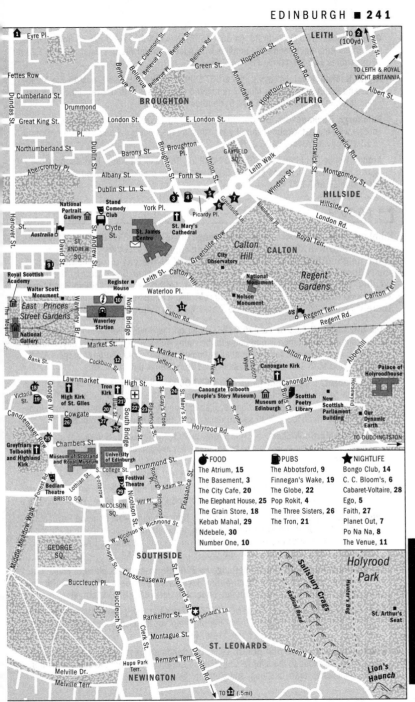

FOOD

The Atrium, **15**
The Basement, **3**
The City Cafe, **20**
The Elephant House, **25**
The Grain Store, **18**
Kebab Mahal, **29**
Ndebele, **30**
Number One, **10**

PUBS

The Abbotsford, **9**
Finnegan's Wake, **19**
The Globe, **22**
Pop Rokit, **4**
The Three Sisters, **26**
The Tron, **21**

NIGHTLIFE

Bongo Club, **14**
C. C. Bloom's, **6**
Cabaret-Voltaire, **28**
Ego, **5**
Faith, **27**
Planet Out, **7**
Po Na Na, **8**
The Venue, **11**

BRITAIN

Gifford House, 103 Dalkeith Rd. (☎667 4688), Newington. Take bus #33 from Princes St. Offers enormous rooms for families with good views of Arthur's Seat. Singles £25-60; doubles £45-80; family £80-140. ❸

Argyle Backpackers, 14 Argyle Pl. (☎667 9991; argyle@sol.co.uk), next to the Meadows and south of the Royal Mile. 2 renovated townhouses with a lovely little back garden. Internet access. Dorms £10-15; doubles £30-40. ❷

Edinburgh Backpackers, 65 Cockburn St. (☎220 2200; www.hoppo.com). Friendly hostel with a great location. Laundry facilities. Internet access. Checkout 10am. Dorms £13-16; private rooms £45-72. ❷

Ardmor House, 74 Pilrig St. (☎554 4944), Pilrig. Take bus #11 from Princes St. A lovely guest house with all rooms ensuite. Excellent Scottish breakfast included. Singles £45-85; doubles £60-100. ❹

🄵 FOOD

Edinburgh boasts an increasingly wide range of cuisines and restaurants. If it's traditional fare you're after, the capital won't disappoint, with everything from haggis at the neighborhood pub to "modern Scottish" at the city's top restaurants. If you're looking for cheap eats, many **pubs** offer student discounts in the early evening. Takeaway shops on **South Clerk Street, Leith Street,** and **Lothian Road** have well-priced Chinese and Indian fare. There's also a **Sainsbury's supermarket,** 9-10 St. Andrew's Sq. (☎225 8400. Open M-Sa 7am-10pm, Su 10am-8pm.)

▨ **The City Cafe,** 19 Blair St. (☎220 0125). Right off the Royal Mile behind the Tron Kirk, this Edinburgh institution is popular with the young and stylish. Relaxed by day, a flashy pre-club spot by night. Incredible shakes immortalized in *Trainspotting*. Burgers £4-6. Food served M-Th 11am-11pm, F-Su 11am-10pm. Drinks until 1am. ❷

▨ **The Basement,** 10a-12a Broughton St. (☎557 0097). Draws a lively mix of locals to its candle-lit cavern. Menu changes daily. Well-known for Mexican fare Sa-Su and Thai cuisine on W nights. Vegetarian options available. 2-course lunch £7. Dinner £10-12. Reservations recommended. Food served daily noon-10pm. Drinks until 1am. ❷

▨ **Restaurant Martin Wishart,** 54 The Shore (☎553 3557), Leith. Showcases exquisite modern French cuisine, which can be sampled in a five-course tasting menu (£48). The three-course lunch special (£19) will also leave you more than satisfied. Make reservations 2 weeks in advance. Open Tu-Sa noon-2pm and 7-9:30pm. ❺

The Atrium, 10 Cambridge St. (☎228 8882). A hot Edinburgh eatery, serving modern Scottish fare. Reservations essential. Open M-F noon-2pm and 6-10pm, Sa 6-10pm. ❹

The Grain Store, 30 Victoria St. (☎225 7635). Only a minute walk from the Royal Mile, The Grain Store offers an extensive wine menu and prepares French cuisine using local Scottish produce. 2-course dinner £20. Reservations recommended. Open M-Th noon-2pm and 6-10pm, F-Sa noon-3pm and 6-11pm, Su 6-10pm. ❹

The Elephant House, 21 George IV Bridge (☎220 5355). A perfect place to chill, chat, or pore over stacks of newspapers. Author J.K. Rowlings made her first notes for the *Harry Potter* series here. Tea and coffee under £5. Open daily 8am-11pm. ❶

La Tasca, 9 South Charlotte St. (☎558 8894). *Tapas* bar with good music and a decor that hits the mark. A native staff will happily help you choose from dozens of small dishes (£2-3 each). Open daily noon-11pm. ❶

Fishers, 1 The Shore (☎554 5666), Leith. Outstandingly fresh seafood, with preparations from the exotic to the simple. Call 24hr. in advance and order the seafood platter, a feast of lobster, crab, scallops, and shellfish. ❸

Ndebele, 57 Home St. (☎221 1141), in Tolcross, 800m south of western Princes St. Named for a South African tribe, this atmospheric cafe serves generous portions of African food for under £5. Open daily 10am-10pm. ❶

Kebab Mahal, 7 Nicolson Sq. (☎667 5214). This hole-in-the-wall offers huge portions of Indian food for under £5. Open M-Th noon-1am, F-Sa noon-2am, Su noon-midnight. ❶

Number One, 1 Princes St. (☎557 6727), underneath the Balmoral Hotel. One of Edinburgh's more exclusive restaurants. Modern Scottish cuisine including local seafood and seasonal game round out the trademark 6-course dinner (£41) that comes with wine. Make reservations at least 1 week in advance. Open M-Th noon-2pm and 7-10pm, F noon-2pm and 7-10:30pm, Sa 7-10:30pm, Su 7-10pm. ❺

🔆 SIGHTS

A boggling array of Edinburgh tour companies tout themselves as "the original" or "the scariest," but the most worthwhile is the ▨**Edinburgh Literary Pub Tour.** Led by professional actors, this alcohol-sodden 2hr. crash course in Scottish literature meets outside the Beehive Inn in the Grassmarket. (☎226 6665. June-Sept. daily 7:30pm; Nov.-Mar. F 7:30pm; Oct. and Apr.-May Th-Su 7:30pm. £8, students £6.) Of the many tours exploring Edinburgh's dark and gristly past, the **City of the Dead Tour** and its promised one-on-one encounter with the MacKenzie Poltergeist is most popular. (40 Candlemaker Row. ☎225 9044. Apr.-Oct. daily 8:30, 9:15, and 10pm; Nov.-Mar. 7:30 and 8:30pm. £6, concessions £5.)

THE OLD TOWN AND THE ROYAL MILE

Edinburgh's medieval center, the fascinating **Royal Mile** defines **Old Town** and passes many classic and worthwhile sights. The Old Town once packed thousands of inhabitants into a scant few square miles, with narrow shop fronts and slum buildings towering to a dozen stories.

▨**EDINBURGH CASTLE.** Perched atop an extinct volcano and dominating the city center, the castle is a testament to Edinburgh's past strategic importance. The castle is the result of centuries of renovation and rebuilding; the most recent additions date to the 1920s. The **One O'Clock Gun** fires daily (except Su) at 1pm. *(Open Apr.-Oct. daily 9:30am-6pm; Nov.-Mar. 9:30am-5pm. Last admission 45min. before closing. £8.50, seniors £6.25, children £2. Under-5 free. Audio tours £3.)*

CASTLE HILL AND LAWNMARKET AREA. The oldest surviving house on the Royal Mile, **Gladstone's Land** (circa 1617) has been carefully preserved and now houses a fine collection of 17th-century Dutch art. *(477b Lawnmarket St. Open Apr.-Dec. M-Sa 10am-5pm, Su 2-5pm. £3.50, students £2.60.)* Nearby, the 17th-century **Lady Stair's House** contains the **Writer's Museum,** featuring memorabilia and manuscripts belonging to three of Scotland's greatest literary figures: Robert Burns, Sir Walter Scott, and Robert Louis Stevenson. *(Lawnmarket St. Open M-Sa 10am-5pm; during festival season M-Sa 10am-5pm, Su 2-5pm. Free.)* For incredible views of the city, try the **Outlook Tower** on Castle Hill. Its 150-year old **camera obscura** captures a moving image of the streets below, while its various illusionary exhibits will certainly entertain. *(Open daily 10am-5pm. Tower and camera obscura £6, concessions £4.60.)*

HIGH STREET AND CANONGATE AREA. Near the Castle, through Mylne's Close, the **Scottish Parliament** convenes in the **Church of Scotland Assembly Hall;** guests are welcome to watch the MPs debate. The **Visitors Centre** is nearby, at the corner of the Royal Mile and the George IV Bridge. *(☎348 5411. Open Sept.-June. Tickets must be reserved in advance. Free. Visitors Centre open M-F 10am-5pm. Free.)* In 2004, Scotland's seat of government will move to the **new Scottish Parliament Building** at Holyrood. The new structure was designed by late Catalan architect

Enric Miralles. *(Off Holyrood Rd. Open daily 10am-4pm. Free.)* At the beautiful ■**High Kirk of St. Giles** (St. Giles Cathedral), Scotland's principal church, John Knox delivered the fiery Presbyterian sermons that drove Mary, Queen of Scots, into exile. Most of the present structure was built in the 15th century, but parts of the the kirk date as far back as 1126. The cathedral now hosts free concerts throughout the year. *(Where Lawnmarket St. becomes High St. Open Easter to mid-Sept. M-F 9am-7pm, Sa 9am-5pm, Su 1-5pm; mid-Sept. to Easter M-Sa 9am-5pm, Su 1-5pm. Suggested donation £1.)* The 17th-century **Canongate Kirk,** on the steep hill at the end of the Mile, is the resting place of economist Adam Smith; royals used to worship here when in residence. *(Same hours as High Kirk. Free.)*

THE PALACE OF HOLYROODHOUSE. This Stewart palace sitting at the base of the Royal Mile beside Holyrood Park remains Queen Elizabeth II's official Scottish residence; as a result, only parts of the ornate interior are open to the public. On the palace grounds lie the 12th-century ruins of **Holyrood Abbey,** which was built by David I in 1128 and was ransacked during the Scottish Reformation. *(Open Apr.-Oct. daily 9:30am-6pm; Nov.-Mar. M-Sa 9:30am-4:30pm; last admission 45min. before closing. Closed during official residences. £7.50, concessions £6. Free audio guide.)*

OTHER SIGHTS IN THE OLD TOWN. The ■**Museum of Scotland** and the connected **Royal Museum,** on Chambers St., just south of the George IV Bridge, are not to be missed. The former houses a definitive collection of Scottish artifacts in a stunning contemporary building; highlights include the working Corliss Steam Engine and the **Maiden,** Edinburgh's pre-French Revolution guillotine. The Royal Museum contains a varied mix of European art and ancient Egyptian artifacts. *(Open M and W-Sa 10am-5pm, Tu 10am-8pm, Su noon-5pm. Free.)* Just across the street stands the statue of Greyfriar's loyal pooch, Bobby, marking the entrance to **Greyfriar's Kirk,** built in 1620 and surrounded by a beautiful and supposedly haunted churchyard. *(Off Candlemaker Row. Gaelic services Su 12:30pm, English 11am. Open Apr.-Oct. M-F 10:30am-4:30pm, Sa until 2:30pm; Nov.-Mar. Th 1:30-3:30pm. Free.)*

THE NEW TOWN

Edinburgh's New Town is a masterpiece of Georgian design. James Craig, a 23-year-old architect, won the city-planning contest in 1767; his rectangular grid of three parallel streets (**Queen, George,** and **Princes**) linking two large squares (**Charlotte** and **St. Andrew**) reflects the Scottish Enlightenment's belief in order.

THE GEORGIAN HOUSE AND THE WALTER SCOTT MONUMENT. The elegantly restored Georgian House gives a fair picture of how Edinburgh's elite lived 200 years ago. *(7 Charlotte Sq. From Princes St., turn right on Charlotte St. and take the second left. Open Apr.-Oct. daily 10am-5pm; Nov.-Dec. and Mar. 11am-3pm. £5, students £3.80.)* The ■**Walter Scott Monument** is a Gothic "steeple without a church"; climb the 287-step staircase for far views stretching out to Princes St., the castle, and the surrounding city. *(On Princes St., between The Mound and Waverley Bridge. Open Mar.-Oct. M-Sa 9am-6pm, Su 10am-6pm; Nov.-Feb. daily 9am-3pm. £2.50.)*

■**ROYAL YACHT BRITANNIA.** Three kilometers northeast of the city center floats one of Edinburgh's top tourist attractions, the Royal Yacht *Britannia.* Used by the Queen and her family from 1953 to 1997, *Britannia* sailed around the world on state visits and royal holidays before going into permanent retirement here. Visitors can follow an audio tour of the entire royal flagship, which remains exactly as it was when decommissioned. *(Entrance on the Ocean Terminal's 3rd fl. Take bus #22 from Princes St. or #35 from the Royal Mile to Ocean Terminal via Leith town center. Open Apr.-Sept. 9:30am-4:30pm; Oct.-Mar. 10am-3:30pm. £8, concessions £4.)*

THE NATIONAL GALLERIES

Edinburgh's National Galleries of Scotland form an elite group, with excellent collections housed in stately buildings and connected by a free shuttle every hour. The flagship is the ◧**National Gallery of Scotland,** on The Mound, which houses a superb collection of works by Renaissance, Romantic, and Impressionist masters, including Degas, Gaugin, Monet, Titian, and Raphael. Be sure not to miss the octagonal room which displays Poussin's entire *Seven Sacrements.* The basement houses a fine spread of Scottish art. The **Scottish National Portrait Gallery,** 1 Queen St., north of St. Andrew Sq., features the faces of famous Scots. Among its notable members are wordsmith Robert Louis Stevenson, renegade Bonny Prince Charlie, and royal troublemaker Mary, Queen of Scots. The gallery also hosts excellent visiting exhibits of contemporary artists. Take the free shuttle, bus #13 from George St., or walk to the **Scottish National Gallery of Modern Art,** 75 Belford Rd., west of town, to see works by Braque, Matisse, and Picasso. The new **Dean Gallery,** 73 Belford Rd., specializes in Surrealist and Dadaist art. *(All open M-W and F-Su 10am-5pm, Th 10am-7pm; longer hours during festival season. Free.)*

GARDENS AND PARKS

Just off the eastern end of the Royal Mile, ◧**Holyrood Park** is a true city oasis, a natural wilderness replete with hills, moorland, and lochs. **Arthur's Seat,** a holy place for Picts and the park's highest point, affords stunning views of the city and countryside. Traces of forts and Bronze Age terraces dot the surrounding hillside. The walk to the summit takes about 45min. Located directly in the city center and affording fantastic views of the Old Town and the castle, the **Princes Street Gardens** are on the site of now-drained Nor'Loch, where Edinburghers used to drown their accused witches. The loch has been replaced with impeccably manicured lawns and stone fountains, and on fine summer days all of Edinburgh eats lunch here. The lovely **Royal Botanic Gardens** are north of the city center. Guided tours wander across the lush grounds and greenhouses. Take bus #23 or 27 from Hanover St. *(Open Apr.-Sept. daily 10am-7pm; Oct. and Mar. 10am-6pm; Nov. and Feb. 10am-4pm. Free.)*

⬛ ENTERTAINMENT

The summer sees an especially joyful string of events—music in the gardens, plays and films, and *ceilidhs*—even before the Festival comes to town. In winter, shorter days and the crush of students promote a flourishing nightlife. For the most up-to-date info on what's going on, check out *The List* (£2.20), a comprehensive bi-weekly guide to events, available from any local newsstand.

THEATER, FILM, AND MUSIC. The **Festival Theatre,** 13-29 Nicholson St., stages ballet and opera, while the affiliated **King's Theatre,** 2 Leven St., hosts comedy, drama, musicals, and opera. Tickets range from £8 matinees to £52 operas. (☎529 6000. Box office open M-Sa 10am-6pm.) **The Stand Comedy Club,** 5 York Pl., has nightly acts. (☎558 7272. Tickets £1-8.) The **Filmhouse,** 88 Lothian Rd., offers quality European, arthouse, and Hollywood cinema. (☎228 2688. Tickets £3.50-5.50.) Thanks to an abundance of students, Edinburgh's live music scene is alive and well. For a run-down of upcoming acts, look to *The List.* Free live jazz can be found at **Henry's Jazz Bar,** 8 Morrison St. (Open W-Su 8pm-3am. £5.) **The Venue,** 15 Calton Rd. (☎557 3073), and **The Liquid Room,** 9c Victoria St. (☎225 2528), often host rock and progressive shows. **Whistle Binkie's,** 4-6 South Bridge, off High St., is a subterranean pub with live music most nights. (Open daily until 3am.)

▨ NIGHTLIFE

PUBS

Edinburgh claims to have the highest density of pubs anywhere in Europe. Pubs directly on the Royal Mile usually attract a mixed crowd, while students tend to loiter in the Old Town just to the south.

▨ **The Tron,** 9 Hunter Sq., behind the Tron Kirk. Wildly popular for its incredible deals. Frequent live music on 3 hopping floors. Students and hostelers get £1 drinks on W nights. A mix of alcoves and pool tables can be found downstairs. Open daily 11:30am-1am.

The Globe, 13 Niddry St. This backpacker's abode is recommended up and down the Royal Mile. A great place to relax and meet fellow travelers. Hosts DJs and karaoke. Open Su-Th 4pm-1am, F-Sa noon-1am.

Finnegan's Wake, 9b Victoria St. Promotes the Irish way with several stouts on tap and live Irish music every weekend. Open daily 1pm-1am.

The Three Sisters, 139 Cowgate. Loads of space for dancing, drinking, and socializing. Three themed bars (Irish, Gothic, and Style) and an outdoor beer garden draw a boisterous, young crowd. Open daily 9am-1am.

Pop Rokit, corner of Broughton St. and Picardy Pl. More London-chic than Edinburgh-cozy, this trendy bar is a favorite pre-club hangout. Open daily 11am-1am.

The Abbotsford, 3 Rose St. The most authentic of the Rose St. pubs. Built in 1902, it retains the era's elegant ambience with a central and ornate wooden bar. Popular with locals. Open daily 11am-11pm.

CLUBS

Club venues are constantly closing down and reopening under new management; consult *The List* for updated info. Clubs cluster around the historically disreputable **Cowgate,** just downhill from and parallel to the Royal Mile; most close at 3am.

Cabaret-Voltaire, 36-38 Blair St. Hosting a wide range of live music, dance, and art, this innovative club throws a great party. Cover free-£15, depending on events.

Bongo Club, 14 New St. A fun and very safe club. Noted for its hip-hop, including the long-running and immensely popular Messenger and Headspin nights, which run on alternate Saturdays from each other. Cover free-£10.

The Venue, 17-23 Calton Rd. 3 dance floors run the musical gamut throughout the month. The Venue also hosts top live gigs. Cover £2-8.

Po Na Na, 26 Frederick St. Moroccan-themed and glamorous, replete with parachute ceilings, red velvet couches, and an eclectic mix of disco and funk music. Cover £2-5.

Faith, 207 Cowgate. This purple-hued club housed in an old church specializes in R&B, and runs the very popular Chocolate Sunday each week. Cover free-£6.

GAY AND LESBIAN

The Broughton St. area of the New Town (better known as the **Broughton Triangle**) is the center of Edinburgh's gay community.

Planet Out, 6 Baxter's Pl. Start off the night at this mellow club. All drinks £1 on M. Open M-F 4pm-1am, Sa-Su 2pm-1am.

C.C. Bloom's, 23-24 Greenside Pl., on Leith St. A friendly gay club with no cover. M-Sa dancing, Su karaoke. Open M-Sa 6pm-3am, Su 8pm-3am.

Ego, 14 Picardy Pl. Hosts several gay nights, including the long-established **Joy** (1 Sa per month). Cover £10.

FESTIVALS

Edinburgh has special events year-round, but the real show is in August when the city is *the* place to be in Europe. What's commonly referred to as "the Festival" actually encompasses a number of independently organized events. For more info on all the festivals, check out www.edinburghfestivals.co.uk. The **Edinburgh International Festival** (Aug. 15-Sept. 4 in 2004), the largest of them all, features a kaleidoscopic program of music, drama, dance, and art. Most tickets (£7-57, 50% discount for students) are sold beginning in April, but you can usually get tickets at the door; look for half-price tickets starting at 9am on performance days at **The HUB**, Edinburgh's Festival Centre, Castlehill. (☎473 2000. Open M-Sa.)

Around the established festival has grown a less formal ■**Fringe Festival** (Aug. 8-30 in 2004), which now includes over 600 amateur and professional companies presenting theater, comedy, children's shows, folk and classical music, poetry, dance, and opera events that budget travelers may find more suitable for their wallets (usually free-£10). Contact the **Fringe Festival Office**, 180 High St. (☎226 0000; www.edfringe.com. Open June-Aug. daily.) Another August festival is the **Military Tattoo** (Aug. 6-28 in 2004), a spectacle of military bands, bagpipes, and drums. For tickets (£9-31), contact the **Tattoo Ticket Sale Office**, 33-34 Market St. (☎225 1188; www.edintattoo.co.uk). The excellent **Edinburgh International Film Festival** is also in August at The Filmhouse (☎229 2550; tickets on sale starting late July), while the **Edinburgh Jazz and Blues Festival** is from July 23 to August 1 in 2004 (☎467 5200; tickets on sale in June). The fun doesn't stop for the long, dark winter: **Hogmanay**, Edinburgh's traditional New Year's Eve festival, is a serious street party with a week of associated events (www.edinburghshogmanay.org).

DAYTRIP FROM EDINBURGH

ST. ANDREWS. Golf overruns the small city of St. Andrews, where the rules of the sport were formally established. The **Old Course** frequently hosts the British Open. (☎(01334) 466 666 for reservations or enter a same-day lottery for starting times. Apr.-Oct. £90 per round; Nov.-Mar. £56.) The budget option, still lovely, is the nine-hole **Balgove Course** for £7-10. If you're more interested in watching than playing, visit the **British Golf Museum**, next to the Old Course, which details the ancient origins of the game. (☎(01334) 460 046. Hours change seasonally; call for info. £4, students £3.) **St. Andrews Cathedral** was the center of

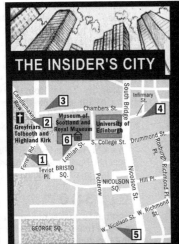

THE INSIDER'S CITY

EDINBURGH UNIVERSITY PUB CRAWL

Oscar Wilde once said that "nothing worth knowing can be taught." For a real Edinburgh education, pick up a thing or two on the *Let's Go* pub crawl.

1 Live folk music at **Sandy Bell's** will prime you for the evening ahead. (25 Forrest Rd. Open daily 11am-1am.)

2 **Greyfriars Bobby** is a student favorite. (34 Candlemaker Row. Open daily 11am-1am.)

3 **Beluga Bar** is *the* spot for the stylish scholar set. (30a Chambers St. Open daily 9am-1am.)

4 **Oxygen Bar** cuts a cool profile with a smart decor. (3-5 Infirmary St. Open M-Sa 10am-1am, Su 11am-1am.)

5 Catch a little sun at **Pear Tree House**'s beer garden. (38 W. Nicolson St. Open daily 11am-midnight, F-Sa until 1am.)

6 Laid-back **Negociants** serves great food until 2:15am. (45-47 Lothian St. Open M-Sa 9am-3am, Su 10am-3am.)

Scottish religion before and during the Middle Ages. The nearby **St. Andrews Castle** hides secret tunnels and bottle-shaped dungeons. (Cathedral and castle open Apr.-Sept. daily 9:30am-6:30pm; Oct.-Mar. 9:30am-4:30pm. Joint ticket £4.)

Trains (☎(08457) 484 590) stop 11km away in Leuchars (1hr., every hr., £8.10), where buses #94 and 96 (£1.60) depart for St. Andrews. **Buses** (☎(01383) 621 249) pull in from Edinburgh (bus #X59 or X60; 2hr.; M-Sa 1-2 per hr. until 6:45pm, fewer on Su; £5.70) and Glasgow (#X24, change at Glenrothes to #X59; 2½hr., M-Sa every hr., £5.50). To get from the bus station to the **tourist office**, 70 Market St., turn right on City Rd. and take the first left. (☎(01334) 472 021; www.standrews.com. Open Apr.-June M-Sa 9:30am-5:30pm, Su 11am-4pm; July-Aug. M-Sa 9:30am-7pm, Su 10:30am-5pm; Sept. M-Sa 9:30am-6pm, Su 11am-4pm; Oct.-Mar. M-Sa 9:30am-5pm.) **Internet** access is across the street at **Costa Coffee**, 83 Market St. (£1 per 20min. Open M-Sa 8am-6pm, Su 10am-5:30pm.) B&Bs line **Murray Place** and **Murray Park** near the bus station. **St. Andrews Tourist Hostel ❷**, St. Mary's Pl., has a great location and has sparkling facilities. (☎(01334) 479 911. Dorms £12; family room £40-48.)

GLASGOW   ☎0141

Scotland's largest metropolitan area, Glasgow (pop. 700,000) has re-invented itself several times, and the mark of each era remains today. It rose to prominence during the Victorian period, exploiting heavy industry to become the world's leading center of shipbuilding and steel production, as evidenced by the soot and cranes that once littered the River Clyde. Yet Glasgow's urbanization had its positive side as well, the legacy of which can be observed in the grand architecture that still characterizes the city centre. Across the river, the daring curves of a new multi-million pound Science Centre shimmer brilliantly. Free museums and international cuisine add cosmopolitan flair, separating the city from its industrial past. At night, Glasgow's pubs explode as Scotland's largest student population and its football-mad locals live up to their national reputation for nighttime fun.

▐ TRANSPORTATION

Flights: Glasgow Airport (GLA; ☎887 1111), 15km west in Abbotsinch. Citylink buses connect to **Buchanan Station** (25min., 6 per hr., £3.30).

Trains: Central Station, on Gordon St. (U: St. Enoch), leave for **London King's Cross** (5-6hr., every hr., £82) and **Stranraer** (2½hr., 3-8 per day, £16). From **Queen St. Station,** on George Sq. (U: Buchanan St.), trains go to: **Aberdeen** (2½hr., 11-24 per day, £31); **Edinburgh** (50min., 2 per hr., £7.40); **Inverness** (3¼hr., 5 per day, £31). Bus #88 runs between the 2 stations (4 per hr., 50p).

Buses: Buchanan Station (☎(0870) 608 2608), on Hanover St., 2 blocks north of Queen St. Station. **Scottish Citylink** (☎(08705) 505 050) to: **Aberdeen** (4hr., every hr., £26); **Edinburgh** (1¼hr., 2-3 per hr., £6); **Inverness** (3½-4½hr., every hr., £26); **Oban** (3hr., 2-3 per day, £12). **National Express** (☎(08705) 808 080) buses arrive daily from **London** (8hr.; every hr.; £22, round-trip £28).

Public Transportation: The circular **Underground** (U) subway line, a.k.a. the "Clockwork Orange," runs M-Sa 6:30am-11pm, Su 11am-5:30pm. 90p. The **Discovery Ticket** is good for one day of unlimited travel. M-F after 9:30am, Su all day. £1.70.

▐ ❼ ORIENTATION AND PRACTICAL INFORMATION

George Square is the center of town. Sections of **Sauchiehall Street, Argyle Street,** and **Buchanan Street** are pedestrian areas. **Charing Cross,** where Bath St. crosses M8 in the northwest, is a useful landmark. The vibrant **West End** revolves around **Byres Road** and **Glasgow University,** 1½km northwest of the city center.

Tourist Office: 11 George Sq. (☎204 4400), south of Queen St. Station, and northeast of Central Station. U: Buchanan St. Books rooms for a £2 fee plus 10% deposit. **Walking tours** depart M-Tu and Th-F 2:30 and 6pm, Su 10:30am (1½hr., £5). Open July-Aug. M-Sa 9am-8pm, Su 10am-6pm; Sept.-June M-Sa 9am-7pm, Su 10am-6pm.

Financial Services: Banks are plentiful and **ATMs** are on every corner. **Thomas Cook,** 15 Gordon St. (☎204 4484), inside Central Station. Open M-Sa 8:30am-5:30pm, Su 10am-4pm. **American Express,** 115 Hope St. (☎(08706) 001 060). Open July-Aug. M-F 8:30am-5:30pm, Sa 9am-5pm; Sept.-June M-F 8:30am-5:30pm, Sa 9am-noon.

Laundromat: Coin-Op Laundromat, 39-41 Bank St. (☎339 8953). U: Kelvin Bridge. Wash £2. Dry 20p per 5min. Open M-F 9am-7:30pm, Sa-Su 9am-5pm.

Emergency: ☎999; no coins required.

Police: 173 Pitt St. (☎532 2000).

Hospital: Glasgow Royal Infirmary, 84-106 Castle St. (☎211 4000).

Internet Access: easyInternet Cafe, 57-61 St. Vincent St. (☎222 2365). £1 per 40min.-3hr. depending on time of day. Open daily 7am-10:45pm.

Post Office: 47 St. Vincent St. (☎204 3688). Open M-F 8:30am-5:45pm, Sa 9am-5:30pm. **Postal Code:** G2 5QX.

ACCOMMODATIONS

Reserve B&Bs and hostels in advance, especially in August. If rooms are booked in Glasgow, consider staying at the **SYHA Loch Lomond** (p. 252). Most B&Bs cluster on **Argyle Street** in the university area or on **Westercraigs Road,** east of the Necropolis.

Bunkum Backpackers, 26 Hillhead St. (☎581 4481). Though located away from the city centre, Bunkum is minutes away from the vibrant West End. Spacious dorms with comfortable beds. Lockers. Laundry £1.50. Dorms £12 per day. ❷

Glasgow Euro Hostel, (☎222 2828; www.euro-hostels.com), on the corner of Clyde St. and Jamaica St. Convenient to the city centre, this hostel also offers a dining room and bar. Breakfast included. Laundry facilities. Internet access. Dorms from £13.80. ❶

Merchant Lodge, 52 Virginia St. (☎552 2424). Originally a tobacco store, this upscale B&B is convenient and comfortable. Singles £35; doubles £55; triples £70. ❸

University of Glasgow, No. 3 The Square, Conference & Visitor Services (☎330 5385). Enter the university from University St. and turn right into the square. Summer housing at several dorms. Office open M-F 9am-5pm. Student dorms £14; B&B £17.50. ❷

Alamo Guest House, 46 Gray St. (☎339 2395), across from Kelvingrove Park at its southern exit. Beautiful location in the West End. Singles £23; doubles £40-46. ❸

McLay's Guest House, 268 Renfrew St. (☎332 4796). With 3 dining rooms and satellite TV, this posh B&B looks and feels more like a hotel. Singles £24, with bath £26; doubles £40/48; family room £55/65. ❸

FOOD

The area bordered by Otago St. in the west, St. George's Rd. in the east, and along Great Western Rd., Woodlands Rd., and Eldon St. brims with cheap kebab-and-curry joints. **Byres Road** and **Ashton Lane,** a tiny cobblestoned alley parallel to Byres Rd., thrive with cheap, trendy cafes.

Ashora, 108 Elderslie St. Just west of several hostels on Berkeley St., this award-winning restaurant features cheap, delicious Indian food. Lunch buffet £2.95, dinner buffet £5.95. Lunch served 11am-2pm. Open daily 11am-midnight. ❶

BRITAIN

THE BIG SPLURGE

GOURMET GLASGOW

During Gourmet Glasgow, a two-week event beginning in mid-July, 19 popular restaurants open their doors to massive crowds, attempting to confirm Glasgow's title as the UK's culinary capital of the north. Each participating restaurant offers an inclusive prix-fixe meal, with at least four courses, wine, and a glass of local malt scotch. Several even include a champagne starter. Though the menus are pricey (most range from £35-60), they are a deal compared to the establishments' everyday charges for similar fare.

In 2003 some of the swankiest participants ranged from traditional Scottish venues like the stylish **City Merchant**, 97-99 Candleriggs (☎553 1577), known for its seafood and sophisticated clientele, to French-influenced **Rococo**, 202 W. George St. (☎221 5004), whose wine list is regarded as one of the city's best. Newcomer **Saint Judes**, 109 Bath St. (☎352 8800), offers modern European fare and is well-liked for its sleek, modern design, while **L'Ariosto**'s, 92-94 Mitchell St. (☎221 0971), Italian dishes have been popular with Glaswegian epicurians for over 20 years.

For more info or to make reservations, pick up *Gourmet Glasgow* (free at the TIC), call the individual restaurant, or visit www.gourmet-glasgow.com.

Willow Tea Rooms, 217 Sauchiehall St. Upstairs from Henderson the Jewellers. A Glasgow landmark. Sip one of 31 kinds of tea. £1.70 per pot. High tea £8.80. Open M-Sa 9am-4:30pm, Su noon-4:15pm. ❷

La Tasca, 39 Renfield St. (☎204 5188), is a popular Spanish *tapas* bar where the *sangria* is not to be missed. *Tapas* £3-8. Open daily noon-midnight. ❶

Cul-de-Sac Restaurant, 44-46 Ashton Ln. Turn from Byres Rd. onto Ashton Ln., and bear right. 3-course dinners include vegetable dishes, meat *cassoulet*, and haggis (£13-20). Open M-Sa noon-10:30pm, Su 12:30-10:30pm. ❸

Henry Healthy, Queen St. (☎227 2791), just south of George Sq. A great place for a quick snack or lunch. Soup 80p. Sandwiches £1.60. Open M-Sa 7:30am-3pm. ❶

🄶 SIGHTS

Glasgow is a budget sightseer's paradise, with splendid architecture, grand museums, and chic galleries that are often free to visitors. Your first stop should be to the Gothic ◼Glasgow Cathedral, the only full-scale cathedral spared the fury of the 16th-century Scottish Reformation. (Open Apr.-Sept. M-Sa 9:30am-6pm, Su 2-5pm; Oct.-Mar. M-Sa 9:30am-4pm, Su 2-4pm. Free.) On the same street is the St. Mungo Museum of Religious Life and Art, 2 Castle St., which surveys every religion from Islam to Yoruba. (Open M-Sa 10am-5pm, Su 11am-5pm. Free.) Behind the cathedral is the spectacular Necropolis, a terrifying hilltop cemetery. (Open 24hr. Free.)

In the West End, Kelvingrove Park lies on the banks of the River Kelvin. In the southwest corner of the park, at Argyle and Sauchiehall St., sits the magnificent Kelvingrove Art Gallery and Museum, which shelters works by van Gogh, Monet, and Rembrandt. Due to renovation, the museum's collection is on display at the new Open Museum, 161 Woodhead Rd., until construction is completed in 2006. (Museum open M-Th and Sa 10am-5pm, F and Su 11am-5pm. Free.) Farther west rise the Gothic edifices of the University of Glasgow. The main building is on University Ave., which runs into Byres Rd. While walking through the campus, stop by the Hunterian Museum, home to the death mask of Bonnie Prince Charlie, or see 19th-century Scottish art at the Hunterian Art Gallery, across the street. (U: Hillhead. Open M-Sa 9:30am-5pm. Free.) Several buildings designed by Charles Rennie Mackintosh, Scotland's most famous architect, are open to the public; the Glasgow School of Art, 167 Renfrew St., reflects a uniquely Glaswegian Modernist style. (Tours July-Aug. M-F 11am and 2pm; Sa-Su 10:30am, 11:30am, and 1pm. Sept.-June M-F 11am and 2pm, Sa 10:30am. £5, students £3.)

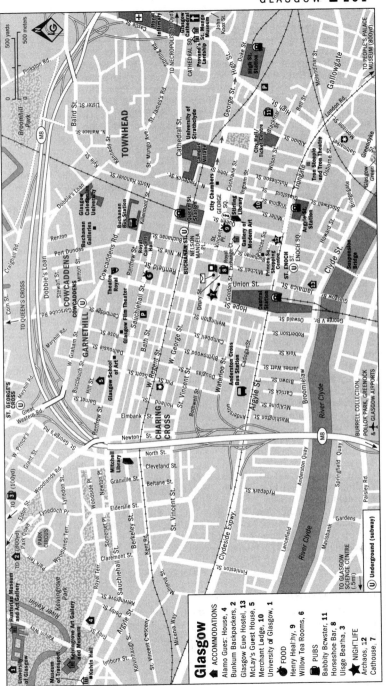

Glasgow

▲ ACCOMMODATIONS
Alamo Gues: House, 4
Bunkum Backpackers, 2
Glasgow Euro Hostel, 13
McLay's Guest House, 5
Merchant Lodge, 10
University of Glasgow, 1

🍴 FOOD
Henry Heal:hy, 9
Willow Tea Rooms, 6

🍺 PUBS
Babbity Bcwster, 11
Horseshoe Bar, 8
Uisge Bea'ha, 3

★ NIGHTLIFE
Archaos, 12
Cathouse, 7

Ⓤ Underground (subway)

BRITAIN

🎵 🎭 ENTERTAINMENT AND NIGHTLIFE

Glaswegians have a reputation for partying hard. *The List* (£2.20 at newsstands) has detailed nightlife and entertainment listings for both Glasgow and Edinburgh. The infamous **Byres Road** pub crawl slithers past the University of Glasgow area, starting at Tennant's Bar and proceeding toward the River Clyde. ⬛**Uisge Beatha,** 232 Woodlands Rd., serves over 100 kinds of malt whiskey. (Whiskey £1.30-1.60. Open M-Th 11am-11pm, F-Sa 11am-midnight, Su 12:30-11pm.) Go to ⬛**Babbity Bowster,** 16-18 Blackfriar St., for football talk and good drinks. (Open M-Sa 10am-midnight, Su 11am-midnight.) **Horseshoe Bar,** 17-21 Drury St., boasts the longest continuous bar in the UK. (Open M-Sa 11am-midnight, Su 12:30pm-midnight.) At the club **Archaos,** 25 Queen St., students drink 2-for-1 whiskeys. (Cover £3-7. Open Su, Tu, and Th-Sa 11pm-3am.) Indie music pleases younger crowds at **Cathouse,** 15 Union St., a 3-story club. (Cover £3-5, student £1-4. Open W-Su 11pm-3am.)

STIRLING
☎01786

The third point of a strategic triangle completed by Glasgow and Edinburgh, Stirling has historically presided over north-south travel in the region; it was once said that "he who controlled Stirling controlled Scotland." At the 1297 Battle of Stirling Bridge, **William Wallace** (of *Braveheart* fame) overpowered the English army, enabling Robert the Bruce to finally overthrow the English at **Bannockburn,** 3km south of town. To reach Bannockburn, take bus #51 or 52 from Murray Pl. in Stirling. (Visitors center open Apr.-Oct. daily 10am-5:30pm; Feb.-Mar. and Nov.-Dec. 10:30am-4pm. £3.50, children £2.60. Battlefield open year-round.) ⬛**Stirling Castle** has superb views of the Forth valley and recalls a history both of royal residence and military might. (Open Apr.-Oct. daily 9:30am-6pm; Nov.-Mar. 9:30am-5pm. £7.50, concessions £5.50.) **Argyll's Lodging,** a 17th-century mansion below the castle has been impressively restored. (Open Apr.-Sept. daily 9:30am-6pm; Oct.-Mar. 9:30am-5pm. £3.30, concessions £2.50. Free with castle admission.) The 19th-century **Wallace Monument Tower,** on Hillfouts Rd., 2.5km from town, offers incredible views. You can also admire the 1.5m sword William Wallace wielded against King Edward I. Take bus #62 or 63 from Murray Pl. (Open July-Aug. daily 9:30am-6pm; Sept. 9:30am-5pm; Oct. and Mar.-May 10am-5pm; Nov.-Feb. 10:30am-4pm; June 10am-6pm. £5, concessions £3.80.)

Trains run from Goosecroft Rd. (☎(08457) 484 950) to: Aberdeen (2hr.; M-Sa every hr., Su 6 per day; £31); Edinburgh (50min., 2 per hr., £5.30); Glasgow (40min., 1-3 per hr., £5.40); Inverness (3hr., 3-4 per day, £31); and London King's Cross (5½hr., every hr., £44-84). **Buses** also run from Goosecroft Rd. to: Edinburgh (1¼hr., every hr., £4); Fort William (2¾hr., daily, £15); Glasgow (40min., 2-3 per hr., £4); and Inverness (3¾hr., every hr., £13). The **tourist office** is at 41 Dumbarton Rd. (☎475 019. Open July-Aug. M-Sa 9am-7:30pm, Su 9:30am-6:30pm; Sept.-Oct. and Apr.-May daily 9am-5pm; Nov.-Mar. M-F 10am-5pm, Sa 10am-4pm.) At the clean and friendly **Willy Wallace Hostel ❷,** 77 Murray Pl., a delightful staff fosters a fun atmosphere. (☎446 773. **Internet** access. Dorms £9-13.) The comfortable **Forth Guest House ❸,** 23 Forth Pl., is near the train station. (☎471 020. All rooms with bath. Singles £20-40; doubles £20-45.) **Postal Code:** FK8 2BP.

LOCH LOMOND
☎01389

Immortalized by the famous ballad, the pristine wilderness surrounding Loch Lomond continues to inspire; lush bays, wooded islands, and bare hills compliment the beauty of Britain's largest lake. Hikers adore the **West Highland Way,** which snakes along the entire eastern side of the Loch and stretches north 152km from Milngavie to Fort William. At the southern tip of the lake is **Balloch,** the area's largest tourist center. Attractions and services at the new **Loch Lomond Shores** in Balloch include a giant-screen film about the loch, a **National Park Gateway Centre,** a tourist office, and bike and canoe rentals. (☎722 406. Shores open June-Sept. 10am-6pm, Oct.-May 10am-5pm. £5.) One of the best introductions to the area is a Sweeney's Cruises **boat tour,** which leaves from the tourist office's side of the River Leven in Balloch (1hr.; every hr. 10am-5:30pm; £5.20, children £2.50).

Trains arrive on Balloch Rd. from Glasgow Queen St. (45min., 2 per hr., £3.20). Scottish Citylink **buses** (☎(08705) 505 050) arrive from Glasgow (45min., 3-5 per day, £3.60). First (☎(0141) 423 6600) buses arrive from Stirling (1½hr., 4 per day, £3.80). **Tourist offices** are at Loch Lomond Shores (see above) and in the Old Station Building. (☎753 533. Open July-Aug. daily 9:30am-6pm; June-Sept. 9:30am-5:30pm; Apr.-May and Oct. 10am-5pm.) The ▧**SYHA Loch Lomond ❷,** 3km north of town, is one of Scotland's largest hostels. From the train station, follow the main road for 800m; at the roundabout, turn right, continue 2.5km, turn left at the sign for the hostel, and it's a short way up the hill. (☎850 226. Dorms £12-14, under-18 £10-12.) Camp at the luxurious **Lomond Woods Holiday Park ❶,** on Old Luss Rd., up Balloch Rd. from the tourist office. (☎750 000. Spa facilities. Bikes £10 per day. Reception 8:30am-8pm. Tent and two people £9-15; additional guests £2.)

THE TROSSACHS   ☎01877

The most accessible tract of Scotland's wilderness, the Trossachs has long been praised for its rich green mountains and misty lochs. The A821 winds through the heart of the area between **Aberfoyle** and **Callander,** the region's main towns. It also passes near **Loch Katrine,** the Trossachs's original lure and the setting of Scott's *The Lady of the Lake.* A pedestrian road traces the loch's shoreline, while the popular Steamship Sir Walter Scott **cruises** from the Trossachs Pier (1-3 per day, round-trip £5.80-6.80). Above the loch hulks **Ben A'an'** (461m); the rocky 1hr. hike up begins a mile from the pier, along A821. The **Rob Roy and Trossachs Visitor Centre** in Callander is a combined tourist office and exhibit on the 17th-century hero who is buried nearby. (☎330 342. Open June-Aug. daily 9am-6pm; Sept. 10am-6pm; Oct.-Dec. and Mar.-May 10am-5pm; Jan.-Feb. Sa-Su 11am-4:30pm. £3.25.)

From Callander, First (☎(01324) 613 777) **buses** run to Stirling (45min., 8 per day, £3) and Aberfoyle (45min., 4 per day, £2.50). **Postbuses** reach some remoter areas of the region; find timetables at tourist offices or call the **Stirling Council Public Transport Helpline** (☎(01786) 442 707). About 2km south of Callander on Invertrossachs Rd. is **Trossachs Backpackers ❷,** a comfortable hostel with an attractive setting. (☎331 100. **Internet** access. Dorms £12.50; singles £15.) Camp at **Trossachs Holiday Park ❶,** outside Aberfoyle. (☎382 614. Open Mar-Oct. £10-14 per person.)

INVERNESS AND LOCH NESS   ☎01463

In 565, St. Columba repelled a savage sea beast as it attacked a monk; whether a prehistoric leftover or cosmic wanderer, the monster has captivated the world's imagination ever since. ▧**Loch Ness** still guards its secrets 7.5km south of Inverness. Tour agencies often are the most convenient ways to see Nessie's home; **Guide Friday** offers a 3hr. bus and boat tour. (☎224 000. May-Sept. daily 10:30am and 2:30pm. £15, students and seniors £12, children £7.) Or let **Kenny's Tours** take you around the entire loch and back to Inverness on a minibus. (☎252 411. Tours 10:30am-5pm. £13, students £10.) Five kilometers south on A82, visit ▧**Urquhart Castle** (URK-hart), one of the largest in Scotland before it was blown up in 1692 to prevent Jacobite occupation. Alleged photos of Nessie have since been taken from the ruins. (☎(01456) 450 551. Open June-Aug. daily 9:30am-6:30pm; Apr.-May and Sept. daily 9:30am-5:45pm; Oct.-Mar. M-Sa 9:30am-3:45pm. Admission £5.) The Jacobite cause died in 1746 on **Culloden Battlefield,** east of Inverness, when Bonny

Prince Charlie lost 1200 men in 40min. To get there, take Highland County bus #12 from the post office at Queensgate (round-trip £2). Just 2.5km south of Culloden, the stone circles and chambered cairns (mounds of rough stones) of the **Cairns of Clava** recall civilizations of the Bronze Age. Bus #12 will also take you to **Cawdor Castle**, home of the Cawdors since the 15th century; don't miss the family maze. (Open May-Sept. daily 10am-5pm. £6.50, students and seniors £5.30.)

Trains (☎(08457) 484 950) run from Academy St. in Inverness's Station Sq. to: Aberdeen (2¼hr., 7-10 per day, £19); Edinburgh (3½-4hr., 5-7 per day, £31); Glasgow (3½hr., 5-7 per day, £31); and London (8hr., 3 per day, £84-110). Scottish Citylink **buses** (☎(08705) 505 050) run from Farraline Park, off Academy St., to Edinburgh and Glasgow (both 4½hr., 10-12 per day, £15). To reach the **tourist office**, Castle Wynd, from the stations, turn left on Academy St. and then right onto Union St. (☎234 353. **Bureau de change** and **Internet** £1 per 20min. Open mid-June to Aug. M-Sa 9am-7pm, Su 9:30am-5pm; Sept. to mid-June M-Sa 9am-5pm, Su 10am-4pm.) **Bazpackers Backpackers Hotel ❶**, 4 Culduthel Rd., has a homey atmosphere and great views of the city. (☎717 663. Reception 7:30am-midnight. Dorms £12; doubles £15.) A minute's walk from the city center, **Felstead ❸**, 18 Ness Bank, is a spacious B&B with comfortable beds. (☎321 634. Singles £28-36; doubles £56-72.) Try the **Lemon Tree ❶**, 18 Inglis St., for fabulously cheap and tasty soups (£1.80) and baked goods. (Open M-Sa 8:30am-5:45pm.)

THE INNER HEBRIDES

ISLE OF SKYE

Often described as the shining jewel in the Hebridean crown, Skye possesses unparalleled natural beauty, from the serrated peaks of the Cuillin Hills to the rugged northern tip of the Trotternish Peninsula.

TRANSPORTATION. The tradition of ferries carrying passengers "over the sea to Skye" ended with the **Skye Bridge**, which links Kyle of Lochalsh, on the mainland, to Kyleakin, on the Isle of Skye. **Trains** (☎(08457) 484 950) arrive at Kyle of Lochalsh from Inverness (2½hr., 2-4 per day, £15). Skye-Ways (☎(01599) 534 328) runs **buses** from: Fort William (2hr., 3 per day, £11); Glasgow (5½hr., 3 per day, £19); and Inverness (2½hr., 2 per day, £11). **Pedestrians** can traverse the Skye Bridge's 2.5km footpath or take the **shuttle bus** (2 per hr., £1.70). **Buses** on the island are infrequent and expensive; pick up the handy *Public Transport Guide to Skye and the Western Isles* (£1) at a tourist office.

KYLE OF LOCHALSH AND KYLEAKIN. Kyle of Lochalsh and Kyleakin (KyLAACK-in) bookend the Skye Bridge. The former, on the mainland, has an **ATM**, tourist office, and train station, making it of practical value to travelers. Kyleakin, though short on amenities, boasts three hostels, countless tours, and a backpackers' atmosphere. ☀**MacBackpackers Skye Trekker Tour,** departing from the hostel in Kyleakin, offers either a 1-day tour emphasizing the history and legends of the of the island and a 2-day eco-conscious hike into the Cuillin hills, with all necessary gear provided. (☎(01599) 534 510. Call ahead. 1-day £15, 2-day £45.) Located between Kyle of Lochalsh and Inverness, **Eilean Donan Castle** is the restored 13th-century seat of the MacKenzie family. If you don't bring a camera, you'll definitely stand out; Eilean Donan Castle is the most photographed monument in Scotland. (☎(01599) 555 202. Open Apr.-Oct. daily 10am-5:30pm; Nov. and Mar. 10am-3pm. £4, students £3.20.) To enjoy the incredible sunset views from the quiet Kyleakin harbor, climb to the memorial on the hill behind the SYHA hostel. A slippery scramble to the west takes you to the small ruins of **Castle Moil**. Cross the bridge behind the hostel, turn left, follow the road to the pier, and take the gravel path. The Kyle of Lochalsh **tourist office** is on the hill above the train station. (☎(01599) 534 276. Open May-Oct. M-Sa 9am-5:30pm.) The friendly owners of **Dun Caan Hostel ❷**, in Kyleakin, have masterfully renovated a 200-year-old cottage. (☎(01599) 534 087. **Bikes** £10 per day. Book ahead. Dorms £10)

SLIGACHAN. Renowned for their hiking and cloud and mist formations, the **Cuillin Hills** (COO-leen), the highest peaks in the Hebrides, are visible from nearly every part of Skye, beckoning hikers and climbers. *Walks from Sligachan and Glen Brittle* (£1), available at tourist offices, hotels, and campsites, suggests routes. West of Kyleakin, the smooth, conical Red Cuillin and the rough, craggy Black Cuillin Hills meet in Sligachan, a hiker's hub in a jaw-dropping setting. Don't be misled by the benign titles 'hills'; the Cuillins are great for experienced hikers, but can be risky for beginners. For accommodations, try the **Sligachan Hotel ❹**, a classic hill-walker and climber's haunt. (☎(01478) 650 204. Breakfast included. Singles £30-40; doubles £60-80.) Camp at **Glenbrittle Campsite ❶**, in Glenbrittle at the foot of the Black Cuillins. Take bus #53 (M-Sa 2 per day) from Portree or Sligachan to Glenbrittle. (☎(01478) 640 404. Open Apr.-Sept. £4 per person.)

PORTREE. The island's capital, Portree, has busy shops and an attractive harbor. **Dunvegan Castle,** the seat of the clan MacLeod, holds the record for the longest-inhabited Scottish castle, with continual residence since the 13th century. The castle holds the **Fairy Flag,** a 1,500-year-old silk, and **Rory Mor's Horn,** capable of holding 2 liters of claret. Traditionally, the new MacLeod chief must drain the horn in one draught. Present lord John MacLeod emptied it in just under two minutes. Buses (1-3 per day) arrive from Portree. (☎(01478) 521 206. Open Apr.-Oct. daily 10am-5:30pm; Nov.-Mar. 11am-4pm. £6. Gardens only £4.) **Buses** to Portree from Kyle of Lochalsh (5 per day, £7.80) stop at Somerled Sq. The **tourist office** is on Bayfield Rd. (☎(01478) 612 137. Open July-Aug. M-Sa 9am-7pm, Su 10am-4pm; Apr.-June and Sept.-Oct. M-F 9am-5pm, Su 10am-4pm; Nov.-Mar. M-Sa 9am-4pm.) The **Portree Independent Hostel ❷**, The Green, has an enthusiastic staff and many amenities. (☎(01478) 613 737. **Internet** £1 per 20min. Dorms £11; doubles £23.)

THE OUTER HEBRIDES

The landscape of the Outer Hebrides is extraordinarily beautiful and astoundingly ancient. Much of its rock is more than half as old as the Earth itself, and long-gone inhabitants have left a collection of tombs, standing stones, and other relics. The culture and customs of the Hebridean people seem equally storied, rooted in religion and a love of tradition. While tourism has diluted some old ways, you're still more likely to get an earful of Gaelic here than anywhere else in Scotland.

▐ TRANSPORTATION. Caledonian MacBrayne (☎(01475) 650 100) **ferries** serve the Western Isles, from Ullapool to Lewis and from Skye to Harris and North Uist. Find schedules in *Discover Scotland's Islands with Caledonian MacBrayne,* free from tourist offices. You'll also want to pick up the *Lewis and Harris Bus Timetables* (40p). Inexpensive **car rental** (from £20 per day) is possible throughout the isles. The terrain is hilly but excellent for **cycling.**

LEWIS AND HARRIS. Despite its 20,000 inhabitants, the island of **Lewis** is desolate; its landscape flat, treeless, and speckled with lochs. Mists shroud miles of moorland and fields of peat, nearly hiding Lewis's many archaeological sites, most notably the **Callanish Stones,** an extraordinary Bronze Age circle. (☎(01851) 621 422. Visitors center open Apr.-Sept. M-Sa 10am-7pm; Oct.-Mar. 10am-4pm. Exhibit £1.80. Stones free.) CalMac **ferries** sail from Ullapool, on the mainland, to **Stornoway**

(pop. 8,000), the largest town in northwestern Scotland (M-Sa 2 per day; £14, round-trip £24). To get to the Stornoway **tourist office,** 26 Cromwell St., turn left from the ferry terminal, then right onto Cromwell St. (☎ (01851) 703 088. Open Apr.-Oct. M-Sa 9am-6pm or until the last ferry; Nov.-Mar. M-F 9am-5pm.) The best place to lay your head is **Fair Haven Hostel ❷,** over the surf shop at the intersection of Francis St. and Keith St. From the pier, turn left onto Shell St., which becomes South Beach, then turn right on Kenneth St. and right again onto Francis St. The meals here are better than in town. (☎ (01851) 705 862. Dorms £10, with three meals £20; doubles £15 per person.)

Harris is technically the same island as Lewis, but they're entirely different worlds. The deserted flatlands of Lewis, in the north, give way to another, more rugged and spectacular kind of desolation—that of Harris's steely gray peaks. Toward the west coast, the **Forest of Harris** (ironically, a treeless, heather-splotched mountain range) descends to yellow beaches bordered by indigo waters and *machair*—sea meadows of soft grass and summertime flowers. Essential *Ordnance Survey* hiking maps can be found at the tourist office in **Tarbert,** the biggest town on Harris. **Ferries** arrive in Tarbert from Uig on Skye (M-Sa 2 per day; £9, round-trip £16). The **tourist office** is on Pier Rd. (☎ (01859) 502 011. Open Apr. to mid-Oct. M-Sa 9am-5pm and for late ferry arrivals; mid-Oct. to Mar. for arrivals only.) **Rockview Bunkhouse ❶,** on Main St., is less than 5min. west of the pier, on the north side of the street. (☎ (01859) 502 211. Dorms £9.)

DENMARK (DANMARK)

Like Thumbelina, the heroine of native son Hans Christian Andersen's fairy tale, Denmark has a tremendous personality crammed into a tiny body. Located between Sweden and Germany, the country is the geographic and cultural bridge between Scandinavia and continental Europe, made up of the Jutland peninsula and the islands of Zealand, Funen, Lolland, Falster, and Bornholm, as well as some 400 smaller islands, some of which are not inhabited. With its Viking past behind it, Denmark now has one of the most comprehensive social welfare structures in the world, and liberal immigration policies have diversified the erstwhile homogeneous population. Today, Denmark has a progressive youth culture that beckons travelers to the hip pub scene in Copenhagen. Contrary to the suggestion of a certain English playwright, very little seems to be rotten in the state of Denmark.

LIFE AND TIMES

HISTORY

The Danes evolved from nomadic hunters to farmers during the Stone Age, then took to the seas as Vikings, sacking the English coast and ruling the North Sea. Denmark, then called **Jutland,** was expanded and Christianized in the 10th century by **King Harald the Bluetooth.** Under the rule of Harald's descendents, Denmark's empire grew, finally comprising all of modern Norway, Iceland, and Sweden. Various disputes plagued the Danish throne, and in 1282 regal power was ultimately made accountable to the **Danehof,** a council composed of high nobles and church leaders. In the 16th century, the **Protestant Reformation** swept through Denmark, and **Lutheranism** was established as the state denomination. Over several centuries, the **Thirty Years War** (1618-1648), the **Napoleonic Wars** (1799-1815), and the **War of 1864,** as well as a series of squabbles with Sweden, resulted in severe financial and territorial losses, and the ultimate establishment of a neutral policy. Denmark's neutrality during WWI proved fiscally beneficial, allowing the country to profit by trading with the warring nations. **World War II** saw the country occupied by Nazis, but Denmark refused to comply with pressure to persecute its Jewish citizens. After WWII, Denmark took its place on the international stage, becoming a founding member of **NATO** (1949) and joining the **European Union** (1972).

SUGGESTED ITINERARIES

THREE DAYS Explore chic and progressive **Copenhagen** (p. 262). Get your kicks in the **Tivoli** amusement park and delight in the **Little Mermaid** statue.

BEST OF DENMARK, 9 DAYS Start in cosmopolitan **Copenhagen** (3 days). Daytrip north to the fabulous **Louisiana** museum (p. 270) and **Elsinore,** Hamlet's castle (p. 271). Take an oar at the Viking Ship museum in **Roskilde** (1 day, p. 272).

Move west to **Funen** island (1 day, p. 274); don't miss **Odense** (p. 274), the hometown of Hans Christian Andersen. Hop a ferry to the idyllic **Ærø** (1 day, p. 276), a throwback to the Denmark of several centuries ago. Cross to **Jutland** to chill with laid-back students in **Aalborg** (1 day, p. 280) and swim off the beautiful beaches in **Skagen** (p. 281). Play with blocks at **Legoland** (p. 277) and stop in **Ribe,** a well-preserved medieval town (1 day, p. 279).

TODAY

Denmark maintains an independent and nationalistic identity. Support for the European Union has been tepid; the country has rejected common defense and the euro, among other EU implementations. Periodic economic setbacks have cultivated support for conservative groups, pitting liberal tradition against a high budget deficit. In 2002, Denmark tempered its long-lauded **social welfare system**, passing a controversial anti-immigration bill that limits spouses' rights of entry and eliminates welfare benefits for recent immigrants. Denmark's unicameral legislature, the Folketing, is led by **Prime Minister Anders Fogh Rasmussen,** while the monarch, **Queen Margrethe II,** remains the nominal head of state.

THE ARTS

Denmark's small size belies its cultural influence. The fairy tales of **Hans Christian Andersen**—from the Little Mermaid to the Ugly Duckling—have delighted children throughout the world for generations. Philosopher and theologian **Søren Kierkegaard** developed the "leap of faith," the idea that religious belief is beyond the bounds of human reason. **Karen Blixen** gained fame under the name **Isak Dinesen,** detailing her life experiences in the book *Out of Africa* (1937). Denmark's most

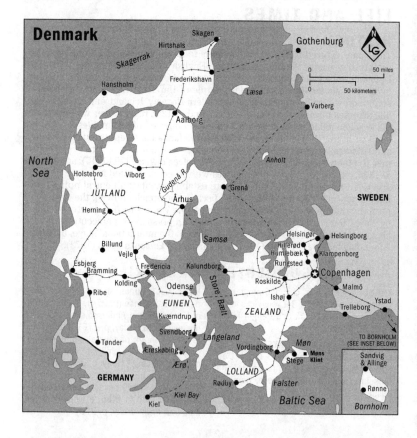

FACTS AND FIGURES

Official Name: Kingdom of Denmark.	**Land Area:** 42,394 sq. km.
Capital: Copenhagen.	**Time Zone:** GMT +1.
Major Cities: Aalborg, Århus, Odense.	**Languages:** Danish, Faroese, and
Population: 5,370,000.	Greenlandic.
	Religions: Evangelical Lutheran (91%).

famous musician, **Carl Nielsen,** composed six symphonies with unusual tonal progressions that won him international recognition (p. 274). Director **Carl Dreyer** explored complex religious themes in his films; the most well-known is *The Passion of Joan of Arc* (1928).

ESSENTIALS

WHEN TO GO

Denmark is best visited May to September, when days are sunny and temperatures average 10-16°C (50-61°F). Winter temperatures average 0°C (32°F). Although temperate for its northern location, Denmark is often windy, and nights can be chilly, even in summer; pack a sweater.

DOCUMENTS AND FORMALITIES

VISAS. EU citizens do not need a visa. Citizens of Australia, Canada, New Zealand, South Africa, and the US do not need a visa for stays of up to 90 days.

EMBASSIES AND CONSULATES: All foreign embassies in Denmark are in Copenhagen (p. 262). Danish embassies abroad include: **Australia,** 15 Hunter St., Yarralumla, Canberra, ACT 2600 (☎(02) 62 73 21 95; fax 62 73 38 64). **Canada,** 47 Clarence St., Ste. 450, Ottawa, ON K1N 9K1 (☎613-562-1811; www.tradecomm.com/danish). **Ireland,** 121 St. Stephen's Green, Dublin 2 (☎(01) 475 64 04; www.denmark.ie). **New Zealand,** 45 Johnston St., PO Box 10874, Wellington (☎(04) 471 05 20; fax 471 05 21). **South Africa,** PO Box 11439, Hatfield, Pretoria 0028 (☎(012) 430 94 30; www.denmark.co.za). **UK,** 55 Sloane St., London SW1X 9SR (☎(020) 7333 0200; www.denmark.org.uk). **US,** 3200 Whitehaven St. NW, Washington, D.C. 20008-3683 (☎202-234-4300; www.denmarkemb.org).

TRANSPORTATION

BY PLANE. Kastrup Airport in Copenhagen (CPH; www.cph.dk) handles international flights from cities around the world, mostly by Air France, British Airways, Delta, Icelandair, KLM, Lufthansa, SAS, and Swiss Air. **Billund Airport** (BLL; ☎76 50 50 50; www.billund-airport.dk) handles flights to other European cities. SAS (Scandinavian Airlines; US ☎800-221-2350; www.scandinavian.net), the national airline company, offers youth, spouse, and senior discounts to some destinations.

BY TRAIN AND BY BUS. The state-run rail line in Denmark is **DSB;** visit www.dsb.dk/journey_planner to use their extremely helpful 🖳**journey planner.** **Eurail** is valid on all state-run routes. The **Scanrail pass,** purchased outside Scandinavia, is good for rail travel through Denmark, Finland, Norway, and Sweden, as well as many discounted ferry and bus rides. The Scanrail pass is also available for purchase within Scandinavia, with restrictions on the number of days spent in the country of purchase. See p. 49 for more info or visit www.scanrail.com or

DENMARK

www.railpass.com/eurail/passes/scanrail.htm. Remote towns are typically served by buses from the nearest train station. The national **bus** network is reliable and fairly cheap. You can take buses or trains over the **Øresund bridge** from Copenhagen to Malmö, Sweden.

BY FERRY. Railpasses include discounts or free rides on many Scandinavian ferries. The free *Vi Rejser* newspaper, at tourist offices, can help you sort out the dozens of smaller ferries that serve Denmark's outlying islands, although the best bet for overcoming language barriers is just to ask at the station. For info on ferries from Copenhagen to Norway, Poland, and Sweden, see p. 263. For more on connections from Bornholm to Germany and Sweden, see p. 273, and from Jutland to England, Norway, and Sweden, see p. 277.

BY CAR. Roads are toll-free, except for the **Storebæltsbro** (Great Belt Bridge; 210kr) and the **Øresund bridge** (around 220kr). Speed limits are 50kph (30mph) in urban areas, 80kph (50mph) on highways, and 110kph (68mph) on motorways. **Service centers** for motorists, called *Info-terias*, are spaced along Danish highways. **Gas** averages 6.50kr per liter. Watch out for bikes, which have the right-of-way. Driving in cities is discouraged by high parking prices and numerous one-way streets. For more info on driving in Denmark, contact the **Forenede Danske Motorejere** (FDM), Firskovvej 32, Box 500, 2800 Kgs. Lyngby (☎70 13 30 40; www.fdm.dk).

BY BIKE AND BY THUMB. Flat terrain, well-marked bike routes, bike paths in the countryside, and raised bike lanes on most streets in towns and cities make Denmark a cyclist's dream. You can rent **bikes** (55-65kr per day) from some tourist offices, rental shops, and a few train stations. The **Dansk Cyklist Forbund** (Danish Cycle Federation), Rømersg. 7, 1362 Copenhagen K (☎33 32 31 21; www.dcf.dk), can hook you up with longer-term rentals. For info on bringing your bike on a train (which costs 50kr or less), pick up *Bikes and Trains* at any train station. **Hitchhiking** on motorways is illegal and uncommon. *Let's Go* does not recommend hitchhiking as a safe means of transport.

TOURIST SERVICES AND MONEY

EMERGENCY **Police:** ☎ 112. **Ambulance:** ☎ 112. **Fire:** ☎ 112.

TOURIST OFFICES. Contact the tourist board in Denmark at Islands Brygge 43, 2300 Copenhagen S (☎32 88 99 00; www.visitdenmark.dt.dk). **Tourist Boards** at home include: **UK**, 55 Sloane St., London SW1X 9SY (☎7259 5959; www.dtb.dt.dk); **US**, 18th fl., 655 3rd Ave., New York, NY 10017 (☎212-885-9700; www.goscandinavia.com). Additional tourist info and helpful ☒**maps** can be found at www.krak.dk.

MONEY. The Danish unit of currency is the **krone** (kr), which is divided into 100 *øre*. The easiest way to get cash is from **ATMs**; cash cards are widely accepted, and many machines give advances on credit cards. Denmark has a high cost of living; expect to pay 85-130kr for a hostel bed, 300-850kr for a hotel room, 75-150kr for a day's groceries, and 40-100kr for a cheap restaurant meal. A barebones day in Denmark might cost 250-350kr; a slightly more comfortable day might cost 400-600kr. The European Union imposes a **value-added tax (VAT)** on goods and services purchased within the EU, which is included in the price (see p. 16). Denmark's VAT is one of the highest in Europe (25%). Non-EU citizens can get a VAT refund upon leaving the country for purchases in any one store that total over 300kr. There are no hard and fast rules for **tipping**, but it's always polite to round up to the nearest 10kr in restaurants and for taxis. In general, service at restaurants is included in the bill, although tipping up to 15% is becoming common in Copenhagen.

DANISH KRONE (KR)		
AUS$1 = 4.44KR	10KR = AUS$2.25
CDN$1 = 4.88KR	10KR = CDN$2.05
EUR€1 = 7.43KR	10KR = EUR€1.35
NZ$1 = 3.98KR	10KR = NZ$2.51
ZAR1 = 0.91KR	10KR = ZAR10.96
UK£1 = 10.73KR	10KR = UK£0.93
US$1 = 6.83KR	10KR = US$1.46

BUSINESS HOURS. Shops are normally open Monday to Thursday from about 9 or 10am to 6pm and Friday until 7 or 8pm; they are usually open Saturday mornings. Shops in Copenhagen stay open all day Saturday. Regular **banking** hours are Monday to Friday 9:30am-4pm, Thursday until 6pm.

COMMUNICATION

PHONE CODES   **Country code: 45. International dialing prefix: 00.**

TELEPHONES. There are no separate city codes; include all digits for local and international calls. Buy phone cards at post offices or kiosks (30kr for 30 units; 50kr for 53 units ; 100kr for 110 units). **Mobile phones** are an increasingly popular and economical alternative (p. 30). For domestic directory info, call ☎118; international info, ☎113; collect calls, ☎141. International direct dial numbers include: **AT&T,** ☎8001 0010; **Canada Direct,** ☎80 01 00 11; **Ireland Direct,** ☎80 01 03 53; **MCI,** ☎8001 0022; **Sprint,** ☎800 10 877; **Telecom New Zealand,** ☎80 01 0064; **Telkom South Africa,** ☎8001 0027; **Telstra Australia,** ☎80 88 0543.

MAIL. Mailing a postcard/letter to Australia, Canada, New Zealand, the US, or South Africa costs 6.25kr; to elsewhere in Europe 5.25kr. Domestic mail costs 4kr.

LANGUAGES. Danish is the official language of Denmark. Faroese is spoken in the Faroe Islands; Greenlandic is spoken in Greenland. The Danish add æ (pronounced like the "e" in "egg"), ø (pronounced like the "i" in "first"), and å (sometimes written as *aa;* pronounced like the "o" in "lord") to the end of the alphabet; thus Århus would follow Viborg in an alphabetical listing of cities. *Let's Go* indexes these under "ae," "o," and "a." Nearly all Danes speak flawless English, but a few Danish words might help break the ice: try *skal* (skoal), or "cheers." Danish has a distinctive glottal stop known as a *stød.* For basic Danish phrases, see p. 1034.

ACCOMMODATIONS AND CAMPING

DENMARK	❶	❷	❸	❹	❺
ACCOMMODATIONS	under 85kr	86-120kr	121-200kr	200-300kr	over 300kr

While Denmark's hotels are generally expensive (300-850kr per night), the country's more than 100 HI youth hostels (*vandrehjem*) are cheap, well-run, and have no age limit. They are also given an official ranking of one to five stars, based on facilities and service. Sheets cost about 45-50kr. Breakfast usually runs 45kr and dinner 65kr. Dorms run about 100kr per night; nonmembers add 25kr. Reception desks normally close for the day around 8 or 9pm, although some are open 24hr. Reservations are highly recommended, especially in summer and near beaches. Many Danish youth hostels are filled by school groups in summer, so it's important to make reservations well in advance. Make sure to arrive before check-in to confirm your reservation. For more info, contact the Danish Youth Hostel Association, Vesterbrog. 39, in Copenhagen. (☎31 31 36 12; www.danhostel.dk. Open M-Th 9am-4pm, F 9am-3pm.) Tourist offices offer the *Danhostel* booklet, which also has more information, and many book rooms in private homes (125-175kr).

Denmark's 525 official **campgrounds** (about 60kr per person) rank from one-star (toilets and drinking water) to three-star (showers and laundry) to five-star (swimming, restaurants, and stoves). You'll need either a **Camping Card Scandinavia**, available at campgrounds (1-year 80kr), or a **Camping Card International**. Campsites affiliated with hostels generally do not require this card. If you only plan to camp for a night, you can buy a 24hr. pass (20kr). The **Danish Camping Council** (*Campingradet;* ☎39 27 80 44) sells the campground handbook *Camping Denmark* and passes. Sleeping in train stations, in parks, or on public property is illegal.

FOOD AND DRINK

DENMARK	❶	❷	❸	❹	❺
FOOD	under 40kr	40-70kr	71-100kr	101-130kr	over 130kr

A "Danish" in Denmark is a *wienerbrød* ("Viennese bread"), found in bakeries alongside other flaky treats. For more substantial fare, Danes favor open-faced sandwiches called *smørrebrød*. Herring is served in various forms, though usually pickled or raw with onions or a curry mayonnaise. For cheap eats, look for lunch specials (*dagens ret*) and all-you-can-eat buffets (*spis alt du kan* or *tag selv buffet*). National beers include Carlsberg and Tuborg; bottled brew tends to be cheaper. A popular alcohol alternative is *snaps* (or *aquavit*), a clear distilled liquor flavored with fiery spices, usually served chilled and unmixed. Many vegetarian (*vegetarret*) options are the result of Indian and Mediterranean influences, but salads and veggies (*grønsager*) can be found on most menus.

HOLIDAYS AND FESTIVALS

Holidays: New Year's (Jan. 1); Easter Holidays (Apr. 8-12); Queen's Birthday (Apr. 16); Worker's Day (May 1); Great Prayer Day (May 7); Ascension Day (May 20); Whit Sunday and Monday (May 30-31); Constitution Day (June 5); Midsummer Eve (June 23); Christmas (Dec. 24-26).

Festivals: Danes celebrate **Fastelavn** (Carnival) in Feb. and Mar. The **Roskilde Festival** is an immense, open-air rock festival held in Roskilde in late June. In early July, the **Copenhagen Jazz Festival** hosts a week of concerts, many free.

COPENHAGEN (KØBENHAVN)

Copenhagen (pop. 1,800,000) combines the swan ponds, gingerbread houses, and *Lille Havfrue* (Little Mermaid) of Hans Christian Andersen's fairy tales with the cosmopolitan style, world-class museums, and round-the-clock nightlife of Europe's largest cities, all the while maintaining a friendly, distinctly Danish charm. Denmark's capital embodies the youthful, laid-back, and progressive attitude that pervades this country of islands.

▐ TRANSPORTATION

Flights: Kastrup Airport (CPH; ☎32 47 47 47; www.cph.dk). **Trains** connect the airport to København H (13min., every 10min., 25kr). RyanAir flies cheaply into nearby **Sturup Airport** in Malmö, Sweden (MMX; ☎+46 40 613 1000) from London and Frankfurt. **Fly-buses** depart for København H 30min. after RyanAir arrivals (45min., 100kr).

Trains: Trains stop at **København H** (Hovedbanegården or Central Station; domestic travel ☎70 13 14 15; international reservations ☎70 13 14 16; info ☎33 14 17 01). For travel within the country, www.dsb.dk is indispensable. Fares depend on seat availability; for the cheapest tickets, book at least 14 days in advance, travel with a partner, or use your Wildcard (under-26 only). Approximate fares to: **Berlin** (9hr., daily, 800kr); **Hamburg** (4½hr., 5 per day, 519kr); **Oslo** (9hr., 3 per day, 800kr); **Stockholm** (5½hr., 4-5 per day, 1100kr). Seat reservations (23-51kr) are mandatory.

Ferries: Scandinavian Seaways (☎33 42 33 42; www.dfds.dk) departs daily for **Oslo** (16hr.; 480-735kr, under-26 315-570kr). **Polferries** (☎33 11 46 45; www.polferries.dk) set out from Ndr. Toldbod, 12A (off Esplanaden) for **Świnoujście, Poland** (10hr.; Su-M and W 8am, Th-F 7:30pm; 340kr, with ISIC 285kr).

Public Transportation: Buses (info ☎36 13 14 15; www.hur.dk) run daily 7am-9:30pm. **Trains** (info ☎33 14 17 01) run 6:30am-11pm. Buses and **S-trains** (subways and suburban trains; M-Sa 5am-12:30am, Su 6am-12:30am) operate on a zone system. To travel any distance, you must buy a minimum of a 2-zone **ticket** (15kr, additional zones 7.50kr). For extended stays or travel in Zealand, the best deal is the **rabatkort** (rebate card; 95kr), available from kiosks and bus drivers, which offers 10 2-zone tickets at a discount; just "clip" the ticket as you embark. For longer travel, you can clip the ticket more than once or purchase a *rabatkort* with more zones. Tickets and clips allow 1hr. of transfers. The **24hr. pass** (90kr), available at any train station, grants unlimited bus and train transport in Northern Zealand, as do both Copenhagen Cards (see below). **Night buses,** marked with an "N," run 12:30-5:30am on limited routes and charge double fare; they also accept the 24hr. pass. Copenhagen's newly renovated **Metro** system is efficient and convenient.

Taxis: ☎35 35 35 35 or 38 77 77 77. Base fare 23kr; add 10-13kr per km. København H to Kastrup Airport costs around 200kr.

Bike Rental: City Bike (www.citybike.dk) lends bikes from 120 racks all over the city for a 20kr deposit. Anyone can return your bike and claim your deposit; lock up your bike or return it to the rack when not in use. **Københavns Cykler**, Reventlowsg. 11 (☎33 33 86 13; www.rentabike.dk), in København H. 75kr per day, 340kr per week; 500kr deposit. Open July-Aug. M-F 8am-5:30pm, Sa 9am-1pm, Su 10am-1pm.

Hitchhiking and Ridesharing: Hitchhiking is not common in Denmark. *Let's Go* does not recommend hitchhiking. For info on ridesharing, check out www.nice.person.dk or www.useit.dk. Always exercise caution when traveling with strangers.

◼️🔢 ORIENTATION AND PRACTICAL INFORMATION

Copenhagen lies on the east coast of the island of **Zealand** (Sjælland), across the Øresund Sound from Malmö, Sweden. The 28km **Øresund bridge and tunnel,** which opened July 1, 2000, established the first "fixed link" between the two countries. Copenhagen's main train station, København H, lies near the city's heart. North of the station, **Vesterbrogade** passes **Tivoli** and **Rådhuspladsen,** the central square, then cuts through the city center as **Strøget** (STROY-yet), the world's longest pedestrian thoroughfare. As it heads east, Strøget goes through a series of names: **Frederiksberggade, Nygade, Vimmelskaftet, Amagertorv,** and **Østergade.**

TOURIST, FINANCIAL, AND LOCAL SERVICES

Tourist Offices: Wonderful Copenhagen, Bernstorffsg. 1 (☎70 22 24 42; www.visitcopenhagen.dk). Head out the main exit of København H and go left, past the back entrance to Tivoli. Open May-Aug. M-Sa 9am-8pm, Su 10am-6pm; Sept.-Apr. M-F 9am-4:30pm, Sa 9am-1:30pm. **Use It,** Rådhusstr. 13 (☎33 73 06 20; www.useit.dk). From the station, follow Vesterbrog., cross Rådhuspl. onto Frederiksbergg., and turn right on Rådhusstr. Indispensable info geared toward budget travelers. Pick up a copy of *Play Time*, a comprehensive budget guide to the city. Provides daytime luggage storage, has free **Internet** access (20min. max.), finds lodgings, and holds mail. Open mid-June to mid-Sept. daily 9am-7pm; mid-Sept. to mid-June M-W 11am-4pm, Th 11am-6pm, F 11am-2pm. The **Copenhagen Card** (24hr. card 159kr), sold in hotels, tourist offices, and train stations, grants free admission to most major sights and discounts on others, but is not worth it unless you're visiting 5 museums or more in one day. The **Copenhagen Card Plus** (72hr. card 395kr) includes even more museums, provides unlimited bus and train travel in Northern Zealand, and offers discounts on ferries to Sweden, but also requires significant museum-hopping to justify the cost.

Budget Travel: Kilroy Travels, Skinderg. 28 (☎ 70 15 40 15). Open M-F 10am-5:30pm, Sa 10am-2pm. **Wasteels Rejser,** Skoubog. 6 (☎33 14 46 33). Open M-F 9am-5pm, Sa 10am-2pm.

Embassies and Consulates: Australia, Dampfaergevej 26, 2nd fl. (☎70 26 36 76). **Canada,** Kristen Bernikowsg. 1 (☎33 48 32 00). **Ireland,** Østerbaneg. 21 (☎35 42 32 33; fax 35 43 18 58). **New Zealanders** should contact their embassy in Brussels (see p. 123). **South Africa,** Gammel Vartovvej 8 (☎39 18 01 55; www.southafrica.dk). **UK,** Kastelsvej 36-40 (☎35 44 52 00). **US,** Dag Hammarskjölds Allé 24 (☎35 55 31 44; www.usembassy.dk).

Currency Exchange: Numerous locations, especially on Strøget. 25kr commission standard. **Forex,** in København H. 20kr commission on cash, 10kr per traveler's check. Open daily 8am-9pm. **The Change Group,** Østerg. 61. 35kr commission minimum. Open May-Sept. M-Sa 8:45am-8pm, Su 10am-6pm; Oct.-Apr. daily 10am-6pm.

Luggage Storage: Free at **Use It** (above) and most hostels. At **København H,** 30kr per bag per day; 10-day maximum. Lockers 25-35kr per 24hr.; 3 day maximum. Open M-Sa 5:30am-1am, Su 6am-1am.

Laundromats: Look for **Vascomat** and **Møntvask** chains. At Borgerg. 2, Nansensg. 39, Vendersg. 13, and Istedg. 45. Wash and dry 40-50kr. Most open daily 7am-9pm.

Bi-Gay-Lesbian Resources: Landsforeningen for Bøsser and Lesbiske (National Association for Gay Men and Women), Teglgårdsstr. 13 (☎33 13 19 48; www.lbl.dk). Open M-F 11am-4pm. The monthly *Out & About,* which lists clubs, cafes, and organizations, is available at gay clubs and the tourist office. Also check out www.copenhagen-gay-life.dk. The city hosts the **Danish Mermaid Parade** (www.danishpride.dk) in August.

EMERGENCY AND COMMUNICATIONS

Emergencies: ☎112. **Police:** ☎33 14 14 48. Headquarters are at Polititorvet.

24-Hour Pharmacy: Steno Apotek, Vesterbrog. 6c (☎33 14 82 66). Open 24hr.; ring the bell. Across from the Banegårdspl. exit of København H.

Medical Assistance: Doctors on Call (☎70 27 57 57). **Emergency rooms** at **Amager Hospital,** Kastrup 63 (☎32 34 32 34), and **Bispebjerg Hospital,** Bispebjerg Bakke 23 (☎35 31 35 31).

Internet Access: Free at **Use It** (above). **Copenhagen Hovedbibliotek** (Central Library), Krystalg. 15 (☎33 73 60 60). Free. Open M-F 10am-7pm, Sa 10am-2pm. **Boomtown,** Axeltorv 1 (☎33 32 10 32). 20kr per 30min., 30kr per hr. Open 24hr.

Post Office: In København H. Address mail to be held: SURNAME Firstname, Post Denmark, Hovedbanegårdens Posthus, Hovedbanegården, **1570** Copenhagen V. DENMARK. Open M-F 8am-9pm, Sa 9am-4pm, Su 10am-4pm. **Use It** (see tourist offices, above) also holds mail. Address mail to: Firstname SURNAME, *Poste Restante,* Use It, 13 Rådhusstr., **1466** Copenhagen K, DENMARK.

DENMARK

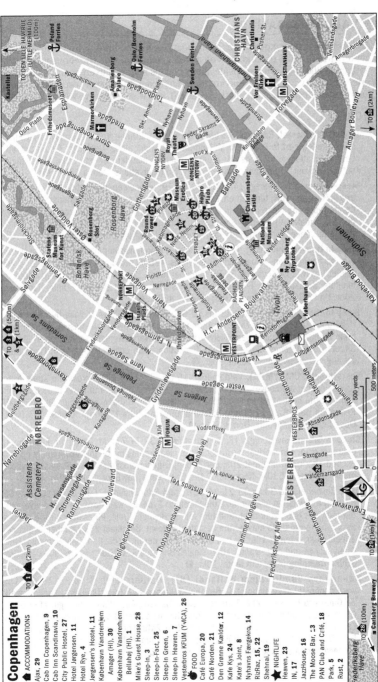

Copenhagen

◆ ACCOMMODATIONS
Ajax, **29**
Cab Inn Copenhagen, **9**
Cab Inn Scandinavia, **10**
City Public Hostel, **27**
Hotel Jørgensen, **11**
Hotel Rye, **4**
Jørgensen's Hostel, **11**
København Vandrerhjem
  Amager (HI), **30**
København Vandrerhem
  Bellahøj (HI), **1**
Mike's Guest House, **28**
Sleep-In, **3**
Sleep-In-Fact, **25**
Sleep-In Green, **6**
Sleep-In Heaven, **7**
Vesterbros KFUM (Y•ICA), **26**

● FOOD
Café Europa, **20**
Café Norden, **21**
Den Grønne Kælder, **12**
Kafe Kys, **24**
Kate's Joint, **8**
Nyhavns Færgekro, **14**
RizRaz, **15, 22**
Shehnai, **19**

★ NIGHTLIFE
Heaven, **23**
IN, **17**
JazzHouse, **16**
The Moose Bar, **3**
PAN Club and Café, **18**
Park, **5**
Rust, **2**

DENMARK

ACCOMMODATIONS

Comfortable and inexpensive accommodations can be hard to find near the city center, where most hostels are converted gymnasiums or warehouses, packed with up to 200 beds. On the upside, many hostels feature a lively social scene. The price jump between hostels and hotels is significant. In summer (especially during holidays and festivals, particularly Roskilde), it is wise to reserve well in advance.

HOSTELS

Jørgensen's Hostel, Rømersg. 11 (☎33 13 81 86), 20min. from København H, 10min. from Strøget, next to Israels Pl. M: Nørreport. Go right along Vendersg.; it's on the left. Central location. 6-12 beds per room. Breakfast included. Sheets 30kr. Max. stay 5 nights. Lockout 11am-3pm. Under-35 only. No reservations. Dorms 135kr. ❸

Sleep-In-Fact, Valdemarsg. 14 (☎33 79 67 79; www.sleep-in-fact.dk). From the main exit of København H, turn left on Vesterbrog., then left again on Valdemarstr. (10min.). Comfortable and clean rooms in a factory-turned-hostel. 30 beds per room. Bikes 50kr per day. Breakfast included. Sheets 30kr. Internet 5kr for first 5min., 20kr per 30min. thereafter. Reception daily 6am-3am. Open late June-Aug. Dorms 120kr. ❸

Sleep-In Heaven, Struenseg. 7 (☎35 35 46 48; morefun@sleepinheaven.com), in Nørrebro. M: Forum. From København H, take bus #250S two stops (dir.: Buddinge; every 10min.) to *H.C. Ørsteds Vej.* 30-86 beds per room. Lively social atmosphere. Close to nightlife. Breakfast 40kr. Free lockers. Sheets 30kr. Internet 20kr per 30min. Reception 24hr. Under-35 only. Dorms 110kr; doubles 450kr. ❷

Sleep-In, Blegdamsvej 132 (☎35 26 50 59). From København H, take bus #1A (dir.: Hellerup; 15min., every 5-7min.) to *Trianglen* and walk down Blegdamsvej. Popular hostel in a huge warehouse. Near lively Østerbro and Nørrebro nightlife. Kitchen available. Sheets 30kr. Internet 6kr per 15min. Reception 24hr. Lockout noon-4pm. Open June 28-Aug. No reservations. Dorms 90kr. ❷

Vesterbros KFUM (YMCA), Valdemarsg. 15 (☎33 31 15 74). Across the street from Sleep-In-Fact (see above). Friendly staff, homey atmosphere, and fewer beds per room come at the cost of an early curfew. Breakfast 25kr. Kitchen available. Sheets 15kr. Reception daily 8:30-11:30am, 3:30-5:30pm, and 8pm-12:30am. Curfew 12:30am. Open late June-early Aug. Dorms 85kr. ❷

Sleep-In Green, Ravnsborgg. 18, Baghuset (☎35 37 77 77). M: Nørreport. From there, take bus #5A. The lackluster exterior belies clean rooms inside this eco-friendly hostel. 30 beds per room. Internet 20kr per 30min. Organic breakfast 30kr. Sheets included; pillow and blanket 30kr. Reception 24hr. Open early May-Sept. Dorms 95kr. ❷

Ajax, Bavnehøj Allé 30 (☎33 21 24 56). From København H, take bus #10 (dir.: CF Richvej) to Bavnehøj Allé. Or, take the S-train to *Sydhavn,* walk north on Enghavevej with the train tracks on your right, and turn left on Bavnehøj Allé. Pleasantly off the beaten track. The rental tents may be the best deal in town. Breakfast 25kr. Kitchen available. Sheets 20kr. Internet 15kr for first 30min., 25kr per hr. Reception daily 8am-midnight. Open July to mid-Aug. Dorms 70kr; singles and doubles 200kr; triples 300kr; quads 350kr. **Camping** 50kr; tent rental 10kr. ❶

København Vandrerhjem Bellahøj (HI), Herbergvejen 8 (☎38 28 97 15; www.danhostel.dk/bellahoej), in Bellahøj. Take bus #2A (dir.: Tingbjerg; 15min., every 5-10min.) to Fuglsang Allé. Turn right onto Fuglsang Allé; it's on the right after 50m. Quiet, clean, and modern hostel 5km from the city center. Breakfast 45kr. Sheets 35kr. Laundry 35kr. Internet 1kr per min. Reception 24hr. Lockout 10am-2pm. Open Feb.-Dec. Dorms 95kr; doubles 300kr; triples 390kr; quads 460kr; 5-person rooms 475kr; six-person rooms 570kr. Nonmembers add 30kr. ❷

City Public Hostel, Absalonsg. 8 (☎33 31 20 70; www.city-public-hostel.dk), in the Vesterbro Youth Center. Proximity to the city center its best feature. 30 beds per room. From the station, walk away from the Rådhuspl. on Vesterbrog. and turn left on Absalonsg. Kitchen and lounge. Breakfast 20kr. Sheets 30kr. Reception 24hr. Open early May-late Aug. Dorms 130kr. ❸

København Vandrerhjem Amager (HI), Vejlandsallé 200 (☎32 52 29 08). M: Bella Center. Ignore the signs and just look for the 2 white flags. Far from civilization in a huge nature reserve. 6 beds per room. Breakfast 45kr. Kitchen available. Sheets 35kr. Laundry 25kr. Lockers 25kr. Reception 7am-1am. Check-in 1-5pm. Open mid-Jan. to Nov. Dorms 95kr; singles and doubles 300kr. Nonmembers add 30kr. ❷

HOTELS

Hotel Jørgensen, Rømersg. 11 (☎33 13 81 86; www.hoteljorgensen.dk). Same ownership and location as Jørgensen's Hostel. Small rooms in a great location. Breakfast included. Reception 24hr. Singles 475-575kr; doubles 575-700kr; triples 900kr. ❺

Cab Inn Scandinavia, Vodroffsvej 55 (☎35 36 11 11, www.cabinn.com). From København H, take bus #2A (dir.: Tingbjerg; 5min., every 5min.) to Vodroffsvej. Sister hotel **Cab Inn Copenhagen** is 5min. away at Danasvej 32-34 (☎33 21 04 00). Small, comfortable, modern rooms. Breakfast 50kr. Reception 24hr. Singles 510kr; doubles 630kr; triples 750kr; quads 870kr. ❺

Hotel Rye, Ryesg. 115 (☎35 26 52 10; www.hotelrye.dk). Take bus #1A (dir.: Hellerup; 15min., every 5-7min.) or 14 to *Trianglen,* then turn right off Osterbrog. onto Ryesg. Cozy hotel that provides a kimono and slippers in your room and homemade buns at breakfast. Shared showers. Breakfast included. Reception daily 8am-9pm. Singles 500kr; doubles 700kr; triples 900kr; quads 1000kr. ❺

Mike's Guest House, Kirkevæng. 13 (☎36 45 65 40). From København H, take bus #26 to *Gl. Jernbanevej* (dir.: Ålholm Pl.; 11min., every 10min.). From there, walk back the way the bus came and turn right onto Kirkevæng.; it's on the left past the church. Call ahead. 4 clean, spacious rooms in Mike's own home. Quiet neighborhood near the Carlsberg Brewery. Singles 200kr; doubles 290kr; triples 400kr. ❸

CAMPING

Bellahøj Camping, Hvidkildevej 66 (☎38 10 11 50), 5km from the city center. Take bus #2A from København H (dir.: Tingbjerg; 15min., every 5-10min.) to Primulavej. Kitchen, cafe, and market. Showers included. Reception 24hr. Open June-Aug. 59kr per person; rental tents 100kr per person. ❶

🍴 FOOD

Among the Viking's legacies is Copenhagen's love-it-or-hate-it pickled herring. Around **Kongens Nytorv,** elegant cafes serve the truly Danish *smørrebrød* (open-faced sandwich) for about 40kr. All-you-can-eat buffets (29-70kr) are popular, especially on Strøget. **Fakta** and **Netto supermarkets** are budget fantasies; there are several in the Nørreport area (S-train: Nørreport) and around the city. (Most open M-F 9am-8pm, Sa 10am-4pm.) Open-air **markets** provide fresh fruits and veggies; try the one at **Israels Plads** near Nørreport Station. (Open M-Th 9am-5:30pm, F 9am-6:30pm, Sa 9am-3pm.) **Fruit stalls** line Strøget and the side streets to the north.

Nyhavns Færgekro, Nyhavn 5. Upscale fisherman's cottage atmosphere along the canal. Lunch on 10 styles of all-you-can-eat herring (89kr) or pick just one style (45kr). Dinner from 150kr. Open daily 9:30am-11:30pm. ❹

DENMARK

Café Norden, Østerg. 61, on Strøget and Nicolaj Pl., in sight of the fountain. A chic cafe in the heart of Strøget. Great for people-watching. Sandwiches 69-89kr. Salads 92-95kr. Brunch 110kr. Kitchen open Su-Th until 9pm, F until 10pm. Open M-Sa 9am-midnight. Su 10am-midnight. ❸

RizRaz, Kompagnistr. 20 and Store Kannikestr. 19. Extensive vegetarian and mediterranean buffet. Lunch buffet 59kr. Dinner 69kr. Open daily 11:30am-midnight. ❷

Kafe Kys, Læderstr. 7, on a quiet street running south of and parallel to Strøget. Plenty of vegetarian options, tasty sandwiches, and salads (48-75kr). Kitchen closes daily at 10:30pm. Open M-Th 11am-1am, F-Sa 11am-2am, Su 11am-midnight. ❷

Shehnai, Vimmelskaftet 39. An Indian restaurant that serves a tasty all-you-can-eat pizza and salad buffet (29kr), in addition to traditional dishes. Tandoori chicken 20kr. Indian buffet 49kr. Open 11am-11pm. ❶

Den Grønne Kælder, Pilestr. 48. Popular vegetarian and vegan dining in a casual atmosphere. Sandwiches 40kr. Lunch 65kr. Dinner 85kr. Open M-Sa 11am-10pm. ❷

Kate's Joint, Blågårdsg. 12. Tasty pan-Asian cuisine in trendy Nørrebro. Entrees 88kr. Open daily 6-10pm. ❸

Café Europa, Amagertorv 1, on Nicolaj Pl. If Norden is the place to see, then trendy Café Europa is the place to be seen. Sandwiches 79-99kr. Gourmet salads 99-119kr. Beer 50kr. Great coffee. Open M-F 9am-midnight, Sa 9am-12:30am, Su 10am-8pm. ❸

🅖 SIGHTS

Compact Copenhagen is best seen on foot or by bike. Various **walking tours** are detailed in *Play Time* (at **Use It**), covering all sections of the city. Opposite Kongens Nytorv is the multi-colored and picturesque Nyhavn, the "new port" where Hans Christian Andersen wrote his first fairy tale. On a nice day, take the the 6.4km walk along the five lakes (*Sø*) that border the western end of the city center. The lakes, as well as the Rosenborg Have, are great places for a **picnic.** Wednesday is the best day to visit museums, as most are free.

CITY CENTER. The first sight you'll see as you exit the train station is **Tivoli,** the famous 19th-century **amusement park.** Christian VIII ordered the creation of the park in 1843, convinced that "when the people are enjoying themselves they forget about politicking." Heed the king and lose yourself in the festive ambience, replete with beautiful fountains, town-fair-style games, and, of course, roller coasters. (*www.tivoligardens.com. Open mid-June to mid-Aug. Su-Th 11am-midnight, F-Sa 11am-1am; off-season reduced hours. Admission 65kr, children 30kr. Rides 15-60kr. Admission with unlimited rides 180kr, children 120kr.*) Across the street from the back entrance of Tivoli, the beautiful 🅜**Ny Carlsberg Glyptotek** boasts a fine collection of ancient and Impressionist art and sculpture, complete with an enclosed Mediterranean garden. (*Dantes Pl. 7. Open Su and Tu-Sa 10am-4pm. 40kr. Free W and Su or with ISIC.*) Follow Denmark's changing face since the beginning of man at the **National Museum.** (*Ny Vesterg. 10. ☎33 13 44 11. Open Su and Tu-Sa 10am-5pm. 50kr, students 40kr. W free.*) **Christiansborg Castle** features subterranean ruins, still-in-use royal reception rooms, and the *Folketing* (Parliament) chambers. To see the magnificent tapestries given to the Queen for her 50th birthday, take the tour. (*Prins Jørgens Gård. ☎33 92 64 92. Ruins open daily 9:30am-3:30pm. 25kr. Required castle tours May-Sept. daily 11am, 1, and 3pm; Oct.-Apr. Su, Tu, Th, and Sa 3pm. 45kr, students 35kr.*) Satisfy your carnal curiosity at the **Museum Erotica,** where various exhibits offer peeks into the sex lives of the famous, the history of prostitution, and kinky art from around the world. (*☎33 12 03 11; www.museumerotica.dk. Open May-Sept. daily 10am-11pm; Oct.-Apr. Su-Th 11am-8pm, F-Sa 10am-10pm.*)

CHRISTIANSHAVN. Climb the awe-inspiring golden spire of **Vor Frelsers Kirke** (Our Savior's Church) for a great view of both the city and the water. *(Sankt Annæg. 29. M: Christianshavn or bus #48. Turn left onto Prinsesseg. Church open Mar.-Nov. daily 11am-4:30pm; Dec.-Feb. 10am-2pm. Free. Tower open Mar.-Nov. M-Sa 11am-4:30pm, Su noon-4:30pm. 20kr.)* The "free city" of **Christiania,** in the southern section of Christianshavn, was founded in 1971 by youthful squatters in abandoned military barracks. Today it is inhabited by a thriving group of artists and alterna-thinkers carrying 70s activism and free love into the new millennium. At Christmas, there is a fabulous **market** with curiosities from all over the world. The aptly named **Pusher Street** features stands that sell all kinds of hash and marijuana. Beware, however, as possession of even small amounts can get you arrested. If you *must,* keep consumption limited to the premises. Always ask before taking pictures, never take pictures on Pusher St. itself, and exercise caution in the area at night. *(Main entrance on Prinsesseg. From København H, take bus #48.)*

FREDERIKSTADEN. Edvard Eriksen's **Lille Havfrue** (Little Mermaid), the tiny but tour-isted statue at the opening of the harbor, honors Hans Christian Andersen's version of the tale. *(S-train: Østerport; turn left out of the station, left on Folke Bernadottes Allé, right on the path bordering the canal, left up the stairs, and then right along the street. Open daily 6am-dusk.)* Head back along the canal and turn left across the moat to reach **Kastellet,** a 17th-century fortress that's now a park. Cross through Kastellet to the fascinating **Frihedsmuseet** (Museum of Danish Resistance), which documents the German occupation from 1940-1945, during which the Danes helped over 7000 Jews escape to Sweden and committed about 4000 acts of sabotage. *(At Churchillparken. ☎ 33 13 77 14. Open May to mid-Sept. Su 10am-5pm, Tu-Sa 10am-4pm; mid-Sept. to Apr. Su 11am-4pm, Tu-Sa 11am-3pm. 40kr, students 30kr. W free. English tours May to mid-Sept. Tu, Th, and Su 2pm. Free.)* From the museum, walk south down Amalieng. to reach the lovely ▨ **Amalienborg Palace,** residence of Queen Margrethe II and the royal family. Most of the interior is closed to the public, but the apartments of Christian VII are open, including the gaudy, original studies of 19th-century Danish kings. The changing of the guard takes place at noon on the brick plaza. *(☎ 33 12 08 08; www.rosenborg-slot.dk. Open May-Oct. daily 10am-4pm; Nov.-Apr. Su and Tu-Sa 11am-4pm. 45kr, students 25kr; combined ticket with Rosenborg Slot (see below) 80kr.)* The gorgeous 19th-century **Marmokirken** (Marble Church), opposite the palace, features an ornate interior, Europe's third-largest dome, and a spectacular view. *(Fredriksg. 4. Open M-Tu and Th 10am-5pm, W 10am-6pm, F-Su noon-5pm. Free. Dome open mid-June to Aug. daily 1 and 3pm; Sept. to mid-June Sa-Su 1 and 3pm. 20kr.)* A few blocks north, **Statens Museum for Kunst** (State Museum of Fine Arts) displays an eclectic collection of Danish and international art in a beautifully designed building. *(Sølvg. 48-50. S-train: Nørreport. Walk up Øster Voldg. ☎ 33 74 84 94; www.smk.dk. Open Su, Tu, and Th-Sa 10am-5pm, W 10am-8pm. 50kr, under-25 35kr. W free.)* Opposite the museum, **Rosenborg Slot,** built from 1606-1634 by King Christian IV as a summer residence, hoards royal treasures, including the **crown jewels.** *(Øster Voldg. 4A. S-train: Nørreport. Walk up Øster Voldg. ☎ 33 15 32 86. Open June-Aug. daily 10am-5pm; May and Sept. 10am-4pm; Oct. 11am-3pm; Nov.-Apr. Su and Tu-Sa 11am-2pm. 60kr, students 30kr.)* Nearby, stroll through the 13,000 plant species in the **Botanisk Have** (Botanical Gardens); make sure to visit the **Palm House.** *(Gardens open June-Aug. daily 8:30am-6pm, Sept.-May Su and Tu-Sa 8:30am-4pm. Palm House open June-Aug. daily 10am-3pm; Sept.-May Su and Tu-Sa 10am-3pm. Free.)*

OTHER SIGHTS. A trip to the **Carlsberg Brewery** will reward you with a wealth of ale-related knowledge and, more importantly, free samples. *(Ny Carlsbergvej 140. Take bus #26 to Bjerregårdsvej (dir.: Ålholm Pl.; 11min., every 10min.) and walk back the way the bus came to turn right onto Ny Carlsbergvej. ☎ 33 27 13 14; www.carlsberg.com. Open Su and Tu-Sa 10am-4pm. Free.)* The hands-on **Experimentarium** it geared toward kids, but great for all ages. *(Tuborg Havnevej 7. Take bus #1A from København H (dir.: Hellerup; 20min., every 5-10min.) to Tuborg Blvd. ☎ 39 27 33 33; www.experimentarium.dk. Open M and W-F 9am-5pm, Tu 9am-9pm, Sa-Su 11am-5pm. 95kr, children 65kr.)*

DENMARK

🎵 🔍 ENTERTAINMENT AND FESTIVALS

For events, consult *Copenhagen This Week*. The **Royal Theater** is home to the world-famous Royal Danish Ballet; the box office is located at Tordenskjoldsg. 7. (Open M-Sa 10am-6pm.) For same-day half-price tickets, head to the **Tivoli ticket office**, Vesterbrog. 3. (☎33 15 10 12. Open mid-Apr. to mid-Sept. daily 10am-8pm; mid-Sept. to mid-Apr. 9am-7pm.) Call **Arte**, Hvidkildevej 64 (☎38 88 22 22), to ask about student discounts. Tickets for a variety of events are sold online at www.billetnet.dk. The relaxed **Kul-Kaféen**, Teglgårdsstr. 5, is a great place to see live performers, listen to stand-up comedy, and grab a bite. (Sandwiches 51kr. Open M 6pm-midnight, Tu-Sa 6pm-2am.) During the world-class **Copenhagen Jazz Festival** (☎33 93 20 13; www.cjf.dk) in mid-July, the city teems with free outdoor concerts. Other festivals include the **Swingin' Copenhagen** festival in late May (www.swinging-copenhagen.dk) and the **Copenhagen Autumn Jazz** festival in early November.

🔊 NIGHTLIFE

In Copenhagen, weekends often begin on Wednesday, clubs rock until 5am, and then the "morning pubs" open up. On Tuesday and Thursday, most bars and clubs have reduced covers and cheap drinks. The city center, **Nørrebro,** and **Østerbro** reverberate with hip, crowded bars. Fancier options abound along **Nyhavn,** but loads of Danes just bring beer and sit on the pier. Copenhagen is known for its progressive view on homosexuality, but its gay and lesbian scene is surprisingly calm.

■ **Park,** Østerbrog. 79, in the Østerbro. An enormous, enormously popular club with 2 packed dance floors, a live music hall, and a rooftop patio. Beer 40kr. Cover Th-Sa 60kr. Restaurant open Tu-Sa 11am-10pm. Club open Th-Sa 11am-5am, Su-Tu 11am-midnight, W 11am-2am.

■ **Rust,** Guldbergsg. 8, in Nørrebro. More intimate than other area nightclubs, with a chic, yet chill ambience. Expect lines after 1am. Cover W 35kr, Th 30kr, F-Sa 50kr. No cover (but no crowd) before 11pm. Open W-Sa 10pm-5am.

The Moose Bar, on Sværtevej. Low on ambiance, high on local spirit. Cheap Happy-Hour specials. Happy Hour Tu, Th, and Sa 9pm-6am. 2 pints 30kr. 2 mixed drinks 25kr. Open Su-M, and W 11am-2am, Tu and Th-Sa 11am-6am.

IN, Nørreg. 1. Steep cover comes with free champagne and wine once inside. Lively and popular club after hours. 18+. Th cover men 130kr, women 80kr; F-Sa 165kr. Open W 10pm-4am, Th 11pm-6am, F 11pm-8am, Sa 11pm-10am.

JazzHouse, Niels Hemmingsens G. 10 (www.jazzhouse.dk). Copenhagen's premier jazz venue. Cover (from 70kr) depends on the performer. Concerts Th 8:30pm, F-Sa 9:30pm. Dance club open Th-Sa midnight-5am.

Heaven, Kompagnistr. 18. Popular and lively gay bar and cafe. Cafe open Sept.-Apr. Th and Su 6-10pm, F-Sa 6-11pm. Bar open Su-Th noon-2am, F-Sa noon-5am.

PAN Club and Café, Knabrostr. 3. Gay cafe, bar, and disco. Cover F-Sa 50kr. Cafe open W-Th 9pm, F-Sa 10pm; disco opens 11pm and gets going around 1am.

🏰 DAYTRIPS FROM COPENHAGEN

Stunning castles and white sand beaches hide in Northern and Central Zealand. Trains offer easy access to many attractive sights within an hour of Copenhagen.

HUMLEBÆK AND RUNGSTED. Humlebæk distinguishes itself with the spectacular ■**Louisiana Museum of Modern Art**, 13 Gl. Strandvej, named for the three wives (all named Louisa) of the estate's original owner. Featuring works by Calder, Lichtenstein, Picasso, and Warhol, Louisiana is an engulfing experience; the building and its sculpture-studded grounds overlooking the sea are themselves worth the trip. Follow signs 1.5km north from the Humlebæk station, or take bus #388 (dir.: Helsingør; every 20min., 15kr) to *Louisiana*. (☎49 19 07 19. Open M-Tu and Th-Su 10am-5pm, W 10am-10pm. 72kr, students 65kr.) The quiet harbor town of **Rungsted** is where Karen Blixen (pseudonym Isak Dinesen) wrote *Out of Africa*. The **Karen Blixen Museum**, Rungsted Strandvej 111, details her life. Follow the street leading out of the train station and turn right on Rungstedsvej, then right again on Rungsted Strandvej; or, take bus #388 and tell the driver your destination. (☎45 57 10 57. Open May-Sept. Su and Tu-Sa 10am-5pm; Oct.-Apr. W-F 1-4pm, Sa-Su 11am-4pm. 35kr. Audioguide 25kr.) Both Humlebæk (45min., every 20min., 53kr or 4 clips) and Rungsted (30min., every 20min., 53kr or 4 clips) are on the Copenhagen-Helsingør **rail** line. The **tourist office** kiosk is on the corner by the museum.

HILLERØD. Hillerød is home of the moated ◪**Frederiksborg Slot;** with its exquisite Baroque gardens, brick ramparts, and dazzling Great Hall, it is the most impressive of Northern Zealand's castles. To get there from the station, cross the street onto Vibekeg. and follow the signs; at the main plaza, walk to the pond and follow it to reach the castle. (☎48 26 04 39. Castle open Apr.-Oct. daily 10am-5pm; Nov.-Mar. 11am-3pm. 60kr, students 50kr. Gardens open May-Aug. daily 10am-9pm; Sept. and Apr. 10am-7pm; Oct. and Mar. 10am-5pm; Nov.-Feb. 10am-4pm. Free.) Hillerød is at the end of **S-train** lines A and E (40min., every 15min., 53kr or 4 clips).

CHARLOTTENLUND AND KLAMPENBORG. Charlottenlund and Klampenborg, on the coastal line, feature topless **beaches.** To get to the beach from the Charlottenlund station, follow the signs for the "Danmark Akvarium," which is next to the beach. The Klampenborg beach is somewhat bigger. Less refined than Tivoli, **Bakken,** the world's oldest amusement park, delivers more thrills. From the Klampenborg train station, turn left, cross the overpass, and head through the park. (☎39 63 73 00; www.bakken.dk. Open late March to late Aug. Hours vary; consult the website. Free admission. Rides 10-35kr each; unlimited rides 199kr.) Bakken borders the **Jægersborg Deer Park,** the royal family's former hunting grounds. It is still home to wooded paths, the **Eremitage** summer chateau, and over 2000 deer. Charlottenlund (18min., every 20min., 23kr or 3 clips) and Klampenborg (22min., every 20min., 30kr or 4 clips) are on **S-train** lines C and F+.

HELSINGØR AND HORNBÆK. Helsingør, 5km from the coast of Sweden, was formerly a strategic Danish stronghold. The fortified 15th-century **Kronborg Slot** was captured and ransacked by the Swedes in 1658, only to be returned two years later. Also known as **Elsinore**, the castle is the setting for Shakespeare's *Hamlet* (although neither the historical "Amled" nor the Bard ever came to visit). A statue of Viking chief Holger Danske sleeps in the castle's spooky casemates; according to legend, he will awake to face any threat to Denmark's safety. The castle also houses the **Danish Maritime Museum,** which contains a sea biscuit from 1852. From the train station, turn right and follow the signs along the waterfront. (☎49 21 30 78; www.kronborg.dk. Open May-Sept. daily 10:30am-5pm; Apr. and Oct. Su and Tu-Sa 11am-4pm; Nov.-Mar. Su and Tu-Sa 11am-3pm. Castle and casemates 40kr. Maritime Museum 30kr. Combination ticket 60kr. Guided 45min. tour of castle daily 2pm. Free.) Helsingør is at the end of the northern **train** line (55min., every 20min., 53kr or 4 clips). The **tourist office,** Havnepl. 3, is in the Kulturhuset, the large brick building across from the station. (☎49 21 13 33. Open mid-June to Aug. M-Th 9am-5pm, F 9am-6pm, Sa 10am-3pm; Sept. to mid-June M-F 9am-4pm, Sa 10am-1pm) To reach the gorgeous beachfront **Helsingør Vandrerhjem Hostel (HI) ❷,** Ndr. Strandvej 24, take bus #340 (8min., every hr.). Or, take the train toward Hornbæk, get off at

Hojstrup, and follow the path across the park; it's on the other side of the street. (☎49 21 16 40; www.helsingorhostel.dk. Breakfast 45kr. Sheets 40kr. Reception daily 8am-noon and 3-9pm. Curfew 11pm. Open Feb.-Nov. Dorms 110kr; doubles 300kr; triples 400kr. Nonmembers add 30kr.)

Hornbæk, a small, untouristed fishing town near Helsingør, offers beautiful beaches. The town hosts a wild harbor festival on the fourth weekend in July. **Bus #340** runs from Helsingør to Hornbæk (25min., every 1-2hr., 23kr). The **tourist office**, Vestre Stejlebakke 2A, in the public library, has a listing of local B&Bs. Turn right from the station onto Havnevej, left onto Ndr. Strandvej, then right through the alley just before the Danske bank. (☎49 70 47 47; www.hornbaek.dk. Open M-Tu and Th 2-7pm, W and F 10am-5pm, Sa 10am-2pm.)

ISHØJ. The small harbor town of Ishøj, just south of Copenhagen, is home to the **Arken Museum of Modern Art**, Skovvej 100, which features temporary exhibitions by notable artists; Edward Munch and Gerhard Richter have both been featured. (☎43 54 02 22; www.arken.dk. Open Su, Tu and Th-Sa 10am-5pm, W 10am-9pm. 55kr, students 35kr.) Take bus #128 (every hr., 14kr) or follow the signs from the station (45min. walk). From Copenhagen take **S-train** lines A or E. **Ishøj Strand Vandrerhjem ❷**, Ishøj Strandvej 13, is near the beach. (☎43 53 50 15. Breakfast 45kr. Sheets 40kr. **Internet** 2kr per min. Reception daily 8am-noon and 2-9:30pm. Dorms 100kr; singles and doubles 370-400kr. **Camping** 62kr per person.)

MØN. To see what Hans Christian Andersen once called the most beautiful spot in Denmark, head south of Copenhagen to the isle of Møn. The gorgeous **Møns Klint** (chalk cliffs) guard the northeastern section of the island. A scenic 3km hike from the cliffs, **Liselund Slot** sits in a beautiful park with peacocks and pastel farm houses. To get to either site, take bus #632 from Stege (30min., 3 per day, 12kr), or hike from the hostel (3km). To get to Møn, take the **train** from Copenhagen to Vordingborg (1½hr., 97kr), then bus #62 or 64 to Stege (45min., 36kr). The **Møns Turistbureau,** Storeg. 2, is next to the bus stop in Stege. (☎55 86 04 00; www.moen-touristbureau.dk. Open June 15-Aug. M-F 9:30am-4:30pm, Sa 9am-6pm, Su 11am-1pm; Sept.-June 14 M-F 9:30am-4:30pm, Sa 9am-noon.) Stay at the lakeside **Youth Hostel (HI) ❷**, Langebjergvej 1. From mid-July to Aug., take the infrequent bus #632 to the campsite stop, backtrack, then take the first road on the right. From Sept. to mid-July, take bus #52 to Magleby and walk 2.5km left down the road. (☎55 81 20 30. Breakfast 45kr. Sheets 30-45kr. Reception daily 8am-noon and 4-8pm. Dorms 100kr; singles and doubles 280kr.)

ROSKILDE ☎46

Roskilde (pop. 53,000), in central Zealand, served as Denmark's capital when King Harald Bluetooth built the country's first Christian church here in AD 980. These days, Roskilde is famous for the ⊠**Roskilde Music Festival,** the largest outdoor concert in Northern Europe, where performers such as Coldplay, REM, U2, Bob Dylan, and Bob Marley have taken the stage. (www.roskilde-festival.dk. July 1-4, 2004.) The ornate sarcophagi of the red-brick ⊠**Roskilde Domkirke,** in Domkirkepl., house the remains of generations of Danish royalty. (☎35 16 24. Open Apr.-Sept. M-F 9am-4:45pm, Sa 9am-noon, Su 1-2pm; Oct.-Mar. Su 12:30-3:45pm, Tu-Sa 10am-3:45pm. 15kr, students 10kr. English tours mid-June to mid-Aug. M-F 11am and 2pm, Sa 11am, Su 2pm.) The **Viking Ship Museum,** Vindeboder 12, near Strandengen along the harbor, houses remnants of five ships sunk circa AD 1060 and salvaged in the late 1960s. From the tourist office, take the pleasant walk downhill through the park or take bus #607 (dir.: Boserup; free with train ticket). Book a ride on an authentic Viking ship, but be prepared to take an oar—conquest is no spectator sport. (☎30 02 00; www.vikingeskibsmuseet.dk. Museum open daily 9am-5pm. In summer 60kr, off-season 45kr. Boat trip 90kr, 50kr with museum ticket.)

Trains depart for Copenhagen (25-30min., every 15min., 52kr). The **tourist office**, Gullandsstr. 15, sells festival tickets and books rooms for a 25kr fee and a 10-15% deposit. From the train station, turn left on Jernbaneg., right on Allehelgansg., and left again on Bredg.; the office is at the corner of Bredg. and Gullandsstr. (☎31 65 65. Open mid-June to Aug. M-F 9am-6pm, Sa 10am-2pm; Apr. to mid-June M-F 9am-5pm, Sa 10am-1pm; Sept.-Mar. M-Th 9am-5pm, F 9am-4pm, Sa 10am-1pm.) The **Youth Hostel (HI) ❷**, Vindeboder 7, is on the harbor next to the Viking Museum shipyard. Book *far* in advance during the festival. (☎35 21 84; www.danhostel.dk/roskilde. Kitchen available. Breakfast 45kr. Sheets 40kr. Reception daily 8am-noon and 4-10pm. Dorms 100kr. Nonmembers add 30kr.) **Roskilde Camping ❶**, Baunehøjvej 7, is on the beach; take bus #603 (15kr) toward Veddelev to *Veddelev Byg*. (☎75 79 96. Reception daily 8am-9pm. Open Apr. to mid-Sept. 64kr per person.)

BORNHOLM

In an area ideal for bikers and nature-lovers, Bornholm's red-roofed cliffside villas may seem Mediterranean, but the flowers and half-timbered houses are undeniably Danish. The unique round churches (half the round churches in Denmark are in Bornholm) were both places of worship and fortresses for waiting out pirate attacks. The sandiest and longest **beaches** are at **Dueodde**, on the island's southern tip. For more info, check out www.bornholm.info.

⌘ TRANSPORTATION. Trains from Copenhagen to Ystad, Sweden are timed to meet the **ferry** from Ystad to Rønne, Bornholm's capital. (Train ☎70 13 14 15; 1¾hr., 5-6 per day; ferry 1½hr.; trip 205kr, under-26 180kr.) A cheaper option is the combo **bus**/ferry route (bus ☎56 95 18 66; 1½hr., 4-6 per day; ferry 1½hr.; trip 195/145kr.) Overnight ferries from Copenhagen to Rønne leave at 11:30pm and arrive in Rønne at 6:30am (224kr, add 76kr for a dorm-style bed). **Bornholmstrafikken** (Rønne ☎56 95 18 66; www.bornholm-ferries.dk) offers the combo train/ferry and bus/ferry routes. **Scandlines** operates ferries from Fährhafen Sassnitz in Germany. (☎+49 383 926 44 20. 3½hr., 1-2 per day, 90-130kr.) Bornholm has an efficient local BAT **bus** service. (☎56 95 21 21. 36-45kr, 24hr. pass 110kr.) Bus #7 makes a circuit of the entire island; it starts at Rønne and end at Hammershus, stopping at Bornholm's towns and attractions along the way. There are numerous well-marked cycling paths between all the major towns; pick up a guide at the tourist office in Rønne (40kr). The **bike** ride from Rønne to Sandvig is about 28km.

NO WORK, ALL PLAY

ROSKILDE ROCKS

In AD 800, Vikings put the small town of Roskilde on the map by sailing to continental Europe and annihilating the feudal order. Over a millennium larter, the tiny town is taking Europe by storm with its annual Roskilde Music Festival, again challenging any semblance of law and order.

Headliners Coldplay, Metallica, REM, U2, Bob Dylan, and Björk have all graced the enormous Orange Stage, but 70,000 international fans don't trek to Roskilde for only the big-name acts. Northern Europe's largest outdoor music festival is not just a concert; it's a week-long, Woodstock-esque musical experience. Although the festival technically begins on Thursday, the gates open four days earlier, offering revelers less hygiene and more hijinks. With five stages showcasing local and international bands, rhythm and communal atmosphere flow non-stop all week.

Attendees wear wrist bands in lieu of tickets, and the most devoted fans sport their bracelets year-round like badges of honor—those boasting 5 years' worth are offered free admission.

At the end of the seven days, unbathed, dehydrated, and sated music-lovers have new friends—and 358 days to recover.

Roskilde reconvenes July 1-4, 2004. For ticket Info, see www.roskilde-festival.dk.

RØNNE. Tiny but charming Rønne (pop. 14,000), on the southwest coast, is Bornholm's principal port of entry. The town serves mainly as an outpost for biking trips through the surrounding fields, forests, and beaches. Rent a **bike** from **Bornholms Cykeludlejning,** next door to the tourist office at Ndr. Kystvej 5. (☎56 95 13 59. Reserve ahead in July. 60kr per day. Open May-Sept. daily 7am-4pm and 8:30-9pm.) The **tourist office,** Ndr. Kystvej 3, books private rooms (140-195kr) for free. (☎56 95 95 00. Open June-Aug. M-Sa 9am-5pm, Su 10am-3pm; Aug.-Feb. M-F 9am-4pm; Mar.-May M-F 9am-4pm, Su 10am-4pm.) The **HI Youth Hostel ❸,** Arsenalvej 12, is in a wooded area near the coastline. From the ferry, walk 3min. down Snellemark to the red BAT terminal and take bus #23 or 24. (☎56 95 13 40. Breakfast 45kr. Kitchen available. Sheets 55kr. Reception daily 8am-noon and 4-5pm. Open mid-June to mid-Aug. Dorms 100kr. Nonmembers add 30kr.) **Galløkken Camping ❶,** Strandvejen 4, is near the city center and the beach. (☎56 95 23 20. Bikes 55kr per day. Reception 7:30am-noon and 2-9pm. Open mid-May to Aug. 58kr per person.) Get groceries at **Kvickly,** opposite the tourist office. (Open mid-June to late Aug. daily 9am-8pm; Sept. to early June M-F 9am-8pm, Sa 8am-5pm, Su 10am-4pm.)

SANDVIG AND ALLINGE. On the tip of the spectacular northern coast, the whitesand and rock beaches in these two small towns attract bikers and bathers. A few kilometers from central Allinge is **Hammershus,** northern Europe's largest castle ruin. Take bus #1, 2, or 7. Set in a field of waving grass, the whitewashed **Østerlars Rundkirke** is the largest of the island's four uniquely fortified round churches. Take bus #3 or 9 to *Østerlars Kirke.* Many pleasant trails originate in Sandvig; the rocky area around **Hammeren,** northeast of the town, is a 2hr. walk that can only be covered on foot. The **Nordbornholms Turistbureau,** Kirkeg. 4, in Allinge, finds rooms. (☎56 48 00 01. Open mid-June to mid-Aug. M-F 10am-5pm, Sa 10am-3pm; mid-Aug. to mid-June 10am-5pm, Sa 10am-noon.) Rent **bikes** at the **Sandvig Cykeludlejning,** Strandvejen 121. (☎56 48 00 60. 55kr per day. Open June-Aug. M-F 9am-4pm, Sa 9am-2pm, Su 10am-1pm.) Many local families rent rooms; look for signs on Strandvejen between Sandvig and Allinge. Just outside Sandvig is the lakeside **Sandvig Vandrerhjem (HI) ❸,** Hammershusvej 94. (☎56 48 03 62. Breakfast 45kr. Sheets 60kr. Reception daily 9-10am and 4-6pm. Open Apr.-Oct. Dorms 100kr; singles 250kr; doubles 350kr.) **Sandvig Familie Camping ❶,** Sandlinien 5, has sites on the sea. (☎56 48 04 47. Bikes 50kr per day, 200kr per week. Reception daily 8am-11pm. Open Apr.-Oct. 50kr per person, 15kr per tent.) **Riccos ❶,** Strandg. 8, a pleasant cafe near the sea, offers free **Internet** access. (Open 7am-10pm.)

FUNEN (FYN)

Situated between Zealand to the east and the Jutland Peninsula to the west, the island of Funen is Denmark's garden. This remote breadbasket is no longer isolated from the rest of Denmark—a bridge and tunnel now connect it to Zealand. Pick up maps (75kr) of the bike paths covering the island at Funen tourist offices.

ODENSE

Most tourists are drawn to Odense (OH-n-sa; pop. 185,000) by the legacy of Hans Christian Andersen and his fairytales. At **Hans Christian Andersen's Hus,** Hans Jensens Str. 37-45, you can learn about the great author's eccentricities, listen to his timeless children's tales, and follow his rags-to-riches rise to fame. From the tourist office, walk right on Vesterg., then turn left on Torveg. and right on Hans Jensens Str. (☎65 51 46 20. Museum open mid-June to Aug. daily 9am-7pm; Sept. to mid-June Su and Tu-Sa 10am-4pm. English performances W-Th 3pm. 40kr.) A few scraps of Andersen's own ugly-duckling childhood are on display at **H. C. Andersen's Barndomshjem** (Childhood Home), Munkemøllestr. 3-5. (☎66 14 88 14. Open mid-June to Aug. daily 10am-4pm; Sept. to mid-June Su and Tu-Sa 11am-3pm. 10kr.) At the **Carl Nielsen Museum,** Claus Bergs G. 11, listen to the works of the most famous Danish musician. (☎66 14 88 14. Open Su noon-4pm, Th-F 4-8pm. 15kr.) Walk down Vesterg. to the eclectic **Brandts Klædefabrik,** Brandts Passage 37 and 43, a former cloth mill that houses the **Museum of Photographic Art,** the **Graphic Arts Museum,** and a **contemporary art** gallery. (☎66 13 78 97. All open July-Aug. daily 10am-5pm; Sept.-June Su and Tu-Sa 10am-5pm. 25-30kr, combination ticket 50kr.)

Trains arrive from Copenhagen (1½hr., 197kr) and from Svendborg via Kværndrup (40min., 55kr). **Buses** depart from behind the train station. The **tourist office,** on Rådhuspl., books rooms for a 35kr fee and sells the **Odense Adventure Pass,** good for admission to museums, discounts on plays, and unlimited public transport (24hr. pass 110kr, 48hr. pass 150kr). From the train station, take Nørreg., which becomes Asylg., and turn left at the end on Vesterg.; it's on the right. (☎66 12 75 20; www.visitodense.com. Open June 15-Aug. M-F 9:30am-7pm, Sa 10am-5pm, Su 10am-4pm; Sept.-June 14 M-F 9:30am-4:30pm, Sa 10am-1pm.) The library in the station has free **Internet,** but you must reserve a slot in advance. (Open Apr.-Sept. M-Th 10am-7pm, F 10am-4pm, Sa 10am-2pm; Oct.-Mar. M-Th 10am-7pm, Sa-Su 10am-4pm.) Rent **bikes** next door to the station at **Rolsted Cykler.** (85kr per day, 300kr deposit. Open M-Th 10am-5:30pm, F 10am-7pm, Sa 10am-2pm.) The fabulous **Danhostel Odense City (HI) ❹** is attached to the station. (☎63 11 04 25. Kitchen available. Breakfast 45kr. Sheets 50kr. Laundry 40kr. Internet 10kr per 15min. Reception daily 8am-noon and 4-8pm. Call ahead. Dorms 115kr; singles 310-360kr; doubles 360-460kr; triples 420-460kr; quads 460kr. Nonmembers add 30kr.) To reach **DCU Camping ❷,** Odensevej 102, take bus #21, 22, or 23 (dir.: Højby) and ask the driver to drop you off. (☎66 11 47 02. Pool. Reception daily 7am-10pm. Open late Mar. to Sept. 58kr per person, 20kr per tent.) Get groceries at **Aktiv Super,** at the corner of Nørreg. and Skulkenborgg. (Open M-F 9am-7pm, Sa 9am-4pm.)

⚡ DAYTRIP FROM ODENSE: KVÆRNDRUP. Just 30min. south of Odense on the Svendborg rail line is Kværndrup, home to ▣**Egeskov Slot,** a stunning 16th-century castle that appears to float on the surrounding lake. Spend at least two hours in the magnificent Renaissance interior and grounds, which include a bamboo labyrinth and motorcycle museum. (Castle open July daily 10am-7pm, W until 11pm; May-June and Aug.-Sept. 10am-5pm. Grounds open July daily 10am-8pm; June and Aug. 10am-6pm; Apr.-May and Sept. 10am-5pm. Grounds, maze, and museums 75kr, with castle 130kr.) Take the Svendborg-bound **train** from Odense to Kværndrup; from the station, go right and continue to Bøjdenvej, the main road. Wait for bus #920 (every hr.; 18kr, free with connecting train ticket); or turn right and walk 2km through wheat fields to the castle. The **tourist office,** Egeskovg. 1, is up the street from the castle. (☎62 27 10 46. Open July daily noon-8pm; June and Aug. noon-6pm; Sept. and Apr.-May noon-5pm.)

SVENDBORG AND TÅSINGE

On Funen's southern coast, an hour from Odense by train, Svendborg (pop. 43,000) is a harbor town and a departure point for ferries to the south Funen islands. On the adjacent island of Tåsinge (pop. 6,000), the regal 17th-century **Valdemars Slot,** built by Christian IV for his son, boasts a yachting museum, Scandinavia's largest hunting museum, a toy museum, and a beach. (☎62 22 61 06. Open May-Aug. daily 10am-5pm; Sept. Su and Tu-Sa 10am-5pm; Apr. and Oct. Sa-Su 10am-5pm. Castle 60kr, combination ticket 110kr.)

Several **trains** from Odense to Svendborg are timed to meet the **ferry** (☎ 62 52 40 00) to Ærøskøbing; ferries depart behind the train station. The **tourist office**, on Centrum Pl., books ferries and rooms. From the train station, go left on Jernbaneg., then right on Brog., which becomes Gerritsg., and right on Kyseborgstr.; it's in the plaza on the right. (☎ 62 21 09 80. Open late June-Aug. M-F 9:30am-6pm, Sa 9:30am-3pm; Sept.-late June M-F 9:30am-5pm, Sa 9:30am-12:30pm.) To get from the station to the **Youth Hostel (HI)** ❷, Vesterg. 45, a five-star on the Danhostel scale, turn left on Jernbaneg. and walk with the coast to your left, then go right onto Valdemarsg., which becomes Vesterg. (☎ 62 21 66 99; dk@danhostel-svendborg.dk. Bikes 50kr per day. Kitchen available. Breakfast 45kr. Sheets 50kr. Laundry 30kr. Reception M-F 8am-8pm, Su 8am-noon and 4-8pm. Dorms 115kr; singles and doubles 375kr. Nonmembers add 30kr.) To get to **Carlsberg Camping** ❶, Sundbrovej 19, take bus #800, 801, or 910 from the ferry terminal to *Bregninge Tasinge*. (☎ 62 22 53 84; www.carlsbergcamping.dk. Reception daily 7:30am-10pm. Open Apr.-Sept. 59kr per person.) Pick up groceries at **Kvickly**, Gerritsg. 33. (Open M-F 9am-8pm, Sa 8am-5pm.) **Postal Code:** 5700.

ÆRØ

The wheat fields, harbors, and hamlets of Ærø (EH-ruh), a small island off the southern coast of Funen, quietly preserve an earlier era of Danish history. Cows, rather than real estate developers, lay claim to the beautiful land, and bikes are the ideal way to explore the Island's three towns, Ærøskøbing, Marstal, and Søby.

▐ TRANSPORTATION. Ferries (☎ 62 52 40 00) run between Ærøskøbing and Svendborg (1¼hr.; 6 per day; one-way 79kr, round-trip 132kr; buy tickets on board). From Mommark, on Jutland, you can sail to Søby (1hr.; 2-5 per day, Oct.-Mar. W-Su only; 85kr; call ahead), on Ærø's northwestern shore. **Bus #990** travels between Ærøskøbing, Marstal, and Søby (20kr, day pass 60kr).

ÆRØSKØBING. Due to economic stagnation followed by conservation efforts, the town of Ærøskøbing appears today almost as it did 200 years ago. Rosebushes, half-timbered houses, and a quaint town center attract German boaters and vacationing Danes. The **tourist office,** Vesterg. 1, opposite the ferry landing, books rooms for a 25kr fee. (☎ 62 52 13 00; www.arre.dk. Open mid-June to Aug. M-F 9am-5pm, Sa 9am-2pm, Su 9:30am-12:30pm; Sept. to mid-June M-F 9am-4pm, Sa 9:30am-12:30pm.) Rent **bikes** from the hostel or **Pilebækken Cykel & Servicestation,** Pilebæken 11. (☎ 62 52 11 10. 45kr per day.) To get to the **Youth Hostel (HI)** ❷, Smedevejen 15, turn left on Smedeg., which becomes Nørreg., Østerg., and finally Smedevejen. (☎ 62 52 10 44. Kitchen available. Breakfast 40kr. Sheets 40kr. Bikes 45kr per day. Reception daily 8am-noon and 4-8pm. Check-in 6pm. Open Apr.-Sept. Dorms 100kr; singles and doubles 260kr. Nonmembers add 30kr. No credit cards.) **Ærøskøbing Camping** ❶, Sygehusvejen 40b, is 10min. to the right along Sygehusvejen, off Vestre Allé as you leave the ferry. (☎ 62 52 18 54. Reception daily 8am-noon and 3-10pm. Open May-Sept. 54kr per person.) Stock up at **Netto,** across from the ferry landing. (Open M-F 9am-7pm, Sa 8am-5pm.) **Postal Code:** 5970.

JUTLAND (JYLLAND)

The Jutland peninsula, homeland of the Jutes who joined the Anglos and Saxons in the conquest of England, is Denmark's largest landmass. Beaches and campgrounds mark the area as prime summer vacation territory, while verdant hills, marshlands, and sparse forests add color and texture.

DENMARK

🌙 FERRIES TO ENGLAND, NORWAY, AND SWEDEN

From **Frederikshavn** (see p. 281), on the northern tip of Jutland, **Stena Line** ferries (☎96 20 02 00; www.stenaline.com) leave for Gothenburg, Sweden (2-3¼hr.; 100-125kr, 50% Scanrail discount) and Oslo, Norway (8½hr.; 145-255kr, with Scanrail 90kr). **Color Line** (☎99 56 20 00; www.colorline.com) sails to Larvik, Norway (6¼hr.; 180-410kr, students and seniors 50% discount). Color Line boats also go from Hirtshals, on the northern tip of Jutland, to Oslo (8-8½hr., 180-410kr) and Kristiansand, Norway (2½-4½hr., 160-350kr).

ÅRHUS

Århus (ORE-hoos; pop. 280,000), Denmark's second-largest city, bills itself as "the world's smallest big city." With small-town charm and a lively downtown, many find that this laid-back student and cultural center fits just right.

🚆📋 TRANSPORTATION AND PRACTICAL INFORMATION. Trains run from

Århus to: Aalborg (1¾hr., 2 per hr., 138kr); Copenhagen (3hr., 2 per hr., 273kr); Fredericia (1hr., 2 per hr., 105kr); and Frederikshavn (2½hr., every hr., 180kr). All major **buses** leave from the train station or from outside the tourist office. To get to the **tourist office,** exit the train station and go left across Banegardspl., then take the first right on Park Allé. They book private rooms (200-300kr) for a 25kr fee and sell the **Århus pass,** which includes unlimited public transit and admission to most museums and sights (1-day 97kr, 2-day 121kr). If you're not going to many museums, consider the **24hr. Tourist Ticket** (50kr), also available at the tourist office, which offers unlimited bus transportation. (☎89 40 67 00; www.visitaarhus.com. Open mid-June to early Sept. M-F 9:30am-6pm, Sa 9:30am-5pm, Su 9:30am-1pm; May to mid-June M-F 9:30am-5pm, Sa 10am-1pm; early Sept.-Apr. M-F 9am-4pm, Sa 10am-1pm.) The main **library,** on Vesterg. 55 in Mølleparken, has free **Internet** access. (Open May-Sept. M-Th 10am-7pm, F 10am-6pm, Sa 10am-2pm; Oct.-Apr. M 10am-10pm, Tu-Th 10am-8pm, F 10am-6pm, Sa 10am-3pm, Su noon-4pm.) After hours, try **Boomtown NetCafe,** Åboulevarden 21, along the canal. (☎89 41 39 30. Open Su-Th 10am-2am, F-Sa 10am-8am. 20kr per 30min., 30kr per hr.) The **post office,** Banegardspl. 1A, is next to the train station. **Postal Code:** 8000.

🛏️🍴 ACCOMMODATIONS AND FOOD. Popular with backpackers, **Århus City Sleep-In ❸,** Havneg. 20, is 10min. from the train station and in the middle of the city's nightlife. From the train station, follow Ryesg., which becomes Sønderg., all the way to the canal. Take the steps or elevator down to Åboulevarden, cross the canal, and turn right; at the end of the canal, turn left on Mindebrog., then left again on Havneg. (☎86 19 20 55; www.citysleep-in.dk. Bikes 50kr per day; deposit 200kr. Kitchen available. Breakfast 40kr. Sheets 40kr; deposit 30kr. Laundry 25kr. Key deposit 50kr. Internet 20kr per hr. Reception 24hr. Dorms 105kr; doubles 320-360kr. Credit card surcharge 4.75%.) **Hotel Guldsmeden ❺,** Guldsmedg. 40, has gorgeous rooms in the center of town. The annex in the back has the cheapest rooms. From the tourist office, continue along Park Allé, which becomes Immervad, and veer left onto Guldsmedg. at the intersection of Vesterg. (☎86 13 45 50; www.hotel-guldmeden.dk. Breakfast included. Reception daily 7am-midnight. Singles 495-895kr; doubles 745-995kr.) **Blommehaven Camping ❶,** Ørneredevej 35, is a camper's resort located in the Marselisborg forest south of the city, near the beach. In summer, take bus #19 from the station to the grounds; off-season, take bus #6 to Ilørhavevej. (☎86 27 02 07; info@blommehaven.dk. Reception daily 8am-noon and 2-10pm. Open Apr.-Aug. 62kr per person, 20kr per site. Add 80kr without camping card.) **Frederiksgade** has a few restaurants with all-you-can-eat buffets. Get groceries at **Netto,** in St. Knuds Torv. (Open M-F 9am-8pm, Sa 8am-5pm.)

🔳🔲 **SIGHTS AND ENTERTAINMENT.** The **Århus Kunstmuseum**, on Vennelyst-parken, houses modern Danish art. (☎86 13 52 55. Open Su and Tu-Sa 10am-5pm, W until 8pm. 40kr, students 30kr.) Just outside town is the **Moesgård Museum of Pre-history**, Moesgård Allé 20, which chronicles Århus's history from 4000 BC through the Viking age and displays the famous mummified ▓**Grauballe Man.** Take bus #6 from the train station to the end. (Open Apr.-Sept. daily 10am-5pm; Oct.-Mar. Su and Tu-Sa 10am-4pm. 45kr, students 35kr.) The **Prehistoric Trail** is a beautiful walk that leads from behind the museum to a sandy **beach** (3km). In summer, bus #19 (last bus 10:18pm) returns from the beach to the Århus station. West of the town center, the open-air **Den Gamle By**, Viborgvej 2, re-create traditional Danish life with actors in authentic garb and original (but relocated) Danish buildings. From the center, take bus #3, 14, 25, or 55. (☎86 12 31 88. Open June-Aug. daily 9am-6pm; off-season reduced hours. 75kr; students 60kr. Grounds free after hours.) The exquisite rose garden of **Marselisborg Slot**, Kongevejen 100, Queen Margrethe II's summer getaway, is open to the public. From the train station, take bus #1, 18, or 19. (Palace and rose gardens closed in July and whenever the Queen is in residence. Changing of the guard daily at noon when the Queen is in residence.) To get to **Tivoli Friheden**, Skovbrynet 1, a smaller version of the amusement park in Copen-hagen, take bus #4 or 19. (☎86 14 73 00; www.friheden.dk. Hours and dates vary, but usually open May to mid-Aug. 1-9pm. 35kr admission; unlimited rides 160kr.)

Århus hosts an acclaimed **jazz festival** (July 10-17, 2004; www.jazzfest.dk). The **Århus Festuge** (☎89 31 82 70; www.aarhusfestuge.dk), from the last week-end in August to early September, is a rollicking celebration of theater, dance, and music. Throughout the year, **Åboulevarden**, in the heart of town, hops with trendy cafes and bars. **Waxies**, Frederiksg. 16, is a popular pub with a young crowd. (Open Su-W 11am-2am, Th-Sa 11am-5am.)

🔁 **DAYTRIP FROM ÅRHUS: BILLUND.** Billund is best known as the home of ▓**Legoland**, an amusement park filled with spectacular sculptures made from over 50 million Lego pieces. "Lego" is an abbreviation of the Danish *leg godt* ("have fun playing"), and young and old will have no trouble doing just that. Don't miss the bone-rattling **Power Builder**, most intense ride in the park. (☎ 75 33 13 33; www.lego-land.com. Park open July to mid-Aug. daily 10am-9pm; June and late Aug. daily 10am-8pm; Apr.-May and Sept.-Oct. reduced hours. Day pass 170kr, under-13 150kr. Free entrance 30min. before rides close.) To get there, take the **train** from Århus to Vejle (45min, every hr.), then take **bus** #912 (dir.: Grinsted) to the park.

SILKEBORG AND RY

Closest to Jutland's wilderness, Silkeborg and Ry both offer a prime base for canoeing, biking, and hiking. Silkeborg (pop. 38,000) is a bit bigger with a bit less charm, but offers more conveniences. The **Silkeborg Museum** boasts the **Tollund Man**, a 2500-year-old body found preserved in a local bog. (Open May to late Oct. daily 10am-5pm; late Oct. to Apr. M-Tu and Th-F 10am-5pm, W and Sa-Su noon-4pm. 40kr.) **Trains** run from Silkeborg to Århus (2 per hr., 39kr) and Ry (2 per hr., 25kr). Visit the **tourist office** for more info on outdoor activities. (☎86 82 19 11; www.silkeborg.com. Open mid-June to Aug. M-F 9am-5pm, Sa 9am-3pm, Su 9:30am-12:30pm; Sept. to mid-June M-F 9am-4pm, Sa 9am-noon.) The **Silkeborg Van-drerhjem (HI) ❶** is near downtown and the water. (☎86 82 36 42. Breakfast 45kr. Sheets 40kr. Laundry. Reception daily 8am-noon and 4-8pm. Dorms June-Aug. only 75kr. Quads 440kr; 6-person rooms 660kr.)

Smaller and more charming, Ry (pop. 4,800) is an excellent, if less developed, base for exploration. Rent canoes from **Ry Kanofart**, Kyhnsvej 20, and bikes from **Ry Mosquito Cykel Center**, Skangerborgvej 19. (Kanofart ☎86 89 11 67. 60kr per hr., full-day 300kr. Open May-Aug. daily 9am-6pm. Cykel Center ☎86 89 14 91. Open M-Th

WHO LET THE BOGS OUT At the beginning of the Iron Age, one quarter of the area that is now Denmark was comprised of bog–an ominous no-man's-land where algae and mist devoured unsuspecting visitors. In these good ole days, these feared quagmires were revered as divine. Accordingly, the early Danes made human sacrifices to appease the bog. Unbeknownst to the Danish ancestors, all bogs contain a sugar compound called sphagnan, which turns skin into a leathery-type substance and can ultimately preserve entire bodies almost completely unscathed. Thus two men sacrificed 2500 years ago, both discovered in the 1950s, are so well-preserved that many of their internal organs are still intact. Visit the Grauballe Man in Århus and the Tollund Man in Silkeborg. Eerily, the bog also preserved the noose with which the Tollund Man was hung.

8am-5:30pm, F 8am-6pm, Sa 8am-noon.) The helpful **tourist office** sells maps, including one to **Himmelbjerget Tower,** one of Denmark's highest points. (☎86 89 34 22; www.visitry.com. Open July M-F 6:15am-4pm, Sa 10am-2pm; June and Aug. M-F 6:15am-4pm, Sa 10am-2pm; Sept.-May M-F 6:15am-4pm, Sa 10am-noon.)

FREDERICIA

Now known primarily as a major railway junction, Fredericia (pop. 49,000) was built between 1650 and 1657 by King Frederik III following his defeat in the Thirty Years War. Convinced the country needed better protection, Frederik outfitted the town with moated and cannon-strewn **ramparts.** In the Battle of Fredericia in 1849, the ramparts helped the Danes ward off enemy troops from the south with sweet vindication. For a great view, climb the **White Water Tower,** across the street from the tourist office. (Open late June to mid-Aug. daily 10am-4pm; May to late June and mid-Aug. to Sept. 11am-4pm. 10kr.)

Trains go to Århus (1¾hr., 105kr) and Copenhagen (2hr., 241kr). To get to the **tourist office,** Danmarksg. 2A, go left across the plaza, and then turn right on Vesterbrog, and right again on Danmarksport. (☎75 92 13 77; www.visitfredericia.dk. Open mid-June to Aug. M-F 9am-6pm, Sa 9am-2pm; Sept. to mid-June M-F 10am-5pm, Sa 10am-1pm.) The library, on the corner of Danmarksg. and Prinsesseg, has free **Internet** access. (Open M-Th 10am-7pm, F 10am-5pm, Sa 10am-2pm.) **Fredericia Vandrerhjem and Kursuscenter (HI) ❷,** Vestre Ringvej 98, is situated on a beautiful lake. From the station, go across the plaza, turn left on Vejlevej, go under the bridge, turn right on the first road past the lake, walk for 10min., then take the path on the right. (☎75 92 12 87; www.fredericia-danhostel.dk. Breakfast 45kr. Sheets 55kr. Reception daily 8am-noon and 4-8pm. Dorms 118kr; doubles 420-472kr. Credit card surcharge 4.75%.) **Postal Code:** 7000.

RIBE

Aware of their town's historic value, the government of Ribe (pop. 8,000) forged preservation laws in 1899 forcing residents to maintain the character of their houses and to live in them year-round. The result is a magnificently preserved medieval town, beautifully situated on the salt plains near Jutland's west coast. For a great view, climb the 248 steps through the clockwork and huge bells of the 12th-century **cathedral tower.** (☎75 42 06 19. Open July to mid-Aug. M-Sa 10am-5:30pm, Su noon-5:30pm; May-June and mid-Aug. to Sept. M-Sa 10am-5pm, Su noon-5pm; Apr. and Oct. M-Sa 11am-6pm, Su noon-4pm; Nov.-Mar. daily 11am-3pm. 12kr.) Next to the *Radhus,* **Von Støckens Plads,** a former debtor's prison, houses a small museum on medieval torture. (☎76 88 11 22. Open June-Aug. daily 1-3pm; May and Sept. M-F 1-3pm. 15kr.) Follow the **night watchman** on his rounds for an English and Danish tour of town beginning in the Torvet. (35min.; June-Aug. 8 and 10pm; May and Sept. 10pm. Free.) South of town, the open-air **Ribe Vikingcenter,** Lustrupvej 4, re-creates a Viking town, complete with a farm and a marketplace. (☎75 41 16 11. Open July-Aug. daily 11am-4:30pm; May-June and Sept. M-F 11am-4pm. 60kr.) Take bus #711 to the **Vadehavscentret** (Wadden Sea Center), Okholmvej 5 in Vestervedsted, which gives *Mandøbus* tours of the marshes on the nearby island of Mandø. (Sea Center ☎75 44 61 61. Open Apr.-Oct. daily 10am-5pm; Feb.-Mar. and Nov. 10am-4pm. 50kr. Tours ☎75 44 51 07. May-Sept. daily. 50kr.)

    Trains run to Bramming (25min., every hr., 30kr) and Esbjerg (40min., every hr., 50kr). The **tourist office,** Torvet 3, books rooms for a 20kr fee. From the train station, walk down Dagmarsg.; it's on the right in the main square. (☎75 42 15 00; www.ribe.dk. Open July-Aug. M-F 9:30am-5:30pm, Sa 10am-5pm, Su 10am-2pm; off-season reduced hours.) Access the **Internet** at **Gamer's Gateway,** Saltg. 20. (☎76 88 03 37. 25kr per hr. Open M-Tu 3pm-midnight, W-Su noon-midnight.) **Ribe Vandrerhjem (HI) ❶,** Sct. Pedersg. 16, offers **bike** rentals (60kr per day). From the station, cross the Viking Museum parking lot, bear right, walk down Sct. Nicolajg. to the end, then turn right on Saltg. and immediately left on Sct. Petersg. (☎75 42 06 20. Breakfast 45kr. Sheets 42kr. Laundry 45kr. Reception daily 8am-noon and 4-6pm. Open Feb.-Nov. Dorms 90kr; singles 250kr; doubles 325kr. Credit card surcharge 4%.) **Ribe Camping ❶,** Farupvej 2, is 1.5km from the town center. Take bus #715 (every 1½hr.) from the station to *Gredstedbro.* (☎75 41 07 77. 65kr per person; 2-person cabins 325kr.) **Seminarievej** is home to a number of supermarkets. Restaurants cluster around the cathedral. **Postal Code:** 6760.

VIBORG

Sights cluster around the cobblestone center of this well-preserved provincial town (pop. 30,000). The mid-19th-century granite **Viborg Cathedral,** Sct. Mogensg. 4, is covered with spectacular, colorful frescoes. (Open June-Aug. M-Sa 10am-5pm, Su noon-5pm; Apr.-May and Sept. M-Sa 11am-4pm, Su noon-4pm; Oct.-Mar. M-Sa 11am-3pm, Su noon-3pm.) A short trip outside of Viborg is the ◪**Mønsted Kalkgruber,** Kalkvaerksvej 8, a beautiful limestone cave shaped by subterranean rivers. Though there is no direct public transportation, the visit is worth the trek. Take bus #28 (every 1-2hr., 20kr) from Viborg to Mønsted and follow the signs for 1.5km. (Open daily Apr.-Oct. 10am-5pm. 45kr.)

    Trains run to Århus (1½hr., every hr., 97kr.). To get to the **tourist office,** Nytorv 9, from the station, go straight across the rotary and onto Jernebaneg., turn right onto Sct. Mathiasg., go through part of the shopping area, and turn left into the main square. (☎87 25 30 75. Open mid-June to Aug. M-F 9am-5pm, Sa 9am-2pm; mid-May to mid-June M-F 9am-5pm, Sa 9:30am-12:30pm; Sept. to mid-May M-F 9am-4pm, Sa 9:30am-12:30pm.) Alongside a lake lie the **Youth Hostel (HI) and Viborg Sø Camping ❷,** Vinkelvej 36. Take bus #707 from the station to *Vinkelvej* and continue walking along the road for 10min. (Hostel ☎86 67 17 81; viborg@danhostel.dk. Kitchen available. Breakfast 45kr. Laundry. Reception daily 7:30am-noon and 2-10pm. Dorms 100kr. Camping ☎86 67 13 11; viborg@dcu.dk.) Pick up groceries at **Netto** on Vesterbrog. (Open M-F 9am-8pm, Sa 8am-5pm.)

AALBORG

Modern Aalborg (OLE-borg; pop. 160,000) is a laid-back student haven located near the remains of the earliest known Viking settlement. **Lindholm Høje,** Vendilavej 11, is the site of 700 ancient Viking graves and a museum detailing life in Viking times. Take bus #6 or 25 (13kr) from outside the tourist office. (☎96 31 04 28. Graves open 24hr. Museum open mid-Apr. to Oct. daily 10am-5pm; Nov. to mid-Apr. M and W-Sa 10am-5pm, Tu 10am-4pm, Su 11am-4pm. 30kr, students 15kr.) The **Budolfi Church,** on Alg., has a brilliantly colored interior. From the tourist office, turn left onto Østeråg. and right on Alg. (Open May-Sept. M-F 9am-4pm, Sa 9am-2pm; Oct.-Apr. M-F 9am-3pm, Sa 9am-noon.) At the corner of Alg. and Molleg., an elevator descends to the ruins of the **Franciscan Friary.** (Open in summer daily 10am-5pm; off-season Su and Tu-Sa 10am-5pm. 20kr.) For a more exhilarating drop, head to the roller coasters at **Tivoliland,** on Karolinelundsvej, a smaller cousin of Copenhagen's famous amusement park. (Open July-Aug. daily 10am-10pm; Sept. and Apr. daily noon-8pm; May-June daily noon-9pm. Entrance 50kr. Rides 10-40kr.) Centuries ago, untamed Aalborg was beyond the northern reach of the king's soldiers and considered "north of law and justice"—at night, watch Aalborg's students carry on the city's wild past in the bars along **Jomfru Ane Gade.**

Trains arrive from Århus (1¾hr., every hr., 140kr) and Copenhagen (5hr., 2 per hr., 300kr). From the station, cross J.F.K. Pl. and turn left on Boulevarden, which becomes Østeråg., to find the **tourist office,** Østeråg. 8. (☎98 12 60 22; www.visitaalborg.com. Open July M-F 9am-5:30pm, Sa 10am-4pm; late June and Aug. M-F 9am-5:30pm, Sa 10am-1pm; Sept. to mid-June M-F 9am-4:30pm, Sa 10am-1pm.) The library has free **Internet** access. (☎99 31 44 00. Open June-Aug. M-F 10am-8pm, Sa 10am-2pm; Sept.-May M-F 10am-8pm, Sa 10am-3pm.) After hours, try **Net City,** Nytorv 13a. (Open Su-Th 11am-3am, F-Sa 11am-8am. 20kr per hour.) **Aalborg Vandrerhjem and Camping (HI) ❷,** Skydebanevej 50, has private cabins and hostel dorms alongside a beautiful fjord. Take bus #8 (dir.: Fjordparken) right to the door, or take bus #2 or 9 and walk. (☎98 11 60 44. Laundry 20kr. Reception daily mid-June to mid-Aug. 7:30am-11pm; mid-Jan. to mid-June and mid-Aug. to mid-Dec. 8am-noon and 4-9pm. Dorms 85-100kr; singles 250-398kr; doubles 325-398kr. Camping 49kr.) **Ved Stranden** is lined with cheap eateries. **Postal Code:** 9000.

FREDERIKSHAVN

Despite noble efforts to woo tourists with its hospitality, Frederikshavn (pop. 35,000) is best known for its **ferry** links (p. 277). The **tourist office,** Skandia Torv 1, is inside the Stena Line terminal south of the rail station. (☎98 42 32 66; www.frederikshavn.dk. Open July to mid-Aug. M-Sa 8:30am-7pm, Su 8:30am-5pm; June and late Aug. daily 8:30am-5pm; Sept.-May M-F 9am-4pm, Sa 11am-2pm.) From the tourist office, walk left to reach the bus and train stations. To get from the station to the **Youth Hostel (HI) ❶,** Buhlsvej 6, walk right on Skipperg. for 10min., then turn left onto Norreg., and follow the signs. (☎98 42 14 75; www.danhostel.dk/frederikshavn. Reception in summer daily 8am-noon and 4-9pm. Call ahead. Closed Jan. Dorms 70-90kr; singles 150-200kr; doubles 210-270kr.) **Postal Code:** 9900.

SKAGEN

Perched on Denmark's northernmost tip, sunny Skagen (SKAY-en; pop. 10,000) is a beautiful summer retreat amid long stretches of sea and white sand dunes. With houses painted in vibrant "Skagen yellow" and roofs covered in red tiles with white edges—supposedly decorated to welcome local fisherman home from sea—Skagen is a colorful and pleasant vacation spot. In nearby **Grenen,** the powerful currents of the North and Baltic Seas violently collide. Stand with one foot in each ocean, but don't try to swim in these dangerous waters; every year people are carried out to sea. To get to Grenen, take bus #99 or 79 from the Skagen station to *Gammel* (12kr) or walk 3km down Fyrvej; turn left out of the train station and bear left when the road forks. About 13km south of Skagen is the spectacular and enormous **Råberg Mile** (MEE-lay; sand dune), formed by a 16th-century storm. The vast faux-desert migrates 15m east each year. Take bus #79 or the train from Skagen to *Hulsig,* then walk along Kandestedvej. From here, you can swim along 60km of **beaches.** Skagen has a large annual **music festival** the last weekend in June.

Nordjyllands Trafikselskab (☎98 44 21 33) runs **buses** and **trains** to Frederikshavn (1hr.; 42kr, with Scanrail 21kr). Biking is by far the best way to experience Skagen's charm, including Grenen and the Råberg Mile; rent **bikes** at **Skagen Cykeludlejning**, Banegardspl., next to the bus station. (☎98 44 10 70. 5kr per day. 200kr deposit. Open daily 8am-8pm.) The **tourist office** is in the station. (☎98 44 13 77; www.skagen.dk. Open July-Aug. M-Sa 9am-6pm, Su 10am-4pm; Sept.-May M 9am-5pm, Tu-Th 9am-4pm, F 9am-3pm, Sa 10am-1pm; June M-Sa 9am-5pm, Su 10am-6pm.) The only **Internet** access is at the Skagen library, Sct. Laurentii Vej 23. (Free. Open M and Th 10am-6pm; Tu-W and F 1-6pm, Sa 10am-1pm.) The **Skagen Ny Vandrerhjem ❷**, Rolighedsvej 2, is popular among vacationing Danish families. From the station, turn right on Chr. X's Vej, which becomes Frederikshavnvej, then left on Rolighedsvej. (☎98 44 22 00; www.danhostelnord.dk/skagen. Breakfast 45kr. Kitchen available. Sheets 50kr. Reception daily 9am-noon and 4-6pm. Open Mar.-Nov. Dorms 115kr; singles 250-400kr; doubles 300-500kr. No credit cards.) Bus #79 passes several **campgrounds**. Get groceries at **Fakta**, Chr. X's Vej.

FRANCE

The French celebrate the senses like no one else: The vineyards of Bordeaux, the savory dishes of Dijon, the sun-soaked shores of the Riviera, and the crisp air of the Alps combine for an exhilarating experience. France welcomes over 70 million visitors to its cities, chateaux, mountains, and beaches each year, making it the most popular tourist destination in the world. Yet to the French, it is only natural that outsiders should flock to their beloved homeland, so steeped in history, rich in art and architecture, and magnificently endowed with diverse landscapes. The fruits of France include the rich literature of Hugo, Proust, and Camus; the visionary art of Rodin, Matisse, and Monet; and the philosophical insight of Voltaire, Sartre, and Derrida. From the ambition of Napoleon to the birth of existentialism and postmodernism, the French occupied the driver's seat of history for many centuries. While France may no longer control the course of world events, it nonetheless remains among the most influential forces in Western history.

LIFE AND TIMES

HISTORY

FROM GAULS TO GOTHS. The graffiti-filled caves of the **Dordogne Valley** (p. 347) and huge stone monuments at **Carnac** were admired by the Celtic **Gauls**, who arrived from the east around 600 BC to trade with Greek colonists settling **Marseilles** (p. 359). Fierce resistance from France's northern Gauls kept the Romans out of their territory until **Julius Caesar**'s victory at Alesia in 52 BC. When Rome fell in AD 476, the Gothic tribes plundered and passed on, leaving

SUGGESTED ITINERARIES

THREE DAYS Don't even think of leaving **Paris, the City of Light** (p. 293). Explore the shops and cafes of the **Latin Quarter**, then cross the **Seine** to reach **Ile de la Cité** to admire **Sainte Chapelle.** Visit the wacky **Centre National d'Art et de Culture Georges Pompidou** before seeing a hotspot of 1789, the **Bastille.** Then swing through **Marais** for food and fun. The next day, stroll down the **Champs-Elysées,** starting at the **Arc de Triomphe,** meander through the **Jardin des Tuileries,** and over the Seine to the **Musée d'Orsay.** Peruse part of the **Louvre** the next morning, then head out for an afternoon at **Versailles.**

ONE WEEK After three days in **Paris,** chug to **Tours** (1 day; p. 343) a great base for exploring explore the **chateaux** of the **Loire Valley** (1 day; p. 341), especially **Chenonceau.** Head to **Rennes** for medieval sights and modern nightlife (1 day; p. 337) before a trip to the dazzling island of **Mont-St-Michel** (1 day; p. 336.)

BEST OF FRANCE, THREE WEEKS Whirl through the **Loire Valley** (3 days), before taking the train to the wine country of **Bordeaux** (2 days; p. 347). Check out **Toulouse** (2 days; p. 352) before sailing through **Avignon** (p. 356), **Aix-en-Provence** (p. 359), and **Nimes** (p. 355) in sunny **Provence** (3 days; p. 355). Let loose your wild side in **Marseilles** and **Nice** (3 days; p. 369), then show off your tan in the **Alps** (p. 383), near **Chamonix** (2 days; p. 385). Party in **Lyon** (2 days; p. 387); and eat your fill in **Dijon** (1 day; p. 396). Experience France with a little German flavor in **Strasbourg** (2 days; p. 397) before returning to Paris via the **Champagne** region (p. 403), visiting the caves in **Reims** (p. 403).

the **Franks** in control. The Frankish king **Clovis** founded the Merovingian dynasty and was baptized a Christian in 507. His empire was succeeded by the Carolingian dynasty of **Charlemagne,** whose **Holy Roman Empire** expanded into Germany, Austria, and Switzerland. Territorial squabbles following the king's death were resolved in 843 with the **Treaty of Verdun.**

FRANCE AND ENGLAND DUKE IT OUT. In the wake of the Carolingians, the noble-elected **Hugh Capet** quickly consolidated power. When his distant descendant, Louis VII's ex-queen, **Eleanor of Aquitaine,** married into the Plantagenet dynasty in the 12th century, a broad swath of land stretching from the Channel to the Pyrenees became English territory. This opened the door to England's **Edward III's** claim to the French throne, triggering the **Hundred Years' War** in 1328. Defeat was near as England crowned **Henry VI** king of France 90 years later, but salvation took the form of a 17-year-old peasant girl, **Jeanne d'Arc** (Joan of Arc). Leading the French army, she won a string of victories before her betrayal; as she burned at the stake in **Rouen** (p. 334), the tide of war swept the English from the continent.

HUGUENOT GETTING ALONG. Fervor and violence made strange bedfellows in the Middle Ages and Renaissance. **Pope Innocent II,** hoping to wrest Jerusalem from the Saracens, proclaimed the first Crusade from **Clermont.** Thousands flocked to take the cross, swayed by the promise of salvation and the probability of plunder. Though few Crusades had any military success, exposure to the advanced civilizations of the East and a revival of international trade helped stir Europe from her intellectual slumber. In the 16th century, religious conflict between **Huguenots** (French Protestants) and **Catholics** initiated the **Wars of Religion.** When the fervently Catholic **Catherine de Médici** claimed the throne, she orchestrated a marriage between her daughter and Huguenot **Henri de Navarre** in 1572. What appeared a peaceful political move became the **St. Bartholomew's Day Massacre,** a murder spree that slaughtered 2000 Huguenots. Henri survived, converted to Catholicism, and ascended the throne as the first **Bourbon** monarch. In 1598 the **Edict of Nantes** granted tolerance for Protestants and quelled religious warfare for a century.

BOURBONS ON THE ROCKS. The Bourbon dynasty peaked in the 17th century as **Louis XIII's** ruthless minister, **Cardinal Richelieu,** consolidated power for the monarchy and created the centralized, bureaucratic administration characteristic of France to this day. The king was succeeded by five-year-old **Louis XIV** who, when he came of age, proclaimed himself the **Sun King** and took the motto *"l'état, c'est moi"* ("I am the state"). He brought the nobility to the extravagant palace of **Versailles** (p. 332) to keep watch over them and avoid any unpleasant uprisings, yet the growing resentment of the monarchy could not be avoided. In 1789 **Louis XVI** called a meeting of the **Estates General** from the three classes of society: Aristocrats, clergy, and the soon-to-be-revolutionary **Third Estate.** A Parisian mob, angered by high bread prices, stormed the **Bastille** on July 14th, and a frenzy of destruction engulfed the nation as peasants burned records of their debts. As the **First Republic** replaced the abolished monarchy, **Maximilien Robespierre** took over the Convention and guillotined the King and his cake-savoring Queen, **Marie-Antoinette.** The Revolution had taken a radical turn. Robespierre leveraged his influence into the **Reign of Terror,** executing rivals before falling to the guillotine himself in 1794. The terror was over and power was entrusted to a five-man **Directory.**

THE LITTLE DICTATOR. Meanwhile, war continued as a young Corsican general, **Napoleon Bonaparte,** swept through northern Italy and into Austria. Riding a wave of public support, he deposed the Directory, ultimately crowning himself **Emperor** in 1804. After a disastrous invasion of Russia, Napoleon lost the support of a war-weary nation; in return for abdicating in 1814, he was given the Mediterranean island of **Elba.** The monarchy was reinstated under **Louis XVIII,** brother of his headless predecessor. The story has a final twist: Napoleon landed with an army at Cannes on March 26th, 1815, marching north as the king fled to England. The ensuing **Hundred Days' War** ended on the field at **Waterloo** in Flanders, Belgium, where the combined Prussian and British forces finally triumphed in a campaign marked by miscalculation on both sides. Napoleon was banished to remote **St. Helena** in the south Atlantic, where he died in 1821. Today, Napoleon is popularly regarded as a hero, and thousands pay their respects in his hometown of **Ajaccio** (p. 381).

WAR AND PEACE, AND MORE WAR. Fifty years of revolution and instability left France with the **Third Republic.** Troubled by the shift in the European power balance from Germany's 1871 unification, a series of treaties forged the **Triple Entente** among France, Britain, and Russia to counter the **Triple Alliance** of Germany, Italy, and the Austro-Hungarian Empire. When **World War I** erupted in 1914, German armies swarmed to France, but a stalemate soon developed as the opposing armies dug trenches along the length of the country. The withdrawal of newly revolutionary Russia in 1917 was offset by the entry of the US, and victory for the West came in 1918. Devastated by four years of fighting and 1.3 million casualties, France won crippling reparations from Germany; these and accompanying humiliations were often invoked by **Adolf Hitler** in his rise to power.

FRANCE

The 1930s found France ill-equipped to deal with Hitler's mobilization across the Rhine. When **World War II** began with Germany's 1939 invasion of Poland, France declared war in response. In May 1940, Germany bypassed the **Maginot Line**, a string of fortresses along the Franco-German border, invading from the north through Belgium and capturing the country by June. With the north under German occupation, a puppet state in the south ruled from **Vichy**. Those that escaped joined the French government-in-exile under **General Charles de Gaulle**. At his insistence, French troops led the **liberation of Paris** on August 25th, 1944.

FOURTH REPUBLIC AND POST-COLONIAL FRANCE. De Gaulle's **Fourth Republic** was proclaimed in 1944, leading to female suffrage and nationalized energy companies. When he quit in 1946, the Fourth lacked a strong replacement, and the next 14 years saw 25 governments. The end of the war also signaled the end of France's 19th-century **colonial empire**. The 1950s witnessed the systematic dismantling of remaining colonies, despite de Gaulle's return to power. In 1962, with a new **constitution** in hand, the nation declared itself the **Fifth Republic.** In May 1968, what started as a student protest grew into a full-scale revolt as 10 million state workers went on strike in support of social reform. The government responded by deploying tank and commando units, and things looked to be heading for revolution yet again. The aging General had lost his magic touch, and he resigned following a referendum defeat in 1969.

THE 1980S AND BEYOND. After de Gaulle's exit, France adopted a less assertive foreign policy. In 1981, Socialist **François Mitterrand** assumed the presidency and the Socialists gained a majority in the Assemblée Nationale. Despite broad social programs created early in the administration, the political collapse of the left forced compromise with the right, and Mitterrand had to appoint the conservative **Jacques Chirac** Prime Minister. **Jean-Marie Le Pen** formed the **Front National (FN)** on an anti-immigration platform to capitalize on blaming France's unemployment woes on foreigners. Meanwhile, in an unprecedented power-sharing relationship known as "cohabitation," Mitterrand withdrew to control foreign affairs, leaving Chirac domestic power. In 1995, Mitterrand chose not to seek reelection, and Chirac was elected president. Facing domestic and international pressure, he was forced to accept his former rival, Socialist **Lionel Jospin,** as Prime Minister in 1998.

Since the 1991 creation of the **European Union** (EU), the French have feared the loss of their national character and autonomy. The **Schengen Agreement** of 1995 created a six-nation zone without border controls, 1999 saw the extension of this zone to the entire EU (barring the UK, Ireland, and Denmark), and 2002 witnessed the birth of the **euro** as the only European legal tender.

TODAY

Facing an increasingly global society, France continues to negotiate the tension between tradition and modernity. Immigration policy remains a prominent issue, with national identity, migrant incorporation and terrorism all factoring into the debate. The 2002 presidential elections shocked the world when far-right nationalist **Jean-Marie Le Pen** edged out Prime Minister Lionel Jospin in the preliminary elections. He was subsequently defeated by Jacques Chirac in an 82% landslide amidst waves of protests pertaining to Le Pen's heavily anti-immigration policies, reputed racism and dismissive remarks about the Holocaust. Still, Le Pen's strong initial showing reflects the continuing weight of the immigration issue. Gay rights have also been a prominent debate in recent years. In 1999, France became the first traditionally Catholic country to legally recognize homosexual unions. The **Civil Solidarity Pact,** known by its acronym, PACS, was designed to extend to homosexual and unmarried heterosexual couples greater welfare, tax, and inheritance rights. While PACS has become so common a term in popular society that it has gained its own noun (*"pacser"*) and adjective (*"pacsé"*), it is has faced a number of detractors. Conservatives seek to keep PACS a strictly legal term, as gay marriage is still a concept unwelcome to many. Gay activists are currently struggling to attain equal rights to adoption and reproductive technologies. In foreign policy, France and Germany's opposition to US-led military action in Iraq made headlines in 2003, causing a rift in their relationship that American President George W. Bush and Jacques Chirac have recently attempted to mend.

THE ARTS

LITERATURE AND PHILOSOPHY

During the 13th century, popular satirical stories called **fabliaux** celebrated the bawdy with tales of cuckolded husbands, saucy wives, and shrewd peasants. **Calvin**'s humanist treaties criticized the Catholic Church and opened the road to the ill-fated Protestant Reformation in France. In his 1637 *Discourse on Method*, **René Descartes** proved his own existence with the catchy deduction, "I think, therefore I am." **La Fontaine**'s *Fables* and **Charles Perrault**'s *Fairy Tales of Mother Goose* explored right and wrong in more didactic ways. **Molière,** the era's comic relief, satirized the social pretensions of his age, and his actors initiated the great **Comédie Française.** The Enlightenment in France was informed by advances in the sciences and aimed at the promotion of reason and tolerance in an often backward and bigoted world. **Denis Diderot**'s *Encylopédie* (1752-1780) took on no smaller ambition than to record the entire body of human knowledge. **Voltaire** gained fame with his satire *Candide* (1758), a refutation of the claim that "all is for the best in the best of all possible worlds." Voltaire's witticisms paled in comparison with **Jean-Jacques Rousseau**'s *Confessions* (1769), which instructed readers to abandon society altogether rather than remaining in a corrupt world. The 19th century saw an emotional reaction against Enlightenment rationality; great novelists like **Stendhal** (*The Red and the Black)* and **Balzac** (*La Comédie Humaine*) penned their masterpieces, but it was **Victor Hugo** who dominated the **Romantic** age with his *The Hunchback of Notre Dame* (1831) .The decadence and social snobbery of the turn of the century was captured by **Marcel Proust** in the seven volumes of *Remembrance of Things Past.* **Jean-Paul Sartre** dominated France's intelligentsia in the years following WWII; his philosophy of **Existentialism** held that life in itself was meaningless–only by committing yourself to a cause could existence take on a purpose. While Sartre worked under censorship in occupied Paris, Algerian-born **Albert Camus** edited the Résistance newspaper *Combat.* He achieved fame with his debut novel *The Outsider* (1942), in which a dispassionate social misfit is condemned to death for murder. Existentialist and feminist **Simone de Beauvoir** made waves with *The Second Sex* (1949), an essay attacking the myth of femininity. Its famous statement, "One is not born, but becomes a woman" inspired a generation of second-wave **feminism** in the 1950s, 1960s, and 1970s. In turn, writers like **Marguerite Duras** (*The Lover*) explored gender identity, challenged Freudian "penis envy," and sparked feminist movements in France and abroad.

THE VISUAL ARTS

ARCHITECTURE. Long before the arrival of the "civilizing" Greeks and Romans, Frenchmen were making their own impressive buildings. The prehistoric murals of **Lascaux** (p. 346) and **Les Eyzies-de-Tayac** (p. 347) testify to the presence of ancient and well-established peoples. No such monuments stand to the ancient Gauls, whose legacy was swept away by Roman conquerors. Rome's leavings are most visible in the arena and temple at **Nîmes** (p. 355). Romanesque churches, like the Basilique St-Sernin in **Toulouse** (p. 352), were designed to accommodate large crowds of worshippers and pilgrims, while the monastery of **Mont St. Michel** (p. 336) provided a secluded religious haven. Louis XIV commissioned the world's largest royal residence, the exorbitantly beautiful palace **Versailles** (p. 332); full of crystal, mirrors, and gold, and surrounded by formal gardens, it is the pinnacle of the Baroque style. Engineering came onto the architectural scene in the latter part of the 19th century, as Gustave Eiffel created the **Eiffel tower** (p. 314), now the best-loved landmark in the country. Charles-Edouard Jeanneret, better known as **Le Corbusier**, was the interwar pioneer in reinforced concrete that dominated much of the rebuilding effort. In the 1980s, Paris became the hub of Mitterrand's 15-billion-franc endeavor known as the **Grands Projets:** The construction of the Musée d'Orsay, the Parc de la Villette, the Institut du Monde Arabe, the Opéra at the Bastille, and I.M. Pei's glass pyramid at the Louvre.

FILM. **François Truffaut's** *The 400 Blows* (1959) and *Jules and Jim* (1961) paved the way for the New Wave movement that dominated French cinema though the 1970s. Recently, the *Three Colors* trilogy (1993-94), *Manon of the Spring* (1987), and *Goodbye Children* (1987) have moved movie-goers around the world. Actor **Gérard Depardieu** (*Cyrano de Bergerac*; 1990, *My Father the Hero*, 1993) is renowned for roles both serious and comic, but **Jean Reno** has had more luck making the transition into Hollywood following the success of **Luc Besson's** *The Professional* (1994), *Fifth Element* (1997), and *Taxi* (1998). On the opposite end of the spectrum from the *belle de jour* fare is the recent spate of **cinéma beur,** second-generation North Africans' brutally honest documentation of life in the HLMs (municipal housing) of suburban Paris. These grafitti-decor films, such as **Mathieu Kassovitz's** *The Hatred* (1995), confront the traumas of urban racism. **Claire Denis's** *Chocolate* (1988) gives a voice to France's tumultuous history of colonialism. Art cinema continues to prosper under **Marcel Hanoun** (*Noise of Love and War*, 1997) and **Jacques Doillon** (*Ponette*, 1997), while the French flock to comedies like **Jean-Marie Poiré's** *The Visitors* (1992). Most recently, the 1999 film *The Taste of Others* has made waves on both sides of the Atlantic, winning a César (French Oscar), several film festival awards, and a nomination for a 2000 Best Foreign Film Oscar.

ON THE CANVAS. France's surviving **medieval art** would instruct the average illiterate 12th- and 13th-century churchgoer on religious themes; stained glass and intricate stone facades, like those at **Chartres** (p. 333), **Reims** (p. 403), and **Sainte-Chapelle** in Paris, served as large reproductions of the Bible. The 11th-century **Bayeux tapestry** (p. 335) unravels a 70-meter-long narrative of the Battle of Hastings. In 1515, **Leonardo da Vinci** trekked up from Florence bearing the smiling **Mona Lisa** in tow; his final home and a number of his sketches can be seen in **Amboise** (p. 343). The French Revolution inspired heroic scenes from its own time; **Jacques-Louis David's** *Death of Marat* paid gory tribute to the Revolutionary leader, while the paintings such as **Eugène Delacroix's** *Liberty Leading the People* (1830) shocked the salons of the 1820s and 1830s. **Edouard Manet** facilitated the transition to **Impressionism** by flattening the fine shading and sharp perspectives of academic art and turning his focus to texture and color; his portrait of a prostitute in *Olympia* scandalized his colleagues. **Claude Monet, Camille Pissarro,** and **Pierre-Auguste Renoir** began to explore Impressionist techniques in the 1860s. Monet's garden at **Giverny** (p. 333), which inspired his monumental *Waterlilies* series, remains a popular daytrip from Paris. Post-Impressionist **Paul Cézanne** created still-lifes, portraits, and geometric landscapes using bold, geometric blocks of color. **Georges Seurat** took fragmentation a step further with **Pointillism:** Thousands of tiny dots merging to form a coherent picture. Dutchman **Vincent van Gogh** migrated to the south of France in search of new light, color, and imagery; the poverty and mental illness that plagued him throughout his life are reflected in his work. Similarly tortured in his art and life, **Henri de Toulouse-Lautrec**'s vibrant posters capture the brilliant and lascivious nightlife of 19th-century Paris. The rich colors and thick contours of **Henri Matisse** anticipated and rivaled Spanish-born **Pablo Picasso**, who developed **Cubism**, a technique of composing the canvas with shaded planes. By reducing everyday objects—fruits, glasses, vases, newspapers—Picasso became arguably the greatest artist of the 20th century, constantly innovating and breaking new ground; his career is chronicled at the **Musée Picasso** in **Paris** (p. 320) and at the beautiful seaside **Musée Picasso** in **Antibes** (p. 368). The loss and disillusionment that pervaded Europe after WWI prompted artists to reject the bourgeois culture that began the war. **Surrealism** and absurdity dominated 20th-century experiments in photography, installation, video, and sculpture; these can be seen in the collections and exhibitions of the **Centre Pompidou** (p. 320) in **Paris**.

ESSENTIALS

WHEN TO GO

In July, Paris starts to shrink; by August it is devoid of Parisians, animated only by tourists and the pickpockets who prey on them. The French Riviera fills with Anglophones from June to September. On the other hand, the rest of France teems with Frenchmen during these months, especially along the Atlantic coast. Early summer and autumn are the best times to visit Paris—the city has warmed up but not completely emptied out. The north and west have cool winters and mild summers, while the less-crowded center and east have a more continental climate. From December to February, the Alps provide some of the best skiing in the world, while the Pyrenees offer a calmer, if less climatically dependable, alternative.

DOCUMENTS AND FORMALITIES

VISAS. For stays shorter than 90 days, only citizens of South Africa need a short-stay visa (30-day visa costs ZAR217; 90-day ZAR260). For stays longer than 90 days, all non-EU citizens need long-stay visas (€95).

EMBASSIES. Foreign embassies in France are in Paris (p. 296). For French embassies at home, contact: **Australia,** Consulate General, Level 26, St. Martins Tower, 31 Market St., Sydney NSW 2000 (☎02 92 61 57 79; www.consulfrance-sydney.org.); **Canada,** Consulate General, 1 pl. Ville Marie, 26th fl., Montréal, QC H3B 4SE (☎514-878-4385; www.consulfrance-montreal.org); **Ireland,** Consulate Section, 36 Ailesbury Rd., Ballsbridge, Dublin 4 (☎01 260 16 66; www.ambafrance.ie); **New Zealand,** 34-42 Manners St., P.O. Box 11-343, Wellington (☎04 384 25 55; www.ambafrance.net.nz); **South Africa,** Consulate General at Johannesburg, 191 Jan Smuts Ave., Rosebank; mailing address P.O. Box 1027, Parklands 2121 (☎011 778 5600, visas 778 5605; www.consulfrance-jhb.org.); **UK,** Consulate General, 21 Cromwell Rd., London SW7 2EN (☎020 7838 2000; www.ambafrance-uk.org.); **US,** Consulate General, 4101 Reservoir Rd. NW, Washington, D.C. 20007 (☎202-944-6195; www.consulfrance-washington.org).

FACTS AND FIGURES

Official Name: French Republic.

Capital: Paris.

Major Cities: Lyon, Marseilles, Nice.

Population: 60,000,000.

Land Area: 547,030 sq. km.

Time Zone: GMT +1.

Language: French.

Religions: Roman Catholic (90%).

MONEY. On January 1, 2002, the **euro** (€) replaced the **franc** as the unit of currency in France. For more information, see p. 14. **Tips** are always included in meal prices in restaurants and cafes, and in drink prices at bars and clubs; look for the phrase *service compris* on the menu or just ask. If service is not included, tip 15-20%. Even when service is included, it is polite to leave a *pourboire* of up to 5% at a cafe, bistro, restaurant, or bar.

TRANSPORTATION

BY PLANE. The two major international airports in Paris are **Roissy-Charles de Gaulle** (CDG; to the north) and **Orly** (ORY; to the south). For information on cheap flights from the UK to Paris, see p. 46.

BY TRAIN. The French national railway company, **SNCF** (☎08 36 35 35 35; www.sncf.fr), manages one of Europe's most efficient rail networks. **TGV** (*train à grande vitesse*, or high-speed) trains, the fastest in the world, run from Paris to major cities in France, as well as to Geneva and Lausanne, Switzerland. **Rapide** trains are slower; local **Express** trains are, oddly, the slowest option. SNCF offers a wide range of discounted round-trip tickets called *tarifs Découvertes*. Get a calendar from a train station detailing *période bleue* (blue period), *période blanche* (white period), and *période rouge* (red period) times and days; blue gets the most discounts, while red gets none. Those under 25 have two great options: The **Découverte 12-25** (€41.20) gives a 25% discount for any blue-period travel; and the **Carte 12-25** (€41.20), valid for a year, is good for 25-50% off all TGV trains, 50% off all non-TGV trips that started during a blue period, and 25% off non-TGV trips starting in a white period. Tickets must be validated in the orange machine at the entrance to the platforms at the *gare* (train station) and revalidated at any connections on your trip. Seat reservations, recommended for international trips, are mandatory on EuroCity (EC), InterCity (IC), and TGV trains. All three require a ticket supplement and reservation fee.

Eurail is valid in France. The SNCF's **France Railpass** grants four days of unlimited rail travel in France in any 30-day period (US$210; companion travelers US$171 each; up to 6 extra days US$30 each); the parallel **Youthpass** provides those under 26 with four days of unlimited travel within a two-month period (US$140; up to 6 extra days US$18 each). The **France Rail 'n' Drive pass** combines three days of rail travel with two days of car rental (US$245; companion travelers US$175 each; extra rail days US$31 each, extra car days US$37).

BY BUS. Within France, long-distance buses are a secondary transportation choice, as service is relatively infrequent. However, in some regions buses are indispensable for reaching out-of-the-way towns. Bus services operated by the SNCF accept railpasses. *Gare routière* is French for "bus station."

BY FERRY. Ferries across the English Channel (*La Manche*) link France to England and Ireland. The shortest and most popular route is between **Dover** and **Calais,** and is run by **P&O Stena Line, SeaFrance,** and **Hoverspeed** (p. 49). Hoverspeed also travels from **Dieppe** to **Newhaven,** England. **Brittany Ferries** (☎08 25 82 88 28; www.brittanyferries.co.uk) travels from **Caen** (p. 335) and **St-Malo** (p. 338) to **Portsmouth.** For more info on English Channel ferries, see p. 49. For info on ferries from **Nice** and **Marseilles** to **Corsica,** see p. 381.

BY CHUNNEL. Traversing 27 miles under the sea, the Chunnel is undoubtedly the fastest, most convenient, and least scenic route from England to France. There are two types of passenger service. **Eurostar** runs a frequent train service from London to Paris and Brussels, with stops at Ashford in England and Calais and Lille in France. Book reservations in UK, by phone, or over the web. (UK ☎0990 186 186; US ☎800-387-6782; elsewhere ☎020 7928 5163; www.eurostar.com.) Eurostar tickets can also be bought at most major travel agencies. **Eurotunnel** shuttles cars and passengers between Kent and Nord-Pas-de-Calais. (UK ☎08705 35 35 35; France ☎03 21 00 61 00; www.eurotunnel.co.uk.)

BY CAR. Unless you are traveling in a group of three or more, you won't save money traveling long distance by car rather than train, thanks to highway tolls, high gasoline cost, and rental charges. If you can't decide between train and car travel, get a **Rail 'n' Drive pass** from railpass vendors (see above). The French drive on the right-hand side of the road; France maintains its roads well, but the landscape itself often makes the roads a menace, especially in twisting Corsica.

BY BIKE AND BY THUMB. Of all Europeans, the French may be alone in loving cycling more than soccer. Drivers usually accommodate bikers on the wide country roads, and many cities banish cars from select streets each Sunday. Renting a bike (€8-19 per day) beats bringing your own if your touring will be confined to one or two regions. Many consider France the hardest country in Europe to get a lift. *Let's Go* does not recommend hitchhiking. In major cities, ride-sharing organizations such as **Eurostop International,** or **Allostop** in France (www.allostop.com), pair drivers and riders, though not all of them screen.

TOURIST SERVICES

TOURIST OFFICES. The extensive French tourism support network revolves around **syndicats d'initiative** and **offices de tourisme;** and in the smallest towns, the **Mairie,** the mayor's office; all of which *Let's Go* labels "tourist office." All three distribute maps and pamphlets, help you find accommodations, and suggest excursions to the countryside. For up-to-date events and regional info, see www.francetourism.com.

COMMUNICATION

TELEPHONES. When calling from abroad, drop the leading zero of the local number. French payphones only accept stylish *Télécartes* (phonecards), available in 50-unit (€7.50) and 120-unit (€15) denominations at *tabacs*, post offices, and train stations. *Décrochez* means pick up; you'll then be asked to *patientez* (wait) to insert your card; at *numérotez* or *composez* you can dial. Use only public France Télécom payphones, as privately owned ones charge more. An expensive alternative is to call collect *(faire un appel en PCV)*; an English-speaking operator can be reached by dialing the appropriate service provider listed below. The information number is ☎12; for an international operator, call ☎00 33 11. For information on purchasing a **cell phone,** see p. 36. International direct dial numbers include: **AT&T,** ☎0 800 99 00 11; **British Telecom,** ☎0 800 99 02 44; **Canada Direct,** ☎0 800 99 00 16 or 99 02 16; **Ireland Direct,** ☎0 800 99 03 53; **MCI,** ☎0 800 99 00 19; **Sprint,** ☎0 800 99 00 87; **Telecom New Zealand,** ☎0 800 99 00 64; **Telkom South Africa,** ☎0 800 99 00 27; **Telstra Australia,** ☎0 800 99 00 61.

EMERGENCY	Police: ☎122. Ambulance: ☎123. Fire: ☎124.
PHONE CODES	**Country code: 33. International dialing prefix: 00.** France has no city codes. From outside France, dial int'l dialing prefix (see inside back cover) + 33 + local number (drop the leading zero).

FRANCE

FRANCE

MAIL. Mail can be held for pickup through *Poste Restante* to almost any city or town with a post office. Address letters to be held according to the following example: SURNAME Firstname, *Poste Restante*, 52 r. du Louvre, 75001 Paris, France. Mark the envelope HOLD.

INTERNET ACCESS. Most major post offices and some branches now offer Internet access at special "cyberposte" terminals; you can buy a rechargeable card that gives you 50min. of access at any post office for €8. Note that *Let's Go* does not list "cyberposte" locations. Most large towns in France have a cybercafe. Rates and speed of connection vary widely; occasionally there are free terminals in technologically-oriented museums or exhibition spaces. **Cybercafé Guide** (www.cyberiacafe.net/cyberia/guide/ccafe.htm#working_france) lists cybercafes in France.

LANGUAGE. Contrary to popular opinion, even flailing efforts to speak French will be appreciated, especially in the countryside. Be lavish with your *Monsieurs*, *Madames*, and *Mademoiselles*, and greet people with a friendly *bonjour* (*bonsoir* in the evening). For basic French vocabulary and pronunciation, see p. 1054.

ACCOMMODATIONS AND CAMPING

FRANCE	❶	❷	❸	❹	❺
ACCOMMODATIONS	under €15	€16-25	€26-35	€36-55	over €55

Hostels generally offer dormitory accommodations in large, single-sex rooms with four to 10 beds, though some have as many as 60. At the other end of the scale, many offer private singles and doubles. In France, a bed in a hostel averages around €7.65-15.25. The **French Hostelling International (HI)** affiliate (p. 24), **Fédéraion Uniedes Auberges de Jeunesse** (FUAJ), operates 178 hostels within France. Some hostels accept reservations through the International Booking Network (p. 24). Two or more people traveling together will often save money by staying in cheap hotels rather than hostels. The French government employs a four-star hotel ratings system. *Gîtes d'étapes* are rural accommodations for cyclists, hikers, and other ramblers in less-populated areas. Expect *gîtes* to provide beds, a kitchen facility, and a resident caretaker. After 3000 years of settled history, true wilderness in France is hard to find. It's illegal to camp in most public spaces, including national parks. Instead, look forward to organized *campings* (campsites), where you'll share your splendid isolation with vacationing families and all manner of programmed fun. Most campsites have toilets, showers, and electrical outlets, though you may have to pay extra for such luxuries (€2-6); you'll often need to pay a fee for your car, too (€3-8). Otherwise, expect to pay €8-15 per site.

FOOD AND DRINK

FRANCE	❶	❷	❸	❹	❺
FOOD	under €5	€6-10	€11-15	€16-25	over €25

French chefs cook for one of the most finicky clienteles in the world. The largest meal of the day is *le déjeuner* (lunch). A complete French meal includes an *apéritif* (drink), an *entrée* (appetizer), a *plat* (main course), salad, cheese, dessert, fruit, coffee, and a *digestif* (after-dinner drink). The French drink wine with virtually every meal; *boisson comprise* entitles you to a free drink (usually wine) with your meal. Most restaurants offer a *menu à prix fixe* (fixed-price meal) that costs less than ordering *à la carte*. The *formule* is a cheaper, two-course version for the hurried luncher. Odd-hour cravings between lunch and dinner can be satisfied at *brasseries*, the middle ground between casual cafes and structured restaurants. *Service compris* means the tip is included in *l'addition* (check). It's easy to get satisfying dinner for under €10 with staples such as cheese, pâté, wine, bread, and chocolate; for a picnic, get fresh produce at a *marché* (outdoor market) and then hop between specialty shops. Start with a *boulangerie* (bakery) for bread, proceed to a *charcuterie* (butcher) for meats, and then *pâtisseries* and *confiseries* (pastry and candy shops) to satisfy a sweet tooth. When choosing a cafe, remember that you pay for its location—those on a major boulevard are more expensive than smaller places a few steps down a side street. Prices are cheaper at the *comptoir* (counter) than in the *salle* (seating area). For supermarket shopping, look for the chains Carrefour, Casino, Monoprix, and Prisunic.

HOLIDAYS AND FESTIVALS

Holidays: New Year's Day (Jan. 1); Easter Monday (Apr. 12); Labor Day (May 1); L'Anniversaire de la Liberation (May 8); Ascension Day (May 20); Whitmonday (May 31); Bastille Day (July 14); Feast of the Assumption (Aug. 15); All Saints' Day (Nov. 1); Armistice Day (Nov. 11); and Christmas (Dec. 25).

Festivals: Most festivals take place in summer. The **Cannes Film Festival** (May; www.festival-cannes.com) is mostly for directors and stars, but provides good people watching. The **Festival d'Avignon** (July-Aug.; www.festival-avignon.com) is famous for its theater. **Bastille Day** (July 14) is marked by military parades and fireworks nationwide. Although you may not be competing in the **Tour de France** (3rd or 4th Su in July; www.letour.fr), you'll enjoy all the hype. A **Vineyard Festival** (Sept., in Nice; www.nice-coteazur.org/americain/tourisme/vigne/index.html) celebrates the grape harvest with music, parades, and wine tastings.

PARIS

City of light, city of love, unsightly city, invisible city—Paris somehow manages to do it all. From alleys that shelter the world's best bistros to broad avenues flaunting the highest of *haute couture*, from the centuries-old stone of Notre Dame's gargoyles to the futuristic motions of the Parc de la Villette, from the masterpieces of the Louvre to the installations of avant-garde galleries, Paris presents itself as both a harbor of tradition and a hotbed of impulse.

Paris has been a center of commerce, culture, and conflict for centuries—and in the midst of it all, this city became the Western world's symbolic capital of romance, revolution, heroism, and hedonism. No wonder it's the world's most heavily touristed city—or that intellectuals in the later 20th century, in inimitable French style, started to question whether "Paris" had become nothing more than a conglomeration of illusions in the imagination of the tourist. You might find yourself wondering the same thing, as you sit in some perfect sidewalk cafe with a view of the Eiffel Tower, sipping an espresso or savoring a croissant, surrounded by beautiful people in brooding black: Can this place exist? But it does. Paris seems, incredibly, to live up to its mythical reputation and to utterly defy it; it is at once a living monument to the past and a city driving the present.

■ INTERCITY TRANSPORTATION

Flights: Aéroport Roissy-Charles de Gaulle (CDG; ☎01 48 62 22 80; www.parisairports.com), 23km northeast of Paris, services most transatlantic flights. For flight info, call the 24hr. English-speaking information center. **Aéroport d'Orly** (ORY; English recording ☎01 49 75 15 15), 18km south of Paris, is used by charters and many continental flights. The cheapest and fastest ways to get into the city are by **RER** or **bus.**

Trains: There are 6 train stations in Paris. Each part of the Métro system services a different geographic region.

Gare d'Austerlitz: To the Loire Valley, southwestern France (Bordeaux, Pyrénées), Spain, and Portugal. TGV to southwestern France leaves from Gare Montparnasse. To Barcelona (9hr., 1 per day, €97) and Madrid (12-13hr., 4 per day, €102).

Gare de l'Est: To eastern France (Champagne, Alsace, Lorraine, Strasbourg), Luxembourg, parts of Switzerland (Basel, Lucerne, Zürich), southern Germany (Frankfurt, Munich), Austria, Hungary, and Prague. To: Luxembourg (4hr., 10 per day, €50); Munich (9hr., 14 per day, €130); Prague (16hr., daily, €180); Strasbourg (4hr., 13 per day, €39); Vienna (13hr., 5 per day, €180); Zürich (6-7hr., 10 per day, €110).

Gare de Lyon: To southern France (Lyon, Provence, Riviera), parts of Switzerland (Bern, Geneva, Lausanne), Italy, and Greece. To: Florence (13hr., 4 per day, €145); Geneva (4hr., 7 per day, €69); Lyon (2hr., 23 per day, €35); Marseilles (4-5hr., 18 per day, €84); Nice (6hr., 8 per day, €60); Rome (15hr., 4-5 per day, €160).

Gare du Nord: Trains to northern France, Belgium, Britain, The Netherlands, Scandinavia, and northern Germany (Cologne, Hamburg). To: Amsterdam (4-5hr., 6 per day, €87); Brussels (1½hr., 28 per day, €66); Cologne (4hr., 7 per day, €78); London (by the Eurostar Chunnel; 3hr., 12-28 per day, up to €299).

Gare Montparnasse: To Brittany and southwestern France on the TGV. To Rennes (2hr., 30 per day, €46).

Gare St-Lazare: To Normandy. To Caen (2hr., 9 per day, €27) and Rouen (1-2hr., 13 per day, €18).

Buses: Gare Routière Internationale du Paris-Gallieni, 28 av. du Général de Gaulle, just outside Paris in Bagnolet. M: Gallieni. **Eurolines** (☎01 43 54 11 99; www.eurolines.fr) sells tickets to most destinations in France and neighboring countries.

▟ ORIENTATION

The **Ile de la Cité** and **Ile St-Louis** sit at the center of the city, while the **Seine,** flowing east to west, splits Paris into two large expanses: The **Rive Gauche (Left Bank)** to the south and the **Rive Droite (Right Bank)** to the north. The Left Bank, with its older architecture and narrow streets, has traditionally been considered bohemian and intellectual, while the Right Bank, with grand avenues and designer shops, is more ritzy. Administratively, Paris is divided into 20 **arrondissements** (districts; e.g. 1er, 6ème) that spiral clockwise around the Louvre. Well-known sites are packed into the central *arrondissements* (1er through 8ème), though the peripheral ones should not be overlooked. Refer also to this book's **color maps** of the city.

RIVE GAUCHE (LEFT BANK). The **Latin Quarter,** encompassing the 5ème and parts of the 6ème around the **Sorbonne** and the **Ecole des Beaux-Arts** (School of Fine Arts), has been home to students for centuries; the animated **boulevard St-Michel** is the boundary between the two *arrondissements*. The lively **rue Mouffetard** in the 5ème is quintessential Latin Quarter. The area around east-west **boulevard St-Germain,** which crosses bd. St-Michel just south of pl. St-Michel in the 6ème, is known as **St-Germain des Prés.** To the west, the gold-domed **Invalides** and the stern Neoclassical **Ecole Militaire,** which faces the **Eiffel Tower** across the **Champ-de-Mars,** recall the military past of the 7ème and northern 15ème, now full of traveling businesspeople. South of the Latin Quarter, **Montparnasse,** in the 14ème, eastern 15ème, and southwestern 6ème, lolls in the shadow of its tower. The glamorous **boulevard du Montparnasse** belies the surrounding residential districts. The eastern Left Bank, the 13ème, is a new hot spot, centered on **place d'Italie.**

RIVE DROITE (RIGHT BANK). The **Louvre** and **rue de Rivoli** occupy the sight- and tourist-packed 1er and the more business-oriented 2ème. The crooked streets of the **Marais**, in the 3ème and 4ème, escaped Baron Haussmann's redesign of Paris and now support many diverse communities. From **place de la Concorde**, at the western end of the 1er, **avenue des Champs-Elysées** bisects the 8ème as it sweeps up toward the **Arc de Triomphe** at **Charles de Gaulle-Etoile.** South of the Etoile, old and new money fills the exclusive 16ème, bordered to the west by the **Bois de Boulogne** park and to the east by the Seine and the **Trocadéro**, which faces the Eiffel Tower across the river. Back toward central Paris, the 9ème, just north of the 2ème, is defined by the sumptuous **Opéra.** East of the 9ème, the 10ème hosts cheap lodgings and the **Gare du Nord** and **Gare de l'Est.** The 10ème, 3ème, and the 11ème, which claims the newest hip nightlife in Paris (in **Bastille**), meet at **place de la République.** South of Bastille, the 12ème surrounds the **Gare de Lyon**, petering out at the **Bois de Vincennes.** East of Bastille, the party atmosphere gives way to the quieter, more residential 20ème and 19ème, while the 18ème is home to the quaint and heavily touristed **Montmartre**, which is capped by the **Sacré-Cœur.** To the east, the 17ème begins in the red-light district of **Pigalle** and bd. de Clichy, and grows more elegant toward the Etoile, the **Opéra Garnier**, and the 16ème. Continuing west along the *grande axe* defined by the Champs-Elysées, the skyscrapers of **La Défense**, Paris's newest quarter, loom across the Seine from Bois de Boulogne.

⌐ LOCAL TRANSPORTATION

Public Transportation: The efficient **Métropolitain**, or **Métro (M)**, runs 5:30am-12:30am. Lines are numbered and are generally referred to by their number and final destinations; connections are called *correspondances*. **Single-fare tickets** within the city €1.30; *carnet* (packet) of 10 €9.60. Buy extras for when ticket booths are closed (after 10pm) and hold onto your ticket until you exit. The **RER** (Réseau Express Régional), the commuter train to the suburbs, serves as an express subway within central Paris; changing to and getting off the RER requires sticking your validated ticket into a turnstile. Watch the signboards next to the RER tracks and check that your stop is lit up before riding. **Buses** use the same €1.30 tickets (bought on the bus; validate in the machine by the driver), but transfer requires a new ticket. Buses run 6:30am-8:30pm; *Autobus de Nuit* until 1am, and *Noctambus* (3-4 tickets) every hr. 1:30-5:30am at stops marked with the bug-eyed moon between the Châtelet stop and the *portes* (city exits). The **Mobilis** pass covers the Métro, RER, and buses only (€5 for a 1-day pass in Zones 1 and 2). A weekly pass (carte orange hebdomadaire) costs €13.75 and expires every Su; photo ID required. Refer to this book's **color maps** of Paris's transit network.

Taxis: Alpha Taxis (☎01 45 85 85 85). **Taxis 7000** (☎01 42 70 00 42). Cabs are expensive and take 3 passengers (there is a €2.45 surcharge for a 4th). The meter starts running when you phone. Cab stands are near train stations and major bus stops.

Car Rental: Rent-a-Car, 79 r. de Bercy (☎01 43 45 98 99). Open M-Sa 8:30am-6pm.

Bike Rental: Paris à velo, 2 r. de Fer-à-Moulin, 5ème (☎01 43 37 59 22). M: Censier-Daubenton. Bike rental €14 per day. Open M-Sa 10am-12:30pm and 2-7pm.

❼ PRACTICAL INFORMATION

TOURIST AND FINANCIAL SERVICES

Tourist Office: Bureau d'Accueil Central, 127 av. des Champs-Elysées, 8ème (☎08 92 68 31 12; www.paristouristoffice.com). M: Georges V. Open in summer daily 9am-8pm; off-season M-Sa 9am-8pm, Su 11am-7pm.

F R A N C E

Embassies: Australia, 4 r. Jean-Rey, 15ème (☎01 40 59 33 00; www.austgov.fr). M: Bir-Hakeim. Open M-F 9:15am-noon and 2-4:30pm. **Canada,** 35 av. Montaigne, 8ème (☎01 44 43 29 00; www.amb-canada.fr). M: Franklin-Roosevelt. Open M-F 9am-noon and 2-5pm. **Ireland,** 12, av. Foch, 16ème (☎01 44 17 67 00; www.irlande-tourisme.fr). M: Trocadéro. Open M-F 9:30am-1pm and 2:30-5:30pm. **New Zealand,** 7ter r. Leonardo de Vinci, 16ème (☎01 45 01 43 43; www.nzembassy.com/france). M: Victor-Hugo. Open July-Aug. M-Th 8:30am-1pm and 2-5:30pm, F 8:30am-2pm; Sept.-June M-F 9am-1pm and 2-5:30pm. **South Africa,** 59 quai d'Orsay, 7ème (☎01 53 59 23 23; www.afriquesud.net). M: Invalides. Open M-F 8:30am-5:45pm; visa services 9am-noon. **UK,** 18bis r. d'Anjou, 8ème (☎01 44 51 31 00; www.amb-grandebretagne.fr). M: St-Augustin. Open M and W-F 9:30am-12:30pm and 2:30-5pm, Tu 9:30am-4:30pm. **US,** 2 r. St-Forentin, 1er (☎01 43 12 22 22; www.amb-usa.fr). M: Concorde. Open M-F 9am-12:30pm and 1-6pm; notarial services Tu-F 9am-noon. Skip the long line; go to the right and tell them you are there for American services.

Currency Exchange: Hotels, train stations, and airports offer poor rates but have extended hours; Gare de Lyon, Gare du Nord, and both airports have booths open 6:30am-10:30pm. Most **ATMs** accept **Visa** ("CB/VISA") and **MasterCard** ("EC"). Crédit Lyonnais ATMs take **AmEx;** Crédit Mutuel and Crédit Agricole ATMs are on the **Cirrus** network; and most Visa ATMs accept **PLUS**-network cards.

American Express: 11 r. Scribe, 9ème (☎01 47 14 50 00), opposite the back of the Opéra. M: Opéra or Auber. Mail held for cardholders and AmEx Traveler's Cheque holders. Open M-Sa 9am-6:30pm; exchange counters open Su 10am-5pm.

LOCAL SERVICES

English-Language Bookstore: Shakespeare and Co., 37 r. de la Bûcherie, 5ème, across the Seine from Notre-Dame. M: St-Michel. A Paris fixture for anglophones, with a quirky, wide selection of new and used books. Open daily noon-midnight.

Gay and Lesbian Services: Centre Gai et Lesbien, 3 r. Keller, 11ème (☎01 43 57 21 47). M: Ledru Rollin or Bastille. Info hub for all gay services and associations in Paris. English spoken. Open M-Sa 2-8pm, Su 2-7pm. **Les Mots à la Bouche,** 6 r. Ste-Croix de la Bretonnerie, 4ème (☎01 42 78 88 30; www.motsbouche.com), is Paris's largest gay and lesbian bookstore and serves as an unofficial info center. M: Hôtel-de-Ville. Open M-Sa 11am-11pm, Su 2-8pm.

Laundromats: Laundromats are everywhere, especially in the 5ème and 6ème. **Arc en Ciel,** 62 r. Arbre Sec, 1er (☎01 42 41 39 39), does dry cleaning. M: Louvre.

EMERGENCY AND COMMUNICATIONS

Emergencies: Ambulance: ☎15. **Fire:** ☎18. **Police:** ☎17. For non-emergencies, head to the local *gendarmerie* (police force) in each *arrondissement.*

Crisis Lines: Rape, SOS Viol (☎08 00 05 95 95). Call free anywhere in France for counseling (medical and legal). Open M-F 10am-7pm. **SOS Help!** (☎01 46 21 46 46). Anonymous, confidential English-speaking crisis hotline. Open daily 3-11pm.

Hospitals: Hôpital Américain de Paris, 63 bd. Hugo, Neuilly (☎01 46 41 25 25). M: Port Maillot, then bus #82 to the end of the line. **Hôpital Franco-Britannique de Paris,** 3 r. Barbès, in the Parisian suburb of Levallois-Perret (☎01 46 39 22 22). M: Anatole France. Has some English speakers, but don't count on it. **Hôpital Bichat,** 46 r. Henri Buchard, 18ème (☎01 40 25 80 80). M: Port St-Ouen. Emergency services.

24 hr. Pharmacies: Every *arrondissement* has a **pharmacie de garde** which opens in emergencies. The locations change, but their names are posted on every pharmacy's door. **Pharmacie Dhéry,** in the Galerie des Champs 84, av. des Champs-Elysées, 8ème (☎01 45 62 02 41). M: George V. Open 24hr. **British & American Pharmacy,** 1 r. Auber, 9ème (☎01 42 65 88 29). M: Auber or Opéra. Open daily 8am-8:30pm.

Telephones: To use the phones, you'll need to buy a **phone card** (télécarte), available at post offices, Métro stations, and *tabacs*. For **directory info**, call ☎ 12.

Internet Access: Internet cafes are widespread throughout the city.

Artefak, 42 r. Volta, 3ème (☎01 44 59 39 58). M: Arts et Metiers or Temple. Early-bird special (before 1pm) €2 per hr.; regular €3 per hr. Open daily 10pm-2am.

Le Jardin de l'Internet, 79 bd. St-Michel, 5ème (☎01 44 07 22 20). RER: Luxembourg. €2.50 per hr. Open daily 9am-11pm.

Le Sputnik, 14-16 r. de la Butte-aux-Cailles, 13ème (☎01 45 65 19 82). M: Place d'Italie. €1 for 15min., €4 per hr.

Taxiphone, 343 r. des Pyrénées, 20ème (☎01 43 15 68 25). M: Pyrénées or Jourdain. €3 per hr. Open daily noon-10pm.

Post Office: Poste du Louvre, 52 r. du Louvre, 1er (☎01 40 28 20 40). M: Louvre. Open 24hr. Address mail to be held: SURNAME Firstname, *Poste Restante*, 52 r. du Louvre, 75001 Paris, FRANCE. **Postal Codes:** 750xx, where "xx" is the *arrondissement* (e.g., 75003 for any address in the 3ème).

⌐ ACCOMMODATIONS

High season in Paris falls around Easter and from May to October, peaking in July and August. Paris's hostels skip many standard restrictions (sheets, curfews, etc.) and tend to have flexible maximum stays. The city's six HI hostels are for members only. The rest of Paris's dorm-style beds are either private hostels or quieter *foyers* (student dorms). Hotels may be the most practical accommodations for the majority of travelers. Expect to pay at least €25 for a single or €35 for a double in the cheapest, luckiest of circumstances. In cheaper hotels, few rooms have private baths; hall showers cost about €2.50 per use. Rooms fill quickly after morning check-out (10am-noon), so arrive early or reserve ahead. Most hostels and *foyers* include the **taxe de séjour** (€1-1.50 per person per day) in listed prices, but some do not. If you haven't reserved ahead, tourist offices (see p. 295) and the organizations below can book rooms.

ACCOMMODATIONS SERVICES

La Centrale de Réservations (FUAJ-HI), 4 bd. Jules Ferry, 11ème. (☎01 43 57 02 60; fax 01 40 21 79 92). M: République. Open daily 8am-10pm.

OTU-Voyage (Office du Tourisme Universitaire), 119, r. St-Martin 4ème (☎08 20 81 78 17 or 01 49 72 57 19 for groups). €1.53 service charge. Open M-F 9:30am-7pm, Sa 10am-noon and 1:30-5pm. Also at 2 r. Malus, 5ème (☎01 44 41 74 74). M: Place Monge. Open M-Sa 9-6pm.

ILE DE LA CITÉ

⚐ Hôtel Henri IV, 25 pl. Dauphine (☎01 43 54 44 53). M: Pont Neuf. One of Paris's best located and least expensive hotels. Showers €2.50. Reserve one month in advance, earlier in the summer. Singles €23; doubles €30, with shower and toilet €54; triples €41, with shower €48; quads €48. ❷

1ER AND 2ÈME ARRONDISSEMENTS

Central to the **Louvre,** the **Tuileries,** the **Seine,** and the ritzy **place Vendôme,** this area still has a few budget hotels. It's best to avoid r. St-Denis.

⚐ Hôtel Montpensier, 12 r. de Richelieu, 1er (☎01 42 96 28 50; fax 01 42 86 02 70). M: Palais-Royal. Clean rooms, lofty ceilings, bright decor. Small elevator. TVs in rooms with shower or bath. Internet €1 per 4min. Breakfast €7. Shower €4. Reserve 2 months in advance in high season. Singles and doubles €57-89. AmEx/DC/MC/V. ❺

FRANCE

Paris Food & Accommodations

🍎 FOOD

404, **16**
L'As du Falafel, **36**
Au Petit Fer à Cheval, **35**
Au Port Salut, **62**
Babylone Bis, **13**
Le Bistro de Gala, **6**
Café de Flore, **51**
Café de l'Industrie, **40**
Café des Lettres, **49**
Le Café Marly, **23**
Le Caveau du Palais, **32**
Le Cheval de Troie, **45**
Chez Janou, **30**
Chez Paul, **44**
La Connivence, **46**
Cosí, **52**
Le Crêpe en L'ile, **43**
La Cucaracha, **14**

Le Divin, **29**
Les Editeurs, **54**
Le Fumoir, **25**
Georges, **27**
Haynes Restaurant
    Américain, **3**
Le Jardin des Pâtés, **65**
Jules, **18**
Lamen Kintaro, **9**
Le Lotus Blanc, **48**
Les Noces de Jeannette, **7**
Le Petit Vatel, **56**
Papou Lounge, **19**
Piccolo Teatro, **37**
Le Rouge et Blanc, **33**
Savannah Café, **63**
La Victoire Suprême
    du Coeur, **26**

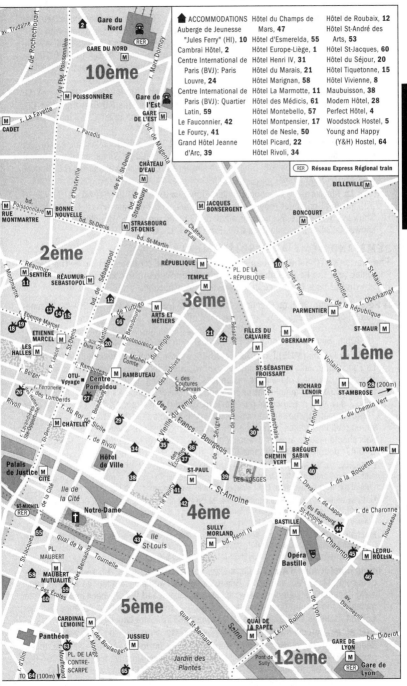

ACCOMMODATIONS
Auberge de Jeunesse "Jules Ferry" (HI), **10**
Cambrai Hôtel, **2**
Centre International de Paris (BVJ): Paris Louvre, **24**
Centre International de Paris (BVJ): Quartier Latin, **59**
Le Fauconnier, **42**
Le Fourcy, **41**
Grand Hôtel Jeanne d'Arc, **39**

Hôtel du Champs de Mars, **47**
Hôtel d'Esmerelda, **55**
Hôtel Europe-Liège, **1**
Hôtel Henri IV, **31**
Hôtel du Marais, **21**
Hôtel La Marmotte, **11**
Hôtel des Médicis, **61**
Hôtel Marignan, **58**
Hôtel Montebello, **57**
Hôtel Montpensier, **17**
Hôtel de Nesle, **50**
Hôtel Picard, **22**
Hôtel Rivoli, **34**

Hôtel de Roubaix, **12**
Hôtel St-André des Arts, **53**
Hôtel St-Jacques, **60**
Hôtel du Séjour, **20**
Hôtel Tiquetonne, **15**
Hôtel Vivienne, **8**
Maubuisson, **38**
Modern Hôtel, **28**
Perfect Hôtel, **4**
Woodstock Hostel, **5**
Young and Happy (Y&H) Hostel, **64**

RER Réseau Express Régional train

FRANCE

■ **Centre International de Paris (BVJ): Paris Louvre,** 20 r. Jean-Jacques Rousseau, 1er (☎01 53 00 90 90). M: Louvre or Palais-Royal. Bright, dorm-style rooms with 2-10 beds per room. English spoken. Internet €1 per 10min. Lockers €2. Weekend reservations up to 1 week in advance; reserve by phone only. Rooms held for only 5-10min. after your expected check-in time; call if you'll be late. Doubles €28 per person; other rooms €25 per person. ❷

Hôtel Tiquetonne, 6 r. Tiquetonne, 2ème (☎01 42 36 94 58; fax 01 42 36 02 94). M: Etienne-Marcel. This affordable 7-story hotel is a study in faux finishes. Breakfast €5. Shower €5. Reserve 2 weeks in advance. Singles €28, with toilet €38; doubles with shower and toilet €46. AmEx/MC/V. ❸

Hôtel Vivienne, 40 r. Vivienne, 2ème (☎01 42 33 13 26; paris@hotel-vivienne.com). M: Grands Boulevards. Adds a touch of refinement to budget digs. Some rooms with balconies. Elevator. Breakfast €6. Singles with shower €50, with shower and toilet €78; doubles €65/80. MC/V. ❹

Hôtel La Marmotte, 6 r. Léopold Bellan, 2ème (☎01 40 26 26 51; fax 01 21 42 96 20). M: Sentier. Quiet rooms with TVs, phones, and free safe-boxes. Breakfast €4. Shower €3. Reserve 2 weeks in advance. Singles and 1-bed doubles €28-35, with shower €42-54; 2-bed doubles €60. Extra bed €12. ❸

3ÈME AND 4ÈME ARRONDISSEMENTS

The Marais's 17th-century mansions now house budget hotels close to the **Centre Pompidou** and the **Ile St-Louis;** the area is also convenient for sampling nightlife, as Paris's night buses converge in the 4ème at M: Châtelet.

■ **Hôtel du Séjour,** 36 r. du Grenier St-Lazare, 3ème (☎/fax 01 48 87 40 36). M: Etienne-Marcel or Rambuteau. This family-run hotel offers clean, bright rooms and a warm welcome. Reserve at least 1 week in advance. 20 rooms. Showers €4. Reception 7am-10:30pm. Singles €31; doubles €43, with shower and toilet €55, third person €23. ❸

■ **Hôtel des Jeunes (MIJE)** (☎01 42 74 23 45; www.mije.com). Books beds in Le Fourcy, Le Fauconnier, and Maubuisson (see below), 3 small hostels located on cobblestone streets in beautiful old Marais residences. No smoking. English spoken. Restaurant. Internet €0.15 per min. Public phones and free lockers (with a €1 deposit). Ages 18-30 only. 7-day max. stay. Reception 7am-1am. Lockout noon-3pm. Curfew 1am. Quiet after 10pm. Breakfast, shower, and sheets included. Arrive before noon the first day of reservation (call in advance if you'll be late). Groups may reserve a year in advance. Individuals should reserve at least 1 week in advance. 5-bed (or more) dorms €24-26; singles €40-47; doubles €60-72; triples €78-93; quads €100-108. ❷

Le Fourcy, 6 r. de Fourcy, 4ème. M: St-Paul or Pont Marie. From M: St-Paul, walk opposite the traffic down r. François-Miron and turn left on r. de Fourcy. The hostel surrounds a large courtyard ideal for meeting travelers. Light sleepers should avoid rooms on the social courtyard.

Le Fauconnier, 11 r. du Fauconnier, 4ème. M: St-Paul or Pont Marie. From M: St-Paul, take r. du Prevôt, turn left on r. Charlemagne, and turn right on r. du Fauconnier. Ivy-covered building steps away from the Seine and Île St-Louis.

Maubuisson, 12 r. des Barres, 4ème. M: Hôtel-de-Ville or Pont Marie. From M: Pont Marie, walk opposite traffic on r. de l'Hôtel-de-Ville and turn right on r. des Barres. A half-timbered former girls' convent on a silent street by the St-Gervais monastery.

Grand Hôtel Jeanne d'Arc, 3 r. de Jarente, 4ème (☎01 48 87 62 11; www.hoteljeanne-darc.com). M: St-Paul or Bastille. Bright, clean hotel with pleasant lounge and breakfast area. Recently renovated rooms with showers, toilets, and TVs. 2 wheelchair-accessible rooms on the ground floor. Breakfast €5.80. Reserve 2-3 months in advance. Singles €55-64; doubles €67-92; triples €107; quads €122. Extra bed €12. MC/V. ❹

Hôtel de Roubaix, 6 r. Greneta, 3ème (☎01 42 72 89 91; fax 01 42 72 58 79). M: Réaumur-Sébastopol. Helpful staff and clean, pleasant rooms. All have shower, toilet, phone, locker, and TV. Breakfast included. Reserve 1 week in advance. Singles €54-60; doubles €65-84; triples €74-83; quads €89; quints €95. Free storage. MC/V. ❹

Hôtel Picard, 26 r. de Picardie, 3ème (☎01 48 87 53 82; fax 01 48 87 02 56). M: République. In a superb location with a friendly, helpful staff. TVs in rooms with showers. Wheelchair accessible. Breakfast €4.50. Hall showers €3. Reserve 2 weeks ahead Apr.-Sept. Singles €33, with shower €41, with shower and toilet €51; doubles €40-43, with shower €52, with bath €63; triples €59-82. 5% Let's Go discount. MC/V. ❸

Hôtel du Marais, 16 r. de Beauce, 3ème (☎01 42 72 30 26; hotelmarais@voila.fr). M: Temple or Filles-de-Calvaire. Simple but spotless rooms in a great location near an open-air market. Take the small stairs above the cafe owned by the same friendly man. Curfew 2am. 3rd fl. showers €3. Singles with sink €25; doubles €33. ❷

Hôtel Rivoli, 44 r. de Rivoli/2 r. des Mauvais Garçons, 4ème (☎01 42 72 08 41). M: Hôtel-de-Ville. Small with basic rooms, but extremely well situated. No entrance from 2-7am. Reserve 1 month in advance. Singles €27, with shower €35; doubles €35/39, with bath and toilet €49; triples €54. Extra bed €9. ❸

5ÈME AND 6ÈME ARRONDISSEMENTS

The lively Latin quarter and St-Germain-des-Prés offer proximity to the **Notre-Dame,** the **Panthéon,** the **Jardin du Luxembourg,** and the bustling student cafe culture.

Young and Happy (Y&H) Hostel, 80 r. Mouffetard, 5ème (☎01 45 35 09 53; www.youngandhappy.fr). M: Monge. A funky, lively hostel with laid-back staff, clean rooms, and commission-free currency exchange. Breakfast included. Sheets €2.50, towels €1. Laundry nearby. Lockout 11am-4pm. Curfew 2am. 25 rooms, a few with showers and toilets. Dorms from €20 per person; doubles from €23 per person; off-season (Jan.-Mar.) prices €2 less per night. ❷

Hôtel de Nesle, 7 r. du Nesle, 6ème (☎01 43 54 62 41; www.hoteldenesle.com). M: Odéon. Walk up r. de l'Ancienne Comédie, take a right onto r. Dauphine, and then take a left on r. du Nesle. Friendly staff and sparkling rooms. Singles €50-69; doubles €69-99. Extra bed €12. AmEx/MC/V. ❹

Hôtel St-André des Arts, 66 r. St-André-des-Arts, 6ème (☎01 43 26 96 16; hsaintand@minitel.net). M: Odéon. Country inn feeling. New bathrooms, free breakfast, and very friendly owner. Reservations recommended. Singles €63; doubles €80-85; triples €100; quads €110. MC/V. ❺

Hôtel St-Jacques, 35 r. des Ecoles, 5ème (☎01 44 07 45 45; hotelstjacques@wanadoo.fr). M: Maubert-Mutualité or RER: Cluny-La Sorbonne. Spacious, faux-elegant rooms with balconies, renovated bathrooms, and TVs. English spoken. Internet access. Breakfast €7. Singles €49, with toilet and shower €75; doubles with toilet and shower €85, some with bath €112. AmEx/MC/V. ❹

Hôtel Marignan, 13 r. du Sommerard, 5ème (☎01 43 54 63 81; www.hotel-marignan.com). M: Maubert-Mutualité. The privacy of a hotel and the welcoming atmosphere of a hostel. Free laundry and kitchen access. Hall showers open until 11pm. Breakfast €3. Internet access. Singles €42-45; doubles €60, with shower and toilet €80-86; triples €90-110; quads €100-130. 15% discount mid-Sept. to Mar. for stays longer than 5 nights. AmEx/MC/V. ❹

Hôtel d'Esmeralda, 4 r. St-Julien-le-Pauvre, 5ème (☎01 43 54 19 20; fax 01 40 51 00 68). M: St-Michel. Rooms are clean but creaky, and tend to have an ancient, professorial feel about them. Great location. Breakfast €6. Singles €35, with shower and toilet €65; doubles €90; triples €110; quads €120. ❸

Centre International de Paris (BVJ): Paris Quartier Latin, 44 r. des Bernardins, 5ème (☎01 43 29 34 80; fax 01 53 00 90 91). M: Maubert-Mutualité. Boisterous, generic hostel with large cafeteria. English spoken. Internet €1 per 10min. Breakfast included. Showers in rooms. Lockers €2. Dorms €25; singles €30; doubles €54; triples €81. ❷

Hôtel des Médicis, 214 r. St-Jacques, 5ème (☎01 43 54 14 66). RER: Luxembourg. Rickety-looking place that shuns right-angles; Jim Morrison crashed here. 1 shower and toilet per floor. Laundromat next door. English spoken. Reception 9am-11pm. Singles €16; larger singles €20; doubles €31; triples €45. ❷

7ÈME AND 8ÈME ARRONDISSEMENTS

■ **Hôtel du Champs de Mars,** 7 r. du Champs de Mars, 7ème (☎01 45 51 52 30; www.hotel-du-champs-de-mars.com). M: Ecole Militaire. Just off av. Bosquet. Elegant rooms. Reserve 1 month ahead and confirm by fax or email. Small elevator. Singles and doubles with shower €68-74; triples with bath €94. MC/V. ❺

■ **Hôtel Montebello,** 18 r. Pierre Leroux, 7ème (☎01 47 34 41 18; fax 01 47 34 46 71). Behind the unremarkable facade are clean, cheery rooms with full baths. Reserve at least 2 weeks in advance. Breakfast €3.50. Singles €37; doubles €42-45. ❸

Hôtel Europe-Liège, 8 r. de Moscou, 8ème (☎01 42 94 01 51; fax 01 43 87 42 18). M: Liège. Clean and fresh rooms and a lovely interior courtyard. Reserve 15 days in advance. All have TV, hair dryer, phone, and shower or bath. 2 wheelchair-accessible rooms on the ground floor. Breakfast €7. Singles €68; doubles €84. AmEx/MC/V. ❺

9ÈME AND 10ÈME ARRONDISSEMENTS

■ **Perfect Hôtel,** 39 r. Rodier, 9ème (☎01 42 81 18 86; perfecthotel@hotmail.com). This hotel almost lives up to its name, with hotel-quality rooms at hostel prices. Breakfast free for *Let's Go* users. Singles €30, with shower and toilet €50; doubles €36/50; triples €53/65. MC/V. ❸

■ **Cambrai Hôtel,** 129bis bd. de Magenta, 10ème (☎01 48 78 32 13; fax 01 48 78 43 55; www.hotel-cambrai.com). M: Gare du Nord. Clean rooms with high ceilings and TVs. Breakfast €5. Showers €3. Singles €30, with toilet €35, with shower €41, with full bath €48; doubles with shower €46, with full bath €54, with twin beds and full bath €60; triples €80; 4-person family suite €90; 5-person €110. AmEx/MC/V. ❷

Woodstock Hostel, 48 r. Rodier, 9ème (☎01 48 78 87 76; www.woodstock.fr). M: Anvers. Funky atmosphere. Communal kitchen and safe-deposit box. International staff; English spoken. Breakfast included. Sheets €2.50, towels €1. Showers on every floor are free (and clean). Internet €1 per 10min. Call ahead to reserve a room. Max. stay 1 week. Curfew 2am. Lockout 11am-4pm. Dorms €20; doubles €23. ❷

11ÈME AND 12ÈME ARRONDISSEMENTS

These hotels are close to hopping bars and clubs, but be careful at night.

■ **Modern Hôtel,** 121 r. de Chemin-Vert, 11ème (☎01 47 00 54 05; www.modern-hotel.fr). M: Père Lachaise. Newly renovated, with spotless marble bathrooms. All rooms have a hair dryer, modem connection, and safe-deposit box. Breakfast €5. Singles €60; doubles €70-75; triples €85; quads €95. Extra bed €15. AmEx/DC/MC/V. ❺

■ **Hôtel Printania,** 91 av. du Dr. Netter, 12ème (☎01 43 07 65 13; fax 01 43 43 56 54). M: Porte de Vincennes. Mini-fridges, large soundproof windows, and faux-marble floors. Breakfast €4.60. Reserve at least 2 weeks in advance; confirm reservations by fax. Doubles with sink and *bidet* €39, with shower and bath €48, with TV €54; triples with shower, bath, and TV €61. AmEx/MC/V. ❷

Auberge de Jeunesse "Jules Ferry" (HI), 8 bd. Jules Ferry, 11ème (☎01 43 57 55 60; auberge@easynet.fr). M: République. Walk east on r. du Faubourg du Temple and turn right on the far side of bd. Jules Ferry. Wonderful location, party atmosphere. Breakfast and showers included. Lockers €1.55. 1 week max. stay. Internet access in lobby. Lockout 10am-2pm. No reservations; arrive by 8am. Dorms €20; doubles €39. MC/V. ❶

Centre International du Séjour de Paris: CISP "Ravel," 6 av. Maurice Ravel, 12ème (☎01 44 75 60 00; www.cisp.asso.fr). M: Porte de Vincennes. Large, clean rooms (most with fewer than 4 beds) with art exhibited all around. Breakfast, sheets, and towels included. Reception 6:30am-1:30am; you can arrange to have the night guard let you in after 1:30am. Reserve at least a month ahead by phone or email. 8-bed dorm with shower and toilet in hall €16; 2-to 4-bed dorm €20; singles with shower and toilet €30; doubles with shower and toilet €48. AmEx/MC/V. ❷

13ÈME TO 15ÈME ARRONDISSEMENTS

Just south of the Latin Quarter, Montparnasse mixes intellectual charm with thriving commercial centers and cafes.

■ **Hôtel de Blois,** 5 r. des Plantes, 14ème (☎01 45 40 99 48; fax 01 45 40 45 62). M: Mouton-Duvernet. Elegant rooms. TVs, hair dryers, and big, clean baths. Breakfast €5. Reserve 10 days ahead. Singles €39, with shower €43, with shower and toilet €45, with bath and toilet €51; doubles €41/45/47/56; triples €61. AmEx/MC/V. ❹

■ **Ouest Hôtel,** 27 r. de Gergovie, 13ème (☎01 45 42 64 99; fax 01 45 42 46 65). M: Pernety. A clean hotel with modest furnishings. Charming dining room. Breakfast €5. Hall shower €5 (sometimes long waits). Singles €22-28; 1-bed doubles €28, with shower €37; 2-bed doubles €34/39. MC/V. ❷

FIAP Jean-Monnet, 30 r. Cabanis, 14ème (☎01 43 13 17 00; reservations ☎01 43 13 17 17; www.fiap.asso.fr). M: Glacière. 500-bed student center offers spotless rooms with phone, toilet, and shower. Breakfast included; add €1.60 for buffet. Curfew 2am. Reserve 2-4 weeks in advance. Be sure to specify if you want a dorm bed or you will be booked for a single. €15 deposit per person per night by check or credit card. Wheelchair accessible. Rooms cleaned daily. Check-in after 2:30pm. Check-out 9am. 3-month maximum stay. Dorms €22; singles €50; doubles €64; quads €112. MC/V. ❷

Three Ducks Hostel, 6 pl. Etienne Pernet, 15ème (☎01 48 42 04 05; www.3ducks.fr). M: Félix Faure. Aimed at young Anglo travelers. Shower and breakfast included. Sheets €2.30, towels €0.75. Internet access in lobby. Reception daily 8am-2am. Lockout daily 11am-5pm. 1 week max. stay. Reserve with credit card a week ahead. Mar.-Oct. dorm beds €22; doubles €50. Nov.-Feb. reduced prices. MC/V. ❷

16ÈME TO 20ÈME ARRONDISSEMENTS

■ **Hôtel Caulaincourt,** 2 sq. Caulaincourt, 18ème (☎01 46 06 46 06; bienvenue@caulaincourt.com). M: Lamarck-Caulaincourt. Friendly establishment in a pleasant, quiet area of Montmartre. TVs and phones in every room. Breakfast €5.50. Reserve up to 1 month in advance. Singles €33, with shower €42, with shower and toilet €50; doubles €44-74; triples with shower €60-75. MC/V. ❸

■ **Eden Hôtel,** 7 r. Jean-Baptiste Dumay, 18ème (☎01 46 36 64 22; fax 01 46 36 01 11). M: Pyrénées. Clean rooms with TVs and toilets. Elevator. Breakfast €4.50. Bath or shower €4. Reserve rooms by fax 1 week in advance. Singles €36, with shower €49; doubles with shower €51-54, 1 double with bath €54. Extra bed €10. MC/V. ❹

Rhin et Danube, 3 pl. Rhin et Danube, 19ème (☎01 42 45 10 13; fax 01 42 06 88 82). M: Danube. Spacious rooms look onto a quaint *place*. Each room has kitchen, fridge, dishes, coffeemaker, hair dryer, shower, toilet, direct phone, and color TV with satellite. Singles €46; doubles €61; triples €73; quads €83; quints €92. MC/V. ❹

◪ FOOD

In Paris, life is about eating. Establishments range from the famous repositories of *haute cuisine* to corner *brasseries*. Inexpensive bistros and *crêperies* offer the breads, cheeses, wines, pâtés, *pôtages*, and pastries central to French cuisine. *Gauche* or gourmet, French or foreign, you'll find it in Paris. **CROUS (Centre Regional des Oeuvres Universitaires et Scolaires),** 39 av. Georges Bernanos, 5ème, has information on university restaurants, which are a cheap way to get a great meal. (M: Port-Royal. Open M-F 9am-5pm.) To assemble a picnic, visit the specialty shops of the **Marché Montorgueil,** 2ème, **rue Mouffetard,** 5ème, or the **Marché Bastille** on bd. Richard-Lenoir (M: Bastille; open Th and Su 7am-1:30pm).

FRANCE

ILE DE LA CITÉ AND ILE ST-LOUIS

▨ **Le Caveau du Palais,** 19 pl. Dauphine, Île de la Cité (☎01 43 26 04 28). M: Cité. A chic, intimate restaurant serving traditional French food from an old-style brick oven. Reservations recommended. Open daily noon-3pm and 7-10:30pm. MC/V. ❹

Le Rouge et Blanc, 26 pl. Dauphine, Île de la Cité (☎01 43 29 52 34). M: Cité. Simple, friendly *provençale* bar and bistro. *Menus* €17 and €22. A la carte *plats* €14-20. On sunny days, tables are set out along the sidewalk. Open M-Sa 11am-3pm and 7-10:30pm. Closed when it rains. MC/V. ❹

La Crêpe en l'Ile, 13 r. des Deux Ponts, Île St-Louis (☎01 43 26 28 68). M: Pont Marie. Just off of the main drag and a bit less crowded than its island siblings. Choose from among 20 *crêpe* options. Incredible selection of unique and flavorful teas. Prices range from €2.50-7.20; 3-course *menu* €8.40. Open in summer daily 11:30am-midnight; off-season 11:30am-11pm. ❷

1ER AND 2ÈME ARRONDISSEMENTS

Cheap options surround **Les Halles,** 1*er* and 2*ème*. Near the **Louvre,** the small streets of the 2*ème* teem with traditional bistros.

▨ **Papou Lounge,** 74 r. Jean-Jacques Rousseau, 1*er* (☎01 44 76 00 03). M: Les Halles. Papou's cuisine is both flavorful (rumsteak €13) and inventive (tuna tartar with strawberries €13.50). Lunch special €10. Beer €3.30. Open daily 10am-2am; food served noon-4:30pm and 7pm-midnight. MC/V. ❸

▨ **Jules,** 62, r. Jean-Jacques Rousseau, 1*er* (☎01 40 28 99 04). M: Les Halles. This restaurant feels like home. Subtle blend of modern and traditional French cooking; selections change by season. 4-course *menu* €21-29 includes terrific cheese course. Open M-Sa noon-2:30pm and 7-10:30pm. AmEx/MC/V. ❹

Les Noces de Jeannette, 14 r. Favart and 9 r. d'Amboise, 2*ème* (☎01 42 96 36 89). M: Richelieu-Drouot. Elegant bistro. 3-course *menu* €28. Reservations recommended. Open daily noon-1:30pm and 7-9:30pm. ❺

La Victoire Suprême du Coeur, 41 r. des Bourdonnais 1*er* (☎01 40 41 93 95). M: Châtelet. All vegetarian, and very tasty. Meals marked with a "V" can be made vegan. 2-course lunch *menu* €11. Open M-F 11:45am-3pm and 6:40-10pm, Sa noon-3pm and 6:40-10pm. MC/V. ❷

Le Fumoir, 6 r. de l'Amiral Coligny, 1*er* (☎01 42 92 05 05). M: Louvre. Decidedly untouristy types drink their chosen beverage in deep leather sofas. Serves one of the best brunches in Paris (€20). Coffee €2.50. Open daily 11am-2am. AmEx/MC/V. ❸

La Cucaracha, 31 r. Tiquetonne, 2*ème* (☎01 40 26 68 36). M: Etienne-Marcel. At this small, Mexican restaurant, flavorful dishes like enchiladas verde or fajitas will run you a reasonable €11-15. Open daily 7-11:30pm. MC/V. ❸

Babylone Bis, 34 r. Tiquetonne, 2*ème* (☎01 42 33 48 35). M: Etienne-Marcel. Antillean and African specialties. With zebra skin on the walls and loud *zouk* playing, this place gets wild. Cocktails €8-13. Dinner served all night. Open daily 8pm-8am. MC/V. ❸

Le Café Marly, cours Napoleon, 1*er* (☎01 49 26 06 60). M: Palais-Royal. One of Paris's classiest cafes, with a terrace facing the Louvre's I.M. Pei pyramids. Main dishes €16-28. Open daily 8am-2am. AmEx/DC/MC/V. ❹

Lamen Kintaro, 24 r. St-Augustin, 2*ème* (☎01 47 42 13 14). M: Opéra. Walk down ave. de l'Opéra and turn left on r. St-Augustin. Delicious and popular Japanese restaurant. Great noodle bowls (€7.80). Sapporo €4.30. Open M-Sa 11:30am-10pm. MC/V. ❷

3ÈME AND 4ÈME ARRONDISSEMENTS

The Marais offers chic bistros, kosher delis, and couple-friendly cafes.

◙ **Chez Janou,** 2 r. Roger Verlomme, 3ème (☎01 42 72 28 41). M: Chemin-Vert. Hip and friendly restaurant lauded for its reasonably priced gourmet food. Main courses such as *thon à la provençale* (€14) are delightful, as are the desserts (€6). Open daily noon-3pm and 8pm-midnight. ❸

◙ **Au Petit Fer à Cheval,** 30 r. Vieille-du-Temple, 4ème (☎01 42 72 47 47). M: Hôtel-de-Ville or St-Paul. An oasis of *chèvre, kir,* and *Gauloises,* and a loyal local crowd. Excellent house salads (€3.50-10). Desserts €4-7. Open daily 10am-2am; food served noon-1:15am. MC/V. ❷

L'As du Falafel, 34 r. des Rosiers, 4ème (☎01 48 87 63 60). M: St-Paul. Amazing falafel; special €5. Tiny but delicious lemonade €3.50 per glass. Open Su-F 11:30am-11:30pm. MC/V. ❶

Piccolo Teatro, 6 r. des Ecouffes (☎01 42 72 17 79). M: St-Paul. A romantic vegetarian hideout. Weekday lunch *menus* at €8.20, €9.90, or €13.30. Entrees €3.60-7.10. *Plats* €7.70-12.50. Open Tu-Sa noon-3pm and 7-11:30pm. AmEx/MC/V. ❷

404, 69 r. des Gravilliers, 3ème (☎01 42 74 57 81). M: Arts et Métiers. Classy, comfortable North African restaurant. Mouth-watering couscous (€13-23) and *tagines* (€13-19). Lunch *menu* €17. Open daily noon-2:30pm and 8pm-midnight. AmEx/MC/V. ❸

Georges, on the 6th fl. of the Centre Pompidou (☎01 44 78 47 99). Ultra-sleek, Zen-cool, in-the-spotlight cafe. Open M and W-Su noon-2am. ❸

Le Divin, 41 r. Ste-Croix-de-la-Bretonnerie (☎01 42 77 10 20). M: Hôtel-de-Ville. Fabulous *Provençal* fare. Vegetarian options available. *Menus* €16 and €21. Open Tu-Su 7-11:30pm. MC/V. ❹

5ÈME AND 6ÈME ARRONDISSEMENTS

The way to the Latin Quarter's heart is through its cafes. Tiny low-priced restaurants and cafes pack the quadrangle bounded by bd. St-Germain, bd. St-Michel, r. de Seine, and the Seine river. **Rue de Buci** harbors Greek restaurants and a street market, and **rue Gregoire de Tours** has cheap, greasy spoons for a quick bite.

◙ **Savannah Café,** 27 r. Descartes (☎01 43 29 45 77). M: Cardinal Lemoine. This cheerful yellow restaurant prides itself on its flavorful Lebanese food. *Entrées* €7-12.50. *Formule* €23. Open M-Sa 7-11pm. MC/V. ❹

Comptoir Méditerranée, 42 r. du Cardinal Lemoine (☎01 43 25 29 08). Savannah's little sister around the corner has takeout and lower prices. Open M-Sa 11am-10pm. ❷

THE HIDDEN DEAL

CAB FARE

When it comes to grabbing a late night snack in Paris, the options are about as plentiful as French millitary victories. The paucity of after-hours dining options exists for good reason: At 2am, perhaps the only people awake are club-goers and taxi-drivers. While the former group stumbles home, the latter group can be found chowing down at a club all their own. If you find yourself roming the streets of Paris in the wee hours with a sudden case of the hunger pangs, join them for some fabulously inexpensive, if culinarily unspectacular, nighttime eats.

Taxi Club ❹, 8 r. Etienne Marcel, 1er, (☎01 42 36 28 30) is at the intersection with r. de Turbigo. Look for the taxis. While far from gourmet, this quirky cafe attracts taxi-drivers with its cheap beer (€2.10-2.30) and cheaper coffee (€1). Customers dig in to breakfast served round-the-clock (omelette paysanne €4), a wide variety of meats (grilled chicken, €4.20), and the most expensive item on the menu: the plat du jour, a whopping €7. As if the cheap grub weren't appealing enough, the club has perfected the tacky-chic look: White Christmas lights, picnic-style table cloths, and mounted objects that were once attached to taxis. As a bonus, once you're done with your midnight munching, a cab driver is just a table away. Open daily 11am-2am. and 4am-6am.

Au Port Salut, 163bis r. St-Jacques (☎01 46 33 63 21). M: Luxembourg. 3 floors of traditional French cuisine. Fabulous 3-course *menus* change with the season (€12.50 and €22). Open Tu-Sa noon-2:30pm and 7-11:30pm. MC/V. ❸

Le Petit Vatel, 5 r. Lobineau (☎01 43 54 28 49). M: Mabillon. Fresh selection of Mediterranean-French specialties like *catalan pamboli* (bread with puréed tomatoes, ham, and cheese), all a very reasonable €10. Non-smoking. Lunch *menu* €11. Vegetarian options always available. Open Tu-Sa noon-2:30pm and 7-10:30pm. ❷

Les Editeurs, 4 carrefour d'Odéon (☎01 43 26 67 76). Les Editeurs pays homage to St-Germain's literary pedigree with books filling its plush red and gold dining rooms. Coffee €2.50, *pressions* €4.50, cocktails €9. *Croque Monsieur* €9.50. Happy Hour daily 6-8pm (cocktails €6-8). Open daily 8am-2am. AmEx/MC/V. ❷

Café de Flore, 172 bd. St-Germain (☎01 45 48 55 26). M: St-Germain-des-Prés. From the Métro, walk against traffic on bd. St-Germain. Sartre composed *Being and Nothingness* here. In the contemporary feud between Café de Flore and Les Deux Magots, Flore reportedly snags more of the local intellectuals. Espresso €4. Pastries €6-10.50. Open daily 7:30am-1:30am. AmEx/MC/V. ❸

Le Jardin des Pâtés, 4 r. Lacépède (☎01 43 31 50 71). M: Jussieu. From the Métro, walk up r. Linné and turn right on r. Lacépède. As calming and pleasant as the Jardin des Plantes around the corner. A menu of organic food is heavy on pâté (€7-12.50), pasta, and vegetables. Open daily noon-2:30pm and 7-11pm. MC/V. ❷

Così, 54 r. de Seine (☎01 46 33 35 36). M: Mabillon. From the métro, walk down bd. St-Germain and make a left onto r. de Seine. Enormous, tasty, inexpensive sandwiches on fresh, brick-oven bread. Sandwiches €5.20-7.60. Open daily noon-11pm. ❷

7ÈME AND 8ÈME ARRONDISSEMENTS

▨ **Le Lotus Blanc,** 45 r. de Bourgogne, 7ème (☎01 45 55 18 89). M: Varenne. Delicious Vietnamese fare. Lunch and all-day *menus* €9-29. Vegetarians will appreciate the great veggie *menu* (€6.50-12.50). Reservations encouraged. Open M-Sa noon-2:30pm and 7-10:30pm. Closed 2 weeks in Aug. AmEx/MC/V. ❸

▨ **Escrouzailles,** 36 r. du Colisée, 8ème (☎01 45 62 94 00). M: Franklin D. Roosevelt. Several comfortable yellow-walled dining rooms; fine yet relaxed dining. Choose from lists of entrees (€8) such as *foie gras*, *plats* (€12) such as the rack of lamb with zucchini, and delicious desserts (€6). Plenty of vegetarian options. Open M-Sa noon-2:30pm and 7:30-10:30pm. MC/V. ❷

Café des Lettres, 53 r. de Verneuil, 7ème (☎01 42 22 52 17). M: Solférino. This Scandinavian cafe offers unique tastes in a fantastic atmosphere. Patrons enjoy platters of smoked salmon and *blindis* (€16) and other Danish seafood dishes (€12.50-20). Coffee €2.50, beer €5-6. Open M noon-3pm, Tu-F noon-11pm, Sa noon-7pm. ❸

Le Paris, 93 av. des Champs-Elysées, 8ème (☎01 47 23 54 37). M: George V. Snobby, but the terrace is the ideal space for people-watching and sipping tea. At night, the cafe turns into a bar with a live DJ. Coffee €3.50, tea €5.50, glass of wine €5.50-7. Sandwiches €10-12.50. Soup €7. Open daily 8am-6pm. ❸

Bagel & Co., 31 r. de Ponthieu (☎01 42 89 44 20). M: Franklin D. Roosevelt. One of the only cheap options in the 8ème. A New York-inspired deli; bagel and specialty sandwiches €3-5. Vegetarian, kosher options. Open M-F 7:30am-9pm, Sa 10am-8pm. AmEx/MC/V. ❶

9ÈME TO 11ÈME ARRONDISSEMENTS

Meals close to the Opéra cater to the after-theater and movie crowd and can be quite expensive. **Rue Faubourg-Montmartre** is packed with cheap eateries.

■ **Haynes Restaurant Américain,** 3 r. Clauzel, 9ème (☎01 48 78 40 63). M: St-Georges. An expat center famous for its "original American Soul Food." Very generous portions, most under €16. Vocal jazz concerts F nights; funk and groove Sa nights (€6 cover). Open Tu-Sa 7pm-12:30am. AmEx/MC/V. ❸

■ **Le Bistro de Gala,** 45 r. du Faubourg-Montmartre, 9ème (☎01 40 22 90 50). M: Grands Boulevards. Spacious bistro lined with film posters; the reputed hangout of some of Paris's theater elite. The price of the *menu* is predictably high (€26-36), but definitely worth it. Reservations recommended. Open M-F noon-2:30pm and 7-11:30pm, Sa 7-11:30pm. AmEx/MC/V. ❺

Chez Paul, 13 r. de Charonne, 11ème (☎01 47 00 34 57). M: Bastille. Paul's fun staff serves a delicious menu. Extensive appetizer list; great *steak au poivre* with *au gratin* potatoes (€13). Reservations are a must during peak hours. Open daily noon-2:30pm and 7pm-2am; food served until 12:30am. AmEx/MC/V. ❸

Cantine d'Antoine et Lili, 95 quai de Valmy, 10ème (☎01 40 37 34 86). M: Gare de l'Est. Canal-side cafe-bistro with tasty, light fare. Pasta salads €6. Salads €6.50. Prices cheaper for takeout. Open Su-Tu 11am-8pm, W-Sa 11am-1am. AmEx/MC/V. ❶

Café de l'Industrie, 16 r. St-Sabin, 11ème(☎01 47 00 13 53). M: Breguet-Sabin. This happening cafe could double as a museum of French colonial history. Quality food, including a €9 lunch *menu*. Coffee €2, *vin chaud* €4. Salads €7-7.50. After 10pm, add €0.60. Open Su-F 10am-2am; lunch served noon-2pm. ❷

12ÈME TO 14ÈME ARRONDISSEMENTS

The 13ème is a budget gourmand's dream, with scores of Asian restaurants packing Paris's **Chinatown,** south of pl. d'Italie on av. de Choisy, and numerous affordable French restaurants in the **Butte-aux-Cailles** area. The 14ème is bordered at the top by the busy **boulevard du Montparnasse,** which is lined with a diverse array of restaurants. Rue du Montparnasse, which intersects with the boulevard, has reasonably priced *crêperies.* **Rue Daguerre** is lined with vegetarian-friendly restaurants. Inexpensive restaurants cluster on **rue Didot, rue du Commerce, rue de Vaugirard,** and **boulevard de Grenelle.**

■ **Café du Commerce,** 39 r. des Cinq Diamants, 13ème (☎01 53 62 91 04). M: Place d'Italie. Traditional food with a twist. Dinner (€15.50) and lunch (€10.50) *menus* both feature options like *boudin antillais* (spiced bloodwurst), and *fromage blanc aux kiwis.* Open daily noon-3pm and 7pm-2am, Sa and Su brunch noon-4pm. Reservations recommended for dinner. AmEx/MC/V. ❸

■ **Tricotin,** 15 av. de Choisy, 13ème (☎01 45 84 74 44). M: Porte de Choisy. This Asian eatery, one of the best in Chinatown, serves delicious food from Cambodia, Thailand, and Vietnam. The *vapeur* foods are specialties here—see if you can eat just one order of steamed shrimp ravioli (€3.40). Open daily 9:30am-11:30pm. MC/V. ❶

Chez Papa, 6 r. Gassendi, 14ème (☎01 43 22 41 19). M: Denfert-Rochereau. Delicious dishes are often served straight from the pot in which they were cooked. Hearty *menu* (€9.20) served M-F until 4pm. Also in the 8ème (29 r. de l'Arcade; ☎01 42 65 43 68), 10ème (206 r. Lafayette; ☎01 42 09 53 87), and 15ème. (101 r. de la Croix Nivert; ☎01 48 28 31 88). Open daily 10am-1am. AmEx/MC/V. ❷

Le Cheval de Troie, 71 r. de Charenton, 12ème (☎01 43 44 24 44). M: Bastille. Savory Turkish food in an appealing setting. Dinner *menu* €16. Open M-Sa noon-2:30pm and 7-11:30pm. MC/V. ❹

La Connivence, 1 r. de Cotte, 12ème (☎01 46 28 49 01). M: Ledru-Rollin. An elegant and intimate restaurant. Lunch *menus* €13-16. Dinner *menus* €17-22. Wine €14-38 per bottle. Mixed drinks €3-6. Open M-Sa noon-2:40pm and 7:40-11pm. MC/V. ❹

15ÈME AND 16ÈME ARRONDISSEMENTS

Thai Phetburi, 31 bd. de Grenelle, 15ème (☎01 41 58 14 88; www.phetburi-paris.com). M: Bir-Hakeim. Award-winning food, friendly service, low prices, and a relaxing atmosphere. Open M-Sa noon-2:30pm and 7-10:30pm. AmEx/MC/V. ❷

La Rotunde de la Muette, 12 Chaussée de la Muette, 16ème (☎01 45 24 45 45). M: La Muette. Hip cafe in a beautiful *fin-de-siècle* building overlooking the tree-lined Chaussée de la Muette. Sandwiches €5-9.60. Salads €4-9.15. AmEx/MC/V. ❷

Byblos Café, 6 r, Guichard, 16ème (☎01 42 30 99 99). M: La Muette. This airy, modern, Lebanese restaurant serves cold *mezzes* (think Middle Eastern *tapas*) that are good for pita-dipping. *Menu* €15. Vegetarian options available. Open daily 11am-3pm and 5-11pm. AmEx/MC/V. ❸

Aux Artistes, 63 r. Falguière, 15ème (☎01 43 22 05 39). M: Pasteur. One of the 15ème's coolest spots, this lively cafe draws a mix of professionals, students, and artists. Lunch *menu* €9.20, dinner *menu* €12.50. Open M-F noon-2:30pm and 7:30pm-midnight, Sa 7:30pm-midnight. ❸

18ÈME TO 20ÈME ARRONDISSEMENTS

In the 18ème, charming bistros and cafes lie near **rue des Abbesses** and **rue Lepic.** The 20ème's **Belleville** offers great traditional dining.

Refuge des Fondues, 17 r. des Trois Frères, 18ème (☎01 42 55 22 65). M: Abbesses. Only 2 main dishes: *Fondue bourguignonne* (meat fondue) and *fondue savoyarde* (cheese fondue). *Menu* €15. Reserve a table or show up early. Open daily 6:30pm-2am (no new diners after 12:30am). Closed Aug. ❸

Café Flèche d'Or, 102 r. de Bagnolet, 20ème (☎01 43 72 04 23; www.flechedor.com). M: Alexandre Dumas. In a defunct train station, this bar/cafe/performance space serves North African, French, Caribbean, and South American cuisine with nightly jazz, ska, folk, salsa, and samba (cover €5-6). Dinner *menus* €12-15. Bar/cafe open daily 10am-2am; dinner daily 8pm-1am. MC/V. ❸

L'Endroit, 67 pl. du Dr. Félix Lobligeois, 17ème (☎01 42 29 50 00). M: Rome. As cool by day as it is at night, L'Endroit must be, well, the place to go in the 17ème. Long menu packed with things like melon and *jambon* (€10.80), salads (€10.70), and toasted sandwiches (€10). Open daily noon-2am. MC/V. ❷

Lao Siam, 49 r. de Belleville, 19ème (☎01 40 40 09 68). M: Belleville. Every bite is worth writing about—you'll forget that you came so far out of your way. Open daily noon-3pm and 6:30-11:30pm. MC/V. ❷

SALONS DE THÉ

Parisian *salons de thé* (tea rooms) fall into three categories: Those stately salons straight out of the last century piled high with macaroons, Seattle-inspired joints for brooding intellectuals, and cafes that simply want to signal they also serve tea.

Angelina's, 226 r. de Rivoli, 1er (☎01 42 60 82 00). M: Concorde or Tuileries. Audrey Hepburn's old favorite. Little has changed here since it's 1903 opening. *Chocolat africain* (hot chocolate; €6.20) and *Mont Blanc* (meringue with chestnut nougat; €6) are the house specialties. Tea €6. Open daily 9am-7pm. AmEx/MC/V.

Mariage Frères, 30 r. du Bourg-Tibourg, 4ème (☎01 42 72 28 11). M: Hôtel-de-Ville. Started by 2 brothers who found British tea shoddy, this salon offers 500 varieties of tea (€7-15). A classic French institution. Tea *menu* includes sandwich, pastry, and tea (€25). Lunch M-Sa noon-3pm; afternoon tea 3-6:30pm; Su brunch 12:30-6:30pm. Open daily 10:30am-7:30pm. AmEx/MC/V.

L'Heure Gourmand, 22 passage Dauphine, 6ème (☎01 46 34 00 40). M: Odéon. A classy, quiet little *salon de thé* with a terrace on a beautiful side street. All teas €4.50, Berthillon ice cream €7-8, pastries €3-6. Open M-Sa noon-9pm, Su noon-7pm. MC/V.

SPECIALTY SHOPS

Food shops, particularly *boulangeries* (bakeries) and *pâtisseries* (pastry shops), are on virtually every street in Paris, or at least it seems like it. Not surprisingly, most of them are excellent; the following listings are some of the best.

Fauchon, 26, pl. de la Madeleine, 8ème (☎01 47 42 60 11). M: Madeleine. Paris's favorite gourmet food shop (complete with gourmet prices), this *traiteur/pâtisserie/épicerie/charcuterie* has it all. Open M-Sa 10am-7pm. MC/V.

Ice Cream: Octave, 138 r. Mouffetard, 5ème (☎01 45 35 20 56). M: Censier-Daubenton. Quite simply the best ice cream you will ever eat. All you taste in each lovely scoop is fresh melon, rich chocolate, soothing cinnamon or one of their many other *parfums*. One scoop €2, two scoops €3. Open Tu-Su 10am-11:30pm, M 2-7:30pm.

Wine: Nicolas, locations throughout Paris. Super-friendly English-speaking staff is happy to help you pick the perfect Burgundy. They will even pack it up in travel boxes with handles. Most branches open M-F 10am-8pm. AmEx/MC/V.

Bakery: Poujauran, 20 r. Jean-Nicot, 7ème (☎01 47 05 80 88). M: La Tour-Maubourg. Sells a wide range of *petit pains*, or miniature breads, alongside their bigger siblings. 2 *petit pains* average €1.50. Open Tu-Sa 8:30am-8:30pm.

Chocolates: La Maison du Chocolat, 8 bd. de la Madeleine, 9ème (☎01 47 42 86 52). M: Madeleine. A whole range of exquisite chocolates, from milk to dark, and a mysterious distilled chocolate essence drink. Box of 2 chocolates €3.30. Also at other locations, including 19 r. de Sèvres, 6ème (☎01 45 44 20 40). Open M-Sa 10am-7pm.

Pastries: Gérard Mulot, 76 r. de Seine, 6ème (☎01 43 26 85 11). M: Odéon or St-Sulpice. Outrageous selection of painstakingly crafted pastries and desserts, from flan to marzipan with virtually any kind of fruit. The *macaron* is heaven on earth (€4.20). Tarts from €2.50, éclairs €2. Open Tu and Th-Su 7am-8pm.

MARKETS

Marché r. Montorgueil, 2ème. M: Etienne-Marcel. From Métro, walk along r. Etienne Marcel away from the river. R. Montorgueil is the 2nd street on your right. A center of food commerce since the 13th century, the marble Mount Pride Market is comprised of wine, cheese, meat, and produce shops. Open Su and Tu-Sa 8am-7:30pm.

Marché Monge, 5ème. M: Monge. In pl. Monge at the Métro exit. A bustling, friendly, and easy-to-navigate market. You'll find everything from cheese to shoes to jewelry and flowers in these stalls. Look for the very popular prepared foods (perfect for a lunch picnic at the Arènes de Lutèce). Open W, F, and Su 8am-1:30pm.

Marché Mouffetard, 5ème. M: Monge. Walk through pl. Monge and follow r. Ortolan to r. Mouffetard. Cheese, meat, fish, produce, and housewares sold here. The bakeries are reputed to be some of the best of all the markets, and don't miss the ice cream at Octave near the far end of the market. Open Tu-Su 8am-1:30pm.

◙ SIGHTS

While seeing all there is to see in Paris is a daunting, if not impossible, task, you can make a solid dent in a reasonable amount of time. In a few hours, you can walk from the heart of the Marais in the east to the Eiffel Tower in the west, passing most major monuments along the way. A solid day of wandering will show you how close the medieval Notre Dame is to the modern Centre Pompidou and the funky Latin Quarter to the royal Louvre, and why you came here in the first place.

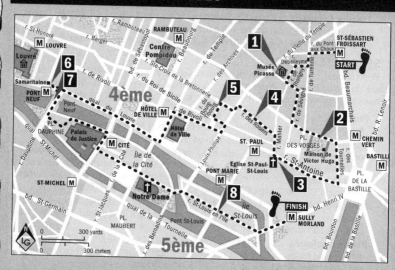

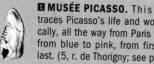

1 MUSÉE PICASSO. This museum traces Picasso's life and work chronologically, all the way from Paris to the Riviera, from blue to pink, from first mistress to last. (5, r. de Thorigny; see p. 320.)

START: M: Odéon.

FINISH: M: St-Michel.

DISTANCE: 6.1km/3¾ mi.

DURATION: 3-4hr.

WHEN TO GO: Start in the afternoon.

2 PLACE DES VOSGES. The exquisite manicured grass of Paris's oldest public square has been tread by the likes of Molière and Victor Hugo (no. 6 is a museum of his life and work), not to mention a good number of royals. An arcade runs around all four of its sides and houses restaurants, art galleries, and shops. (See p. 316.)

3 EGLISE ST-PAUL-ST-LOUIS. This Jesuit cathedral dominates r. St-Antoine and offers the weary traveler a break from the heat and car exhaust on the *rue*. The church's Baroque interior houses Eugène Delacroix's dramatic *Christ in the Garden of Olives* (1826).

4 RUE DES ROSIERS. This quintessential Marais street is filled with bakeries, off-beat boutiques, and kosher restaurants. For lunch, enjoy a delicious falafel sandwich at the perpetually crowded **L'As du Falafel.**, no. 34. (See p. 305.)

5 MARIAGE FRÈRES. This classic and classy *salon de thé* has 500 varieties of tea to choose from. (30, r. du Bourg-Tibourg; see p. 308.)

6 SAMARITAINE. Eleven floors of shopping for him, her, and home are topped off with an unbeatable panoramic view of the city. Markers name every dot on the horizon, making this Art Deco department store worth a visit, even if shopping isn't on the agenda. (67, r. de Rivoli; see p. 326.)

7 PONT NEUF. By way of the very long, very straight, rue de Rivoli and the scenic quai du Louvre, make your way to the Pont Neuf, Paris's oldest bridge (c. 1607). Its gargoyles have seen peddlers and pickpockets, and a whole lot of bubble wrap.

8 RUE ST-LOUIS-EN-ÎLE. Wander down the charming 17th-century-esque main street of the Île St-Louis, popping into a chic boutique or two and stopping for a scoop of **Berthillon** ice cream (no. 34) or gelato at **Amarino** (no. 47). (See p. 312.)

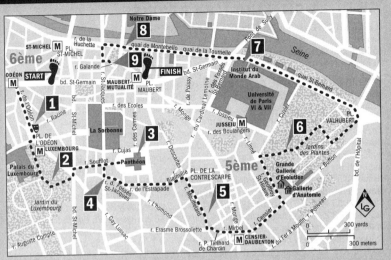

START: M: St-Sébastien Froissart.

FINISH: M: Sully Morland.

DISTANCE: 5.2km/3¼ mi.

DURATION: 3-4hr.

WHEN TO GO: Start in the late morning.

1 THÉÂTRE DE L'ODÉON. When you get off the métro, take a look at the impressive facade of the Odéon, Paris's oldest and largest theater. (See p. 314.)

2 JARDIN DU LUXEMBOURG. Architectural excesses, beautiful lawns, miniature sailboats, and plenty of shady spots make this garden a favorite. (See p. 313.)

3 PANTHÉON. The inscription reads: "To great men from a grateful fatherland." The Panthéon indeed houses some great men (and women): its crypt contains the remains of Emile Zola, Marie Curie, Victor Hugo, and others. And the fatherland must have been grateful to have put them up in a building as beautiful as this one. (See p. 313.)

4 AU PORT SALUT. The traditional 3-course lunch at this boisterous former cabaret is pure gastronomic joy. (163bis, r. St-Jacques; see p. 306.)

5 RUE MOUFFETARD. The Mouff' has held onto its charm since the 2nd century. Hemingway and Paul Verlaine both came to stay. Have some of (arguably) the best ice cream in Paris at **Octave,** no. 138. (See p. 309.)

6 JARDIN DES PLANTES. The Jardin's rare plants and exquisite *roserie* draw visitors. The **Galerie d'Anatomie** is the unlikely star of the garden's many museums. (See p. 314.)

7 INSTITUT DU MONDE ARABE . This modern building has excellent exhibits, striking architecture , and a great (free!) view of the city. (See p. 321.)

8 SHAKESPEARE & CO. Stroll along the Seine until you reach Shakespeare & Co. No visit to the Latin Quarter would be complete without a stop in at this famed bookstore. (37, r. de la Boucherie; see p. 296.)

9 LE CAVEAU DE LA HUCHETTE. This club serves refreshing *digestifs* upstairs and great jazz downstairs. (5, r. de la Huchette.)

ÎLE DE LA CITÉ AND ÎLE ST-LOUIS

ÎLE DE LA CITÉ. If any one place is the heart of Paris, it is this small island. In the 3rd century BC, when it was inhabited by the *Parisii*, a Gallic tribe of hunters, sailors, and fishermen, the Île was all there was to Paris. Today, all distance-points in France are measured from *kilomètre zéro*, a sundial in front of Notre-Dame.

CATHÉDRALE DE NOTRE DAME DE PARIS. This 12th- to 14th-century cathedral, begun under Bishop Maurice Sully, is one of the world's most famous and beautiful examples of medieval architecture. After the Revolution, the building fell into disrepair and was even used to shelter livestock until Victor Hugo's 1831 novel *Notre Dame de Paris* (a.k.a. *The Hunchback of Notre Dame*) inspired citizens to lobby for restoration. The intricately carved, apocalyptic facade and soaring, apparently weightless walls, effects produced by brilliant Gothic engineering and optical illusions, are inspiring even for the most church-weary. The cathedral's biggest draws are its enormous stained-glass **rose windows** that dominate the north and south ends of the transept. A staircase inside the towers leads to a perch from which gargoyles survey the city. (*M: Cité.* ☎01 53 40 60 87; crypt 01 43 29 83 51. *Cathedral open daily 8am-6:45pm. Towers July-Aug. 9am-7:30pm; Sept.-June reduced hours. Admission €6.10, ages 18-25 €4.10. Tours begin at the booth to the right as you enter. In English W-Th noon, Sa 2:30pm; in French M-F noon, Sa 2:30pm. Free. Treasury open M-Sa 9:30am-12:30pm and 1:30-5:30pm, Su 1:30-5:30pm; last ticket at 5pm. €2.50, students €2. Crypt open daily 10am-5:30pm. €3.90, under-27 €2.20.*)

■ **STE-CHAPELLE AND CONCIERGERIE.** Within the courtyard of the **Palais de Justice,** which has housed Paris's district courts since the 13th century, the opulent, Gothic **Ste-Chapelle** was built by Saint Louis (Louis IX) to house his most precious possession, Christ's crown of thorns, now in Notre Dame. No mastery of the lower chapel's dim gilt can prepare the visitor for the **Upper Chapel,** where twin walls of stained glass glow and frescoes of saints and martyrs shine. (*4 bd. du Palais. M: Cité. Within Palais de la Cité. Open daily Apr.-Sept. 9:30am-6pm. €6.10, seniors and ages 18-25 €4.10. Under-18 free.*) Around the corner is the **Conciergerie,** one of Paris's most famous prisons; Marie-Antoinette and Robespierre were imprisoned here during the Revolution. (*Entrance on bd. du Palais, to the right of Palais de Justice. M: Cité. Open daily Apr.-Sept. 9:30am-6:30pm; Oct.-Mar. 10am-5pm. €6.10, students €4.10.*)

ÎLE ST-LOUIS. The Île St-Louis is home to some of Paris's most privileged elite, like the Rothschilds and Pompidou's widow, and formerly Voltaire, Baudelaire, and Marie Curie. Paris's best ice cream is at ■**Berthillon,** 31 r. St-Louis-en-Ile. (*M: Pont Marie. Open Sept. to mid-July; take-out W-Su 10am-8pm; eat-in W-F 1-8pm, Sa-Su 2-8pm.*)

ÉGLISE ST-LOUIS-EN-L'ILE. Louis Le Vau's 17th-century Rococo interior is lit by a surprising number of windows. The third chapel has a splendid gilded wood relief, *The Death of the Virgin.* (*19bis r. St-Louis-en-l'Ile.* ☎01 46 34 11 60. *Open Su and Tu-Sa 9am-noon and 3-7pm. Check with FNAC (www.fnac.com) or call the church for concert details; ticket prices vary, usually around €20 general admission and €15 for students.*)

THE LATIN QUARTER AND ST-GERMAIN-DES-PRÉS: 5ÈME AND 6ÈME ARRONDISSEMENTS

The student population is the soul of the Latin Quarter named for prestigious *lycées* and universities that taught in Latin until 1798. Since the violent student riots in May 1968, many artists and intellectuals have migrated to the cheaper outer *arrondissements*, and the *haute bourgeoisie* have moved in. The *5ème* still presents the most diverse array of bookstores, cinemas, bars, and jazz clubs in the city. Designer shops and cutting edge art galleries lie near **St-Germain-des-Prés.**

BOULEVARD ST-MICHEL AND ENVIRONS. At the center of the Latin Quarter, bd. St-Michel, which divides the 5*ème* and 6*ème*, is filled with cafes, restaurants, bookstores, and clothing boutiques. **Place St-Michel**, to the north, is packed with students, often engaged in a protest of some sort, and lots of tourists. *(M: St-Michel.)*

LA SORBONNE. Founded in 1253 by Robert de Sorbon as a dormitory for 16 poor theology students, the Sorbonne is one of Europe's oldest universities. Visitors can stroll through the **Chapelle de la Sorbonne** (entrance off of the pl. de la Sorbonne), an impressive space which houses temporary exhibitions on the arts and letters. Nearby **place de la Sorbonne**, off bd. St-Michel, boasts a flavorful assortment of cafes, bookstores, and—during term-time—students. *(45-7 r. des Ecoles. M: Cluny-La Sorbonne or RER: Luxembourg. Walk away from the Seine on bd. St-Michel and turn left on r. des Ecoles to see the main building.)*

RUE MOUFFETARD. South of pl. de la Contrescarpe, **rue Mouffetard** plays host to one of the liveliest street markets in Paris, and, along with **rue Monge**, binds much of the Latin Quarter's student social life. *(M: Cardinal Lemoine or Place Monge.)*

JARDIN DU LUXEMBOURG. South along bd. St-Michel, the formal French gardens of the Jardin du Luxembourg are perfect for strolling and reading; they're also home to the most famous *guignol* puppet theater. *(RER: Luxembourg; main entrance is on bd. St-Michel. Open Apr.-Oct. daily 7:30am-9:30pm; Nov.-Mar. 8:15am-5pm.)*

PANTHÉON. The **crypt** of the Panthéon, which occupies the highest point on the Left Bank, houses the tombs of Louis Braille, Victor Hugo, Jean Jaurès, Rousseau, Voltaire, and Emile Zola; you can spy each tomb from behind locked gates. The Panthéon also houses **Foucault's Pendulum**, which proves the rotation of the earth. *(Pl. du Panthéon. M: Cardinal Lemoine. From the Métro, walk down r. Cardinal Lemoine and turn right on r. Clovis; walk around to the front of the building to enter. Open daily in summer 10am-6pm; off-season 10am-6pm; last admission 5:15pm. Admission €7, students €4.50. Under-18 free. Free entrance first Su of every month Oct.-Mar. Guided tours in French leave from inside the main door daily at 2:30 and 4pm.)*

MOSQUÉE DE PARIS. The *Institut Musulman* houses the beautiful Persian gardens, elaborate minaret, and shady porticoes of the Mosquée de Paris, a mosque constructed in 1920 by French architects to honor the role played by the countries of North Africa in WWI. Exhausted travelers can relax in the steam baths at the exquisite *hammam* (Turkish bath) or sip mint tea at the equally soothing cafe. *(M: Jussieu. Behind the Jardin des Plantes at pl. du Puits de l'Ermite. From the métro, walk down r. Daubenton; the mosque is at the end of the street, on the left. ☎01 48 35 78 17. Open June-Aug. daily 10am-noon and 2-6:30pm; Sept.-May reduced hours. Guided tour €3, students €2. Hammam open for men Tu 2-9pm and Su 10am-9pm; women M, W-Th, Sa 10am-9pm and F 2-9pm. €15. 10min. massage €10, 30min. massage €30. MC/V.)*

BOULEVARD ST-GERMAIN. Most famous as the ex-literati hangout of Existentialists (who frequented the Café de Flore, p. 306) and Surrealists like André Breton (who preferred the Deux Magots), the bd. St-Germain is stuck somewhere in between nostalgia for its intellectual cafe-culture past and an unabashed delight with all things fashionable and cutting edge. *(M: St-Germain-des-Prés.)*

ÉGLISE ST-GERMAIN-DES-PRÉS. Scarred by centuries of weather, revolution, and war, the Église St-Germain-des-Prés, begun in 1163, is the oldest standing church in Paris. *(3 pl. St-Germain-des-Prés. From the Métro, walk into pl. St-Germain-des-Prés to enter the church from the front. Open daily 8am-8pm. Info office open M 2:30-6:45pm, Tu-Sa 10:30am-noon and 2:30-6:45pm.)*

JARDIN DES PLANTES. Opened in 1640 to grow medicinal plants for King Louis XIII, the garden now features science museums, rosaries, and a zoo, which Parisians raided for food during the Prussian siege of 1871. (*M: Gare d'Austerlitz or Jussieu.* ☎ *01 40 79 37 94. Open daily 7:30am-8pm; off-season 7:30am-5:30pm.*)

ODÉON. **Cour du Commerce St-André** is one of the most picturesque walking areas in the 6*ème*, with cobblestone streets, centuries-old cafés (including **Le Procope**), and outdoor seating. Just to the south of bd. St-Germain-des-Prés, the **Carrefour d'Odéon**, a favorite Parisian hangout, is a delightful square filled with bistros, cafes, and more outdoor seating. (*M: Odéon.*)

7ÈME ARRONDISSEMENT

EIFFEL TOWER. Gustave Eiffel, its designer, wrote: "France is the only country in the world with a 300m flagpole." Designed in 1889 as the tallest structure in the world, the Eiffel Tower was conceived as a monument to engineering that would surpass the Egyptian pyramids in size and notoriety. Before construction had begun, shockwaves of dismay reverberated through the city. Critics dubbed it a "metal asparagus" and a Parisian tower of Babel. Writer Guy de Maupassant ate lunch every day at its ground-floor restaurant—the only place in Paris, he claimed, from which he couldn't see the offensive thing. Nevertheless, when it was inaugurated in March 1889 as the centerpiece of the Universal Exposition, the tower earned the love of Paris; nearly 2 million people ascended during the event. Today, as an icon of Paris represented on everything from postcards to neckties and umbrellas, Eiffel's wonder still takes the heat from some who see it as Maupassant did: An "excruciating nightmare" overrun with tourists and their trinkets. Don't believe the anti-hype, though. The tower may not be beautiful, but it is a wonder of design and engineering. (*M: Bir-Hakeim or Trocadéro.* ☎ *01 44 11 23 23; www.tour-eiffel.fr. Open daily mid-June through Aug. 9am-midnight; Sept.-Dec. 9:30am-11pm (stairs 9:30am-6pm); Jan. through mid-June 9:30am-11pm (stairs 9:30am-6:30pm). Elevator to 1st fl. €3.70; 2nd fl. €7; 3rd fl. €10.20. Stairs to 1st and 2nd fl. €3. Last access to top 30min. before closing.*)

INVALIDES. The gold-leaf dome of the Hôtel des Invalides shines at the center of the 7*ème*. The green, tree-lined **Esplanade des Invalides** runs from the *hôtel* to the **Pont Alexandre III,** a bridge with gilded lampposts from which you can catch a great view of the Invalides and the Seine. The **Musée de l'Armée, Musée des Plans-Reliefs,** and **Musée de l'Ordre de la Libération** are housed in the Invalides museum complex (see **Museums,** p. 319), as is **Napoleon's tomb,** in the **Église St-Louis.** Enter from either pl. des Invalides or pl. Vauban and av. de Tourville. To the left of the Tourville entrance, the **Jardin de l'Intendant** is a shady break from guns and emperors. (*M: Invalides, Latour Maubourg, or Varenne.*)

LA PAGODE. A pseudo-Japanese pagoda built in 1895 by the Bon Marché department store magnate M. Morin as a gift to his wife, La Pagode is an artifact the 19th-century Orientalist craze in France. When Mme. Morin left her husband just prior to WWI, the building became the scene of Sino-Japanese soirées. In 1931, La Pagode opened its doors to the public, becoming a cinema and cafe where silent screen stars like Gloria Swanson were known to raise a glass. The theater closed during the Nazi occupation, despite its friendliness towards German patrons. It reopened under a private owner in November 2000. (*M: St-François-Xavier. 57bis r. de Babylone.*)

MONTPARNASSE: 13ÈME, 14ÈME, AND 15ÈME ARRONDISSEMENTS

CHINATOWN. Paris's Chinatown is bounded by r. de Tolbiac, bd. Masséna, av. de Choisy, and av. d'Ivry. It is home to large Chinese, Vietnamese, and Cambodian communities, and a host of Asian restaurants and shops. (*M: Tolbiac.*)

BOULEVARD DE MONTPARNASSE. In the early 20th century, Montparnasse became a center for avant-garde artists such as Modigliani and Chagall. Political exiles like Lenin and Trotsky talked strategy over cognac in the cafes, including **Le Dôme, Le Sélect,** and **La Coupole,** along bd. Montparnasse. After WWI, Montparnasse attracted American expatriates and artistic rebels like Calder, Hemingway, and Henry Miller. *(M:Montparnasse-Bienvenue).*

THE CATACOMBS. A series of tunnels 20m below ground and 1.7km in length, the Catacombs were originally excavated to provide stone for building the city. By the 1770s, much of the Left Bank was in danger of caving in and digging promptly stopped. The former quarry was then used as a mass grave, relieving Paris's foul and overcrowded cemeteries. During WWII, the Resistance set up headquarters among the departed. *(M: Denfert-Rochereau. 1 pl. Denfert-Rochereau. ☎01 43 22 47 63. From the Métro, take exit pl. Denfert-Rochereau and cross av. du Général Leclerc; the entrance is the dark green structure straight ahead. Open Tu 11am-4pm, W-Sa 9am-4pm. €5, seniors €3.30, ages 14-26 €2.50. Under-14 free. Tour lasts 45min.)*

LE PARC ANDRÉ CITROËN. The futuristic Parc André Citroën was created by landscapers Alain Provost and Gilles Clément in the 1970s. Rides in the hot-air balloon that launches from the central garden offer spectacular aerial views of the park and all of Paris. *(2 r. de la Montagne de la Fage. ☎01 44 26 20 00; www.volenballon.com. M: Javel-André Citroën or Balard. Open M-F 7:30am-9:30pm, Sa-Su 9am-9:30pm. Balloon rides €12, ages 12-17 €10, ages 3-11 €6. Under-3 free. Tours of the park in English June-Sept. Sa 10:30am; call ☎01 40 71 75 60 for more info. €5.80.)*

LOUVRE AND OPÉRA: 1ER, 2ÈME, AND 9ÈME ARRONDISSEMENTS

LOUVRE AND TUILERIES. World-famous art museum and former residence of kings, the **Louvre** (p. 319) occupies about one-seventh of the 1er *arrondissement.* **Le Jardin des Tuileries,** at the western foot of the Louvre, was commissioned by Catherine de Médicis in 1564 and improved by André Le Nôtre (designer of the gardens at Versailles) in 1649. *(M: Tuileries. ☎01 40 20 90 43. Open daily Apr.-Sept. 7am-9pm; Oct.-Mar. 7:30am-7:30pm. Tours in English from the Arc de Triomphe du Carrousel.)* Three blocks north along r. de Castiglione, **place Vendôme** hides 20th-century offices and luxury shops behind 17th-century facades. Look out for Napoleon on top of the column in the center of the *place*—he's the one in the toga. *(M: Tuileries or Concorde.)*

PALAIS-ROYAL. One block north of the Louvre along r. St-Honoré lies the once regal and racy Palais-Royal, constructed in the 17th century as Cardinal Richelieu's Palais Cardinal. After the Cardinal's death in 1642, Queen Anne d'Autriche moved in, bringing with her a young Louis XIV. In the central courtyard, the controversial **colonnes de Buren,** a set of black-and-white striped pillars, were installed by artist Daniel Buren in 1986. *(Fountain open June-Aug. daily 7am-11pm; Sept. 7am-9:30pm; Oct.-Mar. 7am-8:30pm; Apr.-May 7am-10:15pm. Free.)*

LES HALLES. A sprawling market since 1135, Les Halles received a much-needed face-lift in the 1850s with the construction of large iron-and-glass pavilions to shelter the vendors's stalls. In 1970, when authorities moved the old market to a suburb, planners destroyed the pavilions to build a subterranean transfer-point between the Métro and the new commuter rail and a subterranean shopping mall, the **Forum des Halles,** with over 200 boutiques and three movie theaters. *(M: Les Halles).*

OPÉRA. Located north of the Louvre in the 9ème arrondissement, Charles Garnier's grandiose **Opéra Garnier** was built under Napoleon III in the eclectic style of the Second Empire. Gobelin tapestries, gilded mosaics, a 1964 Marc Chagall ceiling, and a six-ton chandelier adorn the magnificent interior. *(M: Opéra. General info*

FRANCE

☎08 36 69 78 68, tours 01 40 01 22 63; www.opera-de-paris.fr. Concert hall and museum open Sept. to mid-July daily 10am-5pm, last entry 4:30pm; mid-July to Aug. 10am-6pm, last entry 5:30pm. Concert hall closed during rehearsals; call ahead. Admission €6; ages 10-16, students, and over 60 €3. English tours daily at noon and 2pm. €10; students €8.)

PIGALLE. Farther north, at the border of the 18ème, is the infamous area named Pigalle. Stretching along the trash-covered bd. de Clichy from pl. Pigalle to pl. Blanche is a salacious, voracious, and generally pretty naughty neighborhood, the home of famous cabarets-cum-nightclubs like Folies Bergère, Moulin Rouge, and Folies Pigalle. The areas to the north of bd. de Clichy and south of pl. Blanche are comparatively calmer, but visitors should **exercise caution** at all times. (M: Pigalle.)

MARAIS: 3ÈME AND 4ÈME ARRONDISSEMENTS

RUE DES ROSIERS. Until the 13th century, Paris's Jewish community was concentrated in front of Notre Dame. When Philippe-Auguste expelled the Jewish population from the city limits, many families moved to the Marais, just outside the walls. Since then, this quarter has been Paris's Jewish center, with two synagogues at 25 r. des Rosiers and 10 r. Pavée, designed by Art Nouveau architect Hector Guimard. The mix of Mediterranean and Eastern European Jewish cultures gives the area a unique flavor, with kugel and falafel served side by side. Nearby, the corner of **rue Vielle-de-Temple** and **rue St-Croix de la Brettonnerie** is the epicenter of the Marais's gay community, with tons of fun cafes and bars. (M: St-Paul. Four blocks east of Beaubourg, parallel to r. des Francs-Bourgeois.)

MÉMORIAL DU MARTYR JUIF INCONNU. The Memorial to the Unknown Jewish Martyr is the child of a 1956 committee that included de Gaulle, Churchill, and Ben-Gurion; it commemorates European Jews who died at the hands of the Nazis and their French collaborators. Usually located in the 4ème, the memorial is under renovation in 2003; the address below is temporary. (M: St-Paul. 37 r. de Turenne. ☎01 42 77 44 72; fax 01 48 87 12 50. Exposition open M-Th 10am-1pm and 2-5:30pm, F 10am-1pm and 2-5pm. Archives open M-W 11am-5:30pm, Th 11am-8pm.)

HÔTEL DE VILLE. Paris's grandiose city hall dominates a large square with fountains and Belle Époque lampposts. The present edifice is a 19th-century creation built to replace the original medieval structure, a meeting hall for the cartel that controlled traffic on the Seine. (29 r. de Rivoli. M: Hôtel-de-Ville. ☎01 42 76 43 43. Open M-F 9am-6:30pm when there is an exhibit, until 6pm otherwise. Tours given by individual lecturers available for groups with advance reservations; the Hôtel provides a list of lecturers, their dates, and phone numbers; some lecturers offer English tours.)

PLACE DES VOSGES. At the end of r. des Francs-Bourgeois sits the magnificent pl. des Vosges, Paris's oldest public square. The place is one of Paris's most charming spots for a picnic or an afternoon siesta. **Victor Hugo** lived at no. 6, which is now a museum of his life and work. (M: Chemin Vert or St-Paul.)

BASTILLE: 10ÈME, 11ÈME, AND 12ÈME ARRONDISSEMENTS

CANAL ST-MARTIN. Measuring 4.5km, the 1825 canal has several locks, which can be observed on a Canauxrama trip. The canal was built in 1825 as a shortcut for river traffic on the Seine (to which it no longer connects), and it also served as a defense against the upstart eastern arrondissements. This lovely residential area is being rediscovered by Parisians and tourists alike, and is a great place to wander. (M: République or Goncourt will take you to the most beautiful end of the canal.)

THE BASTILLE PRISON. Originally commissioned by Charles V to safeguard the eastern entrance to Paris and later made into a state prison by Louis XIII, the Bastille was hardly the hell-hole the Revolutionaries who tore it down imagined. Titled inmates were allowed to furnish their suites and bring their own servants. Today, the **July Column**, at one corner of the pl. de la Bastille, commemorates the site where the prison once stood. Since the late 19th century, July 14 has been the official state holiday of the French Republic and is usually a time of glorious firework displays and equally glorious alcohol consumption. *(M: Bastille.)*

OPÉRA BASTILLE. Like its namesake, the Opéra Bastille has stirred up a lot of opposition. One of Mitterrand's *Grands Projets*, the Opéra, designed by a Canadian, opened in 1989 to protests over its unattractive design. On the tour (expensive but extremely impressive) you'll see a different side of the largest theater in the world. The immense auditorium seats 2703 people, but 95% of the building is taken up by exact replicas of the stage for rehearsals and workshops. *(M: Bastille. 130 r. de Lyon. ☎01 40 01 19 70; www.opera-de-paris.fr. €10, over-60 €8, students and under-26 €5. 1hr. tour almost every day, usually at 1 or 5pm; call ahead (tours in French, but groups of ten or more can arrange for English.)*

CHAMPS-ELYSÉES AND NEARBY: 8ÈME AND 16ÈME ARRONDISSEMENTS

PLACE DE LA CONCORDE. Paris's most famous public square lies at the eastern end of the Champs-Elysées. Built between 1757 and 1777 as a monument to Louis X, the area soon became the **place de la Révolution,** site of the guillotine that severed 1343 necks from their blue-blooded bodies. After the Reign of Terror, the square was renamed *concorde* (peace). The huge, rose-granite, 13th-century BC **Obélisque de Luxor** depicts the deeds of Egyptian pharaoh Ramses II. Given to Charles X by the Viceroy of Egypt, it is Paris's oldest monument. *(M: Concorde.)*

CHAMPS-ELYSÉES. Stretching west and anchored by the Arc de Triomphe on one end and the pl. de Concorde on the other, the legendary **avenue des Champs-Elysées** is lined with luxury shops, chain stores, cafes, and cinemas. The avenue is the work of Baron Haussmann, who was commissioned by Napoleon III to convert Paris into a grand capital with broad avenues, wide sidewalks, new parks, elegant housing, and sanitary sewers. The city's most elegant shopping is on **avenue Montagne** and **rue Faubourg St-Honoré.**

ARC DE TRIOMPHE. Napoleon commissioned the Arc de Triomphe, at the western terminus of the Champs-Elysées, in 1806 in honor of his Grande Armée. In 1940, Parisians were brought to tears as Nazis goose-stepped through the Arc; on August 26, 1944, British, American, and French troops liberating the city from Nazi occupation marched through to the roaring cheers of thousands. The terrace at the top has a fabulous view. The **Tomb of the Unknown Soldier** has been under the Arc since November 11, 1920. It bears the inscription, "Here lies a French soldier who died for his country, 1914-1918," but represents the 1,500,000 men who died during WWI. *(On pl. Charles de Gaulle. M: Charles-de-Gaulle-Etoile. Open Apr.-Sept. daily 10am-11pm; Oct.-Mar. 10am-10:30pm. €7, ages 18-25 €4.50. Under-17 free.)*

THE MADELEINE. Mirrored by the Assemblée Nationale across the Seine, the Madeleine—formally called **Église Ste-Marie-Madeleine** (Mary Magdalene)—was begun in 1764 by Louis XV and modeled after a Greek temple. Construction was halted during the Revolution, when the Cult of Reason proposed transforming the building into a bank, a theater, or a courthouse. Characteristically, Napoleon decreed that it should become a temple to the greatness of his army, but Louis

FRANCE

XVIII shouted, "It shall be a church!" Completed in 1842, the structure stands alone in the medley of Parisian churches, distinguished by four ceiling domes that light the interior, 52 exterior Corinthian columns, and a curious altarpiece. *(Pl. de la Madeleine. M: Madeleine. ☎01 44 51 69 00. Open daily 7:30am-7pm.)*

PLACE DU TROCADÉRO. In the 1820s, the Duc d'Angoulême built a memorial to his victory in Spain at Trocadéro. Jacques Carlu's modern design for the 1937 World Exposition (which beat out Le Corbusier's plan) for the **Palais de Chaillot** features two white stone wings cradling an austere, Art Deco courtyard that extends from the *place* over spectacular cannon-shaped fountains. The terrace offers brilliant views of the Eiffel Tower and Champs de Mars, particularly at night. Be aware of possible pickpockets as you gaze upward. *(M: Trocadéro.)*

MONTMARTRE AND PERE-LACHAISE: 18ÈME, 19ÈME, AND 20ÈME ARRONDISSEMENTS

MOUNTING MONTMARTRE. Montmartre, comprised mostly of one very large hill, is one of the few Parisian neighborhoods Baron Haussmann left intact when he redesigned the city and its environs. During its Belle Epoque heyday from 1875 to 1905, it attracted bohemians like Toulouse-Lautrec and Erik Satie as well as performers and impresarios like Aristide Bruant. Later, Picasso, Modigliani, Utrillo, and Apollinaire came into its artistic circle. Nowadays, Montmartre is a mix of upscale bohemia (above r. des Abbesses) and sleaze (along bd. de Clichy). The northwestern part of the area retains some village charm, with breezy streets speckled with interesting shops and cafes. *(Funicular runs up and down the hill every 2min. Open 6am-12:30am. €1.30 or Métro ticket. M: Anvers or Abbesses.)*

BASILIQUE DU SACRÉ-COEUR. The Basilique du Sacré-Coeur crowns the butte Montmartre like an enormous white meringue. Its onion dome is visible from almost anywhere in the city, and its 112m bell tower is the highest point in Paris, offering a view that stretches up to 50km. *(35 r. du Chevalier de la Barre. M: Anvers, Abbesses, or Château-Rouge. ☎01 53 41 89 00. Open daily 7am-10:30pm. Wheelchair accessible through back. Free. Dome and crypt open daily 9am-6:45pm. €5.)* Nearby, **place du Tertre** is full of touristy cafes and amateur artists.

BAL DU MOULIN ROUGE. Along the bd. de Clichy and bd. de Rochechouart, you'll find many of the cabarets and nightclubs that were the definitive hangouts of the Belle Epoque, including the infamous cabaret Bal du Moulin Rouge, immortalized by the paintings of Toulouse-Lautrec, the music of Offenbach, and, most recently, Baz Luhrmann's Hollywood blockbuster. *(M: Blanche. 82 bd. de Clichy. Directly across from the métro. ☎01 53 09 82 82; www.moulin-rouge.com. Shows 7, 9, 11pm.)*

PARC DES BUTTES-CHAUMONT. In the south of the 19*ème*, Parc des Buttes-Chaumont is a mix of man-made topography and transplanted vegetation; Napoleon III commissioned it in 1860 out of a longing for London's Hyde Park, where he spent much of his exile. Today's visitors walk the paths surrounded by lush greenery and dynamic hills, and enjoy a great view of the *quartier* from the cave-filled cliffs topped with a Roman temple. Watch out for the ominously-named *Pont des Suicides. (M: Buttes-Chaumont and Botzaris both exit onto the park. Open daily 7am-11pm.)*

CIMETIÈRE PÈRE LACHAISE. The Cimetière Père Lachaise, located in the 20*ème*, holds the remains of Balzac, Sarah Bernhardt, Colette, Danton, David, Delacroix, La Fontaine, Haussmann, Molière, Proust, and Seurat within its peaceful, winding paths and elaborate sarcophagi. Foreigners buried here include Modigliani, Gertrude Stein, and Oscar Wilde, but the most visited grave is that of Jim Morrison. French Leftists make ceremonious pilgrimage to the

Mur des Fédérés (Wall of the Federals), where 147 revolutionaries were executed and buried. *(16 r. du Repos. M: Père-Lachaise. Open Mar.-Oct. M-F 8am-6pm, Sa 8:30am-6pm, Su and holidays 9am-6pm; Nov.-Feb. M-F 8am-5:30pm, Sa 8:30am-5:30pm, Su and holidays 9am-5:30pm. Last entrance 15min. before closing. Free.)*

PERIMETER SIGHTS

LA DÉFENSE. Outside the city limits, west of the 16*ème*, the skyscrapers and modern architecture of La Défense make up Paris's newest (unofficial) *arrondissement*, home to the headquarters of 14 of France's top 20 corporations. The **Grande Arche**, inaugurated in 1989, completes the *axe historique* running through the Louvre, pl. de la Concorde, and the Arc de Triomphe. There's yet another stunning view from the top. Trees, shops, and sculptures by Miró and Calder line the esplanade. *(M/ RER: La Défense. Arch open daily 10am-8pm. €7.50; under-18, students, and seniors €5.50.)*

BOIS DE BOULOGNE. Popular by day for picnics, this 846-hectare (roughly 2,000-acre) park was until recently home to many drug dealers and prostitutes at night and is not the best bet for nighttime entertainment. *(On the western edge of the 16ème. M: Porte Maillot, Sablons, Pont de Neuilly, or Porte Dauphine.)*

🏛 MUSEUMS

The **Carte Musées et Monuments** grants immediate entry to 70 Paris museums (no waiting in line) and will save you money if you plan to visit three or more museums and major sights per day. It's available at major museums and Métro stations. (1-day €22; 3-days €38; 5-days €52.)

MUSÉE DU LOUVRE . A short list of its masterpieces includes the *Code of Hammurabi*, Jacques-Louis David's *The Oath of the Horatii*, Vermeer's *Lacemaker*, and Delacroix's *Liberty Leading the People*. Oh, yeah, and there's that lady with the mysterious smile, too—the *Mona Lisa*. Enter through I.M. Pei's controversial glass **Pyramid** in the Cour Napoléon, or skip lines by entering directly from the Métro. When visiting the Louvre, strategy is everything. The Louvre is organized into three different wings: Sully, Richelieu, and Denon. Each is divided into different sections according to the artwork's date, national origin, and medium. The color-coding and room numbers on the free maps correspond to the colors and numbers on the plaques at the entrances to every room within the wing. *(1er. M: Palais-Royal-Musée du Louvre. ☎01 40 20 51 51; www.louvre.fr. Open M and W 9am-9:30pm, Th-Su 9am-5:30pm. Closed Tu. Last entry 45min. before closing, but people are asked to leave 15-30min. before closing. Admission M and W-Sa 9am-3pm €7.50, M and W-Sa 3pm-close and Su €5. Under-18 and first Su of the month free.)*

MUSÉE D'ORSAY. While considered the premier Impressionist collection, the museum is dedicated to presenting all major artistic movements between 1848 and WWI. On the ground floor, works from Classicism and Proto-Impressionism are on display, including Manet's *Olympia*, a painting that caused a scandal when it was unveiled in 1865. Other highlights include: Monet's *La Gare St-Lazare* and *Cathédrale de Rouen* series, Renoir's *Le bal du Moulin de la Galette* (*The dance at the Moulin de la Galette*), Edgar Dégas's *La classe de danse* (*The Dance Class*), Whistler's *Portrait of the Artist's Mother*, and paintings by Sisley, Pissaro, and Morisot. Over a dozen diverse works by van Gogh follow, including his tormented *Portrait de l'Artiste*. Cézanne's works experiment with the soft colors and geometric planes that would open the door to Cubism. *(62 r. de Lille. 7ème. M: Solférino; RER: Musée d'Orsay. ☎01 40 49 48 14; www.musee-orsay.fr. Open June 20-Sept. 20 Tu-W and F-Su 9am-6pm, Th 9am-*

9:45pm; Sept. 21-June 19 Tu-W and F-Su 10am-6pm, Th 10am-9:45pm. Closed M. Last ticket sales 45min. before closing. €7, ages 18-25 and Su €5. Under-18 and first Su of every month free. Tours in English Tu-Sa 11:30am, 2:30pm. €5.50.)

CENTRE NATIONAL D'ART ET DE CULTURE GEORGES-POMPIDOU. This inside-out building has inspired debate since its opening in 1977. The exterior is a sight, with chaotic colored piping and ventilation ducts, but it's an appropriate shell for the Fauves, Cubists, and Pop and Conceptual works inside. (Pl. Georges-Pompidou, 4ème. M: Rambuteau or Hôtel-de-Ville. ☎01 44 78 12 33. Centre open W-M 11am-10pm; museum open W-M 11am-9pm, last tickets 8pm. Permanent collection €5.50, students and over-60 €3.50. 1st Su of month free.)

MUSÉE RODIN. The 18th-century Hôtel Biron holds hundreds of sculptures by Auguste Rodin (and by his student and lover, Camille Claudel), including the *Gates of Hell*, *The Thinker*, *Burghers of Calais*, and *The Kiss*. (77 r. de Varenne, 7ème. M: Varenne. ☎01 44 18 61 10; www.musee-rodin.fr. Open Tu-Su Apr.-Sept. 9:30am-5:45pm; Oct.-Mar. 9:30am-4:45pm. €5; seniors, 18-25, and Su €3.)

MUSÉE PICASSO. This museum follows Picasso's career from his early work in Barcelona to his Cubist and Surrealist years in Paris and Neoclassical work on the Riviera. (5 r. de Thorigny, 3ème. M: Chemin Vert. ☎01 42 71 63 15. Open Apr.-Sept. M and W-Su 9:30am-6pm; Oct.-Mar. 9:30am-5:30pm; last entrance 30min. before closing. Admission €5.50, Su and ages 18-25 €4. Under-18 free.)

MUSÉE CARNAVALET. Housed in Mme. de Sévigné's 16th-century hôtel parti-culier, this amazing museum traces Paris's history, with exhibits on the city from prehistory and the Roman conquest to 18th-century splendor and Revolu-tion, 19th-century Haussmannization, and Mitterrand's *Grands Projets*. (M: Chemin-Vert. 23 rue de Sévigné, 3ème. ☎01 44 59 58 58; www.paris.fr/musees/musee_carnavalet. Open Tu-Su 10am-5:40pm; last entrance 5:15pm. Admission free. Special exhibits €5.50, students and elderly €4, ages 13-18 €2.50. Under-12 free.)

MUSÉE DE CLUNY. One of the world's finest collections of medieval art, the Musée de Cluny is housed in a medieval monastery built on top of Roman baths. Works include the **La Dame et La Licorne** (The Lady and the Unicorn), a studding medieval tapestry series. (6 pl. Paul Painlevé, 5ème. M: Cluny-La Sor-bonne. ☎01 53 73 78 00. Open M and W-Sa 9:15am-5:45pm; last ticket sold at 5:15pm. €6.70; students, under-25, over-60, and Su €5.20; under-18 free.)

MUSÉE MARMOTTAN MONET. This hunting-lodge-turned-mansion features an eclectic collection of Empire furniture, Impressionist Monet and Renoir can-vases, and medieval illuminations. (2 r. Louis-Boilly, 16ème. M: La Muette. Follow Chaussée de la Muette (which becomes av. Ranelagh) through the Jardin du Ranelagh. ☎01 44 96 50 33. Open Tu-Su 10am-6pm. €6.50, students €4.)

LA VILLETTE. This vast urban renewal project encloses a landscaped park, a science museum, a planetarium, a conservatory, a concert/theater space, a high-tech music museum, and more. (19ème. M: Porte de la Villette or Porte de Pantin. Music museum open Su 10am-6pm, Tu-Sa noon-6pm. €6.10, students €4.60, under-18 €2.30. Science museum open Su 10am-7pm, Tu-Sa 10am-6pm. €7.50, under-25 €5.50.)

INVALIDES MUSEUMS. The resting place of Napoleon also hosts the **Musée de l'Armée,** which celebrates French military history, and the **Musée de l'Ordre de la Libération,** on bd. de Latour-Maubourg, which tells the story of the Resis-tance fighters. (Esplanade des Invalides, 7ème. M: Invalides. ☎01 47 05 04 10. Open daily Apr.-Sept. 10am-6pm; Oct.-Mar. 10am-5pm; last ticket sales 30min. before closing. Admission to all 3 museums €7, students €5. Under-18 free. MC/V.)

PALAIS DE TOKYO. Part of the magnificent Palais houses the **Musée d'Art Moderne de la Ville de Paris,** one of the world's foremost collections of 20th-century art. *(M: Iéna. 11 av. du Président Wilson, 16ème. ☎01 53 67 40 00. Wheelchair-accessible. Open Tu-F 10am-5:30pm, Sa-Su 10am-6:45pm. Admission to permanent exhibitions free; special exhibits admission varies, expect approximately €5, students €2.20-3.)* On the other side, the **site creation contemporaine** displays several exhibits a year of exciting, controversial contemporary art. *(Open Tu-Su noon-midnight. Admission varies with exhibit, expect approximately €5, with reduced student, youth, and senior prices. Free admission for art students.)*

INSTITUT DU MONDE ARABE. Featuring art from the Maghreb and the Near and Middle East, the riverside facade is shaped like a boat, representing the migration of Arabs to France. *(1 r. des Fossés St-Bernard, 5ème. M: Jussieu. From the Métro, walk down r. Jussieu away from the Jardin des Plantes. ☎01 40 51 38 38. M: Jussieu. Open Tu-Su 10am-7pm; library open Tu-Sa 1-8pm. €4.)*

MUSÉE DE LA MODE ET DU COSTUME. With 30,000 outfits and 70,000 accessories, the museum has no choice but to showcase fashions of the past three centuries. A fabulous place to see the history of Parisian fashion, society, and *haute couture.* *(10 av. Pierre I-de-Serbie, 16ème, in the Palais Galliera. M: Iéna. ☎01 56 52 86 00. Open Tu-Su 10am-6pm; last entrance 5:30pm. €7, students and seniors €5.50.)*

MUSÉE JACQUEMART-ANDRÉ. The fantastically ornate former home of Nélie Jacquemart and her husband contains a collection of Renaissance artwork worthy of the most prestigious museums in Paris. *(M: Miromesnil. 158 bd. Haussmann, 8ème. ☎01 45 62 11 59. Open daily 10am-6pm; last entrance at 5:30pm. €8, students and ages 7-17 €6. Under-7 free. English headsets free with admission.)*

MUSÉE D'HISTOIRE NATURELLE. Three museums in one. The **Grande Galerie de l'Evolution** tells the story of evolution via a Genesis-like parade of naturalistic stuffed animals. Next door, the **Musée de Minéralogie** contains some lovely jewels. The **Galeries d'Amatomie Comparée et de Paléontologie,** at the other end of the garden, whose exterior looks like a Victorian house of horrors, is filled with a ghastly collection of fibias, rib-cages, and vertebrae formed into historic and pre-historic animals. *(M: Gare d'Austerlitz. 57 r. Cuvier, in the Jardin des Plantes, 5ème. ☎01 40 79 30 00; www.mnhn.fr. M: Gare d'Austerlitz. Grande Galerie de l'Evolution open M and Su 10am-6pm, Th 10am-10pm. €6.10, students €4.60. Musée de Minéralogie open M and W-Su 10am-6pm. €4.60, students €3. Galeries d'Anatomie Comparée et de Paléontologie open M and W-Su 10am-5pm, Apr.-Oct. Sa-Su until 6pm. €4.60, students €3.)*

MUSÉE D'ART ET D'HISTOIRE DU JUDAISME. Recently renovated and housed in the grand **Hôtel de St-Aignan,** this museum was once a tenement populated by Jews fleeing Eastern Europe. It displays a history of Jews in Europe, France, and North Africa. *(M: Hôtel de Ville. 71 r. du Temple, 3ème. ☎01 53 01 86 60; www.mahj.org. M: Rambuteau. Open M-F 11am-6pm, Su 10am-6pm. Admission €6.10, students and ages 18-26 €3.80. Under-18 free: includes an English audioguide. Wheelchair accessible.)*

GALLERIES. Evidence of its still thriving artistic scene, Paris has dozens of galleries displaying the work of international artists both established and up-and-coming. The highest concentration of hip contemporary art galleries is in the **Marais.** Cutting-edge paintings, sculptures, and photography peek out of store-front windows. The **Champs-Elysée** area in the 8*ème,* on the other hand, is loaded with Old Masters. Galleries near M: Franklin D. Roosevelt on the Champs-Elysées, av. Matignon, r. du Faubourg St-Honoré, and r. de Miromesnil focus on Impressionism and post-Impressionism. The 13*ème* also has a coterie of new galleries along **rue Louise-Weisse** (M: Chevarelet) and the perpendicular **rue Duchefdelaville.** The *Portes Ouvertes* festival (May-June; check *Pariscope* for information) allows visitors to witness artists in action in their studios. Almost all galleries close at lunchtime, on Mondays, and in August.

NO WORK, ALL PLAY

NIGHT MUSIQUE

While the Fête de la Musique is celebrated nationwide on June 21, it should be no surprise that Paris brings in the biggest crowds. We'd love to tell you which part of the city serves as the epicenter for this huge, crazy festival, but there isn't one: the entire city is engulfed.

While you can catch a few acts as early as noon, it isn't until about 8pm that the city really gets humming. Head to one of the major places to see big international acts—2003's lineup included Robbie Williams and Simply Red. After the big shows end, wander whatever area you find yourself in. Every cafe and bar stays open through the night, pumping music into the street. Musicians of all sorts can be found on every corner. Everything is free—including entry into normally pricey venues—and vendors blanket the city with hot dogs and shish kebab sandwiches (€4) and beer (€2). Some subway lines stay open later and night buses run on more regular schedules. For €2.50, you can buy an unlimited métro pass good from the evening of June 21 through the morning of June 22, but you may have a difficult time getting home between midnight and 6am. Consider doing what the Parisians do—stay out and party until the sun comes up. You'll be glad you did (☎01 40 03 94 70).

🎵 ENTERTAINMENT

Paris's cabarets, cinemas, theaters, and concert halls can satisfy all tastes and desires. The bibles of Parisian entertainment, the weekly *Pariscope* and the *Officiel des Spectacles* (both €0.40), on sale at any kiosk or *tabac*, have every conceivable listing. *Pariscope* includes an English-language section.

FREE CONCERTS

For listings of free concerts, check *Paris Selection*, free at tourist offices. Free concerts are often held in churches and parks, especially during summer festivals, and are extremely popular, so plan to arrive at the host venue early. The **American Church in Paris**, 65 quai d'Orsay, 7ème, sponsors free concerts (Sept.-May Su 6pm; ☎01 40 62 05 00; M: Invalides or Alma Marceau). **Église St-Germain-des-Prés** also has free concerts; check the info booth just inside the door for times. **Église St-Merri**, 78 r. St-Martin, 4ème, is also known for its free concerts (Sept.-July Sa 9pm, Su 4pm; M: Hôtel de Ville); contact Accueil Musical St-Merri, 76 r. de la Verrerie, 4ème (☎01 42 71 40 75; M: Châtelet). Concerts take place W-Su in the **Jardin du Luxembourg's** band shell, 6ème (☎01 42 34 20 23); show up early for a seat or prepare to stand. Occasional free concerts are held in the **Musée d'Orsay**, 1 r. Bellechasse, 7ème (☎01 40 49 49 66; M: Solférino).

CONCERT VENUES

Le Bataclan, 50 bd. Voltaire, 11ème (☎01 43 14 35 35). M: Oberkampf. An 800-person concert space and cafe-bar that hosts the likes of Metallica, Oasis, Blur, and Prince, as well as indie rock bands. Tickets start at €15 and vary with show. Call for schedules and reservations. Open Sept.-July. MC/V.

La Cigale, 120 bd. Rochechouart, 18ème (☎01 49 25 89 99). M: Pigalle. One of the 2 large rock clubs in Pigalle, seating 2000 for international indie, punk, and hard-core bands. Also stages modern dance shows. Music starts 8:30pm, box office open M-Sa noon-showtime. Concerts €15-35. MC/V.

L'Olympia, 28 bd. des Capucines, 9ème (☎01 55 27 10 00; www.www.olympiahall.com). M: Opéra. The oldest music hall in Paris. The Beatles and Sinatra played here, and it's still going strong and drawing big-name acts. Box office open M-Sa 9am-7pm. Tickets €25-60. MC/V.

OPERA AND THEATER

Opéra de la Bastille, pl. de la Bastille, 12ème (☎08 92 69 78 68; www.opera-de-paris.fr). M: Bastille. Opera and ballet with a modern spin. Tickets can be purchased by Internet, mail, fax, phone (M-Sa 9am-

7pm), or in person (M-Sa 11am-6:30pm). Rush tickets for students under-25 and seniors 15min. before show. For wheelchair access, call 2 weeks ahead (☎01 40 01 18 08). Tickets €60-105. MC/V.

Opéra Garnier, pl. de l'Opéra, 9ème (☎ 08 92 89 90 90; www.opera-de-paris.fr). M: Opéra. Hosts symphonies, chamber music, and the Ballet de l'Opéra de Paris. Tickets available 2 weeks before shows. Box office open M-Sa 11am-6pm. Last-minute discount tickets available 1hr. before showtime. For wheelchair access, call 2 weeks ahead (☎01 40 01 18 08). Tickets €19-64. AmEx/MC/V.

Opéra Comique, 5 r. Favart, 2ème (☎01 42 44 45 46; www.opera-comique.com). M: Richelieu-Drouot. Operas on a lighter scale—from Rossini to Offenbach. Box office open M-Sa 11am-7pm. Tickets €29-112. Student rush tickets available 15min. before show.

La Comédie Française, 2 r. de Richelieu, 1er (☎01 44 58 15 15; www.comedie-francaise.fr). M: Palais-Royal. Founded by Molière, now the granddaddy of all French theaters. Expect wildly gesticulated slapstick farce; you don't need to speak French to understand the jokes. Tickets €4.50-30, under-27 €4.50-7.50. Rush tickets for students (€9) available 1hr. before show. Handicapped patrons and their guests are asked to make reservations in advance (tickets €11). AmEx/MC/V.

Bouffes du Nord, 37bis bd. de la Chapelle, 10ème (☎01 46 07 34 50; www.bouffes-dunord.com). M: La Chapelle. This experimental theater headed by British director Peter Brook and Stephen Lissner produces cutting-edge performances and concerts and offers occasional productions in English. Closed Aug. Box office open M-Sa 11am-6pm. Concerts €18.50, under 26 and over 60 €12; plays €14-24.50. Wheelchair-accessible, but you must call in advance.

La Cartoucherie, route du Champ de Manoeuvre, 12ème. M: Château de Vincennes; a free shuttle departs every 15min. beginning 1hr. before performances, from the station. This 19th-century weapons factory has housed cutting-edge, socially conscious, and refreshingly democratic theater since 1970. The internationally renowned theater is home to 5 collectives, 2 studios, and 7 performance spaces. Most shows €15-20. For more info, visit www.la-tempete.fr/theatre/cartoucherie.html, or check *Pariscope.*

JAZZ AND CABARET

🅰 **Au Duc des Lombards,** 42 r. des Lombards, 1er (☎01 42 33 22 88; www.jazzvalley.com/duc). M: Châtelet. Still the best in French jazz, with occasional American soloists, and hot items in world music. Three sets each night. Cover €12-23. Beer €5-8. Mixed drinks €9. Music 9:30pm-1:30am. Open M-Sa 8pm-2am. MC/V.

Aux Trois Mailletz, 56 r. Galande, 5ème (☎01 43 54 00 79; before 5pm 01 43 25 96 86). M: St-Michel. Basement houses a crowded cafe featuring world music and jazz vocals. Upper floor is packed with a mix of well-dressed students and forty-somethings. €12.20-19 cover for club on weekends; no cover for bar. Grog €9 at bar. Mixed drinks €12.50. Bar open daily 5pm-dawn; *cave* 10pm-dawn.

Au Lapin Agile, 22 r. des Saules, 18ème (☎01 46 06 85 87). M: Lamarck-Coulaincourt. Picasso, Verlaine, and Renoir; now audiences crowd in for comical poems and songs. Open Tu-Su 9pm-2am. Cover €25; includes 1 drink. Su-F students €18.

CINEMA

There are scores of cinemas throughout Paris, particularly in the Latin Quarter and on the Champs-Elysées. The two big theater chains—**Gaumont** and **UGC**—offer *cartes privilèges* discounts for five visits or more. Most cinemas offer student, senior, and family discounts. On Monday and Wednesday, prices drop by about €1.50 for everyone. Check *Pariscope* or *l'Officiel des Spectacles* (available at any newsstand, €0.40) for weekly film schedules, prices, and reviews.

FRANCE

■ **Cinémathèque Française,** pl. du Trocadéro, 16ème (☎01 45 53 21 86; recorded info 01 47 04 24 24 lists all shows; www.cinemathequefrancaise.com). M: Trocadéro. At the Musée du Cinéma in the Palais de Chaillot; enter through the Jardins du Trocadéro. Also at 42 bd. Bonne Nouvelle, 10eme. M: Bonne Nouvelle. A must for film buffs. 2-3 classics, near-classics, or soon-to-be classics per day. Foreign films usually in V.O. Buy tickets 20min. early. Open W-Su 5-9:45pm. €4.70, students €3.

Les Trois Luxembourg, 67 r. Monsieur-le-Prince, 6ème (☎01 46 33 97 77). M: Cluny. High-quality independent, classic, and foreign films, all in V.O. €6.40, students €5.

La Pagode, 57bis r. de Babylone, 7ème (☎01 45 55 48 48). M: St-François-Xavier. A pseudo-Japanese pagoda built in 1895 and reopened as a cinema in 2000, La Pagode screens foreign and independent films. Stop in at the cafe between shows. Tickets €7.30; over-60, under-21, students and M and W €5.80. MC/V.

☐ SHOPPING

Like its food, nightlife, and conversation, Paris's fashion is an art. From the wild wear near r. Etienne-Marcel to the boutiques of the Marais to the upscale shops of St-Germain-des-Prés, everything Paris touches turns to gold. The great *soldes* (sales) of the year begin after New Year's and at the very end of June, with the best prices at the beginning of February and the end of July. And if at any time of year you see the word *braderie* (clearance sale) in a store window, march in without hesitation.

ETIENNE-MARCEL AND LES HALLES (1ER AND 2ÈME). Fabrics here are cheaper, and the style is younger, especially around **rue Tiquetonne**. A stroll down **rue Etienne-Marcel** will delight shoe fetishists. **Forum Les Halles** and the surrounding streets offer everything you'll need for an urban warrior aesthetic. *(M: Les Halles).*

■ **Le Shop,** 3 r. d'Argout, 2ème (☎01 40 28 95 94). M: Etienne-Marcel. 2 levels, 1200 sq. m and 24 "corners" of sleek Asian-inspired club wear plus a live DJ. Shirts and pants start at around €50. Open M 1-7pm, Tu-Sa 11am-7pm. AmEx/MC/V.

■ **Espace Kiliwatch,** 64 r. Tiquetonne, 2ème (☎01 42 21 17 37). M: Etienne-Marcel. One of the most popular, fun shops in Paris. Pre-owned (*fripe*) shirts from €19, pants from €30. New, pricier clothes, books, furnishings, and other funky stuff also for sale. MC/V.

MARAIS (3ÈME AND 4ÈME). Shopping in the Marais is a complete aesthetic experience: boutiques of all colors and flavors pop out along medieval streets and among welcoming, tree-shaded cafés (M: St-Paul or Hôtel-de-Ville). What the Marais does best is independent designer shops selling truly unique creations, as well as vintage stores that line **rue Vieille-du-Temple, rue de Sévigné, rue Roi de Sicile** and **rue des Rosiers.** The best selection of affordable-chic menswear in Paris can be found here, especially along **rue Ste-Croix-de-la-Bretonnerie,** in stores catering to a largely gay clientele—but anyone who wants to absorb a bit of Euro-style should check them out. Most stores are open on Sundays. *(M: St-Paul or Hôtel de Ville.)*

■ **Culotte,** 7 r. Malher, 4ème (☎01 42 71 58 89). M: St-Paul. Japanese designs ranging from ripped printed tees to 40s-style dresses, all handmade. Funky vintage jewelry. Most items under €100. Open Su 1-7pm, Tu-Sa 11am-7pm. AmEx/MC/V.

Karine Dupont Boutique, 22 r. de Poitou, 3ème (☎01 40 27 84 94). M: St-Sébastien Froissart. From unassuming, waterproof tent material, Karine Dupont makes ingenious bags in every shape imaginable. Most bags €40-80. Open M-Sa noon-7:30pm. MC/V.

Boy'z Bazaar, 5 r. Ste-Croix-de-la-Bretonnerie, 4ème (☎01 42 71 94 00). M: Hôtel-de-Ville. A large selection of all that's elegant and trendy in casual menswear from Energie to Paul Smith. Jeans €100-200. T-shirts €40-50. Athletic-wear branch down the street at no. 38. Open M-Th noon-9pm, F-Sa noon-midnight, and Su 2-8pm. AmEx/MC/V.

Les Antiquaires de la Mode, 11 r. d'Ormesson, 4ème (☎01 42 78 05 45). M: St-Paul. Vintage-trendy boutique offering reincarnated Jackie O.-style dresses (€100), Chanel suits (€150), and the latest line of Playboy Bunny handbags (€60-70). Open Su and Th-Sa 2-7:30pm. MC/V.

LATIN QUARTER AND ST-GERMAIN-DES-PRÉS (5ÈME AND 6ÈME). While you'll find plenty of chain clothing and shoe stores around **boulevard St-Michel** and numerous little boutiques selling chic scarves and jewelry, bookstores of all kinds are where the 5éme really stands out. Post-intellectual, materialistic St-Germain-des-Prés, meanwhile, particularly the triangle bordered by **boulevard St-Germain, rue St-Sulpice,** and **rue des Sts-Pères,** is saturated with high-budget names.

🔳 **Moloko,** 53 r. du Cherche-Midi, 6ème (☎01 45 48 46 79). M: Sèvres-Babylone, St-Sulpice, or Rennes. Simple, Asian-inspired women's clothing with creative twists. Dresses from €120. Open Tu-Sa 11am-1pm and 2-7pm. Closed Aug. MC/V.

Petit Bateau, 26 r. Vavin, 6ème (☎01 55 42 02 53). M: Vavin or Notre-Dame-des-Champs. Other locations throughout the city. A children's store, but the stylish Parisian mothers are not there for their kids—the size for age 16 is about the same as an American 6; sizes go up to age 18. Tees and tanks €6.50. Open Aug. M 2-7pm, T-Sa 10am-7pm; Sept.-July M-Sa 10am-7pm. AmEx/MC/V.

CHAMPS-ELYSÉES AREA (8ÈME). The 8ème is not exactly wallet-friendly, but it is perfect for a day of window shopping. Take a break from the exhausting Champs-Elysées and walk along **avenue Montaigne** to admire the great couture houses; their collections change every season, but are always innovative, gorgeous, and jaw-droppingly expensive—and the window displays won't disappoint. Check out **Chanel** at no. 42, **Christian Dior** at no. 30, **Emanuel Ungaro** at no. 2, and **Nina Ricci** at no. 39. **Rue du Faubourg Saint-Honoré** is home to **Lanvin** at no. 22, **Jean-Paul Gaultier** at no. 30, and other boutiques. Around the **Madeleine,** you'll find **Burberry** and some big American names. Back on the **Champs-Elysées,** you can purchase everything from CDs (check out the **Virgin Megastore,** open until midnight) to perfumes to chocolates, usually until a much later hour than in the rest of Paris. Sale season on the Champs is a great time to pillage the collections and come home with money to spare. *(M: Charles de Gaulle-Etoile or Franklin D. Roosevelt).*

MONTMARTRE (18ÈME). The 18ème has some of the city's most eclectic shopping: Stroll around **rue de Lavieuville** (don't miss **Spree** at no. 16; ☎01 42 23 41 40) for funky independent designer wares. In the **Goutte d'Or** area, meanwhile, cheap fabric and clothing stores abound. *(M: Abbesses).*

OUTLET STORES. *Stock* is French for outlet store, with big name clothes for less—often because they have small imperfections or are from last season. Many are on r. d'Alésia in the 14ème (M: Alésia), including **Cacharel Stock,** no. 114 (☎01 45 42 53 04; open M-Sa 10am-7pm; AmEx/MC/V); **Stock Chevignon,** no. 122 (☎01 45 43 40 25; open M-Sa 10am-7pm; AmEx/MC/V); **S.R. Store** (Sonia Rykiel) at no. 110-112 and no. 64 (☎01 43 95 06 13; open Tu 11am-7pm, W-Sa 10am-7pm; MC/V); **Stock Patrick Gerard,** no. 113 (☎01 40 44 07 40). A large **Stock Kookaï** bustles at 82 r. Réamur, 2ème (☎01 45 08 93 69; open M 11:30am-7:30pm, Tu-Sa 10:30am-7pm); **Apara Stock** sits at 16 r. Etienne Marcel (☎01 40 26 70 04); and **Haut-de-Gomme Stock,** with names like Armani, Khanh, and Dolce & Gabbana, has two locations, at 9 r. Scribe, 9ème (M: Opéra ☎01 40 07 10 20; open M-Sa 10am-7pm) and 190 r. de Rivoli, 1er (M: Louvre-Rivoli ☎01 42 96 97 47; open daily 11am-7pm).

BOOKS. Paris overflows with high-quality bookstores. The 5ème and 6ème are particularly bookish: Interesting shops line every large street in the Latin Quarter, not to mention the endless stalls (*bouquinistes*) along the quais of the Seine. Some specialty bookshops serve as community centers, too. English bookshops like **Shakespeare & Co.** (below) and **The Village Voice**, 6 r. Princesse, 6ème, have bulletin boards for posting events and housing notices. (M: Mabillon. ☎01 46 33 36 47. Open M 2-8pm, Tu-Sa 10am-8pm, Su 2-7pm; Aug. closed Su.) **Les Mots à la Bouche**, 6 r. Ste-Croix de la Bretonnerie, 4ème, carries literature, essays, and art relating to homosexuality, and has info for gays and lesbians. (M: Hôtel-de-Ville. ☎01 42 78 88 30; www.motsbouche.com. Open M-Sa 11am-11pm and Su 2-8pm.) **L'Harmattan**, 21b r. des Ecoles, 5ème, can direct you to Caribbean, Maghrébin, and West African resources. (☎01 46 34 13 71. M: Cluny la Sorbonne. Open M-Sa 10am-12:30pm and 1:30-7pm. MC/V.)

The large, English-language **W.H. Smith**, 248 r. de Rivoli, 1er, has many scholarly works and magazines. The Sunday *New York Times* is available Monday after 2pm. (M: Concorde. ☎01 44 77 88 99. Open M-Sa 9am-7:30pm, Su 1-7:30pm. AmEx/MC/V.) **Brentano's**, 37 av. de l'Opéra, 2ème, is an American and French bookstore with an extensive selection of English literature. (☎01 42 61 52 50. M: Opéra. Open M-Sa 10am-7:30pm. AmEx/MC/V.) **Shakespeare & Co.**, 37 r. de la Bûcherie, 5ème, across the Seine from Notre Dame, is run by *bon vivant* George Whitman. Walt's grandson sells a quirky and wide selection of new and used books, including bargains (€2.50) in bins outside the shop. (M: St-Michel. Open daily noon-midnight.)

MARCHÉ AUX PUCES DE ST-OUEN. This is the granddaddy of all flea markets. The Puces de St-Ouen began in the Middle Ages, when merchants resold the cast-off clothing of aristocrats (crawling with its namesake insects) to peasant-folk. Today it's an overwhelming smorgasbord of stuff. It opens early and shuts down late, and serious hunters should allow themselves the better part of a day in order to cover significant ground, although the market tends to be least crowded before noon. *(Located in St-Ouen, a town just north of the 18ème. M: Porte-de-Clignancourt. Open Sa-M 7am-7:30pm; most vendors only open M 9am-6pm; many of the official stalls close early, but renegade vendors may open at 5am and close at 9pm.)*

DEPARTMENT STORES

Au Printemps, 64 bd. Haussmann, 9ème (☎01 42 82 50 00). M: Chaussée d'Antin-Lafayette or Havre-Caumartin. Also at 30 pl. d'Italie, 13ème (☎01 40 78 17 17), M: Place d'Italie; and 21-25 cours de Vincennes, 20ème (☎01 43 71 12 41), M: Porte de Vincennes. One of the two biggies in the Parisian department store scene. Oo-la-la your way through endless *couture*. Haussmann open M-W and F-Sa 9:35am-7pm, Th 9:35am-10pm. Other locations open M-Sa 10am-8pm. AmEx/MC/V.

Galeries Lafayette, 40 bd. Haussmann, 9ème (☎01 42 82 34 56). M: Chaussée d'Antin. Also at 22 r. du Départ, 14ème (☎01 45 38 52 87), M: Montparnasse. Chaotic (the equivalent of Paris's entire population visits here each month), but carries it all. Haussmann open M-W and F-Sa 9:30am-7:30pm, Th 9:30-9pm; Montparnasse open M-Sa 9:45am-7:30pm. AmEx/MC/V.

Samaritaine, 67 r. de Rivoli, on the quai du Louvre, 1er (☎01 40 41 20 20). M: Pont Neuf, Châtelet-Les Halles, or Louvre-Rivoli. 4 large, historic Art Deco buildings between r. de Rivoli and the Seine, connected by tunnels and bridges. The rooftop observation deck provides one of the best views of the city; take the elevator to the 9th floor and climb the spiral staircase. Open M-W and F-Sa 9:30am-7pm, Th 9:30am-10pm. AmEx/MC/V.

Au Bon Marché, 22 r. de Sèvres, 7ème (☎01 44 39 80 00). M: Sèvres-Babylone. Paris's oldest department store, Bon Marché has it all, from scarves to smoking accessories and designer clothes to home furnishings. Open M-W and F 9:30am-7pm, Th 10am-9pm, Sa 9:30am-8pm. AmEx/MC/V.

⚡ NIGHTLIFE

CAFES AND BARS

LES HALLES AND MARAIS (1ER, 2ÈME, 3ÈME, 4ÈME)

■ **Banana Café**, 13-15 r. de la Ferronnerie, 1er. M: Châtelet. This *très branché* (way cool) evening arena is the most popular gay bar in the 1er, and draws an extremely mixed group. Legendary theme nights. Happy Hour 6-9pm. Beer M-F €5.18, Sa-Su €6.71. Open daily 4pm-dawn. AmEx/MC/V.

■ **Le Champmeslé**, 4 r. Chabanais, 1er. M: Pyramides or Quatre Septembre. This welcoming lesbian bar is Paris's oldest and most famous. Mixed crowd in the front, but women-only in back. Beer €4. Mized drinks €8. Popular cabaret show Th 10pm (first drink is €8). Monthly art exhibits. Open M-Th 2pm-2am, F-Sa 2pm-2am. MC/V.

L'Apparement Café, 18 r. des Coutures St-Gervais, 3ème. M: St-Paul. Beautiful wood and red lounge with games and a calm, young crowd. Late-night meals €10-13.

Chez Richard, 37 r. Vieille-du-Temple, 4ème. M: Hôtel-de-Ville. A hot spot to people-watch on weekends, but during the week it's ideal for chilling, with hip bartenders and smooth beats. Happy Hour 6-8pm for cocktails. Beer €4-6. Mixed drinks €9. Open daily 6pm-2am. AmEx/MC/V.

Lizard Lounge, 18 r. du Bourg-Tibourg, 4ème. M: Hôtel-de-Ville. A happening, split-level space for students and twenty-somethings. Happy Hour upstairs 6-8pm, throughout the bar 8-10pm. Beer €6.20. "Lizard Juice" €7.50. Open daily noon-2am. Serves food noon-3pm and 7-10:30pm, Sa-Su brunch noon-4pm. MC/V.

The Flann O'Brien, 6 r. Bailleul, 1er. M: Louvre-Rivoli. Arguably the best Irish bar in Paris, Flann is often packed, especially on live music nights (F-Su). Go for the Guinness and stay for the reportedly good "crack" downstairs (that's Irish for good fun). Demi €4, full pint €6. Open daily 6pm-5am.

Villa Keops, 58 bd. Sébastopol, 3ème. M: Etienne-Marcel. Stylish, candlelit couch bar where the waiters are as beautiful as the designer drinks. Divine Rose du Nile €8.50. Happy Hour 8-10pm. Open M-Th noon-2am, F-Sa noon-4am, Su 4pm-3am. AmEx/MC/V.

La Belle Hortense, 31 r. Vieille-du-Temple. M: St-Paul. A breath of fresh intellectual air for those worn out by the *hyper-chic* scene along the rest of the *rue*. Varied wine selection from €3 a glass. Frequent exhibits, readings, lectures, signatures, and discussions in the small leather-couch-filled back room. Open daily 5pm-2am. MC/V.

Boobs Bourg, 26 r. de Montmorency. M: Rambuteau. This is where the well-spiked, stylishly punk girls go to find each other. Always lively at night, occasional daytime lectures and discussions. Men welcome accompanied by women. Beer on tap €3.80. Mixed drinks €7. Open Tu-Su 5:30pm-2am. MC/V.

Amnésia Café, 42 r. Vieille-du-Temple, 3ème. M: Hôtel-de-Ville. A largely gay crowd comes to lounge on plush sofas in Amnésia's classy wood-paneled interior. Espresso €2. *Kir* €4. Open daily 10:30am-2am. MC/V.

Le Duplex, 25 r. Michel Le Comte, 3ème. M: Rambuteau. A great place to make friends instead of trouble. Small and intimate atmosphere. Not an exclusively male bar, but few women hang out here. Beer €2.60 until 10pm, €3.50 after. Cocktails €7.30. Open Su-Th 8pm-2am, F-Sa 8pm-4am.

Open Café, 17 r. des Archives. M: Hôtel-de-Ville. The most popular Marais gay bar. Beer €3. Mixed drinks €7. Happy Hour 6-9pm. Open daily 11am-2am. AmEx/MC/V.

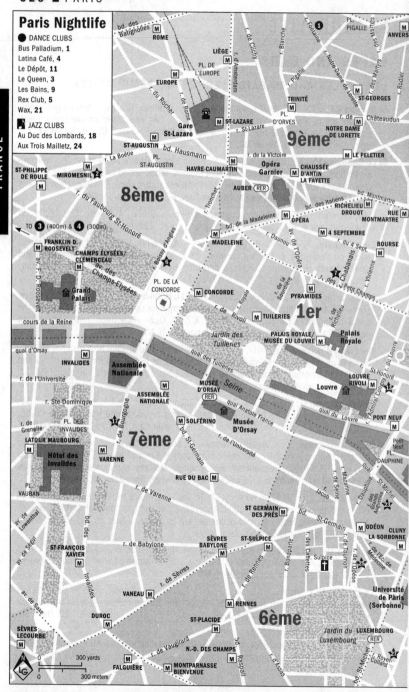

Paris Nightlife

● DANCE CLUBS
Bus Palladium, **1**
Latina Café, **4**
Le Dépôt, **11**
Le Queen, **3**
Les Bains, **9**
Rex Club, **5**
Wax, **21**

◢ JAZZ CLUBS
Au Duc des Lombards, **18**
Aux Trois Mailletz, **24**

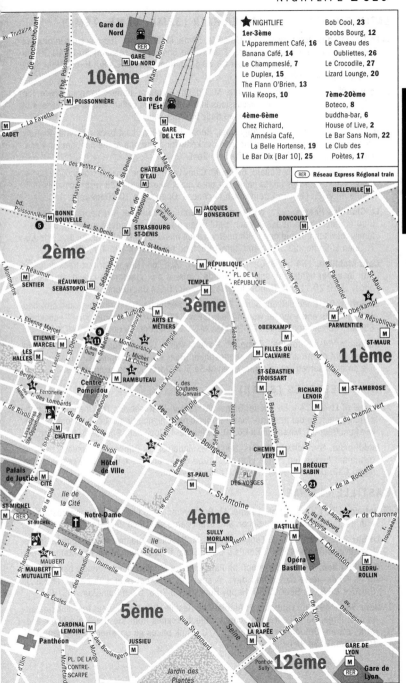

★ NIGHTLIFE

1er-3ème
L'Apparement Café, **16**
Banana Café, **14**
Le Champmeslé, **7**
Le Duplex, **15**
The Flann O'Brien, **13**
Villa Keops, **10**

4ème-6ème
Chez Richard,
  Amnésia Café,
  La Belle Hortense, **19**
Le Bar Dix [Bar 10], **25**

Bob Cool, **23**
Boobs Bourg, **12**
Le Caveau des
  Oubliettes, **26**
Le Crocodile, **27**
Lizard Lounge, **20**

7ème-20ème
Boteco, **8**
buddha-bar, **6**
House of Live, **2**
Le Bar Sans Nom, **22**
Le Club des
  Poètes, **17**

RER Réseau Express Régional train

FRANCE

LATIN QUARTER AND ST-GERMAIN (5ÈME, 6ÈME, 7ÈME)

■ **Le Caveau des Oubliettes,** 52 r. Galande, 5ème. M: St-Michel. Three scenes in one, all with a mellow, funky atmosphere. Free *soirée boeuf* (jam session) Su-Th 10:30pm-1:30am; F-Sa concerts €7.50. Beer €3.70-4.10. Rum cocktail €3.80. Happy Hour daily 5-9pm. Open daily 5pm-2am.

■ **Le Bar Dix,** 10 r. de l'Odéon, 6ème. M: Odéon. A classic student hangout where you might overhear existentialist discussions in the downstairs cellar. After a few glasses of *sangria* (€3), you might join in. Open daily 5:30pm-2am.

■ **Bob Cool,** 15 r. des Grands Augustins, 6ème. M: Odéon. Laid-back clientele, friendly vibe, and a reputation among those in the know for being one of the best bars in Paris. Mexican *mezcal* €8.50. Open daily 5pm-2am.

Le Crocodile, 6 r. Royer-Collard, 6ème. M: Cluny-La Sorbonne. A lively crowd of 20-somethings packs into this unassuming bar on a quiet side street. 238 tasty cocktails (€8, before midnight M-Th €6) from which to choose. Open M-Sa 10:30pm-4am.

Le Club des Poètes, 30 r. de Bourgogne, 7ème. M: Varenne. A restaurant by day, Le Club is transformed at 10pm each night when a troupe of readers, including Rosnay's family, bewitch the audience with poetry. Lunch *menu* €15. Drinks €9, for students €5-7. Open M-Sa noon-2:30pm and 8pm-1am; food served until 10pm. AmEx/MC/V.

Café Mabillon, 164 bd. St-Germain, 6ème. M: Mabillon. This hyper fast-track cafe-bar with lavender lights and snappy attitude draws a hip, glamorous crowd. Drinks are pricey (€10.20-11.50). Happy Hour daily 7-9pm. Open daily 8am-6am. MC/V.

Le Reflet, 6 r. Champollion, 5ème. M: Cluny-La Sorbonne. Small, low-key, and crowded with students and younger working folk. Beer €1.90-2.70 at the bar, *kir* €2, cocktails €5. Also serves food; salads €7-9. Open M-Sa 10am-2am, Su noon-2am. MC/V.

Malone's, 64 av. Bosquet, 7ème. M: Ecole Militaire. Chic mahogany decor and warm candlelight create an easy-going atmosphere. Beer €5. Mixed drinks €8. Tasty snacks like *croques* served until closing. Open M-Sa 5pm-2am, Su 5pm-1am. MC/V.

CHAMPS-ELYSÉES (8ÈME)

■ **House of Live,** 124 r. La Boétie, 8ème. M: Franklin D. Roosevelt. This friendly and happening American bar has first-class live music most nights. Snack bar has good ol' Yankee fare. Beer €6. Mixed drinks €6.80. Coffee €2-4. Open daily 9am-5am. AmEx/MC/V.

buddha-bar, 8 r. Boissy d'Anglas, 8ème. M: Madeleine or Concorde. Gorgeous bar and restaurant frequented by the glitterati. Mixed drinks and martinis €12. Weekday lunch *menu* €32. Open M-F noon-3pm and daily 6pm-2am.

BASTILLE (11ÈME)

■ **Boteco,** 131 r. Oberkampf, 11ème. M: Parmentier. A popular Brazilian bar-restaurant with trendy waitstaff, jungle decor, and avant-garde art. Open daily 9am-2am.

Le Bar Sans Nom, 49 r. de Lappe, 11ème. M: Bastille. Seductive lounge famous for its inventive cocktails (€8.50). Beer €5-6.20. Shots €6.20. Open M-Sa 7pm-2am. MC/V.

Café Charbon, 109 r. Oberkampf. M: Parmentier or Ménilmontant. Proudly bears traces of its *fin-de-siècle* dance hall days. A specialty is sweet beer with *cassis* (€2.30). *Salades* €6-8.50. Beer €2.80. Happy Hour daily 5-7pm. Open 9am-2am. MC/V.

Sanz Sans, 49 r. du Faubourg St-Antoine. M: Bastille. Popular, upbeat bar/club/restaurant. A large, Baroque-framed screen projects scenes from the bar like a black-and-white movie. Outdoor seating; indoor A/C. Drink prices go up after 9pm. Open Su-M 9am-1am, Tu-Sa 9am-5am. MC/V.

MONTPARNASSE (13ÈME, 14ÈME)

■ **L'Entrepôt,** 7-9 r. Francis de Pressensé, 14ème. M: Pernety. Proving that intellectualism and good times go together: Cinema, restaurant, art gallery, and bar. Concerts F-Sa; usually around €5. Beer €2.50. Su brunch 11:30am-4:30pm (€15). Food served noon-3pm and 7:30-11:30pm. Open M-Sa 9am-midnight (though usually stays open later), Su 11:30am-midnight.

Batofar, facing 11 quai François-Mauriac, 13ème. M: Quai-de-la-Gare. This barge/bar/club has made it big with the electronic music crowd and has a friendly vibe. Open Tu-Th 9pm-3am, F-Sa until 4am. Cover €6.50-9.50 usually includes first drink. MC/V.

La Folie en Tête, 33 r. de la Butte-aux-Cailles, 13ème. M: Corvisart. The artsy axis mundi of the 13ème. Crowded concerts on Sa nights, usually Afro-Caribbean music (€8); no concerts July-Aug. Beer €2.50. Happy Hour 6-8pm. Open M-Sa 6pm-2am. MC/V.

Café Tournesol, 9 r. de la Gaîté, 14ème. M: Edgar Quinet. At this ultramodern cafe-bar some of the 14ème's most stylish come out to drink, read, and mingle. Beers €2.30-6; wines €2-3. Open M-Sa 8:30am-1:30am, Su 9:30am-1:30am. MC/V.

Mustang Café, 84 bd. du Montparnasse, 14ème. M: Montparnasse-Bienvenüe. €3.50 beers and all-American good times flow freely all night. Thumping juke box, hordes of Anglophones, and the occasional wet T-shirt contest. Happy Hour M-F 4-8pm. American brunch Sa-Su noon-5pm. Open daily 9am-5am. Food served until 2am. MC/V.

MONTMARTRE AND PIGALLE (9ÈME, 17ÈME, 18ÈME)

■ **L'Endroit,** 67 pl. du Dr. Félix Lobligeois, 17ème. M: Rome. Hip, young 17èmers come for the snazzy bar and idyllic location. Beer €4.50-5.10. Wine €3.50-4. Mixed drinks €6. Open daily noon-2am. MC/V.

Chez Camille, 8 r. Ravignan, 18ème. M: Abbesses. Small, trendy, bright yellow bar on the safe upper slopes of Montmartre. Beer €2.20-3.30. Wine from €2.80. Mixed drinks €6.50. Open M 11am-2pm, Tu-Sa 9am-2am, Su 9am-8pm.

La Fourmi, 74 r. des Martyrs, 18ème. M: Pigalle. Artsy atmosphere with a large zinc bar and industrial decor. Hyper-hip, energetic young crowd. Beer €2.30-3.20. Wine €2.50. Mixed drinks €5.40-10. Open M-Th 8:30am-2am, F-Sa 8:30am-4am, Su 10am-2am.

DANCE CLUBS

LES HALLES AND MARAIS (1ER, 2ÈME, 3ÈME, 4ÈME)

Les Bains, 7 r. du Bourg l'Abbé, 3ème. M: Etienne-Marcel or Réaumur-Sébastopol. Look for the long line of people. Ultra-selective, super-crowded, and expensive. Madonna and Mick Jagger have stopped in. Cover (includes first drink) Su-Th €16, F-Sa €19. Drinks €11. Clubbing daily 11pm-6am. AmEx/MC/V.

Le Dépôt, 10 r. aux Ours, 3ème. M: Etienne-Marcel. A veritable pleasure complex for gay men. Dance for inspiration then take your boy toy of the night to one of the rooms in the downstairs labyrinth. Women welcome after 11pm on the upstairs dance floor. Cover (includes first drink); M-Th €7.50, F €10, Sa €12, Su €10. Open daily 2pm-8am.

Rex Club, 5 bd. Poissonnière, 2ème. M: Bonne-Nouvelle. A non-selective club which presents very selective DJ line-ups. One of the best sound systems in Paris. Large dance floor and lots of seats. Shots €4-5. Beer €5-7. Cover €8-13. Open Th-Sa 11:30pm-6am.

CHAMPS-ELYSÉES (8ÈME)

■ **Latina Café,** 114 av. des Champs-Elysées. M: George V. Draws one of the largest nightclub crowds on the Champs with an energetic world music mix. Drinks €9-11. Women get in free Su-Th, men pay €7 cover which includes a drink. €16 cover F-Sa includes first two drinks. Cafe open daily 7:30pm-2am, club open daily 11:30am-6:30am.

Le Queen, 102 av. des Champs-Elysées. M: George V. Drag queens, superstars, models, moguls, and go-go boys get down to the mainstream rhythms of a 10,000 gigawatt sound system. Cover Su-Th €12, includes one drink. F-Sa €18. All drinks €9. Open daily midnight-dawn. AmEx/MC/V.

BASTILLE (11ÈME)

▨ **Wax,** 15 r. Daval, 11ème. M: Bastille. Always free and fun. Set up in a concrete bunker, with retro orange, red and white couches, this bar/club has DJ competitions and its own magazine. Funk and electronic music. Open daily 6pm-2am. Closed Su in summer months. Drinks €4-9.50. AmEx/MC/V.

Nouveau Casino, 109 r. Oberkampf, 11ème. M: Parmentier or Ménilmontant. This latest hot spot is drawing in the crowds of the 11ème. Each night offers a different form of entertainment, ranging from concerts (rock, electronic, house, or drum and bass), clubbing, video shows, and modern art exhibits.

MONTMARTRE AND PIGALLE (9ÈME, 17ÈME, 18ÈME)

Bus Palladium, 6 r. Fontaine, 9ème. M: Pigalle, Blanche, or St-Georges. Getting past the bouncers can be tough. A trendy, beautiful crowd rocks this rock 'n' roll club. Cover €16. Tu free cover and drinks for ladies. Drinks €13. Open Tu-Sa 11pm-6am. AmEx/V.

Folies Pigalle, 11 pl. Pigalle, 9ème. M: Pigalle. The largest and wildest club in the sleazy Pigalle *quartier*—definitely not for the faint of heart. Popular among both gay and straight clubbers. Very crowded, even at 4am. Open Su 5pm-6am, Tu-Th midnight-6am, F-Sa midnight-noon. €20 cover; includes first drink. Drinks €10. AmEx/MC/V.

▶ DAYTRIPS FROM PARIS

VERSAILLES. Louis XIV, the Sun King, built and held court at Versailles' extraordinary palace, 12km west of Paris. The incredibly lavish chateau embodies the extravagance of the Old Regime, especially in the **Hall of Mirrors** and fountain-filled **gardens.** (Chateau open May-Sept. Tu-Su 9am-6:30pm; Oct.-Apr. Tu-Su 9am-5:30pm. €7.50, over-60 and after 3:30pm €5.30 (entrance A). Audio (1hr., €4) and guided tours at entrances C and D (1-2hr.; €4, under-18 €2.70), respectively. Gardens open dawn-dusk; €3, under 18 and after 6pm free.) A **shuttle** (round-trip €5, ages 3-12 €3) runs behind the palace to the **Grand** and **Petit Trianons,** and to Marie Antoinette's peasant fantasy, the **Hameau.** (Both Trianons Open Nov.-Mar. Tu-Sa noon-5:30pm; Apr.-Oct. noon-6pm. €5. Under-18 free.) Take any RER C5 **train** beginning with a "V" from M: Invalides to the Versailles Rive Gauche station (30-40min., every 15min., round-trip €5). Buy your RER ticket before getting to the platform; a Métro ticket will not get you through the RER turnstiles at Versailles.

CHÂTEAU DE FONTAINEBLEAU. The Château de Fontainebleau achieves the grandeur of Versailles with a unique charm. François I and Napoleon stand out among the parade of post-Renaissance kings who lived here; the former was responsible for the dazzling ballrooms lined with work from Michelangelo's school, the latter restored the post-Revolution dilapidation to a home befitting an emperor. In the long **Galerie de François I,** the most famous room at Fontainebleau, muscular figures by Il Rosso illustrate mythological tales of heroism. Since the 17th century, every queen and empress of France has slept in the gold-and-green **Queen's Bedchamber.** The **Musée Napoléon** features a collection of the Emperor's tiny toothbrush and tiny shoes, as well as his field tent and state gifts. (Open May-Sept. M and W-Su 9:30am-6pm; Oct.-Apr. M and W-Su 9:30am-5pm. Last entry 1hr. before closing. €5.50. Under-18 and first Su of the month free. Invest in a printed guide (€7.50), available down the hall from the ticket booth.) From the Gare de Lyon in Paris, **trains** run to Fontainebleau (45min., every hr., round-trip €14.60). The castle is a 30min. walk or a 10min. bus ride away.

VAUX-LE-VICOMTE. This exquisite chateau was commissioned by Nicolas Fouquet, Louis XIV's Minister of Finance, and assembled by the triumvirate of Le Vau, Le Brun, and Le Nôtre (architect, artist, and landscaper). The king got jealous and, after Fouquet threw a legendary party to celebrate the completion of the chateau, had him arrested and imprisoned for life. The gardens and the inside of the palace are both spectacular. (☎01 64 14 41 90; www.vaux-le-vicomte.com. Open Mar. 23-Nov. 11 daily 10am-6pm; visits by appointment for groups of 20 or more the rest of the year. Admission to chateau, gardens, and carriage museum €12; students and seniors €9.50.) **Trains** run to Melun from Châtelet-Les Halles or Gare de Lyon (45min.; round-trip €13.40). Then take a taxi (at least €15) to the chateau. Be sure to ask the driver to meet you back at the chateau at a certain time, or pay 20 *centimes* for the staff at the exit to phone for you.

CHANTILLY. The name should sound familiar—*crème chantilly* is the French term for "whipped cream," and the creamy concoction was first made in this town. The 14th- to 19th-century Château de Chantilly is a whimsical Baroque amalgam of Gothic extravagance, Renaissance geometry, and flashy Victorian ornamentalism. The triangular-shaped chateau is surrounded by a moat, lakes, canals, and the simple, elegant Le Nôtre gardens (no Versailles fireworks here). With the architecturally masterful Grandes Ecuries (stables) and world-class **Musée Condé**, it's a wonder that this lovely chateau has stayed a hidden treasure for so long. (☎03 44 62 62 62. Open Mar.-Oct. M and W-Su 10am-6pm; Nov.-Feb. M and W-Su 10:30am-12:45pm and 2-5pm. Gardens €3, students €2; to gardens and château €7, students €6.) **Trains** run from the Gare du Nord (Grandes Lignes) to Chantilly Gouvieux (35min., approximately every hr. 5am-midnight, round-trip €12). Free and frequent **navettes** (shuttles) to the chateau: Catch one just to the left as you exit the train station; take direction Senlis. Otherwise, the château is a 30min. walk from the station—your only option Su when the shuttle is not running.

CHARTRES. Chartres's stunning **Cathédrale Notre-Dame** is one of the most beautiful surviving creations of the Middle Ages. Arguably the finest example of early Gothic architecture in Europe, the cathedral retains several of its original 12th-century stained-glass windows; the rest of the windows and the magnificent sculptures on the main portals date from the 13th century, as does the carved floor in the rear of the nave. You can enter the 9th-century **crypt** only from La Crypte, opposite the cathedral's south entrance. (☎02 37 21 75 02; www.cathedrale-chartres.com. Open Easter through Oct. daily 8am-8pm, Nov. through Easter daily 8:30am-7pm. No casual visits during mass. North Tower open May-Aug. M-Sa 9:30am-noon and 2-5:30pm, Su 2-5:30pm; Sept.-Apr. M-Sa 9:30am-noon and 2-4:30pm, Su 2-4:30pm. Tower admission €4, ages 18-25 €2.50. Under-18 and some Su free.) **Trains** run from Paris's Gare Montparnasse (1hr., every hr., €23). From the station, walk straight, turn left into the pl. de Châtelet, turn right on r. Ste-Même, then turn left on r. Jean Moulin.

GIVERNY. Today, Monet's house and gardens in Giverny are maintained by the **Fondation Claude Monet.** From April to July, Giverny overflows with roses, hollyhocks, poppies, and the heady scent of honeysuckle. The water lilies, the Japanese bridge, and the weeping willows seem to be plucked straight from Monet's paintings. Monet's thatched-roof house holds his collection of 18th- and 19th-century Japanese prints. The accompanying **Musée d'Art Américain** houses work by American Impressionists Butler, Breck, and others. (84 r. Claude Monet. ☎02 32 51 28 21; www.fondation-monet.com. Open Apr.-Oct. Tu-Su 9:30am-6:30pm. Admission €5.50, students €4. Gardens €4.) **Trains** run infrequently from Paris-St-Lazare to Vernon, the station nearest Giverny (round-trip €21). When you purchase your ticket, check the timetables or ask for the **bus** schedules for travel from Vernon to Giverny. (Buses ☎02 32 71 06 39. 10min.; 4-6 per day; €2, round-trip €4.)

DISNEYLAND PARIS. It's a small, small world, and Disney is hell-bent on making it even smaller. When EuroDisney opened in 1992, it was met by jeers of French intellectuals and the popular press. However, resistance subsided once they renamed it Disneyland Paris and started serving wine. (www.disneyland-paris.com. Open Apr.-Sept. 9am-11pm; Oct.-Mar. M-F 10am-9pm, Sa-Su 10am-10pm; hours subject to change, especially in winter. Buy *passeports* (tickets) at Disneyland Hotel, at the Paris tourist office, or at RER stations on line A. Early Apr. to early Jan. €38, ages 3-11 €29; early Jan. to early Apr. €29/25.) From Paris, take the RER A4 Marne-la-Vallée to the last stop, Marne-la-Vallée-Chessy (45min., every 30min., round-trip €11); the last train back leaves at 12:20am, but arrives after the Métro closes. Eurailers can take the TGV from Roissy/Charles de Gaulle Airport to the park (15min.).

OTHER DAYTRIPS FROM PARIS

THE LOIRE VALLEY. Between Paris and Brittany stretches the Loire Valley, where renowned chateaux line the celebrated Loire river. Visit Blois, Chambord, or Cheverny (p. 341).

RENNES. If Parisian students will travel out to Rennes for the nightlife, then you should too (p. 337).

NORMANDY (NORMANDIE)

Fertile Normandy is a land of fields, fishing villages, and cathedrals. Vikings seized the region in the 9th century, and invasions have twice secured Normandy's place in military history: in 1066, William of Normandy conquered England; on D-Day, June 6, 1944, Allied armies began the liberation of France on Normandy's beaches.

ROUEN

However strongly Gustave Flaubert may have criticized his home in *Madame Bovary*, Rouen (pop. 108,000) is no provincial town. The pathos of the Joan of Arc story and the Gothic splendor of Rouen's churches have always entranced artists and writers, and today a younger crowd populates the *vieille ville*. The most famous of Rouen's "hundred spires" are those of the ■**Cathédrale de Notre-Dame,** in pl. de la Cathédrale, one of which is the tallest in France (151m). The facade incorporates nearly every style of Gothic architecture. (Open M 2-7pm, Tu-Sa 7:45am-7pm, Su 8am-6pm.) The **Musée des Beaux-Arts,** 26 bis r. Jean Lecanuet, down r. Jeanne d'Arc from the train station, houses a worthwhile collection from the 16th to 20th centuries, including works by Monet and Renoir. (☎02 35 71 28 40. Open M and W-Su 10am-6pm. €3, ages 18-25 and groups €2, under-18 free.) Combining the disparate themes of Flaubert (who was raised on the premises) and medical history, the **Musée Flaubert et d'Histoire de la Médicine,** 51 r. de Lecat, down r. de Crosne from pl. de Vieux Marché, contains strange paraphernalia on both subjects. (☎02 35 15 59 95. Open Tu 10am-6pm, W-Sa 10am-noon and 2-6pm. €2.20, ages 18-25 €1.50, medical students and under-18 free.)

Trains leave r. Jeanne d'Arc for Lille (3hr., 5 per day, €27) and Paris (1½hr., every hr., €17). From the station, walk down r. Jeanne d'Arc and turn left on r. du Gros Horloge to reach pl. de la Cathédrale and the **tourist office,** 25 pl. de la Cathédrale. (☎02 32 08 32 40; fax 02 32 08 32 44. Open May-Sept. M-Sa 9am-7pm, Su 9:30am-12:30pm and 2-6pm; Oct.-Mar. M-Sa 9am-6pm, Su 10am-1pm and 2pm-6pm.) Check email at **Place Net,** 37 r. de la République, near the Église St.-Maclou. (€4 per hr. Open M-Sa 11am-midnight, Su 2-10pm.) ■**Hôtel Normandya ❷,** 32 r. de Courdier, near the train station, is run by a friendly couple and offers comfortable, well-decorated rooms. (☎02 35 71 46 15. Singles €20; doubles €22.) Cheap eateries crowd **place du Vieux-Marché** and the **Gros Horloge** area. **Monoprix** supermarket is at 73-83 r. du Gros Horloge. (Open M-Sa 8:30am-9pm.) **Postal Code:** 76000.

CAEN

Although Allied bombing leveled three-quarters of its buildings during WWII, Caen (pop. 120,000) has skillfully rebuilt itself into a vibrant university town. Its biggest draw is the powerful ▧**Mémorial de Caen.** The best of Normandy's WWII museums, it features footage of the war, displays on pre-war Europe, a haunting testament to the victims of the Holocaust, and a new wing exploring the Cold War. Take bus #2 to *Mémorial.* (☎02 31 06 06 44; www.memorial-caen.fr. Open mid-July to Aug. daily 9am-8pm; Sept. to mid-July reduced hours. €17, students €15.) Flanking the ruined chateau of Caen's most famous denizen, the twin abbeys **Abbaye-aux-Hommes,** off r. Guillaume le Conquérant, and **Abbaye-aux-Dames,** off r. des Chanoines, hold the tombs of William the Conqueror and his wife. (Abbaye-aux-Hommes open 9:15am-noon and 2-6pm; €1.55, students €0.80. Abbaye-aux-Dames open M-Sa 8am-5:30pm, Su 9:30am-12:30pm; free.)

Trains run to: Paris (2½hr., 12 per day, €26); Rennes (3hr., 3 per day, €27); Rouen (2hr., 5 per day, €19); and Tours (3½hr., 2 per day, €27). **Bus Verts** (☎08 10 21 42 14) covers the beaches and the rest of Normandy. The **tourist office,** pl. St-Pierre, offers free maps. (☎02 31 27 14 14; www.ville-caen.fr. Open July-Aug. M-Sa 9am-7pm, Su 10am-1pm and 2-5pm; Sept.-June M-Sa 9:30am-1pm and 2-6pm, Su 10am-1pm.) **Hôtel de l'Univers ❸,** 12 quai Vendeuvre, has reasonable prices and a convenient location. From the train station, follow av. 6 Juin to its end and turn right. All rooms have a telephone, TV, and telephone. (☎02 31 85 46 41. Singles €28, doubles €33. AmEx/V.) **Hôtel du Château ❹,** 5 av. 6 Juin, has large, bright rooms. (☎02 31 86 15 37; fax 02 31 86 58 08. Singles and doubles €35, with shower €45. Oct.-Easter reduced prices. MC/V.) Ethnic restaurants, *crêperies,* and *brasseries* line the **quartier Vaugueux** near the chateau, as well as the streets between **Église St-Pierre** and **Église St-Jean.** Get your groceries at **Monoprix supermarket,** 45 bd. du Maréchal Leclerc. (Open M-Sa 9am-8:30pm.) At night Caen's old streets come to life. **Rue de Bras, rue des Croisiers,** and **rue St-Pierre** are especially popular. **Postal Code:** 14000.

BAYEUX

Relatively untouched by the war, beautiful Bayeux (pop. 15,000) is an ideal base for exploring the nearby D-Day beaches. However, visitors should not miss its 900-year-old ▧**Tapisserie de Bayeux,** 70m of embroidery that relates the tale of William the Bastard's invasion of England and his earning of a more respectable name—"the Conqueror." The tapestry is displayed in the **Centre Guillaume le Conquérant,** on r. de Nesmond. (Open May-Aug. daily 9am-7pm; mid-Mar. to Apr. and Sept. to mid-Oct. 9am-6:30pm; mid-Oct. to mid-Mar. 9:30am-12:30pm and 2-6pm. €7.40, students €3.) Nearby is the original home of the tapestry, the extraordinary **Cathédrale Notre-Dame.** (Open July-Aug. M-Sa 8am-7pm, Su 9am-7pm; Sept.-June M-Sa 8:30am-noon and 2:30-7pm, Su 9am-12:15pm and 2:30-7pm. Free.) The **Musée de la Bataille de Normandie,** bd. Fabian Ware, recounts the D-Day landing and subsequent 76-day battle. (Open May to mid-Sept. 9:30am-6:30pm; mid-Sept. to Apr. 10am-12:30pm and 2-6pm. Closed early Jan. €5.70, students €2.60.) The **British Cemetery** across the street provides a strikingly simple yet moving wartime record.

Trains (☎02 31 92 80 50) leave pl. de la Gare for: Caen (20min., 15 per day, €5.20) and Paris (2½hr., 12 per day, €28). To reach the **tourist office,** pont St-Jean, turn left on the highway (bd. Sadi-Carnot), bear right, follow the signs to the *centre ville,* and follow r. Larcher to r. St-Martin. (☎02 31 51 28 28; www.bayeux-tourism.com.

Open June-Aug. M-Sa 9am-7pm, Su 9am-1pm and 2-6pm; Oct. daily 9:30am-12:30pm and 2-6pm; Nov.-Apr. reduced hours.) From the tourist office, turn right onto r. St-Martin, follow through several name changes, and turn left onto r. Général de Dais for the ▓**Family Home/Auberge de Jeunesse (HI) ❶**, 39 r. Général de Dais. (☎02 31 92 15 22; fax 02 31 92 55 72. Dorms €16. Nonmembers €18.) Follow r. Genas Duhomme to the right and continue straight for **Camping Municipal ❶**, on bd. d'Eindhoven. (☎02 31 92 08 43. Open May-Sept. €3 per person, €3.60 per tent and car.) Get **groceries** at **Champion**, on bd. d'Eindhoven. **Postal Code: 14400.**

D-DAY BEACHES

On June 6, 1944, over one million Allied soldiers invaded the beaches of Normandy in the first of a chain of events that liberated France and led to the downfall of Nazi Europe. Today, reminders of that first devastating battle can be seen in somber gravestones, remnants of German bunkers, and the pockmarked landscape.

📧 **TRANSPORTATION.** Reaching and exploring the D-Day beaches can be difficult without a car. That said, many of the sites are accessible from Caen and Bayeux with **Bus Verts** (☎08 10 21 42 14); ask about the special "D-Day" line. A day pass (€17) takes you to four major sites. **Utah Beach** is accessible only by car or foot from **Ste-Mère-Église**. Take a **train** from Bayeux to Caretan (30min., 10 per day, €6.60) and then a **bus** from Caretan to Ste-Mère-Église (15min.; 12:50pm, return 6:35pm; €2.90). English-language **Victory Tours** leave from behind the Bayeux tourist office. (☎02 31 51 98 14; www.victory-tours.com. 4hr. tour 12:30pm, €31; 8hr. tour 9am, €54. Reserve ahead.)

BEACHES NEAR BAYEUX. At **Utah Beach,** near Ste-Marie du Mont, the Americans headed the western flank of the invasion. The **Musée du Débarquement** here shows how 836,000 troops, 220,000 vehicles, and 725,000 tons of equipment came ashore. (☎02 33 71 53 35. Open June-Sept. daily 9:30am-7pm; Oct.-May reduced hours. €4.50.) The most difficult landing was that of the First US Infantry Division at **Pointe du Hoc.** The Pointe is considered a military cemetery because many who perished are still there, crushed beneath collapsed concrete bunkers. **Omaha Beach,** next to Colleville-sur-Mer and east of the Pointe du Hoc, is perhaps the most famous beach and the severe losses suffered there bestowed the moniker "bloody Omaha." Overlooking the beach, 9387 graves stretch across the American Cemetery. (Open daily 9am-5pm.) Ten kilometers north of Bayeux and just east of Omaha is **Arromanches**, a small town at the center of **Gold Beach,** where the British built the artificial Port Winston in a single day to provide shelter while the Allies unloaded their supplies. The **Arromanches 360° Cinéma** combines images of modern Normandy with those of D-Day. Turn left on r. de la Batterie from the museum and climb the steps to get there. (Open June-Aug. daily 9:40am-6:40pm; Sept.-May reduced hours. Closed Jan. €3.70, students €3.30.)

MONT-ST-MICHEL

Rising like a vision from the sea, the fortified island of Mont-St-Michel (pop. 42) is a dazzling labyrinth of stone arches, spires, and stairways that climb up to the **abbey.** Adjacent to the abbey church, **La Merveille,** a 13th-century Gothic monastery, encloses a seemingly endless web of passageways and chambers. (Open May-Aug. daily 9am-7pm; Sept.-Apr. 9:30am-6pm. €7, ages 18-25 €4.50.) The Mont is most stunning at night, but plan carefully—there is no late-night public transport off the island. Mont-St-Michel is best visited as a daytrip via a Courriers Bretons **bus,** 104 r. Couesnon in Pontorson (☎02 33 60 11 43), from Rennes (1½hr., 3-6 per day, €11) or St-Malo (1½hr., 2-4 per day, €9). Hotels on Mont-St-Michel are expensive, starting at €50 a night. The **Pontorson tourist office**, pl. de l'Église, helps visitors find affordable accommodations (☎02 33 60 20 65; fax 02 33 60 85 67. Open July-Aug. M-F 9am-12:30pm and 2-6:30pm, Sa 10am-12:30pm and 3-6:30pm; Sept.-June reduced hours.) The cheapest beds are at the **Centre Duguesclin (HI)** ❶, r. Général Patton. (☎/fax 02 33 60 18 65. Dorms €8.) **Postal Code:** 50116.

BRITTANY (BRETAGNE)

Lined with spectacular beaches, wild headlands, and cliffs gnawed by the sea into long crags and inlets, Brittany fiercely maintains its Celtic traditions despite Paris's age-old effort to assimilate the province. Britons fled Anglo-Saxon invaders between the 5th and 7th centuries for this beautiful, wild peninsula, and in the 800 years that followed, they defended their independence from Frankish, Norman, French, and English invaders. Breton traditions, dating from centuries of freedom, linger in the pristine islands off the Atlantic coast, and lilting *Brezhoneg* (Breton) is spoken at pubs and ports in the western part of the province.

RENNES

The throbbing heart of Brittany, Rennes (pop. 210,000) has a well-earned reputation as the party capital of northwestern France, but the city is more than just a rocking good time. Its *vielle ville* is as charming as any of France's small medieval towns, cobblestones, half-timbered houses, and all. Unlike many of its neighbors, Rennes is not sagging under history's awesome weight; this is, first and foremost, a city dedicated to life in the moment.

TRANSPORTATION. Trains leave from pl. de la Gare (☎02 99 29 11 92) for: Brest (2¼hr., every hr., €27); Caen (3hr., 8 per day, €28); Paris (2hr., every hr., €47); and St-Malo (1hr., 15 per day, €11). **Buses** (☎02 99 30 87 80) leave the train station for Angers (2½-3hr., 3-4 per day, €16) and Mont-St-Michel (2½hr., 1-2 per day, €12). Local **buses** run daily 5am-8pm; lines in areas with hopping nightlife run as late as midnight. A **métro** line runs through Rennes on the same ticket (€1).

PRACTICAL INFORMATION. To get from the train station to the **tourist office**, 11 r. St-Yves, take av. Jean Janvier to quai Chateaubriand, turn left, walk along the river until you reach r. George Dottin, then turn right onto r. St-Yves. (☎02 99 67 11 11; fax 02 99 67 11 10. Open Apr.-Sept. M-Sa 9am-7pm, Su and holidays 11am-6pm.) Access the **Internet** at **Neurogame**, 2 rue de Dinan. (☎02 99 65 53 85; www.neurogame.com. €3 per hr. Open M-Th 2pm-1am, F-Sa 2pm-3am. The **post office** (☎02 99 01 22 11) is at 27 bd. du Colombier, near the train station. **Postal Code:** 35032.

ACCOMMODATIONS AND FOOD. The **Auberge de Jeunesse (HI)** ❶, 10-12 Canal St-Martin, provides cheap and decent lodging. Take the métro (dir: Kennedy) to *Ste-Anne*. Follow r. St-Malo downhill to the river, bear left onto r. St-Martin, and the hostel will be on the right. (☎02 99 33 22 33; fax 02 99 59 06 21. Breakfast included. Reception 7am-11pm. Dorms €13. MC/V.) **Hotel d'Angleterre** ❷, 19 r. Marechal Joffre, can't be beat for location. Take the métro (dir: Kennedy) to *pl. de la République*, walk towards the river and turn right onto r. Jean Jaurès; the hotel is on the right. (☎02 99 79 38 61; fax 02 99 79 43 85. Breakfast €5. Reception 7am-10:30pm. Singles €21-37; doubles €32-44; triples €41-46. MC/V.) **Camping Municipal des Gayeulles** ❶, deep within Parc les Gayeulles, is packed with activities. Take bus #3 (dir.: St-Laurent) from pl. du Colombier (left of the train station) to *Piscine/Gayuelles*. Follow the paths and signs to the campground. (☎02 99 36 91 22. Reception mid-June to mid-Sept. 7:30am-1pm and 2-8pm; mid-Sept. to mid-June 9am-12:30pm and 4:30-8pm. Electricity €2.60. €3 per person; €1.60 per car. MC/V.) **Rue St-Malo** has many ethnic restaurants. Inside the *vielle ville* are traditional *brasseries* and cheap kebab stands. In general, the best food is found on the outskirts of the city center. The upscale ▨**Café Breton ❷**, 14 r. Nantaise, serves Breton cuisine at reasonable prices. (☎02 99 30 74 95. Open M and Sa noon-4pm, Tu-F noon-3pm and 7-11pm.)

◙ ◪ **SIGHTS AND ENTERTAINMENT.** Excellent examples of medieval architecture are near the tourist office on **rue de la Psalette** and **rue St-Guillaume**. At the end of r. St-Guillaume, turn left onto r. de la Monnaie to visit the imposing **Cathédrale St-Pierre**, which was begun in 1787. The center of attention is its carved and gilded altarpiece depicting the life of the Virgin. (Open daily 9:30am-noon and 3-6pm.) Across the street from the cathedral, the **Portes Mordelaises**, down an alley bearing the same name, are the former entrances to the city and the last vestiges of the medieval city walls. The **Musée des Beaux-Arts**, 20 quai Émile Zola, houses a small but stunningly varied collection. (☎02 99 28 55 85 40. Open Su-M and W-Sa 10am-noon and 2-6pm. €5, students €2.50. Under-18 free.) Across the river and up r. Gambetta is the lush **Jardin du Thabor**, considered to be among the most beautiful gardens in France. Concerts are often held here; a small gallery on the north side exhibits local artwork on a rotating basis. (Open June-Sept. 7:15am-9:30pm.)

With enough bars for a city twice its size and a collection of clubs that draws students from Paris and beyond, Rennes is a partygoer's weekend mecca. Look for action in **place Ste-Anne**, **place St-Michel**, and the radiating streets. ▨**Delicatessen**, 7 allée Rallier du Baty, is tucked around the corner from pl. St-Michel in a former prison, having swapped jailhouse bars for dance cages to become one of Rennes' hottest clubs. (Cover €10 Th-Sa after 1:30am, F-Sa €14 after 1:30am. Open Tu-Sa midnight-5am.) **Le Zing**, 5 pl. des Lices, packs the house with the young and beautiful. (☎02 99 79 64 60. Opens daily at 2pm, active from midnight until 2am.)

ST-MALO

St-Malo (pop. 52,000) manages to merge the best of northern France. Combining miles of warm, sandy beaches and crystal blue waters with a charming, walled *vielle ville* that holds numerous *crêperies*, boutiques, and cafes, St-Malo makes for the ultimate oceanside getaway. To the east of the city is the **Grand Plage**, the most popular beach. The slightly more secluded **Plage de Bon Secours** lies to the west and features the curious **Piscine de Bon-Secours**, three cement walls that hold in a pool's worth of warm salt water even when the tide recedes. The best view of St-Malo is from its **ramparts**, which once kept out invaders but now attract tourists in droves. All entrances to the city have stairs leading up to the old walls; the view from the north side reveals a series of small islands leading out into the sea.

Trains run from pl. de l'Hermine to: Dinan (1hr., 5 per day, €8); Paris (5hr., 3 per day, €50); and Rennes (1hr., 8-12 per day, €11). As you exit the station, cross bd. de la République and follow esplanade St-Vincent to the **tourist office**, near the entrance to the *vielle ville*. (☎02 99 56 64 48; www.saint-malo-tourisme.com. Open July-Aug. M-Sa 9am-7:30pm, Su 10am-6pm; Sept.-June reduced hours.) The 247-bed **Auberge de Jeunesse (HI) ❶**, 37 av. du Révérend Père Umbricht, is near the beach. From the train station, take bus #5 (dir.: Parame or Davier) or bus #1 (dir.: Rotheneuf) to *Auberge de Jeunesse*. (☎02 99 40 29 80; fax 02 99 40 29 02. Reception 24hr. Dorms €13.) Overlooking Plage de Bon Secours, **Les Chiens de Guet ❸**, 4 pl. de Guet, has bright, elegant rooms and a great location within the city walls. (☎02 99 40 87 29; fax 02 99 56 08 75. Breakfast €5. Doubles €31; quads €66. Closed mid-Nov. to Jan. AmEx/MC/V.) The most interesting eateries lie closer to the center of the *vielle ville;* those near the entrances are often generic and overpriced. **Champion supermarket**, on av. Pasteur, is near the hostel. (Open M-F 8:30am-1pm and 3-7:30pm, Sa 8:30am-7:30pm, Su 9:30am-noon.) **Postal Code:** 35400.

DINAN

Perhaps the best-preserved medieval town in Brittany, Dinan's (pop. 10,000) cobblestone streets are lined with 15th-century houses inhabited by traditional artisans. On the ramparts, the 13th-century **Porte du Guichet** is the entrance to the **Château de Dinan,** also known as the **Tour de la Duchesse Anne.** Climb to the terrace to look over the town or inspect the galleries of the 15th-century **Tour de Coëtquen,** which houses a collection of funerary ornaments. (Open June-Sept. daily 10am-6:30pm; Oct.-May reduced hours. €3.90, ages 12-18 €1.50.) On the other side of the ramparts from the chateau is the **Jardin du Val Cocherel,** which holds bird cages and a chessboard scaled for life-sized pieces. (Open daily 8am-7:30pm.) A long, picturesque walk down the steep r. de Petit Fort will lead you to the **Maison d'Artiste de la Grande Vigne,** 103 r. du Quai. This former home of painter Yvonne Jean-Haffen (1895-1993), is a work of art, with exhibitions of her work, murals adorning the walls, and a picturesque garden that would be any artist's dream. (☎ 02 96 87 90 80. Open May 2-6pm, June-Sept. 2-6:30pm. €2.50, students €1.60.)

Trains run from the pl. du 11 Novembre 1918 to Paris (3hr., 8 per day, €50) and Rennes (1hr., 8 per day, €12). To get from the station to the **tourist office,** r. du Château, bear left across pl. 11 Novembre to r. Carnot, turn right on r. Thiers, turn left into the *vielle ville,* and bear right onto r. du Marchix, which becomes r. de la Ferronnerie; it will be on your right. (☎ 02 96 87 69 76; www.dinan-tourisme.com. Open mid-June to mid-Sept. M-Sa 9am-7pm, Su 10am-12:30pm and 2:30-6pm; mid-Sept. to mid-June M-Sa 9am-12:30pm and 2-6pm.) **Internet** access is available at **Arospace Cybercafe,** 9 r. de la Chaux, off r. de l'Horloge. (☎ 02 96 87 04 87. Open Tu-Sa 10am-12:30pm, 1:30-7pm. €1.50 per 15 min.) To reach the **Auberge de Jeunesse (HI)** ❶, in Vallée de la Fontaine-des-Eaux, turn left as you exit the station and cross the tracks, then turn right, and follow the tracks downhill for 1km before turning right again; it will be on your right. (☎ 02 96 39 10 83. Reception 8am-noon and 5-8pm. Curfew 11pm. Dorms €8.50.) **Hôtel du Théâtre** ❶, 2 r. Ste-Claire, is in the heart of the *vielle ville.* (☎ 02 96 39 06 91. Singles €15; doubles €21.) Get **groceries** at **Monoprix** on r. du Marchix. (Open M-Sa 9am-7:30pm.) **Rue de la Cordonnerie** and **place des Merciers** have inexpensive *brasseries.* **Postal Code:** 22100.

ST-BRIEUC

As most locals will tell you, St-Brieuc (pop. 48,000) is much more of a commercial center than a tourist trap. The university students help make the city vibrant; its lively bar scene is one of the best in the region. Situated between the Côte d'Emeraude and the Côte de Granite Rose, it is a perfect base for daytrips to the scenic countryside. **Trains** arrive from Dinan (1hr., 2-3 per day, €8.60) and Rennes (1hr., 15 per day, €15). From the station on bd. Charner, walk straight down r. de la Gare and bear right at the fork to reach pl. de la Résistance and the **tourist office,** 7 r. St-Gouéno. (☎ 02 96 33 32 50; fax 02 96 61 42 16. Open July-Aug. M-Sa 9am-7pm, Su 10am-1pm; Sept.-June M-Sa 9am-noon and 1:30-6pm.) The **Youth Hostel** ❶ is in a 15th-century house 3km from town; take bus #2 (dir.: Centre Commercial les Villages) and get off at the last stop, turn around and take the first left onto r. du Brocéliande; follow it to its end and turn left onto r. du Vau Méno. Turn right onto r. de la Ville Guyomard, where you'll find the hostel on the left. (☎ 02 96 78 70 70. Breakfast included. Reception 9:30am-noon, 2-7pm and 8-8:30pm. Dorms €3. MC/V.) Bars and outdoor cafes cluster in the area

FRANCE

behind the tourist office and along the small **rue Fardel** behind the Cathédrale St-Etienne; **rue des Trois Frères le Goff** is lined with inexpensive Moroccan, Italian, Chinese, Mexican, and Indian restaurants. **Postal Code:** 22000.

CAP FRÉHEL

The rust-hued cliffs of **Cap Fréhel** mark the northern point of the Côte d'Emeraude. Catch a CAT **bus** from St-Brieuc (1½hr.; 3-4 per day; €7.20, students €5.80) and follow the red- and white-striped markers along the **GR34 trail** on the edge of the peninsula. There's also a scenic 1½hr. walk to **Fort La Latte**, a 13th-century castle complete with drawbridges. To reach the **Auberge de Jeunesse Cap Fréhel (HI) ❶**, in La Ville Hadrieux in Kerivet, get off the bus one stop after Cap Fréhel at *Auberge de Jeunesse*, take the only road that branches from the stop, and follow the fir-tree hostel signs. (☎02 96 41 48 98; mid-Sept. to Apr. 02 98 78 70 70. Breakfast €3. Open May-Sept. Dorms or camping €7.)

PAIMPOL

Paimpol (pop. 8200), northwest of St-Brieuc at the end of the Côte de Granite Rose, offers easy access to nearby islands, beaches, and hiking trails. **Trains** (1hr., 4-5 per day, €10) and CAT **buses** (1¼hr.; 8 per day; €7.20, students €5.80) leave av. Général de Gaulle for St-Brieuc. From the station, turn right onto av. de Général de Gaulle and bear left at the roundabout; the **tourist office** will be on the left, and the port will be to the right. (☎02 96 20 83 16; www.paimpol-goelo.com. Open June-Sept. M-Sa 9:30am-7:30pm, Su 10am-6pm; Oct.-May M-Sa 9:30am-12:30pm and 1:30-6:30pm.) **Hôtel Le Goelo ❸**, quai Duguay Trouin, has comfortable rooms, some overlooking the port. From the tourist office, walk towars the water and take the first right; the hotel is just ahead. (☎02 96 20 82 74. Breakfast €4.60. Singles €25, with shower and toilet €31; doubles €34-42; triples €54. MC/V.) **Rue des 8 Patriots** is the best bet for restaurants. **Postal Code:** 22500.

BREST

Brest (pop. 156,000) was transformed into a somber wasteland in 1944 by Allied bombers driving out the occupying German flotilla. However, the city has begun to show signs of life; Brest features a number of pleasant daytime cafes and a new summer concert series, as well as one of the largest aquariums around. Brest's **château** was the only building in the town to survive WWII, and is now the world's oldest active military institution, as well as home to the **Musée de la Marine,** off r. de Château, which highlights the local maritime history. (Open Apr.-Sept. daily 10am-6:30pm; Oct.-Mar. M and W-Su 10am-noon and 2-6pm. €4.60, students €3.) The newly renovated **Océanopolis,** at port de Plaisance, has tropical, temperate, and polar pavilions and a coral reef accessible by a glass elevator. From the Liberty terminal, take bus #7 (dir.: Port de Plaisance; M-Sa every 30min. until 7:30pm; €1) to *Océanopolis.* (☎02 98 34 40 40. Open Apr.-Aug. daily 9am-6pm; Sept.-Mar. Su 10am-6pm, Tu-Sa 10am-5pm. €15.)

Trains (☎02 98 31 51 72) leave pl. du 19*ème* Régiment d'Infanterie for Nantes (4hr., 6 per day, €35); Quimper (30min., 5 per day, €14); and Rennes (1½hr., 15 per day, €27). From the station, av. Georges Clemenceau leads to the intersection of r. de Siam and r. Jean Jaurès, and the **tourist office,** at pl. de la Liberté. (☎02 98 44 24 96. Open July-Aug. M-Sa 9:30am-7pm, Su 10am-noon; Sept.-June M-Sa 9am-12:30pm and 2-6pm.) Access the **Internet** at @cces.cibles, 31 av. Clemenceau. (☎02 98 33 73 07. €3 per hr. Open M-Sa 11am-1am, Su 2-11pm.) For the luxurious ◪**Auberge de Jeunesse (HI) ❶,** 5 r. de Kerbriant, 4km away near Océanopolis, take bus #7 (dir.: Port de Plaisance) from opposite the station to its final stop (M-Sa until 7:30pm, Su until 6pm; €1); with your back to the bus stop, go left toward the beach, take an immediate left, and follow the signs to the hostel. (☎ 02 98 41 90 41. Reception M-F 7-9am and 5-8pm, Sa-Su 7-10am and 6-8pm. Curfew July-Aug. midnight; Sept.-June 11pm; ask for a key. Dorms €12.) **Kelig Hôtel ❷,** 12 r. de Lyon, has clean, relatively spacious rooms. (☎ 02 98 80 47 21. Breakfast €6. Singles €24-37; doubles €27-40; triples €44-47. AmEx/MC/V.) The area at the end of **rue de Siam,** near the port, has a variety of restaurants. **Postal Code:** 29200.

QUIMPER

With a central waterway crisscrossed by pedestrian footbridges decorated with colorful flowers, Quimper (pop. 63,000) has the feel of a mini-Paris. The magnificent dual spires of the **Cathédrale St-Corentin,** built between the 13th and 15th centuries, mark the entrance to the old quarter from quai St-Corentin. (Open M-Sa 8:30am-noon and 1:30-6:30pm, Su 8:30am-noon, except during mass, and 2-6:30pm.) The **Musée Départemental Breton,** 1 r. du Roi Gradlon, through the cathedral garden, offers exhibits on local history, archaeology, and ethnography. (Open June-Sept. daily 9am-6pm; Oct.-May Su 2-5pm, Tu-Sa 9am-noon and 2-5pm. €4, students €2.50.) At night, head to one of the several cafes near the cathedral, or to the Irish pub ▧**Molly Malone's,** pl. St-Mathieu, on r. Falkirk. (☎ 02 98 53 40 42. Beamish stout €3.10, pint €5.40. Open daily 11am-1am.)

Trains go to Brest (1½hr., 4 per day, €14) and Rennes (2¼hr., 10 per day, €28). From the train station, go right onto av. de la Gare and follow the river Odet, keeping it on your right; it will become bd. Dupleix and lead to pl. de la Résistance. The **tourist office** will be on your left. (☎ 02 98 53 04 05; www.quimper-tourisme.com. Open July-Aug. M-Sa 9am-7pm, Su 10am-1pm and 3-5:45pm; Sept.-June reduced hours.) Access the **Internet** at **CyberCopy,** 3 bd. Amiral Kerguelen (☎ 02 98 64 33 99. €4.50 per hr. Open M 1-7pm, Tu-F 9am-7pm, Sa 9am-3pm.) To reach the **Centre Hébergement de Quimper (HI) ❶,** 6 av. des Oiseaux, take bus #1 from pl. de la Résistance (dir: Kermoysan) to *Chaptal* (last bus 7:30pm). The hostel will be 50m up the street on your left. (☎ 02 98 64 97 97; quimper@fuaj.org. Breakfast €3.25. Sheets €3. Dorms €8.40. HI members only.) **Hôtel Le Derby ❸,** 13 av. de la Gare, facing the train station, has well-decorated rooms, all with bath. (☎ 02 98 52 06 91; fax 02 98 53 39 04. Breakfast €5.40. Extra bed €4. Singles €28; doubles €38; Oct.-Apr. €3 discount.) The lively **Les Halles** (covered markets), off r. Kéréon on r. St-François, always has shops with bargains on produce, seafood, meats, and cheeses. (Open M-Sa 7am-8pm, Su 9am-1pm.) **Postal Code** 29200.

LOIRE VALLEY (VAL DE LOIRE)

The Loire, France's longest and most celebrated river, meanders to the Atlantic through a valley overflowing with gentle vineyards and majestic chateaux. Loire vineyards produce some of France's best wines, and the soil is among the country's most fertile. It is hardly surprising that a string of French (and English) kings chose to station themselves in opulent chateaux by these waters rather than in the commotion of their capital cities.

▣ TRANSPORTATION

Faced with such widespread grandeur, many travelers plan over-ambitious itineraries—two chateaux a day is a reasonable limit. Biking is the best way to explore the region, since trains to chateaux are infrequent. The city of Tours is the region's best **rail** hub, although the chateaux Chambord and Cheverny aren't accessible by train. Many stations distribute the invaluable *Châteaux pour Train et Vélo* booklet with train schedules and **bike** and **car rental** information.

FRANCE

ORLÉANS

A pleasant gateway from Paris into the Loire, Orléans (pop. 117,000) clings tightly to its historical connection to Joan of Arc. Most of Orléans's highlights are near **Place Ste-Croix.** Joan of Arc triumphantly marched down nearby **Rue de Bourgogne,** the city's oldest street, in 1429. The **Musée des Beaux-Arts,** 1 r. Ferdinand Rabier, has a fine collection of French, Italian and Flemish works. (☎ 02 38 79 21 55. Open M 1:30-6pm, Tu-Sa 10am-noon and 1:30-6pm. €3, students €1.50.) The **Église St-Paterne,** pl. Gambetta, is a massive showcase of modern stained glass. The stunning windows of **Cathédrale Sainte-Croix,** pl. Ste-Croix, depict Joan's dramatic story. (Open July-Aug. daily 9:15am-7pm; Sept.-June reduced hours.)

Trains arrive at the Gare d'Orléans on pl. Albert 1er from: Blois (30min., every hr. 7am-9pm, €8.40); Paris (1¼hr., 3 per hr., €15); and Tours (1hr., 2 per hr., €14.10). To get from the station to the **tourist office,** 6 r. Albert 1er, go left under the tunnel to pl. Jeanne d'Arc; it's across the street. (☎ 02 38 24 05 05; fax 02 38 54 49 84. Open May-Sept. Tu-Sa 9:30am-1pm and 2-6pm; Oct.-Apr. reduced hours.) To reach the **Auberge de Jeunesse (HI) ❶,** 1 bd. de la Motte Sanguin, take bus RS (dir.: Rosette) or SY (dir.: Concyr/La Bolière) from pl. Jeanne d'Arc to Pont Bourgogne; follow bd. de la Motte and it'll be up on the right. (☎ 02 38 53 60 06. Breakfast €3.40. Sheets €3.20. Reception M-F 8am-7pm, Sa-Su 9-11am and 5-7pm. Dorms €8.) **Les Halles Châtelet,** pl. du Châtelet, is a market attached to the Galeries Lafayette. (Open Su 7am-1pm, Tu-Sa 7am-7pm.) In the back of the mall, buy groceries in **Carrefour** at pl. Jeanne d'Arc. (Open M-Sa 8:30am-9pm.) **Rue de Bourgogne** and **rue Sainte Catherine** have a variety of eateries. **Postal Code:** 45000.

BLOIS

Blois (pop. 50,000) is one of the Loire's most popular and historical cities. Home to monarchs Louis XII and François I, Blois's **chateau** was the Versailles of the late 15th and early 16th centuries; today it exemplifies the progression of French architecture from the 13th to the 17th century. Housed within are excellent museums: The recently renovated **Musée de Beaux-Arts,** featuring a 16th-century portrait gallery; the **Musée d'Archéologie,** showcasing locally excavated glass and ceramics; and the **Musée Lapidaire,** preserving sculpted pieces from nearby chateaux. (☎ 02 54 90 33 33. Open July-Aug. daily 9am-7:30pm; Apr.-June and Sept. 9am-6pm; Oct.-Mar. 9am-12:30pm and 2-5:30pm. €6, students €4.) At night the seemingly tame Blois lights up. Move from the cafes of **Place de la Résistance** to ▊**Le Blue Night,** 15 r. Haute, for a selection of over 100 international beers served in a bar that resembles a medieval chapel. (Open daily 6pm-4am.)

Trains leave pl. de la Gare for: Orléans (30min., 14 per day, €8.40); Paris (1¾hr., 8 per day, €20) via Orléans and Tours (1hr., 13 per day, €8.20). **Transports Loir-et-Cher** (TLC; ☎ 02 54 58 55 44) sends **buses** from the station and pl. Victor Hugo to nearby chateaux (45min.; 2 per day; €10, students €8.). Or, rent a **bike** from **Amster Cycles,** 7 r. de Desfray, one block from the train station, for the hour-long ride to the valley. (☎ 02 54 74 30 13. €13 per day. Open M-Sa 9:15am-1pm and 2-6:30pm, Su 10am-1:30pm and 3-6:15pm.) To reach the **tourist office,** 3 av. Jean Laigret, take a left on av. Jean Laigret out of the train station. (☎ 02 54 90 41 41; www.loiredeschateaux.com. Open Apr.-Oct. Su-M 10am-7pm, Tu-Sa 9am-7pm; Nov.-Mar. reduced hours.) ▊**Hôtel du Bellay ❷,** 12 r. des Minimes, is at the top of porte Chartraine, 2min. above the city center. This family-run establishment offers spotless, comfortable rooms and personal attention. (☎ 02 54 78 23 62; fax 02 54 78 52 04. Breakfast €4.20. Closed Jan. 5-25. Singles and doubles €24; triples €45; quads €55. MC/V.) **Le Pavillon ❷,** 2 av. Wilson, has clean and bright rooms. Take bus line 3A from the station; the hotel can also be reached on foot in 20min. (☎ 02 54 74 23 27; fax 02 54 74 03 36. Breakfast €5.25. Singles €24-38; quads €50. MC/V.) Fragrant *pâtisseries* entice from **rue Denis Papin,** while **rue Drussy, rue St-Lubin,** and **place Poids du Roi** have a number of dining options. **Postal Code:** 41000.

▶ DAYTRIPS FROM BLOIS: CHAMBORD AND CHEVERNY. Built from 1519 to 1545 to satisfy François I's egomania, **Chambord** is the largest and most extravagant of the Loire chateaux. With 440 rooms, 365 fireplaces, and 83 staircases, the chateau rivals Versailles in grandiosity. To cement his claim, François stamped 700 of his trademark stone salamanders throughout this "hunting lodge" and built a spectacular double-helix staircase in the center of the castle. (☎02 54 50 40 00. Open Apr.-Sept. 9am-6:45pm; Oct.-Mar. reduced hours. €7, ages 18-25 €4.50. Under-18 free.) Take TLC **bus** #2 from Blois (45min., 2 per day, €10) or **bike** south from Blois on D956 for 2-3km, and then turn left on D33 (1hr.).

Cheverny and its manicured grounds are unique among the major chateaux. Its magnificent furnishings include elegant tapestries and delicate Delft vases. Fans of Hergé's *Tintin* books may recognize Cheverny's Renaissance facade as the inspiration for Marlinspike, Captain Haddock's mansion. The **kennels** hold 70 mixed English Poitevin hounds who stalk stags in hunting expeditions. (☎02 54 79 96 29. Open July-Aug. daily 9:15am-6:45pm. Hunting Oct.-Mar. Tu and Sa. Off season reduced hours. €6, students €4.) Cheverny is 45min. south of Blois by **bike** and on the route of TLC **bus** #2 (see above).

AMBOISE

Amboise (pop. 11,000) is guarded by the parapets of the 15th-century **chateau** that six security-minded French kings called home. In the **Logis de Roi,** the main part of the chateau, intricate 16th-century Gothic chairs stand over 2m tall to prevent any attacks from behind. The jewel of the grounds is the 15th-century **Chapelle St-Hubert,** the final resting place of **Leonardo da Vinci.** (☎02 47 57 00 98. Open Apr.-Nov. daily 9am-6pm; Dec.-Mar. reduced hours. €7, students €6.) Four hundred meters away is **Clos Lucé** manor, where Leonardo da Vinci spent the last three years of his life. Inside are his bedroom, library, drawing room, and chapel, but the main attraction is a collection of 40 machines created from da Vinci's visionary designs and built with materials contemporaneous to da Vinci's lifetime. (☎02 47 57 62 88. Open Mar.-Oct. daily 9am-7pm; Nov.-Feb. reduced hours. €11, students €9.)

Trains leave bd. Gambetta for: Blois (20min., 20 per day, €5.40); Orléans (1hr., 6 per day, €13); Paris (2½hr., 7 per day, €24); and Tours (20min., 11 per day, €4.30). To reach the **tourist office** on quai du Général de Gaulle, take a left once outside the train station, following r. Jules-Ferry and cross both bridges past the residential Ile d'Or. (☎02 47 57 09 28; fax 02 47 57 14 35. Open July-Aug. M-Sa 9am-8pm, Su 10am-6pm; Sept.-June reduced hours.) The **Centre International de Séjour Charles Péguy (HI) ❶,** on Ile d'Or, sits on an island in the middle of the Loire. Some rooms have a view of the chateau. (☎02 47 30 60 90; fax 02 47 30 60 91. Breakfast €2.60. Sheets €3.10. Reception M-F 3-7pm. Dorms €8.60.) **Postal Code:** 35400.

TOURS

Tours (pop. 253,000) works best as a base for nearby Loire chateaux, but its fabulous nightlife and collection of sights should not be missed. The **Cathédrale St-Gatien,** on r. Jules Simon, has dazzling stained glass and an intricate facade. (Cathedral open daily 9am-7pm. Free. Cloister open Easter-Sept. 9:30am-12:30pm and 2-6pm; Oct.-Mar. Su, W-Sa 9:30am-12:30pm and 2-5pm. €2.50.) At the **Musée du Gemmail,** 7 r. du Murier, works of *gemmail* (a fusion of enameled shards of brightly colored glass) glow in rooms of dark velvet. (Open Apr.-Nov. Su and Tu-Sa 10am-noon and 2-6:30pm. €4.60, students €3.) At night, **place Plumereau** (or just plain pl. Plum) is the place to be, with cheerful students sipping drinks and chatting at cafes and bars.

Trains leave pl. du Général Leclerc for Bordeaux (2½hr., 4 per day, €34) and Paris (2¼hr., 7 per day, €25). To reach the **tourist office**, 78-82 r. Bernard Palissy, from the station, walk through pl. du Général Leclerc, cross bd. Heurteloup and take a right. (☎02 47 70 37 37; www.ligeris.com. Open mid-Apr. to mid-Oct. M-Sa 8:30am-7pm, Su 10am-12:30pm and 2:30-5pm; mid-Oct. to mid-Apr. reduced hours.) Access the **Internet** at **Cyber Gate**, 11 r. de Président Merville. (☎02 47 05 95 94. €1 per 15min., €5 for 1hr. of access, a sandwich, and a beverage. Open M 1-10pm, Tu-Sa 11am-midnight, Su 2-10pm.) The owners of ◨**Hôtel Regina ❸**, 2 r. Pimbert, make you feel like family. It's close to beautiful river strolls and good restaurants. (☎02 47 05 25 36; fax 02 47 66 08 72. Breakfast €4.30. Singles and doubles €20-24; triples €23-36. MC/V.) **Foyer des Jeunes Travailleurs ❷**, 16 r. Bernard Palissy, is centrally located. (☎02 47 60 51 51. Singles €17; doubles €31.) Try **place Plumereau** and **rue Colbert** for great restaurants, cafes, and bars. **La Souris Gourmande ❷**, 100 r. Colbert, is a friendly restaurant specializing in regional cheese dishes and fondues. (Open Tu-Sa noon-2pm and 7-10:30pm.) **Postal Code:** 37000.

▶ **DAYTRIPS FROM TOURS: CHENONCEAU AND LOCHES.** Perhaps the most exquisite chateau in France, Chenonceau arches gracefully over the Cher river. A series of women created the beauty that is the chateau: first Catherine, the wife of a tax collector; then Diane de Poitiers, the lover of Henri II; and then Henri's widowed wife, Catherine de Médici. The part of the chateau bridging the Cher marked the border between occupied and Vichy France during WWII. (☎02 47 23 90 07. Open mid-Mar. to mid-Sept. daily 9am-7pm; off-season reduced hours. €8, students €6.50.) **Trains** from Tours roll into the station in front of the castle. (30min., 6 per day, €5.10). Fil Vert **buses** also leave from Tours (1¼hr, 2 per day, €2.10) and Amboise (20 min., 2 per day, €1).

Surrounded by a walled medieval town that merits a visit in itself, the chateau of **Loches** consists of two structures at opposite ends of a hill. To the north, the 11th-century keep and watchtowers changed roles from keeping enemies out to keeping them in when Charles VII made it a state prison, complete with suspended cages. While the floors in the three-story tower to the south have fallen out, the walls and stairs remain; you can climb the staircase and take in a view of the village below. The **Logis Royal** (Royal Lodge) honors the famous ladies who held court here, including Charles VII's lover Agnès Sorel, the first officially declared Mistress of the King of France. (☎02 47 59 01 32. Open Apr.-Sept. daily 9am-7pm; Oct.-Mar. 9:30am-5pm. Logis Royal €3.80, students €2.70.) **Trains** and **buses** run from Tours to Loches (50 min., 13 per day, €7).

ANGERS

From illustrious aristocratic origins, Angers (pop. 160,000) has grown into a sophisticated modern city. Behind the massive stone walls of the **Château d'Angers**, on pl. Kennedy, the medieval Dukes of Anjou ruled the surrounding area and a certain island across the Channel. The 13th-century chateau remains a well-preserved haven of medieval charm in a city filled with shops and sights. Inside the chateau is the 14th-century **Tapisserie de l'Apocalypse**, the world's largest tapestry. (Open May to mid-Sept. daily 9:30am-7pm; mid-Sept. to Apr. 10am-5:30pm. €5.50, students €3.50.) Angers's other woven masterpiece is the 1930 **Chant du Monde** ("Song of the World"), in the **Musée Jean Lurçat**, 4 bd. Arago. (☎02 41 24 18 45. Open mid-June to mid-Sept. daily 9:30am-6:30pm; mid-Sept. to mid-June Su and Tu-Sa 10am-noon and 2-6pm. €3.50.) The **Musée Cointreau** offers tours of the factory where it makes the famous liqueur, a native of Angers since its creation in 1849, followed by a free tasting. Take bus #7 from the train station to *Cointreau*. (Open July-Aug. daily 10:30am-6:30pm; Sept.-June reduced hours. €5.50)

From r. de la Gare, **trains** leave for Paris (2-4hr., 3 per day, €44) and Tours (1hr., 12 per day, €14). **Buses** run from pl. de la République to Rennes (3hr., 2 per day, €16). To get from the station to the **tourist office**, at pl. du Président Kennedy, exit straight onto r. de la Gare, turn right at pl. de la Visitation on r. Talot, and turn left on bd. du Roi-René; it's on the right, across from the chateau. (☎02 41 23 50 00; www.angers-tourisme.com. Open June-Sept. M-Sa 9am-6:30pm, Su 10am-5pm; Oct.-May reduced hours.) Access the **Internet** at **Cyber Espace**, 25 r. de la Roë. (☎02 41 24 92 71. €3.85 per hr. Open M-Th 9am-10pm, F-Sa 9am-midnight, Su 2-8pm.) **Hôtel de l'Univers ❷**, 2, pl. de la Gare, near the train station, has comfortable rooms. (☎02 41 88 43 58; fax 02 41 86 97 28. Breakfast €5.60. Singles and doubles €25-50.) Walk further down r. de la Gare for the spacious **Royal Hôtel ❷**, 8 bis pl. de la Visitation. (☎02 41 88 30 25; fax 02 41 81 05 75. Breakfast €4.60. Singles and doubles €26-42. AmEx/MC/V.) Cheap food is abundant along **rue St-Laud** and **rue St-Aubin**. Grab groceries in **Galeries Lafayette**, at r. d'Alsace and pl. du Ralliement. (Open M-Sa 9:30am-7:30pm.) **Postal Code:** 49052.

PÉRIGORD AND AQUITAINE

Périgord presents seductive images: green countryside splashed with yellow sunflowers, white chalk cliffs, golden white wines, and plates of black truffles. The region has long been popular; first settled 150,000 years ago, the area around Les Eyzies-de-Tayac has produced more stone-age artifacts than anywhere on earth.

PÉRIGUEUX

Rich with tradition and gourmet cuisine, the lovely old quarters of Périgueux (pop. 65,000) have preserved significant architecture from the city's past, which goes back to Gallo-Roman times. The towering steeple and five massive cupolas of the **Cathédrale St-Front** dominate Périgueux from above the Isle river. Fifteen-hundred years of rebuilding, restoration, rethinking, and revision have produced the largest cathedral in southwestern France. (Open daily 8am-noon and 2:30-7pm.) Just down r. St-Front, the **Musée du Périgord**, 22 cours Tourny, houses one of France's most important collections of prehistoric artifacts, including a set of 2m mammoth tusks. (Open Apr.-Sept. M and W-F 10:30am-6pm, Sa-Su 1-6pm; Oct.-Mar. reduced hours. €4, stu-

THE LOCAL STORY

A MIME IS A TERRIBLE THING TO WASTE

Laure Pierre, 26, has been miming ever since she was old enough to walk. Following an unusually lengthy phase of The Terrible Twos, her parents packed her bags and sent her to the prestigious Ecole Internationale de Mimodrame Marcel Marceau in Paris to teach her the arts of silence, discipline, and finding the way out of an invisible box. She currently performs in Perigueux's annual mime festival, Mimos.

LG: How did you become interested in miming?
A: [silence]

LG: What would you say is the relationship between miming and traditional French theater?
A: [silence]

LG: What's the average day like in the life of a mime?
A: [motions incomprehensibly while jumping on one leg]

LG: How has the art of miming evolved since the great age of Marcel Marceau?
A: [scratches toe against ground, lclucks, runs in circles with arms flapping]

LG: Who is your greatest influence?
A: [walks into an invisible wall]

LG: Do you get a lot of crap about being a professional mime?
A: [single tear runs down cheek]

dents €2. Under-18 free.) The **Musée Gallo-Romain**, 20 r. du 26 Régiment d'Infanterie, has built an intricate walkway over the excavated ruins of the *Domus de
Vésone*, once the home of a wealthy Roman merchant. (Open July-Aug. daily
10am-7pm; Sept.-June Su and Tu-Sa 10am-12:30pm and 2-6pm. €5.50.)

Trains leave r. Denis Papin for: Bordeaux (1½hr., 12 per day, €17); Paris (4-
6hr., 12 per day, €57); and Toulouse (4hr., 8 per day, €33). The **tourist office**, 26
pl. Francheville, has free maps. From the station, turn right on r. Denis Papin,
bear left on r. des Mobiles-de-Coulmierts, which becomes r. du Président Wilson, and take the next right after the Monoprix; it will be on the left. (☎ 05 53 53
10 63; www.ville-perigueux.fr. Open M-Sa 9am-1pm and 2-6pm.) Across from
the train station, **Hôtel des Voyageurs ❶**, 26 r. Denis Papin, has clean, bright
rooms. (☎/fax 05 53 53 17 44. Breakfast €3.20. Singles €13; doubles €15, with
shower €18.) **❷Au Bien Bon ❸**, 15 r. Aubergerie, serves exceptional regional
cuisine. (☎05 53 09 69 91. *Menu* €10-14. Open M 7:30-10pm, Tu-Sa noon-2pm
and 7:30-10pm.) **Monoprix supermarket** is on pl. de la République. (Open M-Sa
8:30am-8pm.) **Postal Code:** 24070.

SARLAT

The golden medieval *vieille ville* of Sarlat (pop. 11,000) has been the focus of
tourist and movie cameras; Gérard Depardieu's *Cyrano de Bergerac* was
filmed here. Today, its narrow 14th- and 15th-century streets fill with flea markets, dancing violinists, and purveyors of *gâteaux aux noix* (cakes with nuts)
and golden Monbazillac wines. **Trains** go to Bordeaux (2½hr., 4 per day, €19)
and Périgueux (3hr., 2 per day, €12). Sarlat **Buses** runs locally on two almost
identical routes around town. Line A stops at the train station; line B at the
roundabout one block away, down r. Dubois. (☎05 53 59 01 48. M-Sa 8:30am-
5pm.) The **tourist office**, r. Tourny in the Ancien Eveche, can arrange accommodations. (☎05 53 31 45 45. Open Apr.-Oct. M-Sa 9am-7pm, Su 10am-noon and 2-
6pm; Nov.-Mar. M-Sa 9am-noon and 2-7pm.) Sarlat's **Auberge de Jeunesse ❶**, 77
av. de Selves, is 40min. from the train station, but only 10min. from the *vieille
ville*. From the *vieille ville*, go straight on r. de la République, which becomes
av. Gambetta, and bear left at the fork onto av. de Selves. (☎05 53 59 47 59.
Reception 6am-8:30pm. Open mid-Mar. to Nov. Reserve ahead. Dorms €10.
Camping €6.) **Champion supermarket** is near the hostel on rte. de Montignac;
continue following av. de Selves away from the *centre ville*. (Open M-Sa 9am-
7:30pm, Su 9am-noon.) **Postal Code:** 24200.

▶ DAYTRIPS FROM SARLAT AND PÉRIGUEUX

CAVE PAINTINGS. The most spectacular cave paintings ever discovered line
the **Caves of Lascaux,** near the town of **Montignac**, 25km north of Sarlat. They
were discovered in 1940 by a couple of teenagers, but were closed in 1963—the
hordes of tourists had fostered algae and micro-stalactites that ravaged the
paintings. **Lascaux II** duplicates the original cave in the same pigments used
17,000 years ago. Although they may lack ancient awe and mystery, the new
caves—filled with paintings of 5m tall bulls, horses, and bison—manage to
inspire a wonder all their own. The **ticket office** (☎05 53 35 50 10) shares a
building with Montignac's **tourist office** (☎05 53 51 82 60), on pl. Bertram-de-
Born. (Ticket office open 9am until sold-out. €7.70.) The **train** station nearest
Montignac is at Le Lardin, 10km away. From there, you can call a **taxi** (☎05 53 50 86
61). During the school year (Sept.-June), **CFTA** (☎05 55 86 07 07) runs buses from
Périgueux (1½hr., 1 per day, €6.10) and Sarlat (20 min., 3 per day, €4.60)

At the **Grotte de Font-de-Gaume,** 1km outside **Les Eyzies-de-Tayac** on D47, amazing 15,000-year-old paintings are still open for viewing. (☎05 53 06 86 00; www.leseyzies.com/grottes-ornees. Open mid-May to mid-Sept. Su-F 9am-5:30pm; mid-Sept. to mid-May reduced hours. Reserve in advance. €6.10, ages 18-25 €4.10. Under-18 free. Tours available in English.) Get more info at the **Point Accueil Prehistoire,** across from the post office, on the main street through town. (☎06 86 66 54 43. Open daily 9:15am-1:30pm and 3-7pm.) The **tourist office** is located at pl. de la Mairie, before the Point Accueil. (☎05 53 06 97 05; www.leseyzies.com. Open July-Aug. M-Sa 9am-8pm, Su 10am-noon and 2-6pm; Sept.-June reduced hours.) From Les Eyzies-de-Tayac, **trains** go to Périgueux (30min., 5 per day, €8.10) and Sarlat (1hr., 3 per day, €9.20) via Le Buisson.

THE DORDOGNE VALLEY. Steep, craggy cliffs and poplar tree thickets overlook the slow-moving turquoise waters of the Dordogne River, 15km south of Sarlat. The town of **Castelnaud-La-Chapelle,** 10km southwest of Sarlat, snoozes in the shadow of its pale yellow **chateau.** (☎05 53 31 30 00. Open July-Aug. daily 9am-8pm; May-June and Sept. 10am-6pm; mid-Nov. to Feb. Su-F 2-5pm. €6.40.) The town of **Domme** was built by King Philippe III in 1280 on a high dome of solid rock. Over 70 Templar Knights were imprisoned by King Philip IV in the **Porte des Tours.** The graffiti they scrawled upon the walls with their bare hands and teeth still remains. Consult the **tourist office,** pl. de la Halle, for tours and more info on exploring the region. (☎05 53 31 71 00. Open July-Aug. daily 10am-7pm; Sept.-June 10am-noon and 2-6pm.) To get to and around the valley, you'll need to rent a car or be prepared for a good bike workout. Many outfits along the Dordogne rent **canoes** and **kayaks.** At the Pont de Vitrac, near Domme, you can find them at **Canoës-Loisirs** (☎05 53 28 23 43) and **Périgord Aventure et Loisirs** (☎05 53 28 23 82).

BORDEAUX

Enveloped by emerald vineyards, Bordeaux (pop. 280,000) toasts the ruby wine that made it famous. Not just a mecca for wine connoisseurs, this spirited, diverse university town also has vibrant nightlife, a stunning opera house, and some of France's best food. Construction of a new transit system currently disrupts the center of the city but is expected to be complete by 2004.

TRANSPORTATION AND PRACTICAL INFORMATION

Trains leave Gare St-Jean, r. Charles Domercq (☎05 56 33 11 06), for: Nice (9-10hr., 5 per day, €70); Paris (3½hr., 15-25 TGV per day, €58); and Toulouse (2-3hr., 11 per day, €27). From the train station, take bus #7 or 8 (dir.: Grand Théâtre) to pl. Gambetta and walk toward the Monument des Girondins to reach the **tourist office,** 12 cours du 30 juillet, which arranges winery tours. (☎05 56 00 66 00; www.bordeaux-tourisme.com. Open July-Aug. M-Sa 9am-7:30pm, Su 9:30am-6:30pm; Oct.-June reduced hours.) **Postal Code:** 33065.

ACCOMMODATIONS

🏨 **Hôtel Studio,** 26 r. Huguerie (☎05 56 48 00 14; www.hotel-bordeaux.com), is a backpacker favorite for good reason. The tiny, clean rooms have phones, toilets, showers, and cable TV. Internet access €2.25 per hr. Breakfast €4. Small singles €16, larger singles €24; doubles €20/27; triples €31; quads and quints €38. MC/V. ❷

Hôtel de la Boétie, 4 r. de la Boétie (☎05 56 81 76 68; fax 05 56 81 24 72). Check-in is at Hôtel Bristol around the corner, 4 r. Bouffard. Run by the same family as Hôtel Studio, La Boétie offers similar amenities. Breakfast €4. Singles €20-25; doubles €28; triples €31; quads and quints €38. AmEx/MC/V. ❷

Hôtel Boulan, 28 r. Boulan (☎05 56 52 23 62; fax 05 56 44 91 65). Take bus #7 or 8 from the train station to cours d'Albret. Right around the corner from the Musée des Beaux Arts. Several of the 16 simple white rooms have hardwood floors, balconies overlooking the quiet street below, and cable TV. Breakfast €3.50. Singles €19-28; doubles €26-31. Extra bed €5. MC/V. ❷

Auberge de Jeunesse (HI), 22 cours Barbey (☎05 56 33 00 70; fax 05 56 33 00 71). Near the station. The hostel is in a seedy neighborhood which can make the 30min. walk from the city center a harrowing experience at night. Large modern rooms are decorated with shiny metal furniture and patches of bright colors. Breakfast included. Handicapped-accessible. Curfew 2am. 2- to 6-person dorm rooms with showers €17. Non-members add €1.60. MC/V. ❶

🍴 FOOD

Bordelais take their food as seriously as their wine. Hunt around **rue St-Remi** and **place St-Pierre** for splendid regional specialties, including oysters, beef braised in wine sauce, and the cake *canelé de Bordeaux*. **La Casuccia ❷,** 49 r. Saint Rémi, is perfect for an intimate dinner or a casual outing. (☎05 56 51 17 70. Open Su 7-11:30pm, Tu-Sa noon-3pm and 7-11:30pm. MC/V.) **Le Valentino ❷,** 6 r. des Lauriers, is a reasonably priced oasis in the expensive quarter of Bordeaux with delicious cuisine and beautiful presentation. (☎05 56 48 11 56. Main course €8-15. Open daily 7-11pm. AmEx/MC/V.) Stock up at **Auchan supermarket,** at the Centre Meriadeck on r. Claude Bonnier. (☎05 56 99 59 00. Open M-Sa 8:30am-10pm.)

👁 SIGHTS

Near the tourist office, on pl. de Quinconces, the elaborate fountains of the **Monument aux Girondins** commemorate the revolutionary leaders from towns bordering the Gironde. Retrace your steps to the breathtaking **Grand Théâtre,** on pl. de la Comédie, to see a performance or take a tour. Possibly the most strictly classical opera house in the world, it is certainly one of the most impressive. (☎05 56 00 66 00. Tours €5, students €4.) Follow r. Ste-Catherine from the pl. de la Comédie, facing the theater, to reach the Gothic **Cathédrale St-André,** in pl. Pey-Berland, which hosted the weddings of Louis VII and Louis XIII. (Open Apr.-Oct. daily 8-11am and 2-5:30pm; Nov.-Mar. W and Sa 2:30-5:30pm. €4, under-25 and seniors €2.50.) Its bell tower, the **Tour Pey-Berland,** juts 50m into the sky. Climb the 229 spiraling steps for a beautiful view of the city. (☎05 56 81 25 26. Open June-Sept. daily 10am-6:30pm; Oct.-May Su and Tu-Sa 10am-noon and 2-5pm. €4, under-25 and seniors €2.50.) The best cityscape of Bordeaux can be seen from the 114m tower of the **Église St-Michel.** (Church open M-Sa 9am-6pm, Su 9am-12:30pm. Free. Tower open June-Sept. daily 2-7pm. €2.50.) Walking toward the river along cours d'Alsace, turn left onto quai Richelieu for the **place de la Bourse,** whose pillars and fountains reflect Bordeaux's grandeur. The impressive **Musée des Beaux Arts,** 20 cours d'Albret, near the cathedral, began as a place to display Napoleon's spoils of war and now contains great works by artists such as Picasso, Seurat, Matisse, and Titian. The permanent collection is held in the two buildings that frame the Hôtel de Ville; the temporary exhibits are across the street in the *Galeries des Beaux Arts.* (Open M and W-Su 11am-6pm. Permanent collection €4, joint pass for permanent and temporary collections €5.50. Students free.)

NIGHTLIFE

A haven for the young, Bordeaux boasts a seemingly endless list of lively bars and nightclubs, including a gay scene rivaled only by that of Paris. For an overview of Bordeaux nightlife, pick up a copy of *Clubs and Concerts* at the tourist office. **Place de la Victoire** and **place Gambetta** are year-round hot spots, mobbed by students during the school year and remaining popular through the summer. **St-Michel** has a more mellow atmosphere, with locals gathering at the cafe tables around 6pm and often staying until midnight. **El Bodegon**, on pl. de la Victoire, has theme nights and free giveaways on weekends. (Beer €2.50. Open M-Sa 7am-2am, Su 2pm-2am.) **Chica Cafe**, 3 r. Duffour Dubergier, in the shadow of the cathedral, has an older crowd during the day but heats up with students at night. The dance floor in the basement stages occasional concerts and dance lessons. (☎05 56 51 70 66. Beer €2. Happy Hour 6-8pm. Open M-Sa 11am-2am.)

DAYTRIP FROM BORDEAUX: ST-ÉMILION. Just 35km northeast of Bordeaux, St-Émilion (pop. 2,850) is home to viticulturists who have been refining their technique since Roman times. Today, they gently crush hectares of grapes to produce 23 million liters of wine annually. Vineyards aside, the medieval-style village itself is a pleasure to visit, with its winding narrow streets and cafe-lined square. The **Église Monolithe** is the largest subterranean church in Europe. The **tourist office**, at pl. des Créneaux, near the church tower, rents **bikes** (€14 per day) and offers guided tours (€9) of the local chateaux. (☎05 57 55 28 28. Open July-Aug. daily 9:30am-8pm; Sept.-June reduced hours.) **Trains** run from Bordeaux to St-Émilion (30min., 4 per day, €7).

THE PAYS BASQUE AND GASCONY

South of Aquitaine, the forests recede and the mountains of Gascony begin, shielded from the Atlantic by the Basque Country. Long renowned as fierce fighters, the Basques continue to struggle to maintain their identity, with some separatists claiming that they are an independent people rather than a part of France or Spain. The Gascons, meanwhile, have long considered themselves French. Today, people come to Gascony to be healed: millions of believers descend on Lourdes hoping for miracle cures, while thousands of others undergo natural treatments in the *thermes* of the Pyrenees.

BAYONNE

The pace of life in Bayonne (pop. 43,000) has not changed for centuries. Here the word for walk is *flâner*, meaning "to stroll," rather than *marcher* or even *se promener*. Towering above it all, the Gothic 13th-century **Cathédrale Ste-Marie** marks the leisurely passing of the time with the tolling of its bells. (Open June-Sept. M-Sa 7:30am-noon and 3-7pm, Su 3:30-8pm; Oct.-May reduced hours.) The **Musée Bonnat,** 5 r. Jacques Laffitte, in Petit-Bayonne, contains works by Degas, El Greco, and Goya. (Open May-Oct. M and W-Su 10am-6:30pm; Nov.-Apr. reduced hours. €5.50, students €3.) The **Harmonie Bayonnaise** orchestra holds traditional Basque **concerts** in pl. de Gaulle. (July-Aug. Th at 9:30pm. Free.)

Trains depart from the station in pl. de la République, running to: Bordeaux (2hr., 9 per day, €22); Toulouse (4hr., 5 per day, €32); and San Sebastián, Spain (1½hr., 6 per day, €8). Local STAB **buses** depart from the Hôtel de Ville for Biarritz (every 30-40min.; last bus M-Sa 8pm, Su 7pm; €1.20). The **tourist office**, on pl. des Basques, finds rooms. From the train station, take the middle fork onto pl. de la République,

FRANCE

IN RECENT NEWS

BASQUE ME NO QUESTIONS

In Bayonne, the capital of France's Basque region, restaurants post signs reading "Euskara badikigu." Years of Latin lessons won't help you discover that this means "Basque spoken here," for Basque is the only non-Indo-European language spoken in Western Europe. Basque might not be the language of Babel, as believed in the 18th century, but Basques are tied to an ancient past—geneticists recently found a link between Basques and Celts. Recent talk of Basque identity, however, has focused on the the the ETA (Basque Homeland and Liberty), a radical movement based in Spain that organizes attacks in the name of independence. As violence continues in Spain, France has cracked down on ETA training cells and imprisoned members for acts of terrorism.

Only 10% of French Basques vote for Basque parties, and even fewer support the ETA's radical ideology. How has France escaped Spain's problems? French Basques did not experience the cultural oppression that their Spanish counterparts did under Franco, and scholars suggest that tolerance toward French Basque culture has actually aided in their assimilation with the larger nation. The Pays Basque remains on the middle ground, balancing its cultural identity between extremes of separatism and assimilation.

veer right over pont St-Esprit, pass through pl. Réduit, cross pont Mayou, and turn right on r. Bernède which becomes av. Bonnat. The tourist office is on the left. (☎05 59 46 01 46; www.bayonne-tourisme.com. Open July-Aug. M-Sa 9am-7pm, Su 10am-1pm; Sept.-June M-F 9am-6:30pm, Sa 10am-6pm.) The █Hôtel Paris-Madrid ❷, on pl. de la Gare, has cozy rooms and friendly proprietors. (☎05 59 55 13 98. Breakfast €4. Reception 6am-12:30am. Singles and doubles €16-22; triples and quads €44.) Get groceries at **Monoprix supermarket,** 8 r. Orbe. (Open M-Sa 8:30am-7:30pm.) **Postal Code:** 64100.

BIARRITZ

A playground for the wealthy since the 19th century, Biarritz (pop. 29,000) can still put a dent in the wallet, but its free **beaches** make it an option for budget travelers as well. Surfers ride the waves and bathers soak up the sun at **Grande Plage,** while bathers repose *au naturel* just to the north at the less-crowded **Plage Miramar.** A short **hike** to **Pointe St-Martin** affords a priceless view of the water.

Trains leave from Biarritz-la-Négresse (☎05 59 23 04 84), 3km from town, for Bordeaux (2hr., 7 per day, €26) and Paris (5hr., 5 TGVs per day, €67). The **tourist office,** 1 sq. d'Ixelles, finds accommodations. (☎05 59 22 37 10; fax 05 59 24 97 80. Open July-Aug. daily 8am-8pm; Sept.-June reduced hours.) The █**Auberge de Jeunesse (HI)** ❶, 8 r. de Chiquito de Cambo, has a friendly staff and lakefront location at the *Francis Jammes* stop on bus line #2. (☎05 59 41 76 00; fax 05 59 41 76 07. **Internet** access €2.50 per 30min. Dorms €13. Amex/MC/V.) **Hôtel Barnetche** ❷, 5 bis r. Charles-Floquet, is one of the best values in the *centre ville*. (☎05 59 24 22 25; www.hotel-barnetche.fr. Breakfast €6. Reception 7:30am-10:30pm. Open May-Sept. Dorms €17; singles €35; doubles €58.) Cheap eateries can be found along **Rue Mazagran** and **Place Clemenceau.** Stock up at **Shopi supermarket,** 2 r. du Centre, is just off r. Gambetta. (Open 9am-12:45pm and 3:30-5pm.) **Postal Code:** 64200.

🔀 DAYTRIP FROM BIARRITZ: ST-JEAN-DE-LUZ.

The vibrant seaport of St-Jean-de-Luz lures visitors with the **Maison Louis XIV,** pl. Louis XIV, which temporarily housed the Sun King. (Open July-Aug. M-Sa 10:30am-12:30pm and 2:30-6:30pm, Su 2:30-6:30pm; Sept.-June closes 5:30pm. €4.50. Tours every 30min.) The village's earlier days of piracy funded its unique buildings, exemplified in the **Église St-Jean-Baptiste,** r. Gambetta, built to resemble a fishing boat. (Open daily 10am-noon and 2-6pm.) **Trains** roll in to bd. du Cdt. Passicot from Biarritz (15min., 10 per day, €2.50) and Bayonne (30min., 7 per day, €3.90). ATCRB **buses** (☎05 59 08 00 33), across from the train station, also run to Bayonne (35min., 7-13 per day, €3.60) and Biarritz (25min., 7-13 per day, €2.80). The **tourist office** is at pl. Foch. (☎05 59 26 03 16 05; fax 05 59 26 21 47. Open July-Aug. M-Sa 9am-7pm, Su 10:30am-1pm and 3-7pm; Sept.-June reduced hours). **Postal Code:** 64500.

LOURDES

In 1858, 14-year-old Bernadette Soubirous saw the first of 18 visions of the Virgin Mary in the Massabielle grotto in Lourdes (pop. 16,300). Today five million visitors from across the globe make the pilgrimage each year. To get to **La Grotte de Massabielle** and the three **basilicas**, follow av. de la Gare, turn left on bd. de la Grotte, and follow it to the right and across the river Gave. Processions depart daily from the grotto at 5pm and 8:45pm. (No shorts or tank tops. Grotto open daily 5am-midnight. Basilicas open Easter to Oct. daily 6am-7pm; Nov.-Easter 8am-6pm.)

Trains leave the station, 33 av. de la Gare, for: Bayonne (2hr., 5 per day, €18); Bordeaux (3hr., 7 per day, €28); Paris (7-9hr., 5 per day, €86); and Toulouse (2½hr., 8 per day, €21). To reach the **tourist office,** on pl. Peyramale, turn right onto av. de la Gare, bear left onto av. Marasin, cross a bridge above bd. du Papacca, and climb uphill. The office is to the right. (☎05 62 42 77 40; lourdes@sudfr.com. Open May-Oct. M-Sa 9am-7pm; Nov.-Apr. reduced hours.) The newly-renovated **Hôtel du Commerce ❸,** 11 r. Basse, faces the tourist office. (☎05 62 94 59 23; hotel-commerce-et-navarre@wanadoo.fr. Breakfast €3.80. July to mid-Oct. singles €32; doubles €38; triples €45; mid-Oct. to June reduced prices. MC/V.) **Camping and Hôtel de la Poste ❶,** 26 r. de Langelle, 2min. from the post office, offers a campground and attached hotel. (☎05 62 94 40 35. Open Easter to mid-Oct. Electricity €2.50. Showers €1.30. €2.50 per person, €3.60 per site.) The cheapest eateries are near the tourist office, away from the touristy main strip. **Postal Code:** 65100.

CAUTERETS

Nestled in a narrow, breathtaking valley on the edge of the **Parc National des Pyrenees Occidentales** is tiny, friendly Cauterets (pop. 1,300). Cauterets's hot sulfuric *thermes* have long been instruments of healing; for more info, contact **Thermes de Cesar,** av. Docteur Domer. (☎05 62 92 51 60. Open M-F 9am-12:30pm and 2-5pm.) Today, most visitors come to ski and hike. For **hiking** info and advice, head to Parc National des Pyrenees (see below). **Skilys,** rte. de Pierrefitte, on pl. de la Gare, rents **bikes** and **skates.** (☎05 62 92 52 10. Bikes €15.30 per day. Open in winter daily 8am-7:30pm; off-season 9am-7pm .)

SNCF **buses** run from pl. de la Gare to Lourdes (1hr., 6 per day, €6). The **tourist office,** on pl. Foch, has free maps of ski trails. (☎05 62 92 50 27; www.cauterets.com. Open July-Aug. daily 9:30am-12:30pm and 1:30-7pm; Sept.-June reduced hours.) ■**Gite d'Etape UCJG ❶,** av. du Docteur Domer, has a great location and friendly staff. From the Parc National office, cross the street and turn left uphill on a footpath underneath the funicular depot. (☎05 62 92 52 95. Open June 15-Sept. 15. Dorms €8; camping and tent rental €6.50.) **Postal Code:** 65110.

🄳 **DAYTRIP FROM CAUTERETS: THE PYRENEES.** The striking **Parc National des Pyrenees** shelters thousands of endangered animals in its snow-capped mountains and lush valleys. Touch base with the friendly and helpful **Parc National Office,** Maison du Parc, pl. de la Gare, before braving the wilderness; they have tons of info on the park and the 15 trails beginning and ending in Cauterets. The trails in the park are designed for wide range of skill levels, from novice hiker to rugged outdoorsman. (☎05 62 92 62 97; www.parc-pyrenees.com. Open June-Aug. daily 9:30am-noon and 3-7pm; Sept.-May M-Tu and

F-Su 9:30am-12:30pm and 3-6pm, Th 3-6pm.) From Cauterets, the **GR10** winds through **Luz-St-Saveur,** over the mountain, and then on to **Gavarnie,** another day's hike up the valley; this is also known as the **circuit de Gavarnie.** One of the most spectacular trails follows the GR10 to the turquoise **Lac de Gaube** and then to the end of the glacial valley (2hr. past the lake) where you can spend the night at the **Refuges Des Oulettes ❶,** the first shelter past the lake. (☎05 62 92 62 97. Open June-Sept. €13.)

LANGUEDOC-ROUSSILLON

An immense region called Occitania once stretched from the Rhône Valley to the foothills of the Pyrenees. It was eventually integrated into the French kingdom, and its Cathar religion was severely persecuted by the Crown and Church. Their *langue d'oc* dialect of French faded, and in 1539, the northern *langue d'oïl* became official. Latent nationalism lingers, however, in vibrant cities like Toulouse and Pérpignan. Many locals speak Catalán, a relative of *langue d'oc,* and feel a stronger cultural connection with Barcelona than Paris.

TOULOUSE

Sassy, headstrong Toulouse—*la ville en rose* (city in pink)—provides a breath of fresh air along with stately architecture and a vibrant twenty-something scene. A rebellious city during the Middle Ages, Toulouse (pop. 350,000) has always retained an element of independence, pushing the frontiers of knowledge as a university town and the prosperous capital of the French aerospace industry.

🚆🚌 TRANSPORTATION AND PRACTICAL INFORMATION. Trains leave Gare Matabiau, 64 bd. Pierre Sémard, for: Bordeaux (2-3hr., 14 per day, €27); Lyon (6½hr., 3-4 per day, €48); Marseilles (4½hr., 8 per day, €39); and Paris (8-9hr., 4 per day, €75). To get from the station to the **tourist office,** r. Lafayette, in sq. Charles de Gaulle, turn left along the canal, turn right on allée Jean Jaurès, bear right around pl. Wilson, and turn right on r. Lafayette; it's in a park near r. d'Alsace-Lorraine. You can also take the métro to *Capitole.* (☎05 61 11 02 22; www.mairie-toulouse.fr. Open Jun.-Sept. M-Sa 9am-7pm, Su 10am-1pm and 2-6pm; Oct.-May reduced hours.) Surf the **Internet** at **Espace Wilson Multimedia,** 7 allée du Président Roosevelt. (€3 per hr. Open M-F 10am-7pm, Sa 10am-6pm.) **Postal Code:** 31000.

🏠🍴 ACCOMMODATIONS AND FOOD. While it lacks a youth hostel, Toulouse has a number of well-located budget hotels. To reach the spacious **▓Hôtel des Arts ❷,** 1bis r. Cantegril off r. des Arts, take the métro (dir: Basso Cambo) to *pl. Esquirol.* Walk down r. de Metz, away from the river; r. des Arts is on the left. (☎05 61 23 36 21; fax 05 61 12 22 37. Breakfast €4. Singles €15-21, with shower €23-25; doubles €25/26-28. MC/V.) Antoine de St-Exupéry always stayed in room #32 at the **Hôtel du Grand Balcon ❸,** 8 r. Romiguières. (☎/fax 05 61 62 77 59. Breakfast €4. Singles and doubles €26, with bath €36; triples with bath €45.) Take bus #59 to *Camping* to **camp** at **Pont de Rupé ❶,** 21 chemin du Pont de Rupé. (☎05 61 70 07 35. €9, €3 per additional person.) **Markets** line **place des Carmes** and **place Victor Hugo.** (Open Su and Tu-Sa 6am-1pm.) A cross between a restaurant, an art gallery and a small theater, **Le Grand Rideau ❸,** 75 r. du Taur, serves regional food in a three-course lunch (€9) and an evening *menu* (€14.) in an eclectic atmosphere. (☎05 61 23 90 19. Open M noon-2pm, Tu-F noon-2pm and 7pm-midnight.)

◙ ➧ SIGHTS AND ENTERTAINMENT. The **Capitole**, the brick palace next door to the tourist office, is the city's most prominent monument. (Open M-F 8:30am-noon and 1:30-7pm, Sa-Su 10am-noon and 2-6pm.) Rue du Taur leads to the **Basilique St-Sernin**, the longest Romanesque structure in the world; its **crypt** houses ecclesiastical relics gathered from Charlemagne's time. (Church open July-Sept. M-Sa 8:30am-6:15pm, Su 8:30am-7:30pm; Oct.-June reduced hours. Free. Crypt open July-Sept. M-Sa 10am-6pm, Su 11:30-6pm; Oct.-June reduced hours. €2.) Backtrack to the pl. du Capitole, take a right on r. Romiguières, and turn left on r. Lakanal to get to the **Réflectoire des Jacobins**, 69 r. Pargaminières, which has exhibitions of archeological artifacts and modern art. (Open daily 10am-7pm. €5.) Nearby on r. Lakanal, a 13th-century southern Gothic **church** holds the remains of St. Thomas Aquinas in an elevated, underlit tomb. (Open daily 9am-7pm.) Retracing your steps on r. de Metz takes you to the restored **Hôtel d'Assézat**, at pl. d'Assézat on r. de

FRANCE

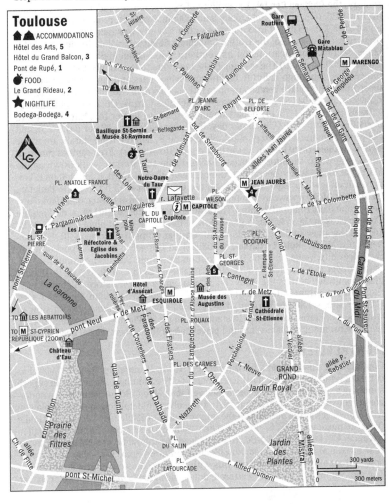

Toulouse

Metz, which houses the **Fondation Bemberg**, an impressive array of Bonnards, Gauguins, and Pisarros. (Open Su, Tu and F-Sa 10am-12:30pm and 1:30-6pm. €2.80.) Toulouse has something to please almost any nocturnal whim, although nightlife is liveliest when students are in town. Numerous cafes flank **place St-Georges** and **place du Capitole**, and late-night bars line **rue St-Rome** and **rue des Filatiers**. The best dancing is at **Bodega-Bodega**, 1 r. Gabriel Péri, just off bd. Lazare Carnot. (Cover €6 Th-Sa 10pm-2am. Open Su-F 7pm-2am, Sa 7pm-6am.)

CARCASSONNE

When approaching breathtaking Carcassonne (pop. 45,000), you realize that Beauty may have fallen in love with the Beast in this fairy-tale city. However, its charm is no secret; the narrow streets of the *cité* are flooded with tourists. Its walls and fortifications date back to the 1st century. Built as a palace in the 12th century, the **Château Comtal**, 1 r. Viollet-le-Duc, became a citadel after royal takeover in 1226. (Open June-Sept. daily 9am-7:30pm; Apr.-Oct. reduced hours. €6.10, under-25 €4.10.) Turned into a fortress after the city was razed during the Hundred Years' War in 1355, the Gothic **Cathédrale St-Michel**, r. Voltaire, in bastide St-Louis, still has fortifications on its southern side. (Open M-Sa 7am-noon and 2-7pm, Su 9:30am-noon.) The evening is the best time to experience the *cité* without the crowds. Although nightlife is limited, several bars and cafes along **boulevard Omer Sarraut** and **place Verdun** are open late. Locals dance all night at **La Bulle**, 115 r. Barbacane. (☎04 68 72 47 70. Cover €9, includes 1 drink. Open F-Sa until dawn.)

Trains (☎04 68 71 79 14) depart behind Jardin St-Chenier for: Marseilles (3hr., every 2hr., €36); Nice (6hr., 5 per day, €47); Nîmes (2½hr., 12 per day, €25); and Toulouse (50min., 24 per day, €14). Shops, hotels, and the train station are in the **bastide St-Louis**, once known as the *basse ville* (lower city). Free **shuttles** run from sq. Gambetta to the more touristed *cité*. From the station, walk down av. de Maréchal Joffre, which becomes r. Clemenceau; after pl. Carnot, turn left on r. Verdun, which leads to sq. Gambetta and the **tourist office**, 15 bd. Camille Pelletan. (☎04 68 10 24 30; www.carcassonne-tourisme.com. Open July-Aug. daily 9am-7pm; Sept.-June 9am-1pm and 2-6pm.) The 🛏**Auberge de Jeunesse (HI) ❶**, r. de Vicomte Trencavel, is in the *cité*, has a great view of the castle late at night. (☎04 68 25 23 16; carcassonne@fuaj.org. Sheets €2.70. **Internet** €3 per hr. Dorms €13. HI members only. MC/V.) **Hôtel Le Cathare ❷**, 53 r. Jean Bringer, is near the post office in the lower city. (☎04 68 25 65 92. Reception 8am-7pm. Singles and doubles €18, with shower €26; triples €46-53. MC/V.) **Camping de la Cité ❷**, rte. de St-Hilaire, 2km from town across the Aude, has a pool and a grocery store. A shuttle runs there from the train station. (☎04 68 25 11 77. Reception 8am-9pm. Open Mar.-Oct. €17 per site, €4.80 per person.) The regional speciality is *cassoulet* (a stew of white beans, herbs, and meat). Restaurants on **rue du Plo** have *menus* under €10, but save room for *crêperies* around **place Marcou** for dessert. **Postal Code:** 11000.

MONTPELLIER

Capital of Languedoc and a bustling college town, Montpellier (pop. 230,000) has earned a reputation as the most light-hearted city in southern France, with superb shopping and nightlife. The gigantic **Musée Fabre**, 39 bd. Bonne Nouvelle, is undergoing renovations until 2006, but part of its substantial collection is on display on a rotating basis at the **pavillion** on the opposite side of Esplanade Charles de Gaulle from the museum. (☎04 67 66 13 46. Open Su and Tu-Sa 1-7pm. Hours vary, call in advance. €3, students €1.) Bd. Henri IV leads to the **Jardin des Plantes**, France's first botanical garden. (Open June-Sept. M-Sa noon-8pm, Oct.-May M-Sa noon-6pm.) At sundown, **rue de la Loge** fills with vendors, musicians, and stilt-walkers. The most animated bars are scattered along **place Jean-Jaurès**. The popular **Barber-**

ousse **"Bar A Shooters,"** 6 r. Boussairolles, just off pl. de la Comédie, sells 73 flavors of rum. (Rum €2. Beer €3. Open M-Sa 6pm-2am.) Gay nightlife is prominent in Montpellier, with establishments scattered throughout the *vielle ville*.

Trains leave pl. Auguste Gibert for Avignon (1¼hr., 10 per day, €13); Marseilles (1¾hr., 9 per day, €21); Paris (3½hr., 12 per day, €84); and Toulouse (2½hr., 10 per day, €29). From the train station, r. Maguelone leads to **place de la Comédie**, Montpellier's modern center. The **tourist office**, 30 allée Jean de Lattre de Tassigny, is to the right. (☎04 67 60 60 60; www.ot-montpellier.fr. Open July-Aug. M-F 9am-7:30pm, Sa 9:30am-6pm, Su 9:30am-1pm and 2:30-6pm; Sept.-May reduced hours.) Access the **Internet** at **Cybercafé www**, 12 bis rue Jules Ferry, across from the train station. (€1.50 per hr. Open daily 9am-1am.) To reach the **Auberge de Jeunesse (HI) ❶**, 2 impasse de la Petite Corraterie, walk from pl. de la Comédie onto r. de la Loge. Turn right onto r. Jacques Cœur and walk until you reach impasse de la Petite Corraterie, just before bd. Louis Blanc, and turn right. The hostel has sunny rooms and large windows. (☎04 67 60 32 22; montpellier@fuaj.org. Breakfast €3. Lockout 10am-1pm. Curfew 2am. Dorms €8.40. MC/V. **Hotel d'Angleterre ❸**, 7 r. Maguelone, is comfortable and centrally located. (☎04 67 58 59 50; www.hotel-d-angleterre.com. Breakfast €5.50. Singles with shower €28; doubles €28-50. Amex/MC/V.) French cuisine dominates Montpellier's *vielle ville*, while a number of ethnic restaurants have taken hold on **rue des Écoles Laïques**. Get groceries at **Supermarket INNO**, in the basement of the Polygone commercial center, just past the tourist office. (Open M-Sa 9am-8:30pm.) **Postal Code:** 34000.

PROVENCE

Carpets of olive groves and vineyards unroll along hills dusted with lavender, sunflowers, and mimosas, while the fierce winds of the *mistral* carry the scent of sage, rosemary, and time well-spent. Generations of writers and artists have found inspiration in Provence's varied landscape—from the Roman arena and cobblestoned elegance of Arles to Cézanne's lingering footsteps in Aix-en-Provence, life unfolds along Provence's shaded paths like a bottomless glass of *pastis*.

NÎMES

Southern France flocks to Nîmes (pop. 132,000) for the *férias*, celebrations featuring bullfights, flamenco dancing, and other hot-blooded fanfare. Yet Nîmes's star attractions are its incredible Roman structures. The magnificent **Les Arènes** is a well-preserved first-century Roman amphitheater that still holds bullfights and concerts. (☎04 66 76 72 77. Open M-F 10am-6pm. €4.50, students €3.20.) North of the arena stands the exquisite **Maison Carrée,** a rectangular temple built in the first century BC. (☎04 66 36 26 76. Open June-Sept. daily 9am-7pm; Oct.-May 10am-6pm.) Across the square, the **Carrée d'Art** houses an excellent collection of contemporary art. (☎04 66 76 35 70. Open Tu-Su 10am-6pm. €4.50, students €3.20.) Along the canals to the left, off pl. Foch, the **Jardins de la Fontaine** hold the Roman ruins of the **Temple de Diane** and the **Tour Magne**. (Garden open Apr.-Sept. daily 7:30am-10pm; Oct.-Mar. 8am-6:30pm; free. Tower open July-Aug. daily 9am-7pm; Sept.-June 9am-5pm; €2.40, students €2.)

Trains chug from bd. Talabot to: Arles (20min., 13 per day, €6.30); Marseilles (1¼hr., 20 per day, €12); and Toulouse (3hr., 8 per day, €30). **Buses** (☎04 66 29 52 00) depart from behind the train station for Avignon (1½hr., 2-8 per day, €6.70). The **tourist office** is at 6 r. Auguste, just off pl. Comédie and near the Maison Carrée. (☎04 66 58 38 00; fax 04 66 58 38 01. Open July-Aug. M-F 8am-8pm, Sa 9am-7pm, Su 10am-6pm; May and Sept. reduced hours.) The newly renovated **⬛Auberge de Jeun-**

esse (HI) ❶ is 4.5km from quai de la Fontaine, at 257 chemin de l'Auberge de la Jeunesse, off chemin de la Cigale. Take bus #2 (dir.: Alès or Villeverte) to *Stade, Route d'Alès* and follow the signs uphill; after buses stop running, call for pick-up. This comfortable, well-kept hostel is well worth the trek. (☎04 66 68 03 20; fax 04 66 68 03 21. Breakfast €3.20. Sheets €2.80 per week. **Internet** access €3.80 per hr. Mar.-Sept. 4- to 6-bed dorms €9.50. **Camping** €5.50. Members only. MC/V.) Stock up at **Marché U supermarket**, 19 r. d'Alès, downhill from the hostel. (Open M-Sa 8am-12:45pm and 3:30-8pm.) **Postal Codes:** 30000 and 30900.

⚡ DAYTRIP FROM NÎMES: PONT DU GARD. In 19 BC, Augustus's close friend and advisor Agrippa built an aqueduct to channel water 50km to Nîmes from the Eure springs near Uzès. The architectural fruit of this 15-year project remains in the Pont du Gard, spanning the gorge of the Gardon River and towering over sunbathers and swimmers. A great way to see the Pont du Gard is to start from **Collias**, 6km toward Uzès. Here **Kayak Vert** rents canoes, kayaks, and bikes. (☎66 22 80 76. Canoes and kayaks €14 per day, kayak/canoe rental and shuttle €16, bikes €17 per day. 15% discount for students or with stay at the hostel in Nîmes.) STDG **buses** (☎04 66 29 27 29) run to the Pont du Gard from Avignon (45min., 7 per day, €5) and Nîmes (30min., 2-5 per day, €4.75). **Camping le Barralet ❶**, r. des Aires in Collias, offers a pool and hot showers. (☎04 66 22 84 52; fax 04 66 22 89 17. Closed Oct.-Feb. €6-8 per person. Mar.-June and Sept reduced prices. MC/V.)

AVIGNON

Known to most as the home of the bridge made famous by the children's song, the city of Avignon (pop. 100,000) also hosts Europe's most prominent theater festival. A reminder of Avignon's brief stint as the center of the Catholic Church, the 14th-century golden ■**Palais des Papes** keeps watch over the city with its gargoyles. Although Revolutionary looting stripped the interior of its lavish furnishings, the giant rooms and their frescoed walls are still remarkable. (☎04 90 27 50 74. Open July-Sept. daily 9am-8pm; Apr.-June and Oct. 9am-7pm; Nov. to Mar. 9:30am-5:45pm. €7.50.) The most prestigious theatrical gathering in Europe, the ■**Festival d'Avignon** appears in at least 30 different venues, from factories to cloisters to palaces. (☎04 90 14 14 14; www.festival-avignon.com. July-early Aug. Tickets up to €30. Some shows free. Reservations accepted from mid-June. Standby tickets available 45min. before shows; 50% student discount.) The also well-established, more experimental **Festival OFF** also takes place in July. (OFFice on pl. du Palais. ☎01 48 05 01 19; www.avignon-off.org. Tickets purchased at the venue or the OFFice; not available over the phone. Tickets €0-16.) Tickets are not necessary to experience the festivals; free theatrical performances often spill into the streets, especially at night. During the festival most eateries stay open late as well. **Place des Corps Saints** has a few lively bars.

Trains (☎04 90 27 81 89) run from porte de la République to: Arles (30min., 19 per day, €5.70); Marseilles (1¼hr., 15 per day, €16); Nîmes (30min., 12 per day, €7.10); and Paris (TGV 3½hr., 13 per day, €80). **Buses** leave from bd. St-Roch, to the right of the train station, for Arles (45min., 5 per day, €7.80) and Marseilles (2hr., 5 per day, €16). From the train station, walk through porte de la République to cours Jean Jaurès to reach the **tourist office**, 41 cours Jean Jaurès (☎04 32 74 32 74; www.ot-avignon.fr. Open Apr.-Sept. M-Sa 9am-6pm, Su 10am-5pm.; Oct.-Mar. reduced hours.) Take an **Internet** break at **Webzone**, 3 r. St-Jean le Vieux, at pl. Pie. (☎04 32 76 29 47. €4 per hr. Open daily 9am-midnight.) Avignon's hotels and *foyers* usually have room; although they fill up fast during festival season; book well ahead or try staying in Arles or Nîmes. The **Foyer YMCA/UCJG ❶**, 7bis chemin de la Justice, is across the river in Villeneuve. From the station, turn left and follow the

FRANCE

Avignon

▲ ACCOMMODATIONS
Foyer YMCA/UCJG, **2**
Hôtel Splendid, **3**
Pont d'Avignon Camping, **1**

N
LG

0   200 yards
0   200 meters

VILLENEUVE

Île de la Barthelasse

Rhône

promenade Antoine Pinay

TO **1** (1km)
2 (1.5km)

PORTE ST-LAZARE
PORTE ST-JOSEPH
PORTE DE LA LIGNE
PORTE ST-DOMINIQUE
PORTE DE L'OULLE
PORTE ST-ROCH
PORTE DE LA RÉPUBLIQUE TO **1** (1.5km)
PORTE ST-MICHEL
PORTE MAGNANEN
PORTE LIMBERT
PORTE THIERS

bd. Limbert
bd. St-Lazare
bd. St-Roch
bd. St-Michel
bd. Raspail

r. du Rempart St-Lazare
r. du Rempart St-Bernard
r. du Rempart St-Roch
r. du Rempart St-Dominique

rte. de Montfavet
rte. de la Trillade

r. Pierre Semard
av. de la Trillade
av. des Sources
av. de l'Arrousaire
av. du 7ème Génie

Université
Shakespeare Bookshop & Tearoom
St-Symphorien
PL. DES CARMES
Église de la Visitation
Palais de Justice
P. P. Sain
PL. PIGNOTTE
Les Halles
Notre Dame des Doms
Rocher des Doms
Palais des Papes
PL. DU PALAIS
Musée du Petit Palais
Pont d'Avignon
Navette Shuttle Boat Port
Maison Jean Vilar
PL. ST-CHÂTAIGNES
Chez Wém
PL. DE L'HORLOGE
Opéra
PL. DE L'OULLE
Esplanade St-Bénézet
PL. CRILLON
PL. ST-JEAN
LE VIEUX
PL. DU CHANGE
PL. DES CORPS SAINTS
PL. ST-DIDIER
PL. DE LA RÉPUBLIQUE
Musée Calvet
Musée Louis Vouland
Collection Lambert
3 Faucons
Laundry
Laundry
TRCA

r. du Pont Trouca
r. Notre Dame des 7 Douleurs
r. de Rascas
r. Muguet
r. St-Bernard
r. de la Carreterie
r. des Infirmières
r. des 3 Colombes
r. Banasterie
r. Palapharnerie
r. de la Croix
r. Ste-Catherine
r. Saluces
r. de l'Oriflamme
Vice Legat
r. Bertrand
r. Pente Rapide
Ste-Anne
r. Louis Pasteur
pl. Louis Pasteur
r. Guillaume Puy
r. Buffon
r. Bourgneuf
r. Philonarde
r. Thiers
r. du Portail Matheron
r. Pourquery
r. des Teinturiers
r. de la Masse
r. Bonneterie
r. Noel Biret
r. du Roi René
r. Petramale
r. des Fourbisseurs
r. Carreterie
r. du Vieux Sextier
r. des Marchands
r. St-Jean LE VIEUX
r. Carnot
r. des Lices
r. Portail Magnanen
r. St-Michel
r. Bon Martinet
r. des Teinturiers
r. Henri-Fabre
r. Perdiguier
r. Mistralveur
r. Labouveur
r. des
r. Sarailleriie
r. Bancasse
r. Viala
r. Racine
r. St-Agricol
r. Petite Fusterie
r. Grande Fusterie
r. Félix Gras
r. de la Calade
r. Joseph Vernet
r. P. Viala
r. St-Étienne
r. des Lices
r. Paul Manivet
r. Bancasse
r. Bouquerie
r. Petite Fusterie
r. d'Annanelle
r. Victor Hugo
r. des Lices
r. des Grottes
r. de la Balance
r. Lanterne
r. Porte-Évêque
r. Vélouterie
r. du Rempart St-Dominique
r. Petit Fusterie
r. St-Charles
r. St-Ruf
cours Jean Jaurès
cours JFK
passage de l'Oratoire
Allées de l'Oulle
av. de Mandela
r. de la Tour de l'Europe
r. de l'Observance
av. de

pont Daladier

PL. ST-JEAN
PL. ST-PIERRE
PL. PIE

city wall, cross pont Daladier and Ile Barthelasse, walk straight ahead, and turn left on chemin de la Justice; it will be up the hill on your left. (☎ 04 90 25 46 20; www.ymca-avignon.com. Reception 8:30am-noon and 1:30-6pm. *Demi-pension* obligatory in July. Dorms €15. AmEx/MC/V.) The **Hôtel Splendid ❸**, 17 r. Perdiguier, near the tourist office, lives up to its name. (☎ 04 90 86 14 46; fax 04 90 85 38 55. Breakfast €5. Reception 7am-11pm. Singles €30-34; doubles €40-46. MC/V.) **Camp at Pont d'Avignon ❶**, 300 Ile de la Barthelasse. (☎ 04 90 80 63 50; fax 04 90 85 22 12. Reception daily 8am-10pm. Open Mar. 27-Oct. 28. €15 per person with tent or car, €4 per extra person. Off-season reduced prices.) **Rue des Teinturiers** hosts a number of restaurants. A **Petit Casino supermarket** is on r. St-Agricol. (Open M-F 8am-8pm, Sa-Su 9am-8pm.) **Postal Code: 84000.**

ARLES

The beauty and ancient history of Arles (pop. 35,000) have made it a Provence favorite. A reminder of Arles's former position as the capital of Roman Gaul, the great Roman arena, **Les Arènes**, is still used for bullfights. (€4, students €3.) The city's Roman past comes back to life in the excellent **Musée d'Arles Antique**, on av. de la 1er D.F.L. (Open daily Mar.-Oct. 9am-7pm; Nov.-Feb. 10am-5pm. €5.40, students €3.80.) The **Fondation Van Gogh**, 26 Rond-Point des Arènes, houses tributes to the master painter by artists, poets, and composers. (Open daily 10am-7pm. €5, students €3.50.) The contemporary **Musée Réattu**, r. du Grand Prieuré, houses 57 drawings with which Picasso honored Arles in 1971. (Open May-Sept. daily 10am-noon and 2-6:30pm; Oct.-Apr. reduced hours. €4, students €3.) The city celebrates **Fête d'Arles** in costume the last weekend in June and the first in July.

Trains leave av. P. Talabot for: Avignon (20min., 17 per day, €5.50); Marseilles (1hr., 20 per day, €11); Montpellier (1hr., 5 per day, €12); and Nîmes (30min., 8 per day, €6.30). **Buses** (☎ 04 90 49 38 01) depart from next to the station for Avignon (45min., M-Sa 6 per day, €8.10) and Nîmes (1hr., M-Sa 6 per day, €5.20). To get to the **tourist office**, esplanade Charles de Gaulle on bd. des Lices, turn left from the station, walk to pl. Lamartine, turn left and follow bd. Emile Courbes to the big intersection, and then turn right on bd. des Lices. (☎ 04 90 18 41 20; fax 04 90 18 41 29. Open daily Apr.-Sept. 9am-6:45pm; Oct.-Mar. reduced hours.) To get from the tourist office to the **Auberge de Jeunesse (HI) ❶**, on av. Maréchal Foch, cross bd. des Lices and follow the signs down av. des Alyscamps. (☎ 04 90 96 18 25; fax 04 90 96 31 26. Breakfast included. Reception 7-10am and 5-11pm. Lockout 10am-5pm. Curfew midnight; in winter 11pm. Reserve ahead Apr.-June. Dorms €14; €12 after 1st night.) **Hôtel le Rhône ❸**, 11 pl. Voltaire, has pastel-painted rooms and an inviting breakfast loft. (☎ 04 90 96 43 70; fax 04 90 93 87 03. Breakfast €5. Singles and doubles €26-39, with shower €30-33; triples with shower €36, with toilet €43. MC/V.) Take the Starlette bus to Clemencau and then take bus #2 (dir.: Pont de Crau) to Hermite for **Camping-City ❶**, 67 rte. de Crau. (☎ 04 90 93 08 86. Reception 8am-8pm. Open Apr.-Sept. €4 per person, €3 per car.) **Monoprix supermarket** is on pl. Lamartine by the station. (Open M-Sa 8:30am-8pm.) **Place du Forum** and **place Voltaire** have many cafes. **Postal Code: 13200.**

⬛ DAYTRIP FROM ARLES: THE CAMARGUE. Between Arles and the Mediterranean coast stretches the Camargue. Pink flamingos, black bulls, and the famous white Camargue horses roam freely across this flat expanse of protected wild marshland. The **Parc Ornithologique de Pont de Gau**, along D570, offers views of birds and grazing bulls. (Open Apr.-Sept. daily 9am-dusk; Oct.-Mar. 10am-dusk. €5.50.) The best way to see the Camargue is on horseback; call the **Association Camarguaise de Tourisme Equestre** (☎ 04 90 97 10 10; €12 per hr, €33 per half-day) for more info. Other options include jeep safaris (☎ 04 90 97 89 33; 2hr. trip €31, 4hr. trip €37) and boat trips (☎ 04 90 97 84 72; 1½hr., 3 per day, €10). Biking is another way to see the area, and informative trail maps are available from the **tourist office** in Stes-Maries-de-la-Mer, 5 av. Van Gogh. (☎04 90 97 82 55. Open July-Aug. daily 9am-8pm; Sept.-June reduced hours.) Arles runs **buses** to Stes-Maries-de-la-Mer (1hr., 5 per day, €4.80), the region's largest town.

AIX-EN-PROVENCE

Famous for festivals, fountains, and former residents Paul Cézanne and Victor Vasarely, Aix (pop. 137,000) caters to tourists without being ruined by them. The **Chemin de Cézanne,** 9 av. Paul Cézanne, features a self-guided walking tour, including the artist's studio. (☎04 42 21 06 53. Open June-Sept. daily 10am-6:30pm; Oct.-May reduced hours. €5.50, students €2.) The **Fondation Vasarely,** av. Marcel-Pagnol, in Jas-de-Bouffan, designed by artist Victor Vasarely, is a must-see for modern art fans. (☎04 42 20 01 09. Open July-Sept. daily 10am-7pm; Oct.-June 10am-1pm and 2-6pm. €7, students €4.) **Cathédrale St-Sauveur,** r. Gaston de Saporta, on pl. de l'Université, is a dramatic mix of Romanesque, Gothic, and Baroque carvings and reliefs. (☎04 42 23 45 65. Open daily 9am-noon and 2-6pm.) In June and July, Aix's **International Music Festival** brings in operas and concerts. (☎04 42 17 34 34; www.aix-en-provence.com/festartlyrique. Tickets from €6.) Aix also hosts a two-week **dance festival** (☎04 42 23 41 24; tickets €10-38). Tickets are available at the tourist office. **Rue Verrerie** is lined with bars and clubs. **The Red Clover,** 30 r. de la Verrerie, is a lively bar with an overflowing international crowd. (Open daily 8am-2am.) **Bistro Aixois,** 37 cours Sextius, packs in students. (Open daily 6:30pm-4am.)

Trains, at the end of av. Victor Hugo, run to Marseilles (35min., 21 per day, €5.70). **Buses** (☎04 42 91 26 80), av. de l'Europe, also run frequently to Marseilles (30min., almost every 10min., €4). From the train station, follow av. Victor Hugo, bearing left at the fork, until it feeds into La Rotonde. On the left is the **tourist office,** 2 pl. du Général de Gaulle, which books rooms for free and stocks maps and guides. (☎04 42 16 11 61; www.aixenprovencetourism.com. Open July-Aug. daily 8:30am-8pm; Sept.-June reduced hours.) You can surf the **Internet** at **Millenium,** 6 r. Mazarine, off cours Mirabeau. (☎04 42 27 39 11. €3 per hr. Open daily 10am-11pm.) The excellent **Hôtel du Globe ❹,** 74 cours Sextius, is 5min. from *centre ville.* (☎04 42 26 03 58; fax 04 42 26 13 68. Singles €35, with bath €40; doubles €50/59; triples €63-69; quads €89.) **Hôtel des Arts ❺,** 69 bd. Carnot, has compact modern rooms. (☎04 42 38 11 77; fax 04 42 26 77 31. Breakfast €4.30. Singles and doubles €31-44. MC/V.) To **camp** at **Arc-en-Ciel ❶,** on rte. de Nice, take bus #3 from La Rotonde to Trois Sautets or Val St-André. (☎04 42 26 14 28. €5.20 per person, €5.80 per tent.) The roads north of **cours Mirabeau** are packed with reasonably priced restaurants, as is **rue Verrerie,** off r. des Cordiliers. You can choose from three **Petit Casinos supermarkets** at: 3 cours d'Orbitelle (open M-Sa 8am-1pm and 4-7:30pm); 16 r. Italie (open M-Sa 8am-7:30pm, Su 8:30am-12:30pm); and 5 r. Sapora (open M and W-Sa 8:30am-7:30pm, Su 8:30am-12:30pm). **Postal Code:** 13100.

MARSEILLES (MARSEILLE)

France's second-largest city, Marseilles (pop. 800,000), is a jumble of color and commotion. The city that Alexandre Dumas once called "the meeting place of the entire world" remains an alluring center of international influence. Although historically similar to many other French cities, complete with Roman ruins, Byzantine churches, and 18th-century art workshops, a walk through the sidestreets is punctuated by the vibrant colors of West African fabrics for sale in markets, the sounds of Arabic music from car stereos, and the smells of North African cuisine wafting out of hole-in-the-wall restaurants. A true immigrant city, Marseille offers a taste of both the ancient and modern cultures of the entire Mediterranean.

FRANCE

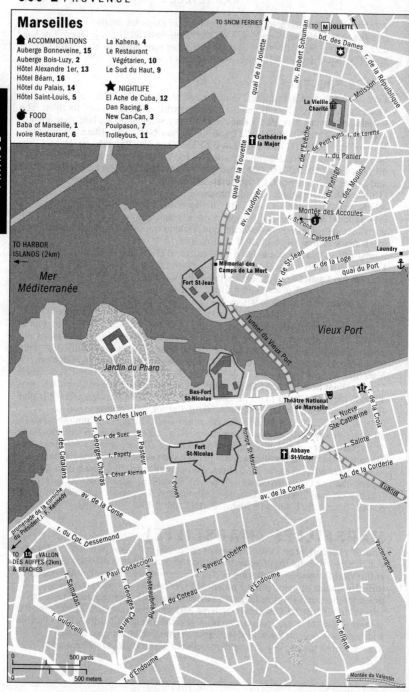

Marseilles

ACCOMMODATIONS
Auberge Bonneveine, 15
Auberge Bois-Luzy, 2
Hôtel Alexandre 1er, 13
Hôtel Béarn, 16
Hôtel du Palais, 14
Hôtel Saint-Louis, 5

FOOD
Baba of Marseille, 1
Ivoire Restaurant, 6

La Kahena, 4
Le Restaurant
  Végétarien, 10
Le Sud du Haut, 9

NIGHTLIFE
El Ache de Cuba, 12
Dan Racing, 8
New Can-Can, 3
Poulpason, 7
Trolleybus, 11

FRANCE

TO SNCM FERRIES

TO M JOLIETTE

bd. des Dames

r. de la République

quai de la Joliette

av. Robert Schuman

r. Moisson

La Vieille
Charité

Cathédrale
la Major

r. de l'Evêché

r. de Petit Puits   r. de Lorette

r. du Panier

r. du Refuge

r. des Moulins

quai de la Tourette

av. Vaudoyer

Montée des Accoules

r. St-Pons

r. Caisserie

Laundry

TO HARBOR
ISLANDS (2km)

Mer
Méditerranée

Mémorial des
Camps de La Mort

Fort St-Jean

av. de St-Jean

r. de la Loge

quai du Port

Tunnel du Vieux Port

Vieux Port

Jardin du Pharo

Bas-Fort
St-Nicolas

Théâtre National
de Marseille

r. de la Croix

r. Nueve
Ste-Catherine

r. Sainte

bd. Charles Livon

r. des Catalans

r. Georges Charas

r. de Suez

r. Papety

av. Pasteur

r. César Aleman

Fort
St-Nicolas

Rampe St-Maurice

Abbaye
St-Victor

bd. de la Corderie

Tunnel

r. Crinas

av. de la Corse

av. de la Corse

promenade de la corniche
du Président J. F. Kennedy

r. du Cpt. Dessemond

TO 15 VALLON
DES AUFFES (2km)
& BEACHES

r. Samatan

r. Paul Codaccioni

r. Georges Charas

r. Saveur Tobelem

r. du Coteau

r. d'Endoume

r. Vauvenargues

bd. Tellène

r. Guidicelli

r. d'Endoume

Montée du Valentin

0   500 yards
0   500 meters

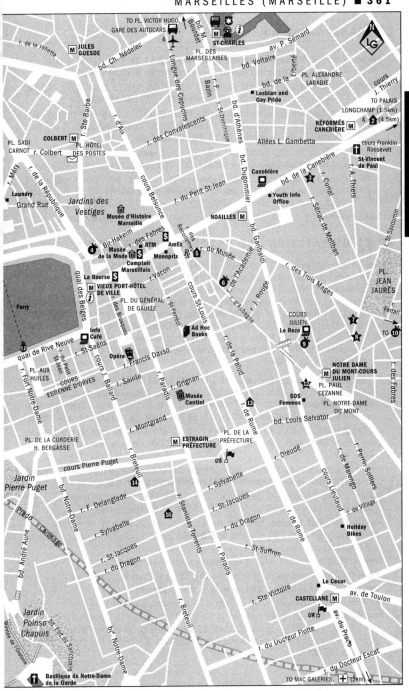

FRANCE

TO PL. VICTOR HUGO,
GARE DES AUTOCARS
ST-CHARLES
PL. DES
MARSEILLAISES
av. P. Sémard

r. de la Joliette
JULES
GUESDE

bd. Ch. Nédelec
bd. M. Bourdet
Longue des Capucins
r. F. Bazin
r. St-Dominique
bd. d'Athènes
bd. Voltaire
bd. de la Liberté
PL. ALEXANDRE
LABADIE

cours J. Thierry
TO PALAIS
LONGCHAMP (1.5km)
(4.5km)

Lesbian and
Gay Pride

r. Ste-Barbe
r. d'Aix
RÉFORMÉS
CANEBIÈRE

COLBERT
PL. HÔTEL
DES POSTES
PL. SADI
CARNOT r. Colbert

r. des Convalescents
bd. Dugommier
Allées L. Gambetta
cours Franklin
Roosevelt
St-Vincent
de Paul

r. Méry
r. de la République

Laundry
Grand Rue

Jardins des
Vestiges
Musée d'Histoire
Marseille

cours Belsunce
r. du Petit St-Jean
Canebière
bd. de la Canebière
r. Curiol
r. A. Thiers
r. St-Savournin

Bir-Hakeim
r. des Fabres
RTM
AmEx
Monoprix
Musée
de la Mode
Comptoir
Marseillais
r. Vacon
La Bourse
quai des Belges
VIEUX PORT–HÔTEL
DE VILLE
Info
Café
r. St-Saëns

NOAILLES
r. des Recolettes
r. du Musée
r. de l'Académie
r. J. Rouge
r. des Trois Mages
r. Sénac de Melhan
bd. Garibaldi

PL.
JEAN
JAURÈS
r. Ferrari

Ferry

PL. DU GÉNÉRAL
DE GAULLE
cours St-Louis
r. St-Ferréol
r. des Brasries
Ad Hoc
Books
r. d'Aubagne
COURS
JULIEN
Le Rezo
TO

Opéra
COURS
ESTIENNE D'ORVES
r. Francis Davso
r. Paradis
r. Grignan
r. Sainte
r. J. Ballard
r. de la Palud
NOTRE DAME
DU MONT–COURS
JULIEN
PL. PAUL
CEZANNE
PL. NOTRE-DAME
DU MONT
r. des Fabres

PL. AUX
HUILES
r. Fort Notre-Dame
r. du Petit
St-Jean

Musée
Cantini
SOS
Femmes
bd. Louis Salvator
cours Lieutaud
r. de Malengo
r. Perrin-Solliers

PL. DE LA CORDERIE
H. BERGASSE
cours Pierre Puget
r. Montgrand
r. Breteuil
ESTRAGIN
PRÉFECTURE
PL. DE LA
PRÉFECTURE
r. Dieudé
r. de Village

Jardin
Pierre Puget
bd. Notre-Dame
r. F. Delanglade
US
r. Sylvabelle
r. St-Jacques
r. du Dragon
r. de Rome
Holiday
Bikes

Prado Carénage
bd. André Aune
r. Sylvabelle
r. St-Jacques
r. du Dragon
r. Stanislas Torrents
r. Paradis
r. St-Suffren
r. Ste-Victoire
Le César
CASTELLANE
av. de Toulon

Jardin
Poinso
Chapuis
bd. du Fort du Sanctuaire
bc. Notre-Dame
UK
av. du Prado
r. du Docteur Flotte

Basilique de Notre-Dame
de la Garde
r. du Docteur Escat
TO MAC GALERIES,
(2km)

⌂ TRANSPORTATION

Flights: Aéroport Marseille-Provence (MRS; ☎04 42 14 14 14). Flights to **Lyon** and **Paris.** Buses connect airport to Gare St-Charles (3 per hr. 5:30am-9:50pm, €8.50).

Trains: Gare St-Charles, pl. Victor Hugo (☎08 36 35 35 35). To: **Lyon** (1½hr., 12 per day, €47); **Nice** (2½hr., 12 per day, €25); **Paris** (3hr., 17 per day, €68).

Buses: Gare Routière, pl. Victor Hugo (☎04 91 08 16 40), ½ a block from the train station. Open M-Sa 6:30am-6:30pm, Su 7:30am-6:30pm. To: **Avignon** (2hr., 5 per day, €15); **Cannes** (2¼-3hr., 4 per day, €21); **Nice** (2¾hr., daily, €23).

Ferries: SNCM, 61 bd. des Dames (☎08 91 70 18 01; www.sncm.fr). Ferries to **Corsica** (€26-52) and **Sardinia** (€41-67). Open M-F 8am-6pm, Sa 8am-noon and 2-5:30pm.

Local Transportation: RTM, 6-8 r. des Fabres (☎04 91 91 92 10). Tickets sold at bus and Métro stations (day pass €3.85; 6- to 12-ride **Carte Liberté** €6.50-13). **Métro** runs M-Th 5am-9pm and F-Su 5am-12:30am.

Taxis: (☎04 91 02 20 20). 24hr. €20-30 from the train station to most hostels.

✴ ⁊ ORIENTATION AND PRACTICAL INFORMATION

Although the city is divided into 16 *arrondissements*, Marseilles is understood by neighborhood names and major streets. **La Canebière** is the main artery, funneling into the **vieux port,** with its upscale restaurants and nightlife, to the west. North of the *vieux port,* working-class residents pile into the hilltop neighborhood of **Le Panier,** east of which lies the **Quartier Belsunce,** the hub of the city's Arab and African communities. A few blocks to the southeast, **Cours Julien** has a younger, countercultural feel to it. Both **Métro** lines go to the train station; line #1 (blue) goes to the *vieux port.* The thorough **bus** system is essential to get to beaches, stretching along the coast southwest of the *vieux port.*

Tourist Office: 4 La Canebière (☎04 91 13 89 00; fax 04 91 13 89 20). Has brochures of walking tours, free maps, accommodations service, and RTM day pass. Offers city tours (€6.50) daily at 10am and 2pm, as well as frequent excursions. Open July-Aug. M-Sa 9am-8pm, Su 10am-6pm; Oct.-June M-Sa 9am-7pm, Su and holidays 10am-5pm.

Consulates: UK, 24 av. du Prado (☎04 91 15 72 10). Open by appt. M-F 9am-noon and 2-5pm. **US,** 12 bd. Paul Peytral (☎04 91 54 92 00). Open by appt. M-F 9am-noon and 2-4pm.

Currency exchange: La Bourse, 3 pl. Général de Gaulle (☎04 91 13 09 00). Good rates and no commission. Open M-F 8:30am-6:30pm, Sa 9am-5:30pm.

Police: 2 r. du Commissaire Becker (☎04 91 39 80 00). Also in the train station on esplanade St-Charles (☎04 91 14 29 97). Dial ☎17 in **emergencies.**

Hospital: Hôpital Timone, bd. Jean Moulin (☎04 91 38 60 00). M: Timone. **SOS Médecins** (☎04 91 52 91 52) and **SOS Dentist** (☎04 91 85 39 39) connect to on-call doctors.

Internet Access: Internet cafes in Marseilles generally run from €2-5 per hr.

Cyber Café de la Canebière, 87 r. de la Canebière. €2 per hr. Open daily 9am-11pm.

Info Café, 1 quai Rive Neuve. €3.80 per hr. Open M-Sa 8:30am-10pm.

Le Rezo, 68 cours Julien. €4.60 per hr. Open M-F 9:30am-8pm, Sa 10am-10pm.

Post Office: 1 pl. Hôtel des Postes (☎04 91 15 47 00). Follow La Canebière toward the sea and turn right onto r. Reine Elisabeth as it becomes pl. Hôtel des Postes. Address mail to be held: Firstname SURNAME, *Poste Restante,* 1 pl. Hotel des Postes, **13001** Marseilles, FRANCE.

ACCOMMODATIONS

Marseilles has a range of hotel options, from the pricey hotels near the *vieux port* to the less reputable but cheap hotels in the Quartier Belsunce. Hotels listed here prioritize safety and location. The two hostels are located far from the city center, which offers an escape from the fast pace of the city, but bus access is infrequent in the summer. Most places fill up quickly on weekends and in the summer, so call at least a week in advance.

■ **Hôtel du Palais,** 26 r. Breteuil (☎04 91 37 78 86; fax 04 91 37 91 19). Kind owner rents large, cheery rooms at a good value. Soundproofed rooms have A/C, TV, and shower. Breakfast €5. Singles €38; doubles €45; triples €53. Extra bed €8. MC/V. ❹

Hôtel Alexandre Ier, 111 r. de Rome (☎04 91 48 67 13; fax 04 91 42 11 14). Located right across from pl. Préfecture. Spacious rooms, all with showers. Breakfast €5. Singles €29; doubles €37-40; triples €48; quads €64. MC/V. ❸

Auberge de Jeunesse Bonneveine (HI), impasse Bonfils (☎04 91 17 63 30; fax 04 91 73 97 23), off av. J. Vidal. From the station, take Métro line #2 to Rond-Point du Prado, and transfer to bus #44 to pl. *Bonnefon.* At the bus stop, walk back toward the traffic circle and turn left at av. J. Vidal, then turn onto impasse Bonfils. A well-organized hostel with an international crowd. Reception 9am-noon. Curfew 1am. Closed Dec. 22-Feb. Dorms €14 first night, €12 thereafter; doubles €17/15. Members only. MC/V. ❶

Auberge de Jeunesse Château de Bois-Luzy (HI), allée des Primevères (☎/fax 04 91 49 06 18). Take bus #8 (dir.: Saint-Julien) from La Canebière to Felibres Laurient, walk uphill and make the first left; the hostel will be on your left. The beautiful, 19th-century chateau used to house a count and countess. Breakfast €3. Dinner €7.50. Sheets €1.80. Reception 7:30am-noon and 5-10:30pm. Lockout noon-5pm. Dorms €11 first night, €8 thereafter; singles €15/12; doubles €12/9. Members only. ❶

Hôtel Béarn, 63 r. Sylvabelle (☎04 91 37 75 83; fax 04 91 81 54 98). On a quiet side street between r. Paradis and r. Breteuil. Adequate rooms with high ceilings and large windows. Internet access €4 per hr. Breakfast €4. Reception 7am-11pm. Singles and doubles €35-40; triples €42. AmEx/MC/V. ❸

Hôtel Saint-Louis, 2 r. des Recollettes (☎04 91 54 02 74; fax 04 91 33 78 59). Pretty, high-ceilinged rooms painted in cheerful colors, just off noisy La Canebière. Some rooms with balcony, nearly all with satellite TV. Breakfast €5. Reception 24hr. Singles €30; doubles €38-45; triples €53. Extra bed €7. AmEx/V. ❸

FOOD

Restaurants in Marseilles reflect the cultural diversity of this dynamic international port city. For the city's famed seafood and North African fare, explore the *vieux port,* especially **place Thiers** and **cours d'Estienne d'Orves,** where one can eat *al fresco* for as little as €9. For a more artsy crowd and cheaper food, head up to **cours Julien,** northeast of the harbor. For groceries, try **Monoprix supermarket,** across from the AmEx office on La Canebière. (Open M-Sa 8:30am-8:30pm.)

Ivoire Restaurant, 57 r. d'Aubagne (☎04 91 33 75 33). This simple restaurant offers a taste of West African cuisine, complete with fresh peanuts and Senegalese beer. A friendly local crowd comes for West African dishes such as Yassa and Maffé (€6-10). Open daily noon-midnight. ❷

Le Sud du Haut, 80 cours Julien (☎04 91 92 66 64). M: Cours Julien. Inviting decor and outdoor seating make this the ideal place for a leisurely meal of tasty, traditional *provençal* cuisine with a modern flair. The *petit légumes provençal* (€9) and the *Saint Marcellin Rôti* (€13) are highly recommended. Funky bathrooms supply markers and paper so patrons can contribute to the wall art. Open W-Sa noon-2am. ❸

THE INSIDER'S CITY

STAYING THE COURS

An eclectic collection of murals, vintage shops, bookstores and cafes, cours Julien is one of Marseille's most interesting neighborhoods and the perfect place to find a bargain.

1 Cartoonish humor and bright colors make up the impressive **murals** on **rue Crudère** and **rue Pastoret** .

2 **Black Music,** 2 r. de la Bibliothèque, has a wide collection of classical and contemporary music by black artists.

3 **Kaleidoscope,** 3 r. des Trois Mages, offers a sweet selection of used records.

4 Tiny **Baluchon Boutique,** 11 r. des Trois Rois, features the best vintage threads.

5 Immerse yourself in paperbacks at **Librairie du Cours Julien** on cours Julien.

6 **La Passerelle,** 26 r. des Trois Mages, features a large selection of comic books and a snappy little cafe-bar.

Baba of Marseille, 14 r. St-Pons (☎04 91 90 66 36). A collision of past and present, the decor underneath the arched stone ceiling of this 14th-century building features hip furniture, eclectic lighting, and photos of past diners. Open W-Sa noon-midnight. ❸

La Kahena, 2 r. de la République (☎04 91 90 61 93). M: Vieux Port. Incredibly spiced couscous dishes (€8-14) are the specialty at this Tunisian restaurant on the corner of the *vieux port.* Blue tile mosaics and smells of warm spices complete its North African aura. Open daily noon-2:30pm and 7:30-11:30pm. MC/V. ❸

Le Restaurant Végétarien, 53 r. St-Pierre (☎04 91 42 75 06). M: Cours Julien. Steps from cours Julien, this quiet outdoor garden offers a respite from the city. Enjoy one of the appetizing *plats du jour* or salads (€9-12) on the full vegetarian menu to the accompaniment of soothing music. Open M-Sa noon-2:30pm and 7:30-11:30pm. ❸

◉ SIGHTS

A walk through the city's streets tops any other sights-oriented itinerary, providing glimpses of the lively African and Arabic communities' influence amid ancient Roman ruins. Check www.museumpaca.org for the latest info on the region's museums. Unless otherwise noted, all the museums listed below have the same hours: June-Sept. Tu-Sa 11am-6pm; Oct.-May Tu-Sa 10am-5pm.

▨ BASILIQUE DE NOTRE DAME DE LA GARDE. A stunning view of the city, surrounding mountains, and stone-studded bay has made this church's hilltop site strategically important for centuries and a must-see for visitors today. The intricate mosaics and intriguing paintings within the basilica are worth the climb. Towering nearly 230m above the city, the golden statue of Madonna cradling the infant Christ, known affectionately as *"la bonne mère,"* is regarded by many as the symbol of Marseilles. (☎04 91 13 40 80. *Open in summer daily 7am-8pm; off-season 7am-7pm.)*

HARBOR ISLANDS. Resembling a child's sandcastle come to life, the **Château d'If** guards the city from its rocky perch outside the harbor. Its dungeon, immortalized in Dumas's *Count of Monte Cristo,* once held a number of hapless Huguenots. Nearby, the **Ile Frioul** quarantined plague infectees for two centuries, beginning in the 1600s. It was only marginally successful, as an outbreak in 1720 killed half of the city's 80,000 citizens. A handful of small shops and restaurants, combined with inlets perfect for swimming, make this an excellent escape from the city. *(Boats depart from quai des Belges for both islands. Call the Groupement des Armateurs Côtiers at ☎04 91 55 50 09. Château ☎04 91 59 02 30. Round-trip 20min.; €9 for each island, €15 for both.)*

LA VIEILLE CHARITÉ. A fine example of the 17th-century work of local architect Pierre Puget, La Charité sheltered orphans, the elderly, and others in need. Now home to many of Marseille's cultural organizations, it contains several of the city's museums, including the Egyptian, prehistoric, and anthropological collections held in the **Musée des Arts Africains, Océaniens et Amérindiens.** *(2 r. de la Charité. ☎04 91 14 58 80. Temporary exhibits €3, permanent collections €2; students with ID half-price.)*

ABBAYE ST-VICTOR. St-Victor, an abbey fortified against pirates and Saracen invaders, is one of the oldest Christian sites in Europe. The eerie 5th-century catacombs and basilica contain both pagan and Christian relics, including the remains of two 3rd-century martyrs. Sarcophagi pile up along the walls; some remain half-embedded in the building's foundations. *(Perched on r. Sainte at the end of quai de Rive Neuve. Follow the signs from the quai. ☎04 96 11 22 60. Open daily 9am-7pm. Crypt €2.)*

MUSÉE CANTINI. This memorable museum chronicles the region's artistic successes of the last century, with major Fauvist and Surrealist collections, including limited works by Henri Matisse and Paul Signac. The works of Auguste Chabaud, a painter from Provence, will be on display until February 2004. *(19 rue Grignan. ☎04 91 54 77 75. €3, students €1.50. Over-65 and under-10 free.)*

MEMORIAL DES CAMPS DE LA MORT. This small but moving museum recalls the death camps of WWII and Marseilles's role in them. In 1943, nearly 2000 buildings housing Jews were destroyed in the *vieux port*. Sobering quotes by Primo Levi, Louis Serre, and Elie Wiesel, and a disturbing collection of ashes are on display. *(Quai de la Tourette. ☎04 91 90 73 15. Free.)*

OTHER SIGHTS. The Musée de la Mode, 11 La Canebière, carries fluctuating exhibits of contemporary fashion. (Free tours in French W and Sa-Su 4pm. €2, students €1. Over 65 free.) The remains of the original port of Marseilles rest peacefully in the quiet Jardin des Vestiges. The grassy harbor, full of limestone stacked like giant Legos, makes a good stop for Classical history buffs. Millennia-old artifacts are displayed in the adjoining Musée d'Histoire de Marseilles, which include pottery pieces and the skeleton of an ancient boat, though there is little explanatory text. *(Enter through the lowest level of the Centre Bourse mall. ☎04 91 90 42 22. €2, students €1, over 65 and under 10 free.)* Bus #83 (dir.: Rond-Point du Prado) takes you from the *vieux port* to Marseilles's **public beaches.** Catch it on the waterfront side of the street and get off just after it rounds the statue of David (20-30min.). Both **plage du Prado** and **plage de la Corniche** offer wide beaches, clear water, and plenty of grass.

🎭 🎟 NIGHTLIFE AND ENTERTAINMENT

Late-night restaurants and a few nightclubs center around **place Thiers,** near the *vieux port.* A more creative crowd unwinds along the **cours Julien.** Tourists should exercise caution at night, particularly on the dimly-lit streets of the quartier Belsunce and bd. d'Athènes. Night buses are scarce, taxis are expensive, and the metro closes early (Su-Th 9pm, F-Sa midnight). Though often overshadowed by the cultural empire of Paris, Marseille's vibrant entertainment scene offers the best of international theater, music, and art. The ticket office at **L'Espace Culture,** 42 r. de la Canebière (☎04 96 11 04 60; www.espaceculture.net), provides detailed information and publications on current cultural events.

El Ache de Cuba, 9 pl. Paul Cézanne. Music blares from the speakers and onto the sidewalk from this little slice of Havana. You must buy a card (€2) to order something, but it's a ticket into the community. Afterwards, drinks run about €2.50, including the "House Punch." Open W-Sa 5pm-2am.

Trolleybus, 24 quai de Rive Neuve. This mega-club, occupying an 18th-century warehouse, has a chic local crowd that gets down to DJs who have been spinning here for 14 years. Beer from €5, drinks €6.50. F nights no cover; Sa cover €10, includes 1 drink. Open July-Aug. W-Sa 11pm-7am; off-season Th-Sa 11pm-7am.

Dan Racing, 17 r. André Poggioli. M: Cours Julien. Patrons speak "the universal language" of music in their own ad hoc performances each night. Drums, guitars, and other music-makers are provided so anyone can join in on stage. Fun auto- and bike-racing decor adds to the atmosphere. Drinks €2.30-3.50. Open W-Sa 10pm-2am.

Poulpason, 2 r. André Poggioli. M: Cours Julien. The underwater theme, complete with a giant octopus reaching out from the wall, creates a cool atmosphere for DJs and live rock. Drinks €2.50-5. Open W-Sa 10pm-2am.

New Can-Can, 3 r. Sénac (☎04 91 48 59 76). A perpetual weekend party for the city's gay community. Cool discotheque setup with red leather couches.Cover F after midnight €13, Sa before midnight €8, €14 thereafter. Open daily 10pm-6am.

FRENCH RIVIERA (CÔTE D'AZUR)

Between Marseilles and the Italian border, the sun-drenched beaches and warm waters of the Mediterranean form the backdrop for this fabled playground of the rich and famous. F. Scott Fitzgerald, Cole Porter, Picasso, Renoir, and Matisse are among those who flocked to the coast in its heyday. Despite the Riviera's glorious past, this choice stretch of sun and sand is a curious combination of high-handed millionaires and low-budget tourists. High society steps out yearly for the Cannes Film Festival and the Monte-Carlo Grand Prix, both in May. Less exclusive are Nice's raucous *Carnaval* in February and various summer jazz festivals.

ST-TROPEZ

Nowhere do the glitz and glamour of the Riviera shine more than in St-Tropez. The "Jewel of the Riviera" unfailingly attracts Hollywood stars and curious backpackers to its exclusive clubs and nude beaches. Unfortunately, the beaches in St-Tropez are difficult to reach without a car. The **shuttle** (*navette municipale*) leaves pl. des Lices for **Les Salins,** a secluded sunspot, and **plage Tahiti** (*Capon-Pinet* stop), the first of the famous **plages des Pampelonne.** (Shuttle runs M-Sa, €1.). Take a break from the sun at the **Musée de l'Annonciade,** pl. Grammont, which showcases Fauvist and neo-Impressionist paintings. (Open June-Sept. M and W-Sa 10am-1pm and 4-9pm; Oct. and Dec.-May reduced hours. €5.50, students €3.50.)

Les Bateaux de St-Raphaël **ferries** (☎04 94 95 17 46), at the old port, serve St-Tropez from St-Raphaël (1hr., 2-5 per day, €10). Sodetrav **buses** (☎04 94 97 88 51) leave av. Général Leclerc for St-Raphaël (2hr., 8-14 per day, €8.40). The **tourist office,** on quai Jean Jaurès, has schedules of the shuttle transport and a *Manifestations* guide that lists local events. (☎04 94 97 45 21; www.ot-saint-tropez.com. Open July-Aug. daily 9:30am-8:30pm; Sept.-June reduced hours.) Budget hotels do not exist in St-Tropez, and the closest youth hostel is in Fréjus (see below). **Camping** is the cheapest option—**Kon Tiki ❶** has a choice location near the northern stretch of the Pampelonne beaches. Campers can soak up sun by day and the beach's wild nightlife (including Kon Tiki's own bar) by night. (☎04 94 55 96 96; fax 04 94 55 96 95. Open Apr. to mid-Oct. July-Aug. two people, tent and car €35; off-season reduced prices.) If you prefer not to camp, one of the most budget-friendly and central hotels is **Lou Cagnard ❸,** 18 av. Paul Roussel. (☎04 94 97 04 24; fax 04 94 97 09 44. Breakfast €8. Open Jan.-Oct. Singles and doubles €43-54, with toilet €55-92. MC/V.) The **vieux port** and the streets behind the waterfront are lined with charmingly pricey restaurants, so create your own meal at **Monoprix supermarket,** 9 av. du Général Leclerc. (Open July-Aug. daily 8am-10pm; Sept.-June 8am-7:50pm.)

Most women who have traveled on the Riviera have a story to tell about men in the big beach towns. Unsolicited pick-up techniques range from subtle invitations to more, uh, bare displays of interest. Brush them off with a biting *"laissez-moi tranquille!"* ("leave me alone") or stony indifference, but don't be shy about enlisting the help of passersby or the police to fend off Mediterranean Don Juans.

ST-RAPHAËL AND FRÉJUS

The twin cities of St-Raphaël and Fréjus provide an excellent base for exploring the Riviera thanks to cheap accommodations, convenient transport, and proximity to the sea. In St-Raphaël, the boardwalk turns into a carnival and golden beaches stretch along the coast, while Fréjus trades sandy shores for Roman ruins. The first weekend in July brings the **Compétition Internationale de Jazz New Orleans** (☎ 04 98 11 89 00). In Fréjus, the **Roman amphitheater**, on r. Henri Vadon, holds frequent concerts and bullfights twice a year. (Open Apr.-Oct. M and W-Sa 10am-1pm and 2:30-6:30pm, Su 8am-7pm; Nov.-Mar. M and W-F 10am-noon and 1:30-5:30pm, Sa 9:30am-12:30pm and 1:30-5:30pm, Su 8am-5pm. Bullfights €22-61. Contact the tourist office for a concert schedule.)

St-Raphaël sends **trains** every 30min. to Cannes (25min., €5.30) and Nice (1hr., €8.80). **Buses** leave from behind the train station in St-Raphaël for Fréjus (25min., every hr., €1.40) and St-Tropez (1½hr., 11 per day, €8.40). The **tourist office**, on r. Waldeck Rousseau, is opposite the train station. (☎ 04 94 19 52 52; www.saint-raphael.com. Open July-Aug. daily 9am-7pm; Sept.-June M-Sa 9am-12:30pm and 2-6:30pm.) Take bus #6 from St-Raphaël to pl. Paul Vernet to get to the **Fréjus tourist office**, 325 r. Jean Jaurès. (☎ 04 94 51 83 83; www.ville-frejus.fr. Open July-Aug. M-Sa 10am-noon and 2:30-6:30pm, Su 10am-noon and 3-6pm; Sept.-June M-Sa 9am-noon and 3-6pm.) Take av. du 15ème Corps d'Armée from the Fréjus tourist office and turn left on chemin de Councillier after the next roundabout to reach the ■**Auberge de Jeunesse de St-Raphaël-Fréjus (HI)** ❶, a clean, friendly hostel with a beautiful, secluded location. (☎ 04 94 52 93 93; youth.hostel.frejus.st.raphael@wanadoo.fr. Sheets €2.70. Reception 8-10am and 6-8pm. Lockout 10am-6pm. Curfew July-Aug. midnight; Sept.-June 10pm. Open Feb.-Nov. Dorms €13. Camping €10 per person with tent.) In St-Raphaël, the **Hôtel les Pyramides** ❸, 77 av. Paul Doumer., is on a calm street just minutes from the waterfront. To get there, leave the station to the left, make a right onto av. Henri Vadon, and take the first left onto av. Paul Doumer. (☎ 04 98 11 10 10; www.saint-raphael.com/pyramides. Breakfast €7. Open Mar. 15-Nov. 15. Reception 7am-9pm; access code after hours. Singles €26; doubles €36-55; triples €56; quads €66. Extra bed €13. MC/V.) St-Raphaël's **Monoprix supermarket** is on 14 bd. de Félix Martin, off av. Alphonse Karr near the train station. (Open M-Sa 8:30am-7:30pm.) **Postal Codes:** St-Raphaël: 83700; Fréjus: 83600.

CANNES

With its legendary **Festival International du Film** each May, Cannes (pop. 70,000) has more associations with stardom than any other place on the coast. None of the festival's 350 screenings are open to the public, but the sidewalk show is free. For the other 11 months of the year, Cannes is among the most approachable of the Riviera's glam-towns. A palm-lined boardwalk, gorgeous sandy beaches, and innumerable boutiques ensure that anyone can sport the famous Cannes style. The best window-shopping along the Riviera lies along **rue d'Antibes** and **boulevard de la Croisette**. Farther west, the **Église de la Castre** and its courtyard stand on the hill on which *vieux Cannes* was built. Of Cannes's three **casinos**, the most accessible is **Le Casino Croisette**, 1 jetée Albert Edouard,

FRANCE

THE LOCAL LEGEND

YOU CANNES NEVER LEAVE

A few short days in celebrity-filled Cannes makes most visitors wish they were just a bit more glamorous. In 1800, however, Cannes was little more than a tiny fishing village, inhabited by the monks of St-Honorat abbey. The city was transformed by the 1834 arrival of Lord Henry Brougham, an member of British Parliament. Lord Brougham was headed to Nice, in hopes that a warm Mediterranean climate would mend his daughter's failing health. He found the city under quarantine due to a sudden cholera epidemic, and was forced to spend the night in Cannes. Thirty-four years later, Brougham was still there. He had built a lovely chateau, planted grass seeds imported from England, and done a fair bit of entertaining. Well-connected Brougham drew both English and French elites to his frequent dinner parties, including Lord Byron and King Louis Philippe of France. Cannes rapidly gained a reputation for being the place for the European aristocracy to winter. Villas and luxury hotels transformed the Croisette from a simple seaside dirt path into a posh boulevard. Guy de Maupassant joked wryly: "I met three princes one after the other on the Croisette!" Cannes transformed from the quiet haunt of monks and fishermen to a playground for the rich and famous in just a few decades, and it has never looked back.

next to the Palais des Festivals. (No shorts, jeans, or t-shirts. Jackets required for men. 18+ with ID. Cover €10. Gambling daily 8pm-4am; slots open at 10am.) If you want to get into one of Cannes's elite nightspots, dress to kill. Just as fun and half the price, cafes and bars near the waterfront stay open all night. Nightlife thrives around **rue Dr. G. Monod.**

Coastal **trains** depart from 1 r. Jean-Jaurès for: Antibes (15min., €2.30); Marseilles (2hr., €23); Monaco (1hr., €7.80); Nice (40min., €5.20); and St-Raphaël (25min., €4.10). The **tourist office**, 1 bd. de la Croisette, helps find accommodations. (☎04 93 39 24 53; www.cannes.fr. Open July-Aug. daily 9am-8pm; Sept.-June M-F 9am-7pm.) There is a **branch** office at the train station. (Open M-Sa 9am-7pm.) Access the **Internet** at **CyberCafé Institut Riviera Langue,** 26 r. de Mimont. (€4 per hr. Open daily 9am-10pm.) Hostels are 10-20min. farther from the beach than other lodgings, but are the cheapest options in town. The **Hostel Les Iris ❷,** 77 bd. Carnot, thrives under the care of friendly, English-speaking owners who have converted an old hotel into a clean, bright hostel with firm beds, a terrace for lounging and dining, and TV. (☎/fax 04 93 68 30 20. Dorms €18. MC/V.) **Hotel Mimont ❸,** 39 r. de Mimont, is two streets behind the train station, off bd. de la République. (☎04 93 39 51 64; fax 04 93 99 65 35. Singles €29; doubles €37; triples €51. AmEx/MC/V.) **Hôtel de Bourgogne ❸,** 11 r. du 24 août, has well-maintained rooms in the heart of town. (☎04 93 38 36 73; fax 04 92 99 28 41. Breakfast €5. Singles €30-50; doubles €40-55; triples €65-80; off-season reduced prices. AmEx/MC/V.) Stock up at **Monoprix supermarket,** in Champion, 6 r. Meynadier. (Open M-Sa 8:30am-7:30pm.) The pedestrian zone around **rue Meynadier** has inexpensive restaurants. **Postal Code:** 06400.

ANTIBES

Blessed with beautiful beaches and a charming *vieille ville*, Antibes (pop. 78,000) is less touristy than Nice and more relaxed than St-Tropez; with access to top-notch nightlife in neighboring **Juan-les-Pins,** it has become an undisputed jewel of the Riviera. The **Musée Picasso,** in the Château Grimaldi, on pl. Mariejol, displays works by the former Antibes resident and his contemporaries. (Open mid-June to mid-Sept. Su and Tu-Sa 10am-6pm; mid-Sept. to mid-June 10am-noon and 2-6pm. €6, students €3.) The two main public **beaches** in Antibes are **Plage du Ponteil** and the adjacent **Plage de la Salis.** Come summer, the young and hip Juan-Les-Pins is synonymous with wild nightlife. Frequent **buses** and **trains** run from Antibes, although walking between the two along bd. Wilson is also an option. Boutiques remain open until midnight, cafes until 2am, and nightclubs past dawn. **Discothèques** are generally open from 11pm to 5am. (Cover approx. €15, usually includes 1 drink.) **▨Milk,** on av. Gallice, fills with a spunky crowd. (Cover €16. Open July-Aug. daily midnight-5am; Sept.-June F-Sa only.) In psychedelic **Whisky à Gogo,** 5 r. Jacques Leonetti, a young crowd dances the night away amid water-filled columns. (Cover €16. Open Apr. to mid-Oct. daily 12:30-5:30am.)

Trains leave av. Robert Soleau for: Cannes (20min., 20 per day, €2.10); Marseilles (2¼hr., 10 per day, €24); Nice (15min., 20 per day, €3.50). **Buses** leave 200 pl. de Gaulle for Cannes (20min., every 20min. €2.50) and Nice (45min., every 20min., €4.10). Exit the station, turn right on av. Robert Soleau, and follow the signs to the **tourist office** at 11 pl. de Gaulle. (☎04 92 90 53 00; www.antibes-juanlespins.com. Open July-Aug. daily 9am-7pm; Sept.-June M-F 9am-12:30pm and 1:30-6pm, Sa 9am-noon and 2-6pm.) For the distant-but-beautiful **▨Relais International de la Jeunesse (Caravelle 60) ❶,** take bus #2A (every 40min. 6:50am-7:30pm, €1.15) from pl. Guynemer in Antibes. (☎04 93 61 34 40. Reception daily 8-10am and 5:30pm-10:30pm. Dorms €14.) Rather than make the trek back to Antibes, crash in Juan-Les-Pins at **Hôtel Parisiana ❹,** 16 av. de L'Estérel, which has bright rooms with excellent amenities. (☎04 93 61 27 03; fax 04 93 67 97 21. Breakfast €5. Singles €35; doubles €49; triples €59; quads €67. Sept.-May reduced prices. AmEx/MC/V.) The **Marché Provençal,** on cours Masséna, is considered one of the best markets on the Côte d'Azur. (Open Su and Tu-Sa 6am-1pm.) **Postal Code:** 06600.

NICE

Sun-drenched and spicy, Nice (pop. 380,000) is the unofficial capital of the Riviera. Its pumping nightlife, top-notch museums, and bustling beaches are unerring tourist magnets. During the annual three-week Carnaval in February, visitors and *Niçois* alike ring in the spring with wild revelry, grotesque costumes, and raucous song and dance. Prepare to have more fun than you'll remember.

▮ TRANSPORTATION

Flights: Aéroport Nice-Côte d'Azur (NCE; ☎08 20 42 33 33). **Air France,** 10 av. Félix Faure (☎08 02 80 28 02), serves **Paris** (€93; under-25, over-60, and couples €46).

Trains: Gare SNCF Nice-Ville (☎04 93 82 62 11), on av. Thiers. Open 5am-12:15am. To: **Cannes** (45min., every 15-45min., €5); **Marseilles** (2¾hr., every 30-90min., €24); **Monaco** (15min., every 10-30min., €3); **Paris** (5½hr., 6 per day, €76).

Buses: 5 bd. Jean Jaurès (☎04 93 85 61 81). Open M-Sa 8am-6:30pm. To: **Cannes** (1½hr., every 20min., €6) and **Monaco** (40min., every 15min., €3.40).

Ferries: Corsica Ferries, Port du Commerce (☎04 92 00 42 93; www.corsicaferries.com). Take bus #1 or 2 (dir.: Port) from pl. Masséna. To **Corsica** (€20-40).

Public Transportation: Sunbus, 10 av. Félix Faure (☎04 93 16 52 10), near pl. Leclerc and pl. Masséna. Individual tickets €1.30. Long treks to museums, the beach, and hostels make passes a bargain (day pass €4, 8-ticket *carnet* €8.30, 7-day pass €17). The tourist office provides **Sunplan** bus maps, schedules, and route info.

Bike and Scooter Rental: JML Location, 34 av. Auber (☎04 93 16 07 00), opposite the train station. Bikes €11 per day, €42 per week. Scooters €37 per day, €196 per week. Credit card deposit required. Open June-Sept. daily 9am-6:30pm; Oct.-May M-Sa 8am-1pm and 2-6.30pm. MC/V.

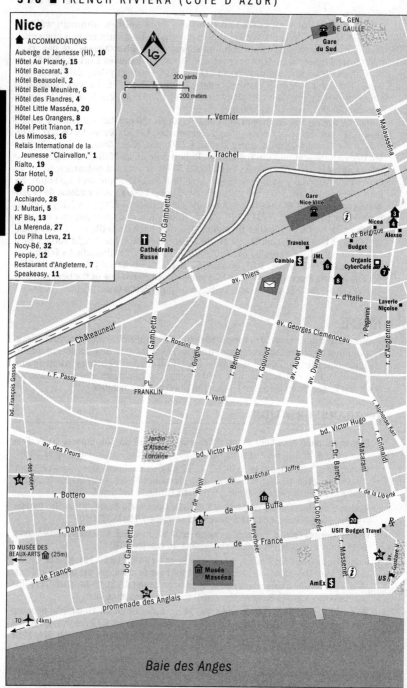

Nice

🏠 **ACCOMMODATIONS**

Auberge de Jeunesse (HI), **10**
Hôtel Au Picardy, **15**
Hôtel Baccarat, **3**
Hôtel Beausoleil, **2**
Hôtel Belle Meunière, **6**
Hôtel des Flandres, **4**
Hôtel Little Masséna, **20**
Hôtel Les Orangers, **8**
Hôtel Petit Trianon, **17**
Les Mimosas, **16**
Relais International de la
   Jeunesse "Clairvallon," **1**
Rialto, **19**
Star Hotel, **9**

🍽 **FOOD**

Acchiardo, **28**
J. Multari, **5**
KF Bis, **13**
La Merenda, **27**
Lou Pilha Leva, **21**
Nocy-Bé, **32**
People, **12**
Restaurant d'Angleterre, **7**
Speakeasy, **11**

Baie des Anges

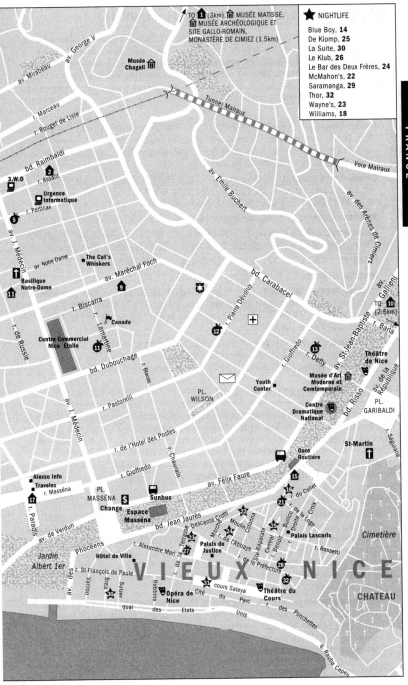

FRANCE

TO ■1 (3km), 🏛 MUSÉE MATISSE,
🏛 MUSÉE ARCHÉOLOGIQUE ET
SITE GALLO-ROMAIN,
MONASTÈRE DE CIMIEZ (1.5km)

★ NIGHTLIFE

Blue Boy, **14**
De Klomp, **25**
La Suite, **30**
Le Klub, **26**
Le Bar des Deux Frères, **24**
McMahon's, **22**
Saramanga, **29**
Thor, **32**
Wayne's, **23**
Williams, **18**

av. George V
av. Mirabeau
r. Marceau
r. Rouget de Lisle
bd. Raimbaldi
Musée Chagall
Tunnel Malraux
Voie Malraux
av. Émile Buchert
av. des Arènes de Cimiez
3.W.0
r. Assalit
Urgence Informatique
r. Pertinax
av. J. Médecin
av. Notre Dame
The Cat's Whiskers
av. Maréchal Foch
bd. Carabacel
r. Pierre Dévoluy
av. St-Jean-Baptiste
av. Gallieni
TO ■10 (2.5km)
Basilique Notre-Dame
r. Biscarra
Canada
Lamartine
r. Blacas
r. Gioffredo
r. Defly
r. Barla
Théâtre de Nice
av. de la République
Centre Commercial Nice Etoile
bd. Dubouchage
Musée d'Art Moderne et Comtemporain
bd. Risso
PL. GARIBALDI
r. de Russie
r. Pastorelli
PL. WILSON
Youth Center
Centre Dramatique National
r. Séguran
St-Martin
r. de l'Hotel des Postes
r. Chauvain
Gare Routière
av. J. Médecin
r. Gioffredo
av. Félix Faure
Alexso Info
Travelex
r. Masséna
r. du Collet
Cimetière
r. Paradis
PL. MASSÉNA
Change
Sunbus
Espace Masséna
bd. Jean Jaurès
Descente Crotti
Marché
Moulin
Colonna
r. de la Loge
Buffa
Central
Droite
r. de la Croix
av. de Verdun
Phocéens
r. Alexandre Mari
r. de la Terrasse
Palais de Justice
r. de l'Abbaye
Ste-Réparate
r. Benoît
Palais Lascaris
r. Rossetti
VIEUX NICE
Jardin Albert 1er
Hôtel de Ville
r. St-François de Paule
Brea
Vanloo
Sulzer
av. des
Robbins
Cité
Opéra de Nice
cours Saleya
du Parc
r. de la Préfecture
Théâtre du Cours
r. des Ponchettes
CHATEAU
quai des Etats - Unis
q. Rauba Capeu

✈️ 🛈 ORIENTATION AND PRACTICAL INFORMATION

Avenue Jean-Médecin, on the left as you exit the train station, and **boulevard Gambetta**, on the right, run directly to the beach. **Place Masséna** is 10min. down av. Jean-Médecin. Along the coast, **promenade des Anglais** is a people-watching paradise. To the southeast, past av. Jean-Médecin and toward the bus station, is **Vieux Nice**. Women should not walk alone after sundown, and everyone should exercise caution at night around the train station, *Vieux Nice*, and promenade des Anglais.

Tourist Office: Av. Thiers (☎08 92 70 74 07; www.nicetourism.com), by the train station. Makes same-day hotel reservations; best chances of getting a room are between 9 and 11am. Ask for *Nice: A Practical Guide*, and a map. Open June-Sept. M-Sa 8am-8pm, Su 9am-6pm; Oct.-May M-Sa 8am-7pm.

Consulates: Canada, 10 r. Lamartine (☎04 93 92 93 22). Open M-F 9am-noon. **UK,** 26 av. Notre Dame (☎04 93 62 13 56). Open M, W, F 9:30-11:30am. **US,** 7 av. Gustave V (☎04 93 88 89 55). Open M-F 9-11:30am and 1:30-4:30pm.

American Express: 11 prom. des Anglais (☎04 93 16 53 53). Open daily 9am-8:30pm.

Laundromat: Laverie Niçoise, 7 r. d'Italie (☎04 93 87 56 50). Beside Basilique Notre-Dame. Open M-Sa 8:30am-12:30pm and 2:30-7:30pm. Wash €4. Dry €2 per 20min.

Police: (☎04 93 17 22 22). At the opposite end of bd. M. Foch from av. Jean-Médecin.

Hospital: St-Roch, 5 r. Pierre Devoluy (☎04 92 03 33 75).

Internet Access: Teknosoft, 16 r. Paganini, (☎04 93 16 89 81), has 14 computers with English keyboards. Open daily 9am-10pm. €2 per 30min. **Alexso Info,** 1 r. de Belgique (☎04 93 88 65 02), has 12 computers and 8 English keyboards. €0.90 per 10min. Open daily 10am-8pm.

Post Office: 21 av. Thiers (☎04 93 82 65 22), near the train station. Open M-F 8am-7pm, Sa 8am-noon. Address mail to be held: Firstname SURNAME, *Poste Restante, Recette Principale,* Nice 06000, FRANCE. **Postal Code:** 06033 Nice Cedex 1.

🏠 ACCOMMODATIONS

To sleep easy, come to Nice with reservations. Hotels fill up quickly, especially in the summertime, so book at least a few weeks in advance. The city has two clusters of budget accommodations—near the train station and near *Vieux Nice*. Those by the station are newer but less centrally located, and the walk home at night can be unsettling for those traveling alone. Hotels closer to *Vieux Nice* are more convenient but tend to be less modern.

HOSTELS

Relais International de la Jeunesse "Clairvallon," 26 av. Scudéri (☎04 93 81 27 63; clajpaca@cote-dazur.com), in Cimiez, 4km out of town. Take bus #15 to Scudéri (dir.: Rimiez; 20min., every 10min.) from the train station or pl. Masséna; after 9pm, take the N2 bus from pl. Masséna. The amenities in this luxurious villa of a deceased marquis include a swimming pool and mini-football field, helping to keep the 160 guests entertained. Laundry €4, dryer €2. Lockout 9:30am-5pm. Curfew 11pm. Dorms €14. ❶

Auberge de Jeunesse (HI), rte. Forestière du Mont-Alban (☎04 93 89 23 64; fax 04 92 04 03 10), 4km from the city center. From the bus station, take #14 (dir: Mont Boron) to l'Auberge (every 30-45min., last bus 7:50pm). From the train station, take #17 and switch to #14 at the Sunbus station. Ultra-clean hostel draws a cool, friendly crowd. Internet with phone card, €5 per 30min., €7 per hr. Breakfast included. Sheets €2.70. Laundry €6. Lockout 10am-5pm. Curfew 12:30am. Dorms €14. ❶

NEAR THE TRAIN STATION

⊠ Hôtel Belle Meunière, 21 av. Durante (☎04 93 88 66 15; fax 04 93 82 51 76), right across from the train station. Birds chirp in the spacious garden courtyard of this former mansion. Luggage storage €2. Laundry €5.50-9.50. Reception 7:30am-midnight, access code after hours. Dorms €14, with shower €19; doubles with shower €48; triples €57; quads €76. MC/V. ❷

Hôtel des Flandres, 6 r. de Belgique (☎04 93 88 78 94; fax 04 93 88 74 90), 100m from the train station and 800m from the beach. With an imposing entrance and large bedrooms and bathrooms, this hotel appears more expensive than it is. Breakfast €5. Singles €35-45; doubles €45-51; triples €60; quads €67. Extra bed €12. MC/V. ❸

Hôtel Notre Dame, 22 r. de Russie (☎04 93 88 70 44; jyung@caramail.com), at the corner of r. d'Italie, 1 block west of av. Jean-Médecin. Friendly owners rent huge, clean rooms in Grecian white and blue. Breakfast €4. Free luggage storage. Reception 24hr. Singles €39; doubles €45; triples €57; quads €60. Extra bed €10. MC/V. ❹

Hôtel Les Orangers, 10bis av. Durante (☎04 93 87 51 41; fax 04 93 82 57 82), across from the station. Behind a beautiful exterior lie bright co-ed dorms with closely packed beds, showers, and fridges. 2-night min. stay. Reception 8am-9pm. Lockout June-Aug. 11am-1pm. Closed Nov. Dorms €16; singles €20-26; doubles €38-40; triples €54; quads €60. MC/V. ❶

Hôtel Beausoleil, 22 r. Assalit (☎04 93 85 18 54; www.beausoleil-hotel.com), a 5min. walk from the train station. In addition to pastel decor, provides attentive service and a modicum of luxury to the budget traveler. Closed Nov.-Feb. Singles July-Aug. €58-65; doubles €75-85; triples €88-98. Prices reduced €10 off-season. AmEx/MC/V. ❹

Hôtel Baccarat, 39 r. d'Angleterre (☎04 93 88 35 73; www.hotel-baccarat.com), 2nd left off r. de Belgique. Offers large rooms with floral bedspreads and comfy mattresses and a secure atmosphere. All rooms with shower and toilet. Free beach mat loan. Breakfast €5. Dorms €18; singles €29; doubles and triples €44; quads €66. MC/V. ❷

NEAR VIEUX NICE AND THE BEACH

Hôtel Petit Trianon, 11 r. Paradis (☎04 93 87 50 46), left off pedestrian r. Masséna. Rooms are small and simple, but elegant chandeliers, pastel decor, and firm beds create a soothing experience. Friendly, English-speaking staff. Reservations essential (8 rooms available). Singles €15; doubles €31, with shower and toilet €39; triples €60. Prices for doubles, triples, and quads higher Apr.-Sept. Extra bed €8. MC/V. ❶

Star Hôtel, 14 r. Biscarra (☎04 93 85 19 03; info@hotel-star.com), in a quiet part of town halfway between the train station and *Vieux Nice*. Offers spacious pastel rooms with charm to spare. May-Sept. Singles €45; doubles with shower €55, with bath €60; triple with bath 70. Prices €10 lowerr Sept.-May. ❹

Hôtel Little Masséna, 22 r. Masséna (☎/fax 04 93 87 72 34). Small, clean rooms with in a boisterous and touristy part of town. Owners are young and friendly. Breakfast €4.50. Reception daily 8am-noon and 2-9pm. Singles and doubles €28, with shower €38, with shower and toilet €48. Oct.-May prices €2-5 lower. MC/V. ❸

Hôtel Au Picardy, 10 bd. Jean Jaurès (☎/fax 04 93 85 75 51), across from the bus station. Ideally located near *Vieux Nice*. Brown paint and a lack of natural light keep the rooms dark. Street-side rooms can be noisy, but the windows are sound-proofed. Breakfast €3. Showers €1.50. Reception 8am-5pm. Singles €19, with shower €28; doubles €24-27, with shower and toilet €33; triples €34-38; quads €38-48. Extra bed €5. ❷

Les Mimosas, 26 r. de la Buffa (☎04 93 88 05 59; fax 04 93 87 15 65). Near the beach and r. Masséna. An impressive staircase leads to 10 small rooms off a single hallway that fill up quickly in the summer with backpackers and a predominantly young clientele. Singles €29-34; doubles €34-49; triples €50-59; quads €60, quads with shower €64-68. MC/V. ❸

Rialto, 55 r. de la Buffa (☎/fax 04 93 88 15 04). A little farther from the big show. More apartment than hotel. 8 bright spacious rooms with baths and sizeable kitchens. Reserve far in advance. Doubles €45; triples €57; quads €72. ❹

🔅 FOOD

Restaurants in Nice range from four-star establishments to outdoor terraces to tiny holes-in-the-wall. *Pâtisseries* and bakeries sell inexpensive local specialties flavored with North African spices, herbs, or olives. Try the round, crusty *pan bagnat,* a loaf of bread garnished with tuna, sardines, vegetables, and olive oil; *pissaladière* pizza topped with onions, anchovies, and olives; *socca,* thin, olive oil-flavored chickpea bread, served hot with pepper; or *bouillabaisse,* a hearty stew of mussels, potatoes, and fish. The famous *salade niçoise* combines tuna, potatoes, tomatoes, and a spicy mustard dressing.

Cafes and food stands along the beach are expensive. The fruit, fish, and flower **market** at cours Saleya is a good place to pick up fresh olives, cheeses, and melons (Tu-Su 6am-1:30pm). A fruit and vegetable market is on av. Maché de la Libération (Tu-Su 6am-12:30pm). Expensive gourmet establishments line r. Masséna, which offer nothing cheaper than a €9 pizza. Av. Jean-Médecin features reasonable *brasseries* and *panini* vendors, and gems hide amid the tourist traps on *Vieux Nice.*

▓ **La Merenda,** 4 r. de la Terrasse. Those lucky enough to get a table can savor the work of a culinary master who left one of the most renowned restaurants in Nice to open this affordable 12-table gem which only stocks enough fresh food to last the day. Nothing about the menu is constant except its exotic flair, evidenced by fried zucchini flowers, stockfish, and veal head. Reserve in the morning, in person, for dinner. Two seatings at 7 and 9pm. Cash only. *Plats* €10-15. Open M-F noon-1:30pm and 7-9:30pm. ❸

▓ **Lou Pilha Leva,** 13 r. du Collet (☎04 93 13 99 08) in *Vieux Nice.* Tourists and locals pack the outdoor wooden benches of this favorite, chowing down on inexpensive and tasty local food. Pizza slice €3, *moules* (mussels) €5. Open daily 8am-11pm. ❶

▓ **Le Restaurant d'Angleterre,** 25 r. d'Angleterre (☎04 93 88 64 49), near the train station. This local favorite serves delicious French specialties in a pleasant, intimate setting. The *menu sâge* includes bread, large salad, main course, side dish, dessert, and an after-dinner cordial (€11.50). Open Tu-Sa 11:30am-1:45pm and 6:45-10pm. ❸

People, 12 r. Pastorelli (☎04 93 85 08 43). Friendly ownership, hearty portions of regional dishes like the delicious *foie gras,* and an excellent wine selection make People well worth the short walk from *Vieux Nice. Plats* €12-17. Open M noon-2:30pm, Tu-Th noon-2:30pm and 7-10:30pm, F-Sa 5pm-midnight. ❸

Acchiardo, 38 r. Droite (☎04 93 85 51 16), in *Vieux Nice.* Simple but appetizing Italian and French dishes served in a charming country setting with gingham, hanging corn husks, grape vines, and bronze pans. Pastas (€6) and classic French meats (house scallop specialty €11.50) are popular with a local clientele loyal to the family-run business. Open M-F noon-1:30pm and 7-10pm. ❶

Speakeasy, 7 r. Lamartine (☎04 93 85 59 50). Alas, there's no illicit liquor here, but there are delectable vegan lunch options, prepared by an American chef/animal-rights activist. Testimonials of famous vegetarians from Gandhi to Martina Navratilova surround the entrance. 2-course meal €11-12. Open M-Sa noon-2:15pm. ❸

J.Multari, 58bis av. Jean-Médecin (☎04 93 92 01 99). This graceful *salon de thé,* bakery, and sandwich shop serves excellent, reasonably priced fare. Try a goat cheese, chicken, or ham sandwich on fresh baguette (€3.10), salad (€3), pizza (€1.50), crepe (€5), or mouth-watering pastry (€1-2). Open M-Sa 6am-8:30pm. ❶

Nocy-Bé, 4-6 r. Jules Gilly (☎ 04 93 85 52 25). Chill out at this mellow Asian tearoom, adorned with low-hanging lamps, comfortable sofas, and inviting floor cushions. Sip one of 45 teas (€2.30-3.80) or relax with a *narguilé* (water pipe) with one of 14 fruit fragrances (€7.60). Open daily July-Sept. 5pm-12:30am; Oct.-June 4pm-12:30am. ❷

KF Bis, 8 r. Delfy (☎ 04 93 80 02 22), next to the Musée d'Art Moderne. Otherwise known as the "fashion lounge cafe," KF Bis fosters a feeling of cool sophistication. Open June-Aug. Tu-F 11:30am-2pm and 7:30-11:30pm, Sa-Su 5:30-11pm; Sept.-May Tu-Su 11:30am-3pm and 5:30-11:30pm. AmEx/V. ❸

🏛 SIGHTS

Many visitors to Nice head straight for the beaches and don't retreat from the sun and water until the day is done. Whatever dreams you've had about Nice's beach, though, the hard reality is an endless stretch of rocks; bring a beach mat if you plan to soak up the sun in comfort. Contrary to popular opinion, there are things in Nice more worthwhile than a long, naked sunbath on a bunch of pebbles.

▧ MUSÉE NATIONAL MESSAGE BIBLIQUE MARC CHAGALL. Chagall founded this extraordinary concrete and glass museum in 1966 to showcase his 17 *Message Biblique* paintings. Twelve of these strikingly colorful canvases illustrate the first two books of the Old Testament, and the remaining five, done all in shades of red, illustrate the Song of Songs. The museum also includes a cursory photobiography of Chagall, a wonderful garden, and a small stained-glass-encircled auditorium decorated by the artist himself, which sometimes stages concerts and lectures. *(Av. du Dr. Ménard. 15min. walk north of the station, or take bus #15 (dir.: Rimiez) to Musée Chagall. ☎ 04 93 53 87 20; www.musee-chagall.fr. Open July-Sept. Su-M and W-Sa 10am-6pm; Oct.-June 10am-5pm. Last tickets sold 30min. before closing. Guided tours in French, English, and Italian by appt. €5.50, under-26 and Su €4. Under-18 and first Su of the month free.)*

▧ MUSÉE MATISSE. Henri Matisse first visited Nice in 1916 and never left its shores. Originally a 17th-century Genoese villa, the museum contains a small collection of paintings and a dazzling exhibit of Matisse's three-dimensional work, including bronze reliefs and dozens of cut-and-paste tableaux. *(164 av. des Arènes de Cimiez. Take bus #15, 17, 20, 22, or 25 to Arènes. Free bus tickets between Musée Chagall and Musée Matisse; ask at either ticket counter. ☎ 04 93 81 08 08. Open M and W-Su Apr.-Sept. 10am-6pm; Oct.-Mar. 10am-5pm. €3.80, students €2.30. Call for info on lectures.)*

MUSÉE D'ART MODERNE ET D'ART CONTEMPORAIN. Enter the concrete, glass, and steel of this museum's minimalist galleries and admire the work of French New Realists and American Pop Artists like Klein, Lichtenstein, and Warhol. The museum showcases European and American avant-garde pieces with a gallery devoted to the statues of Niki de St. Phalle and a reputation for attracting interesting traveling exhibits. *(Promenade des Arts, at the intersection of av. St-Jean Baptiste and Traverse Garibaldi. Take bus #5 (dir.: St-Charles) to Musée Promenade des Arts. The museum is behind the bus station. ☎ 04 93 62 61 62. Open Su and Tu-Sa 10am-6pm. €4, students €2.50.)*

▧ VIEUX NICE. Sprawling southeast from bd. Jean Jaurès, the labarynthine streets of *Vieux Nice* are crowded with tiny pansy-filled balconies, beautiful fountains, public squares, hand-painted awnings, and pristine churches. In the morning, the area hosts bustling **markets,** including a fish frenzy at **place St-François** and a flower market on **cours Salaya.** In the evening, knick-knack stands supplement the cafes, and the quarter becomes the center of Nice's lively nightlife. *(Fish frenzy Tu-Su 6am-1pm; flower market Su 6am-noon, Tu and Th-F 6am-5:30pm, W and Sa 6am-6:30pm.)*

CATHÉDRALE ORTHODOXE RUSSE ST-NICOLAS. Also known as the **Église Russe,** this cathedral was commissioned by Empress Marie Feodorovna, widow of Tsar Nicholas I. Modeled after St-Basil's in Moscow, the onion-domed structure quickly became a spiritual home for exiled Russian nobles. The gilded screen concealing the altar also sets it apart from French cathedrals. There's one hint, however, that the cathedral is influenced by the Riviera: Its dominant colors are Mediterranean light blue and yellow rather than dark and somber blues and grays. (*17 bd. du Tsarevitch, off bd. Gambetta. ☎04 93 96 88 02. Open daily June-Aug. 9am-noon and 2:30-6pm; Sept.-May 9:30am-noon and 2:30-5pm. €1.80.*)

LE CHÂTEAU. At the eastern end of the promenade, Le Château—the formal name for the remains of an 11th-century cathedral—sits in a pleasant green hillside park ornamented by an artificial waterfall. Don't be fooled: There hasn't been a château here since an 8th-century battle. The top does, however, provide a spectacular view of the rooftops of Nice and the sparkling Baie des Anges. The vista can be reached by climbing 400 steps or catching the elevator at the Tour Bellanda. (*Park open daily 7am-8pm. Elevator runs 9am-7:30pm. €1.*)

MUSÉE DES BEAUX-ARTS. The former villa of Ukraine's Princess Kotschoubey has been converted into a celebration of French academic painting, including Van Dongen and Raoul Dufy. Dufy, Nice's second greatest painter, celebrated the spontaneity of his city with sensational pictures of the town at rest and play. (*33 av. Baumettes. Take bus #38 to Chéret or #12 to Grosso. ☎04 92 15 28 28. Open Su and Tu-Sa 10am-noon and 2-6pm. €3.80, students €2.30.*)

MONASTÈRE DE CIMIEZ. This monastery has housed Nice's Franciscans since the 13th century, and a few still call it home. The ancient monastery's former living quarters have been converted to the **Musée Franciscain,** which exhibits illuminated manuscripts, medieval crosses, and a Giotto painting of St. Francis. The complex also includes a church, lovely surrounding gardens, and a large cemetery where Matisse and Dufy are buried. (*Pl. du Monastère. Take bus #15 (dir.: Rimiez) or #17 (dir.: Cimiez) to Monastère, or follow the signs and walk from the Musée Matisse. ☎04 93 81 55 41. Museum open M-Sa 10am-noon and 3-6pm. Church open daily 9am-6pm. Gardens open daily in summer 8am-7pm; off-season 8am-6pm. Cemetery open daily 8am-6pm. Free.*)

MUSÉE ARCHÉOLOGIQUE ET SITE GALLO-ROMAIN. Adjacent to the site of ancient Gallo-Roman baths, this museum displays artifacts discovered on the Côte from the Bronze through the Middle Ages, including excavated coins, jewelry, and sarcophagi. (*160 av. des Arènes de Cimiez. ☎04 93 81 59 57. Take bus #15, 17, 20, 22, or 25 to Arènes. Next to Musée Matisse. Open Apr.-Sept. Su and Tu-Sa 10am-noon and 2-6pm; Oct.-Mar. 10am-1pm and 2-5pm. €3.80, students €2.30.*)

JARDIN ALBERT IER. The central city park, Jardin Albert 1er has the usual repertoire of benches and fountains. In addition, its outdoor Théâtre de Verdun presents jazz and plays in summer. Contact the tourist office for a schedule. (*Between av. Verdun and bd. Jaurès, off promenade des Anglais and quai des Etats-Unis. Box office open daily 10:30am-noon and 3:30-6:30pm.*)

OTHER SIGHTS. Named by the rich English community that commissioned it, the **promenade des Anglais,** a posh, palm-lined seaside boulevard, is Nice's answer to the great pedestrian thoroughfares of Paris, London, and New York. Today the promenade is lined by luxury hotels like the stately **Négresco** (toward the west end), where the staff still don top hats and 19th-century uniforms. Just east of the Négresco, the **Espace Masséna** gives romantic picnickers a lovely shady area in which to woo each other beside lavish fountains. **Private beaches** crowd the seashore between bd. Gambetta and the Opéra, but public strands west of bd. Gambetta compensate for the exclusivity.

NIGHTLIFE

Nice's **Jazz Festival**, in mid-July at the Parc et Arènes de Cimiez near the Musée Matisse, attracts world-famous performers. (☎08 20 80 04 00; www.nicejazzfest.com. €30.) Nice's **Carnaval** in late February gives Rio a run for its money with three weeks of parades, outlandish costumes, fireworks, and parties.

The party crowd swings long after St-Tropez and Antibes have called it a night. The bars and nightclubs around r. Masséna and *Vieux Nice* pulsate with dance and jazz. The dress code at all bars and clubs is simple: Look good. Most pubs will turn you away if they catch you wearing shorts, sandals, or a baseball cap. To experience Nice's nightlife without spending a euro, head down to the **promenade des Anglais**, where street performers, musicians, and pedestrians fill the beach and boardwalk. For more info pick up the free brochure *l'Excés* (www.exces.com) at the tourist office and in some bars.

BARS

▨ **McMahon's**, 50 bd. Jean Jaurès. Join the locals and expats who lap up Guinness and shoot pool at this friendly Irish pub. Happy Hour daily 3-9pm (pints €3, wine €2). Karaoke on Th, request DJ and free shots on Sa. Open daily 3pm-2am.

Thor, 32 cours Saleya. Svelte blonde bartenders pour pints for a youthful crowd in this raucous Scandinavian pub. Daily live music starting at 10pm. Happy Hour 6-9pm (pints €4). Open daily 6pm-2am.

Le Bar Des Deux Frères, 1 r. du Moulin. A young crowd tosses back tequila (€3.10) and beer (€5) amid red curtains and smoky tables at this local favorite. Open Th-Sa 6pm-3:30am, Su-M 10pm-2:30am.

L'Havane, 32 r. de France. This hip Latin bar caters to a mainly local mid-20s crowd and features live salsa bands nightly. Open daily 5pm-2:30am.

De Klomp, 6 r. Mascoinat. 40 types of whiskey (from €6.50) and 18 beers on tap (pints €7). A variety of live music every night. Happy Hour 5:30-9:30pm. Open M-Sa 5:30pm-2:30am, Su 8:30pm-2:30am.

Williams, 4 r. Centrale. When other bars close up, Williams keeps the kegs flowing. Karaoke nights M-Th. Live music F-Sa. Open 9pm-7am.

Wayne's, 15 r. de la Préfecture. The common denominators for this wild, crowded bar: young and on the prowl. Open noon-1am.

CLUBS

▨ **Saramanga,** 45-47 promenade des Anglais. A tropical theme reigns in Nice's hottest club, replete with exotic drinks, Hawaiian shirts, and fire-juggling showgirls. Cover €15. Open F-Sa 11pm-5am.

La Suite, 2 r. Brea. This *petite boite* attracts a funky, well-dressed, moneyed crowd. Cover €13. Open T-Su 11pm-2:30am.

Blue Boy, 9 r. Jean-Baptiste Spinetta, in west Nice. Though far from town, Blue Boy's foam parties make it Nice's most popular gay club. Sa cover €9. Foam parties on W, June-Sept. Open daily 11pm-6am.

Le Klub, 6 r. Halévy. Popular gay club caters to well-tanned crowd. Cover €11. Open T-Su 11:30pm-6am.

DAYTRIPS FROM NICE

THE CORNICHES

Rocky shores, pebble beaches, and luxurious villas glow along the Corniches, between hectic Nice and high-rolling Monaco. More relaxing than their glamorous neighbors, these tiny towns have interesting museums, ancient finds, and breathtaking countryside. The train offers a glimpse of the coast up close, while bus rides on the high roads allow bird's-eye views of the steep cliffs and crashing sea below.

VILLEFRANCHE-SUR-MER. The town's narrow streets and pastel houses have enchanted Aldous Huxley, Katherine Mansfield, and many other artists. Strolling from the train station along quai Ponchardier, a sign to the *vieille ville* points to the spooky 13th-century **rue Obscure,** the oldest street in Villefranche. At the end is the **Chapelle St-Pierre,** decorated by Jean Cocteau, former resident, filmmaker, and jack-of-all-arts. (☎ 04 93 76 90 70. Call ahead for hours. €2.) **Trains** run from Nice. (7min., every hr., €1.30.) To get to the **tourist office** from the train station, exit on quai 1, head inland on av. G. Clemenceau, and continue straight when it becomes av. Sadi Carnot; it will be at the end of the street. (☎ 04 93 01 73 68. Open July-Aug. daily 9am-7pm; Sept.-June reduced hours.)

ST-JEAN-CAP-FERRAT. A lovely town with an even lovelier beach, St-Jean-Cap-Ferrat is the trump card of the Riviera. The **Fondation Ephrussi di Rothschild,** just off av. D. Semeria, is a stunning Italian villa that houses the collections of the Baroness de Rothschild, including Monet canvases, Gobelins tapestries, and Chinese vases. The seven lush gardens reflect different parts of the world. (Open July-Aug. daily 10am-7pm; Sept.-Nov. 1 and Feb. 15-June 10am-6pm; Nov. 2-Feb. 14 M-F 2-6pm, Sa-Su 10am-6pm. €8, students €6.) The town's beautiful **beaches** have earned the area the nickname *"presqu'île des rêves"* (peninsula of dreams). The tiny **tourist office,** 59 av. Denis Séméria, is half-way along the winding street that runs from Nice and Monaco to the port. (☎ 04 93 76 08 90; fax 04 93 76 16 67. Open July-Aug. M-Sa 8:30am-6:30pm; Sept.-June reduced hours.) Two buses per day run from Nice via Villefrance-sur-Mer (9:10 am and 12:15 pm, €1.60).

EZE. Three-tiered Eze owes its fame to the pristine medieval town in the middle tier. It features the **Porte des Maures,** which served as a portal for a surprise attack by the Moors, and the **Église Paroissial,** containing sleek Phonecian crosses mixed with Catholic gilt. (Open daily 9am-7pm.) The best views are 40min. up the **Sentier Friedrich Nietzsche,** a windy trail where its namesake found inspiration; the path begins in Eze Bord-du-Mer, 100m east of the train station and tourist office, and ends near the base of the medieval city, by the **Fragonard parfumerie.** Frequent **trains** run from Nice (15min., every hr., €2).

MONACO AND MONTE-CARLO

Monaco (pop. 7,200) has money—lots of it—invested in ubiquitous surveillance cameras, high-speed luxury cars, and sleek yachts. At Monaco's spiritual heart is its famous casino in Monte-Carlo, a magnet for the wealthy and dissolute since 1885. The sheer spectacle of it all is worth a daytrip from Nice.

CALLING TO AND FROM MONACO	Monaco's country code is 377. To call Monaco from France, dial 00377, then the 8-digit Monaco number. To call France from Monaco, dial 0033, and drop the first zero of the French number.

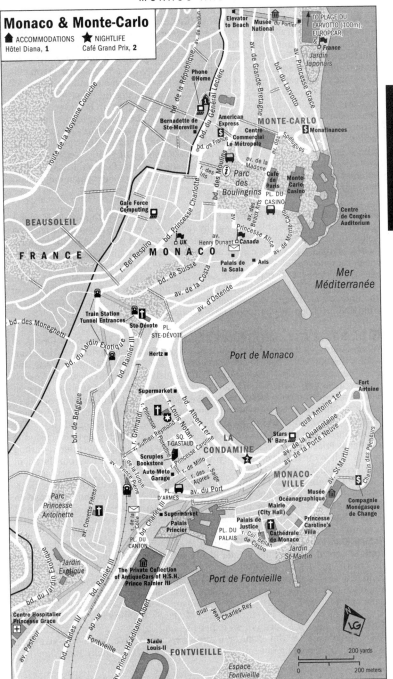

Monaco & Monte-Carlo

🏠 ACCOMMODATIONS   ⭐ NIGHTLIFE
Hôtel Diana, 1   Café Grand Prix, 2

FRANCE

TO PLAGE DU LARVOTTO (100m), EUROPCAR, & P France
Jardin Japonais

Elevator to Beach
Musée National
Musée du Portier

Phone @Home

av. de Verdun
av. de la République
bd. du Général Leclerc
av. de Grande-Bretagne
bd. du Larvotto
av. Princesse Grace

American Express
Bernadette de Ste-Moreville
MONTE-CARLO
Centre Commercial Le Métropole
$ Monafinances
bd. ore France
av. des Spélugues

r. des Iris
r. des Moulins
av. de la Madone
Parc des Boulingrins
Café de Paris
Monte-Carlo Casino
PL. DU CASINO

Gale Force Computing

BEAUSOLEIL

route de la Moyenne Corniche
bd. Princesse Charlotte
av. des Beaux Arts
Centre de Congrès Auditorium

FRANCE
MONACO
UK
av. Henry Dunant Canada
Princesse Alice
Palais de la Scala Avis

bd. de Suisse
av. de la Costa
av. d'Ostende
av. de Monte-Carlo

Mer Méditerranée

bd. des Moneghetti
bd. du Jardin Exotique
bd. de Belgique

Train Station Tunnel Entrances
Ste-Dévote
PL. STE-DÉVOTE
Hertz

bd. Rainier III

Port de Monaco

Fort Antoine

Supermarket
bd. Albert 1er
Louis Notari
Stars N' Bars
quai Antoine 1er
av. de la Quarantaine
av. de la Porte Neuve

r. Grimaldi
r. Suffren Reymond
r. Princesse Caroline
SQ. T-GASTAUD
LA CONDAMINE

Scruples Bookstore
Auto-Moto Garage
r. de Millo
r. des Açores
av. du Port
PL. D'ARMES

MONACO-VILLE
av. St-Martin

Parc Princesse Antoinette
av. Crovetto Frères
av. de la Turbie
av. Prince Pierre

r. de la Colle
bd. Charles III
Supermarket
Palais Princier
PL. DU CANTON

Musée Océanographique
Mairie (City Hall)
Palais de Justice
r. Col. Bellan
de castro
PL. DU PALAIS
Cathédrale de Monaco
Princesse Caroline's Villa
Compagnie Monégasque de Change
$

Jardin St-Martin

Jardin Exotique
bd. du Jardin Exotique
The Private Collection of AntiqueCars of H.S.H. Prince Rainier III

Centre Hospitalier Princesse Grace
bd. Rainier III
av. Pasteur
bd. Charles III

Port de Fontvieille

Stade Louis-II
FONTVIEILLE
av. Prince Héréditaire Albert
Fontvieille
quai Jean-Charles-Rey

Espace Fontvieille

0   200 yards
0   200 meters

FRANCE

■ ⁊ TRANSPORTATION AND PRACTICAL INFORMATION. Trains run to: Antibes (1hr., every 30min., €7); Cannes (65min., every 30min., €7); and Nice (25min., every 30min., €3). **Buses** (☎93 85 61 81) leave av Princesse Alice, near the tourist office, for Nice (45min., every 15min., €3.70). Follow the signs in the new train station for Le Rocher and Fontvieille to the **avenue Prince Pierre** exit; it's close to **La Condamine** quarter, Monaco's port, which has a morning market and cafes. To the right of La Condamine rises the *vieille ville*, **Monaco-Ville.** Leaving the train station onto bd. Princess Charlotte or pl. St-Devote leads to **Monte-Carlo** and the casino. **Bus #4** links the train station to the casino in Monte-Carlo; buy tickets on board. (€1.40, €3.30 for a *carte* of 4). At the **tourist office,** 2a bd. des Moulins, a friendly, English-speaking staff provides city plans, an events guide, and hotel reservations free of charge. (☎92 16 61 16; www.monaco-congres.com. Open M-Sa 9am-7pm, Su 10am-noon.) Access the **Internet** at **Stars 'N' Bars,** 6 quai Antoine 1er. (€5 per 30min. Open daily 10am-midnight.) **Postal Code:** 06500.

■ ◨ ACCOMMODATIONS AND FOOD. There's no need to stay in Monaco, since it is easily accessible from nearby (and less expensive) coastal towns. **Beausoleil,** in France, has several reasonable options and is a 5min. walk from the beach or 10min. from the casino. **Hôtel Diana ❸,** 17 bd. du Général Leclerc, has clean rooms. (☎04 93 78 47 58; www.monte-carlo.mc/hotel-diana-beausoleil. Singles €32; doubles €55; triples €63. Amex/MC/V.) Not surprisingly, Monaco has little budget fare. Fill a picnic basket at the fruit and flower **market** on pl. d'Armes at the end of av. Prince Pierre (open daily 6am-1pm), or atthe huge **Carrefour** in Fontvieille's shopping plaza (☎92 05 57 00; open M-Sa 8:30am-10pm).

◙ ◪ SIGHTS AND ENTERTAINMENT. The extravagant **Monte-Carlo Casino,** at pl. de Casino, is where Richard Burton wooed Elizabeth Taylor and Mata Hari shot a Russian spy. The slot machines open at 2pm, while blackjack, craps, and roulette open at noon (cover €10). The exclusive *salons privés,* where such French games as *chemin de fer* and *trente et quarante* begin at noon, will cost you an extra €10 cover. Next door, the more relaxed **Café de Paris** opens at 10am and has no cover. All casinos have **dress codes** (no shorts, sneakers, sandals, or jeans), and the *salons privés* require coat and tie. Guards are strict about the **21 age minimum;** bring a passport as proof. High above the casino is the **Palais Princier,** the occasional home of Prince Rainier and his tabloid-darling family. When the flag is down, the prince is away and visitors can tour the small but lavish palace, which includes Princess Grace's official state portrait and the chamber where England's King George III died. (☎93 25 18 31. Open June-Sept. 9:30am-6:20pm; Oct. 10am-5pm. €6, students €3.) Next door, the **Cathédrale de Monaco,** at pl. St-Martin, is the burial site of the Grimaldi family and the site of Prince Rainer and Princess Grace's 1956 wedding; Princess Grace lies behind the altar in a tomb marked simply with her Latinized name, "Patritia Gracia." (Open Mar.-Oct. daily 7am-7pm; Nov.-Feb. 7am-6pm.) The **Private Collection of Antique Cars of H.S.H. Prince Rainier III,** on les Terraces de Fontvielle, showcases 105 of the most glamorous cars ever made. (☎92 05 28 56. Open daily 10am-6pm. €6, students and ages 8-14 €3.) The **Musée Océanographique** on av. St-Martin, once directed by Jacques Cousteau, holds the most exotic and bizarre oceanic species. (☎93 15 36 00; www.oceano.mc. Open Apr.-Sept. daily 9am-7pm; Oct.-Mar. 10am-6pm. €11, students €6.) Monaco's nightlife has two centers. **La Condamine,** near the port, is less expensive and caters to a younger clientele. Bars and clubs near the casino are more expensive. **Café Grand Prix,** at 1 quai Antoine 1er, serves up live music to a mixed crowd. (Open daily 10am-5am.)

CORSICA (LA CORSE)

The colorful island of Corsica has a colorful history—having been controlled by Phoenicia, Rome, Carthage, Pisa, and Genoa before becoming part of France. Ever since Corsicans have been divided over the issue of allegiance to France—among those who side with the French was officer Carlo-Maria Buonaparte, father to the island's favorite son, Napoleon. Today a substantial faction still seeks greater autonomy. Many are reluctant, however, as Corsica's economy is highly dependent on France; tourists flock there for summer sun and winter skiing.

⌐ TRANSPORTATION

Air France and its subsidiary Compagnie Corse Méditerranée (CCM) fly to Bastia and Ajaccio from Paris (round-trip from €170, students €140); Nice (€120, students €98); and Marseille (€128, students €104). In Ajaccio, the Air France/CCM office is at 3 bd. du Roi Jérôme (☎08 20 82 08 20). **Ferry** travel between the mainland and Corsica can be a rough trip. High-speed ferries (3½hr.) run between Nice and Corsica. Overnight ferries from Marseille take upwards of 10 hours. The **Société National Maritime Corse Méditerranée** (☎08 91 70 18 01; www.sncm.fr) sends ferries from Marseille (€35-53, under-25 €20-40) and Nice (€30-41, under 25 €15-26) to Bastia and Ajaccio. In summer, nine boats cross between Corsica and the mainland each day, and only three out of season. SNCM schedules and fees are available at travel agencies and ports. **Corsica Ferries** (☎08 25 09 50 95; www.corsicaferries.com) has similar destinations and prices and also crosses from Livorno and Savona in Italy to Bastia (€16-33). **SAREMAR** (☎04 95 73 00 96) and **Moby Lines** (☎04 95 73 00 29) run from Santa Teresa in Sardinia to Bonifacio. (€6.80-15 per person.) **Train** service in Corsica is slow, limited to the half of the island north of Ajaccio, and doesn't accept rail passes. **Buses** provide more comprehensive service; call **Eurocorse Voyages** (☎04 95 21 06 30) for more info.

☒ HIKING

Hiking is the best way to explore the island's mountainous interior. The **GR20** is an extremely difficult 14- to 15-day 200km trail that crosses the island. The popular **Mare e Monti** (10 days) and **Da Mare a Mare Sud** (4-6 days) trails are shorter and less challenging. The **Parc Naturel Régional de la Corse**, 2 Sargent Casalonga, in Ajaccio (☎04 95 51 79 10), publishes maps and a guide to *gîtes d'étapes* (rural lodgings).

AJACCIO (AIACCIU)

One of the few Corsican towns with true urban energy, Ajaccio (pop. 60,000) has excellent museums and nightlife to compliment its palm trees and yellow sunlit buildings. Inside the ▓**Musée Fesch**, 50-52 r. Cardinal Fesch, you'll find an impressive collection of 14th- to 19th-century Italian paintings gathered by Napoleon's uncle Fesch, a merchant during the Revolution who later turned to the cloth and spent his worldly wealth acquiring artistic treasures. Also within the complex is the **Chapelle Impériale**, the final resting place of most of the Bonaparte family—though Napoleon himself is buried in a modest tomb in Paris. (Open July-Aug. M 1:30-6pm, Tu-Th 9am-6:30pm, F 9am-6:30pm and 9pm-midnight, Sa-Su 10:30am-6pm; Sept.-June reduced hours. Museum €5.40, students €3.80; chapel €1.50/0.75.) Napoleon's first home, the **Musée National de la Maison Bonaparte**, r. St-Charles, between r. Bonaparte and r. Roi-de-Rome, is now a warehouse of memorabilia. (Open Apr.-Sept. M 2-6pm, Tu-Su 9am-noon and 2-6pm; Oct.-Mar. M 2-4:45pm, Tu-Su 10am-noon and 2-4:45pm. €4, ages 18-25 €2.60. Under-18 free.) Several lively bars crowd around **boulevard Pascal Rossini**.

FRANCE

Trains (☎04 95 23 11 03) leave pl. de la Gare, for Bastia (4hr., 4 per day, €24) and Corte (2hr., 2 per day, €13). The **tourist office** is at 3 bd. du Roi Jérôme. (☎04 95 51 53 03; www.tourisme.fr/ajaccio. Open July-Aug. M-Sa 8am-8:30pm, Su 9am-1pm and 4-7pm; Sept.-June reduced hours.) The serene and centrally located ■Hôtel **Kallisté** ❹ is at 51 cours Napoléon. (☎04 95 51 34 45; www.cyrnos.com. Singles in Aug. €56; doubles €69; triples €89. Reduced prices off-season. AmEx/MC/V.) To camp at **Les Mimosas ❶**, take bus #4 from cours Napoléon to *Brasilia* and walk straight to the roundabout, take a left on chemin de la Carrossacia and follow the signs. (☎04 95 52 01 17. Electricity €2.80. July-Aug. €4.80 per person, €2 per tent or car. Prices 10% lower Apr.-June and Sept. to mid-Oct.) Pizzerias, bakeries, and one-stop *panini* shops can be found on **rue Cardinal Fesch**; at night, patios on the festive quai offer affordable seafood and pizza. Get groceries at **Monoprix**, 31 cours Napoléon. (Open M-Sa 8am-7:15pm.) **Postal Code: 20000.**

BONIFACIO (BONIFAZIU)

The fortified city of Bonifacio (pop. 3,000) rises like a majestic sand castle atop jagged limestone cliffs; **Marina Croisières** offers **boat tours** of the hidden coves and grottoes. (☎04 95 73 09 77. €11-21.) All the companies by the port run frequent ferries (30min.) to the pristine sands of **Îles Levezzi**, a nature reserve with beautiful reefs perfect for **scuba diving.** To explore the *haute ville*, head up the steep montée Rastello, the wide staircase halfway down the port, where excellent views of the ridged cliffs to the east await. Continue up montée St-Roch to the lookout at **Porte des Gênes**, a drawbridge built by invaders. Then walk to the **place du Marche** to see Bonifacio's famous cliffs and the **Grain de Sable.**

Eurocorse Voyages (☎04 95 21 06 30) runs **buses** to Ajaccio (3½hr., 2-3 per day, €21) as well as Porto Vecchio (30min., 1-4 per day, €6.50), where connections can be made to Bastia. To reach the **tourist office,** at the corner of av. de Gaulle and r. F. Scamaroni, walk along the port and then up the stairs before the *gare maritime*. (☎04 95 73 11 88; www.bonifacio.com. Open May to mid-Oct. daily 9am-8pm; mid-Dec. to Apr. M-F 9am-noon and 2-6pm, Sa 9am-noon.) Finding affordable rooms is difficult in summer; avoid visiting in August, when prices soar. Try **Hôtel des Étrangers ❹**, av. Sylvère Bohn. (☎04 95 73 01 09; fax 04 95 73 16 97. Singles and doubles €50-72; triples €72; quads €82. MC/V.) **Camp** at **L'Araguina,** av. Sylvère Bohn, at the entrance to town between Hôtel des Etrangers and the port. (☎04 95 73 02 96; fax 04 95 73 57 04. Open mid-Mar. to Oct. Electricity €2.80. Laundry €5. €5.30-5.60 per person, €1.90 per car or tent.) **Postal Code:** 20169.

BASTIA

Bastia (pop. 40,000), Corsica's second largest city, constantly bustles with the arrival and departure of ferries from the mainland and Italy. More than just a stop mid-transit, Bastia has some lovely sights of its own in addition to being the perfect gateway to the must-see Cap Corse. The 14th-century **Citadel,** also called Terra Nova, has beautiful views of the sea. The **Oratoire de St-Roch,** on r. Napoleon, is a jewel-box of a church with crystal chandeliers and meticulous *trompe l'oeil* decoration. The neoclassical towers of the **Église St-Jean Baptiste,** pl. de l'Hôtel de Ville, cover an immense interior with gilded domes. **Shuttle buses** leave pl. de la Gare for the **Bastia-Poretta Airport** (30min., €8). **Trains** (☎04 95 32 80 61) also leave pl. de la Gare for Ajaccio (4hr., 4 per day, €24) and Calvi (3hr., 2 per day, €18). Eurocorse **buses** (☎04 95 21 06 30) leave r. Nouveau Port for Ajaccio (3hr., 2 per day, €17). The **tourist office,** pl. St-Nicholas, has indispensible copies of the bus schedule. (☎04 95 54 20 40; fax 04 95 31 81 34. Open daily 8am-noon and 2-6pm.) The **Hôtel Central ❷**, 3 r. Miot, has large, well-kept rooms. (☎04 95 31 71 12; fax 04 95 31 82 40. Breakfast €5.50. Singles €35-50; doubles €40-80. AmEx/MC/V.) To reach **Les**

Orangiers camping ❶, take bus #4 from the tourist office to *Licciola-Miomo.* (☎04 95 33 24 09. Open May to mid-Oct. Electricity €3.50. €4.50 per person, €2.50 per tent, €5 per car.) Inexpensive cafes crowd **place St-Nicolas.**

⚑ DAYTRIP FROM BASTIA: CAP CORSE. North of Bastia stretches the gorgeous Cap Corse peninsula, a necklace of tiny former fishing villages strung together by a narrow road of perilous curves and breathtaking views. The Cap is a dream for **hikers;** every forest and cliff lays claim to some decaying Genoese tower or hilltop chapel. If you don't have access to or funds for a car, the cheapest and most convenient way to see Cap Corse is to take **bus** #4 from pl. St-Nicolas in Bastia, which goes to: Erbalunga (20min., €2); Macinaggio (50min., €6.40); and Marina di Siscu (30min., €2.30). Ask politely and the driver will drop you off wherever you feel the urge to explore. However, most buses serve only the coast; you'll have to hike or hitchhike to the inland villages. While *Let's Go* wholeheartedly endorses hiking, it does not recommend hitchhiking.

CORTE

The most dynamic of Corsica's inland towns, Corte combines breathtaking natural scenery with a boisterous collegiate spirit. Sheer cliffs, snow-capped peaks, and breathtaking gorges create a dramatic backdrop for the island's only university, whose students keep prices surprisingly low. The town's *vieille ville,* with its steep streets and stone **citadel,** has always been a bastion of patriotism. At the top of r. Scolisca is the engaging **La Musée de la Corse,** which also provides entrance to the higher fortifications of the citadel. (Open June-Sept. daily 10am-8pm; Nov.-May reduced hours. Museum and citadel €3-5.30, students €2.30-3.) Corte's mountains and valleys feature numerous spectacular trails. Choose from **hiking** (weather ☎08 92 68 02 20), **biking,** and **horseback riding.** Rent **horses** at **Ferme Equestre Albadu,** 1.5km from town on N193. (☎04 95 46 24 55. €14 per hr., €69 per day.)

Trains (☎04 95 46 00 97) leave from the rotary, where av. Jean Nicoli and N193 meet, for: Ajaccio (2hr., 4 per day, €13) and Bastia (1½hr., 4 per day, €11). Eurocorse Voyages runs **buses** to Ajaccio (1¾hr., M-Sa 2 per day, €12) and Bastia (1¼hr., M-Sa 2 per day, €10). To reach the *centre ville* from the train station, turn right on D14 (av. Jean Nicoli), cross two bridges, and follow the road until it ends at **cours Paoli,** Corte's main drag. A left turn leads to **place Paoli,** the town center; at the *place*'s top right corner, climb the stairs of r. Scolisca to reach the citadel and the **tourist office,** which has hiking maps and info. (☎04 95 46 26 70; www.corte-tourisme.com. Open July-Aug. daily 9am-8pm; May-June and Sept. M-Sa 9am-noon and 2-6pm; Oct.-May M-F 9am-noon and 2-6pm.) The youthful **Hôtel-Residence Porette ❷,** 6 allée du 9 Septembre, offers functional and clean rooms and a nice garden. Bear left from the train station to the stadium and follow it around for another 100m. (☎04 95 45 11 11; fax 04 95 61 02 85. Breakfast €5. Singles €21, with bath €29; doubles €29/39; triples €54.) **Place Paoli** is the spot to find sandwiches and pizza, while **rue Scolisca** and the surrounding citadel streets abound with inexpensive local cuisine. The huge **Casino supermarket** is near the train station, on allée du 9 Septembre. (Open mid-June to Aug. daily 8:30am-7:45pm; Sept. to mid-June M-F 8:30am-12:30pm and 3-7:30pm, Sa 8:30am-7:30pm.) **Postal Code:** 20250.

THE ALPS (LES ALPES)

Nature's architecture is the real attraction of the Alps. The curves of the Chartreuse Valley rise to rugged crags in the Vercors range and ultimately crescendo at Europe's highest peak, Mont Blanc. Winter skiers enjoy some of the world's most challenging slopes. In the summer, hikers take over the mountains for endless vistas and clear air. Skiing arrangements should be made well in advance; Chamonix and Val d'Isère are the easiest bases. TGV trains whisk you from Paris to Grenoble or Annecy; scenic trains and slower buses service Alpine towns from there. The farther into the mountains you want to go, the harder it is to get there, although service is more frequent during ski season (Dec.-Apr.).

GRENOBLE

Grenoble (pop. 156,000) has the eccentric cafes and shaggy radicals of any university town, but also boasts snow-capped peaks and sapphire-blue lakes cherished by athletes and aesthetes alike.

TRANSPORTATION AND PRACTICAL INFORMATION. Trains leave pl. de la Gare for: Annecy (2hr., 18 per day, €14); Lyon (1½hr., 27 per day, €16); Marseilles (2½-4½hr., 15 per day, €33); Nice (5-6½hr., 5 per day, €48); and Paris (3hr., 6 per day, €59-74). **Buses** leave from the left of the station for Geneva, Switzerland (3hr., daily, €26). From the station, turn right into pl. de la Gare, take the third left on av. Alsace-Lorraine, and follow the tram tracks on r. Félix Poulat and r. Blanchard to reach the **tourist office,** 14 r. de la République. (☎04 76 42 41 41; www.grenoble-isere.info. Open M-Sa 9am-6:30pm, Su 10am-1pm and 2-5pm.) **E-toile** has **Internet** access. (☎04 76 00 13 60. €3.50 per hr. Open M-F 10am-11pm, Sa-Su 10am-midnight.) **Postal Code:** 38000.

ACCOMMODATIONS AND FOOD. From the tourist office, follow pl. Ste-Claire to pl. Notre-Dame and take r. du Vieux Temple on the far right to reach **Le Foyer de l'Etudiante ❶,** 4 r. Ste-Ursule, a stately building with large rooms that serves as a dorm during most of the year, but opens to travellers during July and August. (☎04 76 42 00 84; www.multimania.com/foyeretudiante. Sheets €8. Laundry €2.20. Free Internet access. July-Aug. three-night min. for room; five-night max. for dorm. Dorms €8; singles €14; doubles €22.) **Hôtel de la Poste ❷,** 25 r. de la Poste, near the pedestrian zone, has amazing rooms. (☎/fax 04 76 46 67 25. Singles €22-26; doubles €28; triples €32; quads €37. MC/V.) To reach **Camping Les 3 Pucelles ❶,** 58 r. des Allobroges in Seyssins, take hard tram A (dir.: Fontaine-La Poya) to *Louis Maisonnat,* then take bus #51 (dir.: Les Nalettes) to *Mas des Iles;* it's on the left. (☎04 76 96 45 73; fax 04 76 21 43 73. One person, tent, and car €7.50; extra person €2.80.) Grenoble has many affordable restaurants, some with student discounts. Regional restaurants cater to locals around **place de Gordes,** while Asian eateries abound between pl. Notre-Dame and the river and along **rue Condorcet.** *Pâtisseries* and North African joints congregate around **rue Chenoise** and **rue Lionne,** between the pedestrian area and the river. Cafes and restaurants cluster around **place Notre-Dame** and **place St-André,** in the heart of the *vieille ville.* **Monoprix supermarket** is opposite the tourist office. (Open M-Sa 8:30am-7:30pm.)

SIGHTS AND THE OUTDOORS. *Téléphériques* (cable cars) depart from quai Stéphane-Jay every 10min. for the 16th-century **Bastille,** a fort that hovers above town. Enjoy the views from the top, then descend via the **Parc Guy Pape,** which crisscrosses through the fortress and deposits you just across the river from the train station. (Open July-Aug. M 11am-12:15am; Tu-Su 9:15am-12:15am; Sept.-June reduced hours. One-way €3.80, round-trip €5.50; students €3/4.40.) Cross the Pont St-Laurent and go up Montée Chalemont for the **Musée Dauphinois,** 30 r. Maurice Gignoux, with its futuristic exhibits on the people of the Alps and the history of skiing. (Open June-Sept. M and W-Su 10am-7pm; Oct.-May 10am-6pm.

€3.20. Under-25 free.) The **Musée de Grenoble,** 5 pl. de Lavelette, has one of France's most prestigious collections of art. (Open July-Sept. M, Th-Su 10am-6pm, W 10am-9pm; Oct.-June M and Th-Su 11am-7pm, W 11am-10pm. €4, students €2.) Grenoble's proximity to the slopes is another attractive aspect of the city. The biggest and most developed **ski areas** are to the east in **Oisans;** the **Alpe d'Huez** boasts 220km of trails. (Tourist office ☎04 76 11 44 44. €33 per day, €171 per week.) The **Belledonne** region, northeast of Grenoble, has lower elevation and prices. **Chamrousse** is the biggest and most popular ski area (lift tickets €23 per day, €79-113 per week). Only 30min. from Grenoble by **bus** (€8.70), the resort also makes for a hiker's ideal daytrip in summer. Grenoble boasts plenty of funky cafes, bars and clubs; most are in the area between **place St-André** and **place Notre-Dame.**

CHAMONIX

The site of the first winter Olympics in 1924, Chamonix (pop. 10,000) is the ultimate ski town, with soaring mountains and the toughest slopes in the world. The town itself combines the dignity of Mont Blanc, Europe's highest peak (4807m), with the exuberant spirit of energetic travelers.

🖿🚻 TRANSPORTATION AND PRACTICAL INFORMATION. Trains leave av. de la Gare (☎04 50 53 12 98) for: Annecy (2½hr., 7 per day, €17); Geneva, Switzerland (2½hr., 7 per day, €21); Lyon (4hr., 6 per day, €30); and Paris (6½hr., 9 per day, €50-70). Société Alpes Transports **buses** (☎04 50 53 01 15) leave the train station for Annecy (2¼hr., daily, €15) and Geneva, Switzerland (1½hr., 2 per day, €29-32). **Local buses** (€1.50) connect to ski slopes and hiking trails. From the station, follow av. Michel Croz, turn left on r. du Dr. Paccard, and take the first right to reach pl. de l'Église and the **tourist office,** 85 pl. du Triangle de l'Amitié. (☎04 50 53 00 24; www.chamonix.com. Open July-Aug. daily 8:30am-7:30pm; Sept.-June reduced hours.) **Compagnie des Guides,** in Maison de la Montagne facing the tourist office-leads ski trips and hikes. (☎04 50 53 00 88; www.cieguides-chamonix.com. Open Jan.-Mar. and July-Aug. daily 8:30am-noon and 3:30-7:30pm; Sept.-Dec. and Apr.-June reduced hours.) Access the **Internet** at **Cybar,** 80 r. des Moulins. (☎04 50 53 69 70. €1 per 10min. Open daily 11am-1:30am.) **Postal Code:** 74400.

🖿🅲 ACCOMMODATIONS AND FOOD. Chamonix's *gîtes* (mountain hostels) and dorms are cheap, but they fill up fast; call ahead. From the train station, walk down av. Michel Croz and take a right onto r. Joseph Vallot for the ▨**Red Mountain Lodge ❷,** 435 r. Joseph Vallot. The fun-loving, English-speaking staff keeps guests happy with plush furnishings, views of Mont Blanc, and frequent barbeques for €12. (☎04 50 53 94 97; fax 04 50 53 82 64. Reception 8am-noon and 5-7pm. Dorms €16; doubles €40, with bath €50; triples €60/75.) **Gite le Vagabond ❶,** 365 av. Ravanel le Rouge, near the town center, has a friendly atmosphere and a climbing wall. (☎04 50 53 15 43; gitevagabond@hotmail.com. Breakfast €5. Laundry €7.70. Internet €0.15 per min. Reception 8-10:30am. 4- to 8-bunk dorms €13. Credit card deposit. MC/V.) Turn left from the base of the Aiguille du Midi *téléphérique,* continue past the main roundabout, and look right to **camp** at **L'Ile des Barrats ❶,** on rte. des Pélerins. (☎/fax 04 50 53 51 44. Reception July-Aug. daily 8am-10pm; May-June and Sept. 9am-noon and 4-7pm. Open Feb. to mid-Oct. Electricity €2.80. €5 per person, €4.60 per tent, €2 per car.) Restaurants in Chamonix cluster around the town center. **Rue du Docteur Paccard** is a good bet, as is **rue des Moulins,** which also boasts Chamonix's most popular nightclubs and bars. Get groceries at **Super U,** 117 r. Joseph Vallot. (Open M-Sa 8:15am-7:30pm, Su 8:30am-noon.)

⚑⚐ HIKING AND SKIING. Whether you've come to climb up the mountains or ski down them, you're in for a challenge. Wherever you go, be cautious—the mountains here are as wild and steep as they are beautiful. The **Aiguille du Midi** *téléphérique* (cable car) offers a pricey, knuckle-whitening ascent over forests and snowy cliffs to a needlepoint peak at the top, revealing a fantastic panorama from 3842m. (☎04 50 53 40 00. €34.) Bring your passport to continue by gondola to **Helbronner, Italy** for views of three countries and the **Matterhorn** and **Mont Blanc** peaks; pack a picnic to eat on the glacier (May-Sept., round-trip €18). Chamonix has 350km of **hiking;** the tourist office has a map with departure points and estimated length for all trails, some of which are accessible by cable car, which can save time and energy. Hikes generally either head into the north, facing mountains with their jagged peaks and snow fields, or to the south, with wildflowers, blue lakes, and views of Mt. Blanc. Sunken in a valley, Chamonix is surrounded by mountains ideal for skiing. To the south, **Le Tour-Col de Balme,** above the village of **Le Tour,** is ideal for beginner and intermediate skiers (☎04 50 54 00 58. Day pass €25.) On the northern side of the valley, **Les Grands Montets** is the *grande dame* of Chamonix skiing, with advanced terrain and remodeled **snowboarding** facilities. (☎04 50 53 13 18. Day pass €32.)

ANNECY

With narrow cobblestone streets, winding canals, and a turreted castle, Annecy (pop. 50,000) appears more like a fairy-tale fabrication than a modern city. The **Palais de l'Isle,** located in the beautiful *vielle ville,* is a 13th-century chateau that served as a prison for Resistance fighters during World War II. (Open June-Sept. daily 10am-6pm; Oct.-May M and W-Su 10am-noon and 2-5pm. €3.10, students €0.80.) The shaded **Jardins de l'Europe** are the town's pride and joy. Although it may be hard to tear yourself away from the charming city, Annecy's Alpine forests boast excellent **hiking** and **biking trails,** and its clear, crystalline **lake** is a popular spot for windsurfing and kayaking, particularly along the free **plage d'Albigny.** One of the best hikes begins at the **Basilique de la Visitation,** near the hostel. An exquisite 16km scenic *piste cyclable* (bike route) hugs the lake along the eastern coast.

   Trains arrive at pl. de la Gare from: Chamonix (2½hr., 7 per day, €17); Grenoble (2hr., 12 per day, €15); Lyon (2hr., 9 per day, €18); Nice (7hr., 2 per day, €55); and Paris (4hr., 8 per day, €58-73). Autocars Frossard **buses** (☎04 50 45 73 90) leave from next to the station for Geneva, Switzerland. (1¼hr., 6 per day, €9) and Lyon (3½hr., 2 per day, €17). From the train station, take the underground passage to r. Vaugelas, go left and continue for four blocks, and enter the Bonlieu shopping mall to reach the **tourist office,** 1 r. Jean Jaurès, in pl. de la Libération. (☎04 50 45 00 33; www.lac-annecy.com. Open July-Aug. M-Sa 9am-6:30pm, Su 9am-12:30pm and 1:45-6:30pm; Sept.-June daily 9am-12:30pm and 1:45-6pm.) In summer, you can reach the clean and beautifully located ⚑**Auberge de Jeunesse "La Grande Jeanne" (HI)** ❶, on rte. de Semnoz, via the *ligne d'été* (dir.: Semnoz) from the station (€1); otherwise, take bus #1 (dir.: Marquisats) from the station to *Hôtel de Police,* turn right on av. du Tresum, and follow signs pointing to Semnoz. (☎04 50 45 33 19; fax 04 50 52 77 52. Breakfast included. Sheets €2.70. Reception daily 8am-10pm. Dorms €13. AmEx/MC/V.) Caring managers and spacious rooms await at **Hôtel Savoyard** ❷, 41 av. de Cran. From the train station, exit left, walk around the station on r. Brobigny to av. Berthollet, and turn left again on av. de Cran. (☎04 50 57 08 08. Breakfast €4. Open May-Oct. Singles and doubles €20, with bath €27-35; triples €25/31-41; quads with bath €41.) **Camping Bélvédère** ❶, 8 rte. de Semnoz, is near the youth hostel. (☎04 50 45 48 30. Open mid-Apr. to mid-Oct. €13 for 2 people, tent, and car.) **Place Ste-Claire** has morning **markets** (Su, Tu and F 8am-noon) and some of the best restaurants in the city. A **Monoprix supermarket** fills the better part of pl. de Notre-Dame. (Open M-Sa 8:30am-7:30pm.) **Postal Code:** 74000.

LYON

Laid-back Lyon (pop. 1,200,000), usually a stopping point between the north and south, elicits cries of "forget Paris" from weary backpackers. Culinary capital, former center of the silk trade and French Resistance, and ultramodern city, Lyon is friendlier than that other French metropolis. It also has a few more centuries of history, having been a major crossroads since Augustus ordered the construction of roads connecting the provincial capital of Gaul to Italy. *Vieux Lyon* recalls the city's wealthy past with ornate 16th-century townhouses. This city is also a stomping ground for world-renowned chefs and an incubator for new culinary genius. If the way to your heart is through your stomach, Lyon will have you at *bon apètit.*

▐▀ TRANSPORTATION

Flights: Aéroport Lyon-Saint-Exupéry (LYS; ☎04 72 22 72 21), 25km east of Lyon. 50 daily flights to Paris. The TGV stops at the airport, and is cheaper than flying. **Sato-buses/Navette Aéroport** (☎04 72 68 72 17) shuttle passengers to Gare de Perrache, Gare de la Part-Dieu, and subway stops Jean Mace, Grange-Blanche, and Mermoz Pinel (every 20min., €8.20). **Air France** is at 17 r. Victor Hugo, 2ème (☎04 20 82 08 20).

Trains: Trains passing through Lyon stop only at **Gare de la Part-Dieu**, bd. Marius Vivier-Merle (M: Part-Dieu), in the business district on the east bank of the Rhône. Trains terminating at Lyon also stop at **Gare de Perrache**, pl. Carnot (M: Perrache). TGV trains to Paris stop at both. **SNCF** info and reservation desk at Part-Dieu open M-F 9am-7pm, Sa 9am-6:30pm; Perrache open M-Sa 9am-7pm. To: **Dijon** (2hr., 6 per day, €21); **Geneva,** Switzerland (2hr., 13 per day, €19); **Grenoble** (1¼hr., 21 per day, €18); **Marseilles** (3hr., 17 per day, €39); **Nice** (6hr., 12 per day, €48); **Paris** (2hr., 26 TGVs per day, €54-68); and **Strasbourg** (5½hr., 9 per day, €39).

Buses: On the lowest level of the Gare de Perrache, at the train station, and at Gorge de Loup in the 9ème (☎04 72 61 72 61 for all three). Perrache station open daily 5am-12:30am. Domestic companies include **Philibert** (☎04 78 98 56 00) and **Transport Verney** (☎04 78 70 21 01), but it's almost always cheaper, faster, and simpler to take the train. **Eurolines** (☎04 72 56 95 30; fax 04 72 41 72 43) travels out of France.

Local Transportation: TCL (☎04 78 71 70 00), has info offices at both train stations and major *Métro* stops. Pocket maps are available from the tourist office or any TCL branch. Tickets are valid for all methods of mass transport, including the *Métro*, buses, funiculars, and trams. 1hr. single-fare ticket €1.40; carnet of 10 €11, students €9. The *Ticket Liberté* day pass (€3.80) allows unlimited use of all mass transit for the day. The efficient **Métro** runs 5am-midnight. **Buses** run 5am-9pm (a few until midnight).

◼▐ ORIENTATION AND PRACTICAL INFORMATION

Lyon is divided into nine **arrondissements** (districts). The 1er, 2ème, and 4ème lie on the **presqu'île** (peninsula), which juts south toward the **Saône** (to the west) and the **Rhône** (to the east) rivers. Starting in the south, the 2ème (the *centre ville*) includes the **Gare de Perrache** and **place Bellecour**. The 1er houses the nocturnal Terraux neighborhood, with its cafes and popular student-packed bars. Farther north is the 4ème and the **Croix-Rousse**. The main pedestrian roads on the *presqu'île* are **rue de la République** and **rue Victor Hugo**. West of the Saône, **Fourvière Hill** and its basilica overlook **Vieux Lyon** (5ème). East of the Rhône (3ème and 6-8ème) lies the **Part Dieu** train station (3ème) and most of the city's population.

FRANCE

FRANCE

TO MUSÉE D'ART
CONTEMPORAIN (1km)
& PARC DE LA TÊTE D'OR

TO LES HALLES
(MARKET) (100m)

r. Duguesclin

r. de Créqui

r. le Royer

r. Vendôme

Holiday
Bikes

TO
GARE DE LA PART-DIEU
(750m), CENTRE PART-DIEU
& TOUR DU CRÉDIT LYONNAIS

TO M PLACE
GUICHARD
(50m)

r. Moncey

r. Paul
Bert

r. du Maréchal de Saxe

BROTTEAUX

r. de l'Epée

PL. G. PÉRI

r. Garibaldi

r. du Lac

r. de la Part-Dieu

r. Villeroy

r. A. Collomb
Info Service ■
AIDS

TO INSTITUT LUMIÈRE (2km),
LYON ST-EXUPÉRY (9km),
■ HÔPITAL EDOUARD

COURS Gambetta

HERRIOT

r. Robert
r. Fénelon

Cours Lafayette

r. Pierre Corneille

r. Molière

PL. LE
QUINCET

r. Cuvier

r. Bugeaud

quai
du G. Sarrail

Rhône

r. Servient

r. Chaponnay

r. de Bonnel

r. Jean Larrive

r. Duviard

r. Maréchal

r. Montebello
Taxitphone ■
Communications

GUILLOTIÈRE M

PL. A.
JUTARD

r. B. Combaud

Grande r. de
la Guillotière

cours de la Liberté

quai Victor Augagneur

pont de la Guillotière

passerelle
du Collège

r. du Président Carnot

r. Claudia

r. A. Salliès

r. de la Bourse d'Argent

r. Grolée

r. Jussieu

PL. DE LA
RÉPUBLIQUE
PARC
RÉPUBLIQUE

r. Stella

r. Childebert

République

M

SOS
Médecins

quai Jean Moulin

quai Jules Courmont

r. Bellecordière

Hôpital Hôtel Dieu

UK ★

S $

US ★

M

PL. LOUIS
PRADEL

Cinéma ■
Swim 🏊

Opéra

M HÔTEL DE
VILLE

Musée St-Pierre
d'Art Contemporain

PL. DE LA
COMÉDIE

r. d'Algérie

r. de la Poulaillerie

PL. DES
CORDELIERS

CORDELIERS M

PL. DE
LA BOURSE

M

r. Palais Grillet

r. Tupin

r. Thomassin

r. Ferrandière

r. de la

passage de
l'Argue

passage de l'Hôtel
de Ville

PL. DES
JACOBINS

r. des Archers

r. Gasparin

r. Emile
Zola

r. de Savoie

r. Ch. Dullin

r. G. André

r. d'Amboise

Decitre
Bookstore

US

SNCF ■
Boutique

Col. Chambonnet

r. de la Barre

Maison des
Homosexualités ■

Le Cinéma 🎬

Hôtel
de Ville

PL. DES
TERREAUX

Musée des
Beaux-
Arts

TERREAUX

r. Ste-Catherine

r. Paul Chenavard

Maréchal
Centre

PL. D'ALBON

r. Lanterne

r. Longue

r. Mercière

r. de Brest

r. Dubois

quai St-Antoine

quai de la Pêcherie

Connectix
Café

r. G. de
Constantine

Pont
Alphonse
Juin

pont du Palais
de Justice

Palais de
Justice

Théâtre des Célestins

BELLECOUR M

Décitre

r. des
Célestins

PL. DE LA
RÉPUBLIQUE

Palais de
Justice

Cathédrale
St-Jean

r. de la Bombarde

Amphithéâtre
des Trois Gaules

r. des Tables
Claudiennes

r. Burdeau

r. des
Capucins

r. Désirée

r. Romarin

r. St-Brandan

r. de la Martinière

TO MAISON DES CANUTS (550m),
CROIX-ROUSSE AREA, & ①

M ④
TO

r. de l'Annonciade

quai St-Vincent

passerelle
St-Vincent

Saône

quai André Lassagne

quai de la Feuillée

quai Romain Rolland

PL. DU
CHANGE

r. Gadagne

Musée de
la Marionnette

r. St-Jean

PL. St-JEAN

PL.
St-JEAN ℹ

M des
Chazeaux

ROMAN LYON

Basilique
Notre-Dame
de Fourvière

Tour Métallique

Montée
du Rosaire

FOURVIÈRE F

M. Nicolas Lange

M. des Carmes

M. des Carmes

M. St-Barthélemy

r. Juiverie

r. Fr. Vernay

Gare St-Paul

PL. Fr. Vernay

M. St-Vincent

quai de Bondy

TO PARC DE LA TÊTE D'OR (1km)
& CITÉ INTERNATIONALE (1.5km)

FRANCE

Lyon

Rhône

quai Claude Bernard

r. d'Aguesseau
r. de Bonald
r. Montesquieu
r. de l'Université
r. Salomon Reinach
University
r. Chevreul
r. Pasteur
r. de Marseille
r. Bécherellin
r. Janqot
r. G. Du

r. Sébastien Gryphe
TO RESIDENCE LA MADELEINE
av. Berthelot
Centre d'Histoire de la Résistance et de la Déportation
r. du Professeur Grignard
r. Jaboulay
r. Reulin
r. E. Rogron
Raoul Servant
TO MAISON DE LA DANSE

pont de l'Université
pont Galliéni

quai du Dr. Gailleton

PL. BELLECOUR (i)

r. des Marroniers
PL. ANTONIN PONCET
r. de Sala
r. Ch. Biennet
r. de la Charité
r. Laurencin
Laundry
r. Mazard
r. Duhamel
cours de Verdun
r. du Béller

PRESQU'ÎLE
r. Fr. Dauphin
r. A. Comte
Air France
Musée Historique des Tissus & Musée Lyonnais des Arts Décoratifs
r. des Remparts d'Ainay
r. Victor Hugo
r. d'Auvergne
PL. AMPÈRE
AMPÈRE VICTOR HUGO
Canada
r. Henri IV
de Condé
PL. CARNOT
PERRACHE
Gare de Perrache

PL. ANTOINE VOLLAN
r. Ste-Hélène
r. Roissac
Lavadou
r. Jarente
r. Bourgelat
r. Franklin
r. d'Enghien
r. de Castries
r. G. Plessier
cours de Verdun
autoroute A7

r. du Plat
r. A. de St. Exupéry
r. Sala
r. Vaubecour
r. Guynemer
quai du M. Joffre

quai des Célestins
BIJ
quai Tilsitt
Saône
pont Kitchener Marchand
cours de Verdun

pont Bonaparte
pont St-Georges
quai Fulchiron

VIEUX LYON
F M av. A. Max
r. Tramassac
av. du Doyenné
PL. DE LA COMMANDERIE

Montée du Chemin Neuf
r. des Farges
MINIMES
F

Hôpital Antiquaille
r. de l'Antiquaille
r. Cléberg
r. R. Radisson

Musée Gallo-Romain
Théâtres Romains
Parc Archéologique

200 yards
200 meters

ACCOMMODATIONS
Auberge de Jeunesse (HI), 19
Camping Dardilly, 4
Hôtel d'Ainy, 22
Hôtel Iris, 7
Hôtel de Paris, 9
Hôtel St-Vincent, 8
Hôtel Vaubecour, 23

FOOD
L'Assiette St-Jean, 12
Chabert et Fils, 17
Chez Marie-Danielle, 21
Chez Mounier, 16
Chez Paul Bocuse, 1
L'Étoile de l'Orient, 20
Léon de Lyon, 10

Le Nord, 11
Le Sud, 18
La Tour Rose, 13

NIGHTLIFE
Ayers Rock Café, 3
Le Chantier, 5
Le Fish, 15
Le Funambule, 6
La Marquise, 14
Tavern of the Drunken Parrot, 2

(F) Funicular

Tourist Office: In the Tourist Pavilion, at pl. Bellecour, 2ème (☎04 72 77 69 69; fax 04 78 42 04 32). M: Bellecour. Indispensable *Map and Guide*, free hotel reservation office, and SNCF desk. The **Lyon City Card** authorizes unlimited public transport along with admission to 14 museums and various tours. Valid for: 1 day €15, 2 days €25, or 3 days €30. Open May-Oct. M-Sa 9am-7pm; Nov.-Apr. daily 10am-6pm.

Police: 47 r. de la Charité (☎04 78 42 26 56).

Hospital/Medical Service: Hôpital Hôtel-Dieu, 1 pl. de l'Hôpital, 2ème, near quai du Rhône, is the most central. The city hospital line (☎08 20 08 20 09) will direct you.

Internet Access: Taxiphone Communications, 15-17 r. Montebello (☎04 78 14 54 25). €3 per hr. Open daily 8:30am-10:30pm. **Connectix Café,** 19 quai St-Antoine, 2ème (☎04 72 77 98 85). €7 divisible card allows 1hr. of use. Open M-Sa 11am-7pm.

Post Office: Pl. Antonin Poncet 2 (☎04 72 40 65 22), near pl. Bellecour. Address mail to be held: SURNAME Firstname, *Poste Restante*, pl. Antonin Poncet, **69002** Lyon, FRANCE. **Postal Codes:** 69001-69009; last digit indicates *arrondissement*.

⌐ ACCOMMODATIONS

As a financial center, Lyon has fewer empty beds during the work week than on the weekends. Fall is actually the busiest season; it's easier and cheaper to find a place in the summer, but making reservations is still a good idea. Budget hotels cluster east of **place Carnot,** near Perrache. Prices rise as you approach **place Bellecour,** but there are less expensive options north of **place des Terreaux.**

▨ **Hôtel St-Vincent,** 9 r. Pareille, 1er (☎04 78 27 22 56; fax 04 78 30 92 87). Just off quai St-Vincent, north of passerelle St-Vincent. Friendly owners rent simple, elegant rooms within short distances of nightlife. Breakfast €6. Singles with shower €31; doubles €38-48; triples €50-53. MC/V. ❸

Hôtel de Paris, 16 r. de la Platière, 1er (☎04 78 28 00 95; fax 04 78 39 57 64). Bursting with color and character, with rooms ranging from the classic to the futuristic. Breakfast €6.50. Singles €42; doubles €49-75; triples €78. AmEx/MC/V. ❹

Auberge de Jeunesse (HI), 41-45 montée du Chemin Neuf (☎04 78 15 05 50). M: Vieux Lyon. Take the funicular from *Vieux Lyon* to Minimes, walk down the stairs and go left down the hill for 5min. Gorgeous views from the *terrasse* and a lively bar. Sheets €2.70. Laundry €4.50. Internet €2.25 per 15min. Dorms €13. Members only. ❶

Hôtel d'Ainay, 14 r. des Remparts d'Ainay, 2ème (☎04 78 42 43 42; fax 04 72 77 51 90). M: Ampère-Victor Hugo. Basic, sunny rooms. Breakfast €4. Shower €2.50. Reception 6am-10pm. Singles €24-27, with shower €33-38; doubles €28/34-39. MC/V. ❷

Hôtel Iris, 36 r. de l'Arbre Sec (☎04 78 39 93 80; fax 04 72 00 89 91), is a cozy spot filled with return customers thanks to the sunny breakfst room and friendly owner. Breakfast €5.50. Singles €29-40; doubles €32-50. MC/V. ❸

Hôtel Vaubecour, 28 r. Vaubecour, 2ème (☎04 78 37 44 91; fax 04 78 42 90 17). Good budget spot somewhat strangely hidden away on the 3rd floor of an antique building. Breakfast €4. Reception 7am-10pm. Singles from €23; doubles from €26; triples and quads from €55. MC/V. ❷

Grand Hôtel des Terreaux, 16 r. Lanterne, 1er (☎04 78 27 04 10; fax 04 78 27 97 75). Hot spot for a splurge, with tastefully decorated, plush chambers, huge bathrooms, and terry robes. Buffet breakfast €8.50. Singles €73-125; doubles €82-125; triples €92-136. AmEx/MC/V. ❺

Hôtel du Dauphiné, 3 r. Duhamel, 2ème (☎04 78 37 24 19; fax 04 78 92 81 52). Plain, comfortable rooms with showers. English-speaking staff. Breakfast €4.20. Check-out 11:30am. Singles €23-43; doubles €36.50-45; triples and quads €54-56. MC/V. ❷

Hôtel St-Pierre des Terreaux, 8 r. Paul Chenavard, 1er (☎04 78 28 24 61; fax 04 72 00 21 07). M: Hôtel de Ville. This cheery, often-crowded hotel is well-situated. All rooms have baths or showers. Breakfast €5.50. Reserve 10 days ahead. Singles €30-39; doubles €40-43; triples €54. MC/V. ❸

Camping Dardilly, 10km from Lyon in a suburb (☎04 78 35 64 55). From the Hôtel de Ville, take bus #19 (dir.: Ecully-Dardilly) to Parc d'Affaires. Pool, TV, and restaurant. Reception 8am-10pm. Electricity €3. €3 per person; €6 per tent; car free. MC/V. ❶

🍴 FOOD

The galaxy of Michelin stars adorning the city's restaurants confirms what the locals proudly declare—this is the gastronomic capital of the Western world. But if *haute cuisine* doesn't suit your wallet, try one of Lyon's many **bouchons**, cozy restaurants serving local cuisine for low prices. They can be found in the **Terraux** district, along **rue des Marronniers** and **rue Mercière** (both in the *2ème*), and on **rue St-Jean**. Ethnic restaurants are near **rue de la République**, in the *2ème*. Locals take pride in their *cocons* (chocolates wrapped in marzipan), made in Lyon's grandest *pâtisserie*, ▇**Bernachon,** 42 cours F. Roosevelt, *6ème*.

THE PRIDE OF LYON
Dining with the world's most renowned chefs comes with a price—a steep one. However, some of these restaurants have occasional weekend buffet brunches hovering around €30-40; check outside or call.

▇ **Chez Paul Bocuse,** 50 r. de la Plage, 9km out of town (☎04 72 42 90 90), take bus #40 to *Neuville* and tell the driver you are going to "Bocuse." The pinnacle of the *Lyonnais* food scene charges accordingly, with *menus* in excess of €100. Open daily noon-2pm and 8-9:30pm. ❺

Léon de Lyon, 1 r. Pléney, 1er (☎04 72 10 11 12), features the cuisine of master Jean-Paul Lacombe. *Menus* €55-135. Open Tu-Sa noon-2pm and 7:30-10pm. ❺

Tour Rose, 22 r. du Boeuf, 5ème (☎04 78 92 69 11), offers the chance to savor the creations of yet another master chef, Philippe Chavent. *Menus* €53-106. Open M-Sa noon-1pm and 7-9:30pm. ❺

Le Nord, 1 r. Neuve, 2ème (☎04 72 10 69 69). This spin-off restaurant of master Paul Bocuse offers a taste of his famous cuisine and a more reasonable €18 *menu*. Open M-Sa noon-2:30pm and 7-midnight. AmEx/MC/V. ❹

Le Sud, 1 r. Neuve, 2ème (☎04 72 10 69 69). Another Bocuse establishment, Le Sud serves Mediterranean fare in a beautiful setting. Pizzas and pastas from €11. Open M-Sa noon-2:30pm and 7-midnight. AmEx/MC/V. ❸

OTHER FLEURS DES LYON

▇ **Chez Mounier,** 3 r. des Marronniers, 2ème (☎04 78 37 79 26). This tiny place satisfies a discriminating local clientele with generous traditional specialties. 4-course *menus* €9.60-15.10. Open Su noon-2pm, Tu-Sa noon-2pm and 7-10:30pm. ❸

Chabert et Fils, 11 r. des Marronniers, 2ème (☎04 78 37 01 94). One of the better-known *bouchons* in Lyon. For dessert, try the delicious *Guignol*. Lunch *menus* start at €8-12.50. Open daily noon-2pm and 7-11pm. MC/V. ❷

L'Assiette St-Jean, 10 r. St-Jean, 5ème (☎04 72 41 96 20). An excellent *bouchon*, with unusual, somewhat archaic decor. House specialty *gateau de foies de volaille* (chicken liver) €6.60. *Menus* €13-27.50. Open in summer Su and Tu-Sa noon-2pm and 7-10:30pm. Closed Tu in winter. AmEx/MC/V. ❸

Chez Marie-Danielle, 29 r. des Remparts d'Ainay (☎04 72 43 09 25). A refreshing change from the male-dominated chef scene in Lyon—Marie-Danielle has received dozens of awards for her *Lyonnais* fare served in a *brasserie*-style dining hall. Lunch *menu* €14. Dinner *menu* €21.50. Open Tu-Sa noon-2pm and 7:30-10pm. MC/V. ❹

L'Etoile de l'Orient, 31 r. des Remparts d'Ainay, 2ème (☎04 72 41 07 87). M: Ampère-Victor Hugo. Be sure to have some tea at this intimate Tunisian restaurant, run by an exceedingly warm couple. Tajine lamb €11.50. Couscous dishes €11-13. *Menus* €10-25. Open M noon-2pm, Tu-Su noon-2pm and 7-11pm. ❸

 SIGHTS

FRANCE

VIEUX LYON

Stacked against the Saône at the bottom of the Fourvière hill, the narrow streets of *Vieux Lyon* wind between lively cafes, tree-lined squares, and magnificent medieval and Renaissance houses. The colorful *hôtels particuliers*, with their delicate carvings, shaded courtyards, and ornate turrets, sprang up between the 15th and 18th centuries when Lyon controlled Europe's silk and publishing industries.

TRABOULES. The distinguishing features of *Vieux Lyon* townhouses are the **traboules,** tunnels leading from the street through a maze of courtyards, often with vaulted ceilings and statuary niches. Although their original purpose is still debated, later traboules were constructed to transport silk safely from looms to storage rooms. During WWII, the passageways proved invaluable as info-gathering and escape routes for the Resistance (though some *résistants* found their way blocked by Germans at the exits). Many are open to the public at specific hours, especially in the morning. A tour beginning near the Cathédrale is the ideal way to see them, or pick up a list of addresses from the tourist office. *(Tours in summer daily at 2:30pm, hours vary off-season; consult tourist office. €9, students €5.)*

CATHÉDRALE ST-JEAN. The southern end of *Vieux Lyon* is dominated by the Cathédrale St-Jean, with its soaring columns and multicolored stained-glass windows, some of which are relatively new replacements, owing to the destruction caused by Lyon's exploding bridges during the hasty Nazi retreat in 1944. Paris might have been worth a Mass, but Lyon got the wedding cake; it was here that Henri IV met and married Maria de Médici in 1600. Inside, every hour between noon and 4pm, automatons pop out of the 14th-century **astronomical clock** in a charming reenactment of the Annunciation. The clock can calculate Church feast days until 2019. *(Open M-F 8am-noon and 2-7:30pm, Sa-Su 8am-noon and 2-7pm.)*

MUSEUMS IN VIEUX LYON. Down r. St-Jean, turn left at pl. du Change for the **Hôtel de Gadagne,** a typical 16th-century *Vieux Lyon* building, and its relatively minor museums. The better of the two is the **Musée de la Marionnette,** which displays puppets from around the world, including models of **Guignol,** the famed local cynic, and his inebriated friend, Gnaffron. *(Pl. du Petit Collège, 5ème. M: Vieux Lyon. Open Su-M and W-Sa 10:45am-6pm. €3.80, students €2. Under-19 free.)*

FOURVIÈRE AND ROMAN LYON

From the corner of r. du Bœuf and r. de la Bombarde in *Vieux Lyon*, climb the stairs heading straight up to reach **Fourvière Hill,** the nucleus of **Roman Lyon.** From the top of the stairs, continue up via the rose-lined **Chemin de la Rosaire,** a series of switchbacks that leads through a garden to the **esplanade Fourvière,** where a model of the city indicates local landmarks. Most prefer to take the less strenuous **funicular** (known as *la ficelle*) to the top of the hill. It leaves from the head of av. A. Max in *Vieux Lyon*, off pl. St-Jean. The **Tour de l'Observatoire,** on the eastern edge of the hilltop basilica, offers a more acute angle on the city. On a clear day, scan for Mont Blanc, about 200km to the east. *(Jardin de la Rosaire open daily 6:30am-9:30pm. Tour de l'Observatoire open Su-M and W-Sa 10am-noon and 2-6:30pm. €2.)*

▨ **BASILIQUE NOTRE-DAME DE FOURVIÈRE.** Lyon's archbishop vowed to build a church if the city was spared attack during the Franco-Prussian War. His bargain was met, and the bishop followed through. The basilica's white, meringue-like exterior is imposing from a distance—gorgeous or bizarre, depending on taste. The highlights of the ornate interior are the shimmering, gigantic mosaics that depict religious scenes, Joan of Arc at Orléans, and the naval battle of Lepante. The low, heavy crypt, used for mass, was conceived by the architect Pierre Bossan to contrast with the impossibly high and golden Byzantine basilica above. *(Behind the esplanade at the top of the hill. Open 8am-7pm.)*

MUSÉE GALLO-ROMAIN. With rooms and corridors that circle deep into the historic hillside of Fourvière, this brilliant museum houses a collection of arms, pottery, statues, and jewelry. Highlights include six large, luminous mosaics, a bronze tablet inscribed with a speech by Lyon's favorite son, Emperor Claudius, and a huge, half-cracked eggshell pot. Artifacts are labeled in English and French. *(Open Mar.-Oct. Su and Tu-Sa 10am-6pm; Nov.-Feb. 10am-5pm. €3.80, students €2.30. Th free.)*

PARC ARCHÉOLOGIQUE. Just next to the Minimes/Théâtre Romain funicular stop, the Parc holds the almost too well-restored 2000-year-old **Théâtre Romain** and the smaller **Odéon,** discovered when modern developers dug into the hill. Both still function as venues for shows during the **Nuits de Fourvière.** *(Open Apr. 15-Sept. 15 9am-9pm; Sept. 16-Apr. 14 7am-7pm. Free.)*

LA PRESQU'ÎLE AND LES TERREAUX

Monumental squares, statues, and fountains are the trademarks of Presqu'île, the lively area between the Rhône and the Saône. At its heart is **place Bellecour,** from which pedestrian **rue Victor Hugo** unfurls quietly south, lined with boutiques and bladers. To the north, crowded **rue de la République,** or "la Ré," is the urban aorta of Lyon. It runs through **place de la République** and ends at **place Louis Pradel** in the 1*er,* at the tip of the Terreaux district. Once a marshy wasteland, the area was filled with soil, creating dry terraces (*terreaux*) and establishing the neighborhood as the place-to-be for chic locals.

MUSÉE DES BEAUX-ARTS. This unassuming but excellent museum includes a comprehensive archeological wing, a distinguished collection of French, Dutch, and Spanish paintings, works by Picasso, a section devoted to the Italian Renaissance, and a lovely sculpture garden. Surrounded by all-star pre-, post-, and just-plain-Impressionist collections, even the museum's esoteric local works are delightful. A few nice surprises await explorers of the museum, including a Rodin bust of Victor Hugo at the end of his life (1883) and a huge French coin collection. *(20 pl. des Terreaux. Open Su-M, W-Th and Sa 10am-6pm, F 10:30am-8pm. Sculptures closed noon-1pm; paintings closed 1-2pm. €3.80, under-26 €2. Students with ID free.)*

LA CROIX-ROUSSE AND THE SILK INDUSTRY

Lyon is proud of its historical dominance of European silk manufacturing. The 1801 invention of the power loom by *Lyonnais* Joseph Jacquard intensified the sweatshop conditions endured by the silk workers. Unrest came to a head in an 1834 riot, in which hundreds were killed. Mass silk manufacturing is based elsewhere today; Lyon's few remaining silk workers perform delicate handiwork, reconstructing and replicating rare patterns for museum and chateau displays.

MUSÉE HISTORIQUE DES TISSUS. The exhibits about the history of silk trade may be interesting, but everyone comes here for the clothes. In dark rooms, rows of costumes recall skirt-flouting, ruffle-collared, and bosom-baring characters of the past. The collection includes examples of 18th-century elite garb (such as Marie-Antoinette's Versailles winter wardrobe), scraps of luxurious Byzantine textiles, and silk wall-hangings that look like stained-glass windows. Included with admission is the neighboring **Musée des Arts Décoratifs,** housed in an 18th-century **hôtel.** (34 r. de la Charité, 2ème. Tissus open Su and Tu-Sa 10am-5:30pm. Arts Décoratifs open Su and Tu-Sa 10am-noon and 2-5:30pm. €4.60, students with ID €2.30.)

LA MAISON DES CANUTS. Some old silk looms in a tiny back room are all that remain of the weaving techniques of the *canuts* (silk weavers). The shop sells silk made by its own *canuts*. A scarf costs €30 and up, but silk enthusiasts can take home a silkworm cocoon for €7 or less, or a handkerchief for €7. (10-12 r. d'Ivry, 4ème. Open M-F 9am-noon and 2-6:30pm, Sa 9am-noon and 2-6pm. €4, students €2.30.)

EAST OF THE RHÔNE AND MODERN LYON

Lyon's newest train station and monstrous space-age mall form the core of the ultra-modern Part-Dieu district. Locals call the commercial **Tour du Crédit Lyonnais** "le Crayon" for its unintentional resemblance to a giant pencil standing on end. Next to it, the shell-shaped **Auditorium Maurice Ravel** hosts major cultural events.

CENTRE D'HISTOIRE DE LA RÉSISTANCE ET DE LA DÉPORTATION. In a building in which Nazis tortured detainees during the Occupation, the center today houses an impressive but sobering collection of documents, photos, and films of the Resistance, which was based in Lyon. There's also a space set up for children. (14 av. Bertholet, 7ème. M: Jean Macé. Open Su-M and W-Sa 9am-5:30pm. €3.80, students €2. Admission includes an audio guide in French, English, or German.)

MUSÉE D'ART CONTEMPORAIN. This extensive, entertaining mecca of modern art resides in the futuristic **Cité International de Lyon,** a super-modern complex with offices, shops, theaters, and Interpol's world headquarters. All the museum's exhibits are temporary; the walls themselves are built anew for each installation. (Quai Charles de Gaulle, next to Parc de la Tête d'Or, 6ème. Take bus #4 from M: Foch. Open Su-M and W-Sa noon-7pm. €3.80, students €2. Under-18 free.)

INSTITUT LUMIÈRE. A must for film buffs, the museum's exhibits chronicle the exploits of the brothers Lumière, who invented the motion picture in 1895. The relatively small museum is full of intriguing factoids: The brothers also invented postsychronisation, and Louis created a forerunner to holograms in 1920. The Institut's complex also includes a movie theater and a park. (25 r. du Premier-Film, 8ème. M: Monplaisir Lumière. Open Su and Tu-Sa 11am-7pm. €5.50, students €4.50.)

PARC DE LA TÊTE D'OR. Locals gravitate to this massive, completely free park for frisbee, football, and *pique-niques avec vin.* The park, one of the largest in Europe, sprawls over 259 acres. Its name is derived from the legend that a golden head of Jesus lies buried somewhere on its grounds. During the summer, paddle boats are available for a visit to its artificial green lake. Reindeer, elephants, and other animals fill the zoo, and greenhouses encase a botanical garden. The 60,000-bush rose gardens are magnificent. (M: Charpennes or tram T1 from Perrache, dir.: IUT-Feyssine. Open daily mid-Apr. to mid-Oct. 6am-11pm; mid-Oct. to mid-Apr. 6am-9pm.)

🎵 📷 ENTERTAINMENT AND NIGHTLIFE

At the end of June is the two-week **Festival du Jazz à Vienne,** which welcomes jazz masters to Vienne, a medieval town south of Lyon, accessible by bus or train. (☎04 74 85 00 05. Tickets €26, students €24.) **Les Nuits de Fourvière** is a three-month summer music festival held in the ancient Théâtre Romain and Odéon. (☎04 72 32 00 00. Tickets and info at the Théâtre Romain and the FNAC shop on r. de la République. €10-35.) The biennial **Festival de Musique du Vieux Lyon,** 5 pl. du Petit Collège, *5ème*, draws artists worldwide between mid-Nov. and mid-Dec. to perform in the churches of *Vieux Lyon*. (☎04 78 42 39 04. Tickets €15-36.) Nightlife in Lyon is fast and furious; the city is crawling with nightclubs. The best and most accessible late-night spots are a strip of **riverboat dance clubs** by the east bank of the Rhône.

BARS AND CLUBS

▓ **Le Fish,** across from 21 quai Augagneur. Plays salsa, jungle, hip-hop, disco, and house in a swank boat. This club is the choice spot for *Lyonnais* youngsters, with an equally popular deck and dance floor. F-Sa cover €11-13 includes 1st drink, free before 11pm. Open W-Th 10pm-5am, F-Sa 10pm-6am. Students only.

Ayers Rock Café, 2 r. Désirée, is an Aussie bar, and the **Cosmopolitan,** with New York-themed drinks, is right next door. Be sure to stumble over, as both places are usually packed with students. Both have shooters for €3 and cocktails starting at €6. Cosmo is a little darker, a little less international, and a little more restrained. Ayers open daily 6pm-3am; Cosmo open M-Sa 8pm-3am.

Tavern of the Drunken Parrot, next door to Le Chantier, serves potent homemade rum drinks (€2); try the citron or coco. Open daily 6pm-3am.

Le Funambule, 29 r. de l'Arbre Sec. A dimly lit, hip bar for the late-20s crowd. Open Tu-Th 7pm-1am, F-Sa 7pm-3am.

Le Chantier, 20 r. Ste-Catherine, offers 12 tequila shots for €15.25. Slip down a spiral slide to reach the dance floor downstairs. Open Tu-Sa 9pm-3am.

La Marquise, next door to Le Fish. Spends less on the boat but more on big-name jungle and house DJs. Cover €6 for occasional *soirées à thème*. Open W-Sa 11pm-dawn.

GAY AND LESBIAN NIGHTLIFE

The tourist office's city guide lists spots that cater to Lyon's gay community, and *Le Petit Paumé* offers superb tips. The most popular gay spots are in the 1er.

L'United Café, impasse de la Pêcherie, in an alley off quai de la Pêcherie. The weekend club circuit normally starts here around midnight, with American and Latino dance hits. Theme nights throughout the week range from post office to beach party—and there are lip-shaped urinals to boot. Drinks €3-6. Open daily 10:30pm-5am.

DV1, 6 r. Violi, off r. Royale, north of pl. Louis Pradel. Drag queens nightly, with a huge dance floor. A mostly male, mid-20s to mid-30s crowd. Drinks €3.50-4. Open W-Th and Su 10pm-3am, F-Sa 10pm-5am.

CAP Opéra, 2 pl. Louis Pradel. A popular gay pub, with red lights to match the Opéra next door. Occasional *soirées à thème*. Open daily 2pm-3am.

BERRY-LIMOUSIN

Too often passed over for beaches and big cities, Berry-Limousin offers peaceful countryside and and fascinating towns. Bourges served as the capital of France and benefited from King Charles VII's financier, Jacques Coeur, who built a lavish string of chateaux through the area. The region later became an artistic and literary breeding ground, home to Georges Sand, Auguste Renoir, and Jean Giraudoux.

BOURGES

In 1433, Jacques Coeur chose Bourges (pop. 80,000) as the site for one of his many chateaux. You'll see more of the unfurnished **Palais Jacques-Coeur** than he ever did, since he was imprisoned for embezzlement before its completion. (Open July-Aug. daily 9:30am-5:45pm; Sept.-June reduced hours. €6.10, ages 18-24 €4.10, under-18 free.) Inquire at the tourist office about excursions to other chateaux along the **Route Jacques Coeur.** The ▓**Cathédrale St-Etienne,** has stunning stained-glass that illuminates the white marble interior with deep reds and blues. The cathedral is free, but tickets are necessary to enter the simple **crypt** and scenic **tower.** (Open Apr.-Sept. daily 8:30am-7:15pm; Oct.-Mar. 9am-5:45pm. Closed Su morning. Crypt and tower €5.50, students €3.50.) As you exit the cathedral, head right on r. des 3 Maillets and turn left on r. Molière for the **promenade des Remparts,** which offers a quiet stroll past ramparts and flowery gardens.

    Trains leave from the station at pl. Général Leclerc (☎02 48 51 00 00) for Paris (2½hr., 5-8 per day, €24) and Tours (1½hr., 10 per day, €17). From the station, follow av. H. Laudier, which turns into av. Jean Jaurès; bear left onto r. du Commerce, and continue down r. Moyenne to reach the **tourist office,** 21 r. Victor Hugo. (☎02 48 23 02 60; www.ville-bourges.fr. Open Apr.-Sept. M-Sa 9am-7pm, Su 10am-7pm; Oct.-Mar. reduced hours.) **Hôtel St-Jean ❷,** 23 av. Marx-Dormoy, has clean rooms, all with showers, and friendly owners. (☎02 48 24 70 45; fax 02 48 24 79 98. Breakfast €4. Singles €22-28; doubles €26-34; triples €43.) To get to the **Auberge de Jeunesse (HI) ❶,** 22 r. Henri Sellier, bear right from r. du Commerce on to r. des Arènes, which becomes r. Fernault, cross at the intersection to r. René Ménard, follow it to the right, and turn left at r. Henri Sellier. (☎02 48 24 58 09. Breakfast €3.30. Sheets €2.80. Reception daily 8am-noon and 5-10pm. Dorms €8.40.) **Place Gordaine, rue des Beaux-Arts, rue Moyenne,** and **rue Mirabeau** are lined with eateries. The **Leclerc supermarket** is on r. Prado off bd. Juraville. (Open M-F 9:15am-7:20pm, Sa 8:30am-7:20pm.) **Postal Code:** 18000.

BURGUNDY (BOURGOGNE)

What the Loire Valley is to chateaux, Burgundy is to churches. During the Middle Ages, it was the heart of the religious fever sweeping Europe: abbeys swelled in size and wealth, and towns eager for pilgrim traffic built magnificent cathedrals. Today, Burgundy's production of some of the world's finest wines and most delectable dishes, like *coq au vin* and *bœuf bourguignon*, have made this region the homeland of Epicureans worldwide.

DIJON

Dijon (pop. 160,000) isn't just about the mustard. The capital of Burgundy is a charming city with numerous gardens, a couple of good museums, and many fine wines. The diverse **Musée des Beaux-Arts** occupies the east wing of the colossal **Palais des Ducs de Bourgogne,** in pl. de la Libération at the center of the *vieille ville.* (☎03 80 74 52 70. Open May-Oct. W-M 9:30am-6pm; Nov.-Apr. W-M 10am-5pm. €3.40; students with ID free, Su free.) The brightly-tiled **Cathédrale St-Bénigne,** in pl. St-Bénigne, has a spooky circular crypt. (☎03 80 30 39 33. Open 9am-7pm. Crypt €1.) Next door, the **Musée Archéologique,** 5 r. Dr. Maret, features Gallo-Roman sculptures and Neolithic housewares. (☎03 80 30 88 54. Open June-Sept. Tu-Su 9am-6pm; Oct.-May Tu-Su 9am-noon and 2-6pm; €2.20; students free; Su free.) Get your **Grey Poupon** at the Maille Boutique, 32 r. de la Liberté, where *moutarde au vin* has been made since 1747. (☎03 80 30 41 02. Open M-Sa 9am-7pm. MC/V.)

From the train station at cours de la Gare, **trains** chug to: Lyon (2hr., 7 per day, €21); Nice (7-8hr., 6 per day, €57); Paris (1½hr., 20 per day, €26). The **tourist office,** in pl. Guillaume Darcy, is a straight shot down av. Maréchal Foch from the station. (☎03 80 44 11 44. Open May-Oct. daily 9am-7pm; Nov.-Apr. 10am-6pm.) **⊠Hôtel Montchapet ❸,** 26-28 r. Jacques Cellerier, 10min. north of av. Première Armée Française, off pl. Guillaume Darcy, is bright and comfortable. (☎03 80 53 95 00; www.hotelmontchapet.com. Breakfast €5. Reception 7am-10:30pm. Check-out 11am. Singles €26-39; doubles €36-46.) To get to the huge **Auberge de Jeunesse, Centre de Rencontres Internationales (HI) ❶,** 1 av. Champollion, take bus #5 (or night bus A) from pl. Grangier to Epirey. (☎03 80 72 95 20; fax 03 80 70 00 61. Breakfast included. Dorms €15; singles €28. MC/V.) **Rue Amiral Boussin** has charming cafes, while reasonably priced restaurants line **rue Mongue.** Fend for yourself at the **supermarket** in the basement of the Galeries Lafayette department store, 41 r. de la Liberté. (Open M-Sa 8:15am-7:45pm.) **Postal Code:** 21000.

⚡ DAYTRIP FROM DIJON: BEAUNE. Wine has poured out of the well-touristed town of **Beaune** (pop. 24,000), just south of Dijon, for centuries. Surrounded by the famous Côte de Beaune vineyards, the town itself is packed with wineries offering free *dégustations* (tastings). The largest of the cellars belongs to **⊠Patriarche Père et Fils,** 5-7 r. du Collège, a 5km labyrinth of corridors packed with over four million bottles. (☎03 80 24 53 78. Open daily 9:30-11:30am and 2-5pm. €9.) The **tourist office,** 1 r. de l'Hôtel-Dieu, lists *caves* (cellars) that offer tours. (☎03 80 26 21 30; fax 03 80 26 21 39. Open mid-June to mid-Sept. M-Sa 9:30am-8pm, Su 10am-6pm; mid-Sept. to mid-June reduced hrs.) **Trains** run from Dijon (25min., 37 per day, €5.70).

ALSACE-LORRAINE AND FRANCHE-COMTÉ

As first prize in the endless Franco-German border wars, France's northeastern frontier has had a long and bloody history. Heavily influenced by its tumultuous past, the entire region now maintains a fascinating blend of French and German in the local dialects, cuisine, and architecture. Alsace's well-preserved towns offer half-timbered Bavarian houses flanking tiny crooked streets and canals, while Lorraine's elegant cities spread to the west among wheat fields. In Franche-Comté, the Jura mountains offer some of France's finest cross-country skiing.

STRASBOURG

Right near the Franco-German border, Strasbourg (pop. 450,000) has spent much of its history being annexed by one side or another. Today, German is often heard on its streets, and *winstubs* sit next door to *pâtisseries*. It is also the joint center, along with Brussels, of the European Union. With its rich culture and bustling university, Strasbourg combines cosmopolitan elegance with youthful energy.

⚡ TRANSPORTATION AND PRACTICAL INFORMATION. Strasbourg is a major rail hub. **Trains** (☎03 88 22 50 50) go to: Luxembourg (2½hr., 14 per day, €27); Frankfurt (3hr., 18 per day, €47); Paris (4hr., 16 per day, €38); and Zürich (3hr., 18 per day, €35). The **tourist office,** 17 pl. de la Cathédrale, makes hotel reservations for a €1.60 fee plus deposit. (☎03 88 52 28 28. Open daily 9am-7pm.) There is also a branch at pl. de la Gare, near the train station (☎03 88 32 51 49). Get on the **Internet** at **Net computer,** 14 quai des Pêcheurs (€2 per hr. Open M-F 10am-10pm, Sa and Su noon-10pm.) **Postal Code:** 67000.

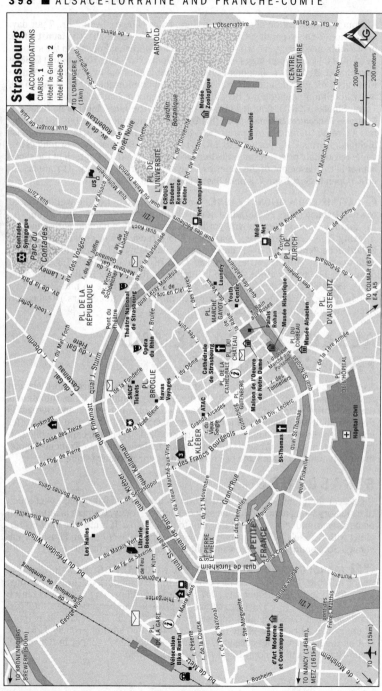

FRANCE

⌐⌐ ACCOMMODATIONS AND FOOD. Make reservations or arrive early to find reasonable accommodations. **⫽CIARUS** (Centre International d'Accueil de Strasbourg) ❷, 7 r. Finkmatt, has large, spotless facilities. From the train station, take r. du Maire-Kuss to the canal, turn left, and follow quais St-Jean, Kléber, and Finkmatt; turn left on r. Finkmatt, and it's on the left. (☎03 88 15 27 88; www.ciarus.com. Breakfast included. Check-in 3:30pm. Check-out 9am. Curfew 1am. Dorms €16-18; singles €38. MC/V.) **Hôtel Kléber** ❹, 29 pl. Kléber, sits on the central pl. Kléber and has spacious, classy rooms. (☎03 88 32 09 53; www.hotel-kleber.com. Breakfast €6. Reception daily 7am-midnight. Singles €32-57; doubles €36-66; triples €66-73. AmEx/MC/V.) **Hôtel le Grillon** ❸, 2 r. Thiergarten, is 1 block from the station toward the city center, has large rooms above a bar where guests get a free drink with *Let's Go.* (☎03 88 32 71 88; www.grillon.com Breakfast €7.50. **Internet** access free for 15min., €1 per 15min. thereafter. Singles €29, with shower €38-53; doubles €37/44-59. D/MC/V.) Informal *Winstubs* serve Alsatian specialties such as *choucroute garnie* (spiced sauerkraut served with meats); try the **La Petite France** neighborhood, especially along r. des Dentelles. Explore **place de la Cathédrale, rue Mercière,** or **rue du Vieil Hôpital** for restaurants, and **place Marché Gayot,** off r. des Frères, for lively cafes. For groceries, swing by the **ATAC,** 47 r. des Grandes Arcades, off pl. Kléber. (Open M-Sa 8:30am-8pm.)

⌐ ⌐ SIGHTS AND ENTERTAINMENT. The tower of the ornate Gothic **⫽Cathédrale de Strasbourg** climbs 142m skyward. Inside, the **Horloge Astronomique** demonstrates the wizardry of 16th-century Swiss clockmakers. While you wait for the clock to strut its stuff—apostles troop out of the clockface while a cock crows to greet Saint Peter daily at 12:30pm—check out the **Pilier des Anges** (Angels' Pillar), a masterpiece of Gothic sculpture. You can climb the **tower** in front of the clock like the young Goethe, who scaled its 330 steps regularly to cure his fear of heights. (Cathedral open M-Sa 7-11:40am and 12:40-7pm, Su 12:45-6pm. Tickets for the clock on sale 8:30am in cathedral and 11:45am at south entrance; €0.80. Tower open Apr.-Oct. M-F 9am-5:30pm; Nov.-Mar. reduced hours. €3, students €1.50.) **Palais Rohan,** 2 pl. du Château, houses three small but excellent museums: the **Musée des Beaux-Arts, Musée des Arts Décoratifs,** and **Musée Archéologique.** (All open M and W-Su 10am-6pm. €4 each, students €2.50.) Take bus #23, 30, or 72 for **L'Orangerie,** Strasbourg's most spectacular park; free concerts play in the summer at the Pavilion Joséphine (Su-Tu and Th-Sa 8:30pm.) **Strasbourg** has bars everywhere. **Pl. Kléber** attracts a student crowd, while **rue des Frères** and the tiny **place du Marché Gayot** wake up with a mixed crowd after 10pm.

LA ROUTE DU VIN

Since the Middle Ages, the wines of Alsace have been highly prized—and priced. The vineyards of Alsace flourish along a 170km corridor known as La Route du Vin (Wine Route) that begins at **Strasbourg** (p. 397) and stretches south along the foothills of the Vosges, passing through 100 towns along the way to Mulhouse. Hordes of tourists are drawn each year to the beautifully preserved medieval villages along the route—and to the free *dégustations* (tastings) along the way.

Colmar (p. 400) and Sélestat (p. 400) offer excellent bases and fascinating sights, but don't miss smaller, less-touristed villages. The most accessible towns from Strasbourg are **Molsheim,** a medieval university center, and **Barr,** an old town with a vineyard trail that leads through the hills. The more famous towns lie to the south: The most visited sight in Alsace, the **Château de Haut Koenigsbourg,** towers over **Kintzheim;** and the 16th-century walled hamlet of **Riquewihr,** the Route's most popular village, with many of Alsace's best-known wine houses. To help plan your tour, pick up the **⫽***Alsace Wine Route* brochure from a tourist office.

FRANCE

◧ TRANSPORTATION. Strasbourg, the northern terminus of the Wine Route, is a major rail hub, easily accessible from France, Germany, and Luxembourg. **Trains** from Strasbourg hit many of the towns along the northern half of the Route, including: Barr (50min., 10 per day, €5.50); Colmar (40min., 36 per day, €10); and Sélestat (30min., 20 per day, €6.50). Trains also run to Colmar from Sélestat, (15min., 20 per day, €3.70). **Bus** lines pepper the southern half of the Route, running from Colmar to Kaysersberg (20min., 1 per hr., €2.30), Riquewihr (30min., 10 per day, €3), and many other small towns on the Route. From Mulhouse, head to nearby Basel, Switzerland (20min., 7 per day, €6.50); go to Paris (4½hr., 8 per day, €45), or return to Strasbourg (1hr., 14 per day, €14).

SÉLESTAT. Sélestat (pop. 17,200), between Colmar and Strasbourg, is a charming town often overlooked by tourists on their way to larger Route cities. The **Bibliothèque Humaniste,** 1 r. de la Bibliothèque, founded in 1452, contains a fascinating collection of ancient documents during Sélestat's 15th-century humanistic boom. (Open July-Aug. M and W-F 9am-noon and 2-6pm, Sa 9am-noon and 2-5pm, Su 2-5pm; Sept.-June closed Su. €3.50, students €2.) The **tourist office,** 10 bd. Général Leclerc, in the Commanderie St-Jean, rents **bikes** (€12.50 per day). From the train station, go straight on av. de la Gare, through pl. Général de Gaulle, to av. de la Liberté. Turn left onto bd. du Maréchal Foch, which veers right and becomes bd. Général Leclerc; the office is a few blocks down on your right.(☎03 88 58 87 20; www.selestat-tourisme.com. Open July-Aug. M-F 9am-noon and 1:30-6:45pm, Sa 9am-noon and 2-5pm, Su 11am-3pm; Sept.-June. reduced hours M-Sa, closed Su.) The ▨**Hôtel de l'Ill ❷,** 13 r. des Bateliers, has bright rooms. (☎03 88 92 91 09. Breakfast €5. Reception daily 7am-3pm and 5-11pm. Singles €23; doubles €38; triples €55. MC/V.) **Camping Les Cigognes ❶** is on the south edge of the *vieille ville.* (☎03 88 92 03 98. Reception July-Aug. 8am-noon and 3-10pm; May-June and Sept.-Oct 8am-noon and 3-7pm. Open May-Oct. July-Aug. €9.20 per person, €13 per for 2 or 3 people; reduced prices Sept.-Oct. and May-June.) The cobbled **rue des Chevaliers** has a wide variety of restaurants. **Postal Code:** 67600.

COLMAR. The bubbling fountains, crooked lanes, and pastel houses of Colmar (pop. 68,000) evoke an intimate charm despite the packs of tourists. The collection of **Musée Unterlinden,** 1 r. d'Unterlinden, ranges from Romanesque to Renaissance, including Grünewald's *Issenheim Altarpiece.* (Open May.-Oct. daily 9am-6pm; Nov.-Apr. M and W-Su 9am-noon and 2-5pm. €7, students €5.) The **Église des Dominicains,** on pl. des Dominicains, has Colmar's other major masterpiece, Schongauer's *Virgin in the Rose Bower.* (Open Apr.-Dec. daily 10am-1pm and 3-6pm. €1.30.) To get to the **tourist office,** 4 r. d'Unterlinden, from the train station, turn left on av. de la République (which becomes r. Kléber) and follow it to the right to pl. Unterlinden. (☎03 89 20 68 92; www.ot-colmar.fr. Open July-Aug. M-Sa 9am-7pm, Su 9:30am-2pm; Sept.-June reduced hours.) To reach the **Auberge de Jeunesse (HI) ❶,** 2 r. Pasteur, take bus #4 (dir.: Logelbach) to *Pont Rouge.* (☎03 89 80 57 39. Breakfast included. Sheets €3.50. Reception July-Aug. daily 7-10am and 5pm-midnight; Sept.-June 7-10am and 5-11pm. Lockout 10am-5pm. Curfew midnight. Open mid-Jan. to mid-Dec. Dorms €12; singles €17; doubles €28. Members only. MC/V.) **Hôtel Kempf ❸,** 1 av. de la République, has large rooms right in the middle of the *vieille ville.* (☎03 89 41 21 72; fax 03 89 23 06 94. Breakfast €6. Shower €2.50. Open early Feb. to mid-Jan; closed two weeks June-July. Singles and doubles €28, with shower €35; triples with bath €55. MC/V.) Take bus #1 (dir.: Horbourg-Wihr) to *Plage d'Ill* for **Camping de l'Ill ❶,** on rte. Horbourg-Wihr. (☎03 89 41 15 94. Reception July-Aug.

daily 8am-10pm; Feb.-June and Sept.-Nov. 8am-8pm. Open Feb.-Nov. Electricity €2.40. €3 per person, €1.80 per child; €3.30 per site.) **Monoprix supermarket** is on pl. Unterlinden. (Open M-F 8am-8pm, Sa 8am-8pm.) **Grand Rue** has a multitude of *brasseries* and other tasty options. **Postal Code:** 68000.

BESANÇON

Surrounded by the river Doubs on three sides and by a steep bluff on the fourth, Besançon (pop. 120,000) has intrigued military strategists from Julius Caesar to the great military engineer Vauban 1800 years later. Today, Besançon boasts a smart, sexy student population and an impressive number of museums and discos. See the city's Renaissance buildings from high up in the Vauban's **citadel,** at the end of r. des Fusilles de la Résistance. Within the citadel, the **Musée de la Résistance et de la Déportation** chronicles the Nazi rise to power and the German occupation of France. Other sights include a natural history museum, a zoo, an aquarium, and a folk arts museum. (☎ 03 81 65 07 54. Open July-Aug. daily 9am-7pm; Sept.-June reduced hours. Closed Tu Nov.-Easter. €7, students €6.) The **Cathédrale St-Jean,** beneath the citadel, holds two treasures: The white marble **Rose de St-Jean** and the intricate 19th-century **Horloge Astronomique.** (Open M and W-Su 9am-6pm. €2.50. Students and under-18 free.) The **Musée des Beaux-Arts et d'Archéologie,** on pl. de la Révolution, houses an exceptional collection ranging from ancient Egyptian mummies to works by Matisse, Picasso, and Renoir. (☎ 03 81 87 80 49. Open M and W-Su 9:30am-12:30pm and 2-6pm. €3. Students free, Su and holidays free.) The area between **rue Claude Pouillet** and **rue Pont Battant** buzzes with nightlife. ▓**Carpe Diem,** 2 pl. Jean Gigoux, is a hotspot that brings together students and non-students for drinks and discussion, with events and concerts held regularly. (☎ 03 81 83 11 18. Beer €2. Open M-Th 7am-1am, F-Sa 7am-2am, Su 8am-11pm. MC/V.) Shoot pool at the surprisingly hip **Pop Hall,** 26 r. Proudhon. (☎ 03 81 83 01 90. Beer €2. Open Su-Th 2pm-1am, F-Sa 2pm-2am.)

Trains pull up at the station on av. de la Paix (☎ 08 36 35 35 35) from: Dijon (1hr., 22 per day, €12); Paris (2hr., 8 per day, €43); and Strasbourg (3hr., 10 per day, €27). Monts Jura **buses,** 9 r. Proudhon (☎ 03 81 21 22 00), go to Pontarlier (1hr., 6 per day, €8). From the station, walk downhill; turn onto av. Maréchal Foch, and continue to the left as it becomes av. de l'Helvétie, until you reach pl. de la Première Armée Française. The *vieille ville* is across the pont de la République; the **tourist office,** 2 pl. de la Première Armée Française, is in

ON THE MENU

THE GOÛT DU VIN

Being in France and drinking wine go hand in hand. Perhaps in a less heralded wine region you could avoid looking like an amateur, but the wine lists along the Route du Vin are a bit more daunting. It's time to learn if that wine was a *première cuvée* or just a bouquet of walnuts and old socks:

Gewurztraminer: This dry, aromatic white wine has been called "The Emperor of Alsatian wines." Drink it as an apéritif with foie gras, pungent cheeses, or Indian, Mexican, or Asian cuisine.

Riesling: Considered one of the world's finest white wines, Riesling is fruity, very dry, and accompanies white meats, *choucroute,* and fish.

Sylvaner: From an Austrian grape, Sylvaner is a light, slightly sparkling white wine that goes well with seafood and salads.

Muscat: A sweet and highly fruity white wine, often an apéritif.

The Pinot family: Pinot Blanc is an all-purpose white wine for chicken, fish, and all sorts of appetizers; **Pinot Gris** is a smoky, strong white wine that can often take the place of a red wine in accompanying rich meats, roasts, and game; and **Pinot Noir,** the sole red wine of the Alsatian bunch, tastes of cherries and complements red meats.

the park to the right. (☎08 20 32 07 82; www.besancon-tourisme.com. Open Apr.-Sept. M 10am-7pm, Tu-Sa 9am-7pm, Su 10am-noon; Oct.-Mar. reduced hours.) Check **email** at **T@cybernet,** 18 r. de Pontarlier. (☎03 81 81 15 74; www.tacybernet.com. €3.60 per hr. Open M-Sa 11am-10pm, Su 2-8pm. MC/V.) For the **Foyer Mixte de Jeunes Travailleurs (HI)** ❷, 48 r. des Cras, take bus #7 or night line A (both €0.90) from pl. Flore (dir.: Orchamps, 3-5 per hr.). To get to pl. Flore bus stop, cross the parking lot of the train station and head down the stairs. Take the road in front of you that heads slightly to the left (av. de la Paix), and keep to the left as the road bends and turns into r. de Belfort. Turn right onto av. Carnot, walk for a block until you see the green lights of the pharmacy in pl. Flore, and take a sharp left onto r. des Chaprais. This friendly hostel has concerts, movies, and other special events, as well as free Internet access in the lobby. (☎03 81 40 32 00; fax 03 81 40 32 01. Singles €17; doubles €25. AmEx/MC/V.) **Hôtel du Nord** ❸, 8-10 r. Moncey, has clean rooms in a quiet but central location. (☎03 81 81 35 56; fax 03 81 81 85 96. Breakfast €4.60. Singles and doubles with shower or bath €30-52; triples and quads with shower €54. AmEx/D/MC/V.) A variety of restaurants line **rue Claude-Pouillet.** Buy groceries at **Monoprix supermarket,** 12 Grande Rue. (Open M-Sa 8:30am-8pm.)

🔁 **DAYTRIP FROM BESANÇON: PONTARLIER AND THE JURA.** The sedate town of **Pontarlier** (pop. 18,400) is a good base from which to explore the oft-overlooked **Haut-Jura Mountains.** The Jura are best known for **cross-country skiing;** nine trails cover every skill level. (Day pass €6, under-17 €3.50; available at the Le Larmont and Le Malmaison trails.) Le Larmont is the closest Alpine ski area (☎03 81 46 55 20). In summer, **fishing, hiking,** and **mountain biking** are popular. Monts Jura **buses** (☎81 39 88 80) run to Besançon (1hr., 6 per day, €8). The **tourist office,** 14 bis r. de la Gare, has guides and maps. (☎03 81 46 48 33; fax 03 81 46 83 32. Open July-Aug. M-Sa 9am-6pm, Su 10am-noon; Sept.-June M-Sa 9am-6pm.) **Postal Code:** 25300.

NANCY

Nancy (pop. 100,000) has always been passionate about beauty: the town that spawned the art-nouveau "Nancy school" is today the artistic and intellectual heart of modern Lorraine. The elaborate ◼**Place Stanislas** houses three neoclassical pavilions, with *son-et-lumière* (sound and light) spectacles held nightly at 10pm in July and August. The collection in the **Musée des Beaux-Arts,** 3 pl. Stanislas, spans from the 14th century to today. (☎03 83 85 30 72. Open Su-M and W-Sa 10am-6pm. €4.80, students €2.30. W and 1st Su of the month students free.) Portals of pink roses lead into the aromatic **Roseraie,** in the relaxing **Parc de la Pépinière,** just north of pl. de la Carrière. (Open May-Sept. 6:30am-11:30pm; Oct.-Apr. reduced hours. Free.) Nancy has a vibrant arts and nightlife scene; check www.nancybynight.com for info on everything from theater to concerts to clubs. **Rue Stanislas** and **Grand Rue** are great places to grab a drink.

Trains (☎03 83 22 12 46) depart from the station at pl. Thiers for Paris (3hr., 14 per day, €36) and Strasbourg (1hr., 17 per day, €19). Follow r. Raymond Poincaré away from the station, through a stone archway, and continue straight to pl. Stanislas and the **tourist office.** (☎03 83 35 22 41; www.ot-nancy.fr. Open Apr.-Sept. M-Sa 9am-7pm, Su 10am-5pm; Oct.-Mar. M-Sa 9am-6pm, Su 10am-1pm.) Access the **Internet** at **E-café,** r. des Quatre Églises. (☎03 83 35 47 34. €5.40 per hr. Open M-Sa 9am-9pm, Su 2-8pm.) **Centre d'Accueil de Remicourt (HI)** ❶, 149 r. de Vandoeuvre, is in Villiers-lès-Nancy, 4km away. From the station, take bus #122 to *St-Fiacre* (dir.: Villiers Clairlieu; 2 per hr.; confirm route with the driver); head downhill from the stop, turn right on r. de la Grange des Moines, which turns into r. de Vandoeuvre. Signs point to Château de Remicourt. (☎03 83 27 73 67. Reception 9am-9pm. Dorms €13; doubles €29. MC/V.) **Hôtel Flore ❸**, 8 r. Raymond Poincaré, near the train station, is bright and homey. (☎03 83 37 63 28. Reception 7:30am-2am. Singles €26-32; doubles €37-40; triples €43. AmEx/MC/V.) Restaurants line **rue des Maréchaux, place Lafayette,** and **place St-Epvre.** A **SHOPI** market sits at 26 r. St-Georges. (Open M-Sa 9am-8pm. MC/V.) **Postal Code: 54000.**

CHAMPAGNE AND THE NORTH

Legend has it that at the moment he discovered Champagne, Dom Perignon exclaimed, "Come quickly, I am drinking the stars!" Since then everyone from Napoleon to John Maynard Keynes has proclaimed its virtues. The term "champagne" is fiercely guarded; the name can only be applied to wines made from regional grapes and produced according to a rigorous, time-honored method. As you head further north to the ferry ports, don't overlook the intriguing Flemish culture of Arras and the world-class art collections of Lille.

REIMS

Reims (pop. 185,000) sparkles with the champagne of its famed caves, the beauty of its architectural masterpieces, and the excitement of its nightlife. The **Cathédrale de Notre-Dame,** built with golden limestone quarried in the Champagne *caves,* features sea-blue stained-glass windows by Marc Chagall. (☎03 26 77 45 25. Open daily 7:30am-7:30pm. €6, students €3.50.) Enter the adjacent **Palais du Tau,** at pl. du Cardinal Luçon, for dazzling 16th-century tapestries. (☎03 26 47 81 79. Open May-Aug. Su and Tu-Sa 9:30am-6:30pm; Sept.-Apr. reduced hours. €6.10, students €4.10.) The firm of **Champagne Pommery,** 5 pl. du Général Gouraud, boasts the largest *tonneau* (vat) in the world, and the best tour of the Champagne caves in Reims. (☎03 26 61 62 56. Tours by reservation. €7, students €3.50.) For good deals on champagne, look for sales on local brands and check prices at supermarkets. Good bottles start at €9.50. The small schoolroom where Germany surrendered to the Allies during WWII is now the **Museé de la Reddition,** 12 r. Franklin Roosevelt, a potent time capsule for the momentous event it witnessed. At night, people congregate in the cafes and bars of **place Drouet d'Erlon.**

Trains (☎03 26 88 11 65) leave bd. Joffre for Épernay (25min., 16 per day, €5.20). Paris (1½hr., 11 per day, €21). To get from the train station to the **tourist office,** 2 r. Guillaume de Machault, follow the right-hand curve of the rotary to pl. Drouet d'Erlon, turn left onto r. de Vesle, turn right on r. du Tresor, and it's on the left before the cathedral. (☎03 26 77 45 00; www.tourisme.fr/reims. Open mid-Apr. to mid-Oct. M-Sa 9am-7pm, Su 10am-6pm; mid-Oct. to mid-Apr. M-F 9am-noon and 2-6pm, Sa 9am-6pm, Su 10am-5pm.) The **🖾Centre International de Séjour/Auberge de Jeunesse (HI) ❶,** on chaussée Bocquaine, has bright, comfortable rooms. Cross the park in front of the station, following the right-hand side of the traffic circle. Turn right onto bd. Général Leclerc, follow it to the canal and cross the first bridge (pont de Vesle) on your left. Bocquaine is the first left. (☎03 26 40 52 60; fax 03 26 47 35 70. Dorms €10; singles €15, with shower €26; doubles €22/30; triples with shower €36. Nonmembers add €2. AmEx/MC/V.) The sunny and spotless **Au Bon Accueil ❷,** 31 r. Thillois, is just off the central pl. d'Erlon. (☎03 26 88 55 74; fax 03 26 05 12 38. Breakfast €4.50. Singles €18-27; doubles €30-39. MC/V.) **Place Drouet d'Erlon** is crowded with cafes, restaurants, and bars. **Monoprix supermarket** is at r. de Vesle and r. de Talleyrand. (Open M-Sa 8:30am-9pm.) **Postal Code: 51100.**

ÉPERNAY

Épernay (pop. 30,000), at the juncture of three wealthy grape-growing regions, is appropriately ritzy. The aptly named **avenue de Champagne** is distinguished by its palatial mansions, lush gardens, and swanky champagne companies. **Moët & Chandon,** 20 av. de Champagne, produces the king of all wines: **Dom Perignon.** (☎03 26 51 20 20. Open late Mar.-early Nov. daily 9:30-11:30am and 2-4:30pm; early Nov. to late Mar. M-F 9:30-11:30am and 2-4:30pm. 1hr. tour with one glass €7.50.) Ten minutes away is **Mercier,** 70 av. de Champagne, the self-proclaimed "most popular champagne in France," which gives tours in rollercoaster-like cars. (☎03 26 51 22 22. Open Mar.-Nov. daily 9:30-11:30am and 2-5pm; Dec. 1-19 and Jan. 13-Mar. Su-M and Th-Sa 9:30-11:30am and 2-4:30pm. 30min. tours €6.)

   Trains leave cour de la Gare for Paris (1¼hr., 18 per day, €18) and Reims (25min., 16 per day, €5.20). From the station, walk straight ahead through pl. Mendès France, go one block up r. Gambetta to the central **place de la République,** and turn left on av. de Champagne to reach the **tourist office,** 7 av. de Champagne. (☎03 26 53 33 00. Open Easter-Oct. 15 M-Sa 9:30am-noon and 1:30-7pm, Su 11am-4pm; Oct. 16-Easter M-Sa 9:30am-5:30pm.) Épernay caters to the champagne set—budget hotels are rare. **⬛Hôtel St-Pierre ❷,** 14 av. Paul-Chandon, is the best budget bet, with spacious, antique-furnished rooms. (☎03 26 54 40 80; fax 03 26 57 88 68. Breakfast €5. Reception 7am-10pm. Singles and doubles €21, with shower €25-32. MC/V.) **Rue Gambetta** has ethnic eateries, while the area around **place des Arcades** and **place Hugues Plomb** is dotted with delis and bakeries. **Postal Code: 51200.**

TROYES

While the city plan of Troyes (pop. 56,000) resembles a champagne cork, this city shares little with its grape-crazy northern neighbors. Gothic churches, 16th-century mansions, and an abundance of museums attest to the city's colorful role in French history, dating back to the Middle Ages. The enormous **Cathédrale St-Pierre et St-Paul,** pl. St-Pierre, down r. Clemenceau past the town hall, has stunning stained glass that has remarkably survived several fires and other disasters. (Open daily 10am-noon and 2-5pm. Closed M morning.) The **Musée d'Art Moderne,** on pl. St-Pierre, has over 2000 works by French artists, including Degas, Rodin, and Seurat. (Open Tu-Su 11am-6pm. €6, students €0.80; W free.) Cinemas and pool halls rub elbows with chic boutiques on **rue Emile Zola.** On warm nights, *Troyens* fill the cafes and taverns of **rue Champeaux** and **rue Mole** near pl. Alexandre Israel.

   Trains run from av. Maréchal Joffre to Paris (1½hr., 14 per day, €8.60). The **tourist office,** 16 bd. Carnot, near the station, helps reserve rooms. (☎03 25 82 62 70; www.ot-troyes.fr. Open M-Sa 9am-12:30pm and 2-6:30pm.) **⬛Les Comtes de Champagne ❸,** 56 r. de la Monnaie, is housed in a 16th-century mansion and has large, airy rooms. (☎03 25 73 11 70; www.comtesdechampagne.com. Reception 7am-10pm. Singles from €28; doubles from €32; triples from €50; quads from €55.) **Camping Municipal ❶,** 2km from Troyes, on N60, has showers and laundry. Take bus #1 (dir.: Pont St-Marie) and ask to be let off at the campground. (☎03 25 81 02 64. Open Apr. to mid-Oct. €4 per person, €5.50 per tent or car.) *Creperies* and inexpensive eateries lie near **rue Champeaux,** in *quartier* St-Jean, and on **rue Général Saussier,** in *quartier* Vauluisant. You can stock up at **Monoprix supermarket,** 78 r. Emile Zola. (Open M-Sa 8:30am-8pm.) **Postal Code: 10000.**

▶ DAYTRIPS FROM TROYES: LES GRANDS LACS. About 30km from Troyes are the freshwater lakes of the Forêt d'Orient. While **Lake Orient** welcomes sunbathers, swimmers, and windsurfers; **Lake Temple** is reserved for fishing and bird-watching; and **Lake Amance** roars with speedboats from **Port Dierville.** The **Comité**

Départmental du Tourisme de l'Aube, 34 quai Dampierre, provides free brochures on various activities. (☎ 03 25 42 50 00; fax 03 25 42 50 88. Open M-F 8:45am-noon and 1:30-6pm.) The Troyes tourist office has bus schedules for the Grands Lacs.

LILLE

A longtime international hub with a rich Flemish ancestry and exuberant nightlife, Lille (pop. 175,000) exudes big-city charm without the hassle. The impressive **Musée des Beaux-Arts,** on pl. de la République, boasts a wide display of 15th- to 20th-century French and Flemish masters. (M: République. Open M 2-6pm, W-Th and Sa-Su 10am-6pm, F 10am-7pm. €4.60, students €3.) Housed in a renovated interior pool, aptly named **La Piscine,** 23 r. de L'Esperance (M: Gare Jean Lebas), has a collection that includes paintings from the 19th and early 20th centuries, vases and stained glass. (Open Tu-Th 11am-6pm, F 11am-8pm, Sa-Su 1-8pm.) The **Vielle Bourse** (Old Stock Exchange), on pl. Général de Gaulle, epitomizing the Flemish Renaissance, houses flower and book markets. (Markets Su and Tu-Sa 9:30am-7:30pm.) At night, students flock to the pubs along **rue Solférino** and **rue Masséna,** while the **vielle ville** has a more sophisticated scene.

Trains leave from Gare Lille Flandres, on pl. de la Gare (M: Gare Lille Flandres), for Brussels, Belgium (1½hr., 20 per day, €22) and Paris (1hr., 21 per day, €34-45). Gare Lille Europe, on r. Le Corbusier (M: Gare Lille Europe; ☎ 08 36 35 35 35), sends **Eurostar** trains to London, Brussels, and Paris and all TGVs to the south of France and Paris. From Gare Lille Flandres, walk straight down r. Faidherbe and turn left through pl. du Théâtre and pl. de Gaulle; behind the huge war monument is the **tourist office,** pl. Rihour (M: Rihour), which offers free maps and currency exchange. (☎ 03 20 21 94 21; fax 03 20 21 94 20. Open M-Sa 9:30am-6:30pm, Su 10am-noon and 2-5pm.) To reach the friendly and spacious **Auberge de Jeunesse (HI) ❶,** 12 r. Malpart, from Gare Lille Flandres, circle left around the station, turn right onto r. du Molinel, take the second left on r. de Paris, and take the 3rd right onto r. Malpart. (☎ 03 20 57 08 94; fax 03 20 63 98 93. M: Mairie de Lille. Sheets €2.75. Key deposit €10. Reception 7-11am and 3pm-1am. Check-out 10am. Curfew 1am. Open Feb. to mid-Dec. Dorms €13.) The spotless **Hôtel Faidherbe ❸,** 42 pl. de la Gare (M: Gare Lille Flandres), is noise-proof. (☎ 03 20 06 27 93; fax 03 20 55 95 38. Singles and doubles €28-42; triples €50. 10% *Let's Go* discount. AmEx/MC/V.) Restaurants and markets line **rue de Béthune, rue Léon Gambetta** and **place du Théâtre.** A huge **Carrefour supermarket** is next to the Gare Lille Europe train station in the EuraLille shopping center. (Open M-Sa 9am-10pm.) **Postal Code:** 59000.

❷ DAYTRIPS FROM LILLE: ARRAS AND VIMY. The town hall of Arras (pop. 80,000), in the gorgeous **Hôtel de Ville,** is built over the eerie **Les Boves** tunnels, which have sheltered both medieval chalk miners and WWI soldiers (Contact tourist office for tours. €3.80, students €2.30.) **Trains** leave pl. Maréchal Foch for Lille (45min., 20 per day, €8.80). From the train station, walk across pl. Foch to r. Gambetta, turn left on r. Desire Delansorne, turn left, and walk two blocks to reach the **tourist office,** on pl. des Héros, in the Hôtel de Ville. (☎ 03 21 51 26 95. Open May-Sept. M-Sa 9am-6:30pm, Su 10am-1pm and 2:30-6:30pm; Oct.-Apr. reduced hours.) The countryside surrounding Arras is dotted with war cemeteries and unmarked graves. The vast limestone **Vimy Memorial,** 12km from Arras, honors the more than 66,000 Canadians killed in WWI. The morbid yet beautiful park, whose soil came from Canada, is dedicated to the crucial victory at Vimy Ridge in 1917. Stay on the marked paths, as there are still undetonated mines in the area. The kiosk by the trenches is the starting point for an **underground tour** of the crumbling tunnels dug by British and Canadian soldiers. (☎03 21 59 19 34. Memorial open dawn-dusk. Tunnel tours Apr. to mid-Nov. 10am-6pm. Free.) The closest town, **Vimy**, is 3km away. **Buses** run from Arras to Vimy (20min., 8 per day M-Sa, €2.40).

CALAIS

Calais (pop. 80,000) is the liveliest of the Channel ports, and with the Chunnel next door, English is spoken as often as French. Rodin's famous sculpture **The Burghers of Calais** stands in front of the **Hôtel de Ville**, at the juncture of bd. Jacquard and r. Royale. Follow r. Royale to the end of r. de Mer for Calais's wide, gorgeous **beaches**. See p. 44 for schedules and prices to **Dover**, England. During the day, free **buses** connect the ferry terminal and train station, Gare Calais-Ville, on bd. Jacquard, from which **trains** leave for: Boulogne (45min., 8 per day, €6.30); Lille (1¼hr., 8 per day, €14); and Paris-Nord (3¼hr., 6 per day, €40). To reach the **tourist office**, 12 bd. Clemenceau, from the train station, turn left, cross the bridge; it's on your right. (☎03 21 96 62 40; fax 03 21 96 01 92. Open M-Sa 9am-7pm, Su 10am-1pm.) The renovated **Centre Européen de Séjour/Auberge de Jeunesse (HI) ❶**, av. Maréchal Delattre de Tassigny, is near the beach. (☎03 21 34 70 20; fax 03 21 96 87 80. Dorms €14.50. Non-members add €1.50.) The quiet **Hotel Bristol ❸**, 13-15 r. du Duc de Guise, is off the main road. (☎03 21 34 53 24. Singles €25; doubles €36. MC/V.) **Markets** are held on pl. Crèvecoeur and on pl. d'Armes (both W and Sa); or look for **Prisunic supermarket**, 17 bd. Jacquard. (Open M-Sa 8:30am-7:30pm, Su 10am-7pm.) **Postal Code:** 62100.

BOULOGNE-SUR-MER

With its refreshing breeze and lavish floral displays, Boulogne (pop. 46,000) is by far the most attractive Channel port. The huge **Château-Musée**, r. de Bernet, houses an eclectic collection that includes Napoleon's second-oldest hat. (Open M and W-Sa 10am-12:30pm and 2-5pm, Su 10am-12:30pm and 2:30-5:30pm. €3.50, students €2.50.) Boulogne also has a huge aquarium, **Le Grand Nausicaa**, bd. Ste-Beuve. (Open July-Aug. daily 9:30am-8pm; Sept.-June reduced hours. €12, students €8.50.) **Trains** leave Gare Boulogne-Ville, bd. Voltaire, for: Calais (30min., 18 per day, €6.40); Lille (2½hr., 11 per day, €18); Paris-Nord (2-3hr., 11 per day, €26-47). From the train station, turn right on bd. Voltaire, turn left on bd. Danou and follow it to pl. Angleterre; continue past pl. de France and pl. Frédéric Sauvage onto r. Gambetta for the **tourist office**, 24 quai Gambetta. (☎03 21 10 88 10; fax 03 21 10 88 11. Open July-Aug. M-Sa 9am-7pm, Su 10am-1pm and 3-6pm; Sept.-June reduced hours.) The fantastic ⛵**Auberge de Jeunesse (HI) ❶**, 56 pl. Rouget de Lisle, is across from the station. (☎03 21 99 15 30; fax 03 21 80 45 62. **Internet** €2 per 40min. Reception in summer daily 8am-1am; off-season 8am-midnight. Curfew 1am. Dorms €15. Nonmembers add €3. MC/V.) **Champion supermarket**, on r. Daunou, is in the Centre Commercial de la Liane mall. (Open M-Sa 8:30am-8pm.) **Postal Code:** 62200.

GERMANY
(DEUTSCHLAND)

Germany is a nation saddled with an incredibly fractured past. Steeped deeply in Beethoven's fiery orchestration and Goethe's Faustian whirlwind, modern Germany must also contend with the legacy of xenophobia and genocide left by Hitler and the Third Reich. Even now, more than a decade after the fall of the Berlin Wall, Germans are still fashioning a new identity for themselves. After centuries of war and fragmentation, Germany finds itself a wealthy nation at the forefront of both European and global politics. Its medieval castles, snow-covered mountains, and funky metropolises make Germany well worth a visit.

LIFE AND TIMES

HISTORY

EARLY HISTORY AND THE FIRST REICH (UNTIL 1400). Early German history—actually, most of German history—can be summed up as alternating unification and fracture. The **Roman Empire** conquered the independent tribes that had formerly occupied the area; Roman ruins can still be seen in **Trier** (p. 486) and **Cologne** (p. 472). When the Empire collapsed, the Germanic tribes separated again, only to be reunified in the 8th century by **Charlemagne** (Karl der Große) in an empire now known as the **First Reich,** or kingdom. Charlemagne established his capital at

---

SUGGESTED ITINERARIES

THREE DAYS Enjoy two days in **Berlin** (p. 418): Stroll along **Unter den Linden** and the **Ku'damm**, gawk at the **Brandenburger Tor** and the **Reichstag**, and explore the **Tiergarten**. Walk along the **East Side Gallery** and visit **Checkpoint Charlie** for a history of the Berlin Wall, then spend an afternoon at **Schloß Sans Soucci** (p. 447). Overnight it to Bavarian **Munich** (p. 492) for a beer-filled last day.

ONE WEEK After scrambling through **Berlin** (3 days), head north to racy **Hamburg** (1 day, p. 460). Take in the cathedral of **Cologne** (1 day, p. 472) before heading to the former West German capital **Bonn** (1 day, p. 477). End your trip in true Bavarian style with castles, churches, and beer galore in **Munich** (1 day)

THREE WEEKS Start in **Berlin** (3 days). Party in **Hamburg** (2 days), stop by **Lübeck** for marzipan (1 day, p. 468), and zip to **Cologne** (1 day). Peek at Charlemagne's remains in **Aachen** (1 day, p. 472), spend a day in glitzy **Frankfurt** (p. 479), and then visit Germany's oldest university in **Heidelberg** (2 days, p. 486). Get lost in the fairy-tale **Schwarzwald** forest (1 day, p. 490), listen to the Glockenspiel in **Munich** (2 days), and marvel at **Neuschwanstein** (1 day, p. 510). Head to the hills above stunning **Berchtesgaden** (1 day, p. 505), tour the wineries of the **Romantic Road** (2 days, p. 508) and take in **Trier** (1 day, p. 486), Germany's oldest city, before ending your trip in **Dresden** (2 days, p. 448).

Aachen (p. 472), where his earthly remains reside today. After Charlemagne's death, the empire was split up again. Without a strong leader, the former empire disintegrated into decentralized **feudalism.** Visit **Rothenburg** (p. 508) for a glimpse into a medieval walled city typical of the time.

THE NORTHERN RENAISSANCE (1400-1517). Inspired by the new ideas of the Italian Renaissance, northern philosophers developed their own concept of **humanism,** focusing particularly on religious reform and a return to Classics (virtues and works). **Johannes Gutenberg** paved the way for widespread dissemination of ideas by inventing the **printing press** in Mainz (p. 484); his Latin printing of the Bible is arguably the world's most seminal publication. This invention allowed rapid production of books, which increased literacy and put information in the hands of the people for the first time.

RELIGION AND REFORM (1517-1700). On All Saints' Day, 1517, **Martin Luther** nailed his **95 Theses** to the door of Wittenberg's church (p. 456), condemning the Catholic Church's extravagance and its practice of selling **indulgences**—certificates that promised to shorten the owner's stay in purgatory. Luther's ideas sparked the **Protestant Reformation,** a period of intense religious conflict. During this time, Luther translated the New Testament from Latin into German, standardizing the German language and allowing lay-people to read the Bible directly for the first time. Rising continent-wide tensions between Catholics and Protestants eventually led to the **Thirty Years' War** (1618-1648). After the fighting, Germany emerged as a group of small, independent territories, each ruled by a local prince, ripe for conquer, separation, and re-conquer.

RISE OF BRANDENBURG-PRUSSIA (1700-1862). Through a series of strategic marriages, the **Hohenzollern** family gained control over a large number of these territories. Their kingdom, Brandenburg-Prussia, became an absolutist state when **Frederick I** crowned himself king in 1701. His grandson, **Frederick the Great,** acquired huge chunks of land and established Prussia as a major world power. When **Napoleon** began nibbling at its borders in the early 1800s, Prussia fractured again, remaining a loose and unstable confederation of states even after its defeat.

THE SECOND REICH (1862-1914). In 1862, worldly aristocrat **Otto von Bismarck** was named chancellor. He believed that "blood and iron" could create a strong and unified German nation. Bismarck consolidated Prussia into a powerful nation through a series of military movements. The culmination was the **Franco-Prussian War** in 1870, when the technologically superior Prussians swept through France. Bismarck besieged Paris, and the king of Prussia, **Wilhelm I,** rose to **Kaiser of the German Reich** at the Palace of Versailles. Bismarck had presented Germany with an offer it couldn't refuse: Unification in exchange for an authoritarian monarchy.

WORLD WAR I (1914-1918). On the eve of **World War I,** Europe was entangled in a complex web of precarious alliances. In 1914, when a Serbian nationalist assassinated **Archduke Franz-Ferdinand,** heir to the Austrian throne, Austria declared war on Serbia. Germany jumped in to help Austria, and the rest of Europe was soon drawn into full-blown war. After four agonizing years of trench warfare, Germany and its allies were defeated. Germany's aggressiveness in France, along with its use of **unrestricted submarine warfare,** allowed the victors to place responsibility for WWI on Germany's shoulders.

THE WEIMAR REPUBLIC (1918-1933). France insisted on a harsh peace agreement with the **Treaty of Versailles,** which imposed staggering reparation payments, drastically reduced the German army, and officially ascribed the blame for the war to Germany. The defeated Germans had little choice but to accept the humiliating terms, and a new republic was set up in **Weimar** (p. 457).

Outstanding war debts and the burden of reparations produced staggering hyperinflation from 1922-1923; paper money was worth more as fireplace fuel than currency. Already smarting from Versailles, the German people needed stability and relief from the post-war hardships, which a charismatic Austrian named **Adolf Hitler** seemed to promise. His party, the **Nazis** (National Socialists), was increasingly associated with über-nationalist ideals.

Hitler's first attempt to seize power, the **Beer Hall Putsch** in Munich (1923), was unsuccessful. But as economic troubles worsened, more and more Germans were drawn to the Nazis and their promises of prosperity and community. Party membership increased to more than a million by 1930. Hitler failed in a presidential bid against the nearly senile war-hero **Paul von Hindenburg** in 1932, but since elections made the Nazis the dominant party in the legislature, Hindenburg reluctantly appointed Hitler chancellor on January 30, 1933.

BEGINNING OF THE THIRD REICH (1933-1939). Hitler's platform, crystallized in his book, **Mein Kampf** (*My Struggle*) provided a scapegoat for WWI losses—the Jews—and played on centuries-old feelings of anti-Semitism. The new government quickly instituted a boycott of Jewish enterprises and expelled Jews from professional and civil service; rival parties that might have opposed the Nazis were outlawed or dissolved. In 1934, after Hindenburg's death, Hitler appropriated presidential powers for himself; that same year, the first of the **Nürnberg Laws** were passed, depriving Jews of German citizenship and preventing intermarriage between Aryan and Jewish Germans—it was felt that the "debased" Jews would taint the pure and "superior" German blood. Nazis destroyed thousands of Jewish businesses, burned synagogues, and killed and deported thousands of Jews on **Kristallnacht** (Night of Broken Glass), November 9, 1938. With the help of **Joseph Goebbels**, his minister of propaganda, Hitler consolidated his power by saturating mass culture—from art to literature to movies to music—with Nazi ideology: The Nazis burned books by Jewish and "subversive" authors at Bebelplatz in Berlin (p. 433), banned American films and music, and destroyed "degenerate" art in favor of propagandist paintings and statues.

Hitler was also busy mounting a war effort. He first freed Germany from making reparations payments by abrogating the Treaty of Versailles. Next, he annexed Austria in an infamous attack known as the **Anschluß** (1938). Other nations, hoping that Hitler would be satisfied with these new acquisitions, followed a policy of **appeasement,** led by British Prime Minster Neville Chamberlain, and allowed Germany to take over the Sudetenland region (now in the Czech Republic). However, it soon became clear that Hitler was after more than small territorial gains.

WORLD WAR II (1939-1945). On September 1, 1939, German tanks rolled into Poland. Britain and France, bound by treaty to defend Poland, immediately declared war on Germany, and the rest of Europe was again dragged into global conflict. Germany's new tactic of **Blitzkrieg** (literally, "lightning war") quickly crushed Poland. Denmark, Norway, Belgium, The Netherlands, and France were soon overwhelmed as well.

The Nazis then began a two-front war, attacking westward with an air-borne offensive in the **Battle of Britain** and eastward in the **invasion of the USSR.** However, daily air raids spurred the British to fight harder rather than submit. Meanwhile, the *Blitzkrieg* faltered in the Russian winter and Hitler sacrificed thousands of German soldiers in his obstinate refusal to retreat. The bloody **Battle of Stalingrad** (1942-1943) marked a critical turning point in the East as the Soviets gained the upper hand. Soon, Germany was retreating on all fronts. The Allied landing in Normandy on **D-Day** (June 6, 1944) preceded an arduous eastward advance across Europe; the Soviet Army rolled westward and took Berlin in April 1945. The Third Reich, which Hitler had boasted would endure for 1000 years, had lasted only 12.

THE HOLOCAUST. By the outbreak of WWII, Jews had lost virtually all rights and were forced to identify themselves with a yellow Star of David patch. The Nazis portrayed Jews as the ultimate influence corrupting the German soul, and Hitler was fixated on his **Final Solution:** Genocide. Seven death camps, including **Buchenwald** (p. 457), were designed for mass extermination; dozens of "labor" camps such as **Dachau** (p. 503) were operating before the war's end. Nearly six million Jews—two-thirds of Europe's Jewish population—mostly from Poland and the Soviet Union, were gassed, shot, starved, worked to death, or killed by exposure. Millions of other victims, including prisoners of war, Slavs, Roma, homosexuals, the mentally disabled, and political dissidents, also died in Nazi camps.

OCCUPATION AND DIVISION (1945-1949). In July 1945, the United States, Great Britain, and the Soviet Union met at **Potsdam** to partition Germany into zones of occupation: The east under the Soviets, the west under the British and Americans, and Berlin under divided control. The Allied program for the **Occupation**—democratization, demilitarization, and de-Nazification—proceeded, but growing animosity between the Soviets and the Western Allies made joint control of Germany increasingly difficult. In 1947, the Allies merged their occupation zones into a single economic unit and began to rebuild a market economy with huge cash infusions under the American **Marshall Plan.** East and West Germany became increasingly distant, especially after the Western Allies introduced the **Deutschmark** into their zones.

THE FEDERAL REPUBLIC OF GERMANY (1949-1989). The Federal Republic of Germany (*Bundesrepublik Deutschland*) was established as the provisional government of Western Germany on May 24, 1949. **Basic Law** safeguarded individual rights and established a system of freely elected parliamentary assemblies. One of the most visionary paragraphs established a **Right of Asylum,** guaranteeing refuge to any person fleeing persecution.

As the only party untainted by the Third Reich, the Social Democratic Party seemed poised to dominate postwar German politics, but the **Christian Democratic Union** (CDP) provided some competition by uniting Germany's historically fragmented conservatives and centrists under a nondenominational platform. With former Cologne mayor **Konrad Adenauer** at the helm, the CDU won a small majority of seats in the Federal Republic's first general election. As chancellor, Adenauer unflaggingly pursued the integration of Germany into a unified Europe; West Germany was aligned with **NATO** (North Atlantic Treaty Organization) in 1955 and became one of the charter members of the European Economic Community (later the **European Union**) in 1957. Speedy fiscal recovery secured the future dominance of the CDU party. In 1982, Christian Democrat **Helmut Kohl** became chancellor and pursued a policy of welfare state cutbacks, tight monetary policy, and military cooperation with the US.

MEANWHILE...IN THE GERMAN DEMOCRATIC REPUBLIC. In spite of pledges to the contrary, the Soviets stopped holding free elections in their sector by 1949. On October 7, 1949, they declared the establishment of the **German Democratic Republic,** with the national capital in Berlin. Constitutional promises of civil liberties and democracy were empty: East Germany became unquestioningly subservient to the Soviet Union. The **Stasi,** or secret police, maintained a network of agents that strove to monitor every citizen from their headquarters in Berlin (p. 437)—one in seven East Germans was a paid informant.

Many East Germans chose to escape oppression by emigrating to West Germany. By 1961, more than three million had illegally crossed the border, and the East German government decided to stop the exodus of young skilled workers. Overnight on August 12, the first barriers of the **Berlin Wall** were laid, and barbed wire and guns dissuaded further attempts to escape, making for a confusing and dangerous barrier between the two halves.

REUNIFICATION (1989). When **Mikhail Gorbachev** took the helm of the USSR in 1985, liberalizing reform spread throughout the Eastern Bloc under his policy of *glasnost* (openness). East Germany, however, remained under tight control. The turning point came in May 1989 when Hungary dismantled its barbed-wire border with Austria, giving East Germans an escape route to the West. In October, Gorbachev announced that the USSR would not interfere with East Germany's domestic affairs, and citizens began to demand free elections, freedom of press, and freedom of travel. The entire East German government resigned on November 8, and a day later, a Central Committee spokesperson announced the opening of all borders to the West.

The destruction of the Wall was the most symbolically significant event for Germans since the end of WWII. The signing of the **Four-Plus-Two Treaty** by the two Germanies and the four occupying powers on September 12, 1990, signaled the **end of a divided Germany.** On October 3, 1990, the Allies forfeited their occupation rights, East Germany ceased to exist, and Germany became one united sovereign nation for the first time in 45 years. However, East and West Germany did not come together on equal terms. The collapse of East Germany's inefficient industries and institutions led to massive unemployment and the Federal Republic's worst-ever recession. Many Westerners resented the inflation and taxes brought on by reunification, while Easterners missed the generous social benefits that Communism had afforded them. Economic frustrations led to the scapegoating of foreigners, especially asylum-seekers from Eastern Europe and immigrant workers. Thankfully, violence has decreased greatly over the past few years.

TODAY

After the dramatic fall of the Berlin Wall in 1989, Helmut Kohl and his CDU party seemed insurmountable. Carrying their momentum into the first all-German elections, the CDU scored a stunning victory. However, Kohl found it difficult to manage the reunification, and his popularity plummeted to the point that Easterners pelted him with eggs during campaign visits. In 1998, left-wing parties ousted the CDU, electing **Gerhard Schroeder** chancellor.

Germany's new place within Europe remains a great political question. The burden of the past makes everyone, including Germans themselves, nervous about Germany's participation in international military operations. Recently, Germans have earned a reputation as a peace-loving people; in the **Kosovo** crisis, for example, Germany played a pivotal role in negotiating a peace accord, and German forces were present both at peacekeeping missions in Yugoslavia and flood relief operations in Africa. Germany has also been one of the most outspoken critics of Anglo-American foreign policy in the wake of the terrorist attack of 9/11, greeting American President George W. Bush's visit to Berlin in May 2002 with widespread rioting, necessitating the largest police presence since the end of WWII. The persistent feeling among Germans now tends toward isolationism, but such a neutral stance may not be possible in the long run for Europe's most populous and economically powerful nation.

THE ARTS

LITERATURE

NARRATIVE. The first significant German novel, **Hans J. C. von Grimmelshausen's** roguish series *Simplicissimus*, was written during the chaos of the Thirty Years' War. By the 18th century, the German literary scene was flourishing. **Johann Wolfgang von Goethe** exemplified the Romantic era with emotional, dramatic masterpieces such as *Faust* (1832), while the **Brothers Grimm** transformed folk tales from an oral tradition into a morbid, child-rearing tool. A rush of realistic political literature emerged in the turbulent mid-19th century; **Heinrich Heine,** as much a poet as a satirist, was one of the finest. In the early 20th century, **Rainer Maria Rilke,** living in Austria-Hungary, produced some of Germany's weepiest poems, and **Franz Kafka** examined the complications of modern existence in *The Metamorphosis* (1915). **Thomas Mann** bore the modern novel to a new height with *The Magic Mountain* (1924) and *Doctor Faustus* (1947), while **Hermann Hesse** experimented with Eastern motifs in *Siddhartha* (1922).

Despite the disruption of WWI, the **Weimar era** was a period of active artistic production. **Erich Maria Remarque**'s *All Quiet on the Western Front* (1929), a blunt account of the horrors of war, became an international bestseller. **Bertolt Brecht**'s dramas and poems presented humankind in all its grotesque absurdity. To nurse German literature back to health after the Nazi book-burning years, several writers, including **Günter Grass** and poet **Paul Celan**, formed **Gruppe 47**, named after the year of its founding. The group coined the term *Nullstunde* ("Zero Hour") to signify that after WWII, culture had to begin again. Much of the ensuing literature dealt with the problem of Germany's Nazi past; the novels of Grass and **Heinrich Böll** and the poetry of **Hans Magnus Enzensberger** turned a critical eye to post-war West Germany's repressive tendencies.

PHILOSOPHY. Germany's philosophical tradition is one of the most respected in the world. Initially, philosophy dealt only with religion. In 1517, **Martin Luther**'s *95 Theses* denied papal infallibility, claiming that only scripture was holy and thus advocating a direct relationship with God; **Gottfried Wilhelm Leibnitz** thought of God as a watchmaker who set the individual's body and soul in motion like two synchronized clocks. During the **Enlightenment**, reason was the key: **Immanuel Kant** argued that ethics can be rationally deduced. **Georg W. F. Hegel** proposed that world history and the development of the individual consciousness could be understood as the synthesis of a thesis and antithesis.

The 19th century brought several controversial but highly influential theories. The founder of modern socialism, **Karl Marx**, asserted that class conflict was the driving force of all history. **Friedrich Nietzsche** developed the idea of the *Übermensch*, a super-man so wise and self-mastered that he could enjoy life even to the point of eternal repetition. **Max Weber** pinpointed the "Protestant Ethic": Work. In the interwar period, **Martin Heidegger** became one of the main exponents of **Existentialism;** his *Being and Time* (1927) examines the crisis of alienation in a world of technical development. After the fall of the Third Reich, thinkers **Theodor Adorno** and **Max Horkheimer** penned the classic *Dialectic of Enlightenment* (1947), which suggests that civilization ultimately culminates in Fascism. More recently, **Jürgen Habermas** has criticized German reunification, citing the danger of joining two nations that have adopted very different cultures.

MUSIC

Johann Sebastian Bach was one of the first great German composers. Bach and his contemporary **Georg Friedrich Händel** composed during the Baroque period of the 17th century, which was known for its extravagant decoration, and popularized the theme-and-variation pattern. Händel's *Messiah* (1741) is still widely performed today—Hallelujah!

The 19th century was an era of German musical hegemony. **Ludwig van Beethoven**'s symphonies and piano sonatas bridged Classicism and Romanticism with rhythmic drives and intense emotional expressionism; he is perhaps best known in popular culture for his dramatic *Fifth* and *Ninth Symphonies* (1808 and 1824, respectively). Meanwhile, **Felix Mendelssohn-Bartholdy** wrote more ethereal works, such as his musical interpretation of Shakespeare's *A Midsummer Night's Dream* (1826). The second generation of Romantic composers included **Johannes Brahms**, who imbued Classical forms with Romantic emotion. *Tristan and Isolde* (1859), *Lohengrin* (1850), and the other (interminably long) operas of **Richard Wagner** express the nationalist sentiments rising in the mid-19th century.

Germany's postwar music scene is mostly transnational; Germans are more likely to listen to American pop than their own countrymen. Nevertheless, they have made important contributions to the field. Germany is best known internationally for pioneering techno with bands like **Kraftwerk,** to the delight of clubgoers worldwide. Since the rise of **Die fantastischen Vier,** the first German rap group, the hip-hop torch has been passed to **Eins, Zwo** and various other numbers.

THE VISUAL ARTS

ARCHITECTURE. Outstanding **Romanesque** cathedrals, featuring a clover-leaf floor plan, numerous towers, and a mitre-like steeple, can be found along the Rhine at **Trier** (p. 486) and **Mainz** (p. 484). The **Gothic** style, with its pointed spires and vaulted roofs, gradually replaced the Romanesque form from 1300-1500; stained-glass windows fill otherwise gloomy interiors with divine light. The cathedral at **Cologne** (p. 472) is one of the most famous German Gothic structures. Secular architecture at the end of the Middle Ages was dominated by the **Fachwerk** (half-timbered) houses that can still be seen in the *Altstadt* (old town) sections of many German cities. **Baroque** ostentation bloomed late (in the 17th century); the **Zwinger** (p. 451) in Dresden is a magnificent example. Baroque developed into the highly decorative **Rococo** style with ornately garnished buildings like **Schloß Sanssouci** (p. 447). A simpler movement, **Neoclassicism,** arose in reaction to the frou-frou Rococo facades; the **Brandenburger Tor** (p. 432) and the buildings along **Unter den Linden** in Berlin use stylistic elements of Classical Greece and Rome. In 1919, Weimar saw the birth of the boxy **Bauhaus** style of architecture, in which form allegedly follows function. The movement later moved to **Dessau,** where a school for design still flourishes.

ON THE WALL. In the Renaissance, **Albrecht Dürer** emerged as a master of engraving and draftsmanship. His *Adam and Eve* still peppers advertisements today, and his *Self-Portrait at 20* (1500) was one of the first self-portraits in Europe. In the 19th century, **Caspar David Friedrich** painted dramatic mountain scenes and billowing landscapes that exemplify the Romantic style. However, it was in the 20th century that German art truly blossomed. The deliberate anti-realism of **German Expressionism** intensified color and object representation to project deeply personal emotions. A 1911 exhibition in Munich entitled **Der Blaue Reiter** (The Blue Rider), led by Russian emigré **Wassily Kandinsky,** displayed some of the first totally non-representational paintings in Western art. In the period between the wars, artists became increasingly political in reaction to the rise of Fascism: **Max Beckmann** painted posed figures whose gestures and symbolism expressed a tortured view of man's condition, and **Max Ernst** started a **Dadaist** group in Cologne, conveying artistic nihilism through collage. During the Nazi era, almost all art was controlled by the state for propagandistic purposes, featuring idealized images of Aryan workers and soldiers. Nevertheless, the German art scene bounced back after the war's end. **Anselm Kiefer** examines Germany's previously unapproachable past in his paintings, while **Josef Beuys**'s innovative art objects and performances challenge artistic conventions.

FACTS AND FIGURES

Official Name: Federal Republic of Germany.

Capital: Berlin.

Major Cities: Cologne, Frankfurt, Hamburg, Munich.

Population: 83,030,000.

Land Area: 357,021 sq. km.

Time Zone: GMT + 1.

Language: German.

Religions: Protestant (38%), Roman Catholic (34%), Muslim (2%), unaffiliated or other (27%).

ESSENTIALS

WHEN TO GO

Germany's climate is temperate, with rain year-round (especially in summer). The cloudy, moderate months of May, June, and September are the best time to go, as there are fewer tourists and the weather is pleasant. Germans head to vacation spots en masse in early July with the onset of school vacations. Winter sports gear up November to April; skiing high-season is mid-December to March.

DOCUMENTS AND FORMALITIES

VISAS. South Africans require a visa. Citizens of Australia, Canada, the EU, New Zealand, and the US do not need a visa for stays of up to 90 days.

EMBASSIES. All foreign embassies are in Berlin (p. 418). German embassies at home include: **Australia,** 119 Empire Circuit, Yarralumla, Canberra, ACT 2600 (☎(02) 62 70 19 11); **Canada,** 1 Waverly St., Ottawa, ON K2P OT8 (☎(613) 232-1101); **Ireland,** 31 Trimleston Ave., Booterstown, Blackrock, Co. Dublin (☎(01) 269 30 11); **New Zealand,** 90-92 Hobson St., Thorndon, Wellington (☎(04) 473 60 63); **South Africa,** 180 Blackwood St., Arcadia, Pretoria, 0083 (☎(012) 427 89 00); **UK,** 23 Belgrave Sq., London SW1X 8PZ (☎(020) 7824 1300); and **US,** 4645 Reservoir Rd., Washington, D.C. 20007 (☎202-298-8140).

TRANSPORTATION

BY PLANE. Most flights land in Frankfurt; Berlin, Munich, and Hamburg also have international airports. **Lufthansa,** the national airline, has the most flights in and out of the country, but they're not always the cheapest option. Flying within Germany is usually more expensive and less convenient than taking the train.

BY TRAIN. The **DB (Deutsche Bahn)** network (in Germany ☎(0180) 599 66 33; www.bahn.de) is Europe's best but also one of its most expensive. **RE** (Regional-Express) and the slightly slower **RB** (RegionalBahn) trains include a number of rail networks between neighboring cities. **IR** (InterRegio) trains, covering larger networks between cities, are speedy and comfortable. **D** trains are foreign trains that serve international routes. **EC** (EuroCity) and **IC** (InterCity) trains zoom between major cities every hour from 6am-10pm. You must purchase a *Zuschlag* (supplement) for IC or EC trains (€3.60). **ICE** (InterCityExpress) trains approach the luxury and kinetics of an airplane, running at speeds up to 280km per hour. On all trains, second-class compartments are clean and comfortable.

Designed for tourists, the **German Railpass** allows unlimited travel for four to 10 days within a four-week period. Non-Europeans can purchase German Railpasses in their home countries and—with a passport—in major German train stations (2nd-class 4-day pass €180, 10-day €316). The **German Rail Youth Pass** is for those under 26 (4-day pass €142, 10-day €216). A **Schönes-Wochenende-Ticket** (€28) gives up to five people unlimited travel on any of the slower trains (RE or RB) from 12:01am Saturday or Sunday until 3am the next day. Single travelers often find larger groups who will share their ticket for a fraction of the purchase cost.

BY BUS. Bus service between cities and to outlying areas runs from the local **ZOB** (*Zentralomnibusbahnhof*), which is usually close to the main train station. Buses are often slightly more expensive than trains for comparable distances. Railpasses are not valid on any buses other than a few run by Deutsche Bahn.

BY CAR. German road conditions are generally excellent. It's true, there is no set speed limit on the *Autobahn*, only a recommendation of 130kph (80mph). Germans drive fast. Watch for signs indicating the right-of-way (usually designated by a yellow triangle). The *Autobahn* is marked by an intuitive "A" on signs; secondary highways, where the speed limit is usually 100kph (60mph), are accompanied by signs bearing a "B." Germans drive on the right side of the road; in cities and towns, speed limits hover around 30-60kph (20-35mph). Germans use mainly unleaded gas; prices run around €4.30 per gallon, or €1.10 per liter. **Mitfahrzentralen** are agencies that pair up drivers and riders for a small fee; riders then negotiate payment for the trip with the driver.

BY BIKE. Cities and towns have designated bike lanes, often on the sidewalk. *Germany by Bike*, by Nadine Slavinski (Mountaineers Books, 1994; US$15), details 20 tours throughout the country.

TOURIST SERVICES AND MONEY

TOURIST OFFICES. Every city in Germany has a tourist office, usually near the *Hauptbahnhof* (main train station) or *Marktplatz* (central square). All are marked by a thick lowercase "i" sign. Many offices book rooms for a small fee. The tourist info website for Germany is www.germany-tourism.de.

MONEY. On January 1, 2002, the **euro** (€) replaced the **Deutschmark** (DM) as the unit of currency in Germany. For more info, see p. 14. As a general rule, it's cheaper to exchange money in Germany than at home. If you stay in hostels and prepare your own food, expect to spend anywhere from €20-40 per person per day. **Tipping** is not practiced as liberally in Germany as elsewhere—most Germans just round up €1. Note that tips in Germany are not left lying on the table, but handed directly to the server when you pay. If you don't want any change, say *"Das stimmt so"* (das SHTIMMT zo). Germans rarely bargain except at flea markets. Most goods and services bought in Germany will automatically include a 7 or 16% **value-added tax (VAT)**; see p. 16 for more information.

COMMUNICATION

TELEPHONES. Most public phones accept only telephone cards. You can pick up a *Telefonkarte* (phone card) in post offices, at kiosks, or at selected Deutsche Bahn counters in major train stations. **Mobile phones** are an increasingly popular and economical alternative (p. 30). There is no standard length for telephone numbers. The smaller the city, the more digits in the city code, while individual phone numbers have between three and 10 digits. International direct dial numbers include: **AT&T**, ☎800 22 55 288; **British Telecom**, ☎800 89 00 49; **Canada Direct**, ☎800 888 00 14; **Ireland Direct**, ☎08000 800 353; **MCI**, ☎800 88 88 000; **Sprint**, ☎800 888 00 13; **Telecom New Zealand**, ☎800 080 00 64; **Telkom South Africa**, ☎800 180 00 27; **Telstra Australia**, ☎800 08 00 061.

MAIL. *Let's Go* lists the addresses for mail to be held (*Postlagernde Briefe*) in the practical information sections of big cities. The mail will go to the main post office unless you specify a post office by street address. Air mail usually takes 3-7 days to North America, Europe, and Australia; 6-12 days to New Zealand.

EMERGENCY	Police: ☎110. Ambulance and Fire: ☎112.
PHONE CODES	Country code: 49. International dialing prefix: 00.

INTERNET ACCESS. Most German cities (as well as a surprising number of smaller towns) have at least one Internet cafe with web access for about €1-5 per 30min. Some German universities have banks of computers hooked up to the Internet in their libraries, though ostensibly for student use.

LANGUAGE. Many people in Western Germany speak English; this is less common in the East and among the older generations. The letter ß is equivalent to a double s. For basic German words and phrases, see p. 1036.

ACCOMMODATIONS AND CAMPING

GERMANY	❶	❷	❸	❹	❺
ACCOMMODATIONS	under €14	€14-19	€20-35	€36-60	over €60

Germany currently has about 600 **hostels**—more than any other nation on Earth. Official hostels in Germany are overseen by **DJH** (*Deutsches Jugendherbergswerk*), Bismarckstr. 8, 32756 Detmold, Germany (☎(05231) 740 10; www.djh.de). DJH has recently initiated a growing number of **Jugendgästehäuser,** youth guest houses that have more facilities and attract slightly older guests. DJH publishes *Jugendherbergen in Deutschland*, a guide to all federated German hostels. The cheapest **hotel-style** accommodations are places with *Pension, Gasthof, Gästehaus,* or *Hotel-Garni* in the name. Hotel rooms start at €20 for singles and €25 for doubles; in large cities, expect to pay nearly twice as much. *Frühstück* (breakfast) is almost always available and often included. The best bet for a cheap bed is often a **Privatzimmer** (a room in a family home). This option works best if you have a rudimentary knowledge of German. Prices generally run €15-30 per person. Travelers over 26 who would pay higher prices at youth hostels will find these rooms within their budget range. Reservations are made through the local tourist office or through a private *Zimmervermittlung* (room-booking office) for free or a €1-4 fee. Germans love **camping;** over 2600 campsites dot the outskirts of even the most major cities. Facilities are well maintained and usually provide showers, bathrooms, and a restaurant or store. Camping costs €3-6 per person, with additional charges for tents and vehicles. Blue signs with a black tent on a white background indicate official sites.

FOOD AND DRINK

GERMANY	❶	❷	❸	❹	❺
FOOD	under €4	€4-6	€7-12	€13-20	over €20

The typical German breakfast consists of coffee or tea with *Brötchen* (rolls), *Wurst* (cold sausage), and *Käse* (cheese). The main meal of the day, *Mittagessen* (lunch), includes soup, broiled sausage or roasted meat, potatoes or dumplings, and a salad or vegetable side dish. *Abendessen* or *Abendbrot* (dinner) is a reprise of breakfast, only beer replaces coffee and the selection of meats and cheeses is wider. Many older Germans indulge in a daily ritual of *Kaffee und Kuchen* (coffee and cake) at 3 or 4pm. To eat on the cheap, stick to the daily *Tagesmenü*, buy food in supermarkets, or, if you have a student ID, head to a university *Mensa* (cafeteria). Fast-food *Imbiß* stands also offer cheap fare; try the delicious Turkish *Döner*, something like a gyro. The average German beer is maltier and more "bread-like" than Czech, Dutch, or American beers; an affectionate German slang term for beer is *Flüßige Brot* ("liquid bread").

HOLIDAYS AND FESTIVALS

Holidays: Epiphany (Jan. 6); Good Friday (Apr. 9); Easter Sunday and Monday (Apr. 11-12); Labor Day (May 1); Ascension Day (May 29); Whit Sunday and Monday (May 30-31); Corpus Christi (June 10); Assumption Day (Aug. 15); Day of German Unity (Oct. 3); All Saints' Day (Nov. 1); Christmas (Dec. 25-26).

Festivals: Check out **Fasching** in Munich (Jan. 7-Feb. 24; p. 492), the **Berlinale Film Festival** (Feb. 5-15; p. 442), **Karneval** in Cologne (Feb. 19-24; p. 477), **Christopher Street Day** in Berlin and other major cities (late June), the **Love Parade** in Berlin (mid-July; p. 7), **Oktoberfest** in Munich (Sept. 18-Oct. 3; p. 492), and the **Christmas Market** in Nuremberg.

BERLIN ☎ 030

Don't wait any longer to see Berlin (pop. 3.4 million). The city is nearing the end of a massive transitional phase, developing from a reunited metropolis reeling in the aftermath of the Cold War to the epicenter of the EU—and the Berlin of five or even two years from now will be radically different from the Berlin of today. Germany is the industrial leader of the continent, and when the Lehrter *Stadtbahnhof* (Europe's largest train station) opens in 2004, this city will essentially become its capital too. However, in the wake of the Nazi regime, some Germans question their own ability—and right—to govern. The problem of "*Mauer im Kopf*" ("wall in the head"), the psychological division between East and West Germany, is felt here more than anywhere else. Still, Berliners have always been more progressive than the rest of their countrymen, a tendency that prompted Hitler's famous proclamation: "Berliners are not fit to be German!" As a result, the atmosphere is the most diverse and tolerant in the country, with a famous gay and lesbian scene and an almost non-existent racial crime rate. But the real reason to visit is the almost palpable tension between past and future. No other city is currently poised to attain such geopolitical importance, and the air is taut with hope and foreboding.

✈ INTERCITY TRANSPORTATION

Berlin is rapidly becoming the hub of the international rail network, with rail and air connections to most other European capitals. Almost all European airlines have service to one of Berlin's three airports.

Flights: For info on all 3 airports, call ☎ (0180) 500 01 86. The city is transitioning from 3 airports to 1 (Flughafen Schönefeld), but for now **Flughafen Tegel** (TXL) remains Berlin's main international airport. Express bus X9 from *Bahnhof Zoo*, bus #109 from *Jakob-Kaiser-Pl.* on U7, bus #128 from *Kurt-Schumacher-Pl.* on U6, or bus TXL from *Potsdamer Platz*. **Flughafen Schönefeld** (SXF), southeast of Berlin, has intercontinental flights. S9 or S45 to *Flughafen Berlin Schönefeld*. **Flughafen Tempelhof** (THF), Berlin's smallest airport, has intra-German and European flights. U6 to *Pl. der Luftbrücke*.

Train Stations: Trains to and from Berlin are serviced by **Zoologischer Garten** (almost always called **Bahnhof Zoo**) in the West and **Ostbahnhof** in the East. Most trains go to both stations, but some connections to cities in former East Germany only stop at *Ostbahnhof*. For info call ☎ (0180) 599 66 33 or visit www.bahn.de. Trains run every hour to: **Cologne** (4¼hr., €98); **Frankfurt** (4hr., €106); **Hamburg** (2½hr., €45); **Leipzig** (2hr., €34); **Munich** (6½-7hr., €102). One per 2hr. to: **Dresden** (2¼hr., €22); **Rostock** (2¾hr., €34). International connections to: **Amsterdam** (6½hr.); **Brussels** (7½hr.); **Budapest** (12hr.); **Copenhagen** (7½hr.); **Kraków** (8½-11hr.); **Moscow** (27-33hr.); **Paris** (9hr.); **Prague** (5hr.); **Rome** (17½-21hr.); **Stockholm** (13-16hr.); **Vienna** (9½hr.); **Warsaw** (6hr.); **Zurich** (8½hr.). Times and prices change frequently—check at the computers in the stations. Under Deutsche Bahn's new pricing system, prices depend on when you book. If you book at the last minute, you'll get the prices we list; for the cheapest tickets, book at least three weeks in advance. The **Euraide** counter has info in English, sells tickets, and often has the shortest lines.

Buses: ZOB, the central bus station (☎301 03 80), by the *Funkturm* near Kaiserdamm. U2 to *Kaiserdamm* or S4, 45, or 46 to *Witzleben*. Open M-F 6am-7:30pm, Sa-Su 6am-noon. Check *Zitty* and *Tip* for deals on long-distance buses. **Gullivers,** Hardenbergpl. 14 (☎0800 4855 4837; www.gullivers.de), by the bus parking lot in *Bahnhof Zoo.* To: **Paris** (14hr., €59) and **Vienna** (10½hr., €49). Open daily 9am-2:30pm and 3-7pm. Buses are slower and less comfortable than trains, but often cheaper.

Mitfahrzentralen: Berlin has many ride-sharing centers; check the magazines *Zitty*, *Tip*, and *030* for addresses and phone numbers. Larger ones include: **Citynetz,** Joachimstaler Str. 17 (☎194 44; www.mtz-citynetz.de). U9 or 15 to *Kurfürstendamm.* To: **Hamburg** or **Hanover** (€17), **Frankfurt** (€29). Open M-F 9am-8pm, Sa-Su 9am-7pm. **Mitfahrzentrale Zoo,** (☎194 40; www.mfzoo.de) on the U2 platform at *Bahnhof Zoo.* Open M-F 9am-8pm, Sa-Su 10am-6pm. **Mitfahr2000,** has branches at Joachimsthaler Str. 1, (☎19 20 00), Yorckstr. 52 (☎194 2000) and Oderberger Str. 45 (☎440 9392; www.mitfahr2000.de). Open daily 8am-8pm.

■ ORIENTATION

Berlin is an immense conglomeration of what were once two separate and unique cities. The former East contains most of Berlin's landmarks and historic sites, as well as an unfortunate number of pre-fab concrete socialist architectural experiments. The former West functioned for decades as a small, isolated, Allied-occupied state and is still the commercial heart of united Berlin. The situation is rapidly changing, however, as businesses and embassies move their headquarters to Potsdamer Pl. and Mitte in the East.

The vast **Tiergarten,** Berlin's beloved park, lies in the center of the city; the grand, tree-lined **Straße des 17. Juni** runs through it from west to east and becomes **Unter den Linden** at the **Brandenburg Gate.** North of the Gate is the **Reichstag,** while south of the Gate **Ebertstraße** winds to glitzy **Potsdamer Platz.** Unter den Linden continues east through **Mitte,** the location of countless historical sites. The street changes names once again, to **Karl-Liebknecht-Straße,** before emptying into **Alexanderplatz,** home to Berlin's most visible landmark, the **Fernsehturm** (TV tower). At the east end of Mitte is the **Museumsinsel** (Museum Island). Cafe- and shop-lined **Oranienburgerstraße** cuts through the area of northeastern Mitte known as **Scheunenviertel,** historically Berlin's center of Jewish life.

The commercial district of West Berlin lies at the southwest end of the Tiergarten, centered around **Bahnhof Zoo** and the **Kurfürstendamm** (**Ku'damm** for short). To the east is **Breitscheidplatz,** marked by the bombed-out **Kaiser-Wilhelm-Gedächtniskirche,** and **Savignyplatz,** one of many pleasant squares in **Charlottenburg,** which is home to cafes, restaurants, and *Pensionen.* Southeast of the Ku'damm, **Schöneberg** is a pleasant residential neighborhood and the traditional nexus of the city's gay and lesbian community. At the southeast periphery of Berlin lies **Kreuzberg,** a district home to an exciting mix of radical leftists and punks as well as a large Turkish population. Northeast of the city is **Prenzlauer Berg,** a former working-class area, and east of Mitte is **Friedrichshain,** the center of Berlin's counterculture and nightlife. Berlin is rightly called a collection of towns, not a homogeneous city, as each neighborhood maintains a strong sense of individual identity: Every year, for example, citizens of Kreuzberg and Friedrichshain battle with vegetables for possession of the Oberbaumbrücke on the border between them.

GERMANY

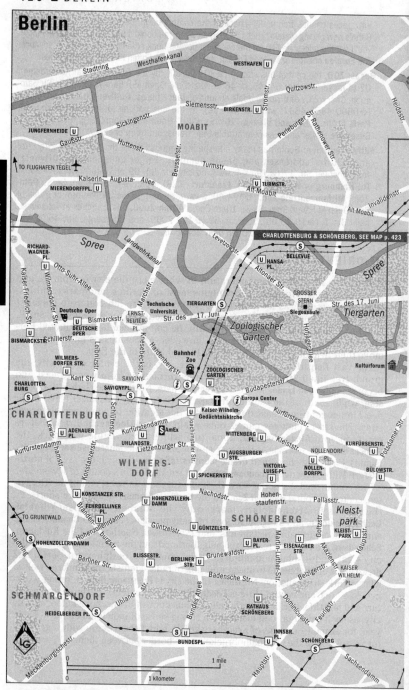

Berlin

CHARLOTTENBURG & SCHÖNEBERG, SEE MAP p. 423

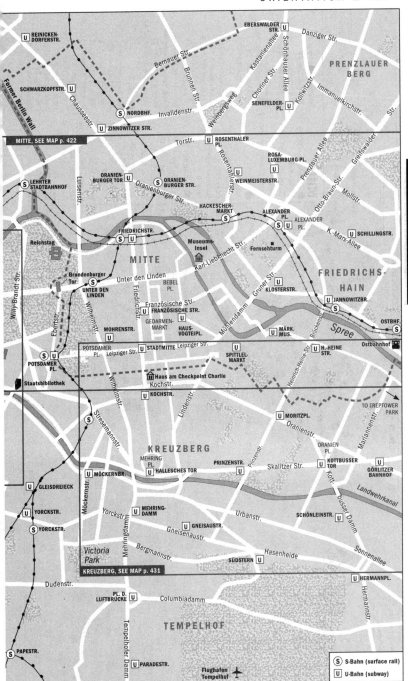

GERMANY

MITTE, SEE MAP p. 422

KREUZBERG, SEE MAP p. 431

PRENZLAUER BERG

MITTE

FRIEDRICHS-HAIN

KREUZBERG

TEMPELHOF

Victoria Park

Reichstag

Staatsbibliothek

Former Berlin Wall

Spree

TO TREPTOWER PARK

Flughafen Tempelhof

Ⓢ S-Bahn (surface rail)
Ⓤ U-Bahn (subway)

GERMANY

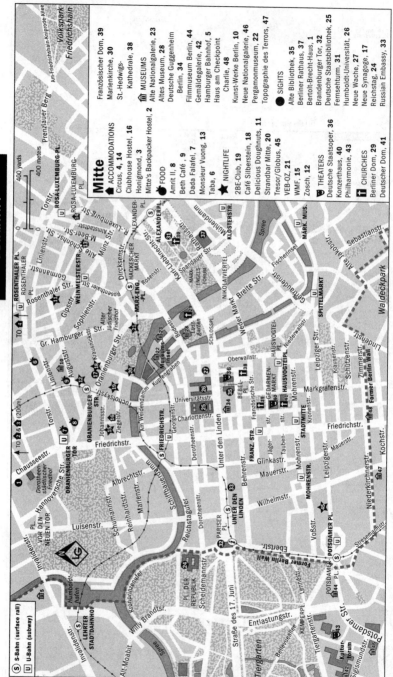

S S-Bahn (surface rail)
U U-Bahn (subway)

Mitte

▲ ACCOMMODATIONS
Circus, 4, 14
Clubhouse Hostel, 16
Honigmond, 3
Mitte's Backpacker Hostel, 2

◆ FOOD
Amrit II, 8
Beth Café, 9
Dada Falafel, 7
Monsieur Vuong, 13
Taba, 6

★ NIGHTLIFE
2BE-Club, 19
Café Silberstein, 18
Delicious Doughnuts, 11
Strandbar Mitte, 20
Tresor/Globus, 45
VEB-OZ, 21
WMF, 15
Zosch, 6

◉ THEATERS
Deutsche Staatsoper, 36
Konzerthaus, 40
Philharmonie, 43

✝ CHURCHES
Berliner Dom, 29
Deutscher Dom, 41

Französischer Dom, 39
Marienkirche, 30
St.-Hedwigs-
Kathedrale, 38

🏛 MUSEUMS
Alte Nationalgalerie, 23
Altes Museum, 28
Deutsche Guggenheim
Berlin, 34
Filmmuseum Berlin, 44
Gemäldegalerie, 42
Hamburger Bahnhof, 5
Haus am Checkpoint
Charlie, 48
Kunst-Werke Berlin, 10
Neue Nationalgalerie, 46
Pergamonmuseum, 22
Topographie des Terrors, 47

● SIGHTS
Alte Bibliothek, 35
Berliner Rathaus, 37
Bertolt-Brecht-Haus, 1
Brandenburger Tor, 32
Deutsche Staatsbibliothek, 25
Fernsehturm, 31
Humboldt-Universität, 26
Neue Wache, 27
Neue Synagoge, 17
Reichstag, 24
Russian Embassy, 33

GERMANY

Charlottenburg & Schöneberg

ACCOMMODATIONS
A&O Hostel, **14**
Charlottenburger Hof, **10**
CVJM-Haus, **20**
Frauenhotel Artemisia, **27**
Hotel-Pension
  Charlottenburg, **18**
Hotel-Pension Hansablick, **4**
Hotel-Pension München, **28**
Jugendgästehaus am Zoo, **6**
Jugendherberge Berlin
  International (HI), **19**
Jugendhotel Berlin City, **32**
Pension Knesebeck, **9**

FOOD
Baharat Falafel, **26**
Café Bilderbuch, **30**
Café Sidney, **24**
Die Feinbeckerei, **33**
Fish and Vegetables, **29**
Mensa TU, **5**
Orchidee, **11**
Restaurant-Café Bleibtreu, **17**
Schwarzes Café, **12**

NIGHTLIFE
A-Trane, **8**
Hafen, **25**
Heile Welt, **21**
Metropol, **22**
Mister Hu, **31**

MUSEUMS
Ägyptisches Museum, **3**
Bauhaus-Archiv, **15**
Gemäldegalerie, **7**
Neue Nationalgalerie, **16**
Sammlung Berggruen, **2**
Schloß Charlottenburg, **1**

Neue Ufer, **34**
Quasimodo, **13**
Slumberland, **23**

S S-Bahn (surface rail)
U U-Bahn (subway)

0   400 yards
0   400 meters

◧ LOCAL TRANPORTATION

Public Transportation: It is impossible to tour Berlin on foot—fortunately, the extensive **bus, Straßenbahn** (streetcar), **U-Bahn** (subway), and **S-Bahn** (surface rail) systems will take you anywhere. Berlin is divided into 3 transit zones. **Zone A** encompasses central Berlin, including Tempelhof airport. Almost everything else falls into **Zone B,** while **Zone C** contains the outlying areas, including Potsdam and Oranienburg. An **AB ticket** is the best deal, as you can buy regional Bahn tickets for the outlying areas. A single ticket (*Einzelfahrschein*) for the combined network is good for 2hr. after validation (Zones AB or BC €2.25, ABC €2.60). However, since single tickets are pricey, it almost always makes sense to buy a pass: a **Tageskarte** (AB €5.60, ABC €6) is good from validation until 3am the next day; the **WelcomeCard** (AB €19) is valid for 72hr.; the **7-Tage-Karte** (AB €23, ABC €29) is good for 7 days; and the **Umweltkarte Standard** (AB €58.50, ABC €72.50) is valid for one calendar month. Tickets may be used on any S-Bahn, U-Bahn, bus, or streetcar. **Bikes** require a supplemental ticket and are permitted on the U- and S-Bahn, but not on buses and streetcars.

Purchasing and Validating Tickets: Buy tickets from *Automaten* (machines), bus drivers, or ticket windows in the U- and S-Bahn stations. When using an *Automat*, make your selection before inserting money; note that the machines will not give more than €10 change and that some machines do not take bills. All tickets must be validated in the box marked *hier entwerfen* before boarding, or you may be slapped with a €40 fine.

Night Transport: U- and S-Bahn lines shut down from 1-4am on weeknights, but **night buses** (preceded by the letter N) run every 20-30min.; pick up the *Nachtliniennetz* map at a *Fahrscheine und Mehr* office. **Clubshuttle** buses connect major clubs and hostels nightly 10pm-6am. A €16 ticket is good one week and includes discounts at 12 clubs.

Taxis: ☎26 10 26, 21 02 02, or 690 22. Call at least 15min. in advance.

Car Rental: Most companies have counters at Tegel and Schönefeld airports and around Bahnhof Zoo, *Ostbahnhof*, Friedrichstr., and the Europa Center at Budapester Str. 39. The latter location has **Hertz** (☎261 10 53) open M-F 7am-8pm, Sa 8am-4pm, Su 9am-1pm; and **Avis** (☎230 93 70) open M-F 7am-7pm, Sa 9am-2pm.

Bike Rental: Fahrradstation, Friedrichstr. 141, is in the Friedrichstr. S-Bahn station. €15 per day. Open M-F 8am-8pm, Sa-Su 10am-4pm. **Prenzleberger Orangebikes,** 37 Kollwitz Pl. U2 to *Senefelderplatz.* €10 per day. Open M-F 2:30-7pm, Sa 10am-7pm. **Deutsche Bahn Call-A-Bikes** (☎0800 522 55 22) are all over the city. Only convenient for those with a cell phone, as you must call both to pick up and drop off.

▊ PRACTICAL INFORMATION

TOURIST AND FINANCIAL SERVICES

The monthly magazine *Berlin Programm* (€1.50) lists opera, theater, and classical music schedules. German-speakers should spring for *Tip* (€2.50) or *Zitty* (€2.30), which have the most comprehensive listings for film, theater, concerts, and clubs. For gays and lesbians, *Siegessäule, Sergej,* and *Gay-yellowpages* have entertainment listings. For info in English, check out www.berlin.de.

Tourist Offices: ▧ **EurAide** (www.euraide.com), in *Bahnhof Zoo,* has excellent travel advice, recommends hostels for free, and makes train and hotel reservations (€4 fee for hotels). Open M-F 8:30am-noon and 1-4pm, Sa 8:30am-noon. **Europa-Center,** on Budapester Str., has city maps (€0.50) and free transit maps. From *Bahnhof Zoo,* walk along Budapester Str. past the Kaiser-Wilhelm-Gedächtniskirche; the office is on the right after about 2 blocks (5min.). Open M-Sa 8:30am-8:30pm, Su 10am-6:30pm. **Branches** at Brandenburg Gate, the Alexanderplatz Television Tower, and KaDeWe.

City Tours: ◪**Terry Brewer's Best of Berlin** (www.brewersberlin.com). Guides Terry and Boris are legendary for their vast knowledge and engaging personalities. 5hr. tours leave daily at 10:30am from the Neue Synagoge on Oranienburger Str., near the intersection with Tucholskystr. (S1, 2, or 25 to *Oranienburger Str.*). The tour picks up guests at hostels Odyssee (p. 428) at 9:15am, Circus (p. 426) at 9:40am and 2pm, and Clubhouse (p. 427) at 10:15am. €10. An abridged version offered Apr.-Oct. at 12:30pm. **Insider Tour** (☎692 31 49) offers a variety of fun, erudite tours that hit the major sights. The 4hr. tour (€9.50) picks up daily at 10am and (in summer) 2:30pm in front of the Zoo Station McDonald's. **Bike tours** meet at Fahrradstation in the Friedrichstr. S-Bahn station at 10:30am and (in summer) 3pm; focus ranges from Communism to club crawls.

Embassies and Consulates: Berlin is building a new embassy complex. As of press time, the locations of the embassies remain in a state of flux. For the latest info, call the **Auswärtiges Amt Dienststelle Berlin** (☎20 18 60) or visit its office on the Werderscher Markt. U2: *Hausvogteipl.* **Australia,** Friedrichstr. 200 (☎880 08 80). U2 or 6 to *Stadtmitte.* Open M-Th 8:30am-1pm and 2-5pm, F 8:30am-1pm and 2-4:15pm. Also Uhlandstr. 181 (☎880 08 80). U15: *Uhlandstr.* Open M-F 8:30am-1pm. **Canada,** Friedrichstr. 95 (☎20 31 20), on the 12th fl. of the International Trade Center. U6: *Friedrichstr.* Open M-F 9-11am. **Irish,** Friedrichstr. 200 (☎22 07 20). Open M-F 9:30am-12:30pm and 2:30-4:45pm. **New Zealand,** Friedrichstr. 60 (☎20 62 10). Open M-Th 9am-1pm and 2-5:30pm; F at 9am-1pm and 2-4:30pm. **South African,** Friedrichstr. 60 (☎22 07 30). South African Consulate: Douglasstr. 9 (☎82 50 11). S7: *Grunewald.* Open M-F 9am-noon. **UK,** Wilhelmstr. 70 (☎20 18 40). U6: *Friedrichstr.* Open M-F 9am-4pm. **US,** Clayallee 170 (☎832 92 33). U1: *Oskar-Helene-Heim.* Open M-F 8:30am-noon. Advice M-F 2-4pm; after hours emergencies, call ☎830 50.

Currency Exchange: The best rates are usually at offices that exclusively exchange currency and traveler's checks—look for **Wechselstube** signs at major train stations and squares. **ReiseBank,** at *Bahnhof Zoo* (open daily 7:30am-10pm) and *Ostbahnhof* (open M-F 7am-10pm, Sa 8am-8pm, Su 8am-noon and 12:30-4pm), has worse rates.

American Express: Main Office, Bayreuther Str. 37 (☎21 47 62 92). U1, 2, or 15 to *Wittenbergpl.* Holds mail and offers banking services. No commission on AmEx traveler's checks. Open M-F 9am-7pm, Sa 10am-1pm. The **branch office,** Friedrichstr. 172 (☎20 45 57 21). U6: *Französische Str.* has the same hours.

LOCAL SERVICES

Luggage Storage: In **Bahnhof Zoo.** Lockers €0.50-2 per day, depending on size. 72hr. max. If lockers are full, try **Gepäckaufbewahrung** (€2 per piece per day). Open daily 6:15am-10:30pm. 24hr. lockers are available at **Ostbahnhof** and **Alexanderplatz.**

Bookstores: Marga Schöler Bücherstube, Knesebeckstr. 33, between Savignypl. and the Ku'damm. S3: *Savignypl.* Off-beat and contemporary reading material in English. Open M-W 9:30am-7pm, Th-F 9:30am-8pm, Sa 9:30am-4pm. **Dussman,** Friedrichstr. 90. U6: *Friedrichstr.* Huge store; books in English on the 2nd fl. Open M-Sa 10am-10pm.

Bi-Gay-Lesbian Resources: Lesbenberatung, Kulmer Str. 20a (☎215 20 00), offers lesbian counseling. Open M-Tu and Th 4-7pm, F 2-5pm. The gay equivalent is **Schwulenberatung,** Mommsenstraße 45 (☎194 46), in Charlottenburg.

Laundromat: Waschcenter Schnell und Sauber has locations in **Charlottenburg,** Leibnizstr. 72 (S3: *Savignypl.*); **Schöneberg,** Wexstr. 34 (U9: *Bundespl.*); **Kreuzberg,** Mehringdamm 32 (U6: *Mehringdamm*); **Mitte,** Torstr. 115 (U8: *Rosenthaler Pl.*). Wash €2-4 for 6kg, dry €0.50 per 15min. Open daily 6am-11pm.

GERMANY

EMERGENCY AND COMMUNICATIONS

Emergency: Police: ☎110. **Ambulance and Fire:** ☎112.

Crisis Lines: American Hotline (☎0177 814 15 10). Crisis and referral service. **Frauenkrisentelefon** (☎614 22 42). Women's crisis line. Open M and W noon-2pm, Th 2-4pm. **Berliner Behindertenverband,** Jägerstraße 63d (☎204 38 47). Advice for the handicapped. Open M-F 8am-4pm.

Pharmacies: Pharmacies are ubiquitous. **Europa-Apotheke,** Tauentzienstr. 9-12 (☎261 41 42), is near *Bahnhof Zoo.* Open M-F 6am-8pm, Sa 9am-4pm.

Medical Assistance: The American and British embassies list English-speaking doctors. **Emergency doctor** (☎31 00 31); **Emergency dentist** (☎89 00 43 33). Both 24hr.

Internet Access: Some cafes have America Online internet stations, free for customers. Also try: **Netlounge,** Auguststr. 89. U-Bahn: *Oranienburgerstr.* €1.50 per hr. Open noon-midnight. **Easy Everything,** the corner of Kurfürstendamm and Meineckestr., fuses Dunkin' Donuts and the Internet (finally!). €1.50-2.50 per hr. Open daily 6am-2:30am. **Com Line,** Innsbrückerstr. 56, in Schöneberg. €1 per hr. Open 24hr.

Post Offices: Joachimstaler Str. 7, down Joachimstaler Str. from *Bahnhof Zoo.* Open M-Sa 8am-midnight, Su 10am-midnight. Most neighborhood branches open M-F 9am-6pm, Sa 9am-noon. Address mail to be held: Firstname SURNAME, *Postlagernde Briefe,* Postamt in der Joachimstaler Str. 7, 10706 Berlin GERMANY.

⛫ ACCOMMODATIONS AND CAMPING

Thanks to the ever-growing hostel and hotel industry, same-day accommodations aren't impossible to find. Failing to make a reservation will, however, limit your options. For longer visits, the various **Mitwohnzentrale** can arrange for you to housesit or sublet an apartment from €250 per month; for more info, contact **Home Company Mitwohnzentrale,** Joachimstaler Str. 17. (☎194 45. U9 or 15 to *Kurfürstendamm.* Open M-F 9am-6pm, Sa 11am-2pm.) For long stays or on weekends, reservations are essential. During the **Love Parade,** call at least two months ahead for a choice of rooms and at least two weeks ahead for any bed at all. Some hostels increase prices that weekend by up to €10 per night.

HOTELS, HOSTELS, AND PENSIONEN

MITTE

▧ **Mitte's Backpacker Hostel,** Chausseestr. (☎102 28 39 09 65). U6: *Zinnowitzer Str.* Look for the giant orange sign on the wall outside. The apex of hostel hipness, with gregarious English-speaking staff and themed rooms. Bikes €10 per day. Kitchen available. Sheets €2.50. Staff does laundry for €5. Internet access €6 per hr. Reception 24hr. Dorms €15-18; singles €20-30; doubles €40-60; €1-2 cheaper in winter. ❷

▧ **Circus,** Rosa-Luxemburg-Str. 39 (☎28 39 14 33). U2: *Rosa-Luxemburg-Pl.* Circus was designed with the English-speaking traveler in mind. Laundry, Internet, info on nightlife, and a disco ball in the lobby. A second **Circus** at Rosenthaler Pl. on Weinbergersweg 1a, has similar facilities and the same prices. Sheets €2. Reception and bar open 24hr. Confirm reservations 1 day before arrival. 6-8 bed dorms €15; 4-5 bed dorms €18; singles €32; doubles €48; triples €60. Cheaper in winter. ❷

Honigmond, Tieckstr. 12 (☎284 45 50). U6: *Zinnowitzer Str.* Old-fashioned and well-furnished rooms with canopy beds. Breakfast €3-9. Check-in 3pm-1am; if checking in after 8pm, call beforehand. Singles €45-70; doubles €65-85, with bath €90-145. ❸

Clubhouse Hostel, Kalkscheunestr. 2 (☎28 09 79 79). U6: *Oranienburger Tor.* Enter the courtyard from Johannisstr. 2 or Kalkscheunestr. In the center of the Oranienburger Str. nightlife. Sheets €2. Internet €0.50 per 5min. Reception and bar open 24hr. 8-10 bed dorms €14; 5-7 bed dorms €17; singles €32; doubles €46. ❷

TIERGARTEN

Jugendherberge Berlin International (HI), Kluckstr. 3 (☎261 10 98). U1 to Kurfürstenstr., then walk up Potsdamer Str., go left on Pohlstr., and right on Kluckstr. Big, clean, and modern. Bikes €10 per day. Large breakfast and sheets included. Internet available. Reception and cafe open 24hr. Dorms €23, under-27 €19. ❷

Hotel-Pension Hansablick, Flotowstr. 6 (☎390 48 00). S3, 5, 7, 9, or 75 to *Tiergarten.* Some rooms have balconies overlooking the Spree; all have bath, minibar, phone, and cable TV. Riverboat tours stop 200m away. Breakfast included. Reception 24hr. Singles €82, doubles €101-121. Mention *Let's Go* for a 5% discount. ❹

SCHÖNEBERG AND WILMERSDORF

Studentenhotel Meininger 10, Meininger Str. 10 (☎78 71 74 14). U4 or bus #146 to *Rathaus Schöneberg.* Walk toward the Rathaus tower on Freiherr-vom-Stein-Str., turn left onto Martin-Luther-Str., then right on Meininger Str. A hostel for the students, by the students. Breakfast included. 24hr. reception. Co-ed dorms €12.50; 3- to 4-bed dorms €21; singles €33; doubles €46. Flash a copy of *Let's Go* for a 5% first night discount. ❶

CVJM-Haus, Einemstr. 10 (☎264 10 88). U1: *Nollendorfpl.* It's fun to stay at the German YMCA, despite its institutional atmosphere. Unlike most hostels, here you usually get your own room. Breakfast included. Sheets €4. Reception M-F 8am-5pm. Quiet time 10pm-7am. Book well ahead. Dorms and singles €21; doubles €42. ❸

Hotel-Pension München, Güntzelstr. 62 (☎857 91 20). U9: *Güntzelstr.* Like visiting a smartly done apartment—the rooms are simple and bright and the halls are pinned with contemporary *Berliner* art. Breakfast included. Singles €40, with bath €56; doubles with bath €70-80; triples €90; quads €105. ❹

Jugendhotel Berlin City, Crellestr. 22 (☎787 02 130). U7 to *Kleistpark.* Sleek little rooms popular with school groups; book well ahead. Breakfast included. Bar serves beer and caipirinha. Dorms €26-28; singles €38, with bath €46; doubles €70/80. ❸

CHARLOTTENBURG

Jugendgästehaus am Zoo, Hardenbergstr. 9a (☎312 94 10), opposite the Technical University Mensa. Bus #145 to *Steinpl.,* or take the short walk from *Bahnhof Zoo* down Hardenbergstr. Push open the front door and hike four flights of stairs—unless the elevator's working. Reception 9am-midnight. Check-in 10am. Check-out 9am. Lockout 10am-2pm. No curfew. Dorms €19, under-27 €16; singles €27/24; doubles €46/43. ❷

A&O Hostel, Joachimstaler Str. 1, (☎0800 2 22 57 22), 40m from *Bahnhof Zoo.* The crowded lobby feels like a cross between a frat and a fast-food restaurant, but the rooms are clean. Sheets €3. Reception 24hr. No curfew. Dorms €10, with shower €18-20; singles €35; doubles €68. Prices lower in winter. ❷

Pension Knesebeck, Knesebeckstr. 86 (☎312 72 55). S3: *Savignypl.* Follow Kantstr. to Savignypl. and go clockwise around the green until Knesebeckstr. on your left. Friendly staff and comfortable *Alt-Berliner* rooms with faux Baroque stylings, couches, and sinks. Hearty breakfast (with Nutella) included. Laundry €4. Reception 24hr. Singles €35-39, with shower €40-45; doubles €55-61/65-72; quads and up €25-30 per person. ❸

GERMANY

Hotel-Pension Charlottenburg, Grolmanstr. 32 (☎880 3296 0). S3: *Savignypl.* Clean simple rooms; the more expensive have private showers. Breakfast included. Check-out 11am. Mention *Let's Go* for the following prices: Singles €30-48, doubles €54-78, triples and up €25 per person. ❸

Charlottenburger Hof, Stuttgarter Pl. 14 (☎32 90 70). U7: *Wilmersdorfer Str.* Mondrian-themed ceilings match the Kandinsky prints on the walls. Every room has a phone, TV, and computer with free Internet (DSL). Pricier rooms have whirlpools. Reception 24hr. Singles €75; doubles €85; quads €125. ❹

Frauenhotel Artemisia, Brandenburgische Str. 18 (☎873 89 05). U7: *Konstanzer Str.* Pricey but rare—an elegant hotel for women only, the first of its kind in Germany. Rooms are named after famous women in the city's history, while a terrace provides a sweeping view of Berlin. The **Speiseraum** upstairs serves breakfast and evening drinks (5-10pm) to a mixed all-female crowd. Reception 6:30-10pm. Singles €59, with bath €79; doubles €89/104; extra bed €23. If you stay three days or more and one day is your birthday, that night is free. "Last-minute, same-day" specials also available. ❹

KREUZBERG

Die Fabrik, Schlesische Str. 18 (☎611 71 16; www.diefabrik.com). U1: *Schlesisches Tor.* This former factory features spacious rooms and easy access to nightlife. Reception 24hr. Dorms €18; singles €36; doubles €49; triples €66; quads €80. ❷

Bax Pax, Skalitzer Str. 104 (☎69 51 83 22). U1: *Görlitzer Bahnhof.* A location at the start of mighty Oranienstr., fuzzy blue carpets, and a bed inside a VW Bug (ask for room 3) make for the mellow good times you'd expect in a Kreuzberg hostel. Kitchen available. Sheets €2.50. Internet €6 per hr. Reception 24hr. Big dorms €15; 6-7 bed dorms €16; 4-5 bed dorms €18; singles €30; doubles and triples €20-30 per person. ❷

Pension Kreuzberg, Großbeerenstr. 64 (☎251 13 62; www.pension-kreuzberg.de). U6 or night bus #N19 to *Mehringdamm.* Gorgeous staircases and a cheery yellow breakfast room. Lively neighborhood, even for Kreuzberg. Breakfast included. Reception 8am-10pm. Singles €40; doubles €52. Larger rooms €22.50 per person. ❸

FRIEDRICHSHAIN

Sunflower Hostel, Helsingforser Str. 17 (☎44 04 42 50). U1: *Warschauer Str.* Turn right out of the station and take your first left coming off the bridge; hug the river for 5min. Airy, relaxed feel. The staff is a trove of insider knowledge. Internet €1.50 per 15min. Reception 24hr. Dorms €13-15; singles €35; doubles €45; triples €57; quads €68. ❷

Odyssee, Grünberger Str. 23 (☎29 00 00 81). U5 to *Frankfurter Tor* or U1 to *Warschauer Str.* A rarity: hip AND spotless. Someone sinks a lot of money into this place, but at €13 a night, it isn't you. Bar open until dawn. 24hr. reception. Dorms €13; doubles €45, with shower €52; triples €57; quads €68. ❷

PRENZLAUER BERG

■ **Lette'm Sleep Hostel**, Lettestr. 7 (☎44 73 36 23). U2: *Eberswalder Str.* Follow the trail of graffiti to the spray-painted gangsta bear on the door. Lette'm Sleep isn't just "tucked between" the bars and cafes on Helmholtzpl.—with its street-level common room and laid back staff, it practically *is* one. Kitchen facilities. Sheets €3 in dorms. Free Internet. Dorms €15-16; doubles €48; triples €57. Lower prices for longer stays. ❷

Alcatraz, Schönhauserallee 133 (☎48 49 68 15). U2: *Eberswalder Str.* The main building has small, graffitied rooms, while the second features airy dorms in an old German brewery. Free bike loan. Kitchen facilities. Internet €3 per hr. Reception 24hr. Dorms €13; singles from €40; doubles from €44; triples from €59; quads from €74. ❶

▐ FOOD

Food in Berlin is less German than it is cosmopolitan; the ethnic food is terrific thanks to Turkish, Indian, Italian, and Thai immigrants. During the early summer, expect an onslaught of *Spargel* (asparagus). Berlin's dearest culinary tradition, however, is breakfast, a gloriously civilized institution served well into the afternoon in cafes. Relax over a *Milchkaffee*, a bowl of coffee with foamed milk.

Typical Berlin street food is Turkish. Their *Imbiß* stands are a late-night lifeline; many are open 24 hours. The *Döner Kebap*—shaved roast lamb or chicken stuffed into toasted flatbread and topped with vegetables—has cornered the fast-food market, with falafel running a close second. Quality Indian and Italian eateries also abound, and of course the city has its share of *Currywurst* and bratwurst.

Aldi, Plus, Edeka, and **Penny Markt** are the cheapest supermarket chains, followed by the pricier **Bolle, Kaiser's,** and **Reichelt.** Supermarkets are usually open M-F 9am-6pm and Sa 9am-4pm, though some are open as late as 8pm on weekdays. *Bahnhof Zoo*'s **open-air market** fires up Saturday mornings on Winterfeldtpl., but almost every neighborhood has one. For cheap veggies and huge wheels of *Fladenbrot*, hit the **Turkish market,** in Kreuzberg along Maybachufer on the Landwehrkanal, every Friday. Take U8 to *Schönleinstr.*

MITTE

▓ **Monsieur Vuong,** Alte Schonhauser Str. 46. U2: *Rosa Luxembourg Platz.* People who live here have this strange obsession with Monsieur Vuong's glass noodle salad (€6.50). It's odd. Really, no one orders anything else. Other things €6-9. Open M-Sa noon-midnight, Su 4pm-midnight. ❷

Taba, Torstr. 164. U8: *Rosenthaler Pl.* A roomy Brazilian restaurant and bar. Dishes are pricey, but the vast, €6.50 buffet on M and Th is tasty and filling. Live music F-Su, occasionally charges cover after 10pm. Open Su and Tu-Sa from 7pm. ❹

Amrit II, Oranienburgerstr. 50. S1: *Oranienburgerstr.* Indian entrees run high (€9) but can be shared. The original location in Kreuzberg, Oranienstr. 202, has same hours. ❸

Dada Falafel, Linienstr. 132. S1 or S2 to *Oranienburgertor.* *"Ich habe soviel getanzt dass ich ganz und gar hungrig bin."* (I have danced so much that I am hungry.) *"Was willst du essen?"* (What do you want to eat?) *"Falafel."* (Falafel.) *"Lass uns zu Dada gehen."* (Then let us go to Dada.) Serves the business crowd by day and the clubgoers by night. Falafel/schwarma sandwiches €3. Open Su-Th 10am-2am, F-Sa until 4am. ❶

Beth Café, Tucholskystr. 40, just off Augustr. S1, 2, or 25 to *Oranienburger Str.* Kosher eats for cheap: Falafel (€3.20) or a bagel with lox and cream cheese (€2.50). Courtyard perfect for afternoon tea. Open M-Th and Su 11am-10pm, F 11am-5pm. ❷

SCHÖNEBERG

▓ **Die Feinbeckerei,** Vorbergstr. 2. U7: *Kleistpark.* The menu has "schwabish" and "not schwabish" sections; *Let's Go* recommends ordering from the schwabish one. Southern German cuisine, unassuming and full of carbohydrates. Try the cheese Spätzle with herbs (€6.50). Open daily noon-midnight. ❸

Baharat Falafel, Winterfeldtstr. 37. U1: *Nollendorfpl.* This ain't no greasy *Döner* stand—it's all about falafel. Five plump chick-pea balls in a fluffy pita, covered with veggies and heavenly sesame, mango, or chili sauce (€3-4). Wash it down with fresh-squeezed *Gute-Laune Saft* (good mood juice). Open daily 8am-4am. Closed the last week in July. ❷

Café Bilderbuch, Akazienstr. 28. U7: *Eisenacher Str.* Fringed lamps, oak bookcases and fat viridian sofas give Café Bilderbuch the feel of a Venetian library. Tasty brunch baskets served around the clock (€8). Oct.-Apr. you can swing or tango at Sunday afternoon *Tantzee.* Open M-Th 9am-1am, F-Sa 9am-2am, Su 10am-1am. ❸

Fish and Vegetables, Goltzstr. 32. U1: *Nollendorfpl.* Generous portions of Thai food (€4-5). Open Su-Th 11am-midnight, F-Sa 11am-1am. ❸

Café Sidney, Winterfeldtstr. 40 (☎216 52 53). U1: *Nollendorfpl.* Enjoy any of a mouth-watering panoply of sandwiches from €5. It gets packed in the evening due to its well-stocked bar and prime Nollendorfpl. locale. Open Su-Th 9am-2am, F-Sa 9am-3am. ❸

KREUZBERG

Café V, Lausitzer Pl. 12. U1: *Görlitzer Bahnhof.* Top-of-the-line, bottom of the food chain. Berlin's oldest vegetarian restaurant also serves fish. Try the *Spinatballchen mit Käse Sauße* (€7) or any of the equally tasty specials (€6-7). Open daily 10am-2am. ❸

Abendmahl, Muskauer Str. 9 (☎612 51 70). U1: *Görlitzer Bahnhof.* A favorite of gay and lesbian Berliners. Sorrel cream soup and fish carpaccio are trumped by fabulously macabre deserts—the "Last Date" is ice cream petit-fours shaped like coffins. If you can't afford the dessert of your choice, buy a postcard of it. Open daily from 6pm. ❹

Weinhaus Hoff, Reichenberger Str. 116 (☎342 08 13). U1: *Gorlitzer Bahnhof.* Delicious Swabian specialties in an out-of-the-way restaurant lined with wine bottles. Pork fillet with mushroom cream and *Spätzle* €7.50. Open M-Sa 4pm-midnight. ❸

Blue Nile, Tempelhofer Ufer 6 (☎25 29 46 55). U1: *Möcknerbrücke.* It's hard to get to and the food takes an age, but with a flask of honey wine (€2.50), you won't mind a bit. All the meals at this Ethiopian restaurant are served on *injera,* a traditional spongy sour-dough bread. Vegetarian or meat combos €7-12. Open 3pm-midnight. ❸

Melek Pastanesi, Oranienstr. 28. U1: *Kottbusser Tor.* Delicious Turkish pastries for pocket change. 100g baklava €0.80. Open 24hr. to satisfy late-night cravings. ❶

Sarod's Thai Restaurant, Friesenstr. 22. U7: *Gneisenaustr.* All-you-can-eat weekdays noon-4pm for €5. Open M-F noon-11:30pm, Sa-Su 2pm-11:30pm. ❷

PRENZLAUER BERG

▨ **Café-Restaurant Miró,** Raumerstr. 29. U2: *Eberswalder Str.* The kind of place where the food looks almost as good as it tastes. Generous portions of delectable Mediterranean cuisine. Breakfast €3-8. Soups €3. Open 10am-midnight. ❸

La Bodeguita del Medio, Husemanstr. 10. U2: *Eberswalderstr.* A Cuban *tapas* bar, decorated by customer scrawlings that cover the tables, walls, and ceilings. Aside from the *tapas* (€4-8) there's not really a menu—they cook new dinner specials every day. Sa-Su dinner buffet (€9.50) starting at 7pm. Open daily 4pm-late. ❸

The Chop Bar, Pappalallee 29. A friendly West African restaurant. Try the *Jassa Djin* (€7), a tasty mackerel dish, or any one of the vegetarian options (€6.50-8). Open Su-Th 4-11pm, F-Sa 4pm-midnight. ❸

Li Do, Knaackstr. 30. U2: *Senefelderpl.* Essential East German chic: The dusty, busted chandelier. Try a blini burger (€8; lox layered with thin buckwheat pancakes) or a more filling pasta special (€5). Open daily 9am-late. ❷

Nosh, Pappelallee 77. U2: *Eberswalder Str.* "Borderless cooking" brings bagels, pad thai (€7), and the Berliner breakfast (€6.30) together on one menu. Pastries so good other cafes sell them. Open daily from 9am, kitchen closes at midnight. ❸

CHARLOTTENBURG

Mensa TU, Hardenbergstr. 34, 10min. from *Bahnhof Zoo.* The mightiest of Berlin's *Mensen.* Vegetarian options. Meals €2-4. Cafeteria downstairs has longer hours and higher prices. *Mensa* open M-F 11:00am-3pm. Cafeteria open M-F 8am-5pm. ❶

Kreuzberg

ACCOMMODATIONS
Bax Pax, 11
Die Fabrik, 16
Pension Kreuzberg, 1

S S-Bahn (surface rail)
U U-Bahn (subway)

NIGHTLIFE
Muvuca, 3
Rose's, 9
Schoko-Café, 8
SchwuZ, 4
SO36, 10
TEK, 6
Wild at Heart, 14

FOOD
Abendmahl, 13
Blue Nile, 2
Café V, 12
Melek Pastanesi, 7
Sarod's Thai Restaurant, 5
Weinhaus Hoff, 15

GERMANY

Schwarzes Café, Kantstr. 148. S3, 5, 7, 9, or 75 to *Savignypl.* Exposed brick walls, curious frescoes, and absinthe on the menu give Schwarzes a bohemian feel, but most notably it's *always* open (except Tu 3am-10am). The bathrooms must be seen to be believed. Breakfast served around the clock (€6-8). ❸

Restaurant-Cafe Bleibtreu, Bleibtreustr. 45. S3: *Savignypl.* Gilt-framed mirrors, classic film posters, and one London phone booth decorate this low-key local favorite. Large portions; many vegetarian options (€5-6). Open daily 9:30am-1am. ❸

Orchidee, Stuttgarter Platz 13. Won tons, satay, pho, and maki all under one roof. Thai, Chinese, Vietnamese, and Japanese tastes unite. Try the coconut juice. M-Sa 11am-midnight, Su 3pm-midnight. ❸

👁 SIGHTS

Most of central Berlin's major sights are along the route of **bus #100,** which travels from *Bahnhof Zoo* to Prenzlauer Berg, passing by the Siegessäule, Brandenburg Gate, Unter den Linden, the Berliner Dom, and Alexanderplatz. There are only a few places to see remnants of the **Berlin Wall:** a narrow band stands in Potsdamer Platz; the popular Haus Am Checkpoint Charlie guards another piece; the sobering Documentation Center in Prenzlauer Berg preserves an entire city block; and an embellished section in Friedrichshain has become the East Side Gallery.

MITTE

Mitte was once the heart of Berlin and has most of the city's imperial architecture. The district was split down the middle by the wall and much of it fell into disrepair, but the wave of revitalization that swept post-wall Berlin hit Mitte first.

UNTER DEN LINDEN

Unter den Linden is one of the best known boulevards in Europe and the spine of Imperial Berlin. During the Cold War it was known as the "idiot's mile" because it was often all that visitors to the East saw, giving them little idea of what the city was really like. Beginning in Pariser Platz in front of Brandenburger Tor, the street runs east through Bebelplatz and the Lustgarten, interspersed with huge dramatic squares. *(S1: Unter den Linden. Bus #100 runs the length of the boulevard every 4-6 minutes.)*

■ **BRANDENBURGER TOR.** Built during the reign of Friedrich Wilhelm II as an image of peace to replace its medieval predecessor, the gate became the enduring symbol of the Cold War East-West division. Situated directly in the center of the city, it was the heart of no-man's land for decades. Today the Brandenburg Gate is the most powerful emblem of reunited Germany and Berlin. The **Room of Silence** in the northern end of the gate provides a place for meditation and reflection.

RUSSIAN EMBASSY. Rebuilding the edifices of the rich and famous wasn't a huge priority in the workers' state. One exception was this massive structure, which covers almost an entire block. While the palace reverted to being just another embassy at the end of the Cold War, you can still marvel at the imposing building from behind the iron fencing. *(Unter den Linden 55.)*

DEUTSCHE STAATSBIBILIOTHEK AND HUMBOLDT-UNIVERSITÄT. The stately library's shady, ivy-covered courtyard, accentuated by serenely lounging intellectuals, provides a pleasant respite from the surrounding urban bustle. *(Unter den Linden 8. Open M-F 9am-9pm, Sa 9am-5pm. €0.50. Free Internet.)* Just beyond the *Staatsbibliothek* lies Humboldt University, which saw the likes of Hegel, Einstein, the Brothers Grimm, Bismarck, and Karl Marx. In the wake of the post-1989 shift, in which "tainted" departments were radically revamped or simply shut down, international scholars have descended upon the university to take part in its dynamic renewal. *(Unter den Linden 6.)*

NEUE WACHE. The New Guardhouse was designed by Prussian architect Karl Friedrich Schinkel in unrepentant Neoclassical style. During the DDR era, it was known as the "Memorial to the Victims of Fascism and Militarism," and, ironically, was guarded by East German soldiers. It was reopened in 1993 as a war memorial. The remains of an unknown soldier and an unknown concentration camp victim are buried inside with earth from Nazi concentration camps as well as dirt from the Stalingrad battlefield. *(Unter den Linden 4. Open daily 10am-6pm.)*

BEBELPLATZ. On May 10, 1933 Nazi students burned nearly 20,000 books here by "subversive" authors such as Heinrich Heine and Sigmund Freud—both Jews. A plaque in the center of the square is engraved with Heine's eerily prescient 1820 quote: *Nur dort wo man Bücher verbrennt, verbrennt man am Ende auch Menschen.* (Wherever books are burned, ultimately people are burned as well.)

The building with the curved facade is the **Alte Bibliothek,** which was once the royal library. On the other side of the square is the **Deutsche Staatsoper,** one of Berlin's three operas, fully rebuilt after the war from original sketches. The distinctive blue dome at the end of the square belongs to the **St.-Hedwigs-Kathedrale.** Completed in 1773 as Berlin's first Catholic church built after the Reformation, it was destroyed by American bombs in 1943 and rebuilt in the 1950s. *(Cathedral open M-Sa 10am-5pm, Su 1-5pm. Free. Organ concerts W at 3pm.)*

TIERGARTEN

Once a hunting ground for Prussian monarchs, the lush **Tiergarten** park greens the center of Berlin from *Bahnhof Zoo* to the Brandenburg Gate. **Straße des 17. Juni,** bisecting the park from west to east, is the site of demonstrations such as the Love Parade in mid-July.

■**THE REICHSTAG.** The Reichstag is the current home of Germany's governing body, the *Bundestag.* History has long been made here, from Philipp Scheidemann's 1918 proclamation "*Es lebe die Deutsche Republik*" ("Long live the German Republic") to the 1933 fire that Adolf Hitler used as an excuse to declare a state of emergency and seize power. Recently, a glass dome has been added to the top; the dome is built around a solar cone that powers the building. A walkway spirals up the inside of the dome, leading visitors around a panoramic view to the top of the cone. *(☎22 72 74 53. Open daily 8am-midnight; last entrance at 10pm. Free.)*

SIEGESSÄULE. In the heart of the Tiergarten, the slender 70m victory column commemorates Prussia's defeat of France in 1870. The statue at the top—the goddess of victory—was made from melted-down French cannons. In a less-than-subtle affront to the French, the Nazis moved the monument here in 1938 in order to increase its height and visibility. Climb its 285 steps for a panorama of the city or leave your mark on the graffiti-covered interior, which has become a favorite forum of expression for the world's touring youth. *(Großer Stern. Take bus #100 or 187 to Großer Stern. Open Apr.-Nov. M 1-6pm, Tu-Su 9am-6pm. €1.20, students €0.60.)*

POTSDAMER PLATZ

Potsdamer Platz, built under Friedrich Wilhelm I in an approximation of Parisian boulevards, was designed with the primary purpose of moving troops. After reunification, Potsdamer Pl. was chosen to become the new commercial center of united Berlin and promptly achieved infamy as the city's largest construction site. Today, its wildly postmodern architectural designs are by turns sickening and sublime. The central complex, overlooking Potsdamer Str., includes the towering **Deutsche Bahn headquarters,** the glossy ■**Sony Center,** and the glass recreation of Mt. Fuji that covers the courtyard. Take in a movie, go window-shopping, or just sit and marvel at the glass and steel. *(U2: Potsdamer Pl.)*

GENDARMENMARKT

Several blocks south of Unter den Linden, this gorgeous Eastern Berlin Platz was considered the French Quarter in the 18th century, when it became the main settlement for Protestant Huguenots. Take U6 to *Französische Str.* During the last week of June and the first week of July, the square becomes an outdoor stage for open-air classical concerts; call ☎ 69 80 75 22 for details.

DEUTSCHER DOM. On the southern end of the square, the Dom is not used as a church but instead houses **Wege Irrwege Umwege** (Milestones, Setbacks, Sidetracks), an exhibition tracing German political history from despotism to democracy. *(Gendarmenmarkt 5. Open Su and W-Sa 10am-7pm, Tu 10am-10pm. Free.)*

FRANZÖSISCHER DOM. Built in the early 18th century by French Huguenots, the Dom is now home to a restaurant and a small museum chronicling the Huguenot diaspora. The tower offers a 360° panorama of the city, as well as a terrific view of the square itself. *(Museum open Su 11am-5pm, Tu-Sa noon-5pm. €2, students €1. Tower open M-Sa 9am-7pm. €2, students €1.50.)*

MUSEUMSINSEL AND ALEXANDERPLATZ

After crossing the Spree, Unter den Linden becomes Karl-Liebknecht-Str. and cuts through the **Museumsinsel** (Museum Island), home to five major museums and the **Berliner Dom.** Take S3, 5, 7, 9, or 75 to *Hackescher Markt.* Karl-Liebknecht-Str. continues into the monolithic **Alexanderplatz.**

BERLINER DOM. This bulky, multi-domed cathedral, one of Berlin's most recognizable landmarks, proves that Protestants can be as excessive as Catholics. Built during the reign of Kaiser Wilhelm II, it recently emerged from 20 years of restoration after being damaged in a 1944 air raid. Look for the Protestant icons (Calvin, Zwingli, and Luther) that adorn the interior, or bask in a glorious view of Berlin from the tower. *(Open M-Sa 9am-8pm, Su noon-8pm; closed during services 6:30-7:30pm. Combined admission to Dom, crypt, tower, and galleries €5, students €3. Free organ recitals W-F at 3pm. Frequent concerts in summer; buy tickets in the church or call ☎ 20 26 91 36.*

ALEXANDERPLATZ. Formerly the frantic heart of Weimar Berlin, the plaza was transformed in East German times into an urban wasteland of concrete-block classics. In the 1970s, the gray drear was interrupted by enormous neon signs with declarations like "Medical Instruments of the DDR—Distributed in All the World!" in order to satisfy the people's need for bright lights. Today chain stores like **Kaufhof** have replaced the signs and serve as a backdrop for the affairs of bourgeois German shoppers, tourists, and punks with their dogs.

MARIENKIRCHE. The church is gothic, the altar and pulpit are rococo, and the tower is neo-romantic. Relatively undamaged during the war, this little church still holds relics from other nearby churches which used it as a shelter. Knowledgeable guides explain them and the painting collection from the Dürer and Cranach schools. *(Open M-Th 10am-4pm, Sa-Su noon-4pm.)*

FERNSEHTURM. The tremendous and bizarre TV tower, the tallest structure in Berlin at 368m, was originally intended to prove East Germany's technological capabilities; as a result, the tower has acquired some colorful politically-infused nicknames, among them the perennial favorite "Walter Ulbricht's Last Erection." Look at the windows when the sun is out to see the cross-shaped glint pattern known as the *Papsts Rache* (Pope's revenge). An elevator whisks tourists up to the view from the spherical node at 203m. *(Open daily Mar.-Oct. 9am-1am; Nov.-Feb. 10am-midnight. €6.50, under-16 €3.)*

GERMANY

BERLINER RATHAUS. Also called the "Roter Rathaus," for its brick color, not the politics of the government that used it in the DDR days. Now the seat of Berlin's municipal government, the building is often mobbed by schoolchildren who come on field trips to watch legislation in action. They are not allowed to vote. *(Rathausstr. 1. M-F 9am-6pm. Free. Call ☎ 90 26 25 23 for guided tours.)*

SCHEUNENVIERTEL AND ORANIENBURGER STRAßE

Northwest of Alexanderpl., around the streets of Oranienburger Str. and Große Hamburger Str., lies the **Scheunenviertel.** Once the center of Berlin's Orthodox Jewish community, the neighborhood harbors evidence of Jewish life back to the 13th century, though the Jews were twice expelled from the city; once for 100 years in in 1573, then again during WWII. Today the Scheunenviertel is better known for its outdoor cafes, but the past few years have seen the opening of several Judaica-oriented bookstores and kosher restaurants. Take U6 to *Oranienburger Tor.*

NEUE SYNAGOGE. This huge, "oriental-style" building, modelled after the Alhambra, was designed by Berlin architect Eduard Knoblauch. The synagogue was destroyed by bombing, but its restoration, largely financed by international Jewish organizations, began in 1988. Exhibits chronicle the history of Berlin's Jews. *(Oranienburger Str. 30. ☎ 88 02 83 00. Open Su-M 10am-8pm, Tu-Th 10am-6pm, F 10am-2pm. Museum €5, students €3. Dome €1.50, students €1.)*

OTHER SIGHTS IN MITTE

BERTOLT-BRECHT-HAUS. If anyone personifies the political and aesthetic contradiction that is Berlin, it is **Bertolt Brecht.** "There is a reason to prefer Berlin to other cities," the playwright once declared, "because it is constantly changing. What is bad today can be improved tomorrow." Brecht lived and worked in the house from 1953 to 1956. The **Brechtforum** sponsors exhibits and lectures. *(Chausseestr. 125. U6: Zinnowitzer Str. Mandatory tour in German every 30min. Tu-F 10-11:30am, Th 10-11:30am and 5-6:30pm, and Sa 9:30am-1:30pm. Tours every hr. Su 11am-6pm. €3, students €1.50.)*

CHARLOTTENBURG

Welcome to Berlin—you're probably in Charlottenburg! Originally a separate town founded around the grounds of Friedrich I's imperial palace, Charlottenburg now has Berlin's main shopping strip, the Ku'damm, heavy with tourist traffic and upscale department stores. Most things in Charlottenburg are expensive, but the sights and tourist services around *Bahnhof Zoo* bring most travelers through.

AROUND BAHNHOF ZOO. During the city's division, West Berlin centered around *Bahnhof Zoo*, the station that inspired U2's "Zoo TV" tour. (The U-Bahn line U2 runs through the station—clever, no?) The surrounding area is a spectacle of department stores and peepshows intermingled with souvenir shops and G-rated attractions. Many of the animals at the renowned **Zoologischer Garten** live in open air habitats, and its flamingo flock is not confined at all. Feeding times are posted at the gate so you can see the creatures chow. The second entrance across from Europa-Center is the famous **Elefantentor,** Budapester Str. 34, a decorated pagoda of pachyderms. *(Open May-Sept. daily 9am-6:30pm; Oct.-Feb. 9am-5pm; Mar.-Apr. 9am-5:30pm. €9, students €7, children €4.50; combo ticket to zoo and aquarium €14/11/7.)* Within the walls of the Zoo, but independently accessible, the **Aquarium** has insects and reptiles as well as miles of fish. Check out the psychedelic jellyfish tanks, filled with translucent sea nettles. *(Budapester Str. 32. €9, students €7, children €4.50.)*

KAISER-WILHELM-GEDÄCHTNISKIRCHE. Nicknamed "the rotten tooth" by Berliners, the jagged edges of this shattered church stand as a reminder of the destruction caused by WWII. Inside, a small exhibit shows pictures of the city in ruins. In the summer, Berlin's street performers, salesmen, foreigners, and young gather in front of the church to hang out, sell watches, and play bagpipes and sitars. (☎218 50 23. *Exhibit open M-Sa 10am-4pm. Church open daily 9am-7pm.*)

SCHLOß CHARLOTTENBURG. Commissioned by Friedrich I, this broad Baroque palace occupies a park in northern Charlottenburg. The grounds include the furnished **Altes Schloß** (*open Tu-F 9am-5pm, Sa-Su 10am-5pm; €8, students €5; Required tour.*); the marbled receiving rooms of the **Neuer Flugel** (*open Tu-F 10am-6pm, Sa-Su 11am-6pm; €5, students €4*); the **Neuer-Pavillon**, a museum dedicated to Prussian architect Karl Friedrich Schinkel (*open Su and Tu-Sa 10am-5pm; €2, €1.50*); the **Belvedere**, a small building with the royal family's porcelain collection (*open Apr.-Oct. Su and Tu-Sa 10am-5pm, Nov.-Mar. Tu-F noon-4pm and Sa-Su noon-5pm; €2, students €1.50*); and the **Mausoleum** (*open Apr.-Oct. Su and Tu-Sa 10am-noon and 1-5pm; €1*). Stroll the **Schloßgarten** (*open Su and Tu-Sa 6am-10pm; free*) behind the main buildings, an elysium of small lakes, footbridges, fountains, and manicured trees. (*U7: Richard-Wagner-Pl, then walk 15min. down Otto-Suhr-Allee. Entire complex €7, students €5. Family card €20.*)

OLYMPIA-STADION. The Olympic Stadium is one of the most prominent legacies of the Nazi architectural aesthetic. It was erected for the 1936 Olympic Games, in which Jesse Owens, an African-American, trounced Nazi racial theories by winning four gold medals. The stadium is under construction until late 2004, but the *Glockenturm* (bell tower) gives a great view of it. (*Glockenturm open April-Oct. 9am-6pm. S5 or 7 to Pichelsburg, turn left onto Shirwindter All and left again onto Passenheimerstr.*)

SCHÖNEBERG

South of the Ku'damm, Schöneberg is a pleasant, middle-class residential district noted for its shopping streets, good restaurants, and lively cafes. It's the kind of place where breakfast is an institution rather than a meal, and locals lounge for hours in laid-back cafes. Nollendorfpl., where even the military store is draped with rainbow flags, is the nexus of Berlin's gay and lesbian community.

GRUNEWALD. The 745-acre birch forest is home to the **Jagdschloß**, a restored royal hunting lodge with paintings by German artists Graff and Cranach. The one-room museum in the building is full of knives, guns, spears, goblets, antlers, and mounted wild boars. (*Am Grunewaldsee 29. U1: Fehrbelliner Pl. Walk west 15min. on Pücklerstr. Open Su and Tu-Sa 10am-1pm and 1:30-5pm. €2, students €1.50.*)

KREUZBERG

Kreuzberg is West Germany's dose of counter-culture. Much of the area was occupied by *Hausbesetzer* (squatters) in the 1960s and 70s, but the city government evicted most of them in the early 80s. Anti-government protests are still frequent and intense; the most prominent is the annual May 1st demonstration. Home to an especially large segment of the city's immigrant and ethnic population, the district has recently seen a wave of gentrification that has brought an influx of prepsters and government workers.

■**HAUS AM CHECKPOINT CHARLIE.** This eccentric museum at the famous border-crossing point has become one of Berlin's most popular attractions. A wonderful clutter of artwork, newspaper clippings, and the devices used to get over, under, or through the wall. The exhibits detail how women curled up in loudspeakers, men attempted to crawl through spiked gates, and student groups dug tunnels with their fingers, all in an attempt to reach the West. Out on the street is the unassuming station itself, overshadowed by two large photos of an American and a Russian soldier looking into "enemy" territory. *(Friedrichstr. 43. U6 to Kochstr. Museum open daily 9am-10pm. €7.50, students €4.50. German-language films every 2hr. from 9:30am.)*

ORANIENSTRAßE. The May Day parades start on Oranienplatz, the site of frequent riots in the 1980s. Revolution-minded radicals jostle shoulders with tradition-oriented Turkish families, while an anarchist punk faction and a boisterous gay population make things interesting after hours (see Nightlife, p. 443). Restaurants, clubs, and shops of staggering diversity beckon to passersby. *(U1: Kottbusser Tor or Görlitzer Bahnhof.)*

FRIEDRICHSHAIN AND LICHTENBERG

As the alternative scene follows the low rents ever eastward, Friedrichshain is becoming the new temple of the unpretentiously hip. Relatively unrenovated since reunification, the district retains its pre-fab apartments and large stretches of the wall. Simon-Dach-Str. is cluttered with outdoor cafes and a crowd of 20-somethings. The grungier area around Rigärstr. is one of the strongholds of Berlin's legendary alternative scene, home to squatter bars, makeshift clubs, and punks lounging with their excitable dogs.

■ **EAST SIDE GALLERY.** The longest remaining portion of the Wall, this 1.3km stretch of cement and asbestos slabs also serves as the world's largest open-air art gallery, unsupervised and open at all hours. The murals are not remnants of Cold War graffiti but rather the efforts of an international group of artists who gathered here in 1989 to celebrate the fall of the wall. It was expected that the wall would be destroyed and the paintings lost, but in 2000, with the wall still standing, many of the same artists reconvened to repaint their work, covering the scrawlings of tourists; unfortunately, the new paintings are again being covered over by other graffiti artists. *(Along Mühlenstr. U1: Warschauer Str., and walk back toward the river.)*

FORSCHUNGS- UND GEDENKSTÄTTE NORMANNENSTRAßE. In the suburb of Lichtenberg is the most hated and feared building of the DDR regime—the headquarters of the East German secret police, the **Staatssicherheit** or **Stasi.** On January 15, 1990, a crowd of 100,000 Berliners stormed and vandalized the building to protest the police state. During the Cold War, some 6 million dossiers on citizens of the DDR, a country of only 16 million people, were kept here. Since a 1991 law made the records public, the "Horror Files" have rocked Germany, exposing informants—and wrecking careers, marriages, and friendships—at all levels of society. Today, German-language exhibits display the tiny microphones and cameras used for survellance and a bizarre Stasi shrine of Lenin busts. *(Ruschestr. 103, Haus 1. U5: Magdalenenstr. From the station's Ruschestr. exit, walk up Ruschestr. and take a right on Normannenstr. Open Su and Sa 2-6pm, Tu-F 11am-6pm. €3, students €1.50.)*

PRENZLAUER BERG

Everything in Prenzlauer Berg used to be something else. Plush brunches unfold every Sunday in what were butcher shops; a former power plant stages exhibitions about furniture; and kids cavort in breweries-turned-nightclubs. The *Bezirk* was largely neglected by the city's reconstruction efforts, leaving Berlin's largest collection of graffiti-covered buildings. Relics of Prenzlberg's past life are disappearing, but cafe owners know shabby chic when they see it: Plenty of advertisements for cabbage and mismatched sofas remain.

■ **DOKUMENTATIONSZENTRUM DER BERLINER MAUER.** A museum, chapel, and entire city block of the Berlin Wall form a controversial memorial to "victims of the communist tyranny." The museum assembles a record of all things related to the wall. *(Bernauer Strasse 111. U8: Bernauer Str. Open Su and W-Sa 10am-5pm. Free.)*

GERMANY

KOLLWITZPLATZ. This little triangle of greenery centers on a statue of famed visual artist **Käthe Kollwitz**. The monument is painted and repainted in acts of affectionate rather than angry vandalism. *(U2: Senefelderpl. Kollwitzstr. forks right off of Schönhauser Allee and hits Kollwitzpl.)*

JÜDISCHER FRIEDHOF. Prenzlauer Berg was one of the major centers of Jewish Berlin, especially during the 19th and early 20th centuries. The ivied Jewish cemetery on Schönhauser Allee contains the graves of composer Giacomo Meyerbeer and painter Max Liebermann. *(Open M-Th 8am-4pm, F 8am-3pm. Men must cover their heads before entering the cemetery.)* Nearby stands the **Synagoge Rykestraße**, one of Berlin's loveliest synagogues. *(Rykestr. 53.)*

🏛 MUSEUMS

Berlin is one of the world's great museum cities, with collections of art and artifacts encompassing all subjects and eras. The **Staatliche Museen zu Berlin (SMB)** runs over 20 museums in four major regions—the **Museumsinsel, Kulturforum, Charlottenburg,** and **Dahlem**—and elsewhere in Mitte and around the Tiergarten. Single admission is €6, €3 for students; the *Drei-Tage-Karte* (€10, students €5) is valid for three consecutive days. Both can be bought at any SMB museum. Admission is free the first Sunday of every month. Unaffiliated museums are smaller and more specialized, dealing with everything from Käthe Kollwitz to the cultural history of marijuana. *Berlin Programm* (€1.60) lists museums and galleries.

SMB MUSEUMS

MUSEUMSINSEL (MUSEUM ISLAND)
The Museumsinsel holds the treasure hoard of the former DDR in five separate museums, separated from the rest of Mitte by two arms of the Spree River. Some are being renovated; the **Bodenmuseum** will be closed until 2005 and the **Neues Museum** until 2008. *(S3, 5, 7, 9 or 75 to Hackescher Markt or bus #100 to Lustgarten. ☎20 90 55 55. All SMB museums open Su and Tu-Sa 10am-6pm, Th until 10pm unless noted. All offer free audio tours in English. Admission to each is €6, students €3. All sell a 3-day card good for admission to every museum; €10, students €5.)*

█ PERGAMONMUSEUM. One of the world's great ancient history museums. The museum is named for Pergamon, the city in present-day Turkey from which the enormous Altar of Zeus (180 BC) in the main hall was taken. The museum features pieces of ancient Mediterranean and Near Eastern history from as far back as the 10th century BC. *(Kupfergraben.)*

ALTE NATIONALGALERIE. After extensive renovations, this renowned museum is again open to art-lovers. Everything from German Realism to French Impressionism and Caspar David Friedrich to Karl Friedrich Schinkel. *(Am Lustgarten.)*

ALTES MUSEUM. This surprisingly untouristed museum contains the *Antikensammlung*, a permanent collection of ancient Greco-Roman decorative art.

TIERGARTEN-KULTURFORUM
The **Tiergarten-Kulturforum** is a complex of museums at the eastern end of the Tiergarten, near the Staatsbibliothek and Potsdamer Pl. Students and local fine arts aficionados throng through the buildings and on the multi-leveled courtyard in front. *(U2: Potsdamer Pl. Walk down Potsdamer Str., the museums will be on your right on Matthäikirchpl. ☎20 90 55 55. Hours and prices same as above.)*

■ **GEMÄLDEGALERIE.** One of Germany's most famous museums, and rightly so. It houses a stunning and enormous collection by Italian, German, Dutch, and Flemish masters, including works by Botticelli, Dürer, Raphael, Rembrandt, Rubens, Titian, and Vermeer. *(Stauffenbergstr. 40. ☎ 266 29 51.)*

■ **HAMBURGER BAHNHOF/MUSEUM FÜR GEGENWART.** Berlin's foremost collection of contemporary art features Warhol, Beuys, Kiefer, and some in-your-face temporary exhibits in the bright, airy spaces of a converted train station. The enormity of the exhibition space lends itself to outrageous sculptures. *(Invalidenstr. 50-51. U6: Zinnowitzer Str. Open Su and Sa 11am-6pm, Tu-F 10am-6pm.)*

NEUE NATIONALGALERIE. This sleek building, designed by Mies van der Rohe, has interesting temporary exhibits and a permanent collection of Ernst, Kirchner, Munch, Warhol, and contemporary art. *(Potsdamer Str. 50, just past the Kulturforum.)*

KUNSTBIBLIOTHEK. A stellar collection of lithographs and drawings by Renaissance masters, including Dürer and Goya, and Botticelli's illustrations for the *Divine Comedy.* *(Library open M 2-8pm, Tu-F 9am-8pm. Tours Su at 3pm. Free.)*

CHARLOTTENBURG

The area surrounding **Schloß Charlottenburg** is home to a number of excellent museums. Take bus #145 to *Luisenpl./Schloß Charlottenburg* or U7 to *Richard-Wagner-Pl.* and walk about 15min. down Otto-Suhr-Allee.

■ **ÄGYPTISCHES MUSEUM.** This stern Neoclassical building contains a famous collection of ancient Egyptian art—hulking sarcophogi, mummified cats, a massive temple gateway, and the famous bust of **Queen Nefertiti** (1350 BC), considered one of the most stunning sculptures on earth. *(Schloßstr. 70. Across Spandauer Damm from the palace. Open Su and Tu-Sa 10am-6pm. €8, students €4.)*

SAMMLUNG BERGGRUEN. A substantial collection of Picasso, Paul Klee, Alberto Giacometti, French Impressionists, and African masks. *(Schloßstr. 1. Across the street from the Ägyptisches Museum. Open Su and Tu-Sa 10am-6pm. €6, students €3.)*

DAHLEM

■ **ETHNOLOGISCHES MUSEUM.** The Ethnology Museum richly rewards a trek to Dahlem. The exhibits are stunning, ranging from huge pieces of ancient Central American stonework to African elephant tusk statuettes to enormous boats from the South Pacific. The smaller **Museum für Indisches Kunst** (Museum for Indian Art), housed in the same building, features ornate shrines and bright murals. The **Museum für Ostasiatisches Kunst** (Museum for East Asian Art) also houses a good collection, including many long tapestries. *(U1 to Dahlem-Dorf and follow the "Museen" signs. ☎ 830 14 38. Open Su-Sa 11am-6pm, Tu-F 10am-6pm. €3, students €1.50.)*

INDEPENDENT (NON-SMB) MUSEUMS

DEUTSCHE GUGGENHEIM BERLIN. A joint venture of Deutsche Bank and the Guggenheim Foundation features rotating exhibits of contemporary art. *(Unter den Linden 13. ☎ 202 09 30. Open daily 11am-8pm. €3, students €2.50. M free.)*

KUNST-WERKE BERLIN. This former margarine factory has studio space, a matrix of rotating contemporary exhibitions, a cafe, and an independent bookstore. *(Auguststr. 69. U6: Oranienburger Tor. ☎ 243 45 90; www.kw-berlin.de. Exhibitions open Su and Tu-Sa noon-6pm, Th until 8pm. €4, students €2.)*

FILMMUSEUM BERLIN. This new museum chronicles the development of German film, with a special focus on older films like *Metropolis* and whole rooms devoted to such superstars as Leni Riefenstahl and Marlene Dietrich. *(Potsdamer Str. 2; 3rd and 4th fl. of the Sony Center. U2: Potsdamer Pl. Tickets sold on the ground floor. Open Su and Tu-Sa 10am-6pm, Th until 8pm. €6, students €4, children €2.50.)*

JÜDISCHES MUSEUM BERLIN. Built from Daniel Libeskind's winning design, the zinc-plated structure that houses this museum is a fascinating architectural experience. None of the walls are parallel, and the jagged hallways end in windows overlooking "the void." Wander through the labyrinthine "Garden of Exile" or experience the chill of being shut in the "Holocaust Tower," a giant concrete room virtually devoid of light and sound. Exhibits feature work by contemporary artists, Holocaust memorials, and a history of Jews in Germany. *(Lindenstr. 9. U6 to Kochstr. or U1, 6, or 15 to Hallesches Tor. Open daily 10am-10pm. €5, students €2.50.)*

BAUHAUS-ARCHIV MUSEUM FÜR GESTALTUNG. Designed by Bauhaus founder Walter Gropius, the museum has changing exhibits of paintings, sculptures, and furniture that would do him proud. *(Klingelhöferstr. 14. Bus #100, 187, 200, or 341 to Nordische Botschaften/Adenauer-Stiftg. Open M and W-Su 10am-5pm. €4, students €2.)*

TOPOGRAPHIE DES TERRORS. In the torture chambers discovered beneath the former Gestapo headquarters, a comprehensive exhibit of photographs, documents, and German texts details the Nazi party's rise to power and the atrocities that occurred during the war. Outside stand 200m of the Berlin Wall, a graffitied memorial to the city's divided past. *(Behind the Martin-Gropius-Bau, at the corner of Niederkirchnerstr. and Wilhelmstr. U2: Potsdamer Pl. Open daily 10am-6pm. Free.)*

🎵 ENTERTAINMENT

Berlin has one of the most vibrant cultural scenes in the world: Exhibitions, concerts, plays, and dance performances. The city still generously subsidizes its art scene, despite recent cutbacks, and tickets are usually reasonable, especially with student discounts. Numerous festivals celebrating everything from Chinese film to West African music spice up the regular offerings; posters proclaiming special events festoon the city well in advance.

Reservations can be made by calling the box office directly. Always ask about student discounts; most theaters and concert halls offer up to 50% off, but only if you buy at the *Abendkasse* (evening box office), which generally opens 1hr. before performance. Other ticket outlets charge 15-18% commissions and do not offer student discounts. There is also a ticket counter in the **KaDeWe** department store, Tauentzienstr. 21. (☎217 77 54. Open M-F 10am-8pm, Sa 10am-4pm). While most theaters accept credit cards, many ticket outlets do not. Most theaters and operas close from mid-July to late August.

CONCERTS, OPERA, AND DANCE
Berlin reaches its musical zenith during the **Berliner Festwochen,** lasting almost all of September and drawing the world's best orchestras and soloists. The **Berliner Jazztage** in November, featuring top-notch jazz musicians, also brings in the crowds. For info about either, contact Berliner Festspiele (☎254 890; www.berlinerfestspiele.de). In mid-July, the **Bachtage** is an intense week of classical music, while every Saturday night in August the **Sommer Festspiele** turns the Ku'damm into a concert hall with punk, steel-drum, and folk groups competing for attention.

Look for concert listings in the pamphlets *Konzerte und Theater in Berlin und Brandenburg* (free), *Berlin Programm* (€1.50), *Zitty*, or *Tip*. Tickets for the *Philharmonie* and the *Oper* are nearly impossible to acquire through conventional channels without writing months in advance. Some people stand out in front before performances with a small sign saying *"Suche Karte"* (seeking ticket)— people unload tickets at the last moment, usually at outrageous prices.

▨ **Berliner Philharmonisches Orchester,** Herbert Von Karajanstr. 1 (☎25 48 81 32; www.berlin-philharmonic.com). U2: *Potsdamer Pl.* and walk up Potsdamer Str. It may look bizarre, but this big yellow building, designed by Scharoun in 1963, is acoustically perfect. The *Berliner Philharmoniker* is one of the world's finest orchestras. It's tough to get a seat; check an hour before concert time or write at least 8 weeks in advance. The *Philharmonie* is closed from the end of June until the start of September. Tickets start at €7 for standing room, €15 for seats. Box office open M-F 3-6pm, Sa-Su 11am-2pm.

Konzerthaus (Schauspielhaus am Gendarmenmarkt), Gendarmenmarkt 2 (☎20 30 90; www.konzerthaus.de). U2: *Stadtmitte.* The opulent home of Berlin's symphony orchestra. Last-minute tickets are somewhat easier to come by. No performances mid-July through August. Box office open M-Sa 11am-7pm, Su noon-4pm.

Deutsche Oper Berlin, Bismarckstr. 35 (☎343 84 01; www.deutscheoperberlin.de). U2: *Deutsche Oper.* Berlin's best and youngest opera, featuring newly commissioned works as well as all the German and Italian classics. Tickets €10-110. 25% student discounts. Box office open M-Sa 11am until 1hr. before performance, Su 10am-2pm. Evening tickets available 1hr. before performance. Open Sept.-June.

Deutsche Staatsoper, Unter den Linden 7 (☎20 35 45 55; www.staatsoper-berlin.de). U6: *Französische Str.* Eastern Berlin's leading opera company is led by Daniel Barenboim (also the conductor of the Chicago Symphony Orchestra). Their big budget leads to grandiose fare. Tours on some Sa-M—check ahead for times. Tickets €5-200. Student tickets €10 1 hr. before show. Box office open M-F 11am-7pm, Sa-Su 2-7pm, and 1hr. before performance. Performs Sept. to mid-July.

THEATER

The pamphlets *Kultur!news, Berlin Programm, 030, Zitty,* and *Tip* have theater listings. In addition to the world's best German-language theater, Berlin also has a lively English-language scene. A number of private companies called "off-theaters" also occasionally feature English-language plays. As with concert halls, look out for summer closings (*Theaterferien* or *Sommerpause*).

▨ **Deutsches Theater,** Schumannstr. 13a (☎28 44 12 25; www.deutsches-theater.berlin.net). U6: *Friedrichstr.* Go north on Friedrichstr., turn left on Reinhardtstr., and then right on Albrechtstr., which curves into Schumannstr. Even western Berlin admits it: this is the best theater in Germany. Max Reinhardt made it great 100 years ago; it now has innovative takes on classics and newer works from Büchner to Mamet to Ibsen. The **Kammerspiel** (☎28 44 12 26) stages smaller, provocative productions. Tickets €4-36, students €8. Box office for both open M-Sa 11am-6:30pm, Su 3-6:30pm.

Hebbel-Theater, Stresemannstr. 29 (☎25 90 04 27). U1: *Hallesches Tor.* The most avant of the avant-garde theaters in Berlin draws talent from all over the world. Committed to producing in the original language, this venue brings in the playwrights to collaborate with the actors. Tickets €11-23, students €11. Box office open daily 4-7pm.

Berliner Ensemble, Bertolt-Brecht-Pl. 1 (☎28 40 81 55). U6: *Friedrichstr.* The famous theater established by Brecht is undergoing a renaissance under the leadership of Claus Peymann. Hip repertoire includes Heiner Müller, young American playwrights, and Brecht himself. Some premieres. Performances Sept.-June. Tickets €6-24, students €5. Box office open M-F 8am-6pm, Sa-Su 11am-6pm, and 1hr. before performance.

Maxim-Gorki-Theater, Am Festungsgraben 1 (☎20 22 10). U6: *Friedrichstr.* Excellent contemporary theater—everything from Schiller to Albee. Tickets €8-26. Box office open M-Sa noon-6:30pm, Su 4-6:30pm and 1hr. before performance.

Friends of Italian Opera, Fidicinstr. 40 (☎691 12 11). U6: *Pl. der Luftbrücke.* The name of Berlin's leading English-language theater is a joking reference to the mafia in *Some Like It Hot.* A smaller, less subsidized venue, this stage still produces new, experimental works and old favorites like Samuel Beckett and Tennessee Williams. Tickets €8-15. Box office opens at 7pm. Most shows at 8pm.

FILM

Berlin is a movie-loving town—it hosts the international **Berlinale** film festival (Feb. 5-15, 2004), and on any night you can choose from over 150 films. *O.F.* next to a movie listing means original version (i.e., not dubbed); *O.m.U.* means original version with German subtitles. Check *Tip* or *Zitty* for theater schedules. Prices are reduced M-W at most theaters. Bring a student ID for discounts.

Arsenal, in the Filmhaus at Potsdamer Pl. (☎26 95 51 00). U2: *Potsdamer Pl.* Indie films and occasional classics. Frequent appearances by guest directors make the theater a popular meeting place for Berlin's filmmakers. Tickets €6.

Progress Studiokino Börse, Burgstr. 27 (☎24 00 35 00). S3: *Hackescher Markt.* Shows the DDR-era *Die Legende von Paul und Paula,* a cult favorite for its poetic storytelling and realistic depiction of East Berlin life. Tickets €6, students €5. Tu and Th €4.

Odeon, Hauptstr. 116 (☎78 70 40 19). U4: *Rathaus Schöneberg.* One of the first English-language theaters in Berlin shows mainstream American and British flicks, generally in English with German subtitles. Tickets F-Su €7, M-Th €4.

CineStar, in the Sony Center, Potsdamer Platz. 4 (☎20 66 62 60). U2: *Potsdamer Pl.* English-language blockbusters in a huge theater. Open 11am-11:30pm. Tickets €4-7.

Freiluftkino (outdoor screenings): **Freiluftkino Hasenheide** (☎30 87 25 10), in Hasenheide park. U7: *Hermannpl.* **Freiluftkino Kreuzberg,** Mariannenpl. 2 (☎24 31 30 30). U1: *Kottbusser Tor.* **Freiluftkino Friedrichshain,** in Volkspark Friedrichshain (☎29 36 16 29). U5: *Straußberger Pl.* Tickets €5.50 for all theaters. Cheaper M and W.

🛍 SHOPPING

The seven-story **KaDeWe department store** on Wittenbergpl. at Tauentzienstr. 21-24, is the largest department store on the continent. The name is an abbreviation of *Kaufhaus des Westens* (Department Store of the West); for product-starved East Germans who flooded Berlin in the days following the opening of the Wall, KaDeWe *was* the West. (☎212 10. Open M-F 9:30am-8pm, Sa 9am-4pm.) The **Kurfürstendamm,** near *Bahnhof Zoo,* has almost every kind of shop imaginable. The classified *Zweite Hand* (second-hand; €2), appears Tu, Th and Sa, and has ads for anything anyone wants to re-sell: plane tickets, silk dresses, cats, and teriffic deals on **bikes.** Kreuzberg's strip for used clothing and cheap antiques is on **Bergmannstraße.** *(U7: Gneisenaustr.)*

The flea market on **Straße des 17. Juni** has the best selection, but the prices are higher. (S3: *Tiergarten.* Open Sa-Su 10am-5pm.) The **Trödelmarkt** on Nostitzstr. 6 in Kreuzberg aims to help the homeless of Berlin. (U6: *Mehringdamm.* Open Tu 5-7pm, Th 11am-1pm and 3-6pm, Sa 11am-3pm.) Other markets are located near **Ostbahnhof** in Friedrichshain (by Erich-Steinfurth-Str.; S3: *Ostbahnhof;* open Sa 9am-3pm, Su 10am-5pm) and on **Am Weidendamm** in Mitte (U2: *Friedrichstr;* open Sa-Su 11am-5pm). If you're looking for used **CDs** or LPs, snoop around the streets near Schlesischesstr. *(U1: Schlesisches Tor.)*

NIGHTLIFE

Berlin's nightlife is absolute madness. Bars typically open around 6pm and get going around midnight, just as the clubs are opening their doors. Bar scenes wind down anywhere between 1am and 6am; meanwhile, dance floors fill up at clubs that groove until dawn, when a variety of after-parties and 24hr. cafes keep up the perpetual motion. From 1-4am, take advantage of the **night buses** and **U-Bahn** 9 and 12, which run all night on F-Sa. The best sources of info about bands and dance venues are *Tip* (€2.50) and the superior *Zitty* (€2.30), available at all newsstands, or the free *030*, distributed in hostels, cafes and bars.

Kreuzberg's reputation as the dance capital of Germany is challenged by clubs sprouting up in **Mitte, Prenzlauer Berg,** southern **Friedrichshain,** and near **Potsdamer Platz** in East Berlin. The largest bar scene sprawls down pricey **Oranienburger Straße** in Mitte. Prenzlauer Berg, originally the edgy alternative to trendy Mitte, has become more expensive, especially around **Kollwitzplatz** and Kastanianallee. Still, areas around Schönhauser Allee and Danziger Str. keep the dream alive, such as the "LSD" zone of Lychener Str., Schliemannstr., and Dunckerstr. **Friedrichshain** has edgier venues and a lively bar scene along Simon-Dach-Str. and Gabriel-Max-Str. Raging dance venues aimed at the young are scattered between the car dealerships and empty lots of Mühlenstr. In western Berlin, gay life centers around **Nollendorfplatz.** The Ku'damm is where businessmen and middle-aged tourists drink.

Try to hit the techno **Love Parade,** usually held in the third weekend of July, when over a million ravers ecstatically converge. Prices are astronomical during this weekend of hedonism and insanity. Counter-movements such as the Hate Parade and the Fuck Parade can provide interesting, cheap party alternatives—ask around.

BARS AND CLUBS

MITTE

■ **Tresor/Globus,** Leipziger Str. 126a. U2 or night bus N5, N29, or N52 to *Potsdamer Pl.* One of the best techno venues in Berlin. Downstairs former bank vaults flicker in strobe light as ravers sweat to hardcore techno; upstairs the music is slower. Cover W €3, F €7, Sa €7-11. Open W and F-Sa 11pm-6am.

Zosch, Tucholskystr. 30. U6: *Oranienburger Tor.* The bright, laid-back bar on the ground floor is like a living room. The basement has live music, fiction and poetry readings, and another, darker bar. Dixieland jazz W. Open M-F from 4pm, Sa-Su from noon.

NO WORK, ALL PLAY

THE LOVE PARADE

Every year on the 3rd weekend in July, the Love Parade brings Berlin to its knees—trains run late, streets fill with litter, and German teenagers dye their hair, drop ecstasy, and get down en masse. What started in 1988 as a DJ's birthday party of 150 people has mutated into an annual corporate-techno-Woodstock—half a million attended in 2004. A huge "parade" takes place on Saturday, involving a procession of tractor-trailers loaded with blasting speakers and topped by gyrating bodies that slowly works it from Ernst-Reuter-Pl. to the Brandenburg Gate. The city-wide party turns the Str. des 17. Juni into a riotous dance floor and the Tiergarten into a den of iniquity. To celebrate the licentious atmosphere, the BVG offers a "No-Limit-Ticket," useful for getting from venue to venue during the weekend's 54hr. of nonstop partying (€5, condom included). Club prices skyrocket as the best DJs are imported for the frantic, beat-thumping weekend.

Some have proclaimed that the Love Parade is dying, down to barely a third of the attendence it enjoyed in the late-90s. But tell that to anyone who's ever been there, they'll tell you it's an experience they'll never forget. Unless they partied too hard, of course.

(The 16th Love Parade will take place the weekend of July 10, 2004.)

WMF, Karl-Marx-Allee 34. U5: *Schillingstr.* In a former East German cabaret, its double-dancefloors fill with electroloungers Th and Sa. Gay night Su. Cover €7-13. Open Th and Sa from 11pm, Su from 10pm.

2BE-Club, Ziegelstr. 23. U6: *Oranienburger Tor.* Reggae and hip-hop in a huge space. F, Sa women free until midnight. Cover €8. Open F-Sa from 11pm.

Strandbar Mitte, Monbijioustr. 3. S3, 5, 7, 9, or 75 to *Hackescher Markt.* In Monbijoupark, across from the Bodemuseum. There's a difference between gimmicks and really awesome gimmicks, and Strandbar's miniature outdoor beach, spread with countless beach chairs, is in the second category. Open in summer only, daily from 10pm.

Delicious Doughnuts, Rosenthaler Str. 9. U8: *Rosenthaler Pl.* This bar's cute, curvacious design draws you through the door into one of the low lounge booths. Foosball and a pocket-sized dance floor. Open daily from 9pm.

Café Silberstein, Oranienburger Str. 27. S1, 2, or 25 to *Oranienburger Str.* Sushi until midnight. Japanese industrial-chic motifs, chairs with 8 ft. high backs, and an intellectual 30-something crowd. Open daily from 10am.

VEB-OZ, Stadtbogen 153. By Monbijoupark under the S-Bahn tracks west of Hackescher Markt. The name stands for *Verkehrsberuhigte Ost Zone,* and it's full of kitschy East German paraphernalia. The new location is a little small and see-through, but still has foosball. Open daily from 6pm.

SCHÖNEBERG

▧ **Slumberland,** Goltzstr. 24. U1: *Nollendorfpl.* See it to believe it: Palm trees, rotating African art, and a sand floor. The secret to the bittersweet frappes is instant coffee crystals. Open Su-Th 6pm-2am, F 6pm-5am, Sa 11am-5am.

Mister Hu, Goltzstr. 39. U1: *Nollendorfpl.* The question: *Wozu?* (Where to?) hangs in neon above the crowd. The answer: Mister Hu. Happy hour 5-8pm. Creative cocktails. Open daily from 5pm, Sa from 11am.

Metropol, Nollendorfpl. 5 (☎217 368 11). U1: *Nollendorfpl.,* or night buses #N5, N19, N26, N48, N52, or N75. Don't tell someone to meet you here without specifying a room and a floor. **Tanz Tempel,** the central dance venue, is vast: 650,000 watts of light, 35,800 watts of sound, and DJs who aren't afraid to use them. Music and hours vary.

KREUZBERG

▧ **Freischwimmer,** vor dem Schlesischen Tor 2. U1: *Schlesischen Tor.* A mess of waterside tables tangled in rose vines—some indoors, some outdoors, some with chubby sofas, some in boats. M poetry reading followed by a party. F a roll of the die determines the cover charge (€1-6). Open M-F from noon, Sa-Su from 11am.

▧ **SO36,** Oranienstr. 190 (☎61 40 13 06). U1, 12, or 15 to *Görlitzer Bahnhof* or night bus #N29 to *Heinrichpl.* Berlin's best mixed club, with a hip hetero, gay, and lesbian clientele. A massive dance packs in a friendly crowd for techno, hip-hop, and ska—often live. Cover for parties €4-8, concerts €7-18. Open from 11pm.

Wild at Heart, Wiener Str. 20 (☎611 70 10). U1: *Görlitzer Bahnhof.* Shrines to Elvis, Chinese lanterns, flaming booths, tiki torches, glowing tigers, and other glittery kitsch. The crowd is pierced and punked. Gritty music every night. Open daily from 8pm.

TEK, Oranienstr. 36. U1: *Kotbussen Tor.* Less outrageous and more genuine than many of its neighbors. Very punk. Movies Su at 8pm. Open F-Sa from 5pm, Su from 4pm.

Muvuca, Mehringhof, Gneisenaustr. 2a (☎693 01 75). U6: *Mehringdamm* or night bus #N4, N19, or N76. A bar, performance space, Afro-Brazilian eatery, and club run by a socialist collective in a steel and concrete courtyard. Also the site of political meetings, lesbian events, and an anarchist bookstore. Open Su and Tu-Sa 3pm-late.

FRIEDRICHSHAIN

Astro-Bar, Simon-Dach Str. 40. Plastic retro space robots and loud electronica. Open daily from 6pm.

Dachkammer Bar (DK), Simon-Dach Str. 39. U5: *Frankfurter Tor.* Rustic themed, with lots of brick, wood, and comfortable nooks. Snacks from €4. Mixed drinks €5-7. Open M-F noon-late, Sa-Su 10am-late.

Paule's Metal Eck, Krossener Str. 15 (☎291 1624; www.paules-metal-eck.de). U5: *Frankfurter Tor.* At the corner of Simon-Dach Str. How do you make your bar stand out on the strip? Chihuahua skeletons! A well-executed fake heavy metal bar—don't let the hooded Goth monk over the door scare you off. Open noon until late.

PRENZLAUER BERG

Morgenrot, Kastanianallee 85. U2: *Eberswalder Str.* By day it's a vegetarian restaurant, by night it serves frosty vodka shots. Th-Su vegetarian brunch buffet 11am-4pm. Open Su and Th-Sa 11am-1am, T-W 3pm-1am, F-Sa until 3am.

August Fengler, Lychener Str. 11 (☎44 35 66 40). U2: *Eberswalder Str.* This hip, homey cafe-bar is very un-Prenzlberg. DJs W-Th, live music F-Sa (reggae, funk, house, jazz, Latin). Open daily from 7pm, music from 10pm.

KulturBrauerei, Knaackstr. 97 (☎441 92 69; www.kulturbrauerei.de). U2: *Eberswalder Str.* Enormous party space in a former East German brewery. This expansive village of *Kultur* houses everything from the popular clubs **Soda** and **Kesselhaus** to a Russian theater to upscale cafes and an art school. Music includes hardcore *Ostrock,* disco, techno, reggae, *Schlager* and more. Cover varies wildly—€1.50-16 or more.

Duncker, Dunckerstr. 64. U2: *Eberswalder Str.* This small, dark, and intense club mixes it up: Su-M Goth, Tu hippie music, W parties, Th live bands, F-Sa varies. Garden with grill in back. Cover €2-4, Th usually free. Partiers show up around 2am.

Knaack, Greifswalderstr. 224 (☎442 7061). Tram #2: *Am Friedrichshain.* 4-floored Knaack plays disco, rock, and punk—anything but techno. Live music on the ground fl., billiards upstairs. Cover varies. Dance floors open F-Su and sometimes W from 11pm.

Icon, Cantianstr. 15 (☎48 49 28 78). U2: *Eberswalder Str.* Dance in underground tunnels. F hip-hop, Sa drum and bass. Cover €5-10. Open from 11:30pm F-Sa.

FROM THE ROAD

CLEANING HOUSE

The art students I met hours ago urge me to—yes—come on inside. This is **Tacheles,** which has been transformed from a luxury hotel to a WWII ruin to a squatters' hive. Recent changes bother my guides. "There used to be this scorched toilet just hanging out of the wall way up there, and a car sticking out of the ground," Holgar says. "Now it's getting gentrified."

On the top floor, overlooking Berlin from a bombed-open room, a DJ spins. "This place is not that cool," says Holgar. I ask him what is. "There was a wreck on my block," he says, "that had a party the night before it was renovated. There was a plank over a hole in the floor that you lowered yourself into. There was a little girl on a folding chair saying, 'Give me five euros.' Then you went down and there was a room of people just smoking, and you went down more and kids were serving beer from crates, and then down more and finally a big thumping techno party. It was just"—he gets wistful—"just completely illegal and against any fire and safety codes."

He sighs and looks out over the city. Berlin's transformation has brought miracles—habitable buildings with central heat in neighborhoods that had none—but it also raises rents. Many still search for the underground party, the unofficial club. If you come soon, and look hard, you just might find it.

—Emily Carmichael

CHARLOTTENBURG (SAVIGNYPLATZ)

Quasimodo, Kantstr. 12a. U2: *Zoologischer Garten.* Beneath a huge cafe, this concert venue showcases soul and jazz. Cover €7-24. Open M-F from 5pm, Sa-Su from 2pm.

A-Trane, Bleibtreustr. 1 (☎313 25 50; www.a-trane.de). S3, 5, 7, 9, or 75 to *Savignypl.* There's little chat: the jazz fans are here for the music. Cover €8-15. Doors open at 9, musicians play 10pm-2am weeknights, later on weekends. Usually closed M and Su.

TREPTOW

Insel der Jugend, Alt-Treptow 6 (☎53 60 80 20). S4, 6, 8, or 9 to *Treptower Park,* then bus #265 or #N65 to *Rathaus Treptow.* The name means "island of youth," but Pinocchio never had it this good. Located in the Spree River, the island is accessible by bridge only. Three winding stories of gyrating youth are complemented by bars, river-side couches, an open-air movie theater and a sweet little cafe. Depending on the night, the top 2 floors spin reggae, hip-hop, ska, and house (sometimes all at once), while the frantic techno scene in the basement claims the casualties of the upper floors. Club cover Th-Sa €4-6, movies €5. Club open W from 8pm, F-Sa from 10pm; cafe open Su and Tu-Sa 3pm-late; movies M, Tu, Th, and Su.

GAY AND LESBIAN NIGHTLIFE

Berlin is one of the most gay-friendly cities on the continent. During the Cold War, thousands of homosexuals flocked to Berlin to take part in its left-wing activist scene as well as to avoid West Germany's *Wehrpflicht* (mandatory military service). Christopher Isherwood lived at Nollendorfstr. 17 in legendarily gay-friendly **Nollendorfplatz** while writing his collection of stories *Goodbye to Berlin,* later adapted as the musical *Cabaret.* The main streets, including Goltzstr., Akazienstr., and Winterfeldtstr., have mixed bars and cafes, while the "Bermuda Triangle" of Motzstr., Fuggerstr., and Eisenacherstr. is more exclusively gay.

Mann-o-Meter, Bülowstr. 106, at the corner of Else-Lasker-Schüler-Str., offers counciling and info on nightlife. (☎216 80 08; www.mann-o-meter.de. Open M-F 5-10pm and Sa-Su 4-10pm.) **Spinnboden-Lesbenarchiv,** Anklamer Str. 38, is the lesbian equivalent. Take U8 to *Bernauer Str.* (☎448 58 48. Open W and F 2-7pm.) For up-to-date event listings, pick up the free *Siegessäule, Sergej* (for men), or *Blattgold* (for women). The second half of June culminates in the ecstatic, champagne-soaked floats of the **Christopher Street Day** (CSD) parade, a six-hour-long street party drawing more than 250,000 revelers (June 26, 2004). The weekend before CSD sees the smaller **Lesbisch-schwules Stadtfest** (city fair) at Nollendorfpl.

SCHÖNEBERG

◪ **Hafen,** Motzstr. 19. U1: *Nollendorfpl.* All its art was made by one of the eight owners, who take turns tending the bar. Mostly male but not restricted. The weekly pub quiz (at 10pm) is in English the first M of each month. Open daily 8pm-late.

Heile Welt, Motstr. 5. U1: *Nollendorfpl.* Despite the recent addition of two enormous, quiet inner sitting rooms, the clientele still packs the bar and spills into the street. Mostly male crowd during "prime time," more mixed in the early evening and early morning. Open 6pm-4am.

Neue Ufer, Hauptstr. 157. U7: *Kleistpark.* Formerly "the other shore," this long-running cafe has become "the new shore." The *Milchkaffee* still flows and the mood is still mellow. M-Th and Su 11am-1am, F and Sa 11am-2am.

KREUZBERG

◪ **Rose's,** Oranienstr. 187 (☎615 65 70). U1: *Görlitzer Bahnhof.* Marked only by "Bar" over the door. It's Liberace meets Cupid meets Satan. A friendly, mixed gay and lesbian clientele packs this intense and claustrophobic party spot at all hours of the night. Margaritas €4. Open daily 10pm-6am.

Schoko-Café, Mariannenstr. 6 (☎615 15 61). Lesbian central; a bright and colorful cafe with billiards, Turkish baths, a cultural center, and innumerable other women-only services. Dancing every second Sa of the month (from 10pm) and cultural events every weekend. Friendly and laid-back. Open daily from 5pm.

SchwuZ, Mehringdamm 61. U6: *Mehringdamm.* Dance floor hidden behind Sundström, a popular gay and lesbian cafe. Semi-famous parties are thrown here, including a lesbian event every second F of the month. Cover €4-8. Open F-Sa from 11pm.

FRIEDRICHSHAIN AND PRENZLAUER BERG

🔳 **Die Busche**, Mühlenstr. 12. U1: *Warschauer Str.* Outside, it looks like an auto yard; inside, Eastern Berlin's largest gay disco is a color-saturated haven of dance, spinning an incongruous rotation of techno, top 40, and *Schlager.* Cover €4-5. Open W and F-Su from 10pm-5am.

Café Amsterdam, Gleimstr. 24. U2: *Schönhauser Allee.* Relaxed and romantic. Good cocoa. Pasta dishes (€6-7) until 11:30pm. Open M-F from 4, Sa-Su brunch from 10am.

🔳 DAYTRIPS FROM BERLIN

KZ SACHSENHAUSEN. The small town of Oranienburg, just north of Berlin, was home to the Nazi concentration camp Sachsenhausen, where more than 100,000 Jews, communists, intellectuals, Roma, and homosexuals were killed between 1936 and 1945. The **Gedenkstätte Sachsenhausen,** a memorial preserving the remains of the camp, was opened by the DDR in 1961. It including some of the original cramped barracks, the cell block where "dangerous" prisoners were kept in solitary confinement and tortured, and a pathology wing where Nazis experimented on inmates. A stone monolith commemorating the camp's victims stands sentinel over the wind-swept grounds and several small museums. *(Str. der Nationen 22. S1: Oranienburg (40min.). Follow the signs from Stralsunderstr., turn right on Bernauer Str., left on Str. der Einheit, and right on Str. der Nationen (20min.). ☎03301 20 00. Free. Audio tour rental €3.50. Open mid-Mar. to mid-Oct. 8:30am-6pm; mid-Oct to mid-Mar. 8:30am-4pm.)*

POTSDAM. Visitors disappointed by Berlin's distinctly unroyal demeanor can get their Kaiserly fix in nearby Potsdam, the glittering city of Friedrich II (the Great). The 600-acre 🔳**Park Sanssouci** is Friedrich's testament to the size of his treasury and the diversity of his aesthetic tastes. For info on the park, stop by the **Visitor's Center** at the windmill. *(Open May-Oct. daily 8:30am-5pm; Nov.-Feb. 9am-4pm.)* **Schloß Sanssouci,** the park's main attraction, was Friedrich's answer to Versailles. German tours are limited to 40 people and leave every 20min., but the final tour (5pm) usually sells out by 2pm, so come early. The tourist office leads English-language tours of the main Schloß only. *(Open Apr.-Oct. Su and Tu-Sa 9am-5pm; Nov.-Mar. Su and Tu-Sa 9am-4pm. Required tour €8, students €5.)* The exotic gold-plated **Chinesisches Teehaus,** complete with a rooftop Buddha toting a parasol, contains 18th-century *chinoiserie* porcelain. Next door is the **Bildergalerie,** whose collection of Caravaggio, van Dyck, and Rubens crams a long hall. *(Open mid-May to mid-Oct. Su and Tu-Sa 10am-12:30pm and 1-5pm. €2, students €1.50. Tour €1 extra.)* The stunning **Sizilianischer Garten** is perhaps the park's most intricate garden. At the opposite end of the park is the largest of the four castles, the 200-room **Neues Palais.** *(Open Apr.-Oct. Sa-Th 9am-5pm; Nov.-Mar. 9am-4pm. €6, students €5; €1 less in winter.)*

Potsdam's second park, **Neuer Garten,** contains several royal residences. **Schloß Cecilienhof,** built in the style of an English Tudor manor, exhibits document the **Potsdam Treaty,** which was signed here in 1945. It was supposed to be the "Berlin Treaty," but the capital was too bombed-out to accommodate the Big Three. *(Take bus #692 to Schloß Cecilienhof. Open Su and Tu-Sa 9am-5pm. €3, students €2. Tours €1.)* The garden also contains the huge, marbled **Marmorpalais,** and odd little buildings like a replica of an Egyptian pyramid. *(Marmorpalais open Apr.-Oct. Su and Tu-Sa 10am-5pm; Nov.-Mar. Sa-Su 10am-4pm. €2, students €1.50. Tours €1.)*

EASTERN GERMANY

Saxony *(Sachsen)* is known primarily for Dresden and Leipzig, the largest cities in Eastern Germany after Berlin. However, the entire region offers fascinating historical and cultural diversity. The castles around Dresden testify to the decadence of Saxony's Electors, while boxy socialist monuments elsewhere recall the GDR aesthetic. Saxony is also home to the Sorbs, Germany's only national minority, who lend a Slavic feel to many of the region's eastern towns.

DRESDEN ☎ 0351

The stunning buildings of Dresden's *Altstadt* look ancient, but most are newly reconstructed—the Allied bombings of February 1945 that claimed over 40,000 lives destroyed 75% of the city center. Its Baroque architecture, world-class museums, and *Neustadt* nightlife make Dresden (pop. 479,000) one of the most celebrated cities its size; backpackers traveling from Berlin to Prague often stop over.

▐ TRANSPORTATION

Flights: Dresden's **airport** (DRS; ☎ 881 33 60) is 9km from the city. S2 runs there from both train stations (20min., 2 per hr. 4am-10:30pm, €1.50).

Trains: Nearly all trains stop at both the **Hauptbahnhof** in the Altstadt and **Bahnhof Dresden Neustadt** across the Elbe. Trains to: **Berlin** (3hr., 1 per hr., €30); **Budapest** (11hr., every 2hr., €64); **Frankfurt** (7hr., 2 per hr., €70); **Leipzig** (1½hr., 1-2 per hr., €17); **Munich** (7 hr., 1 per hr., €27); **Prague** (2½hr., 12 per day, €20); and **Warsaw** (8hr., 8 per day, €27). Buy tickets from the machines in the main halls of both stations or pay less at the *Reisezentrum* desk.

Public Transportation: Most of Dresden is manageable on foot, but **streetcars** cover the whole city. Single ride €1.50; 4 or fewer stops €1. Day pass €4; weekly pass €14. Tickets are available from *Fahrkarten* dispensers at major stops and on the streetcars. For info and maps, go to one of the **Verkehrs-Info** stands in front of the *Hauptbahnhof* or at Postpl. (Open M-F 7am-7pm, Sa 8am-6pm, Su 9am-6pm.) Most major lines run hourly after midnight—look for the moon sign marked *"Gute-Nacht-Linie."*

Taxis: ☎ 211 211 or ☎ 888 88 88.

Bike Rental: In the *Hauptbahnhof.* €6 per day. Open daily 6am-10pm.

Ride-Sharing: Mitfahrzentrale, Dr.-Friedrich-Wolf-Str. 2 (☎ 194 40). On Slesischen Pl., across from Bahnhof Neustadt. Open M-F 9am-8pm, Sa-Su 10am-2pm.

Hitchhiking: *Let's Go* does not recommend hitchhiking as a safe mode of transportation. Hitchers say they stand in front of the *Autobahn* signs at on-ramps. To **Berlin:** Streetcar #3 or 13 to *Liststr.,* then bus #81 to *Am Olter.* To **Prague, Eisenach,** or **Frankfurt am Main:** Bus #72 or 88 to *Luga,* or bus #76, 85, or 96 to *Lockwitz.*

▐ ORIENTATION AND PRACTICAL INFORMATION

Dresden is bisected by the **Elbe** river 60km northwest of the Czech border. The **Hauptbahnhof** is on the same side as the **Altstadt,** south of the river. Many of Dresden's main attractions are between **Altmarkt** and the Elbe. Nightlife is to the north in the **Neustadt,** around Albertplatz.

Tourist Office: There are two main branches: On Prager Str. 3, near the *Hauptbahnhof* (open M-F 9am-7pm, Sa 9am-4pm), and Theaterpl. in the Schinkelwache in front of the Semper Oper (☎49 19 20. Open M-F 10am-6pm, Sa-Su 10am-4pm). Call city hotlines for general info (☎49 19 21 00), reservations (☎49 19 22 22), tours (☎49 19 21 40), and advance ticket purchases (☎49 19 22 33).

Currency Exchange: ReiseBank, in the *Hauptbahnhof*. €1-3 commission, depending on the amount; 1-1.5% for traveler's checks. Open M-F 8am-7pm, Sa 9am-12pm, 12:30-4pm, Su 9am-1pm. Other banks are on Prager Str.

Luggage Storage and Lockers: At all train stations. Lockers €1-2 for 24hr.

Laundromat: "Crazy" Waschsalon, 6 Louisenstr. Wash €2.50, dry €0.50 per 10min. Open M-Sa 7am-11pm.

Emergency: Police ☎110. **Ambulance** and **Fire** ☎112.

Pharmacy: Apotheke Prager Straße, Prager Str. 3 (☎490 30 14). Open M-F 8:30am-7pm, Sa 8:30am-4pm. The *Notdienst* sign outside lists 24hr. pharmacies.

Internet Access: In the bar at **Hostel Mondpalast,** Louisenstr. 77. €3.50 per hr. Open daily 8am-1am. **Groove Station,** Katharinenstr. 11-13. €3 per hr. Open daily 1pm-late.

Post Office: Hauptpostamt, Königsbrücker Str. 21/29 (☎819 13 73), in Neustadt. Open M-F 8am-7pm, Sa 9am-1pm. Address mail to be held: Firstname SURNAME, *Postlagernde Briefe*, Hauptpostamt, **D-01099** Dresden, Germany.

🏠 ACCOMMODATIONS

The *Neustadt* is home to a number of hostels that give revelers proximity to clubs and bars and have late check-out times. Quieter hostels and pricier hotels can be found around the *Altstadt*, closer to the sights. Reservations are a must anywhere.

🏅 Hostel Mondpalast, Louisenstr. 77 (☎563 40 50). With a guestbook full of rave reviews, this hostel has all a backpacker could desire: Good prices, comfortable beds, a large kitchen, a social dining room, and a bar. Sheets €1.50. Internet €3.50 per hr. Reception 24hr. Dorms €13.50-16; singles €29, with bath €39; doubles €37/50. ❷

Pension Raskolnikoff, Böhmische Str. 34 (☎804 57 06). This 6-room pension is squeezed into the same building as the restaurant and gallery of the same name. The distinctly relaxed bohemian atmosphere is a perfect escape from the hostel scene. Singles €31; doubles €41; €8 for each extra person. ❸

Hostel "Louise 20," Louisenstr. 20 (☎889 48 94). Climb the ladder to one of the 20 beds in the dorm attic (€10) in Dresden's newest hostel. Sheets €2.50. 5-bed room €15; 3-4 bed room €16; singles €26; doubles €37. ❶

Lollis Homestay, Seitenstr. 2A (☎799 30 25). From Neustadt station turn left on Dr.-Friedrich-Wolf-Str.; follow it to Bischofsweg and turn left under the tracks. Go right on Rudolf-Leonardstr. and left through the park. Cozy as a German *WG* (shared student flat). Breakfast €3. Sheets €2. Free laundry. Dorms €13; singles €25; doubles €34. ❶

Hostel Die Boofe, Hechtstr. 10 (☎801 33 61). From the Neustadt, take a left and walk parallel to the tracks on Dammweg. Go left on Bischofsweg and right on Hechtstr. Funky hostel has a restaurant downstairs with specials for guests. Sheets €2.75. Reception 6pm-midnight. Dorms €14.50; singles €25; doubles €40, with shower €48. ❷

Jugendgästehaus Dresden (HI), Maternstr. 22 (☎49 26 20). From the *Hauptbahnhof* turn left on Ammonstr. to Rosen Str. Turn right, then take a left onto Maternstr. Come here when everything else is booked—they have 400 beds. Breakfast included. 24hr. reception. Check-in after 4pm. Check-out 9:30am. Dorms €20; singles €8 extra. ❷

FOOD

It's difficult to find anything in the *Altstadt* not targeting tourists; the cheapest eats are at the *Imbiß* stands along **Prager Straße** and around **Postplatz.** The Neustadt area between **Albertplatz** and **Alaunplatz** spawns a new bar every few weeks and is home to most of Dresden's quirky, ethnic, and student-friendly restaurants.

Planwirtschaft, Louisenstr. 20. Attracts political Reds and Greens with neo-German cuisine made with ingredients fresh from local farms. Inventive soups, fresh salads (€3.50-6.50), and entrees from stuffed eggplant to fresh lake fish (€7-10). Breakfast buffet until 4pm. Open Su-Th 9am-midnight, F-Sa 9am-1am. ❸

Café Aha, Kreuzstr. 7. Across the street from Kreuzkirche. Promotes fair trade by introducing food from a different devloping country each month. Often exotic and always delicious. Entrees €3.50-8.40. Open daily 10am-midnight. ❷

El Perro Borracho, Alaunstr. 70. Flowing Spanish wines, *Sekt, sangria,* and tasty *tapas* make happy Dresdeners. Entrees €6-8. Buffet breakfast 10am-3pm on weekends (€8). Open M-F 11:30am-2am, Sa-Su 10am-3am. ❸

Raskolnikoff, Böhmische Str. 34. A Dostoevskian haunt in a pre-war brownstone. Savory fare from all four corners of the globe (€3-14.50). Open daily 10am-2am. ❸

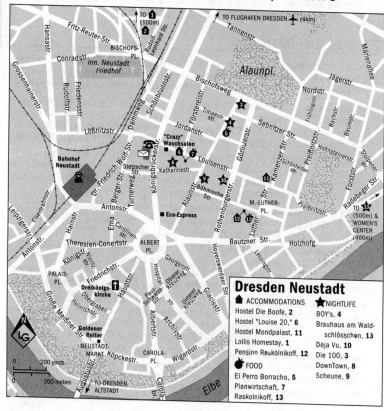

Dresden Neustadt

🔺 ACCOMMODATIONS
Hostel Die Boofe, **2**
Hostel "Louise 20," **6**
Hostel Mondpalast, **11**
Lollis Homestay, **1**
Pension Raskolnikoff, **12**

🍎 FOOD
El Perro Borracho, **5**
Planwirtschaft, **7**
Raskolnikoff, **13**

⭐ NIGHTLIFE
BOY's, **4**
Brauhaus am Wald-
   schlösschen, **13**
Déja Vu, **10**
Die 100, **3**
DownTown, **8**
Scheune, **9**

SIGHTS

The electors of Sachsen once ruled nearly all of central Europe from the banks of the Elbe. Destroyed during WWII and partly rebuilt during Communist times, the *Altstadt* carries the city's legacy as one of the continent's major cultural centers.

ZWINGER. The extravagant collection of August the Strong, Prince Elector of Saxony and King of Poland, is housed in the magnificent Zwinger palace. One of the most successful examples of Baroque design, the palace narrowly escaped destruction in the 1945 bombings. The northern wing was designed by Gottfried Semper, revolutionary activist and master architect. The palace is now home to Dresden's finest museums (see Museums, below).

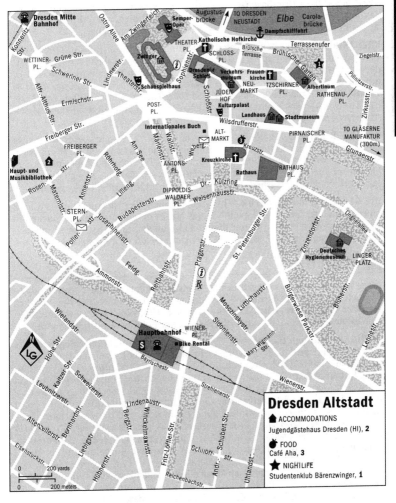

GERMANY

Dresden Altstadt

▲ ACCOMMODATIONS
Jugendgästehaus Dresden (HI), **2**

🍎 FOOD
Café Aha, **3**

★ NIGHTLIFE
Studentenklub Bärenzwinger, **1**

SEMPER-OPER. Dresden's famed opera house luxuriates in the same style as the northern wing of the Zwinger palace. Painstaking restoration has returned the building to its original state, making it one of Dresden's major attractions. Tour the interior any day—or just go to an opera. *(Theaterpl. 2. Check the main entrance for tour times, usually M-F every 30min. 11am-3pm. €5, students €3.)*

DRESDENER SCHLOß. Once the proud home of August the Strong, this palace will regain the lion's share of its notoriety in 2004, when the ▧**Grünes Gewölbe** (Green Vault) returns. From a collection of rare medieval chalices to the most lavish Baroque jewels, the vault dazzles the eyes with some of the finest metal and gem work in Europe. The 100m tall ▧**Hausmannsturm** hosts a collection of sobering photographs of the city after the bombings that, combined with the 360° view from the tower, convey the enormity of the reconstruction project. *(Open Su and Tu-Sa 10am-6pm. €3.50, students and seniors €2.)* To meet the rulers of Saxony from 1123 to 1904, stop by the **Fürstenzug** (Procession of Electors) along Augustsstr., a 102m mural made of 24,000 tiles of Meißen china.

KREUZKIRCHE. After being leveled three times—by fire in 1669; in 1760 by the Thirty Years War; and again in 1897 by fire—the *Kreuzkirche* survived WWII despite the flames that ruined its interior. The tower offers a bird's-eye view of downtown. *(An der Kreuzkirche 6. Open in summer M-Tu and Th-F 10am-5:30pm, W and Sa 10am-4:30pm, Su noon-5:30pm; in winter M-Sa 10am-3:30pm, Su noon-4:30pm. Free. Tower €1.)* The world-class **Kreuzchor** boys' choir is still singing after all these years. *(Concerts Sa 6pm. €4-31, students €3-23.)*

GOLDENER REITER. A gold-plated statue of August the Strong stands just across the Augustusbrücke on Haupstr. August's nickname has two sources: His physical strength, to which a thumbprint on the Brühlische Terasse supposedly attests, and his remarkable virility—legend has it he fathered 365 children, though the official tally is 15. Newly refurbished, August shines with all his former cocky gallantry.

DIE GLÄSERNE MANUFAKTUR. This transparent Volkswagen factory is a bold piece of architecture; Phaetons in various stages of construction are stacked in plain view. Call ahead for a tour that includes an amazingly realistic virtual test drive. *(Lennestr. 1. ☎89 62 68. Tours M-F 8am-8pm every 2 hr. by appointment.)*

⌷ MUSEUMS

After several years of renovations, Dresden's museums are once again ready to compete with the best in Europe. If you plan on visiting more than one in a day, consider a **Tageskarte** (€10, students and seniors €6), which gives one-day admission to the Albertinum museums, the Schloß, most of the Zwinger, and more.

ZWINGER. Through the archway from the Semper-Oper, ▧**Gemäldegalerie Alte Meister** has a world-class collection of predominantly Italian and Dutch paintings from 1400 to 1800. Cranach the Elder's luminous *Adam* and *Eve* paintings, Rubens's *Leda and the Swan*, and Raphael's *Sistine Madonna* are good company. *(Open Su and Tu-Sa 10am-6pm. €6, students €3.50. Tours F and Su at 11am and 4pm, €0.50.)* The nearby **Rüstkammer** shows shiny but deadly toys from the court of the Wettin princes: Ivory-inlaid guns, chain mail, and the wee armor of the Wettin toddlers. *(Open Su and Tu-Sa 10am-6pm. €1.50, students and seniors €1; covered by admission to the Gemäldegalerie Alte Meister.)* With over 20,000 pieces, the **Porzellansammlung** boasts the largest collection of European porcelain in the world. *(Open Su-W and F-Sa 10am-6pm. €1.50, students and seniors €1.)* Europe's oldest "science museum," the **Mathematisch-Physikalischer Salon** is a small room with 16th- to 19th-century scientific instruments that are far more stylish than the ones we use today. *(Open Su-W and F-Sa 10am-6pm. €1.50, students €1.)*

ALBERTINUM. The **Gemäldegalerie Neue Meister** picks up in the 19th century where the Alte Meister gallery leaves off, with such German and French Impressionists as Degas, Monet, Renoir, and hometown hero Caspar David Friedrich. Check out Otto Dix's renowned *War* triptych, along with the Expressionist and *Neue Sachlichkeit* works. *(Open Su-W and F-Sa 10am-6pm. €6, students and seniors €3.50.)* The immense **Skulpturensammlung** collection of classical sculpture was rescued from the basement during the 2002 floods, and will likely fill the void left by the departure of the Grünes Gewölbe in December 2003.

DEUTSCHES HYGIENEMUSEUM. The world's first public health museum is famous for its "Glass Man," a transparent human model with illuminated organs, and its rotating exhibits. *(Lingnerpl. 1; enter from Blüherstr. www.dhmd.de. Open Su and Sa 10am-6pm, Tu-F 9am-5pm. €2.50, students €1.50. Special exhibits €4, students €2.)*

STADTMUSEUM. This museum tells the story of the city since its birth in the 13th century; early history pales before 20th-century memorabilia, including a 1902 replica firefighter with a helmet-sprinkler and a *Volksgasmask* (People's Gas Mask). *(Wilsdruffer Str. 2, near Pirnaischer Pl. Open M-Th and Sa-Su 10am-6pm. €2, students €1.)*

ENTERTAINMENT

For centuries, Dresden has been a focal point of theater, opera, and music. Although most theaters break from mid-July to early September, open-air festivals bridge the gap; movies screen during **Filmnächte am Elbufer** in July and August at 9pm for around €6. (Office at Alaunstr. 62. ☎89 93 20.) Like other area palaces, the **Zwinger** has classical concerts on summer evenings. (Shows start at 6:30pm.)

Sächsische Staatsoper (Semper-Oper), Theaterpl. 2 (☎491 17 05). Opera's finest. Getting a ticket takes work; call ahead. Tickets €3-74.50. Box office at Schinkelwache open M-F 10am-6pm, Sa 10am-1pm, and 1hr. before performances.

Kulturpalast, Am Altmarkt (☎486 66 66). This civic center is home to the **Dresdner Philharmonie** (☎486 63 06) and hosts a wide variety of performances. Tickets at Schloßstr. 2. Main entrance open M-F 10am-7pm, Sa 10am-2pm.

Staatsoperette Dresden, Pirnaer Landstr. 131 (☎207 990). Musical theater and operetta from Lerner and Loewe to Sondheim. Tickets €4-19. Discounted Tu-Th. Ticket office open M 11am-4pm, Tu-Th 10am-7pm, F 11am-7pm, Sa 4-7pm, Su 1hr. before curtain.

projekttheater dresden, Louisenstr. 47 (☎8 10 76 10; www.projekttheater.de.). Cutting-edge, international experimental theater in the heart of the *Neustadt*. Tickets €11, students €7. Box office open 8pm, shows at 9pm.

NIGHTLIFE

It seems like the entire Neustadt spends the day anticipating 10pm. Ten years ago, the area north of Albertpl. was a maze of gray streets lined with crumbling buildings. Now a spontaneous, alternative community has sprung up in the 50 bars crammed onto Königsbrücker Str., Bischofsweg, Kamenzerstr., and Albertpl. *Kneipen Surfer* (free at Neustadt hostels) provides a description of every bar.

DownTown, Katharinenstr. 11. Constantly packed. The music is loud, seating is rare, and the crowd is enthusiastic. The evening here begins upstairs at the bar, billiard hall, and tattoo parlor. Expect pop, Latin, and electronic music. Cover €3.50, students €2.50. Open Tu, Th-Sa 10pm-5am.

Brauhaus am Waldschlösschen, am Brauhaus 8b. Tram 11 to *Waldschlösschen* or walk 25min. up Baunitzerstr. On a hill overlooking the Elbe and the Dresden skyline, this brewery proves Bavaria doesn't have a monopoly on great beer gardens. Beer by the liter (€4.60) and classic German entrees (€6-9).

Scheune, Alaunstr. 36. From Albertpl., walk up Königsbrücker Str. and turn right onto Katharinenstr.; take a left onto Alaunstr. The granddaddy of the *Neustadt* bar scene. Club opens at 8pm. Cover varies. Indian cafe open M-F 5pm-2am, Sa-Su 10am-2pm.

Deja Vu, Rothenburgerstr. 37. From Albertpl., take Bautznerstr. and then a left onto Rothenburgerstr. Tired of beer? Head to this "milkbar" for a milkshake (alcoholic or non) and creamy decor. Open M-F 1pm-1am, Sa-Su 1pm-3am.

Die 100, Alaunstr. 100. With over 250 wines, this quiet *Weinkeller* caters to the *conaisseur* without emptying his *portemonnaie*. Open daily 5pm-3am.

Studentenklub Bärenzwinger, Brühlischer Garten 1, under the garden between the Elbe and the Albertinum. Dresden's former fortress attracts crowds with cheap drinks and student DJs. Beer €1.50. 18+. Cover €3, students €2. Concerts €7-10. Open Tu and F-Sa from 9pm for live shows and dancing.

BOY's, Alaunstr. 30, just beyond the Kunsthof Passage. A half-naked devil mannequin guards one of Dresden's popular gay bars. Drinks €2.70-6. Open daily 8pm-3am.

🔁 DAYTRIP FROM DRESDEN

MEIßEN. In 1710, the Saxon elector contracted severe *Porzellankrankheit* (the porcelain "bug," which still afflicts tourists today) and turned the city's defunct castle into Europe's first porcelain factory. The building was once more tightly guarded than KGB headquarters to prevent competitors from learning its techniques; today, anyone can tour the **Staatliche Porzellan-Manufaktur,** Talstr. 9. Peruse finished products in the **Schauhalle** (€4.50, students €4), but the real fun is the **Schauwerkstatt** (show workshop), in which porcelain artists paint perfectly detailed flowers before your incredulous eyes. (Open May-Oct. daily 9am-6pm; Nov.-Apr. 9am-5pm. €3. English headsets available.) Narrow, romantic alleyways lead up to the **Albrechtsburg** castle and cathedral. (Open Mar.-Oct. daily 9am-6pm; Nov.-Feb. 10am-5pm. €3.50, students €2.50.) From the train station, walk straight onto Bahnhofstr. and follow it over the Elbbrücke. Cross the bridge, continue straight to the Markt, and turn right onto Burgstr. Next door looms the **Meißener Dom,** a Gothic cathedral featuring four 13th-century statues by the Naumburg Master, a triptych by Cranach the Elder, and the metal grave coverings of the Wettins. (Open Apr.-Oct. daily 9am-6pm; Nov.-Mar. 10am-4pm. €2, students €1.50.)

Reach Meißen from Dresden by train (40min. €4.50). The **tourist office,** Markt 3, across from Frauenkirche, finds private rooms for a €3 fee. (☎(03521) 419 40. Open Apr.-Oct. M-F 10am-6pm, Sa-Su 10am-4pm; Nov.-Mar. M-F 10am-5pm, Sa 10am-3pm.) **Postal Code:** 01662.

LEIPZIG
☎0341

Leipzig (pop. 493,000) is one of the few German university cities large enough to have a life outside the academy, but small enough to feel the influence of its students. Every corner is packed with cafes, cabarets, street-musicians, and second-hand stores. Once home to Bach and Mendelssohn, Wagner and Nietzsche, Goethe and Leibniz, central Leipzig is compact and navigable.

🖿🔁 TRANSPORTATION AND PRACTICAL INFORMATION. Leipzig lies on the Berlin-Munich line. **Trains** run to: Berlin (2-3hr., 3 per hr., €26); Dresden (1½hr., 3 per hr., €17); Frankfurt (5hr., 2 per hr., €62); and Munich (7hr., 3 per hr., €68). To find the **tourist office,** Richard-Wagner-Str. 1, cross Willy-Brandt-Pl. in front of the station and turn left at Richard-Wagner-Str. (☎710 42 60. Open M-F 9am-7pm, Sa 9am-4pm, Su 9am-2pm.) **Postal Code:** 04109.

◰▣ ACCOMMODATIONS AND FOOD. To reach **Hostel Sleepy Lion ❷**, Käthe-Kollwitz-Str. 3, take streetcar #1 (dir.: Lausen) to *Gottschedstr*. Run by young locals, it draws an international crowd. All rooms have showers and bath. (☎993 94 80. Sheets €2. **Internet** €2 per hr. Reception 24hr. Dorms €14; singles €24; doubles €36; quads €60.) **Kosmos Hotel ❸**, Gottschedstr. 1, is a 12min. walk from the train station. Cross the street and turn right onto Richard-Wagner-Str.; when it ends, cut left through the parking lot and small park. At the end of the park, keep left on Dittrichring and it'll be ahead on the right. This funky hotel is part of a larger complex that includes a nightclub and restaurant. (☎233 44 20. Breakfast €5. Reception daily 8am-11pm. Singles from €30; doubles from €50.)

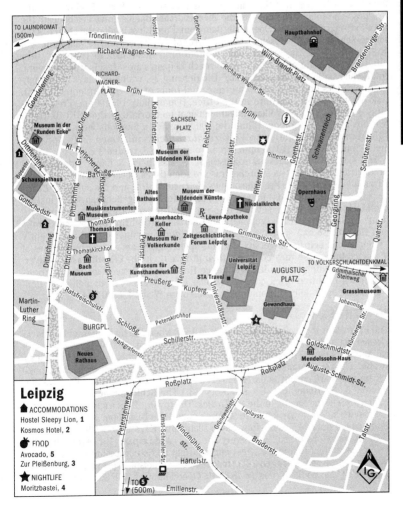

Leipzig

⚑ ACCOMMODATIONS
Hostel Sleepy Lion, **1**
Kosmos Hotel, **2**

🍴 FOOD
Avocado, **5**
Zur Pleißenburg, **3**

★ NIGHTLIFE
Moritzbastei, **4**

The *Innenstadt*, especially **Grimmaischestraße**, is full of *Imbiß* stands, bistros, and bakeries. Outside the city center, **Karl-Liebknecht-Straße** (streetcar #10 or 11 to *Kochstr.*) is packed with cheap *Döner* stands and cafes that double as bars. Vegetarian ◧**Avocado** ❸, Karl-Liebknecht-Str. 79, does big things with goat cheese, forest berries, and its namesake fruit. (Open M-Th and Su 11:30am-1am, F 11:30am-2am, Sa 4pm-2am.) **Zur Pleißenburg** ❷, Schulstr. 2, down Burgstr. from the Thomaskirche, serves hearty fare. (Open daily 9am-5am.) There's a **market** on Richard-Wagner-Pl. at the end of the Brühl. (Open Tu and F 9am-5pm).

◨◨ **SIGHTS AND NIGHTLIFE.** The heart of Leipzig is the **Marktplatz**, a cobblestoned square guarded by the slanted 16th-century **Altes Rathaus**. Head down Grimmaischestr. to the **Nikolaikirche**, where massive weekly demonstrations led to the fall of the GDR. (Open M-Sa 10am-6pm, Su after services. Free.) Backtrack to the *Rathaus* and follow Thomasg. to the **Thomaskirche**; Bach's grave lies beneath the floor in front of the altar. (Open daily 9am-6pm. Free.) Just behind the church is the **Johann-Sebastian-Bach-Museum**, Thomaskirchof 16. (Open daily 10am-5pm. €3, students €2. Free English-language audio tours.) Head back to Thomasg., turn left, then turn right on Dittrichring to reach Leipzig's most fascinating museum, the ◧**Museum in der "Runden Ecke,"** Dittrichring 24, which displays stunningly blunt exhibits on the history, doctrine, and tools of the *Stasi* (secret police). Ask for an English brochure in the office. (Open daily 10am-6pm. Free.) Outside the city ring, the **Völkerschlachtdenkmal** memorializes the 1813 Battle of Nations against Napoleon. Climb the 500 steps for a fabulous view. (Streetcar #15 from the train station to *Völkerschlachtdenkmal*. Open daily Apr.-Oct. 10am-6pm; Nov.-Mar. 10am-5pm. Free. To ascend €3, students €2.)

The **Gewandhaus-Orchester**, Augustuspl. 8, has been a major international orchestra since 1843. Guest orchestras are sometimes free. (☎127 02 80. €12-40, 20% student discount.) Free magazines *Fritz* and *Blitz* and the superior *Kreuzer* (€1.50 at newsstands) fill you in on nightlife. **Barfußgäßchen**, a street just off the Markt, serves as the see-and-be-seen nightlife area for everyone from students to *Schicki-mickis* (yuppies). Just across Dittrichring on **Gottschedstraße** and **Bosestraße** is a similar scene with a slightly younger crowd and slightly louder music. Leipzig university students spent eight years excavating a series of medieval tunnels so they could get their groove on in the ◧**Moritzbastei**, Universitätsstr. 9, which has multi-level dance floors and relaxed bars in cavernous rooms with vaulted brick ceilings. (Cover €4, students €2.50; higher for concerts. Cafe open daily 2pm-midnight. Disco open W and F until late.)

WITTENBERG ☎03491

The Protestant Reformation began here in 1517 when Martin Luther nailed his *95 Theses* to the door of the Schloßkirche; Wittenberg (pop. 48,000) has been fanatical about its native heretic ever since. All the major sights lie around **Collegienstraße**. The ◧**Lutherhalle**, Collegienstr. 54, chronicles the Reformation through letters, texts, art, and artifacts. (☎420 30. Open Apr.-Oct. daily 9am-6pm; Nov.-Mar. Su and Tu-Sa 10am-5pm. €5, students €3.) The **Schloßkirche** allegedly holds Luther's body and a copy of the *95 Theses*. The tower offers a sumptuous view of the countryside. (Down Schloßstr. Church open M-Sa 10am-5pm, Su 11:30am-5pm. Free. Tower open M-F noon-4pm, Sa-Su 10am-4pm. €1, students €0.50.)

Trains leave for Berlin (1½hr., every 2hr., €17) and Leipzig (1hr., every 2hr., €9). From the station, follow the street curving right and continue until Collegienstr., the start of the **pedestrian zone**. The **tourist office**, Schloßpl. 2, provides maps, leads tours (€6), and books rooms. (☎49 86 10. Open Mar.-Oct. M-F 9am-6pm, Sa 10am-

3pm; Su 11am-4pm; Nov.-Feb. M-F 10am-4pm, Sa 10am-2pm, Su 11am-3pm.) The **Jugendherberge (HI) ❷** is in the castle across from the tourist office. (☎40 32 55. Breakfast included. Sheets €3.50. Reception 3-10pm. Dorms €15, under-27 €12.) Cheap eats lie along the Collegienstr.-Schloßstr. strip. **Postal Code:** 06886.

WEIMAR   ☎03643

While countless German towns leap at any excuse to build memorial *Goethe-häuser* (proclaiming that Goethe slept here, Goethe ate here, Goethe once asked for directions here), Weimar (pop. 63,500) features the real thing; the **Goethehaus** and **Goethe-Nationalmuseum,** Frauenplan 1, present the preserved private chambers where the poet entertained, wrote, and ultimately died after 50 years in Weimar. (Open April-Oct. Su and Tu-Sa 9am-6pm; Nov.-Mar. 10am-4pm. Expect a wait on summer weekends. €6, students €4.50.) The **Neuesmuseum,** Weimarpl. 4, has fascinating rotating exhibits of modern art, including an interactive "Terror orchestra," composed of knives, nails, and a hammer and sickle. (Open Apr.-Sept. Su and Tu-Sa 10am-6pm; Oct.-Mar. 10am-4:30pm. €3, students €2.) South of the town center in the **Historischer Friedhof,** Goethe and Schiller rest together in the basement of the **Fürstengruft.** Schiller, who died in an epidemic, was originally buried in a mass grave. Later, Goethe combed through the remains until he identified Schiller and had him interred in a tomb. Skeptics argued that Goethe was mistaken, but a team of Russian scientists verified his claim in the 1960s. (Cemetery open Mar.-Sept. daily 8am-9pm; Oct.-Feb. 8am-6pm. Tomb open April to mid-Oct. M and W-Su 9am-6pm; mid-Oct. to mid-Mar. M and W-Su 10am-4pm. €2, students €1.50.)

Trains run to: Dresden (3½hr., 2 per hr., €30); Frankfurt (3hr., every hr., €40); and Leipzig (1½hr., 2 per hr., €21). To reach **Goetheplatz** (the center of the *Altstadt*) from the station, follow Carl-August-Allee downhill to Karl-Liebknecht-Str., which leads into Goethepl. (15min.). The **tourist office,** Marktstr. 10, across from the *Rathaus,* hands out free maps, books rooms for a €2.55 fee, and offers German-language **walking tours.** The Weimarer Wald desk has lots of info on **outdoor activities** in the area. (☎240 00. Open Apr.-Oct. M-F 9:30am-6pm, Sa-Su 9:30am-3pm; Nov.-Mar. M-F 10am-6pm, Sa-Su 10am-2pm.) To get to the student-run ■**Hababusch Hostel ❶,** Geleitstr. 4, follow Geleitstr. from Goethepl.; after it takes a sharp right, you'll come to a statue on your left. The entrance to the Hababusch is behind the statue. Expect a laid-back atmosphere in the heart of Weimar. (☎85 07 37. Reception 24hr. Dorms €10; singles €15; doubles €24.) In a lovely *Jugendstil* mansion, **Jugendherberge Germania (HI) ❷,** Carl-August-Allee 13, has convenience written all over it. (☎85 04 90. Breakfast and sheets included. Internet access. Dorms €20, under-27 €17.) A combination cafe and gallery, **ACC ❸,** Burgpl. 1-2, is popular with students and vegetarians. (Open daily noon-1am.) The daily **produce market,** at Marktpl., has groceries. (Open M-Sa 7am-5pm.)

◪ DAYTRIP FROM WEIMAR: BUCHENWALD. During WWII, 250,000 Jews, Roma (Gypsies), homosexuals, communists, and political opponents were imprisoned at the Buchenwald labor camp. Although it was not intended as an extermination camp, over 50,000 died here due to harsh treatment by the SS. The **Nationale Mahnmal und Gedenkstätte Buchenwald** (National Monument and Memorial) has two principal sights. **KZ-Lager** refers to the remnants of the camps itself. The large storehouse documents both the history of Buchenwald (1937-1945) and of Nazism in general. The East German **Mahnmal** (monument) is on the other side of the hill; go up the main road that bisects the two large parking lots or take the footpath uphill from the old Buchenwald *Bahnhof* and then continue on the main road. The camp **archives** are open to anyone searching for records of family and friends between 1937 and

ON THE MENU

THE BEST *WURST*

So you're finally in Germany and itching to get your teeth into your first authentic German *Wurst*. With over 1500 varieties, you'll have plenty of choices. All have one thing in common: German law mandates that sausages can only be made of meat and spices—if it has cereal filling, it's not *Wurst*.

Bockwurst: This tasty sausage is common roasted or grilled at street stands, and is usually served dripping with ketchup and mustard in a soft *Brötchen*. Although *Bock* means billy-goat, this *Wurst* is made of finely ground veal with parsley and chives. Complement your Bockwurst with some Bock beer.

Thüringer Bratwurst: Similar to the Bockwurst both in content and presentation, the Bratwurst has a little pork too, plus ginger and nutmeg.

Frankfurter: Unlike the American variety (whose origin is believed to be the *Wienerwurst*), the German Frankfurter can only have this name if made in Frankfurt. It's made of lean pork ground into a paste and then cold smoked, which gives it that orange-yellow coloring.

Knockwurst: Shorter and plumper, this sausage is served with sauerkraut. It's made of lean pork and beef, and a healthy dose of garlic. Pucker up!

Weißwurst: Cream and eggs give this "white sausage" its pale coloring. Weißwurst goes with rye bread and mustard

1945. Schedule an appointment with the curator. (Archives ☎ (03643) 43 01 54; library (03643) 43 01 60. Outdoor camp area open daily until sundown.) Sadly, the suffering at Buchenwald did not end with liberation—Soviet authorities used the site as an internment camp, **Special Camp. No. 2,** where more than 28,000 Germans—mostly Nazi war criminals and opponents of the communist regime—were held until 1950; an exhibit detailing this period opened in 1997.

The best way to reach the camp is by **bus** #6 from Weimar's train station or Goethepl. Check the schedule carefully; some #6 buses go to *Ettersburg* rather than *Gedenkstätte Buchenwald*. (20min.; M-Sa every hr., Su every 2hr.) Buses back to Weimar stop at the *KZ-Lager* parking lot and at the road by the *Glockenturm* (bell tower). There is an **info center** near the bus stop at Buchenwald, which offers a walking tour (€3) and shows an excellent video with English subtitles every hour. (Open May-Sept. Su and Tu-Sa 9am-6pm; Oct.-Apr. 9am-4:30pm.)

EISENACH   ☎03691

Birthplace of Johann Sebastian Bach, Eisenach (pop. 44,000) is also home to one of Germany's most treasured national symbols, ◪**Wartburg castle.** In 1521, the castle protected Martin Luther (disguised as a bearded noble named Junker Jörg) after his excommunication. Much of the castle's interior is not authentically medieval, but the Wartburg is still enchanting and the view from its south tower is spectacular. (Open Mar.-Oct. daily 8:30am-5pm; Nov.-Feb. 9am-3:30pm. Required German tour €6, students and children €3.) According to local tradition, the actual location of Bach's birth in 1685 was the **Bachhaus,** Frauenplan 21. Every 40min., a guide gives a presentation on Bach's life in German and English, complete with musical interludes. (Open Apr.-Sept. M noon-5:45pm, Tu-Su 9am-5:45pm; Oct.-Mar. M 1-4:45pm, Tu-Su 9am-4:45pm. €2.50, students €2.) Bach was baptized at the 800-year-old **Georgenkirche,** just off the Markt, where members of his family were organists for 132 years. (Open M-Sa 10am-12:30pm and 2-5pm, Su after services.) Just up the street is **Lutherhaus,** Lutherpl. 8, Martin's home in his school days. (Open Apr.-Oct. daily 9am-5pm; Nov.-Mar. 10am-5pm. €2.50.)

Trains run frequently to Weimar (1hr., 2 per hr., €11). The **tourist office,** Markt 2, sells maps (€2), offers daily city tours (2pm, €3), and books rooms for free. From the train station, follow Bahnhofstr. through the tunnel and angle left until you turn right onto the pedestrian Karlstr. (☎ 194 33. Open M 10am-6pm, Tu-F 9am-6pm, Sa-Su 10am-2pm.) To reach the recently renovated **Jugendherberge Arthur Becker (HI) ❷,** Mariental 24, take Bahnhofstr. from the station to

Wartburger Allee, which runs into Mariental. (☎ 74 32 59. Breakfast included. Reception daily 8am-11pm. Dorms €18, under-27 €15.) For groceries, head to **Edeka supermarket** on Johannispl. (Open M-F 8am-6:30pm, Sa 8am-12:30pm.) Near the train station, **Café Moritz ❷,** Bahnhofstr. 7, serves Thüringian specialities (€3-9) and sinful ice cream delicacies. (Open May-Oct. M-F 8am-9pm, Sa-Su 10am-9pm; Nov.-Apr. M-F 8am-7pm, Sa-Su 10am-7pm.) **Postal Code:** 99817.

NORTHERN GERMANY

Once a favored vacation spot for East Germans, Mecklenburg-Vorpommern, the northeasternmost portion of Germany, has suffered economic depression in recent years. To the west, Schleswig-Holstein, which borders Denmark, maintains close ties with Scandinavia. Portly Hamburg is by turns rich and radical. To the south, Bremen is Germany's smallest state.

HANOVER (HANNOVER)   ☎ 0511

Despite its relatively small size, Hanover (pop. 516,000) rivals any European city with its art, culture, and landscape. Broad avenues, enormous pedestrian zones, and endless parks and gardens make the city an example of all that is good in urban planning. The gems of Hanover are the three bountiful ◙**Herren-hausen gardens.** The largest, the geometrically trimmed **Großer Garten,** holds the **Große Fontäne,** one of Europe's highest-shooting fountains. (Fountain spurts M-F 11am-noon and 3-5pm, Sa-Su 11am-noon and 2-5pm. Garden open Apr.-Oct. 9am-8pm; Nov.-Mar. 8am-dusk. €2.50.) On the outskirts of the *Altstadt* stands the spectacular **Neues Rathaus;** take the elevator up the tower for a thrilling view of the city. (Open May-Sept. M-F 8am-10pm, Sa-Su 10am-10pm. Elevator €2.) The nearby ◙**Sprengel Museum,** Kurt-Schwitters-Pl., hosts the best of 20th-century art—including Dalí, Picasso, and Magritte. (Open Su and W-Sa 10am-6pm, Tu 10am-8pm. Permanent collection €3.30, students €2; with special exhibits €6, students €3.50.) **Kestner-Museum,** Trammpl. 3, majors in decorative arts, with a focus on chairs. (Open Su, Tu and Th-Sa 11am-6pm, W 11am-8pm. €2.60, students €1.50. F free.)

Trains leave at least every hour for: Amsterdam (4½-5hr., €40); Berlin (2½hr., €40); Frankfurt (3hr., €80); Hamburg (1½hr., €25); and Munich (9hr., €130). To reach the **tourist office,** Ernst-August-Pl. 2, head out the main entrance of the train station; facing the large rear of the king's splendid steed, turn right. (☎ 16 84 97 00. Open M-F 9am-6pm, Sa 9am-2pm.) ◙**Jugendherberge Hannover (HI) ❷,** Ferdinand-Wilhelm-Fricke-Weg. 1, is far from the city center, but definitely worth the trek. Take U3 or 7 to *Fischerhof.* From the stop, backtrack 10m, turn right, cross the tracks, and walk on the path through the school's parking lot; follow the path as it curves, and cross the street. Go over the red footbridge and turn right. (☎ 131 76 74. Breakfast included. Reception daily 7:30am-1am. Dorms €19-30, under-27 €16-28.) To reach **CityHotel am Thielenplatz ❹,** Thielenpl. 2, take a left onto Joachimstr. from the station and go one block to Thielenpl. (☎ 32 76 91 93. Breakfast included. Check-out 11:30am. Singles €40, with shower €57; doubles with shower €75. Weekends cheaper.) **Jalda ❷,** Limmerstr. 97, serves Greek and Middle Eastern dishes for €4-8. (Open M-Th and Su 11:30am-midnight, F-Sa 11:30am-1am.) **Uwe's Hannenfaß Hanover ❷,** Knochenhauerstr. 36, in the center of the *Altstadt,* serves traditional German fare for €5-7 and great house brews for €3. (Open Su-Th 4pm-2am, F 4pm-4am, Sa noon-4am.) There's a **Spar supermarket** by the *Lister Meile* U-Bahn stop. (Open M-F 7am-7pm, Sa 8am-2pm.) **The Loft,** Georgstr. 50b, is packed with students on the weekends. (Disco night F and ladies night Sa have €3.50 covers. Open W-Sa from 8pm.) **Postal Code:** 30159.

HAMBURG ☎ 040

The largest port city in Germany, Hamburg (pop. 1,700,000) radiates an inimitable recklessness. Hamburg gained the status of Free Imperial City in 1618 and proudly retains its autonomy as one of Germany's 16 *Länder* and one of only three German city-states. Restoration and riots determined the post-WWII landscape, but today Hamburg has become a haven for contemporary artists and intellectuals as well as party-goers who live it up in Germany's self-declared "capital of lust."

▐ TRANSPORTATION

Flights: Fuhlsbüttel Airport (HAM; ☎ 507 50) is a hub for **Lufthansa** (☎ 0180 380 3803) and **Air France** (☎ 0180 583 0830). Jasper **buses** (☎ 22 71 06 61) run to the airport from the Kirchenallee exit of the *Hauptbahnhof* (25min., every 20min. 5am-11pm, €5). Or take U1 or S1 to *Ohlsdorf*, and then an **express bus** to the airport (every 10min. 4:30am-11pm, then every 30min. 11pm-1am; €2).

Trains: The *Hauptbahnhof* has hourly connections to: **Berlin** (2½hr., €37); **Copenhagen** (4½hr., €67); **Frankfurt** (5hr., €57); **Hanover** (2¼hr., €25); **Munich** (6hr., €96); and runs frequently to **Amsterdam** (5½, €65). Two other stations, **Dammtor** (near the university) and **Altona** (to the west) service the city; frequent trains and the S-Bahn connect the 3 stations. 24hr. **lockers** available for €1-2 per day.

Buses: The **ZOB** is on Steintorpl. across from the *Hauptbahnhof*, between McDonald's and the Museum für Kunst und Gewerbe. To: **Berlin** (3¼hr., 8 per day, €23); **Copenhagen** (5½hr., 2 per day, €42); **Paris** (12½hr., 1 per day, €61). Open M-F 9am-8pm, Sa 9:30am-1:30pm and 4-8pm, Su 4-8pm.

Public Transportation: HVV operates an efficient U-Bahn, S-Bahn, and bus network. Most single tickets within the downtown cost €1, but prices vary depending on where you go and what transport you take. 1-day ticket €5, 3-day ticket €13. Tickets can be bought at *Automaten*, but consider buying a **Hamburg Card** instead (see below).

Bike Rental: **Fahrradladen St. Georg**, Schmilinskystr. 6, is off Lange Reihe towards the Außenalster. (☎ 24 39 08.) €8 per day, €40 per week. Open M-F 10am-7pm, Sa 10am-1pm.) **Campusrad**, von-Melle-Park 8, is run by students but rents to all at the best price in Hamburg (☎ 41 33 95 59. €2 per day or weekend. Open M-F 9am-5pm.)

■✱▐ ORIENTATION AND PRACTICAL INFORMATION

Hamburg's city center sits between the Elbe River and the two city lakes, **Außenalster** and **Binnenalster**. Most major sights lie between the **St. Pauli Landungsbrücken** port area in the west and the *Hauptbahnhof* in the east. **Mönckebergstraße**, Hamburg's most famous shopping street, runs all the way to Rathausmarkt. North of downtown, the **university** dominates the **Dammtor** area and sustains a vibrant community of students and intellectuals. To the west of the university, the **Schanzenviertel** is a politically active community home to artists, squatters, and a sizeable Turkish population. At the south end of town, an entirely different atmosphere reigns in **St. Pauli**, where the raucous **Fischmarkt** (fish market) is surpassed only by the wilder **Reeperbahn**, home to Hamburg's infamous sex trade and its best discos.

Tourist Offices: The **Hauptbahnhof office**, in the Wandelhalle near the Kirchenallee exit (☎ 30 05 12 01), books rooms for a €4 fee. Open daily 7am-11pm. The **St. Pauli Landungsbrücken office**, between piers 4 and 5 (☎ 300 512 03), is less crowded. Both offices supply free English maps and sell the **Hamburg Card,** which provides unlimited access to public transportation, reduced admission to most museums, and discounts on bus and boat tours. (1-day card €7, 3-day card €15.)

Consulates: Canada, Ballindamm 35 (☎460 02 70). Open M-F 9:30am-12:30pm. **Ireland,** Feldbrunnenstr. 43 (☎441 81 14); U1 to *Hallerstr.* Open M-F 9am-1pm. **New Zealand,** Domstr. 19, 3rd fl. of Zürich-haus (☎442 55 50). Open M-Th 9am-5:30pm, F 9am-4:30pm. **UK,** Harvestehuder Weg 8a (☎448 03 20); U1 to *Hallerstr.* Open M-Th 9am-4pm, F 9am-3pm. **US,** Alsterufer 26-8 (☎41 17 13 50). Open M-F 9am-noon.

Currency Exchange: ReiseBank, on the 2nd fl. of the *Hauptbahnhof* near the Kirchenallee exit, offers Western Union, cashes traveler's checks, and exchanges money for a 4.5% fee. Open daily 7:30am-10pm.

American Express: Rathausmarkt 10, 20095 Hamburg (☎30 39 38 11). Take the S- or U-Bahn to *Jungfernstieg.* Letters held for members up to 5 weeks; all banking services available. Open M-F 9:30am-6pm, Sa 10am-2pm.

Gay and Lesbian Resources: The center of the gay community is in St. Georg. Pick up the free *hinnerk* magazine and *"Friends: The Gay Map"* from **Cafe Gnosa** (p. 464). **Hein und Fiete,** Pulverteich 21 (☎24 03 33). Walk down Steindammstr. away from the *Hauptbahnhof* and turn right on Pulverteich; it's in the rainbow-striped building. Open M-F 4-9pm, Sa 4-7pm.

Laundromat: Schnell und Sauber, Grindelallee 158, in the university district. Take S21 or 31 to *Dammtor.* Wash €3.50. Dry €1 per 15min. Open daily 7am-10:30pm.

Emergency: Police: ☎110. **Fire** and **Ambulance:** ☎112.

Pharmacy: The staff at the **Senator-Apotheke,** Hachmannpl. 14 (☎32 75 27), speaks English. Exit the *Hauptbahnhof* on Kirchenallee. Open M-F 7am-8pm, Sa 8am-6pm.

Internet Access: Teletime, Schulterblatt 39. €0.50 per 10min. Open M-Sa 10am-midnight. **Spiele-Netzwerk,** Kleine Schäferkamp. U3: *Schlump.* €4 per hr. Open daily 10am-2am. **Webdome,** Offenser Hauptstr. 17. S-Bahn to *Altona.* €2 per hr.

Post Office: At the Kirchenallee exit of the *Hauptbahnhof,* 20097 Hamburg. Open M-F 8am-8pm, Sa 9am-6pm. Address mail to be held: Firstname SURNAME, *Postlagernde Briefe,* Post Hamburg-Hauptbahnhof, **20099** Hamburg, GERMANY.

■ ACCOMMODATIONS

The dynamic **Sternschanze** area has the city's two best backpacker hostels. More expensive hotels line the **Binnenalster** and eastern **Außenalster.** Small, relatively cheap pensions line **Steindamm** and the area around the *Hauptbahnhof,* although the prostitutes and wannabe Mafiosi leave something to be desired. **Lange Reihe** has equivalent options in a cleaner neighborhood. For longer stays, try **Mitwohnzentrale Homecompany,** Schulterblatt 112. (☎194 45; www.homecompany.de).

▨ **Schanzenstern Übernachtungs- und Gasthaus,** Bartelsstr. 12 (☎439 84 41). S21 or U3 to *Sternschanze,* turn left onto Schanzenstr., right on Susannenstr., and left onto Bartelsstr. In an electrifying neighborhood of students, working-class Turks, and left-wing dissenters, the hostel maintains order and a tasteful decor. Dorms €17; singles €33; doubles €55; triples €60; quads €73; quints €91. ❷

▨ **Instant Sleep,** Max-Brauer-Allee 277 (☎43 18 23 10). S21 or U3 to *Sternschanze.* Everyone is part of a big happy family in this backpacker hostel; rooms are often left open while guests lounge together, read, or cook dinner in the communal kitchen. Bike rental €4 per 6hr. Sheets €2. Internet €1 for 15min. Reception daily 9am-2pm. Dorms €15; singles €26; doubles €42; triples €57. ❷

Hamburg

🏠 ACCOMMODATIONS

Hotel Annenhof, **12**
Hotel-Pension Schwanenwik, **1**
Instant Sleep, **4**
Jugendherberge auf dem
 Stintfang (HI), **23**
Pension Helga Schmidt, **13**
Schanzenstern Altona, **15**
Schanzenstern Übernachtungs-
 und Gasthaus, **7**

Ⓢ S-Bahn (surface rail)
Ⓤ U-Bahn (subway)

0   300 yards
0   300 meters

Ⓤ HOHELUFTBRÜCKE

HARVESTEHUDE

Binderstr.
Hallerstr.

Grindelberg
Hochallee

Hoha Weide
Schulterblatt

Schäferkampsallee
CHRISTUS-
KIRCHE

G.-Falke-Str.
Beim Schlump
Bundesstr.

Laundromat

Grindelhof
Grindelallee

Schlüterstr.

Ⓤ SCHLUMP
Campus Rad

Spiele-Netzwerk
Kl. Schäferkamp
Schröderstiftstr.

Universität
Heine-Heinrich
Buch

Altonaer Str.

Sternschanzenpark
Rentzelstr.
Grindelallee

STERNSCHANZE Ⓤ Sternschanze
Ⓢ

Verbindungs Bundesbahn
Tiergartenstr.
Moorweidenstr.
E.-Siemers-

Lagerstr.
TV
Turm

Karolinenstr.
St. Petersburger Str.

Wasserlichtkonzerte
Planten un
Blomen

SCHANZENVIERTEL
Max-Brauer-Allee

Susannen-
str.
Bartelsstr.
Schanzenstr.
Sternstr.

Grabenstr.

Botanischer
Garten

Juliusstr.
Buchladen

Marseillenstr.
Jungiusstr.
Musik Pavilion
Gorch-

Stresemannstr.

MESSEHALLEN
Ⓤ

Bei den Kirchhöfen

Glacis
Kleine Wallanlagen
Gorch-Fock-Wall

Bernstorffstr.
Leichenstr.

Marktstr.
Glashüttenstr.

Holsten-
glacis

Dammtorwall
Caffamacherreihe

Drehbahn

Thadenstr.

Laundromat
Neuer Kamp

Haidenstr.

Musikhalle
Ⓤ
Valentins-
kamp

Otzenstr.

Super Walmart

Ⓤ FELDSTR. Feldstr.

SIEVEKING-
PL.

JOHANS-
BRAHMS-PL.

Bäckerbreiten
Speckstr.
Kaiser-Wilhelm-Str.
Fuhlentwiete

Gilbertstr.
Willistrasse
Budapester Str.

PAULINEN
PL.

Glacischaussee
Große Wallanlagen
Holstenwall

Pianuspool
Poolstr.
Neustädtstr.
Kurzestr.

NEUSTADT
Kohlhöfen
Rademachergang

Kornträger
Stadthausbrücke

ST. PAULI
Holstenstr.

TO ALTONA
(1.2km),
&

Paul-Roosen-Str.
Detlev-Bremser-Str.
Budapester Str.

ENCKE-
PL.
Peterstr.
Neanderstr.

Markus-
str.
Thielbek
GROß
NEUMARKT

Wexstr.
Alter Steinweg

Düsternstr.

Große Freiheit
Hamburger Berg
Simon-von-Utrecht-Str.

ST. PAULI Ⓤ
MILLERNTOR-
PL.

Museum für
Hamburgische Geschichte
Neuer Steinweg

Ludwig-Erhard-Str.

Nobistor
Königstr.

REEPERBAHN Ⓢ Reeperbahn

ALBERS
PL.

SpielbudenPl.

Reeperbahn
Elbpark

Gerstäckerstr.

Michaeliskirche
Ost-West-Str.

STADTHAUS-
BRÜCKE Ⓢ

Pepermölenbek

HEIN-
KÖLLISCH-
PL.

Herbertstr.
Davidstr.
Zirkusweg

Erotic
Art
Museum

Rothespodstr.
Böhmkenstr.
Kravenkamp

Neustadtsr.

Teilfeld
Martin-Luther-Str.

Herrengraben
Admiralität str.

Rödings Markt
Stein Hof

Harry's Hamburger
Hafen Basar
Fischmarkt

Erichstr.
Bernhard-Nocht-Str.

Seewartenstr.
Stintfang
Vanusberg

SCHAAR-
MARKT
Schaar-
steinweg

St.-Pauli-Hafenstr.

Fischauctionhalle

St.-Pauli-Fischmarkt
Landungsbrücken

LANDUNGS-
BRÜCKEN Ⓢ

Karpfangerstr.
Neustadt
Neuerweg

Stubbenhuk
Wexkenstr.

Stein Hof

Norderelbe

Old
Elbe
Tunnel

ℹ️

⚓

Windjammer
Rickmer
Rickmers

Johannisbollwerk
Vorsetzen
Baumwall

Hamburg by Air/City Sporthafen

Ⓤ
BAUMWALL

Binnenhafen

GERMANY

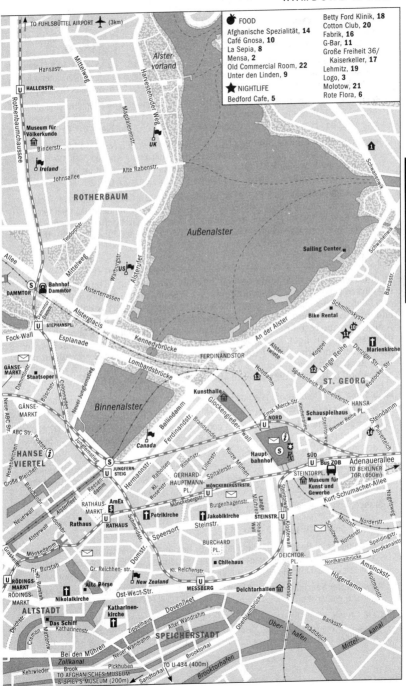

GERMANY

★ **FOOD**
Afghanische Spezialität, **14**
Café Gnosa, **10**
La Sepia, **8**
Mensa, **2**
Old Commercial Room, **22**
Unter den Linden, **9**

★ **NIGHTLIFE**
Bedford Cafe, **5**

Betty Ford Klinik, **18**
Cotton Club, **20**
Fabrik, **16**
G-Bar, **11**
Große Freiheit 36/
  Kaiserkeller, **17**
Lehmitz, **19**
Logo, **3**
Molotow, **21**
Rote Flora, **6**

Pension Helga Schmidt, Holzdamm 14 (☎28 21 19). Welcoming pension only 2 blocks from the *Hauptbahnhof.* Some two room suites; all rooms with TV and phone. Cheaper rooms share a hall shower. Singles €35-37; doubles €55-65; triples €82. ❸

Hotel-Pension Schwanenwik, Schwanenwik 29 (☎220 09 18). U2 to *Munsberg.* Leave the station on Mundsburger Damm, go right on Uhlenhorster and left on Schwanenwik. Beautiful rooms near the lake. Breakfast included. Singles €44-75; doubles €62-90. ❹

Hotel Annenhof, Lange Reihe 23 (☎24 34 26). From the train station's Kirchenallee exit, turn left. Pass the Schauspielhaus, then turn left on Lange Reihe. Simple rooms and soft beds in the gay district. Breakfast €4. Singles €27; doubles €43. ❸

Jugendherberge auf dem Stintfang (HI), Alfred-Wegener-Weg 5 (☎31 34 88). Take U3 or S1, 2, or 3, to *Landungsbrücke,* then head up the hill on the wooded path. Clean and well-furnished rooms look out on the woods or the harbor. Breakfast included. Reception 12:30pm-12:30am. Curfew 2am. Dorms €21-24, under-27 €19-22. ❸

Schanzenstern Altona, (☎39 91 91 91) Kleiner Rainstr. 24. Take the Offenser Hauptstr. exit from the Altona station. After two blocks, turn right on Bahrneldstr., then left on Kleine Rainstr. Just as good as its counterpart in the Schanzenviertel, but further from the center. Dorms €18; singles €40; doubles €55-65; triples €70; quads €80. ❷

🍴 FOOD

Seafood abounds in Hamburg, as you'd expect in a port city. The most interesting part of town from a culinary standpoint is **Sternschanze,** where Turkish fruit and falafel stands and avant-garde cafes entice hungry passersby with good food and great atmosphere. **Schulterblatt, Susannenstraße,** and **Schanzenstraße** have funky cafes and restaurants, while slightly cheaper establishments abound in the **university** area, especially along **Rentzelstraße, Grindelhof,** and **Grindelallee.** In **Altona,** the pedestrian zone leading up to the train station is packed with ethnic food stands and produce shops. The Portuguese community lends its own take on seafood in the area between the Michaelskirche and the river.

🖾 La Sepia, Schulterblatt 36, is a fine Portuguese restaurant with the city's best and most reasonably priced seafood. Lunch €4-6. Dinner €8-14. Open daily 11am-3am. ❸

Unter den Linden, Juliusstr 16. Read complimentary papers over Milchkaffe (€3.20), breakfast (€4-7), or enormous salads (€4-6) in a relaxed atmosphere beneath the linden trees. M-F 11am-11pm, Sa-Su 10am-11pm. ❷

Oma's Apotheke, Schanzenstr. 87. Retro ambiance and portions large enough to make grandma proud. German, Italian and American cuisine. *Schnitzel* platter €7.50. Hamburger with a pound of fries €6.60. Open M-Th and Su 9am-1am, F-Sa 9am-2am. ❷

Mensa, Von-Melle-Park 7. S21 to *Dammtor.* Massive plates of cafeteria food and a bulletin board of university events. Meals €1.50-3 with student ID; non-students add €0.70. Open M-Th 10am-5:30pm, F 10am-4:30pm. ❶

Old Commercial Room, Englische Planke 10. Hamburg-style bacon pancakes with wild cranberries (€11) or lightly salted pork and vegetables (€14.50) right across from St. Michaelskirche. Open daily 10am-midnight. ❹

Afghanische Spezialität, on the corner of Steindamm and Polverteich. Simple Afghan grill and goods shop serves kebabs and rice dishes. Open daily 9am-9pm. ❷

Café Gnosa, Lange Reihe 93. A social focal point for the gay community of St. Georg, Gnosa serves up drinks and dainties to 20-somethings of mixed orientation. Drinks €2-5. Pick up free gay magazine *hinnerk.* Open Su-Th 10am-1am, F-Sa 10am-2am. ❷

👁 SIGHTS

ALTSTADT

GROßE MICHAELSKIRCHE. The gargantuan 18th-century Michaelskirche is the symbol of Hamburg, and with good reason. The turning times that raised the city razed the church as well: Lightning, accidents, and Allied bombs destroyed the church again and again. Restored in 1996, its interior and scalloped walls are reminiscent of a concert hall. The tower, accessible by foot or elevator, is the only one of the city's six spires that may be climbed. On weekends, it is used to project a multimedia presentation about Hamburg's millennial existence onto a 5m-high screen. *(Screenings Th, Sa and Su every hr. 12:30-3:30pm. Organ music Apr.-Aug. daily at noon and 5pm. Church open June-Oct. daily 11am-4:30pm, Nov.-May M-F 11am-4:30pm. Tower €3.)*

RATHAUS. The seat of both city and state government, full of intricate mahogany carvings and two-ton chandeliers, is unquestionably the most richly-ornamented building in Hamburg. The plaza in front hosts political demonstrations and medieval fairs. *(Tours in English every hr. M-Th 10:15am-3:15pm, F-Su 10:15am-1:15pm. €1.)*

NIKOLAIKIRCHE. Devastated by an Allied bomb in 1943, the spire of this hallowed (and hollowed) neo-Gothic ruin pierces the heavens with its dark reminder of war. *(History exhibition open M-F 11am-5pm, Sa-Su 11am-6pm. €2.)* The buildings along nearby **Trostbrücke** sport huge copper models of clipper ships on their spires—a testament to Hamburg's sea-trade wealth. *(Just south of the Rathaus, off Ost-West-Str.)*

MÖNKEBERGSTRAßE. Hamburg's shopping zone stretches from the *Rathaus* to the *Hauptbahnhof* and is punctuated by two spires. The first belongs to **St. Petrikirche,** the oldest church in Hamburg. *(Open M-Tu and Th-F 10am-6:30pm, W 10am-7pm, Sa 10am-5pm, Su 9am-9pm. Free concerts W 5:15pm.)* The second, **St. Jakobikirche,** is known for its 14th-century Arp-Schnittger organ. *(Open M-Sa 10am-5pm.)*

BEYOND THE ALTSTADT

PLANTEN UN BLOMEN. To the west of the Alster, this huge expanse of manicured flower gardens and trees includes the largest Japanese Garden in Europe. *(Open 7am-11pm. Free.)* Daily 3pm performances ranging from Irish step-dancing to Hamburg's police orchestra shake the outdoor **Musikpavillon** from May to September. There are also nightly **Wasserlichtkonzerte,** with a choreographed play of fountains and underwater lights. *(May-Aug. daily 10pm; Sept. 9pm.)* North of the city center, the two **Alster lakes,** bordered by tree-lined paths, provide further refuge from the crowds.

ST. PAULI LANDUNGSBRÜCKEN. Hamburg's harbor lights up at night with ships from all over the world. Take the elevator from the building behind Pier 6 to the old **Elbtunnel,** which was built from 1907 to 1911 and runs 1200m under the Elbe—it's still used by commuters. At the **Fischmarkt,** charismatic vendors haul in and hawk huge amounts of fish, produce, and other goods. Don't shy away if you dislike fish—about 90% of the merchandise is something else. *(U- or S-Bahn to Landungsbrücken or S-Bahn to Königstr. Open April-Oct. Su 5-10am, Nov.-Mar. Su 7-10am.)*

BEYOND THE CENTER

Though outside the city center, two very different testaments to the atrocities of the Nazi regime are accessible by public transportation.

KZ NEUENGAMME. An idyllic agricultural village east of Hamburg provided the backdrop for the Neuengamme concentration camp, where Nazis killed 55,000 prisoners through slave labor. In 1989, the Hamburg senate built a memorial on the site. Banners inscribed with the names and death-dates of the victims hang in the **Haus des Gedenkens,** and **Walther-Werke** has the recorded testimony of survivors. *(Jean-Doldier-Weg 39. S21 to Bergedorf, then bus #227 to Jean-Doldier-Weg. Open May-Oct. Su and Sa 10am-6pm, Tu-F 10am-5pm; Oct.-Mar. Su and Tu-Sa 10am-5pm.)*

GEDENKSTÄTTE BULLENHUSER DAMM UND ROSENGARTEN. Surrounded by warehouses, this schoolhouse is a memorial to 20 Jewish children brought here from Auschwitz for "testing" and murdered by the S.S. only hours before Allied troops arrived. Visitors are invited to plant a rose for the children in the flower garden behind the school, where plaques with the children's photographs line the fence. *(Bullenhuser Damm 92. S21 to Rothenburgsort. Follow the signs to Bullenhuser Damm along Ausschlaeger Bildeich and across a bridge. Open Su 10am-5pm and Th 2-8pm. Free.)*

🏛 MUSEUMS

The **Hamburg Card** provides access to most of these museums, with the exception of the Deichtorhallen, the Hafen Basar, and the Erotic Art Museum. The free newspaper *Museumswelt Hamburg* lists museum exhibitions and events and can be picked up at the tourist offices. Most museums are closed on Mondays.

▧ Hamburger Kunsthalle, Glockengießerwall 1. This sprawling first-rate art museum requires many hours to appreciate in full. The lower level presents the Old Masters and extensive temporary displays of private collections. In the connected four-level **Galerie der Gegenwart,** contemporary art takes a stand, and a loud one at that—check out the pneumatic dancing legs on the top floor. Open Su, Tu-W and F-Sa 10am-6pm, Th 10am-9pm. €7.50, students €5.

Museum für Kunst und Gewerbe, Steintorpl. 1. Handicrafts, china, and furnishings from all corners of the earth fill the applied arts museum. A huge exhibit chronicles the evolution of the modern keyboard with dozens of the world's oldest harpsichords and box pianos. Open Su and Tu-Sa 10am-6pm, Th 10am-8pm. €8.20, students and seniors €4.

Deichtorhallen Hamburg, Deichtorstr. 1-2. Follow signs from the subway station; look for the entwined iron circles. Hamburg's contemporary art scene inhabits these two former fruit warehouses. New exhibits each season showcase up-and-coming artists. Open Su and Tu-Sa 11am-6pm. Each building €6.50, students €4.50.

Erotic Art Museum, Nobistor 10a. S1 or 3 to *Reeperbahn.* Everything from the Kama Sutra to Victorian pornography, from loose sketches to gigantic Russian dolls in varying degrees of undress. Drawings by Picasso add fame and propriety to an otherwise shocking display. Open Su-Th 10am-midnight, F-Sa 10am-2am. €8. Under-16 not admitted.

Hamburger Museum für Völkerkunde, Rothenbaumchaussee 64. U1 to *Hallerstr.* An anthropologist's paradise; Mongolian and Maori huts, African masks, and supermarket placards speak volumes about the cultures of the world. Open Su and Tu-Sa 10am-6pm, Th 10am-9pm. €5, students €2; F €2.50/1.

Harry's Hamburger Hafen Basar, on Balduinstr. After sailing the world and collecting its wares, Harry dropped anchor and set up this cluttered, family-run museum-shop. Collectors will be interested to know that everything besides the shrunken heads and the stuffed leopard is for sale. Open Su and Tu-Sa noon-6pm. €2.50.)

▐♫▐ ▐♪▐ ENTERTAINMENT AND NIGHTLIFE

MUSIC AND FESTIVALS

The **Staatsoper,** Große Theaterstr. 36, houses one of the best opera companies in Germany; the associated **ballet company** is the acknowledged dance powerhouse of the nation. (☎35 68 68. U1 to *Stephanspl.* Open M-Sa 10am-6:30pm.) **Orchestras** abound—the Philharmonie, the Norddeutscher Rundfunk Symphony, and Hamburg Symphonia all perform at the **Musikhalle** on Johannes-Brahms-Pl. (U2 to *Gänsemarkt.*) Live music prospers in Hamburg, satisfying all tastes. Superb traditional **jazz** swings at the **Cotton Club.** On Sunday mornings, good and bad alike play at the **Fischmarkt.** The **West Port Jazz Festival,** Germany's largest, runs in mid-July; call the Koncertskasse (☎32 87 38 54) for info. The most anticipated festival is the **G-Move** (May 25, 2004), dubbed the "Love Parade of the North." Check www.g-move.com for details.

NIGHTLIFE

The Sternschanze and St. Pauli areas play host to Hamburg's unrepressed nightlife. The infamous **Reeperbahn** is the spinal cord of **St. Pauli;** it's lined with sex shops, strip joints, peep shows, and the best bars and clubs in town. Though the Reeperbahn is reasonably safe for both men and women, it is not recommended for women to venture into the adjacent streets. **Herbertstraße,** Hamburg's "official" prostitution strip, runs parallel to the Reeperbahn, and is open only to men over 18. The prostitutes flaunting their flesh on Herbertstr. are licensed professionals required to undergo health inspections, while the streetwalkers elsewhere are venereal roulette wheels.

Students trying to avoid the hypersexed Reeperbahn head north to the trendy streets of the **Schanzenviertel.** Unlike St. Pauli, this area is more cafe than club and more leftist than lustful. Much of Hamburg's **gay scene** is located in the classy **St. Georg** area of the city, near Berliner Tor and along Lange Reihe. In general, clubs open and close late, with some techno and trance clubs remaining open all night. *Szene,* available at newsstands (€2.50), lists events and parties.

▨ **Rote Flora,** Schulterblatt 71. Held together both figuratively and literally by the spray paint and posters that cover all its vertical surfaces, this looming mansion of graffiti serves as the nucleus of the Sternschanze scene. Beer €1.50. Weekend cover from €3-5. Cafe open M-F 6-10pm. Music starts at around 10pm. Crowds come at midnight.

▨ **Große Freiheit 36/Kaiserkeller,** Große Freiheit 36 (☎31 77 780). Everyone from Ziggy Marley to Matchbox Twenty stomps about on the big stage and dance floor upstairs. Live music or DJs usually 10:30pm-5am. Cover €5-6, more for live music. Often entry until 11pm is free—get your hand stamped and return later.

Betty Ford Klinik, Große Freiheit 6. Rehab never hurt so good. Chat on the couches lit by black chandeliers, or head to the atomic den of the most creative DJs and dancers in town. Cover €5-8. Th students free. Open Th 9pm-5am, F-Sa 11pm-6am.

Molotow, Spielbudenpl. 5. This basement lives at the fringes of Hamburg's club scene. Grunge decor, 70's music, great bands, and good dancers keep this small club rocking. Cover usually €3-4, live bands €5-10. Open Th-Sa 10pm-late.

Fabrik, Barnerstr. 36. From the Altona station make a right on Bahrenfeuerstr, and look for the crane. Venue for the likes of AC/DC, Willy Brandt, and Günter Grass. Music most days at 9pm. Tickets €10-20. Live DJ most Sa nights. Cover €6-7.

Bedford Cafe, on the corner of Schulterblatt and Suzannesstr. Easily the most crowded bar of the Schanzenviertel. Beer €2-3.40. Mixed drinks €5-6. Open daily 10am-late.

Logo, Grindelallee 5. Keeps the college crowd cultured with its eclectic lineup of folk, rock, and samba. Cover €5-15. Open daily from 8pm; music from 9pm.

Cotton Club, Alter Steinweg 10. U3 to *Rödingsmarkt.* New Orleans, dixie, swing, and big band jazz in a warmly lit setting. Cover €5 for Hamburg bands, around €10 for guest bands. Shows start at 8:30pm. Open M-Th 8pm-midnight and F-Sa 8pm-1am.

Lehmitz, Reeperbahn 22. Friendly students and hardcore punks gather around the clock for €2 beers. Live, thrashing music W and weekends. Open 24hr.

G-Bar, Lange Reihe 81. Men in skin-tight shirts serve beer (€2-3) and mixed drinks (€7) with a smile in this comfortable, neon-lit gay bar. Open daily noon-2am.

LÜBECK
☎ 0451

Lübeck (pop. 213,000) is easily Schleswig-Holstein's most beautiful city—you'd never guess that most of it was razed in WWII. In its heyday it was the capital of the Hanseatic league, controlling trade across Northern Europe. Although no longer a center of political and commercial influence, Lübeck still churns out delicious marzipan and red-blond Dückstein beer.

⌨️ TRANSPORTATION AND PRACTICAL INFORMATION. Trains run to Berlin (3½hr., 1 per hr., €35) and Hamburg (45min., 2 per hr., €9). Ryanair **flies** cheaply from London to Lübeck (LBC). A privately owned, expensive tourist office is in the train station. The **tourist office** in the *Altstadt,* at Breite Str. 62, is better. (☎ 122 54 20. Open M-F 9:30am-7pm, Sa-Su 10am-3pm.) **Postal Code:** 23552.

⌨️ ACCOMMODATIONS AND FOOD. To reach █**Rucksack Hotel ❶,** Kanalstr. 70, walk past the *Holstentor* from the station, turn left on An der Untertrave and right on Beckergrube; the hostel is on the corner of Kanalstr. (☎ 70 68 92. Breakfast €3. Sheets €3. Reception daily 10am-1pm and 4-9pm. Dorms €13; doubles with bath €40; quads €60, with bath €68.) The **Baltic Hotel ❹,** Hansestr. 11, is across the street from the station. (☎ 855 75. Breakfast included. Reception daily 7am-10pm. Singles €35-45; doubles €58-65; triples from €80.) Lübeck's specialty is **marzipan,** a delectable candy made from almonds. Stop by the famous confectionery █**I.G. Niederegger Marzipan Café ❶,** Breitestr. 89, for marzipan in the shape of pigs, jellyfish, and even the town gate. (Open M-F 9am-7pm, Sa 9am-6pm, Su 10am-4pm.) **Tipasa ❷,** Schlumacherstr. 12, serves pizza, pasta, and vegetarian dishes, and runs a *Biergarten* in back. (Open M-Th and Su noon-1am, F-Sa noon-2am.)

◻ SIGHTS. Between the station and the *Altstadt* stands the massive **Holstentor,** one of Lübeck's four 15th-century gates and the city's symbol. The museum inside deals in equal parts trade and torture. (Open Apr.-Sept. daily 10am-5pm; Oct.-Mar. closed M. €4, students €2.) The city skyline is dominated by the twin brick towers of the **Marienkirche,** a gigantic church housing the largest mechanical organ in the world. (Open in summer daily 10am-6pm; off-season 10am-4pm. Organ concerts Th and Sa at 6:30pm. €3.50, students €2.50.) The **Dom,** on Domkirchhof, shelters a majestic crucifix and is guarded by the trademark lion statue. (Open Apr.-Sept. daily 10am-6pm; Mar. and Oct. 10am-5pm; Nov. 10am-4pm; Dec.-Feb. 10am-3pm. Free. Organ concerts July-Aug. F and Su at 5pm. €3-6, students €1-3.) For a sweeping view of the spire-studded *Altstadt,* take the elevator to the top of **Petrikirche.** (Church open daily 11am-4pm. Tower open Apr.-Oct. 9am-7pm. €2, students €1.20.) The █**Museum für Puppentheater,** Kolk 16, is the largest private puppet collection in the world. (Open daily 10am-6pm. €3, students €2.50.) Dance afloat the **"body and soul"** boat in the water at the corner of Kanalstr. and Höhe Glockenstr. (Cover usually €4. Open Tu and Sa 10pm-late, F 10:30pm-late.)

SCHLESWIG
☎ 04621

With a harbor full of sailboats and a shoreline sprinkled with cafes, Schleswig (pop. 25,000) is a sea town with a royal history. Celebrating 1200 years since its founding as Haithabu, Viking ships set sail to Schleswig for the **Opinn Skjold** festival on the first weekend in August. By the harbor, the 18th-century ◪**Schloß Gottorf** and surrounding buildings comprise the **Landesmuseen**, six museums with enough Danish, Dutch, and German art to fill twenty. The surrounding park is an **outdoor sculpture museum**. (All museums open daily 10am-6pm. €5, students €2.50.) Scale the 240 steps of the **St. Petri Dom** for a striking view of town. (Open May-Sept. M-Sa 9am-5pm, Su 1:30-5pm; Oct.-Apr. M-Sa 10am-4pm, Su 1:30-5pm. €1.)

Schleswig centers around its **bus terminal** rather than its train station. Single rides (€2). The **train station** is 20min. south of the city center; take bus #1, 2, 3, 6, or 7 from the stop outside the bus station. The **tourist office**, Plessenstr. 7, is up the street from the harbor; from the ZOB, walk down Plessenstr. toward the water. (☎ 98 16 16; room reservations ☎ 98 16 17. Open May-Sept. M-F 9:30am-5:30pm, Sa 9:30am-12:30pm; Oct.-Apr. M-Th 10am-4pm, F 10am-1pm.) The **Jugendherberge (HI) ❶**, Spielkoppel 1, is close to the center of town. Take bus #2 from either the train or bus station to *Schwimmhalle;* the hostel is across the street. (☎ 238 93. Breakfast included. Reception daily 7am-1pm and 5-11pm. Curfew 11pm. Dorms €17, under-27 €14; singles €20, under-27 €18.) Nurse cloudy brews at **Asgaard-Brauerei ❸**, Königstr. 27, with descendants of Eric the Red. (Meals €9-10. Open M-Th 5pm-midnight, F 5pm-2am, Sa 11am-2am, Su 11am-midnight.) **Postal Code: 24837.**

CENTRAL AND WEST GERMANY

Lower Saxony (*Niedersachsen*), which stretches from the North Sea to the hills of central Germany, has foggy marshland and broad agricultural plains inland. Just south of Lower Saxony, North Rhine-Westphalia is the most heavily populated and economically powerful area in Germany. While the region's squalor may have inspired the philosophy of Karl Marx and Friedrich Engels, the area's natural beauty and the intellectual energy of Cologne and Düsseldorf inspired the muses of Goethe, Heine, and Böll.

DÜSSELDORF
☎ 0211

As Germany's fashion hub and multinational corporation base, the rich city of Düsseldorf (pop. 571,000) crawls with German patricians and would-be aristocrats. The nation's "Hautstadt"—a pun on *Hauptstadt* (capital) and the French *haute*, as in *haute couture*—is a stately metropolis with an *Altstadt* that features the best nightlife along the Rhine.

◪◪ TRANSPORTATION AND PRACTICAL INFORMATION. Trains run to: Amsterdam (2hr., every hr., €39); Berlin (4½hr., every hr., €93); Frankfurt (2½hr., 3 per hr., €32); Hamburg (3½hr., every hr., €63); Munich (6hr., 2 per hr., €98); and Paris (4½hr., 7 per day, €87). Düsseldorf's S-Bahn is integrated into the mammoth regional **VRR** (*Verkehrsverbund Rhein-Ruhr)* system, which connects most surrounding cities. For schedule info, call ☎ 582 28. The S-Bahn is the cheapest way to get to Aachen and Cologne. On the **public transportation system,** single tickets cost €1-7, depending on distance traveled. The *Tagesticket* (€6.35-17.50) lets up to five people travel for 24hr. on any line. To reach the **tourist office**, Immermannstr. 65, head straight and to the right from the train station; look for the Immermanhof building. It books rooms for a €4 fee. (☎ 172 02 22. Open M-F 8:30am-6pm, Sa 9am-12:30pm.) The **post office**, Konrad-Adenauer-Pl., **40210** Düsseldorf, is just to the right of the tourist office. (Open M-F 8am-6pm, Sa 9am-2pm.)

▐▌▐▌ ACCOMMODATIONS AND FOOD. It's not unusual for hotels in Düsseldorf to double their prices during trade fairs, which happen from August to April. **Jugendgästehaus Düsseldorf (HI) ❷**, Düsseldorfer Str. 1, is just over the Rheinkniebrücke from the *Altstadt*. Take U70, 74, 75, 76, or 77 to *Luegpl.*, then walk 500m down Kaiser-Wilhelm-Ring. (☎55 73 10. Reception daily 7am-1am. Curfew 1am; doors open every hr. 2-6am. Dorms €20; singles €32; doubles €50.) To reach **Hotel Schaum ❸**, 63 Gustav-Poengsen-Str., exit left from the train station on Graf-Adolf-Str., take your first left, and follow the tracks to Gustav-Poengsen-Str. (☎311 65 10. Breakfast included. Singles from €30; doubles from €50.) **Hotel Komet ❹**, Bismarckstr. 93, is straight down Bismarckstr. from the train station and offers bright but snug rooms. (☎17 87 90. Singles from €40; doubles from €55.) To camp at **Kleiner Torfbruch ❶**, take any S-Bahn to *Düsseldorf Geresheim*, then bus #735 (dir.: Stamesberg) to *Seeweg*. (☎899 20 38. €4 per person, €5 per tent.) For a cheap meal, the endless eateries in the *Altstadt* can't be beat; rows of pizzerias, *Döner* stands, and Chinese diners reach from Heinrich-Heine-Allee to the banks of the Rhine. **A Tavola ❸**, Wallstr. 11, has bottomless bread baskets and meticulously prepared pastas. (Open daily noon-3pm and 6-11pm.) The local outlet of the Czech brewery, **Pilsner Urquell ❷**, Gragenstr. 6, specializes in meaty eastern European fare. (Open M-Sa noon-1am, Su 4pm-midnight.) **Otto Mess** is a popular grocery chain; the most convenient location is at the eastern corner of Karlspl. in the *Altstadt*. (Open M-F 8am-8pm, Sa 8am-4pm.)

◪ SIGHTS. The glitzy **Königsallee** (the "Kö"), just outside the *Altstadt*, embodies the vitality and glamor of wealthy Düsseldorf. Midway up is the awe-inspiring **Kö-Galerie**, a marble-and-copper shopping mall showcasing one haughty store after another. (10min. down Graf-Adolf-Str. from the train station.) The Baroque **Schloß Benrath** in the suburbs of Düsseldorf was originally built as a pleasure palace and hunting grounds for Elector Karl Theodor. Strategically placed mirrors and false exterior windows make the castle appear larger than it is, but the enormous French gardens still dwarf it. (S6 (dir.: Köln) to *Schloß Benrath*. Open Su and Tu-Sa 10am-6pm, W until 8pm. Tours every 30min. €4, students €1.75.) The **Heinrich-Heine-Institut** is the official shrine of Düsseldorf's melancholic son. (Bilker Str. 12-14. Open Su and Tu-F 11am-5pm, Sa 1-5pm. €2, students €1.) At the upper end of the Kö is the **Hofgarten park**, the oldest public park in Germany. At the east end of the park, the 18th-century **Schloß Jägerhof** houses the **Goethemuseum**. (Jakobistr. 2. Streetcar #707 or bus #752 to *Schloß Jägerhof*. Open Su and Tu-F 11am-5pm, Sa 1-5pm. €2, students and children €1.) The **Kunstsammlung Nordrhein-Westfalen,** within the black glass edifice west of the Hofgarten, houses works by Expressionists, Surrealists, Picasso, and hometown boy Paul Klee. (Grabbepl. 5. U70, 75, 76, 78, or 79 to *Heinrich-Heine-Allee;* walk north two blocks. Open Su and Sa 11am-6pm, Tu-F 10am-6pm, first W of month until 10pm. €3, students €1.50.)

◪ NIGHTLIFE. Folklore holds that Düsseldorf's 500 pubs make up *die längste Theke der Welt* (the longest bar in the world). Pubs in the *Altstadt* are standing-room-only by 6pm; by nightfall it's nearly impossible to see where one pub ends and the next begins. **Bolkerstraße** is jam-packed with street performers. *Prinz* (€3) gives tips on the scene; it's often free at the youth hostel. *Facolte* (€2), a gay and lesbian nightlife magazine, is available at newsstands. **Pam-Pam**, Bolkerstr 34, plays house, rock, pop, and plenty of American music. (Open F-Sa 10pm-dawn.) **Zur Ül**, Ratinger Str. 16, is the quintessential German pub. (Open M-F 9am-1am, Sa-Su 10am-3am.) **Unique**, Bolkerstr. 30, lives up to its name, drawing a younger, trendier crowd to its red-walled interior. (Cover €5. Open W-Sa 10pm-late.)

GERMANY

Düsseldorf

▲ ACCOMMODATIONS
Hotel Komet, **8**
Hotel Schaum, **9**
Jugendgästehaus
Düsseldorf (HI), **1**
Kleiner Torfbruch, **7**

♦ FOOD
A Tavola, **6**
Pilsner Urquell, **5**

★ NIGHTLIFE
Pam-Pam, **3**
Unique, **4**
Zur Öl, **2**

U U-Bahn (subway)

Worringer Str.
Kölner Str.
Stephaniestr.
Worringer Str.
TO 7 (7km)
Hauptbahnhof
KONRAD-ADENAUER-PL.
U HAUPTBAHNHOF (650m)
& KAISERWERTH (7km)
TO 9

Pempelforter Str.
Cantadorstr.
Leopoldstr.
Am Wehrhahn
Friedrich-Ebert-Str.
Karlstr.
8
Bismarckstr.
Charlottenstr.
Graf-Adolf-Str.

St. Rochus
Prinz-Georg-Str.
Berger Str.
Stiftung Ernst Schneider
Jacobstr.
Tonhallenstr.
Klosterstr.
Immermannstr.
Kreuzstr.
U OSTSTR.
Oststr.
Goppelnstr.

Goethemuseum
Sternstr.
Vagedesstr.
Feldstr.
Rosenstr.
Gartenstr.
Jägerhofstr.
Schadowstr.
Schauspielhaus
Johannes Kirche
Blumenstr.
PLATZ DER DEUTSCHEN EINHEIT
Stresemannstr.
Berliner Allee
Grünstr.

Kaiserstr.
Arnoldstr.
Inselstr.
Hofgarten
U NORDSTR.
Ratinger Tor
Hofgarten
Kunstsammlung N.-Westfalen
Städtische Kunsthalle
Opera
STEINSTR. / KÖNIGSALLEE U
Königstr.
Königs-allee
Königs-allee
Bahnstr.
Breite Str.

Museum Kunst Palast
NRW Forum
U TONHALLE
Tonhalle
Fritz-Roebber-Str.
Kunstakademie
Eiskellerstr.
Ratingel Str.
Max-Weyhe-Allee
Heine-Allee
Neubrückstr.
Hunsrückenstr.
HEINRICH-HEINE-ALLEE
Junges Theater
Grabenstr.
Heinrich-Heine
Benrather Str.
Bastionstr.
Kasernenstr.

Joseph-Beuys-Ufer
Kreuzherrenkirche
Schlossufer
Ritterstr.
ALTSTADT
Mahn-und-Andreas Gedenkstätte
St. Kunsthalle
Kurzestr.
Bolkerstr.
Bolkerstr.-Neander Kirche
Flinger Str.
Walls tr.
5
6
CARLS-PL.
Hohe Str.
Blker Str.
Heinrich-Heine-Institut
Südstr.

St. Lambertus Kirche
BURG-PLATZ
Rathaus
Mühlenstr.
Marktstr.
Rhein. str.
Berger Kirche
St. Maximilian Kirche
Marionetten-theater
Stadtmuseum
TO KUNSTSAMMLUNG IM STÄNDEHAUS (150m)

Heljens- und Film-Museums
Schlossturm
Rheinuferstr.
Citadellstr.
Bäcker str.
Berger Allee
Poststr.
Haroldstr.
Karlstor

Rhine
Oberkasseler Brücke
TO SCHLOSS BENRATH (8km)
Landtag

Rhine
Rheinkniebrücke

Kaiser-Friedrich-Ring
San-Remo-Str.
Theater an der Luegallee
U LUEGPLATZ
Markgrafenstr.
Brend'amoustr.
Kaiser-Wilhelm-Ring
Wildenbruchstr.
Düsseldorfer Str.
1

Rheinallee
LG
0   500 yards
0   500 meters

Rhine

AACHEN

☎ **0241**

Once the capital of Charlemagne's Frankish empire, modern Aachen (pop. 246,000) is a trove of historical treasures and a thriving forum for up-and-coming European artists. The three-tiered dome and dazzling blue-gold mosaics of the **Dom** are in the center of the city; Charlemagne's remains lie in the reliquary behind the altar. (Open M-Sa 11am-7pm, Su 12:30-7pm, except during services.) Around the corner is the **Schatzkammer**, Klosterpl. 2, a treasury of reliquaries containing John the Baptist's hair and ribs, splinters and nails from the cross, and Christ's scourging robe. A silver bust of Charlemagne holds his skull. (Open M 10am-1pm, Tu-W and F-Su 10am-6pm, Th 10am-9pm. €2.50, students €2.) The **Ludwigforum für Internationale Kunst,** Jülicherstr. 97-109, houses a rotating collection of cutting-edge art. (Open Tu and Th 10am-5pm, W and F 10am-8pm, Sa-Su 11am-5pm. Free tours Su 11:30am and 3pm. €3, students €1.50.) **Trains** run to Brussels (2hr., every 2hr., €20) and Cologne (1hr., 2-3 per hr., €11). The **tourist office,** on Friedrich-Wilhelm-Pl. in the Atrium Elisenbrunnen, runs tours and finds rooms for free. From the station, head up Bahnhofstr.; turn left onto Theaterstr., which becomes Theaterpl., then turn right onto Kapuzinergraben, which becomes Friedrich-Wilhelm-Pl. (☎180 29 60. Open M-F 9am-6pm, Sa 9am-2pm.) The **Euroregionales Jugendgästehaus (HI) ❸,** Maria-Theresia-Allee 260, feels more like a hotel than a hostel. From the station, walk left on Lagerhausstr. until it intersects Karmeliterstr. and Mozartstr., then take bus #2 (dir.: Preusswald) to *Ronheide.* (☎71 10 10. Breakfast included. Curfew 1am. Dorms €21; singles €34; doubles €52.) **Hotel Drei König ❸,** Büchel 5, on the corner of Marktpl., is just steps from the *Rathaus.* (☎483 93. Breakfast included. Reception daily 8am-11pm. Singles €45, with bath €65; doubles €65/75; triples €100.) **Pontstraße,** off Marktpl., and the pedestrian zone have a lot of great restaurants. The Mexican cocktail bar and restaurant **Sausalitos ❸,** Markt 47, has become Aachen's most popular place to eat. (Entrees €6-13. Open daily noon-1am.) **Postal Code:** 52064.

COLOGNE (KÖLN)

☎ **0221**

Although most of inner Cologne (pop. 968,000) was destroyed in WWII, the magnificent Gothic *Dom* survived 14 bombings and remains Cologne's main attraction. Today, the city is the largest in North Rhine-Westphalia and its most important cultural center, with a full range of world-class museums and theaters.

▐ TRANSPORTATION

Flights: Flights depart from **Köln-Bonn Flughafen** (CGN); a shuttle to **Berlin** leaves hourly. Bus #170 to the airport leaves from stop #3 at the train station (20min; daily 5:30-6:30am every 30min., 6:30am-8pm every 15min., 8-11pm every 30min.; €4.80).

Trains: To: **Amsterdam** (3hr., €46); **Berlin** (5hr., 1-2 per hr., €67); **Brussels** (2½hr., €43); **Düsseldorf** (40min., 2 per hr., €7); **Frankfurt** (2hr., 3 per hr., €32); **Hamburg** (5hr., 3 per hr., €67); **Munich** (4hr., 1 per hr., €72).

Ride-Sharing: Citynetz Mitfahrzentrale, Maximinstr. 2 (☎194 40). Turn left from the back of the train station. Open daily 9am-7pm.

Ferries: Köln-Düsseldorfer (☎208 83 18) begins its popular Rhine cruises here. Sail upstream to **Koblenz** (€33) or **Bonn** (€11). Eurail valid on most trips.

Public Transportation: VRS (Verkehrsverbund Rhein-Sieg), downstairs in the train station, has free maps of the S- and U-Bahn, bus, and streetcar lines.

Bike Rental: Kölner Fahrradverleihservice, Markmannsgasse (☎0171 629 87 96), in the *Altstadt* on the Rhine. €2 per hr., €10 per day. Open daily 10am-6pm.

✈ ⚅ ORIENTATION AND PRACTICAL INFORMATION

Cologne stretches across the Rhine, but nearly all sights and the city center can be found on the western side. The *Altstadt* is split into **Altstadt-Nord**, near the **Hauptbahnhof**, and **Altstadt-Süd**, south of the **Severinsbrücke** (bridge).

Tourist Office: Verkehrsamt, Unter Fettenhennen 19 (☎194 33), across from the entrance to the *Dom*, provides free city maps and books rooms for a €3 fee. Open May-Oct. M-Sa 9am-9pm, Su 10am-6pm; Nov.-Apr. M-Sa 8am-9pm, Su 9:30am-7pm.

Currency Exchange: Reisebank, in the train station. Open daily 7am-9pm.

Bi-Gay-Lesbian Resources: Schulz Schwulen-und Lesbenzentrum, Kartäuserwall 18 (☎93 18 80 80), near Chlodwigpl. Info, advice, and cafe. The tourist office also offers the *Gay City Map* with listings of gay-friendly hotels, bars, and clubs.

Police: ☎110. **Fire** and **ambulance:** ☎112.

Pharmacy: Apotheke im Hauptbahnhof, near Gleis 12 (☎139 11 12), in the train station. Open M-F 6am-8pm, Sa 9am-8pm.

Internet access: Galeria Kaufhof, Hohe Str. 41 3rd fl. €1.50 per 30min.

Post Office: at the corner of Breite Str. and Tunisstr. in the WDR-Arkaden shopping gallery. Address mail to be held: Postlagernde Briefe für Firstname SURNAME, Hauptpostamt, **50667** Köln, GERMANY. Open M-F 8am-8pm, Sa 8am-4pm.

⌂ ACCOMMODATIONS

Hotels fill up in spring and fall when conventions come to town, and the two hostels are often booked from June to September. The **Mitwohnzentrale, Im Ferkulum 4,** arranges apartments for longer stays. (☎194 45. Open M-F 9am-1pm and 2-4pm.)

▨ **Jansen Pension,** Richard-Wagner-Str. 18 (☎25 18 75). U1, 6, 7, 15, 17, or 19 to *Rudolfpl.* Owned by a welcoming English couple and featuring beautiful high-ceilinged rooms in Victorian style. Breakfast included. Singles €31-39; doubles €57. ❸

▨ **Hotel Heinzelmännchen,** Hohe Pforte 5 (☎21 12 17). Bus #132 to *Waidmarkt*. Or walk down the Hohe Str. shopping zone until it becomes Hohe Pforte. Fairy-tale pictures decorate this family-run hotel. Rooms with TV. Breakfast included. Reception 6am-10pm. Singles €34-38; doubles €60; triples over €70. Discounts for stays over 2 nights. ❸

Station Hostel and Bar, Rheing. 34-36 (☎23 02 47). Clean rooms, a popular bar, and English-speaking staff. Free Internet. Reception 24hr. Reserved rooms held until 6pm. Singles €27; doubles €42; triples €57; quads €70. ❸

Station Hostel for Backpackers, Marzellenstr. 44-48 (☎912 53 01). From the station, walk 1 block along Dompropst-Ketzer-Str. and take the first right on Marzellenstr. Abuzz with backpackers and reggae beats. Breakfast €1.50-2.50. Sheets €1.50. Internet €0.50, plus €0.05 per min. Reception 24hr. Check-in 2pm. Check-out noon. 4- to 6-bed dorms €15-16; singles €27; doubles €40; triples €54. ❷

Jugendherberge Köln-Deutz (HI), Siegesstr. 5a (☎81 47 11), just over the Hohenzollernbrücke. S6, 11, or 12 to *Köln-Deutz*. Exit the station, walk down Neuhöfferstr., and take the 1st right; the hostel is in a courtyard. Newly renovated rooms. Breakfast included. Free laundry. Reception 11am-1am. Curfew 1am. Call ahead. Dorms €20. ❸

Hotel Im Kupferkessel, Probsteigasse 6 (☎13 53 38). From the Dom, follow Dompropst-Ketzer-Str. as it becomes An der Dominikan, Unter Sachenhausen, Gereonstr., and finally Christophstr.; Probsteigasse is on the right. Spacious, comfortable rooms with TV and telephone. Well-stocked breakfast included. Singles €30-41; doubles €66. ❸

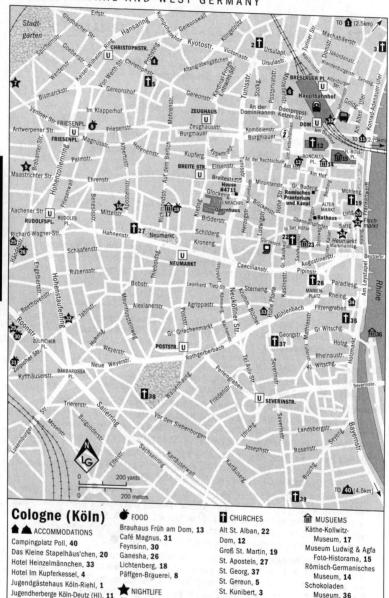

Cologne (Köln)

▲ ▲ ACCOMMODATIONS

Campingplatz Poll, **40**
Das Kleine Stapelhäus'chen, **20**
Hotel Heinzelmännchen, **33**
Hotel Im Kupferkessel, **4**
Jugendgästehaus Köln-Riehl, **1**
Jugendherberge Köln-Deutz (HI), **11**
Jansen Pension, **25**
Station Hostel and Bar, **34**
Station Hostel for
  Backpackers, **6**

🍴 FOOD

Brauhaus Früh am Dom, **13**
Café Magnus, **31**
Feynsinn, **30**
Ganesha, **26**
Lichtenberg, **18**
Päffgen-Brauerei, **8**

★ NIGHTLIFE

Alter Wartesaal, **10**
Das Ding, **32**
Gloria, **16**
Hotel Timp, **24**
M20, **9**
Papa Joe's Jazzlokal, **21**
Stadtgarten, **7**
Vampire, **29**

✝ CHURCHES

Alt St. Alban, **22**
Dom, **12**
Groß St. Martin, **19**
St. Aposteln, **27**
St. Georg, **37**
St. Gereon, **5**
St. Kunibert, **3**
St. Maria im Kapitol, **28**
St. Maria Lyskirchen, **35**
St. Pantaleon, **38**
St. Severin, **39**
St. Ursula, **2**

🏛 MUSUEMS

Käthe-Kollwitz-
  Museum, **17**
Museum Ludwig & Agfa
  Foto-Historama, **15**
Römisch-Germanisches
  Museum, **14**
Schokoladen
  Museum, **36**
Wallraf-Richartz
  Museum, **23**

Ⓢ S-Bahn (surface rail)
Ⓤ U-Bahn (subway)

GERMANY

Das Kleine Stapelhäus'chen, Fischmarkt 1-3 (☎257 78 62). Cross the Altenmarkt from the back of the *Rathaus* and take Lintg. to the Fischmarkt. An old-fashioned, elegant inn overlooking the river. Breakfast included. Singles €39-41, with shower €52-64, with full bath €64-74; doubles €64-74/100-121. ❹

Jugendgästehaus Köln-Riehl (HI), An der Schanz 14 (☎76 70 81), on the Rhine north of the zoo. U16 (dir.: Ebertplatz/Mülheim) to *Boltensternstr.* Breakfast included. Reception 24hr. Call ahead. 4- to 6-bed dorms €21; singles €34. ❸

Campingplatz Poll, Weidenweg (☎83 19 66), on the Rhine, southeast of the *Altstadt*. U16 to *Marenberg* and cross the Rodenkirchener Brücke. Reception daily 8am-noon and 5-8pm. Open mid-Apr. to Oct. €4.50 per person; €2.50 per tent or car. ❶

🍴 FOOD

Cologne cuisine includes scrumptious *Rievekoochen* (slabs of fried potato dunked in applesauce) and smooth Kölsch beer. Cheap restaurants line **Zülpicher-straße,** and **Weidengasse** in the Turkish district. Mid-priced ethnic restaurants toe the perimeter of the *Altstadt*, particularly from **Hohenzollernring** to **Hohenstaufen-ring.** German eateries surround the **Domplatz.** An open-air **market** on **Wilhelmsplatz** takes over the Nippes neighborhood in the morning. (Open M-Sa 8am-1pm.)

Brauhaus Früh am Dom, Am Hof 14 (☎258 03 97). A trip to Cologne isn't complete without a visit. The Kölsch is cheap (€1.35) and the specialties regional (€4-18). Open daily 8am-midnight, menu until 11:45pm. ❸

Lichtenberg, Richmondstr. 13. Take U12 to *Neumarkt.* Chandeliers and a color-coordinated library provide the decor at this hip cafe. Sandwiches €3-4. Entrees €3-11. Open daily 9am-1am. ❷

Päffgen-Brauerei, Friesenstr. 64. Take U6 to *Friesenplatz.* Local favorite since 1883. Kölsch (€1.25) is brewed on the premises and consumed in cavernous halls or in the 600-seat *Biergarten.* Meals €2-16. Open daily 10am-midnight. ❸

Feynsinn, Rathenaupl. 7. U8 to *Zülpicher Platz.* Swank university crowds chatter under a star-studded ceiling. Breakfast until 5pm. Open M-F 9am-1am, Sa-Su 10am-2am. ❸

Café Magnus, Zülpicherstr. 48. Take U8 to *Zülpicher Platz.* Though students dominate the nightly scene, locals of all ages flock to this cafe for funky tunes and artfully prepared meals from €4. Open daily 8am-3am. ❷

Ganesha, Händelstr. 29., at the corner of Richard-Wagner-Str. Take U6 to *Rudolfplatz.* Offers a broad range of Indian specialties, from samosas (€3) to spicy chicken vanda-loo (€6). Most entrees €7-12. Open M-Su 6pm-midnight, Tu-Su also 12:30-3pm. ❸

👁 SIGHTS

DOM. Whether illuminated in a pool of eerie blue floodlighting or eclipsing the sun with its colossal spires, the *Dom*, Germany's greatest cathedral, is the first thing to greet travelers as they enter the city. A chapel inside on the right houses a 15th-century **triptych** that depicts the city's five patron saints. Behind the altar in the center of the choir is the **Shrine of the Magi,** the most sacred element of the cathedral, which reportedly holds the remains of the Three Kings. Before exiting the choir, stop in the **Chapel of the Cross** to admire the 10th-century **Gero crucifix,** which is the oldest intact sculpture of a crucified Christ with his eyes shut. (*Cathedral open daily 6am-7pm. Free. Tours in English M-Sa 10:30am and 2:30pm, Su 2:30pm €4, children €2.*) Fifteen minutes and 509 steps bring you to the top of the **Südturm** tower. (*Open May-*

THE INSIDER'S CITY

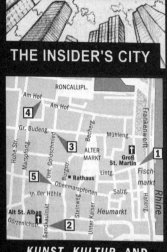

KUNST, KULTUR, AND KÖLSCH

Forever in the shadow of the magnificent Dom, the area surrounding Cologne's Altstadt is underappreciated by most sightseers. But not you.

1 Most of the **Fischmarkt's** colorful *Rheinisch* facades are restorations, but the riverside atmosphere and jolly accordionists are originals.

2 The 15th-century **Gürzenich** hall is still used for festivities. *(Martinstr. 29. ☎92 58 99 90.)*

3 Give thanks for the advent of Roman plumbing at this **sewer** ruin. *(At the intersection of Unter Goldschmied and Kleine Budengasse.)*

4 The **Brauhaus Früh am Dom** has served the best *Kölsch* in town since the 19th century. *(Am Hof 12. ☎258 03 97.)*

5 Though your vision may be blurry from all that beer, don't fret; so is the art at **Wallraf-Richartz-Museum**. *(Martinstr. 39.)*

Sept. 9am-6pm; Nov.-Feb. daily 9am-4pm; Mar.-Apr. and Oct. 9am-5pm. €2, students €1.) Catch your breath at the **Glockenstube**, a chamber with the tower's nine bells, about three-quarters of the way up.

MUSEUMS. ⬛**Heinrich-Böll-Platz** houses two complementary collections: the **Museum Ludwig**, which spans Impressionism through Dalí, Lichtenstein, and Warhol; and the **Agfa Foto-Historama**, which chronicles photography through the last 150 years, including a rotating display of Man Ray's works. *(Bischofsgartenstr. 1. Open Su and Sa 11am-6pm, Tu 10am-8pm, W-F 10am-6pm. €6.40, students €3.20.)* The galleries of the **Wallraf-Richartz Museum** are lined with masterpieces from the Middle Aged to the Post-Impressionist. *(Martinstr. 39. From the Heumarkt, take Gürzenichstr. 1 block to Martinstr. Open Su and Sa 11am-6pm, Tu 10am-8pm, W-F 10am-6pm. €5.10, students €2.60.)* The **Römisch-Germanisches Museum** displays a large array of artifacts documenting the daily lives of Romans rich and poor. *(Roncallipl. 4. Open Su and Tu-Sa 10am-5pm. €3, students €2.)* Four words about the ⬛**Schokoladen Museum** (Chocolate Museum): Willy Wonka made real. It presents every step of chocolate production from the rainforests to the gold fountain that spurts streams of silky chocolate. Resist the urge to drool and wait for the free samples. *(Rheinauhafen 1a, near the Severinsbrücke. From the train station, head for the river, walk along the Rhine heading right, go under the Deutzer Brücke, and take the 1st footbridge. Open M-F 10am-6pm, Sa-Su 11am-7pm. €5.50, students €3.)* The **Käthe-Kollwitz-Museum** houses the world's largest collection of sketches, sculptures, and prints by the brilliant 20th-century artist-activist. *(Neumarkt 18-24. On the top fl. in the Neumarkt-Passage. U12, 14, 16, or 18 to Neumarkt. Open Su and Sa 11am-6pm, Tu-F 10am-6pm. €2.50, students €1.)*

HOUSE #4711. The fabled **Eau de Cologne**, once prescribed as a drinkable curative, gave the town worldwide recognition. Today the house where it was born, labeled #4711 by a Napoleonic system that abolished street names, is a boutique where a corner fountain flows freely with the scented water. Visit the gallery upstairs for a full history of the famous fragrance. *(Glockeng., at the intersection with Tunisstr. From Hohe Str., turn right on Brückenstr., which becomes Glockeng. Open M-F 9:30am-8pm, Sa 9:30am-4pm.)*

RÖMISCHES PRAETORIUM UND KANAL. The excavated ruins of the former Roman military headquarters display remains of Roman gods and an array of rocks left by early inhabitants. *(From the Rathaus, take a right toward the swarm of hotels and then a left onto Kleine Budeng. Open Su and Sa 11am-4pm, Tu-F 10am-4pm. €1.50, students €0.75.)*

🎵 🎭 ENTERTAINMENT AND NIGHTLIFE

Cologne explodes in celebration during **Karneval,** a week-long pre-Lenten festival made up of 50 neighborhood processions in the days before Ash Wednesday. **Weiberfastnacht,** Feb. 19, 2004, is the first major to-do; the mayor mounts the platform at Alter Markt and abdicates leadership to the city's women, who then find their husbands at work and chop off their ties. The weekend builds up to the out-of-control parade on **Rosenmontag** (Feb. 23, 2004), where everyone gets and gives a couple dozen *Bützchen* (Kölsch dialect for a kiss on the cheek). While most revelers nurse their hangovers on Shrove Tuesday, pubs and restaurants set fire to the straw scarecrows hanging out of their windows. For more info, pick up the Karneval booklet at the tourist office.

Roman mosaics dating back to the third century record the wild excesses of the city's early residents; they've toned it down only a bit since. The best way to know what you'll get is to pick up the monthly magazine *Kölner* (€1). The closer to the Rhine or *Dom* you venture, the more quickly your wallet gets emptied. After dark in **Hohenzollernring,** crowds of people move from theaters to clubs and finally to cafes in the early morning. Students congregate in the **Bermuda-Dreieck** (Bermuda Triangle), bounded by Zülpicherstr., Zülpicherpl., Roonstr., and Luxemburgstr. The center of gay nightlife runs up Matthiasstr. to Mühlenbach, Hohe Pforte, Marienpl., and the Heumarkt area by **Deutzer Brücke.** Radiating westward from Friesenpl., the **Belgisches Viertel** has slightly more expensive bars and cafes.

■ **Papa Joes Jazzlokal,** Buttermarkt 37. Papa Joe's reputation for great jazz and good times is legendary. Drinks are pricey, but a Kölsch (€3.60) goes a long way. Grab some peanuts when the sack comes around. Open daily 7pm-3am.

Stadtgarten, Venloerstr. 40. Take U6, 15, 17, or 19 to *Friesenplatz.* Two clubs for the price of one. Downstairs spins techno and house; upstairs, the concert hall is renowned for its live jazz recordings. Cover €4-5. Open M-Th 9pm-1am. F-Sa 9pm-3am.

Das Ding, Hohenstaufenring 30. Smoky and very *noir.* A popular bar and disco for students with varied music and dirt-cheap drink specials (under €1). Cover around €4. Open M and W 9pm-2am, Tu and Th-Su 9pm-3am.

Alter Wartesaal, Johannisstr. 11. In the basement of the train station. Enormous dance floor fills with trendy 20-somethings. Cover €8. Hours vary.

M20, Maastrichterstr. 20. U6 to *Rudolfplatz.* Distinguished DJs deliver some of the city's best drum 'n bass to locals. Open M-Th 10pm-2am, F-Sa 10pm-3am.

GAY AND LESBIAN VENUES

■ **Hotel Timp,** Heumarkt 25 (www.timp.de), right across from the bus stop. This outrageous gay-friendly club and hotel has become a virtual institution in Cologne for travesty theater. Nightly crowds come here to see the gaudy and glitter-filled cabarets. Shows daily from 1-4am. No cover, but your first drink is €8 weeknights or €13 on weekends.

Gloria, Apostelnstr. 11. A former movie theater, this popular cafe and club is at the nexus of the gay and lesbian scene. Cover around €7. Cafe open Tu-Sa 12pm-1am.

Vampire, Rathenaupl. 5 (☎ 240 12 11). Take U7 or 9 to *Zülpicher Platz.* Mostly lesbian bar enchants regulars with its mellow feel and a mysterious drink served in test tubes (€3.50). Open Su and Tu-Th 9pm-2am, F-Sa 9pm-3am.

☎ **0228**

BONN

Once derisively called *Hauptdorf* (capital village) just because it wasn't Berlin, Bonn (pop. 306,000) became the capital of West Germany by chance because Konrad Adenauer, the first chancellor, resided in its suburbs. In 1999, the *Bundestag* packed up and moved back to Berlin, allowing Bonn to be itself again. Today, the streets of the *Altstadt* bustle with notable energy, and Bonn's well-respected university and museums bolster the cultural scene. Bonn is also fast becoming a center for Germany's computer-technology industry and hip cyber-culture.

⌨ TRANSPORTATION AND PRACTICAL INFORMATION. Trains run to: Cologne (20min., 5 per hr., €5); Frankfurt (2hr., 1 per hr., €25); and Koblenz (1hr., 2 per hr., €8). The **tourist office** is at Windeckstr. 2, near the cathedral off Münsterpl. (☎194 33. Open M-F 9am-6:30pm, Sa 9am-4pm, Su 10am-2pm.) Consider buying the **Bonn Regio Welcome Card** (1-day €9, 2-day €14, 3-day €19), which covers transportation (M-F after 9am, Sa-Su 24hr.) and admission to more than 20 museums in Bonn and the surrounding area. The **post office** is at Münsterpl. 17. (Open M-F 9am-8pm, Sa 9am-4pm.) **Postal Code:** 53111.

⌨ ACCOMMODATIONS AND FOOD. Take bus #621 (dir.: Ippendorf Altenheim) to *Jugendgästehaus* to reach the super-modern **Jugendgästehaus Bonn-Venusberg (HI) ❸**, Haager Weg 42. (☎28 99 70. Breakfast included. Laundry €5. Curfew 1am. Dorms €21; singles €34; doubles €48.) Closer to the city center, **Hotel Bergmann ❸**, Kasernenstr. 13 (☎63 38 91) is a small family-run hotel. Follow Poststr. from the station, turn left at Münsterpl. on Vivatsgasse, then right on Kasernenstr. (☎63 38 91. Bath on each floor. Breakfast included. Singles €35; doubles €50.)

The **market** on Münsterpl. teems with vendors selling meat, fruit, and vegetables. At the end of the day voices rise and prices plummet. (Open M-Sa 8am-6pm.) There is also a **supermarket** in the basement of the Kaufhof department store on Münsterpl. (Open M-F 9:30am-8pm, Sa 9am-4pm.) Cheap eats are available at **Mensa ❶**, Nassestr. 11, a 15min. walk from the station along Kaiserstr. (Open M-F noon-2pm and 5:30-7:30pm, Sa noon-2pm.) **Cafe Blau ❷**, Franziskanerstr. 5, across from the university, will sate your hunger without devouring your cash supply. (Chicken or pasta platters €3-5. Open daily 10am-1am.)

⌨ SIGHTS AND NIGHTLIFE. Bonn's lively pedestrian zone is littered with historic nooks. ⌨**Beethovenhaus**, Beethoven's birthplace, hosts a fantastic collection of the composer's personal effects, from his primitive hearing aids to his first violin. (Bonng. 20. Open Apr.-Oct. M-Sa 10am-6pm, Su 11am-4pm; Nov.-Mar. M-Sa 10am-5pm, Su 11am-4pm. €4, students €3.) In its governmental heyday, the transparent walls of the **Bundestag** were meant to symbolize the government's responsibility to the public. (Take U16, 63, or 66 to *Heussallee/Bundeshaus* or bus #610 to *Bundeshaus*.) Students study within the **Kurfürstliches Schloß**, the huge 18th-century palace now serving as the center of Bonn's **Friedrich-Wilhelms-Universität.** To reach Bonn's other palace, follow Poppelsdorfer Allee to the 18th-century **Poppelsdorfer Schloß,** which boasts beautifully manicured **botanical gardens.** (Gardens open Apr.-Oct. M-F 9am-6pm, Su 10am-5pm; Nov.-Mar. M-F 9am-4pm. Free.) The Welcome Card (see Practical Information, above) provides admission to most of Bonn's **Museum Mile.** To start your museum-crawl, take U16, 63, or 66 to *Heussallee* or *Museum König.* ⌨**Haus der Geschichte** (House of History), Willy-Brandt 4, examines post-WWII German history through interactive exhibits. (Open Su and Tu-Sa 9am-7pm. Free.) One block away, **Kunstmuseum Bonn,** Friedrich-Ebert-Allee 2, houses a superb selection of Expressionist and modern German art. (Open Su, Tu and Th-Sa 10am-6pm, W 10am-9pm. €5, students €2.50.)

For club and concert listings, pick up *Schnüss* (€1). The ⌨**Jazz Galerie,** Oxfordstr. 24, hosts jazz and rock concerts as well as a jumping bar and disco. (Cover €3-5. Open Su and Tu-Th 9pm-3am, F-Sa 9pm-4am.) **Pantheon,** Bundeskanzlerpl., caters to eclectic tastes with a disco, concerts, and stand-up comedy; follow Adenauerallee out of the city to Bundeskanzlerpl. (Cover €6.50-8. Open M-Sa 11pm-4am.) **Boba's Bar**, Josephstr. 17, is one of Bonn's most popular gay and lesbian nightspots. (Open Su and Tu-Sa 8pm-3am.)

KASSEL
☎ 0561

Napoleon III was dragged to Kassel (pop. 195,000) as a prisoner of Prussian troops, but today, folks visit this edgy city of their own free will. From Bahnhof Wilhelmshöhe, take streetcar #1 to ■**Wilhelmshöhe**, a hillside park in a time warp. Inside, **Schloß Wilhelmshöhe** is a dressed-down version of the Residenz in Würzburg (p. 509), but more authentically furnished. Uphill, **Schloß Löwenburg** was built by Wilhelm in the 18th century with stones deliberately missing to look like a crumbling medieval castle—he was obsessed with the year 1495 and fancied himself a time-displaced knight. (Both castles open Mar.-Oct. Su and Tu-Sa 10am-5pm; Nov.-Feb. Su and Tu-Sa 10am-4pm. Required tours every hr. €3.50, students €2.50.) All of the park's paths lead up to **Herkules**, Kassel's emblem; visitors can climb up onto Herkules's pedestal and, if they're brave enough, into his club. (Access to the base of the statue free. Pedestal and club open mid-Mar. to mid-Nov. daily 10am-5pm. €2, students €1.25.) The **Brüder-Grimm-Museum**, Schöne Aussicht 2, exhibits Jacob and Wilhelm's handwritten copy of *Kinder- und Hausmärchen*. (Open daily 10am-5pm. €1.50, students €1.)

Kassel has two train stations, Bahnhof Wilhelmshöhe and the Hauptbahnhof; most trains stop only at Wilhelmshöhe. **Trains** run to: Düsseldorf (3½hr., 1 per hr., €37); Frankfurt (2hr., 3 per hr., €27); Hamburg (2½hr., 3 per hr., €51); and Munich (4hr., 1 per hr., €88). The **tourist office**, in Bahnhof Wilhelmshöhe, has free maps and books rooms for a €4 fee. (☎70 77 07. Open M-F 9am-6pm, Sa 9am-1pm.) To reach **Jugendherberge am Tannenwäldchen (HI) ❷**, Schenkendorfstr. 18, take streetcar #4 from the Wilhelmshöhe station to Annastr., backtrack on Friedrich-Ebert-Str., and make a right on Querallee, which becomes Schenkendorfstr. (☎77 64 55. Breakfast included. Sheets €4. Reception daily 9am-11:30pm. Curfew 12:30am. €19, under-26 €18. HI members only.) For **Hotel Kö78 ❸**, Kölnische Str. 78, follow the directions to the Jugendherberge, then walk up Annastr. from the stop and turn right onto Kölnische Str. (☎716 14. Breakfast included. Reception daily 7am-10pm. Singles €32, with shower €41-46; doubles €51/61-75.) **Friedrich-Ebert-Straße**, the upper part of **Wilhelmshöher Allee**, and the area around **Königsplatz** all have supermarkets and cafes sprinkled amongst clothing stores. **Postal Code:** 34117.

FRANKFURT AM MAIN
☎ 069

Frankfurt's role as home to the central bank of the European Union lends it a glitzy vitality—international offices, shiny skyscrapers, and expensive cars define every intersection. Equally important is its role as a major transportation hub for all of Europe. Indeed, Frankfurt (pop. 641,000) first made its appearance as a crossing point for the Main River—the Franks forded the river in early times, and the city's name literally means *ford of the Franks*. Today, the city spends more on cultural attractions and tourism than any other German city. Visitors are drawn by the selection of museums and exhibits—and, of course, the highly trafficked transportation routes that make Frankfurt a likely stop on your itinerary.

▣ TRANSPORTATION

Flights: The airport, **Flughafen Rhein-Main** (FRA; ☎(0180) 53 72 46 36), is connected to the *Hauptbahnhof* (main train station) by S8 and 9 (every 15min.; buy tickets for €3 from the green machines marked *Fahrkarten* before boarding).

GERMANY

Trains: Call ☎(0180) 599 66 33 for schedules, reservations, and info. Frequent trains leave the **Hauptbahnhof** for: **Amsterdam** (4hr., 2 per hr., €80); **Berlin** (5-6hr., 2 per hr., €58-86); **Cologne** (2½hr., 3 per hr., €29-51); **Hamburg** (5hr., 2 per hr., €81); **Munich** (3½-4½hr., 2 per hr., €65); **Paris** (6-8hr., 2 per hr., €59-73).

Public Transportation: Runs daily until about 1am. Single-ride tickets (€1.65, rush hour €1.95) are valid for 1hr. in one direction, transfers permitted. **Eurail** is valid only on S-Bahn. The **Tageskarte** (day pass, valid until midnight of the day of purchase) provides unlimited transportation on the S-Bahn, U-Bahn, streetcars, and buses; buy from machines in any station (€4.60, children €2.70).

Ride-sharing: Mitfahrzentrale, Baseler Str. 7 (☎23 64 44 or 23 64 45). Take a right on Baseler Str. at the side exit of the *Hauptbahnhof* (track 1) and walk 2 blocks. Arranges rides to Berlin (€29), Athens (€110), and everywhere in between. Open M-F 8am-6:30pm, Sa 8am-4pm, Su 10am-4pm.

✴ ⁷ ORIENTATION AND PRACTICAL INFORMATION

The *Hauptbahnhof* lies at the end of Frankfurt's red light district; from the station, the **Altstadt** is a 20min. walk down Kaiserstr. or Münchener Str. To the north, the commercial heart of Frankfurt lies along **Zeil**. Cafes, stores, and services cluster in **Bockenheim** (U6 or 7 to Bockenheimer Warte). Across the Main, **Sachsenhausen** draws pub-crawlers and museum-goers (U1, 2, or 3 to Schweizer Pl.).

Tourist Office: (☎21 23 88 00), in the *Hauptbahnhof*, sells the **Frankfurt Card** (1-day €6.15, 2-day €9.75), which allows unlimited travel on all trains and buses and gives 50% off admission to many sights. Open M-F 8am-9pm, Sa-Su and holidays 9am-6pm.

Currency Exchange: In various airport booths (open daily 7:30am-9pm) or the Hauptbahnhof (open daily 7:30am-9pm). Better rates are available at any bank.

Laundromat: Schnell & Sauber, Wallstr. 8, near the hostel in Sachsenhausen. Wash €3, dry €0.50 per 15min. Soap included. Open M-Sa 6am-11pm.

Emergency: Police: ☎110. **Fire and Ambulance:** ☎112.

Pharmacy: (☎23 30 47), in the Einkaufs passage of the train station. Open M-F 6:30am-9pm, Sa 8am-9pm, Su and holidays 9am-8pm. **Emergencies** ☎192 92.

Internet Access: Alpha, in the *Hauptbahnhof*'s gambling salon, past track 24. €0.50 per 6min. Open M-Sa 6am-12:45am, Su 8am-12:45am. Several Internet cafes are on Elisabethenstr. near the hostel; the cheapest is **Telewave,** Elisabethenstr. 45-47. €1.50 per hr. **CybeRyder Internet Café,** Töngesgasse 31, charges €2.50 per 30min. Open M-Th 9am-11pm, F-Sa 9am-midnight, Su 11am-11pm.

Post Office: Main branch, Zeil 90 (☎13 81 26 21), inside the Karstadt department store. U- or S-Bahn to *Hauptwache.* Open M-Sa 9:30am-8pm. Address mail to be held: Firstname SURNAME, *Postlagernde Briefe,* Hauptpostamt, **60313** Frankfurt, GERMANY.

🏠 ACCOMMODATIONS

🛏 **Hotel-Pension Bruns,** Mendelssohnstr. 42, 2nd fl. (☎74 88 96; www.brunsgallus-hotel.de). Take U4 to Festhalle. In the wealthy Westend area near the *Uni,* Bruns has nine Victorian rooms with high ceilings, hardwood floors, cable TV, and breakfast in bed. Ring the bell. Showers €1.50. Doubles €46-52; triples €63. ❹

Haus der Jugend (HI), Deutschherrnufer 12 (☎610 01 50). Take bus #46 from the main train station to Frankensteiner Pl. Turn left along the river. In the museum district. Popular with student groups. Breakfast included. Reception 24hr. Check-in after 1pm. Check-out 9:30am. Curfew 2am. Reservations by phone recommended. Dorms begin at €20, under-27 €15. ❷

GERMANY

Frankfurt

♠ ACCOMMODATIONS
Fennis Fuchser, **8**
Haus der Jugend (HI), **11**
Hotel-Pension Backer, **1**
Hotel-Pension Bruns, **4**
Hotel-Pension Gölz, **3**

● FOOD
Adolf Wagner, **12**
Capolinea, **10**
Klaane Sachsenhäuser, **13**
Mensa, **2**

★ NIGHTLIFE
Blue Angel, **6**
Der Jazzkeller, **5**
Odeon, **7**
U Bar, **9**

⑤ S-Bahn (surface rail)
Ⓤ U-Bahn (subway)

Universität
Naturmuseum

BEETHOVEN-PL.
Schubertstr.
Corneliusstr.
Arndtstr.
Beethovenstr.
Mendelssohnstr.
Schumannstr.

LUDWIG-ERHARD-ANLAGE
Senkenberger Anlage

TO PALMENGARTEN
& STA TRAVEL (250m)

WESTEND
Bockenheimer Landstr.
Liebigstr.
Lindenstr.
Kettenhofweg
Zimmerweg
Niedstr.

Rothschild-Park
Reuterweg
Bockenheimer Anl.
Oberlindau
Eschenhmr. Landstr.
Querstr.
Blumenstr.
Oederweg
Gärtnerweg
Feldstr.
Frankfurtstr.
Anlage
Leerbachstr.
Hochstr.

ESCHENHEIMER TOR
Stiftstr.
Bleichstr.
Vilbelerstr.

KONSTABLER WACHE
Zeil
Töngesg.
Albusstr.
Klingerstr.
Allerheiligenstr.
Seilerstr.
Battonnstr.
Rechneigrabenstr.
Fischerfeldstr.

Museum für Moderne Kunst
Dom
Schirn Kunst-halle

ALTE OPER
OPERNPLATZ
Große Bockenheimer Str.
Goethestr.
Gr. Bockenheimerstr.
Kleine Bockheimer Str.
Neue Rothofstr.
Junghofstr.

HAUPTWACHE
Goethe Haus
British Bookshop
Alte Oper

TAUNUSANLAGE
Neue Mainzerstr.
Taunusstr.
Taunustor
Gallusanl.
Gr. Gallusstr.
Weißfrauenstr.
Münzg.
Seckb.

GOETHEPL.
AmEx

Paulskirche
Katharinenkirche
Liebfrauenkirche
Römer
RÖMERBERG
Nikolaikirche
Historisches Museum

WILLY-BRANDT-PL.
Die Komödie
Städtische Bühnen
Untermainanl.

Deutsches Filmmuseum
Architektur-museum
Museum der Weltkulturen
Deutsches Museum für Kommunikation
Schweizerstr.
Museum für Angewandte Kunst
Städel

Main

Eiserner Steg
Untermain Brücke
Holbeinsteg

SACHSENHAUSEN
Gartenstr.
Walter-Kolb-Str.
Schulstr.
Schifferstr.
Dreieichstr.
Metzlerstr.
Brückenstr.
Elisabethenstr.
Wallstr.
Laundromat

Museumsufer
Wilhelm-Leuschner-Str.
Windmühlstr.
Wiesenhüttenstr.
Gutleutstr.
Münchener Str.
Kaiserstr.

PLATZ DER REPUBLIK
Düsseldorfer Str.
Savignystr.
Bettinastr.
Rheinstr.
Erlenstr.
Mainzer Landstr.
Baseler Str.
Karlsruher Str.
Stuttgarter Str.
Ludwigstr.
Rudolfstr.
Mannheimer Str.
Hafenstr.
Werftstr.
Heidelberger Str.
Pfafenstr.

HAUPTBHF.
Hauptbahnhof
Am Hauptbahnhof
Bike Rental

FESTHALLE

Main

Tiergarten
Windeckstr.
Zoologischer Garten
ALFRED-BREHM-PLATZ
ZOO
OSTENDSTR.
Uhlandstr.
Grüne Str.
Am Tiergarten
Pfingstweid
Hanauer Landstr.
Oskar-von-Miller-Str.
Sonnemannstr.
Ostendstr.
Deutschherrnufer

Friedberger Anlage
Seilerstr.
Seehofstr.
Supermarket

Obermainanlage
Langestr.
Mainstr.
Schöne Aussicht
Bornheimer Landwehr

Struwelpeter Museum
Schöne Aussicht
Sachsenhäuser Ufer
Deutschherrnufer
FRANKENSTEINER PLATZ

Flösser Brücke
Ignatz Bubis Brücke
Alte Brücke

Karmeliter Kloster
Historisches Museum

FRANKFURT AM MAIN

TO ⑤ & LIEBIGHAUS

200 yards
200 meters

Hotel-Pension Backer, Mendelssohnstr. 92 (☎ 74 79 92). Take U6 or 7 to Westend. Cheap, clean, and near the city center. Breakfast included. If you're on a tight budget, ask for room #1 (€10). Singles €25; doubles €40; triples €45. ❸

Hotel-Pension Gölz, Beethovenstr. 44 (☎ 74 67 35). Take U6 or 7 to *Westend*. Quiet and beautiful rooms with phone, couch, and TV. Big breakfast included. Singles €50; doubles €81; triples €96. ❹

Fennis Fuchser, Mainzer Landstr. 95 (☎ 25 38 55). From the train station, take a left on Düsseldorfer Str., walk 2 blocks, and take a left onto Mainzer Landstr. A convenient place to crash. Enter through the restaurant downstairs. Special rates for stays longer than one night. Singles €20; doubles €40; triples €60. ❸

🅵 FOOD

The cheapest meals surround the university in **Bockenheim** and nearby parts of Westend, and many of the pubs in **Sachsenhausen** serve food at a decent price. Just a few blocks from the youth hostel is a fully stocked **HL Markt,** Dreieichstr. 56 (open M-F 8am-8pm, Sa 8am-4pm); an **Alim Markt,** Münchener Str. 37, is close to the *Hauptbahnhof* (open M-F 8:30am-7:30pm, Su 8am-2pm). **Kleinmarkthalle,** on Haseng. between Berliner Str. and Töngesg., is a three-story warehouse with bakeries, butchers, and fruit and vegetable stands. Cutthroat competition pushes prices way down. (Open M-F 7:30am-6pm, Sa 7:30am-4pm.)

Capolinea, Ziegelgasse 5. The chef *is* the menu: He creates fresh Italian pastas or bruschetta (€8-10) as you like it. Open M-Sa 2pm-1am, Su 6pm-1am. ❸

Mensa, at the university. Take U6 or 7 to Bockenheimer Warte. Follow signs for Palmengarten Universität, then use the exit labeled "Mensa." Go left right before the STA office. It's inside the courtyard to your right. 2 floors of cheap, state-run, cafeteria food. Open M-F 11am-6:30pm. ❶

Klaane Sachsenhäuser, Neuer Wallstr. 11. Let the 5th generation of the Wagner family feed you homemade Ebbelwei (€1.40) and Frankfurt specialties (€7-15). Open M-Sa 4pm-midnight. ❸

Adolf Wagner, Schweizer Str. 71. Sauce-soaked German dishes (€5-17) and mugs of *Äpfelwein* (€1.50 per 0.3L) keep the patrons of this famous corner of old-world Frankfurt jolly and rowdy. Open daily 11am-midnight. ❸

🅶 SIGHTS

Much of Frankfurt's historic splendor lives on only in memories and in reconstructed monuments, since Allied bombing left everything but the cathedral completely destroyed. If you plan on visiting a lot of museums, pick up a **Frankfurt Card,** or visit on Wednesdays, when most museums are free.

🅡ÖMERBERG. Any voyage through Frankfurt should begin in this central area of the *Altstadt,* among the half-timbered homes and medieval-looking fountains that grace most postcards of the city. To celebrate the 13 coronations of German emperors that were held in the city, the statue of Justice in the center of the square once spouted wine. Unfortunately, she has since sobered up. Across from the Römerberg, the **Paulskirche** was the site of the 19th-century attempt at a liberal government over a united Germany; it still holds a memorial to the trials of German democracy. *(Open daily 10am-5pm. Free.)* At the west end of Römerberg, the gables of **Römer** have marked Frankfurt's city hall since 1405. The Kaisersaal, upstairs, is an imperial banquet hall adorned with portraits of the 52 German emperors from Charlemagne to Franz II. *(Entrance from Limpurgergasse. Open daily 10am-1pm and 2-5pm. €2.)* Lone survivor of the WWII bombings, the red sandstone Gothic **Dom** has several elaborate altarpieces. The electors of the Holy Roman Empire selected and coronated the emperors here. *(Open Su and Sa 11am-5pm, Tu-F 10am-5pm. €2, students €1.)*

▨ STÄDEL. One of the few museums to have equally important paintings from nearly every period in the Western tradition. If Beckmann and Kandinsky paintings aren't your thing, the collections of Old Masters and Impressionists are even more extensive. *(Schaumainkai 63, between Dürerstr. and Holbeinstr. Open Su, Tu and F-Sa 10am-5pm, W-Th 10am-8pm. €6, students €5. Tu free.)*

MUSEUM FÜR MODERNE KUNST. The triangular museum (dubbed the "slice of cake") displays an array of modern art by Roy Lichtenstein, Jasper Johns, and emerging talents. *(Domstr. 10. Open Su, Tu and Th-Sa 10am-5pm; W 10am-8pm. €5, students €2.50. W free.)*

GOETHEHAUS. In Frankfurt, the master was born, found his first love (a girl named Gretchen, said to be the inspiration for Margarete in *Faust*), and penned some of his best-known works here, including *The Sorrows of Young Werther*. Unless you're a huge Goethe fan, the house is little more than a typical upper-crust, 18th-century home. *(Großer Hirschgraben 23, a few blocks northwest of the Römer. Open Apr.-Sept. M-F 9am-6pm, Sa-Su 10am-4pm; Oct.-Mar. M-F 9am-4pm, Sa-Su 10am-4pm. English tours must be arranged in advance. €5, students €2.50, family €8.)*

🎵 📷 ENTERTAINMENT AND NIGHTLIFE

Frankfurt's theater and opera are first-rate. The **Alte Oper,** Opernpl. (☎ 134 04 00; U6 or 7 to Alte Oper), offers a full range of classical music. The **Städtische Bühne,** Untermainanlage 11 (☎ 21 23 71 33; U1, 2, 3, or 4 to *Willy-Brandt-Pl.*), hosts ballets and operas. The **English Theatre,** Kaiserstr. 52 (☎ 24 23 16 20) puts on comedies and musicals in English. Shows and schedules are listed in *Fritz* and *Strandgut* (free). For info on tickets at most venues, call **Frankfurt Ticket** (☎ 134 04 00).

Frankfurt has a number of thriving discos and prominent techno DJs, mostly in the commercial district between **Zeil** and **Bleichstraße.** Wear something dressier than jeans if you plan to get past the selective bouncers. For more drinks and less dancing, head to the **Alt-Sachsenhausen** district between Brückenstr. and Dreieichstr., home to a huge number of rowdy pubs and taverns. The complex of cobblestoned streets centering on **Grosse** and **Kleine Rittergaße** teems with cafes, bars, restaurants, and Irish pubs.

▨ U Bar, on Roßmarkt. The old subway station features Frankfurt's best DJs. Cover €6-15. Open M-F 10pm-10am, Sa-Su 10pm-6am.

Der Jazzkeller, Kleine Bockenheimer Str. 18a (☎ 28 85 37, www.jazzkeller.com). An appreciative crowd swings and swigs in this grotto-like mainstay of the jazz scene. Dance mix F. Jazz jam session W. Cover €4-15. Open Su from 8pm, W-Sa from 9pm.

Odeon, Seilerstr. 34. Students dance to house, soul, and hip hop on 2 floors. Cover €5, students €3; Th drinks half-price until midnight and free buffet from 11:30pm. Open Tu-Sa from 10pm.

Blue Angel, Brönnerstr. 17. A Frankfurt institution and one of the liveliest gay men's clubs around. Ring the bell to get in. Cover €5. W and Su free. Open daily 11pm-4am.

GERMANY

SOUTHWEST GERMANY

The Rhine and Mosel river valleys are a feast as much for the eyes as the mouth—the Mosel curls downstream to the Rhine Gorge, a soft shore of castle-backed hills, while dozens of vineyards provide Germany's best wines. Just a bit farther south, the hinterlands of the Black Forest contrast with its modern cities.

RHINE VALLEY (RHEINTAL)

The Rhine River runs from Switzerland to the North Sea, but in the popular imagination it exists only in the 80km Rhine Valley, a region prominent in historical legends, sailors' nightmares, and poets' dreams. The river flows north from Mainz (easily accessible from Frankfurt) through Bacharach and Koblenz to Bonn.

▐ TRANSPORTATION

Two different **train** lines (one on each bank) traverse the Rheintal; the line on the west bank stays closer to the water and provides superior views. Though full of tourists, **boats** are probably the best way to see the sights; the **Köln-Düsseldorfer (KD) Line** covers the Mainz-Koblenz stretch four times per day in summer.

MAINZ. Once the greatest Catholic diocese north of the Alps, Mainz's colossal sandstone **Martinsdom** stands as a memorial to its former ecclesiastic power. (Open Mar.-Oct. Su 1-3pm and 4-6pm, Tu-F 9am-6pm, Sa 9am-2pm; Nov.-Feb. M-F 9am-5pm, Sa 9am-4pm, Su 12:45-3pm and 4-5pm. Free.) The Gothic **Stephanskirche**, south of the Dom, holds stunning stained-glass windows created by artist Marc Chagall. (Stephansberg. Open daily 10am-noon and 2-5pm. Free.) Johannes Gutenberg, the father of movable type, is immortalized at the **Gutenberg-Museum**, which contains a replica of his original press. (Liebfrauenpl. 5, across from the Dom. Open Su 11am-3pm, Tu-Sa 9am-5pm. €3, students €1.50.)

Trains run to: Frankfurt (30min., €6); Heidelberg (1hr., €17); and Koblenz (1hr., €17). **KD ferries** (☎06131 23 28 00) depart from the wharves on the other side of the *Rathaus*. The **tourist office** arranges **tours** (2hr.; July-Aug. daily 2pm, May and Oct. W and F-Sa 2pm; €6) and gives free maps. (☎06131 28 62 10. Open M-F 9am-6pm, Sa 10am-3pm.) To reach the **Jugendgästehaus (HI) ②**, Otto-Brunfels-Schneise 4, take bus #62 (dir.: Weisenau), 63 (dir.: Laubenheim), or 92 (dir.: Ginsheim) to Viktorstift/Jugendherberge and follow the signs. All rooms are clean and come with a private bath. (☎06131 853 32. Breakfast included. Reception daily 7am-10pm. Dorms €17; doubles €44.) On the edge of the *Altstadt*, **Der Eisgrub-Bräu ②**, Weißliliengaße 1a, serves breakfast (€2.90), lunch buffets (€5.10), and its own house beer. (Open Su-Th 9am-1pm, F-Sa 9am-2pm.) For groceries, try **Super 2000**, Am Brand 41, under the Sinn-Leffers department store. (Open M-F 9:30am-8pm, Sa 9am-4pm). **Postal Code:** 55001.

BACHARACH. Bacharach ("Alter of Bacchus") lives up to its name, with *Weinkeller* and *Weinstuben* (wine cellars and pubs) tucked between every other half-timbered house. Try some of the Rhine's best wines and cheeses at **Die Weinstube**, Oberstr. 63. (Open daily from noon.) Nearby is the 14th-century **Wernerkapelle**, the remains of a red sandstone chapel that took 140 years to build but only a few hours to destroy during the Palatinate War of Succession in 1689. The **tourist office**, Oberstr. 45, and the *Rathaus* share a building at one end of the town center. (☎91 93 03. Open Apr.-Oct. M-F 9am-5pm, Sa 10am-4pm; Nov.-Mar. M-F 9am-noon.) Hostels get no better than ▨**Jugendherberge Stahleck (HI) ②**, a gorgeous 12th-century castle that provides a panoramic view of the Rhine Valley. The steep 15min. hike to the hostel is worth every step. Call ahead; they're usually full by 6pm. Make a right out of the station pathway, turn left at the Peterskirche, and take any of the marked paths leading up the hill. (☎ 12 66. Breakfast included. Curfew 10pm. Dorms €14.20; doubles €36.) At ◼**Café Restaurant Rusticana ❸**, Oberstr. 40, a lovely German couple serves up three-course meals (€6-11) and lively conversation. (Open May-Oct. M-W and F-Su 11:30am-9:30pm.) **Postal Code:** 55422.

LORELEI CLIFFS AND CASTLES. Though sailors were once lured to these cliffs by the infamous Lorelei maiden, her hypnotic song is now superfluous; today, hordes of travelers are seduced by scenery alone. The charming towns of **St. Goarshausen** and **St. Goar**, on either side of the Rhine, host the spectacular **Rhein in Flammen** fireworks celebration at the end of every summer (September 19, 2004). St. Goarshausen, on the east bank, provides access by foot to the Lorelei statue and the cliffs. Directly above the town, the fierce **Burg Katz** (Cat Castle) eternally stalks its prey, the smaller **Burg Maus** (Mouse Castle). Burg Maus offers daily falconry demonstrations at 11am and 2:30pm; call ☎76 69 for info or visit St. Goarshausen's **tourist office**, Bahnhofstr. 8. (☎(06771) 76 69. Open Su-M and Sa 9:30am-noon and M, Th and F 2-4pm.) **Trains** run to St. Goarshausen from Cologne (1hr., €18) and Mainz (1hr., €8). The "Lorelei V" **ferry** (M-F 6am-11pm, Sa-Su from 7am; €1, round-trip €1.50) crosses the river to **St.Goar**, which has a spectacular view. St. Goar's **tourist office**, Heerstr. 6, is in the pedestrian zone. (☎(06741) 333. Open M-F 8am-12:30pm and 2-5pm, Sa 10am-noon.) To reach **Jugendheim Loreley ❷**, on the St. Goarshausen side of the Rhine, walk from the cliffs past the parking gate down the road a few hundred meters and turn left. (☎(06771) 26 19. Breakfast included. Curfew 10pm. Dorms €16.) **Postal Code:** 56329.

KOBLENZ
☎**0261**

Koblenz (pop. 108,000) has long been a strategic hotspot; in the 2000 years since its birth, the city has hosted every empire seeking to conquer Europe. The city centers around the **Deutsches Eck** (German Corner), a peninsula at the confluence of the Rhine and Mosel rivers that purportedly witnessed the birth of the German nation in 1216. The **Mahnmal der Deutschen Einheit** (Monument to German Unity) to the right is a tribute to Kaiser Wilhelm I. The ◼**Museum Ludwig im Deutschherrenhaus,** Danziger Freiheit 1, behind the *Mahnmal*, features contemporary French art. (Open Su 11am-6pm, Tu-Sa 10:30am-5pm. €2.50, students €1.50.) Head across the river to the **Festung Ehrenbreitstein**, a fortress at the highest point in the city. Today, it's a youth hostel. (Non-hostel guests €1.05, students €0.60. Tours €2.10.)

Trains run to: Bonn (30min., 4 per hr, €8); Cologne (1hr., 4 per hr., €13.50); Frankfurt (2hr., 1-2 per hr., €17); Mainz (1hr., 3 per hr., €13.50); and Trier (2hr., 1-2 per hr., €16). Directly across from the station is the **tourist office**, Bahnhofpl. 7. (☎30 38 80. Open May-Oct. M-F 9am-7pm, Sa-Su 10am-7pm; Nov.-Apr. M-F 9am-6pm, Sa-Su 10am-6pm.) The best value in town is **Hotel Jan van Werth ❸**, Van-Werth-Str. 9, a classy, family-run, English-speaking establishment. From the station, walk up Bahnhofstr. to the market district and take a right on Van-Werth-Str. (☎365 00. Breakfast included. Reception daily 6:30am-10pm. Singles from €23, with bath €41; doubles from €53/70; triples €60.) **Jugendherberge Koblenz (HI) ❷**, within the fortress, offers breathtaking views of the Rhine and Mosel. Take bus #9 from the stop by the train station on Löhrstr. to *Charlottenstr.* Then take the chairlift up (Mar.-Sept. daily 9am-5:50pm, round-trip €6), or continue along the Rhine side of the mountain on the main road, following the DJH signs, and take the footpath up. (☎97 28 70. Breakfast included. Reception daily 7:15am-10pm. Curfew 11:30pm. Dorms €16; doubles €37.) **Ferries** (€1) cross the Mosel to **Campingplatz Rhein-Mosel**

GERMANY

❶, Am Neuendorfer Eck. (☎827 19. Reception daily 8am-10pm. Open Apr.-Oct. 15. €4 per person, €2.50 per site.) **Marktstübchen** ❷, Am Markt 220, serves authentic German food at budget prices. (Open Su-Tu and Th 11am-midnight, W 11am-2pm, F 4pm-1am, Sa 11am-1am.) **Postal Code:** 65068.

TRIER ☎0651

The oldest town in Germany, Trier (pop. 100,000) has weathered over two millennia in the Mosel Valley. Founded by the Romans, Trier reached its zenith in the 4th century as the capital of the Western Roman Empire and a center for Christianity. A one-day **combination ticket** (€6.20, students €3.10) provides access to all the city's Roman monuments. The most impressive is the massive 2nd-century ▊**Porta Nigra** (Black Gate), one of the best preserved city gates of the ancient world. (Open Apr.-Sept. daily 9am-6pm; Oct.-Mar. 9am-5pm. €2.10, students €1.60.) The nearby **Dom** shelters the *Tunica Christi* (Holy Robe of Christ) and the tombs of many archbishops. (Open Apr.-Oct. daily 6:30am-6pm; Nov.-Mar. 6:30am-5:30pm. Free.) The enormous **Basilika** was originally the location of Emperor Constantine's throne room. (Open M-Sa 10am-6pm, Su noon-6pm. Free.) Near the southeast corner of the city walls are the 4th-century **Kaiserthermen** (Emperor's baths), most memorable for the gloomy underground passages remaining from their ancient sewer network—avoid contact with the walls. (Open daily 9am-5pm. €2.15, students €1.60.) A 10min. walk uphill along Olewiger Str. brings you to the **amphitheater;** once the site of bloody gladiatorial games, it's now a stage for city productions. (Open daily 9am-5pm. €2.10, students €1.60.)

Trains run to Koblenz (1¾hr., 2 per hr., €16). From the station, walk down Theodor-Haus-Allee or Christophstr. to reach the **tourist office,** in the shadow of the Porta Nigra. (☎97 80 80. Open Apr.-Oct. M-Sa 9am-6pm, Su 10am-3pm; Nov.-Dec. and Mar. M-Sa 9am-6pm, Su 10am-1pm; Jan.-Feb. M-F 10am-5pm, Sa 10am-1pm. English city tours Sa 1:30pm. €6, students €5.) The **Jugendhotel/ Jugendgästehaus Kolpinghaus** ❸, Dietrichstr. 42, one block off the Hauptmarkt, is in an unbeatable location. (☎97 52 50. Breakfast included. Sheets €2.50. Dorms €15; singles €22; doubles €42.) Squeezed into the passageway by Miss Maple's, ▊**Astarix** ❸, Karl-Marx-Str. 11, serves excellent tortellini and pizza from €4. (Open M-Th 11:30am-1am, F-Sa 11:30am-2am, Su 2pm-1am.) The **Plus supermarket**, Brotstr. 54, is near the Hauptmarkt. (Open M-F 8:30am-8pm, Sa 8:30am-4pm.) **Postal Code:** 54292.

HEIDELBERG ☎06221

Sun-drenched Heidelberg (pop. 141,000) and its crumbling castle once lured writers and artists, including Twain, Goethe, and Hugo. Today, legions of camera-toting fannypackers fill the length of Hauptstr., where postcards and T-shirts sell like hotcakes and every sign is posted in four languages. But even mass tourism can't mar the experience of Heidelberg's beautiful hillside setting, Germany's oldest university, and its enviable nightlife.

▐ TRANSPORTATION

Trains run to: Frankfurt (50min., 2 per hr., €13) and Stuttgart (40min., 1 per hr., €16); other trains run regularly to towns in the Neckar Valley. On Heidelberg's **public transportation** system, single-ride tickets cost €2; day passes (€5) are available from the tourist office. The Rhein-Neckar-Fahrgastschifffahrt (☎201 81), in front of the *Kongresshaus*, runs **ferries** all over Germany and provides round-trip Neckar cruises to **Neckarsteinach** (3hr., Easter-Oct. 9:30am-3:30pm, €9.50).

⊞🛈 ORIENTATION AND PRACTICAL INFORMATION

Most of Heidelberg's attractions are in the eastern part of the city, along the south bank of the Neckar. From the train station, take any bus or streetcar to Bismarckpl., then walk east down **Hauptstraße**, the city's spine, to the **Altstadt**. The **tourist office**, in front of the station, books rooms for a €2.50 fee and a small deposit. (☎13 88 121. Open Apr.-Oct. M-Sa 9am-7pm, Su 10am-6pm; Nov.-Mar. M-Sa 9am-6pm.) They also sell the 2-day **Heidelberg Card**, which includes unlimited public transit and admission to most sights (€12). Check your email at **Mode Bredl**, Hauptstr. 90, near Bismarckpl. (€3 per 30min. Open M-F 10am-7pm, Sa 10am-6pm.) The **post office** is at Sofienstr. 8-10. (Open M-F 9am-6:30pm, Sa 9:30am-1pm.) **Postal Code:** 69155.

🛏🍴 ACCOMMODATIONS AND FOOD

In summer, reserve rooms ahead or arrive early in the day to spare yourself a headache. To reach the **Jugendherberge (HI) ❷**, Tiergartenstr. 5, take bus #33 (dir.: Zoo-Sportzentrum). Next to the Heidelberg Zoo, one of the biggest in Europe, this hostel also teems with wildlife—schoolchildren. The rooms are large and the basement is a pub. (☎65 11 90. Breakfast and sheets included. Reception daily until 11:30pm. Lockout 9am-1pm. Curfew 11:30pm; stragglers admitted every ½hr. until 2am. Reserve at least a week ahead. Dorms €18, under-27 €15. HI members only.) For rooms with more personality and privacy, head to **Pension Jeske ❸**, Mittelbadgasse 2, in the *Altstadt*. Take bus #33 (dir: Ziegelhausen) to *Rathaus/Kornmarkt*. (☎237 33. Doubles €50, with bath €60; triples €60/90; quints €100. Cash only). At **Hotel-Pension Elite ❹**, Bunsenstr. 15, all rooms have high ceilings, bath, and TV. From the train station, take streetcar #1 to *Poststr*. (☎257 34. Breakfast included. *Let's Go* discounted rates: singles €51; doubles €61; triples €72; quads €83.)

Most of the restaurants on and around Hauptstr. are expensive but the *Imbiße* (fast food stands) are reasonably priced. Just outside this central area, historic student pubs offer good values as well. To reach the student **Mensa ❶**, in the stone fortress on Marstallstr., take bus #35 to *Marstallstr*. You'll find cheap cafeteria fare. (€4, with student ID €2; €1.50 plate deposit; CampusCard required for lunch. Open M-F 11:30am-10pm.) The mood at **Hemingway's Bar-Café-Meeting Point ❷**, Fahrtg. 1, is embodied in the "Ernie" (€5)—a dessert consisting of a shot of brandy and a cigar. (Lunch menu €4.10. Open Su-Th 9am-1am, F-Sa 9am-3am.)

🔄 SIGHTS

▧**HEIDELBERGER SCHLOß.** The jewel in the crown of an already striking city, the castle stands careful watch over the armies (of tourists) that dare approach Heidelberg. Since 1329 it has housed the Prince Electors, whose statues decorate the facade in front of the entrance. Over a period of almost 400 years, the castle's residents commissioned their own distinctive additions, resulting in the conglomeration of styles you see today. The castle **wine cellar** houses the **Großer Faß**, the largest wine barrel ever made, which holds 221,726L. *(Grounds open daily 9am-6pm. €2.50, students €1.50. English tours every 15min. €3.50, students €2.50.)* The *Schloß* is accessible by the **Bergbahn**, one of Germany's oldest cable cars. *(Take bus #11 (dir.: Karlstor) to Bergbahn/Rathaus. Trams leave the parking lot next to the bus stop every 10min. Open 9am-8pm. Round-trip €3.50.)*

GERMANY

Heidelberg

♦ ACCOMMODATIONS
Jugendherberge (HI), **1**
Hotel-Pension Elite, **4**
Pension Jeske, **7**

● FOOD
Hemingway's, **5**
Mensa, **6**

★ NIGHTLIFE
Nachtschicht, **3**
Schwimmbad Musikclub, **2**
Zum Sepp'l, **8**

Karlstor

Wehrsteg

Am Hackteufel

Schlössertunnel

Heidelberger Schloß 🏛

Apothekenmuseum

Molkenkur

Molkenkurweg

TO KÖNIGSTUHL

BERGBAHN

Ziegelhäuser Landstr.

Schlangenweg

Philosophenweg

Philosophen Gärtchen

Neckar

Neuenheimer Landstr.

Karl-Theodor-Br. (Alte Brücke)

Brückentor

MARKT-PL.

Rathaus

KARLS-PL.

Schlossberg

Haspelg.

Untere Str.

Heiliggeist-Kirche

Haus zum Ritter

Zwingerstr.

Seminarstr.

Alte Universität

UNIVERSITÄTS-PL.

Sandg.

Univ. Bibliothek

Grabeng.

Peterskirche

Marstallstr.

Neckarstaden

Schiffg.

Kurpfälzisches Museum 🏛

Theaterstr.

Friedrichstr.

Langefriedstr.

Märzg.

Plöck

Friedrich-Ebert-Anlage

Bootsverleih Simon

Kongresshaus

Ziegelg.

Brunneng.

Hauptstr.

Akademiestr.

Fahrtg.

Familg.

Gaisbergtunnel

Sofienstr.

Bismarckstr.

BISMARCK-PL.

ADENAUERPL.

Laundromat

Gaisbergstr.

Rohrbacherstr.

Bunsenstr.

Bruckenstr.

Theodor-Heuss-Brücke

Uferstr.

Ladenburger Str.

Pesselstr.

Uferstr.

Neckar

Ernst-Walz-Brücke

Berlinerstr.

TO ← (1km) & 2 (1.5km)

Schumannstr.

Thibautstr.

Bergheimer Str.

Poststr.

Vangerowstr.

Bergheimer Str.

Alte Eppelheimer Str.

Kurfürstenanlage

Kurfürstenstr.

RÖMER-KREIS

Römerstr.

Römerstr.

Bahnhofstr.

Blumenstr.

Kaiserstr.

Ringstr.

Kurfürsten-Anlage

Mittermeierstr.

Hauptbahnhof

Häussestr.

Goethestr.

Landhausstr.

400 yards

400 meters

N

UNIVERSITÄT. Heidelberg is home to Germany's oldest and most prestigious university, established in 1386. More than 20 Nobel laureates have called the university home, and it was here that sociology became a legitimate academic subject. The **Museum der Universität Heidelberg** traces the university's long history in a building containing **Alte Aula**, Heidelberg's oldest auditorium. Before 1914, students were exempt from prosecution by civil authorities thanks to the principle of academic freedom; instead, the crimes of naughty youths were tried and punished by the faculty in the **Studentenkarzer** jail. *(Grabeng. 1. Open Apr.-Oct. M-Sa 10am-4pm; Nov.-Mar. Tu-F 10am-2pm. Museum and Studentenkarzer €2.50, students €2.)*

MARKTPLATZ. The center of the *Altstadt* is the cobblestoned *Marktplatz*, where accused witches and heretics were burned at the stake in the 15th century. Some of Heidelberg's oldest structures border the square: the 14th-century **Heiliggeist-kirche** (Church of the Holy Spirit) and the 16th-century **Haus Zum Ritter**, opposite the church. *(Church open M-Sa 11am-5pm, Su 1-5pm. Free. Church tower €0.50.)*

PHILOSOPHENWEG. A high path opposite the Neckar from the *Altstadt*, the Philosophenweg (Philosopher's Way) offers the best views of the city. On the top of Heiligenberg (Holy Mountain) lie the ruins of the 9th-century **St. Michael Basilika**, the 13th-century **Stefanskloster**, and an **amphitheater** built under Hitler in 1934 on the site of an ancient Celtic gathering place. *(To get to the path, take streetcar #1 or 3 to Tiefburg, or use the steep spur trail 10m west of the Karl-Theodor-Brücke.)*

■ NIGHTLIFE

Most popular nightspots fan out from the **Marktplatz**. On the Neckar side of the Heiliggeistkirche, **Unter Straße** boasts the most concentrated—and congested—collection of bars in the city. **Hauptstraße** also harbors a fair number of venues.

Nachtschicht, in Landfried-Komplex (☎43 85 50; www.nachtschicht.com). University students jam to a variety of music in a basement resembling an old factory. Cover €3.50; M and F students €1.50. Open M and Th-Sa 10pm-4am; W 10pm-3am.

Zum Sepp'l, Hauptstr. 213. This age-old student lair, accented by stained glass windows, hosts a loud crowd and piano player M-Tu and F-Sa. Open M-F 5:30pm-midnight, Sa-Su 11am-2:30pm and 5:30pm-1am.

Schwimmbad Musikclub, Tiergartenstr. 13. Convenient for hostelers, but a trek for others. Four levels of live music, dancing, and movies. Open W-Sa 8pm-3am.

⚡ DAYTRIP FROM HEIDELBERG: NECKARSTEINACH. Fourteen kilometers upstream from Heidelberg, Neckarsteinach is a fishing village made famous by its four picture perfect, nearly untouristed castles. The two westernmost castles stand in romantic ruin, while the two to the east are privately occupied and not open to visitors. All lie within 3km of one another along the north bank of the Neckar river and can be reached by foot via the **Burgenweg** (castle path). From the train station, turn right on Bahnhofstr., turn left on Hauptstr., and follow the bend in the road; a red stone cross marks the beginning of the *Schloßsteige* (Castle Stairs), a brick path leading upward to the Burgenweg. Fireworks light the sky above the town on the second Saturday after Pentecost in June and on the last Saturday in July for the **Vierburgenbeleuchtung** (four-castle lighting).

Trains connecting Heidelberg to Heilbronn run through the Neckar valley, a thickly-forested stretch running north through Bad Wimpfen, Burg Guttenberg, Hirschhorn am Neckar, and Neckarsteinach. Castles dot the hilltops of the valley and form part of the Burgenstraße (Castle Road), which stretches from Mannheim to Prague. Local **buses** also traverse the Neckar Valley; often these are faster than the infrequent trains. Schedules are posted at bus stops. The **tourist office,** Hauptstr. 15, has a list of **private rooms.** (☎06229 920 00. Open M-Tu and Th-F 8:30am-12:30pm and 2:30-6pm, W 8:30am-12:30pm, Sa 8:30am-1pm.) **Postal Code:** 69239.

STUTTGART

☎ **0711**

Forget about *Lederhosen*—Porsche, Daimler-Benz, and a host of other corporate thoroughbreds keep Stuttgart (pop. 587,000) speeding along in the fast lane. After almost complete destruction in WWII, Stuttgart was rebuilt in a thoroughly modern and uninspiring style. The city does have amazing **baths** (*Mineralbäder*), fueled by western Europe's most active mineral springs. **Mineralbad Leuze,** Am Leuzebad 2-6, has indoor and outdoor thermal pools. Take U1, or streetcar #2 to *Mineralbäder*. (☎216 42 10. Open daily 6am-9pm. 2hr. soak €6.40, students €4.80.) The superb ⬛**Staatsgallerie Stuttgart,** Konrad-Adenauer-Str. 30-32, houses an excellent collection of modern art in the new wing. (Open Su, Tu-W and F-Sa 10am-6pm; Th 10am-9pm. €4.50, students €3. W free.) The **Mercedes-Benz Museum,** Mercedesstr. 137, is a must for car-lovers. Take S1 to *Daimlerstadion.* (Open Su and Tu-Sa 9am-5pm. Free.)

Stuttgart has direct **trains** to most major German cities, including: Berlin (6hr., 2 per hr., €103); Frankfurt (1½hr., 2 per hr., €43); and Munich (2½-3½hr., 2-3 per hr., €36-43). The tourist office, **tips 'n' trips,** Lautenschlagerstr. 22, has **Internet** access (€3 per hr. W free) and info on the Stuttgart scene. (☎222 27 30. Open M-F noon-7pm, Sa 10am-2pm.) The **post office** is in the station. (Open M-F 8:30am-6pm, Sa 8:30am-12:30pm.) To reach the **Jugendherberge Stuttgart (HI) ❷,** Haußmannstr. 27, take streetcar #15 to *Eugenspl.* and go downhill on Kernerstr. (☎24 15 83. Breakfast included. Sheets €3.10. Reception 24hr. Lockout 9:30am-1pm. Dorms €16, under-26 €14.) **Hotel Espenlaub ❹,** Charlottenstr. 27, has pricey but well-equipped rooms. Take streetcar #15 or U5, 6, or 7 to *Olgaeck.* (☎21 09 10. Breakfast included. Singles €44, with bath €62; doubles €51/87; triples €74/98. MC/V.) The pedestrian zone between Pfarrstr. and Charlottenstr. has many reasonably priced restaurants, while Rotebühlpl. is filled with fast food joints. Nightlife clusters around Eberhardstr., Rotebühlpl., and Calwer Str. **Suite 212,** Theodor-Heuss-Str. 15, has DJs and videotechnique on weekends. (Open M-Th 11am-2am, F-Sa 11am-5am, Su 2pm-2am.) **Postal Code:** 70173.

BLACK FOREST (SCHWARZWALD)

The Black Forest owes its name to the eerie gloom that prevails under its evergreen canopy. Once inspiration for the Grimm Brothers' *Hansel and Gretel,* today the region lures hikers and skiers with more than just gingerbread.

▬ TRANSPORTATION

The gateway to the Black Forest is **Freiburg,** accessible by **train** from Stuttgart and Basel, Switzerland. Most visitors explore the area by bike, as public transportation is sparse. Rail lines encircle its perimeter, but only two **train** lines cut through the region. **Bus** service is more thorough, although slow and infrequent.

FREIBURG IM BREISGAU. Freiburg (pop. 208,000) may be the metropolis of the Schwarzwald, but it has yet to succumb to the hectic pace of city life. Its pride and joy is the majestic **Münster,** a stone cathedral with a 116m spire and a tower whose bell is the oldest in Germany. (Open M-Sa 9:30am-5pm, Su 1-5pm. Tower €1, students €0.50.) The surrounding hills brim with fantastic **hiking** trails; maps (€3.50-6) are available in the tourist office, and paths are clearly marked. **Mountain biking** trails also traverse the hills; look for signs with bicycles to guide you.

Trains run to Basel (1hr., 3 per hr., €9-16) and Stuttgart (2hr., every hr., €38). The **tourist office,** Rotteckring 14, two blocks down Eisenbahnstr. from the station, has maps and books *Privatenzimmer* (rooms in private homes); these are usually the

GERMANY

most affordable accommodations in Freiburg itself. (Open June-Sept. M-F 9:30am-8pm, Sa 9:30am-5pm, Su 10am-noon; Oct.-May M-F 9:30am-6pm, Sa 9:30am-2pm, Su 10am-noon.) To reach the **Jugendherberge (HI) ❷**, Kartäuserstr. 151, take bus #1 to *Lassbergstr.* Take a left and then a right onto Fritz-Geiges-Str., and follow the signs. (☎(0761) 676 56. Breakfast included. Dorms €22, under-27 €19; doubles €48.) The **Freiburger Markthalle ❷**, next to the Martinstor, is home to food-stands serving ethnic specialties for €3-7. (Open M-F 7am-7pm, Sa 7am-4pm.) **Brennessel ❸**, Eschholzstr. 17, behind the train station, stuffs patrons with everything from ostrich-steak to pancakes. (Open M-Sa 8am-1am, Su 5pm-1am.) **Postal Code:** 79098.

TRIBERG. The residents of touristy Triberg (pop. 5,000) brag about the **Gutacher Wasserfall,** the highest in Germany, a series of bright cascades tumbling over moss-covered rocks for 163m. It's more of a mountain stream than a waterfall, but the hike itself is idyllic. (Park open 9am-7pm. €1.50, students €1.20.) Nearby Scho-ach's claim to the world's two largest cuckoo clocks is less tenuous. The signs for **Wallfahrtskirche** lead to the small pilgrimage church, **Maria in der Tanne,** where the pious have, according to legend, been miraculously cured since the 17th century.

Trains run to Freiburg (2-2½hr., 1-2 per hr., €16-25). The **tourist office,** Luisen-str. 10, is on the ground floor of the *Kurhaus;* from the station, turn right and follow the signs, or take any bus to *Marktpl.* (☎(07722) 95 32 30. Open May-Sept. M-F 9am-5pm, Sa 10am-noon; Oct.-Apr. M-F 9am-5pm.)

CONSTANCE (KONSTANZ) ☎07531

Located on the **Bodensee** (Lake Constance), the charming city of Constance (pop. 79,000) has never been bombed; part of the city extends into Switzerland, and the Allies were leery of accidentally striking neutral territory. Now one of Germany's favorite vacation spots, its narrow streets wind around beautiful Baroque and Renaissance facades, gabled and turreted 19th-century houses gleam with a confident gentility along the river promenades, and a palpable jubilation fills the streets. The **Münster** has a 76m Gothic spire and a display of ancient religious objects, but it's being renovated through 2005. (Open M-F 10am-6pm, Sa-Su noon-5pm.) Wander down **Seestraße,** near the yacht harbor on the lake, or **Rheinsteig,** along the Rhine, for picturesque promenades. Constance boasts a number of **public beaches;** all are free and open May to Sept. **Freibad Horn** (bus #5), the largest and most crowded, sports a nude sunbathing section modestly enclosed by hedges.

Trains run from Constance to most cities in southern Germany. BSB **ferries** leave hourly from Constance for all ports around the lake. Buy tickets on board or in the building, Hafenstr. 6, behind the train station. (☎28 13 89. Open Apr.-Oct. daily 7:45am-6:35pm.) The friendly but tiny **tourist office,** Bahnhofspl. 13, to the right of the train station, provides free walking maps and finds rooms for a €2.50 fee. (☎13 30 30. Open Apr.-Oct. M-F 9am-6:30pm, Sa 9am-4pm, Su 10am-1pm; Nov.-Mar. M-F 9:30am-6pm.) In the center of town, **Pension Gretel ❸**, Zollernstr. 6-8, offers bright rooms. In summer, call at least a month ahead. (☎45 58 25. Breakfast included. Singles €29-36; doubles €49-64, with bath €59-74; triples €75-93; quads €87-113. Extra bed €18.) To reach the newly renovated **Jugendherberge Otto-Moericke-Turm (HI) ❷**, Zur Allmannshöhe 18, take bus #4 from the train station to *Jugendherberge;* turn back and head uphill on Zur All-maunshöhe. (☎322 60. Breakfast included. Sheets €3.10. Reception Apr.-Oct. daily 3-10pm; Nov.-Mar. 5-10pm. Lockout 9:30am-noon. Call ahead. Dorms €18, under-26 €15. HI members only.) Camp by the waterfront at **DKV-Campingplatz Bodensee ❶**, Fohren-bühlweg 45. Take bus #1 to *Staad* and walk for 10min. with the lake to your left. (☎330 57. Reception closed daily noon-2:30pm. Showers included. €4 per person, €4 per tent.) For groceries, head to the basement of the **Karstadt** department store, on August-inerpl. (Open M-F 9:30am-8pm, Sa 9am-4pm.) **Postal Code:** 78462.

BAVARIA (BAYERN)

Bavaria is the Germany of Teutonic myth, Wagnerian opera, and the Brothers Grimms' fairy tales. From the Baroque cities along the Danube to mad King Ludwig's castles high in the Alps, the region draws more tourists than any other part of the country. Most foreign notions of Germany are tied to this land of *Biergarten* and *Lederhosen*. Mostly rural, Catholic, and conservative, it contrasts sharply with the rest of the country. Local authorities still use Bavaria's proper name, *Freistaat Bayern*, and its traditions and dialect have been preserved. Residents have always been Bavarians first and Germans second.

MUNICH (MÜNCHEN) ☎089

The capital and cultural center of Bavaria, Munich (pop. 1,228,000) is a sprawling, relatively liberal metropolis in the midst of conservative southern Germany. World-class museums, handsome parks and architecture, a rambunctious arts scene, and an urbane population combine to create a city of astonishing vitality. *Müncheners* party zealously during *Fasching*, Germany's Mardi Gras (Jan. 7-Mar. 4, 2004), shop with abandon during the Christmas Market (Nov. 28-Dec. 24, 2004), and consume unfathomable quantities of beer during the legendary **Oktoberfest** (Sept. 19-Oct. 4, 2004).

▐ TRANSPORTATION

Flights: Flughafen München (☎97 52 13 13). S8 runs between the airport and the *Hauptbahnhof* (40min., every 10min., €8 or 8 stripes on the *Streifenkarte*).

Trains: Munich's **Hauptbahnhof** (☎22 33 12 56) is the transportation hub of southern Germany, with connections to: **Amsterdam** (9hr., every hr., €143); **Berlin** (8hr.; every hr.; €141, or €103 via Leipzig); **Cologne** (6hr., every hr., €101); **Frankfurt** (3½hr., every hr., €76); **Hamburg** (6hr., every hr., €138); **Paris** (10hr., 3 per day, €105); **Prague** (7hr., 2 per day, €60); **Salzburg** (1¾hr., every hr., €25); **Vienna** (5hr., every hr., €59); and **Zurich** (5hr., 4 per day, €61). For 24hr. schedules, fare info, and reservations (in German), call ☎(01805) 99 66 33. **EurAide**, in the station, provides free train info and sells train tickets. **Reisezentrum** info counters open daily 6am-10:30pm.

Public Transportation: MVV, Munich's public transport system, runs Su-Th 5am-12:30am, F-Sa 5am-2am. The S-Bahn to the airport starts running at 3:30am. Eurail, InterRail, and German railpasses are valid on the S-Bahn, but *not* on the U-Bahn, streetcars, or buses.

Tickets: Buy tickets at the blue vending machines and **validate them** in the blue boxes marked with an E before entering the platform. If you jump the fare (*schwarzfahren*), you risk a €30 fine.

Prices: Single ride tickets €2, valid for 3hr. **Kurzstrecke** (short trip) tickets are good for 2 stops on U or S, or 4 stops on a streetcar or bus (€1). A **Streifenkarte** (10-strip ticket; €9) can be used by more than 1 person. Cancel 2 strips per person for a normal ride, or 1 strip per person for a *Kurzstrecke*; beyond the city center, cancel 2 strips per additional zone. A **Single-Tageskarte** (single-day ticket) is valid for 1 day of unlimited travel until 6am the next day (€4.50). The **3-Day Pass** (€11) is also a great deal. Passes can be purchased at the **MVV office** behind tracks 31 and 32 in the *Hauptbahnhof*, or at any of the *Kartenautomats*. Ask at tourist offices about the **Munich Welcome Card** (1-day €6.50, 3-day €15.50), which gives public transportation and various other discounts.

Ride-Sharing: McShare Treffpunkt Zentrale, Klenzestr. 57b or Lämmerstr. 6 (☎194 40; www.mitfahrzentrale.de). Open daily 8am-8pm. At the same location, **Frauenmitfahrzentrale** arranges ride shares for women only. Open M-F 8am-8pm.

Hitchhiking: *Let's Go* does not recommend hitchhiking as a safe mode of transportation. Those looking to share rides scan the bulletin boards in the **Mensa**, Leopoldstr. 13. Otherwise, hitchers try *Autobahn* on-ramps; those who stand behind the blue sign with the white auto **may be fined.** Hitchhikers going to Salzburg take U1 or 2 to Karl-Preis-pl. Those heading to Nürnberg and Berlin take U6 to Studentenstadt and walk 500m to the Frankfurter Ring. Those heading to the Bodensee and Switzerland take U4 or 5 to Heimeranpl., then bus #33 to Siegenburger Str.

Taxis: Taxi-Zentrale (☎216 11 or 194 10) has large stands in front of the train station and every 5-10 blocks in the city center. Women can request a female driver.

Bike Rental: Radius Bikes (☎59 61 13), at the far end of the *Hauptbahnhof*, behind the lockers opposite tracks 30-36. €3 per hr., €14 per day. Deposit €50, passport, or credit card. 10% student, Eurail, and Munich Welcome Card discount. Open July-Aug. M-F 10am-6pm, Sa-Su 9am-8pm; May-Oct. daily 10am-6pm. **Aktiv-Rad,** Hans-Sachs-Str. 7 (☎26 65 06). U1 or 2 to Frauenhofer Str. €12-20 per day. Open M-F 10am-1pm and 2-6:30pm, Sa 10am-1pm.

☀ ORIENTATION

Munich's center is a circle split into four quarters by one horizontal and one vertical line. The east-west and north-south thoroughfares cross at Munich's epicenter, the **Marienplatz,** and connect the traffic rings at **Karlsplatz** (called **Stachus** by locals) in the west, **Isartorplatz** in the east, **Odeonsplatz** in the north, and **Sendlinger Tor** in the south. In the east beyond the Isartor, the **Isar River** flows north-south past the city center. The **Hauptbahnhof** (main train station) is just beyond Karlspl. to the west of the Ring. To get to Marienpl. from the station, use the main exit and head across Bahnhofpl.; keep going east through Karlspl., and Marienpl. will be straight ahead. Or, take any S-Bahn to Marienpl.

The **University** is north of Munich's center, next to the budget restaurants of the **Schwabing** district. East of Schwabing is the **English Garden;** west of Schwabing is the **Olympiapark.** South of town is the **Glockenbachviertel,** filled with all sorts of night hotspots, including many gay bars. The area around the train station is rather seedy, dominated by hotels and sex shops. Oktoberfest is held on the large, open **Theresienwiese,** southeast of the train station on the U4 and 5 lines.

▮ PRACTICAL INFORMATION

Several publications help visitors navigate Munich. The most comprehensive is the monthly English-language *Munich Found* (€3), available at newsstands and bookshops, which provides a list of services, events, and museums.

TOURIST, FINANCIAL, AND LOCAL SERVICES

▨ **EurAide** (☎59 38 89), along track 11 (room 3) of the *Hauptbahnhof*, near the Bayerstr. exit. Books train tickets for free, explains the public transport, and sells maps (€1) and tickets for English tours of Munich. Pick up the free brochure *Inside Track*. Open June-Sept. daily 7:45am-12:45pm and 2-6pm; May 7:45am-12:45pm and 2-4:30pm; Oct. 7:45am-12:45pm and 2-4pm; Nov.-Apr. 8am-noon and 1-4pm.

Main Tourist Office: (☎23 39 65 00), on the front (east) side of the train station, next to the SB-Markt on Bahnhofpl. Books rooms for free with a 10-15% deposit, sells English city maps (€0.30), and offers the **Munich Welcome Card.** Open M-Sa 9:30am-6:30pm, Su 10am-6pm. **Branch office** just inside the entrance to the Neues Rathaus on Marienpl. Open M-F 10am-8pm, Sa 10am-4pm.

Discover Bavaria (☎25 54 39 88), Hochorückenstr., near the rear entrance of the Hofbräuhaus. Helps find rooms for free, rents bikes, and dispenses coupons for a variety of activities. Also sells tickets for the hugely popular Mike's Bike Tours of Munich, Neuschwanstein, and Dachau. Open Apr.-Sept. daily 8:30am-9pm.

Consulates: Canada, Tal 29 (☎219 95 70). Open M-Th 9am-noon and 2-5pm, F 9am-noon and 2-3:30pm. **Ireland,** Dennigerstr. 15 (☎20 80 59 90). Open M-F 9am-noon. **South Africa,** Sendlinger-Tor-Pl. 5 (☎23 11 63 37). Open M-F 9am-noon. **UK,** Bürkleinstr. 10, 4th fl. (☎21 10 90). Open M-F 8:30am-noon and 1-3pm. **US,** Königinstr. 5 (☎288 80). Open M-F 8-11am.

Currency Exchange: ReiseBank, in front of the train station on Bahnhofpl. Open M-Sa 7:30am-7:15pm, Su 9:30am-4:45pm.

Bi-Gay-Lesbian Resources: Gay services information (☎260 30 56). **Lesbian information** (☎725 42 72). Phone staffed M and W 2:30-5pm, Tu 10:30am-1pm, Th 7-9pm. Also see **Gay and Lesbian Munich** (p. 502).

Laundromat: SB Waschcenter, Paul-Heyse-Str. 21, near the train station. Turn right on Bayerstr., then left on Paul-Heyse-Str. Wash €4, dry €0.60 per 10min. Open daily 7am-11pm. **Kingsgard Waschsalon,** Amalienstr. 61, near the university. Wash €3, dry €1.50. Open M-F 8am-6:30pm, Sa 9am-1pm.

EMERGENCY AND COMMUNICATIONS

Police: ☎110. **Ambulance** and **Fire:** ☎112. **Medical service:** ☎192 22.

Pharmacy: Bahnhofpl. 2 (☎59 41 19 or 59 81 19), on the corner outside the train station. Open M-F 8am-6:30pm, Sa 8am-2pm.

Internet Access: Easy Everything, on Bahnhofspl. next to the post office. Prices depend on demand (max. €3 per hr.). Open 24hr. **Internet Cafe,** Marienpl. 20, serves cocktails and food all night. €1 per 30min. Open 24hr.

Post Office: Bahnhofpl. The yellow building across the street from the main train station exit. Open M-F 7:30am-8pm, Sa 9am-4pm. **Postal Code:** 80335.

ACCOMMODATIONS AND CAMPING

Munich's accommodations usually fall into one of three categories: Seedy, expensive, or booked solid. During times like Oktoberfest, when prices usually jump 10-15%, only the latter exists. In summer, book a few weeks in advance or start calling before noon. At most of Munich's hostels you can check in all day, but try to start your search before 5pm. Don't even think of sleeping in any public area, including the *Hauptbahnhof;* police patrol all night long.

HOSTELS AND CAMPING

> **REMINDER.** HI-affiliated hostels in Bavaria generally do not admit guests over age 26 except in families or groups of adults with young children.

 Euro Youth Hotel, Senefelderstr. 5 (☎59 90 88 11). From the *Hauptbahnhof,* make a left on Bayerstr. and a right on Senefelderstr. Friendly and well-informed English-speaking staff. Breakfast buffet €4.90. Reception 24hr. Dorms €18; singles €45; doubles €48, with private shower and breakfast €72; triples €63; quads €84. ❷

4 You München, Hirtenstr. 18 (☎552 16 60), 200m from the *Hauptbahnhof.* Ecological youth hostel with restaurant and bar. Wheelchair accessible. Breakfast buffet €4.35. 12-bed dorms €17; 4-, 6-, or 8-bed dorms €21-29; singles €34; doubles €48. ❷

Jugendlager Kapuzinerhölzl ("The Tent"), In den Kirschen 30 (☎141 43 00). Streetcar #17 from the *Hauptbahnhof* (dir.: Amalienburgstr.) to *Botanischer Garten* (15min.). Follow the signs straight on Franz-Schrank-Str. and turn left at In den Kirschen. Sleep with 250 fellow campers under a big tent on a wooden floor. Laundry €2. Lockers €4. Internet €1 for 15min. Kitchen available. Reception 24hr. Reservations only for groups over 15, but rarely full. Open June-Aug. €8.50 gets you a foam pad, blankets (you can also use your sleeping bag), a shower, and breakfast. Actual beds €11. Camping available for €5.50 per campsite plus €5.50 per person. ❶

Jugendhotel Marienherberge, Goethestr. 9 (☎55 58 05), less than a block from the train station. **Open only to women.** Reduced prices for those under 26. Staffed by merry nuns, the rooms are spacious, cheery, and spotless. Breakfast included. Laundry €1.50. Reception daily 8am-midnight. Curfew midnight. 6-bed dorms €22, over-25 €27; singles €25/30; doubles €40/50; triples €60/75. ❸

Jugendherberge München Neuhausen (HI), Wendl-Dietrich-Str. 20. (☎13 11 56). U1 (dir.: Westfriedhof) to Rotkreuzpl. The most "central" of the HI hostels (3km from the city center). Free safes in the reception area. Bike rental available. Breakfast buffet and sheets included. Sit-down dinner €5. Key deposit €15. Reception 24hr. Check-in starts at 11:30am. Big co-ed dorm (37 beds) €18; 4- to 6-bed dorms €21; doubles €46. ❸

Campingplatz Thalkirchen, Zentralländstr. 49 (☎723 17 07). U1 or 2 to Sendlinger Tor, then U3 to Thalkirchen, and change to bus #57 (20min.). From the bus stop, cross the busy street on the left and take a right onto the footpath. The entrance is down the tree-lined path on the left. Well-run, crowded grounds with jogging and bike paths, TV lounge, groceries, and a restaurant. Showers €1. Laundry facilities (wash €4, dry €0.25 per 11min.). Open mid-Mar. to late Oct. €4.40 per person, €8 per tent. ❶

HOTELS AND PENSIONS

▨ **Hotel Helvetia,** Schillerstr. 6 (☎590 68 50), at the corner of Bahnhofspl. Just beyond the Vereinsbank, to the right as you exit the station. A friendly hotel with newly renovated rooms. Free Internet. Breakfast included. Laundry €6. Reception 24hr. Singles €30-35; doubles €40-55, with shower €50-65; triples €55-69; quads €72-90. ❸

▨ **Creatif Hotel,** Lammerstr. 6 (☎55 57 85). Take the Arnulfstr. exit out of the station, hang a quick right, turn left on Hirtenstr., then right on Lammerstr. Uniquely modern rooms, all with bath, telephone, and TV. Internet €1 per 30min. Reception 24hr. Singles €30-40; doubles €40-65. Extra bed €10. ❸

Pension am Kaiserplatz, Kaiserpl. 12 (☎34 91 90). U3 to Münchener Freiheit. Take the escalator to Herzogstr., then turn left; it's 3 blocks to Viktoriastr. Take a left at Viktoriastr.; it's at the end of the street on the right. A few blocks from nightlife central—a good location if you doubt your sense of direction after a couple of beers. Motherly owner offers elegant rooms, each one in its own style, from Victorian to modern. Breakfast included and served in-room. Reception 7am-8pm. Singles €31, with shower €47; doubles €53/57; triples €63/66; quads €84; quints €105; 6-bed rooms €126. ❸

Pension Locarno, Bahnhofspl. 5 (☎55 51 64). Cozy rooms, all with cable TV and phone. Reception daily 7:30am-5pm. Singles €38; doubles €57; triples €69; quads €81. ❸

Hotel Kurfplaz, Schwanthaler Str. 121 (☎540 98 60). Exit on Bayerstr. from the station, turn right and walk 5-6 blocks down Bayerstr., veer left onto Holzapfelstr., and make a right onto Schwanthaler Str. Or, take streetcar #18 or 19 to Holzapfelstr. and walk from there. TV, phone, and bath in all rooms. Breakfast included. Internet €3 per 30min. Reception 24hr. Singles from €50; doubles from €100. ❹

Hotel-Pension am Markt, Heiliggeiststr. 6 (☎22 50 14), smack dab in the city center, off the Viktualienmarkt. Take any S-Bahn to Marienpl., then walk past the Altes Rathaus and turn right down the little alley behind the Heiliggeist Church. Small but spotless rooms are wheelchair-accessible. Breakfast included. Reception (3rd fl.) daily 7am-9pm. Singles €38, with shower €66; doubles €68/87-92; triples €100/123. ❹

Pension Frank, Schellingstr. 24 (☎28 14 51). U3 or 6 to Universität. Take the Schellingstr. exit, then the 1st right onto Schellingstr. Rooms with balconies in a great location for cafe and bookstore aficionados. Breakfast included. Reception daily 7.30am-10pm. 3- to 6-bed dorms €25; singles €35-40; doubles €52-55. ❸

GERMANY

TO OLYMPISCHE PARK (3km)
& BMW MUSEUM (3km)

THERESIENSTR. U

TO ① (500m)

Theresienstr.

Neue
Pinakothek

Heßstr.

Gabelsbergerstr.

Enhuberstr.

Steinheilstr.

Luisenstr.

Arcisstr.

Alte
Pinakothek

Theresienstr.

Dachauer Str.

Schleißheimer Str.

Rottmanstr.

Volkstheater

Gabelsbergerstr.

Barer Str.

Pinakothek
der Moderne

Nyphenburgerstr.
TO SCHLOSS
NYMPHENBURG,
BOTANISHER
GARTEN (4.5km),
⑨ (2km),
& ⑩ (4.5km)

Cinema

STIGLMAIERPLATZ U

Brienerstr.

Augustenstr.

R.-Wagner-Str.

Hauptschule für
Musik und Theater

Lenbachhaus

Glyptothek

Markuskirche

Seidlstr.

Dachauer Str.

Karlstr.

KÖNIGSPL. U

KÖNIGSPL.

Luisenstr.

Meiserstr.

Antikensammlung

Obelisk

KAROLINENPLATZ

Amerika Haus

Prinz-Ludwig-Str.

Türkenstr.

Universitäts
Hospital

Brienerstr.

Oskar-von-Miller-Ring

Marsstr.

⑪ ⑫

Hirtenstr.

Sophienstr.

Alter
Botanischer
Garten

Barer Str.

Max-Joseph-Str.

Ottostr.

⑯ ☆☆⑰

MAXIMILIANS-
PLATZ

SALVATORPLATZ ⑲

Karld.-Faulhaber-Str.

TO ⑬ (250m) & ⑭ (4.5km)

Arnulfstr. ⑮

Elisenstr.

S HAUPTBHF.

Prielmayerstr.

Justizpalast

U
KARLSPL.

LENBACHPLATZ

Pacellistr.

Pranner-str.

PROMENADEPLATZ
S
AmEx

Bike
Rental

Hauptbahnhof

BAHNHOF-
PLATZ

Schützenstr.

Maxburgstr.

Löwen-grühe

Maffeistr.

$

℞

ⓘ

U HAUPTBHF.

KARLSPLATZ

KARLSPL. S

Neuhauser Str.

Michaelskirche

Frauenkirche

Weinstr.

Bayerstr.

TO ㉑ (500m)

Senefelderstr.

㉕

International
Phone World

Schlosserstr.

Adolf-Kolping Str.

Herzog Str.

Herzogspitalstr.

Herzog-
Wilhelm-
Str.

Eisenmannstr.

Altheimer Eck

Kaufingerstr.

FRAUEN-
PLATZ

ⓘ

Rosenstr.

U
MARIENPL. S

Peterskirche

㉔

㉓

Schwanthalerstr.

Deutsches
Theater

Sonnenstr.

Wilhelm-Str.

Jospehspitalstr.

Brunnstr.

Hackenstr.

Hotterstr.

Dultstr.

Rosental

Rindermarkt

Münchener
Stadtmuseum

TO ㉒ (250m)

Landwehrstr.

Sonnenstr.

Damen-
stiftstr.

Kreuzstr.

Asamkirche

Sendlinger-Str.

Schmidstr.

Hackenstr.

Oberanger

ST. JAKOBS
PLATZ

TO ㉘ (2km)

Goethestr.

Schillerstr.

Pettenkoferstr.

Sendlinger
Tor

Klosterhofstr.

Unterer Anger

Unterer Anger

Blumenstr.

Corneliusstr.

Nußbaumstr.

Lindwurmstr.

SENDLINGER
TOR U

Matthäus-
kirche

Blumenstr.

Kreuzstr.

Blumenstr.

Müllerstr.

Müllerstr.

TO THERESIENWIESE
(250m)

⊞

Thalkirchner Str.

Pestalozzistr.

Hans-Sachs-Str.

Staatstheater
Gärtnerplatz

Fraunhoferstr.

Klenzestr.

Jahnstr.

TO ㉞ (50m)

0   250 yards

0   250 meters

N

LG

TO ㉝ (5km)
& TIERPARK HELLABRUNN ZOO

⑥

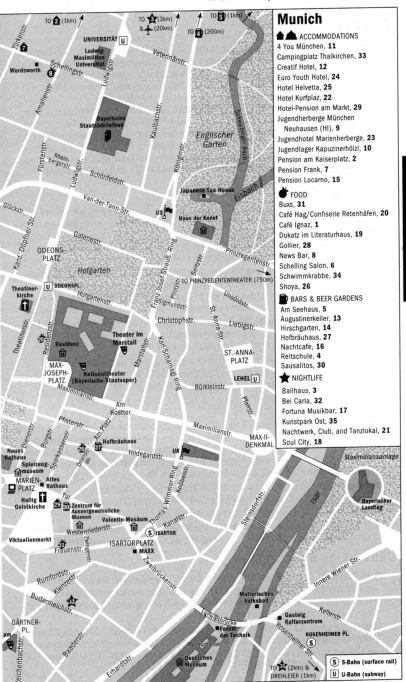

Munich

🏠🏠🔺 ACCOMMODATIONS
4 You München, **11**
Campingplatz Thalkirchen, **33**
Creatif Hotel, **12**
Euro Youth Hotel, **24**
Hotel Helvetia, **25**
Hotel Kurfplaz, **22**
Hotel-Pension am Markt, **29**
Jugendherberge München
  Neuhausen (HI), **9**
Jugendhotel Marienherberge, **23**
Jugendlager Kapuzinerhölzl, **10**
Pension am Kaiserplatz, **2**
Pension Frank, **7**
Pension Locarno, **15**

🍎 FOOD
Buxs, **31**
Café Hag/Confiserie Retenhäfen, **20**
Café Ignaz, **1**
Dukatz im Literaturhaus, **19**
Gollier, **28**
News Bar, **8**
Schelling Salon, **6**
Schwimmkrabbe, **34**
Shoya, **26**

🍺 BARS & BEER GARDENS
Am Seehaus, **5**
Augustinerkeller, **13**
Hirschgarten, **14**
Hofbräuhaus, **27**
Nachtcafe, **16**
Reitschule, **4**
Sausalitos, **30**

⭐ NIGHTLIFE
Ballhaus, **3**
Bei Carla, **32**
Fortuna Musikbar, **17**
Kunstpark Ost, **35**
Nachtwerk, Club, and Tanzlokal, **21**
Soul City, **18**

GERMANY

S-Bahn (surface rail)
U-Bahn (subway)

🗂 FOOD

For an authentic Bavarian lunch, grab a *Brez'n* (pretzel) and spread it with *Leberwurst* (liverwurst) or cheese. **Weißwürste** (white veal sausages) are another native bargain. Don't eat the skin of the sausage, just slice it open and eat the tender meat. **Leberkäs** is a slice of a pinkish, meatloaf-like compound of ground beef and bacon, and **Leberknödel** are liver dumplings, usually served in soup.

The vibrant **Viktualienmarkt,** south of Marienpl., is Munich's gastronomic center. It's fun to browse, but don't plan to do any budget grocery shopping here. (Open M-F 10am-8pm, Sa 8am-4pm.) Birthplace of the **beer garden,** Munich's progeny are everywhere. The university district off **Ludwigstraße** is Munich's best source of inexpensive and filling meals. Many reasonably priced restaurants and cafes cluster on **Schellingstraße, Amalienstraße,** and **Türkenstraße** (U3 or 6 to Universität.)

IN THE CENTER

🍴 **Dukatz im Literaturhaus,** Salvatorpl. 1 (☎291 96 00). Any *Münchener* will tell you this is the place to see and and be seen. The home for small artists serves gourmet food (€6-8) to complement creative drink options (€2-4). Sip a cup of coffee and people watch—not only are entrees among the best in the city, they're also among the most expensive (€16-22). Open daily noon-2:30pm and 6:30-10:30pm. ❹

🍴 **Marché,** Neuhauser Str., between Karlspl. and Marienpl. The top floor offers cafeteria-style food; downstairs, chefs prepare every food imaginable, including great vegetarian selections. You'll get a food card that will be stamped for each item taken; pay at the end. Bottom floor open 11am-10pm; top floor 8am-11pm, until 10pm in off-season. ❷

Café Hag/Confiserie Retenhäfen, Residenzstr. 25-26, across from the Residenz. Specializes in a delectable array of cakes and sweets (€2-4). Serves breakfast (€4-8) and entrees (€5-8). Open M-F 8:45am-7pm, Sa 8am-6pm. ❷

Shoya, Orlandostr. 5, across from the Hofbräuhaus. The most reasonable Japanese restaurant in town. Fill up on rice dishes (€7-9), teriyaki (€4-8), and sushi (€4-10) as you Saki-bomb to Japanese music. Open daily 10:30am-midnight. ❸

ELSEWHERE

Schelling Salon, Schellingstr. 54 (☎272 07 88). Bavarian *Knödel* and billiards since 1872. Rack up at the same tables where Lenin, Rilke, and Hitler once played. Breakfast €3-5. Traditional German entrees €4-11. A free **billiard museum** displays a 200-year-old Polish noble's table and the history of pool back to the pharaohs. Museum open Su night. Restaurant open Su-M and Th-Sa 6:30am-1am. ❸

Schwimmkrabbe, Ickstattstr. 13. U1 or 2 to Frauenhoferstr. This family-run Turkish restaurant is popular with locals. Appetizers €4-9. Meals €8-18. Open daily 5pm-1am. ❹

News Bar, Amalienstr. 55 (☎28 17 87), at the corner of Schellingstr. Trendy cafe teeming with students. Large portions at reasonable prices. Breakfast menu €3-9. A wide assortment of salads, sandwiches, or pasta (€5-9). Open daily 7:30am-2am. ❸

VEGETARIAN RESTAURANTS

Buxs, Frauenstr. 9, on the southern edge of the Viktualienmarkt on the corner of Frauenstr. This upscale cafe provides tasty, artful pastas, salads, soups, and bread in a peaceful indoor/outdoor setting. Self-serve everything, with a weight-based charge at the end. Open M-F 11am-6:45pm, Sa 11am-3pm. ❸

Gollier, Gollierstr. 83. U4 to Heimeranpl. Take a left onto Ridlerstr. and walk 2 blocks north; turn right onto Astallerstr. and then left on Gollierstr. Serves delicious pizzas, casseroles, and crepes (€6-11). Lunch buffet Tu-F 11:30am-2:30pm (€5.50). Open Tu-F 11:30am-3pm and 5-11pm, Sa 5-11pm, Su 10am-11pm. ❸

Café Ignaz, Georgenstr. 67. U2 to Josephspl., then take Adelheidstr. 1 block north and turn right on Georgenstr. Low-key, earth-friendly cafe. Dinners (pasta, pizza, crepes, quiche, and stir-fry) €5-9. Lunch buffet €6. Open M-F 8am-10pm, Sa-Su 9am-10pm. ❷

◎ SIGHTS

MARIENPLATZ. The **Mariensäule,** an ornate 17th-century monument to the Virgin Mary, was built to commemorate the city's survival of the Thirty Years' War. At the neo-Gothic **Neues Rathaus,** the **Glockenspiel** chimes with a display of jousting knights and dancing coopers. *(Daily 11am and noon; in summer also 5pm.)* At 9pm, a mechanical watchman marches out and the Guardian Angel escorts the *Münchner Kindl* (Munich Child) to bed. Be careful; this is a likely spot for pickpocketing. The Neues Rathaus tower offers a sweeping view. *(Tower open M-F 9am-7pm, Sa-Su 10am-7pm. €1.50.)* On the face of the **Altes Rathaus** tower, to the right of the Neues Rathaus, are all but one of Munich's coats of arms—the local government refused to include the swastika-bearing arms from the Nazi era.

PETERSKIRCHE AND FRAUENKIRCHE. Across from the Neues Rathaus is the 12th-century **Peterskirche,** the city's oldest parish church. More than 300 steps scale the tower to a spectacular view of Munich. *(Open daily 10am-7pm. €1.50, students €1.)* From the Marienpl., take Kaufingerstr. one block toward the *Hauptbahnhof* to the onion-domed towers of the 15th-century **Frauenkirche**—one of Munich's most notable landmarks and now the symbol of the city. *(Towers open Apr.-Oct. M-Sa 10am-5pm. €3, students €1.50.)*

RESIDENZ. Down the pedestrian zone from Odeonspl., the richly decorated rooms of the **Residenz** (Palace), built from the 14th to 19th centuries, form the material vestiges of the Wittelsbach dynasty. Behind the Residenz, the beautifully landscaped **Hofgarten** shelters the lovely temple of Diana. The **Schatzkammer** (treasury) contains jeweled baubles, crowns, swords, china, ivory work, and other trinkets. *(Open Apr. to mid-Oct. daily 9am-6pm; mid-Oct. to Mar. 10am-4pm. €4, students €3.)* The **Residenzmuseum** comprises the former Wittelsbach apartments and State Rooms, a collection of European porcelain, and a 17th-century court chapel. The 120 portraits in the **Ahnengalerie** trace the royal lineage in an unusual manner back to Charlemagne. *(Max-Joseph-pl. 3. U3-6 to Odeonspl. Residenz museum open same hours as Schatzkammer. €4, students €3. Combination ticket €7, students €5.50.)*

ENGLISCHER GARTEN. Extending from the city center is the vast **Englischer Garten** (English Garden), Europe's largest metropolitan public park. On sunny days, all of Munich turns out to bike, play badminton, ride horseback, or swim in the Eisbach. The garden includes a Japanese tea house, a Chinese pagoda, a Greek temple, and good old German beer gardens. **Nude sunbathing** areas are designated FKK (*Frei-Körper-Kultur*) on signs and park maps. Daring *Müncheners* surf the rapids of the Eisbach, which flows artificially through the park.

SCHLOß NYMPHENBURG. After 10 years of trying for an heir, Ludwig I celebrated the birth of his son in 1662 by erecting an elaborate summer playground. **Schloß Nymphenburg,** in the northwest of town, hides a number of treasures. Check out Ludwig's "Gallery of Beauties;" whenever a woman caught his fancy, he would have her portrait painted—a scandalous hobby considering many of the women were commoners. Four manors and a few lakes also inhabit the grounds. Finally, learn about the means of 17th-century royal travel in the **Marstallmuseum.** *(Streetcar #17 to Schloß Nymphenburg. All attractions open Apr. to mid-Oct. daily 9am-6pm; late Oct. to Mar. 10am-4pm. Museum and Schloß open Su and Tu-Sa 9am-noon and 1-5pm. Schloß €3.50, students €2.50. Each manor €3/2. Museum €2.50/ 2. Entire complex €7.50/6.)*

GERMANY

OLYMPIAPARK. Built for the 1972 Olympic Games in Munich, the **Olympiapark** contains the architecturally daring, tent-like **Olympia-Zentrum** and the **Olympia Turm** (tower), the highest building in Munich at 290m. Two **tours** in English are available: The "Adventure Tour" of the entire park (Apr.-Oct. daily 2pm, €7) or a tour of just the soccer stadium (Mar.-Oct. daily 11am, €5). The Olympiapark also hosts various events all summer, ranging from concerts to flea markets to bungee jumping. *(U3 to Olympiazentrum. Tower open daily 9am-midnight. €3, students €2. Info Pavilion (Besucherservice) open M-F 10am-6pm, Sa 10am-3pm.)*

🏛 MUSEUMS

Munich is a prime museum city—many of the city's offerings would require days for exhaustive perusal. The *Münchner Volkshochschule* (☎48 00 62 29) offers tours of many city museums for €6. A **day pass** to all of Munich's state-owned museums is sold at the tourist office and many larger museums (€15). All state-owned museums are **free on Sunday.**

■ PINAKOTHEK DER MODERNE. The newest and largest addition to Munich's world of art offers four museums in one. Paintings, drawings, architecture, and design occupy the large building created by *Münchener* Stephan Braunfels. Lose yourself in the works of Picasso, Dalí, Matisse, Warhol, and others. *(Barerstr. 40. U2 to Königspl. Take a right at Königspl., and a left after 1 block onto Meiserstr. Open Su and Tu-Sa 10am-5pm. €5, students €3.50. Day pass for all 3 Pinakotheke €12.)*

■ DEUTSCHES MUSEUM. One of the largest and best museums of science and technology, with fascinating displays, including a mining exhibit that winds through a labyrinth of recreated subterranean tunnels. The museum has over 50 departments covering 17km. *(Museuminsel 1. S1 or 8 to Isartor or streetcar #18 to Deutsches Museum. Open daily 9am-5pm. €7.50, students €3. Guidebooks €4.)*

ALTE PINAKOTHEK AND NEUE PINAKOTHEK. Commissioned in 1826 by King Ludwig I, the world-renowned **Alte Pinakothek** houses Munich's most precious art, including works by da Vinci, Rembrandt, and Rubens. The **Neue Pinakothek** next door displays paintings and sculptures of the 19th to 20th centuries, including van Gogh, Cézanne, and Manet. *(Barerstr. 27-29. U2 to Königspl. Each open W, F, Sa-Su 10am-5pm; Tu-Th 10am-8pm. Each €5, students €3.50; combination ticket €8/5.)*

BMW MUSEUM. The ultimate driving museum features a fetching display of past, present, and future BMW products. The English brochure *Horizons in Time* guides you through the spiral path to the top of the museum. *(Petuelring 130. U3 to Olympiazentrum. Take the Olympiaturm exit and walk a block up Lerchenauer Str.; the museum will be on your left. Open daily 9am-5pm. €3, students €2.)*

ZAM: ZENTRUM FÜR AUSSERGEWÖHNLICHE MUSEEN. Munich's Center for Unusual Museums brazenly corrals—under one roof—such treasures as the Peddle-Car Museum and the Museum of Easter Rabbits. *(Westenriederstr. 41. Any S-Bahn or streetcar #17 or 18 to Isartor. Open daily 10am-6pm. €4, students €3.)*

MÜNCHENER STADTMUSEUM. Exhibitions depict Munich's city life and history through film, fashion, music, weaponry, puppetry, posters, and more. Classic films (€4) nightly at 6 and 9pm, plus 11am and 3pm on Sundays. Foreign films in the original language with German subtitles. Call ☎23 32 41 50 for a program. *(St. Jakobs-pl. 1. S1-8 to Marienpl. Walk down Rindermarkt Str. for 3 blocks; turn left on St.-Jakobs-pl. Open Su and Tu-Sa 10am-6pm. €4, students €2; family pass €6.)*

ENTERTAINMENT

Munich's cultural cache rivals the world's best. Sixty theaters of various sizes are scattered throughout the city; styles range from dramatic classics at the **Residenztheater** and **Volkstheater** to comic opera at the **Staatstheater am Gärtnerplatz** to experimental works at the **Theater im Marstall** in Nymphenburg. Munich's **opera festival** (in July) is held in the ✉**Bayerische Staatsoper** (Bavarian National Theater), Max-Joseph-pl. 2. (Tickets ☎21 85 19 20; recorded info ☎21 85 19 19. Streetcar #19 to Nationaltheater or U3-6 to Odeonspl. Standing-room and student tickets €4-10, sold 1hr. before performance at the side entrance on Maximilian-str. Box office open M-F 10am-6pm, Sa 10am-1pm. No performances Aug. to mid-Sept.) *Monatspro-gramm* (€1.50) and *Munich Found* (€3) both list schedules for Munich's stages, museums, and festivals. Munich reveals its bohemian face in scores of small fringe theaters, cabaret stages, and art cinemas in **Schwabing.**

NIGHTLIFE

Munich's nightlife is a curious collision of Bavarian *Gemütlichkeit* ("warmth") and trendy cliquishness. The odyssey begins at one of Munich's beer gardens or beer halls, which generally close before midnight and are most crowded in the early evening. The alcohol keeps flowing at cafes and bars, which, except for Friday and Saturday nights, close their taps at 1am. Discos and dance clubs, sedate before midnight, throb relentlessly until 4am. The trendy spots along **Leopoldstraße** in **Schwabing** attract tourists from all over Europe. Many of these venues require you to at least attempt the jaded hipster look, and the Munich fashion police generally frown on shorts, sandals, and t-shirts.

BEER GARDENS (BIERGÄRTEN)

The six great Munich labels are *Augustiner, Hacker-Pschorr, Hofbräu, Löwenbräu, Paul-aner,* and *Spaten-Franziskaner;* but most restaurants and *Gaststätte* have picked a side and only serve one brewery's beer. There are four main types of beer served in Munich: **Helles** (light), **Dunkles** (dark), **Weißbier** (cloudy blond beer made from wheat instead of barley), and **Radler** ("cyclist's brew;" half beer and half lemon soda). Saying *"Ein Bier, bitte"* will get you a liter, known as a *Maß* (€4-6). Specify if you want only a *halb-Maß* (€3-4).

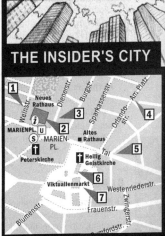

THE INSIDER'S CITY

THE MANY NECTARS OF MUNICH

Munich's Altstadt is not simply for ogling the *Glockenspiel* and other tourist attractions. Small beer gardens and street-side cafes pepper the area, offering an array of local beverages wide enough to suit any palate.

1 Sample the many varieties of *Hacker-Pschorr* beer at **Donisl.**

2 Think Germans only drink beer? The medieval winery in the **Ratskeller** beneath the Neues Rathaus proves otherwise.

3 Down an *Augustiner* at the **Wirthaus zur Weißblauen Rose.**

4 Make merry with hundreds of tourists and locals in *Lederhosen* at the **Hofbräuhaus.**

5 Try out *Schneider Weiße* at the **Weißes Bräuhaus.**

6 Look for the barrel-table of the **Imbiß** to taste a smooth *Paul-aner.*

7 Drink like a lion at the **Löwe am Markt,** home of *Löwenbräu.*

Augustinerkeller, Arnulfstr. 52, at Zirkus-Krone-Str. Any S-Bahn to Hackerbrücke. Founded in 1824, Augustiner is viewed by most *Müncheners* as the finest beer garden in town. Lush grounds, 100-year-old chestnut trees, and the delicious, sharp Augustiner beer (*Maß* €5.70) support their assertion. Open daily 10:30am-1am.

Hirschgarten, Hirschgarten 1. Streetcar #17 (dir.: Amalienburgstr.) to Romanpl. The largest beer garden in Europe (seating 9000) is boisterous and pleasant but somewhat remote, near Schloß Nymphenburg. *Maß* €5.30. Open daily 9am-midnight.

Hofbräuhaus, Platzl 9, 2 blocks from Marienpl. Many tables are reserved for locals—some even keep their personal steins in the hall's safe. To avoid tourists, go in the early afternoon. *Maß* €6. *Weißwürste* with pretzel €3.70. Open daily 9am-midnight.

Am Seehaus, Kleinhesselohe 3. U6 to Dietlindenstr., then bus #44 to Osterwaldstr. Directly on the Kleinhesseloher See in the Englischer Garten. Calmer and less touristy than the Chinesischer Turm. Watch the sun set over the water as you enjoy a *Maß* (€6) and a pretzel (€3.10). Open M-F 11am-midnight, Sa-Su 10am-midnight.

BARS

Nachtcafe, Maximilianspl. 5. U4 or 5 or any S-Bahn to Karlspl. Live jazz, funk, soul, and blues until the wee hours. Very *schicki-micki* (yuppie). Things don't get rolling until midnight. No cover, but prices are outrageous; do your drinking beforehand. Very picky dress code on weekends. Live music 11pm-4am. Open daily 9pm-6am.

Reitschule, Königinstr. 34. U3 or 6 to Giselastr. A sleek bar with marble tables, as well as a cafe with a beer garden out back. *Weißbier* €3. Open daily 9am-1am.

Sausalitos, Im Tal 16. Any U-Bahn to Marienpl. Mexican bar and restaurant hopping with a 20-something crowd. Drinks €6-9. Open daily 11am-late.

CLUBS

Kunstpark Ost, Grafinger Str. 6. U5 or any S-Bahn to Ostbahnhof; follow signs for the Kunstpark Ost exit. A huge complex containing 40 different venues swarming with parties. Try the standard **MilchBar** (open M, W-F); the psychedelic-trance **Natraj Temple** (open F-Sa); the alternative cocktail bar and disco **K41** (open nightly, Th 80s night); or the risque South American rock bar **Titty Twister** (open W-Sa). Hours, cover, and themes vary—check www.kunstpark.de for details.

Nachtwerk, Club, and Tanzlokal, Landesberger Str. 185. Streetcar #18 or 19 or bus #83 to Lautensackstr. **Nachtwerk** spins mainstream dance tunes for sweaty crowds in a packed warehouse. **Club** offers a 2-level dance floor just as tight and swinging as its neighbor. **Tanzlokal** (open F-Sa) has hip-hop on F. Beer €2.50 at all venues. Cover €5.50. Open daily 10pm-4am.

Ballhaus, Domagkstr. 33, in the Alabamahalle. U6 to Heide. Free shuttle from there to the club. On a former military base in Schwabing with 3 other discos. Start out in the beer garden, which opens 8pm. **Alabama** serves free drinks all night Sa and until 1am F (open F 9pm-4am, Sa 10pm-5am). **Tempel Club** has typical pop music (open Sa 10pm-4am) and **Schwabinger Ballhouse** plays international jams. (Drinks €1.50-3. Cover €8. Open F-Sa 10pm-5am.)

GAY AND LESBIAN MUNICH

Although Bavaria has the reputation of being less welcoming to homosexuality, Munich sustains a respectably vibrant gay nightlife. The center of the gay scene is in the **Glockenbachviertel,** stretching from the area south of the Sendlinger Tor through the Viktualienmarkt/Gärtnerpl. area to the Isartor. *Our Munich,* Munich's gay and lesbian leaflet, is available at the tourist office, while *Sergej* is available at many gay locales, including **Max&Milian Bookstore,** Ickstattstr. 2 (open M-F 10:30am-2pm and 3:30-8pm, Sa 11am-4pm).

Bei Carla, Buttermelcherstr. 9. Any S-Bahn to Isartor. Walk 1 block south on Zweibrück-enstr., take a right on Rumfordstr., turn left on Klenzestr., then left again onto Butter-melcherstr. One of Munich's best-kept secrets. Open M-Sa 4pm-1am, Su 6pm-1am.

Soul City, Maximilianspl. 5, at the intersection with Max-Joseph-Str. Purportedly the big-gest gay disco in Bavaria; music ranges from disco to Latin to techno. Straights always welcome. Cover €5-13. Open W-Sa 10pm-late.

Fortuna Musikbar, Maximilianspl. 5. S1-8 to Karlspl. Hip lesbian disco. "Flow Club" electronic on Th; Salsa on F. Cover €5 on F only. Open W-Sa 10pm 6am.

▶ OKTOBERFEST

Every fall, hordes of tourists make an unholy pilgrimage to Munich to drink and be merry in true Bavarian style. From noon on the penultimate Saturday of Septem-ber through early October, it's all about consuming beer, and the numbers for this festival have become truly mindboggling: Participants chug five million liters of beer, but only on a full stomach of 200,000 *Würste.* Oktoberfest is the world's larg-est folk festival—in fact, the festival has gotten so large (and sometimes out of hand) that the city of Munich has stopped advertising it.

Oktoberfest began on October 12, 1810 to celebrate the wedding of crown prince Ludwig (later king Ludwig I of Bavaria) and Princess Theresa von Sachsen-Hildburghausen. Representatives from all over Bavaria met outside the city gates, celebrating with a week of horse racing on fields they named **Theresienwiese** in honor of the bride (U4 or 5 to Theresienwiese). The original reception was such fun that *Müncheners* have repeated the revelry (minus the horses) ever since. An agricultural show, inaugurated in 1811, is still held every three years, and fair fare, from carousels to touristy kitsch, remain to amuse beer-guzzling participants.

The festivities begin with the "Grand Entry of the Oktoberfest Landlords and Breweries," a parade which ends around noon with the drinking of the ceremonial first keg, to the cry of *O'zapft is!* ("it's tapped") by the Lord Mayor of Munich. Other special events include international folklore presentations, a costume and rifleman's parade, and an open-air concert. Each of Munich's breweries sets up tents in the Theresienwiese. The touristy *Hofbräu* tent is the rowdiest; fights break out. Arrive early (by 4:30pm) to get a table; you must have a seat to be served alcohol. Drinking hours are relatively short, about 9am to 10:30pm, depend-ing on the day; fairground attractions and sideshows are open slightly later. For those who share a love of alcohol with their kin, family days have reduced prices.

▶ DAYTRIPS FROM MUNICH

DACHAU. *"Arbeit Macht Frei"* ("work will set you free") was the first thing pris-oners saw as they entered Dachau; it's written over the gate of the **Jourhaus,** for-merly the only entry to the camp. Dachau was primarily a work camp (rather than a death camp, like Auschwitz). During the war, prisoners made armaments in Dachau because the SS knew that the Allies would not bomb a concentration camp. Although Dachau has a **gas chamber,** it was never actually used because the prisoners purposely made mistakes and worked slowly in order to delay comple-tion. Once tightly packed **barracks** are now, for the most part, only foundations; however, survivors ensured that at least two barracks would be reconstructed to teach future generations about the 206,000 prisoners who were interned here from 1933 to 1945. The walls, gates, and crematorium have been restored since 1962 in a chillingly sparse memorial to the victims of Dachau. The **museum,** located in the former administrative buildings, examines pre-1930s anti-Semitism, the rise of Nazism, the establishment of the concentration camp system, and the lives of prisoners through photographs, documents, and artifacts. The thick guide (€26) translates the propaganda posters, SS files, documents, and letters. Most exhibits are accompanied by short captions in English. A **short film** (22min.) is screened in English at 11:30am, 2pm, and 3:30pm. A new display in the **Bunker,** the concentration camp's prison and torture chamber, chronicles the lives of the camp's prisoners and the barbarism of SS guards. Lengthy (2hr.) **tours** in English leave from the museum. (June-Aug. daily 12:30pm; Sept.-May Sa-Su 12:30pm. Free, but donation requested. Camp open Su and Tu-Sa 9am-5pm.)

From Munich, take S2 (dir.: Petershausen) to Dachau (20min.; €4, or 4 stripes on the Streifenkarte), then bus #724 (dir.: Kraütgarten) or 726 (dir.: Kopernikusstr.) to KZ-Gedenkstätte (10min.; €1, or 1 stripe on the Streifenkarte).

GARMISCH-PARTENKIRCHEN ☎ 08821

The **Zugspitze** (2964m), Germany's tallest mountain, is the main attraction in Garmisch-Partenkirchen (pop. 28,000). There are three ways to conquer it, and all of them are weather-dependent. You can take the **cog railway** from the **Zugspitzbahnhof** (behind the Garmisch main station) to *Eibsee* (1¼hr., every hr. 8:15am-3:15pm), then continue on the **Gletscherbahn** or the steeper **Eibsee Seilbahn** cable car to the top (1½hr., every hr. 8am-3:15pm, round-trip with train and either cable car €42). Experienced climbers can make the semi-technical ascent in 10-12hrs., although surrounding peaks may be of more interest.

From Garmisch-Partenkirchen, **trains** run to Munich (1½hr., 1 per hr., €14) and Innsbruck (1½hr., 1 per hr., €10). **Buses** #1084 and 9606 go to Füssen (2hr., 6-7 per day, €7). To get to the **tourist office,** Richard-Strauss-Pl. 2, turn left on Bahnhofstr. from the train station and turn left again onto Von-Brug-Str.; it's the pink building on the square. The staff distributes maps and will help find rooms for free. (☎ 18 07 00. Open M-Sa 8am-6pm, Su 10am-noon.) To reach ▨**Naturfreundehaus ❶,** Schalmeiweg 21, from the station, walk straight on Bahnhofstr. as it becomes Ludwigstr., follow the bend to the right and turn left on Sonnenbergstr., and continue straight as this becomes Prof. Michael-Sachs-Str. and then Schalmeiweg (25min.). At this cozy hostel, you can sleep in attic lofts with up to 16 other backpackers. (☎ 43 22. Kitchen use €0.50. Reception daily 6-8pm. Loft dorm beds €8; 3- to 5-bed dorms €10.) **HL Markt,** at the intersection of Bahnhofstr. and Von-Brug-Str., sells groceries. (Open M-F 8am-8pm, Sa 7:30am-4pm.) **Postal Code:** 82467.

THE CHIEMSEE ☎ 08051

The region's dramatic crescent of mountains and its picturesque islands, forests, and marshland have lured visitors for 2000 years. Today, prices have risen and the area has been overrun by resorts for the German *nouveaux riches.* Prien, the largest lake town, offers easy access to resort paradises Aschau and Sachrang, ski areas of the Kampenwand, and the surrounding curtain of mountains.

PRIEN AM CHIEMSEE. Located on the southwestern corner of the Chiemsee, Prien is a good base for exploring the islands. **Trains** depart from the station, a few blocks from the city center, for Munich (1hr., every hr., €12.40) and Salzburg (50min., 1 per hr., €9). **Ferries** run from Prien to Herreninsel and Fraueninsel (every 40min., 7:15am-7:30pm, €6-7). To get to the ferry port, turn right from the main entrance of the Prien train station and follow Seestr. for 20min., or hop on the green *Chiemseebahn* steam train from the station (10am-6pm, every hr., round-trip €4). The **tourist office,** Alte Rathausstr. 11, dispenses maps and books private rooms for free. (☎ 690 50. Open M-F 8:30am-6pm, Sa 8:30am-noon.) The **Jugendherberge (HI) ❷,** Carl-Braun-Str. 66, is a 20min. walk from the station; go right on Seestr. and turn left on Staudenstr., which becomes Carl-Braun-Str. (☎687 70. Breakfast, showers, and lockers included. Reception 8-9am, 5-7pm, and 9:30-10pm. Open early Feb.-Nov. Dorms €16.) To reach **Campingpl. Hofbauer ❶**, Bernauer Str. 110, from the station, turn left on Seestr., left again at the next intersection, and then walk 25min. along Bernauerstr. heading out of town. (☎41 36. Showers included. Reception 7:30-11am and 2-8pm. Open Apr.-Oct. €6 per person, €5.10 per campsite.) Grab a cheap meal at **Bäckerei/Cafe Müller ❷**, Marktpl. 8. (Open M-F 6:30am-6pm, Sa 6:30am-12:30pm, Su 7:30-10:30am.)

HERRENINSEL AND FRAUENINSEL. Ludwig's palace on ▧**Herreninsel** (Gentlemen's Island), **Königsschloß Herrenchiemsee**, is a shameless attempt to be larger, better, and more extravagant than Louis XIV's Versailles. Ludwig bankrupted Bavaria building this place—a few unfinished rooms (abandoned after funds ran out) contrast greatly with the completed portion of the castle. (Open Apr.-Sept. daily 9am-6pm; Oct. 9:40am-5pm; Nov.-Mar. 9:40am-4pm. Required tour €5.50, students €4.50.) **Fraueninsel** (Ladies' Island) is home to the **Klosterkirche** (Island Cloister), the nunnery that complemented the monastery on Herreninsel. The nuns make their own marzipan, beeswax candles, and five kinds of liqueur, all sold in the convent shop. The 8th-century **Cross of Bischofhofen** and other religious artifacts are displayed in the Michaelskapelle above the **Torhalle** (gate), the oldest surviving part of the cloister. (Open May-Oct. 11am-5pm. €2.)

BERCHTESGADEN. The area's natural beauty and the sinister attraction of **Kehlsteinhaus** ("Eagle's Nest"), Hitler's mountaintop retreat, draw world travelers. The stone resort house, now a restaurant, has a spectacular view from the 1834m peak. From the train station, take bus #38 to *Kehlstein Busabfahrt* (7am-6pm, every 45min.); then catch bus #49 to *Kehlstein Parkpl.* (June-Oct. every 30min. 9:30am-4pm, €15). Be sure to reserve your spot for the return bus when you get off. (Open May-Oct. daily except heavy snow days.) **Trains** run every hr. to Munich (3hr., €25) and Salzburg (1hr., €6.60). The **tourist office**, Königsseerstr. 2, opposite the station, has tips on **hiking** trails in the Berchtesgaden National Park. (☎(08652) 96 71 50. Open mid-June to Oct. M-F 8:30am-6pm, Sa 9am-5pm, Su 9am-3pm; Nov. to mid-June M-F 8:30am-5pm, Sa 9am-noon.) To get to the **Jugendherberge (HI) ❷**, Gebirgsjägerstr. 52, turn right from the station, left on Ramsauer Str., right on Gmündbrücke, and left up the steep gravel path. You can also take bus #39 (dir.: Strub Kaserne). (☎(08652) 943 70. Breakfast included. Reception 6:30-9am and 5-7pm. Check in until 10pm. Curfew midnight. Closed Nov.-Dec. 26. Dorms €16.) For groceries, stop by the **Edeka Markt**, Königsseerstr. 22. (Open M-F 7:30am-6pm, Sa 7:30am-noon.) The nearby **Bäckerei-Konditorei Ernst**, Königser Str. 10, has fresh bread and pastries. (Open M-F 6:30am-6pm, Sa 6:30am-noon.) **Postal Code:** 83471.

▧ **HIKING NEAR BERCHTESGADEN.** From Berchtesgaden, the 5½km path to the **Königssee**—which winds through fields of flowers, across bubbling brooks, and past several beer gardens—affords a heart-stopping view of the Alps. From the train station, cross the street, turn right, and take a quick left over the bridge. Walk to the right of and past the green-roofed building (but not up the hill) and take a left onto the gravel path near the stone wall, then follow the Königssee signs. Alternatively, take bus #41 from the bus station to *Königssee* (round-trip €3.70). Once you arrive in Königstein, walk down Seestr. and look for the *Nationalpark Informationstelle* to your left, which has hiking info. To explore the **Berchtesgaden National Park**, take bus #46 from Berchtesgaden (15min., 6:10am-7:25pm, €2.10). Get off at *Neuhausenbrücke* in Ramsau, and head to the **tourist office**, Im Tal 2, for hiking maps. (☎(08657) 98 89 20. Open July-Sept. M-Sa 8am-noon and 1-5pm, Su 9am-noon and 2-5pm; Oct.-June M-F 8am-noon and 1-5pm.)

PASSAU

☎ **0851**

This beautiful 2000-year-old city (pop. 51,000) embodies the ideal image of Old-World Europe. The capstone of Passau is the Baroque **Stephansdom,** Dompl., where cherubs sprawl across the ceiling and the world's largest church organ, with 17,774 pipes, looms above the choir. (Open in summer daily 6:30am-7pm; off-season 6:30am-6pm. Free. Organ concerts May-Oct. M-F noon, Th also 7:30pm. €3-5, students €1-3.) Behind the cathedral is the **Residenz,** home to the **Domschatz,** an extravagant collection of gold and tapestries. (Enter through the back of the Stephansdom, to the right of the altar. Open Easter-Oct. M-Sa 10am-4pm. €1.50, students €0.50.) The heights of the river during various floods are marked on the outside wall of the 13th-century Gothic **Rathaus.** (Open Apr.-Oct. daily 10am-4pm. €1.50, students €1.) Over the Luitpoldbrücke is the former palace of the bishopric, now home to the **Cultural History Museum.** (Open Apr. to Oct. M-F 9am-5pm, Sa-Su 10am-6pm; Nov.-Mar. Su and Tu-Sa 9am-5pm. €4, students €2.50.)

Trains depart for: Frankfurt (4½hr., every 2hr., €65); Munich (2hr., every 2hr., €27); Nuremberg (2hr., every 2hr., €31); and Vienna (3½hr., 1 per hr., €31). To get to the **tourist office,** Rathauspl. 3, follow Bahnhofstr. from the train station to Ludwigspl., and bear left downhill across Ludwigspl. to Ludwigstr., which becomes Rindermarkt, Steinweg, and finally Große Messerg.; continue straight on Schusterg. and turn left on Schrottg. (☎95 59 80. Open Easter to mid-Oct. M-F 8:30am-6pm, Sa-Su 9:30am-3pm; mid-Oct. to Easter M-Th 8:30am-5pm, F 8:30am-4pm.) High above the Danube in a castle, the **Jugendherberge (HI) ❷,** Veste Oberhaus 125, is 30min. from the station. Cross the bridge downstream from the *Rathaus* and follow the signs. (☎49 37 80. Breakfast included. Dorms €16.) Closer to the center, the homey **Pension Rößner ❸,** Bräug. 19, is downstream from the *Rathaus.* (☎93 13 50. Breakfast included. Singles €35; doubles €50-60.) The student district around **Innstraße,** parallel to the Inn River, is lined with good, cheap places to eat. Pick up groceries at **Normas supermarket,** Bahnhofstr. 16b. Get meat, baked goods, sandwiches, and salads at **Schmankerl Passage ❷,** Ludwigstr. 6. (Open M-F 7:30am-6pm, Sa 7:30am-2pm.) **Postal Code:** 94032.

REGENSBURG

☎ **0941**

Regensburg (pop. 127,000) is teeming with students and the places that feed, souse, and engage them in their idle hours. The city is reputed to have more cafes and bars per square meter than any other city in Europe. The **Dom St. Peter** dazzles with richly colored stained glass. Inside, the **Domschatz** (Cathedral Treasury) displays gold and jewels purchased by the bishops, as well as the preserved hand of Bishop Chrysostomus, who died in AD 407. (Open Apr.-Oct. daily 6:30am-6pm; Nov.-Mar. 6:30am-5pm. Free.) A few blocks away, the **Rathaus** served as capital of the Holy Roman Empire until 1803. Downriver from Regensburg, **Walhalla** is an imitation Parthenon honoring Ludwig I's favorite Germans. Take the ferry or bus #5 from Albertspl. to *Donaustauf Walhallastr.* ▓**Historische Wurstküche,** Thundorfer Str., an 850-year-old beer garden, is ideal for sipping brew (0.5L €2.60) while watching ships drift by on the Danube. Check bulletin boards around campus for student parties, which are usually free and open to all.

Trains to: Munich (1½hr., every hr., €20); Nuremberg (1-1½hr., 1-2 per hr., €14); and Passau (1-1½hr., every hr., €17). The **tourist office** is in the *Altes Rathaus.* From the station, walk down Maximilianstr., turn left on Grasg., turn right at the end onto Obere Bachg., and follow it for 5 blocks. (☎507 44 10. Open Apr.-Oct. M-F 9am-6pm, Sa 9am-4pm, Su 9:30am-4pm; Nov.-March M-F 9am-6pm, Sa 9am-4pm, Su 9:30am-2:30pm.) To get to the **Jugendherberge (HI) ❷,** Wöhrdstr. 60, walk from the station to the end of Maximilianstr., turn right on

Pflugg., and then left at the *Optik* sign onto tiny Erhardig.; at the end, take the steps down, walk left over the bridge, and veer right onto Wöhrdstr. Or, take bus #3, 8, or 9 (€1.50) from the station. (☎574 02. Breakfast included. Reception daily 3pm-midnight. Dorms €17.) **Hinterhaus ❷**, Rote-Hahnen-Gasse 2, serves cheese and meat dishes. (Entrees €4-9. Open daily 6pm-1am.) There's a **supermarket** in the basement of Galeria Kaufhof, on Neupfarrpl. (Open M-F 9am-8pm, Sa 9am-4pm.) **Postal Code:** 93047.

NUREMBERG (NÜRNBERG) ☎0911

Nuremberg (pop. 491,000) once hosted massive Nazi rallies; the Allies later chose it as the site of the post-war tribunals. Today, townspeople have forged a new image for their city as the *Stadt der Menschenrechte* (City of Human Rights). Locally, Nuremberg is known more for its Christmas market (Nov. 26-Dec. 24, 2004), toy fair, sausages, and gingerbread than its politics.

⊟❼ TRANSPORTATION AND PRACTICAL INFORMATION. Trains go to: Berlin (6hr., every 2hr., €78-120); Frankfurt (3½hr., 2 per hr., €36-55); Munich (2½hr., 2 per hr., €38); and Stuttgart (2¾hr., 6 per day, €28). DB Reisezentrum, located in the central hall of the station, sells tickets. (Open daily 6am-9:30pm.) The **tourist office**, Königstr. 93, books rooms for free. Walk through the tunnel from the station to the *Altstadt* and take a right. (☎233 61 31. Open M-Sa 9am-7pm.) **Internet** is available at **Flat-s**, on the second floor of the train station. (€1 per 15min. Open M-Th 7am-11pm, F-Su 24hr.) **Postal Code:** 90402.

❢❒ ACCOMMODATIONS AND FOOD. ▨Jugendgästehaus (HI) ❸, Burg 2, is in a castle above the city. From the tourist office, follow Königstr. through Lorenzerpl. and over the bridge to the Hauptmarkt. Head toward the fountain on the left and go right on Burgstr., then head up the hill. (☎230 93 60. Reception 7am-1am. Dorms €20.) When in town, Hitler would stay at **Deutscher Hof ❹**, Frauentorgraben 29, only 400m from the station. (☎249 40. Breakfast included. Singles €39, doubles €52.) In the southwest corner of the *Altstadt*, **▨Zum Goldener Stern ❷**, Zirkelschmiedgasse 26, is the oldest bratwurst kitchen in the world. (Six bratwurst €6. Open daily 11am-10pm.) **Sushi Glas ❸**, Kornmarkt 7, next to the National Museum, attracts a chic yuppie crowd with delicious Japanese specialties. (Open M-W noon-11pm, Th-Sa noon-midnight, Su 6-11pm.) **Edeka**, Hauptmarkt 12, near Frauenkirche, sells groceries. (Open M-F 8:30am-7pm, Sa 8am-3pm.)

◙⊡ SIGHTS AND ENTERTAINMENT. Allied bombing left little of old Nuremberg for posterity, but its churches, castle, and other buildings have all been reconstructed. The walled-in **Handwerkerhof** near the station is more medieval than mall; head up Königstr. for the real sights. Take a detour to the left for the pillared **Straße der Menschenrechte** ("Avenue of Human Rights") as well as the **Germanisches Nationalmuseum**, Kartäuserg. 1, which chronicles German art from pre-history to the present. (Open Su, Tu and Th-Sa 10am-6pm, W 10am-9pm. €5, students €4. W 6-9pm free.) Across the river is the **Hauptmarktplatz**, site of the annual **Christmas market**. Hidden in the fence of the **Schöner Brunnen** (Beautiful Fountain) in the Hauptmarkt is a seamless gold-colored ring; spinning it brings good luck. Walk uphill to the **Rathaus**; the **Lochgefängnisse** (dungeons) beneath contain medieval torture instruments. (Open Su and Tu-Sa 10am-4:30pm. Required tours every 30min. €2, students €1.) Atop the hill, the **Kaiserburg** (emperor's fortress), Nuremberg's symbol, offers the best vantage point of the city. (Open Apr.-Sept. daily 9am-6pm; Oct.-Mar. 10am-4pm. Required tours every 30min. €5, students €4.)

The ruins of **Reichsparteitagsgelände,** site of the Nazi Party Congress rallies, remind visitors of Nuremberg's darker history. On the far side of the lake is the **Tribüne,** the marble platform where throngs gathered to hear Hitler. The "Fascination and Terror" exhibit, in the ■**Kongresshalle,** at the north end of the park, covers the rise of the Third Reich and the war crimes trials. (Open M-F 9am-6pm, Sa-Su 10am-6pm. €5, students €2.50.) To reach the park, take S2 to *Dutzendteich,* then take the middle of three exits, go down the stairs, and turn left. Walk past the lake on your left, turn left, then turn right to reach the Kongresshalle. On the other side of town, Nazi leaders faced Allied judges during the historic Nuremberg war crimes trials, held in room 600 of the **Justizgebäude,** Fürtherstr. 110. (Take U1 to *Bärenschanze.* Tours Sa-Su 1, 2, 3, and 4 pm. €2, students €1.)

Nuremberg's nightspots are clustered around the *Altstadt;* the most popular are in the west, near the river. **Cine Città,** Gewerbemuseumspl. 3, packs in 16 bars and cafes, 17 cinemas, an IMAX theater, and a disco. Take the U-Bahn to *Wöhrder Wiese.* (Open M-Th and Su until 3am, F-Sa until 4am.) **Frizz,** Weißgerberg. 37, swings to oldies and 80s rock. (Cover men €2. Women free. Open M and Th 8pm-2am, F-Sa 8pm-4am.)

ROMANTIC ROAD

Groomed fields of sunflowers and wheat, vineyards, rolling hills, and dense forests checker the landscape between Würzburg and Füssen. It's beauty was not lost on the German tourist industry, which christened the area the Romantic Road (*Romantische Straße*) in 1950; it's now the most traveled route in Germany.

▐ TRANSPORTATION

Europabus runs daily at 10am from bus platform #13 in Würzburg to Füssen via Rothenburg ob der Tauber. (Reservations ☎089 59 38 89; www.euraide.de/romantic. 10% student discount, 60% Eurail and German Railpass discount.) A more flexible and economical way to travel the Romantic Road is by the frequent trains that connect all the towns.

ROTHENBURG OB DER TAUBER. Rothenburg (pop. 12,000) is *the* Romantic Roadstop. After the Thirty Years' War, the town had no money to modernize; it remained unchanged for 250 years. When it became a tourist destination at the end of the 19th century, new laws protected the integrity of the medieval *Altstadt;* today, Rothenburg is probably your only chance to see a walled medieval city without a single modern building. After the war, the conquering general promised to spare the town from destruction if any local could chug a wine keg (3.25L). The mayor successfully met the challenge, then passed out for several days. The **Meistertrunk** is reenacted each year, and the town clock performs a slow motion version every hour over the Marktpl. For other fascinating tidbits of Rothenburg history, take the 1hr. English tour led by the ■**night watchman,** which starts from the Rathaus. (Easter-Christmas daily 8pm. €3.) The 60m tower of the Renaissance **Rathaus,** on Marktpl., provides a panoramic view of the town. (Open Apr.-Oct. daily 9:30am-12:30pm and 1-5pm; Nov. and Jan.-Mar. noon-3pm, Dec. Sa-Su only noon-3pm. €1.) The ■**Medieval Crime Museum,** Burgg. 3, exhibits tools of torture for anyone who can stomach the thought of iron-maiden justice. (Open Apr.-Oct. daily 9:30am-6pm; Nov. and Jan.-Feb. 2-4pm; Dec. and Mar. 10am-4pm. €3, students €2.) Head to **Christkindlmarkt** (Christ Child Market), Herrng. 2, and **Weihnachtsdorf** (Christmas Village), Herrng. 1, which houses a **Christmas Museum** documenting the evolution of gift-giving. (Open Jan. to mid-May M-F 9am-6:30pm, Sa 9am-4pm; mid-May to Dec. also Su 11am-6pm.)

Trains run to and from Steinach (15min., €1.75), where you can transfer to trains for Würzburg and Munich. The **Europabus** leaves from the *Busbahnhof*, next to the train station. The **tourist office,** Marktpl. 2, books rooms. (☎404 92. Open May-Oct. M-F 9am-noon and 1-6pm, Sa 10am-3pm; Nov.-Apr. M-F 9am-noon and 1-5pm, Sa 10am-1pm.) The cheery, spacious rooms of **Gasthof Goldene Rose ❸,** Spitalgasse 28, are on the main street. (☎(09861) 46 38. Singles €21-23; doubles €36-62.) Many other private rooms are not registered with the tourist office; look for *Zimmer frei* signs and knock on the door to inquire. **Postal Code:** 91541.

WÜRZBURG. The university town of Würzburg is surrounded by vineyard slopes and bisected by the Main River. In 1895, Wilhelm Conrad Röntgen discovered X-rays here and was awarded the first Nobel Prize. Inside the striking **Fortress Marienburg** are the 11th-century **Marienkirche,** the 40m **Bergfried watchtower,** above the Hole of Fear dungeon, and the **Fürstengarten,** built to resemble a ship. Outside the main fortress is the castle arsenal, which now houses the **Mainfränkisches Museum.** (Take bus #9 from the station to *Festung,* or walk 40min. toward the castle on the hill. Tours depart from the main courtyard Apr.-Oct. Tu-F 11am, 2, and 3pm, Sa-Su every hr. 10am-4pm. €2, students €1.50. Museum open Apr.-Oct. Su and Tu-Sa 9am-6pm; Nov.-Mar. 10am-4pm. €2.50/2.) The **Residenz** houses the largest ceiling fresco in the world; the **Residenzhofkirche** inside is a Baroque fantasy of gilding and pink marble. (Open Apr. to mid-Oct. daily 9am-6pm, Th until 8pm; mid-Oct. to Mar. 10am-4pm. €4, students €3. English tours Sa-Su 11am and 3pm.) **Trains** arrive from: Frankfurt (2hr., 2 per hr., €19); Munich (3hr., every hr., €39); Nuremberg (1hr., 2 per hr., €15); and Rothenburg ob der Tauber (1hr., every hr., €9). The **tourist office,** in the yellow Haus zum Falken on the Marktpl., provides maps and helps find rooms. (☎(0931) 37 23 98. Open Apr.-Oct. M-F 10am-6pm, Sa-Su 10am-2pm; Nov.-March M-F 10am-6pm, Sa 10am-2pm.) **Postal Code:** 97070.

FÜSSEN. With its position at the foot of the Romantic Road, in the foothills of the Bavarian Alps, the name Füssen (feet) is apt for this little town. The main attraction of Füssen is its proximity to Ludwig's famed **Königsschlösser** (p. 510). Within the town, the inner walls of the **Hohes Schloß** (High Castle) courtyard feature arresting *trompe-l'oeil* windows and towers, and the **Staatsgalerie** in the castle shelters a collection of regional art. (Open Apr.-Oct. Su and Tu-Sa 11am-4pm; Nov.-Mar. Su and Tu-Sa 2-4pm. €2.50,

TOP TEN LIST

CASTLES OF GERMANY

So **Neuschwanstein** (p. 510) whet your appetite and you want to tour like Teutonic nobility?

10. Jugendherberg Stahleck, Bacharach. Hostels don't get any better than this: Stay in a 12th-century castle overlooking the Rhine for €15 per night (p. 484).

9. Schloß Gottorf, Schleswig. A former Viking stronghold now holds six museums (p. 469).

8. Moritzburg, Dresden. A huge palace full of hunting trophies on a custom made island (p. 448).

7. Wilhelmshöhe, Kassel. A mad prince, artificial ruins, and a 350 ft. statue of Hercules (p. 479).

6. Heidelberger Schloß, Heidelberg. This fortress guards Germany's oldest university and largest wine barrel (p. 486).

5. Burg Rheinfels, St. Goar. Bring a candle to explore the ruined underground passages (p. 485).

4. Schloß Hohenschwangau, Füssen. The royal bedroom is inlaid with thousands of crystals to replicate the night sky (p. 509).

3. Schloß Sanssouci, Potsdam. A French-named English garden near Germany's capitol (p. 447).

2. Wartburg, Eisenach. Deep in the Thuringian forest, this fortress inspired Bach, Goethe, Martin Luther, and Wagner (p. 458).

1. Schloß Linderhof, Oberommergau. The hunting lodge for a king who has everything: Complete with mosque, half-ton chandeliers and a man-made grotto.

students €2.) Inside the **Annakapelle,** macabre paintings depict everyone from the Pope and Emperor to the smallest child engaged in the *Totentanz* (death dance), a public frenzy of despair that overtook Europe during the plague. (Open Apr.-Oct. Su and Tu-Sa 10am-5pm; Nov.-Mar. Su and Tu-Sa 1-4pm. €2.50, students €2.)

Trains run to Munich (2hr., every 2hr., €19). Füssen can also be reached by **bus** #1084 or 9606 from Garmisch-Partenkirchen (2¼hr., 5 per day, €7). To get from the train station to the **tourist office,** Kaiser-Maximilian-Pl. 1, walk the length of Bahnhofstr. and head across the roundabout to the big yellow building on your left. The staff finds **rooms** for free and sells hiking maps. (☎ 08362 93 85 32. Open Apr.-Sept. M-F 8:30am-6:30pm, Sa 9am-12:30pm, Su 10am-noon; Oct.-Mar. M-F 9am-5pm, Sa 10am-noon.) **Postal Code:** 87629.

KÖNIGSSCHLÖßER (ROYAL CASTLES). King Ludwig II, a zany visionary and fervent Wagner fan, used his cash to create fantastic castles. In 1886, a band of nobles and bureaucrats deposed Ludwig, declared him insane, and imprisoned him. Three days later, the King and a loyal advisor were mysteriously discovered dead in a nearby lake. The fairy tale castles that framed Ludwig's life and the enigma of his death still captivate tourists today. The glitzy ◪**Schloß Neuschwanstein** is Germany's most clichéd tourist attraction and was the inspiration for Disney's Sleeping Beauty Castle. The completed chambers (63 remain unfinished) include a Byzantine throne room, a small artificial grotto, and an immense *Sängersaal* (singer's hall) built expressly for performances of Wagnerian operas. For the fairy godmother of all views, hike 10min. up to ◪**Marienbrücke,** a bridge that spans the gorge and waterfall behind the castle. Ludwig summered in the bright yellow, neo-Gothic **Schloß Hohenschwangau** across the valley. (Both open Apr.-Sept. daily 9am-6pm; Oct.-Mar. 10am-4pm. Mandatory tours €7 per castle; combination ticket €13.) Tickets can be purchased at the **Ticket-Service Center,** Alpseestr. 12 (☎ 08362 93 08 30), about 100m south of the Hohenschwangau bus stop.

From Füssen, hop on **bus** #73 or 78 marked Königsschlösser, which departs from the train station (10min., 2 per hr., €1.40). It drops you in front of the info booth (open daily 9am-6pm); the Ticket-Service Center is a short walk uphill on Alpseestr. Separate paths lead up to both Hohenschwangau and Neuschwanstein. A *Tagesticket* (€5.60; buy from the bus driver) gives unlimited regional bus use.

GREECE (Ελλας)

A land where sacred monasteries are mountainside fixtures, three-hour seaside siestas are standard issue, and dancing on tables until daybreak is a summer rite—Greece's treasures are impossibly varied. Much of the history of the Western world owes its character to the philosophical, literary, artistic, and athletic mastery of the ancient Greeks. Schoolkids still dream of Hercules and Medusa, only to long later for Greece's island beaches and its gorgeous natural landscape, once the playground of a pantheon of gods. The all-encompassing Greek lifestyle is a mix of high speed traveling and sun-inspired lounging: Old men hold lively debates in town *plateias*, mopeds skid through the streets around the clock, and unpredictable schedules force a go-with-the-flow approach to life.

LIFE AND TIMES

HISTORY

THE RISE OF THE CITY-STATE. In the aftermath of the Dorian invasion of Mycenaen cities in 1000 BC, the **polis**, or city-state, rose as the major Greek political structure. The heart of the city was the **acropolis**, a fortified citadel and religious center atop the highest point, and the **agora**, the marketplace and the center of commercial and social life. During the **Persian Wars** (490-477 BC), the Greeks overcame overwhelming odds to defeat the Persians in the legendary battles at Marathon, Salamis, and Plataea. The victories ushered in a period of unprecedented prosperity and artistic, commercial, and political success.

SUGGESTED ITINERARIES

THREE DAYS Spend it all in **Athens** (p. 519). Roam the **Acropolis**, gaze at the treasures of the **National Archaeological Museum**, and pay homage to the gods in the fabulous **Parthenon**. Visit the ancient Athenian **Agora**, and run a lap in the **Panathenaic Olympic Stadium**, home of the **Summer 2004 Olympics** (p. 529).

ONE WEEK Begin your week with a sojourn in **Athens** (3 days). Move on to **Corinth** to wander through the 6th-century **Temple of Apollo** (1 day; p. 540). Sprint to **Olympia** to see where the games began—check out the immense **Temple of Zeus** (1 day; p. 536). Take the ferry to **Corfu** (1 day; p. 545) and then soak up Byzantine history in **Thessaloniki** (1 day; p. 540). Ask the **Oracle at Delphi** how to top off your week (1 day; p. 535).

BEST OF GREECE, THREE WEEKS Explore **Athens** (4 days) before strolling among the mansions of **Nafplion** (1 day; p. 539). Race west to **Olympia** (1 day), and then take a ferry from Patras to the immortalized beaches of **Corfu** (2 days). Back on the mainland, wander the streets of **Thessaloniki** (2 days), and then climb to the cliffside monasteries of **Meteora** (1 day, p. 545). Be sure to consult the gods at **Mount Olympus** (1 day; p. 544) and the **Oracle of Delphi** (1 day). A ferry from Athens to **Crete** (3 days; p. 551) will let you discover Europe's largest gorge. Seek respite on **Santorini** (1 day; p. 551), debauchery on **Ios** (1 day; p. 550), and suntanning on **Mykonos** (1 day; p. 548). Finally, repent at the famous temples on **Delos** (1 day; p. 549).

CLASSICAL GREECE. At the end of the Persian Wars, Athens established itself as the head of the **Delian League,** an organization of Greek city-states formed to defend against Persian aggression that actually acted as an Athenian empire. Athens, which prided itself in its commercial, democratic, and cultural achievements, rivaled the agricultural, oligarchical, and martial Sparta in controlling Greece. The competition erupted into violence during the **Peloponnesian War** (431-404 BC), which ended in total defeat for Athens.

MACEDONIAN RULE. The period after the Peloponnesian War was marked by a gradual devolution of city-state power. Macedonia's **King Philip** seized control in 338 BC. After Philip's assassination in 336 BC, his 20-year-old son, Alexander, later known as **Alexander the Great,** took the throne. Alexander ruled Greece with an iron fist and consolidated control of his father's empire. By the time of his sudden death at 33, he ruled Egypt and the entire Persian Empire and had spread Greek culture and language throughout the eastern Mediterranean. The dissolution of Alexander's empire restored a measure of independence to the Greek city-states, but self-rule did not last long. By 27 BC, the upstart Roman Empire had conquered Greece and incorporated it into the province of Achaea.

ROMAN EMPIRE: EAST SIDE. As Rome slowly declined, the empire became dominated by competing halves: An eastern half, centered in Anatolia, the Levant, and Greece, and a western half, centered at Rome. The unusual political arrangement ended in a scramble for power, finally won by **Constantine** in AD 312, who later legalized Christianity within his empire. He gave the Roman Empire a new capital in 324 by founding **Constantinople,** built over the ancient city of Byzantium. While Western Europe was overrun by barbarian invaders, the eastern **Byzantine Empire** became a center of learning, trade, and influence, unrivaled in its time.

NETTLESOME NEIGHBORS. During the 6th century, **Emperor Justinian**'s battles against the Sassanians of Persia overstretched the empire's strength. Power waned under the force of constant raids by Slavs, Mongols, and Avars, and in many areas of the mainland and Peloponnese, Greek culture was wiped out entirely. From 1200 to 1400, the Byzantine Empire was plagued by Norman and Venetian crusaders, who conquered and looted Constantinople in 1204 and imposed western Catholic culture upon the city. On May 29, 1453, the Ottoman Turks overran the much-reduced city, renaming it **İstanbul.** The Muslim Turkish rulers treated their Greek subjects as a **millet**—a separate community ruled by its own religious leaders. The Orthodox Greek church became the moderator of culture and tradition and the foundation of Greek autonomy. By the 19th century, Greeks were pushing for complete independence from the empire.

GREEK NATIONALIST REVOLT. On March 25, 1821, Bishop Germanos of Patras raised a Greek flag at the monastery of Agia Lavra and sparked an empire-wide rebellion. Disorganized but impassioned guerrillas in the Peloponnese and Aegean islands waged sporadic war on the Turkish government for years. Finally, in 1829, with great support from European powers, Greece won its independence. The borders of the new Greece were narrow, including only a fraction of the six million Greeks living under Ottoman rule. For the next century, Greek politics centered around freeing İstanbul from the Turks and uniting all Greeks into one sovereign state, a project called the *Megali Idhea* (the Great Idea).

EXPAND AND CONTRACT. In 1833, the European powers declared Greece a monarchy and handed the crown to a succession of Germanic princes. The 1864 constitution, however, downplayed the power of the king and emphasized the importance of the elected prime minister. In 1919, Prime Minister **Eleftherios Venizelos** ordered an outright invasion of Turkey, but a young Turkish general, Mustafa

Kemal, later called **Atatürk,** crushed the invasion. The **Treaty of Lausanne,** signed in 1923, enacted a population exchange that sent a million Greeks living in Asia Minor to Greece, and 400,000 Turkish Muslims from Greece to Turkey. This ended the *Megali Idhea* but began a series of economic problems for Greece.

THE SECOND WORLD WAR AND THE MODERN GREEK STATE. The 1930s were rocked by political turmoil, as Greeks lived through brief intervals of democracy amid a succession of monarchies and military rule. Although the nation defeated the Italian forces, Greece fell to Germany in 1941 and endured four years of bloody and brutal Axis occupation. The Communist-led resistance was met with broad popular support, and many resistance fighters received aid from the Western powers, which were eager to prevent the formation of a communist Greece.

Civil war broke out in 1944. The left-wing, Soviet-backed Democratic Army eventually lost to the US-supplied anti-communist coalition government. Keeping a visible hand in Greek politics, the US helped place **General Papagos, Constantine Karamanlis,** and the right-wing **Greek Rally Party** in power. When Karamanlis resigned in 1963, left-wing **George Papandreou** came to power, but the right-wing respite was short-lived; the army staged a coup d'etat on April 21, 1967, which resulted in rule by a military junta for seven years. The junta ultimately fell in 1973 after a Turkish invasion of Cyprus and a nationwide student uprising.

Karamanlis returned to power in 1975, instituting parliamentary elections and organizing a referendum on the form of government. Monarchy was defeated by a two-thirds vote, and a new constitution was drawn up in 1975, calling for a parliamentary government with a ceremonial president appointed by the legislature—this system is still in use today.

TODAY

In the 1980s, **Andreas Papandreou,** founder of the leftist **Panhellenic Socialist Movement** (PASOK), steered Greece into the European Economic Community (EEC) and pioneered the passage of women's rights legislation. Fellow socialist **Costas Simitis** took control of the party after the unpopular tenure of **Constantine Mitsotakis,** and has since pursued economic reforms in an attempt to meet the qualifying standards for entry into the **European Union** (EU), which became a reality in January 2001. Also in January 2001, Foreign Minister **George Papandreou** traveled to Turkey, the first such visit in 37 years. While there, he signed four cooperation agreements concerning tourism, the environment, the protection of investments, and terrorism. Talks have even begun regarding Cyprus, which remains divided into Turkish and Greek Cypriot states. Though the discussions have been fruitless so far, the dialogue has brought the nations closer and helped guarantee an extended peace in the Aegean. In the summer of 2004, the **Olympic Games** will return to their birthplace as Athens plays host to the world's athletes and spectators.

THE ARTS

It is impossible to overestimate how much Western culture owes to the architectural and artistic achievements of the ancient Greeks—Augustus Caesar, Michelangelo, Jacques-Louis David, Thomas Jefferson, Constantine Brancusi, and even Salvador Dalí found inspiration in Greek works.

LITERATURE AND DRAMA

The first written Greek did not appear until the 8th century BC, but the Greek literary tradition may have begun as many as 150 years earlier, with the epic songs of **Homer,** including the *Iliad* and *Odyssey,* which most scholars believe survived through oral tradition alone. During the 7th century BC, **Archilochus** of Paros made what is believed to be the first contributions to written poetry in the form of anti-heroic, anti-Homeric elegies. The foundation for modern drama was laid in the 5th century BC, in the *tragodoi* (goat songs) dedicated to the god **Dionysus.** Greek drama began as a religious rite in which all attendants performed in the chorus. Individual acting began when, at a public competition of masked choruses in Dionysus's honor, young **Thespis** stepped out of the crowd to become Athens's first actor—hence the word "thespian." By adding other characters, **Aeschylus** composed the *Oresteia* (458 BC), a trilogy about Agamemnon's ruinous return home from the Trojan War. **Sophocles**'s *Oedipus* trilogy (c. 444-401 BC) arguably founded modern dramatic tragedy.

Greek independence gave rise to the **Ionian School** of modern literature, which dealt with the political and personal issues of the Greek revolution. **Dionysios Solomos** (1798-1857), whose "Hymn to Liberty" became the Greek national anthem, is still referred to as the National Poet. Twentieth-century poets alternately denounced and celebrated nationalism and politics. **Odysseas Elytis,** winner of a 1979 Nobel Prize in Literature, felt that French Surrealism was an integral part of national redemption. The best-known modern Greek author is arguably **Nikos Kazantzakis** (1883-1957). His many novels include *Zorba the Greek* and *The Last Temptation of Christ,* both of which were made into successful films.

Contemporary playwrights like **Iakovos Kambanellis** (b. 1922), **Demitris Kehadis** (b. 1933), and Symiot writer **Eleni Haviara** have delighted audiences with their portrayals of Greek life. Taking advantage of the international attention of the Olympic Games, the **Greek Playwrights Society** (www.eeths.gr) organized a May 2003 festival of modern plays from local writers. But classical theater still dominates, especially at the **Athens Festival** (p. 534) and the **Epidavros Festival** (p. 539).

MUSIC

Rembetika (gutsy blues music with folk influences) first made its appearance in Greece in the late 19th century. After decades of inauthentic performances, interest in traditional *rembetika* has resurfaced, and musicians strumming *bouzouki* (a traditional Greek instrument similar to a mandolin) can be found in several clubs. Trendier venues offer a playlist saturated with Western music, but local band **Pyx Lax** is gaining something of an international following.

THE VISUAL ARTS

ART AND ARCHITECTURE. After the Dark Ages that followed the collapse of Mycenaean civilization, a new artistic style emerged with ceramics as its primary medium and Athens as its major cultural center. During the **Archaic Period** (700-480 BC), artists decorated clay figurines and pottery with geometrical motifs reminiscent of basket-weaving patterns. The Archaic Period also saw the innovation of the **Doric** and **Ionic** architectural orders. Ionic columns were distinguished from their more austere Doric predecessors by their twin **volute** (scrolled spiral) capitals, and their slender, fluted shafts.

The arts flourished as Athens reached the pinnacle of its political and economic power in what is known as the **Classical Period** (480-323 BC). The peerless Athenian **Acropolis** (p. 526), built during this era, embodied "classic" for the entire world; its crown, the **Parthenon,** demonstrates the Greek aesthetic of perfect proportions. Sculptors mastered the representation of the human form during the Classical Period. By the middle of the 5th century BC, they had developed the **severe style,** which elevated the human form to a plane of universal physical perfection, idealizing the athletic heroism praised by Pindar's Olympic odes.

After the death of Alexander the Great, the flamboyant **Hellenistic Period** rose out of the ashes of Classical Greece. Scuttling the simpler Doric and Ionic styles, Eastern Greeks designed ornate, flower-topped **Corinthian** columns. Hellenistic architects worked on a monumental scale, building huge complexes of temples and palaces. Astoundingly precise acoustics graced the enormous amphitheaters like the one at **Epidavros** (p. 539); a coin dropped onstage is audible from the most distant seat. Hellenistic sculpture exuded passion, testing the aesthetic value of ugliness. With the arrival of the Roman Empire, styles shifted to suit Roman tastes.

The art and architecture in Greece under **Byzantine** and **Ottoman** rule belonged more to those imperial cultures than to Greece. Religious Byzantine artistry saw the creation of magnificent mosaics, iconography, and church architecture. Mosaics were composed of **tesserae,** small cubes of stone, glass-covered ceramic, or metallic foil. Sparkling examples can be seen in the churches of **Thessaloniki** (p. 540) and **Meteora** (p. 545) and at the **Monastery of Osios Loukas.**

After Greek independence, nationalist sentiment led the government to subsidize Greek art. King Otto encouraged young artists to study their craft in Munich, and the **Polytechneion,** Greece's first modern art school, was established in 1838. While sculptors still looked to Classical Greece for inspiration, the first wave of post-independence painters showed strong evidence of their German training.

GREECE

Many 20th-century Greek artists contended with European trends, including Impressionism, Expressionism, and Surrealism. Other painters rejected foreign influence, among them the much-adored **Theophilos Chatzimichael** (1873-1934).

Modern Greek art unfortunately tends to be overshadowed by its Classical roots. Current notable artists include **Yiannis Psychopedis** (b. 1945), whose paintings combine social and aesthetic criticism, and the painter **Opy Zouni** (b. 1941), who has won much international acclaim for her geometric art.

FILM. After suffering under the colonels's junta, the Greek film industry rebuilt itself throughout the 1980s and has recently emerged as a distinguished and prolific presence in the international arena. The 1982 reestablishment of the **Greek Film Center,** a state-supported institute, aided this revitalization by funding and producing many of the most highly regarded modern Greek films, including works by **Nikos Perakis, Pantelis Vougaris,** and **Nikos Panayotopoulos,** Greece's most acclaimed filmmaker and winner of the 1998 Cannes Palme d'Or.

FACTS AND FIGURES

Official Name: Hellenic Republic.	**Land Area:** 131,940 sq. km.
Capital: Athens.	**Time:** GMT+2.
Major Cities: Thessaloniki.	**Language:** Greek.
Population: 10,600,000.	**Religion:** Eastern Orthodox (98%).

ESSENTIALS

WHEN TO GO

June through August is high season in Greece; consider visiting during May or September, when the weather is equally beautiful but the crowds are thinner. The low season, from mid-September through May, offers cheaper airfares and lodging, but many sights and accommodations have shorter hours or close altogether. Ferries and trains run considerably less frequently, although ski areas at Mt. Parnassos, Mt. Pelion, and Metsovo beckon winter visitors.

DOCUMENTS AND FORMALITIES

VISAS. EU citizens do not need a visa. Citizens of Australia, Canada, New Zealand, the UK, and the US do not need a visa for stays of up to 90 days, though they are ineligible for employment. South Africans need a visa any stay.

EMBASSIES. Foreign embassies in Greece are in Athens (p. 519). For Greek embassies at home, contact: **Australia,** 9 Turrana St., Yarralumla, Canberra, ACT 2600 (☎02 6273 3011); **Canada,** 80 MacLaren St., Ottawa, ON K2P 0K6 (☎613-238-6271; www.greekembassy.ca); **Ireland,** 1 Upper Pembroke St., Dublin 2 (☎01 676 7254); **South Africa,** 1003 Church St., Hatfield, Arcadia-Pretoria 0028 (☎12 437 3523); **UK,** 1a Holland Park, London W11 3TP (☎020 7229 3850); and **US,** 2221 Massachusetts Ave. N.W., Washington, D.C. 20008 (☎202-939-1300; www.greekembassy.org).

TRANSPORTATION

BY PLANE. The domestic service offered by **Olympic Airways,** Syngrou 96-100, Athens 11741 (☎2810 114 4444; www.olympic-airways.gr), has increased greatly. Their website lists information for every office around the globe. A 1hr. flight from

Athens (€60-90) can get you to almost any island in Greece. Even in the low season, remote destinations are serviced several times per week, while developed areas may have several flights per day.

BY TRAIN. Greece is served by a number of international train routes that connect Athens, Larissa, and Thessaloniki to most European cities. Train service within Greece, however, is limited and sometimes uncomfortable, and no lines go to the western coast. The new express, air-conditioned intercity trains, while slightly more expensive and infrequent, are worth the price. **Eurail** passes are valid on all Greek trains. **Hellenic Railways Organization** (OSE; www.osenet.gr) connects Athens to major Greek cities; from Greece, call ☎ 145 or 147 for schedules and prices.

BY BUS. There are almost no buses running directly from any European city to Greece. **Busabout,** 258 Vauxhall Bridge Rd., London SW1V 1BS (☎ 0207 950 1661; www.busabout.com), is one of the few European bus companies that runs to Greece. Domestic bus service is extensive and fares are cheap. **KTEL** (www.ktel.org) runs most domestic buses; always check with an official source about scheduled departures, as posted schedules are often outdated.

BY FERRY. The most popular way of getting to Greece is by ferry from Italy. Boats travel from Brindisi, Italy, to Corfu (p. 546), Kephalonia (p. 546), and Patras (p. 536), from Ancona, Italy, to Corfu and Patras. The travel agency **Manolopoulos** (☎ 2610 223 621), at Othonos Amalias 35 in Patras, can provide information on ferries to Italy. Ferries also run from Greece to various points on the Turkish coast. There is frequent ferry service to the Greek islands, but schedules are irregular and faulty information is common. Check schedules posted at the tourist office or the *limenarcheio* (port police), or at www.ferries.gr. Make reservations and arrive at least 1-2hr. before your departure time. **Flying Dolphins** (www.dolphins.gr) provides extensive hydrofoil service between the islands at twice the cost and speed as ferries; their routes are listed in the **Transportation** sections where appropriate.

BY CAR AND MOPED. Cars are a luxury in Greece, a country where public transportation is nonexistent after 7pm. Ferries charge a transport fee for cars. Rental agencies may quote low daily rates that exclude the 20% tax and **Collision Damage Waiver** (CDW) insurance; expect to pay €20-40 per day for a rental. Foreign drivers are required to have an **International Driving Permit** and an **International Insurance Certificate** to drive in Greece. The **Automobile and Touring Club of Greece** (ELPA), Messogion 395, Athens 11527, provides assistance and offers reciprocal membership to foreign auto club members. (☎ 210 606 8800. 24hr. emergency roadside assistance ☎ 104. Info line for Athens ☎ 174; elsewhere ☎ 210 606 8838. Open M-F 7am-3pm.) **Mopeds** can be great for exploring, but they also make you extremely vulnerable to the carelessness of other drivers; wear a helmet.

TOURIST SERVICES AND MONEY

EMERGENCY	Police: ☎ 100. Hospital: ☎ 106. Ambulance: ☎ 166.

TOURIST OFFICES. Tourism in Greece is overseen by two national organizations: The **Greek National Tourist Organization** (GNTO) and the **tourist police** *(touristiki astinomia).* The GNTO, Tsoha 7, Athens (☎ 210 870 7000. www.gnto.gr), known as the **EOT** in Greece, can supply general information about sights and accommodations throughout the country. The tourist police (24hr. info ☎ 171) deal with local and immediate problems: Bus schedules, accommodations, lost passports, etc. They are open long hours and are willing to help, but their English may be limited.

MONEY. The official currency of Greece is the **euro.** The Greek drachma can still be exchanged at a rate of 340.75dr to €1. For exchange rates and more information on the euro, see p. 13. If you're carrying more than €1000 in cash when you enter Greece, you must declare it upon entry. A bare-bones day in Greece, staying at hostels, campgrounds, or *domatia* (rooms to let), and buying food at supermarkets or outdoor food stands, costs about €35. A day with more comforts, like accommodation in a nicer *domatia* or budget hotel, and eating one meal per day in a restaurant, runs €50. There is no **tipping** anywhere except restaurants. Generally, **bargaining** is expected for street wares and in other informal venues, but shop owners whose goods are tagged will consider bargaining rude and disrespectful. The European Union imposes a **value-added tax** (VAT) on goods and services purchased within the EU, which is included in the price. For more info, see p. 16.

COMMUNICATION

PHONE CODES	**Country code: 30. International dialing prefix:** 00. The city code must always be dialed, even when calling from within the city. From outside Greece, dial int'l dialing prefix (see inside back cover) + 30 + local number.

TELEPHONES. The only way to use the phone in Greece is with a prepaid phone card. You can buy the cards at *peripteros* (streetside kiosks) in denominations of €3, €12, and €25. Time is measured in minutes or talk units (100 units=30min. of domestic calling). A calling card is the cheapest way to make international phone calls. To place a call with a calling card, contact your service provider's Greek operator: **AT&T** ☎00 800 1311; **British Telecom** ☎00 800 4411; **Canada Direct** ☎00 800 1611; **Ireland Direct** ☎00 155 1174; **MCI** ☎00 800 1211; **Sprint** ☎00 800 1411. Cell phones are an increasingly popular option; for more info, see p. 30.

MAIL. To send a letter weighing up to 50g within Europe costs €0.85; anywhere else in the world costs €0.90. Mail sent to Greece from the Continent generally takes at least 3 days to arrive; from Australia, the US, and South Africa airmail will take 5-10 days. Address mail to be held according to the following example: First name SURNAME, Corfu Town Post Office, Corfu, Greece 8900, POSTE RESTANTE.

INTERNET ACCESS. The availability of the Internet in Greece is rapidly expanding. In all big cities, most small cities and large towns, and most of the touristed islands, you will be able to find Internet access. Expect to pay €3-6 per hour. For lists of cybercafes in Greece, check out http://dmoz.org/Computers/Internet/Cybercafes/Greece/.

ACCOMMODATIONS AND CAMPING

GREECE	❶	❷	❸	❹	❺
ACCOMMODATIONS	under €10	€10-25	€26-40	€41-70	over €70

Lodgings in Greece are a bargain. Tourist offices usually maintain lists of inexpensive accommodations. A bed in a **hostel** averages around €7. Those not currently endorsed by HI are in most cases still safe and reputable. In many areas,

domatia (rooms to let) are an attractive and perfectly dependable option. Often you'll be approached by locals as you enter town or disembark from your boat, a practice that is common, but theoretically illegal. Prices vary; expect to pay €12-20 for a single and €25-35 for a double. Always negotiate with *domatia* owners before settling a price, and never pay more than you would for a hotel in town. If in doubt, ask the tourist police; they may set you up with a room and conduct the negotiations themselves. **Hotel** prices are regulated, but proprietors may try to push you to take the most expensive room. Budget hotels start at €15 for singles and €25 for doubles. Check your bill carefully, and threaten to contact the tourist police if you think you are being cheated. Greece hosts plenty of official **campgrounds,** which run about €4.50 per person, plus €3 per tent. Discreet freelance camping on beaches—though illegal—is common in July and August but may not be the safest way to spend the night.

FOOD AND DRINK

GREECE	❶	❷	❸	❹	❺
FOOD	under €5	€5-10	€11-15	€16-25	over €25

Penny-pinching carnivores will thank Zeus for lamb, chicken, or beef *souvlaki*, stuffed into a pita to make *gyros* (yee-RO). Vegetarians can also eat their fill on the cheap, with *horiatiki* (Greek salad) and savory pastries like *tiropita* (cheese pie) and *spanakopita* (spinach and feta pie). Frothy, iced coffee *frappés* take the edge off the summer heat. *Ouzo*, a powerful, licorice-flavored spirit, is served with *mezedes*, which are snacks of octopus, cheese, and sausage.

Breakfast, served only in the early morning, is generally very simple: A piece of toast with *marmelada* or a pastry. Lunch, a hearty and leisurely meal, can begin as early as noon but is more likely eaten sometime between 2 and 5pm. Dinner is a drawn-out, relaxed affair served late. A Greek restaurant is known as a *taverna* or *estiatorio*; a grill is a *psistaria*. Many restaurants don't offer printed menus.

HOLIDAYS AND FESTIVALS

Holidays: Feast of St. Basil/New Year's Day (Jan. 1); Epiphany (Jan. 6); 1st Monday in Lent (Feb. 23); Greek Independence Day (Mar. 25); Easter (Apr. 11); St. George's Day (Apr. 23); Labor Day (May 1); Ascension (May 20); Pentecost (May 30); Feast of the Assumption of the Virgin Mary (Aug. 15); The Virgin Mary's Birthday (Sept. 8); Feast of St. Demetrius (Oct. 26); Ohi Day (Oct. 28); Christmas Day (Dec. 25).

Festivals: Three weeks of **Carnival** feasting and dancing (starting Feb. 2) precede Lenten fasting. April 23 is **St. George's Day,** when Greece honors the dragon-slaying knight with horse races, wrestling matches, and dances. The **Feast of St. Demetrius** (Oct. 26) is celebrated with particular enthusiasm in Thessaloniki.

ATHENS (Αθηνα) ☎210

Ancient ruins sit quietly amid hectic modern streets as tacit testaments to Athens's rich history, while the Acropolis looms larger than life, a perpetual reminder of ancient glory. Byzantine churches recall an era of foreign invaders, when the city was ruled from Macedonia, Rome, and Constantinople. But the packs of mopeds in Pl. Syndagma prove that Athens refuses to become a museum—over the past two centuries, democracy has revived the city in a wave of madcap construction. The 2004 Olympic Games, to be held in Athens, promises an array of modern landmarks to stand proudly alongside the city's ancient ones.

GREECE

GREECE

Areos Park
Leoforos Alexandras

Filadelfias Khomovitou
Livaniou
Enianos
Khomatianou
M. Smirls
Akharnon
Ioulianou
Metsovou
Skiltsi
Fotifa
Mamouri
M. Voda
Alkiviadou
Aristotelous
Mavromihali
Rethimnou
Psalida
Neof. Metaxa
Fills
Ipirou
Vas. Irakliou
Plapduta
Ioustinianou
Liosson
Makednoias
Tritis Skeptemvriou
Poulkherias
Kritis
Sourmeli
Averof
National
Archeological
Museum
Kountouriotou
EXHARIA
Strefi
Aghrou Pavlou
Politekhniou
Tossitsa
Zbsstmadon
Paleologou
Polytechnic
University/School
of Fine Arts
Zalmi
Notara
Trikoupi
Tsamadou
Ikonomou
Metaxa
Kalidromiou
Iliou
Magker
Solomou
Stournara
Botassi
Soultani
Koleti
Themistokleous
Eressou
Mezonos
Akominatou
PL.
EXARHON
Aghiou
Khiou
Sonlerou
Kapodistriou
Emm. Benaki
Messolognou
Mavromihali
Araklovis
Darverion
Favierou
Aristotelous
Halkokondili
Kaningos
Dervenion
Elefsinion
Deligianni
Laundromat
Veranzerou
PL.
KANINGOS
Talongou
Zoodokhou Pighis
Skoufa
Ippokratous
Asklipiou
Kodratou
Laundromat
Victor Hugo
Psaron
Glad-
stonos
Zoodokhou Pighis
Didotou
Odisseos
Karolou
Satovriandou
Dorou
Gamveta
Har. Trikoupi
Mavromihali
Soonos
Solonos
Didotou
KARAISKAKI
SQ.
OSE
National
Theater
Konstantinou
Fidiou
Emm. Benaki
Cine
Rivera
M. Alexandrou
Aghiou
Nikiforou
Vilara
Zinonos
OMONIA
Santaroza
Aidou
Opera
House
Panepistimiou
Theater
Museum
Massalias
Jassonos
Kolonou
Deligiorgi
Keleri
Voulgari
Likourgou
Efpolidos
KOTZIA
Pesmazoglou
University
Akadimias-Rouxelt
Sina
Omrou
Leonidou
Kolokinthous
Aghisilaou
Menandriou
Geraniou
Sokratous
Kirsthenous
Kratinou
Sofkleous
Armodiou
Oragsaniou
Korai
Papanigopoulou
Vissarionos
Amerikis
El. Venizelou
Valaoritou
Likaviliou
P. Tsaldari - Pireos
PL
THEATROU
Aristoghitonos
Evripidou
Ae. Dimitriou
Praxitelous
Romvis
Stadiou
Smrts
Kriezotou
Epikrou
Aristophanous
Eshilou
Aglon Anaglron
Ae. Mitriou
Polikhtou
Ae. Mikelou
Vissis
Kolokotroni
Leka
National
Historical
Museum
Karageorgi
Servias
Zalokosta
Psaromilingou
Dipliou
Sarf
PSIRI
Pafados
Protoghenous
Aiolou
Evangelistras
Perikleous
Ermou
SYNDAGMA
Vasilissis
Aghlon
Leontou
Lepeniotou
 Nin
Karaiskaki
Ae. Philou
Athinas
Athinaidos
SYNDAGMA
Synagogue
Agia
Assomati
Ermou
MONASTIRAKI
Ploutonos
Deka
Ermou
Mitropoleos
Othonos
Parliament
Building
Amfiktionos
Apostolou Pavlou
Thission
Stoa of
Attalus
Museum
Vrissakou
Pikils
Dexipou
Pandrossou
Adrianou
Aglos
Eleftherios
Mitropoll
Cathedral
Apollonos
Xenofontos
Nikis
Agla
Triada
National
Garden
Iraclidhon
Agora
Ag.
Apostoli
Polignotou
Dioskouron
Kirlstou
Lysiou
Flessa
Apollonos
Nikodimou
Skoufou
Voulis
Filellinon
PLAKA
Pritanios
Metamorphosi
Acropolis
Tetrbah
Ae. Navarhou
Thoukididou
Iperidou
Kydathineon
Zappeion
Exhibition Halls
Nymfon
Hill
Pynx Hill
Parthenon
Acropolis
Museum
Epimenidou
Lissikratous
Frinikhou
Hadrian's
Arch
Leoforos Olgas
Odeon of Herodes
Atticus
Theater of
Dionysus
Dion. Areopaghitou
Thrassilou
Viponos
Leof. Amalias
Philopapou
Hill
Socrates's
Prison
Gkali
Kalisperi
Parthenonos
Mitseon
Makrighlani
Diakou
Rogon
Temple of
Olympian Zeus
Philopappos'
Monument
Garivaldi
Propileon
Elefthtou
Zitrou
Diakou
Syngrou

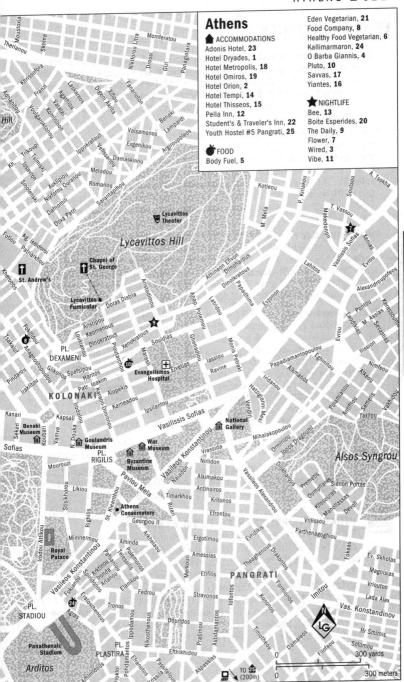

Athens

🏠 **ACCOMMODATIONS**
Adonis Hotel, **23**
Hotel Dryades, **1**
Hotel Metropolis, **18**
Hotel Omiros, **19**
Hotel Orion, **2**
Hotel Tempi, **14**
Hotel Thisseos, **15**
Pella Inn, **12**
Student's & Traveler's Inn, **22**
Youth Hostel #5 Pangrati, **25**

🍎 **FOOD**
Body Fuel, **5**

Eden Vegetarian, **21**
Food Company, **8**
Healthy Food Vegetarian, **6**
Kallimarmaron, **24**
O Barba Giannis, **4**
Pluto, **10**
Savvas, **17**
Yiantes, **16**

⭐ **NIGHTLIFE**
Bee, **13**
Boite Esperides, **20**
The Daily, **9**
Flower, **7**
Wired, **3**
Vibe, **11**

GREECE

▣ TRANSPORTATION

Flights: Eleftherios Venizelou (ATH; ☎210 353 0000; www.aia.gr). Greece's new international airport operates as one massive, yet easily navigable terminal. Arrivals are on the ground floor, departures are on the 2nd. The new **suburban rail,** expected to be finished by summer 2004 for the Olympic Games, will serve the international airport from the city center in 30min. 4 bus lines run from the airport to Athens, Piraeus, and Rafina.

Trains: Hellenic Railways (OSE), Sina 6 (☎210 362 4402; www.ose.gr). **Larisis Train Station** (☎210 529 8837) serves northern Greece and Europe. Ticket office open daily 5am-midnight. Take trolley #1 from El. Venizelou (also known as Panepistimiou) in Pl. Syndagma (every 10min. 5am-midnight, €0.50). Trains depart for **Thessaloniki** (7hr., 5 per day, €15). **Peloponnese Train Station** (☎210 513 1601) serves **Olympia** (express: 5½hr., 2 per day, €4.40), **Patras** (4¼hr., 2 per day, €5.30), and major towns in the Peloponnese. From Larissis, exit to your right and cross the footbridge.

Buses: Terminal A: Kifissou 100 (☎210 512 4910). Take blue bus #051 from the corner of Zinonos and Menandrou near Pl. Omonia (every 15min., €0.50). Buses to: **Corinth** (1½hr., every 45min., €5.70); **Corfu** (10hr., 4 per day, €28); **Patras** (3hr., every 30 min., €13); **Thessaloniki** (6hr., 11 per day, €28). **Terminal B:** Liossion 260 (☎210 831 7153, M-F only). Take blue bus #024 from Amalias outside the National Gardens (45min., every 20min., €0.50). Buses to **Delphi** (3hr., 6 per day, €11).

Public Transportation: KTEL (ΚΤΕΛ) **buses** around Athens and its suburbs are blue and designated by 3-digit numbers. Buy bus/trolley tickets at any street kiosk. Hold on to your ticket—you can be fined €18-30 by police if caught without one. **Trolleys** are yellow and crowded, sporting 1- or 2-digit numbers; they are distinguished from buses by their electrical antennae. The Athens **Metro** consists of 3 lines. **M1** runs from northern Kifissia to the port of Piraeus. **M2** runs from Sepolia to Dafni. **M3** runs from Ethniki Amyna to Monastiraki in central Athens. Trains run 5am-midnight. Buy tickets (€0.30-0.60) in any station. **Tram:** 2 trams are under construction for the 2004 Olympic Games. **Line 1** will run from Zappeio in Athens Centre to Helliniko. **Line 2** will run from Neo Faliro along the Apollo Coast until Glyfada Square.

Car Rental: Try the places on **Singrou.** €35-50 for a small car with 100km mileage (including tax and insurance). Up to 50% student discount. Prices rise in summer.

Taxis: Meters start at €0.80, with an additional €0.30 per km; midnight-5am €0.50 per km. There's a €2 surcharge from the airport and a €0.70 surcharge for trips from bus and railway terminals, plus €0.30 for each piece of luggage over 10kg.

PIRAEUS PORT: FERRIES FROM ATHENS

The majority of ferries from Athens leave from the town of Piraeus Port. Ferries sail to nearly all Greek islands (except the Sporades and Ionian Islands). Ferries to Crete: **Hania** (9½hr., daily, €18); **Iraklion,** (14hr., 3 per day, €21-26); and **Rethymno** (11hr., daily, €22). Additional ferries to: **Chios** (9hr., daily, €19); **Hydra** (3hr., every hr., €15); **Ios** (7½hr., 2-5 per day, €17); **Lesvos** (12hr., daily, €23); **Milos** (7hr., 2-5 per day, €16); **Mykonos** (6hr., 2-5 per day, €17); **Naxos** (6hr., 2-5 per day, €17); **Paros** (6hr., 2-5 per day, €17); **Poros** (2½hr., every hr., €14); **Rhodes** (15hr., 2-5 per day, €27); **Santorini** (9hr., 2-5 per day, €19); and **Spetses** (4½hr., every hr., €21).

ORIENTATION AND PRACTICAL INFORMATION

Athenian geography mystifies newcomers and natives alike. If you lose your bearings, ask for directions back to well-lit **Syndagma** or look for a cab; the **Acropolis** serves as a reference point, as does **Mt. Lycavittos.** Athens's suburbs occupy seven hills in southwest Attica, near the coast. Syndagma, the central *plateia* containing the Parliament building, is encircled by the other major neighborhoods. Clockwise, they are **Plaka, Monastiraki, Psiri, Omonia, Exarhia, Kolonaki,** and **Pangrati.** Plaka, the center of the old city and home to many accommodations, is bounded by the city's two largest ancient monuments—the **Temple of Olympian Zeus** and the Acropolis. Omonia is the site of the city's central subway station. Two parallel avenues, **Panepistimiou** and **Stadiou,** connect Syndagma to Omonia. Omonia's neighbor to the east, progressive Exarhia, sports some of Athens's most exciting nightlife, while nearby Kolonaki, on the foothills of Mt. Lycavittos, has plenty of glitz and swanky shops. Pangrati, southeast of Kolonaki, is marked by several Byzantine churches, a park, the **Olympic Stadium,** and the **National Cemetery.**

Tourist Office: Tsohas 7 (info booth ☎210 870 7181; main desk ☎210 870 7000; www.gnto.gr), off of Vas. Sophias in Ambelokipi. Bus, train, and ferry schedules and prices; lists of museums, embassies, and banks; brochures on travel throughout Greece; and an indispensable Athens map. Open M-F 9am-3:30pm. ■**Philippis Tours,** Akti Tzelepi 3 (☎210 411 7787 or 210 413 3182; filippistours@hotmail.com). Open daily 5:30am-10:30pm. From the Metro, take a left, and walk 200m until you come to Karaskaiki Square. Walk toward the water; it'll be on the left side of the cluster of offices. Sells ferry and plane tickets, helps with accommodations, rents cars, exchanges money, and stores baggage (free for the day with *Let's Go*).

Banks: National Bank of Greece, Karageorgi Servias 2 (☎210 334 0015), in Pl. Syndagma. Open M-Th 8am-2pm, F 8am-1:30pm; open for **currency exchange** only M-Th 3:30-5:20pm, F 3-6:30pm, Sa 9am-3pm, Su 9am-1pm. Currency exchange available 24hr. at the **airport,** but exchange rates and commissions may be unfavorable.

American Express: Ermou 7 (☎210 322 3380), in Pl. Syndagma. Cashes traveler's checks commission-free, exchanges money, and provides travel services for cardholders. Open M-F 8:30am-4pm, Sa 8:30am-1:30pm.

Laundromats: Most *plintirios* have signs reading "Laundry." **National,** Apollonos 17, in Syndagma. Wash and dry €4.50 per kg. Open M-Th 4:30-8:30pm, F 8am-8pm.

Emergencies: Police: ☎100. **Medical:** ☎105 from Athens, 101 elsewhere; line open daily 2pm-7am. **Ambulance:** ☎166. **Fire:** ☎199. **AIDS Help Line:** ☎210 722 2222. *Athens News* lists emergency hospitals. Free emergency health care for tourists.

Tourist Police: Dimitrakopoulou 77 (☎171). English spoken. Open 24hr.

Pharmacies: Identified by a **green cross** hanging over the street. Many are open 24hr.; check *Athens News* for the day's emergency pharmacy.

Hospitals: Emergency hospitals on duty ☎106. **Geniko Kratiko Nosokomio** (Public State Hospital), Mesogion 154 (☎210 720 1211). **Ygeia,** Erithrou Stavrou 4 (☎210 682 7904), is a private hospital in Maroussi. "Hospital" is *nosokomio* in Greek.

Internet Access:

    Berval Travel Internet Access, Voulis 44A (☎210 331 1294), in Plaka near Pl. Syndagma. €6 per hr., students €5 per hr. Open daily 9:30am-8pm.

    Bits 'n Bytes Internet, Akademias 78 in Exarhia (between Em. Benaki and Zoodochou Pigis), Kapnikareas 19 in Plaka, Chremonidou 17 in Pangrati. (☎210 382 2545 or 210 330 6590; www.bnb.gr). Fast-connected flat screens in air-conditioned, black-lit joints. Midnight-9am €1.50 per hr., 9am to midnight €2.50 per hr.

GREECE

easyInternet Cafe: Filellinon 2 (☎210 331 3034) in Syndagma. On the 2nd floor above the Everest fast food eatery, directly across from Pl. Syndagma. 40 high speed, flat screen computers. Rates range from €0.80 to €3 per hr.

Internet Cafe, Stournari 49, in Omonia (☎210 383 8808; www.intergraphics.gr) on 7th floor. Gaze at the city below while checking email (€2 per hr.). Open M-F 9am-9:30pm, Sa 10am-2pm.

Ivis Travel Internet Services, Mitropoleos 3 (☎210 324 3365 or 210 324 3543; fax 210 322 4205). On the 2nd floor of the building across the street from the post office in Syndagma. €2 per hr., €1 min. Open daily 8:30am-10:30pm.

Arcade Internet Cafe, Stadiou 5 (☎210 324 8105; sofos1@ath.forthnet.gr), just up Stadiou from the *plateia* in Syndagma, in a shopping center about 15m from the main thoroughfare. €3 per hr., €0.50 every additional 10min. €1 min. Open M-Sa 9am-11pm, Su 11am-8pm.

Plaka Internet World, Pandrossou 29 (☎210 331 6056; www.internet-greece.gr), on the 4th fl., in **Plaka.** Large screens, fast connection, A/C, and a balcony where you can enjoy cold sodas and a great Acropolis view. €4 per hr. Open daily 10am-10pm.

Museum Internet Cafe, Patission 46 (☎210 883 3418; museum_net_cafe@yahoo.com), on the corner of Vas. Irakliou, in Exarhia. Frothy coffee drinks, A/C, and email at your own personal table. Cappuccino €2.40. Beer €2. €4.40 per hr., €1.50 per 20min. Open daily 9am-3am.

Post Office: Syndagma (☎210 322 6253), on the corner of Mitropoleos. Open M-F 7:30am-8pm, Sa 7:30am-2pm. Branch offices in Omonia, at Aiolou 100, and Exarhia, at the corner of Zaimi and K. Deligiani. **Postal Code:** 10022.

▸ ACCOMMODATIONS

The **Greek Youth Hostel Association,** Damareos 75 in Pangrati, lists hostels in Greece. (☎210 751 9530; y-hostels@ote.net.gr. Open daily M-F 9am-3pm.) The **Hellenic Chamber of Hotels,** Stadiou 24 in Syndagma, provides info and makes reservations for all types of hotels throughout Greece. Reservations require a cash deposit; you must contact them at least one month in advance and inform them of the length of your stay and the number of people. (☎210 323 7193; grhotels@ote-net.gr. Open May-Nov. M-F 8:30am-1:30pm.)

▨ **Student's and Traveler's Inn,** Kydatheneon 16 (☎210 324 4808), in Plaka. Unrivaled location and lively atmosphere with A/C, 24hr. restaurant, and around-the-clock cyber cafe. Reserve ahead and arrive on time. Co-ed dorms €17-22; singles €40, with private bath €50; doubles €58/70; triples €75/90; quads €100/120. ❷

▨ **Pella Inn,** Karaiskaki 1 (☎210 325 0598), in Monastiraki. Walk 10min. down Ermou from Pl. Syndagma; it's two blocks from the Monastiraki subway station. Features a large terrace with impressive views of the Acropolis. Free luggage storage. Dorms €15; doubles €40-50; triples €60; quads €80. ❷

Adonis Hotel, Kodrou 3 (☎210 324 9737), in Plaka. From Syndagma, follow Filellinon; turn right on Nikodimou and left onto Kodrou. A family hotel with a delightful rooftop lounge. Reserve far in advance. All rooms with bath. In summer, singles €41; doubles €56; triples €84. Off-season €29/43/62. A/C €10 extra per person. Discounts for longer stays. ❸

Hotel Tempi, Aiolou 29 (☎210 321 3175), in Monastiraki. Simple rooms with fans. Front-facing rooms are brighter. Luggage storage. Laundry service. Check-out 11am. Singles €32; doubles €42, with bath €48; triples €60. Off-season 20% discount. ❸

Hotel Orion, Em. Benaki 105 (☎210 382 7362), in Exarhia. From Pl. Omonia, walk up Em. Benaki or take bus #230 from Pl. Syndagma. Orion rents small rooms with shared baths. Sunbathers relax on the rooftop. Internet €3 per hr. Laundry €3. Singles €25; doubles €35; triples €40. Bargain for better prices. ❸

Hotel Dryades, Dryadon 4 (☎210 382 7116), in Exarhia. Elegant Dryades offers some of Athens's nicest budget accommodations, with large rooms and private baths. Internet €3 per 30hr. Singles €35; doubles €50; triples €60. ❸

Youth Hostel #5 Pangrati, Damareos 75 (☎210 751 9530). From Omonia or Pl. Syndagma, take trolley #2 or 11 to Filolaou. There's no sign for this cheery hostel, just a green door. Owners speak English. Hot showers €0.50 for 7min. Sheets €0.80; pillowcases €0.50. Laundry €3. Quiet hours 2-5pm and 11pm-7am. Dorms €9. Bring a sleeping bag to stay on the roof (€6). ❶

Hostel Aphrodite, Einardou 12 (☎210 881 0589 or 210 883 9249; www.hostelaphrodite.com), in Omonia. Small, clean rooms with A/C. Free luggage storage. Internet access €6 per hr. Laundry €11 per 6kg. Reception 24hr. Dorms €17; doubles €45; triples €60; quads €72. ❷

Hotel Omiros, Apollonos 15 (☎210 323 5486), near Pl. Syndagma. Relatively spacious rooms have A/C and private baths. Breakfast included. Call ahead. Singles €50; doubles €75; triples €93; quads €111. Bargain for student discounts. ❹

Hotel Metropolis, Mitropoleos 46 (☎210 321 7469; www.hotelmetropolis.gr), in Syndagma. Enjoy full amenities and wonderful views of Cathedral Mitropolis and the Acropolis. Elevator, A/C, TV, and phones. Free luggage storage. Laundry €6 per 5-6kg load. In summer doubles with shared bath €40; doubles with private bath €50. ❷

Hotel Thisseos, Thisseos 10 (☎210 324 5960). Take Karageorgi Servias, which becomes Perikleous; Thisseos is down the street about 20m. Close to Syndagma's sights but far from its noise. Friendly staff speaks English. Kitchen facilities. Common baths. Reception 24hr. Towels and sheets free upon request. Dorms €15; singles €30; doubles €44. To sleep on covered roof in summer, bring a sleeping bag (€10). ❷

Athens International Hostel (HI), Victor Hugo 16 (☎210 523 2049; www.hostelbooking.com), in Omonia. Walk down 30 Septemvriou from Pl. Omonia and take a left on Veranzerou, which becomes Victor Hugo after crossing Marni. Hot water 6-10am and 6-10pm. Laundry service. Sheets included. Common kitchen available. Reservations required. Dorms €8.20; doubles €17. Members only. ❶

◗ FOOD

Athens offers a mix of fast-food stands, open-air cafes, side-street *tavernas*, and intriguing restaurants. Cheap food abounds in **Syndagma** and **Omonia**. Pick up groceries at the markets on **Nikis** in **Plaka.**

▨ **Eden Vegetarian Restaurant,** Lysiou 12, in Plaka. Fantastic dishes like *boureki* pie (zucchini with feta; €5), as well as flavorful mushroom *stifado* with onions and peppers (€8.80). Open Su-M and W-Sa noon-midnight. ❷

▨ **Savvas,** Mitropoleos 86, right off of Plateia Monastiraki, across from the flea market. A budget eater's dream with heavenly, cheap *gyros* (€1.30); just don't sit down—prices skyrocket if you do. *Souvlaki* plate €6.50. Open 8am-4am. ❶

▨ **O Barba Giannis,** Em. Benaki 94, in Exarhia. From Syndagma, walk up Stadiou and make a right on Em. Benaki. Delicious traditional Greek food and outstanding service. *Moussaka* €5.30. Stuffed tomatoes and peppers €4. Ask about the day's choices. In summer, open M-Sa noon-1:30am, Su noon-5:30pm. ❶

Pluto, Plutarchou 38, in Kolonaki. Chic, warm ambience with an international menu. Try the grilled eggplant with feta and tomatoes (€9) or strawberry meringue (€9). Open M-Sa 12:30pm-3am. ❸

ATHENS 2004

DOG DAYS IN ATHENS

In the 1990s, an influx of refugees from unstable Balkan states prompted many Greeks to buy guard dogs. When local anxieties receded, unwanted pets were released into the streets. By 2001, Athens's stray canine population was estimated to be over 3000, and increasing all the time. The animals have become so accustomed to city life that the furry quadrupeds can be seen standing patiently at crosswalks, waiting for the lights to turn green.

On the eve of the Olympic Games, the city has been consumed by spirited debates over how to control this problem. On New Year's Day in 2003, over 60 canine carcasses were found strewn about a city park, the result of a nasty incident of rogue poisoning. Some, believing Olympic conspirators planned the extermination in preparation for the Games, banded together in demonstrations of unprecedented size.

On June 26, 2003, the Athens 2004 Committee announced a new initiative for dealing with the ever burgeoning canine population. The plan involves collecting, vaccinating, and neutering stray animals, before releasing them back onto the city streets. While the debate continues over the fate of Athens's stray population, one thing is certain: these days, more time and energy has been going to the dogs—which may be a good thing.

Food Company, Anagnostopoulou 47, in Kolonaki. Translates the casual, gourmet lunch into an art. Try the lentil salad with goat cheese, parsley, and tomato (€4). Open daily noon-11:30pm. ❸

Healthy Food Vegetarian Restaurant, Panepistimiou 57, in Omonia. Serves huge portions of wholesome, fresh Greek food. Open M-Sa 8am-10pm, Su 10am-4pm. ❷

Body Fuel, Stadiou 3, in Syndagma. A new-age food bar in a sleek setting with fresh and gourmet delights like salmon and vegetable salad (€4.40) or mango, strawberry, and Greek grape fruit salad (€2). Open M-F 10am-8:30pm. ❷

Kallimarmaron, Eforionos 13, in Pangrati. From the old Olympic Stadium (with your back to it), take the closest street on the left and walk 1½ blocks. Some of the best traditional Greek food in the city. Spiced chicken on the spit with raisins is prepared from an ancient recipe (€12). Open daily 8pm-midnight. DC/MC/V. ❹

Furin Kazan, Apollonos 2, in Syndagma. Follow Nikis to Apollonos, which is parallel to Mitropoleos and begins 1 block away from the square. Light Japanese fare. The grilled salmon and vegetable platter (€15) makes a filling meal. Tuna roll €3.50. Open M-Sa 11am-10:30pm. ❸

Yiantes, Valtetsiou 44, next to the movie theater in Exharia. A spacious, open-air oasis for organic and ethnic cuisine accompanied by "chill out" music. *Sougania* (onions stuffed with minted meat, raisins and pine nuts) €6.80. Byzantium chicken €11. Vegetarian options €4-8. Fish €5.80-9. Open Su and Tu-Sa 1:30pm-1:30am. MC/V. ❷

◙ SIGHTS

ACROPOLIS

Looming majestically over the city, the Acropolis complex has been the heart of Athens since the 5th century BC. Although each Greek *polis* had an *acropolis* ("high point of the city"), the buildings atop Athens's central peak outshone their imitators and continue to awe visitors today. Visit as early in the day as possible to avoid crowds and the broiling midday sun. (☎210 321 0219. Open in summer daily 8am-7pm; off-season 8am-2:30pm. Admission includes access to all of the sights below the Acropolis including Hadrian's Arch, the Olympian Temple of Zeus, and the Agora within a 48hr. period; tickets can be purchased at any of the sights. €12, students €6.)

TEMPLE OF ATHENA NIKE. This tiny cliff-side temple was raised during the Peace of Nikias (421-415 BC), a respite from the Peloponnesian War. The temple, known as the "jewel of Greek architecture," is ringed by eight miniature Ionic columns and once housed a statue of the winged goddess of victory, Nike. One day, in a paranoid frenzy, the Athenians were seized by a fear that Nike would flee the city and take peace with her, so they clipped the statue's wings. The remains of the 5m-thick **Cyclopean wall,** predating the Classical Period, lie below the temple.

PARTHENON. The **Temple of Athena Parthenos** (Athena the virgin), more commonly known as the Parthenon, keeps vigil over Athens and the modern world. Ancient Athenians saw their city as the capital of civilization, and the **metopes** (scenes in the open spaces above the columns) on the sides of the Parthenon celebrate Athens's rise. On the far right of the south side—the only side that has not been defaced—the Lapiths battle the Centaurs; on the east side, the Olympian gods defeat the giants; the north depicts the victory of the Greeks over the Trojans; and the west depicts their triumph against the Amazons.

ERECHTHEION. The Erechtheion, to the left of the Parthenon, was completed in 406 BC, just before Sparta defeated Athens in the Peloponnesian War. The building takes its name from the snake-bodied Erechtheus; the eastern half is devoted to the goddess of wisdom, Athena, the western half to the god of the sea, Poseidon.

ACROPOLIS MUSEUM. The museum, which neighbors the Parthenon, houses a superb collection of sculptures, including five of the original Caryatids that supported the south side of the Erechtheion. In Room VIII, notice the space that has been left for the British return of the large part of the Parthenon frieze that was taken: The Elgin marbles. The statues seem to be replicas, but a close look at the folds of their drapery reveals delicately individualized detail. *(Open in summer Su and Tu-Sa 8am-7pm, M 11am-7pm; off-season Su and Tu-Sa 8am-2pm, M 11am-2pm.)*

ELSEWHERE ON THE ACROPOLIS. The southwest corner of the Acropolis looks down over the reconstructed **Odeon of Herodes Atticus,** a functional theater dating from the Roman period (AD 160). See the *Athens News* for a schedule of concerts and plays. *(Entrance on Dionissiou Areopagitou. ☎210 323 2771. Purchase tickets at the door or by phone.)*

OTHER SIGHTS

AGORA. The Agora served as the city's marketplace, administrative center, and hub of daily life from the 6th century BC to AD 500. Here, the debates of Athenian democracy raged; Socrates, Aristotle, Demosthenes, Xenophon, and St. Paul all preached here. Today, visitors have free reign over what is now an archaeological site. The 415 BC ▧**Hephaesteion,** on a hill in the northwest corner of the Agora, is the best-preserved classical temple in Greece, flaunting **friezes** depicting Hercules's labors and Theseus's adventures. The **Stoa of Attalos** was a multi-purpose building filled with shops and home to informal gatherings of philosophers. Reconstructed in the 1950s, it now houses the **Agora Museum,** which contains relics from the site. According to Plato, Socrates's first trial was held at the recently excavated **Royal Stoa,** to the left of the Adrianou exit. *(Enter the Agora off Pl. Thission, from Adrianou, or as you descend from the Acropolis. Open daily 8am-7:20pm. €4, students and EU seniors €2. Under-18 and EU students free.)*

KERAMEIKOS. The Kerameikos's rigidly geometric design is quickly noticeable upon entering the grounds; the site includes a large-scale cemetery and a 40m-wide boulevard that ran through the Agora and the Diplyon Gate and ended at the sanctuary of **Akademos,** where Plato founded his academy. The

Oberlaender Museum displays finds from the burial sites; it houses an excellent collection of highly detailed pottery and sculpture. *(Northwest of the Agora. From Syndagma, walk toward Monastiraki on Ermou for 1km. Open Su and Tu-Sa 8:30am-3pm. €2, students and EU seniors €1. Under-18 and EU students free.)*

TEMPLE OF OLYMPIAN ZEUS AND HADRIAN'S ARCH. Right in the center of downtown Athens, you'll spot the traces of the largest temple ever built in Greece. The 15 Corinthian columns of the Temple of Olympian Zeus mark where it once stood. Started in the 6th century BC, it was completed 600 years later by Roman emperor Hadrian, who attached his name to the effort by adding an arch to mark the boundary between the ancient city of Theseus and Hadrian's own new city. *(Vas. Olgas at Amalias, across from the National Garden. Open Su and Tu-Sa 8:30am-3pm. Temple €2, students and EU seniors €1. Under-18 and EU students free. Arch free.)*

OLYMPIC STADIUM. The Panathenaic Olympic Stadium is wedged between the National Gardens and Pangrati, carved into a hill. The site of the first modern Olympic Games in 1896, the stadium seats 75,000 and will serve as both the finish line of the Marathon events as well as the venue for the sport of archery during the **2004 Summer Olympics.** A new Olympic stadium sits in the northern suburb of Irini; take the M1 Metro line right to it. *(On Vas. Konstantinou. From Syndagma, walk up Amalias 15min. to Vas Olgas, then follow it left. Alternatively, take trolley #2, 4, or 11 from Syndagma. Open daily 8am-8:30pm. Free.)*

AROUND SYNDAGMA. Be sure to catch the changing of the guard in front of the **Parliament** building. Every hour on the hour, two *evzones* (guards) wind up like toy soldiers, kick their tasselled heels in unison, and fall backward into symmetrical guardhouses on either side of the **Tomb of the Unknown Soldier.** Athens's endangered species—greenery and shade—are preserved in the **National Gardens.** Women should avoid strolling here alone.

MT. LYCAVITTOS. Of Athens's seven hills, Lycavittos is the largest and most central. Ascend at sunset to catch a glimpse of Athens's densely packed rooftops in waning daylight and watch the city light up for the night. At the top is the **Chapel of St. George,** a popular spot for weddings. A leisurely stroll around the church provides a view of Athens's panoramic expanse.

■ **NATIONAL ARCHAEOLOGICAL MUSEUM.** This astounding collection deserves a spot on even the most packed itinerary. The museum's highlights include the archaeologist Heinrich Schliemann's treasure, the **Mask of Agamemnon,** the death mask of a king who lived at least three centuries earlier than Agamemnon himself. *(Patission 44. Take trolley #2, 4, 5, 9, 11, 15, or 18 from the uphill side of Syndagma, or trolley #3 or 13 from the north side of Vas. Sofias. Open Apr.-Oct. Su and Tu-Sa 8am-7pm, M 12:30-7pm; Nov.-Mar. 8am-5pm; holidays 8:30am-3pm. €6, students and EU seniors €3. Nov.-Mar. Su and holidays free.)*

NATIONAL GALLERY. The National Gallery (a.k.a. Alexander Soutzos Museum) exhibits the work of Greek artists, with periodic international displays. The permanent collection includes works by El Greco, as well as drawings, photographs, and sculpture gardens. *(Vas. Konstantinou 50. Set back from Vas. Sofias, by the Hilton. ☎ 210 723 5857. Open M and W-Sa 9am-3pm, Su 10am-2pm. €6.50, students and seniors €3.)*

GOULANDRIS MUSEUM OF NATURAL HISTORY. This museum exhibits an impressive array of taxidermied Greek birds and mammals, as well as an overview of insect, reptile, mollusk, and plant biology. *(Levidou 13. Open Su-Th and Sa 9am-2:30pm. €3; students and children 5-18 years €1.20. Children under 5 free.)*

▓ 2004 SUMMER OLYMPIC GAMES

In 776 BC, nearly three millennia ago, the first recorded Olympic Games were held in the olive-shrouded plains of Olympia on the Peloponnese. Two hundred ninety-three *Olympiadas* later, in AD 393, Roman rulers banned the practice in Greece, and the Games did not return to Athens again until 1896. In the summer of 2004, from August 13-29, 5.3 million spectators, along with 4 billion viewers across the globe, will watch the Olympic Games return to the land of their ancient birth.

The city has been busy preparing for the return of the Games. The past few years have seen the revival of the public transport system, featuring a new tram; the construction of a brand new Suburban Rail that will connect the city center's Metro system with the airport, the Peloponnese, and numerous international train lines; and the renovation of the Attiki Odos—a 6-lane, 70km motorway.

The city is ready to accommodate a modern-day audience, and the tone of the Games is being modified to reflect an increasingly interdependent global society. In ancient times, warring city-states would place down their weapons to compete in a nobler medium of human interaction. This year, for the first time in history, the torch relay, intended to inspire all countries to unite in the Olympic Truce, will travel to five continents on the globe.

▓ **TICKETS.** The average ticket for the Athens 2004 Olympic Games goes for €35. Tickets include **free transportation** to and from all competition venues and are available through the National Olympic Committee of an interested party's country or through the official ticketing website: **www.athens2004.com/tickets.** The first phase of ticket sales began and ended in the spring of 2003. **Premium ticket packages** are currently available on a first come, first serve basis. These highly coveted packages include seats to the highest-demand Olympic events (Opening and Closing Ceremonies, the finals of the most popular competitions) and range from €3500 to €71,000. For more information, contact the **Ticketing Call Center** (within Greece: ☎800 11 2004 02, outside of Greece or using mobile: ☎30 210 373 0000). For updates and more information, the official website of the Athens 2004 Olympic Games is: **www.athens2004.com.**

▓ **TRANSPORTATION.** Athens's extended and renovated public transport system will be the primary vessel for movement during the Games. The **Metro,** along with the new **tram** and new **Suburban Rail,** will move approximately one million passengers per day. The largest venue complexes (the Athens Olympic Sports Center, the Hellinikon Olympic Sports Center, and the Faliro Olympic Coastal Zone) will be directly serviced by one or more of these lines, as will many others near and around the city center. Venues not directly serviced by these lines will be accessible through a combination of the public transport system and specially running **Olympic Transport shuttles** that will leave from Metro, tram, and Suburban Rail terminals, using the 210km of new and upgraded roads scheduled to be ready in the Athens area by the start of the Games. Public transportation will be free for all ticketed spectators to and from Olympic venues. **Parking** is also available at a distance from the venues accessible by shuttles.

▓ **ORIENTATION.** Competitions in 28 sports, as well as broadcasting services and accommodations for athletes, will be held in 38 Olympic venues. While the majority are located in and around Athens, events will also be held in Thessaloniki and Volos in Central Greece, Patras in the Peloponnese, and Iraklion on Crete.

GREECE

Olympic Venues

- ═══ Railway   ○ Transport Gates
- ⌇⌇⌇ Suburban Railway
- ━◆━ Metro   ┈┈ Funicular
- ━━━ Olympic Transport Network
- ·········· Marathon Route

Schinias Rowing and Canoeing Centre

Parnitha Mountain Bike Venue

Marathon

Olympic Village

Ano Liossia Hall

Athens Olympic Sports Complex

Peristeri Boxing Hall

Galatsi Hall

MPC IBC

Rafina

Athens Center

Goudi Complex

Nikaia Weightlifting Hall

Panathinaiko Stadium

Piraeus

Faliro Coastal Zone Complex

Saronic Gulf

Hellinikon Complex

Eleftherios Venizelos Airport

Agios Kosmas Sailing Centre

Markopoulo Shooting Centre

Markopoulo Equestrian Centre

Vouliagmeni Centre

0   5 miles
0   5 kilometers

⌐ ACCOMMODATIONS. Preparing to accommodate an influx of 5.3 million spectators, more than double Athens's winter population, has been among the greatest challenges faced by the city and organizing committee. By the time of the Games, there will be a total of 31,000 rooms in new and old hotels throughout the Athens area, but 17,300 of those rooms have already been reserved for use by the press and the family of participants in the Olympics.

A shortage of rooms is almost guaranteed, but there are a number of alternative accommodations options available for the Games. A large number of private residences in the Athens area will open their houses for rental. Two joint venture contractor bodies are officially responsible for putting owners in contact with tenants for the 16 days of the Olympics: **Alpha Philoxenia 2004** (☎30 210 327 7400; fax 210 327 7444; cpallis@alphaastikaakinita.gr) and **Elliniki Philoxenia** (☎210 327 7403 and 327 7406; gmanzavinatos@eurobank.gr).

Eleven conveniently located **cruise liners,** with a combined total of 6489 cabins in the 3-5 star categories, will be docked in the port of Piraeus. Amenities include cinemas, spas, restaurants, swimming pools, libraries, children's play rooms, and Internet cafes. Docked liners will include the German **AIDAvita** (☎49 69 695 801 18; fax 49 69 695 801 30; Heike-Marie.Ebel@DSM-Olympia.de; ask for Mrs. Heike-Marie Ebel); the **MS OOSTERDAM** and **MS ROTTERDAM** (☎30 210 322 1500; fax 30 210 331 6684; sales@sportius.gr; ask for Mrs. Calli Georgiades); the **Olympic Voyager, Olympic Explorer,** and **Olympic Countess** (☎30 210 429 1000; fax 30 210 459 7482; sales@roc.gr; ask for Mr. Evan Pezas); and the luxurious **Queen Mary II** (cruiseships@athens2004.gr).

Accommodations are also available on nearby islands, including **Salamina, Aegina, Hydra, Spetses,** and **Evia,** all of which will be much more frequently serviced by high speed ferries during the Games. Staying in nearby towns and cities in the **Peloponnese,** serviced by the new Suburban Rail, is another viable alternative.

OLYMPIC VILLAGE. The Olympic village, north of Athens at the foot of Mt. Parnitha, is an enormous complex. During the Olympic Games it will accommodate 16,000 athletes and team officials; during the Paralympic Games later in the year, it will house 6000. The facility includes a **Residential Zone,** with over 2200 apartments and training facilities, as well as an **International Zone,** which incorporates the main entrance, **shopping centers,** administrative buildings, and the **Olympic museum.**

ATHENS OLYMPIC SPORTS COMPLEX (OCO). The Athens Olympic Sports Complex is located 9km north of the center of Athens and 11km south of the Olympic Village in Parnitha, where all athletes will stay, is in the residential northern suburb of Marousi. The complex will host 9 sports including track and field, track cycling, swimming, and diving. The jewel of the central complex, the **Olympic Stadium** (STA) has the largest capacity of all the sports venues in Attica and will host a crowd of 75,000 spectators on August 13 for the opening of the Games and on August 29 for its closing. **Track and field** will take place from August 20-28. The stadium is expected to be fully renovated by April 2004.

The vast **Olympic Indoor Hall** (OIH) will hosts 15,000 guests at the **artistic gymnastics** competitions (Aug. 14-19, and 22-23) and **trampoline gymnastics** (Aug. 20). Near the end of the Games, 18,000 fans will flood the hall during the **basketball** finals (Aug. 25-28). The OIH is expected to be up and running by October 2003. An audience of 16,600 is expected at the **Olympic Tennis Center** (TEN) to watch the **tennis** competitions (Aug. 15-18; finals Aug. 19-22). The center boasts 16 courts. The **main court** seats 8000; the **two semifinals courts** 4000 and 2000, respectively; and the 13 others 200 each. TEN was completed at the end of summer of 2003.

The grand **Olympic Aquatic Center** (AQU) is made up of two outdoor pools, the **main pool** (capacity 11,000) and the **synchronized swimming pool** (capacity 5000), as well as an **indoor pool** (capacity 6500). The Indoor Pool will host **diving** (Aug. 14, 16, and 20-28) and the **water polo** preliminaries (Aug. 15-21). **Swimming** (Aug. 14-21) will come to the main pool, which will also host the water polo finals (Aug. 22-27). **Synchronized swimming** (Aug. 23-24 and 26; finals Aug. 25 and 27) will be held in the synchronized swimming pool. The Aquatic Center is expected to be fully renovated by the end of 2003. The sleek and modern **Olympic Velodrome** (VEL), totally overhauled for the Games, will host **track cycling** (Aug. 20-25) for an audience of 5000 anxious onlookers. Renovations will be completed around January 2004. (*Take Metro green line 1 from Omonia toward Kifisia to Eirini. Or, from the Suburban Rail, take blue line 3, get off at Neratziotissa, then board Metro green line 1 toward Piraeus, again getting off at Eirini.*)

FALIRO COASTAL ZONE OLYMPIC COMPLEX (FCO). The stretch of southern Attican coastline between Piraeus and the beach suburbs of Gyfada, Vouliagmeni, and Varkiza was once a neglected sight, covered with piles of old boats and unfinished construction. The addition of the Faliro Coastal Zone Olympic Complex, which will host four of the 28 Olympic sports, has brought beautiful gardens, walkways, and a state-of-the-art marina. The closest venue to the bus-

ATHENS 2004

THE PLEBS' GAMES

The Olympic Committee might be keener on advertising VIP packages to bring in the big bucks, but there are bargains to be found when it comes to the 2004 Olympic Games. One of the most exciting and historically significant events on the schedule, the Athens 2004 Marathon, will be entirely *tzamba* (free). After a 108-year hiatus, the Olympic Marathon will return to Greece to follow the original Marathon route, forged by heroic Phidippides in 490 BC.

To witness the event, find a spot anywhere alongside the runners' path, from a little after where they begin to a little before the finish line. While some pay to watch at the Marathon Finish line and others pay to watch the Marathon's three-second start, anyone willing to wait has the option of viewing the runners from any vantage point along Phidippides' original path. You could even run on the sidewalk alongside your favorite star to share in their agony or lend a little support.

The women's race begins at 6pm on August 22nd; the men's at 6pm on August 29th. The road cycling (men's Aug. 14 12:45pm; women's Aug. 15 3pm) and sailing (in 14 sessions on Aug. 14-26 and 28) events can also be viewed free of charge.

tling docks of Piraeus, the **Peace and Friendship Stadium** (SEF), is a graceful oblong edifice with gently sloping sides. It will be, like the Olympic Stadium, a one-sport stop. The newly renovated stadium, which has been around since the 1980s, is scheduled to host the main **volleyball** event for a crowd of 14,000 fans (Aug. 14-23; finals Aug. 24-29). Renovations are expected to be complete in December 2003. The brand-new **Sports Pavilion** (FSP) can handle up to 8000 spectators for the **handball** preliminaries (Aug. 14-24) and **Taekwondo** events (Aug. 26-29). Construction will be completed by early 2004. Right in front of the sea, the sleek, new **Olympic Beach Volleyball Stadium** (BVF), will host 10,000 **beach volleyball** fans (Aug. 14-21; finals Aug. 22-25). *(Take tram line 1 from Zappeio; switch to tram line 2 at the junction on Poseidonos and continue in the opposite direction to the last stop (Neo Faliro). Alternatively, take Metro green line 1 toward Piraeus and get off at Faliro.)*

HELLINIKON OLYMPIC COMPLEX (HCO). The Hellinikon should be the worldwide symbol of recycling. Once the site of the old airport, parts of many of its buildings are reconstructed using the skeleton of old aviation buildings; in July 2003, an "International Flights" sign still hung from an entrance. The Hellinikon will host 7 sports. The **Olympic Baseball Centre**'s two fields will accommodate 7000 and 12,000 **baseball** fans (Aug. 15-18, 20-22, and 24; finals Aug. 25). The venue for **softball** (Aug. 14-20 and 22; finals Aug. 23), the **Olympic Softball Stadium** has also been built from the ground up. The **Olympic Hockey Centre** (capacity 8000) will host **field hockey** events (Aug. 14-23; finals Aug. 24-27). The neighboring warm-up field (capacity 2000) will be completed in January 2004. The frames of the impressive, high-ceilinged **Indoor Arena** and **Fencing Hall** were modified from what were once the Olympic Airlines hangars of the former airport. The **Indoor Arena** (capacity 15,000) will host **basketball** preliminaries (Aug. 14-24) and then **handball** finals (Aug. 26-29). The two-roomed **Fencing Hall** (capacity 5000 and 3500) will host the age-old sport of **fencing** (Aug. 14-22). The sprawling **Olympic Canoe Kayak Slalom Centre** (capacity 5000), with winding, elevated canoe paths positioned on an incline toward its vast pool, will be used for four consecutive days during the Olympics for **canoe/kayak slalom racing** (Aug. 17 and 19; finals 18 and 20). The surface area of the enormous structure will be larger than almost anything else in the Hellinikon. It will be completed by February 2004. *(Take tram line 1 from Zappeio to the last stop, Helliniko.)*

MARATHON START (MRS). Immediately after running 42km to spread word of the Athenian victory in the 490BC battle of Marathon, Phidippides collapsed and died. During the 2004 Olympics, participants in the **marathon** (women's Aug. 22; men's Aug. 29) will follow the path from Marathon to Athens, starting in a small, newly renovated stadium and ending in the enormous Ancient Panathenaic stadium of central Athens. *(Take Metro green line 1 from Omonia to Neratziotissa and switch to the Olympic shuttle. Marathon is 26 mi/42km from Athens's center.)*

PANATHENAIC/KALLIMARMARO STADIUM (PAN). Ancient aristocrat Herodius Atticus boasted that he could build a stadium entirely out of marble for the Panathenaic Games, and so the elliptical Panathenaic/Kallimarmaro Stadium was built. George Averof refurbished it for the 1896 revival of the Games. **Archery** events (Aug. 15-17; finals Aug. 19-21) will attract an estimated 5500 spectators. The women's marathon finish will be attended by 45,000 spectators on the evening of August 22; the men's on August 29. Renovations should be completed by November of 2003. *(In Athens's center, the Panathenaic is a 7-10min. walk from Syndagma, on the other side of the National Gardens. Stoll down Irodou Atikou to get there.)*

GOUDI OLYMPIC COMPLEX (GOC). Built in the middle of an evergreen thicket of northeastern Athens, Goudi consists of a gymnasium and a **modern pentathlon** center. According to the Athens 2004 Committee, designing the complex was a structural challenge; its completion date is March 2004. In the **Olympic Hall,** the **badminton** competitions (Aug. 14-18; finals Aug. 19-21) will be held before 5000 spectators. The **shooting** and **fencing** disciplines of the modern pentathlon (Aug. 26-27) will take place here before a crowd of 4500. The remaining three disciplines of the modern pentathlon, **swimming, riding,** and **running** (Aug. 26-27), will be held at the **Olympic Modern Pentathlon Centre.** Two thousand fans witness the swimming leg of the pentathlon, while 5000 will watch the riding and running portions. *(Take Metro blue line 3 from Syndagma; get off at Katehaki and catch the Olympic shuttle.)*

VOULIAGMENI OLYMPIC CENTRE (VOU). The **triathlon** (Aug. 25-26) will be held in the beautiful beachside region of Vouliagmeni, farther down the southern coast from most of Athens's crowded summer 2004 chaos. Three thousand fans will behold world-class athletes striving to swim, cycle, and run faster than ever before. **Road race/time trial cycling** (Aug. 18) will use a venue next door called the **Vouliagmeni-Agia Marina Route.** *(Take tram line 1 from Zappeio; switch to line 2 and ride toward Gylfada Sq. (the last stop) from where you can catch the Olympic shuttle.)*

KARAISKAKI STADIUM (ATH). Used over 100 years ago at the Olympic revival games as the velodrome, Karaiskaki was renovated in the 1960s and has been transformed once again into an impressive **soccer** stadium (capacity 35,000). It is the second largest stadium in Athens proper, after the Kallimarmaro. Some of the most important soccer games will take place here (Aug. 14-15; quarterfinals 17-18, 21, and 23; semifinals Aug. 24; finals Aug. 28-29). The completion date for construction is August 2003. *(Take Metro green line 1 from Omonia toward Piraeus and get off at the Faliro stop (in Nea Faliro, just before the Piraeus terminal). You can also take tram line 1 from Zappeio and switch to line 2 toward the terminal in Neo Faliro.)*

PATRAS'S PAMPELOPONNISIAKO STADIUM. Known around the city as the "Jewel of Patras," the new Olympic complex will host **swimming** and **soccer** (Aug. 11-12, 14, 17-18, and 20; quarterfinals Aug. 21 and 23; semifinals Aug. 26) events and also serve as the **athletic training halls.** Added demands from the city, the Greek Athletic Association, and the Athens 2004 Committee have pushed the projected date of completion to February 2004. *(The Suburban Rail runs all the way from Athens to Patras. Trains and buses also run to Patras. When in Patras, take bus #7 (20min., €1) from the Europa Center.)*

VOLOS'S PANTHESSILIKO STADIUM. The stadium (capacity 20,000) will host limited **soccer** (Aug. 11-12, 14-15, 17, and 20) competitions. Another smaller stadium is set next to the Panthessiliko. *(To get to Volos from Athens, take intercity transportation. The stadium is 5km out of Volos's city center, north of the suburb of Nea Ionio.)*

THESSALONIKI'S KAFTANSOGLIO STADIUM. This technologically enhanced stadium (capacity 28,000) will host a smattering of preliminary and semifinal **soccer** matches (Aug. 11-12, 14-15, 17-18, and 20; quarterfinals Aug. 21, 23, and 26). *(To get to Thessaloniki from Athens, take intercity transportation.)*

IRAKLION'S PANKRITIO STADIUM. This venue, seating up to 27,000, will play host to a variety of **soccer** matches (Aug. 11-12, 14-15, 17-18, and 20; quarterfinals Aug. 21 and 23). *(The stadium is located 2km outside Iraklion; follow Kalokerinou through the center of town and the stadium will be on your right.)*

🎵 📷 ENTERTAINMENT AND NIGHTLIFE

The weekly *Athens News* (€1) gives locations, hours, and phone numbers for events, as well as news and ferry information. The **Athens Flea Market**, adjacent to Pl. Monastiraki, is a jumble of second-hand junk and valuable antiques. Sunday is the best day, when it is open from 8am-1pm. Summertime performances are staged in **Lycavittos Theater** as part of the **Athens Festival**, which has included acts from the Greek Orchestra to Pavarotti to the Talking Heads. The **Festival Office**, Stadiou 4, sells tickets. (☎210 322 1459. Open M-Sa 8am-4pm, Su 9am-2pm and 6-9pm. Tickets €10-110. Student discounts available.) The cafe/bar flourishes throughout Athens, especially on **Haritos** in **Kolonaki**. In summertime, chic Athenians head to the seaside clubs of **Glyfada**, past the airport. **Privilege, Venue,** and **Prime,** all along Poseidonos, are perfect places to enjoy the breezy night air. (Dress well; no shorts. Drinks €4-10. Cover €10-15.) Take the A3 or the B3 bus from Vas. Amalias to Glyfada (€0.75), and then catch a cab from there to your club. Taxis to Glyfada run about €8, but the return trip typically costs more.

🎵 **Vibe,** Aristophanous 1, just beyond Pl. Iroön in Monastiraki. Unusual lighting makes for a great atmosphere. Open Su and Tu-Sa 9:30pm-5am.

Boite Esperides, Tholou 6, at the end of Mnisskleous. Young bouzouki players and honey-voiced Greek girls "sing about love and the moon." Ouzo €7.50. Cover €7.50. Open Su and Tu-Sa 10pm-4am.

Bee, at the corner of Miaoli and Themidos, off Ermou; a few blocks from the heart of Psiri in Monastiraki. DJs spin while the friendly staff keeps the booze flowing. Drinks €3-9. Open Su and Tu-Th noon-3am, F-Sa noon-6am.

The Daily, Xenokratous 47. Kolonaki's chic student population converges here to imbibe, listen to Latin and reggae, and watch sports on TV. Fabulous outdoor seating and open-air bar. Drinks €3-6. Open daily 9am-2am.

Wired, Valtetsiou 61, in Exharia. The red parachute on the ceiling and thorn bushes painted on the walls give this rock bar an eerie feel. Varied musical genres each get a turn on the schedule. Drinks €3-5.50. Open Su-Th 11am-1am, F-Sa 11am-3am.

Mo Better, Koleti 32, off Themistokleous, in Exharia. In fall, winter, or spring, find the tall blue wooden door–it's the entrance to the most popular rock bar in Athens. A staple in the nocturnal schedule of alternative *Panepistimio* (university) students. Whiskey, vodka tonic €6. Open Oct.-June Su-Th 10pm-4am, F-Sa 10pm-dawn.

Flower, Dorylaou 2, in Pl. Mavili, in Kolonaki. A popular dive bar with European partiers. Shots €2.50. Mixed drinks €5. Open Su-Th 7pm-4am, F-Sa 7pm-6am.

🔁 DAYTRIPS FROM ATHENS

TEMPLE OF POSEIDON. The **Temple of Poseidon** has been a dazzling white landmark for sailors at sea for centuries. The original temple was constructed around 600 BC, destroyed by the Persians in 480 BC, and rebuilt by Pericles in 440 BC; 16 Doric columns remain. The temple sits on a promontory at ◪**Cape Sounion,** 65km from Athens. (Open daily 10am-sunset. €4, students €2. EU students free.) Two **bus** routes run to Cape Sounion from Athens; the shorter and more scenic route begins at the Mavromateon 14 stop near Areos Park (2hr., every hr., €4.30).

MARATHON. Immediately after running 42km to spread word of the Athenian victory in the 490 BC battle of Marathon, **Phidippides** collapsed and died. Today, runners trace the route between Athens and Marathon twice per year, beginning at a commemorative plaque. The town is just south of **Marathonas Olympic Complex,** which will be the venue for two of the 28 sports during the 2004 Olympic Games. With a car, you can explore nearby sights and beaches. At **Ramnous,** 15km northeast, lie the ruins of the **Temple of Nemesis,** goddess of divine retribution, and **Thetis,** goddess of law and justice. **Schinias** to the north and **Timvos Marathonas** to the south are popular beaches. **Buses** leave Athens for Marathon from the Mavromateon 29 station (1½hr., every hr. 5:30am-10:30pm, €2.50).

DELPHI. Troubled denizens of the ancient world journeyed to the **Oracle of Delphi,** where the priestess of Apollo related the cryptic advice of the gods. Head east out of town to reach the site. (Open 7:30am-6:45pm. Museum closed for renovations until 2004. Site €6, students €3. EU students free.) **Buses** leave Athens for Delphi from Terminal B, Liossion 260 (3hr., 6 per day, €11). Delphi's **tourist office,** Pavlou 12, is in the town hall. (☎ 22650 82 900. Open M-F 8am-2:30pm.) If you spend the night, stay at **Hotel Sibylla ❷,** Pavlou 9, which has rooms with wonderful views and private baths at the best prices in town. (☎ 22650 82 335. Singles €15; doubles €22; triples €27.)

THE PELOPONNESE (Πελοποννεσος)

A hand-shaped peninsula stretching its fingers into the Mediterranean, the Peloponnese is rich in history and folklore that contribute to its otherworldly atmosphere. The majority of Greece's most significant archaeological sites reside here, including Olympia, Mycenae, Messene, Corinth, Mystras, and Epidavros. A world apart from the islands, the serenely beautiful and sparsely populated Peloponnese remembers 5000 years of continuous habitation, making it a bastion of Greek village life.

◧ FERRIES TO ITALY AND CRETE

Boats sail from Patras to destinations in Italy, including Brindisi, Trieste, Bari, Ancona, and Venice. **Manolopoulous,** Othonos Amalias 35, in Patras, sells tickets. (☎ 2610 223 621. Open M-F 9am-8pm, Sa 10am-3pm, Su 5pm-8pm.) Questions about departures from Patras should be directed to the Port Authority (☎ 2610 341 002).

NO WORK, ALL PLAY

PARTY ON THE PORT

The city of Patras plays a great front: a well-populated port city that blends pragmatism with tight-clothed urban flare. But for seven and a half straight weeks, even the most blasé crawl on hands and knees in a city-wide scavenger hunt or are blindsided by fudge in one of Europe's largest chocolate fights. In the pre-Lenten madness of Patras's annual *karnival*, anything goes.

In 1829, the 19th-century merchant Moretis hosted an intimate, VIP-only Carnival ball in Patras. Since then, the festival has grown, and the guest list has been extended to anyone who can fit into the streets from mid-January to Ash Wednesday. In 1966 organizers introduced the treasure hunt game, still one of the most popular events, which unites all of Patras in a quest to unlock clues spread throughout the city.

For adults, there is the *Bourboulia*, a night filled with mystery and seduction. Men pay a "symbolic entrance fee" and arrive at the Apollo Municipal Theater to await their imminent mistresses, dressed in black costumes and masks known as "dominos." For children, the festival offers myriad parades, activities, and games. The Sunday before Ash Wednesday offers a 7hr. Carnival Parade; 72hr. later, on the final night, some 300,000 revelers convene for an all-night harbor-side party including the burning of King Carnival's effigy.

PATRAS (Πατρας)   ☎ 2610

Sprawling Patras (pop. 155,000) Greece's third-largest city and one of the official cities for the 2004 Olympic Games, serves largely as a transport hub for island-bound tourists. During **Carnival** (mid-Jan. to Ash Wednesday), this port city becomes one gigantic dance floor consumed by pre-Lenten madness. During the 2004 Olympics, the **Pampeloponnisiako Stadium**, known around the city as the "Jewel of Patras," will host swimming and soccer events and serve as the athletic training halls. To get there, take bus #7 (20 min., €1) from outside Europa Center. Follow the water to the west end of town to reach **Agios Andreas**, the largest Orthodox cathedral in Greece, which houses magnificent frescoes and St. Andrew's holy head. (Dress modestly. Open daily 7am-dusk.) Sweet black grapes are transformed into Mavrodaphne wine at the ◼**Achaïa Clauss Winery,** the country's most famous vineyard. Take bus #7 (30min., €1) from the intersection of Kolokotroni and Kanakari. (Open daily May-Sept. 11am-8pm; Oct.-Apr. 9am-8pm. Free samples. In summer, free English tours every hr. noon-5pm.)

Trains (☎2610 639 110) leave from Othonos Amalias for: Athens (3½-5hr., 8 per day, €10); Kalamata (5½hr., 2 per day, €5); and Olympia (1½hr., 8 per day, €3-6) via Pyrgos. KTEL **buses** (☎2610 623 886) leave from Othonos Amalias for: Athens (3hr., 33 per day, €13); Ioannina (4hr., 4 per day, €16); Kalamata (4hr., 2 per day, €15); Thessaloniki (8hr., 3 per day, €30); and Tripoli (4hr., 2 per day, €11). **Ferries** go to: Corfu (6-8hr., daily, €21-25); and Italy. The **tourist office** is on Othonos Amalias, between 28 Octovriou and Astingos (☎2610 461 740. Open daily 8am-10pm.) The **Pension Nicos ❷**, Patreos 3, is cheery and conveniently located. (☎2610 623 757. Singles €20; doubles €35; triples €50. Cash only.) The friendly, cafeteria-style ◼**Europa Center ❶**, on Othonos Amalias, serves cheap, large portions. (Entrees €3-7.) **Postal Code:** 26001.

OLYMPIA (Ολυμπια)☎ 26240

In ancient times, every four years city-states would call truces and travel to Olympia for a pan-Hellenic assembly, which was as much about peace and diplomacy as about athletic ability. Modern Olympia (pop. 42,500), though set among meadows and shaded by cypress and olive trees, is anything but relaxed. As the 2004 Olympic Games rapidly approach, this small town is in a frenzy, ready to show the world proudly where it all began. The ancient **Olympic arena**, whose central sanctuary was called the **Altis,** draws hordes of tourists. The gigantic **Temple of Zeus** dominates **Ancient Olympia,** although ▨**Hera's Temple,** dating from the 7th century BC, is better preserved. The ▨**Archaeological Museum** has an impressive sculpture collection that includes the **Nike of Paionios** and the **Hermes of Praxiteles.** Maps, available at the site (€2-4), are essential for navigation. (Site open in summer daily 8am-7pm. Museum open M noon-3pm, Tu-Su 8am-7pm. Site or museum €6, both €9; students and seniors €3/€5; under-18 and EU students free.) The **Museum of the Olympic Games,** or the **Sports Museum,** on Angerinou, two blocks uphill from Kondili, houses a collection of Olympic paraphernalia that includes a silver medal from the 1996 games in Atlanta. (☎ 26240 22 544. Open M-Sa 8am-3:30pm, Su 9am-4:30pm. €2. Children and EU students free.)

Buses run to Tripoli (4hr., 2-3 per day, €8). The **tourist office,** on Kondili, is on the east side of town toward the ruins. (☎ 26240 23 100. Open M-F 9am-4pm.) To reach the **Internet Cafe** (☎ 26240 22 578), turn off Kondili with the youth hostel on your right and walk uphill two blocks. (€3 per hr., €1.50 minimum. Open daily 9:30am-2am.) The friendly **Youth Hostel ❶,** Kondili 18, is cheap. (☎ 26240 22 580. Free hot showers. Check-out 10:30am. Dorms €8; doubles €20.) **New Olympia ❹,** on the road that leads diagonally to the train station, has spacious rooms with A/C, TVs, and large private baths. (☎ 26240 22 506. Buffet breakfast included. Singles €25-52; doubles €45-70; triples €90.) **Minimarkets,** bakeries, and fast-food establishments line **Kondili.** Restaurants on Kondili are overpriced, but a walk toward the railroad station or up the hill leads to inexpensive *tavernas.* **Postal Code:** 27065.

TRIPOLI (Τριπολη)　　　　　　　　　　☎ 2710

The transportation hub of Arcadia, Tripoli (pop. 22,000) is crowded and fast-paced; the *plateias* and huge city park are a break in the city's otherwise urban landscape. The **Archaeological Museum** on Evangelistrias, Pl. Ag. Vasiliou, has a large prehistoric collection, including pottery, jewelry, and weaponry from the Neolithic to the Mycenaean periods. **Trains** arrive from: Athens (4hr., 3 per day, €6); Corinth (2½hr., 4 per day, €3); and Kalamata (2½hr., 2 per day, €5). **Buses** arrive at Pl. Kolokotronis, east of the center of town, from Athens (3hr., 14 per day, €11) and Nafplion (1hr., 5 per day, €3.70). Buses arrive at the KTEL Messenia and Laconia depot, across from the train station, from Kalamata (1½hr., 10 per day, €5.50) and Sparta (1hr., 8 per day, €3.70). **Arcadia Hotel ❸,** in Pl. Kolokotronis, offers old-fashioned rooms with unique color schemes, A/C, and private bath. (☎ 2710 225 551. Singles €30-50; doubles €45-72; triples €80-85.) Try the goat with mushrooms in egg and lemon sauce (€8.20) at ▨**Klimataria ❸,** on Eth. Antistasis, four blocks past the park as you walk from Pl. Petriou. (☎ 2710 222 058. Entrees €10-12.) **Postal Code:** 22100.

KALAMATA (Καλαματα)　　　　　　　　☎ 27210

Kalamata (pop. 50,000) flourishes as a port and beach resort, and also serves as a useful transport hub. Take a bus from Kalamata (1hr., M-Sa 2 per day, €2) to **Ancient Messini** in nearby **Mavromati,** one of Greece's most impressive archaeological sites. (Open daily 8am-8pm. Free.) To reach the train station, walk toward the waterfront in Pl. Georgiou, turn right on Frantzi at the far end of the *plateia,* and walk a few blocks to Sideromikou Stathmou. **Trains** run to: Athens (6½hr., 3 per day, €7) via Tripoli (2½hr., €2.80); Corinth (5¼hr., €5.60); and Patras (5½hr., 3:19pm, €5). **Buses** leave from the station on Artemidos to: Athens (4hr., 12 per day, €16); Patras (4hr., 2 per day, €15); Sparta (2hr., 2 per day, €2.80); and Tripoli (2hr., €5.50). **Tourist information** is available at **D.E.T.A.K.,** Polivou 6, just off Aristomenous near the Old Town.

(☎27210 21 700. Open M-F 7am-2:30pm.) **Hotel Nevada ❷**, Santa Rosa 9, off Faron one block up from the water, offers large, wildly decorated rooms with shared baths and kitchen. (☎27210 82 429. Singles €11-14; doubles €16-19; triples €19-24.) Good meals can be found along the waterfront. Before leaving town, sample the famous Kalamata olives and figs. The immense **New Market**, across the bridge from the bus station, has an assortment of meat, cheese, and fruit shops, and a daily farmer's market. **Postal Code:** 24100.

SPARTA (Σπαρτη) AND MYSTRAS (Μυστρας)   ☎27310

Citizens of today's Sparta (pop. 12,500) make olive oil, not war. Pleasant public gardens and broad, palm-lined boulevards make Sparta hospitable, and it is by far the best base for exploring the Byzantine ruins of Mystras. **Ancient Sparta** is only a 1km walk north down Paleolougou. **Buses** from Sparta go to: Areopolis (1½hr., 2 per day, €4.60); Athens (3½hr., 8 per day, €14) via Corinth (2½hr., €8.30) and Tripoli (1hr., €3.70); and Monemvasia (2hr., 3 per day, €6.80). To reach the town center from the bus station, walk about 10 blocks west on Lykourgou; the **tourist office** is in the *plateia*. (☎24 852. Open M-F 8am-2pm.) **Hotel Cecil ❸**, Paleologou 125, 5 blocks north of Lykourgou toward Ancient Sparta, on the corner of Paleologou and Thermopilion, has pleasant rooms with A/C, phones, private baths, and TVs. (☎24 980. Reservations recommended. Singles €28-33; doubles €33-38.)

Mystras, 4km from Sparta, was once the religious center of all Byzantium and the locus of Constantinople's rule over the Peloponnese. Its extraordinary hillside ruins comprise a city of Byzantine churches, chapels, and monasteries. Modest dress is required at the functioning convent. (Open in summer daily 8am-7pm; offseason 8:30am-3pm. €5. Children and EU students free.) **Buses** leave from the station and from the corner of Lykourgou and Leonidou in Sparta for the top of the ruins (20min., 11 per day, €0.90).

GYTHION (Γυθειο) AND AREOPOLIS (Αρεοπολη)   ☎27330

Near sand and stone beaches, Gythion is the liveliest town in Mani and a good base for visiting other villages. A tiny causeway to the left of the waterfront as you face inland connects it to the island of **Marathonisi**, where Paris and Helen consummated their ill-fated love. **Buses** in Gythion leave from the north end of the waterfront, to the right as you face inland, for: Athens (4hr., 6 per day, €17) via Tripoli (2hr., €6.50); Corinth (3hr., €12); Kalamata (2hr., 2 per day, €6.20) via Itilo (1hr., €3); and Sparta (1hr., €3). **Moto Makis Rent-A-Moped**, on the waterfront near the causeway, rents wheels for exploring. (☎27330 25 111. €16 per day. Open daily 8:30am-1:30pm and 4:30-8:30pm.) ◙**Xenia Karlaftis Rooms ❷**, on the water 20m from the causeway, rents spacious rooms with private baths. (☎27330 22 719. Singles €15; doubles €22; triples €30.) **Postal Code:** 23200.

Although **Areopolis** neighbors both the sea and the mountains, its buildings dominate the scenery: stone tower houses and cobbled streets are framed by the dramatic purple peaks of the Taygetus. Just 11km from Areopolis, the unusual **Vlihada Cave**, part of a subterranean river, is cool, quiet, and strung with tiny crystalline stalagmites; a bus (€0.90) runs from Areopolis at 11am and returns at 12:45pm. (Open daily 8am-3pm. Mandatory 30min. tours. €12, students €7.) **Buses** stop in Areopolis's main *plateia* and go to Athens (6hr., 4 per day, €18) via Gythion (45min., €1.80) and Sparta (2hr., €6.50). To reach **Tsimova ❷**, which rents narrow rooms with tiny doors and windows typical of tower houses, turn left at the end of Kapetan Matapan, the road leading to the Old Town. (☎27330 51 301. Singles €25-32; doubles €35-60.) **Postal Code:** 23062.

MONEMVASIA (Μονεμβασια) AND GEFYRA (Γεφυρα) ☎27320

Despite the tourists, an otherworldly quality shrouds the island of Monemvasia. No cars or bikes are allowed on the island, and pack horses bear residents' groceries into the city. Narrow streets hide tiny doorways and flowered courtyards. At the edge of the cliffs perches the **Agia Sofia**, a 12th-century church; to get there, navigate the maze of streets to the inland edge of town, where a path climbs the side of the cliff to the tip of the rock. Stay in more modern and less expensive **Gefyra**, a 15min. walk down the main road and across the causeway from Monemvasia. An orange **bus** runs between the causeway and Monemvasia's gate (every 15min., 8am-midnight, €0.30). Three **buses** per day leave for: Athens (6hr., €20); Corinth (5hr., €15); Sparta (2½hr., €6.80); and Tripoli (4hr., €11). **Hotel Akrogiali ❷**, Iouliou 23, has private baths, TVs, and a shared fridge. (☎27320 61 360. Singles €20-23; doubles €28-35.) **To Limanaki ❶**, in Gefyra, serves exceptional Greek food, including excellent *pastitsio* (€4) and *moussaka* (€5).

NAFPLION (Ναυπλιο) ☎27520

Beautiful old Nafplion (pop. 10,000) glories in its fortresses, Venetian architecture, and nearby pebble beaches. The town's crown jewel is the 18th-century **Palamidi fortress**, which provides spectacular views of the town and harbor. To get there, walk or take a taxi (€3) up the 3km road; or climb the grueling 999 steps up from Plizoidhou, across the park from the bus station. (Open in summer daily 8am-6:45pm; off-season 8:30am-5:45pm. €4, students €2.) To reach **Bouboulinas,** the waterfront promenade, from the station, go left and follow Syngrou to the harbor and the **Old Town.** Nafplion's small, pebbly beach **Arvanitia** is along the road that curves around the left-hand side of Palamidi; if it gets too crowded on a hot day, follow the footpath for lovely private coves.

Buses leave from Syngrou, near the base of the Palamidi fortress, for Athens (3hr., every hr., €9) via Corinth (2hr., €4). The **tourist office** is on 25 Martiou across from the telephone office. (☎27520 24 444. Open daily 9am-1pm and 4-8pm.) For the Old Town rooftop views from **Dimitris Bekas' Domatia ❷,** turn up the stairs on Kokkinou, following the sign for rooms off Staikopoulou; climb to the top and go up 50 steps. (☎27520 24 594. Singles €16; doubles €20-22.) **To Fanaria ❷,** above the *plateia* on Staikopoulou in a trellised alleyway, serves tantalizing entrees in an intimate atmosphere. (Soups €2.50-3; fish dishes €6-8.) **Postal Code:** 21100.

■ **DAYTRIPS FROM NAFPLION: MYCENAE AND EPIDAVROS.** The head of the Greek world from 1600 to 1100 BC, **Mycenae** (Μυκηνες) was once ruled by the legendary Agamemnon, leader of the attacking forces in the Trojan War. Excavations of ancient Mycenae have persisted for 130 years, turning the area into one of the most visited sites in Greece. Today, backpackers and senior citizens stampede to the famed ruins. The imposing **Lion's Gate,** the portal into the ancient city, has two lions carved in relief above the lintel and is estimated to weigh some 20 tons. The **Tomb of Agamemnon** (also known as the Treasury of Atreus) is the large and impressive *tholos*. (Both sites open Apr.-Sept. daily 8am-7pm; Oct.-Mar. 8am-5pm. €6, students €3. Keep your ticket or pay twice.) The only direct **bus** to Mycenae is from Nafplion (45min., 5 per day, €1.80) via Argos (30min., €0.90). Join the ranks of Claude Debussy, William Faulkner, Allen Ginsberg, and Virginia Woolf by staying at **Belle Helene Hotel ❸,** which doubles as a bus stop on the main road. (☎27510 76 225. Singles €20-30; doubles €40-50; triples €50-55.)

The grandest structure at the ancient site of **Epidavros** (Επιδαυρος) is the **Theater of Epidavros**, built in the early 2nd century BC. The incredible acoustics allow you to stand at the top row of seats—14,000 seats back—and hear a match lit on stage. Near the theater and on the road to the sanctuary's ruins is Epidavros's **museum**. (☎27520 22 009. Open daily 8am-7pm. Ticket office open daily 7:30am-7pm, during festival season also F-Sa 7:30am-9pm. €6, students €3.) From late June to mid-Aug., the **Epidavros Theater Festival** brings performances of classical Greek plays on Friday and Saturday nights. Shows are at 9pm; purchase tickets at the site or by calling the Athens Festival Box Office. (☎210 322 1459. Tickets €17-40, students €9.) **Buses** arrive in Epidavros from Nafplion (45min., 3 per day, €2).

CORINTH (Κορινθος)   ☎27410

Most visitors to the Peloponnese travel to the ruins of **Ancient Corinth**, at the base of the **Acrocorinth**. Majestic columns have endured through the ages around the courtyard of the **Temple of Apollo**, down the stairs to the left of the excellent **Archaeological Museum**. The 2-3hr. hike to the **fortress** at the top of the Acrocorinth is strenuous and dangerous; instead, take a taxi to the summit (☎27410 31 464, €6), which will wait an hour before the drive back down (€10). Explore the surprisingly intact remains of the **Temple to Aphrodite**, where disciples were initiated into the "mysteries of love." (☎27410 31 207. Open summer Tu-F 8am-7pm, Sa-Su 8:30am-3pm; off-season daily 8am-5pm. Museum and site €6, students €3.)

In **New Corinth**, which is both a transportation hub and the logical base for viewing the ruins, **buses** leave from Terminal A, past the train station, for Athens (1½hr., 29 per day, €6). Buses run from Terminal B, on Koliatsou, halfway through the park, to Ancient Corinth (20min., 8 per day 8:10am-9:10pm, €1). Buses leave Terminal C, **Argolis Station** (☎27410 24 403), at the intersection of Eth. Antistasis and Aratou, for: Argos (1hr., €3.20); Mycenae (45min., €2.40); and Nafplion (1½hr., €4). **Trains** go from the station on Demokratias to Athens (normal: 2hr., 7 per day, €2.60; express: 1½hr., 7 per day, €5.70). The **tourist police**, Ermou 51, are located in the city's park and provide tourists with maps, brochures, and other assistance. (☎27410 23 282. Open daily 8am-2pm.) The newly renovated **Hotel Apollon ❷**, Damaskinou 2, in New Corinth, has TVs, A/C, and Internet access. (☎27410 25 920. Singles €40; doubles €60.)

NORTHERN AND CENTRAL GREECE

The last additions to the Greek state, northern and central Greece have a harsh continental climate that makes for a life distinct from that of its Mediterranean counterparts. Forgotten mountain-goat paths lead to glorious vistas, overlooking silvery olive groves, fruit-laden trees, and patchwork farmland.

THESSALONIKI (Θεσσαλονικη)   ☎2310

Thessaloniki (pop. 1,830,000), a jumble of ancient, Byzantine, European, Turkish, Sephardic, and contemporary Greek culture and history, fans out from its hilltop fortress toward the Thermaic Gulf. From its peak, the fortress overlooks the Old Town's placid streets which stretch down to the city's long, congested avenues. Golden mosaics, frescoes, and floating domes still gleam in the industrial city's Byzantine churches. Most travelers spend a couple of days in Thessaloniki checking out the sights, going to clubs, and enjoying the tranquility of countryside hikes.

■ TRANSPORTATION

Ferries: Buy tickets at **Karacharisis Travel and Shipping Agency**, Koundouriotou 8 (☎2310 524 544; fax 2310 532 289), across from the Olympic Airways Office. Open M-F 8:30am-8:30pm, Sa 8:30am-2:30pm. During high season, from mid-June to early Sept., ferries travel to **Chios** (20hr., Su 1am, €31; 9hr., W 9:30am, €62) via **Lesvos** (14hr., Su, €31; 6½hr., W, €62); **Iraklion** (24hr.; Tu 3pm, Th 7:30pm, Sa midnight; €41) via **Mykonos** (15hr., 3 per week, €31); **Naxos** (16hr., 1 per week, €29); **Paros** (17½hr., 2 per week, €31); **Santorini** (19½hr., 3 per week, €33); **Skiathos** (4hr., 2 per week, €16); **Skopelos** (6½hr., 3 per week, €17); **Kos** (20hr., 1 per week, €39), **Samos** (16hr., 2 per week, €32), and **Rhodes** (24hr., 1 per week, €46).

Trains: Main Terminal (☎2310 517 517), on Monastiriou in the western part of the city. Take any bus down Egnatia (€0.50). To **Athens** (8hr., 5 per day, €15). The **Travel Office** (☎2310 598 112) can provide updated schedules.

Buses: Most **KTEL** buses leave from one central, dome-shaped bus station west of the city center. To: **Athens** (☎2310 595 495; 6hr., 11 per day, €28); **Corinth** (☎2310 595 405; 7½hr., 11:30pm, €32); **Patras** (☎2310 595 425; 7hr., 3 per day, €30).

Flights: The **airport** (☎2310 408 400), 16km east of town, can be reached by **bus #78** or from the train station or Pl. Aristotelous, or by **taxi** (€10). There's an EOT **tourist office** branch (☎2310 985 215) at the airport. The **Olympic Airways** office at Koundouriotou 3 (☎2310 368 311), is open M-F 8am-3:45pm. Call for reservations (☎2310 368 666; M-Sa 8am-4:30pm). To: **Athens** (1hr., 9 per day, €90); **Chios** (3hr., 4 per week, €60); **Corfu** (50min., 2 per week, €64); **Iraklion** (2hr., 2 per day, €109); **Lesvos** (2hr., daily, €63); **Rhodes** (3hr., daily, €116); and **Samos** (1hr., 4 per week, €70).

Public Transportation: Local buses cost €0.50 and run throughout the city. Buy tickets at *periptera* or at depot ticket booths. **Taxis** (☎2310 551 525) have specific queues at Ag. Sophia and Mitropoleos.

■ ■ ORIENTATION AND PRACTICAL INFORMATION

Egnatia, an old Roman highway, runs down the middle of town and is home to the cheapest hotels. Running parallel to the water, the main streets are **Ermou, Tsimiski, Mitropoleos**, and **Nikis**, which runs along the waterfront. Inland from Egnatia is **Agios Dimitriou** and the **Old Town** beyond. Intersecting these and leading into town are I. Dragoumi, El. Venizelou, Aristotelous, Ag. Sophias, and Eth. Aminis.

Tourist Office: EOT, inside the port at the Passenger Terminal (☎2310 222 935). Open M-Sa 7:30am-3pm.

Banks: Banks with currency exchange and 24hr. **ATMs** line Tsimiski, including **National Bank**, Tsimiski 11 (☎2310 230 783). Open M-Th 8am-2pm, F 8am-1:30pm.

Tourist Police: Dodekanissou 4, 5th fl. (☎2310 554 871). Free maps and brochures. Open 24hr. For the **local police**, call ☎2310 553 800 or 100.

Telephones: OTE, Karolou Diehl 27 (☎134), at the corner of Ermou, 1 block east of Aristotelous. Open M-F 7am-3pm, W also 7pm-9pm.

Internet Access: There are several small Internet cafes along the western end of Egnatia. **Interspot Cafe**, Tsimiski 43, inside the mall, offers access for €1.50 per hr. **E-Global**, Egnatia 105, one block east of Arch of Galerius, sports over 50 terminals. €2-3 per hr. Open 24hr. **Meganet Internet Cafe**, 5 Pl. Navarinou, overlooking the Palace of Galerius, offers access for €2 per hr. Open 24hr. The **British Council**, Eth. Aminis 9, offers **free access**. Open M-F 9am-1pm.

GREECE

Thessaloniki

ACCOMMODATIONS
Hotel Augustos, 1
Hotel Pella, 2
Hotel Tourist, 4

FOOD
Dore Zythos, 5
Ouzeri Melathron, 3

Gulf of Thessaloniki

0   300 yards
0   300 meters

Post Office: Aristotelous 27, just below Egnatia. Open M-F 7:30am-8pm, Sa 7:30am-2pm, Su 9am-1:30pm. A **branch** office (☎2310 229 324), on Eth. Aminis near the White Tower, is open M-F 7am-8pm. Both offer *Poste Restante.* **Postal Code:** 54101.

📑 ACCOMMODATIONS

Most budget hotels cluster along the western end of Egnatia, between Pl. Dimokratias (500m east of the train station) and Aristotelous. Egnatia can be noisy and gritty, but you'll have to pay more elsewhere.

Hotel Atlantis, Egnatia 14 (☎2310 540 131). Offers standard budget furnishings and well-maintained hallway bathrooms. Singles and doubles €20, with bath €30. ❷

Hotel Augustos, El. Svoronou 4 (☎2310 522 955). Walking down the western end of Egnatia, turn north at the Argo Hotel; Augustos is 20m straight ahead. Cozy rooms. Singles with bath €25; doubles €30, with bath €40; triples with bath €50. ❷

Hotel Pella, Dragoumi 63 (☎2310 524 221). North on Dragoumi 2 blocks up from west Egnatia's budget strip. Comfortable rooms with desk, TV, telephone, and bath. Singles €35; doubles €50. ❸

Hotel Tourist, Mitropoleos 21 (☎2310 270 501). An excellent location. Rooms with TV, telephone, A/C, and bath. Singles €50; doubles €70; triples €90. ❹

🍴 FOOD

Ouzeri can be found in tiny streets off Aristotelous; the innovative places a block down from Egnatia between Dragoumi and El. Venizelou cater to a younger clientele. **Ouzeri Melathron ❷,** Karypi 21-34, in an alleyway at El. Venizelou 23, has a humorous menu and delicious food. (Entrees €3.50-12.) A meal at **Dore Zythos ❷,** Tsiroyianni 7, behind the grassy triangular plot across from the White Tower, includes sea breezes, superb views, and an avant-garde menu. Try the €7 *its pilaf* for an Anatolian treat. (Entrees €6-8.)

🎭 SIGHTS AND ENTERTAINMENT

The streets of modern Thessaloniki are littered with the reminders of its significance during both the Byzantine and Ottoman empires. **Agios Dimitrios,** on Ag. Dimitriou north of Aristotelous, is the city's oldest and most famous church. Although most of its interior was gutted in a 1917 fire, some lovely mosaics remain. (Open daily 6am-10pm.) South of Egnatia, on the square that bears its name, the magnificent domed **Agia Sophia** features a splendid ceiling mosaic of the Ascension. (Open daily 7am-1pm and 5-7pm.) Originally part of a palatial complex designed to honor the Roman Caesar Galerium, the **Rotunda** became the church **Agios Georgiou** in late Roman times. Its walls were once plastered with some of the city's most brilliant mosaics; unfortunately, very few remain. (Open Su and Tu-Sa 8am-7pm.) A colonnaded processional once led south to the **Arch of Galerius,** on the eastern end of Egnatia, which commemorates the Caesar's 397 AD Persian victory. Further west down Egnatia, don't miss **Bey Hamami,** a perfectly preserved 15th-century bath house that served the Ottoman governor and his retinue. (Open daily 8am-9pm. Free.) The **Heptapyrgion,** a 5th-century Byzantine fortress, is the main attraction of the city's modest acropolis. (Open Su and Tu-Sa 8am-7pm.)

All that remains of a 15th-century Venetian seawall, the **White Tower** presides over the eastern edge of the waterfront like an overgrown chess piece. (Tower open M 12:30-7pm, Tu-Su 8am-7pm. Free.) Thessaloniki's **Archaeological Museum,** at the western end of Tsimiski, across from the International Helexpo Fair-grounds, is full of discoveries gleaned from Neolithic tombs, mosaics from Roman houses, and a dazzling display of Macedonian gold. (Open Su and Tu-Sa 8am-7pm, M 12:30-7pm; off-season reduced hours. €4, students €2. EU students free.) Just across the street at Stratou 2, the **Museum of Byzantine Culture** displays an impressive array of artifacts from both the Early and Middle Byzantine eras, from church mosaics and elaborate tombs to 1500-year-old personal effects. (Open Su and Tu-Sa 8am-7pm, M 12:30-7pm; off-season reduced hours. €4, students and seniors €2. EU students and under-18 free.)

There are four main hubs for late-night fun: The bars and cafes of the **Ladadika** district, the renovated mill factories of **Mylos** behind the harbor, the waterfront's cafes, and the open-air discos near the airport exit (€8-9 by taxi). **Rodon 2000,** 11km east of the city along the main highway, is a sophisticated hot spot filled with Greek music. (€10 cover includes 1 drink.)

🔢 DAYTRIP FROM THESSALONIKI

VERGINA. The tombs of Vergina (Βεργινα), final home to ancient Macedonian royalty, lie only 30km from Thessaloniki. The principal sight is the **Great Tumulus,** a huge, man-made mount 12m tall and 110m wide. Check out the bones of **Alexander IV,** son of Alexander the Great, as well as the magnificent **Tomb of Philip II,** Alexander's father. Visitors can stroll into the mound and check out its magnificent burial treasures, intricate gold work, and brilliant frescoes. (Open Su and Tu-Sa 8am-7pm, M noon-7pm; off-season Su and Tu-Sa 8am-7pm. €8, students €4.) **Buses** run from Thessaloniki (1hr., every hr., €4.60) to Veria. From Veria, take the bus to Vergina's *plateia* (20min., 8 per day, €1); follow the signs to the sights.

MOUNT OLYMPUS (Ολυμπος)   ☎ 23520

The impressive height (nearly 3000m) and formidable slopes of the Thermaic Gulf's Mt. Olympus so awed the ancients that they proclaimed it the dwelling place of the gods. A network of well-maintained **hiking** trails now makes the summit accessible to anyone with sturdy legs and a taste for the divine. Two approaches to the peaks begin near **Litochoro** (elev. 340m); the first and most popular starts at **Prionia** (elev. 1100m), 18km from the village, and takes one full day round-trip. The second, a longer and more picturesque route, begins at **Diastavrosi** (also called **Gortsia;** elev. 1300m), 14km away. There is no bus to the trailheads from Litochoro, so you'll have to walk, drive, or take a taxi (from Prionia €20). Unless you're handy with a crampon and an ice axe, make your ascent between May and October. **Mytikas,** the tallest peak, is inaccessible without special equipment before June.

Trains (☎23520 22 522) run to the Litochoro station from Athens (6hr., 4 per day, €15) and Thessaloniki (1½hr., 4 per day, €3); a **taxi** from the train station to the town costs around €6. KTEL **buses** (☎23520 81 271) run from Athens (5½hr., 3 per day, €25) and Thessaloniki (1½hr., 17 per day, €6). The **tourist office** is on Ag. Nikolaou by the park. (☎23520 83 100. Open July-Nov. 8:30am-2:30pm and 5-9pm.) The EOS-run ⬛**Spilos Agapitos ❷** ("Refuge A" or "Zolotas") is about 800m below **Skala** and Mytikas peaks. The English-speaking staff dispenses info over the phone to prospective hikers and can also help reserve spots in other refuges. (☎23520 81 800; zolotam@hol.gr. Meals 6am-9pm. Lights out 10pm. Open mid-May to late-Oct. Dorms €10, members €8. €4.20 to **camp** nearby and use facilities.) Camp at **Olympus Zeus ❷** (☎23520 22 115; sites from €11) on the beach about 5km from town.

METEORA (Μετεωρα)   ☎ 24230

The iron-gray pinnacles of the Meteora rock formations are stunning, offering astonishing views of fields, mountains, and monolithic stone. These wonders of nature are bedecked with 24 gravity-defying, frescoed Byzantine monasteries. (Dress modestly. Open Apr.-Sept. Sa-Su and W 10am-12:30pm and 3:30-5pm; hours vary during the rest of the week. €2 per monastery.) The **Grand Meteoron Monastery** is the oldest, largest, and most touristed of the monasteries. It houses a **folk museum** and the 16th-century **Church of the Transfiguration**, whose dome features a *Pantokrator* (a central image of Christ). To escape the hordes of tourists, venture to **Roussanou**, to the right after the fork in the road. Visible from most of the valley, it is one of the most spectacularly situated monasteries in the area.

Buses leave for Meteora from the fountain in **Kalambaka**, the most popular base for exploring the sight (2 per day, €0.80). **Trains** leave Kalambaka for Athens (4hr., 3 per day, €19.10) and Thessaloniki (5hr., 3 per day, €10.50). **Buses** depart for Athens (5hr., 8 per day, €20) and Patras (6hr., Tu and Th 9:45am and 3pm, €19.40). The large rooms at **Koka Roka ❷** offer views of Meteora; from the central *plateia*, follow Vlachara to its end, bear left, and follow the signs. (☎ 24230 24 554. Singles €15; doubles €27, with bath €32; triples with bath €42.) **Postal Code:** 42200.

IOANNINA (Ιωαννινα)   ☎ 26510

On the shores of Lake Pamvotis lies Epirus's capital and largest city, Ioannina (pop. 100,000). While perhaps not captivating, the city does serve as a useful transport hub between Greece and Italy. Aside from local finds, the highlights of the city's **Archaeological Museum**, off Averof, near the city center, are the lead tablets used by ancients to inscribe their questions to the oracle at Dodoni. (Open Su and Tu-Sa 8:30am-3pm. €2, students free.) Catch a boat from the waterfront (10min., €1) for **Nisi** ("The Island") to explore Byzantine monasteries and the **Ali Pasha Museum** (Open daily 8am-10pm. €0.75.)

Buses run from the terminal at Zossimadon 4 to Athens (6½hr., 10 per day, €27) and Thessaloniki (7hr., 6 per day, €22). To reach the **tourist office,** walk 500m down Leoforos Dodoni; the office is on the left, immediately after the playground. (☎ 26510 46 662. Open July-Sept. M-F 7:30am-2:30pm and 5-8:30pm, Sa 9am-1pm; Oct.-June M-F 7:30am-2:30pm.) **Hotel Tourist ❸**, Kolleti 18, on the right a few blocks up Averof from the kastro, offers baths, telephones, TV, and A/C. (☎ 26510 25 070. Singles €30; doubles €40; triples €50.) **Postal Code:** 45110.

◪ **DAYTRIP FROM IOANNINA: DODONI.** Ancient Dodoni (Δωδωνη), the site of mainland Greece's oldest oracle, is at the base of a mountain 22km southeast of Ioannina. According to myth, **Zeus** answered queries here from the roots of a giant oak tree. There is also a large 3rd-century **amphitheater** at the site (currently undergoing restoration). **Buses** to Dodoni run from Ioannina's smaller station at Bizaniou 21 (30min.; M, W, F 6:30am and 3:30pm; €1.70). Ask to be let off at the theater. The return bus passes by at about 4:45pm; alternatively, you can hire a **taxi** (at least €15).

IONIAN ISLANDS (Νησια Του Ιουιου)

Just to the west of mainland Greece, the Ionian Islands are renowned for their medley of rugged mountains, rolling farmland, shimmering olive groves, and pristine beaches, all surrounded by an endless expanse of clear, blue water. The islands are a favorite among vacationing Brits, Italians, and Germans, as well as ferry-hopping backpackers heading to Italy.

◀ FERRIES TO ITALY

To catch a ferry to Italy, buy your ticket at least a day ahead; be sure to find out if the port tax (€5-6) is included. **International Tours** (☎26610 39 007) and **Ionian Cruises** (☎26610 31 649), both located across the street from the old port on Venizelou, can help with your scheduling woes. Ferries go from Corfu to: Ancona (20hr., daily, €58); Bari (9hr., daily, €46); Brindisi (6-7hr., 3 per day, €30); Trieste (24hr., 4 per week, €52); and Venice (24hr., daily, €57). Schedules vary; call ahead.

CORFU (KERKYRA; Κερκυρα)   ☎26610

Ever since Homer's Odysseus washed ashore and praised its lush beauty, the seas have brought a multitude of conquerors, colonists, and tourists to verdant Corfu. Those who stray from the beaten path, however, will still encounter unspoiled, uncrowded beaches.

CORFU TOWN AND ENVIRONS. Corfu Town (pop. 31,000) enchants with its two fortresses, various museums, churches, and winding streets. South of Corfu Town is the exquisite **Achillion Palace;** take a bus to Gastouri (30min.; M-Sa 6 per day, Su 4 per day; €0.90). The lovely **Paleokastritsa** beach, where Odysseus supposedly washed ashore, lies west of town; take a KTEL bus to Paleokastritsa (45min.; M-Sa 7 per day, Su 5 per day; €1.60). A short walk from there will bring you to the hilltop monastery **Panagia Theotokos.** KTEL buses also run from Corfu Town to **Agios Gordios** (45min.; M-Sa 5 per day, Su 3 per day; €1.50), home to impressive rock formations, a beach, and the **Pink Palace Hotel ❷,** which is immensely popular with American and Canadian backpackers. The Palace has an impressive list of amenities, including tennis courts, a nightclub, massages (€11), clothing-optional cliff-diving (€15), and various water sports. They also run buses to Athens (€38 from Pink Palace, €47 from Athens), that bypass Patras. (☎26610 53 103; www.thepinkpalace.com. Breakfast, dinner, and ferry pick-up included. **Internet** €2 per 30min. Rooms €19, with A/C and bath €25.)

    Ferries run from Corfu Town to Italy (see above) and Patras (6-7hr., 1-2 per day, €25), and high-speed **catamarans** run to Kephalonia (3hr., W and Sa 9am, €38). KTEL inter-city green buses depart from between I. Theotaki and the New Fortress; blue municipal buses leave from Pl. San Rocco. The EOT **tourist office** is at the corner of Rizopaston Voulefton and I. Polila. (☎26610 37 520. Open M-F 8am-1:30pm. Free maps and info.) **The Association of Owners of Private Rooms and Apartments,** I. Polila 24 (☎26610 26 133), has a complete list of rooms in Corfu Town. **Hotel Hermes ❸,** G. Markorka 14, centrally located across the bend from the police station, has a verdant entrance and low rates. (☎26610 39 268. Singles €28, with bath €33; doubles €33/€44; triples €50.) **To Paradosiakon ❶,** Odos Solomou 20, serves traditional food highly recommended by locals. (Open daily 11am-midnight. Entrees €4.10-8.50.) **Restaurant Rex ❸,** Kapodistriou 66, one block back from the Spianada, has long been famed as one of the town's best. (Entrees €7.40-14.) The undisputed epicenter of Corfu Town's nightlife is the **Disco Strip,** on Eth. Antistaseos, 2km west of New Port. **Postal Code:** 49100.

KEPHALONIA (Κεφαλονια)   ☎26710

Mountains, subterranean lakes and rivers, caves, forests, and more than 250km of sand-and-pebble coastline make Kephalonia (pop. 32,000) a nature lover's paradise. Its profound beauty, fought over by the Byzantine, Ottoman, and British Empires draws and humbles a diverse crowd. **Argostoli,** the capital of Kephalonia and Ithaka, is a lively city packed with pastel buildings that climb the hills from the calm waters of the harbor. Argostoli offers good shopping and nightlife, as well as easy access to other points on the island. **Buses** leave from the south end of the waterfront for Sami (2 per day, €3) and Fiskardo (2hr., 2 per day, €4). **Internet** is available at **Cafeland**, on Andrea Choida in Argostoli. (☎ 26710 24 064. €5 per hour, €2.50 min. Open daily 9am-11pm.) **Hotel Tourist ❸**, on the waterfront near the bus station, is a great deal. (☎ 26710 22 510. All rooms have balconies. Singles €30-36; doubles €46-52.) ▓**Mister Grillo ❷**, near the port authority, offers large portions and live Greek music. (Vegetarian options. Entrees €6-14.)

Sami is 24km from Argostoli on the east coast. Stunning views stretch in every direction, from the waves crashing on the beach to the green hills cradling the town. Sami is close to the underground **Melissani Lake** and **Drogarati Cave,** a large cavern filled with stalactites and stalagmites. (Cave open daily until nightfall. €3, children €1.50.) **Fiskardo,** at the northern tip of the island, is the most beautiful of Kephalonia's towns; take a bus from either Sami (1hr., 10:15am, €3) or Argostoli (2hr., 2 per day, €4). Buses from Fiskardo stop at the turn-off for ▓**Myrtos Beach,** one of Europe's best. (Beach 4km from turn-off.) **Ferries** run from Sami to: Patras (2½hr., 2 per day, €12); and Brindisi, Italy (July-Sept. daily, €35). **Hotel Kyma ❷**, in Sami's main *plateia*, has spacious rooms. (☎ 26740 22 064. Singles €18-28; doubles €26-55; triples €31-66.) **Postal Code:** 28100.

THE SPORADES (Σποραδες)

Circling into the azure Aegean, the Sporades form a family of enchanting sea maidens. From wild Skiathos to sophisticated Skopelos to quiet Alonnisos, the islands have beckoned to visitors for millennia. Ancient Athenians and Romans, early Venetians, and modern-day tourists have all basked on their sunlit shores and trod their shaded forests.

▐ TRANSPORTATION

To get to most of the Sporades from Athens, take the bus to Agios Konstantinos (2½hr., every hr., €11), where **Hellas Lines** (☎ 22 209) operates **ferries** to: Alonnisos (5½hr., 2 per week, €14); Skiathos (2hr., 2 per day, €21); and Skopelos (3hr., 2 per day, €27). **Flying Dolphins** leave Agios Konstantinos for: Alonnisos (2¾hr., 1-5 per day, €27); Skiathos (1½hr., 1-5 per day, €21); and Skopelos (2½hr., 1-5 per day, €27). Ferries also shuttle between the islands (see below).

SKIATHOS (Σκιαθος)   ☎ 24270

Having grown up almost overnight from an innocent island daughter to a madcap dancing queen, Skiathos (local pop. 5,000; summer pop. over 50,000) is the tourism hub of the Sporades. Buses leave the port in Skiathos Town for the southern beaches (every 15min., €1.10). The bus route ends in Koukounaries, near the lovely, pine-wooded ▓**Koukounaries Beach and Biotrope** and the nude **Banana Beach** and **Little Banana Beach.** Indulge at the countless bars in **Plateia Papadiamantis** or along **Polytechniou** and **Evangelistra,** then dance all night long at the clubs on the eastern side of the waterfront. Hellas Lines **ferries** (☎ 24270 22 209) run to Alonnisos (2hr., 1-2 per day, €8) and Skopelos (1½hr., 1-3 per day, €5.40). *Domatia* are the best deal in town. The **Rooms to Let Office,** in the wooden kiosk by the port, provides a list of available rooms. (☎ 24270 22 990. Open daily 9am-8pm.) The rooms at ▓**Australia Hotel ❷**, in an alley on Evangelistra off Papadiamantis, have A/C, private baths, fridges, and balconies. (Singles €20; doubles €25-30; triples €36; in Aug. prices increase.) **Primavera ❷** has delicious Italian food. (Entrees €5-10. Open daily 6:30pm-12:30am.) **Postal Code:** 37002.

SKOPELOS (Σκοπελος)   ☎24240

Skopelos (pop. 6,000) sits between the whirlwind of Skiathos and the wilderness of Alonnisos featuring the best elements of both. Hikes and moped rides lead to numerous monasteries, bright beaches, and white cliffs. Buses leave from the right of the waterfront (as you face the sea) for beaches near **Stafylos, Milia,** and **Loutraki.** At night, the waterfront strip closes to traffic and crowds swarm the streets in search of the tastiest *gyros* and the most authentic Greek *taverna.* Hellas Lines (☎22 767) runs **ferries** to: Alonnisos (30min., 1-2 per day, €4.10); Skiathos (1hr., 3-4 per day, €5.50); and Thessaloniki (1 per week, €40). **Thalpos Travel Agency,** 5m to the right of Galanatsiou along the waterfront, provides tourist info. (☎22 947. Open May-Oct. daily 10am-2pm and 6-10pm; Nov.-Apr. info available by phone.) The **Rooms and Apartments Association** can provide a list of current *domatia.* (☎24 567. Open daily 10am-2pm and 6-10pm.) **Pension Sotos ❷,** on the waterfront at the corner of Galanatsiou, has a fantastic location and unbeatable prices. (☎22 549. Singles €22; doubles €32; triples €55.) **Plateia Platanos** abounds with fast, cheap food. **Postal Code:** 37003.

ALONNISOS (Αλοννησος)   ☎24240

Of the 20-odd islands within Greece's new **National Marine Park,** only Alonnisos (pop. 2,000) is inhabited. **Hikers** take to the highland trails in the north; pick up *Alonnisos on Foot* (€9) in **Patitiri** for walking routes. In the south, endless beaches satisfy sun-seeking souls; many are accessible from the island's main road. A 1½hr. walk from Patitiri takes you to **Votsi;** locals dive off the 15-20m cliffs near **Votsi Beach.** Beautiful **Hora** (Χωρα; Old Town) is ideal for both hikers and beachgoers. A **bus** runs between Hora and Patitiri (every hr., €1). **Ferries** run to Skiathos (2hr., 2 per day, €6) and Skopelos (30min., 1-2 per day, €4.10). **Alonissos Travel,** in the center of the waterfront, exchanges currency, finds rooms, books excursions, and sells ferry tickets. (☎65 188. Open daily 8am-11pm.) **Panorama ❷,** down the first alley on the left from Ikion Dolophon, rents bright rooms and studios. (☎65 240. All rooms with bath. Singles €25; doubles €40; 2-bedroom suite with kitchen €40-60.) Locals adore the *ouzeri* **To Kamaki ❶,** on the left side of Ikion Dolophon, past the National Bank. The octopus salad (€8.50) is delicious. (Open daily 11am-2am.) **Postal Code:** 37005.

THE CYCLADES (Κυκλαδες)

When people wax rhapsodic about the Greek islands, chances are they're talking about the Cyclades. Whatever your idea of Greece—cobblestone streets and whitewashed houses, breathtaking sunsets, scenic hikes, all-night revelry—you'll find it here. Although most islands are mobbed in the summer, each has quiet villages and untouched spots.

▣ TRANSPORTATION

Ferries run from: Athens to Mykonos, Naxos, and Santorini; Crete to Naxos and Santorini; and Thessaloniki to Naxos and Ios. Frequent ferries also run between each of the islands in the Cyclades. See below for all ferry information. High-speed ferries and **hydrofoils** typically cover the same routes at twice the cost and speed.

MYKONOS (Μυκονος)   ☎22890

Coveted by pirates in the 18th century, Mykonos is still lusted after by those seeking revelry and excess. Nightlife, both gay and straight, abounds on this island, the expensive playground of chic sophisticates. Ambling in colorful alleyways at dawn or dusk is the cheapest and most exhilarating way to experience the island, especially **Mykonos Town.** All of Mykonos's beaches are nudist, but the degree of bareness varies. **Plati Yialos, Paradise Beach,** and **Super Paradise Beach** are the most daring; **Elia** is a bit tamer. Buses run south from South Station to Plati Yialos (every 30min., €1), where *caïques* (little boats) go to the other beaches (around €1.50); direct buses also run to Paradise from South Station (every 30min., €1) and to Elia from North Station (30min., 8 per day, €1). After 11pm, wild dancing and irresistible hedonism are the norm at **Pierro's** on Matogianni (beer €5). The **Skandinavian Bar** on the waterfront has something for everyone in its two-building party complex. (Beer and shots €3-4. Open Su-F 8:30pm-3am, Sa 8:30pm-4am.)

 Ferries run to: Naxos (3hr., 1-2 per day, €7.10); Santorini (6hr., 3 per week, €14); and Tinos (45min., 3 per day, €4). The helpful **tourist police** are located at the ferry landing. (☎22890 22 482. Open daily 8am-11pm.) Most budget travelers bed down at Mykonos's several festive campsites, which offer a myriad of sleeping options beyond the standard plot of grass. There are **information offices** on the dock, one for **hotels** and one for **camping.** (Hotels ☎22890 24 540; open daily 9am-midnight. Camping ☎22890 23 567; open daily 9am-midnight.) **Hotel Philippi ❷,** Kalogera 25, across from Zorzis Hotel, provides cheerful rooms with bath, fridge, and A/C around a bountiful garden. (☎22890 22 294; chriko@ote-net.gr. Open Apr.-Oct. Singles €35-60; doubles €45-75). The lively ⬛**Paradise Beach Camping ❶,** 6km from the village, is directly on the beach. (☎22890 22 852. €5-7 per person, €2.50-3 per tent, 2-person beach cabin €20-45.) Cheap *creperies* and *souvlaki* joints are on nearly all of Mykonos's streets. **Appaloosa ❸,** one block from Taxi Square on Mavrogeneous, serves mostly Mexican selections. (Entrees €9-11. Open daily 8pm-1:30am.) **Postal Code:** 84600.

⚡ DAYTRIP FROM MYKONOS: DELOS. Delos (Δηλος) is the sacred center of the Cyclades. The **archaeological site,** which occupies much of the small island, takes several days to explore completely, but its highlights can be seen in about three hours. From the dock, head straight to the **Agora of the Competaliasts;** continue in the same direction and turn left onto the wide **Sacred Road** to reach the **Sanctuary of Apollo,** a collection of temples built from Mycenaean times onward. On the right is the biggest and most famous, the **Great Temple of Apollo.** Continue 50m past the end of the Sacred Road to the beautiful **Terrace of the Lions.** The **museum,** next to the cafeteria, contains an assortment of archaeological finds. (Open Su and Tu-Sa 8:30am-3pm. €5, students €2.) A path from the museum leads to the summit of **Mt. Kythnos** (112m), from which Zeus watched Apollo's birth. Excursion **boats** leave the dock near Mykonos Town for Delos (35min., 3 per day, round-trip €10).

PAROS (Παρος) ☎22840

Paros is famed for its slabs of pure white marble, used for many of the great statues and buildings of the ancient world. Today's visitors know the island for its tall mountains and long, golden beaches. Behind the commercial surface of **Parikia** (pop. 3,000), Paros's port and largest city, flower-filled streets wind through archways and past one of the most treasured basilicas of the Orthodox faith, the **Panagia Ekatontapiliani** (Church of Our Lady of 100 Gates). Tradition holds that only 99 of the church's 100 doors are visible—when the 100th appears, Constantinople will again belong to the Greeks. (Dress modestly. Open daily 7am-10pm. Free.) Just 10km south of town is the shady, spring-fed ⬛**Valley of the Butterflies** (a.k.a. *Petaloudes*), where rare *Panaxiaquadripunctaria* moths congregate during the mating season from June to late September. Take the bus from Parikia to Aliki (10min., 8 per day, €0.90) and ask to be let off at Petaloudes. Follow the signs 2km up the road. (Open June-Sept. daily 9am-8pm. €1.50.) The **Parian Experience,** along the waterfront, is a pulsating party complex with a spacious central courtyard and four simultaneous tunes. Follow the spotlight and crowds to the far end of the harbor. (☎22840 21 113. Beer €2-3. Mixed drinks €5-6. €3 discount on first drink.)

Ferries sail to Ios (2½hr., 7-9 per day, €8.30) and Santorini (3½hr., 7-9 per day, €12). The **tourist police** are on the *plateia* behind the telephone office. (☎22840 21 673. Open daily 7am-2:30pm.) Turn left at the dock and take a right after the cemetery ruins to reach the pleasant **Rena Rooms ❷.** (☎22840 22 220. Doubles €18-39; triples €27-45. 20% discount for *Let's Go* readers.) The psychedelic **Happy Green Cow ❸,** a block off the *plateia* behind the National Bank, serves tasty vegetarian fare. (Entrees €8-12. Open Apr.-Nov. daily 7pm-midnight.) **Postal Code:** 84400.

NAXOS (Ναξος)   ☎22850

The ancients believed Naxos (pop. 18,500), the largest of the Cyclades, was the home of Dionysus. Olive groves, wineries, small villages, and chalky white ruins fill its interior, while sandy beaches line its shores. **Naxos Town,** the capital, is crowned by the **Kastro,** a Venetian castle now home to two museums. The 🖼**Venetian Museum** features evening concerts with traditional Greek music, dancing, and shadow theater. (Open daily 10am-4pm and 7-11pm. €5, students and seniors €3.) The **Archaeological Museum** occupies the former Collège Français, which educated Nikos Kazantzakis, author of *The Last Temptation of Christ* and *Zorba the Greek.* (Open Su and Tu-Sa 8:30am-2pm. €3, students €2.) The **Mitropolis Museum,** next to the Orthodox Church, is an architectural achievement in itself, built around the excavated site of a 13th-century BC settlement. (Open Su and Tu-Sa 8:30am-3pm. Free.) The 6th-century BC **Portara** archway, visible from the waterfront, is one of the few archaeological sites in Greece where you can actually climb all over the ruins. To experience the island fully, it's essential to escape Naxos Town. A bus goes from the port to the beaches of **Agia Georgios, Agios Prokopios, Agia Anna,** and **Plaka** (every 30min., €1.20). Buses also run from Naxos Town to **Apiranthos,** a beautiful village with narrow, marble paths (1hr., €2.10). To get to the **Tragea** highland valley, an enormous, peaceful olive grove, take a bus from Naxos Town to Halki (30min., 6 per day, €1.20).

Ferries go from Naxos Town to: Athens (6½hr., 2 per day, €17); Ios (1hr., daily, €8.20); Kos (7hr., 1 per week, €16); Mykonos (3hr., daily, €9); Paros (1hr., 4 per day, €5.50); Rhodes (13hr., 1 per week, €20); Santorini (3hr., 3 per day, €13); and Thessaloniki (14hr., 1 per week, €30). The **tourist office** is 300m up from the dock, by the bus station. (☎22850 24 358. Open daily 8am-11pm.) **Irene's Pension ❷,** about 100m from Ag. Giorgios, is near the center of the town. (☎22850 23 169. All rooms with A/C. Call ahead. Singles €15; doubles €20-30; triples €25-35; 5-person apartments €40-50.) **Panorama ❸,** in Old Naxos, has rooms with fans and fridges. (☎22850 22 330. Doubles from €25.) Naxos has three **camping ❶** options along the beach; look for representatives along the dock. (€5 per person, plus a small tent fee.) **Postal Code:** 84300.

IOS (Ιος)   ☎22860

Ios (pop. 2,000) has everything your mother warned you about—swimming less than 30 minutes after a meal, dancing in the streets, and drinking games all day long on the beach. The **port** (Yialos) is at one end of the island's sole paved road; the **village** (Hora) sits above it on a hill; but the beaches are the place to be. Most spend their days at **Mylopotas Beach,** a 20min. walk downhill from Ios town or a bus ride from the port or village (every 10-20min. 7:20am-midnight, €1). Sunning is typically followed by drinking; **Dubliner,** near the basketball courts, is a good place to start. On Thursday nights, €24 buys you pizza, a drink, and cover immunity at five bars that comprise the ultimate pub crawl. Head up from the *plateia* to reach the **Slammer Bar** for tequila slammers (€3), then run with the pack to **Red Bull** for shots (€2.40). Grind to techno at **Scorpion Disco,** the island's largest club, as you stumble your way back to the beach. (Cover after 1am.) Only a few hours later, crowds begin to gather at the beach, where **Mylopotas Water Sports Center** offers rental and lessons for windsurfing, water-skiing, and snorkeling (€14-40).

Ferries go to: Naxos (1¾hr., at least 3 per day, €8.20) and Santorini (1¼hr., 3 per day, €6.20). The main **tourist office** is next to the bus stop. (☎22860 91 343. Open daily 8am-midnight.) In the village, take the uphill steps to the left in the *plateia* and take the first left to reach ▓**Francesco's ❶,** where you'll find spectacular harbor views and a terrace bar. (☎22860 91 706; www.francescos.net. Dorms €8-14; doubles €10-25.) On the end of Mylopotas Beach, ▓**Far Out Camping ❶** has a pool, plenty of tents, parties, and activities, including bungee jumping. (☎22860 92 301. Open Apr.-Oct. Tent rental €4-7.50; small cabins from €5; bungalows €7-18.) ▓**Ali Baba's ❷,** next to Ios Gym, offers delicious pad thai (€8.50) and burgers (€5.50). On a narrow street off the main church's *plateia,* **Lord Byron's ❸** serves a unique blend of Greek and Smirniki food. (Entrees €9-15.) **Postal Code:** 84001.

SANTORINI (Σαντορινη)   ☎22860

Whitewashed towns balanced on cliffs, black-sand beaches, and deeply scarred hills make Santorini's landscape nearly as dramatic as the volcanic explosion that created it. Despite all the kitsch in touristy **Fira** (pop. 2,500), the island's capital, nothing can ruin the pleasure of wandering the town's cobblestoned streets, browsing its craft shops, and taking in the sunset from its western edge. On the southwestern side of the island, the excavations at **Akrotiri,** a late Minoan city, are preserved under layers of volcanic rock. (Open Su and Tu-Sa 8:30am-3pm. €5, students €3.) Buses run to Akrotiri from Fira (30min., 16 per day, €1.30). Frequent buses also leave Fira for the black-sand **beaches** of Perissa (15min., 30 per day, €0.90) and Kamari (20min., 2-3 per hr., €0.90) to the southeast. The bus stops before Perissa in Pyrgos; from there, you can hike (40min.) to the **Profitis Ilias Monastery,** whose lofty location provides an island panorama, and continue an extra 1½hr. to the ruins of **Ancient Thira.** (Open Su and Tu-Sa 8:30am-2:30pm.)

Ferries from Fira run to: Ios (1½hr., 3-5 per day, €6.30); Iraklion (4hr., daily, €14); Mykonos (7hr., 2 per week, €13); Naxos (4hr., 4-8 per day, €11); and Paros (4½hr., 3-5 per day, €12). Most ferries depart from Athinios harbor; frequent buses (30min., €1.50) connect to Fira. Head 300m north from the *plateia* in Fira to reach the friendly **Thira Youth Hostel ❶,** in an old monastery. (☎22860 22 387. Open Apr.-Oct. Dorms €8-12; doubles €20-40.) Take a bus from Fira to **Oia** (25min., 30 per day, €0.90) for more options; the impeccable rooms at ▓**Youth Hostel Oia ❷** are a good choice. (☎22860 71 465. Breakfast included. Open May-Oct. Dorms €12-14.) The cheery and colorful **Mama's Cyclades Cafe ❷,** north of Fira on the road to Oia, serves up a big breakfast special. (☎22860 23 032. Entrees €5-8. Open daily 8am-midnight.) **Postal Code:** 84700.

CRETE (Κρητη)

According to a Greek saying, a Cretan's first loyalty is to his island, his second to his country. Since 3000 BC, Crete has maintained an identity distinct from the rest of Greece, first expressed in the language, script, and architecture of the ancient Minoans. Despite this insular mind-set, residents are friendly to visitors who come to enjoy their island's inexhaustible trove of mosques, monasteries, mountain villages, gorges, grottoes, and beaches. Crete is divided into four main prefectures: Iraklion, Hania, Rethymno, and Lasithi.

GREECE

▐ TRANSPORTATION

Olympic Airways (☎2810 288 073) and **Air Greece** connect Athens to: Sitia (2-3 per week, €83) in the east; Iraklion (45min., 13-15 per day, €84) in the center; and Hania (4 per day, €53) in the west.

IRAKLION (Ηρακλιον)   ☎2810

Iraklion (pop. 132,000) is Crete's capital and primary port. The chic locals live life in the fast lane, which translates into an urban brusqueness unique among the cities of Crete and the most diverse nightlife on the island. Iraklion's main attraction after Knossos (p. 552) is the superb ▨**Archaeological Museum,** off Pl. Eleftherias. By appropriating major finds from all over the island, the museum has amassed a comprehensive record of the Neolithic and Minoan stages of Cretan history. (Open M noon-7pm, Tu-Su 8am-7pm. €6, students €3. EU students free.) A maze of streets between **Plateia Venizelou** and **Plateia Eleftherias** houses Iraklion's night spots; visit Korai for classy cafes or D. Boufor for posh clubs.

From Terminal A, between the old city walls and the harbor, **buses** leave for Agios Nikolaos (1½hr., 20 per day, €5). Buses leave across from Terminal A for Hania (3hr., 17 per day, €11) and Rethymno (1½hr., 17 per day, €6). The **tourist police** are on Dikeosinis 10. (☎2810 283 190. Open daily 7am-10pm.) **Gallery Games Net,** Korai 14, has **Internet** access. (☎2810 282 804. €3 per hr.) **Rent a Room Hellas ❶,** Handakos 24, two blocks from El Greco Park, has large dorm rooms and a spectacular view. (☎2810 288 851. Dorms €9; doubles €25; triples €36.) The **open-air market** near Pl. Venizelou has stalls piled high with fruit, vegetables, cheeses, and meats. (Open M, W and Sa 8am-2pm, Tu and Th-F 8am-2pm and 5-9pm.) **Prassein Aloga ❷,** Handakos 21, serves fresh Mediterranean dishes in its tree-lined courtyard. (Entrees €6-10. Open M-Sa noon-midnight). **Postal Code:** 71001.

▐ **DAYTRIP FROM IRAKLION: KNOSSOS.** At Knossos (Κνωσσος), the most famous archaeological site in Crete, excavations have revealed the remains of the largest and most complicated of Crete's **Minoan palaces.** Sir Arthur Evans, who financed and supervised the excavations, eventually restored large parts of the palace in Knossos; his work often crossed the line from preservation to artistic interpretation, but the site is nonetheless impressive. (Open in summer daily 8am-7pm; off-season 8am-5pm. €6, students €3; In off-season, Su free.) To reach Knossos from Iraklion, take **bus** #2 from Augustou 25 (€1).

RETHYMNO (Ρεθυμνο)   ☎28310

Crete's many conquerors—Venetians, Ottomans, and even Nazis—have had a profound effect in Rethymno (pop. 25,000). Arabic inscriptions adorn the walls of the narrow streets, minarets highlight the skyline, and the 16th-century **Venetian Fortezza** stands watch over the harbor. Bring a picnic and explore the fortress ruins. (Open M-Th and Sa-Su 8:30am-7pm. €2.90.) Cloistered beaches, steep gorges, and stunning hikes await in the nearby town of **Plakias.** (4 buses from Rethymno per day, €3.30). The **Rethymno-Hania bus station** (☎28310 22 212) is south of the fortress on the water, with service to Hania (1hr., 16 per day, €5.60) and Iraklion (1½hr., 17 per day, €6). Climb the stairs behind the bus station, turn left on Ig. Gavriil, which becomes Kountouriotou, and turn left on Varda Kallergi to reach the waterfront and the **tourist office,** on El. Venizelou. (☎28310 29 148. Open M-F 9am-2pm.) To get from the station to the friendly **Youth Hostel ❶,** Tombazi 41-45, walk down Ig. Gavriil, take the first left at Pl. Martiron; Tombazi is the first right. (☎28310 22 848. Breakfast €1.70. Internet €1 per 15min. Reception 8am-noon and 5-9pm. Dorms €7.) **Postal Code:** 74100.

HANIA (Χανια)   ☎28210

The **Venetian lighthouse** marks the entrance to Hania's (pop. 70,000) stunning architectural relic, the **Venetian Inner Harbor**. The inlet has retained its original breakwater and arsenal; the lighthouse was restored by the Egyptians during their occupation of Crete in the late 1830s. A day is best spent meandering among the narrow Venetian buildings and Ottoman domes on the lively waterfront.

Ferries arrive in the nearby port of Souda; buses connect from the port to Hania's supermarket on Zymvrakakidon (15min., €1). **Buses** (☎28210 93 306) leave from the station on the corner of Kydonias and Kelaidi for Rethymno (17 per day, €5.60). The **tourist office**, Korkidi 16, is just off P. 1866. (☎28210 36 155. Open M-F 8am-2pm.) To get to ◪**Hotel Fidias ❷**, Sarpaki 6, walk toward the harbor on Halidon and turn right onto Athinagora, which then becomes Sarpaki. (☎28210 52 494. Dorms €7-13; singles €13-20; doubles €15-23.) ◪**Anaplous ❷**, near the harbor on Sifaka, is an open-air bistro that serves *pilino*, a pork and lamb creation. (*Pilino* €25; serves three. Entrees €6-8. Open daily 6pm-1am.) **Postal Code:** 73100.

◪ **HIKING NEAR HANIA: SAMARIA GORGE.** The most popular excursion from Hania and Iraklion is the 5-6hr. hike down ◪**Samaria Gorge** (Φαραγγι τηϖ Σαμαριαϖ), a spectacular 16km ravine extending through the White Mountains. Sculpted by rainwater over 14 million years, the gorge—the longest in Europe—retains its allure despite having been trampled by thousands of visitors. Rare native plants peek out from sheer rock walls, wild *agrimi* goats clamber about the hills, and golden eagles and endangered griffin vultures circle overhead. (Open May to mid-Oct. daily 6am-6pm. €3, children under-15 and organized student groups free.) For more info, call **Hania Forest Service** (☎28210 92 287). The trail starts at **Xyloskalo**; take the 6:15am or 8:30am **bus** from Hania to Xyloskalo (1½hr., €5.20) for a day's worth of hiking. The 1:45pm bus from Hania will put you in **Omalos**, ready for the next morning. The trail ends in **Agia Roumeli**, on the southern coast, where you can hop on a **boat** to Hora Sfakion (1¼hr., 3-4 per day, €4.40) or take a return bus to Hania (4 per day, €5.20).

SITIA (Σητεια)   ☎28430

Sitia (pop. 8,500) makes a great base for exploring Crete's east coast. Skip the town's own beach and head to the beautiful **Vai Beach** and its palm tree forest, a 1hr. bus ride away via Palaikastro (€2.10). To reach the **Valley of Death**, a Minoan burial ground that's great for hiking, take a bus from Sitia via Palaikastro and Zakros (1hr., 2 per day, €3.80). The **Minoan Palace** rests at the end of the valley. (Open daily 8am-3pm. €3, students and seniors €2. EU students free.) After midnight, everyone in Sitia heads to **Hot Summer**, 1km down the road to Palaikastro, where a swimming pool replaces the traditional dance floor.

Ferries leave Sitia for: Athens (16-17hr., 5 per week, €24) via Agios Nikolaos (1½hr., €6.30); Karpathos (5hr., €16); and Rhodes (12hr., €22). From the center of town, head east along the water; the **tourist office** will be on your left. (☎28430 28 300. Open M-F 9:30am-2:30pm and 5:30-8:30pm.) **Venus Rooms to Let ❷**, Kondilaki 60, looks out on scenic views; walk up on Kapetan Sifi from the main *plateia* and turn right after the telephone office. (☎28430 24 307. Doubles €25, with bath €30; triples €30/€36.) The **Cretan House ❸**, K. Karamanli 10, off the *plateia* and on the waterfront, serves Cretan meals for €5-8. Ask for the "Cretan Viagra" to heat up your night. (*Staka* €3.30. Open daily 9am-1am.) **Postal Code:** 72300.

EASTERN AEGEAN ISLANDS

The intricate, rocky coastlines and unassuming port towns of the **Northeast Aegean Islands** enclose thickly wooded mountains and unspoiled villages and beaches. Despite their proximity to the Turkish coast and a noticeable military presence, the Northeast Aegean Islands dispense a taste of undiluted Greek culture. **The Dodecanese** are the farthest Greek island group from the mainland. Closer to Asia Minor than to Athens, these islands have experienced more invasions than the central parts of the country—eclectic architecture is the most visible legacy of these comings and goings.

SAMOS (Σαμος) ☎ 22730

Visitors frequently stop in Samos en route to Kuşadası and the ruins of Ephesus on the Turkish coast. *Tavernas* line the crescent-shaped harbor of Samos Town while red roofs speckle the hillsides of **Vathy,** the residential part of town. The ◪**Archaeological Museum,** which sits behind the municipal gardens, houses a comprehensive collection from the Temple of Hera. (Open Su and Tu-Sa 8:30am-3pm. €3, seniors and students €2, EU students free.) The ancient city of **Pythagorion,** once the island's capital, is 14km south of Vathy. Near the town are the magnificent remains of Polykrates's 6th-century BC engineering project, the **Tunnel of Eupalinos,** which supplied water to the city from a natural spring 1.3km away. (Open Su and Tu-Sa 8:45am-2:45pm. €4, students €2, EU students free.) Buses go from Samos Town to Pythagorion (20min., €1.20). Polykrates's greatest feat was the **Temple of Hera,** in Heraion, a 30min. bus ride (€1.60) from Pythagorion. (Open Su and Tu-Sa 8:30am-3pm. €3, students €2.)

Ferries arrive in Samos from: Chios (5hr., 3 per week, €11); Mykonos (6hr., 3 per week, €18); Naxos (6hr., 6 per week, €38); and Rhodes (1 per week, €24). The **tourist office** is on a side street a block before Pl. Pythagoras. (☎22730 28 530. Open July-Aug. M-Sa 7am-2:30pm.) Once an old monastery, **Pension Avli ❸,** Areos 2, offers an elegant, shady courtyard. (☎22730 22 939. Doubles with bath €25-30; triples available.) **Postal Code:** 83100.

CHIOS (Χιος) ☎ 22710

Pine-speckled hills lend an untamed feel to the interior of Chios (pop. 50,000), which offers its visitors charming villages and hot, sandy shores. **Pyrgi,** 25km from Chios Town, is one of Greece's most striking villages, with black-and-white geometric designs covering its buildings. Farther south lies **Emborio** beach, where beige cliffs accentuate the black stones and blue water below. **Buses** run from Chios Town to Pyrgi (4 per day, €2.20). **Ferries** go from Chios Town to: Mykonos (1 per week, €14); Rhodes (2 per week, €28); Samos (4hr., 2 per week, €11); and Tinos (2 per week, €15). To reach the **tourist office,** Kanari 18, turn off the waterfront onto Kanari and walk toward the *plateia.* (☎22710 44 344. Open May-Oct. M-F 7am-2:30pm and 6-10pm, Sa-Su 9am-2pm and 6-10pm; Nov.-Mar. M-F 7am-2:30pm.) The hospitable owners at ◪**Chios Rooms ❷,** Leofores 114, offer large rooms and sparkling-clean bathrooms. (☎22710 20 198. Singles €18-22; doubles €23-25, with bath €30; triples with bath €35.) **Postal Code:** 82100.

LESVOS (Λεσβος) ☎ 22510

Lesvos's (pop. 100,000) cosmopolitan, off-beat culture incorporates horse breeding, *ouzo,* and leftist politics. Huge, geographically diverse, and far from the mainland, the island attracts visitors who spend weeks exploring its therapeutic hot springs, monasteries, petrified forest, sandy beaches, mountain villages, and seaside cliffs. Most travelers pass through the modern **Mytilini,** the capital and central port city. At the new ⊠**Archaeological Museum,** 8 Noemvriou, visitors can walk on preserved mosaic floors dating from Lesvos's Neolithic past. (Open Su and Tu-Sa 8am-3pm. €3, students €2. Under-18 and EU students free.) Only 4km south of Mytilini along El. Venizelou, the village of **Varia** is home to two excellent museums. **Theophilos Museum** features the work of the neo-primitivist Greek painter Theophilos Hadzimichali. (Open Su and Tu-Sa 9am-2:30pm and 6-8pm. €2. Students and under-18 free.) **Musée Tériade** displays lithographs by Chagall, Matisse, Miró, and Picasso. (Open Su and Tu-Sa 9am-2pm and 5-8pm. €2. Students and children free.) The artist colony of **Molyvos** has a quiet charm and is more affordable than the capital; take a bus from Mytilini (1½hr., 5-6 per day, €4.70). **Eftalou** has beautiful pebble and black sand beaches, accessible by frequent buses from Molyvos. A 20-million-year old petrified forest 4km from **Sigri,** one of only two such forests in the world, has fossilized trunks preserved in amazingly precise detail. For more info, call the main parks office in Mytilini. (☎22510 40 132. Park open late July to Aug. daily 8am-7pm; Sept. to early July 8am-4pm. €2. Under-15 free.)

Ferries go from Mytilini to: Chios (3hr., 1-2 per day, €12); Limnos (5hr., 6 per week, €15); and Thessaloniki (13hr., 1 per week, €12). Book ferries at **NEL Lines,** Pavlou Koudourioti 67 (☎22510 46 595), on the far right side of the waterfront facing inland. The **tourist police,** on Aristarchou near the ferry docks, offer brochures and advice. (☎22510 22 776. Open daily 7am-2:30pm.) Mytilini *domatia* are plentiful and well advertised. Be sure to negotiate; doubles should run €20-23. ⊠**Nassos Guest House ❷,** on the hill just into Molyvos, offers cheerful rooms with balconies and a shared kitchen. (☎22510 71 432. Doubles €22-30; triples €24-34; discounts for longer stays.) **Postal Code:** 81100.

RHODES (Ροδος)   ☎22410

The undisputed tourism capital of the Dodecanese, the island of Rhodes (pop. 99,000) has retained a sense of serenity in the sandy beaches along its east coast, the jagged cliffs skirting its west coast, and the green mountains dotted with villages in its interior. The island's most famous sight is one that doesn't exist: the **Colossus of Rhodes,** a 35m bronze statue of Helios was one of the Seven Wonders of the Ancient World. While recent historians have debated the exact stance of the statue, legend says it straddled the island's harbor until it was destroyed by an earthquake in 237 BC. The **Old Town,** constructed by the Knights of St. John, lends **Rhodes Town** a medieval flair. At the top of the hill, a tall, square tower marks the entrance to the pride of the city, the **Palace of the Grand Master,** which features moats, drawbridges, battlements, and 300 rooms. (☎22410 25 500. Open Su and Tu-Sa 8:30am-3pm. €6, students €3. EU students free.) The beautiful halls and courtyards of the **Archaeological Museum,** dominating the **Plateia Argykastrou,** shelter small treasures, including the exquisite *Aphrodite Bathing* from the first-century BC. (Open T-Su 8:30am-2:30pm. €3, students €1.50.) Nightlife in the Old Town focuses around the street of **Militadou,** off Apelou. **Orfanidou,** in the New Town, is popularly known as **Bar Street.** Fifteen kilometers south of the city, **Faliraki** is frequented by rowdy drinkers and beach bathers. Buses run to Faliraki from Rhodes Town (20 per day, €1.60).

Ferries leave Rhodes Town for: Athens (1-4 per day, €30); Karpathos (3 per week, €15); Kos (1-2 per day, €15); Patmos (1-2 per day, €29); Samos (1 per week, €22); and Sitia, Crete (3 per week, €22). There is a **Greek National Tourist**

Office (EOT) up Papgou, a few blocks from Pl. Rimini, at Makariou. ⚑**Mama's Pension ❶**, Menekleous 28, has a kitchen, a *taverna* with live music, and balcony views. (☎22410 25 359. Laundry €3. Dorms €10; doubles €25.) The **Rhodes Youth Hostel ❶**, Ergiou 12, has a cool, quiet courtyard; to reach it, turn onto Fanouriou from Sokratous and follow the signs. (☎22410 30 491. Free luggage storage. Dorms €6; doubles and triples €20.) Fresh shellfish is the specialty at **Nireas ❷**, Sophokleous 22, in the Old Town. Try the *fouskes* (sea snails; €7.50), a local treat. (☎22410 21 703. Entrees €6-8. Open daily 7:30pm-late.) **Postal Code:** 85100.

KOS (Κως)   ☎22420

While the beaches of **Kos Town** (pop. 12,500) draw a young party crowd, rural Kos attracts the traveler in search of serene mountain villages. At the sanctuary of ⚑**Asclepeion,** 4km southwest of Kos Town, Hippocrates opened the world's first medical school in the 5th century BC. In the summer, mini-trains (15 min., every hr., €.50-1.20.) run there from Kos Town. (Open Su and Tu-Sa 8am-6:30pm. €3, students €2.) The island's best beaches stretch along Southern Kos to Kardamene and are all accessible by bus; stops are by request. **Agios Theologos,** south of Limionas, is a pebbly beach perfect for night swimming. Most bars are located in **Exarhia,** in the Old City past Pl. Platonou, or along **Porfirou,** between Averof and Zouroundi. Runway models loom on giant television screens at the **Fashion Club,** Kanari 2, the hottest spot in town. (Cover €10, includes 1 drink. Open daily 11pm-4am.) The **Hamam Club,** inland from the Pl. Diagoras taxi station, is a former bathhouse turned dance club. **Heaven,** on Zouroudi, opposite the beach, is a large, popular disco. (Open Su-Th 10am-4am, F-Sa 10am-dawn.) The island of **Nisryos,** with an active volcano and beaches black with volcanic rock, is an idyllic daytrip; DANE Sea Lines **ferries** run from to Nisryos from **Kos** (1.5 hr., 2 per week, €7.40).

Ferries run to: Athens (11-15hr., 2-3 per day, €16); Patmos (4hr., 1-2 per day, €10); and Rhodes (4hr., 2-3 per day, €16). The **Greek National Tourist Office (EOT)** is at Vas. Georgiou 1. (☎22420 24 460. Open M-F 8am-2:30pm and 5:30-8:30pm.) Take the first right off Megalou Alexandrou to get to ⚑**Pension Alexis ❷**, Irodotou 9, where the hospitable owners offer their guests every service. (☎22420 28 798. Doubles €20-22; triples €28-33.) **Studios Nitsa ❸**, Averof 47, has small rooms with bath and A/C. Take Averof inland from Akti Koundourioti. (☎22420 25 810. Doubles €20.) **Postal Code:** 85300.

PATMOS (Πατμος)   ☎22470

Given that it has recently become a favorite destination of the rich and famous, and that it has also been declared a "Sacred Island" by ministerial decree, Patmos (pop. 25,000) has an interesting blend of visitors. The white houses of **Hora** and the majestic walls of the sprawling **Monastery of St. John the Theologian** are visible from anywhere on the island. (Dress modestly. Monastery open daily 8am-1pm; also Tu, Th, Su 4-6pm.) Buses from **Skala,** the port town, run to Hora (10min., 11 per day, €1); alternatively, take a taxi (€3) or tackle the steep hike. The **Apocalypsis Monastery,** a complex of interconnected buildings between Skala and Hora, is built on the site where St. John stayed while on Patmos. Most visitors come to Patmos to see the **Sacred Grotto of the Revelation,** adjacent to the church of St. Anne, the cave where St. John dictated the Book of Revelation. (Dress modestly. Open daily 8am-1pm; Tu, Th, Su also 4-6pm.)

Ferries arrive in Skala from: Kos (4hr., 2-3 per day, €9.70); Rhodes (8hr., daily, €11); Samos (6 per week, €6); and Thessaloniki (22hr., 1 per week, €37). The **tourist office** is opposite the dock. (☎22470 31 666. Open daily 9am-9pm.) *Domatia* are offered by locals who meet the ferries; expect to pay €15-20 for singles and €20-30 for doubles. To reach **Stefanos Flower Camping at Meloi ❶**, 1.5km northeast of Skala, follow the waterfront road as it wraps along the port. The campground is on the left at the bottom of the hill. (☎22470 31 821. €5 per person.) **To Kyma ❸**, near the campground at Meloi Beach, serves freshly prepared fish. (Fish €20-40 per kg. Open daily 6:30pm-2am.) **Postal Code:** 85500.

GREECE

REPUBLIC OF IRELAND & NORTHERN IRELAND

Travelers who come to Ireland with their heads filled with poetic imagery will not be disappointed—this largely agricultural and sparsely populated island still looks as it did when Celtic bards roamed the land. Windswept scenery is found all along the coast, and untouched mountain chains stretch across the interior bogland. The landscape is punctuated with pockets of civilization, ranging in size from one-street villages to large cities; Dublin and Belfast are cosmopolitan centers whose international populations greatly influence their immediate surroundings. Some fear this threatens the native culture, but the survival of traditional music, dance, and storytelling proves otherwise. The Irish language lives on in small, secluded areas known as *gaeltachts*, as well as on road signs, in national publications, and in a growing body of modern literary works. While non-violence usually prevails in Northern Ireland, recent negotiations hope to ensure peace for future generations. Although the Republic and Northern Ireland are grouped together in this chapter for geographical reasons, no political statement is intended.

LIFE AND TIMES

HISTORY

EARLY CHRISTIANS AND VIKINGS (450-1200). Ireland was Christianized in a piecemeal fashion by a series of hopeful missionaries starting with **St. Patrick** in the 5th century. After the **Dal Cais** clan defeated the Vikings in the epic **Battle of Clontarf**, Ireland was divided between chieftains **Rory O'Connor** and **Dermot MacMurrough**, who then fought for the crown between themselves. Dermot ill-advisedly sought the assistance of Richard de Clare, known popularly as **Strongbow**, who arrived in 1169 and cut a bloody swath through Leinster (eastern and southeastern

SUGGESTED ITINERARIES

THREE DAYS Spend it all in Dublin (p. 568). Wander through **Trinity College,** admire the **Book of Kells,** then have a drink at the **Old Jameson Distillery.** Take a day to visit the **National Museums,** stopping to relax on **St. Stephen's Green.** Get smart at the **James Joyce Centre** and then work your pubbing potential in **Temple Bar** and on **Grafton Street,** stopping by Leopold Bloom's haunt, **Davy Byrnes.**

ONE WEEK From Dublin (2 days) head to historic **Belfast** (1 day; p. 604). Don't miss the beautiful **Giant's Causeway** (1 day; p. 614) before heading to artsy **Galway** (1 day; p. 596). Admire the countryside in the **Ring of Kerry** (1 day; p. 591) and return to civilization in **Cork** (1 day; p. 584).

BEST OF IRELAND, THREE WEEKS Land in **Dublin** (4 days) before taking the train up to **Belfast** (3 days). Catch the bus to **Giant's Causeway** (1 day), and stop at **Derry** (1 days, p. 612). From **Donegal Town,** climb **Slieve League** (1 day, p. 603), Europe's highest seacliffs. Use **Sligo** (2 days; p. 602) as a base for visiting its lakes and mountains. From there, head to **Galway** (2 days), the **Ring of Kerry** (2 days), **Killarney National Park** (1 day; p. 590), and **Cork** (2 day), making a stop at lovely **Kinsale** (1 day; p. 589). On the way back to Dublin, stop by medieval **Kilkenny** (1 day; p. 582).

Ireland). Strongbow married Dermot's daughter Aoife after Dermot's death in 1171 and seemed ready to proclaim an independent Norman kingdom in Ireland. Instead, the turncoat affirmed his loyalty to King Henry II and offered to govern Leinster on England's behalf. Thus began English domination over Irish land.

FEUDALISM (1200-1641). The subsequent feudal period saw constant struggles between English lords of Gaelic and Norman descent. When **Henry VIII** created the Church of England, the Dublin Parliament passed the 1537 **Irish Supremacy Act,** which declared Henry head of the Protestant **Church of Ireland** and effectively made the island property of the Crown. In defiance of the monarchy, **Hugh O'Neill,** an Ulster earl, raised an army of thousands in open rebellion in the late 1590s, supported by Gaelic lords. Their forces were soon demolished, and the rebels left Ireland in 1607 in what is now known as the **Flight of the Earls.** The English took control of land, and parceled it out to Protestants.

PLANTATION AND CROMWELL (1641-1688). The English project of dispossessing Catholics of their land and "planting" Ireland with Protestants was most successful in Ulster, which became known as the **Ulster Plantation.** In response, the now landless Irish natives rebelled in 1641 under a loose-knit group of Gaelic-Irish leaders. In 1642 the rebels formed the **Confederation of Kilkenny,** an uneasy alliance of the Church and Irish and Old English lords. Negotiations between the Confederation and King Charles ended with **Oliver Cromwell**'s victory in England and his arrival in Ireland. Cromwell's army destroyed everything it came across, divvying up confiscated lands among Protestants and soldiers. By 1660, the vast majority of Irish land was owned, maintained, and policed by Protestant immigrants.

THE PROTESTANT ASCENDANCY (1688-1798). Thirty years after the English Civil War, English political disruption again resulted in Irish bloodshed. Deposed Catholic monarch **James II,** driven from England by the "Glorious Revolution" of 1688, came to Ireland to gather military support and reclaim his throne. A war between James and **William of Orange,** the new Protestant king, ended on July 12, 1690 at the **Battle of the Boyne** with James's defeat and exile. The term **"Ascendancy"** was coined to describe the social elite whose distinction depended upon Anglicanism. **Trinity College** was the quintessential institution of the Ascended Protestants.

UNION AND THE FAMINE (1798-1847). The 1801 **Act of Union** dissolved the Dublin Parliament and created The United Kingdom of Great Britain and Ireland; the Church of Ireland was subsumed by the "United Church of England and Ireland." During this time, the potato was the wonder-crop of the rapidly growing Irish population. The potato blight of the **Great Famine** (1847-1851) killed an estimated two to three million people; a million more emigrated. In short, close to half of Ireland's population either died or fled from the blight. In 1858, James Stephens founded the Irish Republican Brotherhood (IRB), commonly known as the **Fenians,** a secret society aimed at the violent removal of the British.

CULTURAL NATIONALISM (1870-1914). In 1870, Isaac Butt founded the **Irish Home Rule Party,** bent on securing autonomous rule for Ireland. Meanwhile, various groups tried to revive an essential "Gaelic" culture, unpolluted by foreign influence; **Arthur Griffin** began a fledgling movement by the name of **Sinn Féin** (SHIN FAYN; "Ourselves Alone"). As the Home Rule movement grew, so did resistance to it. Between 1910 and 1913, thousands of Northern Protestants opposing Home Rule joined a quasi-militia named the **Ulster Volunteer Force (UVF).** Nationalists led by **Eoin MacNeill** responded by creating the **Irish Volunteers.**

IRELAND

THE EASTER RISING (1914-1919). During **World War I,** British Prime Minister Henry Asquith passed a **Home Rule Bill** on the condition that Irishmen would fight for the British army. The Irish Volunteers that remained behind were led by Mac-Neill, who did not know that Fenian leaders were plotting to receive a shipment of German arms for use in a nationwide revolt on **Easter Sunday, 1916.** Although the arms arrived a day too early and were never picked up, Fenian leaders continued to muster support from the Volunteers. On Monday, April 24, about 1000 rebels seized the Dublin **General Post Office** on O'Connell St., holding on through five days of fighting. Fifteen ringleaders then received the death sentence, causing the public to grow increasingly sympathetic to the rebels and anti-British. In 1917, the Volunteers reorganized under Fenian bigwig **Michael Collins.** Collins brought the Volunteers to Sinn Féin, and **Éamon de Valera** became the party president.

INDEPENDENCE AND CIVIL WAR (1919-1922). Extremist Irish Volunteers became known as the **Irish Republican Army (IRA).** The IRA functioned as the military arm of Sinn Féin, winning the **War of Independence** (1919-1921) against the British. Hurried negotiations produced the **Anglo-Irish Treaty,** which created a 26-county Irish Free State, while still recognizing British rule over the northern counties. Sinn Féin, the IRA, and the population split on whether to accept the treaty. Collins said yes; de Valera said no. When the representative parliament voted in favor, de Valera resigned from the presidency and **Arthur Griffith** assumed the position. The capable Griffith and Collins government began the business of setting up a nation. A portion of the IRA, led by **General Rory O'Connor,** opposed the treaty. O'Connor's Republicans occupied the Four Courts in Dublin, took a pro-treaty Army general hostage, and were attacked by the forces of Collins's government. Two years of **civil war** followed. The pro-treaty government won, but Griffith died from the strain of the struggle and Collins was assassinated.

THE DE VALERA ERA (1922-1960). In 1927 de Valera broke with Sinn Féin and the IRA and founded his own political party, **Fianna Fáil.** The party won the 1932 election, and de Valera held power for much of the next 20 years. In 1937, de Valera and the voters approved the Irish Constitution. It declared the state's name to be **Éire,** and established the country's legislative structure, consisting of two chambers with five-year terms. Ireland stayed neutral during **World War II,** despite German air raids on Dublin. Many Irish citizens identified with the Allies, and approximately 50,000 served in the British army. In 1948, the Fine Gael government under **John Costello** had the honor of officially proclaiming "The Republic of Ireland" free, supposedly ending British Commonwealth membership. Britain recognized the Republic in 1949 but declared that the UK would maintain control over Ulster until the Parliament of Northern Ireland consented to join the Republic.

RECENT HISTORY (1960-1990). Ireland's post-war boom didn't arrive until the early 1960s, and economic mismanagement and poor governmental policies kept it short. In an effort to revitalize the nation, the Republic entered the European Economic Community, now the **European Union (EU),** in 1973. EU funds proved crucial to helping Ireland out of a severe mid-80s recession and reducing its dependence on the UK. In 1990, the Republic broke social and political ground when it elected its first female president, **Mary Robinson.**

TODAY

Social reform made further gains when the small, leftist **Labour Party** enjoyed unexpected success in the 1992 elections. The new Taoiseach, or Prime Minister, **Albert Reynolds,** declared that his priority was to stop violence in Northern Ireland. In

August 1994, he announced a cease-fire agreement with Sinn Féin and the IRA. In April of 1998, Taoiseach **Bertie Ahern** helped to produce the **Northern Ireland Peace Agreement.** In May of 1998, in the first island-wide election since 1918, 94% of voters in the Republic voted for the enactment of the Agreement.

The **euro** was formally introduced into the Republic on January 1, 2002. With the money garnered from the EU over the years, increased foreign investment and computer software development, and a flourishing tourism industry, the Irish economy is thriving like never before. According to a 1999 report, the unemployment rate should be reduced to three percent by the year 2005. With each boom comes a bust, however, and some fear the roar of the **Celtic Tiger,** a nickname for the Irish economy, will soon be reduced to a purr.

Ireland:
Republic of Ireland
and Northern Ireland

THE ARTS

LITERATURE

In the 17th century, wit and satire began to characterize emerging Irish literature. **Jonathan Swift** wrote some of the most sophisticated, misanthropic, and marvelous satire in the English language. Besides his masterpiece *Gulliver's Travels* (1726), Swift wrote political essays decrying English cruelty to the native Irish. While Dublin managed to breed talent, gifted young writers like **Oscar Wilde** often headed for London in order to make their names. Wilde wrote many delightful works; his best-known play is *The Importance of Being Earnest* (1895). Fellow playwright **George Bernard Shaw** also moved to London, where he became an active socialist, winning the Nobel Prize for Literature in 1925.

Towards the end of the 19th century, a crop of young Irish writers began to turn to Irish culture for inspiration; this period is known as the **Irish Literary Revival**. The poems of **William Butler Yeats** created an Ireland of loss and legend that won him worldwide fame and a 1923 Nobel Prize. Yet many authors still found Ireland too insular to suit their literary aspirations. **James Joyce** (1882-1942) is without a doubt Ireland's most famous expatriate, and yet his writing never escaped the island. His first novel, *A Portrait of the Artist as a Young Man* (1914), uses the protagonist Stephen Daedalus to describe Joyce's own youth in Dublin. Daedalus reappears in *Ulysses*, Joyce's revolutionary novel of 1922, loosely based on Homer's *Odyssey*. **Samuel Beckett**'s world-famous plays, including *Waiting for Godot* and *Endgame*, both written between 1946-1950, convey a deathly pessimism about language, society, and life. Beckett won the Nobel Prize in 1969, but refused acceptance because Joyce had never received it.

The dirt of Dublin continues to provide fodder for generations of writers. Mild-mannered schoolteacher **Roddy Doyle** wrote the well-known Barrytown trilogy about family life in down-and-out Dublin, as well as the acclaimed *The Woman Who Walked Into Doors* (1996). Doyle won the Booker Prize in 1994 for *Paddy Clarke Ha Ha Ha*. **Frank McCourt** won the Pulitzer Prize in 1996 for a memoir about his poverty-stricken childhood, *Angela's Ashes*, and followed up with a sequel, *'Tis* (2000). Not to be outdone, **Malachy McCourt**, Frank's brother, recently published his own memoir, *A Monk Swimming* (1999). Born in rural County Derry, **Seamus Heaney** was awarded the Nobel Prize for literature in 1995, and is the most prominent living Irish poet. His subject matter ranges from bogs to bombings to archeological remains.

MUSIC

Traditional Irish music, commonly called *trad*, is an array of dance rhythms, cyclical melodies, and embellishments passed down through countless generations of musicians. A traditional musician's training consists largely of listening to and innovating from the work of others. A typical pub session will sample from a variety of styles, including reels, jigs, hornpipes, and slow airs. Many artists put a unique spin on the same basic tune each time it's played.

Best-selling *trad* recording artists include **Altan, De Danann,** and the **Chieftains.** Equally excellent groups include the **Bothy Band** and **Planxty** of the 1970s, and, more recently, **Nomos, Solas, Dervish,** and **Deanta.** These bands have brought Irish music into international prominence, starting with the early recordings of the Chieftains and their mentor **Sean O'Riada,** who fostered the resurrection of *trad* from near-extinction to a national art form. For the best *trad*, find a *fleadh* (FLAH), a musical festival at which musicians' officially scheduled sessions often spill over into nearby pubs. **Comhaltas Ceoltóirí Éireann** (☎01 280 0295; www.comhaltas.com), the national *trad* music association, organizes *fleadhs*.

Currently, Ireland's biggest rock export is ▧U2. From the adrenaline-soaked promise of 1980's *Boy*, the band ascended into the stratosphere, culminating in international fame with *The Joshua Tree* (1987). After a brief turn to techno dance tunes (1997's *Pop*), the recent *All That You Can't Leave Behind* (2000) has been heralded as the band's triumphant return to its roots. Other recent Irish bands to make it off of the isle include **The Corrs, Boyzone,** which recently conquered the UK charts, and their girl-group equivalent, **B*witched.**

THE VISUAL ARTS

FILM. Hollywood discovered Ireland in John Wayne's 1952 film *The Quiet Man*, giving an international audience of millions their first view of the island's beauty, albeit through a stereotypical lens Irish film has long struggled to change. Aside from the garish green of Hollywood technicolor, art-filmmakers have also tried to capture Ireland, including **Robert Flaherty,** who created cinematic Realism in his classic documentary about coastal fishermen, *Man of Aran* (1934).

In the last decade, the government has encouraged a truly Irish film industry. **Jim Sheridan** helped kick off the Irish cinematic renaissance with his universally acclaimed adaptation of Christy Brown's autobiography, *My Left Foot* (1991). More recently, Sheridan has worked with Irish actor **Daniel Day-Lewis** in two films that take a humanitarian approach to the lives of Catholics and Protestants during the Troubles with *In the Name of the Father* (1993) and *The Boxer* (1997). Based on Roddy Doyle's Barrytown Trilogy, *The Commitments* (1991), *The Snapper* (1993), and *The Van* (1996) follow a family from the depressed North Side of Dublin as its members variously form a soul band, have a kid, and get off the dole by running a chipper. Dublin native **Neil Jordan** has become a much-sought-after director thanks to the success of *The Crying Game* (1992), *Michael Collins* (1996), and *The Butcher Boy* (1998). Most recently, the appeal of Irish scenery and accents was demonstrated in the production of two highly Irish sounding and looking films by non-Irish filmmakers: Hollywood produced a film version of Donegal playwright Brian Friel's *Dancing at Lughnasa* (1998), and the government of the Isle of Man sponsored *Waking Ned Devine* (1998), which describes the antics of a village of rustic eccentrics.

REPUBLIC OF IRELAND

ESSENTIALS

WHEN TO GO

Irish weather is subject to frequent changes but relatively constant temperatures. The southeastern coast is the driest and sunniest, while western Ireland is considerably wetter and cloudier. May and June are the sunniest months, July and August the warmest. December and January have the worst weather. Take heart when you wake to clouded, foggy mornings—the weather usually clears by noon. Make sure you bring rain gear, regardless of the season.

FACTS AND FIGURES: REPUBLIC OF IRELAND	
Official Name: Éire.	**Land Area:** 70,280 sq. km.
Capital: Dublin.	**Time Zone:** GMT.
Major Cities: Cork, Galway, Limerick.	**Languages:** English, Irish.
Population: 3,900,000.	**Religion:** Roman Catholic (91.6%).

DOCUMENTS AND FORMALITIES

VISAS. Citizens of Australia, Canada, the EU, New Zealand, South Africa, and the US do not need a visa for stays of up to 90 days.

EMBASSIES. All embassies for the Republic of Ireland are in Dublin (p. 569). For Irish embassies at home, contact: **Australia**, 20 Arkana St., Yarralumla, Canberra ACT 2600 (☎062 73 3022); **Canada**, Suite 1105, 130 Albert St., Ottawa, ON K1P 5G4 (☎613-233-6281); **New Zealand**, Honorary Consul General, 6th fl., 18 Shortland St. 1001, Auckland 1 (☎09 302 2867; www.ireland.co.nz); **South Africa**, 1st fl., Southern Life Plaza, 1059 Shoeman St., Arcadia 0083, Pretoria (☎012 342 5062); **UK**, 17 Grosvenor Pl., London SW1X 7HR (☎020 7235 2171); and **US**, 2234 Massachusetts Ave. NW, Washington, D.C. 20008 (☎202-462-3939).

TRANSPORTATION

BY PLANE. Flying to London and connecting to Ireland is often easier and cheaper than flying direct. A popular carrier to Ireland is its national airline, **Aer Lingus** (☎081 836 5000; US ☎800-474-74247; www.aerlingus.ie), which has direct flights to the US, London, and Paris. **Ryanair** (☎081 836 3030; www.ryanair.ie) is a smaller airline that offers a "lowest-fare guarantee." The web-based phenomenon **easyJet** (UK ☎08706 000 000; www.easyjet.com) has recently began flying from Britain to Belfast. **British Airways** (UK ☎0845 773 3377; Republic ☎800 626 747; US ☎800-247-9297; www.british-airways.com) flies into most Irish airports daily.

BY TRAIN. Iarnród Éireann (Irish Rail; ☎01 836 3333; www.irishrail.ie) is useful only for travel to urban areas. The **Eurail** pass is accepted in the Republic but not in Northern Ireland. The **BritRail** pass does not cover travel in Northern Ireland or the Republic, but the month-long **BritRail+Ireland** pass works in both the North and the Republic, with rail options and round-trip ferry service between Britain and Ireland (€400-570). **Northern Ireland Railways** (☎028 9066 6630; www.nirailways.co.uk) is not extensive but covers the northeastern coastal region well; the major line connects Dublin to Belfast. A valid **Northern Ireland Travelsave** stamp (UK£6), affixed to the back of an ISIC card, will get you up to 33% off all train fares and 15% off bus fares over UK£1.45 within Northern Ireland. The **Freedom of Northern Ireland** ticket allows unlimited travel by train and Ulsterbus (1-day UK£11, 3-day UK£27.50, 7-day UK£40).

BY BUS. Bus Éireann (☎01 836 6111; www.buseireann.ie), the national bus company, reaches Britain and the Continent by working in conjunction with ferry services and the bus company **Eurolines** (www.eurolines.com). Most buses leave from Victoria Station in London (to Belfast: 15hr., €49/UK£31, round-trip €79/UK£51; Dublin: 12hr., €42/UK£27, round-trip €69/UK£45); other major city stops include Birmingham, Bristol, Cardiff, Glasgow, and Liverpool. Services run to Cork, Derry, Galway, Limerick, Tralee, and Waterford, among others. Discounted fares are available in the low-season, as well as for people under 26 or over 60. Bus Éireann operates both long-distance Expressway buses, which link larger cities, and local buses, which serve the countryside and smaller towns.

Ulsterbus (☎028 9033 3000; Belfast ☎028 9032 0011; www.ulsterbus.co.uk) runs extensive routes throughout Northern Ireland. The **Irish Rover** pass covers both Bus Éireann and Ulsterbus services (3 of 8 consecutive days €60/UK£90, children €33/UK£50; 8 of 15 €135/UK£200, children €75/UK£113; 15 of 30 €195/UK£293, children €110/UK£165). The **Emerald Card** offers unlimited travel on Ulsterbus, Northern Ireland Railways, Bus Éireann Expressway, and many local services; for more info, see www.buseireann.ie (8 of 15 consecutive days €168/UK£108, children €84/ UK£54; 15 of 30 €290/UK£187, children €145/UK£94).

BY FERRY. Ferries, more economical than air travel, journey between Britain and Ireland several times per day (€28-55/UK£18-35). Weeknight travel promises the cheapest fares. **An Óige** (HI) members receive up to a 20% discount on fares from Irish Ferries and Stena Sealink, while **ISIC cardholders** with the **TravelSave stamp** receive a 15-17% discount on Stena Line and Irish Ferries. Ferries run from Cork to South Wales and Roscoff, France (p. 581), and from Rosslare Harbour to Pembroke, Wales, and Roscoff and Cherbourg, France (p.581).

BY CAR. Drivers in Ireland use the left side of the road, and their steering wheels are on the right side of the car. Petrol (gasoline) prices are high. Be particularly cautious at roundabouts—give way to traffic from the right. **Dan Dooley** (☎062 53 103, UK ☎0181 995 4551, US ☎800-331-9301; www.dan-dooley.com) is the only company that will rent to drivers between 21 and 24, though such drivers incur an added surcharge. Prices are €150-370/UK£95-235 (plus VAT) per week, including insurance and unlimited mileage. If you plan to drive a car while in Ireland for longer than 90 days, you must have an **International Driving Permit (IDP)**. If you rent, lease, or borrow a car, you will need a **green card** or **International Insurance Certificate** to certify that you have liability insurance and that it applies abroad. It is always significantly less expensive to reserve a car from the US than from Europe.

BY BIKE, FOOT, AND THUMB. Much of Ireland's countryside is well suited for **biking**, as many roads are not heavily traveled. Single-digit N roads in the Republic and M roads in the North are more busily trafficked; try to avoid these. Ireland's mountains, fields, and heather-covered hills make **walking** and **hiking** an arduous joy. The **Wicklow Way** has hostels within a day's walk of each other. Locals do not recommend **hitchhiking** in Northern Ireland, where it is illegal along motorways; some caution against it in Co. Dublin, as well as the Midlands. *Let's Go* does not recommend hitchhiking.

TOURIST SERVICES AND MONEY

TOURIST OFFICES. Bord Fáilte (the Irish Tourist Board; ☎01 602 4000; www.ireland.travel.ie) operates a nationwide network of offices. Most tourist offices book rooms for a small fee and a 10% deposit, but many fine hostels and B&Bs are not on the board's central list. The **Northern Ireland Tourist Board** (☎028 9023 1221; www.discovernorthernireland.com) offers similar services.

MONEY. On January 1, 2002, the **euro** (€) replaced the Irish pound (£) as the unit of currency in the Republic of Ireland. Legal tender in Northern Ireland is the **British pound;** for more info, see p.149. Northern Ireland has its own bank notes, identical in value to English and Scottish notes of the same denominations. Although all of these notes are accepted in Northern Ireland, Northern Ireland notes are not accepted in Britain. As a general rule, it is cheaper to exchange money in Ireland than at home.

| **EMERGENCY** | Police: ☎999. Ambulance: ☎999. Fire: ☎999. |

IRELAND

If you stay in hostels and prepare your own food, expect to spend anywhere from €20-34/UK£12-22 per person per day. Some restaurants in Ireland figure a service charge into the bill; some even calculate it into the cost of the dishes themselves. The menu often indicates whether or not service is included. Most people working in restaurants, however, do not expect a tip, unless the restaurant is targeted exclusively toward tourists. In those incidences, consider leaving 10-15%, depending upon the quality of the service. Tipping is very uncommon for other services, such as taxis and hairdressers, especially in rural areas. In most cases, people are usually happy if you simply round up the bill to the nearest euro. The European Union imposes a **value-added tax (VAT)** on goods and services purchased within the EU, which is included in the price; for more info, see p. 16.

COMMUNICATION

PHONE CODES	**Country code:** 353 (Republic); 44 (Northern Ireland; dial 048 from the Republic). **International dialing prefix:** 00. From outside the Republic of Ireland, dial int'l dialing prefix (see inside back cover) + 353 + city code + local number.

TELEPHONES. Both the Irish Republic and Northern Ireland have public phones that accept coins (€0.20/UK£0.15 for about 4min.) and pre-paid phone cards. In the Republic, dial ☎114 for an international operator, 10 for a national operator, or 11850 for a directory. Mobile phone are an increasingly popular and economical alternative (p. 30). International direct dial numbers in the Republic include: **AT&T,** ☎800 550 000; **British Telecom,** ☎800 550 144; **Canada Direct,** ☎800 555 001; **MCI,** ☎800 551 001; **New Zealand Direct,** ☎800 550 064; **Telkom South Africa,** ☎800 550 027; and **Telstra Australia,** ☎800 550 061. In Northern Ireland, call ☎155 for an international operator, 100 for a national operator, or 192 for a directory. International direct dial numbers in Northern Ireland include: **AT&T,** ☎0800 013 0011; **Canada Direct,** ☎0800 890 016; **MCI,** ☎800 551 001; **New Zealand Direct,** ☎0800 890 064; **Telkom South Africa,** ☎0800 890 027; **Telstra Australia,** ☎0800 856 6161. For more info on making calls to and from Northern Ireland, see p.604.

MAIL. In the Republic, postcards and letters up to 25g cost €0.40 domestically and to the UK, €0.45 to the Continent, and €0.60 to any other international destination. Airmail letters take about 6-9 days between Ireland and North America and cost €0.80. Dublin is the only place in the Republic with postal codes. Even-numbered codes are for areas south of the Liffey, odd-numbered are for those north. The North has the same postal system as the rest of the UK (p.150). Address *Poste Restante* according to the following example: Firstname SURNAME, *Poste Restante*, Enniscorthy, Co. Wexford, Ireland. The mail will go to a special desk in the central post office, unless you specify otherwise.

INTERNET ACCESS. Internet access is available in cafes, hostels, and most libraries. One hour of web time costs about €4-6/UK£2.50-4; an ISIC card often earns you a discount. Look into a county library membership in the Republic (€2.50-3), which gives unlimited access to participating libraries and their Internet terminals. Online listings of cybercafes in Ireland and Britain, updated daily, include the **Cybercafe Search Engine** (http://cybercaptive.com) and **Cybercafes.com** (www.cybercafes.com).

ACCOMMODATIONS AND CAMPING

A **hostel** bed will average €12-18 in the Republic and UK£7-12 in the North. **An Óige** (an OYJ), the **HI** affiliate, operates 32 hostels countrywide. (☎01 830 4555; www.irelandyha.org. One-year membership €25, under-18 €10.50.) Many An

THE REPUBLIC	❶	❷	❸	❹	❺
ACCOMMODATIONS	under €15	€15-24	€25-39	€40-54	over €55

Óige hostels are in remote areas or small villages and were designed primarily to serve hikers, long-distance bicyclists, anglers, and others seeking nature, and do not offer the social environment typical of other European hostels. The North's HI affiliate is **HINI** (Hostelling International Northern Ireland; formerly known as **YHANI**). It operates only eight hostels, all comfortable. (☎028 9031 5435; www.hini.org.uk. One-year membership UK£13, under-18 UK£6.) A number of hostels in Ireland belong to **Independent Holiday Hostels** (**IHH**; ☎01 836 4700; www.hostels-ireland.com). Most of the 140 IHH hostels have no lockout or curfew, accept all ages, require no membership card, and have a comfortable atmosphere that generally feels less institutional than that at An Óige hostels; all are Bord Fáilte-approved. Numerous **B&Bs,** in virtually every Irish town, can provide a luxurious break from hostelling; expect to pay €20-30/UK£12-20 for singles and €35-50/UK£22-32 for doubles. "Full Irish breakfasts" are often filling enough to get you through to dinner. **Camping** in Irish State Forests and National Parks is not allowed; camping on public land is permissible only if there is no official campsite nearby. Sites cost €5-13, depending on the level of luxury. Northern Ireland treats its campers royally; there are well-equipped campsites throughout (£3-8).

FOOD AND DRINK

THE REPUBLIC	❶	❷	❸	❹	❺
FOOD	under €5	€5-9	€10-14	€15-19	over €20

Food in Ireland is expensive, but the basics are simple and filling. Find quick and greasy staples at chippers (fish 'n' chip shops) and takeaways (takeout joints). Most pubs serve food like Irish stew, burgers, soup, and sandwiches. Soda bread is delicious and keeps well, and Irish cheeses are addictive. Guinness, a rich, dark stout, is revered in Ireland with a zeal usually reserved for the Holy Trinity. Known as "the dark stuff" or "the blonde in the black skirt," it was once recommended as food for pregnant mothers, and its head is so thick its rumored that you can stand a match in it. Irish whiskey, which Queen Elizabeth once claimed was her only true Irish friend, is sweeter than its Scotch counterpart. Irish monks invented whiskey, calling it *uisce beatha,* meaning "water of life."

Ordering at an Irish **pub** is a somewhat traditional process. When in a small group, one individual will usually approach the bar and buy a round of drinks for everyone. Once those drinks are downed, another individual will buy the next round. This continues until everyone has bought a round. It's considered poor form to refuse someone's offer to buy you a drink.

HOLIDAYS AND FESTIVALS

Holidays: Holidays for the Republic of Ireland include: New Year's Day (Jan. 1); St. Patrick's Day (Mar. 17); Good Friday; Easter Monday (Apr. 12); and Christmas (Dec. 25-26). There are Bank Holidays in the Republic and Northern Ireland during the summer months; check at tourist offices for dates. Northern Ireland has the same national holidays as the Republic; it also observes Orange Day (July 12).

Festivals: All of Ireland goes green for **St. Patrick's Day** (Mar. 17th). On **Bloomsday** (June 16), Dublin celebrates James Joyce's *Ulysses*. In mid-July, the **Galway Arts Festival** hosts theater, *trad*, rock, and film (p. 598). Many return home happy from the **Lisdoonvarna Matchmaking Festival** in early September (p. 595).

DUBLIN

☎01

In a country known for its relaxed pace and rural sanctity, Dublin stands out with boundless energy and international flair. The city and its suburbs, home to one-third of Ireland's population, are at the vanguard of the country's rapid social evolution. In an effort to stem international and rural emigration, vast portions of the city have undergone renovation and redevelopment, funded by the deep pockets of the EU. Dublin may hardly look like the rustic "Emerald Isle" promoted in tourist brochures, but its people and history still embody the charm and warmth that have made the country famous.

▐ TRANSPORTATION

Flights: Dublin Airport (DUB; ☎814 1111). Dublin **buses** #41, 41B, and 41C run from the airport to Eden Quay in the city center with stops along the way (every 20min., €1.60). The **Airlink shuttle** (☎844 4265) runs non-stop to Busáras Central Bus Station via O'Connell St. (20-25min., every 10min., €5) and on to Heuston Station (50min., €4.50). A **taxi** to the city center costs roughly €15-20.

Trains: The **Iarnród Éireann** travel center, 35 Lower Abbey St. (☎836 6222; www.irishrail.ie), sells tickets for **Irish Rail**. (Open M-Sa 9am-6pm, Su 10am-6pm.) **Connolly Station,** Amiens St. (☎702 2358), is north of the Liffey and close to Busáras Central Bus Station. Buses #20, 20A, and 90 go from the station to destinations south of the river, and the DART (see below) runs to Tara on the south quay. Trains to: **Belfast** (2hr., 5-8 per day, €29); **Sligo** (3hr., 3-4 per day, €22); **Wexford** (3hr., €17). **Heuston Station** (☎703 2132) is south of Victoria Quay, west of the city center (25min. walk from Trinity College). Buses #26, 51, 90, and 79 go to the city center. Trains to: **Cork** (3hr., 6-11 per day, €43); **Galway** (2½hr.; 4-5 per day; €21, F and Su €28); **Limerick** (2½hr., 9 per day, €34); **Waterford** (2½hr., 3-4 per day, €17). Dublin's other train station is and **Pearse Station,** Pearse St. (☎703 3634).

Buses: Info is available at the **Dublin Bus Office,** 59 O'Connell St. (☎872 0000); the Bus Éireann window is open M-F 9am-5pm, Sa 10:30am-2pm. Buses arrive at **Busáras Central Bus Station** (☎836 6111), on Store St., directly behind the Customs House and next to Connolly Station. Bus Éireann runs to: **Belfast** (3hr., 6-7 per day, €18); **Derry** (4¼hr., 5-6 per day, €18); **Donegal Town** (4¼hr., 5-6 per day, €15); **Galway** (3½hr., 13 per day, €13); **Limerick** (3½hr., 7-13 per day, €15); **Rosslare Harbour** (3hr., 7-10 per day, €14); **Sligo** (4hr., 4-5 per day, €14); **Waterford** (3hr., 10 per day, €10); **Wexford** (2¾hr., 7-10 per day, €10).

Ferries: Irish Ferries, 2-4 Merrion Row (☎638 3333; www.irishferries.com), is open M-F 9am-5pm, Sa 9:15am-12:45pm. Ferries arrive from **Holyhead, UK** at the **Dublin Port** (☎607 5665), from which buses #53 and 53A run every hr. to Busáras station (tickets €1). **Norse Merchant Ferries** also dock at the Dublin Port and run a route to **Liverpool, UK** (7½hr.; 1-2 per day; €25-40, with car €105-170); booking for Norse Merchant is only available from **Gerry Feeney,** 19 Eden Quay (☎819 2999). **Stena Line** ferries arrive from **Holyhead** at the Dún Laoghaire ferry terminal (☎204 7777); DART (see below) trains run from Dún Laoghaire to the Dublin city center. Dublin Bus also runs connection buses timed to fit the ferry schedules (€2.50-3.20).

Public Transportation: Dublin Bus, 59 O'Connell St. (☎873 4222). Open M 8:30am-5:30pm, Tu-F 9am-5:30pm, Sa 9am-1pm. The smaller **City Imp** buses run every 8-15min. Dublin Bus runs the **NiteLink** service to the suburbs (M-W at 12:30am and 2am, Th-Sa every 20min. from 12:30am-4:30am; €4). **Travel Wide** passes offer unlimited rides for a day (€5) or a week (€18). **DART** trains serve the suburbs and the coast (every 10-15min. 6:30am-11:30pm, €0.75-1.70).

Taxis: National Radio Cabs, 40 James St. (☎677 2222). €2.75 plus €1.35 per mi. before 10pm, €1.80 per mi. after 10pm. €1.50 call-in charge.

Car Rental: Budget, 151 Lower Drumcondra Rd. (☎837 9611), and at the airport. In summer from €40 per day, €200 per week; off-season €38/165. 23+.

Bike Rental: Cycle Ways, 185-6 Parnell St. (☎873 4748). Open M-W and F-Sa 10am-6pm, Th 10am-8pm. €20 per day, €80 per week; deposit €200.

■ 🛈 ORIENTATION AND PRACTICAL INFORMATION

In general, Dublin is refreshingly compact, though navigation is complicated by the ridiculous number of names a street adopts along its way. Street names are usually posted on the side of buildings at most intersections and never on street-level signs. Buying a map with a street index is a smart idea. Collins publishes the invaluable *Handy Map of Dublin* (€6.50), available at the tourist office. The *Ordnance Survey Dublin Street Map* (€6) is a more detailed, yet heftier, option.

The **River Liffey** forms a natural boundary between Dublin's North and South Sides. Heuston Station and the more famous sights, posh stores, and upscale restaurants are on the **South Side.** Connolly Station and the majority of hostels and the bus station cling to the **North Side.** The North Side hawks merchandise cheaper than in the more touristed South. It also has the reputation of being rougher, especially after sunset. The streets running alongside the Liffey are called **quays** (KEYS); each bridge over the river has its own name, and streets change names as they cross. If a street running parallel to the river is split into "Upper" and "Lower," then the "Lower" is always the part of the street closer to the mouth of the Liffey. **O'Connell Street,** three blocks west of the Busáras Central Bus Station, is the primary link between north and south Dublin. **Henry Street** and **Mary Street** comprise a pedestrian shopping zone that intersects with O'Connell St. after the **General Post Office** (GPO), two blocks from the Liffey. **Fleet Street** becomes **Temple Bar** one block south of the Liffey. **Dame Street** runs parallel to Temple Bar until **Trinity College,** which defines the southern edge of the district. Trinity College is the nerve center of Dublin's cultural activity, with legions of bookshops and student pubs.

TOURIST, FINANCIAL, AND LOCAL SERVICES

Tourist Information: Main Office, Suffolk St. (☎(1850) 230 330). From Connolly Station, turn left down Amiens St., take a right onto Lower Abbey St., and continue until O'Connell St. Turn left, cross the bridge, and walk past Trinity College; Suffolk St. is on the right. Books rooms for a €4 fee plus a 10% non-refundable deposit. Open July-Aug. M-Sa 9am-8:30pm, Su 11am-5:30pm; Sept.-June M-Sa 9am-5:30pm. The **Northern Ireland Tourist Board,** 16 Nassau St. (☎679 1977 or (1850) 230 230), books accommodations in the North. Open M-F 9:15am-5:30pm, Sa 10am-5pm.

Embassies: Australia, 2nd fl., Fitzwilton House, Wilton Terr. (☎676 1517; www.australianembassy.ie); **Canada,** 65/68 St. Stephen's Green (☎478 1988); **South Africa,** 2nd fl., Alexandra House, Earlsfort Terr. (☎661 5553); **UK,** 29 Merrion Rd., Ballsbridge (☎205 3700; www.britishembassy.ie); **US,** 42 Elgin Rd. (☎668 8777). **New Zealanders** should contact their embassy in London.

Banks: Bank of Ireland, AIB, and **TSB** branches with currency exchange and 24hr. **ATMs** cluster on Lower O'Connell St., Grafton St., and in the Suffolk and Dame St. areas. Most bank branches are open M-F 10am-4pm, Th until 5pm.

American Express: Suffolk St., in the main tourist office (☎605 7709). Currency exchange; no commission for AmEx Traveler's Cheques. Open M-Sa 9am-5pm.

Luggage Storage: Connolly Station. €2.50 per item per day. Open M-Sa 7:40am-9:20pm, Su 9:10am-9:45pm. **Heuston Station.** €2-5 per item, depending on size. Open daily 6:30am-10:30pm.

Laundromat: The Laundry Shop, 191 Parnell St. (☎872 3541), near Busáras station. Wash and dry €8-12. Open M-F 8am-7pm, Sa 9am-6pm, Su 11am-5pm.

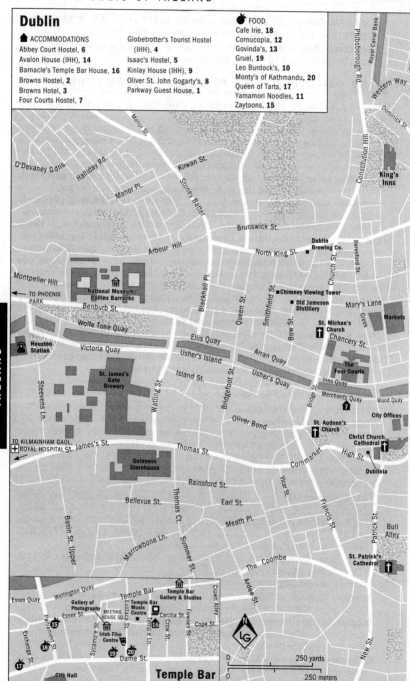

Dublin

ACCOMMODATIONS
Abbey Court Hostel, **6**
Avalon House (IHH), **14**
Barnacle's Temple Bar House, **16**
Browns Hostel, **2**
Browns Hotel, **3**
Four Courts Hostel, **7**
Globetrotter's Tourist Hostel (IHH), **4**
Isaac's Hostel, **5**
Kinlay House (IHH), **9**
Oliver St. John Gogarty's, **8**
Parkway Guest House, **1**

FOOD
Cafe Irie, **18**
Cornucopia, **12**
Govinda's, **13**
Gruel, **19**
Leo Burdock's, **10**
Monty's of Kathmandu, **20**
Queen of Tarts, **17**
Yamamori Noodles, **11**
Zaytoons, **15**

Temple Bar

TO ✈ 　St. George's

Berkeley St.　Blessington St.
Dorset St. Upper
Temple St. N.
Gardiner Pl.
Hill St.
North
MOUNTJOY SQ.
West Middle Gardiner St.
East
South

Mountjoy Sq.

1

Dublin Writers Museum
Hugh Lane Gallery
Denmark St.
N. Great George's St.
Abbey Presbyterian
James Joyce Cultural Centre
Summerhill Rd.
Killarney St.

National Wax Museum
Parnell Sq. N.
Garden of Remembrance
Parnell Sq. E.
Lower Gardiner St.
Sean MacDermott St.
Railway St.

Upper

Bolton St.
Dominick Pl.
PARNELL SQ.
Gate Theatre
Parnell Monument
Moore Ln.
Upper O'Connell St.
Marlborough St.
Corporation St.
Foley St.
2
3
Amiens St.
Main Entrance
DART Trains
Connolly Station

Kings Inn St.
Dominick St. Lower
Parnell Sq. W.

Parnell St.
Jervis St.
Wolf Tone St.
Moore St. Market
Central Library
Henry St.
General Post Office
Moore St.
Tyrone House
Cathedral St.
The Dublin Spire
Talbot St.
Frenchman's Ln.
Beresford Ln.
4
Garda
5
Busaras

Inner Dock

Financial Center
George's Dock

Parnell St.
Jervis Ln.
Mary St.
St. Mary's Church
Prince's St.
Youth Info Centre
Lower Abbey St.
Abbey Theatre
Liberty Hall
Custom House
Beresford Pl.

St. Mary's Abbey
Upper Abbey St.
Liffey St.
Great Strand St.
Middle Abbey St.
Hot Press
Lower O'Connell St.
6
O'Connell Monument
Eden Quay
Custom House Quay

Custom House Quay
River Liffey

Capel St.
Swift Row
Great Strand St.
Lotts
Bachelors Walk
O'Connell Bridge
Burgh Quay
George's Quay
City Quay

Strand St.
Ormond Quay
Millennium Bridge
Ha'Penny Footbridge
Aston Quay
D'Olier St.
Hawkins St.
Tara St.
Tara St. Station
Moss St.
Townsend St.

Grattan Bridge
Wellington Quay
Fleet St.
Westmoreland St.

Essex Quay
Parliament St.
Temple Bar
Anglesea St.
8
Bank of Ireland
College Green
Pearse St.
Garda
Pearse St.

Lord Edward St.
SEE TEMPLE BAR INSET

9

10
Castle St.
City Hall
Andrews Lane Theatre
Suffolk St.
12
Nassau St.

Trinity College
The Old Library

Pearse Station

Dublin Castle & Chester Beatty Library
Dame Ct.
Wicklow St.
Exchequer St.
South Great George's St.
Drury St.
South William St.
Clarendon St.
Grafton St.
Dawson St.
Kildare St.
National Library
National Gallery
Westland Row

Werburgh St.
11
Dublin Civic Museum
Galety Theatre
South King St.
Mansion House
National Museums
National History
Archaeology and History Museum
Leinster House
MERRION SQ.
North

Aungier St.
Mercer St.
13
14
St. Stephen's Green Shopping Centre
York St.
St. Stephen's Green W.
St. Stephen's Green N.
St. Stephen's Green E.
Upper Merrion St.
Baggot St.
#29 Lower Fitzwilliam St.
South

Heytesbury St.
Bishop St.
Kevin St. Lwr.
Wexford St.
Camden Row
Harcourt St.
Garda
St. Stephen's Green S.
St. Stephen's Green
Newman House
Fitzwilliam Ln.
Fitzwilliam St.

TO SANDYMOUNT (1.75mi)

EMERGENCY AND COMMUNICATIONS

Emergency: ☎999 or 112; no coins required.

Police (*Garda*): Dublin Metro Headquarters, Harcourt Terr. (☎666 9500); Store St. Station (☎666 8000); Fitzgibbon St. Station (☎666 8400).

Pharmacy: O'Connell's, 56 Lower O'Connell St. (☎873 0427). Open M-Sa 7:30am-10pm, Su 10am-10pm. **Branches** throughout the city, including 2 on Grafton St.

Hospitals: St. James's Hospital (☎453 7941), on James St. Served by bus #123. **Mater Misericordiae Hospital** (☎830 1122), on Eccles St., off Lower Dorset St. Served by buses #10, 11, 13, 16, 121, and 122.

Internet Access: The Internet Exchange, 146 Parnell St. (☎670 3000). €4 per hour. €2.50 per hr. with €5 membership. Open daily 9am-10:30pm.

Post Office: General Post Office (GPO; ☎705 7000), on O'Connell St. Even-numbered postal codes are for areas south of the Liffey, odd-numbered are for the north. *Poste Restante* pick-up at the *Post Restante* window. Open M-Sa 8am-8pm, Su 10am-6:30pm. **Postal Code:** Dublin 1.

▐▐ ACCOMMODATIONS

Reserve accommodations at least a week in advance, especially during Easter, other holidays, and the summer. **Hostel** dorms range from €10-24 per night. Quality **B&Bs** blanket Dublin and the surrounding suburbs, although prices have risen with housing costs; most charge €20-40 per person.

HOSTELS

Dublin's hostels lean toward the institutional, especially in comparison to their more personable country cousins. The beds south of the river fill up fastest; they also tend to be more expensive than those to the north.

■ **Four Courts Hostel,** 15-17 Merchants Quay (☎672 5839), near O'Donovan Rossa Bridge. First-rate hostel with clean rooms (most with showers) and a very friendly staff. Breakfast included. Internet €1 per 10min. Dorms €15-22; doubles €54-65. ❷

Globetrotter's Tourist Hostel (IHH), 46-7 Lower Gardiner St. (☎878 0700). A dose of luxury awaits the weary in these beautifully designed rooms. Beds are snug, but there's plenty of room to store your stuff. Irish breakfast included. Internet access. Dorms €19-22; singles €60-67; doubles €102-110. ❷

Avalon House (IHH), 55 Aungier St. (☎475 0001). With a good location close to many nightlife spots, Avalon House hums with the energy of transcontinental travelers. Large but not overwhelming, Avalon has top-notch security for its guests. Breakfast included. Internet access. Dorms €15-30; singles €30-37; doubles €56-70. ❷

Kinlay House (IHH), 2-12 Lord Edward St. (☎679 6644). Snuggle into soft couches in the TV room, or gaze at Christ Church Cathedral from your room window. The many icon posters lining the walls offer a crash course in Irish culture. Breakfast included. Laundry €7. Internet €1 per 15min. Dorms €15-26; singles €40-46; doubles €50-60. ❷

Brown's Hostel, 89-90 Lower Gardiner St. (☎855 0034). Glistening decor with closets, A/C, and TV in every room. Dorms are named after Irish rivers; be sure to ask for the Shannon room. Breakfast included. Internet access. Dorms €13-25. ❶

Oliver St. John Gogarty's Temple Bar Hostel, 18-21 Anglesea St. (☎671 1822). Joyce once roomed here with Gogarty. The location is unbeatable if you're frolicking in Temple Bar. Internet access. Laundry €4. Dorms €13-23; doubles €46-56; triples €63-75. ❶

Abbey Court Hostel, 29 Bachelor's Walk, O'Connell Bridge (☎878 0700). Great location and a knowledgeable staff compliment the clean rooms of Abbey Court. Laundry €8. Internet €1 per 15min. Dorms €17-28; doubles €76-88. ❷

Isaac's Hostel, 2-5 Frenchman's Ln. (☎855 6215), off Lower Gardiner St., behind the Custom House. With a bustling cafe next to the lobby, Isaac's attracts a young crowd. Laundry €8. Internet €1 per 15min. Dorms weekdays €13-19, weekends €15-21; doubles €60-64/62-66; triples €78-84/80-86. ❶

Barnacle's Temple Bar House, 19 Temple Ln. (☎671 6277). Right in the hopping (and noisy) heart of Dublin. Crawl home to your bed from Temple Bar pubs. All rooms with bath; some with skylight. Dorms €13-23; doubles €62-74. ❶

Browns Hotel, 90 Lower Gardiner St. (☎855 0034). Elegant Georgian building with newly refurbished rooms and a professional staff. Hot breakfast included. Singles €65-75; doubles €70-100. ❺

BED AND BREAKFASTS

B&Bs with a green shamrock sign out front are registered and approved by Bord Fáilte. On the North Side, B&Bs cluster along Upper and Lower **Gardiner Street,** on **Sheriff Street,** and near **Parnell Square.**

Mona's B&B, 148 Clonliffe Rd. (☎837 4147). Gorgeous house run for 37 years by Ireland's loveliest proprietress. Homemade brown bread accompanies the full Irish breakfast. Singles €35; doubles €66. Open May-Oct. ❸

Parkway Guest House, 5 Gardiner Pl. (☎874 0469). Rooms are high-ceilinged and tidy, and the location is perfectly central. Ask the proprietors for some restaurant and pub advice. Irish breakfast included. Singles €32; doubles €52-60, with bath €60-70. ❸

Mrs. Bermingham, 8 Dromard Terr. (☎668 3861), on Dromard Ave. Take the #2 or 3 bus and get off at Tesco. Soft, comfortable beds. One room has a lovely bay window overlooking the garden. Singles €28; doubles with bath €52. Open Feb.-Nov. ❸

Mrs. Molly Ryan, 10 Distillery Rd. (☎837 4147), off Clonliffe Rd. The unsinkable Mrs. Ryan has never marked her home with a B&B sign. Small rooms, small prices, no breakfast. As honest as they come. Singles €15; doubles €30. ❷

Rita and Jim Casey, Villa Jude, 2 Church Ave. (☎668 4982), off Beach Rd. Take bus #3 to the first stop at Tritonville. The Caseys specialize in royal treatment in this B&B with clean rooms, big breakfasts, and good company. Doubles €45. ❷

CAMPING

Most campsites are far away from the city center, and while it may seem convenient, camping in **Phoenix Park** is both illegal and unsafe.

Camac Valley Tourist Caravan & Camping Park, Naas Rd., Clondalkin (☎464 0644), near Corkagh Park. Accessible by bus #69 (35min. from city center, €1.50). Food shop and kitchen facilities. Laundry €4.50. Hikers €7; 2 people with car €15. ❶

Shankill Caravan and Camping Park, (☎282 0011). The DART and buses #45 and 84 from Eden Quay run to Shankill. Showers €1. €2 per person; €9 per tent. ❶

🄵 FOOD

Dublin's **open-air markets** sell fresh and cheap fixings. On Saturdays, a gourmet open-air market takes place in Temple Bar at the Meeting House Sq. The cheapest **supermarkets** around Dublin are the **Dunnes Stores** chain, with branches at St. Stephen's Green (open M-W and F-Sa 8:30am-7pm, Th 8:30am-9pm, Su noon-6pm), the ILAC Centre off Henry St., and North Earl St. **Temple Bar** has creative eateries catering to every budget.

Cornucopia, 19 Wicklow St. (☎671 2840). If you can find the space, sit down for a rich meal (about €8.50) or snack (€2). Portions at this vegetarian hotspot are huge. Open M-W and F-Sa 8:30am-8pm, Th 9am-9pm. ❷

IRELAND

Queen of Tarts, 3 Cork Hill (☎670 7119). This little red gem offers homemade pastries, scones, cakes, and coffee. Continental breakfast €4-6. Open M-F 7:30am-6pm, Sa 9am-6pm, Su 10am-6pm. ❷

Zaytoons, 14-15 Parliament St. (☎677 3595). Persian food served on big platters of warm bread. Excellent chicken kebab (€6.50). Open M-Sa noon-4am. ❷

Gruel, 68 Dame St. (☎670 7119). Come for a sit-down or takeaway meal made by a world-class chef. Lunch changes daily; go F for roast lamb with apricot chutney (€6). Dinners €6-12. Open daily 8:30am-9:30pm. ❸

Yamamori Noodles, 71-72 S. Great Georges St. (☎475 5001). Exceptional Japanese cuisine. Entrees €12-14. Open M-W and Su 12:30-11pm, Th-Sa 12:30-11:30pm. ❸

Leo Burdock's, 2 Werburgh St. (☎454 0306), up from Christ Church Cathedral. The real deal for fish and chips. A holy ritual for many Dubliners. Takeaway only. Fish €4. Chips €1.50. Open M-Sa noon-midnight, Su 4pm-midnight. ❶

Govinda's, 4 Aungier St. (☎475 0309). Fabulous veggie fare in a bright, airy oasis. Dinner special €7.50. Open M-Sa 11am-9pm. ❷

Cafe Irie, 11 Fownes St. (☎672 5090). Travel up Fownes St. from Temple Bar; it's on the left above the clothing store Sé Si Progressive. A small, hidden eatery with an impressive selecton of sandwiches (€2-4). Open M-Sa 9am-8pm, Su noon-6pm. ❶

The Blue Room, Copperinger Row (☎670 6982). Wonderful, family-friendly cafe. Make sure to try their pesto and homemade cranberry sauce. Sandwiches €6.40. (Open M-F 10am-6:30pm.) ❷

Boulevard Café, 27 Exchequer St. Walk inside to the outside of an Italian street; this funky little place has recreated an Italian boulevard within its walls. Good *tapas* (€5.70) and pastas (€8.30) round out the cuisine. Entrees €14-22. Cafe open daily 10am-6pm. Restaurant open daily 6pm-midnight. ❹

Monty's of Kathmandu, just off Dame St. on the right (☎670 4911). Nepalese food with decor to match. Try the Sekuwa Chatpate Chicken or Begum Bahar (both €14). Open Su 6-11:30pm, M-Sa noon-2:30pm and 6-11:30pm. ❹

⬢ SIGHTS

Most of Dublin's sights lie less than 2km from O'Connell Bridge. The **Historical Walking Tour** provides a 2hr. summary of Irish history, stopping at a variety of sights. Meet at Trinity College's main gate. (☎878 0227. Tours May-Sept. M-F 11am and 3pm; Sa-Su 11am, noon, and 3pm. Oct.-Apr. F-Su noon. €10, students €8.)

TRINITY COLLEGE AND ENVIRONS. The British built Trinity College in 1592 as a Protestant religious seminary that would "civilize the Irish and cure them of Popery." Jonathan Swift, Robert Emmett, Thomas Moore, Edmund Burke, Oscar Wilde, and Samuel Beckett are just a few of the famous Irishmen who studied here. Look for the bullet holes from the Easter Rising that still mar the stone entrance. *(Between Westmoreland and Grafton St. The main entrance is on College Green. Pearse St. runs along the north edge of the college, Nassau St. to its south. Grounds open 24hr. Free.)* **Trinity College Walking Tour** is run by students and concentrates on University lore. *(June-Sept. daily 10:15am-3:40pm; Mar.-May weekends only. Tours leave roughly every 45min. from the info booth inside the front gate. Includes admission to the Old Library. €7, students €6.)* **The Old Library** holds a priceless collection of ancient manuscripts, including the magnificent **Book of Kells,** 9th-century illustrated volumes of the Gospels. *(From Trinity's main gate, go straight; the library is on the south side of Library Sq. Open June-Sept. M-Sa 9:30am-5pm, Su noon-4:30pm; Oct.-May M-Sa 9:30am-5pm, Su noon-4:30pm. €6, students and seniors €5.)* The few blocks south of **College Green** are off-limits to cars, but are ground zero for shopping tourists and residents. **Grafton Street's** street performers range from string octets to jive limboists. Upstairs at the Grafton St. branch of Bewley's Restaurant and inside the chain's former chocolate factory is the **Bewley's Museum,** which includes tea-tasting machines and an overview of the company's history. *(Grafton St. Open daily 7:30am-11pm. Free.)*

KILDARE STREET AND TEMPLE BAR. The ▨**Natural History Museum** displays fascinating examples of classic taxidermy, including enormous Irish deer skeletons *(Upper Merrion St. Open Su 2-5pm and Tu-Sa 10am-5pm. Free.)* The **National Museum of Archaeology and History,** Dublin's largest museum, has extraordinary artifacts spanning the last two millennia, including the **Tara Brooch,** the **Ardagh Hoard,** and other Celtic gold work. Don't miss the bloody vest of nationalist **James Connelly.** *(Kildare St., adjacent to Leinster House. Open Su 2-5pm and Tu-Sa 10am-5pm. Free.)* The **National Gallery** has a collection of over 2400 paintings, including canvases by Bruegel, Caravaggio, Goya, El Greco, Rembrandt, and Vermeer. *(Merrion Sq. West. Open M-W and F-Sa 9:30am-5:30pm, Th 10am-8:30pm, Su noon-5pm. Free.)* The **National Library** chronicles Irish history and exhibits literary goodies in its entrance room. A genealogical research room can help families trace the thinnest roots of their Irish family tree, which will inevitably reach back to the kings of Ireland. *(On Kildare St. Open M-W 10am-9pm, Th-F 10am-5pm, Sa 10am-1pm. Free.)* Visit **Leinster House,** the former home of the Duke of Leinster. Today, the House provides chambers for the **Irish Parliament.** It holds both the **Dail** (DOIL), which does most of the government's work, and the **Seanad** (SHAN-ad), the less powerful upper house. The Dail meets from October to Easter Tu and W 3-9pm, and Th 10am-3pm. Visitors can view the proceedings by contacting the Captain of the Guard, who conducts tours of the galleries. *(☎678 9911. Passport necessary. Tours leave from the adjacent National Gallery on the hour.)* West of Trinity, between Dame St. and the Liffey, the **Temple Bar** neighborhood has rapidly become one of Europe's hottest nightspots. Narrow cobblestone streets link cafes, theaters, rock venues, and used clothing stores. The government-sponsored Temple Bar Properties spent over €40 million to build a fleet of arts-related attractions. Among the most inviting are: **The Irish Film Centre,** which screens specialty and art house film, Ireland's only **Gallery of Photography,** and the **Temple Bar Gallery & Studios.** *(The Irish Film Centre, 6 Eustace St. Gallery of Photography, Meeting House Sq. Temple Bar Gallery & Studios, 5-9 Temple Bar.)*

DAME STREET AND THE CATHEDRALS. King John built **Dublin Castle** in 1204 on top of the Viking settlement of *Dubh Linn.* For 700 years after its construction, it was the seat of British rule in Ireland. As part of the independence movement, fifty insurgents died at the castle's walls on Easter Monday, 1916. Since 1938, each president of Ireland has been inaugurated here. *(On Dame St., at the intersection of Parliament and Castle St. Open M-F 10am-5pm, Sa-Su 2-5pm. €4.50, students and seniors €3.50. Grounds free.)* Housing an eclectic collection including illustrated books by Matisse and Chinese snuff bottles, the **Chester Beatty Library,** behind Dublin Castle, is a truly unique library. Honorary Irish citizen Alfred Chester Beatty was an American rags-to-riches mining engineer who bequeathed his entire collection of Asian art, sacred scriptures, and illustrated texts to Ireland upon his death. Now you can enjoy his library, as well as special exhibits and public lectures held there. *(Open Su 1-5pm, Tu-F 10am-5pm, Sa 11am-5pm. Free.)* **St. Patrick's Cathedral,** Ireland's largest, dates to the 12th century, although Sir Benjamin Guinness remodeled much of it in 1864. Jonathan Swift spent his last years as Dean of St. Patrick's, and his crypt is above the south nave. *(On Patrick St. Take bus #49, 49A, 50, 54A, 56A, 65, 65B, 77, or 77A from Eden Quay. Open Mar.-Oct. daily 9am-6pm; Nov.-Feb. Sa 9am-5pm, Su 9am-3pm. €4. Students, seniors, and children free.)* Sitric Silkenbeard, King of the Dublin

Norsemen, built a wooden church on the site of the **Christ Church Cathedral** around 1038; Strongbow rebuilt it in stone in 1169. Further additions were made in the following century and again in the 1870s. Now, stained glass sparkles above the raised crypts, and fragments of ancient pillars are scattered about like bleached bones. *(At the end of Dame St., across from the castle. Take bus #50 from Eden Quay or 78A from Aston Quay. Open daily 9:45am-5:30pm except during services. Suggested donation €3.)* Finally, stop by **St. Audoen's Church,** High St., Dublin's oldest parish. Don't confuse this Norman-built church with the much more modern (much more Catholic) church of the same name; you might upset the vicar. (Open Sa-Su 2:30-5pm). **St. Audoen's Arch,** built in 1215 and now obscured by a narrow alley, is the only surviving gate from Dublin's medieval city walls.

GUINNESS BREWERY AND KILMAINHAM. Guinness brews its black magic at the St. James Gate Brewery, next door to the ▧**Guinness Storehouse.** In 1759, farsighted Arthur Guinness signed a 9000-year lease for the original 1759 brewery. The lease is displayed in the Storehouse's atrium, an architectural triumph that rises seven floors around a center shaped like a pint glass. View the exhibit on Guinness's infamously clever advertising—and then drink, pilgrim, drink. *(St. James's Gate. From Christ Church Cathedral, follow High St. west through its name changes: Cornmarket, Thomas, and James. Take bus #51B or 78A from Aston Quay or #123 from O'Connell St. Open Apr.-Sept. daily 9:30am-7pm; Oct.-Mar. 9:30am-5pm. €12, students €8, seniors and children €5.30.)* Almost all of the rebels who fought in Ireland's struggle for independence from 1792-1921 spent time at **Kilmainham Gaol.** Tours wind through the chilly limestone corridors of the prison and end in the haunting execution yard. *(Inchicore Rd. Take bus #51 or 79 from Aston Quay or #51A from Lower Abbey St. Open Apr.-Sept. daily 9:30am-4:45pm; Oct.-Mar. M-F 9:30am-4pm, Su 10am-4:45pm. €4.40, seniors €3.10, students and children €1.90.)* Built in 1679 as a hospice for retired and disabled soldiers, **The Royal Hospital Kilmainham,** Military Rd., now houses the **Irish Museum of Modern Art.** The hospital's facade mimics Les Invalides in Paris; the Baroque chapel is also stunning. (Open Su noon-5:30pm, Tu-Sa 10am-5:30pm. Guided tours Su 12:15pm, W, and F 2:30pm. Free.)

O'CONNELL STREET AND PARNELL SQUARE. O'Connell St. is Dublin's biggest shopping thoroughfare, and at 45m it was once Europe's widest street as well. Statues of Irish leaders such as **Daniel O'Connell, Charles Parnell,** and **James Larkin** adorn the street's traffic islands. One monument you won't see is **Nelson's Pillar,** a free standing pillar that commemorated Trafalgar and stood outside the General Post Office for 150 years. In 1966, the IRA celebrated the 50th anniversary of the Easter Rising by blowing the admiral out of the water. Follow O'Connell St. to get to Parnell Sq., home of **The Hugh Lane Municipal Gallery of Modern Art.** In the early 20th century, Dubliners refused to finance the museum that was to hold American artist Lane's collection of French Impressionist paintings; although the gallery was eventually constructed, Yeats lamented his city's provincial attitude in a string of poems. *(Parnell Sq. Buses #3, 10, 11, 13, 16, and 19 all stop near the gallery. Open Su 11am-5pm, Tu-Th 9:30am-6pm, F-Sa 9:30am-5pm. Free.)* Not just a fine place to send a letter, the **General Post Office,** O'Connell St., was the nerve center of the 1916 Easter Rising; Patrick Pearse read the Proclamation of Irish Independence from its steps. When British troops closed in, mailbags became barricades. Outside, a number of bullet nicks are still visible. *(Open Su 10am-6:30pm, M-Sa 8am-8pm.)* The city's rich literary heritage comes to life at **The Dublin Writers' Museum,** which displays rare editions, manuscripts, and memorabilia of Samuel Beckett, Brendan Behan, Patrick Kavanagh, Sean O'Casey, G.B. Shaw, Jonathan Swift, Oscar Wilde, and W.B. Yeats. *(18 Parnell Sq. North. Open June-Aug. M-F 10am-6pm, Sa 10am-5pm, Su 11am-5pm; Sept.-May M-Sa 10am-5pm. €5.50, students and seniors €5. Combined ticket with James Joyce Centre €8.)* The **James Joyce Cultural Centre** features a wide range of Joyceana, including portraits of the individuals who inspired his characters. Call for info on walking tours, and Bloomsday events. *(35 N. Great Georges St. ☎878 8547. Open July-Aug. M-Sa 9:30am-5pm, Su 11am-5pm; Sept.-June M-Sa 9:30am-5pm, Su 12:30-5pm. €4, students and seniors €3.)*

ST. STEPHEN'S GREEN AND MERRION SQUARE. Once a private estate, **St. Stephen's Green** was later bequeathed to the city by the Guinness clan. Today, its 22 acres teem with public life of all sorts, ranging from swans gliding on the artificial lake to punks relaxing by lovely fountains. During the summer, musical and theatrical productions are given near the old bandstand. *(Open Su 10am-dusk, M-Sa 8am-dusk.)* The fully restored **Newman House,** St. Stephan's Green South, was once the seat of **University College Dublin,** the Catholic answer to Trinity. *A Portrait of the Artist as a Young Man* chronicles Joyce's time here. The poet Gerard Manley Hopkins spent the last few years of his life teaching classics at the college. *(Open to individuals only from July-Aug. Tu-F noon-5pm and Sa 2-5pm. Groups admitted throughout the year with advanced booking. Admission €4.)* **Shaw's Birthplace,** 33 Synge St., offers a glimpse at the childhood of author and playwright George Bernard Shaw. His love of music and art is said to have started in his mother's recital room and garden. *(Open May-Sept. M-Sa 10am-5pm, Su 11am-5pm. Admission €5.50, concessions €5; joint ticket with Dublin Writers Museum €7.)*

ALONG THE QUAYS. Not quite the Seine, a walk along the River Liffey can be pleasant enough. To see Dublin's greatest architectural triumph, visit the **Custom House.** The House was built by James Gandon, who gave up the chance to be the Russian state architect in order to settle in Dublin. The building's Roman and Venetian columns and domes hint at what the city's 18th-century Anglo-Irish highbrows wanted Dublin to become. Carved heads along the frieze represent the rivers of Ireland; Liffey is the only lady. *(East of O'Connell St. at Custom House Quay. Visitors's center open mid-Mar. to Nov. M-F 10am-5pm, Sa-Su 12:30-2pm; Nov. to mid-Mar. Su 2-5pm and W-F 10am-5pm. Admission €1.50.)* Another of Gandon's works comes into sight just a few quays west of the Custom House. **Four Courts,** Inn's Quay, has a monumentally impressive facade, and was once seized by members of the IRA, sparking the Irish Civil War when members of the Free State Government attacked the garrison there. The building now houses Ireland's highest national court. *(Open M-F 9am-4:30pm. No scheduled tours. Free.)* Finally, check out fascinating **St. Michan's Church.** The dry atmo-

NO WORK, ALL PLAY

BLOOMSDAY!

Walk around Dublin on a normal day and you'll see plenty of references to James Joyce's famous novel, *Ulysses*. Walk around on June 16, however, and you will encounter Joyceans in Edwardian dress reenacting Leopold Bloom's ordinary-epic journey.

Festivities begin at 8:30am at the James Joyce Center on North Great Georges St., with a breakfast of "the inner organs of beasts and fowls" and pints of "foaming ebon ale." In the Georgian townhouse an engrossed group listens as local actors, musicians, and politicians render selections of the book. Outside, street performers and the Balloonatics Theatre Company perform particularly amusing scenes, encouraging audience participation. Even those who never dared open the tome find it surprisingly accessible.

Events continue around the city, from lunch at Davy Byrnes to tours of Joyce's Dublin, and end well into the night with more performances and music in Wynn's Hotel on Lower Abbey St.

Bloomsday 2004 is especially significant as it marks the centennial of the original Bloomsday: June 16, 1904. Plans are underway for a street-fair with life-size puppets and actors to recreate the red-light district of Edwardian Dublin. Expect the usual festivities as well, including a visual-arts exhibit and film festival. *(For more info, visit www.bloomsday100.org.)*

sphere within the nave has preserved the corpses in the vaults; it was these seemingly-living bodies that inspired Bram Stoker to write about the living dead-man in *Dracula*. Of particular interest is a 6½ ft. tall (dead) crusader and the hanged, drawn, and quartered bodies of two (very dead) 1798 rebels. Fun for the whole family. *(Church St. Open Mar.-Oct. M-F 10am-12:45pm and 2-4:45pm, Sa 10am-12:45pm; Nov.-Feb. M-F 12:30-3:30pm, Sa 10am-12:45pm. Church of Ireland services Su 10am. Admission €2.50, students and seniors €2, under-16 €1.)*

SMITHFIELD AND ELSEWHERE. At the **Old Jameson Distillery,** learn how science, grain, and tradition come together to create the golden fluid called **whiskey.** Be quick to volunteer in the beginning and you'll get to sample a whole tray of different whiskeys. Even the unchosen are blessed, however, with a glass of firewater at the end. *(Bow St. From O'Connell St., turn onto Henry St. and continue straight as the street dwindles to Mary St., then Mary Ln., then May Ln.; the warehouse is on a cobblestone street on the left. Tours daily 9:30am-5:30pm. €7, students and seniors €4.)* Continue your drinking at the nearby **Dublin Brewing Company,** 144-146 N. King St., a small brewing company that runs fun, personal tours with plenty of hops to smell and beer to taste. You get more beer for your money than at that *other* brewery in town, and more often than not, the tour guide partakes as well. *(Tours every hr. from noon-6pm. Tickets €9.)* Outside of the city's center, **Phoenix Park,** Europe's largest enclosed public park, is most famous for the 1882 Phoenix Park murders. The Invincibles, a nationalist splinter group, stabbed the Chief Secretary of Ireland, Lord Cavendish, and his Under-Secretary 180m from the **Phoenix Column.** The 712-hectare park now incorporates the President's residence *(Áras an Uachtaraín)*, cricket pitches, polo grounds, and grazing deer. **Dublin Zoo,** Europe's largest, is in the park. It contains 700 animals and the world's biggest egg. *(Take bus #10 from O'Connell St. or #25 or 26 from Middle Abbey St. Park open 24hr. Free. Zoo open M-Sa 9:30am-6:30pm, Su 10:30am-6:30pm. Closes at sunset in winter. €10, students €8.)*

🎵 🎭 ENTERTAINMENT AND NIGHTLIFE

Whether you fancy poetry or punk, Dublin is equipped to entertain you. The free *Event Guide* is available at the tourist office and Temple Bar restaurants.

THEATER

Dublin's curtains rise on a range of mainstream and experimental theater. There is no true Theater District, but smaller theater companies thrive off Dame St. and Temple Bar. Box office hours are usually for phone reservations. Showtime is generally 8pm.

■ **Abbey Theatre,** 26 Lower Abbey St., Founded in 1904 by Yeats and Lady Gregory to promote Irish culture and modernist theater. Synge's *Playboy of the Western World* was first performed here in 1907. The production generated storms of protest and yet another of Yeats' hard-hitting political poems. Today, the Abbey (like Synge) has gained respectability– it is now Ireland's national theater. (☎878 7222. Box office open M-Sa 10:30am-7pm. Tickets €12-25, M-Th students €10.)

Peacock Theatre, 26 Lower Abbey St., The Abbey's experimental downstairs studio theater offers evening shows in addition to occasional lunchtime plays, concerts, and poetry. (☎878 7222. Box office open M-Sa at 7:30pm. Tickets €17, matinees €13.)

Project Arts Centre, 39 Essex St., sets its sights on the avant-garde and presents every sort of artistic production. The **gallery** hosts rotating visual arts exhibits. Box office and gallery open 11am-7pm. Theater tickets €15, gallery free.

PUBS

James Joyce once proposed that a "good puzzle would be to cross Dublin without passing a pub." A radio station later offered €125 to the first person to solve the puzzle. The winner explained that you could take any route—you'd just have to visit them all on the way. *Let's Go* recommends beginning your journey at the gates of Trinity College, moving onto Grafton St., stumbling onto Camden St., teetering down S. Great Georges St., and, finally, triumphantly crawling into the Temple Bar area. Then again, any port in a storm; drink where ye may.

■ **The Stag's Head,** 1 Dame Ct. This beautiful Victorian pub has stained glass, mirrors, and yes, you guessed it, evidence of deer decapitation, all enjoyed by a largely student crowd. Excellent food abounds. Entrees about €10. Food served M-F noon-3:30pm and 5-7pm, Sa 12:30-2:30pm. Open M-W 11:30am-11:30pm, Th-Sa 11:30am-12:30am.

■ **Whelan's,** 25 Wexford St., down S. Great Georges St. The stage venue in back hosts big-name *trad* and rock groups, with live music every night at 9:30pm (doors open 8pm). Cover €7-12. Open for lunch daily 12:30-2:30pm. Pub open W-Sa until late.

■ **The Brazen Head,** 20 North Bridge St., off Merchant's Quay. Dublin's oldest and one of its liveliest pubs. Brazen Head was established in 1198. The courtyard is quite the pickup scene on summer nights. Open late.

■ **Cobblestones,** King St. North, is by far the best place in the city for *trad* music. No rock here, but live shows every night, a *trad* session in the basement, and many spontaneous performances. Open late.

The Porter House, 16-18 Parliament St. In addition to offering the largest selection of international beers in the country, Porter House also serves 8 self-brewed stouts, ales, and porters. Excellent sampler tray includes a sip of stout made with oysters (€9). Open M-W 10:30am-11:30pm, Th-F 10:30am-1:30am, Sa 10:30am-2am, Su 12:30-11pm.

Mulligan's, 8 Poolbeg St., behind Burgh Quay. Upholds its reputation as one of the best pint-pourers in Dublin. Collect all 6 Guinness coasters to learn how pull a pint yourself. A taste of the typical Irish pub: Low-key and nothing fancy.

Davy Byrnes, 21 Duke St., off Grafton St. A lively, middle-aged crowd fills the pub in which Joyce sets the "Cyclops" chapter of *Ulysses*. Open M-W 11am-11:30pm, Th-Sa 11am-12:30am, Su 11am-11pm.

THE LOCAL STORY

THE PERFECT PINT

Bartender Glenn, of a local Dublin Pub, helps Let's Go resolve the most elusive question of all...

LG: What's the most important thing about pouring a pint

A: The most important thing is to have the keg as close to the tap as possible. The closer, the better.

LG: And why's that?

A: Well, you don't want the Guinness sitting in a long tube while you wait to pour the next pint. You want to pull it straight out of the keg, without any muck in between.

LG: Does stopping to let the Guinness settle make a big difference?

A: Well, you can top it straight off if you want, but you might get too big a head with that. You don't want too small or big a head, so if you stop ¾ of the way, you can adjust the pint until the head is perfect. A true Guinness lover will taste the difference.

LG: Because of the head?

A: No, because of the gas. If you pull the Guinness straight from the tap and get a big head, it means you've gotten too much gas. It kills the taste.

LG: Anything else to look for?

A: Good Guinness leaves a healthy film on the glass. If it doesn't, you didn't get a good Guinness.

LG: Well, Glenn, you sure make pouring pints sound like an art form.

A: Oh aye, but only with Guinness—everything else you just chuck into a glass and hand out.

The Long Stone, 10-11 Townsend St. Old books and handcarved banisters lend a rustic, medieval feel to this pub. Full of interesting rooms, the largest has a huge carving of a bearded man whose mouth serves as a fireplace. Open Su 4-11pm, M-W noon-11:30pm, Th-F 10am-12:30am, Sa 3pm-12:30am.

McDaid's, 3 Harry St., off Grafton St. The center of Ireland's literary scene in the 1950s. Book-covered walls and a gregarious crowd downstairs make up the McDaid's atmosphere, which becomes a tremendous hot spot at nights. Open Su 11am-11pm, M-W 10:30am-11:30pm, Th-Sa 11am-12:30am.

CLUBS

In Dublin's nightlife war, clubs currently have a slight edge over pubs because of their later hours. As a general rule, clubs open at 10:30 or 11pm, but the action really heats up after the 11:30pm pub closings. Clubbing is an expensive way to end the night, since covers run €7-20, and pints are a steep €5. Find a club with an expensive cover but cheap drinks and you'll be set for the night.

The PoD, 35 Harcourt St. Spanish-style decor meets hard core dance music. The brave venture upstairs to **The Red Box,** a separate, more intense club with a warehouse atmosphere. Cover €10-20; Th and Sa €7 with ISIC; Th ladies free before midnight. Cover skyrockets when big-name DJs play. Open until 3am.

Rí-Rá, 1 Exchequer St. Good music that steers clear of pop and house extremes. 2 floors, several bars, lots of nooks and crannies. Cover €7-10. Open daily 11pm-2am.

Gaiety, S. King St., just off Grafton St. This elegant theater shows its wild side late night, with DJs and live music from salsa to soul. Cover from €10. Open F-Sa midnight-4am.

The Shelter, Thomas St., near the Guinness Brewery. Funk, soul, and a little bit of retro sound move a crowd dressed in multiple shades of brown, gray, and black. Live bands and DJs play often. Cover €9. Open Th-Sa until late.

Club M, Blooms Hotel, Anglesea St., in Temple Bar. One of Dublin's largest clubs, attracting a crowd of all ages and styles. Club M boasts an elaborate layout with bars in the back. If at first you don't succeed, grind, grind again. Cover Su-Th €7, ladies free before midnight; F-Sa €12-15.

GAY AND LESBIAN NIGHTLIFE

The gay nightclub scene is alive and well, with gay venues (usually rented-out clubs) just about every night. Keep up-to-date by checking out the queer pages in *In Dublin* for gay-friendly pubs, restaurants, and clubs, or try **Gay Switchboard Dublin** for event info and updates (☎872 1055; Su-F 8-10pm, Sa 3:30-6pm). The following listings are always safe bets.

The George, 89 S. Great Georges St. Dublin's first and most prominent gay bar. All ages gather throughout the day to chat and drink. Hosts frequent theme nights. Su night Drag Bingo offers lots of additional entertainment. Dress well—no effort, no entry. Cover €8-10 after 10pm. The nightclub is open W-Su until 2am.

The Front Lounge, Parliament St. The velvet seats of this gay-friendly bar are popular with a very mixed, very trendy crowd. Open Su 4-11:30pm, M and W noon-11:30pm, Tu and Sa noon-12:30am, F noon-1:30am.

Out on the Liffey, 27 Upper Ormond Quay. Ireland's 2nd gay bar, its name plays on the more traditional Inn on the Liffey just a few doors down. Lots of dark nooks in which to chat and drink. The short hike from the city center ensures a local crowd most nights. Tu drag, W karaoke, F-Sa DJs. No cover. Late bar W-Th until 12:30am, F-Sa until 2am.

▶ DAYTRIPS FROM DUBLIN

HOWTH. Howth (rhymes with "both") dangles from the mainland in Edenic isolation, fewer than 16km from Dublin. A 3hr. **cliff walk** circles the peninsula, passing heather and thousands of seabird nests. The best section of the walk is a 1hr. hike between the harbor and the lighthouse at the southeast tip. To get to the trailhead from town, turn left at the DART station and follow Harbour Rd. around the coast for about 20min. Just offshore is **Ireland's Eye,** a former sanctuary for monks that has become an avian refuge. **Ireland's Eye Boat Trips,** on the East Pier, jets passengers across the water. (☎ (01) 831 4200. Round-trip €8, students and children €4.) To reach the private **Howth Castle,** a charmingly awkward patchwork of architectural styles, turn right as you exit the DART station and then left after 400m, at the entrance to the Deer Park Hotel. To get to Howth, take a northbound DART **train** to the end of the line (30min., 6 per hr., €1.50). Turn left out of the station to get to the **tourist office,** in the Old Courthouse on Harbour Rd. (☎ 844 5976. Open May-Aug. M 11am-1pm, Tu-F 11am-1pm and 1:30-5pm.)

BOYNE VALLEY. The thinly populated Boyne Valley hides Ireland's greatest archaeological treasures. Along the curves of the river between Slane and Drogheda lie no fewer than 40 crypt-like passages constructed by the Neolithics around the 4th millennium BC. **Newgrange** is the most spectacular; a roof box over the entrance allows a solitary beam of sunlight to shine directly into the tomb for 17min. on the winter solstice, a breathtaking experience that is simulated on the tour. You may only enter Newgrange by admission at ▧**Brú na Bóinne Visitors Centre,** near Donore on the south side of the River Boyne, across from the tombs. (☎ (041) 988 0300. Open June to mid-Sept. daily 9am-7pm; late Sept. and May 9am-6:30pm; Oct. and Mar.-Apr. 9:30am-5:30pm; Nov.-Feb. 9:30am-5pm. Center and 1hr. tour €6, students €3.50.) A group of enormous, well-preserved Norman castles—including **Trim Castle,** conquered by Mel Gibson in *Braveheart*—overlooks **Trim** proper on the River Boyne. (Open May-Oct. daily 10am-6pm. Tours every 45min. Limited to 15 people; sign up upon arrival in Trim. Grounds only €1.20. Tour and grounds €3.10, students €1.20.)

SOUTHEAST IRELAND

A base first for the Vikings and then the Normans, the Southeast echoes a fainter Celtic influence than the rest of Ireland. Town and street names in this region reflect Norse, Norman, and Anglo-Saxon influences rather than Gaelic ones. The Southeast's busiest attractions are its beaches, which draw admirers to the coastline stretching from Kilmore Quay to tidy Ardmore.

◀ FERRIES TO FRANCE AND BRITAIN

Irish Ferries (☎ 053 33 158) sails from Rosslare Harbour to Pembroke, Wales (4hr., every day, €28-38) and Roscoff and Cherbourg, France (18hr., every other day). **Eurail** passes grant passage on ferries to France. **Stena Line** (☎ 053 61 567) runs from Rosslare Harbour to Fishguard, Wales (3½hr., €28-35).

THE WICKLOW MOUNTAINS   ☎ 0404

Over 600m tall, carpeted in fragrant heather and pleated by sparkling rivers, the Wicklow summits are home to grazing sheep and scattered villages. Smooth glacial valleys embrace two lakes and the monastic ruins that epitomize the romantic image of pristine rural Ireland. Public transportation is severely limited, so driving is the easiest way to get around. **Glendalough,** a verdant, blessed valley renowned as a medieval monastic village, is most accessible, and draws a steady stream of coach tours from Dublin. The **National Park Information Office,** between the two lakes, is the best source for hiking advice. (☎45 425. Open May-Aug. daily 10am-6pm; Apr.-Sept. Sa-Su 10am-dusk.) **St. Kevin's Bus Service** (☎(01) 281 8119) arrives in Glendalough from St. Stephen's Green in Dublin (2 per day, round-trip €15). The **tourist office** is across from the Glendalough Hotel. (☎45 688. Open from mid-June to Sept. M-Sa 10am-1pm and 2-5:30pm.) Good beds can be found at ▓**The Glendaloch Hostel (An Óige/HI) ❷,** 5min. up the road from the tourist office. Excellent security and an in-house cafe make it by far the best option in the area. (☎45 342. Irish breakfast included. Laundry €5. **Internet** access. Dorms €20-22; singles €23-24; doubles €46-48; off-season €3 discount.) For more affordable food, B&Bs, and groceries, head to **Laragh,** 1.5km up the road.

ROSSLARE HARBOUR   ☎053

Rosslare Harbour is a useful departure point for Wales or France. **Trains** run from the ferry port to Dublin (3hr., 3 per day, €19) and Limerick (2½hr., 1-2 per day, €17) via Waterford (1¼hr., €8.50). **Buses** run from the same office to: Cork (3-5 per day, €9); Dublin (3hr., 10-12 per day, €14); Galway (4 per day, €23) via Waterford; Limerick (3-5 per day, €19); and Tralee (2-4 per day, €23). The Rosslare-Kilrane **tourist office** is 1.5km from the harbor on Wexford Rd. in Kilrane. (☎33 622. Open daily 11am-6pm.) If you need to stay overnight before catching a ferry, try the seaside ▓**Mrs. O'Leary's Farmhouse ❷,** off N25 in Kilrane. It's a 15min. drive from town, so call for pickup. (☎33 134. Singles €30, off-season €27.)

KILKENNY   ☎056

Ireland's best-preserved medieval town, Kilkenny (pop. 25,000) is also a center of great nightlife; nine churches share the streets with 80 pubs. **Tynan Walking Tours** provide the down-and-dirty on Kilkenny's folkloric tradition; hour-long tours depart from the tourist office. (☎(87) 265 1745. €6, students €5.) The 13th-century ▓**Kilkenny Castle** housed the Earls of Ormonde from the 1300s until 1932. The basement shelters the **Butler Gallery**'s modern art exhibitions. (☎21 450. Open June-Aug. daily 9:30am-7pm; Sept. 10am-6:30pm; Oct.-Mar. 10:30am-12:45pm and 2-5pm; Apr.-May 10:30am-5pm. Required tour €4.50, students €2.) Climb the narrow 30m tower of **St. Canice's Cathedral,** up the hill off Dean St., for a panoramic view of the town and its surroundings. (☎64 971. Open Easter-Sept. M-Sa 9am-6pm, Su 2-6pm; Oct.-Easter M-Sa 10am-4pm, Su 2-4pm.) Start your pub crawl at either the top of **John Street** or the end of **Parliament Street.**

Trains (☎22 024) arrive at Dublin Rd. from Dublin (2hr., €16) and Waterford (45min., €8). **Buses** (☎64 933) arrive at Dublin Rd. and the city center from: Cork (3hr., 2-3 per day, €16); Dublin (2hr., 5-6 per day, €10); Galway (5hr., 3-6 per day, €19); Limerick (2½hr., 2-4 per day, €14); Rosslare Harbour (2hr., 2-3 per day, €7); and Waterford (1½hr., 2 per day, €6.40). The **tourist office** is on Rose Inn St. (☎51 500. Open Mar.-Sept. M-F 9am-6pm, Sa 10am-6pm; Oct.-Feb. M-F 9am-5pm.) **B&Bs** are concentrated on **Waterford Road.** Stay in former royal quarters at the 15th-century ▓**Foulksrath Castle (An Óige/HI) ❶,** in Jenkinstown, 12.5km north of town on the N77. Buggy's Buses run to the hostel from the Parade (20min., M-Sa 2 per day, €2) in Kilkenny. (☎67 674. Dorms €11-12.) **Pordylo's ❹,** on Butterslip Ln. between Kieran St. and High St., has excellent world cuisine, including many vegetarian options. (Entrees €17-23. Open daily 6-11pm.) A **Dunnes supermarket** is on Kieran St. (☎61 655. Open M-Tu and Sa 8:30am-7pm, W-F 8:30am-10pm, Su 10am-6pm.)

WATERFORD   ☎051

A skyline of huge metal silos and harbor cranes greets visitors to Waterford. Fortunately, behind this industrial facade lies a city with 10 centuries of fascinating history. Waterford is Ireland's oldest city, founded in AD 914 by the grandson of Viking Ivor the Boneless as a refuge for his longships. Today, traces of early Vadrafjord are still visible in the city's streets, though her harbor is now filled with massive freighters instead of Viking warships. The highlight of Waterford is the ▪Waterford **Crystal Factory,** 3km away on N25 (the Cork road). One-hour tours allow you to witness the transformation of molten glass into polished crystal. Catch the City Imp minibus outside Dunnes on Michael St. and request a stop at the factory (10-15min., every 15-20min., €1.20) or take city bus #1 (2 per hr., €1.20), which leaves across from the Clock Tower. (☎332 500. Gallery open Mar.-Oct. daily 8:30am-6pm; Nov.-Feb. 9am-5pm. Tours Mar.-Oct. daily 8:30am-4pm; Nov.-Feb. M-F 9am-3:15pm. Tours €6.50, students €3.50.) **Reginald's Tower,** at the end of The Quay, has guarded the city's entrance since the 12th century. (☎873 501. Open June-Sept. daily 9:30am-6:30pm; Oct.-May 10am-5pm. €2, students €1.) To get a taste of Vadrafjord, head to **Waterford Treasures** at the Granary, which contains an impressive collection of Viking artifacts as well as the only extant item of Henry VIII's clothing, a velvet hat. (☎304 500. Open June-Aug. M-F 9am-9pm, Sa 9am-6pm, Su 11am-5pm; May and Sept. M-Sa 9:30am-6pm, Su 11am-6pm; Oct.-Apr. M-Sa 10am-5pm, Su 11am-5pm. €6, students €4.50.) The Quay is crowded with pubs; try **T&H Doolan's,** on George's St., which has been serving crowds for 300 years. (Pub food €13-19. *Trad* nightly at 9:30pm.)

Trains (☎876 243) leave from The Quay across the bridge for: Dublin (2½hr., M-F 5-6 per day, €17-21); Kilkenny (40min., 3-5 per day, €8); Limerick (2¼hr., M-Sa 2 per day, €16); and Rosslare Harbour (1hr., M-Sa 2 per day, €10). **Buses** depart from The Quay for: Cork (2½hr., 10-13 per day, €15); Dublin (2¾hr., 6-12 per day, €10); Galway (4¾hr., 5-6 per day, €19); Kilkenny (1hr., daily, €8); Limerick (2½hr., 6-7 per day, €15); and Rosslare Harbour (1¼hr., 3-5 per day, €13). The **tourist office** is on The Quay, across from the bus station. (☎875 823. Open M-F 9am-6pm, Sa 10am-6pm.) There are no hostels in town. Allow Mrs. Ryan of **Beechwood** ❷, 7 Cathedral Sq., to invite you into her charming house. Rooms look directly onto Christ Church Cathedral. (☎876 677. Doubles €50.) ▪**Haricot's Wholefood Restaurant** ❷, 11 O'Connell St., serves healthy and innovative home-cooked meals. The menu changes constantly and is often vegetarian-friendly. (Entrees €8-10. Open M-F 10am-8pm, Sa 10am-6pm.)

CASHEL   ☎062

Cashel sits at the foot of the 90m ▪**Rock of Cashel** (a.k.a. **St. Patrick's Rock**), a huge limestone outcropping topped by medieval buildings. (Open Mar.-Sept. daily 9:30am-5:30pm; Oct.-Feb. M-F 9:30am-5:30pm. Free.) Down the cow path from the Rock lie the ruins of **Hore Abbey,** built by Cistercian monks and presently inhabited by sheep. The **GPA-Bolton Library,** on John St., houses ecclesiastical texts and rare manuscripts, including a 1550 edition of Machiavelli's *Il Principe* and the world's smallest book. (☎62 511. Call for tours.) The internationally acclaimed **Brú Ború Heritage Centre,** at the base of the Rock, stages traditional music and dance performances; participation is encouraged. (☎61 122. Performances mid-June to mid-Sept. Tu-Sa 9pm. €15, with dinner €35.) **Bus Éireann** (☎61 333) leaves from the Bake House on Main St. for: Cork (1½hr., 6 per day, €12); Dublin (3hr., 6 per day, €16); and Limerick (1hr., 5 per day, €12). The **tourist office** is in the City Hall on Main St. (☎61 333. Open June-Sept. M-F 9am-6pm, Su 10am-6pm.) Just out of town on Dundrum Rd. is the outstanding **圏O'Brien's Farmhouse Hostel ❶**. (☎61 003. Laundry €8-10. Dorms €15; doubles €50. **Camping** €7.50 per person.)

SOUTHWEST IRELAND

With a dramatic landscape that ranges from lakes and mountains to stark, ocean-battered cliffs, Southwest Ireland is a land rich in storytellers and history-makers. Outlaws and rebels once lurked in the hidden coves and glens now overrun by visitors. If the tourist mayhem is too much for you, you can always retreat to the placid stretches along the Ring of Kerry and Cork's southern coast.

◀ FERRIES TO FRANCE AND BRITAIN

Swansea-Cork Ferries (☎021 427 1166) go between Cork and Swansea, South Wales (10hr., daily, €30-43). **Brittany Ferries** (☎021 427 7801) sail from Cork to Roscoff, France (14hr., €50-100).

CORK   ☎021

Cork (pop. 150,000), the country's second-largest city, serves as the center of the sports, music, and arts scenes in Southwest Ireland. Cork is a great place to eat and sleep for those who want to explore the surrounding countryside, but the city itself is well worth a visit.

▐▐ TRANSPORTATION AND PRACTICAL INFORMATION

Cork is compact and pedestrian-friendly. **St. Patrick's Street** becomes **Grand Parade** to the west; to the north it crosses **Merchant's Quay,** home of the bus station. Across **St. Patrick's Bridge,** to the north, **McCurtain Street** runs east to **Lower Glanmire Road** and the train station, before becoming the N8 to Dublin, Waterford, and Cobh. Downtown action concentrates on the vaguely parallel **Paul Street, Oliver Plunkett Street,** and St. Patrick's Street. Their connecting north-south avenues are overflowing with shops, and all are largely pedestrian and easy to traverse.

Trains: Kent Station (☎450 6766), on Lower Glanmire Rd., across the river from the city center. Open M-Sa 6:30am-8:00pm, Su 7:50am-8pm. Connections to: **Dublin** (3hr., 5-7 per day, €52); **Killarney** (2hr., 4-7 per day, €26); **Limerick** (1½hr., 4-7 per day, €26); **Tralee** (2½hr., 3 per day, €31).

Buses: (☎450 8188), Parnell Pl., 2 blocks east of St. Patrick's Bridge on Merchant's Quay. Info desk open daily 9am-6pm. **Bus Éireann** (☎450 8188, www.buseireann.ie) goes to: **Dublin** (4½hr., 5-6 per day, €20-33); **Galway** (4hr., 4-7 per day, €17-27); **Killarney** (2hr., 10-13 per day, €13-21); **Limerick** (2hr., 14 per day, €14-21); **Rosslare Harbour** (4hr., 3 per day, €19-30); **Sligo** (7hr., 5 per day, €23-37); **Tralee** (2½hr., 12 per day, €14-22); **Waterford** (2¼hr., 13 per day, €15-23).

Public Transportation: City buses crisscross the city and its suburbs every 10-30min. (M-Sa 7:30am-11:15pm, Su 10am-11:15pm; from €0.95). From downtown, catch buses along St. Patrick St., across from the Father Matthew statue.

Tourist Office: (☎425 5100), on Grand Parade, near the corner of South Mall, along the Lee's south channel. Open June-Aug. M-F 9am-6pm, Sa 9am-5:00pm; Sept.-May M-Sa 9:15am-5:30pm.

Banks: Ulster Bank Limited, 88 St. Patrick's St. (☎427 0618). Open M 10am-5pm and Tu-F 10am-4pm. **Bank of Ireland,** 70 St. Patrick's St. (☎427 7177). Open M 10am-5pm, Tu-F 10am-4pm. Most banks in Cork have 24hr. **ATMs.**

Emergency: ☎999; no coins required. **Police** (*Garda*): (☎452 2000), on Anglesea St.

Pharmacies: Regional Late Night Pharmacy (☎434 4575), on Wilton Rd., opposite the Regional Hospital on bus #8. Open M-F 9am-10pm, Sa-Su 10am-10pm. **Phelan's Late Night,** 9 Patrick St. (☎427 2511). Open M-Sa 9am-10pm, Su 10am-10pm.

Hospital: Mercy Hospital (☎427 1971), on Grenville Pl. €25 fee for emergency room access. **Cork Regional Hospital** (☎454 6400), on Wilton St., on the #8 bus.

Internet Access: ▨ **Web Workhouse** (☎434 3090), on Winthrop St., near the post office. €2.50-5 per hr. Open daily 24hr.

Post Office: (☎427 2000), on Oliver Plunkett St. Open M-Sa 9am-5:30pm.

▛ ACCOMMODATIONS

B&Bs are clustered along **Patrick's Hill,** on **Glanmire Road** rising upward from St. Patrick's Bridge, and on **Western Road** near University College.

▨ **Sheila's Budget Accommodation Centre (IHH),** 4 Belgrave Pl. (☎450 5562; www.sheilashostel.ie). At the intersection of Wellington St. and York St. Helpful, energetic staff. Breakfast €3.20. Internet €1 per 20min. 24hr. reception desk is also a general store. Check-out 10am. Dorms €15-16; singles €30; doubles €40-50. ❶

▨ **Clare D'Arcy B&B,** 7 Sidney Place, Wellington Rd. (☎450 4658; www.darcysguesthouse.com). From St. Patrick's Bridge, start up St. Patrick's Hill, turning right onto Wellington Rd. A luxurious guesthouse with an elegant Parisian interior. Doubles €80. ❹

Cork International Hostel (An Óige/HI), 1-2 Redclyffe, Western Rd. (☎454 3289). A 15min. walk from Grand Parade. Bus #8 stops across the street. Immaculate and spacious bunk rooms in a stately brick Victorian townhouse. All rooms with bath. Breakfast €3.50. Internet €1 per 10min. Reception 10:30am-midnight. Dorms €17-19; doubles €44; under-18, reduced prices. ❷

Kinlay House (IHH), on Bob and Joan Walk (☎450 8966). To the right of Shandon Church. Offers family-sized rooms and a warm atmosphere. Breakfast included. Laundry €7. Internet €1 per 15min. Dorms €14; singles €25-30; triples €54; quads €72. ❶

Acorn House, 14 Patrick's Hill (☎450 2474; www.acornhouse-cork.com). Elegant Georgian townhouse. Streetside rooms are best. Singles €45; doubles €90; off-season prices are negotiable. ❹

Roman House, 3 St. John's Terr., Upper John St. (☎450 3606). Colorfully decorated in decadence, Roman House is Cork's only B&B catering specifically to gay and lesbian travelers (though all are welcome). Bath, oversized armchair, coffee machine, and TV in every room. Vegetarian breakfast option available. Singles €40; doubles €60. ❹

Hotel Isaacs, 48 MacCurtain St. (☎450 0011; www.isaacs.ie). Modern decor that is sleek yet homey. Breakfast included. Standard rooms (most of which have been newly renovated) from €48; superior rooms from €72. ❹

▟ FOOD

Delicious restaurants and cafes abound on the lanes connecting Patrick St., Paul St., and Oliver Plunkett St. **Tesco** (☎427 0791), on Paul St., is the biggest grocery store in town. (Open M-W and Sa 8:30am-8pm, Th-F 8:30am-10pm.)

▨ **Quay Co-op,** 24 Sullivan's Quay (☎431 7660). Delicious vegetarian and vegan meals. Soup €2.80. Entrees around €6.50. Open M-Sa 9am-9pm. ❷

IRELAND

Orrery Rd.
Cathedral Rd.
Mount Nebo Ave.
Gurranbraher Ave.
St. Ann's Rd.
Mary Alkenhead Pl.
Gurranbraher Rd.
Blarney Rd.
Boyce's St.
Glen Ryan Rd.
Old Market Pl.
Blarney St.
Sunday's Well Rd.
North Mall
TO CORK CITY GAOL (100yd)
Convent Ave.
Sunday's Well Rd.
Grenville Pl.
Bachelor's Quay
N. Main
Henry St.
Grattan St.

River Lee (North Channel)

Fitzgerald Park
Cork Museum
Granary Theatre
Dyke Parade
Sheares St.
Liberty St.
Mardyke Walk
Lancaster Quay
Washington St.
TO MARDYKE CENTRE (150yd)
Western Rd.
Hanover St.

R. Lee (South Channel)

Gaol Walk
Donovan's Rd.
Connaught Ave.
Sharman Crawford
University College
College Rd.
Gill Abbey
Bishop's St.
Dean St.
St. Finbarr's Cathedral
Proby's Quay
Elizabethan Fort
Barrack St.

SEE CORK CENTER INSET BELOW

Cork Center

Grattan St.
N. Main St.
Corn Market St.
St. Paul's Ave.
Merchant's Quay
Opera House
Sheares St.
Liberty St.
Castle St.
Coal Quay Market
Paul St.
Crawford Art Gallery
Emmet Pl.
Washington St.
Queens Old Castle
French Church St.
Carey's Lane
Academy
Faulkner
Bowling
William
Merchant St.
Hanover St.
Cinema
Triskel Arts Centre
Grand Parade
St. Patrick's St.
Robert St.
Winthrop
Maylor St.
Web Workhouse
Bishop Lucy Park
English Market
Wandesford Quay
South Main St.
Tuckey St.
Christ Church
Princes St.
Marlboro St.
Cook St.
Morgan St.
Oliver Plunkett St.
Pembroke
South Mall

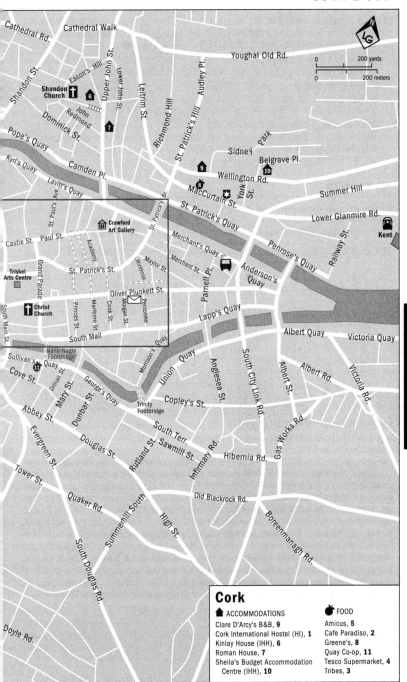

IRELAND

Cork

🏠 ACCOMMODATIONS

Clare D'Arcy's B&B, **9**
Cork International Hostel (HI), **1**
Kinlay House (IHH), **6**
Roman House, **7**
Sheila's Budget Accommodation
    Centre (IHH), **10**

🍎 FOOD

Amicus, **5**
Cafe Paradiso, **2**
Greene's, **8**
Quay Co-op, **11**
Tesco Supermarket, **4**
Tribes, **3**

■ **Tribes,** Tuckey St. (☎427 6070). Keep Bishop Lucy Park on your left and walk to the end of Oliver Plunkett St. The only late-night coffee shop in town. Sandwiches and burgers around €6. Open M-W noon-12:30am, Th-Sa noon-4:30am. ❷

Amicus, 14A French Church St. (☎427 6455). A sophisticated decor. Artistic, delicious dishes. Meals around €15-20. Open M-Sa 10am-10:30pm and Su noon-9pm. ❹

Greene's, 48 MacCurtain (☎455 2279), next to Hotel Isaacs. Warm colors and grand skylights make the atmosphere stunning. Meals range from steak to lamb. Entrees around €22. Open M-Th 6-10pm, F-Sa 6-10:30pm, Su 6-9pm. ❺

Cafe Paradiso, 16 Lancaster Quay (☎427 7939). Award-winning vegetarian meals border on gourmet. Cool Mediterranean feel with a laid-back crowd. Try the watermelon, feta, and cucumber salad (€7). Lunch €7-13. Dinner €9-18. Open Tu-Sa 12:30-3pm and 6:30-10:30pm. ❸

◉ SIGHTS

Cork's sights are loosely divided into three areas: the Old City, the Shandon neighborhood, and the western part of the city, around the university. All can be reached by foot. Pick up the *Cork Area City Guide* at the tourist office (€2).

THE OLD CITY. Looming over Proby's Quay, **St. Finbarr's Cathedral** is a testament to the Victorian obsession with Neo-Gothic bombast. The cathedral was built between 1735 and 1870, and now houses contemporary art exhibits in the summer. *(Bishop St. Open M-Sa 10am-5:30pm. €2.50 requested donation.)* On a nice day, you can get a decent view of Cork (and an unfortunate view of the Beamish Brewery) from **Keyser Hill.** At the top of the stairs leading up the hill is the **Elizabethan Fort,** a star-shaped and ivy-covered remnant of English domination. To access the fort's impressive view, climb the stairs just inside the main gate. *(Follow Main St. away from the city center, cross the South Gate Bridge, turn right onto Proby's Quay, then left onto Keyser Hill. Open 24hr. Free.)* In a city lacking a lot of greenery, the area around steeple-less **Christ Church** provides a quiet spot to rest in Cork. The site, scattered with eclectic statues, suffered the Protestant torch three times between its 1270 inception and its final renovation in 1729. *(Off the Grand Parade just north of Bishop Lucy Park. Open 24hr. Free.)*

SHANDON AND EMMET PLACE. Like Christ Church, **St. Anne's Church** was ravaged by 17th-century pyromaniacal English armies; construction of the current church began in 1722. As a sign of resistance, St. Anne's sandstone- and limestone-striped steeple inspired the red and white "rebel" flag still flying throughout the county. Commonly called Shandon Church, St. Anne's also has the nickname "the four faced liar" because of its four clock faces that are notoriously out of sync. Many an Irishman has blamed St. Anne's for a late arrival at work. *(Walk up Shandon St., take a right on unmarked Church St., and continue straight. Open June-Sept. M-Th and Sa 10am-5pm. €4, students and seniors €3.50.)* Nearby, the monstrous cement **Opera House** was erected two decades ago after the older, more elegant opera house went down in flames. *(Emmet Pl. Gallery open M-Sa 10am-5pm. Free.)* For a more aesthetically pleasing artistic experience, visit the **Crawford Art Gallery,** which runs a program of temporary exhibitions, both Irish and international. The striking main gallery room is filled with marble ghosts of the Venus de Milo and Michelangelo, among other famed artists. *(Off Paul St. Open M-Sa 10am-5pm. Free.)*

WESTERN CORK. Built in 1845, ■**University College Cork's** campus is a collection of brooding Gothic buildings, manicured lawns, and sculpture-studded grounds that make for a great afternoon walk or picnic. One of the newer buildings, **Boole Library** celebrates number-wizard George Boole, mastermind of Boolean logic and model for Sherlock Holmes's arch-nemesis Prof. James Moriarty. *(Main gate on Western Rd. ☎ 490 3000; www.ucc.ie.)* Across the walkway from UCC's front gate, ▓**Fitzgerald Park** is a must-see in Cork, with beautiful rose gardens and art exhibits courtesy of the **Cork Public Museum.** *(From the front gate of UCC, follow the signposted walkway across the street. Museum open Su 3-5pm, M-F 11am-1pm and 2:15-5pm. Sa-Su €1.50. M-F students and seniors free.)* If your time in Cork is tight, make sure you also see the **Cork City Gaol.** The museum offers multimedia tours of the former prison. The disturbingly life-like mannequins are both eerie and thrilling (and also downright amusing with a camera and some goofy friends). A tutorial on Cork's social history includes tidbits about miserable punishments, such as the human treadmill that was used to grind grain. *(Open Mar.-Oct. daily 9:30am-6pm; Nov.-Feb. 10am-5pm. €5, students €4. Audio tour included.)*

▓ NIGHTLIFE

The lively streets of Cork make finding entertainment easy; try **Oliver Plunkett Street, Union Quay,** and **South Main Street** for pubs and live music. To keep on top of the scene, check out *List Cork,* free at local shops.

▓ **The Lobby,** 1 Union Quay. Gave some of Ireland's most famous folk acts their big breaks; it features nightly live music with a view of the river. Occasional cover €2.50-6.40. Open M-Th until 11:30pm, F-Sa until 12:30am, and Su until 11pm.

▓ **An Spailpín Fanac,** 28 South Main St. Live *trad* that complements the decor of this 224-year-old pub. Crowds of visitors and locals come for the live *trad* offered most nights.

▓ **Half Moon,** on Academy Ln., to the left of the Opera House. The most popular dance club in Cork, with a young, hip crowd, *sans* teeny-boppers. 18+. Cover €9. Open daily until 2am. Purchase tickets from the box office across the street.

Bodega, 46-49 Cornmarket St., off the northern end of Grand Parade, is a striking converted warehouse where patrons relax with glasses of wine on velvet couches. Open M-Th until 11:30pm, F-Sa until 12:30am, and Su until 11pm.

Sin E, 8 Coburg St., just left of MacCurtain St., has some of Cork's best live music, especially Th nights. Open M-Th until 11:30pm, F-Sa until 12:30am, and Su until 11pm.

The Savoy, center of Patrick St., is a high brow club "filled with untouchable women," laments Simon the bartender. Dress to impress. Cover €9. Open M-Th until 11:30pm, F-Sa until 12:30am, and Su until 11pm.

▓ DAYTRIPS FROM CORK

BLARNEY. Tourists eager for quintessential Irish scenery and a cold kiss head northwest of Cork to see **Blarney Castle** and its legendary **Blarney Stone,** which confers the gift of persuasion upon those who smooch it while leaning over backwards. The top of the castle provides an airy and stunning view of the countryside. Try to come early in the morning to avoid the ubiquitous crowds. (☎ 438 5252. Open June-Aug. M-Sa 9am-7pm, Su 9:30am-5:30pm; May M-Sa 9am-6:30pm, Su 9:30am-5:30pm; Sept. M-Sa 9am-6:30pm, Su 9:30am-dusk; Oct.-Apr. M-Sa 9am-6pm or dusk, Su 9:30am-5pm or dusk. €4.50, students and seniors €3, children €1.50.) **Buses** run from Cork to Blarney (10-16 per day, round-trip €4.50).

KINSALE. Affluent tourists come to eat at Kinsale's expensive, famed restaurants, known as the **Good Food Circle,** but the town's other attractions are cheap. Follow the coastal **Scilly Walk** 30min. from the end of Pearse St. to reach the star-shaped, 17th-century **Charles Fort,** which offers spectacular views of the town and its watery surroundings. (☎477 2263. Open mid-Mar. to Oct. M-F 10am-6pm; Nov. to mid-Mar. Sa-Su 10am-5pm, M-F by appointment. €3.50, students €1.25.) **Buses** arrive on the pier, at the Esso station, from Cork (40min., 5-11 per day, round-trip €6.50). The **tourist office**, on Emmet Pl., is on the waterfront. (☎477 2234. Open Mar.-Nov. M-Sa 9am-7pm.) Local fishermen roast their catch at ☒**The Spaniard ❸**, a pub with delicious entrees (€7-14).

SCHULL AND THE MIZEN HEAD PENINSULA ☎028

The seaside hamlet of Schull is an ideal base for exploring the craggy and beach-laden southwest tip of Ireland. A calm harbor and numerous shipwrecks make it a diving paradise; the **Watersports Centre** rents gear. (☎28 554. Open Apr.-Oct. M-Sa 9:30am-6pm.) The coastal road winds past the **Barley Coast Beach** and continues on to **Mizen Head.** The Mizen becomes more scenic and less populated the farther west you go from Schull; **Betty Johnson's Bus Hire** offers tours of the area. (☎28 410. Call ahead. €12.) In summer, **ferries** (☎28 138) depart from Schull for Cape Clear Island (June-Sept. 2-3 per day, round-trip €12). **Buses** arrive in Schull from Cork (1-3 per day, €12) and Goleen (1-3 per day, €3.10). There is no other public transportation on the peninsula. Confident **cyclists** can daytrip to Mizen Head (29km from Schull). The immaculate **Schull Backpackers' Lodge (IHH) ❶**, on Colla Rd., has **hiking** and **biking** maps and info. (☎28 681. Bike rental €10 per day. Dorms €12; singles €18; doubles €36.) **The Courtyard ❷**, on Main St., has delicious options for breakfast and lunch; the fruit scones (€0.60) and the sandwiches on fresh ciabatta (€7-9.50) are both worth a try. (Open M-Sa 9:30am-6pm.)

CAPE CLEAR ISLAND ☎028

Although the scenery visible from the ferry landing at Cape Clear Island (*Oileán Chléire*) is desolate and foreboding, the main industry of this beautiful island is farming. Cape Clear provides asylum for gulls, petrels, cormorants, and of course their attendant flocks of ornithologists; the **Cape Clear Bird Observatory** (☎39 181), on North Harbour, is one of the most important observatories in Europe, and offers birdwatching and ecology courses. Those more interested in lovebirds should head to the **Marriage Stones,** on the northeast corner of the island, which were often visited by those seeking the gift of fertility. If the stones fail you, console yourself at **Cléire Goats** (☎39 126), on the steep hill between the harbor and the heritage center, where you can sample rich and delicious goat's milk ice cream for €1.50. **Ferries** (☎28 138) go to Schull (45min., 1-3 per day, round-trip €11.50). There is an **information office** in the pottery shop to the left of the pier that provides a pamphlet detailing all the island's sights. (☎39 100. Open July-Aug. 11am-1pm and 3-6pm; Sept. and June 3-6pm.) **Cléire Lasmuigh (An Óige/HI) ❶** is a 10min. walk from the pier; follow the main road and keep left. (☎39 198. June-Sept. dorms €11-13.) To reach **Cuas an Uisce Campsite ❶**, on the south pier, walk 5min. uphill from the harbor and bear right before Ciarán Danny Mike's; it's 400m down on the left. (☎39 136. Open June-Sept. Tent and one person €10; under-16 €7.50.) Groceries are available at **An Siopa Beag,** on the pier. (Open July-Aug. daily 11am-9pm; June 11am-6pm; Sept.-May 11am-4:30pm.)

KILLARNEY AND KILLARNEY NATIONAL PARK ☎064

The town of Killarney is just minutes from some of Ireland's most glorious natural scenery. The 95 sq. km national park outside of town blends forested mountains with the famous **Lakes of Killarney.** Five kilometers south of Killarney on Kenmare Rd. is **Muckross House,** a massive 19th-century manor with a garden that blooms brilliantly each year. A path leads to the 20m high **Torc Waterfall,** the starting point for several short trails along the beautiful **Torc Mountain.** Walk or drive to the 14th-century **Ross Castle,** the last stronghold in Munster to fall to Cromwell's army, by taking a right on Ross Rd. off Muckross Rd., 3km from Killarney. Alternatively, the footpaths from Knockreer (out of town on New St.) are more scenic. (Open June-Aug. daily 9am-6:30pm; May and Sept. 10am-6pm; Oct. and mid-Mar. to Apr. 10am-5pm. €5, students €2.) Bike around the **Gap of Dunloe,** which borders **Macgilly-cuddy's Reeks,** Ireland's highest mountain range, or hop on a boat from Ross Castle to the head of the Gap (1½hr., €12; book at the tourist office). From **Lord Brandon's Cottage,** on the Gap, head left over the stone bridge, continue cycling 3km to the church, and then turn right onto a winding road. Huff the 2km to the top, and your reward is an 11km coast downhill through the park's most breathtaking scenery. The 13km ride back to Killarney (bear right after Kate Kearney's Cottage, turn left on the road to Fossa, and turn right on Killorglin Rd.) passes the ruins of **Dunloe Castle,** demolished by, you guessed it, Cromwell's armies.

Trains (☎31 067 or (1890) 200 493) arrive at Killarney station, off East Avenue Rd., from: Cork (2hr., 4 per day, €20); Dublin (3½hr., 4 per day, €52); and Limerick (3hr., 4 per day, €20). **Buses** (☎30 011) leave from Park Rd. for: Belfast (2-4 per day, €30); Cork (2hr., 10-14 per day, €13); and Dublin (6hr., 5-6 per day, €20). **O'Sullivan's,** on Bishop's Ln., rents **bikes.** (☎31 282. Free locks and maps. Open daily 8:30am-6:30pm. €12 per day, €70 per week.) The staff at the **tourist office,** Beech St., is extremely helpful. (☎31 633. Open July-Aug. M-Sa 9am-8pm, Su 10am-1pm and 2:15-6pm; June and Sept. M-Sa 9am-6pm, Su 10am-1pm and 2:15-6pm; Oct.-May M-Sa 9:15am-1pm and 2:15-5:30pm.) The immense and immaculate **Neptune's (IHH) ❶,** on Bishop's Ln., up the first walkway off New St. on the right, has an ideal location and professional staff. (☎35 255. Breakfast €2.50. Dorms €11-17; singles €25-35; doubles €16-19.) **Orchard House B&B ❸,** on Fleming's Ln., is near the town center and an unbeatable deal; small rooms are compensated by a lovely proprietress and good amenities. (☎31 879. Singles €25-30; doubles €45-60.) For a delicious variety of quality vegetarian and meat dishes, try ⬛The **Stonechat ❸,** on Fleming's Ln. The low-key but sophisticated atmosphere makes this by far the best restaurant in Killarney. (Lunch €7-9. Dinner €11-14. Open M-Sa 11am-5pm and 6-10pm.) ⬛The **Grand ❷,** on High St., brings together locals and tourists for fantastic food and live music. (No cover before 11pm. Open daily 7pm-3am.)

RING OF KERRY   ☎066

The Southwest's most celebrated peninsula offers picturesque villages, fabled ancient forts, and rugged mountains. Although tour buses often hog the roads, rewards await those who take the time to explore the landscape on foot or by bike.

▣ TRANSPORTATION

The term "Ring of Kerry" usually describes the entire **Iveragh Peninsula,** though it technically refers to the ring of roads circumnavigating it. Hop on the circuit run by **Bus Éireann,** based in Killarney and stopping at the major towns on the Ring (mid-June to Aug., 2 per day), including Cahersiveen (from Killarney 2½hr., €11.50) and Caherdaniel (from Cahersiveen 1hr., €4.30).

CAHERSIVEEN. Although best known as the birthplace of patriot Daniel O'Connell, Cahersiveen (CAR-sah-veen) serves as an excellent base for jaunts to Valentia Island, the Skelligs, and local archeological sites. The ruins of **Bally-carbery Castle,** once held by O'Connell's ancestors, are past the barracks on Bridge St. and over the bridge, off the main road to the left. About 200m past the castle turn-off stands a pair of Ireland's best-preserved stone forts, **Caher-gall Fort** and **Leacanabuaile Fort.** The **tourist office** is directly across from the bus stop, next to the post office. (☎947 2589. Open June to mid-Sept. M-F 9:30am-

THE HIDDEN DEAL

THE EMERALD ISLE'S GOLDEN EGG

Many of Ireland's most tourn-isted sights—its national parks, museums, monuments and gardens—are owned and operated by the Irish Department of Arts and Heritage. While this government-run department keeps the price of admission to these sights quite low, the accumulated cost of visiting each can grow too high for the ordinary budget traveler to afford.

Recently, the Department of Heritage has started to offer discount cards to those wishing to visit multiple sights. Their **Dúchas Heritage Discount Card** may just be Ireland's greatest hidden deal. Not only does the ticket give you access to all of the sights owned and operated by the Department of Heritage, it also gives you one full year of access so that you can return again at your leisure.

There are ten sights in Dublin alone, including the Casino, Kilmainham Gaol, St. Audeon's Church, and the Royal Hospital Kilmainham. Other sights around Ireland include a slew of castles and ruins. The average price to visit one sight is between €2.50-5, so the card—at €19—is a steal.

The Irish Heritage Discount Card. €19.05, students and children €7.62, seniors €12.70, families €45.72. For more info call ☎01 647 2461; or within Ireland ☎1850 600 601; www.heritageireland.ie/en/HeritageCard.

1pm and 2-5:30pm.) The welcoming **Sive Hostel (IHH) ❶** is at 15 East End, Main St. (☎947 2717. Laundry €5.10. Dorms €10.50; doubles €25-32. Camping €5 per person.) **O'Shea's B&B ❸**, next to the post office on Main St., boasts comfortable rooms, some with impressive views. (☎947 2402. Singles €25-30; doubles €50.) **Main Street** has several pubs that harken back to the early 20th century, when establishments served as both watering holes and as the proprietor's main business, be it general store, blacksmithy, or leather shop.

Quiet ■**Valentia Island** is a fantastic daytrip. The little roads of this unspoiled gem are perfect for biking or light hiking. Bridges on either end of the island connect it to the mainland; alternatively, a **ferry** runs during the summer (3min.; Apr.-Sept. 8:15am-10pm, Su 9am-10pm; €1.50, with bike €2.50) from **Reenard Point**, 5km west of Cahersiveen. A taxi to the ferry dock from Cahersiveen is about €7. Another recommended daytrip is to the **Skellig Rocks**, about 13km off the shore of the Iveragh Peninsula. From the boat, **Little Skellig** may appear snow-capped; it's actually covered with 24,000 pairs of crooning birds. Climb 630 steps to reach a **monastery** built by 6th-century Christian monks, whose beehive-like dwellings are still intact. The hostel and campground in Cahersiveen can arrange the **ferry** ride (about 1hr.) for €32-35, including a ride to the dock.

CAHERDANIEL. There's little in the village of **Caherdaniel** to attract the Ring's droves of buses. But nearby **Derrynane National Park**, 2.5km along the shore from the village, holds 3km of gorgeous beach ringed by picture-perfect dunes. Follow the signs for **Derrynane House**, once the residence of Daniel O'Connell. (Open May-Sept. M-Sa 9am-6pm, Su 11am-7pm; Apr. and Oct. Su and Tu-Sa 1-5pm; Nov.-Mar. Sa-Su 1-5pm. €3, students €1.50.) Guests are made to feel at home at **The Travellers' Rest Hostel ❶**. (☎947 5175. Breakfast €4. Dorms €12.50; singles €16.)

DINGLE PENINSULA ☎066

For decades, the Ring of Kerry's undertouristed counterpart has remained more laden with ancient sites than with tour buses. Only recently has the Ring's tourist blitz begun to encroach upon the spectacular cliffs and sweeping beaches of the Irish-speaking Dingle peninsula. Many visitors explore the area by bike, an especially attractive option given the scarcity of public transportation.

TRANSPORTATION. Dingle Town is most easily reached by Bus Éireann from Tralee (1¼hr., 4-6 per day, €8.60); other routes run from Dingle to: Ballydavid (Tu and F 3 per day, round-trip €4.80); Ballyferriter (M-Sa 2 per day, €4.80); and Dunquin (M-Sa 2 per day, €4.80).

DINGLE TOWN. Lively Dingle Town, adoptive home of **Fungi the Dolphin** (now a major focus of the tourist industry), is a good base for exploring the peninsula and a fabulous tourist town in its own right. **Sciúird Archaeology Tours** leave from the pier for 3hr. whirlwind bus tours of the area's ancient spots. (☎915 1606. 2 per day, €15; book ahead.) **Moran's Tours** runs great trips to Slea Head, passing through majestic scenery and stopping at historic sites. (☎915 1155. 2 per day, €15; book ahead.) The **tourist office** is on Strand St. (☎915 1188. Open mid-June to mid-Sept. M-Sa 9am-7pm, Su 10am-5pm; late Sept. to early June daily 9:30am-5:30pm.) ▨**Ballintaggart Hostel (IHH) ❶**, 25min. east of town on Tralee Rd. in a gorgeous stone mansion, is supposedly haunted by the murdered wife of the Earl of Cork. For the less supernaturally-inclined, Ballintaggart's draws are its enormous bedchambers, cobblestone courtyard, and elegant common rooms. (☎915 1454. Dorms €13-20; doubles €48. Camping €11 per tent, €13 per van.) The laid-back **Grapevine Hostel ❶**, on Dykegate St., is just a brief stagger from Dingle's finest pubs. Rooms are small but comfy, and the staff is very accommodating. (☎915 1434. Dorms €13-15.)

VENTRY, SLEA HEAD, AND DUNQUIN. By far the most rewarding way to see Slea Head and Dunquin's cliffs and crashing waves is to **bike** along the predominantly flat **Slea Head Drive.** Past Dingle Town toward Slea Head sits the village of **Ventry** (Ceann Trá), home to a sandy **beach** and the ▨**Celtic and Prehistoric Museum,** 6km from Dingle Town, a massive collection that ranges from sea worm fossils to Millie, a 50,000-year-old woolly mammoth. (☎915 9191. Open Mar.-Nov. daily 9:30am-5:30pm; call ahead Dec.-Feb. €5, students €3.50.) While in Ventry, stay at the marvelous **Ballybeag Hostel ❶**, a secluded, yet convenient, place to unwind. A free shuttle runs to Dingle Town 7 times per day. (☎915 9876. Bike rental €7. Laundry €2. Dorms €10; singles €15.)

North of Slea Head and Ventry, the scattered settlement of Dunquin (Dún Chaoin) consists of stone houses, a pub, and little else. Past Dunquin on the road to Ballyferriter, the ▨**Great Blasket Centre** has outstanding exhibits about the isolated Blasket Islands. (☎915 6444. Open July-Aug. daily 10am-7pm; Easter-June and Sept.-Oct. 10am-6pm. €3.50, students €1.30.) At **An Óige Hostel (HI) ❶**, on the Dingle Way across from the turnoff to the Blasket Centre, each bunk has an ocean view. (☎915 6121. Breakfast €3. Reception 9-10am and 5-10pm. Lockout 10am-5pm. Dorms €13-15; doubles €32.) **Kruger's ❸**, the westernmost pub in Europe, features pub grub, music sessions, and great views. (☎915 6127. Entrees €7-13.)

TRALEE. Tralee (pop. 20,000) is a good departure point for the Ring of Kerry or the Dingle Peninsula, with the hustle and bustle appropriate for the economic and residential capital of County Kerry. ▨**Kerry the Kingdom,** in Ashe Memorial Hall on Denny St., features a high-tech history of Ireland from 8000 BC to the present. (☎712 7777. Open mid-Mar. to Oct. daily 9:30am-6pm; Nov. noon-4:30pm. €8, students €6.50.) During the last week of August, the nationally-known **Rose of Tralee Festival** brings a horde of lovely Irish lasses to town to compete for the title "Rose of Tralee." **Trains** depart from the station on Oakpark Rd. for: Cork (2½hr., 3-4 per day, €25); Dublin (4hr., 3-4 per day, €52); Galway (5-6hr., 3 per day, €52); and Killarney (40min., 4 per day, €7.50). **Buses** leave from the train station for: Cork (2½hr., 10-14 per day, €14); Galway (9-11 per day, €17); Killarney (40min., 5-14 per day, €6); and Limerick (2¼hr., 9 per day, €13). To get from the station to the **tour-**

ist office in Ashe Memorial Hall, head down Edward St., turn right on Castle St., and then left on Denny St. The well-informed staff provides free maps. (☎712 1288. Open July-Aug. M-Sa 9am-7pm, Su 9am-6pm; May-June and Oct. M-Sa 9am-6pm; Nov.-Apr. M-F 9am-5pm.) **Westward Court (IHH) ❷**, Mary St., has spotless dorms and quality showers. (☎718 0081. Breakfast included. Curfew 3am. Dorms €17; singles €24; doubles €44.) **Whitehouse Budget Accommodations and B&B ❸**, Boherboy St., offers incredibly clean rooms with hardwood floors. Relax in the adjoining pub with *trad* on Thursdays. (☎710 2780. Dorms €19; singles €30; doubles €50.)

WESTERN IRELAND

Even Dubliners will tell you that the west is the "most Irish" part of Ireland; in many remote areas you'll hear Gaelic as often as English. The potato famine that plagued the island was most devastating in the west—entire villages emigrated or died. The region still has less than half of its 1841 population. Though miserable for farming, the land from Connemara north to Ballina is great for hiking and cycling, and for those who enjoy the isolation of mountainous landscapes.

LIMERICK   ☎061

Although its 18th-century Georgian streets and parks are both regal and elegant, 20th-century industrial and commercial developments have cursed Limerick (pop. 80,000) with a featureless urban feel. In the past century, what little attention Limerick has received has mostly focused on its squalor—a tradition exemplified by Frank McCourt's celebrated memoir *Angela's Ashes*. Despite the stigma, Limerick is a city on the rise and a fine place to stay en route to points west. The **Hunt Museum**, in the Custom House on Rutland St., has been recognized for its outstanding and diverse collection; among its treasures are a gold crucifix given by Mary Queen of Scots to her executioner and a coin reputed to be one of the infamous 30 pieces of silver paid to Judas by the Romans. (☎312 833. Open M-Sa 10am-5pm, Su 2-5pm. €6, students and seniors €5.) Limerick's student population adds spice to the nightlife scene. The area where **Denmark Street** and **Corn Market Row** intersect is a good place to quench your thirst or listen to live music. **Dolan's**, on Dock Rd., hosts nightly *trad* and rambunctious local patrons.

Trains (☎315 555) leave Parnell St. for: Cork (2½hr., 5-6 per day, €20); Dublin (2hr., 7-10 per day, €37); Ennis (2 per day, €8); Killarney (2½hr., 3-5 per day, €22); and Waterford (2hr., 1-2 per day, €15). **Buses** (☎313 333) leave the train station for: Cork (2hr., 14 per day, €14); Derry (6½hr., 3 per day, €24); Donegal (6hr., 4 per day, €22); Dublin (3½hr., 13 per day, €15); Ennis (45min., 14 per day, €7.50); Galway (2hr., 14 per day, €14); Killarney (2½hr., 3-6 per day, €14); Rosslare Harbour (4hr., 3 per day, €19); Tralee (2hr., 8 per day, €14); and Waterford (2½hr., 7 per day, €15). The **tourist office** is on Arthurs Quay. From the station, walk down Davis St., turn right on O'Connell St., then left at Arthurs Quay Mall. (☎361 555. Open July-Aug. M-F 9am-6pm, Sa-Su 9am-5:30pm; Sept. and May-June M-Sa 9:30am-5:30pm; Oct.-Apr. M-F 9:30am-5:30pm, Sa 9:30am-1pm.) A number of **B&Bs** can be found on Ennis St. or O'Connell St. **Cherry Blossom Budget Accommodation ❶**, several blocks south of the Daniel O'Connell statue, has comfortable and relatively spacious rooms, quality bathrooms, and serves a delicious breakfast. (☎469 449. Singles €20; doubles €40.) Next door, **Alexandra House B&B ❸**, O'Connell St., is a red brick townhouse with a pleasant pastel interior and sunlit upstairs bedrooms. (☎318 472. Irish breakfast included. Singles €26; shared rooms €24-32 per person.) **Dolan's ❷** (see above) is Limerick's best choice for evening meals, serving traditional pub fare. (☎314 483. Entrees €6-10.

Kitchen open during pub hours.) **Furze Bush Cafe Bistro ❷**, on the corner of Catherine St. and Glentworth St., offers delicious crepes (€11.50) and gourmet sandwiches (€7) in an eccentric atmosphere. (☎411 733. Open June-Aug. M-Sa 10:30am-5pm; Sept.-May M-W 10:30am-5pm, Th-Sa 10:30am-5pm and 7-10pm.)

ENNIS AND DOOLIN   ☎065

Ennis's proximity to Shannon Airport and the Burren makes it a common stopover for tourists, who come for a day of shopping followed by a night of pub crawling. At ▨**Cruises Pub**, on Abbey St., local musicians appear nightly for cozy *trad* sessions in one of the oldest buildings in Co. Clare (est. 1658). Those with eclectic tastes should stop by **Glor**, a state-of-the-art music center that features nightly performances of both *trad* and more contemporary music, along with film, theater, and dance performances. (☎684 3103. Box office open M-Sa 9:30am-5:30pm. Tickets €12-22.) **Trains** leave from Station Rd. for Dublin (1-2 per day, €27). **Buses** also leave from Station Rd. for: Cork (3hr., every hr., €14); Dublin (4hr., every hr., €14); Galway (1hr., 5 per day, €10); Limerick (40min., every hr., €6.70); and Shannon Airport (40min., every hr., €7). The **tourist office** is on Arthur's Row, off O'Connell Sq. (☎28 366. Open July-Sept. daily 9am-1pm and 2-6pm; Apr.-June and Oct. M-Sa 9:30am-1pm and 2-6pm; Nov.-Mar. M-F 9:30am-1pm and 2-6pm.) **Abbey Tourist Hostel ❶**, Harmony Row, overflows with flowers, and its rooms are clean and comfortable. (☎682 2620; www.abbeytouristhostel.com. Curfew Su-W 1:30am, Th 2:30am, F-Sa 3am. Dorms €12-15; singles €25; doubles €38.)

Something of a shrine to Irish music, the little village of **Doolin** draws thousands every year to its three pubs. The pubs are commonly known by the mnemonic **MOM:** ▨**McDermott's** (in the Upper Village), **O'Connor's** (in the Lower), and **McGann's** (Upper). All have *trad* sessions nightly at 9:30pm. The ▨**Cliffs of Moher**, 10km south of town, feature a 200m vertical drop into the sea. Take the bus from Doolin (#50; 15min., 1-3 per day). **Buses** leave from Doolin Hostel for Dublin via Ennis and Limerick (#15; 2 per day) and Galway (#50; 1½hr., 1-5 per day). Almost every house on the main road is a **B&B** in Doolin. **Aille River Hostel (IHH) ❶**, halfway between the Upper and Lower villages, has a friendly atmosphere and a gorgeous location. Check out the unofficial beer garden out front, next to the Aille River. (☎707 4260. **Internet** €6 per hr. Dorms €12; doubles €27. **Camping** €6.)

THE BURREN   ☎065

Limestone, butterflies, ruined castles, and labyrinthine caves make the Burren, which covers 260 sq. km, a unique geological experience. ▨**Burren Exposure**, between Kinvara and Ballyvaughn on N67, gives a soaring introduction to the region through films shown on a wall-to-wall screen. (☎707 7277. Open 10am-6pm. Tickets €5, children €3.) The Burren town of **Lisdoonvarna** is synonymous with its **Matchmaking Festival**, a month-long *craic*-and-snogging celebration that attracts over 10,000 singles each September. The **Hydro Hotel ❹** has information on the festival and its own nightly music. (☎707 4005. Open Mar.-Oct. €45 per person.) The Burren is difficult to get around; the surrounding tourist offices (at Kilfenora, Ennis, Corofin, and the Cliffs of Moher) have detailed maps of the region. Hikers can set out on the 40km **Burren Way**, a trail from Liscannor to Ballyvaughan marked by yellow arrows. **Bus Éireann** (☎682 4177) connects Galway to towns in and near the Burren a few times a day in summer but infrequently during winter. In **Ballyvaughan**, stay at **O'Brien B&B ❸**, above a pub and restaurant on Main St., which has pleasing rooms, a plethora of fireplaces, and a hearty Irish breakfast. (☎707 7292. Single €20; doubles €40.) **Fallon's B&B ❸**, in **Kinvara** on the **Quay**, offers spacious rooms. (☎637 483. Breakfast €8-10. Open Apr.-Nov. Singles €35; doubles €60.)

IRELAND

GALWAY
☎**091**

In the past few years, County Galway's reputation as Ireland's cultural capital has brought flocks of young Celtophiles to Galway City (pop. 70,000). Given the 13,000 university students from Galway's two major universities, the large transient population of Europeans in their twenties, and the waves of international backpackers that arrive daily, it is no surprise that Galway is the fastest growing city in Europe. During the day, Galway's greatest draw is its close proximity to the Clare Coast and Connemara; as a starting point for seeing the west, Galway can't be beat. At night, however, the city itself becomes the center of attention, with a mesmerizing pub universe and an incredible music scene.

█ █ TRANSPORTATION AND PRACTICAL INFORMATION

With its many pedestrian-only and one-way streets, Galway is best seen on foot. Other forms of transportation are of use mostly to those staying outside of the city center or planning excursions from the city. **Buses** and **trains** stop near **Eyre Square,** a central block of lawns, monuments, and lounging tourists; the train and bus stations are up the hill on its southeast side. To the northeast of the Square, along **Prospect Hill,** a string of small, cheap B&Bs await your business, while **Forster Street,** to the southeast, takes you to the **tourist office.** The northwest corner of the Sq. is the gateway to the pedestrian center, where daytime sees hordes of shoppers looking for a good coffee, and nighttime sees partiers looking for a pint. From the Sq., **Shop Street** becomes **High Street,** which then becomes **Quay Street.** Without the passing traffic, all three streets feel like a single, long stretch of street-carnival fun. For the more adventurous, head over the bridges into the bohemian **left bank** of the Corrib, where great music and some of Galway's best pubs await.

Trains: Eyre Sq. (☎561 444). Open M-Sa 9am-6pm. Trains to **Dublin** (3hr., 4-5 per day, €21-30) via **Athlone** (€11-14). Transfer at Athlone for lines to all other cities.

Buses: Eyre Sq. (☎562 000). **Bus Éireann** travels to: **Belfast** (7hr., 2-3 per day, €28); **Cork** (4½hr., 13 per day, €16); **Donegal** (4hr., 4 per day, €16); and **Dublin** (4hr., 14 per day, €12). **Citylink, Michael Nee Coaches,** and **P. Nestor Coaches** also run private bus lines to Dublin. Inquire at the station for more info.

Local Transportation: City buses (☎562 000) leave from Eyre Sq. (every 20min, €0.95). Service runs M-Sa 8am-11pm, Su 11am-11pm. **Europa Cycles,** Hunter Buildings, opposite the cathedral, rents **bikes** for €9 per day, €40 per week. Deposit €40. Open M-Sa 9am-6pm, Su 9am-noon and 4-6pm.

Tourist Office: Forster St. (☎537 700), one block south of Eyre Sq. Ask for the free *Galway Tourist Guide* if you don't want to pay for info. **Bureau de change** available. Books accommodations for a €4 fee. Open July-Aug. daily 9:30am-7:45pm; May-June and Sept. daily 9am-5:45pm; Oct.-Apr. Su-F 9am-5:45pm, Sa 9am-12:45pm.

Banks: Bank of Ireland, 19 Eyre Sq. (☎563 181), and **AIB,** Lynch's Castle, Shop St. (☎567 041), both have 24hr. **ATMs** and are open M-F 10am-4pm, Th until 5pm. ATMs can also be found throughout the pedestrian area.

Emergency: ☎999; no coins required. **Police** (*Garda*): (☎538 000), on Mill St.

Pharmacies: Flanagan's, (☎562 924) Shop St. Open M-Sa 9am-6pm. **Matt O'Flaherty's,** (☎566 670) Shop St.

Hospital: University College Hospital, Newcastle Rd. (☎524 222).

Internet Access: Neatsurf, 7 St. Francis St. (☎533 976). €0.75 per 10min. Open M-Sa 9am-11pm, Su 11am-11pm.

Post Office: (☎562 051) Eglinton St. Open M, W-Sa 9am-5:30pm, Tu 9:30am-5:30pm.

ACCOMMODATIONS

In the last few years, the number of accommodations in Galway has tripled. Nevertheless, it's wise to call at least a day ahead in July and August and on weekends. Hostels are spread throughout the city, while most B&Bs are concentrated in the nearby Salthill area.

HOSTELS

Sleepzone, Bóthar na mBán (☎566 999), northwest of Eyre Sq. A comfortable hostel replete with a huge kitchen, big rooms, and free Internet before 10am and after 8pm. Dorms €17-20; singles €40; doubles €54. Weekend and off-season rates vary. ❷

Salmon Weir Hostel, 3 St. Vincent's Ave. (☎561 133), has a homey feel that is reinforced by the laid-back staff and the affable guests. Laundry €6. Curfew 3am. Dorms €9-15; doubles €35. ❶

Kinlay House (IHH), Merchants Rd. (☎565 244), half a block off Eyre Sq. A well-located hostel with all manner of rooms and services. Discounts when you book with their other locations in Cork and Dublin. **Bureau de change** available. Breakfast included. Laundry €7. Dorms €15-19; singles €27; doubles €40, with bath €48. ❷

The Galway Hostel, Eyre Sq. (☎566 959), right across from the station. Despite its tight dorms, this hostel is extremely clean, and has a helpful staff. Breakfast included. Internet €5 per hr. Dorms €15-22; doubles €45-50. ❷

B&BS

St. Martin's, 2 Nun's Island Rd. (☎568 286), at the end of the O'Brien Bridge. Located near Galway's best pubs, St. Martin's also has a gorgeous back garden that sits on the bank of the river. All rooms with bath. Singles €32; doubles €60. ❸

Adria House, 34 Beach Court (☎589 444). Home to a dynamic duo of owners (one is a former chef and the other is a former member of the tourist board), Adria House has nice rooms located between the city center and Salthill. Singles €20-55; doubles €40-110; prices highest in July and Aug. ❸

Ashford Manor, 7 College Rd. (☎563 941). A classy, if pricey, B&B that offers ample amenities. Breakfast included. Singles €45-48; doubles €90-96. ❹

FOOD

The east bank has the greatest concentration of restaurants. Your best budget options are the cafes and pubs around Quay St., High St., and Shop St. On Saturday, an **open market,** on Market St., offers cheap pastries, delicious ethnic foods, and fresh fruit. (Open 8am- 5pm.)

Anton's, Father Griffin Rd. (☎528 067), just over the bridge near the Spanish Arch. A hip eatery with innovative meals. The scrambled eggs with smoked salmon (€5) is delicious. Open M-F 8am-6pm, Sa 10am-5pm. ❶

McDonagh's, 22 Quay St. (☎565 011), has been serving up the best fish and chips in Galway for over a century. The restaurant half of McDonagh's boasts an incredible selection of seafood dishes. Takeaway fish fillet and chips €5.60. (Open daily noon-midnight; takeaway Su 5-11pm.) ❷

Java's, Abbeygate St. (☎567 400). Hip, dimly lit cafe. The New York-style bagels (€4.80) are excellent, as are the brownies. Open daily 10:30am-3am. ❶

Tulsi, Buttermilk Walk (☎564 831), between Middle and High St. This award-winning restaurant serves some of Ireland's best Indian food. The lunch (€7) is cheaper than the nearby fast food joints, and much better. Open daily noon-3pm and 6-10pm. ❷

◎ SIGHTS

NORA BARNACLE HOUSE. The little home of James Joyce's life-long companion has hardly changed since its famous-by-association inhabitant left. Today, a friendly staff happily discusses their favorite author while pointing out his original love letters to Ms. Barnacle. *(8 Bowling Green. ☎ 564 743. Open mid-May to mid-Sept. W-F 10am-1pm and 2-5pm; off-season by appointment. €2.50.)*

LYNCH CASTLE. The Lynch family ruled Galway from the 13th to the 18th century; their 1320 mansion, Lynch's Castle, now houses the Allied Irish Bank. A small display relates a slightly dubious family legend: In the late 1400s, Lynch Jr. killed a Spaniard whom he suspected of trying to steal his potential bride. Junior, sentenced to hang, was so beloved by the populace that no one would agree to hang him. Lynch Sr. was so determined to administer justice that he hanged Junior himself. As various versions of the episodes were passed along, the term **Lynch's Law** came to refer to execution without legal authority, and later came to be known as **lynching**. *(Market St. Exhibit open M-F 10am-4pm, Th until 5pm. Free.)*

CHURCH OF ST. NICHOLAS. With any luck, your prayers will be answered here; St. Nicholas is the patron saint of travelers. A stone marks the spot where Christopher Columbus supposedly stopped to pray before bursting onto the New World scene. Note the three-faced clock on the exterior; local folklore claims that the residents on the fourth side neglected to pay their taxes. *(Market St., near Lynch Castle. Open May-Sept. daily 9am-5:45pm. Free.)*

MENLO CASTLE. For a taste of the natural beauty that surrounds urban Galway, hire a **boat** and row up Lough Corrib to visit the ruined seat of the Blake family. What the castle lacks in majesty it makes up with its breathtaking location. **Frank Dolan**'s boats will take you away from the crowds and up a gorgeous stretch of the lough. *(Dolan's is located at 13 Riverside, Woodquay. ☎ 565 841. Tours €4 per hr.)*

ATLANTAQUARIA. Recently opened as the National Aquarium of Ireland, the museum features all things aquatic, with a particularly interesting tank filled with rays and ridiculous-looking "dabs." For those looking for even greater oddities, check out the jar upstairs holding the gigantic peepers of a fin whale. *(☎ 585 100. Open daily 10am-8pm.)*

🎵 ENTERTAINMENT

The free *Galway Advertiser* provides listings of city-wide events, and can be picked up at the Galway Advertiser office at the top of Eyre Sq. In mid-July, the **Galway Arts Festival** (☎ 583 800) attracts droves of *trad* musicians, rock groups, theater troupes, and filmmakers. Unofficial performers flock to the streets, which are cleared only for incredible parades.

PUBS

With approximately 650 pubs and 70,000 people, Galway maintains an extremely low person to pub ratio. Indeed, the city's intricate constellation of pubs is its number one attraction. In general, Quay St. and Eyre Sq. cater more to tourists, while locals stick to the more *trad*-oriented **Dominick Street** pubs.

▧ **The King's Head,** on High St., has 3 floors and a huge stage devoted to nightly rock. Upstairs music varies, from *trad* to rock cover bands. Su jazz brunch 1-3pm; €12.

▧ **Roisín Dubh** (The Black Rose), Dominick St. An intimate, bookshelved front hides Galway's hottest live music scene. In general, rock artists and singer-songwriters play their stage, but folk and blues musicians put in appearances too. Cover €5-20.

Galway

ACCOMMODATIONS
Adria House, **11**
Ashford Manor, **3**
The Galway Hostel, **4**
Kinlay House (IHH), **6**
St. Martins B&B, **8**
Salmon Weir Hostel, **2**
Sleepzone, **1**

FOOD
Anton's, **10**
Java's, **5**
McDonagh's, **9**
Tulsi, **7**

N59

University College-Galway

University Rd

Riverside Sports Ground

St. Bridger's Pl.

Bóthar na mBán

Prospect Hill

Waterside St.

Waterside

Eglinton Canal

Canal Rd

Presentation Rd

NUNS ISLAND

Salmon Weir Bridge

Gaol Rd.

River Corrib

Cathedral of Our Lady

Town Hall

Courthouse

Neat-surf

St. Vincent's Ave.

Frances St.

Woodquay

St. Brendan's Ave.

Eyre St.

Rosemary Ave.

Bóthar Irwin

St. Patrick's Church

TO **3** (100yd)

Galway Advertiser

Williamsgate St.

Eglinton St.

Mary St.

Eyre Sq.

Forster St.

Station Rd.

Kennedy Park

EYRE SQ.

Bowling Green

Upper Abbeygate

Market St.

Nora Barnacle House

St. Nicholas

Lynch's Castle

Shop St.

Abbeygate St. Lwr.

Medieval Wall

EDWARD SQ.

Victoria Pl.

Merchants Rd.

Queen St.

New Rd.

Mill St.

Nuns Island St.

Lombard St.

Mainguard St.

St. Augustine St.

Middle St.

High St.

An Taibhdhearc

Lower Cross St.

Druid Theatre

Presentation Rd

St. Mary's Rd.

St. Helens St.

Henry St.

Lwr. Dominick St.

O'Brien's Br.

Upper Cross St.

Bridge St.

Quay St.

Flood St.

New Dock St.

Dock Rd.

Lough Atalia Rd.

Raleigh Row

William St. West

Upper Dominick

Wolfetone Br.

Spanish Parade

City Museum

Spanish Arch

The Long Walk

Dock St.

Commercial Dock

Old Dock

Sea Rd.

Munster Ave.

Father Burke Park

THE CLADDAGH

Claddagh Quay

Father Griffin Rd.

Claddagh Hall

St. Nicholas Rd.

Fairhill

River Corrib

Nimmo's Pier

Father Burke Rd.

St. Dominick St.

Beach Court

11

TO SALTHILL (.6mi),
ATLANTAQUARIUM (.5mi)
& SALT HILL CARAVAN PARK

Grattan Rd.

South Park

Galway Bay

0   300 yards
0   300 meters

IRELAND

☒ **The Hole in the Wall,** Eyre Sq. This surprisingly large pub fills up fast with college-age singletons year-round. An ideal place to meet people, offering booths for groups, 3 bars for mingling, and tables to dance on. Music varies, but *craic* is a constant.

The Crane, 2 Sea Rd., is a friendly, musical pub that is one of the best places to hear *trad* in Galway. The 2nd floor hosts live performances that get better and better as musicians filter in throughout the night to join in the jam. *Trad* every night and all day Su. Set dancing Tu.

CLUBS

Between midnight and 12:30am, the pubs drain out and the tireless go dancing. The place to be rotates nightly. The best way to find the hot spot for the night is simply to follow the crowd after last call.

☒ **Cuba,** on Prospect Hill. Far and away the best club, though the top floor live-music venue is superior to the 2nd floor standard dance club. Upstairs provides a little more room, a little less flash, and wonderfully varied but danceable live music. Cover €5-10.

GPO, Eglinton St. A student favorite during term. Monday night "Sheight Night" gives you the chance to dress your sheightiest and dance to Abba's greatest hits. Tu 70s night, W comedy club. Cover around €6.

Karma, Eyre Sq. This club welcomes those who dress to impress; come in sneakers and your night will be over very quickly. A great place to get down with other tourists. Opens Th-Su 11pm until late.

ARAN ISLANDS (OILEÁIN ÁRANN)   ☎099

On the westernmost edge of County Galway, isolated from the mainland by 32km of swelling Atlantic, lie the spectacular Aran Islands (*Oileán Árann*). Their fields are hatched with a maze of limestone, the result of centuries of farmers piling stones into thousands of meters of walls. The tremendous cliff-top forts of the early islanders give the illusion of having sprung from the limestone itself. Of the dozens of ruins, forts, churches, and holy wells that rise from the stony terrain of **Inishmore** (*Inis Mór;* pop. 900), the most amazing is the **Dún Aengus** ring fort, where concentric stones circle a sheer 100m drop. The **Inis Mór Way** is a mostly paved route that passes the majority of the island's sights and is great for biking; pick up a map at the tourist office (€2). Windswept **Inishmaan** (*Inis Meáin;* pop. 300) and **Inisheer** (*Inis Oírr;* pop. 300), the smallest island, also feature paths that pass by the islands' incomparable ruins.

Island Ferries (☎(091) 561 767) go from **Rossaveal,** west of Galway, to Inishmore (2-3 per day) and Inisheer (2 per day). **Queen of Aran II** (☎566 535), based in the islands, also leaves from Rossaveal for Inishmore (4 per day; round-trip €19, student €12). Both companies run **buses** to Rossaveal, which depart from Kinlay House, on Merchant St. in Galway, 1½hr. before ferry departure (€6, students €5). Ferries to Inishmore arrive at **Kilronan.** The **tourist office** stores luggage (€1), changes money, and finds accommodations. (☎61 263. Open July-Sept. daily 10am-6:45pm; Oct. 10am-5pm; Nov.-Mar. 10am-4pm.) ☒**Mainistir House (IHH) ❶,** less than 2km from town on the main road, is a sprawling hostel that was once a haven for musicians and writers. Don't miss the nightly vegetarian buffet (€12), an excellent place to meet other travelers. (☎61 169. Bike rental €10 per day. Laundry €6. Dorms €12; singles €20; doubles €32.) The **Spar Market** in Kilronan functions as an unofficial community center. (Open in summer M-Sa 9am-8pm, Su 10am-6pm; off-season M-Sa 9am-8pm, Su 10am-5pm.)

CONNEMARA

Connemara, a largely Irish-speaking region, is composed of a lacy net of inlets and islands, a gang of inland mountains, and desolate stretches of bog. This thinly populated region of northwest County Galway harbors some of Ireland's most breathtaking scenery, from rocky offshore islands to the green slopes of the area's two major mountain ranges, the **Twelve Bens** and the **Maamturks.**

CLIFDEN (AN CLOCHÁN)   ☎095

Busy, English-speaking Clifden has more amenities than its old-world, Irish-speaking neighbors. Clifden's proximity to the scenic bogs and mountains of Connemara attracts crowds of tourists, who use it as a base for exploring the region. The **Connemara Walking Centre,** on Market St., runs tours of the bogs and explores the history, folklore, and geology of Connemara. (☎21 379. Open Mar.-Oct. M-Sa 10am-6pm. 1-2 tours per day. €19-32.) **Bus Éireann** goes from the library on Market St. to Galway via Oughterard (2hr., 1-6 per day, €9) and Westport via Leenane (1½hr., late June to Aug. M-Sa, 1-3 per day). Michael Nee runs a bus from the courthouse to Galway (June-Sept. 2 per day, €11). Rent a **bike** at **Mannion's,** on Bridge St. (☎21 160. €9 per day, €60 per week; deposit €20. Open Su 10am-1pm and 5-7pm, M-Sa 9:30am-6:30pm.) The **tourist office** is on Galway Rd. (☎21 163. Open July-Aug. M-Sa 9am-6pm, Su noon-4pm; June M-Sa 10am-6pm; Sept.-Oct. and Mar.-May M-Sa 10am-5pm.) **B&Bs** are everywhere and start at €25 per person. **Clifden Town Hostel (IHH) ❶,** on Market St., has great facilities and spotless rooms in a 180-year-old house near the pubs. (☎21 076. Call ahead Nov.-Feb. Dorms €12-15; doubles €32-34; triples €32; quads €56-60.) Tranquil **Shanaheever Campsite ❶** is 1.5km outside Clifden on Westport Rd. (☎21 018. Showers. Laundry €6. €12 per person with tent or trailer.) Most restaurants in Clifden are attached to pubs and serve the standard fare. **Cullen's Bistro & Coffee Shop ❸,** Market St., is a family-run establishment that cooks up hearty meals and delicious desserts. (☎21 983. Thick Irish stew €13. Open daily 11am-10pm.) **O'Connor's SuperValu supermarket** is on Market St. (Open M-F 9am-7pm, Su 10am-6pm.)

CONNEMARA NATIONAL PARK   ☎095

Connemara National Park occupies 12.5 square kilometers of mountainous countryside that thousands of birds call home. Bogs constitute much of the park's terrain, often thinly covered by a deceptive screen of grass and flowers; be prepared to get muddy. The **Snuffaunboy Nature** and **Ellis Wood trails** are easy 20min. hikes. Trails lead from the back of the Ellis Wood trail and along Bog Road onto **Diamond Hill.** Although erosion control efforts have kept Diamond Hill trail closed for the past 2 years, it's worth a call to the Visitors Centre (see below) to check if it's reopened; the 2hr. hike rewards hikers with views of the bog and the harbor. Experienced hikers often head for the **Twelve Bens** (*Na Benna Beola;* the Twelve Pins), a rugged range that reaches 2200m heights. (The range is not recommended for beginning hikers.) A tour of all 12 bens takes experienced hikers about 10hr. **Biking** the 65km circle through Clifden, Letterfrack, and the Inagh Valley is truly captivating, but only appropriate for fit bikers. A guidebook mapping out walks (€6.40) is available at the **Visitors Centre,** where the staff helps plan longer hikes. They'll also explain the differences between hummocks and tussocks. (☎41 054. Open July-Aug. daily 9:30am-6:30pm; June 10am-6:30pm; May and Sept. 10am-5:30pm. €2.50, students €1.25.) Hikers often base themselves at the **Ben Lettery Hostel (An Óige/HI) ❶,** in Ballinafad, 13km east of Clifden. (☎51 136. Dorms €10-12.)

WESTPORT ☎098

Palm trees and steep hills lead down to Westport's busy Georgian streets. Nearby, the conical **Croagh Patrick** rises 650m over Clew Bay. The summit has been revered as a holy site for thousands of years. St. Patrick worked here in AD 441, praying for 40 days and nights to banish snakes from Ireland. Climbers start their excursion from the 15th-century **Murrisk Abbey,** several kilometers west of Westport on R395 toward Louisburgh. Buses go to Murrisk (2-3 per day); for groups, cabs (☎27 171) are cheaper and more convenient. Sheep calmly rule **Clare Island,** a desolate but beautiful speck in the Atlantic. Take a bus to Roonah Pier, 29km from Westport, and then a ferry to the island. (Bus departs from Westport's tourist office at 10am and returns by 6pm; €25 for bus and ferry combined.) **Matt Molloy's,** on Bridge St., is owned by a member of the Irish band the Chieftains and has nightly *trad.* (Open M-W 12:30-11:30pm, Th-Sa 12:30pm-12:30am, Su 12:30-11pm.)

Trains arrive at the Altamont St. Station (☎25 253), a 5min. walk up the North Mall, from Dublin (2-3 per day, €21-23) via Athlone. **Buses** leave Mill St. for Galway (2hr., 4-8 per day, €12). The **tourist office** is on James St. (☎25 711. Open daily 9am-5:45pm.) **B&Bs** cluster on **Altamont Road** and **The Quay.** A conservatory and garden grace ▓**The Granary Hostel ❶,** a 25min. walk from town, just at the bend in The Quay. (☎25 903. Open Apr.-Sept. Dorms €10.) **Altamont House ❶,** Altamont St., has award-winning breakfasts and incredible hospitality that have kept travelers coming back for 36 years. (☎25 226. Singles €25, with bath €27; doubles €50/44.) Restaurants are concentrated on **Bridge Street.** The **SuperValu supermarket** is on Shop St. (Open M-Sa 8:30am-9pm, Su 10am-6pm.)

NORTHWEST IRELAND

The farmland of the upper Shannon stretches northward into County Sligo's mountains, lakes, and ancient monuments. A mere sliver of land connects Co. Sligo to Co. Donegal, the second-largest and most remote of the Republic's counties. Donegal's *gaeltacht* is a storehouse of genuine, unadulterated Irish tradition.

SLIGO ☎071

Since the beginning of the 20th century, Sligo has seen a literary pilgrimage of William Butler Yeats devotees; the poet spent summers in town as a child and set many of his poems around Sligo Bay. **Sligo Town,** the commercial center, is an excellent base from which to explore Yeats's haunts. The well-preserved 13th-century **Sligo Abbey** is on Abbey St. (Open Apr.-Oct. daily 10am-6pm; Nov.-Mar. reduced hours. €1.90, students €0.70.) **The Model Arts Centre and Niland Gallery,** on the Mall, houses one of the finest collections of modern Irish art. (Open June-Oct. Su noon-5:30pm and Tu-Sa 10am-5:30pm; Sept.-Apr. Tu-Sa 10am-5:30pm. Free.) Yeats is buried in **Drumcliffe Churchyard,** on the N15, 6.5km northwest of Sligo. Buses from Sligo to Derry stop at Drumcliffe (10min., 3-7 per day, round-trip €4). Over 70 pubs crowd the main streets of Sligo. The trendy ▓**Shoot the Crows,** on Grattan St., has fairies and skulls dangling from the ceiling.

Trains (☎69 888) go from Lord Edward St. to Dublin (3 hr., 4 per day, €22) via Carrick-on-Shannon and Mullingar. From the same station, **buses** (☎60 066) head to: Belfast (4hr., 2-3 per day, €22); Derry (3hr., 4-7 per day, €15); Dublin (3-4hr., 4-5 per day, €14); Galway (2½hr., 4-6 per day, €12); and Westport (2½hr., 1-4 per day, €13). Turn left on Lord Edward St., then follow the signs right onto Adelaid St. and around the corner to Temple St. to find the **tourist office.** (☎61 201. Open June-Aug. M-Sa 9am-7pm, Su 10am-6pm; Oct.-May M-F 9am-5pm.) **B&Bs** cluster on **Pearse Road,** on the south side. **Eden Hill Holiday Hostel (IHH) ❶,** off Pearse Rd., has Victorian decor and a friendly staff. From the town center, follow Pearse Rd., turn right at the Marymount sign, and take another right after one block. (☎43 204. Laundry facilities. Dorms €13.) A **Tesco supermarket** is on O'Connell St. (☎62 788. Open M-Tu and Sa 8:30am-7pm, W-F 8:30am-9pm, Su 10am-6pm.)

COUNTY DONEGAL AND SLIEVE LEAGUE   ☎073

Tourists are a rarity in County Donegal. Its geographic isolation in the northwest has spared it from the widespread deforestation of the rest of Ireland; vast wooded areas engulf many of Donegal's mountain chains, while the coastline alternates between beaches and cliffs. Travelers use **Donegal Town** as the gateway to the county. **Buses** (☎21 101) stop outside the Abbey Hotel on The Diamond and run to Dublin (4hr., 5-7 per day, €14) and Galway (4hr., 3-4 per day, €14). With your back to the Abbey Hotel, turn right; the **tourist office,** on Quay St., is just outside The Diamond. (☎21 148. Open July-Aug. M-Sa 9am-6pm, Su noon-4pm; Sept.-Oct. and Easter-June M-F 9am-5pm, Sa 10am-2pm.) ▨**Donegal Independent Town Hostel (IHH)** ❶, on Killybegs Rd., is family-run and has a homey atmosphere. (☎(97) 22 805. Call ahead. Dorms €10.50; doubles €24. **Camping** €6.)

The **Slieve League Peninsula**'s rocky cliffs, Europe's highest, jut to the west of Donegal Town. The cliffs and mountains of this sparsely populated area harbor coastal hamlets, untouched beaches, and dramatic scenery. **Glencolmcille** (glen-kaul-um-KEEL), on the western tip of the peninsula, is a parish of several tiny villages wedged between two monstrous cliffs. The villages are renowned for their handmade products, particularly sweaters. On sunny days, visitors to the **Silver Strand** are rewarded with stunning views of the gorgeous beach and rocky cliffs; the trek along the Slieve League coastline begins here. Bus Éireann **buses** run from Donegal Town to Glencolmcille and Dungloe, stopping in tiny **Kilcar** (1-3 per day), the gateway to Donegal's *gaeltacht* and a commercial base for many Donegal tweed weavers. Many Slieve League hikers stay in Kilcar, where they can comfortably drive, bike, or hike to the mountains. The fabulous **Derrylahan Hostel (IHH)** ❶ is 3km from Kilcar on the coast road to Carrick; call for pickup. (☎38 079. Laundry €7. Dorms €10; singles €14; doubles €28. **Camping** €6.) In Glencolmcille, sleep at the hillside ▨**Dooey Hostel (IHO)** ❶, which has an ocean view and a beautiful garden. (☎30 130. Dorms €9.50; doubles €21. **Camping** €5.50.)

LETTERKENNY   ☎074

Letterkenny, although difficult to navigate, is a lively place to make bus connections to the rest of Donegal, the Republic, and Northern Ireland. **Buses** leave from the junction of Port Rd. and Pearse Rd., in front of the shopping center. Bus Éireann (☎912 1309) runs to: Derry (30min., 3-9 per day, €6.50); Dublin (4½hr., 4-6 per day, €15); Galway (4¾hr., 4 per day, €17) via Donegal Town (50min., €7.20); and Sligo (2hr., 4-5 per day, €12). Lough Swilly (☎912 2863) runs to Derry (M-Sa 11 per day, €5.60) and the Inishowen Peninsula (3-4 per day, €5.70). The **Chamber of Commerce Visitors Information Centre** is at 40 Port Rd. (☎24 866. Open M-F 9am-5pm.) **Cove Hill House B&B** ❸, around the corner from the *An Grianan* Theatre, is near the city center and offers numerous amenities. (☎21 038. Singles €25; doubles €50, with bath €56.) There is a **Tesco supermarket** behind the bus station. (Open M-Tu and Sa 8:30am-7pm, W 8:30am-8pm, Th-F 8:30am-9pm, Su noon-6pm.)

NORTHERN IRELAND

Despite its best efforts to present an image of reconciliation and progress in recent years, Northern Ireland still often finds itself associated with the specter of its difficult past. While the aftermath of the Troubles is undeniably visible in much of the North, the sectarian strife that caused it has slowly abated. Today, acts of violence

I R E L A N D

FACTS AND FIGURES: NORTHERN IRELAND

Official Name: Northern Ireland.
Capital: Belfast.
Population: 1,700,000.
Land Area: 14,160 sq. km.

Time Zone: GMT.
Language: English.
Religions: Protestant (40%), Roman Catholic (40%), other (20%).

and extremist fringe groups are less prominent than the division in civil society that sends Protestants and Catholics to separate neighborhoods, separate stores, separate pubs, and often separate schools, with separate, though similar, traditional songs and slang. The 1998 Good Friday Agreement, which granted Home Rule to Northern Ireland with the hope of resolving some of the region's struggles, has been struggling itself. London briefly took the reins again in the summer of 2001, and both sides renewed their efforts to make their country as peaceful as it is beautiful. While everyday life in Northern Ireland may be divided, its landscape and society are for the most part quiet and peaceful.

PHONE CODES	The regional code for all of Northern Ireland is 028. From outside Northern Ireland, dial int'l dialing prefix (see inside back cover) + 44 (from the Republic, 048) + 28 + local number.

BELFAST

☎ 028

Belfast (pop. 330,000), the second-largest city on the island, is the focus of the North's cultural, commercial, and political activity. Acclaimed writers and the annual arts festival in November support Belfast's reputation as a thriving artistic center, with art galleries, coffee shops, and black-clad sub-cultural connoisseurs all contributing to that view. West Belfast's famous sectarian murals are now perhaps the most informative source on the effects of what the locals call the Troubles. Despite the violent associations conjured by the name Belfast, the city feels more neighborly than most international (and even Irish) visitors expect.

⌐ TRANSPORTATION

Flights: Belfast International Airport (BFS; ☎9442 4848; www.belfastairport.com), in Aldergrove. **Airbus** (☎9033 3000) runs from the airport to the Europa and Laganside bus stations (M-Sa every 30min., Su about every hr.; £6). **Trains** connect the **Belfast City Airport** (Sydenham Halt), at the harbor, to Central Station (£1).

Trains: Central Station (☎9066 6630), on East Bridge St., runs trains to: Derry (2hr., 3-9 per day, £8.20) and Dublin (3hr., 5-8 per day, £20). **Centrelink** buses run from the station to the city center (free with rail tickets).

Buses: Europa Station (☎9066 6630), off Great Victoria St., serves the north coast, the west, and the Republic. Buses to Derry (1¾hr., 7-19 per day, £7.50) and Dublin (3hr., 6-7 per day, £12). **Laganside Station** (☎9066 6630), Donegall Quay, serves Northern Ireland's east coast. **Centrelink** buses connect both stations with the city center.

Ferries: SeaCat (☎(08705) 523 523; www.seacat.co.uk) leaves for: Heysham, England (4hr., Apr.-Nov. 1-2 per day); the Isle of Man (2¾hr., Apr.-Nov. M, W, F daily); and Troon, Scotland (2½hr., 2-3 per day). Fares £10-30 without car.

Local Transportation: The red **Citybus Network** (☎9066 6630) is supplemented by **Ulsterbus**'s suburban "blue buses." Travel within the city center £1.10, students and children 55p. **Centrelink** buses traverse the city (every 12min., M-F 7:25am-9:15pm, Sa 8:35am-9:15pm; £1.10, free with bus or rail ticket). Late **Nightlink** buses shuttle to small towns outside the city (F-Sa 1 and 2am; £3, payable on board).

Taxis: **Value Cabs** (☎9080 9080). Residents of West and North Belfast use the huge **black cabs**; some are metered, and some follow set routes.

■↗ ORIENTATION AND PRACTICAL INFORMATION

Buses arrive at the Europa bus station on **Great Victoria Street**. To the northeast is the **City Hall** in **Donegall Square**. South of the Europa bus station, Great Victoria St. meets **Dublin Road** at **Shaftesbury Square**; this stretch of Great Victoria St. between the bus station and Shaftesbury Sq. is known as the **Golden Mile** for its high-brow establishments and Victorian architecture. **Botanic Avenue** and **Bradbury Place** (which becomes **University Road**) extend south from Shaftesbury Sq. into the **Queen's University** area, where cafes, pubs, and budget lodgings await. To get to Donegall Sq. from Central Station, turn left, walk down East Bridge St., turn right on Oxford St., and make the first left on **May Street**, which runs into Donegall Sq.; or, take the Centrelink bus. Divided from the rest of Belfast by the **Westlink Motorway**, working-class **West Belfast** has been more politically volatile; the area is best seen by day. The Protestant neighborhood stretches along **Shankill Road**, just north of the Catholic neighborhood, which is centered around **Falls Road**. The two are separated by the **peace line**. During the week, the area north of City Hall is essentially deserted at night, and it's a good idea to use taxis after dark.

Tourist Office: The Belfast Welcome Centre, 47 Donegall Pl. (☎9024 6609). Has an incredibly helpful and comprehensive free booklet on Belfast and info on surrounding areas. Open June-Sept. M 9:30am-7pm, Tu-Sa 9am-7pm, Su noon-5pm; Oct.-May M 9am-5:30pm, Tu-Sa 9am-7pm.

Banks: Banks and **ATMs** are on almost every corner. **Bank of Ireland**, 54 Donegall Pl. (☎9023 4334). Open M-F 9am-4:30pm.

Laundry: Globe Drycleaners & Launderers, 37-39 Botanic Ave. (☎9024 3956). About £3-4 per load. Open M-F 8am-9pm, Sa-Su noon-6pm.

Emergency: ☎999; no coins required. **Police**, 65 Knock Rd. (☎9065 0222).

Hospitals: Belfast City Hospital, 9 Lisburn Rd. (☎9032 9241). From Shaftesbury Sq., follow Bradbury Pl. and take a right at the fork. **Royal Victoria Hospital**, 12 Grosvenor Rd. (☎9024 0503). From Donegall Sq., take Howard St. west to Grosvenor Rd.

Internet Access: Belfast Central Library, 122 Royal Ave. (☎9050 9150). £1.50 per 30min. Open M and Th 9am-8pm, Tu-W and F 9am-5:30pm, Sa 9:30am-1pm.

Post Office: Central Post Office, 25 Castle Pl. (☎9032 3740). *Poste Restante* mail comes here. Open M-Sa 9am-5:30pm. **Postal Code:** BT1 1NB. **Branch** offices: Botanic Garden, 95 University Rd., across from the university (☎9038 1309; **Postal Code:** BT7 1NG) and Botanic Avenue, 1-5 Botanic Ave. (☎9032 6177; **Postal Code:** BT2 7DA). Branch offices open M-F 8:45am-5:30pm, Sa 10am-12:30pm.

⌂ ACCOMMODATIONS

Despite a competitive hostel market, Belfast's fluctuating tourism and rising rents have shrunk the number of available cheap digs. Most budget accommodations are located near **Queen's University**, south of the city center, which is convenient to pubs and restaurants. Take Citybus #69, 70, 71, 83, 84, or 86 from Donegall Sq. to areas in the south. **B&Bs** occupy virtually every house between **Malone Road** and **Lisburn Road**, just south of Queen's University.

IRELAND

Belfast

⚓ ACCOMMODATIONS

The Ark (IHH), **9**
Arnie's Backpackers (IHH), **11**
Avenue Guest House, **15**
Belfast Hostel (HINI), **4**
Botanic Lodge, **8**
Camera Guest House, **13**
Marine House, **14**
Queen's University
Accommodations, **16**

🍴 FOOD

Azzura, **1**
Benedict's, **5**
Bookfinders, **10**
The Moghul, **6**
The Other Place, **7, 12**
St. George's Market, **3**
Windsor Dairy, **2**

EAST BELFAST

WEST BELFAST

TO A2, HOLYWOOD (10mi),
FOLK AND TRANSPORT
MUSEUM (10mi),
& BELFAST CITY
AIRPORT (2mi)

TO A20,
NEWTOWNARDS,
STORMONT

Maysfield
Leisure
Centre

STENA LINE
TERMINAL (300yds)

Queen's Quay Rd.
Odyssey

RIVER VICTORIA

Lagan Bridge

Dargan Bridge

Seacat
Ferry Terminal

Central
Station

Stewart St.

E. Bridge St.

Waterfront
Hall

Lagan Bank Rd.

Queen Elizabeth
Bridge

Queen's Bridge

Bridge End

Footbridge

Lagan Weir

Donegall Quay

Oxford St.

McAuley St.

Cromac St.

Grace St.

Sinclair
Seamen's
Church

Corporation St.

Tomb St.

Albert St.

Custom
House

Albert
Memorial
Clock

Laganside
Station

Queen's Sq.

Ann St.

Victoria St.

Lagan
Courts

Chichester St.

Royal
Courts

May St.

Hamilton St.

Joy St.

Nelson Rd.

Dunbar Link

Dunbar St.

Gordon St.

Talbot St.

Edward St.

Hill St.

Waring St.

Skipper St.

High St.
Church

Pottinger's
Entry

UK
(Passports)

Victoria Sq.

General
Register
Office

Montgomery St.

Alfred St.

Adelaide St.

Gt. Patrick St.

Frederick St.

York St.

Academy St.

St. Anne's
Cathedral

University
of Ulster

Church St.

Friends
Café

Bridge St.

Rosemary St.

Lombard St.

First Presbyterian
Church

Commarket

Castle Pl.

Castle Ln.

Castle St.

Arthur
St.

Arthur St.

Donegall Sq. E.

Donegall Sq. N.

City
Hall

James St. S.

Craftworks

Linenhall
St.

Ulster
Hall

CARRICK-FERGUS,
ANTRIM COAST RD.

Callender
St.

TO M2,

Donegall St.

Royal Ave.

Royal Ave.

Berry St.

Bank St.

Fountain St.

Donegall Pl.

Donegall Sq. W.

Bedford St.

Clarence St.

Franklin St.

Clifton St.

TO A6, A52,
INTERNATIONAL
AIRPORT
(30mi)

Upper Library St.

Kent St.

North St.

Gresham St.

Library St.

Castlecourt
Shopping
Centre

Chapel Ln.

Queen St.

College St.

Scottish
Provident Inst.

Wellington Pl.

Citybus Kiosk

Wellington St.

Thomas Cooke

Howard St.

Crown
Liquor
Saloon

Belfast
Superbowl

TO M2

Peter's Hill

Samuel St.

West St.

Smithfield
Market

Boyd St.

Marquis St.

Castle St.

College Ct.

College Sq. E.

Old Museum
Arts Centre

Ulster
Historical
Foundation

King St.

Opera
House

Great Victoria St.

Europa
Hotel

Europa
Bus Station

Gardner St.

Brown St.

Millfield

Francis St.

Hamill St.

College Sq. N.

College Sq.

Durham St.

Great
Victoria St.
Rail Station

Westlink

N. Boundary St.

Westlink

TO SHANKILL RD.
(2 blocks)

Divis St.

TO FALLS RD.
(2 blocks)

Grosvenor Rd.

Athol St.

150 yards

150 metres

IRELAND

River Lagan

Ormeau Park

Golf Course

Ormeau Embankment

TO A24, NEWCASTLE (20mi)

Balfour Ave.

Cooke St.

Shaftesbury Ave.

Balfour Ave.

Annadale Embankment

Stranmillis Embankment

Ormeau Rd.

University St.

Fitzroy Ave.

University Ave.

Rugby Ave.

Agincourt Ave.

Lindsay St.

Howard St. S.

Donegall Pass

Elm St.

McClure Street

Vernon Street

Cromwell Rd.

University Ave.

Ormeau Baths Gallery

Ormeau Ave.

Bankmore St.

Maryville St.

Apsley St.

Botanic Rail Station

Globe Drycleaners & Launderers

Wolseley St.

Rugby Rd.

Botanic Gardens

Colenso

UGC Cinemas

Bruce St.

Dublin Rd.

Botanic Ave.

STA Travel

⑥

⑦

⑧

⑨

Queen's Film Theatre

Queen's University

Budget Rent-A-Car

SHAFTESBURY SQ.

Bradbury Pl.

Lower Crescent

Upper Crescent

Mount Charles

University Square

Ulster Museum

Stranmillis Rd.

Avis

Great Victoria St.

Wellwood St.

Albion St.

④

⑤

Crescent Arts Centre

University Rd.

ⓘ Visitors Center

Boyne Bridge

Sandy Row

City Hospital Rail Station

Claremont St.

Camden St.

Fitzwilliam St.

⑪

Malone Rd.

TO LYRIC THEATRE (2mi)

Blythe St.

Donegall Rd.

Lisburn Rd.

Elmwood Ave.

College Gardens

TO ⑯ (5 blocks)

City Hospital ✚

Coolmore St.

Duntice Ave.

Wellesley Ave.

Wellington Park

⑬

Ulsterville Ave.

Lisburn Rd.

⑫

Eglantine Ave.

⑭

⑮

Ashley Ave.

Tate's Ave.

Malone Ave.

TO ROAST COFFEE CO. (2 blocks), A1, & LISBURN

HOSTELS AND UNIVERSITY HOUSING

■ **Arnie's Backpackers (IHH)**, 63 Fitzwilliam St. (☎9024 2867). From Bradbury Pl., turn left onto University Rd.; Fitzwilliam St. is on the right. Friendly atmosphere in the comfort of an antiquated building with a drawing room to match. Luggage storage during the day. Dorms £7-9.50. ❶

Belfast Hostel (HINI), 22 Donegall Rd. (☎9031 5435), off Shaftesbury Sq. Clean and inviting interior is highlighted by colorful rooms and floors. Books tours of Belfast and Giant's Causeway. Breakfast £2. Laundry £3. Reception open 24hr. Dorms £8.50-10.50; singles £17; triples £33. Expect higher prices on the weekend. ❶

The Ark (IHH), 18 University St. (☎9032 9626). Follow Great Victoria St. through Shaftsbury Sq., taking Botanic Ave., and then make a right on University St.; look for the blue grating on the right. The Ark has nice dorm rooms with a bustling, well-stocked kitchen. They also book tours of Belfast (£8) and Giant's Causeway (£16). Weekend luggage storage. Laundry £4. Internet access £1 per 20min. Curfew 2am. Coed dorms £8.50-9.50; doubles £32. ❶

Queen's University Accommodations, 78 Malone Rd. (☎9038 1608). Take bus #71 from Donegall Sq. East. University Rd. runs into Malone Rd.; the residence halls are on your left. Undecorated, institutional dorms provide spacious singles or twin rooms with sinks and desks. Open mid- June to Aug. and Christmas and Easter vacations. Free laundry. Singles £8.50 for UK students, £10 for international students, £12.40 for non-students; doubles £21.40. ❶

BED AND BREAKFASTS

■ **Camera Guesthouse**, 44 Wellington Park (☎9066 0026). A pristine and well-lit family-run guesthouse. The selling point is a fabulous breakfast, with a wide selection of organic options and teas. Singles £25, with bath £40; doubles £48/55. July discounts available. ❸

Botanic Lodge, 87 Botanic Ave. (☎9032 7682). Offers B&B comfort surrounded by many eateries. A short walk to the city center. All rooms with sink and TV, some with bath. Singles £25, with bath £35; doubles £40/45. ❸

Marine House, 30 Elgantine Ave. (☎9066 2828). A mansion with an airy warmth to match its size. Rooms are extremely clean, and come with bath, phone, and TV. Singles £38; doubles £48; triples £66. ❹

Marine House, 30 Elgantine Ave. (☎9068 2814). This comfy roost is especially great for those with cars; secure parking is free. Amazingly hospitable owners and nice amenities round out the deal. Singles £25; doubles £40; triples £55. ❸

Avenue Guest House, 23 Eglantine Ave. (☎9066 5904; fax 9029 1810). Large rooms with excellent beds, a modern decor, and expansive window views. All rooms with bath and TV. Singles £35; doubles £45. ❹

◖ FOOD

Dublin Road, Botanic Avenue, and the **Golden Mile** have a high concentration of restaurants. For dinner in the city center, head to a pub for a cheap meal. If you're in the University area, try one of the many student-filled eateries for a quick fix. Good fruits and vegetables can be had at **St. George's Market,** on East Bridge St., between May St. and Oxford St. (Open F 8am-2pm and Sa 6am-noon.)

■ **Azzura**, 8 Church Ln., has gourmet pizzas, pastas, and sandwiches, with options for both veggie and meat lovers. Chef Sharon often knows what you want to eat before you do. Entrees under £4. Open M-Sa 9am-5pm. ❷

Benedict's, 7-21 Bradbury Pl. (☎9059 1999), is located in a swanky restaurant, but has great meals for reasonable prices. Come between 5:30-7:30pm, and as part of their "Beat the Clock" gimmick the time you order becomes the price you pay. (Open M-Sa 7-10am, noon-2:30pm, and 5:30-10:30pm; Su 5:30-9pm.) ❷

The Moghul, 62A Botanic Ave. (☎9032 6677), overlooking the street from 2nd fl. corner windows. Serves up an outstanding Indian lunch with vegetarian options M-Th noon-2pm (£3), or an all-you-can-eat buffet F noon-2pm (£5). Open for dinner M-W 5-11pm, Th-Sa 5-midnight, Su 5-11pm. ❷

Bookfinders, 47 University Rd. (☎9032 8269). Mismatched dishes mingle with counter-culture paraphernalia bookstore/cafe. Extensive vegetarian and vegan options. Soup and bread £2.80. Sandwiches under £3. Open M-Sa 10am-5:30pm. ❶

Windsor Dairy, 4 College St. (☎9032 7157). This takeaway bakery delights with piles of pastries for 30-50p and daily specials for around £2. Hot food runs out by 3pm, due to hungry locals in the know. Open M-Sa 7:30am-5:30pm. ❶

The Other Place, 79 Botanic Ave. (☎9020 7200), 133 Stranmillis Rd. (☎9020 7100), and 537 Lisburn Rd. (☎9020 7300). Reasonably priced all-day breakfast menu (£3-4) with chalkboard-listed specials. Features huge servings and an array of ethnic foods. Open Su and Tu-Sa 8am-10pm. ❷

🔂 SIGHTS

DONEGALL SQUARE. The most dramatic and impressive piece of architecture in Belfast is appropriately its administrative and geographic center, the **Belfast City Hall.** Neoclassical marble columns and arches figure prominently in A. Brunwell Thomas's 1906 design. Its green copper dome is visible from any point in the city. Check out the forboding **Queen Victoria statue** in front of the main entrance. *(1hr. tour June-Sept. M-F 11am, 2, and 3pm.; Sa 2:30pm; Oct.-May M-F 11am and 2:30pm; Sa 2:30pm. Free.)* The **Linen Hall Library,** 52 Fountain St., contains a comprehensive collection of documents related to the Troubles in Northern Ireland. Note the red hand of Ulster that hangs above its door. *(Open M-F 9:30am-5:30pm, Sa 9:30am-4pm.)*

CORNMARKET AND ST. ANNE'S CATHEDRAL. North of the city center, this shopping district envelops eight blocks around **Castle Street** and **Royal Avenue.** This area, known as Cornmarket after one of its original commodities, has been a marketplace since Belfast's early days. Relics of the old city remain in the **entries,** or tiny alleys. When in Cornmarket, stop by **St. Anne's Cathedral,** also known as the **Belfast Cathedral.** Construction began in 1899, but to keep from disturbing regular worship, it was built around a smaller church already on the site; upon completion of the new exterior, builders extracted the earlier church brick by brick. Each one of the interior pillars of the cathedral names one of Belfast's professions: Agriculture, Art, Freemasonry, Healing, Industry, Music, Science, Shipbuilding, Theology, and "Womanhood." *(Donegall St., near the city center. Open M-Sa 10am-4pm.)*

THE DOCKS AND EAST BELFAST. Although the docks were once the active heart of Belfast, continued commerical development made the area more suitable for industrial machinery than people. However, Belfast's newest mega-attraction, **Odyssey,** 2 Queen's Quay, a gigantic center that houses five different science attractions, promises to bring back the hordes to this previously dilapidated industrial area. The best feature is the **W5 Discovery Centre,** a science and technology museum that beckons geeks of all ages to play with pulley chairs, laser harps, and robots. *(☎9045 1055. Open M-Sa 10am-5pm, Su noon-5pm. £5.50, students and seniors £4.)* For nautical nuts, the **Sinclair Seamen's Church** is sure to please. Here, the minister delivers his sermons from a pulpit carved in the shape of a ship's prow, collections are taken in miniature lifeboats, and an organ with port and starboard lights carries the tune. *(Corporation St. Open W 2-5pm and Su service.)*

THE GOLDEN MILE. This strip along Great Victoria St. contains many of Belfast's jewels. Of these, the **Grand Opera House** is the city's pride and joy, sadly making it a repeated bombing target for the IRA. Recently, it was restored to its original splendor at enormous cost, only to be bombed again. However, more peaceful times have allowed the Grand Opera House to flourish. Enjoy the current calm either by attending a performance or by taking a tour on Saturdays. *(£3, seniors and children £2. Box office open M-Sa 8:30am-6pm. Tours 11am.)* If opera is not your thing, visit the popular **Crown Liquor Saloon,** 46 Great Victoria St., a showcase of carved wood, gilded ceilings, and stained glass recently restored by the National Trust. Finally. check in to the **Europa Hotel,** which has the dubious distinction of being "Europe's most bombed hotel," having survived 32 blasts.

QUEEN'S UNIVERSITY AREA. Charles Lanyon designed the beautiful Tudor-revival brick campus of **Queen's University Belfast** in 1859, modeling it after Magdalen College, Oxford. The Visitor's Centre, in the Lanyon Room to the left of the main entrance, offers Queen's-related exhibits. *(University Rd. Open May-Sept. M-F 10am-4pm, Sa 10am-4pm; Oct.-Mar. M-F 10am-4pm.)* Behind the university, relax in the meticulously groomed **Botanic Gardens,** which offers a welcome respite from the traffic-laden city. Inside the garden lie two 19th-century greenhouses: The toasty **Tropical Ravine House,** and the more temperate Lanyon-designed **Palm House.** *(Open daily 8am-dusk. Tropical House and Palm House open Apr.-Sept. M-F 10am-noon and 1-5pm, Sa-Su 2-5pm; Oct.-Mar. M-F 10am-noon and 1-4pm, Sa-Su 2-4pm. Free.)*

NORTH AND SOUTH BELFAST. Riverside trails, ancient ruins, and idyllic parks south of Belfast make it hard to believe that you're only minutes from the city center. The area can be reached by bus #71 from Donegall Sq. Six kilometers north along the tow path near Shaw's Bridge lies the **Giant's Ring,** an earthen ring with a dolmen in the middle. Scientists estimate that the ring was constructed around 2500 BC. Little is known about the 200m wide circle, but experts speculate that it was built for the same reasons as England's Stonehenge, whatever that reason may be. (Open 24hr. Free.) Like the South, North Belfast is also a pastoral break from the urban grind. **Cave Hill,** long the seat of Ulster rulers, makes for fabulous views. Atop the hill sits **Belfast Castle,** built by the Earl of Shaftsbury in 1934. The castle lacks the history and majesty of its older brethren, but it still offers an amazing view of the Belfast countryside. (Open M-Sa 9am-10:30pm, Su 9am-6pm. Free.)

WEST BELFAST AND THE MURALS. West Belfast is not a "sight" in the traditional sense. The streets display political **murals,** which you will come across quickly as you wander among the houses. Be discreet if photographing the murals. It is illegal to photograph military installations; do so and your film may be confiscated. The Protestant Orangemen's **marching season** (July 4-12) is a risky time to visit the area, since the parades are underscored by mutual antagonism. Cab tours provide a fascinating commentary detailing the murals, paraphernalia, and sights on both sides of the peace line. Michael Johnston of **Black Taxi Tours** has made a name for himself with his witty, objective presentations. (☎0800 052 3914; www.belfasttours.com. £9 per person for groups of 3 or more.)

THE FALLS. On **Divis Street,** a high-rise apartment building marks the site of the **Divis Tower,** an ill-fated housing development built by optimistic social planners in the 1960s. This project soon became an IRA stronghold and saw some of the worst of the Troubles in the 1970s. The British army still occupies the top three floors, and Shankill residents refer to it as "Little Beirut." Continuing west,

Divis St. turns into **Falls Road**. The **Sinn Féin** office is easily spotted: One side of it is covered with an enormous portrait of Bobby Sands and an advertisement for the Sinn Féin newspaper, *An Phoblacht*. Continuing down the Falls there are a number of other murals, generally on side streets and on Beechmont.

SHANKILL. North Street turns into **Shankill Road** as it crosses the **Westlink** and then arrives in Protestant Shankill, once a thriving shopping district. Turning left onto most side roads (coming from the direction of North St.) leads to the **peace line.** The side streets on the right guide you to the **Shankill Estate** and more murals. **Crumlin Road,** through the estate, is the site of the oldest Loyalist murals.

ENTERTAINMENT AND NIGHTLIFE

Belfast's cultural events and performances are covered in the monthly *Arts Council Artslink* (free at the tourist office). The **Grand Opera House,** on Great Victoria St., stages a mix of opera, ballet, musicals, and drama. Buy tickets at the box office, 2-4 Great Victoria St. (☎9024 1919. Tickets from £12.50.) The **Queen's University Festival** (☎9066 7687) in November draws ballet troops, film groups, and opera performances to the city.

PUBS

Pubs were prime targets for sectarian violence at the height of the Troubles. As a result, most of the popular pubs in Belfast are new or restored; those in the city center and university area are quite safe now. Most pubs close early, so start crawling while the sun's still up.

▨ **White's Tavern,** Winecellar Entry, off High St. White's is Belfast's oldest tavern, serving drinks since 1630. W gay-friendly night (£5 after 10pm). Live *trad* music Th-Sa. Open M-Sa 11:30am-11pm.

Katy Daly's Pub, 17 Ormeau Ave., north of Donegall Sq. High-ceilinged, wood-paneled, antique pub with a young crowd. Catch the local bands that frequent it Tu-Th and Sa.

Apartment, 2 Donegall Sq. West, where Belfast's beautiful people come for pre-clubbing cocktails. Spacious, modern layout offers a cafe bar and bistro downstairs and an upscale lounge upstairs. Arrive before 9:30pm on weekends and dress smart. 21+ after 6pm. Open M-F 8am-1am, Sa 9am-1am, Su noon-midnight.

The Botanic Inn, 23 Malone Rd. "The Bot" is an incredibly popular student bar, packed nightly from wall-to-wall. This huge pub is almost an official extracurricular for many students who attend nightly. Get the original "meal deal," a entree with a pint for under £5 (3-8pm). 20+. Cover £2. Open daily 11:30am-1am.

The Duke of York, 7-11 Commercial Ctr. An old boxing venue turned Communist printing press, the building was rebuilt after being bombed by the IRA in the 1960s. The Duke of York is now home to the largest selection of Irish whiskeys in town. 18+. Open M noon-9pm, Tu noon-1am, W noon-midnight, Th-F noon-2am, Sa noon-3am.

CLUBS

When the pubs close, the clubs come alive. Ask the staff at the Queen's University Student Union for info about the latest hot nightspots. You can also consult *The List*, available in the tourist office and hostels.

Milk Club Bar, 10-14 Tomb St. This up-and-coming club indulges in the best kind of fun possible: The slightly cheesy variety. Let loose to pop and club hits on the dance floor, or have a drink at the illuminated bar. (Open daily noon-3am.)

IRELAND

The Fly, 5-6 Lower Crescent. Popular with a young set of partiers and socialites. Check out the fun vodka lounge on the 3rd floor that serves some 60 flavors. Then head to the 1st floor for pint chasers or to the 2nd floor for mingling and dancing. (Open M-Th 9pm-1:30am, F-Sa 9pm-1:45am.)

The Kremlin, 96 Donegall St., is Belfast's hottest gay spot. Free Internet upstairs is upstaged by free condoms downstairs. Theme nights run from foam parties to drag shows. (Bar open M-Th 4pm-3am, F-Su 1pm-3am.)

The Limelight, 17 Ormeau Ave., next door to Katy Daly's Pub. This dark and smokey nightclub is a strong draw for young faces. Tu student night, F Disco night, Sa alternative music night. Cover £2-5. Open 10pm-2am.

DERRY (LONDONDERRY) ☎028

Modern Derry is in the middle of a determined and largely successful effort to cast off the legacy of its political Troubles. Although the landscape was razed by years of bombings and violence still erupts occasionally during the marching season (July 4-12), recent years have been relatively peaceful, and today's rebuilt city looks sparklingly new. Derry's **city walls,** 5.5m high and 6m thick, erected between 1614 and 1619, have never been breached—hence Derry's nickname "the Maiden City." The raised portion of the wall past New Gate was built to protect **St. Columb's Cathedral,** off Bishop St., the symbolic focus of the city's Protestant defenders. (Open Easter-Oct. M-Sa 9am-5pm; Nov.-Mar. M-Sa 9am-4pm. Suggested donation £1.) At Union Hall Place, just inside Magazine Gate, the **Tower Museum**'s engaging exhibits recount Derry's history. (Open July-Aug. M-Sa 10am-5pm, Su 2-5pm; Sept.-June Tu-Sa 10am-5pm. £4.20, students £1.60.) West of the city walls, Derry's residential neighborhoods—both the Protestant **Waterside** and **Fountain Estate** as well as the Catholic **Bogside**—display brilliant murals. After dark, check out ▨**Mullan's,** 13 Little James St., an incredible pub with stained-glass ceilings and bronze lion statues. (Open M-Sa 10am-2am, Su noon-12:30am.)

Trains (☎7134 2228) arrive on Duke St., Waterside, from Belfast (2½hr., 4-9 per day, £8.20). A free Rail-Link bus connects the **train station** and the **bus station,** on Foyle St., between the walled city and the river. **Ulsterbus** (☎7126 2261) goes to Belfast (1½-3hr., 6-16 per day, £8) and Dublin (4¼hr., 4-6 per day, £11). The **tourist office** is at 44 Foyle St. (☎7126 7284. Open July-Sept. M-F 9am-7pm, Sa 10am-6pm, Su 10am-5pm; Nov.-Easter M-F 9am-5pm; Easter-June and Oct. M-F 9am-5pm, Sa 10am-5pm.) Go down Strand Rd. and turn left on Asylum Rd. just before the RUC station to reach the friendly ▨**Derry City Independent Hostel ❶,** 4 Asylum Rd. (☎7137 7989. Breakfast included. Free **Internet.** Dorms £9; singles £13; doubles £26.) At **The Saddler's House (No. 36) ❸,** 36 Great James St., the friendly owners welcome you into their lovely Victorian home, where great breakfasts can be found. (☎7126 9691. Singles £25; doubles £45.) There is a **Tesco supermarket** in the Quayside Shopping Centre, just a short walk from the walled city along Strand Rd. (Open M-Th 9am-9pm, F 8:30am-9pm, Sa 8:30am-8pm, Su 1-6pm.) **Postal Code:** BT48.

GLENS OF ANTRIM ☎028

Glaciers left nine deep scars in the mountainous coastline of northeastern County Antrim. Over the years, water collected in these glens, fostering lush flora not usually found in Ireland. The glens and their mountains and waterfalls are best visited as daytrips from the villages of Glenarm and Cushendall.

◰ TRANSPORTATION. Ulsterbus (☎9032 0011) #162 runs from Belfast to Glenarm (1-7 per day, £3-6) and sometimes continues to Waterfoot, Cushendall, and Cushendun (2-4 per day). Bus #150 runs from Ballymena to Glenariff (M-Sa 5 per day, £2.60), then to Waterfoot, Cushendall, and Cushendun (3-5 per day, £4.30).

GLENARM. Lovely Glenarm was once the chief dwelling place of the MacDonnell Clan. The village is comprised of centuries-old houses and is a starting point for several short walks. The huge arch at the top of Altmore St. marks the entrance to **Glenarm Forest,** where trails trace the river's path. (Open daily 9am-dusk.) The **tourist office** is in the town council building. (☎2884 1087. **Internet** £4 per hr. Open M 10am-4pm, Tu-F noon-7pm, Su 2-6pm.) **Riverside B&B ❷,** Toberwine St., has quaint rooms with lovely baths. (☎2884 1474. £18 per person.)

GLENARIFF. Antrim's broadest (and arguably most beautiful) glen, Glenariff lies 6.5km south of Waterfoot along Glenariff Rd., in the large **Glenariff Forest Park.** Bus #150 stops at the park entrance (3-5 per day); if you're walking from Waterfoot, you can enter the park 2.5km downhill of the entrance by taking the road that branches left toward the Manor Lodge Restaurant. The stunning 5km ▨**Waterfall Trail** follows the fern-lined Glenariff River from the park entrance to the Manor Lodge. (☎2175 8769. Open daily 10am-dusk. £1.50 per pedestrian, £3 per car.)

CUSHENDALL. Cushendall, nicknamed the capital of the Glens, houses a variety of goods, services, and pubs unavailable elsewhere in the region. The **tourist office,** 25 Mill St., is near the bus stop at the northern end of town. (☎2177 1180. Open July-Sept. M-F 10am-5:30pm, Sa 10am-4:30pm; Oct. to mid-Dec. and Feb.-June Tu-Sa 10am-1pm.) A warm welcome and huge rooms await at ▨**Glendale ❷,** 46 Coast Rd., south of town overlooking the sea. (☎2177 1495. £18 per person.)

CUSHENDUN. This minuscule, picturesque seaside village is 8km north of Cushendall on A2. Its white-washed and black-shuttered buildings sit next to a vast beach with wonderful, murky **caves** carved within red sea cliffs. Visitors can choose between the immaculate **B&B ❸** and **camping barn ❶** at **Drumkeerin,** just west of town on the A2 at 201a Torr Rd. (☎2176 1554. B&B singles £20; doubles £35. Camping barn £8.) **Mary McBride's ❶,** 2 Main St., used to hold the *Guinness Book of World Records* title "smallest bar in Europe"—until it expanded. (☎2176 1511. Steak-and-Guinness pie £5. Food served daily noon-9pm.)

CAUSEWAY COAST ☎028

Past Cushendun, the northern coast becomes even more dramatic. Sea-battered cliffs tower 185m over white beaches before giving way to the spectacular geology of **Giant's Causeway,** for which the region is named. Thousands of visitors swarm to the site today, but few venture beyond the visitors center to the stunning and easily accessible coastline that stretches beyond.

▣ **TRANSPORTATION. Ulsterbus** (☎7043 334) #172 runs between Ballycastle and Portrush along the coast (1hr., 3-7 per day, £3.50). The Antrim Coaster #252 runs from Belfast to Portstewart via most small towns along the coast (2 per day). The open-topped Bushmills Bus traces the coast between Coleraine, 8km south of Portrush, and the Causeway (July-Aug. 7 per day).

BALLYCASTLE AND ENVIRONS. The Causeway Coast leaves the sleepy glens behind when it hits **Ballycastle,** a bubbly seaside town that shelters tourists bound for Giant's Causeway. **Ulsterbus** #162A goes to Cushendall via Cushendun (50min., M-F daily, £3), and #131 goes to Belfast (3hr., M-Sa 5-6 per day, £6.10). The **tourist office** is in Sheskburn House, 7 Mary St. (☎2076 2024. Open July-Aug. M-F 9:30am-7pm, Sa 10am-6pm, Su 2-6pm; Sept.-June M-F 9:30am-5pm.) Sleep at the friendly and comfortable **Castle Hostel (IHH) ❶,** 62 Quay Rd. (☎2076 2337. Dorms £7.50.)

Just off the coast of Ballycastle, bumpy, boomerang-shaped **Rathlin Island** ("Fort of the Sea") is home to more puffins (pop. 20,000) than people (pop. 100). A **minibus** drives to the **Kebble Bird Sanctuary,** 7km from the harbor

(20min., every 45min., ₤2.80). Caledonian MacBrayne (☎2076 9299) **ferries** run to the island from the pier at Ballycastle, up the hill from Quay Rd. (45min., 1-3 per day, round-trip ₤8.40).

Eight kilometers west of Ballycastle, the modest village of **Ballintoy** attracts the crowds on their way to the tiny **Carrick-a-rede Island.** From the mainland, cross the fishermen's rope bridge (about 2m wide) over the dizzying 30m drop to rocks and sea below; be extremely careful in windy weather. A sign marks the turn-off for the bridge from the coastal road east of Ballintoy. The island's **Larrybane sea cliffs** are home to a variety of species of gulls. The **Sheep Island View Hostel (IHH)** ❶ is at 42A Main St. in Ballintoy. (☎2076 9391. Continental breakfast ₤3. Laundry ₤2. Dorms ₤10. **Camping** ₤5 per person.)

GIANT'S CAUSEWAY. Geologists believe that the unique rock formations found at ◪**Giant's Causeway** were formed some 60 million years ago. Comprised of over 40,000 perfectly symmetrical hexagonal basalt columns, the site resembles a large descending staircase that leads out from the cliffs to the ocean's floor below. Ulsterbuses #172 to Portrush, the #252 Antrim Coaster, and the Bushmills Bus all drop off visitors at the **Giant's Causeway Visitors Centre.** A minibus (₤1.20) runs from the center to the columns. (Causeway open 24hr. Free. Visitors Centre open July-Aug. daily 10am-7pm; June 10am-6pm; Sept.-Oct. 10am-5pm; Nov.-Feb. 10am-4:30pm; Mar-Apr. M-F 10am-5pm, Sa-Su 10am-5:30pm; May daily 10am-5:30pm.)

ITALY (ITALIA)

One of the few countries whose very geography seems active—it resembles a boot poised to kick Sicily clear across the Mediterranean—Italy has never been inclined to sit back quietly. After bursting onstage as the base for the ambitious Roman empire, it became persecutor and popularizer of an upstart religion called Christianity and later served as center to the artistic and philosophical Renaissance. Today it has emerged as a world power that has changed governments more than 50 times since World War II. Countless invasions have left the land rich with examples of nearly every artistic era; Egyptian obelisks, Etruscan huts, Greek temples, Augustan arches, Byzantine mosaics, Renaissance *palazzi*, Baroque fountains, and postmodern superstructures sprawl across its 20 regions. From perfect pasta to the creation of pizza, Italy knows that the quickest way to a country's happiness is through its stomach. Italy is also the champion of romance—passionate lovers shout their *amore* from the rooftops of southern Italy and Venice. Somewhere between the leisurely gondola rides and the frenetic nightclubs, you too will fall in love with Italy.

LIFE AND TIMES

HISTORY

BEFORE YOU WERE BORN. Although archaeological excavations at Isernia date the earliest inhabitants of Italy to the Paleolithic Era (100,000-70,000 BC), things didn't get swinging until around 1200 BC, when legendary **Aeneas** led his tribe from the ruins of Troy to the Tiber valley, settling down to rule the city of Alba Longa. In 753 BC, two of Aeneas's "descendants," the fratricidal twins **Romulus** and **Remus,** founded Rome. Tyranny ruled for centuries until Lucius Brutus expelled the Tar-

SUGGESTED ITINERARIES

THREE DAYS. Spend it all in the Eternal City of **Rome** (p. 626). Go back in time at the **Ancient City:** be a gladiator in the **Colosseum,** explore the **Roman Forum** and stand in the well-preserved **Pantheon.** Spend the next day admiring the fine art in the **Capitoline Museums** and the **Galleria Borghese,** then satiate your other senses in a disco. Redeem your debauched soul in **Vatican City,** gazing at the ceiling of the **Sistine Chapel,** gaping at **St. Peter's Cathedral** and enjoying the **Vatican Museums.**

ONE WEEK Spend 3 days taking in the sights in **Rome** before heading north to **Florence** (2 days; p. 710) to immerse yourself in Italy's amazing Renaissance art at the Uffizi Gallery. Move to **Venice** (2 days; p. 686) to float through the canals and explore the lagoon islands.

BEST OF ITALY IN 3 WEEKS Begin in **Rome** (3 days), Cheer on horses in **Siena** (1 day; p. 725) then move to **Florence** (3 days). Move up the coast to **Finale Ligure** (1 day; p. 676), and the beautiful **Cinque Terre** (2 days; p. 678). Head to cosmopolitan **Milan** (2 days; p. 662) and visit **Lake Como** for hiking (1 day; p. 672). Find your Romeo or Juliet in **Verona** (1 day; p. 706). Spend time in **Venice** (2 days) before flying south to **Naples** (2 days; p. 731); be sure to visit preserved, ancient **Pompeii** (1 day; p. 738). Then hike and swim along the **Amalfi Coast** (1 day; p. 740), and see the Grotto Azzura on the island of **Capri** (1 day; p. 741).

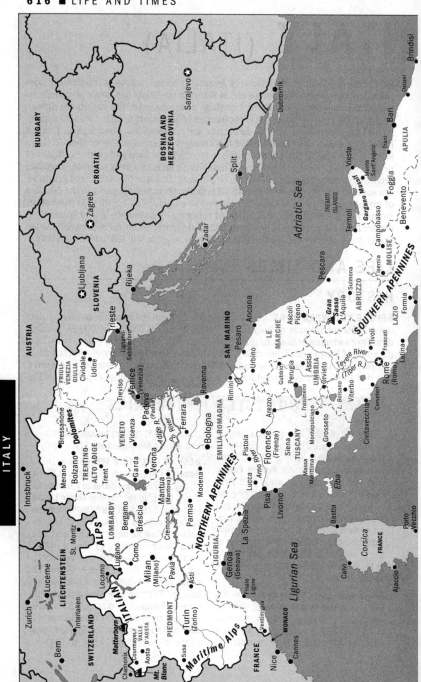

Italy

Leece
Otranto
Gulf of Taranto
Metaponto
Taranto
Matera
Trebisacce
Rossano
Crotone
Potenza
BASILICATA
CALABRIA
Cosenza
Catanzaro
CAMPANIA
Salerno
Paola
Monasterace
Sorrento
Pompeii
Capo Vaticano
Reggio di Calabria
Naples (Napoli)
Capri
Ischia
Gaeta
Taormina
Messina
Catania
Ionian Sea
AEOLIAN (LIPARI) ISLANDS
Cefalù
Mt. Etna▲
PONTINE ISLANDS
Ustica
Palermo
Enna
SICILY
Siracusa
Ragusa
Gela
MALTA
Capo San Vito
Trapani
Agrigento
Marsala
Pantelleria
EGADI ISLANDS

Tyrrhenian Sea
(Mare Tirreno)

Mediterranean Sea
(Mare Mediterraneo)

Costa Smeralda
S. Teresa Gallura
Olbia
Porto Torres
Nuoro
Sassari
Arbatax
Alghero
Oristano
SARDINIA
Cagliari

Tunis
Carthage
TUNISIA
Annaba
ALGERIA

100 miles
100 kilometers

ITALY

quins and established the **Republic** in 509 BC. A string of military victories brought near total unification of the Italian peninsula in 396 BC, and victory in the later **Punic Wars** spread the *Pax Romana* (Roman peace) throughout the Mediterranean. Internal conflict set the stage for **Julius Caesar** to name himself dictator, which lasted all of a year before his assassination on the Ides (15th) of March, 44 BC. Power eluded many would-be successors, like Brutus and Mark Antony. In 31 BC, Octavian, Caesar's adopted heir, a cold and calculating politician, emerged victorious, and had assumed the title of **Augustus** by 27 BC. The Empire made a hobby of Christian persecution until Constantine's **Edict of Milan** declared Christianity the state religion in AD 313. The fall finally came in 476, ushering in the **Dark Ages** while the East continued to thrive as the **Byzantine Empire.**

DEATH AND RESURRECTION. The **Black Death** and the struggle between monarchs and the Papacy dominated the period aptly called the Dark Ages. The fall of Rome had taken its toll on the region, but the 14th century saw a cultural revival unlike any before or since. Fueled by the rediscovery of Greek and Latin texts, the **Renaissance** exposed Italians to the Classical conception of education (rhetoric, grammar, and logic) as the monopoly on knowledge held by the medieval church gradually eroded. Those who had survived the Black Death found themselves in a seller's market and profited from the labor shortage, producing the first merchant middle class. The exalted **Medici family** in Florence rose from obscurity, boasting a pope, a couple of cardinals, and a queen or two. Power in Florence was consolidated under Cosimo and Lorenzo (il Magnifico), who broadened the family's activities from banking and warring to the patronization of the arts. They engaged in a high-stakes battle with Pope Julius II to bring **Michelangelo** to Florence, and would have won if it weren't for that little matter of the Sistine Chapel.

TO THE VICTOR GO THE SPOILS. The 16th to 18th centuries were Italy's punishment for enjoying herself too much during the Renaissance. Weakened by internal conflict, Italy fell to Spanish conquerors. The **Spanish Inquisition** sought to suppress the Protestant Reformation and stamp out all the independent thinkers that the humanist movement had created a century before. In the course of **Napoleon**'s 19th-century march through Europe, the diminutive French Emperor united much of northern Italy into the Italian Republic, conquered Naples, and fostered national sovereignty. In 1804, Napoleon declared himself the monarch of the newly united Kingdom of Italy. After Napoleon's fall in 1815, the **Congress of Vienna** carved up Italy, ceding control to Austria.

TOGETHER AGAIN. Reaction against the arbitrary divisions of Italy culminated in the nationalist **Risorgimento,** a unification movement in 1870. This bit of history is something visitors to Italy cannot afford to ignore; the three primary leaders in the movement, **Giuseppe Mazzini, Giuseppe Garibaldi,** and **Camillo Cavour,** have a namesake boulevard in nearly every city. Once the elation of unification wore off, however, age-old provincial differences reasserted themselves. The North wanted to protect its money from the needs of the agrarian South, and cities were wary of surrendering power to a central administration. The Pope, who had lost power to the kingdom, threatened Catholics who participated in politics with excommunication. Disillusionment increased as Italy became involved in **World War I,** paving the way for the rise of Fascism under the control of **Benito Mussolini,** "Il Duce," who promised order and stability for the young nation. Mussolini established the world's first Fascist regime in 1924 and expelled all opposition parties. As Mussolini initiated domestic development programs and aggressive foreign policy, support for the Fascist leader ran from intense loyalty to increasing discontent. In 1940, Italy entered **World War II** on the side of its Axis ally, Germany. Success came quickly but was short-lived; the Allies landed in Sicily in 1943, prompting Mussolini's fall from power. As a final indignity, he and his mistress were captured and executed by infuriated citizens, their naked bodies left hanging upside down in the public square. By the end of 1943, Italy had formally withdrawn its support from Germany. The Nazis responded by promptly invading their former ally. In 1945, Italy was freed from German domination, and the country was divided between those supporting the monarchy and those favoring a return to Fascism.

POST-WAR POLITICS AND RECOVERY. The end of WWII did little but highlight the intense factionalism of the Italian peninsula. The **Constitution,** adopted in 1948, established the **Republic,** with a caesar, an augustus, and a committee of warring landlords—or, a president, a prime minister (the chief officer), a bicameral parliament, and an independent judiciary. The **Christian Democratic Party** (DC), bolstered by Marshall Plan money and American military aid (as well as rumored Mafia collusion), soon overtook the **Socialist Party** (PSI) as the primary player in the government of the new Republic, as prominent members of the PSI were found to be sleeping with the fishes. Over 300 parties fought for supremacy; none could claim a majority, so they formed tenuous party coalitions. Italy has changed governments 58 times since WWII, none of which has lasted longer than four years.

Italian economic recovery began with 1950s industrialization—skylines of northern cities were quickly dotted with Fiat and Lamborghini billboards and factory smokestacks, along with old cathedral spires and large glowing crucifixes. Despite the **Southern Development Fund,** which was established to build roads, construct schools, and finance industries, the South has lagged behind. Italy's economic inequality has contributed to much of the regional strife that persists today.

Economic success gave way to late-1960s unrest. The *autunno caldo* (hot autumn) of 1969, a season of strikes, demonstrations, and riots (mainly by university students and factory workers) foreshadowed 1970s violence. Perhaps the most shocking episode was the 1978 kidnapping and murder of ex-Prime Minister **Aldo Moro** by a group of left-wing militant terrorists, the *Brigate Rosse* (Red Brigade). Some positive reforms, however, accompanied the horror of the 1970s: divorce was legalized and rights for women expanded. The events of the 1970s had challenged the conservative Social Democrats, however, and **Bettino Craxi** became Italy's first Socialist premier in 1983.

CORRUPTION AND REFORM. It's no secret that Italian government officials have never been adverse to a little grease on their palms. Yet **Oscar Luigi Scalfaro,** elected in 1992, only realized the extent of this when he noticed that his secretary owned a Mercedes and wore a €20,000 diamond-studded Cartier watch. Shortly thereafter, in the *mani pulite* (clean hands) campaign, Scalfaro and **Judge Antonio di Pietro** managed to uncover the **"Tangentopoli"** (Kickback City) scandal. This unprecedented political crisis implicated over 2600 politicians and businessmen in corruption charges. Reactions to the investigation have included the May 1993 bombing of the Uffizi (Florence's premier art museum), the "suicides" of 10 indicted officials, and the murders of anti-Mafia judges and investigators. The elections of 1996 brought the center-left coalition, the **Olive Tree** (l'Ulivo), to power, with **Romano Prodi,** a Bolognese professor, economist, and non-politician, as Prime Minister. Prodi helped stabilize Italian politics. For the first time in modern history, Italy was dominated by two stable coalitions: the center-left l'Ulivo and the center-right **Il Polo.** Despite high hopes, his coalition lost a vote of confidence in October 1998; by the end of the month, his government collapsed, and former Communist **Massimo D'Alema** was sworn in as prime minister. D'Alema and Carlo Ciampi created fiscal reforms and pushed a "blood and tears" budget that qualified Italy for entrance into the European Monetary Union (EMU) in January 1999.

ITALY

TODAY

Italy's tendency toward partisan schisms and quick government turn-over may have been tempered, momentarily at least, by its faith in one individual: **Silvio Berlusconi.** The allure and nonstop drive of Italy's richest man secured his re-election as prime minister in May 2001. Downplaying corruption charges, he won 30% of the popular vote to head Italy's 59th government since WWII with his Forza Italia party. Berlusconi has reaffirmed his commitment to the US, courting President George W. Bush in several meetings and sending 2700 troops to Operation Iraqi Freedom in 2003. In European foreign policy, Berlusconi has focused more on domestic than on integration issues, creating some tension. As his reforms aim to energize the lagging Italian economy, new scandals mar his tenure. He has proposed bills in favor of laxer corruption laws—presenting a clear conflict of interest. Berlusconi breezed through municipal elections in May 2003, as Italy prepared to head the European Union for six months, starting in July.

THE ARTS

LITERATURE

Virgil wrote and wrote but never finished the epic *Aeneid*, about the godly origins of Rome. **Horace**'s (65-8 BC) texts gave a powerful voice to his personal experiences. It is primarily through **Ovid**'s various works that we learn the gory details of Roman mythology: Usually disguised as animals or humans, these gods and goddesses often descended to earth to intervene in human affairs. The Dark Ages put a stop to most literary musings, but three Tuscan writers reasserted the art in the late 13th century. **Dante Alighieri** was one of the first Italian poets to write in the *volgare* (common Italian) instead of Latin. In his infamous epic poem, *The Divine Comedy* (1308-1321), Dante explores the various fires of the afterlife. **Petrarch** restored the popularity of ancient Roman writers by writing love sonnets to a married woman, compiled in *Songbook* (1350). **Giovanni Boccaccio**, a close friend of Petrarch's, composed a collection of 100 bawdy stories in *The Decameron* (1348-1353). Paralleling the scientific exploration of the time, 15th- and 16th-century Italian authors explored new dimensions of the human experience. **Alberti** and **Palladio** wrote treatises on architecture and art theory. **Baldassare Castiglione**'s *The Courtier* (1528) instructed the fastidious Renaissance man on deportment, etiquette, and other fine points of behavior. **Niccolò Machiavelli**'s *The Prince* (1513) gives a timeless, sophisticated assessment of seizing and maintaining political power. The 1800s were an era primarily of *racconti* (short stories) and poetry. **Pellegrino Artusi**'s 1891 cookbook *Science in the Kitchen and the Art of Eating Well* was the first attempt to assemble recipes from regional traditions into a unified Italian cuisine. The 20th century saw a new tradition in Italian literature as Nobel Prize-winning author and playwright **Luigi Pirandello** explored the relativity of truth in works like *Six Characters in Search of an Author* (1921). Literary production slowed in the years preceding WWII, but its conclusion ignited an explosion in antifascist fiction. **Primo Levi** wrote *If This Is a Man* (1947) about his experiences in Auschwitz. Mid-20th-century poets include Nobel Prize winners **Salvatore Quasimodo** and **Eugenio Montale,** who founded the "hermetic movement," characterized by an intimate poetic vision and allusive imagery. More recently, internationally known playwright and satirist **Dario Fo** claimed the 1997 Nobel Prize for literature.

MUSIC

A medieval Italian monk, **Guido d'Arezzo,** is regarded as the originator of musical notation. Religious strains held the day until the 16th century ushered in a new musical extravaganza: **Opera.** Italy's most cherished art form was born in Florence, nurtured in Venice, and revered in Milan. Conceived by the **Camerata,** a circle of Florentine writers, noblemen, and musicians, opera originated as an attempt to recreate ancient Greek drama by setting lengthy poems to music. **Jacobo Peri** composed *Dafne,* the world's first complete opera, in 1597. The first successful opera composer, **Claudio Monteverdi,** drew freely from history, juxtaposing high drama, love scenes, and bawdy humor. **Baroque** music, known for its literal and figurative hot air, took the 17th and 18th centuries by storm. During this period, two main instruments saw their popularity take off: The violin, the shape of which was perfected by Cremona families, including the **Stradivari,** and the piano, created in about 1709 by members of the Florentine **Cristofori** family. **Antonio Vivaldi,** who composed over 400 concertos, triumphed with *The Four Seasons* (1725). With convoluted plots and strong, dramatic music, 19th-century Italian opera continues to dominate modern stages. **Gioacchino Rossini** was the master of the *bel canto* (beautiful song), which consists of long, fluid, melodic lines. **Giuseppe Verdi** remains the transcendent musical and operatic figure of 19th-century Italy. Verdi produced the touching, personal dramas and memorable melodies of *Rigoletto* (1851), *La Traviata* (1853), and *Il Trovatore* (1853) and the grand and heroic conflicts of *Aida* (1871). At the turn of the century, **Giacomo Puccini** created *Madame Butterfly* (1904), *La Bohème* (1896), and *Tosca* (1900).

THE VISUAL ARTS

ARCHITECTURE. The Greeks peppered southern Italy with a large number of **temples** and **theaters.** The best-preserved Greek temples in the world today are found not in Greece, but in Sicily. Most Roman houses incorporated **frescoes,** Greek-influenced paintings on plaster. **Mosaic** was another popular medium. The arch, along with the invention of **concrete,** revolutionized the Roman conception of architecture and made possible such monuments as the **Colosseum** (p. 646) and the **Pantheon** (p. 647), as well as public works like **aqueducts** and **thermal baths.** For fear of persecution, early Christians fled underground to worship; their **catacombs** (p. 651) are now among the most haunting and intriguing of Italian monuments. In the Renaissance, **Filippo Brunelleschi** revolutionized architecture. His mathematical studies of ancient Roman architecture became the cornerstone of all later Renaissance building.

FILM. In the early 20th century, Mussolini created the *Centro Sperimentale della Cinematografia,* a national film school that stifled any true artistic development. The fall of Fascism allowed the explosion of **Neorealist cinema** (1943-1950), which rejected contrived sets and professional actors and sought to produce a candid look at post-war Italy. This new style caught the world's attention and Rome soon became a hotspot for the international jet set. On the heels of these celebrities also came a certain set of photographic stalkers called **paparazzi.** The works of **Roberto Rossellini** and **Vittorio de Sica** best represent *Neorealismo,* with de Sica's 1945 film *The Bicycle Thief* as perhaps the most famous and successful Neorealist film. In the 1960s, post-Neorealist directors like **Federico Fellini** rejected plots and characters for a visual and symbolic world. Fellini's *La Dolce Vita* (*The Sweet Life,* 1960), which was banned by the Pope, is an incisive film scrutinizing 1950s Rome. In a similar

ITALY

vein, **Pier Paolo Pasolini** explored Italy's infamous underworld in films like *Accatone* (*The Beggar*, 1961). Although Italian cinema has fallen into a recent slump, **Bernardo Bertolucci**'s *The Last Emperor* (1987) and Oscar-winners **Giuseppe Tornatore** and **Gabriele Salvatore** have garnered the attention of US and international audiences. Enthusiastic sparkplug **Roberto Benigni** became one of Italy's leading cinematic personalities when his *La Vita e Bella* (*Life is Beautiful*) gained international fame, receiving Best Actor and Best Foreign Film Oscars and a Best Picture Oscar nomination at the 1999 Academy Awards.

ON THE CANVAS. In sculpture, **Donatello** built upon the realistic articulation of the human body in motion. The torch was passed to three exceptional men: Leonardo da Vinci, Michelangelo Buonarroti, and Raphael Santi. **Leonardo da Vinci** was not only an artist but a scientist, architect, engineer, musician, and weapon designer. **Michelangelo** created the illusion of vaults on the flat ceiling of the **Sistine Chapel** (1473-1481), which remains his greatest surviving achievement in painting. Sculpture, however, was his favorite mode of expression, the most classic example being *David* (1501-1504). **Raphael** created technically perfect figures in his paintings. The Italians started to lose their artistic dexterity in the 18th and 19th centuries. **Antonio Canova** explored the formal **Neoclassical** style, which professed a return to the rules of Classical antiquity, while the **Macchiaioli** group, spearheaded by **Giovanni Fattori,** revolted with a unique technique of "blotting." The Italian **Futurist** artists of the 1910s used machines to bring Italy back to the cutting edge of artistry. **Amadeo Modigliani** crafted figures famous for their long oval faces.

FACTS AND FIGURES

Official Name: Italian Republic.

Capital: Rome.

Major Cities: Florence, Milan, Naples, Venice.

Population: 57,000,000

Land Area: 301,230 sq. km.

Time Zone: GMT+1.

Language: Italian; some German, French and Slovenian.

Religions: Roman Catholic (98%).

ESSENTIALS

WHEN TO GO

Traveling to Italy in late May or early September, when the temperature drops to a comfortable 77°F (25°C), will assure a calmer and cooler vacation. Also keep weather patterns, festival schedules, and tourist congestion in mind. Tourism enters overdrive in June, July, and August: Hotels are booked solid, with prices limited only by the stratosphere. During *Ferragosto*, a national holiday in August, all Italians take their vacations and flock to the coast like well-dressed lemmings; northern cities become ghost towns or tourist-infested infernos. Though many visitors find the larger cities enjoyable even during the holiday, most agree that June and July are better months for a trip to Italy.

DOCUMENTS AND FORMALITIES

VISAS. Citizens of Australia, Canada, the EU, New Zealand, South Africa, and the US do not need a visa for stays of up to 90 days. Those wishing to stay in Italy for more than three months must apply for a *permesso di soggiorno* (residence permit) at a police station (*questura*).

EMBASSIES. Foreign embassies are in Rome (p. 626). For Italian embassies at home, contact: **Australia,** 12 Grey St., Deakin, Canberra ACT 2600 (☎02 6273 3333; www.ambitalia.org.au); **Canada,** 275 Slater St., 21st fl., Ottawa, ON K1P 5H9 (☎613-232-2401; www.italyincanada.com); **Ireland,** 63 Northumberland Rd., Dublin (☎01 660 1744; www.italianembassy.ie); **New Zealand,** 34 Grant Rd., Wellington (☎006 4473 5339; www.italy-embassy.org.nz); **South Africa,** 796 George Ave., Arcadia 0083, Pretoria (☎012 430 55 41; www.ambital.org.za); **UK,** 14 Three Kings Yard, London W1K 4EH (☎020 73 12 22 00; www.embitaly.org.uk); and **US,** 3000 Whitehaven St. NW, Washington, D.C. 20008 (☎202 612 4400; www.italyemb.org).

TRANSPORTATION

BY PLANE. Rome's international airport, known as both Fiumicino and Leonardo da Vinci, is served by most major airlines. You can also fly into Milan's Malpensa or Linate airports or Florence's Amerigo Vespucci airport. **Alitalia** (US ☎800-223-5730; UK 870 544 8259; www.alitalia.com) is Italy's national airline and may offer low-season youth fares.

BY TRAIN. The Italian State Railway **Ferrovie dello Stato,** or **FS** (national information line ☎147 88 80 88; www.fs-on-line.com), offers inexpensive and efficient service. There are several types of trains: The *locale* stops at every station on a particular line; the *diretto* makes fewer stops than the *locale;* and the *espresso* stops only at major stations. The air-conditioned *rapido,* an **InterCity** (IC) train, zips along but costs a bit more. Tickets for the fast, pricey **Eurostar** trains require reservations. If you are under 26 and plan to travel extensively in Italy, the **Carta verde** should be your *first* purchase. The card (€26) is valid for one year and gives a 15% discount on state train fare. **Eurail** is valid without a supplement on all trains except Eurostar. For a couple or a family, an **Italian Kilometric Ticket** (€117-181; good for 20 trips or 3000km), can pay off. Otherwise, railpasses are seldom cost effective since regular fares are cheap. For more info, contact the **Italian State Railways** in the US (☎212 730 2121).

BY BUS. Intercity buses serve countryside points inaccessible by train and occasionally arrive in more convenient places in large towns. For city buses, buy tickets in *tabacchi* or kiosks and validate them on board to avoid a fine.

BY FERRY. Portside ferries in Bari, Brindisi, and Ancona (p. 731) connect Italy to Greece. Boats from Trieste (p. 708) serve the Istrian Peninsula down to Croatia's Dalmatian Coast. Ferries also connect Italy's islands to the mainland. For Sardinia, boats go from Genoa (p. 674), La Spezia (p. 680), and Naples (p. 731). Travelers to Sicily (p. 742) take the ferry from Naples (p. 731) or Reggio di Calabria.

BY CAR. There are four kinds of roads: *Autostrada* (superhighways; mostly tollroads); *strade statali* (state roads); *strade provinciali* (provincial); and *strade communali* (local). Italian driving is frightening; congested traffic is common in large cities and in the north. On three-lane roads, be aware that the center lane is for passing. **Mopeds** (€20-31 per day) can be a great way to see the islands and the more scenic areas of Italy, but can be disastrous in the rain and on rough roads. Call the **Automobile Club Italiano** (ACI) at ☎116 if you break down.

BY BIKE AND BY THUMB. Bicycling is a popular national sport, but bike trails are rare, drivers are often reckless, and, except in the Po Valley, the terrain is challenging. *Let's Go* does not encourage hitchhiking. It can be particularly unsafe in Italy, especially in areas south of Rome or Naples.

ITALY

TOURIST SERVICES

EMERGENCY	Police: ☎ 112. Ambulance: ☎ 113. Fire: ☎ 115.

TOURIST OFFICES. In provincial capitals, look for the **Ente Provinciale per il Turismo** (EPT) or **Azienda di Promozione Turistica** (APT) for info on the entire province and the town. Local tourist offices, **Informazione e Assistenza ai Turisti** (IAT) and **Azienda Autonoma di Soggiorno e Turismo** (AAST), are generally the most useful. **Italian Government Tourist Board** (ENIT) has offices in: **Australia,** Level 26, 44 Market St., Sydney NSW 2000 (☎ 02 9262 1666); **Canada,** 175 E. Bloor St., #907 South Tower, Toronto, ON M4W 3R8 (☎ 416 925 4882); **UK,** 1 Princes St., London WIR 2AY (☎ 020 7399 3562); **US,** 630 Fifth Ave., #1565, New York, NY 10111 (☎ 212-245-5618). Visit www.enit.it for a comprehensive list of all ENIT locations.

MONEY. On January 1, 2002, the **euro** (€) replaced the **lira** as the unit of currency in Italy. For more information, see p. 14.

BUSINESS HOURS. Nearly everything closes from around 1 to 3 or 4pm for *siesta*. Most museums are open 9am-1pm and 3-6pm; some are open through lunch, however. Monday is often their *giorno di chiusura* (day of closure).

COMMUNICATION

PHONE CODES	**Country code: 39. International dialing prefix: 00.** The city code must always be dialed, even when calling from within the city. From outside Italy, dial int'l dialing prefix (see inside back cover) + 39 + city code + local number (drop the leading zero).

TELEPHONES. Pre-paid phone cards, available from *tabacchi*, vending machines, and phone card vendors, carry a certain amount of time depending on the card's denomination (€5, €10, or €20). International calls start at €1.05 and vary depending on where you are calling. A collect call is a *contassa a carico del destinatario* or *chiamata collect*. For info on purchasing and using a **cell phone** in Italy, see p. 36. International direct dial numbers include: **AT&T,** ☎ 172 10 11; **British Telecom,** ☎ 172 00 44; **Canada Direct,** ☎ 172 10 01; **Ireland Direct,** ☎ 172 03 53; **MCI,** ☎ 172 10 22; **Sprint,** ☎ 172 18 77; **Telecom New Zealand,** ☎ 172 10 64; **Telkom South Africa,** ☎ 172 10 27; **Telstra Australia,** ☎ 172 10 61.

MAIL. Airmail letters sent from Australia, North America, or the UK to Italy take anywhere from three to seven days. Since Italian mail is notoriously unreliable, it is usually safer and quicker to send mail express (*espresso*) or registered (*raccomandata*). *Fermo Posta* is Italian for *Poste Restante*.

INTERNET ACCESS. Though Italy had initially lagged behind in constructing the information superhighway, it's now playing the catch-up game like a pro. While Internet cafes are still rare in rural and industrial cities, "Internet points" such as bars and even laundromats are becoming common in well-touristed areas. Rates range from €5-8 per hour. For free Internet access, try the local universities and libraries. For a list of Italian cyberspots, check www.cybercaptive.com.

LANGUAGE. Any knowledge of Spanish, French, Portuguese, or Latin will help you understand Italian. The tourist office staff usually speaks some English. For a traveler's survival kit of basic Italian, see p. 1035.

ITALY

ACCOMMODATIONS AND CAMPING

ITALY	❶	❷	❸	❹	❺
ACCOMMODATIONS	under €15	€16-25	€26-40	€41-60	over €60

Associazione Italiana Alberghi per la Gioventù (AIG), the Italian hostel federation, is a Hosteling International (HI) affiliate, though not all Italian hostels (*ostelli per la gioventù*) are part of AIG. A full list is available from most **EPT** and **CTS** offices and from many hostels. Prices start at about €13 per night for dorms. Hostels are the best option for solo travelers (single rooms are relatively scarce in hotels), but curfews, lockouts, distant locations, and less-than-perfect security detract from their appeal. Italian **hotel** rates are set by the state. Hotel owners will need your passport to register you; don't be afraid to hand it over for a while (usually overnight), but ask for it as soon as you think you will need it. Hotel singles (*camera singola*) usually start at around €26-31 per night, and doubles (*camera doppia*) start at €36-42. A room with a private bath (*con bagno*) usually costs 30-50% more. Smaller **pensioni** are often cheaper than hotels. Be sure to confirm the charges before checking in; Italian hotels are notorious for tacking on additional costs at check-out time. The **Azienda di Promozione Turismo** (APT), provides lists of hotels that have paid to be listed; some of the hotels we recommend may not be on the list. **Affittacamere** (rooms for rent in private houses) are another inexpensive option. For more info, inquire at local tourist offices. There are over 1700 **campsites** in Italy; the **Touring Club Italiano,** C. Italia 10-20122, Milan (☎02 852 61; fax 53 59 95 40) publishes numerous books and pamphlets on the outdoors. Rates average €4.20 per person or tent, and €3.70 per car.

FOOD AND DRINK

ITALY	❶	❷	❸	❹	❺
FOOD	under €5	€6-10	€11-15	€16-25	over €25

Breakfast in Italy often goes unnoticed; lunch is the main feast of the day. A *pranzo* (full meal) is a true event, consisting of an *antipasto* (appetizer), a *primo* (first course of pasta or soup), a *secondo* (meat or fish), a *contorno* (vegetable side dish), and then finally *dolce* (dessert or fruit), a *caffè*, and often an after-dinner liqueur. If you don't have a big appetite, you can buy authentic snacks for a picnic at *salumeria* or *alimentari* (meat and grocery shops). A bar is an excellent place to grab a quick bite. They usually offer *panini* (hot and cold sandwiches), drinks with or without alcohol, and *gelato*. Grab a lighter lunch at an inexpensive *tavola calda* (hot table), *Rosticceria* (grill), or *gastronomia* (serving hot prepared dishes). *Osterie, trattorie,* and *ristoranti* are, in ascending order, fancier and more expensive. Many restaurants offer a fixed-price tourist menu *(menu turistico)* that includes *primo, secondo,* bread, water, and wine. Italian dinner is typically a lighter meal. In the north, butter and cream sauces dominate, while Rome and central Italy are notoriously spicy regions. Farther south, tomatoes play a significant role. Coffee is another rich and varied focus of Italian life; for a standard cup of *espresso,* request a *caffè; cappuccino* is the breakfast beverage. *Caffè macchiato* (spotted coffee) has a touch of milk, while *latte macchiato* is heavier on the milk and lighter on the coffee. Wines from the north of Italy, such as the Piedmont's *Asti Spumante* or Verona's *Soave,* tend to be heavy and full-bodied; stronger, fruitier wines come from southern Italy. Almost every shop sells Italy's greatest contribution to civilization: *Gelato* (ice cream).

ITALY

HOLIDAYS AND FESTIVALS

Holidays: New Year's Day (Jan. 1); Epiphany (Jan. 6); Easter Sunday and Monday (Apr. 11 and 12); Liberation Day (Apr. 25); Labor Day (May 1); Assumption of the Virgin (Aug. 15); All Saints' Day (Nov. 1); Immaculate Conception (Dec. 8); Christmas Day (Dec. 25); and Santo Stefano (Dec. 26).

Festivals: The most common excuse for a local festival is the celebration of a religious event—a patron saint's day or the commemoration of a miracle. Most include parades, music, wine, obscene amounts of food, and boisterousness. **Carnevale,** held in February during the 10 days before Lent, energizes Italian towns; in Venice, costumed Carnevale revelers fill the streets and canals. During **Scoppio del Carro,** held in Florence's P. del Duomo on Easter Sunday, Florentines set off a cart of explosives, following a tradition dating back to medieval times. On July 2 and August 16, **Il Palio** hits Siena (p. 725) with a bareback horse race around the central *piazza*.

ROME (ROMA)

Centuries of sporadic growth transformed Rome from a fledgling city-state to the capital of the Western world. At its zenith, the glory of Rome transcended human imagination and touched upon the divine; from its legendary founding in the shadows of pre-history, to the demi-god emperors who reveled in human form, to the modern papacy's global political influence, earthly ideas have proved insufficient to capture the Eternal City. Looking at Rome today, the phrase "decline and fall" seems preposterous—though Rome no longer dictates the course of Western history, its claim upon the modes of culture remains firmly intact. Style. Art. Food. Passion. These form Rome's new empire, tying the city to the living moment, rather than relegating it to stagnate in a museum case.

Today, while the Colosseum crumbles from industrial pollution, Romans celebrate their city: Concerts animate the ancient monuments, children play soccer around the Pantheon, and august *piazze* serve as movie houses for the latest Hollywood costume dramas. In a city that has stood for nearly three thousand years, Rome's glory is not dimmed, merely altered.

⚔ INTERCITY TRANSPORTATION

Flights: da Vinci International Airport (FCO; ☎06 659 51), known as **Fiumicino,** handles most flights. The **Termini line** runs nonstop to Rome's main station, **Termini Station** (30min., 2 per hr., €20). After hours, take the blue **COTRAL bus** to Tiburtina from the ground floor outside the main exit doors after customs (€4.50). From Tiburtina, take bus #40N to Termini. Most charter flights arrive at **Ciampino** (CIA; ☎06 79 49 41). To get to Rome, take the CO.TRA.L bus (every 30min., €1) to Anagnina station.

Trains: From Termini Station to: **Bologna** (2¾-4¼hr., €33); **Florence** (2-3hr., €25); **Milan** (4½-8hr., €47); **Naples** (2-2½hr., €18); **Venice** (5hr., €43). Trains arriving in Rome between midnight and 5am arrive at **Stazione Tiburtina** or **Stazione Ostiense,** which are connected to Termini by the #40N and 20N-21N buses.

🏛 ORIENTATION

Located two blocks north of the **Termini** train station, **Via Nazionale** is the central artery connecting **Piazza della Repubblica** with **Piazza Venezia,** home to the immense wedding-cake-like **Vittorio Emanuele II monument.** A few blocks west of P. Venezia, **Largo Argentina** marks the start of **Corso Vittorio Emanuele,** which leads to Centro

Storico, the medieval and Renaissance tangle of sights around the **Pantheon, Piazza Navona, Campo dei Fiori,** and **Piazza Farnese.** From P. Venezia, V. dei Fori Imperiale leads southeast to the **Forum** and **Colosseum,** south of which are the ruins of the **Baths of Caracalla** and the **Appian Way,** and the neighborhoods of southern Rome: The Aventine, Testaccio, Ostiense, and EUR. **Via del Corso** stretches from P. Venezia north to **Piazza del Popolo.** To the east, fashionable streets border the **Piazza di Spagna** and, to the northeast, the **Villa Borghese.** South and east are the **Fontana di Trevi, Piazza Barberini,** and the **Quirinal Hill.** Across the Tiber to the northwest is the **Vatican City,** and, to the southwest, **Trastevere,** the best neighborhood for wandering. It's impossible to navigate Rome without a map. Pick up a free map from a tourist office. The invaluable **Roma Metro-Bus map** (€4.20) is available at newsstands.

▄ LOCAL TRANSPORTATION

Public Transportation: The 2 **Metropolitana** subway lines (A and B) meet at Termini and run 5:30am-11:30pm. **Buses** run 6am-midnight (with limited late-night routes); validate your ticket in the machine when you board. Buy tickets (€0.80) at *tabacchi*, newsstands, and station machines; they're valid for 1 Metro ride or unlimited bus travel within 75min. of validation. **BIG daily tickets** (€4) and **CIS weekly tickets** (€16) allow for unlimited public transport, including Ostia but not Fiumicino. For a short stay, buy the €11 3-day tourist pass. Be careful; pickpocketing is rampant on buses and trains.

Taxis: Easily located at stands, or flag them down in the street. Ride only in yellow or white taxis, and make sure your taxi has a meter (if not, settle the price before you get in the car). **Surcharges** apply at night (€2.60), on Su (€1), and when heading to or from Fiumicino (€7.25) or Ciampino (€5.50). Fares run about €7.75 from Termini to the Vatican City; between city center and Fiumicino around €35.

Bike and Moped Rental: Bikes generally cost €3 per hr. or €8 per day, but the length of a "day" varies according to the shop's closing time. In summer, try the stands on V. del C. at P. di San Lorenzo and V. di Pontifici. (Open daily 10am-7pm.)

▛ PRACTICAL INFORMATION

TOURIST, FINANCIAL, AND LOCAL SERVICES

▨ **Tourist office: Enjoy Rome,** V. Marghera 8a (☎06 445 18 43; www.enjoyrome.com). From the middle concourse of Termini, exit right, with the trains behind you; cross V. Marsala and follow V. Marghera 3 blocks. Full-service travel agency, booking transportation, tours, and lodgings throughout Italy. Open Apr.-Oct. M-F 8:30am-7pm, Sa 8:30am-2pm; Nov.-Mar. M-F 9:30am-6:30pm, Sa 9am-2pm.

Foreign Consulates: Australia, V. Alessandria 215 (☎06 85 27 21; emergency 800 877 790). Services around the corner at C. Trieste 25. Open M-F 8:30am-12:30pm and 1:30-5:30pm. **Canada,** V. Zara 30 (☎06 44 59 81; www.canada.it). Open M-F 8:30am-4:30pm. **Ireland,** P. Campitelli 3 (☎06 697 91 21; fax 06 69 79 12). Open M-F 10am-12:30pm and 3-4:30pm. **New Zealand,** V. Zara 28 (☎06 441 71 71; fax 06 440 29 84). Open M-F 8:30am-12:45pm and 1:45-5pm. **South Africa,** V. Tanaro 14 (☎06 85 25 41; fax 06 85 25 43). Open M-F 8:30am-4:30pm. **UK,** V. XX Settembre 80/A (☎06 482 54 41; www.grbr.it). Open M-F 8:30am-4:30pm. **US,** V. Veneto 119/A (☎06 467 41; www.usembassy.it/mission). Open M-F 8:30am-5:30pm.

American Express: P. di Spagna 38 (☎06 676 41; lost cards ☎06 722 82). Open Aug. M-F 9am-6pm, Sa 9am-12:30pm; Sept.-July M-F 9am-7:30pm, Sa 9am-3pm.

Luggage Storage: In train station Termini, by track 1.

ITALY

Rome Overview

Circ. Trionfale
Via Trionfale
V. d. Giuliana
Vie. Angelico
Viale delle Milizie
Via Lepanto
Via Cesare
PIAZZA DEL POPOLO
Via Flaminia
Viale G. Washington
Vie. Trinità

PIAZZALE DEGLI EROI
V. Andrea Doria
LGO. TRIONFALE
Via Barletta
Via Leone IV
Via Ottaviano
Via Vespasiano
Viale Giulio
Via F. Massimo
Via Germanico
Via M. A. Colonna
Ponte G. Matteotti
L. Arnaldo da Brescia
Ponte Pietro Nenni
L. Michelangelo
PIAZZA DI LIBERTÀ
Ponte Regina Martherita
L. in Augusta
Via di Ripetta
Via del Babuino
Via Margutta

Via Candia
Via Cola di Rienzo
PIAZZA COLA DI RIENZO
Via Cicerone
PIAZZA CAVOUR
L. Mellini
Ponte Cavour
PIAZZA AUGUSTO IMPERATORE
Via del Corso
Via della
Via Condotti

CITTÀ DEL VATICANO
Via Crescenzio
Castel Sant'Angelo
L. Prati
River
Via Frattina
Via d.

Saint Peter's Basilica
Via d. Conciliazione
Castello
Ponte S. Angelo
Tiber
Ponte Umberto I
L. Marzio
Via d. Scrofa
PIAZZA COLONNA

Viale Vaticano
In Sassia
Ponte P. A. S. Aosta
Ponte V. Emanuele II
V. d. B. di S. Spirito
L. di Tor di Nona
Via dei Coronari
PIAZZA NAVONA
Corso d. Rinascimento
S. Maria d'Anima
Via Giustiani
Pantheon
PZA. DELLA ROTONDA
V. d. Seminario
V. d. Gesù

PIAZZA DELLA ROVERE
L. Gianicolense
V. Staz. di S. Pietro
L. dei Sangallo
Via Giulia
V. d. Monserato
Corso Vittorio Emanuele II
V. Monterone
L. d. Cestari
V. d. Plebiscito

V. Gregorio VII
V. delle Fornaci
Viat Orti d'Alibert
Ponte Mazzini
L. Tebaldi
Palazzo Farnese
v. d. Giubbonari
Via Botteghe Oscure

Via di Cava Aurelia
Viale delle Mura Aurelie
Passeggiata di Gianicolo
Via di S. F. di Sales
L. della Farnesina
L. della Lungara
V. d. Pettinari
Via Arenula
Teatro Marcello

N
LG
0 — 500 yards
0 — 500 meters
MONTE DEL GIANICOLO
Ponte Sisto
V. P. Sisto
L. dei Vallati
L. Sanzio
L. dei Cenci
Ponte Garibaldi
isola Tiberina
Ponte Cestio
V. d. del Pantheon
Via di Marcello

Via Aurelia Antica
Via Garibaldi
Via Garibaldi
PIAZZA S. SONNINO
L. Anguillara
Ponte Palatino
Aventino

Villa Doria Pamphili
Via di S. Pancrazio
Via Luciano Manara
V. d. Genovesi
Via Anicia
Via di S. Michele
L. Ripa

Via Aurelia Antica
Via Giacinto Carini
Via Nicola Fabrizi
Viale Glorioso
V. G. Induno
Via di S. Michele
L. Ripa
Lungotevere
v. d. Porta Lavernale

Via Vitellia
Via Fonteiana
Viale di Villa Pamphili
Viale dei Quattro Venti
Via Dandolo
Viale di Trastevere
Ponte Sublicio
Ponte Grande
Lungotevere Testaccio

Via di Donna Olimpia
V. Ugo Bassi
Via Alessandro Poerio
Via Portuense
L. Portuense
Porto di Pipa Grande
Via Marmorata
Via Giovanni Branca
Nicola Zabaglia
Via Galvani

Parco Testaccio

Villa Torlonia

Villa Borghese

Villa Savoia

PIAZZA FIUME

PZLE. DI PORTA PIA

Porta Pia

PZA. D. CROCE ROSSA

Biblioteca Nazionale

Policlinico Universita

Policlinico

Universita

PIAZZA DI SPAGNA

PIAZZA BARBERINI

PIAZZA DELLA REPUBBLICA

PIAZZA DEI CINQUECENTO

Stazione Termini

PIAZZA SANTA MARIA MAGGIORE

PIAZZA VENEZIA

PIAZZA VITTORIO EMANUELE

PIAZZA DI PTA. MAGGIORE

Forum

CAMPIDOGLIO

Colosseum

MONTE PALATINO

PIAZZA DEL COLOSSEO

Parco del Celio

CELIO

PZA. DI SAN GIOVANNI IN LATERANO

San Giovanni In Laterano

AVENTINO

PZA. DEI RE DI ROMA

Terme di Caracalla

PZA. NUMA POMPILIO

ITALY

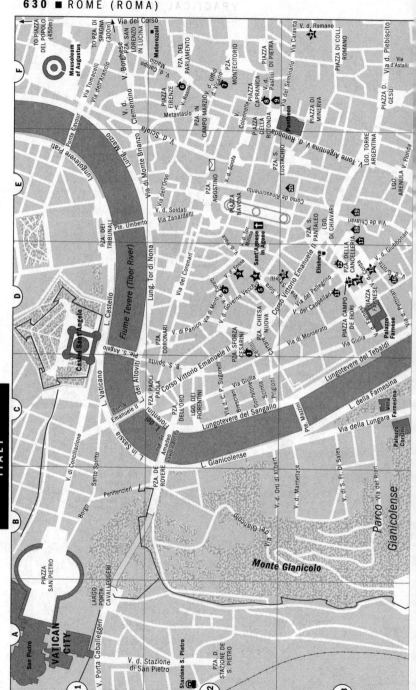

ITALY

Centro Storico & Trastevere

▲ ACCOMMODATIONS

Albergo Abruzzi, 9	F2
Albergo del Sole, 17	E3
Albergo della Lunetta, 18	E3
Albergo Pomezia, 19	E3
Hotel Carmel, 26	C5
Hotel Navona, 20	E3
Hotel Trastevere, 28	C5

🍴 FOOD

Augusto, 24	D4
Dar Poeta, 22	C4
Giolitti, 7	F2
Pizzeria Baffetto, 5	D2
Pizzeria Corallo, 2	D2
Pizzeria San Calisto, 25	C4
Ristorante a Casa di Alfredo, 27	C5
Taverna Lucifero, 11	D3
Tazza d'Oro, 8	F2
Trattoria Da Luigi, 1	D2
Trattoria da Sergio, 16	D3
Trattoria dal Cav. Gino, 7	F2
Zampano, 12	D3

★ NIGHTLIFE

Abbey Theatre, 4	D2
Artu Cafe, 23	C4
The Drunken Ship, 13	D3
Groove, 10	D3
Jonathan's Angels, 3	D2
Sloppy Sam's, 15	D3
Taverna del Campo, 14	D3
Trinity College, 21	F3

ITALY

Bisexual, Gay, and Lesbian Resources: Arci-Gay, V.d. Minzoni 18 (☎051 649 30 55; www.arcigay.it). Membership card (€10) gains admission to gay clubs. **Coordinamento Lesbico Italiano,** V.S. Francesco di Sales 1a (☎06 686 42 01), off V.d. Lungara in Trastevere. **Circolo Mario Mieli di Cultura Omosessuale,** V. Corinto 5 (☎06 541 39 85; www.mariomieli.it). M: B-San Paolo. Walk 1 block to Largo Beato Placido Riccardi, turn left, and walk 1½ blocks to V. Corinto. Open Sept.-July M-F 9am-1pm and 2-6pm.

Laundromat: OndaBlu, V. La Mora 7 (☎800 86 13 46). Locations throughout Rome. Wash €3.20 per 6.5kg load, dry €3.20 per 6.5kg load. Open daily 8am-10pm.

EMERGENCY AND COMMUNICATIONS

Police: ☎113. **Carabinieri:** ☎112. **Emergency:** ☎118. **Fire:** ☎115.

24hr. Pharmacies: Farmacia Internazionale, P. Barberini 49 (☎06 487 11 95). MC/V. **Farmacia Piram,** V. Nazionale 228 (☎06 488 07 54). MC/V.

Hospitals: International Medical Center, V. G. Amendola 7 (☎06 488 23 71; nights and Su 06 488 40 51). Call first. Paramedic crew on call, referral service to English-speaking doctors. General visit €68. Open M-Sa 8:30am-8pm; on-call 24hr. **Rome-American Hospital,** V. E. Longoni 69 (☎06 225 51 for 24hr. service; 22 552 90 for appointments; www.rah.it). Laboratory services, HIV tests, and pregnancy tests. No emergency room. On-call 24hr.

Internet Access: Internet cafes are located throughout the city.

Trevi Tourist Service: Trevi Internet, V.d. Lucchesi 31-32 (☎/fax 06 69 20 07 99). €2.50 per hr., €4 for 2hr. Open daily 9:30am-10pm.

Splashnet, V. Varese 33 (☎06 49 38 20 73), 3 blocks north of Termini. €1.50 per hr. Open in summer daily 9am-1am; off-season daily 9am-11pm.

Freedom Traveller, V. Gaeta 25 (☎06 47 82 38 62; www.freedom-traveller.it). Run by a youth hostel. €2.60 per hr. with card; otherwise €4.13. Open daily 9am-midnight.

Internet Café, V. Cavour 213 (☎06 47 82 30 51). €3.20 per hr. Open daily 9am-1am.

Post Office: Main Post Office (Posta Centrale), P. San Silvestro 19 (☎06 679 50 44 or 06 678 07 88; fax 06 678 66 18). Open M-F 9am-6:30pm, Sa 9am-2pm. **Branch** at V.d. Terme di Diocleziano 30 (☎06 481 82 98), near Termini.

▐ ACCOMMODATIONS

Rome swells with tourists around Easter, from May through July, and in September. Prices vary widely with the time of year, and a proprietor's willingness to negotiate increases with length of stay, number of vacancies, and group size. Termini is swarming with hotel scouts. Many are legitimate and have IDs issued by tourist offices; however, some imposters have fake badges and direct travelers to rundown locations with exorbitant rates, especially at night.

CENTRO STORICO

If being a bit closer to the sights is worth it to you, then choosing Rome's medieval center over the area near Termini may be worth the higher prices.

Albergo del Sole, V.d. Biscione 76 (☎06 68 80 68 73; fax 06 689 37 87). Off Campo dei Fiori. 61 comfortable, modern rooms with phone, fan, TV, and fantastic antique furniture. English spoken. Checkout 11am. Parking garage €15-18. Singles €65, with bath €83; doubles €95/110-140. ❺

Albergo Pomezia, V.d. Chiavari 13 (☎/fax 06 686 13 71; www.hotelpomezia.it). Off C. V. Emanuele II, behind Sant'Andrea della Valle. 3 floors of recently renovated, clean, and quiet rooms with fans. Breakfast included. Handicapped-accessible room on the first floor. Singles €60-105; doubles €80-125; triples €100-160. AmEx/MC/V. ❹

Albergo della Lunetta, P.d. Paradiso 68 (☎06 686 10 80; fax 689 20 28). The 1st right off V. Chiavari from C. V. Emanuele II behind Sant'Andrea della Valle. Clean, well-lit rooms; some face a small, fern-filled courtyard. Great location between Campo dei Fiori and P. Navona. Reservations recommended (with credit card or check). Singles €55, with bath €65; doubles €85/110; triples €115/145. MC/V. ❺

Albergo Abruzzi, P.d. Rotonda 69 (☎06 97 84 13 51). A mere 200 ft. from the Pantheon. Some rooms have a terrific view. Communal bath; rooms have sinks. Singles €75/150; doubles €115/195; triples €170/240. ❺

Hotel "Rosetta," V. Cavour 295 (☎/fax. 06 47 82 30 69). Located just 2 blocks from the Roman Forum, this family-owned hotel offers spacious rooms at unbeatable prices. While the place is not fancy, each room has a TV, phone, fan, and bathroom. Checkout 10:30pm. Singles €60; doubles €80; triples €90; quads €100. AmEx/MC/V. ❹

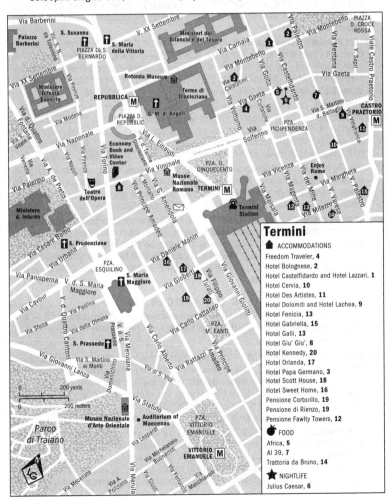

Termini

▲ ACCOMMODATIONS
Freedom Traveler, **4**
Hotel Bolognese, **2**
Hotel Castelfidardo and Hotel Lazzari, **1**
Hotel Cervia, **10**
Hotel Des Artistes, **11**
Hotel Dolomiti and Hotel Lachea, **9**
Hotel Fenicia, **13**
Hotel Gabriella, **15**
Hotel Galli, **13**
Hotel Giu' Giu', **8**
Hotel Kennedy, **20**
Hotel Orlanda, **17**
Hotel Papa Germano, **3**
Hotel Scott House, **18**
Hotel Sweet Home, **16**
Pensione Cortorillo, **19**
Pensione di Rienzo, **19**
Pensione Fawlty Towers, **12**

🍅 FOOD
Africa, **5**
Al 39, **7**
Trattoria da Bruno, **14**

⭐ NIGHTLIFE
Julius Caesar, **6**

ITALY

Hotel Navona, V.d. Sediari 8 1st fl. (☎06 686 42 03; www.hotelnavona.com). Take V.d. Canestrari from P. Navona, cross C. del Rinascimento, and go straight. This recently refurbished building has been used as a *pensione* for over 150 years, and counts Keats and Shelley among its guests. Check-out 10:30am. Breakfast included. A/C €15. Singles €84; doubles €110; triples €150. ❻

NEAR PIAZZA DI SPAGNA

These accommodations might run you a few more euros, but can you really put a price tag on living but a few steps from Prada?

■ **Pensione Panda,** V.d. Croce 35 (☎06 678 01 79; www.webeco.it/hotelpanda), between P.d. Spagna and V.d. Corso. Lovely, immaculate rooms and arched ceilings (some with frescoes). English spoken. Check-out 11am. Reservations recommended. Mar.-Dec. singles €48, with bath €68; doubles €68/98; triples with bath €130; quads with bath €170. Jan.-Feb. €5 less. 5% *Let's Go* discount for cash payments during low season. AmEx/MC/V. ❹

Hotel Pensione Suisse S.A.S., V. Gregoriana 54 (☎06 678 36 49; info@HotelSuisseRome.com). Turn right at the top of the Spanish Steps. Sleek, old-fashioned furniture, comfortable beds, phone, and fan in every room. Internet access and TV available. Breakfast included. All rooms with bath. Singles €90; doubles €140; triples €194; quads €215. Nov.-Feb. 10-15% discount on extended stays. MC/V. ❺

Daphne B&B, V.d. Avignonesi 20 (☎06 47 82 35 29; www.daphne-rome.com) and V.d. San Basilio 55, off P. Barberini. English-speaking owners, full amenities, and a prime location. A/C, maid service, and cell phone rental. Check-in 2pm. Check-out 10am. Reservations strongly recommended. Singles €60-95, with bath €75-120; doubles €70-110/80-160; triples €90-135/105-210; quads €120-160/160-240. MC/V. ❹

Hotel Boccaccio, V.d. Boccaccio 25 (☎06 488 59 62; www.hotelboccaccio.com). M: A-Barberini. Off V.d. Tritone. This quiet, well-situated hotel offers 8 elegantly furnished rooms near many sights. Reception 9am-11pm, late-night access via key. Singles €42; doubles €62, with bath €83; triples €84/112. AmEx/D/MC/V. ❹

Pensione Jonella, V.d. Croce 41 (☎06 679 79 66; www.lodgingitaly.com), between P. di Spagna and V.d. Corso. Four beautiful rooms. Quiet, roomy, and cool in summer. No reception: You must call to arrange for someone to be there. 4th floor location; no elevator. One bathroom. July-Aug. singles €52; doubles €62-68; triples €78; quads €92. Mar.-June €62/72-85/92/110. Off-season €45/45-55/65-75/85. Cash only. Discount for extended stays. ❹

BORGO AND PRATI (NEAR THE VATICAN CITY)

While not the cheapest in Rome, the *pensioni* near the Vatican have all of the sobriety and quiet that one would expect from a neighborhood with this kind of nun-to-tourist ratio.

■ **Colors,** V. Boezio 31 (☎06 687 40 30; www.colorshotel.com). M: A-Ottaviano, or take a bus to P. Risorgimento. V. Cola di Rienzo to V. Terenzio. Wonderful English-speaking staff and guests. 18 beds in rooms painted with a bravado that would put Raphael to shame. Internet €3 per hr. Flower-filled terrace and kitchen open 7:30am-11pm. Coed dorm beds €20; doubles €73-89; triples €83-104. Credit card required for private room reservations; for dorm beds, call at 9pm the night before. ❷

Hotel Florida, V. Cola di Rienzo 243 (☎06 324 18 72; www.hotelfloridaroma.it), on the 1st-3rd floors, reception on 2nd. Floral carpets, bedspreads, and wall decorations. English-speaking staff. A/C (€10 per night), TV, phone, and hair dryer in each of the 18 rooms. Singles €65-82; doubles €90-113; triples €110-135; quads €130-150. Call ahead to reserve; ask about discounts. 5% discount for cash payment. AmEx/MC/V. ❸

Hotel Pensione Joli, V. Cola di Rienzo 243, 6th fl. (☎06 324 18 54; www.hoteljoliroma.com), at V. Tibullo, scala A. A *pensione* with nice beds, ceiling fans, and views of the Vatican. Located on a busy shopping street, Joli also offers rooms that face an interior courtyard. All 18 rooms save a few singles have private baths and telephones. TV available with advance notice. Breakfast 7am-9am. Singles €53, with bath €67; doubles €90-100-; triples €135; quads €165; quints €190. AmEx/MC/V. ❹

Hotel Lady, V. Germanico 198, 4th fl. (☎06 324 21 12; www.hotellady.supereva.it), between V. Fabbio Massimo and V. Paolo Emilio. The 8 rooms, some with beautiful loft-style open wood-work ceilings and tile floors, lack A/C but are cool in the summer. Spacious common room. All rooms with sinks and desks. Singles without bath €75; doubles €90, with bath €100; triples €120. Prices quoted include a *Let's Go* discount, so mention it when you reserve. AmEx/MC/V. ❺

Hotel Isa, V. Cicerone 39 (☎06 321 26 10; www.hotelisa.com). 1 block north of P. Cavour. This 3-star hotel offers all the amenities of a big chain, but with a little more style. Private terraces, phone, cable TV, and minibar. American breakfast buffet included, 7-10:30am. May-Sept. singles €180; doubles €250. Oct.-Apr. singles €130; doubles €180. AmEx/MC/V. ❻

TRASTEVERE

Trastevere is a beautiful old Roman neighborhood famous for its separatism, medieval streets, and pretty-far-from-the-tourist-crowd charm. Hotels here are scattered, most of them too pricey for budget travelers, but the area does offer great nightlife and a location near the Vatican.

Hotel Carmel, V. G. Mameli 11 (☎06 580 99 21; www.hotelcarmel.it). Take a right onto V. E. Morosini (V. G. Mameli), off V.d. Trastevere. A short walk from central Trastevere. This simple hotel has 9 small rooms with bath. A comfortable atrium-like sitting room leads to a lovely garden terrace with breakfast seating. Breakfast included. Singles €80; doubles €100; triples €120; quads €150. AmEx/MC/V. ❺

Hotel Trastevere, V. Luciano Manara 25 (☎06 581 47 13; fax 588 10 16). Take a right off V.d. Trastevere onto V.d. Fratte di Trastevere, which becomes V. Luciano Manara. This homey establishment overlooks P.S. Cosimato. Neighborhood murals give way to 9 simple and airy rooms with bath, TV, and phone. English spoken. Breakfast included. Singles €77; doubles €98-103; triples €129; quads €154. Short-term apartments for 2-6 people with little kitchens and loft beds available. AmEx/D/MC/V. ❺

TERMINI AND SAN LORENZO

Welcome to budget traveler and backpacker central. While Termini is chock-full of traveler's services, the area south of Termini is a little sketchy at night.

🏩 **Pensione Fawlty Towers,** V. Magenta 39, 5th fl. (☎/fax 06 454 359 42; www.fawltytowers.org). Exit Termini to the right, cross V. Marsala onto V. Marghera, and turn right onto V. Magenta. The flower-filled terrace provides a peaceful respite from Termini. Common room with satellite TV, library, refrigerator, microwave, and free Internet. Frequently full, but the reception will help find a room elsewhere. Check-out 9am for dorms, otherwise 10am. Reserve by fax or email. English-speaking staff. No curfew. Dorms €18-20, with bath €23-25; singles €44/51; doubles €62/77; triples €82/90. Cash only. ❷

🏩 **Hotel Papa Germano,** V. Calatafimi 14a (☎06 48 69 19; www.hotelpapagermano.com). From the middle concourse of Termini, exit right; turn left onto V. Marsala, which becomes V. Volturno. V. Calatafimi is the 4th cross-street on the right. Clean rooms with TV and outstanding service. English, French, and Spanish spoken. Internet access €2.60 per hr. Check-out 11am. Dorms €18-25; singles €23-40; doubles €45-70, with bath €52-93; triples €54-78/72-105. Prices vary depending on season. Nov.-Mar. 10% discount. AmEx/MC/V. ❷

ITALY

Hotel Des Artistes, V. Villafranca 20 (☎06 445 43 65; www.hoteldesartistes.com). From the middle concourse of Termini, exit right, turn left onto V. Marsala, right onto V. Vicenza, and then left onto the 5th cross-street. 3-star, 40-room hotel with clean, elegant rooms. Amenities include a rooftop terrace (open until 1am) and lounge with satellite TV. Free Internet. Breakfast included for rooms with a bathroom, otherwise a steep €12. Check-out 11am. Singles €52-62, with bath €99-149; doubles €59-84/109-159; triples €75-112/139-179; quads €96-126/149-199. Off-season prices 20-30% less. €15 discount with cash payment. AmEx/MC/V. ❹

Hotel Dolomiti and **Hotel Lachea,** V.S. Martino della Battaglia 11 (☎06 495 72 56; www.hotel-dolomiti.it). From the middle concourse of Termini, exit right, turn left onto V. Marsala and right onto V. Solferino (V.d. Battaglia). This aging *palazzo* houses two new 3-star hotels with the same reception (on 2nd fl.) and management. Bar and breakfast room. Rooms with bathrooms have satellite TV, minibars, safes, hair-dryers, and A/C. Some with balcony. Breakfast €6. Internet access €2.60 per 30min. A/C €13 per night. Check-out 11am. Check-in 1pm. Singles €37-42, with bath €55-67; doubles €55-68/75; triples €60-73/88; quads €115-135. ❺

Hotel Bolognese, V. Palestro 15 (☎/fax 06 49 00 45). From the middle concourse of Termini, exit right. Walk down V. Marghera and take the 4th left on V. Palestro. In a land of run-of-the-mill *pensioni*, this place is spruced up by the artist-owner's impressive paintings. Some rooms have balconies. Check-out 11am. Singles €31, with bath €43; doubles €47/55; triples €55/70. ❸

Hotel Cathrine, V. Volturno 27 (☎06 48 36 34). From the middle concourse of Termini, exit right, and turn left onto V. Marsala, which becomes V. Volturno. 2 common bathrooms serve the 8 spacious singles and doubles with sinks. There are more rooms at the modern **Affittacamere Aries,** V. XX Settembre 58/a (☎06 420 271 61; www.affi-camereaires.com). Breakfast €2. *Let's Go* discount available, depending on season. Singles €35-45; doubles €47-62, with bath €52-72. Extra bed €15. ❹

Hotel Cervia, V. Palestro 55 (☎06 49 10 57; www.hotelcerviaroma.com). From Termini, exit onto V. Marsala, head down V. Marghera, and take the 4th road on the left. Common TV room, breakfast room with bar, and clean rooms. Rooms with bath include breakfast; otherwise, it's €5. Check-out 11am. Singles €35, with bath €45; doubles €60/95; triples €75/95. In summer, dorm beds available for €20. Ask about the *Let's Go* discount. AmEx/MC/V. ❷

Hotel Gabriella, V. Palestro 88 (☎06 445 02 52). From the middle concourse of Termini, exit right, cross V. Marsala onto V. Marghera and take the 4th right onto V. Palestro. The newly refurbished doubles, with beautifully tiled bathrooms, are an excellent value. All rooms have bathroom, A/C (included in high season price) and television. Shared salon with Internet access. Checkout 10am. Breakfast included (7-9:30am). Singles €50-100; doubles €80-135; triple €100-182. AmEx/MC/V. ❹

Hotel Galli, V. Milazzo 20 (☎06 445 68 59; www.albergogalli.com). From Termini's middle concourse, exit right. Take a right on V. Marsala and the first left on V. Milazzo. 12 clean rooms with tile floors and wrought-iron beds. Kind and helpful family owners. All rooms have bath, phone, TV, A/C, fridge, and safe. Breakfast included. Singles €50; doubles €80; triples €90; quads €110. 10% discount off-season. AmEx/MC/V. ❹

Hotel Fenicia, V. Milazzo 20 (☎/fax 06 49 03 42; www.hotelfenicia.it). Same building as Hotel Galli. 15 sparkling, modern rooms with hardwood floors. Every room with bath, fridge, safe, TV, and A/C. Newly refurbished and spacious room upstairs. Singles €45; doubles €70-85. Extra bed €30. ❹

Freedom Traveller, V. Gaeta 25 (☎06 47 82 38 62; www.freedom-traveller.it). From Termini, exit onto V. Marsala. Walk west down V. Marsala which becomes V. Volturno, and make a right onto V. Gaeta. Though lacking in luxuries, the aging hostel has unbeatable prices. The fun group of guys who run it also organize pub crawls on M and Th nights (€15). Dorms €17-20; doubles €48-60; triples €66-84; quads €80-100. ❷

VIA XX SETTEMBRE AND ENVIRONS

Dominated by government ministries and private apartments, this area is less noisy and touristy than the nearby Termini.

■ **Pensione Monaco**, V. Flavia 84 (☎/fax 06 420 141 80). Go north up V. XX Settembre, turn left onto V. Quintino Sella, and then right onto V. Flavia. The 11 sun-lit rooms, all with bathroom, are kept remarkably clean. Comfortable mattresses and a bright court-yard. Check-out 9am. *Let's Go* discount prices: Singles €37; doubles €60; triples €75; quads €100. 10% discount off-season. ❸

Pensione Tizi, V. Collina 48 (☎06 482 01 28; fax 06 474 32 66). A 10min. walk from the station. Go north up V. XX Settembre, and turn left onto V. Servio Tullio, then right onto V. Flavia, and left on V. Collina. Or take bus #360 or 217. Marble floors and inlaid ceilings adorn spacious and recently renovated rooms. Check-out 11am. Singles €45; doubles €55, with bath €65; triples €80/90; quads €100/110. ❹

Hotel Castelfidardo and **Hotel Lazzari**, V. Castelfidardo 31 (☎06 446 46 38; www.castelfidardo.com). 2 blocks off V. XX Settembre. Both run by the same friendly family. Renovated rooms with soothing pastel walls. 3 floors of modern, comfortable rooms. Check-out 10:30am. English spoken. Singles €44, with bath €55; doubles €64/74; triples €83/96; quads with bath €110. AmEx/MC/V. ❹

Hotel Baltic, V. XX Settembre 89 (☎06 481 47 75). Walk north up V. XX Settembre and continue just past the intersection with V. Castelfidardo. Quiet rooms with high ceilings are well maintained and more like those in a business hotel than a typical *pensione*. All rooms have phone, TV, mini-bar, and safe. A friendly manager and marble lobby sweeten the deal. Breakfast €5. Check-out 11am. Some rooms with A/C for €10. Singles €48-53; doubles €65-70; triples €83-88; quads €110. AmEx/MC/V. ❹

Pensione Piave, V. Piave 14 (☎06 474 34 47; www.albergopiave.it). Going north up V. XX Settembre, turn left onto V. Piave. Recently renovated Piave features key cards, spar-kling floors, and modern decor. All rooms with bathroom, A/C, TV, and phone. Check-in 11:30am. Reservations recommended. Singles €60-90; doubles €75-105. MC/V. ❺

SOUTH AND WEST OF TERMINI

Esquilino (south of Termini) is home to many cheap hotels close to the major sights. The neighborhood west of Termini is slightly more inviting, with busy streets and lots of shopping.

■ **Pensione di Rienzo**, V. Principe Amedeo 79a (☎06 446 71 31; fax 06 446 69 80). A tranquil, family-run retreat with spacious rooms that overlook a courtyard. Extremely friendly English-speaking staff. 20 rooms, with balconies, TVs, and baths. Breakfast €7. Check-out 10am. Singles without bath €20-50; doubles €23-60, with bath €25-70. Prices vary with season. MC/V. ❷

■ **Pensione Cortorillo**, V. Principe Amedeo 79a, 5th fl. (☎06 446 69 34; www.hotelcorto-rillo.it). TVs and A/C in all 14 rooms, and a cheap lobby phone. Breakfast included. Check-out 10am. Singles €30-70, with bath €40-100; doubles €40-80/50-120. Prices vary with season. AmEx/D/MC/V. ❸

Hotel Kennedy, V. Filippo Turati 62-64 (☎06 446 53 73; www.hotelkennedy.net). Clas-sical music in the bar, leather couches and a large color TV in the lounge. Private bath, satellite TV, phone, and A/C. Hearty all-you-can-eat breakfast included. Check-out 11am. Reservations by fax or email only. Singles €60-80; doubles €85-129; triples €100-149. 10% *Let's Go* discount. AmEx/D/MC/V. ❺

Pensione Sandy, V. Cavour 136 4th fl. (☎06 488 45 85; www.sandyhostel.com). Just past the intersection of V.S. Maria Maggiore. Next door to the Hotel Vallet. Free Internet, sheets, and individual lockers (bring a lock) in each room. Simple, hostel-style rooms, usually for 3-5 people. Dorms €12-18. ❶

THE LOCAL STORY

OIL TAKES THE HIGH ROAD

Fabio Parpelli, 27, is the owner and sommelier at Apicius, an oleoteca and wine shop.

LG: How did you get interested in olive oil and wine?
A: I always had good oil at home. My mother taught me a lot. For wine, it started when I was young (about 15). I preferred wine to beer, which I guess is uncommon for young people. I went to stores to buy wines, and tasted the difference. Then I started to study it. I went to the AIS, the only Italian sommelier school in the world that's accredited.

LG: What are some of the challenges of opening a new store in Italy?
A: Well, I think you need to start with an idea of what you want. I wanted to showcase oil, because people usually don't care about it. Until 2 or 3 years ago, people bought bad stuff. I saw that other wine shops sold oil, but they didn't showcase it like they did with their wines. My mother was like a "sommelier" for oil, and so I learned from her. I am very particular about it. When I go into a restaurant, I have to know what I'm using.

LG: What makes a good oil?
A: A good olive oil comes from a small farm that presses olives from their own region, like they did a long time ago.

Hotel Scott House, V. Gioberti 30 (☎06 446 53 79; www.scotthouse.com). Each one of the 34 clean and comfortable rooms features a private bath, A/C, phone, safe box, satellite TV, and brightly painted walls. Breakfast included. Check-out 11am. Singles €35-68; doubles €63-98; triples €75-114; quads €88-129; quints €100-140. Prices vary with season. AmEx/MC/V. ❸

Hotel Il Castello, V. Vittorio Amedeo II 9 (☎06 77 20 40 36; www.ilcastello.com). M: A-Manzoni. Walk down V. San Quintino and take the first left. Spartan rooms, but an eager staff. Continental breakfast €3. Check-out 10:30am. Dorms €20; singles (none with bath) €26-37; doubles €45-82; triples €55-92. MC/V. ❷

Hotel Sweet Home, V. Principe Amedeo 47 (☎/fax 06 488 09 54; www.hotelsweethome.it). The newly renovated rooms are tidy and quite spacious, and the proprietors are very welcoming. Breakfast included. Check-out 11am. Singles €35-45, with bath €45-65; doubles €45-65/55-85. AmEx/D/MC/V. ❸

Hotel Giu' Giu', V.d. Viminale 8 (☎06 482 77 34; www.hotelgiugiu.com). The air-conditioned rooms of this elegant but fading *palazzo* will make you forget the hustle and bustle of Rome. Pleasant breakfast area and 12 quiet rooms. English spoken. Breakfast €7. Check-out 10am. Singles (none with bath) €30-40; doubles €50-70, with bath €60-70; triples with bath €90-105; quads with bath €120-140. ❸

Hotel Orlanda, V. Principe Amedeo 76, 3rd fl. (☎06 488 01 24; www.hotelorlanda.com). At V. Gioberti. Take the stairs in the vestibule. Frequented by Italian businesspeople. Rooms have TV, phone, and sink, but no bathroom. A/C €15.50. Breakfast included. Check-in noon. Check-out 10am. Singles €30-65, with bath €45-70; doubles €52-75/60-100; triples €62-90/80-130; quads €82-110/100-160. AmEx/MC/V. ❷

RELIGIOUS HOUSING

Don't automatically think cheap; some of the most popular religious accommodations run up to €155 for a single. A few still require letters of introduction from local dioceses, but most are open to people of all religious backgrounds. Most are single-sex with early curfews, church services, and light chores.

▧ Domus Nova Bethlehem, V. Cavour 85/A (☎06 478 244 1 or 06 478 825 11; www.suorebambinogesu.it). Walk down V. Cavour from Termini, past P.d. Esquilino on the right. A clean, modern, and centrally located hotel. Curfew 1am. All rooms come with A/C, private bath, safe, TV, and phone. Breakfast included. Singles €70; doubles €100; triples €129; quads €148. AmEx/MC/V. ❺

Santa Maria Alle Fornaci, P.S. Maria alle Fornaci 27 (☎06 393 676 32; ciffornaci@tin.it). Facing St. Peter's Basilica, take a left (through a gate in the basilica walls) onto V.d. Fornace. Take the 3rd right onto V.d. Gasperi, which leads to P.S. Maria alle Fornaci. This *casa per ferie*, in the Trinitarian tradition of hospitality, has 54 rooms, each with a private bath and phone. Simple, small, and clean. No curfew. Breakfast included. Singles €50; doubles €80; triples €110. AmEx/MC/V. ❹

La Fraterna Domus di Roma, V. Monte Brianzo 62 (☎06 68 80 27 27; domusrm@tin.it). From Ponte Umberto, bear left onto V. Monte Brianzo. Take a right on V. Cancello; the entrance is at V. Cancello 6. A safe haven from the noise and commotion of the Centro Storico. Simple rooms with their own bathrooms, and friendly nuns. Breakfast included. Lunch and dinner €12. Curfew 11pm. Singles €48; doubles €78; triples €98. ❹

WOMEN'S HOUSING

YWCA Foyer di Roma, V. C. Balbo 4 (☎06 488 04 60). From Termini, take V. Cavour, turning right onto V. Torino and then the 1st left onto V. C. Balbo. The YWCA (pronounced EEV-kah and known as the *Casa per Studentesse*) is a pretty, clean, and secure hostel. Breakfast included. Tell reception by 10am if you want lunch (served 1-2pm; €11). Reception 7am-midnight. Curfew midnight. Check-out 10am. Singles €37, with bath €47; doubles €62/74; triples €78; quads €104. Extra bed €26. ❸

Associazione Cattolica Internazionale al Servizio della Giovane, V. Urbana 158 (☎06 4890 45 23; www.acisjf.it). From P. Esquilino (in front of Santa Maria Maggiore), walk down V.d. Pretis and turn left. Church-run establishment that arranges housing for women ages 18-25, of any religion. The garden is fantastic, the 10pm curfew (midnight on Sa and Su) less so. Open M-Sa 6:30am-10pm, Su 7am-10pm. 5- or 8-bed dorms €16; doubles €28; triples €57. ❷

▯ FOOD

Traditional Roman cuisine is not generally ranked among the best in Italy, but the city has excellent restaurants specializing in both regional Italian and international cuisine. Lunch is typically the main meal, although some Romans now eat lunch on the go during the week. Restaurants tend to close between 3 and 7:30pm.

ANCIENT CITY

Despite its past glory, this area has yet to discover the noble concept of "affordable food." But along **Via dei Fori Imperiali,** several restaurants offer decent prices.

▧ I Buoni Amici, V. Aleardo Aleardi 4 (☎06 70 49 19 93). From the Colosseum, take V. Labicana to V. Merulana. Turn right, then left onto V.A. Aleardi. The food is worth the walk. Choices include the *linguine all'astice* (linguini with lobster sauce; €6.50). Cover €1. Open M-Sa noon-3pm and 7-11:30pm. AmEx/D/MC/V. ❷

Taverna dei Quaranta, V. Claudia 24 (☎06 700 05 50), off P.d. Colosseo. Shaded by the trees of Celian Park, outdoor dining at this corner *taverna* is a must. The menu changes weekly and often features the sinfully good *oliva ascolane* (olives stuffed with meat and fried; €4). Reservations suggested, especially for a table outside. Open daily 12:30-3:30pm and 7:45pm-midnight. AmEx/D/MC/V. ❷

Hostaria da Nerone, V.d. Terme di Tito 96 (☎06 481 79 52). M: B-Colosseo. Take the stairs to the right (with your back to the Colosseum) and walk up to V.N. Salvi. Turn right, and then left onto V.d. Terme di Tito. Outdoor dining near the Colosseum with views of the Baths of Titus. Traditional specialties like *tegamino di cervello burro e funghi* (brains with butter and mushrooms; €8) make up for the tourist crowd. Pasta €6. Cover €1.30. Open M-Sa noon-3pm and 7-11pm. Closed Aug. AmEx/MC/V. ❷

ITALY

CENTRO STORICO

The twisting streets of Rome's historic center offer many hidden gems, especially just off the main *piazze*.

▨ **Pizzeria Baffetto,** V.d. Governo Vecchio 114 (☎06 686 16 17). At the intersection of V.d. Governo Vecchio and V. Sora. Once a meeting place for 60s radicals, Baffetto now overflows with hungry Romans—be prepared to wait a long time for an outdoor table. Pizza €4.50-7.50. Open daily 8-10am and 6:30pm-1am. Cash only. ❶

Trattoria dal Cav. Gino, V. Rosini 4 (☎06 678 34 34), off V.d. Campo Marzio across from P. del Parlamente. The very affable Gino will greet you at the door. *Tonnarelli alla ciociala* (€7) is the house specialty. Primi €6-7. Secondi under €20. Reservations accepted. Open M-Sa 1-3:30pm and 8-10:30pm. Cash only. ❸

Pizzeria Corallo, V.d. Corallo 10-11 (☎06 68 30 77 03). Off V.d. Governo Vecchio near P. del Fico. This *pizzeria* is a great place to grab a cheap, late dinner. Pizzas €4-9. Excellent *primi* pastas €5-9. Open daily 6:30pm-1am; off-season, closed M. MC/V. ❶

CAMPO DEI FIORI AND THE JEWISH GHETTO

▨ **Trattoria da Sergio,** V.d. Grotte 27 (☎06 654 66 69). Take V.d. Giubbonari and your 1st right. Sergio offers Roman ambience and hearty portions. Try the *Spaghetti Matriciana* (with bacon and spicy tomato sauce; €6). Reservations suggested. Open M-Sa 12:30-3pm and 6:30-11:30pm. MC/V. ❷

▨ **Zampano',** P.d. Cancelleria 83 (☎06 689 70 80), between C. V. Emanuele II and the Campo. This *hostaria* is running out of room for all the awards it has won. Offers creative pizzas (€7-9) and over 200 wines. *Primi* €7-8. *Secondi* €12-13. Finish with a savory dessert (€4.50-6). Open daily noon-2:30pm and 7:30-11pm. AmEx/MC/V. ❷

Trattoria Da Luigi, P.S. Cesarini 24 (☎06 686 59 46), near Chiesa Nuova. Enjoy cuisine such as the delicate *carpaccio di salmone fresco con rughetta* (€8). Bread €1. Open Tu-Su noon-3pm and 7pm-midnight. AmEx/MC/V. ❷

Taverna Lucifero, V.d. Cappellari 28 (☎06 68 80 55 36), off Campo dei Fiori. Pleasant owner knows and greets his guests at the door. The *taverna* offers homemade pastas, tender fillets, and 400 varieties of red wine. Expect to order a full, Roman dinner (€25 without drinks). The white truffles are worth the price (€1-7 per g depending on season). Two seatings: 8:30 and 10:30pm. Call for reservation (2 weeks in advance for Sa). Open Sept.-June daily 8pm-2am. ❺

PIAZZA DI SPAGNA

Although the upscale P.d. Spagna might appear to have little in common with Termini, they both share one thing: Tons of bad, bad food. The difference is that you'll pay €10 more for the atmosphere here. The best food is closer to the Ara Pacis, across V.d. Corso, away from the throngs of tourists.

▨ **Trattoria da Settimio all'Arancio,** V.d. Arancio 50-52 (☎06 687 61 19). Take V.d. Condotti from P.d. Spagna, the 1st right after V.d. Corso, then the 1st left. Order the fried artichokes (€4.50), although the less inhibited might try the squid's ink risotto (€7.50). Bread €1. Open M-Sa 12:30-3pm and 7:30-11:30pm. AmEx/MC/V. ❷

▨ **Vini e Buffet,** P. Toretta 60 (☎06 687 14 45). From V.d. Corso, turn into P.S. Lorenzo in Lucina. Take a left on V. Campo Marzio, then a quick right onto V. Toretta. Popular salads are creative and fresh—the *insalata con salmone* (€8.50) is delightful. Reservations recommended. Open M-Sa 12:30-3pm and 7-11pm. ❷

Il Brillo Parlante, V. Fontanella 12 (☎06 324 33 34), near P. del Popolo. The wood-burning oven, fresh ingredients, and excellent wine attract many lunching Italians. Pizza €5-7.75. Open Su and Tu-Sa 12:30-5:30pm and 7:30pm-1am. MC/V. ❷

PizzaRè, V. di Ripetta 14 (☎06 321 14 68). Take V. di Ripetta 1 block away from P. del Popolo. For those looking for a cheap vacation to the south, PizzaRè serves up Neapolitan-style pizza as well as regional wines and desserts. The "PizzaRè," with buffala mozzarella and cherry tomatoes, is a favorite. **Branch** at V. Oslavia 39a, near P. Mazzini. Open daily 12:45-3:30pm and 7:30pm-12:30am. AmEx/MC/V. ❶

Al Presidente, V. Arcione 95 (☎06 679 73 42). Facing the Trevi Fountain, walk right on V. Lavatore and bear left onto V. Arcione. Fish from the ocean, not from a farm. You can taste the difference in dishes like the toad thighs in seaweed. Try the homemade pasta with truffles. *Primi* €12. *Secondi* €17. Open Tu-Su 7:30-midnight, Sa-Su noon-3pm. ❹

BORGO AND PRATI (NEAR THE VATICAN CITY)

Establishments near the Vatican serve mediocre sandwiches at hiked-up prices, but just a few blocks northeast, food is much better and reasonably priced.

▨ **Franchi,** V. Cola di Rienzo 204 (☎06 687 46 51; www.franchi.it). Delicacies include various croquettes (€1.10), marinated munchies (anchovies, peppers, olives, and salmon, all sold by the kg), and pastas (vegetarian lasagna or *cannellini* stuffed with ricotta and beef; €5.50). Open M-Sa 8:15am-9pm. AmEx/MC/V. ❷

Cacio e Pepe, V. Giuseppe Avezzana 11 (☎06 321 72 68). From P. Mazzini take V. Settembrini to P. dei Martiri di Belfiore, then left on V. Avezzana. Great pasta cheap; no wonder it has been a neighborhood favorite since 1964. All the homemade pasta is delicious, but yes, the *Cacio e Pepe* is their specialty. Lunch under €10. Full dinner around €15. M-F 8-11:30pm, Sa 12:30-3pm. Reservations accepted. Cash only. ❷

"Lo Spuntino" da Guido e Patrizia, V. Borgo Pio 13 (☎06 687 54 91). There's no sign, but you can recognize it by the men playing cards in the sun. Guido holds court behind a counter filled with all the makings of a beautiful *tavola calda*. A full meal (*primi, secondi,* and all the wine you want) will run less than €8. Open M-Sa 9am-8pm. ❷

San Marco, Via Tacito 27-29 (☎06 323 55 96), off P. Cavour. San Marco has been dousing hungry Romans with mozzarella for the past 50 years. Perfect Roman crust and fresh toppings €6-10. The conventional pizzas are delicious, but try their special pies for something more unique—like smoked swordfish (€9.80). Homemade *tiramisu* (€4.10) is heavenly. Open Su-F noon-4pm and 6:30pm-12:30am, Sa 6:30pm-12:30am. ❷

TRASTEVERE

Perhaps one of the best places to enjoy a meal in Rome, Trastevere has fabulous, largely undiscovered restaurants.

▨ **Pizzeria San Calisto,** P.S. Calisto 9a (☎06 581 82 56). Right off P.S. Maria in Trastevere. Simply the best pizza in Rome. Gorgeous thin crust pizzas so large they hang off the plates (€4.20-7.80). Open Tu-Su 7pm-midnight. MC/V. ❶

Ristorante a Casa di Alfredo, V. Roma Libera 5-7 (☎06 588 29 68). Try the *gnocchi tartufo e gamberi* (€8) to start and the grilled calamari (€10.50) or the *filetto a pepe verde* (€13) as a main dish. Open daily noon-3pm and 7:30-11:30pm. AmEx/MC/V. ❸

Augusto, P.d. Renzi 15 (☎06 580 37 98). North of P.S. Maria in Trastevere. Enjoy the daily pasta specials at lunch (around €5), and the *pollo arrosto con patate* (€5.50). The homemade desserts are wonderful. Dinner is chaotic, but lunch features laid-back discussions between waiters and clientele. No reservations. Open M-F 12:30-3pm and 8-11pm, Sa 12:30-3pm. Closed Aug. ❶

Dar Poeta, Vicolo del Bologna 45-46 (☎06 588 05 16; www.darpoeta.it). From P.S. Egidio, head down V. delle Scala and turn right. Hardly a tourist in sight. 18 types of bruschetta (€2) and unusual pizzas amid the old favorites (€4-8.50). Save room for the desserts, homemade daily by owner Marco's mamma (€3.50). Open 7:30pm-1am. AmEx/MC/V. ❶

TERMINI

Tourist traps abound; avoid the torturous €8 "quick lunch" advertised in windows.

▨ **Africa,** V. Gaeta 26-28 (☎06 494 10 77), near P. Independenza. Excellent Eritrean/Ethiopian food. The meat-filled *sambusas* (€2.50) are a flavorful starter; both the *zighini beghi* (roasted lamb in a spicy sauce; €8) and the *misto vegetariano* (mixed veggies; €6) make fantastic entrees. Cover €1. Open M-Sa 8pm-midnight. MC/V. ❷

Al 39, V. Palaestro 39a-41a (☎06 444 12 13). Between the intersection of V. S Martino d. Battaglia and V. Gaeta. The locals' lunch joint. Ingredients are fresh, the waiters friendly, and the food a good value (*bruschetta al pomodoro*, €1.30). Carnivores should try the specialty, *bisteca Al 39* (€10). Vegetarians won't go hungry with the superb *rigatoni vignaroli* (€5). The pizza oven is not wood-fired, but the pizzas (€4-7) are served bubbling. Open M-Sa noon-3:30pm and 7pm-midnight. AmEx/MC/V. ❷

Trattoria da Bruno, V. Varese 29 (☎06 49 04 03). From V. Marsala, next to the train station, walk 3 blocks down V. Milazzo and turn right onto V. Varese. Start with the *tortellini con panna e funghi* (with cream and mushrooms; €6.50). For dessert: The best *crêpes* in town. Open daily noon-3:30pm and 7-10:15pm. Closed Aug. AmEx/MC/V. ❷

SAN LORENZO

Rome's funky university district, San Lorenzo, offers many good, cheap eateries. From Termini, walk south on V. Pretoriano to P. Tiburtino, or take bus #492. Women may find the walk a little uncomfortable at night.

▨ **Il Pulcino Ballerino,** V.d. Equi 66-68 (☎06 494 12 55). Take a right off V. Tiburtina. Dishes include *conchiglione al "Moby Dick"* (shells with tuna, cream, and greens). Open M-Sa 1-3:30pm and 8pm-midnight. Closed mid-Aug. AmEx/MC/V. ❷

▨ **Il Tunnel,** V. Arezzo 11 (☎06 44 23 68 08). From M: B-Bologna, walk down V.d. Provincie, take the 4th right onto V. Padova, and the 2nd left onto V. Arezzo. A bit of a trek, but the locals love it. All pasta dishes (€4-10) are made fresh and the *bisteca alla Fiorentina* is unrivalled in Rome (priced by weight, around €15 per person). Open Tu-Su noon-3pm and 7pm-midnight. Closed Aug. MC/V. ❸

Arancia Blu, V.d. Latini 65 (☎06 445 41 05), off V. Tiburtina. *Tonnarelli con pecorino romano e tartufo* (pasta with sheep cheese and truffles; €6.20) or fried ravioli stuffed with eggplant and smoked *caciocavallo* with pesto sauce (€8.50) make excellent meals. Extensive wine list. Open daily 8:30pm-midnight. ❷

TESTACCIO

This working-class southern neighborhood is the center of Roman nightlife, and eateries here offer food made of just about every animal part imaginable.

▨ **La Cestia,** V. di Piramide Cestia 69. M: B-Piramide. Walk across P. di Porta San Paolo to V. di Piramide Cestia; the restaurant is on the right. Pasta €4.20-7.20. *Secondi* €6.20-11. Open Tu-Su 12:30-3pm and 7:30-11pm. D/MC/V. ❸

Trattoria da Bucatino, V. Luca della Robbia 84-86 (☎06 574 68 86). Take V. Luigi Vanvitelli off V. Marmorata, then the 1st left. The animal entrails you know and love, and plenty of gut-less dishes as well. Heaping mounds of *tripe alla romana* (€7). Pizza €4-7. Cover €1.50. Open Tu-Su 12:30-3:30pm and 6:30-11:30pm. Closed Aug. MC/V. ❷

Volpetti Piu, V. Alessandro Volta (☎06 574 43 06). Take a left onto V.A. Volta off of V. Marmorata. Join the locals at this authentic *gastronomica* for a quick lunch at one of their self-service tables. Fresh salads, pizza, and daily specials from €4. Open M-Sa 10am-10pm. ❶

DESSERT AND COFFEE

Cheap *gelato* is as plentiful on Roman streets as leather pants. Look for *gelato* with very muted (hence natural) colors. Coffee (*espresso*) is Italian for "wash away those early morning hostel lock-out blues."

San Crispino, V.d. Panetteria 42 (☎06 679 39 24). Near the Trevi Fountain. Facing the fountain, turn right onto V. Lavatore and take your 2nd left; it is inset on the right. Crispino is almost universally acknowledged as the best *gelato* in Rome. Every flavor is made from scratch. Cups €1.70-6.30. **Branch** at V. Acaia 56 (☎06 70 45 04 12), in Appio. Both open M, W-Th, and Su noon-12:30am; F-Sa noon-1:30am.

The Old Bridge, V.d. Bastioni di Michelangelo (☎06 39 72 30 26), off P. del Risorgimento, perpendicular to the Vatican museum walls. Huge cups and cones (€1.50-3) filled with your choice of 20 homemade flavors. Open M-Sa 9am-2am, Su 3pm-2am.

Giolitti, V.d. Uffici del Vicario 40 (☎06 699 12 43). 2 blocks north of the Pantheon, find V.d. Maddelena and walk to its end; V.d. Uffici del Vicario is on the right. Makes wonderful *gelato* in dozens of flavors (€1.55-2.60), as well as ices laden with fresh fruit. Festive and crowded at night. Open daily 9am-1am. AmEx/D/MC/V.

Pasticceria Ebraica Boccione, Portico d'Ottavia 1 (☎06 687 86 37). Little fanfare, just long lines of locals who line up for what they all acknowledge to be the best pastries in Rome. *Torta Riccotta Vicciole* and *Torta Ricotta Cioccolate* are the most famous of their creations (€10.30 per kg). Open Su-Th 8am-8pm, F 8am-5:30pm.

Bar Giulia (a.k.a. Caffe Peru), V. Giulia 84 (☎06 686 13 10), near P. V. Emmanuele II. Giulia serves what may be the cheapest (and most delicious) coffee in Rome (€0.70), and they'll add your favorite liqueur at no extra charge. Open M-Sa 4am-9:30pm.

Tazza d'Oro, V.d. Orfani 84-86 (☎06 679 27 68). Facing away from the Pantheon's portico, the yellow-lettered sign is on the right. No seating, but the highest quality coffee in Rome, their signature "regina" arabica. In summer, get the *granita di caffè* with fresh whipped cream (€1.30). Espresso €0.65. Cappuccino €0.80. Open M-Sa 7am-8pm.

ENOTECHE (WINE BARS)

Roman wine bars range from laid-back and local to chic and international. They often serve excellent food to accompany your bottle.

Bar Da Benito, V.d. Falegnami 14 (☎06 686 15 08), off P. Cairoli in the Jewish Ghetto. A *tavola calda* lined with bottles and hungry patrons. Wine from €1; bottles from €5.50. One hot pasta prepared daily (€4.50), along with fresh *secondi* like *prosciutto* with vegetables (€5). Open M-Sa 6:30am-7pm; lunch noon-3:30pm. Closed Aug.

Cul de Sac, P. Pasquino 73 (☎06 68 80 10 94), off P. Navona. Specialty *pates* (such as pheasant and mushroom; €5.40) are exquisite, as are the scrumptious *escargot alla bourguignonne* (€5.10). Open M 7pm-12:30am, Tu-Sa noon-4pm and 6pm-12:30am.

Enoteca Cavour 313, V. Cavour 313 (☎06 678 54 96). A short walk from M: B-Cavour. Wonderful meats and cheeses (€8-9 for a mixed plate) listed by region or type, many fresh salads (€5-7), and rich desserts (€3-5). Massive wine list (€11-260). Open M-Sa 12:30-2:30pm and 7:30pm-1am; kitchen closes 12:30am. Closed Aug.

Trimani Wine Bar, V. Cernaia 37b (☎06 446 96 30), near Termini, perpendicular to V. Volturno. Their shop is around the corner at V. Goito 20. Probably the city's most influential wine bar, at least to those in the know; it is indisputably Rome's oldest. Excellent food includes salads (avocado and feta; €6.90) and filling quiches (try the spiny lobster and leek quiche; €5.50). Wines from just €2.30 a glass. Happy Hour 11:30am-12:30pm and 4-7pm. Open M-Sa 11:30am-12:30pm. AmEx/MC/V.

ITALY

TIME: 3 hr. walk.

DISTANCE: about 3km.

SEASON: Year-round, but spring is best.

A complete tour of the medieval Centro Storico neighborhood.

1 PIAZZA NAVONA. The site of Domitian's stadium, the *piazza* was a special pet project of a number of 17th-century popes. The result was a Baroque masterpiece that today houses Bernini's Fontana dei Quatto Fiumi (p. 647) and pushy vendors alike. The Church of Sant'Agnese in Agone (p. 647) is also worth a look, if for nothing else than the saint's head, which is on prominent display.

2 PANTHEON. A 2000 year old temple currently masquerading under the name Church of Santa Maria ad Martyres. When the ancient Romans dedicated it to all of the pagan gods, they topped the round temple with the largest masonry dome ever constructed. Enter and marvel at the magnificent structure (p. 647).

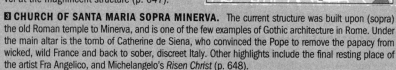

3 CHURCH OF SANTA MARIA SOPRA MINERVA. The current structure was built upon (sopra) the old Roman temple to Minerva, and is one of the few examples of Gothic architecture in Rome. Under the main altar is the tomb of Catherine de Siena, who convinced the Pope to remove the papacy from wicked, wild France and back to sober, discreet Italy. Other highlights include the final resting place of the artist Fra Angelico, and Michelangelo's *Risen Christ* (p. 648).

4 GALLERIA DORIA PAMPHILJ. Taking V.d. Seminario to the east and a right onto V. Sant'Ignazio will lead you directly to the place where the term "nepotism" was first coined. History in the making. The Doria Pamphilj's family's relations with Innocent X are largely responsible for the contents of their palace, which can only be described as opulent. Velasquez's painting of Innocent X is one of the finest papal portraits in Rome (p. 654).

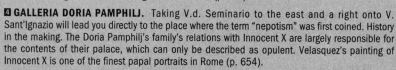

5 TREVI FOUNTAIN. All roads lead to this tourist monstrosity. Just face the facts: you'll end up here at some point, bathed in the flashbulbs of thousands of Kodak disposable cameras, and tossing a coin over your shoulder. If you can, take a moment to enjoy the Neptune fountain, built into the side of a *palazzo* (p. 648). A trip to nearby **San Crispino** (p. 643) is reward enough for being a normal tourist for a night.

6 PIAZZA BARBERINI. Bernini's Fontana del Tritone is the centerpiece of this square, built for Urban VIII (of the same clan of Barberini bees that decorate the bronze canopy in the Vatican). A short walk up V. Veneto to the Capuchin Crypt in the Chiesa Santa Maria della Concezione is a spooky (and cool) way to spend a hot afternoon.

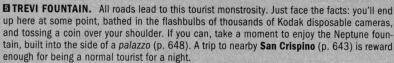

7 SPANISH STEPS. Home of all that's Italian chic, the Spanish Steps are host to a number of overpriced and famous cafes, a couple of decent churches (for the materialistic sinners in Armani that congregate in the nearby *piazze*), and everything that you need to know about international fashion (p. 648).

WALKING TOUR

◎ SIGHTS

Rome wasn't built in a day, and it's not likely that you'll see any substantial portion of it in twenty-four hours, either. Ancient temples and forums, Renaissance basilicas, 280 fountains, and 981 churches—there's a reason, according to Robert Browning, that "everyone sooner or later comes round by Rome."

ANCIENT CITY

What Rome lacks in a "downtown" it more than makes up for in ruins—the downtown Cicero and Catullus knew. The **Umbilicus Urbis**, literally "navel of the world," marked the center of the known universe. And who said Romans were egocentric?

ROMAN FORUM. Here, the pre-Romans founded a thatched-hut shantytown in 753 BC. The entrance ramp leads to V. Sacra, Rome's oldest street, near the **Basilica Aemilia,** built in 179 BC, and the area once known as the Civic Forum. Next to the Basilica stands the Curia (Senate House); it was converted to a church in AD 630 and restored by Mussolini. The broad space in front of the **Curia** was the Comitium, where male citizens came to vote and representatives of the people gathered for public discussion. Bordering the Comitium is the large brick Rostrum (speaker's platform) erected by Julius Caesar in 44 BC, just before his death. The hefty **Arch of Septimius Severus,** to the right of the Rostrum, was dedicated in AD 203 to celebrate Caesar's victories in the Middle East. The **market square** holds a number of shrines and sacred precincts, including the *Lapis Niger* (Black Stone), where Romulus was supposedly murdered by Republican senators. Below the Lapis Niger are the underground ruins of a 6th-century BC altar and the oldest known Latin inscription in Rome. In the square, the **Three Sacred Trees of Rome**—olive, fig, and grape—have been replanted by the Italian state. The newest part of the Forum is the Column of Phocas, erected in AD 608. The three great temples of the **Lower Forum** have been closed off for excavations; however, the eight columns of the 5th-century BC **Temple of Saturn,** next to the Rostrum, have been restored. Around the corner, rows of column bases are all that remain of the **Basilica Julia,** a courthouse built by Julius Caesar in 54 BC. At the far end, three marble columns mark the massive podium of the recently restored **Temple of Castor and Pollux,** built to celebrate the Roman defeat of the Etruscans. The circular building is the **Temple of Vesta,** where Vestal Virgins tended the city's sacred fire, keeping it lit for more than a thousand years.

In the Upper Forum lies the **House of the Vestal Virgins.** For 30 years, the six virgins who officiated over Vesta's rites lived in seclusion here from the ripe old age of seven. Near here, V. Sacra runs over the Cloaca Maxima, the ancient sewer that still drains water from the otherwise marsh-like valley. V. Sacra continues out of the Forum proper to the Velia and the gargantuan Basilica of Maxentius. The middle apse of the basilica once contained a gigantic statue of Constantine with a bronze body and marble head, legs, and arms. The uncovered remains, including a 2m foot, are displayed at the Palazzo dei Conservatori on the Capitoline Hill (p. 647). V. Sacra leads to an exit on the other side of the hill to the Colosseum; the path that crosses before the **Arch of Titus** heads to the Palatine Hill. *(M: B-Colosseo, or bus to P. Venezia. Main entrance is on V.d. Fori Imperiali, at Largo C. Ricci, between P. Venezia and the Colosseum. Open in summer daily 9am-6:30pm; off-season daily 9am-3:30pm. Guided tour €3.50; audioguide in English, French, German, Italian, Japanese, or Spanish; €4.)*

THE PALATINE HILL. The best way to attack the Palatine is from the stairs near the Forum's **Arch of Titus.** Throughout the garden complex, terraces provide breathtaking views. Farther down, excavations continue on the 9th-century BC village, the **Casa di Romulo.** To the right of the village is the podium of the 191 BC **Temple of Cybele.** The stairs to the left lead to the **House of Livia,** which is connected to the **House of Augustus** next door. Around the corner, the long, spooky **Cryptoporticus** connected Tiberius's palace with the buildings nearby. The path around the House of Augustus leads to the vast ruins of a giant palace and is divided into two wings. The solemn **Domus Augustana** was the private space for the emperors; the adjacent wing, the sprawling **Domus Flavia**, once held a gigantic octagonal fountain. Between the Domus Augustana and the Domus Flavia stands the **Palatine Antiquarium**, the museum that houses the artifacts found during the excavations of the Palatine Hill. *(30 people admitted every 20min. starting at 9:10am. Free.)* Outside on the right, the palace's east wing contains the curious **Stadium of Domitian**, or *Hippodrome*, a sunken oval space once surrounded by a colonnade but now decorated with fragments of porticoes, statues, and fountains. The **Arch of Constantine** lies between the Colosseum and the Palatine Hill, marking the tail end of the V. Sacra. One of the best-preserved monuments in the area, it commemorates Constantine's victory over Maxentius at the Milvian Bridge in AD 315. *(The Palatine rises to the south of the Forum. Open in summer daily 9am-7:15pm; off-season 9am-4pm; sometimes closes M-F 3pm, Su and holidays noon. Ticket to the Palatine Hill and the Colosseum €8. 7-day ticket book good for entrance to the 4 Musei Nazionali Romani, the Colosseum, the Palatine Hill, the Terme di Diocleziano, and the Crypti Balbi; €20.)*

FORI IMPERIALI. Across the street from the Ancient Forum are the **Fori Imperiali,** a conglomeration of temples, basilicas, and public squares constructed in the first and second centuries. Excavations will proceed through 2003, so the area is closed off, but you can still get free views by peering over the railing from V.d. Fori Imperiali or V. Alessandrina. Built between AD 107 and 113, the **Forum of Trajan** included a colossal equestrian statue of Trajan and an immense triumphal arch. At one end of the now-decimated forum, 2500 carved legionnaires march their way up the almost perfectly preserved ▧**Trajan's Column,** one of the greatest extant specimens of Roman relief-sculpture. The crowning statue is St. Peter, who replaced Trajan in 1588. The gray tufa wall of the **Forum of Augustus** commemorates Augustus's victory over Caesar's murderers in 42 BC. The aptly named **Forum Transitorium** (also called the **Forum of Nerva**) was a narrow, rectangular space connecting the Forum of Augustus with the Republican Roman Forum. The only remnant of **Vespatian's Forum** is the mosaic-filled **Church of Santi Cosma e Damiano** across V. Cavour, near the Roman Forum. *(Open daily 9am-6:30pm.)*

THE COLOSSEUM. This enduring symbol of the Eternal City—a hollowed-out ghost of marble that dwarfs every other ruin in Rome—once held as many as 50,000 spectators. Within 100 days of its opening in AD 80, some 5000 wild beasts perished in the arena (from the Latin word for sand, *harena*, which was put on the floor to absorb blood). The floor (now partially restored) covers a labyrinth of brick cells, ramps, and elevators used to transport wild animals from cages up to arena level. Beware the men dressed as gladiators: They want to take a picture with you for €5. *(M: B-Colosseo. Open May-Oct. daily 9am-6:30pm; Nov.-Apr. 9am-4pm.)*

DOMUS AUREA. This park houses just a portion of Nero's "Golden House," which once covered a huge chunk of Rome. After deciding that he was a god, Nero had architects build a house worthy of his divinity. The Forum was reduced to a vestibule of the palace; Nero crowned it with the 35m Colossus, a huge statue of himself as the sun. *(On the Oppian Hill. From the Colosseum, walk up V.d. Domus Aurea and make the 1st left. Reservations ☎06 39 96 77 00. Open M and W-Su 9am-7:45pm. Groups of 30 admitted every 20min. €5.)*

VELABRUM. The **Velabrum** is a flat flood plain south of the Jewish Ghetto. At the bend of V. del Portico d'Ottavia, a shattered pediment and a few ivy-covered columns are all that remain of the once magnificent **Portico d'Ottavia.** The stocky, gray **Teatro di Marcello** next door is named for Augustus's nephew, whose early and sudden death remains a mystery. Farther down V. di Teatro di Marcello, **Chiesa di San Nicola in Carcere** incorporates three Roman temples originally dedicated to Juno, Janus, and Spes. (*☎06 686 99 72. Open Sept.-July M-Sa 7:30am-noon and 4-7pm.*) Across the street, the **Chiesa di Santa Maria in Cosmedin** harbors some of Rome's most beautiful medieval decorations. The Audrey Hepburn film *Roman Holiday* made the portico's relief, the **▨Bocca della Verità,** famous; according to legend, the hoary face will chomp on the hand of a liar. (*Open daily 10am-1pm and 3-7pm. Portico open daily 9am-7pm.*)

CAPITOLINE HILL. Home to the original capitol, the **Monte Capitolino** still serves as the seat of the city government. Michelangelo designed its **Piazza di Campidoglio,** now home to the **Capitoline Museums** (p. 653). Stairs lead up to the rear of the 7th-century **Chiesa di Santa Maria in Aracoeli.** The gloomy **Mamertine Prison,** consecrated the **Church of San Pietro in Carcere,** lies down the hill from the back stairs of the Aracoeli. Saint Peter, imprisoned here, baptized his captors with the waters that flooded his cell. (*Open daily 9am-12:30pm and 2:30-6:30pm. Donation requested.*) At the far end of the *piazza,* opposite the stairs, lies the turreted **Palazzo dei Senatori,** the home of Rome's mayor. (*To get to the Campidoglio, take any bus that goes to P. Venezia. From P. Venezia, walk around to the right to P. d'Aracoeli, and take the stairs up the hill.*)

CENTRO STORICO

PIAZZA VENEZIA AND VIA DEL CORSO. The **Via del Corso** takes its name from its days as Rome's premier racecourse, running between P. del Popolo and the rumbling P. Venezia. **Palazzo Venezia** was one of the first Renaissance *palazzi* built in the city; Mussolini used it as an office and delivered his famous orations from its balcony, but today it's little more than a glorified traffic circle dominated by the **Vittorio Emanuele II monument.** Off V. del Corso, the picturesque **Piazza Colonna** was named for the colossal **Colonna di Marco Aurelio,** designed in imitation of Trajan's column. Off the northwest corner of the *piazza* is the **Piazza di Montecitorio,** dominated by Bernini's **Palazzo Montecitorio,** now the seat of the Chamber of Deputies. The opulent **Il Gesu,** mother church of the Jesuit order, makes few concessions towards poverty, chastity, or obedience. (*Take V.C. Battisti from P. Venezia, which becomes V.d. Plebiscito before entering P.d. Gesu. Open daily 6am-12:30pm and 4-7:15pm.*)

THE PANTHEON. Architects still wonder how this 2000-year-old temple was erected; its dome—a perfect half-sphere made of poured concrete without the support of vaults, arches, or ribs—is the largest of its kind. The light that enters the roof was used as a sundial to indicate the passing of the hours and the dates of equinoxes and solstices. In AD 606, it was consecrated as the **Church of Santa Maria ad Martyres.** (*In P. della Rotonda. Open M-Sa 8:30am-7:30pm, Su 9am-6pm.*)

PIAZZA NAVONA. Originally a stadium built in AD 86, the *piazza* once hosted wrestling matches, track and field events, and mock naval battles (in which the stadium was flooded and filled with fleets skippered by convicts). Each of the river god statues in Bernini's **Fountain of the Four Rivers** represents one of the four continents of the globe (as known then): The Ganges for Asia, the Danube for Europe, the Nile for Africa (veiled, since the source of the river was unknown), and the Río de la Plata for the Americas. The **Church of Sant'Agnese in Agone** dominates the *piazza*'s western side. (*Open daily 9am-noon and 4-7pm.*)

OTHER SIGHTS. In front of the temple, the *piazza* centers on Giacomo della Porta's late-Renaissance fountain and an Egyptian obelisk added in the 18th century. Around the left side of the Pantheon, another obelisk marks the center of tiny **Piazza Minerva.** Behind the obelisk, the **Chiesa di Santa Maria sopra Minerva** hides some Renaissance masterpieces, including Michelangelo's *Christ Bearing the Cross*, Antoniazzo Romano's *Annunciation*, and a statue of St. Sebastian recently attributed to Michelangelo. The south transept holds the famous **Carafa Chapel,** home to a brilliant fresco cycle by Filippino Lippi. *(Open M-Sa 7am-7pm, Su 7am-1pm and 3:30-7pm.)* From the upper left-hand corner of P. della Rotonda, V. Giustiniani goes north to intersect V. della Scrofa and V. della Dogana Vecchia at the **Church of San Luigi dei Francesi,** home to three of Caravaggio's most famous paintings: *The Calling of St. Matthew, St. Matthew and the Angel,* and *Crucifixion. (Open Su-W and F-Sa 7:30am-12:30pm and 3:30-7pm, Th 7:30am-12:30pm.)*

CAMPO DEI FIORI

Campo dei Fiori lies across C. V. Emanuele II from P. Navona. During papal rule, the area was the site of countless executions; now the only carcasses that litter the *piazza* are the fish in the colorful produce **market** (M-Sa 6am to 2pm). South of the Campo lie P. Farnese and the huge, stately **Palazzo Farnese,** the greatest of Rome's Renaissance *palazzi*. To the east of the *palazzo* is the baroque facade of the **Palazzo Spada** and the collection of the **Galleria Spada** (p. 591).

THE JEWISH GHETTO. The Jewish community in Rome is the oldest in Europe—Israelites came in 161 BC as ambassadors from Judas Maccabei, asking for help against invaders. The Ghetto, the tiny area to which Pope Paul IV confined the Jews in 1555, was closed in 1870 but is still the center of Rome's vibrant Jewish population of 16,000. In the center of the ghetto are **Piazza Mattei** and the 16th-century **Fontana delle Tartarughe.** Nearby is the **Church of Sant'Angelo in Pescheria;** Jews were forced to attend mass here every Sunday and quietly resisted by stuffing their ears with wax. *(Toward the eastern end of V.d. Portico d'Ottavia. Prayer meetings W 5:30pm, Sa 5pm.)* The **Sinagoga Ashkenazita,** on the Tiber near the Theater of Marcellus, was bombed in 1982; guards now search all visitors. *(Open for services only.)*

PIAZZA DI SPAGNA AND ENVIRONS

■ **THE SPANISH STEPS.** Designed by an Italian, funded by the French, named for the Spaniards, occupied by the British, and currently under the sway of American ambassador-at-large Ronald McDonald, the **Scalinata di Spagna** exude an international air. The pink house to the right of the Steps was the site of John Keats's 1821 death; it's now the **Keats-Shelley Memorial Museum.**

■ **FONTANA DI TREVI.** The extravagant **Fontana di Trevi** emerges from the back wall of **Palazzo Poli.** Legend says that a traveler who throws a coin into the fountain is ensured a speedy return to Rome; a traveler who tosses two will fall in love there. Forget about funding your vacation with an early morning treasure hunt: Several homeless men were arrested in the summer of 2002 and fined €500. Opposite is the Baroque **Chiesa dei Santi Vincenzo e Anastasio,** rebuilt in 1630. The crypt preserves the hearts and lungs of popes from 1590-1903. *(Open daily 7:30am-12:30pm and 4-7pm.)*

PIAZZA DEL POPOLO. P. del Popolo, once a favorite venue for public executions of heretics, is now the lively "people's square." In the center is the 3200-year-old **Obelisk of Pharaoh Ramses II,** which Augustus brought back as a souvenir from Egypt in the first century BC. Behind an early-Renaissance shell, the **Church of Santa Maria del Popolo** contains Renaissance and Baroque masterpieces. Two exquisite Caravaggios, *The Conversion of St. Paul* and *Crucifixion of St. Peter*, are found in the **Cappella Cerasi**. Raphael designed the **Cappella Chigi** for the great Renaissance financier Augustino Chigi. *(Open daily 7am-noon and 4-7pm.)*

VILLA BORGHESE. To celebrate his purchase of a cardinalship, Scipione Borghese built the **Villa Borghese** north of P.d. Spagna and V.V. Veneto. Its huge park houses three art museums: World-renowned **Galleria Borghese**, stark **Galleria Nazionale d'Arte Moderna**, and the intriguing **Museo Nazionale Etrusco di Villa Giulia**. North of the Borghese are the **Santa Priscilla catacombs**. *(M: A-Spagna and follow the signs. Open M-F 9:30am-6pm, Sa-Su 9:30am-7pm. €8.50.)*

THE VATICAN CITY

The Vatican City is the seat of the Catholic Church and was once the mightiest power in Europe. The nation preserves its independence by running a separate postal system and maintaining an army of Swiss Guards. *(M: A-Ottaviano or A-Cipro/ Musei Vaticani. Alternatively, catch bus #64 or 492 from Termini or Largo Argentina, 62 from P. Barberini, or 23 from Testaccio. ☎06 69 82.)*

BASILICA DI SAN PIETRO (ST. PETER'S). A colonnade by Bernini leads from **Piazza San Pietro** to the church. The **obelisk** in the center is framed by two fountains; stand on the round discs set in the pavement and the quadruple rows of the colonnade will visually resolve into one perfectly aligned row, courtesy of the Reformation popes' battery of architects. Above the colonnade are 140 statues; those on the basilica represent Christ, John the Baptist, and the Apostles (except for Peter, naturally). The pope opens the **Porta Sancta** (Holy Door) every 25 years by knocking in the bricks with a silver hammer; the last opening was in 2000, so don't hold your breath. The basilica itself rests on the reputed site of St. Peter's tomb. To the right, Michelangelo's *Pietà* has been protected by bulletproof glass since 1972, when an axe-wielding fiend smashed Christ's nose and broke Mary's hand. Arnolfo di Cambio's *Peter*, in the central nave of the basilica, was not originally malformed, but centuries' worth of pilgrims rubbing his foot have crippled him. The climb to the top of the **Dome** might very well be worth the heart attack it will undoubtedly cause. An elevator will take you up about 300 of the 330 stairs. *(Dress modestly—no shorts, skirts above the knee, sleeveless shirts, or sundresses allowed. Multilingual confession available. Open daily 7am-7pm. Mass M-Sa 9, 10, 11am, noon, and 5pm; Su 9, 10:30, 11:30am, 12:10, 1, 4, and 5:30pm. Dome: From inside the basilica, exit the building, and re-enter the door to the far left with your back to the basilica. €4, by elevator €5. Open Apr.-Sept. daily 7am-5:45pm; Oct.-Mar. 7am-4:45pm.)*

SISTINE CHAPEL. Ever since its completion in the 16th century, the **Sistine Chapel** (named for its founder, Pope Sixtus IV) has served as the chamber in which the College of Cardinals elects new popes. Michelangelo's ceiling, at the pinnacle of artistic creation, gleams from its restoration. The simple compositions and vibrant colors hover above, each section depicting a story from Genesis. The scenes are framed by the famous *ignudi* (young nude males). Contrary to legend, Michelangelo did not paint flat on his back, but standing up and craning backward, and he never recovered from the strain to his neck and eyes. *The Last Judgement* fills the altar wall. The figure of Christ as judge hovers in the upper center, surrounded by his saintly entourage and the supplicant Mary. Michelangelo painted himself as a flayed human skin that hangs symbolically between the realms of heaven and hell. The cycle was completed between 1481 and 1483 by a team of artists under Perugino including Botticelli, Ghirlandaio, Roselli, Pinturicchio, Signorelli, and della Gatta. The frescoes on the side walls predate Michelangelo's ceiling; on the right, scenes from the life of Moses complement parallel scenes of Christ's life on the left. *(Admission included with Vatican Museums, p. 652.)*

ITALY

CASTEL SANT'ANGELO. Built by Hadrian (AD 117-138) as a mausoleum for himself and his family, this mass of brick and stone has served as a fortress, prison, and palace. When the city was wracked with the plague in 590, Pope Gregory the Great saw an angel sheathing his sword at the top of the complex; the plague abated soon after, and the edifice was rededicated to the angel. The fortress offers an incomparable view of Rome and the Vatican. Outside, the marble **Ponte Sant'Angelo,** lined with statues of angels designed by Bernini, is the starting point for the traditional pilgrimage route from St. Peter's to the **Church of San Giovanni in Laterano.** *(Walk along the river with St. Peter's behind you and the towering castle to your left; follow the signs to the entrance. Open Su and Tu-Sa 9am-7pm. €5.)*

TRASTEVERE

Right off the **Ponte Garibaldi** stands the statue of the famous dialect poet G.G. Bellie. On V. di Santa Cecilia, behind the cars, through the gate, and beyond the courtyard full of roses is the **Basilica di Santa Cecilia in Trastevere;** Carlo Maderno's famous statue of Santa Cecilia lies under the altar. *(Open M-Sa 8am-12:30pm and 4:15-6:30pm; Su 9:30-10am, 11:15-noon, and 4:15-6:30pm.)* From P. Sonnino, V. della Lungaretta leads west to P.S. Maria in Trastevere, home to numerous stray dogs, expatriates, and the **Chiesa di Santa Maria in Trastevere,** built in the 4th century. *(Open M-Sa 9am-5:30pm, Su 8:30-10:30am and noon-5:30pm.)* North of the *piazza* are the Rococo **Galleria Corsini,** V. della Lungara 10, and, across the street, the **Villa Farnesina,** the jewel of Trastevere. Atop the Gianicolo hill is the **Chiesa di San Pietro in Montorio,** built on the spot once believed to be the site of St. Peter's upside-down crucifixion. The church contains del Piombo's *Flagellation,* from designs by Michelangelo. Next door in a small courtyard is Bramante's tiny ⬛**Tempietto.** A combination of Renaissance and ancient architecture, it was constructed to commemorate the site of Peter's martyrdom and provided the inspiration for the larger dome of St. Peter's. Rome's **botanical gardens** contain a **garden for the blind** as well as a rose garden that holds the bush from which all the world's roses are supposedly descended. *(Church and Tempietto open daily 9:30am-12:30pm and 4-6pm.)*

NEAR TERMINI

The sights in this urban part of town are concentrated northwest of the station and to the south, near P. V. Emanuele II.

PIAZZA DEL QUIRINALE AND VIA XX SETTEMBRE. Several blocks south of P. Barberini and northeast of P. Venezia, the statues of Castor and Pollux, Rome's protectors, flank yet another obelisk that served as part of Sixtus V's redecoration plan. The **Chiesa di Sant'Andrea al Quirinale,** full of Bernini's characteristic jolly cherubs, highlights the artist's ability to combine architecture and painting for a single, coherent effect—even if that effect is as overdone as most Baroque work. *(Open Sept.-July M and W-Su 8am-noon and 4-7pm; Aug. M and W-Su 8am-noon.)* A Counter-Reformation facade by Maderno marks **Santa Susanna,** the American parish in Rome. The Mannerist frescoes by Croce are worth a look. *(Open daily 9am-noon and 4-7pm.)*

BASILICA OF SANTA MARIA MAGGIORE. As one of the five churches in Rome granted extraterritoriality, this basilica, crowning the Esquiline Hill, is officially part of Vatican City. To the right of the altar, a marble slab marks the **tomb of Bernini.** The 14th-century mosaics in the **loggia** recount the story of the August snowfall that showed the pope where to build the church. *(Dress code strictly enforced. Open daily 7am-7pm. Loggia open daily 9:30am-1pm. Tickets in souvenir shop €2.70.)*

SOUTHERN ROME

The area south of the center is a great mix of wealthy and working-class neighborhoods and is home to the city's best nightlife and some of its grandest churches.

CAELIAN HILL. Southeast of the Colosseum, the Caelian, along with the Esquiline, is the biggest of Rome's seven original hills and home to some of the city's greatest chaos. Split into three levels, each from a different era, the **Chiesa di San Clemente** is one of Rome's most intriguing churches. A fresco cycle by Masolino dating from the 1420s graces the **Chapel of Santa Caterina.** *(M: B-Colosseo. Turn left out of the station and walk east on V. Fori Imperiali. Open M-Sa 9am-12:30pm and 3-6pm, Su and holidays 10am-12:30pm and 3-6pm. €3.)* The immense **Chiesa di San Giovanni in Laterano** was the seat of the pope until the 14th century; founded by Constantine in AD 314, it's Rome's oldest Christian basilica. The two golden reliquaries over the altar contain the heads of St. Peter and St. Paul. Across the street is the **Scala Santa,** which houses what are believed to be the 28 steps used by Jesus outside Pontius Pilate's house. *(Dress code enforced. M: A-San Giovanni or bus #16 from Termini. Open daily 7am-12:30pm and 3:30-7:30pm. €2; museum €1.)*

APPIAN WAY. Since burial inside the city walls was forbidden during ancient times, fashionable Romans made their final resting places along the Appian Way. At the same time, early Christians secretly dug maze-like catacombs under the ashes of their persecutors. *(M: A-San Giovanni. Take bus #218 from P. di S. Giovanni to the intersection of V. Ardeatina and V.d. Sette Chiese.)* **San Callisto,** V. Appia Antica 110, is the largest catacomb in Rome, with nearly 22km of subterranean paths. Its four levels once held 16 popes, St. Cecilia, and 500,000 other Christians. *(Take the private road that runs northeast to the entrance to the catacombs. Open Mar.-Jan. Th-Tu 8:30am-noon and 2:30-5:30pm.)* **Santa Domitilla** houses an intact 3rd-century portrait of Christ and the Apostles. *(Facing V. Ardeatina from the exit of S. Callisto, cross the street and walk up V.d. Sette Chiese. Open Feb.-Dec. M and W-Su 8:30am-noon and 2:30-5pm.)* **San Sebastiano,** V. Appia Antica 136, once held the bodies of Peter and Paul. *(Open Dec.-Oct. M-Sa 8:30am-noon and 2:30-5:30pm. Adjacent church open daily 8am-6pm.)*

AVENTINE HILL. The ▨**Roseto Comunale,** Rome's official rose garden, is host to the annual Premio Roma, the worldwide competition for the best blossom. Entries are sent in May. *(On both sides of V.d. Valle Murcia, across the Circus Maximus from the Palatine Hill. Open daily 8am-7:30pm.)* The **Giardini degli Aranci** nearby is also a pleasant place for an afternoon stroll. *(Open daily dawn to dusk.)* The **Church of Santa Sabina** and its accompanying monastery were home to St. Dominic, Pius V, and St. Thomas Aquinas, and dates from the 5th century. *(At the southern end of Parco Savello. Open daily 6:30am-12:45pm and 3:30-7pm.)* V.S. Sabina continues along the crest of the hill to **Piazza dei Cavalieri di Malta,** home of the crusading order of the Knights of Malta. Through the ▨**keyhole** in the pale yellow gate, the dome of St. Peter's is perfectly framed by hedges.

EUR. South of the city stands a monument to a Roman empire that never was. **EUR** (AY-oor) is an Italian acronym for Universal Exposition of Rome, the 1942 World's Fair that Mussolini intended to be a showcase of Fascist achievements. The new, modern Rome was to shock and impress the rest of the world with its futuristic ability to build lots of identical square buildings. **Via Cristoforo Colombo,** EUR's main street, is the first of many internationally ingratiating addresses like "Viale Asia" and "Piazza Kennedy." It runs north from the Metro station to **Piazza Guglielmo Marconi** and its 1959 **obelisk.** According to legend, when St. Paul was beheaded at the **Abbazia delle Tre Fontane (Abbey of the Three Fountains),** his head bounced three times, creating a fountain at each bounce. *(M: B-Laurentina. Walk north on V. Laurentina and turn right on V. di Acque Salve; the abbey is at the bottom of the hill. Open daily 8am-1pm and 3-7pm.)*

🏛 MUSEUMS

Etruscans, emperors, popes, and *condottiere* have been busily stuffing Rome full of artwork for several millennia, leaving behind a city teeming with galleries. Museums are generally closed holidays, Sunday afternoons, and all day Mondays.

VATICAN MUSEUMS. More or less the content of every art book you've ever seen. The Vatican Museums constitute one of the world's greatest collections of art, with ancient, Renaissance, and modern statues, painting, and papal odds and ends. The museum entrance at V. Vaticano leads to the famous bronze double-helix ramp that climbs to the ticket office. A good place to start a tour is the stellar **Museo Pio-Clementino,** the world's greatest collection of antique sculpture. Two slobbering Molossian hounds guard the entrance to the **Stanza degli Animali,** a marble menagerie that highlights Roman brutality. Among other gems are the ▧**Apollo Belvedere** and the unhappy **Laocoön** family. The last room of the gallery contains the enormous red sarcophagus of Sant'Elena, Constantine's mother. From here, the Simonetti Stairway climbs to the **Museo Etrusco,** filled with artifacts from Tuscany and northern Lazio. Back on the landing of the Simonetti Staircase is the Stanza della Biga (room of an ancient marble chariot) and the Galleria della Candelabra. The long trudge to the Sistine Chapel begins here, passing through the Galleria degli Arazzi (tapestries), the Galleria delle Mappe (maps), the Apartamento di Pio V (where there is a shortcut to *la Sistina,* for all the cheaters out there), the Stanza Sobieski, and the Stanza della Immaculata Concezione. From the Room of the Immaculate Conception, a door leads into the first of the four ▧**Stanze di Rafaele,** apartments built for Pope Julius II in the 1510s. One *stanza* features Raphael's **School of Athens,** painted as a trial piece for Julius, who was so impressed that he fired his other painters, had their frescoes destroyed, and commissioned Raphael to decorate the entire suite. From here, there are two paths: a staircase leading to the brilliantly frescoed Borgia Apartments, the **Museum of Modern Religious Art,** and another route leading to the Sistine Chapel (p. 649). On the way out of the Sistine Chapel, take a look at the **Room of the Aldobrandini Marriage,** which contains a series of rare, ancient Roman frescoes. Finally, the Vatican's painting collection, the **Pinacoteca,** spans eight centuries and is one of the best in Rome. It includes Filippo Lippi's *Coronation of the Virgin,* Perugino's *Madonna and Child,* Titian's *Madonna of San Nicoletta dei Frari,* and Raphael's *Transfiguration. (Walk north from P.S. Pietro along the wall of the Vatican City for about 10 blocks. ☎06 69 88 49 47. Open M-F 8:45am-4:45pm, Sa 8:45am-1:45pm. Last entrance 1hr. before closing. €10. Free last Su of the month 8:45am-1:45pm. Plan to spend at least 4-5hr.)*

GALLERIA BORGHESE. The exquisite Galleria's **Room I,** on the right, houses Canova's sexy statue of **Paolina Borghese** portrayed as Venus triumphant. The next rooms display the most famous sculptures by Bernini: a magnificent **David,** crouching with his slingshot; **Apollo and Daphne;** the weightless body in **Rape of Proserpina;** and weary-looking Aeneas in **Eneo e Anchise.** Don't miss six **Caravaggio** paintings, including his Self Portrait as Bacchus and St. Jerome, which grace the side walls. The collection continues in the pinacoteca upstairs, accessible from the gardens around the back by a winding staircase. **Room IX** holds Raphael's **Deposition** while Sodoma's Pietà graces **Room XII.** Look for self portraits by Bernini, del Conte's Cleopatra and Lucrezia, Rubens's **Pianto sul Cristo Morto,** and Titian's **Amor Sacro e Amor Profano.** *(M: A-Spagna; take the exit labeled "Villa Borghese," walk to the right past the Metro stop to V. Muro Torto and then to P. Porta Pinciana; Viale del Museo Borghese is ahead and leads to the museum. Open daily 9am-7pm. Entrance every hr., visits limited to 2hr. Tickets (including reservation, tour, and bag charge) €8. Audio guide €5. Open M-F 9am-6pm, Sa 9am-1pm.)*

CAPITOLINE MUSEUM. This collection of ancient sculpture is one the largest in the world. The Palazzo Nuovo contains the original statue of **Marcus Aurelius** that once stood in the center of the piazza. The collections continue across the piazza in the Palazzo dei Conservatori. See fragments of the **Colossus of Constantine** and the famous **Capitoline Wolf,** an Etruscan statue that has symbolized the city of Rome since antiquity. At the top of the stairs, the **pinacoteca's** masterpieces include Bellini's *Portrait of a Young Man,* Titan's *Baptism of Christ,* Rubens's *Romulus and Remus Fed by the Wolf,* and Caravaggio's *St. John the Baptist* and *Gypsy Fortune-Teller.* (*On Capitoline Hill behind the Vittorio Emanuele II monument.* ☎06 399 678 00. Open Su and Tu-Sa 9am-8pm. €7.80. Guidebook €7.75, audio guide €4. Guided tours in Italian Sa 5pm, Su at noon and 5pm.)

MUSEO NAZIONALE D'ARTE ANTICA. This collection of 12th- through 18th-century art is split between Palazzo Barberini and Palazzo Corsini, in different parts of the city. **Palazzo Barberini** contains paintings from the medieval through Baroque periods, including works by Lippi, Raphael, El Greco, Carracci, Caravaggio, and Poussin. **Galleria Corsini** holds a collection of 17th- and 18th-century painting, from Dutch masters Van Dyck and Rubens to Italians Caravaggio and Carracci. (*Palazzo Barperini: V. delle Quattro Fontane, 13. M: A-Barberini. Bus #492 or 62.* ☎06 420 036 69. Open Tu-Su 9am-7:30pm. €6. Galleria Corsini: V. della Lungara, 10. Opposite Villa Farnesina in Trastevere. Take the #23 bus and get off between Ponte Mazinni and Ponte Sisto. ☎06 688 023 23. Open Su and Tu-Sa 8:30am-7:30pm. €4. Wheelchair-accessible.)

VILLA FARNESINA. The Villa was the sumptuous home to Europe's one-time wealthiest man, Agostino "il Magnifico" Chigi. To the right of the entrance lies the breathtaking **Sala of Galatea,** mostly painted by the villa's architect, Baldassare Peruzzi, in 1511. The vault displays symbols of astrological signs that add up to a symbolic plan of the stars at 9:30pm on November 29, 1466, the moment of Agostino's birth. The masterpiece of the room is Raphael's **Triumph of Galatea.** The stucco-ceilinged stairway, with its gorgeous perspective detail, ascends to the **Loggia di Psiche,** for which Raphael received the commission. The **Stanza delle Prospettive,** a fantasy room decorated by Peruzzi, offers views of Rome between *trompe l'oeil* columns. The adjacent bedroom, known as the **Stanza delle Nozze** (Marriage Room), is the real reason for coming here. Il Sodoma, who had previously been busy painting the pope's rooms in the Vatican, frescoed this chamber until Raphael showed up and stole the job. Il Sodoma bounced back, making this masterful fresco of Alexander the Great's marriage to the beautiful Roxanne. (*Across from Palazzo Corsini on Lungotevere Farnesina. Bus #23; get off between Ponte Mazinni and Ponte Sisto. At V. della Lungara, 230.* ☎06 6802 7268. Open M-Sa 9am-1pm. €4.50, under-18 €3.50.)

GALLERIA SPADA. Cardinal Bernardino Spada bought a grandiose assortment of paintings and sculpture and commissioned an even more opulent set of great rooms to house them. Time and good luck have left the palatial 17th-century apartments nearly intact—a visit to the gallery offers a glimpse of the luxury surrounding Baroque courtly life. In the first of the gallery's four rooms, the modest cardinal hung portraits of himself by Guercino, Guido Reni, and Cerini. In **Room 2,** look for paintings by the Venetians Tintoretto and Titan and a frieze by Vaga, originally intended for the Sistine Chapel. In **Room 4** are three canvases by the father-daughter team of Orazio and Artemisia Gentileschi. (*From Campo dei Fiori, take any of the small streets leading to P. Farnese. Facing away from Campo dei Fiori, turn left on Capo di Ferro. Bus #64. P. Capo di Ferro, 13, in the Palazzo Spada.* ☎06 687 48 96. Open Su 9am-7:30pm, Tu-Sa 8:30am-7:30pm. Last tickets 7pm. €5. Reservations €1 extra. Guidebooks €10.50. Guided tour Su 10:45am from museum bookshop. Pamphlet guides in English available for each room of the exhibit.)

MUSEI NAZIONALI ROMANI. The fascinating **Museo Nazionale Romano Palazzo Massimo** is devoted to the history of Roman art during the Empire, including the Lancellotti Discus Thrower and a rare mosaic of Nero's. *(Largo di V. Peretti 1. In the left-hand corner of P. dei Cinquecento. ☎06 481 55 76. Open Su and Tu-Sa 9am-7:45pm; ticket office open Su and Tu-Sa 9am-7pm. €6. Audio guide €2.50.)* Nearby, the **Museo Nazionale Romano Terme di Diocleziano,** a beautifully renovated complex partly housed in the huge **Baths of Diocletian** has exhibits devoted to ancient epigraphy (writing) and Latin history through the 6th century BC. *(P. dei Cinquecento 78. Opposite Termini. ☎06 39 96 77 00 for reservations. Open Su and Tu-Sa 9am-7pm. €5. Audioguide €4; guided tour with archaeologist €3.50.)* The Aula Ottogonale, another wing, holds 19 classical sculptures in a gorgeous octagonal space. *(V. Romita 8. ☎06 39 96 77 00. Open Tu-Sa 9am-2pm, Su 9am-1pm. Free.)* Across town is the Renaissance man of the trio, **Museo Nazionale Romano Palazzo Altemps,** displaying Roman sculpture, including the famous 5th-century *Ludovisi Throne. (P. Sant'Apollinare 44. Just north of P. Navona. Museum ☎06 783 35 66. Open Su and Tu-Sa, 9am-7pm. €5. Audioguide €4.)*

EUR MUSEUMS. All of the museums splayed around Mussolini's obelisk are small and manageable, and serve as a break from the usual decadent Classical and Renaissance offerings of Rome's more popular museums. The intimidating facade of the **Museo della Civilita Romana** gives way to a number of scale models of life in ancient Rome. See how the Longobards overran the remains of the Empire in the **Museo dell'Alto Medioevo,** a collection of weapons, jewelry, and household items from Late Antiquity. The **Museo Nazionale delle Arti e Tradizioni Popolari** contains such incongruent items as a Carnevale costume and a wine press. The skull of the famous Neanderthal Guattari Man, discovered near Circeo, is found at the **Museo Preistorico ed Etnografico Luigi Pigorini.** *(M: B-EUR-Palasport or B-EUR-Fermi. Walk north up V. Cristoforo Colombo. Civilita Romana: Open Tu-Sa 9am-6:45pm, Su and holidays 9am-1:30pm. €6.20. Alto Medioevo: Open Tu-Su 9am-8pm. €2. Nazionale delle Arti e Tradizioni Popolari: Open Tu-Su 9am-8pm. Closed holidays. €4. Preistorico ed Etnografico Luigi Pigorini: Open daily 9am-8pm. €4. All museums: under-18 and over-65 free.)*

OTHER RECOMMENDED COLLECTIONS. Montemartini, Rome's first power plant, was converted to hold displaced sculpture from the Capitoline Museums in the 1990s. *(V. Ostiense 106. M: B-Piramide. Open Su and Tu-Sa 9:30am-7pm. €4.20.)* The Doria **Pamphilj** family, whose relations with Pope Innocent X spawned the term "nepotism," still owns its stunning private collection. Titian's *Salome* and Velasquez's portrait of Innocent X alone are worth the visit. *(P. del Collegio Romana 2. Open M-W and F-Su 10am-5pm. €7.30, students and seniors €5.70. Audioguide included.)* After overdosing on "artwork" and "culture," get your aesthetic stomach pumped at the one museum dedicated to crime and punishment, the **Museo Criminologico.** Etchings like *A Smith Has His Brains Beaten Out With a Hammer* hang on the walls along with terrorist, spy, and druggie paraphernalia. *(V. del Gonfalone 27. Open Tu-Th 9am-1pm and 2:30-6:30pm, F-Sa 9am-1pm. €2; under-18 and over-65 €1.)* Despite its disorganization and limited hours, the *Galleria Colonna* remains impressive. The *palazzo* was designed in the 18th century to show off the Colonna family's collection, including Tintoretto's *Narcissus. (V. della Pilotta 17. North of P. Venezia in the centro storico. ☎06 66 78 43 30. Open Sept.-July Sa 9am-1pm. €7, students €5.50, over-65 free. Included tour 11am in Italian and 11:45am in English.)* An eccentric, smallish museum, the **Museo Mario Praz** was the last home of Mario Praz (1896-1982), an equally eccentric and smallish professor of English literature and 18th- and 19th-century art collector. Superstitious neighbors spat or flipped coins when they saw him. *(At the east end of Ponte Umberto, right next to Museo Napoleonico. V. Zanardelli 1, top fl. ☎06 686 10 89. Must visit museum with small tour groups (35-45min.) that leave every hr. in the morning and every half-hr. in the afternoon. Open M 2:30-6:30pm, Tu-Su 9am-1pm and 2:30-6:30pm. Free.)*

🇮🇹 ENTERTAINMENT

Unfortunately, Roman entertainment just ain't what it used to be. Back in the day, you could swing by the Colosseum to watch a man get mauled by a bear; today, Romans seeking diversion are more likely to go to a nightclub than fight a wild beast to the death. Check *Roma C'è* (which has an English-language section) or *Time Out*, available at newsstands, for club, movie, and events listings.

THEATER AND CINEMA

The **Festival Roma-Europa** in late summer brings a number of world-class acts to Rome (consult www.romace.it for more information), but for year-round performances of classic Italian theater, **Teatro Argentina,** Largo di Torre Argentina 52, is the grand matriarch of all Italian venues. (☎06 68 80 46 01. Box office open M-F 10am-2pm and 3-7pm, Sa 10am-2pm. Tickets around €10-26, depending on performance; students €10-21. AmEx/D/MC/V.) **Teatro Colosseo**, V. Capo d'Africa 5a, usually features work by foreign playwrights translated into Italian, but also hosts an English theater night. (☎06 700 49 32. M: B-Colosseo. Box office open Tu-Sa 6-9:30pm. Tickets €10-20. Students €7.80. Closed in summer.)

Most English-language films are dubbed into Italian; check newspapers or *Roma C'è* for listings with a **v.o.** or **l.o.** These indicate that the film is in the original language. For a sure bet, pay a visit to **Il Pasquino**, P. Sant-Egidio 10, off P.S. Maria in Trastevere. Three different screens show English films, and the program changes daily. (☎06 580 36 22. €6.20, students €4.20.) Also, **Nuovo Sacher**, Largo Ascianghi, 1 (☎06 581 81 16) is the famed Italian director Nanni Moretti's theater and shows a host of independent films. (M and Tu films in the original language. Tickets €7, matinee and W €4.50.)

MUSIC

Founded by Palestrina in the 16th century, the **Accademia Nazionale di Santa Cecilia** remains the best in classical music performances. Concerts are held at the Parco della Musicain, V. Pietro di Coubertin, 30, (☎06 80 82 058; http://www.musicaperroma.it/) near P. del Popolo. Box office open 9am-6pm. Regular season runs Oct.-June. €9, students €5. Alexanderplatz Jazz Club, V. Ostia 9, is the current residence of that je ne sais quoi that was expatriate life in Italy during the 50s. Read messages on the wall from old jazz greats, and be prepared to move outside during the summer to the Villa Celimontana. (☎06 39 74 21 71. M: A-Ottaviano, near the Vatican City. Required *tessera* €6.20. Open Sept.-June daily 9pm-2am. Shows start at 10pm.) The **Cornetto Free Music Festival Roma Live** attracts acts like Pink Floyd, The Cure, and the Backstreet Boys at a number of venues throughout the city during the summer. (☎06 592 21 00; www.bbecom.it. Shows start at 9:30pm.)

SPECTATOR SPORTS

While other spectator sports may exist in Rome, it's *calcio* (soccer) that brings the scantily-clad fans and the large-scale riots that the world knows and loves. Rome has two teams in Italy's Serie A: **A.S. Roma** and **S.S. Lazio**. Games are played at the Stadio Olimpico in the Foro Italico (M: A-Ottaviano to bus #32). *Tifosi,* as hardcore fans are called, arrive hours or sometimes days ahead of time for big games, to drink, sing, and taunt rivals. Tickets can be bought at the stadium box office, but are easier to obtain at the **A.S. Roma Store**, P. Colonna 360. (☎06 678 65 14; www.asroma.it. Open daily 10am-10pm, tickets sold 10am-6:30pm. Tickets start at €15.50. AmEx/MC/V.) Italy is also one of the hosts to the **6 Nations Cup,** Europe's premier Rugby Union tournament. Visitors will find that despite rising interest, good seats are readily available from mid-February through March at the Flaminio Stadium (Metro A: Flaminio. Then take the #2 tram to the V. Tiziano stop. For more info visit www.6-nations-rugby.com.)

◘ SHOPPING

Everything you need to know about Italian fashion is summed up in one simple phrase: *la bella figura*. It describes a beautiful, well-dressed, put-together woman, and it is very, very important in Rome. Think whole picture: tinted sunglasses, Ferragamo suit, Gucci pumps with six-inch heels, and, stuffed in your Prada bag, a *telefonino* with a signature ring. For men, a single gorgeous black suit will do the trick. If you're not a Telecom heir or heiress, there are still ways to purchase grace and aplomb. Sales happen twice a year, in mid-January and mid-July, and a number of boutiques, while not as fashionable as their counterparts on the Via Condotti, won't require the sale of a major organ, or even a minor one.

BOUTIQUES

No matter what anti-capitalist mantra you may espouse, you know you've secretly lusted after that Versace jacket. So indulge. If you spend over €155 at one store, you are eligible for a tax refund. (As if you needed another incentive to splurge.)

Bruno Magli, V.d. Gambero 1 (☎06 679 38 02). Open M-Sa 10am-7:30pm.

Dolce & Gabbana, V.d. Condotti 51-52 (☎06 699 249 99). Open M-Sa 10am-7:30pm.

Emporio Armani, V.d. Babuino 140 (☎06 360 021 97). Houses the less expensive end of the Armani line. Same hours as Giorgio Armani.

Ermenegildo Zegna, V. Borgognona 7E-F (☎ 06 678 91 93). M-Sa 10am-7:30pm.

Gianni Versace, Men: V. Borgognona 24-25 (☎06 679 50 37). Women: V. Bocca di Leone, 25-27 (☎06 678 05 21). Open M-Sa 10am-7pm.

Giorgio Armani, V.d. Condotti 75 (☎06 699 14 60). Open M-Sa 10am-7pm.

Gucci, V.d. Condotti, 8 (☎06 678 93 40). Open M 3-7pm, Tu-Sa 10am-7pm, Su 2-7pm.

Laura Biagiotti, V. Borgognona 43-44 (☎06 679 12 05). Open M 3:30-7:30pm, Tu-Sa 10am-1:30pm and 3:30-7:30pm.

Louis Vuitton, V.d. Condotti 15 (☎06 69 94 00 00). Open M-Sa 9:30am-7:30pm, Su 11am-7:30pm.

Max Mara, V.d. Condotti 17-19 (☎06 678 11 44). Open M-Sa 10am-7:30pm, Su 11am-7pm.

Moschino, V. Borgognona, 32a (☎06 699 221 04). Open M noon-8pm, Tu-Sa 9:30am-8pm, Su 10:30am-8pm.

Prada, V.d. Condotti 88-95 (☎06 679 08 97). Open M 3-7pm, Tu-Sa 10am-7pm, Su 1:30-7:30pm.

RoccoBarocco, V. Bocca di Leone 65-66 (☎06 679 79 14). Open M 3:30-7:30pm, Tu-Sa 10am-7:30pm.

Salvatore Ferragamo, men: V.d. Condotti 64-66 (☎06 678 11 30); women: V.d. Condotti, 72-74 (☎06 679 15 65). Open M 3-7pm, Tu-Sa 10am-7pm.

Valentino, V.d. Condotti 13 (☎06 394 20). Open M 3-7pm, Tu-Sa 10am-7pm.

CHEAP AND CHIC

Designer emporiums such as **David Cenci,** V. Campo Marzio 1-7 (☎06 699 06 81; open M 4-8pm, Tu-F 9:30am-1:30pm and 4-8pm, Sa 10am-8pm); **Antonelo & Fabrizio,** C.V. Emanuele 242-243 (☎06 68 80 27 49; open in summer daily 9:30am-1:30pm and 4-8pm; off-season 3:30-7:30pm); and **Discount dell'alta Moda,** V. Agostino Depretis 87 (☎06 47 82 56 72; open M 2:30-7:30pm, Tu-Sa 9:30am-7:30pm) stock many lines of designer clothes and shoes—sometimes at half their normal prices.

Diesel, V.d. Corso 186 (☎06 678 39 33). Off V.d. Condotti. Also at V.d. Babuino 95. *The* label in retro fashion is surprisingly high-octane. Prices are cheaper than elsewhere in the world, so it's worth the visit. Open M-Sa 10:30am-8pm, Su 3:30-8pm.

Mariotti Boutique, V.d. Frezza 20 (☎06 322 71 26). This elegant boutique sells clothes for the modern, sophisticated woman. Prices are steep; watch for the significant sales. Open M-F 10am-7:30pm, Sa 10am-2pm.

David Mayer, V.d. Corso 168 (☎06 69 20 20 97) and V. Cola di Rienzo 185 (☎06 324 33 03; www.davidmayer.com). For the inner *fasionista* in all men, David Mayer offers good-looking attire that doesn't require a trust fund. Short-sleeved button-down shirt €45, sweaters €90, their popular shoes €120. Open daily 10am-8pm.

Ethic, V.d. Corso 85 (☎06 360 021 91) and V.d. Pantheon 46 (☎06 68 30 10 63), and V.d. Carozze, 20. The hip yet less adventurous can find a balance between the avant garde and tasteful. Prices won't break the bank. Open daily 10am-7:30pm.

Max&Co, V.d. Condotti 46-46a (☎06 678 79 46) and V. Nazionale 56. The less expensive line of Max Mara, with more youthful, colorful clothes. Open M-Sa 10am-7:30pm.

SHOES

It's said that a building's only as good as its foundation. In Italy, you're only as good as your shoes. In a city where Birkenstocks are only sold at religious outfitters (Jesus wore sandals), being well-shod is not a luxury, but a way of life. For the pragmatists, **Via Nazionale** is home to a number of larger shoe stores that boast a wide selection, quality products, and reasonable prices.

Trancanelli, P. Cola di Rienzo 84 (☎06 323 45 03). This is where the young and the restless of Rome buy their shoes. A must for anyone looking to return home well-shod, but with their bank account more or less intact (shoes from €65). Open M 3-7:45pm, Tu-Sa 9:30am-7:45pm. AmEx/MC/V.

Bata, V. Nazionale 88a (☎06 679 15 70) and V.d. Due Macelli 45 (☎06 482 45 29). With 250 shops in Italy and 6000 shops world-wide stocked floor to ceiling with functional, affordable shoes that look great. Bonus points for their ability to turn out shoes that look remarkably like Prada's, but can be yours for a fraction of the price. Open M-Sa 9:30am-8pm, Su 4-8pm. AmEx/MC/V.

Mada, V.d. Croce 57 (☎06 679 86 60). A very popular women's shoe store, Mada carries conservative, classic, comfortable shoes. Located in a fashionable shopping district, its (relatively) cheap prices make it a favorite among Roman women. Shoes around €100. Open Tu-F 9:30am-7:30pm, Sa 9:30am-1:30pm. AmEx/MC/V.

Elisheva, V.d. Baullari 19 (☎06 687 17 47), off Campo dei Fiori and P. Irnerio 41 (☎06 66 01 60 77), near V. Aurelia southwest of the Vatican. What's going out in Italy without the right shoes? This small boutique solves your shoe problems with their array of sexy sandals, plus a number of daytime flats (from €40). Also a small selection of women's clothing. Open Su-F 10am-8pm. AmEx/MC/V.

MISCELLANEOUS

Alcozer, V.d. Carozze 48 (☎06 679 13 88). Near P. di Spagna. Gorgeous old-world jewelry at decent prices. Earrings from €20; a jeweled crucifix Lucrezia Borgia would've been proud of for €65. Open M 2-7:30pm, Tu-Sa 10am-7:30pm.

Materozzoli, P.S. Lorenzo in Lucina 5, off V.d. Corso (☎06 68 89 26 86). This old-world *profumeria* carries everything from the exclusive Aqua di Parma line to shaving brushes. Hard-to-find perfumes and colognes. Open M 3:30-7:30pm, Tu-Sa 10am-1:30pm and 3:30-7:30pm. Closed Aug. 10-28.

ITALY

COIN, V. Cola di Rienzo 173 (☎06 36 00 42 98), near Castel San Angelo. Also P. Appio, 7 (☎06 708 00 20), M: A-San Giovanni, and V. Mantova, 1 (☎06 841 58 84), near Porta Pia. By far the most useful of Rome's department stores, COIN carries attractive, functional merchandise at reasonable prices. Good deals, especially on cosmetics. All open daily 9:30am-8pm. AmEx/MC/V.

Campo Marzio Penne, V. Campo Marzio 41 (☎06 68 80 78 77). Fountain pens (from €12) and leather goods, in addition to brightly-colored journals and photo albums (from €25). The small address books (€7) make great presents. Open M-Su 10am-1pm and 2-7pm.

Tedeschi Roma, V. Nazionale 106 (☎06 679 55 75). Good selection of luggage and other bags, convenient to Termini. Large backpacks around €100. Open M-F 10am-7:30pm, Sa 10:30am-2pm. AmEx/MC/V.

Disfunzioni Musicali, V. degli Etruschi 4 (☎06 446 19 84), in San Lorenzo. CDs, cassettes, and LPs available, including excellent selections of rock, avant-garde classical, jazz, and ethnic. Open M 3-8pm, Tu-Sa 10:30am-8pm.

The (Almost) Corner Bookshop, V. del Moro 45 (☎06 583 69 42), in Trastevere. The Corner Bookshop recently acquired the word "almost" in its title after moving a few doors down, but still maintains its hole-in-the-wall charm. They have books in English on just about every topic and can special order anything. Large children's section. Sells early copies of *Wanted in Rome*. Open M-Sa 10am-1:30pm and 3:30-8pm, Su 11am-1:30pm and 3:30-8pm. In Aug., closed Su. AmEx/MC/V.

Porta Portese, in Trastevere at Porta Portese. Tram #8 from Torre Argentina. A surreal experience, with booths selling clothing, shoes, jewelry, bags, toilets, and anything else that you can imagine extending beyond the horizon at this outdoor market. Keep your money close, as this is a notorious spot for pickpockets. Open Su 5am-1pm.

◪ NIGHTLIFE

PUBS

Exactly why the Irish pub became the *de facto* form of Roman nightlife is unclear, but that's the way it is. Rome has more pubs than Dublin, and more are on the way. Not all of Rome's pubs are Irish; some claim to be English, Scottish, American, or Brazilian, and some are distinctly Roman. Nationality is in the eye of the drinker.

▨ **Jonathan's Angels,** V.d. Fossa 14-16. West of P. Navona. Not since Pope Julius II has there been a case of Roman vanity as severe as that of Jonathan, whose face serves as the theme for the decor in this bar. Medium beer on tap €5; delicious cocktails/long drinks €8. Open M-F 5pm-2am, Sa and Su 3pm-2am.

▨ **Trinity College,** V.d. Collegio Romano 6. Off V.d. Corso near P. Venezia. Offers degrees in such diverse curricula as Guinness, Harp, and Heineken. Tuition €5. Happy Hour noon-8pm. Classes held every day 11am-3am. AmEx/MC/V.

▨ **Il Simposio,** V.d. Latini 11. Off V. Tiburtina. Chances are good that on any given night a splattered painter will be hard at work beautifying a discarded refrigerator. With cocktails from €3.50 and a glass of *fragolino* for €2.75, even starving artists can afford the place. Open daily 9pm-2am. Closed late July-Aug.

The Nag's Head, V. IV Novembre 138b. Dance floor inside; live music twice a week. Guinness €5; cocktails €8. Cover €5; F and Sa men €7.80; no cover Su. Open in summer daily 8pm-2am; winter noon-2am. MC/V.

Nuvolari, V. degli Ombrellari 10. Off V. Vittorio. This cocktail bar (serving beer and tropical drinks) also functions as an *enoteca* with wine by the glass (€3.50), a diverse wine list, and the usual salads (choose from 30 at €6 each) and meat and cheese platters (€7.50). Open M-Sa 8pm-2am.

Friend's, V. Piave 71. From P. Independenza take V. Goito, then cross V. XX Settembre onto Via Piave. Plenty of outdoor seating and stainless steel interior. Chill music and all manner of cocktails (€5.50). Beer €4-4.50. Happy Hour 7-9:30pm. Open M-Sa 7:30am-2am, Su 6pm-2am. AmEx/V/MC.

Artu Cafe, Largo Fumasoni Biondi 5. Good selection of drinks. Enjoy specialty cocktails made with fresh juices (€6.20-7.20). Beer €4.50. Wine €3-5.50. Free *apertivi* buffet 6:45-9pm. Open Tu-Su 6pm-2am. MC/V.

Pub Hallo'Ween, P. Tiburtino 31, at the corner of V. Tiburtina and V. Marsala. Plastic skulls and fake spiders and spiderwebs. Beer €3.70-4.20. Mixed drinks €4.20-5.20. Open Sept.-July M-Sa 8:30pm-2:30am, Su 5pm-2:30am.

Shanti, V. dei Conciatori 11. From M: Piramide, head down V. Ostiense; take second street on the right. Yes, these surely are some of the best cocktails (€6-7) to be had in Rome. Great Hookahs (€2.60 per person). Belly dancing Sept.-Mar. W-F 11pm-1am. Open Sept.-July daily 9pm-1am. Closed on Su in July.

ketumbar, V. Galvani 24. A taste of New York decadence in the middle of Italy. It even doubles as a Japanese restaurant (sushi plates €18-36). Wear black; everyone else will. Open Sept.-July M-Sa 8pm-3am. AmEx/MC/V.

Mount Gay Music Bar, V. Galvani 54. Grab a pillow on the floor and sip your cocktail (€8) alongside Rome's young and beautiful. Open daily 11pm-6am. MC/V.

The Proud Lion Pub, Borgo Pio 36. The outside of the pub says "Rome, Borgo Pio," but the beer and scotch says "Hey, I don't forget my Highland roots." Beer and mixed drinks €4. Single malts €4.50-5. Open M-Sa 8:30-late.

The Drunken Ship, Campo dei Fiori 20-21. Because you're tired of meeting Italians. Because you feel the need to have an emotion-free fling with a kindred spirit. Because you're proud to be an American, dammit. Happy Hour daily 5-8pm. W 9-10pm power hour (all you can drink; €6). Open daily 11am-2am. AmEx/MC/V.

Sloppy Sam's, Campo dei Fiori 9-10. The identical twin of the Drunken Ship. Note that once home, wistful stories about that "special someone" you "befriended" at Sloppy Sam's will probably be regarded cynically. Beer €3.50; shots €2.50. Ask about theme nights. Happy Hour 4-8pm. Open M-F 4pm-2am, Sa-Su 11am-2am. AmEx/MC/V.

Night and Day, V.d. Oca 50. Off V. di Ripetta near P. del Popolo. Don't even think of coming until the rest of the bars close. At 2am, Italians who don't let dawn stop their fun stream in. Buy a membership card (€5) for discounts on drinks. Beer €3-5, Guinness €4.50. Happy Hour until midnight. Open daily 7pm-6am. Closed part of Aug.

Taverna del Campo, Campo dei Fiori, 16 (☎06 687 44 02). When munchies strike, head here for the famous shell-peanuts and other great snacks to soak up the alcoholic over-indulgence: *Panini* €4-6; bruschetta €3; salads €5-9. Wine by the glass €2.60-10. Beer €3-4. Mixed drinks €8. Open Tu-Su 8:30am-2am. AmEx/MC/V.

Abbey Theatre, V.d. Governo Vecchio, 51-53 (☎06 686 13 41). One of the only establishments in Rome where you can drop in for a morning Guinness (€5). Stay for lunch (a lot of vaguely Irish dishes, such as beef in Guinness, €6.50). Happy Hour M-F 3:30-8pm. 40min. Internet access and one drink €5. Open daily 11am-3am. AmEx/MC/V.

Morrison's, V. E.Q. Visconti 88. Two blocks north of P. Cavour. Harp, Kilkenny, and Guinness on tap, and an excellent selection of Irish and Scotch whiskey and bourbon. For those in the literary know, the James Joyce (blue curacao and Harp) is a must. Guinness €5. Mixed drinks €6.50. Open daily 6:30pm-2am. AmEx/MC/V.

Julius Caesar, V. Castelfidardo 49. Just north of Termini near P. dell'Indipendenza. Upstairs features beer on tap (€4.50-5.50), while the downstairs is filled with blaring live music most nights (10:30-11:30pm). Happy Hour half-price until 6:30pm. Residents at local hostels receive a 20% discount. Open daily 4:30pm-3am.

Coming Out Pub, V.S. Giovanni in Laterano 8. Right behind the Colosseum, next to the gladiator school. Great BGLTQ hang-out. In winter, pub hosts live music Th, games Tu, and karaoke W. Enjoy a bite to eat (€5-7) before having a satisfying cocktails (€5.50). Open daily 5pm-5am. Cash only.

CLUBS

Although Italian discos can be a flashy, sweaty good time, the scene changes as often as Roman phone numbers. Check *Roma C'è* or *Time Out*. Rome has fewer gay establishments than most cities its size, but those it has are solid and keep late hours. Many gay establishments require an **ARCI-GAY pass** (€10 yearly), available from **Circolo di Cultura Omosessuale Mario Mieli** (☎06 541 39 85).

Chic and Kitsch, V.S. Saba 11a. Uniting the elegant with the eclectic; music (often House or a variant) is selected by resident DJ Giuliano Marchili. Cover: men €13, women €10 includes 1st drink. Open Sept.-July Th-Sa 11:30pm-4am.

Groove, V. Savelli 10. Look for the black door. Lose it to acid jazz, funk, soul, and disco. F-Sa 1-drink min. (€5.16). Open W-Su 10pm-2am. Closed most of Aug.

Alien, V. Velletri 13-19. One of the biggest discos in Rome. As of this writing, the comfy chill-out room had not yet reached 1987. Cover varies (about €15, including a drink). Open Tu-Su 11pm-5:30am. In summer, moves to Fregene.

Piper, V. Tagliamento 9. A popular club that occasionally hosts gay nights. 70s, rock, and disco, as well as house and underground. Gay friendly all the time. Cover €10-18, includes 1st drink. Open F-Sa 11pm-4:30am; in summer Sa-Su 11pm-4:30am.

Black Out, V. Saturnia 18. From the Colosseum, take V. Claudia (V.d. Navicella/V. Gallia) southeast; turn right on V. Saturnia. Punk and Britpop. Occasional bands. Cover €8 (includes 1 drink). Open Sept. to mid-June Th-Su 11pm-4am.

Il Giardini di Adone, V.d. Reti 38a. Off V.d. Sabelli. Though it fancies itself a "spaghetti-pub," the happy students who frequent this little place would remind you that tables are properly used for dancing, not for eating linguine. Cover €6, includes 1st drink. Open Sept. to late July Su and Tu-Sa 8pm-3am.

Charro Cafe, V. di Monte Testaccio 73. So you wanted to go to Tijuana, but got stuck in Rome. Weep no more, *mis amigos:* make a run for Charro, home of the €2.60 tequila. Open daily midnight-3am.

Aquarela, V. di Monte Testaccio 64. You want pottery shards? You got pottery shards. A fine example of urban renewal, Roman-style. Entrance €10, includes 1st drink. Open Su and Tu-Sa 8:30pm-4am.

L'Alibi, V. di Monte Testaccio 40/44. Traditionally a gay club, L'Alibi now draws a mixed crowd. Its two floors host drag queen shows and hip DJs alike. The roof garden, decorated with leopard prints, plays chill music and serves cocktails (€8). Cover F-Sa €13-15. Open W-Su midnight-5am.

Coyote, V. di Monte Testaccio 48b. The newly-opened club sports a Tex-Mex look and caters to the homesick American tourist. Hosts Italian DJs. Its spacious terrace is a welcome escape from the revelry inside. Open daily 9pm-4am.

Radio Londra Caffè, V. di Monte Testaccio 65b. Packed with an energetic, good-looking, young crowd. Pint of beer €4-5. Pizza, *panini*, and hamburgers €4.20-5.20. 1-year membership required (€8; includes one free drink). Open M-Sa 9pm-3am.

Classico Village, V. Libetta 3. M: B-Garbatella. Exit onto V. Argonauti and take a left on V. Libetta. Women probably don't want to travel alone in this area at night. One of the best-known *centri sociali* in Rome—your one-stop shop for all things countercultural. Hosts live music, films, art exhibits, poetry readings, African cuisine tastings, and more. Hours and cover vary (€8-10).

◪ DAYTRIPS FROM ROME

NETTUNO. Following the collapse of the Empire, Roman refugees in flight from marauding Goths installed themselves in the shadows of a coastal temple to Neptune 60km south of Rome. World War II saw the partial destruction of Nettuno and the decimation of nearby Anzio, when amphibious Allied forces emerged from the Tyrrhenian Sea to initiate their advance upon Nazi-occupied Rome. A walk down V. Colombo from the train station takes you to the shore and the perpendicular V. Matteoti. Turn left onto V. Matteoti in order to descend to the marina, teeming with yachts. Entrance to the **beaches** is "free," provided that you rent a beach umbrella and a chair for an easy €15. However, if you continue left past the marina and the church, you will reach the **public beach**, which can get quite crowded in the summer as Romans go on their weekend getaways. Sites of historical and aesthetic interest include a highly touristed medieval quarter: to the right of the marina. A right from V. Colombo onto V. Matteoti will take you to P.S. Francesco, which is dominated by the **Fortezza Sangallo**, a turn-of-the-16th-century fortress that houses the rather musty **Museo dello Sbarco Alleato**, devoted to the Allied landing. (Open Tu-Su 9am-1pm and 2-6pm. Free.)Another reminder of Lazio's unfortunate positioning in the path of the World War II juggernaut is the **Sicily-Rome American Cemetery**, stretching over 77 acres of Italian cypress trees, trickling fountains, and expansive verdant lawns. To reach the cemetery, turn right coming out of the train station and then right again onto V.S. Maria. The memorial at the top of the park contains a chapel, as well as extensive map murals depicting the Allied drive up the peninsula. Americans run the information office to the right of the entrance, and will provide info and help locate graves. (Open daily 9am-5pm.) Take the regional **train** from Termini to Nettuno (1hr., every hr., €2.90.) Pro Loco **tourist office** is in the right corner of marina. (☎06 980 33 35; www.proloconettuno.it. Open M-F 10am-12:30pm and 5-7:30pm, Sa 10am-12:30pm and 6-8pm.)

PONZA. As the largest of the Pontine Islands, Ponza was also the one most susceptible to pirate attacks, which were frequent until the arrival of the fierce and wealthy Bourbon monarchs in 1734. The laid-back island lifestyle has resulted in a happy disregard for signs, street names, and maps. *Isole Pontine*, a comprehensive guide to the islands, is available at newsstands for €6.20. Beaches are the reason for the season in Ponza. **Cala dello Schiavone** and **Cala Cecata** (on the bus line) are the best and most accessible spots. The most spectacular views on the island are available at **Chiaia di Luna,** an expansive, rocky beach set at the bottom of a 200m tufo cliffside. Another point of sunbathing interest is the **Piscine Naturale,** just a quick ride through Ponza's lovely hillside. Take the bus to Le Foma and ask to be let off at the Piscine. Cross the street and make your way down the long, steep path. Spiny sea urchins line the rocks, so take caution. From Rome, take the **train** from Termini to Anzio (1hr., every hr. 6am-11pm, €2.90) and then the Linee Vetor hydrofoil from Anzio to Ponza (1hr., €20-23). The ticket office in Anzio is on the quay (☎06 984 50 85; www.vetor.it.). Pro Loco **tourist office** is on V. Molo Musco, at the right of the port in the long red building. (☎07 718 00 31; prolocoponza@libero.it. Open in summer M-Sa 9am-1pm and 4-8:30pm, Su 9am-1pm.)

FRASCATI. Patrician villas dotting the hillside are a testament to the peculiar power of Frascati and, possibly, of its superb dry white wines. The sculpture-filled gardens of the **Villa Aldobrandini** dominate the hills over P. Marconi, while a 1km walk up on F. Massaia leads to the tiny **Chiesa dei Cappuccini**. A sign above the door announces that you need reservations for marriages, but the **Ethiopian Museum** next door requires no such foresight. It houses a collection of weapons, handmade crafts, and the death mask of the cardinal who collected the artifacts while doing missionary work. (Open daily 9am-noon and 4-6pm. Free.) The town of **Tusculum** was an ancient resort for the who's who of ancient Roman society, including Cicero and Cato. From the entrance of the Villa Aldobrandini, turn right onto V. Tusculo, which climbs 5km over winding country roads to reach the ruins of the collection of villas. The town is a 15min. **bus** ride from Anagnina Station; the bus driver will let you off at the depot in P. Marconi, the town center.

LOMBARDY (LOMBARDIA)

Over the centuries, Roman generals, German emperors, and French kings have vied for control of Lombardy's fertile soil and strategic location. The disputing powers failed to rob Lombardy of her prosperity; the region remains the wealthiest in Italy. While Milan may bask in the cosmopolitan spotlight, equally important are the rich culture and beauty of Bergamo, Mantua, and the foothills of the Alps.

MILAN (MILANO)   ☎02

Since its days as capital of the western Roman Empire from AD 286 to 402, Milan (pop. 1,300,000) has embraced modern life more forcefully than any other major Italian city. The pace of life is quick, and *il dolce di far niente* (the sweetness of doing nothing) is an unfamiliar taste. Although Milan's growth has brought petty crime and drugs, the city remains on the cutting edge of finance, fashion, and fun.

⊏ TRANSPORTATION

Flights: Malpensa Airport (MXP; ☎02 74 85 22 00), 45km from town. Handles intercontinental flights. **Malpensa Express** leaves Cadorna Metro station for the airport (45min., €9). **Linate Airport** (LIN; ☎02 74 85 22 00), 7km away, covers Europe. Take bus #73 from MM1: P.S. Babila (€1).

Trains: Stazione Centrale (☎(01) 47 88 80 88), in P. Duca d'Aosta on MM2. Info office open daily 7am-9:30pm. Every hour to: **Florence** (2½hr., €22); **Genoa** (1½hr., €8); **Rome** (4½hr., €39); **Turin** (2hr., €8); and **Venice** (3hr., €13).

Buses: Stazione Centrale. Intercity buses tend to be less convenient and more expensive than trains. **SAL, SIA, Autostradale,** and other carriers leave from P. Castello and nearby (MM1: Cairoli) for **Bergamo,** the **Lake Country,** and **Turin.**

Public Transportation: The **Metro** (Metropolitana Milanese, or **MM**) runs 6am-midnight. **ATM buses** handle local transportation. Ticket booths (toll free ☎800 01 68 57) are open M-Sa 7:15am-7:15pm. Single-fare tickets €1, day passes €3, 2-day €5.50.

✦ 🛈 ORIENTATION AND PRACTICAL INFORMATION

The layout of the city resembles a giant target, encircled by a series of ancient concentric city walls. In the outer rings lie suburbs built during the 1950s and 60s to house southern immigrants. Within the inner circle are four central squares: **Piazza Duomo,** at the end of V. Mercanti; **Piazza Cairoli,** near the Castello Sforzesco; **Piazza Cordusio,** connected to Largo Cairoli by V. Dante; and **Piazza San Babila,** the business and fashion district along C. Vittorio Emanuele. The **duomo** and **Galleria Vittorio Emanuele** constitute the bull's-eye, roughly at the center of the downtown circle. Radiating from the center are two large parks, the Giardini Pubblici and the Parco Sempione. From the colossal **Stazione Centrale** train station, farther northeast, you can take a scenic ride on bus #60 or the more efficient commute on subway line #3 to the downtown hub. **Via Vito Pisani,** which leads to the mammoth **Piazza della Repubblica,** connects the station to the downtown area.

Tourist Office: APT, V. Marconi 1 (☎02 72 52 43 00; www.milanoinfotourist.com), in the Palazzo di Turismo in P. Duomo. Pick up the comprehensive *Milano e Milano* as well as *Milano Mese* for info on activities and clubs. Open M-Sa 9am-1pm and 3-6pm, Su 9am-1pm and 3-5pm.

American Express: V. Larga 7 (☎02 72 00 36 93), on the corner of V. dell'Orso. Walk through the Galleria, across P. Scala, and up V. Verdi. Holds mail free for AmEx members for 1 month, otherwise €5 per month. Handles wire transfers for AmEx cardholders. Also **exchanges currency.** Open M-F 9am-5:30pm.

Emergencies: ☎118. **Toll-free Operator:** ☎12. **Medical Assistance:** ☎38 83.

Police: ☎113 or 02 772 71. **Carabinieri** (tourist police): ☎112.

Hospital: Ospedale Maggiore di Milano, V. Francesco Sforza 35 (☎02 550 31).

24hr. Pharmacy: Galeria at Stazione Centrale. (☎02 669 07 35).

Internet Access: Enjoy Internet, V. le Tunisia 11 (☎02 36 55 08 05). €2 per hr. Open M-Sa 9am-midnight, Su 9:30am-11:30pm.

Post Office: V. Cordusio 4 (☎02 72 10 41). Address mail to be held: First Name SUR-NAME, *In Fermo Posta,* Ufficio Postale Centrale di Piazza Cordusio 4, Milano **20100,** ITALY. Open M-F 8:30am-7:30pm, Sa 8:30am-1pm.

ACCOMMODATIONS

Every season in Milan is high season—except August. A single room in a decent establishment for under €35 is a real find. For the best deals, try the city's southern periphery or the areas south and east of the train station. When possible, make reservations well ahead of time.

NEAR STAZIONE CENTRALE

Women should use caution in this area when traveling alone at night.

Hotel Sara, V. Sacchini 17 (☎02 20 17 73; www.hotelsara.it). MM1/2: Loreto. From Loreto take V. Porpora; the 3rd street on the right is V. Sacchini. Recently renovated, on a peaceful street, and all rooms with bath. Free Internet. Singles €45-55; doubles €68-85; triples €93-110. AmEx/MC/V. ❹

Hotel Ca 'Grande, V. Porpora 87 (☎02 26 14 40 01; www.hotelcagrande.it). Take tram #33 from Stazione Centrale; it runs along V. Porpora and stops at V. Ampere, near the front door. Spotless rooms over a beautiful garden. Internet €3 per hr. Reception 24hr. Singles €45, with bath €55; doubles €65/75. AmEx/MC/V. ❹

Hotel Ambra, V. Caccianino 10 (☎02 266 54 65). MM1/2: Loreto. V. Caccianino is about a block up on the right from Ca' Grande. Set off on a quiet side street; offers 19 rooms, all with bath, TV, telephone, and balcony. Breakfast €3. Reserve ahead. Singles €42; doubles €68; triples €91. Student discounts July-Aug. AmEx/MC/V. ❹

Hotel Malta, V. Ricordi 20 (☎02 204 96 15; www.hotelmalta.it). MM1/2: Loreto. From Stazione Centrale, take tram #33 to V. Ampere and backtrack along V. Porpora to V. Ricordi. Reserve ahead. Singles €36; doubles €73. ❹

Hotel Oriente, V. Porpora 52 (☎02 236 12 98). From MM1/2: Loreto, take V. Porpora for 10min. Hotel, on the left, has rooms with bath, phone, TV, and fan. Floor-to-ceiling windows with sea-green curtains look out over neighborhood gardens. Singles €45-55, doubles €60-70, triples €85-100. MC/V. ❹

Albergo Villa Maria, V. Sacchini 19 (☎02 29 52 56 18), next to Hotel Sara. The 7 rooms in this family-run hotel have TV, fan, phone, and huge windows. Brightly decorated with strawberry-patterned sheets and sorbet-colored walls. Shared bath. Singles €30, doubles €50. ❸

ITALY

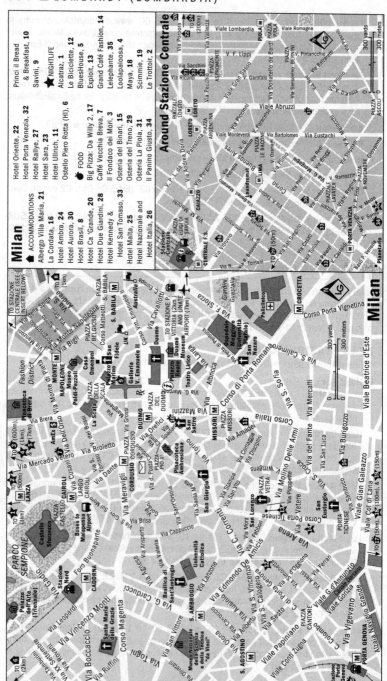

Milan

▲ ACCOMMODATIONS
Albergo Villa Maria, **21**
La Cordata, **16**
Hotel Ambra, **24**
Hotel Aurora, **30**
Hotel Brasil, **8**
Hotel Ca 'Grande, **20**
Hotel Due Giardini, **28**
Hotel Kennedy &
  Hotel San Tomaso, **25**
Hotel Nazionale and
  Hotel Italia, **26**
Hotel Oriente, **22**
Hotel Porta Venezia, **32**
Hotel Rallye, **27**
Hotel Sara, **23**
Hotel Ullrich, **11**
Ostello Piero Rotta (HI), **6**

♥ FOOD
Big Pizza: Da Willy **2, 17**
Caffè Vecchia Breva, **7**
Il Fondaco dei Mori, **3**
Osteria del Binari, **15**
Osteria del Treno, **29**
Osteria La Piola, **31**
Il Panino Giusto, **34**
Princi Il Bread
  & Breakfast, **10**
Savini, **9**

★ NIGHTLIFE
Alcatraz, **1**
Le Biciclette, **12**
BluesHouse, **5**
Exploit, **13**
Grand Café Fashion, **14**
Lelephante, **35**
Loolapaloosa, **4**
Maya, **18**
Scimmie, **19**
Le Trottoir, **2**

Around Stazione Centrale

Milan

NEAR GIARDINI PUBBLICI

Hotel San Tomaso, V. le Tunisia 6, 3rd fl. (☎/fax 02 29 51 47 47). MM1: Porta Venezia. Head to the C. Buenos Aires Metro exit and turn left on V. le Tunisia. One of the cheapest lodgings in Milan. TV, fan, and shared bath. English spoken. Request keys if going out at night. Singles €35; doubles €62. AmEx/DC/MC/V. ❸

Hotel Aurora, C. Buenos Aires 18 (☎02 204 79 60; www.hotelitaly.com/hotels/aurora/index.htm). MM1: Porta Venezia. Exit the station onto C. Buenos Aires, walk straight ahead for 5min.; and it's on the right. Spotless, modern rooms. Singles €41-46, with shower €46-54; doubles with bath €69-82. AmEx/DC/MC/V. ❹

Hotel Due Giardini, V. B. Marcello 47 (☎02 29 52 10 93; duegiardinihotel@libero.it). MM1: Lima. Walk along V. Vitruvio 2 blocks to V. Marcello; turn left on far side of the street. Minty green decor in 11 well-kept rooms, all with bath and TV. Breakfast €4. Internet access. Singles €55; doubles €90-120. MC/V. ❹

Hotel Kennedy, V. Tunisia 6, 6th fl. (☎02 29 40 09 34; raffaelo.bianchi@galactica.it). MM1: Porta Venezia. 3 floors above Hotel San Tomaso. Ask for the room with view of the *duomo*. The street below can be noisy. Check-out 10am. Request keys if going out at night. Singles with shared bath €40; doubles €70, with bath €80; triples €80-110; quads €100-120. AmEx/DC/MC/V. ❹

Hotel Brasil, V. G. Modena 20 (☎/fax 02 749 24 82; www.hotelbrasil.it). MM1: Palestro. From Stazione Centrale, take bus #60 to V. G. Modena. Large rooms with TV and romantic view of the boulevard. Close to clubs. Breakfast in bed €4. Reception closes 12:30am; request keys if going out at night. Singles €39, with shower €44, with bath €57; doubles €52/57/72. AmEx/DC/MC/V. ❹

Hotel Rallye, V. B. Marcello 59 (☎/fax 02 29 53 12 09). MM1: Lima. Walk along V. Vitruvio 2 blocks to V. Marcello and turn left. Homey rooms with phone and TV. Spacious doubles, free parking, and complimentary breakfast under an apricot tree in the garden. Singles €30, with bath €35; doubles €51/67. AmEx/D/MC/V. ❸

Hotel Porta Venezia, V. B. Castaldi 26 (☎02 29 41 42 27; fax 02 20 24 93 97). MM1: P. Venezia. Walk down C. Venezia for 2 blocks, then turn right onto V. B. Castaldi. Simple and tidy rooms come with TV and fan. Singles €31-42, with bath €36-47; doubles €41-62/51-77. MC/V. ❹

Hotel Italia and Hotel Nazionale, V. Vitruvio 44/46 (☎02 669 38 26 or 02 670 59 11; nazionaleitalia@tiscali.it). From the platforms in Stazione Centrale, walk straight into P. Duca D'Aosta; turn left and walk 3 blocks on V. Vitruvio. Hotels are on the left. Run by the same family, their reception on the ground floor of Hotel Italia leads to clean, simple rooms. Singles €33, with bath €52; doubles €49/70; triples €93. AmEx/DC/MC/V. ❸

NEAR THE CITY PERIPHERY

La Cordata, V. Burigozzo 11 (☎02 58 31 46 75; www.lacordata.it). MM3: Missori. From P. Missori, take the tram 2 stops to Italia (Lusardi), walk same direction for 1 block, and turn right on V. Burigozzo. Entrance is around the corner from La Cordata camping store. Founded by a group of educators in the 1980s as a non-profit cooperative, this hostel of sky-blue walls and whimsical murals houses mostly college-aged backpackers. Rooms have bath. Loose curfew 11:30pm. Dorms €16. ❷

Hotel Ullrich, C. Italia 6, 6th fl. (☎02 86 45 01 56; fax 02 80 45 35). MM3: Missori. Near P. Missori. 5min. walk from the *duomo*. Clean rooms with TV. Singles €45-55; doubles €68-78. MC/V. ❹

Ostello Piero Rotta (HI), V. Salmoiraghi 1 (☎02 39 26 70 95), northwest of city. MM1: QT8. Turn right facing the white church outside the Metro. The hostel will be on the right after about 300m. Laundry €5.50. 3-night max. stay. Daytime lockout. Curfew 1am. HI membership required. Closed late Dec. to mid-Jan. Dorms €16. ❷

ITALY

Camping Citta di Milano, V. G. Airaghi 61 (☎02 48 20 01 34). From Stazione Centrale take the Metro to MM1/3: Duomo or MM1/2: Cadorna; from either of these, take bus #62 towards D'Angelli and get off at Vittoria Caldera. Closed Dec.-Jan. Laundry €4.50. €13 per person. ❶

🛱 FOOD

Like its fine *couture*, Milanese cuisine is sophisticated and sometimes over-priced. Specialties include *risotto giallo* (rice with saffron), *cotoletta alla milanese* (breaded veal cutlet with lemon), and *cazzouela* (a mixture of pork and cabbage). *Pasticcerie* and *gelaterie* crowd every block. Sample the Milanese favorite, *panettone*, an Italian fruitcake. **Peck,** V. Cantu 3, off V. Orefici near P. Duomo, has sold delectables like *foie gras* and Black Forest ham since 1883. (Open M 3-7:30pm, Tu-Sa 8:45am-7:30pm.) **Supermarket Pam,** V. Piccinni 2, is off C. Buenos Aires. (Open Su and Tu-Sa 8:30am-9pm, M 3-9pm.)

🔳 Savini, Galleria Vittorio Emanuele II (☎02 72 00 34 33). Opposite the McDonald's—in every way. Italian writer Castellaneta once said, "Savini is as much a part of Milan as the Galleria and La Scala." Pay dearly for exquisite food, superb service, and most of all, bragging rights. *Primi* €14-20. *Secondi* €21-29. Cover €7. Service 12%. Open M-Sa 12:30-2:30pm and 7:30-10:30pm. AmEx/DC/MC/V. ❺

Osteria del Binari, V. Tortona 1 (☎02 89 40 94 28). MM2: Porta Genova. Head to the C. Colombo side of P. Stazione Porta Genova. Cross the train tracks to V. Tortona. Walls knitted from grapevines, an attentive staff, and exquisite regional cuisine render del Binari the perfect setting for an intimate meal. Unless explicitly refused, a platter of *antipasti* (€6) welcomes guests. *Primi* €6. *Secondi* €12. Open M-Sa 7pm-2am. MC/V. ❸

Osteria del Treno, V.S. Gregorio 46/48 (☎02 670 04 79). MM2/3: Centrale F.S. Hearty and reasonably priced food; self-service lunch and *primi* go for €4.20, *secondi* €6.50. In the evening the restaurant is sit-down and prices rise by a euro or two. Open Su-F noon-2:30pm and 7-10:30pm. ❷

Caffé Vecchia Brera, V. Dell'Orso 20 (☎02 86 46 16 95). MM1: Cordusio. From P. Cordusio take V. Broletto until it becomes V. M. Vetero. Creperie is on the left, at the intersection of V. Dell'Orso and V. M. Vetero. This classic in the Brera district serves Parisian chic with an Italian kick. Service 11%. Crepes €3.50-7. Open daily 7am-2am. ❷

Osteria La Piola, V. le Abruzzi 23 (☎02 29 53 12 71). Feast on homemade pasta and flavorful Lombardian cuisine at this *osteria con cucina* (tavern with a kitchen). *Primi* €8-9.50. *Secondi* €12-15. Open M-Sa 12:30-2:30pm and 7:30-11pm. AmEx/D/MC/V. ❹

Il Panino Giusto, V. Malpighi 3 (☎02 29 40 92 97). From MM1: Porta Venezia, turn onto V. Piave, and then take a left on V. Malpighi. Gourmet sandwiches are some of the best in Milan (€3.80-7). ❶

Il Fondaco dei Mori, V. Solferino 33 (☎02 65 37 11). MM2: Moscova. Limited but exquisite Middle Eastern offerings under a richly furnished tent among carpets, cushions, and tapestries. Buffet €12. Appetizers €2.50-4.50. Main courses €10-12. Cover €1.60. Open M-Sa noon-3pm and 7:30pm-midnight. DC/MC/V. ❸

Big Pizza: Da Willy 2, V. G. Borsi 1, along V. A. Sforza (☎02 83 96 77). This student favorite takes its name seriously: Witness the chefs shoving pies of epic proportions into the stone oven. Pizza €5-8. Open M-F 11am-midnight, Sa-Su 6pm-midnight. ❷

Princi Il Bread & Breakfast, V. Speronari 6, (☎02 87 47 97), off P. Duomo. A delicious break from the *duomo's* pricier sit-down options, this busy bakery touts golden *focaccia* slices and luscious *strudel di mele* (strudel with honey; €2.) Open M-Sa 9am-8:30pm. ❶

🎯 SIGHTS

🏛**DUOMO.** The Italian Gothic cathedral is the geographical and spiritual center of Milan and makes a good starting point for any walking tour of the city. The *duomo* is the third-largest church in the world, after St. Peter's and the Seville Cathedral. **Gian Galeazzo Visconti** started building the cathedral in 1386, hoping to flatter the Virgin into granting him a male heir. Construction proceeded sporadically over the next four centuries and was finally completed at Napoleon's command in 1809. In the meantime, the cathedral accumulated more than 3400 statues, 135 spires, and 96 gargoyles. The imposing 16th-century marble tomb of **Giacomo de Médici** in the south transept was inspired by the work of Michelangelo. Climb (or ride) to the top of the cathedral from outside the north transept, where you will find yourself surrounded by a fantastic field of turrets, spires, and statues, along with views of the city and the Alps. *(MM1: Duomo. Cathedral open daily Mar.-Oct. 7am-7pm; Nov.-Feb. 9am-4:15pm. Free. Modest dress required. Roof open daily 9am-5:30pm. €3.50, elevator €5.)* The **Museo del Duomo** displays artifacts relating to the *duomo's* construction. *(P. Duomo 14, to the right as you face the duomo. Open daily 10am-1:15pm and 3-6pm. €6.)*

🎭**TEATRO ALLA SCALA.** Since its founding in 1778, La Scala has established Milan as the opera capital of the world. Its understated Neoclassical facade and lavish interior set the stage for premiers of works by Rossini, Puccini, Mascagni, and Verdi, performed by virtuosos like Maria Callas. The theater's renovation was halted amid controversy in 2002, but it is scheduled to reopen in 2004. *(Through the Galleria Vittorio Emanuele from P. Duomo.)* Visitors can soak up La Scala's historical glow at the **Museo Teatrale alla Scala.** From poster art to a plaster cast of Toscanini's hand, the museum offers a glimpse into the art of opera's premier house. *(C. Magenta 71. MM1: Conciliazione. Open daily 9am-6pm. €5, students €4.)*

🏛**PINACOTECA AMBROSIANA.** The 23 tiny but lovely rooms of the Ambrosiana display exquisite works from the 14th through 19th century, including Botticelli's round *Madonna of the Canopy*, Leonardo's captivating *Portrait of a Musician*, Raphael's cartoon for *School of Athens*, Caravaggio's *Basket of Fruit* (the first still-life painting in Italy), Titian's *Adoration of the Magi*, works by Brueghel and Bril, and several portraits by Hayez. The courtyard is full of statues and busts, and the staircase is decorated with mosaics. *(P. Pio XI 2. ☎02 86 46 29 81. Follow V. Spadari off V. Torino and make a left onto V. Cantù. Open Su and Tu-Sa 10am-5:30pm. €7.50.)*

MUSEO POLDI PEZZOLI. Poldi Pezzoli, an 18th-century nobleman and art collector, bequeathed his house and its outstanding collection to the city "for the enjoyment of the people" in 1879. The museum's masterpieces hang in the Golden Room, overlooking a flower garden. Smaller collections fill Pezzoli's former private chambers, where the decor reflects his imagination and fine taste. Particularly impressive is a tiny but sublime display of Italian military armaments. *(V. Manzoni 12. Open Su and Tu-Sa 10am-6pm. €6.)*

PALAZZO REALE. South of the *duomo*, this structure first served as the town hall in 1138 before becoming the residence of *Milanese* royalty from the 12th to 19th centuries. Giuseppe Piermarini, architect of La Scala, designed its impressive facade with understated Neoclassical touches. Today it houses the **Museo d'Arte Contemporanea,** and a series of temporary exhibits. *(South of the duomo. Wheelchair accessible. Open Su and Tu-Sa 9:30am-7:30pm. €6.20-9.30, depending on the exhibit.)*

ITALY

GALLERIA VITTORIO EMANUELE II. Light pours through an immense glass and steel cupola (48m) and into a five-story arcade of expensive cafes, shops, and offices. Beautiful mosaics representing different continents sieged by the Romans adorn floors and walls and the central octagon's upper portion. Once considered the drawing room of Milan, the statue-bedecked Galleria is now an old and graceful mall. Spin on the mosaic bull clockwise three times for good luck, but gyrate in the opposite direction and the good luck will go bad. *(On the left, facing the duomo. Open M-Sa 10am-11pm, Su 10am-8pm.)*

MUSEO BAGATTI VALSECCHI. This beautifully preserved 19th-century aristocrat's house contains a collection of antique ceramics, frescoes, mosaics, ivory, and weapons in the Italian and Lombard Renaissance style. *(V. Santo Spirito 10. MM3: Napoleone. From V. M. Napoleone, V. Santo Spirito is the 2nd left. Open Su and Tu-Sa 1-5:45pm. M-Tu and Th-Su €6, W €3.)*

NEAR CASTELLO SFORZESCO

■ **CASTELLO SFORZESCO.** Restored after heavy bomb damage in 1943, the Castello Sforzesco is one of Milan's best-known monuments. Constructed in 1368 as a defense against Venice, it was used as an army barrack, a horse stall, and a storage house before da Vinci converted it into a studio. Inside are the **Musei Civici** (Civic Museums), which include the **Museo Degli Instrumenti Musicali** (Musical Instruments Museum) and the **Museo d'Arte Applicata** (Applied Arts Museum). The ground floor contains a sculpture collection most renowned for Michelangelo's unfinished, angular *Pietà Rondanini* (1564), his last work. The Applied Arts Museum showcases ornate household furnishings and stars the *Automa contesta di demonio*. Play puppeteer to the red-eyed wooden demon by cranking the lever below. The underground level has several jeweled mummy cases among a small Egyptian collection. *(MM1: Cairoli. Open Tu-Su 9:30am-7:30pm. Free.)*

PINACOTECA DI BRERA. The Brera Art Gallery presents a superb collection of 14th- to 20th-century paintings, with an emphasis on the Lombard School. Works include Bellini's *Pietà*, Hayez's *The Kiss*, Andrea Mantegna's brilliant *Dead Christ*, Raphael's *Marriage of the Virgin*, Caravaggio's *Supper at Emmaus*, and Piero della Francesca's 15th-century *Sacra Conversazione*. *(V. Brera 280. MM2: Lanza. Wheelchair accessible. Open Su and Tu-Sa 8:30am-7:15pm. €6.20.)*

STADIO GIUSEPPE MEAZZA. Nothing in Milan comes close to the rivalry between its two soccer clubs, Inter and A.C. As passions roil, the city reaches a feverish pitch heightened by political overtones: Inter fans are often left-wing, while A.C. fans tend to be right-wing. The face-off takes place in their shared three-tiered stadium (capacity 85,700), architecturally distinct for its spiralling ramps around the outside. Victory celebrations spill into the streets afterward, marred by occasional bursts of violence. An English-language tour leads through VIP seats, a museum of memorabilia, and the locker rooms. *(MM2: Lotto. Tours M-Sa 10am-6pm. €10, under-18 or over-65 €7. Tickets for either team are available at all Ticket One offices; call ☎02 39 22 61 for locations.)*

CHIESA DI SANTA MARIA DELLA GRAZIE. The church's Gothic nave is dark and elaborately patterned with frescoes, contrasting the splendid, airy Renaissance tribune Bramante added in 1492. The extensive interior renovations allow for a before and after view of the frescoes. Next to the church entrance, in what was once the dining hall, is the **Cenacolo Vinciano** (Vinciano Refectory), home to one of the most important pieces of art in the world: **Leonardo da Vinci's Last Supper.** The painting captures the apostles' reaction to Jesus' prophecy: "One of you will betray me." Make reservations well in advance or risk missing it. *(P. di S. Maria delle Grazie 2, on C. Magenta, off V. Carducci. MM1: Cadorna Cairoli. ☎02 89 42 11 46. Open Su and Tu-F 8am-7:30pm, Sa 8am-11pm. Entrance to Last Supper €6.50.)*

MUSEO NAZIONALE DELLA SCIENZA E DELLA TECNICA "DA VINCI". The brilliance and visionary impact of da Vinci, the first true Renaissance man, in all things technical serves as an ideological foundation for this museum. Tracing innovation from his day through the present, the museum provides a historical view of the precursors of modern technology. The hall of computer technology features an interesting hybrid: A piano converted to a typewriter by Edoardo Hughes of Turin in 1885. The keys have letters pasted to them, and a ribbon receives the letters from a spinning wheel. Another section focuses on applied physics, while wooden models of Leonardo's most visionary inventions fill another room. *(V. San Vittore 21, off V. Carducci. MM2: San Ambrogio. Open Tu-F 9:30am-4:50pm, Sa-Su 9:30am-6:20pm. €6.20.)*

BASILICA DI SANT'AMBROGIO. A prototype for Lombard-Romanesque churches throughout Italy, Sant'Ambrogio is the most influential medieval building in Milan. Ninth-century reliefs in brilliant silver and gold decorate the high altar. St. Ambrose presided over this building between AD 379 and 386. Now visitors may preside over him: Go behind the altar, on either side, and descend into a dim sarcophagus, where the skeletal remains of the saint rest beside those of his eternal bedmate, St. Protasio. The two asymmetrical **belltowers** to the right and left of the facade are not miscalculations, but remains of an 8th century dispute between a group of Benedictine monks and the priests of the church. To make their case, the monks built the belltower on the right. The priests quickly followed up with their own version on the left. The bellringing competition that ensued forced the archbishop to arbitrate over who should ring the bell at what time and for how long. The 4th-century **Cappella di San Vittore in Ciel D'oro,** with exquisite 5th-century mosaics adorning its cupola, lies through the 7th chapel on the right; enter and then turn left. *(MM1: San Ambrogio. Walk up V. G. Carducci, and the church bulwark rises up to the right. Open M-Sa 7:30am-noon and 2:30-7pm, Su 3-7pm. Free. Audio guide €1.)*

NAVIGLI AND CORSO DI PORTA TICINESE

▨ NAVIGLI DISTRICT. The Navigali district, often called the Venice of Lombardy, the Navigli district comes alive at night. Complete with canals, small footbridges, open-air markets, cafes, alleys, and trolleys, the Navigli are part of a medieval canal system (da Vinci designed the original locks) that transported thousands of tons of marble to build the *duomo* and linked Milan to various northern cities and lakes. *(Outside the MM2: Porta Genova station, through the Arco di Porta Ticinese.)*

BASILICA DI SANT'EUSTORGIO. Founded in the 4th century to house the bones of the Magi, the church lost its original function when the dead wise men were spirited off to Cologne in 1164. The present building, erected in 1278, dons a Lombard-Gothic interior of brick ribs, low vaults, and substantial columns. The aesthetic pinnacle of the church, and one of the great masterpieces of early Renaissance art, is the **Portinari Chapel** (1468), attributed to Michelozzo. It holds the Gothic tomb of St. Eustorgious (1339), whose ornate casket rests upon the white marble shoulders of the statues of 8 devotees—one of whom has three faces. Near the front of the church is the 12th-century **Porta Ticinese.** *(P.S. Eustorigio 3, down C. Ticinese from S. Lorenzo Maggiore. Tram #3. Open Su-M and W-Sa 9:30am-noon and 3:30-6pm. Cappella open Su and Tu-Sa 4:30-6:30pm.)*

CHIESA DI SAN LORENZO MAGGIORE. The oldest church in Milan, San Lorenzo Maggiore testifies to the city's 4th-century greatness. To its right lies the **Cappella di Sant'Aquilino,** which contains a 5th-century mosaic of a beardless Christ among his apostles. *(On C. Ticinese. MM2: Porta Genova, then tram #3 from V. Torino. Open daily 7:30am-6:45pm. Cappella €2. Students €1.)*

ITALY

IN THE GIARDINI PUBBLICI

GALLERIA D'ARTE MODERNA. Napoleon lived here with Josephine when Milan was the capital of the Napoleonic Kingdom of Italy (1805-1814). The gallery, reminiscent of Versailles, displays modern Lombardian art as well as works by Impressionists. Of special note are Modigliani's *Beatrice Hastings* (1915), Picasso's *Testa*, Klee's *Wald Bau*, and Morandi's *Natura Morta con Bottiglia*. *(V. Palestro 16, in the Villa Reale. MM1/2: Palestro. Open Su and Tu-Sa 9am-5:30pm. Free.)* Nearby is the **Padiglione D'Arte Contemporanea** (PAC), an extravaganza of video, photographs, multimedia, and painting. *(Across P. Cardorna to Paleocapa, which becomes V. Alemagna. M1: Cardorna. Wheelchair accessible. Open Su-W and F 9:30am-6pm, Th 9:30am-7pm. €8.)*

MUSEO CIVICO DI STORIA NATURALE. Milan's Museum of Natural History holds extensive geological and paleontological collections, including fossils, minerals, and geological and botanical specimen. Though overshadowed by Milan's other attractions, it is a pleasant destination for someone with extra time or interest in the subject. *(C. Venezia 55. Open M-F 9am-6pm, Sa-Su 9:30am-6pm.)*

⬛🅢 SHOPPING AND NIGHTLIFE

If Milan's status as a world-famous fashion capital has lured you here for shopping, don't despair about the prices. If you can tolerate the stigma of being an entire season behind, purchase your famous designer duds from *blochisti* (wholesale clothing outlets), such as **Monitor** on V. Monte Nero (MM3: Porta Romana, then tram #9 or 29) or the well-known **Il Salvagente,** V. Bronzetti 16, off C. XXII Marzo (bus #60 from MM1: Lima or MM2/3: Stazione Centrale). The clothing sold along **Corso Buenos Aires** is more affordable—all the stores are open 10am-12:30pm and 2:30-7pm. Winter sales begin January 10. Shop in late July for end-of-the-summer sales (20-50% off) and a glimpse of the new fall lines. Hard-core window shoppers should head to the world-famous ⬛**fashion district** between **Corso Vittorio Emanuele** near the *duomo* and **Via Monte Napoleone** off P. San Babila. The dresses come straight from the designers and the selection is more up-to-date than anywhere else in the world, including New York and Tokyo. Expect to find high-class places to buy perfume, glasses, leather goods, shoes, and jewelry.

Milan Oltre is a festival of drama, dance and music; call the **Ufficio Informazione del Comune** (☎02 86 46 40 94) for more details. Milan's increasingly popular **Carnevale,** which spans the three days after Ash Wednesday, is the longest festival in Italy. The revelry centers around the *duomo* and spreads throughout the city. Milan's nightlife resembles the sophisticated city: The vibrant, the mellow, the chic, and the wild all live within a few Metro stops. The **Navigali district** is a particularly popular area for nightlife.

- 🔲 **Le Trottoir,** near V. Brera. From MM2: Lanza, take V. Tivoli to the C. Garibaldi intersection. A lively atmosphere with live bands nightly. Open daily 7pm-2:30am.

- 🔲 **Scimmie,** V. Sforza 49. A legendary, energetic bar. Different theme every night and frequent concerts; fusion, jazz, soul, and reggae dominate. Open daily 8pm-3am.

- **Alcatraz,** V. Valtellina 25. MM2: Porta Garibaldi. Take V. Ferrari and go right on C. Farni. After the train tracks, turn left on V. Valtellina. Biggest club and indoor concert venue in Milan. Cover €14 includes 1 drink. Open F-Sa 11pm-3am.

- **Maya,** V. A. Sforza 41. Totem poles, funky geometric figures and highly entertaining drinks (€5) like the *cuccaracha de toro* fuel the easygoing groove. Cover €2. Rowdy Happy Hour 6-9pm (€5). Open M-Su 8pm-2am.

- **Loolapaloosa,** C. Como 15. A wild crowd will have you dancing on the tables. Cover €6, includes 1 drink. Open Su-Th 6pm-3am.

Grand Café Fashion, C. Porta Ticinese, near V. Vetere. A bar/restaurant/dance club with a stunningly beautiful crowd and velour leopard-print couches. €7.80 cover includes 1 drink. Open Su and Tu-Sa 6pm-4am.

Exploit, V. Piopette 3, to the right just before S. Lorenzo Maggiore. A trendy bar and restaurant with cheap beer from €3. Join the crowd of locals around the colonnade. No cover. Open daily noon-3pm and 6pm-3am.

Le Biciclette, V. Conca dei Naviglio 10. A *bici* dangling above the entrance harkens back to the chic but smartly priced bar's predecessor, a bike shop. Beer €4.50. Mixed drinks €5.50. Scrumptious Happy Hour buffet, 6:30-9:30pm. Open daily 7pm-2am.

Blueshouse, V.S. Uguzzone 26. MM1: Villa S. Giovanni. Take V. Vipacco; turn right on V. A. Soffredini and left on V.S. Uguzzone. Good jazz, blues, rock, and tribute bands on a spacious floor. Schedule online. Open Su and W-Sa 9pm-2:30am.

Lelephante, V. Melzo 22. MM2: Porta Venezia; walk up C. Buenos Aires and turn right on V. Melzo. Vaguely 60s gay club with lava lamps. Open Su and Tu-Sa 6:30pm-2am.

MANTUA (MANTOVA)   ☎0376

Mantua (pop. 100,000) owes its literary fame to its celebrated son, the poet Virgil. Its grand *palazzi* and graceful churches come thanks to the Gonzaga family who, after ascending to power in 1328, imported well-known artists to change Mantua's small-town image. Once the largest palace in Europe, the opulent ▓**Palazzo Ducale** towers over **Piazza Sordello,** sheltering the Gothic **Magna Domus** and **Palazzo del Capitano.** Inside, check out a breathtaking array of frescoes, gardens, and facades. Outside the *palazzo*, signs point to the **Castello di San Giorgio** (1390-1406), a formidable fortress before its absorption into the *palazzo* complex. (*Palazzo* open Su and Tu-Sa 8:45am-6:30pm. €6.50, students €3.25. Children and seniors free.) In the far south of the city, down V.P. Amedeo, through P. Veneto, and down Largo Parri, lies the **Palazzo di Te,** built by Giulio Romano in 1534 as a suburban retreat for Federico II Gonzaga. It is widely considered the finest building in the Mannerist style. (Open M 1-6pm, Tu-Su 9am-6pm. €8, students €2.50.) Just south of P. Sordello is the 11th-century Romanesque **Piazza delle Erbe;** opposite the *piazza* is Leon Alberti's **Chiesa di Sant'Andrea,** Mantua's greatest contribution to the Italian Renaissance and one of the first monumental Classical constructions since Imperial Rome. (*Piazza* open daily 10am-12:30pm and 2:30-4:30pm, *Chiesa* open daily 8am-noon and 3-6:30pm. Both free.)

Trains go from P. Don E. Leoni to Milan (2hr., 9 per day, €8) and Verona (40min., 17 per day, €2.30). From the train station, head left on V. Solferino, through P.S. Francesco d'Assisi to V. Fratelli Bandiera, and right on V. Verdi to reach the **tourist office,** P. Mantegna 6, next to Chiesa Sant'Andrea. (☎0376 32 82 53; www.aptmantova.it. Open M-Sa 8:30am-12:30pm and 3-6pm, Su 9:30-12:30pm.) Charming **Hotel ABC ❸,** P. Don E. Leoni 25, is opposite the station. (☎0376 32 33 47; fax 0376 32 23 29. Breakfast included. Singles €44-66; doubles €66-99; triples €77-110.) **Antica Osteria ai Ranari ❷,** V. Trieste 11, down V. Pomponazzo near Porta Catena, specializes in regional dishes. (☎0376 32 84 31. *Primi* €5-7. *Secondi* €5-9. Closed for 3 weeks July-Aug. Open Su and Tu-Sa noon-2pm and 7-11:30pm.) **Postal Code:** 46100.

BERGAMO   ☎035

Bergamo's (pop. 110,000) two sections reflect its colorful history: while the *città alta* (upper city) reveals its origins as a Venetian outpost, the *città bassa* (lower city) is a modern metropolis packed with Neoclassical buildings. **Via Pignolo,** in the *città bassa*, winds past a succession of handsome 16th- to 18th-century palaces. Turning left onto V.S. Tomaso and then right brings you to the **Galleria dell'Accademia Carrara,** which holds works by Breughel, van Dyck, Rubens, and Titian. (Open Apr.-Sept. Su and Tu-Sa 10am-1pm and 3-6:45pm; Oct.-Mar. 9:30am-1pm and 2:30pm-5:45pm. €2.60.) From the Galleria, the cobbled **Via Noca** ascends to the medieval *città alta* through the 16th-century **Porta S. Agostino.** Stroll down V. Porta Dipinta to V. Gambito, which ends in **Piazza Vecchia,** an ensemble of medieval and Renaissance buildings flanked by restaurants and cafes at the heart of the *città alta.* Head through the archway near P. Vecchia to P. del Duomo, and see the fresco-laden **Cappella Colleoni.** (Open Apr.-Oct. daily 9am-12:30pm and 2-6:30pm; Nov.-Feb. Su and Tu-Sa 9am-12:30pm and 2:30-4:30pm.) Immediately left of the Cappella Colleoni is the ⊠**Basilica di Santa Maria Maggiore,** a 12th-century basilica with an ornate Baroque interior and tapestries depicting Biblical scenes. (Open daily Apr.-Oct. 9am-12:30pm and 2:30-6pm; Nov.-Mar. reduced hours.) Climb the **Torre Civica** (Civic Tower) for a marvelous view of Bergamo. (Open May to mid-Sept. Su-Th 10am-8pm, F-Sa 10am-10pm; mid-Sept. to Apr. reduced hours. €1.)

The train station, bus station, and many budget hotels are in the *città bassa.* **Trains** (1hr., every hr., €3.65) and **buses** (every 30min. €4.10) pull into P. Marconi from Milan. To get to the **tourist office,** V. Aquila Nera 2, in the *città alta,* take bus #1a to the top of the *città alta.* (☎035 24 22 26; www.apt.bergamo.it. Open daily 9am-12:30pm and 2-5:30pm.) To get from the train station to **Ostello della Gioventù di Bergamo (HI) ❶,** V.G. Ferraris 1, take bus #9 to *Comozzi,* then take bus #14 to *Leonardo da Vinci* and walk up the hill. (☎/fax 035 36 17 24. **Internet** €5.20 per hr. Lockout 10am-2pm. Curfew midnight. Dorms €14. HI members only. MC/V.) **Locanda Caironi ❷,** V. Toretta 6B, off V. Gorgo Palazzo, is in a quiet residential neighborhood. Take bus #5 or 7 from V. Angelo Maj. (☎ 24 30 83. Singles €20; doubles €38. MC/V.) The friendly, student-run **Cooperativa Città Alta ❶,** has fast service and tasty cuisine. (☎035 21 85 68. Open daily noon-midnight.) **Postal Code:** 24122.

THE LAKE COUNTRY

When Italy's monuments and museums start blurring together, escape to the natural beauty of the northern Lake Country, where clear waters lap the encircling mountains. A young crowd descends upon Lake Garda for its watersports by day and thriving club scene at night; palatial hotels line Lake Maggiore's sleepy beaches, while Lake Como's urbane shore hosts three excellent hostels.

LAKE COMO (LAGO DI COMO)

Although a heavenly magnificence lingers over the reaches of Europe's deepest lake (410m), peaceful Lake Como is more than a figment of your imagination. *Bougainvillea* and lavish villas adorn the lake's craggy backdrop, warmed by the sun and cooled by lakeside breezes. Como, the largest city on the lake, makes an ideal transportation hub. Menaggio, one of the three smaller Centro Lago towns, is an alternate base for exploring the lake, and makes for a more relaxing stay.

⌷ TRANSPORTATION. The only town on the lake accessible by train is Como. **Trains** roll into Stazione San Giovanni (☎0147 88 80 88) from Milan (1hr., every 30min. 4:45am-11:35pm, €4.85) and Venice (4hr., every hr. 4:45am-7:55pm, €22). **Bus** C46 leave P. Matteotti for Bergamo (2hr., every hr., €4.30). From Como, take the C10 near Ferrovia Nord to Menaggio (1hr., every hr. 7:10am-8:30pm, €2.50). Hourly C30 buses also serve Bellagio (1hr., 6:34am-8:14pm, €2.80). Spend the day zipping between stores, gardens, villas, and wineries of the remaining towns by **ferry** (day pass €7-17).

COMO. Situated on the southwest tip of the lake, at the end of the Milan rail line, Como is the lake's token semi-industrial town. For excellent **hiking** and stunning views, head from the far end of Lungo Lario Trieste up to **Brunate.** To get from the train station to the **tourist office,** P. Cavour 16, walk down the steps, turn left on V. Fratelli Ricchi and turn right on V. Fratelli Rosselli, which leads to P. Cavour via Lungo Lario Trento. (☎031 26 97 12; www.lakecomo.org. Open M-Sa 9am-1pm and 2:30-6pm, Su 9:30-1pm.) **Ostello Villa Olmo (HI) ❶,** V. Bellinzona 2, offers clean rooms, great food, and discounts on various sights in Como. From the train station, walk 20min. down V. Borgo Vico, which becomes V. Bellinzona. (☎/fax 031 57 38 00. hostellocomo@tin.it. Breakfast included. Reception 7-10am and 4-11:30pm. Lockout 10am. Strict curfew 11:30pm. Open Mar-Nov. Reserve ahead. Dorms €15) **In Riva al Lago ❷,** P. Matteotti 4, is centrally located with immaculate rooms. (☎031 30 23 33; www.inrivallago.com. Breakfast €2-4. Singles €30-40; doubles €50-60.) The **G.S. supermarket** is at V. Recchi and V. Fratelli Roselli. (Open M 9am-9:30pm, Tu-F 8am-8:30pm, Sa 8am-8pm.) **Postal Code:** 22100.

MENAGGIO. Menaggio is home to historic streets, stunning scenery, and a youth hostel that makes it a perfect northern getaway. From the top of **Rifugio Menaggio,** 1400m above the lake, hikers can make trips to **Monte Grona** and the **Chiesa di S. Amate.** A 1-2hr. hike (each way) leads to the spectacular **Sass Corbee Gorge;** inquire at the **tourist office,** P. Garibaldi 4, for directions and maps. (☎034 43 29 24. infomenaggio@tiscalinet.it. Open M-Sa 9am-noon and 3-6pm.) To get to the resort-like ▨**Ostello La Prinula (HI) ❶,** V. IV Novembre 86, walk along the shore to the main thoroughfare, go past the gas station, and walk up the less steep incline on the right. (☎034 43 23 56; www.menaggiohostel.com. Breakfast included. Lockout 10am-5pm. Curfew 11:30pm. Call ahead to reserve. Open Mar.-Nov. Dorms €13.50; family rooms of 4-6 beds and private bath €14.)

LAKE MAGGIORE (LAGO MAGGIORE)

Lacking the frenzy of its eastern neighbors, Lake Maggiore combines similar temperate mountain waters and idyllic shores. The romantic resort town **Stresa** is only an hour from Milan by **train** (every hr., €5.10). The local **tourist office** is in the ferry building at the dock, in P. Martini. (☎/fax 0323 30 150. Open daily 10am-12:30pm and 3-6:30pm.) To reach **Orsola Meublé ❷,** V. Duchessa di Genova 45, turn right from the station, walk downhill to the intersection and turn left. The affordable blue-tiled rooms have cement balconies. (☎0323 31 087; fax 0323 93 31 21. Breakfast included. Singles €15, with bath €30; doubles €30/40. AmEx/D/MC/V.)

⚡ DAYTRIP FROM LAKE MAGGIORE: BORROMEAN ISLANDS. Stresa is a perfect stepping-stone to the gorgeous Borromean Islands. Daily excursion tickets (€10) allow you to hop back and forth between Stresa and the three islands—**Isola Bella, Isola Superiore dei Pescatori,** and **Isola Madre.** The islands boast lush, manicured botanical gardens and elegant villas. The opulent, Baroque ▨**Palazzo e Giardini Borromeo,** on Isola Bella, features six meticulously designed rooms with priceless masterpieces, tapestries and sculptures. The 10 terraced gardens, punctuated with statues and topped by a unicorn, rise up like a large wedding cake. (Open Mar.-Sept. daily 9am-5:30pm; Oct. 9am-5pm. €8.50.)

LAKE GARDA (LAGO DI GARDA)

Garda has staggering mountains and breezy summers. **Desenzano,** the lake's southern transport hub, is only 30min. from Verona, 1hr. from Milan, and 2hr. from Venice. Sirmione and Gardone Riviera, easily accessible by bus and boat, are best explored as daytrips, as accommodations are scant and pricey.

ITALY

SIRMIONE. Sirmione's beautiful 13th-century castle and Roman ruins make for a leisurely day or a busy afternoon. **Buses** run every hour from Verona (1hr., €2.70). *Battelli* (water steamers) run until 8pm to: Desenzano (20min., €3); Gardone (1¼hr., €5.40); and Riva (4hr., €7.80). The **tourist office,** V. Guglielmo Marconi 2, is in the disc-shaped building. (☎030 91 61 14. Open Apr.-Oct. daily 9am-9pm; Nov.-Mar. reduced hours.) The **Albergo Grifone ❸,** V. Bocchio 4, has country-style rooms, all with bath, and lake views. (☎030 91 60 14; fax 030 91 65 48. Reserve ahead. Singles €32; doubles €55.) **Postal Code:** 25019.

GARDONE RIVIERA. Formerly the playground of the rich and famous, this town is now home to Lake Garda's most famous sight: the villa of 20th-century poet and latter-day Casanova Gabriele D'Annunzio. His quirky mansion, **Il Vittoriale,** sprawls above Gardone. (Villa open Apr.-Sept. Su and Tu-Sa 8:30am-8pm. Gardens open Oct.-Mar. reduced hours. €11.) **Buses** (☎0365 210 61) run to Milan (3hr., 2 per day, €8). The **APT tourist office,** V. Repubblica 8, is in the center of Gardone Sotto. (☎/fax 0365 20 347. Open daily 9am-12:30pm and 3:30-6:30pm.) **Postal Code:** 25083.

RIVA DEL GARDA. Riva's calm pebble beaches are Lake Garda's compromise for the budget traveler. Travelers **swim, windsurf, hike,** and **climb** near the most stunning portion of the lake, where cliffs crash into the water. Riva is accessible by **bus** (☎0464 55 23 23) from Trent (2hr., 10 per day, €3.20) and Verona (2hr., 11 per day, €5). **Ferries** (☎030 914 95 11) leave from P. Matteoti for Gardone (€6.60). The **tourist office,** Giardini di Porta Orientale 8, is near the water. (☎0464 55 44 44; fax 52 03 08. Open M-Sa 9am-noon and 3-6pm, Su 10am-noon and 4-6:30pm.) Snooze at the fabulous **Locanda La Montanara ❷,** V. Montanara 20, off V. Florida. (☎/fax 0464 55 48 57. Breakfast €5. Singles €16; doubles €32-35; triples €49.) **Postal Code:** 38066.

ITALIAN RIVIERA (LIGURIA)

The Italian Riviera stretches 350km along the Mediterranean between France and Tuscany, forming the most famous and most touristed area of the Italian coastline. Genoa divides the crescent-shaped strip into the **Riviera di Levante** ("rising sun") to the east and the **Riviera di Ponente** ("setting sun") to the west. The elegant coast beckons with lemon trees, almond blossoms, and turquoise seas. Especially lovely is the **Cinque Terre** area, just to the west of **La Spezia.**

▐ TRANSPORTATION

The coastal towns are linked by the main **rail** line, which runs west to Ventimiglia (near the French border) and east to La Spezia (near Tuscany), but slow local trains can make short trips take hours. Frequent intercity **buses** pass through all major towns, and local buses run to inland hill-towns. **Boats** connect most resort towns. **Ferries** go from Genoa to Olbia, Sardinia and Palermo, Sicily.

GENOA (GENOVA)   ☎010

Genoa (pop. 640,000), city of grit and grandeur, has little in common with its resort neighbors. A Ligurian will tell you, *"Si deve conosceria per amaria"* (you have to know her to love her). While lacking the intimacy of a small-town resort, Genoa more than makes up for it in its rich cultural history and extravagant sights. Since falling into decline in the 18th century, modern Genoa has turned its attention from industry and trade to the restoration of its bygone splendor, and is once again claiming its position among Italy's most important cultural centers.

TRANSPORTATION. C. **Columbo Internazionale** airport (GOA), in Sesti Ponente, services European destinations. Take **Volabus** #100 from Stazione Brignole to the airport (every 30min., €2) and get off at *Aeroporto*. Most visitors arrive at one of Genoa's two **train stations: Stazione Principe,** in P. Acquaverde, or **Stazione Brignole,** in P. Verdi. **Trains** go to Rome (5hr., 9 per day, €33) and Turin (2hr., 19 per day, €9). AMT **buses** (☎010 558 24 14) run throughout the city. One-way tickets (€1) are valid for 1½hr.; all-day passes cost €3. **Ferries** depart from the Ponte Assereto arm of the port; buy tickets at **Stazione Marittima** in the port.

ORIENTATION AND PRACTICAL INFORMATION. To get to the center of town, **Piazza de Ferrari,** from Stazione Principe, take **Via Balbi** to **Via Cairoli,** which becomes **Via Garibaldi,** and turn right on **Via XXV Aprile** at P. delle Fontane Marose. From Stazione Brignole, turn right onto **Via Fiume,** and right onto **Via XX Settembre.** Or, take bus #19, 20, 30, 32, 35, or 41 from Stazione Principe or bus #19 or 40 from Stazione Brignole to P. de Ferrari in the center of town. The **centro storico** (historic center) contains many of Genoa's monuments. The **tourist office** is on Porto Antico, in Palazzina S. Maria. From the aquarium, walk toward the complex of buildings to the left. (☎010 24 87 11; www.genovatouristboard.net. Open M-Sa 9am-1pm and 2-6pm.) Log on to the **Internet** at **APCA,** V. Colombo 35r. (☎/fax 010 58 13 41. €5.40 per hr. Open M-F 9am-noon.) **Postal Code:** 16121.

ACCOMMODATIONS AND FOOD. Ostello per la Gioventù (HI) ❶, V. Costanzi 120, has a cafeteria, TV, and a view of the city far below. From Stazione Principe, take bus #35 to V. Napoli and transfer to #40, which runs to the hostel. From Stazione Brignole, pick up bus #40 (every 15min.) and ask to be let off at the *ostello.* (☎/fax 010 242 24 57. Breakfast included. Reception 7-11am and 3:30pm-12:30am. No curfew. HI members only. Dorms €13.) **Hotel Balbi ❸,** V. Balbi 21/3, offers large, ornate rooms. (☎/fax 010 25 23 62. Breakfast €4. Singles €30, with bath €45; doubles €55/70; triples €75/85. AmEx/MC/V.) **Camping** is popular; check the tourist office for availability, or try **Genova Est ❶** on V. Marcon Loc Cassa. Take the train from Stazione Brignole to the suburb of Bogliasco (10min., 6 per day, €1); a free bus (5min., every 2hr. 8:10am-6pm) will take you from Bogliasco to the campsite. (☎010 347 20 53. Electricity €1.80 per day. Laundry €3.50 per load. €4.70 per person, €9.60 per tent.) **Trattoria da Maria ❷,** V. Testa d'Oro 14r, off V. XXV Aprile, has new selections every day, with a three-course *menu* for €8. (☎010 58 10 80. Open Su-F noon-2:30pm and 7-9:30pm.)

SIGHTS AND ENTERTAINMENT. Genoa boasts a multitude of *palazzi* built by its famous merchant families. These are best seen along **Via Garibaldi,** on the edge of *centro storico,* and **Via Balbi,** in the heart of the university quarter. The 17th-century **Palazzo Reale,** V. Balbi 10, 10min. west of V. Garibaldi, is filled with Rococo rooms bathed in gold and upholstered in red velvet. (Open Su and Th-Sa 9am-7pm, Tu-W 9am-1:30pm. €4, ages 18-25 €2, under-18 and seniors free.) Follow V. Balbi through P. della Nunziata and continue to L. Zecca, where V. Cairoli leads to **Via Garibaldi,** the most impressive street in Genoa, bedecked with elegant *palazzi* that once earned it the names "Golden Street" and "Street of Kings." The **Galleria di Palazzo Bianco,** V. Garibaldi 11, exhibits Ligurian, Dutch, and Flemish paintings. Across the street, the 17th-century **Galleria Palazzo Rosso,** V. Garibaldi 18, has magnificent furnishings in a lavishly frescoed interior. (Both open Su 10am-6pm, Tu-Sa 9am-7pm. €3.10 each, €5.20 for both. Su free.) The **Villetta Di Negro,** on the hill further down V. Garibaldi, contains waterfalls, grottoes, and terraced gardens. From P. de Ferrari, take V. Boetto to P. Matteotti for the ornate **Chiesa di Gesù.** (Open daily 7:15am-12:30pm and 4-7:30pm.) Head past the Chiesa di

ITALY

Gesù down V. di Porta Soprana to V. Ravecca to reach the medieval twin-towered **Porta Soprana,** the supposed boyhood home of **Christopher Columbus.** Off V.S. Lorenzo lies the **San Lorenzo Duomo,** a church in existence since the 9th century, which boasts a striped Gothic facade with a copiously decorated main entrance and 9th-century carved lions. (Open M-Sa 8am-7pm, Su 7am-7pm.) The **centro storico,** the eerie and beautiful historical center bordered by the port, V. Garibaldi, and P. Ferrari, is a mass of winding and confusing streets containing some of Genoa's most memorable monuments, including the **duomo** and the medieval **Torre Embraici.** However, a dangerous night scene makes visiting the *centro storico* best confined to weekdays when stores are open. From P. Matteotti, go down V.S. Lorenzo toward the water, turn left on V. Chiabrera and left on V. di Mascherona to reach the **Chiesa S. Maria di Castello,** a labyrinth of chapels, courtyards, cloisters, and crucifixes. (Open daily 9am-noon and 3-6pm.) Kids and ocean-lovers will adore the massive **aquarium** on Porto Antico to the right of the APT tourist office. (Open July-Aug. daily 9:30am-11pm; Sept.-June reduced hours. €12.)

RIVIERA DI PONENTE

FINALE LIGURE   ☎019

A beachside plaque proclaims the town of Finale Ligure (pop. 15,000) the place for "*Il riposo del popolo*" (the people's rest). From bodysurfing in choppy waves to browsing through chic boutiques to scaling the 15th-century ruins of **Castello di San Giovanni,** *riposo* takes many forms in Finale Ligure. The city is divided into three sections: **Finalpia** to the east, **Finalmarina** in the center, and **Finalborgo** further inland. The train station and most sights are in Finalmarina. Skip the packed beaches in town and walk east along V. Aurelia through the first tunnel, turning right for a less populated **free beach.** Climb the tough trail to the ruins of **Castel Govone** for a spectacular view. Enclosed within ancient walls, **Finalborgo,** the historic quarter of Finale Ligure proper, is a 1km walk or short ACTS bus ride up V. Bruneghi from the station. **Pilade,** V. Garibaldi 67, features live jazz on Friday nights. (☎019 69 22 20. Open daily 10am-2am.) The towns near Finale Ligure are also worth exploring. SAR **buses** run from the train station to **Borgo Verezzi** (10min., every 15min., €1.50).

Trains leave from P. Vittorio Veneto for Genoa (1hr., every hr., €3.80). The IAT **tourist office,** V.S. Pietro 14, gives out free maps. (☎019 68 10 19; fax 019 68 18 04. Open M-Sa 9am-12:30pm and 3:30-6:30pm, Su 9am-noon.) Check email at **Net Village Internet Cafe,** near the train station. (☎019 681 62 83. Open daily 8:15am-midnight. €5.50 per hr.) **Castello Wuillerman (HI) ❶,** on V. Generale Caviglia, is well worth the hike. From the train station, cross the street and turn left onto V. Raimondo Pertica, then left onto V. Rossi. After passing a church on the left, take a left onto V. Alonzo, and trudge up the daunting steps to a red-brick castle with a stunning view of the sea. (☎019 69 05 15; hostelfinaleligure@libero.it. Breakfast and sheets included. Internet access €4.50 per hr. Reception daily 7-10am and 5-10pm. Curfew 11:30pm. Email reservations. HI members only. Dorms €11.) **Albergo San Marco ❸,** V. della Concezione 22, has spotless rooms, many with balconies. From train station, walk straight ahead down V. Saccone, and turn left on V. della Concezione. (☎019 69 25 33; fax 681 6187. Open Easter-late Sept. Singles €33-39; doubles €45-57. Extra bed €10. AmEx/DC/MC/V.) **Camping Del Mulino ❶,** on V. Castelli, has a restaurant and mini-market on the premises. Take the Calvisio bus from the station to the Boncardo Hotel and follow the brown-and-yellow signs to the campsite entrance. (☎019 60 16 69. Reception Apr.-Sept. 8am-8pm. €4.50-6 per person, €5-7 per tent.) Cheap restaurants lie along **Via Rossi, Via Roma,** and **Via**

Garibaldi. Fill up on huge portions of delicious pasta at **Spaghetteria Il Posto ❷**, V. Porro 21. The **Coop supermarket** is at V. Dante Alighieri 7. (Open M-Sa 8:30am-7:30pm, Su 9am-1pm. MC/V.) **Postal Code:** 17024.

RIVIERA DI LEVANTE

CAMOGLI. Postcard-perfect Camogli shimmers with color. Sun-faded peach houses crowd the hilltop, red and turquoise boats bob in the water, piles of fishing nets cover the docks, and bright umbrellas dot the dark stone beaches. **Trains** run on the Genoa-La Spezia line to Genoa (40min., 38 per day, €1.50) and La Spezia (1½hr., 24 per day, €3.50). Golfo Paradiso **ferries**, V. Scalo 3 (☎0185 77 20 91; www.golfoparadiso.it), near P. Colombo, go to Portofino (round-trip €16) and Cinque Terre (round-trip €20). Buy tickets on the dock, call ahead for the schedule. Turn right from the station to find the **tourist office**, V. XX Settembre 33, which helps find rooms. (☎0185 77 10 66. Open M-Sa 9am-12:30pm and 3:30-7pm, Su 9am-1pm.) Exit the train station, walk down the stairway to the right, and look for the blue sign for the ▨**Albergo La Camogliese ❹**, V. Garibaldi 55, near the beach. (☎0185 77 14 02; fax 77 40 24. **Internet** access €1 per 30min. Singles €51-59; doubles €69-80. 10% *Let's Go* discount with cash payment. AmEx/MC/V.) **Postal Code:** 16032.

SANTA MARGHERITA LIGURE. Santa Margherita Ligure was a calm fishing village until the early 20th century, when it fell into favor with Hollywood stars. Today, glamour and glitz paint the shore, but the serenity of the town's early days still lingers. If ocean waves don't invigorate your spirit, try the holy water in seashell basins at the **Basilica di Santa Margherita**, at P. Caprera. **Trains** along the Pisa-Genoa line go from P. Federico Raoul Nobili, at the top of V. Roma, to Genoa (40min., 2-4 per hr., €2.10) and La Spezia (1½hr., 2 per hr., €4). Tigullio **buses** (☎0185 28 88 34) go from P.V. Veneto to Camogli (30min., 1-2 per hr., €1.20) and Portofino (20min., 3 per hr., €1.50). Tigullio **ferries**, V. Palestro 8/1b (☎0185 28 46 70), have tours to Cinque Terre (July-Sept. W, Th and Sa, daily, €20) and Portofino (every hr., €3.50). Turn right from the train station on V. Roma, left on C. Rainusso, turn left and take a hard right onto V. XXV Aprile from Largo Giusti to find the **tourist office**, V. XXV Aprile 2b, which arranges lodging. (☎0185 28 74 85; fax 28 30 34. Open M-Sa 9am-12:30pm and 3-7:30pm, Su 9:30am-12:30pm and 4:30-7:30pm.) ▨**Hotel Terminus ❹**, P. Nobili 4, is to left as you exit station. The spacious rooms in this 18th-century building give breathtaking view of sea. (Singles €50, with bath €65; doubles with bath €85; triples €105; quads €116. AmEx/MC/V.) **Trattoria Baicin ❸**, V. Algeria 9, has the best pesto in town. (☎0185 28 67 63. Open Su and Tu-Sa noon-3pm and 7pm-midnight. AmEx/MC/V.) **Postal Code:** 16032.

PORTOFINO. As long as you don't buy anything, princes and paupers alike can enjoy the curved shores and tiny bay of Portofino. A 1hr. walk along the ocean road offers the chance to scout out small rocky **beaches**. The area's only sandy beach, **Paraggi** (where the bus stops), is only a small strip. In town, follow the signs uphill from the bay to escape to the cool interior of the **Chiesa di San Giorgio.** A few minutes up the road toward the **castle** is a serene garden with sea views. (Open daily 10am-7pm, off-season reduced hours. €3.50.) To get to town, take the bus to Portofino Mare (*not* Portofino Vetta). From P. Martiri della Libertà, Tigullio **buses** go to Santa Margherita (3 per hr., €1.50); buy tickets at the green kiosk. **Ferries** also go to Camogli (2 per day, €7) and Santa Margherita (every hr. 10:30am-4pm, €3.50). The **tourist office**, V. Roma 35, is on the way to the waterfront from the bus stop. (☎0185 26 90 24. Open daily 10:30am-1:30pm and 2-7:30pm.)

CINQUE TERRE
☎ **0187**

The five bright fishing villages of Cinque Terre are as soothing as they are beautiful. A vast expanse of dazzling turquoise sea laps against the *cittadine* that cling to a stretch of terraced hillsides and steep crumbling cliffs. Tourists journey from around the world to hike between the five villages, climbing through vineyards along dry stone cliffs with breathtaking views of the surrounding seas. Each of these five villages—Monterosso, Vernazza, Corniglia, Manarola, and Riomaggiore—invites the traveler to explore its own unique character. Despite the increasing tourism, the towns of the Cinque Terre still feel untouched by time.

▐ TRANSPORTATION

Trains run along the Genoa-La Spezia line. A **Cinque Terre Tourist Ticket** (€4.20) allows unlimited trips among the five towns and to La Spezia. Monterosso is the most accessible. From the station on V. Fegina, the north end of town, trains run to: Florence (3½hr., every hr., €8), via Pisa (2½hr., every hr., €4.40); Genoa (1½hr., every hr., €3.60); La Spezia (20min., every 30min., €1.20); and Rome (7hr., every 2hr., €27). Frequent local trains connect the 5 towns (5-20min., every 50min., €1-1.50). **Ferries** run to Monterosso from La Spezia (1hr., 2 per day, €18).

▐ ORIENTATION AND PRACTICAL INFORMATION

The five villages stretch along the shore between Levanto and La Spezia, connected by trains, roads (although cars are not allowed inside the towns) and footpaths that traverse the rocky shoreline. **Monterosso** is the northernmost town and the largest, containing most of the services for the area, followed by picturesque **Vernazza**, cliffside **Corniglia**, and the quiet towns of **Manarola** and **Riomaggiore**. The Pro Loco **tourist office** V. Fegina 38 is in Monterosso, below the train station, provides information and accommodations service. (☎0187 81 75 06; fax 0187 81 78 25. Open Apr.-Oct. M-Sa 9am-noon, 2:30-6:30pm, Su 9am-noon.) Each town also has a **Cinque Terre National Park Office** that provides info on hiking and accommodations and sells **5terre Cards,** which give unlimited train, ferry and bus access. The Monterosso office is at P. Garibaldi (☎0187 80 20 53. Open daily 9am-10pm. Cards €14, €5.40 without ferry.) **Postal Codes:** 19016 in Monterosso, 19018 in Corniglia and Vernazza, 19017 in Manarola and Riomaggiore.

▐ ACCOMMODATIONS

Most hotels are in Monterosso. They fill quickly during the summer, so reserve ahead. Try the tourist office for help finding the more plentiful *Affittacamere* (private rooms). For another option for private rooms in Riomaggiore, call **Mar-Mar ❷,** V. Malborghetto 8, an established *Affittacamere* organization. (☎/fax 0187 920 932; www.marmar.5terre.com. Dorms €20, doubles €50-80.)

▧ **Albergo Della Gioventù-Ostello Cinque Terre,** V. B. Riccobaldi 21, Manarola (☎0187 92 02 15; www.hostel5terre.com). Turn right from train station and continue up the hill 300m. Modern hostel has 48 beds, a sweeping terrace on the roof, and music systems on each co-ed floor. Breakfast €3.50. Laundry €4 wash, €3 dry. Ask about kayak, bike, and snorkeling equipment rental. Reception daily 7am-1pm and 5pm-1am. Curfew in summer 1am, off-season midnight. Dorms €17-20. AmEx/MC/V/DC. ❷

Hotel Souvenir, V. Gioberti 24, Monterosso (☎/fax 0187 81 75 95). This quiet, family-run hotel on a charming street has 30 beds, a friendly staff, and an outdoor garden. Most rooms with modern bath. Breakfast €5. Rooms €35 per person; students €25. ❸

Hotel Gianni Franzi, P. Marconi 1, Vernazza (☎0187 82 10 03; www.giannifranzi.it). Run by the town's oldest trattoria, the rooms have lovely antique decor, most with large balconies with views of the town and sea. Single €38; doubles €58-62, with bath €75; triples €96. AmEx/D/MC/V. ❸

Bed and Breakfast La Toretta, Vico Volto 14, Manarola (☎/fax 0187 92 03 27). Spacious, sunny rooms, most with balconies, TV, and AC, all with a view of the sea. Lovely sunbathed solarium offers enchanting vistas. Breakfast included. Doubles €70-90. Reserves one double for students (€36). ❹

Hotel Ca Dei Duxi, V. Colombo 36, Riomaggiore (☎0187 92 00 36; www.duxi.it). Tranquil bed and breakfast in a historic building. Bedrooms are spacious and well-furnished. Breakfast included. Singles €30-50; doubles €60-110; triples €75-130. ❹

◪ FOOD

While Vernazzo is reputed to have the best food in the Cinque Terre, delicious options can be uncovered in all of the towns. Buy groceries at **DiMarket Macelleria** V. Molinelli 21, Monterosso. (Open M-Sa 8am-1pm and 5-7:30pm, Su 8am-1pm.)

▨ **Trattoria Gianni Franzi,** P. Marconi 1, Vernazza (☎0187 82 10 03). Said by many to have the best pesto in the Cinque Terre, Vernazza's oldest *trattoria* has large indoor and outdoor dining areas. *Primi* €4-11. *Secondi* €5-16. Open Su-Tu and Th-Sa noon-3pm, 7:30-9:30pm. AmEx/DC/MC/V. ❷

Focacceria Il Frantoio, V. Gioberti 1, Monterosso (☎0187 81 83 33). The wood-burning oven bakes mouth-watering farinata and *focaccia* stuffed with olives, onions, herbs, and other fillings. Slices €1-2. Open Su-W and F-Sa 9am-2pm and 4-7:30pm. ❶

Ripa del Sole, V. de Casper 282, Riomaggiore (☎0187 92 07 43). Perched on a cliff over the village, this little trattoria serves some of the area's most authentic and flavorful traditional cuisine. Open Su and Tu-Sa noon-2pm and 7-10pm. AmEx/DC/MC/V. ❷

Il Ciliegio, Località Beo, Monterosso (☎0187 81 78 29), near P. Garibaldi. Free taxi service from the historical city center (call ahead). Fantastic food, made fresh daily with ingredients from the owners' garden. Savor your meal and the view from the terrace. *Primi* €6-8. *Secondi* €7-11. Open Su and Tu-Sa 12:30-2:30pm, 7:30-10:30pm. ❸

THE HIDDEN DEAL

LIFE'S A BEACH

In 1873, the first Italian railroad split through the **Guvano** valley surrounding the hill town of Corniglia. Abandoned in 1968, the track left behind a long tunnel that cuts through the mountainside, rendering a sparkling cove and secluded beach newly accessible to the town's inhabitants. Before long, young men and women made the discovery, and soon they turned it into a lawless haven, building bonfires by the tunnel and basking in the buff.

In the 1990s, the local government gave the area over to a group of agricultural workers who cleaned up the beaches, planted vineyards along the coast, and began charging a small entrance fee. The workers are awaiting a license from the state to provide lifeguarding services and sell food and supplies to adventurous swimmers. Though newly scrubbed and supervised, Guvano hasn't lost its naturalist charm. Tourists who discover the tunnel can strut their stuff with the locals down the two pristine coves and take brisk, nude dips in the sea.

To reach Guvano, take a left from the Corniglia train station. Pass the stairs and turn left down the ramp on the other side of the tracks. At the bottom of the ramp, turn right, heading toward town. A 15min. walk through the dark tunnel (don't go alone) delivers you to the cove. Open July-Aug. daily 9am-7pm; June and Sept. Sa-Su 9am-7pm. €5.

�︎ ♫ SIGHTS AND ENTERTAINMENT

The best sightseeing in Cinque Terre consists of exploring the five villages and the gorgeous paths that connect them. Monterosso has the Cinque Terre's largest **free beach,** in front of the historic center, sheltered by a cliff cove. The 17th-century **Chiesa Del Convento dei Cappuccini** perched on a hill in the center of town, yields the most expansive vistas. A chapel on the left contains an impressive crucifix by van Dyck, who traveled here during some of his most productive years. (Open daily 9am-noon and 4-7pm.) The hike between Monterosso and Vernazza is considered the hardest of the four, with steep climbs over dry, rugged cliffs. The trail winds its way through terraced vineyards and past hillside cottages before descending steeply into town. From there, the trip to Corniglia offers breathtaking views of the sea, olive groves, and scents of rosemary, lemon, and lavender. Near Corniglia, the secluded **Guvano Beach** is accessed through a tunnel and popular for nude sunbathing. (Open July-Aug. daily 9am-7pm; June and Sept. Sa-Su 9am-7pm. €5.) The subsequent hike to youthful and vibrant Manarola lacks the picturesque vegetation of the previous two, but retains the sweeping, open views of the turquoise sea. The most famous of the Cinque Terre hikes, the **Via dell'Amore,** between Manarola and Riomaggiore, smallest of the five towns, is a slate-paved walk that features a stone tunnel painted with love scenes. All together the hikes generally take about five hours, not including time spent exploring the towns themselves.

At night, the most popular towns are Monterosso, Manarola, and Riomaggiore. In Monterosso, **Il Casello,** V. Lungo Fessario 70, brings in the backpacking crowd with thumping music and a location near the beach—making it far enough from the town to be the only bar open past 1am. (Beer and mixed drinks from €2.50. Internet access €1 per 15min. Open daily 11am-3am.) **Bar Centrale,** V. C. Colombo 144, Riomaggiore, caters to a young, international backpacking crowd. (Beer €2-4, mixed drinks €4-6. Internet access €1 per 10min. Open daily 7:30am-1am.)

LA SPEZIA. A departure point for Corsica and an important transport hub for Cinque Terre, La Spezia is among Italy's most beautiful ports, with regal palms lining the promenade and citrus trees growing in the parks. The unique collection of the **Museo Navale,** in P. Chiodo, features diving suits from WWII, gargantuan iron anchors, and tiny replicas of Egyptian, Roman, and European vessels. (Open M-Sa 8:30am-1pm and 4:15-9:45pm, Su 8:30am-1:15pm. €1.60.) La Spezia lies on the Genoa-Pisa **train** line. **Navigazione Golfo dei Poeti,** V.d. Minzoni 13, (☎0187 732 987) offers ferries that stop in each village of **Cinque Terre** (one-way €11; round trip M-Sa €19, Su €22). The **tourist office,** V. Mazzini 45, is at the port. (☎0187 77 09 00. Open M-Sa 9:30am-1pm and 3:30-7pm, Su 9:30am-1pm.) **Albergo Il sole ❹,** V. Cavalloti, off V. Prione, offers spacious rooms. (☎0187 73 51 64. Singles €25-36; doubles €39-45, with bath €47-55; triples €53-61/63-74. AmEx/MC/V.) **Postal Code:** 19100.

EAT YOUR HEART OUT, CHEF BOYARDEE

In Italy, the desecration of pasta is a mortal sin. Pasta must be chosen correctly and cooked *al dente* (firm, literally "to the tooth"). To avoid embarrassment, get to know the basics. The *spaghetti* family includes all variations that require twirling, from hollow cousins *bucatini* and *maccheroni* to the more delicate *capellini*. Flat *spaghetti* include *fettuccini, taglierini,* and *tagliatelle.* Short pasta tubes can be *penne* (cut diagonally and occasionally *rigate,* or ribbed), *sedani* (curved), *rigatoni* (wider), or *cannelloni* (usually stuffed). *Fusilli* (corkscrews), *farfalle* (butterflies or bow-ties), and *ruote* (wheels) are fun as well as functional. Don't be alarmed if you see pastry displays labeled "pasta"; the Italian word refers to anything made of dough.

EMILIA-ROMAGNA

Go to Florence, Venice, and Rome to sightsee; come to Emilia-Romagna to eat. Italy's wealthy wheat- and dairy-producing region covers the fertile plains of the Po River Valley, and celebrates the finest culinary traditions on the peninsula. The Romans originally settled here, but the towns later fell under the rule of great Renaissance families whose names adorn every *palazzo* and *piazza* in the region.

BOLOGNA ☎051

Home to Europe's oldest university and rich, flavorful cuisine, Bologna (pop. 500,000) has been known since ancient times as the *grassa* (fat) and *dotta* (learned) city. Today, academic liberalism drives political activism—minority groups, student alliances, and the national gay organization all find a voice (and listening ears) in Bologna. All eyes, however, are on Bologna's art. Priceless works inhabit museums and churches, whose 700-year-old porticoes line the streets.

⌐? TRANSPORTATION AND PRACTICAL INFORMATION

Bologna is a rail hub for all major Italian cities and the Adriatic coast. **Trains** leave the northern tip of the walled city for: Florence (1½hr., every 2hr., €5-€7); Milan (3hr., 2 per hr., €10); Rome (4hr., every hr., €22); and Venice (2hr., every hr., €10). **Buses** #25 and 30 run between the train station and the historic center at **Piazza Maggiore** (€1). The **tourist office**, P. Maggiore 1, is next to the Palazzo Comunale. (☎051 648 76 07; www.comune.bologna.it/bolognaturismo. Open M-Sa 10am-2pm and 3-7pm, Su 10am-2pm.) Check email at **Bar College**, Largo Respighi 6/d (☎051 22 96 24) next to the Teatro Communale. (☎051 22 96 24. €4.50 per hr. Open M-F 8am-3am, Sa 10am-3am, Su 10am-2am.) **Postal Code:** 40100.

⌐ ACCOMMODATIONS

Bologna's hotels are rather pricey; reservations are recommended. Most are located around V. dell'Independenza and V. Marconi.

Albergo Panorama, V. Livraghi 1, 4th fl. (☎051 22 18 02; panorama.hotel@libero.it). Take V. Ugo Bassi from P. del Nettuno, then take the third left. Sparklingly clean hotel in a prime location. Enormous, sunny rooms with high ceilings, hardwood floors, and TVs. Three bathrooms serve all 12 rooms. Curfew 3am. Reception from 7am-3am. Singles €50; doubles €65; triples €80; quads €90; quints €100. AmEx/MC/V. ●

Ostello due Torre San Sisto (HI), V. Viadagola 5 (☎/fax 051 22 49 13), off V. San Donato, in Località di San Sisto, 6km northeast of the center of town. Tourist office has map with directions. Take bus #93 from Marconi St. (available M-Sa, every 30min.) Ask the driver for the San Sisto stop. Exit bus and cross street; hostel is the yellow building on right with yellow-and-green metal fence. Large building in a tranquil setting. Reception 7:30-9am and 3:30-11:30pm. Lockout 10am-3:30pm. Curfew 11:30pm. Dorms €14; doubles €30. Nonmembers add €2.60. AmEx/DC/MC/V. ●

Garisenda, Galleria Leone 1, 3rd fl. (☎051 22 43 69; fax 22 10 07). Down V. Rizzoli and turn right into the gallery mall. Comfortable, homey oasis right in the center of town. Most rooms offer a great view. Singles €45; doubles €65; triples €90. AmEx/MC/V. ●

Pensione Marconi, V. Marconi 22 (☎051 26 28 32). Turn right from station and then left onto V. Amendola, which becomes V. Marconi. Clean, modern rooms, all with bath. Singles €45; doubles €70; triples €93. ●

FOOD

Don't leave without sampling Bologna's signature *spaghetti alla bolognese*. Scout **Via Augusto Righi, Via Piella,** and **Via Saragozza** for traditional *trattorie*. Locals chat over plates of pasta at ▩**Trattoria Da Maro ❷,** V. Broccaindosso 71b, between Strada Maggiore and V.S. Vitale. (☎051 22 73 04. *Primi* €5-6. *Secondi* €5-7. Open Tu-Sa noon-2:30pm and 8-11pm.) **Nuova Pizzeria Gianna ❶,** V.S. Stefano 76A, known to locals simply as "Mamma's," has delicious pizzas crafted by Gianna herself. (☎051 22 25 16. Open M-F 7am-midnight, Sa 7am-10pm. Closed Aug.) **Ristorante Clorofilla ❷,** Strada Maggiore 64C, is a hip, primarily vegetarian spot. (☎051 23 53 43. Salads and hot dishes €5-8. Open M-Sa 12:15-2:45pm and 7:30-11pm.) A **PAM supermarket,** V. Marconi 26, is by the intersection with V. Riva di Reno. (Open M-Sa 7:45am-8pm.)

◉ SIGHTS

Forty kilometers of porticoed buildings line the streets of Bologna in a mix of Gothic, Renaissance, and Baroque styles. The tranquil ▩**Piazza Maggiore** flaunts both Bologna's historical and modern wealth. The cavernous Gothic interior of the city's *duomo,* **Basilica di San Petronio,** was meant to be larger than Rome's St. Peter's, but the jealous Church leadership ordered that the funds be used instead to build the nearby Palazzo Archiginnasio. It hosted both the Council of Trent (when it wasn't meeting in Trent) and the 1530 ceremony in which Pope Clement VII gave Italy to the German King Charles V. The pomp and pageantry of the exercises at the church allegedly inspired a disgusted Martin Luther to reform religion in Germany. (Open M-Sa 7:15am-1pm and 2-6pm, Su 7:30am-1pm and 2-6:30pm.) The **Palazzo Archiginnasio,** behind S. Petronio, was once a university building; the upstairs theater was built in 1637 to teach anatomy to students. (☎051 27 68 11. Open daily 9am-1pm. Closed 2 weeks in Aug.) On the northern side of P. Maggiore is the **Palazzo de Podestà,** remodeled by Fioravanti's son Aristotle, who later designed Moscow's Kremlin. Next to P. Maggiore, **Piazza del Nettuno** contains Giambologna's famous 16th-century fountain, *Neptune and Attendants.* From P. Nettuno, go down V. Rizzoli to **Piazza Porta Ravegana,** where seven streets converge to form Bologna's medieval quarter. Two towers that constitute the city's emblem rise magnificently from the *piazza;* you can climb the 498 steps of the **Torre degli Asinelli** for a breathtaking view of the city. (Open daily 9am-6pm. €3.) From V. Rizzoli, follow V.S. Stefano to P.S. Stefano, where four of the original seven churches of the Romanesque **Piazza Santo Stefano Church Complex** remain. Bologna's patron saint, San Petronio, lies buried under the pulpit of the **Chiesa di San Sepolcro.** (Open daily 9am-noon and 3:30-6pm.) Take Strada Maggiore to P. Aldrovandi to reach the remarkably intact **Chiesa di Santa Mari dei Seru,** whose columns support an unusual combination of arches and ribbed vaulting. (Open daily 7am-1pm and 3:30-8pm.) The **Pinacoteca Nazionale,** V. delle Belle Arti, 56, off V. Zamboni, traces the history of Bolognese artists. (☎051 420 94 11. Open Su and Tu-Sa 9am-6:30pm. €6. Students €3, seniors and under-18 free.)

▣ ♫ ENTERTAINMENT AND NIGHTLIFE

Bologna's hip student population ensures raucous nighttime fun and accounts for the ample number of bars and clubs in the city. **Cluricaune,** V. Zamboni 18/b, is an Irish bar full of students who flock to its pool table and dart boards. (☎051 26 34 19. Pints €4.20. Happy Hour 7-10:30pm features €2.50 pints. Open Su-F 11pm-3am, Sa 4pm-3am.) **Cassero,** in the Porta Saragozza, is a lively gay bar packed with men and women. (☎051 649 44 16. Drinks €3-6. Open daily 10pm-2am.)

Every year from mid-June to mid-September, the city *comune* sponsors an **entertainment festival** of dance, theater, music, cinema, and art shows. Many events are free, but some cost around €5. Visitors to Bologna during the summer should contact the tourist office for a program of events. The **Teatro Comunale**, Largo Respighi 1, hosts operas, symphony concerts, and ballet with world-class performers. (☎051 52 99 99; www.comunalebologna.it. Tickets €5-200. 10% surcharge for pre-order. Box office open M-F 3:30-7pm, Sa 9:30am-12:30pm and 3:30-7pm.)

PARMA   ☎0521

Famous for its *parmigiano* cheese and *prosciutto* ham, Parma's (pop. 200,000) artistic excellence is not confined to the kitchen. 16th-century Mannerist painting came into full bloom here, and native Giuseppe Verdi resided in Parma while composing some of his greatest works. From P. Garibaldi, follow Strada Cavour toward the train station and take the third right on Strada al Duomo to reach the 11th-century Romanesque **duomo**, in P. del Duomo, which is filled with masterpieces. Most spectacular is the dome, where Correggio's *Virgin* ascends to a golden heaven in a spiral of white robes, pink *putti*, and blue sky. The pink-and-white marble **baptistery** was built between the Romanesque and Gothic periods. (*Duomo* open daily 9am-noon and 3-7pm. Baptistery open daily 9am-12:30pm and 3-7pm. €2.70, students €1.50.) Behind the *duomo* is the frescoed dome of the **Chiesa di San Giovanni Evangelista**, P.S. Giovanni, designed by Correggio. (Open M-Sa 8am-11:45am and 3-6:45pm, Su 8am-12:45pm and 3-7:45pm.) From P. del Duomo, follow Strada al Duomo across Strada Cavour, walk one block down Strada Piscane, and cross P. della Pace to reach the 17th-century **Palazzo della Pilotta**, an artistic treasure chest that houses the **Galleria Nazionale**. (Open Su and Tu-Sa 8:30am-2pm. €6, students €3.)

Parma is on the Bologna-Milan rail line. **Trains** go from P. Carlo Alberto della Chiesa to: Bologna (1hr., 2 per hr., €4.20); Florence (3hr., 7 per day, €15); and Milan (1½hr., every hr., €7). Walk left from the station, turn right on V. Garibaldi, and turn left on V. Melloni to reach the **tourist office**, V. Melloni 1a. (☎0521 21 88 89; fax 0521 23 47 35. Open M-Sa 9am-7pm, Su 9am-1pm.) From the station, take bus #9 (€0.75) and get off when the bus turns left on V. Martiri della Libertà for the **Ostello Cittadella (HI) ❶**, on V. Passo Buole, in a corner of a 15th-century fortress with a campground beside it. (☎0521 96 14 34. 3-night max. stay. Lockout 9:30am-5pm. Curfew 11pm. Open Apr.-Oct. HI members only. Dorms €9. Camping €6.50 per person, €11 per site.) **Albergo Leon d'Oro ❸**, V. Fratti 4, off V. Garibaldi, is clean and only two blocks from the train station. (☎0521 77 31 82. Singles €33; doubles €50. AmEx/MC/V.) Look near **Via Garibaldi** for fragrant Parma cuisine. **Pizzeria La Duchessa ❷**, P. Garibaldi 1/B is an excellent *trattoria* with a large variety of pastas and thick-crust pizzas. (☎0521 23 59 62. Pizza €4.20-9.50. *Primi* €5.50-8. *Secondi* €6.50-15. Cover €1.30-1.55. Open Su and Tu-Sa 10am-2pm and 7pm-12:30am. MC/V.) **K2**, Borgo Cairoli 23, next to the Chiesa di San Giovanni Evangelista, has great *gelato*. (Cones from €1.50. Open M-Tu and Th-Su 11am-midnight.) **Dimeglio supermarket** is at V. XXII Luglio 27c. (Open M-W and F-Sa 8:30am-1pm and 4:30-8pm, Th 8:30am-1pm.) **Postal Code:** 43100.

RAVENNA   ☎0544

Ravenna's (pop. 130,000) 15 minutes of historical fame came and went 14 centuries ago, when Justinian and Theodora, rulers of the Byzantine Empire, headquartered their campaign to restore order in the anarchic west here. Take V. Argentario from V. Cavour to reach the 6th-century **▧Basilica di San Vitale**, V.S. Vitale 17. An open courtyard overgrown with greenery leads to the brilliant, glowing mosaics inside; those of the Emperor and Empress adorn the lower left and right panels of the apse. Behind S. Vitale, the city's oldest and most intriguing mosaics cover the glittering interior of the **Mausoleo di Galla Placidia.** (☎0544 21 62 92. Open Apr.-Sept. daily 9am-7pm; Oct.-Mar. 9:30am-5:30pm.) Take bus #4 or 44 across from the train station (€0.70) to Classe, south of the city, to see the astounding mosaics at the **Chiesa di Sant'Apollinare.** (Open M-Sa 8:30am-7:30pm, Su 9am-1pm. €2. Su free.) Much to Florence's dismay, Ravenna is also home to the **Tomb of Dante Alighieri.** In the adjoining **Dante Museum,** his heaven and hell come alive in etchings, paintings, and sculptures. From P. del Popolo, cut through P. Garibaldi to V. Alighieri. (☎0544 302 52. Tomb open daily 9am-7pm. Free. Museum open Apr.-Sept. Su and Tu-Sa 9am-noon and 3:30-6pm; Oct.-Mar. reduced hours. €2.)

Trains (☎0544 21 78 84) leave P. Farini for Ferrara (1hr., every hr., €4) and Bologna (1hr., every 1-2hr., €4). Follow V. Farini from the station to V. Diaz, which runs to the central P. del Popolo and the **tourist office,** V. Salara 8. (☎0544 354 04. Open Apr.-Sept. M-Sa 8:30am-7pm, Su 10am-4pm; Oct.-Mar. reduced hours.) Take bus #1 or 70 from V. Pallavicini at the train station (1-4 per hr., €0.70) to reach **Ostello Dante (HI) ❶,** V. Nicolodi 12. (☎/fax 0544 42 11 64. Breakfast included. Reception 7-10am and 5-11:30pm. Lockout 10am-5pm. Curfew 11:30pm. Dorms €13. MC/V.) Walk down V. Farini, and go right at P. Mameli for the renovated **Albergo Al Giacciglio ❸,** V. Rocca Brancaleone 42. (☎0544 394 03. Breakfast €2-5. Singles €33-36; doubles €42-52; triples €55-65. MC/V.) **Piazza del Popolo** has a number of good restaurants nearby. **Postal Code:** 48100.

FERRARA   ☎0532

Rome has its mopeds, Venice its boats, and Ferrara (pop. 135,000) has its bicycles. Old folks, young folks, and babies perched precariously on handlebars whirl through Ferrara's jumble of major thoroughfares and twisting medieval roads. Take a deep breath of fresh air, hop on a bike, and explore the city.

⊟⁊ TRANSPORTATION AND PRACTICAL INFORMATION. Trains go to: Bologna (30min., 1-2 per hr., €2.80); Padua (1hr., every hr., €4); Ravenna (1hr., 1-3 per hr., €4); Rome (3-4hr., 7 per day, €31); and Venice (2hr., 1-2 per hr., €6). ACFT (☎0532 59 94 92) and GGFP **buses** leave V. Rampari S. Paolo or the train station for Bologna (1½hr., 15 per day, €3.30) and Ferrara's beaches (1hr., 12 per day, €4-5). To get to the center of town, turn left out of the train station, and then veer right on **Viale Costituzione.** This road becomes Viale Cavour and runs to the **Castello Estense** (1km). Or, take bus #2 to *Castello* or bus #1 or 9 to the post office (every 20min., €0.85). The **tourist office** is in Castello Estense. (☎0532 20 93 70. Open M-Sa 9am-1pm and 2-6pm, Su 9:30am-1pm and 2-5:30pm.) Rent **bikes** at **Pirani e Bagni,** P. le Stazione 2. (€7 per day. Open daily 6:30am-1pm and 3:30-7pm.) **Postal Code:** 44100.

⌂❐ ACCOMMODATIONS AND FOOD. Ferrara has plenty of inexpensive and comfortable accommodations. **Pensione Artisti ❷,** V. Vittoria 66, near P. Lampronti, is in the historic center of Ferrara and has a pleasant, attentive staff. (☎0532 76 10 38. Singles €21; doubles €38, with bath €55.) Walk down C. Ercole I d'Este from the *castello,* or take bus #4c from the station to the *castello* stop to reach the central **Ostello della Gioventù Estense (HI) ❶,** C. B. Rossetti 24, with simple, clean rooms. (☎/fax 0532 20 42 27. Breakfast €1.60. **Internet** access. Reception 7-10am and 5-11:30pm. Lockout 10am-5pm. Curfew 11:30pm. Dorms €13.) **Hotel de Prati ❹,** V. Padiglioni 5, is a lovely three-star hotel. (☎0532 24 19 05; www.hoteldeprati.com. Singles €47-70; doubles €70-105; suites €110-140. AmEx/MC/V.) Gorge on local specialties such as triangular meat ravioli served in a broth, or the traditional *Ferrarese* dessert of luscious *pampepato,* chocolate-covered almond and fruit cake. Try delicious *panini* with one of 600 varieties of wine at **Osteria Al Brindisi 11 ❸,** V.G. degli Adelardi 9b, which has wined and dined the likes of Copernicus and Pope John Paul II since opening in 1435. (☎0532 20 91 42. Open Su and Tu-Sa 8:30am-1am.) For picnic supplies, stop by the **Mercato Comunale** on V. Garibaldi. (Open daily 8am-1pm.)

☉▣ SIGHTS AND ENTERTAINMENT. Bike the tranquil, wooded concourse along the city's well-preserved 9km **medieval wall**, which begins at the far end of C. Giovecca. The imposing ▦**Castello Estense** stands precisely in the center of town. C. della Giovecca lies along the former route of the moat's feeder canal, separating the medieval section from the part planned by the d'Este's architect. (☎ 0532 29 92 33. Open Su and Tu-Sa 9:30am-5pm. €7, students €6.) From the *castello*, take C. Martiri della Libertà to P. Cattedrale and the **Duomo San Romano,** which contains the **Museo della Cattedrale.** (*Duomo* open M-Sa 7:30am-noon and 3-6:30pm, Su 7:30am-12:30pm and 4-7:30pm. Museum open Su and Tu-Sa 9am-1pm and 3-6pm. €4.20, students €2.) From the *castello*, cross Largo Castello to C. Ercole I d'Este and walk to the corner of C. Rossetti to reach the gorgeous **Palazzo Diamanti**, built in 1493. Inside, the **Pinacoteca Nazionale** holds many of the best works of the Ferrarese school. (Open Su 9am-1pm, Tu-W and F-Sa 9am-2pm, Th 9am-7pm. €4, students €2.) Follow C. Ercole I d'Este behind the *castello* and go right on C. Porta Mare to find the **Palazzo Massari,** C. Porta Mare 9, which houses both the **Museo d'Arte Moderna e Contemporanea Filippo de Pisis,** and, upstairs, the spectacular **Museo Ferrarese dell'Ottocentro/Museo Giovanni Boldini.** (Both open Su and Tu-Sa 9am-1pm and 3-6pm. Joint ticket €6.70, student €4.20) **Postal Code:** 44100.

THE DOLOMITES (DOLOMITI)

With their sunny skies and powdery, light snow, the Dolomites offer immensely popular downhill skiing. These amazing peaks, which Le Courbusier once called "the most beautiful natural architecture in the world," are also fantastic for hiking and rock climbing.

TRENT ☎ 0461

Between the Dolomites and the Veneto, Trent (pop. 105,000) offers an affordable sampling of northern Italian life with superb restaurants and spectacular hikes set against dramatic scenery. The **Piazza del Duomo,** Trent's center and the heart of its social life, contains the city's best sights. The **Fontana del Nettuno** stands, trident in hand, in the center of the *piazza.* Nearby is the **Cattedrale di San Vigilio,** named for the patron saint of Trent. (Open daily 9:30am-12:15pm and 2:30-7:30pm.) Walk down V. Belenzani and head right on V. Roma to reach the well-preserved **Castello del Buonconsiglio,** which has a series of frescoes depicting medieval life. (Open daily 10am-6pm. €5, students and seniors €2.50.) **Monte Bondone** rises majestically over Trent, making a pleasant daytrip or overnight excursion. Catch the **cable car** (☎ 0461 38 10 00; every 30min., €0.80) to **Sardagna** on Mt. Bondone from V. Lung'Adige Monte Grappa, between the train tracks and the river.

Trains (☎ 0461 98 36 27) leave V. Dogana for: Bologna (3hr., 13 per day, €11); Bolzano (45min., 2 per hr., €3); Venice (3hr., 5 per day, €11); and Verona (1hr., every hr., €4.70). Atesina **buses** (☎ 0461 82 10 00) go from V. Pozzo, next to the train station, to Riva del Garda (1hr., every hr., €3). The **tourist office,** V. Manci 2, offers advice on biking, skiing, and hiking. Turn right as you exit the train station and turn left on V. Roma, which becomes V. Corsi. (☎ 0461 98 38 80; www.apt.trento.it. Open daily 9am-7pm.) The central and clean **Hotel Venezia ❸** is at P. Duomo 45. (☎/ fax 0461 23 41 14. Breakfast €5.20. Singles €40; doubles €59. MC/V.) From the station, turn right on V. Pozzo and left on V. Torre Vanga to get to **Ostello Giovane Europa (HI) ❶,** V. Torre Vanga 11, a white building with new rooms and clean bathrooms. (☎ 0461 26 34 84; fax 0461 22 25 17. Reception 7:30am-11pm. Check-out 10am. Curfew 11:30pm. Dorms €13; singles €25; doubles €40.) Around P. Duomo there are several cafes and a produce market. **Postal Code:** 38100.

THE LOCAL STORY

THE AGE OF JANUARIUS

Dr. Luigi Garlaschelli is an organic chemist at the University of Pavia who, in his spare time, investigates the authenticity of blood relics .

LG: Can you explain the ubiquitousness of relics in Italian churches?

A: In the Middle Ages, it was believed that they would protect the city from its enemies. [Relics include] the feather of the Archangel Michael, the milk of the Virgin Mary, and the fingernails and blood of Christ.

LG: What was your first project?

A: My first work was on the blood of St. Januarius, which is contained in a small vial kept in the duomo in Naples. Januarius was beheaded in 305 AD. The relic appeared in the Middle Ages, 1000 years later. Normally blood taken from a living body will clot only once; the "miracle" of this blood is that it liquefies twice a year during religious ceremonies.

LG: How does that work?

A: Well, using an iron salt, which exists naturally near active volcanoes (like Vesuvius, near Naples, active at the time of the discovery of the blood), kitchen salt, and techniques available in the Middle Ages, we were able to make a substance of the same color and properties as the reputed blood of St. Januarius. The matter would be closed were we to open the vial and take a sample. But, of course, the vial is sealed.

BOLZANO   ☎ 0471

In the tug-of-war between Austrian and Italian cultural influences, Bolzano (pop. 100,000) leans toward Austria's side. The town's prime location beneath vineyard-covered mountains makes it a splendid base for hiking or skiing in the Dolomites. Artwork and numerous frescoes fill the Gothic **duomo**, off P. Walther. (Open M-F 9:45am-noon and 2-5pm, Sa 9:45am-noon.) The fascinating **South Tyrol Museum of Archaeology**, V. Museo 43, near Ponte Talvera, houses the 5000-year-old **Ice Man**. (☎ 0471 98 06 48. Open Tu-F 10am-6pm, Th until 7pm. €8, students €5.50.) **Trains** (☎ 0471 97 42 92) leave P. Stazione for: Milan (3hr., 3 per day, €21); Trent (45min., 2 per hr., €3); and Verona (2hr., 1-2 per hr., €6.80). Walk up V. Stazione from the train station to reach the **tourist office**, P. Walther 8. (☎ 0471 30 70 00; fax 0471 98 01 28. Open M-F 9am-6:30pm, Sa 9am-12:30pm.) **Croce Bianca** ❸, P. del Grano 3, is around the corner from P. Walther. Its homey rooms are the most centrally located budget accomodations in town. (☎ 0471 97 75 52. Singles €28; doubles €47.) Sample some of Bolzano's Austrian-influenced fare around P. Walther and along V. Grappoli. **Postal Code:** 39100.

THE VENETO

From the rocky foothills of the Dolomites to the fertile valleys of the Po River, the Veneto region has a geography as diverse as its historical influences. Once loosely linked under the Venetian Empire, these towns retained their cultural independence, and visitors are more likely to hear regional dialects than standard Italian when neighbors gossip across their geranium-bedecked windows. The tenacity of local culture and custom may be a pleasant surprise for those who come expecting only mandolins and gondolas.

VENICE (VENEZIA)   ☎ 041

There is a mystical quality to Venice's (pop. 265,000) decadence. Her lavish palaces stand proudly on a steadily sinking network of wood, treading in the clouded waters of age-old canals lapping at the feet of her abandoned front doors. Venice's labyrinthine streets lead to a treasury of Renaissance art, housed in scores of palaces, churches, and museums that are themselves architectural delights. But the same streets that once earned the name *La Serenissima* (Most Serene) are now saturated with visitors, as Venice grapples with an economy reliant on the same tourism that forces more and more of the native population away every year. Still, Romanticism dies hard, and the sinking city persists beyond the summer crowds and polluted waters, united by winding canals and the memory of a glorious past.

▐ TRANSPORTATION

The **train station** is on the northwest edge of the city; be sure to get off at **Santa Lucia**, *not* Mestre on the mainland. Buses and boats arrive at **Piazzale Roma,** just across the Canal Grande from the train station. To get from either station to **Piazza San Marco** or the **Ponte di Rialto** (Rialto Bridge), take *vaporetto* #82 or follow the signs for the 40min. walk—from the train station, exit left on Lista di Spagna.

Flights: Aeroporto Marco Polo (VCE; ☎041 260 61 11; www.veniceairport.it), 10km north of the city. Ticket office open daily 5:30am-9:30pm. Take the **ATVO shuttlebus** (☎041 520 55 30) from the airport to P. Roma (30min., every hr., €2.70).

Trains: Stazione Santa Lucia, northwest corner of the city. Open daily 3:45am-12:30am. **Info office** at the left as you exit the platforms. Open daily 7am-9pm. To: **Bologna** (2hr., 1 per hr., €8); **Florence** (3hr., every 2hr., €27); **Milan** (3hr., 1-2 per hr., €13); **Rome** (4½hr., 5 per day, €36-45).

Buses: ACTV (☎041 528 78 86), in P. Roma. Local buses and boats. **ACTV long-distance carrier** runs buses to **Padua** (1½hr., every 30min, €3.50).

Public Transportation: The **Canal Grande** can be crossed on foot only at the Scalzi, Rialto, and Accademia *ponti* (bridges). Most **vaporetti** (water buses) run 5am-midnight, the *Notte* line 11:30pm-5:30am. Single-ride €3.10. 24hr. *biglietto turistico* pass €9.30, 3-day €18.10 (€13 with Rolling Venice Card), 7-day €31. Buy tickets from booths in front of *vaporetti* stops, self-serve dispensers at the ACTV office in P. Roma and the Rialto stop, or from the conductor. Pick up extra *non timbrati* (non-validated) tickets for when the booths aren't open. Validate them yourself before boarding to avoid a fine. **Lines #82** (faster) and **#1** (slower) run from the station down Canale Grande and Canale della Giudecca; **line #52** goes from the station through Canale della Giudecca to Lido and along the city's northern edge, then back to the station; **line #12** runs from Fondamente Nuove to Murano, Burano, and Torcello.

▐ ▐ ORIENTATION AND PRACTICAL INFORMATION

Venice spans 118 bodies of land in a lagoon and is connected to the mainland by a thin causeway. The city is a veritable labyrinth and can confuse even its natives, most of whom simply set off in a general direction and then patiently weave their way. If you follow their example by ungluing your eyes from your map and going with the flow, you'll discover some of the unexpected surprises that make Venice spectacular. A few tips will help you to orient yourself. Locate the following landmarks on a map: **Ponte di Rialto** (the bridge in the center), **Piazza San Marco** (central south), **Ponte Accademia** (the bridge in the southwest), **Ferrovia** (the train station, in the northwest), and **Piazzale Roma** (directly south of the station). The Canal Grande winds through the city, creating six *sestieri* (sections): Cannaregio, Castello, Santa Croce, San Polo, San Marco, and Dorsoduro. Within each *sestiere*, there are no street numbers—door numbers in a section form one long, haphazard set, consisting of around 6000 numbers. While these boundaries are nebulous, they can give you a general sense of location. **Cannaregio** is in the north and includes the train station, Jewish ghetto, and Cà d'Oro; **Castello** extends east toward the Arsenale; **San Marco** fills in the area between the Ponte di Rialto and Ponte Accademia; **Dorsoduro,** across the bridge from S. Marco, stretches the length of Canale della Giudecca and up to Campo S. Pantalon; **San Polo** runs north from Chiesa S. Maria dei Frari to the Ponte di Rialto; and **San Croce** lies west of S. Polo, across the Canal Grande from the train station. If *sestiere* boundaries prove too vague, Venice's **parrochie** (parishes) provide a more defined idea of where you are; *parrochia* signs, like *sestiere* signs, are painted on the sides of buildings.

ITALY

CANNAREGIO

Rio del Battello
Rio d. S. Girolamo
Rio d. Sensa
Rio d.
Rio d. Loredan

Canale di Cannareggio

CAMPO DEL GHETTO
Sinagoga Ebraica
Calle Farnese
C. d. Rabbia
C. d. Masena
C. dell'Orto
Fond.

TO MAINLAND (MESTRE) (6.5km)

Ponte della Libertà

Calle Rielio

Libreria di Demetra

Rio Terrà di S. Leonardo

CAMPO SAN GEREMIA

Lista di Spagna

Casanova

CAMPO SAN MARCUOLA

Canal Grande

Stazione S. Lucia (Ferrovia)

Vela

Ponte Scalzi

Riva d.Biasio

AVA

Lista d. Bari

Fondamenta di Santa Lucia

Fond. di S. Simeon Piccolo

C. Nuova
C. Bergama
Rio Marin
SANTA CROCE

C. Simeona

Berga ma

CAMPO S. GIACOMO DELL'ORIO

Canale di Chiara

Hertz & Expressway Car Rental
ACTV

Fond. S.Simeon Piccolo
C. Muneghe

Corte Canal

Rio della due Torre

Rio d. San

Horus Explorer

C. Contarina

C. Amai

Canale di Chiara

AVA

PIAZZALE ROMA

South Africa

C. Amai

Rio delle

Muneghe

Rio d. San Polo

CAMPO SAN POLO

Rio terra dei Pensieri

Rio Nuovo

Fond. Minotto

C. d. Lacca

S. Maria Gloriosa dei Frari

CAMPO DEI FRARI

Rio d. S. Margherita

CAMPO SAN PANTALON

Rio Foscari

Canal

CAMPO SANTA MARGHERITA

Calle d. Carrozze

Rio d. S. Barnaba

CAMPO SAN BARNABA

C. Lunga San Barnaba

CAMPO SAN STEFANO

Calle Avogaria

DORSODURO

Stazione Marittima

C. Chiesa

Rio d. Ognissanti

UKO

Ponte Accademia

Gallerie dell' Accademia

Zattere Ponto Lungo

CAMPO SAN AGNESE

Rio d. S. Vio

Canale della Giudecca

LA GIUDECCA

Fond. S. Eufemia

Venice Overview

▲ ACCOMMODATIONS
Albergo Adua, **12**
Alloggi Gerotto Calderan, **7**
Domus Civica (ACISJF), **16**
Foresteria Valdese, **18**
Hotel Bernardi-
  Semenzato, **13**
Hotel La Forcola, **4**
Hotel Rossi, **8**
Hotel Tintoretto, **5**
Istituto Canosiano, **26**
La Residenza, **24**
Locanda Cà San
  Marcuola, **9**
Ostello di Venezia (HI), **27**
Ostello Santa Fosca, **3**

🍎 FOOD
Arcimboldo, **20**
Brek, **10**
Gam Gam, **2**
Gelateria Nico, **25**
Pizza al Volo, **21**
Pizzeria La Perla, **15**
Pizzeria/Trattoria
  Al Vecio Canton, **23**
Ristorante Ribó, **17**
Trattoria da Bepi, **14**

★ NIGHTLIFE
Bar Santa Lucia, **6**
Café Blue, **19**
Casanova, **11**
Duchamp, **22**
Paradiso Perduto, **1**

ITALY

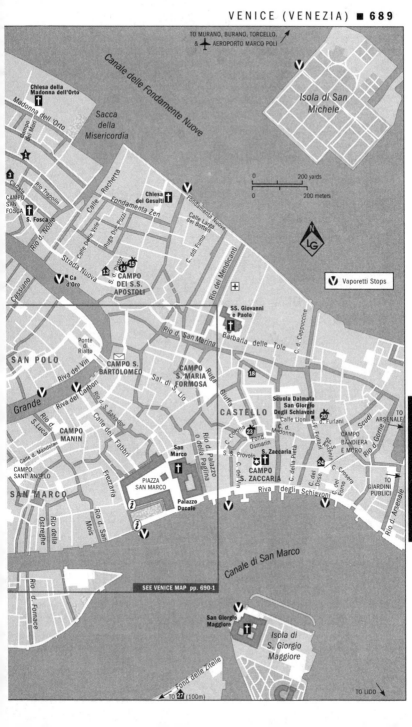

ITALY

Fond. Rio Marin

C. S. Giacomo

CAMPO S. CASSAN

C. Longa

C. dei Botteri

Prim. d. Pettruceria

Rio Terrà

C. dell'Olio

CAMPO DI S. AGOSTIN

C. d. Chiesa

Rio Terrà Rampani

Rio Terrà S. Apponal

C. Vitalba

C. della Vida

C. Bernardo

TO South Africa

CAMPO S. STIN

C. Donà

Rio Terrà San Tomà

Palazzo Corner Mocenigo

CAMPO S. APONAL

CAMPO DI SAN SILVESTRO

C. d. Sbianchesini

C. di Mezzo

CAMPO SAN POLO

Rio Terrà

S. Rocco

CAMPO DEI FRARI

Rio Terrà

San Polo

C. d. Madonnetta

Scuola Grande di S. Rocco

S. Maria Gloriosa dei Frari

Sal. S. Polo

SAN SILVESTRO

Sal. S. Rocco Prima

C. di Christo

CAMPO S. TOMÀ

Scaleter

C. dei Saoneri

Palazzo Grimani di San Luca

C. dei Nomboli

Rio Terrà del Nomboli

C. d. Campaniel

Canal Grande

Crosera S. Pantalon

C. Larga Foscari

C. del Campaniel

C. del Traghetto

Casa dei Goldoni

San Polo

Surf in the Net

SAN TOMÀ

SAN ANGELO

CAMPO S. BENEDETTO

Sal. d. Chiesa e d. Teatro

Teatro Rossini

Palazzo Corner Spinelli

C. Pesaro

Palazzo Pesaro

Rio Terrà d. Mandola

C. d. Mandola

R

CTS ■ Cà Foscari

C. degli Avvocati

C. degli Spezier

Librería Linea D'Acqua

CAMPIELLO DEI SQUELLINI

C. Capelier

Cà Rezzonico (Museo de Settecento Veneziano)

Sal. S. Samuele

C. d. Botteghe

Pisc. S. Samuele

CAMPO SAN ANGELO

C. d. Pestrin

C. d. Verona

C. Bernardo

S. Barnaba

SAN SAMUELE

C. delle Carroze

Sal. Malipiero

S. Samuele

C. d. Teatro

CAMPIELLO NOVO

San Stefano

Net House

CAMPO SAN STEFANO

Teatro la Fenice

C. d.

CÀ REZZONICO

C. del Traghetto

Corte Sforza

C. d. Spezier

C. de Ca'sin

C. del Cerchieri

CAMPO SAN VIDAL

Palazzo Pisani

CAMPO S. MAURIZIO

S. Maria o d. Giglio

C. d. Ostreghe

Fond. Comer Zaguri

CAMPO S. MARIA ZOBENIGO

Palazzo Cavalli

CAMPO SAN VIDAL

ACCADEMIA

UK

CAMPO DI CARITÀ

Ponte dell'Accademia

Cà Grande

SANTA MARIA DEL GIGLIO

C. d. Toletta

Fond. Nani

Fond. Meraviglie

Gallerie dell'Accademia

Ponte dei Sospire

Vaporetti Stops

Canal Grande

CAMPO SAN TROVASO

C. Larga Nani

Rio Terrà d. Carità

Ponte dei Sospiri

CAMPO SAN VIO

Collezione P. Guggenheim

C. d. Bastion

F. di Ca' Bala

Squero Di San Trovaso

Rio Terrà Antonio Foscarini

Piscina del Fomer

Piscina Venier

C. d. Chiesa

Fond. Venier

Fond. Ospedaletto

Numbered markers: 1, 2, 3, 5, 10, 11, 17, 20, 21, 25, 26, 27

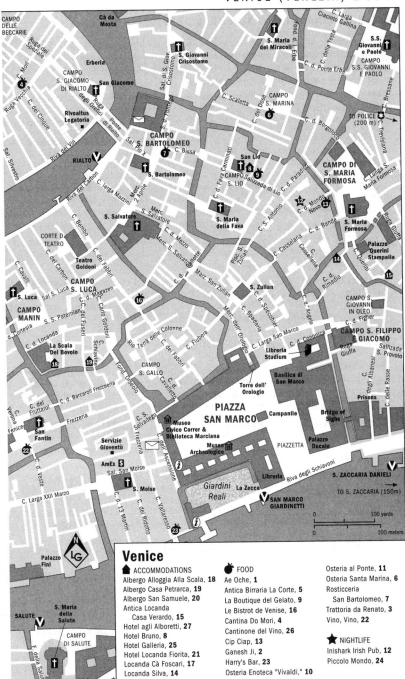

Venice

🏠 **ACCOMMODATIONS**
Albergo Alloggia Alla Scala, **18**
Albergo Casa Petrarca, **19**
Albergo San Samuele, **20**
Antica Locanda
  Casa Verardo, **15**
Hotel agli Alboretti, **27**
Hotel Bruno, **8**
Hotel Galleria, **25**
Hotel Locanda Fiorita, **21**
Locanda Cà Foscari, **17**
Locanda Silva, **14**

🍴 **FOOD**
Ae Oche, **1**
Antica Birraria La Corte, **5**
La Boutique del Gelato, **9**
Le Bistrot de Venise, **16**
Cantina Do Mori, **4**
Cantinone del Vino, **26**
Cip Ciap, **13**
Ganesh Ji, **2**
Harry's Bar, **23**
Osteria Enoteca "Vivaldi," **10**

Osteria al Ponte, **11**
Osteria Santa Marina, **6**
Rosticceria
  San Bartolomeo, **7**
Trattoria da Renato, **3**
Vino, Vino, **22**

⭐ **NIGHTLIFE**
Inishark Irish Pub, **12**
Piccolo Mondo, **24**

ITALY

TOURIST, FINANCIAL, AND LOCAL SERVICES

Tourist Office: APT, Calle della Ascensione, S. Marco 71/F (☎/fax 041 529 87 40; www.tourismovenezia.it), directly opposite the Basilica. Open M-Sa 9:30am-3:30pm. The APT desk at the nearby **Venice Pavilion,** Giardini E Reali, S. Marco 2 (☎041 522 51 50) sells ACTV tickets. Open daily 9am-6pm.

AVA (☎041 171 52 88), in the train station, next to the tourist office. Makes same-day room reservations for a €1 fee. Open daily 9am-10pm. **Branch** offices in P. Roma (☎041 523 13 79) and the airport (☎041 541 51 33). Call for advance reservations.

Rolling Venice Card: Offers discounts on transportation and at over 200 restaurants, cafes, hotels, museums, and shops. Ages 14-29 only. Tourist office provides list of participating vendors. Cards cost €3 and are valid for one year from date of purchase. The card is sponsored by ACTV and can be purchased at the **ACTV VeLa** office (☎041 274 76 50) in P. Roma. Open daily 8:30am-6pm. The card is also available at any APT tourist office, and ACTV VeLa kiosks next to the Ferrovia, Rialto, S. Marco, and Vallaresso *vaporetto* stops.

Budget Travel: CTS, Fondamenta Tagliapietra Dorsoduro, 3252 (☎041 520 56 60; www.cts.it). From Campo S. Barnaba, cross the bridge and follow the road through the piazza. Turn left at the foot of the large bridge. Sells discounted student plane tickets and issues ISIC cards. English spoken. Open M-F 9:30am-1:30pm and 2:30-6pm.

Currency Exchange: Money exchangers charge high prices for service. Use banks whenever possible and inquire about fees beforehand. The streets around S. Marco and S. Polo are full of banks and ATMs. Many 24hr. automatic change machines, outside banks and next to ATMs, offer low commissions and decent rates.

EMERGENCY AND COMMUNICATIONS

Emergency: ☎113. **Ambulance:** ☎118.

Police: ☎113 or 112. **Carabinieri (tourist police):** Campo S. Zaccaria, Castello 4693/A (☎041 27 41 11). **Questura,** V. Nicoladi 24 (☎041 271 55 11). Contact the Questura if you have a serious complaint about your hotel.

Pharmacy: Farmacia Italo Inglese, Calle della Mandola, S. Marco 3717 (☎041 522 48 37), Follow C. Cortesia out of Campo Manin. Open M-F 9am-12:30pm and 3:45-7:30pm, Sa 9am-12:30pm. Late-night and weekend pharmacies rotate; check the list posted in the window of any pharmacy.

Hospital: Ospedale Civile, Campo S.S. Giovanni e Paolo, Castello (☎041 529 41 11).

Internet Access:

Casanova, Lista di Spagna, Cannaregio 158/A (☎041 275 01 99). This hip bar has Internet access on 4 modern, high-speed computers. €7 per hr., students €4. Internet 9am-11:30pm.

Surf In the Net, Calle del Campanile, S. Polo 2898a (☎041 244 02 76). From *vaporetto:* S. Tomà, take Calle del Traghetto, and turn left. €7 per hr., students €5. Open M-Sa 10am-10pm, Su 11am-10pm.

Net House, in Campo S. Stefano, S. Marco 2967-2958 (☎041 227 11 90). €9 per hr., with ISIC or Rolling Venice €6. M-Th 8am-2am, F-Su 24hr.

Post Office: Poste Venezia Centrale, Salizzada Fontego dei Tedeschi, S. Marco 5554 (☎041 271 71 11), off Campo S. Bartolomeo. Open M-Sa 8:30am-6:30pm. **Postal Codes:** S. Marco: 30124; Castello: 30122; S. Polo, S. Croce, and Cannaregio: 30121; Dorsoduro: 30123.

ACCOMMODATIONS

Plan to spend more for a room in Venice than anywhere else in Italy. Always agree on a price before booking, and if possible, make reservations at least one month ahead. Religious institutions around the city offer both dorms and private rooms during the summer for about €25-70. Options include **Casa Murialdo**, Fondamenta Madonna dell'Orto, Cannaregio 3512 (☎041 71 99 33); **Casa Capitania**, S. Croce 561 (☎041 520 30 99; open June-Sept.); **Patronato Salesiano Leone XIII**, Calle S. Domenico, Castello 1281 (☎041 240 36 11); **Domus Cavanis**, Dorsoduro 896 (☎041 528 73 74), near the Accademia Bridge; **Ostello Santa Fosca**, Cannaregio 2372 (☎041 71 57 75); **Instituto Canossiano**, F. delle Romite, Dorsoduro 1323 (☎041 240 97 11); and **Instituto Ciliota**, Calle Muneghe S. Stefano, S. Marco 2976 (☎041 520 48 88).

CANNAREGIO AND SANTA CROCE

The station area, around the Lista di Spagna, has some of Venice's best budget accommodations. Although a 20min. *vaporetto* ride and a 30min. walk from most major sights, at night the streets bustle with young travelers and students.

▨ **Alloggi Gerotto Calderan,** Campo S. Geremia 283 (☎041 71 55 62; www.casagerottocalderan.com). 34 big, bright rooms. Check-out 10am. Curfew 12:30am for dorms, 1am for private rooms. Reserve at least 15 days in advance. Dorms €21; singles €41, with bath €46; doubles €75/93; triples €84/93. ❷

▨ **Locanda Cà San Marcuola,** Campo S. Marcuola, Cannaregio 1763 (☎041 71 60 48; www.casanmarcuola.com). From the Lista di Spagna, follow signs for S. Marcuola. 2 stone lions flank the entrance, next to the "San Marcuola" *vaporetto* stop. This salmon-colored 17th-century abode has completely refurbished rooms and colorful glass lamps lighting the halls. All rooms have bath, A/C, and TV. Free Internet. Singles €70-80; doubles €120-125; triples €150-160; quads €185-200. AmEx/MC/V. ❺

▨ **Hotel Bernardi-Semenzato,** Calle dell'Oca, Cannaregio 4366 (☎041 522 72 57; mtpepoli@tin.it). From *vaporetto*: Cà d'Oro, turn right on Strada Nuova, left on tiny Calle del Duca, then right on Calle dell'Oca. Antiques decorate a renovated annex. Curfew 1am; exceptions made. Singles without bath €30; doubles with bath €95; triples €115; quads €130. 10% Rolling Venice discount on larger rooms. AmEx/MC/V. ❸

Hotel La Forcola, Cannaregio 2353 (☎041 524 14 84; www.laforcolahotel.com). From the station, turn left on Lista di Spagna, which is directly left after 2nd bridge. 23 stately rooms decorated in cream and mahogany in this former Venetian palace. All rooms have bath, A/C, TV, and minibar. Wheelchair accessible. Elaborate buffet breakfast included. Prices vary seasonally. Singles €80-100; doubles €130-165; triples €180-215; quads €200-250. AmEx/MC/V. ❺

Hotel Tintoretto, Santa Fosca, 2316 (☎041 72 15 22; www.hoteltintoretto.com). Head down Lista di Spagna from the station and follow the signs. Cheery rooms with bath, A/C, TV, and minibar, some with canal view. Breakfast included. 24hr. reception. Prices vary seasonally. Singles €41-120; doubles €74-175. AmEx/MC/V. ❹

Ostello Santa Fosca, Fondamenta Canal, Cannaregio, 2372 (☎041 71 57 75; www.santafosca.it). From Lista di Spagna, turn into Campo S. Fosca. Cross the 1st bridge and turn left on Fondamenta Canal. Student-operated, church-affiliated, and quiet. July-Sept. 53 beds available; Oct.-June 31 beds. Internet access available; pay at reception. July-Sept. reception daily 7:30am-noon and 3pm-1am; curfew 12:30am. Oct.-June reception 8am-noon and 5-8pm; no curfew. Singles €21; doubles €42. Dorms €18; €2 discount with ISIC or Rolling Venice. MC/V. ❷

Hotel Rossi, Lista di Spagna, Cannaregio 262 (☎041 71 51 64; rossihotel@interfree.it). 14 rooms with high ceilings and fans in older hotel that shows its age. Currency exchange and drinks available in lobby. June-Sept. reserve at least 1 month ahead. Singles €52, with bath €67; doubles €75/90. Extra bed from €20. 10% Rolling Venice discount. MC/V. ❹

Albergo Adua, Lista di Spagna, Cannaregio 233a (☎041 71 61 84; fax 244 01 62). 22 basic rooms with A/C and TV come at a price. Singles €50, with bath €90; doubles €70 /€100; triples €130 with bath. Cheaper rooms are available through the hotel at a different location; inquire at reception or call for more info. AmEx/MC/V. ❹

Ostello di Venezia (HI), Fondamenta Zitelle, Giudecca 87 (☎041 523 82 11; www.hostelbooking.com). Take *vaporetto* #82, 41, or 42 to Zitelle. Turn right alongside canal. Large and efficient, with a sweeping view of the water. Must book through website; do not call to reserve. Reception 7-9:30am and 1:30-11:30pm. Lockout 9:30am-1:30pm. Curfew 11:30pm. HI members only; cards for sale. Dorms €17. MC/V. ❷

Istituto Canosiano, Ponte Piccolo, Giudecca 428 (☎041 522 21 57). Take *vaporetto* #82 or 41 to Palanca, and cross the bridge on the left. Women only. 35 beds. Sheets included. Reception 3pm-curfew. Lockout noon-3pm. Strict curfew 10:30pm; in winter 10pm. Large dorms €15. ❶

SAN MARCO AND SAN POLO

Surrounded by exclusive shops, souvenir stands, scores of *trattorie* and *pizzerie*, and many of Venice's most popular sights, these accommodations are pricey options for those in search of Venice's showy side.

▨**Albergo San Samuele,** Salizzada S. Samuele, S. Marco 3358 (☎/fax 041 522 80 45, www.albergosansamuele.it). Follow Calle delle Botteghe from Campo S. Stefano and turn left on Salizzada S. Samuele. A crumbling stone courtyard leads to this charming deal. Great location 2min. from *vaporetto* #82 (San Samuele) and 10min. from P.S. Marco. Clean, well-decorated rooms, some with gorgeous balcony views of S. Marco's red rooftops. Singles €26-45; doubles €36-75, with bath €46-105; triples €135. ❸

Albergo Casa Petrarca, Calle Schiavine, S. Marco 4386 (☎/fax 041 520 04 30). From Campo S. Luca, follow C. Fuseri, take 2nd left and then a right. Tiny hotel has 7 small but bright, white rooms. Cheery sitting room with rows of English books and a quaint breakfast room. All rooms with A/C. Singles €45; doubles with bath €90. ❹

Domus Civica (ACISJF), Campiello Chiovere Frari, S. Polo 3082 (☎041 72 11 03; fax 041 522 71 39). From the train station, cross Ponte Scalzi and turn right. Turn left on Fondamenta dei Tolentini and left through the courtyard onto Corte Amai. The hostel is to the right, after the bridge. Simple student housing. Strict curfew 11:30pm. Open June-Sept. 25. Singles €30; doubles €54; triples €81. 15% Rolling Venice discount. ❸

Hotel Locanda Fiorita, Campiello Novo, S. Marco 3457 (☎041 523 47 54; www.locandafiorita.com). From Campo S. Stefano, take Calle del Pestrin and then climb onto the raised *piazza*. A vine-covered courtyard and terrace lead to large doubles with oriental rugs and couches. All rooms have A/C and TV. Singles without bath €78; doubles €103-180. AmEx/MC/V. ❺

Albergo Alloggia Alla Scala, Corte Contarini del Bovolo, S. Marco 4306 (☎041 521 06 29; fax 041 522 64 51). From Campo Manin facing the bridge, turn left on the alley and look for signs to La Scala del Bovolo; the hotel is just beyond, in the alleyway. Superb location. Plain but simple rooms all have bath. Breakfast €9. Singles €55; doubles €77-87; triples €117. AmEx/MC/V. ❹

CASTELLO

Castello is arguably the most beautiful part of Venice, and, as it houses the largest number of Venetians, also the most authentic. A room on the second or third floor with a view of red rooftops and the sculpted skyline is worth the inevitability of getting lost in some of the most narrow and tightly clustered streets in the city.

Foresteria Valdese, Castello 5170 (☎041 528 67 97; www.diaconiavaldese.org/venezia). From Campo S. Maria Formosa, take Calle Lunga S. Marial; it's immediately over the 1st bridge. Frescoed ceilings ornament the 18th-century Palazzo Cavagnis, a guest house of Venice's largest Protestant church. Reception daily 9am-1pm and 6-8pm. Lockout 10am-1pm. Closed 3 weeks in Nov. Dorms €21; doubles €56, with bath €74; quads with bath €102. €1 Rolling Venice discount. MC/V. ❷

La Residenza, Campo Bandiera e Moro Castello 3608 (☎041 528 53 15; www.venicelaresidenza.com). From *vaporetto:* Arsenal, turn left on Riva degli Schiavoni and right on C. del Dose into the *campo.* Luxurious hotel with palatial lobby. Singles €60-95; doubles €100-155. MC/V. ❺

Antica Locanda Casa Verardo, Castello 4765 (☎041 528 61 27; www.casaverardo.it). From the Basilica, take C. Canonica, turn right before the bridge and left over the bridge on Ruga Giuffa into S. Filippo e Giacomo. Follow C. della Chiesa left out of the *campo* until reaching a bridge. Hotel is on the other side. Richly colored rooms in a 15th-century *palazzo.* Singles without A/C €60-75; doubles €80-165. AmEx/MC/V. ❺

Hotel Bruno, Salizzada S. Lio, Castello 5726/A (☎041 523 04 52; www:hoteldabruno.it). From Campo S. Bartolomeo, take Salizzada S. Lio, crossing the bridge. High-ceilinged, beautiful rooms all have bath and A/C. Breakfast included. Singles €60-160; doubles €90-210; triples €120-260. MC/V. ❺

Locanda Silva, Fondamenta del Rimedio Castello 4423 (☎041 522 76 43; albergosilva@libero.it). From P.S. Marco, walk under the clock tower, turn right on Calle Larga S. Marco, left on Calle del Angelo before the bridge, right on Calle Rimedio before next bridge; follow it to the end. Lime-green rooms with 50s decor. Open Feb. to mid-Nov. Singles €40, with bath €60; doubles €70-80/90-105; triples €120-140; quads €140-170. Cash only. ❹

DORSODURO

Spartan facades and still canals trace the quiet, wide streets of Dorsoduro. Here, art museums draw visitors to canal-front real estate, while the interior remains a little-visited residential quarter. Situated near the Grand Canal between Chiesa dei Frari and Ponte Accademia, most hotels here tend to be pricey.

Hotel Galleria, Rio Terra Antonio Foscarini, Dorsoduro 878/A (☎041 523 24 89; www.hotelgalleria.it), on the left facing the Accademia museum. Oriental rugs and art prints lend an elegance appropriate to its location on the Grand Canal. Breakfast in bed included. Singles €70; doubles without bath €95-145. AmEx/MC/V. ❺

Locanda Cà Foscari, Calle della Frescada, Dorsoduro 3887b (☎041 71 04 01; valtersc@tin.it), in a quiet neighborhood. From *vaporetto:* San Tomà, turn left at the dead end, cross the bridge, turn right, then turn left on the alley. Murano glass chandeliers and a private garden embellish this simple, family-run hotel. Closed end of Nov.-Jan. 1. Singles €60; doubles €70-90; triples €87-110; quads €108-130. MC/V. ❹

Hotel agli Alboretti, Accademia 884 (☎041 523 00 58; www.aglialboretti.com). From Accademia *vaporetto,* turn left off the landing, then right along the avenue. Typical old-style Venetian house, now renovated. All rooms have bath and TV. Singles €104; doubles €150-180; triples €210. AmEx/MC/V. ❺

CAMPING

Plan on at least a 20min. boat ride from Venice. In addition to these listings, the **Litorale del Cavallino,** on the Lido's Adriatic side, has multiple beach campsites.

Camping Miramare, Lungomare Dante Alighieri 29 (☎041 96 61 50; www.camping-miramare.it). A 40min. ride on *vaporetto* #14 from P.S. Marco to Punta Sabbioni. Campground is 700m along the beach on the right. 3-night min. stay in high season. Reserve ahead for bungalows with A/C. Open Apr. 1 to Nov. 2. €5 per person, €6 per tent. Bungalows €35 plus €5.50 per person. 15% Rolling Venice discount. ❶

Camping Fusina, V. Moranzani 79 (☎041 547 00 55; www.camping-fusina.com), in Malcontenta. From Mestre, take bus #1. Restaurant, *pizzeria,* laundromat, ATM, Internet access, and satellite TV on premises. Call ahead to reserve cabins. Free hot showers. €4 per person, €7 per tent, €14 per car. Cabins: singles €19; doubles €26. ❶

🍴 FOOD

In Venice, dining well on a budget requires exploration. The best and most affordable restaurants are hidden in the less-traveled alleyways. For an inexpensive and informal option, visit any *osteria* or *bacario* in town and create a meal from the vast array of **cicchetti** (meat- and cheese-filled pastries; €1-3), tidbits of seafood, rice, meat, and *tramezzini* (triangular slices of soft white bread with any imaginable filling). The key ingredients of Venetian cuisine come fresh from the sea. *Spaghetti al vongole* (pasta with fresh clams and spicy vegetables) is served on nearly every menu. Good local wines include the sparkling white *prosecco della Marca* or the red *valpolicella.* **BILLA supermarket,** Strada Nuova, Cannaregio 3660, is near Campo Apostoli. (Open M-Sa 8:30am-8pm, Su 9am-8pm. AmEx/MC/V.)

CANNAREGIO

Trattoria da Bepi, Cannaregio 4550 (☎041 528 50 31). This traditional Venetian restaurant, family-run for 38 years, has copper pots dangling from the ceiling. *Primi* €7-10.50. *Secondi* €9.50-18. Open M-W and F-Su noon-3pm and 7-10pm. MC/V. ❹

Pizzeria La Perla, Rio Terra dei Franceschi, Cannaregio 4615 (☎041 528 51 75). Friendly staff serves over 90 varieties of pizza and pasta in heaping portions. Pizza €4.70-7.90. Pasta €6.10-8.20. Cover €1.10. Service 10%. Open M-Sa noon-2pm and 7-9:45pm. AmEx/MC/V. ❸

Gam Gam, Canale di Cannaregio, Cannaregio 1122 (☎041 71 52 84). The only Jewish restaurant with kosher food in Venice offers a great change of pace from traditional Italian fare. Outdoor seating by canal. *Schnitzel* €11.50. Falafel platter €8.75. Pasta €7.50-9. 10% *Let's Go* discount. Open M-F and Su noon-10pm. ❸

Brek, Lista di Spagna, Cannaregio 124A (☎041 244 01 58). Italian fast-food chain whips up pasta and salad dishes from an extensive array of ingredients. Perfect for a meal on the go. Menu and prices change daily. 10% Rolling Venice discount. *Primi* €2.90-3.90. *Secondi* €4-7. Open daily 8-10:30am and 11:30am-10:30pm. ❷

CASTELLO

🏛 **La Boutique del Gelato,** Salizzada S. Lio, Castello 5727 (☎041 522 32 83). Huge cones, gigantic quality, and miniscule prices. Single scoop €0.80, 2 scoops €1.30. Open daily 10am-8pm, July-Aug. until 10:30pm. ❶

Alle Testiere, Calle del Mondo Novo, Castello 5801 (☎/fax 041 522 72 20). Tiny restaurant mixes old traditions with *nuovo* decor and cuisine. Menu is small but compiled with care; go for the fish entrees. *Primi* €14. *Secondi* €21.50-23. Reservations recommended. Open Tu-Sa noon-3pm and 7pm-midnight. MC/V. ❺

Trattoria Al Vecio Canton, Castello 4738/a (☎041 528 51 76). Tavern-style *trattoria* is famous for its pizza. Try the *Al Vecio Canton* (topped with tomatoes, cheese, olive oil, garlic, and a spritz of lemon; €6). Open M and W-Su noon-3pm and 7pm-midnight. ❸

Arcimboldo, Calle dei Furlani, Castello 3219 (☎041 528 65 69). Paintings by Arcimboldo contribute to a mood of atmospheric irreverence. Try specialty *pesce al forno con verdure di stagione* (baked fish with seasonal vegetables; serves 2; €26). Open M and W-Su noon-3pm and 7pm-midnight. AmEx/MC/V. ❸

Cip Ciap, Calle Mondo Novo, Castello 5799a (☎041 523 66 21). Huge, delicious pizzas from €4.20, with smaller *margherita* for €2.30. Also sold by the slice. Try the *disco volante* (literally, flying saucer), made like a calzone and stuffed with mushrooms, eggplant, ham, egg, and salami (€6.50). Open M and W-Su 9am-9pm. ❷

Osteria Santa Marina, Campo S. Marina, Castello 5911 (☎/fax 041 528 52 39). Splurge to dine with well-dressed locals or just stop by for some *cicchetti* and a glass of *prosecco* at the bar. Restaurant specializes in fish. *Primi* €14. *Secondi* €19-25. Cover €3. Open Su-M 7:30-10pm, Tu-Sa 12:30-2:30pm and 7:30-10pm. MC/V. ❺

SAN MARCO

🏵 **Le Bistrot de Venise,** Calle dei Fabbri, S. Marco 4685 (☎041 523 66 51; www.bistrotdevenise.com). Scrumptious, beautifully presented pasta dishes prepared from 14th-century recipes are overshadowed only by the service. *Primi* from €12. *Secondi* from €17. Service 15%. 10% Rolling Venice discount. Open daily noon-3pm and 7pm-1am. AmEx/MC/V. ❺

Vino, Vino, Ponte delle Veste, S. Marco 2007A. Dark, no-frills wine bar has over 350 varieties of wine. Seafood-focused menu changes daily. *Primi* €5. *Secondi* €9. Open Su-F 10:30am-midnight, Sa 10am-1am. 15% Rolling Venice discount. ❸

Rosticceria San Bartolomeo, Calle della Bissa, S. Marco 5424/A (☎041 522 35 69). A smorgasbord of sandwiches, pasta, and *cicchetti* to be enjoyed on the go or in a window booth. Full-service restaurant upstairs serves lunch. Entrees from €5.90. *Panini* from €1.10. Cover for restaurant €1.30. Open daily 9:30am-9:30pm. AmEx/MC/V. ❶

Harry's Bar, Calle Vallaresso, S. Marco 1323 (☎041 528 57 77). Founded in 1931 by Bostonian Harry Cipriani who believed that Venice suffered a lack of bars, this cafe has been pouring pricey drinks to tourists and notables like Ernest Hemingway, Katharine Hepburn, and Robert DeNiro ever since. Open daily 10:30am-11pm. MC/V. ❹

DORSODURO

🏵 **Cantinone del Vino,** Fondamente Meraviglie, Dorsoduro 992. A spectacular display of wines, ranging in price from €3-200 a bottle. Enjoy a glass (from €0.70) at the bar with some *cicchetti* (from €1). Open M-Sa 8am-2:30pm and 3:15-8:30pm. ❷

Gelateria Nico, Fondamenta Zattere, Dorsoduro 922. Great view of the Giudecca Canal. Try the Venetian specialty *gianduiotto al passagetto* (a slice of dense chocolate-hazelnut ice cream dunked in whipped cream; €2.30). *Gelato* €0.80-6.50. Open daily 6:45am-11pm. ❶

Pizza al Volo, Campo S. Margherita, Dorsoduro 2944 (☎041 522 54 30). Students and locals come for delicious, cheap pizza. Slices from €1.30. Pizza from €3.40. Gigantic pizza for 2 from €6.30. Open daily 11:30am-4pm and 5:30pm-1:30am. ❶

SAN POLO AND SANTA CROCE

Ae Oche, S. Croce 1552a/b (☎041 524 11 61). From Campo S. Giacomo da L'orio, take Calle del Trentor. Not for the indecisive: Over 100 types of pizza (€3.50-10) and a crowd who can take them on. Open daily noon-3pm and 7pm-midnight. MC/V. ❶

Osteria Enoteca "Vivaldi," S. Polo 1457 (☎041 523 81 85). Friendly tavern-style restaurant. *Primi* €8-10. *Secondi* from €10. Cover €1.50. Service 10%. Open daily 11:30am-2:30pm and 6:30-10:30pm. AmEx/MC/V. ❸

Osteria al Ponte, Calle Saoneri, S. Polo 2741/a (☎041 71 08 49). From Campo S. Polo, follow signs to the Accademia; it's immediately across the 1st bridge. Bustling spot serves hungry Venetians at affordable prices. Cover €1.30. *Primi* from €5.50. *Secondi* from €6.50. Open daily 10am-2:30pm and 5:30-10pm. AmEx/MC/V. ❷

Trattoria da Renato, S. Polo 2245/a (☎041 524 19 22). An unassuming facade conceals campy 50's decor. *Primi* €5.50-8. *Secondi* from €8. Cover €1. Open daily 1-3:15pm and 7:15-10:30pm. ❸

Ristorante Ribò, Fondamenta Minotto, S. Croce 158 (☎041 524 24 86). Canal views in an elegant setting with traditional Venetian cuisine. Bright, friendly atmosphere, with garden dining option. *Primi* from €12. *Secondi* €14. Cover €3. Open Su and Tu-Sa 12:15-3pm and 7:15-10:30pm. AmEx/MC/V. ❺

Ganesh Ji, Calle dell'Olio, S. Polo 2426 (☎/fax 041 71 98 04). Indian food served among elephant statues and candy-stripe poles or on a canalfront terrace. Vegetarian lunch €12, regular €13.50. Cover €2.20. 10% Rolling Venice discount. Take-out available. Open Tu-W, F-Su 12:30-2pm and 7pm-midnight, Th 7pm-midnight. MC/V. ❹

Antica Birraria La Corte, Campo S. Polo, S. Polo 2168 (☎041 275 05 70). Housed in a former brewery, the Birraria stays true to its roots with an extensive selection of German hops and a raucous crowd. Beer €1.50-4.30. Pizza €4.50-9. *Primi* €7. Cover €1.80. Open daily 10am-3pm and 6pm-midnight. AmEx/MC/V. ❷

Cantina Do Mori, Calle due Mori, S. Polo 429 (☎041 522 54 01). Tourists gravitate to Venice's oldest wine bar. Aging copperware lining the walls and an uneven stone floor give an antique feel. An elegant place to grab a few *cicchetti* (from €1) or a glass of local wine. Open M-Sa 8:30am-8:30pm, closed some afternoons in summer. ❷

⊚ SIGHTS

AROUND PIAZZA SAN MARCO

■**BASILICA DI SAN MARCO.** The crown jewel of Venice is a spectacular fusion of gold and marble, gracing **Piazza San Marco** with its bulbous symmetrical arches and incomparable mosaic portals. As the city's largest tourist attraction, the **Basilica di San Marco** also has the longest lines. Visit in the early morning for the shortest wait or in late afternoon for the best natural illumination. Begun in the 9th century to house the remains of St. Mark, the interior now sparkles with mosaics from both the 13th-century Byzantine and 16th-century Renaissance periods. Behind the altar, decorated with Renaissance statues of the Apostles, the Virgin Mary, and Mary Magdalene, the gem-encrusted **Pala D'Oro** relief covers the tomb of St. Mark. To the right rests the **Tesoro** (Treasury), containing gold and relics from the Fourth Crusade. Steep stairs in the atrium lead to the **Galleria della Basilica,** which provides a staggering perspective of the interior mosaics, a tranquil vista of the *piazza,* and an intimate view of the original bronze *Horses of St. Mark.* (*Basilica open daily 9:30am-4:30pm. Dress code enforced. Free. Pala D'Oro open daily 9:45am-5pm. €1.50. Treasury open M-Sa 9:45am-5pm. €2. Galleria open daily 9:45am-5pm. €1.50.*)

■**PALAZZO DUCALE (DOGE'S PALACE).** Once the home of Venice's *doge* (mayor), the Palazzo Ducale museum contains spectacular artwork including Veronese's *Rape of Europa.* In the courtyard, Sansovino's enormous sculptures, *Mars* and *Neptune,* flank the **Scala dei Giganti** (Stairs of the Giants), upon which new *doges* would be crowned. On the balcony stands the **Bocca di Leone** (Lion's Mouth), into which the Council of Ten, the *doge's* assistants, who acted as judges and administrators, would drop the names of those they suspected guilty of crimes. The *doge's* private apartments and the magnificent state rooms of the Republic reveal much about the lifestyle and political concerns of the period. Climb the richly decorated **Scala d'Oro** (Golden Staircase) to reach the **Sala del Maggior Consiglio** (Great Council Room), dominated by Tintoretto's *Paradise*, the largest oil painting in the world. Passages lead through the courtrooms of the much-feared Council of Ten and the even-more-feared Council of Three, crossing the covered **Ponte dei Sospiri** (Bridge of Sighs) and continuing into the prisons. Casanova was condemned by the Ten to walk across this bridge, which gets its name from 19th-century Romantic writers' references to the mournful groans of prisoners descending into dank cells. *(Wheelchair accessible. Open Apr.-Oct. daily 9am-7pm; Nov.-Apr. 9am-5pm. €11, students €5.50.)*

■ **PIAZZA SAN MARCO.** Unlike the labyrinthine streets that tangle themselves through most of Venice, P.S. Marco, Venice's only official *piazza*, is a magnificent expanse of light, space, and architectural harmony. Enclosing the *piazza* are the Renaissance **Procuratie Vecchie** (Old Treasury Offices), the Baroque **Procuratie Nuove** (New Treasury Offices), and the Neoclassical **Ala Napoleonica** (also Treasury Offices). The 96m brick **campanile** (belltower), which stands on Roman foundations, provides one of the best views of the city. Though it originally served as a watchtower and lighthouse, savvy Venice took advantage of its location to create a medieval tourist attraction by dangling state prisoners from its top in cages. The practice ceased in the 18th century, but public fascination with the tower did not. In a 1902 restoration project, it collapsed into a mere pile of bricks only to be reconstructed in 1912 with the enlightened addition of an elevator. On a clear day, Croatia and Slovenia are visible from the top. *(Campanile open daily 9am-9pm. €6.)*

PIAZZA SAN MARCO'S MUSEUMS. Beneath the arcade at the short end of P.S. Marco lies the entrance to a trio of museums. The **Museo Civico Correr** contains artifacts from Venice's imperial past. The first part of the museum demonstrates the Neoclassical French influence on Venetian art and then progresses to a medley of works by Bellini and Carpaccio. The **Museo Archeologico** houses a modest but beautiful collection of ancient Greek and Roman sculpture and medallions. Paintings by Veronese, Titian, and Tintoretto adorn the main reading room of the **Biblioteca Nazionale Marciana,** built between 1537 and 1560. *(Open daily Apr.-Oct. 9am-7pm; Nov.-Mar. 9am-5pm. €11, students €5.50. Includes entrance to Palazzo Ducale.)*

LA SCALA DEL BOVOLO. This snow-white marble "staircase of the snails," as it translates into English, is a magnificent flight of architectural fancy. Legend has it that the staircase was designed by Leonardo da Vinci himself and constructed by his assistants. It once led to the top floors of a now-destroyed palace. Today the top only affords views of the next-door neighbor's kitchen. *(From the Campo Manin, facing the bridge, take a left down the alley and look for the signs. Open daily Apr.-Oct. 10am-6pm; Nov.-Mar. 10am-4pm. €3.)*

AROUND THE PONTE RIALTO

THE GRAND CANAL. The Grand Canal is Venice's "main street." Over 3km long and nearly 50m wide, it loops through the city and passes under three bridges: the **Ponte Scalzi, Rialto,** and the **Ponte Accademia.** Coursing past the splendid facades of the *palazzi* that crown its banks, it is a testament to Venice's history and immense wealth. The candy-cane posts used for mooring boats on the canal are called *bricole;* they are painted with the family colors of the adjoining *palazzo*. *(For great facade views, ride vaporetto #82 or the slower #1 from the train station to P.S. Marco. The facades are flood-lit at night, producing a dazzling play of reflections.)*

ITALY

PONTE RIALTO. This impressive architectural construct was named after Rivo Alto, the first colony built in Venice. It was originally built of wood, but after its collapse in the 1500s, Antonio da Ponte designed the current stone structure (1588-91). Today, shops and vendors crowd the top of the bridge.

RIVOALTUS LEGATORIA. Step into Rivoaltus on any given day and hear Wanda Scarpa shouting greetings from the attic, where she has been sewing leather-bound antique style journals for more than three decades. This delightful and reasonably priced shop, run by arguably the nicest husband and wife tandem in Italy, is cluttered with the results of her diligent toiling. Giorgio Scarpa jokes that he chains her there to make her work. Though Venice is now littered with shops advertising handmade journals, Rivoaltus was the first, and sells products of such renowned quality that even movie stars have been known to send their agents specifically to this shop to buy portfolios. Come in for a friendly chat and ask Giorgio for a tour of the shop. *(Ponte di Rialto. Open daily 10am-7:30pm.)*

SAN POLO

■ **SCUOLA GRANDE DI SAN ROCCO.** Venice's most illustrious *scuola*, or guild hall, stands as a monument to Jacopo Tintoretto. The painter, who left Venice only once in 76 years (and refused to take that trip without his wife), set out to combine "the color of Titian with the drawing of Michelangelo." The school commissioned Tintoretto to complete all the paintings in the building, which took 23 years. The *Crucifixion* in the last room upstairs is the collection's crowning glory. Step outside to admire this masterpiece to classical music performed on the street. *(Behind Basilica dei Frari in Campo S. Rocco. Open daily 9:30am-5:30pm. €5.50, students €4.)*

CAMPO SAN POLO. The next-largest *campo* in Venice after P.S. Marco, **Campo San Polo** once hosted bull-baiting matches. During the *carnevale*, authorities would release a wild bull into the crowds, then set dogs on its tail. After the dogs began to tear the bull's flesh, the defeated animal would finally be decapitated before a hooting, jeering mob. A painting depicting the ensuing chaos hangs in the Museo Correr in P.S. Marco. Today, the *campo* is filled with benches, trees, and frolicking children, so visits are rather less intense. *(Between the Ponte Frari and Ponte Rialto. Vaporetto: S. Silvestro.)*

DORSODURO

■ **GALLERIE DELL'ACCADEMIA.** The Accademia houses the most extensive collection of Venetian art in the world. At the top of the double staircase, **Room I**, topped by a ceiling full of cherubim, houses Venetian Gothic art, with a luxurious use of color that influenced Venetian painting for centuries. Among the enormous altarpieces in **Room II**, Giovanni Bellini's *Madonna Enthroned with Child, Saints, and Angels* stands out for its lush serenity. **Rooms IV** and **V** display more Bellinis and **Giorgione's** enigmatic *La Tempesta*. In **Room XX,** works by Gentile Bellini and Carpaccio display Venetian processions and city-scapes so accurately that scholars use them as "photos" of Venice's past. *(Vaporetto: Accademia. Open M 8:15am-2pm, T-Su 9:15am-7:15pm. €6.50.)*

■ **COLLEZIONE PEGGY GUGGENHEIM.** Guggenheim's Palazzo Venier dei Leoni now displays works by Brancusi, Marini, Kandinsky, Picasso, Magritte, Rothko, Ernst, Pollock, and Dalí. The Marini sculpture *Angel in the City*, in front of the *palazzo*, was designed with a detachable penis. Guggenheim occasionally modified this sculpture so as not to offend her more prudish guests. *(Calle S. Cristoforo, Dorsoduro 710. Vaporetto: Accademia. Turn left and follow the yellow signs. Open Su-M and W-F 10am-6pm, Sa 10am-10pm. €8, €5 with Rolling Venice card.)*

ITALY

CÀ REZZONICO. Longhena's great 18th-century Venetian palace houses the newly restored **Museo del Settecento Veneziano** (Museum of 18th-Century Venice). Known as the "Temple of Venetian Settecento," this grand palace features a truly regal ballroom, complete with flowing curtains and Crosato's frescoed ceiling depicting Phoebus with the continents. *(Vaporetto: Cà Rezzonico. Reserve 24hr. ahead. ☎041 241 01 00. Open Apr.-Oct. M and W-Su 10am-6pm, Nov.-Mar. 10am-5pm. €6.50, students and Rolling Venice card holders €4.50.)*

CASTELLO

SCUOLA DALMATA SAN GIORGIO DEGLI SCHIAVONI. Some of Carpaccio's finest paintings, including episodes from the lives of St. George, Jerome, and Tryfon, decorate this early 16th-century building. *(Castello, 3259/A. Vaporetto: S. Zaccaria. Modest dress required. Open Apr.-Oct. Su 9:30am-12:30pm, Tu-Sa 9:30am-12:30pm and 3:30-6:30pm; Nov.-Mar. Su 10am-12:30pm, Tu-Sa 10am-12:30pm and 3-6pm. €3.)*

GIARDINI PUBLICI AND SANT'ELENA. Those who long for trees and grass can stroll through the Public Gardens, installed by Napoleon, or bring a picnic lunch to the shady lawns of Sant'Elena. *(Vaporetto: Giardini or S. Elena. Free.)*

CANNAREGIO

JEWISH GHETTO. In 1516 the *doge* forced Venice's Jewish population into the old cannon-foundry area, creating the first Jewish ghetto in Europe; the word "ghetto" is the Venetian word for "foundry." The oldest *schola* (synagogue), **Schola Grande Tedesca** (German Synagogue), shares a building with the **Museo Ebraica di Venezia** (Hebrew Museum of Venice) in the Campo del Ghetto Nuovo. *(Cannaregio 2899/B. Vaporetto: S. Marcuola. Hebrew Museum open June-Sept. Su-F 10am-7pm; Oct.-May 10am-4:30pm. €3, students €2. Entrance to synagogues by guided tour only (40min.). English tours leave from the museum every hr. June-Sept. 10:30am-5:30pm; Oct.-May 10:30am-3:30pm. Museum and tour €8, students €6.50.)*

CÀ D'ORO AND GALLERIA GIORGIO FRANCHETTI. The most spectacular facade on the Canal Grande and the premiere example of Venetian Gothic, the Cà d'Oro, built between 1425 and 1440, now houses the Giorgio Franchetti collection. For the best view of the palace, take the *traghetto* across the canal to the Rialto Markets. *(Vaporetto: Cà d'Oro. Open daily 9am-2pm. €3.50, students €2.50.)*

CHURCHES

The Foundation for the Churches of Venice sells **mini-passes** that provide access to all of Venice's churches. A three-day pass (€8, students €5) which includes S. Maria dei Miracoli, S. Maria Gloriosa dei Frari, S. Polo, Madonna dell'Orto, Il Redentore, and S. Sebastiano, is available at all participating churches except S. Maria Gloriosa dei Frari. *(For information call ☎041 275 0462.)*

⌗CHIESA DI SAN ZACCARIA (SAN MARCO). Dedicated to the father of John the Baptist and designed in the late 1400s by Coducci, among others, this Gothic-Renaissance church holds Bellini's *Virgin and Child Enthroned with Four Saints*, one of the masterpieces of Venetian Renaissance painting. Its rich tones and meticulous shading are a testament to the Venetian attention to detail. A true find, this church is often overlooked by tourists. *(Vaporetto: S. Zaccaria. Open daily 10am-noon and 4-6pm. Free.)*

CHIESA DI SAN GIACOMO DI RIALTO (SAN POLO). Between the Ponte di Rialto and surrounding markets stands Venice's first church, diminutively called "San Giacometto." An ornate clock-face adorns its *campanile*. Across the *piazza*, a statue called *il Gobbo* (the hunchback) supports the steps. Once the podium from which officials made announcements, it was at the foot of this sculpture that convicted thieves, forced to run naked from P.S. Marco and lashed all the way by bystanders, could finally collapse. *(Vaporetto: Rialto. Cross bridge and turn right. Open daily 10am-5pm. Free.)*

BASILICA DI SANTA MARIA GLORIOSA DEI FRARI (SAN POLO). Franciscans began construction on this enormous Gothic church, also known simply as I Frari, in 1340. Today it is a mausoleum of art, boasting two paintings by Titian as well as the Renaissance master himself, who is entombed within the cathedral's cavernous terracotta walls. His ▨**Assumption** (1516-1518) on the high altar marks the height of the Venetian Renaissance. Like contemporary Roman and Florentine painters, Titian created balanced, harmonious compositions, enlivened with the traditional Venetian reverence for color and sensuality. Titian's elaborate tomb, a triumphal arch, stands diagonally across from the Pesaro altar and directly across from the enormous pyramid in which the sculptor Canova (1757-1822) rests. *(Vaporetto: S. Tomà. Follow signs back to Campo dei Frari. Open M-Sa 9am-6pm, Su 1-6pm. €2.)*

CHIESA DI SANTA MARIA DELLA SALUTE (DORSODURO). This church is central to the architecture of Venice: Its domes are visible from everywhere in the city. The theatrical *Salute* (Italian for "health"), poised at the tip of Dorsoduro, is a prime example of the Venetian Baroque style, which sought to draw spectators more fully into the architectural space. In 1631, the city commissioned Longhena to build the church for the Virgin, whom they believed would return the favor by ending the plague. These days, Venice celebrates the end of the plague on the third Sunday in November by building a wooden pontoon bridge across the Canal and lighting candles in the church. Next to the *Salute* stands the *Dogana*, the old customs house, where ships sailing into Venice were required to stop and pay appropriate duties. Upon leaving the *Dogana*, walk along the *fondamenta* to the tip of Dorsoduro, where a marvelous panorama of the city awaits. *(Vaporetto: Salute. Open daily 9am-noon and 3-5:30pm. Free.)*

CHIESA DI SAN SEBASTIANO (DORSODURO). The Renaissance painter Veronese took refuge in this 16th-century church when he fled Verona in 1555 after allegedly killing a man. By 1565 he had filled the church with an amazing cycle of paintings and frescoes. His breathtaking *Stories of Queen Esther* covers the ceiling, while the artist himself rests under the gravestone by the organ. Also displayed are works by Titian and Paris Bordone. *(Vaporetto: S. Basilio. Continue straight ahead. Open M-Sa 10am-5pm. €2.)*

CHIESA DI SANTISSIMI GIOVANNI E PAOLO (CASTELLO). This terracotta structure, also called San Zanipolo, is primarily built in the Gothic style, but it has a Renaissance-era portal and an arch supported by columns of Greek marble. Inside, monumental salmon-colored brick walls and cream-colored stone ceilings enclose the tombs and monuments of former *doges*. Off the left transept is the **Cappella del Rosario.** After a fire destroyed the chapel in 1867, works by Veronese were brought in to replace the lost paintings. *(Vaporetto: Fond. Nuove. Turn left, then right onto Fond. dei Mendicanti. ☎ 041 523 59 13. Open M-Sa 7:30am-12:30pm and 3:30-7pm, Su 3-6pm. Free.)*

CHIESA DI SANTA MARIA DEI MIRACOLI (CASTELLO). The Lombardi family designed this small Renaissance jewel in the late 1400s. It remains one of Venice's prettiest churches, elegantly faced with polychrome marble and brimming inside with gold reliefs, sculpted figures, and lavish colors. *(From S. S. Giovanni e Paolo, cross Ponte Rosse and continue straight. Open M-Sa 10am-5pm, Su 1-5pm. €2.)*

CHIESA DELLA MADONNA DELL'ORTO (CANNAREGGIO). Tintoretto painted some of his most moving works for his parish church, another Venetian Gothic example. Inside, lofty wood ceilings accommodate ten of his largest paintings.

Near the high altar hang his *Last Judgment,* a spatially intense mass of souls, and *The Sacrifice of the Golden Calf.* On the right apse is the brilliantly shaded *Presentation of the Virgin at the Temple.* A light switch for illuminating the works is at each of the far corners. *(Vaporetto: Madonna dell'Orto. Open M-Sa 10am-5pm. €2.)*

CHIESA SANTA MARIA ASSUNTA (CASTELLO). An excess of green-and-white marble and an extravagant ceiling await within this 18th-century church, which is covered by an equally lavish Baroque facade. Its gilded stucco work is unparalleled in Venice. Titian's *Martyrdom of Saint Lawrence* hangs in the altar to the left at the entrance. *(Vaporetto: Fond. Nuove. Open daily 10am-noon and 4-6pm.)*

SAN GIORGIO MAGGIORE AND GIUDECCA

BASILICA DI SAN GIORGIO MAGGIORE. Standing on its own monastic island, S. Giorgio Maggiore contrasts sharply with most other Venetian churches. Palladio ignored the Venetian fondness for color and instead opted for an austere design. Light fills the enormous open space inside, although unfortunately it does not hit Tintoretto's *Last Supper* by the high altar; a light switch illuminates the wraith-like angels hovering over Christ's table. The beautiful courtyard, to the right of the church, is closed to the public. Take the elevator to the top of the **campanile** for a marvelous view of the city. *(Vaporetto: S. Giorgio Maggiore. Open in summer M-Sa 9am-12:30pm and 2:30-6:30pm; off-season 2:30-5pm. Basilica free. Campanile €3.)*

ISLANDS OF THE LAGOON

▓ **BURANO.** In this traditional fishing village, fishermen haul in their catch every morning while women sit in the doorways of their fantastically colored houses, creating unique knots of Venetian lace. See their handiwork in the small **Scuola di Merletti di Burano** (Lace Museum). The basilica, **Chiesa di San Martino,** sits across from the museum. *(A 40min. boat ride from Venice. Vaporetto #12: Burano from either S. Zaccaria or Fond. Nuove. Museum in P. Galuppi. Open Su-M and W-Sa 10am-5pm. €4.)*

▓ **MURANO.** Famous for its glass since 1292 (when Venice's artisans were forced off Venice proper because their kilns started fires), the island of Murano affords visitors the opportunity to witness the glass-blowing process. Don't be fooled by the vendors near the train station or in P.S. Marco who sell tickets to see glass demonstrations—the studios in Murano are free. Look for signs directing to the *fornace,* concentrated around the Colona, Faro, and Navagero *vaporetti* stops. The speed and grace of these artisans are stunning, and some studios let visitors blow their own glass creations. The **Museo Vetrario** (Glass Museum) houses a splendid collection that features pieces from Roman times. Farther down the street stands the exceptional 12th-century **Basilica di Santa Maria e San Donato,** which displays the supposed bones of the dragon slain by Saint Donatus. *(Vaporetto #12 or 52: Faro from S. Zaccaria. Museo Vetrario: Fond. Giustian 8. ☎041 73 95 86. Open M-Tu and Th-Su 10am-5pm. €5, students €3. Basilica open daily 8am-noon and 4-7pm. Free.)*

TORCELLO. Torcello, a safe haven for early fishermen fleeing barbarians on the mainland, was the most powerful island in the lagoon before Venice usurped its inhabitants and its glory. Today Torcello is a less-visited locale with simple natural beauty that draws visitors seeking a respite from the mainland maelstrom. The island's cathedral, **Santa Maria Assunta,** contains 11th- and 12th-century mosaics depicting the Last Judgment and the Virgin Mary. The **campanile** affords splendid views of the outer lagoon. *(45min. by boat from Venice. Vaporetto #T: Torcello from Burano. Cathedral ☎041 73 01 19. Open daily 10am-6pm. €3. Church and campanile €6.)*

LIDO. Venice's Lido provided the setting for Thomas Mann's classic 14th-century novel *Death in Venice.* Visonti's film version was also shot here at the famous Hotel des Bains, Lungomare Marconi 17. Today, people flock to Lido to enjoy the

ITALY

surf at the crowded **public beach.** An impressive shipwreck looms at one end. The island also offers a casino, horseback riding, and one of Italy's finest golf courses, the Alberoni Golf Club. *(Vaporetto #1 and 82: Lido.)*

ISOLA DI SAN MICHELE. Venice's cemetery island, S. Michele, is home to Coducci's tiny **Chiesa di S. Michele in Isola** (1469), the first Renaissance church in Venice. Enter the grounds through the church's right-hand portal, over which a relief depicting St. Michael slaying the dragon is perched. Beautiful, quiet grounds offer a much-appreciated opportunity for peaceful reflection after the hustle and bustle of Venice. Poet, Fascist sympathizer, and enemy of the state Ezra Pound is buried in the Protestant cemetery, while Russian composer Igor Stravinsky and choreographer Sergei Diaghilev are entombed in the Orthodox graveyard. *(Vaporetto: Cimitero, from Fond. Nuove. Church and cemetery open Apr.-Sept. daily 7:30am-6pm; Oct.-Mar. 7:30am-4pm. Free.)*

🎵 ENTERTAINMENT

The weekly *A Guest in Venice*, free at hotels and tourist offices or online at www.unospitedivenezia.it, lists current festivals, concerts, and gallery exhibits.

GONDOLAS

Admiring the front doors of Venetian houses and *palazzi* via their original canal pathways is an experience only a gondola can provide. Rides are most romantic about 50min. before sunset and most affordable if shared by six people. The rate that a gondolier quotes is negotiable and the most bargain-able gondoliers are those standing by themselves, rather than those in groups at the "taxi-stands" throughout the city. The "official" price starts at €62 per 50min., with a maximum of six people, and prices rise at night.

THEATER, CINEMA, AND ART EXHIBITIONS

Teatro Goldoni, Calle del Teatro, S. Marco 4650/B (☎041 240 20 11; teatrogoldini@libero.it), near the Ponte di Rialto, showcases varying types of productions, often with a seasonal theme. Check with the theater for upcoming listings. The **Mostra Internazionale di Cinema** (Venice International Film Festival), held annually from late August to early September, is a worldwide cinema affair, drawing established names and rising phenoms. Movies are shown in the original language. (☎041 521 88 78. Tickets €20, sold throughout the city. Some late-night outdoor showings are free.) The famed **Biennale di Venezia** (☎041 521 18 98; www.labiennale.org), an international contemporary art exhibition, covers the Giardini Pubblici and the Arsenal with provocative art.

FESTIVALS

Banned by the church for several centuries, Venice's famous **Carnevale** was successfully reinstated in the early 1970s. During the 10 days preceding Ash Wednesday, masked figures jam the streets and outdoor concerts and street performances spring up throughout the city. During **Mardi Gras,** the population of the city doubles. Contact the tourist office in December or January for details and make lodging arrangements far ahead. Venice's second-most colorful festival is the **Festa del Redentore** (3rd Su in July), originally held to celebrate the end of a 16th-century plague. It kicks off with a magnificent fireworks display at 11:30pm the Saturday before. The next day maintenance craftsmen build a pontoon bridge, open to the public, across the Giudecca Canal, connecting **Il Redentore** to the **Zattere.** On the first Sunday in September, Venice stages its classic **regata storica,** a gondola race down the Grand Canal. During the religious **Festa della Salute** (3rd Su in Nov.), which also originated as a celebration of the end of a plague, the city celebrates with the construction of another pontoon bridge, this time over the Grand Canal.

SHOPPING

Be wary of shopping in the heavily touristed P.S. Marco or around the Ponte di Rialto (excluding Rivoaltus). Shops outside these areas often have better quality products and greater selection for about half the price. Interesting clothing, glass, and mask boutiques line the streets leading from the Ponte di Rialto to Campo S. Polo and Strada Nuova and from the Ponte di Rialto toward the station. The map accompanying the Rolling Venice card lists many shops that offer discounts to card holders. The most concentrated and varied selections of Venetian glass and lace require trips to the nearby islands of Murano (p. 703) and Burano (p. 703).

🔊 NIGHTLIFE

Venetian nightlife is quieter and more relaxed than that of other major Italian cities. Most locals would rather spend an evening sipping wine or beer and listening to string quartets in P.S. Marco than gyrating in a disco, but Venice does have a few hot dance spots. Student nightlife is concentrated around **Campo Santa Margherita** in Dorsoduro and the areas around the **Lista di Spagna** in Cannaregio.

🏮 **Paradiso Perduto,** Fondamenta della Misericordia 2540. Students and locals flood this unassuming bar with conversation and laughter, while the young waitstaff doles out large portions of *cicchetti* (mixed plate €11). Live jazz Su. Open Th-Su 7pm-2am.

🏮 **Café Blue,** S. Pantalon, Dorsoduro 3778. Let Johnny from Liverpool flip ice cubes into your drink at this lively, friendly bar. Free Internet available. Live jazz F and Su evening during the winter. Open in summer noon-2am; off-season 9:30am-2am.

Piccolo Mondo, Accademia, Dorsoduro 1056/A. Dance-happy students, locals, and tourists keep the party going at this small but popular *discoteca* where such notables as Michael Jordan, Mick Jagger, and Prince Albert of Monaco have strutted their stuff. Drinks from €7. Open nightly 10pm-4am. AmEx/MC/V.

Duchamp, C. Santa Margherita 3019. Lively place with plenty of outdoor seating for the social, student-heavy crowd that congregates here. Beer €4.30. Wine €1.30. Open Su-F 9pm-2am, Sa 5pm-2am.

Casanova, Lista di Spagna, Cannaregio 158/A. This modern, stylish club claims to be the only real disco in Venice, and modestly-sized crowds mean there's always plenty of room on the dance floor. Enthusiastic dancers make up for the lack of numbers, shaking things up until closing. Cover €10 F-Sa includes 1 drink. Open daily 10pm-4am.

NO WORK, ALL PLAY

LIKE A BRIDGE OVER...VENICE

Every summer, Venetians anticipate the season's biggest party short of Carnivale: The Festa del Redentore, held to honor of the end of a long plague that swept Venice in the late sixteenth century. In an attempt to make amends with God, the Doge of Venice vowed to build a temple on the nearby island of Giudecca. Shortly after the first stone was laid, the plague began to abate, and the Doge proclaimed that Venice had been cured. Venetians built a temporary bridge across the lagoon so the Doge could lead processions to the church.

These days, the celebration begins on the night of the third Saturday in July with a magnificent fireworks display. Venetians crowd the lagoon with their boats, partying all night before journeying out to Lido to watch the sunrise. The other main component of the festival is the reconstruction of the bridge to Giudecca, which is open to the public the night before and the day of the festival. The giant pontoon bridge is quite a feat of construction; it measures 333.7 meters long and 3.6 meters wide, with an opening 4 meters high for water traffic to pass through. During the day, regattas race around Giudecca. Despite the festival's bleak origins, it makes for a fun-filled weekend unlike anything anywhere else in the world.

Inishark Irish Pub, Calle Mondo Novo Castello 5787. Most creative and authentic-looking Irish pub in Venice. Guinness €4.20. Open Tu-Su 6pm-1:30am.

Bar Santa Lucia, Lista di Spagna, Cannaregio 282/B. This tiny bar stays crowded and noisy long into the night with a mix of Italians and tourists. A few outdoor tables available. Guinness €5. Wine €2.10. Open M-Sa 6pm-2am.

PADUA (PADOVA)   ☎049

Ancient Padua (pop. 205,000) was a wealthy center of commerce, but centuries of barbarian attacks and natural disasters left few of her architectural treasures intact. Padua's university, founded in 1222 and second in seniority only to Bologna's, brings book-toting students to the city's statue-lined *piazze*. The ▓**Cappella degli Scrovegni,** P. Eremitani 8, contains Giotto's breathtaking 38-panel fresco cycle, illustrating the lives of Mary and Jesus. Buy tickets at the attached **Musei Civici Erimitani,** which displays an overwhelming art collection, including a beautiful crucifix by Giotto that once adorned the Scrovegni Chapel. (Open Feb.-Oct. daily 9am-7pm; Nov.-Jan. 9am-6pm. €9, students €4.) Thousands of pilgrims are drawn to Saint Anthony's jawbone and well-preserved tongue on display at the **Basilica di Sant'Antonio,** in P. del Santo, a medieval conglomeration of eight domes filled with beautiful frescoes. (Dress code enforced. Open Apr.-Sept. daily 9am-12:30pm and 2:30pm-7pm; Nov.-Mar. reduced hours. €2, students €1.50.) From the basilica, follow signs to **Orto Botanico,** V. Orto Botanico 18, which tempts visitors with water lilies, medicinal herbs, and a 417-year-old palm tree that still offers shade. (Open daily Apr.-Sept. 9am-1pm and 3-6pm; Oct.-Mar. M-F 9am-1pm. €4, students €1) Next to the **duomo,** in P. Duomo, lies the 12th-century **Battistero,** with a dome covered in frescoes. (Open M-Sa 7:30am-noon and 3:45-7:45pm, Su 7:45am-1pm and 3:45-8:30pm. €2.50, students €1.50.) Ancient buildings from the university are scattered throughout the city, especially near **Palazzo Bó.** At night, much of the action is nearby. The **Highlander Pub,** V.S. Martino 69, is a particularly popular establishment. (Open daily 7pm-2am.)

   Trains depart from P. Stazione for: Bologna (1½hr., 1-2 per hr., €6); Milan (2½hr., 1-2 per hr., €17); Venice (30min., 3-4 per hr., €2.30); and Verona (1hr., 1-2 per hr., €4.50). **Buses** (☎049 820 68 11) leave from P. Boschetti for Venice (45min., 2 per hr., €2.20). The **tourist office** is in the train station (☎049 875 20 77. Open M-Sa 9am-7pm, Su 8:30am-12:30pm.) Follow the main street through town from the train station and turn right on V. Rogati. Go to V. Aleardi and turn left; walk to the end of the block and **Ostello Città di Padova (HI) ❶,** V. Aleardi 30, will be on the left. (☎049 875 22 19. **Internet** €5.20 per hr. Reception daily 7-9:30am and 2:30-11pm. Curfew 11pm. Reserve at least 1 week in advance. Dorms €14.) **Locanda la Perla ❸,** V. Cesarotti 67, has large, airy rooms in a great location. (☎049 87 55 89 39. Closed last 2 weeks in Aug. Singles €28, doubles €38.) Join a lively crowd at **Pizzeria Al Borgo ❷,** V.L. Belludi 56, near the Basilica di S. Antonio. (Pizzas from €3.70. Cover €2. Open Su and W-Sa noon-3pm and 7-11:30pm.) **Postal Code:** 35100.

VERONA   ☎045

A glorious combination of majestic Roman ruins, colorful Venetian facades, and orange rooftops, Verona (pop. 245,000) is one of the most beautiful cities in Northern Italy. Gazing at the town from one of its many bridges at sunset sets the tone for romantic evenings befitting the home of *Romeo and Juliet.* Meanwhile, its artistic and historical treasures fill days with rewarding sightseeing.

☞♫ TRANSPORTATION AND PRACTICAL INFORMATION. Trains (☎045 800 08 61) go from P. XXV Aprile to: Bologna (2hr., every hr., €5.80); Milan (2hr., every hr., €7); Trent (1hr., every 2 hr., €4.70); and Venice (1¾hr., every hr., €6). From the train station, walk 20min. up **Corso Porta Nuova**, or take bus #11, 12, 13, 72, or 73 (weekends take #91, 92, or 93) to Verona's heart, the **Arena** in **Piazza Brà**. The **tourist office** is left of the *piazza*. (☎045 806 86 80. Open M-Sa 9am-7pm, Su 9am-3pm.) **Internet Train**, V. Roma 17/a, has modern, high-speed computers. (€2.50 per 30min. Open M-F 11am-10pm, Sa-Su 2-8pm.). **Postal Code:** 37100.

☞♫ ACCOMMODATIONS AND FOOD. Reserve hotel rooms ahead, especially in opera season (June-Sept.). The ▨**Ostello della Gioventù (HI) ❶**, Villa Francescatti, Salita Fontana del Ferro 15, is in a renovated 16th-century villa with gorgeous gardens; from the station, take bus #73 or night bus #90 to P. Isolo, turn right, and follow the yellow signs uphill. (☎045 59 03 60. Lockout 9am-5pm. Curfew 11pm; flexible for opera-goers. No reservations. Dorms €13.) To get to **Locanda Catullo ❹**, V. Catullo 1, walk to V. Mazzini, turn onto V. Catullo, and turn left on Vco. Catullo. (☎045 800 27 86. July-Sept. 3-night min. stay. Singles €40; doubles €55-65; triples €81-96.) Verona is famous for its wines, such as the dry white *soave* and red *valpolicella*. Prices in **Piazza Isolo** are cheaper than those in P. delle Erbe. **Cantore ❸**, V. A. Mario 2, near P. Brà, boasts delicious pizza and pasta dishes. (☎045 803 18 30. Primi €6.80. Secondi €8. Cover €1.50. AmEx/MC/V.) **Pam supermarket** is at V. dei Mutilati 3. (Open M-Sa 8am-8pm and Su 9:30am-1pm and 3-7pm.)

◪ SIGHTS. The physical and emotional heart of Verona is the majestic, pink-marble, first-century ▨**Arena** in P. Brà. (Open M 1:45-6:30pm, Tu-Su 8:30am-6:30pm. €3.10, students €2.10.) From P. Brà, V. Mazzini leads to the markets and stunning medieval of **Piazza delle Erbe,** the former Roman forum. The 83m ▨**Torre dei Lamberti**, in P. dei Signori, offers a stunning view of Verona. (Open M 1:30-5:30pm, Tu-Su 8:30am-7:30pm. €2.60, students €2.10.) The **Giardino Giusti**, V. Giardino Giusti 2, is a magnificent 16th-century garden with a labyrinth of mythological statues. (Open daily 9am-8pm. €5.) The della Scala fortress, **Castelvecchio,** down V. Roma from P. Brà, is filled with walkways, parapets, and an art collection that includes Pisanello's *Madonna and Child*. (Open M 1:30-7:30pm, Tu-Su 8:30am-7:30pm. €5, students €4. Thousands of tourists have immortalized **Casa di Giulietta** (Juliet's House), V. Cappello 23, although the dell Cappello (Capulet) family never really lived there. A balcony overlooks a courtyard full of tourists waiting to rub the bronze statue of Juliet. (Open M 1:30-7:30pm, Tu-Su 8:30am-7:30pm. €3.10, students €2.10.) From late June to early September, tourists and singers from around the world descend on the Arena for the city's annual **Opera Festival.** (☎045 800 51 51. General admission Su-Th €19.50, F-Sa €21.50.)

FRIULI-VENEZIA GIULIA

Friuli-Venezia Giulia traditionally receives less than its fair share of recognition, but this region has served as inspiration to a number of prominent literary figures. James Joyce lived in Trieste for 12 years, during which he wrote most of *Ulysses;* Ernest Hemingway drew part of the plot for *A Farewell to Arms* from the region's role in WWI; and Freud and Rilke both worked and wrote here. The city of Trieste attracts large numbers of tourists to the cheapest beach resorts on the Adriatic.

TRIESTE (TRIEST)   ☎ 040

A long-disputed piece of real estate among Italians, Austrians and Slavs, Trieste (pop. 230,000) finally became part of Italy in 1954, yet it still remains divided between its Slavic and Italian origins. While Trieste's fast-paced center, with Gucci-clad locals and bustling quays, is undeniably urban, the colors of the surrounding Carsoian hillside and the tranquil Adriatic Sea temper the metropolis with stunning natural beauty. The **Città Nuova**, a grid-like pattern of streets lined with crumbling Neoclassical palaces, centers around the **Canale Grande.** Facing the canal from the south is the striking Serbian Orthodox **Chiesa di San Spiridi-one.** (Dress modestly. Open Tu-Sa 9am-noon and 5-8pm.) The ornate **Municipio** complements the **Piazza dell'Unità d'Italia,** the largest *piazza* in Italy. Take bus #24 to the last stop (€0.90) to reach the 15th-century Venetian **Castello di San Giusto,** which presides over **Capitoline Hill,** south of P. Unità (the city's historical center), and includes a museum. From P. Goldoni, you can ascend the hill by the **Scala dei Giganti** (Steps of the Giants), a daunting 265-step climb. (☎ 040 31 36 36. Castle open daily 9am-sunset; free. Museum open daily 9am-1pm; €1.60.) **Piazza della Cattedrale** overlooks the sea and downtown Trieste. The archaeological **Museo di Storia e d'Arte,** V. Cattedrale 15, is down the hill past the *duomo.* (☎ 040 37 05 00. Open Su and Tu-Sa 9am-1pm. €1.70.)

Trains leave P. della Libertà 8, down C. Cavour from the quays, for Budapest, Hungary (12hr., 2 per day, €73) and Venice (2hr., 2 per hr., €8.20). The APT **tourist office** is at P. dell'Unità d'Italia 4/E, near the harbor. (☎ 040 347 83 12; fax 040 347 83 20. Open M-Sa 9am-7pm.) **Hotel Alabarda ❸,** V. Valdirivo 22, is near the city center. All rooms have high ceilings and satellite TV. From P. Oberdan, head down V. XXX Ottobre, and turn right onto V. Valdirivo. (☎ 040 63 02 69; www.hotelalbarda.it. **Internet** access €5.20 per hr. Singles €32-34, with bath €47; doubles €44-49/67. AmEx/MC/V.) To get from the station to **Ostello Tegeste (HI) ❶,** V. Miramare 331, 4km away just south from Castle Miramare, take bus #36 (€0.90), which leaves from across V. Miramare, and ask for the Ostello stop. From there, walk along the Barcola, following the seaside road toward the castle which has a charming view of the Adriatic Sea. (☎/fax 040 22 41 02. Reception daily 8am-11:30pm. Dorms €12. Nonmembers add €3.) For cheap food, stop by **Euro Spesa** supermarket at V. Valdirivo 13/F, off C. Cavour. (Open M-Sa 8am-8pm.) **Postal Code:** 34100.

PIEDMONT (PIEMONTE)

Piedmont has been a politically influential region for centuries, as well as a producer of fine food and wine, which *Piedmontese* insist is the best in Italy, and thus internationally. After native-born Vittorio Emanuele II and Camillo Cavour united Italy, Turin served as the capital from 1861 to 1865.

TURIN (TORINO)   ☎ 011

Turin's (pop. 860,000) elegance is the direct result of centuries of urban planning—graceful, church-lined avenues lead to spacious *piazze.* At the same time, Turin vibrates with modern economic energy as headquarters of the **Fiat Auto Company** and future host of the **2006 Winter Olympics.** The city is also home to one of the more famous relics of Christianity: the **Holy Shroud of Turin** is housed in the **Cattedrale di San Giovanni,** behind the **Palazzo Reale.** The church is undergoing restoration, but remains open. (Open daily 7am-12:30pm and 3-7pm. Free.) The **Museo Egizio,** in the **Palazzo dell'Accademia delle Scienze,** V. dell'Accademia delle Scienze 6, boasts a world-class collection of Egyptian

SHROUD OF MYSTERY Called a hoax by some and a miracle by others, the Holy Shroud of Turin (a 1m by 4.5m piece of linen) was supposedly wrapped around Jesus' body in preparation for burial after his crucifixion. Visible on the cloth are outflows of blood: around the head (supposedly from the Crown of Thorns), all over the body (from scourging), and, most importantly, from the wrists and feet (where the body was nailed to the cross). Although radiocarbon dating places the piece in the 12th century AD, the shroud's uncanny resemblance to that of Christ precludes its immediate dismissal. Scientists agree that the shroud was wrapped around the body of a 5'7" man who died by crucifixion, but whether it was the body of Jesus remains a mystery. For Christian believers, however, the importance of this relic is best described by Pope Paul VI's words: "The Shroud is a document of Christ's love written in characters of blood."

artifacts. (Open Su, Tu and F-Sa 8:30am-2pm; W-Th 2-7:30pm. €4, ages 18-25 €2. Under-18 and over-65 free.) One of Guarini's great Baroque palaces, the **Palazzo Carignano**, V. dell'Accademia delle Scienze 5, houses the **Museo Nazionale del Risorgimento Italiano**, commemorating the 1706-1846 unification of Italy. (Open Su and Tu-Sa 9am-7pm. €4.25, students €2.50.) Begun as a synagogue in 1863, the **Mole Antonelliana**, V. Montebello 20, dominates Turin's skyline. (Open Su and Tu-F 10am-8pm, Sa 10am-11pm. Elevator to the observation deck €3.60.) The **Museo dell'Automobile**, C. Unita d'Italia 40, documents the evolution of the automobile, including prototype models of the Ford, Benz, Peugeot, and homegrown Fiat. From the station, head south along V. Nizza. (Open Su and Tu-Sa 10am-7pm. €2.70.)

Trains leave Porta Nuova on C. Vittorio Emanuele (☎011 531 327) for: Genoa (2hr., every hr., €8); Milan (2hr., every hr., €8); Rome (4½hr., 5 per day, €38); and Venice (4½hr., 3 per day, €31). The **tourist office**, P. Castello 161, has free maps. (☎011 53 51 81. Open M-Sa 9:30am-7pm, Su 9:30am-3:30pm.) To get to the clean and comfortable **Ostello Torino (HI) ❶**, V. Alby 1, take bus #52 (bus #64 on Su) from Stazione Porto Nuova to the 2nd stop past the Po river. Turn right onto C. Lanza, follow the signs to V. Gatti, and climb 200m up the winding road. (☎011 660 29 39; hostelto@tin.it. Reception 7-10am and 3:30-11pm. Curfew 11:30pm; ask for a key if you go out. Closed Dec. 20-Feb. 1. Dorms €12.) **Hotel Canelli ❷**, V.S. Dalmazzo 5b, has clean rooms in a quiet neighborhood. From the train station, take bus #52 to *Cernaia*, turn right down V. Gianone, and then turn left onto V.S. Dalmazzo. (☎011 53 71 66. Singles €24; doubles €32, triples €39.) Turin has grown into one of the great international centers of chocolate; Ferrero Rocher and Nutella are two of its more famous progeny. **Via Mazzini** has cheap fruit, cheese, and bread shops, along with a number of inexpensive eateries. **Postal Code:** 10100.

TUSCANY (TOSCANA)

The vision of Tuscany has inspired countless artists, poets, and hordes of tourists. Its rolling hills, prodigious olive groves, and cobblestone streets beg visitors to slow their frenetic pace, sip some wine, and relax in fields of brilliant sunflowers. Tuscany fostered some of Italy's, and the world's, greatest cultural achievements under the tender care—and devious machinations—of the powerful Médici family, gaining eternal eminence in the arts for its staggering accomplishments during a scant half-century. Today, tourists flock to Tuscany to witness the glory that was, and the wonder that still is, *Toscana*.

FLORENCE (FIRENZE) ☎ 055

The rays of the setting sun shimmer over a sea of burnt-orange roofs and towering domes to reveal the breathtaking concentration of beauty in Florence (pop. 376,000). Once a busy 13th-century wool- and silk-trading town, Florence took a decidedly different path under Medici rule. By the mid-15th century, the city was the undisputed European capital of art, architecture, commerce, and political thought. Present-day Florence is a vibrant mix of young and old: Street graffiti quotes Marx and Malcolm X, businessmen whiz by on Vespas, and children play soccer in front of the *duomo*.

▐ TRANSPORTATION

Flights: Amerigo Vespucci Airport (FLR; ☎ 055 31 58 74), in Peretola. The **ATAF** bus #62 connects the train station to the airport (€1).

Trains: Santa Maria Novella Station, across from S. Maria Novella. Trains depart every hr. for **Bologna** (1hr., €7.80), **Milan** (3½hr., €22), and **Rome** (3½hr., €15-22); and less frequently to **Siena** (1½hr., 10 per day, €5.30) and **Venice** (3hr., 4 per day, €19).

Buses: SITA, V.S. Caterina da Siena 15r (☎ 055 28 46 61). Run to **San Gimignano** (1½hr., 14 per day, €5.70) and **Siena** (1½hr., 2 per day, €6.50). **LAZZI,** P. Adua, 1-4r (☎ 055 35 10 61) sends buses to **Pisa** (every hr., €5.80).

Public Transportation: ATAF (☎ 055 565 02 22), outside the train station, runs orange city buses (6am-1am). 1hr. tickets €1, 3hr. €1.80, 24hr. €4, 3-day €7.20. Buy tickets at any newsstand, *tabacchi,* or automated ticket dispenser before boarding. Validate your ticket using the orange machine on board or risk a €50 fine.

Taxis: ☎ 055 43 90, 055 47 98, or 055 42 42. Outside the train station.

Bike/Moped Rental: Alinari Noleggi, V. Guelfa 85r (☎ 055 28 05 00). Bikes €12-18 per day, mopeds €28-55 per day.

✦▐ ORIENTATION AND PRACTICAL INFORMATION

From the train station, a short walk on V. dei Panzani and a left on V. dei Cerretani leads to the **duomo,** the center of Florence. Major arteries radiate from the *duomo* and its two *piazze.* A bustling walkway, **Via dei Calzaiuoli** runs south from the *duomo* to **Piazza Signoria.** V. Roma leads from P.S. Giovanni through **Piazza della Repubblica** to the **Ponte Vecchio** (Old Bridge), which spans the Arno River to the **Oltrarno** district. Note that most streets change names unpredictably. For guidance through Florence's tangled center, grab a **free map** from the tourist office. Sights are scattered throughout Florence, but few lie beyond walking distance.

AND YOU THOUGHT VENICE WAS CONFUSING. Florence is comprised of streets numbered in red and black sequences. Red numbers indicate commercial establishments and black numbers denote residential addresses (including most sights and hotels). Black addresses appear in *Let's Go* as a numeral only, while red addresses are indicated by a number followed by an "r." If you reach an address and it's not what you're looking for, you've probably got the wrong color sequence. Also making life more complicated, numbers on opposite sides of the street do not necessarily match up.

TOURIST, FINANCIAL, AND LOCAL SERVICES

Tourist Office: Informazione Turistica, P. della Stazione 4 (☎055 21 22 45), across the *piazza* from the main exit. Info on entertainment and cultural events. Be sure to ask for a free map with a street index. Open daily 8:30am-7pm.

Consulates: UK, Lungarno Corsini 2 (☎055 28 41 33). Open M-F 9:30am-12:30pm and 2:30-4:30pm. **US,** Lungarno Amerigo Vespucci 38 (☎055 239 82 76), at V. Palestro, near the station. Open M-F 9am-12:30pm. Others are in Rome or Milan.

Currency Exchange: Local banks offer the best rates. Most are open M-F 8:20am-1:20pm and 2:45-3:45pm. 24hr. **ATMs** abound.

American Express: V. Dante Alighieri 20-22r (☎055 509 81). From the *duomo*, walk down V. dei Calzaiuoli and turn left on V. dei Tavolini. Mail held free for AmEx customers, otherwise €1.55. Open M-F 9am-5:30pm, Sa 9am-12:30pm.

EMERGENCY AND COMMUNICATIONS

Emergency: ☎113. **Fire:** ☎115. **Police:** ☎055 497 71. **Medical Emergency:** ☎118

24-Hour pharmacies: Farmacia Comunale (☎055 28 94 35), at the train station by track #16. **Molteni,** V. dei Calzaiuoli 7r (☎055 28 94 90).

Internet Access: Walk down almost any busy street and you'll find an Internet cafe.

Internet Train. 15 locations listed on www.internettrain.it, including near the train station and *duomo*. €4 per hr., students €3. Most open M-F 9am-midnight, Sa 10am-8pm, Su noon-9pm.

Libreria Edison, P. Repubblica 27r, has great atmosphere and coffee upstairs. €2.50 per hr. Open daily 10am-8pm

Post Office: V. Pellicceria (☎055 21 61 22), off P. della Repubblica. Address mail to be held: Firstname SURNAME, *In Fermo Posta,* L'Ufficio Postale, V. Pellicceria, Firenze, **50100** ITALY. Open M-F 8am-7pm, Sa 8:15am-noon.

■ ACCOMMODATIONS

Lodgings in Florence generally don't come cheap. **Consorzio ITA,** in the train station by track #16, can find rooms for a €2.50-7.75 fee. (☎055 28 28 93. Open daily 8:45am-8pm.) Because of the constant stream of tourists in Florence, it is best to make reservations (*prenotazioni*) in advance, especially if you plan to visit during Easter or summer. If you have any complaints, first talk to the proprietor and then to the **Ufficio Controllo Alberghi,** V. Cavour 37 (☎055 276 01). The municipal government strictly regulates hotel prices; proprietors can charge neither more nor less than the approved range for their category. Rates uniformly increase around 10% every year; the new rates take effect in March or April.

HOSTELS

■ **Ostello Archi Rossi,** V. Faenza 94r (☎055 29 08 04; fax 055 230 26 01). Exit left from the station on V. Nazionale and take the 2nd left on V. Faenza. Patio packed with young travelers. Breakfast €1.60. Laundry €5.20. Free Internet access. Lockout 11:30am-2pm. Curfew 1am. No reservations; in summer, arrive before 8am. Dorms €18-21. ❷

■ **Istituto Gould,** V. dei Serragli 49 (☎055 21 25 76), in the Oltrarno. Take bus #36 or 37 from the train station to the 2nd stop across the river. Spotless rooms. Reception M-F 9am-1pm and 3-7pm, Sa 9am-1pm, Su check-out only. Singles €30, with bath €35; doubles €44/50; triples €56/63; quads €72/80. MC/V. ❸

ITALY

Florence

🏠🏠 ACCOMMODATIONS

Albergo Margaret, **16**
Albergo Sampaoli, **6**
Albergo por S. Maria, **38**
Camping Michelangelo, **54**
Hotel Abaco/
  Hotel Giappone, **24**
Hotel Bellettini, **18**
Hotel Boston, **2**
Hotel Elite, **17**
Hotel Il Perseo, **25**
Hotel La Scaletta, **50**
Hotel Montreal, **11**
Hotel Nazionale, **5**
Hotel Tina, **3**
Hotel Visconti/
  Pensione Ottaviani, **22**
Istituto Gould, **47**
Katti House, **9**

Locanda Orchidea, **33**
Ostello Archi Rossi, **1**
Ostello della Gioventù (HI), **35**
Ostello Santa Monaca, **46**
Pensionato Pio X, **51**
Relais Cavalcanti, **37**
Sorelle Bandini, **48**
Tourist House, **21**
Via Faenza 56, **4**
Via Faenza 69, **7**

🍴 FOOD

Acqua al Due, **40**
Al Lume di Candela, **36**
Amon, **20**
Antica Gelateria il David, **10**
Le Colonnine, **45**
Enoteca Alessi, **26**
Enoteca Fuori Porta, **53**
Gelateria Triangolo delle
  Bermuda, **8**
La Loggia degli Albizi, **32**
La Mangiatoia, **52**
Oltrarno Trattoria
  Casalinga, **49**
Perchè No?, **30**
Trattoria Anita, **43**
Trattoria da Benvenuto, **44**
Trattoria Contadino, **14**
Trattoria da Giorgio, **15**
Tre Merli, **28**
Vivoli, **42**

⭐ NIGHTLIFE

Blob, **42**
Central Park, **13**
The Chequers Pub, **19**
Eby's, **27**
The Fiddler's Elbow, **23**
May Day Lounge, **31**

Rio Grande, **12**
Slowly, **34**
Tabasco, **39**
Yab, **29**

EX FORTEZZA DA BASTO
Viale Filippo Strozzi
Via della Fortezza
PIAZZA DELLA INDIPENDENZA
Via Guelfa
Via Valfonda
Via Faenza
S. Maria Novella Station
LAZZI
Via Fiume
Via Nazionale
Via dell'Ariento
Mercato Centrale
PIAZZA DEL MERCATO CENTRALE
Via Luigi Alamanni
Via S. Antonino
CAP
PIAZZA DELLA STAZIONE
Via della Scala
V. d. Orti Oricellari
Teatro Comunale
Via Magenta
Via Garibaldi
V. Corso Italia
Via Solferino
Via Palestro
Via Rucellai
American Church
Via Palazzuolo
Via dell' Alberno
Via C. C. da Siena
SITA
S. Maria Novella
PIAZZA DELL' UNITA ITALIANA
San Lorenzo
Via de' Panzani
Via de' Cerretani
Via de' Pecori
PIAZZA SANTA MARIA NOVELLA
Via della Scala
Via de' Banchi
Via D. Belle Donne
Via del Sole
Via de' Fossi
US
Via S. Lucia
Borgo Ognissanti
Via Finiguerra
Via Montebello
Lungarno Amerigo Vespucci
Ponte A. Vespucci
Palazzo Rucellai
Via D. Vigna Nuova
PIAZZA DELLA REPUBBLICA
Via Strozzi
Palazzo Strozzi
Via Tornabuoni
V. D. Ancenella
Lungarno S. Rosa
Fiume Arno
Via L. Bartolini
PORTA SAN FREDIANO
Lungarno Soderini
Ponte Alla Carraia
Lungarno Corsini
Santa Trinita
Via Porta Rossa
Viale L. Ariosto
Via dell' Orto
P. dei Nerli
V. d. Cardatori
V. d. Prato D'Ognissanti
V. d. Tessitori
V. d. Leone
Borgo S. Frediano
PIAZZA DEL CARMINE
Via S. Monaca
S. M. del Carmine
Via S. Agostino
Via di S. Spirito
Ponte S. Trinita
Lungarno Acciaiuoli
Ponte Vecchio
Borgo S. Jacopo
Via de' Guicciardini
S. Spirito
PIAZZA SAN SPIRITO
Via Maggio
Via delle Caldaie
Via Mazzetta
Via della Chiesa
Via del Campuccio
V. delle Caldaie
Borgo Tegolaio
Giardino Torrigiani
Via S. Maria
Palazzo Pitti
Giardino di Boboli
Forte Belvedere

ITALY

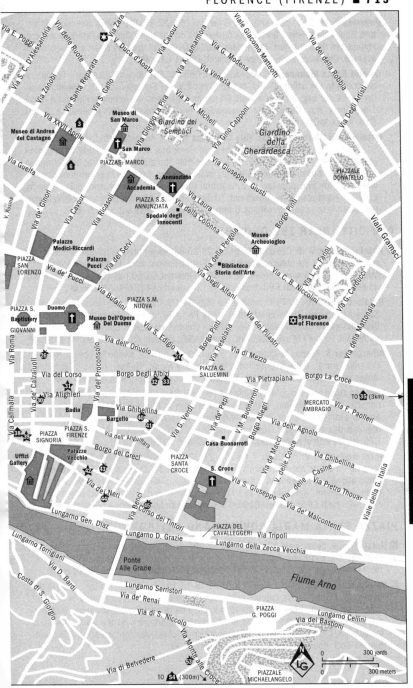

ITALY

Pensionato Pio X, V. dei Serragli 106 (☎/fax 055 22 50 44). Follow directions to Istituto Gould, and walk a few blocks farther; it's on the right. Don't be fazed by the construction in the courtyard. Rooms are nothing fancy, but are very clean and larger than average. Check-out 9am. Curfew midnight. Dorms €16. ❶

Ostello Santa Monaca, V.S. Monaca 6 (☎055 26 83 38; www.ostello.it). Follow the directions to the Istituto Gould, but go right off V. dei Serragli onto V.S. Monaca. Laundry €6.50 per 5kg. Internet access €4 per hr. June-Sept. arrive before 9am for a room. 7-night max. stay. Curfew 1am. Reservations must be made 3 days in advance. Dorms €16. AmEx/MC/V. ❷

Ostello della Gioventù Europa Villa Camerata (HI), V. Augusto Righi 2-4 (☎055 60 14 51; fax 055 61 03 00), northeast of town. Take bus #17 from outside train station (near track #5), or from P. dell'Unità across from the station; get off at the *Salviatino* stop; ask the bus driver when to get off. Walk 8-10min. from the street entrance past a vineyard. Tidy and popular, in a beautiful (if inconveniently located) villa. Laundry €5.20. 3-night max. stay. Check-out 7-10am. Lockout 10am-2pm. Strict midnight curfew. Make reservations in writing. Dorms €15. Nonmembers add €2.60. ❶

OLD CITY (NEAR THE DUOMO)

▨ Hotel Il Perseo, V. de Cerretani 1 (☎055 21 25 04; www.hotelperseo.com), en route to the *duomo* from the station, opposite the Feltrinelli bookstore. Immaculate rooms with fans. Bar and TV lounge. Breakfast included. Internet €1.50 per 15min. Singles €50; doubles €73, with bath €93; triples €97/120; quads €118/140. MC/V. ❹

Relais Cavalcanti, V. Pellicceria 2 (☎055 21 09 62; www.relaiscavalcanti.com). Supreme location just steps from P. della Repubblica, near the central post office. Beautiful gold-trimmed rooms with antique painted wardrobes and large, immaculate baths. Ask for the *Let's Go* discount. Singles €80; doubles €110-120; triples €155. ❺

Albergo Por S. Maria, V. Calimaruzza 3 (☎055 21 63 70). Centrally located between the Uffizi and P. della Repubblica. Pleasant, airy rooms. Bubbly, matronly proprietor strikes up conversations in Italian. Singles €55; doubles €85, with bath €95. ❹

Locanda Orchidea, Borgo degli Albizi 11 (☎/fax 055 248 03 46). Take a left off V. Proconsolo from the *duomo*. Dante's wife was born in this 12th-century *palazzo*, built around a still-intact tower. Friendly and helpful English-speaking management. Graceful rooms with marble floors, some of which open onto a garden. Singles €55; doubles €75; triples with shower €100; quads with shower €120. ❹

Hotel Bellettini, V. de Conti 7 (☎055 21 35 61; www.firenze.net/hotelbellettini). Located on a side street a stone's throw from the Médici Chapels and the *duomo*, Bellettini allows you to see it all without having to hear it. Nicely furnished rooms have soft beds, bathroom, A/C, phone, and TV. Free Internet and breakfast included. Singles €75, with bath €95; doubles €100/130; triples with bath €160. AmEx/MC/V. ❺

PIAZZA SANTA MARIA NOVELLA AND ENVIRONS

▨ Hotel Elite, V. della Scala 12 (☎055 21 53 95). Exit right from the train station onto V. degli orti Oricellari and turn left on V. della Scala. Brass glows in this hotel's lovely rooms. Breakfast €6. Singles €60-75; doubles €90; triples €110; quads €120. ❺

▨ Hotel Abaco, V. dei Banchi 1 (☎/fax 055 238 19 19). From train station, cross to the back of S. Maria Novella church. Walk past church into P.S. Maria Novella and go left onto V. dei Banchi. Seven beautiful rooms, each named after a Renaissance great, feature reproductions of the honored artist's most famous work on the walls. Breakfast included. A/C €5 extra. Laundry €7. Free Internet access. Ask for the *Let's Go* discount. Singles €63; doubles €70, with bath €85. MC/V. ❺

Hotel Giappone, V. dei Banchi, 1 (☎055 21 00 90; fax 29 28 77; www.hotelgiappone.com). Follow directions to Hotel Abaco. 10 clean rooms in a central location. All rooms with phone, TV, A/C and Internet jacks. Singles €45, with shower €47, with bath €55; doubles €65/72/85. Extra bed €26. MC/V. ❹

Hotel Visconti, P. Ottaviani 1 (☎/fax 055 21 38 77). Exit the train station from the left and cross behind the church into P.S. Maria Novella, and walk to the left until you reach tiny P. Ottaviani. Look for huge Grecian nudes. Breakfast included. Singles €40; doubles €60; triples €80; quads €90. ❹

Hotel Montreal, V. della Scala 43 (☎055 238 23 31; www.hotelmontreal.com). Exit train station to right onto V.d. Orti Oricellari, which leads to V. della Scala; take a left. 22 tasteful, wood-furnished rooms, all with phone, TV, A/C. Flexible curfew 1:30am. Singles €40, with bath €55; doubles €65/75; triples €85/105; quads €120. ❹

Albergo Margaret, V. della Scala 25 (☎/fax 055 21 01 38). Follow directions to Hotel Montreal. 7 rooms with eclectic decorations. All rooms with TV and A/C. Curfew midnight. June-Aug. Singles €60; doubles with shower €70, with bath €90. Prices reduced Sept.-May and for longer stays. ❹

Tourist House, V. della Scala 1 (☎055 26 86 75). Extremely friendly proprietors also run Hotel Giappone. Comfortable rooms with bath and TV, some with A/C. Singles €67; doubles €83; quads €124. AmEx/MC/V. ❺

AROUND PIAZZA SAN MARCO

▨ **Hotel Tina,** V.S. Gallo 31 (☎055 48 35 19; hoteltina@tin.it). From P.S. Marco, follow V. XXII Aprile and turn right on V.S. Gallo. *Pensione* with high ceilings, new furniture, and amicable owners. Singles €44; doubles €60-75; triples €83. ❹

Albergo Sampaoli, V.S. Gallo 14 (☎055 28 48 34; www.hotelsampaoli.it). Helpful reception and a large common area with patterned tile floors and ornate wooden furniture. All with fans, some with balconies. Free Internet (30min.). Singles €45, with bath €60; doubles €65/84. AmEx/MC/V. ❹

Hotel San Marco, V. Cavour 50 (☎055 28 18 51; fax 055 28 42 35). 2 floors hold 15 large, bare-walled, airy rooms. Call ahead to reserve the spacious double with a balcony on the top floor at no extra charge. Singles €45, with bath €55; doubles €65/75; triples €105. MC/V. ❹

AROUND VIA NAZIONALE

▨ **Katti House,** V. Faenza 21 (☎/fax 055 21 34 10; www.kattihouse.com). Exit train station onto V. Nazionale; walk 1 block and turn right onto V. Faenza. A jewel among Florence's travel lodgings, it was lovingly renovated by the proprietors and now features 400-year-old antiques and an attentive staff. Large rooms with A/C, TV, and bath. Doubles €95; triples and quads €105. Nov.-Mar prices drop significantly. ❺

Via Faenza 56 houses 5 separate *pensioni*, some of the best deals in the city. From the train station, exit left onto V. Nazionale, walk 1 block, and turn left on V. Faenza.

Pensione Azzi (☎055 21 38 06) has large rooms and a terrace. Breakfast included. Singles €45, with bath €55; doubles €62/80. AmEx/MC/V. ❹

Locanda Paola (☎055 21 36 82) has doubles with views of the surrounding hills. Flexible 2am curfew. Doubles €62. ❹

Albergo Merlini (☎055 21 28 48; www.hotelmerlini.it) has some rooms with views of the *duomo*. Curfew 1am. Doubles €65, with bath €75; triples €90; quads €98. AmEx/MC/V. ❺

Albergo Marini (☎055 28 48 24) boasts spotless rooms. Breakfast €5. Singles €48, with bath €75; doubles €65/96; triples €86/117. ❹

Albergo Armonia (☎055 21 11 46) decorates its rooms with film posters. Singles €42; doubles €65; triples €90; quads €100. ❹

Via Faenza 69 houses no-frills hotels. Same directions as for Via Faenza 56.

Locanda Giovanna (☎055 238 13 53) has basic, well-kept rooms with garden views. Singles €40; doubles €60, with bath €70; triples €80/85. ❹

Hotel Nella/Pina (☎055 265 43 46) has 14 basic rooms and Internet. Singles €47; doubles €62. AmEx/MC/V. ❹

Hotel Nazionale, V. Nazionale 22 (☎055 238 22 03; www.nazionalehotel.it). Exit train station and turn left onto V. Nazionale. 9 sunny and spacious rooms with comfy beds, bath, and A/C. Breakfast included and brought to your room between 8 and 9:30am. Singles €50, with bath €60; doubles €90; triples €97/110. MC/V. ❹

Hotel Boston, V. Guelfa 68 (☎055 47 03 84; fax 055 47 09 34). Exposed wooden-beamed ceilings, intricate tiled floors, and yellow bedspreads spruce up 14 comfortable rooms, all with A/C, TV, and telephone. Enjoy breakfast in the beautiful antique-style dining room or on the patio garden. Singles €50, with bath €70; doubles €80. ❹

OLTRARNO

🏠 **Hotel La Scaletta,** V. Guicciardini 13b (☎055 28 30 28). Turn right onto V. Roma from the *duomo,* cross Ponte Vecchio and walk on V. Guicciardini. Has views of Boboli gardens. Breakfast included. Reception open until midnight. Singles €51, with bath €93; doubles €120; 10% *Let's Go* discount when you pay cash. MC/V. ❹

Sorelle Bandini, P.S. Spirito 9 (☎055 21 53 08; fax 055 28 27 61). From Ponte S. Trinità, continue down V. Maggio and take the 3rd right into P.S. Spirito. 12 rooms on the top two floors of a 500-year-old palace. Spectacular views of the Oltrarno from the huge, wrap-around *loggia* (lodges). Breakfast included. Doubles €108, with bath €130; triples €148/178. ❺

CAMPING

Campeggio Michelangelo, V. Michelangelo 80 (☎055 681 19 77), beneath Piazzale Michelangelo. Take bus #13 from the bus station (15min.; last bus 11:25pm). Crowded, but a great view of Florence. Open Apr.-Nov. €7 per person, €4.70 per tent, €4.30 per car. ❶

🍴 FOOD

Florence's hearty cuisine originated in the peasant fare of the countryside. Specialties include *bruschetta* (grilled bread soaked with olive oil and garlic and topped with tomatoes and basil, anchovy, or liver paste) and *bistecca alla Fiorentina* (thick sirloin steak). Wine is a Florentine staple, and genuine *chianti classico* commands a premium price; a liter costs €3.70-5.20 in Florence's *trattorie*, while stores sell bottles for as little as €2.60. The local dessert is *cantuccini di prato* (almond cookies made with egg yolks) dipped in *vinsanto* (a rich dessert wine made from raisins). Florence's own Buontalenti family supposedly invented *gelato*; true or not, you must sample it. For lunch, visit a *rosticceria gastronomia,* peruse the city's pushcarts, or pick up fresh produce or meat at the **Mercato Centrale,** between V. Nazionale and S. Lorenzo. (Open June-Sept. M-Sa 7am-2pm; Oct.-May M-F 7am-2pm, Sa 7am-2pm and 4-8pm.) To get to **STANDA supermarket,** V. Pietrapiana 1r, turn right on V. del Proconsolo, take the first left on Borgo degli Albizi, and continue straight through P.G. Salvemini; it will be on the left. (Open M-Sa 8am-9pm, Su 9:30am-1:30pm and 3:30-6:30pm.)

OLD CITY (THE CENTER)

■ **Trattoria Anita,** V. del Parlascio 2r (☎055 21 86 98), just behind the Bargello. Dine by candlelight, surrounded by expensive wine bottles on wooden shelves. Traditional Tuscan fare—filling pastas and an array of meat dishes from roast chicken to beefsteak Florentine. *Primi* €4.70-5.20. *Secondi* from €5.20. Fantastic lunch *menu* €5.50. Cover €1. Open M-Sa noon-2:30pm and 7-10pm. AmEx/MC/V. ❷

■ **Acqua al Due,** V. Vigna Vecchia 40r (☎055 28 41 70), behind the Bargello. Popular with young Italians. Serves Florentine specialties, including an excellent *assaggio* (€7.50). *Primi* €6.70; *secondi* from €7-19. Cover €1. Reserve ahead. Open daily 7pm-1am. ❸

Al Lume di Candela, V. delle Terme 23r (☎055 265 65 61), halfway between P.S. Trinità and P. della Signoria. Candlelit tables illuminate the bright yellow walls of this restaurant that serves Tuscan, Venetian, and southern Italian favorites. *Primi* €6-8. *Secondi* €9.60-12. Open daily noon-2:30pm and 7-11pm. AmEx/MC/V. ❸

Le Colonnine, V. dei Benci 6r, north of the Ponte alle Grazie. Delicious traditional fare. Pizza €4.70. Pasta from €7. Famous *paella* for 2 could feed a small army (€18). Open daily noon-3:30pm and 6:30pm-midnight. ❷

Trattoria da Benvenuto, V. della Mosca 16r (☎055 21 48 33). Pastel decor and linen tablecloths make for comfortable dining. *Spaghetti alle vongole* (with clams) €5.50. *Penne* with mushrooms and olives €5.50. *Primi* €4.50-8.50. *Secondi* €6-13. Cover €1.50. 10% service charge. Open M-Sa noon-2:30pm and 7-10:30pm. AmEx/MC/V. ❸

La Loggia degli Albizi, Borgo degli Albizi 39r (☎055 247 95 74). From behind the *duomo*, go right on V. del Proconsolo and take the 1st left onto Borgo degli Albizi. Head 2 blocks down and look right. A hidden treasure, this bakery/cafe offers an escape from the tourist hordes. Pastries and coffee from €0.80 each. Open M-Sa 7am-8pm. ❶

PIAZZE SANTA MARIA NOVELLA AND DEL MERCATO CENTRALE

■ **Tre Merli,** entrances on V. del Moro 11r and V. dei Fossi 12r (☎055 28 70 62). Beautiful red mushroom lights shine on booths for a candlelit meal. *Primi* €7.50-14. *Secondi* €12-19. Cover €2. Lunch *menu* €12. Open daily 11am-11pm. AmEx/MC/V. ❸

■ **Trattoria da Giorgio,** V. Palazzuolo 100r. Generous portions. *Menu* €8-9. Expect a wait. Open M-Sa noon-3:30pm and 7pm-12:30am. ❷

Trattoria Contadino, V. Palazzuolo, 71r (☎055 238 2673). Filling, homestyle meals. Offers fixed price *menu* only that includes *primi*, *secondi*, bread, water, and .25L of house wine for €9.50. Open M-Sa noon-2:30pm and 6-9:30pm. AmEx/MC/V. ❷

Trattoria Antellesi, V. Faenza 9r (☎055 21 69 90). Classic Tuscan *trattoria* tucked just off P. Madonna Aldobrandini. A fine place to sample regional favorites such as *pecorino antipasto* and *bistecca alla Fiorentina* (€16). *Primi* €5.50-7.50. *Secondi* €9.50-16. Cover €1. Open Su-M and W-Sa noon-2:30pm and 7-10:30pm. AmEx/MC/V. ❹

Amon, V. Palazzuolo 28r (☎055 29 31 46). Cheerful owner cooks his own bread and serves scrumptious Middle Eastern food. Try the *mousaka* (pita filled with baked eggplant) or *foul* (spiced beans). Open Su and Tu-Sa noon-3pm and 6-11pm. ❶

OLTRARNO

■ **Oltrarno Trattoria Casalinga,** V. Michelozzi 9r (☎055 21 86 24), near P.S. Spirito. Basic Tuscan dishes and specialties. Good quality for the price. *Primi* €4-6. *Secondi* €5-9. Cover €1.50. Open M-Sa noon-2:30pm and 7-10pm. ❸

■ **La Mangiatoia,** P.S. Felice 8r (☎055 22 40 60). Continue straight on V. Guicciardini from Ponte Vecchio, passing P. dei Pitti. Quality Tuscan fare. *Primi* €3.50-5.50. *Secondi* €4-5. Pizza €4-6.50. Bread and water €3. Open Su and Tu-Sa 11:30am-3pm and 7-10pm. AmEx/MC/V. ❷

ITALY

GELATERIE

Gelato is said to have been invented centuries ago by Florence's Buontalenti family. Before shelling out €1.50 for a *piccolo* cone, assess the quality of an establishment by looking at the banana *gelato:* If it's bright yellow, it's been made from a mix—keep on walking. If it's slightly gray, real bananas were used. *Gelati* in metal bins also tend to be homemade, whereas plastic tubs indicate mass-production. Most *gelaterie* also serve *granite*, flavored ices that are easier on the waistline.

■ **Vivoli,** V. della Stinche 7, behind the Bargello. A renowned Florentine *gelateria* with a huge selection of the self-proclaimed "best ice cream in the world." Cups from €1.50. Open Su and T-Sa 9:30-1am; 7:30am-1am.

■ **Gelateria Triangolo delle Bermuda,** V. Nazionale 61r. Blissful *crema venusiana* has hazelnut, caramel, and meringue. Cones €1.60. Open daily 11am-midnight.

Antica Gelateria il David, V. San Antonino 28r (☎055 21 86 45), off V. Faenza. A hidden gem that's short on variety but big on quality. Large scoops at low prices. Cones from €1.60. Open M-Sa 11am-midnight.

Perchè No?, V. Tavolini 19r (☎055 239 89 69), off V. dei Calzaiuoli. This well-known and centrally located parlor serves some of Florence's finest *gelato*. Excellent coffee crunch, mouth-watering chocolate, and chunky *nocciolosa*. Cones €2. Open Apr.-Oct. daily 11am-12:30am; Nov.-Mar. Su-M and W-Sa 10am-8pm.

Carabè, V. Ricasoli 60r (☎055 28 94 76). Amazing *gelato* with ingredients shipped from Sicily. Cups from €1.60. *Granite* from €2.10. Open May-Sept. daily 10am-midnight; Mar.-Apr. and Oct. noon-midnight.

ENOTECHE (WINE BARS)

Check out an *enoteca* to sample some of Italy's finest wines. A meal can often be made out of the exquisite complementary side-dish sensations (cheeses, olives, toast and spreads, and salami).

Enoteca Alessi, V. della Oche 27/29r (☎055 21 49 66; fax 055 239 69 87), 1 block from the *duomo*. Among Florence's finest, stocking over 1000 wines. Doubling as a chocolate and candy store, it offers delicious nibbles between sips. Spacious, high-ceilinged, and cool. Open M-F 9am-1pm and 4-8pm. AmEx/MC/V. ❷

Enoteca Fuori Porta, V. Monte alle Croce 10r (☎055 234 24 83), in the shadows of S. Miniato. This more casual and off-the-beaten-track *enoteca* serves reasonable meals of traditional Tuscan pasta and *secondi* (from €5.70) in addition to the complimentary snacks. Open M-Sa 10am-2pm and 5-9pm. ❷

◗ SIGHTS

There's enough to see in the center of Florence alone to keep a visitor occupied for years; if you're in the city for only a few days, hit the highlights. Plan well, as the city's art museums are spectacular, but exhausting and expensive. Florence's museums run €3.10-8.50 per venue and no longer offer student discounts. In summer, watch for **Sere al Museo,** evenings when certain museums are free from 8:30-11pm. Also, many of Florence's churches are treasuries of great art.

PIAZZA DEL DUOMO

■ **THE DUOMO (CATTEDRALE DI SANTA MARIA DEL FIORE).** The red brick of Florence's *duomo*, the **Cattedrale di Santa Maria del Fiore,** at the center of P. del Duomo, is visible from virtually every part of the city. Filippo Brunelleschi drew from long-neglected classical methods to come up with his revolutionary double-shelled construction that utilized self-supporting interlocking bricks in order to construct the enormous dome. The *duomo* claims the world's third longest nave, trailing only St. Peter's in Rome and St. Paul's in London. *(Open M-Sa 10am-4:45pm, Su 1:30-4:45pm. Mass daily 7am-12:30pm and 5-7pm.)* Climb the 463 steps inside the dome to ■**Michelangelo's lantern,** which offers an unparalleled view of the city. *(Open M-F 8:30am-7pm, Sa 8:30am-5:40pm. €6.)* The 82m high **campanile,** next to the *duomo,* also has beautiful views. *(Open daily 8:30am-7:30pm. €6.)*

BATTISTERO. The *battistero* (baptistery) next to the *duomo,* built between the 5th and 9th centuries, was the site of Dante's christening; its Byzantine-style mosaics inspired the details of his *Inferno.* The famous **bronze doors** were a product of intense competition among Florentine artists; Ghiberti was commissioned to forge the last set of doors. The products, reportedly dubbed the ■**Gates of Paradise** by Michelangelo, exchanged his earlier 28-panel design for 10 large, gilded squares, each of which employs mathematical perspective to create the illusion of deep space. Under restoration since a 1966 flood, they will soon be housed in the Museo dell'Opera del Duomo. *(Open M-Sa noon-7pm, Su 8:30am-2pm. €3.)*

MUSEO DELL'OPERA DEL DUOMO. Most of the *duomo*'s art resides behind the cathedral in the Museo dell'Opera del Duomo. Up the first flight of stairs is a late *Pietà* by Michelangelo, who, according to legend, destroyed Christ's left arm with a hammer in a fit of frustration; soon after, a diligent pupil touched up the work, leaving visible scars on parts of Mary Magdalene's head. The museum also houses four frames from the baptistery's *Gates of Paradise.* *(P. del Duomo 9, behind the duomo. Open M-Sa 9am-6:30pm, Su 9am-1pm. €6.)*

ORSANMICHELE. Built in 1337 as a granary, the Orsanmichele was converted into a church after a great fire convinced city officials to move grain operations outside the city walls. Secular and spiritual concerns mingle in the statues along the facade. Within these niches, look for Ghiberti's *St. John the Baptist* and *St. Stephen,* Donatello's *St. Peter* and *St. Mark,* and Giambologna's *St. Luke.* Across the street, the **Museo di Orsanmichele** exhibits numerous paintings and sculptures from the original church. *(V. Arte della Lana, between the duomo and P. della Signoria. Museum open daily 9am-noon. Closed 1st and last M of the month. Free.)*

PIAZZA DELLA SIGNORIA AND ENVIRONS

From P. del Duomo, the bustling **Via dei Calzaiuoli,** one of the city's oldest streets, runs south through crowds and chic shops to P. della Signoria.

PIAZZA DELLA SIGNORIA. The destruction of powerful Florentine families' homes in the 13th century created an empty space that cried out *"piazza!"* With the construction of the Palazzo Vecchio in 1299, the square became Florence's civic and political center. In 1497, religious leader and social critic Savonarola convinced Florentines to light the **Bonfire of the Vanities,** a grand roast in the square that consumed some of Florence's best art. A year later, disillusioned citizens sent Savonarola up in smoke on the same spot, marked today by a granite disc. Monumental sculptures cluster in front of the *palazzo,* including a copy of Michelangelo's *David.* The awkward *Neptune* to the left of the Palazzo Vecchio so revolted Michelangelo that he insulted the artist: "Oh Ammannato, Ammannato, what lovely marble you have ruined!" The graceful 14th-century **Loggia dei Lanzi,** built as a stage for civic orators, displays world-class sculpture free of charge.

PALAZZO VECCHIO. Arnolfo del Cambio designed this fortress-like *palazzo* in the late-13th century as the governmental seat. It later became the Médici family home; in 1470, Michelozzo decorated the ■**courtyard** in Renaissance style. Inside are works by Michelangelo, da Vinci, and Bronzino. The **Monumental Apartments,** which house the *palazzo*'s extensive art collections, are accessible as a museum.

ITALY

The **Activities Tour,** well worth the extra €2 (students €1) on top of the cumulative ticket, includes the **Secret Routes,** which reveal hidden stairwells and chambers, and **Invitation to Court,** a reenactment of court life. *(☎ 055 276 84 65; tours ☎ 055 276 82 24. Call ahead for tour reservations. Monumental Apartments €6, ages 18-25 €4.50. Palazzo €5.70. Courtyard free. June-Sept. M and F 9am-11pm, Tu-W and Sa 9am-7pm, Th and Su 9am-2pm; Oct.-May M-W and F-Sa 9am-7pm, Th and Su 9am-2pm.)*

■ **THE UFFIZI.** Vasari designed this palace in 1554 for the offices *(uffizi)* of Duke Cosimo's administration; today, it houses more first-class art per square inch than any other museum in the world. Botticelli, da Vinci, Michelangelo, Raphael, Titian, Giotto, Fra Angelico, Caravaggio, Bronzino, Cimabue, della Francesca, Bellini, even Dürer, Rubens, and Rembrandt—you name it, they have it. To avoid disappointment at the museum, note that a few rooms are usually closed each day and famous works often go on temporary loan, so not all works will be available for viewing. A sign outside the ticket office lists the *sale* that will be closed for the day; ask if they will reopen the next day. *(Extends from P. della Signoria to the Arno River. ☎ 055 21 83 41. Open Su, Tu-Sa 8am-7pm. €8.50.)*

PONTE VECCHIO. From the Uffizi, follow V. Georgofili left and turn right along the river to reach the nearby **Ponte Vecchio** (Old Bridge). The oldest bridge in Florence, it replaced an older Roman version in 1345. In the 1500s, the Médici kicked out the butcheries and tanneries that lined the bridge and installed goldsmiths and diamond-carvers instead. The view of the bridge from the neighboring Ponte alle Grazie at sunset is breathtaking, and the bridge itself buzzes with pedestrians and street performers, particularly at night.

THE BARGELLO AND ENVIRONS

Once the center of medieval Florence, this area now contains a number of sites dating from that period as well as several museums.

BARGELLO. The heart of medieval Florence lies in this 13th-century fortress between the *duomo* and P. della Signoria. Once the residence of the chief magistrate and later a brutal prison with public executions in the courtyard, it was restored in the 19th century and now houses the sculpture-filled **Museo Nazionale.** Donatello's bronze *David*, the first freestanding nude since antiquity, stands opposite the two bronze panels of the *Sacrifice of Isaac*, submitted by Ghiberti and Brunelleschi in the baptistery door competition. Michelangelo's early works, including *Bacchus*, *Brutus*, and *Apollo*, are on the ground floor. *(V. del Proconsolo 4, between duomo and P. della Signoria. ☎ 055 238 86 06. Open daily typically 8:15am-1:50pm. Closed 2nd and 4th M of each month, though hours and off days vary by month. €4.)*

BADIA. The site of medieval Florence's richest monastery, the Badia is now buried in the interior of a residential block; one would never guess the treasures that lie within. Filippino Lippi's stunning *Apparition of the Virgin to St. Bernard*, one of the most famous paintings of the late 15th century, hangs in eerie gloom to the left of the entrance to the church. Note the beautiful, if dingy, frescoes and Corinthian pilasters. If you visit, walk silently among the prostrate, white-robed worshippers. *(Entrance on V. Dante Alighieri, just off V. Proconsolo. Open to tourists M 3-6pm.)*

MUSEO DI STORIA DELLA SCIENZA. After pondering great Italian artists and writers, head to this museum to be awed by the greats of science. This impressive collection boasts scientific instruments from the Renaissance, including telescopes, astrological models, clock workings, and wax models of anatomy and childbirth. The highlight of the museum is **Room 4,** where a number of Galileo's tools are on display, including the objective lens through which he first observed the satellites of Jupiter in 1610. *(P. dei Giudici 1, behind Palazzo Vecchio and the Uffizi. ☎ 055 29 34 93. Open M, W-F 9:30am-5pm; Tu, Sa 9:30am-1pm. Oct.-May also open 2nd Su of each month 10am-1pm. €6.50.)*

CASA DI DANTE. The Casa di Dante is reputedly identical to the house Dante inhabited. Anyone who can read Italian with an interest in Dante will enjoy the displays, which trace the poet's life from youth to exile to the artistic creation that immortalized him. Check out Giotto's early and paradigmatic portrait of Dante on the third floor. Nearby is a facsimile of the abandoned little church where Beatrice, Dante's unrequited love and spiritual guide in *Paradiso*, attended mass. *(Corner of V. Dante Alighieri and V.S. Margherita within 1 block of the Bargello. ☎ 055 21 94 16. Open M and W-Sa 10am-5pm, Su 10am-2pm. €3, groups over 15 €2 per person.)*

PIAZZA DELLA REPUBBLICA AND FARTHER WEST

PIAZZA DELLA REPUBBLICA. The largest open space in Florence, this *piazza* teems with crowds and street performers in the evenings. An enormous arch filling in the gap over V. Strozzi marks the western edge of the square. The rest of the piazza is lined with coffee shops, restaurants, and *gelaterie*. In 1890, the *piazza* replaced the Mercato Vecchio as the site of the city's market. The inscription *"Antico centro della città, da secolare squalore, a vita nuova restituito"* ("The ancient center of the city, squalid for centuries, restored to new life") makes a derogatory reference to the fact that the *piazza* is the site of the old Jewish ghetto, which slowly disappeared as a result of the "liberation of the Jews" in Italy in the 1860s that allowed members of the Jewish community to live elsewhere.

CHIESA DI SANTA MARIA NOVELLA. The wealthiest merchants built their chapels in this church near the train station. Santa Maria Novella was home to the order of Dominicans, or *Domini canes* (Hounds of the Lord), who took a bite out of sin and corruption. The 14th-century *chiesa* boasts a green and white Romanesque-Gothic facade, considered one of the greatest masterpieces of early Renaissance architecture. Thirteenth-century frescoes covered the interior until the Medici commissioned Vasari to paint new ones. Fortunately, Vasari spared Masaccio's powerful ▨**Trinity,** the first painting to use geometric perspective. This fresco, on the left side of the nave, creates the illusion of a tabernacle. *(Open M-Th and Sa 9:30am-5pm, F and Su 1-5pm. €2.50., ages 13-18 €1.50.)*

CHIESA DI SANTA TRINITÀ. To spend an eternity in the company of society's elites, most fashionable *palazzo* owners commissioned family chapels here. The facade, designed by Bernardo Buontalenti in the 16th century, is an exquisite example of late-Renaissance architecture that verges on Baroque in its ornamentation. Scenes from Ghirlandaio's *Life of St. Francis* decorate the **Sassetti chapel** in the right arm of the transept. The famous altarpiece, Ghirlandaio's *Adoration of the Shepherds*, resides in the Uffizi—this one is a convincing copy. *(In P.S. Trinità. Open M-Sa 8am-noon and 4-6pm, Su 4-6pm.)*

MERCATO NUOVO. The *loggie* of the New Market have housed gold and silk traders since 1547 under their Corinthian-columned splendor. Today, vendors sell purses, belts, clothes, fruit, and vegetables, as well as some gold and silk. Pietro Tacca's pleasantly plump statue, *Il Porcellino* (The Little Pig; actually a wild boar)—appeared some 50 years after the market first opened. Reputed to bring good luck, its snout is polished from tourists' rubbing. *(Off V. Calimala, between P. della Repubblica and the Ponte Vecchio. Sellers hawk their wares from dawn until dusk.)*

PALAZZO DAVANZATI. As Florence's 15th-century economy expanded, its bankers and merchants flaunted their new wealth by erecting grand palaces. The great *quattrocento* boom began with construction of the Palazzo Davanzati. Today, the high-ceilinged *palazzo* finds life as the **Museo della Casa Fiorentina Antica.** With reproductions and original furniture, restored frescoes, and wooden doors and ornaments, this museum recreates the 15th-century merchants' life of luxury. *(V. Porta Rossa 13. ☎ 055 238 86 10. Open daily 8:30am-1:50pm. Closed 1st, 3rd, and 5th M and 2nd and 4th Su of each month.)*

ITALY

PALAZZO STROZZI. The modesty of the Palazzo Davanzati's facade gave way to more extravagant *palazzi*. The Palazzo Strozzi, begun in 1489, may be the grandest of its kind, occupying an entire block. Its regal proportions and three-tiered facade, made of bulging blocks of brown stone, embody the Florentine style. The *palazzo* now shelters several cultural institutes, unfortunately not open to the public, and occasionally hosts art exhibits that are open to all, with tickets from €10. The courtyard is open to the public and worth a visit. *(On V. Tornabuoni at V. Strozzi. Enter from P. Strozzi. ☎055 28 53 95.)*

SAN LORENZO AND FARTHER NORTH

BASILICA DI SAN LORENZO. The Médici, who lent the city the funds to build the church (designed in 1419 by Brunelleschi), retained artistic control over its construction. The family cunningly placed Cosimo Médici's grave in front of the high altar, making the entire church his personal mausoleum. Michelangelo designed the exterior but, disgusted by Florentine politics, he abandoned the project to study architecture in Rome. *(☎055 21 66 34. Open daily M-Sa 10am-5pm. €2.50.)*

To reach the ◙**Cappelle dei Médici** (Médici Chapels), walk around to the back entrance on P. Madonna degli Aldobrandini. The **Cappella dei Principi** (Princes' Chapel) is a rare example of Baroque style in Florence, while the **Sacrestia Nuova** (New Sacristy) shows Michelangelo's work and holds two Médici tombs. *(Open daily 8:15am-5pm. Closed the 2nd and 4th Su and the 1st, 3rd, and 5th M of every month. €6.)* The adjacent **Laurentian Library** houses one of the world's most valuable manuscript collections. Michelangelo's famous entrance portico confirms his virtuosity; the elaborate *pietra serena* sandstone staircase is one of his most innovative architectural designs. *(Open daily 8:30am-1:30pm. Free with entrance to San Lorenzo.)*

◙**MUSEO DELLA CHIESA DI SAN MARCO.** Remarkable works by Fra Angelico adorn the Museo della Chiesa di San Marco, one of the most peaceful and spiritual places in Florence. A large room to the right of the lovely courtyard contains some of the painter's major works, including the church's altarpiece. The second floor houses Angelico's most famous *Annunciation*, across from the top of the stairwell, as well as the monks' quarters. Every cell in the convent contains its own Fra Angelico fresco, each painted in flat colors and with sparse detail to facilitate the monks' somber meditation. To the right of the stairwell, Michelozzo's library, modeled on Michelangelo's work in S. Lorenzo, is a fine example of purity and vigor. After visiting, you may want to follow in the footsteps of the convent's patron, Cosimo I, who retired here. In cells 17 and 22, you can see underground artwork through the glass floor, excavated from the medieval period. Towards the exit are two rooms housing the **Museo di Firenze Antica**, which is worth a quick visit. It has numerous archeological fragments on display, most of them from Etruscan and Roman buildings in the area. *(Enter at P. di San Marco, 3. ☎055 238 86 08 or 238 87 04. Open daily 8:15am-6:50pm. Closed 1st, 3rd, and 5th Su and 2nd and 4th M of every month. €4. Over-65 or under-18 free.)*

◙**ACCADEMIA.** Michelangelo's triumphant **David** stands in self-assured perfection under the rotunda designed just for him. In a series of unfortunate incidences, the statue's base was struck by lightning in 1512, damaged by anti-Medici riots in 1527, and was finally moved here from P. della Signoria in 1873 after a stone hurled during a riot broke *David's* left wrist in two places. In the hallway leading up to the *David* are Michelangelo's four *Slaves* and a *Pieta*. The master left these intriguing statues intentionally unfinished. Remaining true to his theories of living stone, he chipped away only enough to show their emerging figures. In addition to the commanding sculptures, check out Botticelli's *Madonna* paintings as well as works by Uccello. *(V. Ricasoli 60 between the churches of San Marco and S.S. Annunziata. Most areas wheelchair accessible. Open Su and Tu-Sa 8:15am-6:50pm. €6.50.)*

PALAZZO MÉDICI RICCARDI. The palace's innovative facade is the work of Michelozzo—it stands as the archetype for all Renaissance *palazzi*. The private chapel inside features Benozzo Gozzoli's beautiful, wrap-around fresco of the ■**Three Magi** and several Médici family portraits. The *palazzo* hosts rotating exhibits ranging from Renaissance architectural sketches to Fellini memorabilia. *(V. Cavour 3. ☎ 055 276 03 40. Open daily 9am-1pm and 3-7pm. €4, children €2.50.)*

MUSEO ARCHEOLOGICO. Unassuming behind its bland, yellow plaster facade and small sign, the archeological museum has a surprisingly diverse collection. Inside, you'll find notable collections of statues and other monuments of the ancient Greeks, Etruscans, and Egyptians. A long, thin, two-story gallery devoted to Etruscan jewelry runs along the length of the plant- and tree-filled courtyard. In almost any other city in the world, this museum would be a major cultural highlight, but in Florence, it's possible to enjoy it without large crowds. *(V. della Colonna 38. Open M 2-7pm, Tu and Th 8:30am-7pm, W and F-Su 8:30am-2pm. €4.)*

PIAZZA SANTA CROCE AND ENVIRONS

■**CHIESA DI SANTA CROCE.** The thrifty Franciscans ironically built the city's most splendid church. Among the luminaries buried here are Machiavelli, Galileo, Michelangelo (who rests in the right aisle in a tomb designed by Vasari), and humanist Leonardo Bruni, shown holding his precious *History of Florence*. Note also Donatello's gilded *Annunciation*. *(Open M-Sa 9:30am-5:30pm, Su and holidays 3-5:30pm.)* Intricate *pietra serena* pilasters and statues of the evangelists by Donatello grace Brunelleschi's small **Cappella Pazzi**, at the end of the cloister next to the church, a humble marvel of perfect proportions and lovely decorations, among them Luca della Robbia's *tondi* of the apostles and Brunelleschi's moldings of the evangelists. *(Enter through the Museo dell'Opera. Open Su-Tu and Th-Sa 10am-7pm. €2.60.)* The **Museo dell'Opera di Santa Croce** forms three sides of the church's peaceful courtyard with gravel paths and cypress trees. *(Enter museum through the loggia in front of Cappella Pazzi. Open Su-Tu and Th-Sa 10am-7pm.)*

SYNAGOGUE OF FLORENCE. This synagogue, also known as the **Museo del Tempio Israelitico,** lies hidden behind gates and walls, waiting to reveal its Sephardic temple's domes, arches, and patterns. David Levi, a wealthy Florentine Jewish business man, donated his fortune in 1870 for the construction of "a monumental temple worthy of Florence," in recognition of the fact that Jews had recently been allowed to live and worship outside the old Jewish ghetto. Architects Micheli, Falchi, and Treves created one of Europe's most beautiful synagogues. *(V. Farini 4, at V. Pilastri. The museum includes free, informative tours every hr.; book in advance. ☎ 055 24 52 52. Open Su-Th 10am-6pm, F 10am-2pm. €4.)*

CASA BUONARROTI. This unassuming little museum houses Michelangelo memorabilia and two of his most important early works, *The Madonna of the Steps* and *The Battle of the Centaurs*. Both pieces are to the left of the second floor landing. He completed these panels, which illustrate his growth from bas-relief to sculpture, when he was only 16 years old. A selection of his sketches is on rotating display from the unusually large collection; before he died, Michelangelo burned most of his sketches and preliminary work "lest he should appear less than perfect." *(V. Ghibellina 70. From P.S. Croce, follow V. dei Pepi and turn right onto V. Ghibellina. ☎ 055 24 17 52. Open Su-M and W-Sa 9:30am-2pm. €6.50, students €4.)*

THE OLTRARNO

Historically disdained by downtown Florentines, the far side of the Arno remains a lively and unpretentious quarter, even in high season.

ITALY

PALAZZO PITTI. Luca Pitti, a wealthy banker of the 15th century, built his *palazzo* east of P.S. Spirito against the Boboli hill. The Médici acquired the *palazzo* and the hill in 1550 and expanded in every way possible. Today, it houses six museums, including the ☒**Galleria Palatina.** The galleria was one of only a few public galleries when it opened in 1833 and today houses Florence's most important art collection after the Uffizi. Works by Raphael, Titian, Andrea del Sarto, Caravaggio, and Rubens line the walls. Other museums display Médici family treasures, costumes, porcelain, carriages, and *Apartamenti Reale* (royal apartments)—lavish reminders of the time when the *palazzo* was the royal House of Savoy's living quarters. *(Open Su and Tu-Sa 8:15am-6.50pm. €6.50.)*

BOBOLI GARDENS. With geometrically sculpted hedges, contrasting groves of holly and cypress trees, and bubbling fountains, the elaborate gardens are an exquisite example of stylized Renaissance landscaping. A large oval lawn is just up the hill from the back of the palace, with an Egyptian obelisk in the middle and marble statues in freestanding niches dotting the hedge-lined perimeter. *(Open June-Aug. daily 8:15am-7:30pm; Sept.-May reduced hours. €4.)*

SAN MINIATO AL MONTE AND ENVIRONS

SAN MINIATO AL MONTE. One of Florence's oldest churches gloriously surveys all of Florence. The inlaid marble facade and 13th-century mosaics provide a prelude to the incredible pavement inside, patterned with lions, doves, and astrological signs. The **Chapel of the Cardinal of Portugal** holds a collection of superlative della Robbia terracottas. Be sure to circle the church and spend a moment in the cemetery, which contains an overwhelming profusion of tombs and mausoleums in many architectural styles. *(Take bus #13 from the station or climb the stairs from Piazzale Michelangelo. ☎055 234 27 31. Open daily 7:30am-7pm.)*

PIAZZALE MICHELANGELO. Laid out in 1860, Piazzale Michelangelo offers a fine panorama of the entire city, which is especially beautiful at sunset. Unfortunately, the *piazza* doubles as a large parking lot, and is home to hordes of tour buses during summer days. It occasionally hosts concerts as well. The stunning photo-op, in addition to the copy of Michelangelo's *David* on an ornate pedestal in the center, make it worth the trek. *(Cross the Ponte Vecchio and turn left, walk through the piazza, and turn right up V. de Bardi. Follow it uphill as it becomes V. del Monte alle Croci, where a staircase to the left heads to the Piazza.)*

🎵 ENTERTAINMENT

In June, the *quartieri* of Florence turn out in costume to play their own medieval version of soccer, known as **calcio storico**, in which two teams of 27 players face off over a wooden ball in one of the city's *piazze*. These games often blur the line between athletic contest and riot. Tickets (around €16) are sold at the box office across from P.S. Croce. Check with the tourist office for times and locations of matches. The **Festival of San Giovanni Battista,** on June 24, features a tremendous fireworks display in P. Michelangelo beginning around 10pm. May starts the summer music festivals with the classical **Maggio Musicale.** The **Estate Fiesolana** (June-Aug.) fills the Roman theater in nearby Fiesole with concerts, opera, theater, ballet, and film events. September brings the **Festa dell'Unità,** a concert series at Campi Bisenzia (take bus #30). The **Festa del Grillo** (Festival of the Cricket), is on the first Sunday after Ascension Day, May 22, when crickets in tiny wooden cages are sold in the Cascine park and then released into the grass.

▌ NIGHTLIFE

For info on hot nightlife, consult the monthly *Firenze Spettacolo* (€2). Begin your nighttime *passeggiata* along V. dei Calzaiuoli and end it with coffee or *gelato* in a ritzy cafe on **Piazza della Repubblica**, where singers prance about the stage in front of **Bar Concerto**. In the Oltrarno, **Piazza San Spirito** has plenty of bars and restaurants, and live music in summer.

BARS

May Day Lounge, V. Dante Alighieri 16r. Aspiring artists display their work on the walls of this eclectic lounge. Play Pong on the early 1980s gaming system or sip mixed drinks (€4.50-€6.50) to the beat of the background funk. Beer €4.50. Happy Hour 8-10pm. Open daily 8pm-2am.

Slowly, V. Porta Rossa 63r. Posh leather booths, sleek black barstools and tables, blaring pop-jazz to a silent four-screen TV, and small mood candles. Lively but casual. Mixed drinks €7. Coffee €3-5. Open daily 7pm-2:30am. MC/V.

Eby's Latin Bar, V. dell'Oriuolo 5r. Eby blends tasty fresh-fruit cocktails with only seasonal ingredients. Fantastic Mexican wraps and the best nachos in Florence are two more reasons to visit. Cocktails €5.50. Beer €3. Happy Hour 6-9pm (drinks €3). Open M-Sa noon-3pm and 6pm-3am.

The Chequers Pub, V. della Scala 7/9r. Of all the pubs in Florence, this one attracts the liveliest Italian crowd. Wide range of beers (pints €4.50). Happy Hour daily 6:30-8pm (pints €2.50). Open daily Apr.-Oct. Su-Th 12:30pm-1:30am, F-Sa 12:20pm-2:30am; Nov.-Mar. Su-Th 6pm-1:30am, F-Sa 6pm-2:30am. AmEx/MC/V.

The Fiddler's Elbow, P.S. Maria Novella 7r. This authentic Irish pub serves cider, Guinness, and other beers (€4.20). Crowded with convivial foreigners. Open daily Su-Th 3pm-1am, F-Sa 2pm-2am.

DISCOS

Rio Grande, V. degli Olmi 1, near Parco delle Cascinè. Among locals and tourists alike, this is the most popular of Florence's discos. Cover €16; includes 1 drink. Special nights include soul, hip-hop, house, and reggae. Open Tu-Sa 11pm-4am. AmEx/MC/V.

Central Park, in Parco della Cascinè. Open-air dance floor pulses with hip-hop, reggae, and rock. Mixed drinks €8. Open M-Tu and Th-Sa 11pm-late. AmEx/MC/V.

Blob, V. Vinegia 21r, behind the Palazzo Vecchio. DJs, movies, foosball, and an evening bar buffet. Mixed drinks €6. 2-for-1 Happy Hour 6-10pm. Open daily until 4am.

Yab, V. Sassetti 5. Another dance club seething with American students and locals. With classic R&B and reggae on Mondays. A very large dance floor is packed by midnight. Mixed drinks €5. Open daily 9pm-1am.

Tabasco Gay Club, P.S. Cecilia 3r from Palazzo Vecchio. Smoke machines and strobe lights on dance floor. Florence's popular gay disco caters primarily to men. 18+. Cover €13, includes 1st drink. Open Tu-Su 10pm-4am. AmEx/MC/V.

SIENA   ☎ 0577

Many travelers rush from Rome to Florence, ignoring gorgeous, medieval Siena (pop. 60,000). The Sienese have a rich history in arts, politics, and trade. One of their proudest celebrations is **Il Palio,** (p. 727) a wild horse race among the city's 17 competing *contrade* (districts).

THE BIG SPLURGE

A VERY NICE CHIANTI

Tuscan rains have swamped the highway, forcing Chianti residents to take clever side-street routes to home and market; even so, on these tiny back roads we don't pass a single car. We make our way to a small hilltop home where a family prepares our lunch, then swing by a private vineyard, unannounced. The manager emerges, and he and our guide exchange cordial waves. Meet Silvio, native and connoisseur of the Chianti region, and host of a unique tour through this land of wine and olives. A long-time friend to many Chianti residents, Silvio has a special rapport with families and vineyard owners. At one home, he borrows a set of keys to the tiny, fresco-filled *chiesa* in the family's private yard. Along the way, he instructs his guests in wine-tasting technique and recounts significant dates and facts with ease. Silvio's day-long tours are each custom designed: he will arrange cooking lessons with a Chianti family or simply host lengthy treks through fields of sunflowers. This increasingly popular part of Tuscany is filled with-tour opportunities, but Silvio's is distinctly enthusiastic, leisurely, and personal. For those who seek a genuine understanding of Chianti and all its richness, this is a special, and comparatively affordable experience.

€420 for 2 people. For info, contact italyinfo1@yahoo.com.

☎ ⚡ TRANSPORTATION AND PRACTICAL INFORMATION. Trains leave P. Rosselli hourly for Florence (1½hr., 12 per day, €5.30) and Rome (3hr., 16 per day, €17) via Chiusi. TRA-IN/SITA **buses** (☎0577 20 42 45) depart from P. Gramsci and the train station for Florence (every hr., €6.50) and San Gimignano (8 per day, €5). From the train station, cross the street and take TRA-IN/SITA buses #3, 4, 7-10, 14, 17, or 77 into the center of town at **Piazza del Sale** or **Piazza Gramsci** (€0.90). The central APT **tourist office** is at Il Campo 56. (☎0577 28 05 51; fax 27 06 76. Open daily mid-Mar. to mid-Nov. 8:30am-7:30pm; mid-Nov. to mid-Mar. 8:30am-1pm and 3-7pm.) **Prenotazioni Alberghiere,** in P.S. Domenico, finds rooms for a €2 fee. (☎0577 28 80 84. M-Sa 9am-7pm.) Check email at **Internet Train,** V. di Citta 121. (€5.20 per hr. Open M-Sa 10am-8pm, Su noon-8pm.) **Postal Code:** 53100.

☎ ⚡ ACCOMMODATIONS AND FOOD. Finding a room in Siena can be difficult from Easter to October. Book months ahead if coming during *Il Palio.* The tastefully furnished **Albergo Tre Donzelle ❸** is at V. Donzelle 5. (☎0577 28 03 58; fax 0577 22 39 38. Curfew 1am. Singles €33; doubles €45-60. AmEx/MC/V.) Take bus #15 from P. Gramsci to reach the **Ostello della Gioventù "Guidoriccio" (HI) ❶,** V. Fiorentina 89, in Località Lo Stellino. (☎0577 522 12. Curfew midnight. Reserve ahead. Dorms €13. MC/V.) **Hotel Alma Domus ❹,** V. Camporegio 37, behind S. Domenico, has spotless rooms with views of the *duomo.* (☎0577 441 77; fax 0577 476 01. Curfew 11:30pm. Singles €42; doubles €55; triples €70; quads €85.) To **camp** at **Colleverde ❶,** Strada di Scacciapensieri 47, take bus #3 or 8 from P. del Sale. (☎0577 28 00 44. Open mid-Mar. to mid-Nov. €8 per person, €8 per tent.)

Siena specializes in rich pastries, of which the most famous is *panforte,* a confection of honey, almonds, and citron; indulge in this treat at **Bar/Pasticceria Nannini,** V. Banchi di Sopra 22-24, the oldest *pasticceria* in Siena. Next to Santuario di S. Caterina is the divine **Osteria La Chiacchera ❷,** Costa di S. Antonio 4, which serves hearty pasta dishes. (☎0577 28 06 31. *Secondi* €4.80-7. Open M, W-Su 12-3:30pm and 7pm-midnight.) **Consortio Agrario supermarket,** V. Pianigiani 5, is off P. Salimberi. (Open M-F 8am-7:30pm.)

⚙ ♬ SIGHTS AND ENTERTAINMENT. Siena offers two **biglietto cumulativi** (cumulative tickets)—the first is good for five days (€7.50) and allows entry into the Museo dell'Opera Metropolitana, baptistery, and Piccolomini library; the second is valid for seven days (€16) and covers four more sights, including the Musco Civico. Both may be purchased at any of the included sights. Siena radiates from ⬛**Piazza del Campo (Il Campo)**, a shell-shaped brick square designed for civic events. At the top of Il Campo is the **Fonte Gaia**, still fed by the same aqueduct used in the 1300s. At the bottom, the **Torre del Mangia** clocktower looms over the graceful Gothic **Palazzo Pubblico**. Inside the *palazzo*, the **Museo Civico** contains excellent Gothic and early Renaissance paintings; also check out the **Sala del Mappamondo** and the **Sala della Pace**. (*Palazzo*, museum, and tower open Mar.-Oct. daily 10am-7pm; Nov.-Feb. reduced hours. Tower €5.50; museum €6.50, students €4; combined ticket with tower €9.50.) From the *palazzo*, take the right-side stairs and cross V. di Città for Siena's Gothic ⬛**duomo**. The apse would have been left hanging in mid-air save for the construction of the lavishly decorated **baptistery** below. (Open mid-Mar. to Oct. M-Sa 7:30am-7:30pm, Su 2-7:30pm; Nov. to mid-Mar. 7:30am-5:30pm and 2:30-5pm, Su 2-5:30pm. Free except when floor is uncovered in Sept. €4-5.50.) The **Libreria Piccolomini**, off the left aisle, holds frescoes and 15th-century scores. (Same hours as *duomo*. €1.50.) The **Museo dell'Opera della Metropolitana**, to the right of the *duomo*, houses overflow art. (Open mid-Mar. to Sept. daily 9am-7:30pm; Nov. to mid-Mar. reduced hours. €5.50.)

Siena's ⬛**Il Palio** (July 2 and Aug. 16) is a traditional bareback horse race around the packed P. del Campo. Arrive three days early to watch the five trial runs and to pick a *contrada* to root for. At *Il Palio*, the jockeys take about 90 seconds to tear around Il Campo three times. To stay in Siena during the Palio, book rooms at least four months in advance, especially budget accommodations—call the APT (see above) in March or April for a list of rented rooms.

🖪 DAYTRIP FROM SIENA: SAN GIMIGNANO. The hilltop village of San Gimignano looks like an illustration from a medieval manuscript. The city's famous 14 towers, which are all that survive of its original 72, earned San Gimignano its nickname as the *Città delle Belle Torri* (City of Beautiful Towers). The **Museo Civico**, on the second floor of **Palazzo del Popolo,** has an amazing collection of Sienese and Florentine artwork. Within the museum is the entrance to the **Torre Grossa**, the tallest remaining tower; climb its 218 steps for a panoramic view of Tuscany. (Open Mar.-Oct. daily 9:30am-7pm; Nov.-Feb. 10am-7pm. €5, students €4.) Not for the faint of heart, ⬛**Museo Della Tortura**, V. del Castello 1, off P. Cisterna, offers a morbidly fascinating history of torture from Medieval Europe to the present. (Open Apr.-Oct. daily 10am-8pm; Nov.-Mar. 10am-6pm. Entrance €8, students €5.50.)

TRA-IN buses leave P. Montemaggio for Siena (1hr., every hr., €5.20) and Florence (1½hr., every hr., €6) via Poggibonsi. From the bus station, pass through the *porta*, climb the hill, following V.S. Giovanni to the city center **Piazza della Cisterna,** which runs into P. del Duomo and the **tourist office,** P. del Duomo 1. (☎0577 94 00 08; fax 0577 94 09 03. Open Mar.-Oct. daily 9am-1pm and 3-7pm; Nov.-Feb. 9am-1pm and 2-6pm.) Accommodations are pricey in San Gimignano—*affitte camere* (private rooms) are a good alternative, with doubles from €50. The tourist office and the **Associazione Strutture Extralberghiere,** P. della Cisterna 6, both find private rooms. (☎0577 94 08 09. Open Mar.-Nov. daily 9:30am-7:30pm.) From the bus stop, enter through Porta S. Giovanni for the quaint **Camere Cennini Gianni ❹,** V.S. Giovanni 21. The reception is at the *passticceria* at V.S. Giovanni 88. (☎0577 94 19 62; www.sangiapartments.com. Reserve ahead. Singles €45; doubles €55; triples €65; quads €75.) **Postal Code:** 53037.

PISA   ☎050

Tourism hasn't always been Pisa's (pop. 96,000) prime industry: during the Middle Ages, the city was a major port with its own Mediterranean empire. But when the Arno River silted up and the tower started leaning, the city's power and wealth declined accordingly. Today the city seems resigned to welcoming tourists and myriad t-shirt and ice cream vendors to the **Piazza del Duomo,** also known as the **Campo dei Miracoli** (Field of Miracles), a grassy expanse enclosing the tower, *duomo,* baptistry, Camposanto, Museo delle Sinopie, and Museo del Duomo. An **all-inclusive ticket** to the Campo's sights–excluding the tower–costs €10.50. Begun in 1173, the famous **Leaning Tower** began to tilt when the soil beneath suddenly shifted. In June of 2001, a multi-year stabilization effort was completed; the tower is presently considered stable. Tours of 30 visitors are permitted to ascend the 300 steps once every 30 minutes. (Make reservations at adjacent tourist office. Tours depart July-Aug. daily 8:30am-10:30pm, 8:30am-7:30pm Sept.-June. €15.) Also on the Campo, the dazzling **duomo,** a treasury of art, is considered one of the finest Romanesque cathedrals in the world. (Open daily 10am-7:30pm. €2.) Next door is the **baptistry,** whose precise acoustics allow an unamplified choir to be heard 2km away. (Open late Apr. to late Sept. daily 8am-8pm; Oct.-Mar. 9am-6pm. €6.) The adjoining **Camposanto,** a cloistered cemetery, has Roman sarcophagi and a series of haunting frescoes by an unidentified 14th-century artist known only as the "Master of the Triumph of Death." (Open late Apr. to late Sept. daily 8am-7:30pm; Mar. and Oct. 9am-5:40pm; Nov.-Feb. 9am-4:40pm. €6.) The **Museo delle Sinopie,** across the *piazza* from the Camposanto, displays preliminary fresco sketches discovered during post-WWII restoration. Behind the tower is the **Museo dell'Opera del Duomo.** (Both open late Apr.-Sept. daily 8am-7:20pm; Oct.-Apr. reduced hours. €6.)

   Trains (☎147 808 88) leave Piazza della Stazione, in the southern part of town, for: Florence (1hr., every hr., €4.90); Genoa (2½hr., €7.90); and Rome (3hr., 12 per day, €24). The **tourist office** is to the left after you exit the train station. (☎050 422 91; www.turismo.toscana.it. Open Apr.-Oct. M-Sa 9am-7pm, Su 9:30am-3:30pm; Nov.-Mar. reduced hours.) To reach the Campo from the train station, take **bus** #3 (€0.75). The **Albergo Helvetia ❸,** V. Don G. Boschi 31, off P. Archivescovado, has large, clean rooms 2min. from the *duomo.* (☎050 55 30 84. Singles €35; doubles €45.) **Centro Turistico Madonna dell'Acqua ❶,** V. Pietrasantina 15, is behind an old Catholic sanctuary 2km from the Tower. Take bus #3 from station (4 per hr., last bus 9:45pm); ask driver to stop at *ostello.* (☎050 89 06 22. Sheets €1. Dorms €15; doubles €42; triples €54; quads €64. MC/V.) Cheap dining options line **Corso Italia,** south of the river, and **Via Santa Maria,** as long as you're not too close to the *duomo,* where prices skyrocket. Try the heavenly *risotto* at the lively ▩**Il Paiolo ❶,** V. Curtatone e Montanara 9. (*Menu* with *primi* and *secondi* €4-6. Open M-F 12:30-3pm and 7:30pm-1am, Sa-Su 7:30pm-2am.) Get groceries at **Superal,** V. Pascoli 6, just off C. Italia. (Open M-Sa 8am-8pm.) **Postal Code:** 56100.

UMBRIA

Umbria is known as the "Green Heart of Italy," a land rich in natural beauty, from wild woods and fertile plains to craggy gorges and tiny villages. Christianity transformed Umbria's architecture and regional identity, turning it into a breeding ground for saints and religious movements; it was here that St. Francis of Assisi shamed the extravagant church with his humility.

PERUGIA ☎075

Perugia (pop. 150,000) may boast the most polite people in Italy. With its gorgeous countryside, big-city vitality, and world-renowned chocolate, this city's residents have much to smile about. Perugia's most popular sights frame **Piazza IV Novembre.** In its center, the **Fontana Maggiore** is adorned with sculptures and bas-reliefs by Nicolà and Giovanni Pisano. At the end of the *piazza,* the imposing

Gothic **duomo** houses the purported wedding ring of the Virgin Mary. (Open M-Sa 9am-12:45pm and 4-5:15pm, Su 4-5:45pm.) The 13th-century **Palazzo dei Priori** presides over the *piazza* and houses the impressive ▩**Galleria Nazionale dell'Umbria,** C. Vannucci 19. (Open daily 8:30am-7:30pm. Closed 1st M each month. €6.50.) At the end of town past the Porta S. Pietro, the ▩**Basilica di San Pietro,** on Borao XX Guigo, has a beautiful garden. (Open daily 8am-noon and 3:30-6:30pm.)

Trains leave **Perugia FS** in P.V. Veneto, Fontiveggio, for: Assisi (25min., every hr., €1.60); Florence (2½hr., 7 per day, €8); and Rome (2½hr., 6 per day, €11) via Terontola or Foligno. From the station, take bus #6, 7, 9, 13d, or 15 to the central P. Italia (€0.80), then walk down C. Vannucci to P. IV Novembre and the **tourist office,** P. IV Novembre 3. (☎075 572 33 27; fax 075 573 93 86. Open M-Sa 8:30am-1:30pm and 3:30-6:30pm, Su 9am-1pm.) ▩**Ostello della Gioventù/Centro Internazionale di Accoglienza per la Gioventù ❶,** V. Bontempi 13, has clean rooms and panoramic views. From the tourist office, walk down C. Vannucci past the *duomo* and P. Danti, take the farthest street directly through P. Piccinino, and turn right on V. Bontempi. (☎/fax 075 572 28 80; www.ostello.perugia.it. Sheets €1.50. Lockout 9:30am-4pm. Curfew midnight. Open mid-Jan. to mid-Dec. Dorms €12. MC/V/AmEx.) **Albergo Anna ❹,** V. dei Priori 48, off C. Vannucci, has cozy 17th-century rooms with great views. (☎/fax 075 573 63 04. Singles €40, with bath €45; doubles €46/€60; triples €70/€85. AmEx/MC/V.) Local favorite **Trattoria Dal Mi Cocco ❸,** provides prompt service and ample food at a reasonable price. (*Menu* €13. Open Su and Tu-Sa 1-3pm and 8:45pm-midnight. MC/V.) The **COOP,** P. Matteotti 15, has groceries. (Open M-Sa 9am-8pm.) **Postal Code:** 06100.

ASSISI ☎079

The undeniable jewel of Assisi (pop. 25,000) is the 13th-century ▩**Basilica di San Francesco.** The subdued art of the lower church celebrates St. Francis' modest lifestyle, while Giotto's renowned *Life of St. Francis* fresco cycle decorates the walls of the upper church, paying tribute to his sainthood and consecration. A no shorts or tank tops dress code is strictly enforced. (Lower basilica open daily 6:15am-6:45pm. Upper basilica open daily 8:30am-6:45pm.) The dramatic fortress **Rocca Maggiore** towers above the town, offering panoramic view of the countryside. (Open daily 10am-dusk. €1.70, students €1.) The pink and white **Basilica of Santa Chiara** houses St. Francis's tunic, sandals, and crucifix. (Open daily 9am-noon and 2-7pm.)

From the station near the Basilica Santa Maria degli Angeli, **trains** go to: Ancona (2hr., 8 per day, €7); Florence (2½hr., 13 per day, €9); and Rome (2½hr., 11 per day, €9). **Buses** run from P. Unita D'Italia to Florence (2½hr., 7am, €6.40) and Perugia (1½hr., 12 per day, €2.70). From P. Matteotti, follow V. del Torrione, bear left in P.S. Rufino, and take V.S. Rufino to **Piazza del Comune,** the town center, and location of the **tourist office.** (☎079 81 25 34; www.umbria2000.it. Open M-F 8am-2pm and 3:30-6:30pm, Sa 9am-1pm and 3:30-6:30pm, Su 9am-1pm.) The lovely ▩**Camere Martini ❷,** V.S. Gregorio 6, has lots of amenities and a friendly atmosphere. (☎/fax 075 81 35 36; cameremartini@libero.it. Singles €23-25; doubles €32-36; triples €48-52; quads €57.) **Ostello Fontemaggio ❶,** V. per L'Eremo delle Carceri 8, has a variety of rooms, camping and a market. Take V. L'Eremo from P. Matteotti about 1.5km. (☎075 81 36 36; fax 075 81 37 49. Curfew 11pm. Camping €5; dorms €18.50; singles €36; doubles €52; quads €86.) **Postal Code:** 06081.

ORVIETO ☎0763

Perched on a plateau of volcanic rock, **Orvieto** (pop. 25,000) has a view of the rolling farmlands of Umbria that provides a perfect complement to a glass of its famous *Orvieto Classico* wine. Below the surface, caves and tunnels attest to the town's long history; Etruscans began burrowing into the hillside in the 7th century BC. Six hundred years of labor went into the construction of the breathtaking ▧ **Duomo**, whose spires, sculptures, and mosaics remain the pride and joy of Orvieto to this day. The **Capella della Madonna di San Brizio**, off the right transept, houses the dramatic Apocalypse frescoes of Luca Signorelli, whose compositions inspired Michelangelo. (*Duomo* open M-Sa 7:30am-12:45pm and 2:30-7pm, Su 2:30-6:45pm. Modest dress required. *Capella* open Apr.-Sept. M-Sa 10am-12:45pm and 2:30-7:15pm, Su 2:30-6pm; Oct.-Mar. reduced hours. €3.) **Underground City Excursions** offers the most complete tour of the ancient Etruscan city buried beneath modern Orvieto. (☎0763 34 48 91. Four 1hr. tours leave the tourist office daily 11:30-5:45pm. €5.50, students €3.50.)

   Trains run hourly to Florence (2½ hr., €9.70) and Rome (2½ hr., €7). From the train station, take a shuttle to the tourist office at P. del Duomo 24. (☎0763 34 17 72; fax 0763 34 44 33. Open M-F 8:15am-1:50pm and 4-7pm, Sa 10am-1pm and 4-7pm, Su 10am-noon and 4-6pm.) Walk up V. Duomo to reach **Hotel Posta ❸**, V. Luca Signorelli 18, situated in a grand old building with antique decorations. (☎0763 34 19 09. Singles €31; doubles €44.) For free tasting of *Orvieto Classico* or another wine that piques your interest, try **Cantina Freddano**, C. Cavour 5. (☎0763 30 82 48. Open daily 9:30am-7:30pm. Bottles from €4.) **Postal Code:** 05018.

THE MARCHES (LE MARCHE)

In the Marches, green foothills separate the gray shores of the Adriatic from the Apennine peaks and traditional hill towns from umbrella-laden beaches. Inland towns, easily accessible by train, rely on agriculture and preserve the region's historical legacy in the architectural remains of Gauls and Romans.

URBINO   ☎0722

With picturesque stone dwellings scattered along steep city streets and a turreted palace ornamenting its skyline, Urbino (pop. 15,000) encompasses all that is classic Italy. The city's most remarkable monument is the imposing Renaissance **Palazzo Ducale**, in P. Rinascimento, though its facade is more thrilling than its interior. The central courtyard is the essence of Renaissance balance and proportion; to the left, stairs lead to the former private apartments of the Duke, which are now home to the **National Gallery of the Marches**. (Open M 8:30am-2pm, Tu-F and Su 8:30am-7:15pm, Sa 8:30am-10:30pm. €4, students €2.) Walk back across P. della Repubblica and continue onto V. Raffaello to Raphael's birthplace, the **Casa di Rafaele**, V. Raffaello 57, now a museum that contains a reproduction of his earliest work, *Madonna e Bambino*. (Open M-Sa 9am-1pm and 3-6pm, Su 10am-1pm. €3.)

   Bucci **buses** (☎0722 13 24 01) go from Borgo Mercatale to Rome (5hr., 1 per day, €19). Blue SOBET **buses** (☎0722 223 33) run to P. Matteotti and the train station in Pesaro, which sends trains on to Ancona (1hr., 4-10 per day, €2.10). From there, a short walk uphill on V.G. Mazzini leads to **P. della Repubblica**, the city center. The **tourist office**, V. Puccinatti 35, is opposite the palace. (☎0722 26 13; fax 0722 24 41. Open M-F 9am-1pm and 3-6pm. Hours change frequently.) **Pensione Fosca ❷**, V. Raffaello 67, has large rooms five doors down from Rafael's birthplace. (☎32 96 22. Singles €21; doubles €40; triples €43.) **Hotel San Giovanni ❷**, V. Barocci 13, has simple, clean rooms. (☎0722 28 27. Open Aug.-June. Singles €23, with bath €33; doubles €34/50.) **Margherita supermarket** is at V. Raffaello 37. (Open M-Sa 7:30am-2pm and 3-8pm.) **Postal Code:** 61029.

ITALY

ANCONA   ☎071

Ancona (pop. 100,000) is Italy's major transportation hub for those heading east. Though industry and transportation are the main functions of this busy town, the old city provides a pleasant atmosphere for those passing through town. The **Piazzale del Duomo**, atop Monte Guasco, offers a view of the red rooftops of the town below. (Open M-Sa 8am-noon and 3-6pm, Su hours vary with Mass schedule.) **Ferries** leave Stazione Marittima for Greece, Croatia, and northern Italy. **Adriatica** (☎071 50 211; www.adriatica.it), **Jadrolinija** (☎071 20 43 05; www.jadrolinija.tel.hr/jadrolinija), and **SEM Maritime Co.** (☎071 20 40 90; www.sem.hr) run to Croatia (from €37). **ANEK** (☎071 207 46; www.anek.gr) and **Blue Star** (Strintzis) (☎071 207 10 68; www.strinzis.gr) ferries go to Greece (from €50). Departure times and frequency vary, so consult a schedule ahead of time. Schedules and tickets are available at the Stazione Marittima. **Trains** arrive at P. Rosselli from: Bologna (2½hr., 1-2 per hr., €12); Milan (5hr., 1-2 per hr., €21); Rome (3-4hr., 9 per day, €15); and Venice (5hr., 3 per day, €15). Take bus #1/4 (€0.80) along the port past Stazione Marittima and up C. Stamira to reach P. Cavour, the city center. The **tourist office** in Stazione Marittima provides ferry info. (☎071 20 11 83. Open June-Sept. Su-M 8am-2pm, Tu-Sa 8am-8pm.) From the train station, cross the *piazza*, turn left, then take the first right and make a sharp right behind the newsstand to reach the **Ostella della Gioventù ❶**, V. Lamaticci 7. (☎071 42 257. Reception daily 6:30-11am and 4:30pm-midnight. Dorms €13.) **CONAD supermarket** is at V. Matteotti 115. (Open M-Sa 8-1:30pm and 5-7:30pm.) **Postal Code:** 60100.

SOUTHERN ITALY

South of Rome, the sun gets brighter, the meals longer, and the passion more intense. The introduction to the *mezzogiorno* (Southern Italy) begins in Campania, the fertile cradle of the Bay of Naples and the Gulf of Salerno. The shadow of Mt. Vesuvius hides the famous ruins of Pompeii, lost to time and a river of molten lava, while the Amalfi Coast cuts a dramatic course down the lush Tyrrhenian shore. The region remains justly proud of its open-hearted populace, strong traditions, classical ruins, and relatively untouristed beaches.

NAPLES (NAPOLI)   ☎081

Italy's third-largest city, Naples (pop. 1,000,000) is also its most chaotic—shouting merchants flood markets, and summer traffic jams clog the broiling city. Striving to shed its bad reputation, Naples has made many improvements in recent years despite continuing problems with poverty and unemployment, including increased efforts to maintain its numerous architectural and artistic treasures. Public art and artisan's workshops abound, as well as some of Italy's most colorful *trattorie*, and of course, Neapolitan *pizzarie*—peerless throughout the world.

⌷ TRANSPORTATION

Flights: Aeroporto Capodichino, V. Umberto Maddalena (NAP; ☎081 789 61 11), northwest of the city. Connects to all major Italian and European cities. A CLP **bus** (☎081 531 16 46) leaves from P. Municipio (20min., 6am-10:30pm, €1.55).

Trains: Ferrovie dello Stato goes from Stazione Centrale to: **Brindisi** (5hr., 5 per day, €19); **Milan** (8hr., 13 per day, €50); **Rome** (2hr., 34 per day, €9.60). **Circumvesuviana** (☎081 772 24 44), heads for **Herculaneum** (€1.55) and **Pompeii** (€1.90).

ITALY

Ferries: Depart from **Molo Angioino** and **Molo Beverello**, at the base of P. Municipio. From P. Garibaldi, take tram #1; from P. Municipio, take the R2 bus. **Caremar,** Molo Beverello (☎081 551 38 82), goes frequently to **Capri** and **Ischia** (both 1½hr., €5). **Tirrenia Lines,** Molo Angioino (☎081 720 11 11), goes to **Palermo, Sicily,** and **Cagliari, Sardinia.** Schedules and prices change frequently, so check *Qui Napoli* (free at the tourist office).

Public Transportation: Giranapoli tickets (€0.80 per 1½hr., full-day €2.35) are valid on **buses, Metro, trams,** and **funiculars.**

Taxis: Free (☎081 551 51 51) or **Napoli** (☎081 556 44 44). Only take metered taxis.

✈🛈 ORIENTATION AND PRACTICAL INFORMATION

The main train and bus terminals are in the immense **Piazza Garibaldi** on the east side of Naples. From P. Garibaldi, broad **Corso Umberto I** leads southwest to P. Bovi, from which V. de Pretis leads left to **Piazza Municipio,** the city center, and **Piazza Trieste e Trento** and **Piazza Plebiscito.** Below P. Municipio lie the **Stazione Marittima** ferry ports. From P. Trieste e Trento, **Via Toledo** (also known as **Via Roma**) leads through the Spanish quarter to **Piazza Dante.** Make a right into the historic **Spaccanapoli** neighborhood, which follows **Via dei Tribunali** through the middle of town. While violence is rare in Naples, theft is fairly common, so exercise caution.

Tourist Offices: EPT (☎081 26 87 79), at Stazione Centrale. Helps with hotels and ferries. Grab ▧**Qui Napoli,** a monthly tourist publication full of schedules and listings. Open M-Sa 9am-8pm. **Branch** at Stazione Mergellina.

Consulates: Canada, V. Carducci 29 (☎081 40 13 38). **South Africa,** C. Umberto 1 (☎081 551 75 19). **UK,** V. dei Mille 40 (☎081 423 89 11). **US,** P. della Repubblica (☎081 583 81 11, emergency 03 37 94 50 83), at the west end of Villa Comunale.

Currency Exchange: Thomas Cook, at the airport (☎081 551 83 99). Open M-F 9:30am-1pm and 3-6:30pm.

Emergency: ☎113. **Police:** ☎113 or 081 794 11 11. English spoken.

Hospital: Cardarelli (☎081 747 28 59), on the R4 line. **Ambulance:** ☎081 752 06 96.

Internet Access: Internet Point, V. Toledo 59A, across from the Bank of Naples (☎081 497 60 90). €2 per hr. Open daily 9:30am-8:30pm. **Internetbar,** P. Bellini 74 (☎081 29 52 37). €3 per hr. Open M-Sa 9am-2am, Su 8am-2am.

Post Office: P. Matteotti (☎081 552 42 33), at V. Diaz on the R2 line. Address mail to be held: First name, SURNAME, *In Fermo Posta,* P. Matteotti, Naples **80100,** ITALY. Open M-F 8:15am-6pm, Sa 8:15am-noon.

▮ ACCOMMODATIONS

Although Naples has some fantastic bargain lodgings, especially near **Piazza Garibaldi,** be cautious when choosing a room. Avoid hotels that solicit customers at the station, never give your passport until you've seen the room, agree on the price *before* unpacking, be alert for unexpected costs, and gauge how secure a lodging seems. The **ACISJF/Centro D'Ascolto,** at Stazione Centrale, helps women find safe rooms. (☎081 28 19 93. Open M-Tu and Th 3:30-6:30pm.) Rooms are scarce in the historic district between P. Dante and the *duomo.*

WATERFRONT

Ostello Mergellina (HI), V. Salita della Grotta, 23 (☎081 761 23 46; fax 081 761 23 91). M: Mergellina. From the Metro station, make 2 sharp rights onto V. Piedigrotta and then a right onto V. Salita della Grotta. Turn right on the long driveway after overpass. Outstanding views of Vesuvius and Capri from terrace area. Laundry €5.20. Lockout 9am-3pm. Strict curfew 12:30am. Dorms €14; doubles €54. ❷

TRAIN STATION

■ **Casanova Hotel,** C. Garibaldi 333 (☎081 26 82 87; www.hotelcasanova.com). From P. Garibaldi, continue down C. Garibaldi and turn right before V. Casanova. Clean, airy rooms, and a rooftop terrace. Breakfast €4. Reserve ahead. Singles €23-26, with bath €26-30; doubles €38-42/47-52; triples €55-68; quads €69-78. 10% *Let's Go* discount. AmEx/MC/V. ❸

■ **Hostel Pensione Mancini,** V. Mancini 33 (☎081 553 67 31; www.hostelpensionemancini.com), off the far end of P. Garibaldi from the train station. Multilingual, friendly owners share their encyclopedic knowledge of Naples. Spacious, newly renovated rooms. Check-in and check-out noon. Dorms €18; singles €35; doubles €45, with bath €55; triples €80; quads €90. ❷

Hotel Zara, V. Firenze 81 (☎081 28 71 25; www.hotelzara.it). Quiet, spacious, newly renovated rooms, all with TV and A/C. Singles €30; doubles €45, with bath €55; triples €75. 5% *Let's Go* discount. ❷

Hotel Ginevra, V. Genova 116 (☎081 28 32 10; www.hotelginevra.it). Exit P. Garibaldi on C. Novara, then turn right on V. Genova; climb the steps to the 2nd floor. A short, well-lit walk from the train station, Ginerva is good for late-night arrivals. Clean, family-run establishment. Singles €25, with bath €45; doubles €45/50; triples €60/75; quads €70/80. 10% *Let's Go* discount when paying cash. AmEx/MC/V. ❸

HISTORIC CENTER

■ **Hostel Soggiorno Imperia,** P. Miraglia 386 (☎081 45 93 47). Take the R2 from the train station, walk up V. Mezzocannone through P.S. Domenico Maggiore, and enter the 1st set of green doors to the left on P. Miraglia. Clean rooms in a 16th-century *palazzo*. Call ahead. Dorms €16; singles €30; doubles €42; triples €60. ❷

6 Small Rooms, V. Diodato Lioy 18 (☎081 790 13 78), up from P. Monteolovieto. Larger rooms than its name suggests in a friendly atmosphere. There is no sign; look for the name on the call button. Dorms €16; singles €21. ❷

Hostel of the Sun, V. Melisurgo 15 (☎/fax 081 420 63 93; www.hostelnapoli.com), across the street from Bella Capri. Buzz #51 to get in. Young owners make this a happening spot. Large dorms and excellent private rooms. Internet access €2.60 per hr. Dorms €18; singles without bath €45; doubles €50, with bath €70; triples €70/90; quads €90/100. 10% *Let's Go* discount. ❷

Pensione Bella Capri, V. Melisurgo 4, door B, 6th fl. (☎081 552 94 94; www.bellacapri.it), at corner of V. Cristofor Colombo, across street from the port. Take the R2 bus to the end of V. de Pretis, cross the street, and turn onto V. Melisurgo. From courtyard enter door B and go to the 6th floor. Less-expensive alternative to the high-priced hotels on the waterfront, with great views of Vesuvius and the port. Singles €70; doubles €80; triples €110; quads €120. 10% *Let's Go* discount. AmEx/MC/V. ❺

Hotel des Artistes, V. Duomo 61 (☎081 44 61 55; www.hoteldesartistesnaples.it). Conveniently located for exploring the historic district's sites. Intimate and inviting, all 11 rooms have balconies and luxurious bedspreads, plus bath, phone, A/C, and TV. Singles €66-80; doubles €80-115; triples €95-120; quads €115-130. 10% *Let's Go* discount. AmEx/MC/V. ❺

HILLTOP

Pensione Margherita, V. Cimarosa 29, 5th fl. (☎081 578 2852; fax 556 7044), in the same building as the Centrale funicular station (go outside and around the corner to the right and buzz to enter). 19 rooms are large and share 6 spotless baths; some rooms with terraces. Endearing management, excellent views of Vesuvius and Capri, and low prices for this posh, peaceful residential area. Check-out 11am. Curfew 1am. Closed Aug. 1-15. Singles €32; doubles €58; triples €82. MC/V. ❸

ITALY

TO CAPODIMONTE (1km)

Via Santa Teresa degli Scalzi

Via Luigi

PIAZZA
CAVOUR

M **CAVOUR**

Via Matteo Imbriani

Via Foria

**Museo
Archeologico
Nazionale**

M

PIAZZA MUSEO
NAZIONALE

Via Salvator Rosa

Via Francesco Saverio Correra

Via S. Tomassi

Via E. Pessina

Via Bellini

Viale L. De Crecchio

Via Santa Maria di Constantinopoli

Via d. Anticaglia

Vico Gigante

Via Pisanelli

Vico San S. Paolo

**San Paolo
Maggiore**

V. D. Sapienza

Via Atri

6

PIAZZA
SAN
GAETANO

Salita Pontecorvo

PIAZZA
BELLINI

7

9

10

PIAZZA
MIRAGLIA

8

Via S. Maggiore

Salita Tarsia

Via Ventaglieri

11

12

**Cappella di
San Severo**

Via Nilo

Via San Biagio

PIAZZA
SANT'
ANGELO

SPACCANAPOLI

PIAZZA
DANTE

M

**Chiesa di
San Domenico
Maggiore**

14

Vico San
Severino

15

MONTESANTO M

Via Montesanto

Via Montesanto

**Stazione
Cumana**

**Chiesa di
Santo Spirito**

Via Toledo

Via San
Sebastiano

**Chiesa di
Gesù Nuovo**

Via Benedetto Croce

PIAZZA
SAN DOMENICO
MAGGIORE

Via Paladino

Via Mezzocannone

TO VOMERO
(500m)

Via P. Scura

Via Capitelli

PIAZZA GESÙ
NUOVO

**Chiesa di
Santa Chiara &
Convent of the Clarisse**

Via Santa Chiara

University

Via Monteoliveto

Via Diocmata

17

PIAZZA
MONTEOLIVETO

**Chiesa di Monteoliveto
Sant'Anna del Lombardi**

Via Santa Maria La Nova

Via Sedile di Portone

**Universial
Books**

Via Francesco Girardi

PIAZZA
CARITÀ

Via Chiostro

Via C. Battisti

Via C. Oberdan

PIAZZA MATTEOTTI

PIAZZA
BOVIO

Via Campodisola

TO CERTOSA DI
SAN MARTINO
& CASTEL
SANT'ELMO
(200m)

Via G. Sanfelice

Rua Catalana

Via A. de Gasperi

Via Cristoforo Colombo

PIAZZA SAN
SEPOLCRO

Corso Vittorio Emanuele

Vico San Sepulcro

Via A. Diaz

Via San Tommaso D'Aquino

Via Medina

Via De Pretis

Via Melisurgo

18

SPANISH QUARTER

Feltrinelli

V. P. di Tappia

Via Cervantes

19

TO VOMERO (500m)

F

**Palazzo
Municipale**

Via P. E. Imbriani

PIAZZA
MUNICIPIO

Via San Mattia

Via Santa Caterina Da Sien

Salita S. A. di Palazzo

**Funicular to
Vomero**

F

**Galleria
Umberto I**

Via Santa
Brigida

Via G. Verdi

Via Vittorio Emanuele III

Via Parco D. Castello

**Castel Nuovo
o Maschio
Angioino**

Molo Beverello

Via Giovanni Nicotera

**Chiesa di
San Fernando**

Via San Carlo

**Teatro
San
Carlo**

PIAZZA TRIESTE
E TRENTO

20

i

Entrance

**Palazzo
Reale**

Via Chiaia

Via Monte

Via Egiziaca a Forcella

PIAZZA
PLEBISCITO

Via Ferdinando Acton

TO VILLA
COMUNALE
(350m)

(1km)

US

**Chiesa di
San Francesco di Paola**

N

LG

ITALY

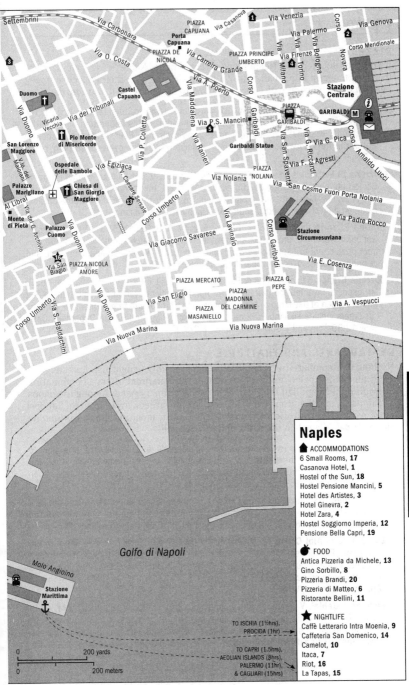

Naples

ACCOMMODATIONS
6 Small Rooms, **17**
Casanova Hotel, **1**
Hostel of the Sun, **18**
Hostel Pensione Mancini, **5**
Hotel des Artistes, **3**
Hotel Ginevra, **2**
Hotel Zara, **4**
Hostel Soggiorno Imperia, **12**
Pensione Bella Capri, **19**

FOOD
Antica Pizzeria da Michele, **13**
Gino Sorbillo, **8**
Pizzeria Brandi, **20**
Pizzeria di Matteo, **6**
Ristorante Bellini, **11**

NIGHTLIFE
Caffè Letterario Intra Moenia, **9**
Caffeteria San Domenico, **14**
Camelot, **10**
Itaca, **7**
Riot, **16**
La Tapas, **15**

▐ FOOD

PIZZERIE

If you ever doubted that Neapolitans invented pizza, Naples's *pizzerie* will take that doubt, beat it into a ball, throw it in the air, spin it on their collective finger, punch it down, cover it with sauce and mozzarella, and serve it *alla margherita*.

▧ **Gino Sorbillo,** V. Tribunali 32 (☎081 44 66 43; www.accademiadellapizza.it). The only *pizzeria* that boasts 21 pizza-making children in this generation alone and a grandfather who invented the *ripieno al forno* (calzone). Peer inside the kitchen to watch the frenzied action and original flame-spewing brick oven. Open daily noon-3:30pm and 7-11:30pm. MC/V. ❶

▧ **Pizzeria Di Matteo,** V. Tribunali 94 (☎081 45 52 62), near V. Duomo. Former President Clinton ate here during the G-7 Conference in 1994. The *marinara* is your best cheap bite (€2). Pies burst with flavor, and the building bursts with pizza aficionados—put your name on the list and expect a short wait. Open M-Sa 9am-midnight. ❶

Antica Pizzeria da Michele, V. Cesare Sersale 1/3 (☎081 553 92 04). From P. Garibaldi, walk up C. Umberto 1 and take the 1st right. Watch sweltering chefs toss pies from pizza-board to flame-licked oven and onto plates–all with superhuman grace and dexterity. Pizza €3.10-4.20. Open M-Sa 10am-11pm. ❶

Pizzeria Brandi, Salita S. Anna di Palazzo 1 (☎081 41 69 28), off V. Chiaia. In 1889, Mr. Esposito invented the *margherita* in Brandi's ancient oven to symbolize Italy's flag with the green of basil, red of tomato sauce, and white of *mozzarella di bufala*. Famous customers include Luciano Pavarotti, Isabella Rossellini, and Gerard Depardieu. Open daily 12:30-3pm and 7:30pm-late. AmEx/MC/V. ❷

RESTAURANTS AND TRATTORIE

Nothing can compare to Neapolitan **seafood;** locally caught fish and shellfish enjoy an exalted place on the city's tables. The **waterfront** offers a combination of traditional Neapolian fare and a change of culinary pace. Among the shops of **downtown,** small options can be found on side streets, away from the louder, more expensive trattorie. Some of the cheapest, most authentic options lie along **Via dei Tribunali** in the heart of Spaccanapoli.

Zorba's, V. Martucci 5 (☎081 66 75 72). M: Mergellina. 2 blocks off P. Amedeo, to the right as you exit the station; turn left at the sign, and it's 3 doors down. A delightful change of pace from the relentless pizza parade, serving good Greek fare. Open Su-F 8pm-1am, Sa 8:30pm-3am. Cash only. ❷

El Bocadillo, V. Martucci 50 (☎081 66 90 30; www.elbocadillo.it). M: Mergellina. Real Brazilian-style barbeque joint, serving tasty, juicy slabs of your favorite animal. The decor won't transport you, but the cuisine just might. Open daily 7pm-3am. ❷

La Cantina di Albi Cocca, V. Ascensione 6 (☎081 41 16 58). Take V. Vittoria Colonna from P. Amedeo, take the 1st right down a flight of stairs, turn right, and then left onto V. Ascensione. Hard to find, but this small, dimly lit restaurant is ideal for a romantic evening out. *Primi* €6-8. *Secondi* €8-10. Cover €1. Open M-Sa 1-3pm and 8pm-midnight. MC/V. ❸

Ristorante Bellini, V. Santa Maria di Constantinopoli 79-80 (☎081 45 97 74), off P. Bellini. Come for obliging service and an evening *al fresco*, surrounded by fragrant flowers and wrought-iron screens. Try the *linguine al cartoccio* (€11) or anything from the *pesce* menu. Open daily 9am-4pm and 7pm-1:30am. Closed Su in summer. MC/V. ❸

🖰 SIGHTS

🖾 MUSEO ARCHEOLOGICO NAZIONALE. Situated in the historical center within a 16th-century *palazzo* and former barracks, one of the world's most important archeological museums houses exquisite treasures from Pompeii and Herculaneum. The mezzanine contains a room filled with mosaics, most noticeably the Alexander Mosaic, which shows a young and fearless Alexander the Great routing a Persian army. A sporadically-open Egyptian Collection quietly inhabits the museum's basement. Peeking out from a beautifully painted sarcophagus is the foot of a real-life mummy. *(M: P. Cavour. Turn right as you exit the station and walk 2 blocks. Open Su-M and Th-Sa 9am-7:30pm. €6.50. Under-18 or over-65 free.)*

SPACCANAPOLI. Naples's most renowned neighborhood is replete with brilliant architecture and merits at least a 30min. stroll. The main sights get lost among ornate banks, *pensioni*, and *pasticcerie*, so watch for the shoebox-sized signs on buildings. Don't lose track of yourself while gaping at picturesque churches, *palazzi*, and alleyways, lest you find yourself staring at an oncoming *motorino*. To get to the Historic Center from P. Dante, walk through **Porta Alba** and past **Piazza Bellini** before turning down **Via dei Tribunali**, the former route of an old Roman road that now contains some of the city's best **pizzerie.**

DUOMO. The main attraction of the 14th-century *duomo* is the **Capella del Tesoro di San Gennaro**, decorated with Baroque paintings. A beautiful 17th-century bronze grille protects the high altar, which possesses a reliquary containing the saint's head and two vials of his coagulated blood. According to legend, disaster will strike the city if the blood does not liquify on the celebration of his **festa** (three times a year); miraculously, it always does. Behind the main altar of the church lies the saint's crypt, decorated with Renaissance carvings in white marble. Visitors can also view the newly opened underground **excavation site**, an intimate tangle of Greek and Roman roads constructed over several centuries. *(Walk 3 blocks up V. Duomo from C. Umberto I or take bus #42 from P. Garibaldi. Open M-F 9am-noon and 4:30-7pm, Sa-Su 8am-3:30pm and 5-7:30pm. Free; excavation site €3.)*

PALAZZO REALE AND CASTEL NUOVO. The 17th-century **Palazzo Reale** contains opulent royal apartments, the **Museo di Palazzo Reale**, and a fantastic view from the terrace of the **Royal Chapel**. The **Biblioteca Nazionale** stores 1.5 million volumes, including the scrolls from the **Villa dei Papiri** in Herculaneum. The **Teatro San Carlo** is reputed to top the acoustics in Milan's La Scala. *(Take the R2 bus from P. Garibaldi to P. Trieste e Trento and go around to the P. Plebiscito entrance. Open M and W-Su 9am-8pm. €4.20.)* From P. Trieste e Trento, walk up V. Vittorio Emanuele III to P. Municipio for the five-turreted **Castel Nuovo**, built in 1286 by Charles II of Anjou. The double-arched entrance commemorates the arrival of Alphonse I of Aragon in Naples. Inside, admire the **Museo Civico.** *(Open M-Sa 9am-7pm. €5.)*

NAPOLI E LA CITTA SOTTERRANEA/NAPOLI SOTTERRANEA. These tours of the subterranean alleys beneath the city are fascinating, but not for the claustrophobic: They will have you crawling through narrow underground passageways, grottoes, and catacombs, spotting Mussolini-era graffiti, and exploring Roman aqueducts. **Napoli e la Città** explores the area underneath Castel Nuovo and downtown, and **Napoli Sotterranea** drags you through the area under the historic center. *(Napoli e la Città office at V.S. Anna di Palazzo. ☎ 081 40 02 56. Tours Th 9pm; Sa 10am and 6pm; Su 10am, 11am, and 6pm. €5. Napoli Sotterranea, P.S. Gaetano 68. Go down V. Tribunali and turn left before San Paolo Maggiore. ☎ 081 29 69 44; www.napolisotterranea.com. Tours every 2hr. M-F noon-4pm; Sa-Su and holidays 10am-6pm. €5.)*

CHIESA DI SAN DOMENICO MAGGIORE. This 13th-century church has been restructured several times over the years, finally settling on a 19th-century Gothic interior. To the right of the altar in the Chapel of the Crucifix hangs the 13th-century painting that allegedly spoke to St. Thomas Aquinas, who lived in the adjoining monastery when Naples was a center of learning in Europe. Fine Renaissance sculptures decorate the side chapels. *(P.S. Domenico Maggiore. Open M-F 8:30am-noon and 5-8pm, Sa-Su 9:30am-1pm and 5-7pm.)*

🎵 🎭 ENTERTAINMENT AND NIGHTLIFE

Neapolitan nightlife is seasonal. Content to groove at the small clubs and discos during the winter, Neapolitans return to the streets and *piazzas* in summer. **Piazza Vanvitelli** in Vomero draws young people to relax and socialize. **Piazza San Domenico Maggiore** is another hotspot. Take the funicular from V. Toledo or bus C28 from P. Vittoria. Outdoor bars and cafes are a popular choice in **Piazza Bellini,** near P. Dante. **ARCI-GAY/Lesbica** (☎ 081 551 82 93) has info on gay and lesbian club nights.

CAFES, BARS, AND PUBS

Caffè Letterario Intra Moenia, P. Bellini 70. Appeals to intellectuals by keeping books amidst the wicker furniture. Outside, vines climb on walls, and the remains of a Roman building lie excavated in the ground. Open daily 10am-2am. AmEx/MC/V.

Itaca, P. Bellini 71. Black decor and eerie trance music will beckon to your dark side. Lip rings don't hinder patrons from guzzling candy-coated cocktails (€6-7). Beer €3-4. Open daily 10am-3am. AmEx/MC/V.

Cafeteria San Domenico, in P. San Domenico Maggiore. Packed every night with throngs of Neapolitan university students. Though there's plenty of outdoor seating, the tables are often packed. Shots €3-4. Mixed drinks €4.50-5.50. Open daily 7am-2am.

La Tapas, V. Paladino 56. A low-key favorite of university students and their professors, close to the bustling nightlife of P.S. Domenico Maggiore. Outdoor seating in an alcove just down V. Nilo from V. dei Tribunali. Enjoy the *sangria* (glass €1.60; liter €9). Open daily 7pm-2:30am.

NIGHTCLUBS AND DISCOTHECHE

Camelot, V.S. Pietro a Majella 8. Just off P. Bellini in the historic center, Camelot has 2 stories of dim lighting, good beer, and fantastically loud pop music. Beer €2.60. Open Sept.-June Tu-Su 10:30pm-5am.

Madison Street, V. Sgambati 47, in Vomero. Large dance floor for weekend revelry. Cover €10. Open Sept.-May F-Su 10pm-4am.

Riot, V.S. Biagio 39, off C. Umberto I. Hear local artists play jazz and sing the blues. Though usually low-key, crowds are often vociferous in support of the live performers. Open Th-Su 10:30pm-3am.

🔆 DAYTRIPS FROM NAPLES

Mount Vesuvius, the only active volcano on the European continent, looms over the area east of Naples. Its infamous eruption in AD 79 buried the nearby Roman city of **Ercolano** (Herculaneum) and neighboring **Pompeii.**

POMPEII. Since 1748, excavations have unearthed a stunningly well-preserved picture of Roman daily life. The site hasn't changed much since then, and neither have the victims, whose ghastly remains were partially preserved by plaster casts in the hardened ash. Walk down V.d. Marina to reach the colonnaded ◪**Forum,**

which was once the civic and religious center of the city. Exit the Forum through the upper end by the cafeteria, and head right on V. della Fortuna to reach the ▨House of the Faun, where a bronze dancing faun and the spectacular Alexander Mosaic (today in the Museo Archeologico Nazionale) were found. Continue on V. della Fortuna and turn left on V. dei Vettii to reach the **House of the Vettii,** on the left, and the most vivid frescoes in Pompeii. Back down V. dei Vettii, cross V. della Fortuna to V. Storto, turn left on V. degli Augustali, and take a quick right to reach a small **brothel** (the Lupenar), still popular after 2000 years. V. dei Teatri, across the street, leads to the oldest standing **amphitheater** in the world (80 BC), which once held up to 12,000 spectators. To get to the ▨**Villa of the Mysteries,** the complex's best-preserved villa, head west on V. della Fortuna, right on V. Consolare, and all the way up Porta Ercolano. (Archaeological site open daily 8:30am-7:30pm. €10.) Take the Circumvesuviana **train** (☎081 772 24 44) from Naples's Stazione Centrale to Pompeii (dir.: Sorrento; 2 per hr., €2.20). To reach the site, head downhill and take your first left to the west (Porta Marina) entrance. To reach the **tourist office,** V. Sacra 1, walk right from the station and continue to the bottom of the hill. (Open M-F 8am-3:30pm, Sa 8am-2pm.) The on-site cafeteria is expensive, so bring lunch.

HERCULANEUM. Herculaneum is 500m downhill from the *Ercolano* stop on the Circumvesuviana **train** from Naples (dir.: Sorrento; 20min., €1.90). Stop at the **tourist office,** V. IV Novembre 84 (☎081 88 12 43), to pick up a free map. The city is less excavated than Pompeii because it was buried much deeper and a modern city sits on top; highlights include the **House of Deer.** (Open daily 8:30am-7:30pm. €10.)

MOUNT VESUVIUS. You can peer into the only active volcano on mainland Europe at Mt. Vesuvius. Trasporti Vesuviani **buses** (buy ticket on board; round-trip €3.10) run from the Ercolano Circumvesuviana station to the crater. Although Vesuvius hasn't erupted since March 31, 1944 (and scientists say volcanoes should erupt every 30 years), experts deem the trip safe.

CASERTA. Few palaces, no matter how opulent, can hold a candle to Caserta's glorious ▨**Reggia**—often referred to as "The Versailles of Naples." A world apart from the brutality of Pompeii, the palace and grounds resonate with a passion for art and beauty. When Bourbon King Charles III commissioned the palace in 1751, he intended it to rival Louis XIV's famously spectacular abode. Completed in 1775, the

THE LOCAL LEGEND

ARE YOU NOT ENTERTAINED?

Before Vesuvius set the city's residents scrambling with her blazing fury in AD 79, the crowds in Pompeii were yelling and stampeding in all directions for an entirely different reason.

The occasion for this melee was a *munera*, (gladiatorial matches). The Pompeiians and the Nucerians (fierce rivals in the Bay of Naples) had packed the amphitheater one hot summer day in AD 59 to see the show, and were now hurling insults at each other, as was their custom.

Such intensity is not surprising to those acquainted with Italy's modern-day sports scene; anyone who has heard the commotion that eminates from bars where soccer matches are televised knows that blood runs hot when foes are joined in close company. For the Pompeiians and the Nucerians it was no different. In fact, historical records suggest that the this rivalry was even more heated. After exhausting their repertoire of insults, the crowds began hurling stones as well, causing the eruption of a massive, no-holds-barred riot. Before it was over, fires had been set, many people were killed, and the city had plunged into a state of complete disarray. The Roman senate, as a punishment for the commotion, decreed that no games should be held for ten years—an awfully long time to wait for people so enthusiastic about them.

vast expanse of lush lawns, fountains, sculptures, and carefully pruned trees culminates in a 75m manmade waterfall—the setting for the final scene of the 1977 *Star Wars*. To the right are the English Gardens, complete with fake ruins inspired by Pompeii and Paestum. The **palazzo** boasts 1200 rooms, 1742 windows, 34 staircases, whose furnishings and decorations are equally grandiose. The Reggia is directly opposite the train station. (Open Su and Tu-Sa 9am-7:30pm. €6.) **Trains** run from Naples (40min., 35 per day, €2.70).

AMALFI COAST

Tucked between the jagged rocks of the Sorrentine peninsula and the azure waters of the Adriatic, the Amalfi Coast has many alluring aspects. Its lush lemon groves bask in the sun, its local population is spirited and lively, and its monuments reflect the area's history as a maritime powerhouse, yet its oldest attribute—the area's natural beauty—remains the region's prime attraction.

▣ TRANSPORTATION. The coast is accessible from Naples, Sorrento, Salerno, and the islands by ferry and blue SITA buses. **Trains** run directly to Salerno from Naples (45min., 42 per day, €5-10) and Rome (2½-3hr., 19 per day, €22-33). Trains also run to Sorrento from Naples (1hr., 29 per day, €3). **Buses** link Paestum and Salerno (1hr., every hr. 7am-7pm, €2.80). From Salerno, Travelmar (☎089 87 31 90) runs **ferries** to Amalfi (35min., 6 per day, €3.60) and Positano (1¼hr., 6 per day, €5.30). From Sorrento, Linee Marittime Partenopee (☎081 807 18 12) ferries (40min., 5 per day 8:30am-4:50pm, €6.50) and **hydrofoils** (20min., 17 per day 7:20am-5:40pm, €9.50) run to Capri.

AMALFI AND ATRANI. Breathtaking natural beauty surrounds the narrow streets and historic monuments of Amalfi. Visitors crowd P. del Duomo to admire the elegant 9th-century **Duomo di Sant'Andrea** and the nearby **Fontana di Sant'Andrea,** a marble nude with water spouting from her breasts. **A'Scalinatella ❶,** P. Umberto 12, has hostel beds and regular rooms all over Amalfi and Atrani. (☎089 87 19 30. Dorms €10-21; doubles €26-50, with bath €40-80.) The tiny beachside village of Atrani is a 15min. walk around the bend from Amalfi. The **Path of the Gods,** a spectacular 3hr. hike, follows the coast from Bomerano to Positano. The 2hr. hike to **Ravello** via Scalla also makes a for a pleasant trip. **Postal Code:** 84011.

RAVELLO. Perched atop 330m cliffs, Ravello has provided a haven for many celebrity artists over the years. The Moorish cloister and gardens of **Villa Rufolo,** off P. Duomo, inspired Boccaccio's *Decameron* and Wagner's *Parsifal*. (Open daily 9am-8pm. €4.) Classical music **concerts** are performed in the gardens of the Villa Rufolo; call the Società di Concerti di Ravello (☎089 85 81 49) for more info. The small road to the right leads to the impressive **Villa Cimbrone,** whose floral walkways and gardens hide temples and statue-filled grottoes. The area also offers magnificent views. (Open daily 9am-7:30pm. €4.50.) **Hotel Villa Amore ❹,** V. dei Fusco 5, has 12 tidy rooms and a garden overlooking the cliffs and sea. (☎/fax 089 85 71 35. Singles €48-60; doubles €74-85. MC/V.) **Postal Code:** 84010.

POSITANO. Today, Positano's most frequent visitors are the wealthy few who can afford the pricey *Positanese* lifestyle, yet the town has its charms for the budget traveler. To see the large *pertusione* (hole) in **Montepertuso,** one of three perforated mountains in the world, hike 45 min. uphill or take the bus from P. dei Mulini. Positano's **beaches** are also popular; the beach at **Fornillo** is a nicer, quieter alternative to the area's main beach, **Spaggia Grande.** The **tourist office,** V. del Saraceno 4, is below the *duomo*. (☎089 87 50 67. Open M-Sa 8am-2pm and 3-8pm;

reduced hours off-season.) **Ostello Brikette ❷**, V.G. Marconi 358, 100m up the main coastal road to Sorrento from Viale Pasitea, has incredible views from two large terraces. (☎089 87 58 57. Dorms €22; doubles €70.) Prices in the town's restaurants reflect the high quality of the food. For a sit-down dinner, thrifty travelers head toward the beach at Fornillo.

SORRENTO. The most heavily touristed town on the peninsula, lively Sorrento makes a convenient base for daytrips around the Bay of Naples. The **tourist office**, L. de Maio 35, is off P. Tasso. (☎081 807 40 33. Open Apr.-Sept. M-Sa 8:45am-7:45pm; Oct.-Mar. reduced hours.) Halfway to the free **beach** at **Punta del Capo** (bus A), **Hotel Elios ❷**, V. Capo 33, has comfy rooms. (☎081 878 18 12. Open Apr.-Oct. Singles €25-30; doubles €45-55.) It's easy to find good, affordable food in Sorrento. ▧**Davide,** V. Giuliani 39, off C. Italia, two blocks from P. Tasso, has divine *gelato* and masterful *mousse*. (Open daily 10am-midnight.) After 10:30pm, a crowd gathers for drinks in the rooftop lemon grove above **The English Inn,** C. Italia 56. (Open daily 9am-1am.) **Postal Code:** 80067.

SALERNO AND PAESTUM. Industrial **Salerno** is best used as a base for daytrips to nearby **Paestum,** the site of spectacularly preserved ▧**Doric temples,** including the **Temple of Ceres** and the **Temple of Poseidon,** as well as a **museum** with artifacts taken from the sites. (Temples open daily 9am-7:30pm. Museum open daily 9am-6:30pm. Reduced hours for both off-season. Both closed 1st and 3rd M each month. €6.50 includes both sites.) To reach the clean and comfortable **Ostello Per La Gioventù ❷,** V. Canali, take C. C. Emanuele into the old district, where it becomes V. dei Mercanti, and head left onto V. Canali. (☎089 23 47 76. Lockout 10:30am-3pm. Curfew 12:30am. Dorms €16; doubles €50.) **Postal Code:** 84100.

BAY OF NAPLES ISLANDS ☎081

CAPRI. There are two towns on the island of Capri—**Capri proper,** near the ports, and **Anacapri,** higher up the mountain. Visitors flock to the renowned **Blue Grotto,** a sea cave whose waters shimmer with neon-blue light. (Open daily 9am-5pm. Boat tour €8.50.) In the summer months crowds and prices increase; the best times to visit are in the late spring and early fall. **Buses** departing from V. Roma make the trip up the mountain to Anacapri every 15 min. until 1:40am. Away from the throngs flitting among Capri's expensive boutiques, Anacapri is home to budget hotels, spectacular vistas, and quiet mountain paths. Upstairs from P. Vittoria in Anacapri, **Villa San Michele** sports lush gardens, ancient sculptures, and a remarkable view. (Open daily 9:30am-6pm. €5.) To appreciate Capri's Mediterranean beauty from higher ground, take the chairlift up **Monte Solaro** from P. Vittoria. (Open Mar.-Oct. daily 9:30am-4:45pm. Round-trip €5.50.) For those who prefer cliff to coastline, Capri's hiking trails lead to stunning panoramas; try the short but strenuous hike to the ruins of Emperor Tiberius's **Villa Jovis,** the largest of his 12 Capri villas. Always the gracious host, Tiberius tossed those who displeased him over the precipice. The view from the **Cappella di Santa Maria del Soccorso,** built onto the villa, is unrivaled. (Open daily 9am-6pm.) In the evenings, dressed-to-kill Italians come out for Capri's nightlife; bars around **Piazza Umberto** in Capri proper keep the music pumping late, while cheaper Anacapri caters to a younger crowd.

Caremar (☎081 837 07 00) **ferries** run from Marina Grande to Naples (1¼hr., 6 per day, €8.50) and Sorrento (50min., 3 per day, €6.50). LineaJet (☎081 837 08 19) runs **hydrofoils** to Naples (40min., 10 per day, €11.50) and Sorrento (20min., €8.50). Ferries and hydrofoils to Ischia and Amalfi run with much less frequency and regularity; check with the lines at Marina Grande for details. The Capri **tourist office** (☎081 837 06 34) sits at the end of Marina Grande; in Anacapri, it's at V. Orlandi 59

ITALY

(☎081 837 15 24), to the right of the P. Vittoria bus stop. (Both open June-Sept. M-Sa 8:30am-8:30pm; Oct.-May M-Sa 9am-1:30pm and 3:30-6:45pm.) ◪**Alla Bussola di Hermes ❷**, V. Traversa La Vigna 14, in Anacapri, has a friendly proprietor and some of the best deals on the island. (☎081 838 20 10; bus.hermes@libero.it. Dorms €20-24 per person; doubles €50-65. AmEx/MC/V.) For more convenient access to the beach and the center of Capri, stay at the **Bed and Breakfast Tirrenia Roberts ❹**, V. Mulo 27. Walk away from P. Umberto on V. Roma and take the stairs on your right just before the fork. (☎081 837 61 19. Reserve well in advance. Doubles €80-105.) Bear right at the fork to reach **Dimeglio supermarket**. (Open M-Sa 8:30am-1:30pm and 5-9pm.) **Postal Codes:** Capri: 80073; Anacapri: 80021.

ISCHIA. Augustus fell in love with Capri's fantastic beauty in 29 BC, but later swapped it for its more fertile neighbor. Ischia, just across the bay, offers sandy beaches, natural hot springs, ruins, forests, vineyards, and lemon groves. Orange SEPSA **buses** #1, CD, and CS (every 20 min.; €1.20, day pass €4.80) depart from the ferry landing and follow the coast in a circular route, stopping at: **Ischia Porto,** a port formed by the crater of an extinct volcano; **Casamicciola Terme,** with a crowded beach and legendary thermal waters; **Lacco Ameno,** the oldest Greek settlement in the western Mediterranean; and popular **Forio,** home to lively bars. The **Motella Gardens,** V. Calese 39, feature acres of tropical plants, manmade streams and gorgeous views of Ischia. (Open daily 9am-7pm. €8).

Caremar **ferries** (☎081 98 48 18) arrive from Naples (1½hr., 14 per day, €6.20). Alilauro (☎081 18 88, www.alilauro.it) runs **hydrofoils** to Sorrento (6 per day; call ahead for prices and schedule). The **tourist office** is on Banchino Porto Salvo, in the main port. (☎081 507 42 31; fax 081 507 42 30. Open in summer daily 8am-2pm and 3-8pm; off-season reduced hours.) **Pensione Di Lustro ❸**, V. Filippo di Lustro 9, is near the beach. (☎081 99 71 63. Singles €34; doubles €50-65.) The **Ostello "Il Gabbiano" (HI) ❷**, Strada Statale Forio-Panza, 162, is accessible by buses #1, CS, and CD. The hostel has beach access as well as a friendly staff. (☎081 90 94 22. Lockout 9:30am-1pm. Curfew 2am. Open Apr.-Sept. Dorms €16.) **Camping Internazionale ❶** is at V. Foschini 22, 15min. from the port. Take V. Alfredo de Luca from V. del Porto; bear right on V. Michele Mazzella at P. degi Eroi. (☎081 99 14 49; fax 99 14 72. Open May-Sept. €6-9 per person, €3-10 per tent.) **Postal Code:** 80077.

SICILY (SICILIA)

Sicily is a land of sensuous sunshine and sinister shadows. Ancient Greek influences lauded the golden island as the second home of the gods; now eager tourists seek it as the home of *The Godfather*. While the *Cosa Nostra* remains a presence in Sicily, it makes up only the smallest part of the vivacious and varied culture.

▐ TRANSPORTATION

Tirrenia Ferries (☎091 33 33 00) offers extensive service. From southern Italy, take a **train** to Reggio di Calabria, then a NGI or Meridiano **ferry** (40min.; NGI: 10-12 per day, €0.55; Meridiano: 11-15 per day, €1.55) or Ferrovie Statale **hydrofoil** (☎096 586 35 40) to Messina, Sicily's transport hub (25min., 12 per day, €2.60). Ferries also go to Palermo from Sardinia (14hr., €42) and Naples (10hr., 2 per day, €38). **SAIS Trasporti** (☎091 617 11 41) and SAIS **buses** (☎091 616 60 28) serve destinations throughout the island. **Trains** head to Messina directly from Naples (4½hr., 7 per day, €22) and Rome (9hr., 7 per day, €30). Trains continue west to Palermo (3½hr., 15 per day, €11) via Milazzo.

PALERMO ☎091

From twisting streets lined with ancient ruins to the shrinking shadow of organized crime, gritty Palermo (pop. 700,000) is a city whose recent history provides shade and texture to a rich cultural heritage. To get to the magnificent **Teatro Massimo**, where the climactic opera scene of *The Godfather: Part III* was filmed, walk up V. Maqueda past the intersection of Quattro Canti and C. Vittorio Emanuele. (Open Su and Tu-Sa 10am-5:30pm. €3.) Up C. Vittorio Emanuele, the **Palazzo dei Normanni** contains the ◪**Cappella Palatina,** full of incredible golden mosaics. (Open M-Sa 9am-noon and 3-4:45pm, Su 9-10am and 11:15am-1pm.) The morbid **Cappuchin Catacombs,** in P. Cappuccini, are only for the strong of stomach. Eight thousand corpses and twisted skeletons line the underground labyrinth. To get there, take buses #109 or 318 from Stazione Centrale to P. Indipendenza and then transfer to bus #327. (Open daily 9am-noon and 3-5:30pm. €1.50.)

Trains leave Stazione Centrale, in P. Giulio Cesare, at V. Roma and V. Maqueda, for Florence (16hr., 3 per day, €46) and Rome (11hr., 8 per day, €42). All four **bus** lines run from V. Balsamo, next to the train station. After purchasing tickets, ask exactly where your bus will arrive and its logo. Ask at an **AMAT** or **Metro** information booth for a combined Metro and bus map. The **tourist office,** P. Castelnuovo 34, is opposite Teatro Politeama; from the train station, take a bus to P. Politeama, at the end of V. Maqueda. (☎091 605 83 51; www.palermotourism.com. Open June-Sept. M-F 8:30am-2pm and 2:30-6pm, Sa-Su 9am-1pm; Oct.-May. M-F 2:30-6pm.) Homey **Hotel Regina ❷,** C. Vittorio Emanuele 316, is off V. Maqueda. (☎091 611 42 16; fax 091 612 21 69. Singles €21, with bath €35; doubles €40/50.) The area around **Teatro Massimo** has a variety of cheap restaurants. **Postal Code:** 90100.

SYRACUSE (SIRACUSA) ☎0931

Never having regained the glory of its golden Grecian days, the modern city of Syracuse (pop. 130,000) takes pride in its extraordinary ruins. Syracuse's one-time role as one of the most powerful cities in the Mediterranean is still evident in the **Archaeological Park,** on the north side of town, which includes several sites. The enormous **Greek theater** is where 20,000 spectators watched Aeschylus premiere his *Persians.* To reach the well-preserved 2nd-century **Roman amphitheater,** follow C. Gelone until it meets V. Teocrito, then walk left down V. Augusto. (Open in summer daily 9am-7pm; off-season reduced hours. €4.50.) More ruins lie over the Ponte Umbertino on

IN RECENT NEWS

LA FAMIGLIA

Powerful because people owed them favors, strong because they supported one another, and feared because they did not hesitate to kill offenders, the Sicilian Mafia founded a brutal tradition that has dominated life since the late 19th century. The Mafia system has its roots in the *latifondi* (agricultural estates) of rural Sicily, where land managers and salaried militiamen protected their turf and people. Today, Sicilians avoid the topic, referring to the Mafia as *Cosa Nostra* (Our Thing). At a grass-roots level, the Mafia is said to have long controlled public works infrastructure, and farmers for years have lived in fear of land seizure and extortion. The Mafia was reported to have capitalized upon a drought in the summer of 2002 by stealing water from private wells and public water systems. Recent local resistance includes a farmers' group, Libera, that sells what it calls "anti-Mafia pasta," made from wheat grown on land seized from the Mafia by the government. Another jailed Mafia don's estate has been converted to a cooperative olive oil production site. Since the mid-80s, government efforts to curtail Mafia influence have had some success. Dozens of members of Mafia strongholds like the Corleone, mythologized by *The Godfather* films, have been arrested, and in August 2002, Palermo police confiscated an estimated €500 million in Mafia property.

Ortigia, the serene island on which the Greeks first landed. The ruined **Temple of Apollo** has a few columns still standing, but those at the **Temple of Diana** are much more impressive. Those who prefer tans to temples take bus #21, 22, or 24 to **Fontane Bianche,** a glitzy beach with plenty of discos.

Trains leave V. Francesco Crispi for Messina (3hr., 16 per day, €8.30) and Rome (12hr., 5 per day, €38). Interbus **buses,** V. Trieste 28 (☎0931 667 10), leave for Palermo (3hr., 5 per day, €14). To get from the train station to the **tourist office,** V.S. Sebastiano 43, take V.F. Crispi to C. Gelone, turn right on V. Teocrite, then left on V.S. Sebastiano; it's on the left. (☎0931 048 12 32. Open M-F 8:30am-1:30pm and 3:30-6:30pm, Sa 8:30am-1:30pm.) **Hotel Centrale ❷,** C. Umberto I 141, has clean rooms with astounding sea views. (☎0931 605 28. Singles €17; doubles €26; triples €35-37.) For cheap food, try places on **Via Savoia** and **Via Cavour,** or the open-air **market** in Ortigia, on V. Trento, off P. Pancali. (Open M-Sa 8am-1pm.)

AEOLIAN ISLANDS (ISOLE EOLIE)

Homer thought the Aeolian Islands to be the second home of the gods, and indeed, these last few stretches of unspoiled seashore border on the divine. Sparkling seas, smooth beaches, and fiery volcanoes testify to the area's stunning beauty.

▐ TRANSPORTATION

The archipelago lies off the Sicilian coast, north of **Milazzo,** the principal and least expensive departure point. Hop off a **train** from Palermo (3hr., €9.20) and onto an orange AST **bus** for the port (10min., every hr., free). Siremar (☎98 60 11) and Navigazione Generale Italiana (NGI; ☎090 98 30 03) **ferries** depart for Lipari (2hr., €6.20); Stromboli (5hr., €9.90); and Vulcano (1½hr., €5.70). **Hydrofoils** *(aliscafi)* make the trip in half the time, but cost twice as much. Both have ticket offices on V. Dei Mille facing the port in Milazzo. Ferries visit the islands less frequently from Molo Beverello port in Naples.

LIPARI. Lipari, the largest and most developed of the islands, is renowned for its amazing beaches and stunning hillside views. To reach the popular beaches of **Spiaggia Bianca** and **Porticello,** take the Lipari-Cavedi bus a few kilometers north to Canneto; Spiaggia Bianca is *the* spot for topless (and sometimes bottomless) sunbathing. Lipari's other offerings include a splendidly rebuilt medieval **castello,** the site of an ancient Greek acropolis. The fortress shares its hill with an **archaeological park,** the **San Bartolo church,** and the superb ▓**Museo Archeologico Eoliano,** up the stone steps off V. Garibaldi. (Open May-Oct. daily 9am-1:30pm and 4-7pm; Nov.-Apr. M-Su 9am-1:30pm and 3-6pm. €4.50.) The **tourist office,** C. Vittorio Emanuele 202, is near the ferry dock. (☎090 988 00 95; www.net-net.it/aasteolie. Open July-Aug. M-F 8am-2pm and 4:30-9:30pm, Sa 8am-2pm; Sept.-June reduced hours.) **Casa Vittorio ❷,** Vico Sparviero 15, is on a quiet street in the center of town. Rooms range from singles to a five-person penthouse. (☎090 981 15 23. €15-40 per person.) **Camp** at **Baia Unci ❶,** V. Marina Garibaldi 2, 2km from Lipari at the entrance to the hamlet of Canneto. (☎090 981 19 09. www.campeggitalia.it/sicilia/baiaunci. Reserve for Aug. Open mid-Mar. to mid-Oct. €8-12 per person, with tent.) Stock up at **UPIM supermarket,** C. Vittorio Emanuele 212. (Open M-Sa 8am-10pm.) ▓**Da Gilberto ❶,** V. Garibaldi 22-24, is known for its sandwiches. (☎090 981 27 56. Sandwiches from €3.50. Open 7am-4am; off-season 7am-2am.) **Postal Code:** 98050.

VULCANO. Black beaches, bubbling seas, and natural mud spas attract visitors from around the world to Vulcano. A steep 1hr. **hike** to the inactive **Gran Cratere** (Grand Crater) snakes between the volcano's noxious yellow fumaroles. On a clear day, you can see all the other islands from the top. The therapeutic **Laghetto di Fanghi** (Mud Pool) is just up V. Provinciale to the right from the port. If you would prefer not to bathe in sulfuric radioactive mud, you can step gingerly into the scalding waters of the **acquacalda,** where underwater volcanic outlets make the sea percolate like a jacuzzi, or visit the nearby black sands and clear waters of **Sabbie Nere.** (Follow the signs off V. Ponente.) To get to Vulcano, take the 10min. **hydrofoil** from the port at nearby Lipari (10min., 8 per day, €2.50). For more info, see the tourist office at V. Provinciale 41. (☎090 985 20 28. Open July-Aug. daily 8am-1:30pm and 3-5pm.) For **private rooms** *(affittacamere),* call ☎090 985 21 42. The Lipari tourist office also has information on Vulcano. **Postal Code:** 98050.

STROMBOLI. If you find luscious beaches and hot springs a bit tame, a visit to Stromboli's active **volcano,** which spews orange cascades of lava and molten rock about every 10min. each night, will quench your thirst for adventure. **Hiking** the *vulcano* on your own is **illegal** and **dangerous,** but **Magmatrek** offers tours, which also should be taken at your own risk. The group runs a 4hr. afternoon trek to the lower craters which emerged December 2002 from a new subterranean magma tunnel that broke through the volcano's crust along the side. As of summer 2003, treks to the top are illegal, but once the situation stabilizes, Magmatrek will resume their 6-7 hour excursions to the pinnacle. (☎/fax 090 986 57 68. Tours depart from V. Vittorio Emanuele. €13.50.) Bring sturdy shoes, a flashlight, snacks, water, and warm clothes; don't wear contact lenses, as the wind sweeps ash and dust everywhere. **Siremar** (☎090 98 60 11) runs an infrequent **ferry** from Milazzo to Stromboli, and boat rentals are readily available. From July to September, you won't find a room without a reservation; your best bet may be one of the non-reservable *affittacamere.* Expect to pay €15-30 for a room. The best value is ▥**Casa del Sole ❷**, on V. Giuseppe Cincotta, off V. Regina at the end of town. At the church of St-Bartholomew, take a right down the stairs and go straight down the alley. Large rooms face a shared terrace. (☎090 986 017. Open Mar.-Oct. €23, off-season reduced prices.) **Postal Code:** 98050.

SARDINIA (SARDEGNA)

When the vanity and cultivation of mainland Italy starts to wear thin, when one more church interior will send you into the path of the nearest speeding Fiat, Sardinia's savage coastline and rugged people will be a reality check for your soul. D. H. Lawrence sought respite here from the "deadly net of European civilization," and he found his escape among the wild horses, wind-carved rock formations, and pink flamingos of this remote island.

▤ TRANSPORTATION

Tirrenia **ferries** (☎081 317 29 99; www.tirrenia.it) run to **Olbia** from Civitavecchia, just north of Rome (6hr., 4 per day, from €30), and Genoa (9hr., 6 per week, from €28). They also chug to **Cagliari** from Civitavecchia (15-18hr., 2 per day, from €26); Genoa (20hr., July-Sept. 2 per week, from €37); Naples (16hr., Jan.-Sept. 1 per week, €26); and Palermo (13½hr., 1 per week, from €24). **Trains** run from Cagliari to Olbia (4hr., daily, €13) via Oristano (1½hr., 16 per day €4.55) and to Sassari (4hr., 2 per day, from €12). From Sassari, trains run to Alghero (40min., 11 per day, €1.80). PANI **buses** connect Cagliari to Oristano (1½hr., €5.80).

CAGLIARI ☎070

Cagliari combines the bustle and energy of a modern Italian city with the endearing rural atmosphere of the rest of the island. Its Roman ruins, medieval towers, and cobblestone streets contrast with the regal tree-lined streets and sweeping beaches downtown. Climb Largo Carlo Felice to reach the city's impressive **duomo,** P. Palazzo 3, with dazzling gold mosaics topping each of its entryways. Open daily 8am-12:30pm and 4-8pm.) The 2nd-century **Roman amphitheater** comes alive with concerts, operas, and classic plays during the summer **arts festival** in July and August. If you prefer to sun-worship, take city bus P, PQ, or PF to **Il Poetto** beach (20min., €0.80), which has pure white sand and turquoise water. The **tourist office** is on P. Matteotti. (☎070 66 92 55; fax 070 66 49 23. Open in summer M-Sa 8:30am-1:30pm and 2:30-7:30pm; off-season reduced hours.) **Albergo Palmas ❷,** V. Sardegna 14 is the town's best budget option. Cross V. Roma and turn right; take the first left on Largo Carlo Felice, and turn right onto V. Sardegna. (☎070 65 16 79. Singles €21; doubles €31-37. AmEx/MC/V.) **Postal Code:** 09100.

ALGHERO ☎079

Vineyards, ruins, and horseback rides are all a short trip away from Alghero's palm-lined parks and twisting medieval streets. The nearby ◪**Grotte di Nettuno,** an eerie, stalactite-filled 70-million-year-old cavern complex in Capo Caccia, can be reached by bus (1hr., 3 per day, round-trip €1.80). Visitors descend 632 steps between massive white cliffs. (Open Apr.-Sept. daily 9am-7pm; Oct. 10am-4pm; Nov.-Mar. 8am-2pm. €10.) The **tourist office,** P. Porta Terra 9, is to the right from the bus stop. (☎079 97 90 54. Open Apr.-Oct. M-Sa 8am-8pm, Su 10am-1pm; Nov.-Mar. M-Sa 9am-1pm.) To get to **Hotel San Francesco ❸,** V. Machin 2, walk straight from the tourist office and take the 3rd right. (☎079 98 03 30; www.sanfrancesco-hotel.com. Singles €35-43; doubles €62-77. MC/V.) **Postal Code:** 07041.

ORISTANO AND THE SINIS PENINSULA ☎0783

The town of Oristano is an excellent base for excursions to the nearby Sinis Peninsula. From the train station, follow V. Vittorio Veneto straight to P. Mariano, then take V. Mazzini to P. Roma to reach the town center (25min.). Rent a moped or car to explore the tranquil beaches, stark white cliffs, and ancient ruins on the mystical Sinis Peninsula. At the tip, 17km west of Oristano, lie the ruins of the ancient Phoenician port of **Tharros.** Take the ARST bus to *San Giovanni di Sinis* (dir.: Is Arutas; 40min., 5 per day, €1.50). Slightly to the north off the road to Cuglieri is **S'Archittu,** where people leap from a 15m limestone arch into the waters of a rocky inlet. ARST buses go to S'Archittu (30min., 7 per day, €1.45). The secluded white quartz sands of **Is Arutas** are well worth the trip. The ARST bus to Is Arutas runs only during July and August (50min., 5 per day, €1.50). The **tourist office,** V. Vittorio Emanuele 8, provides maps. (☎/fax 0783 30 32 12. Open M-F 9am-12:30pm and 4:30-8pm, Sa 9am-12:30pm.) **Piccolo Hotel ❸,** V. Martignano 19, on a quiet side street in the historic center, is spacious and tastefully decorated. (☎0783 71 500. Singles €31; doubles €52.) **Postal Code:** 09170.

LIECHTENSTEIN

A recent tourist brochure amusingly mislabeled the already tiny 160 sq. km country as an even tinier 160 sq. m. That's just about how much most tourists see of the world's only German-speaking monarchy, but the cliff-hugging roads are gateways to unspoiled mountains with great biking and hiking. Above the valley towns, cliff-hanging roads lead to places truly worth visiting—the quiet mountains offer hiking and skiing without the touristy atmosphere of many other alpine resorts.

HISTORY

Liechtenstein's miniscule size and minute population (33,000) belies its long and rich history. The **Romans** invaded in 15 BC, but with the coming of Christianity in the 4th century AD, **Germanic tribes** pushed the Romans out, bringing the area under the control of the German dukedom. Prince **Johann Adam** of Liechtenstein purchased the land and created the Principality of Liechtenstein in 1719, which **Napoleon** conquered in 1806. After the defeat, Liechtenstein became part of the **German Confederacy** in 1815 and was granted a constitution in 1862. It separated from Germany for good in 1866 when the German Confederation dissolved. Two years later Liechtenstein disbanded its army—an intimidating 80-man juggernaut—which it has not re-formed since. In 1938, Prince **Franz Josef** ascended the throne and continued the transformation of Liechtenstein from an impoverished nation into one of the wealthiest (per capita) in Europe. Following the example of the Swiss, Liechtenstein established itself as an extremely desirable tax haven for international companies with its strict banking secrecy policies. The country joined the United Nations in 1990 and the European Economic Area in 1995.

SUGGESTED ITINERARIES

BEST OF (OKAY, ALL OF) LIECHTENSTEIN, TWO SHORT DAYS.

Try to catch a glimpse of the ruling monarch and scope out the art collection at the **Staatliche Kunstmuseum** in capital city **Vaduz** (1 day; p. 748), then scan the Alps from the **Pfälzerhütte** on the sharp ridge above **Malbun** (1 day; p. 749).

ESSENTIALS

Capital: Vaduz.
Major Cities: Malbun, Schaan.
Population: 33,000.
Form of Government: Hereditary constitutional monarchy.

Land Area: 160 sq. km.
Major Exports: Dental products.
Language: German (see p. 1036).
Religions: Roman Catholic (80%), Protestant (7.4%), other (12.6%).

DOCUMENTS AND FORMALITIES. Citizens of Australia, Canada, the EU, New Zealand, South Africa, and the US do not need a visa for stays up to 90 days.

TRANSPORTATION. To enter Liechtenstein, catch a **bus** from **Sargans** or **Buchs** in Switzerland, or from **Feldkirch** just across the Austrian border (20min., 4SFr). Although trains from Austria and Switzerland pass through the country, Liechtenstein itself has no rail system. Instead, it has a cheap, efficient **Post Bus** system that links all 11 villages (short trips 3SFr; long trips 4SFr, students half-price; SwissPass valid). A **one-week bus ticket** (10SFr, students and seniors 5SFr) covers all of Liechtenstein as well as buses to Swiss and Austrian border towns. **Bicycles** are a great way to get around Lower Liechtenstein.

EMERGENCY. Police: ☎117. **Ambulance:** ☎144. **Fire:** ☎118.

MONEY. Liechtenstein uses the **Swiss Franc (SFr).** For currency exchange at acceptable rates, go to Switzerland. (Really.)

SWISS FRANC (SFR)		
	AUS$1 = 0.90SFR	1SFR = AUS$1.11
	CDN$1 = 1.01SFR	1SFR = CDN$0.99
	EUR€1 = 1.54SFR	1SFR = EUR€0.65
	NZ$1 = 0.80SFR	1SFR = NZ$1.24
	ZAR1 = 0.19SFR	1SFR = ZAR5.19
	US$1 = 1.41SFR	1SFR = US$0.71
	UK£1 = 2.23SFR	1SFR = UK£0.45

VADUZ AND LOWER LIECHTENSTEIN. As the national capital, Vaduz (pop. 5,000) attracts the most visitors of any village in Lichtenstein. Above town, the 12th-century **Schloß Vaduz** (Vaduz Castle) is home to Hans Adam II, Prince of Liechtenstein. The interior is off-limits to the masses; however, you can hike up to the castle for a closer look and a phenomenal view of the whole country. The 15min. trail begins down the street from the tourist office, heading away from the post office. Across the street from the tourist office is the **Kunstmuseum Liechtenstein,** Städtle 32. Mainly focusing on modern art, the museum boasts paintings by Dalí, Kandinsky, and Klee, as well as rotating special exhibits and installations. (Open Su, Tu-W and F-Sa 10am-5pm, Th 10am-8pm. 8SFr, students and seniors 5SFr.) Liechtenstein's national **tourist office,** Städtle 37, one block up the hill from the Vaduz Post Bus stop, stamps passports (2SFr), sells **hiking maps** (8-16SFr), and gives hiking advice. (☎232 14 43. Open July-Sept. M-F 8am-5:30pm, Sa-Su 9am-5pm; Oct.-June M-F 8am-noon and 1:30-5:30pm.) Budget lodgings in Vaduz are few and far between, but nearby **Schaan** is more inviting. Liechtenstein's sole **Jugendherberge** ❷, Untere Rüttig. 6, is in Schaan. From Vaduz, take bus #1 to *Mühleholz*, walk toward the intersection with traffic lights, and turn left down Marianumstr. Walk 5min. and follow the signs to this spotless pink hostel on the edge of a farm. (☎232 50 22. Breakfast included. Reception daily 5-10pm. Check-out 10am. Open Feb.-Oct. Dorms 30SFr; doubles 40SFr.) Your best bet for a cheap meal is **Migros supermarket,** Aulestr. 20, across from the tour bus parking lot in Vaduz. (Open M-F 8am-1pm and 1:30-7pm, Sa 8am-6pm.)

UPPER LIECHTENSTEIN. Just when it seems that the roads cannot possibly become any narrower or steeper, they do—welcome to Upper Liechtenstein. These heights are where the real character and beauty of Liechtenstein lie. Even if you're in the country for one day, take the short bus trip to **Triesenberg** or **Malbun** (30min. from Vaduz) for spectacular views of the Rhine Valley below. **Triesenberg** (take bus #10), the principal town, is spanned by a series of switchbacks and foothills 800m above the Rhine. The **tourist office** (☎262 19 26) shares a building with the **Walser Heimatmuseum,** which chronicles the history of the region. (Both open June-Aug. Su 2-5pm, Tu-F 1:30-5:30pm, Sa 1:30-5pm; Sept.-May Tu-F 1:30-5:30pm, Sa 1:30-5pm. Museum 2SFr.) For great hiking, take bus #34 to *Gaflei* (20min., every hr). **Malbun** sits in an alpine valley in the southeastern corner of Liechtenstein. It is undoubtedly the hippest place in the principality, home to approachable people, plenty of hiking, and affordable ski slopes (day-pass 33SFr). Contact the **tourist office** for more info. (☎263 65 77. Open June-Oct. and mid-Dec. to mid-Apr. M-Sa 9am-noon and 1:30-5pm.) The best place to stay for hiking and skiing access is **Hotel Alpen ❸,** which is close to the bus stop and tourist office. (☎263 11 81. Reception daily 8am-10pm. Open mid-May to Oct. and mid-Dec. to Apr. In summer 45-65SFr per person; in winter add 10SFr.)

LIECHTENSTEIN

LUXEMBOURG

Too often overlooked by budget travelers, the tiny Grand Duchy of Luxembourg boasts impressive fortresses and castles as well as beautiful hiking trails. Established in 963, the original territory was called *Lucilinburhuc*, named for the "little fortresses" that saturated the countryside after successive waves of Burgundians, Spaniards, French, Austrians, and Germans had receded. Today, Luxembourg has become a notable European Union member and a prominent international financial center. Judging by their national motto, *"Mir welle bleiwe wat mir sinn"* ("We want to remain what we are"), it seems that the Luxembourgians are pleased with their accomplishments.

LIFE AND TIMES

HISTORY

The Grand Duchy of Luxembourg has a long history of occupation and domination by its larger European neighbors. Ancient history saw Luxembourg inhabited by Belgic tribes and controlled by Romans. In the early Middle Ages, the territory was annexed by the Franks as part of Austrasia, and then claimed by **Charlemagne** as part of the Holy Roman Empire. Luxembourg became an independent region in AD 963, under the control of **Siegfried, Count d'Ardennes.** Siegfried's descendents ruled Luxembourg under the title of Count. The region became a duchy in 1354 by edict of Emperor Charles IV, but in 1443, the Duchess of Luxembourg was forced to give up the property to the Duke of Burgundy. Luxembourg passed into the hands of the Spanish **Habsburgs** in the early 16th century, only to be conquered by France after the devastating **Thirty Years' War** (1618-1648). During the 17th and 18th centuries, Luxembourg was tossed between France, Spain, and Austria. The year after the fall of **Napoleon** at Waterloo in 1814, the **Congress of Vienna** made Luxembourg a grand duchy and gave it to **William I,** King of The Netherlands. After the 1830 Belgian revolt against William, part of Luxembourg was ceded to Belgium, and the remainder was recognized as a sovereign and independent state. A subsequent economic union with Prussia brought industrialization to the previously agrarian country. The 1867 **Treaty of London** reaffirmed Luxembourg's autonomy and declared its neutrality, yet the 20th century found Luxembourg occupied by Germany during both world wars. After being liberated by the Allied powers in 1944, Luxembourg became a member of the **Benelux Economic Union,** along with The Netherlands and Belgium. It relinquished its neutral status in 1948 in order to join various international economic, political, and military

SUGGESTED ITINERARIES

THREE DAYS Spend all of it in **Luxembourg City,** one of Europe's most romantic capitals (p. 753). Marvel at the **Grand Ducal Palace** and wander underground through the **Casemates.**

BEST OF LUXEMBOURG, ONE WEEK Enjoy cosmopolitan **Luxembourg City** (3 days; p. 753), then explore the towns of Luxembourg's verdant **Ardennes** (p. 758). Head to the **Vianden** for a glimpse of the incredible chateau (1 day; p. 759), and then canoe down the Sûre River in **Diekirch** (1 day; p. 758). Finally, check out the moving Family of Man exhibit in little **Clervaux** (1 day; p. 759).

institutions, including **NATO** and the **United Nations.** It was also one of the six founding members of the **European Economic Community,** which later became the **European Union.**

TODAY

Luxembourg is one of the world's most industrialized countries, and it enjoys an economic security evidenced by the highest purchasing power and per capita income in Western Europe. The country is governed by a **constitutional monarchy,** in which the Grand Duke, currently **Henri I,** holds formal authority. The major executive and legislative power is vested in the prime minister, currently **Jean-Claude Juncker,** appointed by the Grand Duke, and in the Chamber of Deputies, elected by popular vote. Luxembourg has the greatest proportion of foreign residents of any Western European country. The Luxembourgian people have been significantly influenced by both German and French culture, but they maintain a distinct national identity.

ESSENTIALS

WHEN TO GO

Anytime between May and mid-Oct. is a good time to visit. Luxembourg has a temperate climate with less rain than Belgium. Temperatures average 17°C (64°F) in summer, and 0°C (32°F) in winter.

DOCUMENTS & FORMALITIES

VISAS. EU citizens do not need a visa. Citizens of Australia, Canada, New Zealand, and the US do not need a visa for stays of up to 30 days. South Africans need a visa for stays of any length. Contact your embassy for more info.

EMBASSIES AND CONSULATES. All foreign embassies are in Luxembourg City (p. 754). Embassies and consulates in other countries include: **Australia,** Level 18, Royal Exchange Bldg., 56 Pitt St., Sydney NSW 2000 (☎(02) 92 41 43 22; fax 92 51 11 13). **Canada,** 3706 St. Hubert St., Montréal, PQ H2L 4A3 (☎514-849-2101). **South Africa,** P.O. Box 357, Lanseria 1748 (☎(011) 659 09 61). **UK,** 27 Wilton Crescent, London SW1X 8SD (☎(020) 7235 6961; fax 7235 9734). **US,** 2200 Massachusetts Ave. NW, Washington, D.C. 20008 (☎202-265-4171; fax 328-8270).

TRANSPORTATION

BY PLANE. The Luxembourg City airport (LUX) is serviced by **Luxair** (☎479 81, reservations ☎4798 42 42) and by flights from the UK and throughout the continent. Cheap last-minute flights on Luxair are available at www.luxair.lu.

LUXEMBOURG

FACTS AND FIGURES

Official Name: Grand Duchy of Luxembourg.
Capital: Luxembourg City.
Population: 430,000.
Land Area: 2,600 sq. km.

Time Zone: GMT +1.
Languages: French, German, Luxembourgian.
Religions: Roman Catholic (90%).

BY TRAIN AND BUS. A **Benelux Tourrail Pass** allows five days of unlimited **train** travel in a one-month period in Belgium, The Netherlands, and Luxembourg (p. 47). The **Billet Réseau** (€4.60, book of 5 €19), a network ticket, is good for one day of unlimited bus and train travel. Even better is the **Luxembourg Card** (p. 757), which includes unlimited transportation. International train routes to Luxembourg include: Brussels (1¾hr.; p. 122) and Liège (2½hr.) in Belgium; Koblenz (2¼hr.; p. 485) and Trier (45min.; p. 486) in Germany.

BY BIKE AND THUMB. **Hiking** and **biking trails** run between Luxembourg City and Echternach, from Diekirch to Echternach and Vianden, and elsewhere. Bikes aren't permitted on buses, but are allowed on many trains for free. *Let's Go* does not recommend **hitchhiking** as a safe means of transport.

TOURIST SERVICES AND MONEY

EMERGENCY   Police: ☎112. Ambulance: ☎112. Fire: ☎112.

TOURIST OFFICES. For general info, contact the **Luxembourg National Tourist Office**, P.O. Box 1001, L-1010 Luxembourg (☎(352) 42 82 82 10; www.etat.lu/tourism). The **Luxembourg Card,** available from Easter to October at tourist offices, hostels, and many hotels and public transportation offices, provides unlimited transportation on national trains and buses and includes admission to 40 tourist sites (1-day €9, 2-day €16, 3-day €22).

MONEY. On January 1, 2002, the **euro** (€) replaced the **Luxembourg Franc** as the unit of currency in Luxembourg. The Luxembourg Franc can still be exchanged at a rate of 40LF to €1. For exchange rates and more info on the euro, see p. 14. The European Union imposes a **value-added tax (VAT)** on goods and services purchased within the EU (p. 16). Luxembourg's VAT (15%) is already included in most prices. Luxembourg's refund threshold (US$85) is lower than most other EU countries; refunds are usually 13% of the purchase price. The cost of living in Luxembourg is moderate to high. **Service** (15-20%) is included in the price; tipping extra for exceptional service is optional. Tip taxi drivers 10%.

BUSINESS HOURS. Most **banks** are open M-F 8:30am-4:30pm, and most **shops** are open M-Sa 10am-6pm with shorter hours on Sunday. However, some banks and shops close at noon for two hours, especially in the countryside.

COMMUNICATION

TELEPHONES. There are no city codes in Luxembourg; from outside the country, dial 352 plus the local number. Most public phones accept phone cards, which are sold at post offices and newspaper stands. **Mobile phones** are an increasingly popular and economical alternative to landlines (p. 30). International direct dial numbers include: **AT&T**, ☎8002 0111; **British Telecom**, ☎0800 89 0352; **Canada Direct**, ☎800 2 0119; **Ireland Direct**, ☎0800 353; **MCI**, ☎8002 0112; **Sprint**, ☎0800 0115; **Telecom New Zealand**, ☎800 20064.

PHONE CODES	Country code: 352. International dialing prefix: 00. Luxembourg has no city codes.

MAIL. Mailing a postcard or a letter (up to 50g) within Luxembourg costs €0.59, within the EU €0.74, and to the rest of the world €1.12.

LANGUAGES. French and German are the administrative languages; since a referendum in 1984, *Letzebuergesch*, a mixture of the two that sounds a bit like Dutch, is the national language. French is most common in the city, while German is more common in smaller towns. English is commonly spoken as a second, third, or fourth language.

ACCOMMODATIONS AND CAMPING

LUXEMBOURG	❶	❷	❸	❹	❺
ACCOMMODATIONS	under €12	€12-16	€17-30	€31-40	over €40

Luxembourg's 12 **HI youth hostels** (*Auberges de Jeunesse*) are often filled with school groups. Check the sign posted in any hostel to find out which hostels are full or closed each day. Prices range from €14-16; nonmembers usually pay €2.75-3 extra. Breakfast and sheets are included, a packed lunch costs €4, and dinner €8. Half of the hostels close from mid-November to mid-December, and the other half close from mid-January to mid-February. Contact **Centrale des Auberges de Jeunesse Luxembourgeoises** (☎ 26 29 35 00; www.youthhostels.lu) for info. **Hotels** generally cost €25-50 or more per night, depending on amenities; make sure you negotiate the price you will pay beforehand. Luxembourg is a **camping** paradise; most towns have campsites close by. Two people with a tent will typically pay €5-9 per night.

FOOD AND DRINK

LUXEMBOURG	❶	❷	❸	❹	❺
FOOD	under €5	€5-9	€10-14	€15-20	over €20

Luxembourgish cuisine combines elements of French and German cooking in a recipe all its own. Regional specialties include **Judd mat Gaardebounen** (smoked neck of pork with beans), **Friture de la Moselle** (fried fish), **Gromperen-kichelchen** (potato cakes), and **Kéiskuch** (cheesecake). **Reisling wines** are produced in the Moselle valley.

HOLIDAYS & FESTIVALS

Holidays: New Year's Day (Jan. 1); Carnival (Feb. 23); Easter (Apr. 11); Easter Monday (Apr. 12); May Day (May 1); Ascension Day (May 20); Whit Sunday and Monday (May 30-31); Grand Duke's Birthday Celebration (June 23); Assumption Day (Aug. 16); All Saints' Holiday (Nov. 1); Christmas (Dec. 25); and Saint Stephen's Day (Dec. 27).

Festivals: Luxembourg City hosts the Luxembourg City Fête (Sept. 6).

LUXEMBOURG CITY

With a medieval fortress perched on a cliff that overlooks lush green river valleys, and high bridges stretching over the downtown area, Luxembourg City (pop. 84,000) is one of the most beautiful and dramatic capitals in Europe. As an international banking capital, it is home to thousands of frenzied foreign business executives; even so, most visitors find it surprisingly relaxed and idyllic.

LUXEMBOURG

▐▀ TRANSPORTATION

Flights: Findel International Airport (LUX), 6km from the city. Bus #9 (€1.20) is cheaper than the Luxair bus (€3.70) and runs the same route every 10-20min.

Trains: Gare CFL, av. de la Gare (toll-free info ☎49 90 49 90; www.cfl.lu), 15min. south of the city center. To: **Amsterdam** (6hr.; every hr.; €45, under-26 €35); **Brussels** (2¾hr., every hr., €25/14); **Ettelbrück** (25min., 2 per hr., €4.60); **Frankfurt** (4½hr., every hr., €46); **Paris** (4hr., every 2hr., €42/31).

Buses: Within the city, buy a *billet courte distance* (short-distance ticket; 1hr. €1.20, package of 10 €9.20) or a *billet réseau* (day pass; €4.60, package of 5 €19). Tickets are valid on buses and trains throughout the country; a day pass is the most economical option for intercity travel. Buses run until midnight; night buses offer limited service.

Taxis: Colux Taxis, ☎48 22 33. €2.04 per km. 10% premium 10pm-6am. €20 from the city center to the airport.

Bikes: Rent from **Vélo en Ville,** 8 r. Bisserwé (☎47 96 23 83), in the Grund. Open daily 10am-noon and 1-8pm. €5 per hr., €13 per half-day, €20 per day, €38 per weekend, €75 per week. Under-26 20% discount.

▚ ▐ ORIENTATION AND PRACTICAL INFORMATION

Five minutes by bus and 15min. by foot from the train station, Luxembourg City's historic center revolves around the **place d'Armes**. Facing the municipal tourist office, located in the commemorative Town Hall, turn right down r. Chimay to reach **Boulevard Roosevelt.**

Tourist Offices: Grand Duchy National Tourist Office (☎42 82 82 20; www.etat.lu/ tourism), in the train station. Open June-Sept. 8:30am-6:30pm, Oct.-May 9:15am-12:30pm and 1:45-6pm. **Municipal Tourist Office,** pl. d'Armes (☎22 28 09; www.ont.lu). Open Apr.-Sept. M-Sa 9am-7pm, Su 10am-6pm; Oct.-Mar. M-Sa 9am-6pm, Su 10am-6pm. Also, look for the helpful, yellow-shirted **"Ask Me"** representatives all over the city—they give out free tourist info. **Centre Information Jeunes,** 26 pl. de la Gare (☎26 29 32 00), inside Galerie Kons across from the train station, is a great service for young people, providing free **Internet** access for students (1hr. max.) and info on everything from hostels to finding jobs. Open M-F 10am-6pm.

Embassies: Ireland, 28 r. d'Arlon (☎45 06 10; fax 45 88 20). Open M-F 10am-12:30pm and 2:30-5pm. **UK,** 14 bd. Roosevelt (☎22 98 64; fax 22 98 67). Open M-F 9am-12:30pm. **US,** 22 bd. Emmanuel Servais (☎46 01 23; www.amembassy.lu). Open M-F 8:30am-5:30pm. **Australians, Canadians, New Zealanders,** and **South Africans** should contact their embassies in France or Belgium.

Currency Exchange: Banks are the only option for changing money or cashing traveler's checks. Most are open M-F 8:30am until 4 or 4:30pm. All are closed on weekends. Expect to pay a commission of €5 for cash and €8.30 for traveler's checks.

Luggage Storage: In train station. €3 per day. Open daily 6:30am-9:30pm.

Laundromat: Quick Wash, 31 r. de Strasbourg, near the station. Wash and dry €10. Open M-Sa 8:30am-6:30pm.

Emergency: Police: ☎113. **Ambulance:** ☎112.

Pharmacy: Pharmacie Goedert, 5 pl. d'Armes (☎22 33 99). Open M 1-6:15pm, Tu-F 8am-6:15pm, Sa 8am-12:30pm. Check pharmacy window for night info.

Medical Services: Doctors and pharmacies on call: ☎112. **Clinique Ste-Therese,** r. Ste-Zithe 36 (☎49 77 61 or 49 77 65).

Internet Access: Center Information Jeunes has free Internet for students. **Cyber-Grund,** 2 r. Saint Ulric (☎26 20 39 55), in the Grund. €2 per 30min., €3 per hr. (50% discount Tu-F 12:30-3:30pm.) Open Tu-F 12:30-6:30pm, Sa 1:30-5pm. **Sp@rky's,** 11a av. Monterey (☎20 12 23), at the pl. d'Armes. €0.10 per min. Open M-Sa 7am-1am.

Post Office: 38 pl. de la Gare, across the street and left of the train station. Open M-F 6am-7pm, Sa 6am-noon. Address mail to be held: Firstname SURNAME, *Poste Restante,* **L-1009** Luxembourg G-I Gare, LUXEMBOURG. **Branch office,** 25 r. Aldringen, near the pl. d'Armes. Open M-F 7am-7pm, Sa 7am-5pm.

▐ ACCOMMODATIONS

The city hostel is the only budget option in Luxembourg City. Hotels are cheaper near the train station than in the city center, but are often a splurge nonetheless.

Youth Hostel (HI), 2 r. du Fort Olisy (☎22 19 20; luxembourg@youthhostels.lu). Take bus #9 and ask to get off at the hostel stop; head under the bridge and turn right down the steep path. Open, but under renovation until 2005. Breakfast and sheets included. 6-night max. stay in summer. Reception 24hr. Dorms €17; singles €25; doubles €39. Nonmembers add €3. ❷

Bella Napoli, 4 r. de Strasbourg (☎48 46 29). Simple rooms with hardwood floors and full bath. Breakfast included. Reception daily 8am-midnight. Singles €38; doubles €45; triples €60. ❹

Hotel Schintgen, 6 r. Notre Dame (☎22 28 44; schintgn@p.lu). One of the cheapest hotels in the Old Center. Breakfast included. Reception daily 7am-11pm. Singles €55-67; doubles €85; triples €90. ❺

Hotel-Restaurant de l'Avenue, 43 ave. de la Liberté (☎40 68 12; hotelav@pt.lu). Small, but nice rooms with cute bathrooms. Singles €47; doubles €70; triples €83. ❻

Camping: Kockelscheuer (☎47 18 15), 7km outside Luxembourg City. Take bus #5 from the station to *Kockelscheuer-Camping.* Showers included. Open Easter-Oct. €3.50 per person, €4 per site. ❶

▐ FOOD

Although the area around the pl. d'Armes teems with a strange mix of fast-food joints and upscale restaurants, there are affordable and appealing alternatives. Stock up on groceries at **Supermarché Boon,** in Galerie Kons across from the train station. (Open M-F 8am-8pm, Sa 8am-6pm, Su 8am-noon.)

▧ Restaurant-Café Chiggeri, 15 r. du Nord (☎22 82 36). Serves divine French food in a fun and funky atmosphere. Wine list offers an amazing 2200 varieties. Free Internet access for all customers, but just 1 computer. Entrees €11-14; more expensive restaurant upstairs. Open M-Th 8am-1am, F-Sa 8am-3am, Su 10am-1am. ❸

Restaurant Bacchus, 32 r. du Marché-aux-Herbes (☎47 13 97), down the street from the Grand Ducal palace. Excellent pizza and pasta (€7.40-12) in a homey environment. Reservations recommended 7-10pm. Open Su and Tu-Sa noon-10pm. ❷

Au Table du Pain, 37 av. de la Liberté (☎29 56 63), on the way to the train station. Serves up soups, salads (€8-10), sandwiches (€4-8), and baked goods on wooden tables in a country-home atmosphere. Open M-F 7am-7pm, Sa 8am-4pm. ❷

Le Beaujolais, 2a r. des Capucins (☎47 45 12), next to the Municipal Tourist Office. Pasta (from €8) and pizza at reasonable prices (€6.50-11). Sit in velvet booths or people watch outside on the pl. d'Armes. Open daily 11:30am-11:30pm. ❷

Daiwelskichen, 4 Grand Rue (☎22 15 08). Although pricey, an authentic place for South American food and margaritas. Meals €12-20. Reservations recommended. Open M noon-3pm, Tu-F noon-3pm and 7-11pm, Sa 7-11pm. ❹

LUXEMBOURG

Schumacher, 18 av. de la Porte-Neuve. Popular spot to grab a sandwich (from €2) and go. Open M-F 7am-6pm, Sa 7am-5pm. ❶

📷 SIGHTS

Luxembourg City is compact enough to be explored without a map; by wandering around you'll bump into most of the major sights. The most spectacular views of the city can be seen from any of the three major bridges connecting to the city center—particularly the bridge closest to the hostel and the Bock Casemates—and from **place de la Constitution.** For guidance, follow the signs pointing out the **Wenzel Walk.** It leads visitors through 1000 years of history as it winds around the old city, from the **chemin de la Corniche** down into the casemates.

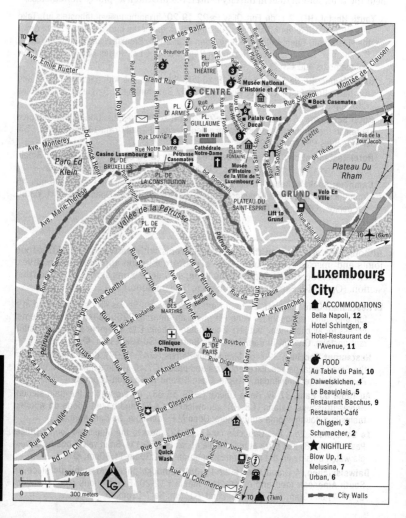

Luxembourg City

⌂ ACCOMMODATIONS
Bella Napoli, **12**
Hotel Schintgen, **8**
Hotel-Restaurant de
  l'Avenue, **11**

🍴 FOOD
Au Table du Pain, **10**
Daiwelskichen, **4**
Le Beaujolais, **5**
Restaurant Bacchus, **9**
Restaurant-Café
  Chiggeri, **3**
Schumacher, **2**

⭐ NIGHTLIFE
Blow Up, **1**
Melusina, **7**
Urban, **6**

━━ City Walls

FORTRESSES AND THE OLD CITY. The 10th-century **Bock Casemates** fortress, part of Luxembourg's original castle, looms over the Alzette River Valley and offers a fantastic view of the **Grund** and the **Clausen.** This strategic stronghold was closed in 1867 and partially destroyed after the country's declaration of neutrality, but was used during WWII to shelter 35,000 people while the rest of the city was ravaged. Of the original 23km, 17 remain today, parts of which are used by banks, schools, and private residences. *(Entrance on r. Sigefroi, just past the bridge leading to the hostel. Open Mar.-Oct. daily 10am-5pm. €1.75, students €1.50.)* The **Pétrusse Casemates** were built by the Spanish in the 1600s to reinforce the medieval structures and were later improved by the Austrians. In the 19th century, a second ring of fortification was extended and a third was begun around the expanding city, lending Luxembourg the nickname "Gibraltar of the North." *(On pl. de la Constitution. Open July-Sept. Tours every hr. 11am-4pm. €1.75, students €1.50.)* Stroll down through the green **Pétrusse** valley, or catch one of the green tourist trains that depart from pl. de la Constitution and meander through the city and into the valley. *(Trains ☎651 16 51. Mid-Mar. to Oct. every 30min. 10am-6pm except 1pm. €6.50.)*

MUSEUMS. The **Luxembourg Card** (p. 751) covers entrance to all museums in the city and free public transportation throughout Luxembourg. The **All-in-One Ticket** covers five museums over three days (€7 at the Municipal Tourist Office). The eclectic collection at the **Musée National d'Histoire et d'Art** chronicles the influences of the various European empires, from ancient to contemporary, that controlled Luxembourg. *(Marché-aux-Poissons, at r. Boucherie and Sigefroi. ☎479 33 01; www.mnha.lu. Open Su and Tu-Sa 10am-5pm. €5, students €3.)* Ignore its name; the only gamble at the **Casino Luxembourg** is on the changing exhibitions of contemporary art. *(41 r. de Notre Dame, near pl. de la Constitution. Exhibition info ☎22 50 45; www.casino-luxembourg.lu. Open M and W-Su 11am-6pm, Th until 8pm. €4, under-26 €3. Under-18 free.)* The **Musée d'Histoire de la Ville de Luxembourg** features quirky exhibits that show the history of the city through an interactive display, accompanied by artifacts and explanations in French. *(14 r. du St-Esprit. ☎47 96 30 61. Open Su and Tu-Sa 10am-6pm, Th until 8pm. €5, students €3.70.)*

OTHER SIGHTS. Built as the city hall in 1574, the Renaissance **Palais Grand Ducal** lies in the heart of the downtown area and became the official city residence of the Grand Duke in 1890. *(Required tours mid-July to Aug. M-F afternoon and Sa morning; tickets sold at the Tourist Office. Reservations ☎22 28 09. English-language tours available. €5.45.)* Nearby, the 17th-century

NO WORK, ALL PLAY

GO HENRI, IT'S YOUR BIRTHDAY

Its petite size doesn't stop Luxembourg from throwing a colossal dusk-till-dawn fête to honor the birthday of its ruling monarch. It's not actually current Grand Duke Henri's birthday; the date, June 23, was set when his grandmother, Duchess Charlotte, deemed her January birth date inopportune for an outdoor celebration of a suitable size.

The action begins in the early evening of June 22nd with a lengthy procession through the old city. At 11pm, fireworks rip through the air, illuminating the city's graceful bridges against the night sky. The procession may have ended—but the real party is just getting started. In an instant, the tiny alleys and narrow streets of this fairy-tale capital are magically transformed into impromptu bars and dance floors. A steady stream of alcohol and universal desire to get down saturate the tiny capital.

The rising sun traditionally breaks up the party, as disheveled revelers stumble to the Place d'Armes for breakfast. Although June 23rd is the official holiday, most Luxembourgers spend the day catching up on sleep missed the night before. The holiday's highlight, for those who can get out of bed, is watching Grand Duke Henri stroll, often with family and without visible security, through the center of what once again feels like a small town.

Cathédrale de Notre Dame incorporates features of the Dutch Renaissance and early Baroque styles, and houses the tomb of John the Blind, the 14th-century King of Bohemia and Count of Luxembourg. *(Entrance at bd. Roosevelt. Open M-F 9am-6:15pm, Sa 9am-6:30pm, Su 9am-10:30am and noon-6pm. Free.)*

🎵 📷 ENTERTAINMENT AND NIGHTLIFE

At night, the **place d'Armes** comes to life with free concerts and stand-up comedy. Pick up a copy of *Nico* at the tourist office for a list of nightlife action and events. On the eve of the **Grand Duke's birthday** (June 23), the city shuts down to honor their beloved Duke with a dusk-til-dawn fiesta filled with fireworks, alcohol, and fun. Nightlife centers on the valley in the **Grund** (by the bottom of the elevator lift on pl. du St-Esprit) and the **Clausen** area. On weekends, dance the night away at **Melusina,** 145 r. de la Tour Jacob (☎43 59 22), a cafe-by-day that becomes a popular student nightspot when the sun sets. (Entrees €7.40-17. Open M-Th 11:30am-2pm and 7-11pm, F-Sa 11:30am-2pm and 7pm-3am.) To get there, cross the bridge from the Grund lift, follow r. de Trèves, and veer left as it becomes r. de la Tour Jacob. At **Blow Up,** 14 av. de la Faiencerie, three rooms pump house, 80s, and Latin music late into the night. (☎43 34 86. Cover €10. Wednesday women free. Open W-Sa nights.) For more drinking and less dancing, try **Urban,** at the corner of r. de la Boucherie and r. du Marché-aux-Herbes, a posh downtown pub and restaurant. (☎264 78 57 80. Open daily noon-1am.)

THE ARDENNES

Six decades ago, the Battle of the Bulge (1944) mashed Luxembourg into the mud. Today, quiet towns, looming castles, and pleasant hiking trails are powerful draws.

ETTELBRÜCK. Ettelbrück's (pop. 7,000) position on the main railway line between Liège, Belgium, and Luxembourg City makes it the transportation hub for the Ardennes. The **General Patton Memorial Museum,** 5 r. Dr. Klein, commemorates Luxembourg's liberation during WWII. (☎81 03 22. Open July to mid-Sept. daily 10am-5pm; mid-Sept. to June Su 2-5pm. €2.50.) **Trains** go to: Clervaux (30min., every hr.); Diekirch (5min., every 20-40min.); and Luxembourg City (25min., 2 per hr.). **Buses** go to Diekirch (10min., every 15-40min., €1.60). To get to the city center from the station, go left on r. du Prince Henri, continue right at the fork, then turn left on Grand Rue and follow it to pl. de l'Église. The **tourist office** is in the train station. (☎81 20 68; site@pt.lu. Open July-Aug. M-F 9am-noon and 1:30-5pm, Sa 10am-noon and 2-4pm; Sept.-May closed Sa.) To get to **Ettelbrück Hostel (HI) ❷,** r. G. D. Josephine-Charlotte, head left out of the station and follow the signs. (☎81 22 69; ettelbruck@youthhostels.lu. Breakfast and sheets included. Lockout 10am-5pm. Dorms €15.) **Camping Kalkesdelt ❶** is at 22 r. du Camping. (☎81 21 85. Open Apr.-Oct. Reception daily 7:30am-noon and 2-10pm. €4.30 per person, €4 per site.) **Delhaize grocery** is close to the center of town. (Open M-F 8am-7pm, Sa 8am-6pm.)

DIEKIRCH. Diekirch (pop. 6,000) was evacuated during WWII in the face of imminent German attack. Today, the only invaders are backpackers and outdoorsy-types. The **National Museum of Military History,** 10 Bamertal, showcases moving relics from WWII's Battle of the Bulge. (☎80 89 08. Open Apr.-Oct. daily 10am-6pm; Jan.-Mar. and Nov.-Dec. daily 2-6pm. €5, students €3.) Rent **bikes** at **Speicher Sport,** 56 r. Clairefontaine (☎80 84 38; speibike@pt.lu. €10 per half-day, €15 per day.) Call ahead to rent **canoes** from **Outdoor Center,** 10 r. de la Sûre. (☎86 91 39. From €17.50 per day.) **Trains** head to Luxembourg City (35min., 2 per hr.) via Ettelbrück (5min.). **Buses** run to: Echternach (40min., every hr.); Ettelbrück (2 per hr., €4.60); and Vianden (#570; 20min., every hr.). To get to the **tourist office,** 3 pl. de la Liberation, turn left out of the station; at the fork, and follow r. du Pont to Grand Rue to pl. de la Liberation. (☎80 30 23; www.diekirch.lu. Open July-Aug. M-F 9am-5pm, Sa-Su 10am-noon and 2-4pm; off-season reduced hours.) **Au Beau-Séjour** ❺, 12 Esplanade, is pricey, but convenient. (80 34 03; beausejour.@pt.lu. Reception daily 8am-midnight. Singles €50; doubles €72.) Pitch your tent at **Camping de la Sûre** ❶, 34 rte. de Gilsdorf. (☎80 94 25; tourisme@diekirch.lu. Open Apr.-Sept. €4.80 per person, €4.30 per tent.) **Match supermarket** is off r. Alexis Heck. (Open M-Th 8:30am-7:30pm, F 8:30am-8pm, Sa 8am-6pm.)

VIANDEN. The village of Vianden (pop. 2,000), is home to one of the most impressive castles in Western Europe. Ride the ■ **télésiège** up to the **chateau,** a mix of Carolingian, Gothic, and Renaissance architecture, filled with armor, furniture, and tapestries. (☎83 41 08. Chateau open Apr.-Sept. daily 10am-6pm. €4.50, students €3.50. Télésiège ☎83 43 23. Open July-Aug. daily 10am-6:30pm; off-season reduced hours. €2.75, students €1.50.) The **Maison Victor Hugo,** 37 r. de la Gare, housed the author of *Les Misérables* during his exile from France. (☎26 87 40 88; www.victor-hugo.lu. Open Jan.-Oct. Su and Tu-Sa 11am-6pm.) **Hikers** enjoy Vianden's many trails; some also **bike** to Diekirch (13km) and Echternach (30km).

Buses head to Ettelbrück (#570; 30min., 2 per hr., €2.40) via Diekirch (20min.). The **tourist office,** 1 r. du Vieux Marché is next to the main bus stop. (☎83 42 57; www.tourist-info-vianden.lu. Open M-F 8am-noon and 1-6pm, Sa 10am-2pm, Su 2-4pm.) To reach the **Youth Hostel (HI)** ❷, 3 Montée du Château, follow Grande Rue away from the river up the hill; turn onto Montée du Château. (☎83 41 77; vianden@youthhostels.lu. Breakfast and sheets included. Reception daily 8-10am and 5-9pm. Lockout 10am-5pm. Curfew 11pm. Open May-Dec. Dorms €15. Nonmembers add €3.) Relax by the fountain at **Hotel Berg en Dal** ❸, 3 r. de la Gare. (☎83 41 27; info@hotel-bergendal.com. Breakfast included. Singles €34, with shower €37, with bath €52; doubles €38/48/74.) **Camp op dem Deich** ❶, r. Neugarten, alongside the Our river, is 5min. downstream from the tourist office. (☎83 43 75. Open Apr.-Sept. €4 per person, €4.50 per site.)

CLERVAUX. You'll see more faces in Clervaux's **chateau** than in the tiny town (pop. 1,000); the castle houses Edward Steichen's moving ■**Family of Man,** an exhibit of 500 photos from 68 countries, depicting milestones of human life, emphasizing the common bonds of the human experience. (☎92 96 57. Open Mar.-Dec. Su and Tu-Sa 10am-6pm. €7, students €3.50.) To get to the chateau and the **Benedictine Abbey,** turn left out of the train station. (Abbey open daily 9am-7pm. Free.) Trains run to: Ettelbrück (25min., every 30min.); Luxembourg City (50min., every hr.); and Liège, Belgium (1¾hr., every 2hr.). The **tourist office,** in the castle, finds rooms. (☎92 00 72; www.tourisme-clervaux.lu. Open July-Aug. daily 9:45-11:45am and 2-6pm; off-season reduced hours.) **Camping Officiel** ❶, 33 Klatzewe, is near the river. (☎92 00 42. Open Apr.-Nov. €4.30 per person, €4.30 per tent.)

THE NETHERLANDS
(NEDERLAND)

The Dutch say that although God created the rest of the world, *they* created The Netherlands. The country is a masterful feat of engineering; since most of it is below sea level, vigorous pumping and many dikes were used to create dry land. What was once the domain of seaweed is now packed with windmills, bicycles, and tulips. The Netherlands's wealth of art and its canal-lined towns draw as many travelers as do the unique hedonism and perpetual partying of Amsterdam.

LIFE AND TIMES

HISTORY AND POLITICS

FROM ROMANS TO HABSBURGS (100 BC TO AD 1579). Julius Caesar, leader of the Roman Empire, invaded the region in the first century BC, displacing obviously disgruntled Celtic and Germanic tribes. The native Germanic tribes had the last laugh in the 4th century as their reconquest swept across the Low Countries—The Netherlands, Belgium, and Luxembourg. Freedom was brief, however; the **Franks** took the place of the Romans from the 5th to the 8th century AD. During this period, towns rose as powerful centers only vaguely connected to each other. The **House of Burgundy** infiltrated the region in the 14th century to establish a more centralized monarchy. By 1482, the Austrian **Habsburgs** had managed to marry into the throne, beginning the long and volatile modern history of The Netherlands. The area quickly came under Spanish control after **Philip I** of the Habsburgs inherited the Spanish crown in 1493.

SUGGESTED ITINERARIES

THREE DAYS Spend all three days finding out what the buzz is in **Amsterdam** (p. 767). Stroll along cobblestone streets and visit the impressive **Museum District** (p. 787) and the **Anne Frank House** (p. 786). Then check out the **Red Light District** (p. 779).

ONE WEEK Begin with **Amsterdam** (2 days), then head to charming **Haarlem** (1 day; p. 795). Stop by the world's largest flower auction in nearby **Aalsmeer** (1 day; p. 794) or tan your whole self on the beaches in **Zandvoort** (1 day; p. 796). From capital city **The Hague** (1 day; p. 797), make your way to student center **Utrecht** (1 day; p. 800).

BEST OF THE NETHERLANDS, TWO WEEKS Chill in **Amsterdam** (4 days). Then take the train to **Haarlem** (1 day) before heading on to **Aalsmeer** (1 day). Catch some rays in **Zandvoort** (1 day) and make your way to **The Hague** (1 day). Swing by ultra-modern **Rotterdam** (1 day; p. 799) and then relax in **Utrecht** (2 days). Visit artsy **Maastricht** (1 day; p. 802) and then head north to hike in **Hoge Veluwe National Park,** using **Arnhem** as your base (1 day; p. 802), before trekking up to trendy **Groningen** (1 day; p. 804).

UTRECHT AND THE WAR WITH SPAIN (1579-1651). The Netherlands was officially founded in 1579 with the **Union of Utrecht,** which aimed to form an independent group of provinces and cities led by a **States-General.** Under Prince **William of Orange,** the Dutch declared independence from Spain in 1580, sparking a prolonged struggle with Spanish forces. The conflict was settled in 1609 with the **Twelve Years' Truce,** which included recognition of The Netherlands's sovereignty. Unfortunately, this peace was short-lived; Spain resumed hostilities in 1621. **Frederick Henry** of the House of Orange led the Dutch to stunning victories, while the Dutch navy trounced the Spanish in battles near Cuba and along the English coast. Shamed by losing to such a tiny country, Spain quickly offered the **Peace of Westphalia** (1648), which not only acknowledged Dutch independence, but also pushed for friendship in order to hedge the growing power of France.

During the **Age of Exploration** in the 17th century, Dutch conquerors fanned out over the globe and gained control of all the major trade routes across Europe. This created incredible wealth for the Dutch—mostly generated by the **Dutch East India Company**—but it also trod on the toes of the British, who resented invasion of their commercial spheres. To protect its trade routes, the company colonized the Cape of Good Hope and other strategic posts. Meanwhile, the **Dutch West India Company** was exploring the New World, creating colonies such as New Amsterdam (modern-day New York). All of this activity created unprecedented growth in Amsterdam, which served as the chief port for The Netherlands.

The Netherlands

WAR GAMES AND POWER STRUGGLES (1651-1795). Neighboring European powers resented the success and power of the Dutch, causing an almost constant period of war and changing alliances for The Netherlands. England began by passing the **Navigation Act,** limiting Dutch involvement in English trade, and then by attacking the Dutch navy. The vastly stronger Brits prevailed, forced peace, and secretly drafted the **Act of Seclusion,** forever banning the Prince of Orange from Dutch politics. Councillor **Johan de Witt** managed to rebuild The Netherlands's military and economy, but when the restored King **Charles II** of England decided to restart the war, the Dutch instantly negotiated an alliance with the French and sabotaged the English fleet.

In 1667, France invaded The Netherlands, which threatened both English and Dutch interests, and caused them to form an alliance. This infuriated King **Louis XIV** of France, as he believed the Dutch had betrayed him, so Louis offered the English a highly subsidized alliance in return. In 1672, The Netherlands found itself in a full-scale war against both countries, but under the leadership of **William III,** it managed to defeat the Franco-English fleets repeatedly. Ironically, William was crowned King of England in 1688, only 14 years after defeating the country in battle, and The Netherlands found itself subordinated to English will. The Dutch grip on international trade quickly eroded with the expansion of French and English colonialism throughout the 18th century.

FRENCH RULE AND INDEPENDENCE (1795-1914). In 1795, **Napoleon Bonaparte** continued the Dutch doormat syndrome by invading and establishing French rule over the country. After Napoleon's defeat at Waterloo, the **Treaty of Vienna** (1815) established the Kingdom of The Netherlands, which included Belgium and Luxembourg. King **William I of Orange** managed to rebuild the economy and trade routes, but Belgium soon revolted against Dutch rule and gained independence in 1839. Under **William,** the Dutch created a constitution establishing The Netherlands as a **constitutional monarchy** in which Parliament held most of the power, and the formation of modern political parties began. William's death in 1890 led to the end of male succession as **Wilhelmina** became queen.

THE WORLD WARS (1914-1945). The outbreak of **World War I** posed a serious threat to The Netherlands, but it managed to remain neutral while focusing its attention on maintaining its trade and economy. After the war, The Netherlands strictly reaffirmed its neutrality despite Belgian attempts to cede Dutch lands (the issue was settled by the **Treaty of Versailles**). The Dutch did not fare as well in **World War II.** Without warning, the Nazis invaded in May 1940 and occupied the nation for almost five years. The Dutch suffered horribly—all acts of resistance were punished, Dutch Jews were sent to concentration camps, and the general population was in near-famine conditions.

THE POSTWAR ERA (1945-1990). After the war, Wilhelmina supported sweeping democratic changes for the nation, granting universal suffrage and proportional representation. The nation also abandoned its policy of neutrality, joining NATO and creating a "closer union" with Belgium and Luxembourg. In order to recover from the destruction of WWII, the government began an economic policy that focused on industrial and commercial expansion.

While the nation experienced relative peace through the 1950s, the 1960s brought years of rioting students and workers in response to economic and political problems. In the 1980s, Dutch politics saw the disintegration of old parties and old alliances. The recent rise of the **Christian Democratic Appeal** (CDA) has provided a new outlet for the major Christian factions. While the established **Labour Party** (PvdA) has managed to avoid ties with extreme leftist groups, it had to form a coalition government with the CDA in 1989.

TODAY

The Netherlands is an integral member of the **European Union (EU)** and has adopted the **euro** as legal tender. The government remains a constitutional monarchy: Parliament holds legislative power while the monarchy **(Queen Beatrix)** retains a symbolic role. Recently, The Netherlands has seen the rise of the conservative CDA. In July of 2002, CDA's **Prime Minister Jan Peter Balkenende** was sworn into office. Among other things, his party is opposed to the country's more liberal sex and drug policies.

THE ARTS

LITERATURE

Dutch literature dates back to the 10th century when the Old Dutch *Wachtendonck Psalm Fragments* were written. The most influential works, however, didn't come until the Dutch Golden Age in the early 17th century. The primary author of the time was **Henric Laurenszoon Spieghel,** whose *Heart-Mirror* (1614) was the first philosophical work written in Dutch. The Reformed Church commissioned the *States Bible* (1620), the first translation of the Bible into Dutch, which further legitimized the language. **Joost van den Vondel** firmly placed the Dutch in the literary world with his dramatic tragedies and satirical treatment of the church and government; his *Lucifer* (1654) depicts an imagined conflict between the angels and God. Dutch literature took a back seat to Dutch imperialism in the 18th century, but in 1839 **Nicolaas Beets** led its revival with *Camera Obscura*, drawing on the humor of Charles Dickens and Laurence Sterne. With the terror of WWI and WWII came a new focus on social and philosophical questions. **Willem Frederik Hermans** examines the hostile environment in *The Dark Room of Damocles* (1958). **Anne Frank** recorded her experience hiding from Nazi soldiers in *The Diary of Anne Frank*. The house in which the Franks lived for two years is now open to the public, a haunting and touching reminder of those who suffered in the The Netherlands's occupation.

VISUAL ARTS

The monumental genius of **Rembrandt** made him a legend in the art world. He made his living as a renowned portrait artist in the 1620s in Amsterdam, but he began to break new artistic ground with **chiaroscuro**—painting in high contrast between light and dark. His paintings are characterized by rich, luxuriant color and texture and sensual brushwork, evidenced in *Judas Returning the Thirty Pieces of Silver* (1629). Later in the 17th century, **Jan Vermeer** explored bold perspectives and aspects of light. In the 19th century, **Vincent van Gogh,** perhaps the most famous **Post-Impressionist** artist, created a masterful collection of paintings in his own intensely personal style, characterized by bright, vibrantly contrasting colors and thick brush strokes, as can be seen in his *Starry Night* (1889). **Piet Mondrian,** the founder of the influential *De Stijl* magazine, formulated the theory of **neoplasticism**, which held that art should not attempt to recreate real life but should instead express universal absolutes. His signature works, characterized by black grids over primary-color blocks, have made their mark all over popular culture, from fashion to interior design.

FACTS AND FIGURES

Official Name: The Kingdom of The Netherlands.

Capital: Amsterdam.

Major Cities: Amsterdam, Maastricht, Rotterdam, Utrecht.

Population: 16,000,000.

Land Area: 41,526 sq. km.

Time Zone: GMT+1.

Language: Dutch.

Religions: Catholic (31%), Protestant (21%), Muslim (4%), unaffiliated (40%).

THE NETHERLANDS

ESSENTIALS

WHEN TO GO

The ideal time to visit is between mid-May and early October, when day temperatures are generally 20-31°C (70-80°F), with nights around 10-20°C (50-60°F). It can be quite rainy; bring an umbrella. The tulip season runs from April to mid-May.

DOCUMENTS AND FORMALITIES

VISAS. South Africans need a visa for stays of any length. Citizens of Australia, Canada, the EU, New Zealand, and the US do not need a visa for stays of up to 90 days.

EMBASSIES. All foreign embassies and most consulates are in The Hague (p. 797). The US has a consulate in Amsterdam (p. 767). For Dutch embassies at home: **Australia,** 120 Empire Circuit, Yarralumla Canberra, ACT 2600 (☎02 62 73 31 11; www.netherlandsembassy.org.au); **Canada,** 350 Albert St., Ste. 2020, Ottawa ON K1R 1A4 (☎6130-237-5030; www.netherlandsembassy.ca); **Ireland,** 160 Merrion Rd., Dublin 4 (☎012 69 34 44; www.netherlandsembassy.ie); **New Zealand,** P.O. Box 840, at Ballance and Featherston St., Wellington (☎04 471 63 90; netherlandsembassy.co.nz); **South Africa,** 825 Arcadia St., Pretoria, P.O. Box 117, Pretoria (☎012 344 3910; www.dutchembassy.co.za); **UK,** 38 Hyde Park Gate, London SW7 5DP (☎020 75 90 32 00; www.netherlands-embassy.org.uk); and **US,** 4200 Linnean Ave., NW, Washington, D.C. 20008 (☎202-244-5300; www.netherlands-embassy.org).

TRANSPORTATION

BY PLANE. Continental, Delta, KLM/Northwest, Martinair, Singapore Airlines, and **United** serve Amsterdam's sleek, glassy Schiphol Airport (AMS).

BY TRAIN. The national rail company is the efficient **Nederlandse Spoorwegen** (NS; Netherlands Railways; www.ns.nl). Train service tends to be faster than bus service. *Sneltreins* are the fastest; *stoptreins* make the most stops. One-way tickets are called *enkele reis;* normal round-trip tickets, *retour;* and same-day round-trip tickets (valid only on day of purchase, but cheaper than normal round-trip tickets), *dagretour.* **Eurail** and **InterRail** are valid in The Netherlands. The **Holland Railpass** (US$52-98) is good for three or five travel days in any one-month period. Although available in the US, the Holland Railpass is cheaper in The Netherlands at DER Travel Service or RailEurope offices. **One-day train passes** cost €35, which is about the equivalent of the most expensive one-way fare across the country. The fine for a missing ticket on Dutch trains is a whopping €90.

BY BUS. A nationalized fare system covers city buses, trams, and long-distance buses. The country is divided into zones; the number of strips on a *strippenkaart* (strip card) required depends on the number of zones through which you travel. A trip between destinations in the same zone costs one strip; a trip that traverses two zones requires two strips. On buses, tell the driver your destination and he or she will cancel the correct number of strips; on trams and subways, stamp your own *strippenkaart* in either a yellow box at the back of the tram or in the subway station. Train and bus drivers sell tickets, but it's cheaper to buy in bulk at public transit counters, tourist offices, post offices, and some tobacco shops and newsstands. *Dagkarten* (day passes) are valid for unlimited use in any zone (€5.20, children and seniors €3.60). Unlimited-use passes are valid for one week in the same zone (€21, seniors and children €13; requires a passport photo and picture ID). Riding without a ticket can result in a €30 fine.

THE NETHERLANDS

BY CAR. The Netherlands has well-maintained roadways. North Americans and Australians need an International Driver's License; if your insurance doesn't cover you abroad, you'll also need a green insurance card. Driving in the Netherlands is expensive. Fuel comes in two types; some cars use benzene (€1.50 per liter), while others use gasoline (€0.90 per liter). The **Royal Dutch Touring Association** (ANWB) offers roadside assistance to members. For more information, contact the ANWB at Wassenaarseweg 220, 2596 EC The Hague (☎070 314 71 47).

BY BIKE AND BY THUMB. Cycling is the way to go in The Netherlands---distances between cities are short, the countryside is absolutely flat, and most streets have separate bike lanes. Bikes run about €7 per day or €30 per week. Bikes are sometimes available at train stations and hostels, and *Let's Go* also lists bike rental shops in many towns. For more info, try www.visitholland.com. Hitchhiking is somewhat effective, but there is cutthroat competition on the roads out of Amsterdam. For more info on hitching, visit www.hitchhikers.org. *Let's Go* does not recommend hitchhiking.

TOURIST SERVICES AND MONEY

EMERGENCY	Police: ☎112. Ambulance: ☎112. Fire: ☎112.

TOURIST OFFICES. VVV (vay-vay-vay) tourist offices are marked by triangular blue signs. The website www.visitholland.com is also a useful resource.

MONEY. On January 1, 2002, the **euro** (€) replaced the guilder (NLG) as the unit of currency in The Netherlands. For more info, see p. 14. A bare-bones day traveling in The Netherlands will cost €30-35; a slightly more comfortable day will run €50-60. Service charges are always included in bills for hotels, shopping, and restaurants. The **value-added tax (VAT)** and service charges are always included in bills for hotels, shopping, taxi fares, and restaurants. If you buy an expensive item like a diamond, you are probably eligible for a tax refund. Keep your receipt and fill out a form at the airport. For more info on VAT, see p. 16. **Tips** for services are accepted and appreciated but not necessary. No waiter expects a 15% tip in Amsterdam, though it would most likely be appreciated. Ten percent is more normal; taxi drivers generally get tipped that much as well. Bouncers in clubs are often tipped €1-2 as patrons leave the club.

COMMUNICATION

TELEPHONES. Pay phones require a **Chipknip** card, which can be bought at hostels, train stations, and tobacconists for as little as €4.50. Even when using a calling card, a Chipknip card is necessary to gain access to the phone system. **Mobile phones** are an increasingly popular and economical alternative (p. 30). For directory assistance, dial ☎09 00 80 08; for collect calls, dial ☎06 04 10. International dial direct numbers include: **AT&T** ☎0800 022 91 11; **Australia Direct** ☎0800 022 20 61; **BT Direct** ☎0800 022 00 44; **Canada Direct** ☎0800 022 91 16; **Ireland Direct** ☎0800 02 20 353; **MCI WorldPhone Direct** ☎0800 022 91 22; **NZ Direct** ☎0800 022 44 64; **Sprint** ☎0800 022 91 19; **Telekom South Africa Direct** ☎0800 022 02 27.

PHONE CODES	**Country code: 31. International dialing prefix:** 00. From outside The Netherlands, dial int'l dialing prefix (see inside back cover) + 31 + city code + local number.

THE NETHERLANDS

MAIL. Post offices are generally open Monday to Friday 9am-6pm, and some are also open Saturday 10am-1:30pm; larger branches may stay open later. Mailing a postcard or letter (up to 20g) in the EU or a postcard outside of Europe costs €0.54; letters to outside of Europe cost €0.75. Mail takes 2-3 days to the UK, 4-6 to North America, 6-8 to Australia and New Zealand, and 8-10 to South Africa. Address mail to be held according to the following example: Firstname SUR-NAME, *Poste Restante*, Museumplein Post Office, 1071 DJ Amsterdam, NL.

INTERNET ACCESS. Email is easily accessible within The Netherlands. In small towns, if Internet access is not listed, try the library or even your hostel.

ACCOMMODATIONS AND CAMPING

NETHERLANDS	❶	❷	❸	❹	❺
ACCOMMODATIONS	under €30	€30-49	€50-69	€70-100	over €100

VVV offices supply accommodation listings and can almost always reserve rooms in both local and other areas (fee around €2). **Private rooms** cost about two-thirds as much as hotels, but they are hard to find; check with the VVV. During July and August, many cities add a tourist tax of €1.15 to the price of all rooms. The country's best values are the 34 **HI youth hostels,** run by **Stayokay International Hostels,** formerly the Dutch Youth Hostel Federation (NJHC). Hostels are divided into four price categories based on quality. Most are exceedingly clean and modern. The VVV has a list of hostels, and the useful *Jeugdherbergen* brochure describes each one (both free). For more information, contact Stayokay at P. O. Box 9191, 1006 AD, Amsterdam (☎010 264 60 64; www.stayokay.com). **Camping** is available across the country, but many sites are crowded and trailer-ridden in summer.

FOOD AND DRINK

NETHERLANDS	❶	❷	❸	❹	❺
FOOD	under €7	€7-10	€11-14	€15-20	over €20

Traditional Dutch cuisine is usually hearty, heavy, meaty, and wholesome. Expect a lot of bread and cheese for breakfast and lunch, and generous portions of meats and fishes for dinner. Popular seafood choices include all sorts of grilled fish and shellfish, fish stews, and raw herring. To round out a truly authentic Dutch meal (especially in May and June), ask for white asparagus, which can be a main dish on its own, served with potatoes, ham, and eggs. The Dutch conception of a light snack often includes *tostjes* (piping hot grilled cheese sandwiches, occasionally with ham), *broodjes* (sandwiches), *oliebollen* (doughnuts), or *poffertjes* (small pancakes). Colonial history has brought Surinamese and Indonesian cuisine to The Netherlands, followed closely by near-relatives from other South American and Asian countries. Indonesian cuisine is probably one of the safest bets for vegetarians and vegans. Wash it all down with a Heineken or Amstel.

CUSTOMS AND ETIQUETTE

DRUGS. The Netherlands' policy towards soft drugs is one of tolerance (not legalization or decriminalization, as many believe), meaning that smoking cannabis or hash *is* an offense, but one that is rarely prosecuted. Smoking up outside coffeeshops is not only illegal, but is considered extremely impolite.

LOVE FOR HIRE. A walk in the Red Light District will make it abundantly clear that prostitution is legal in Amsterdam. All of the prostitutes you see belong to a union called "The Red Thread" and are tested for HIV and STIs, although testing is on a voluntary basis. Do not take photos unless you want to explain yourself to the angriest—and largest—man you'll ever see. Keep in mind that prostitution is an entirely legal enterprise, and windows are a place of business. Show up clean and sober. Prostitutes reserve the absolute right to refuse service to anyone. Specifically state what you get for the money you're paying—that means which sex acts, in what positions, and especially how much time you have in which to do it. Always practice safe sex. A prostitute will never touch a penis without a condom.

HOLIDAYS AND FESTIVALS

Holidays: New Year's Day (Jan. 1); Good Friday (Apr. 9); Easter Sunday and Monday (Apr. 11 and 12); Liberation Day (May 5); Ascension Day (May 9); Whitsunday and Whitmonday (June 3-4); Christmas Day (Dec. 25) and Boxing Day (Dec. 26; also called Second Christmas Day).

Festivals: Koninginnedag (Queen's Day; Apr. 30) turns the country into a huge carnival. The **Holland Festival** (in June) features more than 30 productions in a massive celebration of the arts. **Bloemen Corso** (Flower Parade; first Sa in Sept.) runs from Aalsmeer to Amsterdam. Many historical canal houses and windmills are open to the public for **National Monument Day** (2nd Sa in Sept.). The **Cannabis Cup** (November) celebrates the magical mystery weed that brings millions of visitors to Amsterdam every year.

AMSTERDAM ☎ 020

Amsterdam is not merely the city of garish sin. While the aroma of marijuana smoke does waft out of coffeeshops and prostitutes do pose provocatively behind windows bathed in red light, there is much to savor beyond the city's fabulous excess. Amsterdam has long been a center of varied openness—the same culture of acceptance that tolerates cannabis use and a commercial sex trade has also turned the city into an immigrant capital; countless refugees from Spain to Surinam have called this city home, giving it a multicultural richness rivaled by few places on earth. A Golden Age of art flourished in Amsterdam, and art remains in many forms—Rembrandt's shadowy portraits, Vermeer's luminous women, and the post-Impressionist swirls of van Gogh's brush. And here, history breathes. Renaissance canal houses perch on enchanting waterways, while subtle remnants of WWII Nazi occupation litter the streets. Accordingly, this supremely relaxed capital of northern Europe is alluring for all sorts of guests: Eagerly experimenting youth, pot pilgrims, businesspeople, art aficionados, and history buffs. They all serve as a reminder that, though Amsterdam *is* a place for indulging desires, the best trip to Amsterdam isn't necessarily the one you won't remember.

▐ TRANSPORTATION

Flights: Schiphol Airport (AMS; ☎(0800) 72 44 74 65). Light rail **sneltrains** connect the airport to Centraal Station (20min., every 10min., €3).

Trains: Centraal Station, Stationspl. 1, at the northern end of the Damrak (☎09 00 92 92, €0.30 per min.; www.ns.nl). To: **Brussels** (2½-3hr., 1-2 per hr., €40); **Groningen** (2½hr., 2 per hr., €25); **Haarlem** (20min., 1-2 per hr., €3.10); **Leiden** (35min., 1-6 per hr., €6.60); **Paris** (4hr., 8 per day, €87); **Rotterdam** (1hr., 1-4 per hr, €12); **The Hague** (50min., 1-4 per hr., €8.50); **Utrecht** (30min., 3-6 per hr., €5.60).

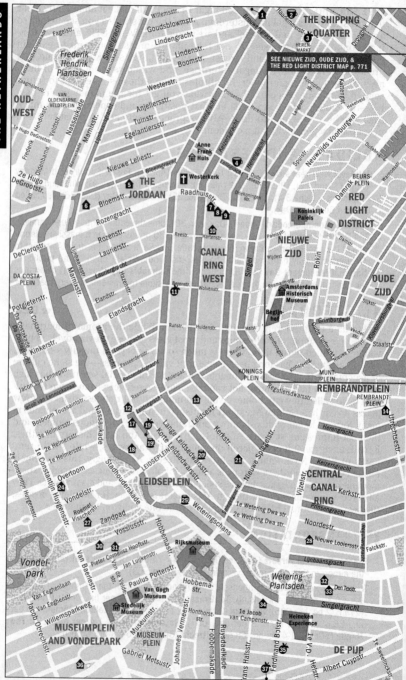

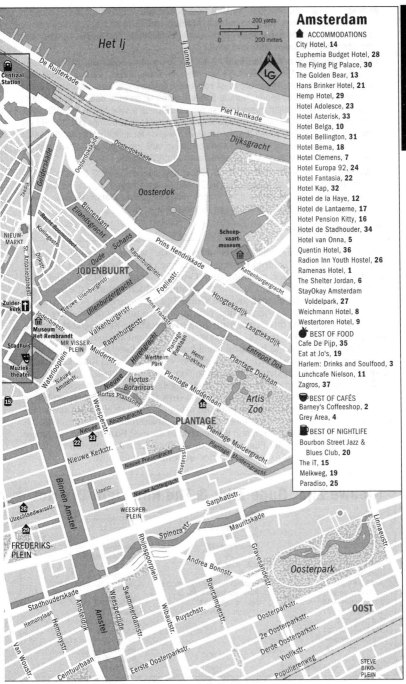

Amsterdam

ACCOMMODATIONS
City Hotel, **14**
Euphemia Budget Hotel, **28**
The Flying Pig Palace, **30**
The Golden Bear, **13**
Hans Brinker Hotel, **21**
Hemp Hotel, **29**
Hotel Adolesce, **23**
Hotel Asterisk, **33**
Hotel Belga, **10**
Hotel Bellington, **31**
Hotel Bema, **18**
Hotel Clemens, **7**
Hotel Europa 92, **24**
Hotel Fantasia, **22**
Hotel Kap, **32**
Hotel de la Haye, **12**
Hotel de Lantaerne, **17**
Hotel Pension Kitty, **16**
Hotel de Stadhouder, **34**
Hotel van Onna, **5**
Quentin Hotel, **36**
Radion Inn Youth Hostel, **26**
Ramenas Hotel, **1**
The Shelter Jordan, **6**
StayOkay Amsterdam
  Voldelpark, **27**
Weichmann Hotel, **8**
Westertoren Hotel, **9**

BEST OF FOOD
Cafe De Pijp, **35**
Eat at Jo's, **19**
Harlem: Drinks and Soulfood, **3**
Lunchcafe Nielson, **11**
Zagros, **37**

BEST OF CAFÉS
Barney's Coffeeshop, **2**
Grey Area, **4**

BEST OF NIGHTLIFE
Bourbon Street Jazz &
  Blues Club, **20**
The iT, **15**
Melkweg, **19**
Paradiso, **25**

Buses: Trains are quicker, but the **GVB** (see below) will direct you to a bus stop for domestic destinations not on a rail line. **Muiderpoort** (2 blocks east of Oosterpark) sends buses east; **Marnixstation** (at the corner of Marnixstr. and Kinkerstr.) west; and the **Stationsplein depot** north and south.

Public Transportation: GVB (☎09 00 92 92, €0.30 per min.) Stationspl. In front of Centraal Station. Open M-F 7am-9pm, Sa-Su 8am-9pm. **Tram, Metro,** and **bus** lines radiate from Centraal Station. Trams are most convenient for inner-city travel; the Metro leads to farther-out neighborhoods. Normal public transportation runs daily 6am-12:30am; from 12:30am-6am, night buses traverse the city—pick up a schedule at the GVB. *Strippenkart* are used on all public transportation in Amsterdam; two strips (€1.40) will get you to almost all sights within the city center and is good for unlimited transportation for one hour. *Strippenkart* are cheaper when bought in bulk (up to bundles of 45) and are available everywhere, especially at newsstands and VVV offices.

Bike Rental: Bike rental runs about €5-12 per day, plus a €30-100 deposit. Try **Frederic Rent a Bike,** Brouwersgr. 78 (☎624 55 09; www.frederic.nl), in the Shipping Quarter. Bikes €10 per day, which includes lock and theft insurance. Reserve online. AmEx/MC/V required for deposit, but pay in cash only.

■ ORIENTATION

Welcome to Amsterdam, the "Venice of the North," whose confusing neighborhoods can be easily explored through its guiding canals. In Amsterdam, water runs in concentric circles, radiating from Centraal Station, the starting point for most visitors. The **Singel** runs around the **Centrum,** which includes the **Oude Zijd,** the infamous **Red Light District,** and the **Nieuwe Zijd.** In a space not even a kilometer in diameter, brothels, bars, clubs, and tourists abound under wafting marijuana smoke. The next three canals are the **Herengracht,** the **Keizersgracht,** and the **Prinsengracht,** lined by streets of the same name. The land around them is known as the **Canal Ring,** home to beautiful canal houses and classy nightlife, including bars and traditional *bruin cafes.* In the eastern end of the Canal Ring, **Rembrandtplein** is the city's gay district and home to some raucous nightlife, while in the western end, at the corner of Leidsegrt. and Singelgrt., **Leidseplein** boasts some of the city's best restaurants and nightlife. Just over the Singelgrt., **Museumplein** is home to the city's most deservedly famous art museums as well as the sprawling **Vondelpark.** Farther out lie the more residential Amsterdam neighborhoods: To the west the **Jordaan, Oud-West,** and **Westerpark;** to the east **Plantage** and the **Jodenbuurt;** and to the south **De Pijp.** Though these districts are populated by dense housing, they still boast excellent eateries and brilliant museums.

Nieuwe Zijd, Oude Zijd, & The Red Light District

🛏 ACCOMMODATIONS
Anna Youth Hostel, **3**
Bob's Youth Hostel, **7**
Durty Nelly's Hostel, **37**
Flying Pig Downtown, **4**
The Greenhouse Effect Hotel, **35**
Hotel Brouwer, **5**
Hotel The Crown, **28**
Hotel Groenendael, **1**
Hotel Monopole, **19**
Hotel Royal Taste, **26**
Old Quarter, **30**
The Shelter City, **23**
StayOkay Amsterdam
 Stadsdoelen, **22**
Tourist Inn, **6**
Young Budget Hotel Kabul, **32**

🍎 FOOD
Aneka Rasa, **31**
Foodism, **8**
Green Planet, **10**
Hoi Tin, **25**
In de Waag, **24**
New Season, **33**
Pannenkoekenhuis Upstairs, **21**
Ristorante Caprese, **15**
Taste of Culture, **27**
Theehuis Himalaya, **34**

☕ COFFEESHOPS
Abraxas, **12**
Conscious Dreams Kokopelli, **29**
Dampkring, **18**
The Essential Seeds Company
 Art and Smart Shop, **2**
Grey Area, **9**
The Magic Mushroom, **14**

⭐ NIGHTLIFE
Absinthe, **13**
Café de Jaren, **20**
Cockring, **36**
Dansen Bij Jansen, **17**
Meander, **16**
NL Lounge, **11**

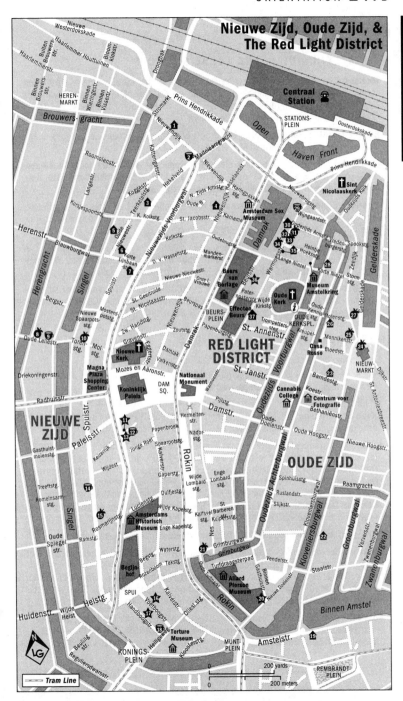

Nieuwe Zijd, Oude Zijd, & The Red Light District

THE NETHERLANDS

🛈 PRACTICAL INFORMATION

TOURIST, FINANCIAL, AND LOCAL SERVICES

Tourist Office: VVV, Stationspl. 10 (☎(0900) 400 40 40, €0.55 per min.), to the left when exiting Centraal Station. Room booking fee €3. Open M-F 9am-5pm. **Branches** inside Centraal Station (open M-Sa 8am-7:45pm, Su 9am-5pm) and Leidsepl. 1 (open M-Th 9am-6pm, F-Sa 9am-7pm, Su 9am-5pm).

Budget Travel: Eurolines, Rokin 10 (☎560 87 88; www.eurolines.nl). Books coach travel throughout Europe. Open M-F 9:30am-5:30pm, Sa 10am-4pm.

Consulates: All foreign embassies are in **The Hague** (p. 797). **American Consulate,** Museumpl. 19 (☎575 53 09; open M-F 8:30am-11:30pm). **British Consulate,** Koningslaan 44 (☎676 43 43; open M-F 9am-noon, and 2-5:30pm).

American Express: American Express, Damrak 66, offers the best rates, no commission on AmEx Traveler's Checks, and a €4 flat fee for all non-euro cash and non-AmEx Traveler's Checks. Open M-F 9am-5pm, Sa 9am-noon.

Bi-Gay-Lesbian Resources: COC, Rozenstr. 14 (☎626 30 87; www.cocamsterdam.nl), is a social network and main source of info. Open M-Tu and Th-F 10am-5pm, W 10am-8pm. **Gay and Lesbian Switchboard** (☎623 65 65) takes calls daily 10am-10pm.

Laundromat: Aquarette, Oudebrugsteeg 22 (☎638 13 97), off Damrak just south of Centraal Station. Self-service 5kg load for €5, dry €1 per 12min. Go to Continental Hotel across the street for doorkey. Open daily 8am-9:30pm. Cash only.

EMERGENCY AND COMMUNICATIONS

Emergency: Medical, Police, and Fire ☎112; no coins required.

Police: Headquarters, Elandsgr. 117 (☎08 00 88 44), at the intersection with Marnixstr. Call here for the **Rape Crisis Department.**

Crisis Lines: General counseling at **Telephone Helpline** (☎675 75 75). Open 24hr. **Rape crisis hotline** (☎612 02 45) staffed M-F 10:30am-11pm, Sa-Su 3:30-11pm. For **drug counseling,** call **Jellinek Clinic** (☎570 22 22). Open M-F 9am-5pm.

Medical Assistance: For hospital care, **Academisch Medisch Centrum,** Meibergdreef 9 (☎566 91 11), is easily accessible by bus #59, 60, 120, or 158 from Centraal Station (ask the driver to announce the medical center). **Kruispost Medisch Helpcentrum,** Oudezijds Voorburgwal 129 (☎624 90 31), is a walk-in clinic offering first aid only to non-insured travelers daily 7am-9pm. For 24hr. medical help, call the English-speaking **Centrale Doktorsdienst** (☎592 34 34). **STD Line,** Groenburgwal 44 (☎555 58 22), offers phone counseling. Free testing clinic. Open for calls M-F 8am-noon, 1-4pm.

24hr. Pharmacy: A hotline (☎694 87 09) will direct you to the nearest pharmacy.

Internet Access: Internet access in Amsterdam leaves much to be desired; the best bet may be a cozy coffeeshop. Try **easyEverything,** Reguliersbreestr. 22 and Damrak 34. (€1 generally buys 26min., but varies according to demand. Open 24hr.) Other cafes include **The Mad Processor,** Bloemgr. 82. (€3 per hr; open daily noon-2am) and **Free World,** Nieuwendijk 30 (€1 per 30min; open M-Th and Su 9am-1am, F-Sa 9am-3am).

Post Office: Singel 250, at Radhuisstr. Address mail to be held: Firstname, SURNAME, *Poste Restante,* Singel 250, Amsterdam, THE NETHERLANDS. Open M-W and F 9am-6pm, Th 9am-8pm, Sa 10am-1:30pm.

ACCOMMODATIONS

Accommodations near **Centraal Station** often take good security measures due to the chaos of the nearby Red Light District. Hostels and hotels near **Museumplein** toward the south and the **Jordaan** out to the west are quieter and safer. Both locations are close to bars, coffeeshops, AND museums and are a mere 2min. by tram from the heart of the city. Museumpl. is also very close to the bustling Leidsepl. The accommodations in the **Red Light District** (surrounded by the Oude Zijd) are often bars with beds over them. Before booking a bed there, consider just how much noise and drug use you can tolerate from your neighbors.

OUDE ZIJD, NIEUWE ZIJD, AND THE RED LIGHT DISTRICT

■ **StayOkay Amsterdam Stadsdoelen,** Kloveniersburgwal 97 (☎624 68 32; www.hostel-booking.com). Clean, drug-free lodgings in a quiet corner of Centrum. Bar on site. Kitchen available. Breakfast and sheets included. Laundry facilities available. Internet €1 per 12min. Reception 7am-1am. Dorms €22; €2.50 HI discount. MC/V. ❶

■ **Hotel Winston,** Warmoesstr. 129 (☎623 13 80; www.winston.nl). Rooms painted by local artists and designers make every room feel like an installation art piece. Club downstairs. Singles €60-72; doubles €74-96; triples €113-128. AmEx/MC/V. ❹

■ **Anna Youth Hostel,** Spuistr. 6 (☎620 11 55). By far the most beautiful hostel in the city. The quiet, drug-free ambience is surprising given its central location in the Nieuwe Zijd. Sheets and lockers included. 2-night min. stay on weekends. Reservations recommended. Closed during part of Dec. Dorms €16-18; doubles €70-80. AmEx/MC/V. ❶

Flying Pig Downtown, Nieuwendijk 100 (☎420 68 22; www.flyingpig.nl). Helpful and professional staff, great location, and colorful decor—a perennial favorite among backpackers. Kitchen available. Breakfast and sheets included. Key deposit €10. Dorms €21-27; singles and doubles €76. AmEx/MC/V. ❶

Hotel Brouwer, Singelgr. 83 (☎624 63 58; www.hotelbrouwer.nl). Eight gorgeously restored rooms each named after a Dutch painter: Rembrandt, Vermeer, and others. Breakfast included. Singles €50; doubles €85. Cash and traveler's checks only. ❷

The Shelter City, Barndesteeg 21 (☎625 32 30; www.shelter.nl). Virtue amid the red lights at this Christian-oriented hostel, but all faiths are welcome. No drugs. Breakfast included. Locker deposit €5. Linens included. Curfew M-Th and Su midnight, F-Sa 1am. Security guard 11:30pm-7:30am. Dorms €16-18. MC/V with 5% surcharge. ❶

Old Quarter, Warmoesstr. 20-22 (☎626 64 29; www.oldquarter.com). Smaller rooms are snug but homey; larger ones clean, classy, and bright. Downstairs *bruin cafe*. Breakfast included. Reception 24hr. Singles €40; doubles €70-100. AmEx/MC/V. ❷

Bob's Youth Hostel, Nieuwezijds Voorburgwal 92 (☎623 00 63). Bare necessities, no-frills living is legendary among backpackers. Breakfast, lockers, and sheets included. 2-night min. weekend stay. Reception 8am-3am. No reservations; arrive before 10am for a room. Dorms €18; doubles €70; triples €80. AmEx/MC/V. ❶

The Greenhouse Effect Hotel, Warmoesstr. 55 (☎624 49 74; www.the-greenhouse-effect.com). Theme rooms like Arabian Nights await your discovery. Singles €60, with bath €75; doubles with bath €90; triples with bath €120-130. AmEx/MC/V ❸

Young Budget Hotel Kabul, Warmoesstr. 38-42 (☎623 71 58; kabulhotel@hotmail.com). Pleasant hostel experience. Breakfast and sheets included. Internet €1 per 15min. Key deposit €15. Dorms €17-23; private rooms €45-95. AmEx/MC/V. ❶

Durty Nelly's Hostel, Warmoesstr. 115/117 (☎638 01 25; http://xs4all.nl/~nellys). Cozy lodgings above an Irish pub with co-ed dorms. Breakfast and sheets included. Lockers €10. Reception 24hr. Internet reservations only. Dorms €25-35. Cash only. ❶

Hotel Royal Taste, Oudezijds Achterburgwal 47 (☎623 24 78; www.hotelroyaltaste.com). Almost-fancy accommodations in the heart of the Red Light District. Breakfast included. Singles €50; doubles €90; triples €135; quads €180. AmEx/MC/V. ❷

Tourist Inn, Spuistr. 52 (☎421 58 41; www.tourist-inn.nl). Clean, friendly, and comfortable. Breakfast and sheets included. Reservations advised. Dorms €25-35; singles €50-100; doubles €65-120; triples €100-150; quads €100-140. AmEx/MC/V. ❶

Hotel Groenendael, Nieuwendijk 15 (☎624 48 22; www.hotelgroenendael.com). Mellow hotel near Centraal Station. Breakfast included. Free safe access. Key deposit €5. Singles €32; doubles €50-55; triples €75. Cash and traveler's checks only. ❷

Hotel The Crown, Oudezijds Voorburgwal 21 (☎626 96 64; www.hotelthecrown.com). This British-owned hotel provides handsome digs in the picturesque end of the Red Light District. Singles €35-50; doubles €70-100; triples €105-150; quads €140-200; quints €175-250. AmEx/MC/V required for reservation confirmation; only cash is accepted for payment. ❷

SHIPPING QUARTER, CANAL RING WEST, AND THE JORDAAN

▨ **Hotel Clemens,** Raadhuisstr. 39 (☎624 60 89; www.clemenshotel.nl). A gem with renovated, elegant suites. Internet and safe in all rooms. Breakfast €7. Key deposit €20. Book well in advance. Min. stay 3 nights on weekends. Singles €55; doubles €70-75; deluxe €110; triples €125/150. Cash only for budget rooms. AmEx/MC/V. ❷

Wiechmann Hotel, Prinsengr. 328-332 (☎626 33 21; www.hotelwiechmann.nl). Three restored canal houses with spacious rooms. Breakfast included. Singles €70-90; doubles with bath €125-135; triples and quads €170-230. MC/V. ❸

Ramenas Hotel, Haarlemmerdijk 61 (☎624 60 30; www.amsterdamhotels.com). Ramenas's rooms are ascetic, but they get the job done. Breakfast included. Reservations via website. Doubles €64-80; triples €96-120; quints €160-200. MC/V. ❶

The Shelter Jordan, Bloemstr. 179 (☎624 47 17; www.shelter.nl). Religious, but not proselytizing, this companionable Christian hostel is a treasure. No smoking or alcohol. Age limit 35. Breakfast included. Lockers €5; free storage for larger bags. Internet €0.50 per 20min. Curfew 2am. Dorms €16.50-18. MC/V. ❶

Hotel van Onna, Bloemgr. 104 (☎626 58 01; www.vanonna.nl). Get a peaceful night's rest in a restored historic building, situated on the prettiest canal in the Jordaan. Small but very comfortable rooms. Breakfast included. Reception 8am-11pm. Singles €40; doubles €80; triples €120; quads €160. Cash only. ❷

Westertoren Hotel, Raadhuisstr. 35b (☎624 46 39; www.hotelwestertoren.nl). Clean, plain surroundings and a friendly staff. Tea and coffee in room. Breakfast included. 3-night min. weekend stay (Su included). Singles €55; doubles €80-90; triples €110-125; family room (4-6 people) €140-205. AmEx/MC/V. ❸

Hotel Belga, Hartenstr. 8 (☎624 90 80; www.hotelnet.nl). Rooms are large and sunny if bland, all with phone and safe. Most rooms with shower and toilet. Breakfast included. Weekend stays include Sa and Su during summer. Singles €41-57; doubles €62-84, with bath €78-118; triples €95-141; quads €134-189. AmEx/MC/V. ❷

LEIDSEPLEIN AND MUSEUMPLEIN

▨ **StayOkay Amsterdam Vondelpark,** Zandpad 5 (☎589 89 96; www.stayokay.com/vondelpark). A palatial, slightly corporate, hostel with many amenities. Breakfast and sheets included. Lockers €2.50. Internet €0.50 per min. Reception 7:30am-midnight. Reserve well in advance. Dorms €21-25; quads €26-28. €2.50 HI discount. MC/V. ❶

🏨 **Quentin Hotel,** Leidsekade 89 (☎626 21 87). You don't have to sacrifice style to get budget accommodations. Each room bears a distinctive motif. Continental breakfast €7. Reception 24hr. Singles €40, with facilities €65; smaller "economy" doubles with facilities €80, regular doubles €100; triples €133. AmEx/MC/V with 5% surcharge. ❷

🏨 **Hotel Bema,** Concertgebouw 19b (☎679 13 96; www.bemahotel.com). Charming 7-room hotel with skylights, a friendly staff, and funky neo-hippie style. Breakfast included. Reception 8am-midnight. Singles €50-65; doubles €68-85; triples €85-120; quads €105-160. AmEx/MC/V with 5% surcharge. ❷

Flying Pig Palace, Vossiusstr. 46-47 (☎400 41 87; www.flyingpig.nl). Laid-back, friendly attitude with views of the park. Ages 18-35 only. Sheets included. Free Internet. Reception 8am-9pm. Dorms €20-38; doubles €63-66. AmEx/MC/V. ❶

Hans Brinker Hotel, Kerkstr. 136 (☎622 06 87; www.hans-brinker.com). Really a massive hostel, with spartan, clean rooms. Guest-only bar. No visitors. Breakfast included. Free Internet. Key deposit €5. Reception 24hr. Dorms €29-35; singles €52; doubles €58-75; triples €90; quads €96. AmEx/MC/V. ❶

Hotel de Lantaerne, Leidsekade 111 (☎623 22 21; www.hotellantaerne.com). Lovely accommodations in 2 converted houses along the Leidsegrt. Breakfast included. Singles €55-75; doubles €85-115; triples €115-150. AmEx/MC/V with 5% surcharge. ❷

Hotel Bellington, P.C Hoftstr. 78-80 (☎671 64 78; www.hotel-bellington.com). From Schiphol Airport, take bus #197 to Hobbemasstr.; from Centraal Station, take tram #2 or 5. A well-groomed hotel on the city's ritziest street. Breakfast included. Reception 8am-11pm. Doubles €60-95; triples €105-115; quads €128. AmEx/MC/V. ❹

Hotel de la Haye, Leidsegr. 114 (☎624 40 44; www.hoteldelahaye.com). Combines the convenience of Leidsepl. proximity and a serene canal view. Breakfast included. Reception 8am-10pm. Singles €57-64; basic doubles €87-95; regular doubles €95-105; triples €105-120; quads €135-175. AmEx/MC/V with 5% surcharge. ❸

CENTRAL CANAL RING AND REMBRANDTPLEIN

🏨 **Hemp Hotel,** Frederikspl. 15 (☎625 44 25; www.hemp-hotel.com). Only 5 rooms, but each is lovingly done up to celebrate one of the world's major hemp-producing regions: Afghanistan, the Caribbean, India, Morocco, and Tibet. Everything is made of hemp—bedclothes, curtains, and even soap. Single €50; doubles €65-70. ❸

Euphemia Budget Hotel, Fokke Simonszstr. 1-9 (☎622 90 45; www.euphemiahotel.com). Welcoming, quiet, and bright budget digs in a former monastery. Gay friendly. Continental breakfast €5. Internet €1 per 15min. Reception 8am-11pm. Dorms €23; doubles €46; triples €69. AmEx/MC/V with 5% surcharge. ❶

The Golden Bear, Kerkstr. 37 (☎624 47 85; www.goldenbear.nl). Opened in 1948, The Golden Bear may be the oldest openly gay hotel in the world. Mainly male couples frequent the hotel, though lesbians are welcome as well. Breakfast included. Singles €57-99; double €78-112. AmEx/MC/V. ❸

City Hotel, Utrechtsestr. 2 (☎627 23 23; www.city-hotel.nl). Classy, spacious accommodations above a pub right on the Rembrandtpl. Rooms immaculately kept. Breakfast included. Reception 24hr. Doubles €80-90, doubles with facilities €90-100; triples €105-135; quads €140-180. AmEx/DC/MC/V. ❹

Hotel Kap, Den Texstr. 5b (☎624 59 08; www.kaphotel.nl). Very personable staff rents clean, comfortable rooms on a quiet, residential street. Breakfast included. Reception 8am-10:30pm. Check-out 11am. Depending on space and facilities, singles €57; doubles €86-109; triples €109-118; quads €136. AmEx/MC/V with 5% surcharge. ❸

Hotel Asterisk, Den Texstr. 16 (☎626 23 96; www.asteriskhotel.nl). Orderly, quiet hotel with clean, bright rooms. All rooms with phone, and safe. Free breakfast if you pay in cash (€8 with credit cards). Singles €44-84; doubles €65-125; triples €130-136; quads €150. MC/V with 4% surcharge. ❷

Radion Inn Youth Hostel, Utrechtsedwarsstr. 79 (☎625 03 45; www.radioinn.nl). Lots of character at this cheerfully idiosyncratic hostel—somewhere between a 70s garage sale and a budget hotel. Housed in an old radio store, the homey lobby is filled with defunct gadgets and 2 cats. Kitchen available 24hr. Free laundry. Dorms €25. Cash only. ❷

Hotel Monopole, Amstel 60 (☎624 62 71; www.monopole.demon.nl). Lovely setting right by the Amstel. Simple but charming rooms with flowered bedspreads and pastel walls. Breakfast included. Some rooms with bath. Singles €85; doubles €95, with facilities €125; triples €160; quads €200; quints €260. MC/V with a 5% surcharge. ❹

DE PIJP, JODENBUURT, AND THE PLANTAGE

▨ **Bicycle Hotel,** Van Ostadestr. 123 (☎679 34 52; www.bicyclehotel.com). Clean digs, spotless bathrooms, and a leafy garden. Bicycle-friendly hotel with a bike garage, trip recommendations, and bike decor. Breakfast included. Free Internet. Double €68-70, with bath €99; triples €90/120; quads with bath €120. Cash only. ❷

Hotel Pension Kitty, Plantage Middenlaan 40 (☎622 68 19). Look out for the small sign. Gentle 80-year-old proprietress provides for those seeking a peaceful respite. Grandmotherly warmth and wonderful tranquility abound. No children. Singles €50; doubles €60-70; triples €75. Cash only. ❷

Hotel De Stadhouder, Stadhouderskade 76 (☎671 84 28). Well-kept rooms, some with patios or canal views. Breakfast and sheets included. Singles €35-65; doubles €40-85; triples €75-100; quads €110/95; quints €125/85. AmEx/MC/V with 5% surcharge. ❸

Hotel Fantasia, Nieuwe Keizersgr. 16 (☎623 82 59; www.fantasia-hotel.com). Clean, friendly, family-owned establishment in an 18th-century house on a quiet canal. Breakfast included. Closed Dec. 14-27 and Jan. 6-Mar. 1. Singles €55-63; doubles €80-90; triples €115; quads €135. AmEx/MC/V with 3% surcharge. ❸

Hotel Adolesce, Nieuwe Keizersgrt. 26 (☎626 39 59; adolesce@xs4all.nl). Pristine hotel located in an old canal house steps away from the Magere Brug ("skinny bridge"). Free coffee/tea all day. No drugs. Reception 8:30am-1am; pay on arrival. Singles €60-€65; doubles €80-85; triples €115. MC/V. ❸

🍴 FOOD

Many cheap restaurants cluster around **Leidseplein, Rembrandtplein,** and the **Spui.** Cafes, especially in the Jordaan, serve inexpensive sandwiches (€1.50-4) and good meat-and-potatoes fare (€5.50-9). Bakeries line **Utrechtsestraat,** south of Prinsengr. Fruit, cheese, flowers, and even live chickens fill the **markets** on **Albert Cuypstraat,** behind the Heineken brewery. (Open M-Sa 9am-6pm.)

NIEUWE ZIJD AND OUDE ZIJD

▨ **In de Waag,** Nieuwmarkt 4 (☎452 77 72; www.indewaag.nl) In the late 1400s, this castle served as the eastern entrance to the city. Today, sandwiches and salads (€4-8.50) are served on the patio for lunch. At night, the restaurant lights 250 candles and patrons pack the medieval behemoth for richly flavored Italian, French, and Norwegian specialties. Entrees €17-22. Open M-Th and Su 10am-midnight, F-Sa 10am-1am; often open until 3am on busy evenings. ❷

Pannenkoekenhuis Upstairs, Grimburgwal 2 (☎626 56 03). This tiny nook boasts the city's best pancakes (€5-9). Open M-F noon-7pm, Sa noon-6pm, Su noon-5pm. ❶

Ristorante Caprese, Spuistr. 259-261 (☎620 00 59). Excellent Italian food accompanied by smooth jazz. Open daily 5-10:45pm. No reservations. ❸

Theehuis Himalaya, Warmoesstr. 56 (☎626 08 99; www.himalaya.nl). The back room houses a Buddhist-themed *theehuis* that serves light vegetarian and vegan lunches as well as 40 varieties of tea. Tasty *tostis* €3-3.50. Pies €3-3.25. Open M 1-6pm, Tu-W and F-Sa 10am-6pm, Th 10am-8:30pm, Su 12:30-5pm. AmEx/MC/V. ❶

Aneka Rasa, Warmoesstr. 25-29 (☎626 15 60). Find elegance amid the seediness of the Red Light District. Indonesian *rijsttafel* (rice table) €16-27 per person. Open daily 5-10:30pm. AmEx/MC/V. ❸

New Season, Warmoesstr. 39 (☎625 61 25). Pan-Asian, family-style, sit-down eatery serves Cantonese, Szechuan, Thai, and Malaysian dishes (€7-10). Vegetarian plates €5-6. Open Su and Tu-Sa 3-11pm. AmEx/MC/V. ❷

Foodism, Oude Leliestr. 8 (☎427 51 03). Swanky, small restaurant serves sandwiches (from €4), soups and salads (from €3.50), and pasta dishes (from €8) on a lovely canal-side street. Open M-Th and Su 11am-10pm, F-Sa 11:30am-11pm. ❷

Taste of Culture, Zeedijk 109 (☎638 14 66). Many an eating contest has been inspired by Taste of Culture's offer: All you can eat in 1hr., €7.50. Open M-W noon-11pm, Th-Su until midnight. Another location at Rokin 152 (☎638 12 49). Cash only. ❶

Green Planet, Spuistr. 122 (☎625 82 80; www.greenplanet.nl). Die-hard vegetarian restaurant with brilliant soups (around €5.50) and other creative vegetarian dishes. Organic wines and beers from €2.50. The only restaurant in The Netherlands to use biodegradable packaging for takeout. Open M-Sa 11am-11pm. ❷

Hoi Tin, Zeedijk 122-124 (☎625 64 51). Remarkably authentic dim sum (11am-5pm) and dinner meals await at this slightly upscale local favorite in Chinatown. Dim sum €2.30-3.80. Entrees €8-14.50. Open daily 11am-11pm. Cash only. ❸

SHIPPING QUARTER, CANAL RING WEST, AND THE JORDAAN

▧ **Harlem: Drinks and Soulfood,** Haarlemmerstr. 77 (☎330 14 98). High-class fusion cuisine blends American-style soul food with Cajun and Caribbean flavors. Entrees €12-17. Soups and sandwiches €4-5. Open M-Th 10am-1am, F-Sa 10am-3am, Su 11am-1am. Kitchen closes 10pm. MC/V. ❸

▧ **Lunchcafe Nielson,** Berenstr. 19 (☎330 60 06). A bright ray of light in an already shining neighborhood. Brilliant breakfast and lunch served all day (€4-10). Open Tu-F 8am-5pm, Sa 8am-6pm, Su 9am-5pm; kitchen closes 30min. before restaurant. ❶

Bolhoed, Prinsengr. 60-62 (☎626 18 03). The best in vegetarian and vegan fare—fresh, flavorful, and lovingly prepared. Pastas, casseroles, and Mexican dishes €12.50-15. Fresh-squeezed juices as well as organic and vegan desserts around €4. Dinner reservations a must. Open M-F and Su 11am-10pm, last reservation 9pm. Cash only. ❸

Cinema Paradiso, Westerstr. 186 (☎623 73 44). Cavernous former cinema with purist Italian food and candle-lit charm. Antipasti €4-10. Pasta €9-15. No reservations; be prepared for a wait. Open Su and Tu-Sa 6-11pm; kitchen closes 11pm. AmEx/MC/V. ❷

Wolvenstraat 23, Wolvenstr. 23 (☎320 08 43). At this trendy spot, lunch means sandwiches (€2-5.20), salads (€6), and omelets (€3-4) and dinner means Cantonese cuisine (around €10). Lunch menu 8am-3:30pm, dinner 6-10:30pm. Open M-Th 8am-1am, F 8am-2am, Sa 9am-2am, Su 10am-1am. Cash only. ❷

De Belhamel, Brouwersgr. 60 (☎622 10 95; www.belhamel.nl). Gloriously luxuriant Art Nouveau setting on a beautiful canal serves elegant Franco-Dutch and Italian Dutch cuisine. Appetizers €8-11. Entrees around €20. Desserts around €8.50. Open M-Th 6-10pm, F-Sa 6-10:30pm. AmEx/MC/V. ❺

Padi, Haarlemmerdijk 50 (☎625 12 80). Locals rave about this Indonesian *eethuis*, lined with Indonesian fans and rustic wood decor. Cheap appetizers (€2-4) and saucy entrees (around €8). Open daily 5-10pm. Cash only. ❷

Top Thai, Herenstr. 22 (☎623 46 33; www.topthai.nl), serves traditional Thai cuisine under Asian sunshades that cover the ceiling. Try the eclectic Top Thai Pearls, a sampler of the restaurant's appetizers (€7). Open daily 4:30-10:30pm. MC/V. ❷

LEIDSEPLEIN AND MUSEUMPLEIN

☒ **Eat at Jo's,** Marnixstr. 409 (☎624 17 77; www.melkweg.nl), inside Melkweg. Multi-ethnic menu that changes daily. Soups (€3.40) and numerous vegetarian options (entrees €10) earn raves. Open Su and W-Sa noon-9pm. Cash only. ❶

Cafe Vertigo, Vondelpark 3 (☎612 30 21; www.vertigo.nl). Vertigo's expansive, tree-lined terrace is the perfect place to relax. Skip the pricier dinner menu in favor of the lunch sandwiches (€4) and tasty pastries (€2). Open daily 10am-1am. MC/V. ❶

Bojo, Lange Leidsedwarsstr. 51 (☎622 74 34). Popular Indonesian eatery with stalwart Javanese chow. Dishes €5.80-11. Try the mini *rijstaffel* sampler (€10.50). Open M-Th 4pm-2am, F 4pm-4am, Sa noon-4am, Su noon-2am. MC/V. ❸

Het Blauwe Theehuis, Vondelpark 5 (☎662 02 54; www.blauwetheehuis.nl). Through the trees in Vondelpark, you may glimpse a linoleum-colored flying saucer full of people having a good time at Het Blauwe Theehuis. Open M-Th and Su 9am-midnight, F-Sa 9am-2am; kitchen closes 10pm. Cash only. ❶

Santa Lucia, Leidsekruisstr. 20-22 (☎623 46 39). Great pizza in a city where decent slices are hard to come by. Hot pies bubbling with cheese (€5) and toppings (mushroom €6.80; pepperoni €7.80). Lasagna €8.50. Open daily noon-11pm. MC/V. ❶

Go Sushi, Johannes Verhulststr. 35 (☎471 00 35). Tram #16 to Jacob Olbrechtstr. Tiny "Japanse Eetwinkel" tucked into a quiet street. 3 pieces of *maki* €1.90-2.60; *nigiri* €1.20-2.95; 10-piece sushi "lunchbox" €9. Open M-F noon-7pm. Cash only. ❷

CENTRAL CANAL RING AND REMBRANDTPLEIN

☒ **Maoz Falafel** Regulierbreestr. 45 (☎624 92 90). Great falafels with all-you-can-stack self-serve salad bar (for any size) make this the best budget deal in the city. Small falafel €2.50. Other locations: Outside Centraal Station; Muntpl. 1; Leidsestr. 85; Ferdinand Bolstr. 67. Open daily at least 11am-11pm; hours vary by location. ❶

Lanskroon, Singel 385 (☎623 77 43). The city's best traditional Dutch pastries and wonderful sorbet. Open Su 10am-5pm, Tu-F 8am-5:30pm, Sa 8am-5pm. Cash only. ❶

Coffee and Jazz, Utrechtsestr. 113 (☎624 58 51). Dutch-Indonesian fusion: Fruity *pannenkoeken* (€4.50-7) share the menu with tender lamb and chicken *satay* (€7-9). Locals say this is the best coffee in town. Open Tu-F 9:30am-8pm, Sa 10am-4pm. ❷

NOA, Leidsegrt. 84 (☎626 08 02; www.withnoa.com). NOA distinguishes itself as much for its elegant design as for its pan-Asian dishes and salads (around €13). Get your cocktail fix here—they make great *caipirinhas,* and *mojitos* (€7-9). AmEx/MC/V. ❹

DE PIJP, JODENBUURT, AND THE PLANTAGE

☒ **Cafe De Pijp,** Ferdinand Bolstr. 17-19 (☎670 41 61). Stylish, but affordable with flavorsome fusion food. Soup of the day €3.90. Appetizers €7.90. Entrees €13-15. Cocktails €5. Open M-Th and Su noon-1am, F-Sa noon-3am. Cash only. ❸

☒ **Zagros,** Albert Cuypstr. 50 (☎670 04 61). Great Kurdish cuisine influenced by the 5 countries spanned by Kurdistan—Armenia, Iran, Iraq, Syria, and Turkey—in a plain but appealing candlelit atmosphere. Hearty, lamb-heavy menu (€10-14) but plenty of veggie options. Open daily 3pm-midnight. AmEx/MC/V. ❷

Cafe Latei, Zeedijk 143 (☎625 74 85). Unique cafe-*cum*-curiosities-shop, with all-day continental breakfast (€6.40). Large sandwiches about €3. Fresh juices €2-4. Call for special food events. Open M-F 8am-6pm, Sa 9am-6pm, Su 11am-6pm. ❶

Abe Veneto, Plantage Kerklaan 2 (☎639 23 64). This homey Italian eatery has food and prices to make any traveler happy. A dizzying selection of freshly made pizzas (€4.50-9.50), pastas (€6.50-9.50), and salads (most under €5). Wine by the bottle or the carafe (half carafe €6.50). Takeout available. Open daily noon-midnight. Cash only. ❷

De Soepwinkel, 1e Sweelinckstr. 19F (☎673 22 93), just off Albert Cuypmarkt. A hip kitchen that elevates soup-making to a fine art form. 6 specialities that change every month, all served with fresh breads (€3.50-9). Non-soup menu features include quiche (€2.10). Open M-F 11am-8pm, Sa 11am-6pm. Cash only. ❶

King Solomon Restaurant, Waterloopl. 239 (☎625 58 60). Run by a hospitable Ortho-dox family, this is the only kosher restaurant in sight of the old Jewish quarter. Serves falafel (€7.25) and gefilte fish (€6.75). Open in summer M-Th and Su noon-10pm, F noon-5pm; off-season Sa 45min. after sundown-10pm. AmEx/MC/V. ❷

Peppino Gelateria, 1e Sweelinckstr. 16 (☎676 49 10). The city's best homemade gelato (from €0.75 per scoop). Flavors include from coconut to banana to pineapple. Excellent cappuccino (€1.80). Open M-F 10am-11pm. Cash only. ❶

Soup En Zo, Jodenbreestr. 94a (☎422 22 43). Let your nose guide you to the amazing broth at this tiny soupery. Several soups and sizes (€2.20-5.50) with free bread and fresh toppings (coriander, dill, cheese, nuts). Check out their new location at Nieuwe Spiegelstr. 54. Open M-F 11am-8pm, Sa 11am-7pm, Su 1-7pm. ❶

Moksie, Ferdinand Bolstr. 21 (☎676 82 64). The name of this mellow Surinamese res-taurant refers to its signature dish, a mixture of chicken, sausage, beef, and pork in soy sauce (€7.50; large €8.80). Open Su 4-10pm, Tu-Sa noon-10pm. Cash only. ❷

◎ SIGHTS

Amsterdam is fairly compact, so tourists can easily explore the area from the Rijksmuseum to the Red Light District on foot. For those not inclined to pedes-trian navigation, the tram system will get you to any of the city's major sights within minutes from any destination (p. 770). For a peaceful trip, **Museumboot Canal Cruise** allows you to hop on and off along its loop from the VVV to the Anne Frank Huis, the Bloemenmarkt, the Rijksmuseum, Waterloopl., and the old ship-yard. (Every 30min. Day ticket €14.30; €12.50 after 1pm.)

OUDE ZIJD, THE RED LIGHT DISTRICT, AND NIEUWE ZIJD

THE RED LIGHT DISTRICT. No trip to Amsterdam would be complete without witnessing the notorious spectacle that is the Red Light District. After dark, the area actually takes on a red radiance—sex theaters throw open their doors, and the main streets are thick with people gawking at the unabashed openness of the window prostitutes; **Warmoesstraat** and **Oudezijds Achterburgwal** boast wall-to-wall brothels. There are also **sex shows,** in which actors perform strictly choreographed fantasies on stage for 1hr.; the most famous live sex show takes place at **Casa Rosso,** Oudezijds Achterburgwal 106-108, where €25 will buy you admission to 8 or 9 consecutive acts and complimentary drinks. The Casa's **marble penis fountain** across from the theater is the Red Light District's most recognizable landmark. (☎627 89 54; www.janot.com. Open daily M-Th 8pm-2am, F-Sa 8pm-3am.)

BEGIJNHOF. You don't have to take vows to enter this secluded courtyard—the 14th-century home of the Beguines, a sect of religiously devoted laywomen—but you will have to get up early. Begijnhof's peaceful, rose-lined gardens, beautifully manicured lawns, and tree-lined walkways afford a much-needed respite from the bustling excesses of the Nieuwe Zijd. The oldest house in Amsterdam, **Het Houten Huys** (The Wooden House), is located on the premises. (Open July-Aug. daily 8-11am; Sept.-May 9am-5pm. Free. Het Houten Huys ☎623 55 54. Open M-F 8-10am. Free.)

To see Amsterdam as locals do, spend a day on **bike.** The nicest biking routes are those that run through through the canal districts; places toward the center of town (especially congested pedestrian walkways near the Red Light District) should always be avoided. Our tour starts and ends at **Frederic Rent a Bike,** Brouwersgr. 78; for more info, see p. 770.

Start off by biking down **Prinsengracht.** Turn left onto **Reestraat,** which becomes **Hartenstraat** and **Gasthuismolensteeg.** Continue over the **Singel** to **Dam Square.**

1 DAM SQUARE. Amsterdam's central square is surrounded by the Nieuwe Kerk, Nationaal Monument, and Koninklijk Paleis, home to the Dutch royal family. Stop and check out the street performers in good weather.

2 SPUI. Head back towards Singel, turn left on Nieuwezijds Voorburgwal and go south for a few minutes to arrive at Spui. The square is home to a Sunday art market, a Friday book market, and is surrounded by bookstores. If you're up early, head into the **Begijnhof** (p. 779), the peaceful residence for observant lay-women. Ride back to the Western Canal Ring via Heistraat. Turn left onto Herengracht and right onto Leidsegracht; the beautiful intersection of the Leidsegracht and Keizersgracht canals is definitely worth a lenghty pause.

3 DE APPEL. Continue down Leidsegracht, turn left at Keizersgracht, and left on Nieuwe Spiegelstraat. Stop at Nieuwe Spiegelstr. 10 to tour Amsterdam's premier space for contemporary art. (p. 787).

4 GOLDEN BEND. After some art-gazing, head over to the stretch of Herengracht between Leidsestraat and Vijzelstraat, known as the "Golden Bend" because of its opulent houses. Officials bent the strict house-width rules for wealthy citizens who were willing to invest in the construction of the Herengracht, or "gentleman's canal."

5 MAGERE BRUG. Turn right at Utrechtsestraat and then left at Prinsengracht. Continue until you hit the Amstel river and turn left; the *Magere Brug* (skinny bridge) is on your right. This is the oldest of the city's pedestrian bridges and the only one operated by hand.

6 NIEUWMARKT. Cross the bridge, turn left, and head north along the Amstel, crossing the bridge at Herengracht. Veer left on the path, go right around the far side of the Stadhuis, and cross the bridge at Staalstraat. When you hit Groenburgwal, turn right, make another right again at Raamgracht, and then left at the first bridge. Cross over, turn left and double back along the far side of Raamgracht. Turn right at Kloveniersburgwal and follow it to Nieuwmarkt, an open-air market on weekends and home to the Waag, Amsterdam's largest surviving medieval building (p. 782). Head back to Frederic's via Zeedijk, which turns into Prins Hendrikkade and passes Centraal Station.

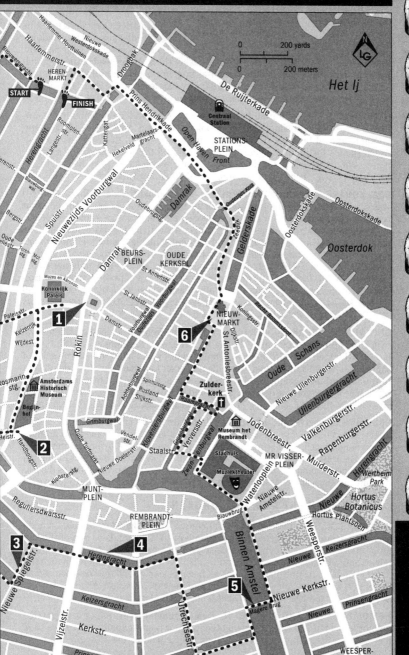

OUDE KERK. The "old church" may come as a welcome, wholesome shock, smack in the middle of the otherwise lurid Red Light District. Oude Kerk is a stunning structure, with an enormous interior and magnificent stained-glass windows. The earliest parish church built in Amsterdam, it is now a center for cultural activities, hosting photography and modern art exhibitions. At the head of the church is the massive Vater-Müller organ, which was built in 1724 and is still played for public concerts. *(Oudekerkspl. 23. ☎625 82 84; www.oudekerk.nl. Open M-Sa 11am-5pm, Su 1-5pm. €4, students €3. Additional admission for exhibitions.)*

NIEUWMARKT. On the border between the Oude Zijd and the Jodenbuurt, Nieuwmarkt is worth a visit simply to take a look at the Waag, Amsterdam's largest surviving medieval building. Dating from the 15th century, the Waag was one of Amsterdam's fortified city gates and later housed the Surgeons Guild's amphiteater. Public dissections and private anatomy lessons were once held there, as Rembrandt's *The Anatomy Lesson of Dr. Tulp* famously depicts.

DAM SQUARE AND KONINKLIJK PALEIS. The **Koninklijk Paleis** (Royal Palace) was completed in 1655 and functioned as the town hall until Louis Napoleon had it renovated and remodeled in 1808 to better serve the function of a royal residence. Today Queen Beatrix still uses the building for official receptions though she makes her home in The Hague. The palace's indisputable highlight is the **Citizen's Hall,** designed to replicate the universe in a single room. Across the large Dam Square is the Dutch **Nationaal Monument,** unveiled on May 4, 1956, to honor Dutch victims of WWII. Inside the 21m white stone obelisk is soil from all twelve of Holland's provinces as well as from the Dutch East Indies. *(Koninklijk Paleis ☎620 40 60; www.kon-paleisamsterdam.nl. Palace open June-Aug. daily 12:30-5pm; off-season hours vary. €4.50, children and seniors €3.60. Under-6 free.)*

SINT NICOLAASKERK. A burst of color emanates from the stained-glass windows over the impressive columned altar of the otherwise forbidding, gray Sint Nicolaaskerk. Erected by A.C. Bleys and completed in 1887 to honor the patron saint of sailors, it replaced a number of Amsterdam's secret Catholic churches from the era of the Alteration. Designed in the neo-Baroque style, the structure houses stern black marble columns, a domed ceiling, and wooden vaults. *(Prins Henrikkade 73. ☎624 87 49. Open M 1-4pm, Tu–F 11am-4pm, Sa noon-3pm. Su mass at 10:30am. Free.)*

SPUI. Pronounced "spow," this tree-lined, cobblestoned square south of the Begijnhof is perfect for quiet lounging on summer afternoons. Spui is home to an art market on Sundays, a book market on Fridays, and is surrounded by bookstores. Look out for **Het Lievertje** (The Little Urchin), a small bronze statue by Carel Kneulman that became a symbol for the Dutch civil action group, the Provos, and was the site of many meetings and riots in the 1960s. *(Tram #4, 9, 14, 16, 20, 24, or 25 to Spui.)*

CANAL RING WEST AND THE JORDAAN

WESTERKERK. This stunning Protestant church was designed by Roman Catholic architect Hendrick de Keyser and completed in 1631. It stands as one of the last structures built in the Dutch Renaissance style, which can be distinguished by its use of both brick and stone. Rembrandt is believed to be buried here, though the exact spot of his resting place has not yet been located. Climb the **Westerkerkstoren** tower in a 45min.-1hr. tour for a great view of the city. *(Prinsengr. 281. ☎624 77 66. Open July-Aug. M-Sa 11am-3pm; Sept. and Apr.-June M-F 11am-3pm. Tours every hr. €3.)*

HOMOMONUMENT AND PINK POINT. Homomonument serves as a tripartite memorial to men and women persecuted for their homosexuality, and since 1987 has stood in the center of Amsterdam as a testament to the strength and resilience of the homosexual community. Karin Daan's design, three pink granite triangles, allude to the signs homosexuals were required to wear in Nazi concentration camps. The Homomonument's neighbor, **Pink Point,** stands as a reminder of everything vibrant and fun about gay life in Amsterdam. The kiosk is a clearinghouse for information on homosexual happenings. Pick up free listings of BGL bars, clubs, restaurants, and cultural life. *(Both in front of Westerkerk. Pink Point:* ☎ *428 10 70; www.pinkpoint.org. Open Apr.-Sept. daily noon-6pm.)*

INSTITUTE FOR WAR DOCUMENTATION. The degree of intricacy in its carvings and other ornamental decoration set this stone mansion apart from other banal canal houses. Nazis occupied the opulent space during WWII, and the building now houses the *Nederlands Instituut voor Oorlogsdocumentatie* (Dutch Library of War Documentation). In addition to a comprehensive collection of Dutch war resources and photographs, the library has English-, French-, and German-language books concerning WWII and other major international conflicts. The study and library are both open to the public. *(Herengrt. 380.* ☎ *523 38 00; www.oorlogsdoc.knaw.nl. Open M 1-5pm; Tu-W, F 9am-5pm; Th 9am-9pm. Free.)*

LEIDSEPLEIN AND MUSEUMPLEIN

LEIDSEPLEIN. Leidseplein proper is a crush of street musicians, blaring neon lights, and open-air urinals. Daytime finds the square packed with shoppers, smokers, and drinkers lining the sidewalks around the square. When night falls, tourists and locals emerge in packs of skin-tight jeans and greased-down hair. **Max Euweplein,** a square along Weteringschans named for the famous Dutch chess master, sports an enormous chess board with people-sized pieces.

VONDELPARK. With meandering walkways, green meadows, several ponds, beautifully maintained rose gardens and a 1.5km paved path for bikers and skaters, this English-style park is a lovely meeting place for children, seniors, soccer players, and stoners. Named after one of Holland's great writers, Joost van den Vondel, Vondelpark is home to an open-air theater—**The Openluchttheater** (☎ 673 14 99; www.openluchttheater.nl)—where visitors can enjoy free concerts during the summer. *(In the southwestern corner of the city, outside the Singelgr. A short walk across the canal and to the left from the Leidsepl. www.vondelpark.org.)*

CENTRAL CANAL RING AND REMBRANDTPLEIN

CENTRAL CANAL RING. You haven't seen Amsterdam until you've spent some time wandering in the Central Canal Ring, the city's highest rent district and arguably its most beautiful. Collectively, **Prinsengracht** (Prince's canal), **Keizersgracht** (Emperor's canal), and **Herengracht** (Gentlemen's canal) are known as the *grachtengordel* (literally "canal girdle"). The Ring is home to some of Amsterdam's most important and breathtaking architecture, particularly on a stretch of the Herengrt. between Leidsegrt. and Vijzelstr. that is known as the **Golden Bend** by virtue of its wide, lavish homes. *(Over the Singel and just south of Centrum.)*

REMBRANDTPLEIN. Rembrandtplein proper consists of a grass rectangle surrounded by scattered flowerbeds. A bronze likeness of the famed master, **Rembrandt van Rijn,** overlooks the scene, but it's what surrounds the greenery that makes this neighborhood unforgettable. Litters of bars and cafes are all packed with lively night owls. In the evening, Rembrandtpl. competes with Leidsepl. for Amsterdam's hippest nightlife, with a concentration of gay hotspots. South and west of the square lies **Reguliersdwarsstraat,** fittingly dubbed "the gayest street in Amsterdam," where good-looking men abound. *(In the northeast corner of the Central Canal Ring, just south of the Amstel.)*

CAT'S CABINET. Housed in the only public building on the Golden Bend, the Cat's Cabinet is a temple to all things feline—including statuary, portraiture, pop art, and assorted knick-knacks. The collection was started by a businessman with an unusually strong 18-year attachment to his cat named J. P. Morgan; check out his feline face gracing the dollar bill in the museum. (*Herengrt. 497.* ☎ *626 53 78; www.kattenkabinet.nl. Open M-F 10am-2pm, Sa-Su 1-5pm. €4.50, under-12 €2.30.*)

DE PIJP, JODENBUURT, AND THE PLANTAGE

HEINEKEN EXPERIENCE. Beer is not made in the Heineken Brewery but plenty is served. The factory stopped producing here in 1988 and has turned the place into an amusement park devoted to their green-bottled beer. In the "Experience," visitors guide themselves past holograms, virtual reality machines, and other multimedia treats. A visit includes three beers and a souvenir glass. (*Heinekenpl.* ☎ *523 96 66; www.heinekenexperince.com. Open Su, Tu-Sa 10am-6pm; last entry at 5pm. Under-18 must be accompanied by a parent. €7.50.*)

PORTUGEES-ISRAELIETISCHE SYNAGOGE. This beautifully maintained Portuguese synagogue dates to 1675, when it was founded by Jews fleeing the Spanish Inquisition. Since then, it has remained largely unchanged and still holds services. (*Mr. Visserpl. 1-3.* ☎ *624 53 51; www.esnoga.com. Open Apr.-Oct. M-F and Su 10am-4pm; Nov.-Mar. M-Th and Su 10am-4pm, F 10am-3pm. €5, under-15 €4.*)

HOLLANDSCHE SCHOUWBURG. This historic building stands today as one of the region's most enduring symbols of freedom, a moving testament to Dutch life before, during, and after Hitler. Hollandsche Schouwburg was founded as a Dutch theater on the edge of the old Jewish quarter. It later underwent a metamorphosis in 1941, when Nazi occupiers converted it into the Joodsche Schouwburg, the city's sole establishment to which Jewish performers and Jewish patrons were granted access. Not long after, the building was changed into an assembly point for Dutch Jews who were to be deported to transit camps in the north. Now Hollandsche Schouwburg houses a memorial to Holocaust victims. (*Plantage Middenlaan 24.* ☎ *626 99 45; www.jhm.nl. Open daily 11am-4pm; closed on Yom Kippur. Free.*)

HORTUS BOTANICUS. With over 6000 species of plants, Hortus, founded in 1638, is one of the oldest gardens of its kind in the world and a refuge for a number of near-extinct plants. It was originally established as "Hortus Medicus," a medicinal garden for the town's physicians. Many of its more exceptional specimens, including a coffee plant whose clippings spawned the Brazilian coffee empire, were gathered by members of the Dutch East India Company. (*Plantage Middenlaan 2A.* ☎ *638 16 70; www.dehortus.nl. Open Apr.-Oct. M-F 9am-5pm, Sa-Su 11am-5pm; Dec.-Mar. M-F 9am-4pm, Sa-Su 11am-4pm. €6, children and seniors €3. Guided tours Su 2pm €1.*)

DE PIJP. De Pijp (pronounced "pipe") is a work in progress, a gentrification project occurring in a neighborhood once known for its immigrant authenticity—citizens from Indonesia, Kurdistan, Morocco, Surinam, and Turkey all live here with would-be bohemians. The neighborhood is now ballooning in popularity as new high-design restaurants and bars get written up in socialite magazines and attract slim fashionistas with the promise of the next big thing. Most of De Pijp is best experienced by wandering around its skinny streets and popping into its cheap, low-end restaurants and shops. The best place to start is amid the crowded, bustling din of the **Albert Cuypmarkt**, a vibrant market and home to some of the best budget-eatery deals in the city—the market is along Albert Cuypstr. between **Ferdinand Bolstraat** (the district's largest thoroughfare) and Van Woustr.

SARPHATIPARK. A short stroll from the Heineken Experience will take you to the lovely, diminutive Sarphatipark, named for the Doctor Samuel Sarphati, a philanthropist who instituted a series of public works programs in the 19th century. Smack in the center of De Pijp, the Sarphatipark is a pleasant stretch of green criss-crossed by a series of paths and a sinuous pond. The park and areas to the south are safe enough by day but should be approached with caution after dark. *(At the corner of Sarphatipark and 1e Swelinckstr.)*

ARCAM (ARCHITECTURE CENTER AMSTERDAM). Staffed by professionals with training in design, ARCAM is a fantastic resource for finding out all you could possibly want to know about Amsterdam's vibrant architecture scene. While the center is not really a museum, it hosts a number of changing exhibitions that provide guests and residents of the city with some insight into what's behind (and inside) Amsterdam's newest and oldest structures. ARCAM also sells a detailed architectural map of the city. *(Oosterdok 14. ☎620 48 78; www.arcam.nl. Open Tu-Sa 1-5pm; closed on bank holidays. Free.)*

🏛 MUSEUMS

OUDE ZIJD, THE RED LIGHT DISTRICT, AND NIEUWE ZIJD

MUSEUM AMSTELKRING "ONS' LIEVE HEER OP SOLDER" ("OUR LORD IN THE ATTIC"). A secret enclave of virtue and piety hides in this 17th-century secret church, built during the Alteration for Catholics who were forbidden to practice their faith. Amstelkring, which once masqueraded as a shop front, contains a stunning little chapel which spans the attics of three adjacent buildings. *(Oudezijds Voorburgwal 40. ☎624 66 04; www.museumamstelkring.nl. Open M-Sa 10am-5pm, Su and holidays 1-5pm. €6, students €4.50, under-18 €1.)*

THE VICES. If it's weed that interests you, far and away your best bet is the staggeringly informative **Cannabis College,** Oudezijds Achterburgwal 124. The center for "higher" education offers info on everything from the uses of medicinal marijuana to facts about the War on Drugs to the creative applications of industrial hemp. For a curated taste of the seaminess that runs down Amsterdam's underbelly, your best bet is to head to the **Amsterdam Sex Museum,** Damrak 18, less than a five-minute walk from Centraal Station. The low admission fee won't leave you feeling burned if you find that walls plastered with pictures of bestiality and S&M are not your thing. *(Cannabis College open daily 11am-7pm. Free. Sex Museum open daily 10am-11:30pm. €2.50.)*

NIEUWE KERK. The extravagant 15th-century brick-red "new church" at the heart of the Nieuwe Zijd now serves a triple role as religious edifice, historical monument, and art museum. Through 2004, the originally Catholic church will open its doors to rotating exhibits from the Stedelijk collection's depository while the Stedelijk is being renovated. *(Adjacent to Dam Sq., beside Koninklijk Palace. ☎638 69 09; www.nieuwekerk.nl. Open M-W, F, and Su, 10am-6pm; Th 10am-10pm. Organ recitals June-Sept. Su 8pm and Th 12:30pm. €8, ages 6-15 and seniors €6.)*

AMSTERDAM HISTORISCH MUSEUM. The Amsterdam Historical Museum offers an introduction to Amsterdam's historical development by way of medieval manuscripts, Baroque paintings, and multimedia displays. Be sure to catch one of the Historical Museum's hidden surprises: In the covered passageway between the museum and Begijnhof there is an extensive collection of large 17th-century paintings of Amsterdam's civic guards. *(Kalverstr. 92, Sint Luciensteeg 27, and Nieuwezijds Voorburgwal 357. ☎523 18 22; www.ahm.nl. Open M-F 10am-5pm, Sa-Su 11am-5pm; closed Apr. 30. €6, seniors €4.50, ages 6-16 €3.)*

AMSTERDAMS CENTRUM VOOR FOTOGRAFIE. The Amsterdam Center for Photography is a brimming forum that emphasizes the talents of young photographers and holds five- to six-week-long exhibitions by up-and-coming, mainly Dutch, artists. The level of talent and breadth of subject matter displayed is highly variable, but there are always some remarkable and vibrant pieces throughout the three floors of open, sunny display rooms. **Gallerie 39,** Bethanienstr. 39, is a newly opened branch of this museum and displays additional photographs by the same artists. *(Bethanienstr. 9.* ☎ *622 48 99. Open W-Sa 1-6pm. Closed July to mid-Aug.)*

BEURS VAN BERLAGE. Architecture buffs will salivate over this old stock-and-commodities exchange, designed by Hendrik van Berlage in 1903. While the restored interior chambers—part of an ongoing project to restore spaces to their original states—provide a fascinating look at the workings of the Dutch economy at the turn of the century, the highlight of the museum may well be the vertiginous ascent up a rickety staircase to the top of the clock tower. Those gutsy enough to brave the climb will be rewarded with a sweeping 360-degree view of the city. The interior space is a gallery featuring displays that focus on architectural models, paintings, and photographs. *(Damrak 277, near Dam Sq.* ☎ *530 41 41; www.beursvanberlage.nl. Open Su and Tu-Sa 11am-5pm. €5, students €3. Under-12 free.)*

CANAL RING WEST AND THE JORDAAN

◼ ANNE FRANK HUIS. A visit to the Anne Frank House is a must for everyone, whether or not you've read the famous diary. The museum chronicles the two years the Frank family and four other Jews spent hiding in the annex of this warehouse on the Prinsengr. The rooms are no longer furnished, but personal objects in display cases and text panels with excerpts from the diary bring the story of the eight inhabitants to life, and the magazine clippings and photos that Anne used to decorate her room still hang on the wall. Footage of interviews with Otto Frank, Miep Gies (who supplied the family with food and other necessities), and childhood friends of Anne provide further information and details. Arrive before 10am and after 4pm for the shortest lines. *(Prinsengr. 267.* ☎ *556 71 00; www.annefrank.nl. Open Apr.-Aug. daily 9am-9pm; Sept.-Mar. daily 9am-7pm. Closed on Yom Kippur. Last admission 30min. before closing. €6.50, ages 10-17 €3. Under-10 free.)*

BIJBELS MUSEUM. The Bible Museum presents info both on the contents and history of the Bible and on the cultural context in which it was written. The collection includes the first Bible ever printed in The Netherlands. *(Herengr. 366-368.* ☎ *624 24 36; www.bijbelsmuseum.nl. Open M-Sa 10am-5pm, Su 11am- 5pm. €5, children €2.50.)*

ELECTRIC LADYLAND: THE FIRST MUSEUM OF FLUORESCENT ART. Endearingly eccentric owner Nick Padalino has collected a singularly impressive assortment of fluorescent objects. These include gorgeous rocks that glow green in black light and an array of everyday objects that reveal hidden shades. Visitors are encouraged to dive into the interactive space and play with the many switches and buttons that turn various lights on and off. *(2e Leliedwarsstr. 5.* ☎ *420 37 76; www.electric-lady-land.com. Open Tu-Sa 1-6pm. €5. Under-12 free.)*

STEDELIJK MUSEUM BUREAU AMSTERDAM. This adjunct of the Stedelijk (see below) devotes itself to exhibiting the newest in Amsterdam art. A pure white space made light and breezy by a vaulted glass ceiling, the museum bureau is something of a testing ground for avant-garde artists and material designers. The temporary shows range from rather traditional forms of painting and sculpture to outrageous attempts at installation, as well as displays of furniture and fashion design. *(Rozenstr. 59.* ☎ *422 04 71; www.smba.nl. Open Su and Tu-Sa 11am-5pm. Free.)*

THE NETHERLANDS

HUIS MARSEILLE. The first locale in the city to curate photography exhibits on a permanent basis, the Marseille is a must for shutterbugs. Every three months, a handful of new displays grace this 1665 canal house—only a few prints are selected from each artist, but their works are invariably expressive, informative, and thoughtfully arranged. The museum also has its own permanent collection of contemporary works by celebrated international photographers whose pieces also branch out into other forms of visual art. *(Keizersgrt. 401.* ☎ *531 89 89; www.huismarseille.nl. Open in summer Tu-W 11am-5pm, Th-F 11am-8pm; off-season Su and Tu-Sa 11am-5pm. €2.80, students €1.40. Under-12 free.)*

MUSEUMPLEIN

■ **VAN GOGH MUSEUM.** This architecturally breathtaking museum houses the largest collection of van Goghs in the world and a diverse group of 19th-century paintings by contemporaries like Gaugin and friend Emile Bernard. Don't miss the substantial collection of Impressionist, post-Impressionist, Realist, and Symbolist art. *(Paulus Potterstr. 7.* ☎ *570 52 52; www.vangoghmuseum.nl. Open daily 10am-6pm; ticket office closes 5:30pm. €9, ages 13-17 €2.50. Under-12 free. Audio guides €4.)*

■ **STEDELIJK MUSEUM OF MODERN ART.** The Stedelijk has amassed a world-class collection that is on par with the Tate Modern or the MoMA. The museum is slated to close in January 2004 for up to three years of renovations, though this repair work may be delayed. If it does undergo renovations, the museum will exhibit selections from its collection in venues around Amsterdam, like the **CoBrA Museum** and the **Nieuwe Kerk** (p. 785); check the website for more up-to-date information. *(Paulus Potterstr. 13.* ☎ *573 27 45; recorded info 573 29 11; www.stedelijk.nl. Open daily 11am-5pm. €7; ages 7-16, over-65 and groups over 15 €3.50. Under-7 free.)*

■ **RIJKSMUSEUM AMSTERDAM.** The "State Museum" has long been known as Amsterdam's preeminent destination for art from the Dutch Golden Age. Even though the main building of the museum will close for renovations in December 2003, the Rijksmuseum is still a mandatory Amsterdam excursion. During restoration, the smaller Philips Wing will remain open to show masterpieces of 17th-century painting, including works by Frans Hals, Rembrandt van Rijn, Jan Steen, and Johannes Vermeer. Unfortunately, while the museum undergoes renovation, much of the collection will not be on display, but you may be able to catch a glimpse of some of the museum's holdings on loan at venues around the city. For details on the locations that will temporarily hold the Rijksmuseum's collection, check the website. *(Stadhouderskade 42.* ☎ *674 70 00; www.rijksmuseum.nl. Open daily 10am-5pm. €8.50. Under-18 free. Audio guides €3.50.)*

FILMMUSEUM. Although the Filmmuseum is dedicated to the celebration and preservation of film, don't come here expecting to find mundane museum exhibits: Most visitors come to see movies. As the national center for cinema in The Netherlands, the museum's collection holds 35,000 titles stretching back to 1898. In addition to screening several films a day, they maintain an information center at 69 Vondelstr. (across the path from the entrance), which houses the largest collection of books and periodicals on film in The Netherlands, many of them in English. You can do film research in the non-circulating archives or on the computerized databases; the staff will help with any requests. *(Vondelpark 3, between the Roemer Visscherstr. and Vondelstr. entrances.* ☎ *589 14 00; www.filmmuseum.nl. Free.)*

CENTRAL CANAL RING

DE APPEL. This contemporary art museum houses a brilliant permanent collection and welcomes compelling, cutting-edge temporary exhibits that make even the Stedelijk look old-fashioned. *(Nieuwe Spiegelstr. 10.* ☎ *625 56 51; www.deappel.nl. Open Su and Tu-Sa 11am-6pm. €2.)*

FOAM PHOTOGRAPHY MUSEUM. Inside a traditional canal house, Foam stages a fearless exploration of modern photography. Every genre of the photographed image is fair game—from the purely aesthetic to the overtly political, from fashion photography to historical exhibits. *(Keizersgr. 609. ☎551 65 00; www.foam.nl. Open daily 10am-5pm. €5, students with ID €4. Cafe open Su and W-Sa 10am-5pm.)*

MUSEUM WILLET-HOLTHUYSEN. Walk into life in the Golden Age. Run by the Amsterdam Historisch Museum, this 17th-century canal house has been preserved as a museum with 18th-century furnishings, so you can see how the wealthy in Amsterdam lived over 300 years ago. In 1895, Sandrina Holthuysen donated the family home she shared with her collector husband Abraham Willet. Now the marble and gilt mansion has been redone in a Baroque, early 18th-century style, with gilt-edged walls, glittering chandeliers, family portraits, Rococo furnishings, and other signs of conspicuous consumption, including Abraham's collection of fine porcelain, crystal, and silver. The French Neoclassical garden out back remains as finely manicured as it was in the Golden Age. *(Herengrt. 605. ☎523 18 70; www.ahm.nl. Open M-F 10am-5pm, Sa-Su 11am-5pm. €4, over-65 €3, ages 6-16 €2. Under-6 free.)*

TORTURE MUSEUM. Just about every means of medieval torture imaginable is displayed at this appropriately dark, claustrophobic museum. Though the racks, guillotines, and thumbscrews lack much context beyond a glib explanation of their use, the sheer intricacy of the darker side of European feudal history is worth a look. *(Singel 449. ☎320 66 42. Open daily 10am-11pm. €5, children €3.50.)*

JODENBUURT AND PLANTAGE

JOODS HISTORISCH MUSEUM. In the heart of Amsterdam's traditional Jewish neighborhood, the Jewish Historical Museum aims to celebrate Jewish culture and document the religion's cultural legacy. Through exhibits by Jewish artists and galleries of historically significant Judaica, the museum presents The Netherlands's most comprehensive picture of Jewish life—photographs, religious artifacts, texts, artwork, and traditional clothing remain in the permanent collection. *(Jonas Daniel Meijerpl. 2-4. ☎626 99 45; www.jhm.nl. Open daily 11am-5pm. Closed Yom Kippur. €6.50, seniors and ISIC holders €4, ages 13-18 €3, ages 6-12 €2. Audio Tour €1.)*

MUSEUM HET REMBRANDT. Dutch master Rembrandt van Rijn's house at Waterloopl. is the home of the artist's impressive collection of 250 etchings. See the inhumanly claustrophobic box-bed in which Rembrandt slept and tour the studio in which he mentored promising painters. *(Jodenbreestr. 4. ☎520 04 00; www.rembrandthuis.nl. Open M-Sa 10am-5pm, Su 1-5pm. €7, with ISIC €5. Under-6 free.)*

TROPENMUSEUM (MUSEUM OF THE TROPICS). The Tropenmuseum takes guests on an anthropological tour of Africa, Asia, the Caribbean, Latin America, and Oceania with ancient artifacts, contemporary objects, and religious pieces. Sponsored by the Dutch Royal Institute of the Tropics, the museum is situated in one of Amsterdam's most awe-inspiring modern buildings—a massive, arched dome slotted with skylights. Most of the works on display were obtained through Dutch colonial expansion; others are contemporary ethnographic studies. *(Linnaeusstr. 2. ☎568 82 15; www.tropenmuseum.nl. Open daily 10am-5pm. €6.80, students and seniors €4.50, ages 6-17 €3.40. Under-6 free.)*

VERZETSMUSEUM (DUTCH RESISTANCE MUSEUM). Though the Nazi-German military quickly overran Dutch armed forces in May, 1940, The Netherlands maintained an active resistance throughout WWII. The Resistance Museum focuses on the members of this secret army, providing visitors with the details of their lives and struggles. Model streets, buildings, and tape-recorded radio reports recreate the rebels' experiences—from smuggling food to issuing anti-propaganda on a printing press. *(Plantage Kerklaan 61. ☎620 25 35; www.verzetsmuseum.org. Open Tu-F 10am-5pm, Sa-M noon-5pm, public holidays noon-5pm. €4.50, ages 7-15 €2.50.)*

NEMO (NEW METROPOLIS). The green hull-like structure rising out of the water is NEMO, a science and creative exploration center geared toward children ages 6-16 and their accompanying adults. The structure, Renzo Piano's modern homage to The Netherlands's seafaring past, spans four stories and is littered with science exhibits just begging to be poked at, jumped on, and experimented with. Don't miss the spectacular view of the shipyard and the historic city; on the eastern side, a staircase traverses the structure's slanted roof. *(Oosterdok 2. East of Centraal Station in/on the Oosterdok. ☎(0900) 919 11 00, €0.35 per min.; www.e-NEMO.nl. Open Su and Tu-Sa 10am-5pm. €10, students €6. Under-4 free.)*

SCHEEPVAARTMUSEUM (MARITIME MUSEUM). For lovers of the sea, the vast three-tiered Maritime Museum leaves no shell unturned in its exploration of The Netherlands's sea-faring history. In addition to the 70 real vessels on display, multiple model ships are spread throughout, including the spectacular Dutch East Indiaman Den Ary, a ship that seems to have sailed straight out of the mythical age of pirates and mermaids. Don't miss the full-size replica of the Dutch East Indian ship "Amsterdam," parked right in front of the museum. On weekends, actors re-create life on board this ship. *(Kattenburgerpl. 1. Follow signs past NEMO. ☎523 22 22; www.scheepvaartmuseum.nl. Open late-Sept. to early-June. Su and Tu-Sa 10am-5pm; mid-June to mid-Sept. daily 10am-5pm. €7, seniors €6, students €5.25, children 6-18 €4.)*

🎭 ENTERTAINMENT

The **Amsterdams Uit Buro** (AUB), Leidsepl. 26, is stuffed with fliers, pamphlets, and guides to help you sift through current events; pick up the free monthly *UITKRANT* at any AUB office to see what's on. The AUB also sells tickets and makes reservations for just about any cultural event. (☎09 00 01 91, €0.55 per min.; www.uitlijn.nl. AUB office open M-W, F-Sa 10am-6pm, Th 10am-9pm, Su noon-6pm.) The VVV **tourist office,** Stationspl. 10, has a theater desk that can also make reservations. (☎(0900) 400 40 40, €0.55 per min. Open M-Sa 10am-5pm.) If you're thirsty for more info on bars, coffeeshops, gay life, and other events, pick up *Shark* (www.underwateramsterdam.com; print versions available throughout the city).

CONCERTS. In the summer, the Vondelpark Openluchttheater hosts free performances of all sorts every Wednesday through Sunday. (☎673 14 99; www.openluchttheater.nl.) The **Royal Concertgebouw Orchestra,** one of the world's finest orchestras, plays in the **Concertgebouw,** Concertgebouwpl. 2-6. Take tram #316 to Museumpl. (☎671 83 45; www.concertegebouw.nl. Tickets from €7. Sept.-June, those under 27 can get last minute tickets for anything that isn't sold out for €7. Free lunchtime concert W 12:30pm, no tickets necessary. Ticket office open daily 10am-7pm. Guided tours Su at 9:30am; €7.)

FILM. Check out www.movieguide.nl for movie listings. In the Vondelpark, head left from the main entrance on Stadhouderskade to see what's on at the stately **Filmmuseum** independent movie theater. (☎589 14 00; www.filmmuseum.nl. Info center open M-F from 10am; Sa-Su box office opens 1hr. prior to first showing. €6.30-7, students and seniors €5.) **The Movies,** Harlemmerstr. 159, is the city's oldest movie theater. (☎624 57 90. €7.50, students and seniors €6.50.)

THE LOCAL STORY

HEMP, PH.D

Lorna Clay volunteers at ■ *Cannabis College (p. 785), the city's foremost authority on all things related to marijuana, hashish, and hemp. Lets Go got her very informed opinion about cannabis in Amsterdam:*

...In the 60s, originally the coffeeshops were known as teahouses. You couldn't buy cannabis, but you could go and buy tea and smoke it there. Then, when the licenses came out, it was just to provide a bit more choice for people and take it away from the criminals. Right off, there only used to be about four or five coffeeshops here, and that was fine for the people that lived here. Then, since the late 70s, Amsterdam's become a mecca for smokers.

...Unfortunately, Amsterdam has seen a big amount of drug tourism and that's been exploited by a lot of horrible owners. They think 'I can sell [tourists] bad cannabis and they'll never come back, and that's fine because I've made my money.' There's 281 coffeeshops in Amsterdam and I can recommend 15, honestly... a lot of the owners don't even smoke. A good thing to look out for are the members of the BCD— basically a union of coffeeshops. We can give you a BCD map.

COFFEESHOPS AND SMART SHOPS

COFFEESHOPS

The coffee at coffeeshops in Amsterdam is rarely the focal point. Places calling themselves coffeeshops sell pot or hash or will let you buy a drink and smoke your own stuff. Look for the green-and-white "Coffeeshop BCD" sticker that certifies a coffeeshop's credibility. Although Amsterdam is known as the **hashish** capital of the world, **marijuana** is increasingly popular. Technically, pot is illegal in The Netherlands; soft drugs are merely tolerated. It is unlikely you'll be punished (though your drugs may be confiscated) if you are carrying 5g of marijuana or hash at any given time. Possession of harder drugs like cocaine and heroin will be severely punished. For info on the legal ins and outs, call the **Jellinek clinic** (☎570 23 55). If your questions pertain only to matters of cannabis or hemp, try the **Cannabis College** (p. 785).

If you do decide to partake, it's a good idea not to get too caught up in Amsterdam's narcotic quirk; use common sense, and remember that any experimentation with drugs can be dangerous. **Never buy drugs from street dealers,** because you have no way of knowing if they are laced with other, more harmful drugs. Coffeeshops are licensed to sell cannabis, and the good ones regulate the quality of their smokeables very carefully. When you walk into a coffeeshop, ask for a menu, because by law they are not allowed to leave menus out on their tables or advertise their products in any way.

Marijuana is the dried, cured flower of the cannabis plant. Different weeds come in and out of favor much like different beers, and are divided into two main strains: Sativa (like the "Haze" or "Kali Mist" breeds) will get you high, giggly, and energized while Indica (like "Afghani Shiva" or "Buddha") will get you really stoned and relaxed. Pot in The Netherlands is incredibly potent; you'll likely need to smoke less to get the same high than marijuana from your home country. Unless otherwise noted, pre-rolled joints are rolled with tobacco, which makes smoking harsher on the lungs; however, pure pre-rolled pot joints are sometimes available. Almost no one smokes out of pipes; while some places provide bongs, usually only tourists use them. Dutch marijuana is the most common and costs anywhere from €3-12 per gram; most coffeeshops sell bags in set amounts (€6, 12, etc.). Staff at coffeeshops are accustomed to explaining the different kinds of pot on the menu. When you move from one coffeeshop to another, you must either buy drugs from the shop or buy a drink if you want to stay and smoke your own stash.

Hashish is made of the resin crystals extracted from the flowers of the cannabis plant, and comes in three varieties: Black (Indian), blonde (Moroccan), and Dutch (also called ice-o-lator hash). These types can run from €4-30 per gram, though the increasingly popular **ice-o-lator hash** tops out at around €20-30 per gram. Typically, the cost of the hash is proportional to its quality and strength. Black hash hits harder than blonde, and ice-o-lator can send even a seasoned smoker off his head.

Spacecakes, Spaceshakes, and **Space Sweets** are cakes and sweets made with hash or weed; hash chocolate, popsicles, and bonbons are also available. Because they need to be digested, they take longer to affect you (up to 1hr.) and longer to rinse out; don't eat another brownie if you don't feel effects immediately.

SMART SHOPS

Smart shops, which peddle a variety of **"herbal enhancers"** and **hallucinogens** that walk the line between soft and hard drugs are also legal. **Magic mushrooms** start to work thirty minutes to an hour after consumption and act on your system for four to eight hours. Different types give different highs: **Mexican** and **Thai** mushrooms are generally used by beginners; they are the least potent and give a laughing, colorful, and speedy high with some visual hallucination. **Philosophers' stones** (which have an Xstasy-like effect) and **Hawaiians** (which give an intensely visual trip similar to LSD) are significantly more intense, and should be taken **only by experienced users.** In certain cases, intake may cause you to panic or have a faster heartbeat. Never look for mushrooms in the wild and never buy from a street dealer; it's extremely difficult to tell the difference between poisonous mushrooms and hallucinogenic mushrooms. Don't mix hallucinogens such as shrooms with alcohol; if you have a bad trip, call ☎122 to go to the hospital or ask someone for help—you won't be arrested, and they've seen it all before.

WHERE TO GO...

Don't smoke at shops right at Centraal Station. The following is a list of well-regarded establishments:

▨ **Barney's Coffeeshop,** Haarlemmerstr. 102. Get a greasy breakfast with your big fat joint. Three-time "best marijuana strain" winner at the Cannabis Cup. Open daily 7am-7pm.

...If a company doesn't even distinguish on their menu between bio or hydro, it's not worth buying. Bio is when weed's grown in soil and hydro is when it's grown in water. Usually when you're growing hydro, you're filling it with artificial chemical nutrients. Good quality coffeeshops will sell good quality hydro but in bad quality coffeeshops, they don't flush the chemicals out of their plants so you get high off the harmful chemicals.

...[In a coffeeshop] don't ask: what's the strongest? It's difficult for someone to answer, because what's strongest for one is not strongest for someone else. Ask them for their most flavorsome, not their strongest. Ask them what they recommend. Never go in and ask for a name because it depends on who grows the particular plant, not the strain. For example, White Widow—it's just been made famous by the name. You will find they will bump up the price. Never ever be afraid to ask the guy or the girl about their weed. Just like if you walk into a wine bar, you want to ask advice about wine. If they give you [a hard time], honestly, turn around and walk straight out... Don't give them your business.

...Know the difference between Sativa and Indica. Sativa will get you high and giggly and energized and that is something that "Haze" or "Kali Mist" will do. When you smoke the Indica, that gets you really stoned and relaxed, and that's like "Afghani Shiva" or "Buddha." The choice is: Do you want to get high or stoned?

■ **Abraxas,** J. Roelensteeg 12-14. Amsterdam's most beautiful coffeeshop. Casual, sophisticated, no-pressure atmosphere. Open daily 10am-1am.

■ **Grey Area,** Oude Leliestr. 2. Where coffeeshop owners go for the best. One of the only owner-operated spots left in the city. The Yankee expat behind the counter will be happy to lend you one of the coffeeshop's bongs. Open Su and Tu-Sa noon-8pm.

The Dolphins, Kerkstr. 39. Enter the beautiful world of coral reefer madness at this ocean-themed coffeeshop. Open M-Th and Su 10am-1am, F-Sa 10am-3pm.

Yo Yo, 2e van der Heijdenstr. 79. So warm it makes smoking nearly wholesome. Famous apple pie, good coffee, and of course, great smokeables. Open daily noon-7pm.

Bluebird, Sint Antoniesbreestr. 71. Fun spot with a vast menu that includes samples of weed and hash for inspection. Open daily 9:30am-1am.

Paradox, 1e Bloemdwarsstr. 2. The owners match the feel of this place: Colorful, free-spirited, and ready to have a good time. Weed, hash, and awesome veggie burgers (€3.50). Kitchen closes at 3pm. Coffeeshop open daily 10am-8pm.

La Tertulia, Prinsengrt. 312. Leafy plants everywhere make for a relaxing time. *Smoker's Guide* praises the special Hawaiian haze. Open Tu-Sa 11am-7pm.

Hill Street Blues, Warmoesstr. 52. Don't let the loud rock music blaring into the street drive you away; it's all about leisurely comfort inside. If you don't want to smoke, the bar serves cheap beer (€2.50). Open M-Th and Su 9am-1am, F-Sa 9am-3am.

Dampkring, Handboogstr. 29. Deep blue, chill subterranean space with experienced, but unpretentious patrons. Open M-Th 10am-1am, F-Sa 10am-2am, Su 11am-1am.

Conscious Dreams Kokopelli, Warmoesstr. 12 (☎421 70 00). This smart shop is perhaps the best place in Amsterdam to begin with psychedelic experimentation. A staff with background in neurobiology and botany gives great information. Open daily 11am-10pm.

The Magic Mushroom, Spuistr. 249. At this museum of a smartshop, procure all the mushrooms, herbal Xstasy, and energy and smart drinks you've ever dreamed existed. Open M-Th and Su 11am-10pm, F-Sa 10am-10pm.

The Essential Seeds Company Art and Smart Shop, Hekelveld 2. Run by knowledgeable Amsterdam natives with 7 varieties of shrooms and specialties like shroom chocolate bars. Open M-W and Su 9am-7pm, Th-Sa 9am-9pm. MC/V.

◪ NIGHTLIFE

The **Leidseplein** and **Rembrandtplein** are the liveliest nightspots, with coffeeshops, loud bars, and tacky clubs galore, but in all locations, bars frequently become more clubby as the night goes on—check listings. Near Leidseplein, pricey discos abound on **Prinsengracht**, near **Leidsestraat**, and on **Lange Leidsedwarsstraat.** Some clubs charge a membership fee in addition to normal cover. Amsterdam's finest cafes are the old, dark, wood-paneled *bruine cafe* (brown cafes) mainly on the **Jordaan;** those lining **Prinsengracht** usually have outdoor seating. In Amsterdam, the concept of a completely "straight" nightlife versus a "gay" nightlife does not really apply. Essentially all establishments are gay-friendly and have a mixed-orientation crowd. Around Rembrandtpl., gay bars almost exclusively for men line **Amstelstraat** and **Reguliersdwarsstraat. Kerkstraat,** five blocks north of Leidseplein, is a gay hotspot. Pick up a wallet-sized *Clu* guide, free at cafes and coffeeshops, for a club map of the city, and *Gay and Night*, a monthly magazine, for more info.

BARS AND CAFES

▨ **Café de Jaren,** Nieuwe Doelenstr. 20-22. This fabulous 2 floor cafe's air of sophistication doesn't quite mesh with its budget-friendly prices. It's a bona fide student haunt as well. Cocktails and beer €1.80-3.10. Open M-Th and Su 10am-1am, F-Sa 10am-2am.

NL Lounge, Nieuwezijds Voorburgwal 169. This is the unmarked destination where some of Amsterdam's slickest, best-dressed, and most savvy insiders hang out. Cocktails (€6). Music varies, but at 1am, the beat invariably switches over to trippy techno. No cover. Open M-Th and Su 10pm-3am, F-Sa 10pm-4am.

Lux, Marnixstr. 403. Kitschy but classy with red plush walls and leopard-print curtains. There's not much dancing, but DJs spinning Th-Su will get you pumped to go hit the clubs later on. Beer €2. Cocktails €4. Open M-Th and Su 8pm-3am, F-Sa 8pm-4am.

Absinthe, Nieuwezijds Voorburgwal 171. With layers of magenta leather couches, Absinthe, bathes in purple light and trancy music. May be more touristy than you'd like. Open M-Th and Su 8pm-3am, F-Sa 8pm-4am.

Cafe de Wilde Zee, Haarlemmerstr. 32. Elegant, black-clad literati congregate in this maroon-colored wine bar to sip Italian espressos (€1.70), and great wines (€2.60-3 per glass), and converse to cool jazz. Open M-Tu 11am-8pm, W-Su 11am-1am.

Cafe Kalkhoven, Prinsengrt. 283. "Old Amsterdam" in all its brown, wooden glory: Old oak barrels on the wall behind the bar, darkly painted ceilings, and food choices all have a markedly Dutch flavor. *Tostis* (ham and cheese sandwich) and *appeltas* (apple strudel) both €1.80. Heineken pint €4. Open daily 11am-1am.

Arc Bar, Reguliersdwarsstr. 44. A hip, cutting-edge spot done up in leather. Cocktails €6.50-7.50. Black tabletops in front are lowered to form dancing platforms later in the evening. Open M-Th and Su noon-1am, F-Sa noon-3am.

Montmartre, Halvemaarsteg 17. Rococo interior bedecked with flowers and rich draperies houses some of the wildest gay parties in the city. Voted best gay bar in Amsterdam by *Gay Krant* 6 years running. Open M-Th and Su 5pm-1am, F-Sa 5pm-3am.

Café 't Smalle, Egelantiersgrt. 12. Founded in 1780 as the tasting room of a neighboring distillery, and one of the most popular cafes in the west end. Summertime canalside seats. Draft beer €2.50. Open M-Th and Su 10am-1am, F-Sa 10am-2am.

CLUBS AND DISCOS

The iT, Amstelstr. 24. This club is the reason why others in Rembrandtpl. are sometimes empty. Amsterdam's beauties come here to dance the night away. Beer €4. Cocktails €7.50. Cover €15. Open Su, Th 11pm-4am, F-Sa, 11pm-6am.

Dansen Bij Jansen, Handboogstr. 11-13. *The* student dance club in Amsterdam, popular with locals from the University of Amsterdam and backpackers. You must show a student ID or be accompanied by a student. A great way to meet local university kids. Beer €1.70-3.30. Cocktails from €3.30. Open M-Th and Su 11pm-4am, F-Sa 11pm-5am.

Escape, Rembrandtpl. 11. Party animals pour into this massive venue—one of Amsterdam's hottest clubs. 2 floors with 6 bars, where scenesters groove to house, trance, disco, and dance classics. Dress well. Beer €2.30. Cocktails €7.50. Cover €10-15. Open Su and Th 11pm-4am, F-Sa 11pm-5am. Cash only.

Meander, Voetboogstr. 3b. Smoky atmosphere, constant din, and dense crowds make for a raucous, high-energy good time. M student night, F-Sa disco. Beer €1.80. Cover €2.50-5. Open M-Th and Su 9pm-3am, F-Sa 9pm-4am.

De Beetles, Lange Leidsedwarsstr. 81. A drink house with a sometimes-hopping dance floor and a mixed crowd. Su reggae, Th rock night, Sa oldies and dance classics. No cover F before midnight; after midnight, €5 includes a €2 drink. Beer and soda €2. Hard liquor €3.50-5. Open Su-Th 9pm-4am, F-Sa 9pm-5am. Cash only.

Cockring, Warmoestr. 90. Somewhere between a sex club and a disco. Dark room in the back where anything goes. Men only. No cover, except for special parties, when it runs around €5. Open M-Th and Su 11pm-4am, F-Sa 11pm-5am.

LIVE MUSIC

■ **Melkweg,** Lijnbaansgrt. 234a (☎531 81 81; www.melweg.nl). Legendary nightspot in an old milk factory, it's one-stop shopping for live music, food (see **Eat At Jo's,** p. 778), films, and dance parties. Concert tickets €9.50-22 plus €2.50 monthly membership fee. Box office open M-F 1-5pm, Sa-Su 4-6pm; show days from 7:30pm to end of show.

■ **Paradiso,** Weteringschans 6-8 (☎626 45 21; www.paradiso.nl). When big-name rock, punk, new-wave, hip-hop, and reggae bands come to Amsterdam, they almost invariably play in this former church. Tickets €5-25; additional mandatory monthly membership fee €2.50. Open until 2am.

■ **Bourbon Street Jazz & Blues Club,** Leidsekruisstr. 6-8 (☎623 34 40; www.bourbonstreet.nl). A slightly older crowd comes for blues, soul, funk, and rock bands. Check the web or posting in the window for events. Beer €2.50. Cover Su and Th €3; F-Sa €5. Free with entry at 10-10:30pm. Open M-Th and Su 10pm-4am, F-Sa 10pm-5am.

⦿ DAYTRIPS FROM AMSTERDAM

TULIP COUNTRY: AALSMEER AND LISSE. Easily accessible by bus, quietly quaint Aalsmeer is home to the world's largest flower auction. With an impressive trading floor that rivals the area of 150 football fields, the **Bloemenveiling Aalsmeer,** Legmeerdijk 313, acts as a central market where growers sell over 19 million flowers annually; the world price of flowers is determined here. (☎297 39 21 85; www.vba-aalsmeer.nl. Open M-F 7:30-11am. €4.) From Amsterdam's Centraal Station, take **bus** #172 (45min., every 15min., 5 strips). Arrive before 9am to witness the busiest trading; buses begin leaving Amsterdam at 6:10am.

To see even more flowers, check out the town of Lisse in late spring. The **Keukenhof Gardens** become a kaleidoscope of color as over 7 million bulbs come to life. Now the world's largest flower garden, Keukenhof boasts impeccably kept grounds and even a petting zoo. (☎252 46 55 55; www.keukenhof.nl. In 2004, open Mar. 25-May 20 daily 8am-7:30pm; tickets on sale until 6pm. €12.) **The Zwarte Tulip Museum** details the historical cultivation and scientific evolution of "bulbiculture". Many call the ongoing quest for the *zwarte* (black) tulip impossible, since the color does not exist naturally. (☎252 41 79 00. Open Su and Tu-Sa 1-5pm. €3.) Take a **train** from Amsterdam's Centraal Station to Leiden (30min., every 30min. until 2:45am, round-trip €12), then catch **bus** #50 or 51 to Lisse (5 strips).

ZAANSE SCHANS. Unleash your inner tourist for a day in delightful Zaanse Schans, a 17th-century town on the River Zaan. In the 1950s, the people of the Zaan region were concerned that industrialization was destroying their historic landmarks, so they transported the prized sights to this pretty plot of land. Duck-filled canals, working windmills, and restored houses make Zaanse Schans feel like a museum village, although a handful of people actually live and work here. The lovely **De Kat Windmill,** Kalverringdijk 29, has been grinding plants into artists' pigments since 1782. (Open Apr.-Oct. daily 9am-5pm; Nov.-Mar. Sa-Su 9am-5pm. €2.) The oldest oil mill in the world is the **De Zoeker Windmill.** (Open Mar.-Oct. daily 9:30am-4:30pm. €2.) The **Cheesefarm Catharina Hoeve** offers free samples of its homemade wares as well as a tour of its workshop. (Open daily 8am-6pm.) Watch craftsmen mold blocks of wood into comfy clogs at **Klompenmakerij de Zaanse Schans,** or see where the ubiquitous Albert Heijn supermarket craze started at the original shop, now the **Albert Heijn Museumwinkel.** Next door you can stop by the **Museum van het Nederlandse Uurwerk** (Museum of the Dutch Clock), Kalverringdijk 3, to view the oldest working pendulum clock in the world. (Open Apr.-Oct. daily 10am-1pm, 2-5pm.

€2.30.) The pint-sized **Museum Het Noorderhuis** features original costumes from the Zaan region. (Open July-Aug. daily 10am-5pm; Sept.-Oct. and Mar.-June Su and Tu-Sa 10am-5pm; Nov.-Feb. Sa-Su 10am-5pm. €1.)

From Amsterdam, take the *stoptrein* (dir: Alkmaar) and get off at Koog Zandijk (20min., €2.25). From there, follow the signs across a bridge to Zaanse Schans (12min.). An **information center** is at Schansend 1. (☎ 616 82 18; www.zaanse-schans.nl. Open July-Aug. daily 8:30am-5:30pm, off-season 8:30am-5pm.)

HAARLEM ☎ 023

Haarlem's narrow cobblestone streets, rippling canals, and fields of tulips make for a great escape from the urban frenzy of Amsterdam. Most visitors come to Haarlem (pop. 150,000) for its Renaissance facades, medieval architecture, and incredible museums, but the city possesses more than just this antiquated charm. Haarlem also bustles with a relaxed energy that befits its urban size. Coffeeshops, bars, and the most restaurants per capita of any Dutch city ensure that there is fun to be had even after the sun goes down.

▐▀▌ TRANSPORTATION AND PRACTICAL INFORMATION. Reach Haarlem from Amsterdam by **train** from Centraal Station (20min.; €3.10, same-day round-trip €5.50) or by **bus** #80 from Marnixstr. (2 per hr., 2 strips). The VVV **tourist office,** Stationspl. 1, just to your right when you walk out of the train station, finds private rooms (from €18.50) for a €5 fee. (☎ (090) 06 16 16 00; www.vvvzk.nl. Open in summer M-F 9am-5:30pm, Sa 10am-3:30pm; off-season Sa 10am-2pm.)

▐▘▐▘ ACCOMMODATIONS AND FOOD. Walk to the Grote Markt and take a right to reach **Joops Innercity Apartments ❶,** Oude Groenmarkt 20, a centrally located hotel with elegant rooms. (☎ 532 2008. Reception M-Sa 7am-11pm, Su 8am-10pm. Singles €28-75; doubles €55-100; triples €95; quads €120.) **Hotel Carillon ❷,** Grote Markt 27, is ideally located right on the town square, to the left of the Grote Kerk. Despite their small size, most rooms include a shower, phone, and TV, and all are extremely clean. (☎ 531 0591; www.hotelcarillon.com. Breakfast included. Reception 7:30am-1am. Singles €30, with bath €55; doubles €55/71; triples €92.) Take bus #2 (dir.: Haarlem-Noord; every 10min. until 6pm, every 15min. 6pm-12:30am) to stay at **Stayokay Haarlem ❶,** Jan Gijzenpad 3. Stayokay is packed with amenities and is home to a laid-back crowd. (☎ 537 3793; www.stay-okay.com/haarlem. Breakfast included. Dorms €22-25, off-season €19-22.) To **camp** at **De Liede ❶,** Lie Over 68, take bus #2 (dir.: Zuiderpolder) and walk 10min. (☎ 535 8666. Single with tent €6, each additional person €2.90. Cash only.) For cheap meals, try cafes in the **Grote Markt** or **Botermarkt;** many offer outdoor patios. **▨Grand Café Doria ❷,** Grote Houtstr. 1a, right in the Grote Markt, special-izes in great Italian fare on an outdoor patio. (☎ 531 3335. Entrees €6-20. Open Su-Th 9am-midnight, Sa-F 9am-2am. **▨Lambermon's ❸,** Spaarne 96, offers Haarlem's best *haute cuisine.* The menu changes nightly, but always mixes fish, meat, and vegetarian options. (☎ 542 7804. Entrees €8. Due to small portions, entrees are usually ordered in groups of 4. Open daily 6:30-10:30pm. Reservations necessary.)

▣ ▥ SIGHTS AND MUSEUMS. The action centers on the **Grote Markt,** Haar-lem's vibrant main square. To get there from the train station, head south along Kruisweg, which becomes Kruisstr. and then Barteljorisstr. The **▨Grote Kerk,** at the opposite end of the Grote Markt, houses a mammoth Müller organ once played by Handel and Mozart. In the nearby **Dog Whipper's Chapel,** check out artist Frans Hals' tomb, marked only by a lantern. (Open M-Sa 10am-4pm. €1.50. Guided tours €2.) Having met the man, now see his work. From the front of the church, take a right on to Warmoestr. and walk three blocks to the ⊠**Frans Hals Museum,** Groot Heiligland 62, which houses a collection of Golden Age paintings in a 17th-century almshouse and orphanage. (Open Su noon-5pm, Tu-Sa 11am-5pm. €5.40. Under-19 free.) A 2min. walk toward the train station from the Grote Markt is the moving ⊠**Corrie Ten Boomhuis,** Barteljorisstr. 19, which served as the headquarters for Corrie Ten Boom's movement to protect Jews during WWII. The savior of an estimated 800 lives, Corrie was caught and sent to a concentration camp but survived to write *The Hiding Place,* which was later made into a film. The **Teyler's Museum,** Spaarne 16, is The Netherlands's oldest museum, and contains an eclectic assortment of scientific instruments, fossils, paintings, and drawings, including works by Michelangelo, Raphael, and Rembrandt; from the church, turn left onto Damstr. and follow it until Spaarne. (Open Su noon-5pm, Tu-Sa 10am-5pm. €5.50.) The **De Hallen Museum,** Grote Markt 16, displays exhibits of modern art housed in a former abattoir. (☎511 5775. Open Su noon-5pm, Tu-Sa 11am-5pm. €4. Under-19 free.)

⧉ DAYTRIPS FROM HAARLEM: ZANDVOORT AND BLOEMENDAAL. A mere seven miles from Haarlem, the seaside town of **Zandvoort** draws sun-starved Nederlanders to its miles of sandy beaches. To find the shore from the train station, follow the signs to the Raadhuis, then head west along Kerkstr. For a different feel, walk 30min. to hip **Bloemendaal,** which has been transformed from a quiet, family-oriented oceanside town to one of the best beach parties in Holland. The hippie-style club ⊠**Woodstock 69** hosts **Beach Bop** the last Sunday of every month (www.beachbop.info), although lower-profile parties go on other nights of the week. The town's clubs, including **Republic, De Zomer,** and **Solaris,** are open only in summer, generally from April to September.

Trains arrive in Zandvoort from Haarlem (10min., round-trip €2.75). The VVV **tourist office,** Schoolpl. 1, is just east of the town square, off Louisdavidstr. (☎571 7947; www.vvvzk.nl. Open M-Sa 9am-5:15pm.) The **Hotel Noordzee ❷,** Hogeweg 15, has cheerful rooms replete with shower and TV just 100m from the beach. (☎571 3127. Doubles €45-65.)

LEIDEN ☎071

Home to one of the oldest and most prestigious universities in Europe, Leiden brims with bookstores, windmills, gated gardens, hidden walkways, and some truly outstanding museums. Rembrandt's birthplace and the site of the first **tulip** cultivation, The Netherlands's third-largest city serves as a gateway to flower country. Follow the signs from the train station to the spacious and modern ⊠**Museum Naturalis,** which explores the history of earth and its inhabitants, providing scientific and anthropological explanations of fossils, minerals, animals, evolution, and astronomy. (☎568 76 00. Open July-Aug. daily 10am-6pm; Sept.-June Su and Tu-Sa 10am-6pm. €8.) Collecting the world's heritage since 1837, the ⊠**Rijksmuseum voor Volkenkunde** (National Museum of Ethnology), Steenstr. 1, has on display Inca sculptures, Chinese paintings, and African bronzes that were all acquired during the height of Dutch imperial power. The museum also houses impromptu re-creations and modern interpretations of past societies in its lush gardens. (☎516 88 00. Open Su and Tu-Sa 10am-5pm. €6.50.) The **Rijksmuseum van Oudheden** (National Antiquities Museum), Rapenburg 28, holds the restored Egyptian Temple of Taffeh, a gift removed from the reservoir basin of the Aswan Dam. (☎516 31 63. Open Su noon-5pm, Tu-F 10am-5pm, Sa noon-5pm. €6.) Sharing a main gate with the Academy building is the university's 400-year-old garden, the **Hortus Botanicus,** Rapenburg 73, where the first Dutch tulips were grown. Its grassy knolls alongside the **Witte Singel** canal make it an ideal picnic spot. (☎527 72 49. Open Apr.-Nov. daily 10am-6pm; Dec.-Mar. M-F and Su 10am-4pm. €4.) Scale steep staircases to inspect the inside of a functioning 18th-century windmill at the **Molenmuseum "De Valk"**, 2e Binnenvestgrt. 1. (☎516 53 53. Open Su 1-5pm, Tu-Sa 10am-5pm. €2.50.) The **Museum De Lakenhal**, Oude Singel 32, exhibits works by Rembrandt and Jan Steen. (☎516 53 60. Open Su noon-5pm, Tu-F 10am-5pm., Sa noon-5pm. €4. Under-18 free.)

Leiden is easily reached by **train** from Amsterdam's Centraal Station (30min., every 30min. until 2:45am, round-trip €12) or The Hague (20min., every 30min. until 3:15am, €4.20). The VVV **tourist office**, Stationsweg 2d, a 5min. walk from the train station, sells maps (€3) and walking tour brochures (€2), and helps find hotel rooms for a €2.30 fee for the first person, €1.80 fee for each additional person. (☎090 02 22 23 33; www.leiden.nl. Open M 11am-5:20pm, T-F 10am-5:20pm, Sa 10am-4:30pm.) The **Hotel Pension Witte Singel ❷**, Witte Singel 80, 5min. from Hortus Botanicus, has immaculate rooms that overlook gorgeous canals and gardens. (☎512 45 92; wvanvriel@pensione-ws.demon.nl. Singles from €31; doubles from €47.) Locals and students pack the popular **de Oude Harmonie ❷**, Breestr. 16, just off Rapenburg, where candlelight and stained glass set the casual mood. (Entrees €6-13. Open M-Th noon-1am, F-Sa noon-2am, Su 3pm-1am.) **Super de Boer supermarket**, Stationsweg 40, is opposite the train station. (Open M-F 7am-9pm, Sa 9am-8pm, Su noon-7pm.)

THE HAGUE (DEN HAAG)   ☎070

In many senses, The Hague (pop. 450,000) is Amsterdam's all-business brother; there are precious few coffeeshops amidst The Hague's intimidating collection of historically significant buildings and monuments. William II moved the royal residence to The Hague in 1248, prompting the creation of Parliament buildings, museums, and sprawling parks. Today, countless diplomats fill designer stores, merging rich history with a bustling metropolis.

🖪🏚 TRANSPORTATION AND PRACTICAL INFORMATION. Trains come from Amsterdam (50min., €8) and Rotterdam (25min., €3.50) to both of The Hague's major stations, **Centraal Station** and **Holland Spoor**. Trams #1, 9, and 12 connect the two stations. The VVV **tourist office**, Kon. Julianapl. 30, just outside the north entrance to Centraal Station and right next to the Hotel Sofitel, books rooms for a €5 fee and sells detailed city maps (€2). Hotel booking by computer is available 24hr. (☎090 03 40 35 05; www.denhaag.com. Open June-Sept. M and Sa 10am-5pm, Tu-F 9am-5:30pm, Su 11am-5pm; Oct.-May M and Sa 10am-5pm, Tu-F 9am-5:30pm.) Most foreign **embassies** are in The Hague: **Australia**, Carnegielaan 4, 2517 KH (☎310 82 00; open M-F 8:45am-4:30pm); **Canada**, Sophialaan 7, 2514 JP (☎311 16 00; open M-F 9am-1pm and 2-5:30pm); **Ireland**, 9 Dr. Kuyperstr., 2514 BA (☎363 09 93; call for hours); **New Zealand**, Carnegielaan 10, 2517 KH (☎346 93 24; open M-F 9am-12:30pm and 1:30-5:30pm); **South Africa**, Wassenaarseweg 40, 2596 CJ (☎392 45 01; open daily 9am-noon); **UK**, Lange Voorhout 10, 2514 ED (☎427 04 27; call for hours); **US**, Lange Voorhout 102, 2514 EJ (☎310 92 09; open M-F 8am-4:30pm).

🖪🗋 ACCOMMODATIONS AND FOOD. The **StayOkay City Hostel Den Haag ❷**, Scheepmakerstr. 27, is near Holland Spoor; turn right from the station, follow the tram tracks, turn right at the big intersection, and Scheepmakerstr. is 3min. down on your right. From Centraal Station, take tram #1 (dir.: Delft), 9 (dir.: Vrederust), or 12 (dir.: Duindrop) to *Rijswijkseplein* (2 strips); cross to the left in front of the tram, cross the intersection, and Scheepmakerstr. is straight ahead. StayOkay is a huge modern hostel that features private baths and a helpful staff. (☎315 78 88; www.njhc.org/denhaag. In-house restaurant/bar. Breakfast included. Dorms €23;

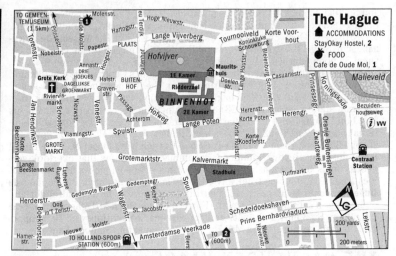

The Hague

🏠 ACCOMMODATIONS
StayOkay Hostel, **2**

🍴 FOOD
Cafe de Oude Mol, **1**

singles €47; doubles €61.) Budget takeaway places line **Lage Poten** and **Korte Poten** near the Binnenhof. 🖪**Cafe de Oude Mol** ❷, Oude Molstr. 61, a few blocks from Grote Halstr., serves up delicious *tapas*, all from €3-5. (☎345 16 23. Open M-W 5pm-1am, Th-Sa 5pm-2am, Su 5pm-1am.)

🖪🔊 **SIGHTS AND ENTERTAINMENT.** The Hague has served as the seat of Dutch government for 800 years; recently, it has also become headquarters for the international criminal justice system. Andrew Carnegie donated the **Peace Palace** (Het Vredespaleis) at Carnegiepl., the opulent home of the International Court of Justice. (www.vredespaleis.nl. Take tram #7 or 8 north from the Binnenhof. Tours M-F 10, 11am, 2, and 3pm. Book through the tourist office. €3.50, under-13 €2.30.) For snippets of Dutch politics, visit the **Binnenhof**, The Hague's Parliament complex. Near the entrance of the Binnenhof, the 17th-century **Mauritshuis**, Korte Vijverberg 8, features an impressive collection of Dutch paintings, including works by Rembrandt and Vermeer. (www.mauritshuis.nl. Open Su 11am-5pm, Tu-Sa 10am-5pm. €7. Under-18 free.) Tours leave from Binnenhof 8a and visit the 13th-century **Ridderzaal** (Hall of Knights) as well as the chambers of the States General. (Open M-Sa 10am-4pm, last tour leaves at 3:45pm. Tour €5. Entrance to courtyard free.) The impressive modern art collection at the **Gemeentemuseum**, Stadhouderslaan 41, displays Piet Mondrian's *Victory Boogie Woogie*. Take tram #10 from Holland Spoor or bus #4 from Centraal Station. (Open Su 11am-5pm, Tu-Sa 11am-5pm. €7.50.) For vibrant nightlife, prowl the Strandweg in nearby **Scheveningen.**

DELFT   ☎015

The lillied canals and stone footbridges that still line the streets of Delft (pop. 95,000) offer the same images that native Johannes Vermeer immortalized in paint over 300 years ago. It's best to visit on Thursdays and Saturdays, when townspeople flood the marketplace. The town is renowned for **Delftware,** blue-on-white earthenware developed in the 16th century. Watch Delftware being made from scratch at **De Candelaer,** Kerkstr. 13a-14, located in the center of town. (Open 9am-6pm.) To see a larger factory, take Tram #1 to *Vrijenbanselaan* and enjoy a free demonstration at **De Delftse Pauw,** Delftweg 133. (Open Apr.-Oct. daily 9am-4:30pm; Nov.-Mar. M-F 9am-4:40pm, Sa-Su 11am-1pm.) Built in 1381, the **Nieuwe Kerk** holds the restored mausoleum of Dutch liberator Willem of Orange. Climb the tower, which holds a 36-bell carillon and offers a magnificent view of old Delft. (Church open Apr.-Oct. M-Sa 9am-6pm; Nov.-Mar. M-F 11am-4pm, Sa 11am-5pm. €2.50. Tower closes 1hr. earlier. €2.) **Nusantra Museum,** St. Agathapl. 4-5, is post-colonialism at its best, housing a small but gorgeous collection of objects from former Dutch colonies. All information is in Dutch, but the friendly staff can answer your questions. (Open Su 1-5pm, Tu-Sa 10am-5pm. €3.50.) Founded in 1200, the **Oude Kerk** has a rich history and a 75m tower that leans 2m out of line. (Open Apr.-Oct. M-Sa 9am-6pm; Nov.-Mar. 11am-4pm, Sa 11am-5pm. €2.50.)

The easiest way into Delft is the 15min. ride on **tram** #1 from The Hague (2 strips) to Delft station. **Trains** also arrive from Amsterdam (1hr., €9). The **Tourist Information Point,** Hippolytusbuurt 4, near the Stadhuis, has lots of free maps and books rooms for free. (☎215 40 15, phone service €0.30 per minute; www.delft.nl. Open M 10am-4pm, T-F 9am-6pm, Sa 9am-5pm, Su 10am-4pm.) There aren't any rock-bottom budget accommodations in Delft; your best bet is to sleep in The Hague, which is 8min. away and has much better deals. **Delftse Hout Recreation Area ❶** has campsites and cabins; take #64 to the end of the line. (☎213 00 40; www.tours.nl/delftsehout. Reception May to mid-Sept. 8:30am-8pm; mid-Sept. to Apr. 9am-6pm. 2-person tent €22.) Restaurants line **Volderstraat** and **Oude Delft.**

ROTTERDAM   ☎010

The second-largest city in The Netherlands and the busiest port city in the world, Rotterdam (pop. 590,000) lacks the quaint, classic feel that characterizes much of The Netherlands. After it was bombed in 1940, experimental architects replaced the rubble with striking (some say strikingly ugly) buildings, creating an urban, industrial conglomerate. Artsy and innovative, yet almost decrepit in its hyper-modernity, the Rotterdam that arose from the ashes—filled with museums, parks, and creative architecture—is now one of the centers of cultural activity in Europe.

🖪 🔢 TRANSPORTATION AND PRACTICAL INFORMATION. Trains run to: Amsterdam (1¼hr., €12); The Hague (25min., €3.60); and Utrecht (45min., €7.50). The VVV **tourist office,** Coolsingel 67, opposite the *Stadhuis,* books rooms for a €2 fee. (Open M-Th 9:30am-6pm, F 9:30am-9pm, Sa 9:30am-5pm.)

🔳🔲 ACCOMMODATIONS AND FOOD. If you've grown tired of Europe, escape to the Middle East, Africa, or South America in one of the many themed rooms of **Hotel Bazar ❸,** Witte de Withstr. 16. For the best value, book the South American floor, which comes with a charming private garden. (☎206 51 51. Singles €60-100; doubles €65-120.) To reach the **StayOkay Rotterdam (HI) ❷,** Rochussenstr. 107-109, take the Metro to *Dijkzigt;* at the top of the Metro escalator, exit onto Rochussentr. and turn left. (☎436 57 63. Breakfast and sheets included. Reception 7am-midnight. Dorms €23; singles €31; doubles €52.) Chinese food and schwarma await along **Witte de Withstraat,** where you can easily grab a meal for under €5. Try **Lijbaan** for its array of pubs, bars, and all their accompanying culinary charm. **Bazar ❷,** on the 1st floor of the hotel of the same name, shines with glittering colored lights, bright blue tables, and amazing Middle Eastern fusion cuisine. (☎206 51 51. Sandwiches and some entrees €4. Open M-Th 8am-1am, F 8am-2am, Sa 10am-2am, Su 10am-midnight.)

◙ 🔳 SIGHTS AND ENTERTAINMENT. The **Netherlands Architecture Institute,** Museumpark 18-20, is one of the most extraordinary buildings in Rotterdam. The multi-leveled glass and steel construction—which traverses a man-made pool and looks out onto the Museumpark—is home to several exhibition spaces, a world-

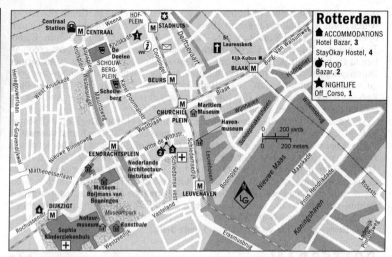

class archive, and a permanent display on Dutch architecture. (Open Su 11am-5pm, Tu-Sa 10am-5pm. €7, students and seniors €5.) For a dramatic example of Rotterdam's eccentric designs, check out the **Kijk-Kubus** (Cube Houses) by Piet Blom. Take tram #1 or the Metro to *Blaak*, turn left, and look up. (Open Mar.-Dec. daily 11am-5pm; Jan.-Feb. F-Su 11am-5pm. €1.80.) Brush up on your knowledge of van Gogh, Magritte, Rembrandt, Rothko, Rubens, and Rubinstein across the street at the **Museum Boijmans van Beuningen,** Museumpark 18-20. (M: Eendractspl. or tram #5. Open Su 11am-5pm and Tu-Sa 10am-5pm. €7.) Restored to its medieval splendor after its bombing, **St. Laurenskerk,** Grote Kerkpl. 15, is home to the largest mechanical organ in Europe. (Open Tu-Sa 10am-4pm. Free.) Step aboard the *De Buffel,* a restored 19th-century turret ship, at the **Maritiem Museum,** Leeuvehaven 1, or peruse hundreds of intricately detailed model ships. (Open July-Aug. M-Sa 10am-5pm, Su 11am-5pm; Sept.-June Su 11am-5pm and Tu-Sa 10am-5pm. €3.50.) Make sure to swing by the powerful **Zadkine Monument,** to the left of the museum. Known as the Monument for the Destroyed City and erected only 11 years after the bombing, it depicts a man with a hole in his heart writhing in agony. **Museumpark** features sculptures, mosaics, and monuments designed by some of the world's foremost artists and architects; take tram #5 to reach the outdoor exhibit.

Coffeeshop-hop along **Oude Binnenweg** and **Nieuwe Binnenweg,** or dance the night away at ▓**Off_Corso,** Kruiskade 22, Rotterdam's hottest club phenomenon. (Beer €2. Mixed drinks €6. Cover €6, €4 with student ID. Open Th-Sa 11pm-5am.)

UTRECHT ☎ 030

Sitting roughly in the center of The Netherlands, Utrecht (pop. 250,000) is a national hub that draws visitors with its lively festivals, numerous museums, young nightlife, and winding, tree-lined canals.

⊟⊡ TRANSPORTATION AND PRACTICAL INFORMATION. Trains arrive in the Hoog Catharijne from Amsterdam (30min., 3-6 per hr., €5.60). To get to the VVV **tourist office,** Vinkenbrugstr. 19, follow the signs to Vredenberg, which leads to the town center. Pick up a map of the city and a complete listing of museums and sights for €2. (☎(0900) 128 87 32; www.utrechtstad.nl. Open M-W and F 9:30am-6:30pm, Th 9:30am-9pm, Sa 9:30am-5pm, Su 10am-2pm.)

⌐⌐ ACCOMMODATIONS AND FOOD. Near the corner of Lucasbolwerk and Nobelstr., ⬛**B&B Utrecht City Centre ❶**, Lucasbolwerk 4, offers a kitchen, sauna, piano, and home video system to its guests. (☎(0650) 43 48 84; www.hostelutrecht.nl. Breakfast 24hr. Free Internet. Dorms €16; singles €55; doubles €65; triples €85; quads €100.) Slightly farther from the city, the same owners run **B&B Utrecht ❶**, Egelantierstr. 25. Take bus #3 to Watertoren (€1), cross the street and head to Anemoonstr., then go two blocks to the end and turn left. The street turns into Egelantierstr. and the hostel is on your left. (☎(0650) 43 48 84; www.hotelinfo.nl. Breakfast 24hr. Free Internet. Dorms €12; singles €40; doubles €45; triples €70; quads €85.) **Strowis Hostel ❶**, Boothstr. 8, has impeccable rooms, shiny darkwood floors, and an outdoor terrace overlooking a garden. (☎38 02 80; www.strowis.nl. Dorms €12-15; doubles €45; triples €55.) For a pastoral setting perfect for recharging, try **Stayokay Ridderhofstad Rhijnauwen (HI) ❷**, Rhijnauwenselaan 14, in nearby Bunnik. Take bus #40, 41, or 43 from Centraal Station (10-15min., round-trip €4.20) and tell the driver to let you off at Bunnik. From the stop, cross the street, backtrack, and turn right on Rhijnauwenselaan. The hostel offers bike rentals and a small bar. (☎656 12 77. Breakfast included. Dorms July-Aug. weeknights €22, weekends €23; doubles €52; triples €64-77; quads €78-€94.)

Sit among a hip crowd, either by the canal or in the cozy lounge area inside **Het Nachtrestaurant ❶**, Oudegr. 158, which serves great *tapas* (€2.40-6.80) and *sangría* (€3.20 per glass) in this "night restaurant." (☎230 30 36. Open M-W 6-11pm, Th 6pm-midnight, F 6pm-1am, Sa 6-10:30pm.) **Toque Toque ❹**, Oudegrt. 138, just off Vinkenburgstr., is an upscale restaurant with a nine page wine list, large salads under €13, and homemade pasta between €11-15. Deep red walls, an aluminum bar, and terrace seats overlooking the canal make this one of the hipper restaurants along the Oudegrt. (☎231 87 87. Open Su-W 1pm-midnight, Th-Sa 10am-1am.) Other cheap meals can be found along the **Nobelstraat,** where a string of pizzarias, pubs, and sandwich shops are clustered together.

◪ SIGHTS. Get info on churches and museums at **RonDom,** Dompl. 9, the Utrecht visitors' center for cultural history. Then make your first stop the awe-inspiring **Domkerk (Dom Church),** which was started in 1254 and finished 250 years later. Initially a Roman Catholic cathedral, the Domkerk has held Protestant services since 1580. (Open May-Sept. M-F 10am-5pm, Sa 10am-3:30pm, Su 2-4pm; Oct.-Apr. M-F 11am-4pm, Sa 11am-3:30pm, Su 2-4pm. Free.) The **Domtoren,** the tallest tower in The Netherlands, was attached to the cathedral until a medieval tornado blew away the nave. (Tickets for tours sold at RonDom. Daily July-Aug. every 30min. 10am-4:30pm; Sept.-June every hr. 10am-4pm. €6, children €3.60.) The **Museum Quarter** contains the core of Utrecht's extended family of museums, with something for everyone. The **Central Museum,** Nicolaaskerkhof 10, is now the oldest municipal museum in The Netherlands. Each of its galleries pays tribute to its national and civic past, with exquisite collections that range from paintings by 17th-century "Utrecht Caravaggists" to 20th-century Dutch masters. (☎236 23 62; www.centraalmuseum.nl. Open Su and T-Sa 11am-5pm. €8. Under-12 free.) At the nearby **Aboriginal Art Museum,** Oude Gracht 176, view contemporary art created by Australian Aborigines. Most info is in Dutch, but ask for the walk-through pamphlet in English. (☎238 01 00. Open Tu-F 10am-5pm, Sa-Su 11am-5pm. Admission €8, seniors and children €5.) Visit **Museum Catherijnconvent,** Lange Nieuwstr. 38, located at the site of a medieval convent, to view an extensive collection of Christian art. (☎231 72 96. Open Tu-F 10am-5pm, Sa-Su 11am-5pm. €6.) The **Nationaal Museum Van Speelklok tot Pierement,** Buurkerkhof 10, traces the history of mechanical musical instruments. Amidst the kitsch, check out the collection of automats from the 17th to 20th centuries. (☎231 27 89. Open Tu-Sa 10am-5pm, Su noon-5pm. €6, under-12 €4. Tours every hr.) If you're an astronomy buff, make sure to check out the **Observatory Son-**

nenborgh Museum, Zonnenburg 2, which is The Netherlands's oldest domed observatory, and has a large collection of antique scientific instruments. (☎230 28 18; www.sonnenbourgh.nl. Hours depend on the cosmos; call or check the web to make a reservation. Generally open M-F 10am-4pm. €3.50, under-14 €2.50.)

⚑ ENTERTAINMENT. Utrecht is The Netherlands's largest college town, and it has the nightlife to prove it. Pick up a copy of *UiLoper* at bars or restaurants to scout out the cultural scene. The big stepping-out nights are usually Wednesday through Friday; on Saturday many university students go home, so plan according. **De Winkel van SInkel,** Oude Gracht 158, is the city's most popular grand-cafe. This huge, mandarin-colored complex has martinis lining the walls for a very chic effect. (Wine €2.60. Beer €2.30. Open Su-F 11am-2am, Sa 11am-5am.) In **'t Oude Pothuys,** Oudegrt. 279, musical instruments hang from the ceiling in a converted cellar that hosts live music every night. (Open daily 10pm-1:30am.) Once the rest of Utrecht has shut down, students can party at fraternity-run **Woolloo Moollo** on Janskerkhof 14. (Student ID required. Cover varies. Open W-Sa 11pm-late.)

HOGE VELUWE NATIONAL PARK ☎0318

The impressive **Hoge Veluwe National Park** (HO-geh VEY-loo-wuh) is a 13,565-acre preserve of woods, heath, dunes, red deer, and wild boars. (☎59 16 27; www.hogeveluwe.nl. Park open June-July daily 8am-10pm; May and Aug. 8am-9pm; Sept. 9am-8pm; Apr. 8am-8pm; Oct. 9am-7pm; Nov.-Mar. 9am-5:30pm. €5, children 6-12 €2.50; 50% discount May-Sept. after 5pm.) Deep in the park, the **▨Rijksmuseum Kröller-Müller** has troves of van Goghs from the Kroller-Muller family's outstanding collection, as well as key works by Giacometti, Gris, Mondrian, Picasso, and Seurat. The museum's striking **sculpture garden,** one of the largest in Europe, has exceptional works by Bourdelle, Rodin, and Serra. (www.kmm.nl. Open Tu-Su 10am-5pm, sculpture garden closes at 4:30pm. €5, children €2.75.) Take one of the free **bikes** in the park and get a map (€2) at the **visitor's center** to explore over 33km of paths. (☎(055) 378 81 19. Open daily 10am-5pm.)

Arnhem (15km from the park) is a good base for exploration; **bus** #107 comes from Arnhem to the park's northwestern Otterlo entrance. Contact the park or either **tourist office** for more information. (☎(0900) 202 40 75; www.vvvarnhem.nl.) To get to the **Stayokay Hostel ❷,** Diepenbrocklaan 27, take bus #3 from the station to Rijnstate Hospital; as you face the hospital turn right, then left on Cattepoelseweg. About 150m ahead, turn right up the brick steps, and at the top turn right. Rooms are exceptionally clean, service is friendly, and the reading room and bar make for a peaceful entree into the park. (☎(026) 442 01 14; www.stayokay.com/arnhem. Breakfast included. Reception 8am-11pm. Dorms €22-23; singles €30-31; doubles €53-55; triples €72-76; quads €91-96.

MAASTRICHT ☎043

Situated on a narrow strip of land between Belgium and Germany, Maastricht's strategic location has made it a frequent target of military conquest throughout history. More recently, however, it has been a symbol of international cooperation, as the Maastricht Treaty created the European Union in 1991. Home of the prestigious **Jan van Eyck Academie of Art,** Maastricht (pop. 125,000) is known for its abundance of art galleries and antique stores.

🛈🚃 TRANSPORTATION AND PRACTICAL INFORMATION. The train station is located on the east side of town, away from most of the action. **Trains** arrive from Amsterdam (2½hr., 2 per hr., €24). You can also arrive by **plane;** KLM (www.klm-excel.com) flies from Amsterdam, London, and Munich. From Amsterdam, round-trip flights cost roughly €96. To get from the train station to the VVV **tourist office,** Kleine Str. 1, walk straight on Station Str., cross the bridge, go one more block, take a right, and walk down a block; the office will be on the right. For a small fee, the VVV books B&B accommodations. (☎325 21 21. Open May-Oct. M-Sa 9am-6pm, Su 11am-3pm; Nov.-Apr. M-F 9am-6pm, Sa 9am-5pm.)

ACCOMMODATIONS AND FOOD. In general, good budget accommodations are difficult to find in Maastricht. **Le Virage ❹,** Cortenstr. 2-2b, offers spotless suites, each complete with bedroom, living room, kitchenette, and bathroom. It's a great option for those traveling in groups. Reception is open Tu-Su 8am-midnight, but hours can be spotty, so make sure you plan your stay in advance. (Breakfast €9. Double apartments €90; triples €112; quads €136.) Spend the night on the centrally located **Botel ❷,** Maasboulevard 95, a boat with tiny cabins and a cozy deckroom lounge. By far, the best budget digs in town, but you get what you pay for. Try to get the rooms above-deck; they're the same price, but much cheerier. (☎321 90 23. Singles €27- 30; doubles €41-43; triples €60.) To get from the train station to **City-Hostel de Dousberg (HI) ❶,** Dousbergweg 4, take bus #11 on weekdays, bus #33 on weeknights after 6pm, and bus #8 or 18 on weekends. Its cinderblock hallways may lack charm, but this hostel makes it up with amenities. Enjoy showers in every room, an indoor and outdoor pool, and a tennis court. (☎346 67 77; www.dousberg.nl. Breakfast included. Dorms €22-25; triples €75.)

Maastricht is known for its *eetcafes,* pubs that serve traditional food along with beer. The **Vrijthof** area is home to many *eetcafes,* but be warned that prices are fairly high in Maastricht across the board. **De Blindgenger ❷,** Koestr. 3, is a warm, red cafe filled with art and mirrors. Their special of the day (€8) or pancakes (€5-8) are cheap ways to fill up. (☎325 06 19. Open daily 11am-11pm.) After a trip to the caves, stop by **Chalet Bergrust ❶,** Luikerweg 71, a good restaurant with beautiful views of the city. Lunch options (sandwiches, pancakes, omelettes) run about €4. (☎325 54 12. Open daily in summer 10am-10pm; in winter M, W, F-Su 11am-8pm.) **L'Hermitage ❸,** St. Bernadusstr. 20, is a favorite with students and locals. Try the cajun *quesadillas* (€9) or vegetarian tacos (€8). French dishes round out the cuisine. (☎325 17 77. Open daily 5-10pm.)

SIGHTS. The striking ◼**Bonnefantenmuseum,** Ave. Ceramique 250, contrasts Maastricht's traditional Dutch brickwork with its futuristic (and slightly dated) rocketship design. The museum houses permanent collections of archaeological artifacts, medieval sculpture, Northern Renaissance painting, and contemporary art. It also makes a concerted effort to collect pieces by up-and-coming Dutch artists, giving it at times a vaguely regional feel. (www.bonnefanten.nl. Open Tu-Su 11am-5pm. €7.) Despite its recent status as the birthplace of modern European unity, Maastricht has seen its share of interstate rivalries; centuries of foreign threats culminated in an innovative subterranean defense system. The ◼**Mount Saint Peter Caves**'s 20,000 underground passages were used as a siege shelter as late as WWII and contain inscriptions and artwork by generations of inhabitants. The man-made "caves" originally began as an old Roman limestone quarry; over time, the Dutch expanded them to the point where the caves could shelter 40,000 people at once. Access to the caves is possible only with a tour guide at two locations: the **Northern System** (Grotten Noord), Luikerweg 71 (tours in Dutch, English available depending on guide; €3.30); and the **Zonneberg Caves,** Slavante 1 (☎325 21 21; call for hours; €3.30). Maastricht's above-ground marvels include the **Basilica of Saint Servatius,** Keizer Karelpl., off the central Vrijthof Sq., which contains ornate ecclesiastical crafts, 11th-century crypts, and the country's largest bell, affectionately known as Grameer (Grandmother). It is also the only Dutch church built over the grave of a saint—not surprisingly, St. Servatius. (Open July-

Aug. daily 10am-6pm; Sept.-June 10am-5pm. €2.) The medieval **Basilica of Our Dear Lady**, O.L. Vrouwepl., honors Mary with a dark interior and colorful stained glass windows; parts of the cruciform church date to the 11th century. (Open Easter-Oct. M-Sa 11am-5pm, Su 1-5pm. Free.) The **Natuurhistorich Museum,** De Bosuetpl. 6-7, features the remains of a newly discovered ancient species, the Montasaurus dinosaur, and giant turtles found fossilized in the stone of the caves. (www.nhm-maastricht.nl. Open M-F 10am-5pm, Sa-Su 2-5pm. €3.10, under-12 €2.30.)

🎵 ENTERTAINMENT. In general, the nightlife in Maastricht is really about pubbing. Marijuana is not accepted here with the same breezy liberality of Amsterdam. Although coffeeshops exist, they tend to be more discreet. Serving over 80 different beers, **Falstaff,** Amorspl. 6, has the best selection in town and is well situated in a beautiful, tree-lined square. (Special Belgian brews €2-2.60. Sandwiches €4. Open Su-Th 10am-2am, F-Sa 10am-3am.) During the school year, students stay out late to drink at **Metamorfoos**, Kleine Gracht 40-42, a *café-brasserie*, where a €12 beer card gets you 10 beers. (Open Su-M, F 3-11pm; Tu-Th, Sa 3pm-5am.)

GRONINGEN ☎ 050

Groningen, easily the most happening city in the northern Netherlands, pulses with new life. More than half of the city's 170,000 inhabitants are under 35, adding to Groningen's reputation as a great party city. Heavily bombed in WWII, Groningen rebuilt itself completely, yet unlike some other Dutch cities, Groningen has managed to keep its old-world appeal.

🚆🛈 TRANSPORTATION AND PRACTICAL INFORMATION. Trains arrive from Amsterdam (2½hr., 2 per hr., €24), occasionally requiring a train switch at Amersfoot; ask the conductor whether you will need to change trains. To get to the **VVV tourist office,** Grote Markt 25, turn right as you exit the station, walk along the canal, turn left at the first bridge, head straight through the Herepl. on Herestr., cross Gedempte Zuiderdiep, and keep on Herestr. until it hits the Grote Markt. The tourist office is in the far corner of the Markt next to the Martinitoren. They book accommodations for free and offer guided walking tours in July and August. (☎313 97 41; www.vvvgroningen.nl. Open M-W 9am-6pm, Th 9am-8pm, F 9am-6pm, Sa 10am-5pm. Walking tours Su 1-3pm, M 2:30-4:30pm. €3.50, under-12 €2.25.)

🛏🍴 ACCOMMODATIONS AND FOOD. A fun crowd hangs out at **Simplon Youthhotel ❶**, Boterdiep 73-2, where a heavy-metal loving staff offers very clean rooms. Take bus #1 from the station (dir.: Korrewegwijk) to Boterdiep; the hostel is through the yellow- and white-striped entranceway. (☎313 52 21; www.xs4all.nl/~simplon. Breakfast €3.40. Free lockers. Sheets €2.50, included in private rooms. Lockout noon-3pm. All-female dorm available. Dorms €11; singles €29; doubles €42; triples €59; quads €76.) **Martini Hotel ❸**, Gedempte Zuiderdiep, about halfway between the train station and Grote Markt, has recently been renovated, with a classy new lobby and private bathrooms all around. (☎312 99 19; www.martini-hotel.nl. TV in every room. Breakfast €7.50. Singles and doubles from €66; triples €75; quads €96.) To get to **Hotel Friesland ❶**, Kleine Pelsterstr. 4, cross the canal at the Groninger Museum and walk up Ubbo Emmiusstr., turn right on Gedempte Zuiderdiep, left on Pelsterstr., and right onto Kleine Pelsterstr. Enjoy friendly service, bright bedrooms with high ceilings, and impeccably clean bathrooms. (☎312 13 07. Breakfast included. Singles €24; doubles €44; triples €60; quads €80.)

Try ▦**De Kleine Moghul** ❷, Nieuwe Boteringstr. 62, an entirely organic Indian restaurant with a beautiful decor. (☎318 89 05. Entrees €8-11. Open daily 5-10pm.) At ▦**Ben'z** ❷, Pepperstr. 17, in the heart of Groningen's party district, dinner is served in a Bedouin tent upon Turkish cushions lit by lantern. Finish your meal off with a puff on the *nargila*, a traditional water pipe. (☎313 79 17; www.restaurantbenz.nl. Special student menu €7.60-9.10. Cash only.) **Eetcafe De 1e Kamer** ❷, Pepperstr. 9, serves some of the cheapest fare in town in a classy setting. Choose between peppersteak or vegetarian stew (€7.20), or fill up on the daily special for just €6. (☎318 1721. Beer €1.50. Kitchen closes at 9:30pm. Open daily 5pm-6am.)

▣ ▧ **SIGHTS AND ENTERTAINMENT.** The town's spectacular ▦**Groninger Museum,** housed in a vibrant, almost entropic building exhibits both modern art and traditional paintings. The multicolored galleries create a futuristic laboratory atmosphere for their contemporary art exhibits. (www.groningermuseum.nl. Open July and Aug. M 1-5pm, Tu-Su 10am-5pm; Sept.-June Tu-Su 10am-5pm. €7, seniors €6, children €3.50.) Admire the city from atop the Grote Markt's **Martinitoren Tower,** a 97m tower that weathered the German attacks during WWII. Built as a Catholic church, the middle section dates from the 13th century. Midway up the tower, you can pull cords to simulate bell ringing. You can also see the bells up close, under which people were occasionally tied for torture. (Open Apr.-Oct. daily 11am-5pm; Nov.-Mar. noon-4pm. €2.50, under-12 €1.50.) A great spot to relax is the serene 16th-century **Prinsenhoftuin** (Princes' Court Gardens); the entrance is on the canal 10min. away from the Martinitorin. (Open Apr. to mid-Oct. daily 10am-dusk.) Inside the gardens, the tiny **Theeschenkerij Tea Hut** offers 130 kinds of tea (€0.80) under charming canopied underpasses. (Open M-F 10-6pm, Sa-Su noon-6pm.) Finally, cool off at **Noorderplantsoen,** a rolling, fountain-filled park that serves as host space to the huge **Noorderzon Festival** of art in late August, Groningen's annual cultural climax.

Groningen parties beyond its size; there are over 160 pubs and discotheques crammed in this medium-sized city. For cheap pitchers of beer and shoulder-to-shoulder packed bars, head to the southeastern corner of the Grote Markt on Poelestr. and Peperstr., where students boast that the bars close when people stop drinking. For the club scene, head to **Vera,** Oosterstr. 44, which bills itself as the "club for the international pop underground." Considering that Vera hosts unmissable parties nearly every night, they may well be right. Pick up a copy of *VeraKrant,* the newsletter in the box outside, for a schedule of events. The intimate, candlelit **de Spieghel Jazz Café,** Peperstr. 11, has two floors of live jazz, funk, or blues every night. Tokers are welcome at this club that caters to a slightly older crowd. (Wine €2.20. Open daily 8pm-4am.) Groningen's coffee-shops offer cheap alternatives to their Amsterdam brethren. **Cafe Dee's,** Papengang 3, is tucked unassumingly in a small alley, but it is just as much a night spot as other shops on the main streets. (Internet €1 per 30min. Open M-W 11am-midnight, Th noon-1am, F 11am-3am, Sa noon-3am.) **The Glory,** Steentilstr. 3, is another super-chill spot with a projection TV, a Bob Marley motif, and theater-style seats. (Open daily 10am-10pm.) **Postal Code:** 9725.

WADDEN ISLANDS (WADDENEILANDEN)

Wadden means "mudflat" in Dutch, but sand is the defining characteristic of these islands: Gorgeous beaches hide behind ridges covered in golden grass. Deserted, tulip-lined bike trails carve through vast, flat stretches of grazing land to the sea. Sleepy and isolated, these islands are truly Holland's best-kept secret.

⌐ TRANSPORTATION

The islands arch clockwise around the northwestern coast of The Netherlands: Texel (closest to Amsterdam), Vlieland, Terschelling, Ameland, and Schiermonnikoog. To reach **Texel**, take the train from Amsterdam to **Den Helder** (1½hr., €11), then grab bus #33 (2 strips), and a ferry to 't Hoorntje, the island's southernmost town (20min., every hr. 6:30am-9:30pm, round-trip €4). **Buses** depart from the ferry dock to various locales throughout the island, though the best way to travel is to rent a **bike** from **Verhuurbedrijf Heijne**, opposite the ferry dock. (From €4.50 per day. Open Apr.-Oct. daily 9am-8pm; Nov.-Mar. 9am-6pm.) To reach the other islands from Amsterdam, grab a **train** from Centraal station to Harlingen Haven (3hr., €26). From Harlingen, **ferries** (☎ (0517) 49 15 00; www.doeksen.nl) depart for Terschelling (1-2 hr., 3-5 per day, €18).

TEXEL. The largest of the Wadden Islands, Texel boasts stunning beaches and museums. **Beaches** lie near De Koog, on the western side of the island. **Nude beaches** beckon the uninhibited; you can bare it all near paal 9 (2km southwest of Den Hoorn) or paal 27 (5km west of De Cocksdorp). Say hi to the playful *zeehonden* (seals) at the **EcoMare Museum and Aquarium**, Ruijslaan 92, in De Koog. (www.ecomare.nl. Open daily 9am-5pm. €7, under-13 €3.50.) The staff can also arrange group tours of the surrounding **nature reserves;** make sure to ask for a guide who speaks English.

A **Texel Ticket** (€3.90) allows one day of unlimited travel on the island's bus system. (Runs mid-June to mid-Sept.). The VVV **tourist office**, Emmaln 66, is located just outside Den Burg, about 300m south of the main bus stop; look for the blue signs. (☎ (0222) 31 47 41; www.texel.net. Open July-Aug. Su 10am-1:30pm, M-Th 9am-6pm, F 9am-9pm, Sa 9am-5:30pm; Sept.-June M-Th 9am-6pm, F 9am-9pm, Sa 9am-5:30pm.) **Campgrounds** cluster south of De Koog and near De Cocksdorp; the tourist office can provide any info you may need.

TERSCHELLING. With 80% of the island covered by protected nature reserves, Terschelling (pop. 4,500) offers secluded **beaches** and green pastures spotted with cows and horses. To explore the island's striking scenery, rent a **bike** from **Haantjes Fietsverhuur**, W. Barentzskade 23 and other locations around the island. (☎ 44 29 29. Bikes at €4.50 per day, €20 per week.)

Both tours can also be booked at the VVV **tourist office**, W. Barentzkade 19, which sits opposite the ferry landing. (☎ (0562) 44 30 00. Open M-Sa 9:30am-5:30pm.) The **Terschelling Hostel (HI) ❶**, van Heusdenweg 39, is located just out of town on the waterfront. (☎ (0562) 44 23 38; www.stayokay.com/terschelling. Breakfast and sheets included. Laundry €7. Reception daily 9am-10pm. Dorms €18-21; ask for the backpacker special.) The best place to grab a bite is in the island's main village, Terschelling West. ▨**The Heartbreak Hotel ❷**, Oosterend, one of Terschelling's best food experiences, also doubles as a shrine to Elvis. Serving great diner-style food (Burning Love Burger €4), the restaurant also hosts free rock n' roll groups every night in July and August. **Zeezicht ❸**, Wm. Barentszkade 20, has enormous dinner portions (€12-16.50) and a sweeping view of the ocean. (Kitchen closes at 9:30pm. Open daily 10am-midnight.) A wild set floods Terschelling on summer nights; head to **Braskoer**, Torenstr. 32, to join a younger crowd on a sweaty, packed dance floor. (Beer €3. Cover €5. Open 10am-2am.) To relax, kick back at **Cafe De Zeevaart**, Torenstr. 22. (Beer €1.80. Open daily 10am-2am.)

PORTUGAL

In the era of Christopher Columbus, Vasco da Gama, and Magellan, Portugal was one of the world's most powerful nations, ruling a wealthy empire that stretched from Africa to America to Asia. Today, it is often overshadowed by its larger neighbor Spain. But while it shares the beaches, nightlife, and strong architectural heritage of the Iberian Peninsula, Portugal is culturally and geographically quite unique. It contains some of the most pristine wilderness areas in all of Europe, and some villages in the northeast have not changed in over 800 years. Despite ongoing modernization, Portugal's rich, age-old traditions seem destined to stay—rows of olive trees give way to ancient castles, and Porto's wines are as fine as ever.

LIFE AND TIMES

HISTORY

EARLY HISTORY. The first clearly identifiable inhabitants of the Iberian peninsula were the **Celts,** who began to settle in northern Portugal and Spanish Galicia in the 8th century BC. The **Greeks** and **Carthaginians** followed them, settling the coasts. After their victory over Carthage in the **Second Punic War** (218-201 BC) and their defeat of the Celts in 140 BC, the **Romans** gained control of central and southern Portugal. Six centuries of Roman rule, which introduced the *Pax Romana* and "Latinized" Portugal's language and customs, paved the way for Christianity.

VISIGOTHS AND ARABIAN KNIGHTS (469-1139). The Iberian Peninsula felt the effects of the Roman Empire's decline in the 3rd and 4th centuries AD. By AD 469, the **Visigoths,** a tribe of migrating Germanic people, had crossed the Pyrenees, and for the next two centuries they dominated the peninsula. In AD 711, however, the Muslims (also known as the **Moors**) invaded Iberia, toppling the Visigoth monarchy. Although these invaders centered their new kingdom of *al-Andalus* in Córdoba, smaller Muslim communities settled along Portugal's

SUGGESTED ITINERARIES

THREE DAYS Make your way through Lisbon's (1 day, p. 814) famous Moorish district, the **Alfama**, up to the **Castelo de São Jorge,** and to the futuristic **Parque das Nações.** By night, listen to *fado* and hit the clubs in **Barrio Alto.** Daytrip to **Sintra's** fairy-tale castles (p. 828) before sipping sweet port in **Porto** (1 day; p. 838).

ONE WEEK From **Lisbon** (2 days) and **Sintra** (1 day), lounge on the beaches of **Lagos** (1 day; p. 831) and **Praia da Rocha** (1 day; p. 836), then move on to the university town of **Coimbra** (1 day; p. 837), and end your week in **Porto** (1 day).

BEST OF PORTUGAL, TWO WEEKS After the sights, sounds, and cafes of **Lisbon** (2 days), daytrip to **Sintra** (1 day). Head down to the infamous beach-and-bar town **Lagos** (2 days), where hordes of visitors dance the night away, and take an afternoon in **Sagres** (p. 835), once considered the end of the world. Check out the bone chapel in **Évora** (1 day; p. 830) and the mysterious convent in **Tomar** (1 day; p. 829). Head north to **Coimbra** (2 days) and **Porto** (2 days), then finish your tour in the impressive squares of **Viana do Castelo** (1 day; p. 841).

southern coast, an area they called the *al-Gharb* (now the Algarve); through nearly four centuries of rule, the Muslims left a significant legacy of agricultural advances, architectural landmarks, and linguistic and cultural customs.

THE CHRISTIAN RECONQUISTA AND THE BIRTH OF PORTUGAL (1139-1415). Though the *Reconquista* officially began in 718, it didn't pick up steam until the 11th century, when Fernando I united Castilla and León and provided a strong base from which to reclaim territory. In 1139, **Afonso Henriques** (Afonso I), a noble from the frontier territory of Portucale (a region centered around Porto), declared independence from Castilla y León. Soon thereafter he named himself the first King of Portugal, though the papacy did not officially recognize the title until 1179.

With the help of Christian military groups like the Knights Templar, the new monarchy battled Muslim forces, capturing Lisbon in 1147. By 1249, the *Reconquista* defeated the last remnants of Muslim power with successful campaigns in the Alentejo and the Algarve. The Christian kings, led by **Dinis I** (Dom Dinis; 1279-1325), promoted the use of the Portuguese language (instead of Spanish) and with the **Treaty of Alcañices** (1297) settled border disputes with neighboring Castilla, asserting Portugal's identity as the first unified, independent nation in Europe.

THE AGE OF DISCOVERY (1415-1580). The reign of **João I** (1385-1433), the first king of the House of Aviz, ushered in unity and prosperity never before seen in Portugal. João increased the power of the crown and in doing so established a strong base for future Portuguese expansion and economic success.

The 15th century was one of the greatest periods in the history of maritime travel and naval advances. Under the leadership of João's son, **Prince Henry the Navigator,** Portugal established itself as a world leader in maritime science and exploration. Portuguese adventurers captured the Moroccan city of Ceuta in 1415, discovered the Madeiras Islands in 1419, happened upon the uninhabited Azores in 1427, and began to exploit the African coast for slaves and riches a few years later.

Bartolomeu Dias changed the world forever when he rounded Africa's Cape of Good Hope in 1488. Dias opened the route to the East and paved the way for Portuguese entrance into the spice trade. The Portuguese monarchs may have turned down **Christopher Columbus,** but they did fund a number of momentous voyages. In 1497, they supported **Vasco da Gama,** who led the first European naval expedition to India; successive expeditions added numerous East African and Indian colonies to Portugal's empire. Three years after da Gama's voyage, **Pedro Álvares Cabral** claimed Brazil, and Portugal established a far-flung empire.

Portugal's monarchy reached its peak with **Manuel the Fortunate** (1495-1521) on the throne. Known to foreigners as "the King of Gold," Manuel controlled a spectacular commercial empire. However, before the House of Aviz lost power in 1580, signs of future decline were already becoming evident, and it was not long before competition from other commercial powers took its toll.

THE HOUSES OF HABSBURG AND BRAGANÇA (1580-1807). In 1580, Habsburg King of Spain **Felipe II** forcibly affirmed his quasi-legitimate claim to the Portuguese throne, and the Iberian Peninsula was briefly ruled by one monarch. For 60 years, the Habsburg family dragged Portugal into several ill-fated wars, including the **Spanish-Portuguese Armada's** crushing loss to England in 1588. By the end of Habsburg rule, Portugal had lost much of its once vast empire. In 1640, during a rebellion against King Felipe IV, the **House of Bragança** assumed control, once again asserting Portuguese independence from Spain.

The momentous **earthquake of 1755** devastated Lisbon and southern Portugal, killing over 15,000 people. Despite the damage, dictatorial minister **Marquês de Pombal** was able to rebuild Lisbon while instituting national economic reform.

Portugal

NAPOLEON'S CONQUEST AND ITS AFTERMATH (1807-1910). Napoleon took control of France in 1801 and had grand designs on much of Europe. His army met little resistance when it invaded Portugal in 1807. Rather than risk death, the Portuguese royal family fled to Brazil. The **Constitution of 1822,** drawn up during the royal family's absence, severely limited the power of the monarchy, and after 1826, the ultimate sibling rivalry exploded into the **War of the Two Brothers** (1826-1834) between constitutionalists (supporting Pedro, the new king of Brazil) and monarchists (supporting Miguel, Pedro's brother).

FROM THE "FIRST REPUBLIC" TO SALAZAR (1910-1974). Portugal spent the first few years of the 20th century trying to recover from the political discord of the previous century. On October 5, 1910, 20-year-old King **Manuel II** fled to England. The new government, known as the **First Republic,** earned worldwide disapproval for its expulsion of the Jesuits and other religious orders, and the conflict between the government and labor movements heightened tensions at home. Portugal's decision to enter **World War I,** though on the side of the victorious Allies, proved economically fatal and internally divisive. The weak republic wobbled and eventually fell in a 1926 military coup. General **António Carmona** took over as leader of the provisional military government, and in the face of financial crisis appointed **António de Oliveira Salazar,** a prominent economics professor, his minister of finance. In 1932 Salazar became prime minister, but he soon evolved into a dictator. His *Estado Novo* (New State) granted suffrage to women but did little else to end the country's authoritarian tradition. While Portugal's international economic standing improved, the regime laid the cost of progress squarely on the shoulders of the working class, the peasantry, and colonial subjects in Africa. A terrifying secret police (PIDE) crushed all opposition to Salazar's rule, and African rebellions were quelled in bloody battles that drained the nation's economy.

REVOLUTION AND REFORM (1974-2000). The slightly more liberal **Marcelo Caetano** dragged on the increasingly unpopular African wars after Salazar's death in 1970. On April 25, 1974, a left-wing military coalition calling itself the **Armed Forces Movement,** under **Francisco da Costa Gomes,** overthrew Caetano in a quick coup. The **Revolution of the Carnations** sent the Portuguese dancing into the streets; today, every town in Portugal has its own **Rua 25 de Abril.** The Marxist-dominated armed forces established a variety of civil and political liberties and withdrew Portuguese claims on African colonies by 1975. The landmark year 1986 brought Portugal into the European Community (now the **European Union**), ending its age-old isolation from affluent northern Europe.

TODAY

The European Union declared Portugal a full member of the EU Economic and Monetary Union (EMU) in 1999, and today the nation strives to economically equal the rest of Western Europe. In 1999, Macau, Portugal's last overseas territory, was ceded to the Chinese.

Portugal has been a republic since 1910. The President represents the nation, serves as commander of the armed forces, and appoints the Prime Minister in accordance with the results of parliamentary elections. **President Jorge Fernando Branco de Sampaio,** of the center-left Socialist Party, won a second term in January of 2001. However, like many European countries, Portugal has recently swung to the right. Socialist Prime Minister Antonio Guterres resigned in December of 2001 after his party suffered heavy losses in parliamentary elections, in which the conservative Popular Party joined with the center-right Social Democratic Party and won the majority. President Sampaio then appointed **Prime Minister Jose Manuel Durao Barroso** as the representative of the newly merged parties. Barroso has pledged to strengthen the Portuguese economy and reduce government spending.

THE ARTS

LITERATURE

Modernist poet **Fernando Pessoa** was Portugal's most famous author at the turn of the 20th century. **José Saramago,** winner of the 1998 Nobel Prize for Literature, is perhaps Portugal's most important living writer. He is best known for *Baltasar and Blimunda* (1982), the story of two lovers who escape the Inquisition in a time machine, and *The Stone Raft* (1986), a satire about Iberia's isolation from the rest of Europe.

THE VISUAL ARTS

ARCHITECTURE. Portugal's signature **Manueline** style celebrates the prosperity and imperial expansion of King Manuel I's reign. Manueline pieces routinely merge Christian images and maritime motifs. Their rich and lavish ornaments reflect a hybrid of Northern Gothic, Spanish Plateresque, and Moorish influences. The Manueline style found its most elaborate expression in the church and tower at Belém (p. 824), built to honor Vasco da Gama. Close seconds are the **Mosteiro dos Jerónimos** in Belém and the **Abadia de Santa Maria de Vitória** in Batalha (p. 824).

ON THE CANVAS. The Age of Discovery (1415-1580) was an era of vast cultural exchange with Renaissance Europe and beyond. High Renaissance artist **Jorge Afonso,** King Manuel's favorite, created realistic portrayals of human anatomy. Afonso's best works hang at the Convento de Cristo in **Tomar** (p. 829). In the 20th century, Cubism, Expressionism and Futurism trickled into Portugal. More recently, **Maria Helena Vieira da Silva** has won international recognition for her abstract works, and **Carlos Botelho** has become world-renowned for his wonderful vignettes about Lisbon life.

ESSENTIALS

WHEN TO GO

Summer is high season, but the southern coast draws tourists March through November. In the low season, many hostels cut their prices by 50% or more, and reservations are seldom necessary. But while Lisbon and some of the larger towns (especially Coimbra with its university) burst with vitality year-round, many smaller towns virtually shut down, and sights cut their hours nearly everywhere.

DOCUMENTS AND FORMALITIES

VISAS. Citizens of Australia, Canada, Ireland, New Zealand, the UK and the US can travel without visas for up to 90 days. As of August 2003, citizens of South Africa need a visa in addition to a valid passport for entrance to Portugal.

FACTS AND FIGURES

Official Name: Portuguese Republic.	**Land Area:** 91,951 sq. km.
Capital: Lisbon.	**Time Zone:** GMT.
Major Cities: Coimbra, Porto.	**Language:** Portuguese.
Population: 10,084,000.	**Religion:** Roman Catholic (94%).

PORTUGAL

EMBASSIES. Most foreign embassies are in Lisbon (p. 815). For Portuguese embassies at home, contact: **Australia,** 23 Culgoa Circuit, O'Malley, ACT 2606, mailing address P.O. Box 9092, Deakin, ACT 2600 (☎612 6290 1733); **Canada,** 645 Island Park Dr., Ottawa, ON K1Y OB8 (☎613 729 0883); **South Africa,** 599 Leyds St., Muckleneuk, Pretoria 0002 (☎27 012 341 5522); **UK,** 11 Belgrave Sq., London SW1X 8PP (☎44 20 7235 5331); and **US,** 2125 Kalorama Rd. NW, Washington, D.C. 20008 (☎202 328 8610). **New Zealanders** should refer to the Australian embassy.

TRANSPORTATION

BY PLANE. Most international airlines serve Lisbon; some serve Porto, Faro, and the Madeiras. **TAP Air Portugal** (Lisbon ☎218 43 11 00; US and Canada ☎800 221 7370; UK ☎845 601 09 32; www.tap.pt) is Portugal's national airline, serving all domestic locations and many major international cities. **Portugália** (www.pga.pt) is a smaller Portuguese airline that flies between Faro, Lisbon, Porto, all major Spanish cities, and other Western European destinations.

BY TRAIN. Caminhos de Ferro Portugueses (☎808 208 208; www.cp.pt) is Portugal's national railway, but for long-distance travel outside of the Braga-Porto-Coimbra-Lisbon line, buses are a better option. The exception is around Lisbon, where local trains are fast and efficient. Trains often leave at irregular hours, and posted schedules (*horarios*) aren't always accurate; check station ticket booths upon arrival. Unless you own a Eurail, **round-trip tickets** must be used before 3am the following day. Don't ride without a ticket; if you're caught *sem bilhete* you'll be fined exorbitantly. Though there is a Portugal Flexipass, it is rarely worth buying.

BY BUS. Buses are cheap, frequent, and connect just about every town in Portugal. **Rodoviária** (national info ☎213 54 57 75), the national bus company, has recently been privatized. Each company name corresponds to a particular region of the country, such as Rodoviária Alentejo or Minho e Douro, with notable exceptions such as EVA in the Algarve. Be wary of non-express buses in small regions like Estremadura and Alentejo, which stop every few minutes. Express coach service (*expressos*) between major cities is especially good; inexpensive city buses often run to nearby villages.

BY CAR. Portugal has the highest rate of automobile accidents per capita in Western Europe. The new highway system (IP) is quite good, but off the main arteries, the narrow, twisting roads are difficult to negotiate. Speed limits are ignored, recklessness is common, and lighting and road surfaces are often inadequate. Buses are safer options. Moreover, parking space in cities borders on nonexistent. **Gas** prices are high by North American standards—€0.60-0.90 per liter. Portugal's national automobile association, the **Automóvel Clube de Portugal** (ACP), Shopping Center Amoreiras, Lojas 1122, Lisbon (☎213 71 20), provides breakdown and towing service and first aid.

BY THUMB. Hitchhikers are rare in Portugal. Rides are easiest to come by at gas stations near highways and rest stops. *Let's Go* does not recommend hitchhiking.

TOURIST SERVICES AND MONEY

TOURIST OFFICES. The official tourism website is www.portugalinsite.pt. When in Portugal, stop by municipal and provincial tourist offices for maps and advice.

EMERGENCY   Dial ☎**112** for police, medical, or fire.

MONEY. On January 1, 2002, the **euro** (€) replaced the **escudo** as the unit of currency in Portugal. For more info, see p. 13. **Taxes** are included in all prices in Portugal and are not redeemable like those in Spain, even for EU citizens. **Tips** are customary only in fancy restaurants or hotels. Some cheaper restaurants include a 10% service charge; if they don't and you'd like to leave a tip, round up and leave the change. Taxi drivers do not expect a tip unless the trip was especially long. **Bargaining** is not customary in shops.

COMMUNICATION

PHONE CODES	**Country code: 351. International dialing prefix: 00.** From outside Portugal, dial int'l dialing prefix (see inside back cover) + 351 + local number.

TELEPHONES. Pay phones are either coin-operated or require a phone card. The basic unit for all calls is €0.10. Telecom phone cards are most common in Lisbon and Porto. Credifone cards are sold at drugstores, post offices, and locations posted on phone booths, and are most useful outside these two big cities. City codes all begin with a 2, and local calls do not require dialing the city code. **Calling cards** probably remain the best method of making international calls. For info on using a **cell phone** in Portugal, see p. 30.

MAIL. Air mail (*via aerea*) can take from one to two weeks (or longer) to reach the US or Canada. It is slightly quicker for destinations in Europe and longer for Australia, New Zealand, and South Africa. **Surface mail** (*superfície*), for packages only, takes up to two months. **Registered** or **blue mail** takes five to eight business days but is roughly three times the price of air mail. **EMS** or **Express Mail** will probably get there in three to four days for more than double the blue mail price.

INTERNET ACCESS. Cybercafes are common in cities and most smaller towns. When in doubt, try the library, where there is often at least one computer with Internet access.

ACCOMMODATIONS AND CAMPING

SYMBOL	❶	❷	❸	❹	❺
ACCOMMODATIONS	under €15	€15-25	€26-35	€36-50	over €50

Movijovem, Av. Duque de Ávila 137, 1069 Lisbon (☎707 20 30 30; www.pousadasjuventude.pt), the Portuguese Hostelling International affiliate, oversees the country's HI hostels. All bookings can be made through them. A bed in a *pousada da juventude* (not to be confused with plush *pousadas*) costs €10-15 per night; slightly less in the low season. To reserve a bed in the high season, obtain an **International Booking Voucher** from Movijovem (or your country's HI affiliate) and send it from home to the desired hostel four to eight weeks in advance. In the low season (Oct.-Apr.), double-check to see if the hostel is open. **Hotels** tend to be pricey. When business is weak, try bargaining down in advance. **Quartos** are rooms in private residences, similar to Spain's *casas particulares*. These rooms may be the only option in smaller towns or the cheapest one in bigger cities; tourist offices can usually help you. There are over 150 official **campgrounds** (*parques de campismo*) with an array of amenities. Police are strict about illegal camping—especially near official campgrounds. Tourist offices stock the free *Portugal: Camping and Caravan Sites,* an official campgrounds guide. Or, write the **Federação Portuguesa de Campismo e Caravanismo,** Av. Coronel Eduardo Galhardo 24D, 1199-007 Lisbon (☎218 12 68 90; www.fpcampismo.pt).

FOOD AND DRINK

SYMBOL	❶	❷	❸	❹	❺
FOOD	under €6	€6-10	€11-15	€16-25	over €25

Dishes are seasoned with olive oil, garlic, herbs, and sea salt, but few spices. The fish selection includes *chocos grelhados* (grilled cuttlefish), *linguado grelhado* (grilled sole), and *peixe espada* (swordfish). Portugal's renowned *queijos* (cheeses) are made from the milk of cows, goats, and ewes. For dessert, try *pudim*, or *flan* (caramel custard). The hearty *almoço* (lunch) is eaten between noon and 2pm and *jantar* (dinner) is served between 9pm and midnight. *Meia dose* (half-portions) are often adequate; full portions may satisfy two. The *prato do dia* (special of the day) or *ementa* (menu) of appetizer, bread, entree, and dessert is filling. *Vinho do porto* (port) is a dessert in itself. *Madeira* wines have a unique "cooked" flavor. Coffees include *bica* (black espresso), *galão* (with milk, served in a glass), and *café com leite* (with milk, in a cup).

HOLIDAYS AND FESTIVALS

Holidays: New Year's Day (Jan. 1); Good Friday (Apr. 9); Easter (Apr. 11); Liberation Day (Apr. 25); Labor Day (May 1); Feast of the Assumption (Aug. 15); Republic Day (Oct. 5); All Saints' Day (Nov. 1); Feast of the Immaculate Conception (Dec. 8); Christmas (Dec. 25).

Festivals: All of Portugal celebrates **Carnival** (Mar. 4) and **Holy Week** (Apr. 4-11). Coimbra holds the **Burning of the Ribbons** festival in early May, and Lisbon hosts the **Feira Internacional de Lisboa** in June. Coimbra's **Feira Popular** takes place the 2nd week of July. For more information on Portuguese festivals, see www.portugal.org.

LISBON (LISBOA)   ☎21

Once the center of the world's richest and farthest-reaching empire, Lisbon (pop. 1,971,000) hit its peak at the end of the 15th century when Portuguese navigators pioneered explorations of Asia, Africa, and South America. Aching with *saudade* for its past, the city works to preserve its rich history, continually renovating its monuments and meticulously maintaining its black-and-white mosaic sidewalks, pastel facades, and cobbled medieval alleys. In 1998, Lisbon hosted the World Expo, sparking a citywide face-lift and beginning a movement to reclaim its place as one of Europe's grandest cities.

▄ TRANSPORTATION

Flights: Aeroporto de Lisboa (LIS; ☎218 41 35 00), on the city's northern edge. **Buses** #44 and 45 (15-20min., every 12-15min., €1) and the express **AeroBus** #91 (15min., every 20min., €1) go to Pr. dos Restauradores from outside the terminal. A **taxi** to downtown costs about €6, plus a €1.50 luggage fee.

Trains: Caminhos de Ferro Portuguêses (☎800 20 09 04; www.cp.pt). Four main stations, each serving different destinations. Portuguese trains are usually quite slow; buses are often a better choice.

Estação do Barreiro, across the Rio Tejo, goes south. Station accessible by ferry from the Terreiro do Paço dock off Pr. do Comércio (30min., every 30min., price included in train ticket). Trains to **Évora** (2½hr., 7 per day, €7.50) and **Lagos** (5½hr., 5 per day, €14).

Estação Cais do Sodré (☎213 47 01 81), to the right of Pr. do Comércio when walking from Baixa. M: Cais do Sodré. To **Estoril** and **Cascais** (30min., every 20min., €1).

Estação Rossio (☎213 46 50 22), serves points west. M: Rossio or Restauradores. To **Sintra** (45min., every 15-30min., €1.30) via **Queluz** (€0.80).

Estação Santa Apolónia (☎218 88 40 25), on Av. Infante Dom Henrique, east of the Alfama on the Rio Tejo, runs the international, northern, and eastern lines. Take bus #9, 39, 46, or 90 to Pr. dos Restauradores and Estação Rossio. To: **Coimbra** (2½hr., 8 per day, €16); **Madrid** (10hr., 10pm, €52); **Porto** (4½hr., 8 per day, €21).

Buses: Arco do Cego, Av. João Crisóstomo, around the block from M: Saldanha. All "Saldanha" buses (#36, 44, 45) stop in the *praça* (€0.60). Fast **Rede Expressos** buses (☎213 10 31 11; www.rede-expressos.pt) go to many destinations, including: **Coimbra** (2½hr., 16 per day, €9.40); **Évora** (2hr., 13 per day, €9.80); **Lagos** (5hr., 9 per day, €15); **Porto** (4hr., 7 per day, €14), via **Leiria.**

Public Transportation: CARRIS (☎213 61 30 00; www.carris.pt) operates **buses, trams,** and **funiculars** (each €1); *passe turístico* (tourist pass) good for unlimited CARRIS travel. 1-day pass €2.40, 3-day pass €5.70, 4-day pass €10, 7-day pass €15. The **Metro** (☎213 55 84 57; www.metrolisboa.pt) covers downtown and the modern business district. Individual tickets €0.65; book of 10 tickets €5.10. **Trains** run daily 6:30am-1am; some stations close earlier.

Taxis: Rádio Táxis de Lisboa (☎218 11 90 00), **Autocoope** (☎217 93 27 56), and **Teletáxis** (☎218 11 11 00) all line up along Av. da Liberdade and Rossio.

✦🔢 ORIENTATION AND PRACTICAL INFORMATION

The city center is **Baixa,** the old business area, between **Bairro Alto** and **Alfama.** Baixa's grid of mostly pedestrian streets is bordered to the north by Rossio (a.k.a. Praça Dom Pedro IV), adjacent to **Praça dos Restauradores** (at the tourist office and airport bus stop); **Avenida da Liberdade** runs north, uphill from Pr. dos Restauradores. At Baixa's southern end is the **Praça do Comércio,** on the **Rio Tejo** (River Tagus). Along the river are the Expo '98 grounds, now called the **Parque das Nações** (Park of Nations), and the fast-growing **Alcântara** and **Docas** (docks) districts. **Alfama,** a labyrinth of narrow alleys and stairways beneath the Castelo de São Jorge, is the city's oldest district. Across Baixa from Alfama is **Bairro Alto** and its upscale shopping district, the **Chiado,** which is traversed by R. do Carmo and R. Garrett, near much of the city's nightlife.

TOURIST, FINANCIAL, AND LOCAL SERVICES

Tourist Offices: Palácio da Foz, Pr. dos Restauradores (☎213 46 33 14). M: Restauradores. The mother of all Portuguese tourist offices, this houses info about the entire country. The **Welcome Center,** Pr. do Comércio (☎210 31 28 10), is the office for the city of Lisbon. Both offices open daily 9am-8pm. Office at the **Aeroporto de Lisboa** (☎218 45 06 60) is just outside the baggage claim area. Open daily 8am-2am.

Embassies: Australia, Av. da Liberdade 200-2 (☎213 10 15 00; austemb@oninet.pt); **Canada,** Av. da Liberdade 198-200, 3rd fl. (☎213 16 46 00; lsbon-cs@dfait-maeci.gc.ca); **Ireland,** R. Imprensa à Estrela, 4th fl. (☎213 92 94 40; fax 97 73 63); **New Zealand** (consulate), R. do S. Felix 13-2 (☎213 50 96 90); **South Africa,** Av. Luis Bivar 10 (☎213 19 22 00; safrica@mail.eunet.pt); **UK,** R. São Bernardo 33 (☎213 92 40 00; www.uk-embassy.pt); **US,** Av. das Forças Armadas (☎217 27 33 00; www.american-embassy.pt).

Currency Exchange: Cota Câmbio, Pr. Dom Pedro IV 41 (☎213 22 04 80). Open M-Sa 9am-8pm. The main post office, most banks, and travel agencies also change money. Exchanges line the streets of Baixa. Ask about fees first—they can be exorbitant.

American Express: Top Tours, Av. Duque de Loulé 108 (☎213 19 42 90). M: Marquês de Pombal. Exit the Metro stop and walk up Av. da Liberdade toward the Marquês de Pombal statue, then turn right; the office is 2 blocks up on the left side of the street. Handles all AmEx functions. English spoken. Open M-F 9:30am-1pm and 2:30-6:30pm.

Luggage Storage: Estação Rossio and **Estação Santa Apolónia.** Lockers €4.50 for 24hr. Open daily 6:30am-1am.

English Bookstore: Livraria Británica, R. Luís Fernandes 14-16 (☎213 42 84 72), in the Bairro Alto. Open M-F 9:30am-7pm.

Laundromat: Lavatax, R. Francisco Sanches 65A (☎218 12 33 92). Wash, dry, and fold €2 per 5kg. Open M-F 8:30am-1pm and 3-7pm, Sa 8:30am-1pm.

EMERGENCY AND COMMUNICATIONS

Emergency: ☎112. **Ambulance:** ☎219 42 11 11.

Police: R. Capelo 13. ☎213 46 61 41. English spoken.

24hr. Pharmacy: Call directory assistance ☎118. Rotates; check the list posted on the door of any pharmacy.

Medical Services: Hospital Inglês, R. Saraiva de Carvalho 49 (☎213 95 50 67). **Cruz Vermelha Portuguesa,** R. Duarte Galvão 54 (☎217 71 40 00).

Internet Access: Web C@fe, R. Diário de Notícias 126 (☎213 42 11 81). €2 per 15min., €2.50 per 30min., €4 per hr. Open daily 4pm-2am. **Abracadabra,** Pr. Dom Pedro IV 66. €1 per 15min., €3 per hr. Open daily 8am-9:30pm. **Cyber.bica,** R. Duques Bragança 7 (☎213 22 50 04), close to Lgo. Chiado, down R. Raiva de Andrade. €0.80 per 15min., €3 per hr. Open M-Th 11am-midnight, F 11am-2am.

Post Office: Marked by red *Correios* signs. **Main** office (☎213 23 89 71), Pr. dos Restauradores. Open daily 8am-7pm. **Branch** office (☎213 22 09 21) at Pr. do Comércio. Open M-F 8:30am-6:30pm. Credit cards not accepted. **Postal Code:** 1100 for central Lisbon.

▐ ACCOMMODATIONS

Several hotels are in the center of town on **Avenida da Liberdade,** while many convenient budget hostels are in **Baixa** along the **Rossio** and on **Rua da Prata, Rua dos Correeiros,** and **Rua do Ouro.** Lodgings near the **Castelo de São Jorge** are quieter and closer to the sights. If central accommodations are full, head east to the hostels along **Avenida Almirante dos Reis.** At night, be careful in Baixa, Bairro Alto, and especially Alfama; many streets are isolated and poorly lit.

Casa de Hóspedes Globo, R. Teixeira 37 (☎/fax 213 46 22 79), across from the Parque São Pedro de Alcântara. From the park entrance, cross the street and go 1 block on Tv. da Cara, then turn right onto R. Teixeira. Popular with young travelers. All rooms newly renovated with phones. Laundry €10 per load. Singles €20, with bath €23; doubles with bath €30; triples with bath €40. ❷

Pousada da Juventude de Lisboa (HI), R. Andrade Corvo 46 (☎213 53 26 96). M: Picoas. Exit the Metro station, turn right, and walk 1 block; the hostel is on your left. HI card required. Due to finish renovations in March 2004. June-Sept. dorms €15; doubles with bath €35. Oct.-May dorms €13; doubles €25. MC/V. ❶

Pensão Londres, R. Dom Pedro V 53, 2nd-5th fl. (☎213 46 22 03; www.pensaolondres.com.pt). From the top of the Elevador Glória, turn right onto R. São Pedro de Alcântara and continue past the park; the *pensão* is on the corner of R. da Rosa. All rooms with phone, some with panoramic views of the city. Breakfast included. Singles €29, with bath €48; doubles €40/67; triples €76; quads €86. MC/V. ❸

Pensão Estação Central, Calçada da Carmo 17, 2nd-3rd fl. (☎213 42 33 08), a block from the central station, across the Lg. Duque Cadaval. M: Rossio. Small, plain rooms in a central location. Rooms without full bath have shower. June-Sept. singles €15, with bath €20; doubles €30/35. Oct.-May €5 less. ❷

Pensão Beira Mar, Lgo. do Terreiro do Trigo 16 (☎218 87 15 28). Probably the cheapest option in Alfama for solo travelers. Rooms with river views cost a bit more. June-Aug. singles €15; doubles €30-40; quads €60. Oct.-May €10/15-20/40. ❶

Pensão Royal, R. do Crucifixo 50, 3rd fl. (☎213 47 90 06). M: Baixa/Chiado. Take a right out of the station on R. do Crucifixo; it's on the left before the intersection with R. São Nicolau. This new *pensão* offers airy rooms with hardwood floors, TV, and bath. May-Oct. dorms €15; singles €20; doubles €30. Nov.-Apr. €5 less. ❶

Residencial Duas Nações, R. da Vitória 41 (☎213 46 07 10), on the corner of R. Augusta, 3 blocks from M: Baixa/Chiado. Hotel-style lodging with large rooms that look out onto the main pedestrian street of Baixa. Breakfast included. May-Sept. singles €20, with bath €35; doubles €25/45; triples with bath €55. Oct.-Apr. €15/30/20/40/45. AmEx/MC/V. ❷

Residencial Florescente, R. Portas de Santo Antão 99 (☎213 42 66 09), 1 block from Pr. dos Restauradores. M: Restauradores. Marble baths and rooms with French doors and small terraces. All rooms with phone and TV. June-Sept. singles €25, with bath €40; doubles €30/45-60; triples €45/60. Oct.-May €5 less. AmEx/MC/V. ❸

Pensão Ninho das Águias, Costa do Castelo 74 (☎218 85 40 70), behind the Castelo. From Pr. da Figueira, take R. da Madalena to Largo Adelino Costa, then head uphill to Costa do Castelo. Canary-filled garden looks out over the old city. Singles €25; doubles €38, with bath €40; triples €50. ❸

Pensão Estrela, R. dos Bacalhoeiros 8 (☎218 86 95 06), in the lower part of Alfama. Breezy rooms with the basic amenities look out onto the busy square below. Checkout 11am. June-Sept. singles €20; doubles €30; triples €45. Oct.-May €5-7 less. ❷

Hospedagem Estrela da Serra, R. dos Fanqueiros 122, 4th fl. (☎218 87 42 51), at the end of R. São Nicolau, on the edge of Baixa toward the Alfama. Worth the five-floor hike; half the rooms have terraces with a view of Baixa. June-Aug. singles €15; doubles €20. Sept-May €5 less. ❶

Parque de Campismo Municipal de Lisboa (☎217 62 31 00), on the road to Benfica. Take bus #14 to the Parque Florestal Monsanto; the campsite is at the entrance of the park and extends throughout the forest. Pool and supermarket. Reception daily 9am-9pm. July-Aug. €4.80 per person, €5 per tent, and €3.20 per car. Off-season prices vary according to month.❶

🍴 FOOD

Lisbon has some of the best wine and least expensive restaurants of any European capital. Dinner costs about €10 per person; the *prato do dia* (daily special) is often only €5. Head to the **Calçada de Sant'Ana** and **Rua dos Correeiros** to find small, authentic restaurants that cater to locals. The city's culinary specialties include *amêjoas à bulhão pato* (steamed clams), *creme de mariscos* (seafood chowder with tomatoes), and *bacalhau cozido com grão e batatas* (cod with chickpeas and boiled potatoes, doused in olive oil). Snack on surprisingly filling and incredibly cheap Portuguese pastries; *pastelarias* (pastry shops) are everywhere. For groceries, look for any **Pingo Doce** supermarket. (Most open M-Sa 8:30am-9pm.)

Lua da Mel, R. Prata 242, on the corner of R. Santa Justa. If it can be caramelized, this diner-style pastry shop has done it. Pastries €0.60-1. Try the house specialty *Lua da Mel*. They also serve affordable meals (€7-9), and the daily specials are a great value (€5-6). Open M-Sa 7am-midnight. ❶

Restaurante Tripeiro, R. dos Correeiros 70A, serves some of the best Portuguese meals to be found on the lower streets of Baixa. Specializes in fish but also offers large portions of non-seafood dishes. Entrees €6-9. Open M-Sa noon-3pm and 7-10pm. ❷

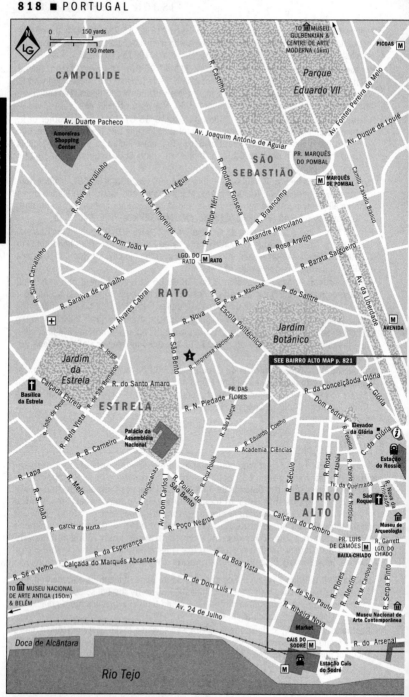

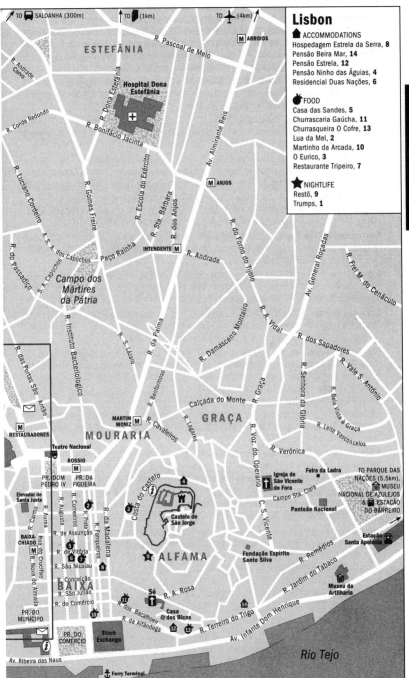

TO 🚆 SALDANHA (300m)   TO 🚌 (1km)   TO ✈ (4km)

ESTEFÂNIA

M ARROIOS

R. Pascoal de Melo

R. Andrade Corvo

R. Dona Estefânia

Hospital Dona Estefânia

R. Conde Redondo

R. Bonifácio Jacinta

Av. Almirante Reis

R. Luciano Cordeiro

R. Gomes Freire

R. Escola do Exército

R. Sta. Bárbara

R. dos Anjos

M ANJOS

R. do Forno do Tijolo

A. S. A. dos Capuchos

S. A. Capuchos

Paço Rainha

INTENDENTE M

R. Andrade

Av. General Roçadas

R. Frei M. do Cenáculo

R. do Passadiço

Campo dos Mártires da Pátria

R. Instituto Bacteriológico

R. S. Lázaro

R. da Palma

R. Damasceno Monteiro

R. A. Vidal

R. dos Sapadores

R. Vale S. António

R. das Portas São Antão

M RESTAURADORES

R. Benformoso

R. Cavaleiros

Calçada do Monte

R. Lagares

GRAÇA

R. Graça

R. Senhora da Glória

R. Bela Vista à Graça

R. Leite Vasconcelos

MARTIM MONIZ M

MOURARIA

Teatro Nacional

ROSSIO M

R. Verónica

PR. DOM PEDRO IV

PR. DA FIGUEIRA

Elevador de Santa Justa

R. Áurea

R. Correeiros

R. Augusta

R. Prata

R. da Madalena

Costa do Castelo

ℹ

4

Castelo de São Jorge

Igreja de São Vicente de Fora

Feira da Ladra

Campo Sta. Clara

C. S. Vicente

Panteão Nacional

TO PARQUE DAS NAÇÕES (5.5km), MUSEU NACIONAL DE AZULEJOS & ESTAÇÃO DO BÁRREIRO

BAIXA-CHIADO M

R. do Crucifixo

R. Nova da Almada

R. de Assunção

5

6 7

R. de Vitória

R. São Nicolau

8

R. Fanqueiros

9 ALFAMA

Fundação Espírito Santo Silva

R. Remédios

Estação Santa Apolónia

PR. DO MUNICÍPIO

R. Conceição

BAIXA

R. São Julião

R. do Comércio

11

Sé

R. A. Rosa

R. dos Bacalhoeiros

Casa dos Bicos

12 13

10

R. da Alfândega

Stock Exchange

R. Terreiro do Trigo

14

R. Jardim do Tabaco

Museu da Artilharia

PR. DO COMÉRCIO

ℹ

Av. Ribeira das Naus

⚓ Ferry Terminal

Av. Infante Dom Henrique

Rio Tejo

Lisbon

🏠 **ACCOMMODATIONS**
Hospedagem Estrela da Serra, **8**
Pensão Beira Mar, **14**
Pensão Estrela, **12**
Pensão Ninho das Águias, **4**
Residencial Duas Nações, **6**

🍎 **FOOD**
Casa das Sandes, **5**
Churrascaria Gaúcha, **11**
Churrasqueira O Cofre, **13**
Lua da Mel, **2**
Martinho da Arcada, **10**
O Eurico, **3**
Restaurante Tripeiro, **7**

⭐ **NIGHTLIFE**
Restô, **9**
Trumps, **1**

PORTUGAL

Martinho da Arcada, Pr. do Comércio 3, just outside the *praça,* to the far right with your back to the river. Founded in 1782, this is the oldest restaurant in Lisbon. Contains photos and poems of the restaurant's most celebrated regular, the renowned Portuguese poet Fernando Pessoa. Adjacent cafe has excellent lunch special. Entrees €11-15. *Pratos do dia* €4. Open M-Sa 7am-10pm. AmEx/MC/V. ❷

Antiga Confeitaria de Belém, R. de Belém 84-92. Since 1837, this pastry shop has served world-famous *pastéis de Belém;* only 3 people are privy to the secret recipe. Most pastries sold in one day: 52,000. *Pastéis* €0.80. ❶

Churrasqueira O Cofre, R. dos Bacalhoeiros 2C-D, at the foot of the Alfama near Pensão Estrela. A display case at the entrance shows everything available for grilling. Entrees €6-11. Open daily 9am-midnight, meals noon-4pm and 7-11:30pm. AmEx/MC/V. ❷

Sul, R. do Norte 13. Dark-wood paneling, tree-trunk bar stools, and candlelight give this restaurant and wine bar a romantic feel. Food tastes as good as it looks. Converts to a bar at 10pm. International entrees €7.50-14. Open Su and Tu-Sa 7:30pm-midnight. ❸

Restaurante Calcuta, R. do Norte 17, near Lg. Camões. Indian restaurant with wide selection of vegetarian entrees (€5). Meat entrees €6.50-9. Fixed price *menú* €13. Open M-F noon-3pm and 7-11pm, Sa-Su 7-11pm. AmEx/MC/V. ❷

Restaurante Ali-a-Papa, R. da Atalaia 95. Serves generous helpings of traditional Moroccan food in a quiet atmosphere. Vegetarian options. Entrees €7.50-12. Open M-Sa 7-11pm. AmEx/MC/V. ❷

A Brasileira, R. Garrett 120-122. A former romping ground of early 20th century poets and intellectuals, the *esplanade* out front is a hot gathering spot day and night. Mixed drinks €5. Specialty is *bife à brasileira* (€11). Open daily 8am-2am. ❸

Casa das Sandes, R. da Vitória 54, between R. dos Correeiros and R. Augusta. This restaurant's baguette sandwiches are becoming a local tradition. Outdoor terrace seating. Large sandwich €3-5. Open daily 10am-10pm. ❶

Pastelaria Anunciada, Lg. da Anunciada 1-2, on the corner of R. de S. José, 2 blocks from Pr. dos Restauradores. Specialties include *bacalhau à minhota* (codfish; €7) and *cozida à portuguesa* (boiled carrots, meats, potatoes, and more; €5). Open daily 6:30am-10pm, serves meals noon-10pm. ❷

Restaurante Bomjardim, Tv. Santo Antão 10 and 11, off Pr. dos Restauradores. Self-proclaimed *Rei dos Frangos* (king of chicken) and *Rei da Brasa* (king of the grill) rules the roost with its savory roast chicken (€8.50) and other grilled meats (€7-9). Open daily noon-11:30pm. AmEx/MC/V. ❷

O Eurico, Lgo. de S. Cristóvão 3-4, on C. do Marques de Tancos. Since 1969, this simple restaurant has served generous portions of grilled meats. Packed at lunchtime. Entrees €5-7. Open M-F 9am-10pm, meals noon-4pm and 7-10pm, Sa lunch only. ❷

Churrascaria Gaúcha, R. Bacalhoeiros 26C-D, 1 block from the river toward Alfama, near Pr. do Comércio. South American-style *churrasco* (grilled meat) dishes. Entrees €7-10. Open M-Sa 9am-midnight. AmEx/MC/V. ❷

Trimar, Av. da Liberdade, just up from Pr. dos Restauradores, to your left with your back to the *praça.* Cafe occupying a little park. Outdoor seating amidst fountains, statues, and trees. Coffee €0.50-1.70. Sandwiches €1.80-3. Restaurant inside. Entrees €5.50-13. Open daily 8am-2am. AmEx/MC/V. ❷

◎ SIGHTS

BAIXA

Although Baixa features few historic sights, the lively atmosphere and dramatic history surrounding the neighborhood's three main *praças* make it a monument in its own right.

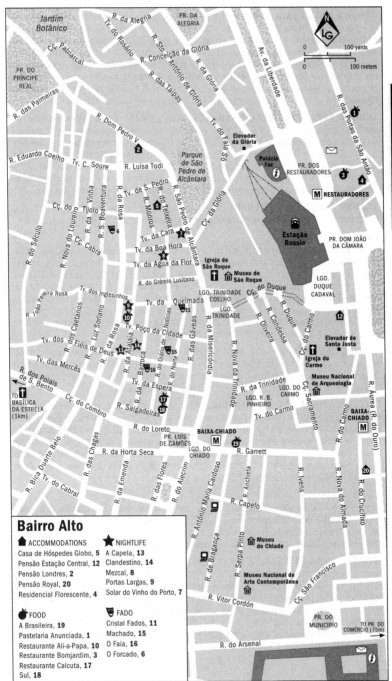

Bairro Alto

🏠 ACCOMMODATIONS
Casa de Hóspedes Globo, 5
Pensão Estação Central, 12
Pensão Londres, 2
Pensão Royal, 20
Residencial Florescente, 4

⭐ NIGHTLIFE
A Capela, 13
Clandestino, 14
Mezcal, 8
Portas Largas, 9
Solar do Vinho do Porto, 7

🍎 FOOD
A Brasileira, 19
Pastelaria Anunciada, 1
Restaurante Ali-a-Papa, 10
Restaurante Bomjardim, 3
Restaurante Calcuta, 17
Sul, 18

🎭 FADO
Cristal Fados, 11
Machado, 15
O Faia, 16
O Forcado, 6

AROUND THE ROSSIO. Start at the heart of Lisbon, the **Rossio** (also known as the **Praça Dom Pedro IV**). Once a cattle market, the site of public executions, a bullfighting arena, and carnival ground, the *praça* is now the domain of drink-sipping tourists and honk-happy traffic, which whizzes around a statue of Dom Pedro IV. A statue of Gil Vicente—Portugal's first great dramatist—peers from the top of the **Teatro Nacional de Dona Maria II** (easily recognized by its large columns) at one end of the *praça*. Adjoining the Rossio is the elegant **Praça da Figueira,** which lies on the border of the hilly streets of the Alfama district.

AROUND PRAÇA DOS RESTAURADORES. Just past the Rossio train station, an obelisk and a sculpture of the "Spirit of Independence" commemorate Portugal's independence from Spain in 1640. The tourist office, numerous shops, and the *Elevador Glória* all line the *praça*, which serves as the start of **Avenida da Liberdade,** Lisbon's most imposing, elegant promenade. Modeled after the wide boulevards of 19th-century Paris, this shady mile-long thoroughfare ends at **Praça do Marquês de Pombal;** from there, an 18th-century statue of the Marquês overlooks the city.

AROUND PRAÇA DO COMÉRCIO. On the other side of the Rossio from Pr. dos Restauradores, Praça do Comércio's grid of pedestrian streets invites wandering.

BAIRRO ALTO

In the Bairro Alto, the only place in Lisbon that never sleeps, pretentious intellectuals mix with teens and idealistic university students. Though the bairro is known for its celebrated *casas de fado* and scores of hip bars and clubs, there is still enough to behold in the daylight hours to warrant a separate visit. At the center of the neighborhood is **Praça Luís de Camões,** which adjoins **Largo Chiado** at the top of R. Garrett, a good place to rest and orient yourself while sightseeing. *(To reach R. Garrett and the heart of the chic Chiado neighborhood from the Rossio, take R. do Carmo uphill; R. Garrett is the 1st street on the right.)*

AROUND THE ELEVADOR DE SANTA JUSTA. The **Elevador de Santa Justa,** a 1902 elevator in a Gothic wrought-iron tower, once served as transportation up to Bairro Alto. Today, it takes tourists up to see the fantastic view and then back down again. *(Elevator runs M-F 7am-11pm, Sa-Su 9am-11pm. €1.)*

MUSEU NACIONAL DE ARTE ANTIGA. The Museum Nacional de Arte Antiga hosts a large collection of Portuguese art as well as a survey of European painting dating back as far as the 12th century and ranging from Gothic primitives to 18th-century French masterpieces. *(R. das Janelas Verdes, Jardim 9 Abril. 30min. down Av. Infante Santo from the Elevador de Santa Justa. Buses #40 and 60 stop to the right of the museum exit. Tram #15, from Pr. Figueria or Pr. do Comércio, also stops nearby. Open Su and W-Sa 10am-6pm, Tu 2-6pm. €3, students €1.50. Su before 2pm free.)*

RATO

Across from the **Basílica** on Lg. da Estrela, the wide paths of the ◼**Jardim da Estrela** wind through flocks of pigeons and lush flora and make a perfect spot for a stroll. *(M: Rato. With your back to the Metro stop, take the 2nd road from the left, R. Pedro Álvares Cabral; follow it 10min. until it runs into the garden. Open daily 8am-9pm.)*

◼**BASÍLICA DA ESTRELA.** Built in 1796, the basilica's dome, poised behind a pair of tall belfries, peaks out from surrounding buildings and trees to take its place in the Lisbon skyline. Half-mad Maria I, desiring a male heir, made fervent religious vows promising God everything if she were granted a son. When a baby boy was finally born, she built this church, and admirers of beautiful architecture and ornate wall paintings have been grateful ever since. Ask the sacristan to show you the 10th-century manger scene. *(On Pr. da Estrela. Accessible by Metro or by tram #28 from Pr. do Comércio. Open daily 8am-12:30pm and 3-7:30pm. Free.)*

ALFAMA

Alfama, Lisbon's medieval quarter, was the lone neighborhood to survive the infamous 1755 earthquake. The area descends in tiers from the dominating **Castelo de São Jorge** facing the Rio Tejo. Between Alfama and Baixa is the quarter known as the **Mouraria** (Moorish quarter), ironically established after Dom Afonso Henriques and the Crusaders expelled the Moors in 1147. Here, Portuguese grandmothers gossip and school boys play soccer amidst the few camera-toting tourists. Muggers make nighttime visits imprudent; even during the day, handbags should be left securely in hotels or lockers. Though sightseeing by foot in Alfama can be fun, visitors can also hop on tram #28 from Pr. do Comércio (€1), which winds up through the neighborhood past most of its sights.

THE LOWER ALFAMA. While any of the small uphill streets east of Baixa lead to Alfama's maze of streets, perhaps the best way to see the neighborhood is by climbing up R. da Madalena, which begins two blocks away from Pr. do Comércio. Veer right when you see the **Igreja da Madalena** in the Lgo. da Madalena on the right. Take R. de Santo António da Sé, and follow the tram tracks to the small **Igreja de Santo António,** built in 1812 over the beloved saint's alleged birthplace. The construction was funded with money collected by the city's children, who fashioned miniature altars bearing images of the saint to place on doorsteps—a custom reenacted annually on June 13, the saint's feast day and Lisbon's largest holiday. *(Open daily 8am-7pm. Mass daily 11am, 5, and 7pm.)*

■ **CASTELO DE SÃO JORGE.** Near the top of the Alfama lies the **Castelo de São Jorge,** which offers spectacular views of Lisbon and the ocean. Built in the 5th century by the Visigoths and enlarged in the 9th century by the Moors, this castle was again improved and converted into a playground for the royal family between the 14th and 16th centuries. Wander around the ruins, soak in the views, explore the ponds, or gawk at the exotic birds in the gardens. For shoppers, the castle also includes a string of souvenir shops and restaurants. *(From the cathedral, follow the brown and yellow signs for the castle on a winding uphill walk. Castle open daily Apr.-Sept. 9am-9pm; Oct.-Mar. 9am-6pm. Free.)*

GRAÇA

The construction of the ■ **Panteão Nacional** (formerly the Igreja de Santa Engrácia) began in 1680 and continued some 280 years, as the church changed hands between Catholic monks, enterprising factory owners, and ultimately, the dictatorial regime of Salazar. At its completion in 1966, the dome was dedicated as a burial for illustrious statesmen. Today, it houses the remains of such national figures as queen of *fado* Amália Rodrigues. *(To reach Graça and the Panteão, take bus #12 or tram #28 from the bottom of R. dos Correiros. Open Su and Tu-Sa 10am-5pm. €2.)*

SÃO SEBASTIÃO

Home to Lisbon's first **Corte Inglés,** this section of town marks the entrance to two excellent art museums.

■ **MUSEU CALOUSTE GULBENKIAN.** When oil tycoon Calouste Gubenkian died in 1955, he left his extensive art collection to his beloved Portugal. Though the philanthropist was of Armenian descent and a British citizen, it was Portugal he chose to call home. The collection is divided into sections of ancient art—Egyptian, Greek, Roman, Islamic, and Oriental—and European pieces from the 15th to 20th centuries. Highlights include works by Monet, Rembrandt, Renoir, and Rodin. *(Av. Berna 45. M: São Sebastião. Bus # 18, 46, or 56. Open Su and Tu-Sa 10am-6pm. €3. Seniors, students, and teachers free.)*

CENTRO DE ARTE MODERNA. Though not as famous as its neighbor, this museum, also funded by Mr. Gulbenkian's foundation, houses an extensive modern collection dedicated to promoting Portuguese talent. Don't miss the sculpture gardens that separate the two museums. *(R. Dr. Nicolau Bettencourt. M: São Sebastião. From the station, head downhill; the museum is tucked among the trees. Bus #16, 31, or 46. Open Su and Tu-Sa 10am-5pm. €3. Seniors, students, and teachers free.)*

BELÉM

Belém is more of a suburb than a neighborhood of Lisbon, but its concentration of monuments and museums makes it a crucial stop on any tour of the capital. The town epitomizes the Portuguese tradition in all its glory with its unbelievable pastries, a religious structure that redefines ornamentation, and a slew of monuments and museums that showcase the seafaring discoverers of centuries past. *(To reach Belém, take tram #15 from Pr. do Comércio (15min.) or bus #28 or 43 from Pr. da Figueira (15min.) to Mosteiro dos Jerónimos, one stop beyond the regular Belém stop. Or, take the train from Estação Cais do Sodré (10min., every 15min., €1). From the train station, cross the tracks, then cross the street and go left. The Padrão dos Descobrimentos will be on the highway to your left, while the Mosteiro dos Jerónimos will be to the right, through the public gardens.)*

■ **MOSTEIRO DOS JERÓNIMOS.** Established in 1502 to give thanks for the success of Vasco da Gama's expedition to India, the Mosteiro dos Jerónimos was granted UN World Heritage status in the 1980s. The country's most refined celebration of the Age of Discovery, it showcases Portugal's native Manueline style, combining Gothic forms with minute Renaissance detail. The main door of the church, to the right of the monastery entrance, is a sculpted anachronism; Prince Henry the Navigator mingles with the Twelve Apostles on both sides of the central column. The symbolic tombs of Luís de Camões and navigator Vasco da Gama lie in two opposing transepts. Inside the monastery, the octagonal cloisters of the courtyard, carved with exquisite detail, surround simple rose gardens. *(Open Su and Tu-Sa 10am-5pm. €3, students €1.50. Su 10am-2pm free.)*

■ **TORRE DE BELÉM.** The best known tower in all of Portugal, the Torre de Belém rises from the north bank of the Rio Tejo and is surrounded by the ocean on three sides. Built under Manuel I from 1515-1520 as a harbor fortress, it originally sat directly on the shoreline; today, due to the receding beach, it is only accessible by a small bridge. This symbol of Portuguese grandeur and member of UNESCO's World Heritage list offers panoramic views of Belém, the Rio Tejo, and the Atlantic beyond. *(A 10min. walk along the water from the monastery in the opposite direction of Lisbon. Take the underpass by the gardens to cross the highway. Open Su and Tu-Sa 10am-6pm. €3, students and seniors €1.50.)*

PADRÃO DOS DESCOBRIMENTOS. Along the river is the Padrão dos Descobrimentos, built in 1960 on the 500-year anniversary of Prince Henry the Navigator's death. The great, white monument features Henry leading his compatriates, including Vasco da Gama and Diogo Cão, and celebrates the centuries of Portuguese adventurers who set sail around the world under Henry's inspiration. Take the elevator 50m up to the small terrace for an excellent view. *(Across the highway from the monastery. Open Su and Tu-Sa 9am-5pm. €2, students €1.)*

■ PARQUE DAS NAÇÕES

The **Parque das Nações** (Park of Nations) inhabits the former Expo '98 grounds 6km from downtown. Until the mid-1990s, the area was a muddy wasteland with a few run-down factories and warehouses along the banks of the Rio Tejo. A few years later, the city transformed the land, preparing the grounds for the 1998 World Exposition. After Expo '98, the government pumped millions into converting the grounds into the Parque das Nações. Today, the park is packed day and night with people enjoying everything from the park's enormous movie theater to its indoor neighborhood of restaurants to its science museum. The park entrance leads through the Centro Vasco de Gama **shopping mall** (open daily 10am-midnight) to the center of the grounds, where information kiosks provide maps and offer free luggage storage (open daily 9:30am-8pm). Those weary of walking can use the cable cars, which connect one end of the park to the other (8min.; M-F 11am-7pm, Sa-Su 10am-8pm; €3, under-18 or over-65 €1.50). *To reach the park from Lisbon, take the Metro to the Oriente stop at the end of the red line (€0.70). The Oriente stop has escalators rising up to the park's main entrance at the Centro Vasco de Gama. Alternatively, city buses #5, 10, 19, 21, 25, 28, 44, 50, 68, and 114 all stop at the Oriente station (€1).*

OCEANÁRIO. The enormous new aquarium is both the park's biggest attraction and the largest oceanarium in Europe. Interactive sections showcase the four major oceans complete with sounds and smells; every section connects to the main tank, which houses fish, sharks, and other sea creatures. Visitors can get within a meter of playful sea otters and penguins. The multilevel design allows for unique views of sea life from underneath the tank. *(Open daily Apr.-Sept. 10am-7pm, Oct.-Mar. 10am-6pm. €9, under-13 or over-65 €5.)*

PAVILIONS. The numerous pavilions scattered around the park appeal to a variety of interests to suit any visitor's fancy. The **Pavilhão do Conhecimento** (Pavilion of Knowledge) hosts an interactive science museum *(open Tu-F 10am-6pm, Sa-Su 11am-7pm. €5, under-18 or over-65 €2.50)* while the **Virtual Reality Pavilion** holds a ride to challenge the senses. The **Atlantic Pavilion** hosts many of Lisbon's concerts, and the **International Fairgrounds** accommodate rotating exhibits during the year.

TORRE VASCO DE GAMA. As the city's tallest building, this 145m structure grabs visitors's attention with its striking, 21st-century architecture. The entire city can be seen from the observation tower. *(Open daily 10am-8pm. €2.50, under-18 or over-65 €1.30.)*

ENTERTAINMENT

Agenda Cultural and *Follow Me Lisboa* have information on arts events and bullfights; both are free at kiosks in the Rossio, on R. Portas de Santo Antão, and at the tourist office.

FADO
Lisbon's trademark is **fado**, an art combining singing and narrative poetry that expresses sorrowful *saudade* (nostalgia). The Bairro Alto has many *fado* joints off R. da Misericórdia and on streets by the Igreja de São Roque, but the prices alone may turn a knife in your heart. Various bars offer free performances.

Machado, R. do Norte 91. Founded in 1937, Machado is one of the larger *fado* restaurants and features some of the most well-known *cantadeiras* and guitarists. Dinner may cost your daily budget. Entrees €19-30. Min. purchase €15. Open Su and Tu-Sa 8pm-3am; *fado* starts at 9:15pm. AmEx/MC/V.

O Faia, R. Barroca 56, between R. Atalaia and R. do Diário de Notícias. Elegant and expensive. Some of Portugal's better known *fadistas* perform nightly. Min. purchase €18, includes 2 drinks. Entrees from €18. *Menú* €35. Open M-Sa 8pm-2am; *fado* starts at 9:30pm. AmEx/MC/V.

O Forcado, R. da Rosa 221. A traditional restaurant that features *fado* from Coimbra and Lisbon, as well as folk music and dance. Decorated with bullfighting pictures and *azulejos*. Min. purchase €15. Entrees €18-20. Open Su-Tu and Th-Sa 8pm-1:30am; *fado* starts at 9:15pm. AmEx/MC/V.

THE LOCAL STORY

SUCH SWEET SORROW

Lisbon's trademark is fado, an art combining singing and narrative poetry. The Bairro Alto has several fado joints off R. da Misericórdia and on streets by the Igreja de São Roque. Here, fado singer Sara Reis describes her interpretation of the musical genre for Let's Go.

Fado comes from the Latin, *fatum*, which means destiny. It's a feeling that is born with us. Either you understand it or you don't. I do because I was born in the middle of *fadistas*. At home I never heard Rock 'n' Roll, and by the time I reached age 7, I was already singing *fado*. To feel *fado* in its totality is to understand life—its love, death, birth, passion, hatred. It's very complex. In order to really feel *fado*, you have to have reached a certain level of maturity and suffering. There you have it. *Fado* is nostalgia. In my opinion, it is one of the most revolutionary kinds of music. It was created by and for the people...I have already heard young girls no older than 16 sing about life in a way that would move you with emotion. And, on the other hand, I've heard old *fado* singers 50 years old sing from here (points to her head). It all depends on the sensibility and ability of the person.

Cristal Fados, Tv. da Queimada 9, on the corner of R. do Norte. With less famous singers and less luxurious meals, have dinner without blowing your budget. Min. purchase €7. Entrees €8-11. Open daily 8:30pm-1am; *fado* Su and Th-Sa. AmEx/MC/V.

FESTIVALS

In June, the people of Lisbon spill into the city for a summer's worth of revelry. Open-air *feiras* (fairs)—smorgasbords of eating, drinking, live music, and dancing—fill the streets. After savoring *farturas* (Portuguese pastries) and Sagres beer, few hesitate to join in traditional Portuguese dancing. On the night of June 12, the streets explode in song and dance in honor of St. Anthony during the **Festa de Santo António.** Banners are strung between streetlights, confetti falls like snow during a parade along Av. da Liberdade, and young crowds pack the streets of Alfama for grilled *sardinhas* (sardines), *ginginha*, and merriment. Lisbon also has a number of commercial *feiras*. From late May to early June, bookworms burrow for three glorious weeks during the **Feira do Livro** in the Parque Eduardo VII behind Pr. Marques do Pombal. The **Feira Internacional de Lisboa,** which has moved to the Parque das Nações, occurs every few months, while in July and August the **Feira de Mar de Cascais** and the **Feira de Artesania de Estoril** (celebrating famous Portuguese pottery) take place near the casino. Year-round *feiras* include the **Feira de Oeiras** (antiques) on the fourth Sunday of every month and the **Feira de Carcanelos** for clothes (Th 8am-2pm). Packrats should catch the **Feira da Ladra** (flea market), held behind the Igreja de São Vicente de Fora in Graça (Tu and Sa 7am-3pm). To get there, take bus #104 or #105 or tram #28.

■ NIGHTLIFE

Bairro Alto is the first place to go for nightlife, where a plethora of small bars and clubs fills the side streets. In particular, **Rua do Norte, Rua do Diário Notícias,** and **Rua Atalaia** have many small clubs packed into three short blocks, making club-hopping as easy as crossing the street. Several gay and lesbian clubs are found between Pr. de Camões and Tv. da Queimada, as well as in the **Rato** area near the edge of Bairro Alto. During the later hours, **Avenida 24 de Julho** and the **Rua das Janelas Verdes** in the **Santos** area have some of the most popular bars and clubs. Newer hot spots include the area along the river across from the **Santa Apolo'nia** train station. There's no reason to arrive before midnight; crowds flow in around 2am and stay until dawn.

Lux, Av. Infante D. Henrique A. Take a taxi to the area across from the St. Apolo'nia train station. In a class of its own, Lux continues to be the hottest spot in Lisbon since its opening in 1998. Beer €1.50-2.50. Min. purchase €10. Open Tu-Sa 6pm-6am; arrive after 2am.

Speakeasy, Docas de St. Amaro, between the *Santos* and *Alcântara* stops, next to the river. More of a concert with waiters and beer than a bar, Speakeasy is Lisbon's premiere jazz and blues center. Live shows every night, with famous national and international performers once a month. Beer €3. Open M-Sa 8pm-4am.

Salsa Latina, Gare Marítima de Alcântara, across the parking lot from the cluster at Doca de Santo Amaro. Sophisticated crowds come for the live salsa on weekends. Terrace with a view of the river. Min. purchase €10. Open M-Th 8-11pm, F-Sa 8pm-4am.

Trumps, R. Imprensa Nacional 104B, in the Bairro Alto. Lisbon's biggest gay club features several bars in addition to a massive dance floor. Min. purchase €10. Open Su and Tu-Th 11:30pm-4:30am, F-Sa midnight-6:30am.

Clandestino, R. da Barroca 99. Cavernous bar with messages scrawled by former patrons on its rock walls. Beer €1.50. Mixed drinks €3. Open Su and Tu-Sa 10pm-2am.

A Capela, R. Atalaia 45. A spacious bar with gold walls and red velvet cushions. Popular in the late hours. Beer €3. Mixed drinks €5. Open daily 9pm-2am.

Restô, R. Costa do Castelo 7. Huge outdoor patio with the best view of the city. Restaurant serves Argentine steaks (€12), New Zealand lamb chops (€15), and Spanish *tapas* (€4). At night, fills with a young crowd. Live Portuguese guitar F-Su. *Caipirinhas* €4. Beer €1.30. Open daily 7:30pm-2am.

Suave, R. do Diário de Notícias 4-6. Well-dressed guests schmooze to jazz and soul on weekends and a mix during the week. Beer €2. Open daily 10pm-2am.

Indochina, R. Cintura do Porto de Lisboa, Armazém H, next to the train tracks. A 10-min. walk from the Santos station. Far East decorations give it a classy feel. Open Th-Sa 11:30pm-6am.

OP Art, R. da Cozinha Economia 11, under the 25 de Abril bridge. The only café/bar/disco right on the river. Beer €3. Open Su and Tu-Sa noon-4:00am.

Portas Largas, R. Atalaia 105, at the end of Tv. da Queimada. Mixed crowd. Popular with Bairro's gay community. Portuguese music before midnight and techno afterward. Open July-Sept. 7pm-3:30am; Oct.-June 8pm-3:30am.

Kapital, Av. 24 de Julho 68. The classiest club in Lisbon, with a ruthless door policy that makes admission a competitive sport. 3 floors, with a nice terrace on top and a dance floor. Cover €15. Open M-Sa 11pm-6am.

Kremlin, Escandinhas da Praia 5, off Av. 24 de Julho next to Kapital. Harsh door policy. Set in a former bishop's residence, Kremlin has giant plastic statues and 3 rooms with throbbing house and dance music. Cover €5 for women and €10 for men, includes 1 drink. Open Tu-W midnight-6am, Th midnight-8am, and F-Sa midnight-9:30am.

Mezcal, on the corner of Tv. Agua da Flor and R. do Diário de Notícias. Tiny Mexican bar with the cheapest drinks in Bairro Alto. Tacos, burritos, and nachos €2-4. *Sangria* €1.80. *Caipirinhas* €2.80. Shots €2. Margaritas €2. Open daily 7pm-2am.

Solar do Vinho do Porto, R. São Pedro de Alcântara 45, at the top of the steps through the large doorway. Sip port and eat fancy cheese served by a tuxedoed wait staff. Port from €1 to €20, depending on age and quality. Open M-Sa 2pm-midnight.

Mahjong, R. Atalaia 3. Located at the corner of R. Atalaia and Tv. das Mercês. The artistically inclined come for the cheap shots (€2). Open daily 9:30pm-4am.

PORTUGAL

▶ DAYTRIPS FROM LISBON

SINTRA. With fairy-tale castles, enchanting gardens, and spectacular mountain vistas, Sintra (pop. 20,000) is a favorite among backpackers. Perched on the mountain overlooking the Old Town, the **Castelo dos Mouros** provides stunning views of the mountains and coast. Follow the blue signs 3km up the mountain or take bus #434 (15min., every 30min., day pass €4), which runs to the top from the tourist office. The awestruck are also usually sun-struck; a bottle of water is recommended. (Open June-Sept. 9am-8pm; Oct.-May 9am-7pm. €3, seniors €1.) A mix of Moorish, Gothic, and Manueline styles, the **Palácio Nacional de Sintra**, in Pr. da República, was once the summer residence of Moorish sultans and their harems. (☎219 10 68 40. Open Su-Tu and Th-Sa 10am-5:30pm. Buy tickets by 5pm. €3, seniors €1.50.) Farther uphill is the **Palácio da Pena**, a Bavarian castle decorated with Arabic minarets, Gothic turrets, Manueline windows, and a Renaissance dome. (Open July-Sept. Su and Tu-Sa 10am-6:30pm; Oct.-June Su and Tu-Sa 10am-5pm. €5, seniors and students €3.50.)

Trains (☎219 23 26 05) arrive at Av. Dr. Miguel Bombarda from Lisbon's Estação Rossio (45min., every 15min. 6am-2am, €1.30). **Stagecoach buses** leave from outside the train station for Cascais (#417; 40min., every hr. 7:20am-8:30pm, €2.80) and Estoril (#418; 40min., every hr. 6:50am-midnight, €2.50). Down the street, **Mafrense buses** go to Ericeira (50min., every hr. 7:30am-8:30pm, €2.30). The **tourist office,** Sintra-Vila Pr. da República 23, is in the historic center. From the bus station, turn left on Av. Bombarda, which becomes the winding Volta do Duche. Continue straight into the Pr. da República; the tourist office is to the left. (☎219 23 11 57. Open June-Sept. daily 9am-8pm; Oct.-May 9am-7pm.) To reach the **Pousada da Juventude de Sintra (HI) ❶**, on Sta. Eufémia, take bus #434 from the train station to São Pedro (15min., €1.20), and then hike 2km, or hail a taxi (weekdays €9; weekends €10) in front of the train station. (☎219 24 12 10. Reservations recommended. June 16-Sept. 15 dorms €11 per person; doubles €24, with bath €25. Sept. 16-June 15 €8.50/20/24. Members only. MC/V.)

ESTORIL AND CASCAIS. Glorious beaches draw sun-loving tourists and locals alike to Estoril (pop. 24,000) and neighboring Cascais (pop. 33,000). For the beach-weary, the marvelous (and air-conditioned) **Casino Estoril**, Europe's largest casino, is a welcome relief. (☎214 66 77 00; www.casino-estoril.pt. No swimwear, tennis shoes, jeans, or shorts. Slots and game room 18+. Passport required. Open daily 3pm-3am.)

Trains from Lisbon's Estação do Sodré stop in Cascais via Estoril (30min., every 20min. 5:30am-2:30am, €1.10). Estoril and Cascais are only a 20min. stroll along the coast or Av. Marginal from each other. **Bus** #418 to Sintra departs from Av. Marginal, in front of Estoril's train station (35min., every hr. 6:10am-11:40pm, €2.30). From the station, cross Av. Marginal and head to the Estoril **tourist office**, which is to the left of the Casino on Arcadas do Parque, for a free map of both towns. (☎214 66 38 13. Open M-Sa 9am-7pm, Su 10am-6pm.) Ask for help finding a room at the Cascais **tourist office**, Av. Dos Combatantes da Grande Guerra 25. From the Cascais train station, cross the square and take a right onto Av. Valbom. Look for a small sign at Av. Dos Combatantes. (☎214 86 82 04. Open M-Sa 9am-7pm, Su 10am-6pm.)

MAFRA. Sleepy Mafra (pop. 11,300) is home to one of Portugal's most impressive sights and one of Europe's largest historical buildings, the **Palácio Nacional de Mafra**. The massive 2000-room palace, including a cathedral-sized church, a monastery, and a library, took 50,000 workers 30 years to complete. (Open Su-M and W-Sa 10am-5pm; last entrance 4pm. €3, students and seniors €1.50.

Under-14 free. Su 10am-1:30pm free. Daily 1hr. tours in English 11am and 2:30pm.) The entrance to the recently renovated **tourist office** is inside the palace compound. (☎261 81 71 70. Open M-F 9am-7pm, Sa-Su 9:30am-1pm and 2:30-6pm.) Frequent Mafrense **buses** run from Lisbon's Campo Grande (M: Campo Grande) to Mafra (1-1½hr., every hr., €2.80) and stop in front of the palace.

ERICEIRA. Primarily a fishing village, Ericeira is known for its spectacular beaches and surfable waves. The main beaches, **Praia do Sul** and **Praia do Norte,** crowd quickly; for something more secluded, stroll down the Largo da Feira toward Ribamar until you reach the stunning sand dunes of **Praia da Ribeira d'Ilhas.** Frequent Mafrense **buses** run from Lisbon's Campo Grande (M: Campo Grande) to Ericeira (1½hr., every hr., €4.) and from Mafra to Ericeira (25min., every hr., €1.50). If you stay, ask about rooms at the **tourist office,** R. Eduardo Burnay 46. (☎261 86 31 22. Open July-Sept. daily 9:30am-midnight; Oct.-June Sa 9:30am-10pm, Su-M 9:30am-7pm.)

CENTRAL PORTUGAL

Jagged cliffs and whitewashed fishing villages line the Costa de Prata of Estremadura, with beaches that rival even those in the Algarve. In the fertile region of the Ribatejo (Banks of the Rio Tejo), lush greenery surrounds historic sights.

LEIRIA ☎244

Capital of the surrounding district and an important transport hub, prosperous and industrial Leiria (pop. 43,000) fans out from a fertile valley, 22km from the coast. Chosen to host the Euro 2004 soccer finals, Leiria is preparing itself for the crowds that will flood the city. The city's most notable sight is its **Castelo de Leiria,** a granite fort built by Dom Afonso Henriques atop the crest of a volcanic hill after he snatched the town from the Moors. The terrace opens onto a panoramic view of the town and river. (Castle open Apr.-Sept. M-F 9am-6:30pm, Sa-Su 10am-6:30pm; Oct.-Mar. M-F 9am-5:30pm, Sa-Su 10am-5:30pm. €1.) Nearby **beaches** include **Vieira, Pedrógão,** and **São Pedro de Muel,** all accessible by bus.

Leiria makes a practical base for exploring the nearby region. **Trains** (☎88 20 27) run from the station 3km outside town to Coimbra (2hr., 6 per day, €3.60) and Lisbon (1¾hr., 9 per day, €7.60-8.50). **Buses** (☎81 15 07), just off Pr. Paulo VI, next to the main park and close to the tourist office, run to: Batalha (20min., 9 per day, €1.20-2); Coimbra (1hr., 11 per day, €6.50); Lisbon (2hr., 11 per day, €7.80); Porto (3½hr., 10 per day, €10.20); and Tomar (1½hr., 6 per day, €3.10-6.70). Buses also run between the train station and the **tourist office** (15min., every hr. 7am-7:20pm, €0.80), in the Jardim Luís de Camões. (☎244 84 87 70. Open May-Sept. daily 10am-1pm and 3-7pm; Oct.-Apr. 10am-1pm and 2-6pm.) If you're going to spend the night, try **Pousada da Juventude de Leiria (HI) ❶,** on Largo Cândido dos Reis 9. (☎/fax 83 18 68. Dorms €8.50-11; doubles €21-27.) **Postal Code:** 2400.

TOMAR ☎249

For centuries, the Knights Templar plotted crusades from a celebrated convent-fortress high above the small town of Tomar (pop. 22,000). The ▨**Convento de Cristo** complex, built by the Moors and fortified by the Knights Templar in 1160, was the Knights' powerful and mysterious headquarters. The **Claustro dos Felipes** is a Renaissance masterpiece. (☎31 34 81. Complex open June-Sept. daily 9am-6pm; Oct.-May 9am-5pm. €3. Under-14 free.) **Trains** (☎72 07 55) run from Av. Combatentes da Grande Guerra, at the southern edge of town, to: Coimbra (2½hr., 8 per day, €5.60-6.40); Lisbon (2hr., 18 per day, €5.60-6.40) and Porto (4½hr., 7 per day, €8.50-9.50). Rodoviária Tejo **buses** (☎968 94 35 50) leave from Av. Combatentes da Grande Guerra, by the train station, for: Coimbra (2½hr., 7am, €9.20); Leiria (1hr.; M-F 7:15am and 5:45pm, Sa 7am; €3.10); Lisbon (2hr., 4 per day, €6.50); and Porto (4hr., 7am, €12). From the bus or train station, head down Av. General Bernardo Faria toward the city three blocks; turn left and follow Av. Cândido Madureira to the **tourist office.** (☎32 24 27. Open July-Sept. daily 10am-8pm; Oct.-June 10am-6pm.) **Postal Code:** 2300.

BATALHA   ☎244

The centerpiece of Batalha is the gigantic ▉**Mosteiro de Santa Maria da Vitória.** Built by Dom João I in 1385, the complex of cloisters and chapels remains one of Portugal's greatest monuments. To get to the monastery, enter through the church. (Open Apr.-Sept. daily 9am-6pm; Oct.-Mar. 9am-5pm. €3, under-25 €1.50. Under-14 and Su before 2pm free.) **Buses** run from across from the monastery to: Leiria (20min., 10 per day, €1.20-1.50); Lisbon (2hr., 6 per day, €6.60); and Tomar (1½hr.; 8am, noon, and 6pm; €3). The **tourist office,** on Pr. Mouzinho de Albuquerque, stands opposite the monastery. (☎76 51 80. Open May-Sept. daily 10am-1pm and 3-7pm; Oct.-Apr. 10am-1pm and 2-6pm.) **Postal Code:** 2440.

NAZARÉ   ☎262

In Nazaré (pop. 10,000), it's hard to tell where authenticity stops and tourism begins. Fishermen in traditional garb go barefoot while the day's catch dries in the hot sun. But if Nazaré is part theater, at least it puts on a good show—and everyone gets front row seats on its glorious **beach.** For an evening excursion, take the **funicular** (3min., every 15min. 7:15am-9:30pm, €0.70), which runs from R. Elevador off Av. da República to the **Sítio,** a clifftop area replete with uneven cobbled streets, weathered buildings, and wonderful views of the town and ocean. Around 6pm, fishing boats return to the **port** beyond the far left end of the beach; head over to watch fishermen at work and eavesdrop as local restaurateurs bid for the most promising catches at the **fish auction** (M-F 6-9:30pm). **Cafes** in Pr. Souza Oliveira teem with people after midnight. Nazaré is on the revolving schedule that brings **bullfights** to a different city in the province each summer weekend. (Usually Sa 10pm; tickets from €27.)

Nazaré is only accessible by **bus** (☎800 20 03 70). Buses run to: Coimbra (2hr., 5 per day 6:25am-7:25pm, €8.80); Lisbon (2hr., 8 per day 6:50am-8pm, €7.30); Porto (3½hr., 7 per day 6:25am-7:25pm, €9); and Tomar (1½hr. 3 per day 7am-5:10pm, €5). The **tourist office** is beachside on Av. da República. (☎56 11 94. Open July-Aug. daily 10am-10pm; Sept. 10am-8pm; Oct.-Mar. 9:30am-1pm and 2:30-6pm; Apr.-June 10am-1pm and 3-7pm.) Try Pr. Dr. Manuel de Arriaga and Pr. Sousa Oliveira for the best deals on accommodations. **Vila Turística Conde Fidalgo ❸,** Av. da Independência Nacional 21-A, is three blocks uphill from Pr. Sousa Oliveira. (☎/fax 55 23 61. July singles €30; doubles €35; Aug. €40/45. Sept.-June singles €15-20; doubles €25-30.) For **camping,** head to **Vale Paraíso ❶,** on Estrada Nacional 242, 2.5km out of town; they also rent bungalows and apartments. Take the bus (10min., 12 per day 7am-7pm) to Alcobaça or Leiria. (☎56 18 00. June-Sept. €4 per person, €3-5 per tent, €3 per car. Oct.-May €3/2.50-3.70/2.50.) Supermarkets line **Rua Sub-Vila,** parallel to Av. da República. **Postal Code:** 2450.

ÉVORA   ☎266

Named a UNESCO World Heritage site, Évora (pop. 44,000) is justly known as the "Museum City." Moorish arches line the streets of this picture-perfect town, which boasts a Roman temple, an imposing cathedral, and a 16th-century university.

🖭🏛 TRANSPORTATION AND PRACTICAL INFORMATION. Trains (☎266 70 21 25) run from Av. dos Combatentes de Grande Guerra to Lisbon (2½hr., 5 per day, €8.10) and Porto (6½hr., 3 per day, €14). **Buses** (☎266 76 94 10) go from Av. Sebastião to Lisbon (3hr., every 1-1½hr., €8.80) and Faro (4½hr., 4 per day, €12). The **tourist office** is at Pr. Giraldo 65. (☎266 70 26 71. Open Apr.-Sept. M-F 9am-7pm, Sa-Su 9am-5:30pm; Oct.-Mar. daily 9am-6pm.) Free **Internet** access is available at **Instituto Português da Juventude**, R. da República 105. (Open M-F 9am-11pm.) **Postal Code:** 7000.

🏠🍴 ACCOMMODATIONS AND FOOD. *Pensões* cluster around **Praça do Giraldo.** Take a right out of the tourist office, and then the first right onto R. Bernardo Mato to get to the warm **Casa Palma ❷,** R. Bernardo Mato 29A, which has quality rooms at competitive prices. (☎266 70 35 60. Singles €15, with bath €25; doubles €25/30.) Or, cross Pr. Giraldo and take a right on R. da República, then turn left on R. Miguel Bombarda to reach **Pousada da Juventude (HI) ❶,** R. Miguel Bombarda 40, which has a terrace with a view of the city. (☎266 74 48 48; fax 266 74 48 43. June 16-Sept. 15 dorms €13; doubles with bath €35. Sept. 16-June 15 €10/28.) Many budget restaurants are near Pr. Giraldo, particularly along **Rua Mercadores.** The cozy **Restaurante Burgo Velho ❷,** R. de Burgos 10, serves large portions of local dishes. (Entrees €5-9. Open M-Sa noon-3pm and 7-10pm.) From Pr. Giraldo, walk up R. 5 de Outubro and take a right onto R. Diogo Cão to reach the only real Italian restaurant in Évora, **Pane & Vino ❷,** Páteo do Salema. (Entrees €5-8. Open Su and Tu-Sa noon-3pm and 6:30-11pm.)

🎭🎶 SIGHTS AND ENTERTAINMENT. Attached to the pleasant **Igreja Real de São Francisco,** the bizarre 🖾**Capela dos Ossos** (Chapel of Bones) was built by three Franciscan monks using the bones of 5000 people. From Pr. Giraldo, follow R. República; the church is on the right and the chapel is around back to the right of the main entrance. (Open M-Sa 9am-1pm and 2:30-6pm, Su 10am-1pm. €1.) According to legend, the second-century **Templo Romano,** on Largo Conde do Vila Flor, was built for the goddess Diana. Facing the temple is the **Igreja de São João Evangelista;** its interior is covered with dazzling tiles. (Open Su and Tu-Sa 10am-12:30pm and 2-6pm. €2.50.) From Pr. Giraldo, head up R. 5 de Outubro to the colossal 12th-century **cathedral;** the 12 apostles on the doorway are masterpieces of medieval Portuguese sculpture. Climb the stairs of the cloister for an excellent view of the city. The **Museu de Arte Sacra,** above the nave, has religious artifacts. (Cathedral open daily 9am-12:30pm and 2-5pm. Cloisters open daily 9am-noon and 2-4:30pm. Museum open Su and Tu-Sa 9am-noon and 2-4:30pm. Cathedral free. Cloisters and museum €2.50.) A country fair accompanies the **Feira de São João** festival the last week of June. After sunset, head to 🖾**Jonas,** R. Serpa Pinto 115, to discover a cavernous underground lounge with a mellow bar. (Open M-Sa 10:30am-3am.)

ALGARVE

Nearly 3000 hours of sunshine per year have transformed the Algarve, a desert on the sea, into a popular vacation spot. In July and August, sun-seeking tourists mob the resorts, packing the bars and discos from sunset until way past dawn. In the off season, the resorts become pleasantly de-populated.

LAGOS   ☎282

As the town's countless international expats will attest, Lagos (pop. 17,400) is a black hole: Come for two days and you'll stay for two months. Lagos keeps you soaking in the view from the cliffs, the sun on the beach, and the drinks at the bars.

PORTUGAL

TRANSPORTATION

Trains: ☎282 79 23 61. Across the river (over the pedestrian suspension bridge) from the main part of town. To **Évora** (6hr., 8:20am and 5:15pm, €13) and **Lisbon** (4-4½hr., 5-6 per day, €14).

Buses: The **EVA** bus station (☎282 76 29 44), off Av. Descobrimentos, is across the channel from the train station. To: **Lisbon** (5hr., 12 per day, €15) and **Sagres** (1hr., 17 per day, €2.80).

Taxis: Lagos Central Taxi (☎282 76 24 69). 24hr. service to Lagos and environs.

Car Rental: Min. age 21 for vehicles, 16 for motorbikes.

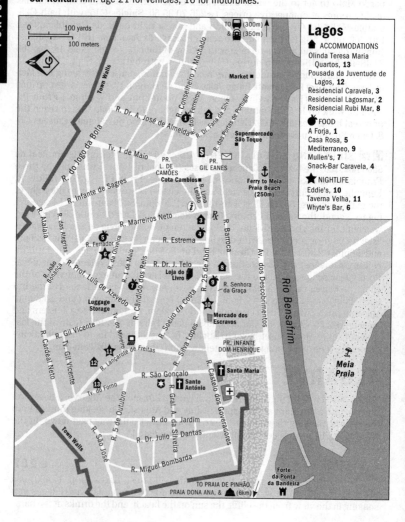

Lagos

♠ ACCOMMODATIONS
Olinda Teresa Maria Quartos, **13**
Pousada da Juventude de Lagos, **12**
Residencial Caravela, **3**
Residencial Lagosmar, **2**
Residencial Rubi Mar, **8**

♦ FOOD
A Forja, **1**
Casa Rosa, **5**
Mediterraneo, **9**
Mullen's, **7**
Snack-Bar Caravela, **4**

★ NIGHTLIFE
Eddie's, **10**
Taverna Velha, **11**
Whyte's Bar, **6**

Marina Rent A Car, Av. Descobrimentos 43 (☎282 76 47 89). July-Aug. cars start at €45 per day; May-June and Sept. €35; Oct.-Apr. €30; tax and insurance included. Rent for two days and get a third free. AmEx/MC/V.

Motoride, R. José Afonso lote 23-C (☎282 76 17 20). Rents bikes (€10 per day) and scooters (€28 per day; min. age 16; must have license). Open daily 9:30am-7pm.

Hertz-Portuguesa, Rossio de S. João Ed. Panorama 3 (☎282 76 98 09), behind the bus station off Av. Descobrimentos. Cars start at €45 per day, tax and insurance included. MC/V.

▓⚹🛈 ORIENTATION AND PRACTICAL INFORMATION

Running the length of the channel, **Avenida dos Descobrimentos** is the main road that carries traffic to and from Lagos. From the **train station,** walk through the pastel pink marina and cross the channel over the pedestrian suspension bridge; turn left onto Av. Descobrimentos. From the **bus station,** walk straight until you hit Av. Descobrimentos, then turn right. After 15m, take another right onto R. Porta de Portugal to reach **Praça Gil Eanes,** the center of the old town. The local **tourist office** is on the corner of R. Lima Leitão, which extends from Pr. Gil Eanes. A cluster of restaurants and accommodations surround the statue of Dom Sebastião in the square. From Praça Gil Eanes, bars and hostels line **Rua Afonso Dalmeida, Rua 25 de Abril,** and **Rua Silva Lopes.** Follow R. Silva Lopes to R. General Alberto Silveira to reach the grotto-lined beach of **Praia Dona Ana.**

Tourist Office: R. Vasco de Gama (☎282 76 30 31), a 25min. walk from the bus station. Open July-Aug. M-Sa 10am-8pm; Sept.-June M-F 10am-6pm.

Emergency: ☎112. **Police:** (☎282 76 29 30), R. General Alberto Silva.

Medical Services: Hospital (☎282 77 01 00), R. Castelo dos Governadores.

Internet Access: The Em@il Box (Ciaxa de Correio), R. Cândido dos Reis 112 (☎282 76 89 50). €3.50 per hr. Open M-F 9:30am-8pm, Sa-Su 10am-3pm.

Luggage Storage: Futebol Mania, R. Professor Luís de Azevedo 4 (☎962 74 63 42), off of R. Cândido dos Reis. €5 per day.

Laundromat: Lavandaria Miele, Av. Descobrimentos 27 (☎282 76 39 69). Wash and dry €6.50 per 5kg. Open M-F 9am-1pm and 3-7pm, Sa 9am-1pm.

Pharmacy: Farmácia Silva, R. 25 de Abril 9 (☎282 76 28 59).

Post Office: R. Portas de Portugal (☎282 77 02 50), between Pr. Gil Eanes and the river. Open M-F 9am-1pm and 3-6pm. **Postal Code:** 8600.

▐ ACCOMMODATIONS

In the summertime, *pensões* (and the youth hostel) fill up quickly and cost a bundle. Reserve rooms over a week in advance. Rooms in *casas particulares* run around €15-20 per person in summer.

▧ **Pousada da Juventude de Lagos (HI),** R. Lançarote de Freitas 50 (☎282 76 19 70; www.hostalbooking.com), off R. 25 de Abril. Friendly staff and lodgers congregate in the courtyard. Breakfast included. In summer, book through the central **Movijovem** office (☎213 59 60 00). June 16-Sept. 15 dorms €15; doubles with bath €42. Sept. 16-June 15 €10/28. MC/V. ❶

▧ **Olinda Teresa Maria Quartos,** R. Lançarote de Freitas 37 (☎282 08 23 29; cell 966 32 40 41), across the street from the youth hostel. Offers doubles or dorm rooms with shared kitchen, terrace, and bath. If the owner is not in, check at the youth hostel. June 16-Sept. 15 dorms €15; doubles €24. Sept. 16-June 15 €10/30. ❶

Residencial Rubi Mar, R. Barroca 70 (☎282 76 31 65; fax 282 76 77 49), off Pr. Gil Eanes toward Pr. Infante Dom Henrique. July-Oct. doubles €40, with bath €45; quads €75. Nov.-June €28/33/50. Prices vary, call ahead. ❹

Residencial Lagosmar, R. Dr. Faria da Silva 13 (☎282 76 37 22), up from Pr. Gil Eanes. Friendly 24hr. reception. July-Aug. singles €60; doubles €70; extra bed €22. June and Sept. €35/40/13. Nov.-Feb. €22/25/9. Mar.-May and Oct. €30/35/11. ❺

Residencial Caravela, R. 25 de Abril 8 (☎282 76 33 61), just up the street from Pr. Gil Eanes. Singles €24; doubles €33, with bath €36; triples €50. ❷

Camping Trindade (☎282 76 38 93), just outside of town. Follow Av. Descobrimentos toward Sagres. The way most Europeans experience the Algarve. €3 per person; €3.50 per tent, €4 per car. ❶

Camping Valverde (☎282 78 92 11), 6km outside Lagos and 1.5km west of Praia da Luz. Showers, grocery, and pool. €4.80 per person; €4 per tent, €6 per car. ❶

☐ FOOD

Peruse multilingual menus around **Praça Gil Eanes** and **Rua 25 de Abril**. The **market,** on Av. Descobrimentos, 5min. from the town center, is cheap (open Sa). **Supermercado São Toque,** R. Portas de Portugal 61, is opposite the post office. (Open July-Sept. M-F 9am-8pm, Sa 9am-7pm; Oct.-June M-F 9am-7:30pm, Sa 9am-7pm.)

▨ Casa Rosa, Tv. Ferrador 22. Hordes of backpackers enjoy €3.50 meals. Many vegetarian options. Open daily 6pm-midnight. ❶

Mediterraneo, R. Senhora da Graça 2. Mediterranean and Thai cuisine. Entrees €7.50-9. Open Tu-Sa. ❸

Mullen's, R. Cândido dos Reis 86, serves Portuguese and international cuisine. Try the duck in orange sauce or the spicy *frango grelhado*. Entrees €7-10. Open noon-2:30pm, 7:30-10pm and midnight-2am. ❷

Snack-Bar Caravela, R. 25 de Abril 14, just off Pr. Gil Eanes. The pizza is the best in town. Pizzas and pasta €4.50-7.10. Try the supreme strawberry ice cream. Open June-Sept. daily 9am-midnight; Oct.-Mar. 9am-11pm. AmEx/MC/V. ❷

A Forja, R. dos Ferreiros 17 (☎282 76 85 88). Traditional Portuguese restaurant that locals swear by. Serves Algarvian seafood with all its tricks but *sans* the steep prices. Entrees €5.50-13. Open noon-3pm and 6:30-10pm. ❷

◉ ☐ SIGHTS AND BEACHES

Although sunbathing and non-stop debauchery have long erased memories of Lagos's rugged, sea-faring past, it's worth taking some time away from the beach or bars to visit the city's 16th-century fortifications and a few other interesting sights. The **Fortaleza da Ponta da Bandeira,** a 17th-century fortress which holds maritime exhibitions, overlooks the marina. (☎282 76 14 10. Open Tu-Sa 10am-1pm and 2-6pm, Su 10am-1pm. €1.90, students €1. Under-13 free.) Also on the waterfront is the old **Mercado de Escravos** (slave market), where the first sale of African slaves in Portugal took place in 1441. Opposite the **Mercado dos Escravos** is a museum, located inside the **Igreja de Santo António,** which houses artifacts from several ruling powers in Lagos, from the Neolithic age to the Republic. The mural painted on the ceiling of the chapel depicts the life of the church patron, St. Anthony. (Open Su and Tu-Sa 9:30am-12:30pm and 2-5pm. €2.)

Today, the waterfront and marina offer jet-ski rentals, scuba diving lessons, sailboat trips, and motorboat tours of the coastal rocks and grottoes. Flat, smooth sands can be found at the 4km-long **Meia Praia,** across the river from town. Hop on the 30-second ferry near Pr. República (€0.50 each way). For beautiful cliffs that plunge into the sea with less-crowded beaches and caves, follow Av. Descobrimentos toward Sagres to **Praia de Pinhão** (20min.). A bit farther, **Praia Dona Ana** features the sculpted cliffs and grottoes that grace the majority of Algarve postcards.

⚓ WATER SPORTS AND ACTIVITIES

Lagos offers a wide variety of outdoor sports—from scuba diving to surfing to (booze) cruising.

Grotto Boat Tours: Companies offering tours of the coastal cliffs and grottoes set up shop on Av. dos Descobrimentos. Most tours are 45min. and start at €25 for 2 people. Smaller boats are preferable, as they can maneuver into rock caves and formations.

Surfing: Surf Experience, R. dos Ferreiros 21 (☎282 76 19 43; www.surf-experience.com). 1- or 2-week surfing trips including lessons, transportation, and accommodations in Lagos. All levels welcome. Daytrips when space available. Apr.-Nov. 1-week €435; 2-week €747. Dec.-Mar. €388/700. Board and wet suit rental €78 per week; €117 per 2 weeks.

Booze Cruise: This extremely popular cruise offers swimming, snorkeling, tours of the nearby grottoes (caves), a live DJ, and, of course, cheap drinks. Cruises on M, W, and Sa. €15, depending on the length of the cruise. For tickets call ☎963 01 26 92, or purchase them at the youth hostel.

🍷 NIGHTLIFE

The streets of Lagos pick up as the sun dips down, and by midnight the city's walls are shaking. The area between **Praça Gil Eanes** and **Praça Luis de Camões** is filled with cafes. For late-night bars and clubs, try **Rua Cândido dos Reis** and **Rua do Ferrador,** as well as the intersection of R. 25 de Abril, R. Silva Lopes, and R. Soeiro da Costa. Staggered Happy Hours make drinking easy on the tightest of budgets.

Three Monkeys, R. Lançarote de Freitas. One of the newest bars in Lagos; quickly becomes packed. Open daily 1pm-2am. Beer €2-3. Mixed drinks €4. Happy Hour 1-9pm. Open daily 1pm-2am.

Eddie's, R. 25 de Abril 99. An easy-going bar popular with backpackers. Beer €2. Open M-Sa 4pm-2am, Su 8pm-2am.

Taverna Velha (The Old Tavern), R. Lançarote de Freitas 34, down the street from Pousada da Juventude. The only air-conditioned bar in Lagos. Beer €1.25-2.50. Open M-Sa 4pm-2am, Su 8pm-2am.

Whyte's Bar, R. Ferrador 7. A Lagos institution. Has a live DJ and the 9 Deadly Sins shot drinking contest. Beer €3. Mixed drinks €2.50-3.50. Open July-Sept. daily 7pm-2am; Oct.-June 8pm-2am.

⚑ DAYTRIPS FROM LAGOS

SAGRES. Marooned atop a desert plateau at the most southwestern point in Europe, desolate Sagres and its cape were once considered the edge of the world. Near the town lurks the ∎**Fortaleza de Sagres,** the fortress where Prince Henry stroked his beard, decided to map the world, and founded his famous **school of navigation.** (Open May-Sept. daily 10am-8:30pm; Oct.-Apr. 10am-6:30pm. €3, under-25 €1.50.) Six kilometers west lies the dramatic **Cabo de São Vicente,** where the second-most powerful lighthouse in Europe shines over 100km out to sea. To get there on weekdays, take the bus from the bus station on R. Comandante Matos near the tourist office (10min.; 11:15am, 12:30 and 4:15pm; €1). Alternatively, hike 1½hr. past the several fortresses perched atop the cliffs. The most notable **beach** in the area is **Mareta,** at the bottom of the road from the town center. The nearby coves of **Salema** and **Luz** are intimate and picturesque. At night, a young crowd fills lively **Rosa dos Ventos,** famous for its *sangria,* in Pr. República. (Beer €1. Open Su-Tu and Th-Sa 10am-2am.) EVA **buses** (☎282 76 29 44) run from Lagos (1hr., 17 per day, €2.60). The **tourist office,** on R. Comandante Matoso, is up the street from the bus stop. (☎282 62 48 73. Open Tu-Sa 9:30am-1pm and 2-5:30pm.)

PRAIA DA ROCHA. A short jaunt from Lagos, this grand beach is perhaps the very best the Algarve has to offer. With vast expanses of sand, surfable waves, rocky red cliffs, and plenty of secluded coves, Praia da Rocha has a well-deserved reputation and the crowds to match. From Lagos, take a bus to Portimão (40min., 14 per day, €1.80), then switch to the Praia da Rocha bus (10min., every 30min. 7:30am-8:30pm, €1.30). The **tourist office** is at the end of R. Tomás Cabreina. (☎282 41 91 32. Open May-Sept. daily 9:30am-7pm; Oct.-Apr. M-F 9:30am-12:30pm and 2-5:30pm, Sa-Su 9:30am-12:30pm.)

TAVIRA ☎281

Tavira (pop. 11,000) invites its visitors with whitewashed houses and cobble-stone streets. The **Castelo de Tavira,** begun in the Neolithic period and later improved by the Phoenicians, Moors, and Christians, sits next to **Igreja de Santa Maria do Castelo.** (Castle open M-F 8am-5pm and Sa-Su 10am-7pm. Church open daily 9:30am-12:30pm and 2-5pm. Free.) ■**Moinha da Rocha** is a beautiful hidden waterfall located 5km outside of town at the source of the Rio Gilão. To reach the golden shores of **Ilha da Tavira,** an island 2km away, take the ferry from the end of Estrada das 4 Aguas (round-trip €1.20).

Trains (☎281 32 23 54) leave Tavira for Faro (40min., 15-20 per day, €1.80) and Vila Real de Santo António (30min., 9-13 per day, €1.20). EVA **buses** (☎281 32 25 46) leave from the station upriver from Pr. República for Faro (1hr., 12-13 per day, €2.50). The town is a short 5-10min. walk down Av. Dr. Teixeira de Azevedo from the train station, or you can catch the local **TUT bus** to the town center (10min., every 30min., €0.50). **Postal Code:** 8800.

FARO ☎289

The Algarve's capital, largest city, and transportation hub, Faro (pop. 55,000) is untouristed despite its charm. Its **cidade velha,** a medley of museums, handi-craft shops, and ornate churches, begins at the **Arco da Vila,** a stone arch. In Largo Carmo is the **Igreja de Nossa Senhora do Carmo** and its **Capela dos Ossos** (Chapel of Bones), a macabre bonanza of bones and skulls "borrowed" from the adjacent cemetery. (Open May-Sept. daily 10am-1pm and 3-6pm; Oct.-Apr. M-F 10am-1pm and 3-5pm, Sa 10am-1pm. Chapel €0.80. Church free.) Faro's **beach** hides on an islet off the coast. Take bus #16 from the bus station or the stop in front of the tourist office (5-10min., every hr., €1).

Trains (☎289 82 64 72) run from Largo Estação to: Évora (5hr., 9am and 5:30pm, €11); Lagos (2hr., 6 per day 8am-9pm, €4.10); and Lisbon (5-6hr., 6 per day 7:20am-11pm, €14). EVA **buses** (☎289 89 97 00) go from Av. República to: Lagos (2hr., 8 per day 7:30am-5:30pm, €4) and Tavira (1hr., 11 per day 7:15am-7:30pm, €2.40). **Renex** (☎289 81 29 80), across the street, provides express long-distance bus service to: Braga (8½hr., 8 per day 5:30am-1:30am, €21); Lisbon (4hr., 11-15 per day 5:30am-1:30am, €15); and Porto (7½hr., 6-13 per day 5:30am-1:30am, €20). From the stations, turn right down Av. República along the harbor, then turn left past the garden to reach the **tourist office,** R. da Misericórdia 8, at the entrance to the old town. (☎289 80 36 04. Open May-Sept. daily 9:30am-7pm; Oct.-Apr. 9:30am-5:30pm.) Travelers sleep easy at **Pousada da Juventude (HI) ❶,** R. Polícia de Segurança Pública, opposite the police station. (☎/fax 289 82 65 21. Dorms €9.50; doubles €23, with bath €27. AmEx/MC/V.) Enjoy coffee and the local marzipan at cafes along **Rua Conselheiro Bívar** and **Praça Dr. Francisco Gomes.**

NORTHERN PORTUGAL

The unspoiled Costa da Prata (Silver Coast), the plush greenery of the interior, and the rugged peaks of the Serra Estrela comprise the Three Beiras region. Beyond trellised vineyards, *azulejo*-lined houses grace charming streets.

COIMBRA   ☎239

Home to the country's only university from the mid-16th to the early 20th century, vibrant Coimbra (pop. 103,000) continues to be a mecca for backpackers and youth around the world.

◪◪ TRANSPORTATION AND PRACTICAL INFORMATION. Trains (☎808 20 82 08) from other regions stop only at Estação Coimbra-B (Velha), 3km northwest of town, while regional trains stop at both Coimbra-B and Estação Coimbra-A (Nova), two blocks from the lower town center. A train connects the two stations, departing after trains arrive (4min., €0.70). Trains run to Lisbon (3hr., 23 per day, €8.50-9.50) and Porto (2hr., 21 per day, €5.60-9.40). **Buses** (☎239 82 70 81) go from Av. Fernão Magalhães, past Coimbra-A on the university side of the river, to Lisbon (2½hr., 17 per day, €9.40) and Porto (1½hr., 10 per day, €8.10). From the bus station, turn right, follow the avenue to Coimbra-A, then walk to Largo Portagem to reach the **tourist office.** (☎239 85 59 30. Open June-Sept. M-F 9am-7pm, Sa-Su 10am-1pm and 2:30-5:30pm; Oct.-May M-F 9am-6pm, Sa-Su 10am-1pm and 2:30-5:30pm.) Check **email** at **Central Modem,** Escada de Quebra Costas, down the stairs from Lg. da Sé Velha. (€0.60 per 15min. Open M-F 11am-11pm.) **Postal Code:** 3000.

◪◪ ACCOMMODATIONS AND FOOD. With both newly renovated and older rooms, **Residencial Vitória ❷,** R. da Sota 11-19, across from Coimbra-A has prices to suit any budget. (☎239 82 40 49; fax 84 28 97. Reception 24hr. Singles €10-25; doubles €20-40; triples €45. MC/V.) **Residência Lusa Atenas ❸,** Av. Fernão Magalhães 68, between Coimbra-A and the bus station, next to Pensão Avis, has rooms with bath, phone, A/C, and cable TV in a classic aristocratic building. (☎239 82 64 12. Reception 8am-midnight. July-Aug. singles €20-25; doubles €30-40; triples €45-50; quads €50-60. Sept.-Apr. €18-20/25-30/38-40/40-50. May-June €20/30/38/50.) The best cuisine in Coimbra lies off Pr. 8 de Maio around **Rua Direita,** on the side streets between the river and Largo Portagem, and around **Praça República** in the university district. **Supermercado Minipreço,** R. António Granjo 6C, is in the lower town center. (Open M-Sa 8:30am-8pm, Su 9am-1pm and 3-7pm.)

◪◪ SIGHTS AND ENTERTAINMENT. Take in the sights in **Old Town** by climbing from the river up the narrow stone steps to the university. Begin your ascent at the **Arco de Almedina,** a remnant of the Moorish town wall, one block uphill from Largo da Portagem. The looming 12th-century Romanesque **Sé**

THE LOCAL LEGEND

FOWL PLAY?

One evening many years ago, a rich landowner hosted a magnificent banquet. The evening turned sour when he discovered that someone had stolen his silver. He accused an innocent guest, who was tried in court and, with a great deal of evidence against him, declared guilty and sentenced to death. The accused man maintained his innocence and pleaded with the town magistrate for one last chance to save himself. Moved by the man's resoluteness, the magistrate agreed. Upon seeing a tray with a roasted rooster on it, the man declared, "If I am innocent, the cock will crow!"

And crow it did. Just before being hanged, the prisoner's life was spared.

The legendary rooster, known as *O Galo de Barcelos*, has become the national symbol of Portugal, representing honesty, integrity, trust, and honor. Today, the Portuguese commemorate the merciful animal with hundreds of rooster statues and statuettes. Vendors sell rooster key chains and trinkets decorated with red and yellow flowers and hearts; likewise, artisans create roosters with original patterns and coloring that are displayed in homes and museums. Though the Portuguese no longer call upon *O Galo* in desperate times, they continue to respect and value the bird who, when faced with an opportunity to speak for justice, certainly was no chicken.

Velha (Old Cathedral) is at the top. (Open M-Th 10am-noon and 2-7:30pm, F-Su 10am-1pm. Cloister €0.75.) Follow signs to the late 16th-century **Sé Nova** (New Cathedral), built by the Jesuits (open Tu-Sa 9am-noon and 2-6:30pm; free), just a few blocks from the 16th-century **University of Coimbra.** The **Porta Férrea** (Iron Gate), off R. São Pedro, opens onto the old university, whose buildings constituted Portugal's royal palace when Coimbra was the kingdom's capital. (Open May-Sept. daily 9am-7:30pm; Oct.-Apr. 9:30am-12:30pm and 2-5:30pm.) The stairs to the right lead to the **Sala dos Capelos,** which houses portraits of Portugal's kings, six of whom were Coimbra-born. (Open daily 9:30am-12:30pm and 2-5:30pm. €2.50.) The **university chapel** and the mind-boggling, entirely gilded 18th-century **Biblioteca Joanina** (University Library) lie past the Baroque clock tower. (Open May-Sept. daily 9am-7:30pm; Oct.-Apr. 9:30am-noon and 2-5:30pm. €2.50. Students free. Ticket to all university sights €4; buy tickets in the main quad.) Cross the bridge in front of Largo Portagem to find the 14th-century **Convento de Santa Clara-a-Velha** and the 17th-century **Convento de Santa Clara-a-Nova.** (Closed indefinitely for renovations and repairs.)

Nightlife in Coimbra gets highest honors. **Bar Quebra Costas,** R. Quebra Costas, blasts jazz and funk. (☎239 821 661. Beer €1-3. Mixed drinks €4-5. Open daily noon-4:00am.) The recently renovated **Pitchclub,** Lgo. da Sé Velha 4-8, one of Coimbra's newest dance spots, pulses with house, Brazilian, African, and pop. (Beer €1. Mixed drinks €2.50. Open June-Sept. 15 M-Sa 11am-4am; Sept. 16-May M-Sa 9pm-4am.) **Via Latina,** R. Almeida Garrett 1, around the corner and uphill from Pr. República, is hot in all senses of the word. (Beer €1.50. Open M-Sa 11pm-7am.) In early May, university graduates burn the narrow ribbons they got as first-years and get wide ones in return during Coimbra's week-long **Queima das Fitas.**

PORTO (OPORTO)   ☎22

Porto (pop. 264,200) is famous for its namesake product—a strong, sugary wine. Developed by English merchants in the early 18th century, the port industry is at the root of the city's successful economy. But there's more to Porto than just port; the country's second-largest city retains traditional charm with granite church towers, orange-tiled houses, and graceful bridges, and also hosts a sophisticated lifestyle that won Porto its title as a Cultural Capital of Europe in 2001.

⚫🔢 TRANSPORTATION AND PRACTICAL INFORMATION. Most trains pass through Porto's main station, Estação Campanhã (☎225 36 41 41), on R. da Estação. **Trains** run to: Coimbra (2hr., 17 per day, €5.60); Lisbon (3½-4½hr., 14 per day, €15-21); and Madrid (13-14hr., daily 6:10pm, €60). Estação São Bento (☎222 00 27 22), Pr. Almeida Garrett, located one block off Pr. Liberdade, is the terminus for trains with local and regional routes. Rede Expresso **buses,** R. Alexandre Herculano 366 (☎222 05 24 59), in the Garagem Atlântico, travel to Coimbra (1½hr., 11 per day, €7.50) and Lisbon (4hr., 12 per day, €14). REDM, R. Dr. Alfredo Magalhães 94 (☎222 00 31 52), two blocks from Pr. República, sends buses to Braga (1hr., 9-26 per day, €3.30). Buy tickets for the **intracity buses** and **trams** from small kiosks around the city, or at the **STCP office,** Pr. de Almeida Garrett 27, downhill and across the street from Estação São Bento (pre-purchased single ticket €0.60, day pass €2.10). The **tourist office,** R. Clube dos Fenianos 25, is off Pr. da Liberdade. (☎223 39 34 72. Open July-Sept. daily 9am-7pm; Oct.-June M-F 9am-5:30pm, Sa-Su 9:30am-4:30pm.) Check **email** at **Portweb,** Pr. Gen. Humberto Delgado 291, near the tourist office. (€1.20 per hour. Open M-Sa 10am-2am, Su 3pm-2am.) The **post office** is on Pr. Gen. Humberto Delgado. (☎223 40 02 00. Open M-F 8:30am-9pm, Sa-Su 9am-6pm.) **Postal Code:** 4000.

⚫🔢 ACCOMMODATIONS AND FOOD. For good accommodation deals, look west of **Avenida dos Aliados** or on **Rua Fernandes Tomás** and **Rua Formosa,** perpendicular to Av. dos Aliados. Popular with young travelers from around the world, **Pensão Duas Nações ❷,** Pr. Guilherme Gomes Fernandes 59, offers a variety of rooms at low rates. (☎222 08 96 21. Internet €0.50 per 15min. Reserve ahead. Singles €13, with bath €20; doubles €22/25-30; triples €30/35; quads €40/45.) From the tourist office, climb the hill past the Igreja de Trinidade and turn left on the second street to reach **Hospedaria Luar ❷,** R. Alferes Malheiro 133, which offers spacious rooms with private baths. (☎222 08 78 45. Singles €20-25; doubles €25-30.) **Pensão Douro ❶,** R. do Loureiro 54, offers huge rooms close to the river. (☎222 05 32 14. Singles €12, with bath €15-20; doubles €18/20-30.) Take bus #6, 50, 54, or 87 (at night #50 or 54) from Pr. Liberdade to **camp** at **Prelada ❶,** on R. Monte dos Burgos, in Quinta da Prelada, 4km from the town center. (☎228 31 26 16. Reception 8am-11pm. €3 per person, €3-3.50 per tent, €2.60 per car.) Look near the river in the **Ribeira** district on C. Ribeira, R. Reboleira, and R. Cima do Muro for great restaurants. The **Confeitaria Império ❶,** R. de Santa Catarina 149-151, serves excellent pastries and inexpensive lunch specials. (Open M-Sa 7:30am-8:30pm.) Across the street, the **Majestic Café ❷,** R. de Santa Catarina 112, is the oldest, most famous cafe in Porto. (Open M-Sa 9:30am-midnight.)

⚫🔢 SIGHTS AND ENTERTAINMENT. Your first brush with Porto's rich stock of fine artwork may be the celebrated collection of *azulejos* (tiles) in the **São Bento train station.** Walk past the station and uphill on Av. Afonso Henriques to reach Porto's pride and joy, the 12th- to 13th-century Romanesque **cathedral.** (Open M-Sa 9am-12:30pm and 2:30-6pm, Su 2:30-6pm. Cloister €1.30.) From the station, follow signs downhill on R. Mouzinho da Silveira to R. Ferreira Borges and the ▨ **Palácio da Bolsa** (Stock Exchange), the epitome of 19th-century elegance. The ornate **Sala Árabe** (Arabian Hall) took 18 years to decorate. (Open Apr.-Oct. daily 9am-7pm; Nov.-Mar. 9am-1pm and 2-6pm. Tours every 30min. €5, students €3.) Next door, the Gothic **Igreja de São Francisco** glitters with an elaborately gilded wooden interior, belying the thousands of human bones stored under the floor. (Open daily 9am-6pm. €3, students €1.50.) Up R. dos Clérigos from Pr. Liberdade rises the **Torre dos Clérigos** (Tower of Clerics), adjacent to the 18th-cen-

THAT TOOK GUTS When native son Henry the Navigator geared up to conquer Cueta in the early 15th century, Porto's residents slaughtered their cattle, gave the meat to Prince Henry's fleet, and kept only the entrails. This dramatic generosity came in the wake of the Plague, when food supplies were crucial. The dish *tripàs a moda do Porto* commemorates their culinary sacrifice; to this day, the people of Porto are known as *tripeiros* (tripe-eaters). If you're feeling adventurous, try some of the tripe dishes, which locals—and few others—consider quite a delicacy.

tury **Igreja dos Clérigos**, which is adorned with Baroque carvings. (Tower open Aug. 9:30am-7pm; Sept.-July daily 9:30am-1pm and 2:30-7pm. €1. Church open M-Th 10am-noon and 2-5pm, Sa 10am-noon and 2-8pm, Su 10am-1pm. Free.) From there, head up R. da Restauração, turn right on R. Alberto Gouveia, and go left on R. Dom Manuel II to reach the **Museu Nacional de Soares dos Reis**, R. Dom Manuel II 44. This former royal residence now houses an exhaustive collection of 19th-century Portuguese painting and sculpture. (Open Su and W-Sa 10am-6pm, Tu 2-6pm. €3, students €1.50.) Bus #78 from Av. dos Aliados runs several kilometers out of town to the **Museu de Arte Contemporânea**, which hosts an exhibit of contemporary art and an impressive park with sculpted gardens and fountains. (Open Tu-W, F and Sa 10am-7pm; Th 10am-10pm; Su 10am-8pm. Park closes at 7pm. Museum and park €5. Su before 2pm free.) To get to Porto's rocky and polluted (but popular) **beach**, in the ritzy Foz district, take bus #1 from the São Bento train station.

But we digress—back to the wine. Fine and bounteous port wines are available for tasting at 20-odd **port wine cellars**, usually *gratuito* (free). The cellars are across the river in **Vila Nova da Gaia**; from the Ribeira district, cross the lower level of the large bridge. Most cellars are open daily 10am-6pm. With costumed guides, **Sandeman**, Lgo. Miguel Bombardo 3, is a good place to start (tours €2.50). ■**Taylor's**, R. do Choupelo 250, has a terrace with views of the city and no entrance fee.

BRAGA ☎253

Braga (pop. 160,000) originally served as the capital of a region founded by Celtic tribes in 300 BC. The city's beautiful gardens, plazas, museums, and markets earned it the nickname "Portuguese Rome." In Portugal's oldest **cathedral**, the treasury showcases the archdiocese's most precious paintings and relics, including a collection of *cofres cranianos* (brain boxes), one of which contains the 6th-century cortex of São Martinho Dume, Braga's first bishop. (Cathedral and treasury open June-Aug. daily 8:30am-6pm; Sept.-May 8:30am-5pm. Cathedral free. Treasury €2.) Braga's most famous landmark, **Igreja do Bom Jesús**, is actually 5km outside of town. To visit Bom Jesús, take the bus labeled "#02 Bom Jesús" from in front of Farmacia Cristal, 571 Av. da Liberdade (€1.10). At the site either take the 285m ride on the antique funicular (8am-8pm; €1), or walk 25-30min. up the granite-paved pathway that leads to a 365-step zig-zagging staircase.

Buses (☎253 61 60 80) leave Central de Camionagem for: Coimbra (3hr., 6-9 per day, €8); Guimarães (1hr., every 30min., €2); Lisbon (5¼hr., 8-9 per day, €12); and Porto (1¾hr., every 45min., €3.80). The **tourist office** is on 1 Av. da Liberdade. (☎253 26 25 50. Open July-Sept. M-F 9am-7pm, Sa-Su 9am-12:30pm and 2-5:30pm; Oct.-June M-F 9am-7pm, Sa 9am-12:30pm and 2-5:30pm.) **Postal Code:** 4700.

▶ **DAYTRIP FROM BRAGA: GUIMARÃES.** Ask any Portugal native about the city of Guimarães (pop. 60,000), and they will tell you it was the birthplace of the nation. It is home to one of Portugal's most gorgeous palatial estates, the ■**Paço dos Duques de Bragança** (Ducal Palace), which is modeled after the manor houses of northern Europe. Guimarães is best reached by **bus** from Braga. REDM buses (☎253 51 62 29) run frequently between the cities (40min., €2.20). The **tourist office** is on Alameda de São Dâmaso 83, facing Pr. Toural. (☎253 41 24 50. Open June-Sept. M-Sa 9:30am-7pm; Oct.-May M-Sa 9:30am-6pm.)

VIANA DO CASTELO ☎258

Situated in the northwestern corner of the country, Viana do Castelo (pop. 20,000) is one of the loveliest coastal cities in all of Portugal. Visited mainly as a beach resort, Viana also has a lively historic district centered around the **Praça da República.** Diagonally across the plaza, granite columns support the flowery facade of the **Igreja da Misericórdia.** Known for its *azulejo* interior, the ▓**Monte de Santa Luzia,** overlooking the city, is crowned by magnificent Celtic ruins and the **Templo de Santa Luzia,** an early 20th-century neo-Byzantine church. The view from the hill is fantastic. For more views of the harbor and ocean, visit the **Castelo de São Tiago da Barra,** built by Felipe I of Spain. Viana do Castelo and the surrounding coast feature excellent beaches. The most convenient are **Praia Norte,** at the end of Av. do Atlántico at the west end of town, and **Praia da Argaçosa,** on Rio Lima.

　　Trains (☎258 82 13 15) run from the station at the top of Av. Combatentes da Grande Guerra to Porto (2hr., 13-14 per day, €4.10). **Buses** run to: Braga (1½hr., 4-9 per day, €3.20); Lisbon (5½hr., 2-3 per day, €18); and Porto (2hr., 4-9 per day, €3.50-6). The **tourist office,** R. do Hospital Velho, at the corner of Pr. Erva, has a helpful English-speaking staff and offers maps and accommodation listings. (☎258 82 26 20. Open Aug. daily 9am-7pm; May-July and Sept. M-Sa 9am-1pm and 2:30-6pm, Su 9:30am-1pm; Oct.-Apr. M-Sa 9am-12:30pm and 2-5pm.) The ▓**Pousada de Juventude de Viana do Castelo (HI) ❶,** R. de Limia, off of R. da Argaçosa, is right on the marina, off Pr. de Galiza; its balconies have great views. (☎258 80 02 60. Reception 8am-midnight. Checkout 10:30am. Reservations recommended. Mid-June to mid-Sept. dorms €13, doubles with bath €35; mid-Sept. to mid-June €10/28.)

PORTUGAL

SPAIN (ESPAÑA)

Fiery flamenco dancers, noble bullfighters, and a rich history blending Christian and Islamic culture set Spain apart from the rest of Europe and draw almost 50 million tourists each year. The raging nightlife of Madrid, Barcelona, and the Balearic Islands has inspired the popular saying "Spain never sleeps," yet the afternoon siestas of Andalucía attest the country's laid-back, easy-going approach to life. Spain houses stunning Baroque, Mudejar, and Mozarabic cathedrals and palaces; hangs the works of Velasquez, Dalí, and Picasso on its hallowed walls; and offers up a backyard of beauty with long sunny coastlines, snowy mountain peaks, and the dry, golden plains wandered by Don Quixote. You can do Spain in one week, one month, or one year. But you must do it at least once.

LIFE AND TIMES

HISTORY

IN THE BEGINNING (UNTIL AD 711). Spain was colonized by a succession of civilizations that have left their cultural mark—**Basque** (considered indigenous), **Tartesian, Iberian, Celtic, Greek, Phoenician,** and **Carthaginian**—before the **Romans** crashed the party in the 3rd century BC. Over nearly seven centuries, the Romans drastically altered the face and character of Spain, introducing their agricultural techniques and architecture, as well as the Latin language. A slew of Germanic tribes, including the Swabians and Vandals, swept over the region in the early 5th century AD, but the **Visigoths,** newly converted Christians, emerged above the rest. The Visigoths established their court at Barcelona in 415 and effectively ruled Spain for the next 300 years.

SUGGESTED ITINERARIES

THREE DAYS Soak in **Madrid's** (p. 854) blend of art and cosmopolitan life. Walk through the **Retiro's** gardens, peruse the famed halls of the **Prado, Thyssen-Bornemisza,** and **Nacional Centro de Arte Reina Sofía.** By night, move from the *tapas* bars of **Santa Anna** to **Malasaña** and **Chueca.** Daytrip to **Segovia** (p. 879) or somber **Valle de los Caídos** (p. 873).

ONE WEEK Begin in southern Spain, exploring the Alhambra's Moorish palaces in **Granada** (1 day; p. 906) and the mosque in **Córdoba** (1 day; p. 887). After two days in **Madrid,** travel east to **Barcelona** (2 days; p. 916) and the beaches of **Costa Brava** (1 day; p. 939).

BEST OF SPAIN, THREE WEEKS Begin in **Madrid** (3 days), with daytrips to **El Escorial** (p. 873) and **Valle de los Caídos** (p. 873). Take the high-speed train to **Córdoba** (2 days), and on to **Seville** (2 days; p. 887). Catch the bus to the white town of **Arcos de la Frontera** (1 day; p. 903) before heading south on the Costa del Sol, **Marbella** (1 day, p. 905). Head inland to **Granada** (2 days). Move along the coast to **Valencia** (1 day; p. 916). Then it's up the coast to **Barcelona** (2 days), where worthwhile daytrips in Cataluña include **Montserrat** (p. 938) and **Figueres** (p. 939). From Barcelona, head to the beaches and *tapas* of **San Sebastián** (2 days; p. 946) and **Bilbao** (1 day; p. 956), home of the world-famous Guggenheim Museum.

MOORISH OCCUPATION (711-1469). Following Muslim unification and a victory tour through the Middle East and North Africa, a small force of Arabs, Berbers, and Syrians invaded Spain in 711. The Moors encountered little resistance, and the peninsula soon fell under the dominion of the caliphate of Damascus. These events precipitated the infusion of Muslim influence, which peaked in the 10th century. The Moors set up their Iberian capital in **Córdoba** (p. 887). During **Abderramán III**'s rule in the 10th century, some considered Spain the wealthiest and most cultivated country in the world. Abderramán's successor, **Al Mansur,** snuffed out all opposition within his extravagant court and undertook a series of military campaigns that climaxed with the destruction of **Santiago de Compostela** (p. 959), a Christian holy city, in 997.

The turning point in Muslim-Christian relations came when Al Mansur died, leaving a power vacuum in Córdoba. At this point, the caliphate's holdings shattered into petty states called *taifas*. With power less centralized, Christians were able to gain the upper hand. The Christian policy was official toleration of Muslims and Jews, which fostered a culture and even a style of art, **Mudéjar.** Later, though, countless Moorish structures were ruined in the **Reconquest,** and numerous mosques were replaced by churches (like Córdoba's **Mezquita,** p. 890).

THE CATHOLIC MONARCHS (1469-1516). In 1469, the marriage of **Ferdinand de Aragón** and **Isabella de Castilla** joined Iberia's two mightiest Christian kingdoms. By 1492, the dynamic duo had captured **Granada** (p. 906), the last Moorish stronghold, and shuttled **Christopher Columbus** off to explore the New World. By the 16th century, the pair had made Spain the world's most powerful empire. The Catholic monarchs introduced the **Inquisition** in 1478, executing and burning heretics. The Spanish Inquisition's aims were to strengthen the Church and unify Spain.

THE HABSBURG DYNASTY (1516-1713). The daughter of Ferdinand and Isabella, **Juana la Loca** (the Mad), married **Felipe el Hermoso** (the Fair) of the powerful Habsburg dynasty. Felipe (who died playing a Basque ball game called *cesta punta* or *jai-alai*) and Juana (who refused to believe that he had died and dragged his corpse through the streets) produced **Carlos I.** Carlos, who went by **Charles V** in his capacity as the last official Holy Roman Emperor, reigned over an empire comprising modern-day Austria, Belgium, parts of Germany and Italy, the Netherlands, Spain, and the American colonies. Carlos did his part: as a good Catholic, he embroiled Spain in a war with Protestant France; as an art patron of superb taste, he nabbed Titian as his court painter; as a fashion plate, he introduced Spain to the Habsburg fashion of wearing only black.

But trouble was brewing among Protestants in the Netherlands. After Carlos I died, his son **Felipe II** was left to grapple with a multitude of rebellious territories. He annexed Portugal after its ailing King Henrique died in 1580. One year later the Dutch declared their independence from Spain, and Felipe began warring with the Protestants, spurring further tensions with England. The war with the British ground to a halt when **Sir Francis Drake** and bad weather buffeted the not-so-invincible **Invincible Armada** in 1588. His enthusiasm and much of his European empire sapped, Felipe retreated to his grim, newly built palace, **El Escorial** (p. 873), and remained there through the last decade of his reign.

Felipe III, preoccupied with both religion and the finer aspects of life, allowed his favorite adviser, the **Duque de Lerma,** to hold the governmental reins. In 1609, Felipe III and the Duke expelled nearly 300,000 of Spain's remaining Moors. **Felipe IV** painstakingly held the country together through his long, tumultuous reign. Emulating his great-grandfather Carlos I, Felipe IV patronized the arts and architecture. Then the **Thirty Years' War** (1618-1648) broke out over Europe, and

Spain

defending Catholicism drained Spain's resources; the war ended with the marriage of Felipe IV's daughter, María Teresa, and Louis XIV of France. Felipe's successor **Carlos II,** the *"hechizado"* (bewitched), was epileptic and impotent, the product of inbreeding. From then on, little went right: Carlos II died, Spain fell into a depression, and cultural bankruptcy ensued.

KINGS, LIBERALS, AND DICTATORS (1713-1931). The 1713 **Treaty of Utrecht** seated **Felipe V,** a Bourbon family member and grandson of French King Louis XIV, on the Spanish throne. Felipe built huge, showy palaces (to mimic Versailles in France) and cultivated a flamboyant, debauched court. Despite his undisciplined example, the Bourbons who followed Felipe administered the Empire well, at last beginning to regain control of Spanish-American trade. They also constructed scores of new canals, roads, and organized settlements, and instituted agricultural reform and industrial expansion. **Carlos III** was probably Madrid's finest leader, founding academies of art and science and generally beautifying the capital. Spain's global standing recovered enough for it to team up with France to help the American colonies gain independence from Britain.

In 1808, **Napoleon** invaded Spain. The ensuing battles were particularly bloody. The French occupation ended when the Protestant Brits defeated the Corsican's troops at Waterloo (1814). This victory led to the restoration of arch-reactionary **Ferdinand VII.** Galvanized by Ferdinand's ineptitude and inspired by liberal ideas in the new constitution, most of Spain's Latin American empire soon threw off its yoke, and declared independence. Lingering dreams of an empire were further curbed by the loss of the Philippines, Puerto Rico, and Cuba to the US in the **Spanish-American War** of 1898. Upon Fernando VII's death, parliamentary liberalism was restored and would dominate Spanish politics until **Primo de Rivera** came along in 1923. Rivera was brought to power in a military coup d'état, after which he promptly dissolved Parliament and suspended the constitution. For almost a decade, he ruled Spain as dictator, but in 1930, having lost the support of his own army, he resigned.

SECOND REPUBLIC AND THE CIVIL WAR (1931-1939). In April 1931, **King Alfonso XIII,** disgraced by his support for Rivera, shamefully fled Spain, thus giving rise to the **Second Republic** (1931-1936). Republican Liberals and Socialists established safeguards for farmers and industrial workers, granted women's suffrage, assured religious tolerance, and chipped away at traditional military dominance. National euphoria, however, faded fast. The 1933 elections split the Republican-Socialist coalition, in the process increasing the power of right-wing and Catholic parties. By 1936, radicals, anarchists, Socialists, and Republicans had formed a loosely federated alliance to win the next elections. But the victory was short-lived. Once **Generalísimo Francisco Franco** snatched control of the Spanish army, militarist uprisings ensued, and the nation plunged into war. The three-year **Civil War** (1936-1939) ignited worldwide ideological passions. Germany and Italy dropped troops, supplies, and munitions into Franco's lap, while the stubbornly isolationist US and the war-weary European states were slow to aid the Republicans. The Soviet Union called for a **Popular Front** of Communists, Socialists, and other leftist sympathizers to battle Franco's fascism. Soon, however, aid from the Soviet Union waned as Stalin began to see the benefits of an alliance with Hitler. Without international aid, Republican forces were cut off from supplies. Bombings, executions, combat, starvation, and disease took nearly 600,000 lives, and in 1939 Franco's forces marched into Madrid and ended the war.

FRANCO AND THE TRANSITION TO DEMOCRACY (1939-1998). Brain drain (as leading scientists, artists, and intellectuals emigrated or were assassinated en masse), worker dissatisfaction, student unrest, and international isolation characterized the first few decades of Franco's dictatorship. In his old age, Franco tried to smooth international relations by joining **NATO** and encouraging tourism, but the "national tragedy" (as it was later called) did not officially end until Franco's death in 1975. **King Juan Carlos I,** grandson of Alfonso XIII and a nominal Franco protégé, carefully set out to undo Franco's damage. In 1978, Spain adopted a constitution that led to the restoration of parliamentary government and regional autonomy.

After serving five years, Prime Minister Adolfo Suárez resigned in 1981, leaving the country vulnerable for an attempted coup d'etat on February 23, when a group of rebels took over Congress in an effort to impose a military-backed government. King Juan Carlos used his personal influence to convince the rebels to stand down, and order was restored. Charismatic **Felipe González** led the **Spanish Socialist Worker's Party** (PSOE) to victory in the 1982 elections. González opened the Spanish economy and championed consensus policies, overseeing Spain's integration into the European Community (now the **European Union**) in 1986. The years 1986 to 1990 were outstanding for Spain's economy, as the nation enjoyed an average annual growth rate of 3.8%. By the end of 1993, however, recession had set in, and González and the PSOE only barely maintained a majority in Parliament over the increasingly popular conservative **Partido Popular** (PP). Revelations of large-scale corruption led to the defeat of the Socialist party at the hands of the PP in 1994.

TODAY

The last several years have seen mixed progress in one of Spain's most pressing areas of concern, Basque nationalism and terrorism. The militant Euskadi Ta Askatasuma (ETA) has committed numerous acts of terror in what they say is an effort to secure autonomy for Basque Country. On September 12, 1998, the federal government called for an open dialogue between all parties and was endorsed by the Basque National Party (PNV). Six days later, ETA publicly declared a truce with the national government. On December 3, 1999, however, ETA announced an end to the 14-month cease-fire due to lack of progress with negotiations. The past few years have seen instances of arson and a return of periodic terrorist murders of PP and PSOE members, journalists and army officers. In June 2002, authorities seized 288 pounds of dynamite near Valencia and charged that ETA was planning to strike tourist spots along the Mediterranean coast. That same month, controversy ensued when the Spanish Parliament moved to ban Batasuna, a pro-independence Basque political party that Aznar claimed is allied with ETA.

On a brighter note, the Spanish economy is currently improving. Over the past several years, unemployment has dropped drastically. Aznar envisions "a new Spain" in which the unemployment rate is even lower and more women join the workforce.

THE ARTS

LITERATURE

Spain's literary tradition first blossomed in the late Middle Ages (1000-1500). **Fernando de Rojas**'s *The Celestina* (1499), a tragicomic dialogue most noted for its folkloric witch character, helped pave the way for picaresque novels like *Lazarillo of Tormes* (1554) and *Guzmán of Alfarache* (1599), rags-to-riches stories about mischievous boys with good hearts. This literary form surfaced during Spain's **Golden Age** (1492-1650). Poetry particularly thrived in this era. Some consider the sonnets and romances of **Garcilaso de la Vega** the most perfect ever written in Castilian. This period also produced outstanding dramas, including works

SPAIN

from **Calderón de la Barca** and **Lope de Vega,** who wrote nearly 2000 plays combined. Both espoused the **Neoplatonic** view of love, claiming that love always changes one's life dramatically and eternally. The most famous work of Spanish literature is **Miguel de Cervantes**'s two-part *Don Quixote de la Mancha* (1605-15), which relates the satiric parable of the hapless Don Quixote and his sidekick, Sancho Panza, who think themselves bold *caballeros* (knights) out to save the world.

The 19th century bred a multiplicity of styles, from **José Zorrilla**'s romantic poems such as *Don Juan Tenorio* (1844) to the naturalistic novels of **Leopoldo Alas** ("Clarín"). The modern literary era began with the **Generación del 1898,** a group led by essayist **Miguel de Unamuno** and cultural critic **José Ortega y Gasset.** These nationalistic authors argued, through essays and novels, that each individual must spiritually and ideologically attain internal peace before society can do the same. The **Generación del 1927,** a clique of experimental lyric poets who used Surrealist and vanguard poetry to express profound humanism included **Jorge Guillén, Federico García Lorca** (assassinated at the start of the Civil War), **Rafael Alberti,** and **Luis Cernuda.** In the 20th century, the Nobel Committee has honored playwright and essayist **Jacinto Benavente y Martínez** (1922), poet **Vicente Aleixandre** (1977), and novelist **Camilo José Cela** (1989). Since the fall of the Fascist regime in 1975, an avant-garde spirit—known as *La Movida*—has been reborn in Madrid. **Ana Rossetti** and **Juana Castro** led a new generation of erotic poets into the 1980s. With this newest group of poets, women are at the forefront of Spanish literature for the first time.

THE VISUAL ARTS

ARCHITECTURE. Scattered **Roman ruins** testify to six centuries of colonization. The **aqueduct** in Segovia (p. 879) is one of the finest examples of remaining ruins. After the invasion of 711, the **Moors** constructed mosques and palaces throughout southern Spain. Because the Koran forbade representations of humans and animals, architects lavished buildings with stylized geometric designs, red-and-white horseshoe arches, ornate tiles called *azulejos,* courtyards, pools, and fountains. The spectacular 14th-century **Alhambra** in Granada (p. 906) and the **Mezquita** in Córdoba (p. 887) epitomize the Moorish style.

The combination of Islam and Christianity created two architectural movements unique to Spain: **Mozarabic** and **Mudéjar.** The former describes Christians under Muslim rule (Mozarabs) who adopted Arab devices like the horseshoe-shaped arch and the ribbed dome. The more common Mudéjar architecture was created by Moors during their occupation. Extensive use of brick and elaborately carved wooden ceilings typify Mudéjar style, which reached its height in the 14th century with **alcázars** (palaces) in Seville (p. 887) and Segovia (p. 879) and **synagogues** in Toledo (p. 874) and Córdoba (p. 887).

The first Gothic cathedral in Spain was built in Burgos in 1221, followed closely by cathedral construction in Toledo and León. The **Spanish Gothic** style brought pointed arches, flying buttresses, slender walls, airy spaces, and stained-glass windows. New World riches inspired the **Plateresque** style, an embellishment of Gothic that transformed wealthier parts of Spain. Intricate stonework and extravagant use of gold and silver splashed 15th- and 16th-century buildings, most notably in **Salamanca** (p. 881), where the university practically drips with ornamentation. In the late 16th century, **Italian Renaissance** innovations in perspective and symmetry arrived in Spain to sober up the Plateresque style. **El Escorial,** Felipe II's palace, was designed by **Juan de Herrera,** one of Spain's most prominent architects, and best exemplifies unadorned Renaissance style (p. 873).

Opulence took over in 17th- and 18th-century **Baroque** Spain. The **Churriguera** brothers pioneered this style—called, appropriately, **Churrigueresque**—which is equal parts ostentatious, ornamental, and difficult to pronounce. Elaborate works with extensive detail and twisted columns, like the altar of the **cathedral** in Toledo (p. 874), help distinguish this period in Spanish architecture.

In the late 19th and early 20th centuries, Catalán's **Modernistas** burst onto the scene in Barcelona, led by the eccentric genius of **Antoni Gaudí, Luis Domènech i Montaner,** and **José Puig i Caldafach.** Modernista structures defy previous standards with their voluptuous curves and abnormal textures. Spain's outstanding architectural tradition continues to this day with such new buildings as the Guggenheim (p. 954) in Bilbao, designed by **Santiago Calatrava.**

FILM. Franco's regime (1939-1975) defined Spanish film during and after his rule. Censorship stifled most creative tendencies and left the public with nothing to watch but cheap westerns and bland spy flicks. As government supervision slacked in the early 1970s, Spanish cinema began to show signs of life, led by **Carlos Saura**'s subversive hits such as *The Garden of Delights* (1970).

In 1977, when domestic censorship laws were revoked in the wake of Franco's death, depictions of the exuberant excesses of liberated Spain gained increasing international attention. **Pedro Almodovar**'s *Law of Desire* (1986), featuring **Antonio Banderas** as a homosexual, perhaps best captures the risqué themes of transgression most often treated by contemporary Spanish cinema. Almodovar's *All About My Mother* won the Best Foreign Film Oscar in 2000. Other influential Spanish directors in Spain include **Bigas Luna,** director of the controversial *Jamón Jamón* (1992), and **Fernando Trueba,** whose *Belle Epoque* won an Oscar in 1994.

ON THE CANVAS. Residents of the Iberian peninsula were creating art as early as 13,000 BC, the birth date of the fabulous cave paintings at Altamira. In the 11th and 12th centuries AD, fresco painters and manuscript illuminators decorated churches and their libraries along the Camino de Santiago and in León (p. 885) and Toledo (p. 874). **Pedro Berruguete**'s use of traditional gold backgrounds in his religious paintings exemplifies the Italian-influenced style of early Renaissance works. Berruguete's style is especially evident in his masterpiece, the altarpiece of San Tomás in Ávila (1499-1503). Not until after Spain's imperial ascendancy in the 16th century did painting reach its Golden Age (roughly 1492-1650). Felipe II imported foreign art and artists in order to jump-start native production and embellish his palace, El Escorial. Although he came to Spain seeking a royal commission, **El Greco** was rejected by Felipe II for his shocking and intensely personal style. Setting up camp in Toledo, El Greco graced the Iglesia de Santo Tomé with his masterpiece *The Burial of Count Orgaz* (1586-1588; p. 877).

Felipe IV's foremost court painter, **Diego Velázquez,** is considered one of the world's greatest artists. Whether depicting Felipe IV's family or lowly court jesters and dwarves, Velázquez painted with the same naturalistic precision. Nearly half of this Sevillian artist's works reside in the **Prado,** including his famous *Las Meninas* (Maids of Honor; 1656; p. 868).

Francisco de Goya, official court painter under the degenerate Carlos IV, ushered European painting into the modern age. Goya's depictions of the royal family come close to caricature, as Queen María Luisa's cruel jawline in the famous *The Family of Charles IV* (1800) can attest. Goya's later paintings graphically protest the lunacy of warfare. The Prado houses an entire room of his chilling *Black Paintings* (1820-1823; p. 868).

It is hard to imagine an artist who has had as profound an effect upon 20th-century painting as Andalucían-born **Pablo Picasso.** A child prodigy, Picasso headed for Barcelona, which was a breeding ground for Modernist architecture and political activism. Picasso's **Blue Period,** beginning in 1900, was characterized by somber depictions of social outcasts. His permanent move to Paris in 1904 initiated his **Rose Period,** during which he probed the curiously engrossing lives of clowns and acrobats. With his French colleague Georges Braque, he founded **Cubism,** a method of painting objects simultaneously from multiple perspectives.

Catalán painter and sculptor **Joan Miró** created simplistic, almost child-like shapes in bright primary colors. His haphazard, undefined creations became a statement against the authoritarian society of Fascist Spain. By contrast, fellow Catalán **Salvador Dalí** scandalized both high society and leftist intellectuals in France and Spain by supporting the Fascists. Dalí's name is virtually synonymous with **Surrealism.** The painter tapped into dreams and the unconscious for images like the melting clocks in *The Persistence of Memory* (1931). His haunting *Premonition of the Civil War* (1936) envisioned war as a distorted monster of putrefying flesh. A shameless self-promoter (he often spoke of himself only in the third person), Dalí founded the **Teatre-Museo Dalí** (p. 939) in Figueres, which defines Surrealism in its collection, its construction, and its very existence.

Since Franco's death in 1975, a new generation of artists, including the unorthodox collage artist **Antonio Tapieshas** and hyperrealist painter **Antonio Lopez Garcia,** have thrived. With impressive museums in Madrid, Barcelona, Valencia, Seville, and Bilbao, Spanish artists once again have a national forum for their work.

BULLFIGHTING. The national spectacle that is bullfighting dates, in its modern form, back to the early 1700s. A bullfight is divided into three principal stages: first, *picadors* (lancers on horseback) pierce the bull's neck; next, assistants on foot thrust *banderillas* (decorated darts) into the back; and finally, the *torero* (bullfighter) performs the kill. If a *torero* has shown special skill and daring, the audience waves white handkerchiefs to implore the bullfight's president to reward the coveted ears (and, very rarely, the tail) to the *torero*. Although bullfighting has always had its critics—the Catholic church in the 17th century felt that the risks made it equivalent to suicide—the late 20th century has seen an especially strong attack from animal rights' activists. Whatever its faults, however, bullfighting is an essential element of the Spanish national consciousness.

ESSENTIALS

WHEN TO GO

Summer is high season for the coastal and interior regions. In many parts of the country, high season includes *Semana Santa* (Holy Week; mid-April) and festival days. Tourism peaks in August; the coastal regions overflow while inland cities empty out, leaving behind closed offices, restaurants, and lodgings. Traveling in the low season has the advantage of noticeably lighter crowds and lower prices, but smaller towns virtually shut down, and tourist offices and sights cut their hours nearly everywhere.

FACTS AND FIGURES

Official Name: Kingdom of Spain.
Capital: Madrid.
Major Cities: Barcelona, Granada, Seville, Valencia.
Population: 40,000,000.

Land Area: 499,542 sq. km.
Time Zone: GMT+1.
Language: Spanish (Castilian), Catalan, Valencian, Basque, Galician dialects.
Religions: Roman Catholic (94%).

DOCUMENTS AND FORMALITIES

VISAS. EU citizens do not need a visa. Citizens of Australia, Canada, New Zealand, South Africa, the UK, and the US do not need a visa for stays of up to 90 days. As of August 2003, citizens of South Africa need a visa in addition to a valid passport for entrance into Spain.

EMBASSIES. Foreign embassies are in Madrid (p. 858); all countries have consulates in Barcelona (p. 920). Australia, the UK, and the US also have consulates in Seville (p. 892). Another Canadian consulate is in Málaga; UK consulates are also in Alicante, Bilbao, Ibiza, Málaga, and Palma de Mallorca; more US consulates are in Las Palmas and Valencia. For Spanish embassies at home, contact: **Australia**, 15 Arkana St., Yarralumla, ACT 2600, mailing address P.O. Box 9076, Deakin, ACT 2600 (☎612 6273 3918; www.embaspain.com); **Canada,** 74 Stanley Ave., Ottawa, ON K1M 1P4 (☎613-747-2252; www.docuweb.ca/SpainInCanada); **Ireland,** 17A Merlyn Park, Ballsbridge, Dublin 4 (☎353 269 1640); **South Africa,** 169 Pine St., Arcadia, P.O. Box 1633, Pretoria 0083 (☎27 12 344 3875); **UK,** 39 Chesham Pl., London SW1X 8SB (☎44 207 235 5555); and **US,** 2375 Pennsylvania Ave. NW, Washington, D.C. 20037 (☎202-738-2330; www.spainemb.org).

TRANSPORTATION

BY PLANE. Airports in Madrid and Barcelona handle most international flights; Seville also has a major international airport. Iberia (US and Canada ☎800-772-4642; UK ☎45 601 28 54; Spain ☎902 40 05 00; South Africa ☎11 884 92 55; Ireland ☎1 407 30 17; www.iberia.com), the national carrier, serves all domestic locations and all major international cities. For more info on flying to Spain, see p. 38.

BY TRAIN. Spanish trains are clean, relatively punctual, and reasonably priced, but tend to bypass many small towns. Spain's national railway is **RENFE** (www.renfe.es). Avoid *transvía, semidirecto,* or *correo* trains—they are very slow. *Alta Velocidad Española* (AVE) trains are the fastest between Madrid, Córdoba, and Seville. *Talgos* are almost as fast; there are lines from Madrid to Algeciras, Cádiz, Huelva, and Málaga. *Intercity* is cheaper, but still fairly fast. *Estrellas* are slow night trains with bunks. *Cercanías* (commuter trains) go from cities to suburbs and nearby towns. There is rarely a good reason to buy a **Eurail** if you are planning on traveling only within Spain and Portugal. Trains are cheap, so a pass saves little money; moreover, buses are an easier and more efficient means of traveling around Spain. However, there are several RailEurope passes that cover travel within Spain. (US ☎1-800-4EURAIL; www.raileurope.com.) **Spain Flexipass** offers three days of unlimited travel in a two-month period (first-class €211, 2nd-class €164). The **Iberic Railpass** is good for three days of unlimited first-class travel in Spain and Portugal (€217). The **Spain Rail 'n' Drive** pass is good for three days of unlimited first-class train travel and two days of unlimited mileage in a rental car (€250-343).

BY BUS. In Spain, buses are cheaper and provide far more comprehensive routes than trains. In addition, bus routes also provide the only public transportation to many isolated areas. Spain has numerous private companies; the lack of a centralized bus company may make itinerary planning an ordeal. **ALSA** (☎902 42 22 42; www.alsa.es) serves Madrid, Asturias, Castilla y León, and Galicia, as well as international destinations in France, Italy, Morocco, Poland and Portugal. **Auto-Res/Cunisa, S.A.** (☎902 02 09 99; www.auto-res.net) serves Madrid, Castilla y León, Extremadura, Galicia, and Valencia.

SPAIN

BY CAR. Gas prices average €1.50-1.60 per liter. Speeders beware: police can "photograph" the speed and license plate of your car and issue a ticket without pulling you over. **Renting a car** in Spain is cheaper than in many other Western European countries. Try **Atesa** (☎902 10 01 01; www.atesa.es), Spain's largest national rental agency. The Spanish automobile association is **Real Automóbil Club de España** (RACE), C. José Abascal 10, Madrid (☎915 94 74 75).

BY BIKE AND BY THUMB. With hilly terrain and extremely hot summer weather, hiking is difficult. Renting a bike should be easy, especially in the flatter southern region. Hitchers report that Castilla y León, Andalucía, and Madrid are long, hot waits. The Mediterranean Coast and the islands are much more promising, but *Let's Go* does not recommend hitchhiking.

TOURIST SERVICES AND MONEY

EMERGENCY	Emergency: ☎112. Local Police: ☎092. National Police: ☎091. Ambulance: ☎124.

TOURIST OFFICES. The Spanish Tourist Office operates an extensive official website (www.tourspain.es) and has 29 offices abroad. Municipal tourist offices, called *oficinas de turismo*, are a good stop to make upon arrival in a town; they usually have free maps and region-specific advice for travelers.

MONEY. On January 1, 2002, the **euro** (€) replaced the **peseta** as the unit of currency in Spain. For more info, see p. 14. As a general rule, it is cheaper to exchange money in Spain than at home. **Santander Central Hispano** often provides good exchange rates. **Tipping** is not very common in Spain. In restaurants, all prices include a service charge. Satisfied customers occasionally toss in some spare change—usually no more than 5%—but this is purely optional. Many people give train, airport, and hotel porters €1 per bag; taxi drivers sometimes get 5-10%. **Bargaining** is common only at flea markets and with street vendors.

Spain has a 7% **value-added tax,** known as IVA, on all restaurants and accommodations. The prices listed in *Let's Go* include IVA unless otherwise mentioned. Retail goods bear a much higher 16% IVA, although listed prices are usually inclusive. Non-EU citizens who have stayed in the EU fewer than 180 days can claim back the tax paid on purchases at the airport. Ask the shop where you made the purchase to supply you with a tax return form.

HEALTH AND SAFETY

While Spain is a relatively stable country, travelers should beware that there is some terrorist activity; the militant Basque separatist group **ETA** has carried out attacks on government officials and tourist destinations. Though the attacks are ongoing, the threat is relatively small. Travelers should be aware of current levels of tension in the region and exercise appropriate caution. Recreational **drugs** are illegal in Spain. Any attempt to buy or sell marijuana could land you in jail or with a heavy fine.

COMMUNICATION

TELEPHONES. The central Spanish phone company is *Telefónica*. The best way to make local calls is with a phone card, issued in denominations of €6 and €12 and sold at tobacconists (*estancos* or *tabacos*) and most post offices. You can also ask tobacconists for calling cards known as *Phonepass*. (To US, €6 per hr.) The best way to call home is with an international calling card issued by your phone company. For info on using a **cell phone** in Spain, see p. 30.

PHONE CODES	Country code: 34. **International dialing prefix:** 00. From outside Spain, dial int'l dialing prefix (see inside back cover) + 34 + local number.

MAIL. Air mail (*por avión*) takes five to eight business days to reach the US or Canada; service is faster to the UK and Ireland and slower to Australia and New Zealand. Standard postage is €0.70 to North America. Surface mail (*por barco*), while less expensive than air mail, can take over a month, and packages take two to three months. Registered or express mail (*registrado* or *certificado*) is the most reliable way to send a letter or parcel home and takes four to seven business days. Address mail to be held (*Poste Restante*) according to the following example: SUR-NAME, First Name; Lista de Correos; City Name; Postal Code; SPAIN; AIR MAIL.

INTERNET ACCESS. Email is easily accessible within Spain and much quicker and more reliable than the regular mail system. An increasing number of bars offer Internet access for a fee of €1.20-4.50. Cybercafes are listed in most towns and all cities. In small towns, if Internet access is not listed, check the library or the tour-ist office. The website www.tangaworld.com lists nearly 200 cybercafes in Spain.

ACCOMMODATIONS AND CAMPING

SYMBOL	❶	❷	❸	❹	❺
ACCOMMODATIONS	under €15	€15-25	€26-35	€36-50	over €50

The cheapest and barest options are *casas de huéspedes* and *hospedajes*, while *pensiones* and *fondas* tend to be a bit nicer. All are essentially just boarding houses. Higher up the ladder, *hostales* generally have sinks in bed-rooms and provide sheets and lockers, while *hostal-residencias* are similar to hotels in overall quality. The government rates *hostales* on a two-star system; even establishments receiving one star are typically quite comfortable. The system also fixes *hostal* prices, posted in the lounge or main entrance. **Red Española de Albergues Juveniles** (REAJ), C. Galera 1a, Seville 41001 (☎954 21 68 03; www.reaj.com), the Spanish Hostelling International (HI) affiliate, runs 165 youth hostels year-round. Prices depend on location (typically some distance away from the town center) and services offered, but are generally €9-15 for guests under 26 and higher for those 26 and over. Breakfast is usually included; lunch and dinner are occasionally offered at an additional charge. Hostels usually lock guests out around 11:30am and have curfews between midnight and 3am. As a rule, don't expect much privacy—rooms typically have four to 20 beds in them. To reserve a bed in high season (July-Aug. and during festivals), call in advance. A national **Youth Hostel Card** is usually required. **Campgrounds** are generally the cheapest choice for two or more people. Most charge separate fees per person, per tent, and per car; others charge for a *par-cela* (a small plot of land), plus per-person fees. Tourist offices can provide more info, including the *Guía de Campings*.

FOOD AND DRINK

SYMBOL	❶	❷	❸	❹	❺
FOOD	under €6	€6-10	€11-15	€16-25	over €25

Spanish food has tended to receive less international attention than the country's beaches, bars, and discos. Taste often ranks above appearance, preparation is rarely complicated, and many of the best meals are served not in expensive restaurants but in private homes or streetside bars. All of this has started to change as Spanish food becomes increasingly sophisticated and cosmopolitan, but fresh local ingredients are still an integral part of the cuisine, varying according to each region's climate, geography, and history. Most experts, in fact, argue that one can speak of Spanish food only in local terms. Spaniards breakfast lightly and wait for a several-course lunch, served between 2 and 3pm. Supper at home (*la cena*) tends to be light while eating out begins anywhere between 9pm and midnight. Some restaurants are "open" from 8am until 1 or 2am, but most serve meals only from 1 to 4pm and from 8pm until midnight. Prices for a full meal start at about €4 in the cheapest *bar-restaurantes*. Many places offer a *plato combinado* (main course, side dishes, bread, and sometimes a beverage) or a *menú del día* (two or three set dishes, bread, beverage, and dessert) for roughly €5-9. If you ask for a *menú*, this is what you may receive; *carta* is the word for menu. *Tapas* (savory meats and vegetables cooked according to local recipes) are truly tasty and in some regions complimentary with beer or wine. *Raciones* are large *tapas* served as entrees. *Bocadillos* are sandwiches on hunks of bread. Spanish specialties include *tortilla de patata* (potato omelette), *jamón serrano* (smoked ham), *calamares fritos* (fried squid), *arroz* (rice), *chorizo* (spicy sausage), *gambas* (shrimp), *lomo* (pork), *paella* (steamed saffron rice with seafood, chicken, and vegetables), and *gazpacho* (cold tomato-based soup). Vegetarians should learn the phrase *"yo soy vegetariano"* (I am a vegetarian) and specify that means no *jamón* (ham) or *atún* (tuna). *Vino blanco* is white wine and *tinto* is red. Beer is *cerveza;* Mahou and Cruzcampo are the most common brands. *Sangría* is red wine, sugar, brandy, and fruit.

HOLIDAYS & FESTIVALS

Holidays: New Year's Day (Jan. 1); Epiphany (Jan. 6); Maundy Thursday (Apr. 8); Good Friday (Apr. 9); Easter (Apr. 11); Labor Day (May 1); Assumption Day (Aug. 15); National Day (Oct. 12); All Saints' Day (Nov. 1); Constitution Day (Dec. 6); Feast of the Immaculate Conception (Dec. 8); Christmas (Dec. 25).

Festivals: Nearly everything closes during festivals. Almost every town has several, and in total there are more than 3000. All of Spain celebrates **Carnaval** March 4; the biggest parties are in Cataluña and Cádiz. Valencia hosts the annual **Las Fallas** in mid-March. From April 4-11, the entire country honors the Holy Week, or **Semana Santa.** Seville's **Feria de Abril** takes place in late April. Pamplona's **San Fermines** (Running of the Bulls) breaks out from July 6 to 14. For more fiesta info, see www.tourspain.es, www.SiSpain.org, or www.planetware.com/national/E/HOLIDAYS.HTM.

MADRID   ☎ 91

After Franco's death in 1975, young *madrileños* celebrated their liberation from totalitarian repression with raging, all-night parties in bars and on streets across the city. This revelry became so widespread that it defined an era, and *la Movida* (the Movement) is recognized as a world-famous nightlife renaissance. While the newest generation is too young to recall the Franco years, it has kept the spirit of *la Movida* alive. Not particularly cognizant of the city's historic landmarks nor preoccupied with the future, young people have taken over the streets, shed their parents' decorous reserve, and captured the present. Bright lights and a perpetual stream of cars and people blur the distinction between 4pm and 4am, and infinitely energized party-goers crowd bars and discos until dawn. Madrid's sights and culture equal its rival European capitals and have twice the intensity.

⊠ INTERCITY TRANSPORTATION

Flights: All flights land at **Aeropuerto Internacional de Barajas** (MAD; general info ☎913 05 83 43, 44, 45, or 46), 20min. northeast of Madrid. The Barajas **Metro** line connects the airport to all of Madrid (€1.10). Another option is the green **Bus-Aeropuerto #89** (look for EMT signs just outside the airport doors), which leaves the national and international terminals and runs to the city center (every 15min., €2.50). The bus stops underground beneath the Jardines del Descubrimiento in Plaza de Colón. Serving national and international destinations, **Iberia** is at Santa Cruz de Marcenado 2, M: San Bernardo. (Office ☎915 87 47 47. 24hr. reservations and info ☎902 40 05 00. Open M-F 9:30am-2pm and 4-7pm.)

Trains: Two *Largo Recorrido* (long distance) **RENFE** stations connect Madrid to the rest of Europe. Call RENFE (☎913 28 90 20; www.renfe.es) for reservations and info. Try the **Main Office,** C. Alcalá 44, at Gran Vía (M: Banco de España) for schedules.

Estación Chamartín: 24hr. info international ☎934 90 11 22, domestic ☎902 24 02 02; Spanish only. M: Chamartín. Bus #5 runs to Sol (45min.). Ticket windows open 8am-10:30pm. Most *cercanías* (local) trains stop at Atocha and Chamartín. To: **Barcelona** (7-10½hr., 10 per day, €33-44); **Lisbon** (9½hr., 10:45pm, €48-67); **Paris** (13½hr., 7pm, €119-131).

Estación Atocha (☎913 28 90 20). M: Atocha-Renfe. Ticket windows open 7:15am-10pm. Trains to Andalucía, Castilla y León, Castilla-La Mancha, El Escorial, Extremadura, Sierra de Guadarrama, Toledo, and Valencia. AVE service (☎915 34 05 05) to **Córdoba** (1¾hr., 20 per day, €35-47) and **Seville** (2½hr., 20 per day, €57-64).

Intercity Buses: Numerous private companies, each with its own station and set of destinations, serve Madrid; many buses pass through the **Estación Sur de Autobuses.**

Estación Sur de Autobuses: C. Méndez Álvaro (☎914 68 42 00). M: Méndez Álvaro. Info open daily 7am-11pm. **Continental-Auto** (☎915 27 29 61) to **Toledo** (1½hr.; every 30min.; €4).

Estación Auto Res: C. Fernández Shaw 1 (☎902 02 09 99). M: Conde de Casal. To: **Cuenca** (3hr.; M-F 8-10 per day, Sa-Su 5-6 per day 8am-8pm; €9); **Salamanca** (2½-3hr., 20 per day, €10-15); **Trujillo** (3¼hr., 11-12 per day, €14); **Valencia** (4-5hr., 14 per day 1am-2pm, €20-24).

Estación La Sepulvedana: Po. de la Frontera 16 (☎915 30 48 00). M: Príncipe Pío (via extension from M: Ópera). To **Segovia** (1½hr., every 30min. 6:30am-10:15pm, €5.60).

Empressa Larrea: ☎915 30 48 00. To **Ávila** (1½hr.; M-F 8 per day, Sa-Su 4 per day; €6.30).

⊞ ORIENTATION

Marking the epicenter of both Madrid and Spain, "Kilometro 0" in **Puerta del Sol** ("Sol" for short) is within walking distance of most sights. To the west are the **Plaza Mayor,** the **Palacio Real,** and the **Ópera** district. East of Sol lies **Huertas,** the heart of cafe, theater, and museum life, which is centered around Pl. Santa Ana and bordered by C. Alcalá to the north, Po. Prado to the east, and C. Atocha to the south. The area north of Sol is bordered by **Gran Vía,** which runs northwest to **Plaza de España.** North of Gran Vía are three club and bar-hopping districts, linked by Calle de Fuencarral: **Malasaña, Bilbao,** and **Chueca.** Modern Madrid is beyond Gran Vía and east of Malasaña and Chueca. East of Sol, the tree-lined thoroughfares **Paseo de la Castellana, Paseo de Recoletos,** and **Paseo del Prado** split Madrid in two, running from Atocha in the south to **Plaza Castilla** in the north, passing the Prado, the fountains of **Plaza Cibeles,** and **Plaza Colón.** Refer to the **color map** of Madrid's Metro. Madrid is safer than its European counterparts, but Sol, Pl. España, Pl. Chueca, and Malasaña's Pl. Dos de Mayo are still intimidating late at night. As a general rule, travel in groups, avoid the parks and quiet streets after dark, and always watch for thieves and pickpockets in crowds.

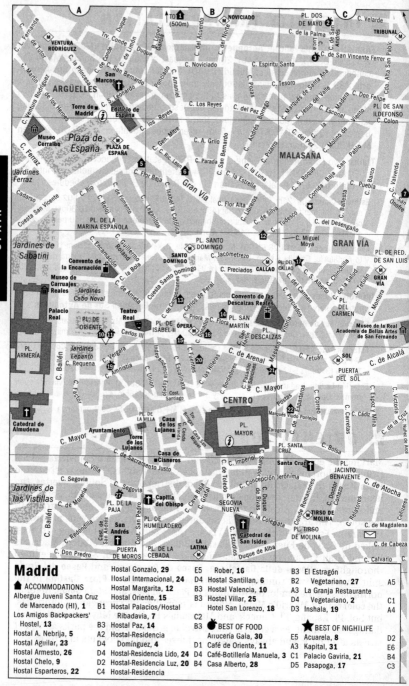

Madrid

ACCOMMODATIONS

Albergue Juvenil Santa Cruz de Marcenado (HI), **1**	B1	
Los Amigos Backpackers' Hostel, **13**	B3	
Hostal A. Nebrija, **5**	A2	
Hostal Aguilar, **23**	D4	
Hostal Armesto, **26**	D4	
Hostal Chelo, **9**	D2	
Hostal Esparteros, **22**	C4	
Hostal Gonzalo, **29**	E5	
Hostal Internacional, **24**	D4	
Hostal Margarita, **12**	B3	
Hostal Oriente, **15**	B3	
Hostal Palacios/Hostal Ribadavia, **7**	C2	
Hostal Paz, **14**	B3	
Hostal-Residencia Domínguez, **4**	D1	
Hostal-Residencia Lido, **24**	D4	
Hostal-Residencia Luz, **20**	B4	
Hostal-Residencia		
Rober, **16**	E5	
Hostal Santillan, **6**	A3	
Hostal Valencia, **10**	B3	
Hostel Villar, **25**	B3	
Hotel San Lorenzo, **18**	D3	

BEST OF FOOD

Arrocería Gala, **30**	B3	
Café de Oriente, **11**	A3	
Café-Botillería Manuela, **3**	C1	
Casa Alberto, **28**	D5	

El Estragón, **27**	A5	
Vegetariano, **27**		
La Granja Restaurante		
Vegetariano, **2**	C1	
Inshala, **19**	A4	

BEST OF NIGHTLIFE

Acuarela, **8**	D2	
Kapital, **31**	E6	
Palacio Gaviria, **21**	B4	
Pasapoga, **17**	C3	

SPAIN

⊑ LOCAL TRANSPORTATION

Public Transportation: Madrid's **Metro** (☎902 44 44 03; www.metromadrid.es) puts most major subway systems to shame. Individual Metro tickets cost €1.10, a **bonotransporte** (ticket of 10 rides for Metro or bus system) is €5.20. Buy both at machines in any Metro stop, *estanco* (tobacco shop), or newsstand. Keep your ticket; Metro officials often board and ask to see them, and travelers without tickets get fined. **Bus** info ☎914 06 88 10 (Spanish only). 6am-midnight, €1.10. *Buho* (owl), the **night bus** service, runs every 20min. midnight-3am, every hr. 3-6am, and is the cheapest form of transportation for late-night revelers. Look for buses N1-20.

Taxis: Call ☎914 05 12 13, 914 47 51 80, or 913 71 37 11. A *libre* sign in the window or a green light indicates availability. Base fare €1.40, plus €0.70-0.90 per km.

Car Rental: There is hardly reason to rent a car in Madrid. Don't drive unless you're planning to leave the city; even then bus and train fares will likely be cheaper. Tobacco shops sell parking permits. **Europcar,** Estación de Atocha, AVE terminal (☎915 30 01 94; reservations ☎902 10 50 30; www.europcar.com). M: Atocha Renfe. 21+.

Moped Rental: Motocicletas Antonio Castro, C. Conde Duque 13 (☎915 42 06 57). M: San Bernardo. 21+. Mopeds from €26 per day (8am-8pm) or €120 per week, including unlimited mileage and insurance. Deposit for 1-day rental €390, for week-long rental €450. Open M-F 8am-1:30pm and 5-8pm.

🔽 PRACTICAL INFORMATION

TOURIST AND FINANCIAL SERVICES

Tourist Offices: Municipal, Plaza Mayor 3 (☎/fax 913 66 54 77), will be expanding and relocating to a location across the Plaza Mayor. M: Sol. Open M-Sa 10am-8pm, Su 10am-3pm. **Regional/Provincial Office of the Comunidad de Madrid,** Duque de Medinacelia 2 (☎914 29 49 51; www.comadrid.es/turismo). **Branches** at Estación Chamartín and the airport.

Websites: www.comadrid.es/turismo; www.madrid.org; www.tourspain.es; www.cronica-madrid.com; www.guiadelocio.com; www.madridman.com; www.red2000.com/spain/madrid; www.descubremadrid.munimadrid.es.

Budget Travel: Viajes TIVE, C. Fernando el Católico 88 (☎915 43 74 12; fax 915 44 00 62). M: Moncloa. Exit the Metro at C. Isaac Peral, walk straight down C. Arcipreste de Hita, and turn left on C. Fernando el Católico; it'll be on your left. Organizes group excursions and language classes. Lodgings and student residence info. ISIC €6; HI card €5, over-30 €11, non-Spaniards €19. Open M-F 9am-2pm. Arrive early to avoid long lines.

Embassies: Australia, Pl. Descubridor Diego de Ordás 3 (☎914 41 60 25; www.embaustralia.es). **Canada,** C. Núñez de Balboa 35 (☎914 23 32 50; www.canada-es.org). **Ireland,** Po. Castellana 46, 4th fl. (☎914 36 40 93; fax 914 35 16 77). **New Zealand,** Pl. Lealtad 2, 3rd fl. (☎915 23 02 26; fax 915 23 01 71). **South Africa,** Claudio Coello 91, 6th fl. (☎914 36 37 80; fax 915 77 74 14). **UK,** C. Fernando el Santo 16 (☎917 00 82 00; fax 917 00 82 72). **US,** C. Serrano 75 (☎915 87 22 00; www.embusa.es).

Currency Exchange: In general, credit and ATM cards offer the best exchange rates. Avoid changing money at airport and train station counters; they tend to charge exorbitant commissions on horrible rates. **Santander Central Hispano** charges no commission on cash or traveler's checks up to €600. **Main branch,** Pl. Canalejas 1 (☎915 58 11 11). M: Sol. Follow C. San Jeronimo to Pl. Canalejas. Open Apr.-Sept. M-F 8:30am-2pm; Oct.-Mar. M-Th 8:30am-4:30pm, F 8:30am-2pm, Sa 8:30am-1pm.

American Express: Pl. Cortés 2 (traveler services ☎917 43 77 40; currency exchange ☎917 43 77 55). M: Banco de España. Traveler services open M-F 9am-7:30pm, Sa 10am-2pm; currency exchange M-F 9am-7:30pm, Sa 9am-2pm. 24hr. Express Cash machine outside.

LOCAL SERVICES

Luggage Storage: Barajas Airport. Follow the signs to *consigna*. One day €3; 2-15 days €3-5 per day; after day 15, €0.60-1.40 per day. **Estación Chamartín** and **Estación Atocha.** Lockers €2.40-4.50 per day. Open daily 6:30am-10:15pm.

Bi-Gay-Lesbian Resources: Most establishments in the Chueca area carry *Shanguide*, a free guide to gay nightlife in Spain. **Colectivo de Gais y Lesbianas de Madrid (COGAM),** C. Fuencarral 37 (☎/fax 915 22 45 17). M: Gran Vía. Provides a wide range of services and activities, including an HIV support group (M-F 6-10pm). Reception daily M-Sa 5:30-9pm. Free counseling M-Th 7-9pm.

Laundromat: Lavandería Ondablu, C. León 3 (☎913 69 50 71). M: Antón Martín, Sol, or Sevilla. Open daily 9am-10:30pm. Just up the street is **Lavandería Cervantes,** C. León, 6. Wash €2, dry €1. Open daily 9am-9pm.

EMERGENCY AND COMMUNICATIONS

Emergency: ☎112. **Ambulance:** ☎061. **National police:** ☎091. **Local police:** ☎092.

Police: C. de los Madrazo 9 (☎915 41 71 60). M: Sevilla. From C. Alcalá take a right onto C. Cedacneros and a left onto C. de los Madrazo. To report crimes committed in the **Metro,** go to the office in the Sol station (open daily 8am-11pm). **Guardia Civil** (☎062 or 915 34 02 00). **Protección Civil** (☎915 37 31 00).

Rape Hotline: ☎915 74 01 10. Open M-F 10am-2pm and 4-7pm.

Medical Services: Equipo Quirúrgico Municipal No. 1, C. Montesa 22 (☎915 88 51 00). M: Manuel Becerra. **Hospital Ramón y Cajal,** Ctra. Colmenar Viejo (☎913 36 80 00). Bus #135 from Pl. Castilla. For non-emergency concerns, **Anglo-American Medical Unit,** Conde de Aranda 1, 1st fl. (☎914 35 18 23), is quick and friendly.

Internet Access: New Internet cafes are surfacing everywhere. While the average is a reasonable €2 per hr., small shops in apartments charge even less; keep a lookout.

 ■ **Easy Everything,** C. Montera 10 (☎915 21 18 65; www.easyeverything.com). M: Sol. From the Plaza del Sol, look for C. Montera, which goes toward Gran Vía. Open daily 8am-1am, with hundreds of computers, fast connections, good music, and a cafe. Access from €0.50.

Conéctate, C. Isaac Peral 4 (☎915 44 54 65; www.conectate.es). M: Moncloa. Over 300 flat-screens and some of the lowest prices in Madrid. Open 24hr.

Yazzgo Internet, Gran Vía 84 & 69 (☎915 22 11 20; www.yazzgo.com). M: San Bernado or Pl. de España. Also locations at Puerta del Sol 6, Gran Vía 60, Estación Chamartín, and Estación Méndez Álvaro. A growing chain; check their website for new locations. Most branches open daily 8:30am-10:30pm; Gran Vía 69 branch open 8:30am-1am.

Post Office: Palacio de Comunicaciones, C. de Alcala 51, on Pl. Cibeles (☎902 19 71 97). M: Banco de España. Windows open M-Sa 8:30am-9:30pm, Su 9am-2pm for stamp purchases, certified mail, telex, and fax service. **Poste Restante** (Lista de Correos) at windows 80-82; passport required. **Postal Code:** 28080.

READ THIS. The *Guía del Ocio*, at any news kiosk, should be your first purchase in Madrid (€1). It has concert, theater, sports, cinema, and TV schedules. It also lists exhibits, restaurants, bars, and clubs. Although it is in Spanish, the alphabetical listings of clubs and restaurants are invaluable even to non-speakers. For an English magazine with articles on finds in and around the city, pick up *In Madrid*, distributed free at tourist offices and restaurants.

⚓ ACCOMMODATIONS

Make reservations for summer visits. Expect to pay €17-€50 per person, depending on location, amenities, and season. Tourist offices provide information about the 13 or so **campsites** within 50km of Madrid. **Centro**, the triangle between Puerta del Sol, Opera, and Plaza Mayor, is full of *hostales*, but you'll pay for the prime location. The cultural hotbed of **Huertas**, framed by C. San Jeronimo, C. las Huertas, and C. Atocha, is almost as central and more fun. Festive **Malasaña** and **Chueca**, bisected by C. Fuencarral, host cheap rooms in the heart of the action, but the sleep-deprived should beware; the party doesn't quiet down for rest. *Hostales*, like temptations, are everywhere among **Gran Vía's** sex shops and scam artists.

EL CENTRO: SOL, ÓPERA, AND PLAZA MAYOR

🏠 **Hostal Paz,** C. Flora 4, 1st and 4th fl. (☎915 47 30 47). M: Ópera. Located on a quiet street, parallel to C. Arenal, off C. Donados or C. Hileras. Peaceful rooms with large windows are sheltered from street noise and lavished with amenities. Reservations advised. Singles €20; doubles €30-36; triples €45. MC/V. ❷

🏠 **Hostal-Residencia Luz,** C. Fuentes 10, 3rd fl. (☎915 42 07 59 or 915 59 74 18; fax 42 07 59), off C. Arenal. M: Ópera. Neck and neck with Hostal Paz for the best digs in Madrid. Newly redecorated rooms with hardwood floors and elegant furniture ooze comfort. Singles €15; doubles €34-39; triples €39-45. ❷

Hostal-Residencia Rober, C. Arenal 26, 5th fl. (☎915 41 91 75). M: Ópera. Brilliant balcony views down Arenal. Singles with double bed and shower €24, with bath €34; doubles with bath €39; triples with bath €59. Discounts for longer stays. ❸

Hostal Valencia, Pl. Oriente 2, 3rd fl. (☎915 59 84 50). M: Ópera. Narrow glass elevator leads to elegant rooms. Singles €42; doubles €72; master suite €92. ❹

Los Amigos Backpackers' Hostel, C. Campomanes 6, 4th fl. (☎915 47 17 07; www.losamigoshostel.com), off Pl. de Isabel II. M: Ópera. One of very few standard hostels in Madrid. Brightly decorated dorms and clean shared baths. Kitchen and festive common room. Breakfast included. Sheets €5. Laundry €5. Internet €1 per 30min. 24hr. reception. Dorms €15 (includes breakfast). MC/V. ❷

Hostal Oriente, C. Arenal 23, 1st fl. (☎915 48 03 14; www.hostaloriente.com), just off Pl. de Isabel II. M: Ópera. Classy newly renovated hostel with friendly owners and inviting reception. 14 spotless rooms have TV, telephone, A/C, safe, and private bath. Singles €33, doubles €50, triples €66. ❸

Hostal Esparteros, C. Esparteros 12, 4th fl. (☎/fax 915 21 09 03). M: Sol. Sparkling rooms with balcony or large windows; some have private bath. English-speaking owner. Laundry €7. Singles €25; doubles €35; triples €42. 10% discount for longer stays. ❷

HUERTAS

🏠 **Hostal Gonzalo,** C. Cervantes 34, 3rd fl. (☎914 29 27 14; fax 914 20 20 07). M: Antón Martín. Off C. León, which is off C. Atocha. A budget traveler's dream: renovated rooms, pristine baths, TVs, and fans in the summer. Singles €38; doubles €47; triples €60. ❸

Hostal Internacional, C. Echegaray 5, 2nd fl. (☎914 29 62 09). M: Sol. Rooms renovated in 2002. Nice common room. Singles €25-30; doubles €40. ❸

Hostal-Residencia Lido, C. Echegaray 5, 2nd fl. (☎914 29 62 07). M: Sol or Sevilla. Across from Internacional, Lido showcases new rooms with comfy beds, TVs, and complete baths. Singles €22-25, with bath €25-30; doubles €35-40. ❷

Hostal Villar, C. Príncipe 18, 1st-4th fl. (☎915 31 66 00; www.arrakis.es/~h-villar). M: Sol. From the Metro, follow C. San Jerónimo and turn right on C. Príncipe. Feels secluded despite its busy location. Singles €22, with bath €25; doubles €30/40; triples €42/56. ❷

Hostal Aguilar, C. San Jerónimo 32, 2nd fl. (☎914 29 59 26 or 914 29 36 61; www.hostalaguilar.com). M: Sol or Sevilla. Clean and expansive rooms with A/C and safe. Hemingway purportedly spent many nights in room 107. Singles €33; doubles €45; triples €60; quads €73. MC/V. ❸

Hostal Sardinero, C. Prado 16, 3rd fl. (☎914 29 57 56, ☎/fax 914 29 41 12), a few blocks from Plaza Santa Ana. An upscale hostel with all the creature comforts of a hotel, sparkling rooms have A/C, TV, safe, and private baths. Singles €50; doubles €60. 24hr. reception. MC/V. ❹

Hostal Armesto, C. San Agustín 6, 1st fl. (☎914 29 90 31). M: Antón Martín. In front of Pl. Cortés. This *hostal* offers exceptional hospitality and a quiet night's sleep. All rooms with private bath and A/C. Older crowd. Singles €45; doubles €50; triples €54. ❹

GRAN VÍA

Hostal A. Nebrija, Gran Vía 67, 8th fl., elevator A (☎915 47 73 19). M: Pl. España. Pleasant, spacious rooms offering magnificent views of the city landscape. Singles €26; doubles €36; triples €49. AmEx/MC/V. ❸

Hostal Santillan, Gran Vía 64, 8th fl. (☎/fax 915 48 23 28). M: Pl. España. Friendly management. Simple rooms all have showers, sinks, TVs, fans, and safes. Singles €30; doubles €45; triples €60. MC/V. ❸

Hostal Margarita, Gran Vía 50, 5th fl. (☎/fax 915 47 35 49). M: Callao. Simple rooms with large windows and TV; most with street views. Singles €25; doubles €36, with bath €38; triples with bath €48. MC/V. ❷

MALASAÑA AND CHUECA

▨ **Hostal-Residencia Domínguez**, C. Santa Brígida 1, 1st fl. (☎/fax 915 32 15 47). M: Tribunal. Go down C. Fuencarral toward Gran Vía, turn left on C. Santa Brígida, and climb up a flight. Hospitable young owner ready with tips on local nightlife. English spoken. Singles €22, with bath €30; doubles with bath and A/C €40. ❷

Hostal Chelo, C. Hortaleza 17, 3rd fl. (☎915 32 70 33; www.chelo.com). M: Gran Vía. Great location, hospitable and helpful staff. Rooms are spacious, with complete bath. Singles €30; doubles €38. ❸

Hostal Palacios and **Hostal Ribadavia**, C. Fuencarral 25, 1st-3rd fl. (☎915 31 10 58 or ☎915 31 48 47). M: Gran Vía. Both run by the same cheerful family. Singles €20, with bath €30; doubles €30/36; triples €45/51. AmEx/MC/V. ❷

Hotel San Lorenzo, C. Clavel 8 (☎915 21 30 57; www.hotel/sanlorenzo.com). M: Gran Vía. From the Metro, walk down Gran Vía and make a left on C. Clavel. New furniture, modern bathrooms, and soundproof windows. Reservations recommended. Singles €50; doubles €75-85. AmEx/MC/V. ❹

ELSEWHERE AND CAMPING

Budget lodgings are rare near the **Chamartín** train station, as is the case in most of the residential districts located away from the city center. Near the **Madrid-Atocha** train station are a handful of hostels, the closest of which are down Po. Santa María de la Cabeza. Tourist offices can provide info about the 13 campsites within 50km of Madrid. Similar info is in the *Guía Oficial de Campings* (official camping guide), a large book they'll gladly let you peruse. For further camping info, contact the **Consejería de Educación de Juventud** (☎915 22 29 41).

Albergue Juvenil Santa Cruz de Marcenado (HI), C. de Santa Cruz de Marcenado 28 (☎915 47 45 32; fax 48 11 96). M: Argüelles. From the Metro, walk 1 block down C. Alberto Aguilera away from C. de la Princesa, turn right on C. de Serrano Jóver, then left on C. de Santa Cruz de Marcenado. Separate floors for men and women. Breakfast included. Lockers €2. Sheets provided. Laundry €3. 3-day max. stay. Quiet hours after midnight. Reception daily 9am-10pm. Curfew 1:30am. Reserve in advance by mail, fax, or in person. Dorms €12, under-26 €7.80. Nonmembers add €3.50. ❶

Camping Alpha (☎916 95 80 69; fax 83 16 59), on a tree-lined site 12km down Ctra. de Andalucía in Getafe. M: Legazpi. From the Metro station take bus #447 (10min., every 30min. until 10pm, €1.30); cross the bridge and walk 1.5km back toward Madrid along a busy highway; camping signs lead the way. Pool, showers, and laundry facilities. €5 per person, €5.30 per tent, €5.20 per car. ❶

◪ FOOD

In Madrid, it's not hard to fork it down without forking over too much. Most restaurants offer a *menú del día*, which includes bread, one drink, and one choice from each of the day's selection of appetizers, main courses, and desserts (€7-9). Many small eateries line **Calles Echegaray, Bentura de la Vega,** and **Manuel Fernández González** in Huertas; **Calle Agurrosa** at Lavapiés has some funky outdoor cafes, and there are good restaurants up the hill toward Huertas; **Calle Fuencarral** in Gran Vía is lined with cheap eats. **Bilbao,** the area north of Glorieta de Bilbao, is the place to go for ethnically diverse culinary choices. Bars along **Calle Hartzenbusch** and **Calle Cisneros** offer cheap *tapas*. Keep in mind the following essential buzz words for quicker, cheaper *madrileño* fare: *bocadillo* (a sandwich on a long, hard roll, €2-2.80); *ración* (a large *tapa,* served with bread €2-3.80); and *empanada* (a puff pastry with meat fillings, €1.30-2). Vegetarians should check out the *Guía del Ocio,* which has a complete listing of Madrid's vegetarian havens under the section *"Otras Cocinas,"* or the website www.mundovegetariano.com. For groceries, **%Dia** and **Simago** are the cheapest supermarket chains. More expensive are **Mantequerías Leonesas, Expreso,** and **Jumbo.**

■ **Inshala,** C. Amnistia 10 (☎915 48 26 32). M: Ópera. Eclectic menu filled with delicious Spanish, Mexican, Japanese, Italian, and Moroccan dishes. Weekday lunch *menú* €8. Dinner *menú* €8-€15. Reservations strongly recommended for both lunch and dinner. Open M-Th noon-2pm, F-Sa until 3am. ❸

■ **Arrocería Gala,** C. Moratín 22 (☎914 29 25 62). Down the hill from C. Atocha on C. Moratín. The decor is as colorful and varied as the house *paella* (€14). Reserve on weekends. Open daily 1:30-5pm and 9-11pm. ❸

■ **El Estragón Vegetariano,** Pl. de la Paja 10 (☎913 65 89 82). M: La Latina. Perhaps the best medium-priced restaurant—of any kind—in Madrid, with vegetarian food that could convert even the most die-hard carnivores. Try the delicious *menú* (M-F €9; Sa-Su and evenings €18). Open daily 1:30-4:30pm and 8pm-1am. AmEx/MC/V. ❹

■ **La Granja Restaurante Vegetariano,** C. San Andrés 11 (☎915 32 87 93), off Pl. 2 de Mayo. M: Tribunal or Bilbao. Dimmed yellow lights glow above intricately tiled walls in this Arabic-themed restaurant. Youthful crowd, friendly owner, and big portions. *Menú* €7.50. Open daily 1:30-4:15pm and 8:30pm-midnight. MC/V. ❷

Al-Jaima, Cocina del Desierto, C. Barbieri 1 (☎915 23 11 42). M: Gran Vía or Chueca. Lebanese, Moroccan, and Egyptian food in intimate North African setting. Specialties include the *pastela,* couscous, *shish kebabs,* and *tajine* (€4-8). Open daily 1:30-4pm and 9pm-midnight. Dinner reservations recommended. AmEx/MC/V. ❷

Osteria Il Regno di Napoli, C. San Andrés 21 (☎914 45 63 00). From Glorieta de Bilbao, head one block down C. Carranza, then turn left onto C. San Andrés. Delicious Italian cuisine in a hip environment. Lunch *menú* €10; dinner entrees €8-12. Reservations recommended. Open M-F 2-4pm and 9pm-midnight, Sa 9pm midnight, Su 2-4pm. AmEx/MC/V. ❷

Restaurante Casa Botín, C. de Cuchilleros 17 (☎913 66 42 17), off Plaza Mayor. The "oldest restaurant in the world," founded in 1725, serves filling Spanish dishes (€7-25). Reservations recommended. Lunch daily 1-4pm, dinner 8pm-midnight. ❸

Ananias, C. Galileo 9 (☎914 48 68 01). M: Argüelles. From C. Alberto Aguilera, take a left onto C. Galileo. Swirling waiters serve Castilian dishes with a flourish. Entrees €7-15. Open Su 1-4pm; M-Tu and Th-Sa 1-4pm and 9pm-midnight. AmEx/MC/V. ❸

La Finca de Susana, C. Arlaban 4 (☎913 69 35 57). M: Sevilla. Probably the most popular lunch place in Madrid; fine dining at an extremely low price (*menú* €7). Be prepared to wait in line. Open daily 1-3:45pm and 8:30-11:45pm. ❷

TAPAS

Not so long ago, bartenders in Madrid used to *tapar* (cover) drinks with saucers to keep the flies out. Later, servers began putting little sandwiches on top of the saucers, and there you have it: *tapas*. Hopping from bar to bar gobbling *tapas* is an active alternative to a full sit-down meal. Most *tapas* bars (*tascas* or *tabernas*) are open noon-4pm and 8pm-midnight or later; many cluster around **Plaza Santa Ana** and **Plaza Mayor.** Authentic bars pack **Calle Cuchilleros** and **Calle de la Cruz.**

■ **Casa Alberto,** C. Huertas 18 (☎914 29 93 56). M: Antón Martín. Interior dining room decorated with bullfighting and Cervantine relics; Cervantes wrote the second part of *El Quijote* here. The *tapas* are all original house recipes. Get the feel of their *gambas al ajillo* (shrimp with garlic and hot peppers; €8.40) or the *canapés* (€2). Sit-down dinner is a bit pricey. Open Tu-Sa noon-5:30pm and 8pm-1:30am. AmEx/MC/V. ❸

■ **Los Gabrieles,** C. Echegaray 17 (☎914 29 62 61). M: Sol. The tiled mural at the back depicts famous artists—from Velázquez to Goya—as stumble-drunks. Serves *tapas* by afternoon and drinks by night. Flamenco Tu night. Open daily 1pm-late. ❶

La Toscana, C. Manuel Fernández González 10-12 (☎914 29 60 31). M: Sol or Sevilla. A local crowd hangs out over *tapas* of *morcilla asado* (€8). Spacious bar jam-packed on weekends. Open Tu-Sa 1-4pm and 8pm-midnight. ❷

Casa Amadeo, Pl. de Cascorro 18 (☎913 65 94 39). M: La Latina. The jovial owner of 60 years supervises the making of house specialty *caracoles* (snails; *tapas* €4.80, *ración* €12) and *chorizo* made with snails (€4.80). Other *raciones* €2-5.50. Open Su and Tu-Sa 10:30am-4pm and 7-10:30pm. ❷

ON THE MENU

WHAT YOU'RE IN FOR

Tapas menus can often be cryptic and indecipherable—and that's if the bar bothered to print them in the first place. To make sure you don't end up eating the stewed parts of the ox you rode in on, just keep the following words in mind.

Servings come in three sizes:

— *pincho* (normally eaten with toothpicks between sips of beer)

— *tapa* (small plate)

— *ración* (sizable meal portion)

Among the standard offerings on any *tapas* menu, you'll find:

— *Aceitunas* (olives)

— *albondigas* (meatballs)

— *anchoas* (anchovies)

— *callos* (tripe)

— *chorizo* (sausage)

— *croquetas* (breaded and fried combos)

— *gambas* (shrimp)

— *jamón* (ham)

— *patatas alioli y bravas* (potatoes with sauces)

— *pimentos* (peppers)

— *pulpo* (octopus)

— *tortilla* (potato omelette)

🔡 CAFES

Spend an afternoon lingering over a *café con leche* and soak up Madrilenian culture in historic cafes.

🔳 **Café-Botillería Manuela,** C. de San Vicente Ferrer 29. M: Tribunal. Upbeat music and contemporary artwork contrast with late 19th-century decor. Specialty international cocktails €3-5. Traditional *tapas* menu €2-8. Story-telling and live music Sa 9:30pm. Open July-Aug. Su and Tu-Sa 6pm-2:30am; Sept.-June daily 4pm-2am.

🔳 **Café de Oriente,** Pl. del Oriente 2. M: Ópera. An old-fashioned cafe catering to a ritzy, older crowd. Spectacular view of the Palacio Real from the *terraza*, especially at night when floodlights illuminate the facade. Specialty coffees (€1.80-5.60) live up to their price. Open Su-Th 8:30am-1:30am, F-Sa 8:30am-12:30am.

Café Gijón, Po. de Recoletos 21. M: Colón. Enjoy thought-provoking conversation and good coffee in this historic landmark. Popular with intellectuals. A perfect stop during a walking tour of the *paseos*. Coffee from €2.60. Open Su-Th 7am-1:30am, F-Sa 7am-2am. AmEx/MC/V.

Café Comercial, Glorieta de Bilbao 7. M: Bilbao. Founded in 1887, Madrid's oldest cafe boasts high ceilings, cushioned chairs, and huge mirrors perfect for people-watching. Coffee €1.10 at the bar, €1.80 at a table. Open M-Th 7:30am-1:30am, F-Sa 8am-2am, Su 10am-1am.

👁 SIGHTS

Madrid, large as it may seem, is a walker's city. Its fantastic public transportation system should only be used for longer distances, or between the day's starting and ending points. Although the word *paseo* refers to a major avenue (such as *Paseo de la Castellana* or *Paseo del Prado*), it literally means "a stroll." Do just that from Sol to Cibeles and from Plaza Mayor to the Palacio Real—sights will kindly introduce themselves. The city's art, architecture, culture, and atmosphere convince wide-eyed walkers that it was once the capital of the world's greatest empire. While Madrid is perfect for walking, it also offers some of the world's best places to relax. Whether soothing tired feet after perusing the *triángulo de arte* or seeking shelter from the summer's sweltering heat, there's nothing better than a shaded sidewalk cafe or a romantic park.

EL CENTRO

The area known as El Centro, spreading out from the Puerta del Sol ("Door of the Sun"), is the gateway to the history and spirit of Madrid. Although several rulers carved the winding streets, the Habsburg and Bourbon families left behind El Centro's most celebrated monuments. As a result, El Centro is divided into two major sections: Madrid de los Habsburgs and Madrid de los Borbones. All directions are given from the Puerta del Sol.

PUERTA DEL SOL

Kilómetro 0, the origin of six national highways, marks the center of the city (and the country) in the most chaotic of Madrid's plazas. Puerta del Sol (Gate of Sun) blazes with taxis, bars, and street performers. The statue **El Oso y el Madroño,** a bear and strawberry tree, is a popular meeting place. *(M: Sol.)*

HABSBURG MADRID

"Old Madrid," the city's central neighborhood, is densely packed with both monuments and tourists. In the 16th century, the Habsburgs built **Plaza Mayor** and the **Catedral de San Isidro.** When Felipe II moved the seat of Castilla from Toledo to Madrid in 1561, he and his descendants commissioned the court architects (including Juan de Herrera) to update many of Madrid's buildings to the latest styles. In 1620, the plaza was completed for Felipe III; his statue, installed in 1847, still graces its center.

PLAZA MAYOR

Juan de Herrera, architect of El Escorial, also designed this plaza. Its elegant arcades, spindly towers, and open verandas, erected for Felipe III in 1620, came to define "Madrid-style" architecture and inspired every peering balcón thereafter. Toward evening, Plaza Mayor awakens as madrileños resurface, tourists multiply, and cafes fill with lively patrons. Live flamenco performances are a common treat. *(M: Sol. From Pta. Sol, walk down C. Mayor. The plaza is on the left.)*

CATEDRAL DE SAN ISIDRO

Designed in the Jesuit Baroque style at the beginning of the 17th century, the cathedral received San Isidro's remains in 1769. During the Civil War, rioting workers burned the exterior and damaged much of the cathedral—only the primary nave and a few Baroque decorations remain from the original. *(M: Latina. From Pta. Sol, take C. Mayor to Plaza Mayor, cross the plaza, and exit onto C. Toledo. Open for Mass only.)*

PLAZA DE LA VILLA

Plaza de la Villa marks the heart of what was once old Madrid. Though only a few medieval buildings remain, the plaza still features a stunning courtyard (around the statue of Don Alvara de Bazón), beautiful tile-work, and eclectic architecture. Across the plaza is the 17th-century **Ayuntamiento (Casa de la Villa)**, designed in 1640 by Juan Gomez de Mora as both the mayor's home and the city jail. *(M: Sol. From Pta. Sol, go down C. Mayor, past Plaza Mayor.)*

BOURBON MADRID

Weakened by plagues and political losses, the Habsburg era in Spain ended with the death of Carlos II in 1700. Felipe V, the first of Spain's Bourbon monarchs, ascended the throne in 1714 after the 12-year War of the Spanish Succession. Bankruptcy, industrial stagnation, and widespread disillusionment compelled Felipe V to embark on a crusade of urban renewal. The lavish palaces, churches, and parks that resulted are the most touristed in Madrid.

PALACIO REAL

The luxurious Palacio Real lies at the western tip of central Madrid, overlooking the Río Manzanares. Felipe V commissioned Giovanni Sachetti to replace the Alcázar, which had burned down in 1734, with a palace that would dwarf all others—he succeeded. Today, the unfinished palace is only used by King Juan Carlos and Queen Sofía on special occasions. The palace's most impressive rooms are decorated in the Rococo style. The **Salón de Gasparini,** site of the king's ceremonial dressing before the court, houses Goya's portrait of Carlos IV and a Mengs ceiling fresco. The **Salón del Trono** (Throne Room) also contains a ceiling fresco, painted by Tiepolo, that outlines the qualities of the quintessential ruler. The **Biblioteca** shelves first editions of *Don Quixote*. Also open to the public is the **Real Armería** (Armory), which displays the armor of Carlos V and Felipe II. *(M: Sol. From Pta. Sol, take C. Mayor and turn right on C. Bailen. Open Apr.-Sept. M-Sa 9am-6pm, Su 9am-3pm; Oct.-Mar. M-Sa 9:30am-5pm, Su 9am-2pm. €7, students €3.30. Tours €8. W free for EU citizens.)* Next door to the palace is the **Cathedral de Nuestra Señora de la Almudena,** begun in 1879 and finished a century later. The cathedral's modern interior stands in contrast to the gilded Palacio Real. *(M: Sol. From Pta. Sol, go down C. Mayor and it's just across C. Bailén. Open daily 9am-9pm. Free.)*

PLAZA DE ORIENTE. A minor architectural miscalculation was responsible for this sculpture park. Most of the statues here were designed for the palace roof, but because they were too heavy (and the queen had a nightmare about the roof collapsing), they were placed in this shady plaza instead. Treat yourself to pricey coffee on one of the elegant *terrazas* that fringe the plaza. The **Jardines de Sabatini**, just to the right as you face the palace, is the romantic's park of choice. *(From Pta. Sol, take C. Arenal to the plaza. Free.)*

PARQUE DE LAS VISTILLAS. This park was named for its gorgeous *vistillas* (views) of Palacio Real, Nuestra Señora de la Almudena, and the surrounding countryside. Be careful at night, as it can be dangerous. *(In Pl. Gabriel Miró. Facing the palace, turn left on C. Bailén, and then right on C. Don Pedro into the plaza.)*

HUERTAS

The area east of Sol is a wedge bounded by C. de Alcalá to the north, C. Atocha to the south, and Po. Prado to the east. Huertas's sights, from authors' houses to famous cafes, reflect its artistic focus. Home to Cervantes, Góngora, Quevedo, Calderón, and Moratín in the "Siglo de Oro" (Golden Age), Huertas enjoyed a fleeting return to literary prominence when Hemingway frequented the neighborhood in the 1920s. **Plaza Santa Ana** and its *terrazas* are the center of this old literary haunt. **Casa de Lope de Vega** is the home where the prolific playwright and poet spent the last 25 years of his life and wrote over two-thirds of his plays. The highlights include the simple garden described in his works and the library filled with crumbling, aromatic books. Among the more interesting tidbits revealed on the required tour are the tangible signs of affection Vega would leave for his young daughters. *(C. de Cervantes 11. With your back to Pl. de Santa Ana, turn left on C. del Prado, right on C. de León, and left on C. de Cervantes. ☎914 29 92 16. Open Th-F 9:30am-2pm, Sa 10am-2pm. Call ahead for definite schedules and prices.)*

GRAN VÍA

Urban planners paved the Gran Vía in 1910 to link C. Princesa with Pl. Cibeles. Madrid gained wealth as a neutral supplier during World War I, and then funneled much of its earnings into making the Gran Vía one of the world's great thoroughfares. At Gran Vía's highest elevation in **Plaza de Callao** (M: Callao). C. Postigo San Martín splits off southward, where you'll find the famed **Convento de las Descalzas Reales.** Westward from Pl. Callao, the Gran Vía makes its descent toward **Plaza de España** (M: Pl. España), where a statue commemorates Spain's most prized fictional duo: Cervantes' Don Quixote and Sancho Panza, riding horseback and muleback respectively.

MALASAÑA AND CHUECA

Devoid of the numerous historic monuments and palaces that characterize most of Madrid, the labyrinthine streets of Malasaña and Chueca house countless undocumented "sights," from platform-shoe stores to spontaneous street performances. Chueca in particular remains an ideal area for people-watching and fabulous boutique shopping. While the area between **Calle de Fuencarral** and **Calle de San Bernardo** contains some of Madrid's most avant-garde architecture and contemporary art exhibitions, most of this neighborhood's scenery lies in its residents.

ARGÜELLES

The area known as Argüelles and the zone surrounding Calle San Bernardo form a cluttered mixture of elegant middle-class houses, student apartments, and bohemian hangouts, all brimming with cultural activity. Heavily bombarded during the

Civil War, Argüelles inspired Chilean poet Pablo Neruda, then a resident, to write *España en el corazón*. By day, families and joggers roam the city's largest park, **Casa del Campo;** night brings curious but unsafe activity.

The **Parque de la Montaña** is home to Spain's only Egyptian temple. Built by Pharaoh Zakheramon in the 4th century BC, the **Temple de Debod** was a gift from the Egyptian government commemorating the Spanish archaeologists who helped rescue monuments in the Aswan dam floods. *(M: Ventura Rodríguez. From the Metro, walk down C. Ventura Rodríguez into the Parque de la Montaña; the temple is on the left. Open April 1-Sept. 31 Tu-F 10am-2pm and 4-8pm, Sa-Su 10am-2pm; Oct. 1-March 31 Tu-F 9:45am-1:15pm and 4:15-5:45pm, Sa-Su 9:45am-1:45pm. Free.)* Although out of the way, the **Ermita de San Antonio de la Florida** is worth the trouble. The Ermita contains Goya's pantheon—a frescoed dome arches above his buried corpse. Goya's skull, apparently stolen by a phrenologist, was missing when the corpse arrived from France. *(M: Príncipe Pío. From the Metro, go left on C. de Buen Altamirano, walk through the park, and turn left on Po. Florida; the Ermita is at the end of the street. Open Tu-F 10am-2pm and 4-8pm, Sa-Su 10am-2pm. Free.)* The **Faro de Moncloa** is a 92m-tall metal tower that offers views of the city. *(Av. Arco de la Victoria. Open Su and Tu-Sa 10am-2pm and 5-8pm. Tower adults €1, over-65 and under-11 €0.50.)*

OTHER SIGHTS

▨ RETIRO

Join an array of vendors, palm-readers, soccer players, and sunbathers in what Felipe IV converted from a hunting ground into a *buen retiro* (nice retreat). The finely landscaped 300-acre Parque del Buen Retiro is centered around a rectangular lake and a magnificent monument to King Alfonso XII. Dubbed **Estanque Grande,** this central location is popular among casual rowers. Built by Ricardo Velázquez to exhibit Filipino flowers, the exquisite steel-and-glass **Palacio de Cristal** hosts a variety of art shows. *(Open Apr.-Sept. M and W-Sa 11am-8pm, Su 11am-6pm; Oct.-Mar. M and W-Sa 10am-6pm, Su 10am-4pm. Free.)* All artists should dream of having their art displayed in the **Palacio de Velázquez,** with its billowing ceilings, marble floors, and ideal lighting. *(Past the Estanque, turn left on Paseo del Venezuela. Open Apr.-Sept. M and W-Sa 11am-8pm, Su 11am-6pm; Oct.-Mar. M and W-Sa 10am-6pm, Su 10am-4pm. Closed Tu. Free.)* Avoid venturing into the park alone after dark.

EL PARDO

Built as a hunting lodge for Carlos I in 1547, El Pardo was enlarged by generations of Habsburgs and Bourbons. El Pardo gained attention in 1940 when Franco made it his home, in which he resided until his death in 1975. It is renowned for its collection of tapestries—several of which were designed by Goya—but the palace also holds paintings by Velázquez and Ribera. *(Take bus #601 (15min., €1) from the stop in front of the Ejército del Aire building. M: Moncloa. Palace open Apr.-Sept. M-Sa 10:30am-6pm, Su 9:20am-1:40pm; Oct.-Mar. M-Sa 10:30am-5pm, Su 9:50am-1:40pm. Required 45min. guided tour in Spanish. €3, students €1.50. W EU citizens free.)*

🏛 MUSEUMS

Madrid's great museums need no introduction. If you're not a student and plan on visiting the big three, your best bet is the **Paseo del Arte** ticket (€7.66), which grants admission to the Museo del Prado, Museo Thyssen-Bornemisza, and Museo Centro de Arte Reina Sofía. The pass is available at all three museums.

■ MUSEO DEL PRADO

The Prado is Spain's pride and joy, as well as one of Europe's finest museums. Its 7000 pieces from the 12th-17th centuries are the result of hundreds of years of Bourbon art collecting. Each room is numbered and described in the museum's free guide. On the second floor, keep an eye out for unforgiving realism and use of light in the works of **Diego Velázquez** (1599-1660), which resonate even in the 20th century. Several of his most famous paintings are here, including *Los Borrachos* (*The Drunkards*) and *Las Lanzas* (*The Spears* or *The Surrender of Breda*). Velazquez's technique, called illusionism, climaxed in his magnum opus *Las Meninas* (*The Maids of Honor*).

The court portraitist **Francisco de Goya y Lucientes** (1746-1828) created the stark *Dos de Mayo* and *Fusilamientas de Tres de Mayo*, which depict the terrors of the Revolution of 1808. Goya painted the *Pinturas Negras* (*Black Paintings*) at the end of his life, deaf and alone. *Saturno devorando a su hijo* (*Saturn Devouring His Son*) stands out among the *Pinturas Negras*, a reminder from an ailing artist that time eventually destroys its creations. The Prado also displays many of **El Greco**'s religious paintings. *La Trinidad* (*The Trinity*) and *La adoración de los pastores* (*The Adoration of the Shepherds*) are characterized by luminous colors, elongated figures, and mystical subjects. On the second floor are other works by Spanish artists, including **Murillo, Ribera**, and **Zurbarán.**

The Prado also has a collection of **Italian** works, including pieces by Titian, Raphael, Tintoretto, Botticelli, and Rubens. As a result of the Spanish Habsburgs' control of the Netherlands, the **Flemish** holdings are also top-notch. Works by **van Dyck** and **Albrecht Durer** are here, including **Peter Breugel the Elder**'s *The Triumph of Death*, in which death drives a carriage of skulls on a decaying horse. **Hieronymus Bosch**'s moralistic *The Garden of Earthly Delights* depicts hedonism and the destiny that awaits its practitioners. *(Po. del Prado at Pl. Cánovas del Castillo. M: Banco de España or Atocha. ☎/fax 913 30 28 00; http://museoprado.mcu.es. Open Su and Tu-Sa 9am-7pm. €3, students €1.50. Under-18, over-65, and Su free.)*

■ MUSEO THYSSEN-BORNEMISZA

Unlike the Prado and the Reina Sofía, the Thyssen-Bornemisza covers a wide range of periods and media, with exhibits ranging from 14th-century canvases to 20th-century sculptures. Baron Heinrich Thyssen-Bornemisza donated his collection in 1993, and today the museum, with over 775 pieces, is the world's most extensive private showcase. To view the collection in chronological order and observe the evolution of styles and themes, begin on the top floor and work your way down—the organization provokes natural comparisons across centuries. The top floor is dedicated to the **Old Masters** collection, which includes such notables as Hans Holbein's austere *Portrait of Henry VIII* and El Greco's *Annunciation*. In both variety and quality, the Thyssen-Bornemisza's **Baroque** collection, including pieces by Caravaggio, José de Ribera, and Claude Lorraine, outshines that of the Prado. The **Impressionist** and **Post-Impressionist** collections explode with texture and color—look for works by Cézanne, Degas, Manet, Matisse, Monet, Pisarro, Renoir, Toulouse-Lautrec, and van Gogh. The highlight of the museum is the **20th-century** collection, on the first floor. The modern artists showcased include Chagall, Dalí, Ernst, Gorky, Hopper, Kandinsky, Klee, Léger, Miró, Mondrian, O'Keefe, Picasso, Pollack, and Rothko. *(On the corner of Po. del Prado and C. San Jerónimo. M: Banco de España. Bus #6, 14, 27, 37, or 45. ☎913 69 01 51; www.museothyssen.org. Open Su and Tu-Sa 10am-7pm. Last entrance 6:30pm. €4.80, students with ISIC and seniors €3. Under-12 free.)*

■ MUSEO NACIONAL CENTRO DE ARTE REINA SOFÍA

Since Juan Carlos I decreed this renovated hospital the national museum in 1988, the Reina Sofía's collection of **20th-century art** has grown steadily. Rooms dedicated to Juan Gris, Salvador Dalí, and Joan Miró display Spain's vital contributions to the Surrealist movement. Picasso's masterwork **Guernica** is the centerpiece of the Reina Sofía's permanent collection. It depicts the Basque town (see p. 956) bombed by the Germans at Franco's request during the Spanish Civil War. Picasso denounced the bloodshed in a huge, colorless work of contorted, agonized figures. When asked by Nazi officials whether he was responsible for this work, Picasso answered, "No, you are." He gave the canvas to New York's Museum of Modern Art on the condition that they return it to Spain when democracy was restored. The subsequent move to the Reina Sofía sparked an international controversy—Picasso's other stipulation had been that the painting hang only in the Prado, to affirm his equivalent status with artists like Titian and Velázquez. *(C. Santa Isabel 52. M: Atocha. ☎914 67 50 62 or 68 30 02; http://museoreinasofia.mcu.es. Open M and W-Sa 10am-9pm, Su 10am-2:30pm. €3, students €1.50. Sa after 2:30pm, Su, and holidays free.)*

OTHER MUSEUMS

MUSEO DE AMÉRICA. This under-appreciated museum documents the cultures of America's pre-Columbian civilizations and the legacy of the Spanish conquest. *(M: Moncloa. Av. Reyes Católicos 6, next to the Faro de Moncloa. Open Su and Tu-Sa 9:30am-3pm. €3, students €1.50. Under-18, over-65, and Su free.)*

MUSEO DE LA REAL ACADEMIA DE BELLAS ARTES DE SAN FERNANDO. An excellent collection of the Old Masters, surpassed only by the Prado. *(M: Sol. C. Alcalá 13. Open Tu-F 9am-7pm, Sa-M 9am-2:30pm. €2.50, students €1.25. W free.)*

⚑ ENTERTAINMENT

🔲 EL RASTRO (FLEA MARKET)

For hundreds of years, El Rastro has been a Sunday morning tradition in Madrid. The market begins in La Latina at Pl. Cascorro off C. Toledo and ends at the bottom of C. Ribera de Curtidores. Get lost in the insanity and the excitement as your senses become overwhelmed with sights, sounds, and smells from every direction. Seek out that souvenir you've been dying for since your first day in Madrid and haggle for it until you're blue in the face. In El Rastro you can find anything, from pots to jeans to antique tools to pet birds. As crazy as the market seems, it is actually thematically organized. The main street is a labyrinth of cheap jewelry, incense, and sunglasses, branching out into side streets, each with its own concert of vendors and wares. Antique-sellers contribute their peculiar mustiness to C. del Prado. *Tapas* bars and small restaurants line the streets and provide an air-conditioned respite for market-weary bargain-hunters. The flea market is a pickpocket's paradise, so leave your camera in your room, bust out with the money belt, or turn that backpack into a frontpack. Police are everywhere if you have any problems. *(El Rastro is open Sundays and holidays from 9am to 2pm.)*

MUSIC AND FLAMENCO

Anyone interested in live entertainment should stop by the **Círculo de Bellas Artes,** C. Alcala 42 *(M: Sevilla or Banco de España. ☎913 60 54 00; www.circulobellasartes.com).* Their magazine, *Minerva,* is indispensable. Check the *Guía del Ocio* for information on the city-sponsored movies, plays, and concerts. **Flamenco** in Madrid is tourist-oriented and expensive. A few nightlife spots are authentic, but pricey. **Casa Patas,** C. Cañizares 10, is good quality for less than usual. *(☎913 69 04 96; www.casapatas.com. M: Antón Martín.)* At **Corral de la Morería,** C. Morería 17, shows start at 9:45pm and last until 2am. *(☎913 65 84 46. M: Ópera or La Latina. Cover €30.)*

FÚTBOL

Spanish sports fans go ballistic for **fútbol** (soccer to Americans). Every Sunday and some Saturdays from September to June, one of two local teams plays at home. **Real Madrid** plays at Estadio Santiago Bernabéu, Po. Castellana 104. *(☎914 57 11 12. M: Lima.)* **Atlético de Madrid** plays at Estadio Vicente Calderón, C. Virgen del Puerto 67. *(☎913 66 47 07. M: Pirámides or Marqués de Vadillos. Tickets €18-42.)*

BULLFIGHTS

Bullfighters are either loved or loathed. So, too, are the bullfights themselves. Nevertheless, bullfights are a Spanish tradition, and locals joke that they are the only things in Spain ever to start on time. Hemingway-toting Americans and true fans of a contorted struggle between man and beast clog Pl. de las Ventas for the heart-pounding, albeit gruesome, events.

From May 15-May 22 every year, the **Fiestas de San Isidro** provide a daily *corrida* (bullfight) with top *matadores* and the fiercest bulls. The festival is nationally televised; those without tickets crowd into bars. There are also bullfights every Sunday from March to October and less frequently throughout the rest of the year. Look for posters in bars and cafes for upcoming *corridas* (especially on C. Victoria, off C. San Jerónimo). **Plaza de las Ventas,** C. de Alcalá 237, is the biggest ring in Spain. (☎913 56 22 00; *www.las-ventas.com. M: Ventas. A seat costs €5-92, depending on location in the sun (sol) or shade (sombra); shade is more expensive. Tickets are available the Friday and Saturday before and the Sunday of the bullfight.)* **Plaza de Toros Palacio de Vista Alegre,** a new ring in town, hosts bullfights and cultural events. (☎914 22 07 80. M: Vista Alegre. Call ahead for schedule and prices.) To watch amateurs, head to the **bullfighting school,** which has its own *corridas.* (☎914 70 19 90. M: Batán. Open Sa 7:30pm. Tickets €7, children €3.50.)

FESTIVALS

The city bursts with street fiestas, dancing, and processions during **Carnaval** in February, culminating on Ash Wednesday with the beginning of Lent and the burial of the Sardine in the Casa de Campo. In late April, the city bubbles with the renowned **International Theater Festival.** The Comunidad de Madrid celebrates its struggle against the French invasion of 1808 during the **Fiestas del 2 de Mayo** with bullfights and concerts. Starting May 15, the month-long **Fiestas de San Isidro** honor Madrid's patron saint with a pilgrimage to the saint's meadow, various concerts, parades, and Spain's best bullfights. At the end of June, Madrid goes mad with **Orgullo Gay** (Gay Pride). Outrageous floats filled with drag queens and muscle boys shut down traffic between El Retiro and Puerta del Sol on the Saturday of Pride Weekend. The weekend is filled with free concerts in Pl. Chueca and Pl. de Vázquez de Mella and bar crawls among the congested streets of Chueca. Throughout the summer, the city sponsors the **Veranos de la Villa,** an outstanding and varied set of cultural activities, including concerts by internationally-renowned artists of all styles, free classical music concerts, open-air movies, plays, art exhibits, an international film festival, opera, *zarzuela* (light Spanish opera), ballet, and sports. The **Festivales de Otoño** (Autumn Festivals), from September to November, also bring an impressive array of music, theater, and film. On November 1, **Todos los Santos** (All Saints' Day), an International Jazz Festival entices great musicians to Madrid. On New Year's Eve, **El Fin del Año,** crowds gather around Puerta del Sol to countdown to the new year and eat 12 *uvas* (grapes), one by one, as the clock strikes midnight. The brochure *Las Fiestas de España,* available at tourist offices and bigger hotels, contains comprehensive info on Spain's festivals.

▊ NIGHTLIFE

Spaniards average one hour less sleep a night than other Europeans, and *madrileños* claim to need even less than that. Proud of their nocturnal offerings—they'll say with a straight face that Paris or New York bored them—they don't retire until they've "killed the night" and a good part of the morning. As the sun sets, *terrazas* and *chiringuitos* (outdoor cafes/bars) spill across sidewalks. *Madrileños* start in the *tapas* bars of **Huertas,** move to the youthful scene in **Mala-**

saña, and end at the crazed parties of **Chueca** or late-night clubs of **Gran Vía**. Students fill the streets of **Bilbao** and **Moncloa**. Madrid's gay scene, centered on **Plaza Chueca**, is fantastic. Most clubs don't heat up until around 2am; don't be surprised by a line waiting outside at 5:30am. The *entrada* (cover) can be as high as €12, but usually includes a drink. Bouncers on power trips love to make examples; dress well to avoid being overcharged or denied. Women may not be charged at all.

EL CENTRO: SOL, ÓPERA, AND PLAZA MAYOR

In the middle of Madrid and at the heart of the action are the grandiose and spectacular clubs of El Centro. With multiple floors, swinging lights, cages, and disco balls, they meet even the wildest clubber's expectations. The mainstream clubs found amid these streets are often tourist hotspots; as a result, a night of fun here is the most expensive in the city. El Centro includes more territory than Madrid's other neighborhoods, so make a plan for the night and bring a map.

■ **Palacio Gaviria**, C. Arenal 9. M: Sol or Ópera. A grand red carpet leads to two huge ballrooms-turned-club-spaces with dancers and blazing light shows; it's the most exceptional of Madrid's grandiose *discotecas*. Cover €9-15. Open M-W 11pm-4am, Th 10:30pm-6am, F-Sa 11pm-6am, Su 9pm-2:30am.

Suite, Virgen de los Peligros 4, off C. de Alcalá. M: Sevilla. Classy restaurant, bar, and club boasts nouveau *tapas* by day and sleek drinks (€6) by night. Mixed crowd. Open daily 1-5pm and 8pm-3:30am.

Joy Madrid, C. del Arenal 11. M: Sol or Ópera. A well-dressed crowd parties the night away to disco, techno, and R&B on a 3-tiered dance floor. Cover Su-W €12, Th-Sa €15. Open daily 11:30pm-6am.

El Barbu, C. Santiago 3. M: Ópera. Chill to lounge music in a 3-room brick interior. Cover €8. Open June-Aug. M-Th 10:30pm-4am, F-Sa 10:30pm-5:30am; Sept.-May Tu-Sa 8pm-4am.

Kathmandú, C. de Señores de Luzón 3. Right off C. Mayor from Puerta del Sol, after Plaza Mayor and facing the Ayuntamiento. M: Ópera. Jammed with locals dancing to high-energy techno and acid jazz until the wee hours of the morning. Cover €7, includes 1 drink. Open Th midnight-5am, F-Sa midnight-6am.

■ HUERTAS

Although *madrileños* have never settled on a nickname for this neighborhood, the area between C. San Jerónimo and C. de las Huertas is generally referred to as Huertas. Once a seedy area and a Hemingway hangout, Huertas has shaped up to be a cultural hotbed of food and drink. Though quieter than El Centro, Malasaña, and Chueca, **Plaza Santa Ana, Calle del Príncipe,** and **Calle de Echegaray** offer some of the best bars in Madrid.

■ **Kapital**, C. Atocha 125. M: Atocha. *Thumba la casa* (bring down the house) on 7 floors of *discoteca* insanity. Dress to impress the bouncer. Cover €12, includes 1 drink. Mixed drinks €9. Open Th-Su midnight-6am and afternoons F–Su 5:30-11pm.

El Café de Sheherezade, C. Santa María 18. M: Antón Martín. Surrounded by Middle Eastern music and decor, groups cluster around *pipas* (pipes; €7-10) that filter sweet smoke through whiskey or water. Open in summer Su-Th 6pm-2:30am, F-Sa 6pm-3:30am; off-season Su-Th 5pm-2am, F-Sa 5pm-3am.

Ananda, Estación Atocha 2, Esq. Av. Ciudad de Barcelona. Large outdoor *terraza* equipped with multiple bars and a 20-something crowd. Check out the white room indoors for a dance. W and Su transform Ananda into a Sundance party packed with crowds to rival weekend nights. Cover €10. Mixed drinks €8. Open daily 11pm-dawn.

Cardamomo, C. de Echegaray 15. M: Sevilla. Flamenco music spins all night. A local crowd dances flamenco occasionally, but come W nights to see professionals do it. Mondays bump with Brazilian and other exotic beats. Open 9pm-4am.

No Se Lo Digas a Nadie, C. de Ventura de la Vega 7. Next to Pl. de Santa Ana. M: Sevilla. Head through the garage doors onto the packed dance floor and squeeze in some dancing along your bar crawl, or play a game of pool upstairs. Mixed drinks €3-5. Open Tu-W until 3:30am, Th-Sa until 6am.

Trocha, C. de las Huertas 55. M: Antón Martín or Sol. Come here for Brazilian *caipirinhas* (lime, mint, rum, and sugar drinks; €4.80). The delicious and potent drinks (ask for *flor de caña*) are served in a chill setting with jazz tunes and cushioned wicker couches. Open Su-Th 6pm-3am, F-Sa 6pm-4am.

GRAN VÍA

The deepest drum and bass pounds in the boisterous landmark clubs on the side streets of Gran Vía well into the early morning. Subtlety has never been a strong suit for this area, nor is it known for its safety; exercise caution as Gran Vía is less than ideal for late-night wandering.

▨ Pasapoga, Gran Vía 37. M: Callao. Around the corner from Pl. Callao. Gay nightlife explodes here on the weekends, especially on Saturdays. Beautiful interior, beautiful people. Cover €15. Open Su and Tu-Sa 6pm-dawn.

Cool, C. de Isabel la Católica 6. M: Santo Domingo. Heavenly drag performances and the occasional underworldly goth party for a wild, mixed crowd. Mesmerizing video projections. Mix of locals and tourists yell to be heard over the latest house. Special Shangay Tea Dance for primarily gay crowd on Sundays. Mixed drinks €5-8. Cover varies, usually includes 1 drink. Open F-Sa midnight-late, Su 9pm-late. With flyer before 9:30pm free.

MALASAÑA AND CHUECA

Malasaña and Chueca come to life in the early evening, especially in Pl. de Chueca and Pl. Dos de Mayo. By sunset, these plazas are social meccas: places to hang out, meet your friends, and get drunk. The area is ideal for bar-hopping until 2 or 3am, when it's time to hit the clubs near Sol, Centro, and Gran Vía.

▨ Acuarela, C. Gravina 10. M: Chueca. A welcome alternative to the club scene. Buddhas and candles surround antique furniture, inspiration for good conversation and a good buzz. Coffees and teas €2-6. Liqueur €4. Open daily 3pm-3am.

Why Not?, C. San Bartolome 7. M: Chueca. Small, downstairs bar packed almost every night of the week with a wild, mixed crowd. Open daily 10pm-6am.

El Clandestino, C. del Barquillo 34. M: Chueca. A chill 20-something crowd drinks at the bar upstairs, then heads down to the caves to nod and dance along with the DJ's acid jazz, fusion, and funk selections. Live music most Th-Sa at 11 or 11:30pm. Open M-Sa 6:30pm-3am.

Mama Ines, C. de Hortaleza 22. M: Chueca. Chic cafe/bar with perfect diva lighting. Great for drinks and conversation. Good desserts, light meals, and teas. Open Su-Th 10am-2am, F-Sa 10am-3am.

BILBAO

In the student-filled streets off **Glorieta de Bilbao**, it's easy to find a cheap drink and even easier to find someone to drink it with. Boisterous customers sip icy Mahou on **Plaza de Olavide, Calle de Fuencarral,** and **Calle de Luchana.**

El Carabinero, C. Cardenal Cisneros 33. Don't worry if you can't get a table at this festive local right away: pass the time at the bar with *sangría* and some *tapas*. *Raciones* €4.50-18. *Menú* €7.50. Open M-Sa 1-5pm and 8pm-1am. ❷

Arepas con Todo, C. Hartzenbusch 19, off C. Cardenal Cisneros from C. de Luchana. Hanging gourds and waitresses in festive dress fill this classic Colombian restaurant. A rotating *menú* (€10-12), plus 60 fixed dishes (€11-14.50). Only the live music repeats itself. For dinner, make reservations. Open daily 2pm-1am. MC/V. ❸

⚡ DAYTRIPS FROM MADRID

EL ESCORIAL. The **Monasterio de San Lorenzo del Escorial** was a gift from Felipe II to God, the people, and himself, commemorating his victory over the French at the battle of San Quintín in 1557. Near the town of **San Lorenzo,** El Escorial is filled with artistic treasures, two palaces, two pantheons, a church, and a magnificent library. Don't come on Monday, when the complex and most of the town shut down. To avoid crowds, enter via the gate on C. Floridablanca, on the west side. The adjacent **Museo de Arquitectura and Pintura** chronicles the construction of El Escorial and includes masterpieces by Bosch, El Greco, Titian, Tintoretto, Velázquez, Zurbarán, and van Dyck. The **Palacio Real,** lined with 16th-century *azulejos* (tiles), includes the majestic **Salón del Trono** (Throne Room), Felipe II's spartan 16th-century apartments, and the luxurious 18th-century rooms of Carlos III and Carlos IV. The macabre **Panteón Real** is filled with tombs of monarchs and glitters with gold-and-marble designs. (Complex ☎918 90 59 03. Open Apr.-Sept. Su-Tu-Sa 10am-6pm; Oct.-Mar. 10am-5pm. Last admission 1hr. before closing. Monastery €7, students and seniors €3.50.) Autocares Herranz **buses** arrive from Madrid's Moncloa Metro station. (50min.; every 15min. M-F 7am-11:30pm, Sa 9am-10pm, Su 9am-11pm; last return 1hr. earlier; €3.)

EL VALLE DE LOS CAÍDOS. In a valley of the Sierra de Guadarrama, Franco built the overpowering **Santa Cruz del Valle de los Caídos** (Valley of the Fallen) as a memorial to those who died during the Civil War. The granite cross was meant to honor only those who died "serving *Dios* and *España*" (ie., the Fascist Nationalists). Many of those forced to build the monument died during its construction. Beneath the high altar, underneath the cross, lies the body of Franco himself. It is accessible only via El Escorial. (Mass M-Sa 11am; Su 11am, 12:30, 1, and 5:30pm. Entrance gate open Su and Tu-Sa 10am-6pm. €5, seniors and students €2.50. EU citizens free on W. Funicular to the cross €2.50.) An Autocares Herranz **bus** runs to the monument from El Escorial, C. Juan de Toledo. (20min.; Su and Tu-Sa 3:15pm, return 5:30pm; round-trip plus admission €7.70.)

CENTRAL SPAIN

Medieval cities and olive groves fill Castilla La Mancha, the land south and east of Madrid. Castilla y León's dramatic cathedrals stand testament to its glorious history. Farther west, bordering Portugal, stark Extremadura was birthplace to hundreds of world-famous explorers.

CASTILLA LA MANCHA

Although Castilla La Mancha is one of Spain's least-developed regions, you don't need Don Quixote's imagination to fall in love with this battered, windswept plateau; its austere beauty surfaces through its tumultuous history, gloomy medieval fortresses, and awesome crags.

TOLEDO

☎ 925

Cossío called Toledo (pop. 66,000) "the most brilliant and evocative summary of Spain's history." Today, the city may be marred by armies of tourists and caravans of kitsch, but this former capital of the Holy Roman, Visigoth, and Muslim empires remains a treasure trove of Spanish culture. The city's numerous churches, synagogues, and mosques share twisting alleyways, emblematic of a time when Spain's three religions coexisted peacefully.

▇▇ TRANSPORTATION AND PRACTICAL INFORMATION

Trains: Po. Rosa 2 (RENFE info ☎902 24 02 02), in an exquisite neo-Mudéjar station just over the Puente de Azarquiel. 1 line to Madrid to either **Atocha** or **Chamartin** (1-1½hr., 9-10 per day, €5-5.50), usually via Aranjuez (35min., 8-9 per day, €2.50).

Buses: Av. Castilla-La Mancha (☎925 21 58 50), 5min. from **Puerta de Bisagra**, the city gate. From Pl. de Zocodóver, take C. Armas and its extension to Puerta de Bisagra; as you exit the old city turn right following Ronda de Granada l to the next traffic circle. Just before the bridge, take a left, and the station is straight ahead (15-20min. walk). Information booth open daily 7am-11pm. Despite multiple companies, destinations are few. **Continental-Auto** (in Toledo ☎925 22 36 41; in Madrid ☎915 27 29 61) runs to **Madrid-Estación Sur** (1½hr., every 30min., €4). **Alsina** (in Toledo ☎925 21 58 50; in Valencia ☎963 49 72 30) goes to **Valencia** (5½hr., M-F 3pm, €17).

Public Transportation: Buses #5 and 6 get you to and from several city points, mainly the bus and train stations and the central **Plaza de Zocodóver.** Buses stop to the right of the train station, underneath and across the street from the bus station (€0.80).

Taxis: Radio Taxi and **Gruas de Toledo** (☎925 25 50 50 or 925 22 70 70.)

Tourist Office: The **regional office** (☎925 22 08 43; fax 925 25 26 48) is just outside Puerta Nueva de Bisagra, on the north side of town. From Pl. de Zocodóver, take C. Armas downhill and through the Puerta de Bisagra gates. The office is across the intersection (10min.). From the train station, turn right and take the busy right-hand fork across the bridge (Puente de Azarquiel), following the city walls until you reach the second traffic circle; the office is across the road, outside the walls. English-speaking staff offers handy maps. Open July-Sept. M-Sa 9am-7pm, Su 9am-3pm; Oct.-June M-F 9am-6pm, Sa 9am-7pm, Su 9am-3pm.

Emergency: ☎112. **Police:** ☎092, where Av. Reconquista and Av. Carlos III meet.

Internet Access: Options are extremely limited, but access is available at **Zococentro,** C. Silleria 14 (☎925 22 03 00), located just off Pl. de Zocodóver. Open summer 10:30am-7pm; off-season until 6pm.

▇ ACCOMMODATIONS

Toledo is chock-full of accommodations, but finding a bed during the summer can be a hassle, especially on weekends. Reservations are strongly recommended, especially during the summer. Last-minute planners should try the tourist office for help. There are several camping grounds around Toledo. Out of town sites bring quiet and shade, while those in town trade convenience for noise.

▓ **Residencia Juvenil San Servando (HI),** on Castillo San Servando (☎925 22 45 54), uphill from the train station. Sits inside a 14th-century castle. Dorms €11, under-26 €8.50. Members only. ❶

Hostal Centro, C. Nueva 13 (☎925 25 70 91), toward C. Comercio on Pl. de Zocodóver. Offers clean, spacious rooms in a central location. Singles €30; doubles €42; triples €60. MC/V. ❸

Toledo

ACCOMMODATIONS
Hostal Centro, 9
Hostal Descalzos, 1
Pensión Castilla, 7
Pensión Nuncio Viejo, 3
Residencia Juvenil San
Servando (HI), 11

FOOD
La Abadía, 6
Market, 5
Pastucci, 4
Restaurante-Mesón
Palacios, 2

NIGHTLIFE
Enebro, 10
O'Brien's Irish Pub, 8

SPAIN

Pensión Castilla, C. Recoletos 6 (☎925 25 63 18). From Pl. de Zocodóver, take C. Armas downhill, then the first left. Clean, basic rooms in a great location. Singles €15; doubles with bath €25. ❷

Hostal Descalzos, C. Descalzos 30 (☎925 22 28 88). Down the steps off Po. del Tránsito, near the Sinagoga del Tránsito. Recently refurbished, with stunning views. Apr.-Oct. singles €30-42; doubles €47-53. Oct.-Mar. €25-36/40-45. MC/V. ❸

Pensión Nuncio Viejo, C. Nuncio Viejo 19, 3rd fl. (☎925 22 81 78). 7 rooms close to the cathedral are cramped, but bright and clean. The motherly owner is a great cook. Breakfast €1.50. Other meals €7.50. Singles €19; doubles €30, with bath €34. ❷

Camping El Greco (☎925 22 00 90), 1.5km from town on Ctra. CM-4000, km0.7. Bus #7 (from Pl. de Zocodóver) stops at the entrance. Shady, wooded site. Open year-round. €4.40 per person, €4.24 per tent, €4.24 per car. IVA not included. ❶

 FOOD

Toledo grinds almonds into marzipan of every shape and size, from colorful fruity nuggets to half-moon cookies; *pastelería* windows beckon on every corner. Alternatively, grab fresh fruit and the basics at **Alimentación Pantoja,** C. Arrabal 30, inside the Puerta de Bisagra and across from the tourist office. (Open June-Aug. M-Sa 9am-11pm, Su 9am-3pm; Sept.-May M-Sa 9am-10pm, Su 9am-3pm.) The **market** is in Plaza Mayor, behind the cathedral. (Open M-Sa 9am-8pm.)

La Abadía, Pl. San Nicolás 3 (☎925 25 11 40). Dine in a maze of cave-like, underground rooms. The delicious lunch *menú* is a steal (€8.50). Open M-Th 8am-12:30am, F 8am-1:30am, Sa-Su noon-1:30am. AmEx/MC/V. ❸

Pastucci, C. Sinagoga 10 (☎925 25 77 42). From Pl. de Zocodóver take C. Comercio through the underpass. Pastas €5.50-8. Small pizza €6.10-8.50. Open in summer M-Th 12:15pm-midnight, F-Su noon-4pm and 8pm-midnight; off-season noon-4pm and 7pm-midnight. 10% discount with a *Let's Go* guide. MC/V. ❶

Restaurante-Mesón Palacios, C. Alfonso X El Sabio 3 (☎925 21 59 72), off C. Nuncio Viejo. Two daily *menús* (€6-11). Try Toledo's famous partridge dish. Entrees €4-12. Open M-Sa 1-4pm and 7-11pm, Su noon-4pm. Closed Su in Aug. AmEx/MC/V. ❷

 SIGHTS

Toledo's vast collection of museums, churches, synagogues, and mosques make the city impossible to see in one day. Within the fortified walls, Toledo's attractions form a belt around its middle. There is an east-west tour beginning in Pl. Zocodóver. Most sights are closed Mondays.

CATHEDRAL. Built between 1226 and 1498, Toledo's cathedral boasts five naves, delicate stained glass, and unapologetic ostentation. Noteworthy pieces include the 14th-century Gothic *Virgen Blanca* by the entrance, El Greco's *El Espolio*, and Narciso Tomés's *Transparente*, a Spanish-Baroque whirlpool of architecture, sculpture, and painting. In the **Capilla Mayor,** the massive Gothic altarpiece stretches to the ceiling. The tomb of Cardinal Mendoza, founder of the Spanish Inquisition, lies to the left. Beneath the dome is the **Capilla Mozárabe,** the only place where the ancient Visigoth Mass (in Mozarabic) is still held. The **treasury** flaunts interesting ornamentation, including a replica of one of Columbus's ships and a 400-pound, 16th-century gold monstrosity lugged through the streets during the annual Corpus Christi procession. The **sacristy** is home to 18 El Grecos and two Van Dycks, along with a portrait of every archbishop of Toledo. The red hats hanging from the ceiling mark cardinals's tombs. *(At Arco de Palacio, up C. Comercio from Pl. de Zocodóver.* ☎*925 22 22 41. Cathedral open daily 10am-noon and 4-6pm. The cathedral is free, but it's worth the extra money to see the sacristy and the capillas, open June-Aug. M-Sa 10:30am-6:30pm, Su 2-6pm; Sept.-May M-Sa 10:30am-6pm, Su 2-6pm. €5. €2.70 for the audio guide available in English, French, and Italian. Tickets sold at the store opposite the entrance. Modest dress required.)*

■ **ALCÁZAR.** Toledo's most formidable landmark, the Alcázar served as a military stronghold for the Romans, Visigoths, Moors, and Spaniards. Much of the building was reduced to rubble during the Civil War, when Fascist troops used it as their refuge. Don't miss the room detailing Colonel Moscardó's refusal to surrender the Alcázar, even at the cost of his son's life. Visit the dark, windowless basement refuge where over 500 civilians hid during the siege. The rooms above ground have been turned into a national military museum complete with armor, swords, guns, knives, and comparatively benign dried plants. *(Cuesta Carlos V 2, a block down from Pl. de Zocodóver.* ☎*925 22 16 73. Open Tu-Su 9:30am-2:30pm. €2. Free W.)*

EL GRECO. Greek painter Doménikos Theotokópoulos, commonly known as El Greco, spent most of his life in Toledo. Some of his works are displayed throughout town, but the majority of his masterpieces have been carted off to the Prado and other big-name museums. On the west side of town, the **Iglesia de Santo Tomé** houses his famous **El entierro del Conde de Orgaz** (*The Burial of Count Orgaz*). The stark figure staring out from the back is El Greco himself, and the boy is his son, Jorge Manuel, who built Toledo's city hall. *(Pl. Conde 1.* ☎*925 25 60 98. Open daily Mar.-Oct. 15 10am-6:45pm; Oct.16-Feb. 10am-5:45pm. €1.50.)* Downhill and to the left lies the **Casa Museo de El Greco,** which contains 19 works, including a copy of the detailed *Vista y plano de Toledo.* *(C. Samuel Leví 2.* ☎*925 22 40 46. Open Tu-Sa 10am-2pm and 4-6pm, Su 10am-2pm. €2.40. Students, under-18, and over-65 free. Sa-Su afternoons free.)* Outside handsome Puerta Nueva de Bisagra, the 16th-century **Hospital de Tavera** displays five El Grecos as well as several works by his mentor, Titian. *(C. Duque de Lerma 2.* ☎*925 22 04 51. Near the tourist office. Open daily 10:30am-1:30pm and 3:30-6pm. €3.10.)*

THE OLD JEWISH QUARTER. Only two of Toledo's many synagogues have been preserved. Samuel Ha Leví, diplomat and treasurer to Pedro el Cruel, built the **Sinagoga del Tránsito** (1366). Its simple exterior hides an ornate sanctuary with Mudéjar plasterwork and an *artesonado* (intricately designed wood) ceiling. The Hebrew-inscripted walls are mostly taken from the Psalter. Inside, the **Museo Sefardí** is packed with artifacts, including a Torah (parts of which are over 400 years old) and a beautiful set of Sephardic wedding costumes. *(C. Samuel Leví.* ☎*925 22 36 65. Closed for renovations in summer 2003; call ahead. Open Tu-Sa 10am-2pm and 4-6pm, Su 10am-2pm. €2.40, students and under-18 €1.20. Free Sa after 4pm and Su.)* **Sinagoga de Santa María la Blanca,** down the street to the right, was originally built to be a mosque, but was then purchased by Jews and used as the city's principal synagogue; in the early 16th century, it was converted into a church. Now secular, its Moorish arches and tranquil garden make for a pleasant retreat. *(C. Reyes Católicos 2.* ☎*925 22 72 57. Open June-Aug. daily 10am-2pm and 3:30-7pm; Sept.-May 10am-2pm and 3:30-6pm. €1.50.)*

MONASTERIO DE SAN JUAN DE LOS REYES. At the far western edge of the city stands the Franciscan Monasterio, commissioned by Isabella and Ferdinand to commemorate their victory over the Portuguese in the Battle of Toro (1476). The cloister, covered with the initials of the *Reyes Católicos*, melds Gothic and Mudéjar architecture. The Catholic monarchs planned to use the church as their burial place but changed their minds after the victory over Granada. *(*☎*925 22 38 02. Open Apr.-Sept. daily 10am-1:45pm and 3:30-6:45pm; Oct.-Mar. 10am-2pm and 3:30-6pm. €1.50.)*

OTHER SIGHTS. Toledo was the seat of Visigoth rule and culture for three centuries prior to the 711 Muslim invasion. The **Museo del Taller del Moro**, on C. Bulas near Iglesia de Santo Tomé, features outstanding woodwork, plasterwork, and tiles. *(C. Taller de Moro 3. ☎925 22 71 15. Open Tu-Sa 10am-2pm and 4-6:30pm, Su 10am-2pm. €0.60.)* The exhibits at the **Museo de los Concilios y de la Cultura Visigótica** pale in comparison to their beautiful setting in a 13th-century Mudéjar church. *(C. San Clemente 4. ☎925 22 78 72. Open Tu-Sa 10am-2pm and 4-6:30pm, Su 10am-2pm. €0.60, students €0.30.)* The impressive and untouristed **Museo de Santa Cruz** (1504) exhibits a handful of works by El Greco in its eclectic art collection, which also includes the remains from archeological digs throughout the province. *(C. Cervantes 3, off Pl. de Zocodóver. ☎925 22 10 36. Open Tu-Sa 10am-6:30pm, Su 10am-2pm. €1.20.)*

▓ NIGHTLIFE

For nightlife, head through the arch and to the left from Pl. Zocodóver to **Calle Santa Fé,** which brims with beer and local youth. **Enebro,** on Pl. Santiago Balleros off C. Cervantes, serves free *tapas* in the evenings. (Open daily 11am-4pm and 7pm-1:30am.) For more upscale bars and clubs, try **Calle Sillería** and **Calle Alfileritos,** west of Pl. de Zocodóver. **O'Brien's Irish Pub,** C. Armas 12 has live music on Thursdays. (Open Su-Th noon-2:30am, F-Sa noon-4am.)

CUENCA ☎969

Cuenca (pop. 50,000) is a hilltop city flanked by two rivers and the stunning rock formations they created. The enchanting ▓**old city** safeguards most of Cuenca's unique charm, including the famed *casas colgadas* (hanging houses) that dangle high above the Río Huécar, on C. Obispo Vaero off Plaza Mayor. Cross the San Pablo bridge to **Hoz del Huécar** for a spectacular view of the *casas* and cliffs. Many of the *casas* house museums; on Pl. Ciudad de Ronda is the excellent **Museo de Arte Abstracto Español.** (Open Tu-F 11am-2pm and 4-6pm, Sa 11am-2pm and 4-8pm, Su 11am-2pm. €3, students and seniors €1.50.) The perfectly square **Cathedral de Cuenca** sits in the Plaza Mayor. (Open daily 9am-2pm and 4-6pm. Free.)

Trains (☎902 24 02 02) run to Madrid (2½-3hr., 5-6 per day, €9) and Valencia (3-4hr., 3-4 per day, €10). **Buses** (☎22 70 87) depart from C. Fermín Caballero for: Barcelona (9hr., 1-2 per day, €30); Madrid (2½hr., 8-9 per day, €8.20-11); and Toledo (2½hr., 3 per day, €10). To get to Plaza Mayor from either station take a left onto C. Fermín Caballero, following it as it becomes C. Cervantes and C. José Cobo and then bearing left through Pl. Hispanidad. The **tourist office** is in Plaza Mayor. (☎23 21 19; www.aytocuenca.org. Open July-Sept. M-Sa 9am-9pm, Su 9am-2pm; Oct.-June M-Sa 9am-2pm and 4-6pm, Su 9am-2pm.) ▓**Posada de San José ❷,** C. Julián Romero 4, a block up from the left side of the cathedral, has gorgeous views and a friendly staff. (☎21 13 00. July-Nov. and F-Sa year-round singles €20, with bath €41; doubles €31/61; triples with sink €42; quads with bath €97. *Semana Santa* increased prices; off-season reduced prices.) To reach **Pensión Tabanqueta ❸,** C. Trabuco 13, head up C. San Pedro from the cathedral past Pl. Trabuco. (☎21 12 90. Singles €12; doubles €24; triples €36.) Budget eateries line **Calle Cervantes** and **Calle República Argentina.** Grab groceries at %**Día,** on Av. Castilla La Mancha and Av. República Argentina. (Open M-Th 9:30am-2pm and 5:30-8:30pm, F-Sa 9am-2:30pm and 5:30-9pm.) **Postal Code:** 16004.

CASTILLA Y LEÓN

Castilla y León's cities rise like green oases from a desert of burnt sienna. The aqueduct of Segovia, the majestic Gothic cathedrals of Burgos and León, the slender Romanesque belfries along Camino de Santiago, the sandstone of Salamanca, and the city walls of Ávila have emblazoned themselves as regional and national images.

SEGOVIA ☎921

Legend has it that the devil built Segovia's (pop. 56,000) famed aqueduct in one night, in an effort to win the soul of a Segovian water-seller named Juanilla. Devil or not, Segovia's attractions and winding alleyways entice their share of Spanish and international tourists, as well as students seeking to practice their *español*. In the 12th and 13th centuries, Segovia had more Romanesque monuments than anywhere else in Europe. Today, its remaining cathedrals and castles represent Castilla at its finest—a labyrinthine town of twisted alleys and old-town charm. However, pleasure has its price: food and accommodations are more expensive than in Madrid. In the Sierra de Guadarrama, 88km northwest of Madrid, Segovia is close enough to the capital to be a daytrip but definitely warrants a longer stay.

▋⚡ **TRANSPORTATION AND PRACTICAL INFORMATION. Trains** (☎921 42 07 74), Po. Obispo Quesada, run to Madrid (2hr.; 7-9 per day M-F 5:55am-8:55pm, Sa-Su 8:55am-8:55pm; €5). **Buses** run from Estacionamiento Municipal de Autobuses, Po. Ezequiel González 12, at the corner of Av. Fernández Ladreda. **La Sepulvedana** (☎921 42 77 07) sends buses to Madrid (1½hr.; M-F every 30min. 6am-9:30pm, Sa 7:30am-9:30pm, Su 8:30am-10:30pm; €6). **Linecar** (☎921 42 77 06) sends buses to Salamanca (3hr.; 4 per day M-F 8:50am-5:45pm; Sa 8:50am, 1:30, 5:45pm; Su 5:45pm; €8.50). From the train station, take any bus (€.70) to the **Plaza Mayor,** the city's historic center and site of the regional **tourist office.** Segovia is impossible to navigate without a map, so pick one up here. (Open June-Aug. Su-Th 9am-8pm, F-Sa 9am-9pm; Sept.-May M-F 9am-2pm and 5-7pm, Sa-Su 9am-2pm and 5-8pm.) The Po. del Salón **bus** (M-F every 30min. 7:45am-10:15pm) runs directly to the steps of **Puerta del Sol.** To access the **Internet,** try **Locutorio Mundo 2000,** Pl. de Azoguejo 4, between Horno de Asar and the Jimena clothing store. (€0.90 per 30min., €1 per 1 hr. Open daily 11am-11pm.)

▋▐ **ACCOMMODATIONS AND FOOD.** Reservations are a must for any of Segovia's hotels, especially those in or around major plazas. Budget travelers should prepare to pay €21 or more for a single and arrive early to ensure space. The pensiones are significantly cheaper, but rooms tend to be on the less comfortable side of "basic." To reach ▌**Hospedaje El Gato ❷,** Pl. del Salvador 10, which has beautiful rooms and individual bathrooms, TV, and A/C, follow the aqueduct up the hill, turning left on C. Ochoa Ondategui; it meets San Alfonso Rodríguez which leads into Pl. del Salvador. (☎921 42 32 44; fax 921 43 80 47. Doubles €35; triples €49.) **Hotel Las Sirenas ❸,** C. Juan Bravo 30, down C. Cervantes, has luxurious rooms with TV, shower, telephone, and A/C. (☎921 46 26 63; fax 921 46 26 57. Singles €36-45, with bath €42-50; doubles with bath €55-65. AmEx/MC/V.) For a fortifying experience, try the stone walls and rustic rooms of the **Pensión Ferri ❶,** C. Escuderos 10, off the Plaza Mayor. (☎921 46 09 57. Showers €2. Singles €13; doubles €19.) From Pl. Azoguejo, follow the aqueduct down C. Teodosio and turn left; around the bend and up the slope is **Hostal Don Jaíme ❷,** Ochoa Ondátegui 8. This *hostal* has rooms with wood paneling and large mirrors. (☎921 44 47 87. Singles €22, with bath €30; doubles with bath €40; triples with bath €50. MC/V.) **Camping**

Acueducto ❶, C. Borbón 49/Ctra. Nacional 601, km 112, is 2km toward La Granja. Take the AutoBus Urbano (€0.65) from Pl. Azoguejo to Nueva Segovia. (☎/fax 921 42 50 00. Open *Semana Santa*-Sept. €4.30 per person, per tent, and per car.)

Sample Segovia's famed lamb, *cochinillo asado* (roast suckling pig), or *sopa castellana* (soup with bread, eggs, and garlic), but steer clear of pricey Plaza Mayor and Pl. Azoguejo. Buy groceries at **%Día,** C. Gobernador Fernández Giménez 3, off C. Fernández Ladreda. (Open M-Th 9:30am-8:30pm, F-Sa 9am-9pm). At the casual but classy ⊠**Bar-Meson Cueva de San Esteban ❸,** C. Vadelaguila 15, off Pl. Esteban and C. Escuderos, the owner knows his wines, and the service is friendly. (☎ 921 46 09 82. Lunch *menús* M-F €8, Sa-Su €10. Entrees €7-14. Wines €1-3. Open daily 10am-midnight. MC/V.) At ⊠**Mesón El Cordero ❸,** C. del Carmen 4-6, spreads of wine, meats, and other specials are a feast for the eyes and the stomach. (Selection of *menús* from €9. Entrees €9-15. Open M-Sa 12:30-4:30pm and 8pm-midnight, Su 12-6pm.) For tasty vegetarian options (€3.60-9) as well as meat entrees (€6-10), try **Restaurante La Almuzara ❷,** C. Marqués del Arco 3, past the cathedral. (Open Tu 8pm-midnight, W-Su 12:45-4pm and 8pm-midnight.)

◎ 🎵 **SIGHTS AND ENTERTAINMENT.** Segovia rewards the wanderer. Its picturesque museums, palaces, churches, and streets beg closer observation. The serpentine ⊠**Roman aqueduct,** built in 50 BC, commands the entrance to the old city. Supported by 128 pillars that span 813m and reach a height of 29m near Pl. Azoguejo, the two tiers of 163 arches were constructed out of some 20,000 blocks of granite—without any mortar to hold them together. This spectacular feat of engineering, restored by the monarchy in the 15th century, can transport 30 liters of water per second and was used until the late 1940s. The **cathedral,** commissioned by Carlos V in 1525, towers over the Plaza Mayor. Inside, the **Sala Capitular,** nicknamed "The Lady of all Cathedrals," displays intricate tapestries. (Open Apr.-Oct. daily 9am-6:30pm; Nov.-Mar. 9:30am-6pm. €2.) The **Alcázar,** a late-medieval castle and site of Isabel's coronation in 1474, dominates the northern end of the old quarter. In the **Sala de Solio** (throne room), an inscription reads: *Tanto monta, monta tanto* ("she mounts, as does he"). Get your mind out of the gutter—this simply means that Ferdinand and Isabella had equal authority as sovereigns. The 140 steps up a nausea-inducing spiral staircase to the top of the **Torre de Juan II** (80m high) afford a marvelous view of Segovia and the surrounding plains.

Though the city isn't particularly known for its sleepless nights, native Segovians know how to party. Packed with bars and cafes, the **Plaza Mayor** is the center of nightlife. Club headquarters are on **Calle Ruiz de Alda,** off Pl. Azoguejo. You can count on a party every night at **La Luna,** C. Puerta de la Luna 8, where a young crowd downs cheap shots and Heineken. (Shots €1. Beer €1.50. Open daily 4:30pm-4am.) From June 24-29, Segovia celebrates a **fiesta,** complete with free open-air concerts, dances, and fireworks, in honor of San Juan and San Pedro.

🗲**DAYTRIP FROM SEGOVIA: LA GRANJA DE SAN ILDEFONSO.** The royal palace and grounds of **La Granja,** 9km southeast of Segovia, were commissioned by Philip V, the first Bourbon King. Of the four royal summer retreats (the others being El Pardo, El Escorial, and Aranjuez), this "Versailles of Spain" is by far the most extravagant. Marble, lace curtains, lavish crystal chandeliers, and a world-class collection of Flemish tapestries enliven the palace, while manicured gardens and a forest envelop it. (Open daily Apr.-Sept. Tu-Su 10am-6pm; Oct.-Mar. Tu-Sa 10am-1:30pm and 3-5pm, Su 10am-2pm. €5, students and EU seniors €2.50. W free for EU citizens. Mandatory guided tours in Spanish depart every 15min.) **Buses** run to La Granja from Segovia (20min., 9-12 per day, round-trip €1.50).

SALAMANCA ☎923

For centuries, the gates of Salamanca (pop. 152,600) have welcomed scholars, saints, rogues, and royals. The bustling city is famed for its exquisite silver filigree and golden sandstone architecture as well as its university—the oldest in Spain, and once one of the "four leading lights of the world" along with the universities of Bologna, Paris, and Oxford.

▐▛ TRANSPORTATION AND PRACTICAL INFORMATION

Trains run from Po. de la Estación (☎902 24 02 02) to Lisbon (6hr., 4:50am, €35) and Madrid (2½hr., 5-6 per day 6am-7:50pm, €14). **Buses** run from Av. Filiberto Villalobos 71-85 (☎923 23 67 17) to: León (2½hr.; M-F 3 per day 11am-6:30pm, Sa 11am, Su 10pm; €11); Madrid (3hr., M-Sa 16 per day, €10-15); and Segovia (3hr., 2 per day, €9). Visit the **tourist office** at Plaza Mayor 32. (☎923 21 83 42. Open M-Sa 9am-2pm and 4:30-6:30pm, Su 10am-2pm and 4:30-6:30pm.) Access the **Internet** at **CiberPlaza,** Plaza Mayor 10. (Open daily 10:30am-2am. 10:30am-9pm €1.20 per hr., 9pm-2am €0.90 per hr.)

▐ ACCOMMODATIONS

Reasonably priced *hostales* and *pensiones* cater to the floods of student visitors, especially off Plaza Mayor and C. Meléndez.

Pensión Las Vegas, C. Meléndez 13, 1st fl. (☎923 21 87 49). Friendly owners. Singles with shower €18; doubles €24, with bath €30-36; triples with bath €45. MC/V.) ❷

Pensión Villanueva, C. San Justo 8, 1st fl. (☎923 26 88 33). Sra. Manuela shares local lore and gossip. Exit Plaza Mayor via Pl. Poeta Iglesias, cross the street, and take the first left. Singles €13; doubles €26. ❶

Hostal Anaya, C. Jesús 18, steps away from Plaza Mayor (☎923 27 17 73). Clean rooms, heating, and friendly service. Singles €24; doubles with shared bath €36, with private bath €42; triples €54; quads €72. ❷

Pension Los Angeles, Plaza Mayor 10, 2nd and 3rd fl. (☎923 21 81 66). Unbeatable location right in Plaza Mayor. English spoken. Singles €15-16; doubles €28-30, with bath €30-32; triples €45. ❷

Pensión Lisboa, C. Meléndez 1 (☎923 21 43 33). Pink stucco walls in rooms with sinks, some with rooftop city views. Singles €16; doubles €32. ❶

Hostal Emperatriz, R. Mayor 16 (☎/fax 923 21 87 83). This hostel operates out of the 2-star hotel next door. To register, go to the hotel lobby. Spacious rooms include full bathroom and telephone. Singles €24; doubles €33; triples €44. ❷

Hotel Emperatriz, R. Mayor 18 (☎923 21 91 56). Offers well-lit rooms replete with medieval charm. Singles €36; doubles €51. ❹

Camping: Regio on Ctra. Salamanca (☎923 13 88 88), 4km toward Madrid. Albertur buses run from Gran Vía every 30min. First-class sites with hot showers. €3 per person, €5.50 per tent, and €2.90 per car. MC/V. ❶

▐ FOOD

Cafes and restaurants surround **Plaza Mayor,** where three course meals run about €8. **Champion,** C. Toro 64, has a supermarket. (Open M-Sa 9:15am-9:15pm.)

El Patio Chico, C. Meléndez 13 (☎923 26 51 03). Crowded at lunch and dinner, but the large and delicious portions are worth the wait. *Menú* €11. Entrees €4-8. *Bocadillos* €2-3. Open daily 1-4pm and 8pm-midnight. ❷

Mesón Las Conchas, R. Mayor 16 (☎923 21 21 67). The quintessential *bar español*. *Menú* €11. *Raciones* €6-14. Open daily 1-4pm and 8pm-midnight. MC/V. ❸

La Fábrica, C. Libreros 47 and 49 (☎923 26 85 69), directly across from the University's library. With wooden floors and 80s music, La Fábrica is popular among students. *Menú* €8.50, *bocadillos* €3-6. Open M-F 9am-2am, Sa-Su 9am-4am. ❷

Restaurante El Bardo, C. Compañía 8 (☎923 21 90 89), between the Casa de Conchas and the Clerecía. Traditional Spanish food and low prices keep the tiled tables full. *Menú* €9. Entrees €6-13. Open daily 1:30-4pm and 9-11:30pm. MC/V. ❷

Restaurante Isidro, Pozo Amarillo 19 (☎923 26 28 48), a block from Plaza Mayor. Prompt, courteous service and large portions. *Menú* €8.40. Entrees €3-9. Open daily 1-4pm and 8pm-midnight. MC/V. ❷

◉ SIGHTS

■ **PLAZA MAYOR.** Salamanca's Plaza Mayor, designed by Alberto Churriguera, has been called one of the most beautiful squares in Spain. Hundreds of tables ring the center, where street performers and musicians entertain and couples stroll hand in hand. Shaped from the majestic sandstone that pervades Salamanca's architecture, the plaza appears golden under the afternoon sun or when the lights come up to collective gasps of admiration at night. Built between 1729 and 1755, the plaza contains 88 towering arches, the **Ayuntamiento,** and three pavilions dedicated to historical figures. The **Pabellón Real,** to the right of the Ayuntamiento, honors the Spanish monarchy, including the controversial 20th-century dictator Franco; the **Pabellón del Sur,** in front of the Ayuntamiento, is dedicated to famous Spanish conquistadors; and the **Pabellón del Oeste,** to the left of the Ayuntamiento, pays homage to important *salmantinos* like San Juan de Sahagún, Santa Teresa, Unamuno, and Cervantes, who studied at the city's university. Before the pavilions were built, the square served as the town bullring; today, more wide-eyed tourist groups than bulls flood the plaza.

■ **THE UNIVERSITY.** The great university, established in 1218, is the focal point of Salamanca. Best entered from C. Libreros, the university's entryway is one of the greatest examples of Spanish Plateresque, a style named for the delicate filigree work of *plateros* (silversmiths). The central medallion represents Ferdinand and Isabella, while the one up higher is generally thought to represent the Pope. Hidden in the sculptural work lies a tiny frog; according to legend, those who can spot the frog without assistance will be blessed with good luck and even marriage.

The old lecture halls inside are open to the public; entering the cool stone foyer feels like stepping into another era. The **Paraninfo** (auditorium) contains Baroque tapestries and a portrait of Carlos IV attributed to Goya. Along with red curtains, red velvet chairs, and a red altar, the 18th-century **chapel** contains the burial sight of Fray Luis de León. Located on the second floor atop a magnificent Plateresque staircase is the spectacular **Antigua Biblioteca,** one of Europe's oldest libraries. The staircase is generally thought to represent the ascent of the young student through playfulness, *amor*, and adventure to the true love of knowledge.

Facing the university entrance is the **Patio de las Escuelas,** which contains a statue of Fray Luis, a university professor and one of the most respected literati of the Golden Age. A Hebrew scholar and classical Spanish stylist, Fray

Luis was arrested by the Inquisition for translating Solomon's *Song of Songs* into Castilian and for preferring the Hebrew version of the Bible to the Latin one. After five years of imprisonment, he returned to the university and began his first lecture, *"Como decíamos ayer..."* ("As we were saying yesterday..."). Don't miss the **University Museum**, which is through the hallway on the left corner of the patio. The reconstructed **Cielo de Salamanca**, the library's famous 15th-century fresco of the zodiac painted on the ceiling by the celebrated Fernando Gallego, is preserved here in all its splendor. Take a peek at the intricate strongbox with its many locks. *(From Plaza Mayor follow R. Mayor, veer right onto R. Antigua, then left onto C. Libreros; the university is on the left. University ☎ 923 29 44 00. Museum ☎ 923 29 12 25. Open M-F 9:30am-1:30pm and 4-7:30pm, Sa 9:30am-1:30pm and 4-7pm, Su 10am-1:30pm. University and museum €2.40, students and seniors €1.20.)*

CATEDRAL NUEVA. It took 220 years to build this striking Gothic Spanish building (1513-1733). Its architects combined the original late Gothic style with touches from later periods, most notably to its Baroque tower, one of the tallest in Spain. Inside, the cathedral is separated into several small chapels that are dedicated to various saints or important locals. The chapels surround a center chapel and an enormous organ, whose pipes rise up toward the high ceiling. The cathedral was recently renovated, and the architects left their marks: Look for the astronaut and a dragon eating an ice cream cone on the left side of the main door. *(From Plaza Mayor, walk down R. Mayor into Pl. Anaya; the Catedral Nueva will be in front of you. Open Apr.-Sept. daily 9am-2pm and 4-8pm; Oct.-Mar. 9am-1pm and 4-6pm. Free.)*

CATEDRAL VIEJA. The smaller Catedral Vieja (1140) was built in the Romanesque style. The cupola, assembled from intricately carved miniature pieces, is one of the most detailed in Spain. Above the high altar, apocalyptic angels separate the sinners from the saved. The oldest original part of the cathedral is the **Capilla de San Martín**, with brilliant frescoes dating from 1242. Look for the image of the Virgen de la Vega, Salamanca's patron saint. The **museum** features a paneled ceiling by Fernando Gallego and houses the Mudéjar Salinas organ, one of the oldest in Europe. Be sure to check out the famed **Patio Chico**, behind the cathedral, where students congregate to chat and play music. It offers splendid views of both cathedrals. *(Enter through the Catedral Nueva. Museum ☎ 923 21 74 76. Cathedral open Apr.-Sept. daily 10am-1:30pm and 4-7:30pm. Cathedral, cloister, and museum €3, students €2.25, children €1.50.)*

CASA LIS MUSEO ART NOUVEAU Y ART DECO. Salamancan industrialist Miguel de Lis collaborated with modernist architect Joaquín Vargas to design the building, which now showcases Lis's eclectic art collection. Exhibits range from the elegant (fans signed by such noteworthies as Salvador Dalí) to the odd (porcelain dolls with two faces), to the racy (small sculptures of animals and people in compromising positions). *(C. Gibraltar 14, behind the cathedrals. ☎ 923 12 14 25. Open Apr.-Oct. 15 Tu-F 11am-2pm and 5-9pm, Sa-Su 11am-9pm; Oct. 16-Mar. Tu-F 11am-2pm and 4-7pm, Sa-Su 11am-8pm. €2.10, students €1.50. Children and Tu mornings free.)*

CASA DE LAS CONCHAS. From Plaza Mayor, follow R. Mayor until you reach a plaza with a water fountain. Take a right, and then take a gander at the 15th-century Casa de las Conchas (House of Shells), with over 300 large scallop halves, one of Salamanca's most famous landmarks. Pilgrims who journeyed to Santiago de Compostela wore shells to commemorate their visit to the tomb of St. James. According to legend, the owner of the *casa* created this monument either to honor the renowned pilgrimage or to honor his wife, whose family shield was decorated with scallops. Legend has it that when the Jesuits leveled every house in the area to build the college, the Casa de las Conchas was the only one that was not bought, despite the Jesuits's offer of one gold coin for every sandstone shell. The building now serves as a public library and houses the provincial tourist office. *(C. Compañía 39. Library ☎923 26 93 17. Open M-F 9am-9pm, Sa-Su 9am-2pm and 4-7pm. Free.)*

PUENTE ROMANO. This 2000-year-old Roman bridge, spanning the scenic Río Tormes at the edge of the city, was once part of an ancient Roman road called the *Camino de la Plata* (Silver Way). The *Camino* ran from Mérida in Extremadura to Astorga and was heavily traveled during the Roman occupation of Spain. In medieval times, the *Camino* was the route most Andalucian and Castilian Christians took to complete their pilgrimage to Santiago de Compostela. The bridge is guarded at its end by a headless granite bull called the **Toro Ibérico.** Though it dates back to pre-Roman times, the bull gained fame in the 16th century when it appeared in *Lazarillo de Tormes*, the prototype of the picaresque novel and a predecessor of *Don Quijote;* in one episode the novel's hero gets his head slammed into the bull's stone ear after he cheats his employer.

🎵 🎭 ENTERTAINMENT AND NIGHTLIFE

According to Salamantinos, Salamanca is the best place in Spain to party; it is said that there is one bar for every one hundred people living in the city. There are *chupiterias* (shot bars), *barres*, and *discotecas* on nearly every street, and while some close at 4am, others go all night. Nightlife centers on **Plaza Mayor** and spreads out to Gran Vía, Calle Bordadores, and side streets. **Calle Prior** and **Rúa Mayor** are also full of bars. Intense partying occurs off **Calle Varillas.**

Bar La Chupitería, Pl. Monterrey, at the intersection of C. Prior and Bordadores. Serves inexpensive shots (€0.90 each) and slightly larger *chupitos* (€1 each).

Duende Bar, Pl. San Juan Bautista 7. A typical *bar de copas* where Salamantino students begin their nights of partying. *Litros* of beer or *sangría* €3.

Birdland, C. Azafranal 57, facing Pl. España. Drink to modern funk and jazz. Beer €1.50-2.40. Mixed drinks €3-6. Open in summer Su-Th 6:30pm-3am, F-Sa 6:30pm-4:30am; off-season Su-Th 4pm-3am, F-Sa 4pm-4:30am.

Gatsby, C. Bordadores 6. African masks and a disco beat draw visitors and locals alike. Beer €1.80. *Sangría* €2.10. Open Su-Th 10pm-4am, F-Sa 7pm-6:30am.

Cum Laude, C. Prior 5. On this bar's dance floor, a replica of the Plaza Mayor, partying starts at 11pm and doesn't stop until 4:30am. Mixed drinks €5-8.

Camelot, C. Bordadores 3. This monastery-turned-club shakes to techno beats. Mixed drinks from €3.

Trastevere, Pl. Monterrey 8. A young, late-night spills in from nearby Bar La Chupiteria. Beer €4, *Copas* from €5. Open M-W 8pm-4am, Th 8pm-5am, F-Su 8pm-7am.

Dolce Via, Gran Vía 48. Groove on Gran Vía to Latin American salsa and pop in a Hollywood-themed disco. Beer €3. Mixed drinks from €5. Open daily 10pm-4:30am.

▶ DAYTRIP FROM SALAMANCA: ZAMORA.

Perched atop a rocky cliff over the Río Duero, Zamora (pop. 70,000) is an intriguing mix of the modern and the medieval; 15th-century palaces harbor Internet cafes and luxury hotels. Zamora's foremost monument is its Romanesque **cathedral,** built between the 12th and 15th centuries. Highlights include its intricately carved choir stalls (complete with seated apostles laughing and singing) and the main altar, an ornate structure of marble, gold, and silver. Inside the cloister, the **Museo de la**

BULLBOARDS Gazing out the window of your preferred mode of transportation, you may notice rather unusual monuments along the highway: massive black paper silhouettes of solitary bulls. Once upon a time (in the 1980s) these cutouts were advertisements for Osborne Sherry. In the early 1990s, however, billboards were prohibited on national roads. A plan was drafted to take the bulls down, but Spaniards protested, as the lone bull towering along the roadside had become an important national symbol. After considerable clamoring and hoofing, the bulls were painted black and left to loom proudly against the horizon. The familiar shape now decorates t-shirts and pins in souvenir shops, but the real thing is still impressive.

Catedral features the priceless 15th-century *Black Tapestries*, which tell the story of Achilles's defeat during the Trojan War. (☎980 53 06 44. Cathedral and museum open Su and Tu-Sa 10am-2pm and 5-8pm. Mass daily at 10am, also Sa 6pm and Su 1pm. Cathedral free, museum €2.) All in all, twelve handsome Romanesque churches remain within the walls of the old city, gleaming in the wake of recent restoration. Most visitors follow the **Romanesque Route,** a self-guided tour of all of the churches available from the **tourist office,** 6 Pl. Arias Gonzalo. (☎987 53 36 94. Open Apr.-Sept. daily 10am-2pm and 4-7pm, Oct.-Mar. 10am-2pm and 5-8pm.) The ▨**Museo de Semana Santa,** in sleepy Pl. Santa María La Nueva 9, is a rare find. Hooded mannequins stand guard over elaborately sculpted floats depicting the stations of the *Vía Crucis.* (Open M-Sa 10am-2pm and 5-8pm, Su 10am-2pm. €2.70.) Linea Regular **buses** run from Avenida Alfonsa Peña to Salamanca. (1hr., 10-15 per day, €3.60.)

LEÓN   ☎987

Formerly the center of Christian Spain, today León (pop. 145,000) is best known for its 13th-century Gothic ▨**cathedral,** arguably the most beautiful in Spain. Its spectacular stained-glass windows have earned the city the nickname *La Ciudad Azul* (The Blue City) and alone warrant a trip to León. The cathedral's **museum** displays gruesome wonders, including a sculpture depicting the skinning of a saint. (Cathedral open in summer daily 8:30am-2:30pm and 5-7pm; off-season 8:30am-1:30pm and 4-7pm. Free. Museum open in summer daily 9:30am-1:30pm and 4-6:30pm; off-season M-F 9:30am-1pm and 4-6pm, Sa 9:30am-1:30pm. €3.50.) The **Basílica San Isidoro,** dedicated in the 11th century to San Isidoro of Seville, houses the bodies of countless royals in the impressive *Panteón Real.* From Pl. Santo Domingo, walk up C. Ramón y Cajal; the basilica is up the flight of stairs on the right just before C. La Torre. (Open M-Sa 9am-1:30pm and 4pm-6:30pm, Su 9am-1:30pm. €3.) For nearby bars, discos, and techno music, head to the *barrio húmedo* (drinker's neighborhood) around **Plaza de San Martín** and **Plaza Mayor.** After 2am, the crowds weave to **Calle Lancia** and **Calle Conde de Guillén,** both heavily populated with discos and bars.

Trains (☎902 24 02 02) run from Av. Astorga 2 to Madrid (4½hr.; M-Sa 6 per day, Su 2 per day; €22-32). **Buses** (☎987 21 00 00) leave from Po. Ingeniero Sáenz de Miera for Madrid (4½hr.; M-F 12 per day 2:30am-10:30pm, Sa-Su 8 per day 2:30am-7:30pm; €18-30). Av. Palencia (a left out of the main entrance of the bus station and then a right onto the bridge, or a right out of the main entrance of the train station) leads across the river to **Plaza Glorieta Guzmán el Bueno,** which after the rotary becomes **Avenida de Ordoño II** and leads to León's cathedral and the adjacent **tourist office,** Pl. Regla 3. (☎987 23 70 82. Open M-F 9am-2pm and 5-7pm, Sa-Su 10am-2pm and 5-8pm.) Many accommodations cluster on **Avenida de Roma, Avenida Ordoño II,** and **Avenida República Argentina,**

SPAIN

which lead into the old town from Pl. Glorieta Guzmán el Bueno. **Hostal Orejas ❸**, C. Villafranca 6, 2nd fl., is just down Av. República Argentina from Pl. Glorieta Guzmán el Bueno. Each brand-new room comes with bath, shower, and cable TV. (☎987 25 29 09; janton@usarios.retecal.es. Free Internet access. Singles €30; doubles €39-49; triples €62; extra bed €10.) Inexpensive eateries fill the area near the cathedral and on the small streets off C. Ancha; also check **Plaza San Martín**, near Plaza Mayor. **Postal Code:** 24004.

🗗 DAYTRIP FROM LEÓN: ASTORGA. Astorga's fanciful ▨**Palacio Episcopal**, designed by Antoni Gaudí in the late-19th century, now houses the **Museo de los Caminos**. (☎987 61 88 82. Open July-Sept. Su 10am-2pm, Tu-Sa 10am-2pm and 4-8pm; Oct.-June Su 11am-2pm, Tu-Sa 11am-2pm and 4-6pm. €2.50.) Opposite the *palacio* is Astorga's cathedral and museum. (Both open daily 10am-2pm and 4-8pm. Cathedral free. Museum €2.50.) Astorga is most easily reached by **bus** from Po. Ingeniero Saenz de Miera in León (45min.; M-F 16 per day 6am-9:30pm, Sa-Su 6-7 per day 8:30am-8:30pm; €3).

EXTREMADURA

Arid plains bake under the intense summer sun, relieved only by scattered patches of glowing sunflowers. This land of harsh beauty and cruel extremes hardened New World conquistadors such as Hernán Cortés and Francisco Pizarro.

TRUJILLO   ☎927

The gem of Extremadura, hill-perched Trujillo (pop. 10,000) is an enchanting old-world town. It's often called the "Cradle of Conquistadors" because the city produced over 600 explorers of the New World. Scattered with medieval palaces, Roman ruins, Arabic fortresses, and churches of all eras, Trujillo is a glorious hodgepodge of histories and cultures. Its most impressive monument is its tallest: A 10th-century **Moorish castle** that offers a panoramic view of the surrounding plains. The **Plaza Mayor** was the inspiration for the Plaza de Armas in Cuzco, Perú, which was constructed after Francisco Pizarro defeated the Incas. Festooned with stork nests, **Iglesia de San Martín** dominates the northeastern corner of the plaza. (Open M-Sa 10am-2pm and 4:30-7:30pm, Su 10am-2pm and 4:30-7pm. €1.30. Mass M-Sa at 7:30pm, Su 1 and 7:30pm. Free.)

Buses run from the corner of C. de las Cruces and C. del M. de Albayada to Madrid (2½hr., 14-16 per day, €14). To get to Plaza Mayor, turn left up C. de las Cruces as you exit the station, right on C. de la Encarnación, then left on C. Chica; turn left on C. Virgen de la Guia and right on C. Burgos, continuing on to the Plaza (15min.). The **tourist office** is across the plaza and posts info in its windows when closed. (☎927 32 26 77. Open June-Sept. daily 9:30am-2pm and 4:30-7:30pm; Oct.-May 9:30am-2pm and 4-7pm.) **Camas Boni ❶**, C. Domingo Ramos 117, is off Plaza Mayor on the street directly across from the church. (☎927 32 16 04. Singles €12; doubles €21, with bath €30.) Try **Hostal Trujillo ❷**, C. de Francisco Pizarro 4-6. From C. de las Cruces, turn right on C. de la Encarnación, then right again onto C. de Francisco Pizarro. (☎/fax 927 32 22 74; www.hostaltrujillo.com. Singles €24; doubles €40.) The **Plaza Mayor** teems with tourist eateries. **Meson Alberca ❹**, C. Victoria 8, has an interior garden and an excellent three-course *menú* for €14-19. (Open Su-Tu and Th-Sa 11am-5pm and 8:30pm-1am.) **Postal Code:** 10200.

SOUTHERN SPAIN (ANDALUCÍA)

Andalucía is all that you expect Spain to be—flamenco shows, bullfighting, tall pitchers of *sangría*, white-washed villages, and streets lined with orange trees. The Moors arrived in AD 711 and bequeathed the region with far more than the flamenco music and gypsy ballads proverbially associated with southern Spain, sparking the European Renaissance and reintroducing the wisdom of Classical Greece and the Near East. Under their rule, Seville and Granada reached the pinnacle of Islamic arts and Córdoba matured into the most culturally influential Islamic city. Despite (or perhaps because of) the poverty and high unemployment in their homeland, Andalucians have always maintained a passionate, unshakable dedication to living the good life. The never-ending *festivales*, *ferias*, and *carnavales* of Andalucía are world-famous for their extravagance.

CÓRDOBA ☎957

Charming Córdoba (pop. 310,000), perched on the south bank of the Río Guadalquivir, was once the largest city in Western Europe. Córdoba remembers its heyday with amazingly well-preserved Roman, Jewish, Islamic, and Catholic monuments; the city's mosques, synagogues, and cathedrals accentuate each other with their befuddling proximity. Today, springtime festivals, flower-filled patios, and a steady nightlife make it one of Spain's most beloved cities.

▐ TRANSPORTATION

Trains: Plaza de las Tres Culturas, Av. América (☎957 24 02 02). To: **Cádiz** (2½-3½hr., 5 per day, €16-32); **Madrid** (2-4hr., 22-31 per day, €24-47); **Málaga** (2-3hr., 10-12 per day, €13-19); and **Seville** (45-60min., 20-29 per day, €7-24).

Buses: Estación de Autobuses, Av. América (☎957 40 40 40), across from the train station. **Alsina Graells Sur** (☎957 27 81 00) covers most of Andalucía. To: **Cádiz** via Seville (4-5hr.; daily 6pm, M-F also 10am; €18); **Granada** (3hr., 8-9 per day, €11); **Málaga** (3-3½hr., 5 per day, €11); and **Seville** (2hr., 10-13 per day, €9). **Bacoma** (☎957 45 65 14) runs to **Barcelona** (10hr., 3 per day, €69). **Secorbus** (☎902 22 92 92) sends cheap buses to **Madrid** (4½hr., 6-7 per day, €11). **Empresa Rafael Ramírez** (☎957 42 21 77) runs buses to nearby towns and camping sites.

✳▐ ORIENTATION AND PRACTICAL INFORMATION

Córdoba is split into two parts: the **old city** and the **new city.** The modern and commercial northern half extends from the train station on Av. de América down to **Plaza de las Tendillas,** the center of the city. The old section in the south is a medieval maze known as the **Judería** (Jewish quarter). The easiest way to reach the old city from the adjacent train and bus stations is to take bus #3 to **Campo Santo de los Mártires** (€0.80). Or to walk (20min.), exit left from the station, cross the parking plaza and make a right onto Av. de los Mozárabes. When you reach the Roman columns, turn left and cross Gta. Sargentos Provisionales. Make a right on Paseo de la Victoria and continue until you reach Puerto Almodóvar and the old city.

Tourist Offices: Oficina Municipal de Turismo y Congresos, currently in Pl. de las Tendillas and Campo Santo de los Martires (☎957 20 05 22) while the old office at Pl. Judá Leví, next to the youth hostel, undergoes renovations. Open M-F 8:30am-2:30pm. **Tourist Office of Andalucía,** C. Torrijos 10 (☎957 47 12 35), in the Junta de Andalucía, across from the Mezquita. From the train station, take bus #3 along the river until a stone arch appears on the right. Office is 1 block up C. Torrijos. General information on Andalucía. Open May-Sept. M-F 9:30am-8pm, Sa 10am-7pm, Su 10am-2pm; Oct.-Apr. M-F 9:30am-6pm, Su 10am-2pm.

Currency Exchange: Santander Central Hispano, Pl. de las Tendillas 5 (☎957 49 79 00). No commission up to €600. Open M-F 8:30am-2pm.

Emergency: ☎092. **Police:** Av. Doctor Flemming 2 (☎957 59 45 80).

Ambulance: urgent ☎902 505 061, main line ☎957 767 359.

Medical Assistance: Emergencies ☎061. **Red Cross Hospital,** Po. de la Victoria (urgent ☎957 22 22 22, main line 957 42 06 66). M-F 9am-1:30pm and 4:30-5:30pm.

24hr. Pharmacy: On a rotating basis. Refer to the list posted outside the pharmacy in Pl. Tendillas or the local newspaper.

Internet Access: In the old city, try **NavegaWeb,** Pl. Judá Leví 1 (☎957 29 30 89. €1.20 per hr.) Enter through the HI youth hostel. In the new city, check out **e-Net,** C. Garcia Lovera 10 (☎957 48 14 62). Leave Pl. Tendillas on C. Claudio Marcelo, take 2nd left. €1.20 per hr. Open daily 9am-2pm and 5-10pm.

Post Office: C. Cruz Conde 15 (☎957 47 97 96), 2 blocks up from Pl. Tendillas. **Lista de Correos.** Open M-F 8:30am-8:30pm, Sa-Su 9:30am-2pm. **Postal Code:** 14070.

ACCOMMODATIONS AND CAMPING

Most accommodations cluster around the whitewashed walls of the Judería, and in old Córdoba between the Mezquita and C. de San Fernando, a quieter and more residential area. Call up to several months before *Semana Santa* and summer.

■ **Residencia Juvenil Córdoba (HI),** Pl. Judá Leví (☎957 29 01 66; informacion@inturjoven.junta.andalucia.es), unbeatable location in the Judería and a 2min. walk from the Mezquita. A backpacker's utopia. Internet cafe inside hostel. Reception 24hr. Reservations recommended. Under-26 €14; over-26 €18. ❶

Hostal El Triunfo, Corregidor Luis de la Cerda 79 (☎957 49 84 84; www.htriunfo.com), across from the southern side of the Mezquita. All rooms have A/C, phone, TV, bath, and a safe. Singles €27-40; doubles €46-59. ❸

Hostal-Residencia Séneca, C. Conde y Luque 7 (☎/fax 957 47 32 34). Follow C. Céspedes 2 blocks from the Mezquita. Beautiful garden courtyard. Breakfast included. Reservations recommended. Singles with sink €21-22, with bath €31-34; doubles €32-36/41-43; triples €40-48/54-58. ❷

Hostal Rey Heredía, C. Rey Heredía 26 (☎957 47 41 82). From C. Cardenal Herrero on the northeast side of the Mezquita, take C. Encarnación to C. Rey Heredía; turn right and the hostel will be half a block down on the right. Singles €12; doubles €24. ❶

Hostal Maestre, C. Romero Barros 4-5 (☎/fax 957 47 53 95), off C. San Fernando. Immaculate and pleasantly decorated rooms. All with private bath, most with TV. 2 pretty courtyards. Singles €22; doubles €33; triples €42. ❷

Camping Municipal, Av. Brillante 50 (☎957 40 38 36). From the train station, turn left on Av. América, left on Av. Brillante, and walk uphill for about 20min; or, take bus #10 or 11 from Av. Cervantes. Pool, supermarket, restaurant, and laundry service. Camping equipment for rent. 1 person and tent €8; 2 people and tent €12. ❶

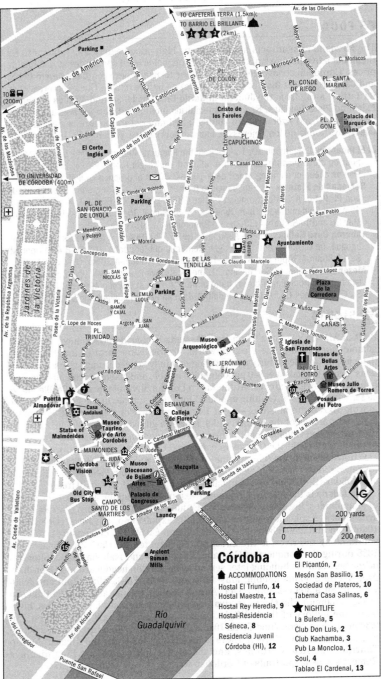

Córdoba

ACCOMMODATIONS

Hostal El Triunfo, 14
Hostal Maestre, 11
Hostal Rey Heredia, 9
Hostal-Residencia Séneca, 8
Residencia Juvenil Córdoba (HI), 12

FOOD

El Picantón, 7
Mesón San Basilio, 15
Sociedad de Plateros, 10
Taberna Casa Salinas, 6

NIGHTLIFE

La Bulería, 5
Club Don Luis, 2
Club Kachamba, 3
Pub La Moncloa, 1
Soul, 4
Tablao El Cardenal, 13

▸ FOOD

The Mezquita area attracts nearly as many high-priced eateries as tourists to fill them, but a five-minute walk in any direction yields local specialties at reasonable prices. Córdobans converge on the outdoor *terrazas* between **Calle Severo Ochoa** and **Calle Dr. Jiménez Díaz** for drinks and *tapas* before dinner. Cheap eateries cluster farther away from the Judería in **Barrio Cruz Conde**, around **Avenida Menéndez Pidal** and **Plaza Tendillas**. Regional specialties include *salmorejo* (a gazpacho-like cream soup) and *rabo de toro* (bull's tail simmered in tomato sauce). **El Corte Ingles**, Av. Ronda de los Tejeres 30, has a grocery store. (Open M-Sa 10am-10pm.)

▨ **El Picantón**, C. F. Ruano 19, 1 block from the Puerta de Almodóvar. Take ordinary *tapas*, pour on *salsa picante*, stick it in a roll, and you've got lunch (€1-3). There's nothing else as cheap or as filling. Open daily 10am-3:30pm and 8pm-midnight. ❶

Sociedad de Plateros, C. San Francisco 6 (☎957 47 00 42), between C. San Fernando and Pl. Potro. A Córdoba mainstay since 1872. Entrees €2.60-6.20. Kitchen open 1-4pm and 8pm-midnight. Open June-Aug. M-Sa 8am-4:30pm and 8pm-midnight; Sept.-May Su and Tu-Sa 8am-4:30pm and 8pm-midnight. MC/V. ❶

Taberna Casa Salinas, Puerto Almodóvar (☎957 29 08 46). A few blocks from the synagogue, up C. Judíos and to the right. Romantic outdoor patio. (€3.60-8.40.) Open M-Sa 11:30am-4:30pm and 8:30pm-12:30am, Su 11:30am-4:30pm. Closed in Aug. ❷

Mesón San Basilio, C. San Basilio 19. The locals love it, and so will you. Dine on one of two floors surrounding a breezy patio or have a drink at the bar. *Menús* M-F €6.50, Sa-Su €10. Entrees €6.50-14. Open daily 1-4pm and 8pm-midnight. AmEx/MC/V. ❷

▸ SIGHTS

Built in AD 784, Córdoba's famous ▨**Mezquita** is considered the most important Islamic monument in the Western world. Visitors enter through the **Patio de los Naranjos,** an arcaded courtyard featuring carefully spaced orange trees and fountains; inside the mosque, 850 pink-and-blue marble and alabaster columns support hundreds of striped arches. At the far end of the Mezquita lies the **Capilla Villaviciosa,** where Caliphal vaulting appeared for the first time. In the center, intricate marble Byzantine mosaics—a gift from Emperor Constantine VII—shimmer across the arches of the **Mihrab,** which houses a gilt copy of the Qur'an. Although the town rallied violently against the proposed erection of a **cathedral** in the center of the mosque, after the Crusaders conquered Córdoba in 1236 the towering **crucero** (transept) and **coro** (choir dome) were built. (☎957 47 05 12. Transept closed for renovations. Open July-Oct. daily 10am-7pm; Apr.-June M-Sa 10am-7:30pm, Su and holidays 2-7:30pm; Nov.-Mar. daily 10am-6pm. €6.50. Under-10 free.)

The **Judería** is the historic area northwest of the Mezquita. Just past the statue of Maimonides, the small **Sinagoga,** on C. Judíos, is one of Spain's few remaining synagogues, a solemn reminder of the 1492 expulsion of the Jews. (Open M-Sa 10am-2pm and 2:30-5:30pm, Su 10am-1:30pm. €0.50. EU citizens free.) To the south, along the river, is the ▨**Alcázar,** constructed for Catholic monarchs in 1328 during the conquest of Granada. Ferdinand and Isabella bade Columbus *adios* here and the building later served as Inquisition headquarters. (Open July-Aug. Tu-Su 8:30am-2:30pm; May-June and Sept. Tu-Sa 10am-2pm and 5:30-7:30pm, Su 9:30am-2:30pm; Oct.-Apr. Tu-Sa 10am-2pm and 4:30-6:30pm, Su 9:30am-2:30pm.) The **Museo Taurino y de Arte Cordobés,** on Pl. Maimónides, highlights the history of the bullfight. (Open July-Aug. Tu-Sa 8:30am-2:30pm, Su 9:30am-2:30pm; Sept.-June Tu-Sa 10am-2pm and 5:30-7:30pm, Su 9:30am-2:30pm. €3, students €1.50. F frec.) There is a **combined ticket** for the Alcázar, Museo Taurino y de Arte Cordobés, and the **Museo Julio Romero,** which displays Romero's sensual portraits of Córdoban women (€7.10, students €3.60).

🎵 🎭 ENTERTAINMENT AND NIGHTLIFE

For the latest cultural events, pick up a free copy of the *Guía del Ocio* at the tourist office. Hordes of tourists flock to see the flamenco dancers at the **Tablao El Cardenal**, C. Torrijos 10, facing the Mezquita. The price is high, but a bargain compared to similar shows in Seville and Madrid. (€18 includes 1 drink. Shows M-Sa 10:30pm.) **La Bulería**, C. Pedro López 3, is even less expensive. (€11 includes 1 drink. Daily 10:30pm.) Close to town is ⬛**Soul**, C. Alfonso XIII 3, a hip and relaxed bar with cozy tables and dreadlock-sporting bartenders. (Beer €1.20. Mixed drinks €4.50. Open Sept.-June 9am-3am.) Starting in June, the **Barrio Brillante**, uphill from Av. América, is packed with young, well-dressed *córdobeses* hopping between packed outdoor bars and dance clubs. Bus #10 goes to Brillante from the train station until about 11pm, but the bars don't wake up until around 1am (most stay open until 4am); a lift from **Radio Taxi** (☎957 76 44 44) should cost €4-6. If you're walking, head up Av. Brillante, passing along the way **Pub BSO**, C. Llanos de Pretorio and **Brujas Bar** right around the corner. Once in Barrio Brillante, where C. Poeta Emilia Prados meets C. Poeta Juan Ramón Jiménez, stop at **Cafetería Terra** before hitting the bars. A string of popular nightclubs run along Av. Brillante, including **Pub La Moncloa, Club Don Luis,** and **Club Kachamba.**

Of Córdoba's festivals, floats, and parades, **Semana Santa** in early April is the most extravagant. During the **Festival de los Patios** in the first two weeks of May, the city erupts with classical music concerts, flamenco dances, and a city-wide patio decorating contest. Late May brings the **Feria de Nuestra Señora de la Salud** (*La Feria*), a week of colorful garb, live dancing, and nonstop drinking.

🎫 DAYTRIP FROM CÓRDOBA

MADINAT AL-ZAHRA. Legend says that Madinat al-Zahra was built by Abd al-Rahman III for his favorite concubine, Zahra. The ruins of this 10th-century medina, considered one of the greatest cities of its time, were discovered in the mid-19th century and excavated in the early 20th century. Today, it's one of Spain's most impressive archaeological finds. (Open May to mid-Sept. Tu-Sa 10am-8:30pm, Su 10am-2pm; mid-Sept. to Apr. Su and Tu-Sa 10am-2pm. €1.50. EU citizens free.) **Córdoba Vision**, C. Doctor Maranon 1, offers transportation and a 2½hr. guided visit to the site in English. (☎957 76 02 41. €18.) Reaching Madinat Al-Zahra takes some effort if you don't go with an

THE HIDDEN DEAL 🗝

CLEAN IN CÓRDOBA

Under the caliphate, Arab culture flowered in Córdoba, complete with marketplaces (*souks*), public fountains, and public baths (*baños árabes*, or *hammam* in Arabic). As Catholics did not have a tradition of public bathing, most of these baths were abandoned, destroyed, or left to ruin after *la Reconquista*, which ended in the 14th century.

In recent past, many baths around the country have been restored and opened for public usage, allowing visitors to escape temporarily to 11th century Andalucía. The rich Arabic decor, combined with gracious service, make the Córdoban baths a fine spot to relax and wash away your travels. Like any traditional Arab bath, there is a dressing room, cold room, temperate room, and two hot rooms. You can proceed through the rooms in ceremonial order or choose your own sudsy adventure. For further indulgence, try a massage or tea in the tea-drinking room, which offers music, Moorish pastries, and even belly dancing. *Baños Árabes, Hammam, Medin Caliphal. C. Corredor Luis de la Cerda 51, 14003.* ☎*957 48 47 46, fax 47 99 17; medinacaliphal@grupoandalus.com. Open daily. Baths every other hour from 10am-midnight. One bath €12; four baths €34; bath, massage, aromatherapy, and tea €21; bath and massage with student ID €16. Reservations required.*

organized tour. The O8 **bus** leaves every hour from Av. República Argentina in Córdoba for Cruce Madinat Al-Zahra; from there, walk 45min. to the palace. (☎957 25 57 00. €0.80.) A taxi from Córdoba should cost about €26.

SEVILLE (SEVILLA)   ☎954

Site of a Roman acropolis, capital of the Moorish empire, focal point of the Spanish Renaissance, and guardian of traditional Andalusian culture, the charming and romantic Seville (pop. 700,000) never disappoints. Flamenco, *tapas*, and bullfighting are at their best here, and Seville's cathedral is among the most impressive in Spain. But it's the city's infectious, vivacious spirit that defines it, and fittingly, the local *Semana Santa* and *Feria de Abril* celebrations are among the most extravagant in all of Europe.

▮ TRANSPORTATION

Flights: All flights arrive at **Aeropuerto San Pablo** (SVQ; ☎954 44 90 00), 12km out of town on Ctra. Madrid. A taxi ride to the town center costs about €13. **Los Amarillos** (☎954 98 91 84) runs a bus to the airport from outside the Hotel Alfonso XIII at the Pta. Jerez (1-2 per hr. 6:15am-11pm, €2.30).

Trains: Estación Santa Justa (☎954 41 41 11), on Av. Kansas City. Near Pl. Nueva is the **RENFE** office, C. Zaragoza 29 (☎954 54 02 02). Open M-F 9am-1:15pm and 4-7pm. **AVE** trains run to **Córdoba** (45min., 18-20 per day, €15-17) and **Madrid** (2½hr., 18-20 per day, €62). **Talgo** trains run to: **Barcelona** (12hr., 3 per day, €53); **Cádiz** (2hr., 7-12 per day, €8.10); **Córdoba** (1½hr., 6 per day, €8); **Granada** (3hr., 5 per day, €17); **Málaga** (2½hr., 4-7 per day, €14); **Valencia** (8½hr., 4 per day, €36).

Buses: The old bus station at Prado de San Sebastián, C. Manuel Vázquez Sagastizabal (☎954 41 71 11), mainly serves Andalucía:

Transportes Alsina Graells (☎954 41 88 11). To: **Córdoba** (2hr., 10-12 per day, €9); **Granada** (3hr., 10 per day, €16); **Málaga** (3hr., 11 per day, €13).

Transportes Comes (☎954 41 68 58). To **Cádiz** (1½hr., 14 per day 7am-10pm, €9.40) and **Jerez de la Frontera** (1½hr., 9-10 per day 9am-10pm, €5.70).

Los Amarillos (☎954 98 91 84). To **Arcos de la Frontera** (2hr., 8am and 4:30pm, €6.40) and **Marbella** (3hr., 3 per day 8am-8pm, €14).

Linesur (☎954 98 82 20). To **Jerez de la Frontera** (1½hr., 8-12 per day 6am-9pm, €5.40), with connections to **Algeciras** (5hr., 7 per day 6:30am-9pm, €14).

Public Transportation: TUSSAM (☎900 71 01 71), the city bus network. Most lines run every 10min. (6am-11:15pm) and converge on Pl. Nueva, Pl. Encarnación, or in front of the cathedral. Night service departs from Pl. Nueva (every hr. midnight-2am). Fare €1, *bonobús* (10 rides) €4.50. Particularly useful are C3 and C4, which circle the center, and 34, which hits the youth hostel, university, cathedral, and Pl. Nueva.

Taxis: TeleTaxi (☎954 62 22 22). **Radio Taxi** (☎954 58 00 00). Base rate €2.20, Su 25% surcharge. Extra charge for luggage and night taxis.

Car Rental: Hertz, at the airport (☎954 25 42 98) or train station (☎954 53 39 14). General info and reservations ☎902 40 24 05. 21+. From €53 per day. Open daily 8am-midnight. AmEx/MC/V. **ATA,** C. Almirante Lobo 2 (☎954 22 09 58). 21+. Manual shift only. From €36 per day plus tax. Open M-F 9am-2pm and 4:30-8:30pm, Sa 9am-2pm. MC/V.

Moped Rental: Alkimoto, C. Fernando Tirado 5 (☎954 58 49 27). €21 per day. Open M-F 9am-1:30pm and 5-8pm.

✈ ❼ ORIENTATION AND PRACTICAL INFORMATION

The **Río Guadalquivir** flows roughly north to south through the city. Most of the touristed areas of Seville, including the **Barrio de Santa Cruz** and **El Arenal**, are on the east bank. The **Barrio de Triana**, the **Barrio de Santa Cecilia, Los Remedios**, and the Expo '92 fairgrounds occupy the west bank. The cathedral, next to Barrio de Santa Cruz, is Seville's centerpiece. If you're disoriented, look for the conspicuous **Giralda** (the minaret-turned-bell-tower). **Avenida de la Constitución**, home of the tourist office, runs alongside the cathedral. **El Centro**, a busy commercial pedestrian zone, lies north of the cathedral, starting where Av. Constitución hits **Plaza Nueva**, site of the Ayuntamiento. **Calle Tetuan**, a popular street for shopping, runs northward from Pl. Nueva through El Centro.

Tourist Offices: Centro de Información de Sevilla, Po. de las Delicias 9 (☎954 23 44 65; www.turismo.sevilla.org), near the university and the river. The main office for Seville. English spoken. Maps, info on flamenco and hostels. Open M-F 8am-7pm. **Turismo Andaluz, S.A.**, Av. Constitución 21B (☎954 22 14 04; fax 22 97 53), 1 block from the cathedral. Info on all of Andalucía. English spoken. Open M-F 9am-7pm, Sa 10am-2pm and 3-7pm, Su 10am-2pm. **Info booths** at the train station and Pl. Nueva.

Currency Exchange: Santander Central Hispano, C. la Campaña 19 (☎902 24 24 24). Open M-F 8:30am-2pm, Sa 8:30am-1pm.

American Express: Pl. Nueva 7 (☎954 21 16 17). Open M-F 9:30am-1:30pm and 4:30-7:30pm, Sa 10am-1pm.

Luggage Storage: At Pr. San Sebastián bus station (€1 per bag per day; open 6:30am-10pm) and the train station (€3 per day).

Bi-Gay-Lesbian Resources: COLEGA (Colectiva de Lesbianas y Gays de Andalucía) (☎954 50 13 77; www.colegaweb.net). Pl. Encarnación 23, 2nd fl. Look for the sign in the window; the door is not marked. Open M-F 10am-2pm.

Laundromat: Lavandería Auto-servicio, C. Castelar 2 (☎954 21 05 35). Wash and dry €6. Open M-Sa 9:30am-1:30pm and 5-8:30pm.

Emergency: Medical: ☎061. **Police:** Po. Concordia (local ☎092; national ☎091).

24hr. Pharmacy: Check list posted at any pharmacy for those open 24hr.

Medical Assistance: Red Cross (☎913 35 45 45). **Ambulatorio Esperanza Macarena** (☎954 42 01 05). **Hospital Universitario Virgen Macarena** (☎954 24 81 81), Av. Dr. Fedriani. English spoken.

Internet Access: Seville Internet Center, C. Almirantazgo 2, 2nd fl., across from the cathedral. €3 per hr., €1.80 per hr. with prepaid cards. Open M-F 9am-10pm, Sa-Su 10am-10pm. **CiberBoston**, C. San Fernando 23. €2 per hr.; Sa special €1 per hr. Open M-F 9am-1am, Sa-Su noon-midnight. **The Email Place**, C. Sierpes 54. €2.20 per hr. Open June-Sept. M-F 10am-10pm, Sa-Sa noon-9pm; Oct.-May M-F 10am-11pm, Sa-Su noon-9pm.

Post Office: Av. Constitución 32 (☎954 21 64 76), opposite the cathedral. *Lista de Correos* and fax. Open M-F 8:30am-8:30pm, Sa 9:30am-2pm. **Postal Code:** 41080.

⌂ ACCOMMODATIONS

Rooms vanish and prices soar during *Semana Santa* and the *Feria de Abril;* reserve ahead. The narrow streets east of the cathedral around **Calle Santa María la Blanca** are full of cheap, centrally located hostels. Hostels by the **Plaza de Armas** bus station, mostly on C. Gravina, are convenient for visits to **El Centro** and the lively C. Betis on the west bank of the river.

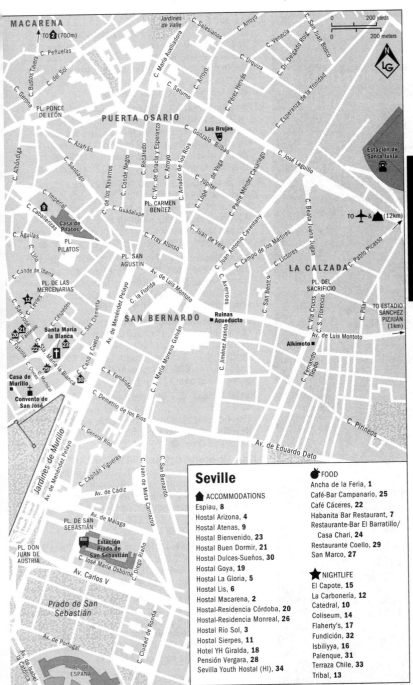

Seville

🏠 ACCOMMODATIONS

Espiau, **8**
Hostal Arizona, **4**
Hostal Atenas, **9**
Hostal Bienvenido, **23**
Hostal Buen Dormir, **21**
Hostal Dulces-Sueños, **30**
Hostal Goya, **19**
Hostal La Gloria, **5**
Hostal Lis, **6**
Hostal Macarena, **2**
Hostal-Residencia Córdoba, **20**
Hostal-Residencia Monreal, **26**
Hostal Río Sol, **3**
Hostal Sierpes, **11**
Hotel YH Giralda, **18**
Pensión Vergara, **28**
Sevilla Youth Hostal (HI), **34**

🍅 FOOD

Ancha de la Feria, **1**
Café-Bar Campanario, **25**
Café Cáceres, **22**
Habanita Bar Restaurant, **7**
Restaurante-Bar El Barratillo/
  Casa Chari, **24**
Restaurante Coello, **29**
San Marco, **27**

⭐ NIGHTLIFE

El Capote, **15**
La Carbonería, **12**
Catedral, **10**
Coliseum, **14**
Flaherty's, **17**
Fundición, **32**
Isbiliyya, **16**
Palenque, **31**
Terraza Chile, **33**
Tribal, **13**

THE HIDDEN DEAL

THE BARGAIN OF SEVILLE

Seville is home to gorgeous *artesanía* and hundreds of people anxious to sell it. Avoid the over-priced tourist shops by the cathedral, and head to the specialty stores for authentic merchandise.

1. **Abanicos de Sevilla,** Pl. San Francisco 7. Largest selection of hand-painted fans in town. Open June-Aug. M-F 9:30am-1:30pm and 5-8:30pm, Sa 9:30am-2pm; Sept.-May M-Sa 9:30am-1:30pm and 5-8:30pm. MC/V.

2. **Martian Cerámica Sevillana,** C. las Sierpes 74. Colorful hand-painted ceramics, all made in Seville. Tiny trays and vases start at €3; larger ones cost €20-30. Open M-Sa 10am-2pm and 5-8:30pm. MC/V.

3. **Artesanía Textil,** C. las Sierpes 70. Authentic, hand-sewn silk shawls. Prices start at €56. Open June-Aug. M-F 10am-1:30pm and 5:15-8:15pm, Sa 10am-1:30pm; Sept.-May M-Sa 10am-1:30pm and 5:15-8:15pm. MC/V.

4. **Diza,** C. Tetuán 5. Fans, some dating back to the 19th-century, from €4. June-Aug. M-F 9:30am-1:30pm and 5-8:30pm, Sa 9:30am-2pm; Sept.-May M-Sa 9:30am-1:30pm and 5-8:30pm. MC/V.

5. **Trajes Sevillanos,** Modas Muñoz, C. Cerrajería 5. Colorful, high-quality *flamenco* costumes (from €120) and accessories (fans, flowers). Open M-F 10am-1:30pm and 5-8:30pm, Sa 10am-1:30pm. MC/V.

Espiau, C. Pérez Galdós 1A (☎954 21 06 82), between Pl. Alfalfa and Pl. Encarnación. Friendly Spanish and British couple keep the most beautiful *hostal* in town. Rooms with high ceilings and full-length tiled mirrors surround huge, sunny living room. Singles €22; doubles €42, with bath €48; triples €54. Discounts for longer stays. ❷

Pensión Vergara, C. Ximénez de Enciso 11, 2nd fl. (☎954 21 56 68), at C. Mesón del Moro. Beautiful rooms of varying size with lace bedspreads, antique-style furniture, and a sitting room with book swap. Singles, doubles, triples, and quads available; all have fans. Towels provided on request. €18 per person. ❷

Hostal Lis, C. Escarpín 10 (☎954 21 30 88), in an alley near Pl. Encarnación. Cozy, tiled rooms in a traditional Sevilian house. Owner is in the process of adding A/C to all rooms and a rooftop terrace. Free Internet access. Laundry service. Singles with shower €21; doubles with bath €42; triples with bath €63. MC/V. ❷

Hostal Macarena, C. San Luis 91 (☎954 37 01 41). Curtains, tiles, wooden furniture, and quilted bedspreads make Macarena's rooms homey and welcoming. All rooms with A/C. Singles €20; doubles €30, with bath €40; triples €51. MC/V. ❷

Hostal Buen Dormir, C. Farnesio 8 (☎954 21 06 82). Quilted bedspreads, tiled walls, and sunny rooms, all with A/C, make Hostal "Good Sleep" one of the best deals in town. Rooftop terrace. Laundry €6. Singles €18; doubles €30, with shower €35, with bath €40; triples with shower €50, with bath €55. ❷

Hostal Arizona, C. Pedro del Toro 14 (☎954 21 60 42), off C. Gravina. Some rooms have balconies. Mar.-Oct. singles €20; doubles €30, with bath €36. Nov.-Apr. €15/30/36. Prices higher for *Semana Santa* and *Feria.* ❶

Hotel YH Giralda, C. Abades 30 (☎954 22 83 24). This 2-star hotel features spacious, sparkling, mauve-and-white painted rooms. Simplistic, modern, but trendy style with iron-post beds and marble-floored patio. All rooms with private bath, A/C, and Internet jacks. July 15-Oct. and Dec. doubles €80; Nov. and Jan.-July 14 €65. AmEx/MC/V. ❹

Hostal Dulces-Sueños, C. Puerta de la Carne 21 (☎954 41 93 93). Comfortable rooms, some with A/C. Prices with *Let's Go:* Singles €20; doubles €40, with bath €50; one triple with bath €65. ❷

Hostal Atenas, C. Caballerizas 1 (☎954 21 80 47; fax 22 76 90), near Pl. Pilatos. Slightly pricier than other options, but with good reason—all sunny, orange-painted rooms come with private baths and A/C. Singles €29; doubles €55; triples €70. Prices higher during *Semana Santa* and *Feria.* MC/V. ❸

Hostal Bienvenido, C. Archeros 14 (☎954 41 36 55), off C. Santa Maria la Blanca. Simple, but cheap rooms. 5 rooftop rooms surround a social patio; downstairs ones overlook an inner atrium. Very international backpacker crowd. Singles €20; doubles €30-37 depending on room; triples and quads €15-16 per person. ❷

Hostal La Gloria, C. San Eloy 58, 2nd fl. (☎954 22 26 73), at the end of a lively shopping street. Spotless rooms. One of the best deals in the center. Singles €18; doubles €30, with bath €36; limited triples available €45. *Semana Santa* and *Feria* prices substantially higher. ❷

Hostal Río Sol, C. Márquez de Parada 25 (☎954 22 90 38), 1 block from Pl. de Armas bus station. Circular staircase leads to cheap and clean rooms. Singles €15, with bath €21; doubles with bath, TV, and A/C €43. MC/V. ❷

Sevilla Youth Hostel (HI), C. Isaac Peral 2 (☎954 61 31 50; reservas@inturjoven.juntaandalucia.es). Take bus #34 across from the tourist office near the cathedral; the 5th stop is behind the hostel. Isolated and difficult to find. A/C. Many private baths. Breakfast included. Mar.-Oct. dorms €17, under-26 €13; Nov.-Feb. €15, under-26 €11. ❶

Hostal-Residencia Córdoba, C. Farnesio 12 (☎954 22 74 98). Immaculate and spacious air-conditioned rooms are worth the extra euros. A/C functions from 4pm-4am, 3pm-5am when the summer meltdown strikes. Curfew 3am. Singles €27, with bath €33; doubles €41/50. *Semana Santa* and *Feria* €36/48/56/65. ❸

Hostal Goya, C. Mateos Gago 31 (☎954 21 11 70; fax 56 29 88). Almost hotel-like. Outside-facing rooms are worth the splurge; inner rooms are dimmer. Spacious, sparkling-clean rooms have A/C and private baths. June-Mar. singles €40; doubles €65; triples €91; quads €107. Apr.-May and *Semana Santa* €45/75/105/123. MC/V. ❹

Hostal Sierpes, C. Corral del Rey 22 (☎954 22 49 48; fax 21 21 07). Lace-canopied lobby and beautiful common spaces belie boring but clean rooms. All rooms with baths, many with A/C. Parking €12. Mar.-June and Aug.-Dec. singles €40; doubles €59; triples €77; quads €96. Holidays and festivals €65/85/111/141. Jan.-Feb. and July €31/43/55/67. ❹

Hostal-Residencia Monreal, C. Rodrigo Caro 8 (☎954 21 41 66). Rooms with bath are spacious and beautiful; those without are basic. Ask for one overlooking the plaza. The downstairs cafe caters to backpackers. Breakfast €2.50-4. Singles €20; doubles €40, with bath €60. MC/V. ❷

Camping Sevilla, Ctra. Madrid-Cádiz km 534 (☎954 51 43 79), near the airport. From Pr. San Sebastián, take bus #70 (stops 800m away at Parque Alcosa). Hot showers, supermarket, and pool. €3 per person, €3 per car, €2.50 per tent. ❶

🖸 FOOD

Seville, which claims to be the birthplace of *tapas*, keeps its cuisine light. *Tapas* bars cluster around **Plaza San Martín** and along **Calle San Jacinto.** Popular venues for *el tapeo* (*tapas*-barhopping) are **Barrio Santa Cruz** and **El Arenal.** Locals imbibe Seville's own Cruzcampo beer, a light, smooth pilsner. **Mercado del Arenal,** near the bullring on C. Pastor y Leandro, has fresh meat and produce. (Open M-Sa 9am-2pm.) For a supermarket, try **%Día,** C. San Juan de Ávila, near El Corte Inglés. (Open M-F 9:30am-2pm and 6:30-9pm, Sa 9am-1pm.)

🖼 Restaurante-Bar El Baratillo/Casa Chari, C. Pavía 12 (☎954 22 96 51), on a tiny street off C. Dos de Mayo. Hospitable owner will help you practice your Spanish. Order at least an hour in advance for the *tour-de-force*: Homemade *paella* (vegetarian options available) with a jar of wine, beer, or *sangría* (2 jars €18). *Menú* €4-9. Open M-F 10am-10pm, Sa 10am-5pm; stays open later when busy. ❷

Habanita Bar Restaurant, C. Golfo 3 (☎606 71 64 56; www.andalunet.com/habanita), on a tiny street off C. Perez Galdos, next to Pl. Alfalfa. Exquisite Cuban fare, including yucca and *tostones* (fried bananas). Full or half-entree €4.80-10. Open daily 12:30-4:30pm and 8pm-12:30am. Closed Su night. MC/V. ●

San Marco, C. Mesón del Moro 6 (☎954 21 43 90), several blocks from the cathedral. Amazing pizzas, pastas, and Italian desserts in an 18th-century house and 17th-century Arab baths. Other locations in equally impressive settings at C. Betis 68 (☎954 28 03 10), and at C. Santo Domingo de la Calzada 5 (☎954 58 33 43). Entrees €5-7.50. Open Su and Tu-Sa 1:15-4:30pm and 8:15pm-12:30am. MC/V. ❷

Ancha de la Feria, C. Feria 61 (☎954 90 97 45). Snack on delicious homemade *tapas* in this bright and airy local bar/restaurant. Old sherry barrels line the walls and ceiling. *Tapas* €1.50-2. *Raciones* from €4. Great *menú del día* €5.80, served M-F afternoons only. Open Tu-Sa 9am-4pm and 9pm-1am, Su 9am-4pm. ●

Café-Bar Campanario, C. Mateos Gago 8 (☎954 56 41 89), ½ block from the cathedral, on the right. Newer and shinier than most *tapas* bars. Mixes the best (and strongest) jugs of *sangría* around (½L €7.30, 1L €9.70). *Tapas* €1.50-2. *Raciones* €6-8.40. Open daily 10:30am-12:30am. ❷

Restaurante Coello, C. Doncella 8 (☎954 42 10 82), on a tiny street off C. Santa María la Blanca. Dine in the bright yellow interior or outside on the narrow cobblestone street. Splurge on their delicately prepared *a la carte* meat and fish entrees (€10-15). *Menú* €8. Appetizers €4-10. Open daily noon-midnight. MC/V. ❸

Café Cáceres, C. San José 24 (☎954 21 51 31). The closest thing to a buffet-style breakfast in Seville. Choose from a spread of cheeses, jams, countless condiments, fresh orange juice, and numerous omelets. *Desayuno de la casa* (orange juice, coffee, ham, eggs, and toast) €4.50. Open M-Sa 7:30am-8pm, Su 7:30am-4pm. ●

⊙ SIGHTS

The tourist office has a detailed map of the winding alleys, wrought-iron gates, and courtyards of Santa Cruz. Its monuments form the most vivid images in the mosaic that is Seville, and harken its history as the one-time *judería*.

■ **CATEDRAL.** Legend has it that in 1401 the *reconquistadores* wished to demonstrate their religious fervor by constructing a church so great, they said, that "those who come after us will take us for madmen." With 44 individual chapels, the cathedral of Seville is the third largest in the world, after St. Peter's Basilica in Rome and St. Paul's Cathedral in London, and the biggest Gothic edifice ever constructed. Not surprisingly, it took more than a century to build. In 1401, a 12th-century Almohad mosque was destroyed to clear space for the massive cathedral. All that remains is the **Patio de Los Naranjos,** where the faithful would wash before prayer, the Puerta del Perdón entryway from C. Alemanes, and the famed **La Giralda** minaret built in 1198. The tower and its twins in Marrakesh and Rabat are the oldest and longest-surviving Almohad minarets. There are 35 ramps inside leading to the tower's top that once allowed the *muezzin* to climb up on his horse for the call to prayer; today, they enable tourists to take pictures.

In the center of the cathedral, the **Capilla Real,** built in Renaissance style, stands opposite **choirstalls** made of mahogany recycled from a 19th-century Austrian railway. The ■**retablo mayor,** one of the largest in the world, is a golden wall of intricately wrought saints and disciples. Nearby is the **Sepulcro de Cristóbal Colón** (Columbus's tomb), which supposedly holds the explorer's remains, brought back to Seville after Cuba's independence in 1902 (the tomb had been located in Havana's cathedral). The black-and-gold pallbearers represent the eternally grateful monarchs of Castilla, León, Aragón, and Navarra. Farther on and to the right stands the **Sacristía Mayor** (treasury), which holds gilded panels of Alfonso X el Sabio, done by Juan de Arefe, works by Ribera and Murillo, and a glittering Corpus Christi icon, **La Custodia Processional.** A small, disembodied head of John the Baptist eyes visitors who enter the gift shop. It overlooks keys presented to the city of Seville by Jewish leaders after King Fernando III ousted the Muslims in 1248. In the northwest corner of the cathedral lies the architecturally stunning **Sala de Las Columnas.** Each year, expenses on the cathedral alone total over €3.8 million. (☎ 954 21 49 71. Entrance by the Pl. de la Virgen de los Reyes. Open M-Sa 11am-5pm, Su 2:30-6pm. Last entrance 1hr. before closing. €6, seniors and students €1.50. Under-12 and Su free. Mass held in the Capilla Real M-Sa 8:30, 10am, noon; Su 8:30, 10, 11am, noon, 1pm.)

■**ALCÁZAR.** The oldest European palace still used as a private residence for royals, Seville's Alcázar is nothing short of magnificent. Like the Alhambra in Granada, Seville's Alcázar has Moorish architecture and gardens, and although the Alhambra gets more press, the Alcázar is equally, if not more, impressive. Constructed by the Moors in the 7th century, the palace was embellished greatly during the 15th century and now displays an interesting mix of Moorish and Christian architecture, seen most prominently in the *mudéjar* style of many of the arches, tiles, and ceilings. Ferdinand and Isabella of Portugal are the palace's most well-known former residents; Carlos V also lived here and married his cousin Isabella of Portugal in the **Salón Techo Carlos V.** Visitors enter through the **Patio de la Montería,** directly across from the intricate Almohad facade of the Moorish palace. Through the archway lie the Arabic residences, including the **Patio del Yeso,** used by Moorish governors before the palace itself was even built, and the exquisitely carved **Patio de las Muñecas** (Patio of the Dolls), so named because of miniature faces carved into the bottom of one of the room's pillars. Originally a courtyard, the Patio de las Muñecas served as a private area for Moorish kings, with an escape path (no longer in existence) so that in case of an attack the king would not have to cross the open space. Of the Christian additions, the most notable is the **Patio de las Doncellas** (Patio of the Maids). Court life in the Alcázar revolved around this colonnaded quadrangle, which is encircled by archways adorned with glistening tile-work. The golden-domed **Salón de los Embajadores** (Embassadors' Room) is allegedly the site where Ferdinand and Isabella welcomed Columbus back from the New World. Several beautiful silk tapestries adorn the walls of the appropriately named **Sala de Tapices.** The son of Ferdinand and Isabella, Prince Juan, was born in the red-and-blue tiled **Cuarto del Príncipe;** the room was named for him after his untimely death, supposedly of a broken heart.

The **private residences** upstairs, the official home of the king and queen of Spain, and where they stay when they visit Seville, have been renovated and redecorated throughout the centuries; most of the furniture today dates from the 18th and 19th centuries. These residences are accessible only by 25min. guided tours (see info below). Peaceful **gardens** stretch from the residential quarters in all directions. (Pl. del Triunfo 7. ☎ 954 50 23 23. Open Tu-Sa 9:30am-7pm, Su 9:30am-5pm. €5. Students, handicapped, residents, over-65, and under-16 free. Tours of the upper palace living quarters every 30min. June-July 10am-1:30pm, Aug.-May 10am-1:30pm and 3:30-5:30pm; €3. Fifteen people max. per tour, so buy tickets in advance. Worthwhile audioguides give anecdotes, historical info, and a clearly marked route through the complex; €3.)

■**MUSEO PROVINCIAL DE BELLAS ARTES.** Cobbled together from decommissioned convents in the mid-1800s, this museum contains Spain's finest collection of works by painters of the *Sevillana* School, notably Murillo, Valdés Leal, and Zurbarán, as well as El Greco and Dutch master Jan Breughel. Although the art

SPAIN

(displayed more or less chronologically as well as thematically) is heavily biased toward religious themes, later works include some landscape paintings and portraits depicting Seville, its environs, and residents. The building itself is a work of art; take time to sit in the shady gardens. *(Pl. del Museo 9. ☎954 22 07 90. Open Tu 3-8pm, W-Sa 9am-8pm, Su 9am-2pm. €1.50. EU citizens free.)*

PLAZA DE TOROS DE LA REAL MAESTRANZA. Home to one of the two great bullfighting schools (the other is in Ronda), Plaza de Toros de la Real Maestranza fills to capacity for weekly fights and the 13 *corridas* of the *Feria de Abril*. The museum inside has costumes, paintings, and antique posters. *(Open non-bullfight days 9:30am–7pm, bullfight days 9:30am-3pm. Tours every 20min., €4.)*

BARRIO DE SANTA CRUZ. King Fernando III forced Jews fleeing Toledo to live in the Barrio de Santa Cruz, now a neighborhood of weaving alleys and courtyards. Beyond C. Lope de Rueda, off C. Ximénez de Enciso, is the **Plaza de Santa Cruz.** South of the plaza are the **Jardines de Murillo,** a shady expanse of shrubbery. Pl. Santa Cruz's church houses the grave of the artist Murillo, who died after falling from a scaffold while painting ceiling frescoes in a Cádiz church. Nearby, **Iglesia de Santa María la Blanca,** built in 1391, contains Murillo's *Last Supper*. *(Church open M-Sa 10-11am and 6:30-8pm, Su 9:30am-2pm and 6:30-8pm. Free.)*

LA MACARENA. This area northwest of El Centro is named for the Virgin of Seville. A stretch of 12th-century **murallas** (walls) runs between the Pta. Macarena and the Pta. Córdoba on the Ronda de Capuchinos. At the west end is the **Basílica Macarena,** whose venerated image of *La Virgen de la Macarena* is paraded through town during *Semana Santa*. A **treasury** within glitters with the virgin's jewels and other finery. *(C. Béquer 1. Basilica open M-Sa 9am-2pm and 5-9pm, Su 9:30am-2pm and 5-9pm. Free. Treasury open daily 9:30am-2pm and 5-8pm. €3, students and over-65 €1.50. Sa free.)* Toward the river is the **Iglesia de San Lorenzo y Jesús del Gran Poder,** with Montañés's remarkably lifelike sculpture *El Cristo del Gran Poder*. Worshipers kiss Jesus's ankle through an opening in the bulletproof glass for luck. *Semana Santa* culminates in a procession honoring the statue. *(Pl. San Lorenzo. Open M-Th 8am-1:30pm and 6-9pm, F 7:30am-10pm, Sa-Su 8am-2pm and 6-9pm. Free.)*

🎵 ENTERTAINMENT

The tourist office distributes *El Giraldillo*, a free monthly magazine with complete listings on music, art exhibits, theater, dance, fairs, and film. Get your flamenco fix at **Los Gallos,** Pl. Santa Cruz 11, on the west edge of Barrio Santa Cruz. (Cover €27, includes 1 drink. Shows daily 9 and 11:30pm.) If you're going to see a **bullfight** somewhere in Spain, Seville is probably the best place to do it; the bullring here is generally considered the most beautiful in the country. The cheapest place to buy bullfight tickets is at the ring on Po. Marqués de Contadero; or try the booths on C. Sierpes, C. Velázquez, or Pl. Toros (€18-75).

BULLFIGHTING

Seville's bullring hosts bullfights from *Semana Santa* through October. The cheapest place to buy tickets is at the ring on Po. Alcalde Marqués de Contadero. However, when there's a good *cartel* (line-up), the booths on C. las Sierpes, C. Velázquez, and Pl. de Toros might be the only source of advance tickets. Ticket prices, depending on the quality of both seat and torero, can run from €18 for a *grada de sol* (nosebleed seat in the sun) to €75 for a *barrera de sombra* (front-row seat in the shade). Scalpers usually add 20% to the ticket price. *Corridas de toros* (bullfights) and *novilladas* (apprentice bullfighters with younger bulls) are held in the 13 days around the *Feria de Abril* and into May, every Sunday April to June and September to October, more often during Corpus Cristi in June and early July, and during the *Feria de San Miguel* near the end of September. During July and August, *corridas* occur on occasional Thursdays at 9pm; check posters around town. Some of the most popular *sevillano* bullfighters include **El Juli, Joselito,** and **José Tomás.** (For current info and ticket sales, call ☎954 50 13 82.)

SHOPPING

Seville is a great place to find Andalusian crafts such as hand-embroidered silk and lace shawls and traditional *flamenco* wear, albeit often at somewhat inflated tourist prices. C. las Sierpes is in the center of the main shopping area. Its environs, including C. San Eloy, C. Velázquez, and C. Francos, have a wide array of crafts, as well as modern clothing, shoe stores, and jewelry. In January and June, all the stores hold huge **rebajas** (sales), where everything is marked down 30-70%. A large, eclectic **flea market** is held Thursday 9am-2pm, extending from C. Feria to C. Regina in La Macarena.

◘ FESTIVALS

Seville swells with tourists during its fiestas, and with good reason: They are insanely fun. If you're in Spain during any of the major festivals, head straight to Seville—you won't regret it. If you can remember it, that is. Reserve a room weeks or months in advance, and expect to pay up to twice the normal rate.

■ **SEMANA SANTA.** Seville's world-famous *Semana Santa* lasts from Palm Sunday to Easter Sunday (Apr. 13-20 in 2004). In each neighborhood of the city, thousands of penitents in hooded cassocks guide *pasos* (stunning, extravagant floats) through the streets, illuminated by hundreds of candles. The climax is Good Friday, when the entire city turns out for the procession along the bridges and through the oldest neighborhoods. Book rooms well in advance and expect to pay double the usual price. The tourist office has a helpful booklet on where to eat and sleep during the week's festivities.

■ **FERIA DE ABRIL.** Two or three weeks after *Semana Santa*, the city rewards itself for its Lenten piety with the *Feria de Abril* (Apr. 27-May 2 in 2004). Begun as part of a 19th-century revolt against foreign influence, the *Feria* has grown into a massive celebration of all things Andalusian. Circuses, bullfights, and *flamenco* shows roar into the night in a showcase of local customs and camaraderie. A spectacular array of flowers and lanterns decorates over 1000 kiosks, tents, and pavilions, collectively called *casetas*. Each has the elements necessary for a rollicking time: Small kitchen, bar, and dance floor. Locals stroll from one to the next, sharing drinks and food amid the lively music and dance. Most *casetas* are privately owned, and the only way to get invited is by making friends with the locals. There are a few large public *casetas* with drinks and dancing though. Either way, people-watching from the sidelines can be almost as exciting, as costumed girls dance *sevillanas* and men parade on horseback through the streets. The city holds bullfights daily during the festival; buy tickets in advance. *(The fairgrounds are on the southern end of Los Remedios.)*

◘ NIGHTLIFE

Seville's reputation for gaiety is tried and true—most clubs don't get going until well after midnight, and the real fun often starts after 3am. Popular bars can be found around **Calle Mateos Gago** near the cathedral, **Calle Adriano** by the bullring, and **Calle Betis** across the river in Triana.

▓ **La Carbonería,** C. Levies 18, off C. Santa María La Blanca. Popular bar with free live flamenco and a massive outdoor patio replete with banana trees, picnic tables, and gui-
tar-strumming Romeos. *Tapas* €1.50-2. Beer €1.50. Mixed drinks €4.50. Open July-
Aug. M-Sa 8pm-4am, Su 8pm-2:30am; Sept.-May M-Sa 8pm-4am, Su 7pm-3am.

▓ **El Capote,** next to Pte. Isabel II, at C. Arjona and C. Reyes Católicos. Popular summertime bar, full of tables overlooking the river. Young *sevillanos* and tourists mingle amidst
upbeat live music or recorded American and Latin pop. Beer €1.50 during the day, €2
at night. Mixed drinks €5. Open June-Sept. 15 daily noon-4am.

Flaherty's, C. Alemanes 7, across from the cathedral. Friendly, sprawling Irish pub popular among tourists, ex-pats, and foreign and local students. 4 beers on tap, including
Guinness. Serves international food daily until 11:30pm. *Entrees* and sandwiches €5-
10. Beer €2. Mixed drinks €4.60. Open daily 11am-3am.

Tribal, next to Pte. de la Barqueta. Popular *discoteca,* playing American hip-hop and
Latin favorites. Outdoor patio overlooking the river. W hip-hop nights are the most pop-
ular with backpacker crowd. Beer €3.50. Mixed drinks €5.50. No cover before 1am.
After 1am cover €6-10, includes 1 drink. Open W-Sa 10pm-6am.

Palenque, Av. Blas Pascal, on the grounds of Cartuja '93. Gigantic dance club, complete
with 2 dance floors and a small ice skating rink (€3, including skate rental). F-Sa dress
to impress. Mainly *sevillano* university crowd. Beer €3. Mixed drinks €5. Cover €7 F-Sa.
Open June-Sept. Th-Sa midnight-7am.

Fundición, C. Betis 49-50, at the end of the hallway. Popular bar among American
exchange students. American music and decor fill the huge interior. Beer €2.50. Mixed
drinks €5. Open M-Sa 10pm-5am. Closed July 15-Aug. 30.

Isbiliyya, Po. de Colon 2, across from Pte. Isabel II. Popular riverfront gay, straight, and
lesbian bar with outdoor seating and an ample dance floor. Beer €2-2.50. Open daily
8pm-6am.

Terraza Chile, Po. de las Delicias. Loud salsa and pop keep this small, breezy dance
club packed and pounding throughout the early morning hours. Young *sevillano* professionals mingle with Euro-chic American exchange students. Beer €1.50. Mixed drinks
€5. Open June-Sept. daily 8am-5am; Oct.-May Th-Sa 8pm-5am.

Coliseum, across from Tribal. A chill cross between a summer *terraza* and a disco.
Upscale 20-somethings sip drinks at tables overlooking the river or crowd the small
dance floor. Beer €3. Mixed drinks €5.50. Cover €7, includes 1 drink; look for free
admission coupons from promoters in town. Open May-Sept. Su and W-Sa 10pm-late.

Catedral, Cuesta del Rosario 12. Underground disco with a metal, stone, and wood
decor. No cover for women and those with coupons. Cover for men €6, includes 1
mixed drink or 2 beers. Open Sept.-June W-Sa midnight-6am.

▶ DAYTRIPS FROM SEVILLE

CÁDIZ. Founded by the Phoenicians in 1100 BC, Cádiz (pop. 155,000) is
thought to be the oldest inhabited city in Europe. **Carnaval** is perhaps Spain's
most dazzling party (Feb. 19-29 in 2004), but year-round the city offers golden
sand **beaches** that put its pebble-strewn eastern neighbors to shame. **Playa de la
Caleta** is the most convenient, but better sand awaits in the new city; take bus
#1 from Pl. España to Pl. Glorieta Ingeniero (€0.80), or walk along the *paseo*
by the water (20-30min. from behind the Cathedral) to reach ▓**Playa de la Victoria,** which has earned the EU's *bandera azul* for cleanliness. Back in town, the
gold-domed, 18th-century **cathedral** is considered the last great cathedral built
by colonial riches. To get there from Pl. San Juan de Dios, follow C. Pelota.
(Cathedral and museum open Tu-F 10am-1:30pm and 4:30-7:30pm, Sa 10am-1:30pm.
€3.) From the train station, walk two blocks past the fountain with the port on
your right, and look left for **Plaza San Juan de Dios,** the town center.

Transportes Generales Comes **buses** (☎956 22 78 11) arrive at Pl. Hispanidad from Seville (2hr., 11-14 per day, €9.40). From the bus station, walk 5min. down Av. Puerto with the port on your left; Pl. de San Juan de Dios will be after the park on your right. The **tourist office** is at #11 Pl. de San Juan de Dios. (☎ 956 24 10 01. Office open M-F 9am-2pm and 5-8pm. Kiosk in front of office open June-Sept. Sa-Su and holidays 10am-1pm and 5-7:30pm; Oct.-May 10am-1:30pm and 4-6pm.) Most *hostales* huddle in and around Pl. de San Juan de Dios and around the harbor. **Hostal Marques ❷**, C. Marques de Cádiz 1, off Pl. de San Juan de Dios, offers clean and spacious rooms with balconies that surround an enclosed inner courtyard. (☎956 28 58 54. Singles €18; doubles €25, with bath €35; triples €35.)

ARCOS DE LA FRONTERA. With castles and Roman ruins at every turn, Arcos (pop. 33,000) is a historic and romantic gem. Wander the winding alleys of ruins and hanging flowers in the **old quarter,** and marvel at the stunning view from 🖼**Plaza Cabildo.** In the square is the **Basilica de Santa María de la Asunción,** a mix of Baroque, Renaissance, and Gothic styles. To reach the old quarter from the bus station, exit left, follow the road and turn left, and continue 20min. uphill on C. Muñoz Vásquez as it changes names. **Buses** (☎956 70 49 77) run from C. Corregidores to Cádiz (1½hr., 6 per day, €4.60) and Seville (2hr., 7am and 5pm, €6.20). The **tourist office** is on Pl. Cabildo. (☎956 70 22 64. Open Mar. 15-Oct. 15 M-Sa 10am-2pm and 4-8pm; Oct. 16-Mar. 14 M-Sa 10am-2pm and 3:30-7:30pm.) **Pensión Callejon de las Monjas ❷**, C. Dean Espinosa 4, shaded by the Iglesia de Sta. María, offers a restaurant, barbershop, and hostel with spotless rooms and A/C. (☎956 70 23 02. Singles €18, with bath €22; doubles €27/33, with large terrace €39; quads €66.) Cheap cafes and *tapas* bars huddle along the bottom end of **C. Corredera** between the bus station and the old quarter.

RONDA. Picturesque Ronda (pop. 38,000) has all the charm of a small, medieval town with the amenities and cultural opportunities of a thriving city. Ancient bridges, picturesque views, and old dungeons—not to mention the famed bull-ring—attract many visitors to Ronda, the birthplace of modern bullfighting. A precipitous 100m gorge, carved by the Río Guadalevín, dips below the **Puente Nuevo,** opposite Pl. España. The views from the Puente Nuevo, and its neighboring **Puente Viejo** and **Puente San Miguel,** are unparalleled. Bullfighting aficionados charge over to Ronda's **Plaza de Toros,** Spain's oldest bullring (est. 1785) and cradle of the modern *corrida.* Descend the steep stairs of the **Casa Del Rey Moro** into the 14th-century water mine for an otherworldly view of the river ravine.

Trains (☎902 24 02 02) depart from Av. Alferez Provisional for: Algeciras (2hr., 4 per day, €5.80); Granada (3hr., 3 per day, €11); Madrid (4½hr., 2 per day, €49); and Málaga (2hr., 7:50am, €7.55). **Buses** (☎952 18 70 61) go from Pl. Concepción García Redondo 2, near Av. Andalucía, to: Cádiz (3hr., 3 per day, €11.50); Málaga (2½hr., 9 per day, €7.60); Marbella (1½hr., 5 per day, €4.30); and Seville (2½hr., 3-5 per day, €9). The **tourist office** is at Pl. España 1. (☎952 87 12 72. Open Sept.-May M-F 9am-7pm, Sa-Su 10am-2pm.; June-Aug. M-F 9am-8pm, Sa-Su 10am-2pm.) **Pensión La Purisima ❶**, C. Seville 10, offers bright rooms. (☎952 87 10 50. Singles €15; doubles €28-30, with bath €30-33; triples with bath €45.) **Postal Code:** 29400.

GIBRALTAR

From the morning mist just off the southern shore of Spain emerges the Rock of Gibraltar. Bastion of empire and Jerusalem of Anglophilia, this rocky peninsula is among history's most contested plots of land. Ancient seafarers called "Gib" one of the Pillars of Hercules, believing it marked the end of the world. After numerous squabbles between Moors, Spaniards, and Turks, the English successfully stormed Gibraltar in 1704 and have remained in possession ever since.

| PHONE CODE | ☎350 from the UK or the US; ☎9567 from Spain. |

S P A I N

C⁷ TRANSPORTATION AND PRACTICAL INFORMATION. Buses arrive in the Spanish border town of **La Línea** from: Algeciras (40min., every 30min., €1.60); Cádiz (3hr., 4 per day, €10); and Granada (5hr., 2 per day, €17). From the bus station, walk directly toward the Rock; the border is 5min. away. Once through Spanish customs and Gibraltar's passport control, catch bus #9 or 10 or walk across the airport tarmac into town (20min.). Stay left on Av. Winston Churchill when the road forks at Corral Lane; Gibraltar's **Main Street**, a commercial strip lined with most services, begins at the far end of a square, past the Burger King on the left.

The **tourist office,** Duke of Kent House, Cathedral Sq., is across the park from the Gibraltar Museum. (☎450 00; tourism@gibraltar.gi. Open M-F 9am-5:30pm.) Although **euros** are accepted almost everywhere (except pay phones and public establishments), the **pound sterling (£)** is preferred. Merchants sometimes charge a higher price in euros than in the pound's exchange equivalent. Change is often given in English currency rather than euros. As of press date, **1£ = €1.45.**

◐ SIGHTS. About halfway up the Rock is the infamous **Apes' Den,** where barbary monkeys cavort on the sides of rocks, the tops of taxis, and the heads of tourists. At the northern tip of the Rock facing Spain are the **Great Siege Tunnels.** Originally used to fend off a combined Franco-Spanish siege at the end of the American Revolution, the underground tunnels were later expanded during WWII to span 33 miles. The eerie chambers of **St. Michael's Cave,** located 0.5km from the siege tunnels, were cut into the rock by thousands of years of water erosion. (Cable car to above sights every 10min. daily 9:30am-5:15pm. Combined admittance ticket, including one-way cable car ride, £7.50/€12.50.)

⌂◖ ACCOMMODATIONS AND FOOD. Gibraltar is best seen as a daytrip. The few accommodations in the area are often full, especially in the summer, and camping is illegal. **Emile Youth Hostel Gibraltar ❷,** Montague Bastian, behind Casemates Sq., has bunk beds in cheerfully painted rooms with clean communal bathrooms. (☎511 06. Breakfast included. Lock-out 10:30am-4:30pm. Dorms and singles £15/€25; doubles £30/€50.) International restaurants are easy to find, but you may choke on the prices. **The Viceroy of India ❸** serves both vegetarian and meat dishes. (Entrees £4-10. Open M-F noon-3pm and 7-11pm, Sa 7-11pm. MC/V.) For groceries, try the **Checkout** supermarket on Main St., next to Marks & Spencer. (Open M-F 8:30am-8pm, Sa 10am-6pm, Su 1am-3pm. MC/V.)

ALGECIRAS
☎956

Hidden beyond Algeciras's (pop. 101,000) seedy port is a more serene old neighborhood, worthy of a visit for those with a few hours to spare. However, for most itinerary-bound travelers, this is a city seen only in transit. RENFE **trains** (☎902 24 02 02) run from C. Juan de la Cierva to Granada (4hr., 3 per day, €16) and Ronda (1½hr., 4 per day, €5.80). Empresa Portillo **buses** (☎956 65 43 04) leave from Av. Virgen del Carmen 15 for: Córdoba (6hr., 2 per day, €20); Granada (4hr., 4 per day, €18); Málaga (3hr., 8-9 per day, €9.40); and Marbella (1hr., 8-9 per day, €5.20). Transportes Generales Comes (☎956 65 34 56) goes from C. San Bernardo 1 to Cádiz (2½hr., 10 per day, €8.60). La Línea runs to: Gibraltar (45min., every 30min. 7am-9:45pm, €1.60); Madrid (8hr., 4 per day, €23); and Seville (4hr., 5 per day, €14.30). To reach the **ferries** from the bus and train stations, follow C. San Bernardo to C. Juan de la Cierva and turn left at its end; the port entrance will be on your right. The **tourist office** is on C. Juan de la Cierva. (☎956 57 26 36. Open M-F 9am-2pm.) Hostels cluster around **Calle José Santacana.** Clean rooms all with phones, TV, and bathrooms can be found at **Hostal Residencia Versailles ❷,** C. Moutero Rios 12, off C. Cayetano del Toro (☎/fax 956 65 42 11. Singles with shower €18; doubles €30.) **Postal Code:** 11203.

COSTA DEL SOL

The Costa del Sol mixes rocky beaches with chic promenades and swank hotels. While some spots have been over-developed and can be hard on the wallet, the coast's stunning natural beauty has elsewhere been left untouched. Summer brings swarms of tourists, but nothing takes away from the main attraction: eight months of spring and four months of summer.

MÁLAGA. Once celebrated by Hans Christian Andersen, Málaga (pop. 550,000) is the largest Andalucian city on the coast and the birthplace of Pablo Picasso. Today this transportation hub offers a charming *casco antiguo* (old town) and beautiful nearby beaches like the whitewashed Nerja. (Buses run from Málaga, 1½hr., 12-18 per day, €3.20.) The ■**Alcazaba,** the city's most imposing sight, exudes a medieval tranquility and offers views of the harbor. (Open June-Aug. Su and Tu-Sa 9:30am-8pm; Sept.-May Tu-Sa 8:30am-7pm. €1.80, students €.60). Málaga's breathtaking **cathedral,** C. Molina Larios 4, blends Gothic, Renaissance, and Baroque styles and contains more than 15 side chapels. (☎952 22 03 45. Open M-F 10am-6:45pm, Sa 10am-5:45pm. €3.)

Buses run from Po. Tilos (☎952 35 00 61), one block from the RENFE station along C. Roger de Flor, to: Cádiz (5hr., 5 per day, €18); Córdoba (3hr., 5 per day, €11); Granada (2hr., 17 per day, €8.10); Madrid (7hr., 12 per day, €18); Marbella (1½hr., every hr., €4.20); and Seville (3hr., 11-12 per day, €14). The **tourist office** is at Av. Cervantes 1 (☎/fax 952 60 44 10. Open M-F 8:15am-2pm and 4:30-7pm, Sa-Su 9:30am-1:30pm). **Hostal La Palma** ❷, C. Martínez 7, off C. Marqués de Larios, has a great family atmosphere and rooms with A/C, mini-terraces and private baths. (☎952 22 67 72. Singles €21-25.) ■**Vegetariano Cañadú** ❶, Pl. de la Merced 21, serves hearty meatless entrees. (☎952 22 90 56. Open Su-Th 1:30-4pm and 8-11pm, F-Sa 1:30-4pm and 8pm-midnight. AmEx/MC/V.) **Postal Code:** 29080.

MARBELLA. Like your vacation spots shaken, not stirred? Scottish smoothie Sean Connery and a host of other jet-setters choose **Marbella** (pop. 116,000; 500,000+ in summer) as their vacation home. While there may be more yachts here than hostels, it's still possible to have a budgeted good time. The beaches beckon with 320 days of sunshine per year, but no visit would be complete without a stroll through the *casco antiguo* (old town), a maze of cobblestone streets and white-washed facades trimmed with wild roses. With 22km of beach, Marbella offers a variety of settings. Stroll the 7km from Marbella center to chic and trendy **Puerto Banús,** where beautiful, clean beaches are buffered by white yachts. Beaches to the east of the port are popular with British backpackers; those to the west attract a more posh crowd.

From the station atop Av. Trapiche (☎952 76 44 00), buses go to: Algeciras (1½hr., 17 per day, €5.20); Cádiz (4hr., 6 per day, €14); Granada (3½hr., 7 per day, €13); Madrid (7½hr., 7 per day, €20); Málaga (1½hr., 2 per hr., €4.20); and Seville (4hr., 2-3 per day, €14). The **tourist office** is on Pl. Naranjos. (☎952 82 35 50. Open June-Aug. M-F 9:30am-9pm, Sa 10am-2pm.) The area in the *casco antiguo* around Pl. Naranjos offers quick-filling hostels. Once a 17th-century inn run by monks for traveling pilgrims, today ■**Hostal del Pilar** ❶, C. Mesoncillo 4, is centrally located off of C. Peral and is clean and comfortable. (☎952 82 99 36. Dorms €15.) The excellent **Albergue Juvenil (HI)** ❶, Av. Trapiche 2, downhill from the bus station, has a social atmosphere and huge pool. (☎952 77 14 91. June 15-Sept. 15 Dorms €18, under-26 €14; Apr.-June 15, Sept. 15-Oct. 15 €16/12; Nov.-Mar. €12/9.) ■**El Gallo,** C. Lobatas 44, offers local cuisine in huge portions. (*Tapas* from €1.50. Entrees €2.50-8. Open Su-M and W-Sa 1-4:30pm and 7-11:30pm.) Nightlife in Marbella begins and ends late. A mellow ambience suffuses the ■**Townhouse Bar,** C. Alamo 1, tucked down an alley off C. Nueva. Ask for a shot (€1.50) of Apple Pie. (Open daily 10pm-3am.) **Postal Code:** 29600.

SPAIN

GRANADA ☎958

Legend says that in 1492, when Moorish ruler Boabdil fled Granada (pop. 240,000), the last Muslim stronghold in Spain, his mother berated him for casting a longing look back at the Alhambra. "You do well to weep as a woman," she told him, "for what you could not defend as a man." A spectacular palace celebrated by poets and artists throughout the ages, the Alhambra continues to inspire melancholy in those who must leave its timeless beauty. The Albaicín, an enchanting maze of Moorish houses and twisting alleys, is Spain's best-preserved Arab quarter and the only part of the Muslim city to survive the *Reconquista*.

◰ TRANSPORTATION

Trains: RENFE Station, Av. Andaluces (☎902 24 02 02). To: **Algeciras** (5-7hr., 3 per day 7am-6pm, €16); **Madrid** (5-6hr., 7:55am and 4:40pm, €28-44); **Seville** (4-5hr., 4 per day 3am-8pm, €16).

Buses: Major bus routes originate from the **bus station** on the outskirts of Granada on Ctra. Madrid, near C. Arzobispo Pedro de Castro. **Alsina Graells** (☎958 18 54 80) runs to **Córdoba** (3hr., 10 per day 7:30am-8pm, €11) and **Seville** (3hr., 10 per day 7:30am-8pm, €16). **ALSA** (☎902 42 22 42) goes to **Alicante** (6hr., 8 per day, €23), **Barcelona** (14hr., 7 per day, €57), and **Valencia** (10hr., 7 per day, €35). All ALSA buses run from 2:15am-11:30pm.

Public Transportation: From the bus station take bus #10 to the youth hostel, C. de Ronda, C. Recogidas, or C. Acera de Darro or bus #3 to Av. Constitución, Gran Vía, or Pl. de Isabel la Católica. From Pl. Nueva catch #30 to the Alhambra or #31 to the Albaicín. Rides €0.85, *bonobus* (10 tickets) €5. Free map at tourist office.

▊ ▐ ORIENTATION AND PRACTICAL INFORMATION

The geographic center of Granada is the small **Plaza de Isabel la Católica,** at the intersection of the city's two main arteries, **Calle de los Reyes Católicos** and **Gran Vía de Colón.** To reach Gran Vía and the **cathedral** from the train station, walk three blocks up Av. Andaluces and take bus #3-6, 9, or 11 from Av. Constitución; from the bus station, take bus #3. Two blocks uphill on C. Reyes Católicos sits **Plaza Nueva.** Downhill on C. Reyes Católicos lies Pl. Carmen, site of the **Ayuntamiento** and Puerta Real. The **Alhambra** commands the steep hill above Pl. Nueva.

Tourist Office: Oficina Provincial, Pl. Mariana Pineda 10 (☎958 24 71 28; www.dipgra.es). From Pta. Real, turn right onto C. Angel Ganivet, then take a right 2 blocks later to reach the plaza. Open M-F 9am-8pm, Sa 10am-7pm, Su 10am-4pm.

American Express: C. Reyes Católicos 31 (☎958 22 45 12), between Pl. de Isabel la Católica and Pta. Real. Open M-F 9am-1:30pm and 2-9pm, Sa 10am-1pm.

Luggage Storage: 24hr. storage at the train station.

Laundromat: C. La Paz 19. From Pl. Trinidad, take C. Alhóndiga, turn right on C. La Paz, and walk 2 blocks. Wash €5, dry €1 per 15min. Open M-F 10am-2pm and 5-8pm.

Emergency: ☎112. **Police:** C. Duquesa 21 (☎958 24 81 00). English spoken.

Medical Assistance: Clínica de San Cecilio, C. Dr. Oloriz 16 (☎958 28 02 00 or 27 20 00), on the road to Jaén. **Ambulance:** ☎958 28 44 50.

Internet Access: Net (☎958 22 69 19) has 2 locations: Pl. de los Girones 3, up C. Pavaneras from Pl. de Isabel la Católica; and C. Buensucesco 22, 1 block from Pl. Trinidad. €0.75 per hr. Both open M-F 9am-11pm, Sa-Su 10am-11pm.

Post Office: Pta. Real (☎958 22 48 35; fax 22 36 41), on the corner of Carrera del Darro and C. Angel Ganivet. **Lista de Correos** and **fax** service. Wires money M-F 8:30am-2:30pm. Open M-F 8am-9pm, Sa 9:30am-2pm. **Postal Code:** 18009.

Granada

▲ ACCOMMODATIONS
Albergue Juvenile
  Granada (HI), **27**
Hospedaje Almohada, **22**
Hostal Antares, **18**
Hostal Goméz, **10**
Hostal Gran Vía, **14**
Hostal Landazuri, **11**
Hostal Macia Plaza, **7**
Hostal Residencia Britz, **8**
Hostal-Residencia Lisboa, **26**
Hostal-Residencia
  Londres, **13**
Hostal Venecia, **9**
Hostal Zurita, **24**
Pensión Olympia, **15**

● FOOD
Botánico Café, **23**
Los Italianos, **20**
El Ladrillo II, **2**
Naturi Albaicín, **6**
La Nueva Bodega, **17**
Restaurante Asador Corrala
  del Carbón, **25**
Restaurant Sonymar, **12**
Taberna Salinas, **19**

★ NIGHTLIFE
El Ángel Azul, **28**
Camborio, **1**
Eshavira, **4**
Fondo Reservado, **3**
Granada 10, **16**
Granero, **21**
Kasbah, **5**
Planta Baja, **29**

S P A I N

ACCOMMODATIONS

Hostels line **Cuesta de Gomérez, Plaza Trinidad,** and **Gran Vía.** Call ahead during *Semana Santa.*

Hostal Venecia, Cuesta de Gomérez 2, 3rd fl. (☎958 22 39 87), near Pl. Nueva. Wake up to a soothing cup of tea and a hint of incense. Singles €15; doubles €26; triples €39. ❶

Hospedaje Almohada, C. Postigo de Zarate 4 (☎958 20 74 46). From Pl. Trinidad, follow C. Duquesa and take a right on C. Málaga; it's the red door with the small sign on your right. A successful experiment in communal living. Dorms €14; singles €16; doubles €30; triples €40. ❶

Hostal Residencia Britz, Cuesta de Gomérez 1 (☎/fax 958 22 36 52), on the corner of Pl. Nueva. Singles €18; doubles €28, with bath €38. Show the reception your copy of *Let's Go* for a 6% discount. MC/V. ❷

Hostal Antares, C. Cetti Meriém 10 (☎958 22 83 13), on the corner of C. Elvira, 1 block from the cathedral. TV and A/C. Singles €18; doubles €30, with bath €36. ❷

Albergue Juvenil Granada (HI), Ramon y Cajal 2 (☎958 00 29 00). From the bus station take #10. Across from "El Estadio de la Juventud," on the left. Dorms €14-16, under-26 €10-12. Nonmembers add €3.50. ❶

Hostal Macia Plaza, Pl. Nueva 4 (☎958 22 75 36), centrally located on the Plaza. Carpeted rooms with marble baths and A/C. Singles €47; doubles €70; triples €90. ❹

Hostal-Residencia Lisboa, Pl. Carmen 29 (☎958 22 14 13 or 22 14 14; fax 22 14 87). Take C. Reyes Católicos from Pl. de Isabel la Católica; Pl. Carmen is on the left. Singles €18, with bath €30; doubles €27/40; triples €33/50. MC/V. ❷

Hostal Gomérez, Cuesta de Gomérez 10 (☎958 22 44 37). Simple rooms with hall baths. Multilingual owner will assist guests planning longer stays. Laundry €6 per load. Singles €15; doubles €24; triples €30. ❷

Hostal Landazuri, Cuesta de Gomérez 24 (☎958 22 14 06). Colorfully decorated rooms and a rooftop terrace with splendid views of the Alhambra and Sierra Nevada. Singles €20, with bath €28; doubles €24/36; large suite for 2-3 €40. ❷

Hostal Zurita, Pl. Trinidad 7 (☎958 27 50 20). Bright rooms and A/C. Singles €17; doubles €29, with bath €36; triples €40/50. ❷

Hostal-Residencia Londres, Gran Vía 29, 6th fl. (☎958 27 80 34), perched atop a fin-de-siècle edifice with multiple patios. Great views. English spoken. Singles €18; doubles €27, with bath €35. Each additional person €10. ❷

Pensión Olympia, Alvaro de Bazán 6 (☎958 27 82 38). From Pl. Isabel, walk 6 blocks down Gran Vía and turn right. Singles €15; doubles €20, with shower €25, with bath €30. MC/V. ❶

Hostal Gran Vía, Gran Vía 17 (☎958 27 92 12), 4 blocks from Pl. de Isabel la Católica. Singles with shower €17; doubles with shower €25, with bath €33; triples €35/45. ❷

FOOD

Cheap North African cuisine can be found around the Albaicín, while more typical *menú* fare awaits in Pl. Nueva and Pl. Trinidad. The adventurous eat well in Granada—try *tortilla sacromonte* (omelette with calf's brains, bull testicles, ham, shrimp, and veggies). Get groceries at **Supermercado T. Mariscal,** C. Genil, next to El Corte Inglés. (Open M-F 9:30am-2pm and 5-9pm, Sa 9:30am-2pm.)

▨ **El Ladrillo II,** C. Panaderos 13. Sumptuous food. Entrees €6.60-12. Open daily 12:30pm-1:30am. MC/V. ❷

▨ **Naturi Albaicín,** C. Calderería Nueva 10. Excellent vegetarian cuisine in a serene Moroccan ambience. No alcohol served. *Menú* €6.90-8.30. Open M-Th and Sa-Su 1-4pm and 7-11pm, F 7-11pm. ❷

Restaurant Sonymar, Pl. Boquero 6 (☎958 27 10 63). Relish in the nouveau Moorish decor and amazing service of this secluded neighborhood eatery. *Menú* €6. Entrees €7.20-12.60. Open daily 1-4pm and 8-11:30pm. AmEx/V. ❷

Taberna Salinas, C. Elvira 13 (☎958 22 14 11). Rustic tavern that serves generous portions. Entrees €7-18. Open daily 12:30pm-2am. ❸

La Nueva Bodega, C. Cetti Meriém 9 (☎958 22 59 34), at the corner of C. Cetti Meriém and C. Elvira. Pleases locals and tourists alike with hearty traditional cuisine. *Menú* €4.20-9. *Tapas* €4. Open daily noon-midnight. ❶

Restaurante Asador Corrala del Carbón, C. Mariana Pineda 8 (☎958 22 38 10). Savor traditional Andalucian grilled meat in an indoor re-creation of an old neighborhood courtyard. Entrees €8-17. Open daily 1-4pm and 8:30pm-midnight. ❸

Botánico Café, C. Málaga 3 (☎958 27 15 98), 2 blocks from Pl. Trinidad. This hip cafe is a major student hangout which brings new life to traditional Spanish dishes. Entrees €4.80-9. Open Su-Th noon-1am, F-Sa noon-2am. ❷

Los Italianos, Gran Vía 4 (☎958 22 40 34). Popular *gelato* parlor with 26 heavenly flavors draws nightly crowds. 2 scoops €1, ice cream sundaes €1.20-2.50. Cold drinks (lemonade and *leche fria*) €1.20. Open daily 9am-3am. ❶

◎ SIGHTS

▨ **THE ALHAMBRA.** From the streets of Granada, the Alhambra, meaning "the red one" in Arabic, appears simple, blocky, faded—a child's toy castle planted in the foothills of the Sierra Nevada. Up close, however, you will discover an elaborate and detailed piece of architecture; one that magically unites water, light, wood, stucco, and ceramics to create a fortress-palace of rich aesthetic and symbolic grandeur. Celebrated by poets and artists throughout the ages, the Alhambra continues to inspire those who visit with its timeless beauty, and many would argue that the age-old saying: "*Si mueres sin ver la Alhambra, no has vivido*" (If you die without seeing the Alhambra, you have not lived) still holds true. (*Walk up C. Cuesta de Gomérez from Pl. Nueva (20min.), or take the quick Alhambra-Neptuno microbus from Pl. Nueva (every 5min., €1). ☎958 22 15 03; reservations ☎902 22 44 60; online reservations www.alhambratickets.com. Admission is limited, so arrive early or reserve tickets in advance at local banks (reservation fee €0.75) or BBVA branches around Spain. Enter the Palace of the Nasrids (Alcázar) during the time specified on your ticket. Open Apr.-Sept. daily 8:30am-8pm; Oct.-Mar. M-Sa 9am-5:45pm. Nighttime visits June-Sept. Tu, Th, Sa 10-11:30pm; Oct.-May Sa 8-10pm. All visits €8. The handicapped and under-8 free. Moonlit tours June-Sept. Tu, Th, Sa 10-11:30pm; Oct.-May Sa 8-10pm; inquire for details at the info desk at the Alhambra; €8. Audioguides narrated by "Washington Irving" in Spanish, English, French, German, and Italian; €3.*)

THE ALCÁZAR. Follow signs to the *Palacio Nazaries* to see the Alcázar, a 14th-century royal palace full of dripping stalactite archways, multicolored tiles, and sculpted fountains. The magnificently carved walls of the **Patio del Cuarto Dorado** (Patio of the Gilded Hall) are topped by the shielded windows of the women's chambers, such that they could see out but no one could see in. In the elaborate **Sala de los Embajadores** (Hall of Ambassadors) Granada was formally surrendered to the Catholic Monarchs, and Ferdinand and Columbus discussed finding

S P A I N

a new route to India. A fountain supported by 12 marble lions babbles in the center of the **Patio de los Leones** (Courtyard of the Lions). The **Sala de los Abencerrajes** is where Boabdil had the throats of 16 sons of the Abencerrajes family slit after one of them had allegedly had amorous encounters with the sultana Zorahayda. The rust-colored stains in the basin are said to mark the indelible traces of the butchering; evidently, none of this bothered the Emperor Charles V, who dined here during the construction of his neighboring *palazzo*. Light streams into the room through the intricate domed ceiling, which features an eight-pointed star—a design said to represent terrestrial and heavenly harmony.

THE ALCAZABA. The Christians drove the first Nasrid King Alhamar from the Albaicín to this more strategic hill, where he built the series of rust-colored brick towers which form the Alcazaba (fortress). A dark, spiraling staircase leads to the **Torre de la Vela** (watchtower), where visitors get a splendid 360° view of Granada and the surrounding mountains. The tower's bells were rung to warn of impending danger and to coordinate the Moorish irrigation system. Every January 1st, during the annual commemoration of the Christian conquest of Granada, an old legend holds that any local girl who scrambles up the tower and rings the bell by hand before the first day of the actual new year will receive a wedding proposal within 365 days. Exit through the **Puerta del Vino**, the original entrance to the medina, where inhabitants of the Alhambra once bought tax-free wine (alas, no more).

EL GENERALIFE. Over a bridge, across the **Callejón de los Cipreses** and the shady **Callejón de las Adelfas,** are the vibrant blossoms, towering cypresses, and streaming waterways of El Generalife, the sultan's vacation retreat. In 1313 Arab engineers changed the Darro's flow by 18km and employed dams and channels to prepare the soil for Aben Walid Ismail's design of El Generalife. Over the centuries, the estate passed through private hands until it was finally repatriated in 1931. The two buildings of El Generalife, the **Palacio** and the **Sala Regia,** connect across the **Patio de la Acequia** (Courtyard of the Irrigation Channel), embellished with a narrow pool fed by fountains that form an aquatic archway. Honeysuckle vines scale the back wall, and shady benches invite long rests. An old oak tree stands here at the place where the sultana Zorahayda apparently had several amorous encounters with a nobleman from the Abencerrajes tribe.

PALACIO DE CARLOS V. After the *Reconquista* drove the Moors from Spain, Ferdinand and Isabella restored the Alcázar. Little did they know that two generations later Emperor Charles V would demolish part of it to make way for his Palacio, a Renaissance masterpiece by Pedro Machuca (a disciple of Michelangelo). Although it is incongruous with the surrounding Moorish splendor, scholars concede that the palace is one of the most beautiful Renaissance buildings in Spain. A square building with a circular inner courtyard wrapped in two stories of Doric colonnades, it is Machuca's only surviving design. Inside, the small but impressive **Museo de La Alhambra** contains the only original furnishings remaining from the Alhambra. (☎ 958 22 62 79. *Open Tu-Sa 9am-2:30pm. Free.*) Upstairs, the **Museo de Bellas Artes** displays religious sculptures and paintings of the Granada School dating from the 16th century to the present. (☎ 958 22 48 43. *Open Apr.-Sept. Tu 2:30-6pm, W-Sa 9am-6pm, Su 9am-2:30pm; Oct.-Mar. Tu 2:30-7:45pm, W-Sa 9am-7:45pm, Su 9am-2:30pm. €1.50.*)

IN THE CATHEDRAL QUARTER

■ **CAPILLA REAL.** Downhill from the Alhambra's Arab splendor, through the Pta. Real off Gran Vía de Colon, on C. Oficios, the Capilla Real (Royal Chapel), Ferdinand and Isabella's private chapel, exemplifies Christian Granada. During their prosperous reign, the Catholic Monarchs funneled almost a quarter of the royal income into the chapel's construction (which lasted from 1504 to 1521) to build a proper burial place. Their efforts did not go unrewarded; intricate Gothic masonry and meticulously rendered figurines, as well as **La Reja,** the gilded iron grille of Master Bartolomé, grace the couple's resting place. Behind La Reja lie the almost lifelike marble figures of the royals themselves. Ferdinand and Isabella are on the right, when facing the altar; beside them sleeps their daughter Juana la Loca (the Mad) and her husband Felipe el Hermoso (the Fair). Much to the horror of the rest of the royal family, Juana insisted on keeping the body of her husband with her for an unpleasantly long time after he died. The lead caskets, where all four monarchs were laid to rest, lie directly below the marble sarcophagi in a crypt down a small stairway on the left. The smaller, fifth coffin belongs to the hastily buried child-king of Portugal, Miguel, whose death allowed Charles V to ascend the throne. (☎ 958 22 92 39. Open M-Sa 10:30am-1pm and 4-7pm, Su 11am-1pm and 4-5pm; €2.50.)

SACRISTY. Next door in the sacristy, Isabel's private **art collection,** the highlight of the chapel, favors Flemish and German artists of the 15th century. The glittering **royal jewels**—the queen's golden crown and scepter and the king's sword—shine in the middle of the sacristy. Nearby are the Christian banners which first fluttered in triumph over the Alhambra. (☎ 958 22 92 39. Open M-Sa 10:30am-1pm and 4-7pm, Su 11am-1pm and 4-5pm; €2.50. Free with admission to Capilla Real.)

CATHEDRAL. Behind the Capilla Real and the sacristy is Granada's cathedral. Construction of the cathedral began after *la Reconquista* upon the smoldering embers of Granada's largest mosque and was not completed until 1704. The first purely Renaissance cathedral in Spain, its massive Corinthian pillars support a 45m vaulted nave. (☎ 958 22 29 59. Open Apr.-Sept. M-Sa 10:45am-1:30pm and 4-7pm, Su 4-7pm; Oct.-Mar. M-Sa 10:30am-1:30pm and 3:30-6:30pm, Su 11am-1:30pm. €2.50.)

■**THE ALBAICÍN.** A labyrinth of steep streets and narrow alleys, the Albaicín was the only Moorish neighborhood to escape the torches of the *Reconquista* and remains a key stop in Granada. After the fall of the Alhambra, a small Muslim population remained here until being expelled in the 17th century. Today, with its abundance of North African cuisine, outdoor bazaars blasting Arabic music, teahouses, and the presence of a mosque near Pl. San Nicolás, the Albaicín attests to the persistence of Islamic influence in Andalucía. Spectacular sunsets over the surrounding mountains can be seen from C. Cruz de Quirós, above C. Elvira. Although generally safe, the Albaicín is disorienting and should be approached with caution at night. (Bus #12 runs from beside the cathedral to C. Pagés at the top of the Albaicín.)

The best way to explore this maze is to proceed along Carrera del Darro off Pl. Santa Ana, climb the Cuesta del Chapiz on the left, then wander through Muslim ramparts, cisterns, and gates. On Pl. Santa Ana, the 16th-century **Real Cancillería** (or **Audiencia**), with its beautiful arcaded patio and stalactite ceiling, was the Christians' Ayuntamiento. Farther uphill are the 11th-century **Arab baths.** (Carrera del Darro 31. ☎ 958 02 78 00. Open Tu-Sa 10am-2pm. Free.) The **Museo Arqueológico** showcases funerary urns, classical sculpture, Carthaginian vases, Muslim lamps, and beautiful ceramics. (Carrera del Darro 41. ☎ 958 22 56 40. Open Tu 3-8pm, W-Sa 9am-8pm, Su 9am-2:30pm. €1.50. EU members free.) The ■**mirador** (lookout terrace) adjacent to **Iglesia de San Nicolás** in the heart of the Albaicín affords the city's best view of the Alhambra, especially in winter when snow adorns the Sierra Nevada behind it. From C. Elvira, go up C. Calderería Nueva to C. San Gregorio and continue uphill on this street past Pl. Algibe Trillo, where it becomes Cta. Algibe de Trillo. At Pl. Camino, make a left on Cta. Tomasa and another left on Atarazana Cta. Cabras. The mirador will be on your right.

🎵 🎷 ENTERTAINMENT AND NIGHTLIFE

The *Guía del Ocio*, sold at newsstands (€0.85), lists clubs, pubs, and cafes. The most boisterous nightspots belong to **Calle Pedro Antonio de Alarcón**, running from Pl. Albert Einstein to Ancha de Gracia, while hip new bars and clubs line **Calle Elvira** from Cárcel to C. Cedrán. **Gay bars** cluster around Carrera del Darro.

Eshavira, C. Postigo de la Cuna, in an alley off C. Azacayes, between C. Elvira and Gran Vía. Flamenco and jazz in a smoky, intimate setting. (1 drink min.)

Camborio, Camino del Sacromonte 48. Scantily clad clubbers replace the highwaymen that once roamed the caves of Sacromonte. Cover F-Sa €4.50. Open Tu-Sa 11pm-dawn.

Granero, Pl. Luis Rosales, near Pl. de Isabel la Católica. A New-Age barn bulging with grooving Spanish yuppies. Open daily 10pm-dawn.

Granada 10, C. Carcel Baja 3, is a movie theater by evening and a raging dance club by night. Th-Sa cover €6; includes 1 drink. Open daily.

Planta Baja, C. Horno de Abad 11. Live bands play regularly within the concrete confines of this techno dance club. Wildly popular with students. Beer €1.80. Cover €3. Open from fall until early July Th-Sa 10pm-6am.

Kasbah, C. Calderería Nueva 4. Relax amidst the comforts of this candlelit cafe. Arab pastries and an exhaustive selection of Moroccan teas (€1.80). Open daily 3pm-3am.

Fondo Reservado, Cuesta de Sta. Inés, left off Carrera del Darro, far beyond Pl. Santa Ana. A popular gay bar with a mixed crowd that parties hard. Beer €2.60. Mixed drinks €3.60. Open daily 11pm-late.

El Angel Azul, C. Lavadero de las Tablas 15. Well established gay bar with a basement dance floor and curtained booths. Monthly drag shows and striptease contests. Beer €2.40. Open daily midnight-5am.

🏔 HIKING AND SKIING NEAR GRANADA: SIERRA NEVADA

The peaks of **Mulhacén** (3481m) and **Veleta** (3470m), Spain's highest, sparkle with snow and buzz with tourists for most of the year. **Ski** season runs from December to April. The rest of the year, tourists hike, parasail, and take jeep tours. Call **Cetursa** (☎958 24 91 11) for info on outdoor activities. The Autocares Bonal **bus** (☎958 27 31 00), between the bus station in Granada and Veleta, is a bargain (9am departure, 5pm return; €5.40).

EASTERN SPAIN

Valencia's rich soil and famous orange groves, fed by Moorish irrigation systems, have earned it the nickname *Huerta de España* (Spain's Orchard). Dunes, sandbars, jagged promontories, and lagoons mark the grand coastline, while lovely fountains and pools grace carefully landscaped public gardens in Valencian cities. The famed rice dish *paella* was born in this region.

ALICANTE (ALICANT) ☎965

Sun-drenched Alicante has it all: relaxing beaches, fascinating historical sites, and an unbelievable collection of bars and port-side discos. High above the rows of bronzed beach-goers, the ancient *castillo*, spared by Franco, guards the tangle of streets in the cobblestone *casco antiguo*.

⚡ 🚊 TRANSPORTATION AND PRACTICAL INFORMATION. RENFE trains (☎902 24 02 02) run from Estación Término on Av. Salamanca, at the end of Av. Estación, to: **Barcelona** (4½-6hr., 9 per day, €43-67); **Madrid** (4hr., 9 per day, €36); and **Valencia** (1½hr., 10 per day, €9-32). Trains from **Ferrocarriles de la Generalitat Valenciana,** Estació Marina, Av. Villajoyosa 2 (☎965 26 27 31), on Explanada d'Espanya, serve the Costa Blanca. **Buses** run from C. Portugal 17 (☎965 13 07 00), to: **Barcelona** (7hr., 13 per day, €34); **Granada** (6hr., 9 per day, €23); and **Madrid** (5hr., 9 per day, €23). The **tourist office** is on Rbla. de Méndez Nuñez 23. (☎965 20 00 00. Open June-Aug. M-F 10am-8pm; Sept.-May M-F 10am-7pm, Sa 10am-2pm and 3-7pm.) Use the **Internet** at **Fundación Ban-Caja,** Rbla. Méndez Nuñez 4, on the corner of C. San Fernando, 2nd fl. (Open M-F 10am-2pm and 5-9pm, Sa 9am-2pm.) **Postal Code:** 03070.

🏠 🍴 ACCOMMODATIONS AND FOOD. The ▨**Habitaciones México ❶**, C. General Primo de Rivera 10, off the end of Av. Alfonso X El Sabio, has a friendly atmosphere and small, cozy rooms. (☎965 20 93 07. Free Internet access. Singles €12-15; doubles €27; triples €33.) **Hostal Les Monges Palace ❷**, C. San Agustín 4, behind the Ayuntamiento, up the hill from Pl. Santísima Faz., is luxurious, with bath, TV, and sometimes A/C. (☎965 21 50 46. Singles €24-35; doubles €27-29; triples €44-46.) Take bus #21 to camp at **Playa Mutxavista ❶**. (☎965 65 45 26. June-Sept. €4 per person, €12 per tent; Oct.-May €2/8.) Try the family-run *bar-restaurantes* in the *casco antiguo*, between the cathedral and the castle steps. ▨**Kebap ❶**, Av. Dr. Gadea 5, serves heaping portions of Middle Eastern cuisine. (Open daily 1-4pm and 8pm-midnight.) Buy basics at **Supermarket Mercadona,** C. Alvarez Sereix 5, off Av. Federico Soto. (Open M-Sa 9am-9pm.)

🎭 🎶 SIGHTS AND ENTERTAINMENT. The ancient Carthaginian **Castell de Santa Bárbara,** complete with drawbridges, dark passageways, and hidden tunnels, keeps silent guard over Alicante's beach. A paved road from the old section of Alicante leads to the top, but most people take the **elevator** rising from a hidden entrance on Av. Jovellanos, just across the street from Playa Postiguet, near the white pedestrian overpass. (Castle open Apr.-Sept. daily 10am-7:30pm; Oct.-Mar. 9am-6:30pm. Elevator €2.40.) The **Museu de Arte del Siglo XX La Asegurada,** Pl. Santa María 3, at the east end of C. Mayor, showcases modern art pieces, including works by Picasso and Dalí. (Open mid-May to mid-Sept. T-F 10am-2pm and 5-9pm, Sa-Su 10:30am-2:30pm; mid-Sept. to mid-May T-F 10am-2pm and 4-8pm, Sa-Su 10:30am-2:30pm.) Alicante's **Playa del Postiguet** attracts beach lovers, as do nearby **Playa de San Juan** (TAM bus #21, 22, or 31) and **Playa del Mutxavista** (TAM bus #21). (Buses depart every 15min., €0.80.) Most begin their night bar-hopping in the *casco antiguo;* the complex of bars that overlook the water in Alicante's **main port** and the discos on **Puerto Nuevo** tend to fill up a little later. For an even crazier night, the **Trensnochador** night train (July-Aug. F-Sa every hr. 9pm-5am, Su-Th 4 per night 9pm-5am; round-trip €0.90-4.20) runs from Estació Marina to *discotecas* and other stops along the beach, where places are packed until dawn. Try **Pachá, Ku, KM,** and **Space** (open nightly until 9am) at the *Disco Benidorm* stop. During the hedonistic **Festival de Sant Joan** (June 20-29), *fogueres* (satiric effigies) are erected around the city and then burned in the streets during *la Cremà;* afterwards, firefighters soak everyone during *la Banyà*, and the party continues until dawn.

VALENCIA
☎963

Stylish and cosmopolitan, Valencia (pop. 750,000) presents a striking contrast to the surrounding orchards and mountain range. Valencia seems to possess all the best of its sister cities: the bustling energy of Madrid, the vibrant spirit of Alicante, the off-beat sophistication of Barcelona, the friendly warmth of Seville. Despite its cosmopolitan style, Valencia retains a small-town charm.

⭐️ TRANSPORTATION AND PRACTICAL INFORMATION. Trains arrive at C. Xàtiva 24 (☎963 52 02 02). **RENFE** (24hr. ☎902 24 02 02) runs to: Alicante (2-3hr., 9 per day, €10-25); Barcelona (3hr., 12 per day, €34); and Madrid (3½hr., 9 per day, €18-37). **Buses** (☎963 49 72 22) go from Av. Menéndez Pidal 13 to: Alicante via the Costa Blanca (4½hr., 13 per day, €13-15); Barcelona (4½hr., 15 per day, €21); Madrid (4hr., 13 per day, €20-24); and Seville (11hr., 4 per day, €41-48). Bus #8 (€0.90) connects to Pl. Ayuntamiento and the train station. Trasmediterránea **ferries** (☎902 45 46 45) sail to the Balearic Islands (p. 956).

The main **tourist office**, C. Paz 46-48, has branches at the train station and Pl. Ayuntamiento. (☎963 98 64 22. Open M-F 9am-7pm and Sa 10am-7pm.) **Internet** access is at **Ono**, C. San Vicente 22, around the corner from Pl. Ayuntamiento. (☎963 28 19 02. €1.80 per 45 min. 9am-2pm, €1.80 per 30 min. 2-10pm, €1.80 per hour 10pm-1am. Open M-Sa 9am-1am, Su 10am-1am.) The **post office** is at Pl. Ayuntamiento 24. (Open M-F 8:30am-8:30pm, Sa 9:30am-2pm.) **Postal Code:** 46080.

⭐️ ACCOMMODATIONS AND FOOD. The best lodgings are around **Plaza del Ayuntamiento** and **Plaza del Mercado**. The **Home Youth Hostel ❶**, C. Lonja 4, is directly behind the Lonja, on a side street off Pl. Dr. Collado. Brightly painted rooms, a spacious common living room, and a kitchen create a homey atmosphere for road-weary guests. (☎963 91 62 29; www.likeathome.net. Laundry €5.50. Internet €0.50 per 15min. Dorms €14; singles €21; doubles €32; triples €48; quads €64.) **Hostal Alicante ❷**, C. Ribera 8, is centrally located on the pedestrian street off Pl. Ayuntamiento. Its clean, well-lit rooms and firm beds are hugely popular with backpackers. (☎963 51 22 96. Singles €20, with bath and A/C €28; doubles €29/37. MC/V.) From Pl. Ayuntamiento, turn right at C. Barcas, left at C. Poeta Querol, and take the second right onto C. Salvá to reach **Pensión Paris ❸**, C. Salvá 12, which has spotless, sunny rooms with balconies. (☎963 52 67 66. Singles €18; doubles €27, with shower €30; triples €34/39.) To get to **Hostal Antigua Morellana ❸**, C. En Bou 2, walk past Pl. Dr. Collado; it's on the small streets behind the Lonja. Quiet and comfortable rooms with bath and A/C cater to an older crowd. (☎/fax 963 91 57 73. Singles €30; doubles €45.)

Paella is the most famous of Valencia's 200 rice dishes; try as many of them as you can before leaving. Buckets of fresh fish, meat, and fruit (including Valencia's famous oranges) are sold at the **Mercado Central**, on Pl. Mercado. (Open M-Sa 7am-3pm.) For groceries, stop by the basement of **El Corte Inglés**, C. Colon, or the fifth floor of the C. Pintor Sorilla building. (Open M-Sa 10am-10pm.)

⭐️ SIGHTS. Touring Valencia on foot is a good test of stamina. Most of the sights line Río Turia or cluster near Pl. Reina, which is linked to Pl. Ayuntamiento by C. San Vicente Mártir. EMT bus #5, dubbed the **Bus Turistic** (€1), makes a loop around the old town sights. Head toward the beach along the riverbed off C. Alcalde Reig. or take bus #35 from Pl. Ayuntamiento to reach the modern, airy, and thoroughly fascinating ▓**Ciudad de las artes y las ciencias.** This mini-city has created quite a stir; it's become the fourth biggest tourist destination in Spain. The complex is divided into four large attractions, only two of which are currently completed: **Palau de les Arts** and **L'Oceanografic** will not open until at least 2004. The ▓**Museu de Les Ciencias Principe Felipe** is an interactive playground for science and technology fiends; **L'Hemisfèric** has an IMAX theater and planetarium. (www.cac.es. Museum open June 15-Sept. 15 daily 10am-9pm, Sept. 16-June 14 M-F and Su 10am-8pm, Sa 10am-9pm. €6, M-F students €4.30. IMAX shows €6.60, M-F students €4.80.) The 13th-century ▓**cathedral,** in Pl. Reina, was built on the site of an Arab mosque. The **Museo de la Catedral** squeezes several treasures into three tiny rooms. (Cathedral open in summer daily 7:30am-

1pm and 4:30-8:30pm; off-season reduced hours. Free. Museum open Mar.-Nov. M-Sa 10am-1pm and 4:30-6pm; Dec.-Feb. 10am-1pm €1.20.) Across the river, the **Museu Provincial de Belles Artes**, on C. Sant Pius V, displays superb 14th- to 16th-century Valencian art. Its collection includes El Greco's *San Juan Bautista*, Velázquez's self-portrait, and a slew of works by Goya. (Open Su and Tu-Sa 10am-8pm. Free.) West across the old river, the **Institut Valenciá d'Art Modern** (IVAM), C. Guillem de Castro 118, has works by 20th-century sculptor Julio González. (Open Su and Tu-Sa 10am-10pm. €2.10, students €1. Su free.)

🎭 🎬 **ENTERTAINMENT AND NIGHTLIFE.** The most popular **beaches** are **Las Arenas** and **Malvarrosa**—buses #20, 21, 22, and 23 all pass through. To get to the more attractive **Salér**, 14km from the center of town, take an Autobuses Buñol **bus** (☎963 49 14 25) from the corner of Gran Vía de Germanias and C. Sueca (25min., every 30min. 7am-10pm, €0.90). Bars and pubs abound in the El Carme district. Follow C. Bolsería out of Pl. Mercado, bearing right at the fork, to guzzle *agua de Valencia* (orange juice, champagne, and vodka) in Pl. Tossal. **Carmen Sui Generis**, C. Caballeros 38, is an upscale lounge in an 18th-century palace with eclectic decor and chic clientele. (Cocktails €5-6. Open W-Sa 11pm-3am.) The loud **Cafe Negrito**, Pl. del Negrito 1, off C. Caballeros, is wildly popular with locals. (Small pitcher of *agua de Valencia* €6. Open daily 10pm-3am.) **Rumbo 144**, Av. Blasco Ibañez 144, plays a wide variety of music, from Spanish pop to house. (Cover €9. Open Th-Sa midnight-7am.) For more info, consult the weekly *Qué y Dónde* (€1), available at newsstands, or the weekly entertainment supplement *La Cartelera* (€0.75). The most famed festival in Valencia is **Las Fallas** (Mar. 12-19), which culminates with the burning of gigantic (up to 30m) papier-mâché effigies.

COSTA BLANCA

You could while away a lifetime touring the charming resort towns of the Costa Blanca. The "white coast" that extends through Dénia, Calpe, and Alicante derives its name from its fine white sands. ALSA **buses** (☎902 42 22 42) run from Valencia to: Alicante (2-4hr., 12-15 per day, €13-15); Altea and Calpe (3-4½ hr., 8-10 per day 6am-5pm, €9.40-11); and Gandía (1 hr., 9-11 per day, €5.10). From Alicante buses run to: Altea (1¼hr., 11 per day, €3.80) and Calpe (1½hr., 11 per day 6:30am-8pm, €5.95). Going to **Calpe** (Calp) is like stepping into a Dalí landscape. The town cowers beneath the **Peñón d'Ifach** (327m), which drops straight to the sea, making it one of the most picturesque coastal set-

ON THE MENU

RICE IS NICE

Paella is known throughout the world as a quintessentially Spanish dish, but any *valenciano* can tell you where it all started—here. From the region's rice fields to the factories where it is carefully processed to the tables of the best restaurants, rice is the spice of life in Valencia. The techniques of preparation have been perfected for years by rice cultivators, processors, and *paelleros* (traditionally male). And don't call it all *paella;* there are hundreds of different rice dishes, each distinct in ingredients and preparation.

Paella, for example, is the Valenciano word for the typical pan in which the rice *paella* dish (originally called *arroz en paella*) is cooked. *Arroz a banda*, while similar to *paella*, is traditionally a more humble dish enjoyed by fishermen, who cook the fish separately (*a banda*) from the rice, saffron, garlic, and tomato.

If you prefer your rice baked, try *arroz al horno*, very popular in la Ribera and la Huerta for its mixes of meats and vegetables and slightly less complicated recipe. If you don't prefer rice at all, try *fideuá*, the cousin of *paella*, made with noodles instead of rice. Whichever you choose, you are certain not to be disappointed, so long as you go for the authentic version. Avoid the more touristy restaurants bearing pictures of pre-made *paellas* on sandwich boards; what you see is what you get, and it's not the real thing.

tings in Spain. Peaceful **Gandía** has fine sand **beaches.** The **tourist office,** Marqués de Campo, is opposite the train station. (☎962 87 77 88. Open June-Aug. M-F 9:30am-1:30pm and 4:30-7:30pm, Sa 10am-1:30pm; Sept.-May M-F 9:30am-1:30pm and 4-7pm, Sa 10am-1pm.) Buses depart from outside the train station for **Platja de Piles** (M-Sa 4-9 per day, €0.80). To sleep at the fantastic **Alberg Mar i Vent (HI) ❶** in Platja, follow the signs down C. Dr. Fleming. The beach is out the back door. (☎962 83 17 48. Sheets €1.80. 3-day max. stay, flexible if uncrowded. Curfew Su-F 2am, Sa 4am. Closed until March 2004 for renovations. Dorms €9-11, under-26 €6-9.)

NORTHEAST SPAIN

Northeastern Spain encompasses the country's most avidly regionalistic areas and is home to some of its best cuisine. Cataluña is justly proud of its treasures, from mountains to beaches to hip Barcelona. However, Cataluña isn't the only reason to head northeast. The area is also home to the glorious mountains of the Pyrenees, the running bulls of Navarra, the industrious cities of Aragón, the beautiful coasts of Basque Country, and the crazy parties of the Balearic Islands.

CATALUÑA

From rocky Costa Brava to chic Barcelona, the prosperous Cataluña is graced with the nation's richest resources. Catalán is the official language (though most everyone is bilingual), and local cuisine is lauded throughout Spain.

BARCELONA ☎93

Barcelona loves to indulge in the fantastic. From the urban carnival that is Las Ramblas to buildings with no straight lines, from wild festivals to even wilder nightlife, the city pushes the limits of style and good taste in everything it does—and with amazing results. The center of the whimsical and daring *Modernisme* architectural movement, and once home to the most well-known Surrealist painters—Salvador Dalí, Pablo Picasso, and Joan Miró—even Barcelona's art is grounded in an alternate reality. In the quarter-century since Spain was freed from Franco's oppressive regime, Barcelona has led the autonomous region of Cataluña in the resurgence of a culture so esoteric and unique it is puzzling even to the rest of Spain. The result is a vanguard city where rooftops drip toward the sidewalk, serpentine park benches twist past fairytale houses, and an unfinished cathedral captures imaginations around the world.

✈ INTERCITY TRANSPORTATION

Flights: El Prat de Llobregat Airport (BCN; ☎932 98 38 38), 12km southwest of Barcelona. To get to the central Pl. Catalunya, take the **Aerobus** (40min.; every 15min.; to Pl. Catalunya M-F 6am-midnight, Sa-Su 6:30am-midnight; to the airport M-F 5:30am-11:15pm, Sa-Su 6am-11:20pm; €3.30) or a RENFE **train** (40min.; every 30min.; from airport 6:10am-11:15pm, from Estació Barcelona-Sants 5:30am-11:20pm; €2.20).

Trains: Barcelona has 2 main train stations. For general info about trains and train stations, call ☎902 24 02 02. **Estació Barcelona-Sants,** in Pl. Països Catalans (M: Sants-Estació) is the main terminal for domestic and international traffic. **Estació França,** on Av. Marquès de l'Argentera. M: Barceloneta. Services regional destinations, including Girona Tarragona and Zaragoza, and some international arrivals.

Ferrocarrils de la Generalitat de Cataluña (FGC; ☎932 05 15 15; www.fgc.catalunya.net), has commuter trains with main stations at Pl. Catalunya and Pl. Espanya.

RENFE (☎902 24 02 02; international ☎934 90 11 22; www.renfe.es). RENFE has extensive service in Spain and Europe. Popular connections include: **Bilbao** (8-9hr., 5 per day, €30-32); **Madrid** (7-8hr., 7 per day, €31-42); **San Sebastián** (8-9hr., 5 per day, €31); **Seville** (11-12hr., 6 per day, €47-51); **Valencia** (3-5hr., 15 per day, €28-32). International destinations include **Milan, Italy** (via Figueres and Nice), and **Montpellier, France** with connections to Geneva, Paris, and various stops along the French Riviera. 20% discount on round-trip tickets.

Buses: Most buses arrive at the **Barcelona Nord Estació d'Autobuses,** C. Ali-bei 80 (☎932 65 61 32). M: Arc de Triomf. **Sarfa** (☎902 30 20 25; www.sarfa.com) goes to **Cadaqués** (2½hr., 11:15am and 8:25pm, €16) and **Tossa del Mar** (1½hr., 10 per day, €8). **Linebús** (☎932 65 07 00) travels to **Paris** (13hr.; M-Sa 8pm; €80, under-26 reduced prices), southern France, and Morocco. **Alsa Enatcar** (☎902 42 22 42; www.alsa.es) goes to: **Alicante** (9hr., 3 per day, €33); **Madrid** (8hr., 13 per day, €22); **Naples** (24hr., 5:15pm, €113); **Valencia** (4hr., 16 per day, €21); **Zaragoza** (3½-4½hr., 20 per day, €18).

Ferries: Trasmediterránea (☎902 45 46 45), in Estació Marítima-Moll Barcelona, Moll de Sant Bertran. In the summer months only to: **Ibiza** (10-11hr., daily M-Sa, €46); **Mahón** (10½hr., daily starting mid-June, €46); **Palma** (3½hr., daily, €65).

ORIENTATION

Barcelona's layout is simple. Imagine yourself perched on Columbus's head at the **Monument a Colom** (on Passeig de Colom, along the shore), viewing the city with the sea at your back. From the harbor, the city slopes upward to the mountains. From the Monument a Colom, **Las Ramblas,** the main thoroughfare, runs from the harbor up to **Plaça de Catalunya** (M: Catalunya), the city's center. The **Ciutat Vella** (Old City) is the heavily touristed historical neighborhood, which centers around Las Ramblas and includes the Barri Gòtic, La Ribera, and El Raval. The **Barri Gòtic** is east of Las Ramblas (to the right, with your back to the sea), enclosed on the other side by **Vía Laietana.** East of V. Laietana lies the maze-like neighborhood of **La Ribera,** which borders Parc de la Ciutadella and the Estació França (train station). To the west of Las Ramblas (to the left, with your back to the sea) is **El Raval.** Beyond La Ribera—farther east, outside the Ciutat Vella—is **Poble Nou** and **Port Olímpic,** with its twin towers (the tallest buildings in Barcelona) and an assortment of discos and restaurants. Beyond El Raval (to the west) rises **Montjuïc,** crammed with gardens, museums, the 1992 Olympic grounds, and a stunning castle. Directly behind your perch on the Monument a Colom is the **Port Vell** (Old Port) development, where a wavy bridge leads across to the ultra-modern shopping and entertainment complexes **Moll d'Espanya** and **Maremàgnum.** Beyond the Ciutat Vella is **l'Eixample,** the gridded neighborhood created during the expansion of the 1860s, which runs from Pl. Catalunya toward the mountains. **Gran Vía de les Corts Catalanes** defines its lower edge, and the **Passeig de Gràcia,** l'Eixample's main street, bisects the neighborhood. **Avinguda Diagonal** marks the border between l'Eixample and the **Zona Alta** ("Uptown"), which includes Pedralbes, Gràcia, and other older neighborhoods in the foothills. The peak of **Tibidabo,** the northwest border of the city, offers the most comprehensive view of Barcelona.

LOCAL TRANSPORTATION

Public Transportation: ☎010. Pick up a *Guia d'Autobusos Urbans de Barcelona* for Metro and bus routes. **Buses** run 5am-10pm and cost €1 per ride. The **Metro** (☎934 86 07 52; www.tmb.net) runs M-Th 5am-midnight, F-Sa 5am-2am, Su and holidays 6am-midnight. Buy tickets at vending machines and ticket windows. Tickets cost €1.10 per *sencillo* (ride). A **T1 Pass** (€5.80) is valid for 10 rides on the bus or Metro; a **T-DIA Card** entitles you to unlimited bus and Metro travel for 1 (€4.40) or 3 days (€11.30).

Barcelona

🔺 **ACCOMMODATIONS**
Albergue de Juventud
  Kabul, **44**
Barcelona Mar Youth
  Hostel, **25**
California Hotel, **39**
Casa de Huéspedes
  Mari-Luz, **48**
Gothic Point Youth
  Hostal, **41**
Hostal Avinyó, **63**
Hostal Benidorm, **59**
Hostal Campi, **12**
Hostal de Ribagorza, **16**
Hostal Levante, **47**
Hostal Malda, **23**
Hostal Nuevo Colón, **58**
Hostal Opera, **29**
Hostal Parisien, **21**
Hostal Plaza, **5**
Hostal Residencia
  Lausanne, **11**
Hostal Residencia
  Rembrandt, **20**
Hostal San Remo, **7**
Hotel Peninsular, **28**
Hotel Toledano/Hostal
  Residencia Capitol, **10**
Ideal Youth Hostel, **32**
Mare Nostrum, **30**
Pensión Ciutadella, **57**
Pensión Dalí, **31**
Pensión Fernando, **36**
Pensión L'Isard, **2**

🍴 **FOOD**
L'Antic Bocoi del Gòtic, **49**
Arc Café, **65**
The Bagel Shop, **13**
Bar Ra, **19**
Café de l'Ópera, **33**
Los Caracoles, **61**
La Colmena, **38**
Comme-Bio, **1**
Irati, **22**
Laie Llibreria Café, **3**
Mi Burrito y Yo, **40**
El Pebre Blau, **53**
Pla dels Angels, **9**
Els Quatre Gats, **14**
Les Quinze Nits, **45**
El Salón, **64**
Terrablava, **15**
Va de Vi, **50**
Xaloc, **24**
Xampanyet, **52**

⭐ **NIGHTLIFE**
El Born, **56**
El Bosq de les Fades, **66**
Casa Almirall, **8**
El Copetin, **54**
Fonfone, **62**
Glaciar Bar, **46**
Jamboree, **43**
London Bar, **42**
Lupino, **18**
Margarita Blue, **67**
Marsella Bar, **27**

Molly's Fair City, **34**
Muebles Navarro
  (El Café que Pone), **17**
New York, **60**
Palau Dalmases, **51**
La Paloma, **4**
Pitin Bar, **55**
Salvation, **6**
Sant Pau 68, **26**
Schilling, **35**
Vildsvin, **37**

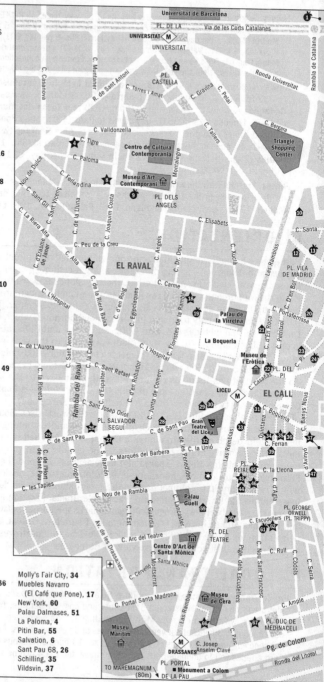

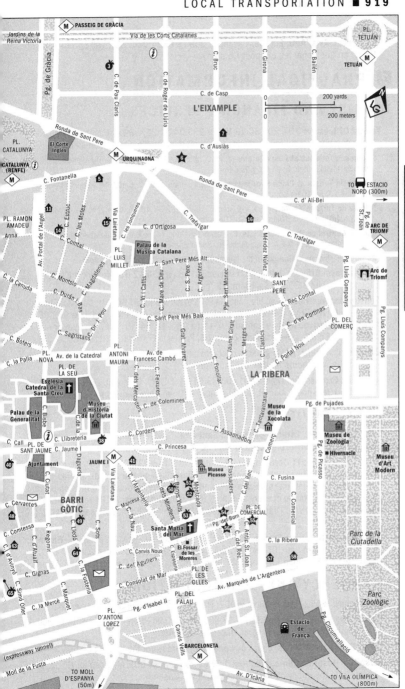

SPAIN

Taxis: ☎933 30 03 00.

Car Rental: Avis/Auto Europe, Casanova 209 (☎932 09 95 33). Will rent to ages 21-25 for an additional fee of about €5 a day.

⏻ PRACTICAL INFORMATION

TOURIST AND FINANCIAL SERVICES

Tourist Offices: (☎010, 906 30 12 82, or 933 04 34 21; www.barcelonaturisme.com.) Barcelona has 4 main tourist offices and numerous mobile information stalls.

Informacio Turistica at Plaça Catalunya, Pl. Catalunya 17S. M: Catalunya. The biggest, best, and busiest tourist office. Open daily 9am-9pm.

Informacio Turista at Plaça Sant Jaume, Pl. Sant Jaume 1, off C. Ciutat. M: Jaume I. Open M-Sa 10am-8pm, Su 10am-2pm.

Oficina de Turisme de Catalunya, Pg. Gràcia 107 (☎932 38 40 00; www.gencat.es/probert). M: Diagonal. Open M-Sa 10am-7pm, Su 10am-2pm.

Estació Central de Barcelona-Sants, Pl. Països Cataláns, in the Barcelona-Sants train station. M: Sants-Estació. Open M-F 4:30am-midnight, Sa-Su 5am-midnight.

Aeroport El Prat de Llobregat, in the international terminal. Open daily 9am-9pm.

Budget Travel Offices: Usit, Ronda Universitat 16 (☎934 12 01 04; www.unlimited.es). Open M-F 10am-8:30pm, Sa 10am-1:30pm.

Consulates: Australia, Gran Vía Carlos III 98, 9th fl. (☎933 30 94 96); **Canada,** Elisenda de Pinos 8 (☎932 04 27 00); **New Zealand,** Traversa de Gràcia 64, 4th fl. (☎932 09 03 99); **South Africa,** Teodora Lamadrid 7-11 (☎934 18 64 45); **UK,** Av. Diagonal 477 (☎933 66 62 00; www.ukinspain.com); **US,** Pg. Reina Elisenda 23 (☎932 80 22 27).

Currency Exchange: ATMs give the best rates; the next best rates are available at banks. General banking hours are M-F 8:30am-2pm.

American Express, Pg. Gràcia 101 (☎933 01 11 66). M: Diagonal. Open M-F 9:30am-6pm, Sa 10am-noon. Also at Las Ramblas 74. Open daily 9am-8pm.

LOCAL SERVICES

Luggage Storage: Estació Barcelona-Sants. M: Sants-Estació. Large lockers €4.50. Open daily 5:30am-11pm. **Estació França.** M: Barceloneta. Open daily 7am-10pm.

Department Store: El Corte Inglés, Pl. Catalunya 14 (☎933 06 38 00). M: Catalunya. Behemoth department store. **Free map** of Barcelona at the info desk. Has English books, salon, cafeteria, supermarket, and the *oportunidades* discount department. Open M-Sa and first Su of every month 10am-10pm. **Branches:** Av. Portal de l'Angel 19-2 (M: Catalunya); Av. Diagonal 471-473 (M: Hospital Clínic); Av. Diagonal 617 (M: Maria Cristina).

Laundromat: Tintorería Ferrán, C. Ferrán 11. M: Liceu. Open M-F 9am-8pm. **Tintorería San Pablo,** C. San Pau 105 (☎933 29 42 49). M: Paral·lel. Wash, dry, and fold €10; do-it-yourself €7.30. Open July-Sept. M-F 9am-2pm; Oct.-June M-F 9am-2pm and 4-8pm.

EMERGENCY AND COMMUNICATIONS

Emergency: ☎112. Local police: ☎092. National police: ☎091. Medical: ☎061.

Police: Las Ramblas 43 (☎933 44 13 00), across from Pl. Reial and next to C. Nou de La Rambla. M: Liceu. Multilingual officers. Open 24hr.

24hr. Pharmacy: Rotates; check any pharmacy window for the nearest on duty.

Hospital: Hospital Clínic, Villarroel 170 (☎932 27 54 00). M: Hospital Clínic. Main entrance at the intersection of C. Roselló and C. Casanova.

Internet Access:

■ **EasyEverything,** Las Ramblas 31. M: Liceu. About €1.20 per 40min. Open 24hr. **Branch** at Ronda Universitat 35, right next to Pl. Catalunya.

Bcnet (Internet Gallery Café), Barra de Ferro 3. Right down the street from the Picasso museum. M: Jaume I. €3 per hr., 10hr. ticket €20. Open daily 10am-1am.

Cybermundo Internet Centre, Bergara 3 and Balmes 8. M: Catalunya. Just off Pl. Catalunya, behind the Triangle shopping mall. Allows uploading of disks. €1 per hr. Open daily 9am-1am.

Workcenter, Av. Diagonal 441. M: Hospital Clínic or Diagonal. Another **branch** is at C. Roger de Lluria 2. M: Urquinaona. €0.52 per 10min. Open 24hr.

CiberOpción, Gran Vía 602. M: Universitat. €0.60 per 30min. Open M-F 9am-1am, Sa-Su 11am-1am.

Post Office: Pl. de Antoni López (general info ☎902 19 71 97). M: Jaume I or Barceloneta. Fax and **lista de correos.** Open M-F 8:30am-9:30pm. A little shop in the back of the post office building, across the street, wraps packages for mailing (about €2). Shop open M-Sa 9am-2pm and 5-8pm. **Postal Code:** 08003.

ᴨ ACCOMMODATIONS

While accommodations in Barcelona are easy to spot, finding a room can be more difficult. During the busier travel months (June-September or December), just wandering up and down Las Ramblas looking for a place to stay can quickly turn into a frustrating experience. If you want to stay in the touristy areas—**Barri Gòtic** or **Las Ramblas**—make reservations weeks, or even months, in advance. Consider staying outside the tourist hub of the Ciutat Vella; there are plenty of great hostels in **l'Eixample** and **Gràcia** that will have more vacancies.

Hostels in Spain are generally not of the dorm variety, but rather a private, basic room, with or without a private bathroom. Because heat and electricity are expensive in Spain, travelers should not assume that rooms have A/C, TV, or phone unless specified; most come with fans only in the summer and some places do not have heat in the winter.

LOWER BARRI GÒTIC

■ **Hostal Levante,** Baixada de San Miguel 2 (☎933 17 95 65; www.hostallevante.com). M: Liceu. The best deal in Barri Gòtic. Singles €30; doubles €50-60. MC/V. ❸

■ **Pensión Fernando,** C. Ferran 31 (☎/fax 933 01 79 93; www.barcelona-on-line.es/fernando). M: Liceu. Fills from walk-in requests. Dorms with lockers. In summer dorms €19, with bath €20; doubles €45/58; triples with bath €68. MC/V. ❷

Hostal Benidorm, Las Ramblas 37 (☎933 02 20 54). M: Drassanes. The best value on Las Ramblas, with phones and complete baths in each of the very clean rooms, balconies overlooking Las Ramblas, and excellent prices. Singles €30; doubles €45-53; triples €65; quads €75; quints €85-90. ❸

Casa de Huéspedes Mari-Luz, C. Palau 4 (☎/fax 933 17 34 63; pensionmariluz@menta.net). M: Liceu. Tidy 4- to 6-person dorm rooms and a few comfortable doubles. Reservations require a credit card. In summer dorms €16; doubles €41. Off-season reduced prices. MC/V. ❷

Hostal Avinyó, C. Avinyó 42 (☎933 18 79 45; www.hostalavinyo.com). M: Drassanes. Rooms with couches, high ceilings, fans, safes, and stained-glass windows. Singles €22; doubles €34, with bath €47; triples €48/66. ❷

Albergue de Juventud Kabul, Pl. Reial 17 (☎933 18 51 90; www.kabul-hostel.com). M: Liceu. Legendary among backpackers; squeezes in up to 200 frat boys at a time. Key deposit €10. Laundry €2.50. No reservations. Dorms €20. ❷

Hotel Toledano/Hostal Residencia Capitol, Las Ramblas 138 (☎933 01 08 72; www.hoteltoledano.com). M: Catalunya. Rooms come with cable TV and phones. 4th-floor hotel, with bath: singles €35; doubles €57; triples €72; quads €81. 5th-floor hostal: singles €28; doubles €39; triples €51; quads €58. AmEx/MC/V. ❸

California Hotel, C. Rauric 14 (☎933 17 77 66). M: Liceu. Enjoy one of the 31 clean, sparkling rooms, all with TV, phone, full bath, and A/C. Convenient location. Singles €52; doubles €82; triples €102. AmEx/MC/V. ❹

Hostal Parisien, Las Ramblas 114 (☎933 01 62 83). M: Liceu. Well-kept rooms keep young guests happy. Quiet hours after midnight. Prices vary, but generally singles €30; doubles with bath €54; triples with bath €57. ❸

UPPER BARRI GÒTIC

Between C. Fontanella and C. Ferran, accommodations are pricier but more serene than in the lower Barri Gòtic. Early reservations are obligatory in summer. The nearest Metro stop is Catalunya, unless otherwise specified.

■ **Hostal-Residencia Rembrandt,** C. Portaferrissa 23 (☎/fax 933 18 10 11; hostrembrandt@yahoo.es). M: Liceu. Biggest rooms in the area; ask for a balcony. Fans €2 per night. Singles €25, with bath €35; doubles €42/50; triples €60/65. MC/V. ❷

■ **Hostal Plaza,** C. Fontanella 18 (☎/fax 933 01 01 39; www.plazahostal.com). Savvy, super-friendly Texan owners; fun, brightly painted rooms with wicker furniture; and great location. Laundry €9. Internet €1 per 15min. Singles €60, with bath €75; doubles €65/75; triples €86/96. 10% discount Nov. and Feb. AmEx/MC/V. ❺

■ **Hostal Campi,** C. Canuda 4 (☎/fax 933 01 35 45; hcampi@terra.es). A great bargain with large balconies. Call ahead to reserve 9am-8pm. Prices vary, but generally doubles €42, with bath €49; triples €58/68. ❷

Hotel Lloret, Las Ramblas 125 (☎933 17 33 66). M: Catalunya. New rooms include large bathrooms, tasteful furniture, A/C, heat, TV, and phone. Worth the cost. Singles €45-48; doubles €75-81; triples €89-95; quads €105. AmEx/MC/V. ❹

Hostal Malda, C. Pi 5 (☎933 17 30 02), inside a shopping center. M: Liceu. Keeps rooms occupied year-round by offering quality rooms at an unbeatable price. Reservations recommended. Singles €13; doubles €26; triples with shower €36. Cash only. ❶

Hostal Residencia Lausanne, Av. Portal de l'Angel 24 (☎933 02 11 39). M: Catalunya. Small hostel includes a posh lounge with TV and vending machines. Doubles €48, with bath €65. Cash only. ❷

Pensión Dalí, C. Boquería 12 (☎933 18 55 90; pensiondali@wanadoo.es). M: Liceu. Designed as a religious house by Domènech i Montaner and originally run by a friend of Dalí. All rooms have TVs. In the high season, doubles €47, with bath €53; triples with bath €75; quads with bath €85. MC/V. ❹

Mare Nostrum, Las Ramblas 67 (☎933 18 53 40; fax 934 12 30 69). M: Liceu. The swankiest hotel on the strip. All rooms have A/C and satellite TV. Breakfast included. Singles €57, with bath €72; doubles €66/76; triples €88/100; quads €99/114. ❺

LA RIBERA

■ **Hostal de Ribagorza,** C. Trafalgar 39 (☎/fax 933 19 19 68). M: Urquinaona. Rooms in a Modernist building complete with marble staircase and tile floors. TVs, fans, and homey decorations. During high season, doubles €38-50. ❷

Pensión Ciutadella, C. Comerç 33. (☎933 19 62 03). M: Barceloneta. Small hostel with spacious rooms, each with fan, TV, and balcony. Family feel. Doubles only. Nov.-Feb. €36, with bath €40; June-Sept. €36-40, with bath €50. ❸

Hostal Nuevo Colón, Av. Marqués de l'Argentera 19 (☎933 19 50 77; www.hostalnuevocolon.com). M: Barceloneta. Modern rooms and a common area with TV. Singles €35; doubles €48, with bath €62. 6-person apartments with kitchen €150 per day. ❸

Gothic Point Youth Hostel, C. Vigatans 5 (☎932 68 78 08; badia@intercom.es). M: Jaume I. Lobby area with free Internet access and large TV. 150 beds in rooms with A/C. Breakfast included. In high season dorms €20; off-season €17. AmEx/MC/V. ❷

EL RAVAL

Be careful in the areas near the port and farther from Las Ramblas.

■ **Pensión L'Isard,** C. Tallers 82 (☎/fax 933 02 51 83). M: Universitat. A clean find with enough closet space for even the worst over-packer. Singles €20; doubles €36, with bath €52; triples €52. ❷

■ **Ideal Youth Hostel,** C. la Unió 12 (☎933 42 61 77; www.idealhostel.com). M: Liceu. One of the best deals in the city. Breakfast included. Free Internet access in the swanky lobby area. Sheets €2.50. Laundry €4. Dorms €16. ❷

Hostal Opera, C. de Sant Pau 20 (☎933 18 82 01; info@hostalopera.com). M: Liceu. Recently renovated rooms feel like new. Bath, telephone, and A/C in every room. Internet access in the common room. Singles €35; doubles €55; triples €80. MC/V. ❸

Hotel Peninsular, C. de Sant Pau 34 (☎933 02 31 38). M: Liceu. This building is now one of the sights on the *Ruta del Modernisme*. Rooms come with telephones and A/C. Breakfast included. Singles €30, with bath €50; doubles €50/70. MC/V. ❸

Barcelona Mar Youth Hostel, C. de Sant Pau 80 (☎933 24 85 30; www.youthostel.com). M: Paral·lel. This new hostel crams 120 dorm-style beds into rooms with A/C. All beds come with a safe for personal belongings. Laundry facilities. Internet €1 per 30min. Breakfast included. In summer, dorms €21-23; off-season €14-18. ❷

L'EIXAMPLE

■ **Hostal Residencia Oliva,** Pg. de Gràcia 32, 4th fl. (☎934 88 01 62 or 934 88 17 89; www.lasguias.com/hostaloliva). M: Pg. de Gràcia. Elegant wood-worked bureaus, mirrors, ceilings, and a light marble floor give this hostel a classy ambience. Singles €26; doubles €48, with bath €55; triple with bath €78. ❸

■ **Pensión Fani,** València 278 (☎932 15 36 45). M: Catalunya. Oozes quirky charm. Rooms rented by month; single nights also available. Singles €280 per month; doubles €500 per month; triples €780 per month. One-night stay €20 per person. ❷

■ **Hostal Eden,** C. Balmes 55 (☎934 52 66 20; http://hostaleden.net). M: Pg. Gràcia. Modern rooms are equipped with TVs and fans; most have big, new bathrooms. May-Oct. singles €29, with bath €39; doubles €39/60. Nov.-Apr. singles €23/32; doubles €29/45. AmEx/MC/V. ❸

Hostal Qué Tal, C. Mallorca 290 (☎/fax 934 59 23 66; www.quetalbarcelona.com), near C. Bruc. M: Pg. Gràcia or Verdaguer. This quality gay-and-lesbian friendly hostel has one of the best interiors in the city. Singles €39; doubles €58, with bath €78. ❹

Hostal San Remo, C. Bruc 20 (☎933 02 19 89; www.hostalsanremo.com). M: Urquinaona. All rooms have TV, A/C, and soundproof windows. Reserve early. Singles €30; doubles €42, with bath €55. Nov. and Jan.-Feb. reduced prices. MC/V. ❸

Pensión Aribau, C. Aribau 37 (☎/fax 934 53 11 06). M: Pg. de Gràcia. All rooms with TV, most with A/C. Reservations recommended. Singles €36; doubles €45, with bath €60; triples with bath €70. Off-season reduced prices. AmEx/MC/V. ❹

Hostal Residencia Windsor, Rambla de Catalunya 84 (☎932 15 11 98). M: Pg. de Gràcia. Rooms come equipped with comfy sleep sofas and heat in winter. Singles €25, with bath €42; doubles €52/60. Extra beds €10. ❷

GRÀCIA

■ **Hostal Lesseps,** C. Gran de Gràcia 239 (☎932 18 44 34). M: Lesseps. Spacious, classy rooms sport red velvet wallpaper. All 16 rooms have TV and bath; 4 have A/C (€5.60 extra). Singles €38; doubles €60; triples €75; quads €90. MC/V. ❹

Pensión San Medín, C. Gran de Gràcia 125 (☎932 17 30 68; www.sanmedin.com). M: Fontana. Embroidered curtains and ornate tiling adorn this family-run pensión. Common room with TV. Singles €30, with bath €39; doubles €48/60. MC/V. ❸

SPAIN

Albergue Mare de Déu de Montserrat (HI), Pg. Mare de Déu del Coll 41-51 (☎932 10 51 51; www.tujuca.com). This gorgeous 220-bed hostel is a great way to meet other backpackers. Breakfast included. Flexible 3-day max. stay. Dorms €18, under-26 €14. Members only. AmEx/MC/V. ❶

CAMPING

El Toro Bravo, Autovía de Castelldefells km 11 (☎936 37 34 62; www.eltorobravo.com). Offers beach access, laundry facilities, currency exchange, 3 pools, 2 bars, a restaurant, and a supermarket. Reception 8am-7pm. Electricity €4. Open Sept.-June 14. €5 per person, €5 per site, €5 per car. AmEx/MC/V. ❶

◘ FOOD

The *Guia del Ocio* (available at newsstands; www.guiadelociobcn.es; €1) is an invaluable source of culinary suggestions. **Port Vell** and **Port Olímpic** are known for seafood. The restaurants on **Calle Aragó** by Pg. Gràcia have great lunchtime *menús*, and the **Passeig de Gràcia** has beautiful outdoor dining. Gràcia's **Plaça Sol** and La Ribera's **Santa Maria del Mar** are the best places to head for *tapas*. If you want to live cheap and do as the Barcelonese do, buy your food fresh at a *mercat* (marketplace). For wholesale fruit, cheese, and wine, head to **La Boqueria** (Mercat de Sant Josep), outside M: Liceu. For groceries, try **Champion Supermarket**, Las Ramblas 11. (M: Liceu. Open M-Sa 10am-10pm.)

BARRI GÒTIC

▧ **Café de l'Opera**, Las Ramblas 74 (☎933 17 75 85). M: Liceu. A drink here used to be a post-opera bourgeois tradition. Hot chocolate €1.70. *Churros* €1.20. *Tapas* €2-4. Salads €2-8. Open Su 10am-2:30am, M-Th 9am-2:30am, F-Sa 9am-2:45am. ❷

▧ **Mi Burrito y Yo**, C. del Pas de l'Ensenyanca 2 (☎933 18 27 42). M: Jaume I. Not a Mexican joint (burrito here means "little donkey"), but rather inviting and lively. Live music 9:30pm. Entrees €12-20. Open daily 1pm-midnight. AmEx/MC/V. ❹

▧ **L'Antic Bocoi del Gòtic**, Baixada de Viladecols 3 (☎933 10 50 67). M: Jaume I. Formed in part by an ancient first-century Roman wall. Tiny and romantic. Excellent salads (€4.25-7.60), *pâtés* (€8-12), and cheeses (€10-12). Reservations recommended. Open M-Sa 8:30pm-midnight. AmEx/MC/V. ❷

▧ **Les Quinze Nits**, Pl. Reial 6 (☎933 17 30 75). M: Liceu. One of the most popular restaurants in Barcelona. Scrumptious Catalán entrees at unbeatable prices (€3-7). No reservations. Open daily 1-3:45pm and 8:30-11:30pm. AmEx/MC/V. ❶

Los Caracoles, C. Escudellers 14 (☎933 01 20 41). M: Drassanes. What started as a snail shop has evolved into a delicious Catalán restaurant. Specialties include *caracoles* (snails; €8) and rabbit (€11). Open daily 1pm-midnight. AmEx/MC/V. ❸

Terrablava, V. Laietana 55 (☎933 22 15 85). An all-you-can-eat buffet of veggies, pasta, pizza, meat dishes, fruit, coffee, and one of the most extensive salad bars in the area. Buffet €8.40. Open daily 12:30pm-1am. Cash only. ❷

Els Quatre Gats, C. Montsió 3 (☎933 02 41 40). M: Catalunya. Picasso's old hangout. Entrees €12-18. Live piano and violin 9pm-1am. Open daily 1pm-1am. Closed Aug. AmEx/MC/V. ❸

Irati, C. Cardenal Casañas 17 (☎933 02 30 84). M: Liceu. An excellent Basque *tapas* bar. Keep your toothpicks to figure out your bill. Bartenders pour *sidra* (cider) behind their backs. Entrees €13-20. Open daily noon-1am. AmEx/MC/V. ❹

La Colmena, Pl. de l'Angel 12 (☎933 15 13 56). M: Jaume I. This divine pastry and candy shop tempts all; don't walk in unless you're prepared to buy. Pastries €1-4. Open daily 9am-9pm. AmEx/MC/V. ❶

Xaloc, C. de la Palla 13-17 (☎933 01 19 90). M: Liceu. This classy delicatessen is centered around a butcher counter with pig legs hanging from the high ceiling. Meat and poultry sandwiches on tasty baguettes €3-7. Open daily 9am-midnight. AmEx/MC/V. ❶

The Bagel Shop, C. Canuda 25 (☎933 02 41 61). M: Catalunya. Barcelona meets New York City. Diverse bagel selection (€0.60 each), bagel sandwiches (€3-5), and varied spreads, from cream cheese to caramel (€3-6). Open July-Aug. M-Sa 9:30am-9:30pm; open Sept-June. M-Sa 9:30am-9:30pm, Su 11am-4pm. ❶

El Salón, C. l'Hostal d'en Sol 6-8 (☎933 15 21 59). M: Jaume I. A mellow bar-bistro serving *gnocchi*, chicken, pork, and fish (€8-15). *Menú* €9.50. Wine €2-6. Cocktails €4.50. Open M-Sa 1:30pm-2:30am. AmEx/MC/V. ❷

Arc Café, C. Carabassa 19 (☎933 02 52 04). M: Drassanes. Away from the crowds, this gay-friendly cafe serves creative soups and salads. Entrees €5-8. Lunch *menú* €7.50. Open M-Th 9am-1am, F 9am-3am, Sa 11am-3am, Su 11am-1am. ❷

ELSEWHERE IN BARCELONA

🍴 **Xampanyet,** C. Montcado 22 (☎933 19 70 03). M: Jaume I. This *tapas* bar serves house *cava* at a colorful bar. Glasses €1. Bottles €7 and up. Open Sept.-July Tu-Sa noon-4pm and 7-11:30pm, Su 7-11:30pm. ❶

🍴 **Va de Vi,** C. Banys Vells 16 (☎933 19 29 00). M: Jaume I. Romantic, medieval wine bar in a 16th-century building. Wine €1.60-4 per glass. Cheeses €4-16. *Tapas* €2-13. Open Su-Th 6pm-2am, F-Sa 6pm-3am. ❷

🍴 **Bar Ra,** Pl. Garduña (☎933 01 41 63). M: Liceu. This place exudes cool. Dinner by reservation. Excellent duck (€10) and vegetarian lasagna (€8). Open M-Sa 9pm-midnight, Su brunch noon-6pm. AmEx/MC/V. ❷

🍴 **OvUm,** C. Encarnacio 56. M: Joanic. Follow C. Escorial for 2 blocks and turn left on C. Encarnacio. True to its name, this charming dimly-lit restaurant features egg specialties and vegetarian options with a Catalán twist. Open Su and Tu-Sa noon-1pm and 8:30-midnight. Closed 1st week of Aug. AmEx/MC/V. ❷

El Pebre Blau, C. Banys Vells 21 (☎933 19 13 08). M: Jaume I. Gourmet dishes creatively fuse Mediterranean, Oriental, and Sephardic flavors. Try the *foie gras* with apricots and honeyed sauce. Open daily 8:30pm-midnight. MC/V. ❹

El Racó d'en Baltá, C. Aribau 125 (☎934 53 10 44). M: Hospital Clínic. Offers creative Mediterranean dishes. Fish and meat entrees €12-17. Open Su 9-10:45pm, Tu-Sa 1-3:30pm and 9-10:45pm, F-Sa until 11pm. AmEx/MC/V. ❸

La Gavina, C. Ros de Olano 17 (☎934 15 74 50). M: Fontanao. Enjoy delicious Italian food in this pizzeria, complete with a life-size patron saint and confessional candles. Pizzas serving several people €7.50-16. Open Su and Tu-Th 6pm-1am, F-Sa 6pm-2am. ❸

Pla dels Angels, C. Ferlandina 23 (☎934 43 31 03). M: Universitat. The funky decor of this eatery is fitting for its proximity to the contemporary art museum. Try *gnocchi* with curry sauce and raisins (€4). Open M-Th 1-4pm and 9-11:30pm, F-Sa 9pm-midnight. ❷

Thai Gardens, C. Diputació 273 (☎934 87 98 98). M: Catalunya. Extravagant decor. Weekday *menú* €11. Pad Thai €6. Entrees €9-14. Open Su-Th 1-4pm and 8pm-midnight, F-Sa 1:30-4pm and 8pm-1am. ❸

Agua, Pg. Marítim de la Barceloneta 30 (☎932 25 12 72; www.grupotragaluz.com). Delicate seafood and rice dishes served on a shady terrace. Entrees €5.50-27. Open daily 1:30-4pm and 8:30pm-midnight. Reservations recommended. AmEx/MC/V. ❸

Comme-Bio, Av. Gran Vía 603 (☎933 01 03 76). The antithesis of traditional Catalán food, this place has hummus, tofu, and yogurt. Restaurant and small grocery store. Veggie pizzas, pasta, and rice €9. Salads €6-8. Open daily 9am-11:30pm. ❷

Zahara, Pg. Joan de Borbó 69 (☎932 21 37 65; www.zahara.com). This hip cocktail bar is a diamond in the rough. Salads €8-9. Sandwiches €4-5. Cocktails €6-9. Beer €2.50. Open daily 10am-3am. MC/V. ❷

Laie Llibreria Café, C. Pau Claris 85 (☎933 02 63 10; www.laie.es). M: Urquinaona. This urban oasis offers a fresh, plentiful all-you-can-eat buffet (€8.30). Internet €1 per 15min. Open M-F 9am-1am, Sa 10am-1am. AmEx/MC/V. ❷

Mandalay Café, C. Provença 330 (☎934 58 60 17; www.mandalaycafe.net). Exotic pan-Asian cuisine, including gourmet dim sum and elegant salads. F-Sa night trapeze artist around 11pm. Entrees €9-13. Open Tu-Sa 8:30pm-midnight. AmEx/MC/V. ❸

◉ SIGHTS

Barcelona is defined by its unique *Modernisme* architecture. The tourist areas are **Las Ramblas,** a bustling avenue smack in the city center, and the **Barri Gòtic,** Barcelona's "old city." But don't neglect vibrant La Ribera and El Raval, the upscale Modernist avenues of l'Eixample, the panoramic city views from Montjuïc and Tibidabo, Gaudi's Park Güell, and the harborside Port Olímpic. The **Ruta del Modernisme** pass is the cheapest and most flexible option for those with a few days and an interest in seeing all the biggest sights. Passes (€3.60; students, over-65, and groups of 11 or more €2.60) are good for a month and give holders discounts on entrance to Palau Güell, La Sagrada Família, Palau de la Música Catalana, Casa-Museu Gaudí, Fundació Antoni Tàpies, the Museu d'Art Modern, tours of El Hospital de la Santa Creu i Sant Pau, tours of the facades of La Manzana de la Discòrdia, and other attractions. You can purchase passes at **Casa Amatller,** Pg. Gràcia 41. (☎934 88 01 39; www.rutamodernisme.com. M: Pg. de Gràcia.)

LAS RAMBLAS

Las Ramblas, a pedestrian-only median strip, is a cosmopolitan cornucopia of street performers, fortune-tellers, human statues, vendors, and artists, all for the benefit of the visiting droves of tourists. A stroll along this bustling avenue can be an adventure at almost any hour, day or night. The wide, tree-lined thoroughfare dubbed Las Ramblas is actually composed of five (six if you count the small Rambla de Mar) distinct ramblas (promenades) that together form one boulevard, about 1km long, starting at Pl. Catalunya and the **Font de Canaletes** (more a pump than a fountain)—visitors who wish to eventually return to Barcelona are supposed to sample the water. Halfway down Las Ramblas, **Joan Miró**'s pavement mosaic brightens up the street. Pass the **Monument a Colom** on your way out to the Rambla de Mar and a beautiful view of the Mediterranean.

GRAN TEATRE DEL LICEU. Once one of Europe's leading stages, the Liceu has been ravaged by anarchists, bombs, and fires. It is adorned with palatial ornamentation, gold facades, sculptures, and grand side rooms—including a fantastic Spanish hall of mirrors. (*Las Ramblas 51-59, by C. de Sant Pau. Office open M-F 2-8:30pm and 1hr. before performances.* ☎934 85 99 13. *Tours M-F 10am, by reservation only. €5.*)

CENTRE D'ART DE SANTA MONICA. One can only imagine what the nuns of this former convent would have thought of the edgy art installations (recently "How Difficult it is to Sleep Alone" and "Transsexual Express") that rotate through this gallery, which is definitely worth a visit for modern art fans. (*Las Ramblas 7. M: Drassanes.* ☎933 16 27 27. *Open M-F 11am–2pm and 5-8pm. Call for info on exhibitions. Free.*)

Suggested Time: 5hr.

Distance: 3.2km (2 mi.)

When to go: A weekday morning.

Start: M: Liceu, L3.

End: M: Drassanes, L3.

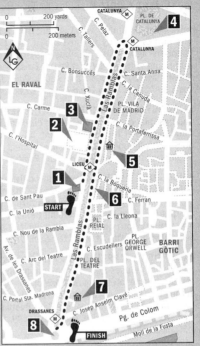

o visit to Barcelona is complete (or even possible) without traversing the famous Las Ramblas. Translated as "The Promenades," Las Ramblas is a series of five individual walkways strung together. Although they are generally referred to as one collective rambla, each has its own distinct character and plenty of built-in entertainment.

GRAN TEATRE DEL LICEU. Get off the Metro at Liceu, you can't miss it. Start your morning with the 10am guided tour of Barcelona's premier stage, and bask in the history of one of Europe's greatest opera houses (tours M-F; see p. 926)

LA BOQUERIA. Check out the famous market housed in an all-steel Modernist structure. Choose a late-morning snack from this wondrous bounty of fresh food (see p. 928).

PALAU DE LA VIRREINA. Wander in the courtyard of this 18th-century Rococo palace and see if any exhibitions are going on. If not, visit the building's Cultural Events Office or admire the upscale souvenirs in the giftshop (see p. 928).

PLAÇA CATALUNYA. Now you've come to the city's main hub. Every tourist wanders through at least once; can you tell by the crowds? The busy *plaça* makes a great place to people-watch or just relax. Check out the enormous El Corte Inglés and do some serious shopping. It is also where the old city meets the new; turn south to catch the rest of this walking tour, but if you continue farther north you can chart your own course through l'Eixample (see p. 931).

MUSEU DE L'ERÒTICA. Swing back around the *plaça* and head back down the left side of Las Ramblas. If you dare, check out Spain's only erotica museum. (see p. 928).

CAFÉ DE L'OPERA. Enjoy a cup of coffee at the famous cafe (see p. 924). But don't expect to order to go; Europeans like to enjoy their coffee by sipping it leisurely.

MUSEU DE CERA. Peruse over 300 different wax recreations of famous politicians, celebrities, fictional characters, and European royalty. While many of the figures are difficult to recognize, the scenes of death in the horror room are straightforward enough to appreciate (see p. 928).

MONUMENT A COLOM. End your tour with a visit to the 60m statue of the man Spanish cities love to claim as their own, Christopher Columbus. Sevilla purports that he is buried in their city (he's not). Barcelona claims that he was born in Catalunya (he wasn't). Christopher Columbus may have been elusive in birth and death, but at least Barcelona has captured the prophet in a moment of inspiration, pointing valiantly, heroically, epically... the wrong way. You can take an elevator to the top of the statue for a stunning view of the city (see p. 928).

MONUMENT A COLOM. Ruis i Taulet's Monument a Colom towers at the port end of Las Ramblas. Nineteenth-century *Renaixença* enthusiasts convinced themselves that Columbus was Catalán, from a town near Girona. The fact that Columbus points proudly toward Libya, not the Americas, doesn't help the claim; historians agree that Columbus was from Italy. Take the elevator to the top to enjoy a stunning view. *(Portal de la Pau. M: Drassanes. Elevator open daily June-Sept. 9am-8:30pm; Oct.-Mar. M-F 10am-1:30pm and 3:30-6:30pm, Sa-Su 10am-6:30pm; Apr.-May M-F 10am-2pm and 3:30-7:30pm, Sa-Su 10am-7:30pm. €1.80, children and over-65 €1.20.)*

LA BOQUERIA (MERCAT DE SANT JOSEP). Besides being one of the cheapest and best places to get food in the city, La Boqueria is a sight in itself: A traditional Catalán market located in a giant, all-steel Modernist structure. Specialized vendors sell delicious produce, fish, and meat from one of a seemingly infinite number of independent stands inside. *(Las Ramblas 95. M: Liceu. Open M-Sa 8am-8pm.)*

MUSEU DE L'ERÒTICA. As Spain's only erotica museum, the exhibits attract many of Barcelona's most intrepid tourists. The random assortment spans human history (somewhat unevenly) and depicts a variety of seemingly impossible sexual acrobatics that push the limits of human flexibility. The seven-foot wooden phallus is an irresistible photo op. *(Las Ramblas 96. M: Catalunya, L1/3. ☎933 18 98 65. Open June-Sept. 10am-midnight; Oct.-May 11am-9pm. €7.50, students €6.50.)*

PALAU DE LA VIRREINA. Once the residence of a Peruvian viceroy, this 18th-century palace houses temporary photography, music, and graphics exhibits. Also on display are the latest incarnations of the 10-15 foot tall dolls which have taken part in the city's Carnival celebrations since 1399. Be sure to check out the famous rainbow stained-glass facade of the **Casa Beethoven** next door at Las Ramblas 97, now a well-stocked music store. *(Las Ramblas 99. M: Liceu. ☎933 16 10 00. Open Tu-Sa 11am-8:30pm, Su 11am-3pm. Free.)*

MUSEU DE CERA (WAX MUSEUM). Some 300 wax figures form an endless parade of celebrities, fictional characters, and European historical figures; the most recognizable are generally ones with distinctive facial hair, like Fidel Castro, and Chewbacca from *Star Wars*. *(Las Ramblas 4. M: Drassanes. ☎933 17 26 49. Open July-Sept. daily 10am-8pm; Oct.-June M-F 10am-1:30pm and 4-7:30pm, Sa-Su and holidays 11am-2pm and 4:30-8:30pm. €6.70, ages 5-11 €3.80.)*

BARRI GÒTIC

While the ancient cathedrals and palaces gives the impression that this neighborhood's time has passed, the area is still very much alive, as evident in the ever-crowded streets. As the oldest part of Barcelona, the Barri Gòtic came into existence well before the inception of the grid layout (found in l'Eixample), which took form during Roman times and continued to develop during the medieval period.

ESGLÉSIA CATEDRAL DE LA SANTA CREU. This cathedral is one of Barcelona's most popular monuments. Beyond the choir are the altar with the bronze cross designed by Frederic Marès in 1976 and the sunken Crypt of Santa Eulalia, one of Barcelona's patron saints. The cathedral museum holds Bartolomé Bermejo's *Pietà*. Catch a performance of the sardana in front of the cathedral on Sunday after Mass. *(M: Jaume I. In Pl. Seu, up C. Bisbe from Pl. St. Jaume. Cathedral open daily 8am-1:30pm and 4-7:30pm. Cloister open 9am-1:15pm and 4-7pm. Elevator to the roof open M-Sa 10:30am-12:30pm and 4:30-6pm. €1.40. Mass Su noon and 6:30pm. Choir area open M-F 9am-1pm and 4-7pm, Sa-Su 9am-1pm. €1. English audioguide €1.)*

PLAÇA DE SANT JAUME. Plaça de Sant Jaume has been Barcelona's political center since Roman times. Two of Cataluña's most important buildings have dominated the square since 1823: The **Palau de la Generalitat,** the headquarters of Cataluña's government, and the **Ajuntament,** the city hall. *(Generalitat open 2nd and 4th Su of every month 10:30am-1:30pm. Closed Aug. Mandatory tours in Catalán, Spanish, or English every 30min. starting at 10:30am. Free. Ajuntament open Su 10am-1:45pm. Free.)*

MUSEU D'HISTÒRIA DE LA CIUTAT. There are two components to the Museu d'Història de la Ciutat (Museum of the History of Barcelona): The Palau Reial Major and the subterranean excavations of the Roman city Barcino. Built on top of the fourth-century city walls, the **Palau Reial Major** served as the residence of the Catalán-Aragonese monarchs. When restoration of the building began, the **Saló de Tinell** (Throne Room) was discovered wholly intact under a Baroque chapel. The huge Gothic room is believed to be the place where Ferdinand and Isabella received Columbus after his journey to America. Today, it houses year-long temporary exhibitions. The second part of the museum lies underground; this 4000 sq. meter ▓**archeological exhibit** was excavated from 1930 to 1960 and displays incredibly intact first- to 6th-century remains of the Roman city of Barcino. *(Pl. del Rei. M: Jaume I. ☎ 933 15 11 11. Open June-Sept. Su 10am-3pm, Tu-Sa 10am-8pm; Oct.-May Su 10am-3pm, Tu-Sa 10am-2pm and 4-8pm. Museum €4, students €2.50. Exhibition €3.50, students €2. Combined museum and exhibition €6, students €4. Pamphlets available in English.)*

EL CALL (JEWISH QUARTER). Although today there is little indicating the Jewish heritage of this area, for centuries El Call was the most vibrant center of intellectual and financial activity in all of Barcelona. One Jewish synagogue was turned into a church, the **Església de Sant Jaume** (C. Ferran 28). However, the only remaining tangible evidence of Jewish inhabitants in El Call is the ancient **Hebrew plaque** in tiny C. Marlet. *(M: Liceu.)*

SANTA MARIA DEL PI. The Església de Santa Maria del Pi is a small 14th-century church with exquisite Gothic stained-glass windows. *(M: Liceu. Open M-F 8:30am-1pm and 4:30-8:30pm, Sa 8:30am-1pm and 4-9pm, Su 9am-2pm and 5-9pm. Free.)*

PLAÇA REIAL. This is the most crowded, happening *plaça* in the entire Barri Gòtic, where tourists and locals congregate to eat and drink at night, and to buy and sell at the Sunday morning flea market. Francesc Daniel Milona designed the *plaça,* replacing decrepit Barri Gòtic streets with this large, architecturally cohesive *plaça* in the 1850s. Near the fountain in the center of the square there are two street lamps designed by Antoni Gaudí. *(M: Liceu or Drassanes.)*

LA RIBERA

This neighborhood has recently evolved into Barcelona's bohemian nucleus, with art galleries, chic eateries, and exclusive bars.

▓**MUSEU PICASSO.** The most-visited museum in Barcelona traces the development of Picasso as an artist, with the world's best collection of work from his formative Barcelona period. *(C. Montcada 15-19. M: Jaume I. Open Tu-Sa 10am-8pm, Su 10am-3pm. €5, students and seniors €2.50. Under-16 free. First Su of each month free.)*

▓**PALAU DE LA MÚSICA CATALANA.** In 1891, the Orfeó Catalán choir society commissioned Modernist Luis Domènech i Montaner to design this must-see concert venue. The music hall glows with tall stained-glass windows, an ornate chandelier, marble reliefs, intricate woodwork, and ceramic mosaics. Concerts given at the Palau include symphonic and choral music in addition to more modern pop, rock, and jazz. *(C. Sant Francesc de Paula 2. ☎ 932 95 72 00;*

www.palaumusica.org. M: Jaume I. Mandatory tours in English every hr. Reserve 1 day in advance. Open daily Aug. 10am-6pm; Sept.-July 10am-3:30pm. €5, students and seniors €4. Check the Guía del Ocio for concert listings. Concert tickets €6-150. MC/V.)

■ **MUSEU DE LA XOCOLATA (CHOCOLATE MUSEUM).** Arguably the most delectable museum in Spain, with gobs of information about the history, production, and ingestion of chocolate. Perhaps more interesting are the exquisite chocolate sculptures, particularly the edible version of La Sagrada Família. A small cafe offers workshops on cake baking and chocolate tasting. (Pl. Pons i Clerch. M: Jaume I. Open M and W-Sa 10am-7pm, Su 10am-3pm. €3.80, students and seniors €3.30. Reservations required. Workshops from €6.)

PARC DE LA CIUTADELLA. Host of the 1888 Universal Exposition, the park harbors several museums, well-labeled horticulture, the wacky Cascada fountains, a pond, and a zoo. Buildings of note include Domènech i Montaner's Modernista **Castell dels Tres Dragons** (now the Museu de Zoología), the geological museum, and Josep Amergós's **Hivernacle.** In the **Parc Zoològic** (M: Ciutadella. Open May-Aug. 9:30am-7:30pm; Apr. and Sept. 10am-7pm; Mar. and Oct. 10am-6pm; Nov.-Feb. 10am-5pm. €12.) ■**Floquet de Neu** (a.k.a. *Copito de Nieve;* Little Snowflake), the world's only known albino gorilla, lounges in the sun. The nearby **Museu d'Art Modern** houses a potpourri of works by 19th-century Catalán artists. (Pl. D'Armes. Open Tu-Sa 10am-7pm, Su 10am-2:30pm. €3, students €2. First Th of every month free.)

SANTA MARIA DEL MAR. This 14th-century architectural wonder was built in a quick 55 years. Standing 13m apart, the supporting columns span a width greater than any other medieval building in the world. It's a fascinating example of the limits of Gothic architecture—were it 2ft. taller, the roof would collapse from structural instability. (Pl. Santa Maria 1. M: Jaume 1. Open M-Sa 9am-1:30pm and 4:30-8pm, Su 9am-2pm and 5-8:30pm. Free.)

EL FOSSAR DE LES MORERES. The Catalans who resisted Felipe V's conquering troops in 1714 were buried here in a mass grave, commemorated by mulberry trees (*les moreres*) and a plaque with a verse by the poet Sefari Pitarra: "In the Mulberry Cemetery no traitors are buried. Even though we lose our flags, this will be the urn of honor." Demonstrators and patriots converge on Catalán National Day, September 11th, to commemorate the siege of Barcelona and the subsequent ban on displays of Catalán nationalism. (Off C. de Santa Maria and next to the church's back entrance.)

EL RAVAL

■ **PALAU GÜELL.** Gaudí's Palau Güell (1886)—the Modernist residence built for patron Eusebi Güell (of Park Güell fame)—has one of Barcelona's most spectacular interiors. Güell spared no expense on this house, considered to be the first where Gaudí's unique style truly showed. (C. Nou de La Rambla 3-5. M: Liceu. Open Mar.-Oct. Su 10am-2pm, M-Sa 10am-8pm, last tour at 6:15pm; Nov.-Dec. M-Sa 10am-6pm. €3, students €1.50. Mandatory tour every 15min.)

MUSEU D'ART CONTEMPORANI (MACBA). This monstrosity of a building was constructed with the idea that sparse decor would allow the art to speak for itself. The MACBA has received worldwide acclaim for its focus on avantgarde art between the two world wars, as well as Surrealist and contemporary art. (Pl. dels Angels 1. M: Catalunya. Open July-Sept. M, W, and F 11am-8pm; Th 11am-9:30pm; Sa 10am-8pm; Su 10am-3pm. Oct.-June M and W-F 11am-7:30pm, Sa 10am-8pm, Su 10am-3pm. €7, students €3. Under-17 free.)

FAR-OUT FACADE Gaudí was a religious man, and his plans for La Sagrada Família called for elaborate and deliberate symbolism in almost every single decorative element of the church. The cypress tree on the **Nativity Facade**, according to one theory, symbolizes the stairway to heaven (cypress trees do not put down deeper roots with time but only grow increasingly taller); the tree is crowned with the word "Tau," the Greek word for God. Similarly, the top of each of the eight finished towers carries the first letter of one of the names of the apostles (and the words "Hosanna" and "Excelsis" are written in a spiral up the sides of the towers). Inside, on the **Portal of the Rosary**, overt references to modern life lurk amongst more traditional religious imagery: the Temptation of Man is represented in one carving by the devil handing a bomb to a terrorist and in another by his waving a purse at a prostitute.

Suberachs, Gaudí's successor, continued the religious symbolism in his **Passion Facade**. To the left, a snake lurks behind Judas, symbolizing the disciple's betrayal of Jesus. The 4x4 box of numbers next to Him contains 310 possible combinations of four numbers, each of which adds up to 33, Christ's age when He died. The faceless woman in the center of the facade, **Veronica**, represents the Biblical woman with the same name and the miraculous appearance of Christ's face on the cloth with which she compassionately wiped his face.

CENTRE DE CULTURA CONTEMPORÀNIA DE BARCELONA (CCCB). The center stands out for its mixture of architectural styles, consisting of an early 20th-century theater and its 1994 addition, a sleek wing of black glass. The institute shows a variety of temporary exhibits, including film screenings and music performances; check the *Guía del Ocio* for scheduled events. *(Casa de Caritat. C. Montalegre 5. M: Catalunya or Universitat. ☎ 933 06 41 00. Open Tu, Th, and F 11am-2pm and 4-8pm; W and Sa 11am-8pm; Su and holidays 11am-7pm. €4, students €3, W €3 for all. Children free.)*

L'EIXAMPLE

The Catalán Renaissance and the growth of Barcelona during the 19th century pushed the city past its medieval walls and into modernity. Ildefons Cerdà drew up a plan for a new neighborhood where people of all social classes could live side by side; however, l'Eixample (pronounced luh-SHOMP-luh) did not thrive as a utopian community but rather as a playground for the bourgeois. Despite the gentrification, the original Modernist architecture remains truly idealistic.

■ **LA SAGRADA FAMÍLIA.** Although Antoni Gaudí's unfinished masterpiece is barely a shell of the intended finished product, La Sagrada Família is without a doubt the world's most visited construction site. Despite the fact that only eight of the eighteen planned towers have been completed (and those the shortest, at that) and the church still doesn't have an "interior," millions of people make the touristic pilgrimage to witness its work-in-progress majesty. Of the three proposed facades, only the Nativity Facade was finished under Gaudí. A furor has arisen over recent additions, especially sculptor Josep Subirachs's Cubist Passion Facade, which is criticized for being inconsistent with Gaudí's plans. *(C. Mallorca 401. M: Sagrada Família. Open Apr.-Sept. daily 9am-8pm, elevator open 9:30am-7:45pm; Oct.-Mar. 9am-6pm, elevator open 9:30am-5:45pm. Entrance €8, students €5. Cash only. ■ Guided tours Apr.-Sept. daily every hour 11am-5pm; Oct. 11am-3pm; Nov.-Mar. Su-M and F-Sa 11am-1pm. €3.)*

■ **LA MANZANA DE LA DISCÒRDIA.** A short walk from Pl. Catalunya, the odd-numbered side of Pg. de Gràcia between C. Aragó and Consell de Cent is popularly known as *la manzana de la discòrdia* (block of discord), referring to the stylistic clashing of three buildings. Regrettably, the bottom two floors of **Casa Lleó i Morera,** by Domènech i Montaner, were destroyed to make room for a fancy store, but you can buy the **Ruta del Modernisme pass** there and take a short tour of the upper floors, where sprouting flowers, stained glass, and legendary doorway sculptures adorn the interior. Puig i Cadafalch opted for a geometric, Moorish-influenced pattern on the facade of **Casa Amatller** at #41. Gaudí's balconies ripple like water, and tiles sparkle in blue-purple glory on **Casa Batlló,** #43. The most popular interpretation of Casa Batlló is that the building represents Cataluña's patron Sant Jordi (St. George) slaying a dragon; the chimney plays the lance, the scaly roof is the dragon's back, and the bony balconies are the remains of his victims. (*Open M-Sa 9am-2pm, Su 9am-8pm. €8, students €6.*)

■ **CASA MILÀ (LA PEDRERA).** Modernism buffs argue that the spectacular Casa Milà apartment building, an undulating mass of granite popularly known as *La Pedrera* (the Stone Quarry), is Gaudí's most refined work. Note the intricate ironwork around the balconies and the irregularity of the front gate's egg-shaped window panes. The roof sprouts chimneys that resemble armored soldiers, one of which is decorated with broken champagne bottles. Rooftop tours provide a closer look at these Prussian helmets. The winding brick attic has been transformed into the **Espai Gaudí,** a multimedia presentation of Gaudí's life and works. (*Pg. Gràcia 92. Open daily 10am-8pm. €7; students and over-65 €3.50. Free guided tours in English M-F 4pm, Sa-Su 11am.*)

HOSPITAL DE LA SANTA CREU I SANT PAU. Designated a UNESCO monument in 1997, the brilliant Modernist Hospital de la Santa Creu i Sant Pau was Domènech i Montaner's lifetime masterpiece. The entire complex covers nine full l'Eixample blocks (320 acres) and the pavilions are whimsically decorated, resembling gingerbread houses. The outdoor spaces are an oasis in the desert of urban gridding; they once included a small forest and still boast more than 300 different types of plants, as well as plenty of shaded paths. (*Sant Antoni M. Claret 167. M: Hospital de St. Pau, L5. ☎ 934 88 20 78. Hospital grounds open 24hr. 50min. guided tours Sa-Su every 30min 10am-2pm. Last tour leaves 1:30pm. €4.30, students and over-65 €3.*)

FUNDACIÓ ANTONI TÀPIES. Antoni Tàpies is one of Cataluña's best-known artists; his works often defy definition, springing from Surrealism and Magicism. Tàpies's massive and bizarre wire sculpture (*Cloud with Chair*) atop Domènech i Montaner's red brick building announces this collection of contemporary abstract art. The top floor of the foundation is dedicated to famous Catalans, particularly Tàpies, while the other two floors feature temporary exhibits of other modern artists' work. (*C. Aragó 255. M: Pg. de Gràcia. ☎ 934 87 03 15. Museum open Su and Tu-Sa 10am-8pm. €4.20, students and seniors €2.10.*)

WATERFRONT

■ **MUSEU MARÍTIM.** The *Drassanes Reiales de Barcelona* (Royal Shipyards of Barcelona) are considered the world's greatest standing example of Civil (i.e., non-religious) Gothic architecture and are currently awaiting nomination as a UNESCO World Heritage Site. The complex consists of a series of huge indoor bays with slender pillars, in which entire ships could be constructed and stored over the winter. Since 1941, the building has housed the Maritime Museum, which traces the evolution of shipbuilding and life on the high seas. (*Av. Drassanes, off the rotary around the Monument a Colom. M: Drassanes, L3. ☎ 933 42 99 20. Open daily 10am-7pm. €5.40; under-16, students, and seniors €2.70.*)

■ **L'AQUÀRIUM DE BARCELONA.** Barcelona's aquarium—the largest in Europe—is an aquatic wonder, featuring a large number of octopi and penguins. The highlight is a 75m glass tunnel through an ocean tank of sharks and sting rays, as well as one two-dimensional fish. *(Moll d'Espanya, next to Maremàgnum. M: Drassanes. Open July-Aug. daily 9:30am-11pm; Sept.-June 9:30am-9pm. €13, students €12, under-12 and seniors €9.)*

■ **TORRE SAN SEBASTIÀ.** One of the easiest and best ways to view the city is on these cable cars, which span the entire Port Vell, connecting beachy Barceloneta with mountainous Montjuïc. The full ride, which takes about 10min. each way and makes an intermediate stop at the Jaume I tower near Colom, gives an aerial perspective of the entire city. *(Pg. Joan de Borbo. M: Barceloneta. In Port Vell, as you walk down Joan de Borbo and see the beaches to the left, stay right and look for the high tower. To Jaume I round-trip €7.50; to Montjuïc one-way €7.50, round-trip €9.50. Open daily 11am-8pm.)*

VILA OLÍMPICA. The Vila Olímpica, beyond the east side of the zoo, was built to house 15,000 athletes and entertain millions of tourists for the 1992 Summer Olympics. It's home to several public parks, a shopping center, and business offices. In the area called **Barceloneta,** beaches stretch out from the port. *(M: Ciutadella/Vila Olímpica. Walk along the waterfront on Ronda Litoral toward the two towers.)*

MONTJUÏC

Throughout Barcelona's history, whoever controlled Montjuïc (Hill of the Jews) controlled the city. Dozens of rulers have modified the **fortress,** built atop an ancient Jewish cemetery; Franco made it one of his "interrogation" headquarters, rededicating it to the city in 1960. A huge stone monument expresses Barcelona's (forced) gratitude for its return; the three statues symbolize the three seas surrounding Spain. *(M: Espanya, then bus #50 (every 10min.) from Av. Reina María Cristina.)*

■ **FUNDACIÓ MIRÓ.** Designed by Miró's friend Josep Luís Sert and tucked into the side of Montjuïc, the Fundació links interior and exterior spaces with massive windows and outdoor patios. Skylights illuminate an extensive collection of statues and paintings from Miró's career. His best-known pieces in the museum include *El Carnival de Arlequin, La Masia,* and *L'or de L'azuz.* Room 13 displays experimental work by young artists. The Fundació also sponsors music and film festivals. *(Av. Miramar 71-75. Take the funicular from M: ParaHel. Open July-Aug. Tu-W and F-Sa 10am-8pm, Th 10am-9:30pm, Su 10am-2:30pm; Oct.-June Tu-W and F-Sa 10am-7pm, Th 10am-9:30pm, Su 10am-2:30pm. €7.20, students and seniors €4.)*

■ **MUSEU NACIONAL D'ART DE CATALUNYA (PALAU NACIONAL).** Designed by Enric Catá and Pedro Cendoya for the 1929 International Exposition, the beautiful Palau Nacional has housed the Museu Nacional d'Art de Catalunya (MNAC) since 1934. Its main hall is a public event space, while the wings are home to the world's finest collection of Catalán Romanesque art and a wide variety of Gothic pieces. The Romanesque frescoes, now integrated as murals into dummy chapels, were salvaged in the 1920s from their original, less protected locations in northern Cataluña's churches. The museum's Gothic art corridor displays paintings on wood, the medium of choice during that period. The chronological tour of the galleries underlines the growing influence of Italy over Cataluña's artistic development, and ends with a breathtaking series of paintings by Gothic master Bernat Martorell. Behind the building, the **Fonts Luminoses** (the Illuminated Fountains) are dominated by the central **Font Mágica,** which are employed in weekend laser shows during the summer. *(From M: Espanya, walk up Av. Reina María Cristina, away from the two brick towers, and take the escalators to the top. Open Su 10am-2:30pm, Tu-Sa 10am-7pm. €4.80; with temporary exhibits €6; temporary exhibits only €4.20. 30% discount for students and seniors.)*

S P A I N

CASTELL DE MONTJUÏC. A visit to this historic fortress and its **Museum Militar** is a great way to get an overview of the city's layout and history. From the castle's exterior *mirador*, gaze over the city. Enjoy coffee at the cafe while cannons stare you down. *(From M: Paral·lel, take the funicular to Av. Miramar and then the Teleféric de Montjuïc cable car to the castle. Teleféric open M-Sa 11:15am-9pm. One-way €3.20, round-trip €4.50. Or, walk up the steep slope on C. Foc, next to the funicular station. Open Mar. 15-Nov. 15 9:30am-8pm; Nov. 16-Mar. 14 9:30am-5pm. Castle and mirador €1.)*

ZONA ALTA

PARK GÜELL. This fantastic park was designed entirely by Gaudí but—in typical Gaudí fashion—was not completed until after his death. Gaudí intended Park Güell to be a garden city with dwarfish buildings and sparkling ceramic-mosaic stairways. Two mosaic staircases flank the park, leading to a towering Modernist pavilion that Gaudí originally designed as an open-air market. The longest park bench in the world, a multicolored serpentine wonder made of tile shards, decorates the top of the pavilion. In the midst of the park is the **Casa-Museu Gaudí.** *(Bus #24 from Pl. Catalunya stops at the upper entrance. Park free. Open May-Sept. daily 10am-9pm; Mar.-Apr. and Oct. 10am-7pm; Nov.-Feb. 10am-6pm. Museum open daily Apr.-Sept. 10am-8pm; Oct.-Mar. 10am-6pm. €4, students €3.)*

MUSEU DEL FÚTBOL CLUB BARCELONA. A close second to the Picasso Museum as Barcelona's most-visited museum, the FCB museum merits all the attention it gets. Sports fans will appreciate the storied history of the team. The high point is the chance to enter the stadium and take in the enormity of Camp Nou. *(C. Aristides Maillol, next to the stadium. M: Collblanc. Enter through access gates 7 or 9. Open M-Sa 10am-6:30pm, Su 10am-2pm. €5, under-13 €3.50.)*

🎵 ■ ENTERTAINMENT AND FESTIVALS

For tips on entertainment, nightlife, and food, pick up the *Guía del Ocio* (www.guiadelociobcn.es) at any newsstand. Most of Barcelona's galleries are in **La Ribera** around C. Montcada. The best shopping in the city is on the posh **Passeig de Gràcia** in l'Eixample. Grab face paint to join Barça at the Nou Camp stadium for **fútbol.** (☎934 96 36 00. Box office C. Aristedes Maillol 12-18.) Join in the **sardana,** Cataluña's regional dance, in front of the cathedral after mass on Sundays (noon and 6:30pm). Bullfights are held at the **Plaça de Toros Monumental,** on C. Castillejos 248. (☎932 45 58 04. Tickets €16-90.) Take advantage of **Barceloneta** or **Poble Nou's** easy access to the Mediterranean. In addition to tons of sand for topless-tanning, there are plenty of places to rent sailboats and other water-sport equipment. Head up to Montjuïc and take advantage of the **Olympic Facilities** which are now open for public use, including **Piscines Bernat Picornell,** the gorgeous pool complex.

Outdoor activities in this bustling cosmopolitan city are not exactly abundant. However, the **Parc de Collserola** in Zona Alta has hiking, biking, and horseback riding. (☎932 80 35 52. Open daily 9:30am-3pm.) Also, the Catalán Pyrenees and Islas Baleares are easily accessible from the city.

Festivals in Barcelona, as in the rest of Spain, occur often; if you are in the city for more than a week, chances are that some sort of celebration will be happening. Remember to double check sight and museum hours during festival times as well as during the Christmas season and during *Semana Santa* (Holy Week; the week before Easter). The **Festa de Sant Jordi** (St. George; Apr. 24) celebrates Cataluña's patron saint with a feast. Men give women roses, and women give men books. On August 15-21, city folk jam at Gràcia's **Festa Mayor;** lights blaze in *plaças* and music plays all night. The **Sónar** music festival comes to town in mid-June, attracting renowned DJs and electronic enthusiasts from all over the world for three days of concerts and partying. The **Festa de Música** (July 1), a city-wide celebration of music, comes soon afterward, during which free concerts are held all over Barcelona. During July and August the **Grec Festival** hosts dance and concert performances, as well as film screenings, in different concert venues. On September 11th, the **Fiesta Nacional de Cataluña** is celebrated with traditional costumes, dancing, and Catalán flags hanging from balconies.

⚑ NIGHTLIFE

Nightlife in Barcelona needs no introduction: Whether you're looking for psychedelic absinthe shots, a great place for grunge rock, a sunrise foam party, or just someplace quiet to sit back and enjoy a drink, the city has it all. Things don't get going until late (don't bother showing up at a club before 1am) and keep going till dawn. Check the *Guía del Ocio*, available at newsstands, for up-to-date listings.

BARRI GÒTIC

In this neighborhood, cookie-cutter *cervecerías* and *bar-restaurantes* can be found every five steps. The Barri Gòtic is perfect for chit-chatting your night away, sipping *sangría*, or scoping out your next dance partner.

Fonfone, C. Escudellers 24. M: Liceu or Drassanes. Atmospheric lighting and cool sounds draw 1-3am crowds. Different DJs every night from all over the world. Beer €3.20. Mixed drinks €6. Open Su-Th 9:30pm-2:30am, F-Sa 9:30pm-3am.

Molly's Fair City, C. Ferran 7. M: Liceu. The place to go if you're looking to meet English-speaking tourists in the Barri Gòtic, guzzling pricey but strong mixed drinks. Guinness on tap €5. Bottled beer €4. Mixed drinks €7. Open Su-Th 8pm-2:30am, F-Sa 7pm-3am.

Jamboree, Pl. Reial 17. M: Liceu. In the corner immediately to your right coming from Las Ramblas. What was once a convent now serves as one of the city's most popular live music venues. Daily jazz or blues performances. Cover M-F €6, Sa-Su €9-12; includes 1 drink. Open daily 11pm-1am. Upstairs, the attached club **Tarantos** hosts flamenco shows (€25). Open M-Sa 9:30pm-midnight.

Schilling, C. Ferran 23. M: Liceu, L3. One of the more chill and spacious bars in the area. Mixed gay and straight crowd. Excellent *sangría* (pitcher €14). Mixed drinks €5. Wine and beer €2. Open daily 10am-2:30am.

Vildsvin, C. Ferran 38. M: Liceu. Oysters and international beers (€4-8) are the specialties at this Norwegian bar. *Tapas* €3-5. Desserts €3.50-5. *Entrees* €8-14. Open M-Th 9am-2am, F-Sa 9am-3am. AmEx/MC/V.

El Bosq de les Fades, (☎933 17 26 49). M: Drassanes, near the Wax Museum. This bar is a mystical, complete with gnarly trees and gnomes. A good place to hang before hitting up a club. Open M-Th 10am-1:30am, F-Sa 10am-2:30am.

Glaciar Bar, Pl. Reial 3. M: Liceu. A hidden treasure in a sea of indistinguishable tourist bars. Plenty of outside tables. Beer €1.50-2. Mixed drinks €4. Liter of *sangría* €10. Open Su 8am-2:30am, M-Sa 4pm-2:30am. Cash only.

New York, C. Escudellers 5. M: Drassanes. Once a strip joint, New York is now the biggest club in the Barri Gòtic. Crowds don't arrive until after 3am; music includes reggae and British pop. Cover 11:30pm-2am €6 (includes 1 beer); 2-5am €13 (includes any drink). Open Th-Sa midnight-5am. Cash only.

Margarita Blue, C. J. A. Clavé 6. M: Drassanes. This Mexican-themed bar draws a 20- and 30-something crowd. Blue margaritas €3. W night drag queen performances. Open Su-W 7pm-2am, Th 7pm-2:30am, F-Sa 7pm-3am.

LA RIBERA

El Copetin, Pg. del Born 19. M: Jaume I. Cuban rhythm infuses everything in this casual nightspot. *Mojitos* €5. Open Su-Th 7pm-2:30am, F-Sa 7pm-3am.

El Born, Pg. del Born 26. M: Jaume I. Sit at the marble counter over the basins where fish were once sold or follow spiral staircase upstairs for a meal. Fondues €12-15. Excellent cocktails €4-6. Open Su-Th 6pm-2am, F-Sa 6pm-3am.

Palau Dalmases, C. Montcada 20. M: Jaume I. A self-labeled "Baroque space" in a 17th-century palace. Live opera performances Th at 11pm (€18, includes one drink). Drinks €6-10. Open Su 6-10pm, Tu-Sa 10pm-2am.

Pitin Bar, Pg. del Born 34. M: Barceloneta. Trippy lounge music will put you in the mood for absinthe (€2.70). Mixed drinks €4.50-8. Open daily 6pm-3am.

EL RAVAL

These streets are densely packed with a place for every variety of bar-hopper—Irish pubbers, American backpackers, absinthe aficionados, social drinkers, lounge lizards, and foosball maniacs will find themselves at home in El Raval.

■ **Casa Almirall,** C. Joaquim Costa 33. M: Universitat. This cavernous space, with weathered couches, is Barcelona's oldest bar, founded in 1860. The staff will walk you through your first glass of *absenta* (absinthe; €4.50)—and cut you off after your second. Beer €2. Mixed drinks €5. Open Su-Th 6:30pm-2:30am, F-Sa 6:30pm-3am.

Muebles Navarro (El Café que pone), C. la Riera Alta 4-6. Enjoy the mellow ambience and watch friends get friendlier as they sink into the comfy couches together. Beer and wine €2-3. Mixed drinks €5-7. Open Tu-Th 6pm-2am, F-Sa 6pm-3am.

London Bar, C. Nou de la Rambla 34, off Las Ramblas. M: Liceu. Rub shoulders with unruly, fun-loving expats at this Modernist tavern. Live music nightly. Beer, wine, and absinthe €2-3. Open Su and Tu-Th 7:30pm-4:30am, F-Sa 7:30pm-5am. AmEx/MC/V.

Sant Pau 68, C. de Sant Pau 68. M: Liceu. One of the hippest bars in El Raval. Drinks €2-5. Open Tu-Th 8pm-2:30am, F-Sa 8pm-3am. Cash only.

La Paloma, C. Tigre 27. M: Universitat. This dance hall, with its theater-like interior, was a factory until 1903. Live salsa and popular Spanish music keep a mature clientele dancing throughout the night. Mixed drinks €7. Cover €7. Open Su and Th 6-9:30pm, F 6-9:30pm and 11:30pm-4am, Sa 6-9:30pm and 11:30pm-5am.

Marsella Bar, C. de Sant Pau 65. M: Liceu. Religious figurines grace the walls; perhaps they're praying for the absinthe drinkers (€3.40) who frequent the place. Mixed drinks €2-6. Open M-Th 10pm-2:30am, F-Sa 10pm-3:30am.

Lupino, C. Carme 33. M: Catalunya. Ultra-chic lounge combines atmospheric lighting and sophisticated furnishing into a stylish haven for fashionable people. Cocktails €5.50. Open Su-Th 9pm-2:30am, F-Sa 9pm-3am.

L'EIXAMPLE

L'Eixample has upscale bars and some of the best gay nightlife in Europe, as evidenced by the area's nickname, "Gaixample."

■ **Buenavista Salsoteca,** C. Rosselló 217. FGC: Provença. This over-the-top salsa club manages to attract a laid-back, mixed crowd. Free salsa and merengue lessons W-Th at 10:30pm. F-Sa cover €9, includes 1 drink. Open W-Th 11pm-4am, F-Sa 11pm-5am, Su 8pm-2am.

■ **Dietrich,** C. Consell de Cent 255. M: Pg. Gràcia. A rather unflattering painting of Marlene Dietrich in the semi-nude greets a mostly gay crowd. Nightly drag/strip/dance shows. Beer €3.50. Mixed drinks €5-8. Open Su-Th 10:30pm-2:30am, F-Sa 10:30pm-3am.

La Fira, C. Provença 171. M: Hospital Clìnic. Bartenders serve a hip crowd dangling from carousel swings and surrounded by creepy fun-house mirrors. DJs spin funk, disco, and oldies. Open M-Th 10pm-3am, F-Sa 10pm-4:30am, Su 6pm-1am.

Fuse, C. Roger de Llúria 40. M: Tetuán or Pg. Gràcia. A cutting-edge Japanese-Mediterranean restaurant, cocktail bar, dance club. Mixed gay and straight crowd. Beer €3. Mixed drinks €6. Restaurant open M-Sa 8:30pm-1am. Bar open Th-Sa 1-3am. MC/V.

Les Gens que J'Aime, C. València 286. M: Pg. de Gràcia. Travel back to Gaudí's time in this intimate bar. Background soul, funk, and jazz soothes patrons. Beer €3. Half-bottles of wine €9. Open June-Aug. daily 7pm-3am; Sept.-May 6pm-3am.

Luz de Gas, C. Muntaner 246. M: Diagonal. Chandeliers and deep red walls set the mood in this hip club. Live music every night. Beer €6. Mixed drinks €9. Live music concerts €15; check the *Guía del Ocio* for listings and times. July-Aug. open M-Sa 11pm-5am; Sept.-June daily 11pm-5am.

Salvation, Ronda de St. Pere 19-21. M: Urquinaona. A popular gay club. Beer €5. Mixed drinks €8. Cover €11, includes 1 drink. Open Su and F-Sa midnight-6am.

The Michael Collins Irish Pub, Pl. Sagrada Família 4. M: Sagrada Família. 100% Irish, from the waitstaff to the smoky, wooden decor. American and European sports on the TV. Draft beer €4. Mixed drinks €5. Open daily 2pm-3am.

Berlin, C. Muntaner 240. M: Diagonal. A slice of streamlined German style in Barcelona; attracts area hipsters, and hordes of l'Eixample yuppies. Beer €3.50. Cocktails €9. Open M-W 9:30pm-2am, Th-Sa 9:30pm-3am.

domèstic, C. Diputació 215. M: Urgell. Multifaceted *bar-musical* with frequent poetry readings, art expositions, and live music. Beer €3. Mixed drinks €5. Open Su and Tu-Th 7pm-2:30am, F-Sa 8pm-3am.

POBLE NOU AND PORT OLÍMPIC

L'Ovella Negra (Megataverna del Poble Nou), C. Zamora 78. *The* place to come for the first few beers of the night. Foosball games on the 2nd floor are nearly as intense as the real-life FCB/Real Madrid rivalry. Large beers €2. Cocktails from €2. Kitchen open until 12:30am. Open F-Sa 5pm-3am, Su 5-10:30pm.

Club Danzatoria, C. Ramon Trias Fargas 24. The sleek interior makes this one of the hottest places in town. All house music all the time. Cover €15, includes 1 drink. Open Su and Th-Sa midnight-late.

Razzmatazz, C. Pamplona 88. M: Marina. A huge warehouse-turned-entertainment complex, with strobe-lit dance floors and concert space for indy-rock. Cover €9, includes 1 drink. Concert prices vary; call ahead for listings. Beer €3. Cocktails from €5. Open F-Sa and holidays midnight-4am. MC/V.

MAREMAGNUM

Barcelona's biggest mall has a split personality. At night, the complex turns into a tri-level maze of clubs, each playing its own music for a plethora of tourists and the occasional Spaniard. This is not the most "authentic" experience in Barcelona, but it is an experience. No one charges cover; clubs make their money from exorbitant drink prices. Be aware that catching a cab at the end of the night can be extremely difficult; consider leaving clubs 30min. before they close.

MONTJUÏC

Lower Montjuïc is home to Barcelona's epic "disco theme park," **Poble Espanyol,** Av. Marqués de Comillas. Fall in love with the craziest disco experience in all of Barcelona at some of the most popular (and surreal) discos: **La Terrazza** (an outdoor madhouse; open July-Aug. Su midnight-6am; Sept.-June Su and Th-Sa midnight-6am), **Torres de Ávila** (with speedy glass elevators; open Th-Sa midnight-6:30am), and ◼**Tinta Roja** (for tango lovers; open July-Aug. Tu-Th 7pm-1:30am, F-Sa 8pm-3am; Sept.-June also Tu-Th). Dancing starts at 1am and ends after 8am.

ZONA ALTA

The area around C. de Marià Cubí has great nightlife, undiscovered by tourists, but you'll have to take a taxi. For more accessible fun in Gràcia, head to Pl. Sol.

◼ **Otto Zutz,** C. Lincoln 15 (www.ottozutz.com). FGC: Pl. Molina. Groove to house, hip-hop, and funk while Japanimation lights up the top floor. Beer €5. Cover €15, includes 1 drink; email ahead for a discount. Open Tu-Sa midnight-6:30am.

◼ **D_Mer,** C. Plató 13. FCG: Muntaner. A blue-hued heaven for lesbians of all ages. A touch of class, a dash of whimsy, and a ton of fun. Cover €6, includes 1 drink. Beer €3.50. Mixed drinks €6. Open Th-Sa 11pm-3:30am.

Gasterea, C. Verdi 39. M: Fontana. Yellow walls cast a warm glow in this table-less bar. Mixed drinks €5. Su-Tu and Th 7pm-1am, F-Sa 7pm-2am. Cash only.

Bar Marcel, C. Santaló 42. When midnight strikes, locals pack the place in search of cheap booze. Certainly not the fanciest bar in the neighborhood, but possibly the most loved. Beer €1.60. Mixed drinks €5. Prices vary. Open daily 8pm-3am.

Nick Havanna, C. Rosello 208. FGC: Provenca. Trendy Spaniards and tourists converge to grind to pop hits. Dress to impress (no sneakers). Drinks €6-8. Cover €10. Open W-Sa 11:30pm-5am. AmEx/MC/V.

◗ DAYTRIPS FROM BARCELONA

MONTSERRAT. An hour northwest of Barcelona, the mountain of Montserrat is where a wandering 9th-century mountaineer had a blinding vision of the Virgin Mary. In the 11th century, a monastery was founded to worship the Virgin, and the site has since evolved into a major pilgrimage center. The **monastery's** ornate **basilica** is above Pl. Creu. To the right of the main chapel is a route through the **side chapels** that leads to the 12th-century Romanesque **La Moreneta** (the black Virgin Mary), Montserrat's venerated icon. (Walkway open July-Sept. daily 8-10:30am and noon-6:30pm. Nov.-June M-F 8-10:30am, noon-6:30pm, and 7:30-8:15pm. Sa-Su 8-10:30am and noon-6:30pm.) In Pl. Santa María, the **Museo de Montserrat** exhibits a sweeping range of art, from an Egyptian mummy to several Picassos. (Open July-Sept. M-F 10am-7pm, Sa-Su 9:30am-7pm; Nov.-June M-F 10am-6pm, Sa-Su 9:30am-6:30pm. €5.30, students and over-65 €4.50.) The **Santa Cova funicular** descends from Pl. Creu to paths that wind along to ancient hermitages. (Apr.-Oct. daily every 20min. 10am-6pm; Nov.-Mar. Sa-Su 10am-5pm. Round-trip €2.50.) Take the **St. Joan funicular** up for more inspirational views. (Apr.-Oct. daily every 20min. 10am-6pm; Nov.-Mar. M-F 11am-5pm, Sa-Su 10am-5pm. Round-trip €6.10; joint round-trip ticket with the Sta. Cova funicular €7, students and over-65 €6.20.) The dilapidated **St. Joan monastery** and **shrine** are only 20min. from the highest station. The real prize is **St. Jerónim** (1235m), about 2hr. from Pl. Creu (1hr. from the terminus of the St. Joan funicular); after walking 45min., take the sharp left at the little old chapel.

FGC **trains** (☎932 05 15 15) to Montserrat leave from M: Espanya in Barcelona (1hr.; every hr. 8:35am-6:36pm; round-trip including cable car €12); get off at Aeri de Montserrat, not Olesa de Montserrat. From the base of the mountain, the Aeri cable car runs up to the monastery. (July-Aug. every 15min. daily 9:20am-6:30pm; Mar. and Oct. 9:20am-1:40pm and 2:20-6:40pm. Schedules change frequently; call ☎938 77 77 01 to check. €4. Free with FCG.)

THE COSTA BRAVA: FIGUERES AND CADAQUÉS. The Costa Brava's jagged cliffs cut into the Mediterranean Sea from Barcelona to the French border. Though rugged by name, the Brave Coast is tamed in July and August by the planeloads of Europeans dumped onto its once-tranquil beaches.

In 1974, Salvador Dalí chose his native, beachless **Figueres** (pop. 37,000), 36km north of Girona, as the site to build a museum to house his works, catapulting the city into instant fame. His personal tribute is undeniably a masterpiece—and the second most popular museum in Spain. The ▨**Teatre-Museu Dalí** is in Pl. Gala. From La Rambla, take C. Girona, which becomes C. Jonquera, and climb the steps. The museum parades the artist's erotically nightmarish landscapes and bizarre installations. (☎972 67 75 00; www.salvador-dali.org. Open July-Sept. 9am-7:15pm; Oct.-June daily 10:30am-5:15pm. Call ahead about night hours during the summer. €9, students €6.50.) **Trains** (☎902 24 02 02) run to Barcelona (2hr., 23 per day, €8.10) and Girona (30min., 23 per day, €2.40). **Buses** (☎972 67 33 54) run from Pl. Estació to: Barcelona (2¼hr., 2-6 per day, €13); Cadaqués (1¼hr., 2-5 per day, €3.60); and Girona (1hr., 2-6 per day, €3.60). The **tourist office** is in Pl. Sol. (☎972 50 31 55. Open July-Aug. M-Sa 9am-8pm, Su 9am-3pm; Apr.-June and Oct. M-F 9am-3pm and 4:30-8pm, Sa 9:30am-1:30pm and 3:30-6:30pm; Sept. M-Sa 9am-8pm; Nov.-Mar. M-F 9am-3pm.) **Hostal La Barretina ❷**, C. Lasauca 13, is a lesson in luxury. (☎972 67 64 12. Singles €23; doubles €39. AmEx/MC/V.) **Postal Code:** 17600.

The whitewashed houses and rocky beaches of **Cadaqués** (pop. 1,800) have attracted artists, writers, and musicians—not to mention tourists—ever since Dalí built his summer home here. ▨**Casa-Museu Salvador Dalí,** Port Lligat, Dalí's home until 1982, holds with a lip-shaped sofa and pop-art miniature Alhambra. Follow the signs to Port Lligat (bear right with your back to the Statue of Liberty) and then to the Casa de Dalí. (☎972 25 10 15. Open June 15-Sept. 15 daily 10am-8:15pm; Sept. 16-Nov. and Mar. 15-June 14 Su and Tu-Sa 10am-5:10pm. Tours are the only way to see the house; make reservations 1-2 days in advance. Ticket office closes 45min. earlier. €8, students €5.) **Buses** arrive from: Barcelona (2½hr., 11:15am and 4:15pm, €16); Figueres (1hr., 5-7 per day, €4); and Girona (2hr., 1-2 per day, €7). With your back to the Sarfa office at the bus stop, walk right along Av. Caritat Serinyana; the **tourist office,** C. Cotxe 2, is off Pl. Frederic Rahola, opposite the *passeig.* (☎972 25 83 15. Open July-Aug. M-Sa 9:30am-1:30pm and 4-8pm, Su 10:30am-1:30pm; Sept.-June M-Sa 9am-2pm and 4-7pm.) **Postal Code:** 17488.

THE COSTA DORADA: SITGES. A mecca of gay-nightlife, the town of Sitges is perhaps better seen as a night-trip from Barcelona rather than as a day trip. The beaches are roomy and often afford more space than the crowded sands of Barceloneta, but Sitges is more about the party than the tan. The place to be at sundown is **Calle Primer de Maig** (which runs directly from the beach and Pg. Ribera) and its continuation, **Calle Marquès Montroig,** off C. Parellades. Bars and clubs line both sides of the small street, blasting pop and house from 10pm until 3am. Wide-open and accepting, the clubs welcome a vibrant mixed crowd of gay people, straight people, and the occasional drag queen. There's no cover anywhere, making for great bar- and club-hopping. Beers at most places go for about €3, mixed drinks €6. Even crazier is the "disco-beach" **Atlàntida,** in Sector Terramar (☎938 94 26 77; foam parties on Th and Su nights), and the legendary **Pachá,** on Pg. Sant Didac in nearby Vallpineda (☎938 94 22 98). Buses run all night on weekends to the two discos from C. Primer de Maig. Other popular nightspots can be found on **Calle Bonaire** and **Calle Sant Pau,** but most open only on weekends.

RENFE **trains** (☎934 90 02 02) run from Sitges to Barcelona (40min., every 15-30min. 5:20am-11:50pm, €2.20). For a good free map and info on accommodations, stop by the **tourist office,** Sínia Morera 1. (☎938 94 50 04. Open July-Aug. daily 9am-

9pm; Sept.-June Su-M and W-Sa 9am-3pm and 4-6:30pm.) **Hostal Parellades** ❷, C. Parellades 11, offers clean rooms and an airy terrace. (☎938 94 08 01. Singles €24; doubles €40, with bath €45; triples with bath €50. Cash only.) **Izarra** ❷, C. Mayor 24, can be either a quick food fix before a long night of club-hopping. (☎93 894 73 70; open daily 1:30-4pm and 8:30-11pm. MC/V.) **Super Avui**, C. Carbonell 24, has groceries. (Open M-Sa 9am-9pm.) **Postal Code:** 08870.

GIRONA

A world-class city patiently waiting to be noticed, Girona (pop. 70,500) is really two cities in one: A hushed medieval masterpiece on one riverbank and a thriving, modern metropolis on the other. Though founded by the Romans, the city owes more to the renowned *cabalistas de Girona*, who for centuries spread the teachings of Kabbalah (mystical Judaism) in the West. Still a cultural center and university town, Girona is a magnet for artists, intellectuals, and activists.

Most sights are in the old city, across the river from the train station. The **Riu Onyar** separates the new city from the old. The **Pont de Pedra** bridge connects the two banks and heads into the old quarter by way of C. Ciutadans, C. Peralta, and C. Força, which lead to the cathedral and ❖**El Call,** the medieval Jewish neighborhood. A thriving community in the Middle Ages, El Call was virtually wiped out by the 1492 Inquisition and mass expulsion and conversion. The entrance to **Centre Bonastruc Ça Porta,** the site of the last synagogue in Girona (today a museum), is off C. Força, about halfway up the hill. (Center and museum open May-Oct. M-Sa 10am-8pm, Su 10am-3pm; Nov.-Apr. M-Sa 10am-6pm, Su 10am-3pm. Museum €2, students €1.) Uphill and around the corner to the right on C. Força, the Gothic **cathedral** rises a record-breaking 90 Rococo steps from the plaza below. The **Tesoro Capitular** within contains some of Girona's most precious possessions, including the **Tapis de la Creació,** a 15th-century tapestry depicting the creation story. (Both open Mar.-Sept. Su-M 10am-2pm, Tu-Sa 10am-2pm and 4-7pm; Oct.-Mar. Su-M 10am-2pm, Tu-Sa 10am-2pm and 4-6pm. Tesoro and cloister €3.) **La Rambla** and **Plaza de Independéncia** are the places to see and be seen in Girona. The expansive, impeccably designed **Parc de la Devesa** explodes with *carpas*, temporary outdoor bars. Bars in the old quarter draw crowds in the early evening. **Café la Llibreria,** C. Ciutadans 15, serves cocktails (€3.60) and *tapas* (€3) to intellectual types. (Open M-Sa 8:30am-1am, Su 8:30am-midnight. MC/V.)

RENFE **trains** (☎972 24 02 02) depart from Pl. de Espanya to Barcelona (1½hr., 24 per day, €5) and Figueres (30-40min., 23 per day, €2.10). **Buses** (☎972 21 23 19) depart from just around the corner. The **tourist office,** Rambla de la Libertat 1, is on the other side. (☎972 22 65 75. Open in summer M-F 9am-3pm, Sa 9am-2pm; off-season M-F 9am-7pm, Sa 9am-2pm.) Most budget accommodations are in the old quarter and are well-kept and reasonably priced. The **Pensió Viladomat** ❷, C. Ciutadans 5, has well-furnished rooms. (☎972 20 31 76. Singles €16; doubles €32, with bath €55.) Girona abounds with innovative cuisine; **Calle Cort Reial** is the best place to find good, cheap food. **La Crêperie Bretonne** ❶, C. Cort Reial 14, is potent proof of Girona's proximity to France. (☎972 21 81 20. Open Su 8pm-midnight, Tu-Sa 1-4pm and 8pm-midnight. MC/V.) Pick up groceries at **Caprabo,** C. Sequia 10, a block from C. Nou off Gran Vía. (Open M-Sa 9am-9pm.) **Postal Code:** 17070.

THE PYRENEES ☎973

The jagged green mountains, Romanesque churches, and tranquil towns of the Pyrenees draw hikers and skiers in search of outdoor adventures. Spectacular views make driving through the countryside an incredible experience in and of itself. Without a car, transportation is tricky, but feasible.

VAL D'ARAN. Some of the Catalán Pyrenees' most dazzling peaks cluster around Val d'Aran, in the northwest corner of Cataluña. The Val d'Aran is best known for its chic ski resorts: the Spanish royal family's favorite slopes are those of **Baquiera-Beret.** The **Auberja Era Garona (HI) ❶,** Ctra. de Vielha s/n, a few kilometers away in the lovely town of **Salardú,** is accessible by shuttle bus (€0.80) in high-season from Vielha. (☎973 64 52 71; eragarona@aran.org. Breakfast included. May-June and Sept.16-Nov. €12, under-26 €11. Dec.-Apr. Sa and Su and *Semana Santa* €19/16; Dec.-Apr. M-F and July-Sept. 15 €16/13.) While you're in town, don't miss Salardú's impressive 13th-century **church,** or the church's incredible garden view. For skiing info, contact the **Oficeria de Baquiera-Beret** (☎973 64 44 55; fax 64 44 88).

The biggest town in the valley, **Vielha** (pop. 7,000) welcomes hikers and skiers to its lively streets with every service the outdoorsy type might desire. It's only 12km from Baquiera-Beret; **shuttle buses** connect the town two during July and August (schedules at the tourist office). Alsina Graells **buses** (☎973 27 14 70) also run to Barcelona (5½hr., 5:30am and 1:30pm, €24). The **tourist office,** C. Sarriulèra 10, is one block upstream from the *plaça.* (☎973 64 01 10; fax 64 03 72. Open daily 9am-9pm.) Several inexpensive *pensiones* cluster at the end of C. Reiau, off Pg. Libertat (which intersects Av. Casteiro at Pl. Sant Antoni); try **Casa Vicenta ❷** at C. Reiau 3. (☎973 64 08 19. Dec.-*Semana Santa* and July 15-Sept. 15 Singles €25; doubles €40. Off-season €18/30. Closed Oct. and Nov.)

PARQUE NACIONAL DE ORDESA. The beauty of Ordesa's Aragonese Pyrenees will enchant even the most seasoned traveler; its well-maintained trails cut across idyllic forests, jagged rock faces, snow-covered peaks, rushing rivers, and magnificent waterfalls. Pay a cyber visit to www.ordesa.net for more info about the park. The **Visitor Center** is on the left, 1.8km past the park entrance. (Open Apr.-Sept. 15 daily 9am-1:30pm and 3-6pm.) The **Soaso Circle** is the most practical hike; frequent signposts clearly mark the 5hr. journey, which can be cut to a 2hr. loop. Enter the park through the village of **Torla,** where you can buy the indispensable *Editorial Alpina* guide (€7.50). La Oscense (☎974 35 50 60) sends a **bus** from Jaca to Sabiñánigo (20min., 2-3 per day, €1.30). Sabiñánigo is also easily accessible by **train;** all trains on the Zaragoza-Huesca-Jaca line stop here. From there, Compañía Hudebus (☎974 21 32 77) runs to Torla (55min., 1-2 per day, €2.50). During the high season, a bus shuttles between Torla and Ordesa (15min., 6am-7pm, €2). Off-season, you'll have to hike the 8km to the park entrance or catch a Jorge Soler **taxi** (☎974 48 62 43; €12), which also offers van tours for up to 8 people. To exit the park area, catch the bus as it passes through Torla at 3:30pm on its way back to Sabiñánigo. In the park, many *refugios* (mountain huts) allow overnight stays. In Torla, ascend C. Francia one block to reach **Refugio L'Atalaya ❶,** C. Francia 45 (☎974 48 60 22), and **Refugio Lucien Briet ❶** (☎974 48 62 21), across the street. (Both €8 per person.) Stock up at **Supermercado Torla,** on C. a Ruata. (Open May-Oct. daily 9am-2pm and 5-8:30pm; Nov.-Apr. closed Su.)

JACA. For centuries, pilgrims bound for Santiago would cross the Pyrenees into Spain, spend the night in Jaca (pop. 14,000), and be off the next morning. They had the right idea; Jaca is a great launching pad for the exploring the Pyrenees. RENFE **trains** (☎974 36 13 32) run from C. Estación to Madrid (7hr., Su-F 1:45pm, €24) and Zaragoza (3hr., daily 7:30am and 6:45pm, €8.50). La Oscense **buses** (☎974 35 50 60) run to Pamplona (2hr., daily, €5.50) and Zaragoza (2hr., 3-4 per day, €9.50). The **tourist office,** Av. Regimiento de Galicia 2, is one block down from Pl. de Cortes de Aragón. (☎974 36 00 98; www.aytojaca.es. Open July-Aug. M-F 9am-2pm and 4:30-8pm, Sa 9am-1:30pm and 5-8pm, Su 10am-1:30pm; Sept.-June M-F 9am-1:30pm and 4:30-7pm, Sa 10am-1pm and 5-7pm.) From the bus station, cross the park and head right past the church to the next plaza to find **Hostal Paris ❷**, San Pedro 5, one of the best deals in town. (☎974 36 10 20; www.jaca.com/hostalparis. July 15-Sept. 15 and *Semana Santa* singles €19; doubles €30; triples €41. Sept. 16-July 14 €18/28/38.) **Postal Code: 22700.**

NAVARRA

Bordered by Basque Country to the west and Aragón to the east, Navarra's villages—from the rustic Pyrenean pueblos on the French border to bustling Pamplona—are seldom visited apart from the festival of *San Fermines*, and greet non-bullrunning tourists with enthusiasm and open arms.

PAMPLONA (IRUÑA) ☎948

While the lush parks, impressive museums, and medieval churches of Pamplona (pop. 200,000) await exploration, it's an annual, eight-minute event that draws visitors from around the world. Since the publication of Ernest Hemingway's *The Sun Also Rises*, hordes of travelers have come the week of July 6-14 to witness and experience *San Fermines*, the legendary "Running of the Bulls."

⚏🕅 TRANSPORTATION AND PRACTICAL INFORMATION. RENFE trains (☎902 24 02 02) run from off Av. San Jorge to Barcelona (6-8hr., 3-4 per day 12:25pm-12:55am, €29) and Madrid (5hr., 7:15am and 6:10pm, €35). **Buses** go from C. Conde Oliveto, at C. Yanguas y Miranda, to: Barcelona (5½hr.; 8:30am, 4:30pm, and 1am; €20); Bilbao (2hr., 4-6 per day 7am-7pm, €11); Madrid (5hr.; 4-7 per day M-Th and Sa 8am-7:30pm, F and Su 8am-9:30pm; €22); San Sebastián (1hr., 7-12 per day 7am-11pm, €5.50); and Zaragoza (2-3hr., 6-8 per day 7:15am-8:30pm, €11). From Pl. del Castillo, take C. San Nicolás, turn right on C. San Miguel, and walk through Pl. San Francisco to get to the **tourist office,** C. Hilarión Eslava 1. (☎948 20 65 40; www.cfnavarra.es. Open during *San Fermines* daily 8am-8pm; July-Aug. M-Sa 9am-8pm, Su 10am-2pm; Sept.-June M-F 10am-2pm and 4-7pm, Sa 10am-2pm.) During *San Fermines*, **store luggage** at the Escuelas de San Francisco, the big stone building at the end of Pl. San Francisco. (€2 per day. Open 24hr.) Check **email** at **Kuria.Net,** C. Curia 15. (€3 per hr. Open during *San Fermines* daily 9am-11pm; rest of year M-Sa 10am-10pm, Su 1-10pm.) **Postal Code: 31001.**

🕅🕅 ACCOMMODATIONS AND FOOD. And now, a lesson in supply and demand: Smart *San Ferministas* take the bull by the horns and book their rooms up to a year (or at least two months) in advance to avoid paying rates up to four times higher than those listed here. Beware of hawkers at the train and bus stations—quality and prices vary tremendously. Check the newspaper *Diario de Navarra* for **casas particulares.** Many roomless folks are forced to fluff up their sweatshirts and sleep on the lawns of the Ciudadela or on Pl. de los Fueros, Pl. del Castillo, or the banks of the river. Be careful—if you can't store your backpack (storage fills fast), sleep on top of it. During the rest of the year, finding a room in Pamplona is no problem. Budget accommodations line C. San Nicolás and C. San Gregorio off Pl. del Castillo. **Hotel Europa ❺,** C. Espoz y Mina 11, off Pl. del Castillo, offers bright, luxurious rooms away from the noise of C. San Nicolás. One good night's sleep is worth the price. Reservations are recommended, especially for *San Fermines*. (☎948 22 18 00. Year-round singles €65; doubles €74. MC/V.) To reach the impressive 18th-century mansion of **Pensión Santa Cecilia ❷**, C. Navarrería 17, follow C. Chapitela, take the first right onto C. Mercaderes, and make a sharp left. (☎948 22 22 30. *San Fermines* dorms €45. Otherwise singles €20; doubles €30; triples €35. MC/V.) To get to **Camping Ezcaba ❶** in Eusa, take city bus line 4-1 from Pl. de las Merindades (4 per day, €0.70). (☎948 33 03 15. *San Fermines* €9 per person, per tent, or per car. Otherwise €3.50 per person, per tent or per car. AmEx/MC/V.) Look for food near Pensión Santa Cecilia, above **Plaza San Francisco**, and around **Paseo Ronda**. Check out **Calles Navarrería** and **Paseo Sarasate** for *bocadillo* bars. **Vendi Supermarket**, at C. Hilarión Eslava and C. Mayor, has groceries. (Open M-F 9am-2pm and 5:30-7:30pm, Sa 9am-2pm.)

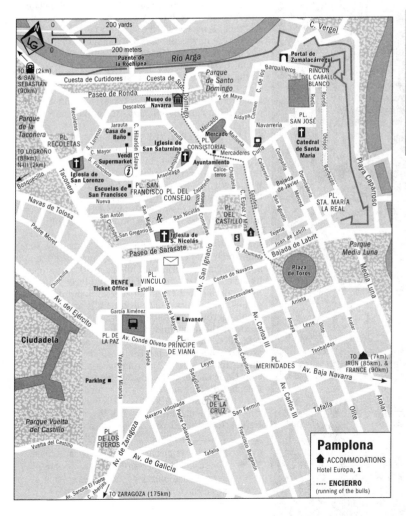

Pamplona

⛺ **ACCOMMODATIONS**
Hotel Europa, **1**

---- **ENCIERRO**
(running of the bulls)

SIGHTS AND NIGHTLIFE. Pamplona's rich architectural legacy is reason enough to visit during the 51 other weeks of the year. The restored 14th-century Gothic **cathedral** is at the end of C. Navarrería. (Open M-F 10am-1:30pm and 4-7pm, Sa 10am-1:30pm. Guided tours €4.) The walls of the pentagonal **Ciudadela** once humbled Napoleon; today the Ciudadela hosts free exhibits and summer concerts. Follow Po. Sarasate to its end, and take a right on Navas de Tolosa; take the next left onto C. Chinchilla, and follow it to its end. (Open M 9:30am-9:30pm; Su and Tu-Sa 7:30am-9:30pm. closed for *San Fermines*. Both free.) Throughout the year, **Plaza del Castillo** is the heart of the social scene. Hemingway's favorite haunt was the **Café-Bar Iruña**, immortalized in *The Sun Also Rises*. (*Menú* €10. Open M-Th 8am-11pm, F 8am-2pm, Sa 9am-2am, Su 9am-11pm.) A young crowd boozes up at bars in the *casco antiguo*, around **Calles de Jarauta, San Nicolás,** and **San Gregorio** before hitting the **Travesia de Bayona,** a plaza of bars and *discotecas* off Av. Bayona.

LOS SAN FERMINES (JULY 6-14). Visitors overcrowd the city as Pamplona delivers an eight-day frenzy of parades, bullfights, parties, dancing, fireworks, concerts, and wine. Pamplonese, clad in white with red sashes and bandanas, literally throw themselves into the merry-making, displaying obscene levels of both physical stamina and tolerance for alcohol. The "Running of the Bulls," called the *encierro*, is the highlight of *San Fermines;* the first *encierro* takes place on July 7 at 8am and it's repeated at 8am every day for the next seven days. Hundreds of bleary-eyed, hungover, hyper-adrenalized runners flee from large bulls as bystanders cheer from barricades, windows, balconies, and doorways. Both the bulls and the mob are dangerous; terrified runners react without concern for those around them. Hemingway had the right idea: Don't run. Instead, arrive at the bullring around 6:45am to watch the *encierro*. Tickets for the Grada section of the ring are available before 7am (M-F €3.60, Sa-Su €4.20). You can watch for free, but the free section is overcrowded, making it hard to see and breathe. To participate in the bullring excitement, line up by the Pl. de Toros well before 7:30am and run in *before* the bulls are in

Although Pamplona is usually very safe, crime skyrockets during *San Fermines*. Beware of assaults and muggings, do not walk alone at night, and take care in the *casco antiguo*.

sight. **Be very careful; follow the tourist office's guidelines for running.** To watch a bullfight, wait in the line that forms at the bullring around 8pm. As one fight ends, the next day's tickets (€15-70) go on sale. Once the running ends, insanity spills into the streets and gathers steam until nightfall, when it explodes with singing in bars, dancing in alleyways, spontaneous parades, and a no-holds-barred party in Pl. del Castillo, Europe's biggest open-air dance floor.

BASQUE COUNTRY (PAÍS VASCO)

Basque Country's varied landscape resembles a nation complete in itself, combining cosmopolitan cities, verdant hills, industrial wastelands, and quaint fishing villages. Many believe that the strongly nationalistic Basques are the native people of Iberia, as their culture and language cannot be traced to any known source.

RUNNING SCARED

So, you're going to run. No one wants to see you end up on evening news programs around the world, so here are a few words of *San Fermines* wisdom:

▨ Research the *encierro* before you run. The tourist office dispenses a pamphlet that outlines the route of the 3min. run and offers tips for inexperienced runners.

▨ Do not stay up all night drinking and carousing. Not surprisingly, hung-over foreigners have the highest rate of injury. Experienced runners get lots of sleep the night before. Access to the course closes at 7:30am.

▨ Give up on getting near the bulls and concentrate on getting to the bullring in one piece. Although some whack the bull with rolled newspapers, runners should never distract or touch the animals; anyone who does is likely to anger the bull and locals alike.

▨ Try not to cower in a doorway; people have been trapped and killed this way.

▨ Be particularly wary of isolated bulls—they seek company in the crowds.

▨ If you fall, **stay down.** Curl up into a fetal position, lock your hands behind your head, and **do not get up** until the clatter of hooves has passed.

Seconds before the signal, a wave of 50 men rushed toward me, clawing past my startled frame and diving between the wooden fences. Two blasts shot through the air. I turned and ran.

About halfway through the seven-minute ordeal, I heard the trampling gait of a bull not far behind. Desparate to escape, I tore past the frightened mob in front of me, drilling through the clog of bodies any way I could. I'll admit it—I kicked, I grabbed, I spit, I punched. And so did anyone else who valued his health.

My mad scrambling was to no avail. The *toro* easily advanced alongside me. It jerked its body around and bucked back its head into my left hip, lifting me off the ground. Airborne, I felt something brush against my leg but was so busy readying for the fall that I didn't notice the horn shredding my left pant leg. As my knee hit the ground, I did my best sprinter-start away. The bull's hooves had slipped out from under him, tossing him sidelong to the ground. It wasn't until the next day, when I saw AP photographs of myself contending with the bull in the newspapers, that I realized how much danger I'd been in.

My head ached, my lungs hurt, and the vinegary aftertaste of last night's *Kalimoxto* burned my throat, but I had never felt better. I spotted another exhausted runner and gave him a victorious smile.

"Mañana," he wheezed. "Otra vez (one more time), eh?"

—Nate Gray

SAN SEBASTIÁN (DONOSTIA)   ☎943

Glittering on the shores of the Cantabrian Sea, coolly elegant San Sebastián (pop. 180,000) is known for its world-famous beaches, bars, and scenery. Locals and travelers down *pintxos* (*tapas*) and drinks in the *parte vieja* (old city), which claims the most bars per square meter in the world. Residents and posters lend a constant reminder: You're not in Spain, you're in Basque Country.

▐ TRANSPORTATION

Trains: RENFE, Estación del Norte (☎902 24 02 02), on Po. Francia, on the east side of Puente María Cristina. Info office open daily 7am-11pm. To: **Barcelona** (9hr., Su-F 10:45am and 11pm, €33); **Madrid** (8hr., 3 per day, €41); **Zaragoza** (4hr., daily 10:45am, €19).

Buses: PESA, Av. Sancho el Sabio 33 (☎902 10 12 10), runs to **Bilbao** (1¼hr., every 30min., €7.50). **Continental Auto,** Av. Sancho el Sabio 31 (☎943 46 90 74), goes to **Madrid** (6hr., 7-9 per day, €25). **La Roncalesa,** Po. Vizcaya 16 (☎943 46 10 64), runs to **Pamplona** (1hr., 9 per day, €5.50). **Vibasa,** Po. Vizcaya 16 (☎943 45 75 00), goes to **Barcelona** (7hr., 3 per day, €23).

Public Transportation: (☎943 28 71 00). Each trip €0.80. **Bus #16** goes from Alameda del Boulevard to the campground and beaches.

Taxis: Santa Clara (☎943 36 46 46), **Vallina** (☎943 40 40 40), or **Donostia** (☎943 46 46 46). Taxis to **Pamplona** take about 45min. and cost around €83.

■ ▐ ORIENTATION AND PRACTICAL INFORMATION

The **Río Urumea** splits San Sebastián. The city center, most monuments, and the two most popular beaches, Playa de la Concha and Playa de Ondaretta, line the peninsula on the west side of the river. At the tip of the peninsula sits **Monte Urgull.** On the east side of the river, Playa de la Zurriola attracts a younger surfing and beach crowd. Inland lies the *parte vieja* (old city), San Sebastián's restaurant, nightlife, and budget accommodation nexus, where you'll find the most tourists. South of the *parte vieja*, at the base of the peninsula, is the commercial district. The **bus station** is south of the city center on Pl. Pío XII, while the RENFE **train stat-ion, Barrio de Gros,** and **Playa de la Zurriola** are across the river from the *parte vieja* east of the city. The river is spanned by four bridges: Puentes Zurriola, Santa Catalina, María Cristina, and de Mundaiz (listed north to south). To get to the *parte vieja* from the train station, head straight to Puente María Cristina, cross the bridge, and turn right at the fountain. Continue four blocks north to Av. Libertad, then take a left and follow it to the port; the *parte vieja* fans out to the right and Playa de la Concha sits to the left.

Tourist Office: Municipal: Centro de Atracción y Turismo, C. Reina Regente 3 (☎943 48 11 66; fax 943 48 11 72), in front of Puente de la Zurriola. From the train station, turn right immediately after crossing Puente María Cristina and continue until Puente de la Zurriola; the office is on the right. From the bus station, start down Av. Sancho el Sabio. At Pl. Centenario, bear right onto C. Prim, follow the river until the 3rd bridge (Puente de la Zurriola), and look for the plaza on your left. Open June-Sept. Su 10am-2pm, M-Sa 8am-8pm; Oct.-May Su 10am-2pm, M-Sa 9am-1:30pm and 3:30-7pm.

Hiking Information: Izadi (☎943 29 35 20), C. Usandizaga 18, off C. Libertad. Sells hiking guides. Open M-F 10am-1pm and 4-8pm, Sa 10am-1:30pm and 4:30-8pm.

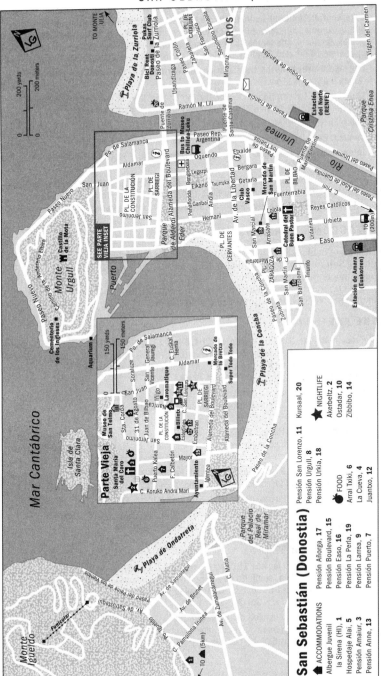

SPAIN

San Sebastián (Donostia)

⚑ ACCOMMODATIONS
Albergue Juvenil
la Sirena (HI), **1**
Hospedaje Alaï, **5**
Pensión Amaiur, **3**
Pensión Anne, **13**

Pensión Añorga, **17**
Pensión Boulevard, **15**
Pensión Easo, **16**
Pensión La Perla, **19**
Pensión Larrea, **9**
Pensión Puerto, **7**

Pensión San Lorenzo, **11**
Pensión Urgull, **8**
Pensión Urkia, **18**

🍴 FOOD
Arrai Txiki, **6**
La Cueva, **4**
Juantxo, **12**

Kursaal, **20**

★ NIGHTLIFE
Akerbeltz, **2**
Ostadar, **10**
Zibbibo, **14**

Bike Rental: Bici Rent Donosti, Po. de la Zurriola 22 (☎943 27 92 60). From Puente de la Zurriola, walk along Playa de la Zurriola. Bici Rent will be on your right. Rents bikes, tandems, and motos (1 week min.). Also provides bike trail maps. Bicycles: €4 per hr., €18 per day. Tandem bicycles: €6 per hr., €36 per day.

Luggage Storage: At the **train station.** €3 per day. Buy tokens at the ticket counter. Open daily 7am-11pm.

Laundromat: Lavomatique, C. Iñigo 14, off C. San Juan in the *parte vieja*. 4kg wash €3.80, dry €2.70. Open M-F 9:30am-2pm and 4-8pm, Sa-Su 10am-2pm.

Emergency: ☎112. **Municipal police:** C. Easo (☎943 45 00 00).

Medical Services: Casa de Socorro, Bengoetxea 4 (☎943 44 06 33).

Internet Access: Zarr@net, C. San Lorenzo 6 (☎943 43 33 81). €0.05 per min., €3 per hr. Also sells phone cards.

Post Office: Po. Francia 13 (☎943 44 68 26), near the RENFE station, just over the Santa Catalina bridge and to the right; look for the yellow trim on the left side of the street. Open M-F 8:30am-8:30pm, Sa 9:30am-2pm. **Postal Code:** 20006.

ACCOMMODATIONS

Desperate backpackers will scrounge for rooms in July and August, particularly during *San Fermines* (July 6-14) and *Semana Grande* (the first Su after Aug. 15); September's film festival is just as booked. Budget options can be found in the *parte vieja* and by the cathedral. The tourist office has lists of accommodations and most hostel owners know of *casas particulares*.

THE PARTE VIEJA

Pensión Amaiur, C. 31 de Agosto 44, 2nd fl. (☎943 42 96 54). From Alameda del Boulevard, follow C. San Jerónimo to its end, turn left. Friendly owner and uniquely decorated rooms. Internet €1 per 18min. July-Sept. and *Semana Santa* dorms €25; May-June and Oct. €22; Nov.-Apr. €18. MC/V. ❷

Pensión San Lorenzo, C. San Lorenzo 2 (☎943 42 55 16), off C. San Juan. Bright, sunny doubles with TV and refrigerator. July-Aug. doubles €45; June and Sept. €36; Oct.-May €24. ❷

Pensión Larrea, C. Narrica 21, 2nd fl. (☎943 42 26 94). Spend time with Mamá and Papá, as the friendly owners are often called, in this comfortable and welcoming *pensión*. July-Aug. singles €24; doubles €36; triples €50. Sept.-June €18/30/45. ❷

Hospedaje Alai, C. 31 de Agosto 16, 3rd fl. (☎943 42 48 06). Comfortable bunks and clean bathrooms. Closed Oct.-May. July-Aug. dorms €25; June and Sept. €12. ❶

Pensión Puerto, C. Puerto 19, 2nd fl. (☎943 43 21 40). Off C. Mayor. Spotless rooms with comfy beds. July-Aug. singles €30; June and Sept. €20-22; Oct.-May €18. ❸

Pensión Urgull, C. Esterlines 10 (☎943 43 00 47). Follow the winding staircase to the 3rd floor. Rooms have balconies and sinks. Prices are not set, so bargain away. July-Aug. doubles €45-50; June and Sept. €28-36; Oct.-May €24. ❷

Pensión Anne, C. Esterlines 15, 2nd fl. (☎943 42 14 38), between C. Narrica and C. San Jerónimo. Plain, comfortable rooms in a convenient location. Private bath €12. July-Sept. singles €36; doubles €45; triples €60. Oct.-June €18/24/34. Oct.-June 10% discount with *Let's Go*. ❹

Pensión Boulevard, Alameda del Boulevard 24 (☎943 42 94 05). Spacious rooms, all with radios, some with balconies. 2 large shared baths for 8 rooms. July-Aug. doubles €50; June and Sept €36-42; Oct.-May €30. ❸

OUTSIDE THE PARTE VIEJA

Most of these places tend to be quieter but just as close to the port, beach, bus and train stations, and no more than 5min. from the *parte vieja*.

Pensión La Perla, C. Loyola 10, 2nd fl. (☎943 42 81 23), on the street directly ahead of the cathedral. English spoken. Private baths and TVs. July-Sept. singles €28-30; doubles €40. Oct.-June €24/32. ❸

Pensión Easo, C. San Bartolomé 24 (☎943 45 39 12; www.pension-easo.com). Head toward the beach on C. San Martín, turn left on C. Easo, and right on C. San Bartolomé. July-Sept. 15 singles €33, with bath €49; doubles €42/61. June and Sept. 15-30 singles €27/40; doubles €33/45. Oct.-May singles €25/33; doubles €30/40. ❸

Pensión Urkia, C. Urbieta 12, 3rd fl. (☎943 42 44 36), located on C. Urbieta between C. Marcial and C. Arrasate. Borders the Mercado de San Martín. All rooms with bath. July-Sept. singles €25; doubles €43; triples €60. Oct.-June €22/30/45. ❸

Pensión Añorga, C. Easo 12 (☎943 46 79 45), at C. San Martín. Shares entryway with 2 other *pensiones*. Spacious rooms have wood floors and comfy beds. July-Aug. singles €25; doubles €34, with bath €43. Sept.-June singles €19, doubles €25/32. ❷

Albergue Juvenil la Sirena (HI), Po. Igueldo 25 (☎943 31 02 68), at the far west end of the city. Take bus #24 or 27 to Av. Zumalacárregui; from there, take Av. Brunet and turn left at its end. Clean rooms, multilingual staff. Breakfast included. Curfew Sept.-May Su-Th midnight, F-Sa 2am. July-Aug. €15, under-25 €13. May 6-Jun. 7 and Apr. 8-31 €12/14. Oct.-Mar. €12/13-15. MC/V. Members only. ❶

Camping Igueldo (☎943 21 45 02), 5km west of town. The 268 spots fill quickly. Beautiful views of the ocean make the drive worth it. Bus #16 ("Barrio de Igueldo-Camping") runs between the site and Alameda del Boulevard (every 30min., €0.80). June-Aug. and *Semana Santa* plots €11, extra person €3.20. Sept.-May €9/€3. MC/V. ❶

▐ FOOD

Pintxos (*tapas*; around €1.50 each), chased down with the fizzy regional white wine *txacoli*, are a religion here; bars in the *parte vieja* spread an array of enticing tidbits on bread. The entire *parte vieja* seems to exist for no other purpose than to feed. **Mercado de la Bretxa,** Alameda del Boulevard at C. San Juan, sells fresh produce. (Open M-Sa 9am-9pm.) **Super Todo Todo,** Alameda del Boulevard 3, across the street from the Mercado de la Brexta, also sells groceries. (Open M-Sa 8:30am-9pm, Su 10am-2pm.)

▨ Kursaal, Po. Zurriola 1. The chef is a legend among locals; enjoy an elegant lunch on the breezy, outdoor patio. *Menú* €13-16. ❷

▨ Arrai Txiki, C. del Campanario 3. Cooks up delicious, healthy cuisine, including an array of vegetarian options, in a simple, elegant setting. Entrees €3-6. Open Su-M and W-Sa 1-4pm and 8-11pm. ❶

Juantxo, C. Esterlines. Best *bocadillos* in San Sebastián. Try the fillete with onions, cheese, and peppers (€3). Wide selection of *bocadillos*, *pintxos*, and *raciones*. *Pintxos* €1-2, Bocadillos €2-3. Open M-Th 9am-11:30pm, F-Su 9am-1:45am. ❶

Bar Intxa, C. Esterlines 12 (☎943 42 48 33), across from Juantxo. Friendly service and great food make Intxa a must. Try the *albóndigas* (meatballs in gravy; €4.10). English, French, and German spoken. Open Su and Tu-Sa 11am-4:30pm and 7pm-midnight. ❶

La Cueva, Pl. Trinidad (☎943 42 54 37), off C. 31 de Agosto. A cavernous restaurant serving traditional seafood cuisine. M-F *menú* €15. Grilled tuna, cod, and squid entrees €6-12. Open Su and Tu-Sa 1-3:30pm and 7-11pm. MC/V. ❸

SAY WHAT? Linguists still cannot pinpoint the origin of *euskera*. Its commonalities with Caucasian and African dialects suggest that prehistoric Basques may have migrated from the Caucasus mountains through Africa. Referred to by other Spaniards as *la lengua del diablo* (the devil's tongue), *euskera* has come to symbolize cultural self-determination. Only half a million natives speak the language, chiefly in País Vasco and northern Navarra. During his regime, Franco banned *euskera* and forbade parents to give their children Basque names (like Iñaki or Estibaliz). Since his death, there has been a resurgence of everything from *euskera* TV shows to Basque schools, and the language is frequently used in the País Vasco.

👁 🏖 SIGHTS AND BEACHES

San Sebastián's most attractive sight is the city itself, with its green walks, grandiose buildings, and the placid bay.

■ **MONTE IGUELDO.** Though the views from both of San Sebastián's mountains are spectacular, those from Monte Igueldo are superior. By day, the countryside meets the ocean in a line of white and blue; by night, Isla Santa Clara seems to float in a halo of light. The sidewalk nearest the mountain ends just before the base of Monte Igueldo with Eduardo Chillida's sculpture *El Peine de los Vientos* (Comb of the Winds). You can walk up the narrow, winding residential road, but you're better off taking the funicular. A small amusement park at the top has bumper cars, water rides, and trampolines, but the view is the real entertainment. (☎ 943 21 02 11. Open daily June-Sept. 10am-10pm; Mar.-June Sa 11am-8pm, Su 11am-9pm; Oct.-Feb. Sa-Su 11am-8pm. Funicular runs every 15min.; €1, round-trip €1.60.)

■ **MONTE URGULL.** Across the bay from Monte Igueldo, the gravel paths on Monte Urgull wind through shady woods, monuments, and stunning vistas. The overgrown **Castillo de Santa Cruz de la Mota** tops the summit with 12 cannons, a chapel, and the statue of the *Sagrado Corazón de Jesús* blessing the city. (4 pathways lead up to the summit from Po. Nuevo; a convenient one is located next to the Museo de San Telmo. Castillo open daily May-Sept. 8am-8pm; Oct.-Apr. 8am-6pm. Free.)

MUSEO CHILLIDA-LEKU. If Monte Igueldo's "Peine de los Vientos" left you wanting more, the Museo Chillida-Leku is a beautiful way to satisfy your craving. Fifteen minutes from the town center, Chillida-Leku is a permanent collection of Eduardo Chillida's work, spread throughout the garden of a restored 16th-century farmhouse. Restored by Chillida, the farmhouse itself is a work of art and houses some of Chillida's earliest pieces. Daily tours are provided, as well as audio tours in five languages. (Autobuses Garayer leaves from C. Oquendo ever half hr. ☎ 943 33 60 06. Bo. Jauregui 66. Drive south on N-1 out of San Sebastián toward Vitoria-Gasteiz. Open July-Aug. and Semana Santa M and W-Sa 10:30am-7pm, Su 10:30am-3pm; Sept.-June Su-M and W-Sa 10:30am-3pm.)

MUSEO DE SAN TELMO. The Museo de San Telmo resides in a Dominican monastery. The serene, overgrown cloister is strewn with Basque funerary relics, and the main museum beyond the cloister displays a fascinating array of pre-historic Basque artifacts, a few dinosaur skeletons, and a piece of contemporary art. (Po. Nuevo. ☎ 943 42 49 70. Open Tu-Sa 10:30am-8:30pm, Su 10:30am-2pm. Free.)

PALACES. When Queen Isabella II started vacationing here in the mid-19th century, fancy buildings sprang up like wildflowers. **El Palacio de Miramar** has passed through the hands of the Spanish court, Napoleon III, and Bismarck; it now serves as the País Vasco University, but anyone can stroll through the adjacent **Parque de Miramar** and contemplate the views of the bay. *(Between Playa de la Concha and Playa de Ondarreta. Open daily June-Aug. 9am-9pm; Sept.-May 10am-5pm. Free.)* The other royal residence, **Palacio de Ayete,** is also closed to the public, but surrounding trails aren't. *(Head up Cuesta de Aldapeta or take bus #19. Grounds open June-Aug. 10am-8:30pm; Sept.-May 10am-5pm. Free.)*

◱ BEACHES AND WATER SPORTS

The gorgeous **Playa de la Concha** curves from the port to the **Pico del Loro,** the promontory home to the Palacio de Miramar. The virtually flat beach disappears during high tide. Sunbathing crowds jam onto the smaller and steeper **Playa de Ondarreta,** beyond the Palacio de Miramar, and surfers flock to **Playa de la Zurrida,** across the river from Mt. Urguel. Picnickers head for the alluring **Isla de Santa Clara** in the center of the bay (motorboat ferry 5min., June-Sept. every 30min., round-trip €2). Check at the portside kiosk for more info.

Several sports-related groups offer a variety of activities and lessons. For **windsurfing** and **kayaking,** call the Real Club Náutico, C. Igentea 9, located on the water and shaped like a small cruise ship. (☎943 42 35 75. Open 10am-1pm and 4-6:30pm. Day courses €30-60.) For **parachuting,** try Urruti Sport, C. José María Soroa 20 (☎943 27 81 96). **Surfers** can check out the Pukas Surf Club, Po. de la Zurriola 23, for rentals and info on lessons. (☎943 42 12 05. Open M-Sa 9:30am-9pm. AmEx/MC/V.) For general info on all sports, pick up a copy of the *UDA-Actividades Deportivas* brochure at the tourist office.

♫ ◪ ENTERTAINMENT AND NIGHTLIFE

For info on **theater** and special events, pick up the weekly *Kalea* (€1.40) from tobacco stands or newsstands. The *parte vieja* pulls out all the stops in July and August, particularly on **Calle Fermín Calbetón,** three blocks in from Alameda del Boulevard. During the year, when students outnumber backpackers, nightlife tends to move beyond the *parte vieja.* Keep an eye out for discount coupons on the street. **Ostadar,** C. Fermín Calbetón 13, attracts locals and tourists alike with its happening dance mix. (Beer €1.80. Mixed drinks €4.50.) **Zibbibo,** Pl. Sarriegi 8, is a hip club with a dance floor and a blend of hits and techno. (Open daily 2pm-4am.) **Akerbeltz,** C. Koruko Andra Mari 9, is a sleek, local bar. (Open M-Th 3pm-2:30am, F-Sa 3pm-3:30am.)

BILBAO (BILBO)   ☎944

Bilbao (pop. 370,000) is a city transformed; what was once industry is now new, avant-garde, and futuristic. 20th-century success showered the city with a new subway system, a new bridge, a stylish riverwalk, and other additions designed by renowned international architects. But above all else, the shining Guggenheim Museum has most powerfully fueled Bilbao's rise to international prominence.

◰ TRANSPORTATION

Flights depart from the **airport** (☎944 86 93 00), 8km from Bilbao. To reach the airport, take the Bizkai bus (☎944 48 40 80) marked *Aeropuerto* from P. Moyua, in front of the Hacienda building (20min.; M-F every 30 min. 6:30am-9pm; Sa-Su every hr. 7am-9pm; €1). Buses return from the airport to Pl. Moyua (M-F every

30min. 6:45am-10:45pm, Sa-Su every hr. 6:30am-10:30pm). **Trains** (☎902 24 02 02) arrive at the Estación de Abando del Norte, Pl. Circular 2, from: Barcelona (9-11hr., Su-F 10:45pm, €43); Madrid (6-9hr., Su-F 4:30 and 8:45pm, €38); and Salamanca (5½hr., 2pm, €24). From Pl. Circular, head right around the station and cross Puente del Arenal to reach Pl. Arriaga, the entrance to the *casco viejo* and Pl. Nueva. Most **bus** companies leave from the Termibús terminal, C. Gurtubay 1 (☎944 39 50 77; M: San Mamés), on the west side of town, for: Barcelona (7¼hr., 4 per day, €35); Madrid (4-5hr.; M-F 10-18 per day, Su 2 per day; €23); Pamplona (2hr., 4-6 per day, €11); and San Sebastián (1¼hr., every hr., €8).

✳ 🛈 ORIENTATION AND PRACTICAL INFORMATION

The city's main thoroughfare, **Gran Vía de Don Diego López de Haro**, or just **Gran Vía**, connects three of Bilbao's main plazas. Heading east from Pl. de Sagrado Corazón, to the central Pl. Moyúa, and ending at Pl. Circular, it is the axis for many important stops and stations. Past Pl. Circular, you will cross the Río de Bilbao on **Puente del Arenal**, which deposits you on **Plaza de Arriaga**, the entrance to the **casco viejo** and **Plaza Nueva**. The **tourist office** is on C. Rodriguez Arias 3. (☎944 79 57 60; www.bilbao.net. Open M-F 9am-2pm and 4-7:30pm, Sa 9am-2pm, Su 10am-2pm.) Surf the **Internet** at **Ciberteca**, C. José Maria Escuza 23, on the corner of C. Simón Bolívar. (€.60 per 10min., €2.10 per hr. Open M-Th 8am-10pm, F-Sa 8am-midnight, Su 10am-10pm.) **Postal Code:** 48008.

🏠 ACCOMMODATIONS

During **Semana Grande** (Aug. 17-25) rates are higher than those listed below. **Plaza Arriaga** and **Calle Arenal** have budget accommodations galore, while upscale hotels line the river or are in the new city off **Gran Vía**.

Hotel Arriaga, C. Ribera 3 (☎944 79 00 01; fax 79 05 16). Large rooms with private bath and A/C. Singles €39; doubles €60; triples €72. AmEx/V. ❹

Pensión Méndez, C. Santa María 13, 4th fl. (☎944 16 03 64). Take C. Bidebbarrieta from Pte. del Arenal; after 2 blocks, take a right onto C. Perro. Turn right on C. Santa María. Rooms insulated from the raging nightlife below. Singles €25; doubles €33. ❷

Pensión Ladero, C. Lotería 1, 4th fl. (☎944 15 09 32). From Pte. del Arenal, take C. Corre; after 3 blocks, take a right onto C. Lotería. Modern common bathrooms and winter heating. Singles €18; doubles €30. ❷

Pensión de la Fuente, C. Sombrería 2 (☎944 16 99 89). From Pte. Arenal, turn right on C. Correo, follow it 2 blocks past Pl. Nueva, and then turn left. Singles €18; doubles €26-28, with bath €36. ❷

Hostal Mardones, C. Jardines 4, 3rd fl. (☎944 15 31 05). From Pte. Arenal, take C. Bidebarrieta, then the 1st right onto C. Jardines; the hostel is on the left. Some rooms with balconies, all with marble sinks. Singles €32, with bath €38; doubles with 1 bed €34, with 2 beds €42, with bath €38-45; triples with bath €45-50. ❸

Albergue Bilbao Aterpetxez (HI), Ctra. Basurto-Kastrexana Errep. 70 (☎944 27 00 54; fax 27 54 79). Take bus #58 from Pl. Circular or Pl. Zabalburu. Internet access, currency exchange, bike rental, and laundry facilities. July-Sept. singles €18, under-26 €16; bed in a double or triple €14, over-25 €16. Oct.-June €1 discount. MC/V. ❶

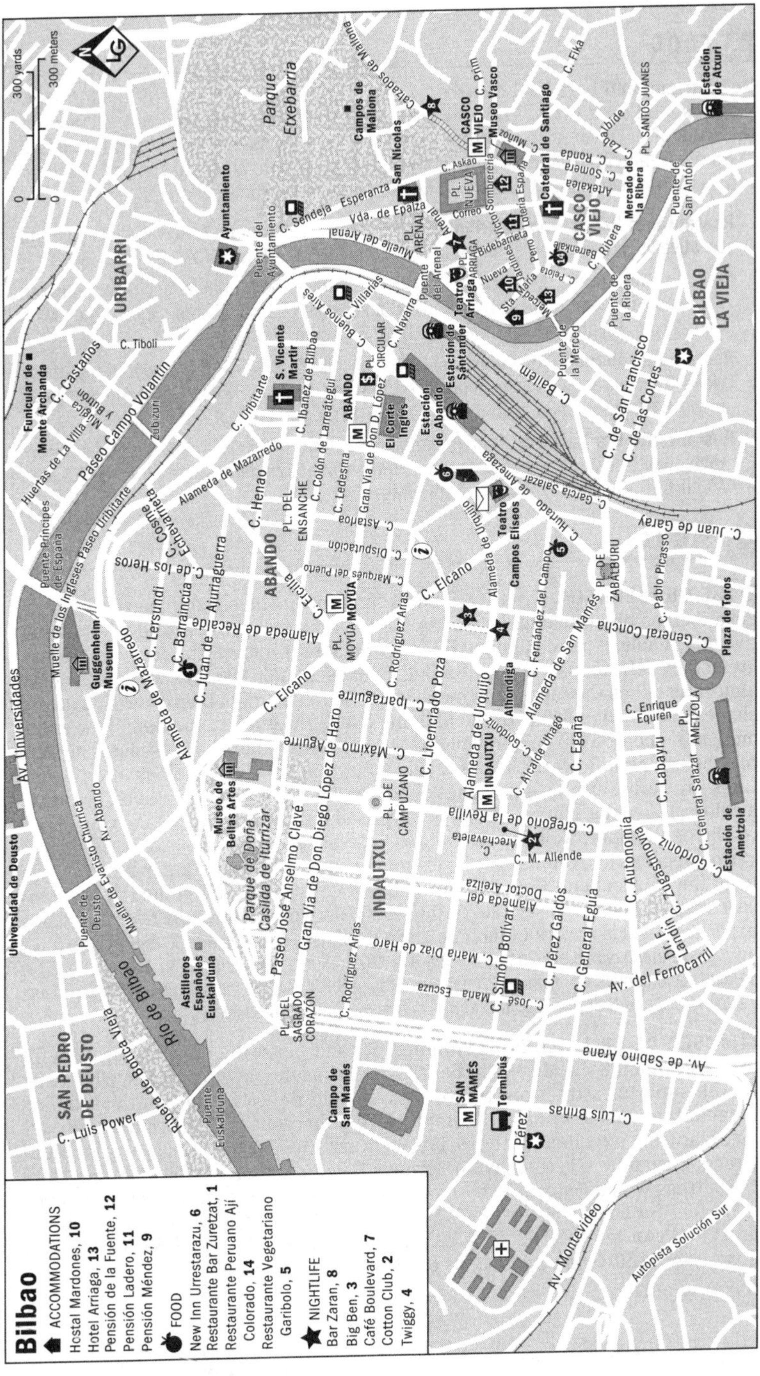
Bilbao
ACCOMMODATIONS
Hostal Mardones, 10
Hotel Arriaga, 13
Pensión de la Fuente, 12
Pensión Ladero, 11
Pensión Méndez, 9
FOOD
New Inn Urrestarazu, 6
Restaurante Bar Zuretzat, 1
Restaurante Peruano Ají Colorado, 14
Restaurante Vegetariano Garibolo, 5
NIGHTLIFE
Bar Zaran, 8
Big Ben, 3
Café Boulevard, 7
Cotton Club, 2
Twiggy, 4
0
300 yards
300 meters
URIBARRI
Ayuntamiento
Parque Etxebarria
Campos de Mallona
San Nicolás
CASCO VIEJO
Museo Vasco
Catedral de Santiago
PL. NUEVA
PL. ARENAL
Teatro Arriaga
Estación de Santander
Estación de Abando
Mercado de la Ribera
BILBAO LA VIEJA
Estación de Atxuri
Funicular de Monte Archanda
Paseo Campo Volantín
S. Vicente Mártir
ABANDO
El Corte Inglés
PL. DEL ENSANCHE
Alameda de Mazarredo
Teatro Campos Elíseos
PL. DE ZABALBURU
Plaza de Toros
PL. AMETZOLA
Estación de Ametzola
Guggenheim Museum
Alameda de Recalde
PL. MOYÚA
MOYÚA
Alhóndiga
INDAUTXU
Museo de Bellas Artes
Parque de Doña Casilda de Iturrizar
PL. DE CAMPUZANO
Gran Vía de Don Diego López de Haro
Universidad de Deusto
Av. Universidades
Astilleros Españoles Euskalduna
Río de Bilbao
SAN PEDRO DE DEUSTO
PL. DEL SAGRADO CORAZÓN
Campo de San Mamés
SAN MAMÉS
Termibús
Av. de Sabino Arana
Av. del Ferrocarril
Av. Montevideo
Autopista Solución Sur

SPAIN

FOOD

Restaurants and bars in the *casco viejo* offer a wide selection of local dishes, *pintxos*, and *bocadillos*. The new city has more variety. **Mercado de la Ribera,** on the bank of the river at the bottom of the *casco viejo*, is the biggest indoor **market** in Spain. (Open M-Th and Sa 8am-2:30pm; F 8am-2:30pm and 4:30-7:30pm.) Pick up groceries at **Champión,** Pl. Santos Juanes. (Open M-Sa 9am-9:30pm.)

Restaurante Vegetariano Garibolo, C. Fernández del Campo 7, serves delicious and creative vegetarian meals. *Menú* €9.80. Open M-Sa 1-4pm. MC/V. ❷

New Inn Urrestarazu, Alameda de Urquijo 9. Features both authentic local cuisine and home-cooked comfort food. Try the Idiazábal cheese (€2.60). Entrees €2-7. Open M-Th 7am-11pm, F 7am-midnight, Sa 8am-1am, Su 10am-10pm. ❶

Restaurante Peruano Ají Colorado, C. Barrencalle 5 (☎944 15 22 09), in the *casco viejo*. Specializes in *ceviche* (marinated raw fish salad; €9.65-11.40). M-F luncheon *menú* €12. Open Tu-Sa 1:30-3:30pm and 9-11:30pm, Su 1:30-3:30pm. MC/V.

Restaurante Bar Zuretzat, C. Iparraguirre 7 (☎944 24 85 05), near the Guggenheim. High-quality seafood. Don't miss the incredibly sweet cinnamon rice pudding (€3.20). *Menú* €10. Open daily 7:30am-11pm. MC/V. ❷

◉ SIGHTS

◪**THE GUGGENHEIM.** Frank O. Gehry's Guggenheim Museum Bilbao can only be described as breathtaking. Lauded in the international press with every superlative imaginable, it has catapulted Bilbao straight into cultural stardom. Visitors are greeted by Jeff Koons's "Puppy," a dog composed of 60,000 flowers and standing almost as tall as the museum. The main attraction is undoubtedly the undulating shapes and flowing forms of the building itself. Sheathed in titanium, limestone, and glass, the US$100 million building is said to resemble an iridescent scaly fish or a blossoming flower. The amazingly light, dramatically spacious interior features a towering atrium and a series of non-traditional exhibition spaces, including a colossal 130m by 30m hall. Don't be surprised if you are asked to take your shoes off, lie on the floor, walk through mazes, or even sing throughout your visit to the various eccentric exhibits. The museum currently hosts rotating exhibits drawn from the Guggenheim Foundation's collection. A cafe on the ground floor serves snacks and drinks; the restaurant on the second floor provides a more decadent dining experience and is a work of modern art in itself. *(Av. Abandoibarra 2. ☎944 35 90 00; www.guggenheim-bilbao.es. Open daily July-Aug. 10am-8pm; Sept.-June Tu-Su 10am-8pm. €10, students and seniors €5. Under-12 free. Audio tour €3.70. Guided tours in English Tu-Su 11am, 12:30, 4:30, and 6:30pm. Sign up 30min. before tour at the info desk.)*

◪**MUSEO DE BELLAS ARTES.** Although it can't boast the name-recognition of the Guggenheim, the Museo de Bellas Artes wins the favor of locals, who insist its superior attraction. Hoarding aesthetic riches behind an unassuming facade, the museum boasts an impressive collection of 12th- to 21st-century art, featuring excellent 15th- to 17th-century Flemish paintings, works by El Greco, Zurbarán, Goya, Gauguin, Francis Bacon, Velázquez, Picasso, and Mary Cassatt, as well as canvases by Basque painters. The sculpture garden in back is perfect for a relaxing stroll. *(Pl. Museo 2. Take C. Elcano to Pl. Museo, or take bus #10 from Pte. Arenal. ☎944 39 60 60, guided visits ☎944 39 61 37. Open Tu-Sa 10am-8pm, Su 10am-2pm. €4.50, seniors and students €3. Under-12 free and W free.)*

MUSEO VASCO. Located appropriately enough in the *casco viejo*, this museum celebrates the region's inhabitants, from prehistoric times to the present, with special attention to Basque craftsmanship. *(Pl. Miguel de Unamuno, 4. From the Pte. Arenal take C. Correo, to the left of Café Boulevard, or 2 blocks, turn left onto C. Sombrería, following it to the end; the museum is on the right side of the plaza. ☎944 15 54 23. Open Tu-Sa 11am-5pm, Su 11am-2pm. Temporary exhibition hours Tu-Sa 11am-8pm, Su 11am-2pm. €3, students €1.50. Seniors, under-12 free and Th free.)*

OTHER SIGHTS. The best view of Bilbao's surrounding landscape and the perfect place for a picnic is at the top of **Monte Archanda,** north of the old town and equidistant from both the *casco viejo* and the Guggenheim. *(Funicular to the top every 15min. M-F 7:15am-10pm, Sa June-Sept. 7:15am-11pm €0.70. Handicap accessible, lift €0.25. With your back to the casco nuevo, turn left from Pl. Arenal and follow the riverside road past the Ayuntamiento. On Po. Campo de Volantín, turn right on C. Mugica Y Butrón and continue until Pl. Funicular.)* A short Metro ride to the north (5-50min.) leads to various **beaches,** including **Getxo, Sopelana,** and **Plencia** (Plentzia). For Getxo, get off at any stop near Neguri or Algorta, then walk ½km to the beach. Along with Sopelana, Getxo attracts a surfer crowd and lies just a little nearer to the Bay of Biscay; its illuminated **Puente Colgante** (a suspension bridge constructed over 100 years ago) spans the river, leading to a plethora of all-night bars.

🎵 🎭 ENTERTAINMENT AND NIGHTLIFE

Bilbao has a thriving bar scene. In the *casco viejo*, revelers spill out into the streets to sip their *txikitos* (chee-KEE-tos; small glasses of wine), especially on **Calle Barrenkalea,** one of the original "seven streets" from which the city of Bilbao has grown. Teenagers and 20-somethings fill **Calle Licenciado Poza** on the west side of town, especially between C. General Concha and Alamede de Recalde, where a covered alleyway connecting C. Licenciado Poza and Alameda de Urquijo teems with bars. Try flower-themed **Twiggy,** across the street from the alley on Alameda de Urquijo, and **Big Ben,** where the dancing is as crazy as the cow on their logo. The **Cotton Club,** C. Gregorio de la Revilla 25 (enter on C. Simón Bolívar), decorated with over 30,000 beer caps, draws a huge crowd on Friday and Saturday nights, while the rest of the week is a little more low-key. (Beer €2-3.50. Over 100 choices of whiskey for €4.50 per *copa.* DJ spins W-Th at 11pm and F-Sa at 1pm. Open M-Th 4:30pm-3am, F-Sa 6:30pm-6am, Su 6:30pm-3am. Cash only.) For a more mellow scene, munch on *pintxos* (€1-1.20) and people-watch at Bilbao's oldest coffee shop, **Café Boulevard** (est. 1871), C. Arenal 3. This Art Deco cafe was once an important site for literary meetings and one of Miguel de Unamuno's favorite haunts. Put on your dancing shoes and get ready to tango on Fridays at 11pm. (☎944 15 31 28. Open M-Th 7:30am-11pm, F-Sa 8am-2am, Su 11am-11pm. MC/V.) Climb your way to a peaceful drink at **Bar Zaran,** C. Calzadas de Mallona 18, towards Campos de Mallona. Ascend the long stone stairway next to the *casco viejo* Metro entrance. Take your drink outside for great views of Bilbao. (Beer €1.40. Red wine €0.40. Cigars €0.40-1. Open daily 8am-12:30am.)

The massive fiesta in honor of *Nuestra Señora de Begoña* takes place during **Semana Grande,** a nine-day party complete with fireworks, concerts, theater beginning the Saturday after August 15. Documentary filmmakers from all over the world gather for a week in October or November for the **Festival Internacional de Cine Documental de Bilbao.** During the summer, the municipal band offers free **concerts** every Sunday morning at the bandstand in Parque Arenal. Pick up a *Bilbao Guide* from the tourist office for event listings.

⚡DAYTRIP FROM BILBAO: GUERNICA (GERNIKA). Founded in 1366, Guernica (pop. 15,600) long served as the ceremonial seat of the Basque country. On April 26, 1937, the Nazi "Condor Legion" released an estimated 29,000kg of explosives on Guernica, obliterating 70% of the city in three hours. The nearly 2000 people who were killed in the bombings were immortalized in Pablo Picasso's stark masterpiece *Guernica*, now in Madrid's Museo Reina Sofía (p. 868). **Trains** (☎902 54 32 10; www.euskotren.es) roll in from Bilbao (45min., every 45min., €2). To reach the **tourist office,** C. Artekalea 8, from the train station, walk two blocks up C. Adolfo Urioste and turn right on C. Barrenkalea. Turn left at the alleyway; the office will be on your right. (☎946 25 58 92; www.gernikalumo.net. Open July-Sept. M-Sa 10am-7pm, Su 10am-2pm; Oct.-June M-Sa 10am-2pm and 4-7pm, Su 10am-2pm.) The office can direct you to several memorial sites, including the newly renovated **⚡Gernika Peace Museum,** Pl. Foru 1, which features an exhibition chronicling the bombardment. **Postal Code:** 48300.

BALEARIC ISLANDS

Every year, discos, ancient history, and beaches—especially beaches—draw nearly two million of the hippest Europeans to the *Islas Baleares*.

▐ TRANSPORTATION

Flights are the easiest way to get to the islands. Those under 26 often get discounts from **Iberia** (☎902 40 05 00; www.iberia.com), which flies to Palma de Mallorca and Ibiza from Barcelona (40min., €60-120) and Madrid (1hr., €150-180). **Air Europa** (☎902 24 00 42; www.air-europa.com) and **SpanAir** (☎902 13 14 15; www.spanair.com) offer budget flights to and between the islands. Most cheap round-trip **charters** include a week's stay in a hotel; some companies called *mayoristas* sell leftover spots on package-tour flights as "seat-only" deals.

    Ferries to the islands are less popular. **Trasmediterránea** (☎902 45 46 45; www.trasmediterranea.com) departs from Barcelona's Estació Marítima Moll and Valencia's Estació Marítima for Mallorca, Menorca, and Ibiza (€38-58). **Buquebus** (☎902 41 42 42) goes from Barcelona to Palma (4hr., 2 per day, €49). Between islands, **ferries** are the most cost-efficient way to travel. **Trasmediterránea** (see above) sails from Palma to Mahón (6½hr., Su only, €23) and Ibiza (2½hr., 7am daily, €37). **Car** rental costs about €36 per day, **mopeds** €18, and **bikes** €6-10.

MALLORCA
☎971

A favorite of Spain's royal family, Mallorca has been popular with the in-crowd since Roman times. Lemon groves and olive trees adorn the jagged cliffs of the northern coast, and lazy beaches sink into calm bays to the east. The capital of the Balearics, **Palma** (pop. 323,000) embraces conspicuous consumption and pleases with its well-preserved old quarter, colonial architecture, and local flavor.

    The tourist office (see below) distributes a list of over 40 nearby **beaches,** many a mere bus ride away; one popular choice is **El Arenal** (*Platja de Palma;* bus #15), 11km southeast of town toward the airport. When the sun sets, **La Bodeguita del Medio,** C. Vallseca 18, keeps its crowd dancing to Cuban rhythms. (Open Su-W 8pm-1am, Th-Sa 8pm-3am.) Follow the Aussie accents down C. Apuntadores to the popular **Bar Latitude 39,** C. Felip Bauza 8, a self-proclaimed "yachtie" bar. (Open M-Sa 7pm-3am.) Palma's clubbers start their night in the *bares-musicales* lining the **Paseo Marítimo** strip; try salsa-happy **Made in Brasil,**

Po. Marítimo 27 (open daily 8pm-4am) or dance-crazy **Salero**, Po. Marítimo 31 (open daily 8pm-6am). The bars and clubs around **El Arenal** overflow with fashion-conscious German disco-fiends, but braving them is well worth the price at **Riu Palace**, one block from the beach. (Cover €15, includes unlimited free drinks. Open daily 10pm-6:30am.) When the bar scene fades at 3am, partiers migrate to Palma's *discotecas*. **Tito's Palace**, Po. Marítimo, is the city's hippest disco. (Cover €15-18. Open daily 11pm-6am.)

From the airport, take bus #1 to **Plaza Espanya** (15min., every 20min., €1.80). To reach the **tourist office**, C. Sant Dominic 11, from Pl. Reina, take C. Conquistador to C. Sant Dominic. (☎971 72 40 90. Open M-F 9am-8pm, Sa 9am-1:30pm.) **Branches** are in Pl. Reina and the Pl. Espanya. **Hostal Cuba ❷**, C. San Magí 1, offers spotless rooms with high ceilings and wood furniture. From Pl. Joan Carles I, turn left and walk down Av. Jaume III, cross the river, and turn left on C. Argentina; the hostel is several blocks down. (☎971 73 81 59. Singles €20; doubles €36.) **Hostal Apuntadores ❶**, C. Apuntadores 8, is in the middle of the action, less than a block from Pl. Reina. (☎971 71 34 91. Dorms €14; singles €25; doubles €33.) Those on a budget tend to head to the side streets off **Passeig Born**, to the cheap cafes along **Avenida Joan Miró**, or to the carbon-copy pizzerias along **Paseo Marítimo**. For groceries, try **Servicio y Precios**, on C. Felip Bauzá. (Open M-F 8:30am-8:30pm, Sa 9am-2pm.)

IBIZA   ☎971

Perhaps nowhere on Earth does style rule over substance (or substances over style) more than on the island of Ibiza (pop. 84,000). Once a 60s hippie enclave, Ibiza has long abandoned her roots for new-age decadence. None of Ibiza's beaches is within quick walking distance of **Eivissa** (Ibiza City), but **Platja de Talamanca**, **Platja des Duros**, **Platja d'en Bossa**, and **Platja Figueredes** are at most a 20min. bike ride away; buses also leave from Av. Isidor Macabich 20 for Platja d'en Bossa (every 30min., €0.75). One of the most beautiful beaches near Eivissa is **Playa de Las Salinas**, where the nude sunbathers are almost as perfect as the crystal-blue water and silky sand. The crowds return from the beaches by nightfall, arriving at the largest party on Earth. The bar scene centers around **Calle Barcelona**, while **Calle Virgen** is the center of gay nightlife. The island's 🏳️‍🌈**discos** (virtually all a mixed gay/straight crowd) are world-famous.

THE LOCAL LEGEND

PRELUDE TO A BREAKUP

Two of Mallorca's most famous vacationers were the Polish composer Frédéric Chopin and his lover, French novelist George Sand, who visited during the winter of 1838-39. Though intended to be a honeymoon of sorts, the excursion was doomed from the outset. Chopin, suffering from tuberculosis, was constantly in pain and prone to black moods. Sand, a passionate freethinker, felt trapped on the island. The presence of the couple, along with Sand's two children from a previous marriage, caused a stir among the townsfolk, who tormented them through the windows of cells #2 and 4 of the Cartoixa Real, where they stayed. Sand documents these incidents in her book *Un Hiver a Majorque* (A Winter in Mallorca), referring to the local villagers as "barbarians and monkeys." Despite (or because of) the less than ideal circumstances, Chopin produced some of his greatest pieces while on the island. At the winter's end, the two realized their personalities were too divergent for the relationship to last. In February of 1839, they boarded the same ship which had taken them to Mallorca less than four months before and, once on the Spanish mainland, parted forever.

Refer to *Ministry in Ibiza* or *DJ*, free at many hostels, bars, and restaurants, for a full list of nightlife options. The **Discobus** runs to and from all the major hot spots (leaves Eivissa from A. Isidoro Macabich every hr. 12:30am-6:30am; schedule available at tourist office and hotels. €1.50). According to the Guinness Book of World Records, wild ▩**Privilege** is the world's largest club. It can fit up to 10,000 bodies, has more than a few bars, and is the place to be Monday nights. (Cover from €40. Open June-Sept. daily midnight-7am.) At **Amnesia,** on the road to San Antonio, you can forget who you are and who you came with. (Foam parties W and Su; cream and MTV parties Th. Cover from €40. Open daily midnight-7am.) Elegant **Pachá,** on Pg. Perimitral, is a 15min. walk or a 2min. cab ride from the port. (Cover €50. Open daily midnight-7:30am.) Cap off your night in **Space,** which starts hopping around 8am, peaks mid-afternoon, and doesn't wind down until 5pm. (Cover €30-40.)

The local paper *Diario de Ibiza* (www.diariodeibiza.es; €0.75) features an *Agenda* page with everything you need to know about Ibiza. The **tourist office,** C. Antoni Riquer 2, is on the water. (☎971 30 19 00. Open M-F 9:30am-1:30pm and 5-7:30pm, Sa 10:30am-1pm.) Email friends about your crazy night while washing the beer out of your clothes at **Wash and Dry,** Av. España 53. (☎971 39 48 22. Wash and dry €4.20 each. Internet €5.40 per hr. Open M-F 10am-3pm and 5-10pm, Sa 10am-5pm.) The letters **"CH"** (*casa de huespedes*) mark many doorways; call the owners at the phone number on the door. **Hostal Residencia Sol y Brisa ❷,** Av. B. V. Ramón 15, parallel to Pg. Vara de Rey, has clean rooms, a central location, and a social atmosphere. (☎971 31 08 18; fax 30 30 32. Singles €24; doubles €42.) **Hostal La Marina ❸,** Puerto de Ibiza, C. Barcelona 7, is across from Estació Marítima, right in the middle of a raucous bar scene. (☎971 31 01 72. Singles €30-62; doubles €41-150.) **Hostal Residencia Ripoll ❸** is at C. Vicente Cuervo 14. (☎971 31 42 75. July-Sept. singles €30; doubles €42; 3-person apartments with patio, kitchen, and TV €78.) For a supermarket, try **Spar,** on the corner of C. d'Avicenna and Pl. des Parc. (Open M-Sa 9am-9pm.)

MENORCA   ☎971

Menorca's (pop. 72,000) 200km coastline of raw beaches, rustic landscapes, and well-preserved ancient monuments draws ecologists, photographers, and wealthy young families. Unfortunately for those on a budget, the island's unique qualities and ritzy patrons have resulted in elevated prices. Atop a steep bluff, **Mahón** (pop. 25,000) is the main gateway to the island. The popular **beaches** outside Mahón are accessible by bus. Transportes Menorca **buses** leave from C. Josep M. Quadrado for ▩**Platges de Son Bou** (6 per day, €1.80), which offers 4km of gorgeous beaches on the southern shore. Autocares Fornells buses leave C. Vasallo in Mahón for the breathtaking views of sandy **Arenal d'en Castell** (30 min., 3-5 per day, €1.70), while TMSA buses go to touristy **Cala'n Porter** (7 per day, €1.10) and its whitewashed houses, orange stucco roofs, and red sidewalks. A 10min. walk away, the ▩ **Covas d'en Xoroi,** caves residing on cliffs high above the sea, are inhabited by a network of bars during the day, and a popular disco at night. (Bar cover €5, includes one drink. Open Apr.-Oct. daily 10:30am-9pm. Disco cover €15. Open daily 11pm-late.)

The **tourist office** is at Sa Rovellada de Dalt 24. (☎971 36 37 90. Open M-F 9am-1:30pm and 5-7pm, Sa 9am-1pm.) **Posada Orsi ❷** is at C. de la Infanta 19; from Pl. s'Esplanada, take C. Moreres, which becomes C. Hannover; turn right at Pl. Constitució, and follow C. Nou through Pl. Reial. (☎971 36 47 51. Breakfast included. Singles €15-21; doubles €26-35, with shower €30-42.) To get to **Hostal La Isla ❷,** C. de Santa Catalina 4, take C. Concepció from Pl. Miranda. (☎/fax 971 36 64 92. Singles €25; doubles €40.)

NORTHWESTERN SPAIN

Northwestern Spain is the country's best-kept secret; its seclusion is half its charm. Rainy **Galicia** hides mysterious Celtic ruins, and on the northern coast tiny **Asturias** allows access to the dramatic Picos de Europa mountain range.

GALICIA (GALIZA)

If, as the Galician saying goes, "rain is art," then there is no gallery more beautiful than the Northwest's misty skies. Often veiled in silvery drizzle, it is a province of fern-laden eucalyptus woods, slate-roofed fishing villages, and endless white beaches. Locals speak *gallego*, a linguistic hybrid of Castilian and Portuguese.

SANTIAGO DE COMPOSTELA   ☎981

Santiago (pop. 140,000) has long drawn pilgrims eager to gaze at one of Christianity's holiest cities. The cathedral marks the end of the *Camino de Santiago*, a pilgrimage believed to halve one's time in purgatory. Today, sunburnt pilgrims, street musicians, and hordes of tourists fill the streets.

■⦿ TRANSPORTATION AND PRACTICAL INFORMATION. Trains (☎981 52 02 02) run from R. Hórreo to Madrid (8hr.; M-F 1:45 and 10:25pm, Sa 10:30pm, Su 9:45am, 1:45, and 10:30pm; €36). A schedule is printed daily in *El Correo Gallego*. To reach the city, take bus #6 to Pr. Galicia or walk up the stairs across the parking lot from the main entrance, cross the street, and bear right onto R. Hórreo, which leads to Pr. Galicia. **Buses** (☎981 58 77 00) run from R. de Rodríguez (20min. from downtown) to: Bilbao (11¼hr., 9am and 9:30pm, €39); Madrid (8-9hr., 4 per day, €31); and San Sebastián (13½hr., 8am and 5:30pm, €44). From the station, take bus #10 to Pr. Galicia. The **tourist office** is at R. do Vilar 43. (☎981 58 40 81. Open M-F 10am-2pm and 4-7pm, Sa 11am-2pm and 5-7pm, Su 11am-2pm.) Check **email** at **CyberNova 50,** R. Nova 50. (9am-10pm €1.20 per hr., 10pm-1am €1 per hr. Open daily 9am-1am.) **Postal Code:** 15701.

⦿◗ ACCOMMODATIONS AND FOOD. Nearly every street in the *ciudad vieja* houses at least one or two *pensiónes*. **Rúa Vilar** and **Rúa da Raíña** are the liveliest and most popular streets. **▨Hospedaje Ramos ❶,** R. da Raíña 18, 2nd fl., above **O Papa Una** restaurant, is in the center of the *ciudad vieja*. (☎981 58 18 59. Singles €14; doubles €25.) **Hospedaje Santa Cruz ❷,** R. Vilar 42, 2nd fl., is close to a myriad of bars and restaurants. (☎981 58 28 15. Singles €15; doubles €25, with bath €40.) Renovated in 2003, **Hostal Barbantes ❸,** Pr. de Fonseca 5, lets big rooms, each with bath. (☎981 57 65 20. Singles €40; doubles €60.) **Hospedaja Fonseca ❶,** R. de Fonseca 1, 2nd fl., offers colorful, sunny rooms with kitchen, TV, and winter heating. (☎981 57 24 79. Singles €12-15; doubles €24-30; triples €36-45; quads €48-60.) Take bus #6 or 9 to get to **Camping As Cancelas ❶,** R. 25 de Xullo 35, 2km from the cathedral on the northern edge of town. (☎981 58 02 66. €4.40 per person, €4.70 per car or per tent.) Bars and cafeterias line the streets, offering a variety of inexpensive *menús;* most restaurants are on R. do Vilar, R. do Franco, R. Nova, and R. da Raíña. Santiago's **market,** between Pl. San Felix and Convento de San Augustín, is a sight of its own right. (Open M-Sa 7:30am-2pm.) **Supermercado Lorenzo Froiz,** Pl. do Toural, is one block from Pr. de Galicia. (Open M-Sa 9am-3pm and 4:30-9pm, Sa 9am-3pm and 5-9pm.)

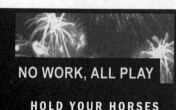

NO WORK, ALL PLAY

HOLD YOUR HORSES

Over 100,000 wild horses inhabit the Galician hills, where they have roamed for nearly 4000 years. Once used as cart-pullers, few are domesticated today. Still, the age-old branding rituals are celebrated each July during *A Rapa das Bestas* ("The Shearing of the Beasts").

"Here, we fight horses for tradition," says one rider, a sweaty, blood-speckled bandana across his hairline. The blood may not be his; for the past two hours he's straddled, head-locked, tail-pulled, herd-surfed, tackled, branded, been kicked and bitten, and—most importantly—sheared numerous feisty steeds. The struggle between man and beast is central to Spanish culture, most famously (and controversially) played out between matador and bull. *A Rapa* gives a new face to the traditional dynamic.

Before the festivities begin, Galician men comb the mountains and valleys gathering wild horses. Then, brave souls, wielding scissors, fight their way into the writhing sea of animals, wrestle one horse at a time to submission, and send thick crops of shiny hair flying to the ground—to be collected later by children as souvenirs.

◨ ◪ SIGHTS AND NIGHTLIFE. Santiago's cathedral has four facades, each a masterpiece from a different era, with entrances opening to four different plazas: Praterías, Quintana, Obradoiro, and Inmaculada. The southern **Praza das Praterías** is the oldest of the facades; the Baroque **Obradoiro** encases the Maestro Mateo's **Pórtico de la Gloria,** considered the crowning achievement of Spanish Romanesque sculpture. The remains of **St. James** (Santiago) lie beneath the high altar in a silver coffer. Inside the **museum** are gorgeous 16th-century tapestries and two poignant statues of the pregnant Virgin Mary. (Cathedral open daily 7am-7pm. Museum open June-Sept. M-Sa 10am-1:30pm and 4-7:30pm, Su 10am-1:30pm; Mar.-June M-Sa 10:30am-1:30pm and 4-6:30pm, Su 10:30am-1:30pm; Oct.-Feb. M-Sa 11am-1pm and 4-6pm, Su 11am-1pm. Museum and cloisters €5, students €3.) Those curious about the Camino de Santiago can head to the **◪Museo das Peregrinacións,** Pl. de San Miguel Dos Agros. (Open Su 10:30am-1:30pm, Tu-F 10am-8pm, Sa 10:30am-1:30pm and 5-8pm. In most of summer free. Off-season €2.40.)

At night, crowds looking for post-pilgrimage consumption flood cellars throughout the city. Take R. Montero Ríos to the bars and clubs off **Praza Roxa** to party with local students. **◪Casa oas Crechas,** Vía Sacra 3, just off Pr. da Quintana, is a smoky pub with a witchcraft theme. (Beer €2. Open daily 4pm-2am or later.) **Xavestre,** R. de San Paolo de Antaltares 31, is packed with 20-somethings. (Mixed drinks €5. Open daily 11am-late.) Students dance the night away at **La Quintana Cafe,** Pr. da Quintana 1. (Beer €3-5. Mixed drinks €4. Open daily 10am-late.)

◪DAYTRIP FROM SANTIAGO: O CASTRO DE BAROÑA. South of the town of **Noia** is a little-known treasure of historical intrigue and mesmerizing natural beauty: The seaside remains of the 5th-century Celtic fortress of **◪O Castro de Baroña.** Its foundations dot the isthmus, ascending to a rocky promontory above the sea and then descending to a crescent **beach,** where clothing is optional. Castromil **buses** from Santiago to Muros stop in Noia (1hr.; M-F 15 per day, Sa 12 per day, Su 8 per day; €3) and Hefsel buses from Noia to Riveira stop at O Castro—tell the driver your destination (30min.; M-F 14 per day, Sa 7 per day, Su 11 per day; €1.30).

ASTURIAS

Spaniards call the tiny land of Asturias a *paraíso natural* (natural paradise). Surrounded by centuries of civilization, its impenetrable peaks and dense alpine forests have remained untouched. Unlike the rest of the country, travelers don't come here to see the sights; they come here to brave them.

PICOS DE EUROPA

This mountain range is home to **Picos de Europa National Park,** the largest national park in Europe. The most popular trails and peaks lie near the **Cares Gorge** (Garganta del Cares). For a list of mountain *refugios* (cabins with bunks but no blankets) and general park info, contact the **Picos de Europa National Park Visitors' Center** in Cangas de Onís. (☎/fax 985 84 86 14. Open May-Sept. M-F 9am-2pm and 5-6:30pm, Sa 9am-2pm and 4-6:30pm, Su 9am-2:30pm; Oct.-Apr. M-Sa 9am-2pm and 4-6:30pm, Su 9am-2:30pm.)

CANGAS DE ONÍS. During the summer months the streets of Cangas (pop. 6,285) are packed with mountaineers and vacationing families looking to spelunk and hang glide in the Picos de Europa National Park. Cangas itself is, if not particularly thrilling, a relaxing town rich in history. The **tourist office,** Jardines del Ayuntamiento 2, is just off Av. de Covadonga, across from the bus stop. (☎985 84 80 05. Open May-Sept. daily 10am-10pm; Oct.-Apr. 10am-2pm and 4-7pm.) ALSA, Av. de Covadonga 18 (☎985 84 81 33), in the Pícaro Inmobiliario building across from the tourist office, runs **buses** to Madrid (7hr., 2:35pm, €26) via Valladolid (5hr., 2 per day, €145).

SPAIN

SWITZERLAND

(SCHWEIZ, SUISSE, SVIZZERA)

The unparalleled natural beauty of Switzerland entices outdoor enthusiasts from around the globe to romp in its Alpine playground. Three-fifths of the country is dominated by mountains: The Jura cover the northwest region bordering France, the Alps stretch gracefully across the entire lower half of Switzerland, and the eastern Rhaetian Alps border Austria. While the stereotypes of Switzerland as a "Big Money" banking and watch-making mecca are to some extent true, its energetic youth culture belies its staid reputation. Although the country is not known for being cheap, the best things—warm Swiss hospitality and the highest peaks in Europe—remain priceless.

LIFE AND TIMES

HISTORY

AGAINST THE EMPIRE (500-1520). Switzerland had been loosely united since 1032 as part of the **Holy Roman Empire,** but when Emperor **Rudolf of Habsburg** tried to assert control over their land in the late 13th century, the Swiss decided to rebel. Three of the Alemanni communities (the Forest Cantons) signed an **Everlasting Alliance** in 1291, agreeing to defend each other from outside attack. The Swiss consider this moment to be the beginning of the **Swiss Confederation.** However, a union of such fiercely independent and culturally distinct states made for an uneasy marriage. The **Swabian War** (1499-1500) against the empire brought virtual independence from the Habsburgs, but domestic struggles based on cultural and religious differences continued.

SUGGESTED ITINERARIES

THREE DAYS Experience the great outdoors at **Interlaken** (1 day, p. 984), and then head to **Lucerne** (1 day, p. 973) for the perfect combination of city culture and natural splendor before jetting to international **Geneva** (1 day, p. 987).

ONE WEEK Begin in **Lucerne** (1 day), where your vision of a typical Swiss city will, strangely, be all too true. Then head to the capital, **Bern** (1 day, p. 968), before getting your adventure thrills in **Interlaken** (1 day). Get a taste of Italian Switzerland in **Locarno** (1 day, p. 996), then traverse northern Italy to reach **Zer**-matt (1 day, p. 986). End your trip in the cosmopolitan city of **Geneva** (2 days).

TWO WEEKS Start in **Geneva** (2 days), then check out **Lausanne** (1 day, p. 993) and **Montreux** (1 day, p. 994). Tackle the Matterhorn in **Zermatt** (1 day) and keep hiking above **Interlaken** (1 day). Bask in **Locarno**'s Mediterranean climate (1 day) then explore the **Swiss National Park** (1 day, p. 984). Head to **Zurich** (2 days, p. 974) and nearby **Lucerne** (1 day). Unwind in tiny, romantic **Stein am Rhein** (2 day, p. 981) and then return to civilization via the capital, **Bern** (1 day).

REFORMATION TO REVOLUTION (1520-1800). With no strong central government to settle quibbles between cantons of different religious faith, the Swiss were split even further by the **Protestant Reformation.** Lutheran **Ulrich Zwingli** of Zurich and **John Calvin** of Geneva instituted reforms, but the rural cantons remained loyal to the Catholic faith. When religious differences between the Protestant city cantons and the Catholic rural cantons escalated into full-fledged battle in the mid-16th century, the Confederation intervened, granting Protestants freedom but prohibiting them from imposing their faith on others. The Confederation remained neutral during the **Thirty Years' War,** escaping the devastation wrought on the rest of Europe. The **Peace of Westphalia,** which ended the war in 1648, granted the Swiss independence from the empire. However, Swiss independence was short lived: **Napoleon** invaded in 1798 and established the **Helvetic Republic.** After Napoleon's defeat at Waterloo in 1815, Swiss neutrality was again officially recognized.

NEUTRALITY AND DIPLOMACY (1815 TO THE 20TH CENTURY). With neutrality established by the **Treaty of Vienna** in 1815, Switzerland could turn its attention to domestic issues. Industrial growth brought relative material prosperity, but religious differences continued to create tension between Catholic and all other cantons. A **civil war** broke out in 1847, but it lasted only 25 days. The Protestant forces were victorious, and the country wrote a new constitution modeled after that of the United States. Once stabilized, Switzerland cultivated its reputation for resolving international conflicts. The **Geneva Convention of 1864** established international laws for conduct during war, and Geneva became the headquarters for the **International Red Cross** (see p. 992).

Switzerland's neutrality was tested in **World War I** as French- and German-speaking Switzerland claimed different cultural loyalties. In 1920, the Allies chose Geneva as the headquarters of the **League of Nations,** solidifying Switzerland's reputation as the center for international mediation. During **World War II,** both sides respected Switzerland (and its banks) as neutral territory. As the rest of Europe cleaned the rubble of two global wars, it nurtured its already sturdy economy; Zurich emerged as a banking and insurance center. Although Geneva became the

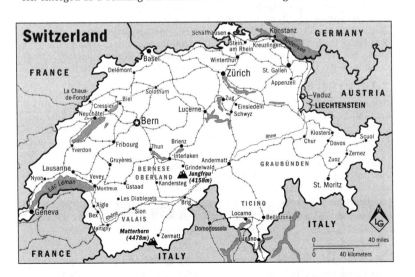

world's most prominent diplomatic headquarters, Switzerland remained isolationist in its relations with the rest of Europe, declining membership in the United Nations (until 2002), NATO, and the European Economic Community.

TODAY

Switzerland has become increasingly wealthy, liberal, and successful since WWII and is still fiercely independent and wary of entanglement with the rest of Europe. The Swiss are remarkably progressive in many areas, electing **Ruth Dreifuss** as their first female president and maintaining one of the world's most stringent ecological policies to protect their fragile Alpine environment. In the past few years, Swiss banks have come under scrutiny for their "blind account" policy, which allowed Holocaust victims and Nazi leaders alike to deposit money and gold during WWII.

In the Swiss government, the 26 cantons are incorporated into the Confederation and its two-chamber legislature, the Federal Assembly. The executive branch consists of a group of seven members—the **Bundesrat** (Federal Council)—elected to four-year terms. The Bundesrat chooses a president from among its ranks. The president holds office for one year; the post is more symbolic than functional. Frequent **referenda** and **initiatives** make political decisions a part of daily life.

THE ARTS

LITERATURE

Jean-Jacques Rousseau, best known for his *Social Contract* (1762), which inspired the French Revolution, was born in Geneva in 1712 and was always proud of his Swiss background—despite the fact that he spent most of his time outside the country and that the Swiss burned his books. When **Romanticism** caught on in Switzerland, J.J. Bodmer and J.J. Breitinger advocated literature in the Swiss-German language, and Gottfried Keller penned the *Bildungsroman* (coming-of-age novel) *Green Henry* (1855). **Conrad Ferdinand Meyer** was a highly influential Swiss poet whose writings united characteristics of Romanticism and Realism.

Carl Jung, whose psychiatric practice in Zurich informed his famous *Symbols of Transformation* (1916), is considered to be the founder of analytical psychology. Switzerland has also produced several respected modern playwrights: Critics laud **Max Frisch** for his Brechtian style and thoughtful treatment of Nazi Germany in works such as *Andorra* (1961), and **Friedrich Dürrenmatt** won renown for his tragicomedic portrayal of human corruptibility in *The Physicists* (1962).

THE VISUAL ARTS

Since the early 20th century, Switzerland has been a prime space for artistic experimentation. One of Switzerland's most famous painters is **Paul Klee,** whose delicately colored watercolors and oil paintings helped shape the beginnings of abstraction, questioning dominant modes of artistic expression. In 1916, Zurich became the birthplace of the **Dada** movement, which rejected traditional aesthetic ideals and attempted to make people reconsider their social values. Later, the country continued to attract liberal artistic thinkers. Switzerland maintains a lively arts scene today; for a glimpse, see Zurich's **Kunsthaus,** p. 980.

FACTS AND FIGURES	
Official Name: Swiss Confederation.	**Land Area:** 41,290 sq. km.
Capital: Bern.	**Time Zone:** GMT + 1.
Major Cities: Basel, Geneva, Zurich.	**Languages:** German, French, Italian.
Population: 7,300,000 (65% German, 18% French, 10% Italian).	**Religions:** Roman Catholic (46%), Protestant (40%), unaffiliated (9%).

ESSENTIALS

WHEN TO GO

November to March is ski season; prices in eastern Switzerland double and travelers need reservations months in advance. The situation is reversed in the summer, when the flatter, western half of Switzerland fills up. Sights and accommodations are cheaper and less crowded in the shoulder season (May-June and Sept.-Oct.); call ahead to check if the Alpine resort areas will be open then.

DOCUMENTS AND FORMALITIES

VISAS. EU citizens do not need a visa. Citizens of Australia, Canada, New Zealand, South Africa, and the US do not need a visa for stays of up to 90 days.

EMBASSIES. Most foreign embassies are in **Bern** (p. 968). Swiss embassies at home include: **Australia,** 7 Melbourne Ave., Forrest, Canberra, ACT 2603 (☎(02) 61 62 84 00); **Canada,** 5 Marlborough Ave., Ottawa, ON K1N 8E6 (☎613-235-1837); **Ireland,** 6 Ailesbury Rd., Ballsbridge, Dublin 4 (☎(353) 12 18 63 82); **New Zealand,** 22 Panama St., Wellington 6001 (☎(04) 472 15 93); **South Africa,** P818 George Ave., Arcadia 0083, 0001 Pretoria (☎(012) 430 67 07); **UK,** 16-18 Montagu Pl., London W1H 2BQ (☎(020) 76 16 60 00); and **US,** 2900 Cathedral Ave. NW, Washington, D.C. 20008 (☎202-745-7900).

TRANSPORTATION

BY PLANE. Major international airports for overseas connections are in Bern (BRN), Geneva (GVA), and Zurich (ZRH). From the UK, **easyJet** (☎(0870) 600 00 00; www.easyjet.com) has flights from London to Geneva and Zurich (UK£47-136). From Ireland, **Aer Lingus** (☎(01) 886 32 00; www.aerlingus.ie) sells round-trip tickets from Dublin to Geneva for €100-300.

BY TRAIN. Federal **(SBB, CFF)** and private railways connect most towns, with frequent trains. For times and prices, check online (www.sbb.ch). **Eurail, Europass,** and **Interrail** are all valid on federal trains. The **SwissPass,** sold worldwide, offers five options for unlimited rail travel: 4, 8, 15, 21, or 30 consecutive days. In addition to rail travel, it entitles you to unlimited transportation within 36 cities and on some private railways and lake steamers. (2nd-class 4-day pass US$160, 8-day US$225, 15-day US$270, 21-day US$315, 1-month US$350.)

BY BUS. **PTT Post Buses,** a barrage of government-run banana-colored coaches, connect rural villages and towns that trains don't service. **SwissPasses** are valid on many buses; **Eurail** passes are not. Even with the SwissPass, you might have to pay a bit extra (5-10SFr) if you're riding one of the direct, faster buses.

BY CAR. With armies of mechanized road crews ready to remove snow at a moment's notice, roads at altitudes of up to 1500m generally remain open throughout winter. The speed limit is 50kph in cities, 80kph on open roads, and 120kph on highways. Many small towns forbid cars to enter; some require special permits, or restrict driving hours. Call ☎140 for roadside assistance.

BY BIKE. Cycling, though strenuous, is a splendid way to see the country; most train stations rent bikes and let you return them at another station. The **Touring Club Suisse,** Chemin de Blandonnet 4, Case Postale 820, 1214 Vernier (☎(022) 417 27 27; www.tcs.ch), is a good source of maps and route descriptions.

SWITZERLAND

TOURIST SERVICES AND MONEY

EMERGENCY	Police: ☎117. Ambulance: ☎144. Fire: ☎118.

TOURIST OFFICES. The **Swiss National Tourist Office,** marked by a standard blue "i" sign, is represented in nearly every town in Switzerland; most agents speak English. The tourist info website for Switzerland is www.myswitzerland.com.

MONEY. The Swiss monetary unit is the **Swiss Franc (SFr/CHF),** which is divided into 100 *centimes* (called *Rappen* in German Switzerland). Coins come in 5, 10, 20, and 50 *centimes* and 1, 2, and 5SFr; bills come in 10, 20, 50, 100, 500, and 1000SFr. Switzerland is not cheap; if you stay in hostels and prepare your own food, expect to spend 45-100SFr per day. As a general rule, it's cheaper to exchange money in Switzerland than at home. There is **no value-added tax (VAT),** although there are frequently tourist taxes of a few SFr for a night at a hostel. **Gratuities** are automatically factored into prices; however, it is polite to round up your bill 1-2SFr as a nod of approval for good service.

SWISS FRANCS		
AUS$1 = 0.90SFR		1SFR = AUS$1.11
CDN$1 = 1.01SFR		1SFR = CDN$0.99
EUR€1 = 1.54SFR		1SFR = EUR€0.65
NZ$1 = 0.80SFR		1SFR = NZ$1.24
ZAR1 = 0.19SFR		1SFR = ZAR5.19
UK£1 = 1.41SFR		1SFR = UK£0.71
US$1 = 2.23SFR		1SFR = US$0.45

COMMUNICATION

TELEPHONES. Whenever possible, use a calling card for international phone calls, as the long-distance rates for national phone services are often exorbitant. For info about using cell phones abroad, see p. 36. Most pay phones in Switzerland accept only prepaid phone cards. Phone cards are available at kiosks, post offices, and train stations. Direct dial access numbers include: **AT&T,** ☎0800 89 00 11; **British Telecom,** ☎0800 55 25 44; **Canada Direct,** ☎0800 55 83 30; **Ireland Direct,** ☎0800 40 00 00; **MCI,** ☎0800 89 02 22; **Sprint,** ☎0800 89 97 77; **Telecom New Zealand,** ☎0800 55 64 11; **Telkom South Africa,** ☎0800 55 85 35.

MAIL. Airmail from Switzerland averages 4-7 days to North America, although times are more unpredictable from smaller towns. Domestic letters take 1-3 days. Address mail to be held according to the following example: Firstname SURNAME, *Postlagernde Briefe,* CH-8021 Zürich, SWITZERLAND.

LANGUAGES. German, French, Italian, and Romansch are the national languages. Most urban Swiss speak English fluently. For basic German words and phrases, see p. 1036; for French, see p. 1035; for Italian, see p. 1038.

PHONE CODES	**Country code: 41. International dialing prefix:** 00. From outside Switzerland, dial int'l dialing prefix (see inside back cover) + 41 + city code + local number.

ACCOMMODATIONS AND CAMPING

SWITZERLAND	❶	❷	❸	❹	❺
ACCOMMODATIONS	under 16SFr	16-35SFr	36-60SFr	61-120SFr	over 120SFr

There are **hostels** (*Jugendherbergen* in German, *Auberges de Jeunesse* in French, *Ostelli* in Italian) in all big cities and in most small towns. **Schweizer Jugendherbergen** (SJH; www.youthhostel.ch) runs HI hostels in Switzerland, where beds are usually 20-34SFr. Non-HI members can stay in any hostel but usually pay a surcharge. The more informal **Swiss Backpackers** (SB) organization (www.backpacker.ch) has 31 hostels for the young, foreign traveler interested in socializing. Most Swiss **campgrounds** are not isolated areas but large plots glutted with RVs. Prices average 6-9SFr per person and 4-10SFr per tent site. **Hotels** and **pensions** tend to charge at least 50-75SFr for a single room, 80-150SFr for a double. The cheapest have *Gasthof*, *Gästehaus*, or *Hotel-Garni* in the name. **Privatzimmer** (rooms in a family home) run about 25-60SFr per person. Breakfast is included at most hotels, pensions, and *Privatzimmer*.

FOOD AND DRINK

SWITZERLAND	❶	❷	❸	❹	❺
FOOD	under 9SFr	9-15SFr	16-24SFr	25-35SFr	over 35SFr

Switzerland is not for the lactose-intolerant. The Swiss are serious about dairy products, from rich and varied **cheeses** to decadent **milk chocolate**—even the major Swiss soft drink, rivella, is dairy. Swiss dishes vary from region to region and what your waiter brings you is most likely related to the language he is speaking. Bernese *Rösti*, a plateful of hash-brown potatoes (sometimes flavored with bacon or cheese), is prevalent in the German regions; cheese or meat **fondue** is popular in the French part. Try Valaisian *raclette*, made by melting cheese over a fire, scraping it onto a baked potato, and garnishing it with meat or vegetables. **Supermarkets** Migros and Co-op double as self-serve cafeterias; stop in for a cheap meal as well as groceries. Each canton has its own local beer—it's relatively cheap, often less expensive than Coca-Cola.

 HIKING AND SKIING. Nearly every town has **hiking trails;** consult the local tourist office. Lucerne (p. 982), Interlaken (p. 984), Grindelwald (p. 986), and Zermatt (p. 986) offer particularly good hiking opportunities. Trails are usually marked with either red-white-red markers (only sturdy boots and hiking poles needed) or blue-white-blue markers (mountaineering equipment needed). **Skiing** in Switzerland is often less expensive than in North America if you avoid pricey resorts. **Ski passes** run 30-50SFr per day, 100-300SFr per week; a week of lift tickets, equipment rental, lessons, lodging, and *demi-pension* (breakfast plus one other meal) averages 475SFr. **Summer skiing** is less common than it once was but is still available in a few towns, such as Zermatt and Saas Fee.

HOLIDAYS AND FESTIVALS

Holidays: New Year's Day (Jan. 1-2); Good Friday (Apr. 9); Easter Monday (Apr. 12); Labor Day (May 1); Swiss National Day (Aug. 1); Christmas (Dec. 25-26).

Festivals: Two raucous festivals are the **Fasnacht** (Carnival; Mar.) in Basel and the **Escalade** (early Dec.) in Geneva. Music festivals occur throughout the summer, including **Open-Air St. Gallen** (late June) and the **Montreux Jazz Festival** (July).

CENTRAL (GERMAN) SWITZERLAND

The cantons in northwest Switzerland are gently beautiful, with excellent museums, a rich Humanist tradition, and charming old town centers. Previously thought of as a financial mecca, the region has begun to change its image with the growing popularity of Interlaken and the cultural attractions of Lucerne.

BERN   ☎ 031

The city (pop. 127,000) has been Switzerland's capital since 1848, but don't expect fast tracks, power politics, or men in suits—the Bernese prefer to focus on the lighter things in life, nibbling the local Toblerone chocolate and lolling along the banks of the serpentine Aare.

▄ TRANSPORTATION

Flights: The Bern-Belp airport (BRN; ☎960 21 11) is 20min. from the city. An airport **bus** runs from the train station 50min. before each flight (10min., 14SFr).

Trains: From the station at Bahnhofpl. to: **Basel** (1¼hr., 4 per hr., 34SFr); **Berlin** (8hr., 14 per day, 245SFr); **Geneva** (2hr., 3 per hr., 47SFr); **Interlaken** (50min., every hr., 23SFr); **Lausanne** (1¼hr., every 30min., 32SFr); **Lucerne** (1½hr., every 30min., 32SFr); **Milan** (3½hr., 6 per day, 72SFr); **Munich** (6hr., 4 per day, 117SFr); **Paris** (4½hr., 4 per day, 109SFr); **Salzburg** (7¼hr., 5 per day, 130SFr); **Zurich** (1¼hr., every 30min., 45SFr). 25% under-27 discount on international fares.

Bike Rental: The small blue **Bernrollt Kiosk** at the train station loans bikes for **free.** A 20SFr deposit and ID required. One-day loan only. Open May-Oct. 7:30am-9:30pm.

▟ ⁊ ORIENTATION AND PRACTICAL INFORMATION

Most of medieval Bern lies in front of the train station and along the Aare River. Bern's main **train station** is a stressful tangle of essential services and extraneous shops. Take extra **caution** around the Parliament park, especially at night.

Tourist Office: (☎328 12 12), on the street level of the train station. In summer, daily **city tours** (14-27SFr) are available by bus, on foot, or by raft. Open June-Sept. daily 9am-8:30pm; Oct.-May M-Sa 9am-6:30pm, Su 10am-5pm.

Embassies: Canada, Kirchenfeldstr. 88 (☎357 32 00). **Ireland,** Kirchenfeldstr. 68 (☎352 14 42). **South Africa,** Alpenstr. 29 (☎350 13 13). **UK,** Thunstr. 50 (☎359 77 00). **US,** Jubiläumstr. 93 (☎357 70 11).

Bi-Gay-Lesbian Resources: Homosexuelle Arbeitsgruppe die Schweiz (HACH), Mühlenpl. 11, is the headquarters of Switzerland's largest gay organization.

Emergency: Police ☎**117, Ambulance** ☎**144.**

Internet Access: Stadtbibliothek (City Library), Münsterg. 61. 4SFr per hr. in the *Medienraum.* Open M-Tu and Th-F 10am-9pm, W noon-9pm, Sa 8am-noon. Basement of **Jäggi Bücher,** Spitalg. on Bubenbergpl. 47-51, in the Loeb department store. 2 computers allow 20min. of **free** access; 4 other terminals cost 5SFr per 30min. Open M-W and F 9am-6:30pm, Th 9am-9pm, Sa 8am-4pm.

Bern

▲ ACCOMMODATIONS
Backpackers Bern/
Hotel Glocke, **6**
Hotel Nydeck, **7**
Jugendherberge (HI), **9**

⊛ FOOD
Kornhaus Keller, **4**
Manora, **8**
Restaurant du Nord, **2**
Restaurant Peking, **3**

★ NIGHTLIFE
Pery Bar, **5**
Reitschule/
Sous Le Pont, **1**

SWITZERLAND

Post Office: Schanzenpost 1, a block from the train station. Open M-F 7:30am-9pm, Sa 8am-4pm, Su 5-9pm. Address mail to be held: Firstname SURNAME, *Postlagernde Briefe*, Schanzenpost 3000, Bern, SWITZERLAND. **Postal Codes:** CH-3000 to CH-3030.

ACCOMMODATIONS

Bern has responded to the influx of backpackers with several new hostels. All offer clean beds with varying services, prices, and personal touches. If the cheaper options are all full, check the tourist office's list of private rooms.

Backpackers Bern/Hotel Glocke, Rathausg. 75 (☎311 37 71). From the train station, cross the tram lines, turn left on Spitalg., continuing onto Marktg; turn left at Kornhauspl., then right on Rathausg. Clean, new, and ideally located. Shoot pool and watch CNN. Internet 2SFr. Reception daily 8-11am and 3-10pm. Dorms 29SFr; singles 75SFr; doubles 120SFr, with bath 150SFr. AmEx/DC/MC/V. ❷

Jugendherberge (HI), Weiherg. 4 (☎311 63 16). From the station, go down Christoffelg; take the stairs to the left of the park entrance gates and go down the steep slope, turn left on Weiherg. Near the river. Breakfast included. Reception June-Sept. daily 7-10am and 3pm-midnight; Oct.-May 7-10am and 5pm-midnight. Closed Jan. Dorms 30SFr; overflow mattresses 22SFr. Nonmembers add 6SFr. MC/V. ❷

Hotel Nydeck, Gerechtigkeitsg. 1 (☎311 86 86), sits above the busy Junkere bar. Take tram #12 to *Nydegg*. Bright pastel rooms include TV, phone, and bathroom. Breakfast 10SFr. Singles 90-110SFr; doubles 130-160SFr. MC/V. ❹

FOOD

Almost every *Platz* overflows with cafes and restaurants. Try one of Bern's hearty specialties: *Gschnätzlets* (fried veal, beef, or pork), *Suurchabis* (a kind of sauerkraut), *Gschwellti* (steamed potatoes), or Toblerone chocolate. **Fruit** and **vegetable markets** sell produce daily at Bärenpl. and every Tuesday and Saturday on Bundespl. (Open May-Oct. 8am-6pm.)

Restaurant du Nord, Lorrainestr. 2, across Lorrainebr. Take bus #20 to *Gewerbeschule*. A diverse crowd smokes and socializes. Creative dishes. Meat entrees 22-32SFr. Pasta plates from 17SFr, Su night Indian specials. Kitchen open M-Sa 11:30am-2pm and 6:30-10pm, Su 6-10pm. Open M-F 8am-12:30am, Sa 9am-12:30am. MC/V. ❸

Restaurant Peking, Speicherg. 27, off Waisenhauspl. Some of the only palatable Chinese takeout in the Germanic world. Takeout 10SFr; sit-down 12-15SFr. Open M-Sa 11am-2:30pm and 6-11:30pm. ❷

Kornhaus Keller, Kornhauspl. 18. Vaulted, frescoed ceilings, golden kegs, and candlelight—all the trappings of gourmet. Try the beef medallions with risotto (39SFr) or mushroom ravioli (24SFr). Open M-Sa 11:45am-2:30pm and 6pm-1:30am, Su 11:45am-2:30pm and 6pm-11:30pm. MC/V. ❹

Manora, Bubenbergpl. 5A, near the station. Self-service chain with big platefuls that are nutritious and cheap. Open M-Sa 6:30am-10:45pm, Su 8:30am-10:45pm. ❶

SIGHTS

THE OLD TOWN. The massive ■**Bundeshaus,** center of the Swiss government, dominates the Aare. *(45min. tour every hr. M-Sa 9-11am and 2-4pm. Free.)* From the Bundeshaus, Kocherg. and Herreng. lead to the 15th-century Protestant **Münster** (cathedral); above the main entrance, a golden sculpture depicts the torments of Hell. For a fantastic view of the city, climb the Münster's 100m spire. *(Open Easter-Oct. Su 11:30am-4:30pm, Tu-Sa 10am-5pm; Nov.-Easter Su 11am-2pm, Tu-F 10am-noon and 2-4pm, Sa 10am-noon and 2-5pm. Tower 3SFr.)* Several walkways lead steeply down from the Bundeshaus to the ⬛**Aare River;** on hotter days, locals dive like lemmings from the banks and the bridges to take a ride on its swift currents, but only experienced swimmers should join in.

KUNSTMUSEUM. Bern's Kunstmuseum includes the world's largest Paul Klee collection and a smattering of big 20th-century names: Giacometti, Ernst Kirchner, Picasso, and Pollock. *(Hodlerstr. 8-12, near Lorrainebrücke. Open Su and W-Sa 10am-5pm, Tu 10am-9pm. 15SFr, students and seniors 10SFr; 7/5SFr for Klee collection only.)*

BEAR PITS AND ROSE GARDEN. Across the Nydeggbr. lie the **Bärengraben** (bear pits), which were recently renovated to provide the bears with trees and rocks to clamber over—perhaps an attempt to make up for the indignity of being on display for the gawking crowds. *(Open June-Sept. daily 9am-5:30pm; Oct.-May 10am-4pm.)* The tourist office here presents **The Bern Show,** a slick recap of Bernese history. *(Every 20min. Free.)* The path snaking up the hill to the left leads to the ⬛**Rosengarten** (Rose Garden), which provides one of the best views of Bern's *Altstadt.*

BERNISCHES HISTORISCHE MUSEUM. Anything and everything relating to Bern's long history, from technology to religious art to 15th-century sculptures, is displayed in this jam-packed museum. *(Helvetiapl. 5. Open Su, Tu and Th-Sa 10am-5pm, W 10am-8pm. 13SFr, students 8SFr, under-16 4SFr.)*

ALBERT EINSTEIN'S HOUSE. This small apartment where Einstein conceived the theory of general relativity is now filled with his photos and letters. *(Kramg. 49. Open Feb.-Nov. Tu-F 10am-5pm, Sa 10am-4pm. 3SFr, students 2SFr.)*

🎵 🎭 ENTERTAINMENT AND NIGHTLIFE

Check out *Bewegungsmelder*, available at the tourist office, for events. July's **Gurten Festival** (www.gurtenfestival.ch) has attracted such luminaries as Bob Dylan, Elvis Costello, and Björk, while jazz-lovers arrive in early May for the **International Jazz Festival** (www.jazzfestivalbern.ch). However, Bern's best-known festival is probably the off-the-wall **onion market** on the fourth Monday in November. The orange grove at **Stadgärtnerei Elfnau** (take tram #19 to Elfnau) has free Sunday concerts in summer. From mid-July to mid-August, **OrangeCinema** (www.orangecinema.ch) screens recently released films in the open air; tickets are available from the tourist office in the train station.

At night, the fashionable folk linger in the *Altstadt*'s bars and cafes while a leftist crowd gathers under the gargoyles of the Lorrainebrücke, behind the station down Bollwerk. **Pery Bar,** Schmiedenpl. 3, is a classic see-and-be-seen bar. (Open M-W 5pm-1:30am, Th 5pm-2:30am, F-Sa 5pm-3:30am.) The **Reitschule,** Neubrückstr. 8, is a cultural center for Bern's counterculture; graffitied **Sous le Pont** serves beer (3.50SFr), indie rock, and hip-hop. From Bollwerk, head left before Lorrainebrücke through the cement park. (Open Tu 11:30am-12:30am, W-Th 11:30am-2:30pm and 6pm-12:30am, F 11:30am-2:30pm and 6pm-2:30am, Sa 6pm-2:30am.)

BASEL (BÂLE)   ☎ 061

Situated on the Rhine near France and Germany, Basel is home to a large medieval quarter as well as one of the oldest universities in Switzerland—graduates include Erasmus and Nietzsche. Visitors can view art from Roman times to the 20th century and be serenaded by musicians on every street corner year-round.

☎🗈 TRANSPORTATION AND PRACTICAL INFORMATION. Basel has three **train stations:** the French (SNCF) and Swiss (SBB) stations on Centralbahnpl., near the Altstadt, and the German (DB) station across the Rhine. **Trains** leave from the SBB to: Bern (1¼hr., every hr. 5:50am-11:50pm, 34SFr); Geneva (3hr., every hr. 6:20am-8:45pm, 71SFr); Lausanne (2½hr., every hr. 6am-10:30pm, 60SFr); Zurich (1hr., every 15-30min. 4:40am-midnight, 30SFr). Make international connections at the French (SNCF) or German (DB) stations. 25% discount on international trips for ages 16-25. To reach the **tourist office,** Schifflände 5, from the SBB station, take tram #1 to Schifflände; the office is on the river, near the Mittlere Rheinbrücke. (☎268 68 68. Open M-F 8:30am-6pm, Sa-Su 10am-4pm.) For information on **bi, gay, and lesbian** establishments, stop by **Arcados,** Rheing. 69, at Clarapl. (☎681 31 32. Open Tu-F noon-7pm, Sa 11am-4pm.) To reach the **post office,** Rüdeng 1., take tram #1 or 8 to Marktpl. and backtrack one block, away from the river. (Open M-W and F 7:30am-6:30pm, Th 7:30am-8pm, Sa 8am-noon.) **Poste Restante:** Postlagernde Briefe für Firstname SURNAME, Rüdengasse, CH-4001 Basel, Switzerland.

🗈🖸 ACCOMMODATIONS AND FOOD. Basel's shortcoming is its lack of cheap lodgings. Call ahead to ensure a spot at the only hostel in town, the **Jugendherberge (HI) ❷,** St. Alban-Kirchrain 10. To get there, take tram #2 to Kunstmuseum; turn right on St. Alban-Vorstadt, then follow the signs. (☎272 05 72. Internet 10SFr per hr. Breakfast included. Laundry 7SFr. Reception Mar.-Oct. 7-10am and 2-11pm; Nov.-Feb. 2-11pm. Check-out 10am. Dorms 29-31SFr; singles 79SFr; doubles 98SFr. Jan.-Feb. 19 and Nov.-Dec. 2.50SFr less. Nonmembers add 6SFr. AmEx/MC/V.) For **Hotel Steinenschanze ❹,** Steinengraben 69, turn left on Centralbahnstr. from the SBB and follow signs for Heuwaage; go up the ramp under the bridge to Steinengraben and turn left. (☎272 53 53. Breakfast included. Reception 24hr. Singles 110-180SFr, under-25 with ISIC 60SFr for up to 3 nights; doubles with shower 160-250SFr, 100SFr. AmEx/MC/V.)

Barfüsserpl., Marktpl., and the streets connecting them are especially full of restaurants. **Wirtshaus zum Schnabel ❷,** Trillengässlein 2, serves tasty German fare. (Open M-Sa 9am-midnight. AmEx/MC/V.) Vegetarians can dine at **Restaurant Gleich ❸,** Leonhardsberg 1. (Open M-F 9am-9:30pm.) Head to **Migros supermarket,** in the SBB station, for groceries. (Open M-F 6am-10pm, Sa-Su 7:30am-10pm.)

🖸 SIGHTS. *Groß-Basel* (Greater Basel) and the train station are separated from *Klein-Basel* (Lesser Basel) by the Rheine. The very red **Rathaus** brightens Marktpl. in *Groß-Basel* with its blinding façade and gold and green statues. Behind the Marktpl. is the 775-year-old **Mittlere Rheinbrücke** (Middle Rhine Bridge) which connects the two halves of Basel. At the other end of Marktpl. is a spectacular **Jean Tinguely Fountain,** also known as the **Fasnachtsbrunnen.** Behind Marktpl. stands the red sandstone **Münster,** where you can visit the tomb of Erasmus or climb the tower for a spectacular view of the city. (Open Easter-Oct.15 M-F 10am-5pm, Sa 10am-4pm, Su 1-5pm; Oct. 16-Easter M-Sa 11am-4pm, Su 2-4pm. Free. Tower closes 30min. before the church. 3SFr.)

MONSTER MADNESS In 1529, Basel's residents spiritedly joined the Reformation and ousted the bishop, keeping his *crozier* (staff) as the town's emblem. The staff shares this honor with the basilisk (Basel-isk), a creature part serpent, part dragon, and part rooster, which caused what may be the world's first and only public trial and execution of a chicken. In 1474, a hen allegedly laid an egg on a dung heap under a full moon, an action sure to hatch the horrible creature. The bird was tried, found guilty, and beheaded, and the egg was ceremonially burnt.

MUSEUMS AND ENTERTAINMENT. Basel has over 30 museums; pick up the comprehensive museum guide at the tourist office. The **Basel Card,** available at the tourist office, provides admission to all museums as well as discounts around town. (24hr. card 25SFr, 48hr. card 33SFr, 72hr. card 45SFr.) The ▨**Kunstmuseum** (Museum of Fine Arts), St. Alban-Graben 16, houses outstanding collections of old and new masters; admission also gives access to the **Museum für Gegenwartskunst** (Modern Art), St. Alban-Rheinweg 60. (Kunstmuseum open Tu and Th-Su 10am-5pm, W 10am-7pm. Gegenwartskunst open Tu-Su 11am-5pm. 10SFr, students 8SFr, first Su of every month free.) At ▨**Museum Jean Tinguely,** Grenzacherstr. 214a, everything rattles and shakes in homage to the Swiss sculptor's vision of metal and movement. Take tram #2 or 15 to Wettsteinpl. and bus #31 or 36 to Museum Tinguely. (Open W-Su 11am-7pm. 7SFr, students 5SFr.) The **Fondation Beyeler,** Baselstr. 101, is one of Europe's finest private art collections, housing works by nearly every major artist. Take tram #6 to Fondation Beyeler. (Open daily 9am-8pm. M-F 16SFr, Sa-Su 20SFr; students 5SFr; 12SFr after 6pm.)

In a year-round party town, Basel's carnival, or **Fasnacht,** still manages to distinguish itself. The festivities commence the Monday before Lent with the *Morgestraich,* a not-to-be-missed, 600-year-old, 72hr. parade beginning at 4am. The goal is to scare away winter (it rarely succeeds). During the rest of the year, head to **Barfüsserplatz** for an evening of bar-hopping. **Atlantis,** Klosterberg 10, is a multi-level, sophisticated bar with reggae, jazz, and funk. (Open Tu-Th 11am-midnight, F 11:30am-4am, Sa 6pm-4am.) **Brauerei Fischerstube,** Rheing. 45, brews the delectably sharp ▨*Hell Spezial* ("light special") beer. (Open M-Th 10am-midnight, F-Sa 10am-1am, Su 5pm-midnight. Full dinner menu from 6pm.)

LUCERNE (LUZERN) ☎041

Lucerne (pop. 60,000) is the Swiss traveler's dream come true. The old city is engaging, the lake is placid, and sunrise over the famous Mt. Pilatus has hypnotized hikers and artists—including Twain, Wagner, and Goethe—for centuries.

TRANSPORTATION AND PRACTICAL INFORMATION. Trains leave Bahnhofpl. for: Basel (1¼hr., 1-2 per hr. 4:40am-11:50pm, 29SFr); Bern (1½hr., 1-2 per hr. 4:40am-11:50pm, 30SFr); Geneva (3½hr., every hr. 4:40am-9:55pm, 64SFr); Interlaken (2hr., every hr. 6:30am-7:35pm, 26SFr); Lausanne (2½hr., every hr. 4:40am-9:55pm, 56SFr); Lugano (3hr., every hr. 6:40am-10:15pm, 56SFr); and Zurich (1hr., 2 per hr. 4:55am-11:10pm, 20SFr). VBL **buses** depart from in front of the station and provide extensive coverage of Lucerne (1 zone 2.40SFr, 2 zones 3.60SFr, 3 zones 5.60SFr; day pass 9SFr); route maps are available at the tourist office. The **tourist office,** in the station, offers free city guides, makes reservations, and sells the **Visitor's Card.** (☎227 17 17. Open May-Oct. daily 9am-6:30pm; Nov.-Apr. M-F 8:30am-5:30pm, Sa-Su 9am-6pm.) **C&A Clothing,** on Hertensteinstr. at the top of the *Altstadt,* has two free but busy **Internet** terminals. (Open M-W 9am-6:30pm, Th-F 9am-9pm, Sa 8:30am-1pm.) The **post office** is by the train station. Address mail to be held: Firstname SURNAME, *Postlagernde Briefe,* Hauptpost, **CH-6000** Luzern 1, SWITZERLAND. (Open M-F 7:30am-6:30pm, Sa 8am-noon.)

ACCOMMODATIONS AND FOOD. Inexpensive beds are limited, so call ahead. To reach ▨**Backpackers ❷,** Alpenquai 42, turn right from the station on Inseliquai and follow it until it turns into Alpenquai (20min.); the hostel is on the right. (☎360 04 20. Bikes 16SFr per day. Internet 10SFr per hr. Reception daily 7:30-10am and 4-11pm. Dorms 27-33SFr.) Until 1998, **Hotel Löwengraben ❷,** Löwengraben ▨8, was a prison; now it's a trendy, clean hostel with a bar, a restaurant, and dance parties every summer Saturday. (☎417 12 12. Breakfast 11SFr. 3- to 4-bed dorms 40SFr; singles 110-160SFr; doubles 160-220SFr.) **Markets** along the river sell cheap, fresh goods on Tuesday and Saturday mornings. There's also a **Migros supermarket** at the train station. (Open M-W and Sa 6:30am-8pm, Th-F 6:30am-9pm, Su 8am-8pm.)

◨◧ **SIGHTS AND NIGHTLIFE.** The *Altstadt*, across the river over Spreuerbrücke from the station, is famous for its frescoed houses; the best examples are those on Hirschenpl. and Weinmarkt. The 14th-century **Kapellbrücke**, a wooden-roofed bridge, runs from left of the train station to the *Altstadt* and is decorated with Swiss historical scenes; further down the river, the **Spreuerbrücke** is decorated by Kaspar Meglinger's eerie *Totentanz* (Dance of Death) paintings. On the hills above the river, the **Museggmauer** and its towers are all that remain of the medieval city's ramparts. Three of the towers are accessible to visitors and provide panoramas of the city; walk along St. Karliquai, head uphill to the right, and follow the brown castle signs. (Open daily 8am-7pm.) To the east is the magnificent **Löwendenkmal** (Lion Monument), the dying lion of Lucerne, which is carved into a cliff on Denkmalstr. The ▨**Picasso Museum**, Am Rhyn Haus, Furreng. 21, displays 200 intimate photographs of Picasso as well as a large collection of his lesser-known works. From Schwanenpl., take Rathausquai to Furreng. (Open Apr.-Oct. daily 10am-6pm; Nov.-Mar. 11am-5pm. 8SFr, students 5SFr.) The ▨**Verkehrshaus der Schweiz** (Swiss Transport Museum), Lidostr. 5, has interactive displays on all kinds of vehicles, but the real highlight is the warehouse of trains. Take bus #6, 8, or 24 to *Verkehrshaus*. (Open Apr.-Oct. daily 10am-6pm; Nov.-Mar. 10am-5pm. 21SFr, students 19SFr, with Eurail 14SFr.)

Lucerne's nightlife is more about lingering than club-hopping, although the candle-lit **Club 57,** Haldenstr. 57, has DJs spin on the weekends. (Beer 4-6SFr. Open daily 8pm-2:30am, F-Sa until 4am.) The mellower **Jazz Cantine,** Grabenstr. 8, is a product of the Jazz School of Lucerne. (Sandwiches 6-8SFr. Open M-Sa 7am-12:30am, Su 4pm-12:30am.) Lucerne attracts big names for its two jazz festivals: **Blue Balls Festival** (July 23-31, 2004) and **Blues Festival** (Nov. 8-14, 2004.)

▣ **DAYTRIPS FROM LUCERNE: MT. PILATUS AND RIGI KULM.** The view of the Alps from the top of **Mt. Pilatus** (2132m) is absolutely phenomenal. For the most memorable trip, catch a boat from Lucerne to Alpnachstad (1½hr.), ascend by the world's steepest **cogwheel train,** then descend by cable car to Krienz and take the bus back to Lucerne (entire trip 80SFr; with Eurail or SwissPass 40-43SFr). For less money and more exercise, take a train or boat to Hergiswill and hike up to Fräkmüntegg (3hr.), then get on the cable car at the halfway point (23SFr round-trip, with Eurail 19SFr.) Fräkmüntegg also operates central Switzerland's longest *Rodelbahn* course; for 7SFr, you whizz down the hillside on a plastic slide that achieves surprising speeds. Across the sea from Pilatus soars the **Rigi Kulm** (1800m), which has a magnificent view of the lake; watching the sunrise from the summit is a Lucerne must. **Ferries** run from Lucerne to Vitznau, where you can catch a cogwheel train to the top. You can also conquer Rigi on foot; it's 5hr. from Vitznau to the top. Return by train, take the cable car from Rigi Kaltbad to Weggis, and head back to Lucerne by boat (round-trip 87SFr; with Eurail 29SFr.)

ZURICH (ZÜRICH) ☎01

Battalions of briefcase-toting executives charge daily through the world's largest gold exchange and fourth-largest stock exchange, pumping enough money into the economy to keep Zurich's upper-crust boutiques thriving. Once the focal point of the Reformation in German Switzerland, 20th-century Zurich (pop. 363,000) enjoyed an avant-garde radicalism that attracted progressive thinkers; while James Joyce wrote *Ulysses* in one corner of the city, an exiled Vladimir Lenin read Marx and dreamt of revolution in another. A walk through Zurich's student quarter immerses you in the energetic counter-culture that encouraged such thinkers, only footsteps away from the deep capitalism of the Bahnhofstr. shopping district.

TRANSPORTATION

Flights: Kloten Airport (☎816 25 00) is a major stop for Swiss International Airlines (☎084 885 20 00). Daily connections to Frankfurt, Paris, London, and New York. Trains connect the airport to the *Hauptbahnhof* in the city center (every 10-20min. 5am-midnight, 5.40SFr; Eurail and SwissPass valid).

Trains: Bahnhofpl. To: **Basel** (1hr., 1-2 per hr., 30SFr); **Bern** (1¼hr., 1-2 per hr., 45SFr); **Geneva** via **Bern** (3hr., every hr. 6am-10pm, 76SFr); **Lucerne** (1hr., 2 per hr. 6am-midnight, 20SFr); **Milan** (4hr., every hr. 6:30am-10pm, 72SFr); **Munich** (5hr., every hour 6am-10pm, 86SFr); **Paris** (5hr., every hour 6:30am-midnight, 133SFr); **Salzburg** (5hr., every hour 6am-7pm, 97SFr); **Vienna** (9hr., every hour 6am-6pm, 124SFr). Under-26 discount on international trains.

Public Transportation: Trams criss-cross the city, originating at the *Hauptbahnhof.* Tickets for rides longer than 5 stops cost 3.60SFr and are valid for one hour (press the blue button on automatic ticket machines); rides less than 5 cost 2.10SFr (yellow button). Policemen won't hesitate to fine you (60SFr) if you try to be a *Schwarzfahrer* (Black Rider) and ride for free. If you plan to ride several times, buy a 24hr. **Tageskarte** (7.20SFr), which is valid on trams, buses, and ferries. **Night buses** run from city center to outlying areas (F-Su 1am-4am).

Taxis: Hail a cab or call ☎777 77 77, 444 44 44, or 222 22 22.

Car Rental: As a rule, try to rent in the city, as renting at the airport involves a 40% tax. The tourist office maintains a special deal with **Europcar** (☎804 46 46; www.europcar.ch) involving a free upgrade to a nicer car. Prices start at 149SFr for 1-2 days. Minimum age 20. **Branches** at the airport (☎813 20 44; fax 813 49 00), Josefstr. 53 (☎271 56 56), and Lindenstr. 33 (☎383 17 47).

Bike Rental: Bike loans are free at **Globus** (☎079 336 36 10); **Enge** (☎079 336 36 12); and **Hauptbahnhof** (☎210 13 88), at the very end of track 18. With passport and 20SFr deposit, same day return. Open daily May-Oct 7:00am-9:30pm.

Hitchhiking: Hitchhiking is illegal on highways. Hitchhikers to Basel, Geneva, or Paris often take tram #4 to *Werdhölzli* or bus #33 to *Pfingstweidstr.* Those bound for Lucerne, Italy, and Austria report taking tram #9 or 14 to *Bahnhof Wiedikon* and walking down Schimmelstr. to Silhölzli. For Munich, hitchhikers have been seen taking S1 or S8 to *Wiedikon* and getting picked up at Seebahnstr. *Let's Go* does not recommend hitchhiking as a safe means of transport.

ORIENTATION AND PRACTICAL INFORMATION

Zurich is in north-central Switzerland, close to the German border, on some of the lowest land in the country. The **Limmat River** splits the city down the middle on its way to the **Zürichsee.** On the west side of the river are the **Hauptbahnhof** and **Bahnhofstraße.** Two-thirds of the way down Bahnhofstr. lies **Paradeplatz,** the town center. On the east side of the river is the University district, which stretches above the narrow **Niederdorfstraße** and pulses with bars, hip restaurants, and hostels.

Tourist Offices: Main office (☎215 40 00; free reservation service ☎215 40 40), in the main train station. An electronic hotel reservation board is at the front of the station. Open April-Oct. M-Sa 8am-8:30pm, Su 8:30am-6:30pm; Nov.-Mar. M-Sa 8:30am-7pm, Su 9am-6:30pm. For bikers and backpackers, the **Touring Club der Schweiz** (TCS), Alfred-Escher-Str. 38 (☎286 86 86), offers maps and travel info.

Currency Exchange: At the main train station. Cash advances with DC/MC/V and photo ID; 200SFr minimum. Open daily 6:30am-10pm. **Credit Suisse,** Bahnhofstr. 53. 2.50SFr commission. Open daily 6am-10pm.

Luggage Storage: At the station one level below ground. Lockers 5-8SFr per day; 72hr. maximum. Luggage watch 7SFr at the *Gepäck* counter. Open daily 6am-10:50pm.

Libraries: Zentralbibliothek, Zähringerpl. 6 (☎268 31 00). Open M-F 8am-8pm, Sa 8am-4pm. **Pestalozzi Bibliothek,** Zähringerstr. 17 (☎261 78 11), has foreign magazines and newspapers. Open M-F 10am-7pm, Sa 10am-4pm. Internet 1SFr per 10min.

Bi-Gay-Lesbian Organizations: Homosexuelle Arbeitsgruppe Zürich (HAZ), Sihlquai 67 (☎271 22 50; www.haz.ch), offers a library, meetings, and the free newsletter *InfoSchwül.* Open Su noon-2pm and 6-11pm, Tu-F 7:30-11pm.

Laundromat: Speed Wash Self Service Wascherei, Weinbergstr. 37 (☎242 99 14). Wash and dry 10.20SFr per 5kg. Open M-Sa 7am-10pm, Su 10:30am-10pm.

Public Showers and Toilets: McClean Toiletten, at the train station. Toilets 1-2SFr. Showers 12SFr for 20min., including 2 towels and shower gel. Open 6am-midnight. Clean enough to eat off the floor, though *Let's Go* does not recommend doing so.

Emergencies: Police, ☎117. **Fire,** ☎118. **Ambulance,** ☎144.

24-Hour Pharmacy: Bahnhofpl. 15 at the main station (☎225 42 42).

Internet Access: The **ETH Library,** Ramistr. 101 (☎631 21 35), in the *Hauptgebäude,* has three free computers. Take tram #6, 9, or 10 to *ETH,* enter the main building, and take the elevator to floor H. Open M-F 8:30am-9pm, Sa 9am-2pm. **Quanta Virtual Fun Space,** Limmatquai 94 (☎260 72 66), at the corner of Muehleg. and Niederdorfstr. Open daily 9am-midnight. **Internet Café,** Uraniastr. 3, (☎210 33 11) in the Urania Parkhaus. 5SFr per 20min. Open M-Sa 9am-midnight, Su 11am-11pm. **Telefon Corner,** downstairs in the station. 6SFr per hr. Open daily 8am-10pm.

Post Office: Main office, Sihlpost, Kasernestr. 97, just behind the station. Open M-F 6:30am-10:30pm, Sa 6am-8pm, Su 11am-10:30pm. Address mail to be held: Firstname, LASTNAME, Sihlpost, Postlagernde Briefe, **CH-8021** Zurich, SWITZERLAND.

▟ ACCOMMODATIONS

The few budget accommodations in Zurich are easily accessible via public transportation. Reserve at least a day in advance, especially in the summer.

Martahaus, Zähringerstr. 36 (☎251 45 50). Three walls and a thick curtain separate you from your neighbors, often American college students. Breakfast and Internet access included. Reception 24hr. Dorms 38SFr. Singles in summer 85SFr, off-season 114SFr; doubles 98/135SFr; quads 200SFr. With private bath add 30-60SFr. AmEx/DC/MC/V. The owners also run the nearby **Luther pension,** a women-only residence that shares reception. Dorms 30SFr, singles 50SFr. ❸

Hotel Foyer Hottingen, Hottingenstr. 31 (☎256 19 19). Take tram #3 (dir.: Kluspl.) to *Hottingenpl.* Families and backpackers fill this renovated house, a block from the Kunsthaus. In-house chapel. Women-only and mixed dorms. Breakfast, lockers, and kitchen included. Reception daily 7am-11pm. Dorms 35SFr; singles 70SFr, with bath 105SFr; doubles 110/150SFr; triples 140/190SFr; quads 180SFr. MC/V. ❷

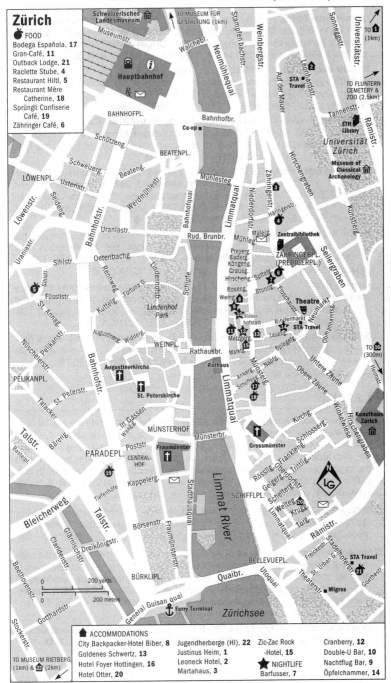

Zürich

FOOD
Bodega Española, 17
Gran-Café, 11
Outback Lodge, 21
Raclette Stube, 4
Restaurant Hiltl, 5
Restaurant Mère
Catherine, 18
Sprüngli Confiserie
Café, 19
Zähringer Café, 6

SWITZERLAND

ACCOMMODATIONS
City Backpacker-Hotel Biber, 8
Goldenes Schwertz, 13
Hotel Foyer Hottingen, 16
Hotel Otter, 20

Jugendherberge (HI), 22
Justinus Heim, 1
Leoneck Hotel, 2
Martahaus, 3

Zic-Zac Rock
-Hotel, 15

★ NIGHTLIFE
Barfusser, 7

Cranberry, 12
Double-U Bar, 10
Nachtflug Bar, 9
Öpfelchammer, 14

Justinus Heim Zürich, Freudenbergstr. 146 (☎361 38 06; justinuszh@bluewin.ch). Take tram #9 to *Seilbahn Rigiblick*, then take the funicular. Quiet, private rooms. Breakfast included. Reception daily 8am-noon and 5-9pm. Singles 35-50SFr, with shower 60SFr; doubles 80-100SFr; triples 120-140SFr; rates reduced for long stays. ❸

The City Backpacker-Hotel Biber, Niederdorfstr. 5 (☎251 90 15). With the Niederdorf nightlife outside, you may not even need to use your bunk-bed. Lockers available; bring a lock. Sheets 3SFr. Internet access 12SFr per hr. Reception daily 8am-noon and 3-10pm. Checkout 10am. Dorms 29SFr; singles 66SFr; doubles 88-92SFr. MC/V. ❷

Hotel Otter, Oberdorfstr. 7 (☎251 22 07), and the swanky **Wuste Bar** below attract not-so-starving-artists. Shared bathrooms. Breakfast included. Reception daily 8am-4pm in hotel, 4pm-midnight in bar. Laundry 15 SFr. Rooms have TV, phone, fridge, and sink. Singles 100SFr; doubles 130-160SFr. AmEx/MC/V. ❹

Jugendherberge Zürich (HI), Mutschellenstr. 114 (☎482 35 44). Take tram #7 to *Morgental* and walk back 5min. past the Migros. Beer on tap; 24-hour snack bar. Breakfast included. Buffet lunch and dinner 13SFr. Internet access 1SFr per 4min. Reception 24hr. Check-in 2pm. Check-out 10am. Dorms 38SFr; singles with bath 58SFr; doubles with bath 99SFr. Nonmembers add 6SFr. AmEx/MC/V. ❷

Zic-Zac Rock-Hotel, Marktg. 17 (☎261 21 81). Each room in this hostel is named after a band, with a slant towards Elvis. Rooms have TV, phone, and sink. Reception 24hr. Singles 75SFr, with shower 90SFr; doubles 120-135/160SFr; triples 156/168SFr; quads with shower 260SFr. 10% ISIC discount. AmEx/DC/MC/V. ❹

Leoneck Hotel, Leonhardstr. 1 (☎254 22 22). Bovine-themed rooms above the **Crazy Cow** restaurant. Serves families and business-people. Rooms include bath, phone, and TV. Currency exchange available. Reception 24hr. Singles 100-140SFr; doubles 150-185SFr; triples 185-240SFr; quads 240-290SFr. AmEx/DC/MC/V. ❹

Goldenes Schwertz, Marktg. 14 (☎266 18 18). Above two gay-friendly discos (free cover if you're staying in the hotel). Breakfast (15SFr) served in-room. Attentive English-speaking staff. Reception 6:30am-11pm. Checkout noon. Singles 130-150; doubles 155-235. AmEx/DC/MC/V. ❺

FOOD

Zurich's over 1300 restaurants run the gamut. The cheapest meals are available at *Würstli* stands for about 5SFr. For heartier appetites, Zurich prides itself on *Geschnetzeltes mit Rösti*, thinly-sliced veal (often liver or kidney) in cream sauce with hash-brown potatoes. Check out the *Swiss Backpacker News* (found at the tourist office, Hotel Biber, and Martahaus) for info on budget meals in Zurich. The **farmer's markets** at Burklipl. (Tu and F 6am-11am) and Rosenhof (Th 10am-8pm and Sa 10am-5pm) sell fruit, flowers, and veggies.

Bodega Española, Münsterg. 15. Catalan delights served by charismatic waiters since 1874. Egg-and-potato tortilla dishes 15.50SFr. Yummy *tapas* 4.80SFr. Kitchen open noon-2pm and 6-10pm. Open daily 10am-midnight. AmEx/DC/MC/V. ❷

Sprüngli Confiserie Café, Paradepl., is a Zurich landmark, founded by one of the original Lindt chocolate makers. Women in matching red business suits assist customers in their quest for the perfect confection. Pick up a handful of the bite-size Luxemburgerli (8SFr per 100g), try the homemade ice cream, or eat a full meal (20-26SFr). Confectionary open M-F 7:30am-8pm, Sa 8am-4pm. Cafe open M-F 7:30am-6:30pm, Sa 8am-6pm, Su 9:30am-5:30pm. AmEx/DC/MC/V. ❸

Gran-Café, Limmatquai 66. Across from the rushing Limmat River. Think *Great Gatsby*. Save room for sundaes (6-8SFr). Open daily 7:30am-11:30pm. AmEx/MC/V. ❷

Restaurant Mère Catherine, Nägelihof 8. Yuppie restaurant hidden on a small street near the Großmünster, in a building constructed in 1565. Serves mainly provençal French dishes (from 22SFr) and wine. Daily fish special from the Zürichsee. Open Su-W 11:30am-10pm, Th-Sa 11:30am-10:30pm. AmEx/DC/MC/V. ❸

Restaurant Hiltl, Sihlstr. 28. Munch carrot sticks with the vegetarian elite. All-day salad buffet (3.90SFr per 100g; 15SFr for large salad), and Indian buffet at night (same price). Open M-Sa 7am-11pm, Su 11am-11pm. AmEx/DC/V/MC. ❷

Raclette Stube, Zähringerstr. 16. Family-oriented Swiss restaurant. All-you-can-eat *raclette* 33SFr per person. Open daily from 6pm to about 11pm. ❹

Zähringer Café, Zähringerpl. 11. Sip coffee, tea, or Italian soda with a young crowd and fill your stomach with stir-fry (from 16SFr). Open M 6pm-midnight, Tu-Th and Su 8am-midnight, F-Sa 8am-12:30am. ❷

Outback Lodge, Stadelhoferstr. 18. Foster's beer on tap (4.20SFr), crocodile dishes (35SFr), and a generally Aussie atmosphere. 18+ after 6pm. Open M-F 9am-midnight, Sa-Su 11:30am-2am. AmEx/V/MC. ❹

🄶 SIGHTS

It's virtually inconceivable to start a tour of Zurich anywhere but the stately **Bahnhofstraße.** This famous causeway of capitalism bustles with shoppers during the day but falls dead quiet at 6pm. At the Zürichsee end of Bahnhofstr., **Bürkliplatz** is a good place to explore the lake shore. The *Platz* itself hosts a colorful Saturday **flea market** (May-Oct. 6am-3pm). On the other side of the river, the pedestrian zone continues on Niederdorfstr. and Münsterg., where shops run from the ritzy to the raunchy. Off of Niederdorfstr., **Spiegelgasse** was once home to Goethe, Buchner, and Lenin. **Fraumünster, Grossmünster,** and **St. Peterskirche** straddle the Limmat.

FRAUMÜNSTER. This 13th-century cathedral's Gothic style is juxtaposed with **Marc Chagall's** stained-glass windows, which depict stories from the Old and New Testament. Outside the church on Fraumünsterstr., a mural decorating the courtyard's archway pictures Felix and Regula—the decapitated patron saints of Zurich—with their heads in their hands. *(Right off Paradepl. Open daily May-Sept. 9am-6pm; Oct. and Mar.-Apr. 10am-5pm; Nov.-Feb. 10am-4pm.)*

GROSSMÜNSTER. The twin Neo-Gothic towers of this mainly Romanesque church can best be viewed on the bridge near the Fraumünster. Considered the mother church of the Swiss-German Reformation, it has become a symbol of Zurich. Below the windows, one of Ulrich Zwingli's Bibles lies in a protected case near his pulpit. Downstairs in the 12th-century crypt are the forbidding statue of Charlemagne and his 2m-long sword. The towers are a great way to orient yourself to the city. *(Church open daily Mar. 15-Oct. daily 9am-6pm; Nov.-Mar. 14 10am-5pm. Tower open Mar.-Oct. daily 1:30-5pm; Nov.-Feb. Sa-Su 9:15am-5pm. Tower 2SFr.)*

ST. PETERSKIRCHE. St. Peterskirche has the largest clock face in Europe. *(Open M-F 8am-6pm, Sa 8am-4pm, Su 10-11am.)* Excavated Roman baths dating from the first century are visible beneath the iron stairway. *(Down Thermeng. from St. Peter's.)*

GARDENS AND PARKS. The lush, picnic-perfect **Rieter-Park,** overlooking the city, creates a romantic backdrop for the Museum Rietberg. *(Take tram #7 to Museum Rietberg and walk in the same direction to Sternenstr. Turn right and follow the signs to the museum. Free.)* The **Stadtgärtnerei** attracts botanists and ornithologists to the aviary, which has artificial streams running through it. The aviary houses 17 species of tropical birds, which whiz freely around the building. *(Sackzeig. 25-27.*

Take tram #3 to Hubertus and head down Gutstr. Open daily 9-11:30am and 1:30-4:30pm. Free.) When the weather heats up, a visit to the bathing parks along the Zürichsee can offer a cool respite. **Strandbad Mythenquai** lies along the western shore. *(Take tram #7 to Brunaustr. and walk in the same direction 2min. until you see a set of stairs. Signs hidden by foliage lead the way. ☎ 201 00 00. Open June to mid-Aug. daily 9am-8pm; May and mid-Aug. to early Sept. daily 9am-7pm. 6SFr. Check out www.badi-info.ch for water quality info and other bathing locations.)*

🏛 MUSEUMS

■ **KUNSTHAUS ZÜRICH.** The Kunsthaus, the largest privately-funded museum in Europe, houses a collection ranging from 21st century American pop art to religious pieces by the Old Masters. Works by Dalí, van Gogh, Gaughin, Picasso, Rubens, Rembrandt, Renoir, and the largest Munch collection outside of Norway highlight a museum that, by itself, is a compelling reason to come to Zürich. The collection is continually expanding: a new wing devoted to Alberto Giacometti opened in May 2002. Future highlights include landscapes by legendary Swiss artist Hodler (Mar.-June 2004) and a contemporary project by Urs Fischer. Renovations from Feb.-Aug. 2004 may reduce the number of works on display. *(Heimpl. 1. Take tram #3, 5, 8, or 9 to Kunsthaus. ☎ 253 84 84; www.kunsthaus.ch. English audio tours and brochures. Bag storage required. Open Su and F-Sa 10am-5pm, Tu-Th 10am-9pm. Admission 12SFr. Students and seniors 6SFr. W free. Free tours W 6:30pm and Sa 3pm.)*

■ **MUSEUM RIETBERG.** In contrast to the Kunsthaus, Rietberg presents an exquisite collection of Asian, African, and other non-European art, housed in two spectacular mansions in the Rieter-Park. **Park-Villa Rieter** features internationally acclaimed exhibits of Chinese, Japanese, and Indian paintings; **Villa Wesendonck** stores most of the permanent sculpture collection. Renovations will close Park-Villa Rieter from spring 2004-2006, while Villa Wesendonck will remain open. *(Gablerstr. 15. Take tram #7 to Museum Rietberg. Villa Wesendonck open Su and Tu-Sa 10am-5pm. Audio guide 5SFr. Park-Villa Rieter open Su 10am-5pm, Tu-Sa 1-5pm. 6SFr, students 3SFr.)*

SCHWEIZERISCHES LANDESMUSEUM. In a castle next to the *Hauptbahnhof*, the Landesmuseum provides fascinating insights into Swiss history. Among the artifacts are 16th-century astrological instruments, Ulrich Zwingli's weapons from the Battle of Kappel (1531) in which he died, and a tiny bejeweled clock with a golden skeleton morbidly indicating the hour. *(Open Su and Tu-Sa 10:30am-5pm. Entrance 5SFr, students and seniors 3SFr. Special exhibits 5-10SFr.)*

🎵🎭 ENTERTAINMENT & NIGHTLIFE

Niederdorfstraße is the epicenter of Zurich's nightlife. Beware the "night club"—it's a euphemism for strip club. Because of these, women may not want to walk alone in this area at night. Other hot spots include **Münsterg.** and **Limmatquai**, both lined with overflowing cafes and bars. Beer in Zurich is pricey (from 6SFr), but a number of cheap bars have established themselves on Niederdorfstr. near Muhleg. Most movies (from 15SFr) are screened in English with German and French subtitles. After July 18, the **Orange Cinema**, an open-air cinema at Zürichhorn (take tram #4 to *Fröhlichstr.*) attracts huge crowds to its lakefront screenings. Every August, the *Street Parade* brings together ravers from all over the world for a giant techno party. For more nightlife info, check **ZüriTipp** (www.zueritipp.ch) or the posters that decorate the streets and cinemas at Bellevuepl. or Hirschenpl.

Double-U (W) Bar, Niederdorfstr. 21, on the 1st floor of Hotel Schafli. Popular with locals and students. Beer (from 10SFr) and mixed drinks (from 14SFr) rise 2SFr in price after midnight. Open Su-F 4pm-2am, Sa 4pm-4am. AmEx/DC/V/MC.

Nachtflug Bar, Café, and Lounge, Stuessihofstatt 4 (☎01 261 99 66), is a popular outdoor bar where laid-back locals mix with backpackers. Occasional live music. Serves wine (from 7SFr), beer (from 4.90SFr), mixed drinks (12-16SFr), as well as cold *tapas* and fresh-squeezed juices (6SFr). Open M-Th 11am-midnight, F-Sa 11am-2am.

Oliver Twist, Rindermarkt 6, welcomes soccer fans, tourists, and ex-pats ready for an American brew in a pub atmosphere that's only somewhat contrived. Beers from 6.50SFr. Wine from 5.50SFr. Pub grub noon-10pm. English breakfast (15.50SFr) available during major sporting events. Open M-Sa 11:30am-midnight.

Öpfelchammer, Rindermarkt 12. This popular Swiss wine bar has low ceilings and wooden crossbeams covered with initials and messages from 200 years of merry-makers. Those who climb the rafters and drink a free glass of wine from the beams get to engrave their names on the furniture. If you decide to try it, be careful; it's harder than it looks. Wine 3-5SFr. Open Tu-Sa 11am-12:30am. Closed from mid-July to mid-August. AmEx/V/MC/DC.

Cranberry, Metzgerg. 3. Gay bar off Limmatquai with a fashionable crowd and a leather lounge upstairs. Mixed drinks 9-14SFr. Open Su-W 5pm-12:30am, Th-Sa 5pm-2am.

Barfusser, Spitalg. 14, off Zähringerpl. Europe's oldest gay bar. Specializes in sushi during the day. Mixed drinks 14-17SFr. Wine 6-9SFr. Open M-W 11-1am, Th 11-2am, F-Sa 11-3am, Su 3pm-1am. AmEx/DC/MC/V.

STEIN AM RHEIN   ☎052

The tiny medieval *Altstadt* of Stein am Rhein (pop. 3,000) is postcard-perfect, with traditional Swiss architecture framed by hills and river. All the houses of the square date back to the 15th century, and are marked by detailed facade paintings depicting the animal or scene after which each house is named. The 12th-century establishment of the **Kloster St. George** first made Stein am Rhein prominent. You can reach the Benedictine monastery by heading up Chirchhofpl. from the Rathauspl. Less austere is the vibrant **Festsaal,** whose yellow-and-green-tiled floor is off-limits to feet. As lights are few and dim, try to go when it is bright outside for the best view of delicate paintings and engravings. (☎741 21 42. Open Mar.-Oct. Su and Tu-Sa 10am-5pm. 3SFr, students 1.50SFr.) The **Rathaus,** at the corner of Rhig. and Rathauspl., is more stately.

THE HIDDEN DEAL

A BED OF STRAW

If crisply-made hotel beds have grown bland, consider making like Heidi and bedding down in an authentic Swiss barn. Started ten years ago to provide back-to-the-roots lodging for cost-conscious Swiss families on vacation, the *Schlaf im Stroh* (sleep in straw) program now involves 240 farms in rural northeastern Switzerland.

Though plots are as hygienic as everything else in Switzerland, bring bug spray and a jacket to ward off pre-dawn chill. Call ahead to tell the host about allergies you have (believe it or not, substantial accommodations can be made). Ammenities range from donkey rides to craft demonstrations, and the sunrises are riveting.

In the vicinity of Stein am Rhein, *Let's Go* recommends the barn run by Frau Ullman, her son, Christian, and their amiable St. Bernard, Leila, who tends the chicken coop.

Contact Frau Ullman through the Stein am Rhein tourist office. To get to her barn, ride the local train to Eschenz. Press the button to get off—the train won't stop if you don't. From the station, make a left; take the bike path and follow the signs. The stay includes a 'farmer's breakfast' with tea from the lindenberry tree and chocolate milk courtesy of the cows. Shower 2SFr. Guests 16+ 20SF; children 11-15 pay by their age; 10 and under 10SFr.) For other barns, check www.abenteuer-stroh.ch/en.

Trains connect Stein am Rhein to Konstanz (40min., every hr. 6:24am-midnight, 10SFr) via Kreuzlingen. **Boats** (☎634 08 88) depart for Schaffhausen (1¼hr., 4 per day, 20SFr); Konstanz (2½hr., 4 per day, 24SFr); and other Bodensee towns. The **tourist office,** Oberstadt. 3, lies on the other side of the *Rathaus*. (☎742 20 90. Open July-Aug. M-F 9:30am-noon and 1:30-5pm, Sa 9:30am-noon and 1:30-4pm, Su 10:30am-12:30pm.; Sept.-June M-F 9:30am-noon and 1:30-5pm.) The family-oriented **Jugendherberge (HI) ❷** is at Hemishoferstr. 87. From the train station, take the bus (#7349, dir.: Singen) to *Strandbad* and walk 5min. farther in the same direction. By foot, the hostel is an enjoyable 20min. stroll along the Rhein from town. (☎052 741 12 55. Breakfast, showers, and sheets included. Reception 8-10am and 5-10pm. Curfew 10:30pm; keys available. Open Mar.-Nov. Dorms 25SFr; doubles 60SFr; family rooms 30SFr per person. Nonmembers add 6SFr. AmEx/DC/MC/V.) The waitresses at the **Rothen Ochsen Wine Bar ❶**, Rathauspl. 9, are dedicated to preserving the traditions of this wooden hall, built in 1466—the oldest public house in the town. Though full meals are not available, their regional soups, appetizers, and wines are sustenance enough. (☎741 23 28. Open Su 10:30am-6pm, Tu-Sa 11:30am-11:30pm.) **Postal Code:** CH-8260.

GRAUBÜNDEN

The largest, least populous, and highest of the Swiss cantons, Graubünden's rugged gorges, fir forests, and eddying rivers give the region a wildness seldom found in ultra-civilized Switzerland. Visitors should plan their trips carefully, especially in ski season, when reservations are absolutely required. Beware: Almost everything shuts down in May and June.

DAVOS   ☎081

Davos (pop. 12,000) sprawls along the valley floor under seven mountains laced with chair-lifts and cable cars. Originally a health resort, the city catered to such *fin de siècle* giants as Robert Louis Stevenson and Thomas Mann, who, while in Davos, wrote *Treasure Island* and *The Magic Mountain*. The influx of tourists in recent decades has given the city an impersonal feel, but the thrill of carving down the famed run from Weißfluhgipfel to Kublis (a 2000m vertical drop) may make up for it. Europe's largest natural **ice rink** (22,000sq. m), between Platz and Dorf, has figure skating, ice dancing, hockey, speed skating, and curling. (☎415 36 04. Open Dec. 15-Feb. 15. M-W and F-Sa 10am-4pm; Th 10am-4pm and 8-10pm. 5SFr. Skate rental 6.50SFr.) For joggers, birdwatchers, and the aspiring windsurfer, the **Davosersee** is the place to be. (Take bus #1 to *Flueelastr.* and follow the yellow signs to the lake.) At the Davosersee Surfcenter, board rentals are 30SFr per hr., 60SFr per day. Classes are also available. (Open mid-June to mid-Sept. daily 11am-6:30pm.) Davos provides direct access to two mountains—**Parsenn** and **Jakobshorn**—and four skiing areas. Parsenn, with long runs and fearsome vertical drops, is the mountain around which Davos built its reputation. (www.fun-mountain.ch. Day pass 60SFr.) Jacobshorn has found a niche with the younger crowd since the opening of a snowboarding park with two half-pipes. (Day pass 55SFr.) In the valley run 75km of cross-country trails, one of which is lit at night. In the summer, ski lifts connect to **hikes,** such as the 2hr. **Panoramweg.** To get a little culture with your sweat, visit the **Kirchner Museum,** on the Promenade. It houses an extensive collection of Ernst Ludwig Kirchner's artwork, whose harsh colors and long figures defined 20th-century German Expressionism. (Take the bus to *Kirchner Museum*. Open Su and Tu-Sa 10am-6pm; Sept.-Dec. 24 and Easter-July 7 Su and Tu-Sa 2-6pm. 10SFr, students 5SFr.)

Davos is accessible by **train** from Chur (1½hr., 7 per day, 25SFr) via Landquart or from **Klosters** (25min., 2 per hr., 8.60SFr) on the Rhätische Bahn lines. The town is divided into two areas, Davos-Dorf and Davos-Platz, each with a train station; Platz has the tourist office, post office, and most places of interest to budget travelers. Dorf is closer to the Davosersee. **Buses** (2.70SFr) run between the two train stations and stop near major hotels and the hostel on the Davosersee. The main **tourist office,** Promenade 67, is up the hill from the *Platz* station. (☎415 21 21. Open Dec. to mid-Apr. and mid-June to mid-Oct. M-F 8:30am-6:30pm, Sa 9am-5pm, and Su 10am-noon, 3-5:30pm; mid-Oct. to Dec. and mid-Apr. to June M-F 8:30am-1:45pm, Sa-Su 8:30am-noon.) At Jakobshorn Ski Mountain's **Snowboardhotel Bolgenschanze ❸,** Skistr. 1, dorm rooms are sold as a package with ski passes (☎414 90 20; www.fun-mountain.ch. Reception Su and M-Th 8:30-11am and 4-7pm. Checkout 10am. Free **Internet** access for guests. 1-night, 2-day ski-pass 125-135SFr, weekend 175-185SFr; 6-night, 7-day pass 570SFr. AmEx/MC/V.) **Postal Code:** CH-7270.

KLOSTERS   ☎081

Davos's sister resort, Klosters, lies across the Gotschna and Parsenn mountains. Though Klosters is 10min. from Davos by train, it's a world away in atmosphere. While Davos makes every effort to be cosmopolitan, Klosters capitalizes on its natural serenity and cozy chalets. Most ski packages include mountains from both towns, and Klosters's main lift leads to a mountain pass where one can ski down to either. In summer, Klosters has better access to fantastic biking trails. **Ski passes** for the Klosters-Davos region run 121SFr for 2 days and 279SFr for 6 days (including public transportation). The **Madrisabahn** leaves from Klosters-Dorf (1-day pass 46SFr, 6-day pass 249SFr). The **Grotschnabahn** gives access to Parsenn and Strela in Davos and Madrisa in Klosters (1-day pass 57SFr, 6-day pass 308SFr). Summer cable car passes (valid on Grotschna and Madrisabahnen) are also available (6-day pass 120SFr). **Bananas,** operated out of Duty Boardsport, Bahnhofstr. 16, gives snowboard lessons. (☎422 66 60. Lessons 70SFr per 4hr. Board and shoes 31SFr per day.) **Ski rental** is also available at **Sport Gotschna,** across from the tourist office. (☎422 11 97. Skis and snowboards 38SFr per day plus 10% insurance, 5 days 123SFr; boots 19/69SFr. Open M-F 8am-noon and 2-6:30pm, Sa 8am-12:30pm and 2-6pm, Su 9am-noon and 3-6pm.) On the luscious green valley floor, **hikers** can make a large loop, from Klosters's Protestant church on Monbielstr. to Monbiel. The route continues to an elevation point of 1488m and turns left, passing through **Bödmerwald, Fraschmardintobel,** and **Monbieler Wald** before climbing to its highest elevation of 1634m and returning to Klosters via **Pardels.** Several adventure companies offer a variety of activities including **river rafting, canoeing, horseback riding, paragliding,** and **glacier trekking.**

Klosters-Platz and Klosters-Dorf are connected to Chur by **train** via Landquart (1¼hr., every hr. 5:30am-9:30pm, 19SFr). The same line connects Klosters and Davos (30min., every hr. 5:30am-11:30pm, 9SFr.) The main **tourist office,** in Platz by the station, sells area hiking (16SFr) and biking (7.50SFr) maps. (Open daily 10am-5pm.) **Andrist Sport** on Gotschnastr, rents **bikes.** (☎410 20 80. 38SFr per day, 6 days 130SFr. Open M-F 9am-noon and 2-6:30pm, Sa 8am-noon and 2-6pm.) To get to **Jugendherberge Soldanella (HI) ❷,** Talstr. 73., from the station, go left uphill past Hotel Alpina to the church, then cross the street and head up the alleyway to the right of the Kirchplatz bus station sign. Walk 10min. along the gravel path. This massive, renovated chalet has a comfortable reading room, couches on a flagstone terrace, and friendly English-speaking owners. (☎422 13 16. Breakfast included. Open mid-Dec. to mid Apr. and late June to mid-Oct. Reception 7-10am and 5-10pm. Checkout 10am. Dorms 28SFr; singles 39SFr; doubles 70SFr. Family rooms 39SFr per person. Nonmembers add 6SFr. AmEx/DC/MC/V.) **Postal Code:** CH-7250.

THE SWISS NATIONAL PARK

The Swiss National Park offers hikes that rival the best in Switzerland, but no other area can match the park's isolation from man-made constructs, which allows hikers to experience the undiluted wildness of the natural terrain. A network of 20 hiking trails runs throughout the park, mostly concentrated in the center. Few of the trails are level; most involve a lot of climbing, often into snow-covered areas. However, all trails are clearly marked, and it is against park rules to wander off the designated trails. Trails that require no mountaineering gear are marked with white-red-white blazes. The Swiss, however, are practically mountain goats, so even some of the no-gear routes can be tricky.

Zernez is the main gateway to the park, and home to the main headquarters of the park, the **National Parkhouse.** The staff provides helpful trail maps as well as up-to-date information on which trails are navigable—take their advice seriously; when they say a trail is too dangerous, they mean it. (☎856 13 78. Open June-Oct. Tu 8:30am-10pm, W-Su 8:30am-6pm.) From Zernez, **trains** and **post buses** run to other towns in the area, including Scuol, Samedan, and S-chanf. The park is closed November through May. The Swiss National Park is one of the most strictly regulated nature preserves in the world. Camping and campfires are prohibited in the park, as is collecting flowers and plants. A team of wardens patrols the park at all times, so it's better not to test the rules. Zernez, Scuol, and S-chanf have campsites right outside the park boundaries. **Phone code:** ☎081

JUNGFRAU REGION

The most famous (and most-visited) region of the Bernese Oberland, the Jungfrau area has attracted tourists for hundreds of years with glorious hiking trails and permanently snow-capped peaks. From Interlaken, the valley splits at the foot of the Jungfrau: The eastern valley contains Grindelwald, with easy access to two glaciers, while the western valley hosts many smaller towns, each with unique hiking opportunities. The two valleys are divided by an easily hikeable ridge.

INTERLAKEN ☎033

Interlaken (pop. 21,000) lies between the Thunersee and the Brienzersee at the foot of the largest mountains in Switzerland. With easy access to these natural playgrounds, Interlaken has earned its rightful place as one of Switzerland's prime tourist attractions and its top outdoor adventure spot.

⬛🔋 TRANSPORTATION AND PRACTICAL INFORMATION. The *Westbahnhof* (☎826 47 50) and *Ostbahnhof* (☎828 73 19) have **trains** to: Basel (5:30am-10:30pm, 56SFr); Bern (6:35am-10:30pm, 24SFr); Geneva (5:30am-9:30pm, 63SFr); Lucerne (5:30am-8:35pm, 26SFr); Lugano/Locarno (5:30am-4:35pm, 87SFr); and Zurich (5:30am-10:30pm, 62SFr). The *Ostbahnhof* also sends trains to Grindelwald (June-Sept. every 30min., Sept.-May every hr. 6:35am-10:35pm; 9.80SFr).

The **tourist office,** Höheweg 37, in Hotel Metropole, has free maps. (☎826 53 00. Open July-Aug. M-F 8am-6pm, Sa 8am-5pm, Su 10am-noon and 5-7pm; Sept.-June M-F 8am-noon and 1:30-6pm, Sa 9am-noon.) Both train stations rent **bikes.** (30SFr per day. Open daily 6am-7pm.) For **snow and weather info,** call ☎828 79 31. In case of emergency, call the **police** ☎117 or the **hospital** ☎826 26 26. **Postal Code:** CH-3800.

🔐🔋 ACCOMMODATIONS AND FOOD. ⬛Backpackers Villa Sonnenhof ❷, Alpenstr. 16, diagonally across the Höhenmatte from the tourist office, is friendly and low-key. (☎826 71 71. Mountain bikes 28SFr per day. Breakfast and lockers included. Laundry 10SFr. **Internet** 10SFr per hr. Reception 7:30-11am and 4-10pm. Dorms 29-32SFr; doubles 82-88SFr; triples 111-120SFr. 5SFr extra for balcony. AmEx/MC/V.) **Balmer's Herberge ❷**, Hauptstr. 23. Switzerland's oldest private hostel (since 1945) is thoroughly American: It is a place to play, not relax. Services include mountain bike rental (35SFr per day), nightly movies, TV, free sleds, and a bar. (☎822 19 61. Breakfast included. **Internet** (20SFr per hr.). Reception summer 6:30am-noon and 4-10pm, winter 6:30-10am and 4:30-10pm. Dorms 20-24SFr; doubles 68SFr; triples 90SFr; quads 120SFr.) **Swiss Adventure Hostel ❷**, in the tiny town of Boltigen, has made this quiet valley a sporty alternative to the party scene in Interlaken. A free shuttle runs to and from Interlaken each day (40min.). Its adventure company offers the same activities as the Interlaken companies, but with a more personal touch. (☎773 73 73. Dorms 20SFr; double with shower 70SFr; quad with shower 100SFr. Special deals if combined with adventure sports.) **Happy Inn ❷**, Rosenstr. 17, lives up to its name with a friendly staff. From *Westbahnhof*, turn left towards the tourist office, then right on Rosenstr. at Centralpl. (☎822 32 25. Reception 7am-6pm. Call early for rooms. Dorms 22SFr; singles 38SFr; doubles 76SFr.) Most hostels serve cheap food, and there are **Migros supermarkets** by both train stations. (Open M-Th 8am-7pm, F 8am-9pm, Sa 7:30am-5pm.)

🔣🔣 OUTDOORS AND HIKING. Interlaken offers a wide range of adrenaline-pumping activities. **Alpin Raft** (☎823 41 00), the most established company in Interlaken, has qualified, personable guides and offers: Paragliding (150SFr); canyoning (110-195SFr); river rafting (95-109SFr); skydiving (380SFr); bungee jumping (125-165SFr); and hang gliding (180SFr). All prices include transportation to and from any hostel in Interlaken. A number of horse and hiking tours, as well as rock-lessons, are also available upon request. **Outdoor Interlaken** (☎826 77 19) offers rock-climbing lessons (89SFr per half-day) and **white-water kayaking** tours (155SFr per half-day). The owner of **Skydiving Xdream**, Stefan Heuser, has been on the Swiss skydiving team for 17 years. (Skydiving 380SFr. ☎079 75 93 48 34. Open Apr.-Oct.)

Interlaken's most traversed trail climbs to the Harder Kulm (1310m). From the *Ostbahnhof*, head toward town, take the first road bridge right across the river, and follow the yellow signs that later give way to white-red-white markings on the rocks. From the top, signs lead back down to the *Westbahnhof*. A funicular runs from the trailhead near the *Ostbahnhof* to the top from May-Oct.

THE LOCAL STORY

BUTTER AND LONG LIFE

Dani Schlaepfer has been playing the alphorn for the last ten years as a part of the Spitzli Trio. He stopped during a concert in Schwaegalp, below Mt. Saentis, to talk with Let's Go.

LG: Tell me about your instrument.
A: Well, my alphorn is 2.5m long; it's a G flat. They come in all different keys—F, A sharp, A flat—depending on horn length.
LG: What is your favorite event to play?
A: Definitely weddings. We do a lot of weddings.
LG: Tell me about your clothing.
A: I am wearing the traditional Appenzeller dress. All of the embroidery is done by hand, along with the tanning of the leather for the belts and suspenders. The gold cows on the belt are also hammered out by hand.
LG: And what's with the earring?
A: All Appenzeller men wear this earring. I got mine when I was five. On the top, there's a horseshoe, which means good and long life. The thing that dangles down on the bottom is a *Rahmkette;* it's what the farmer uses to skim the cream off the top of the milk, which then is made into butter.
LG: Why are they together?
A: It's a symbol—it means that through butter, milk, the cows, and the ways of farming, you will enjoy a long and healthy life.
LG: Do you always wear this symbolic earring?
A: No; normally it is just a cow.

Interlaken's adventure sports industry is thrilling, but accidents do happen. On July 27, 1999, 19 tourists were killed by a sudden flash flood while canyoning. Be aware that you participate in all adventure sports at your own risk.

(2½hr. up, 1½hr. down. May to mid-Oct. 14SFr, round-trip 21SFr; 25% Eurail-pass and SwissPass discount.) For flatter trails, turn left from the train station and left before the bridge, then follow the canal over to the nature reserve on the shore of the Thunersee. The trail winds up the Lombach river and through pastures at the base of the Harder Kulm back toward town (3hr.).

GRINDELWALD
☎033

Grindelwald (pop. 4,500), the launching point to the only glaciers accessible by foot in the Bernese Oberland, crouches beneath the north face of the Eiger. The town has all kinds of hikes, from easy valley walks to challenging peaks for top climbers. The **Bergführerbüro** (Mountain Guides Office), in the sports center near the tourist office, sells hiking maps and coordinates glacier walks, ice climbing, and mountaineering. (☎853 12 00. Open June-Oct. M-F 9am-noon and 2-5pm.) The **Lower Glacier** *(Untere Grindelwaldgletscher)* hike is moderately steep (5hr.). To reach the trailhead, walk up the main street away from the station and follow the signs downhill to Pfinstegg. Hikers can either walk the first forested section of the trail (1hr.), following signs up to Pfinstegg., or take a funicular to the Pfinstegg. hut (July to mid-Sept. 8am-7pm; mid-Sept. to June 8am-4pm; 9.80SFr). From the hut, signs lead up the glacier-filled valley to Stieregg., a hut that offers food.

The **Jungfraubahn** runs to Grindelwald from Interlaken's *Ostbahnhof* (40min., 6:35am-10:30pm, 9.80SFr). The **tourist office**, located in the Sport-Zentrum to the right of the station, provides chairlift information and a list of free guided excursions. (☎854 12 12. Open July-Aug. M-F 8am-6pm, Sa 8am-7pm, Su 9-11am and 2-6pm; Sept.-June M-F 8am-noon and 2-6pm, Sa 8am-noon and 2-5pm.) **Hotel Hirschen ❹**, to the right of the tourist office, offers comfortable beds and a bowling alley. (☎854 84 84. Breakfast included. Reception daily 8am-10pm. Singles 90-135SFr; doubles 150-220SFr.) To reach the **Jugendherberge (HI) ❷**, head left out of the train station for 400m, then cut uphill to the right just before Chalet Alpenblume and follow the steep trail all the way up the hill. (☎853 10 09. Breakfast included. Reception daily 7:30-10am and 3pm-midnight. Dorms 28-30SFr; doubles 70SFr, with toilet and shower 101SFr. Nonmembers add 6SFr. AmEx/MC.) **Hotel Eiger ❷**, near the tourist office, is a huge complex of middle crust eateries and bars. (Open 8:30am-1:30am.) There's a **Co-op supermarket** on Hauptstr., across from the tourist office. (Open M-F 8am-6:30pm, Sa 8am-4pm.) **Postal Code:** CH-3818.

VALAIS

The Valais occupies the deep and wide glacial gorge traced by the Rhône River. Though its mountain resorts can be over-touristed, the region's spectacular peaks and skiing, hiking, and climbing make fighting the traffic worthwhile.

ZERMATT AND THE MATTERHORN
☎027

The shape of the valley blocks out most of the great Alpine summits that ring Zermatt, allowing the monolithic **Matterhorn** (4478m) to rise alone above town. The area has attained mecca status with Europe's longest **ski** run, the 13km trail from Klein Matterhorn to Zermatt, and more **summer ski trails** than any other Alpine ski resort. A one-day ski pass for any of the area's mountains runs 60-

77SFr. The **Zermatt Alpine Center,** which houses both the **Bergführerbüro** (Mountain Guide's Office; ☎966 24 60) and the **Skischulbüro** (Ski School Office; ☎966 24 66), is located past the post office from the station; the Bergführerbüro provides ski passes, four-day weather forecasts, and info on guided climbing. (Open July-Sept. M-F 8:30am-noon and 3:30-7pm, Sa 3:30-7pm, Su 10am-noon and 3:30-7pm; late Dec. to mid-May daily 5-7pm.) Rental prices for skis and snowboards are standardized throughout Zermatt (28-50SFr per day, 123-215SFr per week). **Freeride Film Factory** (☎213 38 07) offers custom **hiking, biking,** and **climbing** expeditions (160-250SFr) that come with a videotape of your trek. ▨**The Pipe Surfer's Cantina,** on Kirchstr., has the craziest "beach parties" in the Alps. Don't leave without downing a shot of Moo (6SFr), their specialty caramel vodka. (www.gozermatt.com/thepipe. Happy Hour daily 7-8pm. Open daily 3:30pm-2:30am.)

To preserve the Alpine air, cars and buses are banned in Zermatt; the only way in is the hourly **BVZ** (Brig-Visp-Zermatt) rail line, which connects to Lausanne (73SFr). The **tourist office,** in the station, sells hiking maps for 26SFr. (☎966 81 00. Open mid-June to mid-Oct. M-F 8:30am-6pm, Sa 8:30am-6:30pm, Su 9:30am-noon and 4-6:30pm; mid-Oct. to mid-Dec. and May to mid-June M-F 8:30am-noon and 1:30-6pm, Sa 8:30am-noon; mid-Dec. to Apr. 8:30am-noon and 1:30-6:30pm, Sa 8:30am-6:30pm, Su 9:30am-noon and 4-6:30pm.) **Hotel Bahnhof ❷,** on Bahnhofstr. to the left of the station, provides hotel housing at hostel rates. (☎967 24 06. Dorms 30SFr; singles 59SFr, with shower 71SFr; doubles 86-96SFr. MC/V.) Treat yourself to filling Swiss fare at **Walliserkanne ❸,** on Bahnhofstr. next to the post office. (Open 9am-midnight. AmEx/MC/V.) Pick up groceries at the **Co-op Center,** opposite the station. (Open M-F 8:15am-12:15pm and 1:45-6:30pm, Sa 8:15am-12:15pm and 1:45-6pm.) **Postal Code:** CH-3920.

FRENCH SWITZERLAND

All around Lac Léman, hills sprinkled with villas and blanketed by patchwork vineyards seem tame and settled—until the haze clears. From behind the hills surge rough-hewn mountain peaks with the energizing promise of unpopulated wilderness and wide, lonely expanses.

GENEVA (GENÈVE)   ☎022

A stay in Geneva will likely change your definition of diversity. As the most international city in Switzerland, Geneva is a brew of 178,000 unlikely neighbors: wealthy businessmen speed past dreadlocked skaters in the street while nuclear families stroll by artists squatting in abandoned factories; only one-third of the city's residents are natives of the canton. Birthplace of the League of Nations and current home to dozens of multinational organizations (including the Red Cross and the United Nations), Geneva emanates worldliness.

⊠ INTERCITY TRANSPORTATION

Flights: Cointrin Airport (GVA; ☎717 71 11, flight info ☎799 31 11) is a hub for **Swiss Airlines** (☎(0848) 85 20 00) and also serves **Air France** (☎827 87 87) and **British Airways** (☎(0848) 80 10 10). Several direct flights per day to Amsterdam, London, New York, Paris, and Rome. Bus #10 runs to the Gare Cornavin (15min., every 5-10min., 2.20SFr). The train provides a shorter trip (6min., every 10min., 4.80SFr).

SWITZERLAND

Trains: Trains run approximately 4:30am-1am. **Gare Cornavin,** pl. Cornavin, is the main station. To: **Basel** (2¾hr., every hr., 71SFr); **Bern** (2hr., every hr., 47SFr); **Interlaken** (3hr., every hr., 63SFr); **Lausanne** (40min., every 20-30min., 19SFr); **Montreux** (1hr., 2 per hr., 29SFr); **Zurich** (3½hr., every hr., 76SFr). Ticket counter open M-F 8:30am-6:30pm, Sa 9am-5pm. **Gare des Eaux-Vives** (☎736 16 20), on av. de la Gare des Eaux-Vives (tram #12 to *Amandoliers SNCF*), connects to France's regional rail through **Annecy** (1½hr., 6 per day, 14SFr) or **Chamonix** (2½hr., 4 per day, 24SFr). Ticket office open M-F 9am-6pm, Sa 11am-5:45pm.

Hitchhiking: Those headed to Germany or northern Switzerland take bus #4 to *Jardin Botanique*. Those headed to France take bus #4 to *Palettes*, then line D to *St. Julien*. *Let's Go* does not recommend hitchhiking.

▣ LOCAL TRANSPORTATION

Carry your passport with you at all times; the French border is never more than a few minutes away and buses frequently cross it. Ticket purchasing is largely on the honor system, but you may be fined 60SFr for evading fares. Much of the city can be explored on foot.

Public Transportation: Geneva has an efficient bus and tram network. **Transport Publics Genevois** (☎308 34 34), next to the tourist office in Gare Cornavin, provides *Le Réseau* (a free map of bus routes) and inexpensive timetables. Open M-Sa 7am-7pm, Su 10am-6pm. **Day passes** 6SFr-12SFr. Stamp multi-use tickets before boarding. Buses run roughly 5:30am-midnight; **Noctambus** (3SFr, 1:30-4:30am) runs when the others don't. SwissPass valid on all buses; Eurail not valid.

Taxis: Taxi-Phone (☎331 41 33). 6.80SFr plus 2.90SFr per km. Taxi from airport to city 30SFr, max. 4 passengers (15-20min.).

Bike Rental: Geneva has well-marked bike paths and special traffic lights for spoked traffic. For routes, get *Itineraires cyclables* or *Tours de ville avec les vélos de location* from the tourist office. Behind the station, **Genève Roule**, pl. Montbrillant 17 (☎740 13 43), has free bikes available (50SFr deposit; hefty fine if bike is lost or stolen). Slightly nicer neon bikes from 5SFr per day. Open daily 7:30am-9:30pm.

◪ ▮ ORIENTATION AND PRACTICAL INFORMATION

The labyrinthine cobbled streets and quiet squares of the historic *vieille ville*, around **Cathédrale de St-Pierre**, make up the heart of Geneva. Across the **Rhône River** to the north, banks and five-star hotels gradually give way to lakeside promenades, **International Hill**, and rolling parks. Across the **Arve River** to the south lies the village of **Carouge**, home to student bars and clubs (take tram #12 or 13 to pl. *du Marché*).

TOURIST, FINANCIAL, AND LOCAL SERVICES

Tourist Offices: Main office, r. du Mont-Blanc 18 (☎909 70 00), in the Central Post Office Building. From Cornavin, walk 5min. toward the Pont du Mont-Blanc. Staff books hotel rooms for a 5SFr fee, leads walking tours, and offers free city maps. Open July-Aug. daily 9am-6pm; Sept.-June M-Sa 9am-6pm. During the summer, head for **Centre d'Accueil et de Renseignements** (☎731 46 47), an office-in-a-bus parked in pl. Mont-Blanc, by the Metro Shopping entrance to Cornavin Station. Lists free performances and makes hotel reservations. Open mid-June to mid-Sept. daily 9am-9pm.

Consulates: Australia, chemin des Fins 2 (☎799 91 00). **Canada,** av. de l'Ariana 5 (☎919 92 00). **New Zealand,** chemin des Fins 2 (☎929 03 50). **South Africa,** r. de Rhône 65 (☎849 54 54). **UK,** r. de Vermont 37 (☎918 24 26). **US,** r. Versonnex 7 (☎840 51 60; recorded info 840 51 61).

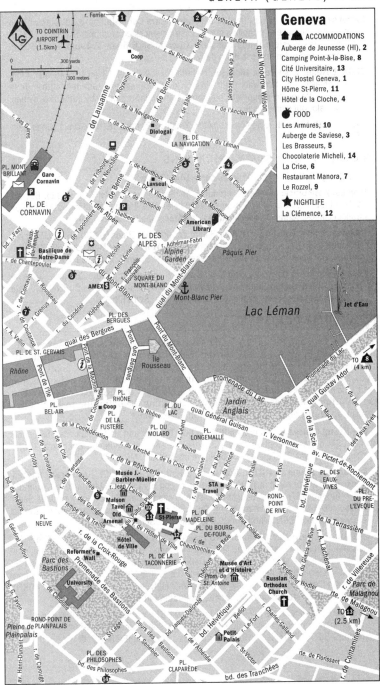

Geneva

■▲ ACCOMMODATIONS

Auberge de Jeunesse (HI), 2
Camping Point-à-la-Bise, 8
Cité Universitaire, 13
City Hostel Geneva, 1
Hôme St-Pierre, 11
Hôtel de la Cloche, 4

🍎 FOOD

Les Armures, 10
Auberge de Saviese, 3
Les Brasseurs, 5
Chocolaterie Micheli, 14
La Crise, 6
Restaurant Manora, 7
Le Rozzel, 9

★ NIGHTLIFE

La Clémence, 12

SWITZERLAND

Currency Exchange: ATMs offer the best rates. **Gare Cornavin** has good rates with no commission on traveler's checks, makes cash advances on credit cards (min. 200SFr), and arranges Western Union transfers. Open M-Sa 6:50am-7:40pm, Su 6:50am-6:40pm. Western Union desk open daily 7am-7pm.

Bi-Gay-Lesbian Resources: Diologai, r. de la Navigation 11-13 (☎906 40 40). From Gare Cornavin, turn left, walk 5min. down r. de Lausanne, and turn right onto r. de la Navigation. Resource group with programs from support groups to outdoor activities. Mostly male, but women welcome.

Laundromat: Lavseul, r. de Monthoux 29. Wash 5SFr, dry 1SFr per 10min. Open daily 7am-midnight.

EMERGENCY AND COMMUNICATIONS

Emergency: Police: ☎117. **Ambulance:** ☎144. **Fire:** ☎118.

Medical Assistance: Hôpital Cantonal, r. Micheli-du-Crest 24 (☎372 33 11). Bus #1 or 5 or tram #12. Door #2 is for emergency care, door #3 for consultations. For info on walk-in clinics, contact the **Association des Médecins** (☎320 84 20).

Internet Access: Point 6, r. de Vieux-Billard 7a, off r. des Bains (☎800 26 00). 5SFr per hr. Open daily noon-midnight. **Connections Net World,** r. de Monthoux 58. 3SFr per 30min., 5SFr per hr. Copier available. Open M-Sa 9:30am-2:30am, Su 1pm-2am.

Post Office: Poste Centrale, r. de Mont-Blanc 18, a block from Gare Cornavin. Open M-F 7:30am-6pm, Sa 8:30am-noon. Address mail to be held: Firstname SURNAME, *Poste Restante,* Genève 1 Mont-Blanc, **CH-1211,** Geneva, SWITZERLAND.

⌂ ACCOMMODATIONS

Geneva is a cosmopolitan city, and its 5-star hotel system is geared toward the international banker. Luckily for the budget traveler, the seasonal influx of university students and interns has created a second network of hostels, pensions, and university dorms moonlighting as summer hotels. The indispensable *Info Jeunes* lists about 50 options; *Let's Go* lists the highlights below. The tourist office publishes *Budget Hotels,* stretching the definition to 120SFr per person. Even for short stays, reservations are a must.

City Hostel Geneva, r. Ferrier 2 (☎901 15 00). TV room and kitchen. Sheets 3SFr. Internet 8SFr per hr. Reception daily 7:30am-noon and 1pm-midnight. Check-out 10am. Single-sex dorms 25SFr; singles 55SFr; doubles 80SFr. MC/V. ❷

Auberge de Jeunesse (HI), r. Rothschild 28-30 (☎732 62 60). Restaurant, kitchen facilities (1SFr per 30min.), TV room, lockers, and library. Breakfast included. Laundry 6SFr. Internet 7SFr per hr. 6-night max. stay. Lockout 10am-3pm. Reception June-Sept. daily 6:30-10am and 2pm-midnight, Oct.-May 6:30-10am and 4pm-midnight. Dorms 25SFr; doubles 70SFr, with bath 80SFr; quads 110SFr. MC/V. ❷

Cité Universitaire, av. Miremont 46 (☎839 22 11). Take bus #3 (dir.: Crets-de-Champel) from the station to the last stop. TV rooms, restaurant, disco (Th and Sa, free to guests), and a small grocery shop. Hall showers. Reception M-F 8am-noon and 2-10pm, Sa 8am-noon and 6-10pm, Su 9-11am and 6-10pm. Check-out 10am. Dorm lockout 11am-6pm. Dorm curfew 11pm. Dorms (July-Sept. only) 20SFr; singles 49SFr; doubles 66SFr; studios with kitchenette and bathroom 75SFr. ❷

Hôtel de la Cloche, r. de la Cloche 6 (☎732 94 81), off quai du Mont-Blanc in a converted mansion. Breakfast included. Reception daily 8am-10pm. Singles 65-70SFr; doubles 85-95SFr; triples 110-140SFr; quads 140SFr. AmEx/MC/V. ❹

Hôme St-Pierre, Cour St-Pierre 4 (☎310 37 07; info@stpierre.ch). Take bus #5 to *pl. Neuve* or walk from the station. This 150-year-old "home" has comfortable beds and a great location. Beware, though, that the church bell rings every 15min. Breakfast M-Sa 7SFr. Showers free. Lockers 5SFr. Reception M-Sa 9am-noon and 4-8pm, Su 9am-noon. Dorms 23SFr; singles 36-45SFr; doubles 50-60SFr. MC/V. ❸

Camping Pointe-à-la-Bise, Chemin de la Bise (☎752 12 96). Take bus #8 to Rive, then bus E north to Bise and walk 10min. to the lake. Reception daily 8am-noon and 2-9pm. Open Apr.-Sept. 6.20SFr per person, 9SFr per site. No tents provided. Beds 15SFr. 4-person bungalows 60SFr. ❶

🍴 FOOD

You can find anything from sushi to *paella* in Geneva, but you may need a banker's salary to foot the bill. Do-it-yourselfers can pick up basics at *boulangeries*, *pâtisseries*, or at the ubiquitous supermarkets. Many supermarkets also have attached cafeterias; try the **Co-op** on the corner of r. du Commerce and r. du Rhône, in the Centre Rhône Fusterie. (Open M 9am-6:45pm, Tu-W and F 8:30am-6:45pm, Th 8:30am-8pm, Sa 8:30am-5pm.) There are extensive dining options in the old city near the cathedral, but you'll pay for the location. In the **Les Paquis** area, bordered by the r. de Lausanne and Gare Cornavin on one side and the Quais Mont-Blanc and Wilson on the other, are a variety of relatively cheap ethnic foods. Around **pl. du Cirque** and **plaine de Plainpalais** are cheap, student-oriented tea rooms. To the south, the village of **Carouge** is known for its cozy pizzerias and funky brasseries.

Chocolaterie Micheli, r. Micheli-du-Crest 1 (☎329 90 06). Take tram #13 to *Plainpalais* and walk up bd. des Philosophes until it intersects r. Micheli-du-Crest. Confectionary masterpieces abound in this chocolate store and cafe *par excellence.* Open Tu-F 8am-7pm, Sa 8am-5pm. MC/V. ❶

Le Rozzel, Grand-Rue 18. Take bus #5 to *pl. Neuve*, then walk up the hill past the cathedral on r. Jean-Calvin to Grand-Rue. Large dinner crepes (4-18SFr). Dessert crepes (5-9SFr). Open M 7am-4pm, Tu-W 7am-7pm, Th-F 7am-10pm, Sa 9am-10pm. ❷

Restaurant Manora, r. de Cornavin 4, to the right of the station in the Placette department store. This huge self-serve restaurant has a varied selection and free water (rare in Switzerland). Entrees from 8SFr. Open M-Sa 7:30am-9:30pm, Su 9am-9:30pm. ❶

Les Armures, r. due Puits-St-Pierre 1, near the main entrance to the cathedral. Elegance in the heart of the *Altstadt.* Fondue 24-26SFr. Pizza 14-17SFr. Entrees run to 45SFr. Open M-F 8am-midnight, Sa 11am-midnight, Su 11am-11pm. ❹

Les Brasseurs, pl. Cornavin 20. Go left from the station. Serves *flammeküchen,* an Alsatian specialty similar to thin crust pizza but topped with cream and onions (11.60-23SFr), and home-brewed towers of beer (31SFr for 2L). Kitchen open 11:30am-2pm and 6-10:45pm. Open M-W 11am-1am, Th-Sa 11am-2am, Su 5pm-1am. ❸

La Crise, r. de Chantepoulet 13. Small but popular snack bar dishes out tasty quiches and soups at reasonable prices. Open M-F 6am-3pm and 5-8pm, Sa 6am-3pm. ❷

Auberge de Saviese, r. des Pâquis 20. Take bus #1 to *Monthoux.* Sip coffee (2.30SFr) with an older crowd in this touristy English-speaking restaurant. Excellent *fondue au cognac* (20SFr), *Raclette* with all the trimmings (31SFr), and regional perch (28SFr). Open M-Sa 10:30am-3pm and 5pm-12:30am, Su 5pm-12:30am. AmEx/DC/MC/V. ❹

⊙ SIGHTS

The city's most interesting historical sites are in a dense, easily walkable space. The tourist office offers 2hr. walking tours. (Mid-June to Sept. M-Sa 10am; Oct. to mid-June Sa 10am. 12SFr, students and seniors 8SFr.)

VIEILLE VILLE. From 1536 to 1564, Calvin preached at the **Cathédrale de St-Pierre.** The **north tower** provides a commanding view of the old town. *(Open June-Sept. daily 9am-7pm; Oct.-May M-Sa 10am-noon and 2-5pm, Su 11am-12:30pm and 1:30-5pm. Tower 3SFr.)* Ruins, including a Roman sanctuary and a 4th-century basilica, rest in an **archaeological site** below the cathedral. *(Open June-Sept. Su 10am-5pm, Tu-Sa 11am–5pm; Oct.-May Su 10am-noon and 2-5pm, Tu-Sa 2-5pm. 5SFr, students 3SFr.)* At the west end of the *vieille ville* sits the 14th-century **Maison Tavel,** which now houses a history museum. *(Open Su and Tu-Sa 10am-5pm. Free.)* Across the street is the **Hôtel de Ville** (town hall), where world leaders met on August 22, 1864, to sign the Geneva Convention that still governs war conduct today. The **Grand-Rue,** which begins at the Hôtel de Ville, is lined with medieval workshops and 18th-century mansions; plaques commemorate famous residents like Jean-Jacques Rousseau, who was born at #40. Below the cathedral, along r. de la Croix-Rouge, the **Parc des Bastions** stretches from pl. Neuve to pl. des Philosophes and includes **Le Mur des Réformateurs** (Reformers' Wall), a sprawling collection of bas-relief figures of the Reformers themselves. The park's center walkway leads to the ▨**Petit-Palais,** Terrasse St-Victor 2, a beautiful mansion containing art by Chagall, Gauguin, Picasso, and Renoir, as well as themed exhibitions. *(Bus #36 to Petit Palais or #1, 3, or 5 to Claparède. Open M-F 10am-6pm, Sa-Su 10am-5pm. 10SFr, students 5SFr.)*

WATERFRONT. As you descend from the cathedral to the lake, medieval lanes give way to wide quais and chic boutiques. Down quai Gustave Ardor, the **Jet d'Eau,** Europe's highest fountain, spews a spectacular 7-ton plume of water 440ft into the air. The **floral clock** in the nearby **Jardin Anglais** pays homage to Geneva's watch industry. It's probably Geneva's most overrated attraction and was once the most hazardous—the clock had to be cut back almost 1m because tourists, intent on taking the perfect photograph, repeatedly backed into oncoming traffic. On the north shore, the beach **Pâquis Plage,** quai du Mont-Blanc 30, is popular with locals. *(Open 9am-8:30pm. 2SFr.)*

INTERNATIONAL HILL. The International Red Cross building contains the moving ▨**International Red Cross and Red Crescent Museum,** Av. de la Paix 17. *(Bus #8 or F to Appia or bus V or Z to Ariana. Open M and W-Su 10am-5pm. 10SFr, students 5SFr.)* The nearby European headquarters of the **United Nations** is in the same building that sheltered the now-defunct League of Nations. The constant traffic of international diplomats (often in handsome non-Western dress) provides more excitement than the dull guided tour. *(Open July-Aug. daily 10am-5pm; Apr.-June and Sept.-Oct. daily 10am-noon and 2-4pm; Nov.-Mar. M-F 10am-noon and 2-4pm. 8.50SFr, seniors and students 6.50SFr.)*

♫ 🎭 ENTERTAINMENT AND NIGHTLIFE

Genève Agenda, available at the tourist office, is your guide to fun, with event listings ranging from major festivals to movies (be warned—a movie runs about 16SFr). In July and August, the **Cinelac** turns Genève Plage into an open-air cinema screening mostly American films. Free **jazz concerts** take place in July and

August in Parc de la Grange. Geneva hosts the biggest celebration of **American Independence Day** outside the US (July 4), and the **Fêtes de Genève** in early August is filled with international music and fireworks. The best party is **L'Escalade** in early December, which lasts a full weekend and commemorates the dramatic repulsion of invading Savoyard troops.

La Jonction, at the junction of the Rhône and Arve rivers, accessible by the #2, 10-20, and D buses, is home to a guerilla artist colony and venues for rockers and ravers. **Place Bourg-de-Four,** in the *vieille ville* below the cathedral, attracts students and professionals to its charming terraces and old-world atmosphere. **Place du Molard,** on the right bank by the pont du Mont-Blanc, offers terrace cafes and big, loud bars and clubs. **Les Paquis,** near Gare Cornavin and pl. de la Navigation, is the city's red-light district, but it also has a wide array of rowdy, low-lit bars, many with an ethnic flavor. **Carouge,** across the river Arve, is a student-friendly locus of nightlife activity. Generations of students have eaten at the famous ▧**La Clémence,** pl. du Bourg-de-Four 20. (Open M-Th 7am-12:30am, F-Sa 7am-1:30am.)

LAUSANNE   ☎021

The unique museums, distinctive neighborhoods, and lazy Lac Léman waterfront of Lausanne (pop. 125,000) make it well worth a stay. In the *vieille ville,* two flights of medieval stairs lead to the Gothic **Cathédrale.** (Open July to mid-Sept. M-F 7am-7pm, Sa-Su 8am-7pm; mid-Sept. to June daily 8am-5:30pm.) Below the cathedral is the **Hôtel de Ville,** on pl. de la Palud, the meeting point for guided tours of the town. (Tours M-Sa 10am and 3pm. 10SFr, students free. English available.) The ▧**Collection de l'Art Brut,** av. Bergières 11, is filled with disturbing and original sculptures, drawings, and paintings by artists on the fringe—institutionalized schizophrenics, uneducated peasants, and convicted criminals. Take bus #2 or 3 to *Jomini.* (Open July-Aug. daily 11am-6pm; Sept.-June Tu-F 11am-1pm and 2-6pm, Sa-Su 11am-6pm. 6SFr, students 4SFr.) The **Musée Olympique,** Quai d'Ouchy 1, is a high-tech temple to modern Olympians with an extensive video collection, allowing visitors to relive almost any moment of the games. Take bus #2 to *Ouchy.* (Open May-Sept. M-W and F-Su 9am-6pm, Th 9am-8pm; Oct.-Apr. closed Mondays. 14SFr, students 9SFr.) In Ouchy, several booths along quai de Belgique and pl. de la Navigation rent **pedal boats** (10SFr per 30min.) and offer water skiing or wake boarding on **Lake Léman** (30SFr per 15min.).

THE LOCAL LEGEND

DO YOU SCHWING?

A summer in Switzerland would not be complete without the institution that is the annual *Schwingfest,* an event dedicated to the arcane sport of *Schwingen.* A form of wrestling, *Schwingen* features two male *Schwingers* faced off in a Sägemuhlring (a ring of sawdust). The men wear leather over-shorts with loops on the back which the other *Schwinger* must grip for leverage at all times. As a *Schwinger,* your goal in life is to throw your opponent down on his back, and to stay within the circle while doing so; matches last around five minutes.

The earliest known reference to the sport is a 13th-century stone carving in the cathedral of Lausanne, which depicts two overshirt-wearing strongmen at loggerheads. The sport's origins lie in Alpine farming regions, where farmhands would compete to see who was the strongest, and everyone presumably wore suspenders. Today, the men are still distinguished by the roots of their training: *Sennen* are farmers and wear traditional blue workshirts; *Turnen* are gym-trained athletes and wear only white.

The *Schwingfest* itself includes more Swiss tradition than just wrestling. Normally, the playing of an *Alphorn* kicks off the first bout, and flag throwers, yodel choirs, and a beer-and-sausage tent provide entertainment on the sidelines. Check www.esv.ch for info on the *Fest* nearest you.

Trains leave from pl. de la Gare 9 for: Basel (2½hr., every hr. 5:25am-9:25pm, 68SFr); Geneva (50min., every 20min. 4:55am-12:45am, 19SFr); Montreux (20min., every 30min. 5:25am-2:25am, 10SFr); Paris (4hr., 4 per day 7:35am-5:50pm, 71SFr); and Zurich (2½hr., 3 per hr. 5:25am-10:25pm, 65SFr). The **tourist office** in the train station reserves rooms. (☎613 73 73. Open daily 9am-5pm.) Home of the world's oldest hotel school, Lausanne has a well-deserved reputation for service-industry excellence. ◪**Lausanne Guesthouse & Backpacker ❷**, chemin des Epinettes 4, is conveniently located and has comfortable rooms. Head left and downhill out of the station on W. Fraisse; take the first right on chemin des Epinettes. (☎601 80 00. Sheets for dorms 5SFr. Reception daily 7am-noon and 3-10pm. 4-bed dorms 29SFr; singles 80SFr, with bathroom 88SFr; doubles 86/98SFr. MC/V.) **Camping de Vidy ❶**, chemin du Camping 3, has a restaurant (open May-Sept. 7am-11pm) and supermarket. Take bus #2 (dir.: *Bourdonnette*) to *Bois-de-Vaux*, cross the street, follow chemin du Bois-de-Vaux past Jeunotel and under the overpass. (☎622 50 00. Showers included. Electricity 3-4SFr. Reception July-Aug. daily 8am-9pm; Sept.-June 8:30am-12:30pm and 4-8pm. 6.50SFr per person, 8-12SFr per tent; 1- to 2-person bungalow 54SFr; 3- to 4-person bungalow 86SFr.) Restaurants, cafes, and bars cluster around place **St-François** and the *vieille ville*, while *boulangeries* sell cheap sandwiches on every street and grocery stores abound. Stop by **Le Barbare ❶**, Escaliers du Marché 27, for a sandwich (7SFr), omelette (8-10SFr), or pizza (12SFr) after trekking to the cathedral. (☎312 21 32. Open M-Sa 8:30am-midnight.)

MONTREUX ☎021

Montreux (pop. 22,500) is a resort town past its Jazz Age heyday. Fortunately, the music still swings; world-famous for drawing and discovering exceptional talent, the ◪**Montreux Jazz Festival** erupts for 15 days starting the first Friday in July (www.montreuxjazz.com; tickets 49-79SFr). Luminaries Neil Young, Bob Dylan, Paul Simon, and Miles Davis have all played here. If you can't get tickets, come anyway for the **Jazz Off**, 500 hours of free, open-air concerts by fledging bands. The **Château de Chillon**, a gloomy medieval fortress on a nearby island, is one of the most visited attractions in Switzerland. It features all the comforts of home: prison cells, a torture chamber, and a weapons room. Take the CGN **ferry** (14SFr) or bus #1 (2.80SFr) to Chillon. (Open Apr.-Sept. daily 9am-6pm; Mar. and Oct. 9:30am-5pm; Nov.-Feb. 10am-4pm. 9SFr, students 7SFr.)

Trains leave the station on av. des Alpes for: Bern (1½hr., 2 per hr. 5:30am-11pm, 37SFr); Geneva (1hr., 2 per hr. 5:30am-11:30pm, 26SFr); and Lausanne (20min., 3-5 per hr. 5:25am-midnight, 9.80SFr). Descend the stairs opposite the station, head left on Grand Rue for 5-10min., and look to the right for the **tourist office**, on pl. du Débarcadère. (☎962 84 84. Open mid-June to mid-Sept. M-F 9:30am-6pm, Sa-Su 10am-5pm; mid-Sept. to mid-June M-F 8:30am-5pm, Sa-Su 10am-3pm.) Cheap rooms in Montreux are scarce year-round and almost nonexistent during the jazz festival, so book ahead. ◪**Riviera Lodge ❷**, pl. du Marché 5, in the neighboring town of Vevey, is worth the commute. Take bus #1 to Vevey (20min., every 10min., 2.80SFr). From the bus stop, head away from the train station on the main road to the open square on the water. Guests get a pass for discounts and free activities in the area, such as waterskiing and a ride up the Vevey funicular. (☎923 80 40. Sheets 5SFr. Laundry 7SFr. **Internet** 7SFr per hour. Reception daily 8am-noon and 5-8pm. Call ahead if arriving late. 4- to 8-bed dorms 24SFr; doubles 80SFr. MC/V.) To get to **Hôtel Pension Wilhelm ❸**, r. du Marché 13-15, take a left on av. des Alpes from the Montreux station, walk uphill 3min., and take a left on r. du Marché. (☎963 14 31. Breakfast included. Reception daily 7am-10pm. Open Mar.-Sept. Singles 60SFr, with shower 70SFr; doubles 100/120SFr.) Grand Rue and ave. de

Casino have reasonably priced markets. **Marché de Montreux,** pl. du Marché, is an open-air food market. (F 7am-1pm.) There's a **Co-op supermarket** at Grand Rue 80. (Open M-F 8am-12:15pm and 2-6:30pm, Sa 8am-5pm.) **Postal Code:** CH-1820.

NEUCHÂTEL   ☎032

Alexandre Dumas once said that Neuchâtel (pop. 164,000) appeared to be carved out of butter. He was referring to its yellow stone architecture, but his comment could easily be taken as a reference to the rich treats in its famous *pâtisseries.* The old town centers around **place des Halles,** a block from **place Pury,** the hub of every bus line. From pl. des Halles, turn left onto r. de Château and climb the stairs on your right to reach **Collégiale church** and the **chateau** that gives the town its name. (Church open Apr.-Sept. daily 9am-8pm; Oct.-Mar. 9am-6:30pm.) You can enter the chateau only on free but dull tours. (Apr.-Sept. M-F every hr. 10am-noon and 2-4pm, Sa 10-11am and 2-4pm, Su 2-4pm.) The nearby **Tour des Prisons** (Prison Tower) on r. Jeanne-Hochberg, has a magnificent view. (Open Apr.-Sept. daily 8am-6pm. 1SFr.) The **Musée d'Histoire Naturelle,** off r. de l'Hôpital, is a more innovative version of the standard natural history museum. Turn right from pl. des Halles onto Croix du Marché, which becomes r. de l'Hôpital. (Open Su and Tu-Sa 10am-6pm. 6SFr, students 3SFr.) The **Musée d'Arts et d'Histoire,** esplanade Léopold-Robert 1, houses an eclectic collection of weapons and textiles. (Open June-Mar. Su and Tu-Sa 10am-6pm; Apr.-May daily 10am-6pm. 7SFr, students 4SFr. W free.)

Trains run to Basel (1¾hr., every hr. 5:30am-10:20pm, 34SFr); Bern (45min., every hr. 5:15am-11:20am, 18SFr); and Geneva (1½hr., every hr. 6am-11:35pm, 40SFr). An underground **tram** runs from the station to the shore area, where you can catch bus #1 to pl. Pury and the **tourist office,** in the same building as the post office. Ask them to find budget pensions. (☎889 68 90. Open M-F 9am-noon and 1:30-6pm, Sa 9am-noon.) Otherwise, try **Hôtel des Arts ❹,** r. Pourtalès 3, for a convenient location near nightlife. From the underground tram exit, walk a block towards the city center on av. du Premier-Mars and turn left onto r. Pourtalès. Most rooms have TVs; all have phones. Ask for a room on the "quiet side" of the building. (☎727 61 61. Breakfast included. Reception 24hr. Check-out noon. Singles 87SFr, with bath 98-126SFr; doubles 112/140-166SFr. AmEx/DC/MC/V.) **Migros,** r. de l'Hôpital 12, sells groceries. (Open M-W 8am-7pm, Th 8am-9pm, F-Sa 7:30am-7pm.) **Postal Code:** CH-2001.

ITALIAN SWITZERLAND

Ever since Switzerland won the Italian-speaking canton of Ticino (Tessin in German and French) from Italy in 1512, the region has been renowned for its mix of Swiss efficiency and Italian *dolce vita*—no wonder the rest of Switzerland vacations here among jasmine-laced villas painted the bright colors of Italian gelato.

LUGANO   ☎091

Set in a valley between two mountains, Lugano (pop. 114,000) draws plenty of visitors with its seamless blend of religious beauty, artistic flair, and natural spectacle. The frescoes of the 16th-century **Cattedrale San Lorenzo,** just south of the train station, are still vivid despite their advanced age. The most spectacular fresco in town, however, is the gargantuan *Crucifixion* in the **Chiesa Santa Maria degli Angiuli,** to the right of the tourist office. Armed with topographic maps and trail guides (sold at the tourist office), hikers can tackle the nearby mountains, **Monte**

Bré (933m) and **Monte San Salvatore** (912m), or the more rewarding **Monte Boglio** (5hr.). Alpine guides at the **ASBEST Adventure Company,** V. Basilea 28 (☎966 11 14), offer everything from snowshoeing and skiing (full-day 90SFr) to paragliding (170SFr) and canyoning (from 90SFr).

Trains leave P. della Stazione for: Locarno (1hr., every 30min. 5:30am-midnight, 17SFr); Milan (45min., every hr. 7am-9:45pm, 21SFr); and Zurich (3hr., 1-2 per hr. 6am-8:35pm, 60SFr). The **tourist office** is across from the ferry station at the corner of p. Rezzonico. (☎913 32 32. Open July-Aug. M-F 9am-7:30pm, Sa 9am-10pm, Su 10am-4pm; Apr.-May and Sept.-Oct. M-F 9am-7:30pm, Sa 9am-5:30pm, Su 10am-4pm; Nov.-Mar. M-F 9am-12:30pm and 1:30-5pm.) ▧**Hotel Montarina ②,** Via Montarina 1, is a palm-tree-enveloped hostel with a swimming pool, kitchen, and terrace. (☎966 72 72. Sheets 4SFr. Laundry 4SFr. Reception daily 8am-10pm. Open Mar.-Oct. Dorms 25SFr; singles 70-80SFr; doubles 100SFr, with bath 120SFr.) The **Migros supermarket,** Via Pretoria 15, also has a food court. (Open M-W and F 8am-6:30pm, Th 8am-9pm, Sa 7:30am-5pm.) **Postal Code:** CH-6900.

LOCARNO   ☎091

A Swiss vacation spot, Locarno (pop. 48,000) gets over 2200 hours of sunlight per year—more than anywhere else in Switzerland. For centuries, visitors have journeyed here solely to see the orange-yellow **Church of Madonna del Sasso** (Madonna of the Rock), founded in 1487. A 20min. walk up the smooth stones of the Via al Sasso leads to the top, passing life-size wooden niche statues along the way. Hundreds of heart-shaped medallions on the church walls commemorate acts of Mary's intervention in the lives of worshipers who have journeyed here. (Grounds open 6:30am-7pm.) Each August (Aug. 4-14, 2004), Locarno swells with pilgrims of a different sort; its world-famous **film festival** draws 150,000 movie-lovers.

Trains run from P. Stazione to: Lucerne (2½hr., every 30min. 6am-9pm, 54SFr); Lugano (50min., every 30min. 5:30am-midnight, 17SFr); and Milan via Bellinzona (2hr., every hr. 5am-9:25pm, 34SFr). The **tourist office,** on P. Grande in the *Kursaal* (casino), makes hotel reservations. (☎791 00 91. Open M-F 9am-6pm, Sa 10am-6pm, Su 2:30-6pm.) To reach **Pensione Città Vecchia ②,** Via Toretta 13, turn right onto Via Toretta from P. Grande. (☎751 45 54. Breakfast included. Reception daily 8am-9pm. Check-in 1-6pm. Dorms 29-37SFr; doubles 70-80SFr; triples 120SFr.) The rooms of **Garni Sempione ③,** Via Rusca 6, are set around an enclosed courtyard. To reach the hotel, walk to the end of the P. Grande, turn right onto Via della Motta, and take the left fork onto Via Rusca. (☎751 30 64. Breakfast included. Reception 8am-9pm. Singles 60SFr, with shower 65SFr; doubles 110/120SFr; triples 150/170SFr; quads 160SFr. AmEx/DC/MC/V.) Left of the station, **Ristorante Manora ①,** Via della Stazione 1, is good, cheap, self-service dining. Salad bar 4.50-10SFr. Pasta buffet 8.50-10SFr. Meat *Menüs* 10.50-16.50SFr. Open Nov.-Feb. M-Sa 8am-9pm, Su 8am-9pm; Mar.-Oct. M-Sa 8am-10pm, Su 8am-9m. Get groceries at the **Aperto** in the station. (Open daily 6am-10pm.) **Postal Code:** CH-6600.

HEADING EAST

During the Cold War, Westerners imposed the name "Eastern Europe" on the Soviet satellites east of the Berlin Wall. The title has always been somewhat of a misnomer, capturing a political rather than geographical reality: Vienna lies farther east than Prague; Croatia sprawls along the Mediterranean; the geometric center of the European continent is in Lithuania; and most of Russia is, quite frankly, in Asia. To understand the remarkable complexity of Eastern Europe is to imagine a map of the region a little over a decade ago: In 1989, there were a total of seven countries behind the Iron Curtain; today, that same area is comprised of 19 independent states. In that time, the region has undergone an astounding political and cultural transformation.

With the exception of the tumultuous Balkans, the former Soviet satellites are progressing, with varying degrees of success, toward democracy and a market economy. In March 1999, the Czech Republic, Poland, and Hungary joined NATO. May 2002 saw the ironic formation of the **NATO-Russia Council,** a strategic alliance between Russia and the organization originally established as a military alliance against Russia. Bulgaria, Estonia, Latvia, Lithuania, Romania, Slovakia, and Slovenia have been invited to join NATO and are expected to become full members by May 2004. That same month, the Czech Republic, Estonia, Latvia, Lithuania, Poland, Hungary, Slovakia, and Slovenia are slated to join the **European Union (EU).** Bulgaria and Romania are expected to become members in 2007.

The region has also recently become the darling of budget travelers. Magnificent cities, pristine national parks, and ridiculously cheap beer lure backpackers seeking bargains and adventure. Prague and Budapest in particular have exploded onto the scene as destinations rivalling the great capitals of Western Europe, while the Dalmatian Coast attracts travelers with azure waters and medieval towns. If Eastern Europe intrigues you further, pick up a copy of *Let's Go: Europe 2004* or *Let's Go: Eastern Europe 2004*.

CZECH REPUBLIC

ESSENTIALS

DOCUMENTS AND FORMALITIES

VISAS. Citizens of Ireland, New Zealand, and the US may visit the Czech Republic without visas for up to 90 days, UK citizens 180 days. Australians, Canadians, and South Africans must obtain 30-day tourist visas. Visas are available at embassies or consulates, but not at the border. Travelers on a visa must **register** with the Czech Immigration Police within three days of arrival; hotels usually register their guests automatically.

CZECH KORUNY		
AUS$1 = 19.11Kč		10Kč = AUS$0.52
CDN$1 = 21.31Kč		10Kč = CDN$0.47
EUR€1 = 32.44Kč		10Kč = EUR€0.31
NZ$1 = 17.07Kč		10Kč = NZ$0.59
UK£1 = 46.59Kč		10Kč = UK£0.21
US$1 = 29.54Kč		10Kč = US$0.34
ZAR1 = 4.03Kč		10Kč = ZAR2.48

SYMBOL	❶	❷	❸	❹	❺
ACCOMMODATIONS	under 320Kč	320-500Kč	501-800Kč	801-1200Kč	over 1200Kč
FOOD	under 80Kč	80-110Kč	111-150Kč	151-200Kč	over 200Kč

EMBASSIES AND CONSULATES. Czech embassies at home include: **Australia,** 8 Culgoa Circuit, O'Malley, Canberra, ACT 2606 (☎02 6290 1386; canberra@embassy.mzv.cz); **Canada,** 251 Cooper St., Ottawa, ON K2P OG2 (☎613-562-3875; ottawa@embassy.mzv.cz); **Ireland,** 57 Northumberland Rd., Ballsbridge, Dublin 4 (☎01 668 1135; dublin@embassy.mzv.cz); **South Africa,** 936 Pretorius St., Arcadia 0083, Pretoria; mail to: P.O. Box 13671, Hatfield 0028, Pretoria 0001 (☎012 431 2380; www.mzv.cz/pretoria); **UK,** 26 Kensington Palace Gardens, London W8 4QY (☎020 7243 1115; www.czechembassy.org.uk); and **US,** 3900 Spring of Freedom St. NW, Washington, D.C. 20008 (☎202-274-9123; www.mzv.cz/washington).

PRAGUE (PRAHA)

According to legend, Countess Libuše stood above the Vltava and declared, "I see a grand city whose glory will touch the stars." Medieval kings, benefactors, and architects fulfilled the prophecy, building soaring cathedrals and lavish palaces that reflected the status of Prague (pop. 1.2 million) as capital of the Holy Roman Empire. Prague's maze of alleys spawned legends of demons and occult forces, giving this "city of dreams" the dark mystique that inspired Franz Kafka's tales of paranoia. Yet since the fall of the Iron Curtain, hordes of foreigners have flooded the city; in summer, tourists pack streets so tightly that crowd-surfing seems a viable method of transportation. Walk a few blocks away from the major sights, however, and you'll be a lone backpacker among cobblestone alleys and looming churches.

⌐ TRANSPORTATION

Flights: Ruzyně Airport (☎220 113 259), 20km northwest of the city. Take bus #119 to Metro A: Dejvická (daily 6am-midnight; 12Kč, luggage 6Kč per bag); buy tickets from kiosks or machines. **Airport buses** (☎220 114 296) run from outside Metro stops (6am-9pm every hr.; Nám. Republiky 90Kč, Dejvická 60Kč). **Cedaz** (☎220 114 296; cedaz@email.cz) offers a shared door-to-door shuttle service. Tickets from the airport are sold at the Cedaz kiosk in the main arrivals hall; tickets to the airport can be booked in advance via phone or email. To/from: central Prague, 360Kč (1-4 people), 720Kč (5-8 people); outer Prague, 720Kč (1-8 people). **Taxis** to the airport are extremely expensive (400-600Kč); try to settle on a price before starting out.

Trains: Domestic ☎224 224 200; International ☎224 615 249; www.cdrail.cz. Prague has 4 main terminals. **Hlavní nádraží** (☎224 224 200; Metro C: Hlavní nádraží) and **Nádraží Holešovice** (☎224 613 249; Metro C: Nádraží Holešovice) are the largest and cover most international service. Domestic trains leave from **Masarykovo nádraží** (☎224 61 51 54; Metro B: Nám. Republiky), on the corner of Hybernská and Havlíčkova, and from **Smíchovské nádraží** (☎224 61 72 55); Metro B: Smíchovské nádraží). International trains run to: **Berlin** (5½hr., 5 per day, 1400Kč); **Bratislava** (4½-5½hr., 7 per day, 450Kč); **Budapest** (7-9hr., 5 per day, 1300Kč); **Kraków** (8½hr., 4 per day, 820Kč); **Moscow** (31hr., daily, 3000Kč); **Munich** (7-9hr., 4 per day, 1650Kč); **Vienna** (4½hr., 4 per day, 900Kč); and **Warsaw** (9½hr., 4 per day, 1290Kč). **BIJ Wasteels** (☎224 617 454; www.wasteels.cz), on the 2nd fl. of Hlavní nádraží, to the right of the stairs, sells discounted international tickets to those under 26, and also books couchettes and bus tickets. Open M-F 8am-6pm, Sa 8am-3pm. Wasteels tickets are also available from the **Czech Railways Travel Agency** (☎224 239 464; fax 224 223 600) at Nádraží Holešovice. Open M-F 9am-5pm, Sa-Su 8am-4pm.

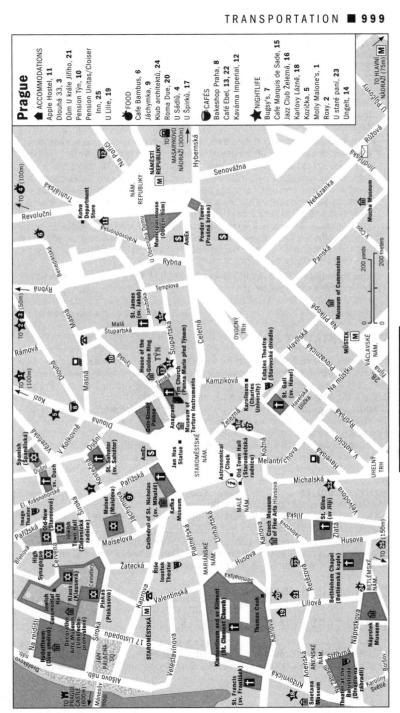

Prague

▲ ACCOMMODATIONS
Apple Hostel, **11**
Dlouhá 33, **3**
Dům U krále Jiřího, **21**
Pension Týn, **10**
Pension Unitas/Cloister Inn, **25**
U Lilie, **19**

◆ FOOD
Cafe Bambus, **6**
Jáchymka, **9**
Klub architektů, **24**
Roma Due, **20**
U Sádlů, **4**
U Špirků, **17**

☕ CAFÉS
Bakeshop Praha, **8**
Café Ebel, **13, 22**
Kavárna Imperial, **12**

★ NIGHTLIFE
Bugsy's, **7**
Cafe Marquis de Sade, **15**
Jazz Club Železná, **16**
Karlovy Lázně, **18**
Kozička, **5**
Molly Malone's, **1**
Roxy, **2**
U staré paní, **23**
Ungelt, **14**

Buses: Schedule info (☎900 149 044; www.jizdnirady.cz or www.vlak.cz). The state-run **ČSAD** (Česká státní automobilová doprava; Czech National Bus Transport; ☎257 319 555) has several bus terminals. The biggest is **Florenc**, Křižíkova 4 (☎ 900 119 041). Metro B or C: Florenc. Info office open daily 6am-9pm. Buy tickets in advance. To: **Berlin** (8hr., daily, 850Kč); **Budapest** (8hr., daily, 1550Kč); **Paris** (18hr., daily, 2200Kč); **Sofia** (26hr., 4 per day, 1600Kč); **Vienna** (8½hr., daily, 600Kč). 10% ISIC discount. The **Tourbus** office (☎224 210 221; www.eurolines.cz), at the terminal, sells tickets for **Eurolines** and airport buses. Open M-F 8am-8pm, Sa 9am-8pm, Su 9am-7pm.

Public Transportation: Buy **Metro, tram,** or **bus** tickets from newsstands, *tabák* kiosks, machines in stations, or **DP** (*Dopravní Podnik;* transport authority) kiosks. The basic 8Kč ticket is good for 15min. on a tram (or 4 stops on the Metro); the 12Kč ticket is valid for 1hr. during the day, with unlimited connections between buses, trams, and Metro in any one direction. Large bags require an extra 6Kč ticket. Validate tickets in machines above escalators or face a 400Kč fine. Before paying a fine, look for the inspector's badge and get a receipt. The three Metro lines run daily 5am-midnight: A is green on maps, B is yellow, C is red. **Night trams** #51-58 and **buses** #501-513 run all night after the last Metro (every 30min.; look for dark blue signs with white lettering at bus stops). The tourist office in the Old Town Hall sells **multi-day passes** valid for the entire network. (Open 24hr. 70Kč, 3-day 200Kč, 7-day 250Kč.)

Taxis: Radiotaxi (☎224 916 666) or **AAA** (☎ 221 111 111). 30Kč flat rate plus 22Kč per km. Hail a cab anywhere on the street, but call one of the above numbers to avoid getting ripped off. To avoid the taxi scams that run rampant throughout the city, always ask for a receipt (*"Prosím, dejte mi paragon"*) with distance traveled and price paid.

✈ ORIENTATION

Shouldering the river **Vltava,** greater Prague is a mess of suburbs and maze-like streets. Fortunately, nearly everything of interest to the traveler lies within the compact downtown. The Vltava runs south-northeast through central Prague, separating **Staré Město** (Old Town) and **Nové Město** (New Town) from **Malá Strana** (Lesser Side). On the right bank of the river, **Staroměstské Náměstí** (Old Town Square) is the heart of Prague. From the square, the elegant **Paížská ulice** (Paris Street) leads north into **Josefov,** the old Jewish ghetto in which only six synagogues and the Old Jewish Cemetery remain. South of Staré Město, Nové Město houses **Václavské Náměstí** (Wenceslas Square), the administrative and commercial core of the city. West of Staroměstské nám., the picturesque **Karlův most** (Charles Bridge) spans the Vltava, connecting the Staré Město with **Malostranské náměstí** (Lesser Town Square). **Pražský Hrad** (Prague Castle) looks over Malostranské nám. from **Hradčany** hill.

Prague's **train station,** Hlavní nádraží, and Florenc bus station lie northeast of Václavské nám. All train and bus terminals are on or near the excellent Metro system. To get to Staroměstské nám., take the Metro A line to *Staroměstská* and head down Kaprova away from the river. Kiosks and bookstores sell an indexed *plán města* (map), which is essential for newcomers to the city.

⚐ PRACTICAL INFORMATION

TOURIST AND FINANCIAL SERVICES

Tourist Offices: Green "i"s mark tourist agencies, which book rooms and sell maps, bus tickets, and guidebooks. **Pražská Informační Služba** (PIS; Prague Info Service; ☎221 714 170; www.pis.cz) is in the Staré Město Hall. Additional branches at Na příkopě 20 and Hlavní nádraží (open in summer M-F 9am-7pm, Sa-Su 9am-5pm; off-season M-F 9am-6pm, Sa 9am-3pm), as well as the tower by the Malá Strana side of the Charles Bridge (open Apr.-Oct., daily 10am-6pm; closed Nov.-Mar.).

Budget Travel: CKM, Manesova 77 (☎222 721 595; www.ckm-praha.cz). Metro A: Jiřího z Poděbrad. Budget air tickets for those under 26. Also books accommodations (dorms from 250Kč). Open M-Th 10am-6pm, F 10am-4pm.

Passport Office: Foreigner Police Headquarters, Olšanská 2 (☎261 441 111). Metro A: Flora. From the Metro, turn right on Jičínská with the cemetery on your right and go right again on Olšanská. Or take tram #9 from Václavské nám. toward Spojovací and get off at Olšanská. For a **visa extension,** get a 90Kč stamp inside. Line up in front of doors #2-12, and prepare to wait up to 2hr. Little English spoken. Open M-Tu and Th 7:30-11:30am and 12:15-3pm, W 8am-12:15pm and 1-5pm, F 7:30-11:30am.

Embassies: Canada, Mickiewiczova 6 (☎272 101 800). Metro A: Hradčanská. Open M-F 8:30am-12:30pm. **Ireland,** Tržiště 13 (☎257 530 061). Metro A: Malostranská. Open M-F 9:30am-12:30pm and 2:30-4:30pm. **South Africa,** Ruská 65 (☎267 311 114). Metro A: Flora. Open M-F 8am-4:30pm. **UK,** Thunovská 14 (☎257 402 111; www.britain.cz). Metro A: Malostranská. Open M-F 9am-noon. **US,** Tržiště 15 (☎257 530 663; emergency ☎253 12 00; www.usembassy.cz). Metro A: Malostranská. Open M-F 9am-4:30pm. **Australia** (☎251 018 350) and **New Zealand** (☎222 514 672) have consuls, but citizens should contact the UK embassy in an emergency.

Currency Exchange: Exchange counters are everywhere and their rates vary wildly. Never change money on the street. **Chequepoints** are convenient and open late, but usually charge commission. **Komerční banka,** Na příkopě 33 (☎222 432 111), buys notes and checks for a 2% commission. Open M-W 9am-6pm, Th-F 9am-5pm. **ATMs** ("Bankomats") abound and can offer the best rates, but sometimes charge large fees.

American Express: Václavské nám. 56 (☎222 432 422). Metro A or C: Muzeum. The **ATM** outside takes AmEx cards. Grants MC/V cash advances for a 3% commission. Open daily 9am-7pm. **Branches** on Mostecká 12 (☎257 313 638; open daily 9:30am-7:30pm), Celetná 17 (☎/fax 224 818 274; open daily 8:30am-7:15pm), and Staroměstské nám. 5 (☎224 818 388; open daily 9am-7:30pm).

LOCAL SERVICES

Luggage Storage: Lockers in all train and bus stations take two 5Kč coins. If these are full, or if you need to store your cargo longer than 24hr., use the luggage offices to the left in the basement of **Hlavní nádraží** (15-30Kč per day; open 24hr.) or halfway up the stairs at **Florenc** (25Kč per day; open daily 5am-11pm).

Laundromat: Laundry Kings, Dejvická 16 (☎233 343 743), 1 block from Metro A: Hradčanská. Cross the tram and railroad tracks, and turn left. Very social. Internet access 55Kč per 30min. Wash 60Kč per 6kg, dry 15Kč per 8min. Open M-F 6am-10pm, Sa-Su 8am-10pm.

EMERGENCY AND COMMUNICATION

Medical Assistance: Na Homolce (Hospital for Foreigners), Roentgenova 2 (☎257 272 142; after-hours 257 772 025; www.homolka.cz). Bus #168 and 184. Open M-F 8am-4pm. 24hr. emergency service. **American Medical Center,** Janovského 48 (☎220 807 756). Major foreign insurance accepted. On call 24hr. Appointments M-F 9am-4pm. Average consultation 50-200Kč.

24hr. pharmacy: U. Lékárna Andwla, Štefánikova 6 (☎257 320 918). Metro B: Anděl.

Telephones: Phone cards sell for 175Kč per 50 units and 320Kč per 100 units at kiosks, post offices, and some exchange places; don't let kiosks rip you off.

Internet Access: Prague is an Internet nirvana. ■ **Bohemia Bagel,** Masna 2 (www.bohemiabagel.cz). Metro A: Staroměstská. 1.5Kč per min. Open M-F 7am-midnight, Sa-Su 8am-midnight. **Cafe Electra,** Rašínovo nábřeží 62 (☎224 922 887; www.electra.cz). Metro B: Karlovo nám. Exit on the Palackého nám. side. Extensive menu. Internet 80Kč per hr. Open M-F 9am-midnight, Sa-Su 11am-midnight.

Post Office: Jindřišská 14 (☎221 131 445). Metro A or B: Můstek. Airmail to the US takes 7-10 days. Open daily 2am-midnight. For *Poste Restante,* address mail to be held: Firstname SURNAME, *Poste Restante,* Jindřišská 14, Praha 1 **110 00,** CZECH REPUBLIC.

▐ ACCOMMODATIONS AND CAMPING

Although hotel prices are through the roof, rates in the glutted hostel market have stabilized at around 300-600Kč per night. Reservations are a must at hotels, which can be booked solid months in advance, and are a good idea at the few hostels that accept them. Most accommodations have 24hr. reception and require check-out by 10am. A growing number of Prague residents rent affordable rooms.

ACCOMMODATIONS AGENCIES

Many room hawkers at the train station offer legitimate deals, but some will rip you off. Apartments go for around 600-1200Kč per day, depending on proximity to the city center. Haggling is possible. If you don't want to bargain on the street, try a **private agency.** Ask where the nearest tram, bus, or Metro stop is, and don't pay until you know what you're getting; ask for details in writing. You can often pay in euros or US dollars, but prices are lower if you pay in Czech crowns. Some travel agencies book lodgings as well (p. 1001). **AveTravel,** on the second floor of Hlavní nádraží, books rooms starting at 800Kč per person and hostels from 290Kč. (☎224 223 226; www.avetravel.cz. Open daily 6am-11pm. AmEx/MC/V.)

HOSTELS

If you tote a backpack in Hlavní nádraží or Holešovice, expect to be bombarded by hostel runners. Many accommodations are university dorms that free up from June to August, and often you'll be offered free transportation. These rooms are convenient options for those arriving in the middle of the night without reservations. If you prefer more than just a place to sleep, smaller establishments are a safer bet. It's a good idea to call as soon as you know your plans, even if only the night before you arrive or at 10am when they know who's checking out. In Prague, the staff typically speaks English, and hostels rarely have curfews.

■ **Hostel Boathouse,** Lodnická 1 (☎241 770 057; www.aa.cz/boathouse), south of the city center. Take tram #21 from Nářodni south toward Sídliště. Get off at Černý Kůň (20min.) and follow the yellow signs. Věra runs the most highly praised staff in Prague. Summer camp vibe. Hot breakfast or dinner 70Kč. Dorms 300-320Kč. ❶

■ **Penzion v podzámčí,** V podzámčí 27 (☎241 444 609; www.sleepinprague.com), south of the city center. From Metro C: Budějovická, take bus #192 to the 3rd stop (*Nad Rybníky*). Homey, with kitchen and laundry. Sept.-June dorms 280Kč, July-Aug. 300Kč; doubles 640/720Kč; triples 900/990Kč. ❶

■ **Dlouhá 33,** (☎224 826 662). Metro B: Nám. Republiky. Follow Revoluční toward the river, turn left on Dlouhá. Unbeatable location in Staré Město; in the same building as the Roxy (p. 1011), but soundproof. Book 2-3 weeks in advance in summer. Open year-round. Dorms 370-430Kč; doubles 1240Kč; triples 1440Kč. ISIC discount 40Kč. ❷

Apple Hostel, Krádlodvorská 16 (☎224 231 050; www.applehostel.cz). Metro B: Nám. Republiky. At the corner of Revoluční and Nám. Republiky, across from Kotva department store. Brand new hostel with a social atmosphere, helpful staff, and a prime location in the heart of Staré Město. Breakfast included. Internet access 1Kč per min. Mar.-Oct. 4-bed dorms 450Kč, Nov.-Feb. 350Kč; 5-bed dorms 440/340Kč; 7-bed dorms 420/320Kč. Singles 1950/1150Kč; doubles 1240/1040Kč. ❷

Hostel U Melounu, Ke Karlovu 7 (☎/fax 224 918 322; www.hostelmelounu.cz), in Nové Město. Metro C: I.P. Pavlova. Follow Sokolská and go right on Na Bojišt then left onto Ke Karlovu. A historic building with great facilities. Breakfast included. Reservations accepted. Dorms 380Kč; singles 500Kč; doubles 840Kč. ISIC discount 30Kč. ❷

Husova 3, (☎222 220 078), in Staré Město. Metro B: Národní třída. Turn right on Spálená (which becomes Na Perštýně after Národní), and again on Husova. Open July-Aug. only. Dorms 400Kč. ❷

Střelecký ostrov, (☎224 932 999), on an island beneath Legií bridge in Staré Město. Metro B: Národní třída. Open mid-June to mid-Sept. Spacious dorms 300Kč. ❶

Ujezd, (☎257 312 403), across Most Legií bridge in Staré Město. Metro B: Národní třída. Sports facilities and park. Open mid-June to mid-Sept. Dorms 220Kč. ❶

Pension Týn, Týnská 19 (☎/fax 224 808 333; backpacker@razdva.cz), in Staré Město. Metro A: Staroměstská. From the Old Town Square, head down Dlouhá, bear right at Masná then right onto Týnská. A quiet getaway located in the center of Staré Město. Immaculate facilities. Dorms 400Kč; doubles 1100Kč. ❷

Welcome Hostel, Zíkova 13 (☎224 320 202; www.bed.cz), outside the center. Metro A: Dejvická. Cheap, tidy, spacious, and convenient university dorm. Near airport shuttle stop. Singles 400Kč; doubles 540Kč. 10% ISIC discount. ❷

Welcome Hostel at Strahov Complex, Vaníčkova 5 (☎233 359 275), outside the center. Take bus #217 or 143 from Metro A: Dejvická to Koleje Strahov. Newly renovated high-rise dorms near Prague Castle. A little far, but there's almost always space. Singles 300Kč; doubles 440Kč. 10% ISIC discount. ❶

HOTELS AND PENSIONS

As tourists colonize Prague, hotels are upgrading their service and their prices; budget hotels are now quite scarce. Call several months ahead to book a room in summer and confirm by fax with a credit card.

▧ **Dům U krále Jiřího,** Liliová 10 (☎222 220 925; www.kinggeorge.cz), in Staré Město. Metro A: Staroměstská. Exit onto Nám. Jana Palacha, walk down Křížovnická toward the Charles Bridge and turn left onto Karlova; Liliová is the first right. Gorgeous rooms with private bath. Breakfast included. May-Dec. singles 2000Kč; doubles 3300Kč. Dec.-May 1500/2700Kč. ❺

U Lilie, Liliová 15 (☎222 220 432; www.pensionville.cz), in Staré Město. Metro A: Staroměstská. See directions for Dům U krále Jiřího (above). Lovely courtyard. Breakfast included. Singles with showers 1850Kč; doubles 2150-2800Kč. ❺

Hotel Kafka, Cimburkova 24 (☎/fax 222 781 333), outside the center. From Metro C: Hlavní nádraží, take tram #5 (dir.: Harfa), 9 (dir.: Spojovací), or 26 (dir.: Nádraží Hostivař); get off at *Husinecká*. Head uphill along Seifertova then on Cimburkova. Locals frequent nearby beer halls. Breakfast included. Apr.-Oct. singles 1700Kč; doubles 2300Kč. Nov.-Mar. 1000/1300Kč. MC/V for 5% commission. ❺

Pension Unitas/Cloister Inn, Bartolomějská 9 (☎224 221 802; www.unitas.cz), in Staré Město. Metro B: Národní třída. Cross Národní, head up Na Perštýně away from Tesco, and turn left on Bartolomějská. Renovated rooms in the cells of the former Communist prison where Václav Havel was incarcerated. Breakfast included. Singles 1100Kč; doubles 1400Kč; triples 1750Kč. ❹

CAMPING

Campsites can be found in both the outskirts and the centrally located Vltava islands. Bungalows must be reserved in advance, but tent space is generally available without prior notice. Tourist offices sell a guide to sites near the city (15Kč).

Sokol Troja, Trojská 171 (☎/fax 233 542 908), north of the center in the Troja district. Metro C: Nádraží Holešovice. Take bus #112 to Kazanka. Similar places line the road. July-Aug. 130Kč per person, 90-180Kč per tent; Oct.-June 70-150Kč per tent. Private rooms available. July-Aug., singles 320Kč; doubles 640Kč. Oct.-June 290/580Kč. ❶

Caravan Park, Císařská louka 599 (☎257 318 681; fax 257 318 387), on the Císařská louka peninsula. Metro B: Smíchovské nádraží, then any of the buses numbered in the 300s to Lihovar. Alternatively, a ferry service leaves every hr. on the hour from the small landing 1 block over from Smíchovské nádraží (10Kč). Small, tranquil camping ground on the banks of the Vltava river. Clean facilities, friendly staff, convenient cafe and currency exchange on premises. 95Kč per person, 90-140Kč per tent. ❶

◘ FOOD

The nearer you are to the center, the more you'll pay. Away from the center, pork, cabbage, dumplings, and a half-liter of beer costs about 50Kč. You will be charged for everything the waiter brings to the table; check your bill carefully. Most restaurants accept only cash. Outlying Metro stops become markets in the summer. **Tesco,** Národní třída 26, has **groceries** right next to metro B: Národní třída. (Open M-F 7am-10pm, Sa 8am-8pm, Su 9am-8pm.) Look for the **daily market** in Staré Město where Havelská and Melantrichova intersect. After a night out, grab a *párek v rohlíku* (hot dog) or a *smažený sýr* (fried cheese sandwich) from a Václavské nám. vendor, or a gyro from a stand on Spálená or Vodíčkova.

RESTAURANTS

▩ **Jáchymka,** Jáchymova 4 (☎224 819 621). From the Old Town Square, walk up Pařížská and take a right on Jáchymova. A favorite among locals, Jáchymka serves heaping portions of traditional Czech cuisine in a lively, informal atmosphere. Try the goulash with dumplings (95Kč) or one of their massive meat escalopes (80-185Kč). Or for lighter fare, try the salmon with pasta and vegetables (195Kč). Open daily 11am-11pm. ❹

▩ **Radost FX,** Bělehradská 120, is both a dance club and a late-night cafe with an imaginative menu and great vegetarian food. Metro C: I.P. Pavlova. Main dishes 105-170Kč. Brunch Sa-Su 95-140Kč. Open daily 11am-late. See also Clubs and Discos, p. 1010. ❸

U Sádlů, Klimentskà 2 (☎224 813 874; www.usadlu.cz). Metro B: Nám. Republiky. From the square, walk down Revoluční toward the river, then go right on Klimentskà. Medieval themed restaurant with bountiful portions; call ahead. Czech-only menu lists traditional meals (115-245Kč). Open daily 11am-midnight. ❸

Klub architektů, Betlémské nám. 52A, in Staré Město. Metro B: Národní třída. A 12th-century cellar with 20th century ambience. Veggie options 90-100Kč. Meat dishes 150-290Kč. Open daily 11:30am-midnight. MC/V. ❸

U Švejků, Újezd 22, in Malá Strana. Metro A: Malostranská. Head down Klárov and go right onto Letenská. Bear left through Malostranské nám. and follow Karmelitská until it becomes Újezd. Named after the lovable Czech cartoon hero from Hasek's novel *The Good Soldier Svejk,* and decorated with scenes from the book. Nightly accordion music after 7pm. Main dishes 98-148Kč. Open daily 11am-midnight. AmEx/MC/V. ❸

Velryba (The Whale), Opatovická 24, in Nové Město. Metro B: Národní třída. Cross the tram tracks and follow Ostrovní, then go left onto Opatovická. Relaxed cafe-restaurant with downstairs art gallery. Entrees 80-140Kč. Open M-Th 11am-midnight, F 11am-2am. Cafe and gallery open M-F noon-midnight, Sa 5pm-midnight, Su 3-10pm. ❷

Kajetanka, Hradcanské nám., in Malá Strana. Metro A: Malostranská. Walk down Letenská through Malostranské nám.; climb Nerudova until it curves to Ke Hradu, continue up the hill. Terrace cafe with a spectacular view. Meat dishes 129-299Kč, salads 49-69Kč. Open in spring and summer daily 10am-8pm; off-season 10am-6pm. ❹

Cafe Bambus, Benediktska 12, in Staré Město. Metro B: Nám. Republiky. An African oasis with an international menu. Entrees 55-228Kč. Czech pancakes 55-75Kč. Open M-Th 10am-1am, F 10am-2am, Sa 11am-2am, Su 11am-11pm. ❷

U Špirků, ul. Kožná 12, in Staré Město. Metro A: Staroměstská. Authentic Czech decor and some of the city's best food at incredibly low prices. Entrees about 100Kč. Open daily 11am-midnight. ❶

Roma Due, Liliová 18. Metro A: Staroměstská. Perfect to cap off a night out. Pasta 89-155Kč until 10pm. Pizza 99-150Kč until 5am. Open 24hr. ❸

CAFES AND TEAHOUSES

🍴 **Cafe Ebel,** Týn 2 (☎224 895 788; www.ebelcoffee.cz). Metro A or B: Staroměstská. Under the Ungelt arches. The best coffee in town and an affordable continental breakfast. Additional location at Retezova 9. Open daily 9am-10pm.

🍴 **Bakeshop Praha,** Kozí 1 (☎222 316 823; info@bakeshop.cz). From the Old Town Square, follow Dlouhá to the intersection of Kozí. Mouthwatering breads, pastries, muffins, salads, sandwiches, and quiches and a multitude of espresso and tea drinks. Additional location at Lázenska 19, off Mostécka in Malá Strana. Open daily 7am-7pm.

🍴 **Kavarná Imperial,** Na Poříčí 15. Metro B: Nám. Republiky. Pillared cafe with a courtly air. Live jazz F-Sa 9pm. Open M-Th 9am-midnight, F-Sa 9am-1am, Su 9am-11pm.

The Globe Coffeehouse, Pštrossova 6. Metro B: Národní třída. At the Globe Bookstore. Exit Metro left on Spálená, turn right on Ostrovní, then left to Pštrossova. Fruit smoothies (45-60Kč), black coffee (25Kč), and English speakers trying to make a love connection (priceless). Open daily 10am-midnight.

U Malého Glena, Karmelitská 23. Metro A: Malostranská. Take tram #12 to Malostranské nám. Their motto is: "Eat, Drink, Drink Some More." Killer margaritas 90Kč. Nightly jazz or blues 9pm. Cover 100-150Kč. Open daily 10am-2am.

U zeleného čaje, Nerudova 19. Metro A: Malostranská. Follow Letenská to Malostranské nám.; stay right of the church. Over 60 varieties of fragrant tea to please the senses and calm the mind. Sandwiches 25-89Kč. Open daily 11am-10pm.

Kavárna Medúza, Belgická 17. Metro A: Nám. Míru. Walk down Rumunská and turn left at Belgická. Cafe masquerading as an antique shop. Fluffed-up Victorian seats and lots of coffee (19-30Kč). Open M-F 11am-1am, Sa-Su noon-1am.

🔄 SIGHTS

One of the only major Central European cities unscathed by WWII, Prague is a well-preserved blend of labyrinthine alleys and Baroque architecture. You can easily escape the crowds by venturing away from **Staroměstské náměstí, Karlův Most** (Charles Bridge), and **Václavské náměstí.** Compact central Prague is best explored on foot. There are plenty of opportunities for exploration in the back alleys of **Josefov,** the hills of **Vyšehrad,** and the maze of streets in **Malá Strana.**

NOVÉ MĚSTO (NEW TOWN)

Established in 1348 by Charles IV, Nové Město has become the commercial center of Prague, complete with American chain stores.

WENCESLAS SQUARE. Not so much a square as a boulevard running through the center of Nové Město, Wenceslas Square (Václavské náměstí) owes its name to the Czech ruler and saint **Wenceslas** (Václav), whose statue is in front of the National Museum (Národní muzeum). Wenceslas has presided over a century of turmoil and triumph, witnessing no fewer than five revolutions from his pedestal: The declaration of the new Czechoslovak state in 1918, the invasion by Hitler's troops in 1939, the arrival of Soviet tanks in 1968, the self-immolation of Jan Palach in protest of the Soviet invasion, and the 1989 Velvet Revolution. The square stretches from the statue past department stores, thumping discos, posh hotels, sausage stands, and glitzy casinos. **Radio Free Europe,** which gives global news updates and advocates peace, has been broadcasting from its glass building behind the National Museum since WWII. *(Metro A or C: Muzeum.)*

FRANCISCAN GARDEN AND VELVET REVOLUTION MEMORIAL. Monks somehow manage to preserve the immaculate and serene **rose garden** (Františkánská zahrada) in the heart of Prague's bustling commercial district. A plaque under the arcades halfway down Národní, across from the Black Theatre, memorializes the hundreds of citizens beaten by police on November 17, 1989. A subsequent wave of mass protests led to the total collapse of Communism in Czechoslovakia during the Velvet Revolution. *(Metro A or B: Můstek. Enter through the arch to the left of Jungmannova and Národní, behind the statue. Open daily mid-Apr. to mid-Sept. 7am-10pm; mid-Sept. to mid-Oct. 7am-8pm; mid-Oct. to mid-Apr. 8am-7pm. Free.)*

THE DANCING HOUSE. American architect Frank Gehry (of Guggenheim-Bilbao fame; p. 979) built the undulating "Dancing House" (Tančící dům) at the corner of Resslova and Rašínovo nábřeží. Since its 1996 unveiling, it has been called an eyesore by some, and a shining example of postmodern design by others. *(Metro B: Karlovo nám. As you walk down Resslova toward the river, the building is on the left.)*

STARÉ MĚSTO (OLD TOWN)

Getting lost among the narrow roads and old-world alleys of Staré Město is probably the best way to appreciate the 1000-year-old neighborhood's charm.

CHARLES BRIDGE. Thronged with tourists and the hawkers who feed on them, the Charles Bridge (Karlův Most) is Prague's most recognizable landmark. On each side of the bridge, defense towers offer splendid views of the city and of the river. Five stars and a cross mark the spot where the St. Jan Nepomucký was tossed over the side of the bridge for guarding the queen's extramarital secrets from a suspicious King Wenceslas IV. *(Metro A: Malostranská on the Malá Strana side and Metro A: Staroměstská on the Staré Město side. Open daily 10am-10pm. 40Kč, students 30Kč.)*

OLD TOWN SQUARE. The heart of Staré Město is Staroměstské náměstí (Old Town Square), surrounded by eight magnificent towers. Next to the grassy knoll stands the **Old Town Hall** (Staroměstské radnice). The multi-facaded building is missing a piece of the front facade where the Nazis partially demolished it in the final week of WWII. Crowds gather on the hour to watch the **astronomical clock** chime, releasing a procession of apostles accompanied by a skeleton symbolizing Death. *(Metro A: Staroměstská or Metro A or B: Můstek. Town Hall open in summer M 11am-5:30pm, Tu-Su 9am-5:30pm. Clock tower open daily 10am-6pm. 40Kč, students 30Kč.)* Opposite the Old Town Hall, the spires of **Týn Church** (Matka Boží před Týnem) rise above a mass of medieval homes. The famous astronomer Tycho Brahe is buried inside. Brahe died when he overindulged at one of Emperor

Rudolf's lavish dinner parties, where it was unacceptable to leave the table unless the Emperor himself did so. Because he was forced to stay seated, his bladder burst. The bronze statue of theologian **Jan Hus,** the country's most famous martyr, stands in the middle of the square. In front of the Jan Hus statue sits the flowery **Goltz-Kinský Palace,** the finest of Prague's Rococo buildings. *(Open Tu-F 10am-6pm; closes early in summer for daily concerts.)*

POWDER TOWER AND MUNICIPAL HOUSE. One of the original eight city gates, the Gothic **Powder Tower** (Prašná Brána) looms at the edge of Nám. Republiky as the entrance to Staré Město. A steep climb to the top rewards you with expansive views. Next door, on the site of a former royal court, is the **Municipal House** (Obecnídům), where the Czechoslovak state declared independence on October 28, 1918. *(Nám. Republiky 5. Metro B: Nám. Republiky. Tower open July-Aug. daily 10am-10pm; Apr.-June and Sept.-Oct. daily 10am-6pm. House open daily 10am-6pm. Guided tours Sa noon and 2pm. 150Kč.)*

JOSEFOV

Josefov, the oldest Jewish settlement in Central Europe, lies north of Staroměstské nám., along Maiselova. In 1180, Prague's citizens built a 12 ft. wall around the area. The closed neighborhood bred exotic tales, many of which centered around Rabbi Loew ben Bezalel (1512-1609) and his legendary *golem*—a mud creature that supposedly came to life to protect Prague's Jews. The city's Jews remained clustered in Josefov until WWII, when the ghetto was vacated as the residents were deported to death camps. Ironically, Hitler's wish to create a "museum of an extinct race" sparked the preservation of Josefov's cemetery and synagogues. Although it's only a fraction of its former size, there's still a Jewish community living in Prague today. *(Metro A: Staroměstská. Synagogues and cemetery open Apr.-Oct. Su-F 9am-6pm; Nov.-Mar. 9am-4:30pm. Closed Jewish holidays. All six synagogues except Starnová charge 250Kč, students 170Kč. Starnová Synagogue 200/140Kč.)*

THE SYNAGOGUES. The **Maisel Synagogue** (Maiselova synagoga) displays artifacts from the Jewish Museum's collections. *(On Maiselova, between Široká and Jáchymova.)* At the time of publication, **Pinkas Synagogue** (Pinkasova) was under repair due to recent flooding. To reach it, turn left down Široká to reach this sobering 16th-century memorial to the 80,000 Czech Jews killed in the Holocaust. Upstairs is an exhibit of drawings made by children in the Terezín camp. Backtrack up Široká and go left on

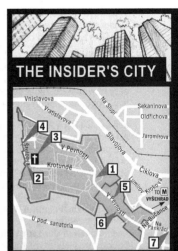

THE INSIDER'S CITY

VYŠEHRAD

The former haunt of Prague's 19th-century Romantics, Vyšehrad is a storehouse of nationalist myths and imperial legends. Quiet paths wind among crumbling stone walls offering respite from Prague's busy streets. (Metro C: Vyšehrad.)

1 Stroll by **St. Martin Rotunda,** Prague's oldest building.

2 Indulge in an elegant Czech meal at **Na Vyšehradě** (open daily 10am-10pm).

3 The **cemetery** holds the remains of the Czech Republic's most famous citizens.

4 Walk along the **castle walls** to enjoy Prague from new heights.

5 Relax in the sun with ice cream from **Obcerstveni Penguin** (open daily 11am-7pm).

6 A small **gallery** exhibits the work of local disabled children (open daily 10am-5pm).

7 Pass through the **Tábor Gate** to reach **Nad Vyšehradem,** a popular beer hall (open M-Th 10am-10pm, F-Su 11am-11pm).

Maiselova to visit the oldest operating synagogue in Europe, the 700-year-old **New Synagogue** (Staronová). Further up Široká on Dušní is the **Spanish Synagogue** (Španělská), which has an ornate Moorish interior.

OLD JEWISH CEMETERY. The Old Jewish Cemetery (Starý židovský hřbitov) remains Josefov's most-visited site. Between the 14th and 18th centuries, 20,000 graves were laid in 12 layers. The striking clusters of tombstones result from a process in which the older stones rose from underneath. Rabbi Loew is buried by the wall opposite the entrance. *(At the corner of Široká and Žatecká.)*

MALÁ STRANA

A seedy hangout for criminals and counter-revolutionaries for nearly a century, the cobblestone streets of Malá Strana have become prized real estate. Malá Strana is centered around **Malostranské Náměstí** and its centerpiece, the Baroque **St. Nicholas's Cathedral** (Chrám sv. Mikuláše), whose towering dome is one of Prague's most prominent landmarks. *(Metro A: Malostranská; follow Letenská to Malostranské nám. Open daily 9am-4:45pm. 50Kč, students 25Kč.)* Along Letenská, a wooden gate opens into the beautiful **Wallenstein Garden** (Valdštejnská zahrada), one of Prague's best-kept secrets. *(Letenská 10. Metro A: Malostranská. Open Apr.-Oct. daily 10am-6pm. Free.)* **Church of Our Lady Victorious** (Kostel Panna Marie Vítězné) is known for the famous wax statue of the **Infant Jesus of Prague,** said to bestow miracles on the faithful. *(Metro A: Malostranská. Follow Letecká through Malostranské nám. and continue onto Karmelitská. Open daily 8:30am-7pm. Museum open M-Sa 9:30am-5:30pm, Su 1-6pm. Free.)*

PRAGUE CASTLE (PRAŽSKÝ HRAD)

Prague Castle has been the seat of the Bohemian government for over 1000 years. From Metro A: Hradčanská, cross the tram tracks and turn left onto Tychonova, which leads to the newly renovated **Royal Summer Palace.** The main castle entrance is at the other end of the lush **Royal Garden** (Královská zahrada), where the Singing Fountain spouts and chimes. Before exploring, pass the main gate to see the **Šternberg Palace,** which houses art from the National Gallery. *(Metro A: Malostranská. Take trams #22 or 23 to Pražský Hrad and go down U Prašného Mostu. Open Apr.-Oct. daily 9am-5pm; Nov.-Mar. 9am-4pm. Buy tickets opposite St. Vitus's Cathedral, inside the castle walls. 1-day ticket valid at Royal Crypt, Cathedral and Powder Tower, Old Royal Palace, and the Basilica. 220Kč, students 110Kč.)*

ST. VITUS'S CATHEDRAL. Inside the castle walls stands the colossal St. Vitus's Cathedral (Katedrála sv. Víta), which looks Gothic but was in fact finished in 1929, 600 years after construction began. To the right of the high altar stands the silver **Tomb of St. Jan Nepomucký.** In the main church, the walls of **St. Wenceslas's Chapel** (Svatováclavská kaple) are lined with precious stones and a painting cycle depicting the legend of Wenceslas. Climb the 287 steps of the **Great South Tower** for the best view of the city, or descend underground to the **Royal Crypt,** which holds the tomb of Charles IV.

OLD ROYAL PALACE. The Old Royal Palace (Starý Královský Palác) is to the right of the cathedral, behind the Old Provost's House and the statue of St. George. The lengthy **Vladislav Hall** once hosted jousting competitions. Upstairs is the **Chancellery of Bohemia,** where the Second Defenestration of Prague took place.

ST. GEORGE'S BASILICA AND ENVIRONS. Behind the cathedral and across the courtyard from the Old Royal Palace stands St. George's Basilica (Bazilika sv. Jiří). The **National Gallery of Bohemian Art,** which has art ranging from Gothic to Baroque, is in the adjacent convent. *(Open Tu-Su 10am-6pm. 100Kč, students 50Kč.)* **Jiřská** street begins to the right of the basilica. Halfway down, tiny **Golden Lane** (Zlatá ulička) heads off to the right; alchemists once worked here, and Kafka later lived at #22.

OUTER PRAGUE

The city's outskirts are packed with greenery, churches, and panoramic vistas, all peacefully tucked away from hordes of tourists. **Vyšehrad** is the former haunt of Prague's 19th-century Romantics; quiet walkways wind between crumbling stone walls to one of the Czech Republic's most celebrated sites, **Vyšehrad Cemetery,** home to the remains of composer Antonin Dvořák. The oldest monastery in Bohemia, **Břevnov Monastery,** was founded in AD993 by King Boleslav II and St. Adalbert, each of whom was guided by a divine dream to build a monastery atop a bubbling stream. The stream leads to a pond to the right of **St. Margaret's Church** (Bazilika sv. Markéty) within the complex. *(From Metro A: Malostranská, take tram #22 uphill to Břevnovský klášter. Church open daily 7:30am-6pm.)* The traditional **Prague Market** (Pražskátrznice) has acres of stalls selling all kinds of wares. *(Take tram #3 or 14 from Nám. Republiky to Vozovna Kobylisy and get off at Pražskátrznice. Open daily.)*

🏛 MUSEUMS

The city's museums often have striking facades but mediocre collections. Still, a few quirky museums are worth a visit.

🖼MUCHA MUSEUM. The museum is devoted to the work of Alfons Mucha, the Czech Republic's most celebrated artist, who composed some of the pioneering brushstrokes of the Art Nouveau movement. *(Panská 7. Metro A or B: Můstek. Walk up Václavské nám. toward the St. Wenceslas statue. Go left onto Jindřišská and again onto Panská. ☎221 451 333; www.mucha.cz. Open daily 10am-6pm. 120Kč, students 60Kč.)*

MUSEUM OF MEDIEVAL TORTURE INSTRUMENTS. The collection and highly detailed explanations are guaranteed to nauseate. *(Mostécka 21. Metro A: Malostranská. Follow Letenská from the Metro and turn left on Mostécka. Open daily 10am-10pm. 120Kč, students 100Kč.)* In the same building, the **Exhibition of Spiders and Scorpions** shows live venomous spiders and scorpions in their natural habitats. *(Open daily 10am-10pm. 100Kč, children 80Kč.)*

NATIONAL GALLERY. The massive collection of the National Gallery (Národní Galerie) is spread around nine different locations; the notable Šternberský palác and Klášter sv. Jiří are in the **Prague Castle** (see p. 1008). The **Trade Fair Palace and the Gallery of Modern Art** (Veletržní palác a Galerie moderního umwní) exhibits an impressive collection of 20th-century Czech and European art. *(Dukelských hrinů 47. Metro C: Holešovice. All open Su and T-Sa 10am-6pm. 150Kč, students 70Kč.)*

MUSEUM OF COMMUNISM. This new gallery is committed to exposing the flaws of the Communist system that suppressed the Czech people from 1948-1989. It features 3-D objects, a model factory, and an interrogation office. *(Na Přikopě 10. Metro A: Můstek. Open daily 9am-9pm. 180Kč, students 140Kč.)*

🎭 ENTERTAINMENT

For concerts and performances, consult *Threshold, Do města-Downtown* (both free at many cafes and restaurants), *The Pill,* or *The Prague Post.* Most performances start at 7pm and offer standby tickets 30min. beforehand. Between mid-May and early June, the **Prague Spring Festival** draws musicians from around the world. For tickets, try **Bohemia Ticket International,** Malé nám. 13, next to Čedok. (☎224 227 832; www.ticketsbti.cz. Open M-F 9am-5pm, Sa 9am-2pm.) The **National Theater** (Národní divadlo), Národní 2/4, stages drama, opera, and ballet. (☎114 901 448. Metro B: Národní třída. Box office open M-F 10am-6pm, Sa-Su 10am-12:30pm, 3-6pm, and 30min. before performances. 100-1000Kč.) **Estates Theater** (Stavovské divadlo), Ovocný trg 1, is on the pedestrian Na Příkopě. (Metro A or B: Můstek.) Mozart's *Don Giovanni* premiered here; shows today are mostly classic theater. Use the National Theater box office, or show up 30min. before the performance. The **Marionette Theater** (Říše loutek), Žatecká 1, stages a hilarious marionette version of *Don Giovanni*. (Metro A: Staroměstská. Performances June-July Su-Tu and Th-Sa 5 and 8pm. Box office open daily 10am-8pm. 490Kč, students 390Kč.)

🅸 NIGHTLIFE

With some of the best beers in the world on tap, it's no surprise that pubs and beer halls are Prague's most popular nighttime hangouts. Tourists have overrun the city center, so authentic pub experiences are now largely restricted to the suburbs and outlying Metro stops. Although dance clubs abound, Prague is not a clubbing city—locals prefer the many jazz and rock hangouts scattered about the city.

BARS

🅼 Vinárna U Sudu, Vodičkova 10. Metro A or B: Můstek. Cross Václavské nám. to Vodičkova and follow the curve left. Infinite labyrinth of cavernous cellars. Red wine 120Kč per 1L. Open M-F 1pm-midnight, Sa-Su 2pm-midnight.

🅼 Kozička (The Little Goat), Kozí 1. Metro A: Staroměstská. This giant cellar bar is always packed; you'll know why after your first 0.5L of *Krušovice* (18Kč). Czech 20-somethings stay all night. Open M-F noon-4am, Sa-Su 6pm-4am.

U Fleků, Křemencova 11. Metro B: Národní třída. Turn right on Spálená away from Národní, right on Myslíkova, and then right again on Křemencova. The oldest beer hall in Prague. Home-brewed beer 49Kč. Open daily 9am-11pm.

Pivnice u Sv. Tomáše, Letenská 12 (☎257 531 835). Metro A: Malostranská. Walk downhill on Letenská. While meat roasts on a spit, the mighty dungeons echo with boisterous revelry and gushing toasts. Order meats a day in advance, 350-400Kč. Beer 40Kč. Live brass band nightly 7-11pm. Open daily 11:30am-midnight. MC/V.

Bugsy's, Parížská 10. Sophisticated, American style speakeasy serving the tastiest mixed drinks in town. Cocktail menu so thick it's hardcover (60-200Kč). When the upscale munchies hit, sushi awaits. Open daily 7pm-2am. Live Jazz M nights.

Cafe Marquis de Sade, Melnicka 5. Metro B: Nám. Republiky. Spacious bar decorated in rich red velvet. Happy Hour M-F 4-6pm. Velvet beer 27-35Kč. Open daily noon-2am.

Zanzibar, Saská 6. Metro A: Malostranská. Head down Mostecká toward the Charles Bridge, turn right on Lázeňská, and turn left on Saská. The tastiest, priciest, and most exotic cocktails this side of the Vltava (110-150Kč). Open daily 5pm-3am.

Molly Malone's, U obecního dvora 4. Metro A: Staroměstská. Overturned sewing machines serve as tables in this pub. Small groups can head to the loft. Guinness 80Kč. Open Su-Th 11am-1am, F-Sa 11am-2am.

Jo's Bar and Garáž, Malostranské nám. 7. Metro A: Malostranská. All-Anglophone with foosball, darts, cards, and a DJ. Beer 30Kč during Happy Hour (6-10pm). Open daily 11am-2am.

CLUBS AND DISCOS

🅼 Radost FX, Bělehradská 120 (www.radostfx.cz). Metro C: I.P. Pavlova. Plays the hippest techno, jungle, and house. Creative drinks. Cover 80-150Kč. Open M-Sa 10pm-late.

Jazz Club Železná, Železná 16. Metro A or B: Staroměstská. Vaulted cellar bar showcases live jazz daily. Beer 30Kč. Cover 120-150Kč. Shows 9-11:30pm. Open daily 3pm-1am. AmEx/MC/V.

Roxy, Dlouhá 33. Metro B: Nám. Republiky. In the same building as the Dlouhá 33 Traveler's Hostel (p. 1002). Experimental DJs and theme nights. Crowds hang out on the huge staircases. Cover 100-350Kč. Open M-Tu and Th-Sa 9pm-late.

Karlovy Lázně, Novotného lávka 1. Four levels of themed dance floors under the Charles Bridge. Cover 100Kč, 50Kč before 10pm and after 4am. Open nightly 9pm-late.

Palác Akropolis, Kubelíkova 27 (www.palacakropolis.cz). Metro A: Jiřího z Poděbrad. Head down Slavíkova and turn right onto Kubelíkova. Live bands several times a week. Top Czech act *Psí vojáci* is an occasional visitor. Open daily 10pm-5am.

U staré paní, Michalská 9. Metro A or B: Můstek. Some of Prague's finest jazz vocalists in a tiny yet classy venue. Shows nightly 9pm-midnight. Cover 160Kč, includes 1 drink. Open for shows 7pm-2am.

Ungelt, Tyn 2. Metro A: Staroměstská. Subterranean vault with live jazz daily from 9pm-midnight. (Cover 160Kč). Or, listen from the pub for free. Open daily noon-midnight.

GAY AND LESBIAN NIGHTLIFE

At any of the places below, you can pick up a copy of *Amigo* (69Kč), the most thorough guide to gay life in the Czech Republic with a lot in English, or *Gaýčko* (60Kč), a glossier piece of work written mostly in Czech.

Friends, Náprstkova 1 (☎221 635 408; www.friends-prague.cz). Lively cellar bar in the heart of Staré Město. Slightly touristy but always busy. Friendly, English-speaking bartenders are good sources for info on hot spots. Czech music party W nights. Internet 2Kč per min (4-8pm). Open daily 3pm-3am.

Tingl Tangl, Karolíny Světlé 12. Metro B: Národní třída. Under the archway on the left, this gay club draws a diverse crowd for its cabarets. Cover 120Kč. Open W-Sa 9pm-5am, with shows after midnight.

A Club, Milíčova 25. Metro C: Hlavní nádraží. Take tram #5, 9, 26, or 55 uphill and get off at Lipsanká. A favorite lesbian nightspot. Men are free to enter, but expect funny looks. Beer 20Kč. Open nightly 7pm-6am.

▶ DAYTRIPS FROM PRAGUE

TEREZÍN (THERESIENSTADT). In 1941, when Terezín became a concentration camp, Nazi propaganda films touted the area as a resort where Jews would live a normal life. In reality, over 30,000 died here, some of starvation and disease, others in death chambers; another 85,000 Jews were transported to death camps further east. The **Ghetto Museum,** around the corner, to the left of the bus stop in town, sets Terezín in the wider context of WWII. (Open Apr.-Sept. daily 9am-6pm; Oct.-Mar. 9am-5:30pm. Tickets to museum, barracks, and small fortress 180Kč, students 160Kč.) Across the river is the **Small Fortress,** which was used as a Gestapo prison. (Open Apr.-Sept. daily 8am-6pm; Oct.-Mar. 8am-4:30pm.) The **cemetery** has tributes left by the victims' descendants. Men should cover their heads when visiting. (Open Mar.-Nov. Su-F 10am-5pm. Free.) The furnaces of the **crematorium** are temporarily closed due to flooding. Terezín has been repopulated to about half of its former size; families now live in the barracks and supermarkets occupy former Nazi offices. A **bus** runs from Prague Florenc station (1hr., 9 per day, 59Kč); get off at the Terezín stop, where the **tourist office** sells a 30Kč map. (Open Su and Tu-Sa 9am-12:30pm and 1-4pm.)

KUTNÁ HORA. East of Prague, the former mining town of Kutná Hora (Mining Mountain) has a history as morbid as the **bone church** that has made the city famous. Founded in the late 13th century when lucky miners hit a vein of silver, the city boomed with greedy diggers, but the Black Plague halted the fortune-seekers dead in their tracks. When the graveyard became overcrowded, the Cistercian Order built a chapel to hold bodies. In a fit of whimsy (or insanity), one monk began designing floral shapes out of pelvises and crania; he never finished, but the artist František Rint eventually completed the project in 1870 with the bones of over 40,000 people, including femur crosses and a grotesque chandelier made from every kind of bone in the human body. (Open Apr.-Oct. daily 8am-6pm; Nov.-Mar. 9am-noon and 1-4pm. 30Kč, students 20Kč.) Take a **bus** (1½hr., 6 per day, 54-64Kč) from Prague Florenc station. Exit left onto Benešova, continue through the rotary until it becomes Vítězná, then go left on Zámecká.

KARLŠTEJN. A gem of the Bohemian countryside, Karlštejn is a turreted fortress built by Charles IV in the 14th century to store his crown jewels and holy relics. (Open July-Aug. Su and Tu-Sa 9am-6pm; May-June and Sept. 9am-5pm; Apr.-Oct. 9am-4pm; Nov.-Mar. 9am-3pm. 7-8 English tours per day; 200Kč, students 100Kč.) The **Chapel of the Holy Cross** is inlaid with precious stones and 129 apocalyptic paintings by medieval artist Master Theodorik. (☎ (02) 74 00 81 54; reservace@spusc.cz. Open Su and Tu-Sa 9am-5pm. Tours by reservation only; 300Kč, students 100Kč.) The area also has beautiful **hiking** trails. A **train** runs to Praha-Hlavní (45min., every hr., 55Kč). To reach the castle, turn right out of the station and go left over the modern bridge; turn right, then walk through the village.

MĚLNÍK. Fertile Mělník is known for its wine-making, supposedly perfected about 1000 years ago when St. Wenceslas, the patron saint of Bohemian wine-makers, was initiated in its vineyards. In one day, you can tour the stately Renaissance castle, sample its homemade wines, and lunch in the old schoolhouse overlooking the Říp Valley. Wine tasting (110Kč) with Martin, the wine master, is available by reservation. (☎ 206 62 21 21; www.lobkowicz-melnik.cz. Castle open daily 10am-6pm. Tours 60K⁻, students 40K⁻.) Buses run from Prague Holešovice (45min., every 30min., 32Kč). From the station, make a right onto Bezručova and head up the left fork onto Kpt. Jaroše, to the town center. Enter the Old Town Square; the castle is down Svatovaclvska to your left.

ČESKÝ RÁJ NATIONAL PRESERVE. The narrow sandstone pillars and deep gorges of **Prachovské skály** (Prachovské Rocks) make for climbs and hikes with stunning views. Prachovské skály also boasts the **Pelíšek** rock pond and the ruins of the 14th-century rock castle **Pařez.** (Open Apr.-Oct. daily 8am-5pm; swimming May-Aug. 25Kč, students 10Kč.) The 588 acres of the park are interwoven by a dense network of **trails;** both green and yellow signs guide hikers to additional sights, while triangles indicate vistas off the main trails. Red signs mark the "Golden Trail," which connects Prachovské skály to **Hrubá Skála** (Rough Rock), a rock town surrounding a hilltop castle from which hikers enjoy the best view of the sandstone rocks. From the Hrubá Skála castle, the red trail leads up to what remains of **Wallenstein Castle** (Valdštejnský hrad). **Buses** run from Prague-Florenc station to **Jičín** (1¾hr., 7 per day, 86Kč), where other buses go to Prachovské Skály and Český Ráj (15min., several per day, 9Kč). Buses to Český Ráj sometimes run less frequently than scheduled; you can also walk from Jičín along a relatively easy 6km trail beginning at Motel Rumcajs, Koněva 331.

HUNGARY

ESSENTIALS

FORINTS	
AUS$1 = 151.88FT	100FT = AUS$0.66
CDN$1 = 169.30FT	100FT = CDN$0.59
EUR€1 = 256.68FT	100FT = EUR€0.40
NZ$1 = 136.08FT	100FT = NZ$0.73
UK£1 = 370.97FT	100FT = UK£0.27
US$1 = 235.70FT	100FT = US$0.42
ZAR1 = 32.25FT	100FT = ZAR3.10

DOCUMENTS AND FORMALITIES

VISAS. Citizens of Canada, Ireland, South Africa, the UK, and the US may visit Hungary without visas for 90 days, provided their passport does not expire within six months of their journey's end. Australians and New Zealanders must obtain 90-day tourist visas from a Hungarian embassy or consulate.

EMBASSIES AND CONSULATES. Hungarian embassies at home include: **Australia**, 17 Beale Crescent, Deakin, ACT 2600 (☎02 6282 3226); **Canada**, 299 Waverley St., Ottawa, ON K2P 0V9 (☎613-230-2717; www.docuweb.ca/hungary); **Ireland**, 2 Fitzwilliam Pl., Dublin 2 (☎01 661 2903; fax 01 661 2880); **New Zealand**, 37 Abbott St., Wellington 6004 (☎04 973 7507); **South Africa**, 959 Arcadia St., Hatfield, Arcadia; P.O. Box 27077, Sunnyside 0132 (☎012 430 3020); **UK**, 35 Eaton Pl., London SW1X 8BY (☎020 7235 5218; www.hunemblon.org.uk); and **US**, 3910 Shoemaker St. NW, Washington, D.C. 20008 (☎202-362-6730; www.hungaryemb.org).

SYMBOL	❶	❷	❸	❹	❺
ACCOMMODATIONS	under 2000Ft	2000-3000Ft	3001-6000Ft	6001-10,000Ft	over 10,000Ft
FOOD	under 400Ft	400-800Ft	801-1300Ft	1301-2800Ft	over 2800Ft

BUDAPEST ☎ 1

Ten times larger than any other Hungarian city, Budapest (pop. 1,900,000) is reassuming its place as a major European capital. Originally two separate cities, Budapest was created in 1872 with the joining of Buda and Pest, soon becoming the most important Habsburg city after Vienna. World War II ravaged the city, but the Hungarians rebuilt it from rubble with the same pride they retained while weathering the Soviet occupation. Neon lights and legions of tourists may draw attention away from the city's cultural and architectural gems—but beneath it all beats a truly Hungarian heart.

▐ TRANSPORTATION

Flights: Ferihegy Airport (BUD; ☎296 9696). **Malév** (Hungarian Airlines; reservations ☎235 3888). From the airport, the cheapest way to reach the city center is to take bus #93 (20min., every 15min. 4:55am-11:20pm, 106Ft), and then take the M3 to Köbanya-Kispest (15min. to Deák tér in downtown Pest).

Trains: There are three main stations: **Keleti pu.**, **Nyugati pu.**, and **Déli pu.** (International ☎461 5500, domestic 461 5400; www.mav.hu). Most international trains arrive at Keleti Pályaudvar, but some from Prague go to Nyugati pu. Each station has schedules for the others; for a complete listing of Hungarian rail schedules, see ⬛ www.bahn.de. To: **Berlin** (12hr., daily, 22,900Ft); **Bucharest** (14hr., 4 per day, 17,400Ft); **Prague** (8hr., 5 per day, 14,000Ft); **Vienna** (3hr., 17 per day, 7000Ft); **Warsaw** (11hr., 2 per day, 13,950Ft). Reservation fees 700-2000Ft. The daily **Orient Express** stops on its way from Paris to Istanbul. Purchase tickets at the **International Ticket Office,** Keleti pu. (Open daily 8am-6pm.) Or, try **MÁV Hungarian Railways,** VI, Andrássy út 35 and at all stations. (☎ 461 5500. Open M-F 9am-5pm. For student or under-26 discount on tickets, say, "*diák*".)

Buses: Most buses to Western Europe leave from **Volánbusz main station,** V, Erzsébet tér (☎117 2966; international tickets ☎485 2162, ext. 211). M1, 2, or 3: Deák tér. Open M-F 6am-6pm, Sa-Su 6am-4pm. Buses to much of Eastern Europe depart from **Népstadion,** Hungária körút 48/52 (☎252 1896). M2: Népstadion. To: **Berlin** (14½hr., 5 per week, 19,900Ft); **Prague** (8hr., 4 per week, 6990Ft); **Vienna** (3-3½hr., 5 per day, 5790Ft).

Commuter Trains: The **HÉV commuter railway** station is at Batthyány tér, across the river from the Parliament, 1 Metro stop past the Danube in Buda. Trains head to **Szentendre** (45min., every 15min. 5am-9pm, 268Ft). Purchase tickets at the station for transport beyond the city limits.

Public Transportation: Subways, buses, and **trams** are cheap, convenient, and easy to navigate. The **Metro** has three lines: yellow (M1), red (M2), and blue (M3). Pick up free **route maps** from hostels, tourist offices, and train stations. Night transit ("É") runs midnight-5am along major routes; buses #7É and 78É follow the M2 route, #6É follows the 4/6 tram line, and #14É and 50É follow the M3 route. **Single-fare tickets** for all public transport (one-way on one line 120Ft) are sold in Metro stations, in *Trafik* shops, and by sidewalk vendors. Punch them in the orange boxes at the gate of the Metro or on buses and trams; punch a new ticket when you change lines, or face a 1500-3000Ft fine. Day pass 925Ft, 3-day 1850Ft, 1-week 2250Ft.

Taxis: Beware of scams; check that the meter is on, and inquire about the rates. **Budataxi** (☎233 3333) charges 135Ft per km if you call. **Fõtaxi** (☎222 2222), **6x6 Taxi** (☎266 6666), and **Tele 5 Taxi** (☎355 5555) are also reliable.

✴ ORIENTATION

Originally Buda and Pest, two cities separated by the **Danube River** (Duna), modern Budapest preserves the distinctive character of each. On the west bank, **Buda** has winding streets, breathtaking vistas, a hilltop citadel, and the Castle District. On the east bank is the city's bustling commercial center, **Pest,** home to shopping boulevards, theaters, Parliament (Országház), and the Opera House. Three main bridges join the two halves: **Széchenyi Lánchíd,** slender **Erzsébet híd,** and green **Szabadság híd.** Just down the north slope of Várhegy (Castle Hill) is **Moszkva tér,** the tram and local bus hub. **Batthyány tér,** opposite Parliament in Buda, is the starting point of the HÉV commuter railway. The city's Metro lines converge at **Deák tér,** next to the main international bus terminal at **Erzsébet tér.** Two blocks west toward the river lies **Vörösmarty tér** and the main pedestrian shopping zone **Váci utca.**

Addresses in Budapest begin with a Roman numeral representing one of the city's 23 **districts.** Central Buda is I; central Pest is V. To navigate Budapest's often-confusing streets, a **map** is essential; pick one up at any tourist office or hostel.

7 PRACTICAL INFORMATION

TOURIST AND FINANCIAL SERVICES

Tourist Offices: All sell the **Budapest Card** (Budapest Kártya), which provides discounts, unlimited public transport, and museum admission (2-day 3950Ft, 3-day 4950Ft). Your first stop should be **Tourinform,** V, Vigadó u. 6 (☎235 4481; www.hungarytourism.hu). M1: Vörösmarty tér. Walk toward the river from the Metro. Open 24hr. **Vista Travel Center,** Paulay Ede 7 (☎429 9950; www.vista.hu), arranges tours and accommodations. Open M-F 9am-8pm, Sa 10am-4pm. ■ **Budapest in Your Pocket** (www.inyour-pocket.com; 750Ft) is an up-to-date guide of the city.

Embassies: Australia, XII, Királyhágó tér 8/9 (☎457 9777; www.ausembbp.hu). M2: Déli pu., then bus #21 or tram #59 to Királyhágó tér. Open M-F 9am-noon. **Canada,** XII, Budakeszi út 32 (☎392 3360; www.canadaeuropa.gc.ca/hungary). Entrance at Zugligeti út. 51-53. Take bus #158 from Moszkva tér to the last stop. Open M-F 8:30-11am and 2-3:30pm. **South Africa,** II, Gárdonyi Géza út 17 (☎392 0999; emergency ☎(0620) 955 8046; www.sa-embassy.hu). **UK,** V, Harmincad u. 6 (☎266 2888), near the intersection with Vörösmarty tér. M1: Vörösmarty tér. Open M-F 9:30am-12:30pm and 2:30-4:30pm. **US,** V, Szabadság tér 12 (☎475 4400; emergency ☎266 28 88 93 31; www.usis.hu). M2: Kossuth tér. Walk 2 blocks down Akademia and turn on Zoltán. Open M-F 8:15am-5pm. **New Zealand** and **Irish** nationals contact the UK embassy.

Currency Exchange: The best rates are at banks. **Citibank,** V, Vörösmarty tér 4 (☎374 5000). M1: Vörösmarty tér. Cashes traveler's checks for no commission and provides MC/V cash advances (passport required).

American Express: V, Deák Ferenc u. 10 (☎235 4330; travel@amex.hu). M2 or 3: Deák tér. Open M-F 9am-5:30pm, Sa 9am-2pm. Cardholders can have mail delivered here.

LOCAL SERVICES

Luggage Storage: Lockers at all three train stations. 150-300Ft.

English-Language Bookstore: Libri Konyvpalota, VII, Rakoczi u. 12 (☎267 6258), is probably the best choice. Open M-F 10am-7:30pm, Sa 10am-3pm. M2: Astoria. MC/V.

Bi-Gay-Lesbian Resources: GayGuide.net Budapest (☎(0630) 932 3334; www.budapest.gayguide.net), maintains a comprehensive website and runs a hotline (daily 4-8pm) with info for gay tourists and gay-friendly accommodations lists.

EMERGENCY AND COMMUNICATIONS

Emergency: ☎112 connects to all. **Police:** ☎107. **Ambulance:** ☎104. **Fire:** ☎105.

Tourist Police: V, Vigadó u. 6 (☎235 4479). M1: Vörösmarty tér. Walk toward the river from the Metro to reach the station, just inside Tourinform. Open 24hr.

24hr. Pharmacies: II, Frankel Leó út 22 (☎212 4406); **III,** Szentendrei út 2/a (☎388 6528); **IV,** Pozsonyi u. 19 (☎389 4079); **VI,** Teréz krt. 41 (☎311 4439); **VII,** Rákóczi út 39 (☎314 3695). At night, call the number on door or ring the bell.

Medical Assistance: Falck (SOS) KFT, II, Kapy út 49/b (☎200 0100 and 275 1535). Open 24hr. The US embassy (see **Embassies,** above) lists English-speaking doctors.

Telephones: Most phones require **phone cards,** available at newsstands, post offices, and Metro stations. 50-unit card 800Ft, 120-unit card 1800Ft. Domestic operator ☎191; info ☎198; international operator ☎190; info ☎199.

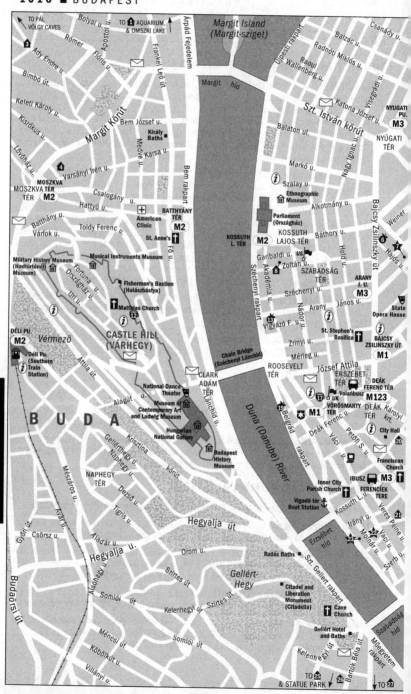

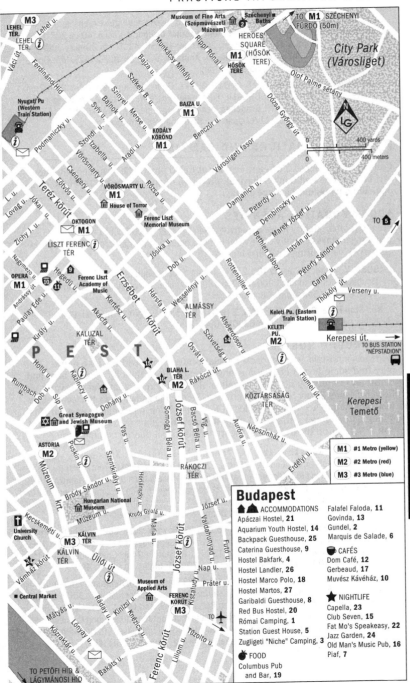

M1 #1 Metro (yellow)
M2 #2 Metro (red)
M3 #3 Metro (blue)

Budapest

🏠🏠 ACCOMMODATIONS
Apáczai Hostel, **21**
Aquarium Youth Hostel, **14**
Backpack Guesthouse, **25**
Caterina Guesthouse, **9**
Hostel Bakfark, **4**
Hostel Landler, **26**
Hostel Marco Polo, **18**
Hostel Martos, **27**
Garibaldi Guesthouse, **8**
Red Bus Hostel, **20**
Római Camping, **1**
Station Guest House, **5**
Zugligeti "Niche" Camping, **3**

🍴 FOOD
Columbus Pub
and Bar, **19**

Falafel Faloda, **11**
Govinda, **13**
Gundel, **2**
Marquis de Salade, **6**

☕ CAFÉS
Dom Café, **12**
Gerbeaud, **17**
Muvész Kávéház, **10**

⭐ NIGHTLIFE
Capella, **23**
Club Seven, **15**
Fat Mo's Speakeasy, **22**
Jazz Garden, **24**
Old Man's Music Pub, **16**
Piaf, **7**

Internet Access: Cybercafes are everywhere, but access can get expensive and long waits are common. Try a wired hostel. **Ami Internet Coffee,** V, Váci u. 40 (☎267 1644; www.amicoffee.hu). M3: Ferenciek tér. 200Ft per 10min., 400Ft per 30min., 700Ft per hr. Open daily 9am-2am. **Eckermann,** VI, Andrássy út 24 (☎269 2542). M1: Opera. Free. Open M-F 8am-10pm, Sa 9am-10pm.

Post Office: V, Városház u. 18 (☎318 4811). Open M-F 8am-9pm, Sa 8am-2pm. Address mail to be held: SURNAME Firstname, *Poste Restante*, V, Városház u. 18, **1052** Budapest, HUNGARY. **Branches** include: Nyugati pu.; VI, Teréz krt. 105/107 and Keleti pu.; VIII, Baross tér 11/c. Open M-F 8am-9pm, Sa 8am-2pm.

▐ ACCOMMODATIONS AND CAMPING

Call ahead in summer. Travelers arriving at Keleti pu. will be swarmed with hawkers; be cautious and don't believe all promises of special discounts, but keep an open mind if you need a place to stay.

ACCOMMODATION AGENCIES

Private rooms, slightly more expensive than hostels (2000-5000Ft per person; less with longer stays), usually offer what hostels can't: Peace, quiet, and private showers. Arrive early, bring cash, and haggle.

IBUSZ, V, Ferenciek tér (☎485 2767; accommodation@ibusz.hu). M3: Ferenciek tér. Doubles 5000Ft; triples 5000-6000Ft. 1800Ft surcharge if staying fewer than 4 nights. Open M-Th 8:15am-4pm, F 8:15am-3pm.

Non-Stop Hotel Service, V, Sütő u. 2 (☎318 3925). M1, 2, or 3: Deák tér. Bus #7 from Keleti pu. Rooms in Pest from 6000Ft. Open 24hr.

YEAR-ROUND HOSTELS

Budapest's hostels are backpacker social centers, each with its own quirks. You may find some hostel common rooms as exciting as the city's expat bars and clubs, and especially if you're traveling alone, they're a great place to whip up instant friends. Many hostels are now run by the **Hungarian Youth Hostels Association,** which operates from an office in Keleti pu. Their representatives wear Hostelling International T-shirts and will—along with legions of competitors—accost you as you get off the train. Take the free transport; it doesn't commit you.

▨ **Backpack Guesthouse,** XI, Takács Menyhért u. 33 (☎209 8406; backpackguest@hotmail.com), in Buda, 12min. from central Pest. From Keleti pu., take bus #7 or 7a toward Buda; get off at Tétenyi u. and walk back under the railway bridge to a sharp left turn. Take the 3rd right at Hamzsabégi út. With a common room full of movies, music, and cheap beer, hostel life doesn't get much better. Internet 15Ft per min. Reception 24hr. Reserve ahead. Dorms 2800Ft; doubles 6600Ft. ❷

▨ **Red Bus Hostel,** V, Semmelweis u. 14 (☎266 0136; www.redbusbudapest.hu), in Pest. New spacious dorms in the heart of downtown Pest. Free luggage storage. Internet 12Ft per min. Breakfast included. Laundry 1000Ft. Reception 24hr. Check-out 10am. 10-bed dorms 2700Ft; singles 6000Ft; doubles 7000Ft; triples 10,000Ft. ❷

Hostel Martos, XI, Stoczek u. 5/7 (☎209 4883; reception@hotel.martos.bme.hu), in Buda. From Keleti pu., take bus #7 to *Móricz Zsigmond Körtér* and walk 300m toward the river on Bartók Béla út. Turn right on Bertalan Lajos and take the 3rd right on Stoczek u.; the hostel is on the corner. A short walk to the outdoor clubs along the river. Free Internet and satellite TV. Reserve ahead. Singles 4000Ft; doubles 5000Ft, with shower 8000Ft; triples 7500Ft; 2- to 4-bed apartments with bath 15,000Ft. ❸

Aquarium Youth Hostel, VII, Alsoérdósor u. 12 (☎322 0502; aquarium@budapesthostels.com), in Pest. A hidden gem—there are no signs outside. Ring buzzer. Close to Keleti pu. and the Metro. Free Internet and kitchen. Laundry 1200Ft. Reception 24hr. 4- to 5-bed dorms 2500Ft; doubles 8000Ft. ❷

Station Guest House (HI), XIV, Mexikói út 36/b (☎221 8864; www.stationguest-house.hu), in Pest. From Keleti pu., take bus #7 or night bus #78É 4 stops to *Hungária körút*, walk under the railway pass, and take an immediate right on Mexikói út. Free billiards, live music, and a friendly staff. Internet 20Ft per min. Reserve ahead. Attic 1900Ft; dorms 2400Ft; quads 2700Ft. All prices drop 100Ft with each night you stay, up to 5 nights. ❶

Hotel Marco Polo, VII, Nyár u. 6 (☎413 2555; www.marcopolohostel.com), in Pest. M2: Astoria or M2: Blaha Lujza tér. Newly renovated, luxurious, and spotless. Internet 500Ft per 30min. Reception 24hr. Book 1-2 days ahead in summer. Dorms 5000Ft; singles 13,900Ft; doubles 17,000Ft. 10% HI and ISIC discount. ❸

SUMMER HOSTELS

Many university dorms moonlight as hostels during July and August. The majority are clustered around Móricz Zsigmond Körtér in district XI.

Hostel Bakfark, II, Bakfark u. 1/3 (☎413 2062), in Buda. M2: Moszkva tér. Comfortable dorms with lofts instead of bunks. Check-out 10am. Call ahead. Open mid-June to late-Aug. Dorms 3300Ft. 10% HI discount. ❸

Apáczai Hostel, V, Papnövelde 4/6 (☎267 0311), in Pest. Great location, clean rooms, and a friendly staff. Open late-June to late-Aug. Dorms 2700Ft; doubles 4300Ft. 10% HI discount. ❷

Hostel Landler, XI, Bartók Béla út 17 (☎463 3621), in Buda. Take bus #7 or 7A across the river and get off at Géllert; take Bartók Béla út away from the river. Comfy dorms. Check-out 9am. Open July 5-Sept. 5. Singles 5850Ft; triples 11,700Ft; quads 15,600Ft. 10% HI discount. ❸

GUESTHOUSES

Guesthouses and private rooms add a personal touch for about the same price as hostels. Owners will usually pick travelers up from the train station or airport.

Garibaldi Guesthouse, V, Garibaldi u. 5 (☎302 3456; garibaldiguest@hotmail.com). M2: Kossuth tér. Charming Ena lets spacious rooms in her apartment and other suites in the building. Some have kitchenette, TV, and shower. Rooms from 3500Ft per person; apartments 6000-10,000Ft. Reduced prices for longer stays. ❸

Caterina Guesthouse and Hostel, VI, Andrássy út 47, 3rd fl., apt. #18; ring bell #11 (☎342 0804; www.extra.hu/caterin), in Pest. M1: Oktogon, or trams #4 and 6. Spotless rooms with fresh linens. Reception 24hr. Check-out 9am. Lockout 10am-2pm. Reserve by email. Dorms 2800Ft; doubles 9000Ft; triples 11,400Ft. ❷

CAMPING

Római Camping, III, Szentendrei út 189 (☎368 6260). M2: Batthyány tér. Take HÉV to Római fürdö; walk 100m toward river. Communal showers and kitchen. Breakfast 880Ft. Laundry 800Ft. Electricity 600Ft. Tents 1950Ft per person; bungalows 1690-15,000Ft. Each person must also pay a personal fee (990Ft, children 590Ft). Tourist tax 3%. 10% HI discount. MC/V. ❷

Zugligeti "Niche" Camping, XII, Zugligeti út 101 (☎/fax 200 8346; www.camping-niche.hu). Take bus #158 from Moszkva tér to *Laszállóhely*, the last stop. Restaurant. Communal showers. Electricity 450Ft. 850Ft per person. Tents 500Ft, large tents 900Ft. Cars 700Ft, caravans 1800Ft. MC/V. ❶

◘ FOOD

Explore the cafeterias beneath "Önkiszolgáló Étterem" signs for something cheap (meat dishes 300-500Ft) or seek out a neighborhood *kifőzés* (kiosk) or *vendéglő* (vendor) for a real taste of Hungary. Corner markets, many of which have 24hr. windows, stock basics. The king of them all, the ◪**Grand Market Hall,** IX, Fövam tér 1/3, next to Szabadság híd (M3: Kálvin tér), was built in 1897; it now boasts 10,000 square meters of stalls, making it a tourist attraction in itself. For a wide array of ethnic restaurants, try the upper floors of **Mammut Plaza,** just outside of the *Moszkva tér* Metro stop in Buda, or the **West End Plaza,** accessible from the *Nyugati* Metro stop in Pest.

RESTAURANTS

◪ **Columbus Pub and Restaurant,** V, Danube prominade below the chain bridge (☎266 9013). If you feel you've neglected the beautiful Danube, enjoy a meal on this moored ship. Open daily noon-1am. AmEx/MC/V. ❸

◪ **Govinda,** V, Vigyázó Ferenc u. 4 (☎269 1625). An Indian vegetarian restaurant, complete with yoga classes. The best deals are the meal plates (big plate 1450Ft, small plate 1150Ft, student plate 520Ft). Yoga classes Sept.-June M 5-6:30pm (500Ft). Open M-Sa noon-9pm. AmEx/MC/V. ❷

◪ **Gundel,** XIV, Allatkerti út 2 (☎468 4040). The most famous restaurant in Hungary. Many think the 7-course meal is worth the splurge (13,000-17,500Ft), but there are also delicious sandwiches outside for 400-600Ft. Su brunch buffet 11:30am-3pm (400Ft). Open daily noon-4pm and 6:30pm-midnight. AmEx/MC/V. ❷

Falafel Faloda, VI, Pauley Ede u. 53 (☎351 1243; www.falafel.hu). M1: Opera. From the Metro, cross Andrássy, head straight on Hajós u., and turn left on Pauley Ede. Make-your-own falafel with tons of ingredients. Falafel 490Ft. Salad 480-580Ft. Open M-F 10am-8pm, Sa 10am-6pm. ❷

Robinson Mediterranean-style Restaurant and Cafe, Városligeti tér (☎422 0222). This spectacularly scenic restaurant overlooking the lake in City Park is infused with charm. Serves favorites like pan-roasted goose liver (2100Ft) and paprika veal (2200Ft). Vegetarian options available. Entrees 1200-5800Ft. Open daily noon-midnight. ❹

Marquis de Salade, VI, Hajós u. 43 (☎302 4086). M3: Arany János. At the corner of Bajcsy-Zsilinszky út, 2 blocks from the Metro. Huge menu with dishes from Azerbaijan, France, India, Italy, Japan, and Hungary. Entrees 1200-2500Ft. Open daily noon-midnight. Cash only. ❹

CAFES

Once the haunts of the literary, intellectual, and cultural elite—as well as political dissidents—the city's cafes boast histories as rich as the pastries they serve.

◪ **Dom Cafe,** I, Szentháromság tér. Atop Castle Hill, with astonishing views of the Danube and Pest. Beer and coffee start at 350Ft. Pastries and sandwiches also served. Open daily 10am-7pm.

Gerbeaud, V, Vörösmarty tér 7 (☎429 9000). M1: Vörösmarty tér. Perhaps Budapest's largest and most famous cafe, this institution has been serving its layer cakes (590Ft) and homemade ice cream (75Ft) since 1858. Open daily 9am-9pm.

Muvész Kávéház, VI, Andrássy út 29 (☎352 1337). M1: Opera. Diagonally across from the Opera. Before or after a show, stop in for a slice of rich cake (290Ft) and a cup of cappuccino (260Ft) at the polished stone tables. Open daily 9am-11:45pm.

SIGHTS

In 1896, Hungary's 1000th birthday bash prompted the construction of what are today Budapest's most prominent sights. Among the works commissioned by the Habsburgs were **Heroes' Square** (Hősök tér), **Liberty Bridge** (Szbadság híd), **Vajdahunyad Castle** (Vajdahunyad vár), and continental Europe's first **Metro** system. Slightly grayer for wear, war, and Communist occupation, these monuments attest to the optimism of a capital on the verge of its Golden Age. See the sights, learn your way around the city, and meet other travelers with **Absolute Walking & Biking Tours.** Their basic tour (3½hr.; 4000Ft, under-27 3500Ft) meets May 16-Sept. 30 daily at 9:30am and 1:30pm on the steps of the yellow church in Déak tér and at 10am and 2pm in Heroes' Sq. They also hold off-season tours Oct.-Jan. 6 and Feb.-May 15 that leave at 10:30am from Déak tér and at 11am from Heroes' Sq. You can also choose from a range of specialized tours that focus on everything from communist Hungary to pub-crawling Budapest. (☎ 211 8861; www.budapesttours.com. Specialized tours 2½-5½hr., 4000-5000Ft.) **Boat tours** of Budapest can also be taken from Vigadó tér piers 6-7. The *Danube Legend*, which runs in the evening, costs 4200Ft (950Ft with Budapest Card). The *Duna Bella*, the daytime boat, costs 3600Ft (850Ft with Budapest Card).

BUDA

On the east bank of the Danube, **Buda** sprawls between the base of **Castle Hill** and southern **Gellért Hill,** rambling into Budapest's main residential areas. Older than Pest, Buda is filled with parks, lush hills, and islands.

CASTLE DISTRICT. Towering above the Danube on Castle Hill, the Castle District has been razed three times in its 800-year history, most recently in 1945. With its winding, statue-filled streets, breathtaking views, and hodge-podge of architectural styles, the UNESCO-protected district now appears much as it did in Habsburg times. Although the reconstructed **Buda Castle** *(Vár)* now houses a number of fine museums (p. 1023), bullet holes in the palace facade recall the 1956 Uprising. (*M1, 2, or 3: Déak tér. From the Metro, take bus #16 across the Danube and up to the castle. Alternatively, take the Metro to M2: Moszkva tér and walk up to the hill on Várfok u. Vienna Gate, or hop on bus #16. Becsi kapu marks the castle entrance.*) Beneath Buda castle are the **Castle Labyrinths** (Budvári Labirinths), caverns that allow for spooky trips through the subterranean world of the city. (*Úri u. 9.* ☎ 212 0207. *Open daily 9:30am-7:30pm. 900Ft, students 700Ft.*)

MATTHIAS CHURCH. The multi-colored roof of Matthias Church (Mátyás templom) is one of Budapest's most popular sights. The church was converted into a mosque in 1541, then reconverted 145 years later when the Habsburgs defeated the Turks. Ascend the spiral staircase to reach the gold-heavy exhibits of the **Museum of Ecclesiastical Art.** (*On Castle Hill. High mass 7, 8:30am, 6pm; Su also 10am and noon. Open M-Sa 9am-5pm, Su 1pm-5pm. Museum 400Ft, students 200Ft. Free.*)

GELLÉRT HILL. When King Stephen, the first Christian Hungarian monarch, was coronated, the Pope sent Bishop Gellért to convert the Magyars. The hill got its name (Gellért-hegy) when those unconvinced by his message hurled the good bishop to his death from the top. The **Liberation Monument** (Szabadság Szobor), created to honor Soviet soldiers who died "liberating" Hungary, looks over Budapest from atop the hill. The view from the adjoining **Citadel,** built as a symbol of Habsburg power after the foiled 1848 revolution, is especially spectacular at night. At the base of the hill sits Budapest's most famous Turkish bath (p. 1024), the **Gellért Hotel and Baths.** *(Take tram #18 or 19, or bus #7, to Hotel Gellért; follow Szabó Verjték u. to Jubileumi Park, continuing on the marked paths to the summit. Or, take bus #27 to the top; get off at Búsuló Juhász and walk 5min. to the peak.)*

PEST

Constructed in the 19th century, the winding streets of Pest now host cafes, corporations, and monuments. The crowded **Belváros** (Inner City) is based around the swarming pedestrian boulevards **Váci utca** and **Vörösmarty tér.**

▦**PARLIAMENT.** Standing 96m tall, a number that symbolizes the date of Hungary's millennial anniversary, the palatial Gothic Parliament (Országház) was modeled after the UK's, right down to the riverside location and churchly facade. The **Hungarian crown jewels,** housed here since 1999, were moved from the National Museum to the center of the Cupola Room amidst national controversy because of the cost of the security required to move them. *(M2: Kossuth Lajos tér. English tours M-F 10am, noon, 2, 2:30, 5, and 6pm; Sa-Su 10am only—come early. 2000Ft, students 1000Ft. Purchase tickets at gate #10 and enter at gate #12.)*

GREAT SYNAGOGUE. The largest synagogue in Europe and the second-largest in the world after Temple Emmanuel in New York City, Pest's Great Synagogue (Zsinagóga) was designed to hold 3000 worshippers. The Moorish building has been under renovation since 1988, and much of its artwork is blocked from view. In the garden is a **Holocaust Memorial** that sits above a mass grave for thousands of Jews killed near the end of the war. The Hebrew inscription reads: "Whose pain can be greater than mine?" with the Hungarian words "Let us Remember" beneath. Each leaf of this enormous metal tree bears the name of a family that perished, but the memorial represents only a fraction of the sufferers. Next door, the **Jewish Museum** (Zsidó Múzeum) documents Hungary's rich Jewish past. *(M2: Astoria. At the corner of Dohány u. and Wesselényi u. Open May-Oct. M-Th 10am-5pm, F 10am-4pm, Su 10am-2pm; Nov.-Apr. M-F 10am-3pm, Su 10am-1pm. Synagogue and museum 600Ft, students with ISIC 200Ft.)*

ST. STEPHEN'S BASILICA. The city's largest church (Sz. István Bazilika) was decimated by Allied bombs in World War II. Its neo-Renaissance facade is still undergoing reconstruction, but the ornate interior attracts both tourists and worshippers. The **Panorama Tower** offers an amazing 360° view. The oddest attraction is St. Stephen's mummified right hand, one of Hungary's most revered religious relics; a 100Ft donation dropped in the box will light up the hand. *(M1-3: Deák tér. Mass M-Sa 7, 8am, 6pm; Su 8:30, 10am, noon, 6pm. Basilica and museum open May-Oct. M-Sa 9am-5pm; Nov.-Apr. M-Sa 10am-4pm. Tower open June-Aug. daily 9:30am-6pm; Sept.-Oct. 10am-5:30pm; Apr.-May 10am-4:30pm. Basilica and museum free. Tower 500Ft, students 400Ft.)*

ANDRÁSSY ÚT AND HEROES' SQUARE. Hungary's grandest boulevard, Andrássy út, extends from Erzsébet tér in downtown Pest to **Heroes' Square** (Hősök tere) to the northeast. The **Hungarian State Opera House** (Magyar Állami Operaház), whose gilded interior glows on performance nights, is a vivid reminder of Budapest's Golden Age. If you can't see an opera, take a tour. *(Andrássy út 22. M1: Opera. Daily English-language tours 3 and 4pm; 2000Ft, students 1000Ft. 20% Budapest Card discount.)* At the Heroes' Sq. end of Andrássy út, the **Millenium Monument** (Millenniumi emlékmű) commemorates the nation's most prominent leaders. Also right off Heroes' Sq. is the **Museum of Fine Arts** (see below).

CITY PARK. The City Park (Városliget) is home to a zoo, a circus, a run-down amusement park, and the lakeside **Vajdahunyad Castle,** whose collage of Romanesque, Gothic, Renaissance, and Baroque styles is intended to chronicle the history of Hungarian architecture. Outside the castle broods the hooded statue of King Béla IV's **anonymous scribe,** to whom we owe much of our knowledge of medieval Hungary. Rent a **rowboat** or **ice skates** on the lake next to the castle, or a **bike-trolley** to navigate the shaded paths. The main road through the park is closed to automobiles on weekends, making the park especially peaceful. *(M1: Széchenyi Fürdő. Park open Apr.-Aug. daily 9am-6pm; Sept.-Mar. 9am-3pm. Pedal boat rentals May-Aug. daily 10am-10pm. Rowboat rental May-Aug. daily 10am-9:30pm. Ice skate rental Oct.-Feb. daily 10am-2pm and 4-8pm.)*

▥ MUSEUMS

▧ **MUSEUM OF FINE ARTS.** A spectacular collection of European art is housed in the magnificent Museum of Fine Arts (Szépművészeti Múzeum). These are paintings you've never seen in books but should not miss, especially those in the El Greco room. *(XIV, Heroes' Sq. M1: Hősök tere. Open Su and Tu-Sa 10am-5:30pm; last entrance 5pm. 500Ft, students 200Ft. Free English tours Tu-F 11am. Camera 300Ft, video 1500Ft.)*

▧ **NATIONAL MUSEUM.** At the National Museum (Nemzeti Múzeum), a well laid-out, extensive exhibition on the second floor chronicles the history of Hungary, extending from the founding of the state through the 20th century. The first floor is reserved for temporary exhibits. *(VIII, Múzeum krt. 14/16. M3: Kálvin tér. ☎ 338 2122; www.origo.hnm.hu. Open Mar. 15-Oct. 15 Su and Tu-Sa 10am-6pm; Oct. 16-Mar. 14 Su and Tu-Sa 10am-5pm; last admission 30min. before closing. 800Ft, students 400Ft.)*

▧ **STATUE PARK.** After the collapse of Soviet rule, the open-air Statue Park museum (Szoborpark Múzeum) was created from statues removed from Budapest's parks and squares. The indispensable English guidebook (1000Ft) explains the statues' past and present locations. *(XXII, on the corner of Balatoni út and Szabadkai út. Take express bus #7 from Keleti pu. to Étele tér and then take the Volán bus from terminal #2 to Diósd (15min., every 10min.). Open in good weather Mar.-Nov. daily 10am-dusk; Dec.-Feb. weekends and holidays only. 600Ft, students 400Ft.)*

MUSEUM OF APPLIED ARTS. (Iparművészeti Múzeum). The Art Nouveau building of the Museum of Applied Arts was designed for Hungary's 1896 millenium celebration. Inside is an eclectic collection of impressive hand-crafted objects, including Tiffany glass and furniture, as well as excellent temporary exhibits highlighting specific crafts. *(IX, Üllői út 33-37. M3: Ferenc körút. Open Mar. 15-Oct. Su and Tu-Sa 10am-6pm; Nov.-Mar. 14 Su and Tu-Sa 10am-4pm. 600Ft, students 300Ft.)*

BUDA CASTLE. Leveled by the Nazis and later by the Soviets, the reconstructed Buda Castle (see **Castle District,** p. 1021) now houses several museums. Wing A contains the **Museum of Contemporary Art** (Kortárs Művészeti Múzeum), as well as the smaller **Ludwig Museum** upstairs, which is devoted to Warhol, Lichtenstein, and other masters of modern art. Wings B-D hold the **Hungarian National Gallery** (Magyar Nemzeti Galéria), a collection of the best in Hungarian painting and sculpture. *(Wings A-D open Su and Tu-Sa 10am-6pm, Th open until 8pm. Wing A 800Ft, students 400Ft. Wings B-D 600/300Ft.)* Artifacts from the 1242 castle are in the **Budapest History Museum** (Budapesti Történéti Múzeum) in Wing E. *(I, Szent György tér 2. M1-3: Deák tér. Take bus #16 across the Danube to the top of Castle Hill. Wing E open mid-May to mid-Sept. daily 10am-6pm; mid-Sept. to Oct. and Mar. to mid-May M and W-Su 10am-6pm; Nov.-Feb. M and W-Su 10am-4pm. 600Ft, students 300Ft.)*

THE BIG SPLURGE

BUCK-NAKED IN BUDAPEST

The city's baths were first built in 1565 by a Turkish ruler who feared that a siege would prevent the population from bathing. Thanks to his anxiety, there's nothing to keep budget travelers from bathing, either: The range of services—from mud baths to massage—is cheap enough to warrant indulgence without guilt.

Although first-time bathers may be intimidated at first, guests at Budapest's baths always receive the royal treatment. Upon arrival, you will probably be handed a bizarre apron no bigger than a dish-rag, which modesty requires that you tie around your waist. In general, women set the apron aside as a towel, while men keep theirs on; bring a bathing suit just in case. Customs vary greatly by establishment, so just do as the locals do—nothing is more conspicuous than a Speedo-clad tourist among naked natives.

Cycle through the sauna and thermal baths a couple times, then enter the massage area. For a good scrubbing, try the sanitary massage (*vízi*); if you're a traditionalist, stick to the medical massage (*orvosi*). Most baths provide a much-needed rest area once the process is complete. Refreshed, smiling, and somewhat sleepy, tip the attendant, lounge over mint tea, and savor your afternoon of guilt-free pampering. (*Baths and pools 700-2000Ft, massages 1000-7500Ft.*)

🎵 ENTERTAINMENT

Budapest Program, Budapest Panorama, Pesti Est and the essential *Budapest in Your Pocket* (750Ft) are the best English-language entertainment guides, listing everything from festivals to cinemas to art showings. All are available at most tourist offices and hotels. The "Style" section of the *Budapest Sun* (www.budapestsun.com; 300Ft) has a comprehensive 10-day calendar and film reviews. (Tickets 550-1000Ft; cinema schedules change on Th.) Many of the world's biggest shows pass through Budapest. Prices are reasonable; check the **Music Mix 33 Ticket Service,** V, Váci ú. 33. (☎317 77 36. Open M-F 10am-6pm, Sa 10am-1pm.)

THEATER, MUSIC, AND DANCE. The ⚑**State Opera House** (Magyar Allami Operaház), VI, Andrássy út 22, one of Europe's leading performance centers, epitomizes the splendor of Budapest's Golden Age. (M1: Opera. ☎332 8197, box office ☎353 0170. Tickets 800-8700Ft. Box office open M-Sa 11am-7pm, Su 4-7pm; cashier closes at 5pm on non-performance days.) The **National Dance Theatre** (Nemzetí Táncszínház), Szinház u. 1-3, hosts a variety of shows—modern, alternative, Latin, ballet—but the Hungarian folklore is the most popular. (On Castle Hill. ☎/fax 201 4407, box office ☎375 8649; www.nemzetitancszinhaz.hu. Most shows 7pm.) Performances in the lovely **Városmajor Open-Air Theater,** XII, Városmajor, include musicals, operas, and ballets. Walk up the big stairs, turn right on Várfok u. and left on Csaba u., then right on Maros u. and left on Szamos u. (M1: Moszkva tér. ☎375 5933. Open June 27-Aug. 18. Box office open Su-M and Th-Sa 3-6pm.) For an eclectic line up of music, go to **Buda Park Stage,** XI, Kosztolányi Dezső tér. (☎466 9894. Tickets 90-350Ft. Box office at V, Vörösmarty tér 1. Open M-F 11am-6pm.)

THERMAL BATHS. To soak away the city grime, sink into a hot, relaxing thermal bath. First built in 1565, their services—from mud baths to massages—are quite cheap. **Széchenyi,** XIV, Állatkerti u. 11/14, is a welcoming bath with beautiful pools. (M1: Hősök tér. Open May-Sept. daily 6am-7pm; Oct.-Apr. M-F 6am-7pm, Sa-Su 6am-5pm. 1700Ft. to enter, 900Ft returned if you leave within 2hr., 600Ft within 3hr., and 300Ft within 4hr.; keep your original receipt. 15min. massage 1200Ft.) Famous **Gellért,** XI, Kelenhegyi út 4/6, one of the most elegant baths, has a rooftop sundeck and an outdoor wave pool. Take bus #7 or tram #47 or 49 to Hotel

Gellért, at the base of Gellért-hegy. (Thermal bath and pool 2000Ft. Pools open daily 6am-7pm, Sa-Su 6am-5pm. 15min. massage 1500Ft., pedicure 1200Ft, foot massage 700Ft. Open M-F 6am-7pm, Sa-Su 6am-5pm.)

🎵 NIGHTLIFE

All-night outdoor parties, elegant after-hours clubs, the nightly thump and grind—Budapest has it all. Pubs and bars bustle until 4am, but the streets themselves are empty and poorly lit. Upscale cafes and restaurants in **VI, Ferencz Liszt tér** (M2: Oktogon) attract Budapest's hip youth.

Undergrass, VI, Ferencz Liszt tér 10. M1: Oktogon. The hottest spot in Pest's trendiest area. A soundproof glass door divides a hip bar from a packed disco. Cover F 300Ft, Sa 1000Ft. Open F-Sa 10pm-4am.

Piaf, VI, Nagymező u. 25. A much-loved lounge, and a good place to meet fellow travelers. Knock on the door to await the approval of the club's matron. Cover 600Ft, includes 1 beer. Open Su-Th 10pm-6am, F-Sa 10pm-7am, but don't come before 1am.

Capella, V, Belgrád rakpart 23 (www.extra.hu/capellacafe). With glow-in-the-dark graffiti and an underground atmosphere, this spot draws a mixed gay and straight crowd. Cover 1000-1500Ft. Open Su and Tu-Sa 9pm-5am. The owners also run the three-level **Limo Cafe** down the street. Open daily noon-5am.

Club Seven, Akácfa u. 7. M2: Blaha Lajos tér. This upscale underground music club is a local favorite and features a casino. Cover for men Sa-Su 2000Ft, women free.

Old Man's Music Pub, VII, Akácfa u. 13. M2: Blaha Lujza tér. Arrive early for nightly blues and jazz from 9-11pm, then relax in the restaurant (open 3pm-3am) or hit the dance floor (11pm-late). Open M-Sa 3pm-4:30am.

Jazz Garden, V, Veres Páiné u. 44a. Although the "garden" is actually a vaulted cellar with Christmas lights, the effect works well. Beer 420-670Ft. Live jazz daily at 9pm. Open Su-F noon-1am, Sa noon-2am.

Fat Mo's Speakeasy, V, Nyári Pal u. 11. M3: Kálvin tér. 14 varieties of draft beer (350-750Ft). Live jazz Su-W 9-11pm. W-Sa DJ after midnight. Open M-F noon-2am, Sa noon-4am, Su 6pm-2am.

NIGHTLIFE SCAM. There have been reports of a mafia-organized scam involving English-speaking Hungarian women who approach foreign men and suggest that they buy her a drink. The bill, accompanied by imposing men, can be US$1000 for a single drink. If he claims not to have money, they conveniently have an ATM inside the bar. The US Embassy (see Embassies, p. 1015) has advised against patronizing a number of establishments in the Váci u. area. More importantly, if a women asks you to come to a bar with her in that area, politely refuse, or take her to a bar of your choice—not the one she suggests. Always check drink prices before ordering at places you are not sure about. The names of these establishments change faster than a two-bit hustle. For the most current list of establishments about which complaints have been received, check with the US Embassy in Budapest or view their list on the web at www.usembassy.hu/conseng/announcements.html. If you are taken in, call the police. You'll probably still have to pay, but get a receipt to issue a complaint at the Consumer Bureau.

◪ DAYTRIPS FROM BUDAPEST: THE DANUBE BEND

North of Budapest, the Danube sweeps in a dramatic arc called the Danube Bend (Dunakanyar), deservedly one of the most beloved tourist attractions in Hungary.

SZENTENDRE. Narrow cobblestone streets in Szentendre (pop. 23,000) brim with upscale art galleries and pricey restaurants. Head up **Church Hill** (Templomdomb) in Fő tér, above the town center, for an amazing view from the 13th-century Roman Catholic church. The **Czóbel Museum,** to the left of the church at Templom tér 1, exhibits the work of Béla Czóbel, Hungary's foremost post-Impressionist painter, including his bikini-clad "Venus of Szentendre." Some English info is provided. (Open Su and Tu-Sa 10am-6pm. 350Ft, students 150Ft.) The popular **Margit Kovács Museum,** Vastagh György u. 1, off Görög u., which branches from Fő tér, displays whimsical ceramic sculptures and tiles by the 20th-century Hungarian artist. (Open Mar.-Oct. daily 10am-6pm; Nov. daily 9am-5pm; Dec.-Feb. Su and Tu-Sa 10am-5pm. 550Ft, students 250Ft.) The real thriller at the **Szabó Marzipan Museum and Confectionery,** Dumtsa Jenő u. 12, is the 80kg white chocolate statue of Michael Jackson. (Open daily 10am-6pm. Desserts 120-1000Ft. 300Ft) The ◪**National Wine Museum** (Nemzeti Bormúzuem), Bogdányi u. 10, is a cellar exhibit of wines from all the wine-making regions in Hungary. (Open daily 10am-10pm. Wine tasting 1500Ft for 8 samples and admission to the exhibition. Exhibition 100Ft.)

HÉV commuter trains travel to Szentendre from Budapest's Batthyány tér (45min., every 10-15min., 335Ft). **Buses** run to: Budapest's Árpád híd Metro station (30min., every 20-40min., 220Ft); Esztergom (1½hr., 476Ft); and Visegrád (45min., 246Ft). The HÉV and bus stations are 10min. from Fő tér; descend the stairs past the end of the HÉV tracks, go through the underpass, and head up Kossuth u. At the fork, bear right onto Dumtsa Jenő u., which leads to the town center. **MAHART boats** leave from a pier 20min. north of the town center. With the river on the right, walk along the water to the sign. **Tourinform,** Dumtsa Jenő u. 22, between the town center and the station, has free maps. (☎ (026) 31 79 65; www.szentendre.hu. Open Mar. 16-Oct. 15 M-F 9am-4:30pm, Sa-Su 10am-2pm; Oct. 16-Mar. 15 M-F 9:30am-4:30pm.) Restaurants are expensive; it's often cheaper to dine in Budapest or Visegrád. Enjoy a pastry (from 350Ft) and cappuccino (from 350Ft) while being serenaded by the opera-singing owners of ◪**Nostalgia Cafe ❷,** Bogdányi u. 2. (Open Su and Th-Sa 10am-10pm.) **Kedvenc Kifőzde ❶,** Bükköspart 21, is a tiny diner with incredible food. (Entrees 300-460Ft. Open M-F noon-5pm, Sa noon-3pm.)

VISEGRÁD. Host to the royal court in medieval times, Visegrád was devastated when the Habsburgs destroyed its 13th-century **citadel** in a struggle against the freedom fighters. This former Roman outpost gives a dramatic view of the Danube and surrounding hills. Hike a strenuous 30min. up Kalvária út, or take the local bus (10-15min.; 9:30am, 12:30, and 3:30pm; 100Ft). Sprawling across the foothills above Fő út are the ruins of King Matthias's **Royal Palace** (Királyi Palota); impressive exhibits inside include a computerized reconstruction of the original castle. (Open Su and Tu-Sa 9am-5pm. 500Ft, students 250Ft.) The palace grounds relive their glory days of parades, jousting, and music during the **Viségrad Palace Games** (☎ (026) 209 34 59) in the mid-July. At the end of Salamontorony u., the **King Matthias Museum,** inside Solomon's Tower (Alsóvár Salamon Torony), displays artifacts from the palace ruins. (Open Apr.-Oct. Su and Tu-Sa 9am-5pm. 460Ft, students 230Ft. Su students free.)

Buses run to Budapest's Árpád híd Metro station (1½hr., 30 per day, 421Ft). The tourist office, **Visegrád Tours,** Rév út 15, has maps (300Ft) for sale. (☎ (026) 39 81 60. Open Apr.-Oct. daily 8am-7pm; Nov.-Mar. M-F 10am-4pm.) Pick up the basics across the street at **CBA Élelmiszer supermarket.** (Open M 7am-6pm, Tu-F 7am-7pm, Sa 7am-3pm, Su 7am-noon.) **Gulás Csárda ❸,** Nagy Lajos u. 4, is a cozy family restaurant. (Entrees 950-1990Ft. Open daily noon-10pm.)

ESZTERGOM. In Esztergom, a millennium of religious history revolves around a solemn hilltop **cathedral,** whose crypt holds the remains of Hungary's archbishops. The ▨**cupola** (200Ft) offers the best view of the Danube Bend. The **Cathedral Treasury** (Kincstáv) to the right of the main altar has Hungary's most extensive collection of ecclesiastical treasures. To the left of the altar is the red marble **Bakócz Chapel,** a masterwork of Renaissance Tuscan craftsmanship. (Open Mar.-Oct. daily 9am-4pm; Nov.-Dec. M-F 11am-3:30pm, Sa-Su 10am-3:30pm. English-language guidebook 100Ft. Cathedral free.)

 Trains go to Budapest (1½hr., 22 per day, 436Ft). From the station, turn left on the main street, Baross Gábor út, and make a right onto Kiss János Altábornagy út, which becomes Kossuth Lajos u., to reach the square. **Buses** run to Szentendre (1½hr., 1 per hr., 476Ft) and Visegrád (45min., 1 per hr., 316Ft). From the bus station, walk up Simor János u. toward the street market to reach Rákóczi tér. MAHART **boats** depart from the pier at Gőzhajó u. on Primas Sziget Island for: Budapest (4hr.; 3 per day; 1200Ft, students 600Ft.); Szentendre (2¾hr.; 1 per hr.; 980Ft, students 490Ft.); and Visegrád (1½hr.; 1 per hr.; 700Ft, students 350Ft). **Grantours,** Széchenyi tér 25, at the edge of Rákóczi tér, sells maps (200Ft-500Ft) and arranges accommodations. (☎(033) 41 17 052; grantour@mail.holop.hu. Open July-Aug. M-F 8am-6pm, Sa 9am-noon; Sept.-June M-F 8am-4pm, Sa 9am-noon.) **Csülök Csárda ❷,** Batthány út 9, offers fine Hungarian cuisine. (Entrees 480-1800Ft. Open daily noon-midnight.)

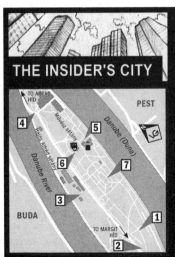

THE INSIDER'S CITY

MARGIT ISLAND

Outdoor enthusiasts will find plenty to do in this gorgeous oasis north of Budapest. Catch the #26 or 26A bus in Pest at Nyugati pu., and take it to the Grand Hotel on the island.

1 Rent bikes, in-line skates, and pedal carts at Bringóvár. (☎329 27 46. Open daily 8am-dusk.)

2 Visit the Palatinus Strandfürdo, dubbed Budapest's Beach. Huge pools and waterslides provide respite from the heat.

3 Stop and have a bite to eat at Europe Grill Kert. (Open daily 11am-10pm.)

4 Stroll or bike through the beautiful Rose Garden.

5 Next to the garden is the Artist's Walk, a sculpture park dedicated to Hungary's cultural icons.

6 King Béla IV once bet on his daughter's freedom and lost; visit St. Margaret's Monastery Ruins which are named after the unfortunate girl.

CROATIA

ESSENTIALS

DOCUMENTS AND FORMALITIES

KUNA	
AUS$1 = 4.39KN	1KN = AUS$0.23
CDN$1 = 4.90KN	1KN = CDN$0.20
EUR€1 = 7.47KN	1KN = EUR€0.13
NZ$1 = 3.91KN	1KN = NZ$0.26
UK£1 = 10.78KN	1KN = UK£0.09
US$1 = 6.86KN	1KN = US$0.15
ZAR1 = 0.93KN	1KN = ZAR1.07

VISAS. Citizens of Australia, Canada, Ireland, New Zealand, the UK, and the US do not need visas for stays of up to 90 days. Visas are required of South African citizens. All visitors must **register** with the police within 48 hours of arrival, regardless of the length of their stay. Hotels, campsites, and accommodations agencies should automatically register you, but those staying with friends or in private rooms must register themselves to avoid fines or expulsion. Police may check passports anywhere. There is no entry fee at the border.

EMBASSIES. Foreign embassies in Croatia are all in Zagreb. Croatian embassies at home include: **Australia,** 14 Jindalee Crescent, O'Malley ACT 2606 (☎02 6286 6988; croemb@bigpond.com.au); **Canada,** 229 Chapel St., Ottawa, ON K1N 7Y6 (☎613-562-7820; www.croatiaemb.net); **New Zealand** (consulate), 291 Lincoln Rd., Henderson, Auckland; mail to: P.O. Box 83-200, Edmonton, Auckland (☎09 836 5581; cro-consulate@xtra.co.nz); **South Africa,** 1160 Church St., Colbyn, 0083; mail to: Pretoria; P.O. Box 11335, Hatfield 0028 (☎012 342 1206; fax 342 1819); **UK,** 21 Conway St., London W1P 5HL (☎020 7387 2022; amboffice@croatianembassy.co.uk; Consular Department ☎020 7387 1144; consulardept@croatianembassy.co.uk); **US,** 2343 Massachusetts Ave. NW, Washington, D.C. 20008 (☎202-588-5899; www.croatiaemb.org).

CROATIA	❶	❷	❸	❹	❺
ACCOMMODATIONS	under 90kn	90-140kn	141-200kn	201-300kn	over 300kn
FOOD	under 30kn	30-60kn	61-120kn	121-200kn	over 200kn

DALMATIAN COAST

After his last visit to Dalmatia, George Bernard Shaw wrote: "The gods wanted to crown their creation and on the last day they turned tears, stars and the sea breeze into the isles of Kornati." Shaw's words speak to the entire Dalmatian Coast—a stunning seascape of unfathomable beauty set against a backdrop of dramatic mountains. With more than 1100 islands, Dalmatia is not only Croatia's largest archipelago, but also has the cleanest and clearest waters in the Mediterranean.

Croatia

TRANSPORTATION

Ferries are the best way to travel along much of the Dalmatian Coast. **Jadrolinija** (www.jadrolinija.hr) sails the Rijeka-Split-Dubrovnik route, with stops at many smaller cities and islands along the way. Ferries also run from Split to Ancona, Italy, and from Dubrovnik to Bari, Italy. A basic ticket provides only a place on the deck. Cheap beds sell out fast, so purchase tickets in advance. If you have a basic ticket, *run* to get a bed. Buses also connect Trogir, Split, and Dubrovnik.

TROGIR
☎ 021

In Trogir (pop. 1,500), made up of tiny Trogir Island and Čiovo Island, medieval buildings crowd into winding streets and palmed promenades open onto well-maintained parks and the calm, blue sea. On Trogir Island, the beautiful Renaissance **North Gate** forms the entrance to **Stari Grad** (Old Town), which earned a coveted place on the UNESCO World Heritage List in 1997. Most sights, including the **Cathedral of St. Lawrence** (Crkva sv. Lovre), are in **Trg Ivana Pavla,** the central square. The **City Museum of Trogir,** which is housed in two buildings, contains many examples of Trogir's storied stone-carving tradition. The **lapidary,** through the arch directly in front of the North Gate, features stone sculpture. (Open M-Sa 9am-noon and 6-9pm. 10kn, students 5kn.) The other part of the museum is in the convent of St. Nicholas, off Kohl-Genscher past Trg Ivana Pavla. (Open M-Sa 9am-12:30pm and 3-7:30pm.) At the tip of the island lie the remains of the **Fortress of Kamerlengo**, which now serves as an open-air cinema. (Open M-Sa 9am-11pm. 10kn. Students free. Movies 20kn.) Trogir's best beaches lie on **Čiovo Island**, accessible from Trogir Island by the Čiovski bridge, past Trg Ivana Pavla.

Buses from Zagreb stop in front of the station on the mainland on their way south to Split (30min., 2-3 per hr., 22kn). Local bus #37 also runs from Trogir to Split (30min., 2-3 per hr., 18kn). Across Čiovski bridge, **Atlas**, Obala kralja Zvonimira 10, has bus schedules. (☎88 42 79. Open M-Sa 8am-9pm, Su 8am-noon.) The **tourist office**, Trg Ivana Pavla 2, gives out free maps of the city. (☎88 14 12. Open M-Sa 8am-9pm, Su 8-noon.) **Čipko ❶**, Gradska 41, across from the cathedral and through an archway, arranges private rooms. (☎88 15 54. Open daily 8am-8pm. July-Aug. singles 84-92kn; tourist tax 7.50kn. May-June and Sept. 70-73/5.50kn.) To reach beachside **Prenocište Saldun ❶**, Sv. Andrije 1, cross Čiovski bridge and take Put Balana up the hill, keeping right; Saldun is at the top. (☎80 60 53. Call ahead. Singles 76kn; tax 6kn.) Luxurious waterfront **Vila Sikaa ❺**, Obala Kralja Zvonimira 13, is across Čiovski Bridge. (☎88 12 23; stjepan.runtic@st.tel.hr. Call ahead. Singles 420-470kn; doubles 450-600kn.) **Bistro Lučica ❸**, Kralja Tomislava, across Čiovski bridge and to the right, grills delightful meat and seafood. (35-120kn. Open M-F 9am-midnight, Sa-Su 4pm-midnight.) **Čiovka supermarket** is next to Atlas. (Open M-Sa 5:30am-9pm, Su 6:30am-8pm.) Cafes line **Kohl-Genscher. Postal Code: 21220.**

SPLIT

☎021

This palatial city by the sea is more of a cultural center than a beach resort; Split boasts a wider variety of activities and nightlife than its neighbors. The **Stari Grad** (Old Town), wedged between a high mountain range and palm-lined waterfront, sprawls around a luxurious **palace** where Roman Emperor Diocletian, known for his violent persecution of Christians, spent his summers. The **cellars** of the city are near the entrance to the palace, across from the taxis on **Obala hrvatskog narodnog preporoda;** turn in either direction to wander around this haunting labyrinth. (Open daily 10am-7pm. 8kn.) Through the cellars and up the stairs is the open-air **peristyle**. The Catholic **cathedral** on the right side of the peristyle is the oldest in the world; ironically, it was once Diocletian's mausoleum. The view from atop the adjoining **Bell Tower of St. Dominus** (Zvonik sv. Duje) is incredible. (Cathedral and tower open daily 8:30am-9:30pm. Tower 5kn.) A 25min. walk away along the waterfront, the **Meštrović Gallery** (Galerija Ivana Meštrovića), Šetaliste Ivana Meštrovića 46, features a collection by Croatia's most famous modern sculptor. (Open June-Aug. Su 9am-2pmTu-Sa 9am-1pm and 5-8pm; Sept.-May Su 10am-2pm, Tu-Sa 10am-4pm. 15kn, students 10kn.)

Buses (☎33 84 83; schedules ☎(050) 32 73 27) go to: Dubrovnik (4½hr., 17 per day, 110kn); Ljubljana (11hr., daily, 236kn); Sarajevo (7½hr., 6 per day, 180kn); and Zagreb (8hr., every 30min., 107-120kn). **Ferries** (☎33 83 33) head from the terminal across from the train and bus stations to Dubrovnik (8hr., 5 per week, 115kn) and Ancona, Italy (10hr., 4 per week, 329kn). From the bus station, follow Obala kneza Domagoja (also called Riva) until it runs into Obala hrvatskog narodnog preporoda, which runs roughly east-west. The **tourist office** is at Obala hrv. 12. (☎34 71 00. Open M-F 8am-9pm, Sa 8am-10pm, Su 8am-1pm.) The **Daluma Travel Agency**, Obala kneza domagoja 1, near the bus and train stations, helps find private rooms. (☎33 84 84; www.tel.hr/daluma-travel. May-Oct. singles 150kn; doubles 240kn; Nov.-Apr. singles 100-120kn. Open M-F 8am-

8pm, Sa 8am-2pm.) To get from the stations to **Prenoćište Slavija ❹**, Buvinova 2, follow Obala hrv., turn right on Trg Braće Radića, then go right on Mihovilova širina; signs lead up the stairs. (☎34 70 53. Breakfast included. Singles 220kn, with shower 280kn; doubles 290/360kn.) There is a **supermarket** at Svačićeva 4. (Open daily 7am-10pm.) To reach ⚫**Jugo Restoran ❷**, Uvala Baluni bb, face the water on Obala hrv. and walk right along the waterfront for 10min., following the curves onto Branimirova Obala. (Entrees 30-65kn. Open daily 9am-midnight.) The closest **beach** to downtown Split is sandy **Bačvice**, a nighttime favorite for local skinny dippers and the starting point of a great strip of waterfront bars. **Postal Code:** 21000.

BRAČ ISLAND: BOL   ☎021

Central Dalmatia's largest island, Brač is an ocean-lover's paradise. Most visitors come here for **Zlatni rat**, a peninsula of white pebble beach and emerald waters, just a short walk from the town center of Bol. The 1475 **Dominican Monastery**, on the eastern tip of Bol, displays Tintoretto's altar painting of the Madonna with Child. (Open daily 10am-noon and 5-7pm. 10kn.) The **ferry** from Split docks at Supetar (1hr., 7-13 per day, 23kn). From there, take a **bus** to Bol (1hr., 5 per day, 15kn). The last bus back to the ferry leaves at 5:50pm. From the bus station, walk left for 5min. to reach the **tourist office,** Porad bolskich pomorca bb, on the far side of the small marina. (☎63 56 38; tzo-bol@st.tel.hr.) **Adria Tours,** Obala Vladimira Nazora 28, to the right facing the sea from the bus station, rents small motorcycles (120kn per half-day, 200kn per day) and cars (400kn per day including mileage), and also books rooms. (☎63 59 66; www.tel.hr/adria-tours-bol. 60-170kn per person. Open daily 8am-9pm.) There are five **campsites** around Bol; the largest is **Kito ❶,** Bračka cesta bb, on the road into town. (☎63 55 51. Open May-Sept. 46kn per person with tent included.) **Postal Code:** 21420.

KORČULA   ☎020

Within sight of the mainland are the macchia thickets and slender cypress trees of Korčula. Marco Polo was born here, among sacred monuments and churches dating from the time of the Apostles. The **Festival of Sword Dances** clangs into town July-Aug. (60kn; tickets available at tourist office). **Buses** from Korčula board a ferry to the mainland and head to: Dubrovnik (3½hr., daily, 75kn); Sarajevo (6½hr., 4 per week, 145kn); Split (5hr., daily, 90kn); and Zagreb (11-13hr., daily, 209kn). **Ferries** run to Dubrovnik (3½hr., 5 per week, 64kn) and Split (4½hr., daily, 74kn). To reach the **tourist office,** face the water and walk left around the peninsula to Hotel Korčula; the office is next door. (Open M-Sa 8am-3pm and 5-9pm, Su 9am-1pm.) **Private rooms** are the only budget lodgings available; shopping around is a good idea. **Marko Polo,** Biline 5, can also arrange rooms. (☎71 54 00; www.korcula.com. Singles 87-150kn; doubles 210-263kn. Open daily 8am-9pm.) ⚫**Adio Mare ❸,** Marka Pola bb, serves authentic local specialties. (Entrees 40-80kn. Open M-Sa 5:30pm-midnight, Su 6pm-midnight.) **Postal Code:** 20260.

DUBROVNIK   ☎020

George Bernard Shaw once wrote: "Those who seek Paradise on earth should come to Dubrovnik." Nearly scarless despite recent wars, the city continues to draw visitors with azure waters and golden sunsets over its 14th-century marble walls. If you make it as far south as Dubrovnik, you might never leave.

TRANSPORTATION AND PRACTICAL INFORMATION. Jadrolinija **ferries** (☎41 80 00) depart from opposite Obala S. Radica 40 for Bari, Italy (9hr., 5 per week, 329kn) and Split (8hr., daily, 115kn). **Buses** (☎35 70 88) run to: Sarajevo (6hr., 2 per day, 160kn); Split (4½hr., 16 per day, 103kn); Trieste (15hr., daily, 325kn); and Zagreb (11hr., 7 per day, 175kn). To reach Stari Grad, walk around the bus station, turn left on Ante Starčevića, and follow it uphill to the Old Town's western gate (25min.). To reach the ferry terminal, head left from the station and then bear right. All local buses *except* #5, 7, and 8 go to Stari Grad's Pile Gate (7kn at kiosks, 10kn from driver.) From the bus stop at Pile Gate, walk up Ante Starčevića away from Stari Grad to reach the **Tourist Board**, Ante Starčevića 7, which has free maps and pamphlets. (☎42 75 91. Open June-Sept. M-Sa 8am-8pm; Oct.-May 8am-3pm.) **Turistička Zajednica Grada Dubrovnika**, Cvijete Zuzoric 1/2, gives out the free, invaluable *City Guide*. (☎32 38 87. Open June-Aug. M-F 8am-4pm, Sa 9am-3pm, Su 9am-noon; Sept.-May M-F 8am-4pm.) **Postal Code:** 20000.

ACCOMMODATIONS AND FOOD. For two people, a **private room** is cheapest; arrange one through the Tourist Board (above; 80-150kn) or **Atlas ❷**, Lučarica 1, next to St. Blasius's Church. (☎44 25 28; www.atlas-croatia.com. Open June-Aug. M-Sa 8am-9pm, Su 8am-1pm; Sept.-May M-Sa 8am-7pm. Singles 100-150kn; doubles 120-180kn.) For cheaper rooms, try haggling with the women

HEADING EAST: CROATIA

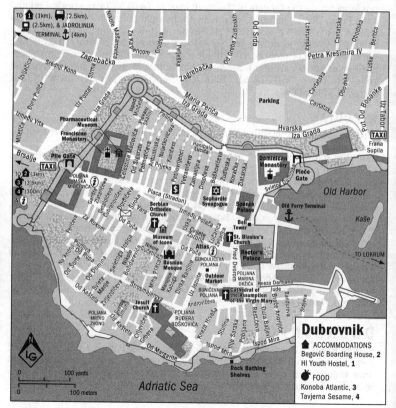

Dubrovnik

⌂ ACCOMMODATIONS
Begović Boarding House, **2**
HI Youth Hostel, **1**

🍴 FOOD
Konoba Atlantic, **3**
Tavjerna Sesame, **4**

around the ferry and bus terminals. To get to cozy ■**Begovic Boarding House** ❷, Primorska 17, from the bus station, take bus #6 toward Dubrava and tell the driver you want to get off at post office Lapad. Facing the pedestrian walkway, turn right at the intersection. Go left at the fork, and take the first right onto Primorska. (☎43 51 91. July-Aug. rooms 100kn; Sept.-June 80kn.) The **HI youth hostel** ❶, b. Josipa Jelačića 15/17 is one of the best in Croatia. From the bus station, walk up Ante Starčevića, turn right at the lights (10min.), take a right on b. Josipa Jelačića, and look for the hidden HI sign on your left. (☎42 32 41. Dorms 70-100kn.) **Konoba Atlantic** ❷, Kardinala Stopinga 42, serves up some of the best pasta in Croatia (28-45kn). To get there, take bus #6 to post office Labad and walk straight on the walkway; take a right on the staircase just before the Hotel Kompas, which will take you up to the restaurant. (Open daily noon-11pm.) **Tavjerna Sesame** ❸, Dante Alighiera bb, specializes in fresh pasta dishes. From Pile Gate, walk on Ante Starčevića toward the hostel. (Entrees 60-95kn. Open M-Sa 8am-11pm, Su 10am-11pm.) Behind St. Blasius's Church, on Gundulićeva Poljana, is an open air **market**. (Open daily 7am-8pm.) **Supermarket Mediator**, Od puča 4, faces the market. (Open M-Sa 6:30am-9pm, Su 7am-9pm.)

 SIGHTS. Stari Grad (Old Town) is full of churches, museums, monasteries, palaces, and fortresses. The most popular sights are along **Placa**. The entrance to the staggering city walls *(gradske zidine)* lies just inside the **Pile Gate**, on the left. Set aside an hour for the 2km walk along the top. (Open daily 9am-7pm. 15kn.) The 14th-century **Franciscan Monastery** (Franjevački samostan), next to the city wall entrance on Placa, houses the oldest working pharmacy in Europe and a pharmaceutical museum. (Open daily 9am-6pm. 6kn.) The **Cathedral of the Assumption of the Virgin Mary** (Riznica Katedrale) dominates Bunićeva Poljana. Its treasury holds religious relics. (Cathedral open daily 6:30am-8pm. Free. Treasury open M-Sa 9am-7pm, Su 11am-5:30pm. 5kn.) To reach the 19th-century **Serbian Orthodox Church** (Pravoslavna Crkva) and its **Museum of Icons** (Muzej Ikona), Od Puča 8, walk from Pile Gate down Placa, go right on Široka, and then turn left on Od Puča. (Church open daily 8am-noon and 5-7pm. Free. Museum open M-Sa 9am-1pm. 10kn.)

> ❗ **WATCH YOUR STEP.** As tempting as it may be to stroll in the hills above Dubrovnik, the area may still contain buried **landmines**. Stick to the paved paths and beach.

APPENDIX
LANGUAGE BASICS

DANISH

ENGLISH	DANISH	PRONOUNCE
yes/no	ano/ne	AH-no/neh
please	vær så venlig	vair soh VEN-li
thank you	tak	tack
Hello	Goddag	go-DAY
Goodbye	Farvel	fah-VEL
Sorry/excuse me	undskyld	UN-scoold
Help!	Hjælp!	yelp
police	politiet	por-lee-TEE-ehth
embassy	ambassade	ahm-ba-SA-theh

ENGLISH	DANISH	PRONOUNCE
ticket	billet	bill-ETT
train/bus	toget/bussen	TOE-et/BOO-sehn
airport	lufthavns	LAYFD-haown
departure	afgang	af-gahng
market	marked	mah-GEHTH
Hotel/Hostel	Hotel/Van-drerhjem	ho-TEL/VAN-drer-yem
pharmacy	apotek	ah-por-TIG
toilet	toilet	toy-LEHD
city center	centrum	SEHN-trum

ENGLISH	DANISH	PRONOUNCE
Where is...?	Hvor er...?	voa air
How do I get to...?	Hvordan kommer jeg til...?	vo-DAN KOM-ah yai tee
How much does this cost?	Hvad koster det?	va KOS-tor dey
I'd like a...	Jeg vil gerne have en...	yai vi GEHR-neh ha en
Do you speak English?	Taler du engelsk?	TAY-luh dou ENG-elsk

DUTCH

ENGLISH	DUTCH	PRONOUNCE
Yes/No	Ja/Nee	ya/nay
Please/You're welcome	Alstublieft	ALs-too-bleeft
Thank you	Dank u wel	dank oo vell
Hello	Hallo	hal-LO
Goodbye	Tot ziens	tot zeens
Sorry/excuse me	Neemt u mij niet/Pardon	naymt oo mi neet/par-DON
Help!	Help!	help
Police	Politie	po-LEET-see
Embassy	Ambassade	am-bass-AH-duh

ENGLISH	DUTCH	PRONOUNCE
Ticket	Kaartje	KAHRT-yuh
Train/Bus	Trein/Bus	trin/boos
Station	Station	staht-see-ohn
Taxi	Taxi	TAX-ee
Grocery	Kruidenier	krow-duh-EER
Tourist office	VVV	fay-fay-fay
Town Center	Centrum	ZEHN-trum
Hotel	Hotel	ho-TEL
Bathroom	Badkamer	BAT-kah-mer

ENGLISH	DUTCH	PRONOUNCE
Where is...?	Waar is...?	vaar is
How do I get to...?	Hoe kom ik in...?	hoo kom ik in
How much does this cost?	Wat kost het?	vat kost het
Do you have...?	Heeft u...?	hayft oo
Do you speak English?	Sprekt u Engels?	spraykt oo EN-gels

In Dutch, "j" is pronounced like the "s" in treasure. A gutteral "g" sound is used for both "g" and "ch." The Dutch "ui" is pronounced "ow," and the dipthong "ij" is best approximated in English as "ah" followed by a long "e." There are two plural endings for nouns: -en (more common) and -s.

FRENCH

ENGLISH	FRENCH	PRONOUNCE
Yes/No	Oui/Non	wee/nohn
Please	S'il vous plaît.	see-voo-PLAY
Thank you	Merci.	mehr-SEE
Hello	Bonjour.	bohn-ZHOOR
Goodbye	Au revoir.	oh re-VWAHR
Excuse me	Excusez-moi!	ex-KU-zay-MWAH
Help!	Au secours!	Help!
Police	la police	Police
Embassy	l'ambassade	Embassy
passport	le passeport	passport
hotel	l'hôtel	LO-tel
hostel	l'auberge de jeunesse	LO-berzh-de-zhun-ESS
single room	une chambre simple	oon-SHAM-bra-samp
double room	une chambre pour deux	oon-SHAM-bra-poor-do
with shower	avec la douche	a-VEK-la-DOO-sh
bathroom	la salle de bain	SAL-de-BAN
open/closed	ouvert/fermé	OO-vert/fer-MAY
left/right	à gauche/ à droite	a-GOsh/a-dwat
straight	tout droit	TOOT-dwat
turn	tournez	toor-NAY
newsstand	le tabac	ta-BAK
cigarette	la cigarette	SEE-gar-et
condom	le préservatif	PRAY-ser-va-teef
bicycle	la vélo	vay-LO
car	la voiture	vwa-TURE

ENGLISH	FRENCH	PRONOUNCE
departure	le départ	DAY-part
one-way	le billet simple	BEE-AY-samp
round-trip	le billet retour	BEE-AY-re-TOOR
reservation	le réservation	rez-va-SHE-on
Ticket	le billet	bee-AY
Train/Bus	le train/le bus	tran/boos
Station	la gare	gahr
Airport	l'aéroport	laehr-O-port
Taxi	le taxi	tax-EE
ferry	le bac	bak
Bank	la banque	bahnk
Exchange	l'échange	lay-SHANZH
Grocery	l'épicerie	lay-PEES–ree
Pharmacy	la pharmacie	far-ma-SEE
Tourist office	le bureau de tourisme	byur-OH-de-toor-EE-sm
Town hall	l'hôtel de ville	LO-tel-de-veel
vegetarian	le végétarien	ve-JAY-ter-REE-en
vegan	le végétaliene	ve-JAY-tal-EE-en
kosher/halal	kascher/halal	ka-SHER/ha-lal
nuts/milk	les caca-houètes/ le lait	CAK-a-hwets/ LAY
change/coins	la monnaie	mon-AY
tip	la service	ser-VEE-s
waiter	le garçon	GAR-son
doctor	le médecin	mehd-SEN
Toilet	les WC	lay-vay-SAY

ENGLISH	FRENCH	PRONOUNCE
Where is...?	Où se trouve...?	OOH-AY
How do I get to...?	Comment peut on aller à...?	KOM-mo-put-on-a-LAY-a
How much does this cost?	Ça fait combien?	sa-FAY-com-BEE-en
Do you have...?	Avez vous...?	ah-VAY-VOO
Do you speak English?	Parlez-vous anglais?	par-LAY-VOO-an-GLAY
I would like ...	Je voudrais...	zhe-VOO-DRAY
I'm allergic to...	Je suis allergique à...	zhe-SWEE-al-er-ZHEEK-a
I love you.	Je t'aime.	zhe-TEM

Le is the masculine singular definite article (the); *la* the feminine; both are abbreviated to *l'* before a vowel, while *les* is the plural definite article for both genders. *Un* is the masculine singular indefinite article (a or an), *une* the feminine; while *des* is the plural indefinite article for both genders ("some").

GERMAN

ENGLISH	GERMAN	PRONOUNCE
Yes/No	Ja/Nein	yah/nain
Please	Bitte	BIH-tuh
Thank you	Danke	DAHNG-kuh
Hello	Hallo	HAH-lo
Goodbye	Auf Wiedersehen	owf VEE-der-zayn
Excuse me	Entschuldigung	ent-SHOOL-di-gung
Help!	Hilfe!	HIL-fuh
Police	Polizei	poh-lit-ZAI
Embassy	Botschaft	BOT-shaft
passport	Reisepass	RY-zeh-pahss
Hotel/Hostel	Hotel/Jugendherberge	ho-TEL/YOO-gend-her-BER-guh
single room	Einzelzimmer	AIN-tsel-tsim-muh
double room	Doppelzimmer	DOP-pel-tsim-muh
dorm	Schlafsaal	SHLAF-zahl
With shower	Mit Dusche	miht DOO-shuh
Bathroom	Badezimmer	BAH-deh-tsim-muh
Open/Closed	Geöffnet/Geschlossen	geh-UHF-net/geh-shlos-sen
left/right	links/rechts	links/rekts
straight	geradeaus	geh-RAH-de-OWS
(to) turn	drehen	DRAY-en
castle	Schloß	shloss
square	Platz	plahtz

ENGLISH	GERMAN	PRONOUNCE
departure	Abfahrt	AHB-fart
one-way	einfache	AYHN-fah-kuh
round-trip	rundreise	RUND-RY-suh
reservation	reservierung	reh-zer-VEER-ung
Ticket	Fahrkarte	FAR-kar-tuh
Train/Bus	Zug/Bus	tsug/boos
Station	Bahnhof	BAHN-hohf
Airport	Flughafen	FLOOG-hahf-en
taxi	Taxi	TAHK-see
Ferry	Fährschiff	FAYHR-shif
Bank	Bank	bahnk
Exchange	Wechseln	VEHK-zeln
Grocery	Lebensmittelgeschäft	LAY-bens-mit-tel-guh-SHEFT
Pharmacy	Apotheke	AH-po-TAY-kuh
Doctor	Arzt	ARTZT
Tourist office	Touristbüro	TOR-ist-byur-oh
city center	Altstadt	AHLT-shtat
vegetarian	vegetarier	veh-geh-TAYR-ee-er
vegan	veganer	VAY-gan-er
kosher/halal	koscher/halaal	KOH-shayr/hah-LAAL
nuts/milk	Nüsse/Milch	NYOO-suh/milch
bridge	Brücke	BROOK-eh

ENGLISH	GERMAN	PRONOUNCE
Where is...?	Wo ist...?	vo ist
How do I get to...?	Wie komme ich nach...?	vee KOM-muh ish NOCK
How much does that cost?	Wieviel kostet das?	VEE-feel KOS-tet das
Do you have...?	Haben Sie...?	HAB-en zee
Do you speak English?	Sprechen Sie English?	SHPREK-en zee EHNG-lish
I would like...	Ich möchte ...	ish MERK-tuh
I'm allergic to...	Ich bin zu ____ allergisch.	ish bihn tsoo ____ ah-LEHR-jish

Every letter is pronounced. Consonants are pronounced as in English with the following exceptions: "j" is pronounced as "y"; "qu" is pronounced "kv"; a single "s" is pronounced "z"; "v" is pronounced "f"; "w" is pronounced as "v"; and "z" is pronounced "ts." "Sch" is "sh"; "st" is "sht"; and "sp" is "shp." The "ch" sound, as in "ich" ("I") and "nicht" ("not"), is tricky; you can substitute a "sh." The letter ß (esstset) is a symbol for a double-S and is pronounced "ss."

GREEK

ENGLISH	GREEK	PRONOUNCE
Yes/No	ναι/οχι	NEH/OH-hee
Please	παρακαλω	pah-rah-kah-LO
Thank you	ευχαριστω	ef-khah-ree-STO
Hello/Good-bye	Γεια σας	YAH-sas
Sorry/Excuse me	Συγνομη	sig-NO-mee
Help!	Βοητηεια!	vo-EE-thee-ah
Police	αστυνομεια	as-tee-no-MEE-a
Embassy	πρεσβεια	prez-VEE-ah
Passport	διαβατηριο	dhee-ah-vah-TEE-ree-o
Open/closed	ανοικτο/κλειστο	ah-nee-KTO/klee-STO
Pharmacy	φαρμακειο	fahr-mah-KEE-o
Doctor	ιατροσ	yah-TROS

ENGLISH	GREEK	PRONOUNCE
Train/Bus	τραινο/λεωφορειο	TREH-no/leh-o-fo-REE-o
Station	σταθμοζ	stath-MOS
Airport	αεροδρομειο	ah-e-ro-DHRO-mee-o
Taxi	ταξι	tax-EE
Ferry	πλοιο	PLEE-o
Bank	τραπεζα	TRAH-peh-zah
Exchange	ανταλλασσω	an-da-LAS-so
Market	αγορα	ah-go-RAH
Tourist office	τουριστικο γραψειο	tou-ree-stee-KO graf-EE-o
Hotel/Hostel	ξενοδοχειο	kse-no-dho-HEE-o
Bathroom	τουαλεττα	tou-ah-LET-ta
Room to let	δωματια	do-MA-shee-ah

ENGLISH	GREEK	PRONOUNCE
Where is...?	Που ειναι...?	pou-EE-neh
How much does this cost?	Ποσπο κανει?	PO-so KAH-nee
Do you have...?	Εχετε...?	Eh-khe-teh
Do you speak English?	Μιλας αγγλικα?	mee-LAHS ahn-glee-KAH
I'd like ...	Θα ηθελα...	tha EE-thel-ah

GREEK ALPHABET

SYMBOL	NAME	PRONUNCIATION	SYMBOL	NAME	PRONUNCIATION
α A	alpha	a as in father	ν N	nu	n as in net
β B	beta	v as in velvet	ξ Ξ	xi	x as in mix
γ Γ	gamma	y as in yo or g as in go	o O	omicron	o as in row
δ Δ	delta	th as in there	π Π	pi	p as in peace
ε E	epsilon	e as in jet	ρ P	rho	r as in roll
ζ Z	zeta	z as in zebra	σ (ς) Σ	sigma	s as in sense
η H	eta	ee as in queen	τ T	tau	t as in tent
θ Θ	theta	th as in three	υ Y	upsilon	ee as in green
ι I	iota	ee as in tree	φ Φ	phi	f as in fog
κ K	kappa	k as in kite	χ X	chi	h as in horse
λ Λ	lambda	l as in land	ψ Ψ	psi	ps as in oops
μ M	mu	m as in moose	ω Ω	omega	o as in go

ITALIAN

ENGLISH	ITALIAN	PRONOUNCE
Yes/No	Sì/No	see/no
Please	Per favore/Per piacere	pehr fah-VOH-reh/pehr pyah-CHAY-reh
Thank you	Grazie	GRAHT-see-yeh
Hello	Ciao	chow
Goodbye	Arrivederci	ah-ree-veh-DAIR-chee
Sorry/Excuse me	Mi dispiace/Scusi	mee dees-PYAH-cheh/SKOO-zee
Help!	Aiuto!	ah-YOO-toh
Police	Polizia	po-LEET-ZEE-ah
Embassy	Ambasciata	ahm-bah-shee-AH-tah
Passport	Il passaporto	eel pahs-sah-POHR-toh
Hotel/Hostel	Albergo	al-BEHR-go
single room	una camera singola	OO-nah CAH-meh-rah SEEN-goh-lah
double room	una camera doppia	OO-nah CAH-meh-rah DOH-pee-yah
With shower	Con doccia	kohn DOH-cha
Bathroom	un gabinetto/un bagno	ooh gah-bee-NEHT-toh/oon BAHN-yoh
Open/Closed	Aperto/Chiuso	ah-PAIR-toh/KYOO-zoh
left/right	sinistra/destra	see-NEE-strah/DEH-strah
straight	sempre diritto	SEHM-pray DREET-toh
turn	gira a	JEE-rah ah

ENGLISH	ITALIAN	PRONOUNCE
departure	partenza	par-TEN-zuh
one-way	solo andata	SO-lo ahn-DAH-tah
round-trip	andata e ritorno	ahn-DAH-tah ey ree-TOHR-noh
reservation	la prenotazione	la pray-no-taht-see-YOH-neh
Ticket	Biglietto	oon beel-YEHT-toh
Train/Bus	Treno/Autobus	TRAY-no/aow-toh-BOOS
Station	Stazione	lah staht-see-YOH-neh
Airport	Aeroporto	AYR-o-PORT-o
Taxi	Tassì	tahs-SEE
Ferry	Traghetto	eel tra-GHEHT-toh
Bank	Banca	bahn-KAH
Exchange	Cambio	CAHM-bee-oh
Grocery	Alimentari	ah-li-mehn-TA-ri
Pharmacy	Farmacia	far-mah-SEE-ah
Tourist office	Azienda Promozione Turistica	ah-tzi-EHN-da pro-mo-tzi-O-nay tur-EES-tee-kah
Doctor	Medico	MEH-dee-koh
vegetarian	vegetariano	ve-ge-tar-i-AN-o
kosher/halal	kasher/halal	KA-sher/HA-lal
nuts/milk	noce/latte	NO-chay/LA-tay

ENGLISH	ITALIAN	PRONOUNCE
Where is...?	Dov'è...?	doh-VEH
How do I get to...?	Come si arriva a...	KOH-meh see ahr-REE-vah ah
How much does this cost?	Quanto costa?	KWAN-toh CO-stah
Do you have...?	Hai...	HI
Do you speak English?	Parla inglese?	PAHR-lah een-GLAY-zeh
I'd like...	Vorrei...	VOH-ray
I'm allergic to...	Ho delle allergie...	OH DEHL-leh ahl-lair-JEE-eh

In many Italian words, stress falls on the next-to-last syllable. When stress falls on the last syllable, accents indicate where stress falls: *città* (cheet-TAH) or *perchè* (pair-KAY). Stress can fall on the first syllable, but this occurs less often.

PORTUGUESE

ENGLISH	PORTUGUESE	PRONOUNCE
Yes/No	Sim/Não	seeng/now
Please	Por favor	pur fah-VOR
Thank you	Obrigado (m)/ Obrigada (f)	oh-bree-GAH-doo/dah
Hello	Olá	oh-LAH
Goodbye	Adeus	ah-DAY-oosh
Sorry/Excuse me	Desculpe	desh-KOOLP
Help!	Socorro!	so-KO-ro!
Police	Polícia	po-LEE-see-ah

ENGLISH	PORTUGUESE	PRONOUNCE
Ticket	Bilhete	beel-YEHT
Train/Bus	Comboio/Auto-carro	kom-BOY-yoo/ OW-to-KAH-roo
Airport	Aeroporto	aye-ro-POR-too
Exchange	Câmbio	CAHM-bee-yoo
Market	Mercado	mer-KAH-doo
Hotel	Pousada	poh-ZAH-dah
Pharmacy	Farmácia	far-MAH-see-ah
Bathroom	Banheiro	bahn-YAY-roo

ENGLISH	PORTUGUESE	PRONOUNCE
Where is...?	Onde é que é ...?	OHN-deh eh keh eh...?
How much does this cost?	Quanto custa?	KWAHN-too KOOSH-tah?
I want...	Quero...	KAY-roo...
Do you speak English?	Fala inglês?	FAH-lah een-GLAYSH?

Vowels with a *til* (ã, õ, etc.) or before "m" or "n" are pronounced with a nasal twang. At the end of a word, "o" is pronounced "oo" as in "room," and "e" is sometimes silent. "S" is pronounced "sh" or "zh" when it occurs before another consonant. "Ch" and "x" are pronounced "sh"; "j" and "g" (before e or i) are pronounced "zh." The combinations "nh" and "lh" are pronounced "ny" and "ly" respectively.

SPANISH

ENGLISH	SPANISH	PRONOUNCE
Yes/No	Si/No	see/noh
Please	Por favor	pohr fah-VOHR
Thank you	Gracias	GRAH-see-ahs
Hello	Hola	OH-lah
Goodbye	Adiós	ah-di-OHS
Sorry/Excuse me	Perdón	pehr-DOHN
Help!	¡Ayuda!	ay-YOOH-duh
Police	Policía	poh-lee-SEE-ah
Embassy	Embajada	em-bah-HA-dah
Passport	Pasaporte	pas-ah-POR-tay
Open/Closed	Abierto(a)/Cer-rado(a)	ah-bee-AYR-toh/ sehr-RAH-doh
Pharmacy	Farmácia	far-MAH-see-ah
Doctor	Médico	MAY-dee-koh

ENGLISH	SPANISH	PRONOUNCE
Ticket	Boleto	boh-LEH-toh
Train/Bus	Tren Autobús	trehn ow-toh-BOOS
Station	Estación	es-tah-see-OHN
Airport	Aeropuerto	ay-roh-PWER-toh
Taxi	Taxi	tahk-SEE
Ferry	Transbordador	trahns-BOR-dah-dohr
Bank	Banco	BAHN-koh
Exchange	Cambio	CAHM-bee-oh
Grocery	Supermercado	soo-pehr-mer-CHAH-doh
Tourist Office	Oficina de tur-ismo	oh-fee-SEE-nah day toor-EEZ-moh
Hotel/Hostel	Hotel/Hostal	oh-TEL/OH-stahl
Dorm	Dormitorio	dor-mih-TOR-ee-oh
Bathroom	Baño	BAHN-yoh

ENGLISH	SPANISH	PRONOUNCE
Where is...?	Dónde está...?	DOHN-day eh-STA
How much does this cost?	Cuánto cuesta...?	KWAN-toh KWEHS-tah
Do you have...?	Usted tiene....?	ooh-STED tee-EN-ay
Do you speak English?	Habla inglés?	AH-blah een-GLAYS
I'd like...	Me gustaría...	may goos-tah-REE-ah

WESTERN EUROPE: A QUICK HISTORY

As you travel through Western Europe, you are bound to encounter the unique political and cultural histories of each country you visit; from architecture to landscapes to the people themselves, the history of Europe is alive and visible. Below is a very brief primer on the major intellectual and political movements that forged Western Europe's identity for four millennia. Use this abridged history along with the historical and cultural introductions at the beginning of each country chapter to truly partake in the delights of Western Europe.

IN THE BEGINNING...(2000 BC-AD 565)

The first Western Europeans were nomads of the Paleolithic and Neolithic periods. Migrating from the East, these Indo-Europeans settled by the Aegean Sea during the 18th and 17th centuries BC. Inter-marriage with the natives gave rise to the **Greeks,** whose culture in turn created the cornerstone of Western European civilization. The Greeks were no strangers to warfare; in the 15th century BC, they defeated the **Minoans;** in 1500 BC, they sacked Troy in the **Trojan War.** Between 337 and 323 BC, **Alexander the Great** expanded the Greek Empire across Europe, and autonomous **city-states** grew in size, power, and cultural influence, with **Athens** and **Sparta** as the two dominant cities. At the height of **Classical Greece** (500-400 BC), Athens produced the art, literature, and philosophy that have come to be hallmarks of Western culture ever since. The military might of the **Romans** eventually proved too great for these sons of Zeus, however; by 133 BC, Greece was essentially under Roman control. Rome expanded its empire over most of Western Europe through the **Punic Wars,** ruling the continent with its distinctive government that borrowed liberally from Greek culture. The general peace that resulted within the empire (often referred to as the **Pax Romana**) fostered transportation between cities on an unprecedented level. Yet as the empire grew, it also became more difficult to control. In AD 293, **Diocletian** tried to strengthen his control over the realm by dividing East and West between himself and a co-emperor. Diocletian's plan backfired when Emperor **Constantine the Great** revoked this agreement and reunited the Roman Empire between 306-337, moving its capital to Byzantium. A converted Christian, Constantine encouraged the growth of Christianity throughout the empire. It would be a course of action that would come to shape the face of European history for the next millennium.

EARLY MIDDLE AGES (AD 476-1000)

There's nothing like 200 years of **Huns, Visigoths,** and **Vandals** to spoil a perfectly good empire. In 476, the last Roman emperor was deposed, and Germanic barbarians began a 150-year political renovation of the Roman Empire, reverting cities to tribal kingdoms. As life became increasingly localized, Western Europe tumbled into the intellectually stagnant **Dark Ages** (AD 500 to 1200). The 9th century saw Pope Leo III crown Frankish king **Charlemagne** as Holy Roman Emperor, in theory uniting eastern and western Christian Europe permanently. Yet following the death of Charlemagne's son, **Louis the Pious,** the Carolingian Empire was divvied among his three sons, thus decentralizing power and leading to the rise of local lords. Europe was now divided into three parts: The **Byzantine Empire** (the East and parts of Italy), **Islamic Europe** (Spain and Portugal), and **Latin Christendom** (Belgium, Britain, France, Germany, and parts of Italy).

HIGH MIDDLE AGES (1000-1300)

When the millennial apocalypse didn't arrive in AD 1000, the first order of business was to establish a stable political system. Carolingian rulers established **feudalism,** a system of local government that subjected agrarian **vassals** to the dictates of their **lords.** Above this political hierarchy, however, reigned the Church, an extremely wealthy and powerful institution that—in light of its absolute power concerning ecclesiastical law—became the de facto adjudicator of secular law as well. With such influence at his disposal, Pope **Innocent III** financed and advised regional kings to advance his goal of Christian unification. The High Middle Ages were marked by costly attempts to extend Christianity.

From 1095 to 1291, Western Europeans launched the **Holy War,** or the seven **Crusades,** against the Islamic East; at the same time, the Church attempted to purge itself of contentious "heretical" factions within Europe itself. As a result, the 13th century saw Christianity become the dominant religion in the Baltic regions, Italy, Prussia, and Spain. Overall, the wars strengthened the might of Christian Europe, despite the abject failures of the Crusades to recapture the Holy Land.

THE RENAISSANCE (1350-1550)

During the 12th and 13th centuries, the Italian writers **Dante** and **Petrarch,** as well as the artist **Giotto,** created works that celebrated the inherent dignity and beauty of humankind. Their work, coupled with a revival of Italian **Classicism,** set the stage for the cultural rebirth known as the **Renaissance.** In the 14th century, sculptors and artists **Donatello, Michelangelo,** and **da Vinci** gave life to **Humanism,** an outlook that treated rhetoric and the Classics as a celebration of human self-respect and preparation for a life of virtue. The optimism of the Renaissance was blemished, however, by the devastation of the **Black Death** (bubonic and pneumonic plague). Between 1347 and 1352, the plague killed 25 million Europeans.

The Renaissance also fostered the **Age of Exploration** that began in the 1490s, with the expansion of Spain's and Portugal's colonial empires. The period featured England's oddly-named **Hundred Years War** with France, which lasted from 1337 to 1453 but saw only 44 years of actual fighting. Although the English won early battles, they were eventually expelled from France. Squabbles within the Roman Catholic Church escalated into **The Great Schism,** during which multiple popes vied for ecclesiastical power from 1378 to 1417. The election of an Italian Cardinal during the **Council of Constance** ended the schism, but papal authority was permanently weakened.

PROTESTANT REFORMATION (1517-1555)

In 1517, **Martin Luther**'s *95 Theses* sparked the Protestant Reformation in Germany. The shocking treatise resulted in Luther's 1521 excommunication, but the Church's condemnation of his work was not enough to prevent its influence. Before the decade's end, the Holy Roman Empire was divided by the issue of reformation. **Henry VIII**'s divorce from **Catherine of Aragon** in 1534 and subsequent second marriage to **Anne Boleyn** severed England from the Roman Catholic Church. With the **Act of Supremacy** in 1534, Henry declared himself not only the head of state, but also head of the new Protestant church as well, instigating the **English Reformation.** Later in the 16th century, **John Calvin** led the **Genevan Reformation** in Switzerland to establish **Calvinism,** which soon became the dominant Protestant force in Europe.

APPENDIX

Yet the movement towards Reformation did not go unchecked. The **Council of Trent** (1545-1563), the 19th ecumenical council of the Roman Catholic Church, formed the keystone of the **Counter-Reformation** argument. While the council refuted all criticism from Protestants, it also made sweeping reforms to correct the many abuses within the Church. Most importantly, the council halted the sale of **indulgences**, which forgave neglected penances or unrepented sins. Despite its earnest attempts to reform, however, the Church had lost its absolute control over Europe's rulers. In 1555, **Charles V** of the Holy Roman Empire granted the princes of Germany the right to establish the religion of their own people, whether that was Catholicism or Protestantism. The **Peace of Augsburg,** as this edict was known, provided a degree of religious freedom never before known in Western Europe, but it came at the cost of future political strife.

REVOLUTION IN THOUGHT (1555-1648)

Unwilling to witness the fracturing of his empire, Charles V abdicated all his titles in 1555. His solution to the already present lack of unity in the Holy Roman Empire was to further divide power; his brother **Ferdinand I** gained control of the Austrian Habsburg lands, while his son **Philip II** ruled Spain and The Netherlands. Under Philip II, Spain entered its Golden Age, **Siglo de Oro,** becoming the greatest power in Europe. Obsessed with the necessity for Catholic reform, Phillip supported the Catholic cause in Western Europe, aiding rebellions against England's Protestant **Queen Elizabeth** and removing French Protestant **Huguenots** from power. Spain's troops and gold ultimately proved insufficient, though. The Spanish were driven out of The Netherlands by **William of Orange** in the **Eighty Years' War** (1568-1648).

From 1618-1648, Germany became the battlefield of Europe, as Protestant forces asserted their independence from the Roman Catholic Church and the Holy Roman Empire during the **Thirty Years' War.** The **Treaty of Westphalia,** signed in 1648, reinforced the Peace of Augsburg's principle of *cuius regio eius religio* (whose region, his religion) and set European political geography for the next century. The havoc of religious strife had redefined the face of Europe—the Holy Roman Empire was severely weakened, Spain fell from grace as Philip II's Catholic crusade crashed in flames, Queen Elizabeth restored the Protestant church, and a Huguenot sat on the throne in France.

The late 17th century exploded with political and intellectual revolutions. England plunged into civil war, and France, under the "Sun King" **Louis XIV,** became the greatest power in Western Europe. The **Scientific Revolution** of the 17th century broke out of the medieval mindset and began to challenge traditional modes of thought. **Descartes, Galileo, Hobbes,** and **Newton** were among the many whose works marked the revolution, each contributing to the belief in harmony, logic, and human abilities. The popularization of scientific thought and the realization of its increasing pertinence to everyday life, medicine, and politics formed the basis for the ideas of the **Age of Enlightenment**.

AGE OF ENLIGHTENMENT (1688-1789)

During the Enlightenment, thinkers such as **Locke, Montesquieu, Rousseau,** and **Voltaire** made the radical proposition that reason and science, rather than a mysterious God, could reveal the truth of life. By reasoning out the universal laws of nature, they claimed, one could achieve freedom and happiness. This age's questioning spirit also affected the conception of the state—**Frederick II** of Prussia, **Catherine the Great** of Russia, and **Joseph II** of the Habsburg empire were monarchs known as the **enlightened despots,** who combined liberal reforms with measures to maintain control over peasants.

APPENDIX

Unfortunately, these utopian ideals didn't halt sparring monarchies. In the **War of the Spanish Succession** (1701-1714), Austria and Britain went to war to keep Louis XIV's son, **Philip V,** from the Spanish throne. This was settled by the **Treaty of Utrecht,** which allowed Philip to take the throne but forbade him from merging the empire with France. The **Seven Years' War** (1756-1763) saw Austria and France ally to fight Prussia and Britain over colonies. War eventually spread to North America, the Caribbean, and India, hinting at the impending wave of imperialism.

FRENCH REVOLUTION AND NAPOLEON (1789-1814)

Louis XIV's full ascension to the French throne in 1661 ushered in an era of aristocratic **absolutism** and excess, perhaps best exemplified by the 14,000-room palace of **Versailles.** Prompted by a financial crisis and a disgruntled population, **Louis XVI** called the first (and last) assembly of the **Estates General** in over 175 years. The assembly was constituted of representatives from France's three classes: Nobility, clergy, and the common people. From this organization, the populace broke away, declaring itself the **National Assembly.** In the midst of this political chaos, the radical **Jacobin** faction seized control. They quickly abolished the monarchy and declared France a Republic, storming the **Bastille** prison on July 14, 1789 to symbolically demonstrate the overturn of the old regime. Yet social order remained elusive. The **Directory,** a representative government established in 1794, lasted only five years; meanwhile, citizens found themselves subject to the **Terror,** a radical phase of the Revolution in which potential enemies of the cause were summarily dispensed by "Madame" Guillotine. Into this political vacuum stepped a little man with a big ego, **Napoleon Bonaparte.** Napoleon's claim to fame was his military success in Egypt and Italy. In 1804, he deposed the Directory and declared himself Emperor and "consul for life."

Soon after his assent, Bonaparte codified the **Napoleonic Code** (a direct result of the Age of Enlightenment ideals), which defined property rights, declared all people equal before the law, and affirmed religious freedoms. Seeking to expand his control, Napoleon abolished the Holy Roman Empire and dismembered Prussia; by 1810, most of Europe was either annexed by or allied to France. After wars with Britain and Spain, Napoleon's **Grand Army** was disastrously defeated in Russia in 1812, after which he abdicated and was sent into exile on **Elba.** Bourbon rule was restored in France in 1814 under Louis XVIII, but the **Congress of Vienna** in 1814 left France without Napoleon's land acquisitions.

INDUSTRIAL REVOLUTION (1760-1848)

With the invention of the steam engine, spinning mill, and **Spinning Jenny** (cotton spinning machine) in the 18th century, the Industrial Revolution was off to a running start. From 1800 to 1850 it spread rapidly throughout Europe, bringing with it **urbanization** and greater life expectancy. **Factories,** especially for textiles and iron, were the Industrial Age's most visible symbol, but the period also saw heightened international trade and the birth of socialist ideology (**St. Simon, Marx,** and **Engels**). Heightened urbanization provided mobility for the peasant class, although conditions in slums remained deplorable.

Industrial changes were harbingers of other social revolutions, as liberal revolts broke out in Germany, Italy, Poland, Portugal, Russia, and Spain from 1815 to 1848. The 19th century also brought new independence for several countries, as Belgium wrested autonomy from The Netherlands in 1830 and the Turks recognized Greek independence in 1832. An 18-year-old **Queen Victoria** ascended the British throne in 1837, giving rise to the era of her name.

NATIONAL UNIFICATION (1851-1867)

During the mid-19th century, European nations, inspired by the "survival of the fittest" theories of **Social Darwinism,** consolidated land and power. Taking the lead from his uncle, President Louis Napoleon dissolved the National Assembly and declared himself **Emperor Napoleon III.** In Italy, the efforts of **Victor Emmanuel II** and **General Giuseppe Garibaldi** from 1859 to 1870 managed to unify Italy despite long-standing regional tensions. Meanwhile, back in Prussia, newly appointed Prime Minister **Otto von Bismarck** unified the German Empire, including the new lands Prussia had garnered as spoils during the **Austro-Prussian** and **Franco-Prussian Wars.** As massive monarchal alliances became trendy, the **Dual Monarchy** of Austria-Hungary was created in 1867, the same year that the **British Reform Bill** doubled the number of English voters by granting suffrage to all household heads.

INVENTION AND IMPERIALISM (1870-1911)

Continuing innovation brought rapid industrialization to Europe with the spread of electricity and the invention of the sewing machine, telephone, and automobile. Railways surged across the continent, standards of living skyrocketed, and the service industry provided many women of the new and expanding middle class gainful employment. Chancellor Bismarck gave the **industrial bourgeoisie** something to cheer about as he enacted the world's first unemployment insurance in 1883. European powers, led by Germany and Britain, extended their long arms to Africa and Asia, establishing dominance during the **Age of Imperialism.** Explorers and missionaries were the first to introduce Europe to Africa, desiring to socialize an otherwise "primitive" continent. **King Leopold II** of Belgium was especially attracted to the potential wealth of Africa, while the British and French also ventured into the "dark continent" to secure political clout and plunder diamonds. The Dutch, British, and Russian imperialists also began to occupy parts of Asia, creating powerful empires while suppressing the revolts of native inhabitants.

WORLD WAR I (1914-1918)

The assassination of the Austro-Hungarian **Archduke Francis Ferdinand** in Serbia in 1914 was the straw that broke Europe's back. Through Bismarck's masterful diplomacy, the continent had become a mess of opposing alliances: Britain and France ended centuries of conflict in 1904 by forming the **Entente Cordiale,** an alliance which Russia later joined to create the **Triple Entente.** At the same time, Austria-Hungary entered into alliance with the recently-unified Germany and Turkey, forming the **Central Powers.** The assassination of Ferdinand prompted Austria-Hungary to issue a military ultimatum to Serbia. The standoff brought Russia into the conflict, prompting Germany to declare war against her and her allies. Germany, seeking to destroy the allied Franco-British threat, advanced quickly through Belgium and France before stalling at the **Battle of the Marne** in 1914, starting four long years of **trench** warfare. The United States was drawn into the war when Germany's practice of **unrestricted submarine warfare** became intolerable, and the American entry in 1917 was followed in short order by the Allied victory on November 11, 1918. In 1919, the **Big Four** (Orlando of Italy, Lloyd George of Britain, Clemenceau of France, and Wilson of the US) forced Germany to accept full responsibility for the Great War in the **Treaty of Versailles**—in the **war guilt clause,** the weak new **Weimar Republic** in Germany was forced to assume the financial burden of the war. The treaty also paved the way for the **League of Nations.**

INTERWAR YEARS (1919-1938)

For Germany, the Treaty of Versailles was disastrous: The Allies demanded enormous reparations, apportioned significant German territory, and limited the size of its standing military. This humiliation, combined with hyperinflation of the 1920s, the **Great Depression,** and alienating urbanization, set the stage for Austrian **Adolf Hitler**'s rise to power. As the leader of the **National Socialist German Workers' Party (NSDAP),** also known as the **Nazis,** Hitler pushed a program of Aryan supremacy (based on anti-Semitism and German racial purity), playing on the post-war insecurities of the Germans. By the 1930s, many European countries were dictatorships, most prominently fascist Italy under **Benito Mussolini,** autarchic Spain, commanded by **General Francisco Franco,** and of course, the newly-created Union of Soviet Socialist Republics, led by **Joseph Stalin.** By 1933, Hitler had been appointed chancellor of Germany; he banned all other parties and created a totalitarian state. The **Kristallnacht** (Night of Broken Glass), on November 9, 1938, saw the destruction of Jewish stores and homes throughout Germany, as well as attacks against (and the imprisonment of) thousands of Jews.

WORLD WAR II (1939-1945)

Continuing German expansion, Hitler, facilitated by British Prime Minister **Neville Chamberlain**'s naïve appeasement policy, moved into Czechoslovakia and then Poland, initiating WWII on September 1, 1939. Britain and France, bound by treaty to help Poland, declared war on Germany. As Germany overran Belgium, Denmark, France, Luxembourg, The Netherlands, and Norway with its **Blitzkrieg** (Lightning-War) offensives, Chamberlain resigned and **Winston Churchill** assumed the British helm. France, despite the elaborate fortifications of the **Maginot Line,** fell to the German offensive, leading to Nazi occupation and the formation of the puppet **Vichy** regime. Russia stayed neutral because of a secret non-aggression pact signed with Hitler. This short-lived treaty only lasted until the Nazis invaded the Soviet Union in 1941; however, German forces were unable to break through during the Russian winter. In the same year, the US, prompted by the Japanese bombing of Pearl Harbor, entered the fray. The Allied landings at **Normandy** on June 6, 1944 **(D-Day),** turned the war's tide and marked the beginning of a bloody, arduous advance across Western Europe. Paris was liberated by Allied forces in September 1944, and Berlin was captured by the Red Army in April 1945. Hitler's **Third Reich,** which he had boasted would last for a thousand years, was dissolved after just twelve. The **Holocaust,** Hitler's "final solution to the Jewish problem," involved establishing mass concentration camps, the most infamous being **Auschwitz-Birkenau.** German forces ultimately killed at least six million Jews and countless other "undesirables," including Catholics, homosexuals, mentally disabled people, political dissidents, Roma (gypsies), and Slavs.

COLD WAR (1946-1989)

In 1945, the US, Britain, and the USSR met at **Yalta** to lay the foundation of the **United Nations,** plan the occupation of Nazi Germany, and determine spheres of influence in post-war Europe. Three **occupation zones** were set up in Germany, with Berlin under joint control. Berlin became the symbol of mounting tension between the Western capitalist world, led by the US, and the communist sphere, controlled by the USSR. East Germany, under the USSR, became known as the **German Democratic Republic. Julius** and **Ethel Rosenberg** helped bring the secrets of the atomic bomb to Russia, paving the way for a 50-year American nuclear **arms race** with the USSR. In 1949, the American, British, and French zones became the **German Federal Republic.** Berlin itself was divided between the two opposing spheres, a division later marked by the construction of the **Berlin Wall** in 1961. The **North Atlantic Treaty Organization (NATO)** was formed in 1949, by a band of 12 nations; it was countered by the Soviet alliance formed by the **Warsaw Pact** (1955). While the US was stricken with McCarthyism and anti-communist fervor, in Western Europe, the foundations for the now vibrant European Union (EU) were laid with the **European Economic Community** (EEC) in 1957—a tariff-free trading zone involving Belgium, France, Luxembourg, Italy, The Netherlands, and West Germany. Britain, Denmark, and Ireland joined in 1973, followed by Austria, Eastern Germany, Finland, Greece, Portugal, Spain, and Sweden over the next 20 years.

WESTERN EUROPE TODAY: EUROPEAN UNION

The fall of the Berlin Wall in November 1989 symbolized the fall of communism and the end of the Cold War in the Western world. At the **Treaty of Maastricht** in 1991, the **European Union** was created from the European Economic Community, eliminating national barriers for the movement of goods, services, workers, and capital. Twelve EU members—Austria, Belgium, Finland, France, Germany, Greece, Ireland, Italy, Luxembourg, The Netherlands, Portugal, and Spain—adopted the **euro** (€) as legal tender on January 1, 2002. And while concerns over xenophobia have been rising, thirteen Eastern European countries are currently undergoing the application processes to join the EU, further signifying the general European movement toward integration.

The Struggle for a European Immigration Policy

In June of 2003, 200 would-be European immigrants believed to have embarked from Libya drowned in the rough waters south of Sicily; that same month, 2666 migrants from Africa survived the journey, landing on the isolated Italian island Lampedusa and creating a study in contrasts in the ongoing EU immigration debate. In the annals of European immigration, tragedies of this caliber are far from rare: The Sicily drowning occurred three years to the month after 58 Chinese refugees were asphyxiated in a container lorry at the English port of Dover. Even the illegal immigrants who beat the odds and the border control do not always escape tragic circumstances. Many are forced into black-market labor, such as prostitution, to pay back smugglers for their passage. While it is fairly clear that current EU immigration policies are harmful to refugees, opening the floodgates on legal immigration is not only in the best interests of those seeking entrance—it now appears that the EU needs immigrants as desperately as immigrants need the EU.

Western European birth-rates have crashed to an all-time low, averaging only 1.5 children per woman, and dipping as low as Spain's scant 1.1. At the other end of things, Europe's aging population has become a major strain on its pension systems. French Parliamentarian Elisabeth Guigou reports that, if present demographic trends continue, without relaxing immigration constraints, the mighty new 25-nation European Union will experience a net decline in population of 50 million people by 2050. Even now Europe is facing shortages in both its skilled and unskilled labor pools, making even more apparent its need for immigrants for economic prosperity to continue.

With so much at stake, it may seem confusing to witness the recent immigration policy swing to the political right experienced by much of Europe. Some of the most developed, prosperous nations, such as Germany and France, worry that an influx of immigrants will destabilize their economies and jeopardize publicly-funded medical and social programs. Tensions have been primarily focused on African and Arab ghettos, commonly seen as drags on the welfare state and

feared to be security threats in the wake of September 11. This explosive combination of fear and uncertainty has fueled the popularity of far-right populist political candidates running on anti-immigration platforms, spawning legislation severely restricting legal immigration.

During June-July 2003 at the Thessaloniki Summit, Germany, Britain, and Italy were the most vocal and influential players in the debate over how to manage illegal immigration while integrating legal immigrants. Some leaders, such as German Interior Minister Otto Schily, think agreements with countires of origin are the best way to curbing illegal immigration. Supporters of such efforts point to Italy's bilateral agreements with Lybia, a hub for human trafficking from Africa to Europe, and Albania as models. In the former scenario, Italy will provide technical assistance to Libya, and the two countries will cooperate on offshore patrols. The 1997 Italian-Albanian cooperation deal contains a simplified repatriation scheme, quotas for seasonal workers, and joint patrols in Albanian waters of the Adriatic Sea that separate Italy and the former Stalinist state.

The stage is set for what promises to be an ongoing debate, as Germany leads the fight to retain autonomous control of its border policies while nations like Britain and Italy attempt to institute centralized, EU-wide control of immigration policy and enforcement. For the moment, a stopgap EU program intended to "promote a tolerant and inclusive society by raising awareness of fundamental European values" and to project accurate information about immigrants' culture, traditions, and religion underscores the two-sided complexity of the situation. By educating immigrants in the cultural, social, and political characteristics of their adoptive state—and providing EU citizens with accurate information about immigrants' cultures—there is hope that some of the elements of mistrust and misunderstanding that have plagued the discussion thus far can be mitigated, and that the frustrated desperation that costs the lives of so many refugees will give way to a peaceful, legal, and mutually beneficial solution.

Derek Glanz is currently earning a Ph.D. in political science and was an editor for Let's Go: Spain and Portugal 1998.

Should Britain Stay in the EU?

Ever since Jean Monnet and Robert Schuman dreamed up the European Coal and Steel Community—the forerunner of today's European Union—back in 1950, the UK has suffered from a prolonged case of attraction/repulsion syndrome towards European integration. Britain only joined the then-European Community in 1973 (which became the EU in 1993), having had its application vetoed twice in the 1960s by de Gaulle's France, thus having been kept out of (or, some say, having missed out on) the formative years of European integration. While having been unable to offer a *yea* or *nay* on fundamental, early efforts at creating the common market may explain Britain's continuing ambivalence (and intermittent obstructiveness) toward the EU, its oft-vaunted 1000 years of independence may go further in illuminating its ongoing love-affair with its sovereignty.

After World War II, Britain's political and economic attachments were felt to lie elsewhere—with its then-empire and within the emerging Commonwealth, as well as in its "special relationship" with the US. Indeed, the fact that Britain arrogantly ignored the developments on the European continent perhaps justified the EC's spiteful rejection of Britain's early attempts at courtship. When Britain finally joined, the Thatcher government almost immediately started to cause trouble, calling into question Britain's significant contribution to the EC's budget and specifically the cherished Common Agricultural Policy (a gargantuan agglomeration of subsidies to Europe's farmers, most of which did not apply to a country like the UK whose agricultural economy is based largely on, well...sheep). Thatcher famously asked for Britain's money back before demanding a massive financial overhaul of Europe, largely provoking the black days when politicians and academics on both sides of the Atlantic questioned whether European integration would ever be attained.

By 1988, Britain had experienced the largest reorientation of its trade toward the EU of all member states—a remarkable demonstration of just how much Britain needed the EU, if it did not really love the idea of it. Britain (with Denmark) nevertheless continues to be Europe's most awkward partner, cherry-picking policies of which it approves and fiercely negotiating opt-outs of those of which it doesn't—most famously, the common travel area and the Euro. Given its reluctance to play like a true European, some even speculate that Britain might be better suited to membership of NAFTA. An all-or-nothing choice between the rapacious capitalism of the North Americans and the mellower mix of mandated job stability, long vacations, and comprehensive social services enjoyed by most European continentals is, however, not a straight-forward one for Britain to make.

Should Britain stay in the EU? Although membership is technically politically reversible, it may not be so economically. Extracting itself from the EU's treaties and legislation adopted to date, as well as from the customs-free European web of trade, would be a Herculean task for Britain. While Britain's pensioners and punters on the street (25% of whom, in a recent poll, didn't even know that Britain was a member of the EU) might proudly rejoice at such a reclamation of self-determination, the City of London's financiers and businessfolk would likely revolt at the idea. The UK's current Labour government has, further, been the most Europhilic in recent times, and is contemplating a referendum on joining the Euro in the year to come. While the advantages of a single currency become evident to Britons as soon as they head out for their next holiday to Spain, France, or Greece, their deep attachment to the Pound Sterling as the last plank of Britishness in a sea of eroding sovereignty still runs high. Continuing to opt out of the Euro, as well as other unwearable policy areas, will keep Britain semi-detached and out of Europe's inner core for some time to come, as well as continue to position the nation as the Euro-Atlantic area's idiosyncratic middle ground. Thus, the question of Britain's membership in the EU may be less one of "should I stay or should I go?", but rather how long its partners in the ever-closer Union will continue to tolerate Britain's consternating fickleness.

Jeremy Faro wrote for Let's Go: Britain & Ireland 1995. He worked in London as a Senior Consultant for Interbrand, and is now a Master's student in European Studies at the University of Cambridge.

The Prevalence of Xenophobia in Modern Europe

In Europe as in America, cultural racism has long been a tale of bodies told as a story about minds—an evaluation of hair and skin behind claims about culture and language. This is evident to every child who, though born and raised in Europe, is perceived as an immigrant because she "looks Middle Eastern" or "looks African."

Anti-immigrant agitators have caused several recent electoral earthquakes. In 1999, the ultra-nationalist party of Jörg Haider shocked the European Union by attracting more than one-fourth of Austria's voters and becoming part of the country's governing coalition. Regimes in Italy, Portugal, and Denmark also depend on the extreme right to maintain parliamentary majorities. Osama bin Laden's September 11th gift to reactionary forces worldwide aided the Dutch Muslim-baiting party of the late Pim Fortuyn as well as France's Jean-Marie Le Pen, who was supported by 17% of the electorate in the first round of the 2002 presidential election.

Political entrepreneurs of the far right fan xenophobic fires by framing immigrants and native workers as rival claimants to material resources and social respect. In a western Europe of advanced general-welfare policies, resources for health-care, education, and housing, as well as unemployment benefits, have been squeezed during recent decades of retrenchment. Some politicians portray immigrants as getting something for nothing, receiving social support without having contributed to society. The immigrants themselves are in a catch-22: they are resented if they are unemployed (and thus seen as living off other people's taxes), but also if they find jobs (seen as taking them from natives).

Support for anti-immigrant parties comes largely from the working classes; bourgeois racism also exists, but wealthy citizens often value the inexpensive labor provided by immigrants even while looking down on them. Working-class opposition to immigration arises above all from the humiliations that workers have suffered. A man who welds fenders eight hours a day at a Renault factory, barely supporting his family in a dreary suburban flat—then finds himself unemployed when production is shifted abroad—is unlikely to welcome a Rwandan refugee, much less to empathize with her own biography of humiliations.

Immigration is also debated as part of Europe's ongoing cultural globalization. Multinational products perceived as American—from food to news to movies—have saturated the continent. Citizens of many countries (not least France) see this development as jeopardizing national integrity. Non-European immigrants may be framed as further eroding an imagined cultural homogeneity due to their different diets, clothing, religion, and language.

The more extreme right-wing politicians supplement economic and cultural discourses with imagery of bodily and sexual danger. As in racisms the world over, men of the disfavored groups are presented as violent, criminal, and predatory toward women—invaders, Le Pen once said, "who want to sleep in my bed, with my wife." In fact, it is the immigrants who are often the victims of crimes, committed largely by the underemployed sons of marginalized workers. Here racism is at its most obvious: those targeted may not be "foreign" at all, but native citizens who happen not to be white.

A politician who opposes anti-immigrant parties and the violence they sometimes condone faces a political obstacle course. How to protect asylum seekers arriving from a war-torn world while at the same time reassuring the public that the nation is strictly guarding its borders? How to reduce unemployment while also encouraging immigration of needed workers in such sectors as high technology and care of the expanding elderly population? How to balance respect for cultural and religious differences with the need to socialize new arrivals in the values and habits of the host society? In the hard-won answers to these questions lies the fate of the European Dream, a vision of an inclusive and egalitarian society extending across a continent.

Dr. Brian Palmer lectures on ethnography and ethics, and Kathleen Holbrook researches globalization and human values. They were voted Harvard's best young faculty member and teaching fellow, respectively, for a course which the New York Times nicknamed "Idealism 101."

INDEX

imagine
U in the UK

Travel, Study and Work in the UK.

**The Festivals. The Clubs.
The Sport. The Pubs. The Heritage.
The Cities. The Countryside.**

Come to the UK and access not just one but four different countries all in one destination. Get off the tourist trail, meet the locals and immerse yourself in the local culture – more than the average traveller gets to do. Get the scoop on what's happening in London, working and studying, visas, the hottest clubs, funky shopping, hippest hot spots, great accommodation, a crash course in the culture and much more.

For your survival guide to the UK
www.visitbritain.com/letsgo

1 2 3 4 5

PRICE RANGES >> WESTERN EUROPE

Our researchers list establishments in order of value from best to worst; our favorites are denoted by the *Let's Go* thumbs-up (🔊). Since the best value does not always come at the cheapest price, we have incorporated a system of price ranges to tell you how an establishment compares to others in the same country on a strictly cost-related basis. Our price ranges are based on a rough estimation of what you will pay. For **accommodations**, we base our price range on the cheapest amount a single traveler can spend for a one-night stay. For **restaurants** and other dining establishments, we approximate the average amount that you will pay for a meal in that restaurant. The table below tells you what you will *typically* find in Western Europe at the corresponding price range; keep in mind that a particularly expensive ice cream stand may still only be marked a ❷, depending on what you will spend.

ACCOMMODATIONS	WHAT YOU'RE *LIKELY* TO FIND
❶	Camping; most dorm rooms, such as you'll find in HI or other hostels, or university dorm rooms. Expect bunk beds and a communal bath; you may have to provide or rent towels and sheets.
❷	Upper-end hostels or small hotels. You may have a private bathroom, or there may be a sink in your room and a communal shower in the hall.
❸	A small room with a private bath. Should have decent amenities, such as a phone and TV. Breakfast may be included in the price of the room.
❹	Similar to 3, but may have more amenities or be in a more convenient or touristed area.
❺	Large hotels or upscale chains. If it's a 5 and it doesn't have the perks you want, you've paid too much.

FOOD	WHAT YOU'RE *LIKELY* TO FIND
❶	Mostly street-corner stands, pizza places, or fast-food joints. Rarely ever a sit-down meal.
❷	Sandwiches, appetizers at a bar, or low-priced entrees. You may have the option of sitting down or getting take-out.
❸	Mid-priced entrees, possibly coming with soup or salad. A tip will bump you up a couple dollars, since you'll probably have a waiter or waitress.
❹	A somewhat fancy restaurant or a steakhouse. Either way, you'll have a special knife. Few restaurants in this range have a dress code, but some may look down on t-shirt and jeans.
❺	Upscale restaurant, generally specializing in regional fare, with a decent wine list. Slacks and dress shirts may be expected.

MAP INDEX

MAP LEGEND

- ■ Point of Interest
- ▲ Accommodation
- ▲ Camping
- 🍴 Food
- ☕ Café
- 🏛 Museum
- ● Sight
- 🍺 Bar/Pub
- ★ Nightlife

- ✈ Airport
- ⌂ Arch/Gate
- $ Bank
- Beach
- 🚌 Bus Station/Stop
- ☉ Capital City
- ♜ Castle
- 🕆 Church
- 🏴 Consulate/Embassy

- ✝ Convent/Monastery
- ⚓ Ferry Landing
- (347) Highway Sign
- ✚ Hospital
- ▣ Internet Café
- ▮ Library/Bookstore
- Ⓜ Ⓜ Metro Station
- ▲ Mountain
- Ⓜ Mosque

- ℞ Pharmacy
- ☒ Police
- ✉ Post Office
- ⛷ Skiing
- ✡ Synagogue
- ☎ Telephone Office
- ♉ Theater
- ⓘ Tourist Office
- 🚂 Train Station

- Park
- Water
- Beach
- Pedestrian Zone
- Stairs
- The Let's Go compass always points NORTH.